THE OFFICIAL®
OVERSTREET
Comic Book
PRICE GUIDE
1990 - 1991

20th Edition

BOOKS FROM 1900—PRESENT INCLUDED

CATALOGUE & EVALUATION GUIDE—ILLUSTRATED

By
Robert M. Overstreet

SPECIAL CONTRIBUTORS TO THIS EDITION

Harry Thomas, Bruce Hamilton, Tom Inge,
and Gary Carter

SPECIAL ADVISORS TO THIS EDITION

*Bruce Hamilton   *Hugh O'Kennon   *Ron Pussell   *Gary M. Carter
*Walter Wang   *John Snyder   *Terry Stroud   *Jon Warren
*Dan Malan   *Steve Geppi   *Gary Colabuono   *Jay Maybruck
*Joe Vereneault   *James Payette   *Harry Matetsky   *Harry Thomas
*Jerry Weist   *John Verzyl   *Joe Mannarino   *Stephen Fishler

THE HOUSE OF COLLECTIBLES
NEW YORK, NEW YORK 10022

Copyright © 1990 by Robert M. Overstreet

Published by the House of Collectibles and distributed to the book trade by Ballantine Books, a division of Random House, Inc., New York and simultaneously in Canada by Random House of Canada Limited, Toronto.

Published and distributed to the collectors' market by Overstreet Publications, Inc., 780 Hunt Cliff Dr. N.W., Cleveland, TN 37311.

Manufactured in the United States of America

Cover Illustration by Carmine Infantino and Murphy Anderson.

ISBN 0-876-37820-3
ISSN 0891-8872
10 9 8 7 6 5 4 3 2 1

20th Edition

TABLE OF CONTENTS

ACKNOWLEDGEMENTS

Larry Bigman (Frazetta-Williamson data); Glenn Bray (Kurtzman data); Dan Malan & Charles Heffelfinger (Classic Comics data); Gary Carter (DC data); J. B. Clifford Jr. (E. C. data); Gary Coddington (Superman data); Wilt Conine (Fawcett data); Dr. S. M. Davidson (Cupples & Leon data); Al Dellinges (Kubert data); Kevin Hancer (Tarzan data); Charles Heffelfinger and Jim Ivey (March of Comics listing); R. C. Holland and Ron Pussell (Seduction and Parade of Pleasure data); Grant Irwin (Quality data); Richard Kravitz (Kelly data); Phil Levine (giveaway data); Fred Nardelli (Frazetta data); Michelle Nolan (love comics); Mike Nolan (MLJ, Timely, Nedor data); George Olshevsky (Timely data); Don Rosa (Late 1940s to 1950s data); Richard Olson (LOA & R. F. Outcault data); Scott Pell ('50s data); Greg Robertson (National data); Frank Scigliano (Little Lulu data); Gene Seger (Buck Rogers data); Rick Sloane (Archie data); David R. Smith, Archivist, Walt Disney Productions (Disney data); Don and Maggie Thompson (Four Color listing); Mike Tiefenbacher & Jerry Sinkovec (Atlas and National data); Raymond True (Classic Comics data); Jim Vadeboncoeur Jr. (Williamson and Atlas data); Kim Weston (Disney and Barks data); Cat Yronwode (Spirit data); Andrew Zerbe and Gary Behymer (M. E. data).

My appreciation must also be extended to Don Maris, John Snyder, Steve Geppi, Bruce Hamilton, Harry Thomas, Gary Carter, and especially to Hugh and Louise O'Kennon for their support and help. Special acknowledgement is also given to Ron Pussell, Ken Mitchell, Michelle Nolan, Garth Wood, Terry Stroud, and Jeremy Dollar for submitting corrective data; to Dr. Richard Olson for rewriting grading definitions; to Larry Breed for his suggestions on re-organizing the introductory section; to Dan Malan for revamping the Classics section; to Terry Stroud, Hugh O'Kennon, Jon Warren, Dave Smith, Rod Dyke, Jay Maybruck, Joe Vereneault, James Payette, John Snyder, Gary Carter, Rick Sloane, Stephen Fishler, Jerry Weist, Walter Wang, Steve Geppi, Joe Mannarino, John Verzyl, Gary Colabuono, Dave Anderson (Okla.) and Ron Pussell, (pricing); to Tom Inge for his "Chronology of the American Comic Book;" to Harry Thomas and Gary Carter for their exciting articles; to Carmine Infantino and Murphy Anderson for their inspired cover art; to Landon Chesney and Dave Noah for their work on the key comic book list; to L. B. Cole, Steve Saffel, and Jerry DeFuccio for their counsel and help; to Bill Spicer and Zetta DeVoe (Western Publishing Co.) for their contribution of data; and especially to Bill for his kind permission to reprint portions of his and Jerry Bails' **America's Four Color Pastime**; and to Walter Presswood, Dave Noah, and Jeff Overstreet for their help in editing this volume.

I will always be indebted to Jerry Bails, Landon Chesney, Bruce Hamilton and Larry Bigman whose advice and concern have helped in making **The Comic Book Price Guide** a reality; to my wife Martha for her encouragement and help in putting this reference work together; and to everyone who placed ads in this edition.

Acknowledgement is also due to the following people who have so generously contributed much needed data for this edition:

Perry A. Albert
Jim Alexander
David Anderson
Alfred Paul Arruda
Jeffrey Backenger
Stephen Baer
Sheila Barnard
Tim Barnes
Stephen Barrington
Jon Berk
Benjamin Bernhart
John H.L. Bernhart

Jeff Birkel
Earl Blair
Marc Brewer
John Brillhart
Paul Broida
Shannon Burns
Steve Carey
Phil Carpenter
Robert N. Cherry, Jr.
Dan Crawford
Jim Crocker
David H. Curtis

Jeremy Dollar
Clayton Emery
Peter Erickson
Gerard Geary
Andrew Gilpin
Keith Gorney
Doug Haines
Jeff Hammons
Terry Harms
David Harper
D.D. Hering
Alex Hloderwski

Duncan Holmes
Joe Hummel III
Bill Hutchison
Ken Kaake
Jason Kirkland
Dan Kurdilla
Frank Lopiccolo, Jr.
Rob Mathis
Derek Matthews
Ken McDaniel
James P. McLaughlin
Wayne Milewski
David Miller
Harry W. Miller
Bill Mills
Ken Mitchell

Bill Mullins
Wayne Mullins
Bob Myers
John Newberry
David Noe
Eric Pavlat
Brian Powell
Donald L. Puff
Juleo F. Reis Jr.
Krishna Sadasivam
Joe Sarno
Randall W. Scott
Sergei Scurfield
Steve R. Sibra
David Sorochty
Mark Steel

Ray Storch
Tom Struck
David E. Taeusch
Francis Tenney
William Tighe
John K. Vavra
Phil Vandrey
M.D. Warner
Lawrence Watt-Evans
David Welch
Mike Welch
Michael Weng
M. Wayne Williams
Garth Wood
LeVar Yuen

PREFACE

Comic book values listed in this reference work were recorded from convention sales, dealers' lists, adzines, and by special contact with dealers and collectors from coast to coast. Prices paid for rare comics vary considerably from one locale to another. We have attempted to list a realistic average between the lowest and highest range observed. The reader should keep in mind that the prices listed only reflect the market just prior to publication. Any new trends that have developed since the preparation of this book would not be shown.

The values listed are based on reports, not estimates. Each new edition of the guide is actually an average report of sales that occurred during the year; not an estimate of what we feel the books will be bringing next year. Even though many prices listed will remain current throughout the year, the wise user of this book would keep abreast of current market trends to get the fullest potential out of his invested dollar.

By the same token, many of the scarcer books are seldom offered for sale in top condition. This makes it difficult to arrive at a realistic market value. Some of the issues in this category are: Action #1, All-American #16, Batman #1, Large Feature Comic #20, Captain America #1, Captain Marvel #1, Detective #27, Double Action #2, the No-# Feature Books, Green Giant #1, March of Comics #4, Marvel #1, More Fun #52, Famous Funnies #1s, Superman #1, Whiz #2 (#1), Amazing Man #5, New Fun #1, and Wow #1.

Some rare comics were published in a complete black and white format; i.e., All-New #15, Blood Is the Harvest, Boy Explorers #2, Eerie #1, If the Devil Would Talk, Is This Tomorrow, Flash #1, Thrill #1 and Stuntman #3. As we have learned in the case of Eerie #1, the collector or investor in these books would be well advised to give due consideration to the possibility of counterfeits before investing large sums of money.

This book is the most comprehensive listing of newsstand comic books ever attempted. Comic book titles, dates of first and last issues, publishing companies, origin and special issues are listed when known.

The Guide will be listing only American comic books due to space limitation. Some variations of the regular comic book format will be listed. These basically include those pre-1933 comic strip reprint books with varying size—usually with cardboard covers, but sometimes with hardback. As forerunners of the modern comic book format, they deserve to be listed despite their obvious differences in presentation. Other books that will be listed are key black and white comics of the 1980s, giveaway comics— but only those that contain known characters, work by known collectible artists, or those of special interest.

All titles are listed as if they were one word, ignoring spaces, hyphens and apostrophes. Page counts listed will always include covers.

IMPORTANT. Prices listed in this book are in U. S. currency and are for your reference only. This book is not a dealer's price list, although some dealers may base their prices on the values listed. The true value of any comic book is what you are willing to pay. Prices listed herein are an indication of what collectors (not dealers) would probably pay. For one reason or another, these collectors might want certain books badly, or else need specific issues to complete their runs and so are willing to pay more. Dealers are not in a position to pay the full prices listed, but work on a percentage depending largely on the amount of investment required and the quality of material offered. Usually they will pay from 20 to 70 percent of the list price depending on how long it will take them to sell the collection after making the investment; the higher the demand and better the condition, the more the percentage. Most dealers are faced with expenses such as advertising, travel, telephone and mailing, rent, employee salaries, plus convention costs. These costs all go in before the books are sold. The high demand books usually sell right away but there are many other titles that are difficult to sell due to low demand. Sometimes a dealer will have cost tied up in this type of material for several years before finally moving it. Remember, his position is that of handling, demand and overhead. Most dealers are victims of these economics.

Black and White comics of the 1980s: In recent years an explosion of new comic book titles has occurred in the direct market. Since many of these books are produced in an inexpensive black & white format, anyone today can become a publisher of comic books; the result has been dozens of new publishers and hundreds of new titles entering the market place. The quality of these publications vary from very poor to excellent. THE PRICE GUIDE'S POSITION: In the past, we have attempted to list all newsstand comic books that qualified for listing. Today, with the advent of the new formatted black and whites, consideration must be given for their inclusion, but obviously all cannot or should not be listed. Just because someone puts out a black and white comic out of their basement does not mean that we should acknowledge its existence in this book. However, there are many collectible and important titles that should and have been listed in this edition. The selection of titles to list was made by our panel of advisors who send in pricing information for the Updates. Of course a much better coverage of these books will be made in the bi-monthly Updates throughout the year.

TERMINOLOGY

Many of the following terms and abbreviations are used in the comic book market and are explained here:

a—Story art; **a(i)**—Story art inks; **a(p)**—Story art pencils; **a(r)**—Story art   reprint.

Annual—A book that is published yearly.

Arrival date—Markings on a comic book cover (usually in pencil) made by either the newsstand dealer or the distributor. These markings denote the date the book was placed on the newsstand. Usually the arrival date is one to two months prior to the cover date.

Ashcan—A publisher's inhouse facsimile of a proposed new title. Most ashcans have black & white covers stapled to an existing coverless comic on the inside. Other ashcans are totally black and white.

B&W—Black and white art.

Bi-monthly—Published every two months.

Bi-weekly—Published every two weeks.

Bondage cover—Usually denotes a female in bondage.

Brittleness—The final stage of paper deterioration.

c—Cover art; **c(i)**—Cover inks; **c(p)**—Cover pencils; **c(r)**—Cover reprint.

Cameo—When a character appears briefly in one or two panels.

CCA—Comics Code Authority.

CCA seal—An emblem that was placed on the cover of all CCA approved comics beginning in April-May, 1955.

Centerfold—The two folded pages in the center of a comic at the terminal end of the staples.

Church, Edgar collection—A large high grade comic book collection discovered by Mile High Comics in Colorado (over 22,000 books).

Colorist—Artist that applies color to the black and white pen and ink art.

Comic book repair—When a tear, loose staple or centerfold has been mended without changing or adding to the original finish of the book. Repair may involve tape, glue or nylon gossamer and is easily detected. It is considered a defect.

Comic book restoration—Any attempt, whether professional or amateur, to enhance the appearance of a comic book. These procedures may include any or all of the following techniques: Recoloring, adding missing paper, stain, ink, dirt, tape removal, whitening, pressing out wrinkles, staple replacement, trimming, re-glossing, etc. Note: Unprofessional work can lower the value of a book. In all cases, a restored book can never be worth the same as an unrestored book in the same condition.

Comics Code Authority—In 1954 the major publishers joined together and formed a committee who set up guide lines for acceptable comic contents. It was their task to approve the contents of comics before publication.

Con—A Convention or public gathering of fans.

Cosmic Aeroplane—Refers to a large collection discovered by Cosmic Aeroplane Books.

Debut—The first time that a character appears anywhere.

Double cover—An error in the binding process which results in two or more covers being bound to a single book. Multiple covers are not considered a defect.

Drug propaganda story—Where comic makes an editorial stand about drug abuse.

Drug use story—Shows the actual use of drugs: shooting, taking a trip, harmful effects, etc.

Fanzine—An amateur fan publication.

File Copy—A high grade comic originating from the publisher's file. Not all file copies are in pristine condition. Note: An arrival date on the cover of a comic does not indicate that it is a file copy.

First app.—Same as debut.

Flashback—When a previous story is being recalled.

Four color—A printing process in which all primary colors plus black are used. Also refers to the Four Color series published by Dell.

Foxing—Tiny orange-brown spots on the cover or pages of a comic book.

G. A.—Golden Age.

Golden Age (G.A.)—The period beginning with Action #1 (June, 1938) and ending with World War II in 1945.

Headlight—Protruding breasts.

i—Art inks.

Infinity cover—Shows a scene that repeats itself to infinity.

Inker—Artist that does the inking.

Intro—Same as debut.

JLA—Justice League of America.

JLI—Justice League International.

JSA—Justice Society of America.

Lamont Larson—Refers to a large high grade collection of comics. Many of the books have Lamont or Larson written on the cover.

Logo—The title of a strip or comic book as it appears on the cover or title page.

LSH—Legion of Super-Heroes.

Marvel chipping—A defect that occurred during the trimming process of 1950s & 1960s Marvels which produced a ragged edge around the comic cover. Usually takes the form of a tiny chip or chips along the right-hand edge of the cover.

Mile High—Refers to a large NM-Mint collection of comics originating from Denver, Colorado (Edgar Church collection).

nd—No date.

nn—No number.

N. Y. Legis. Comm.—New York Legislative Committee to Study the Publication of Comics (1951).

One-shot—When only one issue is published of a title, or when a series is published where each issue is a different title (i.e. Four Color).

Origin—When the story of the character's creation is given.

Over guide—When a comic book is priced at a value over guide list.

p—Art pencils.

Pedigree—A book from a famous collection, e.g. Larson, Church/Mile High, Denver, San Francisco, Cosmic Aeroplane, etc. Note: beware of non-pedigree collections being promoed as pedigree books. Only outstanding famous collections such as those listed qualify.

Penciler—Artist that does the pencils.

POP—**Parade of Pleasure**, book about the censorship of comics.

Post-Code—Comic books published with the CCA seal.

Post-Golden Age—Comic books published between 1945 and 1950.

Post-Silver Age—Comic books published from 1969 to present.

Poughkeepsie—Refers to a large collection of Dell Comics' ''file copies'' believed to have originated from the warehouse of Western Publishing in Poughkeepsie, N. Y.

Pre-Code—Comic books published before the CCA seal.

Pre-Golden Age—Comic books published prior to Action #1 (June, 1938).

Pre-Silver Age—Comic books published between 1950 and Showcase #4 (1956).

Printing defect—A defect caused by the printing process. Examples would include paper wrinkling, mis-cut edges, mis-folded spine, untrimmed pages, off-registered color, off-centered trimming, mis-folded and mis-bound pages. It should be noted that these are defects that lower the grade of the book.

Provenance—When the owner of a book is known and is stated for the purpose of authenticating and documenting the history of the book. Example: A book from the Stan Lee or Forrest Ackerman collection would be an example of a value-adding provenance.

Quarterly—Published every three months.

R or r—Reprint.
Rare—10 to 20 copies estimated to exist.
Reprint comics—Comic books that contain newspaper strip reprints.
Rice paper—A thin, transparent paper commonly used by restorers to repair tears and replace small pieces on covers and pages of comic books.
S. A.—Silver Age.
Scarce—20 to 100 copies estimated to exist.
Silver Age—Officially begins with Showcase #4 in 1956 and ends in 1969.
Silver proof—A black & white actual size print on thick glossy paper given to the colorist to indicate colors to the engraver.
S&K—Simon and Kirby (artists).
SOTI—**Seduction of the Innocent**, book about the censorship of comics. Refer to listing in this guide.
Spine—The area representing the folded and stapled part of a comic book.
Spine roll—A defect caused by improper storage which results in uneven pages and the shifting or bowing of the spine.
Splash panel—A large panel that usually appears at the front of a comic story.
Squarebound—A comic book glue-bound with a square spined cover.
Stress lines—Light, tiny wrinkles occuring along the spine, projecting from the staples or appearing anywhere on the covers of a comic book.
Subscription crease—A center crease caused by the folding of comic books for mailing to subscribers. This is considered a defect.
3-D comic—Comic art that is drawn and printed in two-color layers, producing a true 3-D effect when viewed through special glasses.
3-D Effect comic—Comic art that is drawn to appear 3-D, but isn't.
Under guide—When a comic book is priced at a value less than guide list.
Very rare—1 to 10 copies estimated to exist.
Warehouse copy—Originating from a publisher's warehouse; similar to file copy.
X-over—When one character crosses over into another's strip.
Zine—See Fanzine.

Marvel comic books are cover coded for the direct sales (comic shop), newsstand, and foreign markets. They are all first printings, with the special coding being the only difference. The comics sold to the comic shops have to be coded differently, as they are sold on a no-return basis while newsstand comics are not. The Price Guide has not detected any price difference between these versions. Currently, the difference is easily detected by looking at the front cover bar code (a box located at the lower left). The bar code is filled in for newsstand sales and is left blank or contains a character for comic shop sales. The following emblems were used in the early 1980s.

Direct Sales
(Comic Shops)

Newsstand

Newsstand
Overseas

Marvel Reprints: In recent years Marvel has reprinted some of their comics. There has been confusion in identifying the reprints from the originals. However, in 99 percent of the cases, the reprints will list "reprint," or "2nd printing," etc. in the indicia, along with a later copyright date in some cases. The only known exceptions are a few of the movie books such as *Star Wars*, the *Marvel Treasury Editions*, and tie-in books such as *G. I. Joe*. These books were reprinted and not identified as reprints. The *Star Wars* reprints have a large diamond with no date and a blank UPC symbol on the cover. The other reprints will have some cover variation such as a date missing, different colors, etc.

Gold Key comics were sold with two different labels: Whitman and Gold Key. There are collectors who prefer the Gold Key labels to Whitman, although the Price Guide does not differentiate in the price. Beginning in 1980, all comics produced by Western carried the Whitman label.

Many of the better artists are pointed out. When more than one artist worked on a story, their names are separated by a (/). The first name did the pencil drawings and the second did the inks. When two or more artists work on a story, only the most prominent will be noted in some cases. There has been some confusion in past editions as to which artists to list and which to leave out. We wish all good artists could be listed, but due to space limitation, only the most popular can. The following list of artists are considered to be either the most collected in the comic field or are historically significant and should be pointed out. Artists designated below with an (*) indicate that only their most noted work will be listed. The rest will eventually have all their work shown as the information becomes available. This list could change from year to year as new artists come into prominence.

Adams, Arthur	Everett, Bill	Krenkel, Roy	Rogers, Marshall
Adams, Neal	Feldstein, Al	Krigstein, Bernie	Schomburg, Alex
*Aparo, Jim	Fine, Lou	*Kubert, Joe	Siegel & Shuster
*Austin, Terry	Foster, Harold	Kurtzman, Harvey	Simon & Kirby (S&K)
Baker, Matt	Fox, Matt	Manning, Russ	*Simonson, Walt
Barks, Carl	Frazetta, Frank	McFarland, Todd	Smith, Barry
Beck, C. C.	*Giffen, Keith	*Meskin, Mort	Smith, Paul
*Brunner, Frank	Golden, Michael	Miller, Frank	Stanley, John
*Buscema, John	Gottfredson, Floyd	Moreira, Ruben	*Starlin, Jim
Byrne, John	*Guardineer, Fred	*Morisi, Pete	Steranko, Jim
*Check, Sid	Gustavson, Paul	*Newton, Don	Torres, Angelo
Cole, Jack	*Heath, Russ	Nostrand, Howard	Toth, Alex
Cole, L. B.	Howard, Wayne	Orlando, Joe	Tuska, George
Craig, Johnny	Ingels, Graham	Pakula, Mac	Ward, Bill
Crandall, Reed	Jones, Jeff	*Palais, Rudy	Williamson, Al
Davis, Jack	Kamen, Jack	*Perez, George	Woggon, Bill
Disbrow, Jayson	Kane, Bob	Powell, Bob	Wolverton, Basil
*Ditko, Steve	*Kane, Gil	Raboy, Mac	Wood, Wallace
Eisner, Will	Kelly, Walt	Raymond, Alex	Wrightson, Bernie
*Elder, Bill	Kinstler, E. R.	Ravielli, Louis	
Evans, George	Kirby, Jack	*Redondo, Nestor	

The following abbreviations are used with the cover reproductions throughout the book for copyright credit purposes. The companies they represent are listed here:

ACE—Ace Periodicals	EP—Elliott Publications	QUA—Quality Comics Group
ACG—American Comics Group	ERB—Edgar Rice Burroughs	REAL—Realistic Comics
AJAX—Ajax-Farrell	FAW—Fawcett Publications	RH—Rural Home
AP—Archie Publications	FF—Famous Funnies	S & S—Street and Smith Publishers
ATLAS—Atlas Comics (see below)	FH—Fiction House Magazines	SKY—Skywald Publications
AVON—Avon Periodicals	FOX—Fox Features Syndicate	STAR—Star Publications
BP—Better Publications	GIL—Gilberton	STD—Standard Comics
C & L—Cupples & Leon	GK—Gold Key	STJ—St. John Publishing Co.
CC—Charlton Comics	GP—Gold Key Publications	SUPR—Superior Comics
CEN—Centaur Publications	HARV—Harvey Publications	TC—Tower Comics
CCG—Columbia Comics Group	HILL—Hillman Periodicals	TM—Trojan Magazines
CG—Catechetical Guild	HOKE—Holyoke Publishing Co.	TOBY—Toby Press
CHES—Harry 'A' Chesler	KING—King Features Syndicate	UFS—United Features Syndicate
CLDS—Classic Det. Stories	LEV—Lev Gleason Publications	VITL—Vital Publications
CM—Comics Magazine	ME—Magazine Enterprises	WDC—The Walt Disney Company
DC—DC Comics, Inc.	MEG—Marvel Ent. Group	WEST—Western Publishing Co.
DELL—Dell Publishing Co.	MLJ—MLJ Magazines	WHIT—Whitman Publishing Co.
DMP—David McKay Publishing	NOVP—Novelty Press	WHW—William H. Wise
DS—D. S. Publishing Co.	PG—Premier Group	WMG—William M. Gaines (E. C.)
EAS—Eastern Color Printing Co.	PINE—Pines	WP—Warren Publishing Co.
EC—E. C. Comics	PMI—Parents' Magazine Institute	YM—Youthful Magazines
ENWIL—Enwil Associates	PRIZE—Prize Publications	Z-D—Ziff-Davis Publishing Co.

TIMELY/MARVEL/ATLAS COMICS. "A Marvel Magazine" and "Marvel Group" was the symbol used between December 1946 and May 1947 (not used on all titles/issues during period). The Timely Comics symbol was used between July 1942 and September 1942 (not on all titles/issues during period). The round "Marvel Comic" symbol was used between February 1949 and June 1950. Early comics code symbol (star and bar) was used between April 1952 and February 1955. The Atlas globe symbol was used between December 1951 and September 1957. The M over C symbol (beginning of Marvel Comics) was used between July 1961 until the price increased to 12 cents on February 1962.

TIMELY/MARVEL/ATLAS Publishers' Abbreviation Codes:

ACI—Animirth Comics, Inc.
AMI—Atlas Magazines, Inc.
ANC—Atlas News Co., Inc.
BPC—Bard Publishing Corp.
BFP—Broadcast Features Pubs.
CBS—Crime Bureau Stories
CIDS—Classic Detective Stories
CCC—Comic Combine Corp.
CDS—Current Detective Stories
CFI—Crime Files, Inc.
CmPI—Comedy Publications, Inc.
CmPS—Complete Photo Story
CnPC—Cornell Publishing Corp.
CPC—Chipiden Publishing Corp.
CPI—Crime Publications, Inc.
CPS—Canam Publishing Sales Corp.
CSI—Classics Syndicate, Inc.
DCI—Daring Comics, Inc.
EPC—Euclid Publishing Co.
EPI—Emgee Publications, Inc.

FCI—Fantasy Comics, Inc.
FPI—Foto Parade, Inc.
GPI—Gem Publishing, Inc.
HPC—Hercules Publishing Corp.
IPS—Interstate Publishing Corp.
JPI—Jaygee Publications, Inc.
LBI—Lion Books, Inc.
LCC—Leading Comic Corp.
LMC—Leading Magazine Corp.
MALE—Male Publishing Corp.
MAP—Miss America Publishing Corp.
MCI—Marvel Comics, Inc.
MgPC—Margood Publishing Corp.
MjMC—Marjean Magazine Corp.
MMC—Mutual Magazine Corp.
MPC—Medalion Publishing Corp.
MPI—Manvis Publications, Inc.
NPI—Newsstand Publications, Inc.
NPP—Non-Pareil Publishing Corp.
OCI—Official Comics, Inc.

OMC—Official Magazine Corp.
OPI—Olympia Publications, Inc.
PPI—Postal Publications, Inc.
PrPI—Prime Publications, Inc.
RCM—Red Circle Magazines, Inc.
SAI—Sports Actions, Inc.
SePI—Select Publications, Inc.
SnPC—Snap Publishing Co.
SPC—Select Publishing Co.
SPI—Sphere Publications, Inc.
TCI—Timely Comics, Inc.
TP—Timely Publications
20 CC—20th Century Comics Corp.
USA—U.S.A. Publications, Inc.
VPI—Vista Publications, Inc.
WFP—Western Fiction Publishing
WPI—Warwick Publications, Inc.
YAI—Young Allies, Inc.
ZPC—Zenith Publishing Co., Inc.

YOUR INFORMATION IS NEEDED: In order to make future Guides more accurate and complete, we are interested in any relevant information or facts that you might have. **Relevant and significant data includes:**

Works by the artists named elsewhere. **Caution:** Most artists did not sign their work and many were imitated by others. When submitting this data, advise whether the work was signed or not. In many cases, it takes an expert to identify certain artists—so extreme caution should be observed in submitting this data.

Issues mentioned by Wertham and others in **Seduction, Parade . . .**
Origin issues.
First and last appearances of strips or characters.
Title continuity information.
Beginning and ending numbers of runs.
Atomic bomb, Christmas, Flag and infinity covers.
Swipes.
Photo covers.

To record something in the Guide, **documented** facts are needed. Please send a photo copy of indicia or page in question if possible.

Non-relevent data—Most giveaway comics will not be listed. Literally thousands of titles came out, many of which have educational themes. We will only list significant collectible giveaways such as March of Comics, Disney items, communist books (but not civil defense educational comics), and books that contain illustrated stories by top artists or top collected characters.

Good Luck and Happy Hunting . . .

Robert M. Overstreet

Advertise in the Guide

This book reaches more serious comic collectors than any other publication and has proven ad results due to its world-wide circulation and use. Your ad will pull all year long until the new edition comes out.

Display Ad space is sold in full, half, fourth, and eighth page sizes. Shop listings are sold for the **State Directory**. Ad rates are set in the early fall prior to each edition's release. Write at that time for rates (Between Oct.—Dec.).

PRINTED SIZES

Full Page—8'' long x 5'' wide.   **Half Page**—4'' long x 5'' wide.
Fourth Page—4'' long x 2½'' wide.   **Eighth Page**—2'' long x 2½'' wide.

Classified Ads will be retyped and reduced about one-half. No artwork permitted. Rate is based on your 4'' typed line. **Display Classified Ads:** The use of borders, bold face type, cuts or other decorations change your classified ad to display—rates same as regular display.

NOTE: Submit your ad on white paper in a proportionate version of the actual printed size. All Full to Quarter page advertisers will receive a complimentary copy of the Guide. The **New Guide** will be professionally done throughout . . . so to reflect a consistently high quality from cover to cover, we must ask that all ads be neatly and professionally done. **Full Payment** must be sent with all ads. All but classified ads will be run as is.

AD DEADLINE - COLOR—Dec. 15th
AD DEADLINE - Black & White—Jan. 15th

Overstreet Publications, Inc.
780 Hunt Cliff Dr. N.W.
Cleveland, Tennessee 37311

The **Price Guide** has become the **Standard Reference Work** in the field and is distributed to tens of thousands of comic collectors throughout the world. Don't miss this opportunity to advertise in the Guide.

NOTICE: All advertisements are accepted and placed in the Price Guide in good faith. However, we cannot be held responsible for any losses incurred in your dealings with the advertisers. If, after receiving legitimate complaints, and there is sufficient evidence to warrant such action, these advertisers will be dropped from future editions.

SPECIAL NOTICE

If copyrighted characters are planned for your ad, the following must be done: Send a copy of your ad layout (including characters) to the company(s) or copyright owner(s) involved requesting permission for their use. A copy of this permission must be sent to us with your ad. DC Comics and Marvel Comics have indicated that you will have no problem getting permission, so if you must use their characters . . . write for the permission. For DC, write: Public Relations, DC Comics, Inc. 666 Fifth Ave., New York, NY, 10103. For Marvel, write: Marvel Comics, 387 Park Ave. South, New York, NY 10016. Other companies such as Disney could be more of a problem. At any rate, we cannot accept any ads with copyrighted characters without a copy of the permission.

GRADING COMIC BOOKS

Note: This grading section replaces all previous grading definitions in prior editions of this book.

Before a comic book's true value can be assessed, its condition or state of preservation must be determined. In all comic books the better the condition the more desirable and valuable the book. Comic books in MINT condition will bring several times the price of the same book in POOR condition. Therefore it is very important to be able to properly grade your books. Comics should be graded from the inside out, so the following steps should be taken to properly grade a comic book:

1. Check inside pages. Gently open the comic to the centerfold (except for annuals) and let it lay in the cup of your hand. Check the condition of the paper for suppleness, whiteness/browning/brittleness. Smell paper for freshness/acidity. If the book is brittle or too brown, you may not want to go further; especially check along the spine and outer edges for browning/brittleness. If the paper looks o.k., then proceed and check the following: Centerfold for tightness and secured staples (centerfolds are sometimes replaced from other books—check for trimming and color variations from rest of book); tears or chunks missing from the inside pages; missing pages (count pages); edges for possible trimming (trimmed book edges appear whiter and flatter than normal); soiling, water marks, tape, crayoning, inking or pencilling; repairs, gluing and paper replacement; panels, coupons or pages cut out.

2. Check inside covers. Check the condition of the inside cover paper for suppleness, whiteness/browning/brittleness. Look for unusual whiteness compared to other pages in the book which may indicate the book has been bleached. Look for tears, chunks missing, paper replacement, tear repairs, tape, writing, dirt, water marks, soiling or any noticeable defect that would detract from the grading. Let light reflect off the surface of the cover and check cover edges for pieces replaced.

3. Check inside spine. Check the entire area along the spine, especially where the cover is attached. Look for spine splitting, loose staples that have pulled through the cover, cover & spine paper replacement, tear repairs, gluing, tape repairs, staple reinforcement, recoloring bleed-through from front, spine reinforcement, bleaching or any other noticeable defect.

4. Check outside spine. Check spine for tightness, proper folding (centering & rolled spine), proper stapling and condition of spine corners. Spine corners are easily damaged, so look for rubbing, pieces missing and splitting. Check spine for stress lines and determine the number of stress lines along the spine. Check staple areas for tear repair, recoloring, reinforcement and staple replacement (replaced staples should match the originals as closely as possible) (fraying around staple holes may indicate that the staples had been removed at one time). Look for splitting, paper replacement, recoloring, sewing holes, gluing, tape, soiling, pieces missing or any other defect that would detract from the grade.

5. Check outside covers. Here is where the slightest amount of wear and abuse really shows. The outside appearance of covers subjectively affects grading more than anything else, although inside condition must influence the final grade given a book. Remember, a mint cover with brittle insides is still a brittle book! Check for squareness of trim, sharpness of edges and corners, amount of gloss, color fading, centering and proper placement of staples and centering of cover art. Look for defects such as subscription creases, other creases, tears, corners missing, chips, color flakes, folds, holes, yellowing, soiling, rubbing, writing, color touch-up, paper replacement, tape, retrimming or anything else that would detract from the grade.

After all the above steps have been taken, then the reader can begin to consider an overall grade for his or her book. The grading of a comic book is done by simply looking at the book and describing its condition, which may range from absolutely perfect newsstand condition (MINT) to extremely worn, dirty, and torn (POOR).

Note on understanding terminologies and descriptions: A flaw that is permitted in a higher grade is also permitted in all lower grades, even though the flaw may not be mentioned again in lower grade descriptions. A flaw that is not permitted in a higher grade, but is not noted as being not permitted in the next lower grade, is permitted in that grade and all lower grades. For example, if VF cannot have yellowish pages, but FN does not exclude yellowish pages as a defect, then yellowish pages are allowed in that grade and all lower grades below it.

When a book is described as simply FVF condition, you can expect a book that does not fall abnormally outside of the FVF grade description. When a book is graded as FVF and described as having a 1'' spine split, this means that there is a defect which is not allowed in the FVF grade that is present in this copy, otherwise the appearance of the book is a standard FVF copy. In such case, the value of the book should be reduced to reflect the defect.

Numerous variables (as outlined above) influence the evaluation of a comic's condition and **all** must be considered in the final evaluation. As grading is the most subjective aspect of determining a comic's value, it is very important that the grader must be careful and not allow wishful thinking to influence what the eyes see. It is also very important to realize that older comics in MINT condition are extremely scarce and are rarely advertised for sale; most of the higher grade comics advertised range from VERY FINE to NEAR MINT. To the novice grading will appear difficult at first; but, as experience is gained accuracy will improve. Whenever in doubt, consult with a reputable dealer or experienced collector in your area. The following grading guide is given to aid the collector.

WARNING ABOUT RESTORATION:

Many rare and expensive books are being restored by professionals. These books are not actually higher grades, but are altered lower grade books. It has been brought to our attention that some dealers have been selling these books to unsuspecting collectors/investors—without telling them of the restoration. In some cases these restored books are being priced the same as unrestored books. **Very Important:** Use the guidelines above to examine books very closely for repairing or restoration before purchase. The more expensive the book, the greater the likelihood of restoration. Major things to look for are: bleaching, whitening, trimming, interior spine and tear reinforcement, gluing, restapling, missing pieces replaced, wrinkles pressed out of covers, recoloring and reglossing covers. Dealers should state that a book has been restored and not expect to get as much as a book unrestored in that condition would bring. Any kind of repair or restoration is considered a defect from the original condition of the book.

GRADING DEFINITIONS

The hardest part of evaluating a comic is being honest and objective with yourself, and knowing what characteristics to look for in making your assessment.

VERY IMPORTANT: A book must be graded in its entirety, considering all defects, fairly and honestly. Do not grade just the cover alone. A book in any of the grades listed must be in **ORIGINAL UNRESTORED** condition. **Restored books** must be described as such. The value of an extensively restored book may improve slightly from its original unrestored state. After examining these characteristics a comic may be assigned to one of the following grades:

MINT (M): Absolutely perfect in every way, regardless of age. The cover has full lustre, is crisp, cut square and shows no imperfections of any sort. The cover and all pages are extra white and fresh; the spine is tight, flat, and clean; not even the slightest blemish can be detected around staples, along spine and edges or at corners. Arrival dates pencilled on the cover are usually acceptable. As comics must be truly perfect to be in this grade, they are obviously extremely scarce and seldom are offered for sale. Books prior to 1963 in this grade can bring 20 to 500 per cent more.

NEAR MINT (NM): Like new or newsstand condition, as above, but with very slight loss of lustre, or a slight off-centered cover, or a minor printing error. Could have slight color fading, or a minor blemish that keeps it out of the Mint category, and white to extra white cover and pages. Any defects noticeable would be very minor. This grade is also very rare in books prior to 1963.

VERY FINE (VF): Slight wear beginning to show; possibly a small wrinkle or a minor stress line at staples or where cover has been opened a few times; still clean and flat with most of cover gloss retained. Very slight yellowing acceptable.

FINE (FN): Tight cover with some wear, but still relatively flat, clean and shiny with no subscription crease, writing on cover, yellowed margins or tape repairs. Stress lines around staples and along spine beginning to show; minor color flaking possible at spine, staples, edges or corners. Slight yellowing acceptable.

VERY GOOD (vg): Obviously a read copy with original printing lustre and gloss almost gone; some discoloration, but not soiled; some signs of wear and minor markings, but none that deface the cover; usually needs slight repair around staples and along spine which could be rolled; cover could have a minor tear or crease where a corner was folded under or a loose centerfold; no chunks missing. Slight yellowing acceptable.

GOOD (g): An average used copy complete with both covers and no panels missing; slightly soiled or marked with possible creases, minor tears or splits, rolled spine and small color flaking, but perfectly sound and legible. A well-read copy, but perfectly acceptable with no chunks missing. **Minor** tape repairs usually occur and slight browning (no brittleness) acceptable, although tape repairs should be considered a defect and priced accordingly.

FAIR (f): Very heavily read and soiled, but complete with possibly a small chunk out of cover; tears needing repairs and multiple folds and wrinkles likely; damaged by the elements, but completely sound and legible, bringing 50-70% of good price.

POOR (p): Damaged; heavily weathered; soiled; or otherwise unsuited for collection purposes.

COVERLESS (c): Coverless comics turn up frequently, are usually hard to sell and in many cases are almost worthless. It takes ingenuity and luck to get a good price; e.g., color xerox covers will increase the saleability. A cover of an expensive book is scarcer and worth more. However, certain "high demand" issues could bring up to 30 percent of the good price.

IMPORTANT: Comics in all grades with fresh extra white pages usually bring more. Books with defects such as pages or panels missing, coupons cut, torn or taped covers and pages, brown or brittle pages, restapled, taped spines, pages or covers, watermarked, printing defects, rusted staples, stained, holed, or other imperfections that detract from the original beauty, are worth less than if free of these defects.

Many of the early strip reprint comics were printed in hardback with dust jackets. Books with dust jackets are worth more. The value can increase from 20 to 50 percent depending on the rarity of book. Usually, the earlier the book, the greater the percentage. Unless noted, prices listed are without dust jackets. The condition of the dust jacket should be graded independently of the book itself.

SCARCITY OF COMIC BOOKS RELATED TO GRADE

1900-1933 Comics: Most of these books are bound with thick cardboard covers and are very rare to non-existant in better than fine condition. Due to their extreme age, paper browning is very common. Brittleness could be a problem.

1933-1940 Comics: There are many issues from this period that are very scarce in any condition, especially from the early to mid-1930s. Surviving copies of any particular issue range from a handful to several hundred. Near Mint to Mint copies are extremely rare to virtually non-existant. Known occurences of this grade number 5 or less copies for any particular issue. Most surviving copies are in Fine or less condition. Brittleness or browning of paper is fairly common and could be a problem.

1941-1954 Comics: Surviving comic books would number from less than 100 to several thousand copies of each issue. Near Mint to Mint copies are a little more common, especially during the war years (1942-1945), but are still relatively scarce with only a dozen or so copies in this grade existing of any particular issue. Exceptions would be recent warehouse finds of most Dell comics (6-100 copies, but usually 30 or less), and Harvey comics (1950s-1970s) surfacing. Due to low paper quality of the late 1940s and 1950s, many comics from this period are rare in Near Mint to Mint condition. Browning of paper could be a problem.

1955-1962 Comics: As comic book sales continued to drop during the 1950s, this period probably has some of the rarest comic books published, especially in Very Fine or better condition. Many Atlas and Marvel comics have chipping along the trimmed edges (Marvel chipping) which reduces even more the number of surviving high grade copies.

1963-Recent comics: Early 60s comics are rare in Near Mint to Mint condition today but surviving copies would number in the hundreds to thousands by the late 1960s and 1970s. Of course many of the 1980s comics would number in the hundreds of thousands surviving copies with Near Mint to Mint being very common.

When you consider how few Golden and Silver Age books exist compared to the current market, you will begin to appreciate the true rarity of these early books. In many cases less than 5-10 copies exist of a particular issue in Near Mint to Mint condition, while most of the 1930s books do not exist in this grade at all.

STORAGE OF COMIC BOOKS

Acids left in comic book paper during manufacture are believed to be the primary cause of aging and yellowing, although exposure to atmospheric pollutants can be another factor. Improper storage can accelerate the aging process.

The importance of storage is proven when looking at the condition of books from large collections that have surfaced over the past few years. In some cases, an entire collection has brown or yellowed pages approaching brittleness. Collections of this type were probably stored in too much heat or moisture, or exposed to atmospheric pollution (sulfur dioxide) or light. On the other hand, other collections of considerable age (30 to 50 years) have emerged with creamy white, supple pages and little sign of aging. Thus we learn that proper storage is imperative to insure the long life of our comic book collections.

Store books in a dark, cool place with an ideal relative humidity of 50 percent and a temperature of 40 to 50 degrees or less. Air conditioning is recommended. Do not use regular cardboard boxes, since most contain harmful acids. Use acid-free boxes instead. Seal books in Mylar[1] or other suitable wrappings or bags and store them in the proper containers or cabinets, to protect them from heat, excessive dampness, ultraviolet light (use tungsten filament lights), polluted air, and dust.

Many collectors seal their books in plastic bags and store them in a cool dark room in cabinets or on shelving. Plastic bags should be changed every two to three years, since most contain harmful acids. Cedar chest storage is recommended, but the ideal method of storage is to stack your comics (preferably in Mylar[1] bags) vertically in acid-free boxes. The boxes can be arranged on shelving for easy access. Storage boxes, plastic bags, backing boards, Mylar[1] bags, archival supplies, etc. are available from dealers. (See ads in this edition.)

Some research has been done on deacidifying comic book paper, but no easy or inexpensive, clear-cut method is available to the average collector. The best and longest-lasting procedure involves soaking the paper in solutions or spraying each page with specially prepared solutions. These procedures should be left to experts. Covers of comics pose a special problem in deacidifying due to their varied composition of papers used.

Here is a list of persons who offer services in restoration or archival supplies:

—Bill Cole, P.O. Box 60, Randolph, MA 02368-0060. Archival supplies, storage protection, deacidification solutions.

—The Restoration Lab, Susan Cicconi, P.O. Box 632, New Town Branch, Boston, MA 02258.

—The Art Conservatory, Mark Wilson, P. O. Box 1609, Longview, WA 98632. Restoration.

—Comic Conservation Lab, Jef Hinds, P.O. Box 5L, Bakersfield, CA 93385. PH: (805) 872-8428. Restoration & preservation supplies.

—Lee Tennant Enterprises, P.O. Box 296, Worth, IL 60482. Preservation supplies.

[1]*Mylar is a registered trademark of the DuPont Company.*

1989 MARKET REPORT

by Bob Overstreet[1]

Dramatic increases far beyond expectations were recorded in the comic marketplace during the past year. While the national economy continued it's slow upward expansion, the comic marketplace posted significant gains in most pre-1970 books. By year's end, most DC and Marvel Silver Age books were on fire!

Naturally the release of the Batman movie generated widespread interest in fandom. This led to large increases in all Batman related titles. Nicholson's excellent portrayal of The Joker created unusual demand for all Joker covers and appearances. The Joker has always been one of the most popular DC villains, so don't look for his prices to drop after Batman returns to more normal times.

Surprisingly the largest increases were posted in the Silver Age period. Prices doubled and tripled on many of the key Silver Age issues with no ceiling yet in sight. Books that were considered slow sellers in past years have disappeared from dealer's shelves almost unnoticed. This past year's increases begin to reflect the enormous

[1]*With helpful assistance from Steve Geppi, Hugh O'Kennon, Ron Pussell, Jay Maybruck, Joe Vereneault, Dan Malan, Rick Sloane, John Snyder, Terry Stroud, Gary Colabuono, Walter Wang, James Payette, Jon Warren, Stephen Fishler, Harry Thomas, Bruce Hamilton, John Verzyl, Gary Carter, Mark Wilson and Joe Mannarino.*

attention now given to the Silver Age market by fandom. In the short term, one would expect the growth in the Silver Age market to continue at it's rapid pace. Many collector's from this period are now reaching their prime earning years, and they evidently are not hesitant in spending large amounts to reaquire those fond memories.

Collectables of all types were on the increase with some reaching fever-pitch levels. Disney animation cels and artwork set astounding records with a single black and white cel with background selling for $450,000 in late 1989. Toys, original art, autographs, premiums, Pop culture (Warhol) and baseball memorabilia all experienced heightened awareness and great value appreciation.

While attending some of the major comic conventions last year, it soon became obvious that vintage Batman and related comics could not be touched at anywhere near listed guide prices. We also learned that most '30s and '40s DCs, Timelys and other key books were selling in poor to fair condition at prices way above the listed good value. In year's past, books in good condition had to be priced low to sell. Today they are selling very well in low grade and equally as well in high grade. However, there seems to be some market resistance to books in the middle grades (VG + , Fine, Fine +). This resistance could be caused in part by a tendency to overgrade a VG to a Fine. But, whatever the reason for it, we feel the current general spread of 1-3-7 does not accurately reflect the current market on some titles. For this reason, most important key books have been changed to a 1-2½-6 spread in this edition. Most all high demand '30s and '40s DC and Timely runs have also gone to this spread.

The whole grading section has been updated in this edition. Please note that the highest grade is now just Mint, which means a perfect copy. Terms such as Pristine Mint, Superb Mint, etc. are still being used in the market by some to describe the exceptional. However, no matter how it is described, a perfect book is still just Mint. Today's market has become stricter in grading Mint books, and in 99 per cent of the cases the highest grade observed in vintage books will only be NM, not Mint. In recent years, many dealers and collectors have learned that 1930s to early 1960s books in NM-Mint condition are extremely rare to non-existent. This is why the Mint listing was changed to NM last year, followed by Pristine Mint dropping to Mint this year.

Of course, as we explained last year, true mint books from the 1970s and 1980s do exist, and the NM value listed should be interpreted as a Mint value for these books.

The comic book market enjoyed unprecedented growth in 1989 as the guide's circulation increased by 30 per cent. This expanded exposure of the guide obviously caused several large collections to surface during the year. One such collection was purchased by a Canadian dealer. It consisted of 20,000 comics, pulps and paperbacks from 1935-1985, with around 12,000 pre-1960 books. Virtually all the comic books are high grade, white-paged copies. Books from this collection have been selling at 1.5 and more times guide list. Included in this collection were near complete runs of most DC titles from 1944-up as well as many Timelys, Qualitys, westerns, etc.

Another large collection turned up in Victoria, B.C. containing 1500 books with a retail value of $34,000. In one day, over $30,000 was sold to anxious buyers.

Many other collections entered the market, but demand far outstripped the supply. Late in the year a collection of 1930s *Mickey Mouse Magazines*, 1940s *Walt Disney's Comics & Stories* and Big Little Books surfaced. There were multiple copies of many issues. The market immediately absorbed the whole collection at above guide list prices.

The San Diego Comic Con (largest in the Country) enjoyed a record breaking attendance last year. Comic books of all types, Golden and Silver Age were selling like hot cakes! The dollar volume of sales at this convention was more than has ever been reported in the past. We observed that pedigree books were selling extremely well and setting record prices. Hottest titles were DC with most DC Church copies selling for 4-5 times guide generally. Larson's, San Francisco, Denver, Pennsylvania and other pedigree books were bringing 1.5 to 2 times guide list. It also became obvious this year that demand was way up for all key origin and first appearance issues (all companies) as well as classic covers within runs.

Like San Diego, the earlier Chicago Con was packed with shoulder-to-shoulder crowds. Many rare comics sold at this convention including a Fn Superman #1 for $10,000. Chicago, Atlanta and other Spring to Summer conventions all build to the August San Diego show. The San Diego Convention has become the largest in the country and attracts collectors from all over the U.S. as well as around the world. San Diego today has replaced the 1970s Seuling New York July 4th shows which at that time were the largest in the country.

It has long been known by E.C. fans that Bill Gaines (publisher of E.C.'s) had put back 12 copies of each book published. Each stack of 12 copies were wrapped and sealed in paper and placed in a large box that was also sealed. In August Bob Overstreet was invited to go to New York to participate, along with Russ Cochran, in the opening of these hundreds of small time capsules. We doned white film editor's gloves and began opening the packages and sorting through these beautiful books. We were immediately swept back to 1950. The books were fresh, subtle and had that familiar smell we E.C. fans remember from our childhood. Russ Cochran will be selling these books, probably through auction beginning in 1990.

To sum up, Batman and Joker related comics were the highest in demand causing substantial price increases in this edition.

All early 1960s Silver Age books were on fire, especially DCs and Marvels. High grade copies were not available to meet the tremendous demand, forcing prices up.

There were many record sales covering all genres of comics such as a vf-nm Batman #1 for $16,000; another in nm for $16,500. But the record breaker was the Church copy of Marvel #1 trading for $108,000. This trade was finalized at the San Diego Convention. The books involved in the trade were all pedigree Church, Denver, etc. copies—books that had a real value equal to the dollar amount set.

1930s Titles—Although there has been large price increases in the past few years, inventories continued to decline in this extremely scarce area. Demand still far outpaces supply. DC and Centaur are again the primary leaders, closely followed by early *Famous Funnies*. Most other '30s titles seldom surface in today's market remaining scarce to not-available. Low supply and high demand continued to force prices upward. A few sales of early DC's are: *Action* #1vg(rest.)—$7500, fvf (rep.)—$17000, fn(rest.)—$14000; #2fn—$2000; #4fn—$1400, g+(rest.)—$700; #10vf+—$2300; #11vg+—$395; #16vf+—$750; #18fn+—$300; *Detective* #7,10vg+(rep.)—$500 ea; #18fn+—$900; #22fn—$650; *More Fun* #12g+—$175; #15vf(MH)—$1350; #17fvf(rep.)—$575; #20vf+—$495, g—$115; #21nm—$495; #22nm(MH)—$715; #36vg—$150; #42fn+—$275; #49vg—$138; *Movie* #1fvf—$750; *New Book Of Comics* #2fn+—$500 trade, $250 cash; *New Comics* #2vf+—$2050; #6gvg—$200; #12vf+—$1050; #21fn+—$450; #24vg—$160; #25fn—$210; #31vf—$365, vg—$155; *New Fun* #1fr—$1000, fr—$800, pr, nbc, brittle, pm—$300; #2pr/fr—$850, vg+—$3000, fr+—$850; #3fr—$850, vg/fn(rep.)—$1400; #4fr—$850; #6fr—$1200, pr—$470; *New York World's Fair 1939* vgf—$675; *Superman* #1vg+(rest.)—$8500. Other reported sales: *Ace* #1fn+—$750; *Comics Magazine* #1vf—$2000; *Detective Pict. Stories* #4vf—$450; *Famous Funnies A Carnival Of Comics* #1vf+—$2000, nm—$2250; *Famous Funnies* #1g+(rest.)—$450; *The Funnies* #1fn—$500; *King* #4vf—$350; #5vf—$280; *Single Series* #21fvf—$75.

1940s Titles—First issues and key issues from all publishers were in high demand. All super hero, Fiction House and early Disney titles sold well in all grades. The DC titles were in highest demand followed by Centaur, Timely and Fawcett. With the upcoming release of the Captain America movie, interest has begun to increase in all Captain America related titles. However, it is unlikely that we will see the dramatic increases that accompanied the Batman movie. Good collections remained very difficult to buy due to more and more dealers entering the market. Competition was keen between dealers trying to buy the few collections that did turn up. The very high collector demand for good books and the infrequent opportunity for a dealer to replace books sold is driving prices to higher levels. In many cases, dealers were not anxious to sell their better material, pricing them very high. At the conventions, most material observed was priced at over guide list. At year's end we were beginning to see price ceilings for many of the misc. publishers of this period as demand shifted to the Silver Age.

DC—With the focus on the Batman movie, all Batman and Joker comics took off. This extreme high demand for Batman spilled over into all other DC titles and issues making this company's books the undisputed leader in the collector's market. We observed many issues bringing multiples of guide list which forced prices to even higher levels in this edition. *Green Lantern, All-American, Flash, All-Flash, More Fun* and *All Star* had strong sales, while Superman related titles had some gains. *Wonder Woman, Boy Commandos, Sensation* and *Superboy* were in less demand. *Batman* #1, *Detective* #27 and #168 (origin the Joker) were among the hottest books. *Detective* #27 has now caught up with *Action* #1 as the most valuable comic book. The Denver *Batman* #1NM sold for $16,500 and will probably resell for $20,000 + before this guide is released. Other hot DC books were all *Batman* and *Detective* Joker covers, *Adventure* #40 & 48, *All-American* #16, *Flash Comics* #1, *Green Lantern* #1 and *All-Star* #3. All first appearance and origin issues were in very high demand. A collection of brittle *Batmans* and *Detectives* sold for 2x guide list. Most Batman and related titles were selling for an average of 1.5x guide list. This company's material will continue to perform like blue chip stock in the years ahead and has always been an excellent investment. Reported sales: *Action* #23fn—$475; #123vf + —$150; *Adventure* #40pr—$500; #41gvg—$200; #42(MH)—$2300; #45(MH)—$1800; #47(MH)—$2000; #55vf—$275; #59vf + —$285; #83,85nm—$350; #100vf—$225; *All-American* #16nm + (S.F., coupon replaced)—$9000, fn(rest.)—$6500; #20vf—$750; #44,45,49nm—$500 ea.; #69vf—$110; #95vf + —$250; #100nm—$475; *All Flash* #18vf + —$225; *All Star* #1gvg—$600, vg—$1800; #4fr—$185, vf(rest.)—$1100; #6fr—$165; #9vgf—$325; #31vf—$400; #36fn + —$575; *Batman* #1vf(rep.)—$8500, vg(rep.)—$4300, fr—$1100, fr—$1450, fr(no-c)—$400, vg(rep.)—$6000; #2-10 (set, fn-vf)—1.3x guide; #2vf(rest.)—$2100, g—$550; #3vf + —2750, fr + —$220, g + —$425, vg + —$750; #4fn + —$1200; #5fn + (rest.)—$475; #6vgf—$300, nm + —$1200; #11fn + —$850; #15nm—$900, vf + —$600; #16nm—$2500; #17vf + —$825; #23nm—$450; #24vf—$500; #27vf + —$525;a #42vg—$100;s #47nm—$1000; #100vf + —$800; *Detective* #27vg + (rep.)—$9000, fn—$11000, fn—$11,500; #35nm(Larson)—$2600; #32vgf—$595; #38fn + —$2850; #39g—$300; #40vf + —$1800; #60fn + —$525; #66fvf—$675; #74fvf—$425; #124fn + —$220; #168vg—$650; *Flash* #37nm—$500; #40nm—$450; #87vf + —375; #98vf—$475; #104vf(rep.)—$1200; *Green Lantern* #1vf(rep)—$1300; #10vf + —$400; *Leading* #1g + —$300; #4g—$100; *More Fun* #52vg—$3000; #53fvf—$3200; #54vf—$1800; #56fn—$450; #57gvg(rest.)—$325; #67vf(rest.)—$550; *Star Spangled* #1(MH)—$3000; #3(MH)—$935; *Superman* #1vg + (rest.)—$8500, vf(rest.)—$11,000; #4vg—$550; #6fn(rep.)—$400; #7fvf(rep.)—$600; #11nm—$550; #24vf—$475, vf(rest.)—$400; #76fn + —$250; *New York World's Fair 1940*nm—$1200; *World's Finest* #1-18 (set, vg-nm)—1.2x list.

TIMELY—Low grade copies sold at over guide while high grade sold at around guide. A very popular line of books with solid sales, especially *Captain America*. Anticipation of the Captain America movie due out in 1990 could increase demand. Supplies of all titles were scarce last year and a shift in demand could easily drive up prices. Marvel has several projects in the works to promote their early characters. With the high price increases DC's have enjoyed the past several years, this company's books may be poised to move this year. Reported sales: *All Select* #2nm—$600; *All Winners* #1vf + —$2500; #21fn—$400; *Captain America* #1g + —$1600, vf—$5000, vf—$5250, fn—$2800; #3vf—$1200; #4fvf—$650, vf—$1000; #8vg +—$300; #9nm—$1200, fn +—$425; #45nm +—$575; #52nm +—$500; *Daring* #2vg—$700; *Human Torch* #5nm—$1450; #6,7g—$90; #8nm—$975; #9vf—$450, fn—$250, #23vf +—$275; *Kid Komics* #2m—$700; #4nm—$375; #8,9nm—$275 ea.; *Marvel Mystery* #1vf—$22,000; #9vg(rest.)—$500; #12fn—$500, vg—$265; #18nm—$725; #28nm—$490; #32nm—$550; #44nm—$450; #65vf—$200; #73nm—$325; *Mystic*(1st) #7nm—$1200; *Red Raven* #1fvf—$1600; *Sub-Mariner* #1fn—$1500; #9nm—$600; #18nm—$330; *Tough Kid Squad* #1vf +—1500, fn +—$1400; *USA* #7m—$1200; #14nm—$375; *Young Allies* #1gvg—$325, nm—$1600, nm—$2000; #3nm—$950; #4vf +—$575.

CENTAUR—Remained scarce with continued strong demand. *Arrow* and *Funny Pages* are the most sought-after titles. Reported sales: *Amazing Mystery Funnies* #1vf +—$1500, vf +—$1200; V2#7(MH)—$2400; *Arrow* #1vg +—$400; *Keen Detective* #4(Larson)—$300; #7vf—$420; *Star Rangers* #6(MH)—$750; *Super Spy* #1(Denver)—$650.

FAWCETT—*Captain Marvel* and *Captain Marvel Jr.* enjoyed solid sales last year. *Marvel Family* was very popular with good sales as well as *Captain Midnight, Spy Smasher, Bulletman, Slam Bang* and *Nickel*. All their horror and science fiction titles showed increased demand. The early *Masters* remained scarce, selling very well whenever they surfaced. Reported sales: *America's Greatest* #1vg +—$350; *Captain Marvel* #1g—$850; *Captain Marvel Story Book* #1vf—$135; *Holiday* #1fn—$200; *Master* #1vg—$600; #2vg—$400; #3fn—$500; #21fn +—$600; *Nickel* #1fvf—$450; *Slam Bang* #3vf—$340; *Spy Smasher* #1vg +—$250; *Whiz* #1—$9000 (cash/trade); *Wow* #2vg +—$150.

FOX—*Wonderworld, Mystery Men* and Lou Fine art titles sold well but the supply was very limited. All titles enjoyed small increases due more to scarcity than increased demand. There was increased interest in *Phantom Lady, Blue Beetle* and the jungle titles. Several Church runs of *Rulah, Jo-Jo*, etc. sold for 1.75 to 1.9x guide list. A *Wonder* #1vf sold for $1925. *Wonderworld* #3 (1st Flame) is the book to watch in the upcoming years. Collectors feel this book is scarce and undervalued. Don't be surprised to see this book pass $1000 in the next few years.

GLEASON—Moderate sales overall with early issues of *Daredevil, Boy* and *Silver Streak* remaining very hard to find. The demand centered more around the number ones and keys of this publisher with other issues reaching a plateau and leveling off.

DISNEY—Demand for these titles continued to pick up, especially for the early issues and keys in higher grades. Mid-run issues, e.g. *Comics & Stories* after #100 are still at a plateau in the lower grades. This is due mainly to the enormous print runs of this material and the resulting large supply in today's market. Interest was fueled by the publicity surrounding animation cels and artwork. *Mickey Mouse Magazines, Uncle Scrooge*, pre-Barks *Comics & Stories*, and Mickey Mouse and Donald Duck *Four Color* showed increased demand. Mickey Mouse *Four Color* #16 became the hottest Disney book with few copies surfacing. A damaged and torn file copy sold for $2100 while a very fine copy brought $4200. A vf complete copy of *Mickey Mouse Book* surfaced at year's end and created excitement in the market with offers given at multiples of guide list. Early in the year a high grade collection of books was bought by a dealer who sold them quickly at 1.25x to 1.5x guide list. File copies of *Four Color* #386, 147, 223, 159, 318 sold for 1.5x to 1.75x guide list. Other reported Sales: *Four Color* #9vg +—$500; #16fr—$300; #62gvg—$210; #147nm—$500; #189vf—$210; #178vf +—$325; #199vf +—$330; #214nm—$65; #231nm—$65; #261nm—$66; #223vf +—$300; #308nm—$145; #328vf—$125; *Mickey Mouse Mag.* (1st) #1fn—$1200; *Mickey Mouse Mag.* V5#12fn +—$1800; *Walt Disney's C&S* #1vf—$2400; #2fr—$110; #32g +—$140.

FICTION HOUSE—Reported sales were strong. Early issues of *Jumbo* remained very scarce with sales for low grade recorded at multiples of guide list. *Planet* was highly sought along with *Wings, Rangers, Jungle* and *Jumbo*. Recorded sales: *Jumbo* #8gvg(rest.)—$350; *Planet* #3vg—$300; #6g—$150; #37vf—$140; #53vf—$110; #55vf+ —$145; *Sheena* #10vf—$100; *Wings* #1vf+ —$500.

QUALITY—*Blackhawk, Military* and *Plastic Man* were the most popular with the other titles enjoying average sales. Reported sales: *Hit* #1fn+ —$600; *Military* #3g—$100; #4g—$80; #6,7g—$60; #15vg+ —$75; #31vg—$40; *National* #1vf—$700; #11nm—$275; *Police* #1vg+(rest.)—$500; #5fn—$250; *Smash* #25vf+ —$195; #28vf—$125; *Uncle Sam* #1nm—$750. Low Grade copies of most titles sold very well.

MLJ—There was good demand for *Pep, Zip* and *Top-Notch* and interest in early Archie titles. The solid collector's base and the scarcity of supply has created a slow but steady increase for all early 1940 titles. Low grade copies continued to have strong sales when available. *Katy Keene* reached a plateau with prices leveling off during the year. Recorded sales: *Pep* #17vf—$475.

HARVEY—Early super hero titles such as *Green Hornet* and *Black Cat* sold well as did *Dick Tracy* and strip reprint titles. With the Dick Tracy movie release in 1990, there could be renewed interest in all his collectibles. Other titles registered slow to moderate sales. A nm *Green Hornet* #1 sold for $900.

CLASSICS—Huge demand for high grade issues. These books continued to grow in strength with all editions selling well. Most dealers reported increasing difficulty in replacing depleted stock. Growth in demand for these books should continue in the years ahead with planned projects and books in the works by Dan Malan and others. *Juniors* and *World Around Us* titles also sold very well. An original classics cover painting sold for $1000.

FUNNY ANIMAL—*Looney Tunes* and Bugs Bunny *Four Color* showed moderate sales, especially in high grade. The Church copy of *Looney Tunes* #1 sold for $4500. All DC titles were strong as were the Timely titles. The ACG *Ha Ha, Giggle,* etc. were also in demand. Most Kelly art books were still slow to moderate. All other publishers' titles had moderate sales.

MISCELLANEOUS—Continued strong demand on key or first issues for all publishers. *Shadow Comics* and *Doc Savage* were in high demand with very low supply. *Airboy* and *Air Fighters* still sell extremely well. Nedor Schomburg covers were very popular and sold to anxious buyers in all grades. In fact, all super hero and science fiction titles of the secondary publishers were in demand. Reported sales: *All Negro* #1nm—$500; *Atomic Bomb* #1nm—$100; *Atomic Comics* #1nm—$250; *Air Fighters* #2fn—$550; #5fn+ —$150; *Black Terror* #1nm(Denver)—$860; *Catman* #2nm—$350; #14nm—$133; *Choice* #1(MH)—$1050; *Exciting* #1(MH)—$1500; *Heroic* #1(MH)—$1100; *Hyper Mystery* #1nm—$550; *If The Devil Would Talk* m—$350; *Major Victory* #1fvf—$120; *Miracle* #1fn—$275; *O.K.* #1nm—$260; *Popeye* #2nm—$75; *Power* #1nm—$200; *Prize* #1vf—$200; *Reform School Girl* #1vf—$600; *Red Iceberg* nn—$500, 2nd version fn—$200; *Shadow* #1vf—$800, nm—$1400; V4#2nm—$125, V4#7,9nm—$125; V5#1,9nm—$115; V9#5vf—$150; *Teenage Dope Slaves* #1vg—$125; *Yankee* #1nm—$360.

1950s TITLES—Many different types of books were published in this period and most are very rare in high grade. Whenever nice copies come out, they sell very quickly. A large high grade collection of 700+ books was sold from California late in the year. It had runs of most Atlas and DC titles. The dealer received multiple orders for such titles as *My Greatest Adventure, House of Secrets, Tales of the Unexpected, Amazing Fantasy,* etc. All sold at 2-3x guide list. Other collections surfaced and were absorbed quickly by the market. Most books from this period showed very strong demand which should continue into the years ahead.

ATLAS—Very strong sales for entire runs of all titles, especially in high grade. All western titles were very popular with *Black Rider* and *Whip Wilson* in very high demand. Many sales at multiples of guide were recorded. The pre-hero Atlas/Marvel titles continued to be good investment material.

TV/MOVIE TITLES—All Jay Ward titles (*Rocky & Bullwinkle*, etc.) showed increased interest due to his death in 1989. There were many hot TV titles, especially *Jackie Gleason, Dark Shadows, Howdy Doody, I Love Lucy, Leave It To Beaver, Flintstones, Munsters, Jetsons, Space Ghost, Maverick*, etc. Dell file copies were in very high demand selling at over guide list (when available). The photo cover issues sold the best and all Hanna-Barbera titles were very strong. Unlike Marvel/DC, most comic stores have almost no inventory from this period. All John Wayne movie comics were in high demand selling at over guide list with most Fawcett movie titles having moderate demand. Reported sales: *Captain Nice* #1vf+—$14; *Captain Video* #1nm—$300; *Dark Shadows* #2nm—$30; #5vf—$15; #7nm—$15; *Gidget* #2fn+—$10; *I Love Lucy* #1nm—$75; #26nm—$32; *Munsters* #1vf+—$55; #3vg—$9; #4nm—$30; *Supercar* #1nm—$35.

WESTERNS—All John Wayne comics continued to be very hot. *Sunset Carson* and *Whip Wilson* are also still showing large price increases. The Fawcett and Atlas westerns remained rare in high grade with high demand. Nice copies of most first issues are still very difficult to obtain. *Andy Devine, Bob Steele, Ken Maynard, Lash LaRue* and *Smiley Burnette* are a few examples of popular titles. A *Golden Arrow* #1nm sold for $150; a *John Wayne* #2fvf—$150; #3vf+—$200. There was increased interest in the *Lone Ranger* and *Zorro* with moderate sales in the other Dell titles such as *Roy Rogers, Gene Autry, Red Ryder*, etc. ME's *Ghost Rider, Tim Holt* and *Red Mask* had moderate demand with price reductions occuring in the Frazetta issues of *Durango Kid, Straight Arrow* and other books. Still strong demand for most mint Dell file copies whenever they are offered for sale.

GIANTS—Square-bound books from all publishers were in short supply and high demand. The market is beginning to realize the scarcity of these books in nm condition. Dell file copies continued to sell at above guide list when available.

3-D COMICS—High grade copies of all titles were still in very high demand. Of course, *3-D Batman* was very hot.

DELL/GOLD KEY—Moderate demand for file copies and other high grade copies of most titles. *Little Lulu* has currently reached a plateau compared to previous years. *Popeye* and *Turok* issues enjoyed good sales.

ROMANCE COMICS—Most of these books have been slow sellers laying dormant for the past several years. There seemed to be an increased interest in 1989 and especially in the DC titles. There could be many sleepers in this area as romance comics are still very scarce and have not been as exploited as the other more popular types.

EC COMICS—We had many reports of good sales, especially in the horror titles. The Crypt Keeper appearing on HBO spurred interest in his title *Tales From The Crypt*. A high grade EC collection, near complete, and all vf-nm sold to a collector at around 2x guide list. The earlier (1st 40+) *Mads* remained popular. EC's may begin to have increased demand especially with the high grade Gaines sets appearing on the market beginning in 1990.

ERB COMICS—Tarzan, Korak, etc. continued to show strong demand with good sales all year.

HUMOR COMICS—*Abbott & Costello, The Three Stooges, Sugar & Spike, Bob Hope, Jerry Lewis, Scribbly*, etc. were among the hottest titles. These books had strong sales whenever copies appeared for sale. Most Harvey titles, and *Dennis The Menace* were slow except for early *Richie Rich* issues. *Millie The Model* had moderate sales while all the *Mad* imitators were very strong.

GOOD GIRL-ART COMICS—Strong sales, especially in the Fox titles such as *Rulah, Blue Beetle, Crimes By Women, Women Outlaws*, etc. *Black Cat, Brenda Starr, Undercover Girl* remained popular.

1950s DC—One of the hottest groups of books. Still remained very scarce in high grade. All '50s *Batman* and *Detective* issues were very hot. *Blackhawk* (DC issues) and *Jimmy Olsen* (early issues) were strong. Even most short lived runs such as *Phantom Stranger* and *Romance Trail* were popular. A vfnm run of *Mystery In Space* and *Strange Adventures* sold last year for 2-3x guide list. By year's end all DC horror and science fiction were selling over guide. A *Mystery in Space* #1vf+ sold for $2400. A *House of Mystery* #1vgf brought $100.

HORROR AND CRIME COMICS—All titles from Atlas to Harvey were selling very well. EC horror was up, especially *Tales from the Crypt* and *Vault of Horror*. Grotesque titles such as *Dark Mysteries, The Thing* and *Mysterious Adventures* were popular. Avon titles have been at a plateau for the past several years, but 1989 showed a slight pickup in interest. There were many reported sales of vfnm Atlas, EC, ACG, DC, Charlton and other companies' books bringing 2-3x guide list.

SPORT COMICS—This small area of collecting has been growing every year, primarily due to sports card collecting x-over interest. Fawcett baseball titles are all very hot and remained hard to find driving prices to even higher levels.

ART COMICS—All Kirby books showed strong gains. Frazetta registered a drop in interest, mainly due to the high list price of most of his books. *Thun'da* went down as well as *Durango Kid* and *Straight Arrow* Frazetta issues. Wood, Ditko and Powell were very popular. L.B. Cole books picked up a little while Matt Baker remained slow. Wolverton's *Powerhouse Pepper* showed increased interest.

1960s-1970s TITLES—Marvel: All pre-super hero books were very hot. Of course interest in these books is being held up by the immense popularity of pre-1965 super hero titles. Early issues of all super hero titles registered very strong gains last year becoming explosive by year's end, especially in high grade. DC: Almost everything DC turned to gold. *Batman, JLA, Green Lantern, Atom, Hawkman, Brave and the Bold, Legion* issues, *Metal Men, Showcase, Superman,* 80-pg. *Giants,* etc., etc. were very hot to explosive. The DC war titles such as *Star Spangled War* (Dinosaur issues), *Sgt. Rock, Our Army At War* were also hot. The high interest in Marvel and DC spilled over into all other '60s super hero books. There were many record sales of multiples of guide recorded throughout the year. Don't be surprised to see a $5000 Spiderman #1 in 1990. *Showcase* #4 has now been designated the book that begins the Silver Age, not *Detective* #225. John Jones, although a super hero, never led to anything later and the Flash did. *Detective* #225 however, is still an important key book paving the way for the final coming of the Silver Age.

The early '70s books showed a little pickup in interest, but most mid to late '70s titles remained slow to steady with little price increases needed. Recorded sales: *Action* #252fn+—$200; *Adventure* #247vg+—525; #300vf+—$175; *Advs. of the Jaguar* #1-8nm, 2x guide list; *Advs. of the Fly* #10-20nm, 2x guide list; *Atom* #1nm—$270; #2nm—$90; *Amaz. Spider-Man* #1fn+—$1500; #2fn+ (rest.)—$400; #3vf(rest.)—$250; #129fn+—$125; *Amazing Fantasy* #15fn—$1100, fn+—$2000, vf(rest.)—$1700, $1650, $1200, fn+(rest.)—$1000; *Avengers* #1vf—$450; *Batman* #145nm—2x guide list; Annual #1nm—$275; *Brave and the Bold* #28vf—$700; #43nm—$80; #54nm—$125; *Daredevil* #1vf—$280; *Detective* #225vf(rest.)—$800, vgf—$350; *Fantastic Four* #1nm(rest.)—$2250, vgf(cr.)—$425, vf(rest.)—$1700, vf(rep.)—$1600; #5nm—$500; *Flash* #105fn(rest.)—$370; #123fn+(rest.)—$190; *Green Lantern* #1vf+—$550; #3vf+—$110, #8vf—$44, #16vf—$24; *Hawkman* #1fvf—$40; *Ironman* #1vf—$140, vf—$150, fvf—$130; *Journey Into Mystery* #83vf(rest.)—$430; *Justice League* #1vgf—$300; #9vg+—$40, nm—$125; #13vf+—$40; *Lois Lane Annual* #1nm—$70; *Metal Men* #1vf—$86; *My Greatest Adv.* #80nm—$175; #81nm—$40, fvf—$20; *Mystery In Space* #53frg—$30; *Rip Hunter* #5vf—$20; #2-9nm, 2x list; *Secret Origins* #1('61)vg—$25; *Showcase* #4vf(rest.)—$1900; #8vf(rest.)—$525; #13vf(rest.)—$440; #22vf(rest.)—$625, fr—$45; #34vf+—$290; #37vf—$75; #38nm—$30; *Superman Annual* #5nm—$75; *Tales To Astonish* #27m—$2500; #57nm—$40; *X-Men* #1fn+(rest.)—$580, fvf—$600, nm—$925, vf—$950, $800; #2 vf—$250; #10vf—$65; #25vf—$22.

1980s TITLES—The comic book marketplace of 1989 can be summarized in a single word - Batman. There has never been a phenomenon like it before. The movie opened in late June and shattered virtually every box office record in existence. The country was enveloped in Batmania. The comic book specialty market anticipated this June release with ever increasing sales of Batman and Batman related products beginning in the third quarter of 1989. *Batman* became a bi-weekly for the summer months, Batman appearances in other DC titles sparked increased sales, *Batman* graphic novels and trade paperbacks became the stars of back list sales, a new *Batman* monthly title, *Legends of the Dark Knight* was born and then came *Arkham Asylum*. A $24.95 hardcover featuring The Batman and his arch enemy The Joker, locked in *Arkham Asylum* for the criminally insane. A total retail value in excess of $4,000,000 - and a complete sell-out within 60 days of release. While the national craze became dormant, perhaps until the inevitable sequel to the movie, the comic book specialty market maintained a high pitched interest in Batman with other huge Batman related successes. *Gotham by Gaslight* and *Digital Justice* were two very successful Batman one-shot projects.

While Batman captured most of the headlines, the rest of the DC line also did very well as new readers discovered and old readers rediscovered the entire DC line. DC has shifted more and more towards the series within a series concept, with a clearly defined beginning and end to a particular story line. This format has been very successful in attracting more interest as new readers have frequent opportunities to jump in and start reading.

The industry leader, Marvel Comics had the most successful year in their history in 1989. Because of their dominant position in the comic book marketplace, and their high visibility characters including Spider-Man, Captain America, The Hulk, Thor, Avengers and of course X-Men, Marvel was able to attract their share of sales from the influx of new readers attracted by the Batman phenomenon. Marvel continued to dominate the newsstand sales as DC continued their strategy of turning their new better selling titles into non returnable, guaranteed profits sales through the specialty market. Marvel has chosen to continue to support the traditional returnable sales outlets which sell approximately one third of the copies they put on the racks.

The success of DC and Marvel again came at the expense of many of the smaller publishers. In spite of the infusion of much new money from thousands of new comic book customers, 1989 was a year of financial problems for many of the smaller, less well known publishers. Anything But Comics, Artists Unlimited, Attitude Comics, Blackthorne, Blue Moon Comics, Cat Head Comics, CFW Comics, Double Diamond Comics, Eastern Comics, Greater Mercury Comics, Hero Comics, Jade Graphics, Kid Gang Comics, Lighthouse Comics, Nicotat Comics, Renegade Comics, Triad Comics, Twilight Twins, and Wehner Publications are among the small press publishers who either ceased publication or whose production schedules were drastically curtailed.

The back issue market on the defunct titles continued to decline with many copies going unwanted at deep discounts from cover price as the market continued to pay the price on the black and white glut of 1987, 1988 and to a lesser degree, 1989.

A few of the independent publishers did have strong 1989 fiscal years. First Comics had a smash success in the television tie in, *Beauty and The Beast*. It sold out of its first printing and demand warranted a second printing. Projects such as this did much to bring new readers into our marketplace. *Beauty and The Beast* was used by retailers to attract more women to comic book reading. First Comics will launch what should prove to be a huge new project in 1990. *Classics Illustrated*, co-published with Berkley Publishing will be placed in thousands of book stores as well as thousands of comic shops and should bring our industry much positive media attention and could produce a new generation of Classics collectors. Mirage Studios continued to do very well as the *Teenage Mutant Ninja Turtles* continued their hit series of animated cartoons on television. Back issues of the Turtles should be up in 1990 as the feature length movie opens. Now Comics had an unexpected success with *The Green Hornet*. Excellent art and story combined to capture the attention of the comic marketplace. Dark Horse had major hits with *The Predator* and *Aliens* titles. These books commanded premium prices for first editions in the secondary market. Eclipse's Clive Barker adaptation titled *Tapping The Vein* found an eager audience and went into a second printing. It is becoming the rule rather than the exception that publishers will go to second, third and higher printings if demand continues for back issues. This practice has undoubtedly had a negative impact on the collector market for these particular issues but on the other hand, it has enabled more readers to obtain copies of the issues and thus increase the overall interest in the title.

Most of the independent publications which came out in 1989 were purchased to be read by interested consumers. There was very little interest in back issues of most of these titles and hardly any commanded any premiums. In fact, more than half of these issues could be bought for less than cover price on the secondary market as retailers put unsold copies in their bargain bins rather than bag them, inventory them and charge premium prices for them.

In 1989 the reader/collector continued to be more discriminating in his/her buying practices. The marketplace is more demanding than ever and sub-standard art, writing, pricing, packaging are no longer tolerated. This trend appears to be the force behind the Darwinian processes shaping this evolving marketplace.

INVESTOR'S DATA

The following table denotes the rate of appreciation of the top 50 most valuable Golden Age titles over the past year and the past five years (1985-1990). The retail value for a complete mint run of each title in 1990 is compared to its value in 1989 and 1985. The 1971 values are also included as an interesting point of reference. The rate of return for 1990 over 1989, and the yearly average rate of return for each year since 1985, is given. For example, a complete mint run of *Detective Comics* retails at $194,745 in 1990, $148,016 in 1989, and $65,279 in 1985. The rate of increase of 1990 over 1989 can be easily calculated at 31.6%, while the average yearly increase or rate of return over the past five years is 39.7%. This means that the mint value of this title has increased an average of 39.7% each year over the past five years.

The place in rank is given for each title by year, with its corresponding mint value. This table can be very useful in forecasting trends in the market place. For instance, the investor might want to know which title is yielding the best dividend from one year to the next, or one might just be interested in seeing how the popularity of titles changes from year to year. For instance, *Famous Funnies* was in 8th place in 1971 and has dropped to 18th place in 1990. But this title could be on the move to reclaim its original position, as it has changed from 33rd place to 18th in the past five years and currently continues to show a strong price increase (1990 over 1989).

Batman overtook *Superman* for the number 7 spot, and *Adventure Comics* overtook *Marvel Mystery Comics* for the number 4 spot this year. *Comic Cavalcade* entered the top 50 jumping from 54th to 49th spot. *Green Lantern* increased by 15.8% from 1989, but shows a yearly average increase of 22.1%. *Shadow Comics* was up 35.5% and *Classic Comics* up 17.7%.

The following tables are meant as a guide to the investor and it is hoped that they might aid him in choosing titles in which to invest. However, it should be pointed out that trends may change at anytime and that some titles can meet market resistance with a slowdown in price increases, while others can develop into real comers from a presently dormant state. In the long run, if the investor sticks to the titles that are appreciating steadily each year, he shouldn't go very far wrong.

The Silver Age titles continued to show movement, especially early issues of Marvels and DCs in high grade. Golden & Silver Age titles are continuing to appreciate faster than economic inflationary values during the same period.

TOP THREE TITLES

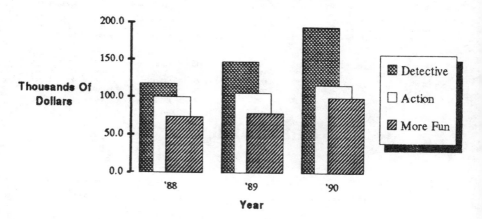

Thousands Of Dollars

Year

Legend: Detective, Action, More Fun

TOP 50 TITLES
TOP 50 TITLES & RATE OF INCREASE OVER 1989 AND 1985 GUIDE VALUES

Title	1990 Guide Rank & Value	%Change From '89 Value	Avg.Yrly. Return '85-'90	1989 Guide Rank & Value		1985 Guide Rank & Value		1971 Guide Rank & Value	
Detective Comics...........1	$194,745	+31.6	+39.7	1	$148,016	2	$65,279	4	$2,747
Action Comics.............2	117,999	+11.0	+14.3	2	106,278	1	68,851	7	2,354
More Fun Comics...........3	100,015	+24.9	+27.8	3	80,066	5	41,855	3	2,816
Adventure Comics..........4	93,768	+28.1	+29.3	5	73,210	7	38,073	2	3,066
Marvel Mystery Comics......5	79,135	+ 3.4	+ 5.4	4	76,530	3	62,265	5	2,584
Four Color................6	76,889	+ 8.6	+13.7	6	70,809	4	45,676	1	4,229
Batman 7	74,357	+58.4	+40.6	8	46,937	10	24,539	19	1,246
Superman.................8	71,416	+11.3	+14.6	7	64,171	6	41,292	13	1,460
Captain America...........9	50,045	+12.3	+13.5	9	44,547	9	29,920	17	1,303
All Star Comics............10	49,975	+13.0	+20.9	10	44,240	11	24,450	10	1,657
All American Comics........11	$48,405	+25.6	+27.1	13	$38,540	16	$20,570	24	$1,189
Flash Comics..............12	47,015	+19.6	+21.7	12	39,300	14	22,565	15	1,344
Whiz Comics..............13	40,578	+ 1.8	+ 5.9	11	39,861	8	31,298	14	1,357
Donald Duck..............14	29,946	+ 2.2	+ 5.3	14	29,300	12	23,714	53	604
World's Fair & Finest........15	29,665	+16.4	+21.5	17	25,496	20	14,280	33	841
Planet Comics.............16	29,162	+13.0	+15.3	16	25,805	18	16,530	50	613
Walt Disney's C & S........17	28,454	+ 4.6	+ 5.1	15	27,194	13	22,691	12	1,487
Famous Funnies...........18	25,855	+21.2	+36.9	20	21,325	25	9,095	8	2,343
Jumbo Comics.............19	25,850	+14.9	+23.7	19	22,495	25	11,842	16	1,320
Mickey Mouse Magazine.....20	24,195	+14.3	+17.6	21	21,164	23	12,880	18	1,252
Police Comics.............21	$23,766	+ 3.8	+ 8.1	18	$22,890	17	$16,924	30	$903
Star Spangled Comics.......22	22,841	+14.1	+19.0	22	20,020	28	11,718	35	830
Captain Marvel Advs........23	21,322	+11.6	+ 8.4	25	19,098	19	15,012	29	1,009
Master Comics.............24	20,922	+ 7.6	+11.4	23	19,451	22	13,329	28	1,021
Green Lantern.............25	20,015	+15.8	+22.1	27	17,280	32	9,505	87	390
Spirit 26	19,327	-0-	- 1.7	24	19,327	15	21,058	44	645
Dick Tracy...............27	18,769	+ 5.4	+11.7	26	17,809	26	11,836	25	1,116
Classic Comics............28	18,740	+17.7	+27.8	31	15,919	42	7,840	189	65
Sensation Comics..........29	18,293	+ 7.9	+12.2	29	16,952	29	11,375	41	681
Pep Comics..............30	18,279	+ 7.5	+11.0	28	17,001	27	11,785	31	880
Human Torch.............31	$18,140	+ 9.1	+ 5.4	30	$16,620	21	$14,275	46	$632
King Comics..............32	16,348	+ 6.7	+24.9	32	15,315	52	7,289	6	2,490
Sub-Mariner 33	16,235	+ 6.8	+ 6.1	33	15,207	24	12,435	54	601
Feature Book.............34	15,682	+ 4.7	+10.1	34	14,976	30	10,435	26	1,069
Wonder Woman...........35	15,533	+ 9.5	+11.4	36	14,184	31	9,900	64	537
Tip Top Comics...........36	15,525	+ 6.6	+18.6	35	14,570	38	8,036	9	2,088
Target Comics............37	15,385	+28.1	+19.8	44	12,008	45	7,730	38	746
Shadow Comics 38	14,575	+35.5	+26.0	50	10,754	59	6,332	72	495
Jungle Comics............39	14,166	+ 5.9	+15.8	37	13,374	40	7,909	32	861
Amazing-Man Comics.......40	14,145	+ 8.5	+18.9	39	13,035	53	7,265	108	314

Title	1990 Guide Rank & Value	%Change From '89 Value	Avg. Yrly. Return '85-'90	1989 Guide Rank & Value		1985 Guide Rank & Value		1971 Guide Rank & Value	
Popular Comics............41	$14,040	+ 7.0	+22.9	38	$13,126	56	$6,547	11	$1,598
Military Comics............42	13,630	+ 9.9	+15.0	42	12,406	44	7,795	68	520
Feature & Feature Funnies...43	13,442	+10.2	+18.7	43	12,198	55	6,949	22	1,214
Silver Streak Comics.......44	13,175	+ 6.1	+11.7	41	12,415	37	8,315	86	394
Marge's Little Lulu.........45	13,028	+ 0.5	+10.2	40	12,957	36	8,619	135	219
Hit Comics................46	12,155	+ 5.9	+ 7.4	45	11,483	35	8,861	67	523
Daredevil Comics..........47	12,090	+11.9	+14.5	49	10,805	54	7,013	45	639
Superboy.................48	11,978	+10.8	+10.3	48	10,815	41	7,895	94	360
Comic Cavalcade..........49	11,913	+20.1	+21.6	54	9,916	62	5,726	93	361
Large Feature Comic.......50	11,672	+ 6.1	+ 6.1	46	10,997	34	8,956	27	1,058

TREND ANALYSIS

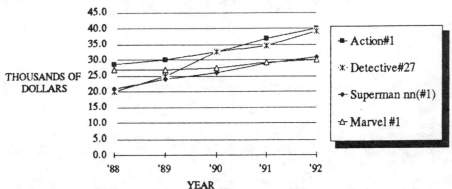

- ■ Action#1
- ✕ Detective#27
- ◆ Superman nn(#1)
- △ Marvel #1

YEAR

The above trend analysis is based on prices from the 1985-1990 Overstreet Price Guide.

The following tables show the rate of return of the 50 most valuable Golden Age books, the 40 most valuable Silver Age titles and the 40 most valuable Silver Age books over the past year. It also shows the average yearly rate of return over the past five years (1990-1985). Comparisons can be made in the same way as in the previous table of the Top 50 titles. Ranking in many cases is relative since so many books have the same value. These books are listed alphabetically within the same value.

50 MOST VALUABLE GOLDEN AGE BOOKS AND RATE OF RETURN

Issue	1990 Guide Rank & Value	%Change From '89 Value	Avg. Yrly. Return '85'90	1989 Guide Rank & Value		1985 Guide Rank & Value	
Action Comics #1.............. 1	$32,500	+ 8.3	+18.2	1	$30,000	2	$17,000
Detective Comics #27........... 1	32,500	+30.0	+45.0	3	25,000	5	10,000
Marvel Comics #1............. 3	27,500	+ 1.9	+ 3.9	2	27,000	1	23,000
Superman #1................. 4	26,000	+ 8.3	+21.6	4	24,000	3	12,500
Whiz Comics #1.............. 5	18,200	-0-	+10.3	5	18,200	4	12,000
Batman #1................... 6	14,500	+48.1	+28.3	7	9,800	6	6,000
Detective Comics #1........... 7	11,400	+14.0	+58.6	6	10,000	18	2,900
All American Comics #16........ 8	10,000	+29.9	+35.6	9	7,700	15	3,600
More Fun Comics #52.......... 9	9,600	+ 6.7	+14.9	8	9,000	8	5,500
Captain America #1............10	9,000	+28.6	+14.6	10	7,000	9	5,200
All Star Comics #3.............11	$7,500	+15.4	+36.1	11	$6,500	23	$2,675
New Fun Comics #1............12	7,200	+28.6	+90.8	15	5,600	73	1,300
Captain Marvel Advs...........13	7,000	+11.1	+ 8.0	13	6,300	10	5,000
Detective Comics #38..........13	7,000	+42.9	+40.9	19	4,900	29	2,300
Flash Comics #1...............13	7,000	+40.0	+38.3	16	5,000	27	2,400
Detective Comics #33...........16	6,500	+32.7	+33.1	19	4,900	26	2,450

Issue	1990Guide Rank & Value		%Change From '89 Value	Avg.Yrly. Return '85'90	1989Guide Rank & Value		1985Guide Rank & Value	
Double Action Comics #2........16		$6,500	-0-	+ 2.4	11	$6,500	7	$5,800
More Fun Comics #53..........18		6,200	+ 6.9	+ 14.4	14	5,800	15	3,600
New Fun Comics #2.............19		5,040	+ 20.0	+ 114.4	24	4,200	—	750
Detective Comics #29...........20		5,000	+ 66.7	+ 38.8	33	3,000	49	1,700
Detective Comics #31...........20		$5,000	+ 70.1	+ 46.7	42	$2,940	58	$1,500
Motion Pic. Funnies Weekly #1....20		5,000	-0-	-0-	16	5,000	10	5,000
Wow Comics #1................20		5,000	-0-	+ 3.8	16	5,000	12	4,200
Action Comics #2..............24		4,800	+ 1.6	+ 4.0	21	4,725	13	4,000
Detective Comics #28...........25		4,600	-0-	+ 11.7	22	4,600	18	2,900
Amazing-Man Comics #5........26		4,500	+ 12.8	+ 32.9	25	3,990	49	1,700
Marvel Mystery Comics #2.......26		4,500	+ 2.3	+ 3.7	23	4,400	14	3,800
Famous Funnies Series #1.......27		4,200	+ 40.0	+ 100.0	33	3,000	—	700
All-Star Comics #1.............28		4,000	+ 10.3	+ 20.0	27	3,625	38	2,000
Batman #2....................28		4,000	+ 42.9	+ 28.5	44	2,800	52	1,650
Action Comics #3..............30		3,800	+ 4.4	+ 6.2	26	3,640	18	2,900
Walt Disney's C&S #1...........31		$3,700	+ 5.7	+ 6.4	28	$3,500	21	$2,800
Adventure Comics #40..........32		3,600	+ 94.6	+ 53.8	88	1,850	111	975
Big Book Of Fun Comics #1......33		3,500	+ 16.7	+ 62.4	33	3,000	—	850
Daring Mystery Comics #1.......33		3,500	+ 16.7	+ 12.9	33	3,000	34	2,125
Detective Comics #2............33		3,500	+ 16.7	+ 38.3	33	3,000	80	1,200
Green Lantern #1..............33		3,500	+ 22.8	+ 28.3	43	2,850	65	1,450
Human Torch #1...............33		3,500	+ 9.4	+ 5.0	30	3,200	21	2,800
Adventure Comics #48..........38		3,400	+ 86.8	+ 49.7	89	1,820	111	975
Superman #2..................38		3,400	+ 5.6	+ 6.2	29	3,220	24	2,600
Jumbo Comics #1..............40		3,300	+ 26.9	+ 40.0	49	2,600	95	1,100
Action Comics #5..............41		$3,200	+ 6.7	+ 6.7	33	$3,000	27	$2,400
Action Comics #7..............41		3,200	+ 7.6	+ 11.2	40	2,975	36	2,050
Action Comics #10.............41		3,200	+ 7.6	+ 11.2	40	2,975	36	2,050
Marvel Mystery Comics #5.......41		3,200	+ 0.5	+ 1.3	31	3,185	17	3,000
Red Raven Comics #1..........41		3,200	+ 6.3	+ 7.8	32	3,010	29	2,300
Famous Funnies #1.............46		3,150	+ 50.0	+ 85.0	67	2,100	—	600
Donald Duck March Of Comics #4.47		3,000	-0-	+ 3.1	33	3,000	24	2,600
New Comics #1................47		3,000	+ 14.3	+ 35.8	48	2,625	98	1,075
Captain America #2............49		2,900	+ 5.0	+ 6.4	46	2,765	31	2,200
Detective Comics #3............49		2,900	+ 16.0	+ 48.2	53	2,500	—	850

TOP TEN ISSUES

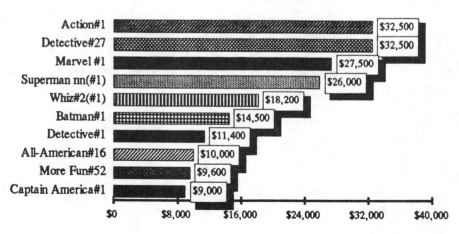

40 MOST VALUABLE SILVER AGE TITLES AND RATE OF INCREASE

Issue	1990 Guide Rank	1990 Guide Value	%Change From '89 Value	Avg.Yrly. Return '85-'90	1989 Guide Rank	1989 Guide Value	1985 Guide Rank	1985 Guide Value
Amaz. Spider-Man	1	$13,109	+66.4	+43.1	2	$7,879	3	$4,158
Showcase	2	12,232	+5089	+27.9	1	8,109	1	5,107
Fantastic Four	3	10,412	+49.7	+24.8	3	6,953	2	4,650
The Flash	4	9,008	+52.9	+34.7	4	5,891	4	3,291
Tales To Astonish/Inc. Hulk	5	6,566	+49.1	+30.5	8	4,404	8	2,601
Brave And The Bold	6	6,375	+29.3	+19.5	6	4,931	5	3,231
X-Men	7	5,979	+18.8	+32.5	5	5,032	9	2,278
Justice League	8	5,781	+25.8	+35.1	7	4,596	10	2,097
Green Lantern	9	5,337	+48.8	+34.0	10	3,586	11	1,975
Sugar & Spike	10	4,731	+10.9	+15.6	9	4,266	7	2,661
Avengers	11	$3,873	+30.7	+ 9.1	11	$2,963	13	$1,852
Journey Into Mystery/Thor	12	3,769	+52.3	+29.7	15	2,475	15	1,516
Challengers Of The Unknown	13	3,706	+28.1	+24.0	12	2,892	14	1,686
Superman's Pal J. Olsen	14	3,144	+16.6	+13.2	14	2,696	12	1,894
Tales Of Suspense/Capt. America	15	2,980	+44.4	+40.1	17	2,063	22	991
Daredevil	16	2,879	+71.4	+35.7	21	1,680	21	1,034
Mystery In Space	17	2,818	+37.1	+26.8	18	2,056	19	1,204
Richie Rich	18	2,744	+ 0.3	+ 0.6	13	2,736	6	2,664
Superman's Girl Friend L. Lane	19	2,621	+25.3	+14.9	16	2,092	17	1,502
Strange Tales	20	2,406	+88.1	+52.0	25	1,279	26	668
Tales Of The Unexpected	21	$2,385	+45.2	+30.9	22	$1,642	24	$938
Cerebus	22	1,876	-8.6	+18.6	19	2,053	23	971
Harvey Hits	23	1,763	+ 1.6	+ 3.4	20	1,736	16	1,508
Iron Man	24	1,530	+74.7	+56.3	30	876	29	401
Our Army At War	25	1,507	+48.3	+20.9	26	1,016	26	737
Atom	26	1,414	+84.8	+84.4	31	765	36	271
Little Archie	27	1,384	+ 0.1	+ 5.0	23	1,383	20	1,106
Sgt. Fury	28	1,313	+79.1	+88.5	32	733	38	242
Advs. Of The Big Boy	29	1,298	-0-	-13.0	24	1,298	18	1,493
G.I. Combat	30	1,213	+29.3	+21.4	28	938	28	586
Aquaman	31	$1,209	+69.1	+54.2	33	$715	31	$326
Doom Patrol	32	1,181	+24.4	+149.9	27	949	46	139
Metal Men	33	1,170	+158.8	+129.0	41	452	43	157
Captain America	34	1,135	+88.5	+60.8	37	602	28	281
Rip Hunter	35	1,105	+66.9	+55.7	34	662	33	294
Hawkman	36	951	+78.8	+44.7	39	532	33	294
Playful Little Audrey	37	897	-0-	+ 2.9	29	897	25	783
Advs. Of The Fly	38	845	+41.5	+24.7	38	597	30	378
Many Loves Of Dobie Gillis	39	805	+25.8	+31.9	36	640	32	310
Conan	40	805	+25.8	+31.9	35	644	27	614

40 MOST VALUABLE SILVER AGE BOOKS AND RATE OF RETURN

Issue	1990 Guide Rank	1990 Guide Value	%Change From '89 Value	Avg.Yrly. Return '85-'90	1989 Guide Rank	1989 Guide Value	1985 Guide Rank	1985 Guide Value
Showcase #4	1	$3,000	+87.5	+34.5	2	$1,600	1	$1,100
Amazing Fantasy #15	2	2,800	+55.6	+30.9	1	1,800	1	1,100
Amaz. Spider-Man #1	3	2,750	+83.3	+53.3	4	1,500	5	750
Fantastic Four #1	4	2,650	+65.6	+28.2	2	1,600	1	1,100
Adventure Comics #247	5	1,600	+14.3	+15.6	5	1,400	4	900
Detective Comics #225	6	1,150	+53.3	+34.1	6	750	9	425
Brave And The Bold #28	7	1,100	+57.1	+42.9	9	700	18	350
X-Men #1	8	990	+32.0	+32.1	6	750	14	380
Incredible Hulk #1	9	950	+35.7	+12.8	9	700	6	580
Justice League #1	10	900	+20.0	+27.4	6	750	14	380
Showcase #8	10	$900	+50.0	+32.9	12	$600	21	$340
Tales Of Suspense #39	12	875	+66.7	+38.3	19	525	24	300
Tales To Astonish #27	13	825	+17.9	+21.3	9	700	12	400
Adventure Comics #210	14	800	+90.5	+60.0	24	420	36	200
Flash #105	14	800	+33.3	+30.0	12	600	22	320
Journey Into Mystery #83	16	750	+29.3	+17.5	14	580	12	400
Avengers #1	17	725	+26.1	+18.2	5	575	4	380
Showcase #22	17	725	+26.1	+28.3	5	575	24	300
Fantastic Four #2	19	700	+21.7	+11.8	15	575	7	440
Amazing Spider-Man #2	20	660	+46.7	+28.9	23	450	28	270

Issue	1990 Guide Rank & Value		%Change From '89 Value	Avg. Yrly. Return '85-'90	1989 Guide Rank & Value		1985 Guide Rank & Value	
Green Lantern #1	20	$660	+ 34.7	+ 27.1	21	$490	26	$280
Superman's Pal J. Olsen #1	22	610	+ 16.2	+ 9.0	19	525	11	420
Fantastic Four #3	23	600	+ 30.4	+ 14.3	22	460	18	350
Showcase #13	23	600	+ 41.2	+ 26.2	26	425	29	260
Showcase #14	23	600	+ 41.2	+ 26.2	26	425	29	260
Brave & The Bold #1	26	575	+ 4.5	+ 7.1	18	550	9	425
Daredevil #1	27	525	+ 50.0	+ 32.5	31	350	36	200
Fantastic Four #4	27	525	+ 47.9	+ 20.4	30	355	29	260
Showcase #6	29	500	+ 33.3	+ 16.4	29	375	27	275
Tales To Astonish #35	29	500	+ 100.0	+ 46.7	47	250	46	150
Showcase #1	31	485	+ 7.8	+ 7.7	23	450	18	350
Fantastic Four #5	32	475	+ 69.6	+ 30.0	40	280	38	190
Amazing Spider-Man #3	33	440	+ 66.0	+ 35.0	43	265	42	160
Brave And The Bold #29	33	440	+ 46.7	+ 53.3	37	300	57	120
Brave And The Bold #30	33	440	+ 46.7	+ 53.3	37	300	57	120
Richie Rich #1	33	440	-0-	-0-	25	440	7	440
Challengers Of The Unknown #1	37	400	+ 14.3	+ 16.4	31	350	34	220
Superman's Girlfriend L. Lane #1	37	400	+ 25.0	+ 12.0	35	320	32	250
Tales Of Suspense #40	37	400	+ 100.0	+ 60.0	55	200	70	100
X-Men #2	40	380	+ 15.2	+ 27.5	34	330	42	160

THE FIRST WAVE OF COMIC BOOKS 1933-1943 (Key books listed and ranked)

The first modern format comic book came out in 1933 and represents the beginning of comic books as we know them today. The impact of these early characters and ideas are today deeply engrained in American folklore and continue to feed and inspire this ever changing industry.

Over the years historians, collectors and bibliofiles have tried to make some sense out of this era. The question 'what are considered to be the most important books?' has been a topic of discussion and debate for many years. With certain criteria considered, how would the top key issues be ranked in order of importance? How would they relate to each other? In an attempt to answer some of these questions, the following list has been prepared. The books are grouped chronologically in the order they were published. The most important books are ranked into seven tiers, with the top six designated with stars. The more important the book is, the more stars it receives. The following criteria were used to determine the importance and placement of each book in each tier:

A. Durability of character(s)
b. Durability of title
c. Popularity of character(s)
d. First app. anywhere of a major character
e. First issue of a title

f. Originality of character (first of a type)
g. First or most significant work of a major artist
h. Starts a trend
i. First of a genre

j. Historical significance
k. First of a publisher
l. First appearance in comic books of a character from another medium

This list was compiled by several people* and represents a collective opinion of all. The list is not perfect, not by any means. Adjustments will be made over time as more input is received. The final ranking of a book depends greatly on the overall importance and impact of that book on the comic book market. Obviously, the further you get away from the top key books, the more difficult it becomes for proper ranking. For this reason, books ranked in the lower numbered tiers could change drastically. The final rating given a book is not based entirely on the quantity of points it receives, but rather the overall weight of the points it does receive. For example, the first appearance of *The Fighting Yank* is not as important as the first appearance of *Superman* who was a trend setting character and long lasting.

In the comics market there are several comics that have become high demand, valuable books due primarily to rarity. A list of the top key books ranked due to value, demand and rarity would look entirely different than what we have here. As we have learned in coins, stamps and other hobbies, rarity is an important factor that affects value and it is not our intention to demean the collectibility of any particular book that is rare. Quite the contrary. There are many rare books that would enhance anyone's collection. Consideration of rarity, for the ranking of books in this list has been kept at a minimum.

The following list covers the period 1933 through 1943 and includes **every** key book of this period of which we are currently aware. Any omissions will be added in future lists. It should be noted that many other issues, although highly collectible, were not considered important for the purpose of this list: i.e., origin issues, early issues in a run, special cover and story themes, etc.

*Special thanks is due **Landon Chesney** who contributed considerable energy and thought to the individual write-ups; to **David Noah** who polished and edited, and to the following people who contributed their time and ideas to the compilation of this list: Hugh O'Kennon, Steve Geppi, Richard Halegua, John Snyder, Joe Tricarichi, Walter Wang, Jon Warren, Bruce Hamilton, Ray Belden and Chuck Wooley

NOTE: All **first issues** are included as well as books that introduce an important new character, or has key significance in some other way.

CHRONOLOGICAL LIST OF KEY COMIC BOOKS FOR PERIOD 1933 - 1943

(All first issues listed)

GENRE CODES (Main theme)

An - Anthology (mixed)
Av - Aviation
Cr - Crime
D - Detective
F - Funny Animal

H - Costumed/Superhero
Hr - Horror
Hm - Humor
J - Jungle
Lit - Literature

Mg - Magic
M - Movie
R - Strip Reprints
Re - Religious
SF - Science Fiction

Sp - Sport
TA - Teen-Age
Tr - True Fact
W - War
Ws - Western

NOTE: The stars signify the ranking of books into seven different tiers of importance. The top (most important) books receive six stars (1st tier), dropping to no star (7th tier) as their significance diminishes. The following information is provided for each comic: 1. Ranking, 2. Title, 3. Issue number, 4. Date, 5. Publisher, 6. Genre code, 7. Description. 8. Criteria codes.

PRE-GOLDEN AGE PERIOD

1933 ■

★ ★ ★ ★ **FUNNIES ON PARADE** nn (1933, Eastern Color, R)-The very first comic book in the modern format reprinting popular strip characters. Given away to test the feasibility of demand for repackaged Sunday newspaper funnies. (An 8-page tabloid folded down to 32 pages).
(a,c,d,e,h,i,j,k,l)

★ ★ ★ ★ **FAMOUS FUNNIES, A CARNIVAL OF COMICS** nn (1933, Eastern Color, R)-The second comic book. Given away to test reader demand. Its success set up another test to come in the following year to see if the public would actually pay 10 cents for this type of product (an 8-page tabloid folded down to 32 pages). The first of three first issues for this title.
(a,b,c,e,f,h,j)

★ **CENTURY OF COMICS** nn (1933, Eastern Color, R)-The third comic book. A 100-pager given away with three times the contents of the previous two books.
(e,j)

1934 ■

★ **SKIPPY'S OWN BOOK OF COMICS** nn (1934, Eastern Color, R)-The fourth comic book. The first to feature a single character-this wasn't tried again until **Superman** No. 1.
(e,j)

★ ★ ★ ★ **FAMOUS FUNNIES, SERIES I** (1934, Eastern Color, R)-The first comic book sold to the general public (through chain stores). The acid test, its unprecedented success set up the beginning of the first continuous series (anthology reprint) title in comics, and started the chain reaction.
(a,b,c,e,f,h,j)

★ ★ ★ ★ ★ **FAMOUS FUNNIES** No. 1 (7/34, Eastern Color, R)-Satisfied with the public response, this issue began the series and was the first comic book sold to the general public through newsstand distribution.
(a,b,c,e,f,h,j)

★ **FAMOUS FUNNIES** No. 3 (9/34, Eastern Color, R)-This issue ushered in the famous and very popular *Buck Rogers* strip reprints. Not trend setting, but important for the survival of the run which lasted 22 years.
(a,b,c,f,i,j,l)

1935 ■

★ ★ ★ ★ **NEW FUN COMICS** No. 1 (2/35, DC, An)-The first prototype of the modern comic in that it featured an anthology format of continuing characters and original rather than reprinted material. First of the DC line and the first tabloid-size book (albeit short-lived), surviving 13 years as *More Fun Comics*.
(b,e,h,i,j,k)

★ **MICKEY MOUSE MAGAZINE** No. 1 (Sum/35, K.K., F)-Magazine-size protocomic introducing the already legendary transfer characters to the fledgling comic book market. This title first appeared in 1933 as a black & white giveaway comic, and after going through format changes, eventually led to the ultimate "funny animal" comic, **Walt Disney's Comics & Stories**, to come five years later.
(a,b,c,e,g,j,k)

★ **NEW COMICS** No. 1 (12/35, DC, An)-DC felt enough confidence in the market to issue a second anthology title featuring original, continuing characters. It was second only to **New Fun** of the DC line. Evolved into **Adventure Comics**, warhorse of the DC line. DC parlayed the second most perfect comic book title (the first is **Action**) into a forty plus year run.
(b,e,h,j)

1936 ■

MORE FUN COMICS No. 7 (1/36, DC, An)-DC cancelled the title **New Fun** due to the appearance of **New Comics**, continuing the series under this changed title.
(b,e,j)

★ ★ ★ **POPULAR COMICS** No. 1 (2/36, Dell, R)-The second anthology format title of continuing reprint strips. First of the Dell line, the third publisher to enter the field. Featuring the first comic book appearance of *Dick Tracy, Little Orphan Annie, Terry & the Pirates* and others, lasting 13 years.
(a,b,c,e,j,k,l)

BIG BOOK OF FUN COMICS (Spr/36, DC, An)-The first annual in comics (56 pages, large size; reprints from **New Fun** No. 1-5).
(e,h,i,j)

★ ★ ★ **KING COMICS** No. 1 (4/36, McKay, R)-Ties as the third continuous series reprint title. The first of a publisher (4th to enter the field). Showcase title of all the King Feature characters-the most popular and widely circulated in the world, featuring Segar's *Popeye* and Raymond's *Flash Gordon* series as the mainstay, lasting 16 years.
(a,b,c,e,j,k,l)

★ ★ ★ **TIP TOP COMICS** No. 1 (4/36, UFS, R)-Ties as the third continuous series reprint anthology title. The first of a publisher (5th to enter the field). Featuring the *Tarzan* and *Li'l Abner* series and surviving 25 years.
(a,b,c,e,j,k,l)

★ **COMICS MAGAZINE, THE** (Funny Pages) No. 1 (5/36, Comics Mag., An)-The third anthology format title of original material. The first of a publisher (6th to enter the field). This book is unique in that its cover and entire contents were purchased from DC. This material created gaps in the story line continuity of DC's titles **More Fun** and **New Adventure** from which it came.
(e,j,k)

WOW COMICS No. 1 (7/36, McKay, An)-The fourth anthology title of original material. McKay's second series (first with original contents), lasting only 4 issues to 11/36. The Unpublished inventory formed the basis of the Eisner/Iger shop.
(e)

NEW BOOK OF COMICS No. 1 (6-8/36, DC, An)-The second annual in comics; 100 pages, reprinting popular strips from *More Fun* and *New Comics*. Second and last issue appeared in Spring of 1938.
(e)

FUNNIES, THE No. 1 (10/36, Dell, R)-Having published this title six years earlier as a tabloid, Dell brought it back as a regular comic book. Featuring more popular strip characters, this became Dell's second comic book title and ran for 6 years.
(b,e)

FUNNY PAGES No. 6 (11/36, Comics Mag., An)-Continued from *The Comics Magazine; introduced The Clock*(?), the first masked hero (detective type, transition hero) in a comic book.
(a,b,c,d,e,f,h,i,j)

FUNNY PICTURE STORIES No. 1 (11/36, Comics Mag., An)-Actually this company's second title, featuring their popular original character, *The Clock*, who appeared on the cover. Title continues for 3 years.
(e)

DETECTIVE PICTURE STORIES No. 1 (12/36, Comic Mag., D)-The first anthology comic title series devoted to a single theme and the first to focus on this subject. Popular in pulps, magazines and films of the time, lasted 7 issues.
(e,h,i,j)

1937 ■

NEW ADVENTURE COMICS No. 12 (1/37, DC, An)-Title change from *New Comics*, continues series.
(e)

STAR COMICS No. 1 (2/37, Chesler, An)-Ties as first of a publisher. Anthology format of continuing original material, but short lived (2½ years). Large-size format.
(e,k)

STAR RANGER No. 1 (2/37, Chesler, Ws)-Ties as first of a publisher, and as the first continuous series western anthology title (see *Western Picture Stories*). Large-size format of original material, lasting only 1 year.
(e,i,j,k)

WESTERN PICTURE STORIES No. 1 (2/37, Comics Mag, Ws)-Ties with *Star Ranger* as the first anthology comic title of original material to focus on this subject, the second of a single theme, not lasting out the year.
(e,i,j)

COMICS, THE No. 1 (3/37, Dell, R)-Dell's third anthology reprint title. The first comic book appearance of *Tom Mix*, lasting only one year.
(e,d)

★ ★ ★ **DETECTIVE COMICS** No. 1 (3/37, DC, D)-Inaugurated the longest run in comics. Initially a pulpy anthology of mystery men and private eyes, it emerged as the first important title on a single theme with the debut of the implacable *Batman* in '39 (Siegel and Shuster's *Slam Bradley* series is a flavorful example of title's '37-'38 period).
(a,b,c,e,f,h,i,j)

ACE COMICS No. 1 (4/37, McKay, R)-Due to the enormous success of McKay's first series, *King Comics*, this companion title was published featuring, among others, Raymond's *Jungle Jim*, lasting 12 years.
(a,b,c,e,j,l)

WESTERN ACTION THRILLERS No. 1 (4/37, Dell, Ws)-The third title devoted to westerns. A one-shot of 100 pages.
(e)

FEATURE BOOK nn (Popeye)(1937, McKay, R)-A new concept. The first series of comic books representing a divergence from the normal anthology format. Each issue in the run is actually a one-shot devoted to a single character. More than one issue in the run can be devoted to the same character. These books began in a B&W, magazine-size format. Improvements on this concept came a year later with UFS's *Single Series* (in color, comic book size), and still a year later with Dell's *Four Color* series, the only one to last.
(a,b,c,e,h,i,j)

FEATURE FUNNIES No. 1 (10/37, Chesler, R)-Another reprint title to add to the list, surviving 13 years as *Feature Comics*; carrying *Joe Palooka, Mickey Finn* and others.
(e)

100 PAGES OF COMICS No. 101 (1937, Dell, R)-Another 100-page reprint anthology book (Dell's 2nd) with a western cover. Only one issue.
(e)

1938 ■

ACE COMICS No. 11 (2/38, McKay, R)-First comic book appearance of *The Phantom*. Premiere mystery man and first costumed hero. The Ghost Who Walks never made the impact in comics that he enjoyed as a syndicated star.
(a,b,c,f,i,j,l)

FUNNY PAGES V2/6 (3/38, Centaur, An)-Ties with *Funny Picture Stories, Star Comics* and *Star Ranger* as first of a publisher. Series picked up from Chesler, ending two years later.
(k)

FUNNY PICTURE STORIES V2/6 (3/38, Centaur, An)-Ties with *Funny Pages, Star Comics*, and *Star Ranger* as first of a publisher. Series picked up from Comics Magazine, ending one year later.
(k)

STAR COMICS No. 10 (3/38, Centaur, An)-Ties with *Funny Pages, Funny Picture Stories*, and *Star Ranger* as first of a publisher. Series picked up from Chesler, ending one year later.
(k)

STAR RANGER V2/10 (3/38, Centaur, Ws)-Ties with *Funny Picture Stories, Star Ranger*, and *Funny Pages* as first of a publisher. Series picked up from Chesler, lasting 2 more issues.
(k)

COMICS ON PARADE No. 1 (4/38, UFS, R)-The second title of this publisher, featuring much the same reprint strips as *Tip Top*, their first. This series survived 17 years.
(a,b,c,e,j)

MAMMOTH COMICS No. 1 (1938, Whitman, R)-First of a publisher, in the same format as the McKay *Feature Books*. Only one issue.
(e,k)

SUPER COMICS No. 1 (5/38, Dell, R)-A dynamic new title, Dell's fourth. Debuted with some of the heavy weights transferred from the already successful *Popular Comics*. This new line-up of *Dick Tracy, Terry & The Pirates*, etc. proved to be a sound marketing strategy, lasting 11 years.
(a,b,c,e,j)

GOLDEN AGE PERIOD

★ ★ ★ ★ ★ **ACTION COMICS** No. 1 (6/38, DC, H)-The ultimate refinement of the anthology, continuing character title. The first appearance of *Superman*, the quintessential hero with extraordinary powers. Arguably the most imitated character in all of fiction. Standard bearer of the DC line.

The most important comic book ever published, and in tandem with **Superman**, one of the most influential, prevailed beyond four decades.
(a,b,c,d,e,f,h,i,j)

CIRCUS COMICS No. 1 (6/38, Globe, An)-A unique short-lived title featuring a top artist line-up. Introduced Wolverton's *Spacehawks*, later to appear in **Target Comics** as *Spacehawk*. First of a publisher.
(d,e,f,j,k)

CRACKAJACK FUNNIES No. 1 (6/38, Dell, R)-A new Dell title, replacing the defunct **The Comics** with a similar but different mix of reprint strips. Lasted 4 years.
(e)

COWBOY COMICS No. 13 (7/38, Centaur, Ws)-Continued from **Star Ranger** and lasted only two issues. The fourth western anthology title.
(e)

KEEN DETECTIVE FUNNIES No. 8 (7/38, Centaur, An)-Continued from **Detective Picture Stories**, this title became one of Centaur's mainstays introducing the *Masked Marvel* one year later, lasting 2 years.
(e)

LITTLE GIANT COMICS No. 1 (7/38, Centaur, An)-Small-size diversion from the regular format and short-lived (4 issues).
(e)

AMAZING MYSTERY FUNNIES No. 1 (8/38, Centaur, An)-Standard bearer of the Centaur line. Top artist line-up due to its production by the Everett shop. Ran for two years.
(e,g)

LITTLE GIANT MOVIE FUNNIES No. 1 (8/38, Centaur, An)-A miniature-sized format comic lasting two issues. A small cartoon panel appears on the right edge of each page giving the illusion of motion when riffled (a flip book) (the cover is set up to represent a movie theater).
(e,i)

★ FUNNY PAGES V2/10 (9/38, Centaur, H)-First appearance of *The Arrow* who is the very first costumed hero originating in the comic book (3 months after *Superman*). A primitive precursor of the more refined archers to come, *The Arrow* executed his adversaries with the medieval bluntness his uniform suggested.
(a,b,d,f,h,i,j)

★★★ JUMBO COMICS No. 1 (9/38, FH, J)-Publisher of the most perused, but least read, of Golden Age comics, Fiction House did not so much initiate a trend as continue the trusty formula that sustained their line of pulps, cheesecake cast against a variety of single theme adventurous backgrounds (aviation, s/f, jungle & war). *Jumbo* was the pilot model of the FH line and the first of the exploitation comics. The debut of *Sheena, Queen of the Jungle* heralded hordes of jungle goddesses to follow. The line overall is perhaps best remembered as a showcase for Matt Baker's patented 'calendar girl' art which, after Caniff and Raymond, was the most pervasive of Golden Age styles, enduring 15 years.
(a,b,c,e,f,h,i,j,k,l)

DETECTIVE COMICS No. 20 (10/38, DC, H)-First appearance of *The Crimson Avenger*, a *Shadow* look-a-like, who was the second comic book costumed hero (4 months after *Superman*).
(b,c,d,f,h,i,j)

LITTLE GIANT DETECTIVE FUNNIES No. 1 (10/38, Centaur, An)-Small-size format only lasting a few issues.
(e)

STAR RANGER FUNNIES No. 15 (10/38, Centaur, An)-Links to **Star Ranger** and **Cowboy Comics**, only lasting a few months. (Packaged by the Iger Shop.)
(e)

★★★ DONALD DUCK nn (1938, Whitman, F)-The first *Donald Duck*, as well as the first Walt Disney comic book; in the format of McKay's **Feature Book** (B&W with color cover), reprinting 1936 & 1937 Sunday comics. The first funny animal comic devoted to a single character. Precursor to great things to come for this character.
(a,b,c,e,f,i,j,l)

★★ SINGLE SERIES nn (Captain & The Kids) (1938, UFS, R)-UFS refined McKay's one-shot **Feature Book** format by adding color and adopting the standard comic book size, resulting in a more marketable package. Dell adopted this format for their **Four Color** series, which started a year later. This is UFS' third continuous series title.
(e,f,h,i,j)

COCOMALT BIG BOOK OF COMICS No. 1 (1938, Chesler, An)-A one-shot mixed anthology Charles Biro creation, packaged by the Chesler shop (top-notch art).
(e)

NICKEL COMICS No. 1 (1938, Dell, An)-A small-size divergent format one-shot, lasting only one issue.
(e)

1939 ■

ALL-AMERICAN COMICS No. 1 (4/39, DC, R)-DC finally bends to the reprint anthology format, but includes some original material for flavor. *Scribbly* by Mayer begins; a ten-year run.
(a,b,c,d,e,j)

NEW YORK WORLD'S FAIR (3-5/39, DC, H)-The first newsstand comic with a commercial tie-in, capitalizing on the enormous publicity of a real life public event, featuring DC's top characters. The thick format, as well as the title segued into **World's Finest Comics** two years later.
(a,c,e,i,j)

★ MOVIE COMICS No. 1 (4/39, DC, M)-A unique but short-lived idea. The notion of adapting films to comics in fumetti form (the panels were half-tones of stills from the films) was a good one, but didn't work any better in '39 than it does today. (The first movie adaptation comic in standard comic book form and probably the first attempt at a fumetti continuity.)
(e,f,j,i)

★★★★★ DETECTIVE COMICS No. 27 (5/39, DC, H)-Reliable but predictable 'funny paper' cops 'n robbers anthology came into focus with the debut of *The Batman*. DC's second powerhouse set another standard for the industry to follow. The 'dynamic' hero—costumed athlete sans extraordinary powers—proved a viable alternative for the burgeoning competition to mimic, but Bob Kane broke the mold. The character's unique personna defied any but the most oblique imitation. **Detective** shared standard bearer honors with **Action** and provided the initials by which the company was known. One of the top four comics.
(a,b,c,d,f,h,j)

KEEN KOMICS V2/1 (5/39, Centaur, An)-A large size mixed anthology comic changing to regular size with number two. Packaged by the Everett shop and lasting only three issues.
(e)

★★ WONDER COMICS No. 1 (5/39, Fox, H)-Salutory effort of Fox (packaged by Eisner/Iger). First, and shortest-lived, of **Superman** imitations. Historically significant because the debut of Fox's *Wonder Man* prompted DC's first attempt to successfully defend their copyright on *Superman*. (A precedent that would prove decisive when the Man of Steel confronted a more formidable courtroom adversary a decade hence). Only one more issue followed.
(d,e,j,k)

★★★ MOTION PICTURE FUNNIES WEEKLY No.1 (5/39? Funnies, Inc., H)-Produced as a theatre giveaway, this title featured the first appearance of *Sub-Mariner*. His official

newsstand debut occurred later in the year in **Marvel Comics** No. 1. Only seven known copies exist.
(a,c,d,e,f,g,h,i,j,k)

FEATURE COMICS No. 21 (6/39, Quality, An)-Continues from **Feature Funnies** of two years earlier. A discreet title change, indicating that original adventure comics were becoming a significant alternative to the formerly dominant reprints.
(b,e,k)

★ ★ **ADVENTURE COMICS** No. 40 (7/39, DC, H)-The *Sandman*, a transition crime fighter who stuck tenaciously to the trusty regalia of the pulp heroes. Finally, the pressure to adopt modern togs was brought to bear. The original mystery man vanished into oblivion, replaced by a swashbuckling Kirby hero.
(a,b,c,d,j)

AMAZING MYSTERY FUNNIES V2/7 (7/39, Centaur, H)-Debut of *The Fantom of the Fair*, mystery man, whose headquarters were under the World's Fair (An unexpected attraction for Fair goers). Destined for extinction with the 1940 wind-up of the Fair. Top artist line-up and exciting cover concepts.
(c,d,j)

COMIC PAGES V3/4 (7/39, Centaur, An)-A mixed anthology series continuing from **Funny Picture Stories** of three years earlier, lasting 3 issues.
(e)

KEEN DETECTIVE FUNNIES V2/7 (7/39, Centaur, H)-The *Masked Marvel*, super sleuth, and his three confederates began a terror campaign against lawless gangs. His big amphibian plane, secret laboratory and projected red shadow were devices used in the strip, lasting one year.
(d,j)

★ ★ ★ **MUTT AND JEFF** nn (Sum/39, DC, R)-This one shot represented a significant departure for DC. Formerly they had avoided the reprint title, preferring to develop their own original characters. This title was obviously a test to see if the market would support an entire book devoted to a single character (or in this case characters). This book has the honor of being the very first *newsstand* comic devoted to a single reprint strip. After a very slow start (four issues in four years), **Mutt and Jeff** was made a quarterly and soon became a popular run lasting 26 astounding years. It was the only successful reprint series of a single character to enjoy a respectible run. The syndicated *Mutt and Jeff* strip was, after *The Katzenjammer Kids*, the oldest continuously published newspaper strip.
(a,b,c,e,j)

★ ★ ★ ★ ★ **SUPERMAN** No. 1 (Sum/39, DC, H)-This landmark issue signaled a major turning point for the industry. Arguably, the second most important comic ever published (*Action* being the first), and possibly the most influential. *Superman* was the first original character promoted from headling an anthology title to starring in a book of his own. More importantly, this tandem exposure demonstrated to the industry that it could survive on its own original material, independent of the proven syndicated stars. As other publishers were attracted to the field in the months to come, they emulated not only *Superman*, but the tandem anthology/headline format that had contributed to his unprecedented success. A double trend setter. Contains reprint material from *Action* No. 1-4. Title has continued beyond four decades.
(a,b,c,e,h,i,j)

WONDERWORLD COMICS No. 3 (7/39, Fox, H)-After the *Wonder Man* debacle, Fox bounces back with a revised title and a new lead character (courtesy of the Iger shop). *The Flame* got off to a brilliant start, but was snuffed out when Iger and Fox parted company, lasting 3 years.
(a,c,d,e,j)

MAGIC COMICS No. 1 (8/39, McKay, R)-King Features' third

reprint anthology (after **King** and **Ace Comics**) featured such popular syndicated stars as *Mandrake, Henry,* and *Blondie*. By 1940 *Blondie* had become the most widely syndicated newspaper strip in the world, and became the prime cover feature for the balance of the run, title enduring 10½ years.
(a,b,c,e,j)

★ **MYSTERYMEN COMICS** No. 1 (8/39, Fox, H)-Fox was on firm ground with a trio of potential contenders: *Wonderworld's The Flame* and, debuting in this title, *The Blue Beetle* and *The Green Mask*. These early products of the Eisner/Iger shop are worth a second look. Potential glows from every page. Soon, due to the E/I and Fox break up, the characters sunk into hack oblivion.
(a,c,d,e,j)

SMASH COMICS No. 1 (8/39, Quality, An)-This is the first title that Quality developed entirely on their own, (previous titles having been purchased from other publishers). The series lacked originality until the debut of Lou Fine's *Ray* which began in issue No. 14.
(b,e,j)

AMAZING MAN COMICS No. 5 (9/39, Centaur, H)-Everett's *A-Man* was launched here, the first Centaur character to headline his own title. The first costumed hero to shrink (*Minimidget*) begins. (This concept was better used later in Quality's *Doll Man*.) Top artist line-up in this series which ended in early 1942. The standard bearer of the Centaur line.
(e,j)

SPEED COMICS No. 1 (10/39, Harvey, H)-First of a publisher. *Shock Gibson* is the main hero. The characters in this series lacked the charisma of the competition's best; had a few bright moments when top artists entered the line-up, surviving as an average run for 7 years.
(a,b,e,k)

BEST COMICS No. 1 (11/39, BP, H)-First of a publisher. Debut of the Red Mask. An experimental large format book that read sideways; it failed to find an audience after four issues and folded.
(e,j,k)

BLUE RIBBON COMICS No. 1 (11/39, MLJ, An)-First of a publisher. Contents unremarkable (*Rang-A-Tang, The Wonder Dog,* for example). An MLJ anthology that failed to survive beyond 1942 despite the influx of super heroes.
(e,j,k)

★ ★ ★ ★ ★ **MARVEL COMICS** No. 1 (11/39, Timely, H)-Timely, the first publisher to hit with a smash twin bill in their inaugural title (courtesy of the Everett shop). From the onset, the formula of iconoclast as hero would prove to be Timely's most successful newsstand strategy. *The Human Torch* and *Sub-Mariner* won immediate reader approval, paving the way for more marvels to come from the pre-eminent Thrill Factory of comicdom. Possibly The most sought after of all Golden Age comics. Title lasted 10 years.
(a,b,c,d,e,f,g,h,i,j,k)

CHAMPION COMICS No. 2 (12/39, Harvey, An)-Early transitional anthology title with a sports theme, changing over to costumed heroes early on. None of the characters caught on enough to sustain the run for more than four years.
(e)

FANTASTIC COMICS No. 1 (12/39, Fox, H)-Biblical character *Samson* debuts. This series is more noted for the Lou Fine covers (Iger Shop). *Stardust* begins, one of the most bizarre super heroes in comics (Almost child-like, almost surrealistic art and plotting). He assassinated wrong doers regularly.
(e)

★ ★ **FEATURE COMICS** No. 27 (12/39, Quality, H)-Debut of the *Dollman* (Quality's first super hero), who was the second, but most significant, with the power to shrink (See

Amazing Man). The stories were generally undistinguished but Quality's high standards of illustration (Eisner in this case) lent the strip a credibility that would have been lacking in lesser hands. This title lasted 11 years.
(a,b,c,d,j)

★ **SILVER STREAK COMICS** No. 1 (12/39, Lev, An)-First of a publisher. Debut of *The Claw*, one of the most bizarre villains in the annals of comics. Standing 100 feet tall with claws and fangs was the ultimate refinement of the 'yellow peril' theme from the pulps. Such a formidable figure had to have an adversary to match (See *Silver Streak* No. 7). The first comic book to display a metallic silver logo to insure prominence on the stands.
(a,c,d,e,f,k)

TOP-NOTCH COMICS No. 1 (12/39, MLJ, H)-*The Wizard*, one of MLJ's top characters debuted. Their second anthology title, lasting 4½ years.
(a,b,c,d,e,j)

LARGE FEATURE COMIC nn (1939, Dell, R)-Black and white, magazine size, one-shot series with color covers (identical to Mckay *Feature Books* of two years earlier), lasting four years.
(a,c,e)

CAPTAIN EASY nn (1939, Hawley, R)-First of a publisher. A one-shot reprint comic devoted to a single character, already proven successful by other publishers.
(a,c,e,k)

★ ★ **FOUR COLOR** No. 1 (Dick Tracy)(1939, Dell, R)-Exact format of UFS's *Single Series* of one year earlier. The most successful of the one-shot continuity titles, lasting 23 years. This series also provided a testing arena for new characters and concepts.
(a,b,c,d,e)

LONE RANGER COMICS, THE nn (1939, giveaway, Ws)-Fifth western title, first of a major character. This one-shot may have had newsstand distribution as price (10 cents) was stamped on cover.
(a,c,e)

1940 ■

★ ★ **BLUE BEETLE, THE** No. 1 (Wint/39-40, Fox, H)-The star of the second continuous series title devoted to a single character exemplified the pioneer 'crime fighter' of the early comics. His uniform was as simple and direct as the four-color medium itself– unadorned, form-fitting chain mail. Disdaining cloak, cape and the cover of night, *Blue Beetle* trounced crime where he found it, usually in the street and in broad daylight. Striking figure made an indelible impression on readers and, had Fox been more committed to long term development, would have doubtless gone the distance. The series eventually succumbed to tepid scripts and lacklustre art, but the character was of sufficient personal appeal to survive, in memory, not only the demise of his title but legions of better produced, longer tenured heroes.

★ ★ ★ ★ ★ **FLASH COMICS** No. 1 (1/40, DC, H)-DC reinforced its arsenal with two more dynamos: *The Flash* (first, and most significant hero with lightning speed), and *The Hawkman* (first and most significant winged hero). Both trend setters, with series lasting beyond 40 years.
(a,b,c,d,e,f,h,i,j)

★ ★ **FLASH COMICS** No. 1 (1/40, Faw, H)-An in-house b&w proof produced to secure pre-publication copyright. Important changes made before the book was officially released were, a title change from *Flash* to *Whiz* (DC had already gone to press with their *Flash Comics*), and the name of the lead character was changed from *Captain Thunder* to *Captain Marvel*. (8 known copies exist.)
(e,f,g,j,k)

THRILL COMICS No. 1 (1/40, Faw, H)-Identical to *Flash Comics* listed above, only a different title. Only three known copies exist.

(e,f,g,j,k)

JUNGLE COMICS No. 1 (1/40, FH, J)-The second single theme anthology series of this subject (cloned from *Jumbo*). The title more perfectly suggested the 'jungle' theme with format selling rather than strong characters. Third series of a publisher, lasting as long as its parent (14½ years), with no competition until six years later.
(a,b,c,d,e,j)

★ ★ **PEP COMICS** No. 1 (1/40, MLJ, H)-Debut of *The Shield*, the first patriotic hero, later eclipsed by Simon & Kirby's *Captain America*, the bombshell of 1941. MLJ's third and longest lasting (over 40 years) anthology title. Archie eventually takes over the series.
(a,b,c,d,e,f,h,i,j)

★ ★ ★ ★ **PLANET COMICS** No. 1 (1/40, FH, SF)-The publisher's fourth anthology title of continuing characters. The first and by far the most successful science fiction run in comics. As with *Jumbo* and *Jungle*, this title had no competition for many years. Fiction House's style of action-packed covers and art made up for the routine plotting, lasting 14 years.
(a,b,c,e,f,h,i,j)

MIRACLE COMICS No. 1 (2/40, Hillman, H)-A mixed anthology series similar to *Rocket Comics* published a month later. First of a publisher. Covers have good eye-appeal, ending with the fourth issue.
(e,k)

★ ★ ★ **MORE FUN COMICS** No. 52,53,(2,3/40, DC, H)-DC modernizes its first anthology title, introducing the ominous *Spectre* in this two-part origin series. This frightening ethereal hero was too much a match for his adversaries, but gave DC an exciting alternative to their swelling ranks of wondermen. A trend setter, lasting 4 years in this title.
(a,b,c,d,f,h,i,j)

SCIENCE COMICS No. 1 (2/40, Fox, SF)-With qualifications, the second science fiction anthology title (very few of the stories dealt with outer space). Aside from the Lou Fine covers (No. 1 & 2), the artwork was not attractive and the series died after eight issues. First *Eagle* (the second winged hero).
(e)

TARGET COMICS No. 1 (2/40, Novelty, H)-First of a publisher. An early Everett shop super hero production. First *White Streak* by Burgos (the second android super hero). Top artist line-up featuring above average covers and stories, lasting 10 years.
(b,e,k)

THRILLING COMICS No. 1 (2/40, Better, H)-The first successful anthology title by this publisher (their second series). Debut of *Dr. Strange*. Logo carried over from the pulp. The Schomburg covers are the highlight of the run. The title lasted 11 years, switching to a jungle theme near the end.
(a,b,c,e,j)

★ ★ ★ ★ ★ **WHIZ COMICS** No. 2 (2/40, Faw, H)-After *Action*, the most significant of all hero/adventure anthologies was this late entry from Fawcett. Origin, first appearance of *Captain Marvel*, humor hero par excellence. The most accessible of miracle men came from behind to eclipse the competition's best. He also founded the industry's first character dynasty (Marvel's *Junior*, *Mary* and even *Bunny*), a tactic that would prove as fundamental to comics' merchandising as DC's hero team concept. Landmark first issue also introduced such secondary stalwarts as *Sivana*, *Old Shazam*, *Spy Smasher* (the definitive aviator/mysteryman), and *Ibis the Invincible*, most memorable of comic book sorcerers. Flagship of the Fawcett line and a perennial favorite for 13 years.
(a,b,c,d,e,f,g,j,k)

ZIP COMICS No. 1 (2/40, MLJ, H)-MLJ's fourth anthology title (featuring *Steel Sterling*). Interesting stylized covers and art. Series lasted four years. With the exception of *Wilbur* (an Archie clone), none of the characters reached their own titles. (a,b,c,d,j)

★ ★ **ADVENTURE COMICS** No. 48 (3/40, DC, H)-Debut of *The Hourman*. A substantial secondary feature that sold a few books for DC, but never received adequate creative support. Interesting premise came to dominate all the stories resulting in monotonous repetition.
(a,b,c,d,e,j)

COLOSSUS COMICS No. 1 (3/40, Sun, H)-An early esoteric book which ties to the esoteric *Green Giant* comic.
(e)

★ ★ ★ **DONALD DUCK FOUR COLOR** No. 4 (3/40?, Dell, F)-The first comic book devoted to this important transfer character. Still confined to one page gag strips. Full potential not yet reached.
(a,b,c,j)

MASTER COMICS No. 1 (3/40, Faw, H)-An experimental format at first (magazine size, priced at 15¢ and 52 pages). Debut of *Master Man*, an imitation of *Superman*, killed by DC after six issues; just in time for *Bulletman* to become the lead figure with issue no. 7, transferred from the defunct *Nickel Comics*.
(b,e,j,k)

MYSTIC COMICS No. 1 (3/40, Timely, H)-Unusual anthology title (their third) in that each issue featured a practically new line-up of costumed heroes. High impact covers and art, lasting only 10 issues.
(e)

PRIZE COMICS No. 1 (3/40, Prize, H)-High quality anthology series with the debut of *Power Nelson*. First of a publisher. Dick Briefer's unique *Frankenstein* was introduced in No. 7 as well as Simon & Kirby's *Black Owl*. The covers have tremendous eye-appeal.
(a,b,e,j,k)

ROCKET COMICS No. 1 (3/40, Hillman, H)-The title is misleading. This is actually a mixed anthology title with science fiction covers; short-lived with only three issues. Companion mag to *Miracle Comics*. The second Hillman title.
(e)

★ **SHADOW COMICS** No. 1 (3/40, S&S, H)-The venerable pulp publisher tested the comic waters with a heavyweight who had dominated both the pulp and radio markets but never quite found his metier in a medium that relied on action over ethereal atmosphere. *Doc Savage*, another renowned pulp character, debuted in this issue. A respectable but undistinguished run (9 years) probably sustained by popularity of radio program.
(a,b,c,e,f,i,j,k,l)

SLAM BANG COMICS No. 1 (3/40, Faw, An)-Fawcett's third title was an ill conceived adventure anthology starring civilian heroes. This formula had gone out two years before with the appearance of *Superman*. The title was retired after 8 issues.
(e)

SUN FUN KOMIKS No. 1 (3/40, Sun, Hm)-An esoteric one-shot printed in black and red. A satire on comic books. The first of its kind not to be fully developed until *Mad* of 12 years hence.
(e,i,j)

★ ★ ★ ★ **DETECTIVE COMICS** No. 38 (4/40, DC, H)-DC initiates yet another breakthrough concept—the apprentice costumed hero. Origin, first appearance of *Robin*, the first and most enduring juvenile aide. For the first time in popular literature, the youthful apprentice was accepted as an equal by his partner. Bob Kane set another standard for the industry to mimic. The foreboding and enigmatic *Batman* was never the same after this issue.
(a,b,c,d,f,h,i,j)

EXCITING COMICS No. 1 (4/40, Better, H)-A sister anthology title to *Thrilling*, becoming Better's second successful series. This title launched *The Black Terror* in No. 9, with Schomburg doing the covers early on (a poor man's Timely). Title lasted 9 years with jungle theme covers at the end.
(b,e,j)

★ ★ **NEW YORK WORLD'S FAIR** (3-5/40, DC, H)-The second comic book produced for a public event, ending the series. The first book to feature *Superman* and *Batman* together on a cover, as well as the first to showcase all of a company's stars, all in one book.
(a,c,j)

SUPERWORLD COMICS No. 1 (4/40, Gernsback, SF)-Following the success of *Planet*, this title takes the honors as the third continuous series science fiction anthology. But Gernsback soon learned that 'raw' science fiction without a unique art style or gimmick (cheesecake) wouldn't sell. Disappeared after only three issues.
(e,k)

WEIRD COMICS No. 1 (4/40, Fox, H)-Another mixed anthology title with costumed heroes. The first to capitalize on this title, which became more common a decade later. Early issues by the Iger shop. First *Birdman* (the third winged hero). First *Thor*, from Greek mythology. Title lasted 2 years.
(e)

BIG SHOT COMICS No. 1 (5/40, CCG, Av)-First *Skyman*, the second aviation hero (noted for his flying wing)(See *Whiz*). The first of a publisher. Mixed anthology series with original and reprint strips (*Joe Palooka*), lasting 9 years.
(a,b,c,d,e,j,k)

CRACK COMICS No. 1 (5/40, Quality, H)-Debut of Fine's *Black Condor* (the fourth winged hero). *Madame Fatal* begins, a bizarre hero who dresses as a woman to fight crime. A top quality series, lasting 9 years.
(a,b,c,d,e)

CRASH COMICS No. 1 (5/40, Tem/Holyoke, H)-The first Simon & Kirby art team-up, whose loose style of action reached maturity a year later with *Captain America*. Kirby was on his way to becoming one of the most influential artists in comics. First of a publisher. A short lived mixed anthology series with costumed heroes, lasting 5 issues.
(e,g,k)

DOC SAVAGE COMICS No. 1 (5/40, S&S, H)-The legendary Man of Bronze headlined Street & Smith's second comic title. But it soon became evident that the original 'super man' was out of his depth. His prose adventures, which crackled with vitality in the pulps, seemed bland and derivative in the four-color medium. Outclassed by the characters he inspired, Doc and his title were retired after 3 years of so-so performance.
(c,e)

HYPER MYSTERY COMICS No. 1 (5/40, Hyper, H)-First of a publisher. A costumed hero anthology title which could not compete with the many heroes on the market at this time, lasting 2 issues.
(e,k)

★ **MORE FUN COMICS** No. 55 (5/40, DC, H)-First *Dr. Fate*, DC's second supernatural hero was given immediate cover exposure. Above average art and stories; colorful costume, lasting 3½ years and not achieving his own title.
(a,b,c,d,j)

★ ★ ★ **NICKEL COMICS** No. 1 (5/40, Faw, H)-Introduced *Bulletman*, Fawcett's third costumed hero. This book was experimental, selling for 5 cents, came out biweekly, and lasting only 8 issues. (After *Bulletman* was moved to *Master Comics*, he won his own title in 1941.)
(a,c,d,e,j)

WAR COMICS No. 1 (5/40, Dell, W)-The first single theme

anthology series devoted to war. The combat genre did not find a significant market until the outbreak of the Korean conflict a decade later.
(e,i,j)

AMAZING ADVENTURE FUNNIES No. 1 (6/40, Centaur, H)-Outstanding collection of Centaur's best characters reprinted from earlier titles. Centaur was increasingly thrown back to all reprint books. Conjecture is that Timely's sudden success pre-empted all of the Everett shop's time.
(c,e)

★ ★ ★ ★ **BATMAN** No. 1 (Spr/40, DC, H)-Has arrival date of 4/25/40. DC's second strongest character achieved stardom and was given his own title. Assembled from *Detective Comics'* inventory, containing the last solo appearance of *The Batman. The Joker* and *The Cat* debut. Title has run uninterrupted over four decades.
(a,b,c,e,j)

BLUE BOLT No. 1 (6/40, Novelty, H)-Second of a publisher. Costumed hero anthology title. Important early Simon & Kirby development began in No. 3. The heroes in this series could not be sustained, with *Dick Cole* eventually taking over, lasting 9 years.
(a,b,c,d,e,j)

CYCLONE COMICS No. 1 (6/40, Bilbara, An)-An anthology title with emphasis on subjects other than costumed hero. First of a publisher, expiring after 5 issues.
(e,j,k)

FUTURE COMICS No. 1 (6/40, McKay, R)-McKay's first new title in about a year. A reprint anthology with a science fiction theme (the fourth ever). This issue is noted for *The Phantom's* origin and science fiction cover. Went down for the count after 4 issues.
(e)

★ ★ ★ **SPIRIT, THE** No. 1 (6/2/40, Eisner, D)-A weekly comic book (the only in comics) featuring the blockbuster strip distributed through newspapers. Notably, one of the best written and illustrated strips ever. A trend setter. Ingenious themes; capital atmospheric art with movie-like continuity and humorous plotting. Focus on special effects, lighting and unusual angles, lasting 12 years and endlessly revived.
(a,b,c,d,e,f,h,i,j)

STARTLING COMICS No. 1 (6/40, Better, H)-Better's third companion anthology series; *Wonder Man* and *Captain Future* begin. *The Fighting Yank* debuted in No. 10. Schomburg covers began early giving the books more impact. Cover theme changed to science fiction at the end.
(a,b,c,e,j)

SURE-FIRE COMICS No. 1 (6/40, Ace, H)-First of a publisher. A super hero anthology title of average quality lasting 4 issues before a title change.
(e,k)

WHIRLWIND COMICS No. 1 (6/40, Nita, H)-First of a publisher. A Three-issue run of mediocre quality with no sustaining characters.
(e,k)

★ ★ ★ ★ **ALL-AMERICAN COMICS** No. 16 (7/40, DC, H)-DC scored with another winning variation on the mystery man/adventure theme. Origin and first appearance of most enduring of DC's magic oriented heroes. The ancient fable of the magic lamp was transformed into a modern and more accessible, more mysterious hero. *The Green Lantern's* chant became a staple of school boy mythology and another great career was launched. Series ended in 1949, although the name continued beyond 4 decades.
(a,b,c,d,j)

★ ★ ★ **ALL-STAR COMICS** No. 1 (Sum/40, DC, H)-The first continuous series showcase comic (see *New York World's Fair*, 1940) for giving more exposure to top characters, who all headlined anthology series but as yet were not strong enough to have titles of their own. (This abundance of

popular characters was unique to DC, forcing them to come up with this new format.)
(a,b,c,e)

FLAME, THE No. 1 (Sum/40, Fox, H)-One of Fox's top characters given prominence, reprinted from *Wonderworld*. Lou Fine art in this issue, but the quality dropped early on, with the title lasting only 1½ years.
(c,e)

GREEN MASK, THE No. 1 (Sum/40, Fox, H)-Fox's emerald mystery man achieved stardom, but was squelched early on due to sub-standard art. An intriguing concept that was resurrected several times over the next 15 years, none of which were successful.
(c,e)

★ **MARVEL MYSTERY COMICS** No. 9 (7/40, Timely, H)-Epic battle issue. The first time in comics that two super heroes appeared together in one story. *Sub-Mariner* and *The Human Torch* each give up their usual space and battle for 22 pages. A coming together of the ancient basic elements, Water and Fire. Ignited newsstands everywhere.
(a,b,c,h,j)

HIT COMICS No. 1 (7/40, Quality, H)-Quality's fourth anthology title. Distinguished primarily by Iger shop graphics (Lou Fine). Non-memorable characters until *Kid Eternity* took over as main feature two years later. Series lasted 10 years.
(a,b,e,j)

NATIONAL COMICS No. 1 (7/40, Quality, H)-Of equal quality to *Hit*, but at his very best (covers and story art). Debut of *Uncle Sam*, Quality's top patriot. Legendary artist line-up with series lasting 9 years.
(a,b,c,d,e,f,j)

OKAY COMICS No. 1 (7/40, UFS, R)-Not having published a new title since 1938 (*Single Series*), United decides to make a comeback. Three new titles are released simultaneously with a fourth the following month. This one-shot issue features *The Captain and the Kids* and *Hawkshaw the Detective*.
(e)

OK COMICS No. 1 (7/40, UFS, H)-United tries their first super hero anthology title, but the characters were not strong enough to endure the stiff competition, lasting only two issues. Their second new title for the month.
(e)

SHIELD-WIZARD COMICS No. 1 (Sum/40, MLJ, H)-MLJ gave their top two characters joint stardom. A unique concept, titling a book after more than one character to insure its survival—a first in comics. The series lasted 4 years (the dual title wasn't enough).
(c,e)

SPARKLER COMICS No. 1 (7/40, UFS, R)-A two-issue reprint anthology series featuring *Jim Hardy* in No. 1 and *Frankie Doodle* in No. 2. United's third new title for the month.
(c,e)

SUPER-MYSTERY COMICS No. 1 (7/40, Ace, H)-Ace's second title, featuring more prominent characters and art, becoming their mainstay run. The series lasted 9 years, sustained by colorful covers and top artists.
(a,b,c,e)

FANTOMAN No. 2 (8/40, Centaur, H)-Centaur's second title reprinting their top characters and lasting three issues. Their second series of repackaged material.
(e)

HEROIC COMICS No. 1 (8/40, Eastern Color, H)-Seven years after introducing *Famous Funnies*, Eastern came out with their second anthology title (their third ever). Original rather than reprinted material. *Hydroman*, a spin-off of the *Sub-Mariner* debuted. Eventually the format was changed to true stories of heroism, lasting 15 years. Top artists in-

cluded throughout the run.
(e)

RED RAVEN COMICS No. 1 (8/40, Timely, H)-A one-shot esoteric super hero book featuring Kirby art. Highly sought after due to its lineage and rarity. Timely's fourth title.
(e)

★ ★ ★ ★ **SPECIAL EDITION COMICS** No. 1 (8/40, Fawcett, H)-Due to the immense popularity of **Whiz's** explosive character, a single theme (Fawcett's first) anthology one-shot of *Captain Marvel* was published. A few months later, he began his own series. Beck cover and story art—high quality throughout.
(a,c,e,j)

UNITED COMICS No. 1 (8/40, UFS, R)-The popular *Fritzi Ritz* strip was featured and sustained the run for 12½ years. United's fourth and only successful title in their recent comeback attempt beginning a month earlier. The first comic book series to focus on the career girl theme (proto-type of *Katy Keene*).
(a,b,c,e)

CRASH COMICS No. 4(9/40, Holyoke, H)-*Catman* debuted for two issues then stayed dormant for six months before appearing in his own title.
(a,c,d,j)

MASKED MARVEL No. 1 (9/40, Centaur, H)-After exposure in *Keen Detective Funnies*, the crimson sleuth was given his own title, lasting only 3 issues.
(e)

★ **MICKEY MOUSE MAGAZINE** V5/12, (9/40, K.K. F)-This historically significant publication was one step removed from becoming the first official funny animal series. As a magazine, it had evolved through various sizes and formats to finally become a full-fledged comic book. The following month, a title change to **Walt Disney's Comics & Stories** completed the transition.
(a,c,h,j)

PRIZE COMICS No. 7 (9/40, Prize, H)-Debut of Dick Briefer's *Frankenstein* series, and *The Black Owl* by Simon & Kirby. Above average strips with eye-catching covers.
(a,b,c,d,j)

★ **RED RYDER COMICS** No. 1 (9/40, Hawley/Dell, Ws)-A one-shot devoted to the popular strip character by Fred Harman, not becoming a continuous series until Dell picked up the title a year later. Ties with *Tom Mix* as the second book devoted to a single western character, but the first to receive widespread newsstand distribution. Lasted 17 years due to popular movie series. The second title of a publisher.
(a,b,c,e,f,h,i,j,l)

★ ★ ★ **SILVER STREAK COMICS** No. 6 (9/40, Lev, H)-High impact cover of *The Claw* by Jack Cole. Debut of *Daredevil* with his unprecedented costume of dichromatic symmetry. (See *Silver Streak* no. 7.)
(a,b,c,d,f,j)

SKY BLAZERS No. 1 (9/40, Hawley, Av)-Ties with *Red Ryder* as 2nd of a publisher. Inspired by the radio show, not lasting beyond 2 issues.
(e)

★ ★ **TOM MIX** No. 1 (9/40, Ralston, Ws)-The first continuous series single theme western comic, but a giveaway by Ralston—not sold on the stands.
(a,b,c,e,j,k)

★ **WINGS COMICS** No. 1 (9/40, FH, Av)-The publisher's fifth single theme anthology title. The first to focus entirely on aviation (a subject of high appeal to boys of the era). With no competition, the series lasted 14 years.
(a,b,c,e,h,i,j)

ALL-AMERICAN COMICS No. 19 (10/40, DC, H)-Debut of *The Atom* (a hero for short people). Good filler material as a back-up to the main feature, who lasted 4½ years.

(a,b,c,d,f,h,j)

ARROW, THE No. 1 (10/40, Centaur, H)-The very first costume hero (pre-*Batman*) was given prominence after a two-year run in *Funny Pages*. Folded after 3 issues (Centaur phasing out).
(e)

BIG 3 No. 1 (Fall/40, Fox, H)-Fox's first showcase anthology title featuring their top characters together in one magazine. A good idea, but not surviving more than 7 issues.
(e)

BILL BARNES COMICS No. 1 (10/40, S&S, Av)-The celebrated pulp ace got his own comic title, but after three years failed to find an audience. Street & Smith's third title.
(c,e,l)

CHAMP COMICS No. 11 (10/40, Harvey, H)-Continued from *Champion*, now featuring super heroes in full swing. Later on the popular and saleable Simon & Kirby art style was copied as an attempt to sustain the run. The title ended in 1944.
(e)

★ ★ ★ **HUMAN TORCH, THE** No. 2(Fall/40, Timely, H)-From the pages of *Marvel Mystery*, the android flys into his own title. Inspired concept. High impact, eye-catching character, making appearances over the next 40 years.
(a,b,c,e,j)

REX DEXTER OF MARS No. 1 (Fall/40, Fox, SF)-A modest success in *Mysterymen*, but not important enough to carry a title of his own. Expired after one issue.
(e)

SAMSON No. 1 (Fall/40, Fox, H)-One of Fox's top characters from *Fantastic* achieves stardom. Lack-luster art leads to the early death of the run the following year.
(e)

SPORT COMICS No. 1 (10/40, S&S, Sp)-A good idea 'real life' comic series featuring notable sport figures and lasting (through a title change) for 9 years. The first comic series devoted entirely to this theme (see *Champion and Fight*).
(b,c,e,h,i,j)

SUPER SPY No. 1 (10/40, Centaur, H)-Late Centaur super hero anthology title, introducing *The Sparkler*. Interesting early vintage comic with only two issues published.
(e)

TOP-NOTCH COMICS No. 9 (10/40, MLJ, H)-Debut of *The Black Hood*, key MLJ hero. One of the few at MLJ to later star in his own title. The costume had eye-appeal which sustained the character, lasting 3 years.
(c,d,j)

★ ★ ★ ★ ★ **WALT DISNEY'S COMICS AND STORIES** No. 1 (10/40, Dell, F)-The first funny animal continuous series comic book title. Miscellaneous collection of proven Disney characters began to come into focus around consistently high quality strips by Taliaferro and Gottfredson, who consistently delivered the goods. The definitive funny animal anthology comic after which all others were modeled. A trend setter. Suspected to have achieved the highest circulation of any comic, lasting beyond 40 years.
(a,b,c,e,h,i,j)

WESTERN DESPERADO COMICS No. 8 (10/40, Fawcett, Ws)-Fawcett's first western theme anthology title, only one issue.
(e)

DETECTIVE EYE No. 1 (11/40, Centaur, H)-More exposure for characters from *Keen Detective Funnies*, lasting 2 issues.
(e)

HI-SPOT COMICS No. 2 (11/40, Hawley, An)-A one-shot book featuring an Edgar Rice Burroughs strip, *David Innes of Pellucidar*.

(c)

WHAM COMICS No. 1 (11/40, Centaur, H)-Another short-lived anthology title, similar to *Super Spy* (reprinting earlier material).
(e)

★ ★ **GREEN HORNET COMICS** No. 1 (12/40, Harvey, H)-The respected radio and movie hero tried his wings in comics. Intriguing concept, with a few high points of good artists in the run. He never excelled in the medium, but did present a respectable run of 9 years—probably sustained by the popularity of the radio program.
(a,b,c,e,l)

LIGHTNING COMICS No. 4 (12/40, Ace, H)-Continued from *Sure-Fire*, becoming Ace's third title. Colorful covers (some exceptional) could not sustain the run beyond 18 months.
(e)

DOUBLE COMICS (1940, Elliot, H)-The first attempt at re-packaging (and remarketing) remaindered comics. First of a publisher. Elliot produced these unique books for four years, taking advantage of the insatiable public demand for comics.
(e,h,j,k)

GREEN GIANT COMICS No. 1 (1940, Funnies, Inc., H)-A very rare one-shot test comic. Conjecture is that its circulation was limited to the New York City area only.
(e,j)

1941 ▪

★ ★ ★ ★ ★ **ALL-STAR COMICS** No. 3 (Wint/40-41, DC, H)-A breakthrough concept, second in importance only to the creation of the super hero. For the first time in comics, top characters came together in one book to form a crime fighting organization *The Justice Society*. A trend setter. Unprecedented in all of literature (the gods of Mt. Olympus weren't on speaking terms; the Knights of the Round Table didn't foregather to confront a common foe). Forerunner of *The Justice League*, and inspiration for many hero groups that followed.
(a,b,c,f,h,i,j)

BUCK ROGERS No. 1 (Wint/40-41, FF, R)-Due to the enormous popularity of the strip in *Famous Funnies*, he earned his own title, which is the first continuous title devoted to a reprint character. Unfortunately, like many other transfer characters, the series didn't last, running only 6 issues.
(a,c,e)

SILVER STREAK COMICS No. 7 (1/41, Lev, H)-Epic clash between *Daredevil* and *The Claw* began in this issue. (Rivaled only by the *Torch-Sub-Mariner* brouhaha). Early enthusiastic work by Jack Cole. *DD's* costume colors change to red and blue, giving him a sinister, demonic appearance (unforgettable). Smash hit series launched *DD* to stardom with own title.
(a,c,f,j)

WOW COMICS No. 1 (Wint/40-41, Faw, H)-Featuring the costumed hero *Mr. Scarlet* (imitation of *Batman*), drawn by Kirby. Included other features with small impact to the comic scene. The major feature of this title was *Mary Marvel*, a *Captain Marvel* clone, who dominated from No. 9 on. This particular issue is highly prized due to its rarity and early Kirby art.
(b,e)

★ ★ ★ **CAPTAIN MARVEL ADVENTURES** nn (1-2/41?, Faw, H)-Following the wake of *Special Edition*, the celebrated character started his own series (this issue illustrated by Kirby), reaching a two-week publication frequency at one point, lasting 13 years.
(a,b,c,e,j)

BLUE RIBBON COMICS No. 9 (2/41, MLJ, H)-Inspired by DC's *The Spectre, Mr. Justice* began this issue and survived to the end of the run (1942).

(d)

★ ★ ★ ★ ★ **CAPTAIN AMERICA COMICS** No. 1 (3/41, Timely, H)-Simon & Kirby's most classic creation; a patriotic paragon (the second but foremost of patriotic heroes) that set the comics market reeling. A trend setter. One of the top ten most sought after books. With a few interruptions, the character has survived beyond 40 years.
(a,b,c,d,e,g,j)

JACKPOT COMICS No. 1 (Spr/41, MLJ, H)-MLJ's first showcase title to give more exposure to their top characters. The mediocre scripts and art could only keep the run alive for 2 years.
(c,e)

★ ★ ★ **SUB-MARINER COMICS** No. 1 (Spr/41, Timely, H)-The aquatic anti-hero is given prominence. The potential of the character was never fully realized. High impact covers, sustaining the run for 8 years.
(a,b,c,e,j)

★ ★ ★ **WORLD'S BEST COMICS** No. 1 (Spr/41, DC, H)-Using the successful format of *The World's Fair* books, DC created this title to feature their top two attractions, *Batman* and *Superman*. This was the first thick format continuous series comic (as *World's Finest*). Series lasted beyond 40 years without interruption.
(a,b,c,e,h,j)

★ ★ ★ **MICKEY MOUSE FOUR COLOR** No. 16 (4/41?, Dell, F)-The first comic devoted to this world renowned character. The subject of this landmark issue was Gottfredson's classic, *The Phantom Blot*.
(a,b,c,j)

★ ★ **ADVENTURE COMICS** No. 61 (4/41, DC, H)-*Starman* was introduced as DC continued to create new characters. Visually, an intriguing alternative with enough appeal to last 3½ years in this run, but not quite strong enough to appear in his own title.
(a,b,c,d,j)

TRUE COMICS No. 1 (4/41, PM, TR)-The second anthology series based on true stories (see *Sport Comics*). The first of a publisher, lasting 9 years.
(b,e,h,i,h,k)

AMERICA'S GREATEST COMICS No. 1 (5/41?, Faw, H)-Fawcett's first showcase anthology title (in thick format) featuring their top characters, lasting 8 issues.
(a,c,e)

ARMY AND NAVY No. 1 (5/41, S&S, W)-S&S's fifth anthology title, the second ever with a war theme, lasting 5 issues.
(e)

CATMAN COMICS No. 1 (5/41, Holyoke, H)-Continued from *Crash*, Catman got his own series. Second of a publisher. Adequate, but unexceptional covers and stories. Expired after 5 years.
(a,b,c,e)

EXCITING COMICS No. 9 (5/41, BP, H)-Debut of *The Black Terror*, nemesis of crime. Editors never adequately capitalized on the tremendous eye-appeal of the character. Indifferent scripts, lack-luster art disappointed more often than not. The indomitable character endured despite lack of staff support. Logical yet striking appearance of costume sustained character.
(a,b,c,d,j)

STARS AND STRIPES COMICS No. 2 (5/41, Centaur, H)-After the failure of Centaur's last flurry of reprint books a year earlier, they tried to make a comeback. Following Timely's newsstand hit, Centaur picked up on the patriotic theme with the first of three books of this type, lasting only 5 issues.
(e)

SUPER MAGIC No. 1 (5/41, S&S, Mg)-A one-shot book featuring *Blackstone the Magician* and *Rex King*. The first

title to focus on magicians. The title was modified to **Super Magician** and the series lasted 6 years.
(b,e,i,j)

LIBERTY SCOUTS No. 2 (6/41, Centaur, H)-Centaur's second patriotic theme series lasted only two issues.
(e)

★ ★ ★ **ALL FLASH COMICS** No. 1 (Sum/41, DC, H)-The hero of speed achieved stardom and was given his own title. Momentarily retired after 6 years.
(a,b,c,e)

★ **ALL WINNERS COMICS** No. 1 (Sum/41, Timely, H)-First Timely showcase title to give more exposure to their top characters. High impact covers and characters sustained run for 5 years.
(a,c,e)

★ ★ **BULLETMAN** No. 1 (7/41, Faw, H)-The hit of **Master Comics**, receives his own title, lasting 5 years. The Raboy cover and silver logo gets the series off to a good start.
(a,c,e)

CAPTAIN BATTLE COMICS No. 1 (Sum/41, Lev, H)-The third patriotic hero (see **Pep Comics** and **Captain America**) from **Silver Streak** is given his own title. Lacked necessary distinctiveness to compete, folding with the second issue.
(e)

★ ★ **DAREDEVIL COMICS** No. 1 (7/41, Lev, H)-High impact cover, inspired costume design and massive support from Biro's strong, complex plotting sustained momentum of "The Greatest Name in Comics" splash debut. Immediately stood out from the hordes of rival strongmen glutting the stands. Series prevailed for 15 years.
(a,b,c,e,j)

EAGLE, THE No. 1 (7/41, Fox, H)-Another publisher on the patriotic band wagon. The Eagle only flew for four issues.
(e)

FUNNIES, THE No. 57 (7/41, Dell, H)-Debut of Captain Midnight, a patriotic aviation hero who was an established attraction on radio. He was also featured in Dell's **Popular Comics** before being picked up by Fawcett as a regular series.
(a,c,d,j)

MINUTEMAN No. 1 (7/41, Faw, H)-Fawcett's answer to a patriotic hero who began in **Master Comics**. This less than distinguished hero only lasted three issues in his own title.
(e)

PEP COMICS No. 17 (7/41, MLJ, H)-Landmark issue. The first time in comics that a major character (The Comet) actually died, and a new character (The Hangman) was created in the same story.
(a,b,c,d,h)

SPARKLER COMICS No. 1 (7/41, UFS, R)-After three years of costumed heroes glutting the stands, UFS tries its second costumed hero series. Debut of Sparkman, a colorful character who eventually gave way to Tarzan and other reprint characters, title proved competitive through 14 years.
(a,b,c,e,j)

★ **YOUNG ALLIES** No. 1 (Sum/41, Timely, H)-The first sidekick group in comics. The Red Skull guest-starred to give the title a good send-off. Proto-type of the more successful Teen Titans of 25 years hence, it managed a respectable run of 5 years.
(e,f,h,i,j)

CAPTAIN FEARLESS No. 1 (8/41, Helnit, H)-Third of a publisher. An interesting mix of super patriots not lasting beyond the second issue.
(e)

★ ★ ★ ★ **MILITARY COMICS** No. 1 (8/41, Qua, Av)-Otherwise predictable war-theme anthology (the third of its kind) sparked by debut of aviation feature of geniune classic proportions. The crack Blackhawk team took command of the series and continued at the helm 9 years after a title change (to **Modern Comics**) indicated the public had grown jaded with war-themes generally. Ace concept (air-borne privateers meet the axis on its own terms) backed by sterling Iger graphics (the shop's piece de resistance) and top-drawer scripting propelled feature into its own title and a phenomenal 40 year run (with interruptions). The introduction of Blackhawk, and Plastic Man later the same month, lifted Quality into the first rank of comics publishers. A masterpiece of collaborative art.
(a,b,c,d,e,f,h,i,j)

OUR FLAG COMICS No. 1 (8/41, Ace, H)-Ace joined the other publishers with a host of patriotic strongmen debuting in this book. High impact patriotic cover. Series lasted 5 issues.
(e,j)

POCKET COMICS No. 1 (8/41, Harv, H)-An experimental pocket size comic book series featuring Harvey's top characters. Most divergent forms didn't last long and this was no exception, expiring after 4 issues.
(e)

★ ★ ★ ★ **POLICE COMICS** No. 1 (8/41, Quality, H)-Debut of one of the most ingenious super heroes in comics, Plastic Man. An original concept, fully exploited by Jack Cole in the ensuing years. Sheer entertainment with the incomparable Cole at the top of his form. Shares standard bearer honors with **Military**, lasting 12 years.
(a,b,c,d,e,f,i,j)

★ **RED RYDER COMICS** No. 3 (8/41, Hawley, Ws)-The first continuous series single theme western comic for newsstand sales. Ties back to a one-shot issue of a year earlier. Title lasted 16 years due to popular movie series.
(a,b,c,e,f,h,i,j)

SPITFIRE COMICS No. 1 (8/41, Harvey, Av)-An experimental aviation pocket size comic book, lasting 2 issues.
(e)

★ **UNCLE SAM QUARTERLY** No. 1 (8/41, Qua, H)-Eisner's version of a patriotic hero, the star of **National Comics**, is given his own book, lasting 8 issues. Usual Iger shop excellence.
(e)

USA COMICS No. 1 (8/41, Timely, H)-Timely, extending the patriotic theme, created another showcase title for introducing new characters. After five issues, their trend setting Captain America was brought in to save the run and it endured 4 years.
(a,c,e)

VICTORY COMICS No. 1 (8/41, Hill, H)-Classic Everett Nazi war cover. Hillman tried their third title, this time with a patriotic costumed hero theme, again unsuccessfully. It lasted only 4 issues.
(e)

BANNER COMICS No. 3 (9/41, Ace, H)-Debut of Captain Courageous, a derivative patriotic hero—not prominent enough to survive more than 3 issues.
(e)

CALLING ALL GIRLS No. 1 (9/41, PMI, TR)-Second of a publisher. The true fact anthology, with biographies of famous persons and sketches of historic events (occasionally mixed with magazine-type photo features), was a comics format pioneered by Parent's Magazine Institute. Here the target audience was adolescent girls. Similar titles were cloned later on. Enjoyed a run of 7 years.
(b,e,f,h,i,j)

FOUR FAVORITES No. 1 (9/41, Ace, H)-Ace's first showcase title featuring their top characters together in one book, lasting 6 years.
(e)

REAL HEROES COMICS No. 1 (9/41, PMI, TR)-With the success of *True Comics*, the publisher attempted another title based on true stories. Their third series, lasting 5 years. *Heroic Comics* was later converted to this theme.
(e)

REAL LIFE COMICS No. 1 (9/41, BP, TR)-Inspired by the newsstand success of PMI's *True Comics*, this publisher came out with their version, lasting 11 years.
(b,e)

STARTLING COMICS No. 10 (9/41, BP, H)-Debut of *The Fighting Yank*, America's super patriot. Interesting variation on the patriotic theme in that he could call up heroes from the American revolution to assist in the modern fight against crime. Tremendous eye-appeal of character never fully realized due to low standard story art. High impact Schomburg covers sustained the run.
(a,b,c,d,j)

SUPER MAGICIAN COMICS No. 2 (9/41, S&S, Mg)-The first continuous series anthology title on the subject of magic, continuing from *Super Magic* and lasting 6 years.
(e,j)

YANKEE COMICS No. 1 (9/41, Chesler, H)-Chesler re-entered the comic market with this patriotic title. Debut of *Yankee Doodle Jones*. Sensational patriotic cover. Despite its visual appeal, it endured only 4 issues.
(e)

★ ★ ★ ★ **CLASSIC COMICS** No. 1 (10/41, Gil, Lit)-First and most enduring of 'educational' theme comics, Gilberton drew on works of great literature for their highly visible newsstand product. One of the few lines that could be endorsed without reservation by parents and educators, its marketing success was not tied to single-theme titles or continuing characters. Variable art quality somewhat diminished the overall impact of the line. The only comic publisher to place each issue into endless reprints while continuing to publish new titles on a monthly basis, lasting 30 years.
(a,b,c,e,f,h,i,j,k)

DOLL MAN No. 1 (Fall/41, Qua, H)-After a successful two-year run in *Feature*, the mighty mite leaped into his own title, lasting 12 years. The proto-type of the Silver Age Atom.
(a,b,c,e,j)

DYNAMIC COMICS No. 1 (10/41, Chesler, H)-Chesler's second patriotic super hero series. Debut of *Major Victory*. Suspended after three issues and brought back with a format change in 1944, lasting four more years.
(e)

★ ★ ★ **GREEN LANTERN** No. 1 (Fall/41, DC, H)-Having headlined *All-American* for one year, one of DC's foremost heroes achieved the distinction of his own title. It ran for 8 years and went on to become one of the key revival characters of the Silver Age.
(a,b,c,e)

★ ★ ★ ★ **LOONEY TUNES & MERRY MELODIES** No. 1 (Fall/41, Dell, F)-The companion title to the enormously successful *WDC&S*. Dell's second funny animal anthology featured *Bugs Bunny*, *Porky Pig* and *Elmer Fudd*. This was the first comic book appearance of Warner Brothers film characters. The series ran for 21 years.
(a,b,c,e,h,j,l)

RANGERS COMICS No. 1(10/41, FH, W)-The publisher's sixth single theme anthology title (war theme). Standard FH style of cheesecake art and covers, lasting 11 years.
(a,b,c,e)

SKYMAN No. 1 (Fall/41, CCG, Av)-After a year's successful run in *Big Shot*, he was given his own title. Second of a publisher, lasting only 4 issues. (He remained the main feature in *Big Shot* for 9 years.)
(a,c,e)

★ ★ **SPYSMASHER** No. 1 (Fall/41, Faw, Av)-Popular war

hero graduating from *Whiz* into his own title, lasting 2 years. Maiden issue featured unusual logo printed in metallic silver.
(a,c,e)

STAR SPANGLED COMICS No. 1(10/41, DC, H)-DC's first patriotic theme title featuring the *Star Spangled Kid*. Due to the weak contents, the title had a dramatic format change with No. 7 when *The Guardian* and *The Newsboy Legion* were introduced.
(b,e)

WORLD FAMOUS HEROES MAGAZINE No. 1 (10/41, Comic Corp, TR)-Similar theme to PMI's *Real Heroes*, and Eastern's *Heroic*, with stories of famous people, lasting 4 issues.
(e)

AIRFIGHTERS COMICS No. 1 (11/41, Hill, Av)-An early attempt at an aviation theme comic (like *Wings*), lasting only one issue. A year later the title was revived more successfully with a new 'dynamic' character in *Airboy*.
(e)

GREAT COMICS No. 1 (11/41, Great, H)-First of a publisher, featuring super heroes. The third and last issue is a classic: *Futuro* takes *Hitler* to hell.
(e,k)

MAN OF WAR No. 1 (11/41, Centaur, H)-Centaur's third and last patriotic theme title, lasting 2 issues. Conjecture is that Centaur itself expired with this book.
(e)

SCOOP COMICS No. 1 (11/41, Chesler, H)-Chesler's third attempt at a comeback with this anthology of super heroes. Debut of *Rocketman* and *Rocketgirl*, lasting 8 issues.
(e)

U.S. JONES No. 1 (11/41, Fox, H)-Fox's second patriotic theme title, lasting 2 issues.
(e)

★ ★ ★ ★ **ALL-STAR COMICS** No. 8 (11-12/41, DC, H)-*Wonder Woman*, the first super-heroine, created by Charles Moulton and drawn by H.G. Peter, debuted in this issue as an 8 page add-on. Her origin continued in *Sensation* No. 1, where she becomes the lead feature. A trend setter.
(a,b,c,d,f,h,i,j)

BANG-UP COMICS No. 1 (12/41, Progressive, H)-A new publisher entered the field. This series was mediocre in its content only surviving 3 issues.
(e,k)

CAPTAIN AERO COMICS No. 7 (12/41, Hoke, Av)-Cashing in on the popularity of *Spy Smasher* and *Captain Midnight*, this publisher began with another aviation hero. With strong, colorful covers, the series lasted 5 years.
(e)

CHOICE COMICS No. 1 (12/41, Great, H)-The publisher's second title. A mixed anthology, lasting 3 issues.
(e)

MASTER COMICS No. 21 (12/41, Faw, H)-*Captain Marvel* and *Bulletman* team-up to fight *Captain Nazi*. A classic battle sequence, rare in comics at this time. High impact (classic) Raboy cover and story art.
(a,b,c)

PIONEER PICTURE STORIES No. 1 (12/41, S&S, TR)-An anthology of true stories about heroes (ala *Heroic Comics*), lasting 9 issues.
(e)

★ ★ ★ ★ **PEP COMICS** No. 22 (12/41, MLJ, TA)-The eternal sophomore and his friends began the first of over forty consecutive terms at Riverdale High. Never rose above pat formula, but survived vagaries of shifting market that did in a host of illustrious predecessors and glut of imitators (many of which originated at MLJ itself). Auxiliary characters achieved stardom with their own titles. Trend setter, lasting

beyond 40 years.
(a,b,c,d,f,h,i,j)

PUNCH COMICS No. 1 (12/41, Chesler, H)-Chesler's fourth attempt to get back into the market. A mixed anthology series with a successful format, lasting 6 years.
(e)

★ ★ ★ **WHIZ COMICS** No. 25 (12/12/41, Faw, H)-*Captain Marvel* was cloned for the second time (see *Lt. Marvels*) into a junior size as *Captain Marvel Jr.* Classic art by Mac Raboy gave the character a slick streamlined 'Raymond' look. He was given immediate headlining in *Master Comics*. This was the first significant character cloned.
(a,b,c,d,j)

X-MAS COMICS No. 1 (12/41, Faw, H)-A new concept. Earlier in the year, Fawcett began over-running certain selected comics with indicias, page numbers, etc. removed. These comics were then bound up into a thick book (324 pgs.) to be sold as a special comic for Christmas. This successful format evolved into several other titles and lasted for 11 years.
(a,b,c,e,f,h,j)

CAPTAIN MARVEL THRILL BOOK nn (1941, Faw, H)-A large-size black & white comic reprinting popular *Captain Marvel* stories, lasting one issue. (Half text, half illustration.)
(e)

DICKIE DARE No. 1 (1941, Eastern, R)-Another single theme anthology title of the popular strip, lasting 4 issues.
(e)

DOUBLE UP nn (1941, Elliott, H)-The same idea as *Double*, except this was a one-shot remarketing of remaindered digest-sized issues of *Speed, Spitfire* and *Pocket*. Probably a special deal to Elliott due to heavy returns?
(e)

FACE, THE No. 1 (1941, CCG, H)-The popular strip from *Big Shot* achieved brief stardom, lasting only two issues.
(e)

KEY RING COMICS (1941, Dell, An)-A special formated comic series of 16 pages each to put in a two-ring binder (sold as a set of five).
(e)

TRAIL BLAZERS No. 1 (1941, S&S, TR)-True fact anthology of heroic deeds, lasting 4 issues.
(e)

USA IS READY No. 1 (1941, Dell, W)-Dell's second war title lasting one issue.
(e)

★ ★ ★ **ANIMAL COMICS** No. 1 (12-1/41-42, Dell, F)-Debut of Walt Kelly's classic character, *Pogo*, which became syndicated in 1948. Dell's third funny animal single theme anthology title following the success of *WDC&S* and *Looney Tunes*. The first funny animal comic with original characters at Dell.
(a,c,d,e,j)

1942 ◼

FOUR MOST No. 1 (Wint/41-42, Novelty, H)-A showcase title featuring Novelty's best characters from *Target* and *Blue Bolt*. Series taken over by *Dick Cole* with No. 3 on. Their third title.
(a,b,c,e)

★ **LEADING COMICS** No. 1 (Wint/41-42, DC, H)-Like *All-Star*, this title provided a showcase for DC's secondary heroes (a poor man's *All-Star*). Series ran 14 issues then changed to a funny animal format for the rest of its 7 year existance.
(e)

★ ★ ★ ★ ★ **SENSATION COMICS** No. 1 (1/42, DC, H)-*Wonder Woman's* origin continued from *All-Star* No. 8 (her first appearance). A very strong character from the onset, achieving stardom instantly as a headline feature of this series. She won her own title within a few months which has run uninterrupted for over 40 years. (One of the few characters to achieve this kind of exposure.)
(a,b,c,e,f,h,j)

SPECIAL COMICS No. 1 (Wint/41-42, MLJ, H)-A one-shot special featuring *The Hangman* from *Pep Comics*. A hit on the stands, the character was launched into his own series with No. 2.
(c,e)

V...- COMICS No. 1 (1/42, Fox, H)-another short-lived title from Fox. His third patriotic theme comic. Introduced *V-Man*, lasted only two issues.
(e)

AMERICA'S BEST COMICS No. 1 (2/42, BP, H)-A showcase title to give more exposure to their top characters. The high impact covers (many by Schomburg) sustained the run, lasting 7 years.
(a,b,c,e)

CAMP COMICS No. 1 (2/42, Dell, Hm)-A mixed (humorous) anthology title with pretty girl photo covers. An unusual format slanted to the soldier boys at camp.
(e)

★ ★ **GENE AUTRY COMICS** No. 1 (2/42, Faw, Ws)-The second newsstand continuous series western title devoted to a single character. *Gene* ties with *Roy Rogers* as the most popular cowboy star of the sound era. Title survived 18 years.
(a,b,c,e,h,j,l)

JINGLE JANGLE COMICS No. 1 (2/42, Eastern Color, Hm)-A young children's comic, containing illustrations and script by George Carlson, a children's book heavyweight (*Uncle Wiggily*). Eastern's second anthology title of original material (see *Heroic*), lasting 7 years.
(a,b,e,j)

TRUE SPORT PICTURE STORIES No. 5 (2/42, S&S, Sp)-Continued from *Sport Comics*, lasting 7 years.
(e)

CAPTAIN COURAGEOUS COMICS No. 6 (3/42, Ace, H)-Introduced in *Banner*, the character was given his own title but lasted only one issue.
(e)

TOUGH KID SQUAD No. 1 (3/42, Timely, H)-Timely's second series devoted to sidekicks (see *Young Allies*). Highly prized due to its rarity.
(e)

★ ★ **BOY COMICS** No. 3 (4/42, Lev, H)-Gleason's second successful title, introducing *Crimebuster*. This series survived 14 years due to Biro's strong, complex plotting.
(a,b,c,d,e,j)

COMEDY COMICS No. 9 (4/42, Timely, H)-The title is misleading. A super hero anthology title changing to a humorous and funny animal format early on.
(e)

HANGMAN COMICS No. 2 (Spr/42, MLJ, H)-The smash hit of *Pep Comics* received his own series, but lasted only 7 issues.
(e)

★ **JOKER COMICS** No. 1 (4/42, Timely, Hm)-First *Powerhouse Pepper* by Wolverton. Wolverton, an original if there ever was one, stood totally aloof from the mainstream of comic art. His effect on later comics ranging from the original *Mad* to the sixties undergrounds, is incalculable. (He tried to fit in, but the effect of playing it straight made his work even more bizzare.)
(a,b,c,d,e,f,g,j)

SHEENA, QUEEN OF THE JUNGLE No. 1 (Spr/42, FH, J)-

After three years exposure in **Jumbo Comics**, *Sheena* finally graduated to her own title, lasting 18 issues spread over 11 years.
(a,b,c,e)

★ ★ **STAR SPANGLED COMICS** No. 7 (4/42, DC, H)-Debut of *The Guardian* and *The Newsboy Legion* by Simon and Kirby (vintage). Title lasted 11 years.
(a,b,c,d,j)

WAMBI, JUNGLE BOY No. 1 (Spr/42, FH, J)-From **Jungle Comics**. Not strong enough to carry his own title which had erratic publishing (18 issues in 11 years).
(e)

★ ★ ★ ★ **CRIME DOES NOT PAY** No. 22 (6/42, Lev, C)-Aside from being the first crime comic, this title was the first of many to be deliberately targeted at the adult reader. Inspired by the widely read **True Detective** - style magazines of the time. Implicit and unsavory subject matter, in the context of what was popularly understood as publications for children, assured the attention and disapproval of Wertham and others. Established conventions of graphically depicted violence that would be exploited to the extreme in the horror comics of a decade later. Arguably the third most influential comic ever published (after **Action** and **Superman**), *CDNP* was a belated trend setter. Gleason had the field all to himself for six years. Then, in 1948 the industry suffered a severe slump in sales. In desperation, publishers turned en masse to the formerly untapped 'crime' market. This move was abetted in part by Gleason himself. In mid-1947 he had begun publishing circulation figures on the covers of *CDNP*, reporting sales of 5 million - 6 million copies (per issue?), an astounding record for a comics periodical and, an open invitation to imitation.
(a,b,c,e,f,h,i,j)

★ **DETECTIVE COMICS** No. 64 (6/42, DC, H)-Simon and Kirby introduce the *Boy Commandos*. A more timely version of the *Newsboy Legion*, this popular series found the Axis plagued with a platoon of wise-cracking juveniles. An immediate hit, the lads were rewarded with a quarterly of their own within a matter of months.
(a,c,d,j)

FAIRY TALE PARADE No. 1 (6-7/42, Dell, F)-Dell's second continuous series funny animal title with original characters. Its popularity was carried entirely by the imaginative illustrative genius of Walt Kelly.
(c,e)

BIG CHIEF WAHOO No. 1 (7/42, Eastern, R)-Popular transfer strip debuts in his own comic series, lasting 23 issues.
(c,e)

DIXIE DUGAN No. 1 (7/42, CCG, R)-Popular strip character given own title, lasting 7 years (13 issues).
(e)

KRAZY KOMICS No. 1 (7/42, Timely, F)-With four funny animal anthology titles on the stands (all by Dell), Timely entered this new developing field. This series had a humorous format with no strong characters, lasting 4 years. The second publisher in this genre.
(e)

NAPOLEON AND UNCLE ELBY No. 1 (7/42), Eastern Color, R)-A one-shot single theme anthology title of the popular transfer strip.
(e)

NEW FUNNIES No. 65 (7/42, Dell, F)-The funny animal fever was catching on as Dell gave stardom to their newly acquired characters, *Andy Panda* and *Woody Woodpecker*. Lantz created these characters who became an instant success for Dell's **The Funnies**. This was Dell's fifth funny animal series (with only six on the stands).
(a,b,c,e,j)

OAKY DOAKS No. 1 (7/42, Eastern Color, R)-A one-shot strip reprint book which couldn't compete on the stands.

(e)

STRICTLY PRIVATE No. 1 (7/42), Eastern Color, R)-A two-issue run of the famous strip, not surviving as a comic book.
(e)

WAR VICTORY ADVENTURES No. 1 (Sum/42, Harv, W)-A unique super hero title produced to promote purchase of war savings bonds, lasting 3 issues.
(e)

★ ★ ★ ★ **WONDER WOMAN** No. 1 (Sum/42, DC, H)-One of the few characters in comics to make her own title just months from her debut in **All-Star** No. 8. The only mythological character to flourish in the comics format, her only concession to the present was adopting a modern costume. The amazing Amazon was a trend setter whose popularity has lasted beyond 40 years.
(a,b,c,e,j)

WAR HEROES No. 1 (7-9/42, Dell, W)-Dell's third war title, lasting 11 issues.
(e)

★ **CAPTAIN MIDNIGHT** No. 1 (9/42, Faw, Av)-This book heralds one of the most changed transfer characters adapted successfully to the comic medium format. Fawcett's version of the character is the most memorable (see **The Funnies** No. 57), lasting 6 years. Kept alive by the long lasting radio series and a movie serial. A spin-off of *Spy Smasher*.
(a,b,c,e)

FIGHTING YANK No. 1 (9/42, BP, H)-After a year's exposure in **Startling**, the colonial hero was given his own series. The outstanding Schomburg covers sustained the run, lasting 7 years.
(a,b,c,e,j)

OUR GANG COMICS No. 1 (9-10/42, Dell, F)-A strong early licensed group from MGM films who didn't quite come across as well in the comic medium due to necessary changes in the stereotyping of *Buckwheat* and others. The comic version is mainly collected due to the outstanding art by Walt Kelly and the back-up strips by Carl Barks.
(a,b,c,e,f,j,l)

★ **COO COO COMICS** No. 1 (10/42, BP, F)-Seeing the stands beginning to swell with Dell's funny animal titles (5), Better got on the band wagon. *Super Mouse* debuted, the first funny animal super hero (cloned from *Superman*). (7 funny animal titles now on the stands.)
(a,b,c,d,e,f,h,i,j)

★ ★ ★ ★ ★ **DONALD DUCK FOUR COLOR** No. 9 (10/42, Dell, F)-Debut of anonymous artist, who breathed life into the character and turned the strip into full-length adventure stories. Carl Barks' successful adaptation won him the position as *Donald Duck's* biographer for almost three decades beginning with **Walt Disney's Comics and Stories** No. 31.
(a,b,c,g,h,j)

★ **JUNGLE GIRL** No. 1 (Fall/42, Faw, J)-Inspired by the popular film serial, *Perils of Nyoka*, this one-shot introduced the jungle heroine to comics. The series was picked up again in 1945 (retitled **Nyoka**), lasting 8 years.
(a,b,c,e,f,j,l)

PICTURE STORIES FROM THE BIBLE No. 1 (Fall/42, DC, TR)-The pilot model of M. C. Gaines' projected 'educational comics' line was laudable in concept but squelched at the stands by abysmal art, pedantic scripting and the normal resistance of kids to anything even remotely preachy. Sustained primarily by lot sales to educators and church groups. Ironically, the first comic ever to bear the EC seal.
(a,c,e,i,j,l)

SUPERSNIPE COMICS No. 6 (10/42, S&S, H)-Probably the best, and certainly the most original comic book character of this pulp publisher. A super hero parody lasting 7 years.
(a,b,c,e,f,j)

★ **TERRY-TOONS COMICS** No. 1 (10/42, Timely, F)-20th Century Fox's characters enter the comic field with this book. Timely's second funny animal anthology series (8 titles are now on the stands). 20th Century Fox's *Mighty Mouse* appeared in films the following year and entered this run with No. 38.
(a,b,c,e,j,l)

★ **AIR FIGHTERS** No. 2 (11/42, Hill, Av)-First appearance of one of the top aviation features also marked Hillman's first successful title. Engaging origin featured air-minded monk who designed and built the premier imaginary aircraft in all of comics. At the controls of the unusual bat-winged orinthopter, dubbed *Birdie*, was the youth who would become known as *Airboy*. He managed to make the standard garb of the pilot—goggles, scarf, flight jacket, et al—look as if they were designed expressly for him. Thoughtful scripting and complimentary art (ala Caniff) propelled this feature through the war years and beyond. Duration 11 years. (*The Heap*, one of the most original characters in comics, began in the next issue.)
(a,b,c,d,j)

★ ★ **CAPTAIN MARVEL JR** No. 1 (11/42, Faw, H)-Fawcett's second most popular hero (from *Master*) was given his own series. Raboy classic covers/story art sustained the run, lasting 11 years.
(a,b,c,e)

MICKEY FINN No. 1 (11/42, Eastern Color, R)-The popular transfer character tried his wings in a title of his own. Like *Sparky Watts*, only 17 issues came out in a 10 year period.
(a,c,e)

SPARKY WATTS No. 1 (11/42, CCG, R)-Humorous, off-beat character (proven in *Big Shot*) is given own title, struggling through 10 issues in 7 years.
(a,c,e)

TOPIX No. 1 (11/42, CG, Re)-The first continuous series comic with a religious theme, lasting 10 years. First of a publisher.
(b,e,i,j,k)

★ **CAPTAIN MARVEL ADVENTURES** No. 18 (12/11/42, Faw, H)-*Captain Marvel* is cloned again. Debut of *Mary Marvel* and *The Marvel Family*. Mary Marvel was given instant stardom in *Wow*.
(a,b,c,d,j)

FAWCETT'S FUNNY ANIMAL COMICS No. 1 (12/42, Faw, F)-The first appearance of *Hoppy The Marvel Bunny*, (cloned from *Captain Marvel*), lasting 13 years. The second funny animal super hero (see *Coo Coo*). Fawcett joined Dell, Timely and Better entering the funny animal market (10 titles now on the stands). (*Captain Marvel* himself introduced *Hoppy* on the cover.)
(a,b,c,d,e,h,j)

FUNNY BOOK No. 1 (12/42, PMI, F)-Another publisher entered the funny animal market with this book. Weak concepts overall, the title lasting 9 issues over 4 years (10 titles now on the stands).
(e)

GIFT COMICS No. 1 (12/42, Faw, H)-Fawcett's second thick-format title containing original comics to be released at Christmas with *Holiday* and *Xmas* for 50¢.
(a,c,e)

HIT COMICS No. 25 (12/42, Qua, H)-*Kid Eternity* debuts. Recurring war-era theme of life after life was given novel twist in this long running series. Youthful hero, dying ahead of his appointed time, was not only miraculously restored to life but granted the ability to call on all the great heroes of the past for assistance in solving crimes (see *The Fighting Yank*). Intriguing concept was given usual stellar Iger shop treatment.
(a,b,c,d,j)

HOLIDAY COMICS No. 1 (12/42, Faw, H)-Fawcett's third thick-format title of original comics to be released at Christmas with *Gift* and *Xmas* for 25¢.
(a,c,e)

SANTA CLAUS FUNNIES No. 1 (12/42, Dell, F)-A special Christmas book illustrated by Kelly. A successful concept that was repeated annually for 20 years.
(a,b,c,e)

AMERICA IN ACTION nn (1942, Dell, W)-A one-shot war anthology book.
(e)

FAMOUS STORIES No. 1 (1942, Dell, Lit)-An educational theme comic, similar to *Classic Comics*, not lasting beyond the 2nd issue.
(e)

JOE PALOOKA No. 1 (1942, CCG, R)-With proven success in *Big Shot* (not to mention syndication), the character became a star in his own title. Early issues boast "over 1,000,000 copies sold." The series lasted 19 years.
(a,b,c,e)

WAR STORIES No. 1 (1942, Dell, W)-Dell's fourth war theme anthology title, lasting 8 issues. *Night Devils*, a mysterious costumed war team debuted in No. 3.
(e)

1943 ∎

ALL NEW COMICS No. 1 (1/43, Harv, H)-A super hero anthology title of mediocre quality, lasting 15 issues.
(e)

★ ★ ★ **ARCHIE COMICS** No. 1 (Wint/42-43, AP, TA)-Early stardom for a non-super hero theme. A successful formula with many spin-off characters, lasting beyond 40 years.
(a,b,c,d,e,h,i,j)

BLACK TERROR No. 1 (Wint/42-43, BP, H)-Fighting his way from *Exciting*, the character begins his own series. Sterling costume. High impact Schomburg covers mislead the buyer as to the quality of the contents. Lasted 7 years.
(a,b,c,e,j)

BOY COMMANDOS No. 1 (Wint/42-43, DC, W)-After *Captain America*, this was the second title that Simon and Kirby had all to themselves. Pat variation of favorite S&K theme: Kid group with adult mentor. Seldom rose above the expected, but S&K were at their loosest and the strip conveys the sense of fun they probably had doing it. Earlier covers, sans redundant blurbs and intrusive dialogue balloons, are superb poster art.
(a,b,c,e,j)

CAPTAIN BATTLE No. 3 (Wint/42-43, Mag. Press, H)-After a year's delay, the character from *Silver Streak* was given another chance, only lasting 3 issues.
(e)

CLUE COMICS No. 1 (1/43, Hill, H)-Hillman's second most successful title. Unusual heroes and bizarre villains sustained run for four years.
(e)

COMIC CAVALCADE No. 1 (Wint/42-43, DC, H)-Following the success of *World's Finest*, DC launched this companion book in thick format featuring their next tier of top characters, *Wonder Woman, The Flash* and *Green Lantern*.
(a,b,c,e)

COMICS DIGEST No. 1 (Wint/42-43, PMI, TR)-A one-shot war theme reprint anthology (pocket size) from *True Comics*.
(e)

FLYING CADET No. 1 (1/43, Flying Cadet, Av)-A true theme World War II aviation anthology (with real photos), lasting 4 years.
(e)

GOLDEN ARROW No. 1 (Wint/42-43, Faw, Ws)-Fawcett's original western character from *Whiz* finally given own title, lasting 6 issues.
(a,e)

HELLO PAL COMICS No. 1 (1/43, Harv, An)-Unusual format featuring photographic covers of movie stars. *Rocketman* and *Rocketgirl* appear (see *Scoop*), lasting 3 issues.
(e)

MISS FURY COMICS No. 1 (Wint/42-43, Timely, H)-A strong transfer character by Tarpe Mills. Noteworthy and unique in that she rarely appeared in costume.
(a,c,e,f,j)

MAJOR HOOPLE COMICS No. 1 (1/43, BP, R)-A one-shot comic of the famous strip character, as Better tried to enter the reprint market.
(e)

REAL FUNNIES No. 1 (1/43, Nedor, F)-The publisher's second funny animal title (11 titles now on stands), only lasting 3 issues. First appearance of *The Black Terrier* (cloned from *The Black Terror*), the third funny animal super hero.
(e)

RED DRAGON COMICS No. 5 (1/43, S&S, An)-Pulpy anthology series not strong enough to last over 5 issues.
(e)

DON WINSLOW OF THE NAVY No. 1 (2/43, Faw, W)-His comic book career was launched here with an introduction by *Captain Marvel* himself. Successful adaptation of this popular transfer character, lasting 12 years.
(a,b,c,e,j,l)

HEADLINE COMICS No. 1 (2/43, Prize, TR)-Taking up the "True" theme of PMI's *True* and *Real Heroes* and Better's *Real Life*, Prize entered the field with this, their second title, which lasted 13 years.
(b,e)

HOPALONG CASSIDY No. 1 (2/43, Faw, Ws)-A one-shot issue continuing as a series three years later. The third continuous series newsstand western title, lasting 16 years. A transfer character kept alive by William Boyd's strong following in the movies and on TV.
(a,b,c,e)

IBIS, THE INVINCIBLE No. 1 (2/43, Faw, Mg)-As a solid back-up feature in *Whiz*, he was invincible, but not invincible enough to support a title of his own. The title expired after 6 issues.
(e)

KID KOMICS No. 1 (2/43, Timely, H)-Timely's third series devoted to sidekicks. The Schomburg covers and guest appearances of secondary characters sustained the run through 10 issues.
(e)

ALL HERO COMICS No. 1 (3/43, Faw, H)-Fawcett's second title that showcased their top characters (see *America's Greatest*). A thick format one-shot.
(a,c,e)

CAPTAIN MARVEL ADVENTURES No. 22 (3/43, Faw, H)-Begins the 25-issue *Mr. Mind* serial which captured nationwide attention at the time. Tremendous and brilliant marketing strategy by Fawcett. An epic by any standard, unmatched before or since.
(c,d,f,h,i,j)

COMEDY COMICS No. 14 (3/43, Timely, F)-The first *Super Rabbit* (the fourth funny animal super hero) (the 12th title on the stands). Given his own title the following year. (An imitation of *Hoppy The Marvel Bunny*.)
(a,c,d,e,j)

FUNNY FUNNIES No. 1 (4/43, BP, F)-A one-shot funny animal title (their third) (13 titles now on stands). No enduring characters.

(e)

★ ★ ★ ★ **WALT DISNEY'S COMICS AND STORIES** No. 31 (4/43, Dell, F)-Anonymous staffer who defined what funny animal continuity is all about began this issue (2nd Barks *DD* story; see *DD Four Color* No. 9). Cinched long-term success of Disney anthology. One of a half-dozen absolute masters of the form, Carl Barks' achievement on individual stories is exceeded only by remarkable consistency of the series over the length of its run (over 40 years).
(a,b,c,j)

GOOFY COMICS No. 1 (6/43, Nedor, F)-Nedor's fourth funny animal title and one of the most enduring, lasting 10 years. No memorable characters. (13 funny animal titles on the stands.)
(b,e)

JOLLY JINGLES No. 10 (Sum/43, MLJ, F)-A new publisher tried their hand at funny animals, introducing *Super Duck* (the fifth funny animal super hero). (A hybrid of *Superman* and *Donald Duck*.) (14 titles on the stands.)
(a,c,d,e,j)

★ ★ **PLASTIC MAN** No. 1 (Sum/43, Qua, H)-After a slow start, this title outlasts *Police Comics*, surviving 13 years. One of the top hero concepts carried by the exciting plotting/art of Jack Cole.
(a,b,c,e)

HAPPY COMICS No. 1 (8/43, Standard, F)-Their fifth funny animal title. No memorable characters, lasting 7 years (14 titles on the stands.)
(b,e)

ALL-SELECT COMICS No. 1 (Fall/43, Timely, H)-Timely's second showcase title featuring their top three characters (see *All Winners*). Series carried by Schomburg covers (a proven sales feature), lasting 3 years.
(a,c,e)

ALL SURPRISE No. 1 (Fall/43, Timely, F)-Timely's fourth funny animal title, giving more exposure to their leading character, *Super Rabbit*, lasting 4 years. (15 titles on the stands.)
(e)

SUPER RABBIT No. 1 (Fall/43, Timely, F)-After his debut in *Comedy Comics*, *Super Rabbit* is given his own title, lasting 5 years. (15 titles on the stands.)
(e)

CAPTAIN BATTLE JR No. 1 (Fall/43, Comic House, H)-Clone of *Captain Battle*. The *Claw* vs. *The Ghost*, lasting 2 issues.
(e)

GIGGLE COMICS No. 1 (10/43, ACG, F)-Ties as first title of a new publisher, reinforcing the trend to funny animals. The quality and style of ACG's whole line was heavily influenced by the mastery of the teacher-artist of Ken Hultgren, the series' artist (beginning in 1944). This title lasted 12 years. (17 titles on the stands.)
(a,b,c,e,j,k)

HA HA COMICS No. 1 (10/43, ACG, F)-Ties as first title of a new publisher, reinforcing the trend to funny animals. A double impact-with sister title on the stands. Ingenious plotting and art by Ken Hultgren begins the following year. This series lasted 12 years. (17 titles on the stands.)
(a,b,c,e,j,k)

SUSPENSE COMICS No. 1 (12/43, Continental, D)-Debut of *The Grey Mask* (imitation of *The Spirit*). Atmospheric radio drama in a comic book form, lasting 3 years.
(e)

AVIATION CADETS nn (1943, S&S, Av)-A World War II aviation anthology one-shot. Navy pre-flight training involving sports.
(e)

COLUMBIA COMICS No. 1 (1943, Wise, R)-More exposure for Columbia's reprint characters, *Joe Palooka, Dixie Duggan*, etc., lasting 4 issues. (e)

POWERHOUSE PEPPER No. 1 (1943, Timely, Hm)-The protagonist of *Joker Comics* of a year earlier, Wolverton's humorous plotting made this character a memorable one. Popular enough to receive his own title. (a,c,e,j)

TINY TOTS COMICS No. 1 (1943, Dell, F)-A one-shot anthology book of funny animals with Walt Kelly art. (e)

TREASURE COMICS nn (1943, Prize, H)-Rebinding of coverless copies of *Prize* No. 7-11 from 1942. A very rare book with only one copy known to exist. (e)

UNITED STATES MARINES nn (1943, Wise, W)-A documentary style war anthology series mixed with magazine-type photo features from the front, surviving one year. The title was resurrected for a brief period after the Korean conflict. (e)

ALL FUNNY COMICS No. 1 (Wint/43-44, DC, Hm)-DC's first all funny anthology title. A popular series with the humorous plotting of *Genius Jones*, lasting 4½ years. (e,j)

BLACK HOOD COMICS No. 9 (Wint/43-44, MLJ, H)-The Man of Mystery graduates from *Top-Notch* into his own title, lasting 11 issues. (e)

CHRONOLOGICAL LIST OF COMIC BOOK TITLES BY PUBLISHER
FOR PERIOD 1933 - 1943
(The indented titles are key books other than No. 1's)

ACE MAGAZINES
Sure-Fire No. 1, 6/40
Super Mystery No. 1, 7/40
Lightning No. 4, 12/40
Our Flag No. 1, 8/41
Banner No. 3, 9/41
Four Favorites No. 1, 9/41
Captain Courageous No. 6, 3/42

AMERICAN COMICS GROUP
Giggle No. 1, 10/43
Ha Ha No. 1, 10/43

BETTER PUBL. (Standard)
Best No. 1, 11/39
Thrilling No. 1, 2/40
Exciting No. 1, 4/40
  Exciting No. 9, 5/41
Startling No. 1, 6/40
Real Life No. 1, 9/41
  Startling No. 10, 9/41
America's Best No. 1, 2/42
Fighting Yank No. 1, 9/42
Coo Coo No. 1, 10/42
Black Terror No. 1, Wint/42-43
Major Hoople No. 1, 1/43
Real Funnies No. 1, 1/43
Funny Funnies No. 1, 4/43
Goofy No. 1, 6/43
Happy No. 1, 8/43

BILBARA PUBLISHING CO.
Cyclone No. 1, 6/40

CENTAUR PUBLICATIONS
Funny Pages V2/6, 3/38
Funny Pic. Stories V2/6, 3/38
Star Comics No. 10, 3/38
Star Ranger No. 10, 3/38
Cowboy No. 13, 7/38
Keen Detective No. 8, 7/38
Little Giant No. 1, 7/38
Amazing Mystery Funnies No. 1, 8/38
Little Giant Movie No. 1, 8/38
  Funny Pages V2/10, 9/38
Star Ranger Funnies No. 15, 10/38
Little Giant Det. No. 1, 10/38
Keen Komics V2/1, 5/39
  Amazing Mystery Funnies V2/7, 7/39
Comic Pages V3/4, 7/39
  Keen Detective V2/7, 7/39
Amazing Man No. 5, 9/39
Amazing Adventure Funnies No. 1, 6/40
Fantoman No. 2, 8/40
Masked Marvel No. 1, 9/40
Arrow, The No. 1, 10/40
Super Spy No. 1, 10/40
Detective Eye No. 1, 11/40
Wham No. 1, 11/40

Stars and Stripes No. 2, 5/41
Liberty Scouts No. 2, 6/41
World Famous Heroes No. 1, 10/41
Man Of War No. 1, 11/41

CATECHETICAL GUILD
Topix No. 1, 11/42

HARRY 'A' CHESLER
Star No. 1, 2/37
Star Ranger No. 1, 2/37
Feature Funnies No. 1, 10/37
Cocomalt Big Book No. 1, 1938
Yankee No. 1, 9/41
Dynamic No. 1, 10/41
Scoop No. 1, 11/41
Punch No. 1, 12/41

COLUMBIA COMICS GROUP
Big Shot No. 1, 5/40
Skyman No. 1, Fall/41
Face, The No. 1, 1941
Dixie Duggan No. 1, 7/42
Joe Palooka No. 1, 1942
Sparky Watts No. 1, 11/42

COMICS MAGAZINE
Comics Magazine No. 1, 5/36
Funny Pages No. 6, 11/36
Funny Picture Stories No. 1, 11/36
Detective Picture Stories No. 1, 12/36
Western Picture Stories No. 1, 2/37

DC COMICS
New Fun No. 1, 2/35
New Comics No. 1, 12/35
More Fun No. 7, 1/36
Big Book of Fun No. 1, Spr/36
New Book of Comics No. 1, 6-8/36
New Adventure No. 12, 1/37
Detective No. 1, 3/37
Action No. 1, 6/38
  Detective No. 20, 10/38
Adventure No. 32, 11/38
All-American No. 1, 4/39
New York World's Fair 3-5/39
Movie No. 1, 4/39
  Detective No. 27, 5/39
  Adventure No. 40, 7/39
Mutt and Jeff No. 1, Sum/39
Superman No. 1, Sum/39
Double Action No. 2, 1/40
Flash No. 1, 1/40
  More Fun No. 52,53, 2,3/40
  Adventure No. 48, 3/40
Batman No. 1, Spr/40
New York World's Fair 3-5/40
  More Fun No. 55, 5/40
  All-American No. 16, 7/40

All-Star No. 1, Sum/40
  All-American No. 19, 10/40
  All-Star No. 3, 10/40-41
  Adventure No. 61, 4/41
World's Best No. 1, Spr/41
All Flash No. 1, Sum/41
World's Finest No. 2, Sum/41
Green Lantern No. 1, Fall/41
Star Spangled No. 1, 10/41
  All-Star No. 8, 11-12/41
Leading No. 1, Wint/41-42
Sensation No. 1, 1/42
  Star Spangled No. 7, 4/42
  Detective No. 64, 6/42
Wonder Woman No. 1, Sum/42
Pic. Stories/Bible No. 1, Fall/42
Boy Commandos No. 1, Wint/42-43
Comic Cavalcade No. 1, Wint/42-43
All Funny No. 1, Wint/43-44

DELL PUBLISHING CO.
Popular No. 1, 2/36
Funnies No. 1, 10/36
Comics No. 1, 3/37
West. Action Thrillers No. 1, 4/37
100 Pages of Comics No. 1, 1937
Super No. 1, 5/38
Crackajack No. 1, 6/38
Nickel No. 1, 1938
Large Feature Comic No. 1, 1939
Four-Color No. 1, 1939
Donald Duck 4-Color No. 4, 3/40?
War No. 1, 5/40
W.D.'s Comics & Stories No. 1, 10/40
Mickey Mouse 4-Color No. 16, 4/41
  Funnies No. 57, 7/41
Red Ryder No. 3, 8/41
Looney Tunes No. 1, Fall/41
Key Ring No. 1, 1941
Large Feature No. 1, 1941
USA Is Ready No. 1, 1941
Animal No. 1, 12-1/41-42
Camp No. 1, 2/42
Fairy Tale Parade No. 1, 6-7/42
New Funnies No. 65, 7/42
War Heroes No. 1, 7-9/42
Our Gang No. 1, 9-10/42
Santa Claus Funnies No. 1, 12/42
America In Action No. 1, 1942
Donald Duck 4-Color No. 9, 1942
Famous Stories No. 1, 1942
War Stories No. 1, 1942
  W.D. Comics & Stories No. 31, 4/43
Tiny Tots No. 1, 1943

EASTERN COLOR
Funnies On Parade nn, 1933
F. F., A Carnival– nn, 1933
Century Of Comics nn, 1933
Skippy's Own Book nn, 1934

Famous Funnies Series 1, 1934
Famous Funnies No. 1, 7/34
Heroic No. 1, 8/40
Buck Rogers No. 1, Wint/40-41
Dickie Dare No. 1, 1941
Big Chief Wahoo No. 1, Wint/41-42
Jingle Jangle No. 1, 2/42
Oaky Doaks No. 1, 7/42
Mickey Finn No. 1, 11/42
Napoleon & Uncle Elby No. 1, 11/42
Strictly Private No. 1, 11/42
Tiny Tots No. 1, 1943

WILL EISNER
Spirit No. 1, 6/2/40

ELLIOT PUBLICATIONS
Double 1940
Double Up 1941

FAWCETT PUBLICATIONS
Flash No. 1, 1/40
Whiz No. 2, 2/40
Master No. 1, 3/40
Slam Bang No. 1, 3/40
Nickel No. 1, 5/40
Special Edition No. 1, 8/40
Western Desperado No. 8, 10/40
Wow No. 1, Wint/40-41
Captain Marvel No. 1, 1-2/41
America's Greatest No. 1, 5/41
Bulletman No. 1, 7/41
Minuteman No. 1, 7/41
Capt. Marvel Thrill Book 1941
Gene Autry No. 1, Fall/41
Spysmasher No. 1, Fall/41
   Master No. 21, 12/41
   Whiz No. 25, 12/12/41
Xmas No. 1, 12/41
Captain Midnight No. 1, 9/42
Jungle Girl No. 1, Fall/42
Captain Marvel Jr. No. 1, 11/42
   Captain Marvel No. 18, 12/11/42
Fawcett's Funny Animals No. 1, 12/42
Gift No. 1, 12/42
Holiday No. 1, 12/42
Golden Arrow No. 1, Wint/42-43
Don Winslow No. 1, 2/43
Hopalong Cassidy No. 1, 2/43
Ibis No. 1, 2/43
All Hero No. 1, 3/43
   Captain Marvel No. 22, 3/43

FICTION HOUSE
Jumbo No. 1, 9/38
Fight No. 1, 1/40
Jungle No. 1, 1/40
Planet No. 1, I/40
Wings No. 1, 9/40
Rangers No. 1, 10/41
Sheena No. 1, Spr/42
Wambi No. 1, Spr/42

FLYING CADET
Flying Cadet No. 1, 1/43

FOX FEATURES SYNDICATE
Wonder No. 1, 5/39
Wonderworld No. 3, 7/39
Mysterymen No. 1, 8/39
Fantastic No. 1, 12/39
Blue Beetle No. 1, Wint/39-40
Science No. 1, 2/40
Weird No. 1, 4/40
Flame, The No. 1, Sum/40
Green Mask No. 1, Sum/40
Big 3 No. 1, Fall/40
Rex Dexter No. 1, Fall/40
Samson No. 1, Fall/40
Eagle, The No. 1, 7/41
U.S. Jones No. 1, 11/41
V-Comics No. 1, 1/42

FUNNIES, INC.
Motion Pic. Funn. Weekly No. 1, 5/39?
Green Giant No. 1, 1940

LEV GLEASON
Silver Streak No. 1, 12/39
   Silver Streak No. 6, 9/40
   Silver Streak No. 7, 1/41
Captain Battle No. 1, Sum/41

Daredevil No. 1, 7/41
Boy No. 3, 4/42
Crime Does Not Pay No. 22, 6/42
Captain Battle No. 3, Wint/42-43
Captain Battle Jr. No. 1, Fall/43

HUGO GERNSBACK
Superworld No. 1, 4/40

GILBERTON PUBLICATIONS
Classic No. 1, 10/41

GLOBE SYNDICATE
Circus No. 1, 6/38

GREAT PUBLICATIONS
Great No. 1, 11/41
Choice No. 1, 12/41

HARVEY PUBL. (Helnit)
Speed No. 1, 10/39
Champion No. 2, 12/39
Champ No. 11, 10/40
Green Hornet No. 1, 12/40
Pocket No. 1, 8/41
War Victory No. 1, Sum/42
All New No. 1, 1/43
Hello Pal No. 1, 1/43

HAWLEY PUBLICATIONS
Captain Easy nn, 1939
Red Ryder No. 1, 9/40
Sky Blazers No. 1, 9/40
Hi-Spot No. 2, 11/40

HILLMAN PERIODICALS
Miracle No. 1, 2/40
Rocket No. 1, 3/40
Victory No. 1, 8/41
Air Fighters No. 1, 11/41
   Air Fighters No. 2, 11/42
Clue No. 1, 1/43

HOLYOKE (Continental)
Crash No. 1, 5/40
   Crash No. 4, 9/40
Catman No. 1, 5/41
Captain Fearless No. 1, 8/41
Captain Aero No. 7, 12/41
Suspense No. 1, 12/43

HYPER PUBLICATIONS
Hyper Mystery No. 1, 5/40

K.K. PUBLICATIONS
Mickey Mouse Mag. No. 1, Sum/35
Mickey Mouse Mag. V5/12, 9/40

DAVID McKAY PUBL.
King No. 1, 4/36
Wow No. 1, 5/36
Ace No. 1, 4/37
Feature Book nn, 1-4/37
Magic No. 1, 8/39
Future No. 1, 6/40

MLJ MAGAZINES
Blue Ribbon No. 1, 11/39
Top-Notch No. 1, 12/39
Pep No. 1, 1/40
Zip No. 1, 2/40
Shield-Wizard No. 1, Sum/40
   Top-Notch No. 9, 10/40
   Blue Ribbon No. 9, 2/41
Jackpot No. 1, Spr/41
   Pep No. 17, 7/41
   Pep No. 22, 12/41
Special No. 1, Wint/41-42
Hangman No. 2, Spr/42
Archie No. 1, Wint/42-43
Jolly Jingles No. 10, Sum/43
Black Hood No. 9, Wint/43-44

NITA PUBLICATIONS
Whirlwind No. 1, 6/40

NOVELTY PUBLICATIONS
Target No. 1, 2/40
Blue Bolt No. 1, 6/40
Four Most No. 1, Wint/41-42

PARENT'S MAGAZINE INST.
True No. 1, 4/41
Calling All Girls No. 1, 9/41
Real Heroes No. 1, 9/41

Funny Book No. 1, 12/42
Comics Digest No. 1, Wint/42-43

PRIZE PUBLICATIONS
Prize No. 1, 3/40
   Prize No. 7, 9/40
Headline No. 1, 2/43
Treasure nn, 1943

PROGRESSIVE PUBLISHERS
Bang-Up No. 1, 12/41

QUALITY COMICS GROUP
Feature No. 21, 6/39
Smash No. 1, 8/39
   Feature No. 27, 12/39
Crack No. 1, 5/40
Hit No. 1, 7/40
National No. 1, 7/40
Military No. 1, 8/41
Police No. 1, 8/41
Uncle Sam No. 1, 8/41
Doll Man No. 1, Fall/41
   Hit No. 25, 12/42
Plastic Man No. 1, Sum/43

RALSTON-PURINA CO.
Tom Mix No. 1, 9/40

STREET AND SMITH PUBL.
Shadow No. 1, 3/40
Doc Savage No. 1, 5/40
Bill Barnes No. 1, 10/40
Sport No. 1, 10/40
Army and Navy No. 1, 5/41
Super Magic No. 1, 5/41
Super Magician No. 2, 9/41
Pioneer Pic. Stories No. 1, 12/41
Trail Blazers No. 1, 1941
True Sport Pic. Stories No. 5, 2/42
Supersnipe No. 6, 10/42
Devil Dogs No. 1, 1942
Remember Pearl Harbor nn, 1942
Red Dragon No. 5, 1/43
Aviation Cadets No. 1, 1943

SUN PUBLICATIONS
Colossus No. 1, 3/40
Sun Fun No. 1, 3/40

TIMELY COMICS (Marvel)
Marvel No. 1, 11/39
Marvel Mystery No. 2, 12/39
Daring Mystery No. 1, 1/40
Mystic No. 1, 3/40
   Marvel Mystery No. 9, 7/40
Red Raven No. 1, 8/40
Human Torch No. 2, Fall/40
Captain America No. 1, 3/41
Sub-Mariner No. 1, Spr/41
All-Winners No. 1, Sum/41
Young Allies No. 1, Sum/41
USA No. 1, 8/41
Tough Kid Squad No. 1, 3/42
Comedy No. 9, 4/42
Joker No. 1, 4/42
Krazy No. 1, 7/42
Terry-Toons No. 1, 10/42
Miss Fury No. 1, Wint/42-43
Kid Komics No. 1, 2/43
   Comedy No. 14, 3/43
All-Select No. 1, Fall/43
All-Surprise No. 1, Fall/43
Super Rabbit No. 1, Fall/43
Powerhouse Pepper No. 1, 1943

UNITED FEATURES SYND.
Tip Top No. 1, 4/36
Comics On Parade No. 1, 4/38
Single Series No. 1, 1938
Okay No. 1, 7/40
O.K. No. 1, 7/40
Sparkler No. 1, 7/40
United No. 1, 8/40
Sparkler No. 1, 7/41

WHITMAN PUBLISHING CO.
Mammoth No. 1, 1937
Donald Duck nn, 1938

WILLIAM H. WISE
Columbia Comics No. 1, 1943
United States Marines No. 1, 1943

COMICS WITH LITTLE IF ANY VALUE

There exists in the comic book market, as in all other collector's markets, items, usually of recent origin, that have relatively little if any value. Why even mention it? We wouldn't, except for one thing—this is where you could probably take your worst beating, investment-wise. Since these books are listed by dealers in such profusion, at prices which will vary up to 500 percent from one dealer's price list to another, determining a realistic "market" value is almost impossible. And since the same books are listed repeatedly, list after list, month after month, it is difficult to determine whether or not these books are selling. In some cases, it is doubtful that they are even being collected. Most dealers must get a minimum price for their books; otherwise, it would not be profitable to handle. This will sometimes force a value on an otherwise valueless item. Most dealers who handle new comics get a minimum price of at least 75 cents to $2.00 per copy. This is the **available** price to obtain a **reading** copy. However, this is not what dealers will pay to restock. Since many of these books are not yet collector's items, their salvage value would be very low. You may not get more than 5 cents to 10 cents per copy selling them back to a dealer. This type of material, from an investment point of view, would be of maximum risk since the salvage value is so low. For this reason, recent comics should be bought for enjoyment as reading copies and if they go up in value, consider it a bonus.

COLLECTING FOREIGN COMICS AND AMERICAN REPRINTS

One extremely interesting source of comics of early vintage—one which does not necessarily have to be expensive—is the foreign market. Many American strips, from both newspapers and magazines, are reprinted abroad (both in English and in other languages) months and even years after they appear in the states. By working out trade agreements with foreign collectors, one can obtain, for practically the cover price, substantial runs of a number of newspaper strips and reprints of American comic books dating back five, ten, or occasionally even twenty or more years. These reprints are often in black and white, and sometimes the reproduction is poor, but this is not always the case. In any event, this is a source of material that every serious collector should look into.

Once the collector discovers comics published in foreign lands, he often becomes fascinated with the original strips produced in these countries. Many are excellent, and have a broader range of appeal than those of American comic books.

CANADIAN REPRINTS (E.C.s: by J. B. Clifford)

Several E.C. titles were published in Canada by Superior Comics from 1949 to at least 1953. Canadian editions of the following E.C. titles are known: (Pre-Trend) *Saddle Romances, Moon Girl, A Moon A Girl. . . Romance, Modern Love, Saddle Justice;* (New-Trend) *Crypt of Terror—Tales From the Crypt, Haunt of Fear, Vault of Horror, Weird Science, Weird Fantasy, Two-Fisted Tales, Frontline Combat,* and *Mad. Crime SuspenStories* was also published in Canada under the title *Weird SuspenStories* (Nos. 1-3 known). No reprints of *Shock SuspenStories* by Superior are known, nor have any "New Direction" reprints ever been reported. No reprints later than January 1954 are known. Canadian reprints sometimes exchanged cover and contents with adjacent numbers (e.g., a *Frontline Combat* 12 with a *Frontline Combat* No. 11 cover). They are distinguished both in cover and contents. As the interior pages are always reprinted poorly, these comics are of less value (about ½) than the U.S. editions; they were printed from asbestos plates made from the original plates. On some reprints, the Superior seal replaces the E.C. seal. Superior publishers took over Dynamic in 1947.

CANADIAN REPRINTS (Dells: by Ronald J. Ard)

Canadian editions of Dell comics, and presumably other lines, began in March-

April, 1948 and lasted until February-March, 1951. They were a response to the great Canadian dollar crisis of 1947. Intensive development of the post-war Canadian economy was financed almost entirely by American capital. This massive import or money reached such a level that Canada was in danger of having grossly disproportionate balance of payments which could drive it into technical bankruptcy in the midst of the biggest boom in its history. The Canadian government responded by banning a long list of imports. Almost 500 separate items were involved. Alas, the consumers of approximately 499 of them were politically more formidable than the consumers of comic books.

Dell responded by publishing its titles in Canada, through an arrangement with Wilson Publishing Company of Toronto. This company had not existed for a number of years and it is reasonable to assume that its sole business was the production and distribution of Dell titles in Canada. There is no doubt that they had a captive market. If you check the publication data on the U. S. editions of the period you will see the sentence "Not for sale in Canada." Canada was thus the only area of the Free World in those days technically beyond the reach of the American comic book industry.

We do not know whether French editions existed of the Dell titles put out by Wilson. The English editions were available nationwide. They were priced at 10 cents and were all 36 pages in length, at a time when their American parents were 52 pages. The covers were made of coarser paper, similar to that used in the Dell Four Color series in 1946 and 1947 and were abandoned as the more glossy cover paper became more economical. There was also a time lag of from six to eight weeks between, say, the date an American comic appeared and the date that the Canadian edition appeared.

Many Dell covers had seasonal themes and by the time the Canadian edition came out (two months later) the season was over. Wilson solved this problem by switching covers around so that the appropriate season would be reflected when the books hit the stands. Most Dell titles were published in Canada during this period including the popular Atom Bomb giveaway, *Walt Disney Comics and Stories* and the *Donald Duck* and *Mickey Mouse* Four Color one-shots. The quality of the Duck one-shots is equal to that of their American counterparts and generally bring about 30 percent less.

By 1951 the Korean War had so stimulated Canadian exports that the restrictions on comic book importation, which in any case were an offense against free trade principle, could be lifted without danger of economic collapse. Since this time Dell, as well as other companies, have been shipping direct into Canada.

CANADIAN REPRINTS (DCs: by Doug A. England)

Many DC comics were reprinted in Canada by National Comics Publications Limited and Simcoe Publishing and Distributing Co., both of Toronto, for years 1948-1950 at least. Like the Dells, these issues were 36 pages rather than the 52 pages offered in the U.S. editions, and the inscription "Published in Canada" would appear in place of "A 52 Page Magazine" or "52 Big Pages" appearing on U.S. editions. These issues contained no advertisements and some had no issue numbers.

HOW TO START COLLECTING

Most collectors of comic books begin by buying new issues in mint condition directly off the newsstand or from their local comic store. (Subscription copies are available from several mail-order services.) Each week new comics appear on the stands that are destined to become true collectors items. The trick is to locate a store that carries a complete line of comics. In several localities this may be difficult. Most panelologists frequent several magazine stands in order not to miss something they want. Even then, it pays to keep in close contact with collectors in other areas. Sooner or later, nearly every collector has to rely upon a friend in Fandom to obtain for him an item that is unavailable locally.

Before you buy any comic to add to your collection, you should carefully inspect its condition. Unlike stamps and coins, defective comics are generally not highly prized. The cover should be properly cut and printed. Remember that every blemish or sign of wear depreciates the beauty and value of your comics.

The serious panelologist usually purchases extra copies of popular titles. He may trade these multiples for items unavailable locally (for example, foreign comics), or he may store the multiples for resale at some future date. Such speculation is, of course, a gamble, but unless collecting trends change radically in the future, the value of certain comics in mint condition should appreciate greatly, as new generations of readers become interested in collecting.

COLLECTING BACK ISSUES

In addition to current issues, most panelologists want to locate back issues. Some energetic collectors have had great success in running down large hoards of rare comics in their home towns. Occasionally, rare items can be located through agencies that collect old papers and magazines, such as the Salvation Army. The lucky collector can often buy these items for much less than their current market value. Placing advertisements in trade journals, newspapers, etc., can also produce good results. However, don't be discouraged if you are neither energetic nor lucky. Most panelologists build their collections slowly but systematically by placing mail orders with dealers and other collectors.

Comics of early vintage are extremely expensive if they are purchased through a regular dealer or collector, and unless you have unlimited funds to invest in your hobby, you will find it necessary to restrict your collecting in certain ways. However you define your collection, you should be careful to set your goals well within your means.

PROPER HANDLING OF COMIC BOOKS

Before picking up an old rare comic book, caution should be exercised to handle it properly. Old comic books are very fragile and can be easily damaged. Because of this, many dealers hesitate to let customers personally handle their rare comics. They would prefer to remove the comic from its bag and show it to the customer themselves. In this way, if the book is damaged, it would be the dealer's responsibility—not the customer's. Remember, the slightest crease or chip could render an otherwise Mint book to Near Mint or even Very Fine. The following steps are provided to aid the novice in the proper handling of comic books: 1. Remove the comic from its protective sleeve or bag very carefully. 2. Gently lay the comic (un-opened) in the palm of your hand so that it will stay relatively flat and secure. 3. You can now leaf through the book by carefully rolling or flipping the pages with the thumb and forefinger of your other hand. Caution: Be sure the book always remains relatively flat or slightly rolled. Avoid creating stress points on the covers with your fingers and be particularly cautious in bending covers back too far on Mint books. 4. After examining the book, carefully insert it back into the bag or protective sleeve. Watch corners and edges for folds or tears as you replace the book.

HOW TO SELL YOUR COMICS

If you have a collection of comics for sale, large or small, the following steps should be taken. (1) Make a detailed list of the books for sale, being careful to grade them accurately, showing any noticeable defects; i.e., torn or missing pages, centerfolds, etc. (2) Decide whether to sell or trade wholesale to a dealer all in one lump or to go through the long laborious process of advertising and selling piece by piece to collectors. Both have their advantages and disadvantages.

OVERSTREET
1990
Publishing Schedule
and
Ad Deadlines For:

*"PRICE UPDATE"*_{TM}

❷

COMICS

Immediate Payment!
Price Guide value!

© Comics Magazine Co.

- We have worked hard to build a reputation of complete customer satisfaction, and welcome any inquiries you may have. We invite you to contact the author of this Price Guide as a reference.

© DC Comics, Inc.

- We are well adept in accurately grading and pricing your books. We use the standards that are written in this Price Guide, and will be happy to go over the grading procedure with you. Don't be afraid to ask questions. We understand that this process might be something you have never done before, so we will not put any pressure on you.

© DC Comics, Inc.

- We offer a TOLL FREE number to call at any time, day or night. (800) 225-4189.
  Our Hours are 8:30 to 5:30 PST, Mon. - Sat.
  When we are not in, a recording will receive your call.

- We travel most ANYWHERE to purchase large collections.

© DC Comics, Inc.

- We buy it all! Comic Books, Big Little Books, Disney Posters, Original Artwork & Animation Cels.

COMICS & COLLECTIBLES
Or Write P.O. Box 1609
Longview, WA 98632

❸

WORLD'S FINEST COMICS & COLLECTIBLES WANTS YOUR BUSINESS!

(206) 423-8673

Here is what we offer:

1. **Selection**-We always have on hand a large selection of Golden Age comics, including DC, Timely, Centaur and prehero. We also sell **Silver Age** comics and Big Little Books.

2. **Accurate Grading**-All books are guaranteed to be in the condition stated or we will give a complete refund. We have built our business on repeat business, and will do all we can to insure complete customer satisfaction.

3. **Exceptional Service**-All books are packaged with extreme care and shipped to you within 24 hours of payment. For an additional charge, we will ship by Federal Express overnight.

4. **Time Payment Plans**-We offer several types of payment plans to assist you in obtaining the book(s) you want. Call us for more information.

5. **Free Catalog**-We offer a free quarterly catalog to all who write and ask. Write for a free copy today.

6. **Want List Service**-Send us a list of which book(s) you need and we will do our best to locate them for you. Give us a try.

SELLING YOUR COMICS?
Nobody pays more or as fast! Payment within 24 hours.

WORLD'S FINEST COMICS & COLLECTIBLES
P.O. Box 1609
Longview, WA 98632

(206) 423-8673

⑥   Action, Adventure, All-American, Detective comic covers above are © DC Comics, Inc. Jumbo Comics cover is © Fiction House.

BATMAN #1 FOR SALE

We are very pleased to offer this copy of **Batman** #1 for sale. This is a truely Near Mint, or better copy. It has white pages, exceptional cover gloss, bright cover colors, sharp corners, a clean tight spine, and virtually perfect edges. On most high grade **Batman** #1's the yellow background is a mustard yellow, which is due to aging. This copy has a bright canary yellow cover, showing almost no signs of aging.

This is the nicest copy of **Batman** #1 for sale. You will not be able to purchase a better copy anywhere.

Price $27,500.00

© DC Comics, Inc.

This copy is from the DENVER collection. A pedigree collection consisting of high grade #1 issues discovered in 1984. Key issues from this collection sell for as much as 2 times the *current market* value.

Call for further details.

Are you interested in other high grade, investment quality comic books? Give us a call, we have many to choose from.
(206) 423-8673

WORLD'S FINEST COMICS & COLLECTIBLES
P.O. Box 1609   Longview, WA 98632   ❼

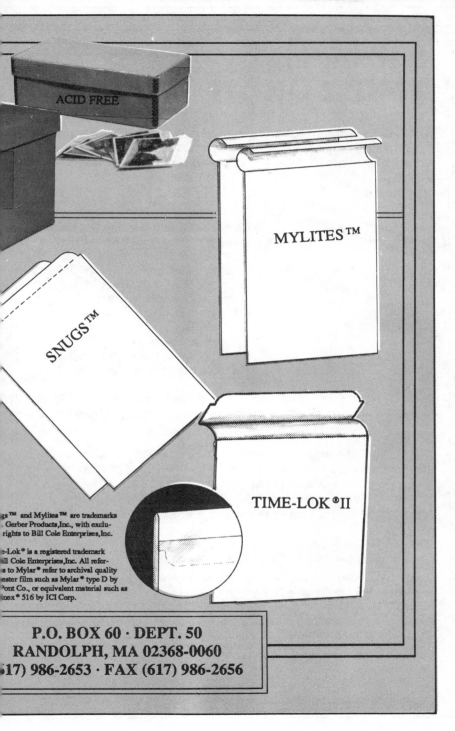

ACID FREE

MYLITES™

SNUGS™

TIME-LOK®II

P.O. BOX 60 · DEPT. 50
RANDOLPH, MA 02368-0060
617) 986-2653 · FAX (617) 986-2656

A-63

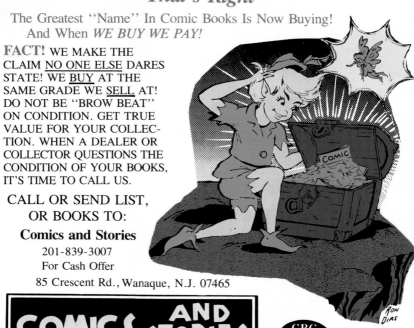

CAPTAIN AMERICA
1940-1990

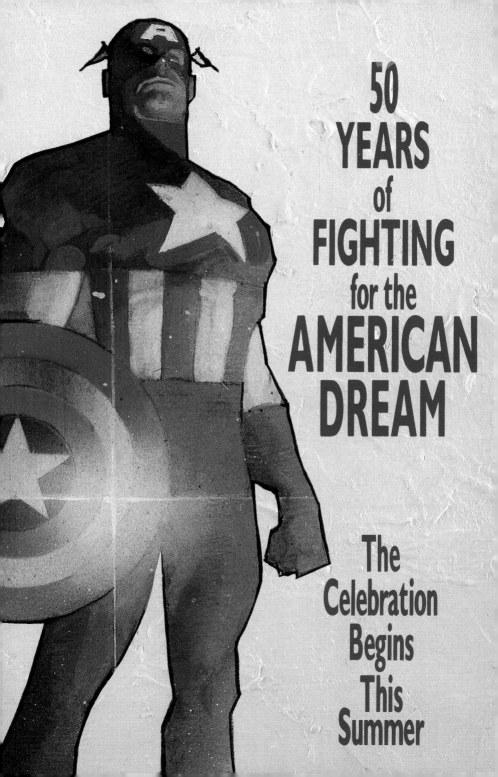

50
YEARS
of
FIGHTING
for the
AMERICAN
DREAM

The
Celebration
Begins
This
Summer

Action Comics #13, 1939, © DC

Adventure Comics #51, 1940, © DC

Advs. Of The Jaguar #1, 1961, © AP

All-American Comics #18, 1940, © DC.
New York World's Fair cover.

Amaz. Mystery Funnies V2#10, 1939, © CEN

Amaz. Spider-Man #14, 1964, © MCG

Andy Devine Western #1, 1950, © FAW

Archie's Mechanics #1, 1954, © AP

The Atom #1, 1962, © DC

The Avengers #4, 1964, © MCG. 1st Silver
Age app. Captain America

Batman #3, 1940, © DC

Big Shot Comics #20, 1941, © CCG

Black Magic #1, 1950, © Headline
Simon & Kirby cover & story art

Brave & The Bold #28, 1960, © DC. 1st
app. The Justice League

Brave & The Bold #34, 1961, © DC. 1st
Silver Age app. Hawkman.

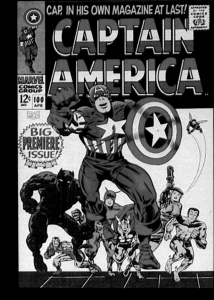

Captain America #100, 1968, © MCG

Captain America #24, 1943, © MCG

Captain Marvel #18, 1942, © FAW. 1st
app. Mary Marvel.

Comedy Comics #9, 1942, © MCG

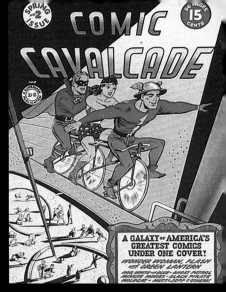

Comic Cavalcade #2, 1943, © DC

The Comics Magazine #1, 1936, © Comics

Cowboy Western #30, 1950, © CC, Sunset

Daredevil #1, 1964, © MCG

Daring Comics #10, 1945, © MCG.
Schomburg cover art.

Dark Shadows #3, 1969, © Dan Curtis.

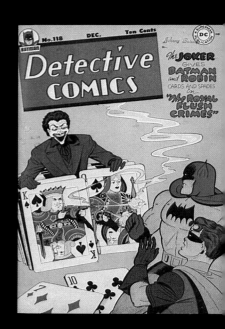

Detective Comics #118, 1946, © DC

Detective Comics #233, 1956, © DC.
1st app. The Bat-Woman.

The Doom Patrol #86, 1964, © DC

80pg. Giant #1, 1964, © DC

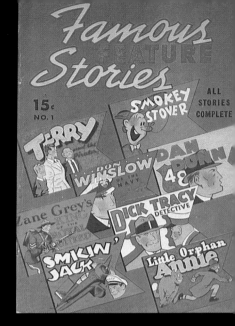

Famous Feature Stories #1, 1938, © DELL

Flash Comics #10, 1940, © DC

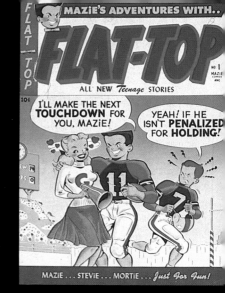

Flat-Top #1, 1953, © HARV

omics #2, 1941, ©

Lantern #24, 19

WANTED

OLD COMICS!!

$CASH REWARD$

FOR THESE AND MANY OTHER ELUSIVE COMIC BOOKS FROM THE GOLDEN AGE. SEEKING WHITE PAGE COLLECTIBLE COPIES IN VG OR BETTER CONDITION. ALSO GOLDEN AGE **BOUND VOLUMES WANTED.**

SERIOUS?

ARTHUR ADAMS © 12-27-88

Serious Business

No one takes comic book collecting more seriously than we do. If you're a hard-core comic book collector, subscribe to Westfield Comics Subscription Service.

Serious Savings

We provide the best in current comics and fan-related materials at 25% to 35% off cover price!

Serious Selection

Choose from comics galore! And buy just the titles and quantities you want on a monthly or biweekly basis.

- All Marvel and DC direct-only titles.
- All mainstream Marvel and DC annuals, limited series and graphic novels.
- An extensive line of the very best independent publishers' titles such as First, Eclipse, Comico and Gladstone.
- A top selection of small press black-and-white comic titles.
- The best specialty magazines and books.
- A growing line of trade paperback collections.

Serious Service

Westfield packs orders to perfection. So comics arrive crisp and clean with no bad scene.

Serious Info

To keep you up on the hottest comic news, we'll send you free promotional materials plus the notorious Westfield Newsletter with each order.

Serious Offer

If you're totally into comics, send us your name, address and a 25¢ stamp. We'll send you a price list and our order form. If you're a new customer, we'll throw in 25 bucks' worth of free comics, preselected, with your first order!

Get Serious

Subscribe to Westfield Comics Subscription Service today! It's the Collectors' Choice! Seriously.

What They're Saying:

"You are truly the best comics mail order company I have ever dealt with."
—Salvatore J. Nardozzi, Jr., Dunmore, PA

"Orders arrive like clockwork, with everything in perfect condition. All this...and great discounts...unbelievable! Thanks from a very satisfied customer."
—Calvin B. Lee, San Francisco, CA

"I really do enjoy collecting comics and with your excellent discounted prices it makes it not only affordable—but fun!"
—Nigel Tickner, Missouri City, TX

"The comics always come in great shape and you do one of the best newsletters in the industry! I know when I tell someone about Westfield, they'll get the best treatment there is."
—Beau Smith, Sales Manager, Eclipse Comics

THE WESTFIELD COMPANY OF WISCONSIN, INC.

8608 University Green • P.O. Box 470 • Middleton, WI 53562 • (608) 836-1945

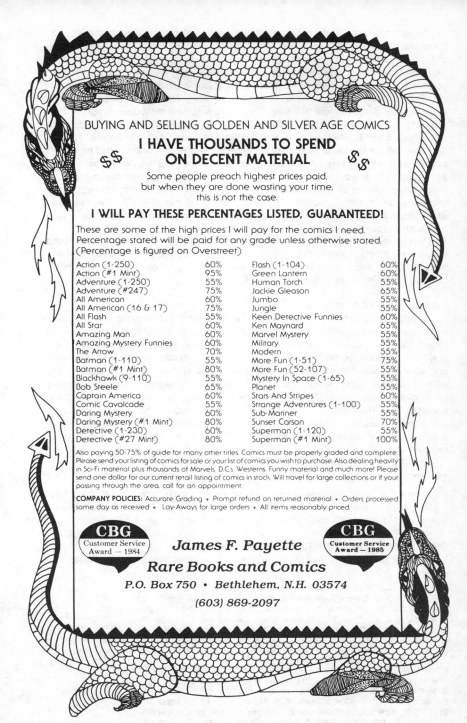

In selling to dealers, you will get the best price by letting everything go at once—the good with the bad—all for one price. Simply select names either from ads in this book or from some of the adzines mentioned below. Send them your list and ask for bids. The bids received will vary depending on the demand, rarity and condition of the books you have. The more in demand, and better the condition, the higher the bids will be.

On the other hand, you could become a "dealer" and sell the books yourself. Order a copy of one or more of the adzines. Take note how most dealers lay out their ads. Type up your ad copy, carefully pricing each book (using the Guide as a reference). Send finished ad copy with payment to adzine editor to be run. You will find that certain books will sell at once while others will not sell at all. The ad will probably have to be retyped, remaining books repriced, and run again. Price books according to how fast you want them to move. If you try to get top dollar, expect a much longer period of time. Otherwise, the better deal you give the collector, the faster they will move. Remember, in being your own dealer, you will have overhead expenses in postage, mailing supplies and advertising cost. Some books might even be returned for refund due to misgrading, etc.

In selling all at once to a dealer, you get instant cash, immediate profit, and eliminate the long process of running several ads to dispose of the books; but if you have patience, and a small amount of business sense, you could realize more profit selling them directly to collectors yourself.

WHERE TO BUY AND SELL

Throughout this book you will find the advertisements of many reputable dealers who sell back-issue comics magazines. If you are an inexperienced collector, be sure to compare prices before you buy. When a dealer is selected (ask for references), send him a small order (under $100) first to check out his grading accuracy, promptness in delivery, guarantees of condition advertised, and whether he will accept returns when dissatisfied. Never send large sums of cash through the mail. Send money orders or checks for your personal protection. Beware of bargains, as the items advertised sometimes do not exist, but are only a fraud to get your money.

The Price Guide is indebted to everyone who placed ads in this volume, whose support has helped in curbing printing costs. Your mentioning this book when dealing with the advertisers would be greatly appreciated.

THE BUYERS GUIDE, Krause Publications, 700 E. State St., Iola, WI 54990 PH:(715) 445-2214

The Price Guide highly recommends the above adzine, which is full of ads buying and selling comics, pulps, radio tapes, premiums, toys and other related items. You can also place ads to buy or sell your comics in the above publication.

COMIC BOOK MAIL ORDER SERVICES

The following offer a mail order service on new comic books. Write for rates and details:

COLLECTOR'S CHOICE, 3405 Keith St., Cleveland, TN 37311
THE COMIC SOURCE, Bruce B. Brittain, P.O. Box 863605, Plano, TX 75086-3605
COMICS TO ASTONISH, 4001-C Country Club Rd., Winston-Salem, NC 27104 (919) 765-0400
COMIX 4-U, INC., 1121 State St., 2nd Floor, Schenectady, NY 12304 (518) 372-6612
DOUG SULIPA'S COMIC WORLD, 374 Donald St., Winnipeg, Man., Canada R3B 2J2
FANTACO ENTERPRISES, INC., 21 Central Ave., Albany, NY 12210-1391. PH: (518) 463-1400.
FRIENDLY FRANK'S Distribution, Inc., 3990 Broadway, Gary IN 46408-2705 (219)884-5052 or 884-5053
    1025 North Vigo, Gary, IN 46403
GEPPI'S SUBSCRIPTION SERVICE, 1720 Belmont Ave., Bay-C, Baltimore, MD 21207
HEROES AREN'T HARD TO FIND, 1214 Thomas Ave., Charlotte, NC 28205
M&M, P.O. Box 6, Orland Park, IL 60462. PH: 312-349-2486
PRESIDENTIAL COMIC BOOK SERVICE, P. O. Box 41, Scarsdale, NY 10583
STYX COMIC SERVICE, 605 Roseberry St., Winnipeg, Manitoba Canada R3H 0T3
LEE TENNANT, THE COMIC SHOP, P.O. Box 296, Worth, IL 60482-(312) 448-2937
THE WESTFIELD COMPANY, 8608 University Green, P.O. Box 470, Middleton, WI 53562 (608)836-1945

COMIC BOOK CONVENTIONS

As is the case with most other aspects of comic collecting, comic book conventions, or cons as they are referred to, were originally conceived as the comic-book counterpart to science-fiction fandom conventions. There were many attempts to form successful national cons prior to the time of the first one that materialized, but they were all stillborn. It is interesting that after only three relatively organized years of existence, the first comic con was held. Of course, its magnitude was nowhere near as large as most established cons held today.

What is a comic con? As might be expected, there are comic books to be found at these gatherings. Dealers, collectors, fans, whatever they call themselves can be found trading, selling, and buying the adventures of their favorite characters for hours on end. Additionally if at all possible, cons have guests of honor, usually professionals in the field of comic art, either writers, artists, or editors. The committees put together panels for the con attendees where the assembled pros talk about certain areas of comics, most of the time fielding questions from the assembled audience. At cons one can usually find displays of various and sundry things, usually original art. There might be radio listening rooms; there is most certainly a daily showing of different movies, usually science-fiction or horror type. Of course there is always the chance to get together with friends at cons and just talk about comics; one also has a good opportunity to make new friends who have similar interests and with whom one can correspond after the con.

It is difficult to describe accurately what goes on at a con. The best way to find out is to go to one or more if you can.

The addresses below are those currently available for conventions to be held in the upcoming year. Unfortunately, addresses for certain major conventions are unavailable as this list is being compiled. Once again, the best way to keep abreast of conventions is through the various adzines. Please remember when writing for convention information to include a self-addressed, stamped envelope for reply. Most conventions are non-profit, so they appreciate the help. Here is the list:

COMIC BOOK CONVENTIONS FOR 1990
(Note: All convention listings must be submitted to us by December 15th of each year)

ATLANTA COMIC BOOK MARKETPLACE—Days Inn, Atlanta North, I-75 at Windy Hill Rd., 10am-5pm. Contact New Dimension Comics, 2609 Central Ave., Charlotte, NC 28205. PH: 704-372-4376.

ATLANTA FANTASY FAIR XVI, Aug. 17-19, 1990, Omni Hotel, Atlanta, GA. Info: Atlanta Fantasy Fair, 691 Spring Forest Dr., Lawrenceville, GA 30243. PH: (404) 961-2347.

ATLANTA SPRING COMICS FAIR IV, (Mar. 3,4 1990), Info: The Atlanta Spring Comics Fair, c/o The Atlanta Fantasy Fair, 691 Spring Forest Dr., Lawrenceville, GA 30243. PH: (404) 961-2347.

BIG-D Super Comic & Collectibles Show (Formally CHILDHOOD TREASURES) July 27-29, 1990-Dallas Sheraton Park Central Hotel, Hwy 635 & Coit Rd. Write Don Maris, Box 111266 Arlington, TX 76007. (817)-261-8745

CAROLINA COMIC BOOK FAIR—For info contact New Dimension Comics, 2609 Central Ave., Charlotte, NC 28205. PH: (704) 372-4376.

    Charlotte, NC show-April 14, 1990—Sheraton Airport Plaza Hotel, I-85 at Billy Graham Pkwy.; June 2/3, 1990-Charlotte Apparel Center, 200 N. College Street; Dec. 1, 1990—Sheraton Airport, Plaza Hotel, I-85 at Billy Graham Pkwy.

    Winston-Salem, NC—May, 4, Oct. 6, 1990—Call about location.

    Columbia, SC—March 17, July 21, Oct. 20/21, 1990—Holiday Inn, Coliseum 630 Assembly Dr.

    Greenville, SC.—March 10, 1990—Phoenix Inn, 246 Pleasantburg Dr. (Hwy. 291).

CAROLINA CON IX—Sept. 15, 1990, Ramada Hotel, 1001 S. Church St., Greenville, SC. Sponsored by The Carolina Pictorial Fiction Assn. Send SASE to Steve Harris, 100 E. Augusta Place, Greenville, SC 29605.

CHICAGO - Baseball Card & Comic Book Show. Held monthly at University of Illinois at Chicago. For more info call Rich at (312) 733-2266.

CHICAGO COMICON—Larry Charet, 1219-A West Devon Ave., Chicago, IL 60660. Phone (312) 274-1832.

CREATION CON—249-04 Hillside Ave., Bellerose, N.Y. 11426. Phone (718) 343-0202. Holds major conventions in the following cities: Atlanta, Boston, Cincinnati, Cleveland, Detroit, London, Los Angeles, Philadelphia, Rochester, San Francisco, and Washington, D.C. Write or call for details.

DALLAS FANTASY FAIR, A Bulldog Prod. Convention. For info: Lary Lankford, P.O. Box 820488, Dallas, TX 75382, PH: (214) 349-3367.

DETROIT AREA COMIC BOOK/BASEBALL CARD SHOWS. Held every 2-3 weeks in Royal Oak and Livonia Mich., write: Michael Goldman, Suite 231, 19785 W. 12 Mile Rd., Southfield, MI 48076. PH: (313) 350-2633.

EL PASO FANTASY FESTIVAL—c/o Rita's Fantasy Shop, No. 34 Sunrise Center, El Paso, TX 79904. PH: (915) 757-1143. Late July-Early August.

FANTACON 1990, Sept. 8,9, 1990, Empire State Plaza Convention Center, between State and Madison, Albany, New York. For info: Tom Skulan, FantaCo Organization Offices, 21 Central Ave., Albany, NY 12210-1391. Please send SASE with inquiry or call (518) 463-1400.

HEROES CONVENTION '90 — June 23-24, 1990, H. Shelton Drum, P.O. Box 9181, Charlotte, NC 28299, (704)-376-5766.

ISLAND NOSTALGIA COMIC BOOK/BASEBALL CARD SHOWS, Hauppauge, N.Y.-Holiday Inn off L.I.E. exit 55, 10-4p.m.1740 Express Drive South, Hauppauge, N.Y., For more info call Dennis (516) 724-7422 or Day of Shows only (516) 234-3030, ext 450.

KANSAS CITY COMIC CONVENTION (Formally MO-KAN COMICS FESTIVAL)—c/o Kansas City Comic Book Club, 734 North 78th St., Kansas City, KS 66112.

LONG ISLAND COMIC BOOK & COLLECTOR'S MARKET CONVENTION—(Held monthly). Rockville Centre Holiday Inn, 173 Sunrise Hwy., Long Island, NY. For info: Cosmic Comics & Books of Rockville Centre, 139 N. Park Ave., Rockville Centre, NY 11570. (516) 763-1133.

LOS ANGELES COMIC BOOK & SCIENCE FICTION CONVENTION, held monthly. For information contact: Bruce Schwartz, 1802 West Olive Ave., Burbank, CA 91506. PH: (818) 954-8432.

MOBI-CON 90, June 1-3, 1990, The Days Inn (I-65 and Airport), Mobile, AL 36608. For more info: Christie Nelson, P.O. Box 161257, Mobile, AL 36616.
Box 161257, Mobile, AL 36616. (205) 342-9073 or 661-4060.

THE ORIGINAL LONG ISLAND MONTHLY COMIC BOOK & BASEBALL CARD SHOW, Held 1st Sunday each month at the Coliseum Motor Inn, 1650 Hempstead Turnpike, East Meadow, Long Island, NY. Contact: Perry Albert, P.O. Box 66, Fredonia, NY 14063. PH: 716-672-2913.

ORLANDO CON, Sept. 22, 23, 1990, International Inn, Orlando, FL. Info: Jim Ivey, 4300 S. Semoran, Suite 109, Orlando, FL 32822-2453, PH: (407) 273-0141.

SAN DIEGO COMIC-CON—Box 17066, San Diego, CA 92117. 1st weekend in Aug., 1990, San Diego Convention Center.

THE SAN FERNANDO VALLEY COMIC BOOK CONVENTION No. 19, Aug., 1989. Write for details: Original Valley Comic Book Con., 11684 Ventura, Bl. #335, Studio City, CA 91604.

THE SCENIC CITY COMICS & COLLECTIBLES FAIR, April 27-29, Chattanooga at Eastgate Mall, Mark Derrick, 3244 Castle Ave., Chattanooga, TN 37412. PH: 615-624-3704.

Schenectady, New York, THE CAPITAL DISTRICT ANNUAL SHOW, S.A.S.E. with inquiry or call Jared Nathanson at 518-372-6612 or write: Comix 4-U, Inc., 1121 State St., 2nd Floor, Schenectady, NY 12304.

SEATTLE CENTER CON, Apr, July, Oct, 1989, Box 2043, Kirkland, Wash. 98033. Phone (206) 822-5709 or 827-5129.

SEATTLE QUEST NORTHWEST, Seattle, Wash. Write: Ron Church or Steve Sibra, P.O. Box 82676, Kenmore, WA 98028.

THE SUNDAY FUNNIES, Will Murray, 334 E. Squantum St., Quincy, MA 02171. Phone (617)328-5224.

COMIC BOOK CLUBS

ALABAMA—The Mobile Panelology Assoc. meets 1st Monday of each month at 2301 Airport Blvd. (Back Bldg. Mobile Recreation Dept.), Mobile, Ala.; 7:00 p.m. to 9:00 p.m. Club business address: 161 West Grant St., Chickasaw, AL 36611. (205) 456-4514. Founded 1973.

CALIFORNIA—The California Comic Book Collectors Club, c/o Matt Ornbaun, 23601 Hwy. 128, Yorkville, CA 95494. Send 50 cents and SASE for information and enrollment.

Alpha Omega—c/o Donald Ensign, 6011 Agnes Ave., Temple City, CA 91780. Puts out bi-monthly pub.

USC Comics Club, University of Southern California Intramural Recreation Dept., Heritage Hall 103, University Park, Los Angeles, CA 90089-0601. PH 213-743-5127.

CONNETICUT—Collectors' Club, c/o Susan Dorne, President, 551 Park Ave., Windsor, CT 06095. Publishes a bi-monthly newsletter.

GEORGIA—The Defenders of Dreams, Inc., c/o Will Rose, 3121 Shady Grove Rd., Carrollton, GA 30117. (Publishes its own clubzine *Excalibur* bi-monthly and a pulpzine *Real Pulp Adventures*.) Send business size SASE for details.

IDAHO—Mr. O's Comic Book Collectors Club, S. 1200 Agate Rd., Coeur D'Alene, Idaho 83814.

MASSACHUSETTS—The Gloo Club, c/o Ron Holmes, 140 Summit St., New Bedford, Mass. 02740. Write for details and send SASE. (This club is both national and international.)

MINNESOTA—The Pogo Fan Club. A mail club dedicated to Walt Kelly's career. Puts out a bi-monthly 'The Fort Mudge Most." Write: Steve Thompson, 6908 Wentworth Ave. So., Richfield, MN 55423.

NEW YORK—Comix 4-U Comic Club, meets 2nd Sunday every month. Write: 1121 State St., 2nd Floor, Schenectady, NY 12304.

OHIO—International Comics Club, meets monthly at Cleveland Hts., University Hts. Library, 2345 Lee Rd., Cleveland Hts., Ohio on 1st Monday of each month, 7p.m. Contact: Richard Bennett, 6204 Fullerton Ave., Apt. 3, Cleveland, OH 44105.

OKLAHOMA—Fandom International. For information, write to: Dan DePalma, 5823 E. 22 St., Tulsa, OK 74114. Phone 834-8035.

TEXAS—The Gulf Coast Comic Collectors' Society (GCCCS). Write to GCCCS Headquarters, c/o Mike Mills, 4318 Iroquois St., Houston, TX 77504.

CANADA—The Collectors' Club. Write: T.M. Maple, Box 1272, Station B., Weston, Ontario M9L 2R9 Canada. Bimonthly newsletter.

THE HISTORY OF COMICS FANDOM

At this time it is possible to discern two distinct and largely unrelated movements in the history of Comics Fandom. The first of these movements began about 1953 as a response to the then-popular, trend-setting EC lines of comics. The first true comics fanzines of this movement were short-lived. Bhob Stewart's EC FAN BULLETIN was a hectographed newsletter that ran two issues about six months apart; and Jimmy Taurasi's FANTASY COMICS, a newsletter devoted to all science-fiction comics of the period, was a monthly that ran for about six months. These were followed by other newsletters, such as Mike May's EC FAN JOURNAL, and George Jennings' EC WORLD PRESS. EC fanzines of a wider and more critical scope appeared somewhat later. Two of the finest were POTRZEBIE, the product of a number of fans, and Ron Parker's HOOHAH. Gauging from the response that POTRZEBIE received from a plug in an EC letter column, Ted White estimated the average age of EC fans to lie in the range of 9 to 13, while many EC fans were in their mid-teens. This fact was taken as discouraging to many of the faneds, who had hoped to reach an older audience. Consequently, many of them gave up their efforts in behalf of Comics Fandom, especially with the demise of the EC groups, and turned their attention to science-fiction fandom with its longer tradition and older membership. While the flourish of fan activity in response to the EC comics was certainly noteworthy, it is fair to say that it never developed into a full-fledged, independent, and self-sustaining movement.

The second comics fan movement began in 1960. It was largely a response to (though it later became a stimulus for) the Second Heroic Age of Comics. Most fan historians date the Second Heroic Age from the appearance of the new FLASH comics magazine (numbered 105 and dated February 1959). The letter departments of Julius Schwartz (editor at National Periodicals), and later those of Stan Lee (Marvel Group) and Bill Harris (Gold Key) were most influential in bringing comics readers into Fandom. Beyond question, it was the reappearance of the costumed hero that sparked the comics fan movement of the sixties. Sparks were lit among some science-fiction fans first, when experienced fan writers, who were part of an established tradition, produced the first in a series of articles on the comics of the forties—ALL IN COLOR FOR A DIME. The series was introduced in XERO No. 1 (September 1960), a general fanzine for science-fiction fandom edited and published by Dick Lupoff.

Meanwhile, outside science-fiction fandom, Jerry Bails and Roy Thomas, two strictly comics fans of long-standing, conceived the first true comics fanzine in response to the Second Heroic Age. The fanzine, ALTER EGO, appeared in March 1961. The first several issues were widely circulated among comics fans, and were to influence profoundly the comics fan movement to follow. Unlike the earlier EC fan movement, this new movement attracted many fans in their twenties and thirties. A number of these older fans had been active collectors for years but had been largely unknown to each other. Joined by scores of new, younger fans, this group formed the nucleus of a new movement that is still growing and shows every indication of being self-sustaining. Although it has borrowed a few of the more appropriate terms coined by science-fiction fans, Comics Fandom of the Sixties was an independent if fledgling movement, without, in most cases, the advantages and disadvantages of a longer tradition. What Comics Fandom did derive from science-fiction fandom it did so thanks largely to the fanzines produced by so-called double fans. The most notable of this type is COMIC ART, edited and published by Don and Maggie Thompson.

HOW TO SELECT FANZINES

In the early 1960s, only a few comic fanzines were being published. A fan could easily afford to subscribe to them all. Today, the situation has radically changed, and it has become something of a problem to decide which fanzines to order.

Fanzines are not all of equal quality or general interest. Even different issues of the same fanzine may vary significantly. To locate issues that will be of interest to you, learn to look for the names of outstanding amateur artists, writers, and editors, and consult fanzine review columns. Although you may not always agree with the judgements of the reviewers, you will find these reviews to be a valuable source of information about the content and quality of the current fanzines.

When ordering a fanzine, remember that print runs are small and the issue you may want may be out of print (OP). Ordinarily in this case, you will receive the next issue. Because of irregular publishing schedules that nearly all fanzines must, of necessity, observe, allow up to 90 days or more for your copy to reach you. It is common courtesy when addressing an inquiry to an ama-publisher to enclose a self-addressed, stamped envelope.

FAN PUBLICATIONS OF INTEREST

NOTE: We must be notified each year by December 1 for listing to be included, due to changes of address, etc. Please send sample copy.

ANNIE PEOPLE, Jon Merrill, P.O. Box 431, Cedar Knolls, NJ 07927. Bi-monthly Little Orphan Annie newsletter.

COMIC ART AND FANTASY—Stephen Barrington, 161 West Grant Street, Chickasaw, AL 36611. Published quarterly for comics, gaming & sf fans. $1.00 for two issues.

COMICS CAREER NEWSLETTER, 601 Clinkscales, Columbia, MO 65203. Information and advice for amateur comics writers and artists who wish to become professionals. Sample copy: $3.00. 12-issue subs.: $24.

COMICS INTERVIEW—c/o Fictioneer Books Ltd., #1 Screamer Mtn., Clayton, GA 30525.

THE COMPLETE EC LIBRARY—Russ Cochran, P. O. Box 437, West Plains, MO 65775. (A must for all EC collectors. Reprinting of the complete EC line is planned. Write for details.)

DITKOMANIA-A quarterly, digest devoted to Steve Ditko's work. Now in its 7th year of continuous publication. $1 per issue. Write: Bill Hall, 556 Main St., Cromwell, CT 05416.

THE DUCKBURG TIMES—Barks/Disney fanzine. Sample copy $1.50, Subscription $6 (Foreign rates double). Dana Gabbard, 3010 Wilshire Blvd., #362, Los Angeles, CA 90010.

FANTACO NOOZ, FantaCo. Enterprises Inc., 21 Central Ave., Albany, NY 12210. Free with SASE.

FCA & ME TOO!—Teresa & William Harper, 301 E. Buena Vista Ave., North Augusta, SC 29841. Covers Golden Age Fawcett and Magazine Enterprises. Sample $1.00. 4 issue sub., $5.

FORT MUDGE MOST, Bi-monthly magazine of the Pogo Fan Club. Subscription: $15/yr. Sample $3. Spring Hollow Books, 6908 Wentworth Ave. So., Richfield, MN 55423.

INSIDE REVIEW on comics—J.E. Essick, Rt. 10, Box 369D, Winston-Salem, NC 27127. Monthly current comics newsletter. Sample 90 cents, 1 year subs-$9. Checks only.

THE YELLOW KID NOTES, The Yellow Kid Society, 103 Doubloon Dr., Slidell, LA 70461. PH: 504-641-5173.

COLLECTING STRIPS

Collecting newspaper comic strips is somewhat different than collecting magazines, although it can be equally satisfying.

Obviously, most strip collectors begin by clipping strips from their local paper, but many soon branch out to strips carried in out-of-town papers. Naturally this can become more expensive and it is often frustrating, because it is easy to miss editions of out-of-town papers. Consequently, most strip collectors work out trade agreements with collectors in other cities in order to get an uninterrupted supply of the strips they want. This usually necessitates saving local strips to be used for trade purposes only.

Back issues of strips dating back several decades are also available from time to time from dealers. The prices per panel vary greatly depending on the age, condition, and demand for the strip. When the original strips are unavailable, it is sometimes possible to get photostatic copies from collectors, libraries, or newspaper morgues.

COLLECTING ORIGINAL ART

In addition to magazines and strips, some enthusiasts also collect the original art for the comics. These black and white, inked drawings are usually done on illustration paper at about 30 percent up (i.e., 30 percent larger than the original printed panels). Because original art is a one-of-a-kind article, it is highly prized and often difficult to obtain.

Interest in original comic art has increased tremendously in the past several years. Many companies now return the originals to the artists who have in turn offered them for sale, usually at cons but sometimes through agents and dealers. As with any other area of collecting, rarity and demand governs value. Although the masters' works bring fine art prices, most art is available at moderate prices. Comic strips are the most popular facet with collectors, followed by comic book art. Once scarce, current and older comic book art has surfaced within the last few years. In 1974 several original painted covers of vintage comic books and coloring books turned up from Dell, Gold Key, Whitman, and Classic Comics.

The following are sources for original art:

Artman, Bruce Bergstrom, 1620 Valley St., Fort Lee, NJ 07024
Cartoon Carnival, 408 Bickmore Dr., Wallingford, PA 19086, PH: 215-566-1292
The Cartoon Museum, Jim Ivey, 4300 S. Semoran, Suite 109, Orlando, FL 32822-2453 (407)273-0141
Russ Cochran, P.O. Box 437, West Plains, MO 65775.
Collectors Paradise Gallery, Harry Kleinman, P.O. Box 1540, Studio City, CA 91604
The Comic Character Shop, Old Firehouse Antiques, 110 Alaskan Way S., Seattle, WA 98104 206-283-0532
Tony Dispoto, Comic Art Showcase, P. O. Box 425, Lodi, NJ 07644
Scott Dunbier, P.O. Box 1446, Gracie Station, New York, NY, 10028
Graphic Collectibles, Mitch Itkowitz, P.O. Box 683, Staten Island, NY 10302, (718)273-3685
Richard Halegua, Comic Art & Graffix Gallery, 2033 Madison Rd., Cincinnati, OH 45208, (513) 321-4208
Steve Herrington, 30 W. 70th St., New York, NY 10023
Carsten Lagua, Havensteinstr. 54, 1000 Berlin 46, West Germany, Tel. 030/7734665.
Museum Graphics, Jerome K. Muller, Box 743, Costa Mesa, CA 92627
Original Artwork, Martin Hilland, AM Josefshaus 6, 4040 Neuss 21, West Germany
San Mateo Comic Books/Original art, 306 Baldwin Ave. San Mateo, CA 94401, (415)344-1536
TRH Gallery (Tom Horvitz), 255 N. Cielo No. 601, Palm Springs, CA 92263, (619) 320-9599.

A Chronology of the Development of
THE AMERICAN COMIC BOOK

By
M. Thomas Inge*

Precursors: The facsimile newspaper strip reprint collections constitute the earliest "comic books." The first of these was a collection of Richard Outcault's **Yellow Kid** from the Hearst **New York American** in March 1897. Commercial and promotional reprint collections, usually in cardboard covers, appeared through the 1920s and featured such newspaper strips as **Mutt and Jeff, Foxy Grandpa, Buster Brown,** and **Barney Google**. During 1922 a reprint magazine, **Comic Monthly**, appeared with each issue devoted to a separate strip, and from 1929 to 1930 George Delacorte published 36 issues of **The Funnies** in tabloid format with original comic pages in color, becoming the first four-color comic newsstand publication.

1933: The Ledger syndicate published a small broadside of their Sunday comics on 7" by 9" plates. Employees of Eastern Color Printing Company in New York, sales manager Harry I. Wildenberg and salesman Max C. Gaines, saw it and figured that two such plates would fit a tabloid page, which would produce a book about 7½" x 10" when folded. Thus 10,000 copies of **Funnies on Parade**, containing 32 pages of Sunday newspaper reprints, was published for Proctor and Gamble to be given away as premiums. Some of the strips included were: **Joe Palooka, Mutt and Jeff, Hairbreadth Harry,** and **Reg'lar Fellas**. M. C. Gaines was very impressed with this book and convinced Eastern Color that he could sell a lot of them to such big advertisers as Milk-O-Malt, Wheatena, Kinney Shoe Stores, and others to be used as premiums and radio give-aways. So, Eastern Color printed **Famous Funnies: A Carnival of Comics**, and then **Century of Comics**, both as before, containing Sunday newspaper reprints. Mr. Gaines sold these books in quantities of 100,000 to 250,000.

1934: The give-away comics were so successful that Mr. Gaines believed that youngsters would buy comic books for ten cents like the "Big Little Books" coming out at that time. So, early in 1934, Eastern Color ran off 35,000 copies of **Famous Funnies, Series 1**, 64 pages of reprints for Dell Publishing Company to be sold for ten cents in chain stores. Selling out promptly on the stands, Eastern Color, in May 1934, issued **Famous Funnies** No. 1 (dated July 1934) which became, with issue No. 2 in July, the first monthly comic magazine. The title continued for over 20 years through 218 issues, reaching a circulation peak of nearly one million copies. At the same time, Mr. Gaines went to the sponsors of Percy Crosby's **Skippy**, who was on the radio, and convinced them to put out a Skippy book, advertise it on the air, and give away a free copy to anyone who bought a tube of Phillip's toothpaste. Thus 500,000 copies of **Skippy's Own Book of Comics** was run off and distributed through drug stores everywhere. This was the first four-color comic book of reprints devoted to a single character.

1935: Major Malcolm Wheeler-Nicholson's National Periodical Publications issued in February a tabloid-sized comic publication called **New Fun**, which became **More Fun** after the sixth issue and converted to the normal comic-book size after issue eight. **More Fun** was the first comic book of a standard size to publish original material and continued publication until 1949. **Mickey Mouse Magazine** began in the summer, to become **Walt Disney's Comics and Stories** in 1940, and combined original material with reprinted newspaper strips in most issues.

1936: In the wake of the success of **Famous Funnies**, other publishers, in conjunction with the major newspaper strip syndicates, inaugurated more reprint comic books: **Popular Comics** (News-Tribune, February), **Tip Top Comics** (United Features, April), **King Comics** (King Features, April), and **The Funnies** (new series, NEA, October). Four issues of **Wow Comics**, from David McKay and Henle Publications, appeared, edited by S. M. Iger and including early art by Will Eisner, Bob Kane, and Alex Raymond. The first non-reprint comic book devoted to a single theme was **Detective Picture Stories** issued in December by The Comics Magazine Company.

1937: The second single-theme title, **Western Picture Stories**, came in February from The Comics Magazine Company, and the third was **Detective Comics**, an offshoot of **More Fun**, which began in March to be published to the present. The book's initials, "D.C.," have long served to refer to National Periodical Publications, which was purchased from Major Nicholson by Harry Donenfeld late this year.

1938: "DC" copped a lion's share of the comic book market with the publication of **Action Comics** No. 1 in June which contained the first appearance of Superman by writer Jerry Siegel and artist Joe Shuster, a discovery of Max C. Gaines. The "man of steel" inaugurated the "Golden Era" in comic book history. Fiction House, a pulp publisher, entered the comic book field in September with **Jumbo Comics**, featuring Sheena, Queen of the Jungle, and appearing in over-sized format for the first eight issues.

1939: The continued success of "DC" was assured in May with the publication of **Detective Comics** No. 27 containing the first episode of Batman by artist Bob Kane and writer Bill Finger. **Superman Comics** appeared in the summer. Also, during the summer, a black and white premium comic titled **Motion Picture Funnies Weekly** was published to be given away at motion picture theatres. The plan was to issue it weekly and to have continued stories so that the kids would come back week after week not to miss an episode. Four issues were planned but only one came out. This book contains the first appearance and origin of the Sub-Mariner by Bill Everett (8 pages) which was later reprinted in **Marvel Comics**. In November, the first issue of **Marvel Comics** came out, featuring the Human Torch by Carl Burgos and the Sub-Mariner reprint with color added.

1940: The April issue of **Detective Comics** No. 38 introduced Robin the Boy Wonder as a sidekick to Batman, thus establishing the "Dynamic Duo" and a major precedent for later costume heroes who would also have boy companions. **Batman Comics** began in the spring. Over 60 different comic book titles were being issued, including **Whiz Comics** begun in February by Fawcett Publications. A creation of writer Bill Parker and artist C. C. Beck, **Whiz's** Captain Marvel was the only superhero ever to surpass Superman in comic book sales. Drawing on their own popular pulp magazine heroes, Street and Smith Publications introduced **Shadow Comics** in March and **Doc Savage Comics** in May. A second trend was established with the summer appearance of the first issue of **All-Star Comics**, which brought several superheroes together in one story and in its third issue that winter would announce the establishment of the Justice Society of America.

1941: Wonder Woman was introduced in the spring issue of **All-Star Comics** No. 8, the creation of psychologist William Moulton Marston and artist Harry Peter. **Captain Marvel Adventures** began this year. By the end of 1941, over 160 titles were being published, including **Captain America** by Jack Kirby and Joe Simon, **Police Comics** with Jack Cole's Plastic Man and later Will Eisner's Spirit, **Military Comics** with Blackhawk by Eisner and Charles Cuidera, **Daredevil Comics** with the original character by Charles Biro, **Air Fighters** with Airboy also by Biro, and **Looney Tunes & Merrie Melodies** with Porky Pig, Bugs Bunny, and Elmer Fudd, reportedly created by Bob Clampett for the Leon Schlesinger Productions animated films and drawn for the comics by Chase Craig. Also, Albert Kanter's Gilberton Company initiated the **Classics Illustrated** series with **The Three Musketeers**.

1942: **Crime Does Not Pay** by editor Charles Biro and publisher Lev Gleason, devoted to factual accounts of criminals' lives, began a different trend in realistic crime stories. **Wonder Woman** appeared in the summer. John Goldwater's character Archie, drawn by Bob Montana, first published in **Pep Comics**, was given his own magazine **Archie Comics**, which has remained popular over 40 years. The first issue of **Animal Comics** contained Walt Kelly's "Albert Takes the Cake," featuring the new character of Pogo. In mid-1942, the undated Dell Four Color title, No. 9, **Donald Duck Finds Pirate Gold**, appeared with art by Carl Barks and Jack Hannah. Barks, also featured in **Walt Disney's Comics and Stories**, remained the most popular delineator of Donald Duck and later introduced his greatest creation, Uncle Scrooge, in **Christmas on Bear Mountain** (Dell Four Color No. 178). The fantasy work of George Carlson appeared in the first issue of **Jingle Jangle Comics**, one of the most imaginative titles for children ever to be published.

1945: The first issue of **Real Screen Comics** introduced the Fox and the Crow by James F. Davis, and John Stanley began drawing the **Little Lulu** comic book based on a popular feature in the **Saturday Evening Post** by Marjorie Henderson Buell from 1935 to 1944. Bill Woggon's Katy Keene appears in issue No. 5 of **Wilbur Comics** to be followed by appearances in **Laugh, Pep, Suzie** and her own comic book in 1950. The popularity of Dick Briefer's satiric version of the Frankenstein monster, originally drawn for **Prize Comics** in 1941, led to the publication of **Frankenstein** by Prize publications.

1950: The son of Max C. Gaines, William M. Gaines, who earlier had inherited his father's firm Educational Comics (later Entertaining Comics), began publication of a series of well-written and masterfully drawn titles which would establish a "New Trend" in comics magazines: **Crypt of Terror** (later **Tales from the Crypt**, April), **The Vault of Horror** (April), **The Haunt of Fear** (May), **Weird Science** (May), **Weird Fantasy** (May), **Crime SuspenStories** (October), and **Two-Fisted Tales** (November), the latter stunningly edited by Harvey Kurtzman.

1952: In October "E.C." published the first number of **Mad** under Kurtzman's creative editorship, thus establishing a style of humor which would inspire other publications and powerfully influence the underground comic book movement of the 1960s.

1953: All Fawcett titles featuring Captain Marvel were ceased after many years of litigation in the courts during which National Periodical Publications claimed that the super-hero was an infringement on the copyrighted Superman.

1954: The appearance of Fredric Wertham's book **Seduction of the Innocent** in the spring was the culmination of a continuing war against comic books fought by those who believed they corrupted youth and debased culture. The U. S. Senate Subcommittee on Juvenile Delinquency investigated comic books and in response the major publishers banded together in October to create the Comics Code Authority and adopted, in their own words, "the most stringent code in existence for any communications media." Before the Code took effect, more than 1,000,000,000 issues of comic books were being sold annually.

1955: In an effort to avoid the Code, "E.C." launched a "New Direction" series of titles, such as **Impact, Valor, Aces High, Extra, M.D.,** and **Psychoanalysis,** none of which lasted beyond the year. **Mad** was changed into a larger magazine format with issue No. 24 in July to escape the Comics Code entirely, and "E.C." closed down its line of comic books altogether.

1956: Beginning with the Flash in **Showcase** No. 4, Julius Schwartz began a popular revival of "DC" superheroes which would lead to the "Silver Age" in comic book history.

1957: Atlas reduced the number of titles published by two-thirds, with **Journey into Mystery** and **Strange Tales** surviving, while other publishers did the same or went out of business. Atlas would survive as a part of the Marvel Comics Group.

1960: After several efforts at new satire magazines (**Trump** and **Humbug**), Harvey Kurtzman, no longer with Gaines, issued in August the first number of another abortive effort, **Help!**, where the early work of underground cartoonists Jay Lynch, Skip Williamson, Gilbert Shelton, and Robert Crumb appeared.

1961: Stan Lee edited in November the first **Fantastic Four**, featuring Mr. Fantastic, the Human Torch, the Thing, and the Invisible Girl, and inaugurated an enormously popular line of titles from Marvel Comics featuring a more contemporary style of superhero.

1962: Lee introduced **The Amazing Spider-Man** in August, with art by Steve Ditko, **The Hulk** in May and **Thor** in August, the last two produced by Dick Ayers and Jack Kirby.

1963: Marvel's **The X-Men**, with art by Jack Kirby, began a successful run in November, but the title would experience a revival and have an even more popular reception in the 1980s.

1965: James Warren issued **Creepy**, a larger black and white comic book, outside Comics Code's control, which emulated the "E.C." horror comic line. Warren's **Eerie** began in September and **Vampirella** in September 1969.

1967: Robert Crumb's **Zap** No. 1 appeared, the first popular underground comic book to achieve wide popularity, although the undergrounds had began in 1962 with **Adventures of Jesus** by Foolbert Sturgeon (Frank Stack) and 1964 with **God Nose** by Jack Jackson.

1970: Editor Roy Thomas at Marvel begins **Conan the Barbarian** based on fiction by Robert E. Howard with art by Barry Smith, and Neal Adams began to draw for "DC" a series of **Green Lantern/Green Arrow** stories which would deal with relevant social issues such as racism, urban poverty, and drugs.

1972: The Swamp Thing by Berni Wrightson begins in November from "DC."

1973: In February, "DC" revived the original Captain Marvel with new art by C. C. Beck and reprints in the first issue of **Shazam** and in October **The Shadow** with scripts by Denny O'Neil and art by Mike Kaluta.

1974: "DC" began publication in the spring of a series of over-sized facsimile reprints of the most valued comic books of the past under the general title of "Famous First Editions," beginning with a reprint of **Action** No. 1 and including afterwards **Detective Comics** No. 27, **Sensation Comics** No. 1, **Whiz Comics** No. 2, **Batman**

No. 1, **Wonder Woman** No. 1, **All-Star Comics** No. 3, **Flash Comics** No. 1, and **Superman** No. 1. Mike Friedrich, an independent publisher, released **Star ★ Reach** with work by Jim Starlin, Neal Adams, and Dick Giordano, with ownership of the characters and stories invested in the creators themselves.

1975: In the first collaborative effort between the two major comic book publishers of the previous decade, Marvel and "DC" produced together an over-sized comic-book version of **MGM's Marvelous Wizard of Oz** in the fall, and then the following year in an unprecedented cross-over produced **Superman vs. the Amazing Spider-Man**, written by Gerry Conway, drawn by Ross Andru, and inked by Dick Giordano.

1976: Frank Brunner's Howard the Duck, who had appeared earlier in Marvel's **Fear** and **Man-Thing**, was given his own book in January, which because of distribution problems became an over-night collector's item. After decades of litigation, Jerry Siegel and Joe Shuster were given financial recompense and recognition by National Periodical Publications for their creation of Superman, after several friends of the team made a public issue of the case.

1977: Stan Lee's **Spider-Man** was given a second birth, fifteen years after his first, through a highly successful newspaper comic strip, which began syndication on January 3 with art by John Romita. This invasion of the comic strip by comic book characters continued with the appearance on June 6 of Marvel's **Howard the Duck**, with story by Steve Gerber and visuals by Gene Colan. In an unusually successful collaborative effort, Marvel began publication of the comic book adaption of the George Lucas film **Star Wars**, with script by Roy Thomas and art by Howard Chaykin, at least three months before the film was released nationally on May 25. The demand was so great that all six issues of **Star Wars** were reprinted at least seven times, and the installments were reprinted in two volumes of an over-sized Marvel Special Edition and a single paperback volume for the book trade. Dave Sim, with an issue dated December, began self-publication of his **Cerebus the Aardvark**, the success of which would help establish the independent market for non-traditional black-and-white comics.

1978: In an effort to halt declining sales, Warner Communications drastically cut back on the number of "DC" titles and overhauled its distribution process in June. The interest of the visual media in comic book characters reached a new high with the Hulk, Spider-Man, and Doctor Strange, the subjects of television shows; with various projects begun to produce film versions of Flash Gordon, Dick Tracy, Popeye, Conan, The Phantom, and Buck Rogers; and with the movement reaching an outlandish peak of publicity with the release of **Superman** in December. Two significant applications of the comic book format to traditional fiction appeared this year: **A Contract with God and Other Tenement Stories** by Will Eisner and **The Silver Surfer** by Stan Lee and Jack Kirby. Eclipse Enterprises published Paul Gulacy's **Sabre**, the first graphic album produced for the direct sales market, and initiated a policy of paying royalties and granting copyrights to comic book creators. Another self-publishing project, Wendy Pini's **Elfquest**, was so popular that it achieved bookstore distribution. The magazine **Heavy Metal** brought to American attention the avant-garde comic book work of European artists.

1980: Publication of the November premier issue of **The New Teen Titans**, with art by George Perez and story by Marv Wolfman, brought back to widespread popularity a title originally published by "DC" in 1966.

1981: The distributor Pacific Comics began publishing titles for direct sales through comic shops with the inaugural issue of Jack Kirby's **Captain Victory and the Galactic Rangers** and offered royalties to artists and writers on the basis of sales. "DC" would do the same for regular newsstand comics in November (with payments retroactive to July 1981), and Marvel followed suit by the end of the year. The first issue of **Raw**, irregularly published by Art Spiegelman and Francoise Mouly, carried comic book art into new extremes of experimentation and innovation with work by

European and American artists. With issue No. 158, Frank Miller began to write and draw Marvel's **Daredevil** and brought a vigorous style of violent action to comic book pages.

1982: The first slick format comic book in regular size appeared, **Marvel Fanfare** No. 1, with a March date. Fantagraphics Books began publication in July of **Love and Rockets** by Mario, Gilbert, and Jaime Hernandez and brought a new ethnic sensibility and sophistication in style and content to comic book narratives for adults.

1983: This year saw more comic book publishers, aside from Marvel and DC, issuing more titles than has existed in the past 40 years, most small independent publishers relying on direct sales, such as Americomics, Capital, Eagle, Eclipse, First, Pacific, and Red Circle, and with Archie, Charlton, and Whitman publishing on a limited scale. Frank Miller's mini-series **Ronin** demonstrated a striking use of sword-play and martial arts typical of Japanese comic book art, and Howard Chaykin's stylish but controversial **American Flagg** appeared with an October date on its first issue.

1984: A publishing, media, and merchandising phenomenon began with the appearance of the first issue of **Teenage Mutant Ninja Turtles** from Mirage Studios by Kevin Eastman and Peter Laird.

1985: Ohio State University's Library of Communication and Graphic Arts hosted the first major exhibition devoted to the comic book May 19 through August 2. In what was billed as an irreversible decision, the silver age superheroine Supergirl was killed in the seventh (October) issue of **Crisis on Infinite Earths**, a limited series intended to reorganize and simplify the DC universe on the occasion of the publisher's 50th anniversary.

1986: In recognition of its twenty-fifth anniversary, Marvel began publication of several new ongoing titles comprising Marvel's "New Universe," a self-contained fictional world. DC attracted extensive publicity and media coverage with its revisions of the character of **Superman** by John Byrne and of **Batman** in the **Dark Knight** series by Frank Miller. **Watchmen**, a limited-series graphic novel by Alan Moore and artist Dave Gibbons, began publication with a September issue from DC and Marvel's **The 'Nam**, written by Vietnam veteran Doug Murray and penciled by Michael Golden, began with its December issue. DC issued guidelines in December for labelling their titles as either for mature readers or for readers of all ages; in response, many artists and writers publicly objected or threatened to resign.

1987: Art Spiegelman's **Maus: A Survivor's Tale** was nominated for the National Book Critics Circle Award in biography, the first comic book to be so honored. A celebration of Superman's fiftieth Birthday began with the opening of an exhibition on his history at the Smithsonian's Museum of American History in Washington, D.C., in June and a symposium on "The Superhero in America" in October.

1988: Superman's birthday celebration continued with a public party in New York and a CBS television special in February, a cover story in **Time** magazine in March (the first comic book character to appear on the cover), and an international exposition in Cleveland in June. With issue number 601 for May 24, **Action Comics** became the first modern weekly comic book, which ceased publication after 42 issues with the December 13 number. In August, DC initiated a new policy of allowing creators of new characters to retain ownership of them rather than rely solely on work-for-hire.

1989: The fiftieth anniversary of Batman was marked by the release of the film **Batman**, starring Michael Keaton as Bruce Wayne and Jack Nicholson as the Joker; it grossed more money in the weekend it opened than any other motion picture in film history to that time.

Note: A special word of thanks is due Gerard Jones for his suggestions and contributions to the above chronology.

IN A LEAGUE OF THEIR OWN!

By

Harry B. Thomas

FOES OF EVIL! ENEMIES OF INJUSTICE! TO THE MIGHTY HEROES OF *THE JUSTICE LEAGUE OF AMERICA* ALL WRONG-DOING IS A MENACE TO BE STAMPED OUT——WHETHER IT COMES FROM OUTER SPACE——FROM THE WATERY DEPTHS OF THE SEVEN SEAS——OR SPRINGS FULL-BLOWN FROM THE MINDS OF MEN! BANDED TOGETHER TO FIGHT ALL FOES OF HUMANITY, THE MIGHTIEST HEROES OF OUR TIME BATTLE THE MENACE OF STARRO THE CONQUEROR!

The Roll Call:

Aquaman — Wonder Woman — Superman — Green Lantern — Batman — Flash — John Jones

Thus began the first of three "tryout" installments for *Justice League of America. Brave and the Bold* No. 28 (February-March, 1960) was a momentous event which shook every comic book rack across the country. Not since the cover of *Showcase* No. 4 dominated newsstands three and one half years earlier, had there been a comic book so breathlessly anticipated by casual readers and fanatic collectors alike. To those born early enough to have enjoyed the exploits of the Justice Society of America in *All Star Comics* (1940-1951), the concept was excitingly familiar. But to the vast army of baby boomers born in the late '40s and early '50s, this totally "new" concept of combining several of one's favorite heroes in a single story....in a single comic book....all pictured on the same unbelievably colorful cover ....Wow!!!!.....Whew!!!! This was the stuff that the most vivid and beloved comic book memories are made from!!!!

Yet it wasn't always this exciting at DC Comics. The years between the last Golden Age appearance of the Flash in *Flash Comics* No. 104 (February, 1949) and the character's revival in *Showcase* No. 4 (September-October, 1956) are considered by most fans as a low ebb in the tide of the super hero comic book genre. DC Comics unleashed a flood of, to say the least, "unlikely" concepts on comic book fans. They included the likes of *Super Baby, Bizzaro, Krypto, Bat Mite,* and *Bat Hound.* There was green, red, blue, gold, white, and rainbow

Brave & The Bold #28. First Justice League app. © DC

kryptonite; even the mildly forgetable chimp detective. DC's line of science fiction, mystery, western, war, teenage humor, funny animal and romance comics often seemed like classics when compared to their super hero storylines.

Over at (what would soon be) Marvel Comics, things weren't a whole lot better. Their specialty was monster comics featuring such often indistinguishable creatures as Trogg, Grogg, Progg, Frogg and Cazoom. Marvel's western and romance titles were equally repetitive.

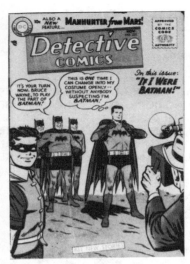

Detective Comics #225. First app. Jonn Jonzz. © DC

Showcase #4. The Silver Age begins! First app. of the new Flash. © DC

A first tiny step toward the light occurred in issue No. 225 (November, 1955) of *Detective Comics*. A new super hero was introduced as a back-up feature to *Batman*. The character Jonn Jonzz Manhunter From Mars, was not truly original in that he was basically a clone of Superman. He could fly, had super strength, and the added ability to make himself invisible. He also had green skin when not in his earth man disguise. While kryptonite did not have any effect on him, fire could destroy him; even a closeness to it could weaken and rob him of his powers. Sound a bit familiar? It sounded familiar to many thousands of readers, too.

J'onn J'onzz' claim to fame is two-fold; first, some comic book historians suggest he was technically the first DC Silver Age super hero. (This is, of course, not technically correct. By definition the Silver Age of comics starts with *Showcase* No. 4. However, *J'onn J'onzz* is a key step toward the Silver Age). Second, he became the only original charter member of the Justice League of America! At the time of J'onn J'onzz' comic book birth, the only costumed heroes still around in their own DC Comics were Superman, Batman, Superboy and Wonder Woman. Superman, Batman and Superboy were also appearing in *Action Comics, Detective Comics* and *Adventure Comics*, respectfully. Ad-

ditionally, Batman and Superman were also appearing in *World's Finest Comics* as a team while such characters as Aquaman, Green Arrow and Congorilla were placed in these same titles as back-up features. If J'onn J'onzz created a crack in the comic book mediocrity of the day, *Showcase* No. 4 in late 1956 busted things wide open!

In the late '50s there were still some staffers at DC Comics who had worked on the Golden Age line-up during the late 1940s and early 1950s. This elite group was comprised of artists, writers, and in particular, one very special editor! The artists still on staff read like a Silver Age "Who's Who:" Joe Kubert, Murphy Anderson, Carmine Infantino, Russ Heath, Gil Kane and Jack Kirby!

A most prominent, prolific, and capable writer from the golden years was Gardner F. Fox, DC's "Dean of Science Fiction." As was to be seen, he (as well as the aforementioned artists) still demonstrated that sense of wonder required to qualify as a truly great comic pro of the '30s and '40s. However, without the guiding hand of a certain editor, it is doubtful (even with all the other talent on hand) that DC or any other company could have manifested one of the most exciting times in comic book history, a rebirth of the comic book hero known as the Silver Age of comics!

Simply put, the genius most responsible for the Silver Age was Julius Schwartz. Schwartz had been around (some say) since the writing of Genesis! He had at least been around since the early '30s, working with science fiction pulp magazines and co-editing the first fan related magazine (fanzine) of that decade, titled *The Time Traveller*! From his experience with science fiction's first fanzine, he moved into the agency business, acting on behalf of some of the finest science fiction writers of the day. By the early '40s, the pulp magazine had declined in popularity and Mr. Schwartz began looking elsewhere to ply a trade.

Through a professional contact, he was recommended to Sheldon Mayer (an editor at DC) in relation to a vacancy. He interviewed, got the job, and 30 plus years later, he is still there! During the first few years at DC, Schwartz had, in one creative way or another, responsibility for some of the company's finest characters—the Flash, Hawkman, Atom, Johnny Thunder, and the most legendary comic team ever produced, *All Star Comics* featuring the Justice Society of America! By the late 1940s, except for the characters noted earlier, most of DC's super heroes had disappeared from the comic racks. For the next few bleak years, DC would struggle with many different concepts in an effort to re-establish sales and excite-

ment in their comic books. Nothing really dynamic would occur until late in 1956.

In March of 1956 DC debued a comic titled *Showcase*, the premise of which was to preview new titles to the market place, check the interest (by measuring sales and reader response), and then determine whether to publish that particular title on an ongoing basis. It was to prove to be one of the best marketing ideas DC would ever develop! This title, along with its sister title *Brave and the Bold* became the proving grounds that launched DC's characters into stardom and began the Silver Age of comics.

The first three issues of *Showcase* (*Fire Fighters, King of the Wild* and *The Frogmen*), although interesting to collectors, gave no clues to prepare comic book fans for the coming revitalization of the industry. And then with issue No. 4, Julius Schwartz came to bat! Comic book history began a new era and the Silver Age was officially born! This would be the issue in which "Julie" Schwartz would rejuvinate and modernize one of the Golden Age's most popular super heroes, the Flash. On hand to assist in this labor of love were the great Carmine Infantino (pencils), the incomparable Joe Kubert (inking) and the ever-consistent Robert Kanigher (writer). The sales on *Showcase* 4 were good enough for a second trial in issue No. 8 and this led to two more tryouts in issues Nos. 13 and 14.

Showcase #8. The 2nd app. of the new Flash. © DC

Showcase #13. The 3rd app. of the new Flash. © DC

Showcase #14. The 4th app. of the new
Flash. © DC

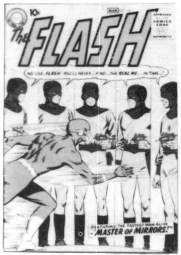

The Flash #105. First issue of the new
series. © DC

DC had a hit and the first real Silver Age hero
was born. It should be noted here that
Showcase No. 4 stands as the single most
historically important comic book event of
the Silver Age and its resounding success
would lead to many more at DC.

Following DC's lead, Archie Comics
would publish *Double Life Of Private Strong*
in June, 1959 introducing the super hero
character the Fly. He immediately won his

The Double Life Of Private Strong #1.
First app. of The Fly by Simon & Kirby.
© AP

wings in *Adventures of the Fly* No. 1 in
August, lasting to 1967 (with several title
changes). *Adventures of the Jaguar*, a companion title, appeared in September, 1961.

Marvel, under the editorship of
showman Stan Lee, would follow quickly
(with *Fantastic Four* No. 1, November,
1961), realizing the super hero was back in
vogue. While DC should be given credit for
starting the Silver Age, Marvel confirmed it
with some of the most original and exciting
characters comicdom would ever know.

DC was relatively cautious about getting
the Flash into his own book after his four
tryout issues in *Showcase*, but eventually the
Flash was given his own magazine. It was
numbered 105 (February-March, 1959), starting the series where his Golden Age
predecessor left off.

With the Flash a hit, his place as a founding member of the JLA was a certainty.
However, it should be noted for comic book
historians that DC had probably not the
slightest clue that *Showcase* No. 4 (and its
star, the Flash) would have such a gigantic
impact on the industry as a whole. Because
of this, an interesting correlation can be suggested between *Action* 1 and *Showcase* 4.
(For many baby boomers who cut their teeth
on the comics of the middle and late '50s,
Showcase 4 was their *Action* 1!!!!)

Showcase #22. First Silver Age Green Lantern. © DC

Showcase #23. 2nd Silver Age Green Lantern. © DC

Moreover, the super hero, backbone of the comics industry, had climbed out of the decline of the early 1950s. The costumed hero was back! Editor Schwartz's staff must have been excited! *The Flash* was a hit, and another costumed hero team book entitled *Challengers of the Unknown* (illustrated by Jack Kirby and edited by Jack Schiff) also looked like a winner. Comics were about to become colorful, fun and imaginative once more. One could feel the fresh air blowing through the industry.

After introducing the Flash, Schwartz again looked to the Golden Age heroes at DC for his next major project. In issue No. 22 of *Showcase*, he introduced a revival of one of the most memorable and novel characters of the '40s, the Green Lantern!

Again, the origin of the character was science fiction oriented, a Julie Schwartz trademark (the Flash had been created by a combination of lightning and chemicals). The Green Lantern obtained his powers via a benevolent group of space beings known as the Guardians of the Universe. Through them, he was given a ring and the power battery needed to charge it. The ring was activated by the wearer's mental concentration. Hal Jordon, the Earth's Green Lantern, was then assigned a certain sector of the universe to patrol and protect.

The artist for *Green Lantern* was a perfect choice. Gil Kane had been around DC since the early '50s where he had begun by illustrating the western strip, Johnny Thunder.

Kane had an action style of illustrating similar to that of Jack Kirby, and his ability to illustrate machinery has yet to be matched. For a series with such a heavy emphasis on science fiction plots, no better artist could have been picked.

Like the Flash, the Green Lantern was an overwhelming success, and after three consecutive tryout issues in *Showcase*, he received his own series. (Actually his success seems to have been a forgone conclusion by DC as they had begun running house ads in their comics for a *Justice League Of America* book and the cover depicted the revived Green Lantern as a member of the team even before he was awarded his own series.)

If *Showcase* No. 4 was the most historically important comic book of the Silver Age, *Brave and the Bold* No. 28 (which came out in 1960) had to have been the most eagerly anticipated comic of the period! No book printed during the early days of the Silver Age created more interest and excitement than did this issue, featuring the introduction of the Justice League of America!

Interestingly enough, the *Brave and the Bold* comic had begun in an adventure format, featuring such characters as the Viking Prince, the Silent Knight and Robin Hood. This anthology/adventure format lasted for 24 issues. With issue No. 25, DC changed the format to their second tryout magazine. This was evidence indeed that the comic book industry was again booming!

By the time the *Brave and the Bold* issue featuring the first appearance of the Justice League Of America (referred to hereafter as the JLA) hit the stands, there was already a fledgling fandom. Many fan magazines of the day that were primarily related to science fiction had begun running comic book related articles. Comic book letter columns enabled fans across the country to discuss the pros and cons of specific stories, read editor feedback directly, and to make contact with other fans and collectors.

It soon became obvious that many fans of the earlier Golden Age were also being caught up in the revivals of their old heroes. The title these older comic book fans recalled most fondly was *All Star Comics* featuring the Justice Society of America.

The Justice Society was a team featuring the more popular DC heroes of the time. In one adventure together, such characters as Green Lantern, Flash, Wonder Woman, Dr. Fate, the Spectre, Hawkman, and the Atom (among others) appeared as members of the elite group. Recalling this brilliant concept (and with the revival of the Flash and the Green Lantern already accomplished) editor Schwartz decided the time was right to bring back this type of book.

Shortly after the Green Lantern's third and last appearance in *Showcase* (No. 24), house ads began to appear in DC comics for *Brave And The Bold* No. 28. The cover depicted the the Justice League of America and proclaimed in the ad copy, "Just imagine, the mightiest heroes of our time have banded together as the Justice League of America to stamp out evil wherever and whenever it appears!"

Fans, collectors and everyday readers of the time were elated! The cover was exciting and colorful, and featured a five-pronged giant starfish with a single huge eye, battling five of DC's top heroes.

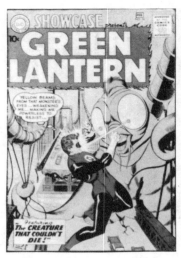

Showcase #24. 3rd app. Silver Age Green Lantern. © DC

Three of the five costumed heroes pictured have already been discussed: Flash, Green Lantern and J'onn J'onzz. The other two charter members of the JLA featured on that first historic cover appearance were Wonder Woman and Aquaman, both of whom had been around in one magazine or another at DC since the early 1940s. These five would make up the active membership for the JLA's first six stories.

While these five members would form the core team for the early JLA issues, there were two other DC heroes that were charter members of the team—Superman and Batman. They would, thankfully, appear only in minor roles until later in the magazine's run. It is generally felt by collectors and fans that the best Justice League stories were those that relegated these two characters to support status and allowed less seen characters at DC to take the limelight.

The writer for the first JLA story was the same one that handled the Justice Society stories of the '40s—Gardner F. Fox. His affinity for the book showed and some of his very best Silver Age work would be done on the JLA series.

Fox set the basic format for the JLA stories right from the start by having the team come together at the beginning of the story, discuss the threat or mystery, hand out specific assignments to members, break up singly or in pairs, handle the assigned task, and meet as a team at story's end to solve the final details as a unit.

Most menaces turned out to be either space aliens or some warped super-genius. In his stories, Fox would deal very little with character development or feuding team members as would later become so popular at Marvel. His stories would be heavy on plot and action and deal primarily with the clash of hero and villain powers.

Fox would rarely continue a story to the next issue, allowing readers the satisfaction of reading the complete plot in one issue. While comic writers today might find that feat nearly an impossibility, Gardner F. Fox did it often and with superb artistic excellence.

It should be mentioned that the team would have a mascot (of sorts...) introduced in their first appearance. Based on a teen heart throb of the time (Ed "Kookie" Byrnes) the teenager, "Snapper" Carr, was so nicknamed because of his continual habit of snapping his fingers, "beatnik style." The reason for his inclusion was for teen identification and, therefore, the hope of added sales. Respectfully, most fans are thankful that his contribution to the JLA was abbreviated.

While the covers would remain outstanding and the writing excellent, the art on the series continues to be a point of controversy among fans. The artist handed the, no doubt, difficult job of drawing all those characters with all those different styles was Mike Sekowsky. (It has been rumored that because of the necessity of illustrating stories with so many different costumed characters, most artists did not want this major chore.)

Sekowsky pencilled the first appearance of the JLA in *Brave and the Bold* No. 28 and would be the regular artist when the JLA got their own magazine. Bernard Sacks would ink Sekowsky's pencils with relative finesse. Murphy Anderson would ink most of the covers for Sekowsky, and actually did many entirely on his own. Sekowsky's fan critiques argue that his "two dimensional," "anatomically avantgarde" style was not appropriate for super heroes.

He had done some nice work on DC's

romance and science fiction titles that seemed much more suited to his special talents, but fans wanted and expected their heroes in the JLA to look just like they did in their regular features. For some reason, DC never caught on to (or chose to ignore) this crucial concept. In spite of this, *JLA* became one of DC's most popular selling books, proving the concept was more important than artistic sentiment.

The membership meld of the JLA was near perfect. While the team was indeed powerful, it was possible to defeat. Unfortunately, this important factor which allowed the book to have such a distinctive personality did not last for long.

J'onn J'onzz, of course, was the team's most powerful active member as for the first ten issues or so, Superman would be mainly a supporting character. However, fire could weaken and destroy him and fire was **much** more common than kryptonite!

Of the other four active members, Green Lantern was an ordinary man armed with his extraordinary, thought-induced power ring, useless against anything yellow. The Flash only had super speed. Aquaman could live under water, communicate with the undersea creatures, and Wonder Woman, though powerful, was not indestructable. So the initial five active members, while a formidable opponent, could be defeated by a writer's imagination.

The vulnerability of the original group allowed the early issues to be fun and rather unpredictable. It also made it relatively easy for writer Fox to come up with villains that could actually present an effective challenge to the team.

The second installment of the JLA in *Brave and the Bold* No. 29 served up more of the same, including a great cover and interesting story. However, this issue did prove the people connected to the Justice League had done their homework on the Golden Age Justice Society, as the cover for this issue was almost a direct swipe of *All Star* No. 43.

The covers were all that was similar, however, because the story in *Brave and the Bold* 29 dealt with a criminal from Earth's future, the Weapon's Master! *All Star* No. 43, on the other hand, sent the Justice Society into a "Dimension Of Gold!"

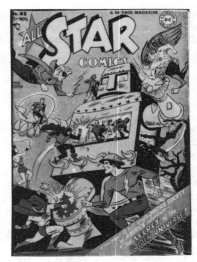

Left: **Brave & The Bold** #29. 2nd app. Justice League. **Right: All Star Comics** #43. Note similarity of both cover layouts.

Brave and the Bold No. 30 featured the outstanding cover of the three *Brave and Bold* tryout stories, depicting one of the best villains ("Amazo") the team would face in its long career. "Amazo" was an android created by a mad genius named Professor Ivo. Ivo proceeded to capture the members of the JLA and transferred their powers to his android. The JLA had to then battle a single being armed with all their combined

Brave & The Bold #30. 3rd app. Justice League. © DC

powers. The story was far and away the best of Fox's first three JLA stories....the first truly classic Silver Age JLA epic.

The three appearances of the JLA in *Brave and the Bold* were instant hits at the newsstands and warranted a near immediate Justice League series in their own magazine. The first issue of *JLA* appeared in late 1960 and featured the same active membership as had been featured in the three *Brave and the Bold* issues. The first issue sported a nice Anderson cover and the story was "sci fi" villain a la Fox.

Issue No. 2 should be noted, as once again the Golden Age Justice Society shed its influence. This time the covers were not similar, but the stories were. In *JLA* No. 2 the Justice League adventure was entitled "Secret of the Sinister Sorcerers" and dealt with the JLA entering a dimension of magic to solve a perplexing problem. (i.e., science no longer working on Earth) Fox admitted to being inspired for this story by a similar one he had written for *All Star* No. 39. "Invasion From Fairyland!" was an off-beat story and contains many comparable concepts to *Brave and the Bold* No. 30.

While nothing that outstanding occured in issue No. 3 except for a nice cover, No. 4 stands as one of the few genuine classic Silver Age comic books. First, the cover was

Justice League Of America #1.
© DC

Justice League Of America #4. The
Green Arrow joins the JLA. © DC

illustrated by Murphy Anderson and is considered the best of the first seven. Second, it featured the first new member to be inducted into the roll call of the JLA.

The Green Arrow had been a perennial favorite at DC for many years. Back in the mid '40s, he had been the cover feature on one of their "Big Eight" anthology books, *More Fun Comics*. From there, he moved on to back-up features in *Adventure Comics* and *World's Finest Comics*. Also in the '40s he had been a member of a team called the "Laws Legionnaires" (also known as the "7 Soldiers of Victory") appearing in *Leading Comics*. This group, illustrated by such top line artists as George Papp and Jack Kirby, was sort of a "second string" Justice Society.

Green Arrow's induction into the JLA

Left: Justice League Of America #6. Right: All Star Comics #42. Note similarity of both cover layouts.

did little to upset the "required vulnerability" needed for effective plot lines, and in that light Green Arrow was the perfect choice!

Because issue No. 4 added the first new member to the JLA, it remains historically important in the JLA saga and is a genuine classic Silver Age book.

The only noteworthy item in issue No. 5 with its story "When Gravity Went Wild" was the fact that this is the first cover to depict Superman and Batman. While they were not prominent on the cover or in the story, it did forebode things to come.

Issue No. 6 "The Wheel Of Misfortune" once again featured a cover reflecting an idea previously suggested by an *All Star* cover. On the cover of issue No. 6 the JLA heroes are shown tied to a wheel of fortune or "misfortune" in this case. On *All Star* No. 42 the Justice Society members are shown attached to a propeller device. Other than the cover, the stories had no similarities.

While issues Nos. 7 and 8 offered up average fare, No. 9 finally got around to telling the origin of the JLA. Except for the fact that it is the origin issue, the book was rather unexceptional.

It's famous cover shows the five original team members, under the influence of a sinister green meteorite, slowly turning into

Justice League Of America #9. The origin of the JLA is given. © DC

trees. Taken from the "space creature genre," the story shows the seven charter members being drawn together for the first time. After the adventure, Batman suggests they should form an ongoing "club" of sorts to be ready to combat such future menaces as needed. The heroes present agreed and the team was formed. Not outstanding, but interesting.

Issue No. 10 featured another distinctive cover by Anderson and was also the first half of the first two-part JLA adventure, with *JLA* No. 11 taking up where No. 10 left off. Interestingly, the two parts of the continued story can actually be read as complete in an of themselves as part one really just leads into the events of part two.

Many fans consider issue No. 10 to be the issue that put the first cracks into the series' strong foundation. It marked the first time Superman and Batman began to take more active rolls in the title. Superman was just too powerful and putting him in a team which already had J'onn J'onzz just made the roll call predictable. And Batman? Well, many have suggested the true quality of his character only works as a "lone" figure, thus rendering him a poor choice for a "team" effort.

With the addition of these two as active members, the roster began to be rather crowded to fit into the standard 25-page comic book. As the membership began to grow, the book began to lose much of its unique personality.

The JLA would have to do a guest appearance in another magazine to finally get the respect art-wise they were due.

At the time of issue No. 11 of their own magazine, over in *Mystery In Space* No. 75, the JLA joined Adam Strange in his book-length adventure "The Planet that came to a standstill." The villain of the story was JLA foe Kanjar-Ro, who had appeared in JLA No. 3.

The art team on Adam Strange at the time was, arguably, done by the best duo of the Silver Age; Carmine Infantino on pencils and Murphy Anderson on inks. For this very special issue, they pulled out all the stops.

The beautiful art done on the JLA in the

Mystery In Space #75. The JLA appears.
© DC

last chapter of this book certainly left fans of the team longing for more of the same. No JLA collection would be complete without *Mystery In Space* No. 75.

JLA Nos. 12 and 13 fall into the "pretty much average issue" category and by this point the JLA began operating more in teams of two or three to accommodate the growing active membership. Fighting a menace

alone as some of the members did in earlier issues was now over. While Fox would still turn out some classic stories for the series before it would collapse into confusion and disarray, the book was just not as much fun as it had been.

Before looking at issue No. 14, time must be taken to look at what had been going on in other areas of the DC universe. Two other Golden Age heroes had been given a new lease on life via DC's two "tryout" titles—the Hawkman in *Brave and the Bold* 34, 35 and 36; the Atom in *Showcase* 34, 35 and 36 (coincidence?).

Both characters were under the editorial guidance of (who else?) Julius Schwartz. For the first time, one of editor Schwartz's revised heroes failed to "fly" as the Hawkman (though well written by Gardner F. Fox and superbly illustrated by Joe Kubert who had illustrated the strip in the '40s) failed to attract buyer support on his tryout issues to warrant his own series. Hope was not lost, though, as Hawkman would be given a second three-issue tryout in *Brave and the Bold* 42, 43 and 44. From there, he would win his own series. As with the other revived Schwartz heroes, the Hawkman strip was science fiction oriented. In this case, the Hawkman (along with his wife Shierra) were visitors from another planet come to Earth

Brave & The Bold #35. 2nd app. of the new Hawkman. © DC

Showcase #34. First app. of the new Atom. © DC

to study our crime solving techniques.

With all its fine points, good writing, fantastic art, the most interesting costume of all the silver age heroes, it remains a mystery why *Hawkman* didn't have instant success.

Over at *Showcase*, the Atom issues did prove successful. The Atom was really a combination of two Golden Age heroes. In name only he was a revival of the former character appearing in DC's *All American Comics* (as well as a member of the Justice Society in *All Star Comics*) and, because of his size-reducing ability, he was an updated edition of the popular Quality Comics hero, Doll Man. As to be expected with a Schwartz hero, the origin was again science fiction in theme.

The Atom gained his powers by being exposed to rays from a meteorite chunk thrown from a white dwarf star. By using a control on the belt of his uniform, the Atom could release these rays to instantly reduce in size from a normal adult to as small as microscopic (though he would normally stop at a few inches in height). Important was the fact that when reduced in size, he retained the strength of a full grown man.

The sales on the "Mighty Mite's" three tryout issues were good enough to win him his own series before Hawkman, the result of which led to his becoming a member of the JLA before the "winged wonder!"

As an aside, it should be noted at this point just how important DC's roll was in creating a new age of interest in the comic book that is still flourishing today! At the time period now being discussed, DC had already successfully introduced such popular characters as the Flash, the Green Lantern, the Challengers of the Unknown, the Justice League of America, Cave Carson, the Suicide Squad, the Atom, and to some extent, the Hawkman. Marvel, to this date, had yet to introduce their first successful Silver Age hero!

JLA No. 14, "Menace of the Atom Bomb," served as a vehicle to induct the Atom into the team's roll call. The Atom had no special powers other than size reduction, so he did little to make the JLA more powerful, but he did add variety. His small size in proportion to the other heroes seemed to be a problem for both illustrator and writer alike. It was a real problem in group scenes and team-up chapters, and it sure made for some ingenious and unusual covers.

With the roster of active JLA members now at nine, things were beginning to get out of hand, in the realms of both art and story. Throw in a couple of villains or so and things really got messy. There were just too many characters for a 25-page comic book. Fans still speculate today as to why Schwartz did not follow the lead set by *All Star Comics*, which kept the membership at a manageable

Brave & The Bold #42. First of the second three tryout issues. © DC

Justice League Of America #14. The Atom joins the JLA. © DC

The Flash #123. The Golden Age Flash
first appears in the Silver Age. © DC

The Flash #129. The second team-up
issue. © DC

level by dropping some members when new
ones were added. That philosophy had kept
All Star fresh and exciting for over 10 years.

Issues 15 through 20 dealt primarily with
alien menaces. However, issues 21 and 22
would wake fans up with one of the most
memorable stories in Silver Age history!

To put these two issues in the proper
perspective, it is important to remember
Flash No. 123, one of the classic stories of
the early Silver Age. The story, "Flash of
Two Worlds," written by Gardner F. Fox
had the modern Flash, through super vibra-
tion, cross dimensions into a world called
"Earth 2." This alternate world was similar
in all aspects to our world except it was here
that the heroes of DC's Golden Age resid-
ed. Earth One's Flash met his name-sake, the
Golden Age Flash of Earth Two, and from
there they shared the first of many adventures
together. The re-introduction of the original
Golden Age Flash marked the first reappearance in the Silver Age of a member of
the Justice Society of America.

The story proved immensely popular
with both new and older fans and a second
team-up of the two heroes appeared in *Flash*
No. 129. In this issue, mention was made of
the original Justice Society. (Note: While
Flash No. 129 was the first official reintroduction of the Justice Society into the

modern DC universe, it was not the team's
first appearance in one of the Schwartz
revival books. A historical reference to the
Justice Society had appeared in the centerfold of *Showcase* No. 34 featuring the Atom.
A reproduction drawn from *All Star* No. 3's
cover was shown and the members were listed
along with their powers.) This teaser got immediate response from fans who demanded
to actually see the group in action once

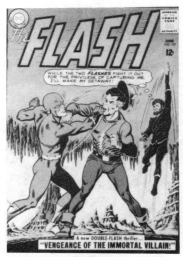

The Flash #137. The third team-up
issue. © DC

more...They got it!!! In the next team-up of the two speedsters in *Flash* No. 137 ("Vengeance of the Immortal Villain"), the Justice Society was brought out of retirement to help the two Flashes do battle with Golden Age villain Vandal Savage.

Fans still wanted more of this very colorful group. They could not seemingly get enough. Even the writers and artists at DC seemed to be caught up in the excitement of the appearance of the JSA. The inevitable happened in *JLA* No. 21; a team-up of the Justice League and the Justice Society!

The book today is justifiably one of the most sought after DC comics of the Silver Age. The cover pencilled by Mike Sekowsky and inked (with inspiration) by Anderson, ranks as one of the very best Silver Age covers ever and only one other *JLA* cover would rival it in impact. The cover shows the JLA members in a seance-like pose around a table with the Justice Society appearing in a cloud of smoke above their heads. It is doubtful any other single issue of the *JLA* in their own series (excluding the *Brave and the Bold* tryout issues) ever created as much excitement as did this single issue.

Fox was inspired in his writing of the story "Crisis On Earth I." The Justice Society members he chose to bring back in their first adventure since *All Star* were: the Flash, Hawkman, Dr. Fate, Black Canary, Hourman, the Atom, and the Green Lantern. The classic tale carried over into issue No. 22 in the story "Crisis On Earth II." These two issues of the *JLA* stand near the top of any Silver Age collector's list of favorites and are bright spots in any comic collection.

Only one other *JLA* book in their own series can top or equal these two exciting issues. The initial appearance of the JLA/JSA team-up proved so popular that it would become an annual affair. The members participating on both teams would vary from annual outing to annual outing. Not much above average would happen in the series until the next pairing of the two groups in issues 29 and 30. While the stories were adequate and there were some nice covers, nothing seemed to quite reach the peak set by the first *JSA* issues. Except for the outstanding cover on No. 29, the second annual team-up issues were a bit of a letdown from issues 21 and 22, a natural consequence of the anticipation for those two issues.

The cover for issue 29, as mentioned above, was another outstanding job from the Sekowsky/Anderson team and was also inspired by a previous *All Star* issue (No. 8, and this time the cover was an almost direct copy). The *All Star* cover has the Justice

Justice League Of America #21. First JLA/JSA team-up. © DC

Justice League Of America #22. "Crisis On Earth II" continues. © DC

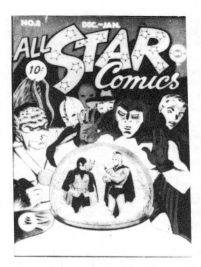

Left: **Justice League Of America** #29. **Right: All Star Comics** #8. Note similarity of both cover layouts.

Society members standing around a crystal ball in which we see two heroes (Starman and Dr. Midnight) who are to be inducted as new members in that issue. On *JLA* No. 29 we see the *JSA* standing over a crystal ball in which appear the members of the *JLA*.

Regrettably, in this issue another alternate Earth is added to the DC universe; Earth III. The two issues entitled "Crisis On Earth III" and "The Most Dangerous Earth Of All" further crowded an already overflowing comics universe.

Earth III had their own costumed counterparts to Earth I and Earth II (in this case things were in reverse of the other two Earths as costumed "Heroes" of Earth III were all criminals). The two issues (*JLA* 29 and 30) were so overcrowded it began to look like a Mack Sennett Keystone Kops comedy! It was a case of "too much of a good thing" carried to its ultimate limit!

JLA No. 31 introduced yet another new member into its roster. The Hawkman had been given a second tryout in *Brave and the Bold* and had finally won his own series. It was now time to award him full membership to the team. With his winged costume he was the League's most visual member, but the timing of his entry was not the most opportune in that the JLA was already overcrowd-

ed. This allowed the character of Hawkman to benefit little from being added to the lineup. His addition, of course, just further log-jammed the already crowded book as his entry brought the active membership to 10.

It became nigh impossible to include the entire membership in one story. Members were left out of some issues and put into others, making it difficult to identify who was where, when and why!!! Hawkman's addition did not seem to meet with the excitement of the inductions of the Green Arrow and the Atom. It appeared that fans had begun to take a bit of a "ho-hum" attitude regarding the continual addition of new members.

Although the "newness" and thrill of the series seemed to be wearing thin, there were still a few bright rays of light that would crack through before the looming dark days of the book would fully take over. Two of these "rays of light" were issues 36 and 41. Back in the '40s the original Justice Society had dealt with social issues in a few of their adventures. In No. 36 the JLA had their first "social issue" adventure.

The story, "Case of the Disabled Justice League," has a villain ("Brain Storm") afflicting members of the JLA with handicaps similar to those of some children they had visited earlier in a hospital. The League then had to do battle against their enemy while afflicted with these handicaps and in so doing see what it was like to be faced with such afflictions. (Note: The JSA in *All Star* No. 27 also dealt with the issue of handicapped children.)

In issue No. 41 a villain by the name of the Key in an adventure entitled "The Key, Master Of The World" uses the members' consciences to influence them to break up the team. This story was also similar in context to two stories Fox had done in *All Star* Nos. 22 and 24 in which he had dealt the importance of conscience in mankind. Though issues 36 and 41 are worthy of more than just passing attention in the context of the *JLA* series, it would be in issue No. 57 that Gardner Fox would really assert himself and do one of the best stories of the Silver Age (and possibly the single best *JLA* story?). Since issue 30, and with the exceptions of issues 36 and 41, not much out of the ordinary occurred until that 57th issue.

The series was on a downhill slide that had (or would) include the pun-filled issues so influenced by the "camp" Batman T.V.

Justice League Of America #41. © DC

show, reprints (the bane of all serious readers), silly guest stars, more reprints, silly covers, so-so stories, even more reprints, and a continually changing active membership that left readers confused as to who was

in the JLA. For all these reasons, issues 36, 41 and 57 remain as outstanding examples of the series.

The cover to *Justice League* No. 57 stands as one of the very best done on any Silver Age comic book by any publisher. It was one of the truly classic covers of the Silver Age, or any age, for that matter. Pencilled by Carmine Infantino and inked by Sid Greene, it depicts the Green Arrow, Flash, and Hawkman standing behind three youths of differing nationalities holding hands in front of a United Nation's symbol. Above all their heads, carved in a granite-like stone, is the story title, "Man Thy Name Is Brother." The background is black, effecting a stunning, vivid and colorful piece of artwork!

The story, as told by the three cover heroes to Snapper Carr, teaches that men are truly brothers regardless of race, creed, or color. The story unravels as each of the stars carry Snapper to different parts of the world to bring their points home. Even Mike Sekowsky seemed inspired in his depiction of the story as was the inking by Sid Greene. Of all the JLA books, this stands as the finest example of what could have been. If one book only could be labeled classic in the JLA series, this would most likely have to be the one. Sad to say, the series would wander from this point into a mire of non-direction.

By the time Fox would write his last JLA adventure in issue No. 65, it had become evident he had lost some enthusiasm (and why not, he had been writing for decades). Writers would come and go, each with their own ideas as to what the characters whould be like, adding and dropping characters in what seemed like arbitrary comic book madness! The series had lost its special distinction. Grown members would squabble and fuss like immature teens in a half- hearted attempt to "copy" Marvel. "Colorful" language would spout from the mouths of drooping and desperate heroic figures.

Characters would be killed off, continuity would become a thing of the past, and art would suffer terribly. Membership would grow to the size of a small army and stories would run on for untold issues. Before its last truly inglorious days, the title would enjoy a few brighter moments, like some nice covers by Neal Adams and Gil Kane, and some really excellent interior art by the talented George Perez. Still, it seemed the book had so lost its personality that even he could not have saved it.

The JLA remains among the most controversial of all the Silver Age, Julius Schwartz- edited, DC titles. That distinction alone will keep the Justice League Of America at the forefront of collector demand and interest for years to come. To gain insight into the title's on-going popularity, one need only look at the current collector's market to see the upwardly escalating demand for, and value of, JLA back issues.

While the JLA was not, perhaps, the artistic perfection "fans" wanted in its later issues, it was intriguing enough to keep readers coming back to the newsstand for over 20 years! Even today JLA International appears to continue the successful format since the demise of the original title with the April, 1987 issue. Consider the fact that the "second series." began in May, 1987, without missing even a single month of publication! You see, the fans just simply love the concept, rather like literary and visual neapolitan ice cream. Remember how you felt the first time you saw all those heroes on the same cover???? Yep, (sigh) so do I . . . . .

THE SILVER AGE...THE BEGINNING

A Comparative Chronology of the First Silver Age Comic Books

By Gary M. Carter

Showcase #4 (The 1st Silver Age wonder). First Flash. © DC

Showcase #22 (The 2nd Silver Age wonder). First Green Lantern. © DC

"Hey kid...this is a drugstore, not a library...either buy it or put it back!" Mr. Corrin, the owner of the pharmacy and newsstand I frequented, knew my seven year old brain would respond to this familiar chastisement. You see, I liked "funny books," but back in 1956, I wasn't too keen on the idea of plunking down a whole dime just to read one. That is, until I saw.....it...across the entire width of Corrin's drug store, up on the highest part of the rack, shining like a red-orange laser-beacon! It was the most beautiful thing I had ever seen. Its gorgeous cover framed an overwhelming red-suited hero with golden winged boots. He seemed to run right off the cover. That "funny book" seized my attention like no comic book had ever done before. Like so many others across the country, I placed my dime on the counter in anticipation of the reading adventure ahead. I had no way of know-

ing it at the time, but that first comic book purchase would profoundly change the rest of my life.

I'm sure editor Julius Schwartz did not intend for *Showcase* No. 4 to siphon off one whole week's worth of my allowance, profoundly change my life, or even to begin the Silver Age of Comics...but it did all three! That's because *Showcase* No. 4, like no 1950s book before it, did something very special and unique in the annals of comic book history. It did not just attempt to recycle a "tried and true" hero that had fallen out of favor with comic book buyers. It applied some of the basic concepts of the Golden Age Flash, yet changed and updated many others, including the origin, the alter ego, and, of course, that incredible uniform. Those important changes incorporated the overriding theme that dominated the media of the '50s. That theme was Science Fiction and *Showcase*

No. 4 perfectly married Super Hero with it. Like myself, most of America's youthful readers likely viewed this "new" Flash with awe and wonder, not realizing that this blast of literary fresh air would change the entire course of comic book publishing forever. In fact, *Showcase* No. 4 might well be considered the first "comic book wonder of the Silver Age world!"

At the age of 10, the second Silver Age wonder came smashing its way into my youthful world. Like the Flash before him, the Silver Age Green Lantern arrived in a September-October issue of *Showcase* with a minimum of fanfare—considering the importance of this blockbuster event. Most periodical distribution houses received *Showcase* No. 22 on July 20, 1959, and delivered it to the stands anywhere from a few days to a few weeks later. When it did finally arrive, enthusiastic readers discovered that, once again, science fiction had converted a well-worn Golden Age hero into a stunning and totally brilliant saga. The cover still gives collectors who purchased it from the stands a severe case of nostalgic chills. *Showcase* No. 22 introduced us to the dying red-skinned Abin-Sur in his sleek green and black uniform. As he searches for an Earthman "deserv-

ing" enough and "totally without fear" to be possessor of the Battery of Power, the reader is treated to a brilliant science fiction scenario worthy of a Shakespearean drama.

The third Silver Age wonder actually starred both Flash and Green Lantern, among others. *The Brave and the Bold* No. 28 tantalized and dazzled comic buyers with magnificent full color ads in advance of its publication with the now-famous quote, "All your favorite heroes in one magazine together." *The Brave and the Bold* No. 28 introduced the Justice League of America to the World with, of all things, an evil alien starfish as the heavy. The JLA debut was so anticipated that many collectors tell a similar story of checking newsstands every day for weeks—waiting to purchase their copy! No Silver Age comic held and delivered so much promise for so many avid readers across the country. Some credit this comic book with being the catalyst which jelled organized fandom and catapulted the hobby of comic book collecting to national status.

DC made the perfect choice when Joe Kubert was given the assignment to draw the rebirth of Hawkman in the fourth wonder of the Silver Age world. And once

Brave & The Bold #28 (The 3rd Silver Age wonder). First Justice League. © DC

Brave & The Bold #34 (The 4th Silver Age wonder). First Hawkman. © DC

Showcase #34 (The 5th Silver Age
wonder). First Atom. © DC

Fantastic Four #1 (The 6th Silver Age
wonder). Marvel enters the arena. © MCG

again, science fiction proved the best foundation upon which to build the Silver Age
Hawkman saga in *The Brave and the Bold*
No. 34 (February-March 1961). From the
details of feathered wings to those blank
but probing white eye slits, Kubert's artwork cast a perfect spell. Hawkman quickly
demonstrated that he was made of the same
great literary quality as Flash and Green
Lantern.

Incredibly, DC's wonders didn't stop
there. In yet another September-October
issue of *Showcase* (No. 34, 1961), DC virtually assaulted the pleasure centers of its
readers with its most beautiful cover of the
decade. Wonder number five (the Atom
saga) was already fantastic enough when
Julius Schwartz decided to "ice the cake"
with a taste of the original Justice Society
of America from the cover of *All-Star* No.
3 just to make sure I would never forget
the day I purchased and read that sensational issue.

But all seven wonders of the Silver Age
world don't belong to DC alone! The sixth
same without warning from this relatively
small publisher whose primary specialty in
the late '50s was strange space monsters.
In late 1961, while comic books were still
ten cents and the supply of monster names

was running low, Stan Lee practiced a little revival magic of his own and refurbish-
ed the Human Torch, as well as inventing
three more never-to-be-forgotten heroes to
boot—Mr. Fantastic, the Invisible Girl, and
the Thing! *Fantastic Four* No. 1 changed
forever the way super heroes are perceived
by the popular culture. The Marvel Age had
arrived!

As though its comic book creativity
was limitless, Marvel sired the seventh
wonder of the Silver Age world when it
converted *Amazing Adult Fantasy* to
Amazing Fantasy with the 15th and final
issue. This phenomenal epic premiered the
innaugural story of the Amazing Spider-
Man, magnificently rendered by Marvel's
avant-garde stylist Steve Ditko. The World
would never be the same.

But what of the rest of the Silver Age
world? To gain a better perspective of the
seven "wonder" comics just mentioned,
their relationship to comic book history,
and their overall place in the scheme of
things, one can utilize a tool known as the
relative chronology (or in simpler terms—a
timeline). With its use, publishing events
prior to, and during, the Silver Age become
easier to understand and to relate to the
"big picture" of comic book publishing

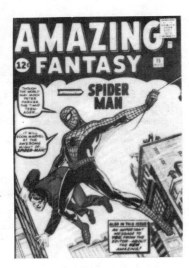

Amazing Fantasy #15 (The 7th Silver Age wonder). First Spider-Man. © MCG

history. This understanding is all the more important when consideration is given to the recent rise in popularity and value of Pre-Silver Age and Silver Age comic books. It is in this regard that the following relative chronology is presented.

As you review the listing, three things should be noted. Firstly, the month of publication shown on the cover or listed in the indicia of a comic book is the primary source of data utilized in this compilation. Given this, it is important to remember that these dates are always 15 to 120 days later than the date the comic actually appeared on the stands. This inconsistency between the month printed on the cover (or in the indicia) and the actual time period the comic was displayed on the racks has been an industry-wide policy almost since the beginning of comics. This is because the date on the cover was generally used by dealers and distributors across the country as an indicator of when to *remove* that particular issue from the sales rack. Understanding this concept is exceptionally important when attempting to pinpoint the date a specific issue was actually displayed.

Secondly, even though DC and Marvel titles clearly dominate this time period (because of collector interest and historical importance), a number of titles represen-

ting other publishing companies have been added to this comparative chronology (especially certain last issues) to provide a clearer picture of related comic book events.

Lastly, the timeline also lists some examples of comic books published previously to September-October 1956, so that a perspective of the events which led up to the Silver Age may be assessed.

I hope, as you explore the data below, you will discover many fascinating and entertaining revelations about **The Silver Age...The Beginning!**

Some of the Events Leading Up to the Silver Age of Comics:

MAY 1951
Mystery in Space No. 1 — "Don't Be Earthbound! Jet Off to Alien Worlds in Every Issue of Mystery in Space. AMAZING Trips Into the Unknown! ASTOUNDING Adventures on Uncharted Planets! Astonishing Experiments of Super-Science! The Magazine That Unlocks the Secrets of the Future." Frazetta's last work at DC ("Spores From Space") and first Knights of the Galaxy.

JUN 1951
Strange Adventures No. 9 — Origin and first appearance of "Captain Comet—First Man of the Future!" by Edgar Ray Merritt.
Strange Tales No. 1 — First of the "big four" Marvel anthology books that survived into the upcoming Silver Age of Comics.

JAN 1952
House of Mystery No. 1 — Now famous "Wanda Was a Werewolf" cover.

JUN 1952
Journey Into Mystery No. 1 — Second of the "big four" Marvel anthology books that survived into the upcoming Silver Age of Comics.

SEP 1952
The Phantom Stranger No. 1 — "Out of the swirling mists of nowhere looms a mysterious figure to shield the innocent from the dark forces of evil...and then to disappear again into the void! Who is the Phantom Stranger?" "Is he man...or ghost?"

APR 1953
Jumbo Comics No. 167 — Last issue.
Master Comics No. 133 — Last issue.
Suspense No. 29 — Last issue.

JUN 1953
Whiz Comics No. 155 — Last issue.
Captain Marvel Jr. No. 119 — Last issue.

JUL 1953
The Phantom Stranger No. 6 — Last issue.

SEP 1953
Batman No. 78 — Ron Kar, the Manhunter From Mars story tells of the first lawman from the planet Mars to visit Earth. Interestingly, he has green skin and appears to be a precurser of Jonn Jonzz who will not appear until approximately two years later.

OCT 1953
Planet No. 73 — Last issue.

Police Comics No. 127 — Last issue.

NOV 1953
Captain Marvel Adventures No. 150 — Last issue.

DEC 1953
Young Men No. 24 — First of five consecutive issues featuring Captain America, Human Torch, and Submariner.
Weird Science No. 22 — Last issue.
Weird Fantasy No. 22 — Last issue.

JAN 1954
Marvel Family No. 89 — Last issue.
Frontline Combat No. 15 — Last issue.

FEB 1954
Young Men No. 25 — Captain America, Human Torch, and Submariner.

MAR 1954
Young Men No. 26 — Captain America, Human Torch, and Submariner.

APR 1954
Young Men No. 27 — Captain America, Human Torch, and Submariner.
Human Torch No. 36 — Third to the last issue.

MAY 1954
Fighting American No. 1 — Classic Simon and Kirby.
Men's Adventures No. 27 — First of two consecutive issues to feature Captain America, Human Torch, and Submariner.
Adventures Into Terror No. 31 — Last issue.

JUN 1954
Young Men No. 28 — Last issue. Captain America, Human Torch, and Submariner appear.
Human Torch No. 37 — Second to the last issue.
Adventures Into Weird Worlds No. 30 — Last issue.

JUL 1954
Men's Adventures No. 28 — Last issue. Captain America, Human Torch, and Submariner.

AUG 1954
Human Torch No. 38 — Last issue.
Jungle Comics No. 163 — Last issue.
World's Finest No. 71 — Superman/Batman team begin. First ten cent issue and first of four consecutive issues to have NOW 10ᶜ on the cover in large print.

SEP 1954
Captain America No. 78 — Last issue.
Congo Bill No. 1 — With Janu the Jungle Boy.

OCT 1954
Superman's Pal, Jimmy Olsen No. 1 — Superman's sidekick got his own signal watch, why not his own magazine? Unlike Lois Lane, Showcase wasn't around quite yet to give Jimmy a tryout.

DEC 1954
Haunt of Fear No. 28 — Last issue.

JAN 1955
Vault of Horror No. 40 — Last issue.
Shock SuspenStories No. 18 — Last issue.

FEB 1955
My Greatest Adventure No. 1 — Although created with an adventure format in mind, the title became a DC science fiction anthology book after the first few issues.
Voodoo No. 19 — Last issue.

MAR 1955
Adventure No. 210 — First appearance of Krypto, Superboy's super dog.
Tales From the Crypt No. 46 — Last issue.
Two Fisted Tales No. 41 — Last issue.
Crime SuspenStories No. 27 — Last issue.

MAY 1955
Mad No. 23 — Last comic book issue.
Fighting American No. 7 — Last issue.
The Black Knight No. 1 — "Men of iron in the age of glorious adventure."
Menace No. 11 — Last issue. A precursor of sorts to Amazing Adult Fantasy, Stan Lee signs and puts his famous "surprise" endings on each and every story in this 11-issue run.

JUN 1955
Heroic Comics No. 97 — Last issue.
Batman No. 92 — First appearance of Ace the Bathound.
Weird Science-Fantasy No. 29 — Last issue.

JUL 1955
Mad No. 24 — First magazine format issue.

SEP 1955
The Brave and the Bold No. 1 — As it boldly and bravely says on the cover, "INVITATION—If you dream of riding in a thundering chariot—if you yearn to explore unknown seas—if you are ready to wield a clashing sword to guard an astounding secret—then—the Golden Gladiator, the Viking Prince, and the Silent Knight invite you to join them in blazing adventures from now on as a member of . . . . . THE BRAVE AND THE BOLD!"
Congo Bill No. 7 — Last issue.
A-1 No. 138 — Last of four issues to feature the Avenger ("The red menace meets America's number one hero . . .")

OCT 1955
Submariner No. 42 — Last issue. Most collectors don't realize how late (in the overall scheme of things) this issue was published!

NOV 1955
Detective No. 225 — Introduction and first appearance the Martian Manhunter. Although tauted to be, this is not actually a Silver Age comic. Jonn Jonzz was, of course, a Silver Age character in that the majority of his most famous appearances (Detective Comics, The Brave and the Bold, House of Mystery, and Justice League of America) did occur in the Silver Age.
The Brave and the Bold No. 2 — Viking Prince cover.
Piracy No. 7 — Last issue.
Psychoanalysis No. 4 — Last issue.

DEC 1955
Aces High No. 5 — Last issue.
Extra No. 5 — Last issue.
Impact No. 5 — Last issue.
Valor No. 5 — Last issue.

JAN 1956
Panic No. 12 — Last issue.
MD No. 5 — Last issue.
The Brave and the Bold No. 3 — Viking Prince uses Thor's hammer to win the day. I wonder if Stan Lee read this DC story? naaaw.

FEB 1956
Wonder Woman No. 80 — Origin Wonder Woman's invisible plane.
Incredible Science Fiction No. 33 — Last issue.

MAR 1956
Tales of the Unexpected No. 1 — Another successful DC science fiction anthology title, the first few issues of which are considered rather scarce by collectors.

APR 1956
Showcase No. 1 — The first page of this famous issue explains "The Story Behind Showcase." "And so was born the most novel idea ever seen in the comic book publishing industry, a magazine inspired by You!". . . "There's a big surprise waiting for you in

the very next issue of *Showcase*. It will introduce a brand-new colorful hero suggested by you!" Although its first feature, "The Firefighters," didn't set the world on fire, the concept of a tryout magazine would later prove to be hot stuff by issue No. 4. This issue starred Fireman Farrell in "Fourth Alarm," "School for Smoke-eaters," and Fire Under the Big Top."

The Black Knight No. 5 — Last issue.
World of Suspense No. 1 — Still another Atlas anthology with excellent stories and art. Companion magazine to *World of Fantasy* and *World of Mystery*.

MAY 1956
World of Fantasy No. 1 — Companion magazine to *World of Suspense* and *World of Mystery*.
The Brave and the Bold No. 5 — Robin Hood begins as a regular feature.

JUN 1956
World of Mystery No. 1 — Companion magazine to *World of Fantasy* and *World of Suspense*.
Showcase No. 2 — Kings of the Wild (animal stories).

JUL 1956
Detective No. 233 — First appearance of Batwoman.

AUG 1956
Tales of the Mysterious Traveler No. 1 — Charlton's rather good "copy" of the Phantom Stranger.
Mysteries of Unexplored Worlds No. 1 — Charlton's most revered science fiction/fantasy anthology title.
Out of This World No. 1 — Charlton's companion title to *Mysteries of Unexplored Worlds*.
Showcase No. 3 — The Frogmen. Great Russ Heath underwater art suggestive of his later work on Sea Devils and various DC war titles.

THE SILVER AGE...THE BEGINNING!

OCT 1956
Showcase No. 4 — Origin and first appearance of the Silver Age Flash, and THE SILVER AGE OF COMICS BEGINS! Considered by historians as the catalyst for and genesis of the Silver Age of Comics. Along with *Fantastic Four* No. 1, collectors view it as one of the two most valuable and sought-after of all Silver Age books and unquestionably the most historically important DC Silver Age comic.
Yellow Claw No. 1 — The "Yellow Menace" theme continued in this truly scarce Atlas contribution.

NOV 1956
Plastic Man No. 64 — Last issue.

DEC 1956
House of Secrets No. 1 — After *House of Mystery* was gradually shifted to a science fiction/fantasy emphasis from its original horror/mystery format, *House of Secrets* was introduced as its "companion" title. DC's "big six" science fiction anthology magazine lineup was now complete. (In chronological order they were *Strange Adventures, Mystery in Space, House of Mystery, My Greatest Adventure, Tales of the Unexpected,* and *House of Secrets*.)
Showcase No. 5 — The Manhunters. Same genre of story as DC's *Gang Busters, Mr. District Attorney,* and *Big Town.* Last diagonal Showcase banner on cover.
Blackhawk No. 107 — Last Quality issue, the end of a great dynasty.

JAN 1957
Blackhawk No. 108 — DC begins publishing the title without skipping a single month.

FEB 1957
Showcase No. 6 — Origin and first appearance of the Challengers of the Unknown by Jack Kirby. Featuring Rocky Davis (Olympic Wrestling Champion), Prof. Haley (Master Skin Diver), Red Ryan (Circus Daredevil), and Ace Morgan (War Hero and Fearless Jet Pilot) in "The Secret of the Sorcerer's Box!"

APR 1957
Showcase No. 7 — Second appearance of the Challengers. "Ultivac Is Loose!" This cover should be on a Marvel comic.

JUN 1957
Showcase No. 8 — Second Silver Age Flash tryout eight months after the first. "Secret of the Empty Box!" and the first Captain Cold story, "The Coldest Man on Earth!"
Spellbound No. 34 — Last issue.
World's Finest No. 88 — Luthor and Joker team up as "Superman's and Batman's Greatest Foes!" Wonderful splash page of Lex Luthor and the Joker cruising downtown Metropolis in the Jokermobile. First villain team-up.

JUL 1957
Adventure Into Mystery No. 8 — Last issue.
World of Mystery No. 7 — Last issue.
World of Suspense No. 8 — Last issue.

AUG 1957
Showcase No. 9 — First Lois Lane tryout. Lois Lane meets Lana Lang in "The Girl From Superman's Past." Also the now classic story where Lois dreams she is "Mrs. Superman."
Mystery Tales No. 54 — Last issue.
Mystic No. 61 — Last issue.
Mystical Tales No. 8 — Last issue.
Marvel Tales No. 159 — Last issue.
Journey Into Unknown Worlds No. 59 — Last issue.
Astonishing No. 63 — Last issue.
Strange Stories of Suspense No. 16 — Last issue.
Strange Tales of the Unusual No. 11 — Last issue.

SEP 1957
Uncanny Tales No. 56 — Last issue.

OCT 1957
Showcase No. 10 — Second and last Lois Lane tryout. Lois Lane gets super powers in "The Forbidden Box From Krypton." Contains a cameo appearance by Jor-el on the planet Krypton.
World's Finest No. 90 — "The Super Batwoman."

NOV 1957
Nyoka, the Jungle Girl No. 22 — Last issue.

DEC 1957
Showcase No. 11 — Third Challengers tryout story, "The Day The Earth Blew Up!", plus two wonderful pages of Virgil Finlay art.

FEB 1958
Showcase No. 12 — Fourth and last Challengers tryout, "Menace of the Ancient Vials!"

MAR 1958
The Brave and the Bold No. 16 — Viking Prince cover.

APR 1958
Showcase No. 13 — Third Silver Age Flash tryout "Around the World in 80 Minutes!" and the villainous Mr. Element in "Master of the Elements!"
Superman's Girl Friend, Lois Lane No. 1 — First *Showcase* feature to be given its own magazine.
Adventure No. 247 — Now famous and sought-after first appearance of the Legion of Super Heroes.

MAY 1958
Challengers of the Unknown No. 1 — Second *Showcase* feature to be given its own magazine.
Outer Space No. 17 — First issue.
The Brave and the Bold No. 17 — Viking Prince

cover and gorgeous Kubert art in the Viking Prince story "The Lady in the Lake."

JUN 1958

Showcase No. 14 — Fourth and last Silver Age Flash tryout with the best of all the *Showcase* Flash stories "Giants of the Time Worlds!" and the return of Mr. Element as Dr. Alchemy in "The Man Who Changed the Earth!"

JUL 1958

Action No. 242 — Origin and first appearance of Brainiac.

Challengers of the Unknown No. 2 — "The Monster Maker!"

AUG 1958

Showcase No. 15 — First Space Ranger tryout.

SEP 1958

The Brave and the Bold No. 19 — Viking Prince cover.

Challengers of the Unknown No. 3 — "The Invisible Challenger!"

OCT 1958

Showcase No. 16 — Second and last Space Ranger tryout.

NOV 1958

Superboy No. 68 — Origin and first appearance of the original Bizarro.

Challengers of the Unknown No. 4 — "The Wizard of Time!"

DEC 1958

Showcase No. 17 — Origin and first appearance of Adam Strange in "Adventures on Other Worlds." Beautiful cover from the lead story "The Planet and the Pendulum."

Strange Worlds No. 1 — Little known companion to Marvel's two other new science fiction anthology titles, *Tales to Astonish* and *Tales of Suspense*.

Forbidden Worlds No. 73 — First appearance of Herbie Popnecker.

JAN 1959

Tales to Astonish No. 1 — Mainstay Marvel science fiction anthology title. Companion to *Tales of Suspense*.

Tales of Suspense No. 1 — "I dared to explore the unknown emptiness!" by Don Heck, "Prisoner of the Satellites" by Steve Ditko, and "The Strangers From Space!" by Al Williamson. Wow—what a lineup! Companion to *Tales to Astonish*.

The Brave and the Bold No. 21 — Viking Prince cover.

Challengers of the Unknown No. 5 — "Riddle of the Star Stone!"

FEB 1959

Showcase No. 18 — Second Adam Strange tryout.

Superman No. 127 — Origin of Titano the Super Ape ("more fantastic than King Kong").

MAR 1959

Flash No. 105 — (No. 1). The Silver Age Flash in his own magazine two and one half years after *Showcase* No. 4. First Mirror Master in "Master of Mirrors!"

Challengers of the Unknown No. 6 — "The Sorcerers of Forbidden Valley!"

APR 1959

Showcase No. 19 — Third and last Adam Strange tryout.

Wonder Woman No. 105 — Wonder Woman's secret origin.

MAY 1959

Challengers of the Unknown No. 7 — "The Isle of No Return!"

The Brave and the Bold No. 23 — The title changes

to a "tryout" format and becomes a companion magazine to *Showcase*. What was the first feature to try for its own magazine? Why, Viking Prince by Kubert, of course! Many collectors erroneously think that issue No. 25 featuring the first Suicide Squad is the innauguration of *Brave and the Bold* as DC's second tryout comic. The format actually changed with issue No. 23. This issue is made even more interesting when you consider it not only has cover-to-cover Viking Prince by Kubert but also has the first of two sensational Kubert covers—and to top it all off, has the origin story of the Viking Prince. All in all, a gem of a comic, both artistically and historically.

Action No. 252 — Origin and first appearance of Supergirl.

Detective No. 267 — First Bat-Mite.

Flash No. 106 — (No. 2). First Pied Piper in "The Pied Piper of Peril!" Also contains the first installment of the "Grodd the Super Gorilla" trilogy and tells of the Flash's first visit to Gorilla City.

JUN 1959

Showcase No. 20 — First Rip Hunter, Time Master tryout issue "Prisoners of 100 Million B.C.!"

Double Life of Private Strong No. 1 — Introduces the Fly by Simon and Kirby, Archie's most successful Silver Age character.

JUL 1959

Action No. 254 — First Bizarro.

Flash No. 107 — (No. 3). "The Amazing Race Against Time!" and the second installment of the Grodd the Super Gorilla trilogy. Amazingly, Grodd was not featured on the cover of either Nos. 106, 107, or 108.

Challengers of the Unknown No. 8 — "Prisoners of Robot Planet!"

The Brave and the Bold No. 24 — Second issue as a tryout magazine. Second Kubert Viking Prince cover. Last Viking Prince.

AUG 1959

The Fly No. 1 — Probably Archie's best contribution to the Silver Age of Comics.

Mystery in Space No. 53 — Adam Strange begins.

Tales of the Unexpected No. 40 — Space Ranger begins.

Strange Worlds No. 5 — Last issue.

World of Fantasy No. 19 — Last issue.

Showcase No. 21 — Second Rip Hunter, Time Master tryout "Secret of the Lost Continent."

SEP 1959

Flash No. 108 — (No. 4). "The Speed of Doom!" and the wonderful third installment of the Grodd the Super Gorilla trilogy.

The Brave and the Bold No. 25 — First mission of the Suicide Squad. "Hitherto locked in the deepest vaults of secrecy are the exploits of Task Force X! Created to combat the perils which defy conventional methods of defense—this unique unit by its utter defiance of danger and startling tactics has earned for itself the code name of the SUICIDE SQUAD. Their first mission will now be revealed to you...as they battle the invincible menace of The Three Waves of Doom!"

Challengers of the Unknown No. 9 — "The Plot to Destroy Earth!"

OCT 1959

Showcase No. 22 — Origin and first appearance of the Silver Age Green Lantern. Considered by many as the second most important Silver Age DC book after *Showcase* No. 4.

Pat Boone No. 1 — Was not submitted for Comics Code Authority approval, hence does not bear Comics Code stamp on cover.

NOV 1959

Flash No. 109 — (No. 5). "Return of the Mirror Master!"

The Brave and the Bold No. 26 — Second mission of the Suicide Squad. First time *Brave and the Bold* editors invite readers to "Write to Suicide Squad, National Comics, 575 Lexington Ave., New York 22, N.Y. if you'd like to read more about the startling reports of the Suicide Squad!"

Challengers of the Unknown No. 10 — "The Four Faces of Doom!"

DEC 1959

Showcase No. 23 — Second Silver Age Green Lantern tryout, "The Invisible Destroyer."

Out of This World No. 16 — Last issue.

Adventure No. 267 — Second appearance of the Legion of Super Heroes.

JAN 1960

Flash No. 110 — (No. 6). "Challenge of the Weather Wizard!" Origin and first appearance of Kid Flash (Wally West).

The Brave and the Bold No. 27 — Third mission of the Suicide Squad, "The Creature of Ghost Lake."

Challengers of the Unknown No. 11 — "The Creatures From the Forbidden World!"

FEB 1960

Showcase No. 24 — Third and last Silver Age Green Lantern tryout, "The Creature That Couldn't Die."

MAR 1960

The Brave and the Bold No. 28 — The World's Greatest Heroes Team Up to Battle "Starro the Conqueror." First appearance of the Justice League of America and the fourth appearance of the Silver Age Green Lantern. (Amazingly, Green Lantern was placed in the JLA before he had his own magazine!)

Flash No. 111— (No. 7). Classic "Invasion of the Cloud Creatures!" Also contains the second appearance of Kid Flash, the first Kid Flash solo adventure and retells Kid Flash's origin.

Challenger of the Unknown No. 12 — "The Challenger From Outer Space!"

APR 1960

Showcase No. 25 — Third Rip Hunter, Time Master. Fabulous dinosaur cover and interior art by Joe Kubert. One of the best covers of the Silver Age.

Space Adventures Vol. 3 No. 33 — First Captain Atom by Ditko.

MAY 1960

The Brave and the Bold No. 29 — A Star-Studded Spectacular... "Challenge of the Weapons Master!" Second tryout of the Justice League of America and fifth appearance of the Silver Age Green Lantern.

Flash No. 112 — (No. 8). "Mystery of the Elongated Man!" Origin and first appearance of the Elongated Man (Ralph Dibney), the only super hero whose alter identity is known to the public. First "Flash Grams" letter column. Third and last of the Kid Flash "tryout" stories.

Star Spangled War Stories No. 90 — "Dinosaurs VS. Tanks!... Who Will Win?... Don't Miss... The Island of Armored Giants!" First of the wonderful dinosaur issues and "The War That Time Forgot."

JUN 1960

Superman Annual No. 1 — "Presenting the greatest Superman stories ever told." First Silver Age DC annual and first 25 cent DC comic since the *Big All American Comic Book* of 1944. Contained a phenomenally beautiful two-page Map of Krypton.

Strange Adventures No. 117 — Origin and first appearance of the Atomic Knights masterfully drawn by Murphy Anderson. Considered by many to be Anderson's finest work. The Atomic Knights made their final appearance in *Strange Adventures* No. 160, January 1964.

Showcase No. 26 — Fourth and last Rip Hunter, Time Master tryout issue. Incredible art by Joe Kubert. "The Aliens From 2000 B.C.!"

JUL 1960

The Brave and the Bold No. 30 — A Star-Studded Spectacular... "The Case of the Stolen Super Powers!" Third and last tryout of the Justice League of America and sixth appearance of the Silver Age Green Lantern. Considered by many collectors as one of the best JLA covers ever published. Introduces Professor Ivo and his android Amazo. First JLA Mail Room letter column, the first letter of which asks about *All-Star Comics* and the Justice Society of America. The editors list the JSA membership from *All-Star* No. 3 and No. 57 (first and last JSA appearances). This is of great historical importance because this was the first time most readers ever realized that many of DC's characters had "former lives" *before* the Silver Age of Comics! Further, the editors hint at the possibility of a Junior Justice League, eventually dubbed the Teen Titans in issue No. 54, June-July 1964.

Flash No. 113 — (No. 9). First Trickster in "Danger in the Air!" Second "Flash Grams" contains explanation of why *Flash Comics* begins with No. 105.

Challengers of the Unknown No. 14 — "Captives of the Alien Beasts!"

AUG 1960

Unknown Worlds No. 1 — Excellent ACG companion to *Forbidden Worlds* and *Adventures Into the Unknown*.

Green Lantern No. 1 — Seventh appearance of the Silver Age Green Lantern, "Menace of the Giant Puppet!"

Flash No. 114 — (No. 10). First Captain Cold in "The Big Freeze!" Fourth Kid Flash.

Adventure No. 275 — "The Origin of the Superman-Batman Team."

Showcase No. 27 — First appearance of the Sea Devils in "The Golden Monster." Phenomenal work by the master of underwater art, Russ Heath.

SEP 1960

The Brave and the Bold No. 31 — First Cave Carson Adventures Inside Earth. This issue sported one of DC's most recognized and remembered Silver Age covers, "The Incredible Lava Creature."

Challengers of the Unknown No. 15 — "The Lady Giant and the Beast!"

Flash No. 115 — (No. 11). "The Day Flash Weighed 1,000 Pounds!"

OCT 1960

Green Lantern No. 2 — "Secret of the Golden Thunderbolts!"

Showcase No. 28 — Second tryout appearance of the Sea Devils in "The Undersea Prison!" "Will This Be the Sea Devils Last Dive?"

Superman Annual No. 2 — "An all star line-up of the greatest super-villains ever featured!"

NOV 1960

Justice League of America No. 1 — Three-eyed Despero of Kalanor plays a for-keeps game of chess with the Flash in one of the most unforgettable stories of the JLA "World of No Return." As the ads read "Just imagine! The mightiest heroes of our time... Superman! Batman! Flash! Green Lantern! Wonder Woman! Aquaman! J'onn J'onzz - Manhunter From Mars!... have banded together as the Justice League of America to stamp out the forces of evil wherever and whenever they appear!"

The Brave and the Bold No. 32 — Second Cave Carson Adventures Inside Earth. "The City 100 Miles Below."

Green Lantern No. 3 — "Amazing Theft of the Power Lamp!"

Challengers of the Unknown No. 16 — "The Incredible Metal Creature!"

Flash No. 116 — (No. 12). "The Man Who Stole Central City!"

DEC 1960

Showcase No. 29 — Third and final tryout appearance of the Sea Devils in "The Last Dive of the Sea Devils." Stunning Russ Heath cover.

Flash No. 117 — (No. 13). "Here Comes Captain Boomerang!"

JAN 1961

Justice League of America No. 2 — "Secret of the Sinister Sorcerers" takes the JLA to Magicland to meet Saturna, the Troll King, and the infamous Simon Magus.

The Brave and the Bold No. 33 — Third Cave Carson Adventures Inside Earth, "The Alien Robots From Inner Space."

Challengers of the Unknown No. 17 — "The Secret of the Space Capsules!"

FEB 1961

Midnight Mystery No. 1 — Short-lived but excellent ACG companion to *Forbidden Worlds, Unknown Worlds,* and *Adventures Into the Unknown.*

Showcase No. 30 — First tryout appearance of Aquaman and Aqualad.

Flash No. 118 — (No. 14). "The Doomed Scarecrow!"

Green Lantern No. 4 — "The Diabolical Missile From Qward!" and "The Secret of Green Lantern's Mask!"

MAR 1961

The Brave and the Bold No. 34 — Introducing the Winged Wonder in "Creature of a Thousand Shapes!" Origin and first appearance of the Silver Age Hawkman and Hawkgirl. One of the greatest, most imaginative super hero comebacks of the Silver Age!

Justice League of America No. 3 — Introduces Kanjar Ro (one of the JLA's best villains), Kromm, Hyathis, Sayyar, and "The Slave Ship of Space."

Challengers of the Unknown No. 18 — Featuring "The Doomed World of Tomorrow" and introducing Cosmo, the Challengers' space pet!

Flash No. 119 — (No. 15). "The Mirror-Master's Magic Bullet!"

APR 1961

Forbidden Worlds No. 94 — Second appearance of Herbie.

Rip Hunter, Time Master No. 1 — "The 1,000-Year-Old Curse!"

Showcase No. 31 — Second tryout appearance of Aquaman and Aqualad. "The Sea Beasts From One Million B.C.!"

Green Lantern No. 5 — "The Power Ring That Vanished!"

MAY 1961

The Brave and the Bold No. 35 — Second Hawkman tryout featuring "The Valley of Vanishing Men!"

Challengers of the Unknown No. 19 — "The Beast From the Fabulous Gem!"

Justice League of America No. 4 — Green Arrow joins the Justice League of America in "Doom of the Star Diamond." Considered one of the best JLA covers ever done (along with *The Brave and the Bold* No. 30). In one famous panel on page 5, Adam Strange and Hawkman are also considered as potential JLA members.

Four Color No. 1173 — First Twilight Zone based on the excellent science fiction anthology television series which was first broadcast October 2, 1959 on CBS (Fridays from 10:00-10:30 P.M.). "There is a fifth dimension beyond that which is known to man.

It is a dimension as vast as space and as timeless as infinity. It is the middle ground between light and shadow, between science and superstition, and it lies between the pit of man's fears and the summit of his knowledge. This is the dimension of imagination. It is an area we call the Twilight Zone."

Flash No. 120 — (No. 16). Flash and Kid Flash team up in "Land of Golden Giants."

JUN 1961

Amazing Adventures No. 1 — First Dr. Droom story five months before *Fantastic Four* No. 1. Some suggest this makes the "good" Doctor the first Marvel-Age hero.

Showcase No. 32 — Third tryout appearance of Aquaman and Aqualad. "The Creature King of the Sea!"

Rip Hunter, Time Master No. 2 — "The Alien Beasts From 500 B.C.!"

Flash No. 121 — (No. 17). "The Trickster Strikes Back!"

Green Lantern No. 6 — "World of Living Phantoms!"

JUL 1961

The Brave and the Bold No. 36 — Third Hawkman tryout, featuring the incredibly superb "Shadow Thief of Midway City."

Justice League of America No. 5 — "When Gravity Went Wild" with its incredible lineup of villains.

Challengers of the Unknown No. 20 — "The Cosmic Powered Creatures!"

AUG 1961

Showcase No. 33 — Fourth and last tryout appearance of Aquaman and Aqualad.

Superman Annual No. 3 — "The Fantastic Faces of Superman."

Rip Hunter, Time Master No. 3 — "The Throne of Doom."

Batman Annual No. 1 — 1,001 Secrets of Batman and Robin.

Secret Origins Annual No. 1 — The ads for this one read "At last the giant comic book you've dreamed about is here. A collection of original origin stories or your favorite super stars...The Superman-Batman Team—Wonder Woman—Flash—Green Lantern—J'onn J'onzz—Challengers of the Unknown—Adam Strange—Green Arrow...All together in one magazine! Don't miss this spectacular issue! You'll treasure it all your life!" They were right—I did and still do. This is the ultimate comic for DC origin fans.

Flash No. 122 — (No. 18). "Beware the Atomic Grenade!"

Green Lantern No. 7 — "The Day 100,000 People Vanished!"

SEP 1961

The Brave and the Bold No. 37 — Fourth tryout for the Suicide Squad. "Back by popular request! In a new top-secret mission...Threat of the Giant Eye!"

Jaguar No. 1 — Second significant Silver Age hero from Archie.

Flash No. 123 — (No. 19). "The Flash of Two Worlds!" Reintroduction of Jay Garrick, the Golden Age Flash. This is the first DC comic in which editor Julius Schwartz proposes the idea of Earth II, a location where DC Golden Age heroes reside. Considered by many as one of the most brilliant and exciting story concepts of the Silver Age.

Justice League of America No. 6 — Professor Fortune injects bad luck charges into JLA members on "The Wheel of Misfortune."

Challengers of the Unknown No. 21 — "The Challengers Space-Pet Ally!"

OCT 1961

Midnight Mystery No. 7 — Last issue.

Sea Devils No. 1 — The Sea Devils Battle the "Octopus Man" and discover "The Secret of the Emerald Whale!" eight months after the last *Showcase* tryout issue. Great Russ Heath art.

Showcase No. 34 — Origin and first appearance of the Silver Age Atom. Interior text illustration shows the Justice Society of America from *All Star Comics* No. 3 to a whole new generation. Along with Flash, Green Lantern, and Hawkman, the Atom becomes the fourth DC character from the Golden Age to be "updated" and reintroduced in the Silver Age. The full page ad said it all: "Big-Big-Big News about a Small-Small-Small Super-Hero the Atom. He can instantly shrink in size from six feet to six inches to six micro-inches (a micro inch is one-millionth of an inch!). He has the explosive power of an atom bomb in his fists! He can speed from place to place by traveling through telephone wires! Don't miss the exciting debut of DC's newest costumed hero in *Showcase*." One of *the* best covers of the Silver Age.

Rip Hunter, Time Master No. 4 — "The Bird-Men of 2,000 B.C.!"

Green Lantern No. 8 — Praised by many as the best cover and story of the title "The Challenge From 5700 A.D.!"

NOV 1961

Fantastic Four No. 1 — Incredible comic that changed the way we think about super heroes forever! Considered by most collectors as one of the two most important and influential comic books of the Silver Age (along with *Showcase* No. 4). Also makes the Human Torch the first Timely character to be recycled from the Golden Age. Human Torch's last appearance (in his own magazine) was only six years earlier!

Justice League of America No. 7 — "The Cosmic Fun House." Last ten cent issue.

The Brave and the Bold No. 38 — Fifth tryout for the Suicide Squad. "Inside an ominous cloud lurks the Suicide Squad's most startling opponent! Master of the Dinosaurs!"

Flash No. 124 — (No. 20). "The Space Boomerang Trap!"

DEC 1961

Showcase No. 35 — Second Atom tryout, "The Dooms From Beyond!"

Amazing Adult Fantasy No. 7 — (No. 1). All Stan Lee and Steve Ditko issue (five stories), "The magazine that respects your intelligence."

Rip Hunter, Time Master No. 5 — "The Secret of the Saxon Traitor!"

Sea Devils No. 2 — The famed divers find themselves in a unique trap in "A Bottle Full of Sea Devils."

Flash No. 125 — (No. 21). "Conquerors of Time!"

Green Lantern No. 9 — Sinestro the renegade Green Lantern in "Battle of the Power Rings!"

JAN 1962

Tales to Astonish No. 27 — "The Man in the Ant Hill!" Scientist Henry Pym's serum reduces him and he begins his adventure with the ants. Just a hint of his future vocation which will begin in September in *Tales to Astonish* No. 35.

Fantastic Four No. 2 — They had taken a deadly oath to destroy the Fantastic Four!! They were merciless! They were inhuman! They had powers far Greater than any earthmen! They were the deadly "Skrulls From Outer Space!"

Justice League of America No. 8 — "For Sale...The Justice League." First 12 cent issue.

The Brave and the Bold No. 39 — Sixth and last tryout for the Suicide Squad. "The Suicide Squad's most astonishing mission turns them into...Prisoners of the Dinosaur Zoo!" At the end of the lead story, the editors write, "Well readers!

This is the Suicide Squad's last issue! If you'd like to see it in action again—Write to: Suicide Squad c/o National Periodical Pub., 575 Lexington Ave., N.Y. 22, N.Y." Guess not enough people wrote in, because their sixth mission turned out to be their last.

Green Lantern No. 10 — "Prisoner of the Power Ring!"

FEB 1962

Aquaman No. 1 — "Now in a magazine of his own" some 20 years after he was introduced in *More Fun* No. 73. Except now he has a kid sidekick, natch!

Showcase No. 36 — Third and last Atom tryout with the famous Atom-on-the-flypaper cover. "Prisoner in a Test Tube!"

Sea Devils No. 3 — The skin-diving daredevils meet their match in "Ghost From the Deep!"

Rip Hunter, Time Master No. 6 — "Secret of the Ancient Seer!"

Batman Annual No. 2 — "Batman and Robin in their most thrilling action roles." Plus a special 1962 giant Batman and Robin pin-up calendar.

Justice League of America No. 9 — Famous story "The Origin of the Justice League." Also contains a full color ad for *JLA* No. 10 stating that it will be published eight times a year beginning with that issue. Eight times a year publication actually begins with issue No. 9.

Magic Agent No. 1 — "See the supernatural powers of America's top secret operative...in blazing action!"

Flash No. 126 — (No. 22). "Doom of the Mirror-Flash!"

MAR 1962

Fantastic Four No. 3 — Finally they get costumes, the amazing Fantasti-car, and an official headquarters. On the cover, Stan Lee suggests for the first time that a Marvel comic is a collector's item, boldly pronounces that *FF* is "THE GREATEST COMIC MAGAZINE IN THE WORLD!!" and the Human Torch gets two left hands. "The Menace of the Miracle Man."

Justice League of America No. 10 — "The Fantastic Fingers of Felix Faust."

The Brave and the Bold No. 40 — Fourth Cave Carson Adventures Inside Earth. "The Three Caverns of Doom!"

Superman Annual No. 4 — Featuring Superman's most famous adventures in Time, Space, and on Alien Worlds!

Batman Annual No. 2 — Batman and Robin's most thrilling action roles!

Flash No. 127 — (No. 23). "Reign of the Super-Gorilla!"

Green Lantern No. 11 — "The Strange Trial of Green Lantern!"

APR 1962

Showcase No. 37 — First appearance of the Metal Men (Gold, Tin, Iron, Mercury, Lead, Platinum, and their non-robot inventor, Dr. Will Magnus) in "The Flaming Doom!" "...Heroes forged out of smoke and flame to battle unique threats! This metal band lives—and dies fighting fantastic furies for mankind..."

Rip Hunter, Time Master No. 7 — "The Lost Wanderers in Time!"

Sea Devils No. 4 — The Sea Devils dive into "the Sea of Sorcery" and are trapped by the "Secret of Volcano Lake!"

Green Lantern No. 12 — "Green Lantern's Statue Goes to War!"

MAY 1962

The Incredible Hulk No. 1 — Loosely based on Dr. Jekyll and Mr. Hyde, Jack Kirby and Stan Lee took a big risk by putting the "jolly green giant" (as he was affectionately known later on) in his own magazine without so much as a tryout. Interestingly, the Hulk's skin was not green, but gray, in issue No. 1. This chromatic inconsistency is the source of the single most common trivia question in the Marvel universe! (If you didn't already, now you know!)

Fantastic Four No. 4 — First appearance of the Sub-Mariner in the Silver Age as Marvel's second Golden Age revival character. Subby's last appearance was only six and one half years earlier in the last issue of his own magazine! "The Coming of the Sub-mariner."

Mystery in Space No. 75 — "The Planet That Came to a Standstill." Sensational sequel to *Justice League of America* No. 3 featuring the infamous insect-eyed Kanjar Ro and his golden Slave Ship of Space along with the Justice League of America.

The Brave and the Bold No. 41 — Fifth Cave Carson Adventures Inside Earth. "Raiders From the Secret World!"

Flash No. 128 — (No. 24). "The Case of the Real-Gone Flash!"

JUN 1962

Sea Devils No. 5 — A strange doom traps the Sea Devils when they uncover the "Vengeful Undersea Ghost."

Lois Lane Annual No. 1 — "Featuring Superman's girl friend in her greatest adventures!"

Rip Hunter, Time Master No. 8 — "The Thieves Who Stole a Genie!"

Showcase No. 38 — Second appearance of the Metal Men. "The Nightmare Menace."

Superman Annual No. 5 — An all-star collection of stories featuring the Superman family on Krypton!

Batman Annual No. 3 — Batman and Robin's most fantastic foes.

Flash No. 129 — (No. 25). Both Flashes star in "Double Danger on Earth!" First Silver Age JSA appearance (cameo flashback) in a story.

Green Lantern No. 12 — Introducing a great new fighting team—Green Lantern and the Flash in "Duel of the Super-Heroes!"

JUL 1962

The Atom No. 1 — The wonderful venus flytrap cover. Collectors across the country are still wondering if Hawkman would ever get his own title.

The Incredible Hulk No. 2 — "The Terror of the Toad Men!" The token "puny earthlings" dialogue required by law in every Stan Lee science fiction plot goes something like this on page 5: "What chance do the puny earthlings have against our invincible magnetic powers?!!!" Actually not much chance without the aid of the HULK!

The Brave and the Bold No. 42 — Fourth fantastic Hawkman tryout, "Menace of the Dragonfly Raiders!" The folks at DC decide to give the Winged Wonder three more trys at his own magazine. With a total of six tryout issues, Hawkman holds the record along with the Suicide Squad.

Fantastic Four No. 5 — "Meet...Doctor Doom!"

AUG 1962

Amazing Fantasy No. 15 — (Shows a September date in the indicia.) World-famous origin and first appearance of the Amazing Spider-Man. While swinging by a web with one hand and holding a crook in the other on this well-known cover, Spidey proclaims, "Though the World may mock Peter Parker, timid teenager...it will soon *Marvel* at the awesome might of Spider-Man!" Inside on the splash page is a rather prophetic prologue: "Like costumed heroes? Confidentially, we in the comic mag business refer to them as 'long underwear characters!' And, as you know, they're a dime a dozen! But, we think you may find our Spider-Man just a bit...different!" I wonder if Stan Lee knew what an understatement

that really was?

Journey Into Mystery No. 83 — Origin and first appearance of the Mighty Thor. "The most exciting super-hero of all time!!" "Begin the saga of Thor in this issue!"

Flash No. 130 — (No. 26). "Who Doomed the Flash!" and "Kid Flash Meets the Elongated Man!"

Rip Hunter, Time Master No. 9 — "The Alien King of 1,000 B.C.!"

Sea Devils No. 6 — The Sea Devils hunt for sunken treasure and instead find "The Flame-Headed Watchmen."

Showcase No. 39 — Third appearance of the Metal Men, "The Deathless Doom!"

SEP 1962

Strange Tales Annual No. 1 — Marvel's first annual, reprinted "pre-hero" science fiction.

The Brave and the Bold No. 43 — Fifth Hawkman tryout. Hawkman battles Manhawk in the high flying adventure, "Masked Marauders of Earth!"

Fantastic Four No. 6 — Dr. Doom and Submariner join forces to battle the Fantastic Four in "The Diabolical Duo Join Forces!"

Tales to Astonish No. 35 — First costumed Ant-Man.

The Incredible Hulk No. 3 — Retells the origin of the Hulk.

Flash No. 131 — (No. 27). The Flash and Green Lantern in "Captives of the Cosmic Ray!"

OCT 1962

Strange Tales No. 101 — First of the Human Torch solo appearances in "The Destroyer Strikes."

Fantastic Four No. 7 — One of the greatest of the early covers, "The Master of Planet X."

Showcase No. 40 — Fourth and last Metal Men tryout issue, "The Day the Metal Men Melted!"

Sea Devils No. 7 — The daring Sea Devils battle "The Human Tidal Wave."

Rip Hunter, Time Master No. 10 — "The Execution of Rip Hunter!"

NOV 1962

Strange Tales No. 102 — Second of the Human Torch solo appearances in "Prisoner of the Wizard."

The Brave and the Bold No. 44 — Sixth and last Hawkman tryout. Armed with a weapon of the past, the Winged Wonder battles against weapons of the future in "The Men Who Moved the World!" One of the more breathtaking Hawkman covers.

Fantastic Four No. 8 — "Prisoners of the Puppet Master!"

The Incredible Hulk No. 4 — "Mongu!! The Gladiator From Space" turns out to be a communist soldier named Boris Monguski inside a large robot. The Kremlin has yet to forgive Stan Lee for the Hulk's immortal line on page 7: "Do those commies think they're playing with kids?" Interestingly, most of the readers were kids.

Flash No. 132 — (No. 28). "The Heaviest Man Alive!"

DEC 1962

Fantastic Four No. 9 — The Submariner plots "The End of the Fantastic Four!"

Sea Devils No. 8 — "The Curse of Neptune's Giant!" a super sea-saga.

Showcase No. 41 — First Tommy Tomorrow of the Planeteers tryout issue. Contains his origin at the West Point of Space. The first appearance of the character Tommy Tomorrow appeared in *Real Fact Comics* No. 6, Jan-Feb 1947, approximately 16 years earlier.

Flash No. 133 — (No. 29). "Plight of the Puppet-Flash!"

JAN 1963

The Incredible Hulk No. 5 — "More Powerful!

More Dangerous! More Uncontrollable Than Ever Before!! Here Comes the Hulk!"

Fantastic Four No. 10 — "The Return of Doctor Doom!"

The Brave and the Bold No. 45 — First Strange Sports Stories—"Challenge of the Headless Baseball Team! Great Infantino artwork. The issue tried out a new style of panel arrangement created to enhance the telling of the story. First to try the novel concept of combining science fiction with sports stories.

FEB 1963

Fantastic Four No. 11 — "The Impossible Man" and "A Day With the Fantastic Four."

Batman Annual No. 4 — The secret adventures of Batman and Robin.

Superman Annual No. 6 — Reprints the Legion of Super Heroes from *Adventure* No. 247.

Showcase No. 42 — Second Tommy Tomorrow of the Planeteers tryout issue. "The Brain Robbers of Satellite X!"

Sea Devils No. 9 — The Sea Devils meet doom in the depths when they uncover the "Secret of the Coral Creature."

Flash No. 134 — (No. 30). "The Man Who Mastered Absolute Zero!"

MAR 1963

The Amazing Spider-Man No. 1 — "The Chameleon Strikes." The most popular super hero of the Silver Age begins his own series.

Fantastic Four No. 12 — "The Fantastic Four Meet the Hulk!"

Tales of Suspense No. 39 — Origin and first appearance of Iron Man by Jack Kirby.

The Incredible Hulk No. 6 — Last issue. The Incredible Hulk vs. "The Metal Master" (the Teen Brigade is formed). This was the only one drawn by the talented Steve Ditko and the contrast to the first five issues is like night and day! Some Marvel afficianados suggest that this was Hulk's finest moment. Others suggest just the opposite. No one disputes that this last issue is scarce and in high demand by Ditko fans.

The Brave and the Bold No. 46 — Second Strange Sports Stories—"Challenge of the Headless Baseball Team!"

Flash No. 135 — (No. 31). Kid Flash gets a new uniform in "Secret of the Three Super-Weapons!"

APR 1963

Sea Devils No. 10 — The Sea Devils meet doom in the depths when they uncover the "Secret of the Coral Creature."

Showcase No. 43 — Internationally-famous James Bond issue.

Fantastic Four No. 13 — "The Red Ghost" and first Watcher.

MAY 1963

The Amazing Spider-Man No. 2 — "Duel to the Death With the Vulture!" and "The Terrible Tinkerer!"

Fantastic Four No. 14 — "The Submariner Strikes."

Metal Men No. 1 — Now in their own spectacular book battling the "Rain of the Missile Men!" In the full page house ad for this issue, DC suggests to potential buyers, ". . .and don't you forget to buy your copy today. . .it may be a Collectors Item!"

The Brave and the Bold No. 47 — Third Strange Sports Stories—"The Phantom Prize Fighter!"

Flash No. 136 — (No. 32). "The Mirror Master's Invincible Bodyguards!"

JUN 1963

My Greatest Adventure No. 80 — Origin and first appearance of the Doom Patrol: Elasti-Girl (Rita Farr), Negative Man (Larry Trainor), Robot Man (Cliff Steele), and the Chief.

Fantastic Four No. 15 — "The Mad Thinker and His Awesome Android."

Superman Annual No. 7 — Silver Anniversary Issue! Featuring the greatest Superman stories published during the last 25 years.

Flash No. 137 — (No. 33). Guest appearance by villain Vandal Savage and the Justice Society of America in "Vengence of the Immortal Villain!" First active revival of the JSA into the Silver Age.

JUL 1963

The Amazing Spider-Man No. 3 — "The Return of Doctor Doom" with special surprise guest star Ant-Man.

The Brave and the Bold No. 48 — Fourth Strange Sports Stories—"The Man Who Drove Through Time!"

Batman Annual No. 5 — "The Strange Lives of Batman and Robin." Reprints the covers of *Batman* No. 1 and *Detective* No. 27 in color on the back cover.

Lois Lane Annual No. 2 — Featuring Superman's girl friend in her greatest adventures!

AUG 1963

Fantastic Four No. 17 — "In the Clutches of Doctor Doom."

Flash No. 138 — (No. 34). "The Pied Piper's Double Doom!"

SEP 1963

The Avengers No. 1 — Something like the Justice League, but not really! As it is so beautifully stated on page 22: "And thus is born one of the greatest super hero teams of all time! Powerful! Unpredictable! Brought together by a strange quirk of fate, the Avengers are on the march, and a new dimension is added to the Marvel Galaxy of Stars!" The "strange quirk of fate" is named Stan Lee. The Fantastic Four make a cameo appearance.

The X-Men No. 1 — X-Men vs. Magneto, Earth's most powerful super villain. The Angel (Warren Worthington III), Cyclops (Slim Summers), Iceman (Bobby Drake), the Beast (Hank McCoy), Marvel Girl (Jean Grey), and Professor Xavier begin.

The Amazing Spider-Man No. 4 — "Nothing Can Stop the Sandman!" Beautiful four-panel cover.

Flash Annual No. 1 — "Famous Flash Firsts." Contains an article by Carmine Infantino entitled "How I Draw the Flash."

Fantastic Four No. 18 — "The All Powerful Super-Skrull."

The Brave and the Bold No. 49 — Fifth Strange Sports Stories—"Gorilla Wonders of the Diamond!"

Flash No. 139 — (No. 35). "Menace of the Reverse Flash!"

OCT 1963

The Amazing Spider-Man No. 5 — "Marked for Destruction by Doctor Doom."

Fantastic Four No. 19 — "At the Mercy of Rama-Tut," the pharoah from the future.

Showcase No. 46 — Third Tommy Tomorrow of the Planeteers tryout issue.

NOV 1963

Fantastic Four No. 20 — "The Mysterious Molecule Man." On the cover, Stan Lee modestly states, "After reading this super-surprise-filled issue, you will clearly understand why fans everywhere are calling this THE MARVEL AGE OF COMICS." Stan was right.

The Brave and the Bold No. 50 — First team-up issue. The Green Arrow and Manhunter From Mars. Has opening page explaining the new team-up series and announcing which two super heroes will team up in the next issue.

Mystery in Space No. 87 — First of four fantastically beautiful Murphy Anderson Hawkman stories. In the letter column (Via Rocket Mail), Joe Kubert writes a letter explaining why he will not be the artist for Hawkman as he was for the six *Brave and the Bold* tryout issues.

The Avengers No. 2 — Ant-Man becomes Giant Man and the Hulk "declines" his membership in the Avengers at the end of "The Space Phantom."

The X-Men No. 2 — "Nothing Can Stop the Vanisher!"

The Amazing Spider-Man No. 6 — "Face to Face With the Lizard."

Flash No. 140 — (No. 36). "The Heat Is On for Captain Cold!"

DEC 1963

The Amazing Spider-Man No. 7 — "The Vulture's Return."

Superman Annual No. 8 — A super collection of untold stories and secret origins.

Batman Annual No. 6 — Batman and Robin's most thrilling mystery cases.

Showcase No. 47 — Fourth and last Tommy Tomorrow of the Planeteers tryout issue.

Flash No. 141 — (No. 37). "The Mystery of Flash's Third Identity!"

JAN 1964

Avengers No. 3 — "This is the issue you've been waiting for!!" "The Hulk and the Submariner Vs. the Avengers!" The X-Men make a cameo appearance in this famous battle issue.

The X-Men No. 3 — "Beware of the Blob!"

The Amazing Spider-Man No. 8 — Special tribute to teenagers issue. "Spider-Man Tackles the Human Torch."

The Brave and the Bold No. 51 — Second team-up issue—Aquaman and Hawkman. "Fury of the Exiled Creature."

FEB 1964

Showcase No. 48 — First Cave Carson tryout in *Showcase*.

The Amazing Spider-Man No. 9 — "The Man Called Electro!"

Flash No. 142 — (No. 38). "Perilous Pursuit of the Trickster!"

MAR 1964

Avengers No. 4 — "A tale destined to become a magnificent milestone in the Marvel age of comics! Bringing you the great super hero which your wonderful avalanche of fan mail demanded!" "Captain America Lives Again," uttering his first Silver Age words, "Bucky, Bucky, look out . . ." The Submariner appears. Cap's last appearance was almost 10 years ago.

The Outer Limits No. 1 — Based on the excellent science fiction anthology television series which was first broadcast September 16, 1963, on ABC (Mondays from 7:30-8:30 P.M.). "There is nothing wrong with your TV set. We are controlling transmission. We can control the vertical. We can control the horizontal. For the next hour we will control all that you see and hear and think. You are watching a drama that reaches from the inner mind to . . . The Outer Limits."

Mystery in Space No. 90 — Wonderful Adam Strange and Hawkman team-up story "Planets in Peril." At the end of the story, DC announces that Hawkman (finally) will get his own magazine.

The Amazing Spider-Man No. 10 — Classic Ditko Spider-Man cover, "The Enforcers."

The X-Men No. 4 — Featuring the return of Magneto in "The Brotherhood of Evil Mutants."

Flash No. 143 — (No. 39). The Flash and Green Lantern in "Trail of the False Green Lanterns!"

APR 1964

The Amazing Spider-Man No. 11 — "The Return of Doctor Octopus."

Daredevil No. 1 — "Here comes the Daredevil, the man without fear!" "Can you guess why Daredevil is different from all other crime fighters?" He made history as the first blind hero.

Showcase No. 49 — Second Cave Carson tryout in *Showcase*.

MAY 1964

Herbie No. 1 — "Make way for the fat fury, Herbie Popnecker."

Hawkman No. 1 — "Now in his own magazine" over three years since his first tryout issue in *The Brave and the Bold* No. 34. Superb Murphy Anderson cover from "Master of the Sky Weapons!"

The Amazing Spider-Man No. 12 — Spider-Man is "Unmasked by Doctor Octopus."

The X-Men No. 5 — See the most unusual teen-agers of all time at their fighting best, when they learn: "The Angel Is Trapped!" Magneto and his evil mutants, more dangerous than ever, strike again!

Detective No. 327 — First "New Look" Batman and Robin. Ralph Dibney, the Elongated Man begins. Hundreds of Batman fans write DC asking for the return of the old Batman. Just as many write in to say they like the new look better. DC decides to kill off Alfred in the next issue.

Avengers No. 5 — "The Invasion of the Lava Men!"

The Brave and the Bold No. 53 — Fourth team-up issue—the Atom and the Flash. "The Challenge of the Expanding World!"

Superboy Annual No. 1 — "Featuring the most fabulous old Superboy and Krypto stories from the Golden Age of comics!"

Flash No. 144 — (No. 40). "Menace of the Man-Missile!"

JUN 1964

The Amazing Spider-Man No. 13 — "Mysterio."

JUL 1964

The X-Men No. 6 — Special guest star issue, "Sub-Mariner Joins the Evil Mutants!"

The Amazing Spider-Man No. 14 — Origin and first appearance of the remarkable Green Goblin. Guest-starring the Hulk.

Avengers No. 6 — "Zemo and His Masters of Evil."

The Brave and the Bold No. 54 — Fifth team-up issue—Kid Flash, Robin, and Aqualad. Origin and first appearance of Teen Titans.

Superman Annual No. 9 — Last annual published independent of the 80 Page Giant series. Featuring Superman's most fabulous imaginary adventures.

Flash No. 145 — (No. 41). "The Weather Wizard Blows Up a Storm!"

Hawkman No. 2 — "Secret of the Sizzling Sparklers!"

AUG 1964

The Amazing Spider-Man No. 15 — "Kraven the Hunter!"

Avengers No. 7 — "Their Darkest Hour."

Flash No. 146 — (No. 42). "The Mirror Master's Master Stroke!"

SEP 1964

The X-Men No. 7 — "The Return of the Blob!"

Avengers No. 8 — "Kang the Conqueror."

The Amazing Spider-Man No. 16 — "Spidey Battles Daredevil."

The Brave and the Bold No. 55 — Sixth team-up issue—Metal Men and the Atom. "Revenge of the Robot Reject."

Flash No. 147 — (No. 43). Mr. Element and the evil Reverse Flash in "Our Enemy, the Flash!"

Hawkman No. 3 — "The Birds in the Gilded Cage!"

OCT 1964

Tales of Suspense No. 58 — Battle issue, Iron Man and Captain America. " . . . why are these two gallant allies battling each other to the bitter end? Mainly to get you to buy this mag and see the answer inside! (If we can't always be clever, we can at least be honest.)"

The Amazing Spider-Man No. 17 — Wow—what a cover! Spider-Man in "The Return of the Green Goblin," guest starring the Human Torch.

Avengers No. 9 — "Marvel proudly introduces 'Wonder Man'."

Showcase No. 52 — Third and last Cave Carson tryout in *Showcase* "Prisoners of the Lost World."

NOV 1964

The Amazing Spider-Man No. 18 — "The End of Spider-Man."

Avengers No. 10 — Featuring the truly different villainy of the evil Immortus! "The Avengers Break Up!"

The X-Men No. 8 — The Uncanny Threat of "Unus the Untouchable!"

The Brave and the Bold No. 56 — Seventh team-up issue—the Flash and the Martian Manhunter. "Raid of the Mutant Marauders" contains a Hawkgirl cameo.

Flash No. 148 — (No. 44). Captain Boomerang in "The Day Flash Went Into Orbit!"

Hawkman No. 4 — The Machine That Magnetized Men!"

DEC 1964

The Amazing Spider-Man No. 19 — *The* classic cover "Spidey Strikes Back!"

Flash No. 149 — (No. 45). The Flash reveals his secret identity in "The Flash's Sensational Risk!"

Special thanks to Kent Lane Carter for help with much of the research. Thanks also to Patrick Calhoun, Greg Ferris, Joe Dungan, Jim Payette, Bob Overstreet, and Lisa and Ryan for their help with research questions, general support, and their genuine love of "funny books" . . . . . *GMC*

DIRECTORY OF COMIC AND NOSTALGIA SHOPS

This is a current up-to-date list, but is not all-inclusive. We cannot assume any responsibility in your dealings with these shops. This list is provided for your information only. When planning your trips, it would be advisable to make appointments in advance. To get your shop included in the next edition, write for rates. Items stocked by these shops are listed just after the telephone numbers and are coded as follows:

(a) Golden Age comics
(b) Silver Age comics
(c) New comics, magazines
(d) Pulps
(e) Paperbacks
(f) Big Little Books
(g) Magazines (old)
(h) Books (old)

(i) Movie posters, lobby cards
(j) Original art
(k) Toys (old)
(l) Records (old)
(m) Gum trading cards
(n) Underground comics
(o) Old radio show tapes
(p) Premiums

(q) Comic related posters
(r) Comic supplies
(s) Role playing games
(t) Star Trek items
(u) Dr. Who items
(v) Japanese animation
items

ALABAMA:

Camelot Books
2201 Quintard Avenue
Anniston, AL 36201
PH:205-236-3474 (a-e,g-k,m-v)

Discount Comic Book Shop
1301 Noble Street
Anniston, AL 36201
PH:205-238-8373 (a-c,e,m,q)

Gold Dragon Comics
3970 Government Blvd.
Mobile, AL 36693
PH:205-661-4060 (a-c,q-s)

Sincere Comics
3738 Airport Blvd.
Mobile, AL 36608
PH:205-342-2603 (a-c,e,i,n,q-u)

ARIZONA:

Atomic Comics
1318 West Southern #9
Mesa, AZ 85202
PH:602-649-0807
(a-c,g,i,j,m,n,q-v)

Books, Comics & Records
535 E. Southern Ave.
Mesa, AZ 85202
PH:602-962-5751 (a-g,k,m,n,q-u)

AAA Best Comics, Etc.
8336 N. Seventh St., B-C
Phoenix, AZ 85020
PH:602-997-4012 (a-c,q-s,v)

All About Books & Comics
529 E. Camelback
Phoenix, AZ 85012
PH:602-277-0757 (a-c,e,g-i,n,q-v)

All About Books & Comics West
4208 W. Dunlap
Phoenix, AZ 85051
PH:602-435-0410
(a-c,e,g-i,m,n,q-v)

CRC Collectibles
3033 North 24th Street
Phoenix, AZ 85016-7800
PH:602-957-8833 (a-c,g,l,m,q,r)

Lost Dutchman Comics
5805 N. 7th Street
Phoenix, AZ 85014
PH:602-263-5249 (a-h,m,n,q-u)

All About Books & Comics III
4000 N. Scottsdale Rd. #102
Scottsdale, AZ 85251
PH:602-994-1812 (a-c,g,n,q-v)

The ONE Book Shop
120-A East University Drive
Tempe, AZ 85281
PH:602-967-3551 (b-e,g-i,m-o,q-v)

The Comic Corner
P. O. Box 58779
Tucson, AZ 85732-8779
PH:602-790-2625 (b,c,e)

Fantasy Comics
6001 E. 22nd St.
Tucson, AZ 85711
PH:602-748-7483 (b,c,n,q,r)

Fantasy Comics
2745 N. Campbell
Tucson, AZ 85719
PH:602-325-9790 (b,c,n,q,r)

ARKANSAS:

Rock Bottom Used Book Shop
418 W. Dickson St.
Fayetteville, AR 72701
PH:501-521-2917 (a-c,e,g,h,n,q,r)

Paperbacks Plus
2207 Rogers Avenue
Fort Smith, AR 72901
PH:501-785-5642 (a-c,e,h,n,q-s)

The Comic Book Store
1400 S. University, Suite #1
Little Rock, AR 72204
PH:501-661-1516 (a-e,h,i,o,q-v)

Pie-Eyes
5223 W. 65th St.
Little Rock, AR 72209
PH:501-568-1414 (a-v)

Collector's Edition Comics
5310 MacArthur Drive
North Little Rock, AR 72118
PH:501-753-2586 (a-e,h,i,o,q-v)

TNT Collectors Hut
503 W. Hale Ave.
Osceola, AR 72370
PH:501-563-5760 (b,c,m,r)

CALIFORNIA:

Comic Heaven
24 W. Main Street
Alhambra, CA 91801
PH:818-289-3945 (a-c,g,j,q-t)

Comic Relief
2138 University Ave.
Berkeley, CA 94704
PH:415-843-5002 (a-d,f-h,n,q,r,v)

Fantasy Kingdom
1802 W. Olive Ave.
Burbank, CA 91506
PH:818-954-8432 (a-c,i,m,n,q,r,t-v)

Graphitti Comics & Games
4325 Overland Ave.
Culver City, CA 90230
PH:213-559-2058
(b,c,n,q-s)

Thrill Books, Comics & Games
629 First Street
Encinitas, CA 92024
PH:619-753-4299 (b-g,m-o,q-v)

Comic Gallery
675-B N. Broadway
Escondido, CA 92025
PH:619-745-5660 (a-c,j,m,n,q-t,v)

The Comic Castle
330 - 5th Street
Eureka, CA 95501
PH:707-444-2665 (b,c,q,r)

Adventureland Comics
106 N. Harbor Blvd.
Fullerton, CA 92632
PH:714-738-3698 (a-c,q,r,v)

Comic Castle
107 W. Amerige
Fullerton, CA 92632
PH:714-879-6160 (a-v)

Comics Unlimited
12913 Harbor Blvd.
Garden Grove, CA 92640
PH:714-638-2040 (a-c,e,g,q-s)

Geoffrey's Comics
15530 Crenshaw Blvd.
Gardena, CA 90249
PH:213-538-3198
(a,c,g,j,m-o,q-s,v)

Shooting Star Comics & Games
700 E. Colorado Blvd.
Glendale, CA 91205
PH:818-502-1535 (a-c,m,o,q-s,v)

Comics Unlimited
21505 Norwalk Blvd.
Hawaiian Gardens, CA 90716
PH:213-865-4474 (a-c,e,g,m,q-t)

The American Comic Book Co.
3972 Atlantic Ave.
Long Beach, CA 90807
PH:213-426-0393 (a-f,j,m,n)

Pacific Fantasy Comics
5622 East Second Street
Long Beach, CA 90803
PH:213-434-5136 (b,c,f,j)

Another World
1615 Colorado Blvd.
Los Angeles, CA 90041
PH:213-257-7757 (b,c,e,q,r,v)

Cheap Comics - 2
7779 Melrose Ave.
Los Angeles, CA 90046
PH:213-655-9323 (a-d,g,i,k,m-v)

Golden Apple Comics
7711 Melrose Ave.
Los Angeles, CA 90046
PH:213-658-6047
(a-c,g,i,j,m-o,q,r,v)

Golden Apple Comics
8934 West Pico Blvd.
Los Angeles, CA 90035
PH:213-274-2008 (b,c,m,q-s,v)

Graphitti-Westwood—UCLA
960 Gayley Ave.
Los Angeles, CA 90024
PH:213-824-3656 (a-c,g-i,m,n,q-t)

**Wonderworld Cards, Comics
and Art**
1579 El Camino
Millbrae, CA 94030
PH:415-871-2674 (a-c,j,m,n,q-s)

Bonanza Books & Comics
Roseburg Square Center
813 W. Roseburg Avenue
Modesto, CA 95350-5058
PH:209-529-0415 (a-f,h-k,m,o-v)

Archive Comics
5148 Colfax Ave.
North Hollywood, CA 91601
PH:818-763-8044 (a-c,e-g,l,q,r)

The Comic Book Store
11517 Burbank Blvd.
North Hollywood, CA 90000
PH:818-509-2901 (a-v)

**Ninth Nebula:
The Comic Book Store**
11517 Burbank Blvd.
North Hollywood, CA 91601
PH:818-509-2901 (a-v)

Golden Apple Comics
8958-8962 Reseda Blvd.
Northridge, CA 91324
PH:818-993-7804
(a-c,g,i,m-o,q,s,v)

Freedonia Funnyworks
350 S. Tustin Ave.
Orange, CA 92666
PH:714-639-5830 (a-c,f,h-k,m-s)

Desert Comics
406 N. Palm Canyon Dr.
Palm Springs, CA 92262
PH:619-325-5805 (c,m,n,q-t,v)

Lee's Comics
3429 Alma St.
(In Alma Plaza)
Palo Alto, CA 94306
PH:415-493-3957 (a-c,e-g,m-o,q-v)

Funtime Comics & Fantasy
147 Pomona Mall East
Pomona, CA 91766
PH:714-629-8860 (a-v)

Galaxy Comics & Cards
1503 Aviation Blvd.
Redondo Beach, CA 90278
PH:213-374-7440 (a-m,o-v)

Markstu Discount Comics
3642 - 7th St.
Riverside, CA 92501
PH:714-684-8544 (a-c,q-u)

**Players Baseball Cards &
Comics**
9462 Magnolia Ave.
Riverside, CA 92503
PH:714-688-5040 (a-c,m,r)

Comic Gallery
4224 Balboa Ave.
San Diego, CA 92117
PH:619-483-4853 (a-c,j,m,n,q-t,v)

Comics and Da-Kind
1643 Noriega St.
San Francisco, CA 94122
PH:415-753-9678 (a-c,m,q,r)

**Com-X & Card-X
The Comic and Card Exchange**
1610 Irving St.
San Francisco, CA 94122
(a-c,g,m,n,q,r)

Gary's Corner Bookstore
1051 So. San Gabriel Blvd.
San Gabriel, CA 91776
PH:818-285-7575 (b,c,e,m,q,r,t,v)

Comics Pendragon
1189 Branham Lane
San Jose, CA 95118
PH:408-265-3323 (a-c,f-j,m-v)

The Comic Shop
2164 E. 14th St.
San Leandro, CA 94577
PH:415-483-0205 (a-c,g,m,q-s)

Lee's Comics
2222 S. El Camino Real
San Mateo, CA 94403
PH:415-571-1489 (a-c,e-g,m-o,q-v)

**San Mateo Wonderworld Cards,
Comics & Art**
106 S. B Street
San Mateo, CA 94401
PH:415-344-1536 (a-c,j,m,n,q-s)

Comic Castle
724 N Street
Sanger, CA 93657
PH:209-875-5160 (c,m,q)

Brian's Books
3225 Cabrillo Ave.
Santa Clara, CA 95127
PH:408-985-7481 (a-g,m,q-t)

R & K Comics
3153 El Camino Real
Santa Clara, CA 95051
PH:408-554-6512
(a-c,f-h,m-o,q,r,u,v)

Atlantis Fantasyworld
610-F Cedar Street
Santa Cruz, CA 95060
PH:408-426-0158 (a-c,e,n,q-u)

Markgraf's Comic Books
440 S. Broadway
Santa Maria, CA 93454
PH:805-925-7470 (a-c,f,g,m,q-s)

Hi De Ho Comics & Fantasy
525 Santa Monica Blvd.
Santa Monica, CA 90401
PH:213-394-2820 (a-j,m-o,q-v)

Superhero Universe VIII
Sycamore Plaza
2955-A5 Cochran St.
Simi Valley, CA 93065
PH:805-583-3027 (a-c,e-v)

Cheap Comics - 1
12123 Garfield Ave.
South Gate, CA 90280
PH:213-408-0900 (a-d,g,i,k,m-v)

Graphitti - The Valley!
12080 Ventura Pl., No. 3
Studio City, CA 91604
PH:818-980-4976 (a-h,l-n,q-t,v)

Superhero Universe IV
18722 Ventura Blvd.
Tarzana, CA 93156
PH:818-774-0969 (a-c,e-v)

J & K Comics and Toys
3535 Torrance Blvd., No. 9
Torrance, CA 90503-4815
PH:213-540-9685 (a-c,e-k,m,p-v)

Silver City Comics
4671 Torrance Blvd. at Anza
Torrance, CA 90503
PH:213-542-8034 (a-g,j,m,n,q-t,v)

Roleplayers
5933 Adobe Rd.
29 Palms, CA 92277
PH:619-367-6282 (c,e,m,n,q-t,v)

Hi De Ho Comics & Fantasy
64 Windward Ave.
Venice, CA 90291
PH:213-399-6206 (a-j,m-o,q-v)

The Second Time Around
391 E. Main St.
Ventura, CA 93001
PH:805-643-3154 (a-i,n,r,s)

Comic Castle
14464 - 7th Street
Victorville, CA 92392
PH:619-245-8006 (a-v)

Graphitti - South Bay!
Airport/Marina Hotel (Rear)
8639 Lincoln Blvd., No. 102
Westchester, L. A., CA 90045
PH:213-641-8661
(b,c,e,g,h,m,n,q-s)

Comics Unlimited
16344 Beach Blvd.
Westminster, CA 92683
PH:714-841-6646 (a-c,e,g,m,n,q-s)

Comics Unlimited
14153 Whittier Blvd.
Whittier, CA 90605
PH:213-945-1733 (a-c,e,m,r,s)

COLORADO:

Colorado Comic Book Co.
220 N. Tejon St.
Colorado Springs, CO 80903
PH:719-635-2516
(a-c,e,n,q-u)

**Colorado Comic Book Co./
Heroes & Dragons**
The Citadel #2158
Colorado Springs, CO 80909
PH:719-550-9570 (b,c,e,o,q-t,v)

CONNECTICUT:

Outer Limit Comic Shop
Rt. 37 - 52½ Pembroke Rd.
Danbury, CT 06811
PH:203-746-1068
(a-c,f,k,m,o,q,r,t,u)

The Bookie
206 Burnside Ave.
East Hartford, CT 06108
PH:203-289-1208 (a-g,j,q,r,t,u)

A Timeless Journey
402 Elm Street
Stamford, CT 06902
PH:203-353-1720 (a-n,q-v)

DELAWARE:

**Captain Blue Hen Comics,
Cards & Games**
Baycourt Plaza, Rte. 113
Dover, DE 19901
PH:302-734-3222 (a-c,e,g,q-s,u)

Comicmania
1616 W. Newport Pike
Stanton, DE 19804
PH:302-995-1971 (a-e,m,q,r,t)

FLORIDA:

The Funny Farm
422 26th St. W.
Bradenton, FL 34205
PH:813-747-7714 (a,b,i,k,m,r)

Time Machine II
Southwood Mall
5748 - 14 Street W.
Bradenton, FL 34207
PH:813-758-3684 (b,c,e,n,o,q-v)

Comics Etc.
1271 Semoran Blvd.,Suite 125
Lake Howell Square
Casselberry, FL 32707
PH:407-679-5665 (b,c,e,m,q-t)

Comics and Cards
7778 Wiles Road
Coral Springs, FL 33071
PH:305-752-0580 (b,c,q,r)

Acevedo's Collectables
4761 S. University Drive
Davie, FL 33328
PH:305-434-0540 (b,c,g,i,k,m,r)

Cliff's Books
209 N. Woodland Blvd. (17-92)
De Land, FL 32720
PH:904-734-6963 (a-h,j-o,q-v)

**Intergalactic Comics &
Collectibles**
109 E. Semoran Blvd.
Fern Park, FL 32720
PH:407-260-0017 (a-m,p-v)

Novel Ideas
804 West University Ave.
Gainesville, FL 32601
PH:904-374-8593 (b,c,e,n,q-s,v)

Novel Ideas
3206 S.W. 35th Blvd.
Butler Plaza
Gainesville, FL 32608
PH:904-377-2694 (b,c,e,n,q-s,v)

Charlie's Comics
1255 West 46th Street
Hialeah, FL 33012
PH:305-557-5994
(b,c,g,i,j,m-o,q-v)

Coliseum of Comics
1180 E. Vine St.
Kissimmee, FL 32741
PH:407-870-5322 (b,c,e,g,m,q-s)

Past—Present—Future Comics
6186 S. Congress Ave., Suite A4
Lantana, FL 33462
PH:407-433-3068 (b,c,q-s)

Geppi's Comic World
2200 East Bay Drive #203
Largo, FL 34641
PH:813-585-0226 (a-c,f)

Phil's Comic Shoppe
614 S. State Rd. 7
Margate, FL 33063
PH:305-977-6947 (a-c,m,n,q,r,t,u)

**Frank's Comic Book & Baseball
Card Store**
2678 S.W. 87 Avenue
Miami, FL 33165
PH:305-226-5072
(a-c,g,j,k,m,o,q,r,t,v)

Comic Warehouse, Inc.
1029 Airport Rd. N., #B-6
Naples, FL 33942
PH:813-643-1020
(b,c,e,g,j,m,o,q-v)

Tropic Comics South, Inc.
742 N.E. 167th St.
N. Miami Beach, FL 33161
PH:305-940-8700 (a-d,j,n,r,v)

Adventure Into Comics
841 Bennett Rd.
Orlando, FL 32803
PH:407-896-4047
(a-c,e,g,j,k,m,o,q-v)

Cartoon Museum
4300 S. Semoran, Suite 109
Orlando, FL 32822-2453
PH:407-273-0141 (a-k,m,o,p,q)

Coliseum of Comics
4103 S. Orange Blossom Trail
Orlando, FL 32809
PH:407-422-5757 (b,c,e,g,m,q-s)

Coliseum of Comics
5306 Silver Star Rd.
Orlando, FL 32808
PH:407-298-9411 (b,c,e,g,m,q-s)

Enterprise 1701
2814 Corrine Drive
Orlando, FL 32803
PH:407-896-1701 (c,e,n,o,q-v)

**Past-Present-Future Comics
North**
4270 Northlake Blvd.
Palm Beach Gardens, FL 33410
(a-c,n,q-t,v)

Sincere Comics, Inc.
Town & Country Plaza
3300 N. Pace Blvd.
Pensacola, FL 32505
PH:904-432-1352 (a-c,e,i,n,q-u)

Tropic Comics, Inc.
313 S. State Rd. 7
Plantation, FL 33317
PH:305-587-8878 (a-d,j,n,q,r,v)

Comics U.S.A.
3231 N. Federal Highway
Pompano Beach, FL 33064
PH:305-942-1455 (a-g,j,k,m,q-t)

Comic & Gaming Exchange
8432 W. Oakland Park Blvd.
Sunrise, FL 33351
PH:305-742-0777 (b-e,g,q-v)

**David T. Alexander's Comic
Books and Baseball Cards**
(By Appointment Only)
P. O. Box 273086
Tampa, FL 33618
PH:813-968-1805 (a,b,d-k,m,n,q)

New England Comics
Northdale Court
15836 N. Dale Mabry Highway
Tampa, FL 33618
PH:813-264-1848 (a-c,m,q-v)

Tropic Comics North, Inc.
1018 - 21st St. (U.S. 1)
Vero Beach, FL 32960
PH:407-562-8501 (a-c,j,n,q-s)

GEORGIA:

Fischer's Book Store
6569 Riverdale Road
Riverdale, GA 30274
PH:404-997-7323 (b,c,e,h,l-n,q-v)

Starbase 1
1517½ N. Ashley St.
Valdosta, GA 31602
PH:1-800-526-5490 (a-c,q-v)

HAWAII:

Jelly's Comics & Books
98-199 Kam. Hwy.
Aiea, HI 96701
PH:808-486-5600
(a-e,g,h,j,l-o,q-t,v)

Jelly's Comics & Books
404 Piikoi St.
Honolulu, HI 96814
PH:808-538-7771 (a-e,g)

Compleat Comics Company
1728 Kaahumanu Avenue
Wailuku, Maui, HI 96793
PH:808-242-5875 (b,c,n,q-s)

IDAHO:

King's Komix Kastle
1706 N. 18th St. (appointments)
Boise, ID 83702
PH:208-343-7142 (a-i,m,n,q,r)

King's Komix Kastle II
2560 Leadville (drop in)
Mail: 1706 N. 18th
Boise, ID 83702
PH:208-343-7055 (a-i,m,n,q,r)

**New Mythology Comics &
Science Fiction**
1725 Broadway
Boise, ID 83706
PH:208-344-6744 (a-e,m,n,q-t)

ILLINOIS:

Friendly Frank's Distribution
(Wholesale Only)
727 Factory Rd.
Addison, IL 60101

Friendly Frank's Comics
11941 S. Cicero
Alsip, IL 60658
PH:312-371-6760 (a-d,f,g,i,j,n,q,r)

All-American Comic Shops 3
9118 Ogden Ave.
Brookfield, IL 60513
PH:708-387-9588 (a-c,e,j,m,q,r)

Moondog's Comicland
1231 W. Dundee Rd.
Plaza Verde
Buffalo Grove, IL 60090
PH:708-259-6060 (a-c,e,m,o,q-v)

Amazing Fantasy
1856 Sibley Blvd.
Calumet City, IL
PH:708-891-2260 (b,c,p-s)

All-American Comic Shops 6
6457 W. Archer Ave.
Chicago, IL 60638
PH:312-586-5090 (a-c,j,m,o,q,r)

Comics for Heroes (Main Store)
1702 W. Foster
Chicago, IL 60640
PH:312-769-4745 (a-c,g,m,n,q-v)

Comics for Heroes
3937 W. Lawrence
Chicago, IL 60625
PH:312-478-8585 (a-c,g,m,n,q-v)

For the Love of Toons
3954 N. Avondale
Chicago, IL 60613
PH:312-549-6430 (b,c,k,q-u)

Larry's Comic Book Store
1219 W. Devon Ave.
Chicago, IL 60660
PH:312-274-1832 (a-c,n,o,u,v)

Larry Laws (by appointment only)
(Call First) (Mail Order)
831 Cornelia
Chicago, IL 60657
PH:312-477-9247 (d,e,g-i,m,o)

Joe Sarno's Comic Kingdom
5941 W. Irving Park Rd.
Chicago, IL 60634
PH:312-545-2231 (a-d,f,j,m,r)

Yesterday
1143 W. Addison St.
Chicago, IL 60613
PH:312-248-8087 (a,b,d-g,i-n,r,t)

All-American Comic Shops 5
1701 N. Larkin Ave.
Hillcrest Shopping Center
Crest Hill, IL 60435
PH:815-744-2094 (b,c,e,m,q,r)

Moondog's Comicland
114 S. Waukegan Rd.
Deerbrook Mall
Deerfield, IL 60015
PH:708-272-6080 (a-c,e,m,o,q-v)

The Paper Escape
205 W. First Street
Dixon, IL 61021
PH:815-284-7567 (b,c,e,g,m,q-t)

GEM Comics
156 N. York Rd.
Elmhurst, IL 60126
PH:708-833-8787 (b,c,q-s)

All-American Comic Shops, Ltd.
3514 W. 95th St.
Evergreen Park, IL 60642
PH:708-425-7555 (a-c,e,j,m,o,q,r)

More Fun Comics
650 Roosevelt Rd., Suite #112
Glen Ellyn, IL 60137
PH:708-469-6141 (a-c,e,m,o,q-v)

Fiction House
Dixie Hwy.
Homewood, IL 60430
PH:708-206-1330 (b,c,m,p-s)

Moondog's Comicland
139 W. Prospect Ave.
Mt. Prospect, IL 60056
PH:708-398-6060 (a-c,e,m,o,q-v)

Moondog's Comicland
Randhurst Shopping Center
Mt. Prospect, IL 60056
PH:708-577-8668 (c,e,m,o,q-v)

All-American Comic Shops 2
14620 S. LaGrange Rd.
Orland Park, IL 60462
PH:708-460-5556 (b,c,e,m,q,r)

All-American Comic Shops 4
22305 S. Central Park
Central Court Plaza
Park Forest, IL 60466
PH:708-748-2509 (b,c,e,m,q,r)

Tomorrow Is Yesterday
5600 N. Second St.
Rockford, IL 61111
PH:815-633-0330 (a-j,m-o,q-v)

Moondog's Comicland
1455 W. Schaumburg Rd.
Schaumburg Plaza
Schaumburg, IL 60194
PH:708-529-6060 (a-c,e,m,o,q-v)

Family Book
3123 So. Dirksen Pkwy.
Springfield, IL 62703
PH:217-529-1709 (a-c,e,q-u)

Unicorn Comics & Cards
216 S. Villa Avenue
Villa Park, IL 60181
PH:708-279-5777
(a-c,e,g,h,j,l-n,q-s)

Heroland Comics
6963 W. 111th St.
Worth, IL 60482
PH:708-448-2937 (a-e,i-s)

INDIANA:

Pen Comics & Entertainment Store
7 North 5th Ave.
Beech Grove, IN 46107
PH:317-782-3450
(a-c,e,i,j,m,n,q-v)

25th Century Five & Dime
106 E. Kirkwood, P.O. Box 7
Bloomington, IN 47402
PH:812-332-0011 (b,c,g,i,n,o,q-s)

The Bookstack
112 W. Lexington Ave.
Elkhart, IN 46516
PH:219-293-3815 (a-c,e,h,r,s)

Spider's Web
51815 State Rd. 19 N.
Elkhart, IN 46514
PH:219-264-9178 (a-c,e,g,h,n,q,r)

Collector's Carnival
2030 E. Morgan
Evansville, IN 47711
PH:812-925-3290 (b,c,e,g,i,k-m,q)

Books, Comics and Things
2212 Maplecrest Rd.
Fort Wayne, IN 46815
PH:219-749-4045 (a-c,e,h,m,q-u)

Books, Comics and Things
5950 W. Jefferson Blvd.
Time Corners
Fort Wayne, IN 46804
PH:219-436-0159 (a-c,e,h,m,q-u)

Broadway Comic Book and Baseball Card Shop
2423 Broadway
Fort Wayne, IN 46807
PH:219-744-1456 (a-c,e-h,m,q-u)

Friendly Frank's Distr., Inc.
(Wholesale only)
3990 Broadway
Gary, IN 46408
PH:219-884-5052 (c,g,n,r,s)

Friendly Frank's Comics
220 Main Street
Hobart, IN 46342
PH:219-942-6020 (a-d,f,g,i,j,n,q,r)

Comic Carnival & Nostalgia Emporium
6265 N. Carrollton Ave.
Indianapolis, IN 46220
PH:317-253-8882 (a-j,m-u)

Comic Carnival & Nostalgia Emporium
5002 S. Madison Ave.
Indianapolis, IN 46227
PH:317-787-3773 (a-j,m-u)

Comic Carnival & Nostalgia Emporium
982 N. Mitthoeffer Rd.
Indianapolis, IN 46229
PH:317-898-5010 (a-j,m-u)

Comic Carnival & Nostalgia Emporium
3837 N. High School Rd.
Indianapolis, IN 46254
PH:317-293-4386 (a-j,m-u)

Tenth Planet
204 Route 30
Schereville, IN
PH:219-322-2902 (b,c,m,p-s)

IOWA:

Oak Leaf Comics
5219 University Ave.
Cedar Falls, IA 50613
PH:319-277-1835 (a-c,m-o,q-u)

Comic World & Baseball Cards
1626 Central Ave.
Dubuque, IA 52001
PH:319-557-1897
(a-c,g,h,m,n,q-u)

Oak Leaf Comics
23 - 5th S.W.
Mason City, IA 50401
PH:515-424-0333 (a-c,e-v)

The Comiclogue
520 Elm St., P.O. Box 65304
West Des Moines, IA 50265
PH:515-279-9006 (a-c,n-r,u)

KANSAS:

Kwality Books, Comics & Games
1111 Massachusetts Street
Lawrence, KS 66044
PH:913-843-7239 (a-c,e,i,q-u)

1,000,000 Comix Inc.
5332 West 95th St.
Prairie Village, KS 66207
PH:913-383-1777
(a-d,f-h,j,m,n,p-v)

Prairie Dog Comics East
Oxford Square Mall
6100 E. 21st St., Suite 190
Wichita, KS 67208
PH:316-688-5576 (a-n,p-s)

Prairie Dog Comics West
Central Heights Mall
7387 West Central
Wichita, KS 67212
PH:316-722-6316 (a-n,p-s)

KENTUCKY:

Comic Book World
7130 Turfway Road
Florence, KY 41042
PH:606-371-9562 (a-c,m,o,q-v)

LOUISIANA:

Comic Book Emporium
5201 Nicholson Dr., Suite H
Baton Rouge, LA 70816
PH:504-767-1227 (b,c,q,r,t,u)

B.T. & W.D. Giles
P. O. Box 271
Keithville, LA 71047
PH:318-925-6654 (a,b,d-f,h)

Bookworm of N.O.E.
7011 Read Rd.
New Orleans, LA 70127
PH:504-242-7608 (a-c,e,g,q,r)

Excalibur Comics, Cards & Games
9066 Mansfield Road
Shreveport, LA 71118
PH:318-686-7076 (a-d,f,g,i,k,m-v)

Comix Plus
637 Carollo Dr.
Slidell, LA 70458
PH:504-649-4376 (b,c,r)

MAINE:

Lippincott Books
624 Hammond St.
Bangor, ME 04401
PH:207-942-4398 (a,b,d-h,m,n,r-u)

Moonshadow Comics
10 Exchange Street
Portland, ME 04101
PH:207-772-3870 (a-c,g,i,j,n,o,q-v)

Moonshadow Comics
The Maine Mall
Maine Mall Road
South Portland, ME 04106
PH:207-772-4605 (a-c,g,i,j,n,o,q-v)

Book Barn
U.S. Route 1
Wells, ME 04090
PH:207-646-4926 (a-c,e,g,h,m,r)

MARYLAND:

Universal Comics
5300 East Drive
Arbutus, MD 21227
PH:301-242-4578
(a-c,e,g,k,m,n,q,r,t)

Comic Book Kingdom, Inc.
4307 Harford Road
Baltimore, MD 21214
PH:301-426-4529 (a-h,k,m,q,r,t)

Geppi's Comic World
7019 Security Blvd.
Hechinger's Square
at Security Mall
Baltimore, MD 21207
PH:301-298-1758 (a-c,f)

Geppi's Comic World
Harbor Place
Upper Level, Light St. Pavilion
301 Light St.
Baltimore, MD 21202
PH:301-547-0910 (a-c,f)

Mindbridge, Ltd. I
1786 Merritt Blvd.
Merritt Park Shopping Center
Baltimore, MD 21222
PH:301-284-7880
(a-c,e-h,j,k,m,n,q-v)

Mike's Clubhouse
108 S. Main Street
Bel Air, MD 21014
PH:301-838-6255 (a-c,g,m,q,r)

Big Planet Comics
4865 Cordell Ave. (2nd Floor)
Bethesda, MD 20814
PH:301-654-6856 (c,j,n,q,r)

The Magic Page
7416 Laurel-Bowie Rd. (Rt. 197)
Bowie, MD 20715
PH:301-262-4735
(b,c,e,m,o,q-s,u,v)

Alternate Worlds
9924 York Road
Cockeysville, MD 21030
PH:301-666-3290 (b,c,g,n,o,q-v)

The Closet of Comics
7319 Baltimore Ave. (U.S. 1)
College Park, MD 20740
PH:301-699-0498 (a-c,g,n,r)

Comic Classics
365 Main Street
Laurel, MD 20707
PH:301-792-4744, 490-9811
(a-c,e,g,m-o,q-v)

Mindbridge, Ltd. II
9847 Belair Road (Route 1)
Perry Hall, MD 21128
PH:301-256-7880 (a-e,g,i-n,q-v)

The Closet of Comics
Calvert Village Shopping Center
Prince Frederick, MD 20678
PH:301-535-4731 (a-c,e,g,n,r)

Geppi's Comic World
8317 Fenton St.
Silver Spring, MD 20910
PH:301-588-2546 (a-c,e,f)

Barbarian
11254 Triangle Lane
Wheaton, MD 20902
PH:301-946-4184
(a-c,e,f,h,m-o,q-v)

MASSACHUSETTS:

New England Comics
168 Harvard Ave.
Allston (Boston), MA 02134
PH:617-783-1848 (a-c,m,n,q-v)

Comically Speaking
1322 Mass. Ave.
Arlington, MA 02174
PH:617-643-XMEN (a-c,f,m,n,q-s)

Bargain Books and Collectibles
247 So. Main St.
Attleboro, MA 02703
PH:508-226-1668
(b,c,e,k,m,o,q,r,t)

Ayer Comics & Baseball Cards
28 Main St.
Ayer, MA 01432
PH:508-772-4994 (b,c,e,g,k,m,q,r)

Superhero Universe III
41 West Street
Boston, MA 02111
(a-c,e-v)

New England Comics
748 Crescent Street
East Crossing Plaza
Brockton, MA 02402
PH:508-559-5068 (a-c,m,q-v)

New England Comics
316 Harvard St.
Brookline, MA 02146
PH:617-566-0115 (a-c,m,n,q-v)

Superhero Universe I
1105 Massachusetts Ave.
Cambridge, MA 02138
PH:617-354-5344 (a-c,e-v)

Michael Richards
P. O. Box 455
Dorchester, MA 02122
PH:617-436-7995 (a-c,j)

World of Fantasy
529 Broadway
Everett, MA 02149
PH:617-381-0411 (a-c,e,g-k,m,q-v)

That's Entertainment
387 Main St.
Fitchburg, MA 01420
PH:508-342-8607 (a-v)

Bop City Comics
80 Worcester Road (Route 9)
Marshalls Mall
Framingham, MA 01701
PH:508-872-2317

New England Comics
12A Pleasant St.
Malden, MA 02148
PH:617-322-2404 (a-c,m,q-v)

New England Comics
714 Washington Street
Norwood, MA 02062
PH:617-769-4552 (a-c,m,q-v)

Imagine That Bookstore
58 Dalton Ave.
Pittsfield, MA 01201
PH:413-445-5934 (a-i,l,m,q-u)

New England Comics
13B Court Street
Plymouth, MA 02360
PH:508-746-8797 (a-c,m,q-v)

New England Comics
1350 Hancock Street
Quincy, MA 02169
PH:617-770-1848 (a-c,m,q-v)

Pages of Reading
25 Harnden Street
Reading, MA 01867
PH:617-944-9613 (b,c,e,h,l,q-u)

Park Nostalgia
1242 Wilbur Avenue
Somerset, MA 02725
PH:508-673-0303 (a-c,m,r)

Blaine's Comics
1 Winter Street
(352 Bldg. Main St.)
Stoneham, MA 02180
PH:617-438-5813 (b,c,m,r,s)

The Outer Limits
457 Moody St.
Waltham, MA 02154
PH:617-891-0444 (a-k,m,n,q-v)

Golden Age Buyers
457 Moody St. Dept. 09
Waltham, MA 02154
PH:617-891-0444 (a,b)

Mayo Beach Bookstore
Kendrick Ave., Mayo Beach
Wellfleet, MA 02667
PH:508-349-3154 (a-i)

Fabulous Fiction Book Store
984 Main St.
Worcester, MA 01603
PH:508-754-8826 (a-e,g,h,o,q-s,u)

That's Entertainment
151 Chandler Street
Worcester, MA 01609
PH:508-755-4207 (a-v)

MICHIGAN:

Dave's II Comics & Collectibles
623 E. William
Ann Arbor, MI 48017
PH:313-665-6969 (a-n,p-r,t-v)

Tom & Terry Comics
508 Lafayette Ave.
Bay City, MI 48708
PH:517-895-5525 (b,c,e,m,q,r,t)

Harley Yee (By appointment)
P. O. Box 19578
Detroit, MI 48219-0578
PH:313-533-2731 (a,b,d,f)

Curious Book Shop
307 E. Grand River Ave.
East Lansing, MI 48823
PH:517-332-0112 (a-k,m-p)

Comix Corner - East
32004 Utica Road
Fraser, MI 48026
PH:313-296-2758 (a-c,q-s)

Argos Book Shop
1405 Robinson Rd. S.E.
Grand Rapids, MI 49506
PH:616-454-0111 (a-h,m,n)

Tardy's Collector's Corner, Inc.
2009 Eastern Ave. S.E.
Grand Rapids, MI 49507
PH:616-247-7828, 247-0245
(a-c,n,q)

Comix Corner - West
861 E. Auburn Road
Rochester Hills, MI 48063
PH:313-852-3356 (a-c,q-s)

Dave's Comics & Collectibles
407 S. Washington
Royal Oak, MI 48067
PH:313-548-1230 (a-n,p-r,t-v)

Book Stop
1160 Chicago Drive S.W.
Wyoming, MI 49509-1004
PH:616-245-0090
(a-c,e,g,j,m-o,q,r,t)

MINNESOTA:

Collector's Connection
21 East Superior Street
Duluth, MN 55802
PH:218-722-9551 (b,c,m,q-s)

College of Comic Book Knowledge
3151 Hennepin Ave. S.
Minneapolis, MN 55408
PH:612-822-2309
(a-c,e-i,k-n,p-r,t-v)

Midway Book & Comic
1579 University Ave.
St. Paul, MN 55104
PH:612-644-7605 (a-h,n,q-u)

MISSISSIPPI:

Gulf Coast Comics
Petit Bois Specialty Center
240 Eisenhower Drive, C-1
Biloxi, MS 39531
PH:601-388-2991 (a-g,m-o,q-v)

Sharon Zocchi's Retail Games and Comics
2803 Pass Rd. (near the airbase)
Biloxi, MS 39531
PH:601-374-6632 (a-c,e,g,l-o,q-v)

Star Store
4212 N. State St.
Jackson, MS 39206
PH:601-362-8001 (a-v)

Spanish Trail Books
1006 Thorn Ave.
Ocean Springs, MS 39564
PH:601-875-1144 (a-h,q,r,t)

MISSOURI:

Parallel Worlds
12th & Virginia, P.O. Box 2802
(Joplin Flea Market)
Joplin, MO 64803
PH:417-781-5130 (c,m,o,q,s,t)

B & R Comix Center
4747 Morganford
St. Louis, MO 63116
PH:314-353-4013 (a-c,g,j,n,q,r)

Mo's Comics and Stories
4530 Gravois
St. Louis, MO 63116
PH:314-353-9500 (a-f,i,m,n,p-r,t,u)

The Book Rack
300 W. Olive
Springfield, MO 65806
PH:417-865-4945 (b-e,h,q,r)

MONTANA:

Marvel-Us Comics
600 15th Street South
Great Falls, MT 59405
PH:406-771-1535 (a-c,m,n,p-r)

The Book Exchange
2335 Brooks
Trempers Shopping Center
Missoula, MT 59801
PH:406-728-6342 (a-c,e-h,n,q-s)

NEBRASKA:

Dragon's Lair
8316 Blondo St.
Omaha, NE 68137
PH:402-399-9141 (a-c,g,h,m,q-t)

Dragon's Lair Too
13826 T Plaza
Omaha, NE 68137
PH:402-895-5653 (b,c,h,m,q-s)

Star Realm
7305 South 85th St.
Omaha, NE 68128
PH:402-331-4844 (c,e,i,r-u)

NEVADA:

Page After Page
1412 E. Charleston Blvd.
Las Vegas, NV 89104
PH:702-384-1690 (a-k,m-v)

Fandom's Comicworld of Reno
2001 East Second St.
Reno, NV 89502
PH:702-786-6663 (a-c,g,o,q,r)

Stella Enterprises
126 "B" Street
P. O. Box 251
Sparks, NV 89432
PH:702-359-7812
(a-c,f,g,j,k,m,q,r)

NEW HAMPSHIRE:

James F. Payette
P. O. Box 750
Bethlehem, NH 03574
PH:603-869-2097 (a,b,d-h)

Comic Store
643 Elm Street
Manchester, NH 03101
PH:603-668-6705 (a-c,j,n,q-v)

Comic Store
300 Main St.
Simoneau Plaza
Nashua, NH 03060
PH:603-881-4855 (a-c,j,n,q-v)

NEW JERSEY:

The Comic Zone
71 Rte. 73 & Day Ave.
Berlin, NJ 08009
PH:609-768-8186 (b,c,e,g,m,n,q-s)

Collector's Cove
27 Watsessing Ave.
Bloomfield, NJ 07003
PH:201-748-9263 (b,c,m)

Rainbow Collectibles
Laurel Hill Plaza
Clementon, NJ 08021
PH:609-627-1711 (a-c,f,g,m,r)

Steve's Comic Relief
1555 St. George Ave. off Rt. 35
Colonia, NJ 07067
PH:201-382-3736 (a-c,j,n,q-v)

Steve's Comic Relief
24 Mill Run Plaza
Off Route 130
Delran, NJ 08075
PH:609-461-1770 (a-c,j,n,q-v)

Thunder Road Comics & Cards
Parkway Plaza
831 Parkway Ave.
Ewing Township, NJ 08618
PH:609-771-1055 (a-c,m,q,r)

Shore Video Comics & Baseball Cards
615 Lacey Road
Forked River, NJ 08731
PH:609-693-3831 (a-c,g,m,o-r)

1,000,000 Comix Inc.
629 Palisade Ave.
Fort Lee, NJ
(call info re phone #)
(a-d,f-h,j,m,n,p-v)

Star Spangled Comics
US Rte. 22 - King George Plaza
Green Brook, NJ 08812
PH: Call information
(a-c,g,h,m,q-s)

Thunder Road Comics & Cards
3694 Nottingham Way
Hamilton Square, NJ 08690
PH:609-587-5353 (a-c,m,q,r)

Steve's Comic Relief
106 Clifton Ave. off Route 9
Lakewood, NJ 08701
PH:201-363-3899 (a-c,j,n,q-v)

Steve's Comic Relief
156-A Mercer Mall off Route 1
Lawrenceville, NJ 08648
PH:609-452-7548 (a-c,j,n,q-v)

The Hobby Shop
Route 34
Strathmore Shopping Center
Matawan, NJ 07747
PH:201-583-0505 (a-f,i,j,m,q-u)

Comic Museum
58 High St.
Mount Holly, NJ 08060
PH:609-261-0996 (a-c,n,q,r,u)

Comicrypt
521 White Horse Pike
Oaklyn, NJ 08107
PH:609-858-3877 (b-e,g,i,j,n,q-s,u)

Passaic Book Center
594 Main Ave.
Passaic, NJ 07055
PH:201-778-6646 (a-h,l-n,r,t,u)

Fantasy Zone Comics
80 Broad Street
Red Bank, NJ 07701
PH:201-842-4940 (b,c,m,n,q,r)

Sparkle City (appointment only)
P. O. Box 67
Sewell, NJ 08080
PH:609-881-1174 (a,b,d,f)

Philip M. Levine and Sons, Rare & Esoteric Books
P. O. Box 246 (appointment only)
Three Bridges, NJ 08887
PH:201-788-0532 (a,b,d-n,p)

Mr. Collector
327 Union Blvd.
Totowa, NJ 07512
PH:201-595-0900 (a-c,g,h,m,r)

TemDee
15 Whitman Square
Black Horse Pike
Turnersville, NJ 08012
PH:609-228-8645
(b-d,f,g,k,i,m,q,s-v)

Comics Plus
Ocean Plaza
Hwy. 35 & Sunset Ave.
Wanamassa, NJ 07712
PH:201-922-3308 (a-c,e,g,k,m,q,r)

1,000,000 Comix Inc.
875 Mantua Pike
Southwood Shopping Centre
Woodbury Heights, NJ 08096
PH:609-384-8844
(a-d,f-h,j,m,n,p-v)

NEW MEXICO:

Over the Rainbow Comics and Cards
1560-F Juan Tabo, N.E.
Albuquerque, NM 87112
PH:505-292-1374 (a-g,j,k,m-v)

Captain Comic's Specialty Shop
109 W. 4th Street
Clovis, NM 88101
PH:505-769-1543 (a-c,q,r)

NEW YORK:

Earthworld Comic Inc.
327 Central Ave.
Albany, NY 12206
PH:518-465-5495 (a-c,k,n-r)

FantaCo Enterprises Inc.
21 Central Avenue - Level Two
Albany, NY 12210
PH:518-463-3667 (e,g,h,m,o)

FantaCo Archival Research Center
21 Central Ave. - Sublevel One
Albany, NY 12210
PH:518-463-1400 (c,e,g-j,l,n,u)

FantaCo Comic Shop
21 Central Avenue - Level One
Albany, NY 12210
PH:518-463-1400
(b,c,e,g,h,j,m-o,q-v)

FantaCon Organization Offices
21 Central Avenue - Level One
Albany, NY 12210
PH:518-463-1400 (a-v)

FantaCo Publications
21 Central Avenue - Level Two
Albany, NY 12210
PH:518-463-3667 (c,e)

FantaCo 1990: Year of the Zombie Headquarters
21 Central Avenue - Level Two
Albany, NY 12210
PH:518-463-3667 (c,e,g,h,o)

Collector's Comics
167 Deer Park Ave.
Babylon, NY 11702
PH:516-321-4347 (a-c,e,n,q-s)

Long Island Comics
1670-D Sunrise Hwy.
Bay Shore, NY 11706
PH:516-665-4342 (a-c,g,j,q-t)

Fordham Comics
390 East Fordham Rd.
Bronx, NY 10458
PH:212-933-9245 (a-c,h,i,m,q-s)

Wow Comics
652 E. 233rd St.
Bronx, NY 10466
PH:212-231-0913 (a-c,m,n,q-s)

Wow Comics
642 Pelham Parkway S.
Bronx, NY 10462
PH:212-829-0461 (a-c,m,n,q-s)

Brain Damage Comics
1289 Prospect Avenue
Brooklyn, NY 11218
PH:718-438-1335
(a-c,e,g,h,m,n,q-s)

Metro Comics
138 Montague St.
Brooklyn, NY 11201
PH:718-935-0911 (a-c,g,j,m-o,q-v)

Metropolis Comics
(by appointment)
P. O. Box 165
Brooklyn, NY 11214
PH:718-837-2538
(a,b,d,g,h,j,k,m,p)

Pinocchio Discounts
1814 McDonald Ave. near Ave. P
Brooklyn, NY 11223
PH:718-645-2573 (a,c,g,m,n,t)

World of Fantasy
737 Long Island Ave. at D.P. Ave.
Deer Park, NY 11729
PH:516-586-7314 (a-f,m-o,q,r)

The Book Stop
384 East Meadow Ave.
East Meadow, NY 11554
PH:516-794-9129 (a-c,e,g,h,n,r,t)

Comics for Collectors
211 West Water St.
Elmira, NY 14901
PH:607-732-2299 (c,m,n,q-v)

Fantazia
2 So. Central Ave.
Hartsdale, NY 10530
PH:914-946-3306 (a-d,f,g,j,m,n,r)

Comics for Collectors
148 The Commons
Ithaca, NY 14850
PH:607-272-3007 (a-c,j,m,n,q-v)

Bush Hobbies
Park Plaza Shopping Center
299-12 Hawkins Ave.
Lake Ronkonkoma, NY 11779
PH:516-981-0253 (b,c,m,r)

Bailey's Comics
106 N. Wellwood Ave.
Lindenhurst, NY 11757
PH:516-957-7276
(a-c,e,g,m,o,q-t,v)

Long Beach Books, Inc.
17 E. Park Ave.
Long Beach, NY 11561
PH:516-432-2265 (a-h,n,r-u)

Comics & Hobbies
156 Mamaroneck Ave.
Mamaroneck, NY 10543
PH:914-698-9473 (a-d,j,m,n,r)

Action Comics
318 E. 84th St.
(Between 1st & 2nd Ave.)
New York, NY 10028
PH:212-249-7344 (a-c,j,k,m,n,q-s)

Big Apple Comics
2489 Broadway (92 - 93 St.)
New York, NY 10025
PH:212-724-0085 (a-d,j,m,n,r)

Forbidden Planet
821 Broadway at 12th St.
New York, NY 10003
PH:212-475-6161
(a-e,g,h,j,k,m-o,q-v)

Forbidden Planet
227 E. 59th St. & 3rd Ave.
New York, NY 10022
PH:212-751-4386
(a-e,g,h,j,k,m-o,q-v)

Funny Business
656 Amsterdam Ave.
(corner 92nd St.)
New York, NY 10025
PH:212-799-9477 (a-c,g,n,o,q,r)

Golden Age Express
2489 Broadway (92-93)
New York, NY 10025
PH:212-769-9570 (a,b,j,r)

Jim Hanley's Universe
At A&S Plaza, 5th & 6th Floors
901 Ave. of Americas (at 33rd)
New York, NY 10001
PH:212-268-7088 (a-c,e-g,n,o,q-v)

Jerry Ohlinger's Movie Material Store, Inc.
242 West 14th St.
New York, NY 10011
PH:212-989-0869 (g,i)

Pinnacle Bag Co.
P.O. Box 6639
Grand Central Sta.
New York, NY 10163
PH:718-539-8603 (r)

St. Mark's Comics
11 St. Mark's Pl.
New York, NY 10003
PH:212-598-9439 or 212-353-3300
(a-c,g,j,m-o,q-v)

West Side Comics & Video
107 West 86 St.
New York, NY 10024
PH:212-724-0432 (a-c,n,o,r)

Corner-Stone Bookshop
110 Margaret St.
Plattsburgh, NY 12901
PH:518-561-0520
(b,c,e,g,h,l,m,q-t)

Fantastic Planet
24 Oak Street
Plattsburgh, NY 12901
PH:518-563-2946 (b-e,g,m,q,r,t-v)

Flash Point — "The Science Fiction & Fantasy Shop"
Harbor Square Mall
134 Main Street
Port Jefferson, NY 11777
PH:516-331-9401 (b,c,e,k,n,q-s)

Amazing Comics
12 Gillette Ave.
Sayville, NY 11782
PH:516-567-8069 (a-c,j,q-s)

Comix 4-U, Inc.
1675 Broadway
Schenectady, NY 12306
PH:518-372-6612, 452-0801
(a-c,e,g,h,n,q,r,t,u)

Electric City Comics
1704 Van Vranken Ave.
Schenectady, NY 12308
PH:518-377-1500 (a-c,g,j,n,q,r,u)

Clearly Chaotic Comix Co.
(By appointment only)
168 Portage Ave.
Staten Island, NY 10314
PH:718-667-9056 (a-c,q,r)

Jim Hanley's Universe
at the Staten Island Mall
2655 Richmond Avenue
Staten Island, NY 10314
PH:718-983-5752 (a-c,e-g,n,o,q-v)

Comic Book Heaven
48-14 Skillman Avenue
Sunnyside, Queens, NY 11104
PH:718-899-4175 (a-c,e,g,k,m,r,s)

Dream Days Comic Book Shop
312 South Clinton St.
Syracuse, NY 13202
PH:315-475-3995 (a-d,f-h,j,n,q,r)

Michael Sagert
P. O. Box 456 - Downtown
Syracuse, NY 13201
PH:315-475-3995 (a,b,d,f,h,j)

Twilight Book & Game Emporium, Inc.
1401 North Salina Street
Syracuse, NY 13208
PH:315-471-3139 (a-c,e,g,m,n,q-v)

Aquilonia Comics
459 Fulton St.
Troy, NY 12180
PH:518-271-1069
(a-c,e,g,m,n,q-u)

Collector's Comics
3247 Sunrise Highway
Wantagh, NY 11793
PH:516-783-8700 (a-c,e,n,q-s)

NORTH CAROLINA:

Super Giant Books
344 Merrimon Ave.
Asheville, NC 28801
PH:704-254-2103 (a-c,e,h,j)

Heroes Aren't Hard to Find
Corner Central Ave. & The Plaza
P. O. Box 9181
Charlotte, NC 28299
PH:704-375-7462
(a-c,g,j,k,m,n,q-t,v)

Heroes Aren't Hard to Find
Carmel Commons Shopping Ctr.
6648 Carmel Rd.
Charlotte, NC 28226
PH:704-542-8842
(a-c,g,j,k,m,n,q-t,v)

Heroes Aren't Hard to Find
Mail Order Subscription & Wholesale
P. O. Box 9181
Charlotte, NC 28299
PH:704-376-5766
(a-c,g,j,k,m,n,q-t,v)

New Dimension Comics
2609 Central Ave.
Charlotte, NC 28205
PH:704-377-4376 (a-v)

New Dimension Comics Whse.
Mailorder-Conventions-Wholesale
2611 Central Ave.
Charlotte, NC 28205
PH:704-372-4376 (a-v)

Heroes Are Here
117 S. Center St.
Goldsboro, NC 27530
PH:919-734-3131 (a-c,e,m,q,r)

Acme Comics
348 S. Elm St.
Greensboro, NC 27401
PH:919-272-5994 (a-c,f,j,n,q,r)

Parts Unknown—The Comic Book Store
The Cotton Mill Square
801 Merritt Dr./Spring Garden St.
Greensboro, NC 27407
PH:919-294-0091 (a-c,g,i,n,q,r)

Heroes Are Here, Too
116 E. Fifth St.
Greenville, NC 27858
PH:919-757-0948 (a-c,m,q,r)

The Nostalgia News Stand
919 Dickinson Ave.
Greenville, NC 27834
PH:919-758-6909 (b,c,e,n,q,r)

Tales Resold
3936 Atlantic Ave.
Raleigh, NC 27604
PH:919-878-8551 (a-c,e,g,h,j,q,r,t)

The Booktrader
121 Country Club Road
Rocky Mount, NC 27801
PH:919-443-3993 (b,c,e,r)

Bargain Bookstore II
Delwood Road
Waynesville, NC 28786
PH:704-452-2539 (b,c,e,h,r,s)

Heroes Aren't Hard to Find
Silas Creek Crossing Shop. Ctr.
3234 Silas Creek Parkway
Winston-Salem, NC 27103
PH:919-765-4370
(a-c,g,j,k,m,n,q,t,v)

NORTH DAKOTA:

Collector's Corner
306 N. 4th St.
Grand Forks, ND 58203
PH:701-772-2518 (a-c,g,m,n,q-t)

OHIO:

C. C. Books
4651 Whipple Ave. N.W.
Canton, OH 44718
PH:216-492-9606 (b,c,m,q-s)

Comics, Cards & Collectables
533 Market Ave. North
Canton, OH 44702
PH:216-456-8907 (a-c,g,k,m,q-s)

Comic Book World
5526 Colerain Ave.
Cincinnati, OH 45239
PH:513-541-8002 (a-c,m,o,q-v)

Collectors Warehouse Inc.
5437 Pearl Road
Cleveland, OH 44129
PH:216-842-2896 (a-i,m-o,q-t)

Bookie Parlor
2920 Wayne Avenue
Dayton, OH 45420
PH:513-256-6806 (a-c,q,r)

Troll and Unicorn Comics and Games
5460 Brandt Pike
Huber Heights, OH 45424
PH:513-233-6535
(a-e,g,i,k,m-o,q-v)

Bigg Fredd's Coins & Collectables
162 West Main St.
(1 Block E. of US 33 on US 22)
Lancaster, OH 43130
PH:614-653-5555 (a-c,e-g,k-n,q-u)

Comic Book City
2601 Hubbard Road
Madison, OH 44057
PH:216-428-4786 (b,c,m,q,s)

L. A. Comics & Collectibles
6672 Pearl Rd.
Parma Heights, OH 44130
PH:216-884-0666
(b-d,f,g,i,m,n,q,r)

Toy Scouts, Inc. (Mail Order)
P. O. Box 268
Seville, OH 44273
PH:216-769-2523 (a,b,i,k,m,p,t)

Monarch Cards & Comics
2620 Airport Hwy.
Toledo, OH 43609
PH:419-382-1451 (b,c,m,q,r)

Funnie Farm Bookstore
328 N. Dixie Drive
Airline Shopping Center
Vandalia, OH 45377
PH:513-898-2794 (a-c,e,m,q-t)

Dark Star Books
231 Xenia Ave.
Yellow Springs, OH 45387
PH:513-767-9400 (a-c,e-h,m,n,q-v)

OKLAHOMA:

Comic Archives
1914 E. Second Street
Edmond, OK 73034
PH:405-348-6800 (a-e,g-i,l,n,q-u)

Comic Archives
Heismen Sq., 1221 E. Alameda
(in Bargain Time Store)
Norman, OK 73071
PH:405-360-6866 (a-e,g-i,l,n,q-u)

Planet Comics & SF
918 W. Main
Norman, OK 73069
PH:405-329-9695
(a-c,e,f,i,m-o,q-v)

New World
6219 N. Meridian Avenue
Oklahoma City, OK 73112
PH:405-721-7634 (a-j,m,n,q-v)

New World
4420 S.E. 44th St.
Oklahoma City, OK 73135
PH:405-677-2559 (a-j,m,n,q-v)

Planet Comics & SF
2112 S.W. 74th
Oklahoma City, OK 73159
PH:405-682-9144 (a-c,e,m-o,q-v)

Comic Empire of Tulsa
3122 S. Mingo Rd.
Tulsa, OK 74146
PH:918-664-5808 (a-d,f,n,q,r,t,u)

Comics, Cards & Collectibles
4618 East 31st Street
Tulsa, OK 74135
PH:918-749-8500 (a-v)

Starbase 21
2130 S. Sheridan Rd.
Tulsa, OK 74129
PH:918-838-3388 (a-e,g-k,m,o-v)

Want List Comics
Box 701932 (appointment only)
Tulsa, OK 74170-1932
PH:918-299-0440 (a-c,f,g,i-m,o-q)

OREGON:

Comic Cave
100 Will Dodge Way
Ashland, OR 97520
PH:503-488-3901 (c,r,s)

Pegasus Books
4390 S.W. Lloyd
Beaverton, OR 97005
PH:503-643-4222 (a-c,e,m,q-v)

Emerald City Comics
770 E. 13th
Eugene, OR 97401
PH:503-345-2568 (a-c,i,j,n,o,q-t)

Nostalgia Collectibles
527 Williamette St.
Eugene, OR 97401
PH:503-484-9202 (a-n,p-r)

House of Fantasy
2005 E. Burnside
P. O. Box 472
Gresham, OR 97030
PH:503-661-1815 (a,c,m,q,s,u)

Nelscott Books
3412 S.E. Hwy. 101
Lincoln City, OR 97367
PH:503-994-3513 (a,b,d-f,h)

More Fun
413 E. Main
Medford, OR 97501
PH:503-776-1200 (b,c,n,r)

The Comic Shop
(Mail Order Service)
P.O. Box 22081
Milwaukie, OR 97222
(a-c,m,q-v)

It Came From Outer Space
10812 S.E. Oak St.
Milwaukie, OR 97222
PH:503-786-0865 (a-c,e,m,q-v)

Pegasus Books & Video
10902 S.E. Main St.
Milwaukie, OR 97222
PH:503-652-2752 (a-c,e,m,o,q-v)

Armchair "Family" Bookstore
3205 S.E. Milwaukie Ave.
Portland, OR 97202
PH:503-238-6680 (a-h,n,o,s)

Future Dreams - Burnside
1800 East Burnside
Portland, OR 97214
PH:503-231-8311
(a-e,g,i,j,n,o,q,r,t-v)

Future Dreams - Gateway
10508 N.E. Halsey
Portland, OR 97220
PH:503-255-5245
(b,c,e,g,n,q,r,t-v)

**Future Dreams Comic Art
Reading Library**
10506 N.E. Halsey
Portland, OR 97220
PH:503-256-1885
(over 14,000 to read free)

Pegasus Books & Video
1401 S.E. Division
Portland, OR 97214
PH:503-233-0768 (a-c,e,m,o,q-v)

Pegasus Books
5015 N.E. Sandy Blvd.
Portland, OR 97213
PH:503-284-4693 (a-c,e,m,q-v)

Rackafratz Comics & Cards
3760 Market
Salem, OR 97301
PH:503-371-1320
(a-c,e,g,m,q,r,t,u)

PENNSYLVANIA:

Cap's Comic Cavalcade
1980 Catasauqua Rd.
Allentown, PA 18103
PH:215-264-5540 (a-c,g,k,m-v)

Dreamscape Comics
404 West Broad St.
Bethlehem, PA 18018
PH:215-867-1178 (a-c,e,m,n,q-s)

Dreamscape Comics
9 East Third St.
Bethlehem, PA 18015
PH:215-865-4636 (a-c,e,m,n,q-s)

Showcase Comics
839 W. Lancaster Ave.
Bryn Mawr, PA 19010
PH:215-527-6236 (a-e,r,s)

Comic Universe
Bazaar of All Nations, Store 228
Clifton Heights, PA 19018
PH:215-259-9943 (a-f,m,n,q-u)

**Mr. Monster's Comic Crypt &
House of Horrors**
1805 Washington Blvd.
Easton, PA 18042
PH:215-250-0659 (c,e,g,i,m,o,q-t)

Comic Universe
446 MacDade Blvd.
Folsom, PA 19033
PH:215-461-7960 (a-f,m,n,q-u)

Comic Universe
395 Lancaster Avenue
Frazer, PA 19355
PH:215-889-3320 (a-f,m,n,q-u)

Golden Unicorn Comics
860 Alter St.
Hazleton, PA 18201
PH:717-455-4645 (b,c,n,q-s)

Ott's Trading Post
201 Allegheny Street
Hollidaysburg, PA 16648
PH:814-696-3494 (a-d,f,g,l,r)

Charlie's Collectors Corner
100-D West Second St.
Hummelstown, PA 17036
PH:717-566-7216 (b,c,m,r)

**Captain Blue Hen Comics,
Cards & Games**
1800 Lincoln Hwy. East
Lancaster, PA 17602
PH:717-397-8011 (a-c,e-g,i,o,q-v)

The Comic Store
Station Square
28 McGovern Ave.
Lancaster, PA 17602
PH:717-397-8737
(a-c,e,g,j,m,n,q-v)

Steve's Comic Relief
4153 Woerner Ave.
Near 5 Points
Levittown, PA 19057
PH:215-945-7954 (a-c,j,n,q-v)

**Chris Bass t/a
Japanimation Super Store**
3407 Kensington Ave.
Philadelphia, PA 19134
PH:215-634-5167 (c,g,i-l,o,q,t-v)

Fat Jack's Comicrypt I
2006 Sansom Street
Philadelphia, PA 19103
PH:215-963-0788
(a-c,e,g,n,q,r,u,v)

Fat Jack's Comicrypt II
7598 Haverford Ave.
Philadelphia, PA 19151
PH:215-473-6333 (b,c,g,n,q,r)

Fat Jack's Comicrypt III
5736 North 5th Street
Philadelphia, PA 19120
PH:215-924-8210 (b,c,g,q,r,t,u)

Sparkle City Comics
Philadelphia, PA
(Philly area by appointment)
PH:609-881-1174 (a,b,d,f)

Adventures in Comics
1368 Illinois Avenue
Pittsburgh, PA 15216
PH:412-531-5644 (a-c,k,q-u)

BEM: The Store
622 South Ave.
Pittsburgh, PA 15221
PH:412-243-2736 (a-h,j,q,r)

Eide's Comics and Records
940 Penn Ave.
Pittsburgh, PA 15222
PH:412-261-3666 (a-r,t-v)

Eide's Comics and Records
2713 Murray Avenue
Pittsburgh, PA 15217
PH:412-422-4666 (a-d,f-r,t-v)

Book Swap
110 South Fraser St.
State College, PA 16801
PH:814-234-6005 (a-c,e,g,h,k,q-v)

The Comic Store - West
Northwest Plaza
915 Loucks Road
York, PA 17404 (b,c,m,n,q-v)

RHODE ISLAND:

The Annex
314 Broadway
Newport, RI 02840
PH:401-847-4607 (a-c,g,m,r)

Starship Excalibur
60 Washington St.
Providence, RI 02903
PH:401-273-8390 (a-c,e,g,m-o,q-v)

Starship Excalibur
834 Hope St.
Providence, RI 02906
PH:401-861-1177 (a-c,g,m-o,q-v)

Superhero Universe II
187 Angell Street
Providence, RI 02906
PH:401-331-5637 (a-c,e-v)

Starship Excalibur
830-832 Post Rd., Warwick Plaza
Warwick, RI 02888
PH:401-941-8890 (a-c,e,g,m-o,q-v)

SOUTH CAROLINA:

Super Giant Comics & Records
Market Place/Cinema Center
3466 Clemson Blvd.
Anderson, SC 29621
PH:803-225-9024 (a-c,e,j,l,q,r)

Silver City
904 Knox Abbott Drive
Cayce, SC 29033
PH:803-791-4021 (a-e,q-t)

Book Exchange
1219 Savannah Hwy.
Charleston, SC 29407
PH:803-556-5051 (a-c,e,g,r)

Final Frontier Comics & Games
1670 Olde Towne Road
Charleston, SC 29407
PH:803-766-9504 (a-c,g,l,k,o,q-t,v)

New Dimension Comics
1930 Main St.
Columbia, SC 29201
PH:803-779-4376 (a-c,g,i,q-v)

Heroes Aren't Hard to Find
1415-A Laurens Rd.
Greenville, SC 29607
PH:803-235-3488 (a-c,g,j,k,m,n,q-t,v)

New Dimension Comics
1608 Laurens Road
Greenville, SC 29607
PH:803-271-1104 (a-c,g,i,q-v)

Haven for Heroes
1131 Dick Pond Rd.
Myrtle Beach, SC 29575
PH:803-238-9975 (a-c,e,m,q,r)

Super Giant Comics
Suite 24 - 660 Spartan Blvd.
Spartanburg, SC 29301
PH:803-576-4990 (a-c,j,q,r)

TENNESSEE:

Comics and Curios #1
3472 Brainerd Rd.
Chattanooga, TN 37411
PH:615-698-1710 (a-c,m,n,q,r-v)

Comics and Curios #2
629 Signal Mountain Rd.
Chattanooga, TN
(a-c,m,q,r-v)

Collector's Choice
3405 Keith St., Shoney's Plaza
Cleveland, TN 37311
PH:615-472-6649 (c,i,m,q-t)

Big D's Baseball Cards & Comics
323 N. Washington Ave.
Cookeville, TN 38501
PH:615-528-6070 (c,m,o,q-s)

Marnello's Comics & Cards
451 E. Elk Avenue
Elizabethton, TN 37643
PH:615-542-6564 (b,c,e,m,q,r)

Gotham City Comics
7869 Farmington Blvd.
Germantown, TN 38138
PH:901-757-9665
(b,c,e,g,k,m,n,q-s)

Comics and Curios #3
5131-B Hixson Pike
Hixson, TN
(a-c,m,q,r-v)

Mountain Empire Collectibles III
1210 N. Roan St.
Johnson City, TN 37602
PH:615-929-8245 (a-c,e,h,i,m,q-t)

Mountain Empire Collectibles II
1451 E. Center St.
Kingsport, TN 37664
PH:615-245-0364 (a-c,e,h,i,m,q-t)

Collector's Choice
2104 Cumberland Ave.
Knoxville, TN 37916
PH:615-546-2665 (c,i,m,q-t)

Comics and Collectibles
4750 Poplar Ave.
Memphis, TN 38117
PH:901-683-7171 (a-e,g,n,q-s)

Memphis Comics & Records
665 So. Highland
Memphis, TN 38111
PH:901-452-1304 (a-v)

Collector's World
1511 East Main St.
Murfreesboro, TN 37130
PH:615-895-1120 (a-c,i,j,l,m,q-v)

Collector's World
5751 Nolensville Rd.
Nashville, TN 37211
PH:615-333-9458 (a-c,f,i,j,m,q-v)

Walt's Paperback Books
2604 Franklin Rd.
Nashville, TN 37204
PH:615-298-2506 (b,c,e,m,o,r)

TEXAS:

Lone Star Comics Books & Games
511 East Abram Street
Arlington, TX 76010
PH:817-Metro 265-0491
(a-c,e,g,h,m,q-s)

Lone Star Comics Books & Games
5721 W. I-20 at Green Oaks Blvd.
Arlington, TX 76016
PH:817-478-5405 (b,c,e,g,h,m,q-s)

Dollar Video
813 Conrad Hilton Ave.
Cisco, TX 76437
PH:817-442-1998 (b,c,i,m-o,q,r)

Lone Star Comics Books & Games
11661 Preston Forest Village
Dallas, TX 75230
PH:214-373-0934 (a-c,e,h,m,n,q-s)

Remember When
2431 Valwood Parkway
Dallas, TX 75234
PH:214-243-3439
(a-c,g,i,j,m,q,r,t,u)

Lone Star Comics Books & Games
3014 West 7th St.
Fort Worth, TX 76107
PH:817-654-0333 (a-c,e,g,h,m,q-s)

B & D Trophy Shop
4404 N. Shepherd
Houston, TX 77018
PH:713-694-8436 (a-c,i,r)

Nan's Games and Comics, Too!
2011 Southwest Freeway (US 59)
Houston, TX 77098-4805
PH:713-520-8700 (a-c,e,g,m-o,q-v)

Third Planet Books
2439 Bissonnet
Houston, TX 77005
PH:713-528-1067 (a-v)

Third Planet Books
3806 S. Shaver
Houston, TX 77587
PH:713-941-1490 (a-v)

Lone Star Comics Books & Games
2550 N. Beltline Road
Irving, TX 75062
PH:214-659-0317 (a-c,e,g,h,m,q-s)

Alan's
2525-B Judson Rd.
Longview, TX 75601
PH:214-753-0493 (a-c,m,q-v)

Lone Star Comics Books & Games
3600 Gus Thomasson, Suite 107
Mesquite, TX 75150
PH:214-681-2040 (b,c,e,m,q-s)

Comics & Records Unlimited
226 Bitters Rd., Suite 102
San Antonio, TX 78216
PH:512-545-9063 (a-c,e,g,i,k-o,q-t)

Comics & Records Unlimited
6856 Ingram Rd.
San Antonio, TX 78238
PH:512-522-9063 (a-c,e-g,i-r,t)

The Book Cellar
2 S. Main St.
Temple, TX 76501
PH:817-773-7545 (a-c,e,h,q,r)

Excalibur Comics, Cards & Games
2811 State Line Ave.
Texarkana, TX 75503
PH:214-792-5767 (a-d,f,g,i,k,m-v)

Bankston's Comics
1321 S. Valley Mills Dr.
Waco, TX 76711
PH:817-755-0070 (a-c,e,g,h,m,q)

UTAH:

The Bookshelf
2456 Washington Blvd.
Ogden, UT 84401
PH:801-621-4752 (b-e,g,h,l,q-v)

Comics Utah
1956 S. 1100 East
Salt Lake City, UT 84105
PH:801-487-5390 (b,c,e,n,q-u)

Comics Utah
2985 W. 3500 South
Salt Lake City, UT 84119
PH:801-966-8581 (b,c,e,n,q-u)

VERMONT:

Comics Outpost
27 Granite St.
Barre, VT 05641
PH:802-476-4553 (a-c,q-t)

Comics City, Inc.
6 No. Winooski Ave.
Burlington, VT 05401
PH:802-865-3828 (b,c,e,m,n,q-v)

Earth Prime Comics
154 Church St.
Burlington, VT 05401
PH:802-863-3666 (a-c,e,f,m,n,q-s)

VIRGINIA:

Capital Comics Center
Storyland, U.S.A.
2008 Mt. Vernon Ave.
Alexandria, VA 22301 (D.C. area)
PH:703-548-3466 (a-c,e,f,m-o,q-u)

Geppi's Crystal City Comics
1675 Crystal Square Arcade
Arlington, VA 22202
PH:703-521-4618 (a-c,f)

Mountain Empire Collectibles I
509 State Street
Bristol, VA 24201
PH:703-466-6337 (a-c,e,h,i,m,q-t)

Burke Centre Books
5741 Burke Centre Pkwy.
Burke, VA 22015
PH:703-250-5114 (b-h,m,q-v)

Fantasia Comics and Records
1419½ University Ave.
Charlottesville, VA 22903
PH:804-971-1029 (b,c,i,l,n,q-v)

Fantasia Comics and Records II
1861 Seminole Trail
Charlottesville, VA 22901
PH:804-974-7512 (b,c,k,l,n,q-v)

Trilogy Shop #3
3580-F Forest Haven Ln.
Chesapeake, VA 23321
PH:804-483-4173 (b,c,m,o,q-v)

Zeno's Books
1112 Sparrow Road
Chesapeake, VA 23225
PH:804-420-2344 (a-j,m-o,q,r)

Hole in the Wall Books
905 West Broad St.
Falls Church, VA 22046
PH:703-536-2511
(b,c,e,g-i,n,o,q-v)

Marie's Books and Things
1701 Princess Anne St.
Fredericksburg, VA 22401
PH:703-373-5196 (a-c,e,h,l,r)

Bender's Books & Cards
22 South Mallory St.
Hampton, VA 23663
PH:804-723-3741 (a-i,m-v)

Franklin Farm Books
13320-I Franklin Farm Rd.
Herndon, VA 22071
PH:703-437-9530 (b-h,m,q-v)

Trilogy Shop #2
700 E. Little Creek Rd.
Norfolk, VA 23518
PH:804-587-2540 (b,c,m,o,q-v)

Ward's Comics
3405 Clifford St.
Portsmouth, VA 23707
PH:804-397-7106 (b,c,q-s)

Dave's Comics
7019-E Three Chopt Rd.
Richmond, VA 23226
PH:804-282-1211 (b,c,m,q-u)

Nostalgia Plus
5610 Patterson Ave.
Richmond, VA 23221
PH:804-282-5532 (a-c,g,k,n,q,r)

B & D Comic Shop
3514 Williamson Rd. N.W.
Roanoke, VA 24012
PH:703-563-4161 (b,c,e,g,m-o,q-v)

Trilogy Shop #1
5773 Princess Anne Rd.
Virginia Beach, VA 23462
PH:804-490-2205 (a-c,m,o,q-v)

Trilogy Shop #4
867 S. Lynnhaven Rd.
Virginia Beach, VA 23452
PH:804-468-0412 (b,c,m,o,q-v)

Zeno's Books
338 Constitution Dr.
Virginia Beach, VA 23462
PH:804-490-1517 (a-j,m-o,q,r)

WASHINGTON:

Psycho 5 Comics & Cards
221 Bellevue Way N.E.
Bellevue, WA 98004
PH:206-462-2869 (a-c,m,q,r)

Paperback Exchange
2100 N. National Ave.
Chehalis, WA 98532
PH:206-748-4792

Geepy's Comics
618 Bridge
Clarkston, WA 99403
No Phone (a,b,g,k,m,r,t)

Everett Comics & Cards
2934½ Colby Ave.
Everett, WA 98201
PH:206-252-8181 (a-c,k,m,n,q-u)

Tales of Kirkland
128-A Park Lane
Kirkland, WA 98033
PH:206-822-7333
(a-c,e,h,j,m,n,q-v)

Olympic Card & Comic Shop
321 S. Sound Center
Lacey, WA 98503
PH:206-459-7721

Coin House
777 Stevens Dr.
Richland, WA 99352
(a-d,f,l,m,q,r,t)

The Comic Character Shop
Old Firehouse Antique Mall
110 Alaskan Way South
Seattle, WA 98104
PH:206-283-0532 (a,b,h,j,k,q)

Corner Comics
6521 N.E. 181st
Seattle, WA 98155
PH:206-486-XMEN (a-c,e,m,n,q-s)

Corner Comics II
5226 University Way N.E.
Seattle, WA 98105
PH:206-525-9394 (b,c,n,q,r)

Gemini Book Exchange and
Comic Center
9614 - 16th Ave. S.W.
Seattle, WA 98106
PH:206-762-5543 (b,c,e,g,m,n,q,r)

Golden Age Collectables, Ltd.
1501 Pike Place Market
401 Lower Level
Seattle, WA 98101
PH:206-622-9799 (a-g,i-k,m-o,q-v)

Psycho 5 Comics & Cards
12513 Lake City Way N.E.
Seattle, WA 98125
PH:206-367-1620 (a-c,m,q,r)

Rocket Comics & Collectibles
119 N. 85th
Seattle, WA 98103
PH:206-784-7300 (a-d,j,m,n,q,r)

Zanadu Comics
1923 3rd Ave.
Seattle, WA 98101
PH:206-443-1316
(a-c,e-h,j,m-o,q-v)

Zanadu Comics
4518 University Way N.E.
2nd Floor Arcade Bldg.
Seattle, WA 98105
PH:206-632-0989
(b,c,e-h,j,m-o,q-v)

The Book Exchange
K-Mart Center, N. 6504 Division
Spokane, WA 99208
PH:509-489-2053 (a-c,e-h,n,q-s)

The Book Exchange
University City East
E. 10812 Sprague
Spokane, WA 99206
PH:509-928-4073 (a-c,e-h,n,q-s)

Lady Jayne's Comics & Books
6611 S. 12th
Tacoma, WA 98465
PH:206-564-6168 (c,e,q-u)

Pegasus Books
813 Grand Blvd.
Vancouver, WA 98661
PH:206-693-1240 (a-c,e,m,q-s,v)

Galaxy Comics
1720 - 5th St., Suite D
Wenatchee, WA 98801
PH:509-663-4330 (b,c,g,q-t)

WEST VIRGINIA:

Downtown Baseball Cards
415 Neville St.
(Mail: 117 Monroe Ave.)
Beckley, WV 25801
PH:304-252-2134 (b,c,m,r)

Cheryl's Comics & Toys
5216½ MacCorkle Ave. S.E.
Charleston, WV 25304
PH:304-925-7269 (a-c,g,i,k,q-u)

Comic World
613 West Lee St.
Charleston, WV 25302
PH:304-343-3874 (a-c,g,k,m,q,r,t)

Comic World
1204 - 4th Avenue
Huntington, WV 25701
PH:304-522-3923 (a-c,g,k,m,q,r,t)

Books and Things
2506 Pike Street
Parkersburg, WV 26101
PH:304-422-0666 (a-c,e,o,q-u)

Triple Play Cards, Comics & Collectibles
335 - 4th Avenue
South Charleston, WV 25303
PH:304-744-2602 (a-c,g,h,m,q,r)

WISCONSIN:

Cover To Cover
511 South Barstow St.
Eau Claire, WI 54701
PH:715-832-4252 (a-c,n,q,r)

River City Cards & Comics
115 South 6th Street
La Crosse, WI 54601
PH:608-782-5540 (a-c,i,m,q-s)

Capital City Comics
1910 Monroe St.
Madison, WI 53711
PH:608-251-8445 (a-c,f,n,q,r,v)

20th Century Books
108 King Street
Madison, WI 53703
PH:608-251-6226
(b-e,g,h,m,n,q-v)

Incredible Comics
4429 W. Lisbon Ave.
Milwaukee, WI 53208
PH:414-445-7006, 786-0112
(a-h,o)

Polaris Comics
4935 W. Center St.
Milwaukee, WI 53210
PH:414-442-0494 (a-c,n,q-s)

CANADA:

ALBERTA:

Another Dimension
324 - 10 Street N.W.
Calgary, Alberta, Can. T2N 1V8
PH:403-283-7078 (b,c,q-t)

Another Dimension
#1 - 3616 - 52 Ave. N.W.
Calgary, Alberta, Can. T2L 1V9
PH:403-282-7120 (b,c,q-t)

Another Dimension
2108B - 33 Ave. S.W.
Calgary, Alberta, Can. T2T 1Z6
PH:403-246-6768 (b,c,q-t)

Another Dimension
7610 Elbow Drive S.W.
Calgary, Alberta, Can. T2V 1K2
PH:403-255-2588 (b,c,q-t)

Comic Legends - Head Office
#205, 908 17th Ave. S.W.
Calgary, Alberta, Can. T2T 0A3
PH:403-245-5884
(a-c,g,m,n,q,r,t,u)

Comic Legends
#8, 10015 Oakfield Dr. S.W.
Calgary, Alberta, Can.
PH:403-251-5964
(a-c,g,m,n,q,r,t,u)

BRITISH COLUMBIA:

L.A. Comics & Books
371 Victoria St.
Kamloops, B.C., Can. V2C 2A3
PH:604-828-1995 (c,e,l-n,q-t)

Page After Page
1763 Harvey Ave.
Kelowna, B.C., Can. V1Y 6G4
PH:604-860-6554 (a,c,e,h,q,r)

Ted's Paperback & Comics
269 Leon Ave.
Kelowna, B.C., Can. V1Y 6J1
PH:604-763-1258 (b,c,e)

Island Fantasy
#29 Market Square
560 Johnson St.
Victoria, B.C., Can. V8W 3C6
PH:604-381-1134 (a-c,f,g,j,n,q-s,v)

MANITOBA:

International Comic Book Co.
Calvin Slobodian
859 - 4th Avenue
Rivers, Man., Can. R0K 1X0
PH:204-328-7846 (a-d,f,g,j,r)

Collector's Slave
156 Imperial Avenue
Winnipeg, Man., Can. R2M 0K8
PH:204-237-4428
(a-c,e-g,i,k,l-n,q,r,t,u)

Comic Factory II
380 Donald St.
Winnipeg, Man., Can. R3B 2J2
PH:204-957-1978 (a-c,g,j,n,q,r,t)

Doug Sulipa's Comic World
374 Donald St.
Winnipeg, Man., Can. R3B 2J2
PH:204-943-3642

NEW BRUNSWICK:

1,000,000 Comix, Inc.
345 Mountain Rd.
Moncton, N.B., Can. E1C 2M4
PH:506-855-0056
(a-d,f-h,j,m,n,p-v)

NOVA SCOTIA:

Members Only Comic Service
(Mail Order Service Only)
6257 Yale St.
Halifax, N.S., Can. B3L 1C9
PH:902-423-MOCS/FAX 423-6627
(c-e,i,j,o,q-v)

1,000,000 Comix, Inc.
6251 Quinpool Rd.
Halifax, N.S., Can. B3L 1A4
PH:902-425-5594
(a-d,f-h,j,m,n,p-v)

ONTARIO:

1,000,000 Comix, Inc.
2400 Guelph Line
Burlington, Ont., Can. L7P 4M7
PH:416-332-5600
(a-d,f-h,j,m,n,p-v)

Starlite Comics and Books
132 Westminster Drive South
Cambridge (Preston),
Ont., Can. N3H 1S8
PH:519-653-6571 (a-h,q,r,t,u)

Comic King
26 King St.
Dryden, Ont., Can.
PH:807-223-3254 (a-c,m,s)

D. Farrell (by appointment only)
2 Dalston Road
Etobicoke, Toronto, Ont., Can.
M8W 4R3
PH:416-251-1659 (a-g,i,j,m,n,q-s)

Lookin' For Heroes
93 Ontario St. S.
Kitchener, Ont., Can. N2G 1W5
PH:519-570-0873 (a-c,m,n,q,r)

Books 'N' Stuff
104 William St. N.
Lindsay, Ont., Can. K9V 4A5
PH:705-328-3491 (a-c,e,g,h,m,q-s)

Bid Time Return
183 Dundas St.
London, Ont., Can. N6A 1G4
PH:519-679-0295
(a-c,e,g,i,m-o,q-v)

Endless Adventure
400 Richmond St.
London, Ont., Can. N6A 3C7
PH:519-660-8521 (o,s-v)

Endless Adventure
White Oaks Mall
1105 Wellington Rd.
London, Ont., Can. N6E 1V4
PH:519-649-4572 (c,i,o,s-v)

1,000,000 Comix, Inc.
2150 Burnhamthorpe Rd.
South Common Mall
Mississauga, Ont., Can. L5L 3A2
PH:416-828-8208
(a-d,f-h,j,m,n,p-v)

Comic King
705 Victoria Ave. East
Victoriaville Mall
Thunder Bay, Ont., Can.
PH:807-623-6499 (a-c,m,s)

Queen's Comics
1009 Kingston Rd.
Toronto, Ont., Can. M4E 1T3
PH:416-698-8757 (c,m,p-s)

Ken Mitchell Comics
(by appointment only)
710 Conacher Drive
Willowdale, Ont., Can. M2M 3N6
PH:416-222-5808 (a,b,f,g)

QUEBEC:

Capitaine Quebec - Dollard
4305 Blvd. St. Jean
D.D.O., Que., Can. H9H 2A4
PH:514-620-1866 (a-c,e,g,m-o,q-v)

Capitaine Quebec - Snowdon
5108 Decarie
Montreal, Que., Can. H3X 2H9
PH:514-487-0970 (a-c,e,g,m-o,q-v)

Capitaine Quebec - Centre-Ville
1837 St. Catherine O.
Montreal, Que., Can. H3H 1M2
PH:514-939-9970 (a-c,e,g,m-o,q-v)

Cosmix
11819 Laurentien Blvd.
Montreal, Que., Can. H4J 2M1
PH:514-337-6183 (a-c,e,n,o,q-t,v)

Komico Inc.
4210 Decarie
Montreal, Que., Can. H4A 3K3
PH:514-489-4009 (a-c,j,o,q,r)

Multinational Comics/Cards
8918A Lajeunesse
Montreal, Que., Can. H2M 1R9
PH: 514-385-6273
(a-c,g,k,m,o,q,r,t)

1,000,000 Comix, Inc.
Corporate Headquarters
6290 Somerled
Montreal, Que., Can. H3X 2B6
PH:514-486-1175
(a-d,f-h,j,m,n,p-v)

1,000,000 Comix, Inc.
372 Sherbrooke St. West
Montreal, Que., Can.
PH:514-844-9313
(a-d,f-h,j,m,n,p-v)

1,000,000 Comix, Inc.
1260 Dollard St., LaSalle
Montreal, Que., Can. H8N 2P2
PH:514-366-1233
(a-d,f-h,j,m,n,p-v)

1,000,000 Comix, Inc.
1539 Van Horne
Montreal, Que., Can.
PH:514-277-5788
(a-d,f-h,j,m,n,p-v)

1,000,000 Comix, Inc.
3846 Jean-Talon
Montreal, Que., Can.
PH:514-725-1355
(a-d,f-h,j,m,n,p-v)

Comix Plus (1,000,000 affil.)
1475 McDonald
St. Laurent, Que., Can.
PH:514-334-0732
(a-d,f-h,j,m,n,p-v)

Capitaine Quebec - Verdun
4422 Wellington
Verdun, Que., Can. H4G 1W5
PH:514-768-1351 (a-c,e,g,m-o,q-v)

Premiere Issue
27 "A" D'Autevil
(Vieux Quebec), Quebec City,
Que., Can. G1R 4B9
PH:418-692-3985 (a-c,e,g,i,q-v)

AUSTRALIA

Nostalgia Old Comic Shop
48 Balmoral Rd.
Mortdale, NSW 2223, Australia
PH: (02) 57-5332 (a,b)

ENGLAND

Stateside Comics
(By Appointment)
P. O. Box 1108
London N11 1RW, England
PH:London 449 5535 & London
368 1837 (a-c,q,r)

DIRECTORY OF ADVERTISERS (Cl = Classified, c = color)

DIRECTORY OF ADVERTISERS (continued)

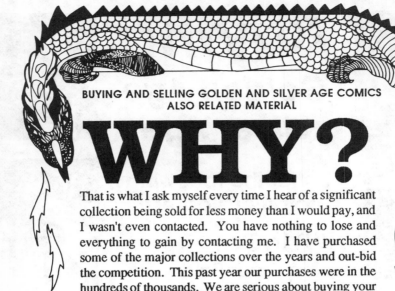

BUYING AND SELLING GOLDEN AND SILVER AGE COMICS
ALSO RELATED MATERIAL

WHY?

That is what I ask myself every time I hear of a significant collection being sold for less money than I would pay, and I wasn't even contacted. You have nothing to lose and everything to gain by contacting me. I have purchased some of the major collections over the years and out-bid the competition. This past year our purchases were in the hundreds of thousands. We are serious about buying your comics and paying you the most for them.

If you have comics or related items for sale please call or send a list for my quote. Or if you would like, just send me your comics and figure them by the percentages below. If your grading is by Overstreets standards you can expect the percentages paid by grade. Before I send any checks I will call to verify your satisfaction with the price. If we cannot reach a price we are both happy and I will ship your books back at my expense that day. Remember, no collection is too large or small, even if it's one hundred thousand or more.

These are some of the high prices I will pay for comics I need. Percentages stated will be paid for any grade unless otherwise stated. Percentages should be based on this guide.

– JAMES F. PAYETTE

Action (1-225)	70%	Detective (#27 Mint)	80%
Action (#1 Mint)	95%	Green Lantern (#1 Mint)	85%
Adventure (247)	75%	Jackie Gleason (1-12)	70%
All American (16 & 17)	75%	Keen Detective Funnies	70%
All Star (3 & 8)	70%	Ken Maynard	70%
Amazing Man	70%	More Fun (7-51)	70%
Amazing Mystery Funnies	70%	New Adventure (12-31)	70%
The Arrow	70%	New Comics (1-11)	70%
Batman (1-125)	70%	New Fun (1-6)	70%
Batman (#1 Mint)	85%	Sunset Carson	70%
Bob Steele	70%	Superman (#1 Mint)	95%
Captain Marvel (#1)	70%	Whip Wilson	70%
Detective (1-225)	70%		

We are paying 65% of guide for the following:

Andy Devine	Funny Picture Stories	Smiley Burnette
Congo Bill	Green Lantern (1st)	Start & Stripes
Detective Eye	Hangman	Tales of the Unexpected
Detec. Picture Stories	Hoot Gibson	Tim McCoy
Funny Pages	Jumbo (1-10)	Wonder Comics (Fox-1&2)

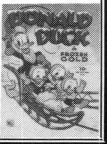

COMIC BOOKS WANTED

The following prices represent a small sample of the prices that we will pay for your comic books. Other dealers say that they will pay top dollar, but when it really comes down to it, they simply do not. If you have comics to sell, we invite you to contact every comic dealer in the country to get their offers. Then come to us to get your best offer. **Metropolis Comics** is not a store. We are a Golden and Silver Age mail-order comic company. If you are looking to buy or sell a copy of Spiderman #129, look elsewhere. We can afford to pay the highest price for your Golden and Silver Age comics because that is all we sell. If you wish to sell us your comic books, please either ship us the books securely via Registered U.S. Mail or UPS. However, if your collection is too large to ship, kindly send us a detailed list of what you have and we well travel directly to you. The prices below are for Mint copies, however, we are interested in **all** grades. Thank You.

Action #1	$61,000
Action #242	$750
Adventure #40	$5,100
Adventure #48	$4,200
Adventure #61	$2,500
Adventure #210	$875
All-American #16	$13,000
All-American #19	$2,100
All-Star #3	$8,000
Amazing Fantasy #15	$5,000
Amaz.Spiderman #1	$4,200
Amaz.Spiderman #6	$600
Arrow #1	$1,000
Atom #1	$275
Batman #1	$19,000
Brave & the Bold #28	$1,600
Brave & the Bold #34	$300
Captain America #1	$10,000
Classic Comics #1	$2,900
Detective #1	$25,000
Detective #27	$65,000
Detective #35	$3,200
Detective #38	$10,000
Detective #40	$2,300
Detective #168	$1,600
Detective #225	$2,000
Detec.Picture Stories #1	$1,500
Donald Duck #9	$2,300
Famous Funnies #1	$4,500

Famous Funnies Series #1. paying $9,000 for Very Fine copy!!!

Fantastic Four #1	$5,000
Fantastic Four #4	$700
Fantastic Four #5	$600
Flash #105	$1,600
Flash #110	$300
Flash Comics #1	$8,000
Funnies On Parade	$3,100
Funny Pages 2#10	$1,500
Green Hornet #1	$1,000
Green Lantern #1(GA)	$4,100
Green Lantern #1 (SA)	$1,500
Human Torch #2(#1)	$3,700
Incredible Hulk #1	$1,400
Journey into Myst. #83	$1,500
Justice League #1	$1,400
Jumbo Comics #1	$6,800
March of Comics #4	$2,100
Marvel Comics #1	$25,000
More Fun #52	$12,000
More Fun #53	$8,000
More Fun #54	$3,100
More Fun #55	$3,200
More Fun #73	$3,000
More Fun #101	$2,200
New Comics #1	$5,000
New Fun #1	$24,000
NY World's Fair '39	$3,000

New Fun #2	$8,000
New Fun #6	$6,000
Planet Comics #15	$1,000
Real Fact Comics #5	$600
Science Fict. Fanzine	$12,000
Showcase #4	$5,000
Showcase #8	$1,700
Showcase #13	$1,450
Showcase #22	$1,500
Showcase #34	$300
Superboy #1	$2,100
Superman #1	$45,000
Superman #14	$1,400
Suspense Comics #3	$645
Tales of Suspense #1	$340
Tales of Suspense #39	$1,500
Tales to Astonish #27	$1,500
Target Comics V1#7	$1,400
Thing #15	$300
Walt Disney C&S #1	$5,100
Weird Fantasy #13(#1)	$550
Whiz #2 (#1)	$20,000
Wonder Woman #1	$3,000
Wow #1 (1936)	$4,000
Young Allies #1	$1,750
X-Men #1	$1,200

The following is a sample of the books we are purchasing:

Action Comics	#1-300
Adventure Comics	#32-320
All-American Comics	#1-102
All-Flash Quarterly	#1-32
All-Select	#1-11
All-Star Comics	#1-57
All-Winners	#1-21
Amazing Spiderman	#1-50
Amazing Man	#5-26
Amaz. Mystery Funnies	#1-24
Avengers	#1-20
Batman	#1-200
Blackhawk	#9-130
Boy Commandos	#1-32
Brave & the Bold	#1-50
Captain America	#1-78
Captain Marvel Advs.	#1-150
Challengers	#1-25
Classic Comics	#1-169
Comic Cavalcade	#1-63
Daredevil Comics	#1-60
Daredevil (MCG)	#1-15
Daring Mystery	#1-8
Detective Comics	#1-350
Donald Duck 4-Colors	#4-up
Fantastic Four	#1-50
Fight Comics	#1-86
Flash	#105-150
Flash Comics	#1-104
Funny Pages	#6-42
Green Lantern (GA)	#1-32
Green Lantern (SA)	#1-59
Hit Comics	#1-65
Human Torch	#2(#1)-38
Incredible Hulk	#1-6
Journey Into Mystery	#1-125
Jumbo Comics	#1-167
Jungle Comics	#1-163
Justice League	#1-50
Mad	#1-30
Marvel Mystery	#1-92
Military Comics	#1-43
More Fun Comics	#7-127
Mystery in Space	#1-75
Mystic Comics	#1-up
New Adventure	#12-31
New Fun Comics	#1-6
Planet Comics	#1-73
Rangers Comics	#1-69
Sensation Comics	#1-116
Showcase	#1-75
Star-Spangled Comics	#1-130
Strange Tales	#1-145
Sub-Mariner	#1-42
Superboy	#1-110
Superman	#1-175
Tales of Suspense	#1-80
Tales to Astonish	#1-80
USA Comics	#1-17
Wings Comics	#1-124
Whiz Comics	#1-155
Wonder Woman	#1-120
World's Finest	#1-100
X-Men	#1-30

METROPOLIS COMICS

7920-19TH AVENUE
BROOKLYN, NY 11214
(718) 837-2538

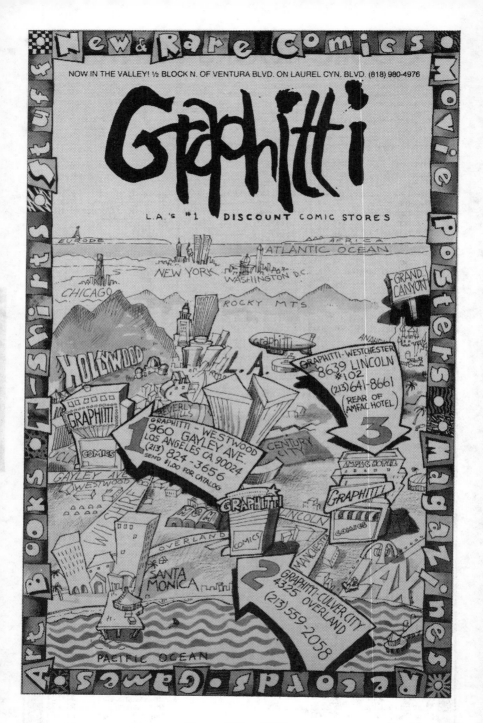

NOTE: ANY BOOKS SENT IN LESS THAN VF SHOULD BE WORTH AT LEAST 3.00 IN THE GRADE THEY ARE IN.

ACTION
51-70 150.00
71-100 115.00,
101-161 100.00
162-201 75.00
202-220 60.00
221-240 45.00
242 225.00
243-251 32.00
252 260.00
253-255 37.00
256-266 15.00
267 130.00
268-275, 277-282 13.00
283-285 18.00
286-290 9.00
291-320 4.00

ADVENTURE
105-120 145.00
121-130 115.00
131-151 100.00
152-209 75.00
210 400.00
211-246 55.00
247 1100.00
248-255, 257-259 32.00
256 120.00
260 75.00
261-266, 268-271 24.00
272-280 17.00
281,284,287-289 14.00
282 45.00
283,285,286,293 23.00
291,292,295-299 12.00
300 135.00
301 45.00
302-305 22.00
306-310 17.00
311-320 14.00
321-340 7.50
341-360 4.00
361-380 2.50

ALL AMERICAN
31-50 165.00

51-70 145.00
71-102 115.00

ALL FLASH
5-10 210.00
11-14 160.00
15-32 125.00

ALL SELECT
3-11 150.00

ALL STAR
9-15,33 600.00
16-24 390.00
25-32 310.00
34-57 235.00

AMAZING SPIDER-MAN
2 425.00
3 270.00
4 235.00
5,6 180.00
7-10,14 130.00
11-13,15 95.00
16-20 55.00
21-30,50 35.00
31-40 22.00
41-49 14.00
51-60 6.00
61-95 4.00
96-98 9.00
100 16.00
101,102 7.00
103-120 2.50
121,122,135 19.00
129 100.00

AQUAMAN
1 80.00   2 29.00
3-5 20.00
6-10 14.00
11-20 7.00
21-20,50-52 4.00

ATOM
1 125.00   2 40.00
3 30.00   4,5 22.00
6-10 16.00
11-15 10.00
21-30 3.50
31-45 2.50

AVENGERS
2,4 170.00   3 115.00
5 70.00   6-10 53.00
11-15 30.00
16-19 22.00
20-30 9.00
31-40 5.00
41-56 3.50
57,58,93,100 12.00
59-92 2.25

BATMAN
6-16 500.00
17-30,47 290.00
31-46 160.00
48-62 140.00
63-89,110 110.00
90-99, 101-109 90.00
111-120 65.00
121-130 50.00
131-145,148 40.00
146,147,149,150 25.00
151-170 20.00
171 100.00
172-187 13.00
188-199,201 8.00
200 65.00
202-219 3.50
222,232,234,237 7.00
235,236,238-242 3.00
243-245 5.00
252-261 3.00 262-300 1.50
301-365,369-399 1.25
366 12.00   368 9.00
400 8.00
401-403, 408-416 1.25
404-407 2.50 417-420 4.00
421-425 1.25 426 18.00

427,428 10.00
429 3.50   430 2.00
431-436 1.00
CULT 1-4 3.50
DARK KNIGHT (1st)
  1 20.00   2 10.00
  3 4.00   4 2.50
KILLING JOKE (1st)
  1 12.00
SON OF THE DEMON
  HARD 26.00
  SOFT (1st) 9.00

BRAVE & BOLD
1 300.00   2 120.00
3-10,23,24 55.00
11-22 40.00
25-27,31-33 15.00
28 850.00
29,30 275.00
34 70.00   35,36 30.00
37-41,50 14.00
42-44 17.00
52,53, 79-86 5.00
54 40.00
57,60 12.00

CAPTAIN AMERICA
(1st)
4-7 550.00
8-10 450.00
11-16 350.00
17-25 225.00
26-40 175.00
41-70 140.00
71-73, 76-78 100.00
  (2nd)
100 70.00
101-111,113 6.00

CAPTAIN MARVEL
6-10 120.00
11-19 75.00
20-35 50.00
36-46 35.00
47-90 22.00
91-150 17.00

CHICAGO
CHICAGO
CHICAGO

MOONDOG'S
MOONDOG'S
MOONDOG'S

Since 1978 Moondog's has been the indisputable, recognized leader in comics retailing in Chicagoland. We sell more new comics, more back issues, more rare high-grade Golden and Silver-Age books, more games, baseball cards, toys, and supplies than any other store in Chicago.

Why?

It's simple. We've got the best service, selection and prices.

If you collect comics seriously or just read them, you owe it to yourself to make Moondog's your comic store. If you live too far away from one of our five conveniently located stores to be a regular weekly customer —no problem—we understand. But you've no excuse not to make it once a month!

Come see why Moondog's Comicland stores are the "Midwest's Finest Shops". We'll be expecting you.

Moondog's
COMICLAND
THE COLLECTOR'S PLACE

139 W. Prospect Ave.
Downtown Mt. Prospect
Mt. Prospect, IL 60056
(708) 398-6060

1231 W. Dundee Rd.
Plaza Verde
Buffalo Grove, IL 60090
(708) 259-6060

1403 W. Schaumburg Rd.
Schaumburg Plaza
Schaumburg, IL 60194
(708) 529-6060

114 S. Waukegan Rd.
Deerbrook Mall
Deerfield, IL 60015
(708) 272-6080

Randhurst Mall
Lower Level
Mt. Prospect, IL 60056
(708) 577-8668

41-93,95-116.....5.00
117-160.........2.50
161-261.........1.50

JUSTICE LEAGUE
(1987) 1,2.......8.00
3,4.............4.00
5-35, up.........1.50

**KAMANDI, LAST BOY
ON EARTH** 1....5.00
2-59............2.00

**KITTY PRYDE &
WOLVERINE**
1-6.............3.00

KORAK (Gold Key)
2-11............6.00
12-45...........3.00

LASSIE
12-69...........5.00

**LEGION OF SUPER-
HEROES** (1973)
1-4.............3.50

**LEGION OF SUPER-
HEROES**
259,285-287.....4.00
260-284.........2.00
288-290,294,300..2.50
291-293,295-299,301-
365, up..........1.50

**LEGION OF SUPER-
HEROES** (1984)
1,37,38,45,50....4.00
2-36,39-44,46-49,51-60,
up..............2.00

LOIS LANE
39-75...........5.00
76-123..........3.50
124-137.........2.50

LONE RANGER (Dell)
44-94...........10.00

MAD (Magazine)
.........please write

MAGIK
1-4............2.00

MARVEL CLASSICS
1-36...........2.00

**MARVEL COMICS
PRESENTS** 1-3...4.00
4-40, up........1.50

MARVEL FANFARE
1,2............6.00
3,4............4.00
5-55, up........2.00

MARVEL PREMIERE
1-4,15,25.......5.00
5-14,16-24......4.00
26-61...........1.50

MARVEL PRESENTS
(1975) 1-12.....2.00

MARVEL SAGA
1-35, up........1.50

MARVEL SPOTLIGHT
(1971-77)
1-4,6-11,28,29...4.50
5..............9.00
12-27,30-33.....2.00

**MARVEL SUPER-
HEROES** (1967)
13,14..........6.00
15-31..........3.00

MARVEL TALES
3-10...........5.00
11-33..........4.00
34-100.........1.50

MARVEL TEAM UP
1..............15.00
2,4............7.50
3,5-10.........5.00
11-19..........4.00
20-29..........2.50
30-52,54-70,75,79.2.00
53.............8.00
71-74,76-78,80-88,90-
116............1.50
89,100,117,150...4.00
118-149........1.50
Annual 1.......12.00
2-7............2.50

MARVEL TWO IN ONE
1..............8.00
2-10...........2.50

11-55,100......1.50
56-99..........1.00
Annual 1,3-7....2.50

MARVEL UNIVERSE
(1983-84), 1-15..2.50

MARVEL UNIVERSE
(1985-up)
1-25, up........2.50

MASTER OF KUNG FU
15.............7.50
16-39..........2.50
40-89..........1.50
90-125.........1.00

**MEPHISTO VS FOUR
HEROES** 1-4.....2.00

METAL MEN
46-56..........2.50

METAMORPHO
2-17...........5.50

MICRONAUTS (1979-
84), 1,37,38....5.00
2-36,39-59.....1.50

MISTER MIRACLE
(1971) 1........6.00
2-8............4.00
9-25...........2.50

MOON KNIGHT (1980)
1..............4.00
2-38...........1.50

MOVIE COMICS (Dell/
Gold Key).please write

MS. MARVEL
1..............5.00
2-23...........2.00

THE NAM
1..............7.50
2-4............4.00
5-35, up........1.50

NEW MUTANTS
1..............5.00
2-17...........2.50
18-50..........1.50
51-85, up.......1.00
Annual 1-5......2.50

NEW GODS (1971)
1..............6.00
2-11...........4.00
12-19..........2.50

NEW TEEN TITANS
(1980) 1.......15.00
2-4............6.00
5-13...........4.00
14-91..........1.50

NEW TEEN TITANS
(1984) 1........2.00
2-49, Annual 1-4..2.00

NIGHTCRAWLER
1-4............2.00

NOVA
1..............5.00
2-25...........2.00

PHANTOM STRANGER
(1969) 1,4......7.50
2,3,5-19........4.00
20-41..........2.00

POWERMAN (Hero
For Hire/Iron Fist)
1..............6.00
2-10...........2.50
11-50..........2.00
51-56,58-125....1.00

POWER PACK
1,19,27........4.00
2-18,20-26,28-50, up
...............1.50

PUNISHER (1987)
16-30, up.......1.50

**PUNISHER WAR
JOURNAL**
8-15, up........2.00

RED RYDER
74-139.........10.00

ROM
1,17,18........4.00
2-16,19-75......1.50

ROY ROGERS
60-80..........10.00

**SAVAGE SWORD OF
CONAN**, 2-9....10.00

10-19..........5.00
20-50..........4.00
51-165, up......3.00

SECRET ORIGINS
(1986), 1-45, up..2.00

SECRET WARS I
1-3............4.00
4-12...........2.50

SECRET WARS II
1-9............2.00

SGT. FURY
30-39..........4.00
40-69..........2.50

SHADOW (1973)
1-12...........4.00

SHADOW - Pulps &
Paperbacks.....write

SHADOW (1987)
1-25, up........2.00

SHAZAM! (1973)
1,8,12-17.......4.00
2-7,9-11,18-35...2.00

SHE HULK (1980)
1..............4.00
2-25...........1.50
1-up (1989).....1.50

SILVER SURFER ('87)
1..............4.00
2-35, up1111111111.50

**SPACE FAMILY RO-
BINSON**, 20-36...4.50

**SPECTACULAR
SPIDER-MAN** (Peter
Parker) 1,27...10.00
2..............6.00
3-10...........4.00
11-26..........2.50
28,64..........7.00
29-63..........2.00
65-68,71-80,84-99
...............1.50
69,70,100......5.00
101-130,133-139,144-
160, up.........1.00
Annual 1-9, up...2.50

SPECTRE (1987)
1-30, up........2.00

SPIDER-MAN (Amaz.)
126-128,130-133,136-
150............4.00
151-160,163-173..2.50
176-199,203-237,240-
251............2.00
252............5.00
253-274,276-283..1.50
286-288,290-292,295-
297,321-330, up..1.50
Annual 10-14,16-24, up
...............2.50
Giant 1-3,5,6....4.00

SPIDER-WOMAN
1,37,38,50......4.00
2-36,39-49......1.50

STAR WARS
1..............7.50
2-10...........4.00
11-44..........2.50
45-107.........1.50

STRANGE ADVENTURES
150-204........4.50
205-216........7.50
217-244........2.50

STRANGE TALES
117-139........10.00
131-139........7.00
140-149........5.00

STRANGE TALES
1-25, up (1987)...1.50

SUB-MARINER (1968)
3-10...........5.00
11-13,15-20.....4.50
21-39..........3.00
40-72..........2.50

SUPERBOY
103-120........5.00
121-150........4.50
151-210........4.00
80 pg. giants on above
...............7.50
211-248........2.50

249-258........2.00

SUPERMAN
165-179........7.50
180-199........6.00
201-254........4.00
80 pg. giants on above
...............7.50
255-350........1.50
351-460, up.....1.00

SUPERMAN (1987)
1..............4.00
2-35, up........1.50

SUPERMAN FAMILY
164-222........2.50

**SUPER TEAM SUPER
VILLAIN TEAM UP**
1..............5.00
2-17...........2.50
Giant Size 1,2...4.00

SWAMP THING ('72)
1..............8.50
2-10...........4.00
11-24..........2.00

SWAMP THING ('82)
1,16-19........4.00
2-15...........1.50
20,21..........15.00
22-29..........4.00
30-40..........2.50
41-90, up.......1.50

TALES OF SUSPENSE
52-56,58-62.....15.00
64,67-69........12.00
70-80..........10.00
81-99..........7.50

TALES TO ASTONISH
51-62..........12.00
63-69..........8.00
70-80..........6.00
81-91,94-99,101..5.00

TARZAN (Gold Key)
170-206........3.00

TARZAN (DC)
207-211,230-235..4.00
212-229,236-258..2.00

TEEN TITANS (1966)
11-44..........5.00
45-53..........2.00

THE THING
1-36...........1.50

THOR (Journey Into
Mystery) 99-109.15.00
110,111,113-119.10.00
123-130........7.50
131-133,136-140..5.00
141-179,182-189..4.50
190-192,194-199..3.00
201-239........2.00
240-336,338-352..1.50
353-420, up.....1.00
Special/Annual
2..............8.00
5-15, up........2.50

TOMB OF DRACULA
1..............7.50
2-10...........4.00
11-50,70.......2.00
51-69..........1.50

TRANSFORMERS
1..............5.00
2-4............3.00
5-55, up........1.50

TV COMICS (Dell/Gold
Key).....please write

TWO FISTED TALES
(EC) 31,34-41...30.00

UNCLE SCROOGE
164-240, up.....2.50

VIGILANTE
1..............4.00
2-50...........2.00

WARLOCK (1972)
1..............5.00
2-9............4.00
10-15..........3.00

WARLORD
1..............14.00
2..............6.00
3-10...........4.50
11-20..........4.00

21-30..........3.00
31-52..........1.50
53-140, up......1.00
Annual 1-6, up...2.50

WATCHMEN
1-12...........3.00

WEB OF SPIDER-MAN
1..............6.00
2,3............4.00
4-10...........2.50
11-20..........2.00
21-28..........1.50
33-60, up.......1.00

WEIRD TALES (pulps)
.........please write

**WEST COAST
AVENGERS** (1985)
1..............6.00
2-10...........2.50
11-55, up.......1.00
Annual 1,3......2.50

WHAT IF? (1977)
1,31...........7.50
2-12,13,27,28,30..4.00
14-26,29,32-47...2.50

WOLVERINE (1987)
11-25, up.......2.00

WONDER WOMAN
204-220........2.50
221-328........1.50

WONDER WOMAN '87
1..............4.00
2-35, up........1.50

WORLD'S FINEST
132-149........6.00
150-174........5.00
177-212,223-228..4.00
213-222,229-243..1.50
244-282........2.50
283-323........1.50

X-FACTOR
1..............6.00
2,3............4.00
4-10...........2.50
11-20..........2.00
21-55, up.......1.00
Annual 1-4, up...2.50

X-MEN
56-65..........15.00
67-93..........4.50
94.............100.00
95.............40.00
96-99,108-111...20.00
100,101,121.....25.00
102,120........20.00
103-107........14.00
112-119,130,137,139-
141............12.00
122-129,131-136,138,
142............8.50
143-171........4.00
172-193........2.50
194-199,201-209..2.00
200,210-213.....4.00
214-260, up.....1.50
Special/Annual
4,5,9,10........4.50
6-8,11-up.......2.50

**X-MEN & ALPHA
FLIGHT** 1,2......3.00

**X-MEN & THE MICRO-
NAUTS** 1-4......2.50

**X-MEN & THE NEW
TEEN TITANS**
1..............5.00

YOUNG ALL STARS
1-30, up........1.50

ZANE GREY (Dell)
.........please write

**WE ALSO BUY!
PLEASE SEND
SASE FOR OUR
BUYING LIST #12**

DIAMOND RETAILERS OVERWHELMINGLY *RECOMMEND OUR SERVICES!*

A WORLDWIDE SURVEY OF ALL DIAMOND COMIC DISTRIBUTORS'
CUSTOMERS REVEALS NEARLY 95%
WOULD RECOMMEND OUR SERVICES
TO OTHER COMIC BOOK RETAIL OUTLETS!

WORLD CLASS SERVICE WORLDWIDE

= DIAMOND WAREHOUSE LOCATIONS

Retailers -
if you aren't
familiar with
Diamond's
dependable
track record,
wide variety of
quality product lines,
and the professional attitude
of our outstanding personnel,
you really should consider
the following points:

BOSTON
NEW YORK
BALTIMORE
COLUMBUS?
CHARLOTTE
ATLANTA
TAMPA
CHICAGO
SPARTA
DALLAS
DENVER
PHOENIX
LOS ANGELES
SAN DIEGO
HAYWARD

A-142

WAREHOUSE MANAGERS

Almost 100% of the surveys rated Diamond warehouse managers:
- Knowledgable about distribution operations
- Friendly
- Helpful
- Respectful of customers

Over 90% of responding retailers think Diamond warehouse managers:
- Earned their respect
- Handled their questions and concerns promptly
- Were accessible when needed

Diamond Comic Distributors is very proud of the outstanding quality of service its warehouse managers provide on a national, and international, scope. Ask a Diamond retailer and find out for yourself!

ACCOUNTS RECEIVABLE

What kind of treatment would you expect from a collections department?
The national survey showed 98% feel Diamond's Accounts Receivable personnel are friendly and fair!
Also, our monthly statements were rated as accurate.

WAREHOUSE SERVICE

100% of the surveys rated Diamond warehouse employees as friendly!

Excellent ratings were received regarding:
- Accurate and timely shipments
- Accurate invoices
- Accurate reorders
- Clean, organized warehouses

MONTHLY ORDERING PACKET

This indispensable monthly mailing provides accurate, easy to use information your business depends on.

Almost all comic book retailers responding to the national survey find Diamond's monthly wholesale catalog (PREVIEWS) and order form:
- Easy to use
- Contains accurate and clear descriptions

Almost 100% of these store owners are very happy with the fliers, posters, and brochures that are included with our catalogs each month.

Aren't these the services and treatment you want and should expect from your distributor?
Find out more about all that Diamond Comic Distributors can do for you!

Call Diamond Customer Service (Bill Neuhaus) at 800-783-2981
1718G Belmont Avenue, Baltimore, MD 21207

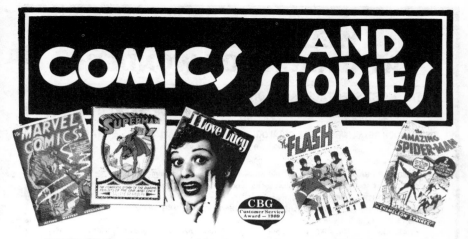

GOLDEN-AGE COMICS / SILVER-AGE COMICS / DISNEY/ DELLS

Comics and Stories features one of the finest selections of all Golden Age comics—DC's, Timelys, Fawcetts, Marvels and of course Dells.

All the Key #1's are our specialty.

We periodically have mail/phone auctions which include prime animation art, BLBs, comic character toys and books, and other prime related material.
Great Opportunities, Great Deals

A "NM" selection of all Dells.

These are the first legal "file" (never distributed) copies available to the public. We are proud to announce that we encompass all the classic Dell & Disney Titles as well as the photo cover T.V. and movie titles.

Remember: I Love Lucy, Maverick, Lawman, Star Trek, The Three Stooges, Lancer, My Favorite Martian, Sergeant Preston, Lost in Space, The Twilight Zone, Sea Hunt, Man from U.N.C.L.E., The Phanthom, Bonanza, Roy Rogers, Gene Autry, Rex Allen, Wild Wild West, Wyatt Earp, Have Gun Will Travel, Bozo, Cisco Kid, Tarzan, Mickey Mouse, Donald Duck & all Disney Titles, Gunsmoke, Howdy Doody, The Jetsons, Lassie, Nancy, Rin Tin Tin, Four Color Comics, Little Lulu, Heroic, Famous Funnies, Raggedy Ann, Jingle Jangle, and all the Hot Hanna-Barbera titles.

WANT LIST SERVICE

We pride ourselves on our ability to find and acquire **prime** and selected pieces. If you have a particular want, take advantage of our computerized Want List service today.

To get on our mailing list for both comic catalogues and auctions send a Want List to the address below.

COMICS & STORIES 85 Crescent Rd., Wanaque, N.J. 07465

(201) 839-3007 • (Viewing By Appointment Only)

WELCOME TO THE
AVALANCHE OF WONDER

▶THE MOST SPECTACULARLY DIVERSE CATALOGUE IN FANDOM
▶60 PLUS TABLOID SIZE PAGES - OVER 100,000 DIFFERENT ITEMS

JOSEPH KOCH RETAIL/WHOLESALE CATALOGUE INCLUDED WITH ALL ORDERS & LIST REQUESTS
(All items available with quantity discounts)

Catalogue Page #

A1-A3...**SUMMER SALE COMICS** - Retail and wholesale; Hot books, Batman, X-Men.

F-1...**SPOTLIGHT MAGAZINES:** Descriptive sections on **EPIC, 2000 AD**, out of print publications featuring **BERNI WRIGHTSON, JOHN BYRNE**, more...

F-2...**WARRIOR** - Home of **ALAN MOORE'S "V FOR VENDETTA" & "MIRACLEMAN;"** all available issues listed with contents & covers.

F-3...**CLASSICS OF COMIC ART** - Reprint publications; relevant fanzines; sections on **EISNER, BELLAMY, KIRBY, WOOD, CANIFF;** more...

F-4...**FURTHER READING:** Journals & reviews. Amazing Heroes, Comics Journal, etc.

F-5...**LIMITED EDITION PORTFOLIOS:** Retail & wholesale.

F-6...**HOUSE OF HAMMER:** Classic British horror mag covers & contents, retail & wholesale.

F-7...**MOVIES & MONSTERS:** Famous Monsters of Filmland, other Warrens pubs, Dr. Who, more.

F-8...**CREEPY, EERIE, WARREN COMIC FORMAT.**

F-9...**STAR TREK GREETING CARDS.**

F-10..**MARVEL MAGAZINES:** Extensive descriptions.

F-11..**BEATLES:** Memorabilia & publications.

F-12..**FILM MAGAZINES:** Starlog, Cinefantastique, Starburst, Etc.

F-14..**WARREN POSTERS.**

JOSEPH KOCH RETAIL CATALOGUE (Included with all retail orders & retail list requests)

Catalogue Page #

11-17...**MARVELS** - 1960's TO PRESENT; **DCs** - 1960's TO PRESENT - INDEPENDENTS.

JOSEPH KOCH SPECIALTY PAGES: Only included upon request (specify catalogue page #) or with orders suggesting an interest in the listed material.
Limited quantity; retail only.

Catalogue Page #
Comics

21-24...**GOLD, SILVER, BRONZE & LEAD AGES: CLASSICS ILLUSTRATED, CLASSIC JR ORIGINAL ART.** Yes, we catalogue Charlton & all "second" line companies.

25...**MOVIE/TV ADAPTATION COMICS** (mostly Dell & Gold Key; mostly photo covers).

26...**GOLD & SILVER AGE DCs; EARLY MARVELS.**

27-28...**HARVEYS, ARCHIES.**

29...**GOLD, SILVER, BRONZE AGE UPDATE.**

FANZINES, MAGAZINES, MISC. PUBLICATIONS RETAIL ONLY; these pages only included upon request.
(specify catalogue page #'s) or with orders suggesting an interest in the listed material.

Catalogue Page #

31...**MOVIES & MONSTERS:** Sci-Fi, Fantasy Film Publications of all kinds; Rock 'N' Roll.

32...**CLASSICS OF COMICS** art-reviewed & reprinted.

33-34...**COMIC FORMAT PUBLICATIONS;** more **FURTHER READING: BLAZING NEW TRAILS** (The Weird & The Wonderful) fanzines & miscellaneous publications of all kinds.

35...**BRITISH TARZAN, UNDERGROUNDS.**

36...**MOVIE/TV PAPERBACKS, STAR WARS, STAR TREK, DOCTOR WHO.**

38-39...**HOLLYWOOD 30s to 60s:** Classic Movie Magazines.

40-41...**PAPERBACKS:** Sci-Fi, Frazetta covers, Jones covers, Cartoon & Comic P/B's Sports.

42-46...**BRITISH ANNUALS:** These are hardbound volumes featuring fictional & real life icons of popular culture - they have been coming out once a year since the 1940s, just about every TV series, cartoon & comic character, pop star has had at least one annual issued in its/his/her name - **this is probably the most extensive sale list in the world.** Cartoons & Heroes, Hollywood, Gerry Anderson, Star Trek, Dr. Who, Disney, Movie/TV/Music.

DO YOU THINK NEW COMICS COST TOO MUCH? THEN DO SOMETHING ABOUT IT.

M & M CORDIALLY INVITES YOU TO STATE OF THE ART COMIC BOOK BUYING.

FEATURING:

—Fully computerized order and invoicing system.
—Monthly credits for late and resolicited books.
—Detailed monthly order form.
—Free promo material with every shipment.
—6 years experience in comic mail order, and mail order is all we do.
—Discounts up to 52%.
—No minimum order.
—Weekly news items on every invoice.
—Expertly packed boxes to ensure your books arrive in great condition.
—Yet get what you order, because we order it for you and only you.
—Customer Satisfaction — we have **never** had a complaint written to any publication we advertise in.

And this is just the tip of the iceberg. WE ARE WITHOUT A DOUBT THE BEST COMIC SERVICE OUT THERE.

If you're not ordering from us, you're probably paying too much and you're not getting everything you ordered.

FIND OUT WHAT YOU'RE MISSING

Send $1.00 for our next order form

M & M

P.O. Box 6
9325 Bradford Lane
Orland Park, IL 60462
312-349-2486
Visa & Mastercard Accepted

THIS YEAR DARK HORSE COMICS WILL GIVE YOU LIBERTY...

Give Me Liberty™ ©1990 Frank Miller & Dave Gibbons

AND A WHOLE LOT MORE!

WORKS BY: BOLTON • BURDEN • CAMPBELL
CHADWICK • DARROW • GEARY • GIBBONS • GIGER
KALUTA • KANE • MILLER • MOEBIUS • PANDER Bros.
STEVENS • VERHEIDEN • VESS • AND MANY OTHERS!

YOUR BEST BET FOR THE 1990s AND BEYOND!

A-161

WANT LIST COMICS

WE FILL WANT LISTS

ATTENTION: COLLECTORS AND INVESTORS

Found those missing comic books **yet**? Are these books **too expensive** or are they just **too difficult** to find? Have local stores and conventions not produced what you want? (**Have you tried us yet?**)

WHAT ARE YOU WAITING FOR?

"The **Batman #1** you sold me was in the **nicest, unrestored condition** I've seen!", **Bob Overstreet, author Overstreet Price Guide.**

"The Golden Age books that you've sold to me **more** than met my standards. They have been **very accurately** described according to condition and **fairly priced**. I've dealt with **several** other dealers and **I wish everyone graded like you do!**" **John Gendall, Orlando, Florida.**

These are just two of the many satisfied customers that have bought books from us in the past. Over the years we have built up a **strong return customer base** because we accurately grade and describe books (in detail if needed) over the phone and through the mail. **Customer references are always available upon request.** If a book is restored we will tell you **up front** so you won't be **UN**pleasantly surprised or deceived. We truly have a fine want list service. For example, **in just 1989 alone**, we purchased the following books for our want list customers: Action 1-5, Batman 1-5, Captain America 1, Detective 27, 28, 30, 31, 35-37, Human Torch 1, Amazing Man 5 and **multiple copies of nearly all** Key Silver Age Marvel and DC issues. As you can see, we are **specialists in Golden Age and Silver Age books** (1933-1969), but do have some later issues also.

We don't claim that we can fill every list all the time, but if anyone can accomplish this, it would **certainly** be us! We can say this with much confidence because we travel to the majority of the 50 states and Canada **plus** attend all major comic book conventions(San Diego, Chicago, New York, Mid Ohio, Oakland, etc.) to uncover books **you** would **not** have the opportunity to find. When we're not on the road we spend **many** hours on the phone locating books from our long list of past and present comic sources we've developed over the years. When sending your want list, please include an **SASE** if possible, **your phone number,** and a good time to reach you. We don't send out catalogs so **please** ask us for **specific** books and conditions desired. We will contact you **when** we find the items you've requested. **WE WILL GLADLY SUGGEST AND PERSONALLY PUT TOGETHER COMIC BOOK INVESTMENT PORTFOLIOS FOR BIG AND SMALL INVESTORS.**

SAVE YOURSELF ALL THE HASSLE AND LET US DO THE LOOKING FOR YOU

SEND US YOUR WANT LIST
YOU HAVE NOTHING TO LOSE AND EVERYTHING ON YOUR WANT LIST TO GAIN!!!

•Competitive pricing • Accurate grading • **Time payments/Layaways possible** • Visa, **Mastercard and American Express accepted for total payment or down payment on books** • No collect calls past 1:00am C.S.T.

918-491-9191
WANT LIST COMICS
BOX 701932
TULSA, OK 74170-1932

PLEASE NOTE: Sometime during mid 1990, our phone number will change to 1-918-299-0440 due to changing locations to expand office and warehouse space. Our mailing address will be unchanged.

A-162

A-164

Capital City Comics

1910 MONROE ST., MADISON, WIS. 53711
MON - FRI: 11-7 SAT: 10-5
PHONE (608) 251-8445

BRUCE AYRES, Owner

DAVID MACEY, Manager

SECOND GENESIS
3 WEST COAST WAREHOUSES FOR RETAILER SERVICE

Complete line of comic book publishers: Marvel,DC, Gladstone, First, Eclipse, Comico, Dark Horse and all the independent publishers.

Specialty products: Trade Paperbacks, T-Shirts, Games, Calendars, Graphic Novels, and more.

Supplies: Long and short comic boxes, magazine boxes, dividers, 9 different sizes of polypropylene bags, baseball sheets, backing boards and mylar products.

Call one of our warehouses for our thick monthly catalog. **Providing wholesale services to retailers since 1976.**

NEW PUBLISHERS: Solicitation material or new product information should go to our Portland Warehouse.

SEATTLE WAREHOUSE
Manager: Al Clover
223 1/2 Ninth Ave. North
Seattle, WA 98109
(206) 624-6210

PORTLAND WAREHOUSE
Main Office
Manager: Kathy Moullet
Catalog Editor: Tim Androes
Controller: Lance Casebeer
5860 NE Going Street
Portland, OR 97218
(503) 281-1821

LOS ANGELES WAREHOUSE
Manager: Glen Quasny
6223 Randolph Street
Commerce, CA 90040
(213) 888-0466

A-172

ANDREW TAYLOR / Daily News

Gerry Ross is shown surrounded by his and Bob Crestohl's Mitchell Moran's mammoth comic book collection purchase for $100,000!

There are many comic book dealers...
There is only one COMIC MASTER.
Gerry Ross is the COMIC MASTER.
$1,000,000
available to purchase at all times!

Paying between **60% - 1000%** of this price guide for accuratly graded Marvels and Golden Age D.C. in fine or better.

In this guide you will read some dealers explaining how everyone but they are "stealing" your collection, or how no one pays as high. Consider that all these big spenders:

1) won't even pay postage costs!

WE PAY ALL POSTAGE COSTS.

2) want to see your collection with no money sent until they "check out the condition".
(If you fall for this you deserve it!)

WE WILL SEND YOU MONEY UP FRONT AS YOUR SECURITY.
BALANCE ON DELIVERY.

3) Where are all the big spenders when big collections or key books surface? (see above)

4) If you don't call us, don't worry, we'll probably buy your books from the other dealers in this guide.
ELIMINATE THE MIDDLE MEN. Get your maximum!

Gerry Ross is an Overstreet update advisor.
Robert Crestohl is a founding father of this hobby and has been active for 20 years.

CALL (514) 630-4518 or send to **Crestohl / Ross**
P.O. Box 4953, St-Laurent, Montreal, Quebec, Canada   H4L 4Z6

A-174

GERRY ROSS   present   ROBERT CRESTOHL

THE COMPLETE MARVEL COLLECTION AT SPECIAL DISCOUNT PRICES!!!

MINI MARKET REPORT. Early Marvels, all titles are booming. Later Marvels have shown tremendous growth in the past year (all titles). Prices reflect a moving average; new price list in 4 months.
HOW TO ORDER: 1) Comics listed by price/condition. GD / VG = good to very good; VG / F = very good to fine; F / VF = fine to very fine; VF / NM = very fine to near mint; M = mint. **2)** Prices listed are for each comic, ex.: Conan #82-99; 1.50 (each issue). **3)** Payment; in U.S. funds by check, money order, MasterCard or Visa (Canadian residents add 20% to Canadian funds. **4)** LIST ALTERNATE CHOICES, and receive a 10% discount!!! **5)** Prices on hot books subject to change. **6)** POSTAGE / HANDLING; add $3.00 if up to 10 comics; $6.00 if more than 11 comics. Overseas orders multiply postage by 3. **7)** Catalog FREE with all orders. **8)** WE TAKE PHONE MASTERCARD AND VISA. HAVE YOUR CARD IN FRONT OF YOU WHEN ORDERING, CALL (514) 630-4518. SPECIAL PHONE DISCOUNT 5% OFF!!! TAKE 15% OFF ALL ORDERS OVER $2000.00 (so long as no two books make up half). **10% DISCOUNT OFF ALL ORDERS WITH ALTERNATE CHOICES** (equal in value to first choices)!!! **We grade accurately. Not responsible for typos. SEND FOR GIANT MARVEL CATALOG $1.00!!! These list prices supercede all catalogs and prior list prices. CALL (514) 630-4518**
MAIL ALL ORDERS/PAYMENT/QUERIES TO: Crestohl/Ross
4732 Circle Rd., DEPT. M, Montreal, Quebec
Canada   H3W 1Z1

[The remainder of the page consists of a dense multi-column price list of Marvel comic back issues with columns: gd/vg, vg/f, f/vf, vf/nm, nm/m, mint. Titles listed include: Amazing Spiderman, Avengers, Brand Echh, Captain America, Captain Marvel (1968), Conan, Daredevil, Defenders, Doctor Strange, Excalibur, Fantastic Four, Fantasy Masterpieces, G.I. Joe, Incredible Hulk, Ironman, Marvel Collector-Item Classics, Marvel Super Heros, Peter Parker (Spectacular Spiderman), Silver Surfer, Strange Tales, Tales of Suspense, Tales to Astonish, Thor (Journey Into Mystery), X-Men, X-Men and Alpha Flight, X-Men and Micronauts, X-Men Classics.]

A-176

OVER 20,000 DIFFERENT COMICS IN STOCK

BUY—SELL—TRADE with Marty Hay or I SMASH!!

Enclose 1 stamp each for Buying or Selling List!

I PAY CASH FOR QUALITY COMICS

FAST CASH FOR SINGLE BOOKS AND LARGE COLLECTIONS. I WANT ALL EARLY MARVELS, SILVER-AGE DC'S, GOLDEN AGE, DISNEY POSTERS & MISC. ANY CONDITION, 50% TO 400% OF GUIDE FOR ITEMS NEEDED! **I WILL PAY MORE THAN ANY BUYING PRICES OFFERED IN THIS GUIDE!** WHY TAKE LESS FOR YOUR VALUED COLLECTIBLES? FAIR PRICES OFFERED EVEN FOR LESSER QUALITY COMICS.

SAMPLE BUYING PRICES (SUBJECT ONLY TO INCREASE!!)
Amazing Fantasy #15 . . . . I Will pay up to $4750
Fantastic Four #1 . . . . Take my cash up to $4200
Spiderman #1 . . . . Worth up to $3750 to me
Showcase #4 . . . . Needed up to $5000 best shape
Flash #105 . . . . Up to $1450 for top quality
Brave & Bold #28 . . . . Your mint is worth $1600 to me
Justice League #1 . . . . Perfection can be worth $1200
Iron Man #1 . . . . $175 offered for choice copies
Showcase #22 . . . . I can use this comic up to $1300
Most Golden Age Comics also worth big money to me!!

MARTY HAY
P.O. Box 359
329 E. Main
Springerville, AZ 85938
☎ (602) 333-2222

Serving Fandom for over 19 Years

A-185

GROWING INTO OUR NAME

There is one publishing house that has risen in stature throughout the 1980s. There is one publishing house whose growing list has captured the imagination of press and public alike. There is one publishing house that is making quality comics as acceptable to read as they are in France,
Italy and Spain.
Welcome to the 1990s. Welcome to **TITAN BOOKS.**

TITAN BOOKS succeeds in four separate areas
- Classic graphic albums featuring *Judge Dredd* and other favourites from *2000 AD*. Collected stories from Britain's bestselling science fiction comic.
- A growing list of originated graphic novels including *Violent Cases, London's Dark* and, coming soon, *The Spiral Cage.*
- Britain's favourite newspaper strips collected into graphic album form - *James Bond, Modesty Blaise, Garth* and *Jeff Hawke.*
- Cult favourites from the worlds of Film and TV - including bestsellers such as *Clive Barker's The Nightbreed Chronicles, Dr Who Scriptbooks, The Complete Gerry Anderson Episode Guide* and many more.

THE LEADING PUBLISHER OF GRAPHIC NOVELS IN THE UK
TITAN BOOKS Ltd,
58 St Giles High Street, London WC2H 8LH

WHEN IT COMES TO DISTRIBUTION HERE AND ABROAD, COMICS UNLIMITED HAS TAKEN THE WORLD BY STORM.

- **Low freight rates from New York**
- **Competitive discounts**
- **Faster service**

These are just some of the benefits of choosing Comics Unlimited for your wholesale distribution. Every week we ship to England, France, Germany and Australia. And we're shipping now, so when it comes to experience and a long history of customer satisfaction, we can make a world of difference. It's simple. We know how to do it. So put the whole world in your reach. Comics Unlimited.

COMICS UNLIMITED

6833 Amboy Rd.
Staten Island, NY 10309
(718) 948-2223
Fax 718-356-1173
(United States outside of N.Y. City) 1-800-729-5704

Comic Books Wanted!

Before you sell, check me out!
Immediate Cash!
Will Travel to View Large Collections

I'm paying the following percentages, GUARANTEED!

(Based on Over Street Price Guide)

Action (1-280)	65	Human Torch	60
Adventure (1-260)	60	Jackie Gleason	75
All American (1-102)	65	John Wayne	70
All Flash	60	Journey into Mystery (1-110)	60
All Select	60	Jumbo	55
All Star	65	Justice League (1-30)	65
All Winners	60	Ken Maynard	65
Avengers (1-20)	60	Marvel Mystery	60
Batman (1-150)	65	Military	60
Blackhawk (9-110)	60	More Fun (1-107)	65
Brave and the Bold (1-44)	65	Mystery Men	55
Captain America	65	Planet	60
Captain Midnight	55	Shadow	65
Centaurs (All)	80	Showcase (1-43)	65
Comic Cavalcade (1-23)	60	Spiderman (1-30)	60
Daredevil (1-10)	60	Star Spangled (1-127)	55
Daring Mystery	65	Strange Tales (1-115)	60
Detective (1-280)	60	Submariner	60
Famous Funnies (1-60)	60	Superman (1-150)	60
Fantastic Four (1-30)	60	Tales of Suspense (1-50)	60
Fight	55	Tales to Astonish (1-40)	60
Flash (1-125)	65	Top Notch	55
Green Lantern (1-38, 1-20)	65	Wings	60
Hulk (1-6)	60	X-Men (1-20)	60

BUYING: Paying high prices, 50-80% for other DC, Timely, Fiction House, Fox, MLJ and Fawcetts. Books must be accurately graded and complete. Send for immediate payment or write.

SELLING: I Offer • Accurate Grading • Reasonable Prices • Large Selection • Satisfaction Guaranteed • Send for Latest List •

HARLEY YEE
P.O. Box 19578
Detroit, MI 48219-0578
Phone: (313) 533-2731

A-194

A-198

#1

ACTION COMICS No. 1
AMAZING FANTASY No. 15
(1st SPIDERMAN)
BATMAN No. 1
FANTASTIC FOUR No. 1
SPIDERMAN No. 1
SUPERMAN No. 1

Sleuthing done dirt cheap!
Can't find that number one (or origin issue)? Then why not try me?
Yes, I have **all** of the **No. 1** issues shown above & other **hard-to-find** comics especially those much sought after **early Marvels** (there are always available in stock a near complete set of all Marvel titles).

And besides this I also have the following:

(A) WALT DISNEY COMICS - all titles: Mickey Mouse, Donald Duck, Uncle Scrooge, and Disney Collectibles.

(B) DC COMICS (Golden Age, Silver Age up to the present-old Flash, Green Lantern, Superman, Batman, and other Super-Heros.

(C) GOLDEN AGE & SILVER AGE) comics. These include Quality, Timely, Fox, Avon, Fiction House, Fawcett, Motion Picture Comics, Dell, Westerns, Funny Animal Comics, Classics, etc.

(D) MAD comics - Panic, Humbug, Trump, Help & Horror, Crime & **EC** comics.

(E) BIG LITTLE BOOKS - all major and minor titles. Also available - the **original** Cupples & Leon comic "books".

(F) Rare **PULPS** - science fiction & pulp hero titles.

(G) ORIGINAL ART - including fine classic as well as modern artists.

(H) SUNDAY COMIC PAGES - Just about every major & minor comic strip character from the early **1900's** to the **1950's**. Strips include: **Little Nemo, Krazy Kat, Mickey Mouse, Donald Duck, Popeye, Tarzan, Flash Gordon, Prince Valiant, Terry & The Pirates, Dick Tracy, Superman** & many, many more too numerous to list here.

I also **BUY & TRADE**, so let me know what you have. For my latest **GIANT** 1990 catalog "Number One Plus", write to the address below enclosing $1.00 in cash (or stamps). Hurry now or you could miss out on getting that issue you've been looking for!

SPECIAL — SPECIAL: MOVIE SALE

A ONCE IN A LIFE-TIME OFFER! Huge Catalog listing hundreds and hundreds of rare (and **ORIGINAL**) movie posters, lobby cards, autographed photos from the 1930's to the 1980's. You'll find your favorite movie stars as: Bogart, Gable, Garbo, Garland, Laurel & Hardy, Presley, Disney Titles & many, many more. Wide selection from B-Westerns, Horror, Science-Fiction, Comedy, Musicals, Etc. Act **NOW** to receive my "1990 **MOVIE CATALOG**".

(NOTE: Those wishing to receive **ONLY** the Movie Catalog **MUST** enclose 50 cents & a self-addressed stamped envelope. Want lists also welcomed. If you wish to receive **BOTH** the Comic & the Movie catalog, send $1.50).

Write: HAL VERB
P.O. BOX 1815
SAN FRANCISCO, CA 94101

WE

OFFER

Comic Heaven
John and Nanette Verzyl
24 W. Main Street
Alhambra, CA 91801
1-818-289-3945

THE

BEST

.................Service
Comic Auctions
Comic Auctions
Comic Auctions
Depth of Inventory
Comic Catalogs
Buying Prices
Selling Prices
Silver Age Comic Books
Golden Age Comic Books
Credit Terms
Investments
Advice
Grading
Selection
D.C.'s
File Copies
Key Issues
Shipping
Church Copies
Timely's
E.C.'s
Pedigree Books

Comic Heaven
John and Nanette Verzyl
24 W. Main Street
Alhambra, CA 91801
1·818·289·3945

A-214

SATISFACTION GUARANTEED

All comics purchased from COMIC HEAVEN may be returned (within 14 days) for a full refund if for any reason you are not satisified.*

Here is what a few happy COMIC HEAVEN customers have to say about us.

"The Mile High Flash #96 you sent me is awsome, I love it." —Pat Kohanek — Pitt, Penn.

Donovan B. says - "I am really happy with the Batman 3, 4, 5 & 6, I got from you. They are the pride of my collection."

Billy M. says - "I get all my comics here, you guys are great."

* Books must be securely wrapped and returned to us in the same condition as they were sent.

Comic Heaven
John and Nanette Verzyl
24 W. Main Street
Alhambra, CA 91801
1·818·289·3945

A BRIEF HISTORICAL NOTE ABOUT "COMIC HEAVEN"

John Verzyl started collecting comic books in 1965, and within ten years, he had amassed thousands of Golden and Silver Age comic books. In 1979, with his wife Nanette, he opened "COMIC HEAVEN", a retail store devoted entirely to the buying and selling of comic books.

Over the years, John Verzyl has come to be recognized as an authority in the field of comic books,. He has served as an advisor to the "Overstreet Price Guide". Thousands of his "mint" comics were photographed for Ernst Gerbers newly-released "Photo-Journal Guide To Comic Books". His tables and displays at the annual San Diego Comic Convention draw customers from all over the country.

The first COMIC HEAVEN AUCTION was held in 1987, and today his Auction Catalogs are mailed out to more then ten thousand interested collectors (and dealers).

Comic Heaven
John and Nanette Verzyl
24 W. Main Street
Alhambra, CA 91801
1·818·289·3945

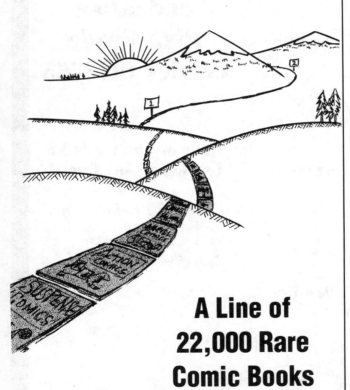

Laid End To End....

It would use <u>27-1/2 Inches</u> of the PHOTO JOURNAL GUIDE TO COMICS Vol. 1 and 2...To Total

<u>22,000</u> <u>Color</u> Photographs of Rare Comic Books.

PLUS...
a bonus of

- 864 Pages in Color
- 13 Pounds: 2 Volumes
- 40,000 Comic Books individually catalogued by:
  —Permanent identification number
  —Scarcity Index
  —Relative Value Index
  —Issue Dates
  —Artists
- Detailed chapters on:
  —Collecting
  —Buying and Selling
  —Grading
  —Value, Investment
  —Storage and Preservation
  —Restoration, Pro and Con
  —Social and Historical Impact
- Specialty Indexes:
  —Artist Index
  —Character Index
  —Title Index

Gerber Publishing Co., Inc.
P.O. Box 906, Minden, NV 89423
(702) 883-4100 (M-S, 9-1) Fax 24 hr. (702) 882-7281

Abbott and Costello #6, © STJ

Ace Comics #144, © ACE

Action Comics #13, © DC

The correct title listing for each comic book can be determined by consulting the indicia (publication data) on the beginning interior pages of the comic. The official title is determined by those words of the title in capital letters only, and not by what is on the cover.

Titles are listed in this book as if they were one word, ignoring spaces, hyphens, and apostrophes, to make finding titles easier.

Comic publishers are invited to send us sample copies for possible inclusion in future guides.

A-1 (See A-One)

ABBIE AN' SLATS (...With Becky No. 1-4) (See Comics On Parade, Fight for Love, Giant Comics Edition 2, Sparkler Comics, Tip Topper, Treasury of Comics, & United Comics)
1940; March, 1948 - No. 4, Aug, 1948 (Reprints)
United Features Syndicate

	Good	Fine	N-Mint
Single Series 25 ('40)	19.00	57.00	135.00
Single Series 28	17.00	51.00	120.00
1 (1948)	9.00	27.00	62.00
2-4: 3 r-/Sparkler #68-72	4.30	13.00	30.00

ABBOTT AND COSTELLO (...Comics)(See Treasury of Comics)
Feb, 1948 - No. 40, Sept?, 1956 (Mort Drucker art in most issues)
St. John Publishing Co.

1	22.00	65.00	154.00
2	11.50	34.00	80.00
3-9 (#8, 8/49; #9, 2/50)	6.50	19.50	45.00
10-Son of Sinbad story by Kubert (new)	13.00	40.00	90.00
11,13-20 (#11, 10/50; #13, 8/51; #15, 12/52)	4.00	12.00	28.00
12-Movie issue	5.50	16.50	38.00
21-30: 28 r-#8. 30-Painted-c	3.00	9.00	21.00
31-40: #33, 38-r	2.30	7.00	16.00
3-D #1 (11/53)-Infinity-c	19.00	57.00	132.00

ABBOTT AND COSTELLO (TV)
Feb, 1968 - No. 22, Aug, 1971 (Hanna-Barbera)
Charlton Comics

1	2.15	6.50	15.00
2-10	1.35	4.00	8.00
11-22	.70	2.00	4.00

ABC (See America's Best TV Comics)

ABRAHAM LINCOLN LIFE STORY (See Dell Giants)

ABSENT-MINDED PROFESSOR, THE (See 4-Color Comics No. 1199)

ABYSS, THE
June, 1989 - No. 2, July, 1989 ($2.25, color, 2 issue series)
Dark Horse Comics

1,2-Movie adaptation; Kaluta, Moebius-a	.40	1.15	2.30

ACE COMICS
April, 1937 - No. 151, Oct-Nov, 1949
David McKay Publications

1-Jungle Jim by Alex Raymond, Blondie, Ripley's Believe It Or Not, Krazy Kat begin	158.00	395.00	950.00
2	50.00	150.00	350.00
3-5	36.00	107.00	250.00
6-10	26.00	77.00	180.00
11-The Phantom begins(In brown costume, 2/38)	32.00	95.00	225.00
12-20	19.00	57.00	135.00
21-25,27-30	16.00	48.00	110.00
26-Origin Prince Valiant (begins series?)	44.00	132.00	310.00
31-40: 37-Krazy Kat ends	11.50	34.00	80.00
41-60	10.00	30.00	70.00
61-64,66-76-(7/43; last 68pgs.)	8.50	25.50	60.00

	Good	Fine	N-Mint
65-(8/42; Flag-c)	9.00	27.00	63.00
77-84 (3/44; all 60pgs.)	7.00	21.00	50.00
85-99 (52 pgs.)	6.00	18.00	42.00
100 (7/45; last 52 pgs.)	7.00	21.00	50.00
101-134: 128-11/47; Brick Bradford begins. 134-Last Prince Valiant (All 36 pgs.)	5.00	15.00	35.00
135-151: 135-6/48; Lone Ranger begins	4.00	12.00	28.00

ACE KELLY (See Tops Comics & Tops In Humor)

ACE KING (See Adventures of the Detective)

ACES
Apr, 1988 - No. 5, Dec, 1988 ($2.95, B&W, Magazine)
Acme Press (Eclipse Comics)

1-5	.50	1.50	3.00

ACES HIGH
Mar-Apr, 1955 - No. 5, Nov-Dec, 1955
E.C. Comics

1-Not approved by code	8.00	24.00	56.00
2	6.50	19.50	45.00
3-5	5.50	16.50	38.00

NOTE: All have stories by *Davis*, *Evans*, *Krigstein*, and *Wood*; *Evans* c-1-5.

ACTION ADVENTURE (War) (Formerly Real Adventure)
V1#2, June, 1955 - No. 4, Oct, 1955
Gillmor Magazines

V1#2-4	1.30	4.00	9.00

ACTION COMICS (See Special Ed.; ...Weekly No. 601 -642)
6/38 - No. 583, 9/86; No. 584, 1/87 - Present
National Periodical Publ./Detective Comics/DC Comics

1-Origin & 1st app. Superman by Siegel & Shuster, Marco Polo, Tex Thompson, Pep Morgan, Chuck Dawson & Scoop Scanlon; intro. Zatara & Lois Lane; Superman story missing 4 pgs. which were included when reprinted in Superman #1. Mentioned in POP, pg. 86

	Good	Fine	Vf-NM
(Only one known copy exists in Mint condition which has not sold)	6,000.00	15,000.00	32,500.00

1-Reprint, Oversize 13½''x10.'' **WARNING:** This comic is an exact reprint of the original except for its size. DC published it in 1974 with a second cover titling it as a **Famous First Edition.** There have been many reported cases of the outer cover being removed and the interior sold as the original edition. The reprint with the new outer cover removed is practically worthless.

	Good	Fine	N-Mint
1(1976,1983)-Giveaway; paper cover, 16pgs. in color; reprints complete Superman story from #1 ('38)	.70	2.00	4.00
1(1987 Nestle Quik giveaway; 1988, 50 cent-c)		.25	.50
2	800.00	2000.00	4800.00
3 (Scarce)	635.00	1590.00	3800.00
4	435.00	1090.00	2600.00
5 (Rare)	535.00	1340.00	3200.00
6-1st Jimmy Olsen (called office boy)	435.00	1090.00	2600.00
7,10-Superman covers	535.00	1340.00	3200.00
8,9	367.00	920.00	2200.00
11,12,14: 14-Clip Carson begins, ends #41	192.00	480.00	1150.00
13-Superman cover; last Scoop Scanlon	267.00	670.00	1600.00
15-Superman cover	267.00	670.00	1600.00
16	148.00	370.00	890.00
17-Superman cover; last Marco Polo	200.00	500.00	1200.00
18-Origin 3 Aces; 1st X-Ray Vision?	140.00	350.00	840.00
19-Superman covers begin	183.00	450.00	1100.00
20-'S' left off Superman's chest; Clark Kent works at 'Daily Star'	168.00	420.00	1000.00
21,22,24,25: 24-Kent at Daily Planet. 25-Last app. Gargantua T. Potts, Tex Thompson's sidekick	105.00	260.00	630.00
23-1st app. Luthor & Black Pirate; Black Pirate by Moldoff; 1st mention of The Daily Planet? (4/40)	153.00	380.00	920.00

ACTION COMICS (continued)	Good	Fine	N-Mint
26-30	82.00	205.00	490.00
31,32	63.00	158.00	375.00
33-Origin Mr. America	75.00	190.00	450.00
34-40: 37-Origin Congo Bill. 40-Intro/1st app. Star Spangled Kid & Stripesy	62.00	155.00	375.00
41	58.00	145.00	350.00
42-Origin Vigilante; Bob Daley becomes Fat Man; origin Mr. America's magic flying carpet; The Queen Bee & Luthor app; Black Pirate ends; not in #41	83.00	210.00	500.00
43-50: 44-Fat Man's i.d. revealed to Mr. America. 45-Intro. Stuff	58.00	145.00	350.00
51-1st app. The Prankster	50.00	125.00	300.00
52-Fat Man & Mr. America become the Ameri-commandos; origin Vigilante retold	58.00	145.00	350.00
53-60: 56-Last Fat Man. 59-Kubert Vigilante begins?, ends #70. 60-First app. Lois Lane as Superwoman	43.00	110.00	255.00
61,63,65-70: 63-Last 3 Aces	39.00	100.00	235.00
64-Intro Toyman	43.00	110.00	255.00
71-79: 74-Last Mr. America	33.00	83.00	200.00
80-2nd app. & 1st Mr. Mxyztplk-c (1/45)	58.00	145.00	350.00
81-90: 83-Intro Hocus & Pocus	33.00	83.00	200.00
91-99: 93-X-Mas-c. 99-1st small logo(7/46)	30.00	75.00	180.00
100	67.00	170.00	400.00
101-Nuclear explosion-c	37.00	92.00	225.00
102-120: 105,117-X-Mas-c	30.00	75.00	180.00
121-126,128-140: 135,136,138-Zatara by Kubert	28.00	70.00	170.00
127-Vigilante by Kubert; Tommy Tomorrow begins	43.00	110.00	225.00
141-157,159-161: 156-Lois Lane as Super Woman. 160-Last 52 pgs.	28.00	70.00	170.00
158-Origin Superman	32.00	80.00	195.00
162-180: 168,176-Used in POP, pg. 90	16.00	48.00	110.00
181-201: 191-Intro. Janu in Congo Bill. 198-Last Vigilante. 201-Last pre-code issue	16.00	48.00	110.00
202-220	13.00	40.00	90.00
221-240: 224-1st Golden Gorilla story	10.00	30.00	70.00
241,243-251: 248-Congo Bill becomes Congorilla. 251-Last Tommy Tomorrow	8.00	24.00	55.00
242-Origin & 1st app. Braniac (7/58); 1st mention of Shrunken City of Kandor	35.00	105.00	245.00
252-Origin & 1st app. Supergirl (5/59); Re-intro Metallo (see Superboy #49 for 1st app.)	51.00	154.00	360.00
253-2nd app. Supergirl	10.00	30.00	70.00
254-1st meeting of Bizarro & Superman	10.00	30.00	70.00
255-1st Bizarro Lois & both Bizarros leave Earth to make Bizarro World	8.50	25.50	60.00
256-260: 259-Red Kryptonite used	4.30	13.00	30.00
261-1st X-Kryptonite which gave Streaky his powers; last Congorilla in Action; origin & 1st app. Streaky The Super Cat	4.30	13.00	30.00
262-266,268-270: 263-Origin Bizarro World	3.60	11.00	25.00
267(8/60)-3rd Legion app; 1st app. Chameleon Boy, Colossal Boy, & Invisible Kid	29.00	86.00	200.00
271-275,277-282: Last 10 cent issue	3.15	9.50	22.00
276(5/61)-6th Legion app; 1st app. Braniac 5, Phantom Girl, Triplicate Girl, Bouncing Boy, Sun Boy, & Shrinking Violet; Supergirl joins Legion	10.00	30.00	70.00
283(12/61)-Legion of Super-Villains app.	4.30	13.00	30.00
284(1/62)-Mon-el app.	4.30	13.00	30.00
285(2/62)-12th Legion app; Brainiac 5 cameo; Supergirl's existance revealed to world	4.30	13.00	30.00
286(3/62)-Legion of Super Villains app.	2.30	7.00	16.00
287(4/62)-14th Legion app.(cameo)	2.30	7.00	16.00
288-Mon-el app.; r-origin Supergirl	2.30	7.00	16.00
289(6/62)-16th Legion app.(Adult); Lightning Man & Saturn Woman's marriage 1st revealed	2.30	7.00	16.00

	Good	Fine	N-Mint
290(7/62)-17th Legion app; Phantom Girl app.	2.30	7.00	16.00
291,292,294-299: 292-2nd app. Superhorse (see Adv. 293). 297-Mon-el app; 298-Legion app.	1.50	4.50	10.00
293-Origin Comet(Superhorse)	3.15	9.50	22.00
300	1.70	5.00	12.00
301-303,305-308,310-320: 306-Brainiac 5, Mon-el app. 307-Saturn Girl app. 314-r-origin Supergirl; J.L.A. x-over. 317-Death of Nor-Kan of Kandor. 319-Shrinking Violet app.	1.00	3.00	6.00
304-Origin & 1st app. Black Flame	1.00	3.00	6.00
309-Legion app.	1.00	3.00	7.00
321-333,335-340: 336-Origin Akvar(Flamebird). 340-Origin, 1st app. Parasite	.70	2.10	4.20
334-Giant G-20; origin Supergirl, Streaky, Superhorse & Legion (all-r)	1.15	3.50	8.00
341-346,348-359	.60	1.75	3.50
347,360-Gnt. Supergirl G-33,G-45; 347-Origin Comet-r; r-origin Supergirl	.90	2.75	5.50
361-372,374-380: 365-Legion app. 370-New facts about Superman's origin. 376-Last Supergirl in Action. 377-Legion begins	.35	1.00	2.00
373-Giant Supergirl G-57; Legion-r	.70	2.00	4.00
381-392: 392-Last Legion in Action. Saturn Girl gets new costume	.25	.75	1.50
393-402-All Superman issues	.25	.75	1.50
403-413: All 52pg. issues; 411-Origin Eclipso-(r). 413-Metamorpho begins, ends #418	.25	.75	1.50
414-424: 419-Intro. Human Target. 421-Intro Capt. Strong; Green Arrow begins. 422/423-Origin Human Target	.25	.75	1.50
425-Adams-a; Atom begins	.35	1.00	2.00
426-436,438,439,442,444-450	.25	.75	1.50
437,443-100pg. giants	.35	1.00	2.00
440-1st Grell-a on Green Arrow	.70	2.00	4.00
441-Grell-a on Green Arrow continues	.40	1.25	2.50
451-499: 454-Last Atom. 458-Last Green Arrow. 487-488, 495,496. 487-1st app. Microwave Man; origin Atom retold	.25	.75	1.50
500-Infinity-c; Superman life story; $1.00 size; 68 pgs.; shows Legion statues in museum		.60	1.20
501-520: 511-514-New Airwave. 513-The Atom begins. 517-Aquaman begins; ends #541		.50	1.00
521-534,537-543,545: 521-Intro. & 1st app. The Vixen. 532-New Teen Titans cameo		.50	1.00
535,536-Omega Men app.; 536-New Teen Titans cameo	.50		1.00
544: (Mando paper); 68pgs.; Origins New Luthor & Brainiac; Omega Men cameo		.50	1.00
546-J.L.A. & New Teen Titans guest		.50	1.00
547-582: 551-Starfire becomes Red-Star		.50	1.00
583-Alan Moore scripts	1.30	4.00	8.00
584-Byrne-a begins; New Teen Titans app.	.25	.75	1.50
585-597,599: 586-Legends x-over. 596-Millennium x-over		.50	1.00
598-1st app. Checkmate	.50	1.50	3.00
600-($2.50, 84 pgs., 5/88)	.70	2.00	4.00
601-642-Weekly issues ($1.50, 52 pgs.); 601-Re-intro The Secret Six. 611-614: Catwoman. 613-618: Nightwing	.25	.75	1.50
643-Superman & monthly issues begin again; Perez-c/a/scripts begin; Cover swipe Superman #1	.25	.75	1.50
644-649		.40	.80
650-$1.50, 52 pgs.	.25	.75	1.50
Annual 1 (10/87)-Art Adams c/a(p)	.60	1.75	3.50
Annual 2 (7/89, $1.75, 68 pgs.)-Perez-c/a(i)	.30	.90	1.75
Wheaties Giveaway (1947, 32 pgs., 6½x8¼", nn)-Vigilante story based on movie serial. NOTE: All copies were taped to Wheaties boxes and never found in mint condition. The mint grade applies to slight tape residue on book.	25.00	75.00	175.00

NOTE: Supergirl's origin in 262, 280, 285, 291, 305, 309. Adams c-356, 358, 359, 361-64, 366, 367, 370-74, 377-79i, 398-400, 402, 404-06, 419p, 466, 468, 473i, 485. Bailey

Action Comics #83, © DC

Action Comics #114, © DC

Action Comics #293, © DC

Advanced Dungeons & Dragons #1, © TSR

Adventure Comics #52, © DC

Adventure Comics #86, © DC

ACTION COMICS (continued)

a-24, 25. **Byrne** a-584-588p, 589i, 594-598p, 599i, 600p; c-596-600. **Grell** a-440-442, 444-446, 450-452, 456-458; c-456. **Guardineer** a-24, 25; c-8, 11, 12, 14-16, 18, 25. **Bob Kane's** Clip Carson-14-41. **Gil Kane** a-493r, 539-541, 544-546, 551-554; c-535p, 540, 541, 544p, 545-49, 551-554. **Meskin** a-42-121(most). **Moldoff** a-23-25. **Perez** a-600i, 643-648p; c-529p, 643-648. **Starlin** a-509. **Leonard Starr** a-597i(part). **Staton** a-525p, 526p, 531p, 535p, 536p. **Toth** a-406, 407, 413, 418, 419, 425, 431. **Tuska** a-486p, 550. **Williamson** a-568i.

ACTION FORCE (Also see G.I. Joe European Missions)
Mar, 1987 - No. 40?, 1988 (Magazine size, $1.00, color, weekly)
Marvel Comics Ltd. (British)

	Good	Fine	N-Mint
1-40: British G.I. Joe series. 3-w/poster insert		.50	1.00

ACTUAL CONFESSIONS (Formerly Love Adventures)
No. 13, October, 1952 - No. 14, December, 1952
Atlas Comics (MPI)

13,14	1.30	4.00	9.00

ACTUAL ROMANCES
October, 1949 - No. 2, Jan, 1950 (52 pgs.)
Marvel Comics (IPS)

1	2.85	8.50	20.00
2	1.50	4.50	10.00

ADAM AND EVE
1975, 1978 (35-49 cents)
Spire Christian Comics (Fleming H. Revell Co.)

By Al Hartley		.25	.50

ADAM-12 (TV)
Dec, 1973 - No. 10, Feb, 1976 (photo covers)
Gold Key

1	1.30	4.00	9.00
2-10	.70	2.00	5.00

ADDAMS FAMILY (TV)
Oct, 1974 - No. 3, Apr, 1975 (Hanna-Barbera)
Gold Key

1	2.00	6.00	12.00
2,3	1.00	3.00	7.00

ADLAI STEVENSON
December, 1966
Dell Publishing Co.

12-007-612-Life story; photo-c	2.35	7.00	16.00

ADOLESCENT RADIOACTIVE BLACK BELT HAMSTERS (See Clint, Laffin Gas)
1986 - No. 9, Jan, 1988 ($1.50, B&W)
Comic Castle/Eclipse Comics

1	.40	1.25	2.50
1-2nd print ($1.50)		.60	1.20
2-9		.60	1.20
3-D 1(7/86) - 4	.30	.90	1.80
2-D 1(Limited edition)	.75	2.25	4.50
2-D 2-4 ($2.50)	.40	1.15	2.30
. . .Massacre The Japanese Invasion #1 (8/89, $2.00)			
	.40	1.20	2.40

ADULT TALES OF TERROR ILL. (See Terror Illustrated)

ADVANCED DUNGEONS & DRAGONS
Dec, 1988 - Present ($1.25, color) (Newsstand #1 is Holiday, 1988-89)
DC Comics

1-Based on role playing game	.70	2.00	4.00
2,3	.35	1.00	2.00
4-14: Later issues $1.50 cover	.25	.75	1.50

ADVENTURE BOUND (See 4-Color Comics No. 239)

ADVENTURE COMICS (Formerly New Adventure)
No. 32, 11/38 - No. 490, 2/82; No. 491, 9/82 - No. 503, 9/83
National Periodical Publications/DC Comics

	Good	Fine	N-Mint
32-Anchors Aweigh (ends #52), Barry O'Neil (ends #60, not in #33), Captain Desmo (ends #47), Dale Daring (ends #47), Federal Men (ends #70), The Golden Dragon (ends #36), Rusty & His Pals (ends #52) by Bob Kane, Todd Hunter (ends #38) and Tom Brent (ends #39) begin	93.00	235.00	560.00
33-38: 37-c-used on Double Action 2	58.00	145.00	350.00
39(1/39)-Jack Wood begins; #42: 1st mention of Marijuana in comics	64.00	160.00	385.00
40-Intro. & 1st app. The Sandman. Socko Strong begins, ends #54	600.00	1500.00	3600.00
41	150.00	375.00	900.00
42-47: 47-Steve Conrad Adventurer begins, ends #76	100.00	250.00	600.00
48-Intro. & 1st app. The Hourman by Bernard Baily	567.00	1420.00	3400.00
49,50: 50-Cotton Carver by Jack Lehti begins, ends #59?	100.00	250.00	600.00
51-60: 53-Intro Jimmy "Minuteman" Martin & the Minutemen of America in Hourman; ends #78. 58-Paul Kirk Manhunter begins, ends #72	93.00	235.00	560.00
61-Intro/1st app. Starman by Jack Burnley	367.00	920.00	2200.00
62-65,67,68: 67-Origin The Mist	75.00	190.00	450.00
66-Origin Shining Knight	102.00	255.00	615.00
69-Intro. Sandy the Golden Boy (Sandman's sidekick) by Bob Kane; Sandman dons new costume	95.00	240.00	570.00
70-Last Federal Men	79.00	200.00	475.00
71-Jimmy Martin becomes costume aide to the Hourman; intro Hourman's Miracle Ray machine	75.00	190.00	450.00
72-1st Simon & Kirby Sandman	300.00	750.00	1800.00
73-Origin Manhunter by Simon & Kirby; begin new series	350.00	875.00	2100.00
74-76: 74-Thorndyke replaces Jimmy, Hourman's assistant	100.00	250.00	600.00
77-Origin Genius Jones; Mist story	100.00	250.00	600.00
78-80-Last Simon & Kirby Manhunter & Burnley Starman	100.00	250.00	600.00
81-90: 83-Last Hourman. 84-Mike Gibbs begins, ends #102	63.00	160.00	375.00
91-Last Simon & Kirby Sandman	56.00	140.00	335.00
92-99,101,102-Last Starman, Sandman, & Genius Jones. Most-S&K-c. 92-Last Manhunter	42.00	105.00	250.00
100	67.00	170.00	400.00
103-Aquaman, Green Arrow, Johnny Quick, Superboy begin; 1st small logo (4/46)	167.00	420.00	1000.00
104	52.00	130.00	315.00
105-110	43.00	110.00	260.00
111-120: 113-X-Mas-c	37.00	92.00	225.00
121-126,128-130: 128-1st meeting Superboy-Lois Lane	30.00	75.00	180.00
127-Brief origin Shining Knight retold	33.00	85.00	200.00
131-140: 132-Shining Knight 1st return to King Arthur time; origin aide Sir Butch	27.00	68.00	160.00
141,143-149	27.00	68.00	160.00
142-Origin Shining Knight & Johnny Quick retold	30.00	75.00	180.00
150,151,153,155,157,159,161,163-All have 6-pg. Shining Knight stories by Frank Frazetta. 159-Origin Johnny Quick	43.00	110.00	260.00
152,154,156,158,160,162,164-169: 166-Last Shining Knight. 168-Last 52 pgs.	20.00	50.00	140.00
170-180	18.50	56.00	130.00
181-199: 189-B&W and color illo in **POP**	17.00	51.00	120.00
200	22.00	64.00	150.00
201-209: 207-Last Johnny Quick (not in 205). 209-Last Pre-code issue;			

ADVENTURE COMICS (continued)	Good	Fine	N-Mint
origin Speedy	22.00	64.00	150.00
210-1st app. Krypto (Superdog)	114.00	343.00	800.00
211-220	13.00	40.00	90.00
221-246: 237-1st Intergalactic Vigilante Squadron (Legion tryout)			
	11.50	34.00	80.00
247(4/58)-1st Legion of Super Heroes app.; 1st app. Cosmic Boy, Lightning Boy (later Lightning Lad in #267), & Saturn Girl (origin)			
	215.00	645.00	1600.00
248-255: All Kirby Green Arrow. 253-1st meeting Superboy-Robin. 255-Intro. Red Kryptonite in Superboy (used in #252 but with no effect)			
	7.00	21.00	50.00
256-Origin Green Arrow by Kirby	25.00	75.00	175.00
257-259	7.00	21.00	50.00
260-Origin Aquaman retold	18.00	54.00	125.00
261-266,268,270: 262-Origin Speedy in Green Arrow. 270-Congorilla begins, ends #281,283			
	5.50	16.50	38.00
267(12/59)-2nd Legion of Super Heroes; Lightning Boy now called Lightning Lad; new costumes for Legion	54.00	161.00	375.00
269-Intro. Aqualad; last Green Arrow (not in #206)			
	9.30	28.00	65.00
271-Origin Luthor	9.30	28.00	65.00
272-275,277-280: 275-Origin Superman-Batman team retold (see World's Finest #94). 279-Intro White Kryptonite in Superboy. 280-1st meeting Superboy-Lori Lemaris	4.00	12.00	28.00
276-(9/60) Re-intro Metallo (3rd app?); story similar to Superboy #49			
	4.00	12.00	28.00
281,284,287-289: 281-Last Congorilla. 284-Last Aquaman in Adv. 287,288-Intro. Dev-Em, the Knave from Krypton. 287-1st Bizarro Perry White & J. Olsen. 289-Legion cameo (statues)			
	3.50	10.50	24.00
282(3/61)-5th Legion app.; intro/origin Star Boy	9.30	28.00	65.00
283-Intro. The Phantom Zone	5.50	16.50	38.00
285-1st Bizarro World story (ends #299) in Adv. (See Action #255)			
	6.50	19.50	45.00
286-1st Bizarro Mxyzptlk	5.15	16.50	36.00
290(11/61)-8th Legion app.; origin Sunboy in Legion (last 10 cent issue)			
	8.50	25.50	60.00
291,292,295-299: 292-1st Bizarro Lana Lang & Lucy Lane. 295-1st Bizarro Titano. 299-1st Gold Kryptonite (8/62)			
	3.00	9.00	21.00
293(2/62)-13th Legion app; Mon-el & Legion Super Pets (intro & origin) app. (1st Superhorse). 1st Bizarro Luthor & Kandor			
	6.00	18.00	42.00
294-1st Bizarro M. Monroe, Pres. Kennedy	4.50	14.00	32.00
300-Legion series begins; Mon-el leaves Phantom Zone (temporarily), joins Legion	26.00	77.00	180.00
301-Origin Bouncing Boy	8.50	25.50	60.00
302-305: 303-1st app. Matter Eater Lad. 304-Death of Lightning Lad in Legion	4.70	14.00	33.00
306-310: 306-Intro. Legion of Substitute Heroes. 307-Intro. Element Lad in Legion. 308-1st app. Lightning Lass in Legion			
	3.70	11.00	26.00
311-320: 312-Lightning Lad back in Legion. 315-Last new Superboy story; Colossal Boy app. 316-Origins & powers of Legion given. 317-Intro. Dream Girl in Legion; Lightning Lass becomes Light Lass; Hall of Fame series begins. 320-Dev-Em 2nd app.			
	2.85	8.50	20.00
321-Intro Time Trapper	2.15	6.50	15.00
322-330: 327-Intro Timber Wolf in Legion. 329-Intro Legion of Super Bizarros	1.85	5.50	13.00
331-340: 337-Chlorophyll Kid & Night Girl app. 340-Intro Computo in Legion	1.70	5.00	12.00
341-Triplicate Girl becomes Duo Damsel	1.15	3.50	8.00
342-345,347,350: 345-Last Hall of Fame; returns in 356,371			
	1.00	3.00	7.00
346-1st app. Karate Kid, Princess Projectra, Ferro Lad, & Nemesis Kid			

	Good	Fine	N-Mint
	1.15	3.50	8.00
348-Origin Sunboy; intro Dr. Regulus in Legion	1.15	3.50	8.00
349-Intro Universo & Rond Vidar	1.15	3.50	8.00
351-1st app. White Witch	1.00	3.00	7.00
352,354-360: 355-Insect Queen joins Legion (4/67)			
	1.00	3.00	6.00
353-Death of Ferro Lad in Legion	1.50	4.50	10.00
361-364,366,368-370: 369-Intro Mordru in Legion	.75	2.25	4.50
365-Intro Shadow Lass; lists origins & powers of L.S.H.			
	.90	2.75	5.50
367-New Legion headquarters	.90	2.75	5.50
371-Intro. Chemical King	.90	2.75	5.50
372-Timber Wolf & Chemical King join	.90	2.75	5.50
373,374,376-380: Last Legion in Adv.	.75	2.25	4.50
375-Intro Quantum Queen & The Wanderers	.90	2.75	5.50
381-389,391-400: 381-Supergirl story. 399-Unpubbed G.A. Black Canary story. 400-New costume for Supergirl			
	.60		1.20
390-Giant Supergirl G-69	.70	2.00	4.00
401,402,404-410: 409-52pg. issues begin; ends #420			
	.60		1.20
403-68pg. Giant G-81	.70	2.00	4.00
411-415: 412-Animal Man reprint/Str. Adv. #180. 413-Hawkman by Kubert; G.A. Robotman-r/Det. 178; Zatanna begins, ends #421			
	.40		.80
416-Giant DC-10. GA-r	.60		1.20
417-Morrow Vigilante; Frazetta Shining Knight r-/Adv. #161; origin The Enchantress	.60		1.20
418-424: Last Supergirl in Adv.	.40		.80
425-New look, content change to adventure; Toth-a, origin Capt. Fear			
	.25	.75	1.50
426-458: 427-Last Vigilante. 428-430-Black Orchid app. 431-440-Spectre app. 435-Mike Grell's 1st comic work ('74). 440-New Spectre origin. 441-452-Aquaman app. 445-447-The Creeper app. 449-451-Martian Manhunter app. 453-458-Superboy app; intro Mighty Girl No. 453. 457,458-Eclipso app.	.40		.80
459-466($1.00 size, 68pgs.): 459-Flash (ends 466), Deadman (ends 466), Wonder Woman (ends 464), Gr. Lantern (ends 460), New Gods begin (ends 460). 460-Aquaman begins; ends 478. 461-Justice Society begins; ends 466; death Earth II Batman (also No. 462)			
		.45	.90
467-490: 467-Starman, Plastic Man begin, end 478. 469,470-Origin Starman. 479-Dial 'H' For Hero begins, ends 490			
	.40		.80
491-499: 491-100pg. issue begins; r-Legion of Super Heroes/Adv. 247 & 267; Spectre, Aquaman, Superboy, S&K Sandman, Bl. Canary-r & new Shazam by Newton begin. 493-Challengers of the Unknown begins by Tuska w/brief origin. 492,495,496,499-S&K Sandman-r/Adventure in all; 494-499-Spectre-r/Spectre 1-3, 5-7. 495,497-499-G.A. Captain Marvel-r. 498-Plastic Man-r begin; origin Bouncing Boy-r/#30	.60		1.20
500-All Star size (Digest size, 148 pgs.)	.60	1.60	
501-503-G.A.-r	.60		1.20

NOTE: Bizarro covers-285, 286, 288, 294, 295. Vigilante app.-420, 426, 427. **Adams** a(r)-495-498i; c-365-369, 371-373, 375-379, 381-383. **Austin** a-449i-451i. **Bernard Baily** c-50, 52-57, 59. **Ditko** a-467p-478p; c-467p. **Giffen** c-491p-494p, 500p. **Grell** a-435-437, 440. **Guardineer** c-34, 45. **Kaluta** c-425. **G. Kane** a-414r, 425; c-494-499, 537. **Kirby** a-250-256. **Kubert** a-413. **Meskin** a-81, 127. **Moldoff** a-494i; c-49. **Morrow** a-413-415, 417, 422, 502r, 503r. **Newton** a-459-461, 464-466, 491p, 492p. **Orlando** a-457p, 458p. **Perez** c-484-486, 490p. **Simon/Kirby** c-73-97, 101, 102. **Starlin** c-471. **Staton** a-445-447i, 456-458p; 459, 460, 461p-465p, 466, 467p-478p, 502p(r); c-458, 461(back). **Toth** a-418, 419, 425, 431, 495p-497p. **Tuska** a-494p.

ADVENTURE COMICS

No date (early 1940s) Paper cover, 32 pgs.

IGA

Two different issues; Super-Mystery reprints from 1941

13.00	40.00	90.00

Adventure Comics #242, © DC

Adventure Comics #277, © DC

Adventure Comics #345, © DC

Adventure Into Mystery #4, © MEG

Adventures Into Terror #11, © MEG

Adventures Into The Unknown #3, © ACG

ADVENTURE IN DISNEYLAND (Giveaway)
May, 1955 (16 pgs., soft-c) (Dist. by Richfield Oil)
Walt Disney Productions

	Good	Fine	N-Mint
nn	3.00	9.00	21.00

ADVENTURE INTO FEAR
1951
Superior Publ. Ltd.

1-Exist?	7.00	21.00	50.00

ADVENTURE INTO MYSTERY
May, 1956 - No. 8, July, 1957
Atlas Comics (BFP No. 1/OPI No. 2-8)

1-Everett-c	9.30	28.00	65.00
2-Flying Saucer story	4.30	13.00	30.00
3,6,8: 3,6-Everett-c	4.00	12.00	28.00
4-Williamson-a, 4 pgs; Powell-a	5.70	17.00	40.00
5-Everett-c/a, Orlando-a	4.00	12.00	28.00
7-Torres-a; Everett-c	4.00	12.00	28.00

ADVENTURE IS MY CAREER
1945 (44 pgs.)
U.S. Coast Guard Academy/Street & Smith

nn-Simon, Milt Gross-a	6.00	18.00	42.00

ADVENTURERS, THE
Aug, 1986 - No. 10, 1987? ($1.50, B&W)
Aircel Comics/Adventure Publ.

1-Peter Hsu-a	1.00	3.00	6.00
1-Cover variant, limited ed.	3.00	9.00	18.00
1-2nd print (1986); 1st app. Elf Warrior	.50	1.50	3.00
2,3	.40	1.25	2.50
0 (#4, 12/86)-Origin	.35	1.00	2.00
4-10	.25	.80	1.60
Book II, regular ed. #1	.25	.80	1.60
Book II, limited ed. #1	.25	.80	1.60
Book II, #2-9	.25	.80	1.60
Book III, #1 (10/89, $2.25)-Regular & limited-c	.40	1.15	2.25
Book III, #2,3	.40	1.15	2.25

ADVENTURES (No. 2 Spectacular... on cover)
11/49 - No. 2, 2/50 (No. 1 ... in Romance on cover)
St. John Publishing Co. (Slightly large size)

1(Scarce); Bolle, Starr-a(2)	11.30	34.00	80.00
2(Scarce)-Slave Girl; China Bombshell app.; Bolle, L. Starr-a	17.00	51.00	120.00

ADVENTURES FOR BOYS
December, 1954
Bailey Enterprises

nn-Comics, text, & photos	2.00	6.00	14.00

ADVENTURES IN PARADISE (See 4-Color No. 1301)

ADVENTURES IN ROMANCE (See Adventures)

ADVENTURES IN SCIENCE (See Classics Illustrated Special Issue)

ADVENTURES IN 3-D
Nov, 1953 - No. 2, Jan, 1954
Harvey Publications

1-Nostrand, Powell-a, 2-Powell-a	10.00	30.00	70.00

ADVENTURES INTO DARKNESS (See Seduction/Innocent 3-D)
No. 5, Aug, 1952 - No. 14, 1954
Better-Standard Publications/Visual Editions

5-Katz c/a; Toth-a(p)	7.00	21.00	50.00
6-Tuska, Katz-a	5.00	15.00	35.00
7-Katz c/a	5.50	16.50	38.00
8,9-Toth-a(p)	6.50	19.50	45.00
10,11-Jack Katz-a	4.00	12.00	28.00

	Good	Fine	N-Mint
12-Toth-a?; lingerie panels	4.30	13.00	30.00
13-Toth-a(p); Cannibalism story cited by T. E. Murphy articles	5.70	17.00	40.00
14	3.15	9.50	22.00

NOTE: *Fawcette* a-13. *Moriera* a-5. *Sekowsky* a-10, 11, 13(2).

ADVENTURES INTO TERROR (Formerly Joker Comics)
No. 43, Nov, 1950 - No. 31, May, 1954
Marvel/Atlas Comics (CDS)

43(#1)	11.00	32.00	75.00
44(2/51)	8.00	24.00	56.00
3(4/51), 4	5.70	17.00	40.00
5-Wolverton-c panel/Mystic #6. Atom Bomb story	6.50	19.50	45.00
6,8: 8-Wolverton text illo r-/Marvel Tales 104	4.50	14.00	32.00
7-Wolverton-a "Where Monsters Dwell", 6 pgs.; Tuska-c	18.50	56.00	130.00
9,10,12-Krigstein-a. 9-Decapitation panels	6.00	18.00	42.00
11,13-20	3.70	11.00	26.00
21-24,26-31	3.00	9.00	21.00
25-Matt Fox-a	5.00	15.00	35.00

NOTE: *Ayers* a-21. *Colan* a-3, 5, 14, 21, 24, 25, 28, 29; c-27. *Colletta* a-30. *Everett* c-13, 21, 25. *Fass* a-28, 29. *Forte* a-28. *Heath* a-43, 44, 4-6, 22, 24, 26; c-43, 9, 11. *Lazarus* a-7. *Maneely* a-7, 10, 11, 21. c-15, 29. *Don Rico* a-4, 5. *Sekowsky* a-43, 3, 4. *Sinnott* a-8, 9, 11, 28. *Tuska* a-14.

ADVENTURES INTO THE UNKNOWN
Fall, 1948 - No. 174, Aug, 1967 (No. 1-33: 52 pgs.)
American Comics Group

(1st continuous series horror comic; see Eerie #1)

1-Guardiner-a; adapt. of 'Castle of Otranto' by Horace Walpole	48.00	145.00	335.00
2	21.50	64.00	150.00
3-Feldstein-a, 9 pgs.	23.00	68.00	160.00
4,5	13.00	40.00	90.00
6-10	10.00	30.00	70.00
11-16,18-20: 13-Starr-a	7.00	21.00	50.00
17-Story similar to movie 'The Thing'	10.00	30.00	70.00
21-26,28-30	6.50	19.50	45.00
27-Williamson/Krenkel-a, 8 pgs.	14.00	42.00	100.00
31-50: 38-Atom bomb panels	4.30	13.00	30.00
51(1/54) - 59 (3-D effect issues). 52-E.C. swipe/Haunt Of Fear 14	10.00	30.00	70.00
60-Woodesque-a by Landau	3.15	9.50	22.00
61-Last pre-code issue (1-2/55)	2.85	8.50	20.00
62-70	2.15	6.50	15.00
71-90	1.50	4.50	10.00
91,95,96(#95 on inside),107,116-All contain Williamson-a	2.85	8.50	20.00
92-94,97-99,101-106,108-115,117-127: 109-113,118-Whitney painted-c	1.35	4.00	8.00
100	2.00	6.00	12.00
128-Williamson/Krenkel/Torres-a(r)/Forbidden Worlds 63	2.00	6.00	12.00
129-150	1.00	3.00	6.00
151-153: 153-Magic Agent app.	.70	2.00	4.00
154-Nemesis series begins (origin), ends #170	1.00	3.00	6.00
155-167,169-174: 157-Magic Agent app.	.70	2.00	4.00
168-Ditko-a(p)	1.00	3.00	6.00

NOTE: "Spirit of Frankenstein" series in 5, 6, 8-10, 12, 16. *Buscema* a-100, 106, 108-110, 158r, 165r. *Craig* a-152, 160. *Goode* a-45, 47, 60. *Landau* a-51, 59-63. *Lazarus* a-48, 51, 52, 58, 79, 87; c-51, 52, 58. *Reinman* a-111, 112, 137, 145, 164. *Whitney* c-most. *Torres/Williamson* a-116.

ADVENTURES INTO WEIRD WORLDS
Jan, 1952 - No. 30, June, 1954
Marvel/Atlas Comics (ACI)

ADVS. INTO WEIRD WORLDS (continued)	Good	Fine	N-Mint
1-Atom bomb panels	12.00	36.00	85.00
2-sci/fic stories (2)	6.50	19.50	45.00
3-9: 7-Tongue ripped out	5.00	15.00	35.00
10-Krigstein, Everett-a	5.00	15.00	35.00
11-20	4.00	12.00	28.00
21-Hitler in Hell story	3.65	11.00	25.00
22-26: 4-Man holds hypo & splits in two	2.85	8.50	20.00
27-Matt Fox end of world story-a; severed head cover	8.50	26.00	60.00
28-Atom bomb story; decapitation panels	3.65	11.00	25.00
29,30	2.65	8.00	18.00

NOTE: Ayers a-8, 26. Everett a-4, 5; c-6, 8, 10-13, 18, 19, 22, 24; a-4, 25. Fass a-7. Forte a-21, 24. Heath a-1, 4, 17, 22; c-7. Rico a-13. Maneely a-3, 11, 20, 22, 23, 25; c-3, 25-27, 29. Reinman a-24, 28. Robinson a-13. Sinnott a-25, 30. Tuska a-1, 12, 15. Whitney a-7. Wildey a-28. Bondage c-22.

ADVENTURES IN WONDERLAND
April, 1955 - No. 5, Feb, 1956 (Jr. Readers Guild)
Lev Gleason Publications

1-Maurer-a	3.50	10.50	24.00
2-4	2.00	6.00	14.00
5-Christmas issue	2.30	7.00	16.00

ADVENTURES OF ALAN LADD, THE
Oct-Nov, 1949 - No. 9, Feb-Mar, 1951 (All 52 pgs.)
National Periodical Publications

1-Photo-c	34.00	100.00	235.00
2-Photo-c	20.00	60.00	140.00
3-6: Last photo-c	16.50	50.00	115.00
7-9	14.00	43.00	100.00

NOTE: Moreira a-3-7.

ADVENTURES OF ALICE
(Also see Alice in Wonderland & . . .at Monkey Island)
1945
Civil Service Publ./Pentagon Publishing Co.

1	5.50	16.50	38.00
2-Through the Magic Looking Glass	4.30	13.00	30.00

ADVENTURES OF BARON MUNCHAUSEN, THE
July, 1989 - No. 4, Oct, 1989 ($1.75, color, mini-series)
Now Comics

1-4: Movie adaptation	.30	.90	1.80

ADVENTURES OF BAYOU BILLY, THE
Sept, 1989 - Present ($1.00, color)
Archie Comics

1-5: Esposito-c/a(i)		.50	1.00

ADVENTURES OF BOB HOPE, THE (Also see True Comics 59)
Feb-Mar, 1950 - No. 109, Feb-Mar, 1968 (#1-10: 52pgs.)
National Periodical Publications

1-Photo-c	50.00	150.00	350.00
2-Photo-c	26.00	77.00	180.00
3,4-Photo-c	17.00	51.00	120.00
5-10	13.00	40.00	90.00
11-20	7.00	21.00	50.00
21-30	5.00	15.00	35.00
31-40	4.00	12.00	28.00
41-50	3.00	9.00	21.00
51-70	2.00	6.00	14.00
71-93,95-105	1.15	3.50	7.00
94-Aquaman cameo	1.50	4.50	9.00
106-109-Adams c/a	2.65	8.00	18.00

NOTE: Kitty Karr of Hollywood in #17-20, 22, 28. Liz in #26, 109. Miss Beverly Hills of Hollywood in #7, 10, 13, 14. Miss Melody Lane of Broadway in #15. Rusty in #23, 25. Tommy in #24. No 2nd feature in #2-4, 6, 8, 11, 12, 28-108.

ADVENTURES OF CAPTAIN JACK, THE
June, 1986 - No. 12, 1988 ($2.00, B&W, Adults)

Fantagraphics Books	Good	Fine	N-Mint
1	.50	1.50	3.00
2	.40	1.25	2.50
3-12	.30	.90	1.80

ADVENTURES OF DEAN MARTIN AND JERRY LEWIS, THE
(The Adventures of Jerry Lewis No. 41 on)
July-Aug, 1952 - No. 40, Oct, 1957
National Periodical Publications

1	36.00	107.00	250.00
2	17.00	51.00	120.00
3-10	9.30	28.00	65.00
11-19: Last precode (2/55)	5.00	15.00	35.00
20-30	3.65	11.00	25.00
31-40	2.85	8.50	20.00

ADVENTURES OF G. I. JOE
1969 (3¼"x7") (20 & 16 pgs.)
Giveaways

First Series: 1-Danger of the Depths. 2-Perilous Rescue. 3-Secret Mission to Spy Island. 4-Mysterious Explosion. 5-Fantastic Free Fall. 6-Eight Ropes of Danger. 7-Mouth of Doom. 8-Hidden Missile Discovery. 9-Space Walk Mystery. 10-Fight for Survival. 11-The Shark's Surprise. Second Series: 2-Flying Space Adventure. 4-White Tiger Hunt. 7-Capture of the Pygmy Gorilla. 12-Secret of the Mummy's Tomb. Third Series: Reprinted surviving titles of First Series. Fourth Series: 13-Adventure Team Headquarters. 14-Search For the Stolen Idol. each.... .30 .60

ADVENTURES OF HAWKSHAW (See Hawkshaw The Detective)
1917 (9-3/4 x 13½", 48 pgs., Color & two-tone)
The Saalfield Publishing Co.

By Gus Mager (only 24 pgs. of strips, reverse of each page is blank)

	18.00	54.00	125.00

ADVENTURES OF HOMER COBB, THE
September, 1947 (Oversized)
Say/Bart Prod. (Canadian)

1-(Scarce)-Feldstein-a	17.00	50.00	120.00

ADVENTURES OF HOMER GHOST (See Homer The Happy Ghost)
June, 1957 - No. 2, August, 1957
Atlas Comics

V1#1, 2	1.50	4.50	10.00

ADVENTURES OF JERRY LEWIS, THE (Advs. of Dean Martin & Jerry Lewis No. 1-40)(See Super DC Giant)
No. 41, Nov, 1957 - No. 124, May-June, 1971
National Periodical Publications

41-60	2.30	7.00	16.00
61-80: 68,74-Photo-c	1.70	5.00	12.00
81-91,93-96,98-100: 89-Bob Hope app.	1.00	3.00	7.00
92-Superman cameo	1.15	3.50	8.00
97-Batman/Robin x-over; Joker-c/sty	2.00	6.00	14.00
101-104-Adams c/a; 102-Beatles app.	2.65	8.00	18.00
105-Superman x-over	1.00	3.00	7.00
106-111,113-116	.70	2.00	4.00
112-Flash x-over	.85	2.50	5.00
117-Wonder Woman x-over	.85	2.50	5.00
118-124	.50	1.50	3.00

ADVENTURES OF LUTHER ARKWRIGHT, THE
Oct, 1987 - No. 9, Jan? 1989 ($2.00, B&W)
Valkyrie Press

1	.40	1.25	2.50
2-9	.30	.90	1.80

ADVENTURES OF MARGARET O'BRIEN, THE
1947 (20 pgs. in color; slick cover; regular size) (Premium)
Bambury Fashions (Clothes)

In "The Big City"-movie adaptation (Scarce) 13.00 40.00 90.00

Adventures Into Weird Worlds #2, © MEG

The Adventures Of Bob Hope #108, © DC

The Adventures Of Jerry Lewis #87, © DC

The Adventures Of Pinky Lee #1, © MEG   The Adventures Of Rex The Wonder Dog #18, © DC   Adventures Of The Fly #2, © AP

ADVENTURES OF MIGHTY MOUSE (Mighty Mouse Advs. No. 1)
No. 2, Jan, 1952 - No. 18, May, 1955
St. John Publishing Co.

	Good	Fine	N-Mint
2	8.50	25.50	60.00
3-5	5.00	15.00	35.00
6-18	3.00	9.00	21.00

ADVENTURES OF MIGHTY MOUSE (2nd Series)
(Two No. 144's; formerly Paul Terry's Comics; No. 129-137 have
nn's)(Becomes Mighty Mouse No. 161 on)
No. 126, Aug, 1955 - No. 160, Oct, 1963
St. John/Pines/Dell/Gold Key

126(8/55), 127(10/55), 128(11/55)-St. John	2.30	7.00	16.00
nn(129, 4/56)-144(8/59)-Pines	1.70	5.00	12.00
144(10-12/59)-155(7-9/62) Dell	1.50	4.50	10.00
156(10/62)-160(10/63) Gold Key	1.50	4.50	10.00

NOTE: Early issues titled "Paul Terry's Adventures of . . . ."

ADVENTURES OF MIGHTY MOUSE (Formerly Mighty Mouse)
No. 166, Mar, 1979 - No. 172, Jan, 1980
Gold Key

166-172	.50	1.50	3.00

ADVS. OF MR. FROG & MISS MOUSE (See Dell Junior Treasury No. 4)

ADVENTURES OF OZZIE AND HARRIET, THE (Radio)
Oct-Nov, 1949 - No. 5, June-July, 1950
National Periodical Publications

1-Photo-c	30.00	90.00	210.00
2	21.00	62.00	150.00
3-5	18.00	54.00	125.00

ADVENTURES OF PATORUZU
Aug, 1946 - Winter, 1946
Green Publishing Co.

nn's-Contains Animal Crackers reprints	1.70	5.00	12.00

ADVENTURES OF PINKY LEE, THE (TV)
July, 1955 - No. 5, Dec, 1955
Atlas Comics

1	10.00	30.00	70.00
2-5	5.70	17.00	40.00

ADVENTURES OF PIPSQUEAK, THE (Formerly Pat the Brat)
No. 34, Sept, 1959 - No. 39, July, 1960
Archie Publications (Radio Comics)

34	2.15	6.50	15.00
35-39	1.30	4.00	9.00

ADVENTURES OF QUAKE & QUISP, THE (See Quaker Oats "Plenty of Glutton")

ADVENTURES OF REX THE WONDER DOG, THE (Rex . . . No. 1)
Jan-Feb, 1952 - No. 45, May-June, 1959; No. 46, Nov-Dec, 1959
National Periodical Publications

1-(Scarce)-Toth-a	50.00	150.00	350.00
2-(Scarce)-Toth-a	25.00	75.00	175.00
3-(Scarce)-Toth-a	20.00	60.00	140.00
4,5	14.00	43.00	100.00
6-10	9.30	28.00	65.00
11-Atom bomb c/story	8.00	24.00	56.00
12-19: Last precode (1-2/55)	5.00	15.00	35.00
20-46	3.15	10.00	22.00

NOTE: Infantino, Gil Kane art in most issues.

ADVENTURES OF ROBIN HOOD, THE (Formerly Robin Hood)
No. 7, 9/57 - No. 8, 11/57 (Based on Richard Greene TV Show)
Magazine Enterprises (Sussex Publ. Co.)

7,8-Richard Greene photo-c. 7-Powell-a	4.30	13.00	30.00

ADVENTURES OF ROBIN HOOD, THE
March, 1974 - No. 7, Jan, 1975 (Disney Cartoon) (36 pgs.)
Gold Key

	Good	Fine	N-Mint
1(90291-403)-Part-r of $1.50 editions	.70	2.00	4.00
2-7: 1-7, part-r	.45	1.25	2.50

ADVENTURES OF SLIM AND SPUD, THE
1924 (3¾''x9¾'')(104 pg. B&W strip reprints)
Prairie Farmer Publ. Co.

nn	9.00	27.00	62.00

ADVENTURES OF STUBBY, SANTA'S SMALLEST REINDEER, THE
nd (early 1940s) 12 pgs.
W. T. Grant Co. (Giveaway)

nn	2.00	6.00	12.00

ADVENTURES OF SUPERMAN (Formerly Superman)
No. 424, Jan, 1987 - Present
DC Comics

424	.45	1.35	2.70
425-435: 426-Legends x-over. 432-1st app. Jose Delgado who becomes Gangbuster in #434		.50	1.00
436-449: 436-Byrne scripts begin. 436,437-Millennium x-over. 438-New Brainiac app.		.50	1.00
450-462: 457-Perez plots		.35	.70
Annual 1 (9/87)-Starlin-c	.25	.70	1.40
Annual 2 (1988)	.25	.70	1.40

ADVENTURES OF THE BIG BOY
1956 - Present (Giveaway)(East & West editions of early issues)
Timely Comics/Webs Adv. Corp./Illus. Features

1-Everett-a	45.00	135.00	315.00
2-Everett-a	22.00	65.00	154.00
3-5	7.00	21.00	50.00
6-10: 6-Sci/fic issue	4.50	13.50	30.00
11-20	2.35	7.00	15.00
21-30	1.35	4.00	8.00
31-50	.70	2.00	4.00
51-100	.35	1.00	2.00
101-150		.50	1.00
151-240		.20	.40
241-376: 266-Superman x-over			.10
1-50 ('76-'84,Paragon Prod.)		.10	.20
Summer, 1959 ish, large size	2.50	7.50	15.00

ADVENTURES OF THE DETECTIVE
No date (1930's) 36 pgs.; 9½x12''; B&W (paper cover)
Humor Publ. Co.

Not reprints; Ace King by Martin Nadle	6.50	19.50	45.00
2nd version (printed in red & blue)	6.50	19.50	45.00

ADVENTURES OF THE DOVER BOYS
September, 1950 - No. 2, 1950 (No month given)
Archie Comics (Close-up)

1,2	3.70	11.00	26.00

ADVENTURES OF THE FLY (The Fly, No. 2; Fly Man No. 32-39; See
The Double Life of Private Strong & Laugh Comics)
Aug, 1959 - No. 30, Oct, 1964; No. 31, May, 1965
Archie Publications/Radio Comics

1-Shield app.; origin The Fly; S&K-c/a	26.00	80.00	185.00
2-Williamson, S&K, Powell-a	14.00	43.00	100.00
3-Origin retold; Davis, Powell-a	9.30	28.00	65.00
4-Adams-a(p)(1 panel); S&K-c; Powell-a; Shield x-over	6.50	19.50	45.00
5-10: 7-Black Hood app. 8,9-Shield x-over. 9-1st app. Cat Girl. 10-Black Hood app.	3.70	11.00	25.00
11-13,15-20: 16-Last 10 cent issue. 20-Origin Fly Girl retold	2.30	7.00	16.00

ADVENTURES OF THE FLY (continued)	Good	Fine	N-Mint
14-Intro. & origin Fly Girl	3.50	10.50	24.00
21-30: 23-Jaguar cameo. 29-Black Hood cameo. 30-Comet x-over in Fly Girl	1.70	5.00	12.00
31-Black Hood, Shield, Comet app.	1.70	5.00	12.00

NOTE: *Tuska a-1. Simon c-2-4.*

ADVENTURES OF THE JAGUAR, THE (See Blue Ribbon Comics, Laugh Comics & Mighty Crusaders)
Sept, 1961 - No. 15, Nov, 1963
Archie Publications (Radio Comics)

1-Origin Jaguar (1st app?)	10.00	30.00	70.00
2,3: 3-Last 10 cent issue	4.30	13.00	30.00
4,5-Catgirl app.	3.15	9.50	22.00
6-10: 6-Catgirl app.	2.30	7.00	16.00
11-15: 13,14-Catgirl, Black Hood app. in both	1.70	5.00	12.00

ADVENTURES OF THE OUTSIDERS, THE (Formerly Batman & The Outsiders; also see The Outsiders)
No. 33, May, 1986 - No. 46, June, 1987
DC Comics

33-46		.35	.70

ADVENTURES OF TINKER BELL (See 4-Color No. 982)

ADVENTURES OF TOM SAWYER (See Dell Junior Treasury No. 10)

ADVENTURES OF WILLIE GREEN, THE
1915 (8½X16, 50 cents, B&W, soft-c)
Frank M. Acton Co.

Book 1-By Harris Brown; strip-r	11.00	32.00	75.00

ADVENTURES OF YOUNG DR. MASTERS, THE
Aug, 1964 - No. 2, Nov, 1964
Archie Comics (Radio Comics)

1,2	.85	2.50	5.00

ADVENTURES OF ZOT! IN DIMENSION 10 ½
Sept, 1987 (One shot, $2.00, B&W)
Eclipse Comics

14 ½	.35	1.00	2.00

ADVENTURES ON THE PLANET OF THE APES
Oct, 1975 - No. 11, Dec, 1976
Marvel Comics Group

1-Planet of the Apes-r in color; Starlin-c		.50	1.00
2-11		.30	.60

NOTE: *Alcala a-6-11r. Buckler c-2p. Nasser c-7. Starlin c-6. Tuska a-1-5r.*

ADVENTURES WITH SANTA CLAUS
No date (early 50's) (24 pgs.) (paper cover) (Giveaway)
Promotional Publ. Co. (Murphy's Store)

Contains 8 pgs. ads	3.00	9.00	21.00
16 page version	3.00	9.00	21.00

AFRICA
1955
Magazine Enterprises

1(A-1 #137)-Cave Girl, Thun'da; Powell-c/a(4)	11.00	32.00	75.00

AFRICAN LION (See 4-Color No. 665)

AFTER DARK
No. 6, May, 1955 - No. 8, Sept, 1955
Sterling Comics

6-8-Sekowsky-a in all	2.65	8.00	18.00

AGAINST BLACKSHARD 3-D (Also see SoulQuest)
August, 1986 ($2.25)
Sirius Comics

1	.40	1.15	2.30

AGGIE MACK
Jan, 1948 - No. 8, Aug, 1949
Four Star Comics Corp./Superior Comics Ltd.

	Good	Fine	N-Mint
1-Feldstein-a, "Johnny Prep"	9.30	28.00	65.00
2,3-Kamen-c	5.00	15.00	35.00
4-Feldstein "Johnny Prep"; Kamen-c	6.50	19.50	45.00
5-8-Kamen c/a	4.50	13.50	32.00

AGGIE MACK (See 4-Color Comics No. 1335)

AIN'T IT A GRAND & GLORIOUS FEELING?
1922 (52 pgs.; 9x9¾''; stiff cardboard cover)
Whitman Publishing Co.

1921 daily strip-r; B&W, color-c; Briggs-a	11.00	32.00	75.00

AIR ACE (Formerly Bill Barnes No. 1-12)
V2#1, Jan, 1944 - V3/8(No. 20), Feb-Mar, 1947
Street & Smith Publications

V2#1	7.00	21.00	50.00
V2#2-12: 7-Powell-a	4.00	12.00	28.00
V3#1-6	2.30	7.00	16.00
V3#7-Powell bondage-c/a; all atomic ish.	6.00	18.00	42.00
V3#8 (V5#8 on-c)-Powell c/a	2.65	8.00	18.00

AIRBOY (Also see Airmaidens, Skywolf, Target: Airboy & Valkyrie)
July, 1986 - No. 50?, 1989 (#1-8, 20pgs., bi-weekly; #9-on, 36pgs, monthly)
Eclipse Comics

1-$1.25-c begins, ends #32 (33-41 are $1.75)	.65	1.90	3.80
2-1st Marisa; Skywolf gets new costume	.35	1.00	2.00
3,4,6-8: 3-The Heap begins	.35	1.00	2.00
5-Valkyrie returns; Dave Stevens-c	.50	1.50	3.00
9-20: 9-Skywolf begins. 11-Origin of G.A. Airboy & his plane Birdie	.25	.80	1.60
21-30	.25	.70	1.40
31-41: 41-r/1st app. Valkyrie from Air Fighters. 38-40-The Heap-r by Infantino. 46,47-part-r/Air Fighters	.25	.80	1.60
42-49: 42-Begins $1.95-c. 48-Black Angel-r/A.F.	.25	.80	1.60
50 ($3.95, 52 pgs.)-Kubert-c	.70	2.00	3.95

NOTE: *Spiegle a-34, 35, 37. Ken Steacy painted-c 33.*

AIRBOY COMICS (Air Fighters Comics No. 1-22)
V2#11, Dec, 1945 - V10#4, May, 1953 (No V3#3)
Hillman Periodicals

V2#11	26.00	77.00	180.00
12-Valkyrie app.	17.00	51.00	120.00
V3#1,2(no #3)	13.00	42.00	100.00
4-The Heap app. in Skywolf	11.50	34.00	80.00
5-8: 6-Valkyrie app;	10.00	30.00	70.00
9-Origin The Heap	11.50	34.00	80.00
10,11	10.00	30.00	70.00
12-Skywolf & Airboy x-over; Valkyrie app.	13.00	40.00	90.00
V4#1-Iron Lady app.	11.50	34.00	80.00
2-Rackman begins	7.00	21.00	50.00
3,12	7.00	21.00	50.00
4-Simon & Kirby-c	8.50	25.50	60.00
5-11-All S&K-a	10.00	30.00	70.00
V5#1-9: 4-Infantino Heap. 5-Skull-c	5.00	15.00	35.00
10,11: 10-Origin The Heap	5.00	15.00	35.00
12-Krigstein-a(p)	6.50	19.50	45.00
V6#1-3,5-12: 6,8-Origin The Heap	5.00	15.00	35.00
4-Origin retold	5.70	17.00	40.00
V7#1-12: 7,8,10-Origin The Heap	5.00	15.00	35.00
V8#1-3,6-12	4.00	12.00	28.00
4-Krigstein-a	6.50	19.50	45.00
5(#100)	5.00	15.00	35.00
V9#1-6,8-12: 2-Valkyrie app.	4.00	12.00	28.00
7-One pg. Frazetta ad	4.50	14.00	32.00

The Adventures Of The Jaguar #1, © AP

Air Ace V3#7, © S & S

Airboy Comics V3#11, © HILL

Air Fighters Comics V1#1, © HILL

Air War Stories #1, © DELL

Alarming Tales #3, © HARV

AIRBOY COMICS (continued)	Good	Fine	N-Mint
V10#1-4	4.00	12.00	28.00

NOTE: *Barry a-V2#3, 7. Bolle a-V4#12. McWilliams a-V3#7, 9. Powell a-V7#2, 3, V8#1, 6. Starr a-V5#1, 12. Dick Wood a-V4#12. Bondage-c V5#8.*

AIRBOY MEETS THE PROWLER
Dec, 1987 (One shot, $1.95, color)
Eclipse Comics

1	.35	1.00	1.95

AIRBOY - MR. MONSTER SPECIAL
Aug, 1987 (One Shot) ($1.75, color)
Eclipse Comics

1	.35	1.00	1.95

AIRBOY VERSUS THE AIR MAIDENS
July, 1988 ($1.95, color)
Eclipse Comics

1	.35	1.00	1.95

AIR FIGHTERS CLASSICS
Nov, 1987 - No. 6, May, 1989 ($3.95, B&W, 68 pgs.)
Eclipse Comics

1-6: r/G.A. Air Fighters #2-7. 1-Origin Airboy	.70	2.00	3.95

AIR FIGHTERS COMICS (Airboy Comics #23 (V2#11) on)
Nov, 1941; No. 2, Nov, 1942 - V2#10, Fall, 1945
Hillman Periodicals

V1#1-(Produced by Funnies, Inc.); Black Commander only app.
	90.00	270.00	630.00
2(11/42)-(Produced by Quality artists & Biro for Hillman); Origin Airboy & Iron Ace; Black Angel, Flying Dutchman & Skywolf begin; Fuje-a; Biro c/a	140.00	420.00	980.00
3-Origin The Heap & Skywolf	71.00	213.00	500.00
4	50.00	150.00	350.00
5,6	37.00	110.00	260.00
7-12	28.00	86.00	200.00
V2#1,3-9: 5-Flag-c; Fuje-a. 7-Valkyrie app.	26.50	80.00	185.00
2-Skywolf by Giunta; Flying Dutchman by Fuje; 1st meeting Valkyrie & Airboy (She worked for the Nazis in beginning)	32.00	95.00	225.00
10-Origin The Heap & Skywolf	32.00	95.00	225.00

NOTE: *Fuje a-V1#2, 5, 7, V2#2, 3, 5, 7-9. Giunta a-V2#2, 3, 7, 9.*

AIRFIGHTERS MEET SGT. STRIKE SPECIAL, THE
Jan, 1988 ($1.95, color, one-shot, stiff-c)
Eclipse Comics

1-Airboy, Valkyrie, Skywolf app.	.35	1.00	2.00

AIR FORCES (See American Air Forces)

AIRMAIDENS SPECIAL
August, 1987 ($1.75, color)(Baxter, One-shot)
Eclipse Comics

1-Marisa becomes La Lupina (origin)	.35	1.00	2.00

AIR POWER (CBS TV & the U.S. Air Force Presents)
1956 (32pgs, 5¼x7¼", soft-c)
Prudential Insurance Co. giveaway

nn-Toth-a? Based on 'You Are There' TV program by Walter Cronkite	5.00	15.00	30.00

AIR RAIDERS
Nov, 1987 - No. 5, Mar., 1988 ($1.00, color)
Star Comics/Marvel #3 on

1-5		.50	1.00

AIR WAR STORIES
Sept-Nov, 1964 - No. 8, Aug, 1966
Dell Publishing Co.

1-Painted-c; Glanzman c/a begins	1.35	4.00	8.00

	Good	Fine	N-Mint
2-8	.70	2.00	4.00

AKIRA
Sept, 1988 - Present ($3.50, color, deluxe, 68pgs.)
Epic Comics (Marvel)

1	.90	2.75	5.50
1,2-2nd printings ('89, $3.95)	.70	2.00	4.00
2	.75	2.25	4.50
3-16	.65	1.90	3.75

ALADDIN (See Dell Junior Treasury No. 2)

ALAN LADD (See The Adventures of . . .)

ALARMING ADVENTURES
Oct, 1962 - No. 3, Feb, 1963
Harvey Publications

1	3.00	9.00	21.00
2,3	2.00	6.00	14.00

NOTE: *Bailey a-1, 3. Crandall a-1, 2. Powell a-2(2). Severin c-1-3. Torres a-2? Tuska a-1. Williamson a-1i, 2i, 3.*

ALARMING TALES
Sept, 1957 - No. 6, Nov, 1958
Harvey Publications (Western Tales)

1-Kirby c/a(4)	5.00	15.00	35.00
2-Kirby-a(4)	5.00	15.00	35.00
3,4-Kirby-a	3.60	11.00	25.00
5-Kirby/Williamson-a	4.30	13.00	30.00
6-Torres-a	3.00	9.00	21.00

ALBEDO
April, 1985 - No. 15?, 1989 (B&W)
Thoughts And Images

0-Yellow cover; 50 copies	24.00	74.00	148.00
0-White cover, 450 copies	22.00	67.00	135.00
0-Blue, 1st printing, 500 copies	12.00	36.00	72.00
0-Blue, 2nd printing, 1000 copies	9.00	27.00	54.00
0-3rd printing	.70	2.05	4.10
0-4th printing	.25	.80	1.60
1-Dark red; 1st app. Usagi Yojimbo	11.20	33.50	67.00
1-Bright red	10.50	31.00	63.00
2	11.20	33.50	67.00
3	1.35	4.05	8.10
4	3.00	9.00	18.00
5	1.10	3.25	6.50
6	1.35	4.05	8.10
7-15	.35	1.05	2.10

(Prices vary widely on this series)

ALBERTO (See The Crusaders)

ALBERT THE ALLIGATOR & POGO POSSUM (See 4-Color Comics No. 105, 148)

ALBUM OF CRIME (See Fox Giants)

ALBUM OF LOVE (See Fox Giants)

AL CAPP'S DOGPATCH (Also see Mammy Yokum)
No. 71, June, 1949 - No. 4, Dec, 1949
Toby Press

71(#1)-R-/from Tip Top #112-114	14.30	43.00	100.00
2-4: 4-R-/from Li'l Abner #73	10.00	30.00	70.00

AL CAPP'S SHMOO (Also see Oxydol-Dreft)
July, 1949 - No. 5, April, 1950 (None by Al Capp)
Toby Press

1	22.00	65.00	155.00
2-5: 3-Sci-fi trip to moon. 4-X-mas-c; origin/1st app. Super-Shmoo	17.00	51.00	120.00

AL CAPP'S WOLF GAL
1951 - No. 2, 1952
Toby Press

	Good	Fine	N-Mint
1,2-Edited-r from Li'l Abner No. 63,64	20.00	60.00	140.00

ALEXANDER THE GREAT (See 4-Color No. 688)

ALF (TV) (See Star Comics Digest)
Mar, 1988 - Present ($1.00, color)
Marvel Comics

1-Post-a; photo-c	1.15	3.50	7.00
2-Post-a	.70	2.00	4.00
3-5	.35	1.00	2.00
6-10: 6-Photo-c		.60	1.20
11-26: 26-Infinity-c		.50	1.00
Annual 1 ($1.75, 68 pgs.)-Evolutionary War	.60	1.75	3.50
Annual 2 (1989, $2.00, 68 pgs.)-Sienkiewicz-c	.35	1.00	2.00
Holiday Special 1 ($1.75, 1988, 68 pgs.)	.30	.90	1.75
Holiday Special 2 ($2.00, 1989, 68 pgs.)	.35	1.00	2.00
...Comics Digest #1 (1988)-Reprints Alf #1,2	.25	.75	1.50
Spring Special 1 (Spr/89, $1.75, 68 pgs.)	.30	.90	1.75

ALGIE
Dec, 1953 - No. 3, 1954
Timor Publ. Co.

1-Teenage	1.60	4.70	11.00
2,3	1.00	3.00	7.00
Accepted Reprint #2(nd)	.70	2.00	5.00
Super Reprint 15	.60	1.80	4.00

ALICE (New Adventures in Wonderland)
No. 10, 7-8/51 - No. 2, 11-12/51
Ziff-Davis Publ. Co.

10-Painted-c (spanking scene); Berg-a	10.00	30.00	70.00
11-Dave Berg-a	4.50	14.00	32.00
2-Dave Berg-a	3.70	11.00	26.00

ALICE AT MONKEY ISLAND (See The Adventures of Alice)
No. 3, 1946
Pentagon Publ. Co. (Civil Service)

3	3.70	11.00	26.00

ALICE IN BLUNDERLAND
1952 (Paper cover, 16 pages in color)
Industrial Services

nn-Facts about big government waste and inefficiency	12.00	36.00	84.00

ALICE IN WONDERLAND (See Advs. of Alice, 4-Color Nos. 331,341, Dell Jr. Treasury No. 1, The Dreamery, Movie Comics, Single Series No. 24, Walt Disney Showcase No. 22, and World's Greatest Stories)

ALICE IN WONDERLAND
1965; 1982
Western Printing Company/Whitman Publ. Co.

...Meets Santa Claus(1950s), nd, 16pgs	2.75	8.00	16.00
Rexall Giveaway(1965, 16 pgs., 5x7¼'') Western Printing (TV-Hanna-Barbera)	2.00	6.00	12.00
Wonder Bakery Giveaway(16 pgs, color, nn, nd) (Continental Baking Co. (1969)	2.00	6.00	12.00
1-(Whitman; 1982)-r/4-Color 331		.40	.80

ALICE IN WONDERLAND MEETS SANTA
nd (16 pgs., 6-5/8x9-11/16'', paper cover)
No publisher (Giveaway)

nn	10.00	30.00	60.00

ALIEN ENCOUNTERS (Replaces Alien Worlds)
June, 1985 - No. 14, Aug, 1987 ($1.75; Baxter) (Mature readers)
Eclipse Comics

1-14: Nudity, strong language	.35	1.00	2.00

ALIEN FIRE
1987 - No. 3, 1987? ($2.00, B&W)
Kitchen Sink Press

	Good	Fine	N-Mint
1-3	.40	1.25	2.50

ALIEN LEGION (See Marvel Graphic Novel #25)
April, 1984 - No. 20, Sept, 1987
Epic Comics (Marvel)

1-$2.00 cover, high quality paper	.60	1.75	3.50
2-5	.35	1.00	2.00
6-10	.30	.85	1.70
11-20	.25	.75	1.50

NOTE: *Austin a-1i, 4i; c-3i-5i.*

ALIEN LEGION (2nd series)
Aug, 1987 (indicia) (10/87 on-c) - Present ($1.25, color)
Epic Comics (Marvel)

V2#1	.35	1.00	2.00
V2#2-15: 7-Begin $1.50 cover	.25	.75	1.50

ALIEN NATION
Dec, 1988 ($2.50; 68 pgs.)
DC Comics

1-Adapts movie; painted-c	.40	1.25	2.50

ALIENS, THE (Captain Johner and...)(Also see Magnus Robot...
Sept-Dec, 1967; No. 2, May, 1982
Gold Key

1-Reprints from Magnus #1,3,4,6-10, all by Russ Manning	1.15	3.50	8.00
2-Magnus-r/#1 by Manning	.40	1.25	2.50

ALIENS
1988 - No. 6, 1989 $1.95, B&W, mini-series)
V2#1, Aug, 1989 - No. 4, 1990 ($2.25, color, mini-series)
Dark Horse Comics

1-Based on movie	2.70	8.00	16.00
1-2nd printing	.40	1.25	2.50
1-3rd & 4th printings; 4th w/new inside front-c	.35	1.00	2.00
2	1.50	4.50	9.00
2-2nd & 3rd printings; 3rd w/new inside f/c	.35	1.00	2.00
3-6	.50	1.50	3.00
V2#1 ($2.25, color)-Adapts sequel	.40	1.25	2.50
2-4	.40	1.15	2.30
...Collection 1 ($10.95)-r/Dark Horse Presents #24 & Aliens #1-6, plus new-a	1.85	5.50	11.00

ALIENS VS. PREDATOR (See Dark Horse Presents #36)
1989 - No. 3, 1990 ($2.50. color, mini-series)
Dark Horse Comics

1-3	.40	1.25	2.50

ALIEN TERROR (See 3-D Alien Terror)

ALIEN WORLDS
12/82; No. 2, 6/83 - No. 7, 4/84; No. 8, 11/84 - No. 9, 1/85
(Baxter paper, $1.50, mature readers on-c)
Pacific Comics No. 1-7/Eclipse No. 8, 9

1-Williamson, Redondo-a; nudity	.60	1.75	3.50
2-7: 4-Nudity scenes	.50	1.50	3.00
8-Williamson-a	.30	.85	1.70
9	.35	1.00	2.00
3-D #1-Art Adams-a	.85	2.50	5.00

NOTE: *Bolton c-5, 9. Brunner a-6p, 9; c-6. Conrad a-1. Corben a-7. J. Jones a-4p. Krenkel a-6. Morrow a-7. Perez a-7. Stevens a-2, 4i; c-2, 4. Williamson/Frazetta a-4r/Witzend No. 1.*

ALIEN WORLDS 3-D (See Eclipse Graphic Album Series #22)

ALIEN WORLDS 3-D (See 3-Dimensional Alien Worlds)

Algie #1, © Timor Publ.

Alien Nation #1, © DC

All-American Comics #61, © DC

All-American Western #107, © DC

Alley Oop #16, © NEA Service

ALL-AMERICAN COMICS (...Western #103-126, ...Men of War #127 on; Also see The Big All-American Comic Book)
April, 1939 - No. 102, Oct, 1948
National Periodical Publications/All-American

	Good	Fine	N-Mint
1-Hop Harrigan, Scribbly, Toonerville Folks, Ben Webster, Spot Savage, Mutt & Jeff, Red White & Blue, Adv. in the Unknown, Tippie, Reg'lar Fellers, Skippy, Bobby Thatcher, Mystery Men of Mars, Daiseybelle, & Wiley of West Point begin			
	217.00	545.00	1300.00
2-Ripley's Believe It or Not begins, ends #24			
	83.00	210.00	500.00
3-5: 5-The American Way begins, ends #10	58.00	145.00	350.00
6,7: 6-Last Spot Savage; Popsicle Pete begins, ends #26, 28.			
7-Last Bobby Thatcher	47.00	120.00	280.00
8-The Ultra Man begins	75.00	190.00	450.00
9,10: 10-X-Mas-c	53.00	135.00	315.00
11-15: 12-Last Toonerville Folks. 15-Last Tippie & Reg'lar Fellars			
	43.00	110.00	260.00
16-(Rare)-Origin & 1st app. Green Lantern, created by Martin Nodell. Inspired by Aladdin's Lamp; the suggested alter ego name Alan Ladd, was never capitalized on. It was changed to Alan Scott before Alan Ladd became a major film star (he was in two films before this issue)	1,670.00	4,180.00	10,000.00
	(Prices vary widely on this book)		
17-(Scarce)	467.00	1170.00	2800.00
18-N.Y. World's Fair-c/story	233.00	585.00	1400.00
19-Origin & 1st app. The Atom; Last Ultra Man			
	367.00	920.00	2200.00
20-Atom dons costume; Hunkle becomes Red Tornado; Rescue on Mars begins, ends #25; 1 pg. origin Green Lantern			
	158.00	395.00	950.00
21-23: 21-Last Wiley of West Point & Skippy. 23-Last Daiseybelle; 3 Idiots begin, end #82	112.00	280.00	670.00
24-Sisty & Dinky become the Cyclone Kids; Ben Webster ends. Origin Dr. Mid-Nite & Sargon, The Sorcerer in text with app.			
	120.00	300.00	720.00
25-Origin & 1st story app. Dr. Mid-Nite by Stan Asch; Hop Harrigan becomes Guardian Angel; last Adventure in the Unknown			
	233.00	585.00	1400.00
26-Origin/1st story app. Sargon, the Sorcerer	133.00	335.00	800.00
27: #27-32 are misnumbered in indicia with correct No. appearing on cover. Intro. Doiby Dickles, Green Lantern's sidekick			
	142.00	355.00	850.00
28-Hop Harrigan gives up costumed i.d.	75.00	190.00	450.00
29,30	75.00	190.00	450.00
31-40: 35-Doiby learns Green Lantern's i.d.	56.00	140.00	335.00
41-50: 50-Sargon ends	49.00	125.00	295.00
51-60: 59-Scribbly & the Red Tornado ends	42.00	105.00	250.00
61-Origin Solomon Grundy	150.00	375.00	900.00
62-70: 70-Kubert Sargon; intro Sargon's helper, Maximillian O'Leary			
	39.00	100.00	235.00
71-Last Red White & Blue	31.00	78.00	185.00
72-Black Pirate begins (not in #74-82); last Atom			
	31.00	78.00	185.00
73-80: 73-Winky, Blinky & Noddy begins, ends #82			
	31.00	78.00	185.00
81-88,90: 90-Origin Icicle	31.00	78.00	185.00
89-Origin Harlequin	38.00	95.00	225.00
91-99-Last Hop Harrigan	31.00	78.00	185.00
100-1st app. Johnny Thunder by Alex Toth	58.00	145.00	350.00
101-Last Mutt & Jeff	44.00	110.00	265.00
102-Last Green Lantern, Black Pirate & Dr. Mid-Nite			
	50.00	125.00	300.00

NOTE: *No Atom in 47, 62-69. Kinstler Black Pirate-89. Stan Aschmeier a-25, 40, 55, 70; c-7. Moldoff c-16-23. Paul Reinman a-55, 70; c-55, 70, 75, 78, 80. Toth a-88, 92, 96, 98-102; c-92, 96-102.*

ALL-AMERICAN MEN OF WAR (Previously All-American Western)
No. 127, Aug-Sept, 1952 - No. 117, Sept-Oct, 1966
National Periodical Publications

	Good	Fine	N-Mint
127 (1952)	25.00	75.00	175.00
128 (1952)	17.00	51.00	120.00
2(12-1/'52-53)-5	14.00	42.00	100.00
6-10	8.50	25.50	60.00
11-18: Last precode (2/55)	7.00	21.00	50.00
19-28	5.15	15.50	36.00
29,30,32-Wood-a	5.70	17.00	40.00
31,33-40	3.50	10.50	24.00
41-50	2.65	8.00	18.00
51-66	1.70	5.00	12.00
67-1st Gunner & Sarge by Andru	2.15	6.50	15.00
68-80	1.00	3.00	7.00
81-100: 82-Johnny Cloud begins, ends #111,114,115			
	.70	2.00	4.00
101-117: 112-Balloon Buster series begins, ends #114,116; 115-Johnny Cloud app.	.50	1.50	3.00

NOTE: *Colan a-112. Drucker a-47,65,74,77. Heath a-27, 32, 47, 95, 112; c-95, 100, 112. Krigstein a-128('52), 2, 3, 5. Kirby a-29, 36, 38, 41, 43, 47, 49, 50, 52, 53, 55, 56, 60, 63, 65, 69, 71-73, 103, 114; c-41, 77, 114. Tank Killer in 69, 71, 76 by Kubert. P. Reinman c-55, 57, 61, 62, 71, 72, 74-76, 80.*

ALL-AMERICAN SPORTS
October, 1967
Charlton Comics

	Good	Fine	N-Mint
1	.35	1.00	2.00

ALL-AMERICAN WESTERN (Formerly All-American Comics; Becomes All-American Men of War)
No. 103, Nov, 1948 - No. 126, June-July, 1952 (103-121: 52 pgs.)
National Periodical Publications

	Good	Fine	N-Mint
103-Johnny Thunder & his horse Black Lightning continues by Toth, ends #126; Foley of The Fighting 5th, Minstrel Maverick, & Overland Coach begin; Captain Tootsie by Beck; mentioned in **Love and Death**	21.50	64.00	150.00
104-Kubert-a	14.00	43.00	100.00
105,107-Kubert-a	12.00	36.00	85.00
106,108-110,112: 112-Kurtzman "Pot-Shot Pete," 1pg.			
	9.30	28.00	65.00
111,114-116-Kubert-a	10.00	30.00	70.00
113-Intro. Swift Deer, J. Thunder's new sidekick; classic Toth-c; Kubert-a	11.50	34.00	80.00
117-120,122-125	8.00	24.00	56.00
121-Kubert-a	8.00	24.00	56.00
126-Last issue	8.00	24.00	56.00

NOTE: *Kubert a-103-105, 107, 111, 112(1 pg.), 113-116, 121. Toth c/a 103-126.*

ALL COMICS
1945
Chicago Nite Life News

	Good	Fine	N-Mint
1	5.50	16.50	38.00

ALLEY OOP (See The Comics, 4-Color No. 3, The Funnies, Red Ryder and Super Book No. 9)

ALLEY OOP
No. 10, 1947 - No. 18, Oct, 1949
Standard Comics

	Good	Fine	N-Mint
10	11.50	34.00	80.00
11-18: 17,18-Schomburg-c	8.50	25.50	60.00

ALLEY OOP
Nov, 1955 - No. 3, March, 1956 (Newspaper reprints)
Argo Publ.

	Good	Fine	N-Mint
1	8.50	25.50	60.00
2,3	6.00	18.00	42.00

ALLEY OOP
12-2/62-63 - No. 2, 9-11/63
Dell Publishing Co.

	Good	Fine	N-Mint
1,2	5.00	15.00	35.00

ALL-FAMOUS CRIME (Becomes Confessions of Love #11 on?)
1949 - No. 10, Nov, 1951
Star Publications

1	6.00	18.00	42.00
2	3.00	9.00	21.00
3-5	2.65	8.00	18.00
6-8,10	2.30	7.00	16.00
9-Used in **SOTI**, illo-"The wish to hurt or kill couples in lovers' lanes is not uncommon perversion;" L.B. Cole-c/a(r)/Law-Crime #3	9.00	27.00	62.00

NOTE: All have **L.B. Cole** covers.

ALL FAMOUS CRIME STORIES (See Fox Giants)

ALL-FAMOUS POLICE CASES
Oct, 1951 - No. 16, Sept, 1954
Star Publications

1	5.70	17.00	40.00
2	3.00	9.00	21.00
3-6,9-16	2.65	8.00	18.00
7-Kubert-a	3.50	10.50	24.00
8-Marijuana story	3.50	10.50	24.00

NOTE: L. B. Cole c-all; a-15, 1pg. **Hollingsworth** a-15.

ALL-FLASH (. . .Quarterly No. 1-5)
Summer, 1941 - No. 32, Dec-Jan, 1947-48
National Periodical Publications/All-American

1-Origin The Flash retold by E. Hibbard	333.00	835.00	2000.00
2-Origin recap	117.00	295.00	700.00
3,4	76.00	190.00	455.00
5-Winky, Blinky & Noddy begins, ends #32	58.00	145.00	350.00
6-10	50.00	125.00	300.00
11-13: 12-Origin The Thinker. 13-The King app.	42.00	105.00	250.00
14-Green Lantern cameo	47.00	120.00	280.00
15-20: 18-Mutt & Jeff begins, ends #22	38.00	95.00	225.00
21-31	32.00	80.00	190.00
32-Origin The Fiddler; 1st Star Sapphire	39.00	100.00	235.00

NOTE: Book length stories in 2-13,16. Bondage c-31, 32.

ALL FOR LOVE (Young Love V3/5-on)
Apr-May, 1957 - V3No.4, Dec-Jan, 1959-60
Prize Publications

V1#1	2.65	8.00	18.00
2-6: 5-Orlando-c	1.50	4.50	10.00
V2#1-6(1/59), 5(3/59)	.90	2.70	6.50
V3#1(5/59), 1(7/59)-4: 2-Powell-a	.75	2.25	4.50

ALL FUNNY COMICS
Winter, 1943-44 - No. 23, May-June, 1948
Tilsam Publ./National Periodical Publications (Detective)

1-Genius Jones, Buzzy (ends #4), Dover & Clover begin; Bailey-a	23.00	70.00	160.00
2	10.00	30.00	70.00
3-10	6.50	19.50	45.00
11-13,15,18,19-Genius Jones app.	5.00	15.00	35.00
14,17,20-23	3.50	10.50	25.00
16-DC Super Heroes app.	12.00	36.00	85.00

ALL GOOD
Oct, 1949 (260 pgs., 50 cents)
St. John Publishing Co.

(8 St. John comics bound together)	43.00	130.00	300.00

NOTE: Also see Li'l Audrey Yearbook & Treasury of Comics.

ALL GOOD COMICS (See Fox Giants)
Spring, 1946 (36 pgs.)
Fox Features Syndicate

	Good	Fine	N-Mint
1-Joy Family, Dick Transom, Rick Evans, One Round Hogan	7.00	21.00	50.00

ALL GREAT (See Fox Giants)
1946 (36 pgs.)
Fox Feature Syndicate

1-Crazy House, Bertie Benson Boy Detective, Gussie the Gob	5.50	16.50	38.00

ALL GREAT
nd (1945?) (132 pgs.)
William H. Wise & Co.

nn-Capt. Jack Terry, Joan Mason, Girl Reporter, Baron Doomsday; Torture scenes	16.50	50.00	115.00

ALL GREAT COMICS (Dagar, Desert Hawk No. 14 on)
No. 14, Oct, 1947 - No. 13, Dec, 1947
Fox Features Syndicate

14-Brenda Starr-r (Scarce)	16.50	50.00	115.00
13-Origin Dagar, Desert Hawk; Brenda Starr (all-r); Kamen-c	14.00	43.00	100.00

ALL-GREAT CONFESSIONS (See Fox Giants)

ALL GREAT CRIME STORIES (See Fox Giants)

ALL GREAT JUNGLE ADVENTURES (See Fox Giants)

ALL HERO COMICS
March, 1943 (100 pgs.) (Cardboard cover)
Fawcett Publications

1-Captain Marvel Jr., Capt. Midnight, Golden Arrow, Ibis the Invincible, Spy Smasher, & Lance O'Casey	68.00	205.00	475.00

ALL HUMOR COMICS
Spring, 1946 - No. 17, December, 1949
Quality Comics Group

1	6.50	19.50	45.00
2-Atomic Tot story; Gustavson-a	3.00	9.00	21.00
3-9: 5-1st app. Hickory? 8-Gustavson-a	2.00	6.00	14.00
10-17	1.30	4.00	9.00

ALL LOVE (. . .Romances No. 26)(Formerly Ernie Comics)
No. 26, May, 1949 - No. 32, May, 1950
Ace Periodicals (Current Books)

26(No. 1)-Ernie, Lily Belle app.	2.65	8.00	18.00
27-L. B. Cole-a	3.00	9.00	21.00
28-32	1.60	4.70	11.00

ALL-NEGRO COMICS
June, 1947 (15 cents)
All-Negro Comics

1 (Rare)	70.00	210.00	495.00

NOTE: Seldom found in fine or mint condition; many copies have brown pages.

ALL-NEW COLLECTORS' EDITION (Formerly Limited . . .)
Jan, 1978 - No. C-62, 1979 (No. 54-58: 76 pgs.)
DC Comics, Inc.

C-53-Rudolph the Red-Nosed Reindeer		.50	1.00
C-54-Superman Vs. Wonder Woman	.25	.75	1.50
C-55-Superboy & the Legion of Super-Heroes	.70	2.00	4.00
C-56-Superman Vs. Muhammad Ali: story & wraparound Adams-c	.35	1.00	2.00
C-58-Superman Vs. Shazam		.60	1.20
C-60-Rudolph's Summer Fun(8/78)		.60	1.20
C-62-Superman the Movie (68 pgs.; 1979)		.60	1.20

ALL-NEW COMICS (. . .Short Story Comics No. 1-3)
Jan, 1943 - No. 14, Nov, 1946; No. 15, Mar-Apr, 1947

All-Famous Police Cases #7, © STAR

All-Flash #32, © DC

All-Negro Comics #1, © All-Negro Comics

All-New Comics #15, © HARV   All-Picture Comedy Carnival #1, © STJ   All Star Comics #14, © DC

ALL-NEW COMICS (continued)
Family Comics (Harvey Publications)

	Good	Fine	N-Mint
1-Steve Case, Crime Rover, Johnny Rebel, Kayo Kane, The Echo, Night Hawk, Ray O'Light, Detective Shane begin; Red Blazer on cover only; Sultan-a	57.00	170.00	400.00
2-Origin Scarlet Phantom by Kubert	27.00	81.00	190.00
3	22.00	65.00	155.00
4,5	19.00	58.00	135.00
6-The Boy Heroes & Red Blazer (text story) begin, end #12; Black Cat app.; intro. Sparky in Red Blazer	21.00	62.00	145.00
7-Kubert, Powell-a; Black Cat & Zebra app.	21.00	62.00	145.00
8-Shock Gibson app.; Kubert, Powell-a; Schomburg bondage-c	21.00	62.00	145.00
9-Black Cat app.; Kubert-a	21.00	62.00	145.00
10-The Zebra app.; Kubert-a(3)	19.00	58.00	135.00
11-Girl Commandos, Man In Black app.	19.00	58.00	135.00
12-Kubert-a	19.00	58.00	135.00
13-Stuntman by Simon & Kirby; Green Hornet, Joe Palooka, Flying Fool app.	21.00	62.00	145.00
14-The Green Hornet & The Man in Black Called Fate by Powell, Joe Palooka app.	21.00	58.00	135.00
15-(Rare)-Small size (5½x8½''); B&W; 32 pgs.). Distributed to mail subscribers only. Black Cat and Joe Palooka app.		Estimated value...$200-250	

NOTE: Also see Boy Explorers No. 2, Flash Gordon No. 5, and Stuntman No. 3. *Powell* a-11. *Schomburg* c-7,8,10,11.

ALL-OUT WAR
Sept-Oct, 1979 - No. 6, Aug, 1980 ($1.00)
DC Comics

1-6: 1-The Viking Commando(origin), Force Three(origin), & Black Eagle Squadron begin		.25	.50

NOTE: *Evans* a-1-6. *Kubert* c-1-6.

ALL PICTURE ADVENTURE MAGAZINE
Oct., 1952 - No. 2, Nov, 1952 (100 pg. Giants, 25 cents, squarebound)
St. John Publishing Co.

1-War comics	13.00	40.00	90.00
2-Horror-crime comics	17.00	51.00	120.00

NOTE: Above comics contain three St. John comics rebound; variations possible. *Baker* art known in both.

ALL PICTURE ALL TRUE LOVE STORY
October, 1952 (100 pages)
St. John Publishing Co.

1-Canteen Kate by Matt Baker	24.00	72.00	165.00

ALL-PICTURE COMEDY CARNIVAL
October, 1952 (100 pages, 25 cents)(Contains 4 rebound comics)
St. John Publishing Co.

1-Contents can vary; Baker-a	24.00	72.00	165.00

ALL REAL CONFESSION MAGAZINE (See Fox Giants)

ALL ROMANCES (Mr. Risk No. 7 on)
Aug, 1949 - No. 6, June, 1950
A. A. Wyn (Ace Periodicals)

1	3.15	9.50	22.00
2	1.60	4.70	11.00
3-6	1.30	4.00	9.00

ALL-SELECT COMICS (Blonde Phantom No. 12 on)
Fall, 1943 - No. 11, Fall, 1946
Timely Comics (Daring Comics)

1-Capt. America, Human Torch, Sub-Mariner begin; Black Widow app.	208.00	520.00	1250.00
2-Red Skull app.	88.00	220.00	525.00
3-The Whizzer begins	58.00	145.00	350.00
4,5-Last Sub-Mariner	49.00	125.00	295.00

	Good	Fine	N-Mint
6-The Destroyer app.	40.00	100.00	240.00
7-9: 8-No Whizzer	40.00	100.00	240.00
10-The Destroyer & Sub-Mariner app.; last Capt. America & Human Torch issue	40.00	100.00	240.00
11-1st app. Blonde Phantom; Miss America app.; all Blonde Phantom-c by Shores	66.00	165.00	395.00

NOTE: *Schomburg* c-1-10. No. 7 & 8 show 1944 in indicia, but should be 1945.

ALL SPORTS COMICS (Formerly Real Sports Comics; becomes All Time Sports Comics No. 4 on)
No. 2, Dec-Jan, 1948-49; No. 3, Feb-Mar, 1949
Hillman Periodicals

2-Krigstein-a(p), Powell, Starr-a	9.30	28.00	65.00
3-Mort Lawrence-a	7.00	21.00	50.00

ALL STAR COMICS (All Star Western No. 58 on)
Summer, 1940 - No. 57, Feb-Mar, 1951; No. 58, Jan-Feb, 1976 - No. 74, Sept-Oct, 1978
National Periodical Publ./All-American/DC Comics

1-The Flash(No.1 by Harry Lampert), Hawkman(by Shelly), Hourman, The Sandman, The Spectre, Biff Bronson, Red White & Blue begin; Ultra Man's only app.	667.00	1670.00	4000.00
2-Green Lantern, Johnny Thunder begin	317.00	795.00	1900.00
3-Origin Justice Society of America; Dr. Fate & The Atom begin, Red Tornado cameo; last Red White & Blue; reprinted in Famous First Edition	1250.00	3125.00	7500.00
4	317.00	795.00	1900.00
5-Intro. & 1st app. Shiera Sanders as Hawkgirl	267.00	670.00	1600.00
6-Johnny Thunder joins JSA	233.00	585.00	1400.00
7-Batman, Superman, Flash cameo; last Hourman; Doiby Dickles app.	233.00	585.00	1400.00
8-Origin & 1st app. Wonder Woman (added as 8pgs. making book 76pgs.; origin cont'd in Sensation #1); Dr. Fate dons new helmet; Dr.Mid-Nite, Hop Harrigan text stories & Starman begin; Shiera app.; Hop Harrigan JSA guest	450.00	1125.00	2700.00
9-Shiera app.	183.00	460.00	1100.00
10-Flash, Green Lantern cameo, Sandman new costume	183.00	460.00	1100.00
11-Wonder Woman begins; Spectre cameo; Shiera app.	175.00	440.00	1050.00
12-Wonder Woman becomes JSA Secretary	175.00	440.00	1050.00
13-15: Sandman w/Sandy in No. 14 & 15; 15-Origin Brain Wave; Shiera app.	158.00	410.00	950.00
16-19: 19-Sandman w/Sandy	117.00	295.00	700.00
20-Dr. Fate & Sandman cameo	117.00	295.00	700.00
21-Spectre & Atom cameo; Dr. Fate by Kubert; Dr. Fate, Sandman end	100.00	250.00	600.00
22,23: 22-Last Hop Harrigan; Flag-c. 23-Origin Psycho Pirate; last Spectre & Starman	100.00	250.00	600.00
24-Flash & Green Lantern cameo; Mr. Terrific only app.; Wildcat, JSA guest; Kubert Hawkman begins	100.00	250.00	600.00
25-27: 25-The Flash & Green Lantern start again. 27-Wildcat, JSA guest	93.00	235.00	560.00
28-32	80.00	200.00	480.00
33-Solomon Grundy, Hawkman, Doiby Dickles app.	150.00	375.00	900.00
34,35-Johnny Thunder cameo in both	73.00	220.00	440.00
36-Batman & Superman app.	158.00	475.00	950.00
37-Johnny Thunder cameo; origin Injustice Society; last Kubert Hawkman	83.00	210.00	500.00
38-Black Canary begins; JSA Death issue	92.00	230.00	550.00
39,40: 39-Last Johnny Thunder	59.00	150.00	355.00
41-Black Canary joins JSA; Injustice Society app.	57.00	145.00	345.00
42-Atom & the Hawkman don new costumes	57.00	145.00	345.00

ALL STAR COMICS (continued)

	Good	Fine	N-Mint
43-49	57.00	145.00	345.00
50-Frazetta art, 3 pgs.	63.00	160.00	380.00
51-56: 55-Sci/fi story	57.00	145.00	345.00
57-Kubert-a, 6 pgs. (Scarce)	67.00	170.00	405.00
58('76)-Flash, Hawkman, Dr. Mid-Nite, Wildcat, Dr. Fate, Green Lantern, Star Spangled Kid, & Robin app.; intro Power Girl		.25	.50
59-74: 69-1st app. Huntress		.25	.50

NOTE: *No Atom-27, 36; no Dr. Fate-13; no Flash-8, 9, 11-23; no Green Lantern-8, 9. 11-23; no Johnny Thunder-5, 36; no Wonder Woman-9, 10, 23. Book length stories in 4-9, 11-14, 18-22, 25, 26, 29, 30, 32-36, 42, 43. Johnny Peril in #42-46, 48, 49, 51, 52, 54-57. Baily a-1-10, 12, 13, 14i, 15-20. Burnley Starman-8-13; c-12, 13. Grell c-58. Kubert Hawkman-24-30, 33-37. Moldoff Hawkman-3-23; c-11. Simon & Kirby Sandman -14-17, 19. Toth a-37(2), 38(2), 40, 41; c-38, 41. Wood a-58i-63i, 64, 65; c-63-65.*

ALL STAR INDEX, THE
Feb, 1987 ($2.00, Baxter)
Independent Comics Group (Eclipse)

1	.35	1.00	2.00

ALL-STAR SQUADRON (See Justice League of America #193)
Sept, 1981 - No. 67, March, 1987
DC Comics

	Good	Fine	N-Mint
1-Original Atom, Hawkman, Dr. Mid-Nite, Robotman (origin), Plastic Man, Johnny Quick, Liberty Belle, Shining Knight begin	.25	.75	1.50
2		.50	1.00
3-24: 5-Danette Reilly becomes new Firebrand. 12-Origin G.A. Hawkman retold. 23-Intro/origin The Amazing Man		.40	.80
25-1st Infinity, Inc.	.50	1.50	3.00
26-Origin Infinity, Inc.	.40	1.25	2.50
27-46,48,49: 31-Origin Freedom Fighters of Earth-X. 41-Origin Starman		.40	.80
47-Origin Dr. Fate; McFarlane-a	.60	1.75	3.50
50-Double size; Crisis x-over	.25	.75	1.50
51-53-Crisis x-over		.50	1.00
54-67: 61-Origin Liberty Belle. 62-Origin The Shining Knight. 63-Origin Robotman. 65-Origin Johnny Quick. 66-Origin Tarantula		.40	.80
Annual 1(11/82)-Retells origin of G.A. Atom, Guardian & Wildcat		.50	1.00
Annual 2(11/83)-Infinity, Inc. app.		.50	1.00
Annual 3(9/84)		.50	1.00

NOTE: *Kubert c-2, 7-18.*

ALL-STAR STORY OF THE DODGERS, THE
April, 1979 (Full Color) ($1.00)
Stadium Communications

1		.50	1.00

ALL STAR WESTERN (Formerly All Star Comics No. 1-57)
No. 58, Apr-May, 1951 - No. 119, June-July, 1961
National Periodical Publications

	Good	Fine	N-Mint
58-Trigger Twins (end #116), Strong Bow, The Roving Ranger & Don Caballero begin	20.00	60.00	140.00
59,60: Last 52 pgs.	9.50	28.00	65.00
61-66: 61,64-Toth-a	8.00	24.00	56.00
67-Johnny Thunder begins; Gil Kane-a	9.50	28.00	65.00
68-81: Last precode, 2-3/55	4.50	14.00	32.00
82-98	3.60	11.00	25.00
99-Frazetta-a r-/Jimmy Wakely #4	5.50	16.00	38.00
100	4.30	13.00	30.00
101-107,109-116,118,119	2.65	8.00	18.00
108-Origin Johnny Thunder	6.50	19.50	45.00
117-Origin Super Chief	4.50	14.00	32.00

NOTE: *Infantino art in most issues. Madame .44 app.-#117-119.*

ALL-STAR WESTERN (Weird Western Tales No. 12 on)
Aug-Sept, 1970 - No. 11, Apr-May, 1972
National Periodical Publications

	Good	Fine	N-Mint
1-Pow-Wow Smith-r; Infantino-a	.50	1.50	3.00
2-Outlaw begins; El Diablo by Morrow begins; has cameos by Williamson, Torres, Gil Kane, Giordano & Phil Seuling	.35	1.00	2.00
3-8: 3-Origin El Diablo. 5-Last Outlaw ish. 6-Billy the Kid begins, ends #8	.35	1.00	2.00
9-Frazetta-a, 3pgs.(r)	.70	2.00	4.00
10-Jonah Hex begins (1st app.)	2.30	7.00	16.00
11	1.00	3.00	6.00

NOTE: *Adams c-1-5; Aparo a-5. G. Kane a-3, 4, 6, 8. Kubert a-4r, 7-9r. Morrow a-2-4, 10, 11. No. 7-11 have 52 pages.*

ALL SURPRISE
Fall, 1943 - No. 12, Winter, 1946-47
Timely/Marvel (CPC)

	Good	Fine	N-Mint
1-Super Rabbit & Gandy & Sourpuss	11.00	32.00	75.00
2	4.50	14.00	32.00
3-10,12	3.15	9.50	22.00
11-Kurtzman "Pigtales" art	5.00	15.00	35.00

ALL TEEN (Formerly All Winners; Teen Comics No. 21 on)
No. 20, January, 1947
Marvel Comics (WFP)

	Good	Fine	N-Mint
20-Georgie, Mitzi, Patsy Walker, Willie app.	3.50	10.50	24.00

ALL THE FUNNY FOLKS
1926 (hardcover, 112 pgs., 11½x3½'') (Full color)
World Press Today, Inc.

	Good	Fine	N-Mint
nn-Barney Google, Spark Plug, Jiggs & Maggie, Tillie The Toiler, Happy Hooligan, Hans & Fritz, Toots & Casper, etc.	20.00	60.00	140.00

ALL-TIME SPORTS COMICS (Formerly All Sports Comics)
V2No. 4, Apr-May, 1949 - V2No. 7, Oct-Nov, 1949
Hillman Periodicals

	Good	Fine	N-Mint
V2#4	6.50	19.50	45.00
5-7: 5-Powell-a. 7-Krigstein-a(p)	4.50	14.00	32.00

ALL TOP
1944 (132 pages)
William H. Wise Co.

	Good	Fine	N-Mint
Capt. V, Merciless the Sorceress, Red Robbins, One Round Hogan, Mike the M.P., Snooky, Pussy Katnip app.	13.00	40.00	90.00

ALL TOP COMICS (My Experience No. 19 on)
1945; No. 2, Sum, 1946 - No. 18, Mar, 1949; 1957 - 1959
Fox Features Synd./Green Publ./Norlen Mag.

	Good	Fine	N-Mint
1-Cosmo Cat & Flash Rabbit begin	10.00	30.00	70.00
2	5.00	15.00	35.00
3-7	3.50	10.50	25.00
8-Blue Beetle, Phantom Lady, & Rulah, Jungle Goddess begin (11/47); Kamen-c	57.00	170.00	400.00
9-Kamen-c	34.00	103.00	240.00
10-Kamen bondage-c	36.00	107.00	250.00
11-13,15-17: 15-No Blue Beetle	26.00	77.00	180.00
14-No Blue Beetle; used in SOTI, illo-"Corpses of colored people strung up by their wrists''	32.00	95.00	225.00
18-Dagar, Jo-Jo app; no Phantom Lady or Blue Beetle	21.50	64.00	150.00
6(1957-Green Publ.)-Patoruzu the Indian; Cosmo Cat on cover only	1.50	4.50	10.00
6(1958-Literary Ent.)-Muggy Doo; Cosmo Cat on cover only	1.50	4.50	10.00
6(1959-Norlen)-Atomic Mouse; Cosmo Cat on cover only	1.50	4.50	10.00

All-Star Squadron #23, © DC

All Star Western #66, © DC

All Top Comics #15, © FOX

All-True Crime #36, © MEG

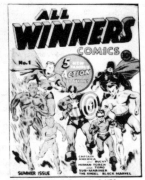

All Winners Comics #1, © MEG

Alpha Flight #7, © MEG

	Good	Fine	N-Mint
ALL TOP COMICS (continued)			
6(1959)-Little Eva	1.50	4.50	10.00
6(Cornell)-Supermouse on-c	1.50	4.50	10.00
NOTE: *Jo-Jo by Kamen-12,18.*			

ALL TRUE ALL PICTURE POLICE CASES
Oct, 1952 - No. 2, Nov, 1952 (100 pages)
St. John Publishing Co.

	Good	Fine	N-Mint
1-Three rebound St. John crime comics	21.50	64.00	150.00
2-Three comics rebound	18.50	56.00	130.00
NOTE: *Contents may vary.*			

ALL-TRUE CRIME (. . .Cases No. 26-35; formerly Official True
Crime Cases)
No. 26, Feb, 1948 - No. 52, Sept, 1952
Marvel/Atlas Comics(OFI No. 26,27/CFI No. 28,29/LCC No. 30-46/LMC
No. 47-52)

	Good	Fine	N-Mint
26(No. 1)	5.35	16.00	38.00
27(4/48)-Electric chair-c	4.50	14.00	32.00
28-41,43-48,50-52: 36-Photo-c	1.70	5.00	12.00
42-Krigstein-a	2.85	8.50	20.00
49-Used in POP, Pg. 79; Krigstein-a	2.85	8.50	20.00
NOTE: *Robinson a-47. Shores c-26. Tuska a-48(3).*			

ALL-TRUE DETECTIVE CASES (Kit Carson No. 5 on)
Feb-Mar, 1954 - No. 4, Aug-Sept, 1954
Avon Periodicals

	Good	Fine	N-Mint
1	10.00	30.00	70.00
2-Wood-a	8.50	25.50	60.00
3-Kinstler-c	3.75	11.25	26.00
4-Wood(?), Kamen-a	7.00	21.00	50.00
nn(100 pgs.)-7 pg. Kubert-a, Kinstler back-c	20.00	60.00	140.00

ALL TRUE ROMANCE (. . .Illustrated No. 3)
3/51 - No. 20, 12/54; No. 22, 3/55 - No. 30?, 7/57; No. 3(#31), 9/57 -
No. 4(#32), 11/57; No. 33, 2/58 - No. 34, 3/58
Artful Publ. #1-3/Harwell(Comic Media) #4-20?/Ajax-Farrell(Excellent
Publ.) No. 22 on/Four Star Comic Corp.

	Good	Fine	N-Mint
1 (3/51)	6.00	18.00	42.00
2 (10/51; 11/51 on-c)	3.50	10.50	24.00
3(12/51) - #5(5/52)	3.00	9.00	21.00
6-Wood-a, 9 pgs. (exceptional)	8.50	25.50	60.00
7-10	2.15	6.50	15.00
11-13,16-19 (2/54)	1.60	4.80	11.00
14-Marijuana story	2.50	7.50	17.00
20-22: Last precode issue (Ajax, 3/55)	1.50	4.50	10.00
23-27,29,30	1.20	3.60	8.40
28 (9/56)-L. B. Cole, Disbrow-a	2.50	7.50	17.00
3,4,33,34 (Farrell, '57-'58)	.70	2.00	5.00

ALL WESTERN WINNERS (Formerly All Winners; becomes Western
Winners with No. 5; see Two-Gun Kid No. 5)
No. 2, Winter, 1948-49 - No. 4, April, 1949
Marvel Comics(CDS)

	Good	Fine	N-Mint
2-Black Rider (Origin & 1st app.) & his horse Satan, Kid Colt & his horse Steel, & Two-Gun Kid & his horse Cyclone begin	18.50	56.00	130.00
3-Anti-Wertham editorial	13.00	40.00	90.00
4-Black Rider i.d. revealed	13.00	40.00	90.00

ALL WINNERS COMICS (All Teen #20)
Summer, 1941 - No. 19, Fall, 1946; No. 21, Winter, 1946-47
(no No. 20) (No. 21 continued from Young Allies No. 20)
USA No. 1-7/WFP No. 10-19/YAI No. 21

	Good	Fine	N-Mint
1-The Angel & Black Marvel only app.; Capt. America by Simon & Kirby, Human Torch & Sub-Mariner begin (#1 was advertised as All Aces)	315.00	790.00	1890.00
2-The Destroyer & The Whizzer begin; Simon & Kirby Captain America	150.00	375.00	900.00

	Good	Fine	N-Mint
3,4	117.00	295.00	700.00
5,6: 6-The Black Avenger only app.; no Whizzer story	78.00	195.00	470.00
7-10	65.00	165.00	390.00
11-18: 12-Last Destroyer; no Whizzer story; no Human Torch #14-16	41.00	105.00	245.00
19-(Scarce)-1st app. & origin All Winners Squad (Capt. America & Bucky, Human Torch & Toro, Sub-Mariner, Whizzer, & Miss America; r-in Fantasy Masterpieces #10	98.00	245.00	590.00
21-(Scarce)-All Winners Squad; bondage-c	91.00	230.00	545.00
NOTE: *Everett Sub-Mariner-1, 3, 4; Burgos Torch-1, 3, 4. Schomburg c-1, 7-18.*			

(2nd Series - August, 1948, Marvel Comics (CDS))
(Becomes All Western Winners with No. 2)

	Good	Fine	N-Mint
1-The Blonde Phantom, Capt. America, Human Torch, & Sub-Mariner app.	68.00	205.00	480.00

ALL YOUR COMICS (See Fox Giants)
Spring, 1946 (36 pages)
Fox Feature Syndicate (R. W. Voight)

	Good	Fine	N-Mint
1-Red Robbins, Merciless the Sorceress app.	6.50	19.50	45.00

ALMANAC OF CRIME (See Fox Giants)

AL OF FBI (See Little Al of the FBI)

ALONG THE FIRING LINE WITH ROGER BEAN
1916 (Hardcover, B&W) (6x17'') (66 pages)
Chas. B. Jackson

	Good	Fine	N-Mint
3-by Chic Jackson (1915 daily strips)	8.50	25.50	60.00

ALPHA AND OMEGA
1978 (49 cents)
Spire Christian Comics (Fleming H. Revell)

	Good	Fine	N-Mint
nn		.30	.60

ALPHA FLIGHT (See X-Men #120,121)
Aug, 1983 - Present (#52-on are direct sale only)
Marvel Comics Group

	Good	Fine	N-Mint
1-Byrne-a begins (52pgs.)-Wolverine & Nightcrawler cameo	.70	2.00	4.00
2-Vindicator becomes Guardian; origin Marrina & Alpha Flight	.40	1.25	2.50
3-5: 3-Concludes origin Alpha Flight	.35	1.10	2.20
6-11: 6-Origin Shaman. 7-Origin Snowbird. 10,11-Origin Sasquatch	.35	1.00	2.00
12-Double size; death of Guardian	.40	1.25	2.50
13-Wolverine app.	.85	2.50	5.00
14-16: 16-Wolverine app.	.25	.75	1.50
17-X-Men x-over; Wolverine cameo	.85	2.50	5.00
18-28: 20-New headquarters. 25-Return of Guardian. 28-Last Byrne issue	.25	.75	1.50
29-32,35-39		.65	1.30
33,34: 33-X-Men (Wolverine) app. 34-Origin Wolverine	.50	1.50	3.00
40-49,51		.65	1.30
50-Double size	.20	.70	1.40
52,53-Wolverine app.	.40	1.25	2.50
54-64		.65	1.30
65-74,76-82: 65-Begin $1.50-c. 71-Intro The Sorcerer (villian). 74-Wolverine, Spider-Man & The Avengers app.	.25	.75	1.50
75-Double size ($1.95, 52 pgs.)	.35	1.00	1.95
Annual 1 (9/86, $1.25)	.30	.90	1.80
Annual 2(12/87, $1.25)		.65	1.30
NOTE: *Austin c-1i, 2i, 53i. Byrne c-81.*			

ALPHA TRACK
Feb, 1986 - No. 2, 1986? ($1.75 cover)
Fantasy General Comics

ALPHA TRACK (continued)	Good	Fine	N-Mint
1,2	.25	.75	1.50

ALPHA WAVE
March, 1987 ($1.75, color, 36 pgs.)
Darkline Comics

	Good	Fine	N-Mint
1	.25	.75	1.50

ALPHONSE & GASTON & LEON
1903 (15x10'' Sunday strip reprints in color)
Hearst's New York American & Journal

	Good	Fine	N-Mint
by Fred Opper	30.00	90.00	210.00

ALTER EGO
May, 1986 - No. 4, Nov, 1986 (mini-series)
First Comics

| 1 | .30 | .90 | 1.80 |
| 2-4 | .20 | .70 | 1.40 |

ALVIN (TV) (See 4-Color Comics No. 1042)
Oct-Dec, 1962 - No. 28, Oct, 1973
Dell Publishing Co.

12-021-212	4.00	12.00	28.00
2	2.30	7.00	16.00
3-10	1.70	5.00	12.00
11-28	1.15	3.50	8.00
Alvin For President (10/64)	1.00	3.00	7.00
...& His Pals in Merry Christmas with Clyde Crashcup & Leonardo 1(02-120-402)-12-2/64, reprinted in 1966 (12-023-604)			
	1.70	5.00	12.00

AMAZING ADULT FANTASY (Formerly Amazing Adventures #1-6; Becomes Amazing Fantasy #15)
No. 7, Dec, 1961 - No. 14, July, 1962
Marvel Comics Group (AMI)

7: Ditko-a No. 7-14; c-7-13	16.00	48.00	110.00
8-Last 10 cent issue	13.00	40.00	90.00
9-14: 12-1st app. Mailbag. 13-Anti-communist story			
	11.00	32.00	75.00

AMAZING ADVENTURE FUNNIES (Fantoman No. 2 on)
June, 1940 - No. 2, Sept. 1940
Centaur Publications

| 1-The Fantom of the Fair by Gustavson (r-/Amaz. Mystery Funnies V2/7, V2/8), The Arrow, Skyrocket Steele From the Year X by Everett (r-/AMF 2); Burgos-a | 100.00 | 300.00 | 700.00 |
| 2-Reprints; Published after Fantoman #2 | 68.00 | 205.00 | 480.00 |

NOTE: *Burgos a-1(2). Everett a-1(3). Gustavson a-1(5), 2(3). Pinajian a-2.*

AMAZING ADVENTURES (Also see Science Comics)
1950 - No. 6, Fall, 1952 (Painted covers)
Ziff-Davis Publ. Co.

1950 (no month given) (8½x11'') (8 pgs.) Has the front & back cover plus Schomburg story used in Amazing Advs. #1 (Sent to subscribers of Z-D s/f magazines & ordered through mail for 10 cents. Used to test market)   Estimated value....190.00

1-Wood, Schomburg, Anderson, Whitney-a	28.50	86.00	200.00
2-5-Anderson-a. 3,5-Starr-a	11.00	32.00	75.00
6-Krigstein-a	15.00	45.00	105.00

AMAZING ADVENTURES (Becomes Amazing Adult Fantasy #7 on)
June, 1961 - No. 6, Nov, 1961
Atlas Comics (AMI)/Marvel Comics No. 3 on

1-Origin Dr. Droom (1st Marvel-Age Superhero) by Kirby; Ditko & Kirby-a in all; Kirby c-1-6	32.00	95.00	225.00
2	21.50	64.00	150.00
3-6: Last Dr. Droom	16.50	50.00	110.00

AMAZING ADVENTURES
Aug, 1970 - No. 39, Nov, 1976
Marvel Comics Group

	Good	Fine	N-Mint
1-Inhumans by Kirby(p) & Black Widow (1st app. in Tales of Suspense #52) begin; Adams-a(p)	.50	1.50	3.00
2-4: Last Kirby Inhumans	.35	1.00	2.00
5-8-Adams-a; 8-Last Black Widow	.60	1.75	3.50
9,10: 10-Last Inhumans (origin-r by Kirby)	.25	.75	1.50
11-New Beast begins(Origin), ends #17; X-Men cameo	.70	2.00	4.00
12-17	.35	1.00	2.00
18-War of the Worlds begins; 1st app. Killraven; Adams-a(p)	.50	1.50	3.00
19-39: 35-Giffen's first story-art, along with Deadly Hands of Kung-Fu #22 (3/76)	.50		1.00

NOTE: *Adams c-6-8. Buscema a-1p, 2p. Colan a-3-5p, 26p. Ditko a-24r. Everett inks-3-5, 7-9. Giffen a-35i, 38p. G. Kane c-11, 25p, 29p. Ploog a-12i. Starlin a-17; c-15p. 16, 17, 27. Sutton a-11-15p.*

AMAZING ADVENTURES
December, 1979 - No. 14, January, 1981
Marvel Comics Group

| V2#1: r-/X-Men No. 1,38 | .35 | 1.00 | 2.00 |
| 2-14: 2,4,6-X-Men-r. 7,8-Origin Iceman | .25 | .75 | 1.50 |

NOTE: *Byrne c-6p, 9p. Kirby a-1-14r; c-7, 9. Steranko a-12r. Tuska a-7-9.*

AMAZING ADVENTURES
July, 1988 ($4.95, One-shot, color, squarebound, 80 pgs.)
Marvel Comics

| 1-Anthology; Austin, Golden-a | .85 | 2.50 | 5.00 |

AMAZING ADVENTURES OF CAPTAIN CARVEL AND HIS CARVEL CRUSADERS, THE (See Carvel Comics)

AMAZING CHAN & THE CHAN CLAN, THE (TV)
May, 1973 - No. 4, Feb, 1974 (Hanna-Barbera)
Gold Key

| 1 | .70 | 2.00 | 4.00 |
| 2-4 | .50 | 1.50 | 3.00 |

AMAZING COMICS (Complete Comics No. 2)
Fall, 1944
Timely Comics (EPC)

| 1-The Destroyer, The Whizzer, The Young Allies, Sergeant Dix; Schomburg-c | 68.00 | 205.00 | 475.00 |

AMAZING CYNICALMAN, THE
June, 1987 ($1.50, B&W)
Eclipse Comics

| 1 | .25 | .75 | 1.50 |

AMAZING DETECTIVE CASES (Formerly Suspense No. 2?)
No. 3, Nov, 1950 - No. 14, Sept, 1952
Marvel/Atlas Comics (CCC)

3	6.50	19.50	45.00
4-6	3.15	9.50	22.00
7-10	2.65	8.00	18.00
11,14: 11-(3/52)-change to horror	3.15	9.50	22.00
12-Krigstein-a	3.50	10.50	24.00
13-Everett-a; electrocution-c/story	4.50	14.00	32.00

NOTE: *Colan a-9. Maneely c-13. Sekowsky a-12. Sinnott a-13. Tuska a-10.*

AMAZING FANTASY (Formerly Amazing Adult Fantasy #7-14)
No. 15, Aug, 1962 (Sept, 1962 shown in indicia)
Marvel Comics Group (AMI)

| 15-Origin & 1st app. of Spider-Man by Ditko; Kirby/Ditko-c | | | |
| | 280.00 | 1120.00 | 2800.00 |

AMAZING GHOST STORIES (Formerly Nightmare)
No. 14, Oct, 1954 - No. 16, Feb, 1955

Alvin #12, © DELL

Amazing Adventures #3 (1961), © MEG

Amazing Fantasy #15, © MEG

Amazing-Man Comics #9, © CEN

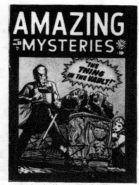

Amazing Mysteries #33, © MEG

The Amazing Spider-Man #1, © MEG

AMAZING GHOST STORIES (continued)
St. John Publishing Co.

	Good	Fine	N-Mint
14-Pit & the Pendulum story by Kinstler; Baker-c			
	11.00	32.00	75.00
15-R/Weird Thrillers #5; Baker-c, Powell-a	7.00	21.00	50.00
16-Kubert reprints from Weird Thrillers #4; Baker-c; Roussos, Tuska, Kinstler-a	8.00	24.00	56.00

AMAZING HIGH ADVENTURE
8/84: No. 2, 10/85; No. 3, 10/86 - No. 5, 1987 (Baxter No. 3,4)
Marvel Comics

1-5	.35	1.00	2.00

NOTE: **Bissette** a-5. **Bolton** c/a-4, 5. **Severin** a-1, 3. **P. Smith** a-2. **Williamson** a-2i.

AMAZING-MAN COMICS (Formerly Motion Picture Funnies Wkly?)
(Also see Stars And Stripes Comics)
No. 5, Sept, 1939 - No. 27, Feb, 1942
Centaur Publications

5(No.1)(Rare)-Origin A-Man the Amazing Man by Bill Everett; The Cat-Man by Tarpe Mills (also No. 8), Mighty Man by Filchock, Minimidget & sidekick Ritty, & The Iron Skull by Burgos begins			
	750.00	1875.00	4500.00
6-Origin The Amazing Man retold; The Shark begins; Ivy Menace by Tarpe Mills app.	217.00	545.00	1300.00
7-Magician From Mars begins; ends #11	133.00	400.00	800.00
8-Cat-Man dresses as woman	84.00	253.00	590.00
9-Magician From Mars battles the 'Elemental Monster', swiped into The Spectre in More Fun 54 & 55	82.00	245.00	575.00
10,11: 11-Zardi, the Eternal Man begins; ends #16; Amazing Man dons costume; last Everett issue	70.00	210.00	490.00
12,13	68.00	204.00	475.00
14-Reef Kinkaid, Rocke Wayburn (ends #20), & Dr. Hypno (ends #21) begin; no Zardi or Chuck Hardy	54.00	160.00	375.00
15,17-20: 15-Zardi returns; no Rocke Wayburn. 17-Dr. Hypno returns; no Zardi	39.00	118.00	275.00
16-Mighty Man's powers of super strength & ability to shrink & grow explained; Rocke Wayburn returns; no Dr. Hypno; Al Avison (a character) begins, ends #18 (a tribute to the famed artist)	42.00	126.00	295.00
21-Origin Dash Dartwell (drug-use story); origin & only app. T.N.T.	39.00	118.00	275.00
22-Dash Dartwell, the Human Meteor & The Voice app; last Iron Skull & The Shark; Silver Streak app.	39.00	118.00	275.00
23-Two Amazing Man stories; intro/origin Tommy the Amazing Kid; The Marksman only app.	42.00	126.00	295.00
24,27: 24-King of Darkness, Nightshade, & Blue Lady begin; end #26; 1st App. Super-Ann	39.00	118.00	275.00
25,26 (Scarce)-Meteor Martin by Wolverton in both; 26-Electric Ray app.	72.00	215.00	505.00

NOTE: **Everett** a-5-11; c-5-11. **Gilman** a-14-20. **Giunta/Mirando** a-7-10. **Sam Glanzman** a-14-16, 18-21, 23. **Louis Glanzman** a-6, 9-11, 14-21; c-13-19, 21. **Robert Golden** a-9. **Gustavson** a-6; c-22, 23. **Lubbers** a-14-21. **Simon** a-10. **Frank Thomas** a-6, 9-11, 14, 15, 17-21.

AMAZING MYSTERIES (Formerly Sub-Mariner No. 31)
No. 32, May, 1949 - No. 35, Jan, 1950
Marvel Comics (CCC)

32-The Witness app; 1st Marvel horror comic			
	24.00	71.00	165.00
33-Horror format	7.00	21.00	50.00
34,35-Change to Crime	5.00	15.00	35.00

AMAZING MYSTERY FUNNIES
Aug, 1938 - No. 24, Sept, 1940 (All 52 pgs.)
Centaur Publications

V1#1-Everett-c(1st); Dick Kent Adv. story; Skyrocket Steele in the Year X on cover only	214.00	535.00	1285.00
2-Everett 1st-a (Skyrocket Steele)	84.00	252.00	590.00

	Good	Fine	N-Mint
3	50.00	150.00	350.00
3(#4, 12/38)-nn on cover, #3 on inside; bondage-c			
	40.00	120.00	280.00
V2#1-4,6: 2-Drug use story. 3-Air-Sub DX begins by Burgos. 4-Dan Hastings, Sand Hog begins (ends #5). 6-Last Skyrocket Steele			
	36.00	107.00	250.00
5-Classic Everett-c	40.00	120.00	280.00
7 (Scarce)-Intro. The Fantom of the Fair; Everett, Gustavson, Burgos-a	170.00	510.00	1190.00
8-Origin & 1st app. Speed Centaur	77.00	230.00	540.00
9-11: 11-Self portrait and biog. of Everett; Jon Linton begins	40.00	120.00	280.00
12 (Scarce)-Wolverton Space Patrol-a (12/39)			
	92.00	275.00	645.00
V3#1(#17, 1/40)-Intro. Bullet; Tippy Taylor serial begins, ends #24 (continued in The Arrow #2)	40.00	120.00	280.00
18,20: 18-Fantom of the Fair by Gustavson	36.00	107.00	250.00
19,21-24-All have Space Patrol by Wolverton			
	65.00	195.00	455.00

NOTE: **Burgos** a-V2#3-9. **Eisner** a-V1#2, 3(2). **Everett** a-V1#2-4, V2#1, 3-6; c-V1#1-4, V2#3, 5, 18. **Filchock** a-V2#9. **Flessel** a-V2#6. **Guardineer** a-V1#4, V2#4-6; **Gustavson** a-V2#4, 5, 9-12, V3#1, 18, 19; c-V2#7, 9, 12, V3#1, 21, 22; **McWilliams** a-V2#9, 10. **Tarpe Mills** a-V2#2, 4-6, 9-12, V3#1. **Leo Morey** (Pulp artist) c-V2#10; text illo-V2#11. **Frank Thomas** c-V2/11. **Webster** a-V2#4.

AMAZING SAINTS
1974 (39 cents)
Logos International

True story of Phil Saint		.20	.40

AMAZING SPIDER-MAN, THE (See All Detergent Comics, Amazing Fantasy, America's Best TV Comics, Aurora, Giant Size Super-Heroes Feat. . . , Marvel Coll. Item Classics, Marvel Fanfare, Marvel Graphic Novel, Marvel Masterworks, Marvel Spec. Ed., Marvel Tales, Marvel Team-Up, Marvel Treasury Ed., Official Marvel Index To . . . , Spectacular. . . , Spider-Man Digest, Spider-Man Vs. Wolverine, Spidey Super Stories, Superman Vs. . . . , Try-Out Winner Book & Web of Spiderman)

AMAZING SPIDER-MAN, THE
March, 1963 - Present
Marvel Comics Group

	Good	Fine	N-Mint
1-Retells origin by Steve Ditko; F.F. x-over; intro. John Jameson & The Chameleon; Kirby-c	275.00	1100.00	2750.00
1-Reprint from the Golden Record Comic set with record	4.30	13.00	30.00
	8.70	26.00	60.00
2-Intro the Vulture & the Terrible Tinkerer	95.00	285.00	660.00
3-Human Torch cameo; intro. & 1st app. Doc Octopus	63.00	189.00	440.00
4-Origin & 1st app. The Sandman; Intro. Betty Brant & Liz Allen	51.00	153.00	360.00
5-Dr. Doom app.	43.00	129.00	300.00
6-1st app. Lizard	48.00	145.00	340.00
7,8,10: 8-Fantastic 4 app. 10-1st app. Big Man & Enforcers	28.00	85.00	200.00
9-1st app. Electro (origin)	32.00	96.00	220.00
11,12: 11-1st app. Bennett Brant	20.00	60.00	140.00
13-1st app. Mysterio	21.50	64.00	150.00
14-Intro The Green Goblin; Hulk x-over	32.00	95.00	225.00
15-Intro Kraven the Hunter	23.00	70.00	160.00
16,18,19: 18-Fant.-4 app; 19-Intro. Ned Leeds	13.00	40.00	90.00
17-2nd app. Green Goblin	18.00	54.00	125.00
20-Intro & origin The Scorpion	14.00	43.00	100.00
21-27,29,30: 22-1st app. Princess Python. 25-1st app. Spencer Smythe. 26-1st app. Crime Master; dies in #27	8.50	25.50	60.00
28-Origin/1st app. Molten Man	10.00	30.00	70.00
31-38: 31-Intro. Harry Osborn, Gwen Stacy & Prof. Warren. 36-1st app. Looter. 37-Intro. Norman Osborn. 38-Last Ditko issue	5.70	17.00	40.00
39,40-Green Goblin in both; origin #40	5.70	17.00	40.00

AMAZING SPIDER-MAN (continued)

	Good	Fine	N-Mint
41,43-49: 41-1st app. Rhino. 46-Intro. Shocker	3.60	11.00	25.00
42-1st app. Mary Jane Watson	4.50	14.00	32.00
50-Intro. Kingpin	11.50	34.00	80.00
51-60: 52-Intro. Joe Robertson. 56-Intro. Capt. George Stacy. 57,58-Ka-Zar app. 59-Intro. Brainwasher (alias Kingpin)	2.15	6.50	15.00
61-80: 67-Intro. Randy Robertson. 73-Intro. Silvermane. 78-Intro. Prowler	1.50	4.50	10.00
81-89: 83-Intro. Schemer & Vanessa (Kingpin's wife)	1.30	4.00	9.00
90-Death of Capt. Stacey	1.70	5.00	12.00
91-93,95,99: 93-Intro. Arthur Stacy	1.30	4.00	9.00
94-Origin retold	2.15	6.50	15.00
96-98-Drug books not approved by CCA	2.85	8.50	20.00
100-Anniversary issue	3.30	13.00	30.00
101-Intro. Morbius	1.70	5.00	12.00
102-Origin Morbius (52 pgs.)	1.70	5.00	12.00
103-112,115-118: 108-Intro. Sha-Shan. 110-Intro. Gibbon	1.15	3.50	7.00
113,114,119,120: 113-Intro. Hammerhead	1.25	3.75	7.50
121,122: 121-Death of Gwen Stacy (r-/in Marvel Tales #98); 122-Death of Green Goblin (r-/in Marvel Tales #99)	4.70	14.00	32.00
123-128: 124-Intro. Man Wolf, origin in #125	1.00	3.00	6.00
129-1st app. The Punisher (2/74)	26.00	79.00	185.00
130-133,136-140: 139-Intro. Grizzly. 140-Intro. Glory Grant	.85	2.50	5.00
134-Punisher cameo; intro Tarantula	1.70	5.00	12.00
135-Punisher app.	5.70	17.00	40.00
141-160: 143-Intro. Cyclone	.70	2.00	4.00
161-Nightcrawler app. from X-Men; Punisher cameo	1.30	4.00	8.00
162-Punisher, Nightcrawler app.	2.00	6.00	14.00
163-173,176-181: 167-1st app. Will O' The Wisp. 171-Nova app. 177-180-Green Goblin app. 181-Origin retold; gives life history of Spider-Man	.50	1.50	3.00
174,175-Punisher app.	1.50	4.50	10.00
182-188	.50	1.50	3.00
189,190-Byrne-a(p)	.60	1.75	3.50
191-193,195-199,203-219: 196-Faked death of Aunt May. 203-2nd Dazzler app. 210-Intro. & 1st app. Madame Web. 212-Intro. Hydro Man	.50	1.50	3.00
194-1st Black Cat	.70	2.00	4.00
200-Giant origin issue	1.00	3.00	6.00
201,202-Punisher app.	1.30	4.00	8.00
220-237: 226,227-Black Cat returns. 236-Tarantula dies. 235-Origin Will-'O-The-Wisp	.40	1.25	2.50
238-1st app. Hobgoblin	2.00	6.00	12.00
239-2nd app. Hobgoblin	1.00	3.00	6.00
240-250: 241-Origin The Vulture	.30	.95	1.90
251-Last old costume	.75	2.20	4.40
252-Spider-Man dons new costume (5/84)	1.05	3.15	6.30
253-1st app. The Rose	.60	1.85	3.70
254	.40	1.20	2.40
255-260: 259-Sp-M back to old costume	.30	.95	1.90
261-274,276-283: 261-Hobgoblin app.	.25	.75	1.50
275-Origin-r ($1.25, double-size)	.55	1.60	3.20
284-Punisher cameo; Gang War story begins	.40	1.20	2.40
285-Punisher app.	1.10	3.30	6.60
286-288: 288-Last Gang War	.30	.90	1.80
289-Double-size, origin Hobgoblin	.85	2.50	5.00
290-292	.25	.75	1.50
293,294-Part 2 & 5 of Kraven story from Web of Spider-Man	.60	1.85	3.70
295-297	.40	1.20	2.40
298-Todd McFarlane-c/a begins, ends #325	1.45	4.40	8.80
299-McFarlane-a	.95	2.80	5.60

	Good	Fine	N-Mint
300 ($1.50, 52 pgs.; 25th Anniversary)-Last black costume	1.25	3.75	7.50
301-305: 301 ($1.00 issues begin). 304-1st bi-weekly issue	.45	1.35	2.70
306-315: 306-Cover swipe from Action #1. 312-Hobgoblin app.	.35	1.10	2.20
316-323,325: 319-Bi-weekly begins again	.25	.70	1.40
324,326-330: 324-McFarlane c/a only. 327-Cosmic Spidey continues from Spect. Spider-Man. 328-Hulk x-over		.50	1.00
Annual 1 (1964)-Origin S-M; Intro. Sinister Six	14.00	43.00	100.00
Annual 2	6.50	19.50	45.00
Special 3,4	2.50	7.50	18.00
Special 5-8 (12/71)	1.35	4.00	8.00
King Size 9 ('73)-Green Goblin app.	.85	2.50	5.00
Giant-Size 1(7/74)-Kirby/Ditko r plus new-a	.80	2.40	4.80
Giant-Size 2(10/74), 3(1/75), 5(7/75), 6(9/75)	.40	1.20	2.40
Giant-Size 4(4/75)-Third Punisher app.	3.70	11.00	26.00
Annual 10(6/76)-Old Human Fly app.	.60	1.85	3.70
Annual 11(9/77), 12(8/78)	.60	1.85	3.70
Annual 13(11/79)-Byrne-a	.80	2.40	4.80
Annual 14(12/80)-Miller c/a(p), 40pgs.	1.00	3.00	6.00
Annual 15(1981)-Miller c/a(p); Punisher app.	1.40	4.25	8.50
Annual 16(12/82)-Origin/1st app. new Capt. Marvel (female heroine)	.40	1.20	2.40
Annual 17(12/83), 18 ('84), 19(11/85)	.40	1.20	2.40
Annual 20(11/86)-Origin Iron Man of 2020	.40	1.20	2.40
Annual 21('87)-Special wedding issue (direct sale, no bar codes)	.75	2.20	4.40
Annual 21-Wedding issue (newsstand)	.60	1.85	3.70
Annual 22('88, $1.75, 68 pgs.)-Intro/1st app. Speedball; Evolutionary War x-over	.60	1.85	3.70
Annual 23 ('89, $2.00, 68 pgs.)-Atlantis Attacks; origin Spider-Man retold; She-Hulk app.; Byrne-c	.35	1.05	2.10
Aim Toothpaste giveaway(36pgs., reg. size)-Green Goblin app.	.35	1.00	2.00
Aim Toothpaste giveaway (16pgs., reg. size)-Dr. Octopus app.		.50	1.00
All Detergent Giveaway ('79, 36 pgs.), nn-Origin-r	.85	2.50	5.00
Giveaway-Acme & Dingo Children's Boots(1980)-Spider-Woman app.		.50	1.00
...& Power Pack ('84, nn)(Nat'l Committee for Prevention of Child Abuse. (two versions, mail offer & store giveaway)-Mooney-a; Byrne-c		.30	.60
...& The Hulk (Special Edition)(6/8/80; 20 pgs.; Chicago Tribune giveaway)	.70	2.00	4.00
...& The Incredible Hulk (1981, 1982; 36 pgs.), Sanger Harris, Dallas Times, Denver Post, Kansas City Star, The Jones Store-giveaway; 16 pgs. (1983)	1.00	3.00	6.00
..., Captain America, The Incredible Hulk, & Spider-Woman ('81) (7-11 Stores giveaway; 36 pgs.)		.30	.60
...: Christmas In Dallas (1983) (Supplement to Dallas Times Herald) giveaway		.30	.60
..., Fire-Star, and Iceman At the Dallas Ballet Nutcracker (1983; supplement to Dallas Times Herald)-Mooney-a		.30	.60
Giveaway-Esquire & Eye Magazines(2/69)-Miniature-Still attached	4.15	12.50	25.00
..., Storm & Powerman ('82; 20 pgs.)(American Cancer Society)-giveaway		.30	.60
...Vs. The Hulk (Special Edition; 1979)(Supplement to Columbus Dispatch)-Giveaway	.50	1.50	3.00
...vs. the Prodigy Giveaway, 16 pgs. in color ('76)-5x6½''-Sex education; (1 million printed;35-50 cents)	.25		.50

NOTE: **Austin** a-248i, Annual 13i; c-188i, 241i, 242i, 248i. **J. Buscema** a(p)-72, 73, 76-81, 84, 85. **Byrne** a-189i, 190p, 206p, Annual 3r, 6r, 7r, 13p, Gnt-Size 1r, 3-5r; c-189p, 268, 296, Annual 12. **Ditko** a-1-38, Annual 1, 2, Gnt-Size 4r; c-1-38. **Gil Kane** a(p)-89-

The Amazing Spider-Man #194, © MEG

The Amazing Spider-Man #300, © MEG

Giant Size Spider-Man #4, © MEG

The American Air Forces #1, © WHW   *America's Best Comics #9, © STD*   *America's Best TV Comics #1, © ABC/MEG*

AMAZING SPIDER-MAN (continued)
105, 120-124, 150, Annual 10, 12i; c-90p, 96, 98, 99, 101-105p, 129p, 131p, 132p, 137-140p, 143p, 148p, 149p, 151p, 153p, 160p, 161p, Annual 10p. **Kirby** a-8. **McFarlane** a-298p, 299p, 300-303, 304-323p, 325p; c-298-325. **Miller** c-218, 219. **Mooney** a-65i, 67-82i, 84-88i, 173i, 178i, 189i, 190i, 192i, 193i, 196-202i, 207i, 211-219i, 221i, 226i, 227i, 229-233i, Annual 11i, 17i. **Nasser** c-228p. **Pollard** a-193-195p, 197p; c-187, 190. **Simonson** c-222. **Starlin** a-113i, 114i, 187p.

AMAZING WILLIE MAYS, THE
No date (Sept, 1954)
Famous Funnies Publ.

	Good	Fine	N-Mint
nn	32.00	95.00	225.00

AMAZING WORLD OF SUPERMAN (See Superman)

AMAZON, THE
Mar, 1989 - No. 3, May, 1989 ($1.95, color, mini-series)
Comico

1-3: Ecological theme	.35	1.00	2.00

AMBUSH (See 4-Color Comics No. 314)

AMBUSH BUG (Also see Son of. . .)
June, 1985 - No. 4, Sept, 1985 (mini-series)
DC Comics

1-Giffen c/a in all		.50	1.00
2-4		.40	.80
. . .Stocking Stuffer (2/86, $1.25)-Giffen c/a		.65	1.30

AMERICA IN ACTION
1942; Winter, 1945 (36 pages)
Dell(Imp. Publ. Co.)/Mayflower House Publ.

1942-Dell-(68 pages)	8.50	25.50	60.00
1(1945)-Has 3 adaptations from American history; Kiefer, Schrotter & Webb-a	5.50	16.50	38.00

AMERICA MENACED!
1950 (Paper cover)
Vital Publications

nn-Anti-communism	estimated value. . . .		125.00

AMERICAN, THE
July, 1987 - No. 8, 1989 ($1.50-$1.75, B&W)
Dark Horse Comics

1 ($1.50)	1.10	3.25	6.50
2	.75	2.20	4.40
3-5	.50	1.50	3.00
6-8	.30	.90	1.75
. . .Color Special #1 (1989, $2.95)	.50	1.50	2.95
. . .Collection ($5.95, B&W)-reprints	1.00	3.00	5.95

AMERICAN AIR FORCES, THE (See A-1 Comics)
Sept-Oct, 1944 - No. 4, 1945; No. 5, 1951 - No. 12, 1954
William H. Wise(Flying Cadet Publ. Co./Hasan(No.1)/Life's Romances/Magazine Ent. No. 5 on)

1-Article by Zack Mosley, creator of Smilin' Jack	5.70	17.00	40.00
2-4	4.00	12.00	28.00

NOTE: *All part comic, part magazine. Art by* **Whitney, Chas. Quinlan, H. C. Kiefer,** *and* **Tony Dipreta.**

5(A-1 45)(Formerly Jet Powers), 6(A-1 54),7(A-1 58),8(A-1 65) 9(A-1 67),10(A-1 74),11(A-1 79),12(A-1 91)	2.15	6.50	15.00

NOTE: *Powell c/a-5-12.*

AMERICAN COMICS
1940's
Theatre Giveaways (Liberty Theatre, Grand Rapids, Mich. known)

Many possible combinations. "Golden Age" superhero comics with new cover added and given away at theaters. Following known: Superman #59, Capt. Marvel #20, Capt. Marvel Jr. #5, Action #33, Classics Comics #8, Whiz #39. Value would vary with book and should be 70-80 percent of the original.

AMERICAN FLAGG! (Also see First Comics Graphic Novel 3, 9, 12, 21 and Howard Chaykin's. . .)
Oct, 1983 - No. 50, Mar, 1988
First Comics

	Good	Fine	N-Mint
1-Chaykin c/a begins	.50	1.50	3.00
2-12	.25	.75	1.50
13-50: 21-27-Alan Moore scripts. 31-Origin Bob Violence		.50	1.00
Special 1 (11/86)	.25	.75	1.50

AMERICAN GRAPHICS
No. 1, 1954; No. 2, 1957 (25 cents)
Henry Stewart

1-The Maid of the Mist, The Last of the Eries (Indian Legends of Niagara) (Sold at Niagara Falls)	3.70	11.00	26.00
2-Victory at Niagara & Laura Secord (Heroine of the War of 1812)	2.65	8.00	18.00

AMERICAN INDIAN, THE (See Picture Progress)

AMERICAN LIBRARY
No. 3, 1944 - No. 6, 1944 (68 pages) (15 cents, B&W, text & pictures)
David McKay Publications

3-6: 3-Look to the Mountain. 4-Case of the Crooked Candle (Perry Mason). 5-Duel in the Sun. 6-Wingate's Raiders	6.50	19.50	45.00

NOTE: *Also see Guadalcanal Diary & Thirty Seconds Over Tokyo (part of series?).*

AMERICA'S BEST COMICS
Feb, 1942 - No. 31, July, 1949
Nedor/Better/Standard Publications

1-The Woman in Red, Black Terror, Captain Future, Doc Strange, The Liberator, & Don Davis, Secret Ace begin	57.00	170.00	400.00
2-Origin The American Eagle; The Woman in Red ends	31.00	95.00	220.00
3-Pyroman begins	22.00	65.00	155.00
4	20.00	60.00	140.00
5-Last Captain Future-not in #4; Lone Eagle app.	17.00	51.00	120.00
6,7: 6-American Crusader app.	16.00	48.00	110.00
8-Last Liberator	12.00	36.00	85.00
9-The Fighting Yank begins; The Ghost app.	12.00	36.00	85.00
10-14: 10-Flag-c. 14-American Eagle ends	11.00	32.00	75.00
15-20	10.00	30.00	70.00
21-Infinity-c	8.50	25.50	60.00
22-Capt. Future app.	8.50	25.50	60.00
23-Miss Masque begins; last Doc Strange	11.50	34.00	80.00
24-Miss Masque bondage-c	10.00	30.00	70.00
25-Last Fighting Yank; Sea Eagle app.	8.50	25.50	60.00
26-The Phantom Detective & The Silver Knight app.; Frazetta text illo & some panels in Miss Masque	11.50	34.00	80.00
27-31: 27,28-Commando Cubs. 27-Doc Strange. 28-Tuska Black Terror. 29-Last Pyroman	8.50	25.50	60.00

NOTE: *American Eagle not in 3, 8, 9, 13. Fighting Yank not in 10, 12. Liberator not in 2, 6, 7. Pyroman not in 9, 11, 14-16, 23, 25-27. Schomburg (Xela) c-5, 7-31. Bondage c-18, 24.*

AMERICA'S BEST TV COMICS (TV)
1967 (Produced by Marvel Comics) (68 pgs. 25 cents)
American Broadcasting Company

1-Spider-Man, Fantastic Four, Casper, King Kong, George of the Jungle, Journey to the Center of the Earth app. (Promotes new TV cartoon show)	2.65	8.00	18.00

AMERICA'S BIGGEST COMICS BOOK
1944 (196 pages) (One Shot)
William H. Wise

1-The Grim Reaper, The Silver Knight, Zudo, the Jungle Boy,

AMERICA'S BIGGEST COMICS BOOK (cont.)	Good	Fine	N-Mint
Commando Cubs, Thunderhoof app.	23.00	70.00	160.00

AMERICA'S FUNNIEST COMICS
1944 - No. 2, 1944 (80 pages) (15 cents)
William H. Wise

nn(#1), 2	10.00	30.00	70.00

AMERICA'S GREATEST COMICS
5?/1941 - No. 8, Summer, 1943 (100 pgs.) (Soft cardboard covers)
Fawcett Publications (15 cents)

1-Bulletman, Spy Smasher, Capt. Marvel, Minute Man & Mr. Scarlet			
begin; Mac Raboy-c	146.00	437.00	875.00
2	62.00	185.00	435.00
3	41.00	124.00	290.00
4-Commando Yank begins; Golden Arrow, Ibis the Invincible & Spy			
Smasher cameo in Captain Marvel	35.00	105.00	245.00
5	35.00	105.00	245.00
6	27.00	81.00	190.00
7-Balbo the Boy Magician app.; Captain Marvel, Bulletman cameo			
in Mr. Scarlet	27.00	81.00	190.00
8-Capt. Marvel Jr. & Golden Arrow app.; Spy Smasher x-over in			
Capt. Midnight; no Minute Man or Commando Yank			
	27.00	81.00	190.00

AMERICA'S SWEETHEART SUNNY (See Sunny, . . .)

AMERICA VS. THE JUSTICE SOCIETY
Jan, 1985 - No. 4, Apr, 1985 (mini-series)
DC Comics

1-Double size; Alcala-a in all	.25	.75	1.50
2-4		.50	1.00

AMERICOMICS
April, 1983 - No. 6, Mar, 1984 (Baxter paper; color)
Americomics

1-Intro/origin The Shade; Intro. The Slayer, Captain Freedom and			
The Liberty Corps; Perez-c	.40	1.25	2.50
2-6: 2-Messenger app., & 1st app. Tara on Jungle Island 3-New &			
old Blue Beetle battle. 4-Origin Dragonfly & Shade. 5-Origin Com-			
mando D. 6-Origin the Scarlet Scorpion	.40	1.25	2.50
Special 1(8/83, $2.00)-Sentinels of Justice (Blue Beetle, Captain			
Atom, Nightshade, & The Question)	.40	1.20	2.50

AMETHYST
Jan, 1985 - No. 16, Aug, 1986
DC Comics

1-16: 8-Fire Jade's i.d. revealed		.50	1.00
Special 1 (10/86, $1.25)		.65	1.30

AMETHYST
Nov, 1987 - No. 4, Feb, 1988 ($1.25, color, mini-series)
DC Comics

1-4		.60	1.25

AMETHYST, PRINCESS OF GEMWORLD
May, 1983 - No. 12, April, 1984 (12 issue maxi-series)
DC Comics

1-60 cent cover	.25	.75	1.50
1-35 cent-tested in Austin & Kansas City	2.00	6.00	12.00
2-35 cent-tested in Austin & Kansas City	2.00	6.00	12.00
2-12: Perez-c(p) #6-11		.50	1.00
Annual 1(9/84)		.65	1.30

ANARCHO DICTATOR OF DEATH (See Comics Novel)

ANCHORS ANDREWS (The Saltwater Daffy)
Jan, 1953 - No. 4, July, 1953 (Anchors the Saltwater. . . No. 4)
St. John Publishing Co.

1-Canteen Kate by Matt Baker, 9 pgs.	8.00	24.00	56.00
2-4	2.15	6.50	15.00

ANDY & WOODY (See March of Comics No. 40,55,76)

ANDY BURNETT (See 4-Color Comics No. 865)

ANDY COMICS (Formerly Scream Comics; becomes Ernie Comics)
No. 20, June, 1948 - No. 21, Aug, 1948
Current Publications (Ace Magazines)

	Good	Fine	N-Mint
20,21-Archie-type comic	2.15	6.50	15.00

ANDY DEVINE WESTERN
Dec, 1950 - No. 2, 1951
Fawcett Publications

1	23.00	70.00	160.00
2	14.00	43.00	100.00

ANDY GRIFFITH SHOW, THE (See 4-Color No. 1252,1341)

ANDY HARDY COMICS (See Movie Comics No. 3 by Fiction House)
April, 1952 - No. 6, Sept-Nov, 1954
Dell Publishing Co.

4-Color 389 (#1)	2.00	6.00	14.00
4-Color 447,480,515,5,6	1.15	3.50	8.00
. . & the New Automatic Gas Clothes Dryer ('52, 16 pgs., 5x7¼")			
Bendix Giveaway (soft-c)	2.00	6.00	14.00

ANDY PANDA (Also see Crackajack Funnies #39, The Funnies, New
Funnies & Walter Lantz . . .)
1943 - No. 56, Nov-Jan, 1961-62 (Walter Lantz)
Dell Publishing Co.

4-Color 25('43)	26.00	77.00	180.00
4-Color 54('44)	16.00	48.00	110.00
4-Color 85('45)	10.00	30.00	70.00
4-Color 130('46),154,198	5.00	15.00	35.00
4-Color 216,240,258,280,297	2.65	8.00	18.00
4-Color 326,345,358	1.70	5.00	12.00
4-Color 383,409	1.15	3.50	8.00
16(11-1/52-53) - 30	.70	2.10	5.00
31-56	.55	1.80	4.00
(See March of Comics No. 5,22,79, & Super Book No. 4,15,27.)			

ANGEL
Aug, 1954 - No. 16, Nov-Jan, 1958-59
Dell Publishing Co.

4-Color 576(#1, 8/54)	1.00	3.00	7.00
2(5-7/55) - 16	.55	1.80	4.00

ANGEL AND THE APE (Meet Angel No. 7) (See Limited Collector's
Edition C-34 & Showcase No. 77)
Nov-Dec, 1968 - No. 6, Sept-Oct, 1969
National Periodical Publications

1-Not Wood-a	1.00	3.00	7.00
2-6-Wood inks in all	.70	2.00	5.00

ANGELIC ANGELINA
1909 (11½x17"; 30 pgs.; 2 colors)
Cupples & Leon Company

By Munson Paddock	14.00	42.00	100.00

ANGEL LOVE
Aug, 1986 - No. 8, Mar, 1987 (mini-series)
DC Comics

1-8		.40	.80
Special 1 (1987, $1.25, 52 pgs.)		.65	1.30

ANGEL OF LIGHT, THE (See The Crusaders)

ANIMAL ADVENTURES
Dec, 1953 - No. 3, Apr?, 1954
Timor Publications/Accepted Publications (reprints)

1	1.60	4.70	11.00
2,3	.90	2.70	6.50
1-3 (reprints, nd)	.80	2.40	5.50

America's Greatest Comics #4, © FAW

Americomics #1, © AC Comics

Angel #3, © DELL

Animal Antics #3, © DC   Annie Oakley And Tagg #8, © DELL   Anthro #2, © DC

ANIMAL ANTICS (Movie Town . . . No. 24 on)
Mar-Apr, 1946 - No. 23, Nov-Dec, 1949
National Periodical Publications

	Good	Fine	N-Mint
1-Raccoon Kids begins by Otto Feur; some-c by Grossman	23.00	68.00	160.00
2	11.00	32.00	75.00
3-10	6.50	19.50	45.00
11-23	4.00	12.00	28.00

NOTE: **Post** a-10,14,15,19; c-10.

ANIMAL COMICS
Dec-Jan, 1941-42 - No. 30, Dec-Jan, 1947-48
Dell Publishing Co.

1-1st Pogo app. by Walt Kelly (Dan Noonan art in most issues)	86.00	257.00	600.00
2-Uncle Wiggily begins	36.00	107.00	250.00
3,5	25.00	75.00	175.00
4,6,7-No Pogo	14.00	42.00	100.00
8-10	17.00	51.00	120.00
11-15	11.00	32.00	75.00
16-20	7.00	21.00	50.00
21-30: 25-30-"Jigger" by John Stanley	5.00	15.00	35.00

NOTE: **Dan Noonan** a-18-30. **Gollub** art in most later issues.

ANIMAL CRACKERS (Also see Adventures of Patoruzu)
1946; No. 31, July, 1950; 1959
Green Publ. Co./Norlen/Fox Feat.(Hero Books)

1-Super Cat begins	5.00	15.00	35.00
2	2.30	7.00	16.00
3-10 (Exist?)	1.15	3.50	8.00
31(Fox)-Formerly My Love Secret	2.30	7.00	16.00
9(1959-Norlen)	.85	2.60	6.00
nn, nd ('50s), no publ.; infinity-c	.85	2.60	6.00

ANIMAL FABLES
July-Aug, 1946 - No. 7, Nov-Dec, 1947
E. C. Comics(Fables Publ. Co.)

1-Freddy Firefly (clone of Human Torch), Korky Kangaroo, Petey Pig, Danny Demon begin	24.00	73.00	170.00
2-Aesop Fables begins	14.00	42.00	100.00
3-6	12.00	36.00	85.00
7-Origin Moon Girl	40.00	120.00	280.00

ANIMAL FAIR (Fawcett's . . .)
March, 1946 - No. 11, Feb, 1947
Fawcett Publications

1	8.50	25.50	60.00
2	4.30	13.00	30.00
3-6	2.85	8.50	20.00
7-11	2.00	6.00	14.00

ANIMAL FUN
1953
Premier Magazines

1-(3-D)	21.00	64.00	150.00

ANIMAL MAN (Also see Strange Adventures #180)
Sept, 1988 - Present ($1.25, color)
DC Comics

1: Bolland c-1-18	1.15	3.50	7.00
2	.85	2.50	5.00
3,4	.50	1.50	3.00
5-10: 6-Invasion tie-in	.30	.90	1.75
11-20		.60	1.25

ANIMAL WORLD, THE (See 4-Color Comics No. 713)

ANIMATED COMICS
No date given (Summer, 1947?)
E. C. Comics

	Good	Fine	N-Mint
1 (Rare)	55.00	165.00	385.00

ANIMATED FUNNY COMIC TUNES (See Funny Tunes)

ANIMATED MOVIE-TUNES (Movie Tunes No. 3)
Fall, 1945 - No. 2, Sum, 1946
Margood Publishing Corp. (Timely)

1,2-Super Rabbit, Ziggy Pig & Silly Seal	7.00	21.00	50.00

ANIMAX
Dec, 1986 - No. 4, June, 1987
Star Comics (Marvel)

1-4: Based on toys		.40	.80

ANNETTE (See 4-Color Comics No. 905)

ANNETTE'S LIFE STORY (See 4-Color No. 1100)

ANNIE
Oct, 1982 - No. 2, Nov, 1982
Marvel Comics Group

1,2-Movie adaptation		.25	.50
Treasury Edition (Tabloid size)	.35	1.00	2.00

ANNIE OAKLEY (Also see Tessie The Typist #19, Two-Gun Kid & Wild Western)
Spring, 1948 - No. 4, 11/48; No. 5, 6/55 - No. 11, 6/56
Marvel/Atlas Comics(MPI No. 1-4/CDS No. 5 on)

1 (1st Series, '48)-Hedy Devine app.	16.00	47.00	110.00
2 (7/48, 52 pgs.)-Kurtzman-a, "Hey Look," 1pg; Intro. Lana; Hedy Devine app; Captain Tootsie by Beck	11.00	32.00	75.00
3,4	8.50	25.50	60.00
5 (2nd Series)(1955)-Reinman-a	5.70	17.00	40.00
6-8: 6,8-Woodbridge-a	4.30	13.00	30.00
9-Williamson-a, 4 pgs.	4.30	13.00	30.00
10,11: 11-Severin-a	3.60	11.00	25.00

ANNIE OAKLEY AND TAGG (TV)
1953 - No. 18, Jan-Mar, 1959; July, 1965 (all photo-c)
Dell Publishing Co./Gold Key

4-Color 438 (#1)	7.00	21.00	50.00
4-Color 481,575	5.00	15.00	35.00
4(7-9/55)-10	4.00	12.00	28.00
11-18(1-3/59)	3.60	11.00	25.00
1(7/65-Gold Key)-Photo-c	3.00	9.00	21.00

NOTE: **Manning** a-13. Photo back c-4, 9, 11.

ANOTHER WORLD (See Strange Stories From . . .)

ANTHRO (See Showcase)
July-Aug, 1968 - No. 6, July-Aug, 1969
National Periodical Publications

1-Howie Post-a in all	1.50	4.50	10.00
2-6: 6-Wood c/a inks	1.00	3.00	6.00

ANTONY AND CLEOPATRA (See Ideal, a Classical Comic)

ANYTHING GOES
Oct, 1986 - No. 6, 1987 (mini-series)(Mature readers, $2.00)
Fantagraphics Books   (#1-4: color & B&W; #5,6: B&W)

1-Flaming Carrot app. (1st in color?)	.60	1.75	3.50
2-4,6: 2-Miller-c(p); Alan Moore scripts. 3-Capt. Jack, Cerebus app.; Cerebus-c by N. Adams. 4-Perez-c	.35	1.00	2.00
5-Teenage Mutant Ninja Turtles app.	.60	1.75	3.50

A-1 COMICS (A-1 appears on covers No. 1-17 only)(See individual title listings. 1st two issues not numbered.)
1944 - No. 139, Sept-Oct, 1955
Life's Romances Publ.-No. 1/Compix/Magazine Ent.

nn-Kerry Drake, Johnny Devildog, Rocky, Streamer Kelly (Slightly large size)	13.00	40.00	90.00
1-Dotty Dripple(1 pg.), Mr. Ex, Bush Berry, Rocky, Lew Loyal			

A-1 COMICS (continued)	Good	Fine	N-Mint
(20 pgs.)	4.50	14.00	32.00
2-8,10-Texas Slim & Dirty Dalton, The Corsair, Teddy Rich, Dotty			
Dripple, Inca Dinca, Tommy Tinker, Little Mexico & Tugboat Tim,			
The Masquerader & others	2.30	7.00	16.00
9-Texas Slim (all)	2.30	7.00	16.00
11-Teena	2.65	8.00	18.00
12,15-Teena	2.00	6.00	14.00
13-Guns of Fact & Fiction (1948). Used in SOTI, pg. 19; Ingels &			
J. Craig-a	12.00	36.00	84.00
14-Tim Holt Western Adventures #1 (1948)	35.00	105.00	245.00
16-Vacation Comics	1.50	4.50	10.00
17-Tim Holt #2. Last issue to carry A-1 on cover (9-10/48)			
	22.00	65.00	155.00
18-Jimmy Durante-Photo-c	13.00	40.00	90.00
19-Tim Holt #3	15.00	45.00	105.00
20-Jimmy Durante-Photo-c	13.00	40.00	90.00
21-Joan of Arc(1949)-Movie adaptation; Ingrid Bergman photo-covers			
& interior photos; Whitney-a	13.00	40.00	90.00
22-Dick Powell(1949)	8.50	25.50	60.00
23-Cowboys 'N' Indians #6	2.65	8.00	18.00
24-Trail Colt #1-Frazetta, r-in Manhunt #13; Ingels-c; L. B. Cole-a			
	27.00	81.00	190.00
25-Fibber McGee & Molly(1949) (Radio)	3.70	11.00	26.00
26-Trail Colt #2-Ingels-c	22.00	65.00	150.00
27-Ghost Rider #1(1950)-Origin G.R.	34.00	103.00	240.00
28-Christmas-(Koko & Kola #6)(1950)	1.50	4.50	10.00
29-Ghost Rider #2-Frazetta-c (1950)	36.00	107.00	250.00
30-Jet Powers #1-Powell-a	16.00	48.00	110.00
31-Ghost Rider #3-Frazetta-c & origin ('51)	36.00	107.00	250.00
32-Jet Powers #2	11.50	34.00	80.00
33-Muggsy Mouse #1('51)	2.15	6.50	15.00
34-Ghost Rider #4-Frazetta-c (1951)	36.00	107.00	250.00
35-Jet Powers #3-Williamson/Evans-a	21.50	64.00	150.00
36-Muggsy Mouse #2; Racist-c	4.30	13.00	30.00
37-Ghost Rider #5-Frazetta-c (1951)	36.00	107.00	250.00
38-Jet Powers #4-Williamson & Wood-a	21.50	64.00	150.00
39-Muggsy Mouse #3	1.15	3.50	8.00
40-Dogface Dooley #1('51)	2.30	7.00	16.00
41-Cowboys 'N' Indians #7	2.00	6.00	14.00
42-Best of the West #1-Powell-a	21.00	62.00	145.00
43-Dogface Dooley #2	1.50	4.50	10.00
44-Ghost Rider #6	11.50	34.00	80.00
45-American Air Forces #5-Powell-c/a	2.15	6.50	15.00
46-Best of the West #2	11.00	32.00	75.00
47-Thun'da, King of the Congo #1-Frazetta-c/a('52)			
	83.00	250.00	580.00
48-Cowboys 'N' Indians #8	2.00	6.00	14.00
49-Dogface Dooley #3	1.50	4.50	10.00
50-Danger Is Their Business #11 (1952)-Powell-a			
	5.00	15.00	35.00
51-Ghost Rider #7 ('52)	11.50	34.00	80.00
52-Best of the West #3	9.50	28.50	65.00
53-Dogface Dooley #4	1.50	4.50	10.00
54-American Air Forces #6(8/52)-Powell-a	2.15	6.50	15.00
55-U.S. Marines #5-Powell-a	2.35	7.00	16.00
56-Thun'da #2-Powell-c/a	12.00	36.00	84.00
57-Ghost Rider #8	10.00	30.00	70.00
58-American Air Forces #7-Powell-a	2.15	6.50	15.00
59-Best of the West #4	9.50	28.50	65.00
60-The U.S. Marines #6-Powell-a	2.35	7.00	16.00
61-Space Ace #5(1953)-Guardineer-a	17.00	51.00	120.00
62-Starr Flagg, Undercover Girl #5 (#1)	20.00	60.00	140.00
63-Manhunt #13-Frazetta reprinted from A-1 #24			
	17.00	51.00	120.00
64-Dogface Dooley #5	1.50	4.50	10.00
65-American Air Forces #8-Powell-a	2.15	6.50	15.00

	Good	Fine	N-Mint
66-Best of the West #5	9.50	28.50	65.00
67-American Air Forces #9-Powell-a	2.15	6.50	15.00
68-U.S. Marines #7-Powell-a	2.35	7.00	16.00
69-Ghost Rider #9(10/52)	10.00	30.00	70.00
70-Best of the West #6	6.50	19.50	45.00
71-Ghost Rider #10(12/52)	10.00	30.00	70.00
72-U.S. Marines #8-Powell-a(3)	2.35	7.00	16.00
73-Thun'da #3-Powell-c/a	9.00	27.00	62.00
74-American Air Forces #10-Powell-a	2.15	6.50	15.00
75-Ghost Rider #11(3/53)	8.00	24.00	55.00
76-Best of the West #7	6.50	19.50	45.00
77-Manhunt #14	11.00	32.00	75.00
78-Thun'da #4-Powell-c/a	9.00	27.00	62.00
79-American Air Forces #11-Powell-a	2.15	6.50	15.00
80-Ghost Rider #12(6/52)	8.00	24.00	55.00
81-Best of the West #8	6.50	19.50	45.00
82-Cave Girl #11(1953)-Powell-c/a; origin (#1)	20.00	60.00	140.00
83-Thun'da #5-Powell-c/a	8.00	24.00	56.00
84-Ghost Rider #13(8/53)	8.00	24.00	55.00
85-Best of the West #9	6.50	19.50	45.00
86-Thun'da #6-Powell-c/a	8.00	24.00	56.00
87-Best of the West #10	6.50	19.50	45.00
88-Bobby Benson's B-Bar-B Riders #20	3.50	10.50	24.00
89-Home Run #3-Powell-a; Stan Musial photo-c			
	8.00	24.00	56.00
90-Red Hawk #11(1953)-Powell-c/a	4.30	13.00	30.00
91-American Air Forces #12-Powell-a	2.15	6.50	15.00
92-Dream Book of Romance #5-photo-c; Guardineer-a			
	2.65	8.00	18.00
93-Great Western #8('54)-Origin The Ghost Rider; Powell-a			
	9.30	28.00	65.00
94-White Indian #11-Frazetta-a(r); Powell-c	16.00	48.00	110.00
95-Muggsy Mouse #4	1.15	3.50	8.00
96-Cave Girl #12, with Thun'da; Powell-c/a	14.00	42.00	100.00
97-Best of the West #11	6.50	19.50	45.00
98-Undercover Girl #6-Powell-c	18.00	54.00	125.00
99-Muggsy Mouse #5	1.15	3.50	8.00
100-Badmen of the West #1-Meskin-a(?)	11.00	32.00	75.00
101-White Indian #12-Frazetta-a(r)	16.00	48.00	110.00
101-Dream Book of Romance #6 (4-6/54); Marlon Brando photo-c;			
Powell, Bolle, Guardineer-a	6.50	19.50	45.00
103-Best of the West #12-Powell-a	6.50	19.50	45.00
104-White Indian #13-Frazetta-a(r)('54)	16.00	48.00	110.00
105-Great Western #9-Ghost Rider app.; Powell-a, 6 pgs.; Bolle-c			
	4.50	14.00	32.00
106-Dream Book of Love #1 (6-7/54)-Powell, Bolle-a; Montgomery			
Clift, Donna Reed photo-c	4.00	12.00	28.00
107-Hot Dog #2	2.65	8.00	18.00
108-Red Fox #15 (1954)-L.B. Cole c/a; Powell 8.50	25.50	60.00
109-Dream Book of Romance #7 (7-8/54). Powell-a; photo-c			
	2.65	8.00	18.00
110-Dream Book of Romance #8 (10/54)	2.65	8.00	18.00
111-I'm a Cop #1 ('54); drug mention story; Powell-a			
	5.50	16.50	38.00
112-Ghost Rider #14 ('54)	8.00	24.00	55.00
113-Great Western #10; Powell-a	4.50	14.00	32.00
114-Dream Book of Love #2-Guardineer, Bolle-a; Peter Lorre, Victor			
Mature photo-c	3.00	9.00	21.00
115-Hot Dog #3	1.50	4.50	10.00
116-Cave Girl #13-Powell-c/a	14.00	42.00	100.00
117-White Indian #14	6.50	19.50	45.00
118-Undercover Girl #7-Powell-c	18.00	54.00	125.00
119-Straight Arrow's Fury #1 (origin); Fred Meagher-c/a			
	5.70	17.00	40.00
120-Badmen of the West #2	6.50	19.50	45.00
121-Mysteries of Scotland Yard #1; r-from Manhunt			

A-1 Comics #21, © ME

A-1 Comics #81, © ME

A-1 Comics #111, © ME

22

Apache Kid #6, © MEG

Appleseed Book One, Volume One, © Eclipse

Aquaman #50, © DC

A-1 COMICS (continued)	Good	Fine	N-Mint
	5.70	17.00	40.00
122-Black Phantom #1(11/54)	16.00	48.00	110.00
123-Dream Book of Love #3(10-11/54)	2.65	8.00	18.00
124-Dream Book of Romance #8(10-11/54)	2.65	8.00	18.00
125-Cave Girl #14-Powell-c/a	14.00	42.00	100.00
126-I'm a Cop #2-Powell-a	2.85	8.50	20.00
127-Great Western #11('54)-Powell-a	4.50	14.00	32.00
128-I'm a Cop #3-Powell-a	2.85	8.50	20.00
129-The Avenger #1('55)-Powell-c	16.00	48.00	110.00
130-Strongman #1-Powell-a	9.30	28.00	65.00
131-The Avenger #2('55)-Powell-c/a	8.50	25.50	60.00
132-Strongman #2	8.00	24.00	56.00
133-The Avenger #3-Powell-c/a	8.50	25.50	60.00
134-Strongman #3	8.00	24.00	56.00
135-White Indian #15	6.50	19.50	45.00
136-Hot Dog #4	1.50	4.50	10.00
137-Africa #1-Powell-c/a(4)	11.00	32.00	75.00
138-The Avenger #4-Powell-c/a	8.50	25.50	60.00
139-Strongman #4-Powell-a	8.00	24.00	56.00

NOTE: Bolle a-110. Photo-c-110.

APACHE
1951
Fiction House Magazines

	Good	Fine	N-Mint
1-Baker-c	8.00	24.00	56.00
I.W. Reprint No. 1	1.00	3.00	6.00

APACHE HUNTER
1954 (18 pgs. in color) (promo copy) (saddle stitched)
Creative Pictorials

	Good	Fine	N-Mint
Severin, Heath stories	13.00	39.00	90.00

APACHE KID (Formerly Reno Browne; Western Gunfighters #20 on)
(Also see Two-Gun Western & Wild Western)
No. 53, 12/50 - No. 10, 1/52; No. 11, 12/54 - No. 19, 4/56
Marvel/Atlas Comics(MPC No. 53-10/CPS No. 11 on)

53(#1)-A. Kid & his horse Nightwind (origin), Red Hawkins by Syd			
Shores begins	8.50	25.50	60.00
2(2/51)	4.50	14.00	32.00
3-5	2.85	8.50	20.00
6-10 (1951-52)	2.30	7.00	16.00
11-19 (1954-56)	2.00	6.00	14.00

NOTE: Heath c-11, 13. Maneely a-53; c-53(#1), 14,16. Powell a-14. Severin c-17.

APACHE MASSACRE (See Chief Victorio's . . .)

APACHE TRAIL
Sept., 1957 - No. 4, June, 1958
Steinway/America's Best

	Good	Fine	N-Mint
1	3.50	10.50	24.00
2-4: 2-Tuska-a	1.70	5.00	12.00

APPLESEED
Sept., 1988 - Present (B&W, $2.50, 52pgs.)
Eclipse Comics

	Good	Fine	N-Mint
Book One, Volume 1 ($2.50)	1.35	4.00	8.00
Book One, Volume 2-5: 5(1/89, $2.75 cover)	.40	1.25	2.50
Book Two, Vol. 1(2/89) -5(7/89): Art Adams-c	.45	1.40	2.75
Book Three, Volume 1(8/89)-5 ($2.75)	.45	1.40	2.75

APPROVED COMICS
March, 1954 - No. 12, Aug, 1954 (All painted-c)
St. John Publishing Co. (Most have no c-price)

	Good	Fine	N-Mint
1-The Hawk #5-r	3.70	11.00	26.00
2-Invisible Boy-r(3/54)-Origin; Saunders-c	7.00	21.00	50.00
3-Wild Boy of the Congo #11-r(4/54)	3.70	11.00	26.00
4-Kid Cowboy-r	3.70	11.00	26.00
5-Fly Boy-r	3.70	11.00	26.00

	Good	Fine	N-Mint
6-Daring Adv.-r(5/54); Krigstein-a(2); Baker-c	5.50	16.50	38.00
7-The Hawk #6-r	3.70	11.00	26.00
8-Crime on the Run; Powell-a; Saunders-c	3.70	11.00	26.00
9-Western Bandit Trails #3-r, with new-c; Baker c/a			
	5.00	15.00	35.00
11-Fightin' Marines #3-r; Kanteen Kate app; Baker-c/a			
	5.50	16.50	38.00
12-North West Mounties #4-r(8/54); new Baker-c			
	5.70	17.00	40.00

AQUAMAN (See Adventure, Brave & the Bold, DC Comics Presents #5, DC Special #28, DC Special Series #1, DC Super Stars #7, Detective, Justice League of America, More Fun #73, Showcase, Super DC Giant, Super Friends, and World's Finest)

AQUAMAN
Jan-Feb, 1962 - No. 56, Mar-Apr, 1971; No. 57, Aug-Sept, 1977 - No. 63, Aug-Sept, 1978
National Periodical Publications/DC Comics

	Good	Fine	N-Mint
1-Intro. Quisp	18.00	54.00	125.00
2	8.50	25.50	60.00
3-5	5.70	17.00	40.00
6-10	4.00	12.00	28.00
11-20: 11-Intro. Mera. 18-Aquaman weds Mera; JLA cameo			
	1.65	8.00	18.00
21-30: 23-Birth of Aquababy. 26-Huntress app.(3-4/66). 29-Intro.			
Ocean Master, Aquaman's step-brother	1.50	4.50	10.00
31,32,34-40	1.50	4.50	10.00
33-Intro. Aqua-Girl	1.70	5.00	12.00
41-47,49	.85	2.50	5.00
48-Origin reprinted	.90	2.70	5.50
50-52-Adams Deadman	1.70	5.00	11.00
53-56('71): 56-Intro Crusader	.60	1.75	3.50
57('77)-63: 58-Origin retold	.35	1.00	2.00

NOTE: Aparo a-40-59; c-57-60, 63. Newton a-60-63.

AQUAMAN
Feb, 1986 - No. 4, May, 1986 (mini-series)
DC Comics

	Good	Fine	N-Mint
1-New costume	.85	2.50	5.00
2-4	.50	1.50	3.00
Special 1 ('88, $1.50, 52 pgs.)	.35	1.00	2.00

AQUAMAN
June, 1989 - No. 5, Oct, 1989 ($1.00, mini-series)
DC Comics

		Good	N-Mint
1-5: Giffen plots/breakdowns; Swan-p		.60	1.20
Special 1 (Legend of . . ., $2.00, 1989, 52 pgs.)-Giffen plots/break-			
downs; Swan-p		.35	1.00	2.00

AQUANAUTS (See 4-Color No. 1197)

ARABIAN NIGHTS (See Cinema Comics Herald)

ARAK/SON OF THUNDER (See Warlord #48)
Sept, 1981 - No. 50, Nov, 1985
DC Comics

1-Origin; 1st app. Angelica, Princess of White Cathay			
		.50	1.00
2-50: 3-Intro Valda, The Iron Maiden. 12-Origin Valda. 20-Origin			
Angelica. 24-$1.00 size. 50-double size		.50	1.00
Annual 1(10/84)		.50	1.00

ARCHIE AND BIG ETHEL
1982 (69 cents)
Spire Christian Comics (Fleming H. Revell Co.)

		Good	N-Mint
nn		.30	.60

ARCHIE AND ME (See Archie Giant Series Mag. 578, 591, 603)
Oct, 1964 - No. 162, 1987
Archie Publications

ARCHIE AND ME (continued)	Good	Fine	N-Mint
1	8.50	25.50	60.00
2	4.30	13.00	30.00
3-5	2.15	6.50	15.00
6-10	1.15	3.50	7.00
11-20	.50	1.50	3.00
21-42: 26-X-Mas-c		.60	1.20
43-63-(All Giants)		.60	1.20
64-162-(Regular size)		.30	.60

ARCHIE AND MR. WEATHERBEE
1980 (59 cents)
Spire Christian Comics (Fleming H. Revell Co.)

nn		.30	.60

ARCHIE...ARCHIE ANDREWS, WHERE ARE YOU? (...Comics
Digest No. 9, 10; ...Comics Digest Mag. No. 11 on)
Feb, 1977 - Present (Digest size, 160-128 pages)
Archie Publications

1	.30	.80	1.60
2,3,5,7-9-Adams-a; 8-r-/origin The Fly by S&K. 9-Steel Sterling-r			
	.35	1.00	2.00
4,6,10-65 ($1.00-$1.50): 17-Katy Keene story		.50	1.00

ARCHIE AS PUREHEART THE POWERFUL
Sept, 1966 - No. 6, Nov, 1967
Archie Publications (Radio Comics)

1	4.30	13.00	30.00
2	2.65	8.00	18.00
3-6	1.50	4.50	10.00

NOTE: Evilheart cameos in all. Title: ...As Capt. Pureheart the Powerful-No. 4,6; ...As
Capt. Pureheart-No. 5.

ARCHIE AT RIVERDALE HIGH (See Archie Giant Series Magazine
573, 586, 604)
Aug, 1972 - No. 114, 1987
Archie Publications

1	2.65	8.00	18.00
2	1.35	4.00	8.00
3-5	.70	2.00	4.00
6-10	.35	1.00	2.00
11-30		.50	1.00
31-114: 96-Anti-smoking issue		.30	.60

ARCHIE COMICS (Archie No. 158 on)(See Christmas & Archie,
Everything's..., Jackpot, Little..., Oxydol-Dreft, and Pep)
(First Teen-age comic)(Radio show 1st aired 6/2/45, by NBC)
Winter, 1942-43 - No. 19, 3-4/46; No. 20, 5-6/46 - Present
MLJ Magazines No. 1-19/Archie Publ.No. 20 on

1 (Scarce)-Jughead, Veronica app.	330.00	830.00	2000.00
2	107.00	320.00	750.00
3 (60 pgs.)	75.00	225.00	525.00
4,5	54.00	162.00	375.00
6-10	37.00	110.00	260.00
11-20: 15,17,18-Dotty & Ditto by Woggon. 16-Woggon-a			
	23.00	70.00	160.00
21-30: 23-Betty & Veronica by Woggon (1st app?). 25-Woggon-a			
	16.00	48.00	110.00
31-40	10.00	30.00	70.00
41-50	7.00	21.00	50.00
51-70 (1954): 51,65-70-Katy Keene app.	4.00	12.00	28.00
71-99: 72-74-Katy Keene app.	2.35	7.00	16.00
100	3.00	9.00	18.00
101-130 (1962)	1.15	3.50	8.00
131-160	.70	2.00	4.00
161-200	.35	1.00	2.00
201-240		.50	1.00
241-282		.30	.60

	Good	Fine	N-Mint
283-Cover/story plugs ''International Children's Appeal'' which was a fraudulent charity, according to TV's 20/20 news program broadcast July 20, 1979		.60	1.25
284-376: 300-Anniversary issue		.25	.50
Annual 1('50)-116 pgs. (Scarce)	75.00	225.00	525.00
Annual 2('51)	40.00	120.00	280.00
Annual 3('52)	22.00	65.00	154.00
Annual 4,5(1953-54)	16.00	48.00	110.00
Annual 6-10(1955-59)	9.00	27.00	62.00
Annual 11-15(1960-65)	4.00	12.00	28.00
Annual 16-20(1966-70)	1.15	3.50	7.00
Annual 21-26(1971-75)	.45	1.25	2.50
Annual Digest 27('75)-55('83-'89)(...Magazine #35 on)			
		.50	1.00
...All-Star Specials(Winter '75)-$1.25; 6 remaindered Archie comics rebound in each; titles: ''The World of Giant Comics,'' ''Giant Grab Bag of Comics,'' ''Triple Giant Comics,'' and ''Giant Spec. Comics''	.50	1.50	3.00
Mini-Comics (1970-Fairmont Potato Chips Giveaway-Miniature)(8 issues-nn's., 8 pgs. each)	1.00	3.00	6.00
Official Boy Scout Outfitter(1946)-9½x6½'', 16 pgs., B. R. Baker Co. (Scarce)	22.00	65.00	154.00
Shoe Store giveaway (1948, Feb?)	7.00	21.00	50.00

ARCHIE COMICS DIGEST (...Magazine No. 37 on)
Aug, 1973 - Present (Small size, 160-128 pages)
Archie Publications

1	2.50	7.50	15.00
2	1.35	4.00	8.00
3-5	.70	2.00	4.00
6-10	.25	.75	1.50
11-33: 32,33-The Fly-r by S&K		.50	1.00
34-98: 36-Katy Keene story; 88-Christmas-c		.40	.80

NOTE: Adams a-1,2,4,5,19-21,24,25,27,29,31,33.

ARCHIE GETS A JOB
1977
Spire Christian Comics (Fleming H. Revell Co.)

nn		.30	.60

ARCHIE GIANT SERIES MAGAZINE
1954 - Present (No No. 36-135, no No. 252-451)
Archie Publications

1-Archie's Christmas Stocking	50.00	150.00	350.00
2-Archie's Christmas Stocking('55)	25.00	75.00	175.00
3-6-Archie's Christmas Stocking('56-'59)	16.00	48.00	110.00
7-10: 7-Katy Keene Holiday Fun(9/60). 8-Betty & Veronica Summer Fun (1/60). 9-The World of Jughead (12/60). 10-Archie's Christmas Stocking (1/61)	11.00	32.00	75.00
11-20: 11-Betty & Veronica Spectacular (6/61). 12-Katy Keene Holiday Fun (9/61). 13-Betty & Veronica Summer Fun (10/61). 14-The World of Jughead (12/61). 15-Archie's Christmas Stocking (1/62). 16-Betty & Veronica Spectacular (6/62). 17-Archie's Jokes (9/62). Katy Keene app. 18-Betty & Veronica Summer Fun (10/62). 19-The World of Jughead (12/62). 20-Archie's Christmas Stocking (1/63)	7.00	21.00	50.00
21-30: 21-Betty & Veronica Spectacular (6/63). 22-Archie's Jokes (9/63). 23-Betty & Veronica Summer Fun (10/63). 24-The World of Jughead (12/63). 25-Archie's Christmas Stocking (1/64). 26-Betty & Veronica Spectacular (6/64). 27-Archie's Jokes (8/64). 28-Betty & Veronica Summer Fun (9/64). 29-Around the World with Archie (10/64). 30-The World of Jughead (12/64)	4.00	12.00	28.00
31-35,136-141: 31-Archie's Christmas Stocking (1/65). 32-Betty & Veronica Spectacular (6/65). 33-Archie's Jokes (8/65). 34-Betty & Veronica Summer Fun (9/65). 35-Around the World with Archie (10/65). 136-The World of Jughead (12/65). 137-Archie's Christmas Stocking (1/66). 138-Betty & Veronica Spectacular (6/66). 139-			

Archie And Me #1, © AP

AMERICA'S LARGEST-SELLING TEEN-AGE MAGAZINE
Archie Comics #73, © AP

Archie Comics #133, © AP

Archie's Jokes (6/66). 140-Betty & Veronica Summer Fun (8/66).

	Good	Fine	N-Mint
141-Around the World with Archie (9/66)	2.85	8.50	20.00
142-Archie's Super-Hero Special (10/66)-Origin Capt. Pureheart, Capt. Hero, and Evilheart	2.65	8.00	18.00

143-160: 143-The World of Jughead (12/66). 144-Archie's Christmas Stocking (1/67). 145-Betty & Veronica Spectacular (6/67). 146-Archie's Jokes (6/67). 147-Betty & Veronica Summer Fun (8/67) 148-World of Archie (9/67). 149-World of Jughead (10/67). 150-Archie's Christmas Stocking (1/68). 151-World of Archie (2/68) 152-World of Jughead (2/68). 153-Betty & Veronica Spectacular (6/68). 154-Archie Jokes (6/68). 155-Betty & Veronica Summer Fun (8/68). 156-World of Archie (10/68). 157-World of Jughead (12/68). 158-Archie's Christmas Stocking (1/69). 159-Betty & Veronica Christmas Spect. (1/69). 160-World of Archie (2/69)

	1.35	4.00	8.00

161-200: 161-World of Jughead (2/69). 162-Betty & Veronica Spectacular (6/69). 163-Archie's Jokes (8/69). 164-Betty & Veronica Summer Fun (9/69). 165-World of Archie (9/69). 166-World of Jughead (9/69). 167-Archie's Christmas Stocking (1/70). 168-Betty & Veronica Christmas Spect. (1/70). 169-Archie's Christmas Love-In (1/70). 170-Jughead's Eat-Out Comic Book Mag. (12/69) 171-World of Archie (2/70). 172-World of Jughead (2/70). 173-Betty & Veronica Spectacular (6/70). 174-Archie's Jokes (8/70) 175-Betty & Veronica Summer Fun (9/70). 176-Li'l Jinx Giant Laugh-Out (8/70). 177-World of Archie (9/70). 178-World of Jughead (9/70). 179-Archie's Christmas Stocking (1/71). 180-Betty & Veronica Christmas Spect. (1/71). 181-Archie's Christmas Love-In (1/71). 182-World of Archie (2/71). 183-World of Jughead (2/71). 184-Betty & Veronica Spectacular (6/71). 185-Li'l Jinx Giant Laugh-Out (6/71). 186-Archie's Jokes (8/71). 187-Betty & Veronica Summer Fun (9/71). 188-World of Archie (9/71). 189-World of Jughead (9/71). 190-Archie's Christmas Stocking (12/71). 191-Betty & Veronica Christmas Spectacular (2/72). 192-Archie's Christmas Love-In (1/72). 193-World of Archie (3/72). 194-World of Jughead (4/72). 195-Li'l Jinx Christmas Bag (1/72). 196-Sabrina's Christmas Magic (1/72). 197-Betty & Veronica Spectacular (6/72). 198-Archie's Jokes (8/72). 199-Betty & Veronica Summer Fun (9/72). 200-World of Archie (10/72)

	.50	1.50	3.00

201-251: 201-Betty & Veronica Spectacular (10/72). 202-World of Jughead (11/72). 203-Archie's Christmas Stocking (12/72) 204-Betty & Veronica Christmas Spectacular (2/73). 205-Archie's Christmas Love-In (1/73). 206-Li'l Jinx Christmas Bag (12/72). 207-Sabrina's Christmas Magic (12/72). 208-World of Archie (3/73). 209-World of Jughead (4/73). 210-Betty & Veronica Spectacular (6/73). 211-Archie's Jokes (8/73). 212-Betty & Veronica Summer Fun (9/73). 213-World of Archie (10/73). 214-Betty & Veronica Spectacular (10/73). 215-World of Jughead (11/73). 216-Archie's Christmas Stocking (12/73). 217-Betty & Veronica Christmas Spectacular (2/74). 218-Archie's Christmas Love-In (1/74). 219-Li'l Jinx Christmas Bag (12/73). 220-Sabrina's Christmas Magic (12/73). 221-Betty & Veronica Spectacular (Advertised as World of Archie) (6/74). 222-Archie's Jokes (Advertised as World of Jughead)(8/74). 223-Li'l Jinx (8/74). 224-Betty & Veronica Summer Fun (9/74). 225-World of Archie (9/74). 226-Betty & Veronica Spectacular (10/74). 227-World of Jughead (10/74). 228-Archie's Christmas Stocking (12/74). 229-Betty & Veronica Christmas Spectacular (2/74). 230-Archie's Christmas Love-In (1/75). 231-Sabrina's Christmas Magic (1/75). 232-World of Archie (3/75). 233-World of Jughead (4/75). 234-Betty & Veronica Spectacular (6/75). 235-Archie's Jokes (8/75). 236-Betty & Veronica Summer Fun (9/75). 237-World of Archie (9/75) 238-Betty & Veronica Spectacular (10/75). 239-World of Jughead (10/75). 240-Archie's Christmas Stocking (12/75). 241-Betty & Veronica Christmas Spectacular (2/75). 242-Archie's Christmas Love-In (1/76). 243-Sabrina's Christmas Magic (1/76). 244-World of Archie (3/76). 245-World of Jughead (4/76). 246-Betty & Veronica Spectacular (6/76). 247-Archie's Jokes (8/76). 248-Betty & Veronica Summer Fun (9/76). 249-World of Archie (9/76). 250-Betty & Veronica Spectacular (10/76). 251-World of Jughead

	.60	1.20	

452-500: 452-Archie's Christmas Stocking (12/76). 453-Betty & Veronica Christmas Spectacular (12/76). 454-Archie's Christmas Love-In (1/77). 455-Sabrina's Christmas Magic (1/77). 456-World of Archie (3/77). 457-World of Jughead (4/77). 458-Betty & Veronica Spectacular (6/77). 459-Archie's Jokes (8/77)-Shows 8/76 in error. 460-Betty & Veronica Summer Fun (9/77). 461-World of Archie (9/77). 462-Betty & Veronica Spectacular (10/77) 463-World of Jughead (10/77). 464-Archie's Christmas Stocking (12/77). 465-Betty & Veronica Christmas Spectacular (12/77). 466-Archie's Christmas Love-In (1/78). 467-Sabrina's Christmas Magic (1/78). 468-World of Archie (2/78). 469-World of Jughead (2/78). 470-Betty & Veronica Spectacular (6/78). 471-Archie's Jokes (8/78). 472-Betty & Veronica Summer Fun (9/78). 473-World of Archie (9/78). 474-Betty & Veronica Spectacular (10/78). 475-World of Jughead (10/78). 476-Archie's Christmas Stocking (12/78). 477-Betty & Veronica Christmas Spectacular (12/78). 478-Archie's Christmas Love-In (1/79). 479-Sabrina's Christmas Magic (1/79). 480-The World of Archie (3/79). 481-World of Jughead (4/79). 482-Betty & Veronica Spectacular (6/79). 483-Archie's

Jokes (8/79). 484-Betty & Veronica Summer Fun (9/79). 485-The World of Archie (9/79). 486-Betty & Veronica Spectacular (10/79). 487-The World of Jughead (10/79). 488-Archie's Christmas Stocking (12/79). 489-Betty & Veronica Christmas Spectacular (1/80) 490-Archie's Christmas Love-in (1/80). 491-Sabrina's Christmas Magic (1/80). 492-The World of Archie (2/80). 493-The World of Jughead (4/80). 494-Betty & Veronica Spectacular (6/80). 495-Archie's Jokes (8/80). 496-Betty & Veronica Summer Fun (9/80) 497-The World of Archie (9/80). 498-Betty & Veronica Spectacular (10/80). 499-The World of Jughead (10/80). 500-Archie's Christmas Stocking (12/80) each....   .40   .80

501-550: 501-Betty & Veronica Christmas Spectacular (12/80). 502-Archie's Christmas Love-in (1/81). 503-Sabrina Christmas Magic (1/81). 504-The World of Archie (3/81). 505-The World of Jughead (4/81). 506-Betty & Veronica Spectacular (6/81). 507-Archie's Jokes (8/81). 508-Betty & Veronica Summer Fun (9/81). 509-The World of Archie (9/81). 510-Betty & Vernonica Spectacular (9/81) 511-The World of Jughead (10/81). 512-Archie's Christmas Stocking (12/81). 513-Betty & Veronica Christmas Spectacular (12/81) 514-Archie's Christmas Love-in (1/82). 515-Sabrina's Christmas Magic (1/82). 516-The World of Archie (3/82). 517-The World of Jughead (4/82). 518-Betty & Veronica Spectacular (6/82). 519-Archie's Jokes (8/82). 520-Betty & Veronica Summer Fun (9/82) 521-The World of Archie (9/82). 522-Betty & Veronica Spectacular (10/82). 523-The World of Jughead (10/82). 524-Archie's Christmas Stocking (1/83). 525-Betty and Veronica Christmas Spectacular (1/83). 526-Betty and Veronica Spectacular (5/83) 527-Little Archie (8/83). 528-Josie and the Pussycats (8/83) 529-Betty and Veronica Summer Fun (8/83). 530-Betty and Veronica Spectacular (9/83). 531-The World of Jughead (9/83) 532-The World of Archie (10/83). 533-Space Pirates by Frank Bolling (10/83). 534-Little Archie (10/83). 535-Archie's Christmas Stocking (1/84). 536-Betty and Veronica Christmas Spectacular (1/84). 537-Betty and Veronica Spectacular (6/84). 538-Little Archie (8/84). 539-Betty and Veronica Summer Fun 8/84). 540-Josie and the Pussycats (8/84). 541-Betty and Veronica Spectacular (9/84). 542-The World of Jughead (9/84). 543-The World of Archie (10/84). 544-Sabrina the Teen-Age Witch (10/84). 545-Little Archie (12/84). 546-Archie's Christmas Stocking (12/84) 547-Betty and Veronica Spectacular (12/84). 548-? 549-Little Archie. 550-Betty and Veronica Summer Fun each....   .40   .80

551-600: 551-Josie and the Pussycats. 552-Betty and Veronica Spectacular. 553-The World of Jughead. 554-The World of Archie 555-Betty's Diary. 556-Little Archie (1/86). 557-Archie's Christmas Stocking (1/86). 558-Betty & Veronica Christmas Spectacular (1/86). 559-Betty & Veronica Spectacular. 560-? 561-Betty & Veronica Summer Fun. 562-Josie and the Pussycats. 563-Betty & Veronica Spectacular. 564-World of Jughead. 565-World of Archie. 566-Little Archie. 567-Archie's Christmas Stocking. 568-Betty & Veronica Christmas Spectacular. 569-Betty & Veronica Spring Spectacular. 570-Little Archie. 571-Josie & The Pussycats 572-Betty & Veronica Summer Fun. 573-Archie At Riverdale High 574-World of Archie. 575-Betty & Veronica Spectacular. 576-Pep 577-World of Jughead. 578-Archie And Me. 579-Archie's Christmas Stocking. 580-Betty and Veronica Christmas Spectacular 581-Little Archie Christmas Special. 582-Betty & Veronica Spring Spectacular. 583-Little Archie. 584-Josie and The Pussycats 585-Betty & Veronica Summer Fun. 586-Archie At Riverdale High 587-The World of Archie (10/88). 588-Betty & Veronica Spectacular. 589-Pep (10/88). 590-The World of Jughead. 591-Archie & Me. 592-Archie's Christmas Stocking. 593-Betty & Veronica Christmas Spectacular. 594-? 595-Betty & Veronica Spring Spectacular. 596-Little Archie. 597-Josie and the Pussycats. 598-Betty & Veronica Summer Fun. 599-The World of Archie (10/89). 600-Betty and Veronica Spectacular   each....   .40   .80

601-607: 601-Pep. 602-The World of Jughead. 603-Archie and Me. 604-Archie at Riverdale High. 605-Archie's Christmas Stocking. 606-Betty and Veronica Christmas Spectacular. 607-Little Archie each....   .40   .80

ARCHIE'S ACTIVITY COMICS DIGEST MAGAZINE
1985 - Present? (Annual, 128 pgs.; digest size)
Archie Enterprises

1-4	.50	1.00

ARCHIE'S CAR
1979 (49 cents)
Spire Christian Comics (Fleming H. Revell Co.)

nn	.30	.60

ARCHIE'S CHRISTMAS LOVE-IN (See Archie Giant Series Mag. No. 169, 181, 192, 205, 218, 230, 242, 454, 466, 478, 490, 502, 514)

ARCHIE'S CHRISTMAS STOCKING (See Archie Giant Series Mag. No. 1-6, 10, 15, 20, 25, 31, 137, 144, 150, 158, 167, 179, 190, 203, 216, 228, 240, 452, 464, 476, 488, 500, 512, 524, 535, 546, 557, 567, 579, 592, 605)

ARCHIE'S CLEAN SLATE
1973 (35-49 cents)
Spire Christian Comics (Fleming H. Revell Co.)

1(Some issues have nn)	.35	1.00	2.00

ARCHIE'S DATE BOOK
1981
Spire Christian Comics (Fleming H. Revell Co.)

	Good	Fine	N-Mint
nn		.30	.60

ARCHIE'S DOUBLE DIGEST QUARTERLY MAGAZINE
1981 - Present ($1.95-$2.25, 256pgs.) (A.D.D. Magazine No. 10 on)
Archie Comics

	Good	Fine	N-Mint
1-46: 6-Katy Keene story	.35	1.10	2.25

ARCHIE'S FAMILY ALBUM
1978 (36 pages) (39 cents)
Spire Christian Comics (Fleming H. Revell Co.)

	Good	Fine	N-Mint
nn		.30	.60

ARCHIE'S FESTIVAL
1980 (49 cents)
Spire Christian Comics (Fleming H. Revell Co.)

	Good	Fine	N-Mint
nn		.30	.60

ARCHIE'S GIRLS, BETTY AND VERONICA (Becomes Betty & Veronica)
1950 - No. 347, 1987
Archie Publications (Close-Up)

	Good	Fine	N-Mint
1	65.00	195.00	455.00
2	32.00	95.00	225.00
3-5	18.00	54.00	125.00
6-10: 10-2pg. Katy Keene app.	14.00	42.00	100.00
11-20: 11,13,14,17-19-Katy Keene app. 20-Debbie's Diary, 2pgs.	9.00	27.00	62.00
21-30: 27-Katy Keene app.	7.00	21.00	50.00
31-50	5.00	15.00	35.00
51-74	3.00	9.00	21.00
75-Betty & Veronica sell souls to Devil	6.00	18.00	42.00
76-99	1.70	5.00	12.00
100	2.30	7.00	16.00
101-140: 118-Origin Superteen. 119-Last Superteen story	.85	2.50	5.00
141-180	.35	1.00	2.00
181-220		.50	1.00
221-347: 300-Anniversary issue		.30	.60
Annual 1 (1953)	40.00	120.00	280.00
Annual 2(1954)	17.00	51.00	120.00
Annual 3-5 ('55-'57)	13.00	40.00	90.00
Annual 6-8 ('58-'60)	9.00	27.00	62.00

ARCHIE SHOE-STORE GIVEAWAY
1944-49 (12-15 pgs. of games, puzzles, stories like Superman-Tim books, No nos. - came out monthly)
Archie Publications

	Good	Fine	N-Mint
(1944-47)-issues	9.00	27.00	62.00
2/48-Peggy Lee photo-c	6.00	18.00	42.00
3/48-Marylee Robb photo-c	6.00	18.00	42.00
4/48-Gloria De Haven photo-c	6.00	18.00	42.00
5/48,6/48,7/48	6.00	18.00	42.00
8/48-Story on Shirley Temple	6.00	18.00	42.00
10/48-Archie as Wolf on cover	6.00	18.00	42.00
5/49-Kathleen Hughes photo-c	4.50	13.50	32.00
7/49	4.50	13.50	32.00
8/49-Archie photo-c from radio show	6.00	18.00	42.00
10/49-Gloria Mann photo-c from radio show	5.50	16.50	38.00
11/49,12/49	4.50	13.50	32.00

ARCHIE'S JOKEBOOK COMICS DIGEST ANNUAL (See Jokebook . .)
ARCHIE'S JOKE BOOK MAGAZINE (See Joke Book . . .)
1953 - No. 3, Sum, 1954; No. 15, Fall, 1954 - No. 288, 11/82
Archie Publications

	Good	Fine	N-Mint
1953-One Shot (#1)	43.00	130.00	300.00
	Good	Fine	N-Mint
2	24.00	72.00	170.00
3 (nn.4-14)	16.00	48.00	110.00
15-20: 15-17-Katy Keene app.	12.00	36.00	84.00
21-30	8.00	24.00	56.00
31-40,42,43	4.00	12.00	28.00
41-1st professional comic work by Neal Adams ('59), 1 pg.	13.00	40.00	90.00
44-47-Adams-a in all, 1-2 pgs.	7.00	21.00	50.00
48-Four pgs. Adams-a	7.00	21.00	50.00
49-60 (1962)	2.00	6.00	14.00
61-80	1.30	4.00	8.00
81-100	.70	2.00	4.00
101-140	.35	1.00	2.00
141-200		.50	1.00
201-288		.30	.60
Drug Store Giveaway (No. 39 w/new-c)	2.00	6.00	14.00

ARCHIE'S JOKES (See Archie Giant Series Mag. No. 17, 22, 27, 33, 139, 146, 154, 163, 174, 186, 198, 211, 222, 235, 247, 459, 471, 483, 495, 519)
ARCHIE'S LOVE SCENE
1973 (35-49 cents)
Spire Christian Comics (Fleming H. Revell Co.)

	Good	Fine	N-Mint
1(Some issues have nn)	.35	1.00	2.00

ARCHIE'S MADHOUSE (Madhouse Ma-ad No. 67 on)
Sept, 1959 - No. 66, Feb, 1969
Archie Publications

	Good	Fine	N-Mint
1-Archie begins	16.00	48.00	110.00
2	8.00	24.00	56.00
3-5	6.00	18.00	42.00
6-10	4.00	12.00	28.00
11-16 (Last w/regular characters)	3.00	9.00	21.00
17-21,23-30 (New format)	1.15	3.50	7.00
22-1st app. Sabrina, the Teen-age Witch (10/62)	4.00	12.00	28.00
31-40	.50	1.50	3.00
41-66: 43-Mighty Crusaders cameo		.50	1.00
Annual 1 (1962-63)	3.00	9.00	21.00
Annual 2 (1964)	1.50	4.50	10.00
Annual 3 (1965)-Origin Sabrina The Teen-Age Witch	.85	2.50	5.00
Annual 4-6('66-69)(Becomes Madhouse Ma-ad Annual No. 7 on)	.40	1.25	2.50

NOTE: Cover title to 61-65 is "Madhouse" and to 66 is "Madhouse Ma-ad Jokes."

ARCHIE'S MECHANICS
Sept, 1954 - No. 3, 1955
Archie Publications

	Good	Fine	N-Mint
1-(15 cents; 52 pgs.)	60.00	180.00	420.00
2-(10 cents)	35.00	105.00	245.00
3-(10 cents)	30.00	90.00	210.00

ARCHIE'S ONE WAY
1972 (35 cents, 39 cents, 49 cents) (36 pages)
Spire Christian Comics (Fleming H. Revell Co.)

	Good	Fine	N-Mint
nn	.35	1.00	2.00

ARCHIE'S PAL, JUGHEAD (Jughead No. 122 on)
1949 - No. 126, Nov, 1965
Archie Publications

	Good	Fine	N-Mint
1	60.00	180.00	420.00
2	30.00	90.00	210.00
3-5	20.00	60.00	140.00
6-10: 7-Suzie app.	12.00	36.00	84.00
11-20	9.00	27.00	62.00
21-30: 23-25,28-30-Katy Keene app. 28-Debbie's Diary app.	5.70	17.00	40.00

Archie's Girls, Betty And Veronica #49, © AP

Archie's Madhouse #43, © AP

Archie's Pal, Jughead #13, © AP

Archie 3000 #1, © AP

Area 88 #2, © Eclipse

Arizona Kid #1, © MEG

ARCHIE'S PAL, JUGHEAD (continued)	Good	Fine	N-Mint
31-50	3.50	10.50	24.00
51-70	2.65	8.00	18.00
71-100	1.50	4.50	9.00
101-126	1.00	3.00	6.00
Annual 1 (1953)	28.00	85.00	200.00
Annual 2 (1954)	17.00	51.00	120.00
Annual 3-5 (1955-57)	12.00	36.00	84.00
Annual 6-8 (1958-60)	8.00	24.00	56.00

ARCHIE'S PALS 'N' GALS
1952-53 - No. 6, 1957-58; No. 7, 1958 - Present
Archie Publications

1-(116 pages)	35.00	105.00	245.00
2(Annual)('53-'54)	20.00	60.00	140.00
3-5(Annual, '54-57)	13.00	40.00	90.00
6-10('58-'60)	7.00	21.00	50.00
11-20	3.50	10.50	24.00
21-40: 29-Beatles satire	1.70	5.00	12.00
41-60	.85	2.50	5.00
61-80	.50	1.50	3.00
81-110	.25	.75	1.50
111-214: Later issues $1.00 cover		.35	.70

ARCHIE'S PARABLES
1973, 1975 (36 pages, 39-49 cents)
Spire Christian Comics (Fleming H. Revell Co.)

nn-By Al Hartley		.40	.80

ARCHIE'S R/C RACERS
Sept, 1989 - Present (95 cents, $1.00, color)
Archie Comics

1-5: Radio control cars		.50	1.00

ARCHIE'S RIVAL REGGIE (Reggie No. 15 on)
1950 - No. 14, Aug, 1954
Archie Publications

1	45.00	135.00	315.00
2	23.00	70.00	160.00
3-5	16.00	48.00	110.00
6-10	10.00	30.00	70.00
11-14: Katy Keene in No. 10-14, 1-2pgs.	8.00	24.00	56.00

ARCHIE'S ROLLER COASTER
1981 (69 cents)
Spire Christian Comics (Fleming H. Revell Co.)

nn		.40	.80

ARCHIE'S SOMETHING ELSE
1975 (36 pages, 39-49 cents)
Spire Christian Comics (Fleming H. Revell Co.)

nn		.40	.80

ARCHIE'S SONSHINE
1973, 1974 (36 pages, 39-49 cents)
Spire Christian Comics (Fleming H. Revell Co.)

nn	.35	1.00	2.00

ARCHIE'S SPORTS SCENE
1983
Spire Christian Comics (Fleming H. Revell Co.)

nn		.40	.80

ARCHIE'S STORY & GAME COMICS DIGEST MAGAZINE
Nov, 1986 - Present (Digest size, $1.25, $1.35, $1.50, 128 pgs.)
Archie Enterprises

1-15		.70	1.35

ARCHIE'S SUPER HERO SPECIAL (See Archie Giant Series Mag. No. 142)

ARCHIE'S SUPER HERO SPECIAL (...Comics Digest Mag. 2)
Jan, 1979 - No. 2, Aug, 1979 (148 pages, 95 cents)
Archie Publications (Red Circle)

	Good	Fine	N-Mint
1-Simon & Kirby r-/Double Life of Pvt. Strong No. 1,2; Black Hood, The Fly, Jaguar, The Web app.		.40	.80
2-Contains contents to the never published Black Hood No. 1; origin Black Hood; Adams, Wood, McWilliams, Morrow, S&K(r)-a; Adams-c. The Shield, The Fly, Jaguar, Hangman, Steel Sterling, The Web, The Fox-r		.40	.80

ARCHIE'S TV LAUGH-OUT
Dec, 1969 - No. 106, 1986
Archie Publications

1	4.00	12.00	28.00
2	1.70	5.00	10.00
3-5	.85	2.50	5.00
6-10	.35	1.00	2.00
11-20		.50	1.00
21-106		.30	.60

ARCHIE'S WORLD
1973, 1976 (39-49 cents)
Spire Christian Comics (Fleming H. Revell Co.)

nn		.40	.80

ARCHIE 3000
May, 1989 - Present (75 & 95 cents, $1.00, color)
Archie Comics

1-8: 6-X-Mas-c		.50	1.00

AREA 88
May 26, 1987 - No. 42?, 1989 ($1.50-$1.75, B&W)
Eclipse Comics/VIZ Comics #37 on

1	.45	1.30	2.60
1-2nd print		.65	1.30
2-5	.30	.85	1.70
2-2nd print		.55	1.10
6-10	.25	.70	1.40
11-36		.55	1.10
37-42: 37 on are $1.75	.25	.75	1.50

ARENA (See Marvel Graphic Novel)

ARION, LORD OF ATLANTIS (Also see Warlord #55)
Nov, 1982 - No. 35, Sept, 1985
DC Comics

1-35: 1-Story cont'd from Warlord #62		.50	1.00
Special #1 (11/85)		.50	1.00

ARISTOCATS (See Movie Comics & Walt Disney Showcase No. 16)

ARISTOCRATIC X-TRATERRESTRIAL TIME-TRAVELING THIEVES
Aug, 1986 - No. 6, 1988? ($1.75, B&W, 28 pgs.)
Fictioneer Books, Ltd.

1-One shot	.40	1.25	2.50
1-2nd print (12/86)	.25	.75	1.50
1-Begin new series (2/87)	.25	.75	1.50
2-6	.25	.75	1.50

ARISTOKITTENS, THE (...Meet Jiminy Cricket No. 1)(Disney)
Oct, 1971 - No. 9, Oct, 1975 (No. 6: 52 pages)
Gold Key

1	1.15	3.50	7.00
2-9	.70	2.00	4.00

ARIZONA KID, THE (Also see The Comics & Wild Western)
March, 1951 - No. 6, Jan, 1952
Marvel/Atlas Comics(CSI)

1	7.00	21.00	50.00
2-4: 2-Heath-a(3)	4.00	12.00	28.00

	Good	Fine	N-Mint
5,6	3.50	10.50	24.00

NOTE: *Heath a-1-3; c-1-3. Maneely c-4-6. Morisi a-4-6.*

ARK, THE (See The Crusaders)

ARKHAM ASYLUM (See Batman: Arkham Asylum)

ARMAGEDDON FACTOR, THE
1987 - No. 2 ($1.95, color)
AC Comics

1,2: Sentinels of Justice, Dragonfly, Femforce	.35	1.00	2.00

ARMOR (AND THE SILVER STREAK; see Revengers Featuring . . .)
Sept, 1985 - Present ($2.00, color)
Continuity Comics

1-Intro. The Silver Streak; Adams c/a	.40	1.25	2.50
2-7	.35	1.00	2.00

ARMY AND NAVY COMICS (Supersnipe No. 6 on)
May, 1941 - No. 5, July, 1942
Street & Smith Publications

1-Cap Fury & Nick Carter	22.00	65.00	154.00
2-Cap Fury & Nick Carter	11.00	32.00	75.00
3,4	8.00	24.00	56.00
5-Supersnipe app.; see Shadow V2#3 for 1st app. Story of Douglas MacArthur	20.00	60.00	140.00

ARMY ATTACK
July, 1964 - No. 4, Feb, 1965; V2#38, July, 1965 - No. 47, Feb, 1967
Charlton Comics

V1#1	.70	2.00	4.00
2-4(2/65)	.35	1.00	2.00
V2#38(7/65)-47 (formerly U.S. Air Force #1-37)	.35	1.00	2.00

NOTE: *Glanzman a-1-3. Montes/Bache a-44.*

ARMY AT WAR (Also see Our Army at War & Cancelled Comic Cavalcade)
Oct-Nov, 1978
DC Comics

1-Kubert-c		.30	.60

ARMY SURPLUS KOMIKZ FEATURING CUTEY BUNNY
1982 - No. 5, 1985 ($1.50, B&W)
Army Surplus Komikz/Eclipse Comics No. 5

1-Cutey Bunny begins	1.50	4.50	9.00
2-5: 5-JLA/X-Men/Batman parody	1.00	3.00	6.00

ARMY WAR HEROES (Also see Iron Corporal)
Dec, 1963 - No. 38, June, 1970
Charlton Comics

1	.50	1.50	3.00
2-20		.50	1.00
21-38: 22-Origin & 1st app. Iron Corporal series by Glanzman. 24-Intro. Archer & Corp. Jack series		.50	1.00
Modern Comics Reprint 36 ('78)		.30	.60

NOTE: *Montes/Bache a-1, 16, 17, 21, 23-25, 27-30.*

AROUND THE BLOCK WITH DUNC & LOO (See Dunc and Loo)

AROUND THE WORLD IN 80 DAYS (See 4-Color Comics No. 784 and A Golden Picture Classic)

AROUND THE WORLD UNDER THE SEA (See Movie Classics)

AROUND THE WORLD WITH ARCHIE (See Archie Giant Series Magazine No. 29, 35, 141)

AROUND THE WORLD WITH HUCKLEBERRY HIS FRIENDS (See Dell Giant No. 44)

ARRGH! (Satire)
Dec, 1974 - No. 5, Sept, 1975
Marvel Comics Group

	Good	Fine	N-Mint
1	.40	.80	
2-5	.25	.50	

NOTE: *Alcala a-2; c-3. Everett a-1r, 2r. Maneely a-4r. Sekowsky a-1p. Sutton a-1.*

ARROW, THE (See Funny Pages)
Oct, 1940 - No. 2, Nov, 1940; No. 3, Oct, 1941
Centaur Publications

1-The Arrow begins(r/Funny Pages)	117.00	350.00	700.00
2-Tippy Taylor serial continues from Amazing Mystery Funnies 24	60.00	180.00	420.00
3-Origin Dash Dartwell, the Human Meteor; origin The Rainbow-r; bondage-c	60.00	180.00	420.00

NOTE: *Gustavson a-1,2; c-3.*

ARROWHEAD (See Black Rider and Wild Western)
April, 1954 - No. 4, Nov, 1954
Atlas Comics (CPS)

1-Arrowhead & his horse Eagle begin	5.00	15.00	35.00
2-4	3.00	9.00	21.00

NOTE:*Forte a-4. Heath c-3. Jack Katz a-3. Maneely c-2. Pakula a-2. Sinnott a-1-4; c-1.*

ASSASSINS, INC.
1987 - No. 2, 1987?($1.95, color)
Silverline Comics

1,2	.35	1.00	2.00

ASTONISHING (Marvel Boy No. 1,2)
No. 3, April, 1951 - No. 63, Aug, 1957
Marvel/Atlas Comics(20CC)

3-Marvel Boy continues	28.00	85.00	200.00
4-6-Last Marvel Boy; 4-Stan Lee app.	22.00	65.00	154.00
7-10	6.00	18.00	42.00
11,12,15,17,20	5.00	15.00	35.00
13,14,16,19-Krigstein-a	5.70	17.00	40.00
18-Jack The Ripper story	5.70	17.00	40.00
21,22,24	4.00	12.00	28.00
23-E.C. swipe-'The Hole In The Wall' from Vault Of Horror #16	5.00	15.00	35.00
25-Crandall-a	5.00	15.00	35.00
26-29: 29-Decapitation-c	3.50	10.50	24.00
30-Tentacled eyeball story	5.70	17.00	40.00
31-37-Last pre-code issue	3.00	9.00	21.00
38-43,46,48-52,56,58,59,61	2.00	6.00	14.00
44-Crandall swipe/Weird Fantasy #22	3.50	10.50	24.00
45,47-Krigstein-a	3.50	10.50	24.00
53-Crandall, Ditko-a	3.00	9.00	21.00
54-Torres-a	3.00	9.00	21.00
55-Crandall, Torres-a	3.50	10.50	24.00
57-Williamson/Krenkel-a, 4 pgs.	4.50	13.50	32.00
60-Williamson/Mayo-a, 4 pgs.	4.50	13.50	32.00
62-Torres, Powell -a	2.30	7.00	16.00
63-Last issue; Woodbridge-a	2.30	7.00	16.00

NOTE: *Ayers a-16. Berg a-36, 53, 56. Cameron a-50. Gene Colan a-12, 20, 29, 56. Ditko a-50, 53. Drucker a-41, 62. Everett a-3-5(3), 6, 10, 12, 37, 47, 48, 58, 61; c-3-5, 13, 15, 16, 18, 29, 47, 51, 53-55, 57, 59-63. Fass a-11, 34. Forte a-53, 58. Fuje a-11. Heath c/a-8; c-9, 26. Kirby a-56. Lawrence a-28, 37, 38, 42. Maneely c-31, 33, 34, 56. Moldoff a-33. Morisi a-10? Morrow a-52, 61. Orlando a-47, 58, 61. Powell a-43, 44, 48. Ravielli a-28. Reinman a-32, 34, 38. Robinson a-20. J. Romita a-18, 24, 43, 57, 61. Roussos a-55. Sale a-28, 38, 59. Sekowsky a-13. Severin c-46. Shores a-16. Sinnott a-11, 30. Ed Win a-20. Canadian reprints exist.*

ASTONISHING TALES (See Ka-Zar)
Aug, 1970 - No. 36, July, 1976
Marvel Comics Group

1-Ka-Zar by Kirby(p) & Dr. Doom by Wood begin	.50	1.50	3.00
2-Kirby, Wood-a	.25	.75	1.50
3-6: Smith-a(p); Wood-a-#3,4. 5-Red Skull app.			

Arrgh! #1, © MEG   The Arrow #2, © CEN   Astonishing #5, © MEG

Astro Boy #1, © NBC   The Atom #10, © DC   Atomic Attack #5, © YM

	Good	Fine	N-Mint
ASTONISHING TALES (continued)	.50	1.50	3.00
7-9: 8-Last Dr. Doom. (52 pgs.)	.25	.75	1.50
10-Smith-a(p)	.40	1.25	2.50
11-Origin Ka-Zar & Zabu	.25	.75	1.50
12-Man-Thing by Adams	.40	1.25	2.50
13-24: 20-Last Ka-Zar. 21-It! the Living Colossus begins, ends #24			
	.50	1.00	
25-Deathlok the Demolisher begins (1st app.); Perez 1st work, 2pgs.			
(8/74)	.50	1.50	3.00
26-30: 29-Origin Guardians of the Galaxy	.50	1.00	
31-36: 31-Wrightson-c(i)	.50	1.00	

NOTE: **Buckler** a-13i, 16p, 25, 26p, 27p, 28, 29p-36p; c-13, 25p, 26-30, 32-35p, 36. **John Buscema** a-9, 12p-14p, 16p; c-4-6p, 12p. **Colan** a-7p, 8p. **Ditko** a-21r. **Everett** a-6i. **G. Kane** a-11p, 15p; c-10p, 11p, 14, 15p, 21p. **McWilliams** a-30i. **Starlin** a-19p; c-16p. **Sutton & Trimpe** a-8. **Tuska** a-5p, 6p, 8p. **Wood** a-1-4.

ASTRO BOY (TV) (Also see March of Comics #285 & The Original. . .)
August, 1965
Gold Key

1(10151-508)	13.00	40.00	90.00

ASTRO COMICS
1969 - 1979 (Giveaway)
American Airlines (Harvey)

nn-Harvey's Casper, Spooky, Hot Stuff, Stumbo the Giant, Little Audrey, Little Lotta, & Richie Rich reprints	.70	2.00	4.00

ATARI FORCE
Jan., 1984 - No. 20, Aug, 1985 (Mando paper)
DC Comics

1-20: 1-1st app. Tempest, Packrat, Babe, Morphea, & Dart			
	.50	1.00	
Special 1 (4/86)	.50	1.00	

NOTE: **Byrne** c-Special 1i. **Giffen** a-12p, 13i. **Rogers** a-18p, Special 1p.

A-TEAM, THE (TV)
March, 1984 - No. 3, May, 1984
Marvel Comics Group

1-3		.30	.60

ATLANTIS, THE LOST CONTINENT (See 4-Color No. 1188)

ATLAS (See First Issue Special)

ATOM, THE (See Action, All-American, Brave & the Bold, D.C. Special Series #1, Detective, Flash Comics #80, Power Of The Atom, Showcase, Super Friends, Sword Of The Atom & World's Finest)

ATOM, THE (. . .& the Hawkman No. 39 on)
June-July, 1962 - No. 38, Aug-Sept, 1968
National Periodical Publications

1-Intro Plant-Master	32.00	95.00	225.00
2	11.00	32.00	75.00
3-1st Time Pool story; 1st app. Chronos (origin)			
	8.50	25.50	60.00
4,5: 4-Snapper Carr x-over	6.50	19.50	45.00
6-10: 7-Hawkman x-over. 8-Justice League, Dr. Light app.			
	5.00	15.00	35.00
11-15	3.50	10.50	24.00
16-20: 19-Zatanna x-over	2.30	7.00	16.00
21-28,30	1.50	4.50	10.00
29-Golden Age Atom x-over	3.50	10.50	24.00
31-38: 31-Hawkman x-over. 36-G.A. Atom x-over. 37-Intro. Major Mynah; Hawkman cameo	1.00	3.00	6.00

NOTE: **Anderson** a-1-11i, 13i; c-inks-1-25, 31-35, 37. **Sid Greene** a-8i-38i. **Gil Kane** a-1p-38p; c-1p-28p, 29, 33p, 34. Time Pool stories also in 6, 9,12, 17, 21, 27, 35.

ATOM AGE (See Classics Illustrated Special Issue)

ATOM-AGE COMBAT
June, 1952 - No. 5, April, 1953; Feb, 1958

St. John Publishing Co.

	Good	Fine	N-Mint
1	19.00	57.00	132.00
2	11.00	32.00	75.00
3,5: 3-Mayo-a, 6 pgs.	8.50	25.50	60.00
4 (Scarce)	10.00	30.00	70.00
1(2/58-St. John)	6.50	19.50	45.00

ATOM-AGE COMBAT
Nov, 1958 - No. 3, March, 1959
Fago Magazines

1	10.00	30.00	70.00
2,3	6.50	19.50	45.00

ATOMAN
Feb, 1946 - No. 2, April, 1946
Spark Publications

1-Origin Atoman; Robinson/Meskin-a; Kidcrusaders, Wild Bill Hickok, Marvin the Great app.	22.00	65.00	154.00
2: Robinson/Meskin-a	16.00	48.00	110.00

ATOM & HAWKMAN, THE (Formerly The Atom)
No. 39, Oct-Nov, 1968 - No. 45, Oct-Nov, 1969
National Periodical Publications

39-45: 43-1st app. Gentlemen Ghost, origin-44	1.00	3.00	6.00

NOTE: **Sid Greene** a-40i-45i. **Kubert** a-40p, 41p; c-39-45.

ATOM ANT (TV)
January, 1966 (Hanna-Barbera)
Gold Key

1(10170-601)	5.00	15.00	35.00

ATOMIC ATTACK (Formerly Attack, first series)
No. 5, Jan, 1953 - No. 8, Oct, 1953
Youthful Magazines

5-Atomic bomb-c	13.00	40.00	90.00
6-8	6.50	19.50	45.00

ATOMIC BOMB
1945 (36 pgs.)
Jay Burtis Publications

1-Airmale & Stampy	11.50	34.00	80.00

ATOMIC BUNNY (Formerly Atomic Rabbit)
No. 12, Aug, 1958 - No. 19, Dec, 1959
Charlton Comics

12	4.50	14.00	32.00
13-19	2.30	7.00	16.00

ATOMIC COMICS
1946 - No. 4, 1946 (Reprints)
Daniels Publications (Canadian)

1-Rocketman, Yankee Boy, Master Key; bondage-c			
	8.50	25.50	60.00
2-4	5.50	16.50	38.00

ATOMIC COMICS
Jan, 1946 - No. 4, July-Aug, 1946
Green Publishing Co.

1-Radio Squad by Siegel & Shuster; Barry O'Neal app.; Fang Gow cover-r/Det. Comics	26.00	77.00	180.00
2-Inspector Dayton; Kid Kane by Matt Baker; Lucky Wings, Congo King, Prop Powers (only app.) begin	17.00	51.00	120.00
3,4: 3-Zero Ghost Detective app.; Baker-a(2) each; 4-Baker-c	10.00	30.00	70.00

ATOMIC MOUSE (TV, Movies) (See Blue Bird, Funny Animals, Giant Comics & Wotalife Comics)
3/53 - No. 54, 6/63; No. 1, 12/84; V2/10, 9/85 - No. 13, ?/86
Capitol Stories/Charlton Comics

1-Origin; Al Fago c/a	9.30	28.00	65.00

ATOMIC MOUSE (continued)	Good	Fine	N-Mint
2	4.30	13.00	30.00
3-10: 5-Timmy The Timid Ghost app.; see Zoo Funnies			
	3.50	10.50	24.00
11-13,16-25	1.85	5.50	13.00
14,15-Hoppy The Marvel Bunny app.	2.65	8.00	18.00
26-(68 pages)	4.00	12.00	28.00
27-40: 36,37-Atom The Cat app.	1.15	3.50	8.00
41-54	.45	1.35	3.00
1 (1984)		.40	.80
V2/10 (10/85) -13-Fago-r. #12(1/86)		.40	.80

ATOMIC RABBIT (Atomic Bunny No. 12 on; see Wotalife Comics)
August, 1955 - No. 11, March, 1958
Charlton Comics

1-Origin; Al Fago-a	8.50	25.50	60.00
2	4.00	12.00	28.00
3-10-Fago-a in most	2.65	8.00	18.00
11-(68 pages)	4.00	12.00	28.00

ATOMIC SPY CASES
Mar-Apr, 1950 (Painted-c)
Avon Periodicals

1-No Wood-a; A-bomb blast panels; Fass-a	13.00	40.00	90.00

ATOMIC THUNDERBOLT, THE
Feb, 1946 - No. 2, April, 1946
Regor Company

1-Intro. Atomic Thunderbolt & Mr. Murdo	12.00	36.00	84.00
2	8.00	24.00	56.00

ATOMIC WAR!
Nov, 1952 - No. 4, April, 1953
Ace Periodicals (Junior Books)

1-Atomic bomb-c	34.00	100.00	235.00
2,3: 3-Atomic bomb-c	23.00	70.00	160.00
4-Used in POP, pg. 96 & illo.	24.00	72.00	168.00

ATOM THE CAT (Formerly Tom Cat)
No. 9, Oct, 1957 - No. 17, Aug, 1959
Charlton Comics

9	3.00	9.00	21.00
10,13-17	1.50	4.50	10.00
11-(64pgs)-Atomic Mouse app., 12(100pgs)	4.00	12.00	28.00

ATTACK
May, 1952 - No. 4, Nov, 1952; No. 5, Jan, 1953 - No. 5, Sept, 1953
Youthful Mag./Trojan No. 5 on

1-(1st series)-Extreme violence	5.50	16.50	38.00
2,3: 3-Harrison c/a	2.65	8.00	18.00
4-Krenkel-a, 7 pgs, Harrison-a. (Becomes Atomic Attack No. 5 on)			
	3.15	9.50	22.00
5-(No. 1, Trojan, 2nd series)	2.65	8.00	18.00
6-8 (No. 2-4), 5	1.85	5.50	13.00

ATTACK
No. 54, 1958 - No. 60, Nov, 1959
Charlton Comics

54(100 pages)	3.50	10.50	24.00
55-60	.70	2.00	4.00

ATTACK!
1962 - No. 15, 3/75; No. 16, 8/79 - No. 48, 10/84
Charlton Comics

nn(#1)-('62) Special Edition	1.00	3.00	6.00
2('63), 3(Fall, '64)	.70	2.00	4.00
V4#3(10/66), 4(10/67)-(Formerly Special War Series #2; becomes Attack At Sea V4#5)	.35	1.00	2.00
1(9/71)		.60	1.20
2-15(3/75): 4-American Eagle app.		.50	1.00
16(8/79) - 47		.40	.80
48(10/84)-Wood-r; S&K-c		.50	1.00
Modern Comics 13('78)-r		.30	.60

ATTACK!
1975 (39, 49 cents) (36 pages)
Spire Christian Comics (Fleming H. Revell Co.)

nn		.40	.80

ATTACK AT SEA (Formerly Attack!, 1967)
V4#5, October, 1968
Charlton Comics

V4#5	.25	.75	1.50

ATTACK ON PLANET MARS (See Strange Worlds #18)
1951
Avon Periodicals

nn-Infantino, Fawcette, Kubert & Wood-a; adaptation of Tarrano the Conqueror by Ray Cummings	43.00	130.00	300.00

AUDREY & MELVIN (Formerly Little . .)
No. 62, September, 1974
Harvey Publications

62		.40	.80

AUGIE DOGGIE (TV) (See Spotlight #2 & Whitman Comic Books)
October, 1963 (Hanna-Barbera)
Gold Key

1	4.00	12.00	28.00

AURORA COMIC SCENES INSTRUCTION BOOKLET
1974 (Slick paper, 8 pgs.)(6¼x9¾'')(in full color)
(Included with superhero model kits)
Aurora Plastics Co.

181-140-Tarzan; Adams-a	.35	1.00	2.00
182-140-Spider-Man; 183-140-Tonto(Gil Kane art); 184-140-Hulk; 185-140-Superman; 186-140-Superboy; 187-140-Batman; 188-140-The Lone Ranger(1974-by Gil Kane); 192-140-Captain America (1975); 193-140-Robin			
each. . . .		.50	1.00

AUTHENTIC POLICE CASES
Feb, 1948 - No. 38, Mar, 1955
St. John Publishing Co.

1-Hale the Magician by Tuska begins	12.00	36.00	84.00
2-Lady Satan, Johnny Rebel app.	8.00	24.00	56.00
3-Veiled Avenger app.; blood drainage story plus 2 Lucky Coyne stories; used in SOTI, illo. from Red Seal #16			
	17.00	51.00	120.00
4,5: 4-Masked Black Jack app. 5-Late 1930s Jack Cole-a(r); transvestism story	7.00	21.00	50.00
6-Matt Baker-c; used in SOTI, illo-''An invitation to learning'', r-in Fugitives From Justice #3; Jack Cole-a; also used by the N.Y. Legis. Comm.	17.00	51.00	120.00
7,8,10-14: 7-Jack Cole-a; Matt Baker art begins #8; Vic Flint in #10-14	7.00	21.00	50.00
9-No Vic Flint	5.70	17.00	40.00
15-Drug c/story; Vic Flint app.; Baker-c	7.00	21.00	50.00
16,18,20,21,23	3.70	11.00	26.00
17,19,22-Baker-c	3.85	11.50	27.00
24-28 (All 100 pages): 26-Transvestism	11.00	32.00	75.00
29,30	2.45	7.25	17.00
31,32,37-Baker-c	2.85	8.50	20.00
33-Transvestism; Baker-c	3.70	11.00	26.00
34-Drug-c by Baker	3.70	11.00	26.00
35-Baker c/a(2)	3.50	10.50	24.00
36-Vic Flint strip-r; Baker-c	2.65	8.00	18.00

Atomic Mouse #16, © CC

Atomic War! #1, © ACE

Authentic Police Cases #4, © STJ

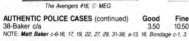

The Avengers #16, © MEG

The Avengers #59, © MEG

The Avengers #200, © MEG

	Good	Fine	N-Mint
AUTHENTIC POLICE CASES (continued)			
38-Baker c/a	3.50	10.50	24.00

NOTE: *Matt Baker c-6-16, 17, 19, 22, 27, 29, 31-38; a-13, 16. Bondage c-1, 3.*

AVENGER, THE (See A-1 Comics)
1955 - No. 4, Aug-Sept, 1955
Magazine Enterprises

	Good	Fine	N-Mint
1(A-1 129)-Origin	16.00	48.00	110.00
2(A-1 131), 3(A-1 133), 4(A-1 138)	8.50	25.50	60.00
IW Reprint #9('64)-Reprints #1 (new cover)	1.30	4.00	9.00

NOTE: *Powell a-2-4; c-1-4.*

AVENGERS, THE (See Kree/Skrull War Starring. . , Marvel Graphic Novel #27, Marvel Super Action, Marvel Super Heroes('66), Marvel Treas. Ed., Marvel Triple Action, Solo Avengers, Tales Of Suspense & West Coast Avengers)

AVENGERS, THE
Sept, 1963 - Present
Marvel Comics Group

	Good	Fine	N-Mint
1-Origin The Avengers (Thor, Iron Man, Hulk, Ant-Man, Wasp)			
	105.00	315.00	725.00
2	40.00	120.00	275.00
3	25.00	75.00	175.00
4-Revival of Captain America who joins the Avengers; 1st Silver Age app. of Captain America (3/64)	47.00	140.00	325.00
4-Reprint from the Golden Record Comic set 2.85		8.50	20.00
With Record. . . .	6.50	19.50	45.00
5-Hulk leaves	16.00	48.00	110.00
6-10: 6-Intro The Masters of Evil. 8-Intro Kang. 9-Intro Wonder Man who dies in same story	12.00	36.00	85.00
11-15: 15-Death of Zemo	8.00	24.00	56.00
16-19: 16-New Avengers line-up (Hawkeye, Quicksilver, Scarlet Witch join; Thor, Iron Man, Giant-Man & Wasp leave.) 19-Intro. Swordsman; origin Hawkeye	5.70	17.00	40.00
20-22: Wood inks	4.00	12.00	28.00
23-30: 28-Giant-Man becomes Goliath	2.65	8.00	18.00
31-40	1.70	5.00	12.00
41-50: 48-Intro/Origin new Black Knight	1.30	4.00	9.00
51,52,54-56: 52-Black Panther joins; Intro The Grim Reaper. 54-Intro new Masters of Evil	1.30	4.00	9.00
53-X-Men app.	1.60	4.80	11.00
57-Intro. The Vision	3.50	10.50	24.00
58-Origin The Vision	2.65	8.00	18.00
59-65: 59-Intro. Yellowjacket. 60-Wasp & Yellowjacket wed. 63-Goliath becomes Yellowjacket; Hawkeye becomes the new Goliath. 65-Last 12 cent issue	1.50	4.50	10.00
66,67: Smith-a	1.50	4.50	10.00
68-70	1.15	3.50	7.00
71-1st Invaders; Black Knight joins	1.10	3.25	6.50
72-80: 80-Intro. Red Wolf	.90	2.75	5.50
81,82,84-91: 87-Origin The Black Panther. 88-Written by Harlan Ellison	.90	2.75	5.50
83-Intro. The Liberators (Wasp, Valkyrie, Scarlet Witch, Medusa & the Black Widow)	1.10	3.25	6.50
92-Adams-c	1.10	3.25	6.50
93-(52 pgs.)-Adams c/a	4.50	13.50	31.00
94-96-Adams c/a	2.75	8.25	18.50
97-G.A. Capt. America, Sub-Mariner, Human Torch, Patriot, Vision, Blazing Skull, Fin, Angel, & new Capt. Marvel x-over			
	1.35	4.00	8.00
98-Goliath becomes Hawkeye; Smith c/a(i)	1.85	5.50	13.00
99-Smith/Sutton-a	1.85	5.50	13.00
100-Smith c/a; featuring everyone who was an Avenger			
	3.70	11.00	25.00
101-106,108,109: 101-Harlan Ellison scripts	.75	2.25	4.50
107-Starlin-a(r)	.85	2.50	5.00
110,111-X-Men app.	1.10 -	3.25	6.50
112-1st app. Mantis	1.00	3.00	6.00

	Good	Fine	N-Mint
113-120: 116-118-Defenders/Silver Surfer app.	.70	2.00	4.00
121-130: 123-Origin Mantis	.60	1.75	3.50
131-133,136-140: 136-Ploog-r/Amaz. Advs. #12	.50	1.50	3.00
134,135-True origin The Vision	.60	1.75	3.50
141-149: 144-Origin & 1st app. Hellcat	.40	1.25	2.50
150-Kirby-a(r); new line-up begins: Capt. America, Scarlet Witch, Iron Man, Wasp, Yellowjacket, Vision & The Beast			
	.40	1.25	2.50
151-163: 151-Wonderman returns with new costume			
	.35	1.15	2.30
164-166-Byrne-a	.75	2.25	4.50
167-180	.35	1.00	2.00
181-191-Byrne-a. 181-New line-up: Capt. America, Scarlet Witch, Iron Man, Wasp, Vision, The Beast & The Falcon. 183-Ms. Marvel joins. 186-Origin Quicksilver & Scarlet Witch			
	.45	1.30	2.60
192-202: Perez-a. 195-1st Taskmaster. 200-Dbl. size; Ms. Marvel leaves	.35	1.00	2.00
203-250: 211-New line-up: Capt. America, Iron Man, Tigra, Thor, Wasp & Yellowjacket. 213-Yellowjacket leaves. 216-Tigra leaves. 221-Hawkeye & She-Hulk join. 227-Capt. Marvel (Female) joins; origins of Ant-Man, Wasp, Giant-Man, Goliath, Yellowjacket, & Avengers. 231-Ironman leaves. 232-Starfox (Eros) joins. 234-Origin Quicksilver, Scarlet Witch. 236-New logo. 238-Double Blackout. 240-Spider-Woman revived		.60	1.20
251-262,264-271,273		.60	1.20
263-1st app. X-Factor (story continues in Fantastic Four #286)			
	.70	2.00	4.00
272-Alpha Flight guest star	.35	1.00	2.00
274-299: 291-$1.00 issues begin. 297-Black Knight, She-Hulk & Thor resign. 298-Inferno tie-in		.60	1.20
300: (68 pgs.)-Thor joins	.30	.90	1.80
301-304,306-314: 302-Re-intro Quasar		.50	1.00
305-Byrne scripts begin	.35	1.00	2.00
Annual 6(11/76)	.60	1.75	3.50
Annual 7(11/77)-Starlin c/a; Warlock dies	1.15	3.50	7.00
Annual 8(10/78)	.50	1.50	3.00
Annual 9(10/79)-Newton-a	.35	1.00	2.00
Annual 10(10/81)-Golden-p; X-Men cameo; 1st app. Rogue (cameo) & Madelyne Pryor	.85	2.50	5.00
Annual 11(12/82), 12(1/84), 13(11/84),	.25	.75	1.50
Annual 14(11/85), 15(10/86), 16(10/87)	.25	.75	1.50
Annual 17(11/88)-Evolutionary War x-over	.40	1.25	2.50
Annual 18(1989, $2.00, 68 pgs.)-Atlantis Attacks	.35	1.00	2.00
Special 1(9/67)	2.85	8.50	20.00
Special 2(9/68), 3(9/69)	1.35	4.00	9.00
Special 4(1/71), 5(1/72)	.85	2.50	5.00
Giant Size 1(8/74)	.75	2.25	4.50
Giant Size 2(11/74)(death of the Swordsman), 3(2/75)			
	.60	1.75	3.50
Giant Size 4(6/75), 5(12/75): 4-Vision marries Scarlet Witch. 5-Reprints Giant Size #1	.40	1.25	2.50

NOTE: *Austin c(i)-157, 167, 168, 170-77, 181, 183-88, 198-201, Annual 8. John Buscema a-41-44p, 46p, 47p, 49, 50, 51-62p, 68-71, 74-77, 79-85, 87-91, 97, 105p, 121p, 124p, 125p, 152, 153p, 255p-279p, 281p-302p; c-41-66, 68-71, 73-91, 97-99, 178, 256p-259p, 261p-279p, 281p-302p. Byrne a-164-66p, 181-191p, 233p, Annual 13, 14p; c-186-190p, 233p, 260, 305p; scripts-305-312. Colan a/c(p)-63-65, 111, 206-208, 210, 211. Guice a-Annual 12p. Kane c-37p, 159p. Kirby a-1-8p. Special 3, 4p; c-1-30, 148, 151-158; layouts-14-16. Miller c-193p. Mooney a-86i, 179p, 180p. Nebres a-178i; c-179i. Newton a-204p, Annual 9p. Perez a(p)-141, 143, 144, 148, 154p, 155p, 160p, 161, 162, 167, 168, 170, 171, 194, 195, 196p, 198-202, Annual 6(p), 8; c-160-162p, 164-166p, 170-74p, 181p, 183-85p, 191p, 192p, 194-201p, Annual 8. Starlin c-121, 135. Staton a-127-134i. Tuska a-47i, 48i, 51i, 53i, 54i, 106p, 107p, 135p, 137-140p, 163p.*

AVENGERS, THE (TV)
Nov, 1968 ("John Steed & Emma Peel" cover title) (15 cents)
Gold Key

	Good	Fine	N-Mint
1-Photo-c	12.00	36.00	84.00

AVENGERS SPOTLIGHT (Formerly Solo Avengers #1-20)
No. 21, Aug, 1989 - Present (.75-$1.00, color)
Marvel Comics

	Good	Fine	N-Mint
21 (75 cents)-Byrne-c/a		.50	1.00
22-30 ($1.00): 26-Acts of Vengeance story		.50	1.00

AVENGERS WEST COAST (Formerly West Coast Avengers)
No. 48, Sept, 1989 - Present ($1.00, color)
Marvel Comics

48-56: Byrne-a & scripts continue. 50-Re-intro original Human Torch			
		.50	1.00

AVIATION ADVENTURES AND MODEL BUILDING
No. 16, Dec, 1946 - No. 17, Feb, 1947 (True Aviation Adv. . .No. 15)
Parents' Magazine Institute

16,17-Half comics and half pictures	3.50	10.50	24.00

AVIATION CADETS
1943
Street & Smith Publications

nn	6.00	18.00	42.00

A-V IN 3-D
Dec, 1984 (28 pgs. w/glasses)
Aardvark-Vanaheim

1-Cerebus, Flaming Carrot, Normalman & Ms. Tree			
	.75	2.25	4.50

AWFUL OSCAR (Formerly & becomes Oscar Comics with No. 13)
No. 11, June, 1949 - No. 12, Aug, 1949
Marvel Comics

11,12	2.65	8.00	18.00

AXA
Apr, 1987 - No. 2, Aug, 1987 ($1.75, color)
Eclipse Comics

1,2	.30	.90	1.75

AXEL PRESSBUTTON (Pressbutton No. 5; see Laser Eraser & Pressbutton)
11/84 - No. 6, 7/85 ($1.50-$1.75, Baxter paper)
Eclipse Comics

1-r/Warrior (British mag.); Bolland-c; origin Laser Eraser & Pressbutton	.30	.90	1.75
2-6	.30	.90	1.75

AZTEC ACE
3/84 - No. 15, 9/85 (Baxter paper, 36 pgs. No. 2 on)
Eclipse Comics

1-$2.25 cover (52 pgs.)	.40	1.25	2.50
2,3-$1.50 cover	.30	.90	1.80
4-15-$1.75-$1.50 cover	.30	.90	1.80

NOTE: **N. Redondo** a-1i-8i, 10i; c-6-8i.

BABE (. . .Darling of the Hills, later issues)(Also see Big Shot and Sparky Watts)
June-July, 1948 - No. 11, Apr-May, 1950
Prize/Headline/Feature

1-Boody Rogers-a	8.00	24.00	56.00
2-Boody Rogers-a	5.00	15.00	35.00
3-11-All by Boody Rogers	3.70	11.00	26.00

BABE AMAZON OF OZARKS
No. 5, 1948
Standard Comics

5-Exist?	3.50	10.50	24.00

BABE RUTH SPORTS COMICS
April, 1949 - No. 11, Feb, 1951
Harvey Publications

	Good	Fine	N-Mint
1-Powell-a	12.00	36.00	84.00
2-Powell-a	10.00	30.00	70.00
3-11: Powell-a in most	8.00	24.00	56.00

BABES IN TOYLAND (See 4-Color No. 1282 & Golden Pix Story Book ST-3)

BABY HUEY AND PAPA (See Paramount Animated. . .)
May, 1962 - No. 33, Jan, 1968 (Also see Casper The Friendly. . .)
Harvey Publications

1	7.00	21.00	50.00
2	3.50	10.50	24.00
3-5	2.00	6.00	14.00
6-10	1.50	4.50	9.00
11-20	.75	2.25	4.50
21-33	.50	1.50	3.00

BABY HUEY DUCKLAND
Nov, 1962 - No. 15, Nov, 1966 (25 cent Giants) (all 68 pgs.)
Harvey Publications

1	4.30	13.00	30.00
2-5	1.85	5.50	12.00
6-15	1.00	3.00	6.00

BABY HUEY, THE BABY GIANT (Also see Blackthorne 3-D Series
#58, Casper, Harvey Hits #22, Harvey Comics Hits #60, & Paramount
Animated Comics)
9/56 - No. 97, 10/71; No. 98, 10/72; No. 99, 10/80
Harvey Publications

1-Infinity-c	20.00	60.00	140.00
2	10.00	30.00	70.00
3-Baby Huey takes anti-pep pills	6.00	18.00	42.00
4,5	4.35	13.00	30.00
6-10	2.15	6.50	15.00
11-20	1.35	4.00	9.00
21-40	1.00	3.00	7.00
41-60	.70	2.00	4.00
61-79(12/67)	.35	1.00	2.00
80(12/68) - 95-All 68 pg. Giants	.50	1.50	3.00
96,97-Both 52 pg. Giants	.50	1.50	3.00
98,99-regular size		.50	1.00

BABY SNOOTS (Also see March of Comics No. 359,371,396,401,
419,431,443,450,462,474,485)
Aug, 1970 - No. 22, Nov, 1975
Gold Key

1	.85	2.50	5.00
2	.35	1.00	2.00
3-22: 22-Titled Snoots, the Forgetful Elefink		.60	1.20

BACHELOR FATHER (TV)
No. 1332, 4-6/62 - No. 2, 1962
Dell Publishing Co.

4-Color 1332 (#1)	4.50	14.00	32.00
2-Written by Stanley	4.50	14.00	32.00

BACHELOR'S DIARY
1949
Avon Periodicals

1(Scarce)-King Features panel cartoons & text-r; pin-up, girl wrestling photos	18.00	54.00	125.00

BAD COMPANY
Aug, 1988 - Present ($1.50, color, high quality paper)
Quality Comics

1-16: 5,6-Guice-c	.25	.75	1.50

BADGE OF JUSTICE
No. 22, 1/55 - No. 23, 3/55; 4/55 - No. 4, 10/55
Charlton Comics

Aviation Cadets No #, © S & S

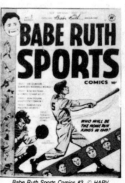

Babe Ruth Sports Comics #3, © HARV

Bad Company #1, © Quality Comics

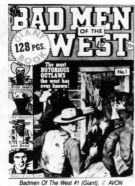

Badmen Of The West #1 (Giant), © AVON

Baffling Mysteries #6, © ACE

The Barker #10, © DC

	Good	Fine	N-Mint
BADGE OF JUSTICE (continued)			
22(1/55)	2.85	8.50	20.00
23(3/55), 1	2.00	6.00	14.00
2-4	1.30	4.00	9.00

BADGER, THE (Also see Coyote #14)
10/83 - No. 4, 4/84; No. 5, 5/85 - Present (Baxter paper)
Capital Comics/First Comics No. 5 on

1-Badger, Ham the Weather Wizard begin	1.00	3.00	6.00
2-4	.75	2.25	4.50
5(5/85)	.70	2.00	4.00
6	.60	1.75	3.50
7-10	.55	1.60	3.20
11-20	.45	1.30	2.60
21-30	.35	1.10	2.20
31-49,51-60	.30	1.00	2.00
50-($3.95, 52 pgs.)	.70	2.00	3.95

BADGER GOES BERSERK
Sept, 1989 - No. 4, Dec, 1989 ($1.95, color, mini-series, Baxter)
First Comics

1-4: 2-Paul Chadwick-c/a(2 pgs.)	.35	1.00	2.00

BADMEN OF THE WEST
1951 (Giant - 132 pages)(Painted-c)
Avon Periodicals

1-Contains rebound copies of Jesse James, King of the Bad Men of Deadwood, Badmen of Tombstone; other combinations possible. Issues with Kubert-a....	17.00	51.00	120.00

BADMEN OF THE WEST! (See A-1 Comics)
1953 - No. 3, 1954
Magazine Enterprises

1(A-1 100)-Meskin-a?	11.00	32.00	75.00
2(A-1 120), 3: 2-Larsen-a	6.50	19.50	45.00

BADMEN OF TOMBSTONE
1950
Avon Periodicals

nn	6.00	18.00	42.00

BAFFLING MYSTERIES (Formerly Indian Braves No. 1-4; Heroes of the Wild Frontier No. 26-on)
No. 5, Nov, 1951 - No. 26, Oct, 1955
Periodical House (Ace Magazines)

5	9.50	28.00	65.00
6,7,9,10: 10-E.C. Crypt Keeper swipe on-c	5.70	17.00	40.00
8-Woodish-a by Cameron	5.70	17.00	40.00
11-24: 24-Last pre-code issue	5.70	17.00	40.00
25-Reprints; surrealistic-c	4.50	13.50	42.00
26-Reprints	2.85	8.50	20.00

NOTE: **Cameron** a-8,16-18,20-22. **Colan** a-5, 11, 25r/5. **Sekowsky** a-5, 6, 22. Bondage c-20. Reprints in 18(1), 19(1), 24(3).

BALBO (See Master Comics #33 & Mighty Midget Comics)

BALDER THE BRAVE
Nov, 1985 - No. 4, 1986 (mini-series)
·Marvel Comics Group

1-4: Simonson c/a		.50	1.00

BALLAD OF HALO JONES, THE
Sept, 1987 - No. 12, Aug, 1988 ($1.25-$1.50, color)
Quality Comics

1-12: Alan Moore scripts in all	.25	.75	1.50

BALOO & LITTLE BRITCHES
April, 1968 (Walt Disney)
Gold Key

1-From the Jungle Book	1.70	5.00	10.00

BALTIMORE COLTS
1950 (Giveaway)
American Visuals Corp.

	Good	Fine	N-Mint
nn-Eisner-c	28.00	85.00	200.00

BAMBI (See 4-Color No. 12,30,186, Movie Classics, Movie Comics, and Walt Disney Showcase No. 31)

BAMBI (Disney)
1941, 1942, 1984
K. K. Publications (Giveaways)/Whitman Publ. Co.

1941-Horlick's Malted Milk & various toy stores - text & pictures; most copies mailed out with store stickers on cover	13.00	40.00	90.00
1942-Same as 4-Color 12, but no price (Same as '41 issue?) (Scarce)	20.00	60.00	140.00
1-(Whitman, 1984; 60 cents)-r/4-Color 186		.30	.60

BAMM BAMM & PEBBLES FLINTSTONE (TV)
Oct, 1964 (Hanna-Barbera)
Gold Key

1	2.15	6.50	15.00

BANANA OIL
1924 (52 pages)(Black & White)
MS Publ. Co.

Milt Gross-a; not reprints	13.00	40.00	90.00

BANANA SPLITS, THE (TV) (See March of Comics No. 364)
June, 1969 - No. 8, Oct, 1971 (Hanna-Barbera)
Gold Key

1	1.15	3.50	8.00
2-8	.70	2.00	4.00

BAND WAGON (See Hanna-Barbera Band Wagon)

BANG-UP COMICS
Dec, 1941 - No. 3, June, 1942
Progressive Publishers

1-Cosmo Mann & Lady Fairplay begin; Buzz Balmer by Rick Yager in all (origin #1)	38.00	115.00	270.00
2,3	22.00	65.00	154.00

BANNER COMICS (Captain Courageous No. 6)
No. 3, Sept, 1941 - No. 5, Jan, 1942
Ace Magazines

3-Captain Courageous & Lone Warrior & Sidekick Dicky begin	50.00	150.00	350.00
4,5: 4-Flag-c	33.00	100.00	230.00

BARBARIANS, THE
June, 1975
Atlas Comics/Seaboard Periodicals

1-Origin, only app. Andrax; Iron Jaw app.		.50	1.00

BARBIE & KEN
May-July, 1962 - No. 5, Nov-Jan, 1963-64
Dell Publishing Co.

01-053-207(#1)-Based on toy dolls	8.50	25.50	60.00
2-5	7.00	21.00	50.00

BARKER, THE (Also see National Comics #42)
Autumn, 1946 - No. 15, Dec, 1949
Quality Comics Group/Comic Magazine

1	7.00	21.00	50.00
2	3.50	10.50	24.00
3-10	2.30	7.00	16.00
11-14	1.70	5.00	12.00
15-Jack Cole-a(p)	2.65	8.00	18.00

NOTE: **Jack Cole** art in some issues.

BARNEY AND BETTY RUBBLE (TV) (Flintstones' Neighbors)
Jan, 1973 - No. 23, Dec, 1976 (Hanna-Barbera)
Charlton Comics

	Good	Fine	N-Mint
1	1.50	4.50	10.00
2-10	.85	2.50	5.00
11-23	.50	1.50	3.00

BARNEY BAXTER (Also see Magic Comics)
1938 - No. 2, 1956
David McKay/Dell Publishing Co./Argo

Feature Books 15(McKay-1938)	17.00	51.00	120.00
4-Color 20(1942)	16.00	48.00	110.00
4,5	8.00	24.00	56.00
1,2(1956-Argo)	3.15	9.50	22.00

BARNEY BEAR HOME PLATE
1979 (49 cents)
Spire Christian Comics (Fleming H. Revell Co.)

nn		.30	.60

BARNEY BEAR LOST AND FOUND
1979 (49 cents)
Spire Christian Comics (Fleming H. Revell Co.)

nn		.30	.60

BARNEY BEAR OUT OF THE WOODS
1980 (49 cents)
Spire Christian Comics (Fleming H. Revell Co.)

nn		.30	.60

BARNEY BEAR SUNDAY SCHOOL PICNIC
1981 (69 cents)
Spire Christian Comics (Fleming H. Revell Co.)

nn		.30	.60

BARNEY BEAR THE SWAMP GANG!
1980 (59 cents)
Spire Christian Comics (Fleming H. Revell Co.)

nn		.30	.60

BARNEY BEAR WAKES UP
1977 (39 cents)
Spire Christian Comics (Fleming H. Revell Co.)

nn		.30	.60

BARNEY GOOGLE AND SPARK PLUG (See Comic Monthly & Giant Comic Album)
1923 - No. 6, 1928 (Daily strip reprints; B&W) (52 pages)
Cupples & Leon Co.

1-By Billy DeBeck	16.50	50.00	115.00
2-6	11.00	32.00	75.00

NOTE: *Started in 1918 as newspaper strip; Spark Plug began 1922, 1923.*

BARNEY GOOGLE & SNUFFY SMITH
1942 - April, 1964
Dell Publishing Co./Gold Key

4-Color 19('42)	24.00	73.00	170.00
4-Color 40('44)	13.00	40.00	90.00
Large Feature Comic 11(1943)	13.00	40.00	90.00
1(10113-404)-Gold Key (4/64)	1.70	5.00	10.00

BARNEY GOOGLE & SNUFFY SMITH
June, 1951 - No. 4, Feb, 1952 (Reprints)
Toby Press

1	5.50	16.50	38.00
2,3	3.50	10.50	24.00
4-Kurtzman-a ''Pot Shot Pete,'' 5 pgs.; reprints/John Wayne #5	4.00	12.00	28.00

BARNEY GOOGLE AND SNUFFY SMITH
March, 1970 - No. 6, Jan, 1971
Charlton Comics

	Good	Fine	N-Mint
1	1.00	3.00	6.00
2-6	.70	2.00	4.00

BARNYARD COMICS (Dizzy Duck No. 32 on)
June, 1944 - No. 31, Sept, 1950; No. 10, 1957
Nedor/Polo Mag./Standard(Animated Cartoons)

1(nn, 52 pgs.)	9.30	28.00	65.00
2 (52 pgs.)	4.30	13.00	30.00
3-5	2.85	8.50	20.00
6-12,16	2.00	6.00	14.00
13-15,17,21,23,26,27,29-All contain Frazetta text illos	3.00	9.00	21.00
18-20,22,24,25-All contain Frazetta-a & text illos	8.00	24.00	56.00
28,30,31	1.15	3.50	8.00
10(1957)(Exist?)	.50	1.50	4.00

BARRY M. GOLDWATER
March, 1965 (Complete life story)
Dell Publishing Co.

12-055-503: Photo-c	2.30	7.00	16.00

BASEBALL COMICS
Spring, 1949 (Reprinted later as a Spirit section)
Will Eisner Productions

1-Will Eisner c/a	37.00	110.00	260.00

BASEBALL HEROES
1952 (One Shot)
Fawcett Publications

nn (Scarce)-Babe Ruth photo-c; baseball's Hall of Fame briographies			
	35.00	105.00	250.00

BASEBALL THRILLS
No. 10, Sum, 1951 - No. 3, Sum, 1952 (Saunders painted-c No.1,2)
Ziff-Davis Publ. Co.

10(No. 1)	17.00	51.00	120.00
2-Powell-a(2)(Late Sum, '51)	11.00	32.00	75.00
3-Kinstler c/a	11.00	32.00	75.00

BASICALLY STRANGE (Magazine)
December, 1982 (B&W, $1.95)
JC Comics (Archie Comics Group)

1-(21,000 printed; all but 1,000 destroyed—pages out of sequence)			
	.30	1.00	2.00
1-Wood, Toth-a; Corben-c. Reprints & new art	.30	1.00	2.00

BASIC HISTORY OF AMERICA ILLUSTRATED
1976 (B&W)
Pendulum Press

07-1999 America Becomes a World Power 1890-1920
07-2251 The Industrial Era 1865-1915
07-226x Before the Civil War 1830-1860
07-2278 Americans Move Westward 1800-1850
07-2286 The Civil War 1850-1876 - Redondo-a
07-2294 The Fight for Freedom 1750-1783
07-2308 The New World 1500-1750
07-2316 Problems of the New Nation 1800-1830
07-2324 Roaring Twenties and the Great Depression 1920-1940
07-2332 The United States Emerges 1783-1800
07-2340 America Today 1945-1976
07-2359 World War II 1940-1945

Softcover		1.50
Hardcover		4.50

BASIL (. . .the Royal Cat)
Jan, 1953 - No. 4, Sept, 1953
St. John Publishing Co.

Barnyard Comics #6, © STD

Barry M. Goldwater No #, © DELL

Baseball Thrills #2, © Z-D

34

Batgirl Special #1, © DC

Batman #11, © DC

Batman #66, © DC

	Good	Fine	N-Mint
BASIL (continued)			
1	2.00	6.00	14.00
2-4	1.00	3.00	7.00
I.W. Reprint 1	.35	1.00	2.00

BASIL WOLVERTON'S GATEWAY TO HORROR
June, 1988 (One-shot, $1.75, B&W)
Dark Horse Comics

1-Wolverton-r	.30	.90	1.75

BASIL WOLVERTON'S PLANET OF TERROR
Oct, 1987 (One-shot, $1.75, B&W)
Dark Horse Comics

1-Wolverton-r	.30	.90	1.75

BATGIRL SPECIAL (See Teen Titans #50)
1988 (One shot, color, $1.50, 52pgs)
DC Comics

1	1.00	3.00	6.00

BAT LASH (See DC Special Series #16, Showcase #76 & Weird Western Tales)
Oct-Nov, 1968 - No. 7, Oct-Nov, 1969
National Periodical Publications

1	.70	2.00	4.00
2-7	.30	1.00	2.00

BATMAN (See Aurora, The Best of DC #2, The Brave & the Bold, Cosmic Odyssey, DC 100-Page Super Spec. #14,20, DC Special, DC Special Series, Detective, Dynamic Classics, 80-Page Giants, Gotham By Gaslight, Greatest Batman Stories Ever Told, Greatest Joker Stories Ever Told, Heroes Against Hunger, The Joker, Justice League of America #250, Justice League Int., Legends of the Dark Knight, Limited Coll. Ed., Man-Bat, Real Fact #5, Saga of Ra's Al Ghul, Shadow of the..., Star Spangled, Super Friends, 3-D Batman, Untold Legend of..., Wanted... & World's Finest)

BATMAN
Spring, 1940 - Present
National Periodical Publ./Detective Comics/DC Comics

1-Origin The Batman retold by Bob Kane; see Detective #33 for 1st origin; 1st app. Joker & The Cat (Catwoman); has Batman story without Robin originally planned for Detective #38. This book was created entirely from the inventory of Detective Comics

	2,420.00	6,050.00	14,500.00

(Prices vary widely on this book)

1-Reprint, oversize 13½"x10". **WARNING**: This comic is an exact duplicate reprint of the original except for its size. DC published it in 1974 with a second cover titling it as a **Famous First Edition**. There have been many reported cases of the outer cover being removed and the interior sold as the original edition. The reprint with the new outer cover removed is practically worthless.

	Good	Fine	N-Mint
2	667.00	1670.00	4000.00
3-1st Catwoman in costume; 1st Puppetmaster app.			
	450.00	1125.00	2700.00
4	367.00	920.00	2200.00
5-1st app. of the Batmobile with its bat-head front			
	280.00	700.00	1680.00
6-10: 8-Infinity-c	205.00	515.00	1230.00
11-Classic Joker-c	225.00	565.00	1350.00
12-15: 13-Jerry Siegel, creator of Superman appears in a Batman story			
	167.00	420.00	1000.00
16-Intro Alfred (4-5/43)	233.00	585.00	1400.00
17-20: 18-Hitler, Hirohito, Mussolini-c	105.00	265.00	630.00
21,22,24,26,28-30: 22-1st Alfred solo	97.00	245.00	580.00
23-Joker-c/story	130.00	325.00	780.00
25-Joker-c; only Joker/Penguin team-up	121.00	305.00	730.00
27-Christmas-c	100.00	250.00	600.00
31,32,34-36,38,39: 32-Origin Robin retold	62.00	155.00	370.00
33-Christmas-c	74.00	185.00	445.00
37,40-Joker-c/stories	83.00	210.00	500.00
41-43,45,46: 45-Christmas-c	52.00	130.00	315.00
44-Joker-c/story	83.00	210.00	500.00

	Good	Fine	N-Mint
47-1st detailed origin The Batman	167.00	420.00	1000.00
48-1000 Secrets of Batcave; r-in #203	56.00	140.00	335.00
49-Joker-c/story; 1st Vicki Vale & Mad Hatter	83.00	210.00	500.00
50-Two-Face impostor app.	52.00	130.00	315.00
51,53,54,56-60: 57-Centerfold is a 1950 calendar			
	47.00	120.00	285.00
52,55-Joker-c/stories	64.00	160.00	385.00
61-Origin Batman Plane II	47.00	120.00	285.00
62-Origin Catwoman	58.00	145.00	350.00
63-65,67-72: 65-Catwoman-c. 68-Two-Face app. 72-Last 52 pgs.			
	37.00	95.00	225.00
66,73-Joker-c/stories	50.00	125.00	300.00
74-Used in POP, pg. 90	37.00	95.00	225.00
75-77,79,80	37.00	95.00	225.00
78-(8-9/53)-Ron Kar, The Man Hunter from Mars story-the 1st lawman of Mars to come to Earth (green skinned)	47.00	120.00	280.00
81-89: 84-Two-Face app. 86-Intro Batmarine (Batman's submarine). 89-Last Pre-Code issue	37.00	95.00	225.00
90,91,93-99	25.00	65.00	150.00
92-1st app. Bat-Hound	28.00	70.00	170.00
100	108.00	270.00	650.00
101-104,106-109	20.00	60.00	140.00
105-1st Batwoman in Batman	25.00	75.00	175.00
110-Joker story	25.00	75.00	175.00
111-120: 113-1st app. Fatman	13.70	41.00	96.00
121,122,124-126,128-130: 129-Origin Robin retold; Bondage-c			
	11.50	34.00	80.00
123,127-Joker stories. 127-Superman cameo	14.00	42.00	100.00
131-135,137-139,141-143: Last 10 cent issue. 131-Intro 2nd Batman & Robin series. 133-1st Bat-Mite in Batman. 134-Origin The Dummy. 139-Intro old Bat-Girl.	8.50	25.50	60.00
136-Joker-c/story	13.00	40.00	90.00
140-Joker story	9.30	28.00	65.00
144-Joker story	9.30	28.00	65.00
145,148-Joker-c/stories	10.00	30.00	70.00
146,147,149,150	6.50	19.50	45.00
151,153-158,160-162,164-170: 164-New Batmobile; New look & Mystery Analysts series begins	4.50	14.00	32.00
152-Joker story	5.15	15.50	36.00
159,163-Joker-c/stories	6.50	19.50	45.00
171-Riddler app.(5/65), 1st since 12/48	25.00	75.00	175.00
172-175,177,178,180,181,183,184: 181-Batman & Robin poster insert; intro. Poison Ivy	2.35	8.50	20.00
176-80-Pg. Giant G-17; Joker-c/story	4.00	12.00	28.00
179-2nd Riddler app.	4.30	13.00	30.00
182,187-80 Pg. Giants G-24, G-30; Joker-c/stories			
	3.50	10.50	24.00
185-80 Pg. Giant G-27	3.15	9.50	22.00
186,188-192,194-197,199: 197-New Bat-Girl app.	1.70	5.00	12.00
193-80 Pg. Giant G-37; Batcave blueprints	2.00	6.00	14.00
198-80-Pg. Giant G-43; Joker-c/story; Origin-r	2.35	7.00	16.00
200-Joker-story; retells origin of Batman & Robin			
	14.00	42.00	100.00
201-Joker story	2.00	6.00	14.00
202,204-207,209,210	1.35	4.00	8.00
203-80 Pg. Giant G-49; r/#48, 61, & Det. 185	1.50	4.50	9.00
208-80 Pg. Giant G-55; New origin Batman by Gil Kane			
	1.50	4.50	9.00
211,212,214-217: 216-Alfred given a new last name-"Pennyworth." (see Det. 96)	1.35	4.00	8.00
213-80-Pg. Giant G-61; origin Alfred, Joker(r/Det. 168), Clayface; new origin Robin	3.50	10.50	24.00
218-80-Pg. Giant G-67	1.50	4.50	9.00
219-Adams-a	2.35	7.00	16.00
220,221,224-227,229-231	1.15	3.50	7.00
222-Beatles take-off	1.70	5.00	12.00

Batman #250, © DC

Batman #300, © DC

Batman #404, © DC

Batman: The Dark Knight Returns #3, © DC   Bat Masterson #3, © ZIV TV Programs   Battle #32, © MEG

BATMAN MINIATURE (See Batman Kellogg's)

BATMAN RECORD COMIC
1966 (One Shot)
National Periodical Publications

	Good	Fine	N-Mint
1-With record	7.00	21.00	50.00
Comic only	1.50	4.50	10.00

BATMAN: SON OF THE DEMON
Sept, 1987 (80 pgs., hardcover, $14.95)
DC Comics

1-Hardcover	10.00	30.00	60.00
Limited signed & numbered hard-c (1,700)	15.00	45.00	90.00
Softcover w/new-c ($8.95)	2.50	7.50	15.00
Softcover, 2nd print (1989, $9.95)-4th print	1.70	5.00	10.00

BATMAN SPECTACULAR (See DC Special Series No. 15)

BATMAN: THE CULT
1988 - No. 4, Nov, 1988 ($3.50, color, deluxe mini-series)
DC Comics

1-Wrightson-a/painted-c in all	3.00	9.00	18.00
2	2.30	7.00	14.00
3,4	2.00	6.00	12.00

BATMAN: THE DARK KNIGHT RETURNS
March, 1986 - No. 4, 1986
DC Comics

1-Miller story & a(p); set in the future	7.50	22.50	45.00
1-2nd printing	1.70	5.00	10.00
1-3rd printing	.70	2.00	4.00
2-Carrie Kelly becomes Robin (female)	4.00	12.00	24.00
2-2nd printing	1.00	3.00	6.00
2-3rd printing	.60	1.80	3.60
3-Death of Joker	1.70	5.00	10.00
3-2nd printing	.70	2.00	4.00
4-Death of Alfred	1.00	3.00	6.00
Hardcover, signed & numbered edition ($40.00)(4000 copies)			
	50.00	150.00	300.00
Hardcover, trade edition	10.85	32.50	65.00
Softcover, trade edition (1st printing)(8 exist)	2.85	8.50	17.00

BATMAN: THE KILLING JOKE
1988 ($3.50, 52pgs. color, deluxe, adults)
DC Comics

1-Bolland-c/a; Alan Moore scripts	4.35	13.00	26.00
1-2nd thru 8th printings	.85	2.50	5.00

BATMAN: THE OFFICIAL COMIC ADAPTATION OF THE WARNER BROS. MOTION PICTURE
1989 ($2.50, $4.95, 68 pgs.) (Movie adaptation)
DC Comics

1-Regular format ($2.50)-Ordway-c/a	.70	2.00	4.00
1-Prestige format ($4.95)-Diff.-c, same insides	.90	2.75	5.50

BATMAN VS. THE INCREDIBLE HULK (See DC Special Series No. 27)

BAT MASTERSON (TV)
Aug-Oct, 1959; Feb-Apr, 1960 - No. 9, Nov-Jan, 1961-62
Dell Publishing Co.

4-Color 1013 (8-10/59)	5.00	15.00	35.00
2-9: Gene Barry photo-c on all	3.00	9.00	21.00

BATS (See Tales Calculated to Drive You Bats)

BATTLE
March, 1951 - No. 70, June, 1960
Marvel/Atlas Comics(FPI No. 1-62/Male No. 63 on)

1	6.00	18.00	42.00
2	2.65	8.00	18.00
3-9: 4-1st Buck Pvt. O'Toole	2.00	6.00	14.00

	Good	Fine	N-Mint
10-Pakula-a	2.00	6.00	14.00
11-20: 11-Check-a	1.50	4.50	10.00
21,23-Krigstein-a	2.30	7.00	16.00
22,24-36: 36-Everett-a	1.15	3.50	8.00
37-Kubert-a (Last precode, 2/55)	1.50	4.50	10.00
38-40,42-48	.85	2.60	6.00
41-Kubert/Moskowitz-a	1.50	4.50	10.00
49-Davis-a	1.70	5.00	12.00
50-54,56-58	.85	2.50	5.00
55-Williamson-a, 5 pgs.	3.00	9.00	21.00
59-Torres-a	1.50	4.50	10.00
60-62: Combat Kelly app.-#60,62; Combat Casey app.-#61			
	.70	2.00	4.00
63-65: 63-Ditko-a. 64,65-Kirby-a	1.70	5.00	12.00
66-Kirby, Davis-a	2.00	6.00	14.00
67-Williamson/Crandall-a, 4 pgs; Kirby, Davis-a			
	3.00	9.00	21.00
68-Kirby/Williamson-a, 4 pgs; Kirby/Ditko-a	3.00	9.00	21.00
69-Kirby-a	1.50	4.50	10.00
70-Kirby/Ditko-a	1.70	5.00	12.00

NOTE: *Andru* a-37. *Berg* a-8, 14, 60-62. *Colan* a-33, 55. *Everett* a-36, 50, 70; c-56, 57. *Heath* a-6, 9, 13, 31, 69; c-6, 9, 26, 35, 37. *Kirby* c-64-69. *Maneely* a-4, 31; c-4, 59, 61. *Orlando* a-47. *Powell* a-53, 55. *Reinman* a-8, 9, 26, 32. *Robinson* a-9, 39. *Romita* a-26. *Severin* a-28, 32-34, 66-69; c-36, 55. *Sinnott* a-33, 37. *Tuska* a-32. *Woodbridge* a-52, 55.

BATTLE ACTION
Feb, 1952 - No. 12, 5/53; No. 13, 11/54 - No. 30, 8/57
Atlas Comics (NPI)

1-Pakula-a	6.00	18.00	42.00
2	2.30	7.00	16.00
3,4,6,7,9,10: 6-Robinson c/a. 7-partial nudity	1.70	5.00	12.00
5-Used in **POP**, pg. 93,94	1.70	5.00	12.00
8-Krigstein-a	2.30	7.00	16.00
11-15 (Last precode, 2/55)	1.50	4.50	10.00
16-26,28,29	1.00	3.00	7.00
27,30-Torres-a	1.50	4.50	10.00

NOTE: *Battle Brady* app. 5-7, 10-12. *Check* a-11. *Everett* a-7; c-13, 25. *Heath* a-8; c-3, 15, 21. *Maneely* a-1. *Reinman* a-1. *Robinson* a-6, 7; c-6. *Shores* a-7. *Woodbridge* a-28, 30.

BATTLE ATTACK
Oct, 1952 - No. 8, Dec, 1955
Stanmor Publications

1	3.00	9.00	21.00
2	1.50	4.50	10.00
3-8: 3-Hollingsworth-a	1.00	3.00	7.00

BATTLE BEASTS
Feb, 1988 - No. 4, 1988 ($1.50, B&W, 4: $1.75, color)
Blackthorne Publishing

1-3 (B&W)-Based on Hasbro toys	.25	.75	1.50
4 (Color)	.30	.90	1.80

BATTLE BRADY (Formerly Men in Action No. 1-9; see 3-D Action)
No. 10, Jan, 1953 - No. 14, June, 1953
Atlas Comics (IPC)

10	3.00	9.00	21.00
11-Used in **POP**, pg. 95 plus B&W & color illos.			
	2.00	6.00	14.00
12-14	1.50	4.50	10.00

BATTLE CLASSICS (See Cancelled Comic Cavalcade)
Sept-Oct, 1978 (44 pages)
DC Comics

1-Kubert-r, new Kubert-c		.40	.80

BATTLE CRY
1952(May) - No. 20, Sept, 1955

BATTLE CRY (continued)
Stanmor Publications

	Good	Fine	N-Mint
1	3.50	10.50	24.00
2	1.70	5.00	12.00
3,5-10: 8-Pvt. Ike begins, ends #13,17	1.15	3.50	8.00
4-Classic E.C. swipe	1.70	5.00	12.00
11-20	.85	2.60	6.00

NOTE: *Hollingsworth a-9; c-20.*

BATTLEFIELD (War Adventures on the. . .)
April, 1952 - No. 11, May, 1953
Atlas Comics (ACI)

1-Pakula, Reinman-a	5.00	15.00	35.00
2-5	2.00	6.00	14.00
6-11	1.00	3.00	7.00

NOTE: *Colan a-11. Everett c-8. Heath a-1, 5p; c-2; 9, 11. Ravielli a-11.*

BATTLEFIELD ACTION (Formerly Foreign Intrigues)
No. 16, Nov, 1957 - No. 62, 2-3/66; No. 63, 7/80 - No. 89, 11/84
Charlton Comics

V2#16	1.15	3.50	8.00
17,20-30	.50	1.50	3.00
18,19-Check-a (2 stories in #18)	.60	1.80	4.00
31-62(1966)		.50	2.00
63-89(1983-'84)		.30	.60

NOTE: *Montes/Bache a-43,55,62. Glanzman a-87r.*

BATTLE FIRE
April, 1955 - No. 7, 1955
Aragon Magazine/Stanmor Publications

1	1.70	5.00	12.00
2	1.15	3.50	8.00
3-7	.70	2.00	5.00

BATTLE FOR A THREE DIMENSIONAL WORLD
May, 1983 (20 pgs., slick paper w/stiff covers, $3.00)
3D Cosmic Publications

nn-Kirby c/a in 3-D; shows history of 3-D	.50	1.50	3.00

BATTLEFORCE
Nov, 1987 - No. 2?, 1988 ($1.75) (#1: color; #2: B&W)
Blackthorne Publishing

1,2-Based on game	.30	.90	1.80

BATTLEFRONT
June, 1952 - No. 48, Aug, 1957
Atlas Comics (PPI)

1-Heath-c	6.50	19.50	45.00
2-Robinson-a(4)	3.00	9.00	21.00
3-5-Robinson-a(4) in each	2.30	7.00	16.00
6-10: Combat Kelly in No. 6-10	2.00	6.00	14.00
11-22,24-28: 22-Teddy Roosevelt & His Rough Riders story. 28-Last			
precode (2/55). Battle Brady in #14,16	1.15	3.50	8.00
23-Check-a	1.50	4.50	10.00
29-39	1.00	3.00	7.00
40,42-Williamson-a	2.85	8.50	20.00
41,44-47	.70	2.00	5.00
43-Check-a	1.30	4.00	9.00
48-Crandall-a	1.50	4.50	10.00

NOTE: *Ayers a-19. Berg a-44. Colan a-21, 22, 33. Drucker a-28, 29. Everett a-44. Heath c-23, 26, 27, 29. Maneely c/a-22, c-13, 35. Morisi a-42. Morrow a-41. Orlando a-47. Powell a-19, 21, 25, 29, 47. Robinson a-1-5; c-4, 5. Robert Sale a-19. Severin c-40. Woodbridge a-45, 46.*

BATTLEFRONT
No. 5, June, 1952
Standard Comics

5-Toth-a	5.00	15.00	35.00

BATTLE GROUND
Sept, 1954 - No. 20, Aug, 1957
Atlas Comics (OMC)

	Good	Fine	N-Mint
1	5.00	15.00	35.00
2-Jack Katz-a	2.65	8.00	18.00
3,4-Last precode (3/55)	1.70	5.00	12.00
5-8,10	1.30	4.00	9.00
9-Krigstein-a	2.30	7.00	16.00
11,13,18-Williamson-a in each	2.85	8.50	20.00
12,15-17,19,20	1.00	3.00	7.00
14-Kirby-a	1.50	4.50	10.00

NOTE: *Colan a-11. Drucker a-7, 12, 13, 20. Heath c-5. Orlando a-17. Pakula a-11. Severin a-5, 12, 19. c-20. Tuska a-11.*

BATTLE HEROES
Sept, 1966 - No. 2, Nov, 1966 (25 cents)
Stanley Publications

1,2	.50	1.50	3.00

BATTLE OF THE BULGE (See Movie Classics)

BATTLE OF THE PLANETS (TV)
6/79 - No. 10, 12/80 (Based on syndicated cartoon by Sandy Frank)
Gold Key/Whitman No. 6 on

1		.40	.80
2-10: Mortimer a-1-4,7-10		.30	.60

BATTLE REPORT
Aug, 1952 - No. 6, June, 1953
Ajax/Farrell Publications

1	2.15	6.50	15.00
2-6	1.00	3.00	7.00

BATTLE SQUADRON
April, 1955 - No. 5, Dec, 1955
Stanmor Publications

1	1.70	5.00	12.00
2-5: 3-Iwo Jima & flag-c	.85	2.50	6.00

BATTLESTAR GALACTICA (TV)(Also see Marvel Super Special #8)
March, 1979 - No. 23, January, 1981
Marvel Comics Group

1		.35	.70
2-23: 1-3-Partial-r		.25	.50

NOTE: *Austin c-9i, 10i. Golden c-18. Simonson a(p)-4, 5, 11-13, 15-20, 22, 23; c-4p, 5p, 11p-15p.*

BATTLE STORIES (See XMas Comics)
Jan, 1952 - No. 11, Sept, 1953
Fawcett Publications

1-Evans-a	5.00	15.00	35.00
2	2.00	6.00	14.00
3-11	1.50	4.50	10.00

BATTLE STORIES
1963 - 1964
Super Comics

Reprints #10-12,15-18; 15-r/American Air Forces by Powell			
	.35	1.00	2.00

BATTLETECH (See Blackthorne 3-D Series #41 for 3-D issue)
Oct, 1987 - Present ($1.75-2.00; #1-color, #2 on-B&W)
Blackthorne Publishing

1-9: Based on game	.30	.90	1.75
Annual 1 ($4.50, B&W)	.75	2.25	4.50

BEACH BLANKET BINGO (See Movie Classics)

BEAGLE BOYS, THE (Walt Disney)(See The Phantom Blot)
11/64; No. 2, 11/65; No. 3, 8/66 - No. 47, 2/79 (See WDC&S #134)
Gold Key

Battle Attack #1, © Stanmor Publ.

Battlefront #17, © MEG

Battle Stories #5, © FAW

38

Beauty And The Beast: Portrait Of Love #1, © First

Behind Prison Bars #1, © AVON

Ben Casey #6, © Bing Crosby Prod.

BEAGLE BOYS (continued)	Good	Fine	N-Mint
1	2.35	7.00	14.00
2-5	1.35	4.00	8.00
6-10	.85	2.50	5.00
11-20: 11,14,19-r	.50	1.50	3.00
21-47: 27-r	.25	.75	1.50

BEAGLE BOYS VERSUS UNCLE SCROOGE
March, 1979 - No. 12, Feb, 1980
Gold Key

1	.25	.80	1.60
2-12: 9-r		.40	.80

BEANBAGS
Winter, 1951 - No. 2, Spring, 1952
Ziff-Davis Publ. Co. (Approved Comics)

1,2	3.50	10.50	24.00

BEANIE THE MEANIE
1958 - No. 3, May, 1959
Fago Publications

1-3	1.30	4.00	9.00

BEANY AND CECIL (TV) (Bob Clampett's . . .)
Jan, 1952 - 1955; July-Sept, 1962 - No. 5, July-Sept, 1963
Dell Publishing Co.

4-Color 368	11.00	32.00	75.00
4-Color 414,448,477,530,570,635(1/55)	8.50	25.50	60.00
01-057-209	8.50	25.50	60.00
2-5	6.50	19.50	45.00

BEAR COUNTRY (Disney) (See 4-Color No. 758)

BEATLES, THE (See Girls' Romances #109, Go-Go, Heart Throbs #101, Herbie #5, Howard the Duck Mag. #4, Laugh #166, Marvel Comics Super Special 4, My Little Margie 54, Not Brand Echh, Strange Tales 130, Summer Love, Superman's Pal Jimmy Olsen #79, Teen Confessions 37, Tippy's Friends & Tippy Teen)

BEATLES, LIFE STORY, THE
Sept-Nov, 1964 (35 cents)
Dell Publishing Co.

1-(Scarce)-Stories with color photo pin-ups	30.00	90.00	210.00

BEATLES YELLOW SUBMARINE (See Movie Comics under Yellow. . .)

BEAUTIFUL STORIES FOR UGLY CHILDREN
1989 - Present ($2.00, B&W, mature readers)
Piranha Press (DC Comics)

Volume 1-3	.35	1.00	2.00

BEAUTY AND THE BEAST, THE
Jan, 1985 - No. 4, Apr, 1985 (Mini-series)
Marvel Comics Group

1-4: Dazzler & the Beast	.25	.75	1.50

BEAUTY AND THE BEAST: PORTRAIT OF LOVE (TV)
May, 1989 ($5.95, 60 pgs., color, squarebound)
First Comics

1-Based on TV show, Wendy Pini-a/scripts	1.00	3.00	6.00

BEAVER VALLEY (See 4-Color No. 625)

BEDKNOBS AND BROOMSTICKS (See Walt Disney Showcase No. 6 & 50)

BEDLAM!
9/85 - No. 2, 9/85 (B&W-r in color)
Eclipse Comics

1,2-Bissette-a	.30	.90	1.80

BEDTIME STORY (See Cinema Comics Herald)

BEEP BEEP, THE ROAD RUNNER (TV)(Also see Daffy)
7/58 - No. 14, 8-10/62; 10/66 - No. 105, 1983
Dell Publishing Co./Gold Key No. 1-88/Whitman No. 89 on

	Good	Fine	N-Mint
4-Color 918	4.00	12.00	28.00
4-Color 1008,1046	2.00	6.00	14.00
4(2-4/60)-14(Dell)	1.50	4.50	10.00
1	1.70	5.00	12.00
2-5	.85	2.60	6.00
6-14	.70	2.00	4.00
15-18,20-40	.35	1.00	2.00
19-w/pull-out poster	1.35	4.00	8.00
41-60		.60	1.20
61-105		.40	.80
Kite Fun Book-Giveaway ('67,'71), 16pgs., soft-c, 5x7¼"	.70	2.00	4.00

NOTE: See March of Comics #351,353,375,387,397,416,430,442,455. #5,8-10,35,53,59-62, 68-r; 96-102, 104 ½-r.

BEETLE BAILEY (Also see Comics Reading Library & Sarge Snorkel)
#459, 5/53 - #38, 5-7/62; #39, 11/62 - #53, 5/66; #54, 8/66 - #65, 12/67; #67, 2/69 - #119, 11/76; #120, 4/78 - #132, 4/80
Dell Publishing Co./Gold Key No. 39-53/King Co. 54-66/Charlton No. 67-119/Gold Key No. 120-131/Whitman No. 132

4-Color 469 (No. 1)-By Mort Walker	5.00	15.00	35.00
4-Color 521,552,622	2.65	8.00	18.00
5(2-4/56)-10(5-7/57)	2.00	6.00	14.00
11-20(4-5/59)	1.30	4.00	9.00
21-38(5-7/62)	.85	2.60	6.00
39-53(5/66)	.70	2.00	4.00
54-119 (No. 66 publ. overseas only?)	.35	1.00	2.00
120-132		.50	1.00
Bold Detergent Giveaway('69)-same as regular issue (No. 67) minus price	.50	1.00	
Cerebral Palsy Assn. Giveaway V2No.71('69)-V2No.73(No. 1), 1/70, Charlton	.50	1.00	
Giant Comic Album(1972, 59 cents, 11x14") Color cover, B&W interior, Modern Promotions (r)	.40	.80	
Red Cross Giveaway, 16pp, 5x7", 1969, paper-c	.40	.80	

BEE 29, THE BOMBARDIER
Feb, 1945
Neal Publications

1-(Funny animal)	6.50	19.50	45.00

BEHIND PRISON BARS
1952
Realistic Comics (Avon)

1-Kinstler-c	14.00	42.00	100.00

BEHOLD THE HANDMAID
1954 (Religious) (25 cents with a 20 cent sticker price)
George Pflaum

nn	2.30	7.00	16.00

BELIEVE IT OR NOT (See Ripley's . . .)

BEN AND ME (See 4-Color No. 539)

BEN BOWIE AND HIS MOUNTAIN MEN
1952 - No. 17, Nov-Jan, 1958-59
Dell Publishing Co.

4-Color 443 (No. 1)	3.00	9.00	21.00
4-Color 513,557,599,626,657	2.00	6.00	14.00
7(5-7/56)-11: 11-Intro/origin Yellow Hair	1.50	4.50	10.00
12-17	1.00	3.00	7.00

BEN CASEY (TV)
June-July, 1962 - No. 10, June-Aug, 1965 (Photo-c)
Dell Publishing Co.

12-063-207	2.30	7.00	16.00
2(10/62)-10: 4-Marijuana & heroin use story	1.30	4.00	9.00

BEN CASEY FILM STORY (TV)
November, 1962 (25 cents) (Photo-c)
Gold Key

	Good	Fine	N-Mint
30009-211-All photos	4.50	14.00	32.00

BENEATH THE PLANET OF THE APES (See Movie Comics)

BEN FRANKLIN KITE FUN BOOK
1975, 1977 (16 pages; 5-1/8''x6-5/8'')
Southern Calif. Edison Co./PG&E('77)

nn	.35	1.00	2.00

BEN HUR (See 4-Color No. 1052)

BEN ISRAEL
1974 (39 cents)
Logos International

nn		.50	1.00

BEOWULF (See First Comics Graphic Novel #1)
April-May, 1975 - No. 6, Feb-Mar, 1976
National Periodical Publications

1		.45	.90
2-6		.25	.50

BERNI WRIGHTSON, MASTER OF THE MACABRE
July, 1983 - No. 5, Nov, 1984 ($1.50; Baxter paper)
Pacific Comics/Eclipse Comics No. 5

1-Wrightson c/a-r begins	.40	1.25	2.50
2-5	.35	1.00	2.00

BERRYS, THE (Also see Funny World)
May, 1956
Argo Publ.

1-Reprints daily & Sunday strips & daily Animal Antics by Ed Nofziger	2.30	7.00	16.00

BEST COMICS
Nov, 1939 - No. 4, 1940 (large size, reads sideways)
Better Publications

1-(Scarce)-Red Mask begins	30.00	90.00	210.00
2-4: 4-Cannibalism story	18.00	54.00	125.00

BEST FROM BOY'S LIFE, THE
Oct, 1957 - No. 5, Oct, 1958 (35 cents)
Gilberton Company

1-Space Conquerors & Kam of the Ancient Ones app.; also No. 3	3.50	10.50	24.00
2,3,5	1.50	4.50	10.00
4-L.B. Cole-a	2.00	6.00	14.00

BEST LOVE (Formerly Sub-Mariner No. 32)
No. 33, Aug, 1949 - No. 36, April, 1950 (Photo-c 33-36)
Marvel Comics (MPI)

33-Kubert-a	4.00	12.00	28.00
34	1.85	5.50	13.00
35,36-Everett-a	2.85	8.50	20.00

BEST OF BUGS BUNNY, THE
Oct, 1966 - No. 2, Oct, 1968
Gold Key

1,2-Giants	2.00	6.00	16.00

BEST OF DC, THE (Blue Ribbon Digest) (See Limited Coll. Ed. C-52)
9-10/79 - No. 71, 4/86 (100-148 pgs; all reprints)
DC Comics

1-17,19-34,36-71: 34-Has #497 on-c from Adv.		.40	.80
18-The New Teen Titans	.25	.80	1.60
35-The Year's Best Comics Stories(148pgs.)	.60	1.20

NOTE: *Adams* a-26, 51. *Aparo* a-9, 14, 26, 30; c-9, 14, 26. *Austin* a-51i. *Buckler* a-40p; c-22. *Giffen* a-50, 52; c-33p. *Grell* a-33p. *Grossman* a-37. *Heath* a-26. *Kaluta* a-40. *G.*
Kane c-40, 44. *Kubert* a-21, 26. *Layton* a-21. *S. Mayer* c-29, 37, 41, 43, 47; a-28, 29, 37, 41, 43, 47, 58, 65, 68. *Moldoff* c-64p. *Morrow* a-40; c-40. *W. Mortimer* a-39p. *Newton* a-5, 51. *Perez* a-24, 50p; c-18, 21, 23. *Rogers* a-14, 51p. *Spiegle* a-52. *Starlin* a-51. *Staton* a-5, 21. *Tuska* a-24. *Wolverton* a-60. *Wood* a-60, 63; c-60, 63. *Wrightson* a-60. New art in No. 14, 18, 24.

BEST OF DENNIS THE MENACE, THE
Summer, 1959 - No. 5, Spring, 1961 (100 pages)
Hallden/Fawcett Publications

	Good	Fine	N-Mint
1 (all reprints; Wiseman-a)	2.65	8.00	18.00
2-5	1.70	5.00	12.00

BEST OF DONALD DUCK, THE
Nov, 1965 (36 pages)
Gold Key

1-Reprints 4-Color 223 by Barks	5.00	15.00	30.00

BEST OF DONALD DUCK & UNCLE SCROOGE, THE
Nov, 1964 - No. 2, Sept, 1967 (25 cent giant)
Gold Key

1(30022-411)('64)-Reprints 4-Color 189 & 408 by Carl Barks; No. 189-c redrawn by Barks	4.50	14.00	32.00
2(30022-709)('67)-Reprints 4-Color 256 & ''Seven Cities of Cibola'' & U.S. 8 by Barks	3.70	11.00	26.00

BEST OF HORROR AND SCIENCE FICTION COMICS
1987 ($2.00, color)
Bruce Webster

1-Wolverton, Frazetta, Powell, Ditko-r	.35	1.00	2.00

BEST OF MARMADUKE, THE
1960 (a dog)
Charlton Comics

1-Brad Anderson's strip reprints	1.00	3.00	7.00

BEST OF MS. TREE, THE
1987 - No. 4, 1988 ($2.00, B&W, mini-series)
Pyramid Comics

1-4	.35	1.00	2.00

BEST OF THE BRAVE AND THE BOLD, THE (See Super DC Giant)
Oct, 1988 - No. 6, Jan, 1989 ($2.50, color, mini-series)
DC Comics

1-6: Adams-r in all	.40	1.25	2.50

BEST OF THE WEST (See A-1 Comics)
1951 - No. 12, April-June, 1954
Magazine Enterprises

1(A-1 42)-Ghost Rider, Durango Kid, Straight Arrow, Bobby Benson begin	21.00	62.00	145.00
2(A-1 46)	11.00	32.00	75.00
3(A-1 52), 4(A-1 59), 5(A-1 66)	9.50	28.50	65.00
6(A-1 70), 7(A-1 76), 8(A-1 81), 9(A-1 85), 10(A-1 87), 11(A-1 97), 12(A-1 103)	6.50	19.50	45.00

NOTE: *Bolle* a-9. *Borth* a-12. *Guardineer* a-5, 12. *Powell* a-1,12.

BEST OF UNCLE SCROOGE & DONALD DUCK, THE
November, 1966 (25 cents)
Gold Key

1(30030-611)-Reprints part 4-Color 159 & 456 & Uncle Scrooge 6,7 by Carl Barks	4.00	12.00	28.00

BEST OF WALT DISNEY COMICS, THE
1974 (In color; $1.50; 52 pages) (Walt Disney)
8½x11'' cardboard covers; 32,000 printed of each
Western Publishing Co.

96170-Reprints 1st two stories less 1 pg. each from 4-Color 62
    1.00   3.00   7.00
96171-Reprints Mickey Mouse and the Bat Bandit of Inferno Gulch
  from 1934 (strips) by Gottfredson 1.00 3.00 7.00
96172-Reprints Uncle Scrooge 386 & two other stories

Best Comics #1, © BP

Best Of The Brave And The Bold #3, © DC

Best Of Uncle Scrooge & Donald Duck #1, © WDC

40

Best Western #59, © MEG

Beware #11 (8/52), © YM

Beware The Creeper #5, © DC

BEST OF WALT DISNEY COMICS (cont.)	Good	Fine	N-Mint
	1.00	3.00	7.00
96173-Reprints "Ghost of the Grotto" (from 4-Color 159) & "Christmas on Bear Mtn." (from 4-Color 178)	1.00	3.00	7.00

BEST ROMANCE
No. 5, Feb-Mar, 1952 - No. 7, Aug, 1952
Standard Comics (Visual Editions)

5-Toth-a; photo-c	5.00	15.00	35.00
6,7-Photo-c	1.60	4.70	11.00

BEST SELLER COMICS (See Tailspin Tommy)

BEST WESTERN (Formerly Terry Toons?) (Western Outlaws & Sheriffs No. 60 on)
No. 58, June, 1949 - No. 59, Aug, 1949
Marvel Comics (IPC)

58,59-Black Rider, Kid Colt, Two-Gun Kid app.	6.00	18.00	42.00

BETTY AND HER STEADY (Going Steady with Betty No. 1)
No. 2, Mar-Apr, 1950
Avon Periodicals

2	5.00	15.00	35.00

BETTY AND ME
Aug, 1965 - Present
Archie Publications

1	7.00	21.00	50.00
2	4.00	12.00	28.00
3-5: 3-Origin Superteen. Superteen in new costume #4-7; dons new helmet #5, ends #8	2.30	7.00	16.00
6-10	1.00	3.00	6.00
11-30	.40	1.20	2.40
31-55 (52 pages #36-55)		.60	1.20
56-182: Later issues $1.00 cover		.30	.60

BETTY AND VERONICA (Also see Archie's Girls . . .)
June, 1987 - Present (75 & 95 cents)
Archie Enterprises

1-30		.40	.75

BETTY & VERONICA ANNUAL DIGEST (. . . Digest Mag. #2-4; . . . Comics Digest Mag. #5 on)
November, 1980 - Present ($1.00 - 1.50)
Archie Publications

1, 2(11/81-Katy Keene story), 3(8/82), 4-6(11/83), 7-42('90)		.40	.80

BETTY & VERONICA ANNUAL DIGEST
Aug?, 1989 - Present ($1.50, 128 pgs.)
Archie Comics

1,2	.25	.75	1.50

BETTY & VERONICA CHRISTMAS SPECTACULAR (See Archie Giant Series Mag.: #159, 168, 180, 191, 204, 217, 229, 241, 453, 465, 477, 489, 501, 513, 525, 536, 547, 558, 568, 580, 593, 606)

BETTY & VERONICA DOUBLE DIGEST MAGAZINE
1987 - Present (Digest size, 256 pgs., $2.25)
Archie Enterprises

1-18: 5-Christmas-c	.35	1.10	2.25

BETTY & VERONICA SPECTACULAR (See Archie Giant Series Mag. #11, 16, 21, 26, 32, 138, 145, 153, 162, 173, 184, 197, 201, 210, 214, 221, 226, 234, 238, 246, 250, 458, 462, 470, 482, 486, 494, 498, 506, 510, 518, 522, 526, 530, 537, 552, 559, 563, 569, 575, 582, 588, 600)

BETTY & VERONICA SPRING SPECTACULAR (See Archie Giant Series Magazine #569, 582, 595)

BETTY & VERONICA SUMMER FUN (See Archie Giant Series Mag. #8, 13, 18, 23, 28, 34, 140, 147, 155, 164, 175, 187, 199, 212, 224, 236, 248, 460, 484, 496, 508, 520, 529, 539, 550, 561, 572, 585, 598)

BETTY BOOP IN 3-D (See Blackthorne 3-D series #11)

BETTY'S DIARY (See Archie Giant Series Mag. No. 555)
April, 1986 - Present (75 & 95 cents)
Archie Enterprises

	Good	Fine	N-Mint
1-32		.40	.75

BEVERLY HILLBILLIES (TV)
4-6/63 - No. 18, 8/67; No. 19; No. 20, 10/70; No. 21, Oct, 1971
Dell Publishing Co.

1	5.70	17.00	40.00
2	2.80	8.50	20.00
3-10	2.15	6.50	15.00
11-21	1.70	5.00	12.00

NOTE: #1-3,5,8-14,17-21 are photo covers. #19 reprints #1.

BEWARE (Formerly Fantastic; Chilling Tales No. 13 on)
No. 10, June, 1952 - No. 12, Oct, 1952
Youthful Magazines

10-Pit & the Pendulum adaptation; Wildey, Harrison-a; atom bomb-c	11.00	34.00	80.00
11-Harrison-a; Ambrose Bierce adapt.	8.50	25.50	60.00
12-Used in SOTI, pg. 388; Harrison-a	9.30	28.00	65.00

BEWARE
No. 13, 1/53 - No. 13, 1/55; No. 14, 3/55, No. 15, 5/55
Trojan Magazines/Merit Publ. No. ?

13(#1)-Harrison-a	10.00	30.00	70.00
14(#2)-Krenkel/Harrison-c; dismemberment, severed head panels	7.00	21.00	50.00
15,16(#3,4)-Harrison-a	5.50	16.50	38.00
5,9,12,13	5.50	16.50	38.00
6-III. in SOTI-"Children are first shocked and then desensitized by all their brutality." Corpse on cover swipe/V.O.H. #26; girl on cover swipe/Advs. Into Darkness #10	14.00	42.00	100.00
7,8-Check-a	8.50	25.50	60.00
10-Frazetta/Check-c; Disbrow, Check-a	30.00	90.00	210.00
11-Disbrow-a; heart torn out, blood drainage	8.50	25.50	60.00
14,15: 14-Fass-c. 15-Harrison-a	7.00	21.00	50.00

NOTE: Fass a-5, 6; c-6, 11, 14. Hollingsworth a-15(3), 16(4), 9; c-16(4), 8, 9. Kiefer a-5, 6, 10.

BEWARE (Tomb of Darkness No. 9 on)
March, 1973 - No. 8, May, 1974 (All reprints)
Marvel Comics Group

1-Everett-c		.50	1.00
2-8: 6-Tuska-a. 7-Torres r-/Mystical Tales #7		.40	.80

BEWARE TERROR TALES
May, 1952 - No. 8, July, 1953
Fawcett Publications

1-E.C. art swipe/Haunt of Fear 5 & Vault of Horror 26	9.30	28.00	65.00
2	6.00	18.00	42.00
3-8: 8-Tothish-a	4.50	14.00	32.00

NOTE: Andru a-2. Bernard Bailey a-1; c-1-5. Powell a-1, 2, 8. Sekowsky a-2.

BEWARE THE CREEPER (See Adventure, Best of the Brave & the Bold, Brave & the Bold, First Issue Special, Showcase, and World's Finest #249)
May-June, 1968 - No. 6, March-April, 1969
National Periodical Publications

1	1.70	5.00	12.00
2-6	1.15	3.50	8.00

NOTE: Ditko a-1-4, 5p; c-1-5. G. Kane c-6. Sparling a-6p.

BEWITCHED (TV)
4-6/65 - No. 11, 10/67; No. 12, 1969? - No. 14, Oct, 1969
Dell Publishing Co.

1	5.70	17.00	40.00
2	3.50	10.50	24.00

BEWITCHED (continued)	Good	Fine	N-Mint
3-14: Photo-c #3-13	2.30	7.00	16.00

BEYOND, THE
Nov, 1950 - No. 30, Jan, 1955
Ace Magazines

	Good	Fine	N-Mint
1-Bakerish-a(p)	13.50	40.00	95.00
2-Bakerish-a(p)	8.00	24.00	56.00
3-10: 10-Woodish-a by Cameron	5.50	16.50	38.00
11-17,19,20	3.70	11.00	26.00
18-Used in POP, pgs. 81,82	3.70	11.00	26.00
21-26,28-30	3.50	10.50	24.00
27-Used in SOTI, pg. 111	4.00	12.00	28.00

NOTE: Cameron a-10, 11p, 12p, 15, 20-27, 30; c-20. Colan a-6, 13, 17. Sekowsky a-2, 3, 5, 7, 11, 14, 27r. No. 1 was to appear as Challenge of the Unknown No. 7.

BEYOND THE GRAVE
7/75 - No. 6, 6/76; No. 7, 1/83 - No. 17, 10/84
Charlton Comics

1-Ditko-a	.30	.80	1.60
2-6-Ditko-a		.60	1.20
7-17: ('83-'84) Reprints		.30	.60
Modern Comics Reprint 2('78)		.20	.40

NOTE: Ditko c-2,3,6. Sutton c-15.

BIBLE TALES FOR YOUNG FOLK (. . .Young People No. 3-5)
Aug, 1953 - No. 5, Mar, 1954
Atlas Comics (OMC)

1	7.00	21.00	50.00
2-Everett, Krigstein-a	5.70	17.00	40.00
3-5: 4-Robinson-c	4.00	12.00	28.00

BIG
March, 1989 ($2.00, color)
Hit Comics (Dark Horse)

1-Paul Chadwick-c; movie adaptation	.35	1.00	2.00

BIG ALL-AMERICAN COMIC BOOK, THE
1944 (One Shot) (132 pages)
All-American/National Periodical Publ.

1-Wonder Woman, Green Lantern, Flash, The Atom, Wildcat, Scribbly, The Whip, Ghost Patrol, Hawkman by Kubert (1st on Hawkman), Hop Harrigan, Johnny Thunder, Little Boy Blue, Mr. Terrific, Mutt & Jeff app.; Sargon on cover only	300.00	750.00	1800.00

BIG BOOK OF FUN COMICS (1st DC Annual)
Spring, 1936 (52 pages, large size) (1st comic book annual)
National Periodical Publications

1 (Very rare)-r-/New Fun No. 1-5	585.00	1470.00	3500.00

BIG BOOK ROMANCES
February, 1950(no date given) (148 pages)
Fawcett Publications

1-Contains remaindered Fawcett romance comics - several combinations possible	14.00	42.00	100.00

BIG BOY (See Adventures of the Big Boy)

BIG CHIEF WAHOO
July, 1942 - No. 23, 1945?
Eastern Color Printing/George Dougherty

1-Newspaper-r (on sale 6/15/42)	20.00	60.00	140.00
2-Steve Roper app.	10.00	30.00	70.00
3-5	7.00	21.00	50.00
6-10	5.00	15.00	35.00
11-23	3.60	11.00	25.00

NOTE: Kerry Drake in some issues.

BIG CIRCUS, THE (See 4-Color No. 1036)

BIG COUNTRY, THE (See 4-Color No. 946)

BIG DADDY ROTH
Oct-Nov, 1964 - No. 4, Apr-May, 1965 (Magazine; 35 cents)
Millar Publications

	Good	Fine	N-Mint
1-Toth-a	8.50	25.50	60.00
2-4-Toth-a	6.50	19.50	45.00

BIG HERO ADVENTURES (See Jigsaw)

BIG JIM'S P.A.C.K.
No date (16 pages)
Mattel, Inc. (Marvel Comics)

Giveaway with Big Jim doll		.15	.30

BIG JOHN AND SPARKIE (Formerly Sparkie, Radio Pixie)
No. 4, 1952
Ziff-Davis Publ. Co.

4	6.50	19.50	45.00

BIG LAND, THE (See 4-Color No. 812)

BIG RED (See Movie Comics)

BIG SHOT COMICS
May, 1940 - No. 104, Aug, 1949
Columbia Comics Group

1-Intro. Skyman; The Face (Tony Trent), The Cloak (Spy Master), Marvelo, Monarch of Magicians, Joe Palooka, Charlie Chan, Tom Kerry, Dixie Dugan, Rocky Ryan begin	65.00	195.00	455.00
2	29.00	87.00	200.00
3-The Cloak called Spy Chief; Skyman-c	24.00	72.00	170.00
4,5	22.00	65.00	154.00
6-10	18.00	54.00	125.00
11-14: 14-Origin Sparky Watts	16.00	48.00	110.00
15-Origin The Cloak	18.00	54.00	125.00
16-20	10.00	30.00	70.00
21-30: 24-Tojo-c. 29-Intro. Capt. Yank; Bo (a dog) newspaper strip reprints by Frank Beck begin, ends #104	8.50	25.50	60.00
31-40: 32-Vic Jordan newspaper strip reprints begin, ends #52; 32-Hitler, Tojo, Musselini-c	7.00	21.00	50.00
41-50: 42-No Skyman. 43-Hitler-c. 50-Origin The Face retold	5.70	17.00	40.00
51-60	4.50	14.00	32.00
61-70: 63 on-Tony Trent, the Face	3.70	11.00	26.00
71-80: 73-The Face cameo. 74,80: The Face app. in Tony Trent. 78-Last Charlie Chan strip reprints	3.50	10.50	24.00
81-90: 85-Tony Trent marries Babs Walsh	2.65	8.00	18.00
91-99,101-104: 69-94-Skyman in Outer Space. 96-Xmas-c	2.30	7.00	16.00
100	3.00	9.00	21.00

NOTE: Mart Bailey art on "The Face"-No. 1-104. Guardineer a-5. Sparky Watts by Boody Rogers-No. 14-42, 77-104, (by others No. 43-76). Others than Tony Trent wear "The Face" mask in No. 46-63, 93. Skyman by Ogden Whitney-No. 1, 2, 4, 12-37, 49, 70-101. Skyman covers-No. 1, 6, 10, 1i, 14, 16, 20, 27, 89, 95, 100.

BIG TEX
June, 1953
Toby Press

1-Contains (3) John Wayne stories-r with name changed to Big Tex	3.70	11.00	26.00

BIG-3
Fall, 1940 - No. 7, Jan, 1942
Fox Features Syndicate

1-Blue Beetle, The Flame, & Samson begin	78.00	235.00	550.00
2	33.00	100.00	230.00
3-5	26.00	78.00	184.00
6-Last Samson; bondage-c	23.00	70.00	160.00
7-V-Man app.	23.00	70.00	160.00

BIG TOP COMICS, THE
1951 - No. 2, 1951 (no month)

The Beyond #3, © ACE

Big Shot Comics #96, © CCG

Big-3 #7, © FOX

Big Town #5, © DC

Bill Boyd Western #2, © FAW

Billy The Kid And Oscar #1, © FAW

BIG TOP COMICS (continued)
Toby Press

	Good	Fine	N-Mint
1,2	2.65	8.00	18.00

BIG TOWN (Radio/TV)
Jan, 1951 - No. 50, Mar-Apr, 1958 (No. 1-9: 52pgs.)
National Periodical Publications

1-Dan Barry-a begins	23.00	70.00	160.00
2	11.00	34.00	80.00
3-10	6.50	19.50	45.00
11-20	3.70	11.00	26.00
21-31: Last pre-code (1-2/55)	2.65	8.00	18.00
32-50	2.00	6.00	14.00

BIG VALLEY, THE (TV)
6/66 - No. 5, 10/67; No. 6, 10/69
Dell Publishing Co.

1: Photo-c #1-5	2.85	8.50	20.00
2-6: 6 r-/#1	1.50	4.50	10.00

BILL BARNES COMICS (. . . America's Air Ace Comics No. 2 on)
(Becomes Air Ace V2No.1 on; also see Shadow Comics)
Oct, 1940(No. month given) - No. 12, Oct, 1943
Street & Smith Publications

1-23 pgs.-comics; Rocket Rooney begins	36.00	107.00	250.00
2-Barnes as The Phantom Flyer app.; Tuska-a			
	21.00	62.00	145.00
3-5	17.00	51.00	120.00
6-12	13.00	40.00	90.00

BILL BATTLE, THE ONE MAN ARMY (Also see Master No. 133)
Oct, 1952 - No. 4, Apr, 1953 (All photo-c)
Fawcett Publications

1	2.85	8.50	20.00
2	1.50	4.50	10.00
3,4	1.15	3.50	8.00

BILL BOYD WESTERN (Movie star; see Hopalong Cassidy & Western Hero)
Feb, 1950 - No. 23, June, 1952 (1-3,7,11,14-on: 36 pgs.)
Fawcett Publications

1-Bill Boyd & his horse Midnite begin; photo front/back-c			
	21.00	64.00	150.00
2-Painted-c	13.00	40.00	90.00
3-Photo-c begin, end #23; last photo back-c	12.00	36.00	84.00
4-6(52pgs.)	9.50	28.50	65.00
7,11(36pgs.)	7.50	22.50	53.00
8-10,12,13(52pgs.)	8.00	24.00	56.00
14-22	6.50	19.50	45.00
23-Last issue	7.00	21.00	50.00

BILL BUMLIN (See Treasury of Comics No. 3)

BILL ELLIOTT (See Wild Bill Elliott)

BILL STERN'S SPORTS BOOK
Spring-Summer, 1951 - V2No.2, Winter, 1952
Ziff-Davis Publ. Co.(Approved Comics)

V1#10(1951)	7.00	21.00	50.00
2(Sum'52-reg. size)	5.00	15.00	35.00
V2#2(1952,96 pgs.)-Krigstein, Kinstler-a	8.50	25.50	60.00

BILLY AND BUGGY BEAR
1958; 1964
I.W. Enterprises/Super

I.W. Reprint #1(early Timely funny animal), #7(1958)			
	.50	1.50	3.00
Super Reprint #10(1964)	.50	1.50	3.00

BILLY BUCKSKIN WESTERN (2-Gun Western No. 4)
Nov, 1955 - No. 3, March, 1956

Atlas Comics (IMC No. 1/MgPC No. 2,3)

	Good	Fine	N-Mint
1-Mort Drucker-a; Maneely-c/a	6.00	18.00	42.00
2-Mort Drucker-a	3.50	10.50	24.00
3-Williamson, Drucker-a	5.00	15.00	35.00

BILLY BUNNY (Black Cobra No. 6 on)
Feb-Mar, 1954 - No. 5, Oct-Nov, 1954
Excellent Publications

1	2.85	8.50	20.00
2	1.50	4.50	10.00
3-5	.85	2.50	6.00

BILLY BUNNY'S CHRISTMAS FROLICS
1952 (100 pages)
Farrell Publications

1	5.50	16.50	38.00

BILLY MAKE BELIEVE (See Single Series No. 14)

BILLY THE KID (Formerly Masked Raider; see Doc Savage Comics & Return of the Outlaw)
No. 9, Nov, 1957 - No. 121, Dec, 1976; No. 122, Sept, 1977 - No. 123, Oct, 1977; No. 124, Feb, 1978 - No. 153, Mar, 1983
Charlton Publ. Co.

9	3.50	10.50	24.00
10,12,14,17-19	2.00	6.00	14.00
11-(68 pgs., origin, 1st app. The Ghost Train)	2.65	8.00	18.00
13-Williamson/Torres-a	3.15	9.50	22.00
15-Origin; 2pgs. Williamson-a	3.15	9.50	22.00
16-Two pgs. Williamson	3.15	9.50	22.00
20-22,25-Severin-a(3-4)	3.15	9.50	22.00
23,24,26-30	1.30	4.00	9.00
31-40	.85	2.60	6.00
41-60	.70	2.00	4.00
61-80: 66-Bounty Hunter series begins. Not in #79,82,84-86			
	.35	1.00	2.00
81-99,101-123: 87-Last Bounty Hunter. 111-Origin The Ghost Train;			
117-Gunsmith & Co., The Cheyenne Kid app.	.50	1.00	
100		.60	1.25
124(2/78)-129		.30	.60
130-153		.30	.60
Modern Comics 109 (1977 reprint)		.15	.30

NOTE: Severin a(r)-121-129,134. Sutton a-111.

BILLY THE KID ADVENTURE MAGAZINE
Oct, 1950 - No. 30, 1955
Toby Press

1-Williamson/Frazetta, 4 pgs; photo-c	14.00	42.00	100.00
2-Photo-c	3.60	11.00	26.00
3-Williamson/Frazetta "The Claws of Death," 4 pgs. plus William-			
son-a	17.00	51.00	120.00
4,5,7,8,10: 7-Photo-c	2.15	6.50	15.00
6-Frazetta story assist on 'Nightmare;'' photo-c			
	7.00	21.00	50.00
9-Kurtzman Pot-Shot Pete; photo-c	5.50	16.50	38.00
11,12,15-20	2.00	6.00	14.00
13-Kurtzman r-/John Wayne 12 (Genius)	2.30	7.00	16.00
14-Williamson/Frazetta; r-of #1, 2 pgs.	5.00	15.00	35.00
21,23-30	1.50	4.50	10.00
22-Williamson/Frazetta r(1pg.)-/#1; photo-c	1.85	8.00	18.00

BILLY THE KID AND OSCAR (Also see Fawcett's Funny Animals)
Winter, 1945 - No. 3, Summer, 1946 (funny animal)
Fawcett Publications

1	5.00	15.00	35.00
2,3	2.65	8.00	18.00

BILLY WEST (Bill West No. 9,10)
1949 - No. 9, Feb, 1951; No. 10, Feb, 1952

BILLY WEST (continued)

Standard Comics (Visual Editions)	Good	Fine	N-Mint
1	4.50	13.50	32.00
2	2.35	7.00	16.00
3-10: 7,8-Schomburg-c	1.70	5.00	12.00

NOTE: *Celardo a-1-6,9; c-1-3. Moreira a-3. Roussos a-2.*

BING CROSBY (See Feature Films)

BINGO (. . .Comics) (H. C. Blackerby)
1945 (Reprints National material)
Howard Publ.

	Good	Fine	N-Mint
1-L. B. Cole opium-c	10.00	30.00	70.00

BINGO, THE MONKEY DOODLE BOY
Aug, 1951; Oct, 1953
St. John Publishing Co.

1(8/51)-by Eric Peters	2.85	8.50	20.00
1(10/53)	2.00	6.00	14.00

BINKY (Formerly Leave It to. . .)
No. 72, 4-5/70 - No. 81, 10-11/71; No. 82, Summer/77
National Periodical Publ./DC Comics

72-81	.35	1.00	2.00
82('77)-(One Shot)		.50	1.00

BINKY'S BUDDIES
Jan-Feb, 1969 - No. 12, Nov-Dec, 1970
National Periodical Publications

1	.85	2.50	5.00
2-12	.50	1.50	3.00

BIONIC WOMAN, THE (TV)
October, 1977 - No. 5, June, 1978
Charlton Publications

1-5		.50	1.00

BIZARRE ADVENTURES (Formerly Marvel Preview)
No. 25, 3/81 - No. 34, 2/83 (#25-33: Magazine-$1.50)
Marvel Comics Group

25-Lethal Ladies. 26-King Kull		.60	1.20
27-Phoenix, Iceman & Nightcrawler app. 28-The Unlikely Heroes; Elektra by Miller; Adams-a	.25	.75	1.50
29-Horror. 30-Tomorrow. 31-After The Violence Stops; new Hangman story; Miller-a. 32-Gods. 33-Horror		.60	1.20
34 ($2.00, Baxter paper, comic size)-Son of Santa; Christmas spec.; Howard the Duck by P. Smith	.25	.75	1.50

NOTE: *Alcala a-27i. Austin a-25i, 28i. J. Buscema a-27p, 29, 30p; c-26. Byrne a-31(2pgs.). Golden a-25p, 28p. Perez a-27p. Reese a-31i. Rogers a-25p. Simonson a-29; c-29. Paul Smith a-34.*

BIZARRE 3-D ZONE (See Blackthorne 3-D Series No. 5)

BLACK AND WHITE (See Large Feature Comic, Series I)

BLACKBEARD'S GHOST (See Movie Comics)

BLACK BEAUTY (See 4-Color No. 440)

BLACK CAT COMICS (. . .West. No. 16-19; . . Mystery No. 30 on)
(See All-New #7,9, The Original Black Cat, Pocket & Speed Comics)
June-July, 1946 - No. 29, June, 1951
Harvey Publications (Home Comics)

1-Kubert-a	25.00	75.00	175.00
2-Kubert-a	14.00	42.00	100.00
3	10.00	32.00	70.00
4-The Red Demons begin (The Demon #4 & 5)	10.00	32.00	70.00
5,6-The Scarlet Arrow app. in ea. by Powell; S&K-a in both. 6-Origin Red Demon	13.00	40.00	90.00
7-Vagabond Prince by S&K plus 1 more story	13.00	40.00	90.00

	Good	Fine	N-Mint
8-S&K-a; Kerry Drake begins, ends #13	11.00	34.00	80.00
9-Origin Stuntman (r-/Stuntman #1)	14.00	43.00	100.00
10-20: 14,15,17-Mary Worth app. plus Invisible Scarlet O'Neil-#15,20, 24	9.00	27.00	62.00
21-26	7.00	21.00	50.00
27-Used in SOTI, pg. 193; X-Mas-c	9.00	27.00	62.00
28-Intro. Kit, Black Cat's new sidekick	9.00	27.00	62.00
29-Black Cat bondage-c; Black Cat stories	8.00	24.00	56.00

BLACK CAT MYSTERY (Formerly Black Cat; . . .Western Mystery #54; . . .Western #55,56; . . .Mystery #57; . . .Mystic #58-62; Black Cat #63-65)
No. 30, Aug, 1951 - No. 65, April, 1963
Harvey Publications

30-Black Cat on cover only	7.00	21.00	50.00
31,32,34,37,38,40	4.50	14.00	32.00
33-Used in POP, pg. 89; electrocution-c	5.70	17.00	40.00
35-Atomic disaster cover/story	6.00	18.00	42.00
36,39-Used in SOTI: #36-Pgs. 270,271; #39-Pgs. 386-388	8.50	25.50	60.00
41-43	4.50	14.00	32.00
44-Eyes, ears, tongue cut out; Nostrand-a	5.00	15.00	35.00
45-Classic "Colorama" by Powell; Nostrand-a	8.50	25.50	60.00
46-49,51-Nostrand-a in all	5.50	16.50	38.00
50-Check-a; Warren Kremer?-c showing a man's face burning away	8.50	25.50	60.00
52,53 (r-#34 & 35)	3.70	11.00	26.00
54-Two Black Cat stories	5.50	16.50	38.00
55,56-Black Cat app.	3.50	10.50	24.00
57(7/56)-Simon?-c	2.85	8.50	20.00
58-60-Kirby-a(4)	5.00	15.00	35.00
61-Nostrand-a; "Colorama" r-/45	4.00	12.00	28.00
62(3/58)-E.C. story swipe	2.85	8.50	20.00
63-Giant(10/62); Reprints; Black Cat app.; origin Black Kitten	4.50	14.00	32.00
64-Giant(1/63); Reprints; Black Cat app.	4.50	14.00	32.00
65-Giant(4/63); Reprints; Black Cat app.	4.50	14.00	32.00

NOTE: *Kremer a-37, 39, 43; c-36, 37, 47. Meskin a-51. Palais a-30, 31(2), 32(2), 33-35, 37-40. Powell a-32-35, 36(2), 40, 41, 43-53, 57. Simon c-63-65. Sparling a-44. Bondage-c No. 32, 34, 43.*

BLACK COBRA
No. 1, 10-11/54; No. 6(No. 2), 12-1/54-55; No. 3, 2-3/55
Ajax/Farrell Publications

1	10.00	30.00	70.00
6(No. 2)-Formerly Billy Bunny	6.50	19.50	45.00
3-(pre-code)-Torpedoman app.	6.50	19.50	45.00

BLACK CROSS SPECIAL (See Dark Horse Presents)
Jan, 1988 ($1.75, B&W, One shot)(Reprints & new-a)
Dark Horse Comics

1-1st and 2nd printings; 2nd has 2 pgs. new-a .30		.90	1.75

BLACK DIAMOND
May, 1983 - No. 5, 1984 (no month) ($2.00-$1.75, color, Baxter)
Americomics

1-Movie adaptation; Colt back up begins	.40	1.25	2.50
2,3-Movie adaptation	.40	1.25	2.50
4,5	.25	.75	1.50

NOTE: *Bill Black a-1i; c-1. Gulacy c-2-5. Photo back-c 1,2.*

BLACK DIAMOND WESTERN (Formerly Desperado No. 1-8)
No. 9, Mar, 1949 - No. 60, Feb, 1956 (No. 9-28: 52 pgs.)
Lev Gleason Publications

9-Origin	8.00	24.00	56.00
10	4.50	14.00	32.00
11-15	3.50	10.50	24.00
16-28-Wolverton's Bing Bang Buster	4.50	14.00	32.00

Billy West #2, © STD

Black Cat Comics #9, © HARV

Black Cobra #6, © AJAX

Black Fury #1, © CC

Blackhawk #11 (1946), © DC

Black Hood Comics #10, © AP

	Good	Fine	N-Mint
BLACK DIAMOND WESTERN (continued)			
29,30,32-40	2.00	6.00	14.00
31-One pg. Frazetta-a	2.30	7.00	16.00
41-50,53-59	1.70	5.00	12.00
51-3-D effect c/story	5.00	15.00	35.00
52-3-D effect story	4.30	13.00	30.00
60-Last issue	2.00	6.00	14.00

NOTE: *Biro c-9-24?. Fass a-58, c-54-56, 58. Guardineer a-18. Morisi a-55. Tuska a-48.*

BLACK DRAGON, THE
5/85 - No. 6, 10/85 (Baxter paper; mini-series; adults only)
Epic Comics (Marvel)

1: Bolton c/a in all	.70	2.00	4.00
2-6	.35	1.00	2.00

BLACK FURY (Becomes Wild West No. 58) (See Blue Bird)
May, 1955 - No. 57, Mar-Apr, 1966 (Horse stories)
Charlton Comics Group

1	2.35	7.00	16.00
2	1.15	3.50	8.00
3-10	.75	2.25	5.00
11-15,19,20	.70	2.00	4.00
16-18-Ditko-a	2.65	8.00	18.00
21-30	.45	1.35	3.00
31-57	.35	1.00	2.00

BLACK GOLD
1945? (8 pgs. in color)
Esso Service Station (Giveaway)

Reprints from True Comics	3.00	9.00	21.00

BLACK GOLIATH
Feb, 1976 - No. 5, Nov, 1976
Marvel Comics Group

1-5: 1-3-Tuska-a(p)		.50	1.00

BLACKHAWK (Formerly Uncle Sam No. 1-8; Also see Military Comics
& Modern Comics)
No. 9, Winter, 1944 - No. 243, 10-11/68; No. 244, 1-2/76 - No. 250,
1-2/77; No. 251, 10/82 - No. 273, 11/84
Comic Magazines(Quality)No. 9-107(12/56); National Periodical Publ.
No. 108(1/57)-250; DC Comics No. 251 on

9 (1944)	103.00	310.00	725.00
10 (1946)	46.00	140.00	325.00
11-15: 14-Ward-a; 13,14-Fear app.	33.00	100.00	235.00
16-20: 20-Ward Blackhawk	28.00	86.00	200.00
21-30	21.00	62.00	145.00
31-40: 31-Chop Chop by Jack Cole	16.00	48.00	110.00
41-49,51-60	11.00	32.00	75.00
50-1st Killer Shark; origin in text	13.50	40.00	95.00
61-Used in **POP**, pg. 91	11.00	32.00	75.00
62-Used in **POP**, pg. 92 & color illo	11.00	32.00	75.00
63-65,67-70,72-80: 70-Return of Killer Shark. 75-Intro. Blackie the			
Hawk	9.50	28.50	65.00
66-B&W and color illos in **POP**	10.00	30.00	70.00
71-Origin retold; flying saucer-c; A-Bomb panels			
	10.00	30.00	70.00
81-86: Last precode, 3/55	8.00	24.00	56.00
87-92,94-99,101-107	5.50	16.50	38.00
93-Origin in text	7.00	21.00	50.00
100	7.00	21.00	50.00
108-Re-intro. Blackie, the Hawk, their mascot; not in #115			
	20.00	60.00	140.00
109-117	5.00	15.00	35.00
118-Frazetta r-/Jimmy Wakely 4, 3 pgs.	6.50	19.50	45.00
119-130	2.30	7.00	16.00
131-142,144-163,165,166: 133-Intro. Lady Blackhawk. 166-Last 10 cent			
issue	1.60	4.80	11.00

	Good	Fine	N-Mint
143-Kurtzman r-/Jimmy Wakely 4	1.70	5.00	12.00
164-Origin retold	1.70	5.00	12.00
167-180	.85	2.50	5.00
181-190	.60	1.75	3.50
191-197,199-202,204-210: Combat Diary series begins. 197-New look			
for Blackhawks	.45	1.30	2.60
198-Origin retold	.60	1.75	3.50
203-Origin Chop Chop	.50	1.50	3.00
211-243(1968): 228-Batman, Green Lantern, Superman, The Flash			
cameos. 230-Blackhawks become superheroes. 242-Return to			
old costumes	.40	1.20	2.40
244 ('76) -250: 250-Chuck dies	.25	.75	1.50
251-264: 251-Origin retold; Black Knights return. 252-Intro Domino.			
253-Part origin Hendrickson. 258-Blackhawk's Island destroyed.			
259-Part origin Chop-Chop		.50	1.00
265-273 (75 cent cover price)		.50	1.00

NOTE: *Chaykin a-260; c-257-60, 262. Crandall a-10, 11, 13, 16, 18-20, 22-26, 30-33, 36(2), 37, 39-44, 46-50, 52-58, 60, 63, 64, 66, 67; c-18-20, 22-on(most). Evans a-244, 245, 246i, 248-250i. G. Kane c-263, 264. Kubert c-244, 245. Newton a-266p. Severin a-257. Spiegle a-261-67, 269-73; c-265-72. Toth a-260p. Ward a-16-27(Chop Chop, 8pgs. ea.); pencilled stories-No. 17-63(approx.). Wildey a-268.*

BLACKHAWK
Mar, 1988 - No. 3, May, 1988 ($2.95, mini-series)
DC Comics

1-3: Chaykin painted c/a	.40	1.25	2.50

BLACKHAWK
March, 1989 - Present ($1.50, color, mature readers)
DC Comics

1-6,8-10	.25	.75	1.50
7-($2.50, 52 pgs.)-story-r/Military #1	.40	1.25	2.50
Annual 1 (1989, $2.95, 68 pgs.)-Recaps origin of Blackhawk, Lady			
Blackhawk, and others	.50	1.50	3.00

BLACKHAWK INDIAN TOMAHAWK WAR, THE
1951
Avon Periodicals

nn-Kinstler-c; Kit West story	7.00	21.00	50.00

BLACK HOLE (See Walt Disney Showcase #54)
March, 1980 - No. 4, September, 1980 (Disney movie)
Whitman Publishing Co.

11295-Photo-c; Spiegle-a		.50	1.00
2,3-Spiegle-a; 3-McWilliams-a; photo-c		.50	1.00
4-Spiegle-a		.40	.80

BLACK HOOD, THE (See Blue Ribbon, Flyman & Mighty Comics)
Jun, 1983 - No. 3, Oct, 1983 (Printed on Mandell paper)
Red Circle Comics (Archie)

1-Morrow, McWilliams, Wildey-a; Toth-c	.60	1.20	
2,3: MLJ's the Fox by Toth, c/a	.50	1.00	

(Also see Archie's Super-Hero Special Digest #2)

BLACK HOOD COMICS (Formerly Hangman #2-8; Laugh Comics
#20 on; also see Black Swan, Jackpot, Roly Poly & Top-Notch #9)
No. 9, Winter, 1943-44 - No. 19, Summer, 1946 (on radio in 1943)
MLJ Magazines

9-The Hangman & The Boy Buddies cont'd	32.00	95.00	225.00
10-The Hangman & Dusty, the Boy Detective app.			
	14.00	42.00	100.00
11-Dusty app.; no Hangman	12.00	36.00	84.00
12-18: 14-Kinstler blood-c	12.00	36.00	84.00
19-I.D. exposed	14.00	42.00	100.00

NOTE: *Hangman by Fuje in 9, 10. Kinstler a-15, c-14-16.*

BLACK JACK (Rocky Lane's . . ., formerly Jim Bowie)
No. 20, Nov, 1957 - No. 30, Nov, 1959
Charlton Comics

BLACK JACK (continued)	Good	Fine	N-Mint
20	2.65	8.00	18.00
21,27,29,30	1.30	4.00	9.00
22-(68 pages)	2.30	7.00	16.00
23-Williamson/Torres-a	3.50	10.50	24.00
24-26,28-Ditko-a	2.65	8.00	18.00

BLACK KISS
June, 1988 - No. 12, July, 1989 ($1.25-1.50, B&W, 16 pgs., adults)
Vortex Comics

1-By Howard Chaykin	1.50	4.50	9.00
1-2nd, 3rd print		.60	1.25
2	.60	1.75	3.50
2-2nd print		.60	1.25
3	.35	1.00	2.00
4-6	.30	.90	1.80
7-12: 10-on are $1.50		.60	1.25

BLACK KNIGHT, THE
May, 1953; 1963
Toby Press

1-Bondage-c	7.00	21.00	50.00
Super Reprint No. 11 (1963)	1.00	3.00	7.00

BLACK KNIGHT, THE (Also see The Avengers #48, Marvel Super Heroes & Tales To Astonish #52)
May, 1955 - No. 5, April, 1956
Atlas Comics (MgPC)

1-Origin Crusader; Maneely c/a	41.00	122.00	285.00
2	27.00	81.00	190.00
3-5: 4-Maneely c/a. 5-Maneely-c, Shores-a	21.50	64.00	150.00

BLACK LIGHTNING (See Brave & The Bold, Cancelled Comic Cavalcade, DC Comics Presents #16, Detective #490 and World's Finest)
April, 1977 - No. 11, Sept-Oct, 1978
National Periodical Publications/DC Comics

1		.40	.80
2-11: 4-Intro Cyclotronic Man		.25	.50

NOTE: *Buckler* c-1-3p, 6-11p.

BLACK MAGIC (...Magazine) (Becomes Cool Cat V8#6 on)
10-11/50 - V4/1, 6-7/53: V4/2, 9-10/53 - V5/3, 11-12/54; V6/1, 9-10/57 -V7/2, 11-12/58: V7/3, 7-8/60 - V8/5, 11-12/61
(V1/1-5, 52pgs.; V1/6-V3/3, 44pgs.)
Crestwood Publ. V1No.1-4,V6No.1-V7No.2/Headline V1No.5-V5No.3, V7No.3-V8No.5

V1/1-S&K-a, 10 pgs.; Meskin-a(2)	20.00	60.00	140.00
2-S&K-a, 17 pgs.; Meskin-a	8.50	25.50	60.00
3-6(8-9/51)-S&K, Roussos, Meskin-a	7.00	21.00	50.00
V2/1(10-11/51),4,5,7(#13),9(#15),12(#18)-S&K-a	5.00	15.00	35.00
2,3,6,8,10,11(#17)	3.50	10.50	24.00
V3/1(#19, 12/52) - 6(#24, 5/53)-S&K-a	4.30	13.00	30.00
V4/1(#25, 6-7/53), 2(#26, 9-10/53)-S&K-a(3-4)	5.00	15.00	35.00
3(#27, 11-12/53)-S&K-a; Ditko-a(1st in comics)	11.50	34.50	80.00
4(#28)-Eyes ripped out/story-S&K, Ditko-a	8.50	25.50	60.00
5(#29, 3-4/54)-S&K, Ditko-a	7.00	21.00	50.00
6(#30, 5-6/54)-S&K, Powell?-a	3.50	10.50	24.00
V5/1(#31, 7-8/54 - 3(#33, 11-12/54)-S&K-a	3.50	10.50	24.00
V6/1(#34, 9-10/57), 2(#35, 11-12/57)	1.70	5.00	12.00
3(1-2/58) - 6(7-8/58)	1.70	5.00	12.00
V7/1(9-10/58) - 3(7-8/60)	1.50	4.50	10.00
4(9-10/60), 5(11-12/60)-Torres-a	2.00	6.00	14.00
6(1-2/61)-Powell-c/a	1.50	4.50	10.00
V8/1(3-4/61)-Powell-c/a	1.50	4.50	10.00
2(5-6/61)-E.C. story swipe/W.F. #22; Ditko, Powell-a	2.00	6.00	14.00
3(7-8/61)-E.C. story swipe/W.F. #22; Powell-a(2)			
4(9-10/61)-Powell-a(5)	1.70	5.00	12.00
5-E.C. story swipe/W.S.F. #28; Powell-a(3)	1.50	4.50	10.00
	1.70	5.00	12.00

NOTE: *Bernard Baily a-V4#6?, V5#3(2). Grandenetti a-V2#3, 11. Kirby c-V1#1-6, V2#1-12, V3#1-6, V4#1, 2, 4-6, V5#1-3. McWilliams a-V3#2i. Meskin a-V1#1(2), 2, 3, 4(2), 5(2), 6, V2#1, 2, 3(2), 4(3), 5, 6(2), 7-9, 11, 12i. V3#1(2), 5, 6, V5#1(2), 2. Orlando a-V6#1, 4, V7#2; c-V6#1-6. Powell a-V5#1?. Roussos a-V1#3-5, 6(2), V2#3(2), 4, 5(2), 6, 8, 9, 10(2), 11, 12i, V3#1(2), 2i, 5, V5#2. Simon a-V2#12, V3#2, V7#5? c-V4#3?, V7#3?, 4, 5?, 6?. V8#1-5. Simon & Kirby a-V1#1, 2(2), 3-6, V2#1, 4, 5, 7, 9, 12, V3#1-6, V4#1(3), 2(4), 3(2), 4(2), 5, 6, V5#1-3; c-V2#1. Leonard Starr a-V1#1. Tuska a-V6#3, 4. Woodbridge a-V7#4.*

BLACK MAGIC
Oct-Nov, 1973 - No. 9, Apr-May, 1975
National Periodical Publications

1-S&K reprints		.30	.60
2-9-S&K reprints		.20	.40

BLACKMAIL TERROR (See Harvey Comics Library)

BLACKMAN
No Date (1981)
Leader Comics Group

V1#1		.30	.60

BLACK ORCHID (See Adventure Comics #428 & Phantom Stranger)
Holiday, 1988-'89 - No. 3, 1989 ($3.50, mini-series, prestige format)
DC Comics

Book 1-3: 2-Batman app.	.60	1.75	3.50

BLACKOUTS (See Broadway Hollywood. . .)

BLACK PANTHER, THE (Also see Avengers #52, Fantastic Four #52 & Jungle Action)
Jan, 1977 - No. 15, May, 1979
Marvel Comics Group

1		.40	.80
2-15		.25	.50

NOTE: *J. Buscema c-15p. Kirby c/a 1-14. Layton c-13i.*

BLACK PANTHER
July, 1988 - No. 4, Oct, 1988 ($1.25, color)
Marvel Comics Group

1-4	.25	.75	1.50

BLACK PHANTOM (See Tim Holt #25, 38)
Nov, 1954 - No. 2, Feb?, 1955 (Female outlaw)
Magazine Enterprises

1 (A-1 122)-The Ghost Rider app.; Headlight c/a	16.00	48.00	110.00
2 (Rare)-Exist?	20.00	60.00	140.00

BLACK PHANTOM, RETURN OF THE (See Wisco)

BLACK RIDER (Formerly Western Winners; Western Tales of Black Rider #28-31; Gunsmoke Western #32 on)(Also see All Western Winners, Best Western, Kid Colt, Outlaw Kid, Rex Hart, Two-Gun Kid, Two-Gun Western, Western Gunfighters, Western Winners, & Wild Western)
No. 8, 3/50 - No. 18, 1/52; No. 19, 11/53 - No. 27, 3/55
Marvel/Atlas Comics(CDS No. 8-17/CPS No. 19 on)

8 (#1)-Black Rider w his horse Satan begin; 36pgs; photo-c	17.00	51.00	120.00
9-52 pgs. begin, end #14	8.50	25.50	60.00
10-Origin Black Rider	11.00	32.00	75.00
11-14(Last 52pgs.)	6.00	18.00	42.00
15-19: 19-Two-Gun Kid app.	5.50	16.50	38.00
20-Classic-c; Two-Gun Kid app.	6.00	18.00	42.00
21-26: 21-23-Two-Gun Kid app. 24,25-Arrowhead app. 26-Kid Colt app.	4.30	13.00	30.00
27-Last issue; last precode. Kid Colt app. The Spider (a villain) burns			

The Black Knight #5, © MEG

Black Magic V1#6, © Headline

Black Rider #19, © MEG

Blackstone, The Magician #2 (5/48), © MEG

Black Terror #3, © STD

Blackthorne 3-D Series #59, © HARV

	Good	Fine	N-Mint
BLACK RIDER (continued)			
to death	4.50	14.00	32.00

NOTE: Ayers c-22. Jack Keller a-15, 26, 27. Maneely a-14; c-16, 17, 25, 27. Syd Shores a-19, 21, 22, 23(3), 24(3), 25-27; c-19, 21, 23. Sinnott a-24, 25. Tuska a-12, 19-21.

BLACK RIDER RIDES AGAIN!, THE
September, 1957
Atlas Comics (CPS)

1-Kirby-a(3); Powell-a; Severin-c	8.50	25.50	60.00

BLACKSTONE (See Super Magician Comics & Wisco Giveaways)

BLACKSTONE, MASTER MAGICIAN COMICS
Mar-Apr, 1946 - No. 3, July-Aug, 1946
Vital Publications/Street & Smith Publ.

1	11.00	32.00	75.00
2,3	8.00	24.00	56.00

BLACKSTONE, THE MAGICIAN
No. 2, May, 1948 - No. 4, Sept, 1948 (No #1)
Marvel Comics (CnPC)

2-The Blonde Phantom begins	22.00	65.00	154.00
3,4-(. . .Detective on cover only). 3,4-Bondage-c			
	16.00	48.00	110.00

BLACKSTONE, THE MAGICIAN DETECTIVE FIGHTS CRIME
Fall, 1947
E. C. Comics

1-1st app. Happy Houlihans	25.00	75.00	175.00

BLACK SWAN COMICS
1945
MLJ Magazines (Pershing Square Publ. Co.)

1-The Black Hood reprints from Black Hood No. 14; Bill Woggon-a; Suzie app.	8.00	24.00	56.00

BLACK TARANTULA (See Feature Presentations No. 5)

BLACK TERROR (See America's Best & Exciting Comics)
Wint, 1942-43 - No. 27, June, 1949
Better Publications/Standard

1-Black Terror, Crime Crusader begin	60.00	180.00	425.00
2	30.00	90.00	210.00
3	22.00	65.00	154.00
4,5	17.00	51.00	120.00
6-10: 7-The Ghost app.	13.00	40.00	90.00
11-19	11.00	34.00	80.00
20-The Scarab app.	11.00	34.00	80.00
21-Miss Masque app.	12.00	36.00	84.00
22-Part Frazetta-a on one Black Terror story	13.00	40.00	90.00
23	11.00	32.00	75.00
24-¼ pg. Frazetta-a	11.00	34.00	80.00
25-27	11.00	32.00	75.00

NOTE: Schomburg (Xela) c-2-27; bondage c-2, 17, 24. Meskin a-27. Moreira a-27. Robinson/Meskin a-23, 24(3), 25, 26. Roussos/Mayo a-24. Tuska a-26, 27.

BLACK TERROR (Also see Total Eclipse)
1989 - No. 3, 1990 ($4.95, color, squarebound, mini-series, 52 pgs.)
Eclipse Comics

1-3: Painted-c/a	.85	2.50	5.00

BLACKTHORNE 3-D SERIES
May, 1985 - Present ($2.25-2.50)
Blackthorne Publishing Co.

1-Sheena In 3-D #1; Dave Stevens-c	.60	1.75	3.50
2-10: 2-MerlinRealm In 3-D #1. 3-3-D Heroes #1. Goldyn In 3-D #1. 5-Bizarre 3-D Zone #1. 6-Salimba In 3-D #1. 7-Twisted Tales In 3-D #1. 8-Dick Tracy In 3-D #1. 9-Salimba In 3-D #2. 10-Gumby In 3-D #1			
	.40	1.25	2.50
11-20: 11-Betty Boop In 3-D #1. 12-Hamster Vice In 3-D #1. 13-Little Nemo In 3-D #1. 14-Gumby In 3-D #2. 15-Hamster Vice #6 In 3-D.			

	Good	Fine	N-Mint
16-Laffin' Gas #6 In 3-D. 17-Gumby In 3-D #3. 18-Bullwinkle and Rocky In 3-D #1. 19-The Flintstones In 3-D #1. 20-G.I. Joe In 3-D #1			
	.40	1.25	2.50
21-30: 21-Gumby In 3-D #4. 22-The Flintstones In 3-D #2. 23-Laurel & Hardy In 3-D #1. 24-Bozo the Clown In 3-D #1. 25-The Transformers In 3-D #1. 26-G.I.Joe In 3-D #2. 27-Bravestarr In 3-D #1. 28-Gumby In 3-D #5. 29-The Transformers In 3-D #2. 30-Star Wars In 3-D #1			
	.40	1.25	2.50
31-40: 31-The California Raisins In 3-D #1. 32-Richie Rich & Casper In 3-D #1. 33-Gumby In 3-D #6. 34-Laurel & Hardy In 3-D #2. 35-G.I. Joe In 3-D #3. 36-The Flintstones In 3-D #3. 37-The Transformers In 3-D #3. 38-Gumby In 3-D #7. 39-G.I. Joe In 3-D #4. 40-Bravestarr In 3-D #2			
	.40	1.25	2.50
41-50: 41-Battletech In 3-D #1. 42-The Flintstones In 3-D #4. 43-Underdog In 3-D #1. 44-The California Raisins In 3-D #2. 45-Red Heat In 3-D #1 (movie adapt.). 46-The California Raisins In 3-D #3. 47,48-Star Wars In 3-D #2,3. 49-Rambo In 3-D #1. 49-Sad Sack In 3-D #1. 50-Bullwinkle For President In 3-D #1			
	.40	1.25	2.50
51-60: 51-Kull In 3-D #1. 52-? 53-? 54-? 55-Waxwork In 3-D #1 (movie adapt.). 56-? 57-Casper In 3-D #1. 58-Baby Huey In 3-D #1. 59-Little Dot In 3-D #1. 60-Solomon Kane In 3-D #1			
	.40	1.25	2.50
61-70: 61-Werewolf In 3-D #1. 62-G.I. Joe In 3-D Annual #1. 63-? 64-To Die For In 3-D #1. 65-Capt. Holo In 3-D #1. 66-Playful Little Audrey In 3-D #1. 67-? 68-? 69? 70-Wendy In 3-D #1			
	.40	1.25	2.50
71-75: 71-? 72? 73? 74-The Noid In 3-D #1. 75-Moonwalker In 3-D #1 (Michael Jackson Movie adapt.)	.40	1.25	2.50

BLACK ZEPPELIN (See Gene Day's. . .)

BLADE OF SHURIKEN
1987 - No. 6? ($1.95, B&W)
Eternity Comics

1-6	.35	1.00	2.00

BLADE RUNNER
Oct, 1982 - No. 2, Nov, 1982
Marvel Comics Group

1-Movie adaptation; Williamson c/a		.30	.60
2-Movie adapt. concludes; Williamson a		.30	.60

BLAKE HARPER (See City Surgeon. . .)

BLAST (Satire Magazine)
Feb, 1971 - No. 2, May, 1971
G & D Publications

1-Wrightson & Kaluta-a	1.70	5.00	10.00
2-Kaluta-a	1.20	3.50	7.00

BLASTERS SPECIAL
1989 ($2.00, one-shot)
DC Comics

1-Invasion spin-off	.35	1.00	2.00

BLAST-OFF (Three Rocketeers)
October, 1965
Harvey Publications (Fun Day Funnies)

1-Kirby/Williamson-a(2); Williamson/Crandall-a; Williamson/Torres/Krenkel-a; Kirby/Simon-c	2.00	6.00	14.00

BLAZE CARSON (Rex Hart No. 6 on)
(See Kid Colt, Tex Taylor, Wild Western, Wisco)
Sept, 1948 - No. 5, June, 1949
Marvel Comics (USA)

1-Shores-c	8.50	25.50	60.00
2	5.70	17.00	40.00
3-Used by N.Y. State Legis. Comm.(Injury to eye splash); Tex			

47

BLAZE CARSON (continued)

	Good	Fine	N-Mint
Morgan app.	7.00	21.00	50.00
4,5: 4-Two-Gun Kid app. 5-Tex Taylor app.	5.70	17.00	40.00

BLAZE THE WONDER COLLIE
No. 2, Oct, 1949 - No. 3, Feb, 1950
Marvel Comics(SePl)

2(#1), 3-photo-c (Scarce)	9.50	28.50	65.00

BLAZING BATTLE TALES
July, 1975
Seaboard Periodicals (Atlas)

1-Intro. Sgt. Hawk & the Sky Demon; Severin; McWilliams, Sparling-a; Thorne-c		.30	.60

BLAZING COMBAT (Magazine)
Oct, 1965 - No. 4, July, 1966 (Black & White, 35 cents)
Warren Publishing Co.

1-Frazetta-c	7.00	21.00	50.00
2-Frazetta-c	2.50	7.50	15.00
3,4-Frazetta-c; 4-Frazetta ½ pg. ad	1.70	5.00	10.00
. . . Anthology (reprints from No. 1-4)	.70	2.00	4.00

NOTE: Above has art by *Colan, Crandall, Evans, Morrow, Orlando, Severin, Torres, Toth, Williamson,* and *Wood.*

BLAZING COMICS
6/44 - #3, 9/44; #4, 2/45; #5, 1945; #5(V2#2), 3/55 - #6(V2#3), 1955?
Enwil Associates/Rural Home

1-The Green Turtle, Red Hawk, Black Buccaneer begin; origin Jun-Gal	20.00	60.00	140.00
2-5: 3-Briefer-a	12.00	36.00	84.00
5(3/55, V2#2-inside)-Black Buccaneer-c, 6(V2#3-inside, 1955)-Indian/Jap-c	3.15	9.50	22.00

NOTE: No. 5 & 6 contain remaindered comics rebound and the contents can vary. Cloak & Daggar, Will Rogers, Superman 64, Star Spangled 130, Kaanga known. Value would be half of contents.

BLAZING SIXGUNS
December, 1952
Avon Periodicals

1-Kinstler c/a; Larsen/Alascia-a(2), Tuska?-a; Jesse James, Kit Carson, Wild Bill Hickok app.	7.00	21.00	50.00

BLAZING SIXGUNS
1964
I.W./Super Comics

I.W. Reprint #1,8,9: 8-Kinstler-c; 9-Ditko-a	.85	2.50	5.00
Super Reprint #10,11,15,16(Buffalo Bill, Swift Deer),17(1964)	.70	2.00	4.00
12-Reprints Bullseye #3; S&K-a	2.00	6.00	12.00
18-Powell's Straight Arrow	.85	2.60	6.00

BLAZING SIX-GUNS (Also see Sundance Kid)
Feb, 1971 - No. 2, April, 1971 (52 pages)
Skywald Comics

1-The Red Mask, Sundance Kid begin, Avon's Geronimo reprint by Kinstler; Wyatt Earp app.		.50	1.00
2-Wild Bill Hickok, Jesse James, Kit Carson-r		.40	.80

BLAZING WEST (Also see The Hooded Horseman)
Fall, 1948 - No. 22, Mar-Apr, 1952
American Comics Group(B&I Publ./Michel Publ.)

1-Origin & 1st app. Injun Jones, Tenderfoot & Buffalo Belle; Texas Tim & Ranger begin, ends #13	7.00	21.00	50.00
2,3	3.70	11.00	26.00
4-Origin & 1st app. Little Lobo; Starr-a	2.65	8.00	18.00
5-10: 5-Starr-a	2.30	7.00	16.00
11-13	1.70	5.00	12.00
14-Origin & 1st app. The Hooded Horseman	4.00	12.00	28.00
15-22: 15,16,19-Starr-a	2.30	7.00	16.00

BLAZING WESTERN
Jan, 1954 - No. 5, Sept, 1954
Timor Publications

	Good	Fine	N-Mint
1-Ditko-a; Text story by Bruce Hamilton	5.00	15.00	35.00
2-4	2.30	7.00	16.00
5-Disbrow-a	2.65	8.00	18.00

BLESSED PIUS X
No date (32 pages); ½ text, ½ comics) (Paper cover)
Catechetical Guild (Giveaway)

nn	2.30	7.00	16.00

BLITZKRIEG
Jan-Feb, 1976 - No. 5, Sept-Oct, 1976
National Periodical Publications

1-Kubert-c on all		.25	.50
2-5		.20	.40

BLONDE PHANTOM (Formerly All-Select #1-11; Lovers #23 on)
(Also see Blackstone, Marvel Mystery, Millie The Model #2, Sub-Mariner Comics #25 & Sun Girl)
No. 12, Winter, 1946-47 - No. 22, March, 1949
Marvel Comics (MPC)

12-Miss America begins, ends #14	46.00	140.00	325.00
13-Sub-Mariner begins	31.00	94.00	220.00
14,15; 14-Male Bondage-c; Namora app. 15-Kurtzman's 'Hey Look'	27.00	81.00	190.00
16-Captain America with Bucky app.; Kurtzman's "Hey Look"	30.00	90.00	210.00
17-22: 22-Anti Wertham editorial	26.00	77.00	180.00

NOTE: *Shores c-12-18.*

BLONDIE (See Ace Comics, Comics Reading Libraries, Dagwood, Daisy & Her Pups, Eat Right to Work. . . , King & Magic Comics)
1942 - 1946
David McKay Publications

Feature Books 12 (Rare)	39.00	118.00	275.00
Feature Books 27-29,31,34(1940)	8.50	25.50	60.00
Feature Books 36,38,40,42,43,45,47	8.00	24.00	56.00
. . .1944, hard-c, 1938-'44 daily strip-r, B&W, 128 pgs.	9.50	28.50	65.00

BLONDIE & DAGWOOD FAMILY
Oct, 1963 - No. 4, Dec, 1965 (68 pages)
Harvey Publications (King Features Synd.)

1	1.70	5.00	12.00
2-4	1.00	3.00	7.00

BLONDIE COMICS (. . . Monthly No. 16-141)
Spring, 1947 - No. 163, Nov, 1965; No. 164, Aug, 1966 - No. 175, Dec, 1967; No. 177, Feb, 1969 - No. 222, Nov, 1976
David McKay No. 1-15/Harvey No. 16-163/King No. 164-175/Charlton No. 177 on

1	10.00	30.00	70.00
2	5.00	15.00	35.00
3-5	3.70	11.00	26.00
6-10	2.85	8.50	20.00
11-15	2.00	6.00	14.00
16-(3/50; 1st Harvey)	2.30	7.00	16.00
17-20	1.70	5.00	12.00
21-30	1.30	4.00	9.00
31-50	1.00	3.00	7.00
51-80	.85	2.60	6.00
81-100	.75	2.50	5.00
101-124,126-130	.70	2.00	4.00
125 (80 pgs.)	1.00	3.00	7.00
131-136,138,139	.50	1.50	3.00
137,140-(80 pages)	.85	2.60	6.00

Blazing Combat #1, © WP

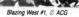

Blazing West #1, © ACG

Blonde Phantom #13, © MEG

Blood Is The Harvest, © CG

The Blue Beetle #55 (Fox), © DC

Blue Beetle #20 (Charlton), © DC

	Good	Fine	N-Mint
BLONDIE COMICS (continued)			
141-166(#148,155,157-159,161-163 are 68 pgs.)	.85	2.60	6.00
167-One pg. Williamson ad	.35	1.00	2.00
168-175,177-222 (no #176)		.50	1.00
Blondie, Dagwood & Daisy 1(100 pgs., 1953)	8.00	24.00	56.00
1950 Giveaway	1.50	4.50	10.00
1962,1964 Giveaway	.50	1.50	3.00
N. Y. State Dept. of Mental Hygiene Giveaway-('50,'56,'61) Regular			
size (Diff. issues) 16 pages; no #	1.00	3.00	6.00

BLOOD
Feb, 1988 - No. 4, Apr, 1988 ($3.25, adults)
Epic Comics (Marvel)

1	.70	2.00	4.00
2-4	.55	1.65	3.30

BLOOD IS THE HARVEST
1950 (32 pages) (paper cover)
Catechetical Guild

(Scarce)-Anti-communism(13 known copies)	64.00	190.00	450.00
Black & white version (5 known copies), saddle stitched	30.00	90.00	200.00
Untrimmed version (only one known copy); estimated value-$600			

NOTE: In 1979 nine copies of the color version surfaced from the old Guild's files plus
the five black & white copies.

BLOOD OF DRACULA
Nov, 1987 - Present ($1.75-$1.95, B&W)
Apple Comics

1-5 ($1.75)	.30	.90	1.75
6-14,16-18: 6-Begin $1.95-c. 10-Chadwick-c. 14-Lost Frankenstein			
pages by Wrightson begins	.35	1.00	2.00
15-Contains stereo flexidisc ($3.75)	.65	1.90	3.80

BLOOD OF THE BEAST
Sum, 1986 - No. 4, 1987? ($2.00, color, mini-series)
Fantagraphics Books

1-4		.35	1.00	2.00

BLOOD OF THE INNOCENT (See Warp Graphics Annual)
1/7/86 - No. 4, 1/28/86 (Weekly mini-series; adults only)
WaRP Graphics

1-4	.50	1.50	3.00
Bound Volume	1.30	4.00	7.95

BLOODSCENT
Oct, 1988 (One-shot, color, $2.00, Baxter paper)
Comico

1-Colan-p	.35	1.00	2.00

BLOOD SWORD, THE
Aug, 1988 - Present ($1.50-1.95, color, 64 pgs.)
Jademan Comics

1-8 ($1.50)-Kung Fu stories	.25	.75	1.50
9-16: ($1.95)	.35	1.00	2.00

BLOOD SWORD DYNASTY
1989 - Present ($1.25, color)
Jademan Comics

1-3: Ties into Blood Sword		.65	1.30

BLUE BEETLE, THE (Also see All Top, Big-3, Mystery Men & Weekly
Comic Magazine)
Winter, 1939-40 - No. 60, Aug, 1950
Fox Publ. No. 1-11, 31-60; Holyoke No. 12-30

1-Reprints from Mystery Men 1-5; Blue Beetle origin; Yarko the			
Great-r/from Wonder/Wonderworld 2-5 all by Eisner; Master			
Magician app.; (Blue Beetle in 4 different costumes)	142.00	355.00	850.00
2-K-51-r by Powell/Wonderworld 8,9	55.00	165.00	385.00

	Good	Fine	N-Mint
3-Simon-c	38.00	115.00	265.00
4-Marijuana drug mention story	28.00	84.00	195.00
5-Zanzibar The Magician by Tuska	24.00	72.00	168.00
6-Dynamite Thor begins; origin Blue Beetle	22.00	65.00	154.00
7,8-Dynamo app. in both. 8-Last Thor	20.00	60.00	140.00
9,10-The Blackbird & The Gorilla app. in both. 10-Bondage/hypo-c			
	18.00	54.00	125.00
11(2/42)-The Gladiator app.	18.00	54.00	125.00
12(6/42)-The Black Fury app.	18.00	54.00	125.00
13-V-Man begins, ends #18; Kubert-a	21.00	62.00	148.00
14,15-Kubert-a in both. 14-Intro. side-kick (c/text only), Sparky			
(called Spunky #17-19)	20.00	60.00	140.00
16-18	15.00	45.00	105.00
19-Kubert-a	18.00	54.00	125.80
20-Origin/1st app. Tiger Squadron; Arabian Nights begin			
	18.00	54.00	125.00
21-26: 24-Intro. & only app. The Halo. 26-General Patton story &			
photo	12.00	36.00	84.00
27-Tamaa, Jungle Prince app.	10.00	30.00	70.00
28-30(2/44)	8.00	24.00	56.00
31(6/44), 33-40: "The Threat from Saturn" serial in #34-38			
	6.50	19.50	45.00
32-Hitler-c	8.00	24.00	56.00
41-45	5.25	15.50	36.00
46-The Puppeteer app.	5.70	17.00	40.00
47-Kamen & Baker-a begin	34.00	100.00	235.00
48-50	27.00	81.00	190.00
51,53	25.00	75.00	175.00
52-Kamen bondage-c	34.00	100.00	235.00
54-Used in **SOTI**. Illo-"Children call these "headlights" comics"			
	54.00	163.00	380.00
55,57(7/48)-Last Kamen issue	25.00	75.00	175.00
56-Used in **SOTI**, pg. 145	23.00	70.00	160.00
58(4/50)-60-No Kamen-a	4.30	13.00	30.00

NOTE: **Kamen** a-47-51, 53, 55-57; c-47, 49-52. **Powell** a-4(2). Bondage-c 9-12, 46, 52.

BLUE BEETLE (Formerly The Thing; becomes Mr. Muscles No. 22
on) (See Charlton Bullseye & Space Adventures)
No. 18, Feb, 1955 - No. 21, Aug, 1955
Charlton Comics

18,19-(Pre-1944-r). 19-Bouncer, Rocket Kelly-r	5.70	17.00	40.00
20-Joan Mason by Kamen	6.50	19.50	45.00
21-New material	4.50	14.00	32.00

BLUE BEETLE (Unusual Tales #1-49; Ghostly Tales #55 on)(Also see
Charlton Bullseye)
V2No. 1, 6/64 - V2No. 5, 3-4/65; V3No. 50, 7/65 - V3No. 54, 2-3/66;
No. 1, 6/67 - No. 5, 11/68
Charlton Comics

V2#1-Origin Dan Garrett-Blue Beetle	2.85	8.50	20.00
2-5, V3#50-54	2.15	6.50	15.00
1(1967)-Question series begins by Ditko	4.30	13.00	30.00
2-Origin Ted Kord-Blue Beetle; Dan Garrett x-over			
	2.00	6.00	14.00
3-5 (#1-5-Ditko-c/a)	1.50	4.50	10.00
1,3(Modern Comics-1977)-Reprints		.15	.30

NOTE: #6 only appeared in the fanzine 'The Charlton Portfolio.'

BLUE BEETLE (Also see Americomics & Crisis On Infinite Earths)
June, 1986 - No. 24, May, 1988
DC Comics

1-Origin retold; intro. Firefist	.25	.75	1.50
2-10: 2-Origin Firefist. 5-7-The Question app.	.50	1.00
11-17: 14-New Teen Titans x-over		.50	1.00
18-24: ($1.00) 20-Justice League app. 20,21-Millennium tie-ins			
		.50	1.00

BLUE BIRD COMICS
Late 1940's - 1964 (Giveaway)
Various Shoe Stores/Charlton Comics

	Good	Fine	N-Mint
nn(1947-50)(36 pgs.)-Several issues; Human Torch, Sub-Mariner app. in some	3.35	10.00	20.00
1959-Li'l Genius, Timmy the Timid Ghost, Wild Bill Hickok (All #1)	.70	2.00	4.00
1959-(6 titles; all #2) Black Fury #1,4,5, Freddy #4, Li'l Genius, Timmy the Timid Ghost #4, Masked Raider #4, Wild Bill Hickok (Charlton)	.70	2.00	4.00
1959-(#5) Masked Raider #21	.70	2.00	4.00
1960-(6 titles)(All #4) Black Fury #8,9, Freddy, Freddy #8,9, Timmy the Timid Ghost #9, Li'l Genius #7,9 (Charlton)	.50	1.50	3.00
1961,1962-(All #10's) Atomic Mouse #12,13,16, Black Fury #11,12, Freddy, Li'l Genius, Masked Raider, Six Gun Heroes, Texas Rangers in Action, Timmy the Ghost, Wild Bill Hickok, Wyatt Earp #3,11-13,16-18 (Charlton)	.35	1.00	2.00
1963-Texas Rangers #17 (Charlton)	.50	1.00	
1964-Mysteries of Unexplored Worlds #18, Teenage Hotrodders #18, War Heroes #18 (Charlton)	.50	1.00	
1965-War Heroes #18	.40	.80	

NOTE: *More than one issue of each character could have been published each year. Numbering is sporadic.*

BLUE BIRD CHILDREN'S MAGAZINE, THE
1957 (16 pages; soft cover; regular size)
Graphic Information Service

	Good	Fine	N-Mint
V1#2-6: Pat, Pete & Blue Bird app.	.40	1.20	2.40

BLUE BOLT
June, 1940 - No. 101 (V10No.2), Sept-Oct, 1949
Funnies, Inc. No. 1/Novelty Press/Premium Group of Comics

	Good	Fine	N-Mint
V1#1-Origin Blue Bolt by Joe Simon, Sub-Zero, White Rider & Super Horse, Dick Cole, Wonder Boy & Sgt. Spook	110.00	330.00	770.00
2-Simon-a	65.00	195.00	455.00
3-1 pg. Space Hawk by Wolverton; S&K-a	50.00	150.00	350.00
4,5-S&K-a in each; 5-Everett-a begins on Sub-Zero	42.00	125.00	295.00
6,8-10-S&K-a	38.00	115.00	265.00
7-S&K c/a	40.00	120.00	280.00
11,12	18.00	54.00	125.00
V2#1-Origin Dick Cole & The Twister; Twister x-over in Dick Cole, Sub-Zero, & Blue Bolt. Origin Simba Karno who battles Dick Cole through V2/5 & becomes main supporting character V2/6 on; battle-c	12.00	36.00	84.00
2-Origin The Twister retold in text	9.00	27.00	62.00
3-5: 5-Intro. Freezum	7.00	21.00	50.00
6-Origin Sgt. Spook retold	6.00	18.00	42.00
7-12: 7-Lois Blake becomes Blue Bolt's costume aide; last Twister	5.00	15.00	35.00
V3#1-3	4.00	12.00	28.00
4-12: 4-Blue Bolt abandons costume	3.50	10.50	24.00
V4#1-Hitler, Tojo, Mussolini-c	4.00	12.00	28.00
V4#2-12: 3-Shows V4#3 on-c, V4#4 inside (9-10/43). 8-Last Sub-Zero	2.65	8.00	18.00
V5#1-8, V6#1-3,5-10, V7#1-12	1.70	5.00	12.00
V6#4-Racist cover	2.30	7.00	16.00
V8#1-6,8-12, V9#1-5,7,8	1.50	4.50	10.00
V8#7,V9#6,9-L. B. Cole-c	2.00	6.00	14.00
V10#1(#100)	1.70	5.00	12.00
V10#2(#101)-Last Dick Cole, Blue Bolt	1.70	5.00	12.00

NOTE: *Everett c-V1#4,11, V2#1,2. Gustavson a-V1#1-12, V2#1-7. Kiefer c-V3#1. Rico a-V6#10, V7#4. Blue Bolt not in V9#8.*

BLUE BOLT (Becomes Ghostly Weird Stories #120 on; continuation of Novelty Blue Bolt) (...Weird Tales #112-119)

No. 102, Nov-Dec, 1949 - No. 119, May-June, 1953
Star Publications

	Good	Fine	N-Mint
102-The Chameleon, & Target app.	10.00	30.00	70.00
103,104-The Chameleon app.; last Target-#104	9.00	27.00	62.00
105-Origin Blue Bolt (from #1) retold by Simon; Chameleon & Target app.; opium den story	21.00	64.00	150.00
106-Blue Bolt by S&K begins; Spacehawk reprints from Target by Wolverton begins, ends #110; Sub-Zero begins; ends #109	17.00	51.00	120.00
107-110: 108-Last S&K Blue Bolt reprint. 109-Wolverton-c(r)/inside Spacehawk splash. 110-Target app.	17.00	51.00	120.00
111-Red Rocket & The Mask-r; last Blue Bolt; 1pg. L. B. Cole-a	19.00	57.00	130.00
112-Last Torpedo Man app.	17.00	50.00	115.00
113-Wolverton's Spacehawk r-/Target V3#7	17.00	50.00	115.00
114,116: 116-Jungle Jo-r	17.00	50.00	115.00
115-Sgt. Spook app.	19.00	57.00	130.00
117-Jo-Jo & Blue Bolt-r	17.00	50.00	115.00
118-"White Spirit" by Wood	19.00	57.00	130.00
119-Disbrow/Cole-c; Jungle Jo-r	17.00	50.00	115.00
Accepted Reprint #103(1957?, nd)	3.50	10.50	24.00

NOTE: *L. B. Cole c-102-108, 110 on. Disbrow a-112(2). 113(3). 114(2?). 115(2?), 116-118. Hollingsworth a-117. Palais a-112r.*

BLUE BULLETEER, THE (Also see Femforce Special)
1989 ($2.25, B&W, one-shot)
AC Comics

	Good	Fine	N-Mint
1-Origin by Bill Black; Bill Ward-a	.40	1.25	2.50

BLUE CIRCLE COMICS (Also see Roly Poly Comic Book)
June, 1944 - No. 6, April, 1945
Enwil Associates/Rural Home

	Good	Fine	N-Mint
1-The Blue Circle begins; origin Steel Fist	9.50	28.50	65.00
2	5.00	15.00	35.00
3-5: 5-Hitler parody-c. 5-Last Steel Fist	3.70	11.00	26.00
6-Colossal Features-r	3.70	11.00	26.00

BLUE DEVIL (See Fury of Firestorm #24)
June, 1984 - No. 31, Dec, 1986
DC Comics

	Good	Fine	N-Mint
1	.25	.75	1.50
2-31: 4-Origin Nebiros. 17-19: Crisis x-over. 27-Godfrey Goose app.			
31-Double size		.50	1.00
Annual 1 (11/85)-Team-ups with Black Orchid, The Creeper, Demon, Madame Xanadu, Man-Bat & Phantom Stranger			
	.25	.70	1.40

BLUE PHANTOM, THE
June-Aug, 1962
Dell Publishing Co.

	Good	Fine	N-Mint
1(01-066-208)-by Fred Fredericks	2.00	6.00	14.00

BLUE RIBBON COMICS (...Mystery Comics No. 9-18)
Nov, 1939 - No. 22, March, 1942 (1st MLJ series)
MLJ Magazines

	Good	Fine	N-Mint
1-Dan Hastings, Richy the Amazing Boy, Rang-A-Tang the Wonder Dog begin; Little Nemo app. (not by W. McCay); Jack Cole-a(3)	118.00	354.00	825.00
2-Bob Phantom, Silver Fox (both in #3), Rang-A-Tang Club & Cpl. Collins begin; Jack Cole-a	50.00	150.00	350.00
3-J. Cole-a	32.00	95.00	225.00
4-Doc Strong, The Green Falcon, & Hercules begin; origin & 1st app. The Fox & Ty-Gor, Son of the Tiger	115.00	300.00	265.00
5-8: 8-Last Hercules; 6,7-Biro, Meskin-a. 7-Fox app. on-c	22.00	65.00	154.00
9-(Scarce)-Origin & 1st app. Mr. Justice	100.00	300.00	700.00
10-12: 12-Last Doc Strong	43.00	130.00	300.00
13-Inferno, the Flame Breather begins, ends #19. Devil-c			

Blue Bolt V1#2, © NOVP

Blue Bolt #105, © STAR

Blue Circle #3, © RH

Blue Ribbon Comics #19, © AP   Bobby Benson's B-Bar-B Riders #11, © ME   Bob Colt #1, © FAW

BLUE RIBBON COMICS (continued)	Good	Fine	N-Mint
	43.00	130.00	300.00
14,15,17,18: 15-Last Green Falcon	38.00	115.00	265.00
16-Origin & 1st app. Captain Flag	70.00	210.00	490.00
19-22: 20-Last Ty-Gor. 22-Origin Mr. Justice retold			
	32.00	95.00	225.00

NOTE: *Biro* c-3-5.

BLUE RIBBON COMICS (Becomes Teen-Age Diary Secrets #6)
Feb, 1949 - No. 6, Aug, 1949 (See Heckle & Jeckle)
Blue Ribbon (St. John)

1,3-Heckle & Jeckle	3.50	10.50	24.00
2(4/49)-Diary Secrets; Baker-c	5.00	15.00	35.00
4(6/49)-Teen-Age Diary Secrets; Baker c/a(2)	6.00	18.00	42.00
5(8/49)-Teen-Age Diary Secrets; Oversize; photo-c; Baker-a(2)- Con-			
tinues as Teen-Age Diary Secrets	7.00	21.00	50.00
6-Dinky Duck(8/49)	1.30	4.00	9.00

BLUE-RIBBON COMICS
Nov, 1983 - No. 14, Dec, 1984
Red Circle Prod./Archie Ent. No. 5 on

1-S&K-r/Advs. of the Fly #1,2; Williamson/Torres-r/Fly #2; Ditko-c		.50	1.00
2-4: 3-Origin Steel Sterling		.50	1.00
5-14: 5-S&K Shield-r. 6,7-The Fox app. 8,11-Black Hood. 12-Thunder			
Agents. 13-Thunder Bunny. 14-Web & Jaguar		.50	1.00

NOTE: *Adams* a(r)-8. *Buckler* a-4i. *Nino* a-2i. *McWilliams* a-8. *Morrow* a-8.

BLUE STREAK (See Holyoke One-Shot No. 8)

BLYTHE (See 4-Color No. 1072)

B-MAN (See Double-Dare Adventures)

BO (Also see Big Shot No. 29; Tom Cat No. 4 on)
June, 1955 - No. 3, Oct, 1955 (a dog)
Charlton Comics Group

1-3-Newspaper reprints by Frank Beck	3.50	10.50	24.00

BOATNIKS, THE (See Walt Disney Showcase No. 1)

BOB & BETTY & SANTA'S WISHING WELL
1941 (12 pages) (Christmas giveaway)
Sears Roebuck & Co.

nn	6.00	18.00	42.00

BOBBY BENSON'S B-BAR-B RIDERS (Radio) (See Best of The West, & Model Fun)
May-June, 1950 - No. 20, May-June, 1953
Magazine Enterprises

1-Powell-a	13.00	42.00	90.00
2	6.50	19.50	45.00
3-5: 4-Lemonade Kid-c	5.00	15.00	35.00
6-8,10	4.00	12.00	28.00
9,11,13-Frazetta-c; Ghost Rider in #13-15 (Ayers-a)			
	14.00	42.00	100.00
12,17-20(A-1 88)	3.50	10.50	24.00
14-Decapitation/Bondage-c & story	5.00	15.00	35.00
15-Ghost Rider-c	5.70	17.00	40.00
16-Photo-c	5.00	15.00	35.00
. . . in the Tunnel of Gold-(1936, 5¼x8''; 100 pgs.) Radio giveaway			
by Hecker-H.O. Company(H.O. Oats); contains 22 color pages of			
comics, rest in novel form	5.00	15.00	35.00
. . .And The Lost Herd-same as above	5.00	15.00	35.00

NOTE: *Ayers* a-13-15, 20. *Powell* a-1-12(4 ea.), 13(3), 14-16(Red Hawk only); c-1-8,10,12. *Lemonade Kid* in most 1-13.

BOBBY COMICS
May, 1946
Universal Phoenix Features

1-by S. M. Iger	4.00	12.00	28.00

BOBBY SHELBY COMICS
1949
Shelby Cycle Co./Harvey Publications

	Good	Fine	N-Mint
nn	1.85	5.50	13.00

BOBBY SHERMAN (TV)
Feb, 1972 - No. 7, Oct, 1972 (Photo-c, 4)
Charlton Comics

1-7-Based on TV show "Getting Together"	1.20	3.50	7.00

BOBBY THATCHER & TREASURE CAVE
1932 (86 pages; B&W; hardcover; 7x9'')
Altemus Co.

Reprints; Storm-a	6.00	18.00	42.00

BOBBY THATCHER'S ROMANCE
1931 (7x8¾'')
The Bell Syndicate/Henry Altemus Co.

nn-By Storm	6.00	18.00	42.00

BOB COLT (Movie star)(See XMas Comics)
Nov, 1950 - No. 10, May, 1952
Fawcett Publications

1-Bob Colt, his horse Buckskin & sidekick Pablo begin; photo front/			
back-c begin	20.00	60.00	140.00
2	13.00	40.00	90.00
3-5	11.50	34.00	80.00
6-Flying Saucer story	10.00	30.00	70.00
7-10: 9-Last photo back-c	8.50	25.50	60.00

BOB HOPE (See Adventures of . . .)

BOB POWELL'S TIMELESS TALES
March, 1989 ($2.00, B&W)
Eclipse Comics

1-Powell-r/Black Cat #5 (Scarlet Arrow), 9 & Race for the Moon #1			
	.35	1.00	2.00

BOB SCULLY, TWO-FISTED HICK DETECTIVE
No date (1930's) (36 pages; 9½x12''; B&W; paper cover)
Humor Publ. Co.

By Howard Dell; not reprints	5.00	15.00	35.00

BOB SON OF BATTLE (See 4-Color No. 729)

BOB STEELE WESTERN (Movie star)
Dec, 1950 - No. 10, June, 1952
Fawcett Publications

1-Bob Steele & his horse Bullet begin; photo front/back-c begin			
	20.00	60.00	140.00
2	13.00	40.00	90.00
3-5: 4-Last photo back-c	11.50	34.00	80.00
6-10: 10-Last photo-c	8.50	25.50	60.00

BOB SWIFT (Boy Sportsman)
May, 1951 - No. 5, Jan, 1952
Fawcett Publications

1	2.85	8.50	20.00
2-5: Saunders painted-c #1-5	1.60	4.70	11.00

BOLD ADVENTURES
Oct, 1983 - No. 3, June, 1984
Pacific Comics

1-Time Force, Anaconda, The Weirdling begin	.30	.90	1.80
2,3: 2-Soldiers of Fortune begins. 3-Spitfire	.25	.75	1.50

NOTE: *Kaluta* c-3. *Nebres* a-3. *Nino* a-2. *Severin* a-3.

BOLD STORIES (Also see Candid Tales & It Rhymes With Lust)
Mar, 1950 - July, 1950 (Digest size; 144 pgs.; full color)
Kirby Publishing Co.

March issue (Very Rare) - Contains "The Ogre of Paris" by Wood

BOLD STORIES (continued)	Good	Fine	N-Mint
	34.00	102.00	240.00
May issue (Very Rare) - Contains "The Cobra's Kiss" by Graham			
Ingels (21 pgs.)	25.00	75.00	175.00
July issue (Very Rare) - Contains "The Ogre of Paris" by Wood			
	27.00	81.00	190.00

BOMBARDIER (See Bee 29, the Bombardier & Cinema Comics Herald)

BOMBA, THE JUNGLE BOY (TV)
Sept-Oct, 1967 - No. 7, Sept-Oct, 1968
National Periodical Publications

1-Infantino/Anderson-c	.85	2.50	5.00
2-7	.50	1.50	3.00

BOMBER COMICS
March, 1944 - No. 4, Winter, 1944-45
Elliot Publ. Co./Melverne Herald/Farrell/Sunrise Times

1-Wonder Boy, & Kismet, Man of Fate begin	17.00	51.00	120.00
2-4: 2-4-Have Classics Comics ad to HRN 20			
	11.50	34.00	80.00

BONANZA (TV)
June-Aug, 1960 - No. 37, Aug, 1970 (All Photo-c)
Dell/Gold Key

4-Color 1110	7.00	21.00	50.00
4-Color 1221,1283, also #01070-207, 01070-210	5.70	17.00	40.00
1(12/62-Gold Key)	5.70	17.00	40.00
2	3.50	10.50	24.00
3-10	2.65	8.00	18.00
11-20	2.00	6.00	14.00
21-37: 29-r	1.30	4.00	9.00

BONGO (See Story Hour Series)

BONGO & LUMPJAW (See 4-Color #706,886, & Walt Disney Showcase #3)

BON VOYAGE (See Movie Classics)

BOOK OF ALL COMICS
1945 (196 pages)
William H. Wise

Green Mask, Puppeteer	21.00	62.00	145.00

BOOK OF COMICS, THE
No date (1944) (132 pages) (25 cents)
William H. Wise

nn-Captain V app.	21.00	62.00	145.00

BOOK OF LOVE (See Fox Giants)

BOOK OF NIGHT, THE
July, 1987 - No. 3, 1987 ($1.75, B&W)
Dark Horse Comics

1-3: Reprints from Epic Illustrated	.30	.90	1.80

BOOSTER GOLD
Feb, 1986 - No. 25, Feb, 1988
DC Comics

1	.35	1.00	2.00
2-5	.25	.75	1.50
6-25: 6-Origin. 24,25-Millennium tie-ins		.50	1.00
NOTE: *Austin* c-22i. *Byrne* c-23i.			

BOOTS AND HER BUDDIES
No. 5, 9/48 - No. 9, 9/49; 12/55 - No. 3, 1956
Standard Comics/Visual Editions/Argo (NEA Service)

5-Strip-r	7.00	21.00	50.00
6,8	4.50	14.00	32.00
7-(Scarce)-Spanking panels(3)	10.00	30.00	70.00
9-(Scarce)-Frazetta-a, 2 pgs.	17.00	51.00	120.00
1-3(Argo-1955-56)-Reprints	1.70	5.00	12.00

BOOTS & SADDLES (See 4-Color No. 919,1029,1116)

BORDER PATROL
May-June, 1951 - No. 3, Sept-Oct, 1951
P. L. Publishing Co.

	Good	Fine	N-Mint
1	3.70	11.00	26.00
2,3	2.30	7.00	16.00

BORDER WORLDS (Also see Megaton Man)
July, 1986 - No. 7, 1987 ($1.95, B&W, adults)
Kitchen Sink Press

1-7: By Donald Simpson	.35	1.00	2.00

BORIS KARLOFF TALES OF MYSTERY (. . .Thriller No. 1,2)
No. 3, April, 1963 - No. 97, Feb, 1980 (TV)
Gold Key

3-8,10-(Two #5's, 10/63,11/63)	1.15	3.50	8.00
9-Wood-a	1.50	4.50	10.00
11-Williamson-a, Orlando-a, 8 pgs.	1.50	4.50	10.00
12-Torres, McWilliams-a; Orlando-a(2)	1.00	3.00	7.00
13,14,16-20	.70	2.00	5.00
15-Crandall,Evans-a	.85	2.60	6.00
21-Jones-a	.85	2.60	6.00
22-30: 23-Reprint; photo-c	.50	1.50	3.00
31-50	.35	1.00	2.00
51-74: 74-Origin & 1st app. Taurus		.60	1.20
75-79,87-97: 78,81-86,88,90,92,95,97-Reprints		.40	.80
80-86-(52 pages)		.40	.80
Story Digest 1(7/70-Gold Key)-All text	.50	1.50	3.00
(See Mystery Comics Digest No. 2,5,8,11,14,17,20,23,26)			
NOTE: *Bolle* a-51-54, 56, 58, 59. *McWilliams* a-12, 14, 18, 19, 80, 81, 93. *Orlando* a-11-15, 21.			

BORIS KARLOFF THRILLER (TV) (Becomes Boris Karloff Tales of Mystery No. 3)
Oct, 1962 - No. 2, Jan, 1963 (80 pages)
Gold Key

1-Photo-c	3.00	9.00	21.00
2	2.50	7.50	20.00

BORIS THE BEAR
Aug, 1986 - No. 23, 1989 ($1.50, B&W)
Dark Horse Comics/Nicotat Comics no. 13 on

1	1.00	3.00	6.00
1-2nd print	.35	1.00	2.00
2	.50	1.50	3.00
3	.30	1.00	2.00
4-6	.30	.90	1.80
7	.25	.75	1.50
8 (44 pgs.)	.35	1.00	2.00
9-23: 13-22 are $1.75, 23-$1.95-c	.25	.75	1.50
Annual 1 ('88, $2.50)	.35	1.10	2.20

BORIS THE BEAR INSTANT COLOR CLASSICS
July, 1987 - No. 3?, 1987 ($1.75-$1.95, color)
Dark Horse Comics

1-3	.30	.90	1.80

BORN AGAIN
1978 (39 cents)
Spire Christian Comics (Fleming H. Revell Co.)

Watergate, Nixon, etc.		.50	1.00

BOUNCER, THE (Formerly Green Mask?)
1944 - No. 14, Jan, 1945
Fox Features Syndicate

nn(1944)-Same as #14	8.00	24.00	56.00
11(#1)(9/44)-Origin; Rocket Kelly, One Round Hogan app.			
	8.00	24.00	56.00
12-14	5.70	17.00	40.00

Bomba, The Jungle Boy #1, © DC

Bonanza #9, © NBC

Boris Karloff Thriller #1, © Estate of B.K.

Boy Comics #60, © LEV

Boy Commandos #11, © DC

Boy Explorers #1, © HARV

BOUNTY GUNS (See 4-Color No. 739)

BOY AND HIS 'BOT, A
Jan, 1987 ($1.95, color)
Now Comics

	Good	Fine	N-Mint
1-A Holiday Special	.35	1.00	2.00

BOY AND THE PIRATES, THE (See 4-Color No. 1117)

BOY COMICS (Captain Battle No. 1 & 2; Boy Illustories No. 43-108)
(Stories by Charles Biro)
No. 3, April, 1942 - No. 119, March, 1956
Lev Gleason Publications (Comic House)

3(No.1)-Origin Crimebuster, Bombshell & Young Robin Hood; Yankee Longago, Case 1001-1008, Swoop Storm, & Boy Movies begin; intro. Iron Jaw	100.00	300.00	700.00
4-Hitler, Tojo, Mussolini-c	43.00	130.00	300.00
5	36.00	107.00	250.00
6-Origin Iron Jaw; origin & death of Iron Jaw's son; Little Dynamite begins, ends #39	68.00	205.00	475.00
7,9: 7-Flag & Hitler, Tojo, Mussolini-c	30.00	90.00	210.00
8-Death of Iron Jaw	34.00	100.00	235.00
10-Return of Iron Jaw; classic Biro-c	43.00	130.00	300.00
11-14	20.00	60.00	140.00
15-Death of Iron Jaw	24.00	73.00	170.00
16,18-20	13.00	40.00	90.00
17-Flag-c	14.00	42.00	100.00
21-26	8.50	25.50	60.00
27-29-(68 pages). 28-Yankee Longago ends	9.30	28.00	65.00
30-Origin Crimebuster retold	11.50	34.00	80.00
31-40: 32(68pgs.)-Swoop Storm, Young Robin Hood ends. 34-Suicide cover/story	4.30	13.00	30.00
41-50	2.85	8.50	20.00
51-59: 57-Dilly Duncan begins, ends #71	2.15	6.50	15.00
60-Iron Jaw returns	2.65	8.00	18.00
61-Origin Crimebuster & Iron Jaw retold	3.50	10.50	24.00
62-Death of Iron Jaw explained	3.70	11.00	26.00
63-72	2.00	6.00	14.00
73-Frazetta 1-pg. ad	2.15	6.50	15.00
74-80: 80-1st app. Rocky X of the Rocketeers; becomes "Rocky X" #101; Iron Jaw, Sniffer & the Deadly Dozen begins, ends #118	1.70	5.00	12.00
81-88	1.70	5.00	12.00
89-92-The Claw serial app. in all	2.00	6.00	14.00
93-Claw cameo; Check-a(Rocky X)	2.85	8.50	20.00
94-97,99	1.70	5.00	12.00
98-Rocky X by Sid Check	3.15	9.50	22.00
100	2.65	8.00	18.00
101-107,109,111,119: 111-Crimebuster becomes Chuck Chandler. 119-Last Crimebuster	1.70	5.00	12.00
108,110,112-118-Kubert-a	2.65	8.00	18.00

(See Giant Boy Book of Comics)

NOTE: *Boy Movies in 3-5,40,41. Iron Jaw app.-3, 4, 6, 8, 10, 11, 13-15; returns-60-62, 68, 69, 72-79, 81-118. Biro c-all. Briefer a-5, 13, 14, 16-20 among others. Fuje a-55, 18 pgs. Palais a-5, 16, 17, 19, 20 among others.*

BOY COMMANDOS (See Detective #64 & World's Finest Comics #8)
Winter, 1942-43 - No. 36, Nov-Dec, 1949
National Periodical Publications

1-Origin Liberty Belle; The Sandman & The Newsboy Legion x-over in Boy Commandos; S&K-a, 48 pgs.	158.00	395.00	950.00
2-Last Liberty Belle; S&K-a, 46 pgs.	64.00	193.00	450.00
3-S&K-a, 45 pgs.	46.00	137.00	320.00
4,5	27.00	80.00	185.00
6-8,10: 6-S&K-a	17.00	51.00	120.00
9-No S&K-a	11.50	34.00	80.00
11-Infinity-c	12.00	36.00	84.00
12-16,18-20	9.50	28.50	65.00
17-Sci/fi c/story	10.00	30.00	70.00

	Good	Fine	N-Mint
21,22,24,25: 22-Judy Canova x-over	6.00	18.00	42.00
23-S&K c/a(all)	8.00	24.00	56.00
26-Flying Saucer story (3-4/48)-4th of this theme	6.50	19.50	45.00
27,28,30	6.00	18.00	42.00
29-S&K story (1)	7.00	21.00	50.00
31-35: 32-Dale Evans app. on-c & story. 34-Intro. Wolf, their mascot	4.30	13.00	30.00
36-Intro The Atomobile c/sci-fi story	5.70	17.00	40.00

NOTE: *Most issues signed by Simon & Kirby are not by them. S&K c-1-9.*

BOY COMMANDOS
Sept-Oct, 1973 - No. 2, Nov-Dec, 1973 (G.A. S&K reprints)
National Periodical Publications

1,2: 1-Reprints story from Boy Commandos #1 & Detective #66 by S&K. 2-Infantino/Orlando-c	.30		.60

BOY DETECTIVE
May-June, 1951 - No. 4, May, 1952
Avon Periodicals

1	8.50	25.50	60.00
2,3: 3-Kinstler-c	5.50	16.50	38.00
4-Kinstler c/a	8.50	25.50	60.00

BOY EXPLORERS COMICS (Terry and The Pirates No. 3 on)
May-June, 1946 - No. 2, Sept-Oct, 1946
Family Comics (Harvey Publications)

1-Intro The Explorers, Duke of Broadway, Calamity Jane & Danny Dixon...Cadet; S&K-c/a, 24 pgs	37.00	110.00	260.00
2-(Scarce)-Small size (5½x8½"; B&W; 32 pgs.) Distributed to mail subscribers only; S&K-a. Estimated value			$250-$400

(Also see All New No. 15, Flash Gordon No. 5, and Stuntman No. 3)

BOY ILLUSTORIES (See Boy Comics)

BOY LOVES GIRL (Boy Meets Girl No. 1-24)
No. 25, July, 1952 - No. 57, June, 1956
Lev Gleason Publications

25(#1)	2.65	8.00	18.00
26,27,29-42: 30-33-Serial, 'Loves of My Life.' 39-Lingerie panels	1.50	4.50	10.00
28-Drug propaganda story	2.35	7.00	16.00
43-Toth-a	3.50	10.50	24.00
44-50: 50-Last pre-code (2/55)	1.15	3.50	8.00
51-57: 57-Ann Brewster-a	.70	2.00	6.00

BOY MEETS GIRL (Boy Loves Girl No. 25 on)
Feb, 1950 - No. 24, June, 1952 (No. 1-17: 52 pgs.)
Lev Gleason Publications

1-Guardineer-a	3.50	10.50	24.00
2	1.70	5.00	12.00
3-10	1.35	4.00	9.00
11-24	1.15	3.50	8.00

NOTE: *Briefer a-24. Fuje c-3,7. Painted c-1,17. Photo-c 19-21,23.*

BOYS' AND GIRLS' MARCH OF COMICS (See March of Comics)

BOYS' RANCH (Also see Western Tales & Witches' Western Tales)
Oct, 1950 - No. 6, Aug, 1951 (No.1-3, 52 pgs.; No. 4-6, 36 pgs.)
Harvey Publications

1-S&K-a(3)	32.00	95.00	225.00
2-S&K-a(3)	26.00	78.00	180.00
3-S&K-a(2); Meskin-a	22.00	65.00	154.00
4-S&K-c/a, 5pgs.	17.00	51.00	120.00
5,6-S&K splashes & centerspread only; Meskin-a	10.00	30.00	70.00
Shoe Store Giveaway #5,6 (Identical to regular issues except S&K centerfold replaced with ad)	8.50	25.50	60.00

NOTE: *Simon & Kirby c-1-6.*

BOZO THE CLOWN (TV) (Bozo No. 7 on)
July, 1950 - No. 4, Oct-Dec, 1963
Dell Publishing Co.

	Good	Fine	N-Mint
4-Color 285	7.00	21.00	50.00
2(7-9/51)-7(10-12/52)	5.00	15.00	35.00
4-Color 464,508,551,594(10/54)	5.00	15.00	35.00
1(nn, 5-7/62) - 4(1963)	2.30	7.00	16.00
Giveaway-1961, 16 pgs., 3½x7¼'', Apsco Products			
	1.50	4.50	10.00

BOZO THE CLOWN IN 3-D (See Blackthorne 3-D Series #24)

BOZZ CHRONICLES, THE
Dec, 1985 - No. 6, 1986 (Adults only)(Mini-series)
Epic Comics (Marvel)

1-6	.35	1.00	2.00

BRADY BUNCH, THE (TV)
Feb, 1970 - No. 2, May, 1970
Dell Publishing Co.

1,2	1.70	5.00	12.00
Kite Fun Book (PG&E, 1976)	1.00	3.00	7.00

BRAIN, THE
Sept, 1956 - No. 7, 1958
Sussex Publ. Co./Magazine Enterprises

1	2.65	8.00	18.00
2,3	1.30	4.00	9.00
4-7	.85	2.60	6.00
I.W. Reprints #1,3,4,8,9,10('63),14	.50	1.50	3.00
I.W. Reprint #2-Reprints Sussex #2 with new cover added			
	.50	1.50	3.00
Super Reprint #17,18(nd)	.50	1.50	3.00

BRAIN BOY
April-June, 1962 - No. 6, Sept-Nov, 1963 (Painted c-5,6)
Dell Publishing Co.

4-Color 1330-Gil Kane-a; origin	4.00	12.00	28.00
2(7-9/62),3-6: 4-origin retold	2.30	7.00	16.00

BRAND ECHH (See Not Brand Echh)

BRAND OF EMPIRE (See 4-Color No. 771)

BRAVADOS, THE (See Wild Western Action)
August, 1971 (52 pages) (One-Shot)
Skywald Publ. Corp.

1-Red Mask, The Durango Kid, Billy Nevada-r	.30		.60

BRAVE AND THE BOLD, THE (See Best Of... & Super DC Giant)
Aug-Sept, 1955 - No. 200, July, 1983
National Periodical Publications/DC Comics

1-Kubert Viking Prince, Silent Knight, Golden Gladiator begin			
	82.00	245.00	575.00
2	37.00	110.00	250.00
3,4	20.00	60.00	140.00
5-Robin Hood begins	14.00	42.00	100.00
6-10: 6-Robin Hood; Golden Gladiator last app.; Silent Knight; no Viking Prince	15.00	45.00	105.00
11-22: 22-Last Silent Knight	11.50	34.00	80.00
23-Kubert Viking Prince origin	14.00	42.00	100.00
24-Last Kubert Viking Prince	14.00	42.00	100.00
25-27-Suicide Squad	5.00	15.00	35.00
28-(2-3/60)-Justice League intro./1st app.; origin Snapper Carr	160.00	480.00	1100.00
29,30-Justice League	63.00	190.00	440.00
31-33-Cave Carson	4.30	13.00	30.00
34-1st app./origin Silver-age Hawkman & Byth by Kubert	19.00	57.00	130.00
35,36-Kubert Hawkman; origin Shadow Thief #36			

	Good	Fine	N-Mint
	7.00	21.00	50.00
37-39-Suicide Squad. 38-Last 10 cent issue	4.00	12.00	28.00
40,41-Cave Carson Inside Earth; #40 has Kubert art			
	4.00	12.00	28.00
42,44-Hawkman by Kubert	5.70	17.00	40.00
43-Origin Hawkman by Kubert	6.50	19.50	45.00
45-49-Infantino Strange Sports Stories	1.00	3.00	6.00
50-The Green Arrow & Manhunter From Mars; team-ups begin			
	4.30	13.00	30.00
51-Aquaman & Hawkman	1.50	4.50	10.00
52-Kubert Sgt. Rock, Haunted Tank, Johnny Cloud, & Mlle. Marie			
	1.35	4.00	8.00
53-Toth Atom & The Flash	1.35	4.00	8.00
54-Kid Flash, Robin & Aqualad; 1st app./origin Teen Titans (6-7/64)			
	12.00	36.00	85.00
55-Metal Men & The Atom	.75	2.25	4.50
56-The Flash & Manhunter From Mars	.75	2.25	4.50
57-Intro & Origin Metamorpho	4.30	13.00	30.00
58-Metamorpho by Fradon	1.50	4.50	10.00
59-Batman & Green Lantern	1.70	5.00	12.00
60-Teen Titans (2nd app.)-1st app. new Wonder Girl (Donna Troy), who joins Titans (6-7/65)	4.00	12.00	28.00
61,62-Origin Starman & Black Canary by Anderson. 62-Huntress app.			
	1.00	3.00	6.00
63-Supergirl & Wonder Woman	.60	1.80	3.60
64-Batman Versus Eclipso	1.30	4.00	8.00
65-Flash & Doom Patrol	.60	1.80	3.60
66-Metamorpho & Metal Men	.60	1.80	3.60
67-Batman & The Flash by Infantino; Batman team-ups begin, end #200	1.00	3.00	6.00
68-Joker/Riddler/Penguin-c/story	1.70	5.00	12.00
69-78: Batman team-ups	1.00	3.00	6.00
79-Batman-Deadman by Adams	2.15	6.50	15.00
80-Batman-Creeper; Adams-a	1.85	5.50	13.00
81-Batman-Flash; Adams-a	1.85	5.50	13.00
82-Batman-Aquaman; Adams-a; origin Ocean Master retold			
	1.85	5.50	13.00
83-Batman-Teen Titans; Adams-a	2.85	8.50	20.00
84-Batman(GA)-Sgt. Rock; Adams-a	1.85	5.50	13.00
85-Batman-Green Arrow; 1st new costume for Green Arrow by Adams	1.85	5.50	13.00
86-Batman-Deadman; Adams-a	1.85	5.50	13.00
87-92: Batman team-ups	.70	2.00	4.00
93-Batman-House of Mystery; Adams-a	1.85	5.50	13.00
94-Batman-Teen Titans	.85	2.50	5.00
95-99: 97-Origin Deadman-r	.70	2.00	4.00
100-Batman-Gr. Lantern-Gr. Arrow-Black Canary-Robin; Deadman by Adams (52 pgs., 25 cents)	1.70	5.00	12.00
101-Batman-Metamorpho; Kubert Viking Prince	.50	1.50	3.00
102-Batman-Teen Titans; Adams-a(p)	.85	2.50	5.00
103-110	.50	1.50	3.00
111-Batman/Joker-c/story	1.35	4.00	8.00
112-117: all 100 pgs.	.70	2.00	4.00
118-Batman/Wildcat/Joker-c/story	1.15	3.50	7.00
119-128	.35	1.00	2.00
129,130-Joker-c/stories	1.35	4.00	8.00
131-140	.35	1.00	2.00
141-Batman vs. Joker c/story	1.15	3.50	7.00
142-190,192-199: 148-XMas-c. 149-Batman-Teen Titans. 179-Legion of Super-Heroes. 196-Origin Ragman retold. 197-Earth II Batman & Catwoman marry	.35	1.00	2.00
191-Batman/Joker-c/story	.85	2.50	5.00
200-Double-sized (64 pgs.); printed on Mando paper; Earth One & Earth Two Batman team-up; Intro/1st app. Batman & The Outsiders	1.00	3.00	6.00

NOTE: **Adams** a-79-86, 93, 100r, 102; c-75, 76, 79-86, 88-90, 93, 95, 99, 100r. **Anderson**

Bozo The Clown #5, © Capitol Records

The Brave And The Bold #28, © DC

The Brave And The Bold #60, © DC

Brenda Starr Reporter #15, © DELL

Brides Romances #3, © QUA

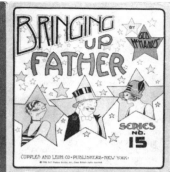
Bringing Up Father #15, © C & L

BRAVE AND THE BOLD (continued)
a-115r; c-72i, 96i. **Aparo** a-98, 100-102, 104-125, 126i, 127-136, 138-145, 147, 148i, 149-152, 154, 155, 157-162, 168-170, 173-178, 180-182, 184, 186-189i, 191-193i, 195, 196, 200; c-105-109, 111-136, 137i, 138-175, 177, 180-184, 186-200. **Austin** a-166i. **Buckler** a-185, 186p; c-137, 178p, 185p, 186p. **Giordano** a-143, 144. **Infantino** a-67p, 72p, 97i, 98r, 172p, 183p, 190p, 194p; c-45-49, 67p, 69p, 70p, 72p, 96p, 98r. **Kaluta** a-115r. **Kubert &/or Heath** a-1-24; reprints-101, 113, 115, 117. **Kubert** c-22-24, 34-36, 40, 42-44, 52. **Mooney** a-114r. **Newton** a-153p, 156p, 165p. **Roussos** a-114r. **Staton** 148p. 52 pgs.-97, 100; 64 pgs.-120; 100 pgs.-112-117.

BRAVE AND THE BOLD SPECIAL, THE (See DC Special Series No. 8)

BRAVE EAGLE (See 4-Color No. 705,770,816,879,929)

BRAVE ONE, THE (See 4-Color No. 773)

BRAVESTARR IN 3-D (See Blackthorne 3-D Series #27, 40)

BREEZE LAWSON, SKY SHERIFF (See Sky Sheriff)

BRENDA LEE STORY, THE
September, 1962
Dell Publishing Co.

	Good	Fine	N-Mint
01-078-209	5.00	15.00	35.00

BRENDA STARR (Also see All Great)
No. 13, 9/47; No. 14, 3/48; V2No.3, 6/48 - V2No.12, 12/49
Four Star Comics Corp./Superior Comics Ltd.

	Good	Fine	N-Mint
V1#13-By Dale Messick	32.00	95.00	225.00
14-Kamen bondage-c	32.00	95.00	225.00
V2#3-Baker-a?	26.00	77.00	180.00
4-Used in SOTI, pg. 21; Kamen bondage-c			
	28.00	85.00	200.00
5-10	21.50	64.00	150.00
11,12 (Scarce)	27.00	80.00	185.00

NOTE: Newspaper reprints plus original material through #6. All original #7 on.

BRENDA STARR (. . . Reporter)(Young Lovers No. 16 on?)
No. 13, June, 1955 - No. 15, Oct, 1955
Charlton Comics

13-15-Newspaper-r	14.00	42.00	100.00

BRENDA STARR REPORTER
October, 1963
Dell Publishing Co.

1	11.00	32.00	75.00

BRER RABBIT (See 4-Color No. 129,208,693, Walt Disney Showcase No. 28, and Wheaties)

BRER RABBIT IN "A KITE TAIL"
1955 (16 pages, 5x7¼", soft-c) (Walt Disney) (Premium)
Pacific Gas & Electric Co./Southern Calif. Edison

(Rare)-Kite fun book	14.00	42.00	100.00

BRER RABBIT IN "ICE CREAM FOR THE PARTY"
1955 (16 pages, 5x7¼", soft-c) (Walt Disney) (Premium)
American Dairy Association

(Rare)	8.00	24.00	56.00

BRIAN BOLLAND'S BLACK BOOK
July, 1985 (One-shot)
Eclipse Comics

1-British B&W-r in color	.25	.75	1.50

BRICK BRADFORD (Also see Ace Comics & King Comics)
No. 5, 1948 - No. 8, 1949 (Ritt & Grey reprints)
King Features Syndicate/Standard

5	8.50	25.50	60.00
6-8: 7-Schomburg-c	6.50	19.50	45.00

BRIDE'S DIARY
No. 4, May, 1955 - No. 10, Aug, 1956
Ajax/Farrell Publ.

4 (#1)	2.65	8.00	18.00

	Good	Fine	N-Mint
5-8	1.70	5.00	12.00
9,10-Disbrow-a	2.50	7.50	17.50

BRIDES IN LOVE (Hollywood Romances & Summer Love No. 46 on)
Aug, 1956 - No. 45, Feb, 1965
Charlton Comics

1	2.30	7.00	16.00
2	1.30	4.00	9.00
3-10	.85	2.50	6.00
11-20	.50	1.50	3.00
21-45	.30	.90	1.80

BRIDES ROMANCES
Nov, 1953 - No. 23, Dec, 1956
Quality Comics Group

1	4.50	14.00	32.00
2	2.15	6.50	15.00
3-10: Last precode (3/55)	1.60	4.70	11.00
11-14,16,17,19-22	1.15	3.50	8.00
15-Baker-a(p); Colan-a	1.30	4.00	9.00
18-Baker-a	1.65	5.00	11.50
23-Baker c/a	2.50	7.50	17.00

BRIDE'S SECRETS
Apr-May, 1954 - No. 19, May, 1958
Ajax/Farrell(Excellent Publ.)/Four-Star Comic

1	4.50	14.00	32.00
2	2.15	6.50	15.00
3-6: Last precode (3/55)	1.50	4.50	10.00
7-19: 12-Disbrow-a. 18-Hollingsworth-a	1.15	3.50	8.00

BRIDE-TO-BE ROMANCES (See True . . .)

BRIGAND, THE (See Fawcett Movie Comics No. 18)

BRINGING UP FATHER (See 4-Color #37 & Large Feature Comic #9)

BRINGING UP FATHER
1917 (16½x5½"; cardboard cover; 100 pages; B&W)
Star Co. (King Features)
(Rare) Daily strip reprints by George McManus (no price on cover)

	30.00	90.00	210.00

BRINGING UP FATHER
1919 - 1934 (by George McManus)
(10x10"; stiff cardboard covers; B&W; daily strip reprints; 52 pgs.)
(No. 22 is 9¼x9½")
Cupples & Leon Co.

1	24.00	70.00	165.00
2-10	11.50	34.00	80.00
11-26 (Scarcer)	18.00	54.00	125.00
The Big Book 1(1926)-Thick book (hardcover); 10¼x10¼", 142pgs.			
	30.00	90.00	210.00
The Big Book 2(1929)	24.00	70.00	165.00

NOTE: The Big Books contain 3 regular issues rebound and probably with dust jackets.

BRINGING UP FATHER, THE TROUBLE OF
1921 (9x15") (Sunday reprints in color)
Embee Publ. Co.

(Rare)	30.00	90.00	210.00

BROADWAY HOLLYWOOD BLACKOUTS
Mar-Apr, 1954 - No. 3, July-Aug, 1954
Stanhall

1	5.00	15.00	35.00
2,3	3.00	9.00	21.00

BROADWAY ROMANCES
January, 1950 - No. 5, Sept, 1950
Quality Comics Group

BROADWAY ROMANCES (continued)	Good	Fine	N-Mint
1-Ward c/a, 9pgs.; Gustavson-a	14.00	42.00	100.00
2-Ward-a, 9pgs., photo-c	8.50	25.50	60.00
3-5: 4,5-Photo-c	3.70	11.00	26.00

BROKEN ARROW (See 4-Color No. 855,947)

BROKEN CROSS, THE (See The Crusaders)

BRONCHO BILL (See Comics On Parade, Sparkler & Tip Top Comics)
1939 - 1940; No. 5, 1?/48 - No. 16, 8?/50
United Features Syndicate/Standard(Visual Editions) No. 5-on

Single Series 2 ('39)	24.00	70.00	170.00
Single Series 19 ('40)(#2 on cvr)	20.00	60.00	140.00
5	4.50	14.00	32.00
6(4/48)-10(4/49)	2.65	8.00	18.00
11(6/49)-16	2.00	6.00	14.00

NOTE: *Schomburg c-6,7,9-13,16.*

BROTHER POWER, THE GEEK
Sept-Oct, 1968 - No. 2, Nov-Dec, 1968
National Periodical Publications

1-Origin; Simon-c(i?)	1.70	5.00	12.00
2	1.15	3.50	8.00

BROTHERS, HANG IN THERE, THE
1979 (49 cents)
Spire Christian Comics (Fleming H. Revell Co.)

nn		.30	.60

BROTHERS OF THE SPEAR (Also see Tarzan)
6/72 - No. 17, 2/76; No. 18, 5/82
Gold Key/Whitman No. 18 on

1	1.00	3.00	6.00
2	.70	2.00	4.00
3-10	.45	1.25	2.50
11-17		.50	1.00
18-Manning-r/No. 2; Leopard Girl-r		.40	.80

NOTE: *Painted-c No. 2-17. Spiegle a-13-17.*

BROTHERS, THE CULT ESCAPE, THE
1980 (49 Cents)
Spire Christian Comics (Fleming H. Revell Co.)

nn		.30	.60

BROWNIES (See 4-Color No. 192, 244, 293, 337, 365, 398, 436, 482, 522, 605 & New Funnies)

BRUCE GENTRY
Jan., 1948 - No. 2, Nov, 1948; No. 3, Jan, 1949 - No. 8, July, 1949
Better/Standard/Four Star Publ./Superior No. 3

1-Ray Bailey strip reprints begin, end #3; E. C. emblem appears as a monogram on stationery in story; negligee panels	20.00	60.00	140.00
2,3	13.00	40.00	90.00
4-8	10.00	30.00	70.00

NOTE: *Kamenish a-2-7; c-1-8.*

BRUTE, THE
Feb, 1975 - No. 3, July, 1975
Seaboard Publ. (Atlas)

1-Origin & 1st app; Sekowsky-a		.40	.80
2,3: 2-Sekowsky-a		.25	.50

BUCCANEER
No date (1963)
I. W. Enterprises

I.W. Reprint #1(r-/Quality #20), #8(r-/#23): Crandall-a in each			
	1.15	3.50	8.00
Super Reprint #12('64, r-/#21)-Crandall-a	1.15	3.50	8.00

BUCCANEERS (Formerly Kid Eternity)
No. 19, Jan, 1950 - No. 27, May, 1951 (No. 24-27: 52 pages)
Quality Comics Group

	Good	Fine	N-Mint
19-Captain Daring, Black Roger, Eric Falcon & Spanish Main begin; Crandall-a	22.00	65.00	154.00
20,23-Crandall-a	16.00	48.00	110.00
21-Crandall c/a	20.00	60.00	140.00
22-Bondage-c	11.50	34.00	80.00
24,26: 24-Adam Peril, U.S.N. begins; last Spanish Main	10.00	30.00	70.00
25-Origin & 1st app. Corsair Queen	10.00	30.00	70.00
27-Crandall c/a	17.00	51.00	120.00

BUCCANEERS, THE (See 4-Color No. 800)

BUCKAROO BANZAI
Dec, 1984 - No. 2, Feb, 1985
Marvel Comics Group

1,2-r/Marvel Super Special		.40	.80

BUCK DUCK
June, 1953 - No. 4, Dec, 1953
Atlas Comics (ANC)

1-(funny animal)	3.00	9.00	21.00
2-4-(funny animal) 2-Ed Win-a(5)	1.70	5.00	12.00

BUCK JONES (Also see Crackajack Funnies & Master Comics #7)
No. 299, Oct, 1950 - No. 850, Oct, 1957 (All Painted-c)
Dell Publishing Co.

4-Color 299(#1)-Buck Jones & his horse Silver-B begin; painted back-c begins, ends #5	8.50	25.50	60.00
2(4-6/51)	4.50	14.00	32.00
3-8(10-12/52)	3.50	10.50	24.00
4-Color 460,500,546,589	3.50	10.50	24.00
4-Color 652,733,850	2.30	7.00	16.00

BUCK ROGERS (In the 25th Century)
1933 (36 pages in color) (6x8'')
Kelloggs Corn Flakes Giveaway

370A-By Phil Nowlan & Dick Calkins; 1st Buck Rogers radio premium (tells origin)	25.00	75.00	175.00

BUCK ROGERS (Also see Famous Funnies, Pure Oil Comics, Salerno Carnival of Comics, 24 Pages of Comics, & Vicks Comics)
Winter, 1940-41 - No. 6, Sept, 1943
Famous Funnies

1-Sunday strip reprints by Rick Yager; begins with strip #190; Calkins-c	121.00	365.00	850.00
2 (7/41)-Calkins-c	72.00	215.00	500.00
3 (12/41), 4 (7/42)	57.00	170.00	400.00
5-Story continues with Famous Funnies No. 80; ½ Buck Rogers, ½ Sky Roads	51.00	152.00	360.00
6-Reprints of 1939 dailies; contains B.R. story ''Crater of Doom'' (2 pgs.) by Calkins not reprinted from Famous Funnies	51.00	152.00	360.00

BUCK ROGERS
No. 100, Jan, 1951 - No. 9, May-June, 1951
Toby Press

100(7)	14.00	42.00	100.00
101(8), 9-All Anderson-a('47-'49-r/dailies)	11.50	34.00	80.00

BUCK ROGERS (. . . in the 25th Century No. 5 on) (TV)
10/64; No. 2, 7/79 - No. 16, 5/82 (no No. 10)
Gold Key/Whitman No. 7 on

1(10128-410)	2.65	8.00	18.00
2(8/79)-Movie adaptation	.35	1.00	2.00
3-9,11-16: 3,4-Movie adaptation; 5-new stories		.50	1.00
Giant Movie Edition 11296(64pp, Whitman, $1.50), reprints GK No.			

Buddies In The U.S. Army #1, © AVON

Buffalo Bill, Jr. #12, © Tie-Ups Co.

Bugs Bunny #29, © Warner Bros.

	Good	Fine	N-Mint
BUCK ROGERS (continued)			
2-4 minus cover; tabloid size	.35	1.00	2.00
Giant Movie Edition 02489(Western/Marvel, $1.50), reprints GK No.			
2-4 minus cover	.35	1.00	2.00

NOTE: *Bolle* a-2p-4p, Movie Ed.(p). *McWilliams* a-2i-4i, 5-11, Movie Ed.(i). Painted-c No. 1-13.

BUCKSKIN (Movie) (See 4-Color No. 1011,1107)

BUCKY O'HARE (Graphic Novel)
1988 ($5.95, color)
Continuity Comics

	Good	Fine	N-Mint
1-Michael Golden-c/a; funny animal	1.00	3.00	5.95

BUDDIES IN THE U.S. ARMY
Nov, 1952 - No. 2, 1953
Avon Periodicals

1-Lawrence-c	6.50	19.50	45.00
2-Mort Lawrence c/a	4.60	14.00	32.00

BUDDY TUCKER & HIS FRIENDS
1906 (11x17'') (In color)
Cupples & Leon Co.

1905 Sunday strip reprints by R. F. Outcault	20.00	60.00	140.00

BUFFALO BEE (See 4-Color No. 957,1002,1061)

BUFFALO BILL (Also see Frontier Fighters, Super Western Comics & Western Action Thrillers)
No. 2, Oct, 1950 - No. 9, Dec, 1951
Youthful Magazines

2	3.50	10.50	24.00
3-9: 3,4-Walter Johnson c/a	1.70	5.00	12.00

BUFFALO BILL CODY (See Cody of the Pony Express)

BUFFALO BILL, JR. (TV) (See Western Roundup under Dell Giants)
Jan, 1956 - No. 13, Aug-Oct, 1959; 1965 (All photo-c)
Dell Publishing Co./Gold Key

4-Color 673 (#1)	3.70	11.00	26.00
4-Color 742,766,798,828,856(11/57)	2.65	8.00	18.00
7(2-4/58)-13	2.00	6.00	14.00
1(6/65-Gold Key)	1.30	4.00	9.00

BUFFALO BILL PICTURE STORIES
June-July, 1949 - No. 2, Aug-Sept, 1949
Street & Smith Publications

1,2-Wildey, Powell-a in each	5.00	15.00	35.00

BUFFALO BILL'S PICTURE STORIES
1909 (Soft cardboard cover)
Street & Smith Publications

nn	10.00	30.00	70.00

BUGALOOS (TV)
Sept, 1971 - No. 4, Feb, 1972
Charlton Comics

1-4	.35	1.00	2.00

NOTE: No. 3(1/72) went on sale late in 1972 (after No. 4) with the 1/73 issues.

BUGHOUSE (Satire)
Mar-Apr, 1954 - No. 4, Sept-Oct, 1954
Ajax/Farrell (Excellent Publ.)

V1#1	6.00	18.00	42.00
2-4	3.70	11.00	26.00

BUGHOUSE FABLES
1921 (48 pgs.) (4x4½'') (10 cents)
Embee Distributing Co. (King Features)

1-Barney Google	8.00	24.00	56.00

BUG MOVIES
1931 (52 pages) (B&W)

Dell Publishing Co.

	Good	Fine	N-Mint
Not reprints; Stookie Allen-a	7.00	21.00	50.00

BUGS BUNNY (See Dell Giants for annuals)
1942 - No. 245, 1983
Dell Publishing Co./Gold Key No. 86-218/Whitman No. 219 on
Large Feature Comic 8(1942)-(Rarely found in fine-mint condition)

	56.00	167.00	390.00
4-Color 33 ('43)	32.00	95.00	220.00
4-Color 51	18.50	56.00	130.00
4-Color 88	11.50	34.00	80.00
4-Color 123('46),142,164	6.50	19.50	45.00
4-Color 187,200,217,233	5.50	16.50	38.00
4-Color 250-Used in SOTI, pg. 309	5.50	16.50	38.00
4-Color 266,274,281,289,298('50)	4.30	13.00	30.00
4-Color 307,317(#1),327(#2),338,347,355,366,376,393			
	3.50	10.50	24.00
4-Color 407,420,432	2.30	7.00	16.00
28(12-1/52-53)-30	1.50	4.50	10.00
31-50	.85	2.60	6.00
51-85(7-9/62)	.75	2.25	5.00
86(10/62)-88-Bugs Bunny's Showtime-(80 pgs.)(25 cents)			
	2.00	6.00	16.00
89-100	.70	2.00	4.00
101-120	.40	1.25	2.50
121-140	.35	1.00	2.00
141-170		.60	1.20
171-228,230-245		.30	.60
229-Swipe of Barks story/WDC&S 223		.35	.70

NOTE: Reprints-100, 102, 104, 123, 143, 144, 147, 167, 173, 175-77, 179-85, 187, 190.

...Comic-Go-Round 11196-(224 pgs.)($1.95)(Golden Press, 1979)			
	.40	1.20	2.40
Kite Fun Book ('60,'68)-Giveaway, 16 pgs., 5x7¼''			
	.85	2.60	6.00
Winter Fun 1(12/67-Gold Key)-Giant	1.50	4.50	12.00

BUGS BUNNY (See The Best of ...; Camp Comics; Comic Album #2, 6, 10, 14; Dell Giant #28, 32, 46; Dynabrite; Golden Comics Digest #1, 3, 5, 6, 8, 10, 14, 15, 17, 21, 26, 30, 34, 39, 42, 47; Large Feature Comic 8; Looney Tunes...; March of Comics #44, 59, 75, 83, 97, 115, 132, 149, 160, 179, 188, 201, 220, 231, 245, 259, 273, 287, 301, 315, 329, 343, 363, 367, 380, 392, 403, 415, 428, 440, 452, 464, 476, 487; Puffed Wheat, Story Hour Series #802, Super Book #14, 26; and Whitman Comic Books)

BUGS BUNNY (Puffed Rice Giveaway)
1949 (32 pages each, 3-1/8x6-7/8'')
Quaker Cereals

A1-Traps the Counterfeiters, A2-Aboard Mystery Submarine, A3- Rocket to the Moon, A4-Lion Tamer, A5-Rescues the Beautiful Princess, B1-Buried Treasure, B2-Outwits the Smugglers, B3-Joins the Marines, B4-Meets the Dwarf Ghost, B5-Finds Aladdin's Lamp, C1-Lost in the Frozen North, C2-Secret Agent, C3-Captured by Cannibals, C4-Fights the Man from Mars, C5-And the Haunted Cave

each....	1.70	5.00	10.00

BUGS BUNNY (3-D)
1953 (Pocket size) (15 titles)
Cheerios Giveaway

each....	5.00	15.00	35.00

BUGS BUNNY & PORKY PIG
Sept, 1965 (100 pages; paper cover; giant)
Gold Key

1(30025-509)	2.50	7.50	17.50

BUGS BUNNY'S ALBUM (See 4-Color No. 498,585,647,724)

BUGS BUNNY LIFE STORY ALBUM (See 4-Color No. 838)

BUGS BUNNY MERRY CHRISTMAS (See 4-Color No. 1064)

BULLETMAN (See Fawcett Miniatures, Master Comics, Mighty Midget Comics, Nickel Comics & XMas Comics)
Sum, 1941 - #12, 2/12/43; #14, Spr, 1946 - #16, Fall, 1946 (nn 13)
Fawcett Publications

BULLETMAN (continued)

	Good	Fine	N-Mint
1	142.00	425.00	850.00
2	70.00	210.00	490.00
3	50.00	150.00	350.00
4,5	41.00	124.00	290.00

6-10: 7-Ghost Stories as told by the night watchman of the cemetery begins; Eisnerish-a | 36.00 | 107.00 | 250.00

11,12,14-16 (nn 13)	30.00	90.00	210.00

...Well Known Comics (1942)-Paper-c, glued binding; printed in red (Bestmaid/Samuel Lowe giveaway) | 12.00 | 36.00 | 72.00

NOTE: *Mac Raboy c-1-3,5,10.*

BULLS-EYE (Cody of The Pony Express No. 8 on)
7-8/54 - No. 5, 3-4/55; No. 6, 6/55; No. 7, 8/55
Mainline No. 1-5/Charlton No. 6,7

1-S&K-c, 2 pages	23.00	70.00	160.00
2-S&K c/a	21.50	64.00	150.00
3-5-S&K c/a(2)	14.00	43.00	100.00
6-S&K c/a	11.50	34.00	80.00
7-S&K c/a(3)	14.00	43.00	100.00

Great Scott Shoe Store giveaway-Reprints #2 with new cover | 8.50 | 25.50 | 60.00

BULLS-EYE COMICS
No. 11, 1944
Harry 'A' Chesler

11-Origin K-9, Green Knight's sidekick, Lance; The Green Knight, Lady Satan, Yankee Doodle Jones app. | 13.00 | 40.00 | 90.00

BULLWHIP GRIFFIN (See Movie Comics)

BULLWINKLE (TV) (...and Rocky No. 20 on; See March of Comics No. 233, and Rocky & Bullwinkle)
3-5/62 - No. 11, 4/74; No. 12, 6/76 - No. 19, 3/78; No. 20, 4/79 - No. 25, 2/80 (Jay Ward)
Dell/Gold Key

4-Color 1270 (3-5/62)	7.00	21.00	50.00
01-090-209 (Dell, 7-9/62)	7.00	21.00	50.00
1(11/62, Gold Key)	5.00	15.00	35.00
2(2/63)	4.00	12.00	28.00
3(4/72)-11(4/74-Gold Key)	1.15	3.50	8.00
12(6/76)-reprints	.70	2.00	4.00
13(9/76), 14-new stories	.85	2.60	6.00
15-25	.70	2.00	4.00

Mother Moose Nursery Pomes 01-530-207 (5-7/62-Dell) | 5.00 | 15.00 | 35.00

NOTE: *Reprints-6, 7, 20-24.*

BULLWINKLE (...& Rocky No. 2 on)(TV)
July, 1970 - No. 7, July, 1971
Charlton Comics

1	1.50	4.50	10.00
2-7	.85	2.60	6.00

BULLWINKLE AND ROCKY
Nov., 1987 - No. 9, Mar, 1989
Star Comics/Marvel Comics No. 3 on

1-9		.50	1.00

BULLWINKLE AND ROCKY IN 3-D (See Blackthorne 3-D Series #18)

BULLWINKLE FOR PRESIDENT IN 3-D (See Blackthorne 3-D Series #50)

BUNNY (Also see Rock Happening)
Dec, 1966 - No. 20, Dec, 1971; No. 21, Nov, 1976
Harvey Publications

1: 68 pg. Giant	2.00	4.00	8.00
2-18: 68 pg. Giants	1.15	3.50	7.00
19-21: 52 pg. Giants	1.00	3.00	6.00

BURKE'S LAW (TV)
1-3/64; No. 2, 5-7/64; No. 3, 3-5/65 (Gene Barry photo-c, all)
Dell Publishing Co.

	Good	Fine	N-Mint
1-Photo-c	2.30	7.00	16.00
2,3-Photo-c	1.50	4.50	10.00

BURNING ROMANCES (See Fox Giants)

BUSTER BEAR
Dec, 1953 - No. 10, June, 1955
Quality Comics Group (Arnold Publ.)

1-Funny animal	2.65	8.00	18.00
2	1.30	4.00	9.00
3-10	.85	2.50	6.00

I.W. Reprint #9,10 (Super on inside) | .50 | 1.50 | 3.00

BUSTER BROWN
1903 - 1916 (11x17") strip reprints in color
Frederick A. Stokes Co.

	Good	Fine	VF
...& His Resolutions (1903) by R. F. Outcault	42.00	125.00	295.00
...Abroad (1904)-86 pgs.; hardback; 8x10¼"; B&W; by R. F. Outcault(76pgs.)	34.00	100.00	240.00
...His Dog Tige & Their Troubles (1904)	34.00	100.00	240.00
...Pranks (1905)	34.00	100.00	240.00
...Antics (1906)-11x17", 30 pages color strip reprints	34.00	100.00	240.00
...And Company (1906)-11x17" in color	34.00	100.00	240.00
...Mary Jane & Tige (1906)	34.00	100.00	240.00
...My Resolutions (1906)-68 pgs.; B&W; hardcover; Sunday panel reprints	34.00	100.00	240.00
Collection of Buster Brown Comics (1908)	34.00	100.00	240.00
Buster Brown Up to Date (1910)	34.00	100.00	240.00
...The Fun Maker (1912)	34.00	100.00	240.00
...The Little Rogue (1916)(10x15¾," 62pp, in color)	25.00	75.00	175.00

NOTE: *Rarely found in fine or mint condition.*

BUSTER BROWN
1906 - 1917 (11x17") strip reprints in color
Cupples & Leon Co./N. Y. Herald Co.

	Good	Fine	VF
(By R. F. Outcault)			
...His Dog Tige & Their Jolly Times (1906)	32.00	95.00	225.00
...Latest Frolics (1906), 58 pgs.	28.00	84.00	195.00
...Amusing Capers (1908)	28.00	84.00	195.00
...And His Pets (1909)	28.00	84.00	195.00
...On His Travels (1910)	28.00	84.00	195.00
...Happy Days (1911)	28.00	84.00	195.00
...In Foreign Lands (1912)	26.00	78.00	180.00
...And the Cat (1917)	25.00	75.00	175.00

NOTE: *Rarely found in fine or mint condition.*

BUSTER BROWN COMICS (Also see My Dog Tige)
1945 - No. 43, 1959 (No. 5: paper cover)
Brown Shoe Co.

	Good	Fine	N-Mint
nn, nd (#1)	9.30	28.00	65.00
2	4.50	14.00	32.00
3-10	2.30	7.00	16.00
11-20	1.85	5.50	13.00
21-24,26-28	1.50	4.50	10.00
25,31,33-37,40-43-Crandall-a in all	3.65	11.00	25.00
29,30,32-"Interplanetary Police Vs. the Space Siren" by Crandall	3.65	11.00	25.00
38,39	1.15	3.50	8.00
...Goes to Mars (2/58-Western Printing), slick-c, 20 pgs., reg. size	2.30	7.00	16.00
...In "Buster Makes the Team!" (1959-Custom Comics)	1.15	3.50	8.00

Bulletman #6, © FAW

Bullwinkle #1 (11/62), © Jay Ward Prod.

Buster Bear #1, © QUA

Buster Crabbe #4, © FF

Buz Sawyer #1, © STD

Calling All Girls #40, © PMI

	Good	Fine	N-Mint
BUSTER BROWN COMICS (continued)			
. . . In The Jet Age ('50s), slick-c, 20 pgs., 5x7¼''			
	2.00	6.00	14.00
. . .Of the Safety Patrol ('60-Custom Comics)	1.15	3.50	8.00
. . .Out of This World ('59-Custom Comics)	1.15	3.50	8.00
. . .Safety Coloring Book (1958)-Slick paper, 16 pages			
	1.15	3.50	8.00

BUSTER BUNNY
Nov, 1949 - No. 16, Oct, 1953
Standard Comics(Animated Cartoons)/Pines

	Good	Fine	N-Mint
1-Frazetta 1 pg. text illo.	3.50	10.50	24.00
2	1.70	5.00	12.00
3-16	1.00	3.00	7.00

BUSTER CRABBE (TV)
Nov, 1951 - No. 12, 1953
Famous Funnies

	Good	Fine	N-Mint
1-Frazetta drug pusher back-c	16.50	50.00	115.00
2-Williamson/Evans-c	20.00	60.00	140.00
3-Williamson/Evans c/a	22.00	65.00	154.00
4-Frazetta c/a, 1pg.; bondage-c	26.00	78.00	180.00
5-Frazetta-c; Williamson/Krenkel/Orlando-a, 11pgs. (per Mr.			
Williamson)	85.00	255.00	600.00
6,8,10-12	4.50	14.00	32.00
7,9-One pg. of Frazetta in each	5.00	15.00	35.00

BUSTER CRABBE (The Amazing Adventures of. .)
Dec, 1953 - No. 4, June, 1954
Lev Gleason Publications

	Good	Fine	N-Mint
1	7.00	21.00	50.00
2,3-Toth-a	10.00	30.00	70.00
4-Flash Gordon-c	7.00	21.00	50.00

BUTCH CASSIDY
June, 1971 - No. 3, Oct, 1971 (52 pages)
Skywald Comics

	Good	Fine	N-Mint
1-Red Mask reprint, retitled Maverick; Bolle-a	.40	.80	
2-Whip Wilson reprint	.30	.60	
3-Dead Canyon Days reprint/Crack Western No. 63; Sundance Kid			
app.; Crandall-a	.30	.60	

BUTCH CASSIDY (. . .& the Wild Bunch)
1951
Avon Periodicals

	Good	Fine	N-Mint
1-Kinstler c/a	9.00	27.00	62.00

NOTE: *Reinman* story; Issue No. on inside spine.

BUTCH CASSIDY (See Fun-In No. 11 & Western Adventure Comics)

BUZ SAWYER
June, 1948 - No. 5, 1949
Standard Comics

	Good	Fine	N-Mint
1-Roy Crane-a	8.50	25.50	60.00
2-Intro his pal Sweeney	5.50	16.50	38.00
3-5	4.30	13.00	30.00

BUZ SAWYER'S PAL, ROSCOE SWEENEY (See Sweeney)

BUZZY (See All Funny Comics)
Winter, 1944-45 - No. 75, 1-2/57; No. 76, 10/57; No. 77, 10/58
National Periodical Publications/Detective Comics

	Good	Fine	N-Mint
1 (52 pgs. begin)	14.00	42.00	100.00
2	7.00	21.00	50.00
3-5	4.35	13.00	30.00
6-10	2.80	8.60	20.00
11-20	2.15	6.50	15.00
21-30	1.70	5.00	12.00
31,35-38	1.30	4.00	9.00

32-34,39-Last 52 pgs. Scribbly by Mayer in all (These four stories

	Good	Fine	N-Mint
were done for Scribbly #14 which was delayed for a year)			
	1.50	4.50	10.00
40-77: 62-Last precode (2/55)	1.00	3.00	7.00

BUZZY THE CROW (See Harvey Hits #18 & Paramount Animated Comics #1)

CADET GRAY OF WEST POINT (See Dell Giants)

CAIN'S HUNDRED (TV)
May-July, 1962 - No. 2, Sept-Nov, 1962
Dell Publishing Co.

	Good	Fine	N-Mint
nn(01-094-207)	1.70	5.00	12.00
2	1.15	3.50	8.00

CALIFORNIA GIRLS
June, 1987 - No. 8, May, 1988 ($2.00, B&W, 40pgs)
Eclipse Comics

	Good	Fine	N-Mint
1-8: All contain color paper dolls	.35	1.00	2.00

CALIFORNIA RAISINS IN 3-D, THE (See Blackthorne 3-D Series #31,44,46)

CALL FROM CHRIST
1952 (36 pages) (Giveaway)
Catechetical Educational Society

	Good	Fine	N-Mint
nn	1.50	4.50	10.00

CALLING ALL BOYS (Tex Granger No. 18 on)
Jan, 1946 - No. 17, May, 1948
Parents' Magazine Institute

	Good	Fine	N-Mint
1	3.70	11.00	26.00
2	2.00	6.00	14.00
3-9,11,14-17: 8-Milton Caniff story. 11-Rin Tin Tin photo-c. 14-J. Edgar			
Hoover photo-c	1.50	4.50	10.00
10-Gary Cooper photo-c	2.35	7.00	16.00
12-Bob Hope photo-c	2.65	8.00	18.00
13-Bing Crosby photo-c	2.00	6.00	14.00

CALLING ALL GIRLS
Sept, 1941 - No. 72, April, 1948 (Part magazine, part comic)
Parents' Magazine Institute

	Good	Fine	N-Mint
1	5.70	17.00	40.00
2	2.85	8.50	20.00
3-Shirley Temple photo-c	4.00	12.00	28.00
4-10: 9-Flag-c	1.70	5.00	12.00
11-20: 11-Photo-c	1.30	4.00	9.00
21-39,41-43(10-11/45)-Last issue with comics	.85	2.60	6.00
40-Liz Taylor photo-c	3.00	9.00	21.00
44-51(7/46)-Last comic book size issue	.70	2.00	4.00
52-72	.50	1.50	3.00

NOTE: *Jack Sparling* art in many issues.

CALLING ALL KIDS (Also see True Comics)
Dec-Jan, 1945-46 - No. 26, Aug, 1949
Parents' Magazine Institute

	Good	Fine	N-Mint
1-Funny animal	3.50	10.50	24.00
2	1.70	5.00	12.00
3-10	1.00	3.00	7.00
11-26	.55	1.65	4.00

CALVIN (See Li'l Kids)

CALVIN & THE COLONEL (TV)
No. 1354, 4-6/62 - No. 2, July-Sept, 1962
Dell Publishing Co.

	Good	Fine	N-Mint
4-Color 1354	4.00	12.00	28.00
2	3.00	9.00	21.00

CAMELOT 3000
12/82 - No. 11, 7/84; No. 12, 4/85 (Direct Sale; Mando paper)
DC Comics (Maxi-series)

	Good	Fine	N-Mint
1-12: 5-Intro Knights of New Camelot	.35	1.00	2.00

CAMELOT 3000 (continued)
NOTE: *Austin a-7i-12i.*

CAMERA COMICS
July, 1944 - No. 9, Summer, 1946
U.S. Camera Publishing Corp./ME

	Good	Fine	N-Mint
nn (7/44)	10.00	30.00	70.00
nn (9/44)	7.00	21.00	50.00
1(10/44)-The Grey Comet	7.00	21.00	50.00
2	5.00	15.00	35.00
3-Nazi WW ll-c; ½ photos	4.50	14.00	32.00
4-9: All ½ photos	3.50	10.50	24.00

CAMP COMICS
Feb, 1942 - No. 3, April, 1942 (All have photo-c)
Dell Publishing Co.

	Good	Fine	N-Mint
1-"Seaman Sy Wheeler" by Kelly, 7 pgs.; Bugs Bunny app.	34.00	100.00	235.00
2-Kelly-a, 12 pgs.; Bugs Bunny app.	25.00	75.00	175.00
3-(Scarce)-Kelly-a	34.00	100.00	235.00

CAMP RUNAMUCK (TV)
April, 1966
Dell Publishing Co.

	Good	Fine	N-Mint
1-Photo-c	1.50	4.50	10.00

CAMPUS LOVES
Dec, 1949 - No. 5, Aug, 1950
Quality Comics Group (Comic Magazines)

	Good	Fine	N-Mint
1-Ward c/a, 9 pgs.	14.00	42.00	100.00
2-Ward c/a	11.00	32.00	75.00
3,4	4.60	14.00	32.00
5-Spanking panels (2)	5.00	15.00	35.00

NOTE: *Gustavson a-1-5. Photo-c-3-5.*

CAMPUS ROMANCE (. . .Romances on cover)
Sept-Oct, 1949 - No. 3, Feb-Mar, 1950
Avon Periodicals/Realistic

	Good	Fine	N-Mint
1-Walter Johnson-a; c-/Avon paperback 348	11.00	32.00	75.00
2-Grandenetti-a; c-/Avon paperback 151	8.50	25.50	60.00
3-c-/Avon paperback 201	8.50	25.50	60.00
Realistic reprint	3.50	10.50	24.00

CANADA DRY PREMIUMS (See Swamp Fox, The & Terry & The Pirates)

CANCELLED COMIC CAVALCADE
Summer, 1978 - No. 2, Fall, 1978 (8½x11"); B&W)
(Xeroxed pages on one side only w/blue cover and taped spine)
DC Comics, Inc.

1-(412 pages) Contains xeroxed copies of art for: Black Lightning #12, cover to #13; Claw #13,14; The Deserter #1; Doorway to Nightmare #6; Firestorm #6; The Green Team #2,3.

2-(532 pages) Contains xeroxed copies of art for: Kamandi #60 (including Omac), #61; Prez #5; Shade #9 (including The Odd Man); Showcase #105 (Deadman), 106 (The Creeper); The Vixen #1; and covers to Army at War #2, Battle Classics #3, Demand Classics #1 & 2, Dynamic Classics #3, Mr. Miracle #26, Ragman #6, Weird Mystery #25 & 26, & Western Classics #1 & 2. (Rare)
(One set sold in 1986 for $550.00)
NOTE: In June, 1978, DC cancelled several of their titles. For copyright purposes, the unpublished original art for these titles was xeroxed, bound in the above books, published and distributed. Only 35 copies were made.

CANDID TALES (Also see Bold Stories & It Rhymes With Lust)
April, 1950(?); June, 1950 (Digest size) (144 pages) (Full color)
Kirby Publishing Co.

	Good	Fine	N-Mint
(Scarce) Contains Wood female pirate story, 15 pgs., and 14 pgs. in June issue; Powell-a	35.00	105.00	245.00

NOTE: *Another version exists with Dr. Kilmore by Wood; no female pirate story.*

CANDY
Fall, 1944 - No. 3, Spring, 1945
William H. Wise & Co.

	Good	Fine	N-Mint
1-Two Scoop Scuttle stories by Wolverton	13.00	40.00	90.00
2,3-Scoop Scuttle by Wolverton, 2-4 pgs.	9.50	28.50	65.00

CANDY (Teen-age)
Autumn, 1947 - No. 64, July, 1956
Quality Comics Group (Comic Magazines)

	Good	Fine	N-Mint
1-Gustavson-a	6.50	19.50	45.00
2-Gustavson-a	3.50	10.50	24.00
3-10	2.30	7.00	16.00
11-30	1.50	4.50	10.00
31-63	1.15	3.50	8.00
64-Ward-c(p)?	1.65	5.00	11.50
Super Reprint No. 2,10,12,16,17,18('63-'64)	.70	2.00	4.00

NOTE: *Jack Cole 1-2 pg. art in many issues.*

CANNONBALL COMICS
Feb, 1945 - No. 2, Mar, 1945
Rural Home Publishing Co.

	Good	Fine	N-Mint
1-The Crash Kid, Thunderbrand, The Captive Prince & Crime Crusader begin	23.00	70.00	160.00
2	15.00	45.00	105.00

CANTEEN KATE (Also see All Picture All True Love Story & Fightin' Marines)
June, 1952 - No. 3, Nov, 1952
St. John Publishing Co.

	Good	Fine	N-Mint
1-Matt Baker c/a	24.00	72.00	170.00
2-Matt Baker c/a	20.00	60.00	140.00
3-(Rare)-Used in POP, pg. 75; Baker c/a; transvestism story	26.00	77.00	180.00

CAP'N CRUNCH COMICS (See Quaker Oats)
1963; 1965 (16 pgs.; miniature giveaways; 2½x6½")
Quaker Oats Co.

	Good	Fine	N-Mint
(1963 titles)-"The Picture Pirates," "The Fountain of Youth," "I'm Dreaming of a Wide Isthmus." (1965 titles)-"Bewitched, Betwitched, & Betweaked," Seadog Meets the Witch Doctor" (another 1965 title suspected)	1.30	4.00	8.00

CAP'N QUICK & A FOOZLE
July, 1985 - No. 3, Nov, 1985 ($1.50; Baxter paper)
Eclipse Comics

	Good	Fine	N-Mint
1-3-Rogers c/a	.25	.75	1.50

CAPTAIN ACTION
Oct-Nov, 1968 - No. 5, June-July, 1969
National Periodical Publications

	Good	Fine	N-Mint
1-Origin; Wood-a; based on Ideal toy	1.00	3.00	7.00
2-5: 2,3,5-Kane/Wood-a	.70	2.00	4.00
. . .& Action Boy('67)-Ideal Toy Co. giveaway	1.15	3.50	7.00

CAPTAIN AERO COMICS (Samson No. 1-6; also see Veri Best Sure Fire & Veri Best Sure Shot Comics)
V1No.7(No.1), Dec, 1941 - V2No.4(No.10), Jan, 1943; V3No.9(No.11), Sept, 1943 - V4No.3(No.17), Oct, 1944; No. 21, Dec, 1944 - No. 26, Aug, 1946 (no no. 18-20)
Holyoke Publishing Co.

	Good	Fine	N-Mint
V1#7(#1)-Flag-Man & Solar, Master of Magic, Captain Aero, Cap Stone, Adventurer begin	46.00	140.00	325.00
8(#2)-Pals of Freedom app.	27.00	81.00	190.00
9(#3)-Alias X begins; Pals of Freedom app.	27.00	81.00	190.00
10(#4)-Origin The Gargoyle; Kubert-a	27.00	81.00	190.00
11,12(#5,6)-Kubert-a; Miss Victory app. in #6	23.00	70.00	160.00
V2#1(#7)	13.00	40.00	90.00
2(#8)-Origin The Red Cross; Miss Victory app.	13.00	40.00	90.00

Camp Comics #2, © DELL

Captain Action #1, © DC

Captain Aero V2#3 (#9), © HOKE

Captain America #113, © MEG

Captain America #333, © MEG

Captain America Comics #4, © MEG

CAPTAIN AERO COMICS (continued)

	Good	Fine	N-Mint
3(#9)-Miss Victory app.	10.00	30.00	70.00
4(#10)-Miss Victory app.	8.00	24.00	56.00
V3#9 - V3#13(#11-15): 11,15-Miss Victory app.	6.00	18.00	42.00
V4#2, V4#3(#16,17)	5.00	15.00	35.00
21-24,26-L. B. Cole covers. 22-Intro/origin Mighty Mite			
	7.00	21.00	50.00
25-L. B. Cole S/F-c	8.50	25.50	60.00

NOTE: *Hollingsworth a-23. Infantino a-23.*

CAPTAIN AMERICA (See All-Select, All Winners, Aurora, Avengers #4, The Invaders, Marvel Double Feature, Marvel Fanfare, Marvel Mystery, Marvel Super-Action, Marvel Super Heroes, Marvel Team-Up, Marvel Treasury Special, USA Comics, Young Allies & Young Men)

CAPTAIN AMERICA (Tales of Suspense #1-99; . . .and the Falcon #134-223)
No. 100, April, 1968 - Present
Marvel Comics Group

	Good	Fine	N-Mint
100-Flashback on Cap's revival with Avengers & Sub-Mariner			
	17.00	51.00	120.00
101	3.60	11.00	25.00
102-108	2.65	8.00	18.00
109-Origin Capt. America	2.85	8.50	20.00
110,111,113-Steranko c/a. 110-Rick becomes Cap's partner. 110-Hulk x-over. 111-Death of Steve Rogers. 113-Cap's funeral			
	4.30	13.00	30.00
112-Origin retold	1.50	4.50	10.00
114-120: 117-1st app. The Falcon	1.15	3.50	8.00
121-130: 121-Retells origin	1.00	3.00	6.00
131-139: 133-The Falcon becomes Cap's partner; origin Modok.			
137,138-Spider-Man x-over	1.00	3.00	6.00
140-Origin Grey Gargoyle retold	1.00	3.00	6.00
141-150: 143-(52 pgs.)	.50	1.50	3.00
151-171,176-199: 155-Origin; redrawn with Falcon added. 164-1st app. Nightshade. 176-End of Capt. America	.50	1.50	3.00
172-175-X-Men x-over	1.15	3.50	7.00
180-200: 180-Intro & origin of Nomad. 181-Intro & origin of new Capt. America. 183-Death of New Cap; Nomad becomes Cap. 186-True origin The Falcon	.40	1.25	2.50
201-240,242-246: 244,245-Miller-c	.35	1.00	2.00
241-Punisher app.; Miller-c	3.35	10.00	20.00
247-255-Byrne-a. 255-Origin; Miller-c	.50	1.50	3.00
256-331: 269-1st Team America. 281-1950s Bucky returns. 282-Bucky becomes Nomad. 284-Patriot (Jack Mace) app. 285-Death of Patriot. 298-Origin Red Skull	.30	.90	1.80
332-Old Cap resigns	1.50	4.50	9.00
333-Intro new Captain	1.00	3.00	6.00
334	.70	2.00	4.00
335-340: 339-Fall of the Mutants	.60	1.75	3.50
341-343,345-349	.25	.75	1.50
344-Double size, $1.50	.35	1.00	2.00
350 (68 pgs., $1.75)	.60	1.75	3.50
351-353,355-368: 351-Nick Fury app.	.55	1.10	
354-Return of Steve Rogers (original Cap) to original costume			
	.50	1.50	3.00
. . .& The Campbell Kids (1980, 36pg. giveaway, Campbell's Soup/ U.S. Dept. of Energy)	.35	1.00	2.00
. . .Meets the Asthma Monster (No #, 1987, giveaway, Your Physician and Glaxo, Inc.)		.30	.60
Giant Size 1(12/75)	.70	2.00	4.00
Special 1(1/71), 2(1/72)	1.15	3.50	7.00
Annual 3(4/76), 4(8/77)-Kirby c/a, 5(1981), 6(11/82), 7('83)			
	.30	.85	1.70
Annual 8(9/86)-Wolverine featured	1.00	3.00	6.00

NOTE: *Austin c-225i, 239i, 246i. Buscema a-115p, 217p; c-136p, 217. Byrne part c-223, 238, 239, 247p-54p, 290, 291, 313; a-247-254p, 255, 313p. Colan a(p)-116-137, 256. Annual 5; c(p)-116-123, 126, 129. Everett a-136i, 137i; c-126i. Gil Kane a-145p; c-147p, 149p, 150p, 170p, 172-174, 180, 181p, 183-190p, 215, 216, 220, 221. Kirby a(p)-100-109, 112,*

CAPTAIN AMERICA COMICS
Mar, 1941 - No. 75, Jan, 1950; No. 76, 5/54 - No. 78, 9/54
(No. 74 & 75 titled Capt. America's Weird Tales)
Timely/Marvel Comics (TCI 1-20/CmPS 21-68/MjMC 69-75/Atlas Comics (PrPI 76-78)

	Good	Fine	N-Mint
1-Origin & 1st app. Captain America & Bucky by S&K; Hurricane, Tuk the Caveboy begin by S&K; Red Skull app. Hitler-c			
	1500.00	3750.00	9000.00
(Prices vary widely on this book)			
2-S&K Hurricane; Tuk by Avison (Kirby splash)			
	483.00	1210.00	2900.00
3-Red Skull app; Stan Lee's 1st text	350.00	875.00	2100.00
4	233.00	585.00	1400.00
5	217.00	545.00	1300.00
6-Origin Father Time; Tuk the Caveboy ends			
	183.00	460.00	1100.00
7-Red Skull app	183.00	460.00	1100.00
8-10-Last S&K issue, (S&K centerfold #6-10)			
	150.00	375.00	900.00
11-Last Hurricane, Headline Hunter; Al Avison Captain America begins, ends #20	117.00	295.00	700.00
12-The Imp begins, ends #16; Last Father Time			
	117.00	295.00	700.00
13-Origin The Secret Stamp; classic-c	125.00	315.00	750.00
14,15	117.00	295.00	700.00
16-Red Skull unmasks Cap	125.00	315.00	750.00
17-The Fighting Fool only app.	100.00	250.00	600.00
18,19-Human Torch begins #19	89.00	225.00	535.00
20-Sub-Mariner app.; no H. Torch	89.00	225.00	535.00
21-25: 25-Cap drinks liquid opium	79.00	200.00	475.00
26-30: 27-Last Secret Stamp; last 68 pg. issue? 28-60 pg. issues begin?	71.00	180.00	425.00
31-36,38-40	64.00	160.00	385.00
37-Red Skull app.	67.00	170.00	400.00
41-45,47: 41-Last Jap War-c. 47-Last German War-c			
	56.00	140.00	335.00
46-German Holocaust-c	56.00	140.00	335.00
48-58,60	52.00	130.00	310.00
59-Origin retold	75.00	190.00	450.00
61-Red Skull c/story	67.00	170.00	400.00
62,64,65: 65-"Hey Look" by Kurtzman	52.00	130.00	310.00
63-Intro/origin Asbestos Lady	56.00	140.00	335.00
66-Bucky is shot; Golden Girl teams up with Captain America & learns his i.d; origin Golden Girl	63.00	160.00	380.00
67-Captain America/Golden Girl team-up; Mxyztplk swipe; last Toro in Human Torch	52.00	130.00	310.00
68,70-Sub-Mariner/Namora, and Captain America/Golden Girl team-up in each. 70-Science fiction c/story	52.00	130.00	310.00
69-Human Torch/Sun Girl team-up	52.00	130.00	310.00
71-Anti Wertham editorial; The Witness, Bucky app.			
	52.00	130.00	310.00
72,73	52.00	130.00	310.00
74-(Scarce)(1949)-Titled "C.A.'s Weird Tales;" Red Skull app.			
	81.00	205.00	485.00
75(2/50)-Titled "C.A.'s Weird Tales;" no C.A. app.; horror cover/ stories	55.00	140.00	330.00
76-78(1954); Human Torch/Toro story	35.00	90.00	210.00
132-Pg. Issue (B&W-1942)(Canadian)-Has blank inside-c and back-c			
	233.00	585.00	1400.00
Shoestore Giveaway #77	16.00	48.00	110.00

NOTE: *Bondage c-3, 7, 15, 16, 34, 38. Crandall a-2i, 3i, 9i. 10i. Kirby c-8p. Rico c-70, 71. Romita c-77, 78. Schomburg c-26-29, 31, 33, 37-39, 41-43, 45-54, 58. Shores c-20-25. 30, 32, 34-36, 40, 59, 61-63. S&K c-1, 2, 5-7, 9, 10.*

193-214, 216, Giant Size 1, Special 1, 2(layouts), Annual 3,4; c-100-109, 112, 126p, 193-214. Miller c-241p, 244p, 245p, 255p, Annual No. 5. Mooney a-149i. Morrow a-144. Perez c-243p, 246p. Roussos a-140i, 168i. Starlin/Sinnott c-162. Sutton a-244i. Tuska a-112i, 215p, Special 2. Williamson a-313i. Wood a-127i.

CAPTAIN AMERICA SPECIAL EDITION
Feb, 1984 - No. 2, Mar, 1984 ($2.00; Baxter paper)
Marvel Comics Group

	Good	Fine	N-Mint
1,2-Steranko-c/a(r)	.40	1.25	2.50

CAPTAIN AND THE KIDS, THE (See Famous Comics Cartoon Books)

CAPTAIN AND THE KIDS, THE (See Comics on Parade, Okay Comics & Sparkler Comics)
1938 -12/39; Sum, 1947 - No. 32, 1955; 4-Color No. 881, Feb, 1958
United Features Syndicate/Dell Publ. Co.

Single Series 1('38)	40.00	120.00	280.00
Single Series 1(Reprint)(12/39-"Reprint" on cover)			
	23.00	70.00	160.00
1(Summer, 1947-UFS)	6.00	18.00	42.00
2	3.50	10.50	24.00
3-10	2.15	6.50	15.00
11-20	1.60	4.70	11.00
21-32(1955)	1.30	4.00	9.00
50th Anniversary issue('48)-Contains a 2 page history of the strip, including an account of the famous Supreme Court decision allowing both Pulitzer & Hearst to run the same strip under different names	3.50	10.50	24.00
Special Summer issue, Fall issue (1948)	2.65	8.00	18.00
4-Color 881 (Dell)	1.60	4.70	11.00

CAPTAIN ATOM
1950 - No. 7, 1951 (5x7¼") (5 cents, 52 pgs.)
Nationwide Publishers

1-Sci/fic	5.00	15.00	35.00
2-7	3.50	10.50	24.00

CAPTAIN ATOM (Formerly Strange Suspense Stories No. 77)
No. 78, Dec, 1965 - No. 89, Dec, 1967 (Also see Space Adventures)
Charlton Comics

78-Origin retold	3.60	11.00	25.00
79-82: 82-Intro. Nightshade	2.65	8.00	18.00
83-86: Ted Kord Blue Beetle in all	2.00	6.00	14.00
87-89-Nightshade by Aparo in all	2.00	6.00	14.00
83-85(Modern Comics-1977)-reprints	.15		.30

NOTE: Aparo a-87-89. Ditko c/a(p) 78-89. #90 only published in fanzine 'The Charlton Bullseye' #1, 2.

CAPTAIN ATOM (Also see Americomics & Crisis On Infinite Earths)
March, 1987 - Present (Direct sale only #35 on)
DC Comics

1-(44 pgs., $1.00)-Origin/1st app. with new costume			
	.35	1.00	2.00
2-10: 5-Firestorm x-over. 6-Intro. new Dr. Spectro			
		.60	1.20
11-16: 11-Millennium tie-in. 14-Nightshade app. 16-Justice League app. 20-Blue Beetle x-over		.60	1.20
17-38: 17-$1.00-c begin; Justice League app.		.60	1.20
Annual 1 (3/88, $1.25)-Intro Major Force	.25	.75	1.50
Annual 2 (12/88, $1.50)	.25	.75	1.50

CAPTAIN BATTLE (Boy No. 3 on) (See Silver Streak Comics)
Summer, 1941 - No. 2, Fall, 1941
New Friday Publ./Comic House

1-Origin Blackout by Rico; Captain Battle begins			
	50.00	150.00	350.00
2	30.00	90.00	210.00

CAPTAIN BATTLE (2nd Series)
No. 3, Wint, 1942-43 - No. 5, Sum, 1943 (#3: 52pgs., nd)(#5: 68pgs.)
Magazine Press/Picture Scoop No. 5

3-Origin Silver Streak-r/SS#3; Origin Lance Hale-r/Silver Streak; Simon-a(r)	25.00	75.00	175.00
4	18.00	54.00	125.00

	Good	Fine	N-Mint
5-Origin Blackout retold	18.00	54.00	125.00

CAPTAIN BATTLE, JR.
Fall, 1943 - No. 2, Winter, 1943-44
Comic House (Lev Gleason)

1-The Claw vs. The Ghost	40.00	120.00	280.00
2-Wolverton's Scoop Scuttle; Don Rico-c/a; The Green Claw story			
	34.00	100.00	235.00

CAPTAIN BRITAIN (Also see Marvel Team-Up No. 65,66)
Oct. 13, 1976 - No. 39, July 6, 1977 (Weekly)
Marvel Comics International

1-Origin; with Capt. Britain's face mask inside	.85	2.50	5.00
2-Origin, conclusion; Capt. Britain's Boomerang inside			
	.60	1.80	3.60
3-Vs. Bank Robbers	.35	1.00	2.00
4-7-Vs. Hurricane	.35	1.00	2.00
8-Vs. Bank Robbers	.35	1.00	2.00
9-13-Vs. Dr. Synne	.30	.90	1.80
14,15-Vs. Mastermind	.30	.90	1.80
16-20-With Capt. America; 17 misprinted & color section reprinted in No. 18	.30	.90	1.80
21-23,25,26-With Capt. America	.30	.90	1.80
24-With C.B.'s Jet Plane inside	.60	1.80	3.60
27-Origin retold	.30	.90	1.80
28-32-Vs. Lord Hawk	.25	.75	1.50
33-35-More on origin	.30	.90	1.80
36-Star Sceptre	.25	.75	1.50
37-39-Vs. Highwayman & Manipulator	.25	.75	1.50
Annual(1978,Hardback,64pgs.)-Reprints No. 1-7 with pin-ups of Marvel characters	1.35	4.00	8.00
Summer Special (1980, 52pp)-Reprints	.35	1.00	2.00

NOTE: No. 1,2, & 24 are rarer in mint due to inserts. Distributed in Great Britain only. Nick Fury-r by Steranko in 1-20, 24-31, 35-37. Fantastic Four-r by J. Buscema in all. New Buscema-a in 24-30. Story from No. 39 continues in Super Spider-Man (British weekly) No. 231-247. Following cancellation of his series, new Captain Britain stories appeared in "Super Spider-Man" (British weekly) No. 231-247. Captain Britain stories which appear in Super-Spider-Man No. 248-253 are reprints of Marvel Team-Up No. 65&66. Capt. Britain strips also appeared in Hulk Comic (weekly) 1, 3-30, 42-55, 57-60, in Marvel Superheroes (monthly) 377-388, in Daredevils (monthly) 1-11, Mighty World of Marvel (monthly) 7-16 & Captain Britain (monthly) 1-present.

CAPTAIN CANUCK
7/75 - No. 4, 7/77; No. 4, 7-8/79 - No. 14, 3-4/81
Comely Comix (Canada) (All distr. in U. S.)

1-1st app. Bluefox	.40	1.25	2.50
2-1st app. Dr. Walker, Redcoat & Kebec	.30	.90	1.80
3(5/7-5/76)-1st app. Heather	.30	.90	1.80
4(1st printing-2/77)-10x14½"; (5.00); B&W; 300 copies serially numbered and signed with one certificate of authenticity	5.00	15.00	30.00
4(2nd printing-7/77)-11x17", B&W; only 15 copies printed; signed by creator Richard Comely, serially #'d and two certificates of authenticity inserted; orange cardboard covers (Very Rare)	8.00	25.00	50.00
4(7-8/79)-1st app. Tom Evans & Mr. Gold; origin The Catman		.40	.80
5-Origin Capt. Canuck's powers; 1st app. Earth Patrol & Chaos Corps		.40	.80
6-14: 8-Jonn 'The Final Chapter'. 9-1st World Beyond. 11-1st 'Chariots of Fire' story		.40	.80
Summer Special 1(7-9/80, 95 cents, 64pgs.)		.50	1.00

NOTE: 30,000 copies of No. 2 were destroyed in Winnipeg.

CAPTAIN CARROT AND HIS AMAZING ZOO CREW
March, 1982 - No. 20, Nov, 1983 (Also see New Teen Titans)
DC Comics

1-Superman app.		.30	.60

The Captain And The Kids #16, © UFS

Captain Atom #78 (12/65), © DC

Captain Battle, Jr. #2, © LEV

Captain Fearless Comics #1, © HOKE

Captain Fleet #1, © Z-D

Captain Gallant #1, © CC

CAPTAIN CARROT (continued)

	Good	Fine	N-Mint
2-20: 3-Re-intro Dodo & The Frog. 9-Re-intro Three Mouseketeers, the Terrific Whatzit. 10,11- Pig Iron reverts back to Peter Porkchops. 20-The Changeling app.		.30	.60

CAPTAIN CARVEL AND HIS CARVEL CRUSADERS (See Carvel Comics)

CAPTAIN COURAGEOUS COMICS (Banner No. 3-5)
No. 6, March, 1942
Periodical House (Ace Magazines)

	Good	Fine	N-Mint
6-Origin & 1st app. The Sword; Lone Warrior, Capt. Courageous app.	37.00	110.00	255.00

CAPT'N CRUNCH COMICS (See Cap'n. . . .)

CAPTAIN DAVY JONES (See 4-Color No. 598)

CAPTAIN EASY (See The Funnies & Red Ryder #3-32)
1939 - No. 17, Sept, 1949; April, 1956
Hawley/Dell Publ./Standard(Visual Editions)/Argo

	Good	Fine	N-Mint
Hawley(1939)-Contains reprints from The Funnies & 1938 Sunday strips by Roy Crane	32.00	95.00	225.00
4-Color 24 (1943)	21.00	62.00	145.00
4-Color 111(6/46)	8.50	25.50	60.00
10(Standard-10/47)	4.00	12.00	28.00
11-17: All contain 1930's & '40's strip-r	2.85	8.50	20.00
Argo 1(4/56)-(r)	2.65	8.00	18.00
NOTE: *Schomburg c-13, 16.*

CAPTAIN EASY & WASH TUBBS (See Famous Comics Cartoon Books)

CAPTAIN ELECTRON
Aug, 1986 ($2.25, color)
Brick Computer Science Institute

	Good	Fine	N-Mint
1-Disbrow-a	.35	1.10	2.25

CAPTAIN EO 3-D (Disney)
July, 1987 (Eclipse 3-D Special #18, $3.50, Baxter)
Eclipse Comics

	Good	Fine	N-Mint
1-Adapts 3-D movie	.60	1.75	3.50
1-2-D limited edition	.85	2.50	5.00
1-Large size (11x17", 8/87)-Sold only at Disney Theme parks ($6.95)	1.20	3.50	7.00

CAPTAIN FEARLESS COMICS (Also see Holyoke One-Shot #6, Old Glory Comics & Silver Streak #1)
August, 1941 - No. 2, Sept, 1941
Helnit Publishing Co. (Holyoke Publishing Co.)

	Good	Fine	N-Mint
1-Origin Mr. Miracle, Alias X, Captain Fearless, Citizen Smith Son of the Unknown Soldier; Miss Victory begins	31.00	92.00	215.00
2-Grit Grady, Captain Stone app.	18.00	54.00	125.00

CAPTAIN FLASH
Nov, 1954 - No. 4, July, 1955
Sterling Comics

	Good	Fine	N-Mint
1-Origin; Sekowsky-a; Tomboy (female super hero) begins; Last pre-code ish	11.50	34.00	80.00
2-4	6.50	19.50	45.00

CAPTAIN FLEET
Fall, 1952
Ziff-Davis Publishing Co.

	Good	Fine	N-Mint
1-Painted-c	6.00	18.00	42.00

CAPTAIN FLIGHT COMICS
Mar, 1944 - No. 10, Dec, 1945; No. 11, Feb-Mar, 1947
Four Star Publications

	Good	Fine	N-Mint
nn	10.00	30.00	70.00
2	5.50	16.50	38.00
3,4: 4-Rock Raymond begins, ends #7	4.30	13.00	30.00
5-Bondage, torture-c; Red Rocket begins; the Grenade app.			

	Good	Fine	N-Mint
	6.50	19.50	45.00
6,7	5.50	16.50	38.00
8-Yankee Girl, Black Cobra begin; intro. Cobra Kid	8.50	25.50	60.00
9-Torpedoman app.; last Yankee Girl; Kinstler-a	8.50	25.50	60.00
10-Deep Sea Dawson, Zoom of the Jungle, Rock Raymond, Red Rocket, & Black Cobra app; L. B. Cole bondage-c	8.50	25.50	60.00
11-Torpedoman, Blue Flame app.; last Black Cobra, Red Rocket; L. B. Cole-c	8.50	25.50	60.00
NOTE: *L. B. Cole c-7-11.*

CAPTAIN FORTUNE PRESENTS
1955 - 1959 (16 pages; 3¼x6-7/8") (Giveaway)
Vital Publications

	Good	Fine	N-Mint
"Davy Crockett in Episodes of the Creek War," "Davy Crockett at the Alamo," "In Sherwood Forest Tells Strange Tales of Robin Hood" ('57), "Meets Bolivar the Liberator"('59), "Tells How Buffalo Bill Fights the Dog Soldiers"('57), "Young Davy Crockett"	.85	2.50	5.00

CAPTAIN GALLANT (. . .of the Foreign Legion) (TV)
(Texas Rangers in Action No. 5 on?)
1955; No. 2, Jan, 1956 - No. 4, Sept, 1956
Charlton Comics

	Good	Fine	N-Mint
Heinz Foods Premium (#1?)(1955; regular size)-U.S. Pictorial; contains Buster Crabbe photos; Don Heck-a	4.00	12.00	28.00
Non-Heinz version (same as above except pictures of show replaces ads) (#1)-Buster Crabbe photo on-c	4.00	12.00	28.00
2-4: Buster Crabbe in all	3.00	9.00	21.00

CAPTAIN HERO (See Jughead as. . .)

CAPTAIN HERO COMICS DIGEST MAGAZINE
Sept, 1981
Archie Publications

	Good	Fine	N-Mint
1-Reprints of Jughead as Super-Guy		.30	.60

CAPTAIN HOBBY COMICS
Feb, 1948 (Canadian)
Export Publication Ent. Ltd. (Dist. in U.S. by Kable News Co.)

	Good	Fine	N-Mint
1	2.65	8.00	18.00

CAPT. HOLO IN 3-D (See Blackthorne 3-D Series #5)

CAPTAIN HOOK & PETER PAN (See 4-Color No. 446 and Peter Pan)

CAPTAIN JET (Fantastic Fears No. 7 on)
May, 1952 - No. 5, Jan, 1953
Four Star Publ./Farrell/Comic Media

	Good	Fine	N-Mint
1-Bakerish-a	6.50	19.50	45.00
2	3.70	11.00	26.00
3-5,6(?)	2.65	8.00	18.00

CAPTAIN JUSTICE
March, 1988 - No. 2, April, 1988
Marvel Comics

	Good	Fine	N-Mint
1,2-Based on TV series, True Colors		.65	1.30

CAPTAIN KANGAROO (See 4-Color No. 721,780,872)

CAPTAIN KIDD (Formerly Dagar; My Secret Story #26 on)(Also see Comic Comics & Fantastic Comics)
No. 24, June, 1949 - No. 25, Aug, 1949
Fox Feature Syndicate

	Good	Fine	N-Mint
24,25	6.50	19.50	45.00

CAPTAIN MARVEL (See All Hero, All-New Collectors' Ed., America's Greatest, Fawcett Min., Gift, Legends, Limited Collectors' Ed., Marvel Family, Master No. 21, Mighty Midget Comics, Shazam, Special Edition Comics, Whiz, Wisco, and XMas)

CAPTAIN MARVEL (. . . Presents the Terrible 5 No. 5)
April, 1966 - No. 4, Nov, 1966 (25 cent Giants)
M. F. Enterprises

	Good	Fine	N-Mint
nn-(#1 on pg. 5)-Origin; created by Carl Burgos	.85	2.50	5.00
2,4	.50	1.50	3.00
3-(#3 on page 4)-Fights the Bat	.50	1.50	3.00

CAPTAIN MARVEL (See Life Of . . ., Marvel Graphic Novel, Marvel
Spotlight & Marvel Super-Heroes #12)
May, 1968 - No. 19, Dec, 1969; No. 20, June, 1970 - No. 21, Aug,
1970; No. 22, Sept, 1972 - No. 62, May, 1979
Marvel Comics Group

	Good	Fine	N-Mint
1	7.00	21.00	50.00
2	1.70	5.00	12.00
3-5	1.50	4.50	10.00
6-10	.85	2.50	5.00
11-Smith/Trimpe-c; Death of Una	.85	2.50	5.00
12-24; 17-New costume	.60	1.80	3.60
25-Starlin c/a	1.35	4.00	8.00
26-Starlin c/a	1.00	3.00	6.00
27-34-Starlin c/a. 29-C.M. gains more powers. 34-C.M. contracts			
cancer which eventually kills him	.75	2.25	4.50
35-62: 36-Origin recap; Starlin-a (3 pgs.). 39-Origin Watcher. 41,43-			
Wrightson part inks; #43-c(i)		.50	1.00
Giant-Size 1 (12/75)	.50	1.50	3.00
Special 1 (11/89, $1.50, one-shot)-Bolle-a	.25	.75	1.50

NOTE: Alcala a-35. Austin a-46i, 49-53i; c-52i. Buscema a-18p-21p. Colan a(p)-1-4;
c(p)-1-4, 8, 9. Heck a-5p-10p, 16p. Gil Kane a-17p-21p, Gnt-Size 1p; c-17p-24p, 37p, 53.
McWilliams a-40i.

CAPTAIN MARVEL
Nov, 1989 ($1.50, color, one-shot, 52 pgs.)
Marvel Comics

	Good	Fine	N-Mint
1-Super-hero from Avengers; new powers	.25	.75	1.50

CAPTAIN MARVEL ADVENTURES (See Special Edition Comics for
pre-No. 1)
1941 - No. 150, Nov, 1953
Fawcett Publications

	Good	Fine	VF-NM
nn(#1)-Captain Marvel & Sivana by Jack Kirby. The cover was			
printed on unstable paper stock and is rarely found in Fine or			
Mint condition; blank inside-c	1167.00	2925.00	7000.00
(Prices vary widely on this book)			

	Good	Fine	N-Mint
2-(Advertised as #3, which was counting Special Edition Comics			
as the real #1); Tuska-a	157.00	470.00	1100.00
3-Metallic silver-c	81.00	245.00	570.00
4-Three Lt. Marvels app.	59.00	178.00	415.00
5	51.00	152.00	355.00
6-10	39.00	118.00	275.00
11-15: 13-Two-pg. Capt. Marvel pin-up. 15-Comic cards on back-c			
begin, end #26	30.00	90.00	210.00
16,17: 17-Painted-c	27.00	81.00	190.00
18-Origin & 1st app. Mary Marvel & Marvel Family; painted-c			
(12/11/42)	41.00	122.00	285.00
19-Mary Marvel x-over; Christmas-c	25.00	75.00	175.00

20,21-Attached to the cover, each has a miniature comic just like
the Mighty Midget Comics #11, except that each has a full
color promo ad on the back cover. Most copies were circulated
without the miniature comic. These issues with miniatures attached are very rare, and should not be mistaken for copies with the
similar Mighty Midget glued in its place. The Mighty Midgets had
blank back covers except for a small victory stamp seal. Only the
Capt. Marvel and Captain Marvel Jr. No. 11 miniatures have
been positively documented as having been affixed to these
covers. Each miniature was only partially glued by its back cover
to the Captain Marvel comic making it easy to see if it's the genuine miniature rather than a Mighty Midget.

	Good	Fine	N-Mint
with comic attached. . . .	65.00	195.00	455.00
20,21-Without miniature	21.50	64.00	150.00
22-Mr. Mind serial begins	39.00	118.00	275.00
23-25	21.00	62.00	145.00
26-30: 26-Flag-c	17.00	51.00	120.00
31-35: 35-Origin Radar	16.00	48.00	110.00
36-40: 37-Mary Marvel x-over	13.00	40.00	95.00
41-46: 42-Christmas-c. 43-Captain Marvel 1st meets Uncle Marvel;			
Mary Batson cameo. 46-Mr. Mind serial ends			
	12.00	36.00	84.00
47-50	11.00	32.00	75.00
51-53,55-60: 52-Origin & 1st app. Sivana Jr.; Capt. Marvel Jr. x-over			
	8.00	24.00	56.00
54-Special oversize 68-pg. issue	10.00	30.00	70.00
61-The Cult of the Curse serial begins	11.00	32.00	75.00
62-66-Serial ends; Mary Marvel x-over in #65. 66-Atomic War-c			
	7.00	21.00	50.00
67-77,79: 69-Billy Batson's Christmas; Uncle Marvel, Mary Marvel,			
Capt. Marvel Jr. x-over. 71-Three Lt. Marvels app. No. 79-Origin			
Mr. Tawny	6.50	19.50	45.00
78-Origin Mr. Atom	7.00	21.00	50.00
80-Origin Capt. Marvel retold	11.50	34.00	80.00
81-84,86-90: 81,90-Mr. Atom app. 82-Infinity-c. 86-Mr. Tawny app.			
	7.00	21.00	50.00
85-Freedom Train issue	8.50	25.50	60.00
91-99: 96-Mr. Tawny app.	5.70	17.00	40.00
100-Origin retold	12.00	36.00	84.00
101-120: 116-Flying Saucer issue (1/51)	5.70	17.00	40.00
121-Origin retold	7.00	21.00	50.00
122-141,143-149: 138-Flying Saucer issue (11/52). 141-Pre-code			
horror story "The Hideous Head-Hunter"	5.70	17.00	40.00
142-Used in POP. pgs. 92,96	5.70	17.00	40.00
150-(Low distribution)	11.00	32.00	75.00
Bond Bread Giveaways-(24 pgs.; pocket size-7¼x3½"; paper cover):			
". . .& the Stolen City ('48)," "The Boy Who Never Heard of			
C.M.,""Meets the Weatherman"-(1950)(reprint)			
each	13.00	40.00	80.00
. . .Well Known Comics (1944; 12 pgs.; 8½x10½")-printed in red &			
in blue; soft-c; glued binding)-Bestmaid/Samuel Lowe Co.			
giveaway	16.00	48.00	96.00

CAPTAIN MARVEL ADVENTURES
1945 (6x8") (Full color, paper cover)
Fawcett Publications (Wheaties Giveaway)

"Captain Marvel & the Threads of Life" plus 2 other stories (32pgs.)			
	16.00	48.00	110.00

NOTE: All copies were taped at each corner to a box of Wheaties and are never found
in Fine or Mint condition.

CAPTAIN MARVEL AND THE GOOD HUMOR MAN
1950
Fawcett Publications

nn	19.00	57.00	132.00

CAPTAIN MARVEL AND THE LTS. OF SAFETY
1950 - 1951 (3 issues - no No.'s)
Ebasco Services/Fawcett Publications

"Danger Flies a Kite"('50)," "Danger Takes to Climbing"('50),			
"Danger Smashes Street Lights"('51)	11.50	34.00	80.00

CAPTAIN MARVEL COMIC STORY PAINT BOOK (See Comic Story. . . .)

CAPTAIN MARVEL, JR. (See Fawcett Miniatures, Marvel Family, Master Comics,
Mighty Midget Comics, Shazam & Whiz Comics)

CAPTAIN MARVEL, JR.
Nov, 1942 - No. 119, June, 1953 (nn 34)
Fawcett Publications
1-Origin Capt. Marvel Jr. retold (Whiz No. 25); Capt. Nazi app.

Captain Marvel, Jr. #10, © FAW

Captain Midnight #24, © FAW

Captain Rocket #1, © P.L. Publ.

CAPTAIN MARVEL, JR. (continued)

	Good	Fine	N-Mint
	110.00	332.00	775.00
2-Vs. Capt. Nazi; origin Capt. Nippon	55.00	165.00	385.00
3,4	41.00	122.00	285.00
5-Vs. Capt. Nazi	31.00	94.00	220.00
6-10: 8-Vs. Capt. Nazi. 9-Flag-c. 10-Hitler-c	24.00	73.00	170.00
11,12,15-Capt. Nazi app.	19.00	58.00	135.00
13,14,16-20: 16-Capt. Marvel & Sivana x-over. 19-Capt. Nazi & Capt.			
Nippon app.	13.50	41.00	95.00
21-30: 25-Flag-c	9.30	28.00	65.00
31-33,36-40: 37-Infinity-c	6.00	18.00	42.00
35-#34 on inside; cover shows origin of Sivana Jr. which is not on			
inside. Evidently the cover to #35 was printed out of sequence			
and bound with contents to #34	6.00	18.00	42.00
41-50	4.30	13.00	30.00
51-70: 53-Atomic Bomb story	3.70	11.00	26.00
71-99,101-103	3.15	9.50	22.00
100	3.70	11.00	26.00
104-Used in POP, pg. 89	3.15	9.50	22.00
105-114,116-119: 119-Electric chair-c	3.15	9.50	22.00
115-Injury to eye-c; Eyeball story w/ injury-to-eye panels			
	4.50	14.00	32.00
...Well Known Comics (1944; 12 pgs.; 8½x10½")(Printed in blue;			
paper-c, glued binding)-Bestmaid/Samuel Lowe Co. giveaway			
	12.00	36.00	72.00

NOTE: **Mac Raboy** c-1-10, 12-14, 16, 19, 22, 25, 27, 28, 30-33, 57 among others.

CAPTAIN MARVEL PRESENTS THE TERRIBLE FIVE
Aug, 1966; V2#5, Sept, 1967 (No #2-4) (25 cents)
M. F. Enterprises

1	.70	2.00	4.00
V2#5-(Formerly Capt. Marvel)	.35	1.00	2.00

CAPTAIN MARVEL'S FUN BOOK
1944 (½" thick) (cardboard covers)
Samuel Lowe Co.

Puzzles, games, magic, etc.; infinity-c	12.00	36.00	84.00

CAPTAIN MARVEL SPECIAL EDITION (See Special Edition)

CAPTAIN MARVEL STORY BOOK
Summer, 1946 - No. 4, Summer?, 1948
Fawcett Publications

1-½ text	26.00	79.00	185.00
2-4	18.00	54.00	125.00

CAPTAIN MARVEL THRILL BOOK (Large-Size)
1941 (Black & White; color cover)
Fawcett Publications

	Good	Fine	VF-NM
1-Reprints from Whiz #8,10, & Special Edition #1 (Rare)			
	142.00	425.00	1000.00

NOTE: Rarely found in Fine or Mint condition.

CAPTAIN MIDNIGHT (Radio, films, TV) (See The Funnies & Popular
Comics) (Becomes Sweethearts No. 68 on)
Sept, 1942 - No. 67, Fall, 1948
Fawcett Publications

	Good	Fine	N-Mint
1-Origin Captain Midnight; Captain Marvel cameo on cover			
	108.00	325.00	650.00
2	46.00	140.00	325.00
3-5	32.00	95.00	225.00
6-10: 9-Raboy-c. 10-Raboy Flag-c	22.00	65.00	155.00
11-20: 11,17-Raboy-c	14.00	43.00	100.00
21-30	11.50	34.00	80.00
31-40	8.50	25.50	60.00
41-59,61-67: 54-Sci/fi theme begins?	6.50	19.50	45.00
60-Flying Saucer issue (2/48)-3rd of this theme; see Shadow Comics			
V7#10 & Boy Commandos #26	10.00	30.00	70.00

CAPTAIN NICE (TV)
Nov, 1967 (One Shot)
Gold Key

	Good	Fine	N-Mint
1(10211-711)-Photo-c	2.65	8.00	18.00

CAPTAIN PARAGON
Dec, 1983 - No. 4, 1985? (#2-4 are in color)
Americomics

1-4: 1-Ms. Victory begins (Intro/1st app.)	.40	1.25	2.50

CAPTAIN PARAGON AND THE SENTINELS OF JUSTICE
April, 1985 - No. 6, 1986? ($1.75, color)
AC Comics

1-Capt. Paragon, Commando D., Nightveil, Scarlet Scorpion,			
Stardust & Atoman begin	.40	1.25	2.50
2-6	.30	.90	1.80

CAPTAIN POWER AND THE SOLDIERS OF THE FUTURE (TV)
Aug, 1988 - No. 2? ($2.00, color)
Continuity Comics

1,2: 1-Neal Adams-c/layouts/i	.35	1.00	2.00

CAPTAIN PUREHEART (See Archie as . . .)

CAPTAIN ROCKET
November, 1951
P. L. Publ. (Canada)

1	16.00	48.00	110.00

CAPTAIN SAVAGE AND HIS LEATHERNECK RAIDERS
Jan, 1968 - No. 19, Mar, 1970 (See Sgt. Fury No. 10)
Marvel Comics Group

1-Sgt. Fury & Howlers cameo	.35	1.00	2.00
2-19: 2-Origin Hydra. 2,3,7-Ayers/Shores-a		.50	1.00

CAPTAIN SCIENCE (Fantastic No. 8 on)
Nov, 1950 - No. 7, Dec, 1951
Youthful Magazines

1-Wood-a; origin	43.00	130.00	300.00
2	19.00	58.00	135.00
3,6,7: 3-Bondage c-swipe/Wings 94	16.00	48.00	110.00
4,5-Wood/Orlando-c/a(2) each	37.00	110.00	260.00

NOTE: Fass a-4. Bondage c-3, 6, 7.

CAPTAIN SILVER'S LOG OF SEA HOUND (See Sea Hound)

CAPTAIN SINDBAD (Movie Adaptation) (See Movie Comics)

CAPTAIN STEVE SAVAGE (. . .& His Jet Fighters, No. 2-13)
1950 - No. 13, 1952? No. 5, 9-10/54 - No. 13, 5-6/56
Avon Periodicals

nn(1st series)-Wood-a, 22 pgs. (titled ". . .Over Korea")			
	19.00	58.00	135.00
1(4/51)-Reprints nn issue (Canadian)	8.50	25.50	60.00
2-Kamen-a	5.00	15.00	35.00
3-11	2.85	8.50	20.00
12-Wood-a, 6pp	5.70	17.00	40.00
13-Check, Lawrence-a	4.00	12.00	28.00

NOTE: Kinstler c-2-5, 7-9, 11. Lawrence a-8. Ravielli a-5, 9.

5(9-10/54-2nd series)(Formerly Sensational Police Cases)			
	3.15	9.50	22.00
6-Reprints nn issue; Wood-a	5.00	15.00	35.00
7-13: 13 reprints cover to #8 (1st series)	1.70	5.00	12.00

CAPTAIN STONE (See Holyoke One-Shot No. 10)

CAPT. STORM
May-June, 1964 - No. 18, Mar-Apr, 1967
National Periodical Publications

1-Origin	.70	2.00	4.00
2-18: 3,6,13-Kubert-a. 12-Kubert-c	.40	1.25	2.50

CAPTAIN 3-D
December, 1953
Harvey Publications

	Good	Fine	N-Mint
1-Kirby/Ditko-a	4.00	12.00	24.00

CAPTAIN THUNDER AND BLUE BOLT
Sept, 1987 - No. 10, 1988 ($1.95, color)
Hero Comics

1-10: 1-Origin Blue Bolt. 3-Origin Capt. Thunder. 6-1st app. Wicket			
8-Champions x-over	.35	1.00	2.00
Book 1 ($9.95, color)	1.70	5.00	9.95

CAPTAIN TOOTSIE & THE SECRET LEGION (Advs. of . .)(Also see
Monte Hale #30,39 & Real Western Hero)
Oct, 1950 - No. 2, Dec, 1950
Toby Press

1-Not Beck-a	11.00	32.00	75.00
2-Not Beck-a	6.50	19.50	45.00

CAPTAIN VENTURE & THE LAND BENEATH THE SEA
Oct, 1968 - No. 2, Oct, 1969
Gold Key (See Space Family Robinson)

1,2: 1-r/Space Family Robinson serial; Spiegle-a in both			
	2.30	7.00	16.00

CAPTAIN VICTORY AND THE GALACTIC RANGERS
Nov, 1981 - No. 13, Jan, 1984 ($1.00) (36-48 pgs.)
Pacific Comics (Sold only through comic shops)

1-13: 1-1st app. Mr. Mind. 3-Adams-a		.50	1.00
Special Issue #1(10/83)-Kirby c/a(p)		.50	1.00
NOTE: *Conrad* a-10, 11. **Ditko** a-6. **Kirby** a-1-13p; c-1-13.			

CAPTAIN VIDEO (TV) (See XMas Comics)
Feb, 1951 - No. 6, Dec, 1951 (No. 1,5,6-36pgs.; 2-4, 52pgs.)
Fawcett Publications

1-George Evans-a(2)	31.50	94.00	220.00
2-Used in **SOTI**, pg. 382	24.00	71.00	165.00
3-6-All Evans-a	20.00	60.00	140.00
NOTE: Minor *Williamson* assist on most issues. Photo c-1, 5, 6; painted c-2-4.			

CAPTAIN WILLIE SCHULTZ (Also see Fightin' Army)
No. 76, Oct, 1985 - No. 77, Jan, 1986
Charlton Comics

76,77		.40	.75

CAPTAIN WIZARD COMICS (Also see Meteor)
1946
Rural Home

1-Capt. Wizard dons new costume; Impossible Man, Race Wilkins			
app.	8.00	24.00	56.00

CARDINAL MINDSZENTY (The Truth Behind the Trial of. . .)
1949 (24 pages; paper cover, in color)
Catechetical Guild Education Society

nn-Anti-communism	4.30	13.00	30.00
Press Proof-(Very Rare)-(Full color, 7½x11¾", untrimmed)			
Only two known copies			120.00
Preview Copy (B&W, stapled), 18 pgs.; contains first 13 pgs. of			
Cardinal Mindszenty and was sent out as an advance promotion.			
Only one known copy		$150.00 - $200.00	
NOTE: Regular edition also printed in French. There was also a movie released in 1949 called "Guilty of Treason" which is a fact-based account of the trial and imprisonment of Cardinal Mindszenty by the Communist regime in Hungary.			

CARE BEARS (TV, Movie)(See Star Comics Magazine)
Nov, 1985 - No. 20, Jan, 1989 ($1.00 #11 on)
Star Comics/Marvel Comics No. 15 on

1-20: Post-a begins		.40	.80

CAREER GIRL ROMANCES (Formerly Three Nurses)
June, 1964 - No. 78, Dec, 1973
Charlton Comics

	Good	Fine	N-Mint
V4#24-31,33-50		.60	1.20
32-Presley, Hermans Hermits, Johnny Rivers line drawn-c			
	1.50	4.50	10.00
51-78		.40	.80

CAR 54, WHERE ARE YOU? (TV)
Mar-May, 1962 - No. 7, Sept-Nov, 1963; 1964 - 1965 (All photo-c)
Dell Publishing Co.

4-Color 1257(3-5/62)	3.50	10.50	24.00
2(6-8/62)-7	2.00	6.00	14.00
2,3(10-12/64), 4(1-3/65)-Reprints #2,3&4 of 1st series			
	1.50	4.50	10.00

CARNATION MALTED MILK GIVEAWAYS (See Wisco)

CARNIVAL COMICS
1945
Harry 'A' Chesler/Pershing Square Publ. Co.

1	5.00	15.00	35.00

CARNIVAL OF COMICS
1954 (Giveaway)
Fleet-Air Shoes

nn-Contains a comic bound with new cover; several combinations			
possible; Charlton's Eh! known	1.00	3.00	7.00

CAROLINE KENNEDY
1961 (One Shot)
Charlton Comics

nn	4.30	13.00	30.00

CAROUSEL COMICS
V1No.8, April, 1948
F. E. Howard, Toronto

V1#8	2.00	6.00	14.00

CARTOON KIDS
1957 (no month)
Atlas Comics (CPS)

1-Maneely c/a; Dexter The Demon, Willie The Wise-Guy, Little			
Zelda app.	2.00	6.00	14.00

CARVEL COMICS (Amazing Advs. of Capt. Carvel)
1975 - No. 5, 1976 (25 cents; #3-5: 35 cents) (#4,5: 3¼x5")
Carvel Corp. (Ice Cream)

1-3		.15	.30
4,5(1976)-Baseball theme	.85	2.50	5.00

CASE OF THE SHOPLIFTER'S SHOE (Perry Mason) (See Feature Book No. 50 McKay)

CASE OF THE WASTED WATER, THE
1972? (Giveaway)
Rheem Water Heating

nn-Neal Adams-a	2.00	6.00	14.00

CASE OF THE WINKING BUDDHA, THE
1950 (132 pgs.; 25 cents; B&W; 5½x7-5½x8")
St. John Publ. Co.

nn-Charles Raab-a; reprinted in Authentic Police Cases No. 25			
	11.00	32.00	75.00

CASES OF SHERLOCK HOLMES
May, 1986 - Present ($1.70-$2.25, B&W)
Renegade Press/Northstar Publishing #16 on

1-15	.35	1.00	2.00
16,17 ($2.25-c)	.40	1.15	2.30

Captain 3-D #1, © HARV

Captain Video #5, © FAW

Career Girl Romances #32, © CC

Casey Crime Photographer #1, © MEG

Casper Cat #1, © I.W.

Casper, The Friendly Ghost #20, © Paramount

CASEY-CRIME PHOTOGRAPHER (Two-Gun Western No. 5 on)
Aug, 1949 - No. 4, Feb, 1950 (Radio)
Marvel Comics (BFP)

	Good	Fine	N-Mint
1: Photo-c	6.00	18.00	42.00
2-4: Photo-c	4.00	12.00	28.00

CASEY JONES (See 4-Color No. 915)

CASPER AND. . .
1987 - Present (All reprints)
Harvey Comics

1-The Ghostly Trio		.40	.75
2-12 ($1.00): 2-Spooky. 3-Wendy. 4-Nightmare. 5-Ghostly Trio. 6-Spooky. 7-Wendy. 8-? 9-? 10-Wendy. 11-Spooky. 12-Ghostly Trio			
		.50	1.00

CASPER AND NIGHTMARE (See Harvey Hits No. 37, 45, 52, 56, 59, 62, 65, 68, 71, 75)

CASPER AND NIGHTMARE (Nightmare & Casper No. 1-5) (25 cents)
No. 6, 11/64 - No. 44, 10/73; No. 45, 6/74 - No. 46, 8/74
Harvey Publications

	Good	Fine	N-Mint
6: 68 pg. Giants begin, ends #32	2.00	6.00	12.00
7-10	1.00	3.00	6.00
11-20	.50	1.50	3.00
21-32	.35	1.00	2.00
33-37: 52 pg. Giants	.35	1.00	2.00
38-46: regular size	.35	1.00	2.00
NOTE: Many issues contain reprints.

CASPER AND SPOOKY (See Harvey Hits No. 20)
Oct, 1972 - No. 7, Oct, 1973
Harvey Publications

1	.85	2.50	5.00
2-7	.35	1.00	2.00

CASPER AND THE GHOSTLY TRIO
Nov, 1972 - No. 7, Nov, 1973
Harvey Publications

1	.85	2.50	5.00
2-7	.35	1.00	2.00

CASPER AND WENDY
Sept, 1972 - No. 8, Nov, 1973
Harvey Publications

1: 52 pg. Giant	.85	2.50	5.00
2-8	.35	1.00	2.00

CASPER CAT (See Dopey Duck)
1958; 1963
I. W. Enterprises/Super

1,7-Reprint, Super No. 14('63)	.50	1.50	3.00

CASPER DIGEST (. . . Magazine #?; . . .Halloween Digest #8, 10)
Oct, 1986 - Present ($1.25-$1.75, digest-size)
Harvey Publications

1-12: 8,10-. . .Halloween Digest		.65	1.30

CASPER DIGEST STORIES
2/80 - No. 4, 11/80 (95 cents; 132 pgs.; digest size)
Harvey Publications

1	.50	1.50	3.00
2-4	.35	1.00	2.00

CASPER DIGEST WINNERS
April, 1980 - No. 3, Sept, 1980 (95 cents; 132 pgs.; digest size)
Harvey Publications

1	.35	1.00	2.00
2,3	.25	.75	1.50

CASPER HALLOWEEN TRICK OR TREAT
January, 1976 (52 pgs.)

Harvey Publications

	Good	Fine	N-Mint
1	.35	1.00	2.00

CASPER IN SPACE (Formerly Casper Spaceship)
No. 6, June, 1973 - No. 8, Oct, 1973
Harvey Publications

6-8	.35	1.00	2.00

CASPER IN 3-D (See Blackthorne 3-D Series #57)

CASPER'S GHOSTLAND
Winter, 1958-59 - No. 97, 12/77; No. 98, 12/79 (25 cents)
Harvey Publications

1: 68 pgs. begin, ends #61	7.00	21.00	50.00
2	4.00	12.00	28.00
3-10	2.85	8.50	20.00
11-20: 13-X-Mas-c	1.70	5.00	12.00
21-40	1.15	3.50	8.00
41-61: Last 68 pg. issue	.85	2.60	6.00
62-77: All 52 pgs.	.50	1.50	3.00
78-98: 94-X-Mas-c	.35	1.00	2.00
NOTE: Most issues contain reprints.

CASPER SPACESHIP (Casper in Space No. 6 on)
Aug, 1972 - No. 5, April, 1973
Harvey Publications

1: 52 pg. Giant	.85	2.50	5.00
2-5	.35	1.00	2.00

CASPER STRANGE GHOST STORIES
October, 1974 - No. 14, Jan, 1977 (All 52 pgs.)
Harvey Publications

1	.70	2.00	4.00
2-14	.35	1.00	2.00

CASPER, THE FRIENDLY GHOST (See America's Best TV Comics, Famous TV Funday Funnies, The Friendly Ghost. . ., Nightmare &. . ., Richie Rich, Tastee-Freez & Treasury of Comics)

CASPER, THE FRIENDLY GHOST (Becomes Harvey Comics Hits No. 61 (No. 6), and then continued with Harvey issue No. 7)
9/49 - No. 3, 8/50; 9/50 - No. 5, 5/51
St. John Publishing Co.

1(1949)-Origin & 1st app. Baby Huey	50.00	150.00	350.00
2,3	27.00	81.00	190.00
1(9/50)	35.00	105.00	245.00
2-5	22.00	65.00	155.00

CASPER, THE FRIENDLY GHOST (Paramount Picture Star. . .)
No. 7, Dec, 1952 - No 70, July, 1958
Harvey Publications (Family Comics)

Note: No. 6 is Harvey Comics Hits No. 61 (10/52)

7-Baby Huey begins, ends #9	17.00	51.00	120.00
8-10: 10-Spooky begins(1st app.), ends #70?	8.50	25.50	60.00
11-19: 19-1st app. Nightmare (4/54)	5.70	17.00	40.00
20-Wendy the Witch begins (1st app, 5/54)	6.50	19.50	45.00
21-30: 24-Infinity-c	4.50	14.00	32.00
31-40	3.75	11.25	26.00
41-50	3.00	9.00	21.00
51-70	2.30	7.00	16.00
American Dental Association (Giveaways):			
. . .'s Dental Health Activity Book-1977	.30	.80	1.60
. . .Presents Space Age Dentistry-1972	.40	1.20	2.40
. . ., His Den, & Their Dentist Fight the Tooth Demons-1974			
	.40	1.20	2.40

CASPER T.V. SHOWTIME
Jan, 1980 - No. 5, Oct, 1980
Harvey Comics

1	.35	1.00	2.00

CASPER T.V. SHOWTIME (continued)

	Good	Fine	N-Mint
2-5		.50	1.00

CASSETTE BOOKS
(Classics Illustrated)
1984 (48 pgs, b&w comic with cassette tape)
Cassette Book Co./I.P.S. Publ.

Note: This series was illegal. The artwork was illegally obtained, and the Classics Illustrated copyright owner, Twin Circle Publ. sued to get an injunction to prevent the continued sale of this series. Many C.I. collectors obtained copies before the 1987 injunction, but now they are already scarce. Here again the market is just developing, but sealed mint copies of comic and tape should be worth at least $25.
 1001 (CI#1-A2)New-PC 1002(CI#3-A2)CI-PC 1003(CI#13-A2)CI-PC
 1004(CI#25)CI-LDC 1005(CI#10-A2)New-PC 1006(CI#64)CI-LDC

CASTILIAN (See Movie Classics)

CAT, T.H.E. (TV) (See T.H.E. Cat)

CAT, THE (See Movie Classics)

CAT, THE
Nov, 1972 - No. 4, June, 1973
Marvel Comics Group

	Good	Fine	N-Mint
1-Origin The Cat; Mooney-a(i); Wood-c(i)/a(i)	.60	1.75	3.50
2-Mooney-a(i), 3-Everett inks	.35	1.10	2.25
4-Starlin/Weiss-a(p)	.35	1.10	2.25

CAT & MOUSE
Dec, 1988 ($1.75, color w/part B&W)
EF Graphics (Silverline)

1-1st printing (12/88, 32 pgs.)	.30	.90	1.75
1-2nd printing (5/89, 36 pgs.)	.30	.90	1.75

CAT FROM OUTER SPACE (See Walt Disney Showcase #46)

CATHOLIC COMICS (See Heroes All Catholic...)
June, 1946 - V3No.10, July, 1949
Catholic Publications

1	8.50	25.50	60.00
2	4.30	13.00	30.00
3-13(7/47)	2.85	8.50	20.00
V2#1-10	1.70	5.00	12.00
V3#1-10: Reprints 10-part Treasure Island serial from Target V2#2-11 (See Key Comics #5)	2.65	8.00	18.00

CATHOLIC PICTORIAL
1947
Catholic Guild

1-Toth-a(2) (Rare)	14.00	42.00	100.00

CATMAN COMICS (Crash Nos. 1-5)
5/41 - No. 17, 1/43; No. 18, 7/43 - No. 22, 12/43; No. 23, 3/44 - No. 26, 11/44; No. 27, 4/45 - No. 30, 12/45; No. 31, 6/46 - No. 32, 8/46
Holyoke Publishing Co./Continental Magazines V2#12, 7/44 on

1(V1#6)-Origin The Deacon & Sidekick Mickey, Dr. Diamond & Rag-Man; The Black Widow app.; The Catman by Chas. Quinlan & Blaze Baylor begin	64.00	192.00	450.00
2(V1#7)	31.00	92.00	215.00
3(V1#8), 4(V1#9)-3-The Pied Piper begins	24.00	73.00	170.00
5(V2#10)-Origin Kitten; The Hood begins (c-redated), 6,7(V2#11,12)	19.00	58.00	135.00
8(V2#13,13/42)-Origin Little Leaders; Volton by Kubert begins (his 1st comic book work)	27.00	80.00	185.00
9(V2#14)	17.00	50.00	120.00
10(V2#15)-Origin Blackout; Phantom Falcon begins	17.00	50.00	120.00
11(V3#1)-Kubert-a	17.00	50.00	120.00
12(V3#2) - 15, 17, 18(V3#8, 7/43)	13.00	40.00	90.00
16 (V3#5)-Hitler, Tojo, Mussolini, Stalin-c	14.00	42.00	100.00

	Good	Fine	N-Mint
19 (V2#6)-Hitler, Tojo, Mussolini-c	14.00	42.00	100.00
20(V2#7) - 23(V2#10, 3/44)	13.00	40.00	90.00
nn(V3#13, 5/44)-Rico-a; Schomburg bondage-c	11.50	34.00	80.00
nn(V2#12, 7/44)	11.50	34.00	80.00
nn(V3#1, 9/44)-Origin The Golden Archer; Leatherface app.;	10.00	30.00	70.00
nn(V3#2, 11/44)-L. B. Cole-c	16.00	48.00	110.00
27-Origin Kitten retold; L. B. Cole Flag-c	17.00	51.00	120.00
28-Catman learns Kitten's I.D.; Dr. Macabre, Deacon app.; L. B. Cole-c/a	19.00	58.00	135.00
29-32-L. B. Cole-c; bondage-#30	16.00	48.00	110.00

NOTE: *Fuje a-11, 29(3), 30. Palais a-11, 29(2), 30Rico a-11(2).*

CAT TALES (3-D)
April, 1989 ($2.95)
Eternity Comics

1-Felix the Cat-r in 3-D	.50	1.50	3.00

CATWOMAN (Also see Action Comics Weekly #611-614 & Batman)
Feb, 1989 - No. 4, May, 1989 ($1.50, mini-series, mature readers)
DC Comics

1	2.00	6.00	12.00
2	1.70	4.00	8.00
3,4: 3-Batman cameo. 4-Batman app.	.60	1.75	3.50

CAUGHT
Aug, 1956 - No. 5, April, 1957
Atlas Comics (VPI)

1	5.00	15.00	35.00
2,4: 4-Severin-c; Maneely-a	2.00	6.00	14.00
3-Torres-a	2.85	8.50	20.00
5-Crandall, Krigstein-a; Severin-c	3.70	11.00	26.00

CAVALIER COMICS
1945; 1952 (Early DC reprints)
A. W. Nugent Publ. Co.

2(1945)-Speed Saunders, Fang Gow	7.00	21.00	50.00
2(1952)	3.50	10.50	24.00

CAVE GIRL (Also see Africa)
No. 11, 1953 - No. 14, 1954
Magazine Enterprises

11(A-1 82)-Origin; all Cave Girl stories	20.00	60.00	140.00
12(A-1 96), 13(A-1 116), 14(A-1 125)-Thunda by Powell in each	14.00	42.00	100.00

NOTE: *Powell c/a in all.*

CAVE GIRL
1988 ($2.95, 44 pgs., 16 pgs. of color, rest B&W)
AC Comics

1-Powell-r/Cave Girl #11; Nyoka photo back-c from movie; Powell/ Black-c; Special Limited Edition on-c	.50	1.50	3.00

CAVE KIDS (TV)
Feb, 1963 - No. 16, Mar, 1967 (Hanna-Barbera)
Gold Key

1	1.70	5.00	12.00
2-5	1.15	3.50	8.00
6-16: 7-Pebbles & Bamm Bamm app.	.70	2.00	5.00

CENTURION OF ANCIENT ROME, THE
1958 (no month listed) (36 pages) (B&W)
Zondervan Publishing House

(Rare) All by Jay Disbrow			
Estimated Value....			200.00

CENTURIONS
June, 1987 - No. 4, Sept, 1987 (mini-series)

Catman Comics #8, © HOKE

Catwoman #1, © DC

Cave Girl #12, © ME

December 2, 1988

Cerebus Bi-Weekly #1, © A-V

Challengers Of The Unknown #12, © DC

Chamber Of Clues #27, © HARV

	Good	Fine	N-Mint

CENTURIONS (continued)
DC Comics
1-4   .40   .75

CENTURY OF COMICS
1933 (100 pages) (Probably the 3rd comic book)
Eastern Color Printing Co.

Bought by Wheatena, Milk-O-Malt, John Wanamaker, Kinney Shoe
Stores, & others to be used as premiums and radio giveaways.
No publisher listed.

nn-Mutt & Jeff, Joe Palooka, etc. reprints   433.00   1085.00   2600.00

CEREBUS BI-WEEKLY
Dec. 2, 1988 - No. 26, Nov. 11, 1989 ($1.25, B&W)
Aardvark-Vanaheim

1-Reprints Cerebus #1   .25   .75   1.50
2-26-Reprints Cerebus #2-26   .60   1.25

CEREBUS JAM
Apr, 1985
Aardvark-Vanaheim

1-Eisner, Austin-a   .85   2.50   5.00

CEREBUS THE AARDVARK (See A-V in 3-D & Nucleus)
Dec, 1977 - Present
Aardvark-Vanaheim

1-2000 print run; most copies poorly printed   60.00   175.00   350.00
Note: There is a counterfeit version known to exist. It can be
distinguished from the original in the following ways: inside cover is
glossy instead of flat, black background on the front cover is blotted
or spotty. These counterfeits sell for between $50.00 and $70.00.

	Good	Fine	N-Mint
2	25.00	75.00	150.00
3-Origin Red Sophia	20.00	60.00	120.00
4-Origin Elrod the Albino	13.50	40.50	81.00
5,6	12.00	36.00	72.00
7-10	8.35	25.00	50.00
11,12: 11-Origin Moon Roach	8.35	25.00	50.00
13-15: 14-Origin Lord Julius	4.85	14.50	29.00
16-20	3.15	9.50	19.00
21-Scarcer	12.50	37.50	75.00
22	3.65	11.00	22.00
23-28	1.85	5.50	11.00
29,30	2.15	6.50	13.00
31-Origin Moonroach	2.50	7.50	15.00
32-40	1.00	3.00	6.00
41-50,52: 52-Cutey Bunny app.	.85	2.50	5.00
51-Not reprinted; Cutey Bunny app.	3.35	10.00	20.00
53-Intro. Wolveroach (cameo)	1.15	3.50	7.00
54-Wolveroach 1st full story	2.00	6.00	12.00
55,56-Wolveroach app.	1.15	3.50	7.00
57-60	.60	1.75	3.50
61,62: Flaming Carrot app.	.85	2.50	5.00
63-68	.70	2.00	4.00
69-75	.55	1.60	3.20
76-79	.50	1.50	3.00
80-85	.45	1.25	2.50
86-128: 104-Flaming Carrot app.	.30	1.00	2.00

CHALLENGE OF THE UNKNOWN (Formerly Love Experiences)
No. 6, Sept, 1950 (See Web Of Mystery No. 19)
Ace Magazines

6-'Villa of the Vampire' used in N.Y. Joint Legislative Comm. Publ;
Sekowsky-a   8.00   24.00   56.00

CHALLENGER, THE
1945 - No. 4, Oct-Dec, 1946
Interfaith Publications/T.C. Comics

nn; nd; 32 pgs.; Origin the Challenger Club; Anti-Fascist with funny

	Good	Fine	N-Mint
animal filler	12.00	36.00	84.00
2-4-Kubert-a; 4-Fuje-a	11.50	34.00	80.00

CHALLENGERS OF THE UNKNOWN (See Showcase, Super DC
Giant, and Super Team Family)
4-5/58 - No.77, 12-1/70-71; No.78, 2/73 - No.80, 6-7/73;
No.81, 6-7/77 - No.87, 6-7/78
National Periodical Publications/DC Comics

	Good	Fine	N-Mint
1-Kirby/Stein-a(2)	57.00	170.00	400.00
2-Kirby/Stein-a(2)	30.00	90.00	210.00
3-Kirby/Stein-a(2)	24.00	73.00	170.00
4-8-Kirby/Wood-a plus c-#8	21.00	62.00	145.00
9,10	10.00	30.00	70.00
11-15: 14-Origin Multi-Man	6.50	19.50	45.00
16-22: 18-Intro. Cosmo, the Challengers Spacepet. 22-Last 10 cent issue	4.50	14.00	32.00
23-30	2.15	6.50	15.00
31-40: 31-Retells origin of the Challengers	1.50	4.50	10.00
41-60: 43-New look begins. 48-Doom Patrol app. 49-Intro. Challenger Corps. 51-Sea Devils app. 55-Death of Red Ryan. 60-Red Ryan returns	.85	2.50	5.00
61-63,66-73: 69-Intro. Corinna	.50	1.50	3.00
64,65-Kirby origin-r, parts 1 & 2	.50	1.50	3.00
74-Deadman by Tuska/Adams	1.30	4.00	8.00
75-87: 82-Swamp Thing begins	.25	.75	1.50

NOTE: **Adams** c-67, 68, 70, 72, 74i, 81i. **Buckler** c-83-86p. **Giffen** a-83-87p. **Kirby**
a-75-80r; c-75, 77, 78. **Kubert** c-64, 66, 69, 76, 79. **Nasser** c/a-81p, 82p. **Tuska** a-73.
Wood r-76.

CHALLENGE TO THE WORLD
1951 (36 pages) (10 cents)
Catechetical Guild

nn   2.30   7.00   16.00

CHAMBER OF CHILLS (. . .of Clues No. 27 on)
No. 21, June, 1951 - No. 26, Dec, 1954
Harvey Publications/Witches Tales

	Good	Fine	N-Mint
21	10.00	30.00	70.00
22,24	6.00	18.00	42.00
23-Excessive violence; eyes torn out	7.00	21.00	50.00
5(2/52)-Decapitation, acid in face scene	7.00	21.00	50.00
6-Woman melted alive	5.70	17.00	40.00
7-Used in SOTI, pg. 389; decapitation/severed head panels	5.00	15.00	35.00
8-10: 8-Decapitation panels	4.30	13.00	30.00
11,12,14	3.50	10.50	24.00
13,15-24-Nostrand-a in all; c-#20. 13,21-Decapitation panels. 18-Atom bomb panels	5.70	17.00	40.00
25,26	3.00	9.00	21.00

NOTE: About half the issues contain bondage, torture, sadism, perversion, gore, can-
nabalism, eyes ripped out, acid in face, etc. **Kremer** a-12, 17. **Palais** a-21(1), 23.
Nostrand/Powell a-13, 15, 16. **Powell** a-21, 23, 24('51), 5-8, 11, 13, 18-21, 23-25.
Bondage-c-21, 24('51), 7. 25 r-No. 5; 26 r-No. 9.

CHAMBER OF CHILLS
Nov, 1972 - No. 25, Nov, 1976
Marvel Comics Group

	Good	Fine	N-Mint
1-Harlan Ellison adaptation		.50	1.00
2-25		.40	.80

NOTE: **Adkins** a-1i, 2i. **Brunner** a-2-4; c-4. **Ditko** r-14, 16, 19, 23, 24. **Everett** a-3i, 11r,
21r. **Heath** a-1r. **Gil Kane** c-2p. **Powell** a-13r. **Russell** a-1p, 2p. **Williamson/Mayo** a-13r.
Robert E. Howard horror story adaptation-2, 3.

CHAMBER OF CLUES (Formerly Chamber of Chills)
No. 27, Feb, 1955 - No. 28, April, 1955
Harvey Publications

	Good	Fine	N-Mint
27-Kerry Drake r-/No. 19; Powell-a	4.30	13.00	30.00
28-Kerry Drake	2.30	7.00	16.00

CHAMBER OF DARKNESS (Monsters on the Prowl #9 on)
Oct, 1969 - No. 8, Dec, 1970
Marvel Comics Group

	Good	Fine	N-Mint
1-Buscema-a(p)	.70	2.00	4.00
2-Adams script	.35	1.00	2.00
3-Smith, Buscema-a	.50	1.50	3.00
4-A Conanesque tryout by Smith; reprinted in Conan #16			
	1.70	5.00	12.00
5,6,8: 5-H.P. Lovecraft adaptation	.25	.75	1.50
7-Wrightson c/a, 7pgs. (his 1st work at Marvel); Wrightson draws			
himself in 1st & last panels	.85	2.50	5.00
1-(1/72-25 cent Special)	.35	1.00	2.00

NOTE: Adkins/Everett a-8. Craig a-5. Ditko a-6-8r. Kirby a(p)-4, 5, 7. Kirby/Everett c-5. Severin/Everett c-6. Wrightson c-7, 8.

CHAMP COMICS (Formerly Champion No. 1-10)
No. 11, Oct, 1940 - No. 29, March, 1944
Worth Publ. Co./Champ Publ./Family Comics(Harvey Publ.)

11-Human Meteor cont'd.	34.00	100.00	235.00
12-18: 14,15-Crandall-c	25.00	75.00	175.00
19-The Wasp app.	25.00	75.00	175.00
20-The Green Ghost app.	25.00	75.00	175.00
21-29: 22-The White Mask app. 23-Flag-c	21.00	62.00	145.00

CHAMPION (See Gene Autry's . . .)

CHAMPION COMICS (Champ No. 11 on)
No. 2, Dec, 1939 - No. 10, Aug, 1940 (no No.1)
Worth Publ. Co.(Harvey Publications)

2-The Champ, The Blazing Scarab, Neptina, Liberty Lads, Jungleman, Bill Handy, Swingtime Sweetie begin			
	46.00	140.00	325.00
3-7: 7-The Human Meteor begins?	25.00	75.00	175.00
8-10-Kirbyish-c; bondage #10	28.00	84.00	195.00

CHAMPIONS, THE
October, 1975 - No. 17, Jan, 1978
Marvel Comics Group

1-The Angel, Black Widow, Ghost Rider, Hercules, Ice Man (The Champions) begin; Kane/Adkins-c; Venus x-over			
	.60	1.75	3.50
2-10,16: 2,3-Venus x-over	.25	.75	1.50
11-15,17-Byrne-a	.50	1.50	3.00

NOTE: Buckler/Adkins c-3. Kane/Layton c-11. Tuska a-3p, 4p, 6p.

CHAMPIONS
June, 1986 - No. 6, Feb, 1987 (limited series)
Eclipse Comics

1-6: Based on role playing game	.25	.75	1.50

CHAMPIONS (Also see New Champions)
Sept, 1987 - Present ($1.95, color)
Hero Comics

1-15: 1-Intro Flare, The Marksman & The Rose. 14-Origin Malice			
	.35	1.00	2.00
Annual 1(1988, $2.75, 52 pgs.)-Origin of Giant	.45	1.40	2.75

CHAMPION SPORTS
Oct-Nov, 1973 - No. 3, Feb-Mar, 1974
National Periodical Publications

1-3		.30	.60

CHAOS (See The Crusaders)

CHARLIE CHAN (See Columbia Comics, Feature Comics & The New Advs. of . . .)

CHARLIE CHAN (The Adventures of . . .) (Zaza The Mystic No. 10 on)
6-7/48 - No.5, 2-3/49; No.6, 6/55 - No.9, 3/56
Crestwood(Prize) No. 1-5; Charlton No. 6(6/55) on

1-S&K-c, 2 pages; Infantino-a	22.00	65.00	150.00
2-S&K-c	13.00	40.00	90.00

	Good	Fine	N-Mint
3-5-All S&K-c	12.00	36.00	85.00
6(6/55-Charlton)-S&K-c	8.50	25.50	60.00
7-9	5.00	15.00	35.00

CHARLIE CHAN
Oct-Dec, 1965 - No. 2, Mar, 1966
Dell Publishing Co.

1-Springer-a	1.70	5.00	10.00
2	1.00	3.00	6.00

CHARLIE CHAPLIN
1917 (9x16''; large size; softcover; B&W)
Essanay/M. A. Donohue & Co.

Series 1, #315-Comic Capers (9¾x15¾'')-18pp by Segar,			
Series 1, #316-In the Movies	44.00	132.00	310.00
Series 1, #317-Up in the Air. #318-In the Army			
	44.00	132.00	310.00
. . .Funny Stunts-(12½x16-3/8'') in color	34.00	100.00	235.00

NOTE: All contain Segar -a; pre-Thimble Theatre.

CHARLIE McCARTHY (See Edgar Bergen Presents. . .)
No. 171, Nov, 1947 - No. 571, July, 1954 (See True Comics #14)
Dell Publishing Co.

4-Color 171	9.30	28.00	65.00
4-Color 196-Part photo-c; photo back-c	8.00	24.00	56.00
1(3-5/49)-Part photo-c; photo back-c	8.00	24.00	56.00
2-9(7/52; No. 5,6-52 pgs.)	3.00	9.00	21.00
4-Color 445,478,527,571	2.30	7.00	16.00

CHARLTON BULLSEYE
1975 - No. 5, 1976 (B&W, bi-monthly, magazine format)
CPL/Gang Publications

1-Jeff Jones, Byrne, Ditko-a; 1st app. new Capt. Atom by Ditko			
	.85	2.50	5.00
2-Capt. Atom by Ditko; Byrne-a	.85	2.50	5.00
3-Wrong Country by Sanho Kim	.50	1.50	3.00
4-Doomsday + 1 by John Byrne	.85	2.50	5.00
5-Doomsday + 1 by Byrne, The Question by Ditko; Neal Adams back-c	.85	2.50	5.00

CHARLTON BULLSEYE
June, 1981 - No. 10, Dec, 1982; Nov, 1986
Charlton Publications

1-Blue Beetle, The Question		.40	.80
2-10: 2-1st app. Neil The Horse. 6-Origin & 1st app. Thunderbunny			
		.30	.60
Special 1(11/86)(½-in B&W)	.35	1.00	2.00
Special 2-Atomic Mouse app. ('87)	.25	.75	1.50

CHARLTON CLASSICS
April, 1980 - No. 9, Aug, 1981
Charlton Comics

1		.30	.60
2-9		.25	.50

CHARLTON CLASSICS LIBRARY (1776)
V10No.1, March, 1973 (One Shot)
Charlton Comics

1776 (title) - Adaptation of the film musical ''1776''; given away at movie theatres	.35	1.00	2.00

CHARLTON PREMIERE (Formerly Marine War Heroes)
V1No.19, July, 1967; V2No.1, Sept, 1967 - No. 4, May, 1968
Charlton Comics

V1#19-Marine War Heroes, V2#1-Trio; intro. Shape, Tyro Team, & Spookman, 2-Children of Doom, 3-Sinistro Boy Fiend; Blue Beetle Peacemaker x-over, 4-Unlikely Tales; Ditko-a	.35	1.00	2.00

Chamber Of Darkness #1, © MEG

Champion Comics #2, © HARV

Charlie Chan #1, © DELL

Checkmate #1, © GK   Cheyenne #22, © Warner Bros.   Cheyenne Kid #11, © CC

CHARLTON SPORT LIBRARY - PROFESSIONAL FOOTBALL
Winter, 1969-70 (Jan. on cover) (68 pages)
Charlton Comics

	Good	Fine	N-Mint
1	.70	2.00	4.00

CHASING THE BLUES
1912 (52 pages) (7½x10''; B&W; hardcover)
Doubleday Page

by Rube Goldberg	30.00	90.00	210.00

CHECKMATE (TV)
Oct, 1962 - No. 2, Dec, 1962
Gold Key

1,2-Photo-c	2.30	7.00	16.00

CHECKMATE (See Action Comics #598)
April, 1988 - Present ($1.25)
DC Comics

1	.60	1.75	3.50
2	.40	1.25	2.50
3-5	.30	.90	1.75
6-24: 13-on are $1.50, new format	.25	.75	1.50

NOTE: *Gil Kane* c-2, 4, 7, 8, 10, 11, 15-19.

CHEERIOS PREMIUMS (Disney)
1947 (32 pages) (Pocket size; 16 titles)
Walt Disney Productions

Set ''W''-Donald Duck & the Pirates	2.65	8.00	18.00
Pluto Joins the F.B.I.	1.50	4.50	10.00
Bucky Bug & the Cannibal King	1.50	4.50	10.00
Mickey Mouse & the Haunted House	2.30	7.00	16.00
Set ''X''-Donald Duck, Counter Spy	2.00	6.00	14.00
Goofy Lost in the Desert	1.50	4.50	10.00
Br'er Rabbit Outwits Br'er Fox	1.50	4.50	10.00
Mickey Mouse at the Rodeo	2.30	7.00	16.00
Set ''Y''-Donald Duck's Atom Bomb by Carl Barks	40.00	120.00	280.00
Br'er Rabbit's Secret	1.50	4.50	10.00
Dumbo & the Circus Mystery	2.00	6.00	14.00
Mickey Mouse Meets the Wizard	2.30	7.00	16.00
Set ''Z''-Donald Duck Pilots a Jet Plane (not by Barks)	2.00	6.00	14.00
Pluto Turns Sleuth Hound	1.50	4.50	10.00
The Seven Dwarfs & the Enchanted Mtn.	2.00	6.00	14.00
Mickey Mouse's Secret Room	2.30	7.00	16.00

CHEERIOS 3-D GIVEAWAYS (Disney)
1954 (Pocket size) (24 titles)
Walt Disney Productions

(Glasses were cut-outs on boxes)

Glasses only....	4.00	12.00	28.00

(Set 1)
1-Donald Duck & Uncle Scrooge, the Firefighters
2-Mickey Mouse & Goofy, Pirate Plunder
3-Donald Duck's Nephews, the Fabulous Inventors
4-Mickey Mouse, Secret of the Ming Vase
5-Donald Duck with Huey, Dewey, & Louie; ...the Seafarers (title on 2nd page)
6-Mickey Mouse, Moaning Mountain
7-Donald Duck, Apache Gold
8-Mickey Mouse, Flight to Nowhere

(per book)....	5.00	15.00	35.00

(Set 2)
1-Donald Duck, Treasure of Timbuktu
2-Mickey Mouse & Pluto, Operation China
3-Donald Duck in the Magic Cows
4-Mickey Mouse & Goofy, Kid Kokonut

5-Donald Duck, Mystery Ship
6-Mickey Mouse, Phantom Sheriff
7-Donald Duck, Circus Adventures
8-Mickey Mouse, Arctic Explorers

	Good	Fine	N-Mint
(per book)....	5.00	15.00	35.00

(Set 3)
1-Donald Duck & Witch Hazel
2-Mickey Mouse in Darkest Africa
3-Donald Duck & Uncle Scrooge, Timber Trouble
4-Mickey Mouse, Rajah's Rescue
5-Donald Duck in Robot Reporter
6-Mickey Mouse, Slumbering Sleuth
7-Donald Duck in the Foreign Legion
8-Mickey Mouse, Airwalking Wonder

(per book)....	5.00	15.00	35.00

CHESTY AND COPTIE
1946 (4 pages) (Giveaway) (Disney)
Los Angeles Community Chest

(Very Rare) by Floyd Gottfredson	17.00	51.00	120.00

CHESTY AND HIS HELPERS
1943 (12 pgs., Disney giveaway, 5½x7¼'')
Los Angeles War Chest

nn-Chesty & Coptie	19.00	57.00	132.00

CHEVAL NOIR
1989 - Present ($3.50, B&W, 68 pgs.)
Dark Horse Comics

1-6: 1-Stevens-c. 2-Bolland, Bolton-a. 4-Bolton-c. 5-Moebius-c. 6-Moebius poster insert	.60	1.75	3.50

CHEYENNE (TV)
No. 734, Oct, 1956 - No. 25, Dec-Jan, 1961-62
Dell Publishing Co.

4-Color 734(#1)-Ty Hardin photo-c begin	6.00	18.00	42.00
4-Color 772,803	4.00	12.00	28.00
4(8-10/57) - 12-Last Ty Hardin photo-c	3.50	10.50	24.00
13-25 (All Clint Walker photo-c)	3.00	9.00	21.00

CHEYENNE AUTUMN (See Movie Classics)

CHEYENNE KID (Formerly Wild Frontier No. 1-7)
No. 8, July, 1957 - No. 99, Nov, 1973
Charlton Comics

8 (No. 1)	2.65	8.00	18.00
9,15-17,19	1.30	4.00	9.00
10-Williamson/Torres-a(3); Ditko-c	5.50	16.50	38.00
11,12-Williamson/Torres-a(2) ea.; 11-(68 pgs.)	5.50	16.50	38.00
13-Williamson/Torres-a, 5 pgs.	3.50	10.50	24.00
14,18-Williamson-a, 5 pgs.?	3.50	10.50	24.00
20-22,25-Severin c/a(3) each	1.70	5.00	12.00
23,24,27-29	.85	2.60	6.00
26,30-Severin-a	1.00	3.00	7.00
31-59	.50	1.50	3.00
60-99: 66-Wander by Aparo begins, ends #87. Apache Red begins #88, origin #89		.40	.80
Modern Comics Reprint 87,89('78)		.20	.40

CHICAGO MAIL ORDER (See C-M-O Comics)

CHIEF, THE (Indian Chief No. 3 on)
No. 290, Aug, 1950 - No. 2, Apr-June, 1951
Dell Publishing Co.

4-Color 290, 2	3.00	9.00	21.00

CHIEF CRAZY HORSE (See Wild Bill Hockok #21)
1950
Avon Periodicals

nn-Fawcette-c	11.00	32.00	75.00

CHIEF VICTORIO'S APACHE MASSACRE
1951
Avon Periodicals

	Good	Fine	N-Mint
nn-Williamson/Frazetta-a, 7 pgs.; Larsen-a; Kinstler-c	25.00	75.00	175.00

CHILDREN OF FIRE
Nov., 1987 - No. 3, 1988 (Color) (Mini-series, $2.00)
Fantagor Press

1-3: by Richard Corben	.35	1.00	2.00

CHILDREN'S BIG BOOK
1945 (68 pages; stiff covers) (25 cents)
Dorene Publ. Co.

Comics & fairy tales; David Icove-a	5.50	16.50	38.00

CHILI (Millie's Rival)
5/69 - No. 17, 9/70; No. 18, 8/72 - No. 26, 12/73
Marvel Comics Group

1	1.15	3.50	8.00
2-5	.70	2.00	4.00
6-17	.50	1.50	3.00
18-26	.30	1.00	2.00
Special 1(12/71)	.50	1.50	3.00

CHILLING ADVENTURES IN SORCERY (. . .as Told by Sabrina No.1, 2) (Red Circle Sorcery No. 6 on)
9/72 - No. 2, 10/72; No. 3, 10/73 - No. 5, 2/74
Archie Publications (Red Circle Prod.)

1,2-Sabrina cameo in both	.50	1.50	3.00
3-Morrow c/a, all	.35	1.00	2.00
4,5-Morrow c/a, 5,6 pgs.	.35	1.00	2.00

CHILLING TALES (Formerly Beware)
No. 13, Dec, 1952 - No. 17, Oct, 1953
Youthful Magazines

13(No.1)-Harrison-a; Matt Fox c/a	13.50	41.00	95.00
14-Harrison-a	8.00	24.00	56.00
15-Has No. 14 on-c; Matt Fox-c; Harrison-a	10.00	30.00	70.00
16-Poe adapt.-'Metzengerstein'; Rudyard Kipling adapt.-'Mark of the Beast,' by Kiefer; bondage-c	8.00	24.00	56.00
17-Matt Fox-c; Sir Walter Scott & Poe adapt.	10.00	30.00	70.00

CHILLING TALES OF HORROR (Magazine)
V1No.1, 6/69 - V1No.7, 12/70; V2No.2, 2/71 - V2No.5, 10/71
(52 pages; black & white) (50 cents)
Stanley Publications

V1#1	.85	2.50	5.00
2-7: 7-Cameron-a	.50	1.50	3.00
V2#2,3,5: 2-Spirit of Frankenstein r-/Adventures into the Unknown #16	.50	1.50	3.00
V2#4-r-9 pg. Feldstein-a from Adventures into the Unknown #3	.70	2.00	4.00

NOTE: *Two issues of V2No.2 exist, Feb, 1971 and April, 1971.*

CHILLY WILLY (See 4-Color 740,852,967,1017,1074,1122,1177,1212,1281)

CHINA BOY (See Wisco)

CHIP 'N' DALE (Walt Disney)(See Walt Disney's C&S #204)
11/53 - No. 30, 6-8/62; 9/67 - No. 83, 1982
Dell Publishing Co./Gold Key/Whitman No. 65 on

4-Color 517	1.70	5.00	12.00
4-Color 581,636	1.30	4.00	9.00
4(12/55-2/56)-10	.75	2.25	5.00
11-30	.55	1.65	4.00
1(Gold Key reprints, 1967)	.70	2.00	4.00
2-10	.35	1.00	2.00
11-20		.60	1.20
21-83		.40	.80

NOTE: *All Gold Key/Whitman issues have reprints except No. 32-35, 38-41, 45-47. No. 23-28, 30-42, 45-47, 49 have new covers.*

CHITTY CHITTY BANG BANG (See Movie Comics)

CHOICE COMICS
Dec, 1941 - No. 3, Feb, 1942
Great Publications

	Good	Fine	N-Mint
1-Origin Secret Circle; Atlas the Mighty app.; Zomba, Jungle Fight, Kangaroo Man, & Fire Eater begin	47.00	140.00	325.00
2	30.00	90.00	210.00
3-Features movie 'The Lost City" classic cover; continues in Great Comics #3	41.00	124.00	290.00

CHOO CHOO CHARLIE
Dec, 1969
Gold Key

1-John Stanley-a (scarce)	5.00	15.00	35.00

CHRISTIAN HEROES OF TODAY
1964 (36 pages)
David C. Cook

nn	.70	2.00	4.00

CHRISTMAS (See A-1 No. 28)

CHRISTMAS ADVENTURE, A (See Classics Comics Giveaways, 12/69)

CHRISTMAS ADVENTURE, THE
1963 (16 pages)
S. Rose (H. L. Green Giveaway)

nn	.85	2.50	5.00

CHRISTMAS ALBUM (See March of Comics No. 312)

CHRISTMAS & ARCHIE ($1.00)
Jan, 1975 (68 pages) (10¼x13¼")
Archie Comics

1	1.70	5.00	10.00

CHRISTMAS AT THE ROTUNDA (Titled Ford Rotunda Christmas Book 1957 on) (Regular size)
Given away every Christmas at one location
1954 - 1961
Ford Motor Co. (Western Printing)

1954-56 issues (nn's)	1.75	5.25	12.00
1957-61 issues (nn's)	1.15	3.50	8.00

CHRISTMAS BELLS (See March of Comics No. 297)

CHRISTMAS CARNIVAL
1952 (100 pages, 25 cents) (One Shot)
Ziff-Davis Publ. Co./St. John Publ. Co. No. 2

nn	8.00	24.00	56.00
2-Reprints Ziff-Davis issue plus-c	5.70	17.00	40.00

CHRISTMAS CAROL, A (See March of Comics No. 33)

CHRISTMAS CAROL, A
No date (1942-43) (32 pgs.; 8¼x10¾"; paper cover)
Sears Roebuck & Co. (Giveaway)

nn-Comics & coloring book	5.00	15.00	30.00

CHRISTMAS CAROL, A
1940s ? (20 pgs.)
Sears Roebuck & Co. (Christmas giveaway)

Comic book & animated coloring book	4.00	12.00	24.00

CHRISTMAS CAROLS
1959 ? (16 pgs.)
Hot Shoppes Giveaway

nn	1.20	3.50	7.00

CHRISTMAS COLORING FUN
1964 (20 pgs.; slick cover; B&W inside)

Chilling Tales #15, © YM

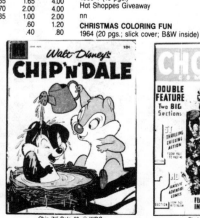

Chip 'N' Dale #6, © WDC

Choice Comics #3, © GP

THE GOLDEN CHRISTMAS TREE
Mickey and Goofy as Santa's Helpers in
SPECIAL DELIVERY

Christmas Parade #4, © WDC   Christmas Parade #1 (2/89), © WDC   Chuckle #1, © R.B. Leffingwell

CHRISTMAS COLORING FUN (continued)
H. Burnside

	Good	Fine	N-Mint
nn	.70	2.00	4.00

CHRISTMAS DREAM, A
1950 (16 pages) (Kinney Shoe Store Giveaway)
Promotional Publishing Co.

nn	1.35	4.00	8.00

CHRISTMAS DREAM, A
1952? (16 pgs.; paper cover)
J. J. Newberry Co. (Giveaway)

nn	1.35	4.00	8.00

CHRISTMAS DREAM, A
1952 (16 pgs.; paper cover)
Promotional Publ. Co. (Giveaway)

nn	1.35	4.00	8.00

CHRISTMAS EVE, A (See March of Comics No. 212)

CHRISTMAS FUN AROUND THE WORLD
No date (early 50's) (16 pages; paper cover)
No publisher

nn	2.00	6.00	12.00

CHRISTMAS IN DISNEYLAND (See Dell Giants)

CHRISTMAS JOURNEY THROUGH SPACE
1960
Promotional Publishing Co.

Reprints 1954 issue Jolly Christmas Book with new slick cover

	1.50	4.50	10.00

CHRISTMAS ON THE MOON
1958 (20 pgs.; slick cover)
W. T. Grant Co. (Giveaway)

nn	1.75	5.25	12.00

CHRISTMAS PARADE (See Dell Giant No. 26, Dell Giants, March of Comics No. 284, & Walt Disney's. . .)
CHRISTMAS PARADE (Walt Disney's)
1/63 (no month) - No. 9, 1/72; Wint/88 (#1,5: 80pgs.; #2-4,7-9: 36pgs.)
Gold Key/Gladstone Publishing

1 (30018-301)-Giant	3.75	11.00	26.00
2-Reprints 4-Color 367 by Barks	4.00	12.00	28.00
3-Reprints 4-Color 178 by Barks	4.00	12.00	28.00
4-Reprints 4-Color 203 by Barks	4.00	12.00	28.00
5-Reprints Christmas Parade 1(Dell) by Barks; giant			
	4.00	12.00	28.00
6-Reprints Christmas Parade 2(Dell) by Barks(64pp)-Giant			
	4.00	12.00	28.00
7,9: 7-Pull-out poster	2.00	6.00	14.00
8-Reprints 4-Color 367 by Barks; pull-out poster			
	4.00	12.00	28.00
1(Winter/88, $2.95, 100pgs, Gladstone): Barks-r/painted-c			
	.50	1.50	3.00
2(Winter/89, $2.95)-Barks-r	.50	1.50	3.00

CHRISTMAS PARTY (See March of Comics No. 256)

CHRISTMAS PLAY BOOK
1946 (16 pgs.; paper cover)
Gould-Stoner Co. (Giveaway)

nn	2.75	8.00	16.00

CHRISTMAS ROUNDUP
1960
Promotional Publishing Co.

Marv Levy c/a	1.00	3.00	7.00

CHRISTMAS STORIES (See 4-Color No. 959,1062)

CHRISTMAS STORY (See March of Comics No. 326)

CHRISTMAS STORY BOOK (See Woolworth's Christmas Story Book)

CHRISTMAS STORY CUT-OUT BOOK, THE
1951 (36 pages) (15 cents)
Catechetical Guild

	Good	Fine	N-Mint
393-½ text, ½ comics	2.75	8.00	16.00

CHRISTMAS TREASURY, A (See Dell Giants & March of Comics No. 227)

CHRISTMAS USA (Through 300 Years) (Also see Uncle Sam's. . .)
1956
Promotional Publ. Co. (Giveaway)

Marv Levy c/a	1.00	3.00	6.00

CHRISTMAS WITH ARCHIE
1973, 1974 (52 pages) (49 cents)
Spire Christian Comics (Fleming H. Revell Co.)

nn		.60	1.20

CHRISTMAS WITH MOTHER GOOSE (See 4-Color No. 90,126,172,201,253)

CHRISTMAS WITH SANTA (See March of Comics No. 92)

CHRISTMAS WITH SNOW WHITE AND THE SEVEN DWARFS
1953 (16 pages, paper cover)
Kobackers Giftstore of Buffalo, N.Y.

nn	3.00	9.00	18.00

CHRISTMAS WITH THE SUPER-HEROES (See Limited Coll. Ed.)
1988; No. 2, 1989 ($2.95, 100 pgs., all reprints)
DC Comics

1-N. Adams-r, Byrne-c; Batman, Superman, JLA, LSH Christmas stories; r-Miller's 1st Batman/DC Special Series #21			
	.50	1.50	2.95
2-Superman by Chadwick, Batman, Wonder Woman, Deadman, Gr. Lantern, Flash app.; Enemy Ace by Byrne	.50	1.50	2.95

CHRISTOPHERS, THE
1951 (36 pages) (Some copies have 15 cent sticker)
Catechetical Guild (Giveaway)

nn-Hammer & sickle dripping blood-c; Stalin as Satan in Hell			
	16.00	48.00	110.00

CHROME
1986 - No. 3, 1986? ($1.50, color)
Hot Comics

1-3	.25	.75	1.50

CHRONICLES OF CORUM, THE (Also see Corum. . .)
Jan, 1987 - No. 12, Nov, 1988 ($1.75-$1.95, deluxe series)
First Comics

1-12: Adapts Michael Moorcock's novel	.35	1.00	2.00

CHRONICLES OF PANDA KHAN, THE (Panda Khan No. 3)
Feb, 1987 - Present? ($1.50, B&W)
Abacus Press

1,2-Character from A Distant Soil	.25	.75	1.50
3,4 ($2.00-c)	.35	1.00	2.00

CHUCKLE, THE GIGGLY BOOK OF COMIC ANIMALS
1945 (132 pages) (One Shot)
R. B. Leffingwell Co.

1-Funny animal	9.30	28.00	65.00

CHUCK NORRIS (TV)
Jan, 1987 - No. 5, Sept, 1987
Star Comics (Marvel)

1-Ditko-a		.40	.80
2-5		.40	.80

CHUCK WAGON (See Sheriff Bob Dixon's. . .)

CICERO'S CAT
July-Aug, 1959 - No. 2, Sept-Oct, 1959
Dell Publishing Co.

	Good	Fine	N-Mint
1,2	1.70	5.00	12.00

CIMARRON STRIP (TV)
January, 1968
Dell Publishing Co.

1	2.30	7.00	16.00

CINDER AND ASHE
May, 1988 - No. 4, Aug, 1988 ($1.75, mini-series)
DC Comics

1-4: Mature readers	.30	.90	1.80

CINDERELLA (See 4-Color No. 272,786, & Movie Comics)

CINDERELLA
April, 1982
Whitman Publishing Co.

nn-r-/4-Color 272		.30	.60

CINDERELLA IN ''FAIREST OF THE FAIR''
1955 (16 pages, 5x7¼, soft-c) (Walt Disney)
American Dairy Association (Premium)

nn	5.00	15.00	30.00

CINDERELLA LOVE
No. 10, 1950; No. 11, 4/51 - No. 12, 9/51; No. 4, 10-11/51 - No. 11,
Fall, 1952; No. 12, 10/53 - No. 15, 8/54; No.25, 12/54 -No.29, 10/55
(No #16-24)
Ziff-Davis/St. John Publ. Co. No. 12 on

	Good	Fine	N-Mint
10 (1st Series, 1950)	4.30	13.00	30.00
11(4/51), 12(9/51)	1.85	5.50	13.00
4-8: 4,7-Photo-c	1.60	4.70	11.00
9-Kinstler-a; photo-c	2.65	8.00	18.00
10-Whitney painted-c	2.15	6.50	15.00
11(Fall/'52)-Crandall-a; Saunders painted-c	3.50	10.50	24.00
12(St. John-10/53) - #14: 13-Painted-c	1.50	4.50	10.00
15 (8/54)-Matt Baker-c	2.65	8.00	18.00
25(2nd Series)(Formerly Romantic Marriage)	1.50	4.50	10.00
26-Baker-c; last precode (2/55)	3.00	9.00	21.00
27,28	1.15	3.50	8.00
29-Matt Baker-c	2.65	8.00	18.00

CINDY COMICS (. . . Smith No. 39,40; Crime Can't Win No. 41 on)
(Formerly Krazy Komics)(See Teen Comics)
No. 27, Fall, 1947 - No. 40, July, 1950
Timely Comics

27-Kurtzman-a, 3 pgs: Margie, Oscar begin	6.50	19.50	45.00
28-31-Kurtzman-a	3.70	11.00	26.00
32-40: 33-Georgie story; anti-Wertham edit.	2.65	8.00	18.00

NOTE: *Kurtzman's ''Hey Look''-#27(3), 29(2), 30(2), 31; ''Giggles 'N' Grins''- #28.*

CINEMA COMICS HERALD
1941 - 1943 (4-pg. movie ''trailers,'' paper-c, 7½x10½'')
Paramount Pictures/Universal/RKO/20th Century Fox/Republic
(Giveaway)

''Mr. Bug Goes to Town''-(1941)	3.35	10.00	20.00
''Bedtime Story''	3.35	10.00	20.00
''Lady For A Night,'' John Wayne, Joan Blondell (1942)			
	3.35	10.50	24.00
''Reap The Wild Wind''-(1942)	3.35	10.00	20.00
''Thunder Birds''-(1942)	3.35	10.00	20.00
''They All Kissed the Bride''	3.35	10.00	20.00
''Arabian Nights,'' nd	3.35	10.00	20.00
''Bombardier''-(1943)	3.35	10.00	20.00
''Crash Dive''-(1943)-Tyrone Power	3.35	10.00	20.00

NOTE: *The 1941-42 issues contain line art with color photos. 1943 issues are line art.*

CIRCUS (. . .the Comic Riot)
June, 1938 - No. 3, Aug, 1938
Globe Syndicate

	Good	Fine	N-Mint
1-(Scarce)-Spacehawks (2 pgs.), & Disk Eyes by Wolverton (2 pgs.), Pewee Throttle by Cole (2nd comic book work; see Star Comics V1#11), Beau Gus, Ken Craig & The Lords of Crillon, Jack Hinton by Eisner, Van Bragger by Kane	200.00	600.00	1400.00
2,3-(Scarce)-Eisner, Cole, Wolverton, Bob Kane-a in each			
	100.00	300.00	700.00

CIRCUS BOY (See 4-Color No. 759,785.813)

CIRCUS COMICS
1945 - No. 2, June, 1945; Winter, 1948-49
Farm Women's Publishing Co./D. S. Publ.

1-Funny animal	4.30	13.00	30.00
2	2.85	8.50	20.00
1(1948)-D.S. Publ.; 2 pgs. Frazetta	13.50	41.00	95.00

CIRCUS OF FUN COMICS
1945 - 1947 (a book of games & puzzles)
A. W. Nugent Publishing Co.

1	5.00	15.00	35.00
2,3	3.00	9.00	21.00

CIRCUS WORLD (See Movie Classics)

CISCO KID, THE (TV)
July, 1950 - No. 41, Oct-Dec, 1958
Dell Publishing Co.

4-Color 292(No.1)-Cisco Kid, his horse Diablo, & sidekick Pancho & his horse Loco begin; painted-c begin	9.30	28.00	65.00
2(1/51)-5	4.50	14.00	32.00
6-10	3.70	11.00	26.00
11-20	3.00	9.00	21.00
21-36-Last painted-c	2.65	8.00	18.00
37-41: All photo-c	5.00	15.00	35.00

NOTE: *Buscema a-40. Ernest Nordli painted-c-5-16,20,35.*

CISCO KID COMICS
Winter, 1944 - No. 3, 1945
Bernard Bailey/Swappers Quarterly

1-Illustrated Stories of the Operas: Faust; Funnyman by Giunta; Cisco Kid begins	20.00	60.00	140.00
2,3	14.00	42.00	100.00

CITIZEN SMITH (See Holyoke One-Shot No. 9)

CITY OF THE LIVING DEAD (See Fantastic Tales No. 1)
1952
Avon Periodicals

nn-Hollingsworth c/a	17.00	51.00	120.00

CITY SURGEON (Blake Harper. . .)
August, 1963
Gold Key

1(10075-308)-Painted-c	1.15	3.50	8.00

CIVIL WAR MUSKET, THE (Kadets of America Handbook)
1960 (36 pages) (Half-size; 25 cents)
Custom Comics, Inc.

nn	1.50	4.50	10.00

CLAIRE VOYANT (Also see Keen Teens)
1946 - No. 4, 1947 (Sparling strip reprints)
Leader Publ./Standard/Pentagon Publ.

nn	26.00	78.00	180.00
2-Kamen-c	20.00	60.00	140.00
3-Kamen bridal-c; contents mentioned in Love and Death, a book by Gershom Legman('49) referenced by Dr. Wertham			
	23.00	70.00	160.00

Cinderella Love #4, © STJ

Circus Of Fun #1, © A.W. Nugent

The Cisco Kid #7, © DELL

CLAIRE VOYANT (continued)	Good	Fine	N-Mint
4-Kamen bondage-c	20.00	60.00	140.00

CLANCY THE COP
1930 - No. 2, 1931 (52 pages; B&W) (not reprints) (10"x10")
Dell Publishing Co. (Soft cover)

	Good	Fine	N-Mint
1,2-Vep-a	7.00	21.00	50.00

CLASSIC COMICS/ILLUSTRATED - INTRODUCTION
by Dan Malan

Further revisions have been made to help in understanding the **Classics** section. **Classics** reprint editions prior to 1963 had either incorrect dates or no dates listed. Those reprint editions should be identified only by the highest number on the reorder list (HRN). Past price guides listed what were calculated to be approximately correct dates, but many people found it confusing for the price guide to list a date not listed in the comic itself.

We have also attempted to clear up confusion about edition variations, such as color, printer, etc. Such variations will be identified by letters. Editions will now be determined by three categories. Original edition variations will be Edition 1A, 1B, etc. All reprint editions prior to 1963 will be identified by HRN only. All reprint editions from 9/63 on will be identified by the correct date listed in the comic.

We have also included new information on four recent reprintings of **Classics** not previously listed. From 1968-1976 Twin Circle, the Catholic newspaper, serialized over 100 **Classics** titles. That list can be found under non-series items at the end of this section. In 1972 twelve **Classics** were reissued as **Now Age Books Illustrated**. They are listed under **Pendulum Illustrated Classics**. In 1982, 20 Classics were reissued, adapted for teaching English as a second language. They are listed under **Regents Illustrated Classics**. Then in 1984, six Classics were reissued with cassette tapes. See the listing under **Cassette Books**.

UNDERSTANDING CLASSICS ILLUSTRATED
by Dan Malan

Since 1982, this book has been listing every **Classics** edition. That became possible because of Charles Heffelfinger's 1978 book, **The Classics Handbook**, detailing and illustrating every **Classics** edition. But there are still some areas of confusion, and this revised and expanded introduction will attempt to alleviate those problem areas.

THE HISTORY OF CLASSICS

The **Classics** series was the brainchild of Al Kanter, who sought for a way to introduce children to quality literature. In October 1941 his Gilberton Co. began the series **Classic Comics** with **The Three Musketeers**, with 64 pages of storyline. The early years saw irregular schedules and numerous printers, not to mention some second-class artwork and liberal story adaptations. With No. 13 the page total was dropped to 56 (except for No. 33, originally scheduled to be No. 9), and with No. 15 the next-issue ad on the outside back cover moved indoors. In 1945 the Iger shop began producing Classics, beginning with No. 23. In 1947 the search for a "classier" logo title produced **Classics Illustrated**, beginning with No. 35, **The Last Days Of Pompeii**. With No. 45 the story length dropped again to 48 pages, which was to become the standard.

What was probably the most important development for the success of the **Classics** series began in 1951 with the introduction of painted covers, instead of the old line drawn covers, beginning with No. 81, **The Odyssey**. That served as a good excuse to raise the cover price from 10 to 15 cents and did not hinder the growth of the series. From 1947 to 1953 **Classics** artwork was dominated by H.C. Kiefer and Alex Blum, together accounting for nearly 50 titles. Their distinctive styles gave real personality to the **Classics** series. **Classics** flourished during the fifties, and they diversified with **Juniors**, **Specials**, and **World Around Us** series.

But in the early sixties financial troubles set in. In 1962 the issuing of new titles ended with No. 167, **Faust**. In 1967 the company was sold to the Catholic publisher, Twin Circle. They issued two new titles in 1969 as part of an attempted revival, but succumbed to major distribution problems.

One of the major trademarks of the **Classics** series was the proliferation of reprint variations. Some titles had as many as 25 reprint editions. Reprinting began in 1943. Some of the **Classic Comic** (CC) reprints (r) had the logo format revised to the banner logo, and had the motto added under the banner. Then, reprints of all the CC titles were changed over to the new logo title, **Classics Illustrated** (CI), but still had line drawn covers (LDC). Nos. 13, 18, 29 and 41 received second covers (LDC2), replacing covers considered too violent. During 1948 and 1949, reprints of title Nos. 13 to 44 had pages reduced to 48 (except for No. 26, which had 48 pages to begin with).

Starting in the mid-fifties, 70 of the 80 LDC titles were reissued with new painted covers (PC). Thirty of them also received new interior artwork (A2). The new artwork was generally higher quality with larger art panels and more faithful but abbreviated storylines. There were also 29 second painted covers (PC2) issued, mostly by Twin Circle. The last reprints were issued in 1971. Altogether there were 199 interior artwork variations (169 (0)s plus 30 A2 editions) and 272 different covers (169 (0)s, four LDC2s, 70 new PCs of LDC (0) titles, and 29 PC2s). It is mildly astounding to realize that there were over 1,350 editions in the U.S. **Classics** series.

FOREIGN CLASSICS ILLUSTRATED

If U.S. **Classics** variations are mildly astounding, the veritable plethora of foreign **Classics** variations will boggle your imagination. While new information is still coming in, we definitely know about series in 22 languages, 25 countries of origin (some with two or three series), and over 30 distribu-

tion countries. There were nearly 300 new **Classics** titles in foreign series and nearly 400 new foreign covers of U.S. titles. Altogether, there were over 4,000 foreign **Classics** editions.

The first foreign **Classics** series consisted of six Canadian **Classic Comic** reprints in 1946. By 1948 series had sprung up in Australia, Brazil, and the Netherlands. But the early series were isolated and often brief. In the mid-fifties, when the U.S. began developing its PC/A2 editions, that U.S. development was coordinated with multi-European country series utilizing the same editions in nine languages at once. This was the main thrust of foreign **Classics**. And when the U.S. stopped issuing new titles in the early sixties, the European series continued with 82 new European titles, which continued until 1976. There were also 88 new Greek History & Mythology titles, and 80 new Brazilian titles, almost all by Brazilian authors. Countries with large numbers of new covers of U.S. titles were Brazil, Mexico, Greece, and the early Australian series. All the rare U.S. titles which never had a painted cover can be found with a new cover in some foreign series.

Here is a chronological list of countries with **Classics** series:

Canada (1946), Australia (1947), Brazil (1948), Netherlands (1948) Italy (1950), Greece (1951), Japan (1951), Hong Kong (1951?) Great Britain (1951), Argentina (1951), Mexico (1951), W. Germany (1952), Norway (1954), New Zealand (1955), Iceland (1956), Denmark (1956), Sweden (1956), Finland (1957), France (1957), Singapore (1962?), India (1964), Ireland (1971), Belgium (1971?), Philippines (1973?)

Other listed distribution countries included Austria, Switzerland, Luxemburg, Spain, Morocco, and South Africa.

REFERENCE WORKS ON CLASSICS

The Classics Handbook (3rd edition - 1986) by Charles Heffelfinger. This work identifies and illustrates all U.S. **Classics** editions. It also has illustrations of all **Juniors**, **Specials** & **World Around Us**, plus information on giveaways, artists, etc.

The Classics Index (1986) by Tom Fisher. This comprehensive subject index covers all **Classics** title stories and filler articles, plus all **Juniors**, **Specials** & **World Around Us**.

The Foreign Classics Handbook (preliminary draft - 1986) by Dan Malan. This draft details over 30 series in 20 countries. It also includes a cross-reference index for all U.S. titles/artwork/covers, and a cross-reference comparison chart for all European country series.

The Complete Guide To Classics Collectibles (1990), by Dan Malan. Contains thousands of illustrations with a market analysis of every facet of U.S. and Foreign **Classics** , books, art and non-series items.

The Classics Collector Magazine, Dan Malan, editor. One of the top zines for Classics collectors the world over. Has information & ads about U.S. and foreign Classics.

Worldwide Classics Newsletter (1987-89) Dan Malan, Editor. With subscribers from 18 countries, **WCN** is the nerve center for all new information about U.S. and foreign **Classics**, related series, and non-series collectible items. It also includes ads and market analysis of all **Classics**-related items. The above two items are available from Dan Malan, 7519 Lindbergh Dr., St. Louis, MO 63117.

IDENTIFYING CLASSICS EDITIONS

HRN: This is the highest number on the reorder list. It is crucial to understanding the various **Classics** editions. It is shown in parentheses.

ORIGINALS (O): This is the all-important First Edition. There is one basic rule and two secondary rules (with exceptions) that apply here.

Rule No. 1: All (O)s and only (O)s have an ad for the next title (issue).
Exceptions: No. 14(15) (reprint) has an ad on the last inside page of the text. No. 14(O) has an ad on the outside back cover and also says 10 cents on the front cover. Nos. 55(75) and 57(75) (reprints) have ads for the next issue. (Rules 2 and 3 apply here.) Nos. 168(O) and 169(O) do not have ads for the next issue. (No. 168 was never reprinted; No. 169(O) has HRN (166), No. 169(169) is the only reprint.)
Rule No. 2: All (O)s and only (O)s (Nos. 1-80) list 10 cents on the front cover. Exceptions: Nos. 37(62), 39(71) and 46(62) (reprints) say 10 cents on the front cover. (Rules 1 and 3 apply here.)
Rule No. 3: All (O)s have HRN very close to the issue No. of that title. Exceptions: A few reprints also have HRN very close to the title number. Some CC(r)s, 58(62), 60(62), 149(149), 152(149), 153(149), (r)s of titles in 160's. (Rules 1 and 2 apply here.)

For information on variations of (O)s, see the next section (TIPS. . .).
DATES: As stated in the new Introduction, many reprints list either incorrect or no dates. **All Reprint Editions Which List Specific Dates Prior To 1963 Are Incorrect!** All HRNs of (167), (166), and (169) with listed dates of 9/63 or later are correct. Otherwise, ignore the listed date and go by the HRN. Trust me, this is like radar!
COVERS: A change from CC to LDC does not indicate a new cover, only a new logo title, while a change from LDC to PC does indicate a new cover. Keep in mind that there are only four new LDC covers—13, 18, 29 and 41. New PCs can be identified by the HRN, and PC2s should be identified by the HRN and the listed date. Remember that many little details can change on a cover and still be listed as the same cover.
NOTES: If a front cover states "15 cents in Canada," that does not necessarily mean that it is a Canadian edition. Check the return address to be certain. An HRN listed in the price guide with a "/" in it means that there are two different reorder lists in the front and back covers. Twin Circle editions have a back cover different from regular **Classics**.

TIPS ON LISTING CLASSICS FOR SALE

It may be easy to just list "Edition 17," but **Classics** collectors think of issues in terms of what the HRN is, and whether it is an (0) or an (r), and whether it is a CC, LDC, PC, A2, PC2, stiff cover, etc.

ORIGINALS: The best way to list Originals is to just say (O), unless there are variations of Originals, such as HRN (Nos. 95, 108, 160), printer (Nos. 51, 61), etc.

REPRINTS: Just list HRN if it is 165 or below; above that, HRN and date. Also, please list type of logo/cover/art for the convenience of buyers. They will appreciate it.

CLASSIC COMICS (See America in Action, Stories by Famous Authors, Story of the Commandos, & The World Around Us)

CLASSIC COMICS (. . .'s Illustrated No. 35 on)
10/41 - No. 34, 2/47; No. 35, 3/47 - No. 169, Spring/69
(Painted-c on original editions #81 on, and reprints of most nos. 1-80)
Gilberton Publications

Abbreviations:
A-Art; C or c—Cover; CC—Classic Comics; CI—Classics Ill.; Ed—Edition; LDC—Line Drawn Cover; PC—Painted Cover; r—Reprint

1. The Three Musketeers

Ed	HRN	Date	Details	A	C	Good	Fine	N-Mint
1	—	10/41	Date listed-1941; Elliot Pub; 68 pgs.	1	1	257.00	770.00	1800.00
2	10	—	10¢ price removed on all (r)s; Elliot Pub; CC-r	1	1	17.00	51.00	120.00
3	15	—	Long Isl. Ind. ed.; CC-r	1	1	13.00	40.00	90.00
4	18/20	—	Sunrise Times Ed.; CC-r	1	1	10.00	30.00	70.00
5	21	—	Richmond Courier Ed.; CC-r	1	1	9.30	28.00	65.00
6	28	1946	CC-r	1	1	7.00	21.00	48.00
7	36	—	LDC-r	1	1	3.50	10.50	24.00
8	60	—	LDC-r	1	1	2.00	6.00	14.00
9	64	—	LDC-r	1	1	1.70	5.00	10.00
10	78	—	C-price 15¢; LDC-r	1	1	1.50	4.50	9.00
11	93	—	LDC-r	1	1	1.50	4.50	9.00
12	114	—	Last LDC-r	1	1	1.50	4.50	9.00
13	134	—	New-c; old-a; 64 pg. PC-r	1	2	1.70	5.00	10.00
14	143	—	Old-a; PC-r; 64 pg.	1	2	1.30	4.00	8.00
15	150	—	New-a; PC-r; Evans/Crandall-a	2	2	1.30	4.00	8.00
16	149	—	PC-r	2	2	1.00	2.00	4.00
17	167	—	PC-r	2	2	1.00	2.00	4.00
18	167	4/64	PC-r	2	2	1.00	2.00	4.00
19	167	1/65	PC-r	2	2	1.00	2.00	4.00
20	167	3/66	PC-r	2	2	1.00	2.00	4.00
21	166	11/67	PC-r	2	2	1.00	2.00	4.00
22	166	Spr/69	C-price 25 ¢; stiff-c; PC-r	2	2	1.00	2.00	4.00
23	169	Spr/71	PC-r; stiff-c	2	2	1.00	2.00	4.00

2. Ivanhoe

Ed	HRN	Date	Details	A	C	Good	Fine	N-Mint
1	(O)	12/41?	Date listed-1941; Elliot Pub; 68 pgs.	1	1	115.00	345.00	800.00
2	10	—	Price & 'Presents' removvd; Elliot Pub; CC-r	1	1	14.00	43.00	100.00
3	15	—	Long Isl. Ind. ed.; CC-r	1	1	11.00	32.00	75.00
4	18/20	—	Sunrise Times ed.; CC-r	1	1	9.30	28.00	65.00

(continued, The Three Musketeers)

						Good	Fine	N-Mint
5	21	—	Richmond Courier ed.; CC-r	1	1	8.50	25.50	60.00
6	28	1946	Last 'Comics'-r	1	1	7.00	21.00	50.00
7	36	—	1st LDC-r	1	1	3.50	10.50	24.00
8	60	—	LDC-r	1	1	2.00	6.00	14.00
9	64	—	LDC-r ·	1	1	1.70	5.00	12.00
10	78	—	C-price 15¢; LDC-r	1	1	1.70	5.00	10.00
11	89	—	LDC-r	1	1	1.50	4.50	9.00
12	106	—	LDC-r	1	1	1.50	4.50	9.00
13	121	—	Last LDC-r	1	1	1.50	4.50	9.00
14	136	—	New-c&a; PC-r	2	2	1.70	5.00	12.00
15	142	—	PC-r	2	2	1.00	2.00	4.00
16	153	—	PC-r	2	2	1.00	2.00	4.00
17	149	—	PC-r	2	2	1.00	2.00	4.00
18	167	—	PC-r	2	2	1.00	2.00	4.00
19	167	5/64	PC-r	2	2	1.00	2.00	4.00
20	167	1/65	PC-r	2	2	1.00	2.00	4.00
21	167	3/66	PC-r	2	2	1.00	2.00	4.00
22	167	3/66	PC-r	2	2	1.00	2.00	4.00
23	166	R/1968	C-Price 25¢; PC-r	2	2	1.00	2.00	4.00
24	169	Win/69	Stiff-c	2	2	1.00	2.00	4.00
25	169	Win/71	PC-r; stiff-c	2	2	1.00	2.00	4.00

3. The Count of Monte Cristo

Ed	HRN	Date	Details	A	C	Good	Fine	N-Mint
1	(O)	3/42	Elliot Pub; 68 pgs.	1	1	83.00	250.00	580.00
2	10	—	Conray Prods; CC-r	1	1	14.00	43.00	100.00
3	15	—	Long Isl. Ind. ed.; CC-r	1	1	10.00	30.00	70.00
4	18/20	—	Sunrise Times ed.; CC-r	1	1	9.30	28.00	65.00
5	20	—	Sunrise Times ed.; CC-r	1	1	9.00	27.00	62.00
6	21	—	Richmond Courier ed.; CC-r	1	1	8.50	25.50	60.00
7	28	1946	CC-r; new Banner logo	1	1	7.00	21.00	50.00
8	36	—	1st LDC-r	1	1	3.50	10.50	24.00
9	60	—	LDC-r	1	1	2.00	6.00	14.00
10	62	—	LDC-r	1	1	2.85	8.50	20.00
11	71	—	LDC-r	1	1	1.50	4.50	9.00
12	87	—	C-price 15¢; LDC-r	1	1	1.50	4.50	9.00
13	113	—	LDC-r	1	1	1.50	4.50	9.00
14	135	—	New-c&a; PC-r	2	2	1.70	5.00	10.00
15	143	—	PC-r	2	2	1.00	2.00	4.00
16	153	—	PC-r	2	2	1.00	2.00	4.00
17	161	—	PC-r	2	2	1.00	2.00	4.00
18	167	—	PC-r	2	2	1.00	2.00	4.00
19	167	7/64	PC-r	2	2	1.00	2.00	4.00
20	167	7/65	PC-r	2	2	1.00	2.00	4.00
21	167	7/66	PC-r	2	2	1.00	2.00	4.00
22	166	R/1968	C-price 25¢;; PC-r	2	2	1.00	2.00	4.00
23	169	Win/69	Stiff-c; PC-r	2	2	1.00	2.00	4.00

4. The Last of the Mohicans

Ed	HRN	Date	Details	A	C	Good	Fine	N-Mint
1	(O)	8/42?	Date listed-1942; Gilberton #4(0) on; 68 pgs.	1	1	65.00	193.00	450.00
2	12	—	Elliot Pub; CC-r	1	1	13.00	40.00	90.00
3	15	—	Long Isl. Ind. ed.; CC-r	1	1	11.50	34.00	80.00
4	20	—	Long Isl. Ind. ed.; CC-r; banner logo	1	1	10.00	30.00	70.00
5	21	—	Queens Home News ed.; CC-r	1	1	8.00	24.00	56.00

Classic Comics #1 (Orig.), © GIL

Classic Comics #2 (HRN-18), © GIL

Classic Comics #3, © GIL

Classic Comics #5 (HRN-36), © GIL

Classic Comics #6 (HRN-20), © GIL

Classics Illustrated #8 (HRN-51), © GIL

CLASSIC COMICS (continued)

				A	C	Good	Fine	N-Mint
6	28	1946	Last CC-r; new	1	1	7.00	21.00	48.00
7	36	—	1st LDC-r	1	1	3.50	10.50	24.00
8	60	—	LDC-r	1	1	2.00	6.00	14.00
9	64	—	LDC-r	1	1	1.70	5.00	12.00
10	78	—	C-price 15¢; LDC-r	1	1	1.50	4.50	9.00
11	89	—	LDC-r	1	1	1.50	4.50	9.00
12	117	—	Last LDC-r	1	1	1.50	4.50	9.00
13	135	—	New-c; PC-r	1	2	1.70	5.00	10.00
14	141	—	PC-r	1	2	1.50	4.50	9.00
15	150	—	New-a; PC-r; Severin, L.B. Cole-a	2	2	1.70	5.00	10.00
16	161	—	PC-r	2	2	1.25	2.50	5.00
17	167	—	PC-r	2	2	1.00	2.00	4.00
18	167	6/64	PC-r	2	2	1.00	2.00	4.00
19	167	8/65	PC-r	2	2	1.00	2.00	4.00
20	167	8/66	PC-r	2	2	1.00	2.00	4.00
21	166	R/1967	C-price 25¢; PC-r	2	2	1.00	2.00	4.00
22	169	Spr/69	Stiff-c; PC-r	2	2	1.00	2.00	4.00

5. Moby Dick

Ed	HRN	Date	Details	A	C	Good	Fine	N-Mint
1	(O)	9/42?	Date listed-1942; Gilberton; 68 pgs.	1	1	78.00	235.00	550.00
2	10	—	Conray Prods; Pg. 64 changed from 105 title list to letter from Editor; CC-r	1	1	14.00	43.00	100.00
3	15	—	Long Isl. Ind. ed.; Pg. 64 changed from Letter to the Editor to Ill. poem-Concord Hymn; CC-r	1	1	11.50	34.00	80.00
4	18/20	—	Sunrise Times ed.; CC-r	1	1	11.50	34.00	80.00
5	20	—	Sunrise Times ed.; CC-r	1	1	10.00	30.00	70.00
6	21	—	Sunrise Times ed.; CC-r	1	1	8.50	25.50	60.00
7	28	1946	CC-r; new banner logo	1	1	7.00	21.00	50.00
8	36	—	1st LDC-r	1	1	3.50	10.50	24.00
9	60	—	LDC-r	1	1	2.00	6.00	14.00
10	62	—	LDC-r	1	1	3.00	9.00	21.00
11	71	—	LDC-r	1	1	1.50	4.50	9.00
12	87	—	C-price 15¢; LDC-r	1	1	1.50	4.50	9.00
13	118	—	LDC-r	1	1	1.50	4.50	9.00
14	131	—	New c&a; PC-r	2	2	1.70	5.00	10.00
15	138	—	PC-r	2	2	1.00	2.00	4.00
16	148	—	PC-r	2	2	1.00	2.00	4.00
17	158	—	PC-r	2	2	1.00	2.00	4.00
18	167	—	PC-r	2	2	1.00	2.00	4.00
19	167	6/64	PC-r	2	2	1.00	2.00	4.00
20	167	7/65	PC-r	2	2	1.00	2.00	4.00
21	167	3/66	PC-r	2	2	1.00	2.00	4.00
22	166	9/67	PC-r	2	2	1.00	2.00	4.00
23	166	Win/69	New-c & c-price 25¢; Stiff-c; PC-r	2	3	1.70	5.00	10.00
24	169	Win/71	PC-r	2	3	1.70	5.00	10.00

6. A Tale of Two Cities

Ed	HRN	Date	Details	A	C	Good	Fine	N-Mint
1	(O)	10/42	Date listed-1942; 68 pgs. Zeckerberg c/a	1	1	64.00	193.00	450.00
2	14	—	Elliot Pub; CC-r	1	1	13.00	40.00	90.00

				A	C	Good	Fine	N-Mint
3	18	—	Long Isl. Ind. ed.; CC-r	1	1	11.50	34.00	80.00
4	20	—	Sunrise Times ed.; CC-r	1	1	10.00	30.00	70.00
5	28	1946	Last CC-r; new banner logo	1	1	7.00	21.00	48.00
6	51	—	1st LDC-r	1	1	3.00	9.00	21.00
7	64	—	LDC-r	1	1	1.70	5.00	10.00
8	78	—	C-price 15¢; LDC-r	1	1	1.50	4.50	9.00
9	89	—	LDC-r	1	1	1.50	4.50	9.00
10	117	—	LDC-r	1	1	1.50	4.50	9.00
11	132	—	New-c&a; PC-r; Joe Orlando-a	2	2	1.70	5.00	12.00
12	140	—	PC-r	2	2	1.00	2.00	4.00
13	147	—	PC-r	2	2	1.00	2.00	4.00
14	152	—	PC-r; very rare	2	2	8.50	25.50	60.00
15	153	—	PC-r	2	2	1.00	2.00	4.00
16	149	—	PC-r	2	2	1.00	2.00	4.00
17	167	—	PC-r	2	2	1.00	2.00	4.00
18	167	6/64	PC-r	2	2	1.00	2.00	4.00
19	167	8/65	PC-r	2	2	1.00	2.00	4.00
20	167	5/67	PC-r	2	2	1.00	2.00	4.00
21	166	Fall/68	New-c & 25¢-c; PC-r	2	3	1.70	5.00	10.00
22	169	Sum-70	Stiff-c; PC-r	2	3	1.70	5.00	10.00

7. Robin Hood

Ed	HRN	Date	Details	A	C	Good	Fine	N-Mint
1	(O)	12/42	Date listed-1942; first Gift Box ad-bc; 68 pgs.	1	1	54.00	160.00	375.00
2	12	—	Elliot Pub; CC-r	1	1	13.00	40.00	90.00
3	18	—	Long Isl. Ind. ed.; CC-r	1	1	11.00	32.00	75.00
4	20	—	Nassau Bulletin ed.; CC-r	1	1	10.00	30.00	70.00
5	22	—	Queens Cty. Times ed.; CC-r	1	1	9.30	28.00	65.00
6	28	—	CC-r	1	1	7.00	21.00	50.00
7	51	—	LDC-r	1	1	3.00	9.00	21.00
8	64	—	LDC-r	1	1	2.00	6.00	14.00
9	78	—	LDC-r	1	1	1.50	4.50	9.00
10	97	—	LDC-r	1	1	1.50	4.50	9.00
11	106	—	LDC-r	1	1	1.50	4.50	9.00
12	121	—	LDC-r	1	1	1.50	4.50	9.00
13	129	—	New-c; PC-r	1	2	1.70	5.00	10.00
14	136	—	New-a; PC-r	2	2	1.70	5.00	10.00
15	143	—	PC-r	2	2	1.00	2.00	4.00
16	153	—	PC-r	2	2	1.00	2.00	4.00
17	164	—	PC-r	2	2	1.00	2.00	4.00
18	167	—	PC-r	2	2	1.00	2.00	4.00
19	167	6/64	PC-r	2	2	1.50	3.00	6.00
20	167	5/65	PC-r	2	2	1.00	2.00	4.00
21	167	7/66	PC-r	2	2	1.00	2.00	4.00
22	166	12/67	PC-r	2	2	1.50	3.00	6.00
23	169	Sum-69	Stiff-c; c-price 25¢; PC-r	2	2	1.00	2.00	4.00

8. Arabian Nights

Ed	HRN	Date	Details	A	C	Good	Fine	N-Mint
1	(O)	2/43	Original; 68 pgs. Lilian Chestney c/a	1	1	121.00	365.00	850.00
2	17	—	Long Isl. ed.; pg. 64 changed from Gift Box ad to Letter from British Medical Worker; CC-r	1	1	57.00	171.00	400.00

CLASSIC COMICS (continued)

Ed	HRN	Date	Details	A C	Good	Fine	N-Mint
3	20	—	Nassau Bulletin; Pg. 64 changed from letter to article-Three Men Named Smith; CC-r	1 1	40.00	120.00	280.00
4	28	1946	CC-r; new banner logo	1 1	28.00	85.00	200.00
5	51	—	LDC-r	1 1	17.00	51.00	120.00
6	64	—	LDC-r	1 1	14.00	42.00	100.00
7	78	—	LDC-r	1 1	13.00	40.00	90.00
8	164	—	New-c&a; PC-r	2 2	11.00	32.00	75.00

9. Les Miserables

Ed	HRN	Date	Details	A C	Good	Fine	N-Mint
1A	(O)	3/43	Original; slick paper cover; 68 pgs.	1 1	46.00	140.00	325.00
1B	(O)	3/43	Original; rough, pulp type-c; 68 pgs.	1 1	46.00	140.00	325.00
2	14	—	Elliot Pub; CC-r	1 1	14.00	42.00	100.00
3	18	3/44	Nassau Pg. 64 changed from Gift Box ad to Bill of Rights article; CC-r	1 1	12.00	36.00	84.00
4	20	—	Richmond Courier ed.; CC-r	1 1	10.00	30.00	70.00
5	28	1946	Gilberton; pgs. 60-64 rearranged/illos added; CC-r	1 1	7.50	22.00	52.00
6	51	—	LDC-r	1 1	3.70	11.00	26.00
7	71	—	LDC-r	1 1	2.65	8.00	18.00
8	87	—	C-price 15¢; LDC-r	1 1	2.15	6.50	15.00
9	161	—	New-c&a; PC-r	2 2	2.00	6.00	14.00
10	167	9/63	PC-r	2 2	1.50	4.50	10.00
11	167	12/65	PC-r	2 2	1.50	4.50	10.00
12	166	R/1968	New-c & price 25¢; PC-r	2 3	1.70	5.00	12.00

10. Robinson Crusoe (Used in SOTI, pg. 142)

Ed	HRN	Date	Details	A C	Good	Fine	N-Mint
1A	(O)	4/43	Original; Violet-c; 68 pgs; Zuckerberg c/a	1 1	46.00	140.00	325.00
1B	(O)	4/43	Original; blue-grey -c, 68 pgs.	1 1	54.00	160.00	375.00
2A	14	—	Elliot Pub; violet-c; 68 pgs; CC-r	1 1	12.00	36.00	85.00
2B	14	—	Elliot Pub; blue-grey -c; CC-r	1 1	13.50	41.00	95.00
3	18	—	Nassau Bul. Pg. 64 changed from Gift Box ad to Bill of Rights article; CC-r	1 1	10.00	30.00	70.00
4	20	—	Queens Home News ed.; CC-r	1 1	9.30	28.00	65.00
5	28	1946	Gilberton; pg. 64 changes from Bill-Rights to WWII article-One Leg Shot Away; last CC-r	1 1	7.00	21.00	50.00
6	51	—	LDC-r	1 1	3.00	9.00	21.00
7	64	—	C-price 15¢; LDC-r	1 1	2.00	6.00	14.00
8	78	—	LDC-r	1 1	1.50	4.50	9.00
9	97	—	LDC-r	1 1	1.50	4.50	9.00
10	114	—	LDC-r	1 1	1.50	4.50	9.00
11	130	—	New-c; PC-r	1 2	1.70	5.00	10.00
12	140	—	New-a; PC-r	2 2	1.70	5.00	10.00
13	153	—	PC-r	2 2	1.00	2.00	4.00
14	164	—	PC-r	2 2	1.00	2.00	4.00
15	167	—	PC-r	2 2	1.00	2.00	4.00
16	167	7/64	PC-r	2 2	1.00	2.00	4.00
17	167	5/65	PC-r	2 2	1.50	4.50	9.00
18	167	6/66	PC-r	2 2	1.00	2.00	4.00
19	166	Fall/68	C-price 25¢; PC-r	2 2	1.00	2.00	4.00
20	166	R/68	(No Twin Circle ad)	2 2	1.50	3.00	6.00
21	169	Sm/70	Stiff-c; PC-r	2 2	1.50	3.00	6.00

11. Don Quixote

Ed	HRN	Date	Details	A C	Good	Fine	N-Mint
1	10	5/43	First (O) with HRN list; 68 pgs.	1 1	50.00	150.00	350.00
2	18	—	Nassau Bulletin ed.; CC-r	1 1	12.00	36.00	85.00
3	21	—	Queens Home News ed.; CC-r	1 1	10.00	30.00	70.00
4	28	—	CC-r	1 1	7.00	21.00	50.00
5	110	—	New-PC; PC-r	1 2	2.35	7.50	16.00
6	156	—	Pgs. reduced 68 to 52; PC-r	1 2	1.50	4.50	9.00
7	165	—	PC-r	1 2	1.50	3.00	6.00
8	167	1/64	PC-r	1 2	1.50	3.00	6.00
9	167	11/65	PC-r	1 2	1.50	3.00	6.00
10	166	R/1968	New-c & price 25¢; PC-r	1 3	1.70	5.00	12.00

12. Rip Van Winkle and the Headless Horseman

Ed	HRN	Date	Details	A C	Good	Fine	N-Mint
1	11	6/43	Original; 68 pgs.	1 1	54.00	160.00	375.00
2	15	—	Long Isl. Ind. ed.; CC-r	1 1	14.00	42.00	100.00
3	20	—	Long Isl. Ind. ed.; CC-r	1 1	11.00	32.00	75.00
4	22	—	Queens Cty. Times ed.; CC-r	1 1	9.30	28.00	65.00
5	28	—	CC-r	1 1	7.00	21.00	50.00
6	60	—	1st LDC-r	1 1	2.65	8.00	18.00
7	62	—	LDC-r	1 1	2.65	8.00	18.00
8	71	—	LDC-r	1 1	1.70	5.00	10.00
9	89	—	C-price 15¢; LDC-r	1 1	1.50	4.50	9.00
10	118	—	LDC-r	1 1	1.50	4.50	9.00
11	132	—	New-c; PC-r	1 2	1.70	5.00	10.00
12	150	—	New-a; PC-r	2 2	1.70	5.00	10.00
13	158	—	PC-r	2 2	1.00	2.00	4.00
14	167	—	PC-r	2 2	1.00	2.00	4.00
15	167	12/63	PC-r	2 2	1.00	2.00	4.00
16	167	4/65	PC-r	2 2	1.50	3.00	6.00
17	167	4/66	PC-r	2 2	1.00	2.00	4.00
18	166	R/1968	New-c&price 25¢; PC-r; stiff-c	2 3	1.70	5.00	10.00
19	169	Sm/70	PC-r; stiff-c	2 3	1.70	5.00	10.00

13. Dr. Jekyll and Mr. Hyde (Used in SOTI, pg. 143)

Ed	HRN	Date	Details	A C	Good	Fine	N-Mint
1	12	8/43	Original 60 pgs.	1 1	57.00	170.00	400.00
2	15	—	Long Isl. Ind. ed.; CC-r	1 1	14.00	42.00	100.00
3	20	—	Long Isl. Ind. ed.; CC-r	1 1	11.00	32.00	75.00
4	28	—	No c-price; CC-r	1 1	8.50	25.50	60.00
5	60	—	New-c; Pgs. reduced from 60 to 52; H.C. Kiefer-c; LDC-r	1 2	2.85	8.50	20.00
6	62	—	LDC-r	1 2	2.85	8.50	20.00
7	71	—	LDC-r	1 2	1.70	5.00	10.00

Classic Comics #10 (HRN-14), © GIL

Classic Comics #12 (HRN-20), © GIL

Classic Comics #13, © GIL

Classic Comics #14 (HRN-21), © GIL   *Classics Illustrated #17 (HRN-60), © GIL*   *Classic Comics #18, © GIL*

CLASSIC COMICS (continued)

					Good	Fine	N-Mint
8	87	—	Date returns (erroneous); LDC-r	1 2	1.70	5.00	10.00
9	112	—	New-c&a; PC-r	2 3	1.70	5.00	12.00
10	153	—	PC-r	2 3	1.00	2.00	4.00
11	161	—	PC-r	2 3	1.00	2.00	4.00
12	167	—	PC-r	2 3	1.00	2.00	4.00
13	167	8/64	PC-r	2 3	1.00	2.00	4.00
14	167	11/65	PC-r	2 3	1.00	2.00	4.00
15	166	R/1968	C-price 25¢; PC-r	2 3	1.50	3.00	6.00
16	169	Wn/69	PC-r; stiff-c	2 3	1.00	2.00	4.00

14. Westward Ho!

Ed	HRN	Date	Details	A C			
1	13	9/43	Original; last outside bc coming-next ad; 60 pgs.	1 1	107.00	321.00	750.00
2	15	—	Long Isl. Ind. ed.; CC-r	1 1	54.00	161.00	375.00
3	21	—	Queens Home News; Pg. 56 changed from coming-next ad to Three Men Named Smith; CC-r	1 1	38.00	114.00	265.00
4	28	1946	Gilberton; Pg. 56 changed again to WWII article-Speaking for America; last CC-r	1 1	30.00	90.00	210.00
5	53	—	Pgs. reduced from 60 to 52; LDC-r	1 1	23.00	68.00	160.00

15. Uncle Tom's Cabin (Used in **SOTI**, pgs. 102, 103)

Ed	HRN	Date	Details	A C			
1	14	11/43	Original; Outside-bc ad: 2 Gift Boxes; 60 pgs.	1 1	43.00	130.00	300.00
2	15	—	Long Isl. Ind. listed-bottom inside-fc; also Gilberton listed bottom-pg. 1; CC-r	1 1	17.00	51.00	120.00
3	21	—	Nassau Bulletin ed.; CC-r	1 1	13.00	40.00	90.00
4	28	—	No c-price; CC-r	1 1	8.50	25.50	60.00
5	53	—	Pgs. reduced 60 to 52; LDC-r	1 1	3.50	10.50	24.00
6	71	—	LDC-r	1 1	2.30	7.00	16.00
7	89	—	C-price 15¢; LDC-r	1 1	2.00	6.00	14.00
8	117	—	New-c/lettering changes; PC-r	1 2	1.70	5.00	10.00
9	128	—	'Picture Progress' promo; PC-r	1 2	1.75	3.50	8.00
10	137	—	PC-r	1 2	1.00	2.00	4.00
11	146	—	PC-r	1 2	1.00	2.00	4.00
12	154	—	PC-r	1 2	1.00	2.00	4.00
13	161	—	PC-r	1 2	1.00	2.00	4.00
14	167	—	PC-r	1 2	1.00	2.00	4.00
15	167	6/64	PC-r	1 2	1.00	2.00	4.00
16	167	5/65	PC-r	1 2	1.00	2.00	4.00
17	166	5/67	PC-r	1 2	1.00	2.00	4.00
18	166	Wn/69	New-stiff-c; PC-r	1 3	1.70	5.00	10.00
19	169	Sm/70	PC-r; stiff-c	1 3	1.70	5.00	10.00

16. Gullivers Travels

Ed	HRN	Date	Details	A C			
1	15	12/43	Original-Lilian Chestney c/a; 60 pgs.	1 1	36.00	107.00	250.00
2	18/20	—	Price deleted; Queens Home News ed; CC-r	1 1	12.00	36.00	84.00
					Good	Fine	N-Mint
3	22	—	Queens Cty. Times ed.; CC-r	1 1	10.00	30.00	70.00
4	28	—	CC-r	1 1	7.00	21.00	50.00
5	60	—	Pgs. reduced to 48; LDC-r	1 1	2.30	7.00	16.00
6	62	—	LDC-r	1 1	2.00	6.00	14.00
7	78	—	C-price 15¢; LDC-r	1 1	1.50	4.50	9.00
8	89	—	LDC-r	1 1	1.50	4.50	9.00
9	155	—	New-c; PC-r	1 2	1.70	5.00	10.00
10	165	—	PC-r	1 2	1.00	2.00	4.00
11	167	5/64	PC-r	1 2	1.00	2.00	4.00
12	167	11/65	PC-r	1 2	1.00	2.00	4.00
13	166	R/1968	C-price 25¢; PC-r	1 2	1.00	2.00	4.00
14	169	Wn/69	PC-r; stiff-c	1 2	1.00	2.00	4.00

17. The Deerslayer

Ed	HRN	Date	Details	A C			
1	16	1/44	Original; Outside-bc ad: 3 Gift Boxes; 60 pgs.	1 1	36.00	107.00	250.00
2A	18	—	Queens Cty Times (inside-fc); CC-r	1 1	12.00	36.00	84.00
2B	18	—	Gilberton (bottom-pg. 1); CC-r; Scarce	1 1	16.00	48.00	110.00
3	22	—	Queens Cty. Times ed.; CC-r	1 1	11.00	32.00	75.00
4	28	—	CC-r	1 1	7.00	21.00	56.00
5	60	—	Pgs.reduced to 52; LDC-r	1 1	2.30	7.00	16.00
6	64	—	LDC-r	1 1	1.70	5.00	12.00
7	85	—	C-price 15¢; LDC-r	1 1	1.75	3.50	7.00
8	118	—	LDC-r	1 1	1.75	3.50	7.00
9	132	—	LDC-r	1 1	1.50	3.00	6.00
10	167	11/66	Last LDC-r	1 1	1.50	3.00	6.00
11	166	R/1968	New-c & price 25¢; PC-r	1 2	1.70	5.00	10.00
12	169	Spr/71	Stiff-c; letters from parents & educators; PC-r	1 2	1.70	5.00	10.00

18. The Hunchback of Notre Dame

Ed	HRN	Date	Details	A C			
1A	17	3/44	Orig.; Gilberton ed; 60 pgs.	1 1	47.00	140.00	325.00
1B	17	3/44	Orig.; Island Pub. Ed.; 60 pgs.	1 1	43.00	130.00	300.00
2	18/20	—	Queens Home News ed.; CC-r	1 1	12.00	36.00	84.00
3	22	—	Queens Cty. Times ed.; CC-r	1 1	10.00	30.00	70.00
4	28	—	CC-r	1 1	7.00	21.00	50.00
5	60	—	New-c; 8pgs. deleted; Kiefer-c; LDC-r	1 2	2.00	6.00	14.00
6	62	—	LDC-r	1 2	1.70	5.00	12.00
7	78	—	C-price 15¢; LDC-r	1 2	1.50	4.50	9.00
8A	89	—	H.C.Kiefer on bottom right-fc; LDC-r	1 2	1.50	4.50	9.00
8B	89	—	Name omitted; LDC-r	1 2	2.00	6.00	14.00
9	118	—	LDC-r	1 2	1.50	4.50	9.00
10	140	—	New-c; PC-r	1 3	2.65	8.00	18.00
11	146	—	PC-r	1 3	2.00	6.00	14.00
12	158	—	New-c&a; PC-r; Evans/Crandall-a	2 4	2.00	6.00	14.00

CLASSIC COMICS (continued)

Ed	HRN	Date	Details	A	C	Good	Fine	N-Mint
13	165	—	PC-r	2	4	1.50	3.00	6.00
14	167	9/63	PC-r	2	4	1.50	3.00	6.00
15	167	10/64	PC-r	2	4	1.50	3.00	6.00
16	167	4/66	PC-r	2	4	1.00	2.00	4.00
17	166	R/1968	New price 25¢; PC-r	2	4	1.00	2.00	4.00
18	169	Sp/70	Stiff-c; PC-r	2	4	1.00	2.00	4.00

19. Huckleberry Finn

Ed	HRN	Date	Details	A	C	Good	Fine	N-Mint
1A	18	4/44	Orig.; Gilberton ed.; 60 pgs.	1	1	31.00	92.00	215.00
1B	18	4/44	Orig.; Island Pub.; 60 pgs.	1	1	36.00	107.00	250.00
2	18	—	Nassau Bulletin ed.; fc-price 15¢-Canada; no coming-next ad; CC-r	1	1	12.00	36.00	84.00
3	22	—	Queens Cty. Times ed.; CC-r	1	1	11.00	32.00	75.00
4	28	—	CC-r	1	1	7.00	21.00	50.00
5	60	—	Pgs. reduced to 48; LDC-r	1	1	2.30	7.00	16.00
6	62	—	LDC-r	1	1	1.70	5.00	12.00
7	78	—	LDC-r	1	1	1.50	4.50	9.00
8	89	—	LDC-r	1	1	1.50	4.50	9.00
9	117	—	LDC-r	1	1	1.50	4.50	9.00
10	131	—	New-c&a; PC-r	2	2	1.70	5.00	10.00
11	140	—	PC-r	2	2	1.00	2.00	4.00
12	150	—	PC-r	2	2	1.00	2.00	4.00
13	158	—	PC-r	2	2	1.00	2.00	4.00
14	165	—	PC-r	2	2	1.00	2.00	4.00
15	167	—	PC-r	2	2	1.00	2.00	4.00
16	167	6/64	PC-r	2	2	1.00	2.00	4.00
17	167	6/65	PC-r	2	2	1.00	2.00	4.00
18	167	10/65	PC-r	2	2	1.00	2.00	4.00
19	166	9/67	PC-r	2	2	1.00	2.00	4.00
20	166	Win/69	C-price 25¢; PC-r; stiff-c	2	2	1.00	2.00	4.00
21	169	Sm/70	PC-r; stiff-c	2	2	1.00	2.00	4.00

20. The Corsican Brothers

Ed	HRN	Date	Details	A	C	Good	Fine	N-Mint
1A	20	6/44	Orig.; Gilberton ed.; bc-price: 4 Gift Boxes; 60 pgs.	1	1	36.00	107.00	250.00
1B	20	6/44	Orig.; Courier ed.; 60 pgs.	1	1	32.00	95.00	225.00
1C	20	6/44	Orig.; Long Island Ind. ed.; 60 pgs.	1	1	32.00	95.00	225.00
1D	20	6/44	Orig.; Both Gilberton & Long Isl. Ind.; 60 pgs.	1	1	41.00	122.00	285.00
2	22	—	Queens Cty. Times ed.; white logo banner; CC-r	1	1	16.00	48.00	110.00
3	28	—	CC-r	1	1	13.00	40.00	90.00
4	60	—	CI logo; no price; 48 pgs.; LDC-r	1	1	10.00	30.00	70.00
5	62	—	LDC-r	1	1	8.50	25.50	60.00
6	78	—	C-price 15¢; LDC-r	1	1	8.00	24.00	56.00
7	97	—	LDC-r	1	1	7.00	21.00	50.00

21. 3 Famous Mysteries ("The Sign of the 4," "The Murders in the Rue Morgue," "The Flayed Hand")

Ed	HRN	Date	Details	A	C	Good	Fine	N-Mint
1A	21	7/44	Orig.; Gilberton ed.;	1	1	56.00	167.00	390.00
1B	21	7/44	Orig. Island Pub. Co.; 60 pgs.	1	1	62.00	186.00	435.00
1C	21	7/44	Original; Courier Ed.; 60 pgs.	1	1	52.00	156.00	365.00
2	22	—	Nassau Bulletin ed.; CC-r	1	1	24.00	71.00	165.00
3	30	—	CC-r	1	1	20.00	60.00	140.00
4	62	—	LDC-r; 8 pgs. deleted; LDC-r	1	1	14.00	42.00	100.00
5	70	—	LDC-r	1	1	12.00	36.00	84.00
6	85	—	C-price 15¢; LDC-r	1	1	11.00	32.00	75.00
7	114	—	New-c; PC-r	1	2	11.00	32.00	75.00

22. The Pathfinder

Ed	HRN	Date	Details	A	C	Good	Fine	N-Mint
1A	22	10/44	Orig.; No printer listed; ownership statement inside fc lists Gilberton & date; 60 pgs.	1	1	27.00	81.00	190.00
1B	22	10/44	Orig.; Island Pub. ed.; 60 pgs.	1	1	23.00	70.00	160.00
1C	22	10/44	Orig.; Queens Cty Times ed. 60 pgs.	1	1	23.00	70.00	160.00
2	30	—	C-price removed; CC-r	1	1	8.00	24.00	56.00
3	60	—	Pgs. reduced to 52; LDC-r	1	1	2.30	7.00	16.00
4	70	—	LDC-r	1	1	1.70	5.00	12.00
5	85	—	C-price 15¢; LDC-r	1	1	1.50	4.50	9.00
6	118	—	LDC-r	1	1	1.50	4.50	9.00
7	132	—	LDC-r	1	1	1.15	3.50	7.00
8	146	—	LDC-r	1	1	1.15	3.50	7.00
9	167	11/63	New-c; PC-r	1	2	2.65	8.00	18.00
10	167	12/65	PC-r	1	2	2.00	6.00	14.00
11	166	8/67	PC-r	1	2	2.00	6.00	14.00

23. Oliver Twist (1st Classic produced by the Iger Shop)

Ed	HRN	Date	Details	A	C	Good	Fine	N-Mint
1	23	7/45	Original; 60 pgs.	1	1	21.00	64.00	150.00
2A	30	—	Printers Union logo on bottom left-fc— same as 23(Orig.) (very rare); CC-r	1	1	14.00	42.00	100.00
2B	30	—	Union logo omitted; CC-r	1	1	7.00	21.00	50.00
3	60	—	Pgs. reduced to 48; LDC-r	1	1	2.30	7.00	16.00
4	62	—	LDC-r	1	1	1.70	5.00	12.00
5	71	—	LDC-r	1	1	1.50	4.50	9.00
6	85	—	C-price 15¢; LDC-r	1	1	1.50	4.50	9.00
7	94	—	LDC-r	1	1	1.50	4.50	9.00
8	118	—	LDC-r	1	1	1.15	3.50	7.00
9	136	—	New-PC, old-a; PC-r	1	2	1.50	4.50	9.00
10	150	—	Old-a; PC-r	1	2	1.30	4.00	8.00
11	164	—	Old-a; PC-r	1	2	1.30	4.00	8.00
12	164	—	New-a; PC-r; Evans/Crandall-a	2	2	1.70	5.00	12.00
13	167	—	PC-r	2	2	1.50	4.50	9.00
14	167	8/64	PC-r	2	2	1.25	2.50	5.00
15	167	12/65	PC-r	2	2	1.25	2.50	5.00
16	166	R/1968	New 25¢-c; PC-r	2	2	1.00	2.00	5.00
17	169	Win/69	Stiff-c; PC-r	2	2	1.00	2.00	4.00

24. A Connecticut Yankee in King Arthur's Court

Ed	HRN	Date	Details	A	C

Classic Comics #19, © GIL

Classic Comics #20, © GIL

Classics Illustrated #22 (HRN-85), © GIL

Classic Comics #24 (Orig.), © GIL

Classics Illustrated #27, © GIL

Classic Comics #29 (Orig.), © GIL

CLASSIC COMICS (continued)

						Good	Fine	N-Mint
1	—	9/45	Original	1	1	21.50	64.00	150.00
2	30	—	Price circle blank; CC-r	1	1	7.00	21.00	50.00
3	60	—	8 pgs. deleted; LDC-r	1	1	2.30	7.00	16.00
4	62	—	LDC-r	1	1	2.30	7.00	16.00
5	71	—	LDC-r	1	1	1.50	4.50	9.00
6	87	—	C-price 15¢; LDC-r	1	1	1.50	4.50	9.00
7	121	—	LDC-r	1	1	1.50	4.50	9.00
8	140	—	New-c&a; PC-r	2	2	1.50	4.50	9.00
9	153	—	PC-r	2	2	1.00	2.00	4.00
10	164	—	PC-r	2	2	1.00	2.00	4.00
11	167	—	PC-r	2	2	1.00	2.00	4.00
12	167	7/64	PC-r	2	2	1.00	2.00	4.00
13	167	6/66	PC-r	2	2	1.00	2.00	4.00
14	166	R/1968	C-price 25¢; PC-r	2	2	1.00	2.00	4.00
15	169	Spr/71	PC-r; stiff-c	2	2	1.00	2.00	4.00

25. Two Years Before the Mast

Ed	HRN	Date	Details	A	C			
1	—	10/45	Original; Webb/ Heames-a&c	1	1	22.00	65.00	155.00
2	30	—	Price circle blank; CC-r	1	1	7.00	21.00	50.00
3	60	—	8 pgs. deleted; LDC-r	1	1	2.30	7.00	16.00
4	62	—	LDC-r	1	1	1.70	5.00	12.00
5	71	—	LDC-r	1	1	1.50	4.50	9.00
6	85	—	C-price 15¢; LDC-r	1	1	1.50	4.50	9.00
7	114	—	LDC-r	1	1	1.50	4.50	9.00
8	156	—	3 pgs. replaced by fillers; new-c; PC-r	1	2	1.50	4.50	9.00
9	167	12/63	PC-r	1	2	1.00	2.00	4.00
10	167	12/65	PC-r	1	2	1.00	2.00	4.00
11	166	9/67	PC-r	1	2	1.00	2.00	4.00
12	169	Win/69	C-price 25¢; stiff-c PC-r	1	2	1.00	2.00	4.00

26. Frankenstein

Ed	HRN	Date	Details	A	C			
1	26	12/45	Orig.; Webb/Brewster a&c; 52 pgs.	1	1	52.00	155.00	365.00
2	30	—	Price circle blank; CC-r	1	1	17.00	51.00	120.00
3	60	—	LDC-r	1	1	4.50	14.00	32.00
4	62	—	LDC-r	1	1	8.00	24.00	56.00
5	71	—	LDC-r	1	1	3.00	9.00	21.00
6	82	—	C-price 15¢; LDC-r	1	1	2.65	8.00	18.00
7	117	—	LDC-r	1	1	1.70	5.00	12.00
8	146	—	New Saunders-c PC-r	1	2	1.70	5.00	12.00
9	152	—	Scarce; PC-r	1	2	2.30	7.00	16.00
10	153	—	PC-r	1	2	1.00	2.00	4.00
11	160	—	PC-r	1	2	1.00	2.00	4.00
12	165	—	PC-r	1	2	1.00	2.00	4.00
13	167	—	PC-r	1	2	1.00	2.00	4.00
14	167	6/64	PC-r	1	2	1.00	2.00	4.00
15	167	6/65	PC-r	1	2	1.00	2.00	4.00
16	167	10/65	PC-r	1	2	1.00	2.00	4.00
17	166	9/67	PC-r	1	2	1.00	2.00	4.00
18	169	Fall/69	C-price 25¢; stiff-c PC-r	1	2	1.00	2.00	4.00
19	169	Spr/71	PC-r; stiff-c	1	2	1.00	2.00	4.00

27. The Adventures of Marco Polo

Ed	HRN	Date	Details	A	C			
1	—	4/46	Original	1	1	21.50	64.00	150.00

						Good	Fine	N-Mint
2	30	—	Last 'Comics' re-print; CC-r	1	1	7.00	21.00	50.00
3	70	—	8 pgs. deleted; no c-price; LDC-r	1	1	1.70	5.00	12.00
4	87	—	C-price 15¢; LDC-r	1	1	1.50	4.50	9.00
5	117	—	LDC-r	1	1	1.50	4.50	9.00
6	154	—	New-c; PC-r	1	2	1.50	4.50	9.00
7	165	—	PC-r	1	2	1.00	2.00	4.00
8	167	4/64	PC-r	1	2	1.00	2.00	4.00
9	167	6/66	PC-r	1	2	1.00	2.00	4.00
10	169	Spr/69	New price 25¢; stiff-c; PC-r	1	2	1.00	2.00	4.00

28. Michael Strogoff

Ed	HRN	Date	Details	A	C			
1	—	6/46	Original	1	1	21.50	64.00	150.00
2	51	—	8 pgs. cut; LDC-r	1	1	6.50	19.50	45.00
3	115	—	New-c; PC-r	1	1	1.70	5.00	12.00
4	155	—	PC-r	1	2	1.25	2.50	5.00
5	167	11/63	PC-r	1	2	1.25	2.50	5.00
6	167	7/66	PC-r	1	2	1.25	2.50	5.00
7	169	Sm/69	C-price 25¢; stiff-c PC-r	1	3	1.70	5.00	10.00

29. The Prince and the Pauper

Ed	HRN	Date	Details	A	C			
1	—	7/46	Orig.; "Horror"-c	1	1	41.00	122.00	285.00
2	60	—	8 pgs. cut; new-c by Kiefer, LDC-r	1	2	2.30	7.00	16.00
3	62	—	LDC-r	1	2	2.30	7.00	16.00
4	71	—	LDC-r	1	2	1.50	4.50	9.00
5	93	—	LDC-r	1	2	1.50	4.50	9.00
6	114	—	LDC-r	1	2	1.50	4.50	9.00
7	128	—	New-c; PC-r	1	3	1.50	4.50	9.00
8	138	—	PC-r	1	3	1.00	2.00	4.00
9	150	—	PC-r	1	3	1.00	2.00	4.00
10	164	—	PC-r	1	3	1.00	2.00	4.00
11	167	—	PC-r	1	3	1.00	2.00	4.00
12	167	7/64	PC-r	1	3	1.00	2.00	4.00
13	167	11/65	PC-r	1	3	1.00	2.00	4.00
14	166	R/1968	C-price 25¢; PC-r	1	3	1.00	2.00	4.00
15	169	Sm/70	PC-r; stiff-c	1	3	1.00	2.00	4.00

30. The Moonstone

Ed	HRN	Date	Details	A	C			
1	—	9/46	Original; Rico c/a	1	1	21.50	64.00	150.00
2	60	—	LDC-r; 8pgs. cut	1	1	3.00	9.00	21.00
3	70	—	LDC-r	1	1	2.00	6.00	14.00
4	155	—	New L.B. Cole-c; PC-r	1	2	5.00	15.00	35.00
5	165	—	PC-r; L.B. Cole-c	1	2	2.00	6.00	14.00
6	167	1/64	PC-r; L.B. Cole-c	1	2	2.00	4.00	8.00
7	167	9/65	PC-r; L.B. Cole-c	1	2	1.50	3.00	6.00
8	166	R/1968	C-price 25¢; PC-r	1	2	1.00	2.00	4.00

31. The Black Arrow

Ed	HRN	Date	Details	A	C			
1	—	10/46	Original	1	1	19.00	58.00	135.00
2	51	—	CI logo; LDC-r 8pgs. deleted	1	1	2.65	8.00	18.00
3	64	—	LDC-r	1	1	1.70	5.00	12.00
4	87	—	C-price 15¢; LDC-r	1	1	1.50	3.50	7.00
5	108	—	LDC-r	1	1	1.50	3.50	7.00
6	125	—	LDC-r	1	1	1.50	3.50	7.00
7	131	—	New-c; PC-r	1	2	1.50	3.00	6.00
8	140	—	PC-r	1	2	1.00	2.00	4.00
9	148	—	PC-r	1	2	1.00	2.00	4.00

CLASSIC COMICS (continued)

Ed	HRN	Date	Details	A	C	Good	Fine	N-Mint
10	161	—	PC-r	1	2	1.00	2.00	4.00
11	167	—	PC-r	1	2	1.00	2.00	4.00
12	167	7/64	PC-r	1	2	1.00	2.00	4.00
13	167	11/65	PC-r	1	2	1.00	2.00	4.00
14	166	R/1968	C-price 25¢; PC-r	1	2	1.00	2.00	4.00

32. Lorna Doone

Ed	HRN	Date	Details	A	C	Good	Fine	N-Mint
1	—	12/46	Original; Matt Baker c&a	1	1	19.00	58.00	135.00
2	53/64	—	8 pgs. deleted; LDC-r	1	1	3.65	11.00	25.00
3	85	—	C-price 15¢; LDC-r; Baker c&a	1	1	3.00	9.00	21.00
4	118	—	LDC-r	1	1	2.00	6.00	14.00
5	138	—	New-c; old-c becomes new title pg.; PC-r	1	2	1.50	4.50	9.00
6	150	—	PC-r	1	2	1.00	2.00	4.00
7	165	—	PC-r	1	2	1.00	2.00	4.00
8	167	1/64	PC-r	1	2	1.00	2.00	4.00
9	167	11/65	PC-r	1	2	1.00	2.00	4.00
10	166	R/1968	New-c; PC-r	1	3	1.70	5.00	12.00

33. The Adventures of Sherlock Holmes

Ed	HRN	Date	Details	A	C	Good	Fine	N-Mint
1	33	1/47	Original; Kiefer-c; contains Study in Scarlet & Hound of the Baskervilles; 68 pgs.	1	1	64.00	193.00	450.00
2	53	—	'A Study in Scarlet' (17 pgs.) deleted; LDC-r	1	1	34.00	100.00	240.00
3	71	—	LDC-r	1	1	26.00	77.00	180.00
4	89	—	C-price 15¢; LDC-r	1	1	21.00	62.00	145.00

34. Mysterious Island

Ed	HRN	Date	Details	A	C	Good	Fine	N-Mint
1	—	2/47	Original; Last 'Classic Comic.' Webb/Heames c&a	1	1	21.50	64.00	150.00
2	60	—	8 pgs. deleted; LDC-r	1	1	2.30	7.00	16.00
3	62	—	LDC-r	1	1	2.00	6.00	14.00
4	71	—	LDC-r	1	1	3.00	9.00	21.00
5	78	—	C-price 15¢ in circle; LDC-r	1	1	1.50	4.50	9.00
6	92	—	LDC-r	1	1	1.50	4.50	9.00
7	117	—	LDC-r	1	1	1.50	4.50	9.00
8	140	—	New-c; PC-r	1	2	1.50	3.00	6.00
9	156	—	PC-r	1	2	1.00	2.00	4.00
10	167	10/63	PC-r	1	2	1.00	2.00	4.00
11	167	5/64	PC-r	1	2	1.00	2.00	4.00
12	167	6/66	PC-r	1	2	1.00	2.00	4.00
13	166	R/1968	C-price 25¢; PC-r	1	2	1.00	2.00	4.00

35. Last Days of Pompeii

Ed	HRN	Date	Details	A	C	Good	Fine	N-Mint
1	—	3/47	Original; 1st 'Classics Illus.;' LDC; Kiefer c/a	1	1	21.50	64.00	150.00
2	161	—	New c&a; 15¢; Jack Kirby-a	2	2	2.30	7.00	16.00
3	167	1/64	PC-r	2	2	1.50	3.00	6.00
4	167	7/66	PC-r	2	2	1.50	3.00	6.00
5	169	Spr/70	New price 25¢; stiff-c; PC-r	2	2	2.00	4.00	8.00

36. Typee

Ed	HRN	Date	Details	A	C	Good	Fine	N-Mint
1	—	4/47	Original	1	1	10.00	30.00	70.00
2	64	—	No c-price; 8 pg. ed.; LDC-r	1	1	2.65	8.00	18.00
3	155	—	New-c; PC-r	1	2	1.50	4.50	9.00
4	167	9/63	PC-r	1	2	1.50	3.50	7.00
5	167	7/65	PC-r	1	2	1.50	3.50	7.00
6	169	Sm/69	C-price 25¢; stiff-c PC-r	1	2	1.50	3.00	6.00

37. The Pioneers

Ed	HRN	Date	Details	A	C	Good	Fine	N-Mint
1	37	5/47	Original; Palais-c/a	1	1	10.00	30.00	70.00
2A	62	—	8 pgs. cut; LDC-r; price circle blank	1	1	2.65	8.00	18.00
2B	62	—	10 cent-c; LDC-r;	1	1	7.00	21.00	50.00
3	70	—	LDC-r	1	1	1.50	4.50	9.00
4	92	—	15 cent-c; LDC-r	1	1	1.50	3.50	7.00
5	118	—	LDC-r	1	1	1.50	3.50	7.00
6	131	—	LDC-r	1	1	1.50	3.50	7.00
7	132	—	LDC-r	1	1	1.50	3.50	7.00
8	153	—	LDC-r	1	1	1.50	3.50	7.00
9	167	5/64	LDC-r	1	1	1.50	3.00	6.00
10	167	6/66	LDC-r	1	1	1.50	3.00	6.00
11	166	R/1968	New-c; 15 cent-c; PC-r	1	2	1.70	5.00	12.00

38. Adventures of Cellini

Ed	HRN	Date	Details	A	C	Good	Fine	N-Mint
1	—	6/47	Original; Froehlich	1	1	19.00	58.00	135.00
2	164	—	New-c&a; PC-r	2	2	1.70	5.00	10.00
3	167	12/63	PC-r	2	2	1.50	3.00	6.00
4	167	7/66	PC-r	2	2	1.50	3.00	6.00
5	169	Spr/70	Stiff-c; new price 25¢; PC-r	2	2	2.00	4.00	8.00

39. Jane Eyre

Ed	HRN	Date	Details	A	C	Good	Fine	N-Mint
1	—	7/47	Original	1	1	16.00	48.00	110.00
2	60	—	No c-price; 8 pgs. cut; LDC-r	1	1	3.00	9.00	21.00
3	62	—	LDC-r	1	1	3.00	9.00	21.00
4	71	—	LDC-r; c-price 10¢	1	1	2.65	8.00	18.00
5	92	—	C-price 15¢; LDC-r	1	1	1.70	5.00	12.00
6	118	—	LDC-r	1	1	1.70	5.00	12.00
7	142	—	New-c; old-a; PC-r	1	2	2.00	6.00	14.00
8	154	—	Old-a; PC-r	1	2	1.70	5.00	12.00
9	165	—	New-a; PC-r	2	2	2.00	6.00	14.00
10	167	12/63	PC-r	2	2	2.00	6.00	14.00
11	167	4/65	PC-r	2	2	1.70	5.00	12.00
12	167	8/66	PC-r	2	2	1.70	5.00	12.00
13	166	R/1968	New-c; PC-r	2	3	4.00	12.00	28.00

40. Mysteries ("The Pit and the Pendulum," "The Advs. of Hans Pfall," "The Fall of the House of Usher")

Ed	HRN	Date	Details	A	C	Good	Fine	N-Mint
1	—	8/47	Original; Kiefer-c/a, Froehlich, Griffiths-a	1	1	48.00	145.00	335.00
2	62	—	LDC-r; 8pgs cut	1	1	17.00	51.00	120.00
3	75	—	LDC-r	1	1	14.00	42.00	100.00
4	92	—	C-price 15¢; LDC-r	1	1	10.00	30.00	70.00

Classics Illustrated #32, © GIL

Classics Illustrated #34 (HRN-167), © GIL

Classics Illustrated #38 (Orig.), © GIL

Classics Illustrated #41 (Orig.), © GIL

Classics Illustrated #43 (Orig.), © GIL

Classics Illustrated #48 (Orig.), © GIL

CLASSICS ILLUSTRATED (continued)

41. Twenty Years After

Ed	HRN	Date	Details	A	C	Good	Fine	N-Mint
1	—	9/47	Original; 'horror'-c	1	1	32.00	95.00	225.00
2	62	—	New-c; no c-price 8 pgs. cut; LDC-r; Kiefer-c	1	2	2.30	7.00	16.00
3	78	—	C-price 15¢; LDC-r	1	2	1.70	5.00	12.00
4	156	—	New-c; PC-r	1	3	1.50	3.50	7.00
5	167	12/63	PC-r	1	3	1.00	2.00	4.00
6	167	11/66	PC-r	1	3	1.00	2.00	4.00
7	169	Spr/70	New price 25¢; stiff-c; PC-r	1	3	1.00	2.00	4.00

42. Swiss Family Robinson

Ed	HRN	Date	Details	A	C	Good	Fine	N-Mint
1	42	10/47	Orig.; Kiefer a&c	1	1	10.00	30.00	70.00
2A	62	—	8 pgs. cut; outside-bc: Gift Box ad; LDC-r	1	1	2.30	7.00	16.00
2B	62	—	8 pgs. cut; outside-bc: Reorder list; scarce; LDC-r	1	1	4.00	12.00	28.00
3	75	—	LDC-r	1	1	1.50	4.50	9.00
4	93	—	LDC-r	1	1	1.50	4.50	9.00
5	117	—	LDC-r	1	1	1.50	4.50	9.00
6	131	—	New-c; old-a; PC-r	1	2	1.70	5.00	10.00
7	137	—	Old-a; PC-r	1	2	1.50	4.50	9.00
8	141	—	Old-a; PC-r	1	2	1.50	4.50	9.00
9	152	—	New-a; PC-r	2	2	1.50	3.00	6.00
10	158	—	PC-r	2	2	1.00	2.00	4.00
11	165	—	PC-r	2	2	1.50	4.50	9.00
12	167	12/63	PC-r	2	2	1.50	3.00	6.00
13	167	4/65	PC-r	2	2	1.50	3.00	6.00
14	167	5/66	PC-r	2	2	1.50	3.00	6.00
15	166	11/67	PC-r	2	2	1.00	2.00	4.00
16	169	Spr/69	PC-r; stiff-c	2	2	1.00	2.00	4.00

43. Great Expectations (Used in SOTI, pg. 311)

Ed	HRN	Date	Details	A	C	Good	Fine	N-Mint
1	—	11/47	Original; Kiefer-a/c	1	1	53.00	159.00	370.00
2	62	—	No c-price; 8 pgs. cut; LDC-r	1	1	32.00	95.00	225.00

44. Mysteries of Paris (Used in SOTI, pg. 323)

Ed	HRN	Date	Details	A	C	Good	Fine	N-Mint
1	44	12/47	Original; 56 pgs.; Kiefer-a/c	1	1	41.00	122.00	285.00
2A	62	—	8 pgs. cut; outside-bc: Gift Box ad; LDC-r	1	1	18.00	54.00	125.00
2B	62	—	8 pgs. cut; outside-bc: reorder list; LDC-r	1	1	18.00	54.00	125.00
3	78	—	C-price 15¢; LDC-r	1	1	14.00	42.00	100.00

45. Tom Brown's School Days

Ed	HRN	Date	Details	A	C	Good	Fine	N-Mint
1	44	1/48	Original; 1st 48pg. issue	1	1	7.00	21.00	50.00
2	64	—	No c-price; LDC-r	1	1	3.00	9.00	21.00
3	161	—	New-c&a; PC-r	2	2	1.50	4.50	9.00
4	167	2/64	PC-r	2	2	1.50	3.50	7.00
5	168	8/66	PC-r	2	2	1.50	3.50	7.00
6	166	R/1968	C-price 25¢; PC-r	2	2	1.50	3.50	7.00

46. Kidnapped

Ed	HRN	Date	Details	A	C

1	47	4/48	Original; Webb-c/a	1	1	7.00	21.00	50.00
2A	62	—	Price circle blank; LDC-r	1	1	2.30	7.00	16.00
2B	62	—	C-price 10¢; rare; LDC-r	1	1	7.00	21.00	50.00
3	78	—	C-price 15¢; LDC-r	1	1	1.50	3.50	9.00
4	87	—	LDC-r	1	1	1.50	4.50	9.00
5	118	—	LDC-r	1	1	1.50	4.50	9.00
6	131	—	New-c; PC-r	1	2	1.50	4.50	9.00
7	140	—	PC-r	1	2	1.00	2.00	4.00
8	150	—	PC-r	1	2	1.00	2.00	4.00
9	164	—	Reduced pg.width; PC-r	1	2	1.00	2.00	4.00
10	167	—	PC-r	1	2	1.00	2.00	4.00
11	67	3/64	PC-r	1	2	1.00	2.00	4.00
12	167	6/65	PC-r	1	2	1.00	2.00	4.00
13	167	12/65	PC-r	1	2	1.00	2.00	4.00
14	166	9/67	PC-r	1	2	1.00	2.00	4.00
15	166	Win/69	New price 25¢; PC-r; stiff-c	1	2	1.00	2.00	4.00
16	169	Sm/70	PC-r; stiff-c	1	2	1.00	2.00	4.00

47. Twenty Thousand Leagues Under the Sea

Ed	HRN	Date	Details	A	C			
1	47	5/48	Orig.; Kiefer-a&c	1	1	8.00	24.00	56.00
2	64	—	No c-price; LDC-r	1	1	2.30	7.00	16.00
3	78	—	C-price 15¢; LDC-r	1	1	1.50	4.50	9.00
4	94	—	LDC-r	1	1	1.50	4.50	9.00
5	118	—	LDC-r	1	1	1.50	4.50	9.00
6	128	—	New-c; PC-r	1	2	1.50	4.50	9.00
7	133	—	PC-r	1	2	1.50	4.50	9.00
8	140	—	PC-r	1	2	1.25	2.50	5.00
9	148	—	PC-r	1	2	1.25	2.50	5.00
10	156	—	PC-r	1	2	1.25	2.50	5.00
11	165	—	PC-r	1	2	1.25	2.50	5.00
12	167	—	PC-r	1	2	1.25	2.50	5.00
13	167	3/64	PC-r	1	2	1.25	2.50	5.00
14	167	8/65	PC-r	1	2	1.00	2.00	4.00
15	167	10/66	PC-r	1	2	1.25	2.50	5.00
16	166	R/1968	C-price 25¢; new-c PC-r	1	3	1.70	5.00	10.00
17	169	Spr/70	Stiff-c; PC-r	1	3	1.70	5.00	10.00

48. David Copperfield

Ed	HRN	Date	Details	A	C			
1	47	6/48	Original; Kiefer a/c	1	1	8.00	24.00	56.00
2	64	—	Price circle replaced by motif of boy reading; LDC-r	1	1	2.30	7.00	16.00
3	87	—	C-price 15¢; LDC-r	1	1	1.50	4.50	9.00
4	121	—	New-c; PC-r	1	2	1.50	4.50	9.00
5	130	—	PC-r	1	2	1.50	3.00	6.00
6	140	—	PC-r	1	2	1.50	3.00	6.00
7	148	—	PC-r	1	2	1.50	3.00	6.00
8	156	—	PC-r	1	2	1.50	3.00	6.00
9	167	—	PC-r	1	2	1.00	2.00	4.00
10	167	4/64	PC-r	1	2	1.00	2.00	4.00
11	167	6/65	PC-r	1	2	1.00	2.00	4.00
12	167	5/67	PC-r	1	2	1.00	2.00	4.00
13	166	R/67	PC-r; C-price 25¢	1	2	1.50	4.50	9.00
14	166	Spr/69	C-price 25¢; stiff-c PC-r	1	2	1.00	2.00	4.00
15	169	Win/69	Stiff-c; PC-r	1	2	1.00	2.00	4.00

49. Alice in Wonderland

Ed	HRN	Date	Details	A	C

				A	C	Good	Fine	N-Mint
1	47	7/48	Original; 1st Blum a & c	1	1	11.50	34.00	80.00
2	64	—	No c-price; LDC-r	1	1	2.65	8.00	18.00
3	85	—	C-price 15¢; LDC-r	1	1	2.00	6.00	14.00
4	155	—	New PC, similar to orig.; PC-r	1	2	2.00	6.00	14.00
5	165	—	PC-r	1	2	1.50	4.50	9.00
6	167	3/64	PC-r	1	2	1.50	4.50	9.00
7	167	6/66	PC-r	1	2	1.50	4.50	9.00
8A	166	Fall/68	New-c; soft-c; 25¢ c-price; PC-r	1	3	2.30	7.00	16.00
8B	166	Fall/68	New-c; stiff-c; 25¢ c-price; PC-r	1	3	5.00	15.00	35.00

50. Adventures of Tom Sawyer (Used in SOTI, pg. 37)

Ed	HRN	Date	Details	A	C			
1A	51	8/48	Orig.; Aldo Rubano a&c	1	1	8.00	24.00	56.00
1B	51	9/48	Orig.; Rubano c&a	1	1	8.50	25.50	60.00
2	64	—	No c-price; LDC-r	1	1	2.30	7.00	16.00
3	78	—	C-price 15¢; LDC-r	1	1	1.50	4.50	9.00
4	94	—	LDC-r	1	1	1.50	4.50	9.00
5	117	—	LDC-r	1	1	1.50	4.50	9.00
6	132	—	LDC-r	1	1	1.50	4.50	9.00
7	140	—	New-c; PC-r	1	2	1.50	4.50	9.00
8	150	—	PC-r	1	2	1.30	4.00	8.00
9	164	—	New-a; PC-r	2	2	1.50	4.50	9.00
10	167	—	PC-r	2	2	1.00	2.00	4.00
11	167	1/65	PC-r	2	2	1.00	2.00	4.00
12	167	5/66	PC-r	2	2	1.00	2.00	4.00
13	166	12/67	PC-r	2	2	1.00	2.00	4.00
14	169	Fall/69	C-price 25¢; stiff-c PC-r	2	2	1.00	2.00	4.00
15	169	Win/71	PC-r	2	2	1.00	2.00	4.00

51. The Spy

Ed	HRN	Date	Details	A	C			
1A	51	9/48	Original; inside-bc illo: Christmas Carol	1	1	7.00	21.00	50.00
1B	51	9/48	Original; inside-bc illo: Man in Iron Mask	1	1	8.00	24.00	56.00
1C	51	8/48	Original; outside-bc full color	1	1	8.00	24.00	56.00
1D	51	8/48	Original; outside-bc: blue & yellow only; scarce	1	1	11.50	34.00	80.00
2	89	—	C-price 15¢; LDC-r	1	1	1.70	5.00	12.00
3	121	—	LDC-r	1	1	1.50	4.50	9.00
4	139	—	New-c; PC-r	1	2	1.50	4.50	9.00
5	156	—	PC-r	1	2	1.00	2.00	4.00
6	167	11/63	PC-r	1	2	1.00	2.00	4.00
7	167	7/66	PC-r	1	2	1.00	2.00	4.00
8A	166	Win/69	C-price 25¢; soft-c; scarce; PC-r	1	2	1.70	5.00	12.00
8B	166	Win/69	C-price 25¢; stiff-c; PC-r	1	2	1.00	2.00	4.00

52. The House of the Seven Gables

Ed	HRN	Date	Details	A	C			
1	53	10/48	Orig.; Griffiths a&c	1	1	7.00	21.00	50.00
2	89	—	C-price 15¢; LDC-r	1	1	1.70	5.00	12.00
3	121	—	LDC-r	1	1	1.50	3.50	7.00
4	142	—	New-c&a; PC-r Woodbridge-a	2	2	1.50	3.50	7.00
5	156	—	PC-r	2	2	1.00	2.00	4.00

						Good	Fine	N-Mint
6	165	—	PC-r	2	2	1.00	2.00	4.00
7	167	5/64	PC-r	2	2	1.00	2.00	4.00
8	167	3/66	PC-r	2	2	1.00	2.00	4.00
9	166	R/1968	C-price 25¢; PC-r	2	2	1.00	2.00	4.00
10	169	Spr/70	Stiff-c; PC-r	2	2	1.00	2.00	4.00

53. A Christmas Carol

Ed	HRN	Date	Details	A	C			
1	53	11/48	Original & only ed; Kiefer-a,c	1	1	10.00	30.00	70.00

54. Man in the Iron Mask

Ed	HRN	Date	Details	A	C			
1	55	12/48	Original; Froehlich-a, Kiefer-c	1	1	7.00	21.00	50.00
2	93	—	C-price 15¢; LDC-r	1	1	1.70	5.00	12.00
3A	111	—	(O) logo lettering; scarce; LDC-r	1	1	3.00	9.00	21.00
3B	111	—	New logo as PC; LDC-r	1	1	1.50	4.50	9.00
4	142	—	New-c&a; PC-r	2	2	1.50	4.50	9.00
5	154	—	PC-r	2	2	1.00	2.00	4.00
6	165	—	PC-r	2	2	1.00	2.00	4.00
7	167	5/64	PC-r	2	2	1.00	2.00	4.00
8	167	4/66	PC-r	2	2	1.00	2.00	4.00
9A	166	Win/69	C-price 25¢; soft-c PC-r	2	2	2.00	6.00	14.00
9B	166	Win/69	Stiff-c	2	2	1.00	2.00	4.00

55. Silas Marner (Used in SOTI, pgs. 311, 312)

Ed	HRN	Date	Details	A	C			
1	55	1/49	Original-Kiefer-c	1	1	8.00	24.00	56.00
2	75	—	Price circle blank; 'Coming Next' ad; LDC-r	1	1	2.30	7.00	16.00
3	97	—	LDC-r	1	1	1.50	4.50	9.00
4	121	—	New-c; PC-r	1	2	1.50	4.50	9.00
5	130	—	PC-r	1	2	1.00	2.00	4.00
6	140	—	PC-r	1	2	1.00	2.00	4.00
7	154	—	PC-r	1	2	1.00	2.00	4.00
8	165	—	PC-r	1	2	1.00	2.00	4.00
9	167	2/64	PC-r	1	2	1.00	2.00	4.00
10	167	6/65	PC-r	1	2	1.00	2.00	4.00
11	166	5/67	PC-r	1	2	1.00	2.00	4.00
12A	166	Win/69	C-price 25¢; soft-c PC-r	1	2	2.00	6.00	14.00
12B	166	Win/69	C-price 25¢; stiff-c PC-r	1	2	1.00	2.00	4.00

56. The Toilers of the Sea

Ed	HRN	Date	Details	A	C			
1	55	2/49	Original; A.M. Froehlich a,c	1	1	11.00	32.00	75.00
2	165	—	New-c&a; PC-r; Angelo Torres-a	2	2	2.65	8.00	18.00
3	167	3/64	PC-r	2	2	2.00	6.00	14.00
4	167	10/66	PC-r	2	2	2.00	6.00	14.00

57. The Song of Hiawatha

Ed	HRN	Date	Details	A	C			
1	55	3/49	Original; Alex Blum a&c	1	1	6.50	19.50	45.00
2	75	—	No c-price; 'Coming Next'ad; LDC-r	1	1	2.30	7.00	16.00
3	94	—	C-price 15¢; LDC-r	1	1	1.50	4.50	9.00
4	118	—	LDC-r	1	1	1.50	4.50	9.00
5	134	—	New-c; PC-r	1	2	1.50	4.50	9.00

Classics Illustrated #50 (Orig.), © GIL

Classics Illustrated #52 (Orig.), © GIL

Classics Illustrated #54 (Orig.), © GIL

Classics Illustrated #61, © GIL

Classics Illustrated #64 (Orig.), © GIL

Classics Illustrated #66 (Orig.), © GIL

CLASSICS ILLUSTRATED (continued)

				A C		Good	Fine	N-Mint
6	139	—	PC-r	1 2		1.00	2.00	4.00
7	154	—	PC-r	1 2		1.00	2.00	4.00
8	167	—	Has orig.date; PC-r	1 2		1.00	2.00	4.00
9	167	9/64	PC-r	1 2		1.00	2.00	4.00
10	167	10/65	PC-r	1 2		1.00	2.00	4.00
11	166	F/1968	C-price 25¢; PC-r	1 2		1.00	2.00	4.00

58. The Prairie

Ed	HRN	Date	Details	A C	Good	Fine	N-Mint
1	60	4/49	Original; Palais c/a	1 1	6.50	19.50	45.00
2	62	—	No c-price; no coming-next ad; LDC-r	1 1	3.50	10.50	24.00
3	78	—	C-price 15¢ in dbl circle; LDC-r	1 1	1.70	5.00	12.00
4	114	—	LDC-r	1 1	1.50	4.50	9.00
5	131	—	LDC-r	1 1	1.50	4.50	9.00
6	132	—	LDC-r	1 1	1.50	4.50	9.00
7	146	—	New-c; PC-r	1 2	1.50	3.00	6.00
8	155	—	PC-r	1 2	1.00	2.00	4.00
9	167	5/64	PC-r	1 2	1.00	2.00	4.00
10	167	4/66	PC-r	1 2	1.00	2.00	4.00
11	169	Sm/69	New price 25¢; stiff-c; PC-r	1 2	1.00	2.00	4.00

59. Wuthering Heights

Ed	HRN	Date	Details	A C	Good	Fine	N-Mint
1	60	5/49	Original; Kiefer a/c	1 1	8.00	24.00	56.00
2	85	—	C-price 15¢; LDC-r	1 1	2.85	8.50	20.00
3	156	—	New-c; PC-r	1 2	1.50	4.50	9.00
4	167	1/64	PC-r	1 2	1.25	2.50	5.00
5	167	10/66	PC-r	1 2	1.25	2.50	5.00
6	169	Sm/69	C-price 25¢; stiff-c; PC-r	1 2	1.00	2.00	4.00

60. Black Beauty

Ed	HRN	Date	Details	A C	Good	Fine	N-Mint
1	62	6/49	Original; Froehlich c/a	1 1	6.50	19.50	45.00
2	62	—	No c-price; no coming-next ad; LDC-r	1 1	7.00	21.00	50.00
3	85	—	C-price 15¢; LDC-r	1 1	2.20	6.50	15.00
4	158	—	New L.B. Cole -c&a; PC-r	2 2	2.65	8.00	18.00
5	167	2/64	PC-r	2 2	1.70	5.00	12.00
6	167	3/66	PC-r	2 2	1.70	5.00	12.00
8	166	R/1968	New-c&price, 25¢; PC-r	2 3	5.00	15.00	35.00

61. The Woman in White

Ed	HRN	Date	Details	A C	Good	Fine	N-Mint
1A	62	7/49	Original; Blum-c/a fc-purple; bc: top illos light blue	1 1	6.50	19.50	45.00
1B	62	7/49	Original; Blum-c/a fc-pink; bc: top illos light violet	1 1	6.50	19.50	45.00
2	156	—	New-c; PC-r	1 2	2.00	6.00	14.00
3	167	1/64	PC-r	1 2	1.70	5.00	12.00
4	166	R/1968	C-price 25¢; PC-r	1 2	1.70	5.00	12.00

62. Western Stories ("The Luck of Roaring Camp" and "The Outcasts of Poker Flat")

Ed	HRN	Date	Details	A C	Good	Fine	N-Mint
1	62	8/49	Original; Kiefer-a,c	1 1	6.50	19.50	45.00
2	89	—	C-price 15¢; LDC-r	1 1	1.70	5.00	12.00

				A C		Good	Fine	N-Mint
3	121	—	LDC-r	1 1		1.50	4.50	9.00
4	137	—	New-c; PC-r	1 2		1.50	4.50	9.00
5	152	—	PC-r	1 2		1.50	3.00	6.00
6	167	10/63	PC-r	1 2		1.50	3.00	6.00
7	167	6/64	PC-r	1 2		.70	2.00	4.00
8	167	11/66	PC-r	1 2		.70	2.00	4.00
9	166	R/1968	New-c&price 25¢; PC-r	1 3		1.70	5.00	12.00

63. The Man Without a Country

Ed	HRN	Date	Details	A C	Good	Fine	N-Mint
1	62	9/49	Original; Kiefer-a,c	1 1	7.00	21.00	50.00
2	78	—	C-price 15¢ in double circle; LDC-r	1 1	2.30	7.00	16.00
3	156	—	New-c, old-a; PC-r	1 2	2.30	7.00	16.00
4	165	—	New-a & text pgs.; PC-r; A. Torres-a	2 2	1.50	4.50	9.00
5	167	3/64	PC-r	2 2	1.00	2.00	4.00
6	167	8/66	PC-r	2 2	1.00	2.00	4.00
7	169	Sm/69	C-price 25¢; stiff-c; PC-r	2 2	1.00	2.00	4.00

64. Treasure Island

Ed	HRN	Date	Details	A C	Good	Fine	N-Mint
1	62	10/49	Original; Blum-a,c	1 1	7.00	21.00	50.00
2	82	—	C-price 15¢; LDC-r	1 1	1.70	5.00	12.00
3	131	—	LDC-r	1 1	1.50	4.50	9.00
4	138	—	New-c; PC-r	1 2	1.50	4.50	9.00
5	146	—	PC-r	1 2	1.00	2.00	4.00
6	158	—	PC-r	1 2	1.00	2.00	4.00
7	165	—	PC-r	1 2	1.00	2.00	4.00
8	167	—	PC-r	1 2	1.00	2.00	4.00
9	167	6/64	PC-r	1 2	1.00	2.00	4.00
10	167	—	PC-r	1 2	1.00	2.00	4.00
11	167	12/65	PC-r	1 2	1.00	2.00	4.00
12A	167	10/67	PC-r	1 2	1.50	4.50	9.00
12B	166	10/67	w/Grit ad stapled in book	1 2	7.00	21.00	50.00
13	169	Spr/69	New price 25¢; stiff-c; PC-r	1 2	1.00	2.00	4.00

65. Benjamin Franklin

Ed	HRN	Date	Details	A C	Good	Fine	N-Mint
1	64	11/49	Original; Kiefer-c Iger Shop-a	1 1	7.00	21.00	50.00
2	131	—	New-c; PC-r	1 2	1.50	4.50	9.00
3	154	—	PC-r	1 2	1.25	2.50	5.00
4	167	2/64	PC-r	1 2	1.25	2.50	5.00
5	167	4/66	PC-r	1 2	1.25	2.50	5.00
6	169	Fall/69	New price 25¢; stiff-c; PC-r	1 2	1.00	2.00	4.00

66. The Cloister and the Hearth

Ed	HRN	Date	Details	A C	Good	Fine	N-Mint
1	67	12/49	Original & only ed; Kiefer-a & c	1 1	14.00	42.00	100.00

67. The Scottish Chiefs

Ed	HRN	Date	Details	A C	Good	Fine	N-Mint
1	67	1/50	Original; Blum-a&c	1 1	6.00	18.00	42.00
2	85	—	C-price 15¢; LDC-r	1 1	1.70	5.00	12.00
3	118	—	LDC-r	1 1	1.50	4.50	9.00
4	136	—	New-c; PC-r	1 2	1.50	4.50	9.00
5	154	—	PC-r	1 2	1.25	2.50	5.00
6	167	11/63	PC-r	1 2	1.25	2.50	5.00
7	167	8/65	PC-r	1 2	1.25	2.50	5.00

CLASSICS ILLUSTRATED (continued)

68. Julius Caesar (Used in SOTI, pgs. 36, 37)

Ed	HRN	Date	Details	A	C	Good	Fine	N-Mint
1	70	2/50	Original; Kiefer-a,c	1	1	6.50	19.50	45.00
2	85	—	C-price 15¢; LDC-r	1	1	1.70	5.00	12.00
3	108	—	LDC-r	1	1	1.50	4.50	9.00
4	156	—	New L.B. Cole-c; PC-r	1	2	2.00	6.00	14.00
5	165	—	New-a by Evans, Crandall; PC-r	2	2	2.00	6.00	14.00
6	167	2/64	Tarzan books inside cover; PC-r	2	2	1.00	2.00	4.00
7	167	10/65		2	2	1.00	2.00	4.00
8	166	R/1967	PC-r	2	2	1.00	2.00	4.00
9	169	Win/69	PC-r; stiff-c	2	2	1.00	2.00	4.00

69. Around the World in 80 Days

Ed	HRN	Date	Details	A	C	Good	Fine	N-Mint
1	70	3/50	Original; Kiefer-a/c	1	1	6.50	19.50	45.00
2	87	—	C-price 15¢; LDC-r	1	1	1.70	5.00	12.00
3	125	—	LDC-r	1	1	1.50	4.50	9.00
4	136	—	New-c; PC-r	1	2	1.50	4.50	9.00
5	146	—	PC-r	1	2	1.00	2.00	4.00
6	152	—	PC-r	1	2	1.00	2.00	4.00
7	164	—	PC-r	1	2	1.00	2.00	4.00
8	167	—	PC-r	1	2	1.00	2.00	4.00
9	167	7/64	PC-r	1	2	1.00	2.00	4.00
10	167	11/65	PC-r	1	2	1.00	2.00	4.00
11	166	7/67	PC-r	1	2	1.00	2.00	4.00
12	169	Spr/69	C-price 25¢; stiff-c; PC-r	1	2	1.00	2.00	4.00

70. The Pilot

Ed	HRN	Date	Details	A	C	Good	Fine	N-Mint
1	71	4/50	Original; Blum-a,c	1	1	5.00	15.00	35.00
2	92	—	C-price 15¢; LDC-r	1	1	1.70	5.00	12.00
3	125	—	LDC-r	1	1	1.50	4.50	9.00
4	156	—	New-c; PC-r	1	2	1.50	4.50	9.00
5	167	2/64	PC-r	1	2	1.25	2.50	5.00
6	167	5/66	PC-r	1	2	1.25	2.50	5.00

71. The Man Who Laughs

Ed	HRN	Date	Details	A	C	Good	Fine	N-Mint
1	71	5/50	Original; Blum-a,c	1	1	9.00	27.00	62.00
2	165	—	New-c&a; PC-r	2	2	6.50	19.50	45.00
3	167	4/64	PC-r	2	2	5.70	17.00	40.00

72. The Oregon Trail

Ed	HRN	Date	Details	A	C	Good	Fine	N-Mint
1	73	6/50	Original; Kiefer-a,c	1	1	5.00	15.00	35.00
2	89	—	C-price 15¢; LDC-r	1	1	1.70	5.00	12.00
3	121	—	LDC-r	1	1	1.50	4.50	9.00
4	131	—	New-c; PC-r	1	2	1.50	4.50	9.00
5	140	—	PC-r	1	2	1.50	3.00	6.00
6	150	—	PC-r	1	2	1.00	2.00	4.00
7	164	—	PC-r	1	2	1.00	2.00	4.00
8	167	—	PC-r	1	2	1.00	2.00	4.00
9	167	8/64	PC-r	1	2	1.00	2.00	4.00
10	167	10/65	PC-r	1	2	1.00	2.00	4.00
11	166	R/1968	C-price 25¢; PC-r	1	2	1.00	2.00	4.00

73. The Black Tulip

Ed	HRN	Date	Details	A	C	Good	Fine	N-Mint
1	75	7/50	1st & only ed.; Alex Blum-a & c	1	1	18.00	54.00	125.00

74. Mr. Midshipman Easy

Ed	HRN	Date	Details	A	C	Good	Fine	N-Mint
1	75	8/50	1st & only edition	1	1	17.00	51.00	120.00

75. The Lady of the Lake

Ed	HRN	Date	Details	A	C	Good	Fine	N-Mint
1	75	9/50	Original; Kiefer-a/c	1	1	5.00	15.00	35.00
2	85	—	C-price 15¢; LDC-r	1	1	1.70	5.00	12.00
3	118	—	LDC-r	1	1	1.50	4.50	9.00
4	139	—	New-c; PC-r	1	2	1.50	4.50	9.00
5	154	—	PC-r	1	2	1.00	2.00	4.00
6	165	—	PC-r	1	2	1.00	2.00	4.00
7	167	4/64	PC-r	1	2	1.00	2.00	4.00
8	167	5/66	PC-r	1	2	1.00	2.00	4.00
9	169	Spr/69	New price 25¢; stiff-c; PC-r	1	2	1.00	2.00	4.00

76. The Prisoner of Zenda

Ed	HRN	Date	Details	A	C	Good	Fine	N-Mint
1	75	10/50	Original; Kiefer-a,c	1	1	4.30	13.00	30.00
2	85	—	C-price 15¢; LDC-r	1	1	1.70	5.00	12.00
3	111	—	LDC-r	1	1	1.50	4.50	9.00
4	128	—	New-c; PC-r	1	2	1.50	4.50	9.00
5	152	—	PC-r	1	2	1.00	2.00	4.00
6	165	—	PC-r	1	2	1.00	2.00	4.00
7	167	4/64	PC-r	1	2	1.00	2.00	4.00
8	167	9/66	PC-r	1	2	1.00	2.00	4.00
9	169	Fall/69	New price 25¢; stiff-c; PC-r	1	2	1.00	2.00	4.00

77. The Iliad

Ed	HRN	Date	Details	A	C	Good	Fine	N-Mint
1	78	11/50	Original; Blum-a,c	1	1	4.30	13.00	30.00
2	87	—	C-price 15¢; LDC-r	1	1	1.70	5.00	12.00
3	121	—	LDC-r	1	1	1.50	4.50	9.00
4	139	—	New-c; PC-r	1	2	1.50	4.50	9.00
5	150	—	PC-r	1	2	1.00	2.00	4.00
6	165	—	PC-r	1	2	1.00	2.00	4.00
7	167	10/63	PC-r	1	2	1.00	2.00	4.00
8	167	7/64	PC-r	1	2	1.00	2.00	4.00
9	167	5/66	PC-r	1	2	1.00	2.00	4.00
10	166	R/1968	C-price 25¢; PC-r	1	2	1.00	2.00	4.00

78. Joan of Arc

Ed	HRN	Date	Details	A	C	Good	Fine	N-Mint
1	78	12/50	Original; Kiefer-a,c	1	1	4.30	13.00	30.00
2	87	—	C-price 15¢; LDC-r	1	1	1.70	5.00	12.00
3	113	—	LDC-r	1	1	1.50	4.50	9.00
4	128	—	New-c; PC-r	1	2	1.50	4.50	9.00
5	140	—	PC-r	1	2	1.00	2.00	4.00
6	150	—	PC-r	1	2	1.00	2.00	4.00
7	159	—	PC-r	1	2	1.00	2.00	4.00
8	167	—	PC-r	1	2	1.00	2.00	4.00
9	167	12/63	PC-r	1	2	1.00	2.00	4.00
10	167	6/65	PC-r	1	2	1.00	2.00	4.00
11	166	6/67	PC-r	1	2	1.00	2.00	4.00
12	166	Win/69	New-c&price, 25¢; PC-r; stiff-c	1	3	1.70	5.00	12.00

79. Cyrano de Bergerac

Ed	HRN	Date	Details	A	C	Good	Fine	N-Mint
1	78	1/51	Orig.; movie promo inside front-c; Blum-a & c	1	1	4.30	13.00	30.00
2	85	—	C-price 15¢; LDC-r	1	1	1.70	5.00	12.00
3	118	—	LDC-r	1	1	1.50	4.50	9.00
4	133	—	New-c; PC-r	1	2	1.70	5.00	10.00
5	156	—	PC-r	1	2	2.00	4.00	8.00
6	167	8/64	PC-r	1	2	2.00	4.00	8.00

Classics Illustrated #71, © GIL

Classics Illustrated #73, © GIL

Classics Illustrated #79 (Orig.), © GIL

Classics Illustrated #83 (HRN-142), © GIL

Classics Illustrated #87 (Orig.), © GIL

Classics Illustrated #91 (HRN-112), © GIL

CLASSICS ILLUSTRATED (continued)

80. White Fang (Last line drawn cover)

Ed	HRN	Date	Details	A	C	Good	Fine	N-Mint
1	79	2/51	Orig.; Blum-a&c	1 1		4.00	12.00	28.00
2	87	—	C-price 15¢; LDC-r	1 1		1.70	5.00	12.00
3	125	—	LDC-r	1 1		1.50	4.50	9.00
4	132	—	New-c; PC-r	1 2		1.50	4.50	9.00
5	140	—	PC-r	1 2		1.00	2.00	4.00
6	153	—	PC-r	1 2		1.00	2.00	4.00
7	167	—	PC-r	1 2		1.00	2.00	4.00
8	167	9/64	PC-r	1 2		1.00	2.00	4.00
9	167	7/65	PC-r	1 2		1.00	2.00	4.00
10	166	6/67	PC-r	1 2		1.00	2.00	4.00
11	169	Fall/69	New price 25¢; PC-r; stiff-c	1 2		1.00	2.00	4.00

81. The Odyssey (1st painted cover)

Ed	HRN	Date	Details	A	C	Good	Fine	N-Mint
1	82	3/51	First 15¢ Original; Blum-c	1 1		3.00	9.00	21.00
2	167	8/64	PC-r	1 1		1.50	4.50	9.00
3	167	10/66	PC-r	1 1		1.50	4.50	9.00
4	169	Spr/69	New, stiff-c; PC-r	1 2		1.70	5.00	10.00

82. The Master of Ballantrae

Ed	HRN	Date	Details	A	C	Good	Fine	N-Mint
1	82	4/51	Original; Blum-c	1 1		3.00	9.00	21.00
2	167	8/64	PC-r	1 1		1.50	4.50	9.00
3	166	Fall/68	New, stiff-c; PC-r	1 2		1.70	5.00	10.00

83. The Jungle Book

Ed	HRN	Date	Details	A	C	Good	Fine	N-Mint
1	85	5/51	Original; Blum-c Bossert/Blum-a	1 1		3.00	9.00	21.00
2	110	—	PC-r	1 1		1.00	2.00	3.00
3	125	—	PC-r	1 1		1.00	2.00	3.00
4	134	—	PC-r	1 1		1.00	2.00	3.00
5	142	—	PC-r	1 1		1.00	2.00	3.00
6	150	—	PC-r	1 1		1.00	2.00	3.00
7	159	—	PC-r	1 1		1.00	2.00	3.00
8	167	—	PC-r	1 1		1.25	2.50	5.00
9	167	3/65	PC-r	1 1		1.25	2.50	5.00
10	167	11/65	PC-r	1 1		1.25	2.50	5.00
11	167	5/66	PC-r	1 1		1.25	2.50	5.00
12	166	R/1968	New c&a; stiff-c; PC-r	2 2		1.50	4.50	10.00

84. The Gold Bug and Other Stories ("The Gold Bug," "The Tell-Tale Heart," "The Cask of Amontillado")

Ed	HRN	Date	Details	A	C	Good	Fine	N-Mint
1	85	6/51	Original; Blum-c/a Palais, Laverly-a	1 1		9.30	28.00	65.00
2	167	7/64	PC-r	1 1		5.00	15.00	35.00

85. The Sea Wolf

Ed	HRN	Date	Details	A	C	Good	Fine	N-Mint
1	85	7/51	Original; Blum-a&c	1 1		2.65	8.00	18.00
2	121	—	PC-r	1 1		1.00	2.00	3.00
3	132	—	PC-r	1 1		1.00	2.00	3.00
4	141	—	PC-r	1 1		1.00	2.00	3.00
5	161	—	PC-r	1 1		1.00	2.00	3.00
6	167	2/64	PC-r	1 1		1.00	2.00	3.00
7	167	11/65	PC-r	1 1		1.00	2.00	3.00
8	169	Fall/69	New price 25¢; stiff-c; PC-r	1 1		1.00	2.00	3.00

86. Under Two Flags

Ed	HRN	Date	Details	A	C

87. A Midsummer Nights Dream

Ed	HRN	Date	Details	A	C	Good	Fine	N-Mint
1	87	8/51	Original; first delBourgo-a	1 1		2.65	8.00	18.00
2	117	—	PC-r	1 1		1.00	2.00	3.00
3	139	—	PC-r	1 1		1.00	2.00	3.00
4	158	—	PC-r	1 1		1.00	2.00	3.00
5	167	2/64	PC-r	1 1		1.00	2.00	3.00
6	167	8/66	PC-r	1 1		1.00	2.00	3.00
7	169	Sm/69	New price 25¢; stiff-c; PC-r	1 1		1.00	2.00	3.00

Ed	HRN	Date	Details	A	C	Good	Fine	N-Mint
1	87	9/51	Original; Blum c/a	1 1		2.65	8.00	18.00
2	161	—	PC-r	1 1		1.25	2.50	5.00
3	167	4/64	PC-r	1 1		1.00	2.00	3.00
4	167	5/66	PC-r	1 1		1.00	2.00	3.00
5	169	Sm/69	New price 25¢; stiff-c; PC-r	1 1		1.00	2.00	3.00

88. Men of Iron

Ed	HRN	Date	Details	A	C	Good	Fine	N-Mint
1	89	10/51	Original	1 1		2.65	8.00	18.00
2	154	—	PC-r	1 1		1.00	2.00	3.00
3	167	1/64	PC-r	1 1		1.00	2.00	3.00
4	166	R/1968	C-price 25¢; PC-r	1 1		1.00	2.00	3.00

89. Crime and Punishment (Cover illo. in POP)

Ed	HRN	Date	Details	A	C	Good	Fine	N-Mint
1	89	11/51	Original; Palais-a	1 1		3.00	9.00	21.00
2	152	—	PC-r	1 1		1.00	2.00	3.00
3	167	4/64	PC-r	1 1		1.00	2.00	3.00
4	167	5/66	PC-r	1 1		1.00	2.00	3.00
5	169	Fall/69	New price 25¢ stiff-c; PC-r	1 1		1.00	2.00	3.00

90. Green Mansions

Ed	HRN	Date	Details	A	C	Good	Fine	N-Mint
1	89	12/51	Original; Blum-a&c	1 1		3.00	9.00	21.00
2	148	—	New L.B. Cole -c; PC-r	1 2		2.00	4.00	8.00
3	165	—	PC-r	1 2		1.00	2.00	3.00
4	167	4/64	PC-r	1 2		1.00	2.00	3.00
5	167	9/66	PC-r	1 2		1.00	2.00	3.00
6	169	Sm/69	New price 25¢; stiff-c; PC-r	1 2		1.00	2.00	3.00

91. The Call of the Wild

Ed	HRN	Date	Details	A	C	Good	Fine	N-Mint
1	92	1/52	Orig.; delBourgo-a	1 1		2.65	8.00	18.00
2	112	—	PC-r	1 1		1.00	2.00	3.00
3	125	—	'Picture Progress' on back-c; PC-r	1 1		1.00	2.00	3.00
4	134	—	PC-r	1 1		1.00	2.00	3.00
5	143	—	PC-r	1 1		1.00	2.00	3.00
6	165	—	PC-r	1 1		1.00	2.00	3.00
7	167	—	PC-r	1 1		1.00	2.00	3.00
8	167	4/65	PC-r	1 1		1.00	2.00	3.00
9	167	3/66	PC-r	1 1		1.00	2.00	3.00
10	166	11/67	PC-r	1 1		1.00	2.00	3.00
11	169	Spr/70	New price 25¢; stiff-c; PC-r	1 1		1.00	2.00	3.00

92. The Courtship of Miles Standish

Ed	HRN	Date	Details	A	C	Good	Fine	N-Mint
1	92	2/52	Original; Blum-a&c	1 1		2.65	8.00	18.00
2	165	—	PC-r	1 1		1.00	2.00	3.00
3	167	3/64	PC-r	1 1		1.00	2.00	3.00
4	166	5/67	PC-r	1 1		1.00	2.00	3.00

Ed	HRN	Date	Details	A	C	Good	Fine	N-Mint
5	169	Win/69	New price 25¢ stiff-c; PC-r	1	1	1.00	2.00	3.00

93. Pudd'nhead Wilson

Ed	HRN	Date	Details	A	C	Good	Fine	N-Mint
1	94	3/52	Orig.; Kiefer-a&c;	1	1	3.00	9.00	21.00
2	165	—	New-c; PC-r	1	2	1.50	3.00	6.00
3	167	3/64	PC-r	1	2	1.50	3.00	6.00
4	166	R/1968	New price 25¢; soft-c; PC-r	1	2	1.50	3.00	6.00

94. David Balfour

Ed	HRN	Date	Details	A	C	Good	Fine	N-Mint
1	94	4/52	Original; Palais-a	1	1	3.00	9.00	21.00
2	167	5/64	PC-r	1	1	2.00	4.00	8.00
3	166	R/1968	C-price 25¢; PC-r	1	1	2.00	4.00	8.00

95. All Quiet on the Western Front

Ed	HRN	Date	Details	A	C	Good	Fine	N-Mint
1A	96	5/52	Orig.; del Bourgo-a	1	1	6.50	19.50	45.00
1B	99	5/52	Orig.; del Bourgo-a	1	1	5.50	16.50	38.00
2	167	10/64	PC-r	1	1	2.00	6.00	14.00
3	167	11/66	PC-r	1	1	2.00	6.00	14.00

96. Daniel Boone

Ed	HRN	Date	Details	A	C	Good	Fine	N-Mint
1	97	6/52	Original; Blum-a	1	1	2.65	8.00	18.00
2	117	—	PC-r	1	1	1.00	2.00	3.00
3	128	—	PC-r	1	1	1.00	2.00	3.00
4	132	—	PC-r	1	1	1.00	2.00	3.00
5	134	—	'Story of Jesus' on back-c; PC-r	1	1	1.00	2.00	3.00
6	158	—	PC-r	1	1	1.00	2.00	3.00
7	167	1/64	PC-r	1	1	1.00	2.00	3.00
8	167	5/65	PC-r	1	1	1.00	2.00	3.00
9	167	11/66	PC-r	1	1	1.00	2.00	3.00
10	166	Win/69	New-c; price 25¢; PC-r; stiff-c	1	2	1.50	4.50	10.00

97. King Solomon's Mines

Ed	HRN	Date	Details	A	C	Good	Fine	N-Mint
1	96	7/52	Orig.; Kiefer-a	1	1	2.65	8.00	18.00
2	118	—	PC-r	1	1	1.50	3.50	7.00
3	131	—	PC-r	1	1	1.00	2.00	4.00
4	141	—	PC-r	1	1	1.00	2.00	4.00
5	158	—	PC-r	1	1	1.00	2.00	4.00
6	167	2/64	PC-r	1	1	1.00	2.00	4.00
7	167	9/65	PC-r	1	1	1.00	2.00	4.00
8	169	Sm/69	New price 25¢; stiff-c; PC-r	1	1	1.25	2.50	5.00

98. The Red Badge of Courage

Ed	HRN	Date	Details	A	C	Good	Fine	N-Mint
1	98	8/52	Original	1	1	2.65	8.00	18.00
2	118	—	PC-r	1	1	1.00	2.00	3.00
3	132	—	PC-r	1	1	1.00	2.00	3.00
4	142	—	PC-r	1	1	1.00	2.00	3.00
5	152	—	PC-r	1	1	1.00	2.00	3.00
6	161	—	PC-r	1	1	1.00	2.00	3.00
7	167	—	Has orig.date; PC-r	1	1	1.00	2.00	3.00
8	167	9/64	PC-r	1	1	1.00	2.00	3.00
9	167	10/65	PC-r	1	1	1.00	2.00	3.00
10	166	R/1968	New-c&price 25¢; PC-r; stiff-c	1	2	1.70	5.00	12.00

99. Hamlet (Used in POP, pg. 102)

Ed	HRN	Date	Details	A	C	Good	Fine	N-Mint
1	98	9/52	Original; Blum-a	1	1	3.00	9.00	21.00

Ed	HRN	Date	Details	A	C	Good	Fine	N-Mint
2	121	—	PC-r	1	1	1.00	2.00	4.00
3	141	—	PC-r	1	1	1.00	2.00	4.00
4	158	—	PC-r	1	1	1.00	2.00	4.00
5	167	—	Has orig.date; PC-r	1	1	1.00	2.00	4.00
6	167	7/65	PC-r	1	1	1.00	2.00	4.00
7	166	4/67	PC-r	1	1	1.00	2.00	4.00
8	169	Spr/69	New-c&price 25¢; PC-r; stiff-c	1	2	1.70	5.00	10.00

100. Mutiny on the Bounty

Ed	HRN	Date	Details	A	C	Good	Fine	N-Mint
1	100	10/52	Original	1	1	2.00	6.00	14.00
2	117	—	PC-r	1	1	1.00	2.00	3.00
3	132	—	PC-r	1	1	1.00	2.00	3.00
4	142	—	PC-r	1	1	1.00	2.00	3.00
5	155	—	PC-r	1	1	1.00	2.00	3.00
6	167	—	Has orig. date; PC-r	1	1	1.00	2.00	3.00
7	167	5/64	PC-r	1	1	1.00	2.00	3.00
8	167	3/66	PC-r	1	1	1.00	2.00	3.00
9	169	Spr/70	PC-r; stiff-c	1	1	1.00	2.00	3.00

101. William Tell

Ed	HRN	Date	Details	A	C	Good	Fine	N-Mint
1	101	11/52	Original; Kiefer-c delBourgo-a	1	1	2.00	6.00	14.00
2	118	—	PC-r	1	1	1.00	2.00	3.00
3	141	—	PC-r	1	1	1.00	2.00	3.00
4	158	—	PC-r	1	1	1.00	2.00	3.00
5	167	—	Has orig.date; PC-r	1	1	1.00	2.00	3.00
6	167	11/64	PC-r	1	1	1.00	2.00	3.00
7	166	4/67	PC-r	1	1	1.00	2.00	3.00
8	169	Win/69	New price 25¢; stiff-c; PC-r	1	1	1.00	2.00	3.00

102. The White Company

Ed	HRN	Date	Details	A	C	Good	Fine	N-Mint
1	101	12/52	Original; Blum-a	1	1	4.00	12.00	28.00
2	165	—	PC-r	1	1	2.00	6.00	14.00
3	167	4/64	PC-r	1	1	2.00	6.00	14.00

103. Men Against the Sea

Ed	HRN	Date	Details	A	C	Good	Fine	N-Mint
1	104	1/53	Original; Kiefer-c, Palais-a	1	1	2.65	8.00	18.00
2	114	—	PC-r	1	1	1.70	5.00	12.00
3	131	—	New-c; PC-r	1	2	1.50	4.50	9.00
4	158	—	PC-r	1	2	1.50	4.50	9.00
5	149	—	White reorder list; came after HRN-158; PC-r	1	2	2.00	6.00	14.00
6	167	3/64	PC-r	1	2	1.00	2.00	4.00

104. Bring 'Em Back Alive

Ed	HRN	Date	Details	A	C	Good	Fine	N-Mint
1	105	2/53	Original; Kiefer c/a	1	1	2.30	7.00	16.00
2	118	—	PC-r	1	1	1.00	2.00	3.00
3	133	—	PC-r	1	1	1.00	2.00	3.00
4	150	—	PC-r	1	1	1.00	2.00	3.00
5	158	—	PC-r	1	1	1.00	2.00	3.00
6	167	10/63	PC-r	1	1	1.00	2.00	3.00
7	167	9/65	PC-r	1	1	1.00	2.00	3.00
8	169	Win/69	New price 25¢; stiff-c; PC-r	1	1	1.00	2.00	3.00

105. From the Earth to the Moon

Ed	HRN	Date	Details	A	C	Good	Fine	N-Mint
1	106	3/53	Original; Blum-a	1	1	2.30	7.00	16.00
2	118	—	PC-r	1	1	1.00	2.00	3.00

Classics Illustrated #95, © GIL

Classics Illustrated #98 (Orig.), © GIL

Classics Illustrated #103, © GIL

Classics Illustrated #105 (HRN-167), © GIL

Classics Illustrated #107 (HRN-167), © GIL

Classics Illustrated #111 (HRN-167), © GIL

CLASSICS ILLUSTRATED (continued)

Ed	HRN	Date	Details	A	C	Good	Fine	N-Mint
3	132	—	PC-r	1	1	1.00	2.00	3.00
4	141	—	PC-r	1	1	1.00	2.00	3.00
5	146	—	PC-r	1	1	1.00	2.00	3.00
6	156	—	PC-r	1	1	1.00	2.00	3.00
7	167	—	Has orig. date; PC-r	1	1	1.00	2.00	3.00
8	167	5/64	PC-r	1	1	1.00	2.00	3.00
9	167	5/65	PC-r	1	1	1.00	2.00	3.00
10A	166	10/67	PC-r	1	1	1.00	2.00	3.00
10B	166	10/67	w/Grit ad	1	1	7.00	21.00	50.00
11	169	Sm/69	New price 25¢; stiff-c; PC-r	1	1	1.00	2.00	3.00
12	169	Spr/71	PC-r	1	1	1.00	2.00	3.00

106. Buffalo Bill

Ed	HRN	Date	Details	A	C	Good	Fine	N-Mint
1	107	4/53	Orig.; delBourgo-a	1	1	2.30	7.00	16.00
2	118	—	PC-r	1	1	1.00	2.00	3.00
3	132	—	PC-r	1	1	1.00	2.00	3.00
4	142	—	PC-r	1	1	1.00	2.00	3.00
5	161	—	PC-r	1	1	1.00	2.00	3.00
6	167	3/64	PC-r	1	1	1.00	2.00	3.00
7	166	7/67	PC-r	1	1	1.00	2.00	3.00
8	169	Fall/69	PC-r; stiff-c	1	1	1.00	2.00	3.00

107. King of the Khyber Rifles

Ed	HRN	Date	Details	A	C	Good	Fine	N-Mint
1	108	5/53	Original	1	1	2.30	7.00	16.00
2	118	—	PC-r	1	1	1.00	2.00	4.00
3	146	—	PC-r	1	1	1.00	2.00	4.00
4	158	—	PC-r	1	1	1.00	2.00	4.00
5	167	—	Has orig.date; PC-r	1	1	1.00	2.00	4.00
6	167	—	PC-r	1	1	1.00	2.00	4.00
7	167	10/66	PC-r	1	1	1.00	2.00	4.00

108. Knights of the Round Table

Ed	HRN	Date	Details	A	C	Good	Fine	N-Mint
1A	108	6/53	Original; Blum-a	1	1	2.65	8.00	18.00
1B	109	6/53	Original; scarce	1	1	4.00	12.00	28.00
2	117	—	PC-r	1	1	1.00	2.00	3.00
3	165	—	PC-r	1	1	1.00	2.00	3.00
4	167	4/64	PC-r	1	1	1.00	2.00	3.00
5	166	4/67	PC-r	1	1	1.00	2.00	3.00
6	169	Sm/69	New price 25¢; stiff-c; PC-r	1	1	1.00	2.00	3.00

109. Pitcairn's Island

Ed	HRN	Date	Details	A	C	Good	Fine	N-Mint
1A	110	7/53	Original; Palais-a	1	1	3.00	9.00	21.00
1B	110	7/53	Original; bc missing red line 'Mail coupon . . .' above coupon (printing error); very rare; Palais-a	1	1	8.00	24.00	56.00
2	165	—	PC-r	1	1	1.50	3.50	7.00
3	167	3/64	PC-r	1	1	1.50	3.50	7.00
4	166	6/67	PC-r	1	1	1.50	3.50	7.00

110. A Study in Scarlet

Ed	HRN	Date	Details	A	C	Good	Fine	N-Mint
1	111	8/53	Original	1	1	8.50	25.50	60.00
2	165	—	PC-r	1	1	5.70	17.00	40.00

111. The Talisman

Ed	HRN	Date	Details	A	C	Good	Fine	N-Mint
1	112	9/53	Original; last H.C. Kiefer-a	1	1	4.30	13.00	30.00
2	165	—	PC-r	1	1	1.00	2.00	3.00
3	167	5/64	PC-r	1	1	1.00	2.00	3.00
4	166	Fall/68	C-price 25¢; PC-r	1	1	1.00	2.00	3.00

112. Adventures of Kit Carson

Ed	HRN	Date	Details	A	C	Good	Fine	N-Mint
1	113	10/53	Original; Palais-a	1	1	4.30	13.00	30.00
2	129	—	PC-r	1	1	1.00	2.00	3.00
3	141	—	PC-r	1	1	1.00	2.00	3.00
4	152	—	PC-r	1	1	1.00	2.00	3.00
5	161	—	PC-r	1	1'	1.00	2.00	3.00
6	167	—	PC-r	1	1	1.00	2.00	3.00
7	167	2/65	PC-r	1	1	1.00	2.00	3.00
8	167	5/66	PC-r	1	1	1.00	2.00	3.00
9	166	Win/69	New-c&price 25¢; PC-r; stiff-c	1	2	1.70	5.00	10.00

113. The Forty-Five Guardsmen

Ed	HRN	Date	Details	A	C	Good	Fine	N-Mint
1	114	11/53	Orig.; delBourgo-a	1	1	5.00	15.00	35.00
2	166	7/67	PC-r	1	1	2.30	7.00	16.00

114. The Red Rover

Ed	HRN	Date	Details	A	C	Good	Fine	N-Mint
1	115	12/53	Original	1	1	5.00	15.00	35.00
2	166	7/67	PC-r	1	1	2.30	7.00	16.00

115. How I Found Livingstone

Ed	HRN	Date	Details	A	C	Good	Fine	N-Mint
1	116	1/54	Original	1	1	5.00	15.00	35.00
2	167	1/67	PC-r	1	1	2.30	7.00	16.00

116. The Bottle Imp

Ed	HRN	Date	Details	A	C	Good	Fine	N-Mint
1	117	2/54	Orig.; Cameron-a	1	1	6.00	18.00	42.00
2	167	1/67	PC-r	1	1	2.30	7.00	16.00

117. Captains Courageous

Ed	HRN	Date	Details	A	C	Good	Fine	N-Mint
1	118	3/54	Orig.; Costanza-a	1	1	4.00	12.00	28.00
2	167	2/67	PC-r	1	1	1.50	4.50	9.00
3	169	Fall/69	New price 25¢; stiff-c; PC-r	1	1	1.50	4.50	9.00

118. Rob Roy

Ed	HRN	Date	Details	A	C	Good	Fine	N-Mint
1	119	4/54	Original; Rudy & Walter Palais-a	1	1	4.50	14.00	32.00
2	167	2/67	PC-r	1	1	2.65	8.00	18.00

119. Soldiers of Fortune

Ed	HRN	Date	Details	A	C	Good	Fine	N-Mint
1	120	5/54	Original Shaffenberger-a	1	1	4.50	14.00	32.00
2	166	3/67	PC-r	1	1	1.50	4.50	9.00
3	169	Spr/70	New price 25¢; stiff-c; PC-r	1	1	1.50	4.50	9.00

120. The Hurricane

Ed	HRN	Date	Details	A	C	Good	Fine	N-Mint
1	121	6/54	Orig.; Cameron-a	1	1	4.50	14.00	32.00
2	166	3/67	PC-r	1	1	3.00	9.00	21.00

121. Wild Bill Hickok

Ed	HRN	Date	Details	A	C	Good	Fine	N-Mint
1	122	7/54	Original	1	1	2.30	7.00	16.00
2	132	—	PC-r	1	1	1.00	2.00	3.00
3	141	—	PC-r	1	1	1.00	2.00	3.00
4	154	—	PC-r	1	1	1.00	2.00	3.00
5	167	—	PC-r	1	1	1.00	2.00	3.00

CLASSICS ILLUSTRATED (continued)

Ed	HRN	Date	Details	A	C	Good	Fine	N-Mint
6	167	8/64	PC-r	1	1	1.00	2.00	3.00
7	166	4/67	PC-r	1	1	1.00	2.00	3.00
8	169	Win/69	PC-r; stiff-c	1	1	1.00	2.00	3.00

122. The Mutineers

Ed	HRN	Date	Details	A	C	Good	Fine	N-Mint
1	123	9/54	Original	1	1	2.30	7.00	16.00
2	136	—	PC-r	1	1	1.00	2.00	3.00
3	146	—	PC-r	1	1	1.00	2.00	3.00
4	158	—	PC-r	1	1	1.00	2.00	3.00
5	167	11/63	PC-r	1	1	1.00	2.00	3.00
6	167	3/65	PC-r	1	1	1.00	2.00	3.00
7	166	8/67	PC-r	1	1	1.00	2.00	3.00

123. Fang and Claw

Ed	HRN	Date	Details	A	C	Good	Fine	N-Mint
1	124	11/54	Original	1	1	2.30	7.00	16.00
2	133	—	PC-r	1	1	1.00	2.00	3.00
3	143	—	PC-r	1	1	1.00	2.00	3.00
4	154	—	PC-r	1	1	1.00	2.00	3.00
5	167	—	Has orig.date; PC-r	1	1	1.00	2.00	3.00
6	167	9/65	PC-r	1	1	1.00	2.00	3.00

124. The War of the Worlds

Ed	HRN	Date	Details	A	C	Good	Fine	N-Mint
1	125	1/55	Orig.; Cameron c/a	1	1	2.65	8.00	18.00
2	131	—	PC-r	1	1	1.00	2.00	3.00
3	141	—	PC-r	1	1	1.00	2.00	3.00
4	148	—	PC-r	1	1	1.00	2.00	3.00
5	156	—	PC-r	1	1	1.00	2.00	3.00
6	165	—	PC-r	1	1	1.00	2.00	3.00
7	167	—	PC-r	1	1	1.00	2.00	3.00
8	167	11/64	PC-r	1	1	1.00	2.00	3.00
9	167	11/65	PC-r	1	1	1.00	2.00	3.00
10	166	R/1968	C-price 25¢; PC-r	1	1	1.00	2.00	3.00
11	169	Sm/70	PC-r; stiff-c	1	1	1.00	2.00	3.00

125. The Ox Bow Incident

Ed	HRN	Date	Details	A	C	Good	Fine	N-Mint
1	—	3/55	Original; Picture Progress replaces reorder list	1	1	2.30	7.00	16.00
2	143	—	PC-r	1	1	1.00	2.00	3.00
3	152	—	PC-r	1	1	1.00	2.00	3.00
4	149	—	PC-r	1	1	1.00	2.00	3.00
5	167	—	PC-r	1	1	1.00	2.00	3.00
6	167	11/64	PC-r	1	1	1.00	2.00	3.00
7	166	4/67	PC-r	1	1	1.00	2.00	3.00
8	169	Win/69	New price 25¢; stiff-c; PC-r	1	1	1.00	2.00	3.00

126. The Downfall

Ed	HRN	Date	Details	A	C	Good	Fine	N-Mint
1	—	5/55	Orig.; 'Picture Progress' replaces re-order list; Cameron c/a	1	1	2.30	7.00	16.00
2	167	8/64	PC-r	1	1	1.50	3.00	6.00
3	166	R/1968	C-price 25¢; PC-r	1	1	1.50	3.00	6.00

127. The King of the Mountains

Ed	HRN	Date	Details	A	C	Good	Fine	N-Mint
1	128	7/55	Original	1	1	2.30	7.00	16.00
2	167	6/64	PC-r	1	1	1.50	3.00	6.00
3	166	F/1968	C-price 25¢; PC-r	1	1	1.50	3.00	6.00

128. Macbeth (Used in POP, pg. 102)

Ed	HRN	Date	Details	A	C	Good	Fine	N-Mint
1	128	9/55	Orig.; last Blum-a	1	1	2.65	8.00	18.00
2	143	—	PC-r	1	1	1.00	2.00	3.00
3	158	—	PC-r	1	1	1.00	2.00	3.00
4	167	—	PC-r	1	1	1.00	2.00	3.00
5	167	6/64	PC-r	1	1	1.00	2.00	3.00
6	166	4/67	PC-r	1	1	1.00	2.00	3.00
7	166	R/1968	C-Price 25¢; PC-r	1	1	1.00	2.00	3.00
8	169	Spr/70	Stiff-c; PC-r	1	1	1.00	2.00	3.00

129. Davy Crockett

Ed	HRN	Date	Details	A	C	Good	Fine	N-Mint
1	129	11/55	Orig.; Cameron-a	1	1	5.70	17.00	40.00
2	167	9/66	PC-r	1	1	3.50	10.50	24.00

130. Caesar's Conquests

Ed	HRN	Date	Details	A	C	Good	Fine	N-Mint
1	130	1/56	Original; Orlando-a	1	1	2.30	7.00	16.00
2	142	—	PC-r	1	1	1.00	2.00	3.00
3	152	—	PC-r	1	1	1.00	2.00	3.00
4	149	—	PC-r	1	1	1.00	2.00	3.00
5	167	—	PC-r	1	1	1.00	2.00	3.00
6	167	10/64	PC-r	1	1	1.00	2.00	3.00
7	167	4/66	PC-r	1	1	1.00	2.00	3.00

131. The Covered Wagon

Ed	HRN	Date	Details	A	C	Good	Fine	N-Mint
1	131	3/56	Original	1	1	2.30	7.00	16.00
2	143	—	PC-r	1	1	1.00	2.00	3.00
3	152	—	PC-r	1	1	1.00	2.00	3.00
4	158	—	PC-r	1	1	1.00	2.00	3.00
5	167	—	PC-r	1	1	1.00	2.00	3.00
6	167	11/64	PC-r	1	1	1.00	2.00	3.00
7	167	4/66	PC-r	1	1	1.00	2.00	3.00
8	169	Win/69	New price 25 cents; stiff-c; PC-r	1	1	1.00	2.00	3.00

132. The Dark Frigate

Ed	HRN	Date	Details	A	C	Good	Fine	N-Mint
1	132	5/56	Original	1	1	2.30	7.00	16.00
2	150	—	PC-r	1	1	1.50	3.00	6.00
3	167	1/64	PC-r	1	1	1.50	3.00	6.00
4	166	5/67	PC-r	1	1	1.50	3.00	6.00

133. The Time Machine

Ed	HRN	Date	Details	A	C	Good	Fine	N-Mint
1	132	7/56	Orig.; Cameron-a	1	1	3.00	9.00	21.00
2	142	—	PC-r	1	1	1.05	2.10	4.20
3	152	—	PC-r	1	1	1.05	2.10	4.20
4	158	—	PC-r	1	1	1.05	2.10	4.20
5	167	—	PC-r	1	1	1.05	2.10	4.20
6	167	6/64	PC-r	1	1	1.05	2.10	4.20
7	167	3/66	PC-r	1	1	1.05	2.10	4.20
8	166	12/67	PC-r	1	1	1.05	2.10	4.20
9	169	Win/71	New price 25 cents; stiff-c; PC-r	1	1	1.50	3.00	6.00

134. Romeo and Juliet

Ed	HRN	Date	Details	A	C	Good	Fine	N-Mint
1	134	9/56	Original; Evans-a	1	1	2.30	7.00	16.00
2	161	—	PC-r	1	1	1.00	2.00	3.00
3	167	9/63	PC-r	1	1	1.00	2.00	3.00
4	167	5/65	PC-r	1	1	1.00	2.00	3.00
5	166	6/67	PC-r	1	1	1.00	2.00	3.00
6	166	Win/69	New c&price 25¢; stiff-c; PC-r	1	2	2.65	8.00	18.00

Classics Illustrated #124 (Orig.), © GIL

Classics Illustrated #127 (Orig.), © GIL

Classics Illustrated #133 (HRN-167), © GIL

Classics Illustrated #138, © GIL

Classics Illustrated #140 (HRN-160), © GIL

Classics Illustrated #148, © GIL

CLASSICS ILLUSTRATED (continued)

135. Waterloo

Ed	HRN	Date	Details	A	C	Good	Fine	N-Mint
1	135	11/56	Orig.; G. Ingels-a	1	1	2.30	7.00	16.00
2	153	—	PC-r	1	1	1.00	2.00	3.00
3	167	—	PC-r	1	1	1.00	2.00	3.00
4	167	9/64	PC-r	1	1	1.00	2.00	3.00
5	166	R/1968	C-price 25 cents; PC-r	1	1	1.00	2.00	3.00

136. Lord Jim

Ed	HRN	Date	Details	A	C			
1	136	1/57	Original; Evans-a	1	1	2.30	7.00	16.00
2	165	—	PC-r	1	1	1.00	2.00	3.00
3	167	3/64	PC-r	1	1	1.00	2.00	3.00
4	167	9/66	PC-r	1	1	1.00	2.00	3.00
5	169	Sm/69	New price 25 cents; stiff-c; PC-r	1	1	1.00	2.00	3.00

137. The Little Savage

Ed	HRN	Date	Details	A	C			
1	136	3/57	Original; Evans-a	1	1	2.30	7.00	16.00
2	148	—	PC-r	1	1	1.00	2.00	3.00
3	156	—	PC-r	1	1	1.00	2.00	3.00
4	167	—	PC-r	1	1	1.00	2.00	3.00
5	167	10/64	PC-r	1	1	1.00	2.00	3.00
6	166	8/67	PC-r	1	1	1.00	2.00	3.00
7	169	Spr/70	New price 25 cents; stiff-c; PC-r	1	1	1.00	2.00	3.00

138. A Journey to the Center of the Earth

Ed	HRN	Date	Details	A	C			
1	136	5/57	Original	1	1	3.00	9.00	21.00
2	146	—	PC-r	1	1	1.00	2.00	3.00
3	156	—	PC-r	1	1	1.00	2.00	3.00
4	158	—	PC-r	1	1	1.00	2.00	3.00
5	167	—	PC-r	1	1	1.00	2.00	3.00
6	167	6/64	PC-r	1	1	1.00	2.00	3.00
7	167	4/66	PC-r	1	1	1.00	2.00	3.00
8	166	R/1968	C-price 25 cents; PC-r	1	1	1.00	2.00	3.00

139. In the Reign of Terror

Ed	HRN	Date	Details	A	C			
1	139	7/57	Original; Evans-a	1	1	2.30	7.00	16.00
2	154	—	PC-r	1	1	1.00	2.00	3.00
3	167	—	Has orig.date; PC-r	1	1	1.00	2.00	3.00
4	167	7/64	PC-r	1	1	1.00	2.00	3.00
5	166	R/1968	C-price 25 cents; PC-r	1	1	1.00	2.00	3.00

140. On Jungle Trails

Ed	HRN	Date	Details	A	C			
1	140	9/57	Original	1	1	2.30	7.00	16.00
2	150	—	PC-r	1	1	1.00	2.00	3.00
3	160	—	PC-r	1	1	1.00	2.00	3.00
4	167	9/63	PC-r	1	1	1.00	2.00	3.00
5	167	9/65	PC-r	1	1	1.00	2.00	3.00

141. Castle Dangerous

Ed	HRN	Date	Details	A	C			
1	141	11/57	Original	1	1	2.30	7.00	16.00
2	152	—	PC-r	1	1	1.00	2.00	3.00
3	167	—	PC-r	1	1	1.00	2.00	3.00
4	166	7/67	PC-r	1	1	1.00	2.00	3.00

142. Abraham Lincoln

Ed	HRN	Date	Details	A	C			
1	142	1/58	Original	1	1	2.30	7.00	16.00
2	154	—	PC-r	1	1	1.00	2.00	3.00
3	158	—	PC-r	1	1	1.00	2.00	3.00
4	167	10/63	PC-r	1	1	1.00	2.00	3.00
5	167	7/65	PC-r	1	1	1.00	2.00	3.00
6	166	11/67	PC-r	1	1	1.00	2.00	3.00
7	169	Fall/69	New price 25 cents; stiff-c; PC-r	1	1	1.00	2.00	3.00

143. Kim

Ed	HRN	Date	Details	A	C			
1	143	3/58	Original; Orlando-a	1	1	2.30	7.00	16.00
2	165	—	PC-r	1	1	1.00	2.00	3.00
3	167	11/63	PC-r	1	1	1.00	2.00	3.00
4	167	8/65	PC-r	1	1	1.00	2.00	3.00
5	169	Win/69	New price 25 cents; stiff-c; PC-r	1	1	1.00	2.00	3.00

144. The First Men in the Moon

Ed	HRN	Date	Details	A	C			
1	143	5/58	Original; Woodbridge/Williamson/Torres-a	1	1	3.00	9.00	21.00
2	153	—	PC-r	1	1	1.00	2.00	3.00
3	161	—	PC-r	1	1	1.00	2.00	3.00
4	167	—	PC-r	1	1	1.00	2.00	3.00
5	167	12/65	PC-r	1	1	1.00	2.00	3.00
6	166	Fall/68	New-c&price 25¢; PC-r; stiff-c	1	2	1.50	3.00	6.00
7	169	Win/69	Stiff-c; PC-r	1	2	1.50	3.00	6.00

145. The Crisis

Ed	HRN	Date	Details	A	C			
1	143	7/58	Original; Evans-a	1	1	2.30	7.00	16.00
2	156	—	PC-r	1	1	1.00	2.00	3.00
3	167	10/63	PC-r	1	1	1.00	2.00	3.00
4	167	3/65	PC-r	1	1	1.00	2.00	3.00
5	166	R/1968	C-price 25¢; PC-r	1	1	1.00	2.00	3.00

146. With Fire and Sword

Ed	HRN	Date	Details	A	C			
1	143	9/58	Original; Woodbridge-a	1	1	2.30	7.00	16.00
2	156	—	PC-r	1	1	1.50	3.50	6.00
3	167	11/63	PC-r	1	1	1.50	3.50	6.00
4	167	3/65	PC-r	1	1	1.50	3.50	6.00

147. Ben-Hur

Ed	HRN	Date	Details	A	C			
1	147	11/58	Original; Orlando-a	1	1	2.30	7.00	16.00
2	152	—	Scarce; PC-r	1	1	2.30	7.00	16.00
3	153	—	PC-r	1	1	1.00	2.00	3.00
4	158	—	PC-r	1	1	1.00	2.00	3.00
5	167	—	Orig.date; but PC-r	1	1	1.00	2.00	3.00
6	167	2/65	PC-r	1	1	1.00	2.00	3.00
7	167	9/66	PC-r	1	1	1.00	2.00	3.00
8A	166	Fall/68	New-c&price 25¢; PC-r; soft-c	1	2	1.70	5.00	12.00
8B	166	Fall/68	New-c&price 25¢; PCpr; stiff-c; scarce	1	2	3.50	10.50	24.00

148. The Buccaneer

Ed	HRN	Date	Details	A	C			
1	148	1/59	Orig.; Evans/Jenny-a; Saunders-c	1	1	2.30	7.00	16.00
2	568	—	Juniors list only PC-r	1	1	1.50	3.00	6.00
3	167	—	PC-r	1	1	1.00	2.00	3.00

CLASSICS ILLUSTRATED (continued)

				A	C	Good	Fine	N-Mint
4	167	9/65	PC-r	1	1	1.00	2.00	3.00
5	169	Sm/69	New price 25¢; PC-r; stiff-c	1	1	1.00	2.00	3.00

149. Off on a Comet

Ed	HRN	Date	Details	A	C			
1	149	3/59	Orig.; G.McCann-a; blue reorder list	1	1	2.30	7.00	16.00
2	155	—	PC-r	1	1	1.00	2.00	3.00
3	149	—	PC-r; white reorder list; no coming-next ad	1	1	1.00	2.00	3.00
4	167	12/63	PC-r	1	1	1.00	2.00	3.00
5	167	2/65	PC-r	1	1	1.00	2.00	3.00
6	167	10/66	PC-r	1	1	1.00	2.00	3.00
7	166	Fall/68	New-c&price 25¢; PC-r	1	2	1.70	5.00	12.00

150. The Virginian

Ed	HRN	Date	Details	A	C			
1	150	5/59	Original	1	1	3.00	9.00	21.00
2	164	—	PC-r	1	1	1.50	4.50	9.00
3	167	10/63	PC-r	1	1	1.50	4.50	9.00
4	167	12/65	PC-r	1	1	1.50	4.50	9.00

151. Won By the Sword

Ed	HRN	Date	Details	A	C			
1	150	7/59	Original	1	1	3.70	11.00	26.00
2	164	—	PC-r	1	1	1.50	3.50	7.00
3	167	10/63	PC-r	1	1	1.50	3.50	7.00
4	166	7/67	PC-r	1	1	1.50	3.50	7.00

152. Wild Animals I Have Known

Ed	HRN	Date	Details	A	C			
1	152	9/59	Orig.; L.B. Cole c/a	1	1	3.00	9.00	21.00
2	149	—	PC-r; white reorder list; no coming-next ad	1	1	1.00	2.00	4.00
3	167	9/63	PC-r	1	1	1.00	2.00	3.00
4	167	8/65	PC-r	1	1	1.00	2.00	3.00
5	169	Fall/69	New price 25¢; stiff-c; PC-r	1	1	1.00	2.00	3.00

153. The Invisible Man

Ed	HRN	Date	Details	A	C			
1	153	11/59	Original	1	1	3.00	9.00	21.00
2	149	—	PC-r; white reorder list; no coming-next ad	1	1	1.00	2.00	3.00
3	167	—	PC-r	1	1	1.00	2.00	3.00
4	167	2/65	PC-r	1	1	1.00	2.00	3.00
5	167	9/66	PC-r	1	1	1.00	2.00	3.00
6	166	Win/69	New price 25¢; PC-r; stiff-c	1	1	1.00	2.00	3.00
7	169	Spr/71	Stiff-c; letters spelling 'Invisible Man' are 'solid' not'invisible;' PC-r	1	1	1.00	2.00	3.00

154. The Conspiracy of Pontiac

Ed	HRN	Date	Details	A	C			
1	154	1/60	Original	1	1	3.00	9.00	21.00
2	167	11/63	PC-r	1	1	1.70	5.00	12.00
3	167	7/64	PC-r	1	1	1.70	5.00	12.00
4	166	12/67	PC-r	1	1	1.70	5.00	12.00

155. The Lion of the North

Ed	HRN	Date	Details	A	C	Good	Fine	N-Mint
1	154	3/60	PC-r	1	1	2.30	7.00	16.00
2	167	1/64	PC-r	1	1	1.50	3.50	7.00
3	166	R/1967	C-price 25¢; PC-r	1	1	1.50	3.50	7.00

156. The Conquest of Mexico

Ed	HRN	Date	Details	A	C			
1	156	5/60	Orig.; Bruno Premiani-a&c	1	1	2.30	7.00	16.00
2	167	1/64	PC-r	1	1	1.25	2.50	5.00
3	167	8/67	PC-r	1	1	1.25	2.50	5.00
4	169	Spr/70	New price 25¢; stiff-c; PC-r	1	1	1.25	2.50	5.00

157. Lives of the Hunted

Ed	HRN	Date	Details	A	C			
1	156	7/60	Orig.; L.B. Cole-c	1	1	3.00	9.00	21.00
2	167	2/64	PC-r	1	1	1.70	5.00	12.00
3	166	10/67	PC-r	1	1	1.70	5.00	12.00

158. The Conspirators

Ed	HRN	Date	Details	A	C			
1	156	9/60	Original	1	1	3.00	9.00	21.00
2	167	7/64	PC-r	1	1	1.70	5.00	12.00
3	166	10/67	PC-r	1	1	1.70	5.00	12.00

159. The Octopus

Ed	HRN	Date	Details	A	C			
1	159	11/60	Orig.; Gray Morrow & Evans-a; L.B. Cole-c	1	1	2.65	8.00	18.00
2	167	2/64	PC-r	1	1	1.50	4.50	9.00
3	166	R/1967	C-price 25¢; PC-r	1	1	1.50	4.50	9.00

160. The Food of the Gods

Ed	HRN	Date	Details	A	C			
1A	159	1/61	Original	1	1	2.65	8.00	18.00
1B	160	1/61	Original; same, except for HRN	1	1	2.00	6.00	14.00
2	167	1/64	PC-r	1	1	1.50	4.50	9.00
3	166	6/67	PC-r	1	1	1.50	4.50	9.00

161. Cleopatra

Ed	HRN	Date	Details	A	C			
1	161	3/61	Original	1	1	3.50	10.50	24.00
2	167	1/64	PC-r	1	1	1.70	5.00	12.00
3	166	8/67	PC-r	1	1	1.70	5.00	12.00

162. Robur the Conqueror

Ed	HRN	Date	Details	A	C			
1	162	5/61	Original	1	1	2.65	8.00	18.00
2	167	7/64	PC-r	1	1	1.50	4.50	9.00
3	166	8/67	PC-r	1	1	1.50	4.50	9.00

163. Master of the World

Ed	HRN	Date	Details	A	C			
1	163	7/61	Original; Gray Morrow-a	1	1	2.65	8.00	18.00
2	167	1/65	PC-r	1	1	1.50	4.50	9.00
3	166	R/1968	C-price 25¢; PC-r	1	1	1.50	4.50	9.00

164. The Cossack Chief

Ed	HRN	Date	Details	A	C			
1	164	(1961)	Original; nd (10/61?)	1	1	3.00	9.00	21.00
2	167	4/65	PC-r	1	1	1.50	4.50	9.00
3	166	Fall/68	C-price 25¢; PC-r	1	1	1.50	4.50	9.00

Classics Illustrated #149 (Orig.), © GIL

Classics Illustrated #160 (Orig.), © GIL

Classics Illustrated #163 (Orig.), © GIL

Classics Illustrated #166 (HRN-167), © GIL   Classics Giveaway 12/44, © GIL   Classics Giveaway 1951, © GIL

CLASSICS ILLUSTRATED (continued)

165. The Queen's Necklace

Ed	HRN	Date	Details	A	C	Good	Fine	N-Mint
1	164	1/62	Original; Morrow-a	1	1	3.00	9.00	21.00
2	167	4/65	PC-r	1	1	1.50	4.50	9.00
3	166	Fall/68	C-price 25¢; PC-r	1	1	1.50	4.50	9.00

166. Tigers and Traitors

Ed	HRN	Date	Details	A	C			
1	165	5/62	Original	1	1	4.30	13.00	30.00
2	167	2/64	PC-r	1	1	2.00	6.00	14.00
3	167	11/66	PC-r	1	1	2.00	6.00	14.00

167. Faust

Ed	HRN	Date	Details	A	C			
1	165	8/62	Original	1	1	8.00	24.00	56.00
2	167	2/64	PC-r	1	1	3.70	11.00	26.00
3	166	6/67	PC-r	1	1	3.70	11.00	26.00

168. In Freedom's Cause

Ed	HRN	Date	Details	A	C			
1	169	Win/69	Original; Evans/ Crandall-a; stiff-c; 25¢; no coming-next ad;	1	1	7.00	21.00	50.00

169. Negro Americans—The Early Years

Ed	HRN	Date	Details	A	C			
1	166	Spr/69	Orig. & last issue; 25¢; Stiff-c; no coming-next ad; other sources indicate pub. date of 5/69.	1	1	7.00	21.00	50.00
2	169	Spr/69	Stiff-c	1	1	4.30	13.00	30.00

NOTE: *Many other titles were prepared or planned but were only issued in British/European series.*

CLASSICS GIVEAWAYS (Arranged in chronological order)

1942—Double Comics containing CC#1 (orig.) (diff. cover) (not actually a giveaway) (very rare) (also see Double Comics; (only one known copy) 135.00 405.00 950.00
12/42—Saks 34th St. Giveaway containing CC#7 (orig.) (diff. cover) (very rare; only 6 known copies) 228.00 685.00 1600.00
2/43—American Comics containing CC#8 (orig.) (Liberty Theatre Giveaway) (diff. cover) (only one known copy) (see American Comics) 71.00 215.00 500.00
12/44—Robin Hood Flour Co. Giveaway - #7-CC(R) (diff. cover) (rare) (edition probably 5 [22]) 86.00 257.00 600.00

NOTE: *How are above editions determined without CC covers? 1942 is dated 1942, and CC#1-first reprint did not come out until 5/43. 12/42 and 2/43 are determined by blue note at bottom of first text page only in original edition. 12/44 is estimate from page width—each reprint edition had progressively smaller page width.*

1951—Shelter Thru the Ages (C.I. Educational Series) (actually Giveaway by the Ruberoid Co.) (16 pgs.) (contains original artwork by H. C. Kiefer) (there are back cover ad variations) (scarce) 54.00 160.00 375.00
1952—George Daynor Biography Giveaway (CC logo) (partly comic book/pictures/newspaper articles) (story of man who built Palace Depression out of junkyard swamp in NJ) (64 pgs.) (very rare; only 2 known copies, one missing-bc) 121.00 364.00 850.00
1953—Westinghouse/Dreams of a Man (C.I. Educational Series) (Westinghouse bio./Westinghouse Co. giveaway) (contains original artwork by H. C. Kiefer) (16 pgs.) (also French/Spanish/Italian versions) (scarce) 47.00 170.00 400.00
NOTE: *Reproductions of 1951, 1952, and 1953 exist — color*

photocopy covers and black & white photocopy interior ("W.C.N. Reprint") 1.50 4.50 10.00
51-53—Coward Shoe Giveaways (all editions very rare) (two variations of back cover Coward Shoe ads) 5 (87), 12 (89), 49 (85), 69 (87), 72 (no HRN), 92 (0), 96 (0), 98 (0), 100 (0), 101 (0), 103 (0), 104 (0), 105 (0), 108 (0), 110 (111), 112 (0). (some above editions recently discovered—some only one copy currently known to exist) 34.00 103.00 240.00
1956—Ben Franklin 5-10 Store Giveaway (#65-PC with back cover ad) (scarce) 19.00 58.00 135.00
1956—Ben Franklin Insurance Co. Giveaway (#65-PC with diff. back cover ad) (very rare) 43.00 130.00 300.00
11/56—Sealtest Co. Edition - #4 (135) (identical to regular edition except for Sealtest logo printed, not stamped, on front cover) (only one copy known to exist) 21.50 64.00 150.00
1958—Get-Well Giveaway containing #15-CI (new cartoon-type cover) (Pressman Pharmacy) (only one copy known to exist) 21.50 64.00 150.00
67-68—Twin Circle Giveaway Editions - all HRN 166, with back cover ad for National Catholic Press.
2(R68), 4(R67), 10(R68), 48(R67) 2.65 8.00 18.00
13(R68), 128(R68) 3.50 10.50 24.00
16(R68), 68(R67), 535(576-R68) 4.50 14.00 32.00
12/69—Christmas Giveaway ("A Christmas Adventure") (reprints Picture Parade #4-1953, new cover) (4 ad variations)
Stacy's Dept. Store 2.00 6.00 14.00
Anne & Hope Store 5.70 17.00 40.00
Gibson's Dept. Store (rare) 5.70 17.00 40.00
"Merry Christmas" & blank ad space . . 2.30 7.00 16.00

CLASSICS ILLUSTRATED GIANTS

October, 1949 (One-Shots - "OS")
Gilberton Publications

These Giant Editions, all with new Kiefer front and back covers, were advertised from 10/49 to 2/52. They were 50 cents on the newsstand and 60 cents by mail. They are actually four classics in one volume. All the stories are reprints of the Classics Illustrated Series. NOTE: *There were also British hardback Adventure & Indian Giants in 1952, with the same covers but different contents: Adventure - 2, 7, 10; Indian - 17, 22, 37, 58. They are also rare.*
"An Illustrated Library of Great Adventure Stories" - reprints of No. 6,7,8,10 (Rare); Kiefer-c 67.00 200.00 470.00
"An Illustrated Library of Exciting Mystery Stories" - reprints of No. 30,21,40,13 (Rare) 70.00 210.00 500.00
"An Illustrated Library of Great Indian Stories" - reprints of No. 4,17, 22,37 (Rare) 63.00 190.00 440.00

INTRODUCTION TO CLASSICS ILLUSTRATED JUNIOR

Collectors of Juniors can be put into one of two categories — those who want any copy of each title, and those who want all the originals. Those seeking every original and reprint edition are a limited group, primarily because Juniors have no changes in art or covers to spark interest, and because reprints are so low in value it is difficult to get dealers to look for specific reprint editions. Anyone interested in information about the full scope of Junior editions should write to **Jim McLoughlin, 28 Mercury Ave., East Patchogue, NY 11772.** He has been doing research in this area for several years.

In recent years it has become apparent that most serious Classics collectors seek Junior originals. Those seeking reprints seek them for low cost. This has made the previous note about the comparative market value of reprints inadequate. Most dealers report difficulty in moving reprints for more than $2-$4 for mint copies. Some may be worth $5-$7, just because of the popularity of the title, such as Snow White, Sleeping Beauty, and Wizard of Oz. Others may be worth $5-$7, because of the scarcity of particular title nos., such as 514, 560, 562, 575 & 576. These particular reprint editions are worth even more. For the 535-Twin Circle edition, see Giveaways. There are also reprint editions of 501 and 503 which have a full-page bc ad for the very rare Junior record. Those may sell as high as $10-$15 in mint. Original editions of 557 and 558 also have that ad.

There are no reprint editions of 577. The only edition, from 1969, is

INTRODUCTION TO CLASSICS ILLUSTRATED JUNIOR (continued)
a 25 cent stiff-cover edition with no ad for the next issue. All other original editions have coming-next ad. But 577, like C.I. #168, was prepared in 1962 but not issued. Copies of 577 can be found in 1963 British/European series, which then continued with dozens of additional new Junior titles.

PRICES LISTED BELOW ARE FOR ORIGINAL EDITIONS, WHICH HAVE AN AD FOR THE NEXT ISSUE.

CLASSICS ILLUSTRATED JUNIOR
Oct, 1953 - Spring, 1971
Famous Authors Ltd. (Gilberton Publications)

	Good	Fine	N-Mint
501-Snow White & the Seven Dwarfs; Alex Blum-a	8.00	24.00	56.00
502-The Ugly Duckling	5.00	15.00	35.00
503-Cinderella	3.00	9.00	21.00
504-The Pied Piper	2.00	6.00	14.00
505-The Sleeping Beauty	2.00	6.00	14.00
506-The Three Little Pigs	2.00	6.00	14.00
507-Jack & the Beanstalk	2.00	6.00	14.00
508-Goldilocks & the Three Bears	2.00	6.00	14.00
509-Beauty and the Beast	2.00	6.00	14.00
510-Little Red Riding Hood	2.00	6.00	14.00
511-Puss-N-Boots	2.00	6.00	14.00
512-Rumpel Stiltskin	2.00	6.00	14.00
513-Pinocchio	3.00	9.00	21.00
514-The Steadfast Tin Soldier	4.00	12.00	28.00
515-Johnny Appleseed	2.00	6.00	14.00
516-Aladdin and His Lamp	3.00	9.00	21.00
517-The Emperor's New Clothes	2.00	6.00	14.00
518-The Golden Goose	2.00	6.00	14.00
519-Paul Bunyan	2.00	6.00	14.00
520-Thumbelina	3.00	9.00	21.00
521-King of the Golden River	2.00	6.00	14.00
522-The Nightingale	1.50	4.50	10.00
523-The Gallant Tailor	1.50	4.50	10.00
524-The Wild Swans	1.50	4.50	10.00
525-The Little Mermaid	1.50	4.50	10.00
526-The Frog Prince	1.50	4.50	10.00
527-The Golden-Haired Giant	1.50	4.50	10.00
528-The Penny Prince	1.50	4.50	10.00
529-The Magic Servants	1.50	4.50	10.00
530-The Golden Bird	1.50	4.50	10.00
531-Rapunzel	2.00	6.00	14.00
532-The Dancing Princesses	1.50	4.50	10.00
533-The Magic Fountain	1.50	4.50	10.00
534-The Golden Touch	1.50	4.50	10.00
535-The Wizard of Oz	4.00	12.00	28.00
536-The Chimney Sweep	1.50	4.50	10.00
537-The Three Fairies	1.50	4.50	10.00
538-Silly Hans	1.50	4.50	10.00
539-The Enchanted Fish	3.00	9.00	21.00
540-The Tinder-Box	3.00	9.00	21.00
541-Snow White & Rose Red	2.00	6.00	14.00
542-The Donkey's Tale	2.00	6.00	14.00
543-The House in the Woods	1.50	4.50	10.00
544-The Golden Fleece	4.00	12.00	28.00
545-The Glass Mountain	2.00	6.00	14.00
546-The Elves & the Shoemaker	2.00	6.00	14.00
547-The Wishing Table	1.50	4.50	10.00
548-The Magic Pitcher	1.50	4.30	10.00
549-Simple Kate	1.50	4.50	10.00
550-The Singing Donkey	1.50	4.50	10.00
551-The Queen Bee	1.50	4.50	10.00
552-The Three Little Dwarfs	2.00	6.00	14.00
553-King Thrushbeard	1.50	4.50	10.00
554-The Enchanted Deer	1.50	4.50	10.00
555-The Three Golden Apples	1.50	4.50	10.00

	Good	Fine	N-Mint
556-The Elf Mound	1.50	4.50	10.00
557-Silly Willy	3.00	9.00	21.00
558-The Magic Dish; L.B. Cole-c; soft and stiff-c exist on (O)			
	3.00	9.00	21.00
559-The Japanese Lantern; 1 pg. Ingels-a; L.B. Cole-c			
	3.00	9.00	21.00
560-The Doll Princess; L.B. Cole-c	3.00	9.00	21.00
561-Hans Humdrum; L.B. Cole-c	1.50	4.50	10.00
562-The Enchanted Pony; L.B. Cole-c	3.00	9.00	21.00
563-The Wishing Well; L.B. Cole-c	1.50	4.50	10.00
564-The Salt Mountain; L.B. Cole-c	1.50	4.50	10.00
565-The Silly Princess; L.B. Cole-c	1.50	4.50	10.00
566-Clumsy Hans; L.B. Cole-c	1.50	4.50	10.00
567-The Bearskin Soldier; L.B. Cole-c	1.50	4.50	10.00
568-The Happy Hedgehog; L.B. Cole-c	1.50	4.50	10.00
569-The Three Giants	1.50	4.50	10.00
570-The Pearl Princess	1.50	4.50	10.00
571-How Fire Came to the Indians	1.70	5.00	12.00
572-The Drummer Boy	1.70	5.00	12.00
573-The Crystal Ball	1.70	5.00	12.00
574-Brightboots	1.70	5.00	12.00
575-The Fearless Prince	2.00	6.00	14.00
576-The Princess Who Saw Everything	3.00	9.00	21.00
577-The Runaway Dumpling	4.00	12.00	28.00

NOTE: *Last reprint - Spring, 1971.* **Costanza & Shaffenberger** *art in many issues.*

CLASSICS ILLUSTRATED SPECIAL ISSUE
Dec, 1955 - July, 1962 (100 pages) (35 cents)
Gilberton Co. (Came out semi-annually)

	Good	Fine	N-Mint
129-The Story of Jesus (titled ...Special Edition) "Jesus on Mountain" cover	3.50	10.50	24.00
"Three Camels" cover(12/58)	5.70	17.00	40.00
"Mountain" cover (1968 re-issue; has black 50 cent circle)			
	2.00	6.00	14.00
132A-The Story of America (6/56)	3.00	9.00	21.00
135A-The Ten Commandments(12/56)	3.70	11.00	26.00
138A-Adventures in Science(6/57)	3.00	9.00	21.00
141A-The Rough Rider (Teddy Roosevelt)(12/57); Evans-a			
	2.30	7.00	16.00
144A-Blazing the Trails West(6/58)- 73 pages of Crandall/Evans plus Severin-a	2.30	7.00	16.00
147A-Crossing the Rockies(12/58)-Crandall/Evans-a			
	4.00	12.00	28.00
150A-Royal Canadian Police(6/59)-Ingels, Sid Check-a			
	4.00	12.00	28.00
153A-Men, Guns & Cattle(12/59)-Evans-a, 26 pgs.; Kinstler-a			
	4.00	12.00	28.00
156A-The Atomic Age(6/60)-Crandall/Evans, Torres-a			
	3.00	9.00	21.00
159A-Rockets, Jets and Missiles(12/60)-Evans, Morrow-a			
	3.00	9.00	21.00
162A-War Between the States(6/61)-Kirby & Crandall/Evans-a; Ingels-a	5.70	17.00	40.00
165A-To the Stars(12/61)-Torres, Crandall/Evans, Kirby-a			
	3.00	9.00	21.00
166A-World War II('62)-Torres, Crandall/Evans, Kirby-a			
	4.00	12.00	28.00
167A-Prehistoric World(7/62)-Torres & Crandall/Evans-a			
	4.30	13.00	30.00

nn Special Issue-The United Nations (1964; 50 cents; scarce); This is actually part of the European Special Series, which continued on after the U.S. series stopped issuing new titles in 1962. This English edition was prepared specifically for sale at the U.N. It was printed in Norway. — 21.50 64.00 150.00

NOTE: *158A appeared as DC's Showcase No. 43, "Dr. No" and was only published in Great Britain as 158A with different cover. There was another U.S. Special Issue*

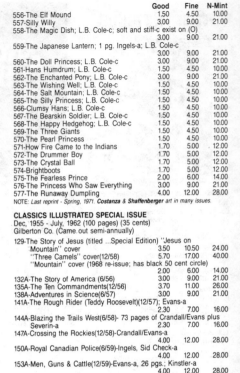

Classics Illustrated Junior #502, © GIL

Classics Illustrated Junior #560, © GIL

Classics Illustrated Special Issue #129A, © GIL

Classic X-Men #1, © MEG   Climax! #1, © Gillmor Magazines   Clown Comics #2, © HARV

CLASSICS ILLUSTRATED JUNIOR (continued)
prepared in 1962 with artwork by Kirby, Crandall & Evans, entitled **World War I**. Unfortunately, it was never issued in any English-language edition. It was issued in 1964 in West Germany, The Netherlands, and other Scandanavian countries, with another edition in 1974 with a new cover.

CLASSIC PUNISHER (Also see Punisher)
Dec, 1989 - Present ($4.95, B&W, deluxe format, 68 pgs.)
Marvel Comics

	Good	Fine	N-Mint
1-R/Marvel Super Action #1 & Marvel Preview #2 plus new story	.85	2.50	5.00

CLASSICS ILLUSTRATED
1990 - Present ($3.75, color)
First Comics

1-7: 1-The Raven and Other Poems; Gahan Wilson-a). 2-Great Expectations. 3-Through the Looking Glass. 4-Moby Dick; Sienkiewicz-a. 5-Hamlet. 6-The Scarlet Letter; Russell scripts. 7-The Count of Monte Cristo; Spiegle-a	.65	1.90	3.80

CLASSICS LIBRARY (See King Classics)

CLASSIC X-MEN
Sept, 1986 - Present (#27 on: $1.25)
Marvel Comics Group

	Good	Fine	N-Mint
1-Begins-r of New X-Men	.85	2.50	5.00
2-4	.50	1.50	3.00
5-10	.40	1.25	2.50
11-15	.35	1.10	2.20
16,18-20	.30	.90	1.80
17-Wolverine-c	.70	2.00	4.00
21-25,27-30: 27-r/X-Men #121	.25	.75	1.50
26-r/X-Men #120; Wolverine app.	.35	1.00	2.00
31-42,44: 35-r/X-Men #129 (1st Kitty Pryde)		.65	1.30
43-$1.75, double-size	.30	.90	1.80

NOTE: **Art Adams** c(p)-1-10, 12-16, 18, 19, 25. **Austin** a-19i. **Bolton** back up stories in many issues. **Williamson** c-12i, 13i.

CLAW THE UNCONQUERED (See Cancelled Comic Cavalcade)
5-6/75 - No. 9, 9-10/76; No. 10, 4-5/78 - No. 12, 8-9/78
National Periodical Publications/DC Comics

1		.50	1.00
2,3: 3-Nudity panel		.40	.80
4-12: 9-Origin		.25	.50

NOTE: **Giffen** a-8-12p. **Kubert** c-10-12. **Layton** a-9i, 12i.

CLAY CODY, GUNSLINGER
Fall, 1957
Pines Comics

1-Painted-c	1.60	4.70	11.00

CLEAN FUN, STARRING "SHOOGAFOOTS JONES"
1944 (24 pgs.; B&W; oversized covers) (10 cents)
Specialty Book Co.

Humorous situations involving Negroes in the Deep South

White cover issue....	2.75	8.00	16.00
Dark grey cover issue....	3.00	9.00	18.00

CLEMENTINA THE FLYING PIG (See Dell Jr. Treasury)

CLEOPATRA (See Ideal, a Classical Comic No. 1)

CLIFF MERRITT SETS THE RECORD STRAIGHT
Giveaway (2 different issues)
Brotherhood of Railroad Trainsmen

...and the Very Candid Candidate by Al Williamson			
	.40	1.20	2.40
...Sets the Record Straight by Al Williamson (2 diff.-c: one by Williamson, the other by McWilliams)	.40	1.20	2.40

CLIFFORD MCBRIDE'S IMMORTAL NAPOLEON & UNCLE ELBY
1932 (12x17"; softcover cartoon book)
The Castle Press

	Good	Fine	N-Mint
Intro. by Don Herod	7.00	21.00	50.00

CLIMAX!
July, 1955 - No. 2, Sept, 1955
Gillmor Magazines

1,2 (Mystery)	5.00	15.00	35.00

CLINT (Also see Adolescent Radioactive Black Belt Hamsters)
Sept, 1986 - No. 2, Jan, 1987 ($1.50, B&W)
Eclipse Comics

1,2	.25	.75	1.50

CLINT & MAC (See 4-Color No. 889)

CLIVE BARKER'S . . . (See Hellraiser and Tapping the Vein)

CLOAK AND DAGGER
Fall, 1952
Ziff-Davis Publishing Co.

1-Saunders painted-c	11.00	32.00	75.00

CLOAK AND DAGGER (Also see Marvel Fanfare)
Oct, 1983 - No. 4, Jan, 1984 (Mini-series)
Marvel Comics Group

1-4-Austin c/a(i) in all. 4-Origin	.25	.75	1.50

CLOAK AND DAGGER (Also see Marvel Graphic Novel #34, Mutant Misadventures Of. . . & Strange Tales, 2nd series)
July, 1985 - No. 11, Jan, 1987
Marvel Comics

1	.25	.75	1.50
2-8,10,11		.50	1.00
9-Art Adams-p	.50	1.50	3.00
...And Power Pack (1990, $7.95, 68 pgs.)	1.35	4.00	8.00

CLONEZONE SPECIAL
1989 ($2.00, B&W)
Dark Horse Comics/First Comics

1-Back-up series from Badger & Nexus	.35	1.00	2.00

CLOSE ENCOUNTERS (See Marvel Special Edition)

CLOSE SHAVES OF PAULINE PERIL, THE (TV?)
June, 1970 - No. 4, March, 1971 (Jay Ward?)
Gold Key

1	1.00	3.00	6.00
2-4	.70	2.00	4.00

CLOWN COMICS (No. 1 titled Clown Comic Book)
1945 - No. 3, Wint, 1946
Clown Comics/Home Comics/Harvey Publ.

nn	3.70	11.00	26.00
2,3	2.15	6.50	15.00

CLUBHOUSE RASCALS (#1 titled . . .Presents?)
June, 1956 - No. 2, Oct, 1956 (Also see Three Rascals)
Sussex Publ. Co. (Magazine Enterprises)

1,2: The Brain app.	1.70	5.00	12.00

CLUB "16"
June, 1948 - No. 4, Dec, 1948
Famous Funnies

1	4.65	14.00	32.00
2-4	2.15	6.50	15.00

CLUE COMICS (Real Clue Crime V2No.4 on)
Jan, 1943 - No. 15(V2No.3), May, 1947
Hillman Periodicals

1-Origin The Boy King, Nightmare, Micro-Face, Twilight, & Zippo			
	42.00	126.00	295.00
2	22.00	65.00	155.00

95

CLUE COMICS (continued)	Good	Fine	N-Mint
3	17.00	51.00	120.00
4	14.00	42.00	100.00
5	12.00	36.00	84.00
6,8,9: 8-Palais-c/a(2)	9.30	28.00	65.00
7-Classic torture-c	13.00	40.00	90.00
10-Origin The Gun Master	10.00	30.00	70.00
11	6.00	18.00	42.00
12-Origin Rackman; McWilliams-a, Guardineer-a(2)			
	8.50	25.50	60.00
V2#1-Nightro new origin; Iron Lady app.; Simon & Kirby-a			
	13.00	40.00	90.00

V2#2-S&K-a(2)-Bondage/torture-c; man attacks & kills people with
| electric iron. Infantino-a | 13.00 | 40.00 | 90.00 |
| V2#3-S&K-a(3) | 13.00 | 40.00 | 90.00 |

CLUTCHING HAND, THE
July-Aug, 1954
American Comics Group
| 1 | 9.30 | 28.00 | 65.00 |

CLYDE BEATTY COMICS (Also see Crackajack Funnies)
October, 1953 (84 pages)
Commodore Productions & Artists, Inc.
1-Photo front/back-c; includes movie scenes and comics
| | 13.00 | 40.00 | 90.00 |
...African Jungle Book('56)-Richfield Oil Co. 16 pg. giveaway,
| soft-c | 5.00 | 15.00 | 35.00 |

CLYDE CRASHCUP (TV)
Aug-Oct, 1963 - No. 5, Sept-Nov, 1964
Dell Publishing Co.
| 1-All written by John Stanley | 4.30 | 13.00 | 30.00 |
| 2-5 | 3.00 | 9.00 | 21.00 |

C-M-O COMICS
1942 - No. 2, 1942 (68 pages, full color)
Chicago Mail Order Co.(Centaur)
1-Invisible Terror, Super Ann, & Plymo the Rubber Man app. (All
| Centaur costume heroes) | 36.00 | 107.00 | 250.00 |
| 2-Invisible Terror, Super Ann app. | 24.00 | 73.00 | 170.00 |

COBALT BLUE (Also see Power Comics)
Sept, 1989 - No. 2, Oct?, 1989 ($1.95, color, mini-series, 28 pgs.)
Innovation Publishing
| 1,2-Gustovich-c/a/scripts | .35 | 1.00 | 2.00 |

COCOMALT BIG BOOK OF COMICS
1938 (Regular size; full color; 52 pgs.)
Harry 'A' Chesler (Cocomalt Premium)
1-(Scarce)-Biro-c/a; Little Nemo by Winsor McCay Jr., Dan Hastings;
| Guardineer, Jack Cole, Gustavson, Bob Wood-a | | | |
| | 83.00 | 210.00 | 500.00 |

CODE NAME: ASSASSIN (See First Issue Special)

CODENAME: DANGER
Aug, 1985 - No. 4, May, 1986 ($1.50 cover)
Lodestone Publishing
| 1-4 | .25 | .75 | 1.50 |

CODENAME SPITFIRE (Formerly Spitfire And The Troubleshooters)
No. 10, July, 1987 - No. 13, Oct, 1987
Marvel Comics Group
| 10-13: 10-Rogers c/a | | .50 | 1.00 |

CODE NAME: TOMAHAWK
Sept, 1986 ($1.75, color, high quality paper)
Fantasy General Comics
| 1-Sci/fi | .30 | .90 | 1.80 |

CODY OF THE PONY EXPRESS (See Colossal Features Magazine)
Sept, 1950 - No. 3, Jan, 1951 (See Women Outlaws)
Fox Features Syndicate
	Good	Fine	N-Mint
1-3 (actually #3-5). 1-Painted-c	5.00	15.00	35.00

CODY OF THE PONY EXPRESS (Buffalo Bill . . .) (Outlaws of the
West #11 on; Formerly Bullseye)
No. 8, Oct, 1955; No. 9, Jan, 1956; No. 10, June, 1956
Charlton Comics
| 8-Bullseye on splash pg; not S&K-a | 2.85 | 8.50 | 20.00 |
| 9,10: 10-Buffalo Bill app. | 1.85 | 5.50 | 13.00 |

CO-ED ROMANCES
November, 1951
P. L. Publishing Co.
| 1 | 2.30 | 7.00 | 16.00 |

COLLECTORS ITEM CLASSICS (See Marvel Collectors Item Classics)

COLOSSAL FEATURES MAGAZINE (Formerly I Loved) (See Cody of
the Pony Express)
No. 33, May, 1950 - No. 34, July, 1950; No. 3, Sept, 1950
Fox Features Syndicate
33,34-Cody of the Pony Express begins (based on Columbia serial).
| 33-Painted-c; 34-Photo-c | 5.00 | 15.00 | 35.00 |
| 3-Authentic criminal cases | 4.30 | 13.00 | 30.00 |

COLOSSAL SHOW, THE (TV)
October, 1969
Gold Key
| 1 | 2.00 | 6.00 | 14.00 |

COLOSSUS COMICS (See Green Giant & Motion Pic. Fun. Wkly)
March, 1940
Sun Publications (Funnies, Inc.?)
1-(Scarce)-Tulpa of Tsang (hero); Colossus app.
| | 93.00 | 280.00 | 650.00 |
NOTE: *Cover by artist that drew Colossus in Green Giant Comics.*

COLT .45 (TV)
No. 924, 8/58 - No. 1058, 11-1/59-60; No. 4, 2-4/60 - No. 9, 5-7/61
Dell Publishing Co.
4-Color 924-Wayde Preston photo-c on all	5.00	15.00	35.00
4-Color 1004,1058; #4,5,7-9	3.70	11.00	26.00
6-Toth-a	5.00	15.00	35.00

COLUMBIA COMICS
1943
William H. Wise Co.
1-Joe Palooka, Charlie Chan, Capt. Yank, Sparky Watts, Dixie
| Dugan app. | 13.00 | 40.00 | 90.00 |

COMANCHE (See 4-Color No. 1350)

COMANCHEROS, THE (See 4-Color No. 1300)

COMBAT
June, 1952 - No. 11, April, 1953
Atlas Comics (ANC)
1	4.30	13.00	30.00
2	2.00	6.00	14.00
3,5-9,11: 9-Robert Q. Sale-a	1.50	4.50	10.00
4-Krigstein-a	2.30	7.00	16.00
10-B&W and color illos. in POP	2.00	6.00	14.00
NOTE: *Combat Casey in 7-11. Heath c-1, 9. Maneely a-1. Pakula a-1. Reinman a-1.*

COMBAT
Oct-Nov, 1961 - No. 40, Oct, 1973 (No #9)
Dell Publishing Co.
| 1 | 1.70 | 5.00 | 12.00 |
| 2-5: 4-John F. Kennedy c/story (P.T. 109) | 1.15 | 3.50 | 8.00 |

Clue Comics V2#1, © HILL

Cocomalt Big Book Of Comics #1, © CHES

Combat #2 (1952), © MEG

Combat Casey #19, © MEG   Comedy Comics #9 (4/42), © MEG   Comic Album #6, © Warner Bros.

	Good	Fine	N-Mint
COMBAT (continued)			
6,7,8(4-6/63), 8(7-9/63)	.70	2.00	4.00
10-27	.50	1.50	3.00
28-40(reprints #1-14). 30-r/#4	.35	1.00	2.00
NOTE: *Glanzman c/a-1-27, 28-40r.*			
COMBAT CASEY (Formerly War Combat)			
No. 6, Jan, 1953 - No. 34, July, 1957			
Atlas Comics (SAI)			
6 (Indicia shows 1/52 in error)	3.50	10.50	24.00
7-Spanking panel	2.30	7.00	16.00
8-Used in **POP**, pg. 94	2.00	6.00	14.00
9	1.50	4.50	10.00
10,13-19-Violent art by R. Q. Sale; Battle Brady x-over #10			
	2.30	7.00	16.00
11,12,20-Last Precode (2/55)	1.15	3.50	8.00
21-34	.85	2.60	6.00
NOTE: *Everett a-6. Heath c-10, 17, 19, 30. Powell a-29(5), 30(5), 34. Severin c-26, 33.*			
COMBAT KELLY			
Nov, 1951 - No. 44, Aug, 1957			
Atlas Comics (SPI)			
1-Heath-a	6.50	19.500	45.00
2	3.00	9.00	21.00
3-10	2.00	6.00	14.00
11-Used in **POP**, pages 94,95 plus color illo.	1.70	5.00	12.00
12-Color illo. in **POP**	1.70	5.00	12.00
13-16	1.00	3.00	7.00
17-Violent art by R. Q. Sale; Combat Casey app.			
	2.65	8.00	18.00
18-20,22-44: 18-Battle Brady app. 28-Last precode (1/55). 38-Green Berets story(8/56)	1.00	3.00	7.00
21-Transvestism-c	2.00	6.00	14.00
NOTE: *Berg a-8, 12-14, 16, 17, 19-23, 25, 26, 28, 31-36, 42-44. Colan a-42. Heath a-4; c-31. Lawrence a-23. Maneely a-4(2), 6, 7(3), 8; c-7, 8, 25. R.Q. Sale a-17, 25. Severin c-41, 42. Whitney a-5.*			
COMBAT KELLY (and the Deadly Dozen)			
June, 1972 - No. 9, Oct, 1973			
Marvel Comics Group			
1-Intro. Combat Kelly; Ayers/Mooney-a; Severin-c	.50		1.00
2-9	.40		.80
COMBINED OPERATIONS (See The Story of the Commandos)			
COMEDY CARNIVAL			
no date (1950's) (100 pages)			
St. John Publishing Co.			
nn-Contains rebound St. John comics	13.00	40.00	90.00
COMEDY COMICS (1st Series) (Formerly Daring Mystery No. 1-8)			
(Becomes Margie Comics No. 35 on)			
No. 9, April, 1942 - No. 34, Fall, 1946			
Timely Comics (TCI 9,10)			
9-(Scarce)-The Fin by Everett, Capt. Dash, Citizen V, & The Silver Scorpion app.; Wolverton-a; 1st app. Comedy Kid; satire on Hitler & Stalin	86.00	257.00	600.00
10-(Scarce)-Origin The Fourth Musketeer, Victory Boys; Monstro, the Mighty app.	61.00	182.00	425.00
11-Vagabond, Stuporman app.	19.00	58.00	135.00
12,13	5.50	16.50	38.00
14-Origin & 1st app. Super Rabbit	21.50	64.00	150.00
15-20	4.50	14.00	32.00
21-32	3.50	10.50	24.00
33-Kurtzman-a, 5 pgs.	4.50	14.00	32.00
34-Wolverton-a, 5 pgs.	6.50	19.50	45.00
COMEDY COMICS (2nd Series)			
May, 1948 - No. 10, Jan, 1950			
Marvel Comics (ACI)			

	Good	Fine	N-Mint
1-Hedy, Tessie, Millie begin; Kurtzman's "Hey Look" (he draws himself)	12.00	36.00	85.00
2	4.50	14.00	32.00
3,4-Kurtzman's "Hey Look"(?&3)	6.50	19.50	45.00
5-10	2.30	7.00	16.00
COMET, THE (See The Mighty Crusaders & Pep Comics #1)			
Oct, 1983 - No. 2, Dec, 1983			
Red Circle Comics			
1,2: 1-Origin The Comet; The American Shield begins; 2-Origin continues	.50		1.00
COMET MAN, THE			
Feb, 1987 - No. 6, July, 1987 (mini-series)			
Marvel Comics Group			
1-6		.50	1.00
COMIC ALBUM			
Mar-May, 1958 - No. 18, June-Aug, 1962			
Dell Publishing Co.			
1-Donald Duck	3.50	10.50	24.00
2-Bugs Bunny	1.50	4.50	10.00
3-Donald Duck	2.85	8.50	20.00
4-Tom & Jerry	1.30	4.00	9.00
5-Woody Woodpecker	1.30	4.00	9.00
6-Bugs Bunny	1.30	4.00	9.00
7-Popeye (9-11/59)	2.30	7.00	16.00
8-Tom & Jerry	1.30	4.00	9.00
9-Woody Woodpecker	1.30	4.00	9.00
10-Bugs Bunny	1.30	4.00	9.00
11-Popeye (9-11/60)	2.30	7.00	16.00
12-Tom & Jerry	1.30	4.00	9.00
13-Woody Woodpecker	1.30	4.00	9.00
14-Bugs Bunny	1.30	4.00	9.00
15-Popeye	2.30	7.00	16.00
16-Flintstones (12-2/61-62)-3rd app.	2.65	8.00	18.00
17-Space Mouse-3rd app.	1.30	4.00	9.00
18-Three Stooges; photo-c	5.00	15.00	35.00
COMIC BOOK (Also see Comics From Weatherbird)			
1954 (Giveaway)			
American Juniors Shoe			
Contains a comic rebound with new cover. Several combinations possible. Contents determines price.			
COMIC BOOK MAGAZINE			
1940 - 1943 (Similar to Spirit Sections)			
(7¾x10¾''; full color; 16-24 pages each)			
Chicago Tribune & other newspapers			
1940 issues	5.00	15.00	35.00
1941, 1942 issues	4.00	12.00	28.00
1943 issues	3.35	10.00	23.00
NOTE: *Published weekly. Texas Slim, Kit Carson, Spooky, Josie, Nuts & Jolts, Lew Loyal, Brenda Starr, Daniel Boone, Captain Storm, Rocky, Smokey Stover, Tiny Tim, Little Joe, Fu Manchu appear among others. Early issues had photo stories with pictures from the movies; later issues had comic art.*			
COMIC BOOKS (Series 1)			
1950 (16 pgs.; 5¼x8½''; full color; bound at top; paper cover)			
Metropolitan Printing Co. (Giveaway)			
1-Boots and Saddles; intro. The Masked Marshal			
	3.35	10.00	23.00
1-The Green Jet; Green Lama by Raboy	20.00	60.00	140.00
1-My Pal Dizzy (Teen-age)	1.70	5.00	12.00
1-New World; origin Atomaster (costumed hero)			
	5.00	15.00	35.00
1-Talullah (Teen-age)	1.70	5.00	12.00

COMIC CAPERS
Fall, 1944 - No. 6, Summer, 1946
Red Circle Mag./Marvel Comics

	Good	Fine	N-Mint
1-Super Rabbit, The Creeper, Silly Seal, Ziggy Pig, Sharpy Fox begin	9.30	28.00	65.00
2	5.00	15.00	35.00
3-6	3.15	9.50	22.00

COMIC CAVALCADE
Winter, 1942-43 - No. 63, June-July, 1954
(Contents change with No. 30, Dec-Jan, 1948-49 on)
All-American/National Periodical Publications

	Good	Fine	N-Mint
1-The Flash, Green Lantern, Wonder Woman, Wildcat, The Black Pirate by Moldoff (also #2), Ghost Patrol, and Red White & Blue begin; Scribbly app., Minute Movies	217.00	545.00	1300.00
2-Mutt & Jeff begin; last Ghost Patrol & Black Pirate; Minute Movies	108.00	270.00	650.00
3-Hop Harrigan & Sargon, the Sorcerer begin; The King app.	80.00	200.00	480.00
4-The Gay Ghost, The King, Scribbly, & Red Tornado app.	67.00	170.00	400.00
5-Christmas-c	67.00	170.00	400.00
6-10: 7-Red Tornado & Black Pirate app.; last Scribbly. 9-X-mas-c	50.00	125.00	300.00
11,12,14-20: 12-Last Red White & Blue. 15-Johnny Peril begins, ends #29. 19-Christmas-c	42.00	105.00	255.00
13-Solomon Grundy app.	72.00	180.00	435.00
21-23	42.00	105.00	255.00
24-Solomon Grundy x-over in Gr. Lantern	50.00	125.00	300.00
25-29: 25-Black Canary app.; X-mas-c. 26-28-Johnny Peril app. 28-Last Mutt & Jeff. 29-Last Flash, Wonder Woman, Green Lantern & Johnny Peril; Wonder Woman invents ''Thinking Machine;'' 1st computer in comics?	32.00	80.00	190.00
30-The Fox & the Crow, Dodo & the Frog & Nutsy Squirrel begin	20.00	60.00	140.00
31-35	9.00	27.00	62.00
36-49	7.00	21.00	48.00
50-62(Scarce)	9.00	27.00	62.00
63(Rare)	16.00	48.00	110.00
Giveaway (1945, 16 pages, paper-c, in color)-Movie ''Tomorrow The World'' (Nazi theme)	36.00	108.00	250.00
Giveaway (c. 1944-45; 8 pgs, paper-c, in color)-The Twain Shall Meet-r/C. Cavalcade	21.50	64.00	150.00

NOTE: *Grossman* a-30-63. *Sheldon Mayer* a(2-3)-40-63. *Post* a-31, 36. *Reinman* a-15, 20. *Toth* a-26-28(Green Lantern); c-23, 27. Atom app.-22, 23.

COMIC COMICS
April, 1946 - No. 10, Feb, 1947
Fawcett Publications

	Good	Fine	N-Mint
1-Captain Kidd	5.00	15.00	35.00
2-10-Wolverton-a, 4 pgs. each. 5-Captain Kidd app.	5.50	16.50	38.00

COMIC CUTS (Also see The Funnies)
5/19/34 - 7/28/34 (5 cents; 24 pages) (Tabloid size in full color)
(Not reprints; published weekly; created for newsstand sale)
H. L. Baker Co., Inc.

	Good	Fine	N-Mint
V1#1 - V1#7(6/30/34), V1#8(7/14/34), V1#9(7/28/34)-Idle Jack strips	7.00	21.00	50.00

COMIC LAND
March, 1946
Fact and Fiction Publ.

	Good	Fine	N-Mint
1-Sandusky & the Senator, Sam Stupor, Sleuth, Marvin the Great, Sir Passer, Phineas Gruff app.; Irv Tirman & Perry Williams art	4.50	14.00	32.00

COMIC MONTHLY
Jan, 1922 - No. 12, Dec, 1922 (32 pgs.)(8½x9'')(10 cents)
(1st monthly newsstand comic publication) (Reprints 1921 B&W dailies)
Embee Dist. Co.

	Good	Fine	N-Mint
1-Polly & Her Pals	33.00	100.00	230.00
2-Mike & Ike	7.00	21.00	50.00
3-S'Matter, Pop?	7.00	21.00	50.00
4-Barney Google	14.00	42.00	100.00
5-Tillie the Toiler	10.00	30.00	70.00
6-Indoor Sports	5.50	16.50	38.00
7-Little Jimmy	5.50	16.50	38.00
8-Toots and Casper	5.50	16.50	38.00
9,10-Foolish Questions	5.50	16.50	38.00
11-Barney Google & Spark Plug in the Abadaba Handicap	5.50	16.50	38.00
12-Polly & Her Pals	5.50	16.50	38.00

COMICO CHRISTMAS SPECIAL
Dec, 1988 ($2.50, 44pgs, color)
Comico

	Good	Fine	N-Mint
1-Rude/Williamson-a; Stevens-c	.40	1.25	2.50

COMICO PRIMER (See Primer)

COMIC PAGES (Formerly Funny Picture Stories)
V3No.4, July, 1939 - V3No.6, Dec, 1939
Centaur Publications

	Good	Fine	N-Mint
V3#4-Bob Wood-a	25.00	75.00	175.00
5,6	17.00	51.00	120.00

COMIC PAINTING AND CRAYONING BOOK
1917 (32 pages)(10x13½'')(No price on cover)
Saalfield Publ. Co.

	Good	Fine	N-Mint
Tidy Teddy by F. M. Follett, Clarence the Cop, Mr. & Mrs. Butt-In. Regular comic stories to read or color	8.00	24.00	56.00

COMICS (See All Good)

COMICS, THE
March, 1937 - No. 11, 1938 (Newspaper strip reprints)
Dell Publishing Co.

	Good	Fine	N-Mint
1-1st Tom Mix in comics; Wash Tubbs, Tom Beatty, Myra North, Arizona Kid, Erik Noble & International Spy w/Doctor Doom begin	64.00	193.00	450.00
2	34.00	103.00	240.00
3-11: 3-Alley Oop begins	28.00	85.00	200.00

COMICS AND STORIES (See Walt Disney's . . .)

COMICS CALENDAR, THE (The 1946. . .)
1946 (116 pgs.) 25 cents)(Stapled at top)
True Comics Press (ordered through the mail)

	Good	Fine	N-Mint
(Rare) Has a ''strip'' story for every day of the year in color	20.00	60.00	140.00

COMICS DIGEST (Pocket size)
Winter, 1942-43 (100 pages) (Black & White)
Parents' Magazine Institute

	Good	Fine	N-Mint
1-Reprints from True Comics (non-fiction World War II stories)	5.00	15.00	35.00

COMIC SELECTIONS (Shoe store giveaway)
1944-46 (Reprints from Calling All Girls, True Comics, True Aviation, & Real Heroes)
Parents' Magazine Press

	Good	Fine	N-Mint
1	1.70	5.00	12.00
2-5	1.30	4.00	9.00

COMICS FOR KIDS
1945 (no month); No. 2, Sum, 1945 (Funny animal)
London Publishing Co./Timely

	Good	Fine	N-Mint
1,2-Puffy Pig, Sharpy Fox	5.00	15.00	35.00

Comic Cavalcade #5, © DC

Comic Comics #7, © FAW

The Comics #5, © DELL

Comics Novel #1, © FAW   Comics On Parade #6, © UFS   Comics Revue #4, © UFS

COMICS FROM WEATHER BIRD (Also see Comic Book, Edward's
Shoes, Free Comics to You & Weather Bird)
1954 - 1957 (Giveaway)
Weather Bird Shoes

Contains a comic bound with new cover. Many combinations possible. Contents would
determine price. Some issues do not contain complete comics, but only parts of comics.
Value equals 40 to 60 percent of contents.

COMICS HITS (See Harvey Comics Hits)

COMICS MAGAZINE, THE (...Funny Pages #3)(Funny Pages #6 on)
May, 1936 - No. 5, Sept, 1936 (Paper covers)
Comics Magazine Co.

	Good	Fine	N-Mint
1: Dr. Mystic, The Occult Detective by Siegel & Shuster (1st episode continues in More Fun #14); 1pg. Kelly-a; Sheldon Mayer-a			
	200.00	500.00	1200.00
2: Federal Agent by Siegel & Shuster; 1pg. Kelly-a			
	90.00	270.00	620.00
3-5	75.00	225.00	525.00

COMICS NOVEL (Anarcho, Dictator of Death)
1947
Fawcett Publications

	Good	Fine	N-Mint
1-All Radar	16.00	48.00	110.00

COMICS ON PARADE (No. 30 on, continuation of Single Series)
April, 1938 - No. 104, Feb, 1955
United Features Syndicate

1-Tarzan by Foster; Captain & the Kids, Little Mary Mixup, Abbie & Slats, Ella Cinders, Broncho Bill, Li'l Abner begin			
	137.00	345.00	825.00
2	57.00	170.00	400.00
3	46.00	137.00	320.00
4,5	34.00	103.00	240.00
6-10	25.00	75.00	175.00
11-20	20.00	60.00	140.00
21-29: 22-Son of Tarzan begins. 29-Last Tarzan issue			
	17.00	51.00	120.00
30-Li'l Abner	12.00	36.00	84.00
31-The Captain & the Kids	9.00	27.00	62.00
32-Nancy & Fritzi Ritz	7.00	21.00	50.00
33-Li'l Abner	10.00	30.00	70.00
34-The Captain & the Kids (10/41)	8.00	24.00	56.00
35-Nancy & Fritzi Ritz	7.00	21.00	50.00
36-Li'l Abner	10.00	30.00	70.00
37-The Captain & the Kids (6/42)	8.00	24.00	56.00
38-Nancy & Fritzi Ritz; infinity-c	7.00	21.00	50.00
39-Li'l Abner	10.00	30.00	70.00
40-The Captain & the Kids (3/43)	8.00	24.00	56.00
41-Nancy & Fritzi Ritz	5.50	16.50	38.00
42-Li'l Abner	10.00	30.00	70.00
43-The Captain & the Kids	8.00	24.00	56.00
44-Nancy & Fritzi Ritz (3/44)	5.50	16.50	38.00
45-Li'l Abner	8.50	25.50	60.00
46-The Captain & the Kids	7.00	21.00	50.00
47-Nancy & Fritzi Ritz	5.50	16.50	38.00
48-Li'l Abner (3/45)	8.50	25.50	60.00
49-The Captain & the Kids	7.00	21.00	50.00
50-Nancy & Fritzi Ritz	5.50	16.50	38.00
51-Li'l Abner	7.00	21.00	50.00
52-The Captain & the Kids (3/46)	4.50	14.00	32.00
53-Nancy & Fritzi Ritz	4.50	14.00	32.00
54-Li'l Abner	7.00	21.00	50.00
55-Nancy & Fritzi Ritz	4.50	14.00	32.00
56-The Captain & the Kids (r-/Sparkler)	4.50	14.00	32.00
57-Nancy & Fritzi Ritz	4.50	14.00	32.00
58-Li'l Abner	7.00	21.00	50.00
59-The Captain & the Kids	4.00	12.00	28.00

	Good	Fine	N-Mint
60-70-Nancy & Fritzi Ritz	4.00	12.00	28.00
71-76-Nancy only	2.85	8.50	20.00
77-99,101-104-Nancy & Sluggo	2.85	8.50	20.00
100-Nancy & Sluggo	3.70	11.00	26.00
Special Issue, 7/46; Summer, 1948 - The Captain & the Kids app.			
	2.85	8.50	20.00

NOTE: Bound Volume (Very Rare) includes No. 1-12; bound by publisher in pictorial
comic boards & distributed at the 1939 World's Fair and through mail order from ads
in comic books (Also see Tip Top)

	160.00	480.00	1120.00

NOTE: Li'l Abner reprinted from Tip Top.

COMICS READING LIBRARIES (Educational Series)
1973, 1977, 1979 (36 pages in color) (Giveaways)
King Features (Charlton Publ.)

	Good	Fine	N-Mint
R-01-Tiger, Quincy		.15	.30
R-02-Beetle Bailey, Blondie & Popeye		.15	.30
R-03-Blondie, Beetle Bailey		.30	.60
R-04-Tim Tyler's Luck, Felix the Cat	1.30	4.00	8.00
R-05-Quincy, Henry		.15	.30
R-06-The Phantom, Mandrake	2.30	7.00	14.00
1977 reprint(R-04)	.85	2.50	5.00
R-07-Popeye, Little King	.85	2.50	5.00
R-08-Prince Valiant(Foster), Flash Gordon	4.00	12.00	24.00
1977 reprint	1.35	4.00	8.00
R-09-Hagar the Horrible, Boner's Ark		.15	.30
R-10-Redeye, Tiger		.15	.30
R-11-Blondie, Hi & Lois		.25	.50
R-12-Popeye-Swee'pea, Brutus	.85	2.50	5.00
R-13-Beetle Bailey, Little King		.15	.30
R-14-Quincy-Hamlet		.15	.30
R-15-The Phantom, The Genius	2.30	7.00	14.00
R-16-Flash Gordon, Mandrake	4.00	12.00	24.00
1977 reprint	1.35	4.00	8.00
Other 1977 editions....		.15	.30
1979 editions(68pgs.)		.20	.40

NOTE: Above giveaways available with purchase of $45.00 in merchandise. Used as a
reading skills aid for small children.

COMICS REVUE
June, 1947 - No. 5, Jan, 1948
St. John Publ. Co. (United Features Synd.)

	Good	Fine	N-Mint
1-Ella Cinders & Blackie	5.50	16.50	38.00
2-Hap Hopper (7/47)	3.50	10.50	24.00
3-Iron Vic (8/47)	2.85	8.50	20.00
4-Ella Cinders (9/47)	3.50	10.50	24.00
5-Gordo No. 1 (1/48)	2.85	8.50	20.00

COMIC STORY PAINT BOOK
1943 (68 pages) (Large size)
Samuel Lowe Co.

	Good	Fine	N-Mint
1055-Captain Marvel & a Captain Marvel Jr. story to read & color; 3 panels in color per page (reprints)	30.00	90.00	210.00

COMIX BOOK (B&W Magazine - $1.00)
Oct, 1974 - No. 5, 1976
Marvel Comics Group/Krupp Comics Works No. 4,5

	Good	Fine	N-Mint
1-Underground comic artists; 2 pg. Wolverton-a			
	.70	2.00	4.00
2-Wolverton-a (1 pg.)	.40	1.20	2.40
3-Low distribution (3/75)	.50	1.50	3.00
4(2/76), 4(5/76), 5	.40	1.20	2.40

NOTE: Print run No. 1-3: 200-250M; No. 4&5: 10M each.

COMIX INTERNATIONAL
July, 1974 - No. 5, Spring, 1977 (Full color)
Warren Magazines

	Good	Fine	N-Mint
1-Low distribution; all Corben remainders from Warren			
	4.00	12.00	24.00

COMIX INTERNATIONAL (continued)	Good	Fine	N-Mint
2-Wood, Wrightson-r	1.20	3.50	7.00
3-5: 4-Crandall-a	.70	2.00	4.00

NOTE: *No. 4 had two printings with extra* **Corben** *story in one.*

COMMANDER BATTLE AND THE ATOMIC SUB
July-Aug, 1954 - No. 7, July-Aug, 1955
American Comics Group (Titan Publ. Co.)

	Good	Fine	N-Mint
1 (3-D effect)	18.00	54.00	125.00
2	6.50	19.50	45.00
3-H-Bomb-c; Atomic Sub becomes Atomic Spaceship	9.30	28.00	65.00
4-7: 4,6,7-Landau-a	6.50	19.50	45.00

COMMANDMENTS OF GOD
1954, 1958
Catechetical Guild

300-Same contents in both editions; different-c	1.70	5.00	10.00

COMMANDO ADVENTURES
June, 1957 - No. 2, Aug, 1957
Atlas Comics (MMC)

1,2-Severin-c; 2-Drucker-a	1.70	5.00	12.00

COMMANDO YANK (See Mighty Midget & Wow Comics)

COMPLETE BOOK OF COMICS AND FUNNIES
1944 (196 pages) (One Shot) (25 cents)
William H. Wise & Co.

1-Origin Brad Spencer, Wonderman; The Magnet, The Silver Knight by Kinstler, & Zudo the Jungle Boy app.	21.50	64.00	150.00

COMPLETE BOOK OF TRUE CRIME COMICS
No date (Mid 1940's) (132 pages) (25 cents)
William H. Wise & Co.

nn-Contains Crime Does Not Pay rebound (includes #22)	50.00	150.00	350.00

COMPLETE COMICS (Formerly Amazing Comics No. 1)
No. 2, Winter, 1944-45
Timely Comics (EPC)

2-The Destroyer, The Whizzer, The Young Allies & Sergeant Dix; Schomburg-c	50.00	150.00	350.00

COMPLETE LOVE MAGAZINE (Formerly a pulp with same title)
V26/2, May-June, 1951 - V32/4(No.191), Sept, 1956
Ace Periodicals (Periodical House)

V26/2-Painted-c (52 pgs.)	2.30	7.00	16.00
V26/3-6(2/52), V27/1(4/52)-6(1/53)	1.50	4.50	10.00
V28/1(3/53), V28/2(5/53), V29/3(7/53)-6(12/53)	1.30	4.00	9.00
V30/1(2/54), V30/1(No. 176, 4/54)-6(No.181, 1/55): 178-Rock Hudson photo-c	1.15	3.50	8.00
V31/1(No.182, 3/55)-Last precode	1.00	3.00	7.00
V31/2(5/55)-6(No.187, 1/56)	.85	2.50	6.00
V32/1(No.188, 3/56)-4(No.191, 9/56)	.80	2.40	5.50

NOTE: *(34 total issues). Photo-c V27/5-on. Painted-c V26/3.*

COMPLETE MYSTERY (True Complete Mystery No. 5 on)
Aug, 1948 - No. 4, Feb, 1949 (Full length stories)
Marvel Comics (PrPI)

1-Seven Dead Men	14.00	42.00	100.00
2-Jigsaw of Doom!	9.30	28.00	65.00
3-Fear in the Night; Burgos-a	9.30	28.00	65.00
4-A Squealer Dies Fast	9.30	28.00	65.00

COMPLETE ROMANCE
1949
Avon Periodicals

1-(Scarce)-Reprinted as Women to Love	22.00	65.00	154.00

COMPLIMENTARY COMICS
No date (1950's)
Sales Promotion Publ. (Giveaway)

	Good	Fine	N-Mint
1-Strongman by Powell, 3 stories	3.35	10.00	20.00

CONAN (See Chamber of Darkness #4, Handbook of . . ., King Conan, Marvel Graphic Novel #19, 28, Marvel Treasury Ed., Robert E. Howard's . . ., Savage Sword of Conan, and Savage Tales)

CONAN SAGA, THE
June, 1987 - Present ($2.00-$2.25, B&W magazine)
Marvel Comics

	Good	Fine	N-Mint
1-Barry Smith-r begin	.35	1.00	2.00
2-27: 13,15-Boris-c. 22-r/Giant-Size Conan 1,2	.35	1.00	2.00
28-36 ($2.25): 31-Red Sonja by N. Adams. 32-Newspaper strip-r begin by Buscema. 33-Smith/Conrad-c	.40	1.15	2.30

CONAN, THE BARBARIAN
Oct, 1970 - Present
Marvel Comics Group

1-Origin/1st app. Conan by Barry Smith; Kull app.	13.50	41.00	95.00
2	5.00	15.00	35.00
3-(low distribution in some areas)	8.00	24.00	55.00
4,5	3.70	11.00	26.00
6-10: 8-Hidden panel message, pg. 14. 10-52 pgs.; Black Knight-r; Kull story by Severin	2.85	8.50	20.00
11-13: 11-52 pgs. 12-Wrightson c(i)	2.15	6.50	15.00
14,15-Elric app.	3.15	9.50	22.00
16,19,20: 16-Conan-r/Savage Tales #1	1.70	5.00	12.00
17,18-No Smith-a	1.15	3.50	7.00
21,22: 22-has r-from #1	1.50	4.50	10.00
23-1st app. Red Sonja	1.85	5.50	13.00
24-1st full story Red Sonja; last Smith-a	1.85	5.50	13.00
25-Buscema-c/a begins	1.15	3.50	7.00
26-30	.70	2.00	4.00
31-36,38-40	.40	1.25	2.50
37-Adams c/a	.85	2.50	5.00
41-43,46-49	.30	.85	1.70
44,45-Adams-i (Crusty Bunkers). 45-Adams-c	.35	1.00	2.00
50-57,60	.30	.85	1.70
58-2nd Belit app.(see Giant-Size 1)	.50	1.50	3.00
59-Origin Belit	.30	.85	1.70
61-99: 87-R/Savage Sword of Conan #3 in color		.60	1.20
100-(52 pg. Giant)-Death of Belit	.40	1.25	2.50
101-114,116-193		.50	1.00
115-Double size		.60	1.20
194-199,201-230: $1.00 cover		.50	1.00
200-Double size ($1.50)	.25	.75	1.50

NOTE: **Adams** *a-116r(i); c-49i.* **Austin** *a-125, 126; c-125i, 126i.* **Brunner** *c-17i. c-40.* **Buscema** *a-25-36p, 38, 39, 41-56p, 58-63p, 65-67p, 68, 70-78p, 84-86p, 88-91p, 93-126p, 136p, 140, 141-44p, 146-58p, 159, 161, 162, 163p, 165p-185p, 187p-190p, Annual 2-5p, 7p; c(p)-26, 36, 44, 46, 52, 56, 58, 59, 64, 65, 72, 78-80, 83-91, 93-103, 105-26, 136-51, 155-159, 161, 162, 168, 169, 171, 172, 174, 175, 178-185, 188, 189.* **Chaykin** *a-79-83.* **Golden** *c-152.* **Kaluta** *c-167.* **Gil Kane** *a-12p, 17p, 18p, 127-30, 131-134p, Gnt-Size 1p-4p; c-12p, 17p, 18p, 23, 25, 27-32, 34, 35, 38, 39, 41-43, 45-51, 53-55, 57, 60-63, 65-71, 73p, 76p, 127-34, Gnt-Size 1, 3, 4.* **Ploog** *a-57.* **Russell** *a-21.* **Simonson** *c-135.* **Smith** *a-1p-11p, 12, 13p-15p, 16, 19-21, 23, 24; c-1-11, 13-16, 19-24p.* **Starlin** *a-64.* **Sutton** *inks-Gnt-Size 1-3.* **Wood** *a-47i. Issues No. 3-5, 7-9, 11, 16-18, 21, 23, 25, 27-30, 35, 37, 38, 42, 45, 52, 57, 58, 65, 69-71, 73, 79-83, 99, 100, 104, 114, Annual 2 have original Robert E. Howard stories adapted. Issues #32-34 adapted from Norvell Page's novel* Flame Winds.

Giant Size 1(9/74)-Smith r-/#3; start adaptation of Howard's "Hour of the Dragon." 1st app. Belit; new-a also #1-4	.70	2.00	4.00
Giant Size 2(12/74)-Smith r-/#5; Sutton-a; Buscema-c	.70	2.00	4.00
Giant Size 3(4/75-Smith r-/#6; Sutton-a), Giant Size 4(6/75; Smith r-/#7), Giant Size 5('75; Smith r-/#14,15; Kirby-c)	.35	1.00	2.00

Commander Battle And The Atomic Sub #3, © ACG

Complete Mystery #2, © MEG

Conan, The Barbarian #6, © MEG

Concrete Color Special #1, © P. Chadwick

Confessions Of Romance #9, © STAR

Congo Bill #5, © DC

CONAN, THE BARBARIAN (continued)

	Good	Fine	N-Mint
King Size 1(9/73-35 cents)-Smith r-/#2,4; Smith-c			
	1.00	3.00	6.00
Annual 2(6/76)-50 cents; new stories	.40	1.25	2.50
Annual 3(2/78)-reprints	.35	1.00	2.00
Annual 4(10/78), 5(12/79)-Buscema-a/part-c	.25	.75	1.50
Annual 6(10/81)-Kane c/a	.25	.75	1.50
Annual 7(11/82), 8(2/84)		.60	1.25
Annual 9(12/84), 10(2/87), 11(2/88)		.60	1.25
Special Edition 1(Red Nails)	.50	1.50	3.00

CONAN THE BARBARIAN MOVIE SPECIAL
Oct, 1982 - No. 2, Nov, 1982
Marvel Comics Group

	Good	Fine	N-Mint
1,2-Movie adaptation; Buscema-a		.25	.50

CONAN THE DESTROYER
Jan, 1985 - No. 2, Mar, 1985 (Movie adaptation)
Marvel Comics Group

	Good	Fine	N-Mint
1,2-r/Marvel Super Special		.40	.80

CONAN THE KING (Formerly King Conan)
No. 20, Jan, 1984 - No. 55, Nov, 1989
Marvel Comics Group

	Good	Fine	N-Mint
20-47		.60	1.20
48-55 ($1.50)	.25	.75	1.50

NOTE: *Kaluta c-20-23, 24i, 26, 27, 50, 52. Williamson a-37i; c-37i, 38i.*

CONCRETE (Also see Dark Horse Presents)
March, 1987 - No. 10, 1989 ($1.50, B&W)
Dark Horse Comics

	Good	Fine	N-Mint
1-Paul Chadwick-c/a in all	1.85	5.50	11.00
1-2nd print	.45	1.40	2.80
2	.90	2.75	5.50
3-Origin	.55	1.65	3.30
4	.45	1.40	2.80
5-10	.35	1.10	2.20
. . . : A New Life 1 ('89, $2.95, B&W)-r/#3,4 plus new-a (11 pgs.)			
	.50	1.50	3.00
. . . : Land And Sea 1 ('89, $2.95, B&W)-r/#1,2	.50	1.50	3.00
. . . Color Special 1 (2/89, $2.95, 44 pgs.)-r/1st two Conrete app. from			
Dark Horse Presents #1,2 plus new-a	.55	1.65	3.30

CONDORMAN (Walt Disney)
Oct, 1981 - No. 3, Jan, 1982
Whitman Publishing

	Good	Fine	N-Mint
1-3: 1,2-Movie adaptation; photo-c		.30	.60

CONFESSIONS ILLUSTRATED (Magazine)
Jan-Feb, 1956 - No. 2, Spring, 1956
E. C. Comics

	Good	Fine	N-Mint
1-Craig, Kamen, Wood, Orlando-a	5.50	16.50	38.00
2-Craig, Crandall, Kamen, Orlando-a	6.50	19.50	45.00

CONFESSIONS OF LOVE
4/50 - No. 2, 7/50 (25 cents; 132 pgs. in color)(7¼x5¼'')
Artful Publ.

	Good	Fine	N-Mint
1-Bakerish-a	17.00	51.00	120.00
2-Art & text; Bakerish-a	10.00	30.00	70.00

CONFESSIONS OF LOVE (Confessions of Romance No. 7 on)
(Formerly All-Famous Crimie #10?)
No. 11, July, 1952 - No. 6, Aug, 1953
Star Publications

	Good	Fine	N-Mint
11	3.50	10.50	24.00
12,13-Disbrow-a	3.50	10.50	24.00
14, 6	2.00	6.00	14.00
4-Disbrow-a	2.75	8.00	18.00
5-Wood/?-a	4.00	12.00	28.00

NOTE: *All have L. B. Cole covers.*

CONFESSIONS OF ROMANCE (Formerly Confessions of Love)
No. 7, Nov, 1953 - No. 11, Nov, 1954
Star Publications

	Good	Fine	N-Mint
7	3.50	10.50	24.00
8	2.35	7.00	16.00
9-Wood-a	6.00	18.00	42.00
10,11-Disbrow-a	3.00	9.00	21.00

NOTE: *L. B. Cole covers on all.*

CONFESSIONS OF THE LOVELORN (Formerly Lovelorn)
No. 52, Aug, 1954 - No. 114, June-July, 1960
American Comics Group (Regis Publ./Best Synd. Features)

	Good	Fine	N-Mint
52 (3-D effect)	10.00	30.00	70.00
53,55	1.70	5.00	12.00
54 (3-D effect)	9.30	28.00	65.00
56-Communist propaganda sty, 10pgs; last pre-code (2/55)			
	2.30	7.00	16.00
57-90	1.15	3.50	8.00
91-Williamson-a	4.00	12.00	28.00
92-99,101-114	.85	2.50	6.00
100	1.00	3.00	7.00

NOTE: *Whitney a-most issues. Painted c-106, 107.*

CONFIDENTIAL DIARY (Formerly High School Confidential Diary;
Three Nurses No. 18 on)
No. 12, May, 1962 - No. 17, March, 1963
Charlton Comics

	Good	Fine	N-Mint
12-17	.40	1.25	2.50

CONGO BILL (See Action Comics & More Fun Comics #56)
Aug-Sept, 1954 - No. 7, Aug-Sept, 1955
National Periodical Publications

	Good	Fine	VF-NM
1-(Scarce)	34.00	100.00	235.00
2-(Scarce)	27.00	80.00	185.00
3-7 (Scarce), 4-Last precode issue	21.50	64.00	150.00

NOTE: *(Rarely found in fine or mint condition.)*

CONNECTICUT YANKEE, A (See King Classics)

CONQUEROR, THE (See 4-Color No. 690)

CONQUEROR COMICS
Winter, 1945
Albrecht Publishing Co.

	Good	Fine	N-Mint
nn	6.50	19.50	45.00

CONQUEROR OF THE BARREN EARTH
Feb, 1985 - No. 4, May, 1985 (Mini-series)
DC Comics

	Good	Fine	N-Mint
1-Back-up series from Warlord		.60	1.20
2-4		.50	1.00

CONQUEST
1953 (6 cents)
Store Comics

	Good	Fine	N-Mint
1-Richard the Lion Hearted, Beowulf, Swamp Fox			
	2.65	8.00	18.00

CONQUEST
Spring, 1955
Famous Funnies

	Good	Fine	N-Mint
1-Crandall-a, 1 pg.; contains contents of 1953 issue			
	2.15	6.50	15.00

CONTACT COMICS
July, 1944 - No. 12, May, 1946
Aviation Press

	Good	Fine	N-Mint
nn-Black Venus, Flamingo, Golden Eagle, Tommy Tomahawk begin			
	13.00	40.00	90.00

CONTACT COMICS (continued)	Good	Fine	N-Mint
2-5: 3-Last Flamingo. 3,4-Black Venus by L. B. Cole. 5-The			
Phantom Flyer app.	9.30	28.00	65.00
6,11-Kurtzman's Black Venus; 11-Last Golden Eagle, last Tommy			
Tomahawk; Feldstein-a	12.00	36.00	85.00
7-10,12: 12-Sky Rangers, Air Kids, Ace Diamond app.			
	8.00	24.00	56.00

NOTE: *L. B. Cole* a-9; c-1-12. *Giunta* a-3. *Hollingsworth* a-5, 7, 10. *Palais* a-11,12.

CONTEMPORARY MOTIVATORS
1977 - 1978 (5-3/8x8")(31 pgs., B&W, $1.45)
Pendelum Press

14-3002 The Caine Mutiny; 14-3010 Banner in the Sky; 14-3029 God Is My Co-Pilot;
14-3037 Guadalcanal Diary; 14-3045 Hiroshima; 14-3053 Hot Rod; 14-3061 Just Dial a
Number; 14-307x Star Wars; 14-3088 The Diary of Anne Frank; 14-3096 Lost Horizon
1.50

NOTE: *Also see Now Age III. Above may have been dist. the same.*

CONTEST OF CHAMPIONS (See Marvel Super-Hero . . .)

COO COO COMICS (. . . the Bird Brain No. 57 on)
Oct, 1942 - No. 62, April, 1952
Nedor Publ. Co./Standard (Animated Cartoons)

1-1st app./origin Super Mouse (cloned from Superman)-The first			
funny animal super hero	10.00	30.00	70.00
2	4.50	14.00	32.00
3-10 (3/44)	2.85	8.50	20.00
11-33: 33-1pg. Ingels-a	2.00	6.00	14.00
34-40,43-46,48-50-Text illos by Frazetta in all	3.50	10.50	24.00
41-Frazetta-a(2)	8.50	25.50	60.00
42,47-Frazetta-a & text illos.	6.00	18.00	42.00
51-62	1.60	4.70	11.00

"COOKIE" (Also see Topsy-Turvy)
April, 1946 - No. 55, Aug-Sept, 1955
Michel Publ./American Comics Group(Regis Publ.)

1	8.00	24.00	56.00
2	4.00	12.00	28.00
3-10	2.65	8.00	18.00
11-20	2.00	6.00	14.00
21-30	1.50	5.00	10.00
31-34,36-55	1.15	3.50	8.00
35-Starlett O'Hara story	1.50	4.50	10.00

COOL CAT (Formerly Black Magic)
V8/6, Mar-Apr, 1962 - V9/2, July-Aug, 1962
Prize Publications

V8#6, nn(V9#1), V9#2	1.30	4.00	9.00

COPPER CANYON (See Fawcett Movie Comics)

COPS (TV)
Aug, 1988 - No. 15, Aug, 1989 ($1.00, color)
DC Comics

1 ($1.50) Based on Hasbro Toys	.35	1.10	2.20
2-7		.60	1.25
8-15: 14-Orlando-c(p)		.50	1.00

CORBEN SPECIAL, A
May, 1984 (One-shot)
Pacific Comics

1-Corben c/a; E.A. Poe Adaptation	.35	1.00	2.00

CORKY & WHITE SHADOW (See 4-Color No. 707)

CORLISS ARCHER (See Meet Corliss Archer)

CORPORAL RUSTY DUGAN (See Holyoke One-Shot #2)

CORPSES OF DR. SACOTTI, THE (See Ideal a Classical Comic)

CORSAIR, THE (See A-1 Comics No. 5,7,10)

CORUM: THE BULL AND THE SPEAR (See Chronicles Of Corum)
Jan, 1989 - No. 4, July, 1989 ($1.95, limited series, color)
First Comics

	Good	Fine	N-Mint
1-4: Adapts Michael Moorcock's novel	.35	1.00	2.00

COSMIC BOOK, THE
Dec, 1986 - No. 2?, 1987 ($1.95, color)
Ace Comics

1-Wood, Toth-a	.35	1.00	2.00
2-(B&W)	.25	.80	1.60

COSMIC BOY (See The Legion of Super-Heroes)
Dec, 1986 - No. 4, Mar, 1987 (mini-series)
DC Comics

1-Legends tie-in, all issues	.25	.75	1.50
2-4		.50	1.00

COSMIC ODYSSEY
1988 - No. 4, 1988 (Squarebound, $3.50, color)
DC Comics

1-Superman, Batman, Green Lantern app.	.70	2.00	4.00
2-4	.70	2.00	4.00

COSMO CAT (Also see Wotalife Comics)
July-Aug, 1946 - No. 10, Oct, 1947; 1957; 1959
Fox Publications/Green Publ. Co./Norlen Mag.

1	7.00	21.00	50.00
2	3.70	11.00	26.00
3-Origin	3.70	11.00	26.00
4-10	2.65	8.00	18.00
2-4(1957-Green Publ. Co.)	1.00	3.00	7.00
2-4(1959-Norlen Mag.)	.85	2.60	6.00
I.W. Reprint #1	.50	1.50	3.00

COSMO THE MERRY MARTIAN
Sept, 1958 - No. 6, Oct, 1959
Archie Publications (Radio Comics)

1-Bob White-a in all	6.50	19.50	45.00
2-6	4.00	12.00	28.00

COTTON WOODS (See 4-Color No. 837)

COUGAR, THE (Cougar No. 2)
April, 1975 - No. 2, July, 1975
Seaboard Periodicals (Atlas)

1-Adkins-a(p)		.40	.80
2-Origin		.25	.50

COUNTDOWN (See Movie Classics)

COUNT DUCKULA (TV)
Nov, 1988 - Present ($1.00, color)
Marvel Comics

1-10: 2-Dangermouse app. 8-Geraldo Rivera photo-c	.50	1.00

COUNT OF MONTE CRISTO, THE (See 4-Color No. 794)

COURAGE COMICS
1945
J. Edward Slavin

1,2,77	3.70	11.00	26.00

COURTSHIP OF EDDIE'S FATHER (TV)
Jan, 1970 - No. 2, May, 1970
Dell Publishing Co.

1,2-Bill Bixby photo-c	1.70	5.00	12.00

COVERED WAGONS, HO (See 4-Color No. 814)

COWBOY ACTION (Formerly Western Thrillers No. 1-4; Becomes
Quick Trigger Western No. 12 on)
No. 5, March, 1955 - No. 11, March, 1956

Coo Coo Comics #46, © DC

Cosmic Odyssey #3, © DC

Cosmo Cat #2, © FOX

Cowboy Action #11, © MEG

Cowboy Western #26, © CC

Cowgirl Romances #1, © FH

COWBOY ACTION (continued)
Atlas Comics (ACI)

	Good	Fine	N-Mint
5	3.70	11.00	26.00
6-10	2.30	7.00	16.00
11-Williamson-a, 4 pgs., Baker-a	4.00	12.00	28.00

NOTE: *Ayers a-8. Drucker a-6. Heath c-6-8. Maneely c/a-5, 6. Severin c-10. Shores a-7.*

COWBOY COMICS (. . .Stories No. 14; formerly Star Ranger)
(Star Ranger Funnies No. 15 on)
No. 13, July, 1938 - No. 14, Aug, 1938
Centaur Publishing Co.

13-(Rare)-Ace and Deuce, Lyin Lou, Air Patrol, Aces High, Lee Trent, Trouble Hunters begin	50.00	150.00	350.00
14	35.00	105.00	245.00

NOTE: *Guardineer a-13, 14. Gustavson a-13, 14.*

COWBOY IN AFRICA (TV)
March, 1968
Gold Key

1(10219-803)-Chuck Connors photo-c	1.70	5.00	12.00

COWBOY LOVE (Becomes Range Busters?)
7/49 - V2/10, 6/50; No. 11, 1951; No. 28, 2/55 - No. 31, 8/55
Fawcett Publications/Charlton Comics No. 28 on

V1#1-Rocky Lane photo back-c	5.70	17.00	40.00
2	2.00	6.00	14.00
V1#3,4,6 (12/49)	1.70	5.00	12.00
5-Bill Boyd photo back-c (11/49)	3.00	9.00	21.00
V2#7-Williamson/Evans-a	4.50	14.00	32.00
V2#8-11	1.50	4.50	10.00
V1#28 (Charlton)-Last precode (2/55) (Formerly Romantic Story?)	1.15	3.50	8.00
V1#29-31 (Charlton; becomes Sweetheart Diary #32 on)	1.15	3.50	8.00

NOTE: *Powell a-10. Photo c-1-11 No. 1-3,5-7,9,10, 52 pgs.*

COWBOY ROMANCES (Young Men No. 4 on)
Oct, 1949 - No. 3, Mar, 1950
Marvel Comics (IPC)

1-Photo-c	8.00	24.00	56.00
2-William Holden, Mona Freeman 'Streets of Laredo' photo-c	5.70	17.00	40.00
3	4.30	13.00	30.00

COWBOYS 'N' INJUNS (. . .'N' Indians No. 6 on)
1946 - No. 5, 1947; No. 6, 1949 - No. 8, 1952
Compix No. 1-5/Magazine Enterprises No. 6 on

1	3.50	10.50	24.00
2-5-All funny animal western	2.00	6.00	14.00
6(A-1 23)-half violent, half funny	2.65	8.00	18.00
7(A-1 41, 1950), 8(A-1 48)-All funny	2.00	6.00	14.00
I.W. Reprint No. 1,7 (reprinted in Canada by Superior, No. 7)	.70	2.00	4.00
Super Reprint #10 (1963)	.70	2.00	4.00

COWBOY WESTERN COMICS (Formerly Jack In The Box; Becomes Space Western No. 40-45 & Wild Bill Hickok & Jingles No. 68 on; title: . . .Heroes No. 47 & 48; Cowboy Western No. 49 on (TV))
No. 17, 7/48 - No. 39, 8/52; No. 46, 10/53; No. 47, 12/53; No. 48 Spr, '54, No. 49, 5-6/54 - No. 67, 3/58 (nn 40-45)
Charlton(Capitol Stories)

17-Jesse James, Annie Oakley, Wild Bill Hickok & Texas Rangers app.	6.00	18.00	42.00
18,19-Orlando c/a	4.00	12.00	28.00
20-25	2.30	7.00	16.00
26-George Montgomery photo-c	4.30	13.00	30.00
27,30-Sunset Carson photo-c	28.00	85.00	200.00
28,29-Sunset Carson app.	10.00	30.00	70.00

	Good	Fine	N-Mint
31-39,47-50 (no #40-45)	1.70	5.00	12.00
46-(Formerly Space Western)-Space western story	7.00	21.00	42.00
51-57,59-66	1.30	4.00	9.00
58 (68 pgs.)-Wild Bill Hickok & Jingles	1.70	5.00	12.00
67-Williamson/Torres-a, 5 pgs.	5.00	15.00	35.00

NOTE: *Many issues trimmed 1'' shorter.*

COWGIRL ROMANCES (Formerly Jeanie Comics)
No. 28, Jan, 1950 (52 pgs.)
Marvel Comics (CCC)

28(#1)-Photo-c	8.00	24.00	56.00

COWGIRL ROMANCES
1950 - No. 12, Winter, 1952-53 (No. 1-3: 52 pgs.)
Fiction House Magazines

1-Kamen-a	13.50	41.00	95.00
2	6.50	19.50	45.00
3-5	5.50	16.50	38.00
6-9,11,12	4.30	13.00	30.00
10-Frazetta?/Williamson-a; Kamen/Baker-a	16.00	48.00	110.00

COW PUNCHER (. . .Comics)
Jan, 1947; No. 2, Sept, 1947 - No. 7, 1949
Avon Periodicals

1-Clint Cortland, Texas Ranger, Kit West, Pioneer Queen begin; Kubert-a; Alabam stories begin	17.00	51.00	120.00
2-Kubert, Kamen/Feldstein-a; Kamen bondage-c	14.00	42.00	100.00
3-5,7; 3-Kiefer story	9.00	27.00	63.00
6-Opium drug mention story; bondage, headlight-c; Reinman-a	11.00	33.00	76.00

COWPUNCHER
1953 (nn) (Reprints Avon's No. 2)
Realistic Publications

Kubert-a	5.00	15.00	35.00

COWSILLS, THE (See Harvey Pop Comics)

COYOTE
June, 1983 - No. 16, Mar, 1986 (Adults only) ($1.50)
Epic Comics (Marvel)

1-10,15,16: 1,2-Origin issues. 7,9-Ditko-p	.25	.75	1.50
11-14-1st Todd McFarlane-a	.50	1.50	3.00

CRACKAJACK FUNNIES (Giveaway)
1937 (32 pgs.; full size; soft cover; full color)(Before No. 1?)
Malto-Meal

Features Dan Dunn, G-Man, Speed Bolton, Freckles, Buck Jones, Clyde Beatty, The Nebbs, Major Hoople, Wash Tubbs

	40.00	120.00	280.00

CRACKAJACK FUNNIES
June, 1938 - No. 43, Jan, 1942
Dell Publishing Co.

1-Dan Dunn, Freckles, Myra North, Wash Tubbs, Apple Mary, The Nebbs, Don Winslow, Tom Mix, Buck Jones, Major Hoople, Clyde Beatty, Boots begin	82.00	245.00	575.00
2	38.00	115.00	270.00
3	27.00	81.00	190.00
4,5	22.00	65.00	154.00
6-8,10	17.00	51.00	120.00
9-(3/39)-Red Ryder strip-r begin by Harman; 1st app. in comics & 1st cover app.	24.00	73.00	170.00
11-14	15.00	45.00	105.00
15-Tarzan text feature begins by Burroughs (9/39); not in #26,35	16.00	48.00	115.00

	Good	Fine	N-Mint
CRACKAJACK FUNNIES (continued)			
16-24	12.00	36.00	84.00
25-The Owl begins; in new costume #26 by Frank Thomas	27.00	81.00	190.00
26-30: 28-Owl-c. 29-Ellery Queen begins	21.00	62.00	145.00
31-Owl covers begin	19.00	57.00	132.00
32-Origin Owl Girl	21.00	62.00	145.00
33-38: 36-Last Tarzan issue	14.00	42.00	100.00
39-Andy Panda begins (intro/1st app.)	16.00	48.00	110.00
40-43: 42-Last Owl cover	13.00	40.00	90.00

NOTE: *McWilliams* art in most issues.

CRACK COMICS (. . .Western No. 63 on)
May, 1940 - No. 62, Sept, 1949
Quality Comics Group

1-Origin The Black Condor begin by Lou Fine, Madame Fatal, Red Torpedo, Rock Bradden & The Space Legion; The Clock, Alias the Spider, Wizard Wells, & Ned Brant begin; Powell-a; Note: Madame Fatal is a man dressed up as a woman	171.00	515.00	1200.00
2	86.00	257.00	600.00
3	63.00	188.00	440.00
4	54.00	163.00	380.00
5-10: 5-Molly The Model begins. 10-Tor, the Magic Master begins	42.00	126.00	295.00
11-20: 18-1st app. Spitfire?	37.00	110.00	260.00
21-24-Last Fine Black Condor	28.00	85.00	200.00
25,26	18.50	56.00	130.00
27-Intro & origin Captain Triumph by Alfred Andriola (Kerry Drake artist)	37.00	110.00	260.00
28-30	16.00	48.00	110.00
31-39: 31-Last Black Condor	9.30	28.00	65.00
40-46	6.50	19.50	45.00
47-57,59,60-Capt. Triumph by Crandall	7.50	22.50	52.00
58,61,62-Last Captain Triumph	5.50	16.50	38.00

NOTE: *Black Condor by Fine:* No. 1, 2, 4-6, 8, 10-24; *by Sultan:* No. 3, 7; *by Fugitani:* No. 9. *Crandall* c-55, 59, 60. *Guardineer* a-17. *Gustavson* a-17. *McWilliams* art-No. 15-21, 23-27.

CRACKED (Magazine) (Satire) (Also see The 3-D Zone #19)
Feb-Mar, 1958 - Present
Major Magazines

1-One pg. Williamson	5.70	17.00	40.00
2-1st Shut-Ups & Bonus Cut-Outs	2.85	8.50	20.00
3-6	1.50	4.50	10.00
7-10: 7-R/1st 6 covers on-c	1.15	3.50	8.00
11-12, 13(nn,3/60), 14-17, 18(nn,2/61), 19,20	.85	2.60	6.00
21-27(11/62), 27(No.28, 2/63; misnumbered), 29(5/63)	.70	2.00	4.00
31-60	.50	1.50	3.00
61-100: 99-Alfred E. Neuman on-c	.35	1.00	2.00
101-245: 234-Don Martin-a begins	.50	1.00	
Biggest. . .(Winter, 1977)	.50	1.50	3.00
Biggest, Greatest. . .nn('65)	1.15	3.50	8.00
Biggest, Greatest. . .2('66) - #12('76)	.70	2.00	4.00
. . .Blockbuster 1,2('88)	.45	1.40	2.75
. . .Digest 1(Fall, '86, 148p) - #5	.35	1.00	2.00
. . .Collectors' Edition ('73; formerly . . .Special)			
4	.70	2.00	4.00
5-70	.25	.75	1.50
71-80	.45	1.40	2.75
. . .Party Pack 1,2('88)	.45	1.40	2.75
. . .Shut-Ups (2/72-'72; Cracked Special #3) 1,2	.70	2.00	4.00
. . .Special 3('73; formerly Cracked Shut-Ups; . . .Collectors' Edition #4 on)	.70	2.00	4.00
Extra Special. . .1('76), 2('76)		.60	1.20
Giant. . .nn('65)	1.15	3.50	8.00
Giant. . .2('66)-12('76), nn(9/77)-48('87)	.70	2.00	4.00

	Good	Fine	N-Mint
King Sized. . .1('67)	1.50	4.50	10.00
King Sized. . .2('68)-11('77)	.70	2.00	5.00
King Sized. . .12-22 (Sum/'86)	.35	1.00	2.00
Super. . .1('68)	1.15	3.50	8.00
Super. . .2('69)-24('88): 2-Spoof on Beatles movie by Severin	.70	2.00	4.00
Super. . .1('87, 100p)-Severin & Elder-a	.45	1.40	2.75

NOTE: *Burgos* a-1-10. *Davis* a-5, 11-17, 24, 40, 80; c-12-14, 16. *Elder* a-5, 6, 10-13; c-10. *Everett* a-1-10, 23-25, 61; c-1. *Heath* a-1-3, 6, 13, 14, 17, 110; c-6. *Jaffee* a-5, 6. *Morrow* a-8-10. *Reinman* a-1-4. *Severin* a-in most all issues. *Shores* a-3-7. *Torres* a-7-10. *Ward* a-22-24, 143, 144, 149, 150, 152, 153, 156. *Williamson* a-1 (1 pg.). *Wolverton* a-10 (2 pgs.), *Giant nn('65). Wood* a-27, 35, 40.

CRACK WESTERN (Formerly Crack Comics; Jonesy No. 85 on)
No. 63, Nov, 1949 - No. 84, May, 1953 (36pgs., 63-68,74-on)
Quality Comics Group

63(#1)-Two-Gun Lil (origin & 1st app.)(ends #84), Arizona Ames, his horse Thunder (sidekick Spurs & his horse Calico), Frontier Marshal (ends #70), & Dead Canyon Days (ends #69) begin; Crandall-a	8.50	25.50	60.00
64,65-Crandall-a	6.00	18.00	42.00
66,68-Photo-c. 66-Arizona Ames becomes A. Raines (ends #84)	6.00	18.00	42.00
67-Randolph Scott photo-c; Crandall-a	7.00	21.00	50.00
69(52pgs.)-Crandall-a	6.00	18.00	42.00
70(52pgs.)-The Whip (origin & 1st app.) & his horse Diablo begin (ends #84); Crandall-a	6.00	18.00	42.00
71(52pgs.)-Frontier Marshal becomes Bob Allen F. Marshal (ends #84); Crandall-c/a	7.00	21.00	50.00
72(52pgs.)-Tim Holt photo-c	6.00	18.00	42.00
73(52pgs.)-Photo-c	4.50	14.00	32.00
74,77,79,80,82	3.00	9.00	21.00
75,76,78,81,83-Crandall-c	4.50	14.00	32.00
84-Crandall c/a	6.50	19.50	45.00

CRASH COMICS (Catman Comics No. 6 on)
May, 1940 - No. 5, Nov, 1940
Tem Publishing Co.

1-The Blue Streak, Strongman (origin), The Perfect Human, Shangra begin; Kirby-a	93.00	280.00	650.00
2-Simon & Kirby-a	43.00	130.00	300.00
3-Simon & Kirby-a	35.00	105.00	245.00
4-Origin & 1st app. The Catman; S&K-a	57.00	170.00	400.00
5-S&K-a	35.00	105.00	245.00

NOTE: *Solar Legion by Kirby No. 1-5 (5 pgs. each).*

CRASH DIVE (See Cinema Comics Herald)

CRASH RYAN
Oct, 1984 - No. 4, Jan, 1985 (Baxter paper, limited series)
Epic Comics (Marvel)

1-4	.25	.75	1.50

CRAZY
Dec, 1953 - No. 7, July, 1954
Atlas Comics (CSI)

1-Everett c/a	7.00	21.00	50.00
2	5.70	17.00	40.00
3-7: 4-I Love Lucy satire. 5-Satire on censorship	4.50	14.00	32.00

NOTE: *Ayers* a-5. *Berg* a-1, 2. *Burgos* c-5, 6. *Drucker* a-6. *Everett* a-1-4. *Heath* a-3, 7; c-7. *Maneely* a-1-7, c-3, 4. *Post* a-3-6.

CRAZY (People Who Buy This Magazine Is. . .) (Formerly This Magazine Is. . .)
V3No.3, Nov, 1957 - V4No.8, Feb, 1959 (Magazine) (Satire)
Charlton Publications

V3#3 - V4#7	.50	1.50	3.00
V4#8-Davis-a, 8 pgs.	1.00	3.00	7.00

Crackjack Funnies #34, © DELL　　　*Crack Comics #8, © QUA*　　　*Crack Western 73, © QUA*

Crime And Justice #5, © CC

Crime And Punishment #66, © LEV

Crime Can't Win #6, © MEG

CRAZY (Satire)
Feb, 1973 - No. 3, June, 1973
Marvel Comics Group

	Good	Fine	N-Mint
1-3-Not Brand Echh-r. 1-Beatles cameo (r)		.30	.60

CRAZY (Magazine) (Satire)
Oct, 1973 - No. 94, Mar, 1983 (40 cents) (Black & White)
Marvel Comics Group

	Good	Fine	N-Mint
1-Wolverton(1 pg.), Ploog, Bode-a; 3 pg. photo story of Adams & Giordano	.35	1.00	2.00
2-Adams-a; Kurtzman's "Hey Look" reprint, 2 pgs.; Buscema-a		.60	1.20
3,5,6,8: 3-Drucker-a		.40	.80
4,7-Ploog-a		.40	.80
9-16-Eisner-a		.40	.80
17-81,83-94: 43-E.C. swipe from Mad 131. 76-Best of. .Super Special		.30	.60
82-Super Special ish; X-Men on-c		.60	1.20
Super Special 1(Summer,'75, 100pgs.)-Ploog, Adams-r	.30	.80	1.60

NOTE: *Austin* a-82i. *Buscema* a-82. *Byrne* c-82p. *Cardy* c-7,8. *Freas* c-1,2,4,6; a-7. *Rogers* a-82.

CRAZY, MAN, CRAZY (Magazine) (Satire)
June, 1956
Humor Magazines

	Good	Fine	N-Mint
V2#2-Wolverton-a, 3pgs.	4.00	12.00	28.00

CREATURE, THE (See Movie Classics)

CREATURES ON THE LOOSE (Tower of Shadows No. 1-9)
No. 10, March, 1971 - No. 37, Sept, 1975
Marvel Comics Group

	Good	Fine	N-Mint
10-First King Kull story; Wrightson-a	1.70	5.00	12.00
11-16: 13-Crandall-a. 16-Origin Warrior of Mars		.50	1.00
17-37: 21,22: Steranko-c; Thongor begins #22, ends #29. 30-Manwolf begins		.50	1.00

NOTE: *Ditko* r-15, 17, 18, 20, 22, 24, 27, 28. *Everett* a-16i(r). *Gil Kane* a-16p(r); c-16, 20, 25, 29, 33p, 35p, 36p. *Morrow* a-20, 21. *Perez* a-33-37; c-34p. *Tuska* a-32p.

CREEPER, THE (See Beware . . . & First Issue Special)

CREEPY (Magazine)(See Warren Presents)
1964 - No. 145, Feb, 1983; No. 146, 1985 (B&W)
Warren Publishing Co./Harris Publ. #146

	Good	Fine	N-Mint
1-Frazetta-a; Jack Davis-c; 1st Warren mag?	1.35	4.00	8.00
2	.70	2.00	4.00
3-13: 7,10-Frazetta-c. 10-Wrightson sketch	.50	1.50	3.00
14-Adams 1st Warren work	.70	2.00	4.00
15-25	.50	1.50	3.00
26-40: 32-Harlan Ellison story	.35	1.00	2.00
41-47,49-54,56-61: 61-Wertham parody	.35	1.00	2.00
48,55-(1973, 1974 Annuals)	.50	1.50	3.00
62-64-145	.35	1.00	2.00
65-($2.95)	.70	2.00	4.00
146	.70	2.00	4.00
Year Book 1968, 1969	.70	2.00	4.00
Year Book 1970-Adams, Ditko-a(r)	.70	2.00	4.00
Annual 1971,1972	.70	2.00	4.00

NOTE: *Above books contain many good artists works: Adams, Brunner, Corben, Craig (Taycee), Crandall, Ditko, Evans, Frazetta, Heath, Jeff Jones, Krenkel, McWilliams, Morrow, Nino, Orlando, Ploog, Severin, Torres, Toth, Williamson, Wood, & Wrightson; covers by Crandall, Davis, Frazetta, Morrow, San Julian, Todd/Bode; Otto Binder's "Adam Link" stories in No. 2, 4, 6, 8, 9, 12, 13, 15 with Orlando art.*

CREEPY THINGS
July, 1975 - No. 6, June, 1976
Charlton Comics

	Good	Fine	N-Mint
1		.50	1.00
2-6		.40	.80

	Good	Fine	N-Mint
Modern Comics Reprint 2-6('77)		.25	.50

NOTE: *Ditko* a-3,5. *Sutton* c-3,4.

CRIME AND JUSTICE (Rookie Cop? No. 27 on)
March, 1951 - No. 26, Sept, 1955
Capitol Stories/Charlton Comics

	Good	Fine	N-Mint
1-Spanking panel	11.50	34.00	80.00
2	2.85	8.50	20.00
3-8,10,11,13: 6-Negligee panels	2.65	8.00	18.00
9-Classic story "Comics Vs. Crime"	6.00	18.00	42.00
12-Bondage-c	3.70	11.00	26.00
14-Color illos in **POP**; gory story of man who beheads women	4.00	12.00	28.00
15-17,19-26	1.70	5.00	12.00
18-Ditko-a	10.00	30.00	70.00

NOTE: *Alascia c-20. Ayers a-17. Shuster a-19-21; c-19. Bondage c-11,12.*

CRIME AND PUNISHMENT (Title inspired by 1935 film)
April, 1948 - No. 74, Aug, 1955
Lev Gleason Publications

	Good	Fine	N-Mint
1-Mr. Crime app. on-c	9.30	28.00	65.00
2	4.00	12.00	28.00
3-Used in **SOTI**, pg. 112; injury-to-eye panel; Fuje-a	5.00	15.00	35.00
4,5	3.15	9.50	22.00
6-10	2.65	8.00	18.00
11-20	2.15	6.50	15.00
21-30	1.70	5.00	12.00
31-38,40-44	1.50	4.50	10.00
39-Drug mention story "The 5 Dopes"	2.85	8.50	20.00
45-"Hophead Killer" drug story	3.25	9.75	22.00
46-One page Frazetta	2.00	6.00	14.00
47-58,60-65,70-74: 58-Used in **POP**, pg. 79	1.30	4.00	9.00
59-Used in **SOTI**, illo-"What comic-book America stands for"	11.00	32.00	75.00
66-Toth c/a(4); 3-D effect issue(3/54)	14.00	42.00	100.00
67-"Monkey on His Back"-heroin story; 3-D effect issue	11.50	34.00	80.00
68-3-D effect issue; Toth-c (7/54)	10.00	30.00	70.00
69-"The Hot Rod Gang"-dope crazy kids	4.35	13.00	30.00

NOTE: *Biro c-most. Everett a-31. Fuje a-3, 12, 13, 17, 18, 26, 27. Guardineer a-2, 3, 10, 14, 17, 18, 26-28, 32, 40-44. Kinstler c-69. McWilliams a-41, 48, 49. Tuska a-28, 30.*

CRIME AND PUNISHMENT MARSHALL LAW TAKES MANHATTAN
1989 ($4.95, color, 52 pgs., direct sale only, mature readers)
Epic Comics (Marvel)

	Good	Fine	N-Mint
nn-Graphic album featuring Marshall Law	.85	2.50	5.00

CRIME CAN'T WIN (Formerly Cindy Smith)
No. 41, 9/50 - No. 43, 2/51; No. 4, 4/51 - No. 12, 9/53
Marvel/Atlas Comics (TCI 41/CCC 42,43,4-12)

	Good	Fine	N-Mint
41(#1)	7.00	21.00	50.00
42	3.50	10.50	24.00
43-Horror story	4.00	12.00	28.00
4(4/51), 5-9,11,12	3.00	9.00	21.00
10-Possible use in **SOTI**, pg. 161	3.00	9.00	21.00

NOTE: *Robinson a-9-11. Tuska a-43.*

CRIME CASES COMICS (Formerly Willie Comics)
No. 24, 8/50 - No. 27, 3/51; No. 5, 5/51 - No. 12, 7/52
Marvel/Atlas Comics(CnPC No.24-8/MJMC No.9-12)

	Good	Fine	N-Mint
24 (52 pgs.)	4.00	12.00	28.00
25,26	2.65	8.00	18.00
27-Morisi-a	2.65	8.00	18.00
5-12: 11-Robinson-a, 12-Tuska-a	2.30	7.00	16.00

CRIME CLINIC
No. 10, July-Aug, 1951 - No. 5, Summer, 1952

CRIME CLINIC (continued)
Ziff-Davis Publishing Co.

	Good	Fine	N-Mint
10-Painted-c; origin Dr. Tom Rogers	10.00	30.00	70.00
11,4,5-Painted-c	6.50	19.50	45.00
3-Used in SOTI, pg. 18	6.50	19.50	45.00

NOTE: Painted covers by Saunders. Starr a-10.

CRIME DETECTIVE COMICS
Mar-Apr, 1948 - V3/8, May-June, 1953
Hillman Periodicals

	Good	Fine	N-Mint
V1#1-The Invisible 6, costumed villains app; Fuje-c	7.00	21.00	50.00
2	2.85	8.50	20.00
3,4,7,10-12	2.30	7.00	16.00
5-Krigstein-a	3.50	10.50	24.00
6-McWilliams-a	2.30	7.00	16.00
8-Kirbyish-a by McCann	2.85	8.50	20.00
9-Used in SOTI, pg. 16 & "Caricature of the author in a position comic book publishers wish he were in permanently" illo.	11.50	34.00	80.00
V2#1,4,7-Krigstein-a	2.85	8.50	20.00
2,3,5,6,8-12 (1-2/52)	1.70	5.00	12.00
V3#1-Drug use-c	2.00	6.00	14.00
2-8	1.50	4.50	10.00

NOTE: Briefer a-V3#1. Kinstlerish -a by McCann-V2#7, V3#2. Powell a-11.

CRIME DETECTOR
Jan, 1954 - No. 5, Sept, 1954
Timor Publications

	Good	Fine	N-Mint
1	5.70	17.00	40.00
2	2.85	8.50	20.00
3,4	2.65	8.00	18.00
5-Disbrow-a (classic)	7.00	21.00	50.00

CRIME DOES NOT PAY (Formerly Silver Streak Comics No. 1-21)
No. 22, June, 1942 - No. 147, July, 1955 (1st crime comic)
Comic House/Lev Gleason/Golfing (Title inspired by film)

	Good	Fine	N-Mint
22(23 on cover, 22 on indicia)-Origin The War Eagle & only app.; Chip Gardner begins; No. 22 rebound in Complete Book of True Crime (Scarce)	82.00	245.00	575.00
23 (Scarce)	46.00	140.00	325.00
24-Intro. & 1st app. Mr. Crime (Scarce)	38.00	115.00	270.00
25-30	21.00	62.00	145.00
31-40	12.00	36.00	84.00
41-Origin & 1st app. Officer Common Sense	8.00	24.00	56.00
42-Electrocution-c	9.30	28.00	65.00
43-46,48-50: 44,45,50 are 68 pg. issues	6.50	19.50	45.00
47-Electric chair-c	9.30	28.00	65.00
51-62,65-70	3.50	10.50	24.00
63,64-Possible use in SOTI, pg. 306. #63-Contains Biro-Gleason's self censorship code of 12 listed restrictions (5/48)	3.50	10.50	24.00
71-99: 87-Chip Gardner begins, ends #99	2.30	7.00	16.00
100	2.65	8.00	18.00
101-104,107-110: 102-Chip Gardner app.	1.70	5.00	12.00
105-Used in POP, pg. 84	1.70	5.00	12.00
106,114-Frazetta, 1 pg.	2.00	6.00	14.00
111-Used in POP, pgs. 80,81 & injury-to-eye story illo	1.70	5.00	12.00
112,113,115-130	1.30	4.00	9.00
131-140	1.15	3.50	8.00
141,142-Last pre-code issue; Kubert-a(1)	2.30	7.00	16.00
143-147-Kubert-a, one each	2.30	7.00	16.00
144-146	1.00	3.00	7.00
1(Golfing-1945)	1.50	4.50	10.00
The Best of... (1944, 128 pgs.)-Series contains 4 rebound issues	28.00	85.00	200.00

	Good	Fine	N-Mint
...1945 issue	24.00	73.00	170.00
...1946-48 issues	20.00	60.00	140.00
...1949-50 issues	15.00	45.00	105.00
...1951-53 issues	13.50	40.00	90.00

NOTE: Many issues contain violent covers and stories. Who Dunnit by Guardineer-39-42, 44-105, 108-110; Chip Gardner by Bob Fujitani (Fuje)-88-103. Alderman a-29, 41-44, 49. Dan Barry a-75. Biro c-1-76, 122, 142. Briefer a-29(2), 30, 33, 37, 39. Fuje c-88, 89, 91-94, 96, 98, 99, 102, 103. Guardineer a-71. Kubert c-143. Landau-a-118. Maurer a-29, 39, 41, 42. McWilliams a-91, 93, 95, 100-103. Palais a-30, 33, 37, 39, 41-43, 44(2), 46, 49. Powell a-146, 147. Tuska a-50(2), 51, 52, 56, 57(2), 60, 61, 63, 64, 66, 67, 71. Painted c-87-102. Bondage c-43, 62, 98.

CRIME EXPOSED
June, 1948; Dec, 1950 - No. 14, June, 1952
Marvel Comics (PPI)/Marvel Atlas Comics (PrPI)

	Good	Fine	N-Mint
1(6/48)	8.50	25.50	60.00
1(12/50)	5.00	15.00	35.00
2	2.85	8.50	20.00
3-9,11,14	2.15	6.50	15.00
10-Used in POP, pg. 81	2.15	6.50	15.00
12-Krigstein & Robinson-a	2.30	7.00	16.00
13-Used in POP, pg. 81; Krigstein-a	2.85	8.50	20.00

NOTE: Maneely c-8. Robinson a-11,12. Tuska a-3, 4.

CRIMEFIGHTERS
April, 1948 - No. 10, Nov, 1949
Marvel Comics (CmPS 1-3/CCC 4-10)

	Good	Fine	N-Mint
1-Some copies are undated & could be reprints	7.00	21.00	50.00
2	3.00	9.00	21.00
3-Morphine addict story	3.00	9.00	21.00
4-10: 6-Anti-Wertham editorial. 9,10-Photo-c	2.30	7.00	16.00

CRIME FIGHTERS (...Always Win)
No. 11, Sept, 1954 - No. 13, Jan, 1955
Atlas Comics (CnPC)

	Good	Fine	N-Mint
11,12: 11-Maneely-a	2.65	8.00	18.00
13-Pakula, Reinman, Severin-a	2.85	8.50	20.00

CRIME FIGHTING DETECTIVE (Shock Detective Cases No. 20 on; formerly Criminals on the Run?)
No. 11, Apr-May, 1950 - No. 19, June, 1952
Star Publications

	Good	Fine	N-Mint
11-L. B. Cole c/a, 2pgs.	3.50	10.50	24.00
12,13,15-19: 17-Young King Cole & Dr. Doom app.; L. B. Cole-c on all	2.65	8.00	18.00
14-L. B. Cole-c/a, r-/Law-Crime No. 2	3.50	10.00	24.00

CRIME FILES
No. 5, Sept, 1952 - No. 6, Nov, 1952
Standard Comics

	Good	Fine	N-Mint
5-Alex Toth-a; used in SOTI, pg. 4 (text)	9.30	28.00	65.00
6-Sekowsky-a	4.00	12.00	28.00

CRIME ILLUSTRATED (Magazine, 25 cents)
Nov-Dec, 1955 - No. 2, Spring, 1956 (Adult Suspense Stories on-c)
E. C. Comics

	Good	Fine	N-Mint
1-Ingels & Crandall-a	7.00	21.00	50.00
2-Ingels & Crandall-a	5.70	17.00	40.00

NOTE: Craig a-2. Crandall a-1, 2; c-2. Evans a-1. Davis a-2. Ingels a-1, 2. Krigstein/Crandall a-1, 2; c-1.

CRIME INCORPORATED (Formerly Crimes Incorporated)
No. 2, Aug, 1950; No. 3, Aug, 1951
Fox Features Syndicate

	Good	Fine	N-Mint
2	7.00	21.00	50.00
3(1951)-Hollingsworth-a	4.50	14.00	32.00

CRIME MACHINE (Magazine)
Feb, 1971 - No. 2, May, 1971 (B&W)

Crime Detective V1#3, © HILL

Crime Does Pay #45, © LEV

Crime Illustrated #2, © WMG

Crime Must Pay The Penalty #47, © ACE

Crime Patrol #16, © WMG

Crimes By Women #6, © FOX

CRIME MACHINE (continued)
Skywald Publications

	Good	Fine	N-Mint
1-Kubert-a(2)(r)(Avon)	1.15	3.50	8.00
2-Torres, Wildey-a; violent c/a	1.15	3.50	8.00

CRIME MUST LOSE! (Formerly Sports Action?)
No. 4, Oct, 1950 - No. 12, April, 1952
Sports Action (Atlas Comics)

	Good	Fine	N-Mint
4-Ann Brewster-a in all; c-used in N.Y. Legis. Comm. documents			
	5.00	15.00	35.00
5-10,12: 9-Robinson-a	2.65	8.00	18.00
11-Used in POP, pg. 89	2.65	8.00	18.00

CRIME MUST PAY THE PENALTY (Formerly Four Favorites;
Penalty No. 47,48)
No. 33, 2/48; No. 2, 6/48 - No. 48, 1/56
Ace Magazines (Current Books)

	Good	Fine	N-Mint
33(2/48)-Becomes Four Teeners #34?	9.30	28.00	65.00
2(6/48)-Extreme violence; Palais-a?	5.70	17.00	40.00
3-'Frisco Mary' story used in Senate Investigation report, pg. 7			
	3.00	9.00	21.00
4,8-Transvestism story	5.00	15.00	35.00
5-7,9,10	2.30	7.00	16.00
11-20	1.70	5.00	12.00
21-32,34-40,42-48	1.50	4.50	10.00
33(7/53)-''Dell Fabry-Junk King''-drug story; mentioned in Love and			
Death	3.00	9.00	21.00
41-Drug story-''Dealers in White Death''	3.00	9.00	21.00

NOTE: Cameron a-30-32,34,39-41. Colan a-20, 31. Kremer a-3, 37r. Palais a-2?, 5?, 37.

CRIME MUST STOP
October, 1952 (52 pgs.)
Hillman Periodicals

	Good	Fine	N-Mint
V1#1(Scarce)-Similar to Monster Crime; Mort Lawrence-a			
	27.00	81.00	190.00

CRIME MYSTERIES (Secret Mysteries No. 16 on; combined with
Crime Smashers No. 7 on)
May, 1952 - No. 15, Sept, 1954
Ribage Publishing Corp. (Trojan Magazines)

	Good	Fine	N-Mint
1-Transvestism story	20.00	60.00	140.00
2-Marijuana story (7/52)	11.50	34.00	80.00
3-One pg. Frazetta	8.50	25.50	60.00
4-Cover shows girl in bondage having her blood drained; 1 pg.			
Frazetta	18.00	54.00	125.00
5-10	8.50	25.50	60.00
11,12,14	7.00	21.00	50.00
13-Angelo Torres 1st comic work; Check-a	10.00	30.00	70.00
15-Acid in face-c	13.00	40.00	90.00

NOTE: Fass c-4. Hollingsworth a-10-12, 15; c-12, 15. Kiefer a-4. Woodbridge a-13. Bondage-c-1, 8, 12.

CRIME ON THE RUN (See Approved Comics)
No. 8, 1949
St. John Publishing Co.

	Good	Fine	N-Mint
8 (Exist?)	3.00	9.00	21.00

CRIME ON THE WATERFRONT (Formerly Famous Gangsters)
No. 4, May, 1952 (Painted cover)
Realistic Publications

	Good	Fine	N-Mint
4	12.00	36.00	84.00

CRIME PATROL (International #1-5; International Crime Patrol #6,
becomes Crypt of Terror #17 on)
No. 7, Summer, 1948 - No. 16, Feb-Mar, 1950
E. C. Comics

	Good	Fine	N-Mint
7-Intro. Captain Crime	31.00	92.00	215.00
8-14: 12-Ingels-a	27.00	81.00	190.00
15-Intro. of Crypt Keeper (inspired by Witches Tales radio show) &			

	Good	Fine	N-Mint
Crypt of Terror; used by N.Y. Legis. Comm.-last pg. Feldstein-a			
	66.00	197.00	460.00
16-2nd Crypt Keeper app.	54.00	163.00	380.00

NOTE: Craig c/a in most.

CRIME PHOTOGRAPHER (See Casey . . .)

CRIME REPORTER
Aug, 1948 - No. 3, Dec, 1948 (Shows Oct.)
St. John Publ. Co.

1-Drug club story	17.00	51.00	120.00
2-Used in SOTI: illo-''Children told me what the man was going to			
do with the red-hot poker;'' r-/Dynamic #17 with editing;			
Baker-c; Tuska-a	34.00	103.00	240.00
3-Baker-c; Tuska-a	13.00	40.00	90.00

CRIMES BY WOMEN
June, 1948 - No. 15, Aug, 1951; 1954
Fox Features Syndicate

1	43.00	130.00	300.00
2	22.00	65.00	154.00
3-Used in SOTI, pg. 234	22.00	65.00	154.00
4,5,7,9,11-15	20.00	60.00	140.00
6-Classic girl fight-c; acid-in-face panel	23.00	70.00	160.00
8-Used in POP	20.00	60.00	140.00
10-Used in POP, pg. 72	20.00	60.00	140.00
54(M.S. Publ.-'54)-Reprint; (formerly My Love Secret)			
	9.00	27.00	62.00

CRIMES INCORPORATED (Formerly My Past)
No. 12, June, 1950 (Crime Incorporated No. 2 on)
Fox Features Syndicate

12	4.30	13.00	30.00

CRIMES INCORPORATED (See Fox Giants)

CRIME SMASHER
Summer, 1948 (One Shot)
Fawcett Publications

1 (Spy Smasher)	15.00	45.00	105.00

CRIME SMASHERS (Secret Mysteries No. 16 on)
Oct, 1950 - No. 15, Mar, 1953
Ribage Publishing Corp.(Trojan Magazines)

1-Used in SOTI, pg. 19,20, & illo-''A girl raped and murdered;''			
Sally the Sleuth begins	30.00	90.00	210.00
2-Kubert-c	14.00	42.00	100.00
3,4	11.50	34.00	80.00
5-Wood-a	17.00	51.00	120.00
6,8-11	9.00	27.00	62.00
7-Female heroin junkie story	10.00	30.00	70.00
12-Injury to eye panel; 1pg. Frazetta	11.00	32.00	75.00
13-Used in POP, pgs. 79,80; 1pg. Frazetta	9.00	27.00	62.00
14,15	9.00	27.00	62.00

NOTE: Hollingsworth a-14. Kiefer a-15. Bondage c-7, 9.

CRIME SUSPENSTORIES (Formerly Vault of Horror No. 12-14)
No. 15, Oct-Nov, 1950 - No. 27, Feb-Mar, 1955
E. C. Comics

15-Identical to #1 in content; #1 printed on outside front cover. #15 (formerly ''The Vault of Horror'') printed and blackened out on inside front cover with Vol. 1, No. 1 printed over it. Evidently, several of No. 15 were printed before a decision was made not to drop the Vault of Horror and Haunt of Fear series. The print run was stopped on No. 15 and continued on No. 1. All of No. 15 were changed as described above.

1	70.00	210.00	495.00
2	55.00	165.00	385.00
3-5	34.00	100.00	235.00
6-10	23.00	70.00	160.00
11,12,14,15	17.00	51.00	120.00
	12.00	36.00	84.00

CRIME SUSPENSTORIES (continued)

	Good	Fine	N-Mint
13,16-Williamson-a	15.00	45.00	105.00
17-Williamson/Frazetta-a, 6 pgs.	17.00	52.00	120.00
18	10.00	30.00	70.00
19-Used in SOTI, pg. 235	10.00	30.00	70.00
20-Cover used in SOTI, illo-"Cover of a children's comic book"	13.00	40.00	90.00
21,25-27	7.00	21.00	50.00
22,23-Used in Senate investigation on juvenile delinquency. 22-Ax decapitation-c	11.00	33.00	76.00
24-'Food For Thought' similar to 'Cave In' in Amazing Detective Cases #13 ('52)	7.00	21.00	50.00

NOTE: *Craig a-1-21; c-1-18,20-22. Crandall a-18-26. Davis a-4, 5, 7, 9-12, 20. Elder a-17, 18. Evans a-15, 19, 21, 23, 25, 27; c-23, 24. Feldstein c-19. Ingels a-1-12, 14, 15, 27. Kamen a-2, 4-18, 20-27; c-25-27. Krigstein a-22, 24, 25, 27. Kurtzman a-1, 3. Orlando a-16, 22, 24, 26. Wood a-1, 3.* Issues No. 11-15 have E. C. "quickie" stories. No. 25 contains the famous "Are You a Red Dupe?" editorial.

CRIMINALS ON THE RUN (Formerly Young King Cole)
(Crime Fighting Detective No. 11 on?)
V4#1, Aug-Sept, 1948 - #10, Dec-Jan, 1949-50
Premium Group (Novelty Press)

	Good	Fine	N-Mint
V4#1-Young King Cole continues	7.00	21.00	50.00
2-6: 6-Dr. Doom app.	5.50	16.50	38.00
7-Classic "Fish in the Face" cover by L. B. Cole	13.00	40.00	90.00
V5#1,2 (#8,9)	5.50	16.50	38.00
10-L. B. Cole-c	5.50	16.50	38.00

NOTE: Most issues have *L. B. Cole* covers. *McWilliams* a-V4#6,7, V5#2; c-V4#5.

CRIMSON AVENGER, THE (See Detective Comics #20 for 1st app.)
(Also see Leading Comics #1 & World's Best/Finest Comics)
June, 1988 - No. 4, Sept, 1988 ($1.00, color, limited series)
DC Comics

1-4		.50	1.00

CRISIS ON INFINITE EARTHS (See Official . . . Index)
Apr, 1985 - No. 12, Mar, 1986 (12 issue maxi-series)
DC Comics

1-1st DC app. Blue Beetle & Detective Karp from Charlton; Perez-c on all	.70	2.00	4.00
2	.50	1.50	3.00
3	.40	1.25	2.50
4-6: 6-Intro Charlton's Capt. Atom, Nightshade, Question, Judomaster, Peacemaker & Thunderbolt	.35	1.00	2.00
7-Double size; death of Supergirl	.40	1.25	2.50
8-Death of Flash	.40	1.25	2.50
9-11: 9-Intro. Charlton's Ghost. 10-Intro. Charlton's Banshee, Dr. Spectro, Image, Punch & Jewellee	.35	1.00	2.00
12-Double size; deaths of Dove, Kole, Lori Lemaris, Sunburst, G.A. Robin & Huntress; Kid Flash becomes new Flash	.50	1.50	3.00

CRITICAL MASS (Graphic Album)
Jan, 1990 - No. 7, July, 1990 ($4.95, limited series, 68 pgs.)
Epic Comics (Marvel) (#1 shows Jan, 1989 by mistake)

1-4: Dr. Zero, Powerline, St. George; Morrow-i	.85	2.50	5.00

CRITTERS (Also see Usagi Yojimbo Summer Special)
1986 - No. 50, 1990 ($1.70/$2.00, B&W)
Fantagraphics Books

1-Cutey Bunny, Usagi Yojimbo app.	1.15	3.50	7.00
2	.70	2.00	4.00
3-Usagi Yojimbo app.	.50	1.50	3.00
4-10: 10-Usagi Yojimbo app.	.40	1.25	2.50
11-Christmas Special (68 pgs.); Usagi Yojimbo	.60	1.75	3.50
12-22,24-49: 14,38-Usagi Yojimbo app. 22-Watchmen parody; two diff. covers exist	.35	1.00	2.00
23-With Alan Moore Flexi-disc ($3.95)	.70	2.00	4.00

	Good	Fine	N-Mint
50 ($4.95, 84 pgs.)-Neil the Horse, Capt. Jack	.85	2.50	5.00
Special 1 (1/88, $2.00)	.35	1.00	2.00

CROSLEY'S HOUSE OF FUN (Also see Tee and Vee Crosley. . .)
1950 (32 pgs.; full color; paper cover)
Crosley Div. AVCO Mfg. Corp. (Giveaway)

Strips revolve around Crosley appliances	1.70	5.00	10.00

CROSS AND THE SWITCHBLADE, THE
1972 (35-49 cents)
Spire Christian Comics/Fleming H. Revell Co.

1(Some issues have nn)		.40	.80

CROSSFIRE
1973 (39,49cents)
Spire Christian Comics (Fleming H. Revell Co.)

nn		.40	.80

CROSSFIRE
5/84 - No. 17, 3/86; No. 18, 1/87 - No. 26, 2/88 (Baxter paper)
Eclipse Comics

1-DNAgents x-over; Spiegle c/a begins	.30	.90	1.80
2-17: 12,13-Death of Marilyn Monroe; 12-Stevens-c	.25	.75	1.50
18-26 (B&W)	.30	.90	1.80

CROSSFIRE AND RAINBOW
June, 1986 - No. 4, Sept, 1986 (mini-series)
Eclipse Comics

1-3: Spiegle-a		.65	1.30
4-Dave Stevens-c	.35	1.00	2.00

CROSSING THE ROCKIES (See Classics Illustrated Special Issue)

CROSSROADS
July, 1988 - No. 5, Nov., 1988 ($3.25, color, deluxe)
First Comics

1-5	.55	1.60	3.25

CROW, THE
Feb, 1989 - No. 5, 1990? ($1.95, B&W, mini-series)
Caliber Press

1	1.35	4.00	8.00
1,2-2nd printings	.35	1.00	2.00
2	.85	2.50	5.00
3-5	.35	1.00	2.00

CROWN COMICS
Winter, 1944-45 - No. 19, July, 1949
Golfing/McCombs Publ.

1-"The Oblong Box"-Poe adaptation	16.00	47.00	110.00
2,3-Baker-a	9.30	28.00	65.00
4-6-Baker c/a; Voodah app. #4,5	9.30	28.00	65.00
7-Feldstein, Baker, Kamen-a; Baker-c	8.00	24.00	56.00
8-Baker-a; Voodah app.	8.00	24.00	56.00
9-11,13-19: Voodah in #10-19	4.30	13.00	30.00
12-Feldstein?, Starr-a	5.00	15.00	35.00

NOTE: *Bolle* a-11, 13-16, 18, 19; c-11p, 15. *Powell* a-19. *Starr* a-11-13; c-11i

CRUSADER FROM MARS (See Tops in Adventure)
Jan-Mar, 1952 - No. 2, Fall, 1952
Ziff-Davis Publ. Co.

1	32.00	95.00	225.00
2-Bondage-c	24.00	72.00	170.00

CRUSADER RABBIT (See 4-Color No. 735,805)

CRUSADERS, THE
1974 - Vol. 16, 1985 (36 pg.) (39-69 cents) (Religious)
Chick Publications

Crime Suspenstories #16, © WMG   Crown Comics #1, © Golfing   Crusader From Mars #2, © Z-D

Crypt Of Terror #17, © WMG

Cyclone Comics #1, © Bilbara Publ.

Dagar, Desert Hawk #20, © FOX

	Good	Fine	N-Mint
THE CRUSADERS (continued)			

Vol. 1-Operation Bucharest('74). Vol. 2-The Broken Cross('74). Vol. 3-Scarface('74). Vol. 4-Exorcists('75). Vol. 5-Chaos('75).

each....		.40	.80

Vol. 6-Primal Man?('76)-(Disputes evolution theory). Vol. 7-The Ark-(Claims proof of existence, destroyed by Bolsheviks). Vol. 8-The Gift-(Life story of Christ). Vol. 9-Angel of Light-(Story of the Devil). Vol. 10-Spellbound?-(Tells how rock music is Satanical & produced by witches). 11-Sabotage?. 12-Alberto. 13-Double-Cross 14-The Godfathers. (No. 6-14 low in distribution; Loaded in religious propaganda.). 15-The Force. 16-The Four Horsemen

		.40	.80

CRUSADERS (Southern Knights No. 2 on)
1982 (Magazine size, B&W)
Guild Publications

1-1st app. Southern Knights	3.35	10.00	20.00

CRYING FREEMAN
1989 - Present ($3.50, B&W)
Viz Comics

1-3: Japanese manga	.60	1.75	3.50

CRYIN' LION, THE
Fall, 1944 - No. 3, Spring, 1945
William H. Wise Co.

1-Funny animal	6.00	18.00	42.00
2,3	3.50	10.50	24.00

CRYPT OF SHADOWS
Jan, 1973 - No. 21, Nov, 1975
Marvel Comics Group

1-Wolverton-a r-/Advs. Into Terror No. 7	.30	.60
2-21		.50

NOTE: *Briefer* a-2r. *Ditko* a-13r, 18-20r. *Everett* a-6, 14r; c-2i. *Heath* a-1r. *Mort Lawrence* a-1r. *Maneely* a-2r. *Moldoff* a-8. *Powell* a-12r, 14r.

CRYPT OF TERROR (Tales From the Crypt No. 20 on; formerly Crime Patrol)
No. 17, Apr-May, 1950 - No. 19, Aug-Sept, 1950
E. C. Comics

17-1st New Trend to hit stands	77.00	230.00	540.00
18,19	57.00	170.00	400.00

NOTE: *Craig* c/a-17-19. *Feldstein* a-17-19. *Ingels* a-19. *Kurtzman* a-18. *Wood* a-18. Canadian reprints known; see Table of Contents.

CUPID
Jan, 1950 - No. 2, Mar, 1950
Marvel Comics (U.S.A.)

1-Photo-c	4.50	14.00	32.00
2-Betty Page photo-c (see My Love #4, Miss America #4)			
	7.00	21.00	50.00

CURIO
1930's(?) (Tabloid size, 16-20 pages)
Harry 'A' Chesler

nn	5.70	17.00	40.00

CURLY KAYOE COMICS
1946 - No. 8, 1950; Jan, 1958
United Features Syndicate/Dell Publ. Co.

1 (1946)	6.50	19.50	45.00
2	3.00	9.00	21.00
3-8	2.15	6.50	15.00
United Presents... (Fall, 1948)	2.15	6.50	15.00
4-Color 871 (Dell, 1/58)	1.70	5.00	12.00

CUSTER'S LAST FIGHT
1950
Avon Periodicals

	Good	Fine	N-Mint
nn-Partial reprint of Cowpuncher #1	8.50	25.50	60.00

CUTEY BUNNY (See Army Surplus Komikz Featuring...)

CUTIE PIE
May, 1955 - No. 3, Dec, 1955; No. 4, Feb, 1956; No. 5, Aug, 1956
Junior Reader's Guild (Lev Gleason)

1	2.30	7.00	16.00
2-5: 4-Misdated 2/55	1.30	4.00	9.00

CYBERPUNK
Sept, 1989 - No. 2, Oct?, 1989 ($1.95, color, mini-series, 28 pgs.)
Innovation Publishing

1,2-Both have Ken Steacy painted-c (Adults)	.35	1.00	2.00

CYBER 7
3/89 - #7, 9/89; V2#1, 10?/89 - Present ($2.00, B&W)
Eclipse Comics

1-7: Stories translated from Japanese	.35	1.00	2.00
Book Two, #1-3	.35	1.00	2.00

CYCLONE COMICS (Also see Whirlwind Comics)
June, 1940 - No. 5, Nov, 1940
Bilbara Publishing Co.

1-Origin Tornado Tom; Volton begins, Mister Q app.			
	43.00	130.00	300.00
2	22.00	65.00	154.00
3-5: 4,5-Mr. Q app.	17.00	51.00	120.00

CYNTHIA DOYLE, NURSE IN LOVE (Formerly Sweetheart Diary)
No. 66, Oct, 1962 - No. 74, Feb, 1964
Charlton Publications

66-74 (#74, exist?)	.40	1.25	2.50

DAFFY (...Duck No. 18 on)(See Looney Tunes)
#457, 3/53 - #30, 7-9/62; #31, 10-12/62 - #145, 1983 (No #132,133)
Dell Publishing Co./Gold Key No. 31-127/Whitman No. 128 on

4-Color 457-Elmer Fudd x-overs begin	2.15	6.50	15.00
4-Color 536,615('55)	1.50	4.50	10.00
4(1-3/56)-11('57)	1.15	3.50	8.00
12-19(1958-59)	.85	2.50	6.00
20-40(1960-64)	.70	2.00	4.00
41-60(1964-68)	.35	1.00	2.00
61-90(1969-73)-Road Runner in most		.60	1.20
91-131,134-145(1974-83)		.40	.80
Mini-Comic 1 (1976; 3¼x6½'')		.25	.50

NOTE: Reprint issues-No.41-46, 48, 50, 53-55, 58, 59, 65, 67, 69, 73, 81, 96, 103-08; 136-142, 144, 145(½-⅔-r). (See March of Comics No. 277, 288, 313, 331, 347, 357, 375, 387, 397, 402, 413, 425, 437, 460).

DAFFYDILS
1911 (52 pgs.; 6x8''; B&W; hardcover)
Cupples & Leon Co.

by Tad	9.00	27.00	62.00

DAFFY TUNES COMICS
June, 1947 - No. 2, Aug, 1947
Four Star Publications

nn	3.50	10.50	24.00
2-Al Fago c/a	2.85	8.50	20.00

DAGAR, DESERT HAWK (Capt. Kidd No. 24-on; formerly All Great)
No. 14, Feb, 1948 - No. 23, Apr, 1949 (No #17,18)
Fox Features Syndicate

14-Tangi & Safari Cary begin; Edmond Good bondage-c/a			
	25.00	75.00	175.00
15,16-E. Good-a; 15-Bondage-c	15.00	45.00	105.00
19,20,22	13.00	40.00	90.00
21-'Bombs & Bums Away' panel in 'Flood of Death' story used in			
SOTI	16.00	48.00	110.00

DAGAR, DESERT HAWK (continued)	Good	Fine	N-Mint
23-Bondage-c	15.00	45.00	105.00

NOTE: *Tangi by Kamen-14-16, 19, 20; c-20, 21.*

DAGAR THE INVINCIBLE (Tales of Sword & Sorcery. . .) (Also see
Dan Curtis & Gold Key Spotlight)
10/72 - No. 18, 12/76; No. 19, 4/82
Gold Key

1-Origin; intro. Villains Olstellon & Scorpio	1.15	3.50	7.00
2-5: 3-Intro. Graylin, Dagar's woman; Jarn x-over			
	.60	1.75	3.50
6-1st Dark Gods story	.40	1.25	2.50
7-10: 9-Intro. Torgus. 10-1st Three Witches sty	.40	1.25	2.50
11-18: 13-Durak & Torgus x-over; story continues in Dr. Spektor			
#15. 14-Dagar's origin retold. 18-Origin retold		.70	1.40
19-Origin-r/#18		.40	.80

NOTE: *Durak app.-7,12,13. Tragg app.-5,11.*

DAGWOOD (Chic Young's) (Also see Blondie Comics)
Sept, 1950 - No. 140, Nov, 1965
Harvey Publications

1	7.00	21.00	50.00
2	3.50	10.50	25.00
3-10	3.00	9.00	21.00
11-30	1.70	5.00	12.00
31-70	1.00	3.00	6.00
71-100	.85	2.50	5.00
101-128,130,135	.70	2.00	4.00
129,131-134,136-140-All are 68-pg. issues	1.00	3.00	6.00

NOTE: *Popeye and other one page strips appeared in early issues.*

DAGWOOD SPLITS THE ATOM (Also see Topix V8No.4)
1949 (Science comic with King Features characters) (Giveaway)
King Features Syndicate

nn-½ comic, ½ text; Popeye, Olive Oyl, Henry, Mandrake, Little			
King, Katzenjammer Kids app.	3.00	9.00	21.00

DAI KAMIKAZE!
June, 1987 - No. 12, Aug, 1988 ($1.75, color)
Now Comics

1-1st app. Speed Racer	.50	1.50	3.00
1-2nd print	.25	.70	1.40
2-12	.25	.75	1.50

DAISY AND DONALD (See Walt Disney Showcase No. 8)
May, 1973 - No. 59, 1984 (no No. 48)
Gold Key/Whitman No. 42 on

1-Barks r-/WDCS 280,308	.50	1.50	3.00
2-5: 4-Barks r-/WDCS 224	.35	1.00	2.00
6-10	.25	.75	1.50
11-20		.50	1.00
21-47,49,50: 32-r-/WDC&S 308. 50-r-/No. 3		.40	.80
51-Barks r-/4-Color 1150		.50	1.00
52-59: 52-r-/No. 2. 55-r-/No. 5		.35	.70

DAISY & HER PUPS (Blondie's Dogs)
No. 21, 7/51 - No. 27, 7/52; No. 8, 9/52 - No. 25, 7/55
Harvey Publications

21-27 (#1-7): 26,27 have No. 6 & 7 on cover but No. 26 & 27 on			
inside	1.00	3.00	6.00
8-25: 19-25-Exist?	.85	2.50	5.00

DAISY COMICS
Dec, 1936 (Small size: 5¼x7½'')
Eastern Color Printing Co.

Joe Palooka, Buck Rogers (2 pgs. from Famous Funnies No. 18),			
Napoleon Flying to Fame, Butty & Fally	16.00	48.00	110.00

DAISY DUCK & UNCLE SCROOGE PICNIC TIME (See Dell Giant #33)

DAISY DUCK & UNCLE SCROOGE SHOW BOAT (See Dell Giant #55)

DAISY DUCK'S DIARY (See Dynabrite Comics, Four Color No. 600,659,743,
858,948,1055,1150,1247 & Walt Disney's Comics & Stories #298)

DAISY HANDBOOK
1946; No. 2, 1948 (132 pgs.)(10 cents)(Pocket-size)
Daisy Manufacturing Co.

	Good	Fine	N-Mint
1-Buck Rogers, Red Ryder	17.00	51.00	120.00
2-Captain Marvel & Ibis the Invincible, Red Ryder, Boy Commandos			
& Robotman; 2 pgs. Wolverton-a; contains 8pg. color catalog			
	17.00	51.00	120.00

DAISY LOW OF THE GIRL SCOUTS
1954, 1965 (16 pgs.; paper cover)
Girl Scouts of America

1954-Story of Juliette Gordon Low	2.15	6.50	15.00
1965	.70	2.00	4.00

DAISY MAE (See Oxydol-Dreft)

DAISY'S RED RYDER GUN BOOK
1955 (132 pages)(25 cents)(Pocket-size)
Daisy Manufacturing Co.

Boy Commandos, Red Ryder, 1 pg. Wolverton-a			
	11.50	34.00	80.00

DAKOTA LIL (See Fawcett Movie Comics)

DAKOTA NORTH
1986 - No. 5, Feb, 1987
Marvel Comics Group

1-5		.40	.80

DAKTARI (Ivan Tors) (TV)
7/67 - No. 3, 10/68; No. 4, 9/69 (Photo-c)
Dell Publishing Co.

1	1.70	5.00	12.00
2-4	1.15	3.50	8.00

DALE EVANS COMICS (Also see Queen of the West. . .)
Sept-Oct, 1948 - No. 24, July-Aug, 1952 (No. 1-19: 52 pgs.)
National Periodical Publications

1-Dale Evans & her horse Buttermilk begin; Sierra Smith begins by			
Alex Toth	23.00	70.00	160.00
2-Alex Toth-a	14.00	42.00	100.00
3-11-Alex Toth-a	12.00	36.00	85.00
12-24	6.50	19.50	45.00

NOTE: *Photo-c-1, 2, 4-14.*

DALGODA
Aug, 1984 - No. 8, Feb, 1986 (Color, high quality paper)
Fantagraphics Books

1-($2.25 cover price). Fujitake c/a in all	.50	1.50	3.00
2-8-($1.50). 2,3-Debut Grimwood's Daughter. 8-Alan Moore story			
	.35	1.00	2.00

DALTON BOYS, THE
1951
Avon Periodicals

1-(No. on spine)-Kinstler-c	8.50	25.50	60.00

DAMAGE CONTROL
May, 1989 - No. 4, Aug, 1989 ($1.00, color, mini-series)
Marvel Comics

1-4: 4-Wolverine app.		.60	1.20

DAMAGE CONTROL
Dec, 1989 - No. 4, March, 1990 ($1.00, color, mini-series)
Marvel Comics

1,2: 2-Punisher app.	.25	.75	1.50
3,4		.50	1.00

Dagwood #8, © KING

Dale Evans Comics #19, © DC

Damage Control #1, © MEG

Danger Is Our Business #1, © TOBY

Dan'l Boone #2, © Sussex

Daredevil #7, © MEG

DAN CURTIS GIVEAWAYS
1974 (24 pages) (3x6'') (in color, all reprints)
Western Publishing Co.

	Good	Fine	N-Mint
1-Dark Shadows, 2-Star Trek, 3-The Twilight Zone, 4-Ripley's Believe It or Not!, 5-Turok, Son of Stone, 6-Star Trek, 7-The Occult Files of Dr. Spektor, 8-Dagar the Invincible, 9-Grimm's Ghost Stories Set...	.50	1.50	3.00

DANDEE
1947
Four Star Publications

	Good	Fine	N-Mint
nn	2.65	8.00	18.00

DAN DUNN (See Crackajack Funnies, Detective Dan & Red Ryder)

DANDY COMICS (Also see Happy Jack Howard)
Spring, 1947 - No. 7, Spring, 1948
E. C. Comics

1-Vince Fago-a in all	17.00	51.00	120.00
2	12.00	36.00	84.00
3-7	10.00	30.00	70.00

DANGER
January, 1953 - No. 11, Aug, 1954
Comic Media/Allen Hardy Assoc.

1-Heck-c/a	5.00	15.00	35.00
2,3,5-7,9-11	2.00	6.00	14.00
4-Marijuana cover/story	5.00	15.00	35.00
8-Bondage/torture/headlights panels	5.50	16.50	38.00

NOTE: *Morisi* a-2,5,6(3); c-2. Contains some-r from Danger & Dynamite.

DANGER (Jim Bowie No. 15 on; formerly Comic Media title)
No. 12, June, 1955 - No. 14, Oct, 1955
Charlton Comics Group

12(#1)	3.50	10.50	24.00
13,14: 14 r-/#12	2.00	6.00	14.00

DANGER
1964
Super Comics

Super Reprint #10-12 (Black Dwarf; #11-r-/from Johnny Danger), #15,16 (Yankee Girl & Johnny Rebel), #17 (Capt. Courage & Enchanted Dagger), #18(nd) (Gun-Master, Annie Oakley, The Chameleon, L.B. Cole-a)	.85	2.50	5.00

DANGER AND ADVENTURE (Formerly This Magazine Is Haunted; Robin Hood and His Merry Men No. 28 on)
No. 22, Feb, 1955 - No. 27, Feb, 1956
Charlton Comics

22-Ibis the Invincible, Nyoka app.	4.00	12.00	28.00
23-Nyoka, Lance O'Casey app.	4.00	12.00	28.00
24-27: 24-Mike Danger & Johnny Adventure begin			
	2.65	8.00	18.00

DANGER IS OUR BUSINESS!
1953(Dec.) - No. 10, June, 1955
Toby Press

1-Captain Comet by Williamson/Frazetta-a, 6 pgs. (Science Fiction)			
	27.00	81.00	190.00
2	3.50	10.50	24.00
3-10	2.85	8.50	20.00
I.W. Reprint #9('64)-Williamson/Frazetta r-/#1; Kinstler-c			
	6.50	19.50	45.00

DANGER IS THEIR BUSINESS (See A-1 Comics No. 50)

DANGER MAN (See 4-Color No. 1231)

DANGER TRAIL (Also see Showcase #50, 51)
July-Aug, 1950 - No. 5, Mar-Apr, 1951 (52 pgs.)
National Periodical Publications

1-King Farraday begins, ends #4; Toth-a	38.00	115.00	265.00
2-Toth-a	28.00	85.00	200.00

	Good	Fine	N-Mint
3-5-Toth-a in all; Johnny Peril app. #5	25.00	75.00	175.00

DANIEL BOONE (See The Exploits of . . ., Fighting . . ., 4-Color No. 1163, Frontier Scout . . ., The Legends of . . . & March of Comics No. 306)

DAN'L BOONE
Sept, 1955 - No. 8, Sept, 1957
Magazine Enterprises/Sussex Publ. Co. No. 2 on

1	4.50	14.00	32.00
2	2.85	8.50	20.00
3-8	2.00	6.00	14.00

DANIEL BOONE (TV) (See March of Comics No. 306)
Jan, 1965 - No. 15, Apr, 1969
Gold Key

1	1.50	4.50	10.00
2-5	.85	2.50	5.00
6-15: 4,6-Fess Parker photo-c	.70	2.00	4.00

DANNY BLAZE (Nature Boy No. 3 on)
Aug, 1955 - No. 2, Oct, 1955
Charlton Comics

1,2	2.65	8.00	18.00

DANNY DINGLE (See Single Series #17 & Sparkler Comics)

DANNY KAYE'S BAND FUN BOOK
1959
H & A Selmer (Giveaway)

nn	2.00	6.00	14.00

DANNY THOMAS SHOW, THE (See 4-Color No. 1180,1249)

DARBY O'GILL & THE LITTLE PEOPLE (See 4-Color No. 1024 & Movie Comics)

DAREDEVIL (. . .& the Black Widow #92-107; see Marvel Advs., Marvel Graphic Novel #24, Marvel Super Heroes, '66 & Spider-Man and . . .)
April, 1964 - Present
Marvel Comics Group

1-Origin Daredevil; r-/in Marvel Super Heroes #1, 1966. Death of Battling Murdock; intro Foggy Nelson & Karen Page			
	75.00	225.00	525.00
2-Fantastic Four cameo	31.00	93.00	215.00
3-Origin, 1st app. The Owl	20.00	60.00	140.00
4,5: 5-Wood-a begins	11.50	34.00	80.00
6,7,9,10: 7-dons new costume	9.30	28.00	65.00
8-Origin & 1st app. Stilt-Man	9.30	28.00	65.00
11-15: 12-Romita's 1st work at Marvel. 13-Facts about Ka-Zar's origin; Kirby-a	5.70	17.00	40.00
16,17-Spider-Man x-over	4.30	13.00	30.00
18-20: 18-Origin & 1st app. Gladiator	3.50	10.50	24.00
21-30	2.65	8.00	18.00
31-40	2.15	6.50	15.00
41-49: 41-Death Mike Murdock. 43-vs. Capt. America			
	1.30	4.00	9.00
50-52-Smith-a	1.60	4.80	11.00
53-Origin retold	1.60	4.80	11.00
54-56,58-60	1.00	3.00	6.00
57-Reveals i.d. to Karen Page	1.15	3.50	7.00
61-99: 62-1st app. Nighthawk. 81-Oversize issue; Black Widow begins	.85	2.50	5.00
100-Origin retold	1.60	4.80	11.00
101-106,108-113,115-120	.35	1.00	2.00
107-Starlin-c	.50	1.50	3.00
114-1st app. Deathstalker	.50	1.50	3.00
121-130,132-137: 124-1st app. Copperhead; Black Widow leaves. 126-1st New Torpedo	.35	1.00	2.00
131-Origin & 1st app. Bullseye	1.00	3.00	6.00

	Good	Fine	N-Mint
DAREDEVIL (continued)			
138-Byrne-a	.50	1.50	3.00
139-157: 142-Nova cameo. 148-30 & 35 cent issues exist. 150-1st app. Paladin. 151-Reveals i.d. to Heather Glenn	.35	1.00	2.00
158-Frank Miller art begins (5/79); origin & death of Deathstalker			
	6.00	18.00	36.00
159	2.50	7.50	15.00
160,161	1.50	4.50	9.00
162-Ditko-a, no Miller	.35	1.00	2.00
163,164: 163-Hulk cameo. 164-Origin	1.35	4.00	8.00
165-167,170	1.00	3.00	6.00
168-Intro/origin Elektra	2.65	8.00	16.00
169-Elektra app.	1.35	4.00	8.00
171-175: 174,175-Elektra app.	.70	2.00	4.00
176-180-Elektra app. 179-Anti-smoking issue mentioned in the Congressional Record	.50	1.50	3.00
181-Double size; death of Elektra	.60	1.75	3.50
182-184-Punisher app. by Miller	1.15	3.50	7.00
185-191: 187-New Black Widow. 189-Death of Stick. 190-Double size; Elektra returns, part origin. 191-Last Miller Daredevil	.25	.75	1.50
192-195,197-210: 208-Harlan Ellison scripts	.60		1.20
196-Wolverine app.	1.00	3.00	6.00
211-225		.50	1.00
226-Frank Miller plots begin	.25	.75	1.50
227-Miller scripts begin	.70	2.00	4.00
228-233-Last Miller script	.35	1.00	2.00
234-240,242-247,250,251,253-256,258,259		.50	1.00
241-Todd McFarlane-a(p)	.35	1.00	2.00
248,249-Wolverine app.	.40	1.25	2.50
252-Double size, 52 pgs. Fall of the Mutants	.40	1.25	2.50
257-Punisher app.	.50	1.50	3.00
260-Double size	.35	1.00	2.00
261-278: 272-Intro Shotgun (villain)		.50	1.00
Giant Size 1 ('75)	.50	1.50	3.00
Special 1(9/67)-new art	1.50	4.50	10.00
Special 2(2/71)(Wood-r), 3(1/72)-r	.85	2.50	5.00
Annual 4(10/76)	.50	1.50	3.00
Annual 4(1989, $2.00, 68 pgs.)-Atlantis Attacks	.40	1.25	2.50

NOTE: *Art Adams* c-238p, 239. *Austin* a-191i; c-151i, 200i. *John Buscema* a-136, 137p, 234p, 235p; c-86p, 136i, 137p, 142, 219. *Byrne* c-200p, 201, 203, 223. *Colan* a(p)-20-49, 53-82, 84-98, 100, 110, 112, 124, 153, 154, 156, 157, Spec. 1p; c(p)-20-42, 44-49, 53-60, 71, 92, 98, 138, 153, 154, 156, 157, Annual 1. *Craig* a-50i, 52i. *Ditko* a-162, 234p, 235p, 264p; c-162. *Everett* a/c-1; inks-21. *Gil Kane* a-141p, 146-148p, 151p; c(p)-85, 90, 91, 93, 94, 115, 116, 119, 120, 125-128, 133, 139, 147, 152. *Kirby* c-2-4, 5p, 12p, 13p, 136p. *Layton* c-202. *Miller* script-168-182, 183(part), 184-191; a-158-161p, 163-184p, 191p; c-158-161p, 163-189, 190p, 191. *Orlando* a-2-4p. *Powell* a-9p, 11p, Special 1r, 2r. *B. Smith* a-83p, 236p. *Smith* c-51p, 52p. *Simonson* c-199. *Starlin* a-105p. *Steranko* c-44i. *Tuska* a-39i, 145p. *Williamson* a-237i, 239i, 240i, 243i, 248-257i, 259-275i; c-237i, 243i, 244i, 248-257i, 259-263i, 265-275i. *Wood* a-5-9i, 10, 11i, Spec. 2i; c-5i, 6-11, 164i.

	Good	Fine	N-Mint
DAREDEVIL AND THE PUNISHER (Child's Play)			
1988 ($4.95, color, squarebound, one-shot)			
Marvel Comics			
1-r/Daredevil #182-184 by Miller	.85	2.50	5.00
Trade Paperback ($4.95)	1.35	4.00	8.00

DAREDEVIL COMICS (See Silver Streak Comics)
July, 1941 - No. 134, Sept, 1956 (Charles Biro stories)
Lev Gleason Publications (Funnies, Inc. No. 1)

(No. 1 titled "Daredevil Battles Hitler")

	Good	Fine	N-Mint
1-The Silver Streak, Lance Hale, Cloud Curtis, Dickey Dean, Pirate Prince team up with Daredevil and battle Hitler; Daredevil battles the Claw; Origin of Hitler feature story. Hitler photo app. on-c	300.00	750.00	1800.00
2-London, Pat Patriot, Nightro, Real American No. 1, Dickie Dean, Pirate Prince, & Times Square begin; intro. & only app. The Pioneer, Champion of America	130.00	390.00	910.00
3-Origin of 13	78.00	238.00	550.00

	Good	Fine	N-Mint
4	64.00	193.00	450.00
5-Intro. Sniffer & Jinx; Ghost vs. Claw begins by Bob Wood, ends #20	57.00	170.00	400.00
6-(#7 on indicia)	50.00	150.00	350.00
7-10: 8-Nightro ends	43.00	130.00	300.00
11-London, Pat Patriot end; bondage/torture-c	38.00	114.00	265.00
12-Origin of The Claw; Scoop Scuttle by Wolverton begins (2-4 pgs.), ends #22, not in #21	57.00	170.00	400.00
13-Intro. of Little Wise Guys	57.00	170.00	400.00
14	28.00	85.00	200.00
15-Death of Meatball	43.00	130.00	300.00
16,17	26.00	80.00	185.00
18-New origin of Daredevil-Not same as Silver Streak #6	57.00	170.00	400.00
19,20	24.00	70.00	165.00
21-Reprints cover of Silver Streak #6(on inside) plus intro. of The Claw from Silver Streak #1	34.00	103.00	240.00
22-30	14.00	42.00	100.00
31-Death of The Claw	25.00	75.00	175.00
32-37: 34-Two Daredevil stories begin, end #68	9.30	28.00	65.00
38-Origin Daredevil retold from #18	19.00	58.00	135.00
39,40	9.30	28.00	65.00
41-50: 42-Intro. Kilroy in Daredevil	5.70	17.00	40.00
51-69-Last Daredevil issue	4.30	13.00	30.00
70-Little Wise Guys take over book; McWilliams-a; Hot Rock Flanagan begins, ends #80	2.65	8.00	18.00
71-79,81: 79-Daredevil returns	2.00	6.00	14.00
80-Daredevil x-over	2.00	6.00	14.00
82,90-One page Frazetta ad in both	2.30	7.00	16.00
83-89,91-99,101-134	1.70	5.00	12.00
100	3.00	9.00	21.00

NOTE: *Wolverton's Scoop Scuttle*-12-20, 22. *Biro* c/a-all?. *Bolle* a-125. *Maurer* a-75. *McWilliams* a-73, 75, 79, 80.

DARING ADVENTURES (Also see Approved Comics)
Nov, 1953 (3-D)
St. John Publishing Co.

	Good	Fine	N-Mint
1 (3-D)-Reprints lead story/Son of Sinbad #1 by Kubert	19.00	58.00	135.00

DARING ADVENTURES
1963 - 1964
I.W. Enterprises/Super Comics

	Good	Fine	N-Mint
I.W. Reprint #1-Disbrow-a(3)	2.00	6.00	14.00
Super Reprint #10,11('63)-r/Dynamic #24,16: 11-Marijuana story; Yankee Boy app.	1.00	3.00	7.00
Super Reprint #12('64)-Phantom Lady from Fox(r/#14,15)	8.00	24.00	56.00
Super Reprint #15('64)-Hooded Menace	5.00	15.00	35.00
Super Reprint #16('64)-r/Dynamic #12	1.00	3.00	6.00
Super Reprint #17('64)-Green Lama by Raboy from Green Lama #3	2.00	6.00	14.00
Super Reprint #18-Origin Atlas	1.00	3.00	6.00

DARING COMICS (Formerly Daring Mystery) (Jeanie No. 13 on)
No. 9, Fall, 1944 - No. 12, Fall, 1945
Timely Comics (HPC)

	Good	Fine	N-Mint
9-Human Torch & Sub-Mariner begin	36.00	107.00	250.00
10-The Angel only app.	32.00	95.00	220.00
11,12-The Destroyer app.	32.00	95.00	220.00

NOTE: *Schomburg* c-9-11.

DARING CONFESSIONS (Formerly Youthful Hearts)
No. 4, 11/52 - No. 7, 5/53; No. 8, 10/53
Youthful Magazines

Daredevil #168, © MEG

Daredevil Comics #14, © LEV

Daring Comics #12, © MEG

Daring Mystery Comics #1, © MEG

The Daring New Adventures Of Supergirl #1, © DC

Dark Mysteries #19, © Merit Publ.

	Good	Fine	N-Mint
DARING CONFESSIONS (continued)			
4-Doug Wildey-a	3.70	11.00	26.00
5-8: 6,8-Wildey-a	2.65	8.00	18.00

DARING LOVE (Radiant Love No. 2 on)
Sept-Oct, 1953
Gilmor Magazines

1	3.00	9.00	21.00

DARING LOVE (Formerly Youthful Romances)
No. 15, 12/52; No. 16, 2/53-c, 4/53-Indicia; No. 17-4/53-c & indicia
Ribage/Pix

15	3.15	9.50	22.00
16,17: 17-Photo-c	2.65	8.00	18.00

NOTE: *Colletta* a-15. *Wildey* a-17.

DARING LOVE STORIES (See Fox Giants)

DARING MYSTERY COMICS (Comedy Comics No. 9 on; title changed to Daring Comics with No. 9)
Jan, 1940 - No. 8, Jan, 1942
Timely Comics (TPI 1-6/TCI 7,8)

1-Origin The Fiery Mask by Joe Simon; Monako, Prince of Magic, John Steele, Soldier of Fortune, Doc Doyle begin; Flash Foster & Barney Mullen, Sea Rover only app; bondage-c	583.00	1460.00	3500.00
2-(Rare)-Origin The Phantom Bullet & only app.; The Laughing Mask & Mr. E only app.; Trojak the Tiger Man begins, ends #6; Zephyr Jones & K-4 & His Sky Devils app., also #4	283.00	710.00	1700.00
3-The Phantom Reporter, Dale of FBI, Breeze Barton, Captain Strong & Marvex the Super-Robot only app.; The Purple Mask begins	200.00	500.00	1200.00
4-Last Purple Mask; Whirlwind Carter begins; Dan Gorman, G-Man app.	133.00	335.00	800.00
5-The Falcon begins; The Fiery Mask, Little Hercules app. by Sa-gendorf in the Segar style; bondage-c	133.00	335.00	800.00
6-Origin & only app. Marvel Boy by S&K; Flying Flame, Dynaman, & Stuporman only app.; The Fiery Mask by S&K; S&K-c	158.00	395.00	950.00
7-Origin The Blue Diamond, Captain Daring by S&K, The Fin by Everett, The Challenger, The Silver Scorpion & The Thunderer by Burgos; Mr. Millions app.	158.00	395.00	950.00
8-Origin Citizen V; Last Fin, Silver Scorpion, Capt. Daring by Borth, Blue Diamond & The Thunderer; S&K-c; Rudy the Robot only app.	125.00	315.00	750.00

NOTE: *Schomburg* c-1-4, 7. *Simon* a-2, 3, 5.

DARING NEW ADVENTURES OF SUPERGIRL, THE
Nov, 1982 - No. 13, Nov, 1983 (Supergirl No. 14-on)
DC Comics

1-Origin retold		.40	.80
2-13: 13-New costume; flag-c		.25	.50

NOTE: *Buckler* c-1p, 2p. *Giffen* c-3p, 4p. *Gil Kane* c-6, 8, 9, 11-13.

DARK CRYSTAL, THE
April, 1983 - No. 2, May, 1983
Marvel Comics Group

1,2-Movie adaptation, part 1&2		.25	.50

DARKEWOOD
1987 - No. 5, 1988 ($2.00, color, 28 pgs., mini-series)
Aircel Publishing

1-5		.35	1.00	2.00

DARK HORSE PRESENTS
July, 1986 - Present ($1.50, $1.75, $1.95, B&W)
Dark Horse Comics

1-1st app. Concrete by Paul Chadwick	2.00	6.00	12.00
1-2nd print	.25	.75	1.50

	Good	Fine	N-Mint
2-Concrete app.	1.50	4.50	9.00
3-Concrete app.	1.00	3.00	6.00
4,5-Concrete app.	.85	2.50	5.00
6,7,9	.40	1.25	2.50
8,10-Concrete app.	.60	1.75	3.50
11-19,21-23: 12-Concrete app.	.35	1.00	2.00
20-Double size ($2.95)-Flaming Carrot app.	.60	1.75	3.50
24-1st app. Aliens; Concrete, Mr. Monster app.	.70	2.00	4.00
25-31,33-35: 28-Concrete app. 34-Aliens story. 35-Concrete, Predator stories ($1.95-c begins)	.40	1.15	2.25
32-($3.50, 68 pgs.)-Annual; Concrete, American	.60	1.75	3.50
36-Aliens Vs. Predator	.70	2.00	4.00
37,38: 38-Concrete story	.35	1.00	2.00

DARK KNIGHT (See Batman: The Dark Knight Returns)

DARKLON THE MYSTIC (Also see Eerie Magazine #79, 80)
Oct, 1983 (One shot)
Pacific Comics

1-Starlin c/a(r)	.35	1.00	2.00

DARK MANSION OF FORBIDDEN LOVE, THE (Becomes Forbidden Tales of Dark Mansion No. 5 on)
Sept-Oct, 1971 - No. 4, Mar-Apr, 1972
National Periodical Publications

1-4: 2-Adams-c. 3-Jeff Jones-c		.40	.80

DARK MYSTERIES
June-July, 1951 - No. 25, 1955
"Master"-"Merit" Publications

1-Wood c/a, 8 pgs.	27.00	81.00	190.00
2-Wood/Harrison c/a, 8 pgs.	22.00	65.00	150.00
3-9: 7-Dismemberment, hypo blood drainage stories	7.00	21.00	50.00
10-Cannibalism story	8.50	25.50	60.00
11-13,15-18: 11-Severed head panels. 13-Dismemberment-c/story	6.50	19.50	45.00
14-Several E.C. Craig swipes	6.50	19.50	45.00
19-Injury to eye panel	8.50	25.50	60.00
20-Female bondage, blood drainage story	7.00	21.00	50.00
21,22-Last pre-code issue, mis-dated 3/54 instead of 3/55	5.00	15.00	35.00
23-25	3.70	11.00	26.00

NOTE: *Cameron* a-1, 2. *Myron Fass* c/a-21. *Harrison* a-3, 7; c-3. *Hollingsworth* a-7-17, 20, 21, 23. *Wildey* a-5. *Woodish* art by *Fleishman*-9; c-10. Bondage-c, 10, 18, 19.

DARK SHADOWS
October, 1957 - No. 3, May, 1958
Steinway Comic Publications (Ajax)(America's Best)

1	4.30	13.00	30.00
2,3	2.85	8.50	20.00

DARK SHADOWS (TV) (See Dan Curtis)
March, 1969 - No. 35, Feb, 1976 (Photo-c, 2-7)
Gold Key

1(30039-903)-with pull-out poster	8.00	24.00	56.00
2	3.70	11.00	26.00
3-with pull-out poster	5.15	15.50	36.00
4-7: Last photo-c	3.50	10.50	24.00
8-10	2.65	8.00	18.00
11-20	2.00	7.00	14.00
21-35: 30-last painted-c	1.50	4.50	10.00
Story Digest 1 (6/70)	1.50	4.50	10.00

DARLING LOVE
Oct-Nov, 1949 - No. 11, 1952 (no month) (52 pgs.)
Close Up/Archie Publ. (A Darling Magazine)

1-Photo-c	5.00	15.00	35.00
2	2.65	8.00	18.00

DARLING LOVE (continued)	Good	Fine	N-Mint
3-8,10,11: 5,6-photo-c	2.00	6.00	14.00
9-Krigstein-a	3.35	10.00	23.00

DARLING ROMANCE
Sept-Oct., 1949 - No. 7, 1951
Close Up (MLJ Publications)

1-Photo-c	5.00	15.00	35.00
2	2.65	8.00	18.00
3-7	2.00	6.00	14.00

DASTARDLY & MUTTLEY IN THEIR FLYING MACHINES (See Fun-In No. 1-4,6)

DASTARDLY & MUTTLEY KITE FUN BOOK (Giveaway)
1969 (16 pages) (5x7''), soft-c) (Hanna-Barbera's)
Florida Power & Light Co./Sou. Calif. Edison/Pacific Gas & Electric

nn	1.00	3.00	6.00

DATE WITH DANGER
No. 5, Dec, 1952 - No. 6, Feb, 1953
Standard Comics

5,6	2.85	8.50	20.00

DATE WITH DEBBI
1-2/69 - No. 17, 9-10/71; No. 18, 10-11/72
National Periodical Publications

1	1.00	3.00	6.00
2-5	.60	1.75	3.50
6-18	.50	1.50	3.00

DATE WITH JUDY, A (Radio/TV, and 1948 movie)
Oct-Nov, 1947 - No. 79, Oct-Nov, 1960 (No. 1-25: 52 pgs.)
National Periodical Publications

1	12.00	36.00	84.00
2	6.00	18.00	42.00
3-10	4.00	12.00	28.00
11-20	2.65	8.00	18.00
21-40	2.00	6.00	14.00
41-45: 45-Last pre-code (2-3/55)	1.50	4.50	10.00
46-79: 79-Drucker c/a	1.15	3.50	8.00

DATE WITH MILLIE, A (Life With Millie No. 8 on)
Oct, 1956 - No. 7, Aug, 1957; Oct, 1959 - No. 7, Oct, 1960
Atlas/Marvel Comics (MPC)

1(10/56)-(1st Series)	7.00	21.00	50.00
2	3.50	10.50	24.00
3-7	2.65	8.00	18.00
1(10/59)-(2nd Series)	4.00	12.00	28.00
2-7	2.00	6.00	14.00

DATE WITH PATSY, A (Also see Patsy Walker)
September, 1957
Atlas Comics

1	3.50	10.50	24.00

DAVID AND GOLIATH (See 4-Color No. 1205)

DAVID CASSIDY (TV?)(See Swing With Scooter #33)
Feb, 1972 - No. 14, Sept, 1973
Charlton Comics

1	1.00	3.00	6.00
2-14: 7,9-Photo-c	.70	2.00	4.00

DAVID LADD'S LIFE STORY (See Movie Classics)

DAVY CROCKETT (See Dell Giants, Fightin. . . , Frontier Fighters, It's Game Time, Western Tales & Wild Frontier)

DAVY CROCKETT
1951
Avon Periodicals

nn-Tuska?, Reinman-a; Fawcette-c	8.00	24.00	56.00

DAVY CROCKETT (. . .King of the Wild Frontier No. 1,2)(TV)
5/55 - No. 671, 12/55; No. 1, 12/63; No. 2, 11/69 (Walt Disney)
Dell Publishing Co./Gold Key

	Good	Fine	N-Mint
4-Color 631-Fess Parker photo-c	3.50	10.50	24.00
4-Color 639-Photo-c	3.50	10.50	24.00
4-Color 664,671(Marsh-a)-Photo-c	4.00	12.00	28.00
1(12/63-Gold Key)-r; Fess Parker photo-c	1.70	5.00	12.00
2(11/69)-r; Fess Parker photo-c	1.00	3.00	7.00
. .Christmas Book (no date, 16pgs, paper-c) Sears giveaway			
	1.70	5.00	12.00
. .In the Raid at Piney Creek (1955, 16pgs, 5x7¼'')American Motors			
giveaway; slick, photo-c	3.50	10.50	24.00
. .Safety Trails (1955, 16pgs, 3¼x7'') Cities Service giveaway			
	3.00	9.00	21.00

DAVY CROCKETT (. . .Frontier Fighter #1,2; Kid Montana #9 on)
Aug, 1955 - No. 8, Jan, 1957
Charlton Comics

1	3.50	10.50	24.00
2	1.70	5.00	12.00
3-8	1.15	3.50	8.00
Hunting With. . .('55, 16 pgs.)-Ben Franklin Store giveaway (Publ.-			
S. Rose)	1.15	3.50	8.00

DAYS OF THE MOB (See In the Days of the Mob)

DAZEY'S DIARY
June-Aug, 1962
Dell Publishing Co.

01-174-208: Bill Woggon-c/a	2.00	6.00	14.00

DAZZLER, THE (Also see Marvel Graphic Novel & X-Men #130)
March, 1981 - No. 42, Mar, 1986
Marvel Comics Group

1,2-X-Men app.	.35	1.00	2.00
3-37,39-42: 21-Double size; photo-c		.50	1.00
38-Wolverine-c/app.; X-Men app.	.40	1.25	2.50

NOTE: No. 1 distributed only through comic shops. *Alcala* a-1i, 2i. *Guice* a-42.

DC CHALLENGE
11/85 - No. 12, 10/86 ($1.25-$2.00; 12 issue maxi-series)
DC Comics

1-11: 1-Colan-a. 4-G. Kane-c/a	.25	.75	1.50
12($2.00)-Perez/Austin-c	.25	.75	1.50

DC COMICS PRESENTS
July-Aug, 1978 - No. 97, Sept, 1986
DC Comics

(Superman team-ups with No. 1-on)			
1-12,14-25,27-40,42,43,45-71,73-84,86-97	.25	.75	1.50
13-Legion of Super Heroes	.40	1.25	2.50
26-(10/80)-Green Lantern; intro Cyborg, Starfire, Raven, New Teen			
Titans; Starlin-c/a; Sargon the Sorcerer back-up; 16 pgs. preview			
of the New Teen Titans	1.15	3.50	7.00
41-Superman/Joker-c/story	.50	1.50	3.00
44-Superman/Joker-c/story	.50	1.50	3.00
72-Joker/Phantom Stranger-c/story	.50	1.50	3.00
85-Swamp Thing; Alan Moore scripts	.35	1.00	2.00
Annual 1(9/82)-G.A. Superman		.60	1.20
Annual 2(7/83)-Intro/origin Superwoman		.60	1.20
Annual 3(9/84)-Shazam		.60	1.20
Annual 4(10/85)-Superwoman		.60	1.20

NOTE: *Adkins* a-2, 54; c-2. *Gil Kane* a-28, 35, Annual 3; c-48p, 56, 58, 60, 62, 64, 68, Annual 2, 3. *Kirby* c/a-84. *Kubert* c/a-66. *Morrow* c/a-65. *Newton* a/c-54p. *Orlando* c-53i. *Perez* a-26p, 61p; c-38, 61, 94. *Starlin* a-26-29p, 36p, 37p; c-26-29, 36, 37, 93. *Toth* a-84. *Williamson* i-79, 85, 87.

DC GRAPHIC NOVEL (Also see DC Science Fiction. . .)
Nov, 1983 - No. 7, 1986 ($5.95, 68 pgs.)

Darling Romance #1, © AP

A Date With Judy #18, © DC

DC Comics Presents #41, © DC

DC 100 Page Super Spectacular #14, © DC

DC Special #17, © DC

Dead-Eye Western V2#7, © HILL

DC GRAPHIC NOVEL (continued)
DC Comics

	Good	Fine	N-Mint
1-Star Raiders	1.00	3.00	6.00
2-Warlords; not from regular Warlord series	1.00	3.00	6.00
3-The Medusa Chain; Ernie Colon story/a	1.00	3.00	6.00
4-The Hunger Dogs; Kirby-c/a	1.00	3.00	6.00
5-Me And Joe Priest	1.00	3.00	6.00
6-Metalzoic	1.20	3.50	7.00
7-Space Clusters	1.00	3.00	6.00

DC 100 PAGE SUPER SPECTACULAR (50 cents)
(Title is 100 Page. . .No. 14 on)(Square bound) (Reprints)
1971 - No. 13, 6/72; No. 14, 2/73 - No. 22, 11/73 (No #1-3)
National Periodical Publications

	Good	Fine	N-Mint
4-Weird Mystery Tales-Johnny Peril & Phantom Stranger; cover & splashes by Wrightson; origin Jungle Boy of Jupiter	.35	1.00	2.00
5-Love stories; Wood Inks, 7pgs.	.35	1.00	2.00
6-''World's Greatest Super-Heroes''-JLA, JSA, Spectre, Johnny Quick, Vigilante, Wildcat & Hawkman; Adams wrap-around-c	.40	1.25	2.50
7-(See Superman #245),8-(See Batman #238)			
9-(See Our Army at War #242),10-(See Adventure #416)			
11-(See Flash #214),12-(See Superboy #185)			
13-(See Superman #252)			
14-Batman-r/Det. 31,32	.70	2.00	4.00
15-22: 20-Batman-r; origin Two-Face. 21-r/Showcase 54. 22-r/All Flash 13	.50	1.00	

NOTE: *Anderson a-11, 14, 18i, 22. B. Baily a-18r, 20r. Burnley a-18r, 20r. Crandall a-14p(r), 20r. Drucker a-4r. Infantino a-17, 20, 22. G. Kane a-18. Kubert a-6, 7, 16, 17; c-16,19. Meskin a-4, 22. Mooney a-15r, 21r. Toth a-17, 20r.*

DC SCIENCE FICTION GRAPHIC NOVEL
1985 - No. 7, 1987 ($5.95)
DC Comics

	Good	Fine	N-Mint
SF1-Hell on Earth by Robert Bloch, SF2-Nightwings by Robert Silverberg, SF3-Frost & Fire by Bradbury	1.00	3.00	6.00
SF4-Merchants of Venus	1.00	3.00	6.00
SF5-Demon With A Glass Hand by Ellison; M. Rogers-a. SF6-The Magic Goes Away by Niven, SF7-Sandkings by George R.R. Martin	1.00	3.00	6.00

DC SPECIAL (Also see Super DC. . .)
10-12/68 - No. 15, 11-12/71; No. 16, Spr/75 - No. 29, 8-9/77
National Periodical Publications

	Good	Fine	N-Mint
1-All Infantino issue; Flash, Batman, Adam Strange-r (68 pgs., 25 cents)	.85	2.50	5.00
2-29: 5-All Kubert issue; Viking Prince, Sgt. Rock-r. 12-Viking Prince; Kubert-c/a. 15-G.A. Plastic Man origin r/Police #1; origin Woozy by Cole; Last 68 pg. issue. 16-Super Heroes Battle Super Gorillas. 28-Earth Shattering Disaster Stories; Legion of Super-Heroes story. 29-Secret Origin of the Justice Society	.35	1.00	2.00

NOTE: *Adams c-3, 4, 6, 11, 29. Grell a-20; c-17. Heath a-12r. G. Kane a-6p, 13r; 17r, 19-21r. Kubert a-6r, 12r, 22. Meskin a-10. Moreira a-10. Staton a-29p. Toth a-13, 20r.*

DC SPECIAL BLUE-RIBBON DIGEST
Mar-Apr, 1980 - No. 24, Aug, 1982
DC Comics

	Good	Fine	N-Mint
1-24: All reprints?		.50	1.00

NOTE: *Adams a-16(6)r, 17r, 23r; c-16. Aparo a-6r, 24r; c-23. Grell a-8, 10; c-10. Heath a-14. Kaluta a-17r. Gil Kane a-22r. Kirby a-23r. Kubert a-3, 18r, 21r; c-7, 12, 14, 17, 18, 21, 24. Morrow a-24r. Orlando a-17r, 22r; c-1, 20. Perez c-19p. Toth a-21r, 24r. Wood a-3, 17r, 24r. Wrightson a-16r, 17r; 24r.*

DC SPECIAL SERIES
9/77 - No. 16, Fall, 1978; No. 17, 8/79 - No. 27, Fall, 1981
(No. 23 & 24 - digest size; No. 25-27 - over-sized)
National Periodical Publications/DC Comics

	Good	Fine	N-Mint
1-Five-Star Super-Hero Spectacular; Atom, Flash, Green Lantern, Aquaman, Batman, Kobra app.; Adams-c; Staton, Nasser-a	.40	1.25	2.50
2(#1)-Original Swamp Thing Saga, The(9-10/77)-reprints Swamp Thing No. 1&2 by Wrightson; Wrightson wrap-around-c	.35	1.00	2.00
3-20,22-24: 6-Jones-a. 10-Origin Dr. Fate, Lightray & Black Canary	.25	.75	1.50
21-Miller-a (1st on Batman)	1.35	4.00	8.00
25-Superman II The Adventure Continues (Sum '81); photos from movie($2.95) (Same as All-New Coll. Ed. C-64?)	.40	1.25	2.50
26-Superman and His Incredible Fortress of Solitude (Sum '81) ($2.50) (Same as All-New Co.. Ed. C-63?)	.40	1.25	2.50
27-Batman vs. The Incredible Hulk($2.50)	.40	1.25	2.50

NOTE: *Golden a-15. Heath a-12i, 16. Kubert c-13. Rogers c/a-15. Starlin c-12.*

DC SPOTLIGHT
1985 (50th anniversary special)
DC Comics (giveaway)

	Good	Fine	N-Mint
1		.40	.80

DC SUPER-STARS
March, 1976 - No. 18, Winter, 1978 (No.3-18: 52 pgs.)
National Periodical Publications/DC Comics

	Good	Fine	N-Mint
1-Re-intro Teen Titans	.25	.75	1.50
2-9,11-16,18: 2-Adam Strange begins		.50	1.00
10-Batman/Joker-c	.70	2.00	4.00
17-Secret Origins of Super-Heroes(origin of The Huntress); origin Green Arrow by Grell; Legion app.	.60	1.20	

NOTE: *Aparo c-7, 14, 17, 18. Austin a-11i. Buckler a-14p; c-10. Grell a-17. G. Kane a-1r, 10r. Kubert c-15. Layton c-16i, 17i. Mooney a-4r, 6r. Morrow c/a-11r. Nasser a-11. Newton c/a-16p. Staton a-17; c-17. No. 10, 12-18 contain all new material; the rest are reprints.*

D-DAY (Also see Special War Series)
Sum/63; No. 2, Fall/64; No. 4, 9/66; No. 5, 10/67; No. 6, 11/68
Charlton Comics (no No. 3)

	Good	Fine	N-Mint
1(1963)-Montes/Bache-c	.85	2.60	6.00
2(Fall,'64)-Wood-a(3)	1.15	3.50	8.00
4-6('66-'68)-Montes/Bache-a #5	.70	2.00	4.00

DEAD END CRIME STORIES
April, 1949 (52 pages)
Kirby Publishing Co.

	Good	Fine	N-Mint
nn-(Scarce)-Powell, Roussos-a	22.00	65.00	154.00

DEAD-EYE WESTERN COMICS
Nov-Dec, 1948 - V3#1, Apr-May, 1953
Hillman Periodicals

	Good	Fine	N-Mint
V1#1(52 pgs.)-Krigstein, Roussos-a	6.50	19.50	45.00
V1#2,3(52 pgs.)	3.50	10.50	24.00
V1#4-12	2.00	6.00	14.00
V2#1,2,5-8,10-12: 6,7-52 pgs.	1.50	4.50	10.00
3,4-Krigstein-a (52 pgs.)	3.00	9.00	21.00
9-One pg. Frazetta ad	1.70	5.00	12.00
V3#1	1.30	4.00	9.00

NOTE: *Briefer a-V1No.8. Kinstleresque stories by McCann-12, V2No.1,2, V3No.1.*

DEADLIEST HEROES OF KUNG FU
Summer, 1975 (Magazine)
Marvel Comics Group

	Good	Fine	N-Mint
1	.30	.90	1.80

DEADLY HANDS OF KUNG FU, THE (See Master of Kung Fu)
April, 1974 - No. 33, Feb, 1977 (75 cents) (B&W - Magazine)
Marvel Comics Group

1(V1#4 listed in error)-Origin Sons of the Tiger; Shang-Chi, Master

DEADLY HANDS OF KUNG FU (continued) | Good | Fine | N-Mint

	Good	Fine	N-Mint
of Kung Fu begins; Bruce Lee photo pin-up	.40	1.25	2.50
2,3,5	.30	.90	1.80
4-Bruce Lee painted-c by Adams; 8 pg. biog of Bruce Lee			
	.40	1.25	2.50
6-14	.30	.90	1.80
15-(Annual 1, Summer '75)	.30	.90	1.80
16-19,21-27,29-33: 17-1st Giffen-a (1 pg.; 11/75). 19-1st White Tiger.			
22-1st Giffen story-a	.60		1.20
20-Origin The White Tiger; Perez-a	.30	.90	1.80
28-Origin Jack of Hearts; Bruce Lee life story	.40	1.25	2.50
Special Album Edition 1(Summer, '74)-Adams-i	.30	.90	1.80

NOTE: *Adams* c-1, 2-4, 11, 12, 14, 17. *Giffen* a-22p, 24p. *G. Kane* a-23p. *Kirby* a-5r. *Perez* a(p)-6-14, 16, 17, 19, 21. *Rogers* a-32, 33. *Starlin* a-1, 2r, 15r. *Staton* a-28p, 31, 32. Sons of the Tiger in 1, 3, 4, 6-14, 16-19.

DEADMAN (See The Brave and the Bold & Phantom Stranger #39)
May, 1985 - No. 7, Nov, 1985
DC Comics

1-Deadman-r by Infantino, Adams	.35	1.00	2.00
2-7	.30	.90	1.80

DEADMAN
Mar, 1986 - No. 4, June, 1986 (mini-series)
DC Comics

1-4-Lopez-c/a; 4-Byrne-c(p)		.45	.90

DEADMAN: LOVE AFTER DEATH
1989 - No. 2, 1990 ($3.95, 2 issue series, mature readers, 52 pgs.)
DC Comics

Book One, Two: 1-Contains nudity	.70	2.00	4.00

DEAD OF NIGHT
Dec, 1973 - No. 11, Aug, 1975
Marvel Comics Group

1-Reprints		.30	.60
2-11: 11-Kane/Wrightson-c		.25	.50

NOTE: *Ditko* a-7r, 10r. *Everett* c-2.

DEADSHOT
Nov, 1988 - No. 4, Feb, 1989 ($1.00, color, mini-series)
DC Comics

1-4		.50	1.00

DEAD WHO WALK, THE (Also see Strange Myst., Super-r #15,16)
1952 (One Shot)
Realistic Comics

nn	22.00	65.00	154.00

DEADWOOD GULCH
1931 (52 pages) (B&W)
Dell Publishing Co.

By Gordon Rogers	7.00	21.00	50.00

DEAN MARTIN & JERRY LEWIS (See Adventures of . . .)

DEAR BEATRICE FAIRFAX
No. 5, Nov, 1950 - No. 9, Sept, 1951 (Vern Greene art)
Best/Standard Comics(King Features)

5	3.00	9.00	21.00
6-9	1.85	5.50	13.00

NOTE: *Schomburg* air brush-c-5-9.

DEAR HEART (Formerly Lonely Heart)
No. 15, July, 1956 - No. 16, Sept, 1956
Ajax

15,16	1.70	5.00	12.00

DEAR LONELY HEART (. . .Illustrated No. 1-6)
Mar, 1951; No. 2, Oct, 1951 - No. 8, Oct, 1952
Artful Publications

	Good	Fine	N-Mint
1	8.00	24.00	56.00
2	3.70	11.00	26.00
3-Matt Baker Jungle Girl story	8.00	24.00	56.00
4-8	3.35	10.00	23.00

DEAR LONELY HEARTS (Lonely Heart #9 on)
Aug, 1953 - No. 8, Oct, 1954
Harwell Publ./Mystery Publ. Co. (Comic Media)

1	3.15	9.50	22.00
2-8	1.70	5.00	12.00

DEARLY BELOVED
Fall, 1952
Ziff-Davis Publishing Co.

1-Photo-c	7.00	21.00	50.00

DEAR NANCY PARKER
June, 1963 - No. 2, Sept, 1963
Gold Key

1,2-Painted-c	1.50	4.50	10.00

DEATH OF CAPTAIN MARVEL (See Marvel Graphic Novel #1)

DEATH RATTLE (Formerly an Underground)
V2#1, 10/85 - No. 18, 1988 ($1.95, Baxter)(Mature readers)
Kitchen Sink Press

V2#1-Corben-c	.35	1.00	2.00
2-5: 2-Unpubbed Spirit story by Eisner. 5-Robot Woman by			
Wolverton-r	.35	1.00	2.00
6-18: 6-B&W issues begin. 16-Wolverton Spacehawk-r			
	.35	1.00	2.00

DEATH'S HEAD
Dec, 1988 - No. 10, Dec, 1989 ($1.75, color)
Marvel Comics

1-10: Spin-off from Dragon's Claws. 9-Simonson-c(p)			
	.30	.90	1.75

DEATH VALLEY
Oct, 1953 - No. 6, Aug, 1954?
Comic Media

1-Old Scout	4.00	12.00	28.00
2	2.30	7.00	16.00
3-6	1.70	5.00	12.00

NOTE: *Discount* a-5. *Morisi* a-1, 3, 5.

DEATH VALLEY (Becomes Frontier Scout, Daniel Boone No.10-13)
No. 7, 6/55 - No. 9, 10/55 (Cont. from Comic Media series)
Charlton Comics

7-9: 8-Wolverton-a (½ pg.)	1.70	5.00	12.00

DEBBIE DEAN, CAREER GIRL
April, 1945 - No. 2, 1945
Civil Service Publ.

1,2-Newspaper reprints by Bert Whitman	7.00	21.00	50.00

DEBBI'S DATES
Apr-May, 1969 - No. 11, Dec-Jan, 1970-71
National Periodical Publications

1	.70	2.00	5.00
2-11: 4-Adams text illo.	.50	1.50	3.00

DEEP, THE (Movie)
November, 1977
Marvel Comics Group

1-Infantino c/a		.40	.80

DEFENDERS, THE (TV)
Sept-Nov, 1962 - No. 2, Feb-Apr, 1963
Dell Publishing Co.

Deadman #5 (9/85), © DC

Dear Lonely Heart #3, © Artful Publ.

Dear Nancy Parker #2, © GK

The Defenders #8, © MEG

Dell Giant Comics #31, © Hanna-Barbera

Bugs Bunny's Christmas Funnies #4, © Warner Bros.

	Good	Fine	N-Mint
THE DEFENDERS (continued)			
12-176-211(#1), 304(#2)	1.50	4.50	10.00

DEFENDERS, THE (Also see Marvel Feature & Marvel Treas. Ed.; The New. . . #140-on)
Aug, 1972 - No. 152, Feb, 1986
Marvel Comics Group

	Good	Fine	N-Mint
1-The Hulk, Doctor Strange, & Sub-Mariner begin	2.00	6.00	12.00
2-5: 4-Valkyrie joins	.70	2.00	4.00
6-10: 9,10-Avengers app. 10-Thor-Hulk battle	.70	2.00	4.00
11-50: 31,32-Origin Nighthawk. 35-Intro. New Red Guardian. 44-Hellcat joins. 45-Dr. Strange leaves	.35	1.00	2.00

51-151: 55-Origin Red Guardian. 77-Origin Omega. 100-Double size. 106-Death of Nighthawk. 125-Dbl size; 1st app. Mad Dog; intro. new Defenders. 129-New Mutants cameo. 150-Dbl size; origin

	Good	Fine	N-Mint
Cloud	.50		1.00
152-Double size; ties in with X-Factor & Secret Wars II	.30	.90	1.75

NOTE: Art Adams c-142p. Austin a-53i; c-65i, 119i, 145i. Frank Bolle a-7i, 10i, 11i. Buckler c(p)-34, 38, 76, 77, 79-86, 90, 91. J. Buscema c-66. Ditko a-Gnt-Size 1-4r. Everett r-Gnt-Size 1-4. Giffen a-42-49p, 50, 51p, 52p, 53p, 54p. Golden a-53p, 54p; c-94, 96. Guice c-129. G. Kane c(p)-13, 16, 18, 19, 21-26, 31-33, 35-37, 40, 41, 52, 55, Gnt-Size 2, 4. Kirby c-42-45. Mooney a-3i, 31-34i, 62i, 63i, 85i. Nasser c-88p. Perez c(p)-51, 53, 54. Rogers c-98. Starlin c-110. Tuska a-57p. Silver Surfer in No. 2, 3, 6, 8-11, 92, 98-101, 107, 112-115, 122-125.

	Good	Fine	N-Mint
Annual 1(11/76)	.35	1.00	2.00
Giant Size 1(7/74)-Silver Surfer app.; Starlin-a; Everett, Ditko, & Kirby-r	.50	1.50	3.00
Giant Size 2(10/74)-G. Kane-a; Everett, Ditko-r	.50	1.00	
Giant Size 3(1/75)-Starlin, Newton, Everett-a	.50	1.00	
Giant Size 4(4/75), 5(7/75)-Guardians app.	.50	1.00	

DEFENDERS OF THE EARTH (TV)
Jan, 1987 - No. 5, Sept, 1987
Star Comics (Marvel)

	Good	Fine	N-Mint
1-5: The Phantom, Mandrake The Magician, Flash Gordon begin	.45		.90

THE DEFINITIVE DIRECTORY OF THE DC UNIVERSE (See Who's Who . . .)

DELECTA OF THE PLANETS (See Don Fortune & Fawcett Miniatures)

DELLA VISION (Patty Powers #4 on)
April, 1955 - No. 3, Aug, 1955
Atlas Comics

	Good	Fine	N-Mint
1	6.50	19.50	45.00
2,3	4.30	13.00	30.00

DELL GIANT COMICS
No. 21, Sept, 1959 - No. 55, Sept, 1961 (Most 84 pages, 25 cents)
Dell Publishing Co.

	Good	Fine	N-Mint
21-M.G.M.'s Tom & Jerry Picnic Time (84pp, stapled binding)	4.30	13.00	30.00
22-Huey, Dewey & Louie Back to School(10/59, 84pp, square binding begins)	3.50	14.00	35.00
23-Marge's Little Lulu & Tubby Halloween Fun (10/59)-Tripp-a	7.00	28.00	70.00
24-Woody Woodpecker's Family Fun (11/59)	2.50	10.00	25.00
25-Tarzan's Jungle World(11/59)-Marsh-a	4.50	18.00	45.00
26-Christmas Parade-Barks-a, 16pgs.(Disney; 12/59)-Barks draws himself on wanted poster pg. 13	8.00	32.00	80.00
27-Man in Space r-/4-Color 716,866, & 954 (100 pages, 35 cents) (Disney)(TV)	3.50	14.00	35.00
28-Bugs Bunny's Winter Fun (2/60)	3.00	12.00	30.00
29-Marge's Little Lulu & Tubby in Hawaii (4/60)-Tripp-a	7.00	28.00	70.00
30-Disneyland USA(6/60)-Reprinted in Vacation in Disneyland	4.50	18.00	45.00

	Good	Fine	N-Mint
31-Huckleberry Hound Summer Fun (7/60)(TV)	7.00	28.00	70.00
32-Bugs Bunny Beach Party	2.50	10.00	25.00
33-Daisy Duck & Uncle Scrooge Picnic Time (9/60)	4.00	16.00	40.00
34-Nancy & Sluggo Summer Camp (8/60)	3.00	12.00	30.00
35-Huey, Dewey & Louie Back to School (10/60)	3.50	14.00	35.00
36-Marge's Little Lulu & Witch Hazel Halloween Fun(10/60)-Tripp-a	7.00	28.00	70.00
37-Tarzan, King of the Jungle(11/60)-Marsh-a	4.00	16.00	40.00
38-Uncle Donald & His Nephews Family Fun (11/60)	3.50	14.00	35.00
39-Walt Disney's Merry Christmas(12/60)	3.50	14.00	35.00
40-Woody Woodpecker Christmas Parade(12/60)	2.50	10.00	25.00
41-Yogi Bear's Winter Sports (12/60)(TV)	5.50	22.00	55.00
42-Marge's Little Lulu & Tubby in Australia (4/61)	7.00	28.00	70.00
43-Mighty Mouse in Outer Space (5/61)	8.00	32.00	80.00
44-Around the World with Huckleberry & His Friends (7/61)(TV)	6.00	24.00	60.00
45-Nancy & Sluggo Summer Camp (8/61)	3.00	12.00	30.00
46-Bugs Bunny Beach Party (8/61)	2.50	10.00	25.00
47-Mickey & Donald in Vacationland (8/61)	3.50	14.00	35.00
48-The Flintstones (No. 1)(Bedrock Bedlam)(7/61)(TV)	8.00	32.00	80.00
49-Huey, Dewey & Louie Back to School (9/61)	3.50	14.00	35.00
50-Marge's Little Lulu & Witch Hazel Trick 'N' Treat (10/61)	7.00	28.00	70.00
51-Tarzan, King of the Jungle by Jesse Marsh (11/61)	4.00	16.00	40.00
52-Uncle Donald & His Nephews Dude Ranch (11/61)	3.50	14.00	35.00
53-Donald Duck Merry Christmas(12/61)-Not by Barks	3.50	14.00	35.00
54-Woody Woodpecker Christmas Party(12/61)-issued after No. 55	2.50	10.00	25.00
55-Daisy Duck & Uncle Scrooge Showboat (9/61)-1st app. Daisy Duck's nieces, April, May & June	5.00	20.00	50.00

NOTE: All issues printed with & without ad on back cover.

(OTHER DELL GIANT EDITIONS)

	Good	Fine	N-Mint
Abraham Lincoln Life Story 1(3/58, 100p)	3.00	12.00	30.00
Bugs Bunny Christmas Funnies 1(11/50, 116p)	8.00	32.00	80.00
. . .Christmas Funnies 2(11/51, 116p)	5.00	20.00	50.00
. . .Christmas Funnies 3-5(11/52-11/54, 100p)-Becomes Christmas Party No. 6	3.50	14.00	35.00
. . .Christmas Funnies 7-9(12/56-12/58, 100p)	3.00	12.00	30.00
. . .Christmas Party 6(11/55, 100p)-Formerly B.B. Christmas Funnies #5	3.50	14.00	35.00
. . .County Fair 1(9/57, 100p)	3.50	14.00	35.00
. . .Halloween Parade 1(10/53, 100p)	6.00	24.00	60.00
. . .Halloween Parade 2(10/54, 100p)-Trick 'N' Treat Halloween Fun No. 3-on	4.00	16.00	40.00
. . .Trick 'N' Treat Halloween Fun 3,4(10/55-10/56, 100p)-Formerly Halloween Parade 2	3.50	14.00	35.00
. . .Vacation Funnies 1(7/51, 112p)	8.00	32.00	80.00
. . .Vacation Funnies 2('52, 100p)	5.00	20.00	50.00
. . .Vacation Funnies 3-5('53-'55, 100p)	3.50	14.00	35.00
. . .Vacation Funnies 6-9('54-6/59, 100p)	3.00	12.00	30.00
Cadet Gray of West Point 1(4/58, 100p)-Williamson-a, 10pgs. Buscema-a, photo-c	4.00	16.00	40.00
Christmas In Disneyland 1(12/57, 100p)-Barks-a, 18pgs.	8.00	32.00	80.00
Christmas Parade 1(11/49)-Barks-a, 25pgs; r-in G.K. Christmas			

DELL GIANTS (continued)	Good	Fine	N-Mint
Parade 5	33.00	130.00	325.00

Christmas Parade 2('50)-Barks-a, 25pgs; r-in G.K. Christmas

| Parade 6 | 19.00 | 76.00 | 190.00 |
| Christmas Parade 3-7('51-'55, 116-100p) | 4.00 | 16.00 | 40.00 |

Christmas Parade 8(12/56, 100p)-Barks-a, 8pgs.

| | 8.00 | 32.00 | 80.00 |
| Christmas Treasury, A 1(11/54, 100p) | 5.00 | 20.00 | 50.00 |

Davy Crockett, King Of The Wild Frontier 1(9/55, 100p)-Photo-c;

| Marsh-a | 10.00 | 40.00 | 100.00 |

Disneyland Birthday Party 1(10/58, 100p)-Barks-a, 16pgs.

| | 7.00 | 28.00 | 70.00 |

Donald and Mickey In Disneyland 1(5/58, 100p)

	3.50	14.00	35.00
Donald Duck Beach Party 1(7/54, 100p)	6.00	24.00	60.00
...Beach Party 2('55, 100p)	4.00	16.00	40.00
...Beach Party 3-5('56-'58, 100p)	3.50	14.00	35.00
...Beach Party 6(8/59, 84p)-Stapled	2.50	10.00	25.00

Donald Duck Fun Book 1,2('53-10/54, 100p)-Games, puzzles,

comics & cut-outs (Rare)	14.00	56.00	140.00
Donald Duck In Disneyland 1(9/55, 100p)	3.50	14.00	35.00
Golden West Rodeo Treasury 1(10/57, 100p)	4.50	18.00	45.00

Huey, Dewey and Louie Back To School 1(9/58, 100p)

| | 4.00 | 16.00 | 40.00 |
| Lady and The Tramp 1(6/55, 100p) | 4.50 | 18.00 | 45.00 |

Life Stories of American Presidents 1(11/57, 100p)-Buscema-a

| | 3.00 | 12.00 | 30.00 |

Lone Ranger Golden West 3(8/55, 100p)-Formerly Lone Ranger

| Western Treasury | 7.00 | 28.00 | 70.00 |

Lone Ranger Movie Story nn(3/56, 100p)-Origin Lone Ranger in

| text; Clayton Moore photo-c | 17.00 | 68.00 | 170.00 |

...Western Treasury 1(9/53, 100p)-Origin L. Ranger, Silver,

| & Tonto | 12.00 | 48.00 | 120.00 |

...Western Treasury 2(8/54, 100p)-Becomes Lone Ranger Golden

| West #3 | 6.50 | 26.00 | 65.00 |

Marge's Little Lulu & Alvin Story Telling Time 1(3/59)-r/#2,5,3,11,

| 30,10,21,17,8,14,16; Stanley-a | 8.00 | 32.00 | 80.00 |
| ...& Her Friends 4(3/56, 100p)-Tripp-a | 6.50 | 26.00 | 65.00 |

...& Her Special Friends 3(3/55, 100p)-Tripp-a

| | 6.50 | 26.00 | 65.00 |

...& Tubby At Summer Camp 5(10/57, 100p)-Tripp-a

| | 6.50 | 26.00 | 65.00 |

...& Tubby At Summer Camp 2(10/58, 100p)-Tripp-a

| | 6.50 | 26.00 | 65.00 |

...& Tubby Halloween Fun 6(10/57, 100p)-Tripp-a

| | 6.50 | 26.00 | 65.00 |

...& Tubby Halloween Fun 2(10/58, 100p)-Tripp-a

| | 7.00 | 30.00 | 75.00 |
| ...& Tubby In Alaska 1(7/59, 100p)-Tripp-a | 7.00 | 30.00 | 75.00 |

...On Vacation 1(7/54, 100p)-r/4C-110,14,4C-146,5,4C-97,4,4C-158,3,1;

| Stanley-a | 11.00 | 44.00 | 110.00 |

...& Tubby Annual 1(3/53, 100p)-r/4C-165,4C-74,4C-146,4C-97,4C-158,

| 4C-139,4C-131; Stanley-a | 16.00 | 64.00 | 160.00 |

...& Tubby Annual 2('54, 100p)-r/4C-139,6,4C-115,4C-74,5,4C-97,3,

| 4C-146,18; Stanley-a | 14.00 | 56.00 | 140.00 |

Marge's Tubby & His Clubhouse Pals 1(10/56, 100p)-1st app.
Gran'pa Feeb, written by Stanley; 1st app. Janie; Tripp-a

| | 9.00 | 36.00 | 90.00 |

Mickey Mouse Almanac 1(12/57, 100p)-Barks-a, 8pgs.

| | 10.00 | 40.00 | 100.00 |

...Birthday Party 1(9/53, 100p)-r-/entire 48pgs. of Gottfredson's
"M.M. in Love Trouble" from WDC&S 36-39. Quality equal to
original. Also reprints one story each from 4-Color 27, 29, &
181 plus 6 panels of highlights in the career of Mickey Mouse

| | 15.00 | 60.00 | 150.00 |

	Good	Fine	N-Mint

...Club Parade 1(12/55, 100p)-R-/4-Color 16 with some art redrawn
by Paul Murry & recolored with night scenes turned into day;

| quality much poorer than original | 12.00 | 48.00 | 120.00 |
| ...In Fantasy Land 1(5/57, 100p) | 6.00 | 24.00 | 60.00 |

...In Frontier Land 1(5/56, 100p)-Mickey Mouse Club issue

| | 5.00 | 20.00 | 50.00 |

...Summer Fun 1(8/58, 100p)-Mobile cut-outs on back-c; becomes

| Summer Fun No. 2 | 5.00 | 20.00 | 50.00 |

Moses & The Ten Commandments 1(8/57, 100p)-Not based on

| movie; Dell's adaptation; Sekowsky-a | 3.00 | 12.00 | 30.00 |
| Nancy & Sluggo Travel Time 1(9/58, 100p) | 3.50 | 14.00 | 35.00 |

Peter Pan Treasure Chest 1(1/53, 212p)-Disney; contains movie

| adaptation plus other stories | 28.00 | 110.00 | 280.00 |

Picnic Party 6,7(7/55-6/56, 100p)(Formerly Vacation Parade)-Uncle

| Scrooge, Mickey & Donald | 3.50 | 14.00 | 35.00 |
| Picnic Party 8(7/57, 100p)-Barks-a. 6pgs. | 6.00 | 24.00 | 60.00 |

Pogo Parade 1(9/53, 100p)-Kelly-a(r-/Pogo from Animal Comics in

| this order: #11,13,21,14,27,16,23,9,18,15,17) | 20.00 | 80.00 | 200.00 |
| Raggedy Ann & Andy 1(2/55, 100p) | 5.50 | 22.00 | 55.00 |

Santa Claus Funnies 1(11/52, 100p)-Dan Noonan -A Christmas

| Carol adaptation | 5.00 | 20.00 | 50.00 |

Silly Symphonies 1(9/52, 100p)-r/Chicken Little, M. Mouse "The
Brave Little Tailor," Mother Pluto, Three Little Pigs, Lady, Bucky
Bug, Wise Little Hen, Little Hiawatha, Pedro, The Grasshopper &

| The Ants | 11.00 | 44.00 | 110.00 |

Silly Symphonies 2(9/53, 100p)-r/M. Mouse-"The Sorcerer's
Apprentice," Little Hiawatha, Peculiar Penguins, Lambert The
Sheepish Lion, Pluto, Spotty Pig, The Golden Touch, Elmer

| Elephant, The Pelican & The Snipe | 7.00 | 28.00 | 70.00 |

Silly Symphonies 3(2/54, 100p)-r/Mickey & The Beanstalk
(4-Color 157), Little Minnehaha, Pablo, The Flying Gauchito,

| Pluto, & Bongo | 6.50 | 26.00 | 65.00 |

Silly Symphonies 4(8/54, 100p)-r/Dumbo (4-Color 234), Morris
The Midget Moose, The Country Cousin, Bongo, & Clara Cluck

| | 5.50 | 22.00 | 55.00 |

Silly Symphonies 5(2/55, 100p)-r/Cinderella (4-Color 272), Bucky
Bug, Pluto, Little Hiawatha, The 7 Dwarfs & Dumbo, Pinocchio

| | 5.50 | 22.00 | 55.00 |

Silly Symphonies 6(8/55, 100p)-r/Pinocchio(WDC&S 63), The 7
Dwarfs & Thumper (WDC&S 45), M. Mouse-"Adventures With
Robin Hood," Johnny Appleseed, Pluto & Peter Pan, & Bucky

| Bug; Cut-out on back-c | 5.50 | 22.00 | 55.00 |

Silly Symphonies 7(2/57, 100p)-r/Reluctant Dragon (4-Color 13),
Ugly Duckling, M. Mouse & Peter Pan, Jiminy Cricket, Peter &
The Wolf, Brer Rabbit, Bucky Bug; Cut-out on back-c

| | 6.00 | 24.00 | 60.00 |

Silly Symphonies 8(2/58, 100p)-r/Thumper Meets The 7 Dwarfs
(4-Color 19), Jiminy Cricket, Niok, Brer Rabbit; Cut-out on back-c

| | 5.00 | 20.00 | 50.00 |

Silly Symphonies 9(2/59, 100p)-r/Paul Bunyan, Humphrey Bear,
Jiminy Cricket, The Social Lion, Goliath II; Cut-out on back-c

| | 5.00 | 20.00 | 50.00 |
| Sleeping Beauty 1(4/59, 100p) | 9.00 | 36.00 | 90.00 |

Summer Fun 2(8/59, 100p)(Formerly Mickey Mouse...)-Barks-a(2),

| 24 pgs. | 6.00 | 24.00 | 60.00 |

Tales From The Tomb (See Tales From The Tomb)

| Tarzan's Jungle Annual 1(8/52, 100p) | 6.00 | 24.00 | 60.00 |
| ...Annual 2(8/53, 100p) | 5.00 | 20.00 | 50.00 |

...Annual 3-7('54-9/58, 100p)(two No. 5s)-Manning-a-No. 3,5-7;

Marsh-a in No. 1-7	4.00	16.00	40.00
Tom And Jerry Back To School 1(9/56, 100p)	3.50	14.00	35.00
...Picnic Time 1(7/58, 100p)	3.00	12.00	30.00

...Summer Fun 1(7/54, 100p)-Droopy written by Barks

	7.00	28.00	70.00
...Summer Fun 2-4(7/55-7/57, 100p)	3.00	12.00	30.00
...Toy Fair 1(6/58, 100p)	3.50	14.00	35.00

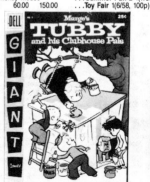

Donald Duck Beach Party #6, © WDC   Marge's Tubby And His Clubhouse Pals #1, © WEST

Silly Symphonies #1, © WDC

Tom And Jerry Winter Carnival #2, © M.G.M.

Vacation Parade #3. © WDC

Dennis The Menace #1. © STD

	Good	Fine	N-Mint
DELL GIANTS (continued)			
...**Winter Carnival** 1(12/52, 100p)-Droopy written by Barks			
	9.00	36.00	90.00
...**Winter Carnival** 2(12/53, 100p)-Droopy written by Barks			
	5.00	20.00	50.00
...**Winter Fun** 3(12/54, 100p)	3.50	14.00	35.00
...**Winter Fun** 4-7(12/55-11/58, 100p)	3.00	12.00	30.00
Treasury of Dogs, A 1(10/56, 100p)	2.50	10.00	25.00
Treasury of Horses, A 1(9/55, 100p)	2.50	10.00	25.00
Uncle Scrooge Goes To Disneyland 1(8/57, 100p)-Barks-a, 20pgs.			
	8.00	32.00	80.00
Universal Presents-Dracula-The Mummy & Other Stories			
02-530-311 (9-11/63, 84p)-R-/Dracula 12-231-212, The Mummy			
12-437-211 & part of Ghost Stories No. 1	3.50	14.00	35.00
Vacation In Disneyland 1(8/58, 100p)	4.00	16.00	40.00
Vacation Parade 1(7/50, 130p)-Donald Duck & Mickey Mouse;			
Barks-a, 55 pgs.	50.00	200.00	500.00
Vacation Parade 2(7/51, 100p)	8.00	32.00	80.00
Vacation Parade 3-5(7/52-7/54, 100p)-Picnic Party No. 6 on			
	4.00	16.00	40.00
Western Roundup 1(6/52, 100p)-Photo-c; Gene Autry, Roy Rogers,			
Johnny Mack Brown, Rex Allen, & Bill Elliott			
begin, end No. 14,16,18	10.00	40.00	100.00
Western Roundup 2(2/53, 100p)-Photo-c	6.00	24.00	60.00
Western Roundup 3-5(7-9/53 - 1-3/54)-Photo-c	5.50	22.00	55.00
Western Roundup 6-10(4-6/54 - 4-6/55)-Photo-c			
	5.00	20.00	50.00
Western Roundup 11-13,16,17(100p)-Photo-c; Manning-a. 11-Flying			
A's Range Rider, Dale Evans begin	4.00	16.00	40.00
Western Roundup 14,15,25(1-3/59; 100p)-Photo-c			
	4.00	16.00	40.00
Western Roundup 18(100p)-Toth-a; last photo-c; Gene Autry ends			
	4.50	18.00	45.00
Western Roundup 19-24(100p)-Manning-a; 19-Buffalo Bill Jr. begins.			
21-Rex Allen, Johnny Mack Brown end. 22-Jace Pearson's .			
Texas Rangers, Rin Tin Tin, Tales of Wells Fargo & Wagon			
Train begin	3.50	14.00	35.00
Woody Woodpecker Back To School 1(10/52, 100p)			
	3.50	14.00	35.00
...**Back To School** 2-4,6('53-10/57, 100p)-County Fair No. 5			
	2.50	10.00	25.00
...**County Fair** 5(9/56, 100p)-Formerly Back To School			
	2.50	10.00	25.00
...**County Fair** 2(11/58, 100p)	2.50	10.00	25.00
DELL JUNIOR TREASURY (15 cents)			
June, 1955 - No. 10, Oct, 1957 (All painted-c)			
Dell Publishing Co.			
1-Alice in Wonderland-Reprints 4-Color 331 (52 pgs.)			
	6.50	19.50	45.00
2-Aladdin & the Wonderful Lamp	5.00	15.00	35.00
3-Gulliver's Travels(1/56)	3.70	11.00	26.00
4-Advs. of Mr. Frog & Miss Mouse	4.50	14.00	32.00
5-The Wizard of Oz(7/56)	5.00	15.00	35.00
6-Heidi (10/56)	3.70	11.00	26.00
7-Santa and the Angel	3.70	11.00	26.00
8-Raggedy Ann and the Camel with the Wrinkled Knees			
	3.70	11.00	26.00
9-Clementina the Flying Pig	4.00	12.00	28.00
10-Adventures of Tom Sawyer	4.50	14.00	32.00
DEMON, THE (See Detective Comics No. 482-485)			
8-9/72 - No. 16, 1/74; 1/87 - No. 4, 4/87			
National Periodical Publications			
1-Origin; Kirby-c/a in 1-16	.35	1.00	2.00
2-16		.55	1.10
1-4('87)-Mini series		.60	1.20

	Good	Fine	N-Mint
DEMON DREAMS			
Feb, 1984 - No. 2, May, 1984			
Pacific Comics			
1,2-Mostly r-/Heavy Metal	.25	.75	1.50
DEMON-HUNTER			
September, 1975			
Seaboard Periodicals (Atlas)			
1-Origin; Buckler c/a		.30	.60
DEN			
1988 - No. 10, Dec?, 1989 ($2.00, color)			
Fantagor Press			
1-10: Corben-c/a. 9,10-Alex Nino-a	.35	1.00	2.00
DENNIS THE MENACE (Becomes ...Fun Fest Series; See The Best			
of . . . & The Very Best of . . .)			
8/53 - #14, 1/56; #15, 3/56 - #31, 11/58; #32, 1/59 - #166, 11/79			
Standard Comics/Pines No.15-31/Hallden (Fawcett) No.32 on			
1-1st app. Mr. & Mrs. Wilson, Ruff & Dennis' mom & dad; Wise-			
man-a, written by Fred Toole-most issues	21.50	65.00	150.00
2	11.00	32.00	75.00
3-10	5.70	17.00	40.00
11-20	3.50	10.50	24.00
21-30: 22-1st app. Margaret w/blonde hair	1.70	5.00	12.00
31-40: 31-1st app. Joey	1.15	3.50	8.00
41-60	.85	2.60	6.00
61-90	.60	1.75	3.50
91-166	.30	1.00	2.00
...& Dirt('59,'68)-Soil Conservation giveaway; r-No. 36; Wiseman-c/a			
	.25	.70	1.40
...Away We Go('70)-Caladayl giveaway	.25	.70	1.40
...Coping with Family Stress-giveaway		.30	.60
...Takes a Poke at Poison('61)-Food & Drug Assn. giveaway;			
Wiseman c/a	.35	1.00	2.00
...Takes a Poke at Poison-Revised 1/66, 11/70, 1972, 1974, 1977, 1981			
		.30	.60
NOTE: Wiseman c/a-1-46, 53, 68, 69			
DENNIS THE MENACE (Giants) (No. 1 titled Giant Vacation Special;			
becomes Dennis the Menace Bonus Magazine No. 76 on)			
(#1-8,18,23,25,30,38: 100 pgs.; rest to #41: 84 pgs.; #42-75: 68 pgs.)			
Summer, 1955 - No. 75, Dec, 1969			
Standard/Pines/Hallden(Fawcett)			
nn-Giant Vacation Special(Summ/55-Standard)	5.00	15.00	40.00
nn-Christmas issue (Winter '55)	3.75	11.25	30.00
2-Giant Vacation Special (Summer '56-Pines)			
3-Giant Christmas issue (Winter '56-Pines)			
4-Giant Vacation Special (Summer '57-Pines)			
5-Giant Christmas issue (Winter '57-Pines)			
6-In Hawaii (Giant Vacation Special)(Summer '58-Pines)-Reprinted			
Summer '59 plus 3 more times			
6-Giant Christmas issue (Winter '58)			
each....	3.25	9.75	26.00
7-In Hollywood (Winter '59-Hallden)			
8-In Mexico (Winter '60, 100 pgs.-Hallden/Fawcett)			
8-In Mexico (Summer '62, 2nd printing)			
9-Goes to Camp (Summer '61, 84 pgs., 2nd printing-Summer '62)-			
1st CCA approved issue			
10-X-Mas issue (Winter '61)			
11-Giant Christmas issue (Winter '62)			
12-Triple Feature (Winter '62)			
each....	2.75	8.25	22.00
13-Best of Dennis the Menace (Spring '63)-Reprints			
14-And His Dog Ruff (Summer '63)			
15-In Washington, D.C. (Summer '63)			
16-Goes to Camp (Summer '63)-Reprints No. 9			

DENNIS THE MENACE (continued)
17-& His Pal Joey (Winter '63)
18-In Hawaii (Reprints No. 6)
19-Giant Christmas issue (Winter '63)

	Good	Fine	N-Mint
20-Spring Special (Spring '63) each....	1.50	4.50	12.00
21-40	1.00	3.00	7.00
41-75	.70	2.00	4.00

NOTE: *Wiseman c/a-1-8, 12, 14, 15, 17, 20, 22, 27, 28, 31, 35, 36, 41, 49.*

DENNIS THE MENACE
Nov, 1981 - No. 13, Nov, 1982
Marvel Comics Group

1-13: 1,2-New art. 3-Part-r. 4,5-r	.25	.50

NOTE: *Hank Ketcham c-most; a-3, 12. Wiseman a-4, 5.*

DENNIS THE MENACE AND HIS DOG RUFF
Summer, 1961
Hallden/Fawcett

1-Wiseman c/a	2.50	7.50	20.00

DENNIS THE MENACE AND HIS FRIENDS
1969; No. 5, Jan, 1970 - No. 46, April, 1980 (All reprints)
Fawcett Publications

	Good	Fine	N-Mint
Dennis T.M. & Joey No. 2 (7/69)	1.35	4.00	8.00
Dennis T.M. & Ruff No. 2 (9/69)	1.00	3.00	6.00
Dennis T.M. & Mr. Wilson No. 1 (10/69)	1.00	3.00	6.00
Dennis & Margaret No. 1 (Winter '69)	.50	1.50	3.00
5-10: No. 5-Dennis T.M. & Margaret. No. 6-& Joey. No. 7-& Ruff. No. 8-& Mr. Wilson	.25	.70	1.40
11-20	.25	.70	1.40
21-37		.60	1.20
38(begin digest size, 148 pgs., 4/78, 95 cents) - 46		.60	1.20

NOTE: *Titles rotate every four issues, beginning with No. 5.*

DENNIS THE MENACE AND HIS PAL JOEY
Summer, 1961 (10 cents) (See Dennis the Menace Giants No. 45)
Fawcett Publications

1-Wiseman c/a	2.85	8.50	20.00

DENNIS THE MENACE AND THE BIBLE KIDS
1977 (36 pages)
Word Books

1-Jesus. 2-Joseph. 3-David. 4-The Bible Girls. 5-Moses. 6-More About Jesus. 7-The Lord's Prayer. 8-Stories Jesus told. 9-Paul, God's Traveller. 10-In the Beginning each....	.25	.50

NOTE: *Ketcham c/a in all.*

DENNIS THE MENACE BIG BONUS SERIES
No. 10, 1980 - No. 11, 1980
Fawcett Publications

10,11	.50	1.00

DENNIS THE MENACE BONUS MAGAZINE (Formerly Dennis the Menace Giants Nos. 1-75)
No. 76, 1/70 - No. 194, 10/79; (No. 76-124: 68 pgs.; No. 125-163: 52 pgs.; No. 164 on: 36 pgs.)
Fawcett Publications

	Good	Fine	N-Mint
76-90	.30	.90	1.80
91-110		.60	1.20
111-140		.40	.80
141-194		.30	.60

DENNIS THE MENACE COMICS DIGEST
April, 1982 - No. 3, Aug, 1982 (Digest Size, $1.25)
Marvel Comics Group

1-3-Reprints	.20	.60	1.25

NOTE: *Hank Ketcham c-all. Wiseman a-all. A few thousand No. 1's were published with a DC emblem on cover.*

DENNIS THE MENACE FUN BOOK
1960 (100 pages)
Fawcett Publications/Standard Comics

	Good	Fine	N-Mint
1-Part Wiseman-a	3.00	9.00	24.00

DENNIS THE MENACE FUN FEST SERIES (Formerly Dennis The Menace #166)
No. 16, Jan, 1980 - No. 17, Mar, 1980 (40 cents)
Hallden (Fawcett)

16,17-By Hank Ketcham	.20	.40

DENNIS THE MENACE POCKET FULL OF FUN!
Spring, 1969 - No. 50, March, 1980 (196 pages) (Digest size)
Fawcett Publications (Hallden)

1-Reprints in all issues	.70	2.00	4.00
2-10	.35	1.00	2.00
11-28		.50	1.00
29-50: 35,40,46-Sunday strip-r		.40	.80

NOTE: *No. 1-28 are 196 pgs.; No. 29-36: 164 pgs.; No. 37: 148 pgs.; No. 38 on: 132 pgs. No. 8, 11, 15, 21, 25, 29 all contain strip reprints.*

DENNIS THE MENACE TELEVISION SPECIAL
Summer, 1961 - No. 2, Spring, 1962 (Giant)
Fawcett Publications (Hallden Div.)

1	2.50	7.50	20.00
2	1.50	4.50	12.00

DENNIS THE MENACE TRIPLE FEATURE
Winter, 1961 (Giant)
Fawcett Publications

1-Wiseman c/a	2.00	6.00	16.00

DEPUTY, THE (See 4-Color No. 1077,1130,1225)

DEPUTY DAWG (TV) (Also see New Terrytoons)
Oct-Dec, 1961 - No. 1, Aug, 1965
Dell Publishing Co./Gold Key

4-Color 1238,1299	5.00	15.00	35.00
1(10164-508)	4.30	13.00	30.00

DEPUTY DAWG PRESENTS DINKY DUCK AND HASHIMOTO-SAN
August, 1965 (TV)
Gold Key

1(10159-508)	4.00	12.00	28.00

DESIGN FOR SURVIVAL (Gen. Thomas S. Power's...)
1968 (36 pages in color) (25 cents)
American Security Council Press

nn-Propaganda against the Threat of Communism-Aircraft cover	3.00	9.00	18.00
Twin Circle edition-cover shows panels from inside	1.70	5.00	10.00

DESPERADO (Black Diamond Western No. 9 on)
June, 1948 - No. 8, Feb, 1949
Lev Gleason Publications

1-Biro-c	5.70	17.00	40.00
2	3.00	9.00	21.00
3-Story with over 20 killings	2.65	8.00	18.00
4-8	2.15	6.50	15.00

NOTE: *Barry a-2. Kida a-3-7. Fuje a-4, 8. Guardineer a-6, 7. Ed Moore a-4, 6.*

DESTINATION MOON (See Fawcett Movie Comics, Space Adventures #20, 23, & Strange Adventures #1)

DESTROY!!
1986 (One shot, B&W, Magazine size, $4.95)
Eclipse Comics

1	.85	2.50	5.00
3-D Special 1-r-/#1 ($2.50)	.40	1.25	2.50

Dennis The Menace And His Pal Joey #1, © FAW

Desperado #1, © LEV

Destroy! 3-D #1, © Eclipse

Detective Comics #40, © DC   Detective Comics #65, © DC   Detective Comics #140, © DC

DESTROYER, THE
Nov, 1989 - Present ($2.25, B&W, magazine, 52 pgs.)
Marvel Comics

	Good	Fine	N-Mint
1-5: Based on Remo Williams movie & paperbacks; 2-Williamson part inks. 3-Mortimer part inks	.40	1.15	2.30

DESTROYER DUCK
1982 (no number) - No. 7, 5/84 (2-7: Baxter paper) ($1.50)
Eclipse Comics

1-Origin D. Duck; 1st app., origin Groo	1.15	3.50	7.00
2-7: 2-Starling back-up begins	.25	.75	1.50

NOTE: Adams c-1i. Kirby a-1-5p; c-1-5p. Miller c-7.

DESTRUCTOR, THE
February, 1975 - No. 4, Aug, 1975
Atlas/Seaboard

1-Origin; Ditko/Wood-a; Wood-c(i)		.60	1.20
2-4: 2-Ditko/Wood-a. 3,4-Ditko-a(p)		.40	.80

DETECTIVE COMICS (See Special Edition)
March, 1937 - Present
National Periodical Publications/DC Comics

	Good	Fine	Vf-NM
1-(Scarce)-Slam Bradley & Spy by Siegel & Shuster, Speed Saunders by Guardineer, Flat Foot Flannigan by Gustavson, Cosmo, the Phantom of Disguise, Buck Marshall, Bruce Nelson begin; Chin Lung-c from 'Claws of the Red Dragon' serial; Flessel-c (1st?)			
	1900.00	4750.00	11,400.00

(No copy is known to exist beyond NM condition)

	Good	Fine	
2 (Rare)	583.00	1460.00	3500.00
3 (Rare)	483.00	1210.00	2900.00

	Good	Fine	N-Mint
4,5: 5-Larry Steele begins	267.00	670.00	1600.00
6,7,9,10	180.00	450.00	1080.00
8-Mister Chang-c	228.00	570.00	1370.00
11-17,19: 17-1st app. Fu Manchu in Det.	153.00	385.00	920.00
18-Fu Manchu-c	200.00	500.00	1200.00
20-The Crimson Avenger begins (intro. & 1st app.)			
	217.00	545.00	1300.00
21,23-25	108.00	270.00	650.00
22-1st Crimson Avenger-c (12/38)	150.00	375.00	900.00
26	125.00	315.00	750.00
27-The Batman & Commissioner Gordon begin (1st app.) by Bob Kane (5/39); Batman-c (1st)	**Good**	**Fine**	**Vf-NM**
	6,000.00	15,000.00	32,500.00

(Only one copy known to exist beyond VF-NM condition which sold in 1988 for $35,000. Prices vary widely on this book)

27-Reprint, Oversize 13½''x10''. **WARNING:** This comic is an exact duplicate reprint of the original except for its size. DC published in 1974 with a second cover titling it as Famous First Edition. There have been many reported cases of the outer cover being removed and the interior sold as the original edition. The reprint with the new outer cover removed is practically worthless.

	Good	Fine	N-Mint
27(1984)-Oreo Cookies giveaway (32 pgs., paper-c, r-/Det. 27, 38 & Batman No. 1 (1st Joker)	1.15	3.50	7.00
28	767.00	2200.00	4600.00
29-Batman-c; Doctor Death app.	833.00	2100.00	5000.00
30,32: 30-Dr. Death app. 32-Batman uses gun			
	350.00	875.00	2100.00
31-Classic Batman-c; 1st Julie Madison, Bat Plane (Bat-Gyro) & Batarang	833.00	2100.00	5000.00
33-Origin The Batman; Batman gunholster-c			
	1083.00	2710.00	6500.00
34-Steve Malone begins; 2nd Crimson Avenger-c			
	300.00	750.00	1800.00
35-37: 35-Batman-c begin. 35-Hypo-c. 36-Origin Hugo Strange. 37-Cliff Crosby begins	333.00	835.00	2000.00
38-Origin/1st app. Robin the Boy Wonder (4/40)			

	Good	Fine	N-Mint
	1000.00	2500.00	7000.00
39	283.00	710.00	1700.00
40-Origin & 1st app. Clay Face (Basil Karlo); 1st Clay Face cover app.			
	283.00	710.00	1700.00
41-Robin's 1st solo	183.00	450.00	1100.00
42-44: 44-Crimson Avenger-new costume	133.00	335.00	800.00
45-1st Joker story in Det. (3rd app.)	200.00	500.00	1200.00
46-50: 48-1st time car called Batmobile; Gotham City 1st mention.			
49-Last Clay Face	122.00	305.00	735.00
51-57,59: 59-Last Steve Malone; 2nd Penguin; Wing becomes Crimson Avenger's aide	100.00	250.00	600.00
58-1st Penguin app.; last Speed Saunders	183.00	450.00	1100.00
60-Intro. Air Wave	108.00	270.00	650.00
61,63: 63-Last Cliff Crosby; 1st app. Mr. Baffle			
	92.00	230.00	550.00
62-Joker-c/story (1st Joker-c)	120.00	300.00	720.00
64-Origin & 1st app. Boy Commandos by Simon & Kirby; Joker app.			
	250.00	625.00	1500.00
65-Boy Commandos-c	125.00	315.00	750.00
66-Origin & 1st app. Two-Face	167.00	420.00	1000.00
67,70	78.00	195.00	470.00
68-Two-Face-c/story	83.00	210.00	500.00
69-Joker-c/story	103.00	260.00	620.00
71-Joker-c/story	93.00	235.00	560.00
72-75: 73-Scarecrow-c/story. 74-1st Tweedledum & Tweedledee; S&K-a	70.00	175.00	420.00
76-Newsboy Legion & The Sandman x-over in Boy Commandos; S&K-a; Joker-c/story	108.00	270.00	650.00
77-79: All S&K-a	70.00	175.00	420.00
80-Two-Face app.; S&K-a	73.00	185.00	440.00
81,82,84,86-90: 81-1st Cavalier app. 89-Last Crimson Avenger			
	63.00	160.00	380.00
83-1st ''Skinny'' Alfred; last S&K Boy Commandos? Most issues #84 on signed S&K are not by them	71.00	180.00	425.00
85-Joker-c/story; Last Spy	83.00	210.00	500.00
91,102-Joker-c/story	78.00	195.00	470.00
92-99: 96-Alfred's last name 'Beagle' revealed, later changed to 'Pennyworth'-Batman 214	58.00	145.00	350.00
100 (6/45)	83.00	21.00	500.00
101,103-108,110-113,115-117,119,120: 114-1st use small logo(8/46)			
	53.00	135.00	320.00
109,114,118-Joker-c/stories	72.00	180.00	430.00
121-123,125-127,129,130: 126-Electrocution-c	51.00	128.00	305.00
124,128-Joker-c/stories	67.00	170.00	400.00
131-136,139: 137-Last Air Wave	43.00	110.00	260.00
137-Joker-c/story	58.00	145.00	350.00
138-Origin Robotman (See Star Spangled No. 7, 1st app.); series ends No. 202	75.00	190.00	450.00
140-1st app. The Riddler (10/48)	133.00	335.00	800.00
141,143-148,150: 150-Last Boy Commandos	43.00	110.00	260.00
142-2nd Riddler app.	67.00	170.00	400.00
149-Joker-c/story	56.00	140.00	335.00
151-Joker & 1st app. Pow Wow Smith	46.00	115.00	275.00
152,154,155,157-160: 152-Last Slam Bradley	43.00	110.00	260.00
153-1st Roy Raymond app.; origin The Human Fly			
	46.00	115.00	275.00
156(2/50)-The new classic Batmobile	54.00	135.00	325.00
161-167,169-176: Last 52 pgs.	46.00	115.00	275.00
168-Origin the Joker	158.00	395.00	950.00
177-189,191-199,201-204,206-212,214-216: 185-Secret of Batman's utility belt. 187-Two-Face app. 202-Last Robotman & Pow Wow Smith. 216-Last precode (2/55)	30.00	75.00	180.00
190-Origin Batman retold	47.00	120.00	280.00
200	43.00	110.00	260.00
205-Origin Batcave	45.00	115.00	270.00
213-Origin Mirror Man	42.00	105.00	250.00

DETECTIVE COMICS (continued)	Good	Fine	N-Mint
217-224	28.00	70.00	170.00

225-(11/55)-Intro. & 1st app. Martian Manhunter-John Jones, later
changed to J'onn J'onzz; also see Batman #78

	165.00	495.00	1150.00
226-Origin Martian Manhunter continued	44.00	132.00	310.00
227-229	27.00	81.00	190.00
230-1st app. Mad Hatter	32.00	96.00	225.00
231-Origin Martian Manhunter retold	21.00	63.00	145.00
232,234,236-240	18.00	54.00	125.00
233-Origin & 1st app. Batwoman	42.00	125.00	295.00
235-Origin Batman & his costume	26.00	77.00	180.00

241-260: 246-Intro. Diane Meade, J. Jones' girl. 257-Intro. & 1st app.
Whirly Bats

| | 13.50 | 40.00 | 95.00 |

261-264,266,268-270: 261-1st app. Dr. Double X. 262-Origin Jackal

	10.00	30.00	70.00
265-Batman's origin retold	14.00	43.00	100.00
267-1st app. Bat-Mite	11.00	32.00	75.00
271-280: 276-2nd Bat-Mite	8.00	24.00	55.00

281-297: 287-Origin J'onn J'onzz retold. 292-Last Roy Raymond.
293-Aquaman begins, ends #300. 297-Last 10 cent issue (11/61)

| | 5.70 | 17.00 | 40.00 |
| 298-1st modern Clayface (Matt Hagen) | 8.00 | 24.00 | 55.00 |

299-327,329,330: 311-Intro. Zook in John Jones; 1st app. Catman.
322-Batgirl's 1st app. in Det. 326-Last J'onn J'onzz; intro. Idol-
Head of Diabolu. 327-Elongated Man begins, ends 383; new
Batman costume

| | 3.15 | 9.50 | 22.00 |
| 328-Death of Alfred | 4.70 | 14.00 | 33.00 |

331,333-340,342-358,360-364,366-368,370: 345-Intro The Block Buster.
351-Elongated Man new costume. 355-Zatanna x-over in
Elongated Man. 356-Alfred brought back in Batman

	1.85	5.50	13.00
332,341,365-Joker-c/stories	2.85	8.50	20.00
359-Intro/origin new Batgirl	2.85	8.50	20.00
369-Adams-a	3.15	9.50	22.00
371-386,389,390	1.50	4.50	9.00
387-R/1st Batman story from #27; Joker-c	2.85	8.50	20.00
388-Joker-c/story	2.15	6.50	15.00
391-394,396,398,399,401,403,405,406,409: 392-1st app. Jason Bard.			
401-2nd Batgirl/Robin team-up	1.15	3.50	7.00
395,397,402,404,407,408,410-Adams-a	1.85	5.50	13.00

400-First app & 1st app. Man-Bat; 1st Batgirl/Robin team-up; Adams-a

| | 2.65 | 8.00 | 18.00 |

411-420: 414-52 pgs. begin, end #424. 418-Creeper x-over

| | 1.15 | 3.50 | 7.00 |

421-436: 424-Last Batgirl; 1st She-Bat. 426-Elongated Man begins,
ends #436. 428,434-Hawkman begins, ends #467

| | 1.00 | 3.00 | 6.00 |

437-New Manhunter begins by Simonson, ends #443

| | 1.00 | 3.00 | 6.00 |
| 438,439(100 pgs.)- 439-Origin Manhunter | 1.15 | 3.50 | 7.00 |

440(100 pgs.)-G.A. Manhunter, Hawkman, Dollman, Gr. Lantern;
Toth-a

| | 1.15 | 3.50 | 7.00 |
| 441(100 pgs.)-G.A. Plastic Man, Batman, Ibis-r | 1.15 | 3.50 | 7.00 |

442(100 pgs.)-G.A. Newsboy Legion, Bl. Canary, Elongated Man, Dr.
Fate-r

| | 1.15 | 3.50 | 7.00 |

443(100 pgs.)-Origin The Creeper-r; death of Manhunter; G.A. Green
Lantern, Spectre-r

| | 1.15 | 3.50 | 7.00 |

444,445(100 pgs.): 444-G.A. Kid Eternity-r. 445-G.A. Dr. Midnite-r

	1.15	3.50	7.00
446-460: 457-Origin retold & updated	.85	2.50	5.00
461-465,469,470,480	.85	2.50	5.00

466-468,471-474,478,479-Rogers-a; 478-1st app. 3rd Clayface (Preston
Payne)

	1.50	4.50	9.00
475,476-Joker-c/stories; Rogers-a	2.70	8.00	16.00
477-Adams-a(r); Rogers-a, 3pgs.	1.70	5.00	10.00

481-(Combined with Batman Family, 12/78-1/79)(Begin $1.00 issues)

	Good	Fine	N-Mint
	1.35	4.00	8.00
482-Starlin/Russell, Golden-a; origin Demon-r	.85	2.50	5.00

483-40th Anniversary issue; origin retold; Newton Batman begins

	1.00	3.00	6.00
484-495: 485-Death of Batwoman. 487-The Odd Man by Ditko. 490-			
Black Lightning begins. 491(492 on inside)	.60	1.80	3.60
496-499,501-503,505-523: 519-Last Batgirl. 521-Green Arrow series			
begins	.60	1.80	3.60
500-($1.50)-Batman/Deadman team-up	1.00	3.00	6.00
504-Joker-c/story	1.00	3.00	6.00
524-2nd app. Jason Todd (cameo)(3/83)	.70	2.00	4.00
525-3rd app. Jason Todd (See Batman #357)	.50	1.50	3.00
526-Batman's 500th app. in Detective Comics (68 pgs., $1.50);			
Joker-c/story	1.50	4.50	9.00
527-531,533,534,536-565,567,568,571: 554-1st new Black Canary.			
567-Harlan Ellison scripts	.40	1.25	2.50
532,566,569,570-Joker-c/stories	.85	2.50	5.00
535-Intro new Robin (Jason Todd)-1st app. in Batman			
	.85	2.50	5.00
572 (60 pgs., $1.25)-50th Anniversary	.60	1.80	3.60
573	.40	1.25	2.50
574-Origin Batman & Jason Todd retold	.70	2.00	4.00
575-Year 2 begins, ends #578	2.50	7.50	15.00
576-578: McFarlane-c/a	2.00	6.00	12.00
579-597,601-607: 579-New logo. 595-free 16 pg. Batman story. 604-			
607-Mudpack storyline; 604,607-contain Batman mini-poster			
	.25	.75	1.50
598-Double-size, $2.95; "Blind Justice" storyline begins by Batman			
movie writer Sam Hamm, ends 600	1.70	5.00	10.00
599	1.35	2.00	4.00
600-($2.95, 84 pgs.)-50th Anniversary issue; 1 pg. Adams pin-up,			
among others	.85	2.50	5.00
608-612		.50	1.00
Annual 1(9/88, $1.50)	.85	2.50	5.00
Annual 2(1989, $2.00, 68 pgs.)	.60	1.80	3.60

NOTE: *Adams* c-369, 370, 372, 383, 385, 389, 391, 392, 394-422, 439. *Aparo* a-437, 438. 444-46, 500; c-430, 437, 440-46, 448, 468-70, 480, 484(back), 492-9, 500-02, 508, 509, 515, 518-22. *Austin* a-450i, 451i, 463i-68i, 471i-76i; c-474-76i, 478i. *Baily* a-443r. *Buckler* a-434, 446p, 479p; c-467p, 482p, 505p, 506p, 511p, 513-16p, 518p. *Colan* a(p)-510, 512, 517, 523, 528-38, 540-64, 565-64, 567; c(p)-510, 512, 528, 530-35, 537, 538, 540, 541, 543-45, 556-58, 560-64. *J. Craig* a-488. *Ditko* a-443r, 483-85, 487. *Golden* a-482p. *Grell* a-445, 455, 463p, 464p; c-455. *Gustavson* a-441r. *Kaluta* c-423, 424, 426-28, 431, 434, 438, 484, 486, 572. *Bob Kane* a-Most early ish. *Kubert* c-91, 297r, 438-40r, 442r, 443r. *Gil Kane* a(p)-368, 370-74, 384, 385, 388-407, 438r, 439r, 520. *Kubert* a-438r, 439r, 500; c-348-500. *McFarlane* c/a(p) 576-578. *Meskin* a-420r. *Mooney* a-444r. *Moreira* a-153-300, 419r, 444r, 445r. *Newton* a(p)-480, 481, 483-99, 501-09, 511, 513-16, 518-20, 524, 526, 539; c-526p. *Robinson* a-part; 66, 68, 71-73; all; 74-76, 79, 80; c-62, 64, 66, 68-74, 76, 79, 82, 86, 88, 442r, 443r. *Rogers* a-467, 478p, 479p, 481p; c-471p, 472p, 473, 474-479p. *Roussos* Airwave-76-105(most). *Russell* a-481i, 482i. *Simon/Kirby* a-440r, 442r. *Simonson* a-437-43, 450, 469, 470, 500. *Starlin* a-481p, 482p; c-503, 504, 567p. *Starr* a-441r. *Toth* a-414r, 416r, 418r, 424r, 440-44r. *Tuska* a-486p, 490p. *Wrightson* c-425.

DETECTIVE DAN, SECRET OP. 48
1933 (36 pgs.; 9½x12") (B&W; Softcover)
Humor Publ. Co.

| By Norman Marsh; forerunner of Dan Dunn | 7.00 | 21.00 | 50.00 |

DETECTIVE EYE (See Keen Detective Funnies)
Nov, 1940 - No. 2, Dec, 1940
Centaur Publications

1-Air Man & The Eye Sees begins; The Masked Marvel app.			
	86.00	257.00	600.00
2-Origin Don Rance and the Mysticape; Binder-a; Frank Thomas-c			
	64.00	193.00	450.00

DETECTIVE PICTURE STORIES (Keen Detective Funnies No. 8 on?)
Dec, 1936 - No. 7, 1937 (1st comic of a single theme)
Comics Magazine Company

| 1 | 125.00 | 375.00 | 875.00 |

Detective Comics #225, © DC

Detective Comics #483, © DC

Detective Comics #578, © DC

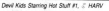
Devil Kids Starring Hot Stuff #1, © HARV

Diary Secrets #20, © STJ

Dickie Dare #1, © EAS

	Good	Fine	N-Mint
DETECTIVE PICTURE STORIES (continued)			
2-The Clock app.	57.00	170.00	400.00
3,4: 4-Eisner-a	52.00	156.00	365.00
5-7: 5-Kane-a	47.00	140.00	325.00

DETECTIVES, THE (See 4-Color No. 1168,1219,1240)

DETECTIVES, INC. (See Eclipse Graphic Album Series)
April, 1985 - No. 2, April, 1985 (Both have April dates)
Eclipse Comics

	Good	Fine	N-Mint
1,2: 2-Nudity	.35	1.00	2.00

DETECTIVES, INC.: A TERROR OF DYING DREAMS
June, 1987 - No. 3, Dec, 1987 ($1.75, duo-tone, mini-series)
Eclipse Comics

	Good	Fine	N-Mint
1-3: Adapts movie; Colan-c/a	.30	.90	1.80

DEVIL DINOSAUR
April, 1978 - No. 9, Dec, 1978
Marvel Comics Group

	Good	Fine	N-Mint
1-9		.25	.50

NOTE: *Byrne* a(i)-4-8. All Kirby c/a. *Kirby/Byrne* c-9.

DEVIL-DOG DUGAN (Tales of the Marines No. 4 on)
July, 1956 - No. 3, Nov, 1956
Atlas Comics (OPI)

	Good	Fine	N-Mint
1-Severin-c	3.15	9.50	22.00
2-Iron Mike McGraw x-over; Severin-c	2.00	6.00	14.00
3	1.60	4.70	11.00

DEVIL DOGS
1942
Street & Smith Publishers

	Good	Fine	N-Mint
1-Boy Rangers, U.S. Marines	10.00	30.00	70.00

DEVILINA
Feb, 1975 - No. 2, May, 1975 (Magazine) (B&W)
Atlas/Seaboard

	Good	Fine	N-Mint
1,2: 1-Reese-a	.50	1.50	3.00

DEVIL KIDS STARRING HOT STUFF
July, 1962 - No. 107, Oct, 1981 (Giant-Size #41-55)
Harvey Publications (Illustrated Humor)

	Good	Fine	N-Mint
1	6.75	20.00	45.00
2	3.35	10.00	21.00
3-10 (1/64)	2.35	7.00	14.00
11-20	1.35	4.00	8.00
21-30	1.00	3.00	6.00
31-40 ('71)	.70	2.00	4.00
41-50: All 68 pg. Giants	.85	2.50	5.00
51-55: All 52 pg. Giants	.70	2.00	4.00
56-70	.40	1.20	2.40
71-90	.30	.80	1.60
91-107		.30	.60

DEXTER COMICS
Summer, 1948 - No. 5, July, 1949
Dearfield Publ.

	Good	Fine	N-Mint
1	3.15	9.50	22.00
2	2.00	6.00	14.00
3-5	1.30	4.00	9.00

DEXTER THE DEMON (Formerly Melvin The Monster)
No. 7, Sept, 1957 (Also see Cartoon Kids & Peter the Little Pest)
Atlas Comics (HPC)

	Good	Fine	N-Mint
7	1.50	4.50	10.00

DIARY CONFESSIONS (Formerly Ideal Romance)
No. 9, May, 1955 - No. 14, April, 1955
Stanmor/Key Publ.

	Good	Fine	N-Mint
9	2.65	8.00	18.00

	Good	Fine	N-Mint
10-14	1.70	5.00	12.00

DIARY LOVES (Formerly Love Diary #1; G. I. Sweethearts #32 on)
No. 2, Nov, 1949 - No. 31, April, 1953
Quality Comics Group

	Good	Fine	N-Mint
2-Ward c/a, 9 pgs.	8.50	25.00	60.00
3 (1/50)	3.00	9.00	21.00
4-Crandall-a	4.85	14.50	34.00
5-7,10	2.15	6.50	15.00
8,9-Ward-a 6,8 pgs. plus Gustavson-#8	5.70	17.00	40.00
11,13,14,17-20	1.70	5.00	12.00
12,15,16-Ward-a 9,7,8 pgs.	4.85	14.50	34.00
21-Ward-a, 7 pgs.	4.00	12.00	28.00
22-31: 31-Whitney-a	1.30	4.00	9.00

NOTE: *Photo c-3-5, 8, 12-27.*

DIARY OF HORROR
December, 1952
Avon Periodicals

	Good	Fine	N-Mint
1-Hollingsworth c/a; bondage-c	16.00	48.00	110.00

DIARY SECRETS (Formerly Teen-Age Diary Secrets)
No. 10, Feb, 1952 - No. 30, Sept, 1955
St. John Publishing Co.

	Good	Fine	N-Mint
10	6.50	19.50	45.00
11-Spanking panel	6.50	19.50	45.00
12-16,18,19	4.85	14.50	34.00
17,20-Kubert-a	5.70	17.00	40.00
21-30: 28-Last precode (3/55)	3.00	9.00	21.00
(See Giant Comics Ed. for Annual)			

NOTE: *Baker c/a most issues.*

DICK COLE (Sport Thrills No. 11 on)(See Blue Bolt & Four Most #1)
Dec-Jan, 1948-49 - No. 10, June-July, 1950
Curtis Publ./Star Publications

	Good	Fine	N-Mint
1-Sgt. Spook; L. B. Cole-c; McWilliams-a; Curt Swan's 1st work	7.00	21.00	50.00
2	4.30	13.00	30.00
3-10	3.70	11.00	26.00
Accepted Reprint #7(V1#6 on-c)(1950's)-Reprints #7			
L.B. Cole-c	2.15	6.50	15.00
Accepted Reprint #9(nd)-(Reprints #9 & #8-c)	2.15	6.50	15.00

NOTE: *L. B. Cole a-all; c 1,3,4,6-10. Dick Cole in 1-9.*

DICKIE DARE
1941 - No. 4, 1942 (#3 on sale 6/15/42)
Eastern Color Printing Co.

	Good	Fine	N-Mint
1-Caniff-a, Everett-c	18.00	56.00	130.00
2	11.00	32.00	75.00
3,4-Half Scorchy Smith by Noel Sickles who was very influential in			
Milton Caniff's development	11.50	34.00	80.00

DICK POWELL (See A-1 Comics No. 22)

DICK QUICK, ACE REPORTER (See Picture News #10)

DICK'S ADVENTURES IN DREAMLAND (See 4-Color No. 245)

DICK TRACY (See Blackthorne 3-D Series #8, Harvey Comics Library, Limited Collectors' Ed., Mammoth Comics, Merry Christmas, Popular Comics, Super Book No. 1, 7, 13, 25, Super Comics & Tastee-Freez)

DICK TRACY
May, 1937 - Jan, 1938
David McKay Publications

	Good	Fine	N-Mint
Feature Books - 100 pgs., part reprinted as 4-Color No. 1 (appeared before Large Feat. Comics, 1st Dick Tracy comic book)			
(Very Rare-three known copies)			
Estimated Value....	467.00	1400.00	2800.00
Feature Books 4 - Reprints nn issue but with new cover added	72.00	215.00	500.00

DICK TRACY (continued)	Good	Fine	N-Mint
Feature Books 6,9	60.00	180.00	420.00

DICK TRACY
1939 - No. 24, Dec, 1949
Dell Publishing Co.

	Good	Fine	N-Mint
Large Feat. Comic 1(1939)	86.00	257.00	600.00
Large Feat. Comic 4	46.00	140.00	325.00
Large Feat. Comic 8,11,13,15	42.00	125.00	295.00
4-Color 1(1939)('35-r)	128.00	385.00	900.00
4-Color 6(1940)('37-r)-(Scarce)	76.00	230.00	535.00
4-Color 8(1940)('38-'39-r)	50.00	150.00	350.00
Large Feature Comics 3(1941)	40.00	120.00	280.00
4-Color 21('41)('38-r)	44.00	132.00	310.00
4-Color 34('43)('39-'40-r)	32.00	95.00	220.00
4-Color 56('44)('40-r)	24.00	72.00	165.00
4-Color 96('46)('40-r)	18.00	54.00	125.00
4-Color 133('47)('40-'41-r)	15.00	45.00	105.00
4-Color 163('47)('41-r)	12.00	36.00	84.00
4-Color 215('48)-Titled "Sparkle Plenty," Tracy-r	7.00	21.00	50.00
Buster Brown Shoes giveaway-36 pgs. in color (1938,'39-r)-by Gould	24.00	72.00	168.00

Gillmore Giveaway-(See Super Book)
...Hatful of Fun(no date, 1950-52)-32 pgs.; 8½x10''-Dick Tracy hat promotion; Dick Tracy games, magic tricks. Miller Bros. premium

	6.00	18.00	42.00

Motorola Giveaway('53)-Reprints Harvey Comics Library No. 2

	3.00	9.00	21.00

Popped Wheat Giveaway('47)-'40-r; 16 pgs. in color; Sig Feuchtwanger publ.; Gould-a

	.85	2.50	5.00

...Presents the Family Fun Book-Tip Top Bread Giveaway, no date, number (1940); 16 pgs. in color; Spy Smasher, Ibis, Lance O'Casey app. Fawcett Publ.

	25.00	75.00	175.00
Same as above but without app. of heroes & Dick Tracy on cover only	7.50	22.50	45.00

Service Station giveaway(1958)-16 pgs. in color, regular size; Harvey Info. Press(slick cover)

	1.70	5.00	12.00

Shoe Store Giveaway (1939, 16p)-Gould-a

1(1/48)('34-r)	10.00	30.00	70.00
	38.00	115.00	265.00
2,3	20.00	60.00	140.00
4-10	17.00	51.00	120.00
11-18: 13-Bondage-c	13.00	40.00	90.00
19-1st app. Sparkle Plenty, B.O. Plenty & Gravel Gertie in a 3-pg. strip not by Gould	14.00	42.00	100.00
20-1st app. Sam Catchem c/a not by Gould	11.50	34.00	80.00
21-24-Only 2 pg. Gould-a in each	11.50	34.00	80.00

NOTE: No. 19-24 have a 2 pg. biography of a famous villain illustrated by Gould: 19-Little Face; 20-Flattop; 21-Breathless Mahoney; 22-Measles; 23-Itchy; 24-The Brow.

DICK TRACY (Continued from Dell series)
No. 25, Mar, 1950 - No. 145, April, 1961
Harvey Publications

25	14.00	42.00	100.00
26-28,30: 28-Bondage-c	11.50	34.00	80.00
29-1st app. Gravel Gertie in a Gould-r	14.00	42.00	100.00
31,32,34,35,37-40	10.00	30.00	70.00
33-"Measles the Teen-Age Dope Pusher"	11.50	34.00	80.00
36-1st app. B.O. Plenty in a Gould-r	11.50	34.00	80.00
41-50	8.50	25.50	60.00
51-56,58-80: 51-2pgs Powell-a	8.00	24.00	56.00
57-1st app. Sam Catchem, Gould-r	10.00	30.00	70.00
81-99,101-140	6.00	18.00	42.00
100	6.50	19.50	45.00
141-145 (25 cents)	5.70	17.00	40.00

NOTE: Powell a(1-2pgs.)-43, 44, 104, 145. No. 110-120, 141-145 are all reprints from earlier issues.

DICK TRACY & DICK TRACY JR. CAUGHT THE RACKETEERS, HOW
1933 (88 pages) (7x8½'') (Hardcover)
Cupples & Leon Co.

	Good	Fine	N-Mint
2-(numbered on pg. 84)-Continuation of Stooge Viller book (daily strip reprints from 8/3/33 thru 11/8/33)			
(Rarer than No. 1)	38.00	115.00	265.00
with dust jacket....	60.00	180.00	420.00
Book 2 (32 pgs.; soft-c; has strips 9/18/33-11/8/33)	19.00	57.00	132.00

DICK TRACY & DICK TRACY JR. AND HOW THEY CAPTURED "STOOGE" VILLER (See Treasure Box of Famous Comics)
1933 (7x8½'') (Hard cover; One Shot; 100 pgs.)
Reprints 1932 & 1933 Dick Tracy daily strips
Cupples & Leon Co.

nn(No.1)-1st app. of "Stooge" Viller	27.00	81.00	190.00
with dust jacket....	42.00	125.00	295.00

DICK TRACY, EXPLOITS OF
1946 (Strip reprints) (Hardcover) ($1.00)
Rosdon Books, Inc.

1-Reprints the complete case of "The Brow" from early 1940s	19.00	57.00	132.00
with dust jacket....	32.00	95.00	225.00

DICK TRACY MONTHLY/WEEKLY
May, 1986 - Present ($2.00, B&W) (becomes Weekly #26 on)
Blackthorne Publishing

1-99: Gould-r. 30,31-Mr. Crime app.	.35	1.00	2.00
100-Double-size issue, $3.95	.70	2.00	4.00
101-112 ($2.50-c)	.40	1.25	2.50

DICK TRACY SHEDS LIGHT ON THE MOLE
1949 (16 pgs.) (Ray-O-Vac Flashlights giveaway)
Western Printing Co.

Not by Gould	5.00	15.00	35.00

DICK TRACY SPECIAL
Jan, 1988 - Present? ($2.95, B&W)
Blackthorne Publishing

1,2: 1-Origin Dick Tracy	.50	1.50	3.00

DICK TRACY UNPRINTED STORIES
Sept, 1987 - No. 4? ($2.95, B&W)
Blackthorne Publishing

1-4	.50	1.50	3.00

DICK TURPIN (See Legend of Young...)

DICK WINGATE OF THE U.S. NAVY
1951; 1953 (no month)
Superior Publ./Toby Press

nn-U.S. Navy giveaway	1.30	4.00	9.00
1(1953, Toby)	2.00	6.00	14.00

DIE, MONSTER, DIE (See Movie Classics)

DIG 'EM
1973 (16 pgs.) (2-3/8x6'')
Kellogg's Sugar Smacks Giveaway

4 different		.50	1.00

DILLY (Dilly Duncan from Daredevil Comics; see Boy Comics #57)
May, 1953 - No. 3, Sept, 1953
Lev Gleason Publications

1-Biro-c	2.30	7.00	16.00
2,3-Biro-c	1.30	4.00	9.00

DILTON'S STRANGE SCIENCE
May, 1989 - Present (.75-$1.00, color)

Dick Tracy Popped Wheat Giveaway, © N.Y. News Synd.

Dick Tracy #19, © N.Y. News Syndicate

Dick Tracy Special #1, © N.Y. News Syndicate

Dilton's Strange Science #1, © AP

Dirty Pair #1, © Eclipse

Disney's Ducktales #5, © WDC

DILTON'S STRANGE SCIENCE (continued)
Archie Comics

	Good	Fine	N-Mint
1-6		.50	1.00

DIME COMICS
1945; 1951
Newsbook Publ. Corp.

1-Silver Streak app.; L. B. Cole-c	13.00	40.00	90.00
1(1951), 5	2.00	6.00	14.00

DINGBATS (See First Issue Special)

DING DONG
Summer?, 1946 - No. 5, 1947 (52 pgs.)
Compix/Magazine Enterprises

1-Funny animal	4.00	12.00	28.00
2 (11/46)	2.00	6.00	14.00
3 (Wint '46-'47) - 5	1.50	4.50	10.00

DINKY DUCK (Paul Terry's. . .) (See Blue Ribbon & New Terrytoons)
11/51 - No. 16, 9/55; No. 16, Fall/'56; No. 17, 5/57 - No. 19, Summer/'58
St. John Publishing Co./Pines No. 16 on

1	3.50	10.50	24.00
2	1.70	5.00	12.00
3-10	1.15	3.50	8.00
11-16(9/55)	.85	2.60	6.00
16(Fall,'56) - 19	.55	1.65	4.00

DINKY DUCK & HASHIMOTO-SAN (See Deputy Dawg Presents. . .)

DINO (TV)(The Flintstones)
Aug, 1973 - No. 20, Jan, 1977
Charlton Publications

1	.50	1.50	3.00
2-20		.50	1.00

DINO RIDERS
Feb, 1989 - No. 3, 1989 ($1.00, color)
Marvel Comics

1-3: Based on toys		.50	1.00

DINOSAUR REX
1986 - No. 3, 1986 (mini-series; $2.00)
Upshot Graphics (Fantagraphics Books)

1-3	.35	1.00	2.00

DINOSAURS FOR HIRE
Mar, 1988 - No. 9?, 1989 ($1.95, B&W)
Eternity Comics

1-9; 1-1st & 2nd printings	.35	1.00	2.00
. . .Fall Classic 1 (11/88, $2.25, B&W, 52 pgs.)	.40	1.15	2.30
. . .3-D 1 (10/88, $2.95)	.50	1.50	3.00

DINOSAURUS (See 4-Color No. 1120)

DIPPY DUCK
October, 1957
Atlas Comics (OPI)

1-Maneely-a	2.30	7.00	16.00

DIRECTORY TO A NONEXISTENT UNIVERSE
Dec, 1987 ($2.00, B&W)
Eclipse Comics

1	.35	1.00	2.00

DIRTY DOZEN (See Movie Classics)

DIRTY PAIR
Dec, 1988 - No. 4, April, 1989 ($2.00, B&W, mini-series)
Eclipse Comics

1-4: Japanese manga with original stories	.35	1.00	2.00

DIRTY PAIR II
June, 1989 - No. 5, Feb?, 1990 ($2.00, B&W, mini-series)
Eclipse Comics

	Good	Fine	N-Mint
1-5: 3-Indicia is misnumbered as #1	.35	1.00	2.00

DISHMAN
Sept, 1988 - Present ($2.50, B&W, 52pgs)
Eclipse Comics

1,2	.40	1.25	2.50

DISNEYLAND BIRTHDAY PARTY (Also see Dell Giants)
Aug, 1985 ($2.50)
Gladstone Publishing Co.

1-R-/Dell Giant with new-photo-c	.40	1.25	2.50
. . .Comics Digest #1-(Digest)		.60	1.25

DISNEYLAND, USA (See Dell Giant No. 30)

DISNEY'S DUCKTALES (TV)
Oct, 1988 - Present (1,2,9-11: $1.50; 3-10: 95 cents, color)
Gladstone Publishing

1-Barks-r	.40	1.25	2.50
2,3: 2-Barks-r	.25	.80	1.60
4,5: 4,5-Barks-r	.25	.75	1.50
6-8: 6-Barks-r. 7-Barks-r(1 pg.)		.50	1.00
9-11: ($1.50, 52 pgs.) 9-11-Barks-r	.25	.75	1.50
12 ($1.95, 68 pgs.)	.35	1.00	2.00

DISTANT SOIL, A
Dec, 1983 - No. 10? ($1.50, B&W)
WaRP Graphics

1-Panda Khan app.	.50	1.50	3.00
2-5	.35	1.00	2.00
6-10	.25	.75	1.50
Graphic Novel ($6.95)	1.20	3.50	7.00
Graphic Album 2 ($12.95)	2.15	6.50	12.95

DIVER DAN (TV)
Feb-Apr, 1962 - No. 2, June-Aug, 1962
Dell Publishing Co.

4-Color 1254, 2	3.00	9.00	21.00

DIXIE DUGAN (Also see Columbia Comics & Feature Funnies)
July, 1942 - No. 13, 1949
McNaught Syndicate/Columbia/Publication Ent.

1-Joe Palooka x-over by Ham Fisher	13.00	40.00	90.00
2	6.50	19.50	45.00
3	5.00	15.00	35.00
4,5(1945-46)	3.50	10.50	24.00
6-13(1948-49)	2.30	7.00	16.00

DIXIE DUGAN
Nov, 1951 - V4/4, Feb, 1954
Prize Publications (Headline)

V3No.1	3.50	10.50	24.00
2-4	2.15	6.50	15.00
V4No.1-4(No.5-8)	1.60	4.70	11.00

DIZZY DAMES
Sept-Oct, 1952 - No. 6, July-Aug, 1953
American Comics Group (B&M Distr. Co.)

1	3.70	11.00	26.00
2	2.30	7.00	16.00
3-6	1.50	4.50	10.00

DIZZY DON COMICS
1942 - No. 22, Oct, 1946 (B&W)
F. E. Howard Publications/Dizzy Don Ent. Ltd (Canada)

1	2.65	8.00	18.00
2	1.30	4.00	9.00

DIZZY DON COMICS (continued)	Good	Fine	N-Mint
3-21	1.00	3.00	7.00
22-Full color, 52pgs.	2.00	6.00	14.00

DIZZY DUCK (Formerly Barnyard Comics)
No. 32, Nov, 1950 - No. 39, Mar, 1952
Standard Comics

32	3.50	10.50	24.00
33-39	1.70	5.00	12.00

DNAGENTS (The New DNAgents V2/1 on)(Also see Surge)
March, 1983 - No. 24, July, 1985 ($1.50, Baxter paper)
Eclipse Comics

1-Origin	.50	1.50	3.00
2-10: 4-Amber app.	.40	1.25	2.50
11-24: 18-Infinity-c	.35	1.00	2.00
NOTE: *Spiegle a-9. Dave Stevens c-24.*

DOBERMAN (See Sgt. Bilko's Private. . .)

DOBIE GILLIS (See The Many Loves of . . .)

DOC CARTER VD COMICS
1949 (16 pages in color) (Paper cover)
Health Publications Institute, Raleigh, N. C. (Giveaway)

nn	17.00	51.00	120.00

DOC SAVAGE
November, 1966
Gold Key

1-Adaptation of the Thousand-Headed Man; James Bama-c r-/'64			
Doc Savage paperback	2.65	8.00	18.00

DOC SAVAGE
Oct, 1972 - No. 8, Jan, 1974
Marvel Comics Group

1	.30	.90	1.80
2-8: 2,3-Steranko-c		.50	1.00
Giant-Size 1(1975)-Reprints No. 1 & 2		.50	1.00
NOTE: *Mooney a-1i, Gnt-Size 1r. No. 1, 2 adapts pulp story "The Man of Bronze," No. 3, 4 adapts "Death in Silver," No. 5, 6 adapts "The Monsters," No. 7, 8 adapts "The Brand of The Werewolf."*

DOC SAVAGE (Magazine)
Aug, 1975 - No. 8, Spr, 1977 (Black & White)
Marvel Comics Group

1-Cover from movie poster	.25	.75	1.50
2-8		.50	1.00
NOTE: *John Buscema a-1, 3.*

DOC SAVAGE
Nov, 1987 - No. 4, Feb, 1988 ($1.75, mini-series)
DC Comics

1-4: Adam & Andy Kubert c/a	.35	1.00	2.00

DOC SAVAGE
Nov, 1988 - Present ($1.75, color)
DC Comics

1	.35	1.00	2.00
2-18	.30	.90	1.75
Annual 1 (1989, $3.50, 68 pgs.)	.60	1.75	3.50

DOC SAVAGE COMICS (Also see Shadow Comics)
May, 1940 - No. 20, Oct, 1943 (1st app. in Doc Savage pulp, 3/33)
Street & Smith Publications

1-Doc Savage, Cap Fury, Danny Garrett, Mark Mallory, The Whisperer, Captain Death, Billy the Kid, Sheriff Pete & Treasure Island begin; Norgil, the Magician app.	133.00	335.00	800.00
2-Origin & 1st app. Ajax, the Sun Man; Danny Garrett, The Whisperer end	57.00	170.00	400.00
3	46.00	140.00	320.00

	Good	Fine	N-Mint
4-Treasure Island ends; Tuska-a	34.00	103.00	240.00
5-Origin & 1st app. Astron, the Crocodile Queen, not in #9 & 11; Norgil the Magician app.	28.00	85.00	200.00
6-9: 6-Cap Fury ends; origin & only app. Red Falcon in Astron story.			
8-Mark Mallory ends; Charlie McCarthy app. on cover. 9-Supersnipe app.	23.00	70.00	160.00
10-Origin & only app. The Thunderbolt	23.00	70.00	160.00
11,12	17.00	51.00	120.00
V2#1-8(#13-20): 16-The Pulp Hero, The Avenger app. 17-Sun Man ends; Nick Carter begins	17.00	51.00	120.00

DOC STEARN. . .MR. MONSTER (See Mr. Monster)

DR. ANTHONY KING, HOLLYWOOD LOVE DOCTOR
1952(Jan.) - No. 3, May, 1953; No. 4, May, 1954
Minoan Publishing Corp./Harvey Publications No. 4

1	4.50	13.50	32.00
2-4: 4-Powell-a	3.00	9.00	21.00

DR. ANTHONY'S LOVE CLINIC (See Mr. Anthony's. . .)

DR. BOBBS (See 4-Color No. 212)

DOCTOR BOOGIE
1987 ($1.75, color)
Media Arts Publishing

1-Airbrush wraparound-c; Nick Cuti-i	.30	.90	1.75

DR. FATE (See First Issue Special, The Immortal. . ., Justice League, More Fun #55, & Showcase)

DOCTOR FATE
July, 1987 - No. 4, Oct, 1987 ($1.50, mini-series, Baxter)
DC Comics

1-Giffen c/a begins	.35	1.10	2.20
2-4	.30	.90	1.80

DOCTOR FATE
Winter, 1988-'89 - No. 13, Jan, 1990 ($1.25-$1.50, color)
DC Comics

1-13: 5-Begin $1.50-c	.25	.75	1.50
Annual 1(1989, $2.95, 68 pgs.)-Sutton-a	.50	1.50	3.00

DR. FU MANCHU (See The Mask of. . .)
1964
I.W. Enterprises

1-Reprints Avon's "Mask of Dr. Fu Manchu;" Wood-a	5.70	17.00	40.00

DOCTOR GRAVES (Formerly The Many Ghosts of. . .)
No. 73, Sept, 1985 - No. 75, Jan, 1986
Charlton Comics

73-75		.40	.75

DR. JEKYLL AND MR. HYDE (See A Star Presentation & Supernatural Thrillers #4)

DR. KILDARE (TV)
No. 1337, 4-6/62 - No. 9, 4-6/65 (All Richard Chamberlain photo-c)
Dell Publishing Co.

4-Color 1337('62)	3.50	10.50	24.00
2-9	2.30	7.00	16.00

DR. MASTERS (See The Adventures of Young. . .)

DOCTOR SOLAR, MAN OF THE ATOM
10/62 - No. 27, 4/69; No. 28, 4/81 - No. 31, 3/82
Gold Key/Whitman No. 28 on (Painted-c No. 1-27)

1-Origin Dr. Solar (1st Gold Key comic-No. 10000-210)	4.30	13.00	30.00
2-Prof. Harbinger begins	2.15	6.50	15.00
3-5: 5-Intro. Man of the Atom in costume	1.70	5.00	12.00
6-10	1.30	4.00	9.00

Doc Savage Comics #12, © S & S

Doctor Fate #1 (7/87), © DC

Doctor Solar #1, © GK

Doctor Strange #1 (6/74), © MEG

The Dodo & The Frog #86, © DC

Doll Man #2, © QUA

	Good	Fine	N-Mint
DOCTOR SOLAR (continued)			
11-14,16-20	1.00	3.00	7.00
15-Origin retold	1.30	4.00	9.00
21-27	.85	2.50	5.00
28-31: 29-Magnus Robot Fighter begins. 31-The Sentinel app.		.40	.80

NOTE: *Frank Bolle* a-6-19, 29-31; c-29i, 30i. *Bob Fugitani* a-1-5. *Spiegle* a-29-31. *Al McWilliams* a-20-23.

DOCTOR SPEKTOR (See The Occult Files of . . .)

DOCTOR STRANGE (Strange Tales No. 1-168) (Also see The Defenders, Marvel Fanfare, Marvel Graphic Novel, Marvel Premiere, Marvel Treas. Ed. and Strange Tales, 2nd Series)
No. 169, 6/68 - No. 183, 11/69; 6/74 - No. 81, 2/87
Marvel Comics Group

	Good	Fine	N-Mint
169(#1)-Origin; panel swipe/M.D. #1-c	4.30	13.00	30.00
170-183: 177-New costume	1.70	5.00	12.00
1(6/74)-Brunner c/a	1.50	4.50	10.00
2-5	.50	1.50	3.00
6-26: 21-Origin-r/Str. Tales #169	.30	.90	1.80
27-81: 56-Origin retold	.60		1.20

NOTE: *Adkins* a-169, 170, 171i; c-169-71, 172i, 173. *Adams* a-4i. *Austin* a-48-60i, 66i, 68i, 70i; c-38i, 47-53i, 55i, 58-60i, 70i. *Brunner* a-1-5p; c-1-6, 22, 28-30, 33. *Colan* a(p)-172-78, 180-83, 6-18, 36-45, 47; c(p)-172, 174-83, 11-21, 23, 27, 35, 36, 47. *Ditko* a-179r, 3r. *Everett* c-183i. *Golden* a-46p, 55p; c-42-44, 46, 55p. *G. Kane* c(p)-8-10. *Miller* c-46p. *Nebres* a-20, 22, 23, 24i, 26i, 32i; c-32i, 34. *Rogers* a-48-53p; c-47p-53p. *Russell* a-34i, 46i, Annual 1. *B. Smith* c-179. *Paul Smith* a-54p, 56p, 65, 66p, 68p, 69, 71-73; c-56, 65, 66, 68, 71. *Starlin* a-23p, 26; c-25, 26. *Sutton* a-27-29p, 34p.

	Good	Fine	N-Mint
Annual 1(1976)-Russell-a	.35	1.00	2.00
Giant Size 1(11/75)-Str. Tales-r	.35	1.00	2.00
. . ./Silver Dagger (Special Edition)(3/83)($2.50, Baxter paper)-r-/ Dr. Strange 1,2,4,5 & Strange Tales 127; Wrightson/-a			
	.35	1.00	2.00

DOCTOR STRANGE CLASSICS
Mar, 1984 - No. 4, June, 1984 ($1.50 cover price; Baxter paper)
Marvel Comics Group

1-4: Ditko reprints	.25	.75	1.50

DOCTOR STRANGE, SORCERER SUPREME
Nov, 1988 - Present (Mando paper, $1.25-1.50, direct sales only)
Marvel Comics

1 ($1.25)	.65	1.90	3.80
2-14 ($1.50): 3-New Defenders app. 5-Guice-a(p) begins. 11-Hobgoblin app.	.25	.75	1.50

DR. TOM BRENT, YOUNG INTERN
Feb, 1963 - No. 5, Oct, 1963
Charlton Publications

1	.85	2.50	5.00
2-5	.50	1.50	3.00

DR. VOLTZ (See Mighty Midget Comics)

DOCTOR WHO (Also see Marvel Premiere #57-60)
Oct, 1984 - No. 23, Aug, 1986 ($1.50, Direct sales, Baxter paper)
Marvel Comics Group

1-($1.50 cover)-British-r	.40	1.25	2.50
2-23	.35	1.00	2.00

DR. WHO & THE DALEKS (See Movie Classics)

DOCTOR ZERO
April, 1988 - No. 8, Aug, 1989 ($1.25/$1.50, color)
Epic Comics (Marvel)

1-8: 1-Sienkiewicz-c. 6,7-Spiegle-a	.25	.75	1.50

DO-DO
1950 - No. 7, 1951 (5x7¼'' Miniature) (5 cents)
Nation Wide Publishers

1 (52 pgs.); funny animal	2.30	7.00	16.00

	Good	Fine	N-Mint
2-7	1.50	4.50	10.00

DODO & THE FROG, THE (Formerly Funny Stuff)
9-10/54 - No. 88, 1-2/56; No. 89, 8-9/56; No. 90, 10-11/56; No.91, 9/57; No. 92, 11/57 (See Comic Cavalcade)
National Periodical Publications

	Good	Fine	N-Mint
80-Doodles Duck by Sheldon Mayer	5.70	17.00	40.00
81-91: Doodles Duck by Sheldon Mayer in #81,83-90			
	3.00	9.00	21.00
92-(Scarce)-Doodles Duck by S. Mayer	5.00	15.00	35.00

DOGFACE DOOLEY
1951 - No. 5, 1953
Magazine Enterprises

1(A-1 40)	2.30	7.00	16.00
2(A-1 43), 3(A-1 49), 4(A-1 53), 5(A-1 64)	1.50	4.50	10.00
I.W. Reprint #1('64), Super Reprint #17	.70	2.00	4.00

DOG OF FLANDERS, A (See 4-Color No. 1088)

DOGPATCH (See Al Capp's. . . & Mammy Yokum)

DOINGS OF THE DOO DADS, THE
1922 (34 pgs.; 7¾x7¾''; B&W) (50 cents)
(Red & White cover; square binding)
Detroit News (Universal Feat. & Specialty Co.)

Reprints 1921 newspaper strip ''Text & Pictures'' given away as prize in the Detroit News Doo Dads contest; by Arch Dale

	8.00	24.00	56.00

DOLLFACE & HER GANG (See 4-Color No. 309)

DOLL MAN (Also see Feature Comics #27 & Freedom Fighters)
Fall, 1941 - No. 7, Fall, '43; No. 8, Spring, '46 - No. 47, Oct, 1953
Quality Comics Group

1-Dollman (by Cassone) & Justin Wright begin			
	100.00	300.00	700.00
2-The Dragon begins; Crandall-a(5)	52.00	155.00	365.00
3	37.00	110.00	260.00
4	27.00	80.00	190.00
5-Crandall-a	24.00	73.00	170.00
6,7(1943)	19.00	58.00	135.00
8(1946)-1st app. Torchy by Bill Ward	21.50	64.00	150.00
9	16.50	50.00	115.00
10-20	13.00	40.00	90.00
21-30	11.50	34.00	80.00
31-36,38,40: Jeb Rivers app. #32-34	9.30	28.00	65.00
37-Origin Dollgirl; Dollgirl bondage-c	12.00	36.00	85.00
39-''Narcotics...the Death Drug''-c-/story	10.00	30.00	70.00
41-47	6.50	19.50	45.00
Super Reprint #11('64, r-#20),15(r-#23),17(r-#28): Torchy app.-#15,17			
	1.35	4.00	8.00

NOTE: *Ward* Torchy in 8, 9, 11, 12, 14-24, 27; by *Fox*-#30, 35-47. *Crandall* a-2,5,10,13 & Super #11,17,18. *Guardineer* a-3. Bondage-c #27,37,38,39.

DOLLY
No. 10, 1951 (Funny animal)
Ziff-Davis Publ. Co.

10	1.70	5.00	12.00

DOLLY DILL
1945
Marvel Comics/Newsstand Publ.

1	7.00	21.00	50.00

DOLLY DIMPLES & BOBBY BOONCE'
1933
Cupples & Leon Co.

nn	7.00	21.00	50.00

DOMINION
1990 - No. 6, 1990 ($2.00, B&W, mini-series)

Eclipse Comics	Good	Fine	N-Mint
1-6	.35	1.00	2.00

DOMINO CHANCE
May/June, 1982 - No. 9, May, 1985 (B&W)
Chance Enterprises

	Good	Fine	N-Mint
1	2.00	6.00	12.00
1-Reprint, May 1985	.50	1.50	3.00
2-6.9		.50	1.00
7-1st app. Gizmo, 2 pgs.	1.35	4.00	8.00
8-1st full Gizmo story	2.00	6.00	12.00

DONALD AND MICKEY IN DISNEYLAND (See Dell Giants)

DONALD AND MICKEY MERRY CHRISTMAS (Formerly Famous
Gang Book Of Comics)
1943 - 1949 (20 pgs.)(Giveaway) Put out each Christmas; 1943 issue
titled ''Firestone Presents Comics'' (Disney)
K. K. Publ./Firestone Tire & Rubber Co.

1943-Donald Duck reprint from WDC&S #32 by Carl Barks
    50.00 150.00 350.00
1944-Donald Duck reprint from WDC&S #35 by Barks
    48.00 144.00 335.00
1945-''Donald Duck's Best Christmas,'' 8 pgs. Carl Barks; intro. &
   1st app. Grandma Duck in comic books 61.00 184.00 430.00
1946-Donald Duck in ''Santa's Stormy Visit,'' 8 pgs. Carl Barks
    46.00 137.00 320.00
1947-Donald Duck in ''Three Good Little Ducks,'' 8 pgs. Carl Barks
    38.00 115.00 265.00
1948-Donald Duck in ''Toyland,'' 8 pgs. Carl Barks
    36.00 107.00 250.00
1949-Donald Duck in ''New Toys,'' 8 pgs. Carl Barks
    43.00 130.00 305.00

DONALD AND THE WHEEL (See 4-Color No. 1190)

DONALD DUCK (See Cheerios, Disney's Ducktales, Dynabrite Comics, Gladstone
Comic Album, Mickey Mouse Mag., Story Hour Series, Uncle Scrooge, Walt Disney's
Comics & Stories, Wheaties & Whitman Comic Books)

DONALD DUCK
1935, 1936 (Linen-like text & color pictures; 1st book ever devoted to
Donald Duck; see The Wise Little Hen for earlier app.) (9½x13'')
Whitman Publishing Co./Grosset & Dunlap/K.K.

978(1935)-16 pgs.; story book   71.00 215.00 500.00
nn(1936)-36 pgs.; reprints '35 edition with expanded ill. & text
    50.00 150.00 350.00
  with dust jacket....   64.00 193.00 450.00

DONALD DUCK (Walt Disney's) (10 cents)
1938 (B&W) (8½x11½'') (Cardboard covers)
Whitman/K.K. Publications

(Has Donald Duck with bubble pipe on front cover)
            Good Fine VF-NM
nn-The first Donald Duck & Walt Disney comic book; 1936 & 1937
   Sunday strip-r(in B&W); same format as the Feature Books;
   1st strips with Huey, Dewey & Louie from 10/17/37
    100.00 300.00 700.00
   (Prices vary widely on this book)

DONALD DUCK (Walt Disney's. . .#262 on; see 4-Color listings for
titles & 4-Color No. 1109 for origin story)
1940 - No. 84, 9-11/62; No. 85, 12/62 - No. 245, 1984;
No. 246, 10/86 - Present
Dell Publishing Co./Gold Key No. 85-216/Whitman No. 217-245/
Gladstone Publishing No. 246 on   Good Fine N-Mint
4-Color 4(1940)-Daily 1939 strip-r by Al Taliaferro
    328.00 985.00 2300.00

            Good Fine N-Mint
Large Feature Comic 16(1/41?)-1940 Sunday strips-r in B&W
    157.00 470.00 1100.00
Large Feature Comic 20('41)-Comic Paint Book, r-single panels from
   Large Feat. 16 at top of each page to color; daily strip-r across
   bottom of each page 215.00 645.00 1500.00
4-Color 9('42)-''Finds Pirate Gold.''-64 pgs. by Carl Barks & Jack
   Hannah (pgs. 1,2,5,12-40 are by Barks, his 1st comic book work;
   © 8/17/42) 370.00 1115.00 2600.00
4-Color 29(9/43)-''Mummy's Ring'' by Carl Barks; reprinted in Uncle
   Scrooge & Donald Duck #1('65), W. D. Comics Digest #44('73)
   & Donald Duck Advs. #14 243.00 730.00 1700.00
   (Prices vary widely on all above books)
4-Color 62(1/45)-''Frozen Gold;'' 52 pgs. by Carl Barks, reprinted in
   The Best of W.D. Comics & Donald Duck Advs. #4
    120.00 360.00 840.00
4-Color 108(1946)-''Terror of the River;'' 52 pgs. by Carl Barks; reprinted in Gladstone Comic Album #2 90.00 270.00 630.00
4-Color 147(5/47)-in ''Volcano Valley'' by Carl Barks
    60.00 180.00 420.00
4-Color 159(8/47)-in ''The Ghost of the Grotto;'' 52 pgs. by Carl
   Barks-reprinted in Best of Uncle Scrooge & Donald Duck #1
   ('66) & The Best of W.D. Comics & D.D. Advs. #9; two Barks
   stories 54.00 160.00 375.00
4-Color 178(12/47)-1st Uncle Scrooge by Carl Barks; reprinted in
   Gold Key Christmas Parade No. 3 & The Best of W.D. Comics
    64.00 192.00 450.00
4-Color 189(6/48)-by Carl Barks; reprinted in Best of Donald Duck &
   Uncle Scrooge #1('64) & D.D. Advs. #19 54.00 160.00 375.00
4-Color 199(10/48)-by Carl Barks; mentioned in Love and Death;r/in
   Gladstone Comic Album #5 54.00 160.00 375.00
4-Color 203(12/48)-by Barks; reprinted as Gold Key Christmas
   Parade #4 36.00 108.00 250.00
4-Color 223(4/49)-by Barks; reprinted as Best of Donald Duck #1 &
   Donald Duck Advs. #3 50.00 150.00 350.00
4-Color 238(8/49), 256(12/49)-by Barks; No. 256-reprinted in Best of
   Donald Duck & Uncle Scrooge #2('67), Gladstone Comic Album
   #16 & W.D. Comics Digest #44('73) 27.00 81.00 190.00
4-Color 263(2/50)-Two Barks stories; r-in D.D. #278
    27.00 81.00 190.00
4-Color 275(5/50), 282(7/50), 291(9/50), 300(11/50)-All by Carl Barks;
   #275,282 reprinted in W.D. Comics Digest #44('73). #275 r/in
   Gladstone Comic Album #10. #291 r/in Donald Duck Advs. #16
    25.00 75.00 175.00
4-Color 308(1/51), 318(3/51)-by Barks; #318-reprinted in W.D. Comics
   Digest #34 & D.D. Advs. #2,19 21.00 63.00 147.00
4-Color 328(5/51)-by Carl Barks 23.00 70.00 160.00
4-Color 339(7-8/51), 379-not by Barks 4.35 13.00 30.00
4-Color 348(9-10/51), 356,394-Barks-c only 6.00 18.00 42.00
4-Color 367(1-2/52)-by Barks; reprinted as Gold Key Christmas
   Parade #2 & #8 20.00 60.00 140.00
4-Color 408(7-8/52), 422(9-10/52)-All by Carl Barks. #408-R/in Best of
   Donald Duck & Uncle Scrooge #1('64) & Gladstone Comic Album
   #13 20.00 60.00 140.00
26(11-12/52)-In ''Trick or Treat''(Barks-a, 36pgs.) 1st story r-/Walt Disney Digest #16 & Gladstone C.A. #23 22.00 65.00 154.00
27-30-Barks-c only 4.30 13.00 30.00
31-40 2.65 8.00 18.00
41-44,47-50 2.00 6.00 14.00
45-Barks-a, 6 pgs. 7.00 21.00 50.00
46-''Secret of Hondorica'' by Barks, 24 pgs.; reprinted in Donald
   Duck #98 & 154 8.00 24.00 56.00
51-Barks, ½ pg. 1.70 5.00 12.00
52-''Lost Peg-Leg Mine'' by Barks, 10 pgs. 6.50 19.50 45.00
53,55-59 1.60 4.80 11.00
54-''Forbidden Valley'' by Barks, 26 pgs. 7.50 22.00 52.00
60-''D.D. & the Titanic Ants'' by Barks, 20 pgs. plus 6 more pgs.

Donald And Mickey Merry Christmas 1943, © WDC

Donald Duck Four Color #108, © WDC

Donald Duck Four Color #318, © WDC

Donald Duck #26, © WDC

Donald Duck Adventures #3, © WDC

Donald Duck's Surprise Party, © WDC

DONALD DUCK (continued)	Good	Fine	N-Mint
	6.50	19.50	45.00
61-67,69,70	1.30	4.00	9.00
68-Barks-a, 5 pgs.	3.75	11.25	26.00
71-Barks-r, ½ pg.	1.50	4.50	10.00
72-78,80,82-97,99,100: 96-Donald Duck Album	1.15	3.50	8.00
79,81-Barks-a, 1pg.	1.50	4.50	10.00
98-Reprints #46 (Barks)	2.15	6.50	15.00
101-133: 112-1st Moby Duck	.85	2.50	6.00
134-Barks-r/#52 & WDC&S 194	1.00	3.00	7.00
135-Barks-r/WDC&S 198, 19 pgs.	.70	2.00	5.00
136-153,155,156,158	.50	1.50	3.00
154-Barks-r(#46)	.70	2.00	5.00
157,159,160,164: 157-Barks-r(#45). 159-Reprints/WDC&S #192 (10 pgs.). 160-Barks-r(#26). 164-Barks-r(#79)	.40	1.25	2.50
161-163,165-170	.25	.75	1.50
171-173,175-187,189-191		.60	1.20
174-Reprints 4-Color #394	.35	1.00	2.00
188-Barks-r/#68	.35	1.00	2.00
192-Barks-r(40 pgs.) from Donald Duck #60 & WDC&S #226,234 (52 pgs.)	.40	1.25	2.50
193-200,202-207,209-211,213-218: 217 has 216 on-c	.50	1.00	
201,208,212: 201-Barks-r/Christmas Parade #26, 16pgs. 208-Barks-r/#60 (6 pgs.). 212-Barks-r/WDC&S #130	.35	1.00	2.00
219-Barks-r/WDC&S #106,107, 10 pgs. ea.		.60	1.20
220-227,231-245		.35	.70
228-230: 228-Barks-r/F.C. #275. 229-Barks-r/F.C. #282. 230-Barks-r/#52 & WDC&S #194	.25	.75	1.50
246-(1st Gladstone)-Barks-r/FC #422	1.10	3.25	6.50
247-249: 248-Barks-r/DD #54. 249-Barks-r/DD #26	.40	1.25	2.50
250-Barks-r/4-Color #9, 64 pgs.	.85	2.50	5.00
251-256: 251-Barks-r/'45 Firestone. 254-Barks-r/FC #328. 256-Barks-r/FC #147	.35	1.00	2.00
257-Barks-r/Vac. Parade #1 (52 pgs.)	.35	1.00	2.00
258-260	.25	.75	1.50
261-277: 261-Barks-r/FC #300. 275-Kelly-r/FC #92	.50	1.00	
278 ($1.95, 68 pgs.)-Rosa-a; Barks-r/FC 263	.35	1.00	2.00
Mini-Comic #1(1976)-(3¼x6½''); R/D.D. #150			.10

NOTE: **Carl Barks** wrote all issues he illustrated, but #117, 126, 138 contain his script only. Issues 4-Color #189, 199, 203, 223, 238, 256, 263, 275, 282, 308, 348, 356, 367, 394, 408, 422, 26-30, 35, 44, 46, 52, 55, 57, 60, 65, 70-73, 77-80, 83, 101, 103, 105, 106, 111, 126, 246r, 266r, 268r, 271r, 275r all have **Barks** covers. **Barks** r-263-267, 269-278. #96 titled "Comic Album," #99-"Christmas Album." New art issues (not reprints)-106-46, 148-63, 167, 169, 170, 172, 173, 175, 178, 179, 196, 209, 223, 225, 236.

DONALD DUCK
1944 (16 pg. Christmas giveaway)(paper cover)(2 versions)
K. K. Publications

Kelly cover reprint	37.00	110.00	260.00

DONALD DUCK ADVENTURES (Walt Disney's. . .#4 on)
Nov, 1987 - Present
Gladstone Publishing

1	.50	1.50	3.00
2-r/F.C. #308	.35	1.00	2.00
3,4,6,7,9-11,13,15-18: 3-r/F.C. #223. 4-r/F.C. #62. 9-r/F.C. #159. 16-r/F.C. #291; Rosa-c. 18-r/F.C. #318; Rosa-c	.25	.75	1.50
5,8-Don Rosa-a	.35	1.00	2.00
12($1.50, 52pgs)-Rosa-c/a w/Barks poster	.35	1.00	2.00
14-r/F.C. #29, "Mummy's Ring"	.35	1.00	2.00
19 ($1.95, 68 pgs.)-Barks-r/F.C. #199	.35	1.00	2.00

NOTE: **Barks** a-1-19r; c-10r, 14r.

DONALD DUCK ALBUM (See Comic Album 1,3 & Duck Album)
5-7/59 - F.C. No. 1239, 10-12/61; 1962; 8/63 - No. 2, Oct, 1963
Dell Publishing Co./Gold Key

	Good	Fine	N-Mint
4-Color 995,1182, 01204-207 (1962-Dell)	2.00	6.00	14.00
4-Color 1099,1140,1239-Barks-c	2.30	7.00	16.00
1(8/63-Gold Key)-Barks-c	2.00	6.00	14.00
2(10/63)	1.00	3.00	7.00

DONALD DUCK AND THE BOYS (Also see Story Hour Series)
1948 (Hardcover book; 5¼x5½'') 100pgs., ½art, ½text
Whitman Publishing Co.

845-Partial r-/WDC&S No. 74 by Barks	17.00	51.00	120.00
(Prices vary widely on this book)			

DONALD DUCK AND THE RED FEATHER
1948 (4 pages) (8½x11'') (Black & White)
Red Feather Giveaway

nn	4.60	14.00	32.00

DONALD DUCK BEACH PARTY (Also see Dell Giants)
Sept, 1965 (25 cents)
Gold Key

1(#10158-509)-Barks-r/WDC&S #45	3.00	9.00	21.00

DONALD DUCK BOOK (See Story Hour Series)

DONALD DUCK COMIC PAINT BOOK (See Large Feature Comic No. 20)

DONALD DUCK COMICS DIGEST
Nov, 1986 - No. 5, July, 1987 ($1.25-$1.50, 96 pgs.)
Gladstone Publishing

1-3: 1-Barks c/a-r		.60	1.25
4,5	.25	.75	1.50

DONALD DUCK FUN BOOK (See Dell Giants)

DONALD DUCK IN DISNEYLAND (See Dell Giants)

DONALD DUCK IN ''THE LITTERBUG''
1963 (16 pgs., 5x7¼'', soft-c) (Disney giveaway)
Keep America Beautiful

nn	2.00	6.00	14.00

DONALD DUCK MARCH OF COMICS
No. 4, 1947 - No. 69, 1951; No. 263, 1964 (Giveaway) (Disney)
K. K. Publications

nn(No.4)-''Maharajah Donald;'' 30 pgs. by Carl Barks-(1947)	428.00	1285.00	3000.00
20-''Darkest Africa'' by Carl Barks-(1948); 22 pgs.	257.00	770.00	1800.00
41-''Race to South Seas'' by Carl Barks-(1949); 22 pgs.(On Disney's band list)	200.00	600.00	1400.00
56-(1950)-Barks-a on back-c	22.00	65.00	140.00
69-(1951)-Not by Barks; Barks-a on back-c	19.00	57.00	125.00
263-Not by Barks	6.00	18.00	36.00

DONALD DUCK MERRY CHRISTMAS (See Dell Giant No. 53)

DONALD DUCK PICNIC PARTY (See Picnic Party under Dell Giants)

DONALD DUCK ''PLOTTING PICNICKERS''
1962 (16 pgs., 3¼x7'', soft-c) (Disney)(Also see Ludwig Von Drake & Mickey Mouse)
Fritos Giveaway

nn	2.30	7.00	16.00

DONALD DUCK'S SURPRISE PARTY
1948 (16 pgs.) (Giveaway for Icy Frost Twins Ice Cream Bars)
Walt Disney Productions

(Rare)-Kelly c/a	100.00	300.00	700.00

DONALD DUCK TELLS ABOUT KITES
11/54 (Giveaway) (8 pgs. - no cover) (Disney)
Southern California Edison Co./Pacific Gas & Electric Co./Florida Power & Light Co.

Fla. Power, S.C.E. & version with blank label issues-Barks pencils-8

D. DUCK TELLS ABOUT KITES (continued) **Good Fine N-Mint**
pgs.; inks-7 pgs. (Rare) 285.00 850.00 1800.00
P.G.&E. issue-7th page redrawn changing middle 3 panels to show
P.G.&E. in story line; (All Barks; last page Barks pencils only)
(Scarce) 250.00 750.00 1600.00
(Prices vary widely on above books)
NOTE: These books appeared one month apart in the Fall and were distributed on the West and East Coasts.

DONALD DUCK, THIS IS YOUR LIFE (See 4-Color No. 1109)

DONALD DUCK XMAS ALBUM (See regular Donald Duck No. 99)

DONALD IN MATHMAGIC LAND (See 4-Color No. 1051, 1198)

DONATELLO, TEENAGE MUTANT NINJA TURTLE
Aug, 1986 (One-shot, 1.50, B&W, 44 pgs.)
Mirage Studios
1 1.00 3.00 6.00

DONDI (See 4-Color No. 1176,1276)

DON FORTUNE MAGAZINE
Aug, 1946 - No. 6, Feb, 1947
Don Fortune Publishing Co.
1-Delecta of the Planets by C. C. Beck in all 8.00 24.00 56.00
2 5.00 15.00 35.00
3-6: 3-Bondage-c 3.50 10.50 24.00

DON NEWCOMBE
1950 (Baseball)
Fawcett Publications
nn 17.00 51.00 120.00

DON'T GIVE UP THE SHIP (See 4-Color #1049)

DON WINSLOW OF THE NAVY (See Crackajack Funnies, 4-Color #2,22, Popular Comics & Super Book #5,6)

DON WINSLOW OF THE NAVY (See TV Teens; Movie, Radio, TV)
2/43 - #64, 12/48; #65, 1/51 - #69, 9/51; #70, 3/55 - #73, 9/55
(Fightin' Navy No. 74 on)
Fawcett Publications/Charlton No. 70 on
1-(68 pgs.)-Captain Marvel on cover 42.00 125.00 290.00
2 21.00 62.00 145.00
3 14.00 42.00 100.00
4,5 11.50 34.00 80.00
6-Flag-c 9.30 28.00 65.00
7-10: 8-Last 68pg. issue? 7.00 21.00 50.00
11-20 5.00 15.00 35.00
21-40 3.50 10.50 24.00
41-63 2.65 8.00 18.00
64(12/48)-Matt Baker-a 2.85 8.50 20.00
65(1/51) - 69(9/51): All photo-c. 65-Flying Saucer attack
3.70 11.00 26.00
70(3/55)-73: 70-73 r-/#26,58 & 59 2.30 7.00 16.00

DOOM PATROL, THE (My Greatest Adv. No. 1-85; see Brave and the Bold, DC Special Blue Ribbon Digest 19, Official...Index & Showcase No. 94-96)
No. 86, 3/64 - No. 121, 9-10/68; 2/73 - No. 124, 6-7/73
National Periodical Publications
86-1pg. origin 6.00 18.00 42.00
87-99: 88-Origin The Chief. 91-Intro. Mento. 99-Intro. Beast Boy who later became the Changeling in the New Teen Titans
4.30 13.00 30.00
100-Origin Beast Boy; Robot-Maniac series begins
5.25 16.00 37.00
101-110: 102-Challengers/Unknown app. 105-Robot-Maniac series ends. 106-Negative Man begins (origin) 2.35 7.00 16.00
111-120 1.85 5.50 13.00
121-Death of Doom Patrol; Orlando-c 5.85 17.50 41.00
122-124(reprints) .35 1.00 2.00

DOOM PATROL
Oct, 1987 - Present
DC Comics
	Good	Fine	N-Mint
1	.40	1.25	2.50
2-9: 3-1st app. Lodestone. 4-1st app. Karma		.50	1.00
10-18 ($1.00): 15,16-A. Adams-c(i). 18-Invasion		.50	1.00
19-30: 19-New format, direct sale begins($1.50)	.25	.75	1.50
...And Suicide Squad Special 1($1.50,3/88)	.35	1.00	2.00
Annual 1 ('88, $1.50)	.25	.75	1.50

DOOMSDAY + 1
7/75 - No. 6, 6/76; No. 7, 6/68 - No. 12, 5/79
Charlton Comics
1	1.00	3.00	6.00
2	.75	2.25	4.50
3-6: 4-Intro Lor	.70	2.00	4.00
V3#7-12 (reprints #1-6)	.30	.80	1.60
5 (Modern Comics reprint, 1977)		.20	.40
NOTE: Byrne c/a-1-12; Painted covers-2-7.

DOOMSDAY SQUAD, THE
Aug, 1986 - No. 7, Feb, 1987 ($2.00)
Fantagraphics Books
1,2: Byrne-a in all. 1-3-new Byrne-c .35 1.00 2.00
3-Usagi Yojimbo app. (1st in color) .70 2.00 4.00
4-7: 4-N. Adams-c. 5-7-Gil Kane-c .35 1.00 2.00

DOORWAY TO NIGHTMARE (See Cancelled Comic Cavalcade)
Jan-Feb, 1978 - No. 5, Sept-Oct, 1978
DC Comics
1-5-Madame Xanadu in all. 4-Craig-a .30 .60
NOTE: Kaluta covers on all. Merged into The Unexpected with No. 190.

DOPEY DUCK COMICS (Wacky Duck No. 3) (See Super Funnies)
Fall, 1945 - No. 2, April, 1946
Timely Comics (NPP)
1,2-Casper Cat, Krazy Krow 8.00 24.00 56.00

DOROTHY LAMOUR (Formerly Jungle Lil)(Stage, screen, radio)
No. 2, June, 1950 - No. 3, Aug, 1950
Fox Features Syndicate
2,3-Wood-a(3) each, photo-c 10.00 30.00 70.00

DOT AND DASH AND THE LUCKY JINGLE PIGGIE
1942 (12 pages)
Sears Roebuck Christmas giveaway
Contains a war stamp album and a punch out Jingle Piggie bank
3.50 10.50 24.00

DOT DOTLAND (Formerly Little Dot Dotland)
No. 62, Sept, 1974 - No. 63, November, 1974
Harvey Publications
62,63 .60 1.20

DOTTY (...& Her Boy Friends) (Formerly Four Teeners; Glamorous Romances, No. 41 on)
No. 35, July, 1948 - No. 40, May, 1949
Ace Magazines (A. A. Wyn)
35 3.70 11.00 26.00
36,38-40 2.00 6.00 14.00
37-Transvestism story 2.30 7.00 16.00

DOTTY DRIPPLE (Horace & Dotty Dripple No. 25 on)
1946 - No. 24, June, 1952 (See A-1 No. 1-8, 10)
Magazine Ent.(Life's Romances)/Harvey No. 3 on
nn (nd) (10 cent) 3.00 9.00 21.00
2 1.50 4.50 10.00
3-10: 3,4-Powell-a 1.00 3.00 7.00
11-24 .75 2.25 5.00

Double Action Comics #2. : DC   Down With Crime #1. FAW   Dracula #2. DELL

DOTTY DRIPPLE AND TAFFY
No. 646, Sept, 1955 - No. 903, May, 1958
Dell Publishing Co.

	Good	Fine	N-Mint
4-Color 646	1.70	5.00	12.00
4-Color 691,718,746,801,903	1.30	4.00	9.00

DOUBLE ACTION COMICS
No. 2, Jan, 1940 (Regular size; 68 pgs.; B&W, color cover)
National Periodical Publications

2-Contains original stories(?); pre-hero DC contents; same cover as
Adventure No. 37. (Five known copies) (not an ashcan)
Estimated value 6500.00

NOTE: The cover to this book was probably reprinted from Adventure #37. #1 exists as
an ash can copy with B&W cover; contains a coverless comic on inside with 1st & last
page missing.

DOUBLE COMICS
1940 - 1944 (132 pages)
Elliot Publications

	Good	Fine	N-Mint
1940 issues; Masked Marvel-c & The Mad Mong vs. The White Flash			
covers known	117.00	295.00	700.00
1941 issues; Tornado Tim-c, Nordac-c, & Green Light covers known			
	71.00	215.00	500.00
1942 issues	57.00	170.00	400.00
1943,44 issues	46.00	140.00	325.00

NOTE: Double Comics consisted of an almost endless combination of pairs of remaindered,
unsold issues of comics representing most publishers and usually mixed publishers in the
same book; e.g., a Captain America with a Silver Streak, or a Feature with a Detective, etc.,
could appear inside the same cover. The actual contents would have to determine its price.
Prices listed are for average contents. Any complete rare origin or first issues are worth
much more. Covers also vary in same year. Value would be approximately 50 percent of
contents.

DOUBLE-CROSS (See The Crusaders)

DOUBLE-DARE ADVENTURES
Dec, 1966 - No. 2, March, 1967 (35-25 cents, 68 pgs.)
Harvey Publications

	Good	Fine	N-Mint
1-Origin Bee-Man, Glowing Gladiator, & Magic-Master; Simon/			
Kirby-a	.85	2.50	6.00
2-Williamson/Crandall-a; r-/Alarming Adv. #3('63)			
	1.15	3.50	8.00

NOTE: Powell a-1. Simon/Sparling c-1,2.

DOUBLE LIFE OF PRIVATE STRONG, THE
June, 1959 - No. 2, Aug, 1959
Archie Publications/Radio Comics

	Good	Fine	N-Mint
1-Origin The Shield; Simon & Kirby c/a; intro./1st app. The Fly			
	25.00	75.00	175.00
2-S&K c/a; Tuska-a; The Fly app.	16.00	48.00	110.00

DOUBLE TALK (Also see Two-Faces)
No date (1962?) (32 pgs.; full color; slick cover)
Christian Anti-Communism Crusade (Giveaway)
Feature Publications

	Good	Fine	N-Mint
nn	8.50	25.50	60.00

DOUBLE TROUBLE
Nov, 1957 - No. 2, Jan-Feb, 1958
St. John Publishing Co.

	Good	Fine	N-Mint
1,2	1.70	5.00	12.00

DOUBLE TROUBLE WITH GOOBER
No. 417, Aug, 1952 - No. 556, May, 1954
Dell Publishing Co.

	Good	Fine	N-Mint
4-Color 417	1.50	4.50	10.00
4-Color 471,516,556	1.00	3.00	7.00

DOUBLE UP
1941 (200 pages) (Pocket size)
Elliott Publications

	Good	Fine	N-Mint
1-Contains rebound copies of digest sized issues of Pocket Comics,			
Speed Comics, & Spitfire Comics	43.00	130.00	300.00

DOVER BOYS (See Adventures of the . . .)

DOVER THE BIRD
Spring, 1955
Famous Funnies Publishing Co.

	Good	Fine	N-Mint
1	1.70	5.00	12.00

DOWN WITH CRIME
Nov, 1952 - No. 7, Nov, 1953
Fawcett Publications

	Good	Fine	N-Mint
1	9.00	27.00	62.00
2,4-Powell-a each	5.00	15.00	35.00
3-Used in POP, pg. 106	5.70	17.00	40.00
5-Bondage-c	5.70	17.00	40.00
6-Used in POP, pg. 80	3.50	10.50	24.00
7	3.50	10.50	24.00

DO YOU BELIEVE IN NIGHTMARES?
Nov, 1957 - No. 2, Jan, 1958
St. John Publishing Co.

	Good	Fine	N-Mint
1-Ditko c/a(most)	12.00	36.00	84.00
2-Ayers-a	5.70	17.00	40.00

D.P. 7
Nov, 1986 - No. 32, June, 1989 (26 on: $1.50)
Marvel Comics Group

		Good	Fine	N-Mint
1-32			.60	1.20
Annual #1 (11/87)-Intro. The Witness			.65	1.30

NOTE: Williamson a-9i. 11i. c-9i.

DRACULA (See Tomb of . . . Marvel Graphic Novel & Movie Classics under Universal Presents as well as Dracula)

DRACULA (See Movie Classics for No. 1)
11/66 - No. 4, 3/67; No. 6, 7/72 - No. 8, 7/73 (No No.5)
Dell Publishing Co.

	Good	Fine	N-Mint
2-Origin Dracula (11/66)	.85	2.60	6.00
3,4-Intro. Fleeta #4('67)	.70	2.00	4.00
6-('72)-r-/#3, w/origin	.35	1.00	2.00
7,8: 7 r-/#3, 8-r/#4		.50	1.00

DRACULA (Magazine)
1979 (120 pages) (full color)
Warren Publishing Co.

	Good	Fine	N-Mint
Book 1-Maroto art; Spanish material translated into English			
	1.00	3.00	6.00

DRACULA LIVES! (Magazine)
1973(no month) - No. 13, July, 1975 (B&W) (75 cents)
Marvel Comics Group

	Good	Fine	N-Mint
1-3: 2-Origin	.50	1.50	3.00
4-Ploog-a	.45	1.25	2.50
5(V2#1)-13: 5-Dracula series begins	.35	1.00	2.00
Annual 1('75)	.35	1.00	2.00

NOTE: Adams a-2. 3i. 10i. Annual 1r; 2, 3i. Alcala a-9. Buscema a-3p. 6p. Colan a(p)-1.
2. 5. 6. 8. Evans a-7. Heath a-1r. 13. Pakula a-6r. Starlin a-2.

DRAFT, THE
1988 (One shot, $3.50, color, squarebound)
Marvel Comics

		Good	Fine	N-Mint
1-Sequel to "The Pitt"		.60	1.75	3.50

DRAG 'N' WHEELS (Formerly Top Eliminator)
No. 30, Sept, 1968 - No. 59, May, 1973
Charlton Comics

		Good	Fine	N-Mint
30-40-Scot Jackson begins		.35	1.00	2.00
41-50			.60	1.25

Dragonlance #1, © TSR

Dragonring #6, Aircel Publ.

Dreadstar #1, First Comics

The Durango Kid #5.   ME   Dynamic Comics #16.   CHES   Dynamite #6.   Comic Media

DUDLEY DO-RIGHT (TV)
Aug, 1970 - No. 7, Aug, 1971 (Jay Ward)
Charlton Comics

	Good	Fine	N-Mint
1	2.85	8.50	20.00
2-7	2.00	6.00	14.00

DUKE OF THE K-9 PATROL
April, 1963
Gold Key

1 (10052-304)	1.75	5.25	12.00

DUMBO (See 4-Color #17,234,668, Movie Comics, & Walt Disney Showcase #12)
DUMBO (Walt Disney's. . .)
1941 (K.K. Publ. Giveaway)
Weatherbird Shoes/Ernest Kern Co.(Detroit)

16 pgs., 9x10'' (Rare)	22.00	65.00	154.00
52 pgs., 5½x8½'', slick cover in color; B&W interior; half text, half reprints/4-Color No. 17	13.00	40.00	90.00

DUMBO COMIC PAINT BOOK (See Large Feature Comic No. 19)
DUMBO WEEKLY
1942 (Premium supplied by Diamond D-X Gas Stations)
Walt Disney Productions

1	10.00	30.00	60.00
2-16	5.00	15.00	30.00

NOTE: A cover and binder came separate at gas stations. Came with membership card.

DUNC AND LOO (1-3 titled ''Around the Block with Dunc and Loo'')
Oct-Dec, 1961 - No. 8, Oct-Dec, 1963
Dell Publishing Co.

1	5.00	15.00	35.00
2	3.50	10.50	24.00
3-8	2.30	7.00	16.00

NOTE: Written by John Stanley; Bill Williams art.

DUNE
April, 1985 - No. 3, June, 1985
Marvel Comics

1-3-r/Marvel Super Special; movie adaptation	.40	.80

DUNGEONEERS, THE
1987 - No. 5? ($1.50, B&W)
Silverwolf Comics

1-5	.25	.80	1.60

DURANGO KID, THE (Also see Best of the West, Great Western & White Indian) (Charles Starrett starred in Columbia's Durango Kid movies)
Oct-Nov, 1949 - No. 41, Oct-Nov, 1955 (All 36pgs.)
Magazine Enterprises

1-Charles Starrett photo-c; Durango Kid & his horse Raider begin; Dan Brand & Tipi (origin) begin by Frazetta & continue through #16	37.00	110.00	260.00
2(Starrett photo-c)	25.00	75.00	175.00
3-5(All-Starrett photo-c)	21.50	64.00	150.00
6-10	11.50	34.00	80.00
11-16-Last Frazetta issue	8.50	25.50	60.00
17-Origin Durango Kid	11.00	32.00	75.00
18-Fred Meagher-a on Dan Brand begins	5.50	16.50	38.00
19-30: 19-Guardineer c/a(3) begin; end #41. 23-Intro. The Red Scorpion	5.50	16.50	38.00
31-Red Scorpion returns	4.50	14.00	32.00
32-41-Bolle/Frazetta-a (Dan Brand)	6.00	18.00	42.00

NOTE: •6,8,14,15 contain Frazetta art not reprinted in White Indian. Ayers c-18. Guardineer a(3)-19-41. c-19-41. Fred Meagher a-18-29 at least.

DWIGHT D. EISENHOWER
December, 1969
Dell Publishing Co.

	Good	Fine	N-Mint
01-237-912 - Life story	2.00	6.00	12.00

DYNABRITE COMICS
1978 - 1979 (69 cents; 48 pgs.)(10x7-1/8''; cardboard covers)
(Blank inside covers)
Whitman Publishing Co.

11350 - Walt Disney's Mickey Mouse & the Beanstalk (4-C 157)
11350-1 - Mickey Mouse Album (4-C 1057,1151,1246)
11351 - Mickey Mouse & His Sky Adventure (4-C 214,343)
11352 - Donald Duck (4-C 408, Donald Duck 45,52)-Barks
11352-1 - Donald Duck (4-C 318, 10 pg. Barks/WDC&S 125,128)-Barks-c(r)
11353 - Daisy Ducks Diary (4-C 1055,1150) - Barks-a
11354 - Goofy: A Gaggle of Giggles
11354-1 - Super Goof Meets Super Thief
11355 - Uncle Scrooge (Barks-a/U.S. 12,33)
11355-1 - Uncle Scrooge (Barks-a/U.S. 13,16) - Barks-c(r)
11356 - Bugs Bunny(?)
11357 - Star Trek (r-Star Trek 33 & 41)
11358 - Star Trek (r-Star Trek 34,36)
11359 - Bugs Bunny-r
11360 - Winnie the Pooh Fun and Fantasy (Disney-r)
11361 - Gyro Gearloose & the Disney Ducks (4-C 1047,1184)-Barks-c(r)

each	.50	1.00

DYNAMIC ADVENTURES
No. 8,9, 1964
I. W. Enterprises

8-Kayo Kirby by Baker?	1.20	3.50	7.00
9-Reprints Avon's ''Escape From Devil's Island''-Kinstler-c	1.35	4.00	8.00
nn(no date)-Reprints Risks Unlimited with Rip Carson, Senorita Rio	1.20	3.50	7.00

DYNAMIC CLASSICS (See Cancelled Comic Cavalcade)
Sept-Oct, 1978 (44 pgs.)
DC Comics

1-Adams Batman, Simonson Manhunter-r	.50	1.00

DYNAMIC COMICS (No #4-7)
Oct, 1941 - No. 3, Feb, 1942; No. 8, 1944 - No. 25, May, 1948
Harry 'A' Chesler

1-Origin Major Victory by Charles Sultan (reprinted in Major Victory #1), Dynamic Man & Hale the Magician; The Black Cobra only app.	60.00	180.00	425.00
2-Origin Dynamic Boy & Lady Satan; intro. The Green Knight & sidekick Lance Cooper	30.00	90.00	210.00
3	24.00	70.00	165.00
8-Dan Hastings, The Echo, The Master Key, Yankee Boy begin; Yankee Doodle Jones app.; hypo story	24.00	70.00	165.00
9-Mr. E begins; Mac Raboy-c	25.00	75.00	175.00
10	20.00	60.00	140.00
11-15: 15-The Sky Chief app.	14.00	42.00	100.00
16-Marijuana story	16.00	48.00	110.00
17(1/46)-Illustrated in SOTI, ''The children told me what the man was going to do with the hot poker,'' but Wertham saw this in Crime Reporter #2	21.50	64.00	150.00
18,19,21,22,24,25	9.30	28.00	65.00
20-Bare-breasted woman-c	13.00	40.00	90.00
23-Yankee Girl app.	10.00	30.00	70.00
I.W. Reprint #1,8('64): 1-r/#23	.85	2.50	5.00

NOTE: Kinstler c-IW #1. Tuska art in many issues. #3, 9, 11, 12, 16, 19. Bondage c-16.

DYNAMITE (Johnny Dynamite No. 10 on)
May, 1953 - No. 9, Sept, 1954
Comic Media/Allen Hardy Publ.

1-Pete Morisi-a; r-as Danger No. 6	6.50	19.50	45.00
2	3.70	11.00	26.00
3-Marijuana story; Johnny Dynamite begins by Pete Morisi	5.00	15.00	35.00
4-Injury-to-eye, prostitution; Morisi-a	5.70	17.00	40.00

	Good	Fine	N-Mint
DYNAMITE (continued)			
5-9-Morisi-a in all. 6-Morisi-c	3.50	10.50	24.00

DYNAMO (Also see Tales of Thunder & T.H.U.N.D.E.R. Agents)
Aug. 1966 - No. 4. June, 1967 (25 cents)
Tower Comics

	Good	Fine	N-Mint
1-Crandall/Wood, Ditko/Wood-a; Weed series begins; NoMan & Lightning cameos; Wood c/a	3.00	9.00	21.00
2-4: Wood c/a in all	2.00	6.00	14.00

NOTE: *Adkins/Wood a-2. Ditko a-4. Tuska a-2,3.*

DYNAMO JOE (Also see First Adventures & Mars)
May. 1986 - No. 15, Jan. 1988 (#12-15: $1.75)
First Comics

1	.35	1.10	2.20
2-15: 4-Cargonauts begin	.25	.75	1.50
Special 1(1/87)-Mostly-r/Mars	.25	.75	1.50

DYNOMUTT (TV)(See Scooby-Doo, 3rd series)
Nov. 1977 - No. 6, Sept. 1978
Marvel Comics Group

1-6		.50	1.00

EAGLE, THE (1st Series) (See Science Comics & Weird Comics #8)
July. 1941 - No. 4, Jan. 1942
Fox Features Syndicate

1-The Eagle begins; Rex Dexter of Mars app. by Briefer			
	60.00	180.00	425.00
2-The Spider Queen begins (origin)	32.00	95.00	225.00
3,4: 3-Joe Spook begins (origin)	25.00	75.00	175.00

EAGLE (2nd Series)
Feb-Mar. 1945 - No. 2. Apr-May. 1945
Rural Home Publ.

1-Aviation stories	8.00	24.00	56.00
2-Lucky Aces	6.50	19.50	45.00

NOTE: *L. B. Cole c/a in each.*

EAGLE
Sept. 1986 - Present ($1.50/1.75/1.95, B&W)
Crystal Comics/Apple Comics #17 on

1	.70	2.00	4.00
1-Signed and limited	.85	2.50	5.00
2-11,13-26	.35	1.00	2.00
12-Origin issue ($2.50)	.40	1.25	2.50

EARTH MAN ON VENUS (An . . .) (Also see Strange Planets)
1951
Avon Periodicals

nn-Wood-a, 26 pgs.; Fawcette-c	68.00	205.00	475.00

EASTER BONNET SHOP (See March of Comics No. 29)

EASTER WITH MOTHER GOOSE (See 4-Color No. 103,140,185,220)

EAT RIGHT TO WORK AND WIN
1942 (16 pages) (Giveaway)
Swift & Company

Blondie. Henry, Flash Gordon by Alex Raymond, Toots & Casper. Thimble Theatre (Popeye). Tillie the Toiler. The Phantom, The Little King, & Bringing Up Father - original strips just for this book - (in daily strip form which shows what foods we should eat and why)

	18.00	54.00	125.00

EB'NN THE RAVEN
Oct. 1985 - No. 10, 1987 ($1.50, B&W)
Crowquill Comics/Now Comics #3 on

1 (44 pgs.)	.75	2.25	4.50
2 (44 pgs.)	.50	1.50	3.00
3 (52 pgs.)	.35	1.00	2.00
4,5	.30	.90	1.80
6-9	.25	.75	1.50

	Good	Fine	N-Mint
10-(Color)		.60	1.20

E. C. CLASSIC REPRINTS
May, 1973 - No. 12, 1976 (E. C. Comics reprinted in color minus ads)
East Coast Comix Co.

1-The Crypt of Terror #1 (Tales From the Crypt #46)			
	.70	2.00	4.00
2-Weird Science #15('52)	.50	1.50	3.00
3-Shock SuspenStories #12	.35	1.00	2.00
4-12: 4-Haunt of Fear #12. 5-Weird Fantasy #13('52). 6-Crime SuspenStories #25. 7-Vault of Horror #26. 8-Shock SuspenStories #6 9-Two-Fisted Tales #34. 10-Haunt of Fear #23. 11-Weird Science #12(#1). 12-Shock SuspenStories #2	.35	1.00	2.00

EC CLASSICS
1985 - Present? (High quality paper; r-/8 stories in color)
Russ Cochran

(All #1)-Shock Suspenstories, Two-Fisted Tales, Vault of Horror, Weird Fantasy	.85	2.50	4.95

ECHO OF FUTUREPAST
May, 1984 - No. 8?, 1986 (52 pgs., $2.95)
Pacific Comics/Continuity Comics

1-Adams c/a begins	.60	1.80	3.50
2-8	.50	1.50	3.00

NOTE: *Adams a-1-6; c-1-3. 5p. 8. Golden a-1-6. c-6. Toth a-6. 7.*

ECLIPSE GRAPHIC ALBUM SERIES
Oct. 1978 - Present (8½x11'') (B&W #1-5)
Eclipse Comics ·

1-Sabre (10/78, B&W, 1st print.)	1.35	4.00	8.00
1-Sabre (2nd printing, 1/79)	1.35	4.00	8.00
1-Sabre (3rd printing)	1.00	3.00	5.95
2-Night Music (11/79, B&W)-Russell-a	.85	2.50	5.00
3-Detectives, Inc. (5/80, B&W)-Rogers-a	1.15	3.50	7.00
4-Stewart The Rat ('80, B&W)-G. Colan-a	1.15	3.50	7.00
5-The Price (10/81, B&W)-Starlin-a	2.00	6.00	12.00
6-I Am Coyote (11/84, color)-Rogers c/a	1.35	4.00	8.00
7-The Rocketeer (9/85, color)-Stevens-a	1.70	5.00	10.00
7-The Rocketeer (2nd print.)	1.35	4.00	7.95
7-The Rocketeer, signed & limited hardcover	10.00	30.00	60.00
8-Zorro In Old California ('86, color)	1.35	4.00	8.00
8-Hard cover	2.00	6.00	11.95
9-Sacred And The Profane ('86)-Steacy-a	2.70	8.00	16.00
9-Hard cover	4.00	12.50	24.95
10-Somerset Holmes ('86, color)-Adults, soft-c	2.70	8.00	16.00
10-Hard cover	4.00	12.50	24.95
11-Floyd Farland, Citizen of the Future ('87, B&W)			
	.70	2.00	4.00
12-Silverheels ('87, color)	1.50	4.50	9.00
12-Hard cover	2.50	7.50	14.95
12-Hard cover, signed & #'d	4.00	12.50	24.95
13-The Sisterhood of Steel ('87, color)	1.70	5.00	10.00
14-Samurai, Son of Death ('87, B&W)	.85	2.50	5.00
14-Samurai, Son of Death (2nd print.)	.70	2.00	3.95
15-Twisted Tales (11/87, color)-Stevens-c	.70	2.00	3.95
16-See Airfighters Classics #1			
17-Valkyrie, Prisoner of the Past ('88, color)-soft-c			
	.70	2.00	3.95
18-See Airfighters Classics #2			
19-Scout: The Four Monsters ('88, color)-r/Scouts #1-7; soft-c	2.50	7.50	14.95
20-See Airfighters Classics #3			
21-XYR-Multiple ending comic ('88, B&W)	.70	2.00	3.95
22-Alien Worlds #1 (5/88, $3.95)	.70	2.00	3.95
23-See Airfighters Classics #4			
24-Heartbreak ($4.95, B&W)	.85	2.50	4.95

Dynamo #4, © TC

The Eagle #1 (7/41), © FOX

Eclipse Graphic Album Series #15. © Eclipse

Edgar Bergen Presents C. McCarthy #764, © E. Bergen

Eerie #2, © AVON

Eerie #60, © WP

ECLIPSE GRAPHIC ALBUM SERIES (cont.)

	Good	Fine	N-Mint
25-Alex Toth's Zorro Vol. 1 ($10.95, B&W)	1.85	5.50	10.95
26-Alex Toth's Zorro Vol. 2 ($10.95, B&W)	1.85	5.50	10.95
27-Fast Fiction (She) ($5.95, B&W)	1.00	3.00	5.95
28-Miracleman Book I ($5.95)	1.00	3.00	5.95
29-Real Love: The Best of the Simon and Kirby Romance Comics ($12.95)	2.15	6.50	12.95
30-Brought To Light; Alan Moore scripts	1.85	5.50	10.95
30-Limited hardcover ed. ($29.95)	5.00	15.00	29.95
31-Pigeons From Hell by Robert E. Howard	1.35	4.00	7.95
31-Signed & Limited Edition ($29.95)	5.00	15.00	30.00

ECLIPSE MONTHLY
8/83 - No. 10, 7/84 (Baxter paper); 1-3: 52 pgs., $2.00)
Eclipse Comics

1-3: ($2.00)-Cap'n Quick and a Foozle by Rogers, Static by Ditko, Dope by Trina Robbins, Rio by Doug Wildey, The Masked Man by Boyer begin. 3-Ragamuffins begins	.30	.90	1.80
4-8 ($1.50 cover)	.30	.90	1.80
9,10-($1.75 cover)	.30	.90	1.80

NOTE: *Boyer* c-6. *Ditko* a-1-3. *Rogers* a-1-4; c-2, 4. *Wildey* a-1, 2, 5, 9, 10; c-5, 10.

E. C. 3-D CLASSICS (See Three Dimensional . . .)

EDDIE STANKY (Baseball Hero)
1951 (New York Giants)
Fawcett Publications

nn-Photo-c	10.00	30.00	70.00

EDGAR BERGEN PRESENTS CHARLIE McCARTHY
No. 764, 1938 (36 pgs.; 15x10½''; in color)
Whitman Publishing Co. (Charlie McCarthy Co.)

764 (Scarce)	40.00	120.00	280.00

EDGE OF CHAOS
July, 1983 - No. 3, Jan, 1984
Pacific Comics

1-3-Morrow c/a; all contain nudity	.35	1.00	2.00

EDWARD'S SHOES GIVEAWAY
1954 (Has clown on cover)
Edward's Shoe Store

Contains comic with new cover. Many combinations possible. Contents determines price. 50-60 percent of original. (Similar to Comics From Weatherbird & Free Comics to You)

ED WHEELAN'S JOKE BOOK STARRING FAT & SLAT (See Fat & Slat)

EERIE (Strange Worlds No. 18 on)
No. 1, Jan, 1947; No. 1, May-June, 1951 - No. 17, Aug-Sept, 1954
Avon Periodicals

1(1947)-1st horror comic; Kubert, Fugitani-a; bondage-c	38.00	115.00	265.00
1(1951)-Reprints story/'47 No. 1	21.50	64.00	150.00
2-Wood c/a; bondage-c	24.00	70.00	165.00
3-Wood-a, Kubert, Wood/Orlando-a	24.00	70.00	165.00
4,5-Wood-c	21.50	64.00	150.00
6,13,14	8.00	24.00	56.00
7-Wood/Orlando-c; Kubert-a	14.00	42.00	100.00
8-Kinstler-a; bondage-c; Phantom Witch Doctor story	8.50	25.50	60.00
9-Kubert-a; Check-c	10.00	30.00	70.00
10,11-Kinstler-a	8.00	24.00	56.00
12-25-pg. Dracula story from novel	11.00	32.00	75.00
15-Reprints No. 1('51)minus-c(bondage)	5.00	15.00	35.00
16-Wood-a r-/No. 2	6.50	19.50	45.00
17-Wood/Orlando & Kubert-a; reprints #3 minus inside & outside Wood-c	8.50	25.50	60.00

NOTE: *Hollingsworth* a-9-11; c-10,11.

EERIE
1964
I. W. Enterprises

	Good	Fine	N-Mint
I.W. Reprint #1(1964)-Wood-c(r)	1.20	3.50	7.00
I.W. Reprint #2,6,8: 8-Dr. Drew by Grandenetti from Ghost #9	.85	2.50	5.00
I.W. Reprint #9-From Eerie #2(Avon); Wood-c	1.35	4.00	8.00

EERIE (Magazine)(See Warren Presents)
No. 1, Sept, 1965; No. 2, Mar, 1966 - No. 139, Feb, 1983
Warren Publishing Co.

1-24 pgs., black & white, small size (5¼"x7¼"), low distribution; cover from inside back cover of Creepy No. 2; stories reprinted from Creepy No. 7, 8. At least three different versions exist.

First Printing - B&W, 5¼'' wide x 7¼'' high, evenly trimmed. On page 18, panel 5, in the upper left-hand corner, the large rear view of a bald headed man blends into solid black and is unrecognizable. Overall printing quality is poor.

	14.00	42.00	100.00

Second Printing - B&W, 5¼''x7¼'', with uneven, untrimmed edges (if one of these were trimmed evenly, the size would be less than as indicated). The figure of the bald headed man on page 18, panel 5 is clear and discernible. The staples have a ¼'' blue stripe.

	7.00	21.00	50.00

Other unauthorized reproductions for comparison's sake would be practically worthless. One known version was probably shot off a first printing copy with some loss of detail; the finer lines tend to disappear in this version which can be determined by looking at the lower right-hand corner of page one, first story. The roof of the house is shaded with straight lines. These lines are sharp and distinct on original, but broken on this version.

	1.35	4.00	8.00

NOTE: *The Official Overstreet Comic Book Price Guide recommends that, before buying, you consult an expert.*

2-Frazetta-c	1.00	3.00	7.00
3-Frazetta-c, 1 pg.	.85	2.50	5.00
4-10: 4-Frazetta-c (½ pg.). 9-Headlight-c	.70	2.00	4.00
11-25	.50	1.50	3.00
26-41,43-45	.50	1.50	3.00
42-(1973 Annual)	.70	2.00	4.00
46-50,52,53,56-78: 78-The Mummy-r	.30	1.00	2.00
51-(1974 Annual)	.70	2.00	4.00
54,55-Color Spirit story by Eisner, 12/21/47 & 6/16/46	.50	1.50	3.00
79,80-Origin Darklon the Mystic by Starlin	.30	1.00	2.00
81-139	.25	.75	1.50
Year Book 1970-Reprints	1.00	3.00	6.00
Year Book 1971-Reprints	1.00	3.00	6.00
Year Book 1972-Reprints	.85	2.50	5.00

NOTE: *The above books contain art by many good artists: Adams, Brunner, Corben, Craig (Taycee), Crandall, Ditko, Eisner, Evans, Jeff Jones, Kinstler, Krenkel, McWilliams, Morrow, Orlando, Ploog, Severin, Starlin, Torres, Toth, Williamson, Wood, and Wrightson; covers by Bode', Corben, Davis, Frazetta, Morrow, and Orlando. Annuals from 1973-on are included in regular numbering. 1970-74 Annuals are complete reprints. Annuals from 1975-on are in the format of the regular issues.*

EERIE ADVENTURES (Also see Weird Adventures)
Winter, 1951
Ziff-Davis Publ. Co.

1-Powell-a(2), Kinstler-a; used in SOTI; bondage-c; Krigstein back-c	10.00	30.00	70.00

NOTE: *Title dropped due to similarity to Avon's Eerie & legal action*

EERIE TALES (Magazine)
1959 (Black & White)
Hastings Associates

1-Williamson, Torres, Tuska, Powell(2), & Morrow(2)-a	4.50	14.00	32.00

EERIE TALES
1964
Super Comics

Super Reprint No. 10,11,12,18: Purple Claw in No. 11,12; No. 12

EERIE TALES (continued)

	Good	Fine	N-Mint
r-Avon Eerie No. 1('51)	.70	2.00	4.00
15-Wolverton-a, Spacehawk-r/Blue Bolt Weird Tales No. 113; Disbrow-a	2.00	6.00	14.00

EGBERT
Spring, 1946 - No. 20, 1950
Arnold Publications/Quality Comics Group

	Good	Fine	N-Mint
1-Funny animal; intro Egbert & The Count	9.00	27.00	62.00
2	4.30	13.00	30.00
3-10	2.65	8.00	18.00
11-20	1.70	5.00	12.00

EH! (. . . Dig This Crazy Comic) (From Here to Insanity No. 8 on)
Dec, 1953 - No. 7, Nov-Dec, 1954 (Satire)
Charlton Comics

	Good	Fine	N-Mint
1-Davisish-c/a by Ayers, Woodish-a by Giordano; Atomic Mouse app.	9.30	28.00	65.00
2-Ayers-c/a	6.50	19.50	45.00
3-7: 4,6-Sexual innuendo-c. 6-Ayers-a	5.70	17.00	40.00

80 PAGE GIANT (. . . Magazine No. 1-15) (25 cents)
8/64 - No. 15, 10/65; No. 16, 11/65 - No. 89, 7/71 (All reprints)
National Periodical Publications (#1-56: 84 pgs.; #57-89: 68 pages)

	Good	Fine	N-Mint
1-Superman Annual	8.15	24.50	65.00
2-Jimmy Olsen	3.50	10.50	28.00
3-Lois Lane	2.00	6.00	16.00
4-Flash-G.A.-r; Infantino-a	2.00	6.00	16.00
5-Batman; has Sunday newspaper strip; Catwoman-r; Batman's Life Story-r (25th anniversary special)	3.00	9.00	24.00
6-Superman	2.00	6.00	16.00
7-Sgt. Rock's Prize Battle Tales; Kubert c/a	2.00	6.00	16.00
8-More Secret Origins-origins of JLA, Aquaman, Robin, Atom, & Superman; Infantino-a	7.50	22.50	60.00
9-Flash(reprints Flash #123)-Infantino-a	2.00	6.00	16.00
10-Superboy	2.00	6.00	16.00
11-Superman-All Luthor issue	2.00	6.00	16.00
12-Batman; has Sunday newspaper strip	2.50	7.50	20.00
13-Jimmy Olsen	2.00	6.00	16.00
14-Lois Lane	2.00	6.00	16.00
15-Superman and Batman; Joker-c/story	3.00	9.00	24.00

Continued as part of regular series under each title in which that particular book came out, a Giant being published instead of the regular size. Issues No. 16 to No. 89 are listed for your information. See individual titles for prices.

16-JLA #39 (11/65), 17-Batman #176, 18-Superman #183, 19-Our Army at War #164, 20-Action #334, 21-Flash #160, 22-Superboy #129, 23-Superman #187, 24-Batman #182, 25-Jimmy Olsen #95, 26-Lois Lane #68, 27-Batman #185, 28-World's Finest #161, 29-JLA #48, 30-Batman #187, 31-Superman #193, 32-Our Army at War #177, 33-Action #347, 34-Flash #169, 35-Superboy #138, 36-Superman #197, 37-Batman #193, 38-Jimmy Olsen #104, 39-Lois Lane #77, 40-World's Finest #170, 41-JLA #58, 42-Superman #202, 43-Batman #198, 44-Our Army at War #190, 45-Action #360, 46-Flash #178, 47-Superboy #147, 48-Superman #207, 49-Batman #203, 50-Jimmy Olsen #113, 51-Lois Lane #86, 52-World's Finest #179, 53-JLA #67, 54-Superman #212, 55-Batman #208, 56-Our Army at War #203, 57-Action #373, 58-Flash #187, 59-Superboy #156, 60-Superman #217, 61-Batman #213, 62-Jimmy Olsen #122, 63-Lois Lane #95, 64-World's Finest #188, 65-JLA #76, 66-Superboy #222, 67-Batman #218, 68-Our Army at War #216, 69-Adventure #390, 70-Flash #196, 71-Superboy #165, 72-Superman #227, 73-Batman #223, 74-Jimmy Olsen #131, 75-Lois Lane #104, 76-World's Finest #197, 77-JLA #85, 78-Superman #232, 79-Batman #228, 80-Our Army at War #229, 81-Adventure #403, 82-Flash #205, 83-Superboy #174, 84-Superman #239, 85-Batman #233, 86-Jimmy Olsen #140, 87-Lois Lane #113, 88-World's Finest #206, 89-JLA #93

87TH PRECINCT (TV)
Apr-June, 1962 - No. 2, July-Sept, 1962
Dell Publishing Co.

	Good	Fine	N-Mint
4-Color 1309; Krigstein-a	5.70	17.00	40.00
2	4.50	14.00	32.00

EINHERJAR: THE CHOSEN
1987 (Color, $1.50)
Vanguard Graphics (Canadian)

	Good	Fine	N-Mint
1	.25	.75	1.50

EL BOMBO COMICS
1946
Standard Comics/Frances M. McQueeny

	Good	Fine	N-Mint
nn(1946)	5.00	15.00	35.00
1(no date)	5.00	15.00	35.00

EL CID (See 4-Color No. 1259)

EL DIABLO (See All-Star Western #2 & Weird Western Tales #12)
Aug., 1989 - Present ($1.50, color)
DC Comics

	Good	Fine	N-Mint
1 ($2.50, 52 pgs.)-Masked hero	.40	1.25	2.50
2-6 ($1.50)	.25	.75	1.50

EL DORADO (See Movie Classics)

ELECTRIC UNDERTOW (See Strikeforce Morituri: Electric Undertow)

ELECTRIC WARRIOR
May, 1986 - No. 18, Oct, 1987 (Baxter paper)
DC Comics

	Good	Fine	N-Mint
1	.40	1.25	2.50
2-18	.25	.75	1.50

ELEKTRA: ASSASSIN
Aug, 1986 - No. 8, Mar, 1987 (limited series)(Adults)
Epic Comics (Marvel)

	Good	Fine	N-Mint
1-Miller scripts in all	.85	2.50	5.00
2	.70	2.00	4.00
3-8	.50	1.50	3.00
Signed & numbered hardcover (Graphitti Designs, $39.95, 2000 print run)-reprints 1-8	6.75	20.00	40.00

ELEKTRA SAGA, THE
Feb, 1984 - No. 4, June, 1984 ($2.00 cover; Baxter paper)
Marvel Comics Group

	Good	Fine	N-Mint
1-4-r/Daredevil 168-190; Miller c/a	1.00	3.00	6.00

ELEMENTALS, THE (Also see The Justice Machine)
June, 1984 - No. 29, Sept, 1988; V2#1, Mar, 1989 - Present
Comico The Comic Co. ($1.50, Baxter paper)

	Good	Fine	N-Mint
1-Willingham c/a, 1-8	1.35	4.00	8.00
2	.70	2.00	4.00
3	.50	1.50	3.00
4-7	.45	1.35	2.70
8-10: 9-Bissette-a(p)	.30	.90	1.80
11-29	.25	.80	1.60
V2#1-3 ($1.95)	.35	1.00	1.95
V2#4-10 ($2.50)	.40	1.25	2.50
Special 1 (3/86)-Willingham-a(p)	.30	.90	1.80
Special 2 (1/89, $1.95)	.35	1.00	1.95

ELFLORD
1986 - No. 30?, 1989 ($1.70, B&W, V2#1 on are $2.00 & color)
Aircel Publishing

	Good	Fine	N-Mint
1	1.00	3.00	6.00
1-2nd print	.25	.75	1.50
2	.40	1.25	2.50
2-2nd print	.25	.75	1.50
3	.45	1.35	2.70
4-6: Last B&W issue	.25	.80	1.60
V2#1-(color begins)	.40	1.25	2.50
2-20	.25	.80	1.60
21-Double size, $4.95	.75	2.25	4.50
22-30: 22-New cast; 25-Begin B&W, $1.95-c	.30	.90	1.80

ELFQUEST (Also see Fantasy Quarterly & Warp Graphics Annual)
No. 2, Aug, 1978 - No. 21, Feb, 1985 (All magazine size)
No. 1, April, 1979
WaRP Graphics, Inc.

NOTE: *Elfquest* was originally published as one of the stories in Fantasy Quarterly #1.

Eh! #7, © CC

80 Page Giant #9, © DC

El Diablo #2, © DC

Elfquest: Siege At Blue Mountain #2, © Apple Comics

Ellery Queen #1, © SUPR

Elsie The Cow #1, © D.S. Publ.

ELFQUEST (continued)
When the publisher went out of business, the creative team, Wendy and Richard Pini, formed WaRP Graphics and continued the series, beginning with Elfquest #2. Elfquest #1, which reprinted the story from Fantasy Quarterly, was published about the same time Elfquest #4 was released. Thereafter, most issues were reprinted as demand warranted, until Marvel announced it would reprint the entire series under its Epic imprint (Aug., 1985).

	Good	Fine	N-Mint
1(4/79)-Reprints Elfquest story from Fantasy Quarterly No. 1			
1st printing ($1.00 cover)	5.50	16.50	33.00
2nd printing ($1.25 cover)	1.70	5.00	10.00
3rd printing ($1.50 cover)	.85	2.50	5.00
2(8/78)-5: 1st printing ($1.00 cover)	3.35	10.00	20.00
2nd printing ($1.25 cover)	.85	2.50	5.00
3rd printing ($1.50 cover)	.50	1.50	3.00
6-9: 1st printing ($1.25 cover)	1.50	4.50	9.00
2nd printing ($1.50 cover)	.70	2.00	4.00
3rd printing ($1.50 cover)	.35	1.00	2.00
10-21: ($1.50 cover); 16-8pg. preview of A Distant Soil			
	1.00	3.00	6.00

ELFQUEST
Aug., 1985 - No. 32, Mar, 1988
Epic Comics (Marvel)

1-Reprints in color the Elfquest epic by WaRP Graphics			
	.85	2.50	5.00
2-5	.50	1.50	3.00
6-10	.40	1.15	2.25
11-20	.30	.90	1.80
21-32	.25	.75	1.50

ELFQUEST
1989 - No. 4, 1989 ($1.50, B&W)
WaRP Graphics

1-4: Reprints original Elfquest series	.25	.75	1.50

ELFQUEST: SIEGE AT BLUE MOUNTAIN
3/87 - No. 8, 12/88 (mini-series)($1.75/$1.95, B&W)
WaRP Graphics/Apple Comics

1-Staton-a(i) in all	1.10	3.25	6.50
1-2nd printing	.35	1.00	2.00
2	.70	2.00	4.00
2-2nd printing	.30	.90	1.80
3-8	.40	1.25	2.50

ELF WARRIOR (See Adventurers)
1987 - No. 4, 1988 ($1.95, B&W)
Adventure Publications

1-4	.35	1.00	2.00

ELLA CINDERS (See Comics On Parade, Comics Revue #1,4, Famous Comics Cartoon Book, Sparkler Comics, Tip Top & Treasury of Comics)

ELLA CINDERS
1938 - 1940
United Features Syndicate

Single Series 3(1938)	22.00	65.00	154.00
Single Series 21(#2 on-c, #21 on inside), 28('40)			
	17.00	51.00	120.00

ELLA CINDERS
March, 1948 - No. 5, 1949
United Features Syndicate

1	8.00	24.00	56.00
2	3.70	11.00	26.00
3-5	2.65	8.00	18.00

ELLERY QUEEN
May, 1949 - No. 4, Nov, 1949
Superior Comics Ltd.

1-Kamen c; L.B. Cole-a; r-in Haunted Thrills	19.00	57.00	135.00

	Good	Fine	N-Mint
2,4	11.50	34.00	80.00
3-Drug use stories(2)	12.00	36.00	84.00

NOTE: *Iger shop art-all issues.*

ELLERY QUEEN (TV)
1-3/52 - No. 2, Summer/52 (Saunders painted covers)
Ziff-Davis Publishing Co.

1-Saunders-c	20.00	60.00	140.00
2-Saunders bondage, torture-c	17.00	51.00	120.00

ELLERY QUEEN (See 4-Color No. 1165,1243,1289)

ELMER FUDD (Also see Camp Comics & Daffy)
May, 1953 - No. 1293, Mar-May, 1962
Dell Publishing Co.

4-Color 470,558,628,689('56)	1.15	3.50	8.00
4-Color 725,783,841,888,938,977,1032,1081,1131,1171,1222,1293('61)			
	.85	2.50	6.00

(See Super Book #10,22)

ELMO COMICS
January, 1948 (Daily strip-r)
St. John Publishing Co.

1-By Cecil Jensen	5.00	15.00	35.00

ELRIC OF MELNIBONE (See First Comics Graphic Novel #6)
Apr, 1983 - No. 6, Apr, 1984 ($1.50, Baxter paper)
Pacific Comics

1-6: Russell c/a(i) in all	.35	1.00	2.00

ELRIC: SAILOR ON THE SEAS OF FATE
June, 1985 - No. 7, June, 1986 (Limited series; $1.75 cover)
First Comics

1-7: Adapts Michael Moorcock's novel	.30	.90	1.80

ELRIC: THE BANE OF THE BLACK SWORD
Aug, 1988 - No. 6, June, 1989 ($1.75-$1.95, color, limited series)
First Comics

1-4: Adapts Michael Moorcock's novel	.30	.90	1.80

ELRIC: THE VANISHING TOWER
Aug, 1987 - No. 6, June, 1988 ($1.75, color)
First Comics

1-6: Adapts Michael Moorcock's novel	.30	.90	1.75

ELRIC: WEIRD OF THE WHITE WOLF
Oct, 1986 - No. 5, June, 1987 (limited series)
First Comics

1-5: Adapts Michael Moorcock's novel	.35	1.00	2.00

EL SALVADOR - A HOUSE DIVIDED
March, 1989 ($2.50, B&W, Baxter paper, stiff-c, 52 pgs.)
Eclipse Comics

1-Gives history of El Salvador	.40	1.25	2.50

ELSIE THE COW
Oct-Nov, 1949 - No. 3, July-Aug, 1950
D. S. Publishing Co.

1-(36 pages)	11.50	34.00	80.00
2,3	8.50	25.50	60.00
Borden Milk Giveaway-(16 pgs., nn) (3 issues, 1957)			
	3.00	9.00	21.00
Elsie's Fun Book(1950; Borden Milk)	4.50	13.50	31.00
Everyday Birthday Fun With...(1957; 20 pgs.)(100th Anniversary);			
Kubert-a	3.50	10.50	24.00

ELSON'S PRESENTS
1981 (100 pgs., no cover price)
DC Comics

Series 1-6: Repackaged 1981 DC comics; Superman, Action, Flash

Elvira's House Of Mystery #1, © DC

E-Man #1 (4/83), © First

Enchanting Love #1, © Kirby Publ.

Escape From Devil's Island #1, © AVON

The Eternals #2 (8/76), © MEG

Exciting Comics #2, © STD

ESCAPADE IN FLORENCE (See Movie Comics)

ESCAPE FROM DEVIL'S ISLAND
1952
Avon Periodicals

	Good	Fine	N-Mint
1-Kinstler-c; r/as Dynamic Adv. #9	16.00	47.00	110.00

ESCAPE FROM FEAR
1956, 1962, 1969 (8 pages full color) (On birth control)
Planned Parenthood of America (Giveaway)

1956 edition	10.00	30.00	70.00
1962 edition	7.00	21.00	50.00
1969 edition	3.50	10.50	24.00

ESCAPE TO WITCH MOUNTAIN (See Walt Disney Showcase No. 29)

ESPERS
July, 1986 - No. 5, April, 1987 ($1.25-$1.75, color, Mando paper, color)
Eclipse Comics

1-3 ($1.25)		.65	1.30
4,5 ($1.75)	.30	.90	1.80

ESPIONAGE (TV)
May-July, 1964 - No. 2, Aug-Oct, 1964
Dell Publishing Co.

1,2	1.30	4.00	9.00

ETC
1989 - No. 5, 1989 ($4.50, color, mini-series, adults, 60 pgs.)
Piranha Press (DC Comics)

Book 1-5: Conrad scripts/layouts in all	.75	2.25	4.50

ETERNAL BIBLE, THE
1946 (Large size) (16 pages in color)
Authentic Publications

1	5.00	15.00	35.00

ETERNALS, THE
July, 1976 - No. 19, Jan, 1978
Marvel Comics Group

1-19: 1-Origin. 2-1st app. Ajak & The Celestials		.50	1.00
Annual 1(10/77)		.30	.60

NOTE: *Kirby c/a(p) in all. Price changed from 25 cents to 30 cents during run of #1.*

ETERNALS, THE
Oct, 1985 - No. 12, Sept, 1986 (Maxi-series, mando paper)
Marvel Comics Group

1-11: 1-($1.25), 2-11-(75 cents)		.50	1.00
12-Double size ($1.25)-Williamson-a(i)		.50	1.00

ETERNITY SMITH
Sept, 1986 - No. 5, May, 1987 (Color, 36 pgs.)
Renegade Press

1 ($1.25)-1st app. Eternity Smith		.65	1.30
2-5 ($1.50): 5-Death of Jasmine	.25	.75	1.50

ETERNITY SMITH
Sept, 1987 - No. 9?, 1988 ($1.95, color)
Hero Comics

V2#1-9: 8-Indigo begins	.30	.95	1.90
Book 1 ($7.95)	1.35	4.00	8.00

ETTA KETT
No. 11, Dec, 1948 - No. 14, Sept, 1949
King Features Syndicate/Standard

11	4.50	14.00	32.00
12-14	3.00	9.00	21.00

EVANGELINE (Also see Primer)
2/84 - #2, 6/84; V2#1, 5/87 - V2#12, Mar, 1989 (Color; Baxter paper)
Comico/First Comics V2/1 on/Lodestone Publ.

1	1.00	3.00	6.00

	Good	Fine	N-Mint
2	.50	1.50	3.00
V2#1 (5/87) - 12	.35	1.00	2.00
Special #1 ('86, $2.00, color)-Lodestone Publ.	.35	1.00	2.00

EVA THE IMP
1957 - No. 2, Nov, 1957
Red Top Comic/Decker

1,2	1.30	4.00	9.00

EVEL KNIEVEL
1974 (20 pages) (Giveaway)
Marvel Comics Group (Ideal Toy Corp.)

nn		.40	.80

EVERYBODY'S COMICS (See Fox Giants)

EVERYTHING HAPPENS TO HARVEY
Sept-Oct, 1953 - No. 7, Sept-Oct, 1954
National Periodical Publications

1	10.00	30.00	70.00
2	5.70	17.00	40.00
3-7	4.50	14.00	32.00

EVERYTHING'S ARCHIE
May, 1969 - Present (Giant issues No. 1-20)
Archie Publications

1	4.65	14.00	32.00
2	2.30	7.00	16.00
3-5	1.30	4.00	9.00
6-10	.85	2.50	5.00
11-20	.35	1.00	2.00
21-40		.50	1.00
41-150		.30	.60

EVERYTHING'S DUCKY (See 4-Color No. 1251)

EWOKS (TV) (See Star Comics Magazine)
June, 1985 - No. 15, Sept, 1987
Star Comics (Marvel)

1-13: 10-Williamson-a		.35	.70
14,15($1.00)		.50	1.00

EXCALIBUR (Also see Marvel Comics Presents #31)
Apr, 1988; Oct, 1988 - Present ($1.50, Baxter)
Marvel Comics

1($1.50, 10/88)-X-Men spin-of	1.15	3.50	7.00
2	.70	2.00	4.00
3,4	.50	1.50	3.00
5-10	.40	1.25	2.50
11-20: 10,11-Rogers/Austin-a	.35	1.00	2.00
...The Sword Is Drawn nn ($3.25, 4/88)	1.70	5.00	10.00
...The Sword Is Drawn nn ($3.50, 10/88)-2nd printing	.60	1.75	3.50
...The Sword Is Drawn nn ($4.50, 12/89)-3rd printing	.75	2.25	4.50
...Mojo Mayhem nn ($4.50, 12/89)-Art Adams/Austin-c/a	.75	2.25	4.50

EXCITING COMICS
April, 1940 - No. 69, Sept, 1949
Nedor/Better Publications/Standard Comics

1-Origin The Mask, Jim Hatfield, Sgt. Bill King, Dan Williams begin	64.00	193.00	450.00
2-The Sphinx begins; The Masked Rider app.	28.50	85.00	200.00
3	24.00	73.00	170.00
4	19.00	57.00	135.00
5	15.00	45.00	105.00
6-8	12.00	36.00	84.00

EXCITING COMICS (continued)

	Good	Fine	N-Mint
9-Origin/1st app. of The Black Terror & sidekick Tim, begin series			
	64.00	193.00	450.00
10-13	27.00	81.00	190.00
14-Last Sphinx, Dan Williams	17.00	51.00	120.00
15-The Liberator begins (origin)	22.00	65.00	154.00
16-20: 20-The Mask ends	12.00	36.00	84.00
21,23-30: 28-Crime Crusader begins, ends #58			
	11.50	34.00	80.00
22-Origin The Eaglet; The American Eagle begins			
	12.00	36.00	84.00
31-38: 35-Liberator ends, not in 31-33	11.00	32.00	75.00
39-Origin Kara, Jungle Princess	16.00	48.00	110.00
40-50: 42-The Scarab begins. 49-Last Kara, Jungle Princess. 50-			
Last American Eagle	13.00	40.00	90.00
51-Miss Masque begins	17.00	51.00	120.00
52-54: Miss Masque ends	13.00	40.00	90.00
55-Judy of the Jungle begins(origin), ends #69; 1 pg. Ingels-a			
	17.00	51.00	120.00
56-58: All airbrush-c	16.00	48.00	110.00
59-Frazetta art in Caniff style; signed Frank Frazeta (one t), 9 pgs.			
	21.50	64.00	150.00
60-65: 60-Rick Howard, the Mystery Rider begins			
	12.00	36.00	84.00
66-Robinson/Meskin-a	12.00	36.00	84.00
67-69	8.00	24.00	56.00

NOTE: **Schomburg (Xela)** c-28-68; airbrush c-57-66. Black Terror by **R. Moreira**-#65.
Roussos a-62. Bondage-c 9, 12, 13, 20, 23, 25, 30, 59.

EXCITING ROMANCES
1949 (nd); No. 2, Spring, 1950 - No. 5, 10/50; No. 6 (1951, nd), No. 7,
9/51 - No. 14, 1/53
Fawcett Publications

	Good	Fine	N-Mint
1(1949)-Photo-c	3.70	11.00	26.00
2-5-(1950): 4-Photo-c	2.85	8.50	20.00
6-14	1.60	4.70	11.00

NOTE: **Powell** a-8-10. Photo c-1, 4-7, 11, 12.

EXCITING ROMANCE STORIES (See Fox Giants)

EXCITING WAR (Korean war)
No. 5, Sept, 1952 - No. 8, May, 1953; No. 9, Nov, 1953
Standard Comics (Better Publ.)

	Good	Fine	N-Mint
5	2.65	8.00	18.00
6,7,9	1.50	4.50	10.00
8-Toth-a	3.50	10.50	24.00

EX-MUTANTS
Aug, 1986 - Present ($1.80-1.95, B&W)
Eternity Comics/Amazing Comics/Eternity Comics

	Good	Fine	N-Mint
1	.45	1.35	2.70
2	.40	1.15	2.25
3-15	.35	1.00	1.95
Special 1	.30	.90	1.80
Graphic Novel 1	1.00	3.00	5.95
Graphic Novel 1-2nd & 3rd print w/new text	1.15	3.50	6.95
Graphic Novel 2 ('88, $7.95)	1.35	4.00	7.95
Pin-Up Book ($1.95, color)	.35	1.00	1.95
Winter Special 1 (2/89, $1.95)	.35	1.00	1.95

EX-MUTANTS: THE SHATTERED EARTH CHRONICLES
Apr, 1988 - No. 7?, ($1.95, B&W)
Eternity Comics

	Good	Fine	N-Mint
1-7	.35	1.00	1.95

EXORCISTS (See The Crusaders)

EXOTIC ROMANCES (Formerly True War Romances)
No. 22, Oct, 1955 - No. 31, Nov, 1956
Quality Comics Group (Comic Magazines)

	Good	Fine	N-Mint
22	3.70	11.00	26.00
23-26,29	2.00	6.00	14.00
27,31-Baker c/a	3.85	11.50	27.00
28,30-Baker-a	3.50	10.50	24.00

EXPLOITS OF DANIEL BOONE
Nov, 1955 - No. 6, Sept, 1956
Quality Comics Group

	Good	Fine	N-Mint
1	7.00	21.00	50.00
2	3.50	10.50	24.00
3-6	2.85	8.50	20.00

EXPLOITS OF DICK TRACY (See Dick Tracy)

EXPLORER JOE
Winter, 1951 - No. 2, Oct-Nov, 1952
Ziff-Davis Comic Group (Approved Comics)

	Good	Fine	N-Mint
1-Saunders painted-c	5.50	16.50	38.00
2-Krigstein-a	6.50	19.50	45.00

EXPOSED (...True Crime Cases)
Mar-Apr, 1948 - No. 9, July-Aug, 1949
D. S. Publishing Co.

	Good	Fine	N-Mint
1	7.00	21.00	50.00
2-Giggling killer story with excessive blood; two eye injury panels			
	8.00	24.00	56.00
3,8,9	3.70	11.00	26.00
4-Orlando-a	4.00	12.00	28.00
5-Breeze Lawson, Sky Sheriff by E. Good	4.00	12.00	28.00
6-Ingels-a; used in **SOTI**, illo.-"How to prepare an alibi"			
	16.00	48.00	110.00
7-Illo. in **SOTI**, "Diagram for housebreakers"; used by N.Y. Legis.			
Comm.	15.00	45.00	105.00

EXTRA
1948
Magazine Enterprises

	Good	Fine	N-Mint
1-Giant; consisting of rebound ME comics. Two versions known:			
(1)-Funny Man by Siegel & Shuster, Space Ace, Undercover Girl,			
& (2)-All Funnyman	22.00	65.00	154.00

EXTRA!
Mar-Apr, 1955 - No. 5, Nov-Dec, 1955
E. C. Comics

	Good	Fine	N-Mint
1	7.00	21.00	50.00
2-5	5.00	15.00	35.00

NOTE: **Craig, Crandall, Severin** art in all.

FACE, THE (Tony Trent, the Face No. 3 on)
1941 - No. 2, 1941? (See Big Shot Comics)
Columbia Comics Group

	Good	Fine	N-Mint
1-The Face; Mart Bailey-c	30.00	90.00	210.00
2-Bailey-c	20.00	60.00	140.00

FACULTY FUNNIES
June, 1989 - Present (75 & 95 cents, color)
Archie Comics

	Good	Fine	N-Mint
1-(75 cents)-The Awesome Four app.		.40	.80
2-6 (95 cents): 2-The Awesome Four app.		.50	1.00

FAIRY TALE PARADE (See Famous Fairy Tales)
June-July, 1942 - No. 121, Oct, 1946 (Most all by Walt Kelly)
Dell Publishing Co.

	Good	Fine	N-Mint
1-Kelly-a begins	81.00	245.00	570.00
2(8-9/42)	46.00	137.00	320.00
3-5 (10-11/42 - 2-4/43)	29.00	88.00	205.00
6-9 (5-7/43 - 11-1/43-44)	22.00	70.00	160.00
4-Color 50('44)	21.50	64.00	150.00
4-Color 69('45)	18.50	56.00	130.00

Exploits Of Daniel Boone #5, © QUA

Extra! #3, © WMG

The Face #2, © CCG

Fairy Tales #11, © Z-D

Falling In Love #1, © DC

Famous Crimes #5, © FOX

	Good	Fine	N-Mint
FAIRY TALE PARADE (continued)			
4-Color 87('45)	16.50	50.00	115.00
4-Color 104,114('46)-Last Kelly issue	14.00	42.00	100.00
4-Color 121('46)-Not Kelly	8.50	25.50	60.00

NOTE: #1-9, 4-Color #50,69 have Kelly c/a; 4-Color #87, 104, 114-Kelly art only. #9 has a redrawn version of The Reluctant Dragon. This series contains all the classic fairy tales from Jack In The Beanstalk to Cinderella.

	Good	Fine	N-Mint
FAIRY TALES			
No. 10, 1951 - No. 11, June-July, 1951			
Ziff-Davis Publ. Co. (Approved Comics)			
10,11-Painted-c	7.00	21.00	50.00
FAITHFUL			
November, 1949 - No. 2, Feb, 1950 (52 pgs.)			
Marvel Comics/Lovers' Magazine			
1,2-Photo-c	2.85	8.50	20.00
FALCON (Also see Avengers #181 & Captain America #117 & 133)			
Nov, 1983 - No. 4, Feb, 1984 (mini-series)			
Marvel Comics Group			
1-4: 1-Paul Smith c/a(p). 2-P. Smith-c	.50	1.00	
FALLEN ANGELS			
April, 1987 - No. 8, Nov, 1987 (mini-series)			
Marvel Comics Group			
1	.50	1.50	3.00
2-8	.25	.80	1.60
FALLING IN LOVE			
Sept-Oct, 1955 - No. 143, Oct-Nov, 1973			
Arleigh Publ. Co./National Periodical Publications			
1	12.00	36.00	84.00
2	5.70	17.00	40.00
3-10	3.50	10.50	24.00
11-20	2.00	6.00	14.00
21-40	1.50	4.50	10.00
41-46: 46-Last 10 cent issue	1.00	3.00	7.00
47-100	.70	2.00	4.00
101-107,109-143	.50	1.50	3.00
108-Wood-a, 4pgs. (7/69)	.70	2.00	4.00

NOTE: Colan c/a-75, 81. 52 pgs.-#125-133.

FALL OF THE HOUSE OF USHER, THE (See Corben Special, A)

FALL OF THE ROMAN EMPIRE (See Movie Comics)

	Good	Fine	N-Mint
FAMILY AFFAIR (TV)			
Feb, 1970 - No. 4, Oct, 1970 (25 cents)			
Gold Key			
1-Pull-out poster; photo-c	2.30	7.00	16.00
2-4: 3,4-Photo-c	1.50	4.50	10.00
FAMILY FUNNIES			
No. 9, Aug-Sept, 1946			
Parents' Magazine Institute			
9	2.30	7.00	16.00
FAMILY FUNNIES (Tiny Tot Funnies No. 9 on)			
Sept, 1950 - No. 8, April?, 1951			
Harvey Publications			
1-Mandrake	3.50	10.50	24.00
2-Flash Gordon, 1 pg.	2.35	7.00	16.00
3-8: 4,5,7-Flash Gordon, 1 pg.	2.00	6.00	14.00
1(black & white)	1.20	3.50	8.00

FAMOUS AUTHORS ILLUSTRATED (See Stories by. . .)

FAMOUS COMICS (Also see Favorite Comics)
No date; Mid 1930's (24 pages) (paper cover)
Zain-Eppy/United Features Syndicate

Reprinted from 1934 newspaper strips in color; Joe Palooka, Hair-

	Good	Fine	N-Mint
breadth Harry, Napoleon, The Nebbs, etc.	19.00	57.00	132.00
FAMOUS COMICS			
1934 (100 pgs., daily newspaper reprints)			
(3½x8½''; paper cover) (came in a box)			
King Features Syndicate (Whitman Publ. Co.)			
684(#1)-Little Jimmy, Katzenjammer Kids, & Barney Google	16.00	48.00	110.00
684(#2)-Polly, Little Jimmy, Katzenjammer Kids	16.00	48.00	110.00
684(#3)-Little Annie Rooney, Polly, Katzenjammer Kids	16.00	48.00	110.00
. . . .Box price. . . .	6.00	24.00	60.00
FAMOUS COMICS CARTOON BOOKS			
1934 (72 pgs.; 8x7¼''; daily strip reprints)			
Whitman Publishing Co. (B&W; hardbacks)			
1200-The Captain & the Kids (1st app?); Dirks reprints credited to Bernard Dibble	11.00	32.00	75.00
1202-Captain Easy (1st app?) & Wash Tubbs by Roy Crane	16.00	48.00	110.00
1203-Ella Cinders (1st app?)	11.00	32.00	75.00
1204-Freckles & His Friends (1st app?)	8.50	25.50	60.00

NOTE: Called Famous Funnies Cartoon Books inside.

FAMOUS CRIMES
June, 1948 - No. 19, Sept, 1950; No. 20, Aug, 1951
Fox Features Syndicate/M.S. Dist. No. 51,52

	Good	Fine	N-Mint
1-Blue Beetle app. & crime story r-/Phantom Lady #16; Hollingsworth-a	14.00	42.00	100.00
2-Shows woman dissolved in acid; lingerie-c/panels	11.50	34.00	80.00
3-Injury-to-eye story used in SOTI, pg. 112; has two electrocution stories	14.00	42.00	100.00
4-6	5.70	17.00	40.00
7-''Tarzan, the Wyoming Killer'' used in SOTI, pg. 44; drug trial/possession story	12.00	36.00	84.00
8-20: 17-Morisi-a	4.00	12.00	28.00
51(nd, 1953)	4.35	13.00	30.00
52	2.65	8.00	18.00

FAMOUS FAIRY TALES
1943 (32 pgs.); 1944 (16 pgs.) (Soft covers)
K. K. Publ. Co. (Giveaway)

	Good	Fine	N-Mint
1943-Reprints from Fairy Tale Parade No. 2,3; Kelly inside art	40.00	120.00	260.00
1944-Kelly inside art	28.00	85.00	180.00

FAMOUS FEATURE STORIES
1938 (68 pgs., 7½x11'')
Dell Publishing Co.

	Good	Fine	N-Mint
1-Tarzan, Terry & the Pirates, King of the Royal Mtd., Buck Jones, Dick Tracy, Smilin' Jack, Dan Dunn, Don Winslow, G-Man, Tailspin Tommy, Mutt & Jeff, & Little Orphan Annie reprints - all illustrated text	43.00	130.00	300.00

FAMOUS FIRST EDITION (See Limited Collectors' Edition)
($1.00; 10x13½''-Giant Size)(72pgs.; No.6-8, 68 pgs.)
1974 - No. 8, Aug-Sept, 1975; C-61, Sept, 1978
National Periodical Publications/DC Comics

	Good	Fine	N-Mint
C-26-Action No. 1	1.00	3.00	7.00
C-28-Detective No. 27	5.00	15.00	30.00
C-30-Sensation No. 1(1974)	1.00	3.00	7.00
F-4-Whiz No. 2(No.1)(10-11/74)-Cover not identical to original	1.00	3.00	7.00
F-5-Batman No. 1(F-6 on inside)	5.00	15.00	30.00
F-6-Wonder Woman No. 1	.85	2.50	6.00
F-7-All-Star Comics No. 3	1.00	3.00	7.00

FAMOUS FIRST EDITION (continued)

	Good	Fine	N-Mint
F-8-Flash No. 1(8-9/75)	.85	2.50	6.00
C-61-Superman No. 1(9/78)	1.35	4.00	8.00
Hardbound editions w/dust jackets ($5.00) (Lyle Stuart, Inc.)			
C-26,C-28,C-30,F-4,F-6 known	1.75	5.25	12.00

Warning: The above books are almost **exact** reprints of the originals that they represent except for the Giant-Size format. None of the originals are Giant-Size. The first five issues and C-61 were printed with two covers. Reprint information can be found on the outside cover, but not on the inside cover which was reprinted exactly like the original (inside and out).

FAMOUS FUNNIES
1933 - No. 218, July, 1955
Eastern Color

	Good	Fine	Vf-NM
A Carnival of Comics (probably the second comic book), 36 pgs., no date given, no publisher, no number; contains strip reprints of The Bungle Family, Dixie Dugan, Hairbreadth Harry, Joe Palooka, Keeping Up With the Jones, Mutt & Jeff, Reg'lar Fellers, S'Matter Pop, Strange As It Seems, and others. This book was sold by M. C. Gaines to Wheatena, Milk-O-Malt, John Wanamaker, Kinney Shoe Stores, & others to be given away as premiums and radio giveaways (1933).	300.00	900.00	2100.00

Series 1-(Very rare)(nd-early 1934)(68 pgs.) No publisher given (Eastern Color Printing Co.); sold in chain stores for 10 cents. 35,000 print run. Contains Sunday strip reprints of Mutt & Jeff, Reg'lar Fellers, Nipper, Hairbreadth Harry, Strange As It Seems, Joe Palooka, Dixie Dugan, The Nebbs, Keeping Up With the Jones, and others. Inside front and back covers and pages 1-16 of Famous Funnies Series 1, #s 49-64 reprinted from **Famous Funnies, A Carnival of Comics**, and most of pages 17-48 reprinted from **Funnies on Parade**. This was the first comic book sold.

	600.00	1800.00	4200.00

No. 1 (Rare)(7/34-on stands 5/34) - Eastern Color Printing Co. First monthly newsstand comic book. Contains Sunday strip reprints of Toonerville Folks, Mutt & Jeff, Hairbreadth Harry, S'Matter Pop, Nipper, Dixie Dugan, The Bungle Family, Connie, Ben Webster, Tailspin Tommy, The Nebbs, Joe Palooka, & others.

	450.00	1350.00	3150.00
2 (Rare)	150.00	375.00	900.00
3-Buck Rogers Sunday strip reprints by Rick Yager begins, ends # 218; not in No. 191-208; the number of the 1st strip reprinted is pg. 190, Series No. 1	200.00	500.00	1200.00

	Good	Fine	N-Mint
4	71.00	215.00	500.00
5	57.00	170.00	400.00
6-10	46.00	140.00	325.00
11,12,18-Four pgs. of Buck Rogers in each issue, completes stories in Buck Rogers #1 which lacks these pages; #18-Two pgs. of Buck Rogers reprinted in Daisy Comics #1	40.00	120.00	280.00
13-17,19,20: 14-Has two Buck Rogers panels missing. 17-1st Christmas-c on a newsstand comic	29.00	90.00	205.00
21,23-30: 27-War on Crime begins	21.00	62.00	145.00
22-Four pgs. of Buck Rogers needed to complete stories in Buck Rogers #1	23.00	70.00	160.00
31,32,34,36,37,39,40	16.00	48.00	110.00
33-Careers of Baby Face Nelson & John Dillinger traced	16.00	48.00	110.00
35-Two pgs. Buck Rogers omitted in Buck Rogers #2	17.00	51.00	120.00
38-Full color portrait of Buck Rogers	16.00	48.00	110.00
41-60: 55-Last bottom panel, pg. 4 in Buck Rogers redrawn in Buck Rogers #3	11.00	32.00	75.00
61-64,66,67,69,70	9.30	28.00	65.00
65,68-Two pgs. Kirby-a-"Lightnin & the Lone Rider"	10.00	30.00	70.00
71,73,77-80: 80-Buck Rogers story continues from B. R. #5	8.00	24.00	56.00
72-Speed Spaulding begins by Marvin Bradley (artist), ends #88. This series was written by Edwin Balmer & Philip Wylie and later appeared as film & book "When Worlds Collide"	8.50	25.50	60.00
74-76-Two pgs. Kirby-a in all	7.00	21.00	50.00
81-Origin Invisible Scarlet O'Neil; strip begins #82, ends #167	6.00	18.00	42.00
82-Buck Rogers-c	7.00	21.00	50.00

	Good	Fine	N-Mint
83-87,90: 87 has last Buck Rogers full page-r. 90-Bondage-c	6.00	18.00	42.00
88-Buck Rogers in "Moon's End" by Calkins, 2 pgs.(not reprints). Beginning with #88, all Buck Rogers pages have rearranged panels	6.50	19.50	45.00
89-Origin Fearless Flint, the Flint Man	6.50	19.50	45.00
91-93,95,96,98-99,101-110: 105-Series 2 begins (Strip Page #1)	4.50	14.00	32.00
94-Buck Rogers in "Solar Holocaust" by Calkins, 3 pgs.(not reprints)	5.50	16.50	38.00
97-War Bond promotion, Buck Rogers by Calkins, 2 pgs.(not reprints)	5.50	16.50	38.00
100	5.50	16.50	38.00
111-130	3.70	11.00	26.00
131-150: 137-Strip page No. 110½ omitted	2.65	8.00	18.00
151-162,164-168	2.30	7.00	16.00
163-St. Valentine's Day-c	2.85	8.50	20.00
169,170-Two text illos. by Williamson, his 1st comic book work	5.50	16.50	38.00
171-180: 171-Strip pgs. 227,229,230, Series 2 omitted. 172-Strip Pg. 232 omitted	2.30	7.00	16.00
181-190: Buck Rogers ends with start of strip pg. 302, Series 2	1.85	5.50	13.00
191-197,199,201,203,206-208: No Buck Rogers	1.60	4.70	11.00
198,202,205-One pg. Frazetta ads; no Buck Rogers	2.00	6.00	14.00
200-Frazetta 1 pg. ad	2.15	6.50	15.00
204-Used in POP, pgs. 79,99	2.15	6.50	15.00
209-Buck Rogers begins with strip pg. 480, Series 2; Frazetta-c	24.00	73.00	170.00
210-216: Frazetta-c. 211-Buck Rogers ads by Anderson begins, ends #217. #215-Contains B. Rogers strip pg. 515-518, series 2 followed by pgs. 179-181, Series 3	24.00	73.00	170.00
217,218-Buck Rogers ends with pg. 199, Series 3	2.15	6.50	15.00

NOTE: **Rick Yager** did the Buck Rogers Sunday strips reprinted in Famous Funnies. The Sundays were formerly done by Russ Keaton and Lt. Dick Calkins did the dailies, but would sometimes assist Yager on a panel or two from time to time. Strip No. 169 is Yager's first full Buck Rogers page. Yager did the strip until 1958 when **Murphy Anderson** took over. **Tuska** art from 4/26/59 - 1965. Virtually every panel was rewritten for Famous Funnies. Not identical to the original Sunday page. The Buck Rogers reprints run continuously through Famous Funnies issue No. 190 (Strip No. 302) with no break in story line. The story line has no continuity after No. 190. The Buck Rogers newspaper strips came out in four series: Series 1, 3/30/30 - 9/21/41 (No. 1 - 600); Series 2, 9/28/41 -10/21/51 (No. 1 -525)(Strip No. 110½ (½ pg.) published in only a few newspapers); Series 3, 10/28/51 -2/9/58 (No. 100-428)(No No. 1-99); Series 4, 2/16/58 - 6/13/65 (No numbers, dates only). **Everett** c-86. **Moulton** a-100.

FAMOUS FUNNIES
1964
Super Comics

Reprint No. 15-18	.50	1.50	3.00

FAMOUS GANG BOOK OF COMICS (Becomes Donald & Mickey Merry Christmas 1943 on)
Dec, 1942 (32 pgs.; paper cover) (Christmas giveaway)
Firestone Tire & Rubber Co.

(Rare)-Porky Pig, Bugs Bunny, Sniffles; r-/Looney Tunes	67.00	200.00	500.00

FAMOUS GANGSTERS (Crime on the Waterfront No. 4)
April, 1951 - No. 3, Feb, 1952
Avon Periodicals/Realistic

1-Capone, Dillinger; c-/Avon paperback 329	14.00	42.00	100.00
2-Wood-c/a (1 pg.); r-/Saint #7 and retitled "Mike Strong"	15.00	45.00	105.00
3-Lucky Luciano & Murder, Inc; c-/Avon paperback #66	15.00	45.00	105.00

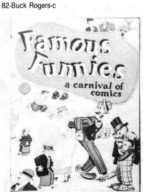

Famous Funnies (A Carnival Of Comics), © EAS

Famous Funnies #27, © EAS

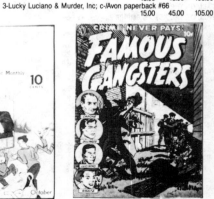

Famous Gangsters #1, © AVON

Famous Stars #1, © Z-D

Fantastic Comics #4, © FOX

Fantastic Four #1, © MEG

FAMOUS INDIAN TRIBES
July-Sept, 1962; No. 2, July, 1972
Dell Publishing Co.

	Good	Fine	N-Mint
12-264-209 (The Sioux)	1.00	3.00	7.00
2(7/72)-Reprints above	.25	.75	1.50

FAMOUS STARS
Nov-Dec, 1950 - No. 6, Spring, 1952 (All photo covers)
Ziff-Davis Publ. Co.

	Good	Fine	N-Mint
1-Shelley Winters, Susan Peters, Ava Gardner, Shirley Temple	13.00	40.00	90.00
2-Betty Hutton, Bing Crosby, Colleen Townsend, Gloria Swanson; Everett-a(2)	9.30	28.00	65.00
3-Farley Granger, Judy Garland's ordeal, Alan Ladd	8.50	25.50	60.00
4-Al Jolson, Bob Mitchum, Ella Raines, Richard Conte, Vic Damone; Crandall-a, 6pgs.	8.00	24.00	56.00
5-Liz Taylor, Betty Grable, Esther Williams, George Brent; Krigstein-a	11.00	32.00	75.00
6-Gene Kelly, Hedy Lamarr, June Allyson, William Boyd, Janet Leigh, Gary Cooper	8.00	24.00	56.00

NOTE: *Whitney* a-1, 3.

FAMOUS STORIES (. . . Book No. 2)
1942 - No. 2, 1942
Dell Publishing Co.

	Good	Fine	N-Mint
1-Treasure Island	14.00	42.00	100.00
2-Tom Sawyer	14.00	42.00	100.00

FAMOUS TV FUNDAY FUNNIES
Sept, 1961
Harvey Publications

1-Casper the Ghost	3.00	9.00	21.00

FAMOUS WESTERN BADMEN (Formerly Redskin)
No. 13, Dec, 1954 - No. 15, 1953
Youthful Magazines

13	4.30	13.00	30.00
14,15	2.65	8.00	18.00

FANTASTIC (Formerly Captain Science; Beware No. 10 on)
No. 8, Feb, 1952 - No. 9, April, 1952
Youthful Magazines

8-Capt. Science by Harrison; decapitation, shrunken head panels	12.00	36.00	84.00
9-Harrison-a	7.00	21.00	50.00

FANTASTIC ADVENTURES
1963 - 1964 (Reprints)
Super Comics

9,10,12,15,16,18: 16-Briefer-a. 18-r/Superior Stories #1	1.15	3.50	8.00
11-Wood-a; r/Blue Bolt #118	1.70	5.00	12.00
17-Baker-a(2) r-/Seven Seas #6	1.50	4.50	10.00

FANTASTIC COMICS
Dec, 1939 - No. 23, Nov, 1941
Fox Features Syndicate

1-Intro/origin Samson; Stardust, The Super Wizard, Space Smith, Sub Saunders (by Kiefer), Capt. Kidd begin	120.00	360.00	835.00
2-Powell text illos	59.00	178.00	415.00
3-5: 3-Powell text illos	48.00	145.00	340.00
6-9: 6,7-Simon-c	38.00	115.00	270.00
10-Intro/origin David, Samson's aide	29.00	88.00	205.00
11-17: 16-Stardust ends	23.00	70.00	160.00
18-Intro. Black Fury & sidekick Chuck; ends #23	26.00	77.00	180.00
19,20	23.00	70.00	160.00

	Good	Fine	N-Mint
21-The Banshee begins(origin); ends #23. Hitler-c	26.00	77.00	180.00
22	23.00	70.00	160.00
23-Origin The Gladiator	26.00	77.00	180.00

NOTE: *Lou Fine* a-3-5, 8. Bondage c-6, 8, 9.

FANTASTIC COMICS (Fantastic Fears #1-9; Becomes Samson #12)
No. 10, Nov-Dec, 1954 - No. 11, Jan-Feb, 1955
Ajax/Farrell Publ.

10,11	4.00	12.00	28.00

FANTASTIC FEARS (Formerly Captain Jet) (Fantastic Comics #10 on)
No. 7, May, 1953 - No. 9, Sept-Oct, 1954
Ajax/Farrell Publ.

7(5/53)	10.00	30.00	70.00
8(7/53)	6.50	19.50	45.00
3,4	5.00	15.00	35.00
5-1st Ditko story is written by Bruce Hamilton reprinted in Weird V2#8	23.00	70.00	160.00
6-Decapitation of girl's head with paper cutter (classic)	13.00	40.00	90.00
7(5-6/54), 9(9-10/54)	4.50	14.00	32.00
8(7-8/54)-Contains story intended for Jo-Jo; name changed to Kaza; decapitation story	6.50	19.50	45.00

FANTASTIC FOUR (See America's Best TV. . ., Giant Size Super-Stars, Marvel Collectors Item Classics, Marvel Masterworks, Marvel's Greatest, Marvel Treasury Ed., Marvel Triple Action & Official Marvel Index to. . .)

FANTASTIC FOUR
Nov, 1961 - Present
Marvel Comics Group

1-Origin & 1st app. The Fantastic Four (Reed Richards: Mr. Fantastic, Johnny Storm: The Human Torch, Sue Storm: The Invisible Girl, & Ben Grimm: The Thing); origin The Mole Man	265.00	1060.00	2650.00
1-Golden Record Comic Set-r	3.60	11.00	25.00
with record	8.00	24.00	55.00
2-Vs. The Skrulls (last 10 cent issue)	100.00	300.00	700.00
3-Fantastic Four don costumes & establish Headquarters; brief 1pg. origin. intro The Fantasticar. H. Torch drawn w/two left hands on-c	85.00	255.00	600.00
4-1st Silver Age Sub-Mariner app.	75.00	225.00	525.00
5-Origin & 1st app. Doctor Doom	68.00	205.00	475.00
6-Sub-Mariner, Dr. Doom team up; 1st Marvel villain team-up	47.00	140.00	325.00
7-10: 7-1st app. Kurrgo. 8-1st app. Puppet-Master & Alicia Masters	35.00	105.00	250.00
11-Origin The Impossible Man	27.00	81.00	190.00
12-Fantastic Four Vs. The Hulk	27.00	81.00	190.00
13-Intro. The Watcher; 1st app. The Red Ghost	23.00	70.00	160.00
14-19: 17-Early Ant-Man app. (7/63. 18-Origin The Super Skrull. 19-Intro. Rama-Tut	16.00	48.00	110.00
20-Origin The Molecule Man	17.00	51.00	120.00
21-24,27: 21-Intro. The Hate Monger	8.50	25.50	60.00
25,26-The Thing vs. The Hulk	16.00	48.00	110.00
28-X-Men app.	11.00	32.00	75.00
29,30: 30-Intro. Diablo	5.70	17.00	40.00
31-40: 31-Avengers x-over. 33-1st app. Attuma. 35-Intro/1st app. Dragon Man. 36-Intro/1st app. Madam Medusa & the Frightful Four (Sandman, Wizard, Paste Pot Pete). 39-Wood inks on Daredevil	4.50	14.00	32.00
41-47: 41-43-Frightful Four app. 44-Intro. Gorgan. 45-Intro. The Inhumans	3.15	9.50	22.00
48-Intro/1st app. The Silver Surfer, & Galactus (3/66)	16.00	48.00	110.00
49,50-Silver Surfer x-over	6.50	19.50	45.00

143

FANTASTIC FOUR (continued)	Good	Fine	N-Mint
51-54: 52-Intro. The Black Panther; origin-#53. 54-Inhumans cameo			
	2.15	6.50	15.00
55-60: Silver Surfer x-over. 59,60-Inhumans cameo			
	2.85	8.50	20.00
61-65,68-70: 61-Silver Surfer cameo	1.70	5.50	12.00
66,67-1st app. & origin Him (Warlock)	1.85	5.50	13.00
71,73,78-80	1.15	3.50	7.00
72,74-77: Silver Surfer app.	1.85	5.50	13.00
81-88: 81-Crystal joins & dons costume. 82,83-Inhumans app. 84-87-Dr. Doom app. 88-Last 12 cent ish.	1.15	3.50	7.00
89-99,101,102: 94-Intro. Agatha Harkness. 102,108-Last Kirby issues			
	.85	2.50	5.00
100	3.15	9.50	22.00
103-111	.85	2.50	5.00
112-Hulk Vs. Thing	2.00	6.00	12.00
113-120: 116-(52 pgs.)	.85	2.50	5.00
121-123-Silver Surfer x-over	1.00	3.00	6.00
124-127,129-140: 126-Origin F.F. retold. 129-Intro. Thundra. 130-Sue leaves F.F. 132-Thundra Vs. Thing			
	.50	1.55	3.10
128-Four pg. insert of F.F. Friends & Fiends	.70	2.00	4.00
141-149,151-154,158-160: 142-Kirbyish-a by Buckler begins. 151-Origin Thundra. 159-Medusa leaves, Sue rejoins	.50	1.55	4.00
150-Crystal & Quicksilver's wedding	.70	2.00	4.00
155-157: Silver Surfer in all	.70	2.00	4.00
161-180: 164-The Crusader (old Marvel Boy) revived; origin #165. 176-Re-intro Impossible Man; Marvel artists app.	.35	1.05	2.10
181-199: 190-191-F.F. breaks up	.25	.80	1.60
200-Giant size-FF re-united	.70	2.00	4.00
201-208,219		.65	1.30
209-216,218,220,221-Byrne-a. 209-1st Herbie the Robot. 220-Brief origin	.25	.80	1.60
217-Dazzler app. by Byrne	.45	1.35	2.70
222-231		.65	1.30
232-Byrne-a begins	.50	1.55	3.10
233-235,237-249: Byrne-a. 238-Origin Frankie Ray	.40	1.25	2.50
236-20th Anniversary issue(11/81, 64pgs., $1.00)-Brief origin F.F.	.50	1.55	3.10
250-Double size; Byrne-a; Skrulls impersonate New X-Men	.50	1.55	3.10
251-259: Byrne c/a. 252-Reads sideways; Annihilus app.	.40	1.15	2.30
260-Alpha Flight app.	.50	1.55	3.10
261-285: 261-Silver Surfer. 262-Origin Galactus	.35	1.05	2.10
286-2nd app. X-Factor cont./Avengers #263	.60	1.80	3.60
287-295		.50	1.00
296-Barry Smith c/a; Thing rejoins	.35	1.05	2.10
297-305,307-318, 320-330: 312-X-Factor x-over. 327-Mr. Fantastic & Invisible Girl return. 337-Simonson-a begins		.50	1.00
306-New team begins	.25	.75	1.50
319-Double size	.35	1.00	2.00
331-338: 334-Simonson-c/scripts begin. 337-Simonson-c/a/scripts begin		.50	1.00
Giant-Size 2(8/74) - 4: Formerly Giant-Size Super-Stars			
	.85	2.50	5.00
Giant-Size 5(5/75), 6(8/75)	.50	1.50	3.00
Annual 1('63)-Origin F.F.; Ditko-i	20.00	60.00	140.00
Annual 2('64)-Dr. Doom origin & x-over	13.00	40.00	90.00
Annual 3('65)-Reed & Sue wed	6.50	19.50	45.00
Special 4(11/66)-G.A. Torch x-over & origin retold			
	2.15	6.50	15.00
Special 5(11/67)-New art; Intro. Psycho-Man; Silver Surfer, Black Panther, Inhumans app.	1.70	5.00	10.00
Special 6(11/68)-Intro. Annihilus; no reprints; birth of Franklin Richards	1.70	5.00	10.00

	Good	Fine	N-Mint
Special 7(11/69)	1.70	5.00	10.00
Special 8(12/70), 9(12/71), 10('73)	.55	1.70	3.40
Annual 11(6/76), 12(2/78), 13(10/78), 14(1/80)	.40	1.15	2.30
Annual 15(10/80), 16(10/81), 17(9/83)	.40	1.15	2.30
Annual 18(11/84), 19(11/85), 20(9/87)	.40	1.15	2.30
Annual 21(9/88)-Evolutionary War x-over	.55	1.70	3.40
Annual 22(1989, $2.00, 64pg.)-Atlantis Attacks x-over; Sub-Mariner & The Avengers app. Buckler-a	.35	1.00	2.00
Special Edition 1 (5/84)-r/Annual #1; Byrne c/a	.35	1.05	2.10
Giveaway (nn, 1981, 32pgs., Young Model Builders Club)			
	.25	.80	1.60

NOTE: *Austin* c(i)-232-236, 238, 240-42, 250i, 286i. *John Buscema* a(p)-107,108 (w/Kirby & Romita),109-130, 132, 134-141, 160, 173-175, 202, 296p-309p, Annual 11, 13, Gnt-Size 1-4; c(p)-107-122, 124-129, 133-139, 202, Annual 12p, Special 10. *Byrne* a-209-218p, 220p, 221p, 232-65, 266i, 267-73, 274-93p, Annual 17; c-211-14p, 220p, 232-236p, 237, 238p, 239, 240-42p, 243-49, 250p, 251-67, 269-77, 275p-81p, 283p, 284, 285, 286p, 288-293, Annual 17. *Ditko* a-13i, Gnt Size 2r, Annual 16. *G. Kane* c-150p, 160p. *Kirby* a-1-102p, 108, 180i, 189r, 236p(r), Special 1-10, Giant-Size 5, 6r; c-1-101, 164, 167, 171-177, 180, 181, 190, 200, Annual 11, Giant-Size 5, Special 1-7, 9. *Marcos* a-Annual 14i. *Mooney* a-118i, 152i. *Perez* a-164-167, 170-172, 176-178, 184-188, 191p, 192p, Annual 14p, 15p; c(p)-183-88, 191, 192, 194-197. *Simonson* c-212, 334-337. *Steranko* c-130-132p.

FANTASTIC FOUR INDEX (See Official...)

FANTASTIC FOUR ROAST
May, 1982 (One Shot, Direct Sale)
Marvel Comics Group

1-Celebrates 20th anniversary of Fantastic Four No. 1; Golden, Miller, Buscema, Rogers, Byrne, Anderson, Austin-c(i)			
	.60	1.80	3.60

FANTASTIC FOUR VS. X-MEN
Feb, 1987 - No. 4, Jun, 1987 (mini-series)
Marvel Comics

	Good	Fine	N-Mint
1	.60	1.75	3.50
2-4: 4-Austin-a(i)	.40	1.25	2.50

FANTASTIC GIANTS (Konga No. 1-23)
V2#24, September, 1966 (25 cents, 68 pgs.)
Charlton Comics

V2#24-Origin Konga & Gorgo reprinted; two new Ditko stories			
	2.65	8.00	18.00

FANTASTIC TALES
1958 (no date) (Reprint)
I. W. Enterprises

1-Reprints Avon's ''City of the Living Dead''	1.35	4.00	8.00

FANTASTIC VOYAGE (See Movie Comics)
Aug, 1969 - No. 2, Dec, 1969
Gold Key

1,2 (TV)	1.70	5.00	12.00

FANTASTIC VOYAGES OF SINDBAD, THE
Oct, 1965 - No. 2, June, 1967
Gold Key

1,2-Painted-c	2.30	7.00	16.00

FANTASTIC WORLDS
No. 5, Sept, 1952 - No. 7, Jan, 1953
Standard Comics

5-Toth, Anderson-a	12.00	36.00	84.00
6-Toth story	11.00	32.00	75.00
7	6.50	19.50	45.00

FANTASY FEATURES
1987 - No. 2, 1987 ($1.75, color)
Americomics

1,2	.30	.90	1.80

Fantasy Masterpieces #9, © MEG

Fargo Kid V11#3, © PRIZE

Fatman, The Human Flying Saucer #3, © Lightning

FANTASY MASTERPIECES (Marvel Super Heroes No. 12 on)
Feb, 1966 - No. 11, Oct, 1967; Dec, 1979 - No. 14, Jan, 1981
Marvel Comics Group

	Good	Fine	N-Mint
1-Photo of Stan Lee	2.15	6.50	15.00
2	.70	2.00	4.00
3-G.A. Captain America-r begin; 1st Giant	.70	2.00	4.00
4-6-Capt. America-r	.70	2.00	4.00
7-Begin G.A. Sub-Mariner, Torch-r/M. Mystery	.70	2.00	4.00
8-Torch battles the Sub-Mariner r-/Marvel Mystery #9			
	.70	2.00	4.00
9-Torch Human Torch r-/Marvel Comics #1	.85	2.50	5.00
10-Reprints origin/1st app. All Winners Squad from All Winners #19			
	.70	2.00	4.00
11-Reprints origin of Toro & Black Knight	.70	2.00	4.00
V2#1(12/79)-52 pgs.; 75 cents; r-/origin Silver Surfer from S. Surfer #1 with editing; J. Buscema-a	.30	.90	1.80
2-14-Silver Surfer-r	.60	1.20	

NOTE: *Buscema* c-V2No.7-9(in part). *Ditko* a-1-3r, 7r, 9r. *Everett* a-9r. *Matt Fox* a-9(r). *Kirby* a-2-4r, 8r, 11r. *Starlin* a-8-13r. Some direct sale V2No14's had a 50 cent cover price.

FANTASY QUARTERLY (Also see Elfquest)
Spring, 1978 (B&W)
Independent Publishers Syndicate

	Good	Fine	N-Mint
1-1st app. Elfquest (2nd printing exist?)	10.00	30.00	60.00

FANTOMAN (Formerly Amazing Adventure Funnies)
No. 2, Aug, 1940 - No. 4, Dec, 1940
Centaur Publications

	Good	Fine	N-Mint
2-The Fantom of the Fair, The Arrow, Little Dynamite-r begin; origin The Ermine by Filchock; Burgos, J. Cole, Ernst, Gustavson-a			
	70.00	210.00	495.00
3,4: Gustavson-a(r). 4-Bondage-c	50.00	150.00	350.00

FARGO KID (Formerly Justice Traps the Guilty)
V11No3(No.1), June-July, 1958 - V11No.5, Oct-Nov, 1958
Prize Publications

	Good	Fine	N-Mint
V11#3(#1)-Origin Fargo Kid, Severin-c/a; Williamson-a(2)			
	8.00	24.00	56.00
V11#4,5-Severin c/a	4.50	14.00	32.00

FARMER'S DAUGHTER, THE
2-3/54 - No. 3, 6-7/54; No. 4, 10/54
Stanhall Publ./Trojan Magazines

	Good	Fine	N-Mint
1-Lingerie, nudity panel	7.00	21.00	50.00
2-4(Stanhall)	3.70	11.00	26.00

FASHION IN ACTION
Aug, 1986 - Feb, 1987 (Color, Baxter paper)
Eclipse Comics

	Good	Fine	N-Mint
. . .Summer Special 1 ($1.75)	.30	.90	1.80
. . .Winter Special 1(2/87, $2.00)	.35	1.00	2.00

FASTEST GUN ALIVE, THE (See 4-Color No. 741)

FAST FICTION (. . .Action) (Stories by Famous Authors Ill. #6 on)
Oct, 1949 - No. 5, Mar, 1950 (All have Kiefer-c)(48 pgs.)
Seaboard Publ./Famous Authors Ill.

	Good	Fine	N-Mint
1-Scarlet Pimpernel; Jim Lavery-a	20.00	60.00	140.00
2-Captain Blood; H. C. Kiefer-a	18.00	54.00	125.00
3-She, by Rider Haggard; Vincent Napoli-a	23.00	70.00	160.00
4-(52pgs, 1/50)-The 39 Steps; Lavery-a	14.00	42.00	100.00
5-Beau Geste; Kiefer-a	14.00	42.00	100.00

NOTE: *Kiefer* a-2, 5; c-2, 3, 5. *Lavery* a-1, 4; c-1, 4. *Napoli* a-3.

FAST WILLIE JACKSON
October, 1976 - No. 7, 1977
Fitzgerald Periodicals, Inc.

		Fine	N-Mint
1		.50	1.00
2-7		.40	.80

FAT ALBERT (. . .& the Cosby Kids) (TV)
March, 1974 - No. 29, Feb, 1979
Gold Key

	Good	Fine	N-Mint
1	.35	1.00	2.00
2-29		.40	.80

FAT AND SLAT (Ed Wheelan) (Gunfighter No. 5 on)
Summer, 1947 - No. 4, Spring, 1948
E. C. Comics

	Good	Fine	N-Mint
1-Intro/origin Voltage, Man of Lightning	16.00	48.00	110.00
2,4	12.00	36.00	84.00
3	10.00	30.00	70.00

FAT AND SLAT JOKE BOOK
Summer, 1944 (One Shot, 52 pages)
All-American Comics (William H. Wise)

	Good	Fine	N-Mint
nn-by Ed Wheelan	12.00	36.00	84.00

FATE (See Hand of Fate, & Thrill-O-Rama)

FATHER OF CHARITY
No date (32 pgs.; paper cover)
Catechetical Guild Giveaway

	Good	Fine	N-Mint
nn	1.50	4.50	10.00

FATHOM
May, 1987 - No. 3, July, 1987 ($1.50, mini-series, color)
Comico

	Good	Fine	N-Mint
1-3	.25	.75	1.50

FATIMA...CHALLENGE TO THE WORLD
1951, 36 pgs. (15 cent cover)
Catechetical Guild

	Good	Fine	N-Mint
nn (not same as 'Challenge to the World')	1.70	5.00	12.00

FATMAN, THE HUMAN FLYING SAUCER
April, 1967 - No. 3, Aug-Sept, 1967 (68 pgs.)
Lightning Comics(Milson Publ. Co.) (Written by Otto Binder)

	Good	Fine	N-Mint
1-Origin Fatman & Tinman by C. C. Beck	3.00	9.00	21.00
2-Beck-a	2.30	7.00	16.00
3-(Scarce)-Beck-a	4.50	14.00	32.00

FAUNTLEROY COMICS (Superduck Presents . . .)
1950 - No. 3, 1952
Close-Up/Archie Publications

	Good	Fine	N-Mint
1	4.00	12.00	28.00
2,3	2.15	6.50	15.00

FAUST
1989 - Present ($2.00-$2.25, B&W, adults)
Northstar Publishing

	Good	Fine	N-Mint
1	1.85	5.50	11.00
2	2.00	6.00	12.00
3,4: 3-Begin $2.25-c	.70	2.00	4.00
5,6	.40	1.15	2.30

FAVORITE COMICS (Also see Famous Comics)
1934 (36 pgs.)
Grocery Store Giveaway (Dif Corp.) (detergent)

	Good	Fine	N-Mint
Book #1-The Nebbs, Strange As It Seems, Napoleon, Dixie Dugan, Joe Palooka, S'Matter Pop, Hairbreadth Harry, etc. reprints			
	17.00	51.00	120.00
Book #2,3	15.00	45.00	105.00

FAWCETT MINIATURES (See Mighty Midget)
1946 (12-24 pgs.; 3¾x5'') (Wheaties giveaways)
Fawcett Publications

	Good	Fine	N-Mint
Captain Marvel-''And the Horn of Plenty;'' Bulletman story			
	2.65	8.00	18.00
Captain Marvel-''& the Raiders From Space;'' Golden Arrow story			
	2.65	8.00	18.00

FAWCETT MINIATURES (continued)   Good   Fine   N-Mint
Captain Marvel Jr.-"The Case of the Poison Press!" Bulletman story
                 2.65   8.00   18.00
Delecta of the Planets-C. C. Beck art; B&W inside; 12 pgs.; 3
   printing variations (coloring) exist   8.50   25.50   60.00

FAWCETT MOTION PICTURE COMICS (See Motion Picture Comics)

FAWCETT MOVIE COMIC
1949 - No. 20, Dec, 1952 (All photo-c)
Fawcett Publications
nn-"Dakota Lil"-George Montgomery & Rod Cameron('49)
                 23.00   70.00   160.00
nn-"Copper Canyon"-Ray Milland & Hedy Lamarr('50)
                 17.00   51.00   120.00
nn-"Destination Moon"-(1950)   50.00   150.00   350.00
nn-"Montana"-Errol Flynn & Alexis Smith('50) 17.00   51.00   120.00
nn-"Pioneer Marshal"-Monte Hale(1950)   17.00   51.00   120.00
nn-"Powder River Rustlers"-Rocky Lane(1950) 18.50   55.00   130.00
nn-"Singing Guns"-Vaughn Monroe & Ella Raines(1950)
                 16.00   48.00   110.00
7-"Gunmen of Abilene"-Rocky Lane; Bob Powell-a(1950)
                 18.50   55.00   130.00
8-"King of the Bullwhip"-Lash LaRue; Bob Powell-a(1950)
                 29.00   85.00   200.00
9-"The Old Frontier"-Monte Hale; Bob Powell-a(2/51); mis-dated
2/50)   17.00   51.00   120.00
10-"The Missourians"-Monte Hale(4/51)   17.00   51.00   120.00
11-"The Thundering Trail"-Lash LaRue(6/51) 24.00   73.00   170.00
12-"Rustlers on Horseback"-Rocky Lane(8/51) 18.50   55.00   130.00
13-"Warpath"-Edmond O'Brien & Forrest Tucker(10/51)
                 13.00   40.00   90.00
14-"Last Outpost"-Ronald Reagan(12/51)   35.00   105.00   245.00
15-(Scarce)-"The Man From Planet X"-Robert Clark; Shaffenberger-a
(2/52)   150.00   450.00   1050.00
16-"10 Tall Men"-Burt Lancaster   10.00   30.00   70.00
17-"Rose of Cimarron"-Jack Buetel & Mala Powers
                 6.50   19.50   45.00
18-"The Brigand"-Anthony Dexter; Shaffenberger-a
                 7.00   21.00   50.00
19-"Carbine Williams"-James Stewart; Costanza-a
                 9.00   27.00   62.00
20-"Ivanhoe"-Liz Taylor   13.00   40.00   90.00

FAWCETT'S FUNNY ANIMALS (No. 1-26, 80-on titled "Funny
Animals;" Li'l Tomboy No. 92 on?)
12/42 - #79, 4/53; #80, 6/53 - #83, 12?/53; #84, 4/54 - #91, 2/56
Fawcett Publications/Charlton Comics No. 84 on

1-Capt. Marvel on cover; intro. Hoppy The Captain Marvel Bunny,
   cloned from Capt. Marvel; Billy the Kid & Willie the Worm begin
                 26.00   77.00   180.00
2-Xmas-c   12.00   36.00   84.00
3-5   8.50   25.50   60.00
6,7,9,10   5.70   17.00   40.00
8-Flag-c   6.50   19.50   45.00
11-20   3.70   11.00   26.00
21-40: 25-Xmas-c. 26-St. Valentines Day-c   2.30   7.00   16.00
41-88,90,91   1.60   4.70   11.00
89-Merry Mailman issue   2.00   6.00   14.00
NOTE: Marvel Bunny in all issues to at least No. 68 (not in 49-54).

FAZE ONE FAZERS
1986 - No. 4, Sept, 1986 (Color, mini-series)
Americomics (AC Comics)
1-4   .25   .75   1.50

F.B.I., THE
April-June, 1965
Dell Publishing Co.

          Good   Fine   N-Mint
1-Sinnott-a   1.00   3.00   7.00

F.B.I. STORY, THE (See 4-Color No. 1069)

FEAR (Adventure into. . .)
Nov, 1970 - No. 31, Dec, 1975 (No.1-6: Giant Size)
Marvel Comics Group
1-Reprints Fantasy & Sci-Fi stories   .35   1.00   2.00
2-9,13-18   .50   1.00
10-Man-Thing begins; Morrow c/a(p)   .70   2.00   4.00
11-Adams-c   .25   .75   1.50
12-Starlin/Buckler-a   .25   .75   1.50
19-Intro. Howard the Duck; Val Mayerick-a   1.70   5.00   10.00
20-31: 20-Morbius, the Living Vampire begins, ends #31; Gulacy-a(p)
                     .50   1.00

NOTE: *Bolle* a-13i. *Brunner* c-15-17. *Colan* a-23r. *Craig* a-10p. *Ditko* a-6-8r. *Evans* a-30. *Everett* a-9, 10i, 21r. *Gil Kane* a-21p; c(p)-20, 21, 23-28, 31. *Kirby* a-8r, 9r. *Maneely* a-24r. *Mooney* a-11i, 26r. *Paul Reinman* a-14r. *Russell* a-23p, 24p. *Severin* c-8. *Starlin* c-12p.

FEARBOOK
April, 1986 (One shot) ($1.75, color, adults)
Eclipse Comics
1-Scholastic Mag.-r; Bissette-a   .30   .90   1.80

FEAR IN THE NIGHT (See Complete Mystery No. 3)

FEARLESS FAGAN (See 4-Color No. 441)

FEATURE BOOK (Dell) (See Large Feature Comic)

FEATURE BOOKS (Newspaper-r, early issues)
May, 1937 - No. 57, 1948 (B&W; Full color, 68 pgs. begin #26 on)
David McKay Publications
nn-Popeye & the Jeep (#1, 100 pgs.); reprinted as Feature Books
#3 (Very Rare; only 3 known copies, 1-vf, 2-in low grade)
       Estimated value. . . .   467.00   1400.00   2800.00
nn-Dick Tracy (#1)-Reprinted as Feature Book #4 (100 pgs.) & in part
as 4-Color #1 (Rare, less than 10 known copies)
       Estimated value. . . .   467.00   1400.00   2800.00
NOTE: *Above books were advertised together with different covers from Feature Books No. 3 & 4.*

1-King of the Royal Mtd. (#1)   41.00   122.00   285.00
2-Popeye(6/37) by Segar   54.00   160.00   375.00
3-Popeye(7/37) by Segar; same as nn issue but a new cover added
                 45.00   135.00   315.00
4-Dick Tracy(8/37)-Same as nn issue but a new cover added
                 72.00   215.00   500.00
5-Popeye(9/37) by Segar   37.00   110.00   260.00
6-Dick Tracy(10/37)   60.00   180.00   420.00
7-Little Orphan Annie (#1) (Rare)   75.00   225.00   525.00
8-Secret Agent X-9-Not by Raymond   28.00   85.00   170.00
9-Dick Tracy(1/38)   60.00   180.00   420.00
10-Popeye(2/38)   37.00   110.00   260.00
11-Little Annie Rooney (#1)   19.00   57.00   135.00
12-Blondie (#1) (4/38) (Rare)   39.00   118.00   275.00
13-Inspector Wade   11.50   34.00   80.00
14-Popeye(6/38) by Segar (Scarce)   50.00   150.00   350.00
15-Barney Baxter (#1) (7/38)   17.00   51.00   120.00
16-Red Eagle   11.00   32.00   75.00
17-Gangbusters (#1)   24.00   73.00   170.00
18,19-Mandrake   24.00   73.00   170.00
20-Phantom (#1)   43.00   130.00   300.00
21-Lone Ranger   43.00   130.00   300.00
22-Phantom   36.00   107.00   250.00
23-Mandrake   24.00   73.00   170.00
24-Lone Ranger(1941)   43.00   130.00   300.00
25-Flash Gordon (#1)-Reprints not by Raymond
                 54.00   163.00   380.00
26-Prince Valiant(1941)-Harold Foster-a; newspaper strips reprinted,

Fawcett Movie Comic #8, © FAW

Fawcett's Funny Animals #9, © FAW

Feature Book #25, © KING

Feature Comics #38, © QUA

Feature Stories Magazine #3, © FOX

Felix The Cat #12, © KING

FEATURE BOOKS (continued)	Good	Fine	N-Mint
pgs. 1-28,30-63. Color, 68pg. issues begin	73.00	218.00	510.00
27-29,31,34-Blondie	8.50	25.50	60.00
30-Katzenjammer Kids (#1)	9.30	28.00	65.00
32,35,41,44-Katzenjammer Kids	7.00	21.00	50.00
33(nn)-Romance of Flying-World War II photos			
	7.00	21.00	50.00
36('43),38,40('44),42,43,45,47-Blondie	8.00	24.00	56.00
37-Katzenjammer Kids; has photo & biog of Harold H. Knerr(1883-			
1949) who took over strip from Rudolph Dirks in 1914			
	8.50	25.50	60.00
39-Phantom	26.00	77.00	180.00
46-Mandrake in the Fire World-(58 pgs.)	20.00	60.00	140.00
48-Maltese Falcon by Dashiell Hammett('46)	41.00	124.00	290.00
49,50-Perry Mason	13.00	40.00	90.00
51,54-Rip Kirby c/a by Raymond; origin-#51	20.00	60.00	140.00
52,55-Mandrake	17.00	51.00	120.00
53,56,57-Phantom	20.00	60.00	140.00

NOTE: All Feature Books through #25 are over-sized 8½x11-3/8" comics with color covers and black and white interiors. The covers are rough, heavy stock. The page counts, including covers, are as follows: nn, #3,4-100 pgs.; #1,2-52 pgs.; #5-25 are all 76 pgs. #33 was found in bound set from publisher.

FEATURE COMICS (Formerly Feature Funnies)
No. 21, June, 1939 - No. 144, May, 1950
Quality Comics Group

	Good	Fine	N-Mint
21-Strips continue from Feature Funnies	23.00	70.00	160.00
22-26: 23-Charlie Chan begins	17.00	51.00	120.00
26-(nn, nd)-c-in one color, (10 cents, 36pgs.; issue No. blanked out.			
2 variations exist, each contain half of the regular #26)			
	5.50	16.50	38.00
27-(Rare)-Origin/1st app. Dollman by Eisner	135.00	405.00	945.00
28-1st Fine Dollman	65.00	195.00	455.00
29,30	40.00	120.00	280.00
31-Last Clock & Charlie Chan issue	32.00	95.00	225.00
32-37: 32-Rusty Ryan & Samar begin. 34-Captain Fortune app. 37-			
Last Fine Dollman	25.00	75.00	175.00
38-41: 38-Origin the Ace of Space. 39-Origin The Destroying Demon,			
ends #40. 40-Bruce Blackburn in costume	18.00	54.00	125.00
42-USA, the Spirit of Old Glory begins	12.00	36.00	84.00
43,45-50: 46-Intro. Boyville Brigadiers in Rusty Ryan. 48-USA ends			
	12.00	36.00	84.00
44-Dollman by Crandall begins, ends #63; Crandall-a(2)			
	17.00	51.00	120.00
51-60: 56-Marijuana story in "Swing Session." 57-Spider Widow			
begins. 60-Raven begins, ends #71	10.00	30.00	70.00
61-68 (5/43)	9.50	28.50	65.00
69,70-Phantom Lady x-over in Spider Widow	10.00	30.00	70.00
71-80: 71-Phantom Lady x-over. 72-Spider Widow ends			
	6.50	19.50	45.00
81-99	5.50	16.50	38.00
100	6.50	19.50	45.00
101-144: 139-Last Dollman. 140-Intro. Stuntman Stetson			
	4.50	14.00	32.00

NOTE: Celardo a-37-43. Crandall a-44-60, 62, 63-on(most). Gustavson a-(Rusty Ryan)-32-134. Powell a-34, 64-73.

FEATURE FILMS
Mar-Apr, 1950 - No. 4, Sept-Oct, 1950 (Photo-c 2,3)
National Periodical Publications

	Good	Fine	N-Mint
1-"Captain China" with John Payne, Gail Russell, Lon Chaney &			
Edgar Bergen	29.00	88.00	205.00
2-"Riding High" with Bing Crosby	24.00	73.00	170.00
3-"The Eagle & the Hawk" with John Payne, Rhonda Fleming &			
D. O'Keefe	24.00	73.00	170.00
4-"Fancy Pants"-Bob Hope & Lucille Ball	27.00	81.00	190.00

FEATURE FUNNIES (Feature Comics No. 21 on)
Oct, 1937 - No. 20, May, 1939

Harry 'A' Chesler

	Good	Fine	N-Mint
1(V9/1-indicia)-Joe Palooka, Mickey Finn, The Bungles, Jane Arden,			
Dixie Dugan, Big Top, Ned Brant, Strange As It Seems, & Off the			
Record strip reprints begin	138.00	412.00	825.00
2-The Hawk app. (11/37); Goldberg-c	57.00	170.00	400.00
3-Hawks of Seas begins by Eisner, ends #12; The Clock begins;			
Christmas-c	40.00	120.00	280.00
4,5	28.00	85.00	195.00
6-12: 11-Archie O'Toole by Bud Thomas begins, ends #22			
	23.00	70.00	160.00
13-Espionage, Starring Black X begins by Eisner, ends #20			
	25.00	75.00	175.00
14-20	20.00	60.00	140.00

FEATURE PRESENTATION, A (Feature Presentations Mag. #6)
(Formerly Women in Love) (Also see Startling Terror Tales #11)
No. 5, April, 1950
Fox Features Syndicate

	Good	Fine	N-Mint
5-Black Tarantula	15.00	45.00	105.00

FEATURE PRESENTATIONS MAGAZINE (Formerly A Feature
Presentation #5; becomes Feature Stories Mag. #3 on)
No. 6, July, 1950
Fox Features Syndicate

6-Moby Dick; Wood-c	13.00	40.00	90.00

FEATURE STORIES MAGAZINE (Formerly Feat. Present. Mag. #6)
No. 3, Aug, 1950 - No. 4, Oct, 1950
Fox Features Syndicate

3-Jungle Lil, Zegra stories; bondage-c	11.00	32.00	75.00
4	8.00	24.00	56.00

FEDERAL MEN COMICS (See Adventure Comics #32, The Comics
Magazine, New Adv. Comics, New Book of Comics & New Comics)
No. 2, 1945 (DC reprints from 1930's)
Gerard Publ. Co.

2-Siegel & Shuster-a; cover redrawn from Detective #9; spanking			
panel	11.00	32.00	75.00

FELIX'S NEPHEWS INKY & DINKY
Sept, 1957 - No. 7, Oct, 1958
Harvey Publications

1-Cover shows Inky's left eye with 2 pupils	4.00	12.00	28.00
2-7	1.75	5.25	12.00

NOTE: Contains no Messmer art.

FELIX THE CAT
1931 (24 pgs.; 8x10¼")(1926,'27 color strip reprints)
McLoughlin Bros.

260-(Rare)-by Otto Messmer	62.00	185.00	435.00

FELIX THE CAT (See Cat Tales 3-D, The Funnies, March of Comics
#24,36,51, New Funnies & Popular Comics)
1943 - No. 118, 11/61; 9-11/62 - No. 12, 7-9/65
Dell Publ. No.1-19/Toby No.20-61/Harvey No.62-118/Dell

4-Color 15	40.00	120.00	280.00
4-Color 46('44)	28.00	84.00	195.00
4-Color 77('45)	24.00	72.00	170.00
4-Color 119('46)	18.00	54.00	125.00
4-Color 135('46)	14.00	42.00	100.00
4-Color 162(9/47)	11.00	32.00	75.00
1(2-3/48)(Dell)	14.00	42.00	100.00
2	7.00	21.00	50.00
3-5	5.50	16.50	38.00
6-19(2-3/51-Dell)	4.00	12.00	28.00
20-30(Toby): 28-2/52 some copies have #29 on cover, #28 on inside			
	3.50	10.50	24.00
31,34,35-No Messmer-a	1.70	5.00	12.00
32,33,36-61(6/55-Toby)-Last Messmer issue	2.30	7.00	16.00

FELIX THE CAT (continued)	Good	Fine	N-Mint
62(8/55)-100 (Harvey)	1.00	3.00	7.00
101-118(11/61)	.85	2.50	6.00
12-269-211(9-11/62)(Dell)	1.50	4.50	10.00
2-12(7-9/65)(Dell, TV)	.75	2.25	5.00
3-D Comic Book 1(1953-One Shot)	20.00	60.00	140.00
Summer Annual 2('52)-Early 1930s Sunday strip-r (Exist?)			
	17.00	51.00	120.00
Summer Annual nn('53, 100 pgs., Toby)-1930s daily & Sunday-r			
	17.00	51.00	120.00
Winter Annual 2('54, 100 pgs., Toby)-1930s daily & Sunday-r			
	11.50	34.00	80.00
Summer Annual 3('55) (Exist?)	10.00	30.00	70.00

NOTE: 4-Color No. 15, 46, 77 and the Toby Annuals are all daily or Sunday newspaper reprints from the 1930's drawn by Otto Messmer, who created Felix in 1915 for the Sullivan animation studio. He drew Felix from the beginning under contract to Pat Sullivan. In 1946 he went to work for Dell and wrote and pencilled most of the stories and inked some of them through the Toby Press issues. No. 107 reprints No. 71 interior; No. 110 reprints No. 56 interior.

FELIX THE CAT & HIS FRIENDS
Dec, 1953 - No. 4, 1954
Toby Press

1	3.50	10.50	24.00
2-4	2.30	7.00	16.00

FEM FANTASTIQUE
Aug, 1988 ($1.95, B&W)
AC Comics

V2#1-By Bill Black; Betty Page pin-up	.45	1.40	2.75

FEMFORCE (Also see Untold Origin of the Femforce)
Apr, 1985 - Present ($1.75/1.95/2.25; in color; B&W #12? on)
Americomics

1: Black-a in all; Nightveil, Ms. Victory begin	.85	2.50	5.00
2	.50	1.50	3.00
3-15: 12-15 are $1.95 cover	.40	1.25	2.50
16-21: 16-19($2.25), 20-on($2.50)	.40	1.25	2.50
Special 1 (Fall, '84)(B&W, 52pgs.)-1st app. Ms. Victory, She-Cat, Blue Bulleteer, Rio Rita & Lady Luger	.35	1.00	2.00
In the House of Horror 1 ('89, $2.50, B&W)	.40	1.25	2.50
Out of the Asylum Special 1 ('87, B&W, $1.95)	.35	1.00	2.00

FERDINAND THE BULL (See Mickey Mouse Magazine V4/3)
1938 (10 cents)(Large size; some color, rest B&W)
Dell Publishing Co.

nn	8.00	24.00	56.00

FIBBER McGEE & MOLLY (See A-1 Comics No. 25)

55 DAYS AT PEKING (See Movie Comics)

FIGHT AGAINST CRIME (Fight Against the Guilty #22,23)
May, 1951 - No. 21, Sept, 1954
Story Comics

1	9.30	28.00	65.00
2	4.00	12.00	28.00
3,5: 5-Frazetta, 1 pg.	3.50	10.50	24.00
4-Drug story-"Hopped Up Killers"	5.70	17.00	40.00
6,7: 6-Used in POP, pgs. 83,84	3.50	10.50	24.00
8-Last crime format issue	3.50	10.50	24.00

NOTE: No. 9-21 contain violent, gruesome stories with blood, dismemberment, decapitation, E.C. style plot twists and several E.C. swipes. Bondage c-4,6,18,19.

9-11,13	7.00	21.00	50.00
12-Morphine drug story-"The Big Dope"	9.30	28.00	65.00
14-Tothish art by Ross Andru; electrocution-c	7.00	21.00	50.00
15-B&W & color illos in POP	7.00	21.00	50.00
16-E.C. story swipe/Haunt of Fear No. 19; Tothish by Ross Andru; bondage-c	9.30	28.00	65.00
17-Wildey E.C. swipe/Shock SuspenStories No. 9; knife through			

neck-c (1/54)	9.30	28.00	65.00
18,19: 19-Bondage/torture-c	6.50	19.50	45.00
20-Decapitation cover; contains hanging, ax murder, blood & violence	16.00	48.00	120.00
21-E.C. swipe	8.00	24.00	56.00

NOTE: Cameron a-4, 5. Hollingsworth a-3, 4, 9, 10, 13. Wildey a-15, 16.

FIGHT AGAINST THE GUILTY (Formerly Fight Against Crime)
No. 22, Dec, 1954 - No. 23, Mar, 1955
Story Comics

22-Tothish-a by Ross Andru; Ditko-a; E.C. story swipe; electrocution-c			
	7.00	21.00	50.00
23-Hollingsworth-a	4.50	14.00	32.00

FIGHT COMICS
Jan, 1940 - No. 86, Summer, 1953
Fiction House Magazines

1-Origin Spy Fighter, Starring Saber; Fine/Eisner-c; Eisner-a			
	90.00	270.00	625.00
2-Joe Louis life story	39.00	118.00	275.00
3-Rip Regan, the Power Man begins	36.00	107.00	250.00
4,5: 4-Fine-c	27.00	81.00	190.00
6-10: 6,7-Powell-c	22.00	65.00	154.00
11-14: Rip Regan ends	20.00	60.00	140.00
15-1st Super American	26.00	80.00	185.00
16-Captain Fight begins; Spy Fighter ends	26.00	80.00	185.00
17,18: Super American ends	23.00	70.00	160.00
19-Captain Fight ends; Senorita Rio begins (origin & 1st app.); Rip Carson, Chute Trooper begins	23.00	70.00	160.00
20	17.00	51.00	120.00
21-30	11.50	34.00	80.00
31,33-35: 31-Decapitation-c	10.00	30.00	70.00
32-Tiger Girl begins	11.00	32.00	75.00
36-47,49,50: 44-Capt. Fight returns	10.00	30.00	70.00
48-Used in Love and Death by Legman	10.00	30.00	70.00
51-Origin Tiger Girl; Patsy Pin-Up app.	16.00	48.00	110.00
52-60	8.00	24.00	56.00
61-Origin Tiger Girl retold	10.00	30.00	70.00
62-65-Last Baker issue	8.00	24.00	56.00
66-78: 78-Used in POP, pg. 99	7.00	20.00	48.00
79-The Space Rangers app.	7.00	20.00	48.00
80-85	5.70	17.00	40.00
86-Two Tigerman stories by Evans; Moreira-a	7.00	20.00	48.00

NOTE: Bondage covers, Lingerie, headlights panels are common. Tiger Girl by Baker-#36-60,62-65; Kayo Kirby by Baker-#52-64, 67. Eisner c-1-3, 5, 10, 11. Kamen a-54?, 57?. Tuska a-1, 5, 8, 10, 21, 29.

FIGHT FOR FREEDOM
1949, 1951 (16 pgs.) (Giveaway)
National Association of Mfgrs./General Comics

Dan Barry-c/a; used in POP, pg. 102	5.00	15.00	30.00

FIGHT FOR LOVE
1952 (no number)
United Features Syndicate

nn-Abbie & Slats newspaper-r	6.50	19.50	45.00

FIGHTING AIR FORCE (See United States Fighting Air Force)

FIGHTIN' AIR FORCE (Formerly Sherlock Holmes?; Never Again? War and Attack #54 on)
No. 3, Feb, 1956 - No. 53, Feb-Mar, 1966
Charlton Comics

V1#3	1.50	4.50	10.00
4-10	.70	2.00	5.00
11(68 pgs.)(3/58)	1.15	3.50	8.00
12 (100 pgs.)	1.50	4.50	10.00
13-30	.50	1.50	3.00

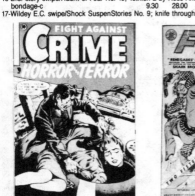

Fight Against Crime #20, © Story Comics

Fight Comics #2, © FH

Fight Comics #52, © FH

Fighting American #2, © PRIZE   Fightin' Army #24, © CC   Fightin' Marines #11, © STJ

	Good	Fine	N-Mint
FIGHTIN' AIR FORCE (continued)			
31-50: 50-American Eagle begins	.35	1.00	2.00
51-53	.25	.75	1.50

NOTE: *Glanzman a-13, 24; c-24.*

FIGHTING AMERICAN
Apr-May, 1954 - No. 7, Apr-May, 1955
Headline Publications/Prize

1-Origin Fighting American & Speedboy; S&K c/a(3)			
	73.00	220.00	515.00
2-S&K-a(3)	37.00	110.00	255.00
3,4-S&K-a(3)	31.00	94.00	220.00
5-S&K-a(2), Kirby/?-a	31.00	94.00	220.00
6-Four pg. reprint of origin, plus 2 pgs. by S&K			
	28.00	85.00	200.00
7-Kirby-a	26.00	79.00	185.00

NOTE: *Simon & Kirby covers on all.*

FIGHTING AMERICAN
October, 1966 (25 cents)
Harvey Publications

1-Origin Fighting American & Speedboy by S&K-r; S&K-c/a(3); 1 pg. Adams ad	1.50	4.50	10.00

FIGHTIN' ARMY (Formerly Soldier and Marine Comics; see Captain Willy Schultz)
No. 16, 1/56 - No. 127, 12/76; No. 128, 9/77 - No. 172, 11/84
Charlton Comics

16	1.15	3.50	8.00
17-19,21-23,25-30	.50	1.50	3.00
20-Ditko-a	1.15	3.50	8.00
24 (68 pgs., 3/58)	1.15	3.50	8.00
31-45	.35	1.00	2.00
46-60		.50	1.00
61-80: 75-The Lonely War of Willy Schultz begins, ends #92			
		.40	.80
81-172: 89,90,92-Ditko-a; Devil Brigade in #79,82,83			
		.30	.60
108(Modern Comics-1977)-Reprint		.15	.30

NOTE: *Aparo c-154. Montes/Bache a-48,49,51,69,75,76, 170r.*

FIGHTING DANIEL BOONE
1953
Avon Periodicals

nn-Kinstler c/a, 22 pgs.	8.00	24.00	56.00
I.W. Reprint #1-Kinstler c/a; Lawrence/Alascia-a			
	1.00	3.00	6.00

FIGHTING DAVY CROCKETT (Formerly Kit Carson)
No. 9, Oct-Nov, 1955
Avon Periodicals

9-Kinstler-c	3.50	10.50	24.00

FIGHTIN' 5, THE (Formerly Space War; also see The Peacemaker)
7/64 - No. 41, 1/67; No. 42, 10/81 - No. 49, 12/82
Charlton Comics

V2#28-Origin Fightin' Five	.70	2.00	4.00
29-39,41	.40	1.25	2.50
40-Peacemaker begins	.50	1.50	3.00
42-49: Reprints		.30	.60

FIGHTING FRONTS!
Aug, 1952 - No. 5, Jan, 1953
Harvey Publications

1	1.70	5.00	12.00
2-Extreme violence; Nostrand/Powell-a	2.30	7.00	16.00
3-5: 3-Powell-a	1.20	3.50	8.00

FIGHTING INDIAN STORIES (See Midget Comics)

FIGHTING INDIANS OF THE WILD WEST!
Mar, 1952 - No. 2, Nov, 1952
Avon Periodicals

	Good	Fine	N-Mint
1-Kinstler, Larsen-a	7.00	21.00	50.00
2-Kinstler-a	4.60	14.00	32.00
100 Pg. Annual(1952, 25 cents)-Contains three comics rebound			
	15.00	45.00	105.00

FIGHTING LEATHERNECKS
Feb, 1952 - No. 6, Dec, 1952
Toby Press

1-"Duke's Diary"-full pg. pin-ups by Sparling	5.50	16.50	38.00
2-"Duke's Diary"	3.70	11.00	26.00
3-5-"Gil's Gals"-full pg. pin-ups	3.70	11.00	26.00
6-(Same as No. 3-5?)	2.65	8.00	18.00

FIGHTING MAN, THE (War)
May, 1952 - No. 8, July, 1953
Ajax/Farrell Publications(Excellent Publ.)

1	2.65	8.00	18.00
2	1.30	4.00	9.00
3-8	1.00	3.00	7.00
Annual 1 (100 pgs, 1952)	12.00	36.00	84.00

FIGHTIN' MARINES (Formerly The Texan; see Approved Comics)
No. 15, 8/51 - No. 12, 3/53; No. 14, 5/55 - No. 132, 11/76;
No. 133, 10/77 - No. 176, 9/84 (No #13?)
St. John(Approved Comics)/Charlton Comics No. 14 on

15(No.1)-Matt Baker c/a "Leatherneck Jack;" slightly large size; Fightin' Texan No. 16 & 17?	9.30	28.00	65.00
2-1st Canteen Kate by Baker; slightly large size			
	12.00	36.00	84.00
3-9-Canteen Kate by Matt Baker; Baker c-No. 2,3,5-10			
	6.50	19.50	45.00
10-Baker-c	1.60	4.70	11.00
11,12-No Baker; 12-Last St. John issue?	1.15	3.50	8.00
14 (5/55; 1st Charlton issue; formerly?)-Canteen Kate by Baker			
	5.00	15.00	35.00
15-Baker-c	1.60	4.70	11.00
16,18-20-Not Baker-c	1.00	3.00	7.00
17-Canteen Kate by Baker	5.00	15.00	35.00
21-24	.70	2.00	4.00
25-(68 pgs.)(3/58)-Check-a?	1.50	4.50	10.00
26-(100 pgs.)(8/58)-Check-a(5)	2.65	8.00	18.00
27-50	.50	1.50	3.00
51-81,83-100: 78-Shotgun Harker & the Chicken series begin			
	.30	1.00	2.00
82-(100 pgs.)	.70	2.00	4.00
101-122: 122-Pilot issue for "War" title (Fightin' Marines Presents War)		.50	1.00
123-176		.30	.60
120(Modern Comics reprint, 1977)		.20	.40

NOTE: *No. 14 & 16 (CC) reprint St. John issues; No. 16 reprints St. John insignia on cover. Colan a-3, 7. Glanzman c/a-92, 94. Montes/Bache a-48, 53, 55, 64, 65, 72-74, 77-83, 176r.*

FIGHTING MARSHAL OF THE WILD WEST (See The Hawk)

FIGHTIN' NAVY (Formerly Don Winslow)
No. 74, 1/56 - No. 125, 4-5/66; No. 126, 8/83 - No. 133, 10/84
Charlton Comics

74	1.15	3.50	8.00
75-81	.75	2.50	5.00
82-Sam Glanzman-a	.70	2.00	4.00
83-99,101-105,106-125('66)	.40	1.25	2.50
100	.45	1.40	2.80
126-133('84)		.30	.60

NOTE: *Montes/Bache a-109. Glanzman a-131r.*

149

FIGHTING PRINCE OF DONEGAL, THE (See Movie Comics)

FIGHTIN' TEXAN (Formerly The Texan & Fightin' Marines?)
No. 16, Oct, 1952 - No. 17, Dec, 1952
St. John Publishing Co.

	Good	Fine	N-Mint
16,17-Tuska-a each. 17-Cameron-c/a	2.85	8.50	20.00

FIGHTING UNDERSEA COMMANDOS (See Undersea Fighting...)
1952 - No. 5, April, 1953
Avon Periodicals

1	4.30	13.00	30.00
2	2.85	8.50	20.00
3-5: 3-Ravielli-c. 4-Kinstler-c	2.65	8.00	18.00

FIGHTING WAR STORIES
Aug, 1952 - No. 5, 1953
Men's Publications/Story Comics

1	2.00	6.00	14.00
2	1.15	3.50	8.00
3-5	.85	2.60	6.00

FIGHTING YANK (See America's Best & Startling Comics)
Sept, 1942 - No. 29, Aug, 1949
Nedor/Better Publ./Standard

1-The Fighting Yank begins; Mystico, the Wonder Man app; bondage-c	60.00	180.00	420.00
2	28.00	85.00	200.00
3	19.00	58.00	135.00
4	14.00	42.00	100.00
5-10: 7-The Grim Reaper app.	12.00	36.00	84.00
11-The Oracle app.	10.00	30.00	70.00
12-17: 12-Hirohito bondage-c	10.00	30.00	70.00
18-The American Eagle app.	10.00	30.00	70.00
19,20	10.00	30.00	70.00
21,23,24: 21-Kara, Jungle Princess app. 24-Miss Masque app.	11.50	34.00	80.00
22-Miss Masque-c/story	14.00	42.00	100.00
25-Robinson/Meskin-a; strangulation, lingerie panel; The Cavalier app.	14.00	42.00	100.00
26-29: All-Robinson/Meskin-a. 28-One pg. Williamson-a	11.50	34.00	80.00

NOTE: *Schomburg (Xela) c-4-29; airbrush c- 28, 29. Bondage c-4, 8, 11, 15, 17.*

FIGHT THE ENEMY
Aug, 1966 - No. 3, Mar, 1967 (25 cents)
Tower Comics

1-Lucky 7 & Mike Manly begin	1.50	4.50	10.00
2-Boris Vallejo, McWilliams-a	1.70	5.00	12.00
3-Wood-a ½pg; McWilliams, Bolle-a	.85	2.50	6.00

FILM FUNNIES
Nov, 1949 - No. 2, Feb, 1950 (52 pgs.)
Marvel Comics (CPC)

1-Krazy Krow	7.00	21.00	50.00
2	5.00	15.00	35.00

FILM STARS ROMANCES
Jan-Feb, 1950 - No. 3, May-June, 1950
Star Publications

1-Rudy Valentino story; L. B. Cole-c; lingerie panels	14.00	42.00	100.00
2-Liz Taylor/Robert Taylor photo-c	16.00	48.00	110.00
3-Photo-c	12.00	36.00	84.00

FINAL CYCLE, THE
July, 1987 - No. 4, 1988 (Mini-series, color)
Dragon's Teeth Productions

1-4	.35	1.00	2.00

FIRE AND BLAST
1952 (16 pgs.; paper cover) (Giveaway)
National Fire Protection Assoc.

	Good	Fine	N-Mint
nn-Mart Baily A-Bomb cover; about fire prevention	12.00	35.00	70.00

FIRE BALL XL5 (See Steve Zodiac & The ...)

FIRE CHIEF AND THE SAFE OL' FIREFLY, THE
1952 (16 pgs.) (Safety brochure given away at schools)
National Board of Fire Underwriters (produced by American Visuals Corp.) (Eisner)

(Rare) Eisner c/a	30.00	90.00	210.00

FIREHAIR COMICS (Pioneer West Romances #3-6; also see Rangers Comics)
Winter/48-49 - No. 2, Spr/49; No. 7, Spr/51 - No. 11, Spr/52
Fiction House Magazines (Flying Stories)

1	20.00	60.00	140.00
2	10.00	30.00	70.00
7-11	7.00	21.00	50.00
I.W. Reprint 8-Kinstler-c; reprints Rangers #57; Dr. Drew story by Grandenetti (nd)	.85	2.60	6.00

FIRESTAR
March, 1986 - No. 4, June, 1986 (From Spider-Man TV series)
Marvel Comics Group

1-X-Men & New Mutants app.	.35	1.00	2.00
2,4: 2-Wolverine-c/story	.25	.75	1.50
3-Wolverine-c by Art Adams (p)	.50	1.50	3.00

FIRESTONE (See Donald And Mickey Merry Christmas)

FIRESTORM (See Cancelled Comic Cavalcade, DC Comics Presents, Flash #289 & The Fury of... & Justice League of America #179)
March, 1978 - No. 5, Oct-Nov, 1978
DC Comics

1-Origin & 1st app.	.50	1.50	3.00
2-5: 2-Origin Multiplex. 3-Origin Killer Frost. 4-1st app. Hyena	.35	1.00	2.00

FIRESTORM, THE NUCLEAR MAN (Formerly Fury of Firestorm)
No. 65, Nov, 1987 - Present
DC Comics

65-94: 66-1st app. Zuggernaut. 71-Death of Capt. X. 67,68-Millennium tie-ins	.50		1.00
Annual 5 (10/87)-1st app. new Firestorm	.65		1.30

FIRST ADVENTURES
Dec, 1985 - No. 5, Apr, 1986 ($1.25, color)
First Comics

1-5: 1-Blaze Barlow, Whisper & Dynamo Joe begin	.65		1.30

FIRST AMERICANS, THE (See 4-Color No. 843)

FIRST CHRISTMAS, THE (3-D)
1953 (25 cents) (Oversized - 8¼x10¼'')
Fiction House Magazines (Real Adv. Publ. Co.)

nn-(Scarce)-Kelly Freas-c; Biblical theme, birth of Christ; Nativity-c	26.00	78.00	180.00

FIRST COMICS GRAPHIC NOVEL
Jan, 1984 - Present (52-176 pgs, high quality paper)
First Comics

1-Beowulf ($5.95)	1.00	3.00	6.00
1-2nd printing	1.15	3.50	7.00
2-Time Beavers ($5.95)	1.00	3.00	6.00
3($11.95, 100 pgs.)-American Flagg! Hard Times. (2 printings)	2.00	6.00	12.00
4-Nexus ($6.95)-r/B&W 1-3	1.30	4.00	8.00

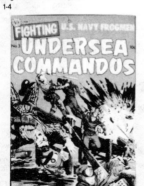

Fighting Undersea Commandos #3, © AVON

Fighting Yank #6, © STD

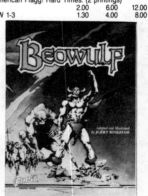

First Comics Graphic Novel #1, © First

First Romance Magazine #1, © HARV

The Flame #6, © FOX

Flaming Carrot #16, © Bob Burden

FIRST COMICS GRAPHIC NOVEL (cont.)	Good	Fine	N-Mint
5-The Enchanted Apples of Oz ($7.95, 52pp)-Intro by Harlan Ellison (1986)	1.35	4.00	8.00
6-Elric of Melnibone ($14.95, 176pp)-r with new color	2.50	7.50	15.00
7-The Secret Island Of Oz ($7.95)	1.35	4.00	8.00
8-Teenage Mutant Ninja Turtles Book I(132 pgs., r-/TMNT #1-3 in color w/12 pgs. new-a ($9.95)-Origin	1.70	5.00	10.00
9-Time 2: The Epiphany by Chaykin, 52 pgs. ($7.95)	1.35	4.00	8.00
10-Teenage Mutant Ninja Turtles Book II	1.70	5.00	10.00
11-Sailor On The Sea of Fate	2.50	7.50	15.00
12-American Flagg! Southern Comfort	2.00	6.00	12.00
13-The Ice King Of Oz	1.35	4.00	8.00
14-Teenage Mutant Ninja Turtles Book III	1.70	5.00	10.00
15-Hex Breaker: Badger (64 pgs., $7.95)	1.35	4.00	8.00
16-The Forgotten Forest of Oz ($8.95)	1.50	4.50	9.00
17-Mazinger (64pgs., $8.95)	1.50	4.50	9.00
18-Teenage Mutant Ninja Turtles Book IV	1.70	5.00	10.00
19-The Original Nexus Graphic Novel ($7.95, 104pgs)-Reprints First Comics Graphic Novel #4 ($7.95)	1.35	4.00	8.00
20-American Flagg! State of the Union; r/A.F. 7-9 ($11.95)	2.00	6.00	12.00

1ST FOLIO (The Joe Kubert School Presents. . .)
March, 1984 ($1.50, color)
Pacific Comics

1-Kubert-c/a(2pgs.); Adam & Andy Kubert-a	.25	.75	1.50

FIRST ISSUE SPECIAL
April, 1975 - No. 13, April, 1976
National Periodical Publications

1-Intro. Atlas; Kirby c/a		.50	1.00
2-7: 2-Green Team (See Cancelled Comic Cavalcade). 3-Metamorpho. 4-Lady Cop. 5-Manhunter; Kirby c/a. 6-Dingbats; Kirby c/a, 7-The Creeper		.50	1.00
8-The Warlord (origin); Grell c/a	1.70	5.00	10.00
9-Dr. Fate; Kubert-c; Simonson-a		.50	1.00
10-13: 10-The Outsiders. 11-Code Name: Assassin; Redondo-a. 12-Origin/1st app. new Starman. 13-Return of the New Gods		.50	1.00

FIRST KISS
Dec, 1957 - No. 40, Jan, 1965
Charlton Comics

V1#1	1.00	3.00	7.00
V1#2-10	.50	1.50	3.00
11-40	.25	.75	1.50

FIRST LOVE ILLUSTRATED
2/49 - No. 9, 6/50; No. 10, 1/51 - No. 86, 3/58; No. 87, 9/58 - No. 88, 11/58; No. 89, 11/62, No. 90, 2/63
Harvey Publications(Home Comics)(True Love)

1-Powell-a(2)	4.00	12.00	28.00
2-Powell-a	2.30	7.00	16.00
3-''Was I Too Fat To Be Loved'' story	2.85	8.00	20.00
4-10	2.00	6.00	14.00
11-30: 30-Lingerie panel	1.15	3.50	8.00
31-34,37,39-49: 49-Last pre-code (2/55)	1.00	3.00	7.00
35-Used in SOTI, illo-''The title of this comic book is First Love''	8.00	24.00	56.00
36-Communism story, ''Love Slaves''	1.30	4.00	9.00
38-Nostrand-a	2.30	7.00	16.00
50-90	.70	2.00	4.00

NOTE: *Disbrow* a-13. *Orlando* c-87. *Powell* a-1, 3-5, 7, 10, 11, 13-17, 19-24, 26-29, 33, 35-41, 43, 45, 46, 50, 54, 55, 57, 58, 61-63, 65, 71-73, 76, 79r, 82, 84, 88.

FIRST MEN IN THE MOON (See Movie Comics)

FIRST ROMANCE MAGAZINE
8/49 - #6, 6/50; #7, 6/51 - #50, 2/58; #51, 9/58 - #52, 11/58
Home Comics(Harvey Publ.)/True Love

	Good	Fine	N-Mint
1	4.00	12.00	28.00
2	2.30	7.00	16.00
3-5	2.00	6.00	14.00
6-10	1.50	4.50	10.00
11-20	1.15	3.50	8.00
21-27,29-32: 32-Last pre-code issue (2/55)	.85	2.60	6.00
28-Nostrand-a(Powell swipe)	2.00	6.00	14.00
33-52	.70	2.00	4.00

NOTE: *Powell* a-1-5, 8-10, 14, 18, 20-22, 24, 25, 28, 36, 46, 48, 51.

FIRST TRIP TO THE MOON (See Space Advs. No. 20)

FISH POLICE
Dec, 1985 - No. 11, Nov, 1987 ($1.50, B&W)
V2#5, April, 1988 - V2#17, May, 1989 ($1.75, color)
No. 18, Aug, 1989 - Present ($2.25, B&W)
Fishwrap Productions/Comico V2#5-17/Apple Comics #18 on

1	.85	2.50	5.00
1-2nd print (5/86)	.30	.90	1.80
2	.30	1.00	2.00
2-2nd print	.25	.75	1.50
3-11	.25	.75	1.50
V2#5-17(Color): V2#5-11-r/V1#5-11. 12-17, new-a	.40	1.25	2.50
18-22 ($2.25-c, B&W) 18-Origin Inspector Gill	.40	1.15	2.30
Special 1 ($2.50, 7/87, Comico)	.40	1.25	2.50
Graphic Novel: The Hairball Saga (r/1-4, color)	1.35	4.00	8.00

FIST OF THE NORTH STAR, THE
1989 - No. 8, 1989 ($2.95, B&W, mini-series, 52 pgs.)
Viz Comics

1-8: Martial arts super-hero	.50	1.50	3.00

5-STAR SUPER-HERO SPEC. (See DC Special Series No. 1)

FLAME, THE (See Big 3 & Wonderworld Comics)
Summer, 1940 - No. 8, Jan, 1942 (#1,2, 68 pgs; #3-8, 44 pgs.)
Fox Features Syndicate

1-Flame stories from Wonderworld #5-9; origin The Flame; Lou Fine-a, 36 pgs., r-/Wonderworld 3,10	142.00	425.00	850.00
2-Fine-a(2). Wing Turner by Tuska	59.00	176.00	410.00
3-8-Powell-a	32.00	95.00	225.00

FLAME, THE (Formerly Lone Eagle)
No. 5, Dec-Jan, 1954-55 - No. 4, June-July, 1955
Ajax/Farrell Publications (Excellent Publ.)

5(#1)	11.50	34.00	80.00
2-4	8.50	25.50	60.00

FLAMING CARROT (Also see Junior Carrot Patrol)
Summer-Fall, 1981 (One Shot) (Large size, 8½x11'')
Kilian Barracks Press

1-By Bob Burden	12.00	36.00	85.00

FLAMING CARROT (Also see Anything Goes, Cerebus & Visions)
5/84 - No. 5, 1/85; No. 6, 3/85 - Present ($1.70-$2.00, B&W)
Aardvark-Vanaheim/Renegade Press #6-17/Dark Horse #18 on

1-Bob Burden story/art	7.00	21.00	50.00
2	4.30	13.00	30.00
3	3.70	11.00	22.00
4-6	2.50	7.50	15.00
7-9	1.50	4.50	9.00
10-12	.75	2.25	4.50
13-15	.70	2.00	4.00
16-23: 18-1st Dark Horse issue	.50	1.50	3.00

FLAMING LOVE
Dec, 1949 - No. 6, Oct, 1950 (Photo covers No. 2-6)

FLAMING LOVE (continued)
Quality Comics Group (Comic Magazines)

	Good	Fine	N-Mint
1-Ward-c, 9 pgs.	16.00	48.00	110.00
2	7.00	21.00	50.00
3-Ward-a, 9 pgs.; Crandall-a	11.00	32.00	75.00
4-6: 4-Gustavson-a	5.50	16.50	38.00

FLAMING WESTERN ROMANCES
Nov-Dec, 1949 - No. 3, Mar-Apr, 1950
Star Publications

	Good	Fine	N-Mint
1-L. B. Cole-c	12.00	36.00	84.00
2-L. B. Cole-c	8.50	25.50	60.00
3-Robert Taylor, Arlene Dahl photo-c with biographies inside; L. B. Cole-c; spanking panel	18.50	56.00	130.00

FLARE (Also see Champions for 1st app.)
Nov, 1988 - Present ($2.75, color, 52pgs)
Hero Comics

	Good	Fine	N-Mint
1-4: 4-Origin The Black Enchantress	.60	1.75	3.50

FLASH, THE (See Adventure, The Brave and the Bold, Crisis On Infinite Earths, DC Comics Presents, DC Special, DC Special Series, DC Super-Stars, Green Lantern, Justice League of America, Showcase, Super Team Family, & World's Finest)

FLASH, THE (Formerly Flash Comics)
No. 105, Feb-Mar, 1959 - No. 350, Oct, 1985
National Periodical Publications/DC Comics

	Good	Fine	N-Mint
105-Origin Flash(retold), & Mirror Master	115.00	345.00	800.00
106-Origin Grodd & Pied Piper	47.00	140.00	330.00
107	23.00	70.00	160.00
108,109	19.00	57.00	135.00
110-Intro/origin The Weather Wizard & Kid Flash who later becomes Flash in Crisis On Infinite Earths #12	25.00	75.00	175.00
111	11.00	32.00	75.00
112-Intro & origin Elongated Man	11.50	34.00	80.00
113-Origin Trickster	10.00	30.00	70.00
114-Origin Captain Cold	10.00	30.00	70.00
115-120: 117-Origin Capt. Boomerang. 119-Elongated Man marries Sue Dearborn	8.00	24.90	55.00
121,122: 122-Origin & 1st app. The Top	5.70	17.00	40.00
123-Re-intro. Golden Age Flash; origins of both Flashes; 1st mention of an Earth II where DC Golden Age heroes live	37.00	110.00	260.00
124-Last 10 cent issue	5.00	15.00	35.00
125-128,130: 128-Origin Abra Kadabra	3.15	9.50	22.00
129-G.A. Flash x-over; J.S.A. cameo in flashback	9.35	28.00	65.00
131-136,138-140: 136-1st Dexter Miles. 139-Origin Prof. Zoom. 140-Origin & 1st app. Heat Wave	3.15	9.50	22.00
137-G.A. Flash x-over; J.S.A. cameo (1st real app. since 2-3/51); 1st Silver Age app. Vandall Savage	8.00	24.00	55.00
141-150	1.50	4.50	10.00
151-159: 151-G.A. Flash x-over	1.35	4.00	8.00
160-80-Pg. Giant G-21-G.A.-r Flash & Johnny Quick	1.50	4.50	10.00
161-168,170: 165-Silver Age Flash weds Iris West. 167-new facts about Flash's origin. 170-Dr. Mid-Nite, Dr. Fate, G.A. Flash x-over	1.15	3.50	7.00
169-80-Pg. Giant G-34	1.50	4.50	9.00
171-177,179,180: 171-JLA, Green Lantern, Atom Guest-stars. 173-G.A. Flash x-over. 174-Barry Allen reveals I.D. to wife. 175-2nd Superman/Flash race; JLA cameo	1.00	3.00	6.00
178-80-Pg. Giant G-46	1.35	4.00	8.00
181-186,188-190: 186-Re-intro. Sargon	.70	2.00	4.00
187,196: 68-Pg. Giants G-58, G-70	1.00	3.00	6.00
191-195,197-200	.70	2.00	4.00
201-204,206-210: 201-New G.A. Flash story. 208-52 pg. begin, end #213,215,216. 206-Elongated Man begins	.35	1.00	2.00

	Good	Fine	N-Mint
205-68-Pg. Giant G-82	.85	2.50	5.00
211-213,216,220: 211-G.A. Flash origin (#104). 213-All-r	.35	1.00	2.00
214-Giant DC-11; origin Metal Men-r; 1st pubbed G.A. Flash story	.70	2.00	4.00
215 (52 pgs.)-Flash-r/Showcase 4; G.A. Flash x-over, r-in #216	.35	1.00	2.00
217-219: Adams-a in all. 217-Green Lantern/Green Arrow series begins. 219-Last Green Arrow	1.00	3.00	6.00
221-225,227,228,230,231	.25	.75	1.50
226-Adams-a	.60	1.75	3.50
229,232,233-(100 pgs. each)	.40	1.25	2.50
234-274,277-288,290: 243-Death of The Top. 246-Last Green Lantern. 256-Death of The Top retold. 267-Origin of Flash's uniform. 270-Intro The Clown. 286-Intro/origin Rainbow Raider	.60	1.20	
275,276-Iris West Allen dies	.35	1.00	2.00
289-Perez 1st DC art; new Firestorm series begins, ends #304	.35	1.00	2.00
291-299,301-305: 291-Intro/origin Colonel Computron. 298-Intro/origin Shade. 301-Atomic Bomb-c. 303-The Top returns. 305-G.A. Flash x-over	.50	1.00	
300-52pgs.; origin Flash retold	.35	1.00	2.00
306-Dr. Fate by Giffen begins, ends #313	.35	1.00	2.00
307-313-Giffen-a. 309-Origin Flash retold	.25	.75	1.50
314-349: 324-Death of Reverse Flash (Prof. Zoom). 328-Iris West Allen's death retold. 344-Origin Kid Flash	.50	1.00	
350-Double size ($1.25)	.55	1.60	3.20
Annual 1(10-12/63, 84pgs.)-Origin Elongated Man & Kid Flash-r; origin Grodd, G.A. Flash-r	18.00	54.00	125.00

NOTE: **Adams** c-194, 195, 203, 204, 206-208, 211, 213, 215, 246. **Austin** a-233i, 234i, 246i. **Buckler** a-271p, 272p; c(p)-247-50, 252, 253p, 255, 256p, 258, 262, 265-267, 269-271. **Giffen** a-306p-313p; c-310p, 315. **Sid Greene** a-167-174i, 229i(r). **Grell** a-237p, 238p, 240-243p; c-236. **G. Kane** a-195p, 197-199p, 229r, 232r; c-197-199, 312p. **Kubert** a-108p, 215i(r); c-189-191. **Lopez** c-272. **Meskin** a-229r, 232r. **Perez** a-289-293p; c-293. **Starlin** a-294-296p. **Staton** c-263p, 264p. Green Lantern x-over-131, 143, 168, 171, 191.

FLASH
June, 1987 - Present (75 cents, $1.00 #17 on)
DC Comics

	Good	Fine	N-Mint
1-Guice c/a begins; New Teen Titans app.	1.15	3.50	7.00
2	.85	2.50	5.00
3-Intro. Kilgore	.50	1.50	3.00
4-6: 5-Intro. Speed McGee	.50	1.00	2.00
7-10: 7-1st app. Blue Trinity. 8,9-Millennium tie-ins. 9-1st app. The Chunk	.25	.75	1.50
11-20: 12-Extra 16pg. Dr. Light story	.55	1.10	
21-36: 28-Capt. Cold app. 29-New Phantom Lady app.	.50	1.00	
Annual 1 (9/87, $1.25), 2 (10/88, $1.50)	.35	1.00	2.00
Annual 3 (7/89, $1.75, 68 pgs.)-Gives history of G.A., Silver Age, & new Flash in text	.30	.90	1.75

NOTE: **Guice** a-1-9p, 11p, Annual 1p; c-1-9p, Annual 1p.

FLASH COMICS (Whiz Comics No. 2 on)
Jan, 1940 (12 pgs., B&W, regular size)
(Not distributed to newsstands; printed for in-house use)
Fawcett Publications

NOTE: **Whiz Comics #2** was preceded by two books, **Flash Comics** and **Thrill Comics**, both dated Jan, 1940, (12 pgs, B&W, regular size) and were not distributed. These two books are identical except for the title. It is believed that the complete 68 page issue of Fawcett's **Flash** and **Thrill Comics #1** was finished and ready for publication with the January date. Since D.C. Comics was also about to publish a book with the same date and title, Fawcett hurriedly printed up the black and white version of **Flash Comics** to secure copyright before D.C. The inside covers are blank, with the covers and inside pages printed on a high quality uncoated paper stock. The eight page origin story of Captain Thunder is composed of pages 1-7 and 13 of the Captain Marvel story essentially as they appeared in the first issue of **Whiz Comics**. The balloon dialogue on page thirteen was relettered to tie the story into the end of page seven in **Flash** and **Thrill Comics** to produce a shorter version of the origin story

Flaming Love #5, © QUA

The Flash #137, © DC

The Flash #324, © DC

Flash Comics #6, © DC   Flash Comics #102, © DC   Flash Gordon #13 (Charlton), © KING

FLASH COMICS (continued)

for copyright purposes. Obviously, D.C. acquired the copyright and Fawcett dropped **Flash** as well as **Thrill** and came out with **Whiz Comics** a month later. Fawcett never used the cover to **Flash** and **Thrill #1**, designing a new cover for **Whiz Comics**. Fawcett also must have discovered that Captain Thunder had already been used by another publisher. All references to Captain Thunder were relettered to Captain Marvel before appearing in **Whiz**.

1 (nn on-c, #1 on inside)-Origin & 1st app. Captain Thunder. Eight copies of **Flash** and three copies of **Thrill** exist. All 3 copies of Thrill sold in 1986 for between $4,000-$10,000 each. A NM copy of Thrill sold in 1987 for $12,000. A vg copy of Thrill sold in 1987 for $9000 cash; another copy sold in 1987 for $2000 cash, $10,000 trade.

FLASH COMICS (The Flash No. 105 on) (Also see All-Flash)
Jan, 1940 - No. 104, Feb, 1949
National Periodical Publications/All-American

	Good	Fine	N-Mint
1-Origin The Flash by Harry Lampert, Hawkman by Gardner Fox, The Whip, & Johnny Thunder by Stan Asch; Cliff Cornwall by Moldoff, Minute Movies begin; Moldoff (Shelly) cover; 1st app. Shiera Sanders who later becomes Hawkgirl, #24; reprinted in Famous First Edition	1170.00	2925.00	7000.00
2-Rod Rian begins, ends #11	300.00	750.00	1800.00
3-The King begins, ends #41	233.00	585.00	1400.00
4-Moldoff (Shelly) Hawkman begins	200.00	500.00	1200.00
5	175.00	440.00	1050.00
6,7	142.00	355.00	850.00
8-10	108.00	270.00	650.00
11-20: 12-Les Watts begins; "Sparks" #16 on. 17-Last Cliff Cornwall	83.00	210.00	500.00
21-23	70.00	175.00	420.00
24-Shiera becomes Hawkgirl	82.00	205.00	490.00
25-30: 28-Last Les Sparks. 29-Ghost Patrol begins(origin, 1st app.), ends #104	58.00	145.00	350.00
31-40: 35-Origin Shade	50.00	125.00	300.00
41-50	44.00	110.00	265.00
51-61: 59-Last Minute Movies. 61-Last Moldoff Hawkman	37.00	95.00	225.00
62-Hawkman by Kubert begins	50.00	125.00	300.00
63-70: 66-68-Hop Harrigan in all	39.00	98.00	235.00
71-80: 80-Atom begins, ends #104	39.00	98.00	235.00
81-85	39.00	98.00	235.00
86-Intro. The Black Canary in Johnny Thunder; rare in Mint due to black ink smearing on white cover	100.00	250.00	600.00
87-90: 88-Origin Ghost. 89-Intro villain Thorn	50.00	125.00	300.00
91,93-99: 98-Atom dons new costume	63.00	160.00	380.00
92-1st solo Black Canary	96.00	240.00	575.00
100 (10/48),103(Scarce)-52 pgs. each	103.00	260.00	620.00
101,102(Scarce)	83.00	210.00	500.00
104-Origin The Flash retold (Scarce)	200.00	500.00	1200.00
Wheaties Giveaway (1946, 32 pgs., 6½x8¼")-Johnny Thunder, Ghost Patrol, The Flash & Kubert Hawkman app. NOTE: All known copies were taped to Wheaties boxes and are never found in mint condition. Copies with light tape residue bring the listed prices in all grades	28.00	84.00	195.00

NOTE: *Infantino a-86p, 90, 93-95, 99-104. Kinstler a-87, 89(Hawkman). Chet Kozlak c-77, 79, 81. Krigstein a-94. Kubert a-62-76, 83, 85, 86, 88-104; c-63, 65, 67, 70, 71, 73, 75, 83, 85, 86, 88, 89, 91, 94, 96, 98, 100, 104. Moldoff a-3; c-3, 7, 9, 17, 21, 23, 25, 27, 29, 31, 33, 37, 43, 55, 57. #8-Male bondage-c.*

FLASH DIGEST, THE (See DC Special Series #24)

FLASH GORDON (See Defenders Of The Earth, Eat Right to Work..., Feature Book #25 (McKay), King Classics, King Comics, March of Comics #118, 133, 142, The Phantom #18, Street Comix & Wow Comics, 1st series)

FLASH GORDON
No. 10, 1943 - No. 512, Nov, 1953
Dell Publishing Co.

	Good	Fine	N-Mint
4-Color 10(1943)-by Alex Raymond; reprints/"The Ice Kingdom"	55.00	165.00	385.00
4-Color 84(1945)-by Alex Raymond; reprints/"The Fiery Desert"	33.00	100.00	230.00
4-Color 173,190: 190-Bondage-c	11.50	34.00	80.00
4-Color 204,247	9.00	27.00	62.00
4-Color 424	6.50	19.50	45.00
2(5-7/53-Dell)-Evans-a	3.50	10.50	24.00
4-Color 512	3.50	10.50	24.00
Macy's Giveaway(1943)-(Rare)-20 pgs.; not by Raymond	60.00	160.00	320.00

FLASH GORDON (See Tiny Tot Funnies)
Oct, 1950 - No. 4, April, 1951
Harvey Publications

	Good	Fine	N-Mint
1-Alex Raymond-a; bondage-c	17.00	51.00	120.00
2-Alex Raymond-a	13.00	40.00	90.00
3,4-Alex Raymond-a; 3-bondage-c	12.00	36.00	80.00
5-(Rare)-Small size-5½x8½"; B&W; 32 pgs.; Distributed to some mail subscribers only Estimated value....		$200.00—$300.00	

(Also see All-New No. 15, Boy Explorers No. 2, and Stuntman No. 3)

FLASH GORDON
1951 (Paper cover; 16 pgs. in color; regular size)
Harvey Comics (Gordon Bread giveaway)

	Good	Fine	N-Mint
1 (1938-r), 2(1941-r?)-Reprints by Raymond each....	2.15	6.50	15.00

NOTE: *Most copies have brittle edges.*

FLASH GORDON
June, 1965
Gold Key

	Good	Fine	N-Mint
1 (1947 reprint)-Painted-c	2.00	6.00	14.00

FLASH GORDON (Also see Comics Reading Libraries)
9/66 – #11, 12/67; #12, 2/69 – #18, 1/70; #19, 10-11/78 – #37, 3/82
(Painted covers No. 19-30, 34)
King #1-11/Charlton #12-18/Gold Key #19-23/Whitman #24 on

	Good	Fine	N-Mint
1-Army giveaway(1968)("Complimentary" on cover)(Same as regular #1 minus Mandrake story & back-c)	1.30	4.00	9.00
1-Williamson c/a(2); E.C. swipe/Incred. S.F. 32. Mandrake story	1.70	5.00	12.00
2-Bolle, Gil Kane-c/a; Mandrake story	1.30	4.00	9.00
3-Williamson-c	1.50	4.50	10.00
4-Secret Agent X-9 begins, Williamson-c/a(3)	1.50	4.50	10.00
5-Williamson c/a(2)	1.50	4.50	10.00
6,8-Crandall-a. 8-Secret Agent X-9-r	2.00	6.00	14.00
7-Raboy-a	1.50	4.50	10.00
9,10-Raymond-r. 10-Buckler's 1st pro work (11/67)	1.70	5.00	12.00
11-Crandall-a	1.15	3.50	8.00
12-Crandall c/a	1.30	4.00	9.00
13-Jeff Jones-a	1.30	4.00	9.00
14-17: 17-Brick Bradford story	.70	2.00	4.00
18-Kaluta-a (1st pro work?)	.85	2.50	5.00
19(9/78, G.K.), 20-30(10/80)	.35	1.00	2.00
30 (7/81; re-issue)		.30	.60
31-33: Movie adaptation; Williamson-a		.50	1.00
34-37: Movie adaptation		.40	.80

NOTE: *Aparo a-8. Bolle a-21, 22. Buckler a-10. Crandall c-6. Estrada a-3. Gene Fawcette a-29, 30, 34, 37. McWilliams a-31-33, 36.*

FLASH GORDON
June, 1988 - No. 9, Holiday, 1988-'89 ($1.25, color, mini-series)
DC Comics

	Good	Fine	N-Mint
1-Painted-c	.35	1.00	2.00
2-9: 5-Painted-c	.25	.75	1.50

153

FLASH GORDON GIANT COMIC ALBUM
1972 (11x14''; cardboard covers; 48 pgs.; B&W; 59 cents)
Modern Promotions, N. Y.

	Good	Fine	N-Mint
Reprints 1968, 1969 dailies by Dan Barry	.25	.70	1.40

FLASH GORDON THE MOVIE
1980 ($1.95. color, 68pgs)
Western Publishing Co.

11294-Williamson-c/a; adapts movie	.35	1.00	2.00

FLASH SPECTACULAR, THE (See DC Special Series No. 11)

FLATTOP
11/53 - No. 3, 5/54; No. 4, 3/55 - No. 6, 7/55
Mazie Comics/Harvey Publ.(Magazine Publ.) No. 4 on

1-Teenage	1.70	5.00	12.00
2,3	1.00	3.00	7.00
4-6	.70	2.00	5.00

FLESH AND BONES
June, 1986 - No. 4, Dec, 1986 (Color, mini-series)
Upshot Graphics (Fantagraphics Books)

1-Dalgoda by Fujitake-r; Alan Moore scripts	.40	1.25	2.50
2-4: Alan Moore scripts	.35	1.00	2.00

FLINTSTONE KIDS, THE (TV; See Star Comics Digest)
Aug, 1987 - No. 11, April, 1989
Star Comics/Marvel Comics #5 on

1-11		.50	1.00

FLINTSTONES, THE (TV)(See Dell Giant #48 for No. 1)
No. 2, Nov-Dec, 1961 - No. 60, Sept, 1970 (Hanna-Barbera)
Dell Publ. Co./Gold Key No. 7 (10/62) on

2	3.70	11.00	26.00
3-6(7-8/62)	2.65	8.00	18.00
7 (10/62; 1st GK)	2.65	8.00	18.00
8-10: Mr. & Mrs. J. Evil Scientist begin?	2.30	7.00	16.00
11-1st app. Pebbles (6/63)	3.00	9.00	21.00
12-15,17-20	2.00	6.00	14.00
16-1st app. Bamm-Bamm (1/64)	2.30	7.00	16.00
21-30: 24-1st app. The Grusomes app.	1.70	5.00	12.00
31-33,35-40: 31-Xmas-c. 33-Meet Frankenstein & Dracula.			
39-Reprints	1.50	4.50	10.00
34-1st app. The Great Gazoo	2.00	6.00	14.00
41-60: 45-Last 12 cent issue	1.30	4.00	9.00
At N. Y. World's Fair('64)-J.W. Books(25 cents)-1st printing; no date			
on-c (29 cent version exists, 2nd print?)	2.30	7.00	16.00
At N. Y. World's Fair (1965 on-c; re-issue). NOTE: Warehouse find in			
1984	.50	1.50	3.00
Bigger & Boulder 1(#30013-211) (Gold Key Giant, 11/62, 25 cents,			
84 pgs.)	3.70	11.00	26.00
Bigger & Boulder 2-(25 cents)(1966)-reprints B&B No. 1			
	3.15	9.50	22.00
...With Pebbles & Bamm Bamm(100 pgs., G.K.)-30028-511 (paper-			
c, 25 cents)(11/65)	3.15	9.50	22.00

NOTE: (See Comic Album #16, Bamm-Bamm & Pebbles Flintstone, Dell Giant 48, March of Comics #229, 243, 271, 289, 299, 317, 327, 341, Pebbles Flintstone, and Whitman Comic Books.)

FLINTSTONES, THE (TV)(. . .& Pebbles)
Nov, 1970 - No. 50, Feb, 1977 (Hanna-Barbera)
Charlton Comics

1	1.70	5.00	12.00
2	1.00	3.00	6.00
3-7,9,10	.85	2.50	5.00
8-''Flintstones Summer Vacation,'' 52 pgs. (Summer, 1971)			
	1.00	3.00	6.00
11-20	.70	2.00	4.00
21-50: 37-Byrne text illos (1st work). 42-Byrne-a, 2pgs.			

	Good	Fine	N-Mint
	.50	1.50	3.00

(Also see Barney & Betty Rubble, Dino, The Great Gazoo, & Pebbles & Bamm-Bamm)

FLINTSTONES, THE (TV)(See Yogi Bear, 3rd series)
October, 1977 - No. 9, Feb, 1979 (Hanna-Barbera)
Marvel Comics Group

1-9: Yogi Bear app. 4-The Jetsons app.		.50	1.00

FLINTSTONES CHRISTMAS PARTY, THE (See The Funtastic World of Hanna-Barbera No. 1)

FLINTSTONES IN 3-D, THE (See Blackthorne 3-D Series #19, 22, 36, 42)

FLIP
April, 1954 - No. 2, June, 1954 (Satire)
Harvey Publications

1,2-Nostrand-a each. 2-Powell-a	8.50	25.50	60.00

FLIPPER (TV)
April, 1966 - No. 3, Nov, 1967 (Photo-c)
Gold Key

1	2.30	7.00	16.00
2,3	1.70	5.00	12.00

FLIPPITY & FLOP
12-1/51-52 - No. 46, 8-10/59; No. 47, 9-11/60
National Periodical Publ. (Signal Publ. Co.)

1	11.50	34.00	80.00
2	5.70	17.00	40.00
3-5	4.30	13.00	30.00
6-10	3.70	11.00	26.00
11-20: 20-Last precode (3/55)	2.65	8.00	18.00
21-47	1.60	4.70	11.00

FLOYD FARLAND (See Eclipse Graphic Album Series #11)

FLY, THE (Also see Blue Ribbon Comics)
May, 1983 - No. 9, Oct, 1984 (See The Advs. of . . .)
Archie Enterprises, Inc.

1-Mr. Justice app; origin Shield		.50	1.00
2-9: 2-Flygirl app.		.40	.80

NOTE: Buckler a-1, 2. Ditko a-2-9; c-4p-8p. Nebres c-4, 5i, 6, 7i. Steranko c-1-3.

FLY BOY (Also see Approved Comics)
Spring, 1952 - No. 4, 1953
Ziff-Davis Publ. Co. (Approved)

1-Saunders painted-c	5.70	17.00	40.00
2-Saunders painted-c	3.70	11.00	26.00
3,4-Saunders painted-c	2.65	8.00	18.00

FLYING ACES
July, 1955 - No. 5, March, 1956
Key Publications

1	1.70	5.00	12.00
2-5: 2-Trapani-a	1.00	3.00	7.00

FLYING A'S RANGE RIDER, THE (TV) (See Western Roundup under Dell Giants)
#404, 6-7/52; #2, June-Aug, 1953 - #24, Aug, 1959 (All photo-c)
Dell Publishing Co.

F.C. 404(#1)-Titled ''The Range Rider''	5.50	16.50	38.00
2	4.00	12.00	28.00
3-10	3.50	10.50	24.00
11-16,18-24	3.00	9.00	21.00
17-Toth-a	3.70	11.00	26.00

FLYING CADET (WW II Plane Photos)
Jan, 1943 - V2#8, 1947 (½ photos, ½ comics)
Flying Cadet Publishing Co.

V1#1	5.70	17.00	40.00
2	2.85	8.50	20.00

The Flintstones #16 (Gold Key), © Hanna-Barbera

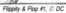

Flippity & Flop #1, © DC

Fly Boy #1, © Z-D

Football Thrills #1, © Z-D   Forbidden Love #2, © QUA   Forbidden Worlds #1, © ACG

	Good	Fine	N-Mint
FLYING CADET (continued)			
3-9 (Two #6's, Sept. & Oct.)	2.30	7.00	16.00
V2#1-7(#10-16)	1.70	5.00	12.00
8(#17)-Bare-breasted woman-c	5.70	17.00	40.00
FLYIN' JENNY			
1946 - No. 2, 1947 (1945 strip reprints)			
Pentagon Publ. Co.			
nn	5.50	16.50	40.00
2-Baker-c	6.50	19.50	45.00
FLYING MODELS			
V61#3, May, 1954 (16 pgs.) (5 cents)			
H-K Publ. (Health-Knowledge Publs.)			
V61#3 (Rare)	3.50	10.50	24.00
FLYING NUN (TV)			
Feb, 1968 - No. 4, Nov, 1968			
Dell Publishing Co.			
1	1.70	5.00	12.00
2-4: 2-Sally Fields photo-c	1.15	3.50	8.00
FLYING NURSES (See Sue & Sally Smith...)			
FLYING SAUCERS			
1950 - 1953			
Avon Periodicals/Realistic			
1(1950)-Wood-a, 21 pgs.; Fawcette-c	36.00	110.00	255.00
nn(1952)-Cover altered plus 2 pgs. of Wood-a not in original			
	34.00	100.00	235.00
nn(1953)-Reprints above	18.50	56.00	130.00
FLYING SAUCERS (Comics)			
April, 1967 - No. 4, Nov, 1967; No. 5, Oct, 1969			
Dell Publishing Co.			
1	1.00	3.00	7.00
2-5	.70	2.00	4.00
FLY MAN (Formerly Adventures of The Fly; Mighty Comics #40 on)			
No. 32, July, 1965 - No. 39, Sept, 1966 (Also see Mighty Crusaders)			
Mighty Comics Group (Radio Comics) (Archie)			
32,33-Comet, Shield, Black Hood, The Fly & Flygirl x-over; re-intro.			
Wizard, Hangman #33	1.50	4.50	10.00
34-36: 34-Shield begins. 35-Origin Black Hood. 36-Hangman x-over			
in Shield; re-intro. & origin of Web	1.50	4.50	10.00
37-39: 37-Hangman, Wizard x-over in Flyman; last Shield issue. 38-			
Web story. 39-Steel Sterling story	1.50	4.50	10.00
FOES			
1989 - No. 8 ($1.95, color, mini-series)			
Ram Comics			
1-3	.35	1.00	2.00
FOLLOW THE SUN (TV)			
May-July, 1962 - No. 2, Sept-Nov, 1962 (Photo-c)			
Dell Publishing Co.			
01-280-207(No.1), 12-280-211(No.2)	2.30	7.00	16.00
FOODINI (TV)(The Great...; see Jingle Dingle & Pinhead &...)			
March, 1950 - No. 5, 1950			
Continental Publications (Holyoke)			
1 (52 pgs.)	5.70	17.00	40.00
2	2.85	8.50	20.00
3-5	2.00	6.00	14.00
FOOEY (Magazine) (Satire)			
Feb, 1961 - No. 4, May, 1961			
Scoff Publishing Co.			
1	1.50	4.50	10.00
2-4	.85	2.60	6.00

	Good	Fine	N-Mint
FOOFUR (TV)			
Aug, 1987 - No. 6, June, 1988			
Star Comics/Marvel Comics No. 5 on			
1-6		.50	1.00
FOOTBALL THRILLS (See Tops In Adventure)			
Fall-Winter, 1951-52 - No. 2, Fall, 1952			
Ziff-Davis Publ. Co.			
1-Powell a(2); Saunders painted-c. Red Grange, Jim Thorpe app.			
	10.00	30.00	70.00
2-Saunders painted-c	6.50	19.50	45.00
FOR A NIGHT OF LOVE			
1951			
Avon Periodicals			
nn-Two stories adapted from the works of Emile Zola; Astarita,			
Ravielli-a; Kinstler-c	16.00	48.00	110.00
FORBIDDEN LOVE			
Mar, 1950 - No. 4, Sept, 1950			
Quality Comics Group			
1-(Scarce)Classic photo-c; Crandall-a	50.00	150.00	350.00
2,3(Scarce)-Photo-c	22.00	65.00	150.00
4-(Scarce)Ward/Cuidera-a; photo-c	24.00	72.00	170.00
FORBIDDEN LOVE (See Dark Mansion of...)			
FORBIDDEN TALES OF DARK MANSION (Dark Mansion of Forbid-			
den Love #1-4)			
No. 5, May-June, 1972 - No. 15, Feb-Mar, 1974			
National Periodical Publications			
5-15: 13-Kane/Howard-a		.25	.50
NOTE: *Adams* c-9. *Alcala* a-9-11, 13. *Chaykin* a-7,15. *Evans* a-14. *Kaluta* c-7-11, 13. *G.*			
Kane a-13. *Kirby* a-6. *Nino* a-8, 12, 15. *Redondo* a-14.			
FORBIDDEN WORLDS			
7-8/51 - No. 34, 10-11/54; No. 35, 8/55 - No. 145, 8/67			
(No. 1-5: 52 pgs.; No. 6-8: 44 pgs.)			
American Comics Group			
1-Williamson/Frazetta-a, 10pgs.	55.00	165.00	385.00
2	22.00	65.00	155.00
3-Williamson/Wood/Orlando-a, 7pgs.	26.00	77.00	180.00
4	12.00	36.00	85.00
5-Williamson/Krenkel-a, 8pgs.	21.50	65.00	150.00
6-Harrison/Williamson-a, 8pgs.	19.00	58.00	135.00
7,8,10	8.50	25.50	60.00
9-A-Bomb explosion story	9.30	28.00	65.00
11-20	5.70	17.00	40.00
21-33: 24-E.C. swipe by Landau	4.00	12.00	28.00
34(10-11/54)(Becomes Young Heroes #35 on)-Last pre-code issue;			
A-Bomb explosion story	4.00	12.00	28.00
35(8/55)-62	2.15	6.50	15.00
63,69,76,78-Williamson-a in all; w/Krenkel #69	3.50	10.50	24.00
64,66-68,70-72,74,75,77,79-90	1.50	4.50	10.00
65-"There's a New Moon Tonight" listed in #114 as holding 1st			
record fan mail response	1.70	5.00	12.00
73-Intro./1st app. Herbie by Whitney	14.00	42.00	100.00
91-93,95,97-100	1.00	3.00	7.00
94-Herbie app.	4.00	12.00	24.00
96-Williamson-a	2.00	6.00	14.00
101-109,111-113,115,117-120	.85	2.50	5.00
110,114,116-Herbie app. 114 contains list of editor's top 20 ACG			
stories	2.00	6.00	14.00
121-124: 124-Magic Agent app.	.70	2.00	4.00
125-Magic Agent app.; intro. & origin Magicman series, ends #141			
	1.00	3.00	7.00
126-130	.85	2.50	5.00
131,132,134-141: 136-Nemesis x-over in Magicman. 140-Mark Mid-			
night app. by Ditko	.70	2.00	4.00

FORBIDDEN WORLDS (continued) Good Fine N-Mint
133-Origin & 1st app. Dragonia in Magicman (1-2/66); returns #138
.70 2.00 4.00
142-145 .50 1.50 3.00
NOTE: *Buscema* a-75, 79, 81, 82, 140r. *Disbrow* a-10. *Ditko* a-137p, 138, 140. *Landau* a-24, 27-29, 31-34, 48, 86r, 96, 143-45 *Lazarus* a-18, 23, 24, 57. *Moldoff* a-27, 31, 139r. *Whitney* a-115, 116, 137; c-40, 46, 57, 60, 68, 78, 79, 90, 93, 94, 100, 102, 103, 106-108, 114, 129.

FORCE, THE (See The Crusaders)

FORCE OF BUDDHA'S PALM THE
Aug, 1988 - Present ($1.50-$1.95, color, 64 pgs.)
Jademan Comics

1-8 ($1.50)-Kung Fu stories .25 .75 1.50
9-18 ($1.95) .35 1.00 2.00

FORD ROTUNDA CHRISTMAS BOOK (See Christmas at the Rotunda)

FOREIGN INTRIGUES (Formerly Johnny Dynamite; Battlefield Action No. 16 on)
No. 13, 1956 - No. 15, Aug, 1956
Charlton Comics

13-15-Johnny Dynamite continues 2.00 6.00 14.00

FOREMOST BOYS (See Four Most)

FOREST FIRE (Also see Smokey The Bear)
1949 (dated-1950) (16 pgs., paper-c)
American Forestry Assn.(Commerical Comics)

nn-Intro/1st app. Smokey The Forest Fire Preventing Bear; created by Rudy Wendelein; Wendelein/Sparling-a; 'Carter Oil Co.' on back-c of original 10.00 30.00 70.00

FOREVER, DARLING (See 4-Color No. 681)

FOREVER PEOPLE
Feb-Mar, 1971 - No. 11, Oct-Nov, 1972
National Periodical Publications

1-Superman x-over; Kirby-c/a begins .90 2.75 5.50
2-11: 4-G.A.-r begin, end No. 9 .40 1.25 2.50
NOTE: *Kirby* c/a(p)-1-11; #4-9 contain Sandman reprints from Adventure #85, 84, 75, 80, 77, 74 in that order. #1-3, 10-11 are 36pgs; #4-9 are 52pgs.

FOREVER PEOPLE
Feb, 1988 - No. 6, July, 1988 ($1.25, mini-series)
DC Comics

1-6 .25 .75 1.50

FOR GIRLS ONLY
Nov, 1953 (Digest size, 100 pgs.)
Bernard Bailey Enterprises

1-½ comic book, ½ magazine 6.00 18.00 42.00

FORGOTTEN FOREST OF OZ, THE (See First Comics Graphic Novel #16)

FORGOTTEN REALMS
Sept, 1989 - Present ($1.50, color)
DC Comics

1-8: Based on TSR role-playing game .25 .75 1.50

FORGOTTEN STORY BEHIND NORTH BEACH, THE
No date (8 pgs.; paper cover)
Catechetical Guild

nn 3.00 9.00 18.00

FOR LOVERS ONLY (Formerly Hollywood Romances)
No. 60, Aug, 1971 - No. 87, Nov, 1976
Charlton Comics

60-87 .25 .50

40 BIG PAGES OF MICKEY MOUSE
1936 (44 pgs.; 10¼x12½''; cardboard cover)
Whitman Publishing Co.

945-Reprints Mickey Mouse Magazine #1, but with a different cover. Ads were eliminated and some illustrated stories had expanded text. The book is ¾'' shorter than Mickey Mouse Mag. #1, but the reprints are the same size. (Rare) 50.00 150.00 350.00

48 FAMOUS AMERICANS
1947 (Giveaway) (Half-size in color)
J. C. Penney Co. (Cpr. Edwin R. Stroh)

Simon & Kirby-a 6.75 20.00 40.00

FOR YOUR EYES ONLY (See James Bond . . .)

FOUR COLOR
Sept?, 1939 - No. 1354, Apr-June, 1962
Dell Publishing Co.
NOTE: *Four Color only appears on issues #19-25, 1-99,101. Dell Publishing Co. filed these as Series I, #1-25, and Series II, #1-1354. Issues beginning with #710? were printed with and without ads on back cover. Issues without ads are worth more.*

SERIES I:
	Good	Fine	N-Mint
1(nn)-Dick Tracy	128.00	385.00	900.00
2(nn)-Don Winslow of the Navy (#1) (Rare) (11/39?)	72.00	215.00	500.00
3(nn)-Myra North (1/40?)	32.00	95.00	225.00
4-Donald Duck by Al Taliaferro('40)(Disney) (3/40?)	328.00	985.00	2300.00
(Prices vary widely on this book)			
5-Smilin' Jack (#1) (5/40?)	42.00	125.00	290.00
6-Dick Tracy (Scarce)	76.00	230.00	535.00
7-Gang Busters	21.50	65.00	150.00
8-Dick Tracy	50.00	150.00	350.00
9-Terry and the Pirates-r/Super #9-29	43.00	130.00	300.00
10-Smilin' Jack	39.00	116.00	270.00
11-Smitty (#1)	24.00	71.00	165.00
12-Little Orphan Annie	34.00	100.00	235.00
13-Walt Disney's Reluctant Dragon('41)-Contains 2 pages of photos from film; 2 pg. foreword to Fantasia by Leopold Stokowski; Donald Duck, Goofy, Baby Weems & Mickey Mouse (as the Sorcerer's Apprentice) app. (Disney)	82.00	245.00	575.00
14-Moon Mullins (#1)	21.00	62.00	145.00
15-Tillie the Toiler (#1)	21.00	62.00	145.00

	Good	Fine	VF-NM
16-Mickey Mouse (#1) (Disney) by Gottfredson	343.00	1030.00	2400.00
(Prices vary widely on this book)			

	Good	Fine	N-Mint
17-Walt Disney's Dumbo, the Flying Elephant (#1)(1941)-Mickey Mouse, Donald Duck, & Pluto app. (Disney)	82.00	245.00	575.00
18-Jiggs and Maggie (#1)(1936-'38-r)	21.50	64.00	150.00
19-Barney Google and Snuffy Smith (#1)-(1st issue with Four Color on the cover)	24.00	73.00	170.00
20-Tiny Tim	21.00	62.00	145.00
21-Dick Tracy	44.00	132.00	310.00
22-Don Winslow	17.00	51.00	120.00
23-Gang Busters	16.50	50.00	115.00
24-Captain Easy	21.00	62.00	145.00
25-Popeye	41.00	121.00	285.00

SERIES II:
	Good	Fine	N-Mint
1-Little Joe	29.00	85.00	200.00
2-Harold Teen	16.50	50.00	115.00
3-Alley Oop (#1)	34.00	100.00	240.00
4-Smilin' Jack	31.00	92.00	215.00
5-Raggedy Ann and Andy (#1)	34.00	102.00	235.00
6-Smitty	13.00	40.00	90.00
7-Smokey Stover (#1)	22.00	65.00	155.00
8-Tillie the Toiler	13.00	40.00	90.00
9-Donald Duck Finds Pirate Gold, by Carl Barks & Jack Hannah			

Forever People #8 (1st series), © DC

Four Color #11 (1st series), © N.Y. News Synd.

Four Color #16 (1st series), © WDC

Four Color #10 (2nd series), © KING

Four Color #20 (2nd series), © KING

Four Color #88, © Warner Bros.

	Good	Fine	N-Mint
FOUR COLOR (continued)	370.00	1115.00	2600.00
(Disney) (c. 8/17/42)			
(Prices vary widely on this book)			
10-Flash Gordon by Alex Raymond; r-/from ''The Ice Kingdom''			
	55.00	165.00	385.00
11-Wash Tubbs	19.00	58.00	135.00
12-Walt Disney's Bambi (#1); reprinted in Gladstone Comic Album #9			
	34.00	102.00	240.00
13-Mr. District Attorney (#1)-See The Funnies #35 for 1st app.			
	16.00	48.00	110.00
14-Smilin' Jack	25.00	75.00	175.00
15-Felix the Cat (#1)	40.00	120.00	280.00
16-Porky Pig (#1)(1942)-''Secret of the Haunted House''			
	38.00	114.00	265.00
17-Popeye	34.00	100.00	235.00
18-Little Orphan Annie's Junior Commandos; Flag-c			
	25.00	75.00	175.00
19-Walt Disney's Thumper Meets the Seven Dwarfs (Disney); r-in			
Silly Symphonies	37.00	110.00	260.00
20-Barney Baxter	16.00	48.00	110.00
21-Oswald the Rabbit (#1)(1943)	22.00	65.00	154.00
22-Tillie the Toiler	10.00	30.00	70.00
23-Raggedy Ann and Andy	24.00	73.00	170.00
24-Gang Busters	16.50	50.00	115.00
25-Andy Panda (#1) (Walter Lantz)	26.00	77.00	180.00
26-Popeye	31.00	92.00	215.00
27-Walt Disney's Mickey Mouse and the Seven Colored Terror			
	50.00	150.00	350.00
28-Wash Tubbs	14.00	42.00	100.00
29-Donald Duck and the Mummy's Ring, by Carl Barks (Disney)			
(9/43)	243.00	730.00	1700.00
(Prices vary widely on this book)			
30-Bambi's Children(1943)-Disney	34.00	102.00	235.00
31-Moon Mullins	12.00	36.00	84.00
32-Smitty	11.00	32.00	76.00
33-Bugs Bunny ''Public Nuisance #1''	32.00	95.00	220.00
34-Dick Tracy	32.00	95.00	220.00
35-Smokey Stover	11.50	34.00	80.00
36-Smilin' Jack	14.00	42.00	100.00
37-Bringing Up Father	12.00	36.00	84.00
38-Roy Rogers (#1, c. 4/44)-1st western comic with photo-c			
	50.00	150.00	350.00
39-Oswald the Rabbit('44)	16.00	48.00	110.00
40-Barney Google and Snuffy Smith	13.00	40.00	90.00
41-Mother Goose and Nursery Rhyme Comics (#1)-All by Kelly			
	18.00	54.00	125.00
42-Tiny Tim (1934-r)	11.50	34.00	80.00
43-Popeye (1938-'42-r)	21.00	62.00	145.00
44-Terry and the Pirates ('38-r)	26.00	78.00	185.00
45-Raggedy Ann	20.00	60.00	140.00
46-Felix the Cat and the Haunted Castle	28.00	84.00	195.00
47-Gene Autry (© 6/16/44)	34.00	100.00	240.00
48-Porky Pig of the Mounties by Carl Barks (7/44)			
	70.00	210.00	490.00
49-Snow White and the Seven Dwarfs (Disney)			
	28.00	84.00	195.00
50-Fairy Tale Parade-Walt Kelly art (1944)	21.50	64.00	150.00
51-Bugs Bunny Finds the Lost Treasure	18.50	56.00	130.00
52-Little Orphan Annie	19.00	57.00	135.00
53-Wash Tubbs	10.00	30.00	70.00
54-Andy Panda	16.00	48.00	110.00
55-Tillie the Toiler	8.00	24.00	56.00
56-Dick Tracy	24.00	72.00	165.00
57-Gene Autry	28.00	84.00	195.00
58-Smilin' Jack	14.00	42.00	100.00
59-Mother Goose and Nursery Rhyme Comics-Kelly c/a			
	16.00	48.00	110.00

	Good	Fine	N-Mint
60-Tiny Folks Funnies	10.00	30.00	70.00
61-Santa Claus Funnies(11/44)-Kelly art	20.00	60.00	140.00
62-Donald Duck in Frozen Gold, by Carl Barks (Disney) (1/45)			
	120.00	360.00	840.00
63-Roy Rogers-Photo-c	34.00	100.00	235.00
64-Smokey Stover	8.50	25.50	60.00
65-Smitty	8.50	25.50	60.00
66-Gene Autry	28.00	84.00	195.00
67-Oswald the Rabbit	11.00	32.00	75.00
68-Mother Goose and Nursery Rhyme Comics, by Walt Kelly			
	16.00	48.00	110.00
69-Fairy Tale Parade, by Walt Kelly	18.50	56.00	130.00
70-Popeye and Wimpy	17.00	51.00	120.00
71-Walt Disney's Three Caballeros, by Walt Kelly(c. 4/45)-(Disney)			
	60.00	180.00	420.00
72-Raggedy Ann	16.50	50.00	115.00
73-The Gumps (No.1)	6.50	19.50	45.00
74-Marge's Little Lulu (No.1)	90.00	270.00	630.00
75-Gene Autry and the Wildcat	23.00	70.00	165.00
76-Little Orphan Annie	16.00	48.00	110.00
77-Felix the Cat	24.00	72.00	170.00
78-Porky Pig and the Bandit Twins	14.00	42.00	100.00
79-Walt Disney's Mickey Mouse in The Riddle of the Red Hat by Carl			
Barks(8/45)	64.00	193.00	450.00
80-Smilin' Jack	11.50	34.00	80.00
81-Moon Mullins	6.50	19.50	45.00
82-Lone Ranger	28.50	86.00	200.00
83-Gene Autry in Outlaw Trail	23.00	70.00	165.00
84-Flash Gordon by Alex Raymond-Reprints from ''The Fiery			
Desert''	33.00	100.00	230.00
85-Andy Panda and the Mad Dog Mystery	10.00	30.00	70.00
86-Roy Rogers-Photo-c	25.00	75.00	175.00
87-Fairy Tale Parade by Walt Kelly; Dan Noonan cover			
	16.50	50.00	115.00
88-Bugs Bunny's Great Adventure	11.50	34.00	80.00
89-Tillie the Toiler	7.00	21.00	50.00
90-Christmas with Mother Goose by Walt Kelly (11/45)			
	15.00	45.00	105.00
91-Santa Claus Funnies by Walt Kelly (11/45)	14.00	42.00	100.00
92-Walt Disney's The Wonderful Adventures Of Pinocchio(1945);			
Donald Duck by Kelly, 16 pgs. (Disney)	25.00	75.00	175.00
93-Gene Autry in The Bandit of Black Rock	19.00	58.00	135.00
94-Winnie Winkle (1945)	8.50	25.50	60.00
95-Roy Rogers Comics-Photo-c	25.00	75.00	175.00
96-Dick Tracy	18.00	54.00	125.00
97-Marge's Little Lulu (1946)	47.00	140.00	330.00
98-Lone Ranger, The	23.50	71.00	165.00
99-Smitty	7.00	21.00	50.00
100-Gene Autry Comics-Photo-c	19.00	58.00	135.00
101-Terry and the Pirates	17.00	51.00	120.00

NOTE: No. 101 is last issue to carry ''Four Color'' logo on cover; all issues beginning with No. 100 are marked ''...O. S.'' (One Shot) which can be found in the bottom left-hand panel on the first page; the numbers following ''O. S.'' relate to the year/month issued.

	Good	Fine	N-Mint
102-Oswald the Rabbit-Walt Kelly art, 1 pg.	9.50	28.50	65.00
103-Easter with Mother Goose by Walt Kelly	14.00	42.00	100.00
104-Fairy Tale Parade by Walt Kelly	14.00	42.00	100.00
105-Albert the Alligator and Pogo Possum (No.1) by Kelly (4/46)			
	57.00	171.00	400.00
106-Tillie the Toiler	5.70	17.00	40.00
107-Little Orphan Annie	13.00	40.00	90.00
108-Donald Duck in The Terror of the River, by Carl Barks (Disney)			
(c. 4/16/46)	90.00	270.00	630.00
109-Roy Rogers Comics	19.00	57.00	135.00
110-Marge's Little Lulu	33.00	100.00	230.00
111-Captain Easy	8.50	25.50	60.00

	Good	Fine	N-Mint
FOUR COLOR (continued)			
112-Porky Pig's Adventure in Gopher Gulch	8.50	25.50	60.00
113-Popeye	9.30	28.00	65.00
114-Fairy Tale Parade by Walt Kelly	14.00	42.00	100.00
115-Marge's Little Lulu	33.00	100.00	230.00
116-Mickey Mouse and the House of Many Mysteries (Disney)	17.00	51.00	120.00
117-Roy Rogers Comics-Photo-c	14.00	42.00	100.00
118-Lone Ranger, The	23.50	71.00	165.00
119-Felix the Cat	18.00	54.00	125.00
120-Marge's Little Lulu	30.00	90.00	210.00
121-Fairy Tale Parade-(not Kelly)	8.50	25.50	60.00
122-Henry (No.1)(10/46)	5.50	16.50	40.00
123-Bugs Bunny's Dangerous Venture	6.50	19.50	45.00
124-Roy Rogers Comics-Photo-c	14.00	42.00	100.00
125-Lone Ranger, The	17.00	51.00	120.00
126-Christmas with Mother Goose by Walt Kelly (1946)	12.00	36.00	84.00
127-Popeye	9.30	28.00	65.00
128-Santa Claus Funnies-''Santa & the Angel'' by Gollub; ''A Mouse in the House'' by Kelly	12.00	36.00	84.00
129-Walt Disney's Uncle Remus and His Tales of Brer Rabbit (No.1) (1946)	12.00	36.00	84.00
130-Andy Panda (Walter Lantz)	5.00	15.00	35.00
131-Marge's Little Lulu	30.00	90.00	210.00
132-Tillie the Toiler('47)	5.70	17.00	40.00
133-Dick Tracy	15.00	45.00	105.00
134-Tarzan and the Devil Ogre	40.00	120.00	280.00
135-Felix the Cat	14.00	42.00	100.00
136-Lone Ranger, The	17.00	51.00	120.00
137-Roy Rogers Comics-Photo-c	14.00	42.00	100.00
138-Smitty	6.50	19.50	45.00
139-Marge's Little Lulu (1947)	27.00	81.00	190.00
140-Easter with Mother Goose by Walt Kelly	12.00	36.00	84.00
141-Mickey Mouse and the Submarine Pirates (Disney)	16.00	48.00	110.00
142-Bugs Bunny and the Haunted Mountain	6.50	19.50	45.00
143-Oswald the Rabbit & the Prehistoric Egg	4.30	13.00	30.00
144-Roy Rogers Comics ('47)-Photo-c	14.00	42.00	100.00
145-Popeye	9.30	28.00	65.00
146-Marge's Little Lulu	27.00	81.00	190.00
147-Donald Duck in Volcano Valley, by Carl Barks (Disney)(5/47)	60.00	180.00	420.00
148-Albert the Alligator and Pogo Possum by Walt Kelly (5/47)	47.00	141.00	330.00
149-Smilin' Jack	8.50	25.50	60.00
150-Tillie the Toiler (6/47)	4.30	13.00	30.00
151-Lone Ranger, The	14.00	42.00	100.00
152-Little Orphan Annie	9.30	28.00	65.00
153-Roy Rogers Comics-Photo-c	11.50	34.00	80.00
154-Walter Lantz Andy Panda	5.00	15.00	35.00
155-Henry (7/47)	4.30	13.00	30.00
156-Porky Pig and the Phantom	6.50	19.50	45.00
157-Mickey Mouse & the Beanstalk (Disney)	16.00	48.00	110.00
158-Marge's Little Lulu	27.00	81.00	190.00
159-Donald Duck in the Ghost of the Grotto, by Carl Barks (Disney) (8/47)	54.00	160.00	375.00
160-Roy Rogers Comics-Photo-c	11.50	34.00	80.00
161-Tarzan and the Fires Of Tohr	35.00	105.00	245.00
162-Felix the Cat (9/47)	11.00	32.00	75.00
163-Dick Tracy	12.00	36.00	84.00
164-Bugs Bunny Finds the Frozen Kingdom	6.50	19.50	45.00
165-Marge's Little Lulu	27.00	81.00	190.00
166-Roy Rogers Comics-52 pgs.,Photo-c	11.50	34.00	80.00
167-Lone Ranger, The	14.00	42.00	100.00
168-Popeye (10/47)	9.30	28.00	65.00
169-Woody Woodpecker (No.1)-''Manhunter in the North''; drug use			
story	7.00	21.00	50.00
170-Mickey Mouse on Spook's Island (11/47)(Disney)-reprinted in Mickey Mouse No. 103	13.00	40.00	90.00
171-Charlie McCarthy (No.1) and the Twenty Thieves	9.30	28.00	65.00
172-Christmas with Mother Goose by Walt Kelly (11/47)	12.00	36.00	84.00
173-Flash Gordon	11.50	34.00	80.00
174-Winnie Winkle	5.00	15.00	35.00
175-Santa Claus Funnies by Walt Kelly ('47)	12.00	36.00	84.00
176-Tillie the Toiler (12/47)	4.30	13.00	30.00
177-Roy Rogers Comics-36 pgs, Photo-c	11.50	34.00	80.00
178-Donald Duck ''Christmas on Bear Mountain'' by Carl Barks; 1st app. Uncle Scrooge (Disney)(12/47)	64.00	192.00	450.00
179-Uncle Wiggily (No.1)-Walt Kelly-c	9.00	27.00	62.00
180-Ozark Ike (No.1)	6.00	18.00	42.00
181-Walt Disney's Mickey Mouse in Jungle Magic	13.00	40.00	90.00
182-Porky Pig in Never-Never Land (2/48)	6.50	19.50	45.00
183-Oswald the Rabbit (Lantz)	4.30	13.00	30.00
184-Tillie the Toiler	4.30	13.00	30.00
185-Easter with Mother Goose by Walt Kelly (1948)	11.50	34.00	80.00
186-Walt Disney's Bambi (4/48)-Reprinted as Movie Classic Bambi #3('56)	8.00	24.00	56.00
187-Bugs Bunny and the Dreadful Dragon	5.50	16.50	38.00
188-Woody Woodpecker (Lantz, 5/48)	5.00	15.00	35.00
189-Donald Duck in The Old Castle's Secret, by Carl Barks (Disney) (6/48)	54.00	160.00	375.00
190-Flash Gordon ('48)	11.50	34.00	80.00
191-Porky Pig to the Rescue	6.50	19.50	45.00
192-The Brownies (No.1)-by Walt Kelly (7/48)	11.50	34.00	80.00
193-M.G.M. Presents Tom and Jerry (No.1)(1948)	8.00	24.00	56.00
194-Mickey Mouse in The World Under the Sea (Disney)-Reprinted in Mickey Mouse No. 101	13.00	40.00	90.00
195-Tillie the Toiler	3.70	11.00	26.00
196-Charlie McCarthy in The Haunted Hide-Out	8.00	24.00	56.00
197-Spirit of the Border (No.1) (Zane Grey) (1948)	6.00	18.00	42.00
198-Andy Panda	5.00	15.00	35.00
199-Donald Duck in Sheriff of Bullet Valley, by Carl Barks; Barks draws himself on wanted poster, last page; used in **Love & Death** (Disney) (10/48)	54.00	160.00	375.00
200-Bugs Bunny, Super Sleuth (10/48)	5.00	15.00	35.00
201-Christmas with Mother Goose by Walt Kelly	11.00	32.00	76.00
202-Woody Woodpecker	3.00	9.00	21.00
203-Donald Duck in the Golden Christmas Tree, by Carl Barks (Disney) (12/48)	36.00	108.00	250.00
204-Flash Gordon (12/48)	9.00	27.00	62.00
205-Santa Claus Funnies by Walt Kelly	11.00	32.00	76.00
206-Little Orphan Annie	5.70	17.00	40.00
207-King of the Royal Mounted	11.50	34.00	80.00
208-Brer Rabbit Does It Again (Disney)(1/49)	7.00	21.00	50.00
209-Harold Teen	2.30	7.00	16.00
210-Tippie and Cap Stubbs	2.30	7.00	16.00
211-Little Beaver (No.1)	3.00	9.00	21.00
212-Dr. Bobbs	2.30	7.00	16.00
213-Tillie the Toiler	3.70	11.00	26.00
214-Mickey Mouse and His Sky Adventure (2/49)(Disney)-Reprinted in Mickey Mouse No. 105	10.00	30.00	70.00
215-Sparkle Plenty (Dick Tracy reprints by Gould)	7.00	21.00	50.00
216-Andy Panda and the Police Pup (Lantz)	2.65	8.00	18.00

Four Color #119, © KING

Four Color #140, © DELL

Four Color #208, © WDC

Four Color #227, © WDC

Four Color #247, © KING

Four Color #303, © Warner Bros.

FOUR COLOR (continued)

	Good	Fine	N-Mint
217-Bugs Bunny in Court Jester	5.50	16.50	38.00
218-3 Little Pigs and the Wonderful Magic Lamp (Disney)(3/49)	6.50	19.50	45.00
219-Swee'pea	6.50	19.50	45.00
220-Easter with Mother Goose by Walt Kelly	11.00	32.00	76.00
221-Uncle Wiggily-Walt Kelly cover in part	7.00	21.00	50.00
222-West of the Pecos (Zane Grey)	5.00	15.00	35.00
223-Donald Duck ''Lost in the Andes'' by Carl Barks (Disney-4/49) (square egg story)	50.00	150.00	350.00
224-Little Iodine (No.1), by Hatlo (4/49)	4.30	13.00	30.00
225-Oswald the Rabbit (Lantz)	2.65	8.00	18.00
226-Porky Pig and Spoofy, the Spook	4.30	13.00	30.00
227-Seven Dwarfs (Disney)	7.00	21.00	50.00
228-Mark of Zorro, The (No.1) ('49)	16.00	48.00	110.00
229-Smokey Stover	3.00	9.00	21.00
230-Sunset Pass (Zane Grey)	5.00	15.00	35.00
231-Mickey Mouse and the Rajah's Treasure (Disney)	10.00	30.00	70.00
232-Woody Woodpecker (Lantz, 6/49)	3.00	9.00	21.00
233-Bugs Bunny, Sleepwalking Sleuth	5.50	16.50	38.00
234-Dumbo in Sky Voyage (Disney)	5.70	17.00	40.00
235-Tiny Tim	3.70	11.00	26.00
236-Heritage of the Desert (Zane Grey)('49)	5.00	15.00	35.00
237-Tillie the Toiler	3.70	11.00	26.00
238-Donald Duck in Voodoo Hoodoo, by Carl Barks (Disney) (8/49)	27.00	81.00	190.00
239-Adventure Bound (8/49)	2.30	7.00	16.00
240-Andy Panda (Lantz)	2.65	8.00	18.00
241-Porky Pig, Mighty Hunter	4.30	13.00	30.00
242-Tippie and Cap Stubbs	1.70	5.00	12.00
243-Thumper Follows His Nose (Disney)	5.70	17.00	40.00
244-The Brownies by Walt Kelly	10.00	30.00	70.00
245-Dick's Adventures in Dreamland (9/49)	3.00	9.00	21.00
246-Thunder Mountain (Zane Grey)	3.70	11.00	26.00
247-Flash Gordon	9.00	27.00	62.00
248-Mickey Mouse and the Black Sorcerer (Disney)	10.00	30.00	70.00
249-Woody Woodpecker in the Globetrotter (10/49)	3.00	9.00	21.00
250-Bugs Bunny in Diamond Daze-Used in **SOTI**, pg. 309	5.50	16.50	38.00
251-Hubert at Camp Moonbeam	2.30	7.00	16.00
252-Pinocchio(Disney)-not Kelly; origin	6.50	19.50	45.00
253-Christmas with Mother Goose by Walt Kelly	9.50	28.50	65.00
254-Santa Claus Funnies by Walt Kelly; Pogo & Albert story by Kelly (11/49)	11.00	32.00	76.00
255-The Ranger (Zane Grey) (1949)	3.70	11.00	26.00
256-Donald Duck in ''Luck of the North'' by Carl Barks (Disney) (12/49)-Shows No. 257 on inside	27.00	81.00	190.00
257-Little Iodine	3.50	10.50	24.00
258-Andy Panda and the Balloon Race (Lantz)	2.65	8.00	18.00
259-Santa and the Angel (Gollub art-condensed from No. 128) & Santa at the Zoo (12/49)-two books in one	3.50	10.50	24.00
260-Porky Pig, Hero of the Wild West(12/49)	4.30	13.00	30.00
261-Mickey Mouse and the Missing Key (Disney)	10.00	30.00	70.00
262-Raggedy Ann and Andy	3.70	11.00	26.00
263-Donald Duck in ''Land of the Totem Poles'' by Carl Barks (Disney)(2/50)-has two Barks stories	27.00	81.00	190.00
264-Woody Woodpecker in the Magic Lantern (Lantz)	3.00	9.00	21.00
265-King of the Royal Mounted (Zane Grey)	8.00	24.00	56.00
266-Bugs Bunny on the Isle of Hercules''(2/50)-Reprinted in Best of Bugs Bunny No. 1	4.30	13.00	30.00
267-Little Beaver-Harmon c/a	2.00	6.00	14.00

	Good	Fine	N-Mint
268-Mickey Mouse's Surprise Visitor (1950) (Disney)	10.00	30.00	70.00
269-Johnny Mack Brown (No.1)-Photo-c	12.00	36.00	84.00
270-Drift Fence (Zane Grey) (3/50)	3.70	11.00	26.00
271-Porky Pig in Phantom of the Plains	4.30	13.00	30.00
272-Cinderella (Disney)(4/50)	4.65	14.00	32.00
273-Oswald the Rabbit (Lantz)	2.65	8.00	18.00
274-Bugs Bunny, Hare-brained Reporter	4.30	13.00	30.00
275-Donald Duck in ''Ancient Persia'' by Carl Barks (Disney) (5/50)	25.00	75.00	175.00
276-Uncle Wiggily	4.00	12.00	28.00
277-Porky Pig in Desert Adventure (5/50)	4.30	13.00	30.00
278-Bill Elliott Comics (No.1)-Photo-c	10.00	30.00	70.00
279-Mickey Mouse and Pluto Battle the Giant Ants (Disney); r-/in Mickey Mouse No. 102 & 245	8.50	25.50	60.00
280-Andy Panda in The Isle Of Mechanical Men (Lantz)	2.65	8.00	18.00
281-Bugs Bunny in The Great Circus Mystery	4.30	13.00	30.00
282-Donald Duck and the Pixilated Parrot by Carl Barks (Disney) (c. 5/23/50)	25.00	75.00	175.00
283-King of the Royal Mounted (7/50)	8.00	24.00	56.00
284-Porky Pig in The Kingdom of Nowhere	4.30	13.00	30.00
285-Bozo the Clown and His Minikin Circus (No.1)(TV)	7.00	21.00	50.00
286-Mickey Mouse in The Uninvited Guest (Disney)	8.50	25.50	60.00
287-Gene Autry's Champion in The Ghost Of Black Mountain (No.1)-Photo-c	5.70	17.00	40.00
288-Woody Woodpecker in Klondike Gold (Lantz)	3.00	9.00	21.00
289-Bugs Bunny in ''Indian Trouble''	4.30	13.00	30.00
290-The Chief	3.00	9.00	21.00
291-Donald Duck in ''The Magic Hourglass'' by Carl Barks (Disney) (9/50)	25.00	75.00	175.00
292-The Cisco Kid Comics (No.1)	9.30	28.00	65.00
293-The Brownies-Kelly c/a	9.50	28.50	65.00
294-Little Beaver	2.00	6.00	14.00
295-Porky Pig in President Porky (9/50)	4.30	13.00	30.00
296-Mickey Mouse in Private Eye for Hire (Disney)	8.50	25.50	60.00
297-Andy Panda in The Haunted Inn (Lantz, 10/50)	2.65	8.00	18.00
298-Bugs Bunny in Sheik for a Day	4.30	13.00	30.00
299-Buck Jones & the Iron Horse Trail (No.1)	8.50	25.50	60.00
300-Donald Duck in ''Big-Top Bedlam'' by Carl Barks (Disney) (11/50)	25.00	75.00	175.00
301-The Mysterious Rider (Zane Grey)	3.70	11.00	26.00
302-Santa Claus Funnies (11/50)	2.30	7.00	16.00
303-Porky Pig in The Land of the Monstrous Flies	3.00	9.00	21.00
304-Mickey Mouse in Tom-Tom Island (Disney) (12/50)	5.70	17.00	40.00
305-Woody Woodpecker (Lantz)	2.00	6.00	14.00
306-Raggedy Ann	3.00	9.00	21.00
307-Bugs Bunny in Lumber Jack Rabbit	3.50	10.50	24.00
308-Donald Duck in ''Dangerous Disguise'' by Carl Barks (Disney) (1/51)	21.00	63.00	147.00
309-Betty Betz' Dollface and Her Gang ('51)	2.30	7.00	16.00
310-King of the Royal Mounted (1/51)	5.00	15.00	35.00
311-Porky Pig in Midget Horses of Hidden Valley	3.00	9.00	21.00
312-Tonto (No.1)	8.00	24.00	56.00
313-Mickey Mouse in The Mystery of the Double-Cross Ranch (No. 1) (Disney) (2/51)	5.70	17.00	40.00
314-Ambush (Zane Grey)	3.70	11.00	26.00
315-Oswald the Rabbit (Lantz)	1.70	5.00	12.00

	Good	Fine	N-Mint
316-Rex Allen (No.1)-Photo-c; Marsh-a	11.50	34.00	80.00
317-Bugs Bunny in Hair Today Gone Tomorrow (No.1)			
	3.50	10.50	24.00
318-Donald Duck in "No Such Varmint" by Carl Barks (No. 1)			
Indicia shows #317 (Disney, c. 1/23/51)	21.00	63.00	147.00
319-Gene Autry's Champion	3.00	9.00	21.00
320-Uncle Wiggily (No. 1)	3.00	9.00	21.00
321-Little Scouts (No.1)	1.70	4.00	9.00
322-Porky Pig in Roaring Rockets (No.1)	3.00	9.00	21.00
323-Susie Q. Smith (3/51)	1.50	4.50	10.00
324-I Met a Handsome Cowboy (3/51)	4.35	13.00	30.00
325-Mickey Mouse in The Haunted Castle (No. 2)(Disney)(4/51)			
	5.70	17.00	40.00
326-Andy Panda (No. 1, Lantz)	1.70	5.00	12.00
327-Bugs Bunny and the Rajah's Treasure (No. 2)			
	3.50	10.50	24.00
328-Donald Duck in Old California (No.2) by Carl Barks-Peyote drug use issue (Disney) (5/51)	23.00	70.00	160.00
329-Roy Roger's Trigger (No.1)(5/51)-Photo-c	7.00	21.00	50.00
330-Porky Pig Meets the Bristled Bruiser (No.2)			
	3.00	9.00	21.00
331-Alice in Wonderland (Disney) (1951)	7.00	21.00	50.00
332-Little Beaver	2.00	6.00	14.00
333-Wilderness Trek (Zane Grey) (5/51)	3.70	11.00	26.00
334-Mickey Mouse and Yukon Gold (Disney) (6/51)			
	5.70	17.00	40.00
335-Francis the Famous Talking Mule (No.1)	1.70	5.00	12.00
336-Woody Woodpecker (Lantz)	2.00	6.00	14.00
337-The Brownies-not by Walt Kelly	2.65	8.00	18.00
338-Bugs Bunny and the Rocking Horse Thieves			
	3.50	10.50	24.00
339-Donald Duck and the Magic Fountain-not by Carl Barks (Disney)			
(7-8/51)	4.35	13.00	30.00
340-King of the Royal Mounted (7/51)	5.00	15.00	35.00
341-Unbirthday Party with Alice in Wonderland (Disney) (7/51)			
	7.00	21.00	50.00
342-Porky Pig the Lucky Peppermint Mine	2.30	7.00	16.00
343-Mickey Mouse in The Ruby Eye of Homar-Guy-Am (Disney)-			
Reprinted in Mickey Mouse No. 104	4.30	13.00	30.00
344-Sergeant Preston from Challenge of The Yukon (No.1)(TV)			
	5.70	17.00	40.00
345-Andy Panda in Scotland Yard (8-10/51)(Lantz)			
	1.70	5.00	12.00
346-Hideout (Zane Grey)	3.70	11.00	26.00
347-Bugs Bunny the Frigid Hare (8-9/51)	5.00	15.00	24.00
348-Donald Duck "The Crocodile Collector"-Barks-c only (Disney)			
(9-10/51)	5.00	15.00	35.00
349-Uncle Wiggily	3.00	9.00	21.00
350-Woody Woodpecker (Lantz)	2.00	6.00	14.00
351-Porky Pig and the Grand Canyon Giant (9-10/51)			
	2.30	7.00	16.00
352-Mickey Mouse in The Mystery of Painted Valley (Disney)			
	4.30	13.00	30.00
353-Duck Album (No.1)-Barks-c (Disney)	3.00	9.00	21.00
354-Raggedy Ann & Andy	3.00	9.00	21.00
355-Bugs Bunny Hot-Rod Hare	3.50	10.50	24.00
356-Donald Duck in "Rags to Riches"-Barks-c only (Disney)			
	5.00	15.00	35.00
357-Comeback (Zane Grey)	3.00	9.00	21.00
358-Andy Panda (Lantz)(11-1/52)	1.70	5.00	12.00
359-Frosty the Snowman (No.1)	3.00	9.00	21.00
360-Porky Pig in Tree of Fortune (11-12/51)	2.30	7.00	16.00
361-Santa Claus Funnies	2.30	7.00	16.00
362-Mickey Mouse and the Smuggled Diamonds (Disney)			
	4.30	13.00	30.00
363-King of the Royal Mounted	4.00	12.00	28.00

	Good	Fine	N-Mint
364-Woody Woodpecker (Lantz)	1.70	5.00	12.00
365-The Brownies-not by Kelly	2.65	8.00	18.00
366-Bugs Bunny Uncle Buckskin Comes to Town (12-1/52)			
	3.50	10.50	24.00
367-Donald Duck in "A Christmas for Shacktown" by Carl Barks			
(Disney) (1-2/52)	20.00	60.00	140.00
368-Bob Clampett's Beany and Cecil (No.1)	11.00	32.00	75.00
369-The Lone Ranger's Famous Horse Hi-Yo Silver (No.1); Silver's			
origin	5.50	16.50	38.00
370-Porky Pig in Trouble in the Big Trees	2.30	7.00	16.00
371-Mickey Mouse in The Inca Idol Case ('52) (Disney)			
	4.30	13.00	30.00
372-Riders of the Purple Sage (Zane Grey)	3.00	9.00	21.00
373-Sergeant Preston (TV)	3.70	11.00	26.00
374-Woody Woodpecker (Lantz)	1.70	5.00	12.00
375-John Carter of Mars (E. R. Burroughs)-Jesse Marsh-a; origin			
	12.00	36.00	84.00
376-Bugs Bunny, "The Magic Sneeze"	3.50	10.50	24.00
377-Susie Q. Smith	1.50	4.50	10.00
378-Tom Corbett, Space Cadet (No.1)(TV)-McWilliams-a			
	7.00	21.00	50.00
379-Donald Duck in "Southern Hospitality"-not by Barks (Disney)			
	4.35	13.00	30.00
380-Raggedy Ann & Andy	3.00	9.00	21.00
381-Marge's Tubby (No.1)	11.00	36.00	84.00
382-Snow White and the Seven Dwarfs (Disney)-origin; partial reprint			
of 4-Color No. 49 (Movie)	5.00	15.00	35.00
383-Andy Panda (Lantz)	1.15	3.50	8.00
384-King of the Royal Mounted (3/52)(Zane Grey)			
	4.00	12.00	28.00
385-Porky Pig in The Isle of Missing Ships (3-4/52)			
	2.30	7.00	16.00
386-Uncle Scrooge No. 1 by Carl Barks (Disney) in "Only a Poor Old			
Man" (3/52)	60.00	180.00	420.00
387-Mickey Mouse in High Tibet (Disney) (4-5/52)			
	4.30	13.00	30.00
388-Oswald the Rabbit (Lantz)	1.70	5.00	12.00
389-Andy Hardy Comics (No.1)	2.00	6.00	14.00
390-Woody Woodpecker (Lantz)	1.70	5.00	12.00
391-Uncle Wiggily	2.65	8.00	18.00
392-Hi-Yo Silver	2.85	8.50	20.00
393-Bugs Bunny	3.50	10.50	24.00
394-Donald Duck in Malayalaya-Barks-c only (Disney)			
	5.00	15.00	35.00
395-Forlorn River (Zane Grey) (1952)-First Nevada (5/52)			
	3.00	9.00	21.00
396-Tales of the Texas Rangers (No.1)(TV)-Photo-c			
	5.50	16.50	38.00
397-Sergeant Preston of the Yukon (TV)(5/52)	3.70	11.00	26.00
398-The Brownies-not by Kelly	2.65	8.00	18.00
399-Porky Pig in The Lost Gold Mine	2.30	7.00	16.00
400-Tom Corbett, Space Cadet (TV)-McWilliams c/a			
	5.70	17.00	40.00
401-Mickey Mouse and Goofy's Mechanical Wizard (Disney) (6-7/52)			
	3.50	10.50	24.00
402-Mary Jane and Sniffles	7.00	21.00	50.00
403-Li'l Bad Wolf (Disney) (6/52)	2.00	6.00	14.00
404-The Range Rider (No.1)(TV)-Photo-c	6.00	18.00	42.00
405-Woody Woodpecker (Lantz) (6-7/52)	1.70	5.00	12.00
406-Tweety and Sylvester (No.1)	1.70	5.00	12.00
407-Bugs Bunny, Foreign-Legion Hare	2.30	7.00	16.00
408-Donald Duck and the Golden Helmet by Carl Barks (Disney)			
(7-8/52)	20.00	60.00	140.00
409-Andy Panda (7-9/52)	1.15	3.50	8.00
410-Porky Pig in The Water Wizard (7/52)	2.30	7.00	16.00
411-Mickey Mouse and the Old Sea Dog (Disney) (8-9/52)			

Four Color #329, © Roy Rogers

Four Color #346, © DELL

Four Color #408, © WDC

Four Color #419, © Sgt. Preston   Four Color #458, © W. Lantz   Four Color #493, © DELL

FOUR COLOR (continued)	Good	Fine	N-Mint
	3.50	10.50	24.00
412-Nevada (Zane Grey)	3.00	9.00	21.00
413-Robin Hood (Disney-Movie) (8/52)-Photo-c	3.00	9.00	21.00
414-Bob Clampett's Beany and Cecil (TV)	8.50	25.50	60.00
415-Rootie Kazootie (No.1)(TV)	4.30	13.00	30.00
416-Woody Woodpecker (Lantz)	1.70	5.00	12.00
417-Double Trouble with Goober (No.1; 8/52)	1.50	4.50	10.00
418-Rusty Riley, a Boy, a Horse, and a Dog (No.1)-Frank Godwin-a			
(strip reprints) (8/52)	2.00	6.00	14.00
419-Sergeant Preston (TV)	3.70	11.00	26.00
420-Bugs Bunny in The Mysterious Buckaroo (8-9/52)			
	2.30	7.00	16.00
421-Tom Corbett, Space Cadet (TV)-McWilliams-a			
	5.70	17.00	40.00
422-Donald Duck and the Gilded Man, by Carl Barks (Disney)			
(9-10/52) (No.423 on inside)	20.00	60.00	140.00
423-Rhubarb, Owner of the Brooklyn Ball Club (The Millionaire Cat)			
(No.1)	1.15	3.50	8.00
424-Flash Gordon-Test Flight in Space (9/52)	6.50	19.50	45.00
425-Zorro, the Return of	8.50	25.50	60.00
426-Porky Pig in The Scalawag Leprechaun	2.30	7.00	16.00
427-Mickey Mouse and the Wonderful Whizzix (Disney) (10-11/52)-			
reprinted in Mickey Mouse No. 100	3.50	10.50	24.00
428-Uncle Wiggily	2.30	7.00	16.00
429-Pluto in "Why Dogs Leave Home" (Disney)(10/52)			
	3.00	9.00	21.00
430-Marge's Tubby, the Shadow of a Man-Eater			
	7.00	21.00	50.00
431-Woody Woodpecker (10/52)(Lantz)	1.70	5.00	12.00
432-Bugs Bunny and the Rabbit Olympics	2.30	7.00	16.00
433-Wildfire (Zane Grey)	3.00	9.00	21.00
434-Rin Tin Tin-"In Dark Danger" (No.1)(TV)(11/52)-Photo-c			
	5.00	15.00	35.00
435-Frosty the Snowman	2.30	7.00	16.00
436-The Brownies-not by Kelly (11/52)	2.30	7.00	16.00
437-John Carter of Mars (E. R. Burroughs)-Marsh-a			
	10.00	30.00	70.00
438-Annie Oakley (No.1) (TV)	7.00	21.00	50.00
439-Little Hiawatha (Disney) (12/52)	2.30	7.00	16.00
440-Black Beauty (12/52)	1.70	5.00	12.00
441-Fearless Fagan	1.15	3.50	8.00
442-Peter Pan (Disney) (Movie)	5.00	15.00	35.00
443-Ben Bowie and His Mountain Men (No.1)	3.00	9.00	21.00
444-Marge's Tubby	7.00	21.00	50.00
445-Charlie McCarthy	2.30	7.00	16.00
446-Captain Hook and Peter Pan (Disney) (Movie) (1/53)			
	5.00	15.00	35.00
447-Andy Hardy Comics	1.15	3.50	8.00
448-Bob Clampett's Beany and Cecil (TV)	8.50	25.50	60.00
449-Tappan's Burro (Zane Grey) (2-4/53)	3.00	9.00	21.00
450-Duck Album-Barks-c (Disney)	2.65	8.00	18.00
451-Rusty Riley-Frank Godwin-a (strip reprints) (2/53)			
	1.70	5.00	12.00
452-Raggedy Ann & Andy ('53)	3.00	9.00	21.00
453-Susie Q. Smith (2/53)	1.30	4.00	9.00
454-Krazy Kat Comics-not by Herriman	2.30	7.00	16.00
455-Johnny Mack Brown Comics(3/53)-Photo-c	3.50	10.50	24.00
456-Uncle Scrooge Back to the Klondike (No.2) by Barks (3/53)			
(Disney)	29.00	86.00	200.00
457-Daffy (No.1)	2.15	6.50	15.00
458-Oswald the Rabbit (Lantz)	1.15	3.50	8.00
459-Rootie Kazootie (TV)	3.50	10.50	24.00
460-Buck Jones (4/53)	3.50	10.50	24.00
461-Marge's Tubby	6.50	19.50	45.00
462-Little Beaver	.85	2.50	6.00
463-Petunia (4/53)	1.30	4.00	9.00

	Good	Fine	N-Mint
464-Bozo (4/53)	5.00	15.00	35.00
465-Francis the Famous Talking Mule	1.00	3.00	7.00
466-Rhubarb, the Millionaire Cat	.85	2.50	6.00
467-Desert Gold (Zane Grey) (5-7/53)	3.00	9.00	21.00
468-Goofy (No.1) (Disney)	3.00	9.00	21.00
469-Beetle Bailey (No.1)(5/53)	5.00	15.00	35.00
470-Elmer Fudd	1.15	3.50	8.00
471-Double Trouble with Goober	1.00	3.00	7.00
472-Wild Bill Elliott (6/53)-Photo-c	4.00	12.00	28.00
473-Li'l Bad Wolf (Disney)(6/53)	2.00	6.00	14.00
474-Mary Jane and Sniffles	6.00	18.00	42.00
475-M.G.M.'s The Two Mouseketeers (No.1)	1.50	4.50	10.00
476-Rin Tin Tin (TV)-Photo-c	3.70	11.00	26.00
477-Bob Clampett's Beany and Cecil (TV)	8.50	25.50	60.00
478-Charlie McCarthy	2.30	7.00	16.00
479-Queen of the West Dale Evans (No.1)	7.00	21.00	50.00
480-Andy Hardy Comics	1.15	3.50	8.00
481-Annie Oakley And Tagg (TV)	5.00	15.00	35.00
482-Brownies-not by Kelly	2.30	7.00	16.00
483-Little Beaver (7/53)	1.70	5.00	12.00
484-River Feud (Zane Grey) (8-10/53)	3.00	9.00	21.00
485-The Little People-Walt Scott (No.1)	2.30	7.00	16.00
486-Rusty Riley-Frank Godwin strip-r	1.70	5.00	12.00
487-Mowgli, the Jungle Book (Rudyard Kipling's)			
	2.65	8.00	18.00
488-John Carter of Mars (Burroughs)-Marsh-a	10.00	30.00	70.00
489-Tweety and Sylvester	1.00	3.00	7.00
490-Jungle Jim (No.1)	2.65	8.00	18.00
491-Silvertip (No.1) (Max Brand)-Kinstler-a (8/53)			
	4.00	12.00	24.00
492-Duck Album (Disney)	2.00	6.00	14.00
493-Johnny Mack Brown-Photo-c	3.50	10.50	24.00
494-The Little King (No.1)	3.50	10.50	24.00
495-Uncle Scrooge (No.3)(Disney)-by Carl Barks (9/53)			
	26.00	77.00	180.00
496-The Green Hornet	10.00	30.00	70.00
497-Zorro (Sword of . . .)	8.50	25.50	60.00
498-Bugs Bunny's Album (9/53)	1.70	5.00	12.00
499-M.G.M.'s Spike and Tyke (No.1)(9/53)	1.30	4.00	9.00
500-Buck Jones	3.50	10.50	24.00
501-Francis the Famous Talking Mule	1.00	3.00	7.00
502-Rootie Kazootie (TV)	3.50	10.50	24.00
503-Uncle Wiggily (10/53)	2.30	7.00	16.00
504-Krazy Kat-not by Herriman	2.30	7.00	16.00
505-The Sword and the Rose (Disney) (10/53) (TV)-Photo-c			
	3.50	10.50	24.00
506-The Little Scouts	.85	2.50	6.00
507-Oswald the Rabbit (Lantz)	1.15	3.50	8.00
508-Bozo (10/53)	5.00	15.00	35.00
509-Pluto (Disney) (10/53)	3.00	9.00	21.00
510-Son of Black Beauty	1.70	5.00	12.00
511-Outlaw Trail (Zane Grey)-Kinstler-a	3.50	10.50	24.00
512-Flash Gordon (11/53)	3.50	10.50	24.00
513-Ben Bowie and His Mountain Men	2.00	6.00	14.00
514-Frosty the Snowman (11/53)	2.00	6.00	14.00
515-Andy Hardy	1.15	3.50	8.00
516-Double Trouble With Goober	1.00	3.00	7.00
517-Chip 'N' Dale (No.1)(Disney)	1.70	5.00	12.00
518-Rivets (11/53)	1.15	3.50	8.00
519-Steve Canyon (No.1)-not by Milton Caniff	4.00	12.00	28.00
520-Wild Bill Elliott-Photo-c	4.00	12.00	28.00
521-Beetle Bailey (12/53)	2.65	8.00	18.00
522-The Brownies	2.30	7.00	16.00
523-Rin Tin Tin (TV)-Photo-c (12/53)	3.70	11.00	26.00
524-Tweety and Sylvester	1.00	3.00	7.00
525-Santa Claus Funnies	1.70	5.00	12.00

FOUR COLOR (continued)	Good	Fine	N-Mint
526-Napoleon	1.15	3.50	8.00
527-Charlie McCarthy	2.30	7.00	16.00
528-Queen of the West Dale Evans-Photo-c	5.00	15.00	35.00
529-Little Beaver	1.70	5.00	12.00
530-Bob Clampett's Beany and Cecil (TV) (1/54)			
	8.50	25.50	60.00
531-Duck Album (Disney)	2.00	6.00	14.00
532-The Rustlers (Zane Grey) (2-4/54)	3.00	9.00	21.00
533-Raggedy Ann and Andy	3.00	9.00	21.00
534-Western Marshal (Ernest Haycox's)-Kinstler-a			
	3.00	9.00	21.00
535-I Love Lucy (No. 1)(TV) (2/54)-photo-c	14.00	42.00	100.00
536-Daffy (3/54)	1.50	4.50	10.00
537-Stormy, the Thoroughbred... (Disney-Movie) on top ⅔ of each page; Pluto story on bottom ⅓ of each page (2/54)			
	2.00	6.00	14.00
538-The Mask of Zorro-Kinstler-a	9.30	28.00	65.00
539-Ben and Me (Disney) (3/54)	1.50	4.50	10.00
540-Knights of the Round Table (3/54) (Movie)-Photo-c			
	3.50	10.50	24.00
541-Johnny Mack Brown-Photo-c	3.50	10.50	24.00
542-Super Circus Featuring Mary Hartline (TV) (3/54)			
	2.65	8.00	18.00
543-Uncle Wiggily (3/54)	2.30	7.00	16.00
544-Rob Roy (Disney-Movie)-Manning-a; photo-c			
	5.00	15.00	35.00
545-The Wonderful Adventures of Pinocchio-Partial reprint of 4-Color #92 (Disney-Movie)	3.00	9.00	21.00
546-Buck Jones	3.50	10.50	24.00
547-Francis the Famous Talking Mule	1.00	3.00	7.00
548-Krazy Kat-not by Herriman (4/54)	2.00	6.00	14.00
549-Oswald the Rabbit (Lantz)	1.15	3.50	8.00
550-The Little Scouts	.85	2.50	6.00
551-Bozo (4/54)	5.00	15.00	35.00
552-Beetle Bailey	2.65	8.00	18.00
553-Susie Q. Smith	1.30	4.00	9.00
554-Rusty Riley (Frank Godwin strip-r)	1.75	5.25	12.00
555-Range War (Zane Grey)	3.00	9.00	21.00
556-Double Trouble With Goober (5/54)	1.00	3.00	7.00
557-Ben Bowie and His Mountain Men	2.00	6.00	14.00
558-Elmer Fudd (5/54)	1.15	3.50	8.00
559-I Love Lucy (No. 2)(TV)-Photo-c	11.00	32.00	75.00
560-Duck Album (Disney)(5/54)	2.00	6.00	14.00
561-Mr. Magoo (5/54)	5.00	15.00	35.00
562-Goofy (Disney)	2.30	7.00	16.00
563-Rhubarb, the Millionaire Cat (6/54)	.85	2.50	6.00
564-Li'l Bad Wolf (Disney)	1.70	5.00	12.00
565-Jungle Jim	2.00	6.00	14.00
566-Son of Black Beauty	1.75	5.25	12.00
567-Prince Valiant (No.1)-by Bob Fuje (Movie)-Photo-c			
	5.70	17.00	40.00
568-Gypsy Colt (Movie)	2.30	7.00	16.00
569-Priscilla's Pop	1.30	4.00	9.00
570-Bob Clampett's Beany and Cecil (TV)	8.50	25.50	60.00
571-Charlie McCarthy	2.30	7.00	16.00
572-Silvertip (Max Brand)(7/54); Kinstler-a	3.00	9.00	21.00
573-The Little People by Walt Scott	1.70	5.00	12.00
574-The Hand of Zorro	8.50	25.50	60.00
575-Annie Oakley and Tagg(TV)-Photo-c	5.00	15.00	35.00
576-Angel (No.1) (8/54)	1.00	3.00	7.00
577-M.G.M.'s Spike and Tyke	1.00	3.00	7.00
578-Steve Canyon (8/54)	3.50	10.50	24.00
579-Francis the Famous Talking Mule	1.00	3.00	7.00
580-Six Gun Ranch (Luke Short-8/54)	2.30	7.00	16.00
581-Chip 'N' Dale (Disney)	1.30	4.00	9.00
582-Mowgli Jungle Book (Kipling)(8/54)	2.30	7.00	16.00

	Good	Fine	N-Mint
583-The Lost Wagon Train (Zane Grey)	3.00	9.00	21.00
584-Johnny Mack Brown-Photo-c	3.50	10.50	24.00
585-Bugs Bunny's Album	1.70	5.00	12.00
586-Duck Album (Disney)	2.00	6.00	14.00
587-The Little Scouts	.85	2.50	6.00
588-King Richard and the Crusaders (Movie) (10/54) Matt Baker-a; photo-c	8.00	24.00	56.00
589-Buck Jones	3.50	10.50	24.00
590-Hansel and Gretel; partial photo-c	3.50	10.50	24.00
591-Western Marshal (Ernest Haycox's)-Kinstler-a			
	3.00	9.00	21.00
592-Super Circus (TV)	2.65	8.00	18.00
593-Oswald the Rabbit (Lantz)	1.15	3.50	8.00
594-Bozo (10/54)	5.00	15.00	35.00
595-Pluto (Disney)	2.30	7.00	16.00
596-Turok, Son of Stone (No.1)	24.00	73.00	170.00
597-The Little King	2.85	8.50	20.00
598-Captain Davy Jones	1.50	4.50	10.00
599-Ben Bowie and His Mountain Men	2.00	6.00	14.00
600-Daisy Duck's Diary (No.1)(Disney)(11/54)	2.00	6.00	14.00
601-Frosty the Snowman	2.00	6.00	14.00
602-Mr. Magoo and Gerald McBoing-Boing	5.00	15.00	35.00
603-M.G.M.'s The Two Mouseketeers	1.00	3.00	7.00
604-Shadow on the Trail (Zane Grey)	3.00	9.00	21.00
605-The Brownies-not by Kelly (12/54)	2.30	7.00	16.00
606-Sir Lancelot (not TV)	6.50	19.50	45.00
607-Santa Claus Funnies	1.70	5.00	12.00
608-Silvertip-"Valley of Vanishing Men" (Max Brand)-Kinstler-a			
	3.00	9.00	21.00
609-The Littlest Outlaw (Disney-Movie) (1/55)-Photo-c			
	2.65	8.00	18.00
610-Drum Beat (Movie); Alan Ladd photo-c	7.00	21.00	50.00
611-Duck Album (Disney)	2.00	6.00	14.00
612-Little Beaver (1/55)	1.30	4.00	9.00
613-Western Marshal (Ernest Haycox's) (2/55)-Kinstler-a			
	3.00	9.00	21.00
614-20,000 Leagues Under the Sea (Disney) (Movie) (2/55)			
	3.00	9.00	21.00
615-Daffy	1.50	4.50	10.00
616-To the Last Man (Zane Grey)	3.00	9.00	21.00
617-The Quest of Zorro	8.50	25.50	60.00
618-Johnny Mack Brown-Photo-c	3.50	10.50	24.00
619-Krazy Kat-not by Herriman	2.00	6.00	14.00
620-Mowgli Jungle Book (Kipling)	2.30	7.00	16.00
621-Francis the Famous Talking Mule	1.00	3.00	7.00
622-Beetle Bailey	2.65	8.00	18.00
623-Oswald the Rabbit (Lantz)	.85	2.50	6.00
624-Treasure Island (Disney-Movie) (4/55)-Photo-c			
	2.65	8.00	18.00
625-Beaver Valley (Disney-Movie)	1.70	5.00	12.00
626-Ben Bowie and His Mountain Men	2.00	6.00	14.00
627-Goofy (Disney) (5/55)	2.30	7.00	16.00
628-Elmer Fudd	1.15	3.50	8.00
629-Lady and the Tramp with Jock (Disney)	2.00	6.00	14.00
630-Priscilla's Pop	1.15	3.50	8.00
631-Davy Crockett, Indian Fighter (No.1)(Disney)(5/55)(TV)- Fess Parker photo-c	3.50	10.50	24.00
632-Fighting Caravans (Zane Grey)	3.00	9.00	21.00
633-The Little People by Walt Scott (6/55)	1.70	5.00	12.00
634-Lady and the Tramp Album (Disney) (6/55)	1.70	5.00	12.00
635-Bob Clampett's Beany and Cecil (TV)	8.50	25.50	60.00
636-Chip 'N' Dale (Disney)	1.30	4.00	9.00
637-Silvertip (Max Brand)-Kinstler-a	3.00	9.00	21.00
638-M.G.M.'s Spike and Tyke (8/55)	1.00	3.00	7.00
639-Davy Crockett at the Alamo (Disney) (7/55)(TV)-Fess Parker photo-c	3.50	10.50	24.00

Four Color #559, © Lucille Ball & Desi Arnaz

Four Color #581, © WDC

Four Color #635, © Bob Clampett

WANTED

OLD COMICS!!

$CASH REWARD$

FOR THESE AND MANY OTHER ELUSIVE COMIC BOOKS FROM THE GOLDEN AGE. SEEKING WHITE PAGE COLLECTIBLE COPIES IN VG OR BETTER CONDITION. ALSO GOLDEN AGE **BOUND VOLUMES** WANTED.

Green Lantern #40, 1965, © DC. 1st Silver Age app. Golden Age Green Lantern.

The Hangman #3, 1942, © MLJ

Happy Comics #1, 1943, © NEDOR

Hello Pal Comics #1, 1943, © HARV. Rocketman & Rocketgirl begin.

Hit Comics #22, 1942, © QUA

House Of Mystery #143, 1964, © DC. J'onn J'onzz series begins.

The Incredible Hulk #1, 1962, © MCG

Iron Man #1, 1968, © MCG

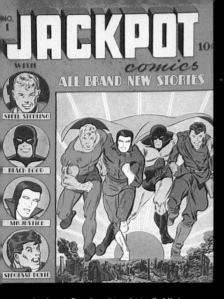

Jackpot Comics #1, 1941, © MLJ

Jumbo Comics #16, 1940, © FH

Justice League #4, 1961, © DC

Justice League #21, 1963, © DC. Re-intro

Kewpies #1, 1949, © Will Eisner.
Eisner cover and art.

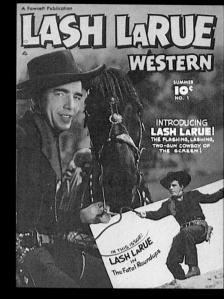

Lash LaRue #1, 1949, © FAW

Lightning Comics V2#3, 1941, © ACE

Marmaduke Mouse #1, 1946, © QUA

Bringing

you the

best

comics

in the

1980s—

and

into

the 1990s

DC Comics

Four Color #651, © DELL

Four Color #694, © DELL

Four Color #721, © DELL

FOUR COLOR (continued)	**Good**	**Fine**	**N-Mint**
640-Western Marshal (Ernest Haycox's)-Kinstler-a			
	3.00	9.00	21.00
641-Steve Canyon ('55)-by Caniff	3.50	10.50	24.00
642-M.G.M.'s The Two Mouseketeers	1.00	3.00	7.00
643-Wild Bill Elliott-Photo-c	3.50	10.50	24.00
644-Sir Walter Raleigh (5/55)-Based on movie "The Virgin Queen"-Photo-c	4.00	12.00	28.00
645-Johnny Mack Brown-Photo-c	3.50	10.50	24.00
646-Dotty Dripple and Taffy (No.1)	1.70	5.00	12.00
647-Bugs Bunny's Album (9/55)	1.70	5.00	12.00
648-Jace Pearson of the Texas Rangers (TV)-Photo-c			
	3.50	10.50	24.00
649-Duck Album (Disney)	2.00	6.00	14.00
650-Prince Valiant - by Bob Fuje	3.50	10.50	24.00
651-King Colt (Luke Short)(9/55)-Kinstler-a	3.00	9.00	21.00
652-Buck Jones	2.30	7.00	16.00
653-Smokey the Bear (No.1) (10/55)	2.65	8.00	18.00
654-Pluto (Disney)	2.30	7.00	16.00
655-Francis the Famous Talking Mule	1.00	3.00	7.00
656-Turok, Son of Stone (No.2) (10/55)	17.00	51.00	120.00
657-Ben Bowie and His Mountain Men	2.00	6.00	14.00
658-Goofy (Disney)	2.30	7.00	16.00
659-Daisy Duck's Diary (Disney)	1.70	5.00	12.00
660-Little Beaver	1.30	4.00	9.00
661-Frosty the Snowman	2.00	6.00	14.00
662-Zoo Parade (TV)-Marlin Perkins (11/55)	2.30	7.00	16.00
663-Winky Dink (TV)	3.50	10.50	24.00
664-Davy Crockett in the Great Keelboat Race (TV) (Disney)(11/55)-Fess Parker photo-c	4.00	12.00	28.00
665-The African Lion (Disney-Movie) (11/55)	2.00	6.00	14.00
666-Santa Claus Funnies	1.70	5.00	12.00
667-Silvertip and the Stolen Stallion (Max Brand) (12/55)-Kinstler-a			
	3.00	9.00	21.00
668-Dumbo (Disney) (12/55)	3.50	10.50	24.00
668-Dumbo (Disney) (1/58) different cover, same contents			
	3.50	10.50	24.00
669-Robin Hood (Disney-Movie) (12/55)-reprint of No. 413-Photo-c			
	2.00	6.00	14.00
670-M.G.M's Mouse Musketeers (No.1)(1/56)-Formerly the Two Mouseketeers	1.00	3.00	7.00
671-Davy Crockett and the River Pirates (TV) (Disney) (12/55)-Jesse Marsh-a; Fess Parker photo-c	4.00	12.00	28.00
672-Quentin Durward (1/56)(Movie)-Photo-c	3.50	10.50	24.00
673-Buffalo Bill, Jr. (No.1)(TV)-Photo-c	3.70	11.00	26.00
674-The Little Rascals (No.1) (TV)	2.00	6.00	14.00
675-Steve Donovan, Western Marshal (No.1)(TV)-Kinstler-a; photo-c			
	4.00	12.00	28.00
676-Will-Yum!	1.15	3.50	8.00
677-Little King	2.65	8.00	18.00
678-The Last Hunt (Movie)-Photo-c	3.50	10.50	24.00
679-Gunsmoke (No.1) (TV)	6.00	18.00	42.00
680-Out Our Way with the Worry Wart (2/56)	1.30	4.00	9.00
681-Forever, Darling (Movie) with Lucille Ball & Desi Arnaz (2/56)-Photo-c	5.70	17.00	40.00
682-When Knighthood Was in Flower (Disney-Movie)-Reprint of No. 505-Photo-c	2.85	8.50	20.00
683-Hi and Lois (3/56)	1.00	3.00	7.00
684-Helen of Troy (Movie)-Buscema-a; photo-c	7.00	21.00	50.00
685-Johnny Mack Brown-Photo-c	3.50	10.50	24.00
686-Duck Album (Disney)	2.00	6.00	14.00
687-The Indian Fighter (Movie)-Kirk Douglas Photo-c			
	3.00	9.00	21.00
688-Alexander the Great (Movie) (5/56) Buscema-a; photo-c			
	3.70	11.00	26.00
689-Elmer Fudd (3/56)	1.15	3.50	8.00
690-The Conqueror (Movie) - John Wayne photo-c			

	Good	**Fine**	**N-Mint**
	10.00	30.00	70.00
691-Dotty Dripple and Taffy	1.30	4.00	9.00
692-The Little People-Walt Scott	1.70	5.00	12.00
693-Song of the South (Disney)(1956)-Partial reprint of No. 129			
	2.00	6.00	14.00
694-Super Circus (TV)-Photo-c	2.65	8.00	18.00
695-Little Beaver	1.30	4.00	9.00
696-Krazy Kat-not by Herriman (4/56)	2.00	6.00	14.00
697-Oswald the Rabbit (Lantz)	.85	2.50	6.00
698-Francis the Famous Talking Mule (4/56)	1.00	3.00	7.00
699-Prince Valiant-by Bob Fuje	3.50	10.50	24.00
700-Water Birds and the Olympic Elk (Disney-Movie)(4/56)			
	2.35	7.00	16.00
701-Jiminy Cricket (No.1)(Disney)(5/56)	2.35	7.00	16.00
702-The Goofy Success Story (Disney)	2.00	6.00	14.00
703-Scamp (No.1) (Disney)	1.70	5.00	12.00
704-Priscilla's Pop (5/56)	1.15	3.50	8.00
705-Brave Eagle (No.1) (TV)-Photo-c	2.00	6.00	14.00
706-Bongo and Lumpjaw (Disney)(6/56)	1.50	4.50	10.00
707-Corky and White Shadow (Disney)(5/56)-Mickey Mouse Club (TV)-Photo-c	2.30	7.00	16.00
708-Smokey the Bear	2.00	6.00	14.00
709-The Searchers (Movie) - John Wayne photo-c			
	14.00	42.00	100.00
710-Francis the Famous Talking Mule	1.00	3.00	7.00
711-M.G.M.'s Mouse Musketeers	.85	2.50	6.00
712-The Great Locomotive Chase (Disney-Movie) (9/56)-Photo-c			
	3.00	9.00	21.00
713-The Animal World (Movie) (8/56)	2.65	8.00	18.00
714-Spin and Marty (No.1)(TV)(Disney)-Mickey Mouse Club (6/56)-Photo-c	4.00	12.00	28.00
715-Timmy (8/56)	1.50	4.50	10.00
716-Man in Space (Disney-Movie)	2.30	7.00	16.00
717-Moby Dick (Movie)-Photo-c	5.00	15.00	35.00
718-Dotty Dripple and Taffy	1.30	4.00	9.00
719-Prince Valiant - by Bob Fuje (8/56)	3.50	10.50	24.00
720-Gunsmoke (TV)-Photo-c	4.00	12.00	28.00
721-Captain Kangaroo (TV)-Photo-c	8.00	24.00	56.00
722-Johnny Mack Brown-Photo-c	3.50	10.50	24.00
723-Santiago (Movie)-Kinstler-a(9/56); Alan Ladd photo-c			
	7.00	21.00	50.00
724-Bugs Bunny's Album	1.70	5.00	12.00
725-Elmer Fudd (9/56)	.85	2.50	6.00
726-Duck Album (Disney)	1.70	5.00	12.00
727-The Nature of Things (TV) (Disney)-Jesse Marsh-a			
	2.30	7.00	16.00
728-M.G.M.'s Mouse Musketeers	.85	2.50	6.00
729-Bob Son of Battle (11/56)	1.70	5.00	12.00
730-Smokey Stover	1.70	5.00	12.00
731-Silvertip and The Fighting Four (Max Brand)-Kinstler-a			
	3.00	9.00	21.00
732-Zorro, the Challenge of (10/56)	8.50	25.50	60.00
733-Buck Jones	2.30	7.00	16.00
734-Cheyenne (No.1)(TV)(10/56)-Photo-c	6.00	18.00	42.00
735-Crusader Rabbit (No. 1) (TV)	7.00	21.00	50.00
736-Pluto (Disney)	1.70	5.00	12.00
737-Steve Canyon-Caniff-a	3.50	10.50	24.00
738-Westward Ho, the Wagons (Disney-Movie)-Fess Parker photo-c			
	2.30	7.00	16.00
739-Bounty Guns (Luke Short)-Drucker-a	2.30	7.00	16.00
740-Chilly Willy (No.1)(Walter Lantz)	1.15	3.50	8.00
741-The Fastest Gun Alive (Movie) (9/56)-Photo-c			
	3.50	10.50	24.00
742-Buffalo Bill, Jr. (TV)-Photo-c	2.65	8.00	18.00
743-Daisy Duck's Diary (Disney) (11/56)	1.70	5.00	12.00
744-Little Beaver	1.30	4.00	9.00

	Good	Fine	N-Mint
745-Francis the Famous Talking Mule	1.00	3.00	7.00
746-Dotty Dripple and Taffy	1.30	4.00	9.00
747-Goofy (Disney)	2.30	7.00	16.00
748-Frosty the Snowman (11/56)	1.70	5.00	12.00
749-Secrets of Life (Disney-Movie)-Photo-c	2.30	7.00	16.00
750-The Great Cat Family (Disney-Movie)	2.65	8.00	18.00
751-Our Miss Brooks (TV)-Photo-c	4.00	12.00	28.00
752-Mandrake, the Magician	4.00	12.00	28.00
753-Walt Scott's Little People (11/56)	1.70	5.00	12.00
754-Smokey the Bear	2.00	6.00	14.00
755-The Littlest Snowman (12/56)	2.15	6.50	16.00
756-Santa Claus Funnies	1.70	5.00	12.00
757-The True Story of Jesse James (Movie)-Photo-c	5.00	15.00	35.00
758-Bear Country (Disney-Movie)	2.30	7.00	16.00
759-Circus Boy (TV)-The Monkees' Mickey Dolenz photo-c (12/56)	6.50	19.50	45.00
760-The Hardy Boys (No. 1) (TV) (Disney)-Mickey Mouse Club-Photo-c	4.50	14.00	32.00
761-Howdy Doody (TV) (1/57)	4.50	14.00	32.00
762-The Sharkfighters (Movie)(1/57)(Scarce); Buscema-a; photo-c	8.00	24.00	56.00
763-Grandma Duck's Farm Friends (No. 1) (Disney)	2.30	7.00	16.00
764-M.G.M's Mouse Musketeers	.85	2.50	6.00
765-Will-Yum!	1.00	3.00	7.00
766-Buffalo Bill, Jr. (TV)-Photo-c	2.65	8.00	18.00
767-Spin and Marty (TV)(Disney)-Mickey Mouse Club (2/57)	3.70	11.00	26.00
768-Steve Donovan, Western Marshal (TV)-Kinstler-a; photo-c	3.50	10.50	24.00
769-Gunsmoke (TV)	4.00	12.00	28.00
770-Brave Eagle (TV)-Photo-c	1.50	4.50	10.00
771-Brand of Empire (Luke Short)(3/57)-Drucker-a	2.30	7.00	16.00
772-Cheyenne (TV)-Photo-c	4.00	12.00	28.00
773-The Brave One (Movie)-Photo-c	2.30	7.00	16.00
774-Hi and Lois (3/57)	1.00	3.00	7.00
775-Sir Lancelot and Brian (TV)-Buscema-a; photo-c	6.00	18.00	42.00
776-Johnny Mack Brown-Photo-c	3.50	10.50	24.00
777-Scamp (Disney)(3/57)	1.15	3.50	8.00
778-The Little Rascals (TV)	1.70	5.00	12.00
779-Lee Hunter, Indian Fighter (3/57)	2.65	8.00	18.00
780-Captain Kangaroo (TV)-Photo-c	7.00	21.00	50.00
781-Fury (No.1)(TV)(3/57)-Photo-c	5.00	15.00	35.00
782-Duck Album (Disney)	1.70	5.00	12.00
783-Elmer Fudd	.85	2.50	6.00
784-Around the World in 80 Days (Movie) (2/57)-Photo-c	3.50	10.50	24.00
785-Circus Boy (TV) (4/57)-The Monkees' Mickey Dolenz photo-c	6.50	19.50	45.00
786-Cinderella (Disney) (3/57)-Partial reprint of No. 272	2.00	6.00	14.00
787-Little Hiawatha (Disney) (4/57)	1.70	5.00	12.00
788-Prince Valiant - by Bob Fuje (4/57)	3.50	10.50	24.00
789-Silvertip-Valley Thieves (Max Brand) (4/57)-Kinstler-a	3.00	9.00	21.00
790-The Wings of Eagles (Movie) (John Wayne) Toth-a; John Wayne photo-c; 10 & 15 cent editions exist	11.50	34.00	80.00
791-The 77th Bengal Lancers (TV)-Photo-c	3.70	11.00	26.00
792-Oswald the Rabbit (Lantz)	.85	2.50	6.00
793-Morty Meekle	1.50	4.50	10.00
794-The Count of Monte Cristo (5/57) (Movie)-Buscema-a	5.70	17.00	40.00
795-Jiminy Cricket (Disney)	2.00	6.00	14.00

	Good	Fine	N-Mint
796-Ludwig Bemelman's Madeleine and Genevieve	2.00	6.00	14.00
797-Gunsmoke (TV)-Photo-c	4.00	12.00	28.00
798-Buffalo Bill, Jr. (TV)-Photo-c	2.65	8.00	18.00
799-Priscilla's Pop	1.15	3.50	8.00
800-The Buccaneers (TV)-Photo-c	4.30	13.00	30.00
801-Dotty Dripple and Taffy	1.30	4.00	9.00
802-Goofy (Disney) (5/57)	2.30	7.00	16.00
803-Cheyenne (TV)-Photo-c	4.00	12.00	28.00
804-Steve Canyon-Caniff-a (1957)	3.50	10.50	24.00
805-Crusader Rabbit (TV)	6.00	18.00	42.00
806-Scamp (Disney) (6/57)	1.15	3.50	8.00
807-Savage Range (Luke Short)-Drucker-a	2.30	7.00	16.00
808-Spin and Marty (TV)(Disney)-Mickey Mouse Club-Photo-c	3.70	11.00	26.00
809-The Little People-Walt Scott	1.70	5.00	12.00
810-Francis the Famous Talking Mule	1.00	3.00	7.00
811-Howdy Doody (TV) (7/57)	4.50	14.00	32.00
812-The Big Land(Movie); Alan Ladd photo-c	7.00	21.00	50.00
813-Circus Boy (TV)-The Monkees' Mickey Dolenz photo-c	6.50	19.50	45.00
814-Covered Wagons, Ho! (Disney)-Donald Duck (TV)(6/57); Mickey Mouse app.	2.00	6.00	14.00
815-Dragoon Wells Massacre (Movie)-photo-c	4.30	13.00	30.00
816-Brave Eagle (TV)-photo-c	1.50	4.50	10.00
817-Little Beaver	1.30	4.00	9.00
818-Smokey the Bear (6/57)	2.00	6.00	14.00
819-Mickey Mouse in Magicland (Disney) (7/57)	2.00	6.00	14.00
820-The Oklahoman (Movie)-Photo-c	5.00	15.00	35.00
821-Wringle Wrangle (Disney)-Based on movie "Westward Ho, the Wagons"-Marsh-a; Fess Parker photo-c	3.50	10.50	24.00
822-Paul Revere's Ride with Johnny Tremain (TV)(Disney)-Toth-a	6.50	19.50	45.00
823-Timmy	1.15	3.50	8.00
824-The Pride and the Passion (Movie)(8/57)-Frank Sinatra & Cary Grant photo-c	4.30	13.00	30.00
825-The Little Rascals (TV)	1.70	5.00	12.00
826-Spin and Marty and Annette (TV)(Disney)-Mickey Mouse Club-Annette Funicello photo-c	8.50	25.50	60.00
827-Smokey Stover (8/57)	1.70	5.00	12.00
828-Buffalo Bill, Jr. (TV)-Photo-c	2.65	8.00	18.00
829-Tales of the Pony Express (TV) (8/57)-Painted-c	2.00	6.00	14.00
830-The Hardy Boys (TV)(Disney)-Mickey Mouse Club (8/57)-Photo-c	4.00	12.00	28.00
831-No Sleep 'Til Dawn (Movie)-Carl Malden photo-c	3.50	10.50	24.00
832-Lolly and Pepper (No.1)	1.70	5.00	12.00
833-Scamp (Disney) (9/57)	1.15	3.50	8.00
834-Johnny Mack Brown-Photo-c	3.50	10.50	24.00
835-Silvertip-The Fake Rider (Max Brand)	2.30	7.00	16.00
836-Man in Flight (Disney) (TV)(9/57)	2.30	7.00	16.00
837-All-American Athlete Cotton Woods	2.30	7.00	16.00
838-Bugs Bunny's Life Story Album (9/57)	2.00	6.00	14.00
839-The Vigilantes (Movie)	3.70	11.00	26.00
840-Duck Album (Disney)(9/57)	1.70	5.00	12.00
841-Elmer Fudd	.85	2.50	6.00
842-The Nature of Things (Disney-Movie)('57)-Jesse Marsh-a (TV series)	2.65	8.00	18.00
843-The First Americans (Disney)(TV)-Marsh-a	2.65	8.00	18.00
844-Gunsmoke (TV)-Photo-c	4.00	12.00	28.00
845-The Land Unknown (Movie)-Alex Toth-a	10.00	30.00	70.00
846-Gun Glory (Movie)-by Alex Toth-photo-c	8.50	25.50	60.00
847-Perri (squirrels) (Disney-Movie)-Two different covers published	1.50	4.50	10.00

Four Color #766, © Tie-Ups Co.

Four Color #784, © DELL

Four Color #813, © DELL

Four Color #851, © Warner Bros. Four Color #891, © WDC Four Color #921, © Wyatt Earp Ent.

FOUR COLOR (continued)	Good	Fine	N-Mint
848-Marauder's Moon	3.00	9.00	21.00
849-Prince Valiant-by Bob Fuje	3.50	10.50	24.00
850-Buck Jones	2.30	7.00	16.00
851-The Story of Mankind (Movie) (1/58)-Hedy Lamarr & Vincent			
Price photo-c	3.50	10.50	24.00
852-Chilly Willy (2/58)(Lantz)	.85	2.50	6.00
853-Pluto (Disney) (10/57)	1.70	5.00	12.00
854-The Hunchback of Notre Dame (Movie)-Photo-c			
	8.00	24.00	56.00
855-Broken Arrow (TV)-Photo-c	2.65	8.00	18.00
856-Buffalo Bill, Jr. (TV)-Photo-c	2.65	8.00	18.00
857-The Goofy Adventure Story (Disney) (11/57)			
	2.00	6.00	14.00
858-Daisy Duck's Diary (Disney) (11/57)	1.70	5.00	12.00
859-Topper and Neil (TV)(11/57)	1.30	4.00	9.00
860-Wyatt Earp (No.1)(TV)-Manning-a; photo-c	7.00	21.00	50.00
861-Frosty the Snowman	1.70	5.00	12.00
862-The Truth About Mother Goose (Disney-Movie) (11/57)			
	3.50	10.50	24.00
863-Francis the Famous Talking Mule	1.00	3.00	7.00
864-The Littlest Snowman	2.15	6.50	16.00
865-Andy Burnett (TV) (Disney) (12/57)-Photo-c			
	4.00	12.00	28.00
866-Mars and Beyond (Disney-Movie)	2.30	7.00	16.00
867-Santa Claus Funnies	1.70	5.00	12.00
868-The Little People (12/57)	1.70	5.00	12.00
869-Old Yeller (Disney-Movie)-Photo-c	2.65	8.00	18.00
870-Little Beaver (1/58)	1.30	4.00	9.00
871-Curly Kayoe	1.70	5.00	12.00
872-Captain Kangaroo (TV)-Photo-c	7.00	21.00	50.00
873-Grandma Duck's Farm Friends (Disney)	2.00	6.00	14.00
874-Old Ironsides (Disney-Movie with Johnny Tremain) (1/58)			
	2.30	7.00	16.00
875-Trumpets West (Luke Short) (2/58)	2.30	7.00	16.00
876-Tales of Wells Fargo (No.1) (TV) (2/58)-Photo-c			
	5.00	15.00	35.00
877-Frontier Doctor with Rex Allen (TV)-Alex Toth-a; photo-c			
	7.00	21.00	50.00
878-Peanuts (No.1)-Schulz-c only (2/58)	5.70	17.00	40.00
879-Brave Eagle (TV)(2/58)-Photo-c	1.50	4.50	10.00
880-Steve Donovan, Western Marshal-Drucker-a (TV)-Photo-c			
	2.30	7.00	16.00
881-The Captain and the Kids (2/58)	1.60	4.70	11.00
882-Zorro (Disney)-1st Disney issue by Alex Toth (2/58)-Photo-c			
	7.00	21.00	50.00
883-The Little Rascals (TV)	1.70	5.00	12.00
884-Hawkeye and the Last of the Mohicans (TV) (3/58)			
	3.50	10.50	24.00
885-Fury (TV) (3/58)-Photo-c	3.70	11.00	26.00
886-Bongo and Lumpjaw (Disney, 3/58)	1.30	4.00	9.00
887-The Hardy Boys (Disney)(TV)-Mickey Mouse Club (1/58)-Photo-c			
	4.00	12.00	28.00
888-Elmer Fudd (3/58)	.85	2.50	6.00
889-Clint and Mac (Disney)(TV)-Alex Toth-a (3/58)-Photo-c			
	6.50	19.50	45.00
890-Wyatt Earp (TV)-by Russ Manning; photo-c			
	4.00	12.00	28.00
891-Light in the Forest (Disney-Movie) (3/58)-Fess Parker photo-c			
	2.65	8.00	18.00
892-Maverick (No.1) (TV) (4/58)-James Garner/Jack Kelly photo-c			
	7.00	21.00	50.00
893-Jim Bowie (TV)-Photo-c	3.00	9.00	21.00
894-Oswald the Rabbit (Lantz)	.85	2.50	6.00
895-Wagon Train (No.1)(TV)(3/58)-Photo-c	5.70	17.00	40.00
896-The Adventures of Tinker Bell (Disney)	3.00	9.00	21.00
897-Jiminy Cricket (Disney)	2.00	6.00	14.00

	Good	Fine	N-Mint
898-Silvertip (Max Brand)-Kinstler-a (5/58)	3.00	9.00	21.00
899-Goofy (Disney)(5/58)	2.00	6.00	14.00
900-Prince Valiant-by Bob Fuje	3.50	10.50	24.00
901-Little Hiawatha (Disney)	1.70	5.00	12.00
902-Will-Yum!	1.00	3.00	7.00
903-Dotty Dripple and Taffy	1.30	4.00	9.00
904-Lee Hunter, Indian Fighter	2.00	6.00	14.00
905-Annette (Disney,TV, 5/58)-Mickey Mouse Club; Annette Funicello			
photo-c	12.00	36.00	84.00
906-Francis the Famous Talking Mule	1.00	3.00	7.00
907-Sugarfoot (No.1)(TV)Toth-a; photo-c	8.50	25.50	60.00
908-The Little People and the Giant-Walt Scott (5/58)			
	1.70	5.00	12.00
909-Smitty	1.50	4.50	10.00
910-The Vikings (Movie)-Buscema-a; Kirk Douglas photo-c			
	5.70	17.00	40.00
911-The Gray Ghost (TV)(Movie)-Photo-c	4.30	13.00	30.00
912-Leave It to Beaver (No.1)(TV)-Photo-c	12.00	36.00	84.00
913-The Left-Handed Gun (Movie) (7/58); Paul Newman photo-c			
	7.00	21.00	50.00
914-No Time for Sergeants (Movie)-Photo-c; Toth-a			
	6.00	18.00	42.00
915-Casey Jones (TV)-Photo-c	3.00	9.00	21.00
916-Red Ryder Ranch Comics	1.60	4.70	11.00
917-The Life of Riley (TV)-Photo-c	7.00	21.00	50.00
918-Beep Beep, the Roadrunner (No.1)(7/58)-Two different back			
covers published	4.00	12.00	28.00
919-Boots and Saddles (No.1)(TV)-Photo-c	5.00	15.00	35.00
920-Zorro (Disney-TV)(6/58)Toth-a; photo-c	7.00	21.00	50.00
921-Wyatt Earp (TV)-Manning-a; photo-c	4.00	12.00	28.00
922-Johnny Mack Brown by Russ Manning-Photo-c			
	4.00	12.00	28.00
923-Timmy	1.15	3.50	8.00
924-Colt .45 (No.1)(TV)(8/58)-Photo-c	5.00	15.00	35.00
925-Last of the Fast Guns (Movie) (8/58)-Photo-c			
	3.70	11.00	26.00
926-Peter Pan (Disney)-Reprint of No. 442	2.00	6.00	14.00
927-Top Gun (Luke Short) Buscema-a	2.30	7.00	16.00
928-Sea Hunt (No.1) (TV)-Lloyd Bridges photo-c			
	5.70	17.00	40.00
929-Brave Eagle (TV)-Photo-c	1.50	4.50	10.00
930-Maverick (TV) (7/58)-James Garner/Jack Kelly photo-c			
	5.00	15.00	35.00
931-Have Gun, Will Travel (No.1) (TV)-Photo-c	6.00	18.00	42.00
932-Smokey the Bear (His Life Story)	2.00	6.00	14.00
933-Zorro (Disney)-by Alex Toth (9/58)	7.00	21.00	50.00
934-Restless Gun (No.1)(TV)-Photo-c	5.70	17.00	40.00
935-King of the Royal Mounted	3.00	9.00	21.00
936-The Little Rascals (TV)	1.70	5.00	12.00
937-Ruff and Reddy (No.1)(TV)(1st Hanna-Barbera comic book)			
	3.00	9.00	21.00
938-Elmer Fudd (9/58)	.85	2.50	6.00
939-Steve Canyon - not by Caniff	3.00	9.00	21.00
940-Lolly and Pepper (10/58)	1.30	4.00	9.00
941-Pluto (Disney) (10/58)	1.70	5.00	12.00
942-Pony Express (TV)	2.00	6.00	14.00
943-White Wilderness (Disney-Movie) (10/58)	2.65	8.00	18.00
944-The 7th Voyage of Sindbad (Movie) (9/58)-Buscema-a			
	10.00	30.00	70.00
945-Maverick (TV)-James Garner/Jack Kelly photo-c			
	5.00	15.00	35.00
946-The Big Country (Movie)-Photo-c	3.50	10.50	24.00
947-Broken Arrow (TV)-Photo-c (11/58)	2.65	8.00	18.00
948-Daisy Duck's Diary (Disney) (11/58)	1.70	5.00	12.00
949-High Adventure (Lowell Thomas')(TV)-Photo-c			
	2.65	8.00	18.00

FOUR COLOR (continued)

	Good	Fine	N-Mint
950-Frosty the Snowman	1.70	5.00	12.00
951-The Lennon Sisters Life Story (TV)-Toth-a, 32pgs.-Photo-c			
	8.50	25.50	60.00
952-Goofy (Disney) (11/58)	2.00	6.00	14.00
953-Francis the Famous Talking Mule	1.00	3.00	7.00
954-Man in Space-Satellites (Disney-Movie)	2.30	7.00	16.00
955-Hi and Lois (11/58)	1.00	3.00	7.00
956-Ricky Nelson (No.1)(TV)-Photo-c	12.00	36.00	84.00
957-Buffalo Bee (No.1)(TV)	3.70	11.00	26.00
958-Santa Claus Funnies	1.50	4.50	10.00
959-Christmas Stories-(Walt Scott's Little People)(1951-56 strip re-prints)	1.70	5.00	12.00
960-Zorro (Disney)(TV)(12/58)-Toth art	7.00	21.00	50.00
961-Jace Pearson's Tales of the Texas Rangers (TV)-Spiegle-a; photo-c	3.50	10.50	24.00
962-Maverick (TV) (1/59)-James Garner/Jack Kelly photo-c			
	5.00	15.00	35.00
963-Johnny Mack Brown-Photo-c	3.50	10.50	24.00
964-The Hardy Boys (TV)(Disney)-Mickey Mouse Club (1/59)-Photo-c	4.00	12.00	28.00
965-Grandma Duck's Farm Friends (Disney) (1/59)			
	2.00	6.00	14.00
966-Tonka (starring Sal Mineo; Disney-Movie)-Photo-c			
	3.50	10.50	24.00
967-Chilly Willy (2/59)(Lantz)	.85	2.50	6.00
968-Tales of Wells Fargo (TV)-Photo-c	4.00	12.00	28.00
969-Peanuts (2/59)	5.00	15.00	35.00
970-Lawman (No.1)(TV)-Photo-c	6.50	19.50	45.00
971-Wagon Train (TV)-Photo-c	3.70	11.00	26.00
972-Tom Thumb (Movie)-George Pal (1/59)	7.00	21.00	50.00
973-Sleeping Beauty and the Prince (Disney) (5/59)			
	4.00	12.00	28.00
974-The Little Rascals (TV)(3/59)	1.70	5.00	12.00
975-Fury (TV)-Photo-c	3.70	11.00	26.00
976-Zorro (Disney)(TV)-Toth-a; photo-c	7.00	21.00	50.00
977-Elmer Fudd (3/59)	.85	2.50	6.00
978-Lolly and Pepper	1.30	4.00	9.00
979-Oswald the Rabbit (Lantz)	.85	2.50	6.00
980-Maverick (TV) (4-6/59)-James Garner/Jack Kelly photo-c			
	5.00	15.00	35.00
981-Ruff and Reddy (TV)(Hanna-Barbera)	2.00	6.00	14.00
982-The New Adventures of Tinker Bell (TV-Disney)			
	3.00	9.00	21.00
983-Have Gun, Will Travel (TV) (4-6/59)-Photo-c			
	4.00	12.00	28.00
984-Sleeping Beauty's Fairy Godmothers (Disney)			
	4.00	12.00	28.00
985-Shaggy Dog (Disney-Movie)-Photo-c	2.65	8.00	18.00
986-Restless Gun (TV)-Photo-c	4.30	13.00	30.00
987-Goofy (Disney) (7/59)	2.00	6.00	14.00
988-Little Hiawatha (Disney)	1.70	5.00	12.00
989-Jiminy Cricket (Disney) (5-7/59)	2.00	6.00	14.00
990-Huckleberry Hound (No.1)(TV)(Hanna-Barbera)			
	3.00	9.00	21.00
991-Francis the Famous Talking Mule	1.00	3.00	7.00
992-Sugarfoot (TV)-Toth-a; photo-c	8.50	25.50	60.00
993-Jim Bowie (TV)-Photo-c	3.00	9.00	21.00
994-Sea Hunt (TV)-Lloyd Bridges photo-c	4.50	14.00	32.00
995-Donald Duck Album (Disney) (5-7/59)	2.00	6.00	14.00
996-Nevada (Zane Grey)	2.30	7.00	16.00
997-Walt Disney Presents-Tales of Texas John Slaughter (No. 1) (TV-Disney)-Photo-c	3.00	9.00	21.00
998-Ricky Nelson (TV)-Photo-c	12.00	36.00	84.00
999-Leave It to Beaver (TV)-Photo-c	11.00	32.00	75.00
1000-The Gray Ghost (Movie) (6-8/59)-Photo-c	4.50	14.00	32.00
1001-Lowell Thomas' High Adventure (TV) (8-10/59)-Photo-c			

	Good	Fine	N-Mint
	2.65	8.00	18.00
1002-Buffalo Bee (TV)	2.85	8.50	20.00
1003-Zorro (TV) (Disney)-Photo-c	5.70	17.00	40.00
1004-Colt .45 (TV) (6-8/59)-Photo-c	3.70	11.00	26.00
1005-Maverick (TV)-James Garner/Jack Kelly photo-c			
	5.00	15.00	35.00
1006-Hercules (Movie)-Buscema-a	7.00	21.00	50.00
1007-John Paul Jones (Movie)-Robert Stack photo-c			
	2.65	8.00	18.00
1008-Beep Beep, the Road Runner (7-9/59)	2.00	6.00	14.00
1009-The Rifleman (No.1) (TV)-Photo-c	8.50	25.50	60.00
1010-Grandma Duck's Farm Friends (Disney)-by Carl Barks			
	6.00	18.00	42.00
1011-Buckskin (No.1)(TV)-Photo-c	5.00	15.00	35.00
1012-Last Train from Gun Hill (Movie) (7/59)-Photo-c			
	4.50	14.00	32.00
1013-Bat Masterson (No.1) (TV) (8/59)-Gene Barry photo-c			
	5.00	15.00	35.00
1014-The Lennon Sisters (TV)-Toth-a; photo-c	8.00	24.00	56.00
1015-Peanuts-Schulz-c	5.00	15.00	35.00
1016-Smokey the Bear Nature Stories	1.30	4.50	10.00
1017-Chilly Willy (Lantz)	.85	2.50	6.00
1018-Rio Bravo (Movie)(6/59)-John Wayne; Toth-a; John Wayne, Dean Martin & Ricky Nelson photo-c	14.00	42.00	100.00
1019-Wagon Train (TV)-Photo-c	3.70	11.00	26.00
1020-Jungle Jim-McWilliams-a	1.70	5.00	12.00
1021-Jace Pearson's Tales of the Texas Rangers (TV)-Photo-c			
	3.00	9.00	21.00
1022-Timmy	1.15	3.50	8.00
1023-Tales of Wells Fargo (TV)-Photo-c	3.70	11.00	28.00
1024-Darby O'Gill and the Little People (Disney-Movie)-Toth-a; Photo-c	6.00	18.00	42.00
1025-Vacation in Disneyland (8-10/59)-Carl Barks-a (Disney)			
	6.00	18.00	42.00
1026-Spin and Marty (TV)(Disney)-Mickey Mouse Club (9-11/59)-Photo-c	3.50	10.50	24.00
1027-The Texan (TV)-Photo-c	3.70	11.00	26.00
1028-Rawhide (No.1)(TV)-Clint Eastwood photo-c			
	14.00	42.00	100.00
1029-Boots and Saddles (9/59, TV)-Photo-c	3.50	10.50	24.00
1030-Spanky and Alfalfa, the Little Rascals (TV)			
	1.50	4.50	10.00
1031-Fury (TV)-Photo-c	3.70	11.00	26.00
1032-Elmer Fudd	.85	2.50	6.00
1033-Steve Canyon-not by Caniff; photo-c	3.00	9.00	21.00
1034-Nancy and Sluggo Summer Camp (9-11/59)			
	1.70	5.00	12.00
1035-Lawman (TV)-Photo-c	4.30	13.00	30.00
1036-The Big Circus (Movie)-Photo-c	2.65	8.00	18.00
1037-Zorro (Disney)(TV)-Tufts-a; Annette Funicello photo-c			
	8.00	24.00	56.00
1038-Ruff and Reddy (TV)(Hanna-Barbera)('59)	2.00	6.00	14.00
1039-Pluto (Disney) (11-1/60)	1.70	5.00	12.00
1040-Quick Draw McGraw (No.1)(TV)(Hanna-Barbera)(12-2/60)			
	3.70	11.00	26.00
1041-Sea Hunt (TV)-Toth-a; Lloyd Bridges photo-c			
	6.50	19.50	45.00
1042-The Three Chipmunks (Alvin, Simon & Theodore) (No.1)(TV) (10-12/59)	.85	2.50	6.00
1043-The Three Stooges (No.1)-Photo-c	7.00	21.00	50.00
1044-Have Gun, Will Travel (TV)-Photo-c	4.00	12.00	28.00
1045-Restless Gun (TV)-Photo-c	4.30	13.00	30.00
1046-Beep Beep, the Road Runner (11-1/60)	2.00	6.00	14.00
1047-Gyro Gearloose (No.1)(Disney)-Barks c/a	6.50	19.50	45.00
1048-The Horse Soldiers (Movie) (John Wayne)-Sekowsky-a			
	13.00	40.00	90.00

Four Color #951, © DELL

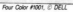

Four Color #1001, © DELL

Four Color #1026, © WDC

Four Color #1056, © Warner Bros.

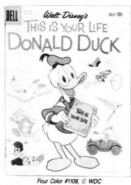

Four Color #1109, © WDC

Four Color #1130, © DELL

FOUR COLOR (continued)	Good	Fine	N-Mint
1049-Don't Give Up the Ship (Movie) (8/59)-Jerry Lewis photo-c			
	3.70	11.00	26.00
1050-Huckleberry Hound (TV)(Hanna-Barbera)(10-12/59)			
	2.30	7.00	16.00
1051-Donald in Mathmagic Land (Disney-Movie)			
	3.70	11.00	26.00
1052-Ben-Hur (Movie) (11/59)-Manning-a	5.70	17.00	40.00
1053-Goofy (Disney) (11-1/60)	2.00	6.00	14.00
1054-Huckleberry Hound Winter Fun (TV)(Hanna-Barbera)(12/59)			
	2.30	7.00	16.00
1055-Daisy Duck's Diary (Disney)-by Carl Barks (11-1/60)			
	5.00	15.00	35.00
1056-Yellowstone Kelly (Movie)-Clint Walker photo-c			
	2.65	8.00	18.00
1057-Mickey Mouse Album (Disney)	1.70	5.00	12.00
1058-Colt .45 (TV)-Photo-c	3.70	11.00	26.00
1059-Sugarfoot (TV)-Photo-c	5.00	15.00	35.00
1060-Journey to the Center of the Earth (Movie)-Photo-c			
	8.00	24.00	56.00
1061-Buffalo Bee (TV)	2.85	8.50	20.00
1062-Christmas Stories-(Walt Scott's Little People strip-r)			
	1.50	4.50	10.00
1063-Santa Claus Funnies	1.50	4.50	10.00
1064-Bugs Bunny's Merry Christmas (12/59)	1.70	5.00	12.00
1065-Frosty the Snowman	1.70	5.00	12.00
1066-77 Sunset Strip (No.1)(TV)-Toth-a (1-3/60)-Photo-c			
	6.50	19.50	45.00
1067-Yogi Bear (No.1)(TV)(Hanna-Barbera)	4.00	12.00	28.00
1068-Francis the Famous Talking Mule	1.00	3.00	7.00
1069-The FBI Story (Movie)-Toth-a; James Stewart photo-c			
	7.00	21.00	50.00
1070-Solomon and Sheba (Movie)-Sekowsky-a; photo-c			
	5.70	17.00	40.00
1071-The Real McCoys (No.1)(TV)-Toth-a; photo-c			
	7.00	21.00	50.00
1072-Blythe (Marge's)	2.00	6.00	14.00
1073-Grandma Duck's Farm Friends-Barks c/a (Disney)			
	6.00	18.00	42.00
1074-Chilly Willy (Lantz)	.85	2.50	6.00
1075-Tales of Wells Fargo (TV)-Photo-c	4.00	12.00	28.00
1076-The Rebel (No.1)(TV)-Sekowsky-a; photo-c	7.00	21.00	50.00
1077-The Deputy (No.1)(TV)-Buscema-a; Henry Fonda photo-c			
	7.00	21.00	50.00
1078-The Three Stooges (2-4/60)-Photo-c	5.00	15.00	35.00
1079-The Little Rascals (TV)(Spanky & Alfalfa)	1.50	4.50	10.00
1080-Fury (TV) (2-4/60)-Photo-c	3.70	11.00	26.00
1081-Elmer Fudd	.85	2.50	6.00
1082-Spin and Marty (Disney)(TV)-Photo-c	3.50	10.50	24.00
1083-Men into Space (TV)-Anderson-a; photo-c	3.00	9.00	21.00
1084-Speedy Gonzales	1.30	4.00	9.00
1085-The Time Machine (H.G. Wells) (Movie) (3/60)-Alex Toth-a			
	8.50	25.50	60.00
1086-Lolly and Pepper	1.30	4.00	9.00
1087-Peter Gunn (TV)-Photo-c	5.00	15.00	35.00
1088-A Dog of Flanders (Movie)-Photo-c	2.30	7.00	16.00
1089-Restless Gun (TV)-Photo-c	4.30	13.00	30.00
1090-Francis the Famous Talking Mule	1.00	3.00	7.00
1091-Jacky's Diary (4-6/60)	2.30	7.00	16.00
1092-Toby Tyler (Disney-Movie)-Photo-c	2.30	7.00	16.00
1093-MacKenzie's Raiders (Movie)-Photo-c	3.70	11.00	26.00
1094-Goofy (Disney)	2.00	6.00	14.00
1095-Gyro Gearloose (Disney)-Barks-c/a	5.50	16.50	38.00
1096-The Texan (TV)-Rory Calhoun photo-c	3.70	11.00	26.00
1097-Rawhide (TV)-Manning-a; Clint Eastwood photo-c			
	11.00	32.00	75.00
1098-Sugarfoot (TV)-Photo-c	5.00	15.00	35.00

	Good	Fine	N-Mint
1099-Donald Duck Album (Disney) (5-7/60) - Barks-c			
	2.30	7.00	16.00
1100-Annette's Life Story (Disney-Movie)(5/60)-Annette Funicello			
photo-c	13.00	40.00	90.00
1101-Robert Louis Stevenson's Kidnapped (Disney-Movie) (5/60);			
photo-c	3.50	10.50	24.00
1102-Wanted: Dead or Alive (No.1)(TV) (5-7/60); Steve McQueen			
photo-c	7.00	21.00	50.00
1103-Leave It to Beaver (TV)-Photo-c	11.00	32.00	75.00
1104-Yogi Bear Goes to College (TV)(Hanna-Barbera)(6-8/60)			
	3.00	9.00	21.00
1105-Gale Storm (Oh! Susanna) (TV)-Toth-a; photo-c			
	8.00	24.00	56.00
1106-77 Sunset Strip (6-8/60)-Toth-a; photo-c			
	5.70	17.00	40.00
1107-Buckskin (TV)-Photo-c	3.70	11.00	26.00
1108-The Troubleshooters (TV)-Keenan Wynn photo-c			
	3.50	10.50	24.00
1109-This Is Your Life, Donald Duck (Disney)(TV)(8-10/60)-Gyro flash-			
back to WDC&S 141. Origin Donald Duck (1st told)			
	7.00	21.00	50.00
1110-Bonanza (No.1) (TV) (6-8/60)-Photo-c	7.00	21.00	50.00
1111-Shotgun Slade (TV)	3.70	11.00	26.00
1112-Pixie and Dixie and Mr. Jinks (No.1)(TV)(Hanna-Barbera)(7-9/60)			
	3.00	9.00	21.00
1113-Tales of Wells Fargo (TV)-Photo-c	4.00	12.00	28.00
1114-Huckleberry Finn (Movie) (7/60)-Photo-c	2.65	8.00	18.00
1115-Ricky Nelson (TV)-Manning-a; photo-c	12.00	36.00	84.00
1116-Boots and Saddles (TV)(8/60)-Photo-c	3.50	10.50	24.00
1117-Boy and the Pirates (Movie)-Photo-c	3.70	11.00	26.00
1118-The Sword and the Dragon (Movie) (6/60)-Photo-c			
	4.50	14.00	32.00
1119-Smokey the Bear Nature Stories	1.50	4.50	10.00
1120-Dinosaurus (Movie)-Painted-c	3.00	9.00	21.00
1121-Hercules Unchained (Movie)(8/60)-Crandall/Evans-a			
	5.70	17.00	40.00
1122-Chilly Willy (Lantz)	.85	2.50	6.00
1123-Tombstone Territory (TV)-Photo-c	5.00	15.00	35.00
1124-Whirlybirds (No.1) (TV)-Photo-c	5.00	15.00	35.00
1125-Laramie (No.1)(TV)-Photo-c	5.50	16.50	38.00
1126-Sundance (TV) (8-10/60)-Earl Holliman photo-c			
	5.70	17.00	40.00
1127-The Three Stooges-Photo-c	5.00	15.00	35.00
1128-Rocky and His Friends (No.1)(TV) (Jay Ward) (8-10/60)			
	10.00	30.00	70.00
1129-Pollyanna (Disney-Movie)-Photo-c	6.50	19.50	45.00
1130-The Deputy (TV)-Buscema-a; Henry Fonda photo-c			
	5.70	17.00	40.00
1131-Elmer Fudd (9-11/60)	.85	2.50	6.00
1132-Space Mouse (Lantz)(8-10/60)	1.50	4.50	12.00
1133-Fury (TV)-Photo-c	3.70	11.00	26.00
1134-Real McCoys (TV)-Toth-a; photo-c	7.00	21.00	50.00
1135-M.G.M.'s Mouse Musketeers	.85	2.50	6.00
1136-Jungle Cat (Disney-Movie) (9-11/60)-Photo-c			
	3.50	10.50	24.00
1137-The Little Rascals (TV)	1.50	4.50	10.00
1138-The Rebel (TV)-Photo-c	5.70	17.00	40.00
1139-Spartacus (Movie) (11/60)-Buscema-a; photo-c			
	7.00	21.00	50.00
1140-Donald Duck Album (Disney)	2.30	7.00	16.00
1141-Huckleberry Hound for President (TV)(Hanna-Barbera)(10/60)			
	2.30	7.00	16.00
1142-Johnny Ringo (TV)-Photo-c	4.50	14.00	32.00
1143-Pluto (Disney) (11-1/61)	1.70	5.00	12.00
1144-The Story of Ruth (Movie)-Photo-c	7.00	21.00	50.00
1145-The Lost World (Movie)-Kane-a; photo-c	7.00	21.00	50.00

FOUR COLOR (continued)

	Good	Fine	N-Mint
1146-Restless Gun (TV)-Photo-c; Wildey-a	4.30	13.00	30.00
1147-Sugarfoot (TV)-Photo-c	5.00	15.00	35.00
1148-I Aim at the Stars-the Wernher Von Braun Story (Movie) (11-1/61)-Photo-c	3.00	9.00	21.00
1149-Goofy (Disney) (11-1/61)	2.00	6.00	14.00
1150-Daisy Duck's Diary (Disney) (12-1/61) by Carl Barks	5.00	15.00	35.00
1151-Mickey Mouse Album (Disney) (11-1/61)	1.70	5.00	12.00
1152-Rocky and His Friends (Jay Ward) (TV) (12-2/61)	8.00	24.00	56.00
1153-Frosty the Snowman	1.50	4.50	10.00
1154-Santa Claus Funnies	1.50	4.50	10.00
1155-North to Alaska (Movie) - John Wayne-Photo-c	11.50	34.00	80.00
1156-Walt Disney Swiss Family Robinson (Movie) (12/60)-Photo-c	3.50	10.50	24.00
1157-Master of the World (Movie) (7/61)	3.50	10.50	24.00
1158-Three Worlds of Gulliver (2 issues with different covers)(Movie); Photo-c	3.50	10.50	24.00
1159-77 Sunset Strip (TV)-Toth-a; photo-c	5.70	17.00	40.00
1160-Rawhide (TV)-Clint Eastwood photo-c	11.00	32.00	75.00
1161-Grandma Duck's Farm Friends (Disney) by Carl Barks (2-4/61)	6.00	18.00	42.00
1162-Yogi Bear Joins the Marines (TV)(Hanna-Barbera)(5-7/61)	3.00	9.00	21.00
1163-Daniel Boone (3-5/61); Marsh-a	2.65	8.00	18.00
1164-Wanted: Dead or Alive (TV); Steve McQueen photo-c	6.00	18.00	42.00
1165-Ellery Queen (No.1)(3-5/61)	6.00	18.00	42.00
1166-Rocky and His Friends (Jay Ward) (TV)	8.00	24.00	56.00
1167-Tales of Wells Fargo (TV)-Photo-c	4.00	12.00	28.00
1168-The Detectives (TV)-Robert Taylor photo-c	4.50	14.00	32.00
1169-New Adventures of Sherlock Holmes	11.00	32.00	75.00
1170-The Three Stooges-Photo-c	5.00	15.00	35.00
1171-Elmer Fudd	.85	2.50	6.00
1172-Fury (TV)-Photo-c	3.70	11.00	26.00
1173-The Twilight Zone (No.1)-Crandall/Evans-c/a (TV) (5/61)	5.70	17.00	40.00
1174-The Little Rascals (TV)	1.50	4.50	10.00
1175-M.G.M.'s Mouse Musketeers (3-5/61)	.85	2.50	6.00
1176-Dondi (Movie)-Origin; photo-c	2.00	6.00	14.00
1177-Chilly Willy (Lantz)(4-6/61)	.85	2.50	6.00
1178-Ten Who Dared (Disney-Movie) (12/60)	2.65	8.00	18.00
1179-The Swamp Fox (TV)(Disney)-Leslie Nielson photo-c	3.50	10.50	24.00
1180-The Danny Thomas Show (TV)-Toth-a; photo-c	10.00	30.00	70.00
1181-Texas John Slaughter (TV)(Disney)(4-6/61)-Photo-c	2.30	7.00	16.00
1182-Donald Duck Album (Disney) (5-7/61)	2.00	6.00	14.00
1183-101 Dalmatians (Disney-Movie) (3/61)	2.85	8.50	20.00
1184-Gyro Gearloose; Barks c/a (Disney) (5-7/61) Two variations exist	5.50	16.50	38.00
1185-Sweetie Pie	1.50	4.50	10.00
1186-Yak Yak (No.1) by Jack Davis (2 versions - one minus 3-pg. Davis-c/a)	4.50	14.00	32.00
1187-The Three Stooges (6-8/61)-Photo-c	5.00	15.00	35.00
1188-Atlantis, the Lost Continent (Movie) (5/61)-Photo-c	7.00	21.00	50.00
1189-Greyfriars Bobby (Disney-Movie, 11/61)-Photo-c	3.00	9.00	21.00
1190-Donald and the Wheel (Disney-Movie) (11/61); Barks-c	3.50	10.50	24.00
1191-Leave It to Beaver (TV)-Photo-c	11.00	32.00	75.00
1192-Ricky Nelson (TV)-Manning-a; photo-c	12.00	36.00	84.00
1193-The Real McCoys (TV)(6-8/61)-Photo-c	5.70	17.00	40.00

	Good	Fine	N-Mint
1194-Pepe (Movie) (4/61)-Photo-c	2.00	6.00	14.00
1195-National Velvet (No.1)(TV)-Photo-c	2.65	8.00	18.00
1196-Pixie and Dixie and Mr. Jinks (TV)(Hanna-Barbera)(7-9/61)	2.30	7.00	16.00
1197-The Aquanauts (TV)(5-7/61)-Photo-c	3.50	10.50	24.00
1198-Donald in Mathmagic Land - reprint of No. 1051 (Disney-Movie)	3.70	11.00	26.00
1199-The Absent-Minded Professor (Disney-Movie) (4/61)-Photo-c	3.50	10.50	24.00
1200-Hennessey (TV) (8-10/61)-Gil Kane-a; photo-c	3.70	11.00	26.00
1201-Goofy (Disney) (8-10/61)	2.00	6.00	14.00
1202-Rawhide (TV)-Clint Eastwood photo-c	11.00	32.00	75.00
1203-Pinocchio (Disney) (3/62)	2.00	6.00	14.00
1204-Scamp (Disney)	.85	2.50	6.00
1205-David and Goliath (Movie) (7/61)-Photo-c	3.00	9.00	21.00
1206-Lolly and Pepper (9-11/61)	1.30	4.00	9.00
1207-The Rebel (TV)-Sekowsky-a; photo-c	5.70	17.00	40.00
1208-Rocky and His Friends (Jay Ward) (TV)	8.00	24.00	56.00
1209-Sugarfoot (TV)-Photo-c	5.00	15.00	35.00
1210-The Parent Trap (Disney-Movie)(8/61)-Haley Mills photo-c	7.00	21.00	50.00
1211-77 Sunset Strip (TV)-Manning-a; photo-c	4.50	14.00	32.00
1212-Chilly Willy (Lantz)(7-9/61)	.85	2.50	6.00
1213-Mysterious Island (Movie)-Photo-c	4.50	14.00	32.00
1214-Smokey the Bear	1.50	4.50	10.00
1215-Tales of Wells Fargo (TV) (10-12/61)-Photo-c	4.00	12.00	28.00
1216-Whirlybirds (TV)-Photo-c	4.00	12.00	28.00
1218-Fury (TV)-Photo-c	3.70	11.00	26.00
1219-The Detectives (TV)-Robert Taylor & Adam West photo-c	3.50	10.50	24.00
1220-Gunslinger (TV)-Photo-c	4.00	12.00	28.00
1221-Bonanza (TV) (9-11/61)-Photo-c	5.70	17.00	40.00
1222-Elmer Fudd (9-11/61)	.85	2.50	6.00
1223-Laramie (TV)-Gil Kane-a; photo-c	4.30	13.00	30.00
1224-The Little Rascals (TV)(10-12/61)	1.50	4.50	10.00
1225-The Deputy (TV)-Henry Fonda photo-c	5.70	17.00	40.00
1226-Nikki, Wild Dog of the North (Disney-Movie) (9/61)-Photo-c	2.00	6.00	14.00
1227-Morgan the Pirate (Movie)-Photo-c	6.00	18.00	42.00
1229-Thief of Baghdad (Movie)-Evans-a; photo-c	7.00	21.00	50.00
1230-Voyage to the Bottom of the Sea (#1)(Movie)-Photo insert on-c	4.00	12.00	28.00
1231-Danger Man (TV)(9-11/61); Patrick McGoohan photo-c	4.00	12.00	28.00
1232-On the Double (Movie)	2.30	7.00	16.00
1233-Tammy Tell Me True (1961)	3.70	11.00	26.00
1234-The Phantom Planet (Movie) (1961)	3.50	10.50	24.00
1235-Mister Magoo (12-2/62)	4.00	12.00	28.00
1235-Mister Magoo (3-5/65) 2nd printing - reprint of '61 issue	2.35	7.00	16.00
1236-King of Kings (Movie)-Photo-c	4.50	14.00	32.00
1237-The Untouchables (No.1)(TV)-not by Toth; photo-c	5.00	15.00	35.00
1238-Deputy Dawg (TV)	5.00	15.00	35.00
1239-Donald Duck Album (Disney) (10-12/61)-Barks-c	2.30	7.00	16.00
1240-The Detectives (TV)-Tufts-a; Robert Taylor photo-c	3.50	10.50	24.00
1241-Sweetie Pie	1.50	4.50	10.00
1242-King Leonardo and His Short Subjects (No.1)(TV)(11-1/62)	5.00	15.00	35.00
1243-Ellery Queen	4.50	14.00	32.00
1244-Space Mouse (Lantz)(11-1/62)	1.50	4.50	10.00

Four Color #1162, © Hanna-Barbera

Four Color #1199, © WDC

Four Color #1219, © DELL

Four Color #1249, © DELL

Four Color #1341, © Mayberry Ent.

Four Favorites #11, © ACE

FOUR COLOR (continued)	Good	Fine	N-Mint
1245-New Adventures of Sherlock Holmes	11.00	32.00	75.00
1246-Mickey Mouse Album (Disney)	1.70	5.00	12.00
1247-Daisy Duck's Diary (Disney) (12-2/62)	1.70	5.00	12.00
1248-Pluto (Disney)	1.70	5.00	12.00
1249-The Danny Thomas Show (TV)-Manning-a; photo-c			
	9.30	28.00	65.00
1250-The Four Horsemen of the Apocalypse (Movie)-Photo-c			
	3.70	11.00	26.00
1251-Everything's Ducky (Movie) (1961)	2.65	8.00	18.00
1252-The Andy Griffith Show (TV)-Photo-c; 1st show aired 10/3/60			
	8.50	25.50	60.00
1253-Space Man (No.1) (1-3/62)	3.50	10.50	24.00
1254-"Diver Dan" (TV) (2-4/62)-Photo-c	3.00	9.00	21.00
1255-The Wonders of Aladdin (Movie) (1961)	3.50	10.50	24.00
1256-Kona, Monarch of Monster Isle (No.1)(2-4/62)-Glanzman-a			
	2.85	8.50	20.00
1257-Car 54, Where Are You? (No.1) (TV) (3-5/62)-Photo-c			
	3.50	10.50	24.00
1258-The Frogmen (No.1)-Evans-a	3.50	10.50	24.00
1259-El Cid (Movie) (1961)-Photo-c	3.50	10.50	24.00
1260-The Horsemasters (TV, Movie - Disney) (12-2/62)-Annette			
Funicello photo-c	5.00	15.00	35.00
1261-Rawhide (TV)-Clint Eastwood photo-c	11.00	32.00	75.00
1262-The Rebel (TV)-Photo-c	5.70	17.00	40.00
1263-77 Sunset Strip (TV) (12-2/62)-Manning-a; photo-c			
	4.50	14.00	32.00
1264-Pixie and Dixie and Mr. Jinks (TV)(Hanna-Barbera)			
	2.30	7.00	16.00
1265-The Real McCoys (TV)-Photo-c	5.70	17.00	40.00
1266-M.G.M.'s Spike and Tyke (12-2/62)	.85	2.50	6.00
1267-Gyro Gearloose; Barks c/a, 4 pgs. (Disney) (12-2/62)			
	4.00	12.00	28.00
1268-Oswald the Rabbit (Lantz)	.85	2.50	6.00
1269-Rawhide (TV)-Clint Eastwood photo-c	11.00	32.00	75.00
1270-Bullwinkle and Rocky (No.1)(Jay Ward)(TV)(3-5/62)			
	7.00	21.00	50.00
1271-Yogi Bear Birthday Party (TV)(Hanna-Barbera)(11/61)			
	2.30	7.00	16.00
1272-Frosty the Snowman	1.50	4.50	10.00
1273-Hans Brinker (Disney-Movie)-Photo-c	3.00	9.00	21.00
1274-Santa Claus Funnies	1.50	4.50	10.00
1275-Rocky and His Friends (Jay Ward) (TV)	8.00	24.00	56.00
1276-Dondi	1.50	4.50	10.00
1278-King Leonardo and His Short Subjects (TV)			
	5.00	15.00	35.00
1279-Grandma Duck's Farm Friends (Disney)	2.00	6.00	14.00
1280-Hennessey (TV)-Photo-c	3.50	10.50	24.00
1281-Chilly Willy (Lantz)(4-6/62)	.85	2.50	6.00
1282-Babes in Toyland (Disney-Movie) (1/62); Annette Funicello			
photo-c	6.00	18.00	42.00
1283-Bonanza (TV) (2-4/62)-Photo-c	5.70	17.00	40.00
1284-Laramie (TV)-Heath-a; photo-c	4.30	13.00	30.00
1285-Leave It to Beaver (TV)-Photo-c	11.00	32.00	75.00
1286-The Untouchables (TV)-Photo-c	5.00	15.00	35.00
1287-Man from Wells Fargo (TV)-Photo-c	3.70	11.00	26.00
1288-The Twilight Zone (TV) (4/62)-Crandall/Evans c/a			
	4.50	14.00	32.00
1289-Ellery Queen	4.50	14.00	32.00
1290-M.G.M.'s Mouse Musketeers	.85	2.50	6.00
1291-77 Sunset Strip (TV)-Manning-a; photo-c	4.50	14.00	32.00
1293-Elmer Fudd (3-5/62)	.85	2.50	6.00
1294-Ripcord (TV)	3.50	10.50	24.00
1295-Mister Ed, the Talking Horse (No.1)(TV)(3-5/62)-Photo-c			
	5.70	17.00	40.00
1296-Fury (TV) (3-5/62)-Photo-c	3.70	11.00	26.00
1297-Spanky, Alfalfa and the Little Rascals (TV)			

	Good	Fine	N-Mint
	1.50	4.50	10.00
1298-The Hathaways (TV)-Photo-c	2.65	8.00	18.00
1299-Deputy Dawg (TV)	5.00	15.00	35.00
1300-The Comancheros (Movie) (1961)-John Wayne			
	11.50	34.00	80.00
1301-Adventures in Paradise (TV) (2-4/62)	2.30	7.00	16.00
1302-Johnny Jason, Teen Reporter (2-4/62)	1.15	3.50	8.00
1303-Lad: A Dog (Movie)-Photo-c	2.65	8.00	18.00
1304-Nellie the Nurse (3-5/62)-Stanley-a	5.00	15.00	35.00
1305-Mister Magoo (3-5/62)	4.00	12.00	28.00
1306-Target: the Corruptors (TV) (3-5/62)	2.30	7.00	16.00
1307-Margie (TV) (3-5/62)	2.30	7.00	16.00
1308-Tales of the Wizard of Oz (TV) (3-5/62)	7.00	21.00	50.00
1309-87th Precinct (TV) (4-6/62)-Krigstein-a; photo-c			
	5.70	17.00	40.00
1310-Huck and Yogi Winter Sports (TV)(Hanna-Barbera)(3/62)			
	2.30	7.00	16.00
1311-Rocky and His Friends (Jay Ward) (TV)	8.00	24.00	56.00
1312-National Velvet (TV)-Photo-c	2.30	7.00	16.00
1313-Moon Pilot (Disney-Movie)-Photo-c	2.65	8.00	18.00
1328-The Underwater City (Movie)-Evans-a (1961)-Photo-c			
	4.00	12.00	28.00
1330-Brain Boy (No.1)-Gil Kane-a	4.00	12.00	28.00
1332-Bachelor Father (TV)	4.50	14.00	32.00
1333-Short Ribs (4-6/62)	2.65	8.00	18.00
1335-Aggie Mack (4-6/62)	2.00	6.00	14.00
1336-On Stage - not by Leonard Starr	2.65	8.00	18.00
1337-Dr. Kildare (No.1) (TV)-Photo-c	3.50	10.50	24.00
1341-The Andy Griffith Show (TV) (4-6/62)-Photo-c			
	8.50	25.50	60.00
1348-Yak Yak (No.2)-Jack Davis c/a	4.00	12.00	28.00
1349-Yogi Bear Visits the U.N. (TV)(Hanna-Barbera)(1/62)-Photo-c			
	2.30	7.00	16.00
1350-Comanche (Disney-Movie)(1962)-Reprints 4-Color 966 (title			
change from "Tonka" to "Comanche")(4-6/62)-Sal Mineo			
photo-c	2.30	7.00	16.00
1354-Calvin & the Colonel (TV)(4-6/62)	4.00	12.00	28.00

NOTE: Missing numbers probably do not exist.

4-D MONKEY, THE
1988 - Present ($1.80, color, 52 pgs.)
Leung's Publications

1-Karate Pig, Ninja Flounder & 4-D Monkey (48 pgs., centerfold is a			
Christmas card	.30	.90	1.80
2-4 (52 pgs.)	.30	.90	1.80

FOUR FAVORITES (Crime Must Pay the Penalty No. 33 on)
Sept, 1941 - No. 32, Dec, 1947
Ace Magazines

1-Vulcan, Lash Lightning, Magno the Magnetic Man & The Raven			
begin; Flag-c	45.00	135.00	315.00
2-The Black Ace only app.	21.50	64.00	150.00
3-Last Vulcan	18.50	56.00	130.00
4,5: 4-The Raven & Vulcan end; Unknown Soldier begins, ends			
#28. 5-Captain Courageous begins, ends #28; not in #6			
	17.00	51.00	120.00
6-8: 6-The Flag app.; Mr. Risk begins	14.00	42.00	100.00
9,11-Kurtzman-a; 11-Hitler, Mussolini, Hirohito-c; L.B. Cole-a			
	19.00	58.00	135.00
10-Classic Kurtzman c/a	21.50	64.00	150.00
12-L.B. Cole-a	11.00	32.00	75.00
13-20: 18,20-Palais c/a	9.30	28.00	65.00
21-No Unknown Soldier; The Unknown app.	6.50	19.50	45.00
22-Captain Courageous drops costume	6.50	19.50	45.00
23-26: 23-Unknown Soldier drops costume. 26-Last Magno			
	6.50	19.50	45.00

FOUR FAVORITES (continued)	Good	Fine	N-Mint
27-32: 29-Hap Hazard app.	5.50	16.50	38.00

NOTE: *Jim Mooney* c-3. *Palais* c-18, 20, 24, 25.

FOUR HORSEMEN, THE (See The Crusaders)

FOUR HORSEMEN OF THE APOCALYPSE, THE (See 4-Color No. 1250)

FOUR MOST (. . .Boys No. 32-41)
Winter, 1941-42 - V8#5(#36), 9-10/49; #37, 11-12/49 - #41, 6-7/50
Novelty Publications/Star Publications No. 37-on

V1#1-The Target by Sid Greene, The Cadet & Dick Cole begin with			
origins retold; produced by Funnies Inc.	45.00	135.00	315.00
2-Last Target	21.50	64.00	150.00
3-Flag-c	18.50	56.00	130.00
4-1pg. Dr. Seuss(signed)	14.00	42.00	100.00
V2#1-4, V3#1-4	3.50	10.50	24.00
V4#1-4	2.65	8.00	18.00
V5#1-The Target & Targeteers app.	2.30	7.00	16.00
2-5	2.30	7.00	16.00
V6#1-White Rider & Super Horse begins	2.30	7.00	16.00
2-4,6	2.30	7.00	16.00
5-L. B. Cole-c	3.70	11.00	26.00
V7#1,3,5, V8#1	2.30	7.00	16.00
2,4,6-L. B. Cole-c. 6-Last Dick Cole	3.70	11.00	26.00
V8#2,3,5-L. B. Cole c/a	5.00	15.00	35.00
4-L. B. Cole-a	3.00	9.00	21.00
37-41: 38,39-L.B. Cole-c. 38-Johnny Weismuller life story			
	3.00	9.00	21.00
Accepted Reprint 38-40 (nd); L.B. Cole-c	2.00	6.00	14.00

FOUR-STAR BATTLE TALES
Feb-Mar, 1973 - No. 5, Nov-Dec, 1973
National Periodical Publications

1-All reprints		.30	.60
2-5: 5-Krigstein-a(r)		.25	.50

NOTE: *Drucker* a-1,3-5r. *Heath* a-2r, 5r; c-1. *Kubert* a-4r; c-2.

FOUR STAR SPECTACULAR
Mar-Apr, 1976 - No. 6, Jan-Feb, 1977
National Periodical Publications

1-Reprints begin		.30	.60
2-6: 2-Infinity cover		.25	.50

NOTE: *All contain DC Superhero reprints. No. 1 has 68 pages; No. 2-6, 52 pages. No. 1,4-Hawkman app.; No. 2-Flash app.; No. 3-Green Lantern app; No. 4-Wonder Woman, Superboy app; No. 5-Gr. Arrow, Vigilante app; No. 6-Blackhawk G.A.-r.*

FOUR TEENERS (Formerly Crime Must Pay The Penalty?; Dotty No. 35 on)
No. 34, April, 1948 (Teen-age comic)
A. A. Wyn

34	2.15	6.50	15.00

FOX AND THE CROW (Stanley & His Monster No. 109 on)
(See Comic Cavalcade & Real Screen Comics)
Dec-Jan, 1951-52 - No. 108, Feb-Mar, 1968
National Periodical Publications

1	50.00	150.00	350.00
2(Scarce)	24.00	73.00	170.00
3-5	14.00	42.00	100.00
6-10	10.00	30.00	70.00
11-20	6.50	19.50	45.00
21-40: 22-Last precode (2/55)	4.00	12.00	28.00
41-60	2.65	8.00	18.00
61-80	1.70	5.00	12.00
81-94	1.15	3.50	8.00
95-Stanley & His Monster begins(origin)	1.70	5.00	12.00
96-99,101-108	.85	2.50	6.00
100	1.15	3.50	8.00

NOTE: Many covers by *Mort Drucker.*

FOX AND THE HOUND, THE (Disney)
Aug, 1981 - No. 3, Oct, 1981
Whitman Publishing Co.

	Good	Fine	N-Mint
11292 ('81)-Based on animated movie		.30	.60
2,3		.30	.60

FOX GIANTS
1944 - 1950 (132 - 196 pgs.)
Fox Features Syndicate

Album of Crime nn(1949, 132p)	26.00	77.00	180.00
Album of Love nn(1949, 132p)	19.00	58.00	135.00
All Famous Crime Stories nn('49, 132p)	26.00	77.00	180.00
All Good Comics 1(1944, 132p)(R.W. Voigt)-The Bouncer, Purple			
Tigress, Puppeteer, Green Mask; Infinity-c	19.00	58.00	135.00
All Great nn(1944, 132p)-Capt. Jack Terry, Rick Evans, Jaguar Man			
	19.00	58.00	135.00
All Great nn(Chicago Nite Life News)(1945, 132p)-Green Mask, Boun-			
cer, Puppeteer, Rick Evans, Rocket Kelly	24.00	71.00	165.00
All-Great Confessions nn(1948, 132p)	19.00	58.00	135.00
All Great Crime Stories nn('49, 132p)	26.00	77.00	180.00
All Great Jungle Adventures nn('49, 132p)	26.00	77.00	180.00
All Real Confession Mag. 3 (3/49, 132p)	19.00	58.00	135.00
All Real Confession Mag. 4 (4/49, 132p)	19.00	58.00	135.00
All Your Comics 1(1944, 132p)-The Puppeteer, Red Robbins, &			
Merciless the Sorcerer	19.00	58.00	135.00
Almanac Of Crime nn(1948, 148p)	26.00	77.00	180.00
Almanac Of Crime 1(1950, 132p)	26.00	77.00	180.00
Book Of Love nn(1949, 132p)	19.00	58.00	135.00
Burning Romances 1(1949, 132p)	24.00	71.00	165.00
Crimes Incorporated nn(1950, 132p)	24.00	71.00	165.00
Daring Love Stories nn(1950, 132p)	19.00	58.00	135.00
Everybody's Comics 1(1944, 196p)-The Green Mask, The Puppeteer,			
The Bouncer; (50 cents)	23.00	70.00	160.00
Everybody's Comics 1(1946, 196p)-Green Lama, The Puppeteer			
	19.00	58.00	135.00
Everybody's Comics 1(1946, 196p)-Same as '45 Ribtickler			
	16.00	48.00	110.00
Everybody's Comics nn(1947, 132p)-Jo-Jo, Purple Tigress, Cosmo			
Cat, Bronze Man	19.00	58.00	135.00
Exciting Romance Stories nn('49, 132p	19.00	58.00	135.00
Intimate Romances nn(1950, 132p)	19.00	58.00	135.00
Journal Of Crime nn(1949, 132p)	24.00	71.00	165.00
Love Problems nn(1949, 132p)	19.00	58.00	135.00
Love Thrills nn(1950, 132p)	19.00	58.00	135.00
March of Crime nn('48, 132p)-female w/rifle-c	24.00	71.00	165.00
March of Crime nn('49, 132p)-cop w/pistol-c	24.00	71.00	165.00
March of Crime nn(1949, 132p)-coffin & man w/machine-gun-c			
	24.00	71.00	165.00
Revealing Love Stories nn(1950, 132p)	19.00	58.00	135.00
Ribtickler nn(1945, 196p, 50¢)-Chicago Nite Life News; Marvel Mutt,			
Cosmo Cat, Flash Rabbit, The Nebbs app.	19.00	58.00	135.00
Romantic Thrills nn(1950, 132p)	19.00	58.00	135.00
Secret Love nn(1949, 132p)	19.00	58.00	135.00
Secret Love Stories nn(1949, 132p)	19.00	58.00	135.00
Strange Love nn(1950, 132p)-Photo-c	24.00	71.00	165.00
Sweetheart Scandals nn(1950, 132p)	19.00	58.00	135.00
Teen-Age Love nn(1950, 132p)	19.00	58.00	135.00
Throbbing Love nn(1950, 132p)-Photo-c	24.00	71.00	165.00
Truth About Crime nn(1949, 132p)	24.00	71.00	165.00
Variety Comics 1(1946, 132p)-Blue Beetle, Jungle Jo			
	19.00	58.00	135.00
Variety Comics nn(1950, 132p)	19.00	58.00	135.00
Western Roundup nn(1950, 132p)-Hoot Gibson	19.00	58.00	135.00

NOTE: Each of the above usually contain four remaindered Fox books minus covers. Since these missing covers often had the first page of the first story, most Giants therefore are usually incomplete. Approximate values are listed. Books with appearances of Phantom Lady, Rulah, Jo-Jo, etc. could bring more.

Four Most V3#1, © NOVP

Fox And The Crow #12, © DC

Fox Giant (Love Problems), © FOX

Foxhole #1, © PRIZE

Frank Buck #70, © FOX

Frankenstein Comics #19, © PRIZE

FOXHOLE (Becomes Never Again #8?)
9-10/54 - No. 4, 3-4/55; No. 5, 7/55 - No. 7, 3/56
Mainline/Charlton Comics No. 5 on

	Good	Fine	N-Mint
1-Kirby-c	5.70	17.00	40.00
2-Kirby c/a(2)	5.70	17.00	40.00
3,5-Kirby-c only	2.65	8.00	18.00
4,7	1.00	3.00	7.00
6-Kirby c/a(2)	5.00	15.00	35.00
Super Reprints #10-12,15-18	.35	1.00	2.00

NOTE: Kirby a(r)-Super #11,12. Powell a(r)-Super #15,16.

FOXY FAGAN COMICS
Dec, 1946 - No. 7, Summer, 1948
Dearfield Publishing Co.

1-Foxy Fagan & Little Buck begin	5.70	17.00	40.00
2	2.65	8.00	18.00
3-7	2.00	6.00	14.00

FOXY GRANDPA (Also see The Funnies, 1st series)
1901 - 1916 (Hardcover; strip reprints)
N. Y. Herald/Frederick A. Stokes Co./M. A. Donahue & Co./Bunny
Publ.(L. R. Hammersly Co.)

	Good	Fine	VF-NM
1901-9x15'' in color- N. Y. Herald	30.00	90.00	210.00
1902-''Latest Larks of . . .,'' 32 pgs. in color, 9½x15½''	30.00	90.00	210.00
1902-''The Many Advs. of . . .,'' 9x15'', 148pgs. in color (Hammersly)	38.00	115.00	265.00
1903-''Latest Advs.,'' 9x15'', 24 pgs. in color, Hammersly Co.	30.00	90.00	210.00
1903-''. . .'s New Advs.,'' 10x15'', 32 pgs. in color, Stokes	30.00	90.00	210.00
1904-''Up to Date,'' 10x15'', 28 pgs. in color, Stokes	30.00	90.00	210.00
1905-''& Flip Flaps,'' 9½x15½'', 52 pgs., in color	30.00	90.00	210.00
1905-''The Latest Advs. of,'' 9x15'', 28 pgs., in color, M.A. Donahue Co.; re-issue of 1902 ish	19.00	57.00	130.00
1905-''Merry Pranks of,'' 9½x15½'', 52 pgs. in color, Donahue	19.00	57.00	130.00
1905-''Latest Larks of,'' 9½x15½'', 52 pgs. in color, Donahue; re-issue of 1902 issue	19.00	57.00	130.00
1905-''Latest Larks of,'' 9½x15½'', 24 pg. edition in color, Donahue; re-issue of 1902 issue	19.00	57.00	130.00
1906-''Frolics,'' 10x15'', 30 pgs. in color, Stokes	19.00	57.00	130.00
1907	17.00	51.00	120.00
1908?-''Triumphs,'' 10x15''	17.00	51.00	120.00
1908?-''& Little Brother,'' 10x15''	17.00	51.00	120.00
1911-''Latest Tricks,'' r-1910,1911 Sundays in color-Stokes Co.	18.00	54.00	125.00
1914-9½x15½'', 24 pgs., 6 color cartoons/page, Bunny Publ.	14.00	52.00	100.00
1916-''Merry Book,'' 10x15'', 30 pgs. in color, Stokes	14.00	42.00	100.00

FOXY GRANDPA SPARKLETS SERIES
1908 (6½x7¾''; 24 pgs. in color)
M. A. Donahue & Co.

''. . . Rides the Goat,'' ''. . .& His Boys,'' ''. . .Playing Ball,''
''. . .Fun on the Farm,'' ''. . .Fancy Shooting,'' ''. . .Show the Boys
Up Sports,'' ''. . .Plays Santa Claus''

each. . .	19.00	57.00	130.00
900-. . .Playing Ball; Bunny illos; 8 pgs., linen like pgs., no date	12.00	36.00	84.00

FRACTURED FAIRY TALES (TV)
October, 1962 (Jay Ward)
Gold Key

	Good	Fine	N-Mint
1 (10022-210)	5.00	15.00	35.00

FRAGGLE ROCK (TV)
4/85 - No. 8, 9/86; V2#1, 4/88 - No. 6, 9/88
Star Comics (Marvel)/Marvel V2#1 on

1-8		.40	.80
V2#1-6($1.00): Reprints 1st series		.50	1.00

FRANCIS, BROTHER OF THE UNIVERSE
1980 (75 cents) (52 pgs.) (One Shot)
Marvel Comics Group

nn-Buscema/Marie Severin-a; story of Francis Bernadone celebrating his 800th birthday in 1982		.30	.60

FRANCIS THE FAMOUS TALKING MULE (All based on movie) (See 4-Color
No. 335, 465, 501, 547, 579, 621, 655, 698, 710, 745, 810, 863, 906, 953, 991, 1068, 1090)

FRANK BUCK (Formerly My True Love)
No. 70, May, 1950 - No. 3, Sept, 1950
Fox Features Syndicate

70-Wood a(p)(3)-Photo-c	8.50	25.50	60.00
71-Wood a? (9 pgs.), 3-Painted-c	5.00	15.00	35.00

FRANKENSTEIN (See Movie Classics)
Aug-Oct, 1964; No. 2, Sept, 1966 - No. 4, Mar, 1967
Dell Publishing Co.

1(12-283-410)(1964)	1.15	3.50	8.00
2-Intro. & origin super-hero character (9/66)	.70	2.00	4.00
3,4	.35	1.00	2.00

FRANKENSTEIN (The Monster of . . .; also see Monsters Unleashed & Psycho)
Jan, 1973 - No. 18, Sept, 1975
Marvel Comics Group

1-Ploog-a begins		.50	1.00
2-18: 8,9-Dracula app.		.40	.80
Power Record giveaway-(12¼x12¼''; 16 pgs.); Adams, Ploog-a	.25	.75	1.50

NOTE: Adkins c-17i. Buscema a-7-10p. Ditko a-12r. G. Kane c-15p. Orlando a-8r. Ploog a-1-3, 4p, 5p, 6; c-1-6. Wrightson c-18i.

FRANKENSTEIN COMICS (Also See Prize Comics)
Sum, 1945 - V5/5(No.33), Oct-Nov, 1954
Prize Publications (Crestwood/Feature)

1-Frankenstein begins by Dick Briefer (origin); Frank Sinatra parody	32.00	95.00	225.00
2	14.00	42.00	100.00
3-5	12.00	36.00	84.00
6-10: 7-S&K a(r)/Headline Comics. 8(7-8/47)-Superman satire	11.00	32.00	75.00
11-17(1-2/49)-11-Boris Karloff parody c/story. 17-Last humor issue	8.00	24.00	56.00
18(3/52)-New origin, horror series begins	11.00	32.00	75.00
19,20(V3No.4, 8-9/52)	6.50	19.50	45.00
21(V3/5), 22(V3/6)	6.50	19.50	45.00
23(V4/1) - #28(V4/6)	5.50	16.50	38.00
29(V5/1) - #33(V5/5)	5.50	16.50	38.00

NOTE: Briefer c/a-all. Meskin a-21, 29.

FRANKENSTEIN, JR. (. . . .& the Impossibles) (TV)
January, 1967 (Hanna-Barbera)
Gold Key

1	1.30	4.00	9.00

FRANK FRAZETTA'S THUNDA TALES
1987 ($2.00, color, one shot)
Fantagraphics Books

1-Frazetta-r	.35	1.00	2.00

FRANK FRAZETTA'S UNTAMED LOVE (Also see Untamed Love)
Nov, 1987 ($2.00, color, one shot)
Fantagraphics Books

	Good	Fine	N-Mint
1-Frazetta-r from 1950s romance comics	.35	1.00	2.00

FRANKIE COMICS (. . .& Lana No. 13-15) (Formerly Movie Tunes; becomes Frankie Fuddle No. 16 on)
No. 4, Wint, 1946-47 - No. 15, June, 1949
Marvel Comics (MgPC)

4-Mitzi, Margie, Daisy app.	5.00	15.00	35.00
5-8	2.65	8.00	18.00
9-Transvestism story	2.85	8.50	20.00
10-15: 13-Anti-Wertham editorial	1.85	5.50	13.00

FRANKIE DOODLE (See Single Series #7 and Sparkler, both series)

FRANKIE FUDDLE (Formerly Frankie & Lana)
No. 16, Aug, 1949 - No. 17, Nov, 1949
Marvel Comics

16,17	2.15	6.50	15.00

FRANK LUTHER'S SILLY PILLY COMICS (See Jingle Dingle. . .)
1950 (10 cents)
Children's Comics

1-Characters from radio, records, & TV	2.65	8.00	18.00

FRANK MERRIWELL AT YALE (Speed Demons No. 5 on?)
June, 1955 - No. 4, Jan, 1956 (Also see Shadow Comics)
Charlton Comics

1	2.15	6.50	15.00
2-4	1.30	4.00	9.00

FRANTIC (Magazine) (See Ratfink & Zany)
Oct, 1958 - V2#2, April, 1959 (Satire)
Pierce Publishing Co.

V1#1,2	.85	2.60	6.00
V2#1,2: 1-Burgos-a, Severin-c/a	.50	1.50	3.00

FRECKLES AND HIS FRIENDS (See Crackajack Funnies, Famous Comics Cartoon Book, Honeybee Birdwhistle. . . & Red Ryder)

FRECKLES AND HIS FRIENDS
No. 5, 11/47 - No. 12, 8/49; 11/55 - No. 4, 6/56
Standard Comics/Argo

5-Reprints	4.00	12.00	28.00
6-12-Reprints; 11-Lingerie panels	2.00	6.00	14.00

NOTE: Some copies of No. 8 & 9 contain a printing oddity. The negatives were elongated in the engraving process, probably to conform to page dimensions on the filler pages. Those pages only look normal when viewed at a 45 degree angle.

1(Argo,'55)-Reprints (NEA Service)	2.30	7.00	16.00
2-4	1.30	4.00	9.00

FREDDY (Formerly My Little Margie's Boy Friends)
June, 1958 - No. 47, Feb, 1965 (Also see Blue Bird)
Charlton Comics

V2#12	.85	2.50	6.00
13-15	.50	1.50	3.00
16-47	.35	1.00	2.00
Schiff's Shoes Presents. . . No. 1(1959)-Giveaway	.35	1.00	2.00

FREDDY
May-July, 1963 - No. 3, Oct-Dec, 1964
Dell Publishing Co.

1-3	.55	1.65	4.00

FRED HEMBECK DESTROYS THE MARVEL UNIVERSE
July, 1989 ($1.50, One-shot)
Marvel Comics

1-Punisher app.; Staton-i (5 pgs.)	.25	.75	1.50

FREE COMICS TO YOU FROM. . . (name of shoe store) (Has clown on cover & another with a rabbit) (Like comics from Weather Bird & Edward's Shoes)
Circa 1956, 1960-61
Shoe Store Giveaway

Contains a comic bound with new cover - several combinations possible; Some Harvey titles known. contents determines price.

FREEDOM AGENT (Also see John Steele)
April, 1963
Gold Key

	Good	Fine	N-Mint
1 (10054-304)-Painted-c	1.00	3.00	7.00

FREEDOM FIGHTERS (See Justice League of America No. 107,108)
Mar-Apr, 1976 - No. 15, July-Aug, 1978
National Periodical Publications/DC Comics

1-Uncle Sam, The Ray, Black Condor, Doll Man, Human Bomb, & Phantom Lady begin		.35	.70
2-15: 7-1st app. Crusaders. 10-Origin Doll Man. 11-Origin The Ray. 12-Origin Firebrand. 13-Origin Black Condor. 14,15-Batgirl & Batwoman app. 15-Origin Phantom Lady		.25	.50

NOTE: Buckler c-5-11p, 13p, 14p.

FREEDOM TRAIN
1948 (Giveaway)
Street & Smith Publications

Powell-c	1.70	5.00	10.00

FRENZY (Magazine) (Satire)
April, 1958 - No. 6, March, 1959
Picture Magazine

1	.85	2.50	5.00
2-6	.50	1.50	3.00

FRIDAY FOSTER
October, 1972
Dell Publishing Co.

1	1.00	3.00	6.00

FRIENDLY GHOST, CASPER, THE (See Casper. . .)
8/58 - No. 224, 10/82; No. 225, 10/86 - Present
Harvey Publications

1-Infinity-c	14.00	42.00	100.00
2	7.00	21.00	50.00
3-10: 6-X-Mas-c	4.00	12.00	28.00
11-20: 18-X-Mas-c	2.65	8.00	18.00
21-30	1.20	3.50	8.00
31-50	.70	2.00	5.00
51-100: 54-X-Mas-c	.55	1.60	3.20
101-159		.60	1.20
160-163: All 52 pg. Giants	.25	.75	1.50
164-238: 173,179,185-Cub Scout Specials. 238-on $1.00 issues		.35	.70
239-252 ($1.00)		.50	1.00
American Dental Assoc. giveaway-Small size (1967, 16 pgs.)	.50	1.50	3.00

FRIGHT
June, 1975 (August on inside)
Atlas/Seaboard Periodicals

1-Origin The Son of Dracula; Frank Thorne c/a		.40	.80

FRIGHT NIGHT
Oct, 1988 - Present ($1.75, color)
Now Comics

1-18: 1-3-Adapts movie. 8,9-Evil Ed horror photo-c from movie		.30	.90	1.75

FRIGHT NIGHT II
1989 ($3.95, color, 52 pgs.)

Frank Merriwell At Yale #4, © CC

Freckles And His Friends #4 (6/56), © NEA Service

The Friendly Ghost Casper #2, © Paramount

Frisky Fables V2#6, © NOVP   The Frogmen #3, © DELL   Frontier Romances #1, © AVON

FRIGHT NIGHT II (continued)
Now Comics

	Good	Fine	N-Mint
1-Adapts movie sequel	.70	2.00	4.00

FRISKY ANIMALS (Formerly Frisky Fables)
No. 44, Jan, 1951 - No. 58, 1954
Star Publications

44-Super Cat	5.70	17.00	40.00
45-Classic L. B. Cole-c	9.30	28.00	65.00
46-51,53-58-Super Cat	5.00	15.00	35.00
52-L. B. Cole c/a, 3pgs.	5.70	17.00	40.00

NOTE: All have **L. B. Cole-c**. No. 47-No Super Cat. **Disbrow** a-49,52. **Fago** a-51.

FRISKY ANIMALS ON PARADE (Formerly Parade Comics; becomes Superspook)
Sept, 1957 - No. 3, Dec/Jan, 1957-1958
Ajax-Farrell Publ. (Four Star Comic Corp.)

1-L. B. Cole-c	4.30	13.00	30.00
2-No L. B. Cole-c	2.00	6.00	14.00
3-L. B. Cole-c	3.00	9.00	21.00

FRISKY FABLES (Frisky Animals No. 44 on)
Spring, 1945 - No. 44, Oct-Nov, 1949
Premium Group/Novelty Publ.

V1/1-Al Fago c/a	5.70	17.00	40.00
2,3(1945)	3.00	9.00	21.00
4-7(1946)	2.00	6.00	14.00
V2/1-9,11,12(1947)	1.30	4.00	9.00
10-Christmas-c	1.50	4.50	10.00
V3/1-12(1948): 4-Flag-c. 9-Infinity-c	1.15	3.50	8.00
V4/1-7	1.15	3.50	8.00
36-44(V4/8-12, V5/1-4)-L. B. Cole-c; 40-X-mas-c	5.00	15.00	35.00
Accepted Reprint No. 43 (nd); L.B. Cole-c	2.00	6.00	14.00

FRITZI RITZ (See Comics On Parade, Single Series #5,1(reprint), Tip Top & United Comics)

FRITZI RITZ
Fall/48 - No. 42, 1/55; No. 43, 1955 - No. 55, 9-11/57; No. 56, 12-2/57-58 - No. 59, 9-11/58
United Features Synd./St. John No. 41-55/Dell No. 56 on

nn(1948)-Special Fall issue	6.00	18.00	42.00
2	2.85	8.50	20.00
3-5	2.30	7.00	16.00
6-10: 6-Abbie & Slats app. 7-Lingerie panel	1.85	5.50	13.00
11-19,21-28	1.50	4.50	10.00
20-Strange As It Seems; Russell Patterson Cheesecake-a; negligee panel	1.85	5.50	13.00
29-Five pg. Abbie & Slats; 1 pg. Mamie by Russell Patterson	1.50	4.50	10.00
30-59: 36-1 pg. Mamie by Patterson. 43-Peanuts by Schulz	1.00	3.00	7.00

NOTE: Abbie & Slats in #6-8, 11, 18, 20, 27-31. Li'l Abner in #33, 35, 36. Peanuts in #31, 43, 58, 59.

FROGMAN COMICS
Jan-Feb, 1952 - No. 11, May, 1953
Hillman Periodicals

1	4.30	13.00	30.00
2	2.30	7.00	16.00
3,4,6-11: 4-Meskin-a	1.70	5.00	12.00
5-Krigstein, Torres-a	3.50	10.50	24.00

FROGMEN, THE
No. 1258, 2-4/62 - No. 11, 11-1/1964-65 (Painted-c)
Dell Publishing Co.

4-Color 1258-Evans-a	3.50	10.50	24.00
2,3-Evans-a; part Frazetta inks in #2,3	4.00	12.00	28.00
4,6-11	1.30	4.00	9.00

	Good	Fine	N-Mint
5-Toth-a	2.30	7.00	16.00

FROM BEYOND THE UNKNOWN
10-11/69 - No.25, 11-12/73 (No.7-11: 64 pgs.; No.12-17: 52 pgs.)
National Periodical Publications

1	.35	1.00	2.00
2-10: 7-Intro. Col. Glenn Merrit		.50	1.00
11-25: Star Rovers-r begin #18,19. Space Museum in #23-25		.40	.80

NOTE: **Adams** c-3, 6, 8, 9. **Anderson** c-2, 4, 5, 10, 11i, 15-17, 22; reprints-3, 4, 6-8, 10, 11, 13-16, 24, 25. **Infantino** reprints-1-5, 7-19, 23-25; c-11p. **Kaluta** c-18,19. **Kubert** c-1, 7, 12-14. **Toth** a-2r. **Wood** a-13i. Photo-c 22.

FROM HERE TO INSANITY (Satire) (Eh No. 1-7)
(See Frantic & Frenzy)
No. 8, Feb, 1955 - V3#1, 1956
Charlton Comics

8	4.00	12.00	28.00
9	2.85	8.50	20.00
10-Ditko-c/a, 3 pgs.	6.00	18.00	42.00
11,12-All Kirby except 4 pgs.	7.00	21.00	50.00
V3#1(1956)-Ward-c/a(2)(signed McCartney); 5 pgs. Wolverton; 3 pgs. Ditko; magazine format	13.50	40.50	95.00

FRONTIER DAYS
1956 (Giveaway)
Robin Hood Shoe Store (Brown Shoe)

1	1.35	4.00	8.00

FRONTIER DOCTOR (See 4-Color No. 877)

FRONTIER FIGHTERS
Sept-Oct, 1955 - No. 8, Nov-Dec, 1956
National Periodical Publications

1-Davy Crockett, Buffalo Bill by Kubert, Kit Carson begin (Scarce)	23.00	70.00	160.00
2	15.00	45.00	105.00
3-8	12.00	36.00	84.00

NOTE: Buffalo Bill by **Kubert** in all.

FRONTIER ROMANCES
Nov-Dec, 1949 - No. 2, Feb-Mar, 1950 (Painted-c)
Avon Periodicals/I. W.

1-Used in **SOTI**, pg. 180(General reference) & illo. "Erotic spanking in a western comic book"	33.00	100.00	230.00
2 (Scarce)	17.00	51.00	120.00
1-I.W.(reprints Avon's #1)	2.75	8.00	16.00
I.W. Reprint #9	1.35	4.00	8.00

FRONTIER SCOUT: DAN'L BOONE (Formerly Death Valley; The Masked Raider No. 14 on)
No. 10, Jan, 1956 - No. 13, Aug, 1956; No. 14, March, 1965
Charlton Comics

10	2.65	8.00	18.00
11-13(1956)	1.50	4.50	10.00
V2No.14(3/65)	.70	2.00	4.00

FRONTIER TRAIL (The Rider No. 1-5)
No. 6, May, 1958
Ajax/Farrell Publ.

6	1.50	4.50	10.00

FRONTIER WESTERN
Feb, 1956 - No. 10, Aug, 1957
Atlas Comics (PrPI)

1	5.70	17.00	40.00
2,3,6-Williamson-a, 4 pgs. each	5.00	15.00	35.00
4,7,9,10: 10-Check-a	2.00	6.00	14.00
5-Crandall, Baker, Wildey, Davis-a; Williamson text illos			

FRONTIER WESTERN (continued)	Good	Fine	N-Mint
	3.70	11.00	26.00
8-Crandall, Morrow, & Wildey-a	2.30	7.00	16.00

NOTE: *Colan* a-2. *Drucker* a-3,4. *Heath* c-5. *Maneely* a-2,7. c-2. *Romita* a-7. *Severin* c-6,8,10. *Tuska* a-2. Ringo Kid in No. 4.

FRONTLINE COMBAT
July-Aug, 1951 - No. 15, Jan, 1954
E. C. Comics

1	36.00	110.00	255.00
2	24.00	73.00	170.00
3	18.00	54.00	125.00
4-Used in **SOTI**, pg. 257; contains "Airburst" by Kurtzman which is			
his personal all-time favorite story	15.00	45.00	105.00
5	13.00	40.00	90.00
6-10	11.00	32.00	75.00
11-15	8.50	25.50	60.00

NOTE: *Davis* a-in all; c-11,12. *Evans* a-10-15. *Heath* a-1. *Kubert* a-14. *Kurtzman* a-1-5; c-1-9. *Severin* a-5-7, 9, 13, 15. *Severin/Elder* a-2-11; c-10. *Toth* a-8, 12. *Wood* a-1-4, 6-10, 12-15; c-13-15. Special issues: No. 7 (Iwo Jima), No. 9 (Civil War), No. 12 (Air Force). (Canadian reprints known; see Table of Contents.)

FRONT PAGE COMIC BOOK
1945
Front Page Comics (Harvey)

1-Kubert-a; intro. & 1st app. Man in Black by Powell; Fuje-c			
	16.00	48.00	110.00

FROST AND FIRE (See DC Science Fiction Graphic Novel)

FROSTY THE SNOWMAN
No. 359, Nov, 1951 - No. 1272, Dec-Feb?/1961-62
Dell Publishing Co.

4-Color 359	3.00	9.00	21.00
4-Color 435	2.30	7.00	16.00
4-Color 514,601,661	2.00	6.00	14.00
4-Color 748,861,950,1065	1.70	5.00	12.00
4-Color 1153,1272	1.50	4.50	10.00

FRUITMAN SPECIAL
Dec, 1969 (68 pages)
Harvey Publications

1-Funny super hero	1.00	3.00	6.00

F-TROOP (TV)
Aug, 1966 - No. 7, Aug, 1967 (All have photo-c)
Dell Publishing Co.

1	3.00	9.00	21.00
2-7	1.70	5.00	12.00

FUGITIVES FROM JUSTICE
Feb, 1952 - No. 5, Oct, 1952
St. John Publishing Co.

1	6.50	19.50	45.00
2-Matt Baker-a; Vic Flint strip reprints begin, end No. 5			
	6.00	18.00	42.00
3-Reprints panel from Authentic Police Cases that was used in			
SOTI with changes; Tuska-a	6.00	18.00	42.00
4	2.85	8.50	20.00
5-Bondage-c	3.70	11.00	26.00

FUGITOID
1985 (One shot, B&W, magazine size)
Mirage Studios

1-Ties into Teenage Mutant Ninja Turtles #5	.90	2.75	5.50

FULL COLOR COMICS
1946
Fox Features Syndicate

nn	5.50	16.50	38.00

FULL OF FUN
Aug, 1957 - No. 2, Nov, 1957; 1964
Red Top (Decker Publ.)(Farrell)/I. W. Enterprises

	Good	Fine	N-Mint
1(1957)-Dave Berg-a	2.00	6.00	14.00
2-Reprints Bingo, the Monkey Doodle Boy	1.30	4.00	9.00
8-I.W. Reprint('64)	.35	1.00	2.00

FUN AT CHRISTMAS (See March of Comics No. 138)

FUN CLUB COMICS (See Interstate Theatres. . .)

FUN COMICS (Mighty Bear No. 13 on)
No. 9, Jan, 1953 - No. 12, Oct, 1953
Star Publications

9(Giant)-L. B. Cole-c	6.50	19.50	45.00
10-12-L. B. Cole-c	3.70	11.00	26.00

FUNDAY FUNNIES (See Famous TV. . . , and Harvey Hits No. 35,40)

FUN-IN (TV)(Hanna-Barbera)
Feb, 1970 - No. 10, Jan, 1972; No. 11, 4/74 - No. 15, 12/74
Gold Key

1-Dastardly & Muttley in Their Flying Machines; Perils of Penelope			
Pitstop in 1-4; It's the Wolf in all	.85	2.60	6.00
2-4,6-Cattanooga Cats in 2-4	.60	1.75	3.50
5,7-Motormouse & Autocat, Dastardly & Muttley in both; It's the			
Wolf in #7	.50	1.50	3.00
8,10-The Harlem Globetrotters, Dastardly & Muttley in #10			
	.50	1.50	3.00
9-Where's Huddles?, Dastardly & Muttley, Motormouse & Autocat			
app.	.50	1.50	3.00
11-15: 11-Butch Cassidy. 12,15-Speed Buggy. 13-Hair Bear Bunch.			
14-Inch High Private Eye	.35	1.00	2.00

FUNKY PHANTOM, THE (TV)
Mar, 1972 - No. 13, Mar, 1975 (Hanna-Barbera)
Gold Key

1	1.00	3.00	7.00
2-5	.70	2.00	4.00
6-13	.50	1.50	3.00

FUNLAND
No date (25 cents)
Ziff-Davis (Approved Comics)

Contains games, puzzles, etc.	6.00	18.00	42.00

FUNLAND COMICS
1945
Croyden Publishers

1	6.00	18.00	42.00

FUNNIES, THE (Also see Comic Cuts)
1929 - No. 36, 10/18/30 (10 cents; 5 cents No.22 on) (16 pgs.)
Full tabloid size in color; not reprints; published every Saturday
Dell Publishing Co.

1-My Big Brudder, Johnathan, Jazzbo & Jim, Foxy Grandpa, Sniffy,			
Jimmy Jams & other strips begin; first four-color comic news-			
stand publication; also contains magic, puzzles & stories			
	27.00	81.00	190.00
2-21 (1930, 30 cents)	10.00	30.00	70.00
22(nn-7/12/30-5 cents)	7.00	21.00	50.00
23(nn-7/19/30-5 cents), 24(nn-7/26/30-5 cents), 25(nn-8/2/30), 26(nn-8/9/30), 27(nn-8/16/30), 28(nn-8/23/30), 29(nn-8/30/30), 30(nn-9/6/30), 31(nn-9/13/30), 32(nn-9/20/30), 33(nn-9/27/30), 34(nn-10/4/30), 35(nn-10/11/30), 36(nn, no date-10/18/30)			
each. . . .	7.00	21.00	50.00

FUNNIES, THE (New Funnies No. 65 on)
Oct, 1936 - No. 64, May, 1942
Dell Publishing Co.

1-Tailspin Tommy, Mutt & Jeff, Alley Oop (1st app?), Capt. Easy, Don

Frontline Combat #12, © WMG

Fugitives From Justice #1, © STJ

Funland Comics #1, © Croyden Publ.

The Funnies #64, © DELL

Funny Films #4, © ACG

Funny Pages V3#7, © CEN

THE FUNNIES (continued)	Good	Fine	N-Mint
Dixon begin	92.00	230.00	550.00
2-Scribbly by Mayer begins	39.00	118.00	275.00
3	34.00	100.00	235.00
4,5: 4-Christmas-c	28.00	84.00	195.00
6-10	22.00	65.00	155.00
11-20: 16-Christmas-c	19.00	58.00	135.00
21-29	16.50	50.00	115.00
30-John Carter of Mars (origin) begins by Edgar Rice Burroughs			
	50.00	150.00	350.00
31-44: 33-John Coleman Burroughs art begins on John Carter. 35-			
(9/39)-Mr. District Attorney begins-based on radio show			
	28.00	84.00	195.00
45-Origin Phantasmo, the Master of the World & intro. his sidekick			
Whizzer McGee	22.00	65.00	155.00
46-50: 46-The Black Knight begins, ends #62	19.00	58.00	135.00
51-56-Last ERB John Carter of Mars	19.00	58.00	135.00
57-Intro. & origin Captain Midnight	48.00	145.00	335.00
58-60	20.00	60.00	140.00
61-Andy Panda begins by Walter Lantz	21.50	65.00	150.00
62,63-Last Captain Midnight cover	19.00	57.00	135.00
64-Format change; Oswald the Rabbit, Felix the Cat, Li'l Eight Ball			
app.; origin & 1st app. Woody Woodpecker in Oswald; last Capt.			
Midnight	39.00	118.00	275.00

NOTE: **Mayer** c-26, 48. **McWilliams** art in many issues on "Rex King of the Deep."

FUNNIES ANNUAL, THE
1959 ($1.00)(B&W; tabloid-size; approx. 7x10'')
Avon Periodicals

1-(Rare)-Features the best newspaper comic strips of the year: Archie, Snuffy Smith, Beetle Bailey, Henry, Blondie, Steve Canyon, Buz Sawyer, The Little King, Hi & Lois, Popeye, & others. Also has a chronological history of the comics from 2000 B.C. to 1959.
23.00 70.00 160.00

FUNNIES ON PARADE (Premium)
1933 (Probably the 1st comic book) (36 pgs.; slick cover)
No date or publisher listed
Eastern Color Printing Co.

nn-Contains Sunday page reprints of Mutt & Jeff, Joe Palooka, Hairbreadth Harry, Reg'lar Fellers, Skippy, & others (10,000 print run). This book was printed for Proctor & Gamble to be given away & came out before Famous Funnies or Century of Comics.
300.00 900.00 2100.00

FUNNY ANIMALS (See Fawcett's Funny Animals)
Sept, 1984 - No. 2, Nov, 1984
Charlton Comics

1,2-Atomic Mouse-r		.30	.60

FUNNYBONE
1944 (132 pages)
La Salle Publishing Co.

nn	10.00	30.00	70.00

FUNNY BOOK (. . . Magazine) (Hocus Pocus No. 9)
Dec, 1942 - No. 9, Aug-Sept, 1946
Parents' Magazine Press

1-Funny animal; Alice In Wonderland app.	7.00	21.00	50.00
2	3.50	10.50	24.00
3-9	2.30	7.00	16.00

FUNNY COMICS (7 cents)
1955 (36 pgs.; 5x7''; in color)
Modern Store Publ.

1-Funny animal	.80	2.25	4.50

FUNNY COMIC TUNES (See Funny Tunes)

FUNNY FABLES
Aug, 1957 - V2No. 2, Nov, 1957
Decker Publications (Red Top Comics)

	Good	Fine	N-Mint
V1No.1	1.70	5.00	12.00
V2No.1,2	1.00	3.00	7.00

FUNNY FILMS
Sept-Oct, 1949 - No. 29, May-June, 1954 (No. 1-4: 52 pgs.)
American Comics Group(Michel Publ./Titan Publ.)

1-Puss An' Boots, Blunderbunny begin	7.00	21.00	50.00
2	3.50	10.50	24.00
3-10	2.30	7.00	16.00
11-20	1.70	5.00	12.00
21-29	1.30	4.00	9.00

FUNNY FOLKS (Hollywood . . . on cover only No. 16-26; becomes
Hollywood Funny Folks No. 27 on)
April-May, 1946 - No. 26, June-July, 1950 (52 pgs., #16 on)
National Periodical Publications

1-Nutsy Squirrel begins (1st app.) by Rube Grossman	18.00	54.00	125.00
2	8.50	25.50	60.00
3-5	6.50	19.50	45.00
6-10	4.50	14.00	32.00
11-26: 16-Begin 52 pg. issues (10-11/48)	3.15	9.50	22.00

NOTE: **Sheldon Mayer** a-in some issues.

FUNNY FROLICS
Summer, 1945 - No. 5, Dec, 1946
Timely/Marvel Comics (SPI)

1-Sharpy Fox, Puffy Pig, Krazy Krow	8.00	24.00	56.00
2	4.30	13.00	30.00
3,4	3.50	10.50	24.00
5-Kurtzman-a	4.30	13.00	30.00

FUNNY FUNNIES
April, 1943 (68 pages)
Nedor Publishing Co.

1 (Funny animals)	10.00	30.00	70.00

FUNNYMAN
Dec, 1947; No. 1, Jan, 1948 - No. 6, Aug, 1948
Magazine Enterprises

nn(12/47)-Prepublication B&W undistributed copy by Siegel & Shuster-(5¾x8''), 16 pgs.; Sold in San Francisco in 1976 for $300.00

1-Siegel & Shuster-a in all	14.00	42.00	100.00
2	11.00	32.00	75.00
3-6	8.50	25.50	60.00

FUNNY MOVIES (See 3-D Funny Movies)

FUNNY PAGES (Formerly The Comics Magazine)
No. 6, Nov, 1936 - No. 42, Oct, 1940
Comics Magazine Co./Ultem Publ.(Chesler)/Centaur Publications

V1#6 (nn, nd)-The Clock begins (2 pgs., 1st app.), ends #11			
	46.00	140.00	325.00
7-11	28.00	85.00	200.00
V2#1 (9/37)(V2#2 on-c; V2#1 in indicia)	23.00	70.00	160.00
V2#2 (10/37)(V2#3 on-c; V2#2 in indicia)	23.00	70.00	160.00
3(11/37)-5	23.00	70.00	160.00
6(1st Centaur, 3/38)	36.00	110.00	250.00
7-9	26.00	77.00	180.00
10(Scarce)-1st app. of The Arrow by Gustavson (Blue costume)			
	117.00	295.00	700.00
11,12	50.00	150.00	350.00
V3#1-6	50.00	150.00	350.00
7-1st Arrow-c; 9/39	61.00	182.00	425.00
8	50.00	150.00	350.00
9-Tarpe Mills jungle-c	50.00	150.00	350.00
10-2nd Arrow-c	55.00	165.00	385.00

FUNNY PAGES (continued)

	Good	Fine	N-Mint
V4#1(1/40, Arrow-c)-(Rare)-The Owl & The Phantom Rider app.; origin Mantoka, Maker of Magic by Jack Cole. Mad Ming begins, ends #42. Tarpe Mills-a	60.00	180.00	420.00
35-Arrow-c	43.00	130.00	300.00
36-38-Mad Ming-c	43.00	130.00	300.00
39-42-Arrow-c. 42-Last Arrow	43.00	130.00	300.00

NOTE: *Burgos* c-V3#10. *Jack Cole* a-V2#3, 7, 8, 10, 11, V3#2, 6, 9, 10, V4#1, 37. *Eisner* a-V1#7, 8, 10. *Ken Ernst* a-#7. *Everett* a-V2#11 (illos). *Gill Fox* a-V2#11. *Sid Greene* a-39. *Guardineer* a-V2#2, 3, 5. *Gustavson* a-V2#5, 11, 12, V3#1-10, 35, 38-42; c-V3#7, 35, 39-42. *Bob Kane* a-V3#1. *McWilliams* a-V2#12, V3#1, 3-6. *Tarpe Mills* a-V3#8-10, V4#1; c-V3#9. *Ed Moore Jr.* a-V2#12. *Bob Wood* a-V2#2, 3, 8, 11, V3#6, 9, 10; c-V2#6, 7.

FUNNY PICTURE STORIES (Comic Pages V3#4 on)
Nov, 1936 - V3#3, May, 1939
Comics Magazine Co./Centaur Publications

	Good	Fine	N-Mint
V1#1-The Clock begins (c-feature)(See Funny Pages for 1st app.)	108.00	270.00	650.00
2	41.00	125.00	290.00
3-9: 4-Eisner-a; Christmas-c	28.00	85.00	200.00
V2#1 (9/37); V1#10 on-c; V2#1 in indicia)-Jack Strand begins	23.00	70.00	160.00
2 (10/37; V1#11 on-c; V2#2 in indicia)	23.00	70.00	160.00
3-5: 4-Xmas-c	20.00	60.00	140.00
6-(1st Centaur, 3/38)	34.00	100.00	235.00
7-11	21.50	65.00	150.00
V3#1-3	18.50	56.00	130.00
Giveaway (16-20 pgs., 1930s)-slick-c	8.50	25.50	60.00

NOTE: *Biro* c-V2#1. *Guardineer* a-V1#11. *Bob Wood* c/a-V1#11, V2#2.

FUNNY STUFF (Becomes The Dodo & the Frog No. 80)
Summer, 1944 - No. 79, July-Aug, 1954
All-American/National Periodical Publications

	Good	Fine	N-Mint
1-The Three Mouseketeers & The "Terrific Whatzit" begin-Sheldon Mayer-a	45.00	135.00	315.00
2-Sheldon Mayer-a	21.50	65.00	150.00
3-5	13.00	40.00	90.00
6-10 (4)	8.50	25.50	60.00
11-20: 18-The Dodo & the Frog begin?	5.70	17.00	40.00
21,23-30: 24-Infinity-c	4.30	13.00	30.00
22-Superman cameo	14.00	42.00	100.00
31-79: 75-Bo Bunny by Mayer	2.85	8.50	20.00
Wheaties Giveaway(1946, 6½x8¼'') (Scarce)	8.50	25.50	60.00

NOTE: *Mayer* a-1-8, 55, .57, 58, 61, 62, 64, 65, 68, 70, 72, 74-79; c-2, 5, 6, 8.

FUNNY STUFF STOCKING STUFFER
March, 1985 (52 pgs.)
DC Comics

	Good	Fine
1-Almost every DC funny animal featured	.60	1.25

FUNNY 3-D
December, 1953
Harvey Publications

	Good	Fine	N-Mint
1	7.00	21.00	50.00

FUNNY TUNES (Animated Funny Comic Tunes No. 16-22; Funny Comic Tunes No. 23, on covers only; formerly Human Torch; Oscar No. 24 on)
No. 16, Summer, 1944 - No. 23, Fall, 1946
U.S.A. Comics Magazine Corp. (Timely)

	Good	Fine	N-Mint
16-Silly, Ziggy, Krazy Krow begin	5.50	16.50	38.00
17 (Fall/'44)-Becomes Gay Comics #18 on?	3.70	11.00	26.00
18-22: 21-Super Rabbit app.	3.15	9.50	22.00
23-Kurtzman-a	4.00	12.00	28.00

FUNNY TUNES
July, 1953 - No. 3, Dec-Jan, 1953-54
Avon Periodicals

	Good	Fine	N-Mint
1-Space Mouse begins	3.50	10.50	24.00

	Good	Fine	N-Mint
2,3	2.00	6.00	14.00

FUNNY WORLD
1947 - No. 3, 1948
Marbak Press

	Good	Fine	N-Mint
1-The Berrys, The Toodles & other strip reprints begin	4.30	13.00	30.00
2,3	3.00	9.00	21.00

FUNTASTIC WORLD OF HANNA-BARBERA, THE (TV)
Dec, 1977 - No. 3, June, 1978 ($1.25) (Oversized)
Marvel Comics Group

	Good	Fine	N-Mint
1-The Flintstones Christmas Party(12/77); 2-Yogi Bear's Easter Parade(3/78); 3-Laff-a-lympics(6/78) each....	.35	1.00	2.00

FUN TIME
1953: No. 2, Spr, 1953; No. 3(nn), Sum, 1953; No. 4, Wint, 1953-54
Ace Periodicals

	Good	Fine	N-Mint
1	1.70	5.00	12.00
2-4 (100 pgs. each)	4.50	13.50	32.00

FUN WITH SANTA CLAUS (See March of Comics No. 11,108,325)

FURTHER ADVENTURES OF INDIANA JONES, THE (Also see Indiana Jones and the Temple of Doom)
Jan, 1983 - No. 34, Mar, 1986
Marvel Comics Group

	Good	Fine
1-Byrne/Austin-a	.55	1.10
2-34: 2-Byrne/Austin-c/a	.55	1.10

NOTE: *Austin* a-6i, 9i; c-1i, 2i, 6i, 9i. *Chaykin* a-6p; c-6p, 8p-10p. *Ditko* a-21p, 25, 26, 34. *Simonson* c-9.

FURTHER ADVENTURES OF NYOKA, THE JUNGLE GIRL, THE
1988 - No. 5?, 1989 ($1.95, color; $2.25-$2.50, B&W)(See Nyoka)
AC Comics

	Good	Fine	N-Mint
1,2 ($1.95, color)-Bill Black-a plus reprints	.35	1.00	2.00
3,4 ($2.25, B&W) 3-Photo-c. 4-Krigstein-r	.40	1.15	2.30
5 ($2.50, B&W)-Reprints plus movie photos	.40	1.25	2.50

FURY (Straight Arrow's Horse...) (See A-1 No. 119)

FURY (TV) (See March Of Comics #200)
No. 781, Mar, 1957 - Nov, 1962 (All photo-c)
Dell Publishing Co./Gold Key

	Good	Fine	N-Mint
4-Color 781	5.00	15.00	35.00
4-Color 885,975	3.70	11.00	26.00
4-Color 1031,1080,1133,1172,1218,1296, 01292-208(#1-'62)	3.70	11.00	26.00
10020-211(11/62-G.K.)-Crandall-a	3.70	11.00	26.00

FURY OF FIRESTORM, THE (Becomes Firestorm The Nuclear Man #65 on; also see Firestorm)
June, 1982 - No. 64, Oct, 1987 (#19-on: 75 cents)
DC Comics

	Good	Fine	N-Mint
1-Intro The Black Bison; brief origin	.40	1.25	2.50
2	.25	.80	1.60
3-18: 17-1st app. Firehawk		.65	1.30
19-40: 21-Death of Killer Frost. 22-Origin. 23-Intro. Byte. 24-1st app. Blue Devil & Bug (origin); origin Byte. 34-1st app./origin Killer Frost II. 39-Weasel's i.d. revealed		.50	1.00
41,42-Crisis x-over		.60	1.20
43-64: 48-Intro. Moonbow. 53-Origin/1st app. Silver Shade. 55,56-Legends x-over. 58-1st app./origin Parasite		.45	.90
61-Test cover	7.50	22.50	45.00
Annual 1(11/83), 2(11/84), 3(11/85), 4(10/86)		.65	1.30

NOTE: *Colan* a-19p, Annual 4p. *Giffen* a-Annual 4p. *Gil Kane* c-30. *Nino* a-37. *Tuska* a-17p, 18p, 32p, 45p.

Funny Stuff #27, © DC

Funny Tunes #16, © MEG

The Further Adventures Of Indiana Jones #10, © MEG

Future Comics #1, © DMP

Gang Busters #14, © DC

Gangsters And Gun Molls #3, © AVON

FUSION
Jan, 1987 - No. 16, July, 1989 ($2.00, B&W, Baxter paper)
Eclipse Comics

	Good	Fine	N-Mint
1	.40	1.25	2.50
2-16	.35	1.00	2.00

FUTURE COMICS
June, 1940 - No. 4, Sept, 1940
David McKay Publications

	Good	Fine	N-Mint
1-Origin The Phantom; The Lone Ranger, & Saturn Against the Earth begin	128.00	320.00	770.00
2	57.00	170.00	400.00
3,4	47.00	141.00	330.00

FUTURE WORLD COMICS
Summer, 1946 - No. 2, Fall, 1946
George W. Dougherty

1,2	10.00	30.00	70.00

FUTURE WORLD COMIX (Warren Presents... on cover)
September, 1978
Warren Publications

1		.50	1.00

FUTURIANS, THE (See Marvel Graphic Novel #9)
Sept, 1985 - No. 3, 1985 ($1.50, color)
Lodestone Publishing/Eternity Comics

1-Indicia title "Dave Cockrum's..."	.50	1.50	3.00
2	.35	1.00	2.00
3	.25	.75	1.50
Graphic Novel 1 ($9.95, Eternity)-r/#1-3, plus never published #4 issue	1.70	5.00	9.95

G-8 (See G-Eight)

GABBY (Formerly Ken Shannon) (Teen humor)
No. 11, July, 1953; No. 2, Sept, 1953 - No. 9, Sept, 1954
Quality Comics Group

11(#1)(7/53)	2.85	8.50	20.00
2	1.50	4.50	10.00
3-9	1.00	3.00	7.00

GABBY GOB (See Harvey Hits No. 85, 90, 94, 97, 100, 103, 106, 109)

GABBY HAYES ADVENTURE COMICS
Dec, 1953
Toby Press

1-Photo-c	6.00	18.00	42.00

GABBY HAYES WESTERN (Movie star) (See Monte Hale, Real Western Hero & Western Hero)
Nov, 1948 - No. 50, Jan, 1953; No. 51, Dec, 1954 - No. 59, Jan, 1957
Fawcett/Toby Press/Charlton Comics No. 51 on

1-Gabby & his horse Corker begin; Photo front/back-c begin	23.00	70.00	165.00
2	11.50	34.00	80.00
3-5	8.50	25.50	60.00
6-10	7.00	21.00	50.00
11-20: 19-Last photo back-c?	5.00	15.00	35.00
21-49	3.50	10.50	24.00
50-(1/53)-Last Fawcett issue; last photo-c?	3.70	11.00	26.00
51-(12/54)-1st Charlton issue; photo-c	3.70	11.00	26.00
52-59(Charlton '55-57): 53,55-Photo-c	2.15	6.50	15.00
Quaker Oats Giveaway nn(#1-5, 1951) (Dell?)	2.50	7.50	17.00

GAGS
July, 1937 - V3No.10, Oct, 1944 (13¾x10¾")
United Features Synd./Triangle Publ. No. 9 on

1(7/37)-52 pgs.; 20 pgs. Grin & Bear It, Fellow Citizen	4.00	12.00	28.00

	Good	Fine	N-Mint
V1#9 (36 pgs.) (7/42)	2.30	7.00	16.00
V3#10	1.70	5.00	12.00

GALACTIC WAR COMIX (Warren Presents... on cover)
December, 1978
Warren Publications

nn-Wood, Williamson-r		.50	1.00

GALLANT MEN, THE (TV)
October, 1963 (Photo-c)
Gold Key

1(10085-310)-Manning-a	1.15	3.50	8.00

GALLEGHER, BOY REPORTER (TV)
May, 1965 (Disney)
Gold Key

1(10149-505)-Photo-c	1.15	3.50	8.00

GAMMARAUDERS
Jan, 1989 - No. 10, Dec, 1989 ($1.25, $1.50, $2.00, color)
DC Comics

1-Based on TSR game	.40	1.25	2.50
2-10	.35	1.00	2.00

GANDY GOOSE (See All Surprise, Paul Terry's & Terry-Toons)
Mar, 1953 - No. 5, Nov, 1953; No. 5, Fall, 1956 - No. 6, Sum/58
St. John Publ. Co./Pines No. 5,6

1	3.00	9.00	21.00
2	1.50	4.50	10.00
3-5(1953)(St. John)	1.15	3.50	8.00
5,6(1956-58)(Pines)	.85	2.50	6.00

GANG BUSTERS (See Popular Comics #38)
1938 - 1943
David McKay/Dell Publishing Co.

Feature Books 17(McKay)('38)	24.00	73.00	170.00
Large Feature Comic 10('39)-(Scarce)	29.00	87.00	205.00
Large Feature Comic 17('41)	19.00	56.00	130.00
4-Color 7(1940)	21.50	65.00	150.00
4-Color 23,24('42-43)	16.50	50.00	115.00

GANG BUSTERS (Radio/TV)
Dec-Jan, 1947-48 - No. 67, Dec-Jan, 1958-59 (No. 1-23: 52 pgs.)
National Periodical Publications

1	31.00	92.00	215.00
2	13.00	40.00	90.00
3-8	8.00	24.00	56.00
9,10-Photo-c	9.30	28.00	65.00
11-13-Photo-c	7.00	21.00	50.00
14,17-Frazetta-a, 8 pgs. each. 14-Photo-c	18.00	54.00	125.00
15,16,18-20	5.00	15.00	35.00
21-30: 26-Kirby-a	3.70	11.00	26.00
31-44: 44-Last Pre-code (2-3/55)	2.85	8.50	20.00
45-67	2.00	6.00	14.00

NOTE: *Barry* a-6, 8, 10. *Drucker* a-51. *Moreira* a-48, 50, 59. *Roussos* a-8.

GANGSTERS AND GUN MOLLS
Sept, 1951 - No. 4, June, 1952 (Painted-c)
Avon Periodical/Realistic Comics

1-Wood-a, 1 pg; c-/Avon paperback 292	20.00	60.00	140.00
2-Check-a, 8 pgs.; Kamen-a	14.00	42.00	100.00
3-Marijuana mention story; used in POP, pg. 84-85	13.00	40.00	90.00
4	11.00	32.00	75.00

GANGSTERS CAN'T WIN
Feb-Mar, 1948 - No. 9, June-July, 1949
D. S. Publishing Co.

1	11.00	32.00	75.00

GANGSTERS CAN'T WIN (continued)

	Good	Fine	N-Mint
2	5.50	16.50	38.00
3-6: 4-Acid in face story	6.50	19.50	45.00
7-9	3.15	9.50	22.00

NOTE: *Ingles a-5,6. McWilliams a-5. 7. Reinman c-6.*

GANG WORLD
No. 5, Nov, 1952 - No. 6, Jan, 1953
Standard Comics

5-Bondage-c	7.00	21.00	50.00
6	4.50	14.00	32.00

GARGOYLE
June, 1985 - No. 4, Sept, 1985 (Limited series)
Marvel Comics Group

1-Character from The Defenders; Wrightson-c .25	.75	1.50
2-4		.50	1.00

GARRISON'S GORILLAS (TV)
Jan, 1968 - No. 4, Oct, 1968; No. 5, Oct, 1969 (Photo-c)
Dell Publishing Co.

1	1.70	5.00	12.00
2-5: 5-Reprints #1	1.15	3.50	8.00

GASOLINE ALLEY (Also see Popular & Super Comics)
1929 (B&W daily strip reprints)(7x8¾''; hardcover)
Reilly & Lee Publishers

By King (96 pgs.)	9.30	28.00	65.00

GASOLINE ALLEY
Sept-Oct, 1950 - No. 2, 1950 (Newspaper reprints)
Star Publications

1-Contains 1 pg. intro. history of the strip (The Life of Skeezix); reprints 15 scenes of highlights from 1921-1935, plus an adventure from 1935 and 1936 strips; a 2-pg. filler is included on the life of the creator Frank King, with photo of the cartoonist.

	10.00	30.00	70.00
2-(1936-37 reprints)-L. B. Cole-c	11.00	32.00	75.00

(See Super Book No. 21)

GASP!
March, 1967 - No. 4, Aug, 1967 (12 cents)
American Comics Group

1-L.S.D. drug mention	1.30	4.00	9.00
2-4	.85	2.60	6.00

GAY COMICS (Honeymoon No. 41)
Mar, 1944 (no month); No. 18, Fall, 1944 - No. 40, Oct, 1949
Timely Comics/USA Comic Mag. Co. No. 18-24

1-Wolverton's Powerhouse Pepper; Tessie the Typist begins; Millie The Model & Willie app. (One Shot)	19.00	58.00	135.00
18-(Formerly Funny Tunes #17?)-Wolverton-a	10.00	30.00	70.00
19-29-Wolverton-a in all. 24,29-Kurtzman-a	8.00	24.00	56.00
30,33,36,37-Kurtzman's ''Hey Look''	2.65	8.00	18.00
31-Kurtzman's ''Hey Look''(1), Giggles 'N' Grins (1½)	2.65	8.00	18.00
32,35,38-40: 35-Nellie The Nurse begins?	2.00	6.00	14.00
34-Three Kurtzman's ''Hey Look''	3.50	10.50	24.00

GAY COMICS (Also see Smile, Tickle, & Whee Comics)
1955 (52 pgs.; 5x7¼''; 7 cents)
Modern Store Publ.

1	.50	1.50	3.00

GAY PURR-EE (See Movie Comics)

GEEK, THE (See Brother Power...)

G-8 AND HIS BATTLE ACES
October, 1966
Gold Key

1 (10184-610)-Painted-c	1.75	5.25	12.00

GEM COMICS
April, 1945 (52 pgs.) (Bondage-c)
Spotlight Publishers

	Good	Fine	N-Mint
1-Little Mohee, Steve Strong app.	8.50	25.50	60.00

GENE AUTRY (See March of Comics No. 25,28,39,54,78,90,104,120,135,150, & Western Roundup under Dell Giants)

GENE AUTRY COMICS (Movie, Radio star; singing cowboy)
(Dell takes over with No. 11)
1941 (On sale 12/31/41) - No. 10, 1943 (68 pgs.)
Fawcett Publications

1 (Rare)-Gene Autry & his horse Champion begin	142.00	355.00	850.00
2	48.00	145.00	335.00
3-5	36.00	110.00	255.00
6-10	31.00	92.00	215.00

GENE AUTRY COMICS (...& Champion No. 102 on)
No. 11, 1943 - No. 121, Jan-Mar, 1959 (TV - later issues)
Dell Publishing Co.

11,12(1943-2/44)-Continuation of Fawcett series (60pgs. each); #11-photo back-c	34.00	100.00	240.00
4-Color 47(1944, 60 pgs.)	34.00	100.00	240.00
4-Color 57(11/44),66('45)(52 pgs. each)	28.00	84.00	195.00
4-Color 75,83('45, 36 pgs. each)	23.00	70.00	165.00
4-Color 93,100('45-46, 36 pgs. each)	19.00	58.00	135.00
1(5-6/46, 52 pgs.)	34.00	100.00	240.00
2(7-8/46)-Photo-c begin, end #111	17.00	51.00	120.00
3-5: 4-Intro Flapjack Hobbs	13.00	40.00	90.00
6-10	9.30	28.00	65.00
11-20: 12-Line drawn-c. 20-Panhandle Pete begins	6.50	19.50	45.00
21-29(36pgs.)	5.00	15.00	35.00
30-40(52pgs.)	5.00	15.00	35.00
41-56(52pgs.)	4.00	12.00	28.00
57-66(36pgs.): 58-X-mas-c	2.65	8.00	18.00
67-80(52pgs.)	3.00	9.00	21.00
81-90(52pgs.): 82-X-mas-c. 87-Blank inside-c	2.30	7.00	16.00
91-99(36pgs. No. 91-on). 94-X-mas-c	1.70	5.00	12.00
100	2.65	8.00	18.00
101-111-Last Gene Autry photo-c	1.70	5.00	12.00
112-121-All Champion painted-c	1.15	3.50	8.00
...Adventure Comics And Play-Fun Book ('40s)-36 pgs., 8x6½''; games, comics, magic	12.00	36.00	84.00
Pillsbury Premium('47)-36 pgs., 6½x7½''; games, comics, puzzles	12.00	36.00	84.00
Quaker Oats Giveaway(1950)-2½x6¾''; 5 different versions; ''Death Card Gang, Phantom of the Cave, Riddle of Laughing Mtn., Secret of Lost Valley, Bond of Broken Arrow'' (came in wrapper) each...	5.50	16.50	38.00
3-D Giveaway(1953)-Pocket-size; 5 different	5.50	16.50	38.00

NOTE: *Photo back-c, 4-18, 20-45, 48-65. Manning a-118. Jesse Marsh art: 4-Color No. 66, 75, 93, 100, No. 1-25, 27-37, 39, 40.*

GENE AUTRY'S CHAMPION (TV)
No. 287, 8/50; No. 319, 2/51; No. 3, 8-10/51 - No. 19, 8-10/55
Dell Publishing Co.

4-Color 287('50, 52pgs.)-Photo-c	5.70	17.00	40.00
4-Color 319('51), 3-(Painted-c begin)	3.00	9.00	21.00
4-19: 19-Last painted-c	1.30	4.00	9.00

GENE AUTRY TIM (Formerly Tim) (Becomes Tim in Space)
1950 (Half-size) (Black & White Giveaway)
Tim Stores

Several issues (All Scarce)	5.00	15.00	35.00

GENE DAY'S BLACK ZEPPELIN
April, 1985 - No. 5, Oct, 1986 ($1.70, B&W)

Gasoline Alley #2, © STAR

Gay Comics #22, © MEG

Gene Autry Comics #7 (Dell), © Gene Autry

George Pal's Puppetoons #19, © FAW

Get Lost #3, © Mikeross Publ.

Ghost #10, © FH

GENE DAY'S BLACK ZEPPELIN (continued)
Renegade Press

	Good	Fine	N-Mint
1-5	.30	.90	1.80

GENERAL DOUGLAS MACARTHUR
1951
Fox Features Syndicate

nn	10.00	30.00	70.00

GENERIC COMIC, THE
April, 1984 (One-shot)
Marvel Comics Group

1		.30	.60

GENTLE BEN (TV)
Feb, 1968 - No. 5, Oct, 1969 (All photo-c)
Dell Publishing Co.

1	1.50	4.50	10.00
2-5: 5-Reprints #1	.85	2.60	6.00

GEORGE OF THE JUNGLE (TV)(See America's Best TV Comics)
Feb, 1969 - No. 2, Oct, 1969 (Jay Ward)
Gold Key

1,2	3.00	9.00	21.00

GEORGE PAL'S PUPPETOONS
Dec, 1945 - No. 18, Dec, 1947; No. 19, 1950
Fawcett Publications

1-Captain Marvel on cover	20.00	60.00	140.00
2	10.00	30.00	70.00
3-10	6.50	19.50	45.00
11-19	4.30	13.00	30.00

GEORGIE COMICS (. . .& Judy Comics #20-35?; see All Teen & Teen Comics)
Spring, 1945 - No. 39, Oct, 1952
Timely Comics/GPI No. 1-34

1-Dave Berg-a	8.00	24.00	56.00
2	4.00	12.00	28.00
3-5,7,8	2.65	8.00	18.00
6-Georgie visits Timely Comics	3.15	9.50	22.00
9,10-Kurtzman's "Hey Look" (1 & ?); Margie app.			
	3.70	11.00	26.00
11,12: 11-Margie, Millie app.	2.30	7.00	16.00
13-Kurtzman's "Hey Look", 3 pgs.	3.50	10.50	24.00
14-Wolverton art, 1 pg. & Kurtzman's "Hey Look"			
	3.70	11.00	26.00
15,16,18-20	1.70	5.00	12.00
17,29-Kurtzman's "Hey Look," 1 pg.	2.65	8.00	18.00
21-24,27,28,30-39: 31-Anti-Wertham editorial	1.30	4.00	9.00
25-Painted cover by classic pin-up artist Peter Driben			
	3.15	9.50	22.00
26-Logo design swipe from Archie Comics	1.30	4.00	9.00

GERALD McBOING-BOING AND THE NEARSIGHTED MR. MAGOO
(TV)(Mr. Magoo No. 6 on)
Aug-Oct, 1952 - No. 5, Aug-Oct, 1953
Dell Publishing Co.

1	5.00	15.00	35.00
2-5	4.00	12.00	28.00

GERONIMO
1950 - No. 4, Feb, 1952
Avon Periodicals

1-Indian Fighter; Maneely-a; Texas Rangers r-/Cowpuncher No. 1; Fawcette-c	9.00	27.00	62.00
2-On the Warpath; Kit West app.; Kinstler c/a	5.50	16.50	38.00
3-And His Apache Murderers; Kinstler c/a(2); Kit West, drug story r-Cowpuncher No. 6	5.50	16.50	38.00

	Good	Fine	N-Mint
4-Savage Raids of; Kinstler c/a(3)	4.30	13.00	30.00

GERONIMO JONES
Sept, 1971 - No. 9, Jan, 1973
Charlton Comics

1		.50	1.00
2-9		.30	.60
Modern Comics Reprint #7('78)		.20	.40

GETALONG GANG, THE
May, 1985 - No. 6, March, 1986
Star Comics (Marvel)

1-6: Saturday morning TV stars		.35	.70

GET LOST
Feb-Mar, 1954 - No. 3, June-July, 1954 (Satire)
Mikeross Publications

1	8.00	24.00	56.00
2-Has 4 pg. E.C. parody featuring "the Sewer Keeper"			
	5.70	17.00	40.00
3-John Wayne 'Hondo' parody	4.30	13.00	30.00

GET SMART (TV)
June, 1966 - No. 8, Sept, 1967 (All have Don Adams photo-c)
Dell Publishing Co.

1	4.00	12.00	28.00
2-Ditko-a	3.50	10.50	24.00
3-8: 3-Ditko-a(p)	2.65	8.00	18.00

GHOST (. . .Comics #9)
1951(Winter) - No. 11, Summer, 1954
Fiction House Magazines

1	27.00	80.00	190.00
2	13.00	40.00	90.00
3-9: 3,6,7,9-Bondage-c	11.00	32.00	75.00
10,11-Dr. Drew by Grandenetti in each, reprinted from Rangers; Evans-a-No. 11	13.00	40.00	90.00

GHOST BREAKERS (Also see Racket Squad in Action, Red Dragon & (CC) Sherlock Holmes Comics)
Sept, 1948 - No. 2, Dec, 1948 (52 pages)
Street & Smith Publications

1-Powell-c/a(3); Dr. Neff (magician) app.	14.00	42.00	100.00
2-Powell-c/a(2); Maneely-a	11.50	34.00	80.00

GHOSTBUSTERS (TV)(Also see Real . . . & Slimer and the Real . . .)
Feb, 1987 - No. 6, Aug, 1987 ($1.25, color)
First Comics

1-6: Based on new animated TV series		.65	1.30

GHOSTBUSTERS II
Oct, 1989 - No. 3, Dec, 1989 ($1.95, color, mini-series)
Now Comics

1-3: Movie adaptation	.35	1.00	2.00

GHOST CASTLE (See Tales of . . .)

GHOSTLY HAUNTS (Formerly Ghost Manor)
#20, 9/71 - #53, 12/76; #54, 9/77 - #55, 10/77; #56, 1/78 - #58, 4/78
Charlton Comics

20-58: 27-Dr. Graves x-over. 39-Origin & 1st app. Destiny Fox.

42-Newton c/a		.50	1.00
40,41(Modern Comics-r, 1977, 1978)		.15	.30

NOTE: *Ditko* a-22-28, 31-34, 36-41, 43-48, 50, 52, 54, 56r; c-22-27, 30, 33-37, 47, 54, 56. *Glanzman* a-20. *Howard* a-27, 30, 35, 42. *Staton* a-35; c-46. *Sutton* c-33, 39.

GHOSTLY TALES (Blue Beetle No. 50-54)
No. 55, 4-5/66 - No. 124, 12/76; No. 125, 9/77 - No. 169, 10/84
Charlton Comics

55-Intro. & origin Dr. Graves	.50	1.50	3.00

179

GHOSTLY TALES (continued)

	Good	Fine	N-Mint
56-70-Dr. Graves ends	.25	.75	1.50
71-106,108-113,115-169		.60	1.20
107,114: 107-Sutton, Wood-a. 114-Newton-a		.60	1.20

NOTE: *Ditko* a-55, 57, 58, 60, 61, 67, 69-73, 75-90, 92-97, 99-118, 120-122, 125r, 126r, 131-33r, 136-41r, 143r, 144r; 152, 155, 161, 163; c-67, 69, 73, 77, 78, 83, 84, 86-90, 92-97, 99, 102, 109, 111, 118, 120-22, 125, 131-33, 163. *Glanzman* a-167. *Howard* a-95, 98, 99, 117; c-98, 107, 120, 121, 161. *Newton* a-115. *Staton* a-161; c-117. *Sutton* a-112-114.

GHOSTLY WEIRD STORIES (Formerly Blue Bolt Weird)
No. 120, Sept, 1953 - No. 124, Sept, 1954
Star Publications

120-Jo-Jo-r	11.00	32.00	75.00
121-Jo-Jo-r	8.00	24.00	56.00
122-The Mask-r/Capt. Flight 5; Rulah-r; has 1pg. story 'Death and the Devil Pills'-r/Western Outlaws 17	8.00	24.00	56.00
123-Jo-Jo; Disbrow-a(2)	8.00	24.00	56.00
124-Torpedo Man	8.00	24.00	56.00

NOTE: *Disbrow* a-120-124. L. B. Cole covers-all issues (#122 is a sci-fi cover).

GHOST MANOR (Ghostly Haunts No. 20 on)
July, 1968 - No. 19, July, 1971
Charlton Comics

1	.50	1.50	3.00
2-5	.25	.75	1.50
6-12,17		.50	1.00
13-16,18,19-Ditko-a; c-15,18,19		.60	1.20

GHOST MANOR (2nd Series)
Oct, 1971 - No. 32, Dec, 1976; No. 33, Sept, 1977 - No. 77, 11/84
Charlton Comics

1	.25	.75	1.50
2-7,9,10		.50	1.00
8-Wood-a	.35	1.00	2.00
11-56,58-77: 18,20-Newton-a. 22-Newton c/a. 21-E-Man, Blue Beetle, Capt. Atom cameos. 28-Nudity panels. 40-Torture & drug use		.35	.70
57-Wood, Ditko, Howard-a		.40	.80
19(Modern Comics reprint, 1977)		.20	.40

NOTE: *Ditko* a-4, 8, 10, 11(2), 13, 14, 18, 20-22, 24-26, 28, 29, 31, 37r, 38r, 40r, 42-44r, 46r, 47, 51r, 52r, 57, 60, 62(4), 64r, 71; c-2-7, 9-11, 14-16, 28, 31, 37, 38, 42, 43, 46, 47, 51, 52, 60, 62, 64. *Howard* a-4, 8, 19-21, 57. *Newton* a-64. *Sutton* a-19; c-8.

GHOST RIDER (See A-1 Comics, Best of the West, Black Phantom, Bobby Benson, Great Western, Red Mask & Tim Holt)
1950 - No. 14, 1954
Magazine Enterprises

NOTE: The character was inspired by Vaughn Monroe's "Ghost Riders in the Sky," and Disney's movie "The Headless Horseman."

1(A-1 27)-Origin Ghost Rider	34.00	103.00	240.00
2(A-1 29), 3(A-1 31), 4(A-1 34), 5(A-1 37)-All Frazetta-c only	36.00	107.00	250.00
6(A-1 44), 7(A-1 51)	11.50	34.00	84.00
8(A-1 57)-Drug use story, 9(A-1 69)-L.S.D. story	10.00	30.00	70.00
10(A-1 71)-vs. Frankenstein	10.00	30.00	70.00
11(A-1 75), 12(A-1 80, bondage-c), 13(A-1 84), 14(A-1 112)	8.00	24.00	55.00

NOTE: *Dick Ayers* art in all; c-1, 6-14.

GHOST RIDER, THE (See Night Rider & Western Gunfighters)
Feb, 1967 - No. 7, Nov, 1967 (Western hero)
Marvel Comics Group

1-Origin Ghost Rider; Kid Colt-r begin	2.15	6.50	15.00
2-7: 6-Last Kid Colt-r	.85	2.50	5.00

GHOST RIDER (See The Champions & Marvel Spotlight)
Sept, 1973 - No. 81, June, 1983 (Super-hero)
Marvel Comics Group

1	1.00	3.00	6.00

	Good	Fine	N-Mint
2-19: 10-Ploog-a; origin-r/Marvel Spotlight 5	.35	1.00	2.00
20-Byrne-a	.70	2.00	4.00
21-81: 50-Double size. 68-Origin		.50	1.00

NOTE: *Anderson* c-64p. *Infantino* a(p)-43, 44, 51. *G. Kane* a-21p; c(p)-1, 2, 4, 5, 8, 9, 11-13, 19, 20, 24, 25. *Kirby* c-21-23. *Mooney* a-2-9p, 30i. *Nebres* c-26i. *Newton* a-23i. *Perez* c-26p. *J. Sparling* a-62p, 64p, 65p. *Starlin* a(p)-35. *Sutton* a-1p, 44i, 64i, 65i, 66, 67i. *Tuska* a-13p, 14p, 16p.

GHOSTS (Ghost No. 1)
Sept-Oct, 1971 - No. 112, May, 1982 (No. 1-5: 52 pgs.)
National Periodical Publications/DC Comics

1,2: 2-Wood-a		.40	.80
3-112: 97-99-The Spectre app. 100-Infinity-c		.25	.50

NOTE: *Ditko* a-77. *DeZuniga* a-104p, 106p, 111p. *Giffen* a-104p, 106p, 111p. *Golden* a-88. *Kaluta* c-7, 93, 101. *Kubert* c-89, 105-08, 111. *Sheldon Mayer* a-111. *McWilliams* a-99. *Win Mortimer* a-89, 91, 94. *Newton* a-92p, 94p. *Nino* a-35, 37, 57. *Orlando* a-74i; c-80. *Redondo* a-8, 13, 45. *Sparling* a-90p, 93p, 94p. *Spiegle* a-103, 105.

GHOSTS SPECIAL (See DC Special Series No. 7)

GHOST STORIES (See Amazing Ghost Stories)

GHOST STORIES
Sept-Nov, 1962; No. 2, Apr-June, 1963 - No. 37, Oct, 1973
Dell Publishing Co.

1-2-295-211-Written by John Stanley	2.30	7.00	16.00
2	1.15	3.50	8.00
3-10: Two No. 6's exist with different c/a(12-295-406,12-295-503)	.70	2.00	5.00
11-20	.50	1.50	3.00
21-37	.35	1.00	2.00

NOTE: #21-34, 36, 37 all reprint earlier issues.

GHOUL TALES (Magazine)
Nov, 1970 - No. 5, July, 1971 (52 pages) (B&W)
Stanley Publications

1-Aragon pre-code reprints; Mr. Mystery as host; bondage-c	.85	2.60	6.00
2-(1/71)Reprint/Climax #1	.50	1.50	3.00
3-(3/71)	.50	1.50	3.00
4-(5/71)Reprints story "The Way to a Man's Heart" used in SOTI	1.30	4.00	9.00
5-ACG reprints	.50	1.50	3.00

NOTE: No. 1-4 contain pre-code Aragon reprints.

GIANT BOY BOOK OF COMICS (See Boy)
1945 (Hardcover) (240 pages)
Newsbook Publications (Gleason)

1-Crimebuster & Young Robin Hood	50.00	150.00	350.00

GIANT COMIC ALBUM
1972 (52 pgs.; 11x14"; B&W; 59 cents)
King Features Syndicate

Newspaper reprints: Little Iodine, Katzenjammer Kids, Henry, Mandrake the Magician ('59 Falk), Popeye, Beetle Bailey, Barney Google, Blondie, Flash Gordon ('68-69 Dan Barry), & Snuffy Smith   each...   1.00   3.00   6.00

GIANT COMICS
Summer, 1957 - No. 3, Winter, 1957 (100 pgs.) (25 cents)
Charlton Comics

1-Atomic Mouse, Hoppy app.	8.00	24.00	56.00
2,3-Atomic Mouse, Rabbit, Christmas Book, Romance stories known	5.70	17.00	40.00

NOTE: The above may be rebound comics; contents could vary.

GIANT COMICS (See Wham-O Giant Comics)

GIANT COMICS EDITION (See Terry-Toons)
1947 - No. 17, 1950 (All 100-164 pgs.) (25 cents)
St. John Publishing Co.

1-Mighty Mouse	21.50	65.00	150.00

Ghostly Weird Stories #124, © STAR

Ghost Rider #11, © ME

Ghost Stories #6, © DELL

Giant Comics Edition #14, © Terrytoons

Giant-Size Chillers #1, © MEG

G. I. Combat #5, © DC

GIANT COMICS EDITION (continued)

	Good	Fine	N-Mint
2-Abbie & Slats	10.00	30.00	70.00
3-Terry-Toons Album; 100 pgs.	15.00	45.00	105.00
4-Crime comics; contains Red Seal No. 16, used & illo. in SOTI	25.00	75.00	175.00
5-Police Case Book(4/49)-Contents varies; contains remaindered St. John books - some volumes contain 5 copies rather than 4, with 160 pages; Matt Baker-c	23.00	70.00	160.00
5A-Terry-Toons Album, 132 pgs.	15.00	45.00	105.00
6-Western Picture Stories; Baker-c/a(3); The Sky Chief, Blue Monk, Ventrilo app.; Tuska-a	22.00	65.00	154.00
7-Contains a teen-age romance plus 3 Mopsy comics	15.00	45.00	105.00
8-The Adventures of Mighty Mouse (10/49)	15.00	45.00	105.00
9-Romance and Confession Stories; Kubert-a(3); Baker-a; photo-c	22.00	65.00	154.00
10-Terry-Toons	15.00	45.00	105.00
11-Western Picture Stories-Baker c/a(4); The Sky Chief, Desperado, & Blue Monk app.; another version with Son of Sinbad by Kubert	20.00	60.00	140.00
12-Diary Secrets; Baker prostitute-c; 4 St. John romance comics; Baker-a	43.00	130.00	300.00
13-Romances; Baker, Kubert-a	22.00	65.00	154.00
14-Mighty Mouse Album	15.00	45.00	105.00
15-Romances (4 love comics)-Baker-c	22.00	65.00	154.00
16-Little Audrey, Abbott & Costello, Casper	15.00	45.00	105.00
17(nn)-Mighty Mouse Album (nn, no date, but did follow No. 16); 100 pgs. on cover but has 148 pgs.	15.00	45.00	105.00

NOTE: The above books contain remaindered comics and contents could vary with each issue. No. 11,12 have part photo mag. insides.

GIANT COMICS EDITIONS
1940's (132 pages)
United Features Syndicate

	Good	Fine	N-Mint
1-Abbie & Slats, Abbott & Costello, Jim Hardy, Ella Cinders, Iron Vic	20.00	60.00	140.00
2-Jim Hardy & Gordo	14.00	43.00	100.00

NOTE: Above books contain rebound copies; contents can vary.

GIANT GRAB BAG OF COMICS (See Archie All-Star Specials under Archie Comics)

GIANTS (See Thrilling True Stories of . . .)

GIANT-SIZE (Avengers, Captain America, Captain Marvel, Conan, Daredevil, Defenders, Fantastic Four, Hulk, Invaders, Iron Man, Kid Colt, Man-Thing, Master of Kung Fu, Power Man, Spider-Man, Super-Villain Team-Up, Thor, Werewolf, and X-Men are listed under their own titles.)

GIANT-SIZE CHILLERS (Giant-Size Dracula No. 2)
June, 1974; Feb, 1975 - No. 3, Aug, 1975 (35 cents)
Marvel Comics Group

		Fine	N-Mint
1-(6/74)-Curse of Dracula (52 pgs.); Origin & 1st app. Lilith, Dracula's daughter; Heath-a(r)		.50	1.00
1-(2/75)(50 cents)(68 pgs.)-Alcala-a		.40	.80
2-(5/75)-All-r		.30	.60
3-(8/75)-Wrightson c/a; Smith-a(r)		.50	1.00

NOTE: Everett reprint/No. 2/Advs. Into Weird Worlds No. 10.

GIANT SIZE CREATURES (Giant-Size Werewolf No. 2)
July, 1974 (52 pgs.) (35 cents)
Marvel Comics Group

		Fine	N-Mint
1-Werewolf, Tigra app.; Crandall-a(r)		.30	.60

GIANT-SIZE DRACULA (Formerly Giant-Size Chillers)
No. 2, Sept, 1974 - No. 5, June, 1975 (50 cents)
Marvel Comics Group

		Fine	N-Mint
2		.50	1.00
3-Fox-a/Uncanny Tales #6		.40	.80
4-Ditko-a(2)(r)		.30	.60
5-1st Byrne-a at Marvel	.70	2.00	4.00

GIANT-SIZE SUPER-HEROES FEATURING SPIDER-MAN
June, 1974 (35 cents) (52 pgs.)
Marvel Comics Group

	Good	Fine	N-Mint
1-Spider-Man vs. Man-Wolf; Morbius, The Living Vampire app. Ditko-a(r); G. Kane-a(p)	1.00	3.00	6.00

GIANT-SIZE SUPER-STARS (Giant-Size Fantastic Four No. 2)
May, 1974 (35 cents) (52 pgs.)
Marvel Comics Group

		Fine	N-Mint
1-Fantastic Four, Thing, Hulk by Buckler (p); Kirbyish-a	.85	2.50	5.00

GIANT SPECTACULAR COMICS (See Archie All-Star Special under Archie Comics)

GIANT SUMMER FUN BOOK (See Terry-Toons . . .)

G. I. COMBAT
Oct, 1952 - No. 43, Dec, 1956
Quality Comics Group

	Good	Fine	N-Mint
1-Crandall-c	14.00	42.00	100.00
2	5.70	17.00	40.00
3-5,10-Crandall c/a	5.70	17.00	40.00
6-Crandall-a	5.00	15.00	35.00
7-9	3.70	11.00	26.00
11-20	2.30	7.00	16.00
21-31,33,35-43	2.00	6.00	14.00
32-Nuclear attack-c	4.00	12.00	28.00
34-Crandall-a	3.60	11.00	25.00

G. I. COMBAT
No. 44, Jan, 1957 - No. 288, Mar, 1987
National Periodical Publications/DC Comics

	Good	Fine	N-Mint
44	13.50	40.00	95.00
45	7.00	21.00	50.00
46-50	4.30	13.00	30.00
51-60	2.85	8.50	20.00
61-66,68-80	2.00	6.00	14.00
67-1st Tank Killer	4.00	12.00	28.00
81,82,84-86	1.35	4.00	8.00
83-1st Big Al, Little Al, & Charlie Cigar	2.00	6.00	14.00
87-1st Haunted Tank	4.00	12.00	28.00
88-90: Last 10 cent issue	.85	2.50	5.00
91-113,115-120	.50	1.50	3.00
114-Origin Haunted Tank	1.35	4.00	8.00
121-137,139,140	.35	1.00	2.00
138-Intro. The Losers (Capt. Storm, Gunner/Sarge, Johnny Cloud) in Haunted Tank	.40	1.25	2.50
141-259: 151,153-Medal of Honor series by Maurer. 201-245,247-259 are $1.00 size. 232-Origin Kana the Ninja. 244-Death of Slim Stryker; 1st app. The Mercenaries. 246-(72 pgs., $1.50)-30th Anniversary issue. 257-Intro. Stuart's Raiders	.25	.75	1.50
260-281 ($1.25 size). 264-Intro Sgt. Bullet and the Bravos of Vietnam; origin Kana	.25	.80	1.60
282-288 (75 cents)		.70	1.40

NOTE: Adams c-168, 201, 202. Check a-168, 173. Drucker a-48, 61, 63, 66, 71, 72, 76, 134, 140, 141, 144, 147, 148, 153. Evans a-135, 138, 158, 164, 166, 201, 202, 204, 205, 215, 256. Giffen a-267. Glanzman a-most issues. Kubert/Heath a-most issues; Kubert covers most issues. Morrow a-159-161(2 pgs.). Redondo a-189, 240i, 243i. Sekowsky a-162p. Severin a-147, 152. Simonson c-169. Thorne a-152, 156. Wildey a-153. Johnny Cloud app.-No. 112, 115, 120. Mlle. Marie app.-No. 123, 132, 200. Sgt. Rock app-#111-113, 116, 120, 125, 141, 146, 147, 149, 200. USS Stevens by Glanzman-#145, 150-153, 157.

G. I. COMICS (Also see Jeep & Overseas Comics)
1945 (distributed to U. S. armed forces)
Giveaways

	Good	Fine	N-Mint
1-49-Contains Prince Valiant by Foster, Blondie, Smilin' Jack, Mickey Finn, Terry & the Pirates, Donald Duck, Alley Oop, Moon Mullins & Capt. Easy strip reprints	4.00	12.00	28.00

GIDGET (TV)
April, 1966 - No. 2, Dec, 1966
Dell Publishing Co.

	Good	Fine	N-Mint
1,2: 1-Sally Field photo-c	2.85	8.50	20.00

GIFT (See The Crusaders)

GIFT COMICS (50 cents)
1942 - No. 4, 1949 (No.1-3: 324 pgs.; No. 4: 152 pgs.)
Fawcett Publications

	Good	Fine	N-Mint
1-Captain Marvel, Bulletman, Golden Arrow, Ibis the Invincible, Mr. Scarlet, & Spy Smasher app. Not rebound, remaindered comics, printed at same time as originals	125.00	375.00	880.00
2	89.00	270.00	625.00
3	63.00	190.00	440.00
4-The Marvel Family, Captain Marvel, etc.; each issue can vary in contents	42.00	125.00	295.00

GIFTS FROM SANTA (See March of Comics No. 137)

GIGGLE COMICS (Spencer Spook No. 100) (Also see Ha Ha)
Oct, 1943 - No. 99, Jan-Feb, 1955
Creston No.1-63/American Comics Group No. 64 on

1	14.00	42.00	100.00
2	6.50	19.50	45.00
3-5: Ken Hultgren-a begins?	4.50	14.00	32.00
6-10: 9-1st Superkatt	3.70	11.00	26.00
11-20	2.30	7.00	16.00
21-40	1.85	5.50	13.00
41-54,56-59,61-99: 95-Spencer Spook app.	1.50	4.50	10.00
55,60-Milt Gross-a	1.85	5.50	13.00

G-I IN BATTLE (G-I No. 1 only)
Aug, 1952 - No. 9, July, 1953; Mar, 1957 - No. 6, May, 1958
Ajax-Farrell Publ./Four Star

1	2.65	8.00	18.00
2	1.30	4.00	9.00
3-9	1.00	3.00	7.00
Annual 1(1952, 100 pgs.)	12.00	36.00	84.00
1(1957-Ajax)	1.70	4.00	12.00
2-6	.85	2.60	6.00

G. I. JANE
May, 1953 - No. 11, Mar, 1955 (Misdated 3/54)
Stanhall/Merit No. 11

1	4.30	13.00	30.00
2-7(5/54)	2.15	6.50	15.00
8-10(12/54, Stanhall)	1.70	5.00	12.00
11 (3/55, Merit)	1.50	4.50	10.00

G. I. JOE (Also see Advs. of . . ., Showcase #53,54 & The Yardbirds)
No. 10, 1950; No. 11, 4-5/51 - No. 51, 6/57 (52pgs.: 10-14,6-17?)
Ziff-Davis Publ. Co. (Korean War)

10(#1, 1950)-Saunders painted-c begin	4.30	13.00	30.00
11-14(10/51)	2.65	8.00	18.00
V2#6(12/51)-17-(Last 52pgs.?)	2.30	7.00	16.00
18-(100 pg. Giant-'52)	8.00	24.00	56.00
19-30: 21-The Yardbirds app.	2.00	6.00	14.00
31-47,49-51	1.70	5.00	12.00
48-Atom bomb story	2.00	6.00	14.00

NOTE: Powell a-V2#7, 8, 11. Norman Saunders painted c-10-14, V2#6-14, 26, 30, 31, 35, 38, 39. Tuska a-7. Bondage c-29, 35, 38.

G. I. JOE (America's Movable Fighting Man)
1967 (36 pages) (5-1/8"x8-3/8")
Custom Comics

Schaffenberger-a		.40	.80

G. I. JOE AND THE TRANSFORMERS
Jan, 1987 - No. 4, Apr, 1987 (mini-series)

Marvel Comics Group

	Good	Fine	N-Mint
1	.40	1.15	2.25
2-4	.25	.80	1.60

G. I. JOE, A REAL AMERICAN HERO
June, 1982 - Present
Marvel Comics Group

1-Printed on Baxter paper	3.00	9.00	18.00
2-Printed on reg. paper	4.50	13.50	27.00
3-5	1.80	5.40	10.80
6,8	1.95	5.85	11.70
7,9,10	1.65	4.95	9.90
2-10 (2nd printing)	.30	.90	1.80
11-Intro Airborne	1.20	3.60	7.20
12	1.80	5.40	10.80
13-15	1.50	4.50	9.00
14 (2nd printing)	.30	.90	1.80
16	1.35	4.05	8.10
17-20	.90	2.70	5.40
17-19 (2nd printing)	.25	.70	1.40
21,22	1.15	3.40	6.80
23-25	.60	1.80	3.60
21,23,25 (2nd printing)	.25	.70	1.40
26-Origin Snake-Eyes; ends #27	.90	2.70	5.40
27	1.05	3.15	6.30
26,27 (2nd printing)		.45	.90
28-30	.60	1.80	3.60
29,30 (2nd printing)		.45	.90
31-35: 33-New headquarters	.50	1.55	3.10
36-40	.40	1.25	2.50
34,35,36,37 (2nd printing)		.45	.90
41-49	.30	.95	1.90
50-Double size; intro Special Missions	.55	1.70	3.40
51-59: 59-$1.00 issues begin	.25	.75	1.50
51 (2nd printing)		.35	.70
60-Todd McFarlane-a	.30	.90	1.80
61-98: 94-96-Snake-Eyes app.		.45	.90
Special Treasury Edition (1982)-r/#1	1.20	3.60	7.20
...Yearbook 1 ('84)-r/#1	1.05	3.15	6.30
...Yearbook 2 ('85)	.60	1.80	3.60
...Yearbook 3 ('86, 68 pgs.)	.45	1.35	2.70
...Yearbook 4 (2/88)	.25	.80	1.60

NOTE: Golden c-23. Heath a-24. Rogers a-75p, 77-84p, 86p.

G. I. JOE COMICS MAGAZINE
Dec, 1986 - No. 13, 1988 ($1.50, digest-size)
Marvel Comics Group

1-G.I. Joe-r	.30	.90	1.80
2-13	.25	.75	1.50

G.I. JOE EUROPEAN MISSIONS (Action Force in indicia)
June, 1988 - No. 15, 1989 ($1.50/$1.75 #12 on, color)
Marvel Comics Ltd. (British)

1-15: Reprints Action Force	.25	.75	1.50

G.I. JOE IN 3-D (See Blackthorne 3-D Series #20, 26, 35, 39, 62)

G. I. JOE ORDER OF BATTLE, THE
Dec, 1986 - No. 4, Mar, 1987 (mini-series)
Marvel Comics Group

1	.55	1.60	3.20
2-4	.30	.90	1.80

G. I. JOE SPECIAL MISSIONS
Oct, 1986 - No. 28, Dec, 1989 ($1.00, color)
Marvel Comics Group

1	.50	1.50	3.00
2	.30	.90	1.80
3-10	.25	.75	1.50

Giggle Comics #51, © ACG

G. I. Jane #1, © Stanhall

G. I. Joe, A Real American Hero #3, © MEG

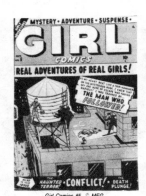

Girl Comics #5, © MEG

The Girl From U.N.C.L.E. #1, © M.G.M.

Girls' Love Stories #2, © DC

	Good	Fine	N-Mint
G.I. JOE SPECIAL MISSIONS (continued)			
11-28		.50	1.00
G. I. JUNIORS (See Harvey Hits No. 86, 91, 95, 98, 101, 104, 107, 110, 112, 114, 116, 118, 120, 122)			
GILGAMESH II			
1989 - No. 4, 1989 ($3.95, mini-series, prestige format)			
DC Comics			
1-4: Starlin-c/a, scripts; mature readers	.70	2.00	4.00
GIL THORP			
May-July, 1963			
Dell Publishing Co.			
1-Canifish-a	2.00	6.00	14.00
GINGER (Li'l Jinx No. 11 on?)			
1951 - No. 10, Summer, 1954			
Archie Publications			
1	6.50	19.50	45.00
2	3.50	10.50	24.00
3-6	2.35	7.00	16.00
7-10-Katy Keene app.	3.70	11.00	26.00
GINGER FOX			
Sept, 1988 - No. 4, Dec, 1988 ($1.75, color, mini-series)			
Comico			
1-4: 1-4-part photo-c	.30	.90	1.80
G.I. R.A.M.B.O.T.			
April, 1987 - No. 2? ($1.95, color)			
Wonder Color Comics/Pied Piper #2			
1,2	.35	1.00	2.00
GIRL COMICS (Girl Confessions No. 13 on)			
Nov, 1949 - No. 12, Jan, 1952 (Photo-c 1-4)			
Marvel/Atlas Comics(CnPC)			
1 (52 pgs.)	7.00	21.00	50.00
2-Kubert-a	3.70	11.00	26.00
3-Everett-a; Liz Taylor photo-c	5.00	15.00	35.00
4-11	2.00	6.00	14.00
12-Krigstein-a	3.50	10.50	24.00
GIRL CONFESSIONS (Formerly Girl Comics)			
No. 13, Mar, 1952 - No. 35, Aug, 1954			
Atlas Comics (CnPC/ZPC)			
13-Everett-a	3.70	11.00	26.00
14,15,19,20	2.00	6.00	14.00
16-18-Everett-a	2.65	8.00	18.00
21-35	1.50	4.50	10.00
GIRL FROM U.N.C.L.E., THE (TV) (Also see Man From . . .)			
Jan, 1967 - No. 5, Oct, 1967			
Gold Key			
1-McWilliams-a; photo-c	3.00	9.00	21.00
2-5-Leonard Swift-Courier No. 5	2.00	6.00	14.00
GIRLS' FUN & FASHION MAGAZINE (Formerly Polly Pigtails)			
V5No.44, Jan, 1950 - V5No.47, July, 1950			
Parents' Magazine Institute			
V5#44	2.15	6.50	15.00
45-47	1.15	3.50	8.00
GIRLS IN LOVE			
May, 1950 - No. 2, July, 1950			
Fawcett Publications			
1,2-Photo-c	4.35	13.00	30.00
GIRLS IN LOVE (Formerly G. I. Sweethearts No. 45)			
No. 46, Sept, 1955 - No. 57, Dec, 1956			
Quality Comics Group			

	Good	Fine	N-Mint
46	2.85	8.50	20.00
47-56: 54-'Commie' story	1.50	4.50	10.00
57-Matt Baker c/a	3.35	10.00	23.00
GIRLS IN WHITE (See Harvey Comics Hits No. 58)			
GIRLS' LIFE			
Jan, 1954 - No. 6, Nov, 1954			
Atlas Comics (BFP)			
1-Patsy Walker	3.70	11.00	26.00
2	2.00	6.00	14.00
3-6	1.30	4.00	9.00
GIRLS' LOVE STORIES			
Aug-Sept, 1949 - No. 180, Nov-Dec, 1973 (No. 1-13: 52 pgs.)			
National Comics(Signal Publ. No.9-65/Arleigh No.83-117)			
1-Toth, Kinstler-a, 8 pgs. each; photo-c	19.00	58.00	135.00
2-Kinstler-a?	9.30	28.00	65.00
3-10: 1-9-Photo-c	5.50	16.50	38.00
11-20	3.50	10.50	24.00
21-33: 21-Kinstler-a. 33-Last pre-code (1-2/55)	2.30	7.00	16.00
34-50	1.70	5.00	12.00
51-99: 83-Last 10 cent issue	1.00	3.00	7.00
100	1.15	3.50	8.00
101-146: 113-117-April O'Day app.	.70	2.00	4.00
147-151-''Confessions'' serial	.40	1.25	2.50
152-180: 161-170, 52 pgs.	.25	.75	1.50
GIRLS' ROMANCES			
Feb-Mar, 1950 - No. 160, Oct, 1971 (No. 1-11: 52 pgs.)			
National Periodical Publ.(Signal Publ. No.7-79/Arleigh No.84)			
1-Photo-c	19.00	58.00	135.00
2-Photo-c; Toth-a	9.30	28.00	65.00
3-10: 3-6-Photo-c	5.50	16.50	38.00
11,12,14-20	3.50	10.50	24.00
13-Toth-c	4.00	12.00	28.00
21-31: 31-Last pre-code (2-3/55)	2.30	7.00	16.00
32-50	1.70	5.00	12.00
51-99: 80-Last 10 cent issue	1.00	3.00	7.00
100	1.15	3.50	8.00
101-108,110-120	.70	2.00	4.00
109-Beatles c/story	2.30	7.00	16.00
121-133,135-140	.50	1.50	3.00
134-Adams-c	.70	2.00	5.00
141-160: 159,160-52 pgs.	.25	.75	1.50
G. I. SWEETHEARTS (Formerly Diary Loves; Girls In Love #46 on)			
No. 32, June, 1953 - No. 45, May, 1955			
Quality Comics Group			
32	2.65	8.00	18.00
33-45: 44-Last pre-code (3/55)	1.50	4.50	10.00
G. I. TALES (Sgt. Barney Barker No. 1-3)			
No. 4, Feb, 1957 - No. 6, July, 1957			
Atlas Comics (MCI)			
4-Severin-a(4)	2.00	6.00	14.00
5	1.00	3.00	7.00
6-Orlando, Powell, & Woodbridge-a	1.50	4.50	10.00
G. I. WAR BRIDES			
April, 1954 - No. 8, June, 1955			
Superior Publishers Ltd.			
1	2.65	8.00	18.00
2	1.30	4.00	9.00
3-8: 4-Kamenesque-a; lingerie panels	1.00	3.00	7.00
G. I. WAR TALES			
Mar-Apr, 1973 - No. 4, Oct-Nov, 1973			
National Periodical Publications			

G. I. WAR TALES (continued)	Good	Fine	N-Mint
1,3-Reprints		.15	.30
2,4: 2-Adams-a(r), 4-Krigstein-a(r)		.15	.30

NOTE: *Drucker a-3r, 4r. Heath a-4r. Kubert a-2, 3; c-4r.*

GIZMO (Also see Domino Chance)
May-June, 1985 (B&W, one shot)
Chance Ent.

1	1.70	5.00	10.00

GIZMO
1986 - No. 6, July, 1987 ($1.50, B&W)
Mirage Studios

1	.70	2.00	4.00
2-6	.30	.90	1.80

GLADSTONE COMIC ALBUM
1987 - Present (8½x11")($5.95)
Gladstone Publishing

1-10: 1-Uncle Scrooge, Barks-r; Beck-c. 2-Donald Duck, Barks-r, F.C. #108. 3-Mickey Mouse-r by Gottfredson. 4-Uncle Scrooge-r by Barks, F.C. #456. 5-Donald Duck Advs. r/F.C. #199. 6-Uncle Scrooge-r by Barks. 7-Donald Duck-r by Barks. 8-Mickey Mouse-r. 9-Bambi, r/F.C. #12. 10-Donald Duck Advs., r/F.C. #275			
	1.00	3.00	6.00
11-20: 11-Uncle Scrooge, r/U.S. #4. 12-Donald And Daisy, r/F.C. #1055, WDC&S. 13-Donald Duck Advs., r/F.C. #408. 14-Uncle Scrooge, Barks-r/U.S #21. 15-Donald And Gladstone, Barks-r. 16-Donald Duck Advs., r/F.C. #238. 17-Mickey Mouse strip-r (The World of Tomorrow, The Pirate Ghost Ship). 18-Donald Duck and the Junior Woodchucks; Barks-r. 19-Uncle Scrooge; r/U.S. #12; Rosa-c. 20-Uncle Scrooge; r/F.C. #386; Barks-c/a(r)			
	1.00	3.00	6.00
21-24: 21-Donald Duck Family; Barks-c/a(r). 22-Mickey Mouse strip-r. 23-Donald Duck; Barks-r/D.D. #26. 24-Uncle Scrooge; Barks-r, Rosa-c	1.00	3.00	6.00
Special 1 (1989, $9.95)-Donald Duck Finds Pirate Gold; r/F.C. #9	1.70	5.00	10.00
Special 2 (1989, $8.95)-Uncle Scrooge and Donald Duck; Barks-r/ Uncle Scrooge #5; Rosa-c	1.50	4.50	9.00
Special 3 (1990, $8.95)-Mickey Mouse-r	1.50	4.50	9.00

GLAMOROUS ROMANCES (Formerly Dotty)
No. 41, Sept, 1949 - No. 90, Oct, 1956 (Photo-c 68-90)
Ace Magazines (A. A. Wyn)

41-Dotty app.	2.30	7.00	16.00
42-72,74-80: 50-61-Painted-c. 80-Last pre-code (2/55)			
	1.15	3.50	8.00
73-L.B. Cole-a(r)-/All Love #27	1.65	5.00	11.50
81-90	1.00	3.00	7.00

GLOBAL FORCE
1987 - No. 2? ($1.95, color)
Silverline Comics

1,2	.35	1.00	2.00

GNOME MOBILE, THE (See Movie Comics)

GOBBLEDYGOOK
1984 - No. 2, 1984 (B&W)(1st Mirage comic, both pubbed same time)
Mirage Studios

1,2-24 pgs., early TMNT	17.00	50.00	100.00

GOBBLEDYGOOK
Dec, 1986 (One shot, $3.50, B&W, 100 pgs.)
Mirage Studios

1-New 10 pg. TMNT story	.85	2.50	5.00

GOBLIN, THE
June, 1982 - No. 4, Dec, 1982 (Magazine, $2.25)
Warren Publishing Co.

	Good	Fine	N-Mint
1-The Gremlin app; Golden-a(p)	.35	1.10	2.25
2-4: 2-1st Hobgoblin	.35	1.10	2.25

GODFATHERS, THE (See The Crusaders)

GOD IS
1973, 1975 (35-49 Cents)
Spire Christian Comics (Fleming H. Revell Co.)

By Al Hartley		.40	.80

GODS FOR HIRE
Dec, 1986 - No. 3? ($1.50, color)
Hot Comics

1-3	.25	.75	1.50

GOD'S HEROES IN AMERICA
1956 (nn) (68 pgs.) (25-35 cents)
Catechetical Guild Educational Society

307	1.15	3.50	8.00

GOD'S SMUGGLER (Religious)
1972 (39 & 49 cents)
Spire Christian Comics/Fleming H. Revell Co.

1-Two variations exist		.40	.80

GODZILLA
August, 1977 - No. 24, July, 1979
Marvel Comics Group

1-Mooney-i	.55	1.65	3.25
2-10: 3-Champions x-over; 4,5-Sutton-a	.35	1.10	2.20
11-24	.30	.90	1.80

GODZILLA
May, 1988 - No. 6, 1988 ($1.95, B&W, mini-series)
Dark Horse Comics

1	.50	1.50	3.00
2-6	.40	1.25	2.50
King Of The Monsters Special (8/87, $1.50)-Origin; Bissette-c/a	.40	1.25	2.50

GO-GO
June, 1966 - No. 9, Oct, 1967
Charlton Comics

1-Miss Bikini Luv begins; Rolling Stones, Beatles, Elvis, Sonny & Cher, Sinatra, Bob Dylan parody; Herman's Hermits pin-ups			
	2.85	8.50	20.00
2-Ringo Starr, David McCallum, Beatles photo cover; Beatles story and photos	2.85	8.50	20.00
3,4: 3-Blooperman begins, ends No. 6	1.15	3.50	8.00
5-Super Hero & TV satire by J. Aparo & Grass Green begin			
	1.15	3.50	8.00
6-9: 6-8-Aparo-a. 6-Petulia Clark photo-c	1.15	3.50	8.00

GO-GO AND ANIMAL (See Tippy's Friends....)

GOING STEADY (Formerly Teen-Age Temptations)
No. 10, 1954 - No. 13, June, 1955; No. 14, Oct, 1955
St. John Publishing Co.

10(1954)-Matt Baker c/a	6.50	19.50	45.00
11(2/55, last precode), 12(4/55)-Baker-c	3.15	9.50	22.00
13(6/55)-Baker c/a	4.35	13.00	30.00
14(10/55)-Matt Baker-c/a, 25 pgs.	4.65	14.00	33.00

GOING STEADY (Formerly Personal Love)
V3#3, Feb, 1960 - V3#6, Aug, 1960; V4#1, Sept-Oct, 1960
Prize Publications/Headline

V3#3-6, V4#1	.70	2.00	4.00

GOING STEADY WITH BETTY (Betty & Her Steady No. 2)
Nov-Dec, 1949
Avon Periodicals

Glamorous Romances #71, © ACE

Godzilla #2, © MEG

Going Steady With Betty #1, © AVON

Golden Arrow Well Known Comics, © FAW

Golden Lad #4, © Spark Publ.

Golden Picture Story Book ST-3, © WDC

	Good	Fine	N-Mint
GOING STEADY WITH BETTY (continued)			
1	6.00	18.00	42.00

GOLDEN ARROW (See Fawcett Miniatures, Mighty Midget & Whiz Comics)

GOLDEN ARROW (. . .Western No. 6)
Wint, 1942-43 - No. 6, Spring, 1947
Fawcett Publications

1-Golden Arrow begins	16.00	48.00	110.00
2	7.00	21.00	50.00
3-5	5.00	15.00	35.00
6-Krigstein-a	5.70	17.00	40.00
. . .Well Known Comics (1944; 12 pgs.; 8½x10½"; paper-c; glued binding)-Bestmaid/Samuel Lowe giveaway; printed in green			
	6.00	18.00	42.00

GOLDEN COMICS DIGEST
May, 1969 - No. 48; Jan, 1976
Gold Key

NOTE: *Whitman editions exist of many titles and are generally valued less.*

1-Tom & Jerry, Woody Woodpecker, Bugs Bunny	1.15	3.50	8.00
2-Hanna-Barbera TV Fun Favorites; Space Ghost app.			
	.85	2.50	5.00
3-Tom & Jerry, Woody Woodpecker	.50	1.50	3.00
4-Tarzan; Manning & Marsh-a	1.70	5.00	12.00
5,8-Tom & Jerry, W. Woodpecker, Bugs Bunny	.35	1.00	2.00
6-Bugs Bunny	.35	1.00	2.00
7-Hanna-Barbera TV Fun Favorites	.70	2.00	4.00
9-Tarzan	1.50	4.50	10.00
10-17: 10-Bugs Bunny. 11-Hanna-Barbera TV Fun Favorites. 12-Tom & Jerry, Bugs Bunny, W. Woodpecker Journey to the Sun. 13-Tom & Jerry. 14-Bugs Bunny Fun Packed Funnies. 15-Tom & Jerry, W. Woodpecker, Bugs Bunny. 16-Woody Woodpecker Cartoon Special. 17-Bugs Bunny	.50	1.50	3.00
18-Tom & Jerry; Barney Bear-r by Barks	.70	2.00	4.00
19-Little Lulu	1.70	5.00	12.00
20-22: 20-Woody Woodpecker Falltime Funtime. 21-Bugs Bunny Showtime. 22-Tom & Jerry Winter Wingding	.50	1.50	3.00
23-Little Lulu & Tubby Fun Fling	1.70	5.00	12.00
24-26,28: 24-Woody Woodpecker Fun Festival. 25-Tom & Jerry. 26-Bugs Bunny Halloween Hulla-Boo-Loo; Dr. Spektor article, also #25. 28-Tom & Jerry	.50	1.50	3.00
27-Little Lulu & Tubby in Hawaii	1.50	4.50	10.00
29-Little Lulu & Tubby	1.50	4.50	10.00
30-Bugs Bunny Vacation Funnies	.50	1.50	3.00
31-Turok, Son of Stone; r/4-Color #596,656	1.15	3.50	8.00
32-Woody Woodpecker Summer Fun	.50	1.50	3.00
33,36: 33-Little Lulu & Tubby Halloween Fun; Dr. Spektor app. 36-Little Lulu & Her Friends	1.70	5.00	12.00
34,35,37-39: 34-Bugs Bunny Winter Funnies. 35-Tom & Jerry Snow-time Funtime. 37-Woody Woodpecker County Fair. 38-The Pink Panther. 39-Bugs Bunny Summer Fun	.50	1.50	3.00
40,43: 40-Little Lulu & Tubby Trick or Treat; all by Stanley. 43-Little Lulu in Paris	1.70	5.00	12.00
41,42,44,45,47: 41-Tom & Jerry Winter Carnival. 42-Bugs Bunny. 44-Woody Woodpecker Family Fun Festival. 45-The Pink Panther. 47-Bugs Bunny	.35	1.00	2.00
46-Little Lulu & Tubby	1.50	4.50	10.00
48-The Lone Ranger	.70	2.00	4.00

NOTE: *#1-30, 164 pages; #31 on, 132 pages.*

GOLDEN LAD
July, 1945 - No. 5, June, 1946
Spark Publications

1-Origin Golden Lad & Swift Arrow	27.00	81.00	190.00
2-Mort Meskin-c/a	13.00	40.00	90.00
3,4: 3-Mort Meskin-a	12.00	36.00	84.00

	Good	Fine	N-Mint
5-Origin Golden Girl; Shaman & Flame app.	13.00	40.00	90.00

NOTE: *All have Robinson, Meskin, and Roussos art.*

GOLDEN LEGACY
1966 - 1972 (Black History) (25 cents)
Fitzgerald Publishing Co.

1-Toussaint L'Ouverture (1966), 2-Harriet Tubman (1967), 3-Crispus Attucks & the Minutemen (1967), 4-Benjamin Banneker (1968), 5-Matthew Henson (1969), 6-Alexander Dumas & Family (1969), 7-Frederick Douglass, Part 1 (1969), 8-Frederick Douglass, Part 2 (1970), 9-Robert Smalls (1970), 10-J. Cinque & the Amistad Mutiny (1970), 11-Men in Action: White, Marshall J. Wilkins (1970), 12-Black Cowboys (1972), 13-The Life of Martin Luther King, Jr. (1972), 14-The Life of Alexander Pushkin (1971), 15-Ancient African Kingdoms (1972), 16-Black Inventors (1972)			
each	.25	.75	1.50
1-10,12,13,15,16(1976)-Reprints	.25		.50

GOLDEN LOVE STORIES (Formerly Golden West Love)
No. 4, April, 1950
Kirby Publishing Co.

4-Powell-a; Glenn Ford/Janet Leigh photo-c	7.00	21.00	50.00

GOLDEN PICTURE CLASSIC, A
1956-1957 (Text stories w/illustrations in color; 100 pgs. each)
Western Printing Co. (Simon & Shuster)

CL-401: Treasure Island	7.00	21.00	50.00
CL-402: Tom Sawyer	6.00	18.00	42.00
CL-403: Black Beauty	6.00	18.00	42.00
CL-404: Little Women	6.00	18.00	42.00
CL-405: Heidi	6.00	18.00	42.00
CL-406: Ben Hur	4.00	12.00	28.00
CL-407: Around the World in 80 Days	4.00	12.00	28.00
CL-408: Sherlock Holmes	5.00	15.00	35.00
CL-409: The Three Musketeers	4.00	12.00	28.00
CL-410: The Merry Advs. of Robin Hood	4.00	12.00	28.00
CL-411: Hans Brinker	5.00	15.00	35.00
CL-412: The Count of Monte Cristo	5.00	15.00	35.00

(Both soft & hardcover editions are valued the same)

NOTE: *Recent research has uncovered new information. Apparently #s 1-6 were issued in 1956 and #7-12 in 1957. But they can be found in five different series listings: CL-1 to CL-12 (softbound); CL-401 to CL-412 (also softbound); CL-101 to CL-112 (hardbound); plus two new series discoveries: A GOLDEN READING ADVENTURE, publ. by Golden Press; edited down to 60 pages and reduced in size to 6"x9"; only #s discovered so far are #381 (CL-4), #382 (CL-6) & #387 (CL-3). They have no reorder list and new have covers different from GPC. There have also been found British hardbound editions of GPC with dust jackets. Copies of all five listed series vary from scarce to very rare. Some editions of some series have not yet been found at all.*

GOLDEN PICTURE STORY BOOK
Dec, 1961 (52 pgs.; 50 cents; large size)
Racine Press (Western)

ST-1-Huckleberry Hound (TV)	4.30	13.00	30.00
ST-2-Yogi Bear (TV)	4.30	13.00	30.00
ST-3-Babes in Toyland (Walt Disney's. . .)-Annette Funicello photo-c	4.30	13.00	30.00
ST-4-(. . .of Disney Ducks)-Walt Disney's Wonderful World of Ducks (Donald Duck, Uncle Scrooge, Donald's Nephews, Grandma Duck, Ludwig Von Drake, & Gyro Gearloose stories)			
	4.30	13.00	30.00

GOLDEN RECORD COMIC (See Amazing Spider-Man #1, Avengers #1, Fantastic Four #1, Journey Into Mystery #83)

GOLDEN WEST LOVE (See Golden Love Stories No. 4)
Sept-Oct, 1949 - No. 3, Feb, 1950 (All 52 pgs.)
Kirby Publishing Co.

1-Powell-a in all; Roussos-a; painted-c	7.00	21.00	50.00
2,3: 3-Photo-c	5.50	16.50	38.00

GOLDEN WEST RODEO TREASURY (See Dell Giants)

GOLDILOCKS (See March of Comics No. 1)

GOLDILOCKS & THE THREE BEARS
1943 (Giveaway)

GOLDILOCKS & THE THREE BEARS (continued)
K. K. Publications

	Good	Fine	N-Mint
nn	6.75	20.00	40.00

GOLD KEY CHAMPION
Mar, 1978 - No. 2, May, 1978 (52 pages) (50 cents)
Gold Key

1-Space Family Robinson; ½-r		.40	.80
2-Mighty Samson; ½-r		.40	.80

GOLD KEY SPOTLIGHT
May, 1976 - No. 11, Feb, 1978
Gold Key

1-Tom, Dick & Harriet		.60	1.20
2-5,7: 2-Wacky Advs. of Cracky. 3-Wacky Witch. 4-Tom, Dick & Harriet. 5-Wacky Advs. of Cracky. 7-Wacky Witch & Greta Ghost		.50	1.00
6,8,9: 6-Dagar the Invincible; Santos-a; origin Demonomicon. 8-The Occult Files of Dr. Spektor, Simbar, Lu-sai; Santos-a. 9-Tragg			
		1.50	3.00
10,11: 10-O. G. Whiz. 11-Tom, Dick & Harriet		.50	1.00

GOLD MEDAL COMICS
1945 (132 pages)
Cambridge House

nn-Captain Truth by Fugitani, Crime Detector, The Witch of Salem, Luckyman, others app.	10.00	30.00	70.00
2	6.50	19.50	45.00
3-5	5.00	15.00	35.00

GOLDYN IN 3-D (See Blackthorne 3-D Series No. 4)

GOMER PYLE (TV)
July, 1966 - No. 3, Jan, 1967
Gold Key

1-Photo front/back-c	3.50	10.50	24.00
2,3	2.85	8.50	20.00

GOODBYE, MR. CHIPS (See Movie Comics)

GOOFY (Disney)(See Dynabrite Comics, Mickey Mouse Magazine V4/7, Walt Disney Showcase #35 & Wheaties)
No. 468, May, 1953 - Sept-Nov, 1962
Dell Publishing Co.

4-Color 468	3.00	9.00	21.00
4-Color 562,627,658,747,802	2.30	7.00	16.00
4-Color 899,952,987,1053,1094,1149,1201	2.00	6.00	14.00
12-308-211(Dell, 9-11/62)	2.00	6.00	14.00

GOOFY ADVENTURE STORY (See 4-Color No. 857)

GOOFY COMICS (Companion to Happy Comics)
June, 1943 - No. 48, 1953
Nedor Publ. Co. No. 1-14/Standard No. 14-48(Animated Cartoons)

1	11.00	32.00	75.00
2	5.50	16.50	38.00
3-10	3.70	11.00	26.00
11-19	2.85	8.50	20.00
20-35-Frazetta text illos in all	4.30	13.00	30.00
36-48	2.00	6.00	14.00

GOOFY SUCCESS STORY (See 4-Color No. 702)

GOOSE (Humor magazine)
Sept, 1976 - No. 3, 1976 (52 pgs.) (75 cents)
Cousins Publ. (Fawcett)

1-3		.50	1.00

GORDO (See Comics Revue No. 5)

GORGO (Based on movie) (See Return of. . .)
May, 1961 - No. 23, Sept, 1965
Charlton Comics

	Good	Fine	N-Mint
1-Ditko-a, 22 pgs.	13.00	40.00	90.00
2,3-Ditko c/a	6.50	19.50	45.00
4-10: 4-Ditko-c	4.30	13.00	30.00
11,13-16-Ditko-a	3.00	9.00	21.00
12,17-23: 12-Reptisaurus x-over; Montes/Bache-a-No. 17-23. 20-Giordano-c	1.15	3.50	8.00
Gorgo's Revenge('62)-Becomes Return of Gorgo			
	2.30	7.00	16.00

GOSPEL BLIMP, THE
1973, 1974 (36 pgs.) (35, 39 cents)
Spire Christian Comics (Fleming H. Revell Co.)

nn		.50	1.00

GOTHAM BY GASLIGHT
1989 ($3.95, one-shot, squarebound, 52 pgs.)
DC Comics

nn-Mignola/Russell-a; Batman story	.70	2.00	4.00

GOTHIC ROMANCES
January, 1975 (B&W Magazine) (75 cents)
Atlas/Seaboard Publ.

1-Adams-a	.30	.90	1.80

GOVERNOR & J. J., THE (TV)
Feb, 1970 - No. 3, Aug, 1970 (Photo-c)
Gold Key

1	2.30	7.00	16.00
2,3	1.70	5.00	12.00

GRANDMA DUCK'S FARM FRIENDS (See 4-Color No. 763, 873, 965, 1010, 1073, 1161, 1279, Walt Disney's Comics & Stories #293 & Wheaties)

GRAND PRIX (Formerly Hot Rod Racers)
No. 16, Sept, 1967 - No. 31, May, 1970
Charlton Comics

16: Features Rick Roberts	.60	1.75	3.50
17-20	.35	1.00	2.00
21-31	.25	.75	1.50

GRAY GHOST, THE (See 4-Color No. 911,1000)

GREAT ACTION COMICS
1958 (Reprints)
I. W. Enterprises

1-Captain Truth	1.00	3.00	6.00
8,9-Phantom Lady No. 15 & 23	6.00	18.00	42.00

GREAT AMERICAN COMICS PRESENTS - THE SECRET VOICE
1945 (10 cents)
Peter George 4-Star Publ./American Features Syndicate

1-All anti-Nazi	7.00	21.00	50.00

GREAT AMERICAN WESTERN, THE
1987 - No. 4? ($1.75-$2.95, B&W with some color)
AC Comics

1 ($1.75)-Western-r plus Bill Black-a	.30	.90	1.80
2,3 ($2.95) 3-Billy the Kid-r by Severin	.50	1.50	3.00
4 ($3.50)-Photo-c & interior photos; Fawcett-r	.60	1.75	3.50

GREAT CAT FAMILY, THE (See 4-Color No. 750)

GREAT COMICS
Nov, 1941 - No. 3, Jan, 1942
Great Comics Publications

1-Origin The Great Zarro; Madame Strange begins	45.00	135.00	315.00
2	26.00	77.00	180.00
3-Futuro Takes Hitler to Hell; movie story cont'd./Choice No. 3	46.00	140.00	325.00

Goofy Comics #2, © STD

Gorgo #3, © CC

Great Comics #3, © Great Comics Publ.

Great Western #8, © ME

Green Arrow #1 (5/83), © DC

Green Giant Comics #1, © Funnies, Inc.

GREAT COMICS
1945
Novack Publishing Co./Jubilee Comics

	Good	Fine	N-Mint
1-The Defenders, Capt. Power app.; L. B. Cole-c	8.00	24.00	56.00
1-Same cover; Boogey Man, Satanas, & The Sorcerer & His Apprentice	5.70	17.00	40.00

GREAT DOGPATCH MYSTERY (See Mammy Yokum & the...)

GREATEST BATMAN STORIES EVER TOLD, THE
1988 (Color reprints) (Greatest Stories Vol. 2)
DC Comics

Softcover ($15.95)-Simonson-c	3.00	9.00	18.00
Hardcover ($24.95) with dust jacket	8.35	25.00	50.00

GREATEST JOKER STORIES EVER TOLD, THE
1988 (Color reprints) (Greatest Stories Vol. 3)
DC Comics

Softcover ($14.95)-Brian Bolland Joker-c	2.70	8.00	16.00
Hardcover ($19.95) with dust jacket	6.70	20.00	40.00

GREAT EXPLOITS
October, 1957
Decker Publ./Red Top

1-Krigstein-a(2) (re-issue on cover); reprints/Daring Advs. #6 (Approved Comics)	3.70	11.00	26.00

GREAT FOODINI, THE (See Foodini)

GREAT GAZOO, THE (The Flintstones)(TV)
Aug, 1973 - No. 20, Jan, 1977 (Hanna-Barbera)
Charlton Comics

1	.50	1.50	3.00
2-20		.50	1.00

GREAT GRAPE APE, THE (TV)(See TV Stars #1)
Sept, 1976 - No. 2, Nov, 1976 (Hanna-Barbera)
Charlton Comics

1,2	.35	1.00	2.00

GREAT LOCOMOTIVE CHASE, THE (See 4-Color No. 712)

GREAT LOVER ROMANCES (Young Lover Romances #4,5)
3/51; #2, 1951(nd); #3, 1952 (nd); #6, Oct?, 1952 - No. 22, May, 1955
Toby Press   (Photo-c #1-3,13,17)

1-Jon Juan-r/J.J. #1 by Schomburg; Dr. Anthony King app.	5.50	16.50	38.00
2-Jon Juan, Dr. Anthony King app.	2.65	8.00	18.00
3,7,9-14,16-22 (no #4,5)	1.30	4.00	9.00
6-Kurtzman-a (10/52)	2.85	8.50	20.00
8-Five pgs. of ''Pin-Up Pete'' by Sparling	3.70	11.00	26.00
15-Liz Taylor photo-c	2.65	8.00	18.00

GREAT PEOPLE OF GENESIS, THE
No date (64 pgs.) (Religious giveaway)
David C. Cook Publ. Co.

Reprint/Sunday Pix Weekly	1.50	4.50	10.00

GREAT RACE, THE (See Movie Classics)

GREAT SACRAMENT, THE
1953 (36 pages, giveaway)
Catechetical Guild

nn	1.50	4.50	10.00

GREAT SCOTT SHOE STORE (See Bulls-Eye)

GREAT WEST (Magazine)
1969 (52 pages) (Black & White)
M. F. Enterprises

V1#1	.25	.75	1.50

GREAT WESTERN
No. 8, Jan-Mar, 1954 - No. 11, Oct-Dec, 1954
Magazine Enterprises

	Good	Fine	N-Mint
8(A-1 93)-Trail Colt by Guardineer; Powell Red Hawk-r/Straight Arrow begins, ends #11	9.30	28.00	65.00
9(A-1 105), 11(A-1 127)-Ghost Rider, Durango Kid app.	4.50	14.00	32.00
10(A-1 113)-The Calico Kid by Guardineer-r/Tim Holt #8; Straight Arrow, Durango Kid app.	4.50	14.00	32.00
I.W. Reprint #1,2 9: Straight Arrow in #1,2	.85	2.50	5.00
I.W. Reprint #8-Origin Ghost Rider(Tim Holt #11); Tim Holt app.; Bolle-a	1.20	3.50	8.00

NOTE: *Guardineer* c-8. *Powell* a(r)-8-11 (from Straight Arrow).

GREEN ARROW (See Action #440, Adventure, Brave & the Bold, DC Super Stars #17, Detective #521, Flash #217, Green Lantern #76, Justice League of America #4, Leading, More Fun, and World's Finest)

GREEN ARROW
May, 1983 - No. 4, Aug, 1983 (Mini-series)
DC Comics

1-Origin; Speedy cameo	.50	1.50	3.00
2-4	.35	1.00	2.00

GREEN ARROW
Feb, 1988 - Present ($1.00, mature readers)(Painted-c #1-3)
DC Comics

1-Mike Grell scripts in all	.75	2.25	4.50
2	.45	1.40	2.75
3	.35	1.10	2.20
4,5	.30	.90	1.75
6-12	.25	.75	1.50
13-28: 27,28-Warlord app.		.60	1.25
Annual 1 ('88)-No Grell scripts	.35	1.00	2.00
Annual 2 ('89, $2.50, 68 pgs.)-No Grell scripts; recaps origin Green Arrow, Speedy, Black Canary & others	.40	1.25	2.50

NOTE: *Grell* c-1-4, 10p.

GREEN ARROW: THE LONG BOW HUNTERS
Aug, 1987 - No. 3, Oct, 1987 ($2.95, color, mature readers)
DC Comics

1-Grell c/a	2.00	6.00	14.00
1-2nd printing	.50	1.50	3.00
2	1.35	4.00	8.00
2-2nd printing	.50	1.50	3.00
3	.85	2.50	5.00
Trade paperback (1989, $12.95) reprints #1-3	2.15	6.50	12.95

GREEN BERET, THE (See Tales of...)

GREEN GIANT COMICS (Also see Colossus Comics)
1940 (no price on cover)
Pelican Publications (Funnies, Inc.)

1-Dr. Nerod, Green Giant, Black Arrow, Mundoo & Master Mystic app; origin Colossus. (Rare, only 10-20 copies exist)	357.00	1070.00	2500.00

NOTE: The idea for this book came about by a stroll through a grocery store. Printed by Moreau Publ. of Orange, N.J. as an experiment to see if they could profitably use the idle time of their 40-page Hoe color press. The experiment failed due to the difficulty of obtaining good quality color registration and Mr. Moreau believes the book never reached the stands. The book has no price or date which lends credence to this. Contains five pages reprinted from Motion Picture Funnies Weekly.

GREENHAVEN
1988 - No. 3, 1988 ($2.00, color, 28pgs, mini-series)
Aircel Publishing

1-3	.35	1.00	2.00

GREEN HORNET, THE (TV)(See Four Color 496)
Feb, 1967 - No. 3, Aug, 1967 (All have photo-c)
Gold Key

THE GREEN HORNET (continued)	Good	Fine	N-Mint
1-All have Bruce Lee photo-c	6.50	19.50	45.00
2,3	5.00	15.00	35.00

GREEN HORNET, THE
Nov., 1989 - Present ($1.75, color)
Now Comics

	Good	Fine	N-Mint
1 ($2.95, double-size)-Steranko painted-c; G.A. Green Hornet	.60	1.75	3.50
2-4: Green Hornet & Kato from '60s TV show	.35	1.00	2.00
5-7: 6-Intro new Kato	.30	.90	1.80

GREEN HORNET COMICS (. . . Racket Buster #44) (Radio, movies)
Dec, 1940 - No. 47, Sept, 1949 (See All New #13,14)
Helnit Publ. Co.(Holyoke) No. 1-6/Family Comics(Harvey) No. 7-on

	Good	Fine	N-Mint
1-Green Hornet begins(1st app.); painted-c	117.00	350.00	820.00
2	54.00	160.00	375.00
3	43.00	130.00	300.00
4-6 (8/41)	34.00	100.00	235.00
7 (6/42)-Origin The Zebra; Robin Hood & Spirit of 76 begin	30.00	90.00	210.00
8-10	24.00	70.00	165.00
11,12-Mr. Q in both	20.00	60.00	140.00
13-20	18.50	56.00	130.00
21-30: 24-Sci-fic-c	16.50	50.00	115.00
31-The Man in Black Called Fate begins	17.00	51.00	120.00
32-36: 36-Spanking panel	14.00	42.00	100.00
37-Shock Gibson app. by Powell; S&K Kid Adonis reprinted from Stuntman No. 3	16.00	48.00	110.00
38-Shock Gibson, Kid Adonis app.	14.00	42.00	100.00
39-Stuntman story by S&K	18.50	56.00	130.00
40,41	10.00	30.00	70.00
42-45,47-Kerry Drake in all. 45-Boy Explorers on cover only	10.00	30.00	70.00
46-''Case of the Marijuana Racket'' cover/story; Kerry Drake app.	10.00	30.00	70.00

NOTE: *Fuje* a-23, 24, 26. *Kubert* a-20, 30. *Powell* a-7-10, 12, 14, 16-21, 30, 31(2), 32(3), 33, 34(3), 35, 36, 37(2), 38. *Robinson* a-27. *Schomburg* c-15, 17-23. *Kirbyish* c-7, 9, 15. *Bondage* c-8, 14, 18, 26, 36.

GREEN JET COMICS, THE (See Comic Books, Series 1)

GREEN LAMA (Also see Comic Books, Series 1, Daring Adventures #17 & Prize Comics #7)
Dec, 1944 - No. 8, March, 1946
(Formerly a pulp hero who began in 1940)
Spark Publications/Prize No. 7 on

	Good	Fine	N-Mint
1-Intro. The Green Lama, Lt. Hercules & The Boy Champions; Mac Raboy-c/a #1-8	55.00	165.00	385.00
2-Lt. Hercules borrows the Human Torch's powers for one panel	38.00	115.00	270.00
3,6-8: 7-Christmas-c	27.00	81.00	190.00
4-Dick Tracy take-off in Lt. Hercules story by H. L. Gold (sci-fiction writer)	27.00	81.00	190.00
5-Lt. Hercules story; Little Orphan Annie, Smilin' Jack & Snuffy Smith take-off	27.00	81.00	190.00

NOTE: *Robinson* a-3-5.

GREEN LANTERN (1st Series) (See All-American, All Flash Quarterly, All Star Comics, The Big All-American & Comic Cavalcade)
Fall, 1941 - No. 38, May-June, 1949
National Periodical Publications/All-American

	Good	Fine	N-Mint
1-Origin retold	583.00	1460.00	3500.00
2-1st book-length story	250.00	625.00	1500.00
3	192.00	480.00	1150.00
4	133.00	335.00	800.00
5	106.00	265.00	635.00
6-8: 8-Hop Harrigan begins	92.00	230.00	550.00
9,10: 10-Origin Vandal Savage	79.00	200.00	475.00

	Good	Fine	N-Mint
11-17,19,20: 12-Origin Gambler	67.00	170.00	400.00
18-Christmas-c	75.00	190.00	450.00
21-29: 27-Origin Sky Pirate	56.00	140.00	335.00
30-Origin/1st app. Streak the Wonder Dog by Toth	56.00	140.00	335.00
31-35	47.00	120.00	285.00
36-38: 37-Sargon the Sorcerer app.	56.00	140.00	335.00

NOTE: *Book-length stories #2-8. Paul Reinman* c-11, 12, 15, 16, 18, 19, 22. *Toth* a-28, 30, 31, 34-38; c-28, 30, 34, 36-38.

GREEN LANTERN (2nd Series) (See Action Comics Weekly, Adventure, Brave & the Bold, DC Special, DC Special Series, Flash, Justice League of America, Showcase & Tales of The . . . Corps; Gr. Lant. Corps #206 on)
7-8/60 - No. 89, 4-5/72; No. 90, 8-9/76 - No. 205, 10/86
National Periodical Publications/DC Comics

	Good	Fine	N-Mint
1-Origin retold; Gil Kane-a begins	95.00	285.00	660.00
2-1st Pieface	43.00	130.00	300.00
3	25.00	75.00	175.00
4,5: 5-Origin & 1st app. Hector Hammond; 1st 5700 A.D. story	20.00	60.00	140.00
6-10: 6-Intro Tomar-re the alien G.L. 7-Origin Sinestro. 9-1st Jordan Brothers; last 10 cent issue	11.50	34.50	80.00
11-15: 13-Flash x-over. 14-Origin Sonar	8.50	25.50	60.00
16-20: 16-Origin Star Sapphire. 20-Flash x-over	7.00	21.00	50.00
21-30: 21-Origin Dr. Polaris. 23-1st Tattooed Man. 24-Origin Shark. 29-JLA cameo; 1st Blackhand	5.70	17.00	40.00
31-39	3.60	11.00	25.00
40-1st app. Crisis; 1st solo G.A. Green Lantern in Silver Age; origin The Guardians	30.00	90.00	200.00
41-44,46-50: 42-Zatanna x-over. 43-Flash x-over	2.30	7.00	16.00
45-G.A. Green Lantern x-over	3.60	11.00	25.00
51,53-58	1.50	4.50	10.00
52-G.A. Green Lantern x-over	2.15	6.50	15.00
59-1st app. Guy Gardner	11.00	32.00	75.00
60,62-75: 69-Wood inks	1.35	4.00	8.00
61-G.A. Green Lantern x-over	1.50	4.50	10.00
76-Begin Green Lantern/Green Arrow series by Neal Adams	7.00	21.00	50.00
77	2.85	8.50	20.00
78-80	2.15	6.50	15.00
81-84: 82-One pg. Wrightson inks. 83-G.L. reveals i.d. to Carol Ferris. 84-Adams/Wrightson-a, 22pgs.	1.60	4.80	11.00
85,86(52 pgs.)-Drug propaganda books. 86-G.A. Green Lantern-r; Toth-a	2.50	7.50	17.00
87(52 pgs.)-2nd app. Guy Gardner (cameo)	1.50	4.50	9.00
88(52 pgs.,'72)-Unpubbed G.A. Gr. Lantern story; Gr. Lant.-r/Showcase #23. Adams-a(1 pg.)	.40	1.25	2.50
89(52 pgs.)-G.A. Green Lantern-r	1.15	3.50	7.00
90('76)-99	.35	1.00	2.00
100(Giant)-1st app. new Air Wave	.50	1.50	3.00
101-119: 108-110 (44pgs)-G.A. Gr. Lant. 111-Origin retold; G.A. Green Lant. app. 112-G.A. Gr. Lant. origin retold	.25	.75	1.50
120-135,138-140,144-149: 131,132-Tales of the G.L. Corps. 132-Adam Strange begins new series, ends 147. 144-Omega Men cameo. 148-Tales of the G.L. Corps begins, ends #173	.60	1.20	
136,137-1st app. Citadel	.35	1.00	2.00
141-1st app. Omega Men	.50	1.50	3.00
142,143-The Omega Men app.; Perez-c	.35	1.00	2.00
150-Anniversary issue, 52 pgs.	.25	.75	1.50
151-170: 159-Origin Evil Star. 160,161-Omega Men app.	.50	1.00	
171-194,196,197,199,201-210: (75– cover). 174-Book-length stories begin. 194-Crisis x-over	.50	1.00	
195-Guy Gardner becomes Green Lantern. 195-Crisis x-over			

Green Hornet Comics #17, © HARV

Green Lantern #33 (1st series), © DC

Green Lantern #45 (2nd series), © DC

The Green Mask #2, © FOX

The Green Planet, © CC

Grimjack #12, © First Comics

GREEN LANTERN (continued)	Good	Fine	N-Mint
	.70	2.00	4.00
198,200: 198-Crisis x-over. 200-double-size	.35	1.00	2.00
Annual 1-3: (See Tales Of The. . .)			
Special 1 (1988), 2 (1989)-(Both $1.50, 52 pgs.)	.25	.75	1.50

NOTE: **Adams** a-76, 77p-87p, 89; c-63, 76-89 **Austin** a-93i, 94i, 171i. **Greene** a-39-49i, 58-63i; c-54-58i. **Grell** a-90, 91, 92-100p, 106p, 108-110p; c-90, 93-100, 101p, 102-106, 108-112 **Gil Kane** a-1-49p, 50-57, 58-61p, 68-75p, 85p(r), 87p(r), 88p(r), 156, 177, 184p; c-1-52, 54-61p, 67-75, 123, 154, 156, 165-171, 177, 184. **Newton** a-148p, 149p, 181 **Perez** c-132p, 141-144 **Sekowsky** a-65p, 170p **Sparling** a-63p; **Starlin** c-129, 133 **Staton** a-117p, 123-127p, 128, 129-131p, 132-139, 140p, 141-146, 147p, 148-150, 151-155p; c-107p, 117p, 135(i), 136p, 145p, 146, 147, 148-152p, 155p **Toth** a-86r, 171p **Tuska** a-166-68p, 170p.

GREEN LANTERN CORPS (Formerly Green Lantern)
No. 206, Nov, 1986 - No. 224, May, 1988
DC Comics

206-223: 220,221-Millennium tie-ins		.50	1.00
224-Double size last issue	.25	.75	1.50
. .Corps Annual 2 (12/86)-Moore scripts	.25	.75	1.50
. .Corps Annual 3 (8/87)-Moore scripts; Byrne-a	.25	.75	1.50

NOTE: **Austin** a-Annual 31. **Gil Kane** a-223, 224p; c-223, 224. **Staton** a-207p-213p, 217p, 221p, 222p, Annual #3; c-207p-213p, 217p, 221p, 222p. **Willingham** a-213p, 219p, 220p, 218p, 219p, Annual 2, 3p; c-218p, 219p.

GREEN LANTERN: EMERALD DAWN
Dec, 1989 - No. 6, May, 1990 ($1.00, color, mini-series)
DC Comics

1-6: 1-Origin retold		.50	1.00

GREEN LANTERN/GREEN ARROW (Also see The Flash #217)
Oct, 1983 - No. 7, April, 1984 (52-60 pgs.)
DC Comics

1-7: Reprints Green Lantern #76-89	.50	1.50	3.00

NOTE: **Adams** r-1-7, c-1-4. **Wrightson** r-4, 5.

GREEN MASK, THE (The Bouncer No. 11 on? See Mystery Men)
Summer, 1940 - No. 9, 2/42; No. 10, 8/44 - No. 11, 11/44;
V2/1, Spr, 1945 - No. 6, 10-11/46
Fox Features Syndicate

V1/1-Origin The Green Mask & Domino; reprints/Mystery Men No.

1-3,5-7: Lou Fine-c	93.00	278.00	650.00
2-Zanzibar The Magician by Tuska	44.00	133.00	310.00
3-Powell-a; Marijuana story	27.00	81.00	190.00
4-Navy Jones begins, ends No. 6	22.00	65.00	154.00
5	19.00	58.00	135.00
6-The Nightbird begins, ends No. 9; bondage/torture-c			
	16.50	50.00	115.00
7-9	13.00	40.00	90.00
10,11: 10-Origin One Round Hogan & Rocket Kelly			
	11.50	34.00	80.00
V2/1	8.50	25.50	60.00
2-6	6.50	19.50	45.00

GREEN PLANET, THE
1962 (One Shot)
Charlton Comics

nn	2.65	8.00	18.00

GREEN TEAM (See Cancelled Comic Cavalcade & First Issue Special)

GREETINGS FROM SANTA (See March of Comics No. 48)

GRENDEL (Also see Primer No. 2 and Mage)
Mar, 1983 - No. 3, Feb, 1984 (B&W)
Comico

1-Origin Hunter Rose	8.00	24.00	48.00
2,3: 2-Origin Argent	6.35	19.00	38.00

GRENDEL
Oct, 1986 - Present ($1.50-$1.95-$2.50, color) (Mature readers)
Comico

	Good	Fine	N-Mint
1	.70	2.00	4.00
1-2nd printing	.25	.75	1.50
2	.45	1.30	2.60
2-2nd printing	.25	.75	1.50
3-5	.35	1.10	2.20
6-10	.35	1.00	2.00
11-15: 13-15-Ken Steacy-c	.30	.90	1.80
16-Re-intro Mage	.70	2.00	4.00
17-32: 18-26-$1.75-c; 27-32-$1.95-c	.35	1.00	2.00
33-($2.75, 44 pgs.)	.45	1.40	2.75
34-38: Begin $2.50 cover price	.40	1.25	2.50
Devil the Deed (Graphic Novel, 10/86, $5.95, 52 pgs.)-r/Grendel			
back-ups/Mage 6-14; Alan Moore intro.	1.15	3.50	7.00
Devil's Legacy ($14.95, 1988, Graphic Novel)	2.50	7.50	15.00

GREY
Oct, 1988 - No. 9, June?, 1989 ($2.95, B&W, mini-series, 72 pgs.)
Viz Comics

1-7: Japanese manga set in future	.50	1.50	3.00
8,9 ($3.25)	.55	1.65	3.30

GREYFRIARS BOBBY (See 4-Color No. 1189)

GREYLORE
12/85 - No. 5, Sept, 1986 ($1.50-$1.75, full color, high quality paper)
Sirius Comics

1-5	.25	.75	1.50

GRIM GHOST, THE
Jan, 1975 - No. 3, July, 1975
Atlas/Seaboard Publ.

1-Origin		.40	.80
2,3-Heath-c		.30	.60

GRIMJACK (Also see Starslayer)
Aug, 1984 - Present
First Comics

1	.40	1.20	2.40
2-5	.35	1.00	2.00
6-10	.25	.80	1.60
11-25: 20-Sutton c/a begins		.70	1.40
26-2nd color Teenage Mutant Ninja Turtles	.70	2.00	4.00
27-38: 30-Dynamo Joe x-over; 31-Mandrake c/a begins			
		.65	1.30
39-70	.35	1.00	1.95

GRIMM'S GHOST STORIES (See Dan Curtis)
Jan, 1972 - No. 60, June, 1982 (Painted-c No. 1-56)
Gold Key/Whitman No. 55 on

1	.50	1.50	3.00
2-4,6,7,9,10	.25	.75	1.50
5,8-Williamson-a	.40	1.25	2.50
11-16,18-35: 32,34-Reprints		.50	1.00
17-Crandall-a	.35	1.00	2.00
36-55,57-60: 43,44-(52 pgs.)		.40	.80
56-Williamson-a		.50	1.00
Mini-Comic No. 1 (3¼x6½'', 1976)		.30	.60

NOTE: Reprints-#32?, 34?, 39, 43, 44, 47?, 53; 56-60(½). **Bolle** a-23-25, 27, 29(2), 33, 35, 43r, 45(2), 48(2), 50, 52. **Lopez** a-24, 25. **McWilliams** a-33, 44r, 48, 58. **Win Mortimer** a-31, 33, 49, 51, 55, 56, 58(2), 59, 60. **Roussos** a-25, 30. **Sparling** a-23, 24, 28, 30, 31, 33, 43r, 45, 51(2), 52, 56, 58, 59(2), 60.

GRIN (The American Funny Book) (Magazine)
Nov, 1972 - No. 3, April, 1973 (52 pgs.) (Satire)
APAG House Pubs

1		.60	1.20
2,3		.40	.80

GRIN & BEAR IT (See Gags & Large Feature Comic No. 28)

189

GRIPS (Extreme violence) Sept. 1986 - No. 4, 1986? ($1.50, B&W) Silverwolf Comics	Good	Fine	N-Mint
1	1.15	3.50	7.00
2	.50	1.50	3.00
3	.35	1.00	2.00
4	.25	.75	1.50

GRIT GRADY (See Holyoke One-Shot No. 1)

GROO CHRONICLES, THE
1989 - No. 6, Feb, 1990 ($3.50, color, squarebound, 52 pgs.)
Epic Comics (Marvel)

Book 1-6: r/all Pacific issues & Eclipse one-shot w/new Aragones' covers (front & back) & some new-a	.60	1.75	3.50

GROO SPECIAL
Oct. 1984 ($2.00, 52 pgs., Baxter paper)
Eclipse Comics

1	5.00	15.00	30.00

GROO THE WANDERER (See Destroyer Duck & Starslayer)
Dec, 1982 - No. 8, March, 1984
Pacific Comics

1-Aragones c/a(p) in all	2.85	8.50	20.00
2	2.00	6.00	12.00
3-7	1.70	5.00	10.00
8	2.00	6.00	12.00

GROO THE WANDERER (Sergio Aragones'. . .) (See Marvel Graphic
Novel #27)
March, 1985 - Present
Epic Comics (Marvel)

1-Aragones c/a begins	2.00	6.00	12.00
2	1.50	4.50	9.00
3-5	1.00	3.00	6.00
6-10	.75	2.25	4.50
11-20	.50	1.50	3.00
21-26	.35	1.00	2.00
27-35 ($1.00-c)	.35	1.00	2.00
36-48 ($1.50-c)	.25	.75	1.50
49,51-62 ($1.00-c)		.50	1.00
50-$1.50, double-size	.25	.75	1.50
Graphic Novel "Death of Groo" (1988, $6.95)	1.35	4.00	8.00

GROOVY (Cartoon Comics - not CCA approved)
March, 1968 - No. 3, July, 1968
Marvel Comics Group

1-Monkees, Ringo Starr photos	1.15	3.50	8.00
2,3	1.00	3.00	7.00

GROUP LARUE, THE
1989 - No. 4, 1990 ($1.95, color, mini-series)
Innovation Publishing

1-4: By Mike Baron	.35	1.00	2.00

GUADALCANAL DIARY (Also see American Library)
1945 (One Shot) (See Thirty Seconds Over Tokyo)
David McKay Publishing Co.

nn-B&W text & pictures; painted-c	14.00	42.00	95.00

GUERRILLA WAR (Formerly Jungle War Stories)
No. 12, July-Sept, 1965 - No. 14, Mar, 1966
Dell Publishing Co.

12-14	.70	2.00	5.00

GUILTY (See Justice Traps the Guilty)

GULF FUNNY WEEKLY (Gulf Comic Weekly No. 1-4)
1933 - No. 422, 5/23/41 (in full color; 4 pgs.; tabloid size to
2/3/39; 2/10/39 on, regular comic book size)(early issues undated)

Gulf Oil Company (Giveaway)	Good	Fine	N-Mint
1	10.00	30.00	60.00
2-30	4.00	12.00	24.00
31-100	3.00	9.00	18.00
101-196	2.00	6.00	12.00
197-Wings Winfair begins(1/29/37); by Fred Meagher beginning in 1938	15.00	45.00	90.00
198-300 (Last tabloid size)	7.00	20.00	40.00
301-350 (Regular size)	3.35	10.00	20.00
351-422	2.35	7.00	14.00

GULLIVER'S TRAVELS (See Dell Jr. Treasury No. 3)
Sept-Nov, 1965 - No. 3, May, 1966
Dell Publishing Co.

1	1.70	5.00	12.00
2,3	1.15	3.50	8.00

GUMBY IN 3-D (See Blackthorne 3-D Series #10, 14, 17, 21, 28, 33, 38)

GUMBY'S SUMMER FUN SPECIAL
July, 1987 ($2.50, color)
Comico

1-Art Adams-c/a, B. Burden story	.75	2.25	4.50

GUMBY'S WINTER FUN SPECIAL
Dec, 1988 ($2.50, 44pgs.)
Comico

1-Art Adams-c/a	40	1.25	2.50

GUMPS, THE
1918 - No. 8, 1931 (10x10'')(52 pgs.; black & white)
Landfield-Kupfer/Cupples & Leon No. 2

Book No.2(1918)-(Rare); 5¼x13⅓''; paper cover; 36 pgs. daily strip reprints by Sidney Smith	17.00	51.00	120.00
nn(1924)-by Sidney Smith	11.00	32.00	75.00
2,3	9.30	28.00	65.00
4-7	8.50	25.50	60.00
8-(10x14''); 36 pgs.; B&W; National Arts Co.	8.50	25.50	60.00

GUMPS, THE (See Merry Christmas..., Popular & Super Comics)
1945 - No. 5, Nov-Dec, 1947
Dell Publ. Co./Bridgeport Herald Corp.

4-Color 73 (Dell)(1945)	6.50	19.50	45.00
1 (3-4/47)	6.50	19.50	45.00
2-5	4.00	12.00	28.00

GUNFIGHTER (Fat & Slat #1-4) (Becomes Haunt of Fear #15 on)
No. 5, Summer, 1948 - No. 14, Mar-Apr, 1950
E. C. Comics (Fables Publ. Co.)

5,6-Moon Girl in each	31.50	95.00	220.00
7-14: 14-Bondage-c	21.00	62.00	145.00

NOTE: *Craig & H. C. Kiefer art in most issues. Craig c-5, 6, 13, 14. Feldstein/Craig
a-10. Feldstein a-7-11. Harrison/Wood a-13, 14. Ingels a-5-14; c-7-12.*

GUNFIGHTERS, THE
1963 - 1964
Super Comics (Reprints)

10,11(Billy the Kid), 12(Swift Arrow), 15(Straight Arrow-Powell-a), 16,18-All reprints	.50	1.50	3.00

GUNFIGHTERS, THE (Formerly Kid Montana)
No. 51, 10/66 - No. 52, 10/67; No. 53, 6/79 - No. 85, 7/84
Charlton Comics

51,52	.40	1.25	2.50
53,54-Williamson a(r)/Wild Bill Hickok		.40	.80
55,57-85		.30	.60
56-Williamson/Severin-c/a; r-Sheriff of Tombstone		.40	.80
85-S&K-r/1955 Bullseye		.40	.80

GUN GLORY (See 4-Color No. 846)

Groo The Wanderer #1 (Pacific), © S. Aragones

Gumby's Winter Fun Special #1, © Comico

The Gumps #1 (3-4/47), © News Synd.

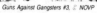
Guns Against Gangsters #3, © NOVP

Gunsmoke #21 (Dell), © CBS

Ha Ha Comics #12, © ACG

GUNHAWK, THE (Formerly Whip Wilson)(See Wild Western)
No. 12, Nov, 1950 - No. 18, Dec, 1951
Marvel Comics/Atlas (MCI)

	Good	Fine	N-Mint
12	5.70	17.00	40.00
13-18: 13-Tuska-a. 18-Maneely-c	4.50	14.00	32.00

GUNHAWKS (Gunhawk No. 7)
October, 1972 - No. 7, October, 1973
Marvel Comics Group

1-Reno Jones, Kid Cassidy	.25	.75	1.50
2-7: 6-Kid Cassidy dies. 7-Reno Jones solo		.50	1.00

GUNMASTER (Judo Master No. 89 on; formerly Six-Gun Heroes)
9/64 - No. 4, 1965; No. 84, 7/65 - No. 88, 3-4/66; No. 89, 10/67
Charlton Comics

V1#1	.70	2.00	5.00
2-4,V5#84-86: 4-Blank inside-c	.60	1.75	3.50
V5#87-89	.40	1.25	2.50

NOTE: Vol. 5 was originally cancelled with #88 (3-4/66). #89 on, became Judo Master, then later in 1967, Charlton issued #89 as a Gunmaster one-shot.

GUNS AGAINST GANGSTERS
Sept-Oct, 1948 - V2No.2, 1949
Curtis Publications/Novelty Press

1-Toni Gayle begins by Schomburg	10.00	30.00	70.00
2	6.50	19.50	45.00
3-6, V2#1,2: 6-Toni Gayle-c	6.00	18.00	42.00

NOTE: L. B. Cole c-1-6, V2#1, 2; a-1,2,3(2),4-6.

GUNSLINGER (See 4-Color No. 1220)

GUNSLINGER (Formerly Tex Dawson . . .)
No. 2, April, 1973 - No. 3, June, 1973
Marvel Comics Group

2,3		.30	.60

GUNSMOKE
Apr-May, 1949 - No. 16, Jan, 1952
Youthful Magazines

1-Gunsmoke & Masked Marvel begin by Ingels; Ingels bondage-c			
	18.50	56.00	130.00
2-Ingels c/a(2)	9.30	28.00	65.00
3-Ingels bondage-c/a	8.00	24.00	56.00
4-6: Ingels-c	5.70	17.00	40.00
7-10	3.70	11.00	26.00
11-16	2.65	8.00	18.00

GUNSMOKE (TV)
No. 679, 2/56 - No. 27, 6-7/61; 2/69 - No. 6, 2/70
Dell Publishing Co./Gold Key (All have James Arness photo-c)

4-Color 679(No. 1)	6.00	18.00	42.00
4-Color 720,769,797,844	4.00	12.00	28.00
6(11-1/57-58), 7	4.00	12.00	28.00
8,9,11,12-Williamson-a in all, 4 pgs. each	5.00	15.00	35.00
10-Williamson/Crandall-a, 4 pgs.	5.00	15.00	35.00
13-27	3.70	11.00	26.00
Gunsmoke Film Story (11/62-G.K. Giant) No. 30008-211			
	4.00	12.00	28.00
1 (G.K.)	2.15	6.50	15.00
2-6('69-70)	1.15	3.50	8.00

GUNSMOKE TRAIL
June, 1957 - No. 4, Dec, 1957
Ajax-Farrell Publ./Four Star Comic Corp.

1	3.50	10.50	24.00
2-4	2.00	6.00	14.00

GUNSMOKE WESTERN (Formerly Western Tales of Black Rider)
No. 32, Dec, 1955 - No. 77, July, 1963
Atlas Comics No. 32-35(CPS/NPI); Marvel No. 36 on

	Good	Fine	N-Mint
32	5.00	15.00	35.00
33,35,36-Williamson-a in each: 5,6 & 4 pgs. plus Drucker No. 33			
	5.50	16.50	38.00
34-Baker-a, 3pgs.	2.30	7.00	16.00
37-Davis-a(2); Williamson text illo	2.65	8.00	18.00
38,39	1.70	5.00	12.00
40-Williamson/Mayo-a, 4 pgs.	4.30	13.00	30.00
41,42,45-49,51-55,57-60: 49,52-Kid From Texas story. 57-1st Two Gun Kid by Severin. 60-Sam Hawk app. in Kid Colt			
	1.15	3.50	8.00
43,44-Torres-a	1.70	5.00	12.00
50,61-Crandall-a	1.70	5.00	12.00
56-Matt Baker-a	1.70	5.00	12.00
62-77: 72-Origin Kid Colt	1.00	3.00	7.00

NOTE: Colan a-36, 37, 72, 76. Davis a-37, 52, 54, 55; c-50, 54. Ditko a-56, 66. Jack Keller a-40, 60, 72; c-72. Kirby a-47, 50, 51, 59, 62(3), 63-67, 69, 71, 73, 77; c-56(w/Ditko),57, 58, 60, 61(w/Ayers), 62, 63, 66, 68, 69, 71-77. Severin a-60; 61; c-42, 43. Wildey a-10, 37, 42, 57. Kid Colt in all. Two-Gun Kid in No. 57, 59, 60-63. Wyatt Earp in No. 45, 48, 49, 52, 54, 55, 58.

GUNS OF FACT & FICTION (See A-1 Comics No. 13)

GUN THAT WON THE WEST, THE
1956 (24 pgs.; regular size) (Giveaway)
Winchester-Western Division & Olin Mathieson Chemical Corp.

nn-Painted-c	2.30	7.00	16.00

GYPSY COLT (See 4-Color No. 568)

GYRO GEARLOOSE (See Dynabrite Comics, Walt Disney's C&S #140 & Walt Disney Showcase #18)
No. 1047, Nov-Jan/1959-60 - May-July, 1962 (Disney)
Dell Publishing Co.

4-Color 1047 (No. 1)-Barks c/a	6.50	19.50	45.00
4-Color 1095,1184-All by Carl Barks	5.50	16.50	38.00
4-Color 1267-Barks c/a, 4 pgs.	4.00	12.00	28.00
No. 01-329-207 (5-7/62)-Barks-c only	2.65	8.00	18.00

HAGAR THE HORRIBLE (See Comics Reading Libraries)

HA HA COMICS (Teepee Tim No. 100 on) (Also see Giggle)
Oct, 1943 - No. 99, Jan, 1955
Scope Mag.(Creston Publ.) No. 1-80/American Comics Group

1	14.00	42.00	100.00
2	6.50	19.50	45.00
3-5: Ken Hultgren-a begins?	4.50	14.00	32.00
6-10	3.70	11.00	26.00
11-20: 14-Infinity-c	2.30	7.00	16.00
21-40	1.85	5.50	13.00
41-94,96-99: 49-XMas-c	1.50	4.50	10.00
95-3-D effect-c	5.70	17.00	40.00

HAIR BEAR BUNCH, THE (TV) (See Fun-In No. 13)
Feb, 1972 - No. 9, Feb, 1974 (Hanna-Barbera)
Gold Key

1	.85	2.50	5.00
2-9	.50	1.50	3.00

HALLELUJAH TRAIL, THE (See Movie Classics)

HALL OF FAME FEATURING THE T.H.U.N.D.E.R. AGENTS
May, 1983 - No. 3, Dec, 1983
JC Productions(Archie Comics Group)

1-3: T.H.U.N.D.E.R. Agents-r		.45	.90

HALLOWEEN HORROR
Oct, 1987 (Seduction of the Innocent #7)($1.75, color)
Eclipse Comics

1-Pre-code horror-r	.30	.90	1.80

HALO JONES (See The Ballad of . . .)

191

HAMMER OF GOD
Feb, 1990 - No. 4, May, 1990 ($1.95, color, limited series)
First Comics

	Good	Fine	N-Mint
1-4	.35	1.00	2.00

HAMSTER VICE IN 3-D (See Blackthorne 3-D Series #12 & 15)

HANDBOOK OF THE CONAN UNIVERSE, THE (See Official . . .)

HAND OF FATE (Formerly Men Against Crime)
No. 8, Dec, 1951 - No. 26, March, 1955
Ace Magazines

8: Surrealistic text story	11.50	34.00	80.00
9,10	6.50	19.50	45.00
11-18,20,22,23	4.30	13.00	30.00
19-Bondage, hypo needle scenes	5.50	16.50	38.00
21-Necronomicon story; drug belladonna used	6.50	19.50	45.00
24-Electric.chair-c	8.00	24.00	56.00
25(11/54), 25(12/54)	4.35	13.00	30.00
26-Nostrand-a	5.00	15.00	35.00

NOTE: *Cameron* art-No. 9, 10, 18-25; c-13. *Sekowsky* a-8, 9, 13, 14.

HAND OF FATE
Feb, 1988 - No. 3, Apr, 1988 ($1.75, color, Baxter paper)
Eclipse Comics

1,2 (color, $1.75)	.30	.90	1.75
3 (B&W, $2.00)	.35	1.00	2.00

HANDS OF THE DRAGON
June, 1975
Seaboard Periodicals (Atlas)

1-Origin; Mooney inks		.50	1.00

HANGMAN COMICS (Special Comics No. 1; Black Hood No. 9 on)
(Also see Flyman, Mighty Comics, Mighty Crusaders & Pep Comics)
No. 2, Spring, 1942 - No. 8, Fall, 1943
MLJ Magazines

2-The Hangman, Boy Buddies begin	71.00	215.00	500.00
3-8	36.00	107.00	250.00

NOTE: *Fuje* a-7(3), 8(3); c-3. *Reinman* c-3. Bondage c-3.

HANK
1946
Pentagon Publications

nn-Coulton Waugh's newspaper reprint	4.00	12.00	28.00

HANNA-BARBERA (See Golden Comics Digest No. 2,7,11)

HANNA-BARBERA BAND WAGON (TV)
Oct, 1962 - No. 3, April, 1963
Gold Key

1,2-Giants, 84 pgs.	3.50	10.50	28.00
3-Regular size	2.00	6.00	14.00

HANNA-BARBERA HI-ADVENTURE HEROES (See Hi-Adventure . . .)

HANNA-BARBERA PARADE (TV)
Sept, 1971 - No. 10, Dec, 1972
Charlton Comics

1	1.30	4.00	9.00
2-10: 7-"Summer Picnic"-52 pgs.	.85	2.50	5.00

NOTE: *No. 4 (1/72) went on sale late in 1972 with the January 1973 issues.*

HANNA-BARBERA SPOTLIGHT (See Spotlight)

HANNA-BARBERA SUPER TV HEROES (TV)
April, 1968 - No. 7, Oct, 1969 (Hanna-Barbera)
Gold Key

1-The Birdman, The Herculoids(ends #2), Moby Dick, Young Samson & Goliath(ends #2,4), and The Mighty Mightor begin; Spiegle-a in all	5.00	15.00	35.00
2-The Galaxy Trio app.; Shazzan begins	3.50	10.50	24.00

	Good	Fine	N-Mint
3-7: The Space Ghost app. in all	3.00	9.00	21.00

HANNA-BARBERA (TV STARS) (See TV Stars)

HANS BRINKER (See 4-Color No. 1273)

HANS CHRISTIAN ANDERSEN
1953 (100 pgs. - Special Issue)
Ziff-Davis Publ. Co.

nn-Danny Kaye (movie)-Photo-c	9.00	27.00	62.00

HANSEL & GRETEL (See 4-Color No. 590)

HANSI, THE GIRL WHO LOVED THE SWASTIKA
1973, 1976 (39-49 cents)
Spire Christian Comics (Fleming H. Revell Co.)

nn	.35	1.00	2.00

HANS UND FRITZ
1917 (10x13½"); 1916 strip-r in B&W; 1929 (28 pgs.; 10x13½")
The Saalfield Publishing Co.

nn-by R. Dirks	28.00	84.00	195.00
193-(Very Rare)-By R. Dirks; contains B&W Sunday strip reprints of Katzenjammer Kids & Hawkshaw the Detective from 1916	28.00	84.00	195.00
. . .The Funny Larks Of 2(1929)	28.00	84.00	195.00

HAP HAZARD COMICS (Real Love No. 25 on)
1944 - No. 24, Feb, 1949
Ace Magazines (Readers' Research)

1	5.50	16.50	38.00
2	2.85	8.50	20.00
3-10	1.85	5.50	13.00
11-13,15-24	1.30	4.00	9.00
14-Feldstein-c (4/47)	3.50	10.50	24.00

HAP HOPPER (See Comics Revue No. 2)

HAPPIEST MILLIONAIRE, THE (See Movie Comics)

HAPPINESS AND HEALING FOR YOU (Also see Oral Roberts'. . .)
1955 (36 pgs.) (slick cover) (Oral Roberts Giveaway)
Commercial Comics

nn	7.00	20.00	40.00

NOTE: *The success of this book prompted Oral Roberts to go into the publishing business himself to produce his own material.*

HAPPI TIM (See March of Comics No. 182)

HAPPY COMICS (Happy Rabbit No. 41 on)
Aug, 1943 - No. 40, Dec, 1950 (Companion to Goofy Comics)
Nedor Publ./Standard Comics (Animated Cartoons)

1	11.50	34.00	80.00
2	5.50	16.50	38.00
3-10	3.70	11.00	26.00
11-19	2.15	6.50	15.00
20-31,34-37-Frazetta text illos in all; 2 in #34&35, 3 in #27,28,30	3.50	10.50	24.00
32-Frazetta-a, 7 pgs. plus two text illos; Roussos-a	10.00	30.00	70.00
33-Frazetta-a(2), 6 pgs. each (Scarce)	17.00	51.00	120.00
38-40	1.60	4.70	11.00

NOTE: *Al Fago* a-27.

HAPPY DAYS (TV)
March, 1979 - No. 6, Feb, 1980
Gold Key

1	.35	1.00	2.00
2-6		.50	1.00
. . .With the Fonz Kite Fun Book(6¾x5¼"; '78)-PG&E	.35	1.00	2.00

Hangman Comics #5, © AP

Hap Hazard Comics #1, © ACE

Happy Comics #12, © STD

Harvey Comics Hits #57. HARV   Harvey Comics Library #1. HARV   Harvey Hits #9. HARV

HAPPY HOLIDAY (See March of Comics No. 181)

HAPPY HOOLIGAN (See Alphonse. . .)
1903 (18 pgs.) (Sunday strip reprints in color)
Hearst's New York American-Journal

	Good	Fine	N-Mint
Book 1-by Fred Opper	30.00	90.00	210.00
50 Pg. Edition(1903)-10x15'' in color	35.00	105.00	245.00

HAPPY HOOLIGAN (Handy. . .) (See The Travels of. . .)
1908 (32 pgs. in color) (10x15''; cardboard covers)
Frederick A. Stokes Co.

nn	25.00	75.00	175.00

HAPPY HOOLIGAN (Story of. . .)
1932 (16 pgs.; 9½x12''; softcover)
McLoughlin Bros.

281-Three-color text, pictures on heavy paper	8.00	24.00	56.00

HAPPY HOULIHANS (Saddle Justice No. 3 on; see Blackstone, The Magician Detective)
Fall, 1947 - No. 2, Winter, 1947-48
E. C. Comics

1-Origin Moon Girl	25.00	75.00	175.00
2	12.00	36.00	84.00

HAPPY JACK
August, 1957 - No. 2, Nov. 1957
Red Top (Decker)

V1#1,2	1.60	4.80	11.00

HAPPY JACK HOWARD
1957
Red Top (Farrell)/Decker

nn-Reprints Handy Andy story from E. C. Dandy Comics No. 5, renamed "Happy Jack"	1.85	5.50	13.00

HAPPY RABBIT (Formerly Happy Comics)
No. 41, Feb. 1951 - No. 48, April, 1952
Standard Comics (Animated Cartoons)

41	2.85	8.50	20.00
42-48	1.50	4.50	10.00

HARDY BOYS, THE (See 4-Color No. 760,830,887,964-Disney)

HARDY BOYS, THE (TV)
April, 1970 - No. 4, Jan. 1971
Gold Key

1	.85	2.50	5.00
2-4	.40	1.25	2.50

HARLEM GLOBETROTTERS (TV) (See Fun-In No. 8,10)
April, 1972 - No. 12, Jan. 1975 (Hanna-Barbera)
Gold Key

1	.50	1.50	3.00
2-12	.25	.75	1.50

NOTE: #4, 8, and 12 contain 16 extra pages of advertising.

HAROLD TEEN (See 4-Color #2, 209, Popular Comics, Super Comics & Treasure Box of Famous Comics)

HAROLD TEEN (Adv. of . . .)
1929-31 (36-52 pgs.) (Paper covers)
Cupples & Leon Co.

B&W daily strip reprints by Carl Ed	9.00	27.00	62.00

HARVEY
Oct. 1970 - No. 2, 12/70; No. 3, 6/72 - No. 6, 12/72
Marvel Comics Group

1	.50	1.50	3.00
2-6	.25	.75	1.50

HARVEY COLLECTORS COMICS (Richie Rich Collectors Comics
#10 on, cover title only)
9/75 - No. 15, 1/78; No. 16, 10/79 (52 pgs.)
Harvey Publications

	Good	Fine	N-Mint
1-Reprints Richie Rich #1,2	.70	2.00	4.00
2-10	.40	1.20	2.40
11-16: 16-Sad Sack-r		.50	1.00

NOTE: All reprints: Casper-#2, 7, Richie Rich-#1, 3, 5, 6, 8-15, Wendy-#4, #6 titled 'Richie Rich' on inside.

HARVEY COMICS HITS
No. 51, Oct. 1951 - No. 62, Dec. 1952
Harvey Publications

51-The Phantom	11.00	34.00	80.00
52-Steve Canyon	6.35	19.00	44.00
53-Mandrake the Magician	10.00	30.00	70.00
54-Tim Tyler's Tales of Jungle Terror	6.50	19.50	45.00
55-Mary Worth	3.35	10.00	23.00
56-The Phantom; bondage-c	10.00	30.00	70.00
57-Rip Kirby-"Kidnap Racket;" entire book by Alex Raymond	9.25	28.00	65.00
58-Girls in White	3.00	9.00	21.00
59-Tales of the Invisible Scarlet O'Neil	6.50	20.00	45.00
60-Paramount Animated Comics No.1(2nd app. Baby Huey); 1st Harvey app. Baby Huey	17.00	51.00	120.00
61-Casper the Friendly Ghost; 1st Harvey Casper	17.00	51.00	120.00
62-Paramount Animated Comics	7.00	21.00	50.00

HARVEY COMICS LIBRARY
April, 1952 - No. 2, 1952
Harvey Publications

1-Teen-Age Dope Slaves as exposed by Rex Morgan, M.D.; drug propaganda story; used in SOTI, pg. 27 (Prices vary widely on this book)	50.00	150.00	350.00
2-Sparkle Plenty (Dick Tracy in "Blackmail Terror")	11.50	34.50	80.00

HARVEY COMICS SPOTLIGHT
Sept, 1987 - No. 4? (#1-3: 75 cents, #4: $1.00)
Harvey Comics

1-3: 1-Sad Sack, 2-Baby Huey, 3-Little Dot		.40	.75
4-Little Audrey		.50	1.00

HARVEY HITS
Sept, 1957 - No. 122, Nov. 1967
Harvey Publications

1-The Phantom	13.00	40.00	90.00
2-Rags Rabbit(10/57)	1.35	4.00	8.00
3-Richie Rich(11/57)-r/Little Dot; 1st book devoted to Richie Rich; see Little Dot for 1st app.	54.00	160.00	340.00
4-Little Dot's Uncles	8.00	24.00	48.00
5-Stevie Mazie's Boy Friend	1.35	4.00	8.00
6-The Phantom; Kirby-c; 2pg. Powell-a (2/58)	6.50	19.50	45.00
7-Wendy the Witch	8.00	24.00	48.00
8-Sad Sack's Army Life	2.75	8.00	16.00
9-Richie Rich's Golden Deeds-r (2nd book devoted to Richie Rich)	26.00	78.00	180.00
10-Little Lotta	5.70	17.00	40.00
11-Little Audrey Summer Fun (7/58)	4.00	12.00	28.00
12-The Phantom; Kirby-c; 2pg. Powell-a (8/58)	4.30	13.00	30.00
13-Little Dot's Uncles (9/58); Richie Rich 1pg.	5.50	16.50	38.00
14-Herman & Katnip (10/58)	1.35	4.00	8.00
15-The Phantom (12/58)-1 pg. origin	4.50	14.00	32.00
16-Wendy the Witch (1/59)	4.00	12.00	24.00
17-Sad Sack's Army Life (2/59)	1.35	4.00	8.00
18-Buzzy & the Crow	1.35	4.00	8.00
19-Little Audrey (4/59)	2.75	8.00	16.00

HARVEY HITS (continued)	Good	Fine	N-Mint
20-Casper & Spooky	4.00	12.00	24.00
21-Wendy the Witch	3.00	9.00	18.00
22-Sad Sack's Army Life	1.00	3.00	6.00
23-Wendy the Witch (8/59)	3.00	9.00	18.00
24-Little Dot's Uncles (9/59); Richie Rich 1pg.	4.00	12.00	24.00
25-Herman & Katnip (10/59)	1.00	3.00	6.00
26-The Phantom (11/59)	4.50	14.00	32.00
27-Wendy the Good Little Witch	3.00	9.00	18.00
28-Sad Sack's Army Life	.50	1.50	3.00
29-Harvey-Toon (No.1)('60); Casper, Buzzy	2.00	6.00	12.00
30-Wendy the Witch (3/60)	2.75	8.00	16.00
31-Herman & Katnip (4/60)	.70	2.00	4.00
32-Sad Sack's Army Life (5/60)	.50	1.50	3.00
33-Wendy the Witch (6/60)	2.75	8.00	16.00
34-Harvey-Toon (7/60)	1.00	3.00	6.00
35-Funday Funnies (8/60)	.70	2.00	4.00
36-The Phantom (1960)	2.65	8.00	18.00
37-Casper & Nightmare	2.00	6.00	12.00
38-Harvey-Toon	1.35	4.00	8.00
39-Sad Sack's Army Life (12/60)	.50	1.50	3.00
40-Funday Funnies	.50	1.50	3.00
41-Herman & Katnip	.50	1.50	3.00
42-Harvey-Toon (3/61)	.80	2.30	4.60
43-Sad Sack's Army Life (4/61)	.50	1.50	3.00
44-The Phantom (5/61)	2.65	8.00	18.00
45-Casper & Nightmare	1.70	5.00	10.00
46-Harvey-Toon	.80	2.30	4.60
47-Sad Sack's Army Life (8/61)	.50	1.50	3.00
48-The Phantom (9/61)	2.65	8.00	18.00
49-Stumbo the Giant (See Hot Stuff for 1st app.)	5.00	15.00	35.00
50-Harvey-Toon (11/61)	.80	2.30	4.60
51-Sad Sack's Army Life (12/61)	.50	1.50	3.00
52-Casper & Nightmare	1.70	5.00	10.00
53-Harvey-Toons (2/62)	.70	2.00	4.00
54-Stumbo the Giant	2.65	8.00	18.00
55-Sad Sack's Army Life (4/62)	.50	1.50	3.00
56-Casper & Nightmare	1.70	5.00	10.00
57-Stumbo the Giant	2.65	8.00	18.00
58-Sad Sack's Army Life	.50	1.50	3.00
59-Casper & Nightmare (7/62)	1.70	5.00	10.00
60-Stumbo the Giant (9/62)	2.65	8.00	18.00
61-Sad Sack's Army Life	.50	1.50	3.00
62-Casper & Nightmare	1.35	4.00	8.00
63-Stumbo the Giant	2.65	8.00	18.00
64-Sad Sack's Army Life (1/63)	.50	1.50	3.00
65-Casper & Nightmare	1.35	4.00	8.00
66-Stumbo The Giant	2.65	8.00	18.00
67-Sad Sack's Army Life (4/63)	.50	1.50	3.00
68-Casper & Nightmare	1.35	4.00	8.00
69-Stumbo the Giant (6/63)	2.65	8.00	18.00
70-Sad Sack's Army Life (7/63)	.50	1.50	3.00
71-Casper & Nightmare (8/63)	.40	1.20	2.40
72-Stumbo the Giant	2.65	8.00	18.00
73-Little Sad Sack (10/63)	.50	1.50	3.00
74-Sad Sack's Muttsy... (11/63)	.50	1.50	3.00
75-Casper & Nightmare	1.00	3.00	6.00
76-Little Sad Sack	.50	1.50	3.00
77-Sad Sack's Muttsy...	.50	1.50	3.00
78-Stumbo the Giant	2.65	8.00	18.00
79-87: 79-Little Sad Sack (4/64). 80-Sad Sack's Muttsy... (5/64). 81-Little Sad Sack. 82-Sad Sack's Muttsy... 83-Little Sad Sack (8/64). 84-Sad Sack's Muttsy... 85-Gabby Gob (No.1)(10/64). 86-G. I. Juniors (No.1). 87-Sad Sack's Muttsy... (12/64)	.50	1.50	3.00
88-Stumbo the Giant (1/65)	2.65	8.00	18.00

	Good	Fine	N-Mint
89-122: 89-Sad Sack's Muttsy... 90-Gabby Gob. 91-G. I. Juniors. 92-Sad Sack's Muttsy... (5/65). 93-Sadie Sack (6/65). 94-Gabby Gob. 95-G. I. Juniors. 96-Sad Sack's Muttsy... (9/65). 97-Gabby Gob. 98-G. I. Juniors (11/65). 99-Sad Sack's Muttsy... (12/65). 100-Gabby Gob. 101-G. I. Juniors (2/66). 102-Sad Sack's Muttsy... (3/66). 103-Gabby Gob. 104-G. I. Juniors. 105-Sad Sack's Muttsy... 106-Gabby Gob (7/66). 107-G. I. Juniors (8/66). 108-Sad Sack's Muttsy... 109-Gabby Gob. 110-G. I. Juniors (11/66). 111-Sad Sack's Muttsy... (12/66). 112-G. I. Juniors. 113-Sad Sack's Muttsy... 114-G. I. Juniors. 115-Sad Sack's Muttsy... 116-G. I. Juniors. 117-Sad Sack's Muttsy... 118-G. I. Juniors. 119-Sad Sack's Muttsy... (8/67). 120-G. I. Juniors (9/67). 121-Sad Sack's Muttsy... (10/67). 122-G. I. Juniors	.50	1.50	3.00

HARVEY HITS COMICS
Nov. 1986 - No. 6. Oct. 1987
Harvey Publications

	Good	Fine	N-Mint
1-6: Little Lotta, Little Dot, Wendy, & Baby Huey app.		.40	.75

HARVEY POP COMICS (Teen Humor)
Oct., 1968 - No. 2. Nov. 1969 (Both are 68 pg. Giants)
Harvey Publications

	Good	Fine	N-Mint
1,2-The Cowsills	1.00	3.00	7.00

HARVEY 3-D HITS (See Sad Sack)

HARVEY-TOON (...S) (See Harvey Hits No. 29,34,38,42,46,50,53)

HARVEY WISEGUYS (...Digest #? on)
Nov. 1987 - Present (98 pgs., digest-size, $1.25-$1.75)
Harvey Comics

	Good	Fine	N-Mint
1-Hot Stuff, Spooky, etc.		.60	1.25
2 (11/88, 68 pgs.)		.60	1.25
3 (4/89, $1.75) - 6 (3/90)	.30	.90	1.75

HATARI (See Movie Classics)

HATHAWAYS, THE (See 4-Color No. 1298)

HAUNTED (See This Magazine Is Haunted)

HAUNTED
9/71 - No. 30. 11/76; No. 31. 9/77 - No. 75. 9/84
Charlton Comics

	Good	Fine	N-Mint
1	.25	.75	1.50
2-5		.50	1.00
6-21		.40	.80
22-75: 64,75-r		.30	.60

NOTE: *Aparo* c-45. *Ditko* a-1-8, 11-16, 18, 23, 24, 28, 30, 34r, 36r, 39-42r, 47r, 49-51r, 57, 60, c-1-7, 11, 13, 14, 16, 30, 41, 47, 49-51. *Howard* a-18, 22, 32. *Morisi* a-13. *Newton* a-17, 21, 59r; c-21,22(painted). *Staton* a-18, 21, 22, 30, 33; c-18, 33. *Sutton* a-21, 22, 38; c-17, 64r. #51 reprints #1; #49 reprints Tales/Myst. Traveler #4.

HAUNTED LOVE
April, 1973 - No. 11, Sept. 1975
Charlton Comics

	Good	Fine	N-Mint
1-Tom Sutton-a, 16 pgs.		.50	1.00
2,3,6-11		.30	.60
4,5-Ditko-a		.40	.80
Modern Comics #1(1978)		.20	.40

NOTE: *Howard* a-8i. *Newton* c-8,9. *Staton* a-5.

HAUNTED THRILLS
June, 1952 - No. 18, Nov-Dec, 1954
Ajax/Farrell Publications

	Good	Fine	N-Mint
1: r-r/Ellery Queen 1	11.50	34.00	80.00
2-L. B. Cole-a r-r/Ellery Queen 1	7.00	21.00	50.00
3-5: 3-Drug use story	5.70	17.00	40.00
6-12: 12-Webb-a	4.50	14.00	32.00
13,16-18: 18-Lingerie panels	3.50	10.50	24.00
14-Jesus Christ apps. in story by Webb	3.50	10.50	24.00

Harvey Hits #48, © HARV

Haunted #17, © CC

Haunted Thrills #8, © AJAX

Haunt Of Fear #8. © WMG

Hawk And Dove #1 (10/88). © DC

Hawkman #8 (7/65). © DC

	Good	Fine	N-Mint
HAUNTED THRILLS (continued)			
15-Jo-Jo-r	4.00	12.00	28.00

NOTE: *Kamenish art in most issues.*

HAUNT OF FEAR (Formerly Gunfighter)
No. 15, May-June, 1950 - No. 28, Nov-Dec, 1954
E. C. Comics

15(#1, 1950)	110.00	332.00	775.00
16	56.00	170.00	395.00
17-Origin of Crypt of Terror, Vault of Horror, & Haunt of Fear; used in			
SOTI, pg. 43; last pg. Ingels-a used by N.Y. Legis. Comm.			
	56.00	170.00	395.00
4	43.00	130.00	300.00
5-Injury-to-eye panel, pg. 4	32.00	95.00	225.00
6-10	22.00	65.00	155.00
11-13,15-18	16.00	48.00	110.00
14-Origin Old Witch by Ingels	22.00	65.00	155.00
19-Used in SOTI, ill.-"A comic book baseball game" & Senate invest-			
igation on juvenile delinq. bondage/decapitation-c			
	21.00	62.00	150.00
20-Feldstein r-/Vault of Horror #12	14.00	42.00	100.00
21,22,25,27: 27-Cannibalism story	9.30	28.00	65.00
23-Used in SOTI, pg. 241	11.00	32.00	75.00
24-Used in Senate Investigative Report, pg.8	10.00	30.00	70.00
26-Contains anti-censorship editorial, 'Are you a Red Dupe?'			
	10.00	30.00	70.00
28-Low distribution	11.50	34.00	80.00

NOTE: *(Canadian reprints known; see Table of Contents). Craig a-15-17, 5, 7, 10, 12, 13; c-15-17, 5-7. Crandall a-20, 21, 26, 27. Davis a-4-26, 28. Evans a-15-19, 22-25, 27. Feldstein a-15-17, 20: c-4, 8-10. Ingels a-16, 17, 4-28; c-11-28. Kamen a-16, 4, 6, 7, 9-11, 13-19, 21-28. Krigstein a-28. Kurtzman a-15/1, 17/3. Orlando a-9, 15/1, 16, 4-6.*

HAUNT OF HORROR, THE (Magazine)
5/74 - No. 5, 1/75 (75 cents) (B&W)
Cadence Comics Publ. (Marvel)

1	.85	2.50	5.00
2,4: 2-Origin & 1st app. Gabriel the Devil Hunter; Satana begins. 4-			
Adams-a	.70	2.00	4.00
3,5: 5-Evans-a(2)	.50	1.50	3.00

NOTE: *Alcala a-2. Colan a-2p. Heath r-1. Krigstein r-3. Reese a-1. Simonson a-1.*

HAVE GUN, WILL TRAVEL (TV)
No. 931, 8/58 - No. 14, 7-9/62 (All Richard Boone photo-c)
Dell Publishing Co.

4-Color 931 (#1)	6.00	18.00	42.00
4-Color 983,1044	4.00	12.00	28.00
4 (1-3/60) - 14	3.70	11.00	26.00

HAVOK AND WOLVERINE
Mar. 1989 - No. 4, Oct, 1989 ($3.50, mini-series, squarebound)
Epic Comics (Marvel)

1-Mature readers, violent	.85	2.50	5.00
2-4	.60	1.75	3.50

HAWAIIAN EYE (TV)
July, 1963 (Troy Donahue, Connie Stevens photo-c)
Gold Key

1 (10073-307)	2.65	8.00	18.00

HAWAIIAN ILLUSTRATED LEGENDS SERIES
1975 (B&W)(Cover printed w/blue, yellow, and green)
Hogarth Press

1-Kalelealuaka, the Mysterious Warrior	.60	1.20	
2,3(Exist?)	.40	.80	

HAWK, THE (Also see Approved Comics #1,7 & Tops In Adventure)
Wint/51 - No. 3, 11-12/52; No. 4, 1953 - No. 12, 5/55
Ziff-Davis/St. John Publ. Co. No. 4 on

1-Anderson-a	8.50	25.50	60.00

	Good	Fine	N-Mint
2-Kubert, Infantino-a; painted-c	5.00	15.00	35.00
3-8,10-11: 8-Reprints #3 with diff.-c. 10-Reprints one story/#2.			
11-Buckskin Belle & The Texan app.	3.70	11.00	26.00
9-Baker c/a; Kubert-a(r)/#2	4.00	12.00	28.00
12-Baker c/a; Buckskin Belle app.	4.00	12.00	28.00
3-D 1(11/53)-Baker-c	18.50	56.00	130.00

NOTE: *Baker c-8, 9, 11. Tuska a-9. 12. Painted c-1, 7.*

HAWK AND DOVE
Oct, 1988 - No. 5, Feb, 1989 ($1.00, color, mini-series)
DC Comics

1	.75	2.25	4.50
2	.50	1.50	3.00
3-5	.35	1.00	2.00

HAWK AND DOVE
June, 1989 - Present ($1.00, color)
DC Comics

1	.25	.75	1.50
2-10		.50	1.00

HAWK AND THE DOVE, THE (See Showcase #75 & Teen Titans)
Aug-Sept, 1968 - No. 6, June-July, 1969
National Periodical Publications

1-Ditko c/a	2.00	6.00	14.00
2-6: 5-Teen Titans cameo	1.50	4.50	10.00

NOTE: *Ditko c/a-1, 2. Gil Kane a-3p, 4p, 5, 6p; c-3-6.*

HAWKEYE (See The Avengers #16 & Tales Of Suspense #57)
Sept, 1983 - No. 4, Dec, 1983 (Mini-series)
Marvel Comics Group

1-4: 1-Origin Hawkeye. 3-Origin Mockingbird	.35	1.00	2.00

HAWKEYE & THE LAST OF THE MOHICANS (See 4-Color No. 884)

HAWKMAN (See Atom & Hawkman. The Brave & the Bold. DC Comics Presents. Detective, Flash Comics. Justice League of America 31. Mystery in Space. Shadow War Of . . . , Showcase & World's Finest)

HAWKMAN
Apr-May, 1964 - No. 27, Aug-Sept, 1968
National Periodical Publications

1	17.00	51.00	120.00
2	8.00	24.00	55.00
3-5: 4-Zatanna x-over(origin-1st app.)	5.00	15.00	35.00
6-10: 9-Atom cameo; Hawkman & Atom learn each other's I.D.;			
2nd app. Shadow Thief	3.15	9.50	32.00
11-15	1.70	5.00	12.00
16-27: Adam Strange x-over #18, cameo #19. 25-G.A. Hawkman-r			
	1.15	3.50	8.00

NOTE: *Anderson a-1-21; c-1-21. Kubert c-27. Moldoff a-25r.*

HAWKMAN
Aug, 1986 - No. 17, Dec, 1987
DC Comics

1	.30	.90	1.75
2-17: 10-Byrne-c		.50	1.00
Special #1 ('86, $1.25)	.25	.75	1.50
Trade paperback (1989, $19.95)-r/Brave and the Bold #34-36,42-44 by			
Kubert; Kubert-c	3.35	10.00	20.00

HAWKMOON: COUNT BRASS
Feb, 1989 - No. 4, Aug, 1989 ($1.95, limited series, color)
First Comics

1-4: Adapts novel by Michael Moorcock	.35	1.00	2.00

HAWKMOON: THE JEWEL IN THE SKULL
May, 1986 - No. 4, Nov, 1986 ($1.75, limited series, Baxter)
First Comics

1-4: Adapts novel by Michael Moorcock	.30	.90	1.80

HAWKMOON: THE MAD GOD'S AMULET
Jan. 1987 - No. 4, July, 1987 ($1.75, limited series, Baxter)
First Comics

	Good	Fine	N-Mint
1-4: Adapts novel by Michael Moorcock	.30	.90	1.80

HAWKMOON: THE RUNESTAFF
June. 1988 - No. 4, Dec, 1988 ($1.75-1.95, limited series, Baxter)
First Comics

1,2: ($1.75) Adapts novel by Michael Moorcock	.30	.90	1.80
3,4 ($1.95)	.35	1.00	2.00

HAWKMOON: THE SWORD OF DAWN
Sept. 1987 - No. 4, Mar, 1988 ($1.75 limited series, Baxter)
First Comics

1-4: Adapts novel by Michael Moorcock	.30	.90	1.80

HAWKSHAW THE DETECTIVE (See Advs. of . . ., Hans Und Fritz & Okay)
1917 (24 pgs.; B&W; 10½x13½'') (Sunday strip reprints)
The Saalfield Publishing Co.

By Gus Mager	9.00	27.00	62.00

HAWKWORLD
1989 - No. 3. 1989 ($3.95, prestige format, mini-series)
DC Comics

Book 1-3: Hawkman app.; Truman-c/a/scripts	.70	2.00	4.00

HAWTHORN-MELODY FARMS DAIRY COMICS
No date (1950's) (Giveaway)
Everybody's Publishing Co.

Cheerie Chick, Tuffy Turtle, Robin Koo Koo, Donald & Longhorn Legends	.85	2.50	5.00

HAYWIRE
Oct. 1988 - No. 13, Sept, 1989 ($1.25, color, mature readers)
DC Comics

1	.30	.90	1.80
2-13	.25	.75	1.50

HEADLINE COMICS (. . .Crime No. 32-39)
Feb. 1943 - No. 22, Nov-Dec, 1946; No. 23, 1947 - No. 77, Oct, 1956
Prize Publications

1-Yank & Doodle x-over in Junior Rangers	18.00	54.00	125.00
2	7.00	21.00	50.00
3-Used in POP. pg. 84	6.50	19.50	45.00
4-7,9,10: 4,9,10-Hitler stories	5.00	15.00	35.00
8-Classic Hitler-c	8.00	24.00	56.00
11,12	3.50	10.50	24.00
13-15-Blue Streak in all	3.70	11.00	26.00
16-Origin Atomic Man	8.00	24.00	56.00
17,18,20,21: 21-Atomic Man ends	4.30	13.00	30.00
19-S&K-a	11.00	32.00	75.00
22-Kiefer-c	2.30	7.00	16.00
23,24: (All S&K-a). 24-Dope-crazy killer story	11.00	32.00	75.00
25-35-S&K c/a. 25-Powell-a	7.00	21.00	50.00
36-S&K-a	5.00	15.00	35.00
37-One pg. S&K, Severin-a	2.85	8.50	20.00
38,40-Meskin-a	2.00	6.00	14.00
39,41-43,45,48,50-55: 51-Kirby-c. 45-Kirby-a	1.15	3.50	8.00
44-S&K-c; Severin/Elder, Meskin-a	3.50	10.50	24.00
49-Meskin-a	1.50	4.50	10.00
56-S&K-a	2.85	8.50	20.00
57-77: 72-Meskin c/a(i)	1.15	3.50	8.00

HEAP, THE
Sept. 1971 (52 pages)
Skywald Publications

1-Kinstler-a, r-/Strange Worlds No. 8	.50	1.50	3.00

HEART AND SOUL
April-May, 1954 - No. 2, June-July, 1954
Mikeross Publications

	Good	Fine	N-Mint
1,2	2.30	7.00	16.00

HEART THROBS (Love Stories No. 147 on)
8/49 - No. 8, 10/50; No. 9, 3/52 - No. 146, Oct, 1972
Quality/National No. 47(4-5/57) on (Arleigh No. 48-101)

1-Classic Ward-c, Gustavson-a, 9pgs.	18.50	56.00	130.00
2-Ward c/a, 9 pgs; Gustavson-a	11.00	32.00	75.00
3-Gustavson-a	4.00	12.00	28.00
4,6,8-Ward-a, 8-9 pgs.	6.50	19.50	45.00
5,7	2.15	6.50	15.00
9-Robert Mitchum, Jane Russell photo-c	3.00	9.00	21.00
10,15-Ward-a	4.65	14.00	32.00
11-14,16-20: 12 (7/52)	1.50	4.50	10.00
21-Ward-c	3.65	11.00	25.00
22,23-Ward-a(p)	2.65	8.00	18.00
24-33: 33-Last pre-code (3/55)	1.15	3.50	8.00
34-39,41-46 (12/56; last Quality issue)	1.00	3.00	7.00
40-Ward-a; r-7 pgs./#21	2.00	6.00	14.00
47-(4-5/57; 1st DC)	4.30	13.00	30.00
48-60	1.70	5.00	12.00
61-70	1.15	3.50	8.00
71-100: 74-Last 10 cent issue	.70	2.00	5.00
101-The Beatles app. on-c	2.30	7.00	16.00
102-120: 102-123-(Serial)-Three Girls, Their Lives, Their Loves.			
120-Adams-c	.40	1.25	2.50
121-146: #133-142, 52 pgs.		.50	1.00

NOTE: Gustavson a-8. Photo-c 8-10, 15, 17. Tuska a-128.

HEATHCLIFF (See Star Comics Mag.)
Apr, 1985 - Present (#16-on, $1.00)
Star Comics/Marvel Comics No. 23 on

1-44: Post-a most issues. 43-X-Mas issue		.50	1.00
Annual 1 ('87)		.60	1.20

HEATHCLIFF'S FUNHOUSE
May, 1987 - No. 10, 1988
Star Comics/Marvel Comics No. 6 on

1-10		.50	1.00

HECKLE AND JECKLE (See Blue Ribbon, Paul Terry's & Terry-Toons Comics)
10/51 - No. 24, 10/55; No. 25, Fall/56 - No. 34, 6/59
St. John Publ. Co. No. 1-24/Pines No. 25 on

1	16.00	48.00	110.00
2	8.00	24.00	56.00
3-5	5.50	16.50	38.00
6-10	4.00	12.00	28.00
11-20	2.65	8.00	18.00
21-34	1.70	5.00	12.00

HECKLE AND JECKLE (TV) (See New Terrytoons)
11/62 - No. 4, 8/63; 5/66; No. 2, 10/66 - No. 3, 8/67
Gold Key/Dell Publishing Co.

1 (11/62; Gold Key)	2.00	6.00	14.00
2-4	1.15	3.50	8.00
1 (5/66; Dell)	1.50	4.50	10.00
2,3	1.00	3.00	7.00

(See March of Comics No. 379,472,484)

HECKLE AND JECKLE 3-D
1987 - No. 2? ($2.50; color)
Spotlight Comics

1,2	.40	1.25	2.50

HECTOR COMICS
Nov, 1953 - No. 3, 1954

Hedy Of Hollywood #36. : MEG

Hellblazer #1. : DC

Herbie #19. : ACG

HECTOR COMICS (continued) Key Publications	Good	Fine	N-Mint
1	2.35	7.00	16.00
2,3	1.30	4.00	9.00

HECTOR HEATHCOTE (TV)
March, 1964
Gold Key

	Good	Fine	N-Mint
1 (10111-403)	2.35	7.00	16.00

HEDY DEVINE COMICS (Formerly All Winners #21?; Hedy of Hollywood #36 on; also see Annie Oakley, Comedy & Venus)
No. 22, Aug, 1947 - No. 50, Sept, 1952
Marvel Comics (RCM)/Atlas #50

	Good	Fine	N-Mint
22	4.00	12.00	28.00
23,24,27-30: 23-Wolverton-a, 1 pg; Kurtzman's "Hey Look," 2 pgs.			
24,27-30-"Hey Look" by Kurtzman, 1-3 pgs.	5.50	16.50	38.00
25-Classic "Hey Look" by Kurtzman-"Optical Illusion"			
	6.00	18.00	42.00
26-"Giggles & Grins" by Kurtzman	3.70	11.00	26.00
31-34,36-50: 32-Anti-Wertham editorial	2.00	6.00	14.00
35-Four pgs. "Rusty" by Kurtzman	3.70	11.00	26.00

HEDY-MILLIE-TESSIE COMEDY (See Comedy)

HEDY WOLFE
August, 1957
Atlas Publishing Co. (Emgee)

1	2.65	8.00	18.00

HEE HAW (TV)
July. 1970 - No. 7, Aug, 1971
Charlton Press

1	.70	2.00	4.00
2-7	.50	1.50	3.00

HEIDI (See Dell Jr. Treasury No. 6)

HELEN OF TROY (See 4-Color No. 684)

HELLBLAZER
Jan. 1988 - Present ($1.25-1.50, Adults)
DC Comics

1	.45	1.25	2.50
2-5	.35	1.00	2.00
6-10	.30	.90	1.80
11-26	.25	.75	1.50
Annual 1 ('89, $2.95, 68 pgs.)	.50	1.50	3.00

HELLO, I'M JOHNNY CASH
1976 (39-49 cents)
Spire Christian Comics (Fleming H. Revell Co.)

nn		.40	.80

HELL ON EARTH (See DC Science Fiction Graphic Novel)

HELLO PAL COMICS (Short Story Comics)
Jan. 1943 - No. 3, May, 1943 (Photo-c)
Harvey Publications

1-Rocketman & Rocketgirl begin; Yankee Doodle Jones app.;			
Mickey Rooney cover	27.00	81.00	190.00
2-Charlie McCarthy cover	19.00	58.00	135.00
3-Bob Hope cover	20.00	60.00	140.00

HELLRAISER (Clive Barker's)
1989 - Present ($4.95, color, mature readers, 68 pgs., quarterly)
Epic Comics (Marvel)

1-Based on Hellraiser & Hellbound movies; Bolton-c/a; Spiegle &			
Wrightson-a (graphic album)	.85	2.50	5.00

HELL-RIDER (Magazine)
Aug. 1971 - No. 2, Oct, 1971 (B&W)

Skywald Publications	Good	Fine	N-Mint
1-Origin & 1st app.; Butterfly & Wildbunch begins			
	.80	2.40	3.60
2	.70	2.00	3.00

NOTE: #3 advertised in Psycho #5 but did not come out. **Buckler** a-1,2. **Morrow** c-3.

HE-MAN (See Masters Of The Universe)

HE-MAN (Also see Tops In Adventure)
Fall, 1952
Ziff-Davis Publ. Co. (Approved Comics)

1-Kinstler-c; Powell-a	5.70	17.00	40.00

HE-MAN
May, 1954 - No. 2, July, 1954 (Painted-c)
Toby Press

1	5.70	17.00	40.00
2	4.30	13.00	30.00

HENNESSEY (See 4-Color No. 1200,1280)

HENRY
1935 (52 pages) (Daily B&W strip reprints)
David McKay Publications

1-by Carl Anderson	8.00	24.90	56.00

HENRY (See Magic Comics)
No. 122, Oct, 1946 - No. 65, Apr-June, 1961
Dell Publishing Co.

4-Color 122	5.60	16.50	40.00
4-Color 155 (7/47)	4.30	13.00	30.00
1 (1-3/48)	4.30	13.00	30.00
2	2.15	6.50	15.00
3-10	1.50	4.50	10.00
11-20: 20-Infinity-c	1.15	3.50	8.00
21-30	.85	2.50	6.00
31-40	.55	1.65	4.00
41-65	.40	1.25	3.00

HENRY (See Giant Comic Album and March of Comics No. 43. 58. 84. 101. 112. 129. 147. 162. 178. 189)

HENRY ALDRICH COMICS (TV)
Aug-Sept, 1950 - No. 22, Sept-Nov, 1954
Dell Publishing Co.

1-Part series written by John Stanley; Bill Williams-a			
	4.50	14.00	32.00
2	2.30	7.00	16.00
3-5	2.00	6.00	14.00
6-10	1.70	5.00	12.00
11-22	1.30	4.00	9.00
Giveaway (16p, soft-c, 1951)-Capehart radio	2.00	6.00	14.00

HENRY BREWSTER
Feb, 1966 - V2No.7, Sept, 1967 (All Giants)
Country Wide (M.F. Ent.)

1	.35	1.00	2.00
2-6(12/66)-Powell-a in most	.25	.75	1.50
V2#7		.60	1.20

HERBIE (See Forbidden Worlds)
April-May, 1964 - No. 23, Feb, 1967
American Comics Group

1	8.00	24.00	56.00
2-4	4.00	12.00	28.00
5-Beatles, Dean Martin, F. Sinatra app.	5.00	15.00	35.00
6,7,9,10	2.65	8.00	18.00
8-Origin The Fat Fury	3.70	11.00	26.00
11-22: 14-Nemesis & MagicMan app. 17-R-1st Herbie/F.W. #73			
	1.60	4.70	11.00
23-R-2nd Herbie/F.W. #94	1.60	4.70	11.00

197

HERBIE (continued)
NOTE: Most have *Whitney* c/a.

HERBIE GOES TO MONTE CARLO, HERBIE RIDES AGAIN (See Walt Disney Showcase No. 24, 41)

HERCULES (See Hit Comics #1-21, Journey Into Mystery Annual, Marvel Premiere #26 & The Mighty   )

HERCULES
Oct. 1967 - No. 13, Sept. 1969; Dec. 1968
Charlton Comics

	Good	Fine	N-Mint
1-Thane of Bagarth series begins; Glanzman, Aparo-a	.85	2.60	6.00
2-13: 3-5,7,9,10-Aparo-a	.70	2.00	4.00
8-(Low distribution)(12/68)-35 cents; magazine format; B&W-r	2.50	7.50	17.50
Modern Comics reprint 10('77), 11('78)		.20	.40

HERCULES, PRINCE OF POWER (Also see The Champions)
9/82 - No. 4, 12/82; 3/84 - No. 4, 6/84
Marvel Comics Group

1-4	.25	.75	1.50
V2#1 (Mini-series)	.25	.75	1.50
2-4		.50	1.00

NOTE: *Layton* a-1, 2, 3p, 4p. V2#1-4; c-1-4, V2#1-4.

HERCULES UNBOUND
Oct-Nov. 1975 - No. 12, Aug-Sept. 1977
National Periodical Publications

1-Wood inks begin		.40	.80
2-5		.30	.60
6-12: 10-Atomic Knights x-over		.25	.50

NOTE: *Buckler* c-7p. *Layton* inks-No. 9, 10. *Simonson* a-7-10p. 11, 12. c- 8p. 9-12. *Wood* inks-1-8. c-7i, 8i.

HERCULES UNCHAINED (See 4-Color No. 1006, 1121)

HERE COMES SANTA (See March of Comics No. 30,213,340)

HERE IS SANTA CLAUS
1930s (16 pgs., 8 in color) (stiff paper covers)
Goldsmith Publishing Co. (Kann's in Washington, D.C.)

nn	3.50	10.50	24.00

HERE'S HOW AMERICA'S CARTOONISTS HELP TO SELL U.S. SAVINGS BONDS
1950? (16 pgs.; paper cover)
Harvey Comics giveaway

Contains: Joe Palooka, Donald Duck, Archie, Kerry Drake, Red Ryder, Blondie & Steve Canyon	12.00	35.00	80.00

HERE'S HOWIE COMICS
Jan-Feb. 1952 - No. 18, Nov-Dec. 1954
National Periodical Publications

1	11.00	32.00	75.00
2	5.00	15.00	35.00
3-5	4.00	12.00	28.00
6-10	3.15	9.50	22.00
11-18	2.30	7.00	16.00

HERMAN & KATNIP (See Harvey Hits #14,25,31,41 & Paramount Animated Comics #1)

HERO ALLIANCE, THE
Dec. 1985 - No. 2, Sept. 1986 (No. 2, $1.50)
Sirius Comics

1,2	.25	.75	1.50
The Special Edition 1 (7/86)-Full color	.25	.75	1.50

HERO ALLIANCE
May, 1987 ($1.95, color)
Wonder Color Comics

1	.35	1.00	2.00

HERO ALLIANCE
Sept. 1989 - Present ($1.95, color, 28 pgs.)
Innovation Publishing

	Good	Fine	N-Mint
V2#1-6: 1,2-Ron Lim-a	.35	1.00	2.00

HERO ALLIANCE: END OF THE GOLDEN AGE
July, 1989 - No. 3, Aug. 1989 ($1.75, bi-weekly mini-series, color)
Innovation Publishing

1-3: By Bart Sears & Ron Lim-r & new-a	.30	.90	1.80

HEROES AGAINST HUNGER
1986 (One shot) ($1.50) (For famine relief)
DC Comics

1-Superman, Batman app.; Adams-c(p); includes many artists work	.40	1.20	2.50

HEROES ALL CATHOLIC ACTION ILLUSTRATED
1943 - V6No.5, March 10, 1948 (paper covers)
Heroes All Co.

V1#1,2-(16 pgs., 8x11'')	4.00	12.00	28.00
V2#1(1/44)-3(3/44)-(16 pgs., 8x11'')	2.50	7.50	17.50
V3#1(1/45)-10(10/45)-(16 pgs., 8x11'')	2.00	6.00	14.00
V4#1-35 (12/20/46)-(16 pgs.)	1.50	4.50	10.00
V5#1(1/10/47)-8(2/28/47)-(16 pgs.)	1.15	3.50	8.00
V5#9(3/7/47)-20(11/25/47)-(32 pgs.)	1.15	3.50	8.00
V6#1(1/10/48)-5(3/10/48)-(32 pgs.)	1.15	3.50	8.00

HEROES FOR HOPE STARRING THE X-MEN
Dec. 1985 ($1.50, One Shot, 52 pgs.)
Marvel Comics Group

1-Proceeds donated to famine relief; Harlan Ellison, Stephen King scripts; Wrightson, Corben-a; Art Adams-c	.60	1.75	3.50

HEROES, INC. PRESENTS CANNON
1969 - No. 2, 1976 (Sold at Army PX's)
Wally Wood/CPL/Gang Publ. No. 2

nn-Wood/Ditko-a	1.35	4.00	8.00
2-Wood-c; Ditko, Byrne, Wood-a; 8½x10½''; B&W; $2.00	.70	2.00	4.00

NOTE: First issue not distributed by publisher, 1,800 copies were stored and 900 copies were stolen from warehouse. Many copies have surfaced in recent years.

HEROES OF THE WILD FRONTIER (Formerly Baffling Mysteries)
No. 26, 3/55; No. 27, 1/56 - No. 2, 4/56
Ace Periodicals

26(No.1)	2.35	7.00	16.00
27,28,2: 28-Exist?	1.30	4.00	9.00

HERO FOR HIRE (Power Man No. 17 on)
June, 1972 - No. 16, Dec. 1973
Marvel Comics Group

1-Origin Luke Cage retold; Tuska-a(p)	.65	1.90	3.75
2-16: 2,3-Tuska-a(p). 3-1st app. Mace. 4-1st app. Phil Fox of the Bugle. 14-Origin retold. 15-Everett Subby-r('53). 16-Origin Stilletto; death of Rackham	.25	.80	1.60

HERO HOTLINE (1st app. in Action Comics Weekly #637)
April, 1989 - No. 6, Sept. 1989 ($1.75, mini-series)
DC Comics

1-6: Super-hero humor; Schaffenberger-i	.30	.90	1.75

HEROIC ADVENTURES (See Adventures)

HEROIC COMICS (Reg'lar Fellers. . .#1-15; New Heroic #41 on)
Aug. 1940 - No. 97, June, 1955
Eastern Color Printing Co./Famous Funnies(Funnies, Inc. No. 1)

1-Hydroman(origin) by Bill Everett, The Purple Zombie(origin) & Mann of India by Tarpe Mills begins	50.00	150.00	350.00
2	25.00	75.00	175.00
3,4	21.50	64.00	150.00

Hercules #11.   CC

Hero Alliance #1.   Innovation

Hero For Hire #1.   MEG

Heroic Comics #50. EAS

Hi-Ho Comics #2. Four Star

Hillbilly Comics #1. CC

HEROIC COMICS (continued)	Good	Fine	N-Mint
5,6	16.00	48.00	110.00
7-Origin Man O'Metal, 1 pg.	18.50	56.00	130.00
8-10: 10-Lingerie panels	11.00	32.00	75.00
11,13: 13-Crandall/Fine-a	9.30	28.00	65.00
12-Music Master(origin) begins by Everett, ends No. 31; last Purple Zombie & Mann of India	11.00	32.00	75.00
14-Hydroman x-over in Rainbow Boy; also in No. 15; origin Rainbow Boy	11.00	32.00	75.00
15-Intro. Downbeat	11.00	32.00	75.00
16-20: 17-Rainbow Boy x-over in Hydroman. 19-Rainbow Boy x-over in Hydroman & vice versa	7.00	21.00	50.00
21-30:25-Rainbow Boy x-over in Hydroman. 28-Last Man O'Metal. 29-Last Hydroman	4.30	13.00	30.00
31,34,38	1.60	4.70	11.00
32,36,37-Toth-a. 3-4 pgs.	2.85	8.50	20.00
33,35-Toth-a. 8 & 9 pgs.	3.15	9.50	22.00
39-42-Toth, Ingels-a	3.15	9.50	22.00
43,46,47,49-Toth-a, 2-4 pgs. 47-Ingels-a	2.15	6.50	15.00
44,45,50-Toth-a. 6-9 pgs.	2.65	8.00	18.00
48,53,54	1.15	3.50	8.00
51-Williamson-a	3.50	10.50	24.00
52-Williamson-a (3 pg. story)	1.70	5.00	12.00
55-Toth-a	2.15	6.50	15.00
56-60-Toth-c. 60-Everett-a	1.85	5.50	13.00
61-Everett-a	1.30	4.00	9.00
62,64-Everett-c/a	1.50	4.50	10.00
63-Everett-c	1.00	3.00	7.00
65-Williamson/Frazetta-a; Evans-a 2 pgs.	5.00	15.00	35.00
66,75,94-Frazetta-a, 2 pgs. each	2.00	6.00	14.00
67,73-Frazetta, 4 pgs. each	2.85	8.50	20.00
68,74,76-80,84,85,88-93,95-97	.85	2.60	6.00
69,72-Frazetta-a (6 & 8 pgs. each)	5.00	15.00	35.00
70,71,86,87-Frazetta, 3-4 pgs. each; 1 pg. ad by Frazetta in #70	2.65	8.00	18.00
81,82-One pg. Frazetta art	1.30	4.00	9.00
83-Frazetta-a. ½ pg.	1.30	4.00	9.00

NOTE: *Evans a-64. 65. Everett a-(Hydroman-c/a-No. 1-9), 44. 60-64. c-1-9. 62-64. Sid Greene a-38-43. 46. Guardineer a-42(3). 43. 44. 45(2). 49(3). 50. 60. 61(2). 65. 67(2). 70-72. Ingels c-41. Kiefer a-46. 48. c-19-22. 24. 44. 46. 48. 51-53. 65. 67-69. 71-74. 76. 77. 79. 80. 82. 85. 88. 89. Mort Lawrence a-45. Tarpe Mills a-2(2). 3(2). 10. Ed Moore a-49. 52-54. 56-63. 65-69. 72-74. 76. 77. 87. H.G. Peter a-58-74. 76. 77. 87. Paul Reinman a-49. Rico a-31. Captain Tootsie by Beck-31. 32. Painted-c #16 on.*

HERO SANDWICH
Feb. 1987 - Present ($1.50-1.75, B&W)
Slave Labor Graphics

1-4 ($1.50)	.25	.75	1.50
5-8 ($1.75)	.30	.90	1.80

HEX (Replaces Jonah Hex)
Sept. 1985 - No. 18, Feb. 1987
DC Comics

1-Hex in post-atomic war world; origin	.25	.75	1.50
2-9,14-18: 6-Origin Stiletta		.50	1.00
10-13: All contain future Batman storyline. 13-Intro The Dogs of War (Origin #15)	.35	1.00	2.00

HEXBREAKER (See First Comics Graphic Novel #15)

HEY THERE, IT'S YOGI BEAR (See Movie Comics)

HI-ADVENTURE HEROES (Hanna-Barbera)(TV)
May. 1969 - No. 2, Aug, 1969
Gold Key

1-Three Musketeers, Gulliver, Arabian Knights stories	1.15	3.50	8.00
2-Three Musketeers, Micro-Venture, Arabian Knights	.85	2.60	6.00

HI AND LOIS (See 4-Color No. 683,774,955)

HI AND LOIS
Nov, 1969 - No. 11, July, 1971
Charlton Comics

	Good	Fine	N-Mint
1	.75	2.25	4.50
2-11	.50	1.50	3.00

HICKORY (See All Humor Comics)
Oct, 1949 - No. 6. Aug, 1950
Quality Comics Group

1-Sahl c/a in all; Feldstein?-a	6.50	19.50	45.00
2	3.15	9.50	22.00
3-6	2.35	7.00	16.00

HIDDEN CREW, THE (See The United States Air Force Presents:)

HIDE-OUT (See 4-Color No. 346)

HIDING PLACE, THE
1973 (35-49 cents)
Spire Christian Comics/Fleming H. Revell Co.

nn		.40	.80

HIGH ADVENTURE
October, 1957
Red Top(Decker) Comics (Farrell)

1-Krigstein-r from Explorer Joe (re-issue on cover)	2.00	6.00	14.00

HIGH ADVENTURE (See 4-Color No. 949,1001)

HIGH CHAPPARAL (TV)
August, 1968 (Photo-c)
Gold Key

1 (10226-808)-Tufts-a	2.65	8.00	18.00

HIGH SCHOOL CONFIDENTIAL DIARY (Confidential Diary #12 on)
June, 1960 - No. 11, March, 1962
Charlton Comics

1	1.00	3.00	7.00
2-11	.70	2.00	4.00

HI-HO COMICS
nd (2/46?) - No. 3, 1946
Four Star Publications

1-Funny Animal; L. B. Cole-c	7.00	21.00	50.00
2,3: 2-L. B. Cole-c	5.00	15.00	35.00

HI-JINX (See Teen-age Animal Funnies)
July-Aug, 1947 - No. 7, July-Aug, 1948
B&I Publ. Co.(American Comics Group)/Creston/LaSalle Publ. Co.

1-Teen-age, funny animal	6.50	19.50	45.00
2,3	3.50	10.50	24.00
4-7-Milt Gross	4.30	13.00	30.00
132 Pg. issue, nn, nd ('40s)(LaSalle)	8.00	24.00	56.00

HI-LITE COMICS
Fall, 1945
E. R. Ross Publishing Co.

1-Miss Shady	5.70	17.00	40.00

HILLBILLY COMICS
Aug. 1955 - No. 4, July, 1956 (Satire)
Charlton Comics

1	3.15	9.50	22.00
2-4	1.60	4.80	11.00

HIP-ITTY HOP (See March of Comics No. 15)

HI-SCHOOL ROMANCE (...Romances No. 41 on)
Oct, 1949 - No. 5, June, 1950; No. 6, Dec, 1950 - No. 73, Mar. 1958; No. 74, Sept, 1958 - No. 75, Nov, 1958
Harvey Publications/True Love(Home Comics)

Hi-School Romance #1. HARV

Hit Comics #2. QUA

Holiday Comics #6. STAR

Hollywood Pictorial #3. STJ

Hollywood Secrets #1. QUA

Holyoke One-Shot #1. HOKE

HOLLYWOOD FILM STORIES (continued)
Feature Publications/Prize

	Good	Fine	N-Mint
1-"Fumetti" type movie comic	8.50	25.50	60.00
2-4	5.50	16.50	38.00

HOLLYWOOD FUNNY FOLKS (Formerly Funny Folks; Nutsy Squirrel #61 on)
No. 27, Aug-Sept, 1950 - No. 60, July-Aug, 1954
National Periodical Publications

27	4.30	13.00	30.00
28-40	2.65	8.00	18.00
41-60	1.85	5.50	13.00

NOTE: *Sheldon Mayer* a-27-35, 37-40, 43-46, 48-51, 53, 56, 57, 60.

HOLLYWOOD LOVE DOCTOR (See Doctor Anthony King...)

HOLLYWOOD PICTORIAL (...Romances on cover)
No. 3, January, 1950
St. John Publishing Co.

3-Matt Baker-a; photo-c	9.00	27.00	62.00

(Becomes a movie magazine - Hollywood Pictorial Western with No. 4)

HOLLYWOOD ROMANCES (Formerly Brides In Love; becomes For Lovers Only #60 on)
#46, 11/66; #47, 10/67; #48, 11/68; #49, 11/69 - #59, 6/71
Charlton Comics

V2#46-Rolling Stones c/story	1.00	3.00	7.00
V2#47-59: 56-"Born to Heart Break" begins	.40	1.25	2.50

HOLLYWOOD SECRETS
Nov. 1949 - No. 6, Sept, 1950
Quality Comics Group

1-Ward-c/a, 9pgs.	18.00	54.00	125.00
2-Crandall-a, Ward c/a, 9 pgs.	11.00	32.00	75.00
3-6: All photo-c; 5-Lex Barker (Tarzan)-c	4.50	14.00	32.00
...of Romance, I.W. Reprint #9; Kinstler-c; Ward, Crandall-a	.85	2.50	5.00

HOLYOKE ONE-SHOT
1944 - No. 10, 1945 (All reprints)
Holyoke Publishing Co. (Tem Publ.)

1-Grit Grady (on cover only), Miss Victory, Alias X (origin)-All reprints from Captain Fearless	6.00	18.00	42.00
2-Rusty Dugan (Corporal); Capt. Fearless (origin), Mr. Miracle (origin). app.	6.00	18.00	42.00
3-Miss Victory-Crash #4-r; Cat Man (origin), Solar Legion by Kirby app.; Miss Victory on cover only (1945)	13.00	40.00	90.00
4-Mr. Miracle-The Blue Streak app.	5.50	16.50	38.00
5-U.S. Border Patrol Comics (Sgt. Dick Carter of the...), Miss Victory (story matches cover #3), Citizen Smith, & Mr. Miracle app.	6.00	18.00	42.00
6-Capt. Fearless, Alias X, Capt. Stone (splash used as cover-#10); Diamond Jim & Rusty Dugan (splash from cover-#2)	5.50	16.50	38.00
7-Z-2, Strong Man, Blue Streak (story matches cover-#8)-Reprints from Crash #2	6.50	19.50	45.00
8-Blue Streak, Strong Man (story matches cover-#7)-Crash reprints	5.50	16.50	38.00
9-Citizen Smith, The Blue Streak, Solar Legion by Kirby & Strongman. the Perfect Human app.; reprints from Crash #4 & 5; Citizen Smith on cover only-from story in #5(1944-before #3)	8.50	25.50	60.00
10-Captain Stone (Crash reprints); Solar Legion by S&K	8.50	25.50	60.00

HOMER COBB (See Adventures of)

HOMER HOOPER
July, 1953 - No. 4, Dec., 1953
Atlas Comics

	Good	Fine	N-Mint
1	2.85	8.50	20.00
2-4	2.00	6.00	14.00

HOMER, THE HAPPY GHOST (See Adventures of...)
3/55 - No. 22, 11/58; V2No.1, 11/69 - V2No.5, 7/70
Atlas(ACI/PPI/WPI)/Marvel Comics

V1#1	3.70	11.00	26.00
2	2.00	6.00	14.00
3-10	1.50	4.50	10.00
11-22	1.15	3.50	8.00
V2#1 - V2#5 (1969-70)	.70	2.00	4.00

HOME RUN (See A-1 Comics No. 89)

HOME, SWEET HOME
1925 (10¼×10'')
M.S. Publishing Co.

nn-By Tuthill	10.00	30.00	70.00

HONEYBEE BIRDWHISTLE AND HER PET PEPI (Introducing)
1969 (24 pgs.; B&W; slick cover)
Newspaper Enterprise Association (Giveaway)

nn-Contains Freckles newspaper strips with a short biography of Henry Fornhals (artist) & Fred Fox (writer) of the strip	3.00	9.00	21.00

HONEYMOON (Formerly Gay Comics)
No. 41, January, 1950
A Lover's Magazine(USA) (Marvel)

41	3.00	9.00	21.00

HONEYMOONERS, THE (TV)
Oct, 1986 ($1.50, color)
Lodestone Publishing

1-Jackie Gleason photo-c	.50	1.50	3.00

HONEYMOONERS, THE (TV)
Sept, 1987 - No. 24 ($2.00, color)
Triad Publications

1	.50	1.50	3.00
2,4-8,10-12	.35	1.00	2.00
3 ($3.50, X-Mas Special, squarebound)	.60	1.75	3.50
9 ($3.95)-Jack Davis-c	.70	2.00	3.95
13-Comic book size	.40	1.25	2.50
13-Magazine size	.35	1.00	2.00

HONEYMOON ROMANCE
April, 1950 - No. 2, July, 1950 (25 cents) (digest size)
Artful Publications(Canadian)

1,2-(Rare)	17.00	51.00	120.00

HONEY WEST (TV)
September, 1966 (Photo-c)
Gold Key

1 (10186-609)	6.00	18.00	42.00

HONG KONG PHOOEY (Hanna-Barbera)(TV)
June, 1975 - No. 9, Nov, 1976
Charlton Comics

1-9		.40	.80

HOODED HORSEMAN, THE (Also see Blazing West)
No. 21, 1-2/52 - No. 27, 1-2/53; No. 18, 12-1/54-55 - No. 27, 6-7/56
American Comics Group (Michel Publ.)

21(1-2/52)-Hooded Horseman. Injun Jones continues	6.50	19.50	45.00
22	3.70	11.00	26.00
23-25,27(1-2/53)	2.85	8.50	20.00
26-Origin/1st app. Cowboy Sahib	3.70	11.00	26.00
18(12-1/54-55)(Formerly Out of the Night)	2.85	8.50	20.00

THE HOODED HORSEMAN (continued)	Good	Fine	N-Mint
19-3-D effect-c; last precode, 1-2/55	6.00	18.00	42.00
20-Origin Johnny Injun	2.85	8.50	20.00
21-24,26,27(6-7/56)	2.65	8.00	18.00
25-Cowboy Sahib on cover only; Hooded Horseman i.d. revealed			
	2.85	8.50	20.00

NOTE: *Whitney c/a-21(52). 20-22.*

HOODED MENACE, THE (Also see Daring Adventures)
1951 (One Shot)
Realistic/Avon Periodicals

nn-Based on a band of hooded outlaws in the Pacific Northwest, 1900-1906; r-/in Daring Advs. #15	32.00	95.00	225.00

HOODS UP
1953 (16 pgs.) (15 cents) (Eisner c/a in all)
Fram Corp. (Dist. to service station owners)

1-(Very Rare: only 2 known)	33.00	100.00	230.00
2-6-(Very Rare: only 1 known of 3-4, 2 known of #2)			
	33.00	100.00	230.00

NOTE: *Convertible Connie gives tips for service stations, selling Fram oil filters.*

HOOT GIBSON'S WESTERN ROUNDUP (See Western Roundup under Fox Giants)

HOOT GIBSON WESTERN (Formerly My Love Story)
No. 5, May, 1950 - No. 3, Sept, 1950
Fox Features Syndicate

5,6(#1,2): 5-Photo-c	10.00	30.00	70.00
3-Wood-a	13.00	40.00	90.00

HOPALONG CASSIDY (Also see Bill Boyd Western, Master Comics, Real Western Hero, Six Gun Heroes & Western Hero; Bill Boyd starred as H. Cassidy in the movies; H. Cassidy in movies, radio & TV)
Feb. 1943: No. 2, Summer, 1946 - No. 85, Jan, 1954
Fawcett Publications

1 (1943. 68pgs.)-H. Cassidy & his horse Topper begin (On sale 1/8/43)-Captain Marvel on-c	125.00	315.00	750.00
2-(Sum, '46)	37.00	110.00	260.00
3,4: 3-(Fall, '46, 52pgs. begin)	19.00	57.00	135.00
5-"Mad Barber" story mentioned in SOTI, pgs. 308,309			
	18.00	54.00	125.00
6-10	14.00	42.00	100.00
11-19: 11,13-19-Photo-c	11.00	32.00	76.00
20-29 (52pgs.)-Painted/photo-c	8.50	25.50	60.00
30,31,33,34,37-39,41 (52pgs.)-Painted-c	5.50	16.50	38.00
32,40 (36pgs.)-Painted-c	4.50	14.00	32.00
35,42,43,45 (52pgs.)-Photo-c	5.50	16.50	38.00
36,44,48 (36pgs.)-Photo-c	4.50	14.00	32.00
46,47,49-51,53,54,56 (52pgs.)-Photo-c	5.00	15.00	35.00
52,55,57-70 (36pgs.)-Photo-c	3.70	11.00	26.00
71-84-Photo-c	2.85	8.50	20.00
85-Last Fawcett issue; photo-c	3.50	10.50	24.00

NOTE: *Line-drawn c-1-10. 12*

Grape Nuts Flakes giveaway(1950,9x6'')	7.00	21.00	50.00
& the Mad Barber(1951 Bond Bread giveaway)-7x5''; used in SOTI, pgs. 308,309	17.00	51.00	120.00
in the Strange Legacy	6.00	18.00	42.00
Meets the Brend Brothers Bandits	6.00	18.00	42.00
White Tower Giveaway (1946, 16pgs., paper-c)	6.00	18.00	42.00

HOPALONG CASSIDY (TV)
No. 86, Feb, 1954 - No. 135, May-June, 1959 (All-36pgs.)
National Periodical Publications

86-Photo covers continue	12.00	36.00	84.00
87	6.50	19.50	45.00
88-90	4.50	14.00	32.00
91-99 (98 has #93 on-c & is last precode issue, 2/55)			
	3.70	11.00	26.00

	Good	Fine	N-Mint
100	5.00	15.00	35.00
101-108-Last photo-c	3.15	9.50	22.00
109-135: 124-Painted-c	3.15	9.50	22.00

NOTE: *Gil Kane art-1956 up. Kubert a-123*

HOPE SHIP
June-Aug, 1963
Dell Publishing Co.

1	1.35	4.00	8.00

HOPPY THE MARVEL BUNNY (See Fawcett's Funny Animals)
Dec, 1945 - No. 15, Sept, 1947
Fawcett Publications

1	12.00	36.00	84.00
2	5.70	17.00	40.00
3-15: 7-Xmas-c	4.30	13.00	30.00
Well Known Comics (1944,8½x10½'',paper-c) Bestmaid/Samuel Lowe (Printed in red or blue)	6.75	20.00	40.00

HORACE & DOTTY DRIPPLE (Dotty Dripple No. 1-24)
No. 25, Aug, 1952 - No. 43, Oct, 1955
Harvey Publications

25-43	.70	2.00	5.00

HORIZONTAL LIEUTENANT, THE (See Movie Classics)

HORRIFIC (Terrific No. 14 on)
Sept, 1952 - No. 13, Sept, 1954
Artful/Comic Media/Harwell/Mystery

1	10.00	30.00	70.00
2	5.00	15.00	35.00
3-Bullet in head-c	8.00	24.00	56.00
4,5,7,9,10	3.50	10.50	24.00
6-Jack The Ripper story	3.70	11.00	26.00
8-Origin & 1st app. The Teller(E.C. parody)	5.00	15.00	35.00
11-13: 11-Swipe/Witches Tales #6,27	2.85	8.50	20.00

NOTE: *Don Heck a-8; c-3-13. Hollingsworth a-4. Morisi a-8. Palais a-5. 8. 11.*

HORROR FROM THE TOMB (Mysterious Stories No. 2 on)
Sept, 1954
Premier Magazine Co.

1-Woodbridge/Torres, Check-a	10.00	30.00	70.00

HORRORS, THE
No. 11, Jan, 1953 - No. 15, Apr, 1954
Star Publications

11-Horrors of War; Disbrow-a(2)	6.50	19.50	45.00
12-Horrors of War; color illo in POP	6.00	18.00	42.00
13-Horrors of Mystery; crime stories	6.00	18.00	42.00
14,15-Horrors of the Underworld	6.00	18.00	42.00

NOTE: *All have L. B. Cole covers. a-12. Hollingsworth a-13 Palais a-13r.*

HORROR TALES (Magazine)
V1#7, 6/69 - V6#6, 12/74; V7#1, 2/75; V7#2, 5/76 - V8#5, 1977; V9#3, 8/78; (V1-V6: 52 pgs.; V7, V8#2: 112 pgs.; V8#4 on: 68 pgs.) (No V5#3, V8#1,3)
Eerie Publications

V1#7	.70	2.00	5.00
V1#8,9	.50	1.50	3.00
V2#1-6('70), V3#1-6('71)	.35	1.10	2.20
V4#1-3,5-7('72)	.25	.75	1.50
V4#4-LSD story reprint/Weird V3#5	.85	2.50	5.00
V5#1,2,4,5(6/73),5(10/73),6(12/73)	.25	.75	1.50
V6#1-6('74),V7#1,2,4('76)	.25	.75	1.50
V7#3('76)-Giant issue	.25	.75	1.50
V8#2,4,5('77),V9#3(8/78, $1.50)	.25	.75	1.50

NOTE: *Bondage-c-V6#1, 3. V7#2.*

Hoot Gibson Western #3. : FOX

Hopalong Cassidy #19. : FAW

Horrific #4. : Comic Media

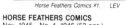

Horse Feathers Comics #1.   LEV

Hot Rod And Speedway Comics #5.   HILL

The House Of Mystery #143.   DC

HORSE FEATHERS COMICS
Nov. 1945 - No. 4, 1946 (52 pgs.)
Lev Gleason Publications

	Good	Fine	N-Mint
1-Wolverton's Scoop Scuttle, 2 pgs.	9.00	27.00	62.00
2	3.50	10.50	24.00
3.4	2.65	8.00	18.00

HORSEMASTERS, THE (See 4-Color No. 1260)

HORSE SOLDIERS, THE (See 4-Color No. 1048)

HORSE WITHOUT A HEAD, THE (See Movie Comics)

HOT DOG
June-July, 1954 - No. 4, Dec-Jan, 1954-55
Magazine Enterprises

1(A-1 107)	2.65	8.00	18.00
2.3(A-1 115).4(A-1 136)	1.50	4.50	10.00

HOTEL DEPAREE - SUNDANCE (See 4-Color No. 1126)

HOT ROD AND SPEEDWAY COMICS
Feb-Mar. 1952 - No. 5, Apr-May, 1953
Hillman Periodicals

1	7.00	21.00	50.00
2-Krigstein-a	5.00	15.00	35.00
3-5	2.00	6.00	14.00

HOT ROD COMICS (See XMas Comics)
Nov. 1951 (no month given) - V2No.7, Feb. 1953
Fawcett Publications

nn (V1#1)-Powell-c/a in all	9.30	28.00	65.00
2 (4/52)	4.50	14.00	32.00
3-6. V2#7	3.00	9.00	21.00

HOT ROD KING
Fall. 1952
Ziff-Davis Publ. Co.

1-Giacoia-a: painted-c	8.00	24.00	56.00

HOT ROD RACERS (Grand Prix No. 16 on)
Dec. 1964 - No. 15. July. 1967
Charlton Comics

1	1.00	3.00	7.00
2-5	.60	1.75	3.50
6-15	.35	1.00	2.00

HOT RODS AND RACING CARS
Nov. 1951 - No. 120. June. 1973
Charlton Comics (Motor Mag. No. 1)

1	5.70	17.00	40.00
2	2.65	8.00	18.00
3-10	1.70	5.00	12.00
11-20	1.30	4.00	9.00
21-34.36-40	.85	2.60	6.00
35 (68 pgs.; 6/58)	1.30	4.00	9.00
41-60	.60	1.75	3.50
61-80	.30	.90	1.80
81-100	.25	.75	1.50
81-120		.50	1.00

HOT SHOT CHARLIE
1947 (Lee Elias)
Hillman Periodicals

1	2.85	8.50	20.00

HOTSPUR
June. 1987 - No. 3. Oct. 1987 ($1.75, color, Baxter paper)
Eclipse Comics

1-3	.30	.90	1.80

HOT STUFF CREEPY CAVES
Nov. 1974 - No. 7, Nov. 1975
Harvey Publications

	Good	Fine	N-Mint
1	.55	1.60	3.20
2-5	.25	.80	1.60
6,7		.40	.80

HOT STUFF SIZZLERS
July. 1960 - No. 59. March. 1974
Harvey Publications

1: 68 pgs. begin	5.00	15.00	35.00
2-5	1.70	5.00	12.00
6-10	1.15	3.50	8.00
11-20	.85	2.50	5.00
21-45: Last 68 pgs.	.50	1.50	3.00
46-52: All 52 pgs.	.40	1.20	2.40
53-59	.35	1.00	2.00

HOT STUFF, THE LITTLE DEVIL (Also see Devil Kids & Harvey Hits)
10/57 - No. 141. 7/77; No. 142. 2/78 - No. 164. 8/82; No. 165.
10/86 - No. 171. 11/87; No. 172. 11/88 - Present
Harvey Publications (Illustrated Humor)

1	13.00	40.00	90.00
2-1st app. Stumbo the Giant	8.00	24.00	56.00
3-5	6.00	18.00	42.00
6-10	3.00	9.00	21.00
11-20	1.50	4.50	10.00
21-40	.70	2.00	5.00
41-60	.55	1.60	3.20
61-105	.25	.80	1.60
106-112: All 52 pg. Giants	.35	1.00	2.00
113-174 (10/89)-Later issues $1.00-c		.40	.80
Shoestore Giveaway('63)	.50	1.50	3.00

HOT WHEELS (TV)
Mar-Apr. 1970 - No. 6. Jan-Feb. 1971
National Periodical Publications

1	1.70	5.00	12.00
2.4.5	1.00	3.00	6.00
3-Adams-c	2.00	6.00	12.00
6-Adams c/a	2.50	7.50	15.00

NOTE: **Toth** a-1p. 2-5: c-1p. 4. 5.

HOUSE OF MYSTERY (See Brave and the Bold #93. Limited Collectors' Edition & Super DC Giant)

HOUSE OF MYSTERY, THE (Also see Elvira's...)
Dec-Jan, 1951-52 - No. 321. Oct. 1983 (No. 199-203: 52 pgs.)
National Periodical Publications/DC Comics

1	46.00	137.00	320.00
2	20.00	60.00	140.00
3	16.00	48.00	110.00
4.5	13.00	40.00	90.00
6-10	11.00	32.00	75.00
11-15	9.00	27.00	62.00
16(7/53)-35(2/55)-Last pre-code ish: #30-Woodish-a	5.70	17.00	40.00
36-49	3.00	9.00	21.00
50-Text story of Orson Welles' War of the Worlds broadcast	2.30	7.00	16.00
51-60	1.70	5.00	12.00
61.63.65.66.70.72.76.84.85-Kirby-a	1.70	5.00	12.00
62.64.67-69.71,73-75.77-83.86-99	1.30	4.00	9.00
100	1.50	4.50	10.00
101-116: Last 10 cent issue. 109-Toth. Kubert-a	1.00	3.00	7.00
117-119.121-130	.70	2.00	4.00
120-Toth-a	.75	2.25	5.00
131-142	.50	1.50	3.00
143-J'onn J'onzz, Manhunter begins. ends #173 (6/64); story cont./			

203

THE HOUSE OF MYSTERY (continued)

	Good	Fine	N-Mint
Detective #326	3.60	11.00	25.00
144	2.15	6.50	15.00
145-155,157-160: 149-Toth-a. 158-Origin/1st app. Diabolu Idol-Head in J'onn J'onzz. 160-Intro Marco Xavier (Martin Manhunter) & Vulture Crime Organization; ends #173	1.30	4.00	9.00
156-Robby Reed begins (Origin), ends #173	1.50	4.50	10.00
161-173: 169-Origin/1st app. Gem Girl	1.00	3.00	7.00
174-177,182: 174-Mystery format begins. 182-Toth-a	.30	.85	1.70
178-Adams-a	.70	2.00	4.00
179-Adams/Orlando, Wrightson-a (1st pro work. 3 pgs.)	1.10	3.30	6.60
180,181,183: Wrightson-a (3, 10, & 3 pgs.). 180,183-Wood-a	.45	1.40	2.80
184-Kane/Wood, Toth a	.35	1.10	2.20
185-Williamson/Kaluta-a; 3 pgs. Wood-a	.70	2.00	4.00
186-Adams-a; Wrightson-a, 10 pgs.	.70	2.00	4.00
187,190: 190-Toth-a(r)	.30	.85	1.70
188,191,195-Wrightson-a (8, 3 & 10 pgs.)	.70	2.00	4.00
189-Wood-a	.35	1.10	2.20
192-194,196-198,200: 194-Toth, Kirby-a; 48 pgs. begin, end #198	.30	.85	1.70
199-Wood. Kirby-a; 52pgs. begin, end 203	.45	1.40	2.80
201-203,205,206,208-220	.30	.85	1.70
204-Wrightson-a, 9 pgs.	.45	1.40	2.80
207-Wrightson, Starlin-a	.35	1.10	2.20
221-Wrightson/Kaluta-a, 8 pgs.	.35	1.10	2.20
222,223,225,227	.30	.85	1.70
224-Adams/Wrightson-a(r); begin 100 pg. issues; Phantom Stranger-r	.55	1.65	3.30
226-Wrightson-r; Phantom Stranger-r	.30	.85	1.70
228-Adams inks; Wrightson-r	.45	1.40	2.80
229-321: 229-Wrightson-a(r); Toth-r; last 100 pg. issue. 230-68 pgs. 251-259, 84 pgs. 251-Wood-a	.30	.85	1.70

NOTE: **Adams** a-236i; c-175-192, 197, 199, 251-254. **Aragones** a-186, 251. **Baily** a-279p. **Colan** a-202r. **Craig** a-263, 275, 295, 300. **Ditko** a-236, 247, 254, 258, 276; c-277. **Drucker** a-37. **Evans** c-218. **Giunta** a-199. **Golden** a-257, 259. **Heath** a-194r; c-203. **Howard** a-182, 187, 196, 229r, 247i, 254, 279i. **Kaluta** a-195, 200. 250r; c-200-202i. 210, 212, 233, 260, 261, 263, 265, 267, 268, 273, 276, 284, 287, 288, 293-295, 300, 302, 304, 305, 309-319, 321. **Bob Kane** a-84. **Gil Kane** a-196p, 253p, 300p. **Kirby** a-194r, 199r; c-65, 76, 78, 79, 85. **Kubert** c-282, 283, 285, 286, 289-292, 297-99, 301, 303, 306-308. **Mayer** a-317p. **Meskin** a-52-144 (most), 224r, 229r; c-63, 66, 124, 127. **Mooney** a-160. **Moreira** a-3, 20-50, 58, 59, 62, 68, 77, 79, 90, 123, 201r, 228; c-44, 47, 50, 54, 59, 62, 64, 68, 70, 73. **Morrow** a-192, 196, 255, 320i. **Mortimer** a-204. **Nasser** a-278. **Newton** a-259, 272. **Nino** a-204, 212, 213, 220, 224, 225, 245, 250, 252-256, 283. **Orlando** a-175(2 pgs.), 178; c-240, 256p, 262, 264p, 270p, 271, 272, 274, 275, 278, 296i. **Redondo** a-194, 195, 197, 202, 203, 207, 211, 214, 217, 219, 226, 227, 229, 235, 241, 287(layout), 302p, 303i, 308; c-229. **Reese** a-195, 200, 205i. **Rogers** a-254, 274, 277. **Roussos** a-65, 84, 224i. **Sekowsky** a-282p. **Sparling** a-203. **Starlin** a-207(2 pgs.), 282p; c-281. **Leonard Starr** a-9. **Staton** a-300p. **Sutton** a-271, 290, 291, 293, 295, 297-99, 302, 303, 306-09, 310-13i, 314. **Tuska** a-293p, 294p, 316p. **Wrightson** c-193-195, 204, 207, 209, 211, 213, 214, 217, 221, 231, 236, 255, 256.

HOUSE OF SECRETS
11-12/56 - No. 80, 9-10/66; No. 81, 8-9/69 - No. 140, 2-3/76; No. 141, 8-9/76 - No. 154, 10-11/78
National Periodical Publications/DC Comics

	Good	Fine	N-Mint
1-Drucker-a; Moreira-c	34.00	102.00	240.00
2-Moreira-a	15.00	45.00	105.00
3-Kirby c/a	13.00	40.00	90.00
4,8-Kirby-a	6.50	19.50	45.00
5-7,9-11	4.50	14.00	32.00
12-Kirby c/a	5.70	17.00	40.00
13-15	3.50	10.50	24.00
16-20	2.85	8.50	20.00
21,22,24-30	2.15	6.50	15.00
23-Origin Mark Merlin	2.30	7.00	16.00
31-47,49,50: Last 10 cent issue	1.50	4.50	10.00
48-Toth-a	1.85	5.50	13.00

	Good	Fine	N-Mint
51-60,62: 58-Origin Mark Merlin retold	.75	2.25	4.50
61-First Eclipso	2.15	6.50	15.00
63-67-Toth-a	.75	2.25	4.50
68-81,84,86,88,89: 73-Mark Merlin ends. Prince Ra-Man begins. 80-Eclipso, Prince Ra-Man end. 81-Mystery format begins	.25	.75	1.50
82,85: 82-Adams-c(i). 85-Adams-a(i)	.60	1.75	3.50
83,91: 83-Toth-a. 91-Wood-i	.50	1.50	3.00
87-Wrightson & Kaluta-a	.60	1.75	3.50
90-Buckler (1st pro work)/Adams-a	.60	1.75	3.50
92-Intro. Swamp Thing; Wrightson-a (6-7/71); J. Jones part inks	5.00	15.00	35.00
93,96,98-Toth-a(r). 96-Wood-a	.25	.75	1.50
94-Wrightson inks; Toth-a(r)	.60	1.75	3.50
95,97,99,100	.25	.75	1.50
101-154: 140-Origin The Patchworkman	.50		1.00

NOTE: **Adams** c-81, 82, 84-88, 90, 91. **Colan** a-63. **Ditko** a-139p, 148. **Evans** a-118. **Finlay** a-7. **Glanzman** a-91. **Golden** a-151. **Kaluta** a-87, 98, 99; c-98, 99, 101, 102, 151, 154. **Bob Kane** a-85p. **Kirby** c-11. **Kubert** a-39. **Meskin** a-2-68 (most); c-55-60. **Moreira** a-7, 8, 102-104, 106, 108, 113, 116, 118, 121, 123, 127; c-2, 7-9. **Morrow** a-86, 89, 90; c-89, 146-148. **Nino** a-101, 103, 106, 109, 115, 117, 126, 128, 131, 147, 153. **Redondo** a-95, 99, 102, 104p, 113, 116, 134, 139, 140. **Reese** a-85. **Starlin** c-150. **Sutton** a-154. **Toth** a-63-67, 123. **Tuska** a-90, 104. **Wrightson** c-92-94, 96, 100, 103, 106, 107, 135, 139.

HOUSE OF TERROR (3-D)
October, 1953 (1st 3D horror comic)
St. John Publishing Co.

	Good	Fine	N-Mint
1-Kubert, Baker-a	16.00	48.00	110.00

HOUSE OF YANG, THE (See Yang)
July, 1975 - No. 6, June, 1976; 1978
Charlton Comics

	Good	Fine	N-Mint
1-Opium propaganda story		.40	.80
2-6		.30	.60
Modern Comics #1,2(1978)		.30	.60

HOUSE II: THE SECOND STORY
1987
Marvel Comics

	Good	Fine	N-Mint
1-Adapts movie	.35	1.00	2.00

HOWARD CHAYKIN'S AMERICAN FLAGG! (Formerly Amer. Flagg!)
V2#1, May, 1988 - V2#12, April, 1989 ($1.75-$1.95, Baxter paper)
First Comics

	Good	Fine	N-Mint
V2#1-5: ($1.75)-Chaykin-c(p) in all	.30	.90	1.75
6-9,11,12: ($1.95)	.30	.90	1.75
10-Elvis Presley photo-c	.40	1.25	2.50

HOWARD THE DUCK (See Bizarre Adventures #34, Fear, Man-Thing, & Marvel Treasury Edition)
1/76 - No. 31, 5/79; No. 32, 1/86; No. 33, 9/86
Marvel Comics Group

	Good	Fine	N-Mint
1-Brunner c/a; Spider-Man x-over (low distribution)	1.15	3.50	7.00
2-Brunner c/a (low distr.)	.25	.75	1.50
3-11: 3-Buscema-a	.25	.75	1.50
12-1st app. Kiss	.70	2.00	4.00
13-Kiss app.	.85	2.50	5.00
14-33: 16-Album issue; 3pgs. comics		.40	.80
Annual 1(9/77)		.40	.80

NOTE: **Austin** c-29i. **Bolland** c-33. **Brunner** a-1p, 2p; c-1, 2. **Buckler** c-3p. **Buscema** a-3p. **Colan** a(p)-4-15, 17-20, 24-27, 30, 31; c(p)-4-31. Annual 1. **Leialoha** a-1-13i; c(i)-3-5, 8-11. **Mayerik** a-22, 23, 33. **P. Smith** a-30p.

HOWARD THE DUCK MAGAZINE
October, 1979 - No. 9, March, 1981 (B&W)
Marvel Comics Group

	Good	Fine	N-Mint
1		.50	1.00

The House Of Mystery #199. © DC

House Of Secrets #7. © DC

Howard The Duck #7. © MEG

Howdy Doody #16. : Kagran Corp.

Huckleberry Hound #7 (Dell). : Hanna-Barbera

Huey, Dewey, & Louie Junior Woodchucks #2. WDC

	Good	Fine	N-Mint
HOWARD THE DUCK MAGAZINE (continued)			
2,3,5-9: 7-Has poster by Byrne		.30	.60
4-Beatles, John Lennon, Elvis, Kiss & Devo cameos; Hitler app.		.40	.80

NOTE: *Buscema* a-4. *Colan* a-1-5p. 7-9p. *Davis* c-3. *Golden* a-1. 5p. 6p(51pgs.). *Rogers* a-7. 8. *Simonson* a-7.

HOWARD THE DUCK: THE MOVIE
Dec, 1986 - No. 3, Feb, 1987 (mini-series)
Marvel Comics Group

1-3: Movie adaptation; r/Marv. Super Special		.40	.80

HOW BOYS AND GIRLS CAN HELP WIN THE WAR
1942 (One Shot) (10 cents)
The Parents' Magazine Institute

1-All proceeds used to buy war bonds	12.00	36.00	84.00

HOWDY DOODY (TV)(See Poll Parrot)
1/50 - No. 38, 7-9/56; No. 761, 1/57; No. 811, 7/57
Dell Publishing Co.

1-Photo-c; 1st TV comic?	18.00	54.00	125.00
2-Photo-c	8.50	25.50	60.00
3-5: All photo-c	5.70	17.00	40.00
6-Used in **SOTI**, pg. 309; painted-c begin	5.00	15.00	35.00
7-10	4.50	14.00	32.00
11-20	3.50	10.50	24.00
21-38	2.30	7.00	16.00
4-Color 761,811	4.50	14.00	32.00

HOW IT BEGAN (See Single Series No. 15)

HOW SANTA GOT HIS RED SUIT (See March of Comics No. 2)

HOW STALIN HOPES WE WILL DESTROY AMERICA
1951 (16 pgs.) (Giveaway)
Joe Lowe Co. (Pictorial News)

nn	34.00	103.00	240.00

(Prices vary widely on this book)

HOW THE WEST WAS WON (See Movie Comics)

HOW TO DRAW FOR THE COMICS
No date (1942?) (64 pgs.; B&W & color) (10 Cents) (No ads)
Street and Smith

nn-Art by Winsor McCay, George Marcoux(Supersnipe artist), Vernon Greene(The Shadow artist), Jack Binder(with biog), Thorton Fisher, Jon Small, & Jack Farr. Has biographies of each artist	12.00	36.00	84.00

H. R. PUFNSTUF (TV) (See March of Comics 360)
Oct, 1970 - No. 8, July, 1972
Gold Key

1	.85	2.50	5.00
2-8	.35	1.00	2.00

HUBERT (See 4-Color No. 251)

HUCK & YOGI JAMBOREE (TV)
March, 1961 (116 pgs.; $1.00) (B&W original material)
(6¼x9''; cardboard cover; high quality paper)
Dell Publishing Co.

nn	3.00	9.00	21.00

HUCK & YOGI WINTER SPORTS (See 4-Color No. 1310)

HUCK FINN (See The New Adventures of . . .)

HUCKLEBERRY FINN (See 4-Color No. 1114)

HUCKLEBERRY HOUND (See Dell Giant No. 31.44. Golden Picture Story Book. March of Comics No. 199,214,235. Spotlight No. 1 & Whitman Comic Books)

HUCKLEBERRY HOUND
No. 990, 5-7/59 - No. 43, 10/70 (Hanna-Barbera)
Dell/Gold Key No. 18 (10/62) on

	Good	Fine	N-Mint
4-Color 990	3.00	9.00	21.00
4-Color 1050,1054 (12/59)	2.30	7.00	16.00
3(1-2/60) - 7 (9-10/60)	2.30	7.00	16.00
4-Color 1141 (10/60)	2.30	7.00	16.00
8-10	2.00	6.00	14.00
11-17 (6-8/62)	1.30	4.00	9.00
18,19 (84pgs.); 18-20 titled . . .Chuckleberry Tales)			
	3.50	10.50	28.00
20-30: 20-Titled Chuckleberry Tales	1.00	3.00	7.00
31-43: 37-reprints	.85	2.60	6.00
. . .Kite Fun Book('61)-16 pgs.; 5x7¼'', soft-c	2.00	6.00	14.00

HUCKLEBERRY HOUND (TV)
Nov, 1970 - No. 8, Jan, 1972 (Hanna-Barbera)
Charlton Comics

1	.85	2.60	6.00
2-8	.60	1.75	3.50

HUEY, DEWEY, & LOUIE (See Donald Duck. 1938 for 1st app. Also see Mickey Mouse Magazine V4#2, V5#7)

HUEY, DEWEY, & LOUIE BACK TO SCHOOL (See Dell Giant #22.35.49 & Dell Giants)

HUEY, DEWEY AND LOUIE JUNIOR WOODCHUCKS (Disney)
Aug, 1966 - No. 81, 1984 (See Walt Disney's C&S #125)
Gold Key No. 1-61/Whitman No. 62 on

1	2.65	8.00	18.00
2,3(12/68)	1.70	5.00	12.00
4,5(4/70)-Barks-r	1.70	5.00	12.00
6-17-Written by Barks	1.15	3.50	8.00
18,27-30	.70	2.00	4.00
19-23,25-Written by Barks. 22,23,25-Barks-r	.85	2.50	5.00
24,26-Barks-r	.85	2.50	5.00
31-57,60-81: 41,70,80-Reprints	.25	.75	1.50
58,59-Barks-r	.35	1.00	2.00

NOTE: *Barks* story reprints-No. 22-26.35.42.45.51.

HUGGA BUNCH (TV)
Oct, 1986 - No. 6, Aug, 1987
Star Comics (Marvel)

1-6		.45	.90

HULK, THE (See The Incredible Hulk)

HULK, THE (Formerly The Rampaging Hulk)
No. 10, 8/78 - No. 27, June, 1981 (Magazine)($1.50)(in color)
Marvel Comics Group

10-12: (B&W)-11-Moon Knight begins by Colan		.60	1.20
13-27: 13-Color issues begin. 23-Anti-Gay issue		.60	1.20

NOTE: *Alcala* a(i)-15. 17-20. 22. 24-27. *Buscema* a-23; c-26. *Chaykin* a-21-25. *Colan* a(p)-11. 17. 19. 24-27. *Golden* a-20. *Nebres* a-16. *Simonson* a-27; c-23.

HUMAN FLY
1963 - 1964 (Reprints)
I.W. Enterprises/Super

I.W. Reprint No. 1-Reprints Blue Beetle No. 44('46)			
	.70	2.00	4.00
Super Reprint No. 10-Reprints Blue Beetle No. 46('47)			
	.70	2.00	4.00

HUMAN FLY, THE
Sept, 1977 - No. 19, Mar, 1979
Marvel Comics Group

1-Origin; Spider-Man x-over		.40	.80
2-19: 9-Daredevil x-over; Byrne/Austin-c		.25	.50

NOTE: *Austin* c-4i. *Elias* a-1. 3p. 4p. 7p. 10-12p. 15p. 18p. 19p. *Layton* c-19.

HUMAN TORCH, THE (Red Raven #1)(See All-Select, All Winners, Marvel Mystery, Men's Advs., Mystic Comics (2nd series), Sub-

THE HUMAN TORCH (continued)
Mariner, USA & Young Men)
No. 2. Fall, 1940 - No. 15, Spring, 1944 (becomes Funny Tunes);
No. 16, Fall, 1944 - No. 35, Mar, 1949 (becomes Love Tales);
No. 36, April, 1954 - No. 38, Aug, 1954
Timely/Marvel Comics (TP 2,3/TCI 4-9/SePI 10/SnPC 11-25/CnPC
26-35/Atlas Comics (CPC 36-38))

	Good	Fine	N-Mint
2(#1)-Intro & Origin Toro; The Falcon, The Fiery Mask, Mantor the Magician, & Microman only app.; Human Torch by Burgos, Sub-Mariner by Everett begin (origin of each in text)	583.00	1460.00	3500.00
(Prices vary widely on this book)			
3(#2)-40pg. H.T. story; H.T. & S.M. battle over who is best artist in text-Everett or Burgos	233.00	585.00	1400.00
4(#3)-Origin The Patriot in text; last Everett Sub-Mariner; Sid Greene-a	175.00	440.00	1050.00
5(#4)-The Patriot app; Angel x-over in Sub-Mariner. (Summer, 1941)	125.00	315.00	750.00
5-Human Torch battles Sub-Mariner (Fall,'41)	200.00	500.00	1200.00
6,7,9	82.00	205.00	490.00
8-Human Torch battles Sub-Mariner; Wolverton-a, 1 pg.	133.00	335.00	800.00
10-Human Torch battles Sub-Mariner; Wolverton-a, 1 pg.	100.00	250.00	600.00
11-15	63.00	160.00	380.00
16-20: 20-Last War issue	50.00	125.00	300.00
21-30	42.00	105.00	250.00
31-Namora x-over in Sub-Mariner (also #30); last Toro	33.00	83.00	200.00
32-Sungirl. Namora app.; Sungirl-c	33.00	83.00	200.00
33-Capt. America x-over	35.00	90.00	210.00
34-Sungirl solo	33.00	83.00	200.00
35-Captain America & Sungirl app. (1949)	35.00	90.00	210.00
36-38(1954)-Sub-Mariner in all	25.00	63.00	150.00

NOTE: *Burgos* c-36. *Everett* a-1-3, 27, 28, 30, 37, 38. *Powell* a-36. *Schomburg* c-1-3,
5-23. *Shores* c-27. *Mickey Spillane* text 4-6. *Bondage-c* #2, 12, 19. Since there is a six
month delay between #15 & 16, it is believed that Funny Tunes #16 continued after
Human Torch #15.

HUMAN TORCH, THE (Also see Fantastic Four, The Invaders &
Strange Tales #101)
Sept. 1974 - No. 8, Nov, 1975
Marvel Comics Group

1		.40	.80
2-8		.25	.50

NOTE: *Golden age Torch-r No. 1-8. Kirby/Ayers* a-1-5,8r.

HUMBUG (Satire by Harvey Kurtzman)
8/57 - No. 9, 5/58; No. 10, 6/58; No. 11, 10/58
Humbug Publications

1	8.00	24.00	56.00
2	3.70	11.00	26.00
3-9: 8-Elvis in Jailbreak Rock	2.85	8.50	20.00
10,11-Magazine format. 10-Photo-c	2.85	8.50	20.00
Bound Volume(#1-6)-Sold by publisher	20.00	60.00	140.00
Bound Volume(#1-9)	24.00	72.00	170.00

NOTE: *Davis* a-1-11. *Elder* a-2-4, 6-9, 11. *Heath* a-2, 4-8, 10. *Jaffee* a-2, 4-9. *Kurtzman*
a-11. *Wood* a-1.

HUMDINGER
May-June, 1946 - V2#2, July-Aug, 1947
Novelty Press/Premium Group

1-Jerkwater Line, Mickey Starlight by Don Rico, Dink begin	4.50	14.00	32.00
2	2.65	8.00	18.00
3-6, V2#1,2	1.70	5.00	12.00

HUMOR (See All Humor Comics)

HUMPHREY COMICS (Also see Joe Palooka)
October, 1948 - No. 22, April, 1952
Harvey Publications

	Good	Fine	N-Mint
1-Joe Palooka's pal (r); (52 pgs.)-Powell-a	5.70	17.00	40.00
2,3: Powell-a	2.65	8.00	18.00
4-Boy Heroes app.; Powell-a	3.50	10.50	24.00
5-8,10: 5,6-Powell-a. 7-Little Dot app.	2.00	6.00	14.00
9-Origin Humphrey	2.65	8.00	18.00
11-22	1.60	4.70	11.00

HUNCHBACK OF NOTRE DAME, THE (See 4-Color No. 854)

HUNK
August, 1961 - No. 11, 1963
Charlton Comics

1	.75	2.25	4.50
2-11	.35	1.10	2.25

HUNTED (Formerly My Love Memoirs)
No. 13, July, 1950 - No. 2, Sept, 1950
Fox Features Syndicate

13(#1)-Used in **SOTI**, pg. 42 & illo.-''Treating police contemptuously'' (lower left); Hollingsworth bondage-c	17.00	51.00	120.00
2	5.70	17.00	40.00

HUNTRESS, THE (See All-Star Comics #69, DC Super Stars #17, In-
finity, Inc. #1 & Sensation Comics #68)
April, 1989 - Present ($1.00, color)
DC Comics

1-12: Staton-c/a(p) in all		.50	1.00

HURRICANE COMICS
1945 (52 pgs.)
Cambridge House

1-(Humor, funny animal)	5.00	15.00	35.00

HYPER MYSTERY COMICS
May, 1940 - No. 2, June, 1940 (68 pgs.)
Hyper Publications

1-Hyper, the Phenomenal begins	52.00	155.00	365.00
2	40.00	120.00	280.00

I AIM AT THE STARS (See 4-Color No. 1148)

I AM COYOTE (See Eclipse Graphic Album Series)

IBIS, THE INVINCIBLE (See Fawcett Min., Mighty Midget & Whiz)
1943 (Feb) - No. 2, 1943; No. 3, Wint, 1945 - No. 6, Spring, 1948
Fawcett Publications

1-Origin Ibis; Raboy-c; on sale 1/2/43	75.00	225.00	525.00
2-Bondage-c	37.00	110.00	260.00
3-Wolverton-a #3-6 (4 pgs. each)	30.00	90.00	210.00
4-6: 5-Bondage-c. 6-Beck-c	23.50	71.00	165.00

ICE KING OF OZ, THE (See First Comics Graphic Novel #13)

ICEMAN (Also see The Champions & X-Men #94)
Dec, 1984 - No. 4, June, 1985 (Limited series)
Marvel Comics Group

1	.35	1.00	2.00
2-4: 3-X-Men x-over	.25	.75	1.50

IDAHO
June-Aug, 1963 - No. 8, July-Sept, 1965
Dell Publishing Co.

1	1.15	3.50	8.00
2-8: 5-Painted-c	.75	2.25	5.00

IDEAL (. . . a Classical Comic) (2nd Series) (Love Romances No. 6?)
July, 1948 - No. 5, March, 1949 (Feature length stories)
Timely Comics

1-Antony & Cleopatra	14.00	42.00	100.00

The Human Torch #2 (#1). MEG

Hyper Mystery Comics #1. Hyper Publ.

Ibis, The Invincible #6. FAW

Illustrated Stories Of The Operas (Faust). © B. Baily

I Love Lucy #5. © Lucille Ball & Desi Arnaz

The Incredible Hulk #2. © MEG

	Good	Fine	N-Mint
IDEAL (continued)			
2-The Corpses of Dr. Sacotti	13.00	40.00	90.00
3-Joan of Arc; used in **SOTI**, pg. 308-'Boer War'			
	11.00	32.00	75.00
4-Richard the Lion-hearted; titled ''. . .the World's Greatest			
Comics;'' The Witness app.	16.00	48.00	110.00
5-Ideal Love & Romance; photo-c	6.50	19.50	45.00

IDEAL COMICS (1st Series) (Willie Comics No. 5 on)
Fall, 1944 - No. 4, Spring, 1946
Timely Comics (MgPC)

	Good	Fine	N-Mint
1-Super Rabbit in all	7.00	21.00	50.00
2	5.00	15.00	35.00
3,4	4.00	12.00	28.00

IDEAL LOVE & ROMANCE (See Ideal, A Classical Comic)

IDEAL ROMANCE (Formerly Tender Romance)
No. 3, April, 1954 - No. 8, Feb, 1955 (Diary Confessions No. 9 on)
Key Publications

3	3.00	9.00	21.00
4-8	1.50	4.50	10.00

I DREAM OF JEANNIE (TV)
April, 1965 - No. 2, Dec, 1966 (Photo-c)
Dell Publishing Co.

1,2	3.50	10.50	24.00

IF THE DEVIL WOULD TALK
1950; 1958 (32 pgs.; paper cover; in full color)
Roman Catholic Catechetical Guild/Impact Publ.

nn-(Scarce)-About secularism (20-30 copies known to exist); very low

distribution	50.00	150.00	350.00
1958 Edition-(Rare)-(Impact Publ.); art & script changed to meet			
church criticism of earlier edition; only 6 known copies exist			
	50.00	150.00	350.00
Black & White version of nn edition; small size; only 4 known copies			
exist	30.00	90.00	200.00

NOTE: The original edition of this book was printed and killed by the Guild's board of directors. It is believed that a very limited number of copies were distributed. The 1958 version was a complete bomb with very limited, if any, circulation. In 1979, 11 original, 4 1958 reprints, and 4 B&W's surfaced from the Guild's old files in St. Paul, Minnesota.

ILLUSTRATED GAGS (See Single Series No. 16)

ILLUSTRATED LIBRARY OF. . ., AN (See Classics Illustrated Giants)

ILLUSTRATED STORIES OF THE OPERAS
1943 (16 pgs.; B&W) (25 cents) (cover-B&W & red)
Baily (Bernard) Publ. Co.

nn-(Rare)-Faust (part-r in Cisco Kid #1)	33.00	100.00	230.00
nn-(Rare)-Aida	33.00	100.00	230.00
nn-(Rare)-Carmen; Baily-a	33.00	100.00	230.00
nn-(Rare)-Rigoleito	33.00	100.00	230.00

ILLUSTRATED STORY OF ROBIN HOOD & HIS MERRY MEN, THE
(See Classics Giveaways, 12/44)

ILLUSTRATED TARZAN BOOK, THE (See Tarzan Book)

I LOVED (Formerly Rulah; Colossal Features Magazine No. 33 on)
No. 28, July, 1949 - No. 32, Mar, 1950
Fox Features Syndicate

28	4.00	12.00	28.00
29-32	2.65	8.00	18.00

I LOVE LUCY COMICS (TV) (Also see The Lucy Show)
No. 535, Feb, 1954 - No. 35, Apr-June, 1962 (All photo-c)
Dell Publishing Co.

4-Color 535(#1)	14.00	42.00	100.00
4-Color 559 (5/54)(#2)	11.00	32.00	75.00
3 (8-10/54) - 5	7.00	21.00	50.00
6-10	6.00	18.00	42.00

	Good	Fine	N-Mint
11-20	5.50	16.50	38.00
21-35	4.50	14.00	32.00

I LOVE YOU
June, 1950 (One shot)
Fawcett Publications

1-Photo-c	5.50	16.50	38.00

I LOVE YOU (Formerly In Love)
No. 7, 9/55 - No. 121, 12/76; No. 122, 3/79 - No. 130, 5/80
Charlton Comics

7-Kirby-c, Powell-a	3.70	11.00	26.00
8-10	1.15	3.50	8.00
11-16,18-20	1.00	3.00	7.00
17-68 pg. Giant	1.30	4.00	9.00
21-25,27-50	.55	1.65	4.00
26-Torres-a	1.00	3.00	7.00
51-59	.35	1.10	2.20
60(1/66)-Elvis Presley drawn c/story	5.70	17.00	40.00
61-85		.60	1.20
86-130		.40	.80

I'M A COP
1954 - No. 3, 1954?
Magazine Enterprises

1(A-1 111)	5.50	16.50	38.00
2(A-1 126), 3(A-1 128)	2.85	8.50	20.00

NOTE: Powell c/a-1-3.

I'M DICKENS - HE'S FENSTER (TV)
May-July, 1963 - No. 2, Aug-Oct, 1963 (Photo-c)
Dell Publishing Co.

1,2	2.00	6.00	14.00

I MET A HANDSOME COWBOY (See 4-Color No. 324)

IMMORTAL DOCTOR FATE, THE
Jan, 1985 - No. 3, Mar, 1985 (Mini-series)
DC Comics

1-3: 1-Simonson c/a. 2-Giffen c/a(p)	.35	1.00	2.00

IMPACT
Mar-Apr, 1955 - No. 5, Nov-Dec, 1955
E. C. Comics

1	8.00	24.00	56.00
2	5.50	16.50	38.00
3-5: 4-Crandall-a	5.00	15.00	35.00

NOTE: Crandall a-1-4. Davis a-2-4. c-1-5. Evans a-1, 4, 5. Ingels a-in all. Kamen a-3. Krigstein a-1, 5. Orlando a-2, 5.

INCAL, THE
Nov, 1988 - No. 3, Jan, 1989 ($9.95, adults)
Epic Comics (Marvel)

1-3: Moebius-c/a; sexual content	1.70	5.00	10.00

INCREDIBLE HULK, THE (See Aurora, The Avengers #1, The Defenders #1, Marvel Coll. Item Classics, Marvel Comics Presents #26, Marvel Fanfare, Marvel Treas. Ed. & Rampaging Hulk)

INCREDIBLE HULK, THE
May, 1962 - No. 6, Mar, 1963; No. 102, Apr, 1968 - Present
Marvel Comics Group

1-Origin & 1st app.	135.00	405.00	950.00
2	50.00	150.00	350.00
3-Origin retold	37.00	110.00	260.00
4-6: 4-Brief origin retold. 6-Intro. Teen Brigade			
	30.00	90.00	210.00
102-(Formerly Tales to Astonish)-Origin retold	11.00	32.00	75.00
103-105: 105-1st Missing Link	5.00	15.00	35.00
106-108	3.15	9.50	22.00

NOTE: *Adkins* a-111-16i. *Austin* a(i)-350, 351, 353, 354; c-302i, 350i. *J. Buscema* c-202p. *Byrne* a-314p-319p; c-314-316, 318, 319, 359. *Colan* a-363. *Ditko* a-2, 6, 249. Annual 2r(3), 3r, 9p; c-2i, 6, 235, 249. *Everett* c-133i. *Golden* c-248, 251. *Kane* c(p)-193, 194, 196, 198. *Kirby* a-1-5, Special 2, 3p, Annual 5p; c-1-5, Annual 5. *McFarlane* a-330p-334p, 336p-339p, 340-343, 344p-346p; c-330p, 340p, 341-343, 344p, 345, 346p. *Miller* c-258p, 261, 264, 268. *Mooney* a-230p, 287i, 288i. *Powell* a-Special 3r(2). *Severin* a(i)-108-110, 131-33, 141-51, 153-55; c(i)-109, 110, 132, 142, 144-55. *Simonson* c-283, 364, 365. *Starlin* a-222p; c-217. *Staton* a(i)-187-89, 191-209. *Tuska* a-102i, 105i, 106i, 218p. *Williamson* a-310i; c-310i, 311i. *Wrightson* c-197.

INCREDIBLE HULK AND WOLVERINE, THE
Oct, 1986 (One shot, $2.50, color)

INCREDIBLE MR. LIMPET, THE (See Movie Classics)

INCREDIBLE SCIENCE FICTION (Formerly Weird Science-Fantasy)
No. 30, July-Aug, 1955 - No. 33, Jan-Feb, 1956
E. C. Comics

NOTE: *Davis* a-30, 32, 33; c-30-32. *Krigstein* a-in all. *Orlando* a-30, 32, 33("Judgement Day" reprint). *Wood* a-30, 31, 33; c-33.

INDIANA JONES (See Further Adventures of . . .)

INDIANA JONES AND THE LAST CRUSADE
1989 - No. 4, 1989 ($1.00, color, limited series)
Marvel Comics

INDIANA JONES AND THE TEMPLE OF DOOM
Sept, 1984 - No. 3, Nov, 1984
Marvel Comics Group

INDIAN BRAVES (Baffling Mysteries No. 5 on)
March, 1951 - No. 4, Sept, 1951
Ace Magazines

INDIAN CHIEF (White Eagle . . .) (Formerly The Chief)
No. 3, July-Sept, 1951 - No. 33, Jan-Mar, 1959 (All painted-c)
Dell Publishing Co.

INDIAN CHIEF (See March of Comics No. 94,110,127,140,159,170,187)

INDIAN FIGHTER, THE (See 4-Color No. 687)

INDIAN FIGHTER
May, 1950 - No. 11, Jan, 1952
Youthful Magazines

NOTE: *Walter Johnson* c-1, 3, 4, 6. *Wildey* a-2-4; c-2, 5.

INDIAN LEGENDS OF THE NIAGARA (See American Graphics)

INDIANS
Spring, 1950 - No. 17, Spring, 1953
Fiction House Magazines (Wings Publ. Co.)

INDIANS OF THE WILD WEST
Circa 1958? (no date) (Reprints)

The Incredible Hulk #180, © MEG

Indian Chief #22, © DELL

Indians #1, © FH

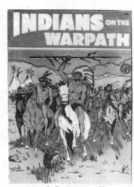
Indians On The Warpath. STJ

The Inferior Five #6. DC

Inside Crime #3. FOX

INDIANS OF THE WILD WEST (continued)
I. W. Enterprises

	Good	Fine	N-Mint
9-Kinstler-c; Whitman-a	.50	1.50	3.00

INDIANS ON THE WARPATH
No date (Late 40s, early 50s) (132 pages)
St. John Publishing Co.

nn-Matt Baker-c; contains St. John comics rebound. Many combinations possible	14.00	42.00	100.00

INDIAN TRIBES (See Famous Indian Tribes)

INDIAN WARRIORS (Formerly White Rider and Super Horse)
No. 7, June, 1951 - No. 11, 1952
Star Publications

	Good	Fine	N-Mint
7-White Rider & Superhorse continue; L.B. Cole-c	3.70	11.00	26.00
8-11: 11-L. B. Cole-c	2.65	8.00	18.00
3-D 1(12/53)-L. B. Cole-c	17.00	51.00	120.00
Accepted Reprint(nn)(inside cover shows White Rider & Superhorse #11)-R-/cover/#7; origin White Rider & . . . L. B. Cole-c	1.70	5.00	12.00
Accepted Reprint #8 (nd); L.B. Cole-c	1.70	5.00	12.00

INDOORS-OUTDOORS (See Wisco)

INDOOR SPORTS
nd (64 pgs.; 6x9''; B&W reprints; hardcover)
National Specials Co.

By Tad	3.50	10.50	24.00

INFERIOR FIVE, THE (Inferior 5 on No. 11,12) (See Showcase)
3-4/67 - No. 10, 9-10/68; No. 11, 8-9/72 - No. 12, 10-11/72
National Periodical Publications

1-Sekowsky-a(p)	1.70	5.00	12.00
2-Plastic Man app.; Sekowsky-a(p)	1.00	3.00	6.00
3-10: 10-Superman x-over	.85	2.50	5.00
11,12-Orlando c/a; both r-/Showcase #62,63	.85	2.50	5.00

INFINITY, INC. (See All-Star Squadron #25)
3/84 - No. 53, 8/88 ($1.25; Baxter paper; 36 pgs.)
DC Comics

1-Brainwave, Jr., Fury, The Huntress, Jade, Northwind, Nuklon, Obsidian, Power Girl, Silver Scarab & Star Spangled Kid begin	.60	1.75	3.50
2-5: 2-Dr. Midnite, G.A. Flash, W. Woman, Dr. Fate, Hourman, Gr. Lantern, Wildcat app. 5-Nudity panels	.35	1.10	2.20
6-10	.30	.95	1.90
11-13,38-49,51-53: 46,47-Millennium tie-ins	.25	.80	1.60
14-Todd McFarlane-a, 5/85	.75	2.20	4.40
15-37-McFarlane-a (20,23,24: 5 pgs. only; 33: 2 pgs.); 18-22-Crisis x-over. 21-Intro new Hourman & Dr. Midnight. 26-New Wildcat app. 31-Star-Spangled Kid becomes Skyman. 32-Green Fury becomes Green Flame. 33-Origin Obsidian	.45	1.30	2.60
50 ($2.50, 52 pgs.)	.40	1.25	2.50
Annual 1 (12/85)-Crisis x-over	.35	1.00	2.00
Annual 2 (1988, $2.00)	.35	1.00	2.00
Special 1 ('87, $1.50)	.25	.75	1.50

NOTE: **Kubert** r-4 **McFarlane** a-14-37p: c(p)-14, 15, 17-19, 22, 25, 26, 31-33, 37. **Newton** a-12p. 13p(last work 4/85) **Tuska** a-11p. JSA app. 3-10.

INFORMER, THE
April, 1954 - No. 5, Dec, 1954
Feature Television Productions

1-Sekowsky-a begins	4.00	12.00	28.00
2	2.65	8.00	18.00
3-5	2.00	6.00	14.00

IN HIS STEPS
1973, 1977 (39, 49 cents)
Spire Christian Comics (Fleming H. Revell Co.)

	Good	Fine	N-Mint
nn	.40	.80	

INHUMANOIDS, THE (TV)
Jan, 1987 - No. 4, July, 1987
Star Comics (Marvel)

1-4: Based on Hasbro toys	.50	1.00	

INHUMANS, THE (See Amazing Adventures, Fantastic Four #45, Marvel Graphic Novel & Thor #146)
Oct, 1975 - No. 12, Aug, 1977
Marvel Comics Group

1	.35	1.00	2.00
2-12: 9-Reprints	.60	1.20	

NOTE: **Buckler** c-2-4p, 5. **Gil Kane** a-5-7p; c-1p, 7p, 8p. **Kirby** a-9r. **Mooney** a-11i. **Perez** a-1-4p, 8p.

INKY & DINKY (See Felix's Nephews . . .)

IN LOVE (I Love You No. 7 on)
Aug-Sept, 1954 - No. 6, July, 1955 ('Adult Reading' on-c)
Mainline/Charlton No. 5 (5/55)-on

1-Simon & Kirby-a	8.00	24.00	56.00
2-S&K-a; book-length novel	3.70	11.00	26.00
3,4-S&K-a. 3-Last pre-code (12-1/54-55)	2.85	8.50	20.00
5-S&K-c only	1.70	5.00	12.00
6-No S&K-a	1.30	4.00	9.00

IN LOVE WITH JESUS
1952 (36 pages) (Giveaway)
Catechetical Educational Society

nn	2.00	6.00	14.00

INSANE
Feb, 1988 - No. 2? ($1.75, B&W)
Dark Horse Comics

1,2: 1-X-Men, Godzilla parodies. 2-Concrete	.30	.90	1.80

IN SEARCH OF THE CASTAWAYS (See Movie Comics)

INSIDE CRIME (Formerly My Intimate Affair)
No. 3, July, 1950 - No. 2, Sept, 1950
Fox Features Syndicate (Hero Books)

3-Wood-a, 10 pgs.; L. B. Cole-c	11.00	32.00	75.00
2(9/50)-Used in **SOTI**, pg. 182-3; r-/Spook #24	8.50	25.50	60.00
nn(no publ. listed, nd)	3.50	10.50	24.00

INSPECTOR, THE (Also see The Pink Panther)
July, 1974 - No. 19, Feb, 1978
Gold Key

1	.60	1.75	3.50
2-5	.30	.90	1.80
6-19: 11-Reprints	.50	1.00	

INSPECTOR WADE (See Feature Books No. 13, McKay)

INTERFACE
Dec, 1989 - Present ($1.95, color, printed on coated paper)
Epic Comics (Marvel)

1,2: Based on ESPers; painted-c/a	.35	1.00	2.00

INTERNATIONAL COMICS (. . . Crime Patrol No. 6)
Spring, 1947 - No. 5, Nov-Dec, 1947
E. C. Comics

1	34.00	100.00	235.00
2	25.00	75.00	175.00
3-5	22.00	65.00	154.00

INTERNATIONAL CRIME PATROL (Formerly International Comics No. 1-5; becomes Crime Patrol No. 7 on)
No. 6, Spring, 1948
E. C. Comics

	Good	Fine	N-Mint
INTERNATIONAL CRIME PATROL (cont.)			
6-Moon Girl app.	34.00	100.00	235.00

INTERSTATE THEATRES' FUN CLUB COMICS
Mid 1940's (10 cents on cover) (B&W cover) (Premium)
Interstate Theatres

Cover features MLJ characters looking at a copy of Top-Notch Comics, but contains an early Detective Comic on inside; many combinations possible

	Good	Fine	N-Mint
	5.35	16.00	24.00

IN THE DAYS OF THE MOB (Magazine)
Fall, 1971 (Black & White)
Hampshire Dist. Ltd. (National)

	Good	Fine	N-Mint
1-Kirby-a; has John Dillinger wanted poster inside	.70	2.00	4.00

IN THE PRESENCE OF MINE ENEMIES
1973 (35-49 cents)
Spire Christian Comics/Fleming H. Revell Co.

nn		.50	1.00

INTIMATE (Teen-Age Love No. 4 on)
December, 1957 - No. 3, May, 1958
Charlton Comics

1-3	1.00	3.00	7.00

INTIMATE CONFESSIONS (See Fox Giants)

INTIMATE CONFESSIONS
July-Aug, 1951 - No. 7, Aug, 1952; No. 8, Mar, 1953 (All painted-c)
Realistic Comics

	Good	Fine	N-Mint
1-Kinstler-c/a; c/Avon paperback 222	50.00	150.00	350.00
2	9.00	27.00	60.00
3-c/Avon paperback 250; Kinstler-c/a	12.00	36.00	80.00
4-c/Avon paperback 304; Kinstler-c	9.00	27.00	60.00
5	9.00	27.00	60.00
6-c/Avon paperback 120	9.00	27.00	60.00
7-Spanking panel	10.00	30.00	70.00
8-c/Avon paperback 375; Kinstler-a	9.00	27.00	60.00

INTIMATE CONFESSIONS
1964
I. W. Enterprises/Super Comics

I.W. Reprint #9,10	.70	2.00	4.00
Super Reprint #12,18	.70	2.00	4.00

INTIMATE LOVE
No. 5, 1950 - No. 28, Aug, 1954
Standard Comics

	Good	Fine	N-Mint
5	2.30	7.00	16.00
6-8-Severin/Elder-a	3.00	9.00	21.00
9	1.15	3.50	8.00
10-Jane Russell, Robert Mitchum photo-c	2.65	8.00	18.00
11-18,20,23,25,27,28	1.00	3.00	7.00
19,21,22,24,26-Toth-a	3.50	10.50	24.00

NOTE: Celardo a-8, 10. Colletta a-23. Moreira a-13(2). Photo-c-6, 7, 10, 12, 14, 15, 18-20, 24, 26, 27.

INTIMATE SECRETS OF ROMANCE
Sept. 1953 - No. 2, April, 1954
Star Publications

1,2-L. B. Cole-c	4.50	14.00	32.00

INTRIGUE
January, 1955
Quality Comics Group

1-Horror; Jack Cole reprint/Web of Evil	9.00	27.00	62.00

INVADERS, THE (TV)
Oct. 1967 - No. 4, Oct, 1968 (All have photo-c)
Gold Key

	Good	Fine	N-Mint
1-Spiegle-a in all	3.50	10.50	24.00
2-4	2.65	8.00	18.00

INVADERS, THE (Also see The Avengers No. 71)
August, 1975 - No. 40, May, 1979; No. 41, Sept, 1979
Marvel Comics Group

	Good	Fine	N-Mint
1-Captain America, Sub-Mariner & Human Torch begin	.70	2.00	4.00
2-10: 2-1st app. Mailbag & Brain-Drain. 3-Intro U-Man. 6-Liberty Legion app; intro/1st app. Union Jack. Two cover prices, 25 & 30 cents. 7-Intro Baron Blood; Human Torch origin retold. 9-Origin Baron Blood. 10-G.A. Capt. America-r	.60		1.20
11-19: 11-Origin Spitfire; intro The Blue Bullet. 14-1st app. The Crusaders. 16-Re-intro The Destroyer. 17-Intro Warrior Woman. 18-Re-intro The Destroyer w/new origin	.60		1.20
20-Reprints Sub-Mariner story/Motion Picture Funnies Weekly with color added & brief write-up about MPFW	.60		1.20
21-41: 21-r/Marvel Mystery #10. 22-New origin Toro. 24-r/Marvel Mystery #17. 28-Intro new Human Top & Golden Girl. 29-Intro Teutonic Knight. 34-Mighty Destroyer joins. 41-Double size	.60		1.20
Giant Size . . 1(6/75)-50 cents; origin; GA Sub-Mariner r-/Sub-Mariner 1; intro Master-Man	.25	.75	1.50
Annual 1(9/77)-Schomburg, Rico stories; Schomburg-c; Avengers app; re-intro The Shark & The Hyena	.25	.75	1.50

NOTE: Buckler a-5. Everett a-21r(1940). 24r. Annual 1r. Gil Kane c(p)-13, 17, 18, 20-27. Kirby c(p)-3-12, 14-16, 32, 33. Mooney a-5, 16, 22.

INVASION
Holiday, 1988-'89 - No 3, Jan, 1989 ($2.95, 84pgs, mini-series)
DC Comics

	Good	Fine	N-Mint
1-McFarlane/Russell-a	.60	1.75	3.50
2,3: 2-McFarlane/Russell-a. 3-Russell-i	.50	1.50	3.00

INVINCIBLE FOUR OF KUNGFU & NINJA
April, 1988 - Present? ($2.75, color)
Leung Publications

1	.45	1.40	2.75

INVISIBLE BOY (See Approved Comics)

INVISIBLE MAN, THE (See Superior Stories No. 1 & Supernatural Thrillers #2)

INVISIBLE SCARLET O'NEIL (Also see Famous Funnies #81 & Harvey Comics Hits 59)
Dec, 1950 - No. 3, April, 1951
Famous Funnies (Harvey)

	Good	Fine	N-Mint
1	9.50	28.00	65.00
2,3	6.50	19.50	45.00

IRON CORPORAL, THE (See Army War Heroes)
No. 23, Oct, 1985 - No. 25, Feb, 1986
Charlton Comics

23-25: Glanzman-a(r)		.40	.75

IRON FIST (Also see Marvel Premiere & Power Man)
Nov, 1975 - No. 15, Sept, 1977
Marvel Comics Group

	Good	Fine	N-Mint
1-McWilliams-a(i); Iron Man app.	1.85	5.50	11.00
2	1.00	3.00	6.00
3-5	.75	2.25	4.50
6-10: 8-Origin retold	.60	1.80	3.60
11-13: 12-Capt. America app.	.45	1.40	2.80
14-1st app. Saber Tooth	2.85	8.50	17.00
15-New X-Men app., Byrne-a	3.00	9.00	18.00
15 (35 cent edition)	4.15	12.50	25.00

NOTE: Adkins a-8p, 13i; c-8i. Byrne a-1-15p; c-8p, 15p. G. Kane c-4-6p.

IRON HORSE (TV)
March, 1967 - No. 2, June, 1967

The Invaders #4.   MEG

Invasion #1.   DC

Iron Fist #6.   MEG

Iron Man #2. MEG   Iron Man Special #1. MEG   I Spy #2. Three F Prod.

IRON HORSE (continued)
Dell Publishing Co.

	Good	Fine	N-Mint
1,2	1.15	3.50	8.00

IRON JAW (Also see The Barbarians)
Jan., 1975 - No. 4, July, 1975
Atlas/Seaboard Publ.

1-Adams-c; Sekowsky-a(p)	.25	.75	1.50
2-Adams-c		.50	1.00
3,4: 4-Origin		.30	.60

IRON MAN (Also see The Avengers #1, Marvel Collectors Item Classics, Marvel Double Feature, Marvel Fanfare & Tales of Suspense)
May, 1968 - Present
Marvel Comics Group

1-Origin	28.00	85.00	200.00
2	11.00	32.00	75.00
3	8.00	24.00	55.00
4,5	5.70	17.00	40.00
6-10	3.60	11.00	25.00
11-15: 15-Last 12 cent issue	2.85	8.50	20.00
16-20	1.70	5.00	12.00
21-40: 22-Death of Janice Cord. 27-Intro Fire Brand. 33-Intro Spymaster	1.50	4.50	9.00
41-46,48-50: 43-Intro The Guardsman. 46-The Guardsman dies. 50-Princess Python app.	1.15	3.50	7.00
47-Origin retold; Smith-a(p)	1.85	5.50	11.00
51-54	.90	2.70	5.50
55,56-Starlin-a; 55-Starlin-c	1.35	4.00	8.00
57-67,69,70: 65-Origin Dr. Spectrum	.85	2.50	5.00
68-Starlin-c; origin retold	.90	2.70	5.50
71-99: 76 r-/#9. 86-1st app. Blizzard. 87-Origin Blizzard	.70	2.00	4.00
100-Starlin-c	1.35	4.00	8.00
101-117: 101-1st app. new Crimson Dynamo. 110-Origin Jack of Hearts retold	.50	1.50	3.00
118-Byrne-a(p)	.85	2.50	5.00
119,120,123-128-Tony Stark recovers from alcohol problem	.60	1.75	3.50
121,122,129-149: 122-Origin	.35	1.00	2.00
150-Double size	.40	1.25	2.50
151-168: 152-New armor. 161-Moon Knight app. 167-Tony Stark alcohol problem starts again	.25	.75	1.50
169-New Iron Man (Jim Rhodes replaces Tony Stark)	1.25	3.75	7.50
170	.70	2.00	4.00
171	.35	1.00	2.00
172-199: 186-Intro Vibro. 191-Tony Stark new armor	.25	.75	1.50
200-Double size ($1.25)	.60	1.75	3.50
201-224: 213-Intro new Dominic Fortune	.25	.70	1.40
225-Double size	.85	2.50	5.00
226-243: 231-New armor. 233-Ant-Man app; intro new Iron Man. 243-Tony Stark looses use of legs	.25	.70	1.40
244-($1.50, 52pgs.)-New Armor makes him walk	.70	2.00	4.00
245-249,251-254: 247-Hulk x-over	.25	.70	1.40
250 ($1.50, 52 pgs.)	.25	.75	1.50
Giant Size 1('75)-Ditko-a(r)	.70	2.00	4.00
Special 1(8/70)-Everett-c	1.35	4.00	8.00
Special 2(11/71)	.85	2.50	5.00
Annual 3(6/76)-Man-Thing app.	.50	1.50	3.00
Annual 5(12/82), 6(11/83), 7(10/84)	.35	1.00	2.00
Annual 8(10/86)-X-Factor app.	.35	1.00	2.00
Annual 9(12/87)	.35	1.00	2.00
Annual 10(8/89, $2.00, 68 pgs.)-Atlantis Attacks x-over; P. Smith-a; Layton/Guice-a; Sub-Mariner app.	.50	1.50	3.00
King Size 4(8/77)-Newton-a(i)	.35	1.00	2.00

	Good	Fine	N-Mint
Graphic Novel: Crash (1988, $12.95, Adults, 76 pgs?)-Computer generated art & color; violence & nudity	2.15	6.50	12.95

NOTE: **Austin** c-105i, 109-111i, 151i. **Byrne** a-118p; c-109p. **Colan** a-Special 1p(3). **Craig** a-1i, 2-4, 5-13i, 14, 15-19i, 24p, 25p, 26-28i; c-2-4. **Ditko** a-160p. **Guice** a-233p-241p. **G. Kane** c(p)-52-54, 63, 67, 72-75, 77, 78, 88, 98. **Kirby** a-Special 1p; c-80p, 90, 92-95. **Mooney** a-40i, 47i. **Perez** c-103p. **Simonson** c-Annual 8. **B. Smith** a-229, 232p, 243i; c-229, 232. **P. Smith** a-159p, 245p. Annual 10p; c-159. **Starlin** a-53p, 55p, 56p; c-55p, 160, 163. **Tuska** a-5-13p, 15-23p, 24i, 32p, 38-46p, 48-54p, 57-61p, 63-69p, 70-72p, 78p, 86-92p, 95-106p. Annual 4p. **Wood** a-Special 1i.

IRON MAN & SUB-MARINER
April, 1968 (One Shot) (Pre-dates Iron Man #1)
Marvel Comics Group

1-Colan/Craig-a-Iron Man; Colan/Everett-c	10.00	30.00	70.00

IRON VIC (See Comics Revue No. 3)
1940; Aug, 1947 - No. 3, 1947
United Features Syndicate/St. John Publ. Co.

Single Series 22	14.00	42.00	100.00
2,3(St. John)	2.65	8.00	18.00

IRONWOLF (See Weird Worlds #8)
1986 ($2.00, one shot)
DC Comics

1	.35	1.00	2.00

ISIS (TV) (Also see Shazam)
Oct-Nov, 1976 - No. 8, Dec-Jan, 1977-78
National Periodical Publications/DC Comics

1-Wood inks		.40	.80
2-8: 5-Isis new look. 7-Origin		.25	.50

ISLAND AT THE TOP OF THE WORLD (See Walt Disney Showcase 27)

ISLAND OF DR. MOREAU, THE (Movie)
October, 1977 (52 pgs.)
Marvel Comics Group

1-Gil Kane-c		.50	1.00

I SPY (TV)
Aug, 1966 - No. 6, Sept, 1968 (Photo-c)
Gold Key

1-Bill Cosby, Robert Culp photo covers	4.30	13.00	30.00
2-6: 3,4-McWilliams-a	2.65	8.00	18.00

IS THIS TOMORROW?
1947 (One Shot) (3 editions) (52 pages)
Catechetical Guild

1-Theme of communists taking over the USA; (no price on cover) Used in **POP**, pg. 102	10.00	30.00	70.00
1(10 cents on cover)	14.00	42.00	100.00
1-Has blank circle with no price on cover	14.00	42.00	100.00
Black & White advance copy titled "Confidential"-(52 pgs.)-Contains script and art edited out of the color edition, including one page of extreme violence showing mob nailing a Cardinal to a door; (only two known copies)	43.00	130.00	300.00

NOTE: The original color version first sold for 10 cents. Since sales were good, it was later printed as a giveaway. Approximately four million in total were printed. The two black and white copies listed plus two other versions as well as a full color untrimmed version surfaced in 1979 from the Guild's old files in St. Paul, Minnesota.

IT! (See Astonishing Tales No. 21-24 & Supernatural Thrillers No. 1)

IT HAPPENS IN THE BEST FAMILIES
1920 (52 pages) (B&W Sundays)
Powers Photo Engraving Co.

By Briggs	8.00	24.00	56.00
Special Railroad Edition(30 cents)-r-/strips from 1914-1920	7.00	21.00	50.00

IT REALLY HAPPENED
1944 - No. 11, Oct, 1947

IT REALLY HAPPENED (continued)	Good	Fine	N-Mint
William H. Wise No. 1,2/Standard (Visual Editions)			
1-Kit Carson story	6.50	19.50	45.00
2	3.50	10.50	24.00
3,4,6,9	2.65	8.00	18.00
5-Lou Gehrig story	3.50	10.50	24.00
7-Teddy Roosevelt story	3.00	9.00	21.00
8-Story of Roy Rogers	5.50	16.50	38.00
10-Honus Wagner story	3.50	10.50	24.00
11-Baker-a	4.35	13.00	30.00

NOTE: *Guardineer a-7(2). 8(2). 11. Schomburg c-1-7. 9-11*

IT RHYMES WITH LUST (Also see Bold Stories & Candid Tales)
1950 (Digest size) (128 pages)
St. John Publishing Co.

(Rare)-Matt Baker & Ray Osrin-a	27.00	81.00	190.00

IT'S ABOUT TIME (TV)
January, 1967
Gold Key

1 (10195-701)-Photo-c	2.65	8.00	18.00

IT'S A DUCK'S LIFE
Feb. 1950 - No. 11, Feb, 1952
Marvel Comics/Atlas(MMC)

1-Buck Duck, Super Rabbit begin	5.70	17.00	40.00
2	2.85	8.50	20.00
3-11	1.70	5.00	12.00

IT'S FUN TO STAY ALIVE (Giveaway)
1948 (16 pgs.) (heavy stock paper)
National Automobile Dealers Association

Featuring: Bugs Bunny, The Berrys, Dixie Dugan, Elmer, Henry, Tim Tyler, Bruce Gentry, Abbie & Slats, Joe Jinks, The Toodles, & Cokey; all art copyright 1946-48 drawn especially for this book.

	11.50	34.00	80.00

IT'S GAMETIME
Sept-Oct, 1955 - No. 4, Mar-Apr, 1956
National Periodical Publications

1-(Scarce)-Infinity-c; Davy Crockett app. in puzzle			
	25.00	75.00	175.00
2-4(Scarce): 2-Dodo & The Frog	21.50	64.00	150.00

IT'S LOVE, LOVE, LOVE
November, 1957 - No. 2, Jan, 1958 (10 cents)
St. John Publishing Co.

1,2	2.15	6.50	15.00

IVANHOE (See Fawcett Movie Comics No. 20)

IVANHOE
July-Sept, 1963
Dell Publishing Co.

1 (12-373-309)	2.65	8.00	18.00

IWO JIMA (See Spectacular Features Magazine)

JACE PEARSON OF THE TEXAS RANGERS (Tales of the Texas Rangers 4-Color 396; ...'s Tales of ... #11-on)(See Western Roundup under Dell Giants)
No. 396, 5/52 - No. 1021, 8-10/59 (No #10) (All-Photo-c)
Dell Publishing Co.

4-Color 396 (#1)	5.50	16.50	38.00
2(5-7/53)	3.50	10.50	24.00
3-9(2-4/55)	3.50	10.50	24.00
4-Color 648(9/55)	3.50	10.50	24.00
11(11-2/55/56) - 14,17-20(6-8/58)	3.00	9.00	21.00
15,16-Toth-a	4.00	12.00	28.00
4-Color 961-Spiegle-a	3.50	10.50	24.00
4-Color 1021	3.00	9.00	21.00

JACK & JILL VISIT TOYTOWN WITH ELMER THE ELF
1949 (16 pgs.) (paper cover)

Butler Brothers (Toytown Stores Giveaway)	Good	Fine	N-Mint
nn	1.70	5.00	10.00

JACK ARMSTRONG (Radio)(See True Comics)
11/47 - No. 9, 9/48; No. 10, 3/49 - No. 13, Sept, 1949
Parents' Institute

1	11.00	32.00	75.00
2	5.50	16.50	38.00
3-5	4.30	13.00	30.00
6-13	3.50	10.50	24.00
12-Premium version(distr. in Chicago only); Free printed on upper right-c; no price (Rare)	10.00	30.00	70.00

JACK HUNTER
July, 1987 - No. 4? ($1.25, color)
Blackthorne Publishing

1-4		.60	1.25

JACKIE GLEASON (TV) (Also see The Honeymooners)
1948 - No. 2, 1948; Sept, 1955 - No. 5, Jan, 1956?
St. John Publishing Co.

1(1948)	33.00	100.00	230.00
2(1948)	21.50	64.00	150.00
1(1955)(TV)-Photo-c	22.00	65.00	154.00
2-5: 5-Exist?	16.00	48.00	110.00

JACKIE GLEASON AND THE HONEYMOONERS (TV)
June-July, 1956 - No. 12, Apr-May, 1958
National Periodical Publications

1	41.00	122.00	285.00
2	25.00	75.00	175.00
3-11	19.00	58.00	135.00
12 (Scarce)	23.00	70.00	165.00

JACKIE JOKERS (Also see Richie Rich & ...)
March, 1973 - No. 4, Sept, 1973
Harvey Publications

1-4: 2-President Nixon app.		.20	.40

JACKIE ROBINSON (Famous Plays of ...) (Also see Negro Heroes #2 & Picture News #4)
May, 1950 - No. 6, 1952 (Baseball hero) (All photo-c)
Fawcett Publications

nn	30.00	90.00	210.00
2	20.00	60.00	140.00
3-6	17.00	51.00	120.00

JACK IN THE BOX (Formerly Yellowjacket Comics No. 1-10)
(Cowboy Western Comics No. 17 on)
Feb, 1946; No. 11, Oct, 1946 - No. 16, Nov-Dec, 1947
Frank Comunale/Charlton Comics No. 11 on

1-Stitches, Marty Mouse & Nutsy McKrow	5.00	15.00	35.00
11-Yellowjacket	5.50	16.50	38.00
12,14,15	2.00	6.00	14.00
13-Wolverton-a	9.00	27.00	62.00
16-12pg. adapt. of Silas Marner; Kiefer-a	3.50	10.50	24.00

JACK OF HEARTS
Jan, 1984 - No. 4, April, 1984 (Mini-series)
Marvel Comics Group

1-4		.50	1.00

JACKPOT COMICS (Jolly Jingles No. 10 on)
Spring, 1941 - No. 9, Spring, 1943
MLJ Magazines

1-The Black Hood, Mr. Justice, Steel Sterling & Sgt. Boyle begin; Biro-c	117.00	295.00	700.00

It's Gametime #3. © DC

Jace Pearson Of The Texas Rangers #12. © DELL

Jackie Robinson #2. © FAW

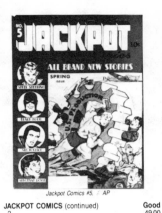

Jackpot Comics #5. : AP

Jeanie Comics #16. : MEG

Jeep Comics #2.   R.B. Leffingwell

JACKPOT COMICS (continued)	Good	Fine	N-Mint
2	49.00	148.00	345.00
3	38.00	115.00	270.00
4-Archie begins (on sale 12/41)-(Also see Pep Comics No. 22);			
Montana-c	114.00	342.00	800.00
5-Hitler-c	49.00	148.00	345.00
6-9: 6,7-Bondage-c	43.00	130.00	300.00

JACK Q FROST (See Unearthly Spectaculars)

JACK THE GIANT KILLER (See Movie Classics)

JACK THE GIANT KILLER (New Advs. of. . .)
Aug-Sept, 1953
Bimfort & Co.

V1#1-H. C. Kiefer-c/a	9.30	28.00	65.00

JACKY'S DIARY (See 4-Color No. 1091)

JADEMAN KUNG FU SPECIAL
1988 ($1.50, color, 64pgs.)
Jademan Comics

1	.25	.75	1.50

JAGUAR, THE (See The Adventures of   )

JAKE THRASH
1988 - No. 3, 1988 ($2.00, color)
Aircel Publishing

1-3	.35	1.00	2.00

JAMBOREE
Feb. 1946(no mo. given) - No. 3, April, 1946
Round Publishing Co.

1-Funny animal	6.00	18.00	42.00
2,3	4.30	13.00	30.00

JAMES BOND FOR YOUR EYES ONLY
Oct. 1981 - No. 2, Nov, 1981
Marvel Comics Group

1,2-Movie adapt.; r-/Marvel Super Spec. #19		.30	.60

JAMES BOND: LICENCE TO KILL (See Licence To Kill)

JAMES BOND: PERMISSION TO DIE
1989 - No. 3, 1990 ($3.95, color, mini-series, squarebound, 52 pgs.)
Eclipse Comics/ACME Press

1-3: Mike Grell-c/a/scripts	.70	2.00	4.00

JAM: SUPER COOL COLOR INJECTED TURBO ADVENTURE #1 FROM HELL!, THE
May, 1988 ($2.50, 44pgs. color)
Comico

1	.40	1.25	2.50

JANE ARDEN (See Feature Funnies & Pageant of Comics)
March, 1948 - No. 2, June, 1948
St. John (United Features Syndicate)

1-Newspaper reprints	9.30	28.00	65.00
2	5.50	16.50	38.00

JANN OF THE JUNGLE (Jungle Tales No. 1-7)
No. 8, Nov. 1955 - No. 17, June, 1957
Atlas Comics (CSI)

8(#1)	9.30	28.00	65.00
9,11-15	5.00	15.00	35.00
10-Williamson/Colleta-c	6.00	18.00	42.00
16,17-Williamson/Mayo-a(3), 5 pgs. each	8.50	25.50	60.00

NOTE: Everett c-15-17 Heck a-8, 15: 17 Shores a-8.

JASON & THE ARGONAUTS (See Movie Classics)

JAWS 2 (See Marvel Super Special. A)

JCP FEATURES
Feb, 1982-c; Dec, 1981-indicia ($2.00, One-shot, B&W)
J.C. Productions (Archie)

	Good	Fine	N-Mint
1-T.H.U.N.D.E.R. Agents; Black Hood by Morrow & Adams			
	.35	1.00	2.00

JEANIE COMICS (Cowgirl Romances No. 28) (Formerly Daring)
No. 13, April, 1947 - No. 27, Oct. 1949
Marvel Comics/Atlas(CPC)

13-Mitzi, Willie begin	6.50	19.50	45.00
14,15	4.00	12.00	28.00
16-Used in Love and Death by Legman; Kurtzman's "Hey Look"			
	5.70	17.00	40.00
17-19,22-Kurtzman's "Hey Look," 1-3 pgs. each			
	3.70	11.00	26.00
20,21,23-27	2.65	8.00	18.00

JEEP COMICS (Also see G.I. and Overseas Comics)
Winter, 1944 - No. 3, Mar-Apr, 1948
R. B. Leffingwell & Co.

1-Capt. Power, Criss Cross & Jeep & Peep (costumed) begin			
	9.30	28.00	65.00
2	5.50	16.50	40.00
3-L. B. Cole-c	6.50	19.50	45.00
1-29(Giveaway)-Strip reprints in all; Tarzan, Flash Gordon, Blondie, The Nebbs, Little Iodine, Red Ryder, Don Winslow, The Phantom, Johnny Hazard, Katzenjammer Kids; distr. to U.S. Armed Forces in mid 1940's	3.35	10.00	20.00

NOTE: L. B. Cole c-3.

JEFF JORDAN, U.S. AGENT
Dec, 1947 - Jan, 1948
D. S. Publishing Co.

1	5.00	15.00	35.00

JEMM, SON OF SATURN
9/84 - No. 12, 8/85 (12 part maxi-series; mando paper)
DC Comics

1-12: Colan p-all; c-1-5p,7-12p: 3-Origin		.50	1.00

JERRY DRUMMER (Formerly Soldier & Marine V2No.9)
No. 10, Apr, 1957 - No. 12, Oct. 1957
Charlton Comics

V2#10, V3#11,12	1.30	4.00	9.00

JERRY IGER'S CLASSIC SHEENA (Also see Sheena 3-D Special)
April, 1985 (One-shot)
Blackthorne Publishing

1	.25	.75	1.50

JERRY IGER'S FAMOUS FEATURES
July, 1984 (One-shot)
Pacific Comics

1-Unpub. Flamingo & Wonder Boy by Baker	.25	.75	1.50

JERRY IGER'S GOLDEN FEATURES
1986 - No. 7? ($2.00, B&W) (All reprints)
Blackthorne Publishing

1-7: 2-Wonder Boy by Baker. 3-South Sea Girl & Lucky Wings by Iger; Phantom Lady. 4-Feiffer/Kirby-r	.35	1.00	2.00

JERRY LEWIS (See Adventures of   )

JESSE JAMES (See 4-Color No. 757 & The Legend of   )

JESSE JAMES (See Badmen of the West & Blazing Sixguns)
Aug., 1950 - No. 29, Aug-Sept, 1956
Avon Periodicals

1-Kubert Alabam r-/Cowpuncher #1	11.00	33.00	76.00
2-Kubert-a(3)	8.50	25.50	60.00
3-Kubert Alabam r-/Cowpuncher #2	7.00	21.00	50.00

JESSE JAMES (continued)	Good	Fine	N-Mint
4,9,10-No Kubert	2.85	8.50	20.00
5,6-Kubert Jesse James-a(3); one pg. Wood-a, #5			
	7.00	21.00	50.00
7-Kubert Jesse James-a(2)	6.00	18.00	42.00
8-Kinstler-a(3)	4.00	12.00	28.00
11-14 (Exist?)	2.15	6.50	15.00
15-Kinstler r-/#3	2.15	6.50	15.00
16-Kinstler r-/#3 & Sheriff Bob Dixon's Chuck Wagon #1 with name			
changed to Sheriff Tom Wilson	2.65	8.00	18.00
17-19,21: 17-Jesse James r-/#4; Kinstler-c idea from Kubert splash in			
#6. 18-Kubert Jesse James r-/#5. 19-Kubert Jesse James-r. 21-Two			
Jesse James r-/#4, Kinstler r-/#4	1.70	5.00	12.00
20-Williamson/Frazetta-a; r-Chief Vic. Apache Massacre; Kubert			
Jesse James r-/#6	8.50	25.50	60.00
22,23-No Kubert	1.60	4.80	11.00
24-New McCarty strip by Kinstler plus Kinstler r-/#9			
	1.60	4.80	11.00
25-New McCarty Jesse James strip by Kinstler; Kinstler J. James r-/			
#7,9	1.60	4.80	11.00
26,27-New McCarty J. James strip plus a Kinstler/McCann Jesse			
James-r	1.60	4.80	11.00
28,29: 28-Reprints most of Red Mountain, Featuring Quantrells			
Raiders	1.60	4.80	11.00
Annual(nn; 1952; 25 cents)-''...Brings Six-Gun Justice to the West''			
(100 pgs.)-3 earlier issues rebound; Kubert, Kinstler-a(3)			
	17.00	51.00	120.00

NOTE: Mostly reprints #10 on. *Fawcette* c-1, 2. **Kinstler** a-3, 4, 7-9, 15r, 16r(2), 21-27; c-3, 4, 9, 17, 18, 20-27. Painted c-5, 6.

JESSE JAMES
July, 1953
Realistic Publications

nn-Reprints Avon's #1, same cover, colors different			
	5.00	15.00	35.00

JEST (Kayo No. 12) (Formerly Snap)
No. 10, 1944; No. 11, 1944
Harry 'A' Chesler

10-Johnny Rebel & Yankee Boy app. in text	5.00	15.00	35.00
11-Little Nemo in Adventure Land	5.50	16.50	38.00

JESTER
No. 10, 1945
Harry 'A' Chesler

10	4.50	14.00	32.00

JESUS
1979 (49 cents)
Spire Christian Comics (Fleming H. Revell Co.)

nn		.40	.80

JET (See Jet Powers)
JET ACES
1952 - No. 4, 1953
Fiction House Magazines

1	5.00	15.00	35.00
2	3.50	10.50	24.00
3,4	2.65	8.00	18.00

JET DREAM (...& Her Stuntgirl Counterspies)
June, 1968
Gold Key

1	1.70	5.00	12.00

JET FIGHTERS (Korean War)
No. 5, Nov, 1952 - No. 7, Mar, 1953
Standard Magazines

5,7-Toth-a	5.00	15.00	35.00

	Good	Fine	N-Mint
6-Celardo-a	1.85	5.50	13.00

JET POWERS (American Air Forces No. 5 on)
1950 - No. 4, 1951
Magazine Enterprises

1(A-1 30)-Powell-c/a begins	16.00	48.00	110.00
2(A-1 32)	11.50	34.00	80.00
3(A-1 35)-Williamson/Evans-a	21.50	64.00	150.00
4(A-1 38)-Williamson/Wood-a: ''The Rain of Sleep'' drug story			
	21.50	64.00	150.00
I.W. Reprint 1,2(1963)-r-/#1,2	1.70	5.00	12.00

JET PUP (See 3-D Features)

JETSONS, THE (TV)(See March of Comics 276,330,348, Spotlight 3)
Jan, 1963 - No. 36, Oct, 1970 (Hanna-Barbera)
Gold Key

1	8.00	24.00	56.00
2	4.50	14.00	32.00
3-10	3.15	9.50	22.00
11-20	2.65	8.00	18.00
21-36	2.30	7.00	16.00

JETSONS, THE (TV) (Hanna-Barbera)
Nov, 1970 - No. 20, Dec, 1973
Charlton Comics

1	3.70	11.00	26.00
2	2.15	6.50	15.00
3-10	1.60	4.80	11.00
11-20	1.15	3.50	8.00

JETTA OF THE 21ST CENTURY
No. 5, Dec, 1952 - No. 7, Apr, 1953 (Teen-age Archie type)
Standard Comics

5	6.50	19.50	45.00
6,7	3.70	11.00	26.00

JEZEBEL JADE (Hanna-Barbara)
Oct, 1988 - No. 3, Dec, 1988 ($2.00, color, mini-series)
Comico

1-3: Jonny Quest spin-off	.35	1.00	2.00

JIGGS & MAGGIE (See 4-Color No. 18)

JIGGS & MAGGIE
No. 11, 1949(Aug.) - No. 21, 2/53; No. 22, 4/53 - No. 27, 2-3/54
Standard Comics/Harvey Publications No. 22 on

11	6.50	19.50	45.00
12-15,17-21	3.50	10.50	24.00
16-Wood text illos.	4.30	13.00	30.00
22-25,27: 22-24-Little Dot app.	2.30	7.00	16.00
26-Four pgs. partially in 3-D	9.50	28.00	65.00

NOTE: Sunday page reprints by **McManus** loosely blended into story continuity. Based on Bringing Up Father strip. Advertised on covers as 'All New.'

JIGSAW (Big Hero Adventures)
Sept, 1966 - No. 2, Dec, 1966 (36 pgs.)
Harvey Publications (Funday Funnies)

1-Origin; Crandall-a, 5pgs.	.85	2.50	5.00
2-Man From S.R.A.M.	.50	1.50	3.00

JIGSAW OF DOOM (See Complete Mystery No. 2)

JIM BOWIE (Formerly Danger; Black Jack No. 20 on)
No. 15, 1955? - No. 19, April, 1957
Charlton Comics

15	2.65	8.00	18.00
16-19	1.50	4.50	10.00

JIM BOWIE (See 4-Color No. 893,993, & Western Tales)

Jesse James #26. AVON

Jet Powers #1. ME

Jigsaw #1. HARV

Jimmy Wakely #6. DC

Jingle Jangle Comics #42. EAS

Joe Louis #2. FAW

JIM DANDY
May, 1956 - No. 3, Sept, 1956 (Charles Biro)
Dandy Magazine (Lev Gleason)

	Good	Fine	N-Mint
1	2.85	8.50	20.00
2,3	1.50	4.50	10.00

JIM HARDY (Also see Sparkler & Treasury of Comics No. 2&5)
1939; 1942; 1947 - No. 2, 1947
United Features Syndicate/Spotlight Publ.

Single Series 6 ('39)	20.00	60.00	140.00
Single Series 27('42)	14.00	42.00	100.00
1('47)-Spotlight Publ.	5.50	16.50	38.00
2	2.85	8.50	20.00

JIM HARDY
1944 (132 pages, 25 cents) (Tip Top, Sparkler-r)
Spotlight/United Features Syndicate

(1944)-Origin Mirror Man; Triple Terror app.	20.00	60.00	140.00

JIMINY CRICKET (See 4-Color No. 701,795,897,989, Mickey Mouse Mag. V5/3 & Walt Disney Showcase #37)

JIMMY (James Swinnerton)
1905 (10x15'') (40 pages in color)
N. Y. American & Journal

nn	18.00	54.00	125.00

JIMMY DURANTE (See A-1 Comics No. 18,20)

JIMMY OLSEN (See Superman's Pal   )

JIMMY WAKELY (Cowboy movie star)
Sept-Oct. 1949 - No. 18, July-Aug, 1952 (1-13: 52pgs.)
National Periodical Publications

1-Photo-c. 52pgs. begin; Alex Toth-a; Kit Colby Girl Sheriff begins	32.00	95.00	225.00
2-Toth-a	22.00	65.00	154.00
3,6,7-Frazetta-a in all, 3 pgs. each; Toth-a in all. 7-Last photo-c?	23.50	70.00	165.00
4-Frazetta-a. 3pgs.; Kurtzman ''Pot-Shot Pete,'' 1pg; Toth-a	23.50	70.00	165.00
5,8-15,18-Toth-a; 12,14-Kubert-a. 3 & 2 pgs.	17.00	51.00	120.00
16,17	12.00	36.00	84.00

JIM RAY'S AVIATION SKETCH BOOK
Feb. 1946 - No. 2. May-June, 1946
Vital Publishers

1,2-Picture stories about planes and pilots	12.00	36.00	84.00

JIM SOLAR (See Wisco/Klarer)

JINGLE BELLS (See March of Comics No. 65)

JINGLE BELLS CHRISTMAS BOOK
1971 (20 pgs.; B&W inside; slick cover)
Montgomery Ward (Giveaway)

nn		.40	.80

JINGLE DINGLE CHRISTMAS STOCKING COMICS
V2No.1. 1951 (no date listed) (100 pgs.; giant-size)(25 cents)
Stanhall Publications (Publ.-annually)

V2#1-Foodini & Pinhead, Silly Pilly plus games & puzzles	6.50	19.50	45.00

JINGLE JANGLE COMICS (Also see Puzzle Fun)
Feb. 1942 - No. 42, Dec. 1949
Eastern Color Printing Co.

1-Pie-Face Prince of Old Pretzleburg, & Jingle Jangle Tales by George Carlson, Hortense, & Benny Bear begin	22.00	65.00	154.00
2,3-No Pie-Face Prince	10.00	30.00	70.00
4-Pie-Face Prince cover	10.00	30.00	70.00
5	8.50	25.50	60.00

	Good	Fine	N-Mint
6-10: 8-No Pie-Face Prince	8.00	24.00	56.00
11-15	5.00	15.00	35.00
16-30: 17,18-No Pie-Face Prince. 30-XMas-c	3.70	11.00	26.00
31-42: 36,42-Xmas-c	2.65	8.00	18.00

NOTE: **George Carlson** a-(2) in all except No. 2, 3, 8, 17, 18; c-1-6. **Carlson** 1 pg. puzzles in 9, 10, 12-15, 18, 20. **Carlson** illustrated a series of Uncle Wiggily books in 1930's.

JING PALS
Feb. 1946 - No. 4, Aug?, 1946 (Funny animal)
Victory Publishing Corporation

1-Wishing Willie, Puggy Panda & Johnny Rabbit begin	5.50	16.50	38.00
2-4	3.00	9.00	21.00

JINKS, PIXIE, AND DIXIE (See Whitman Comic. . .)
1965 (Giveaway) (Hanna-Barbera)
Florida Power & Light

nn	.50	1.50	3.00

JOAN OF ARC (See A-1 Comics No. 21 & Ideal a Classical Comic)

JOAN OF ARC
No date (28 pages)
Catechetical Guild (Topix) (Giveaway)

nn	7.00	21.00	50.00

NOTE: Unpublished version exists which came from the Guild's files.

JOE COLLEGE
Fall, 1949 - No. 2, Winter, 1950
Hillman Periodicals

1,2-Powell-a; 1-Briefer-a	3.50	10.50	24.00

JOE JINKS (See Single Series No. 12)

JOE LOUIS (See Fight Comics 2, Picture News 6 & True Comics 5)
Sept, 1950 - No. 2, Nov, 1950 (Photo-c) (Boxing champ)
Fawcett Publications

1-Photo-c; life story	24.00	73.00	170.00
2	17.00	51.00	120.00

JOE PALOOKA
1933 (B&W daily strip reprints) (52 pages)
Cupples & Leon Co.

nn-(Scarce)-by Fisher	47.00	140.00	330.00

JOE PALOOKA (1st Series)(Also see Big Shot. Columbia Comics & Feature Funnies)
1942 - No. 4, 1944
Columbia Comic Corp. (Publication Enterprises)

1-1st to portray American president; gov't permission required	30.00	90.00	210.00
2 (1943)-Hitler-c	17.00	51.00	120.00
3,4	12.00	36.00	84.00

JOE PALOOKA (2nd Series) (Battle Adv. #68-74;   . Advs. #75,77-81,83-85,87; Champ of the Comics #76,82,86,89-93) (See All-New)
Nov, 1945 - No. 118, Mar, 1961
Harvey Publications

1	20.00	60.00	140.00
2	10.00	30.00	70.00
3,4,6	6.50	19.50	45.00
5-Boy Explorers by S&K (7-8/46)	9.50	28.00	65.00
7-1st Powell Flyin' Fool, ends #25	5.70	17.00	40.00
8-10	5.00	15.00	35.00
11-14,16-20: 19-Freedom Train-c	4.00	12.00	28.00
15-Origin Humphrey; Super heroine Atoma app. by Powell	5.00	15.00	35.00
21-30: 30-Nude female painting	3.00	9.00	21.00
31-61: 35-1st app. Little Max? 44-Joe Palooka marries Ann Howe			

JOE PALOOKA (continued)	Good	Fine	N-Mint
	2.30	7.00	16.00
62-S&K Boy Explorers-r	3.00	9.00	21.00
63-80: 66,67-'commie' torture story	1.70	5.00	12.00
81-99,101-115	1.50	4.50	10.00
100	1.75	5.25	12.00
116-S&K Boy Explorers (r) (Giant, '60)	2.85	8.50	20.00
117,118-Giants	2.65	8.00	18.00
Body Building Instruction Book (1958 Sports Toy giveaway, 16 pgs. 5¼x7'')-Origin	5.00	15.00	35.00
Fights His Way Back (1945 Giveaway, 24 pgs.) Family Comics	14.00	42.00	100.00
in Hi There! (1949 Red Cross giveaway, 12 pgs., 4¾x6'')	5.00	15.00	35.00
in It's All in the Family (1945 Red Cross giveaway, 16 pgs., regular size)	6.50	19.50	45.00
Visits the Lost City (1945)(One Shot)(nn)(50 cents)-164 page continuous story strip reprint. Has biography & photo of Ham Fisher; possibly the single longest comic book story published (159 pgs.?)	55.00	165.00	385.00

NOTE: *Nostrand/Powell* a-73. *Powell* a-7, 8, 10, 12, 14, 17, 19, 26-45, 47-53, 70, 73 at least. Black Cat text stories #8, 12, 13, 19. Bondage c-50.

JOE YANK
No. 5, March, 1952 - No. 16, 1954
Standard Comics (Visual Editions)

5-Celardo, Tuska-a	2.15	6.50	15.00
6-Toth, Severin/Elder-a	4.00	12.00	28.00
7	1.30	4.00	9.00
8-Toth-c	2.65	8.00	18.00
9-16: 12-Andru-a	1.00	3.00	7.00

JOHN BOLTON'S HALLS OF HORROR
June, 1985 - No. 2, June, 1985 ($1.75 cover, color)
Eclipse Comics

1,2-British-r; Bolton c/a	.30	.90	1.80

JOHN CARTER OF MARS (See 4-Color No. 375,437,488, The Funnies, Tarzan #207 & Weird Worlds)

JOHN CARTER OF MARS
April, 1964 - No. 3, Oct., 1964
Gold Key

1(10104-404)-Reprints 4-Color 375; Jesse Marsh-a	2.85	8.50	20.00
2(407), 3(410)-Reprints 4-Color 437 & 488; Marsh-a	2.30	7.00	16.00

JOHN CARTER OF MARS
1970 (72 pgs.; paper cover; 10½x16½''; B&W)
House of Greystoke

1941-42 Sunday strip reprints; John Coleman Burroughs-a	2.65	8.00	18.00

JOHN CARTER, WARLORD OF MARS
June, 1977 - No. 28, Oct., 1979
Marvel Comics Group

1-Origin by Gil Kane		.50	1.00
2-10-Last Kane issue		.30	.60
11-17,19-28: 11-Origin Dejah Thoris		.25	.50
18-Miller-a(p)	.35	1.00	2.00
Annual 1(10/77), 2(9/78), 3(10/79)		.40	.80

NOTE: *Austin* c-24i. *Gil Kane* a-1-10p; c-1p, 2p, 3, 4-9p, 10, 15p. Annual 1p. *Layton* a-17i. *Miller* c-25, 26p. *Nebres* a-2-4i, 8-16i; c(i)-6-9, 11-22, 25. Annual 1. *Perez* c-24p. *Simonson* a-15p. *Sutton* a-7i.

JOHN F. KENNEDY, CHAMPION OF FREEDOM
1964 (no month) (25 cents)
Worden & Childs

nn-Photo-c	3.50	10.50	24.00

JOHN F. KENNEDY LIFE STORY
Aug.-Oct., 1964; Nov., 1965; June, 1966 (12 cents)
Dell Publishing Co.

	Good	Fine	N-Mint
12-378-410	2.30	7.00	16.00
12-378-511 (reprint, 11/65)	1.70	5.00	12.00
12-378-606 (reprint, 6/66)	1.30	4.00	9.00

JOHN FORCE (See Magic Agent)

JOHN HIX SCRAP BOOK, THE
Late 1930's (no date) (68 pgs.; reg. size; 10 cents)
Eastern Color Printing Co. (McNaught Synd.)

1-Strange As It Seems (resembles Single Series books)	12.00	36.00	84.00
2-Strange As It Seems	10.00	30.00	70.00

JOHN LAW DETECTIVE (See Smash Comics #3)
April, 1983 ($1.50, color, Baxter paper)
Eclipse Comics

1-Three Eisner stories originally drawn in 1948 for the never publ- lished John Law No. 1; original cover pencilled in 1948 & inked in 1982 by Eisner	.35	1.00	2.00

JOHNNY APPLESEED (See Story Hour Series)

JOHNNY CASH (See Hello, I'm ___)

JOHNNY DANGER
1950
Toby Press

1-Photo-c; Sparling-a	7.00	21.00	50.00

JOHNNY DANGER PRIVATE DETECTIVE
1954 (Reprinted in Danger No. 11 (Super))
Toby Press

1-Opium den story	5.50	16.50	38.00

JOHNNY DYNAMITE (Formerly Dynamite No. 1-9)
No. 10, 6/55 - No. 12, 10/55 (Foreign Intrigues No. 13 on)
Charlton Comics

10-12	2.30	7.00	16.00

JOHNNY HAZARD
No. 5, Aug., 1948 - No. 8, May, 1949; No. 35, date?
Best Books (Standard Comics) (King Features)

5-Strip reprints by Frank Robbins	8.00	24.00	56.00
6,8-Strip reprints by Frank Robbins	5.50	16.50	38.00
7-New art, not Robbins	4.00	12.00	28.00
35	4.00	12.00	28.00

JOHNNY JASON (. . .Teen Reporter)
Feb-Apr., 1962 - No. 2, June-Aug., 1962
Dell Publishing Co.

4-Color 1302, 2(01380-208)	1.15	3.50	8.00

JOHNNY JINGLE'S LUCKY DAY
1956 (16 pgs.; 7¼x5-1/8'') (Giveaway) (Disney)
American Dairy Association

nn	2.35	7.00	14.00

JOHNNY LAW, SKY RANGER
Apr., 1955 - No. 3, Aug., 1955; No. 4, Nov., 1955
Good Comics (Lev Gleason)

1-Edmond Good-c/a	3.50	10.50	24.00
2-4	2.00	6.00	14.00

JOHNNY MACK BROWN (TV western star; see Western Roundup under Dell Giants)
No. 269, Mar, 1950 - No. 963, Feb, 1959 (All Photo-c)
Dell Publishing Co.

4-Color 269(3/50, 52pgs.)-J. Mack Brown & his horse Rebel begin;

Joe Palooka #62, © HARV

EDGAR RICE BURROUGHS
John Carter Of Mars #1 (G.K.), © ERB

Johnny Law, Sky Ranger #1, © LEV

216

John Wayne Adventure Comics #9. TOBY   The Joker #2. DC   Joker Comics #3. MEG

JOHNNY MACK BROWN (continued)	Good	Fine	N-Mint
photo front/back-c begin; Marsh-a begins, ends #9	12.00	36.00	84.00
2(10-12/50, 52pgs.)	6.50	19.50	45.00
3(1-3/51, 52pgs.)	4.30	13.00	30.00
4-10 (9-11/52)(36pgs.)	3.50	10.50	24.00
4-Color 455,493,541,584,618	3.50	10.50	24.00
4-Color 645,685,722,776,834,963	3.50	10.50	24.00
4-Color 922-Manning-a	4.00	12.00	28.00

JOHNNY NEMO
Sept, 1985 - No. 3, Feb, 1986 (Mini-series)
Eclipse Comics

1,2 ($1.75 cover)	.30	.90	1.75
3 ($2.00 cover)	.35	1.00	2.00

JOHNNY RINGO (See 4-Color No. 1142)

JOHNNY STARBOARD (See Wisco)

JOHNNY THUNDER (Also see World's Best/Finest Comics)
Feb-Mar, 1973 - No. 3, July-Aug, 1973
National Periodical Publications

1-Johnny Thunder & Nighthawk-r begin	.25	.75	1.50
2,3: 2-Trigger Twins app.		.50	1.00

NOTE: *Drucker a-2r, 3r. G. Kane a-2r, 3r. Toth a-1r, 3r; c-1r, 3r. Also see All-American, All-Star Western, Flash Comics, Western Comics, World's Best & World's Finest.*

JOHN PAUL JONES (See Four Color No. 1007)

JOHN STEED & EMMA PEEL (See The Avengers. Gold Key series)

JOHN STEELE SECRET AGENT (Also see Freedom Agent)
December, 1964 (Freedom Agent)
Gold Key

1	1.50	4.50	10.00

JOHN WAYNE ADVENTURE COMICS (Movie star; See Big Tex, Oxydol-Dreft, Tim McCoy & With The Marines. . .#1)
Winter, 1949 - No. 31, May, 1955 (Photo-c: 1-12,17,25-on)
Toby Press

1 (36pgs.)-Photo-c begin	41.00	122.00	285.00
2 (36pgs.)-Williamson/Frazetta-a(2) (one r-/Billy the Kid #1), 6 & 2 pgs; photo back-c	41.00	125.00	290.00
3 (36pgs.)-Williamson/Frazetta-a(2), 16 pgs. total; photo back-c	41.00	125.00	290.00
4 (52pgs.)-Williamson/Frazetta-a(2), 16 pgs total	41.00	125.00	290.00
5 (52pgs.)-Kurtzman-a-(Alfred "L" Newman in Potshot Pete)	28.50	85.00	200.00
6 (52pgs.)-Williamson/Frazetta-a, 10 pgs; Kurtzman a-'Pot-Shot Pete,' 5pgs.; & "Genius Jones." 1 pg.	39.00	120.00	275.00
7 (52pgs.)-Williamson/Frazetta-a, 10 pgs.	32.00	95.00	225.00
8 (36pgs.)-Williamson/Frazetta-a(2), 12 & 9 pgs.	39.00	120.00	275.00
9-11: Photo western-c	20.00	60.00	140.00
12-Photo war-c; Kurtzman-a, 2pgs. "Genius"	21.00	62.00	145.00
13-15: 13-Line-drawn-c begin, end #24	16.00	48.00	110.00
16-Williamson/Frazetta r-/Billy the Kid #1	22.00	65.00	155.00
17-Photo-c	20.00	60.00	140.00
18-Williamson/Frazetta-a r-/#4 & 8, 19 pgs.	27.00	81.00	190.00
19-24: 23-Evans-a?	15.00	45.00	105.00
25-Photo-c return; end #31; Williamson/Frazetta-a r-/Billy the Kid #3	27.00	81.00	190.00
26-28,30-Photo-c	18.00	54.00	125.00
29,31-Williamson/Frazetta-a in each, r-/#4,2	25.00	75.00	175.00

NOTE: *Williamsonish art in later issues by Gerald McCann.*

JO-JO COMICS (. . .Congo King #7-29; My Desire #30 on)
(Also see Fantastic Fears and Jungle Jo)
1945 - No. 29, July, 1949 (two No.7's; no No. 13)

Fox Feature Syndicate	Good	Fine	N-Mint
nn(1945)-Funny animal, humor	5.50	16.50	38.00
2(Sum,'46)-6: Funny animal; 2-Ten pg. Electro story	2.85	8.50	20.00
7(7/47)-Jo-Jo, Congo King begins	27.00	81.00	190.00
7(No.8) (9/47)	21.00	62.00	145.00
8-10(No.9-11): 8-Tanee begins	17.00	51.00	120.00
11,12(No.12,13),14,16	14.00	42.00	100.00
15-Cited by Dr. Wertham in 5/47 Saturday Review of Literature	16.00	48.00	110.00
17-Kamen bondage-c	16.00	48.00	110.00
18-20	14.00	42.00	100.00
21-29	13.00	40.00	90.00

NOTE: *Many bondage-c/a by Baker/Kamen/Feldstein/Good. No. 7's have Princesses Gwenna. Geesa. Yolda. & Safra before settling down on Tanee.*

JO-JOY (Adventures of. . .)
1945 - 1953 (Christmas gift comic)
W. T. Grant Dept. Stores

1945-53 issues	2.00	6.00	14.00

JOKEBOOK COMICS DIGEST ANNUAL (. . .Mag. No. 5 on)
10/77 - No. 13, 10/83 (Digest Size)
Archie Publications

1(10/77)-Reprints; Adams-a		.60	1.20
2(4/78)-13		.60	1.20

JOKER, THE (See Batman, Batman: The Killing Joke, Brave & the Bold, Detective & Justice League Annual #2)
May, 1975 - No. 9, Sept-Oct, 1976
National Periodical Publications

1-Two-Face app.	2.85	8.50	20.00
2,3	1.70	5.00	12.00
4-6	1.50	4.50	10.00
7,8	1.15	3.50	8.00
9	1.30	4.00	9.00

JOKER COMICS (Adventures Into Terror No. 43 on)
April, 1942 - No. 42, August, 1950
Timely/Marvel Comics No. 36 on (TCI/CDS)

1-(Rare)-1st app. Powerhouse Pepper by Wolverton; Stuporman app. from Daring	78.00	235.00	550.00
2-Wolverton-a continued; 1st app. Tessie the Typist	33.00	100.00	230.00
3-5-Wolverton-a	23.00	70.00	160.00
6-10-Wolverton-a	16.00	48.00	110.00
11-20-Wolverton-a	13.00	40.00	90.00
21,22,24-27,29,30-Wolverton cont'd. & Kurtzman's "Hey Look" in #24-27	10.00	30.00	70.00
23-1st "Hey Look" by Kurtzman; Wolverton-a	12.00	36.00	84.00
28,32,34,37-41	2.00	6.00	14.00
31-Last Powerhouse Pepper; not in #28	8.00	24.00	56.00
33,35,36-Kurtzman's "Hey Look"	3.15	9.50	22.00
42-Only app. 'Patty Pinup,' a clone of Millie the Model	2.30	7.00	16.00

JOLLY CHRISTMAS, A (See March of Comics No. 269)

JOLLY CHRISTMAS BOOK (See Christmas Journey Through Space)
1951; 1954; 1955 (36 pgs.; 24 pgs.)
Promotional Publ. Co.

1951-(Woolworth giveaway)-slightly oversized; no slick cover; Marv Levy c/a	2.00	6.00	14.00
1954-(Hot Shoppes giveaway)-regular size-reprints 1951 issue; slick cover added; 24 pgs.; no ads	2.00	6.00	14.00
1955-(J. M. McDonald Co. giveaway)-regular size	1.50	4.50	10.00

JOLLY COMICS
1947
Four Star Publishing Co.

	Good	Fine	N-Mint
1	3.15	9.50	22.00

JOLLY JINGLES (Formerly Jackpot Comics)
No. 10, Sum. 1943 - No. 16, Wint, 1944/45
MLJ Magazines

	Good	Fine	N-Mint
10-Super Duck begins (origin & 1st app.). Woody The Woodpecker begins. (not same as Lantz character)	17.00	51.00	120.00
11 (Fall. '43)	8.00	24.00	56.00
12-16: 12-Hitler-c	4.00	12.00	28.00

JONAH HEX (See All-Star Western, Hex and Weird Western Tales)
Mar-Apr. 1977 - No. 92, Aug, 1985
National Periodical Publications/DC Comics

	Good	Fine	N-Mint
1	.50	1.50	3.00
2-6,8-10: 9-Wrightson-c		.50	1.00
7-Explains Hex's face disfigurement	.25	.75	1.50
11-20: 12-Starlin-c		.40	.80
21-92: 31,32-Origin retold		.25	.50

NOTE: Aparo c-76p. Ayers a(p)-35-37, 41,44-53, 56, 58-82. Kubert c-43-46. Morrow a-90-92; c-10 Spiegle(Tothish) a-34, 38, 40, 49, 52.

JONAH HEX AND OTHER WESTERN TALES (Blue Ribbon Digest)
Sept-Oct. 1979 - No. 3, Jan-Feb, 1980 (100 pgs.)
DC Comics

	Good	Fine	N-Mint
1-3: 1-Origin Scalphunter-r; painted-c. 2-Weird Western Tales-r; Adams, Toth, Aragones, Gil Kane-a		.40	.80

JONAH HEX SPECTACULAR (See DC Special Series No. 16)

JONESY (Formerly Crack Western)
No. 85, Aug, 1953; No. 2, Oct, 1953 - No. 8, Oct, 1954
Comic Favorite/Quality Comics Group

	Good	Fine	N-Mint
85(#1)-Teen-age humor	3.00	9.00	21.00
2	1.70	5.00	12.00
3-8	1.15	3.50	8.00

JON JUAN (Also see Great Lover Romances)
Spring, 1950
Toby Press

	Good	Fine	N-Mint
1-All Schomburg-a (signed Al Reid on-c); written by Siegel; used in **SOTI**, pg. 38	11.50	34.00	80.00

JONNI THUNDER
Feb, 1985 - No. 4, Aug, 1985 (Mini-series)
DC Comics

	Good	Fine	N-Mint
1-4: 1-Origin		.45	.90

JONNY QUEST (TV)
December, 1964 (Hanna-Barbera)
Gold Key

	Good	Fine	N-Mint
1 (10139-412)	8.00	24.00	55.00

JONNY QUEST (TV)
June, 1986 - No. 31, Dec, 1988 (Hanna-Barbera)
Comico

	Good	Fine	N-Mint
1	.70	2.00	4.00
2	.45	1.30	2.60
3,5-Dave Stevens-c	.45	1.40	2.75
4,6-10	.25	.75	1.50
11-31: #15 on, $1.75. 30-Adapts TV episode		.60	1.25
Special 1(9/88, $1.75), 2(10/88, $1.75)	.25	.75	1.50

NOTE: Pini a-2. Rude a-1. Sienkiewicz c-11. Spiegle a-12; c-21. Staton a-11. Stevens a-4i; c-3, 5. Wildey a-1, c-1, 7, 12. Williamson a-4i; c-4i.

JONNY QUEST CLASSICS (TV)
May, 1987 - No. 3, July, 1987 ($2.00, color) (Hanna-Barbera)
Comico

	Good	Fine	N-Mint
1-3: Wildey c/a	.35	1.00	2.00

JON SABLE, FREELANCE (Also see Mile Grell's Sable & Sable)
6/83 - No. 56, 2/88 (#1-17, $1; #18-33, $1.25; #34-on, $1.75)
First Comics

	Good	Fine	N-Mint
1-Created, story/a&c by Mike Grell	.70	2.00	4.00
2-5: 3-5-Origin, parts 1-3	.40	1.25	2.50
6-10: 6-Origin, part 4	.35	1.00	2.00
11-20: 14-Mando paper begins	.30	.90	1.80
21-33: 25-30-Shatter app.	.25	.75	1.50
34-56: 34-Deluxe format begins ($1.75)	.25	.70	1.40

NOTE: Aragones a-33. Grell a-1-43; c-1-52, 53p, 54-56.

JOSEPH & HIS BRETHREN (See The Living Bible)

JOSIE (She's. . . #1-16) (. . . & the Pussycats #45 on) (See Archie Giant Series 528,540,551,562,571,584,597)
Feb, 1963 - No. 106, Oct, 1982
Archie Publications/Radio Comics

	Good	Fine	N-Mint
1	9.00	27.00	62.00
2	4.30	13.00	30.00
3-5	2.65	8.00	18.00
6-10	1.70	5.00	12.00
11-20	1.15	3.50	8.00
21,23-30	.75	2.25	5.00
22-Mighty Man & Mighty (Josie Girl) app.	.75	2.25	5.00
31-54	.45	1.35	3.00
55-74(52pg. issues)		.50	1.00
75-106		.35	.70

JOURNAL OF CRIME (See Fox Giants)

JOURNEY
1983 - No. 14, 9/84; No. 15, 4/85 - No. 27, 7/86 (B&W)
Aardvark-Vanaheim #1-14/Fantagraphics Books #15-on

	Good	Fine	N-Mint
1	2.00	6.00	12.00
2	1.10	3.25	6.50
3	.60	1.75	3.50
4-27	.25	.75	1.50

JOURNEY INTO FEAR
May, 1951 - No. 21, Sept, 1954
Superior-Dynamic Publications

	Good	Fine	N-Mint
1-Baker-a(2)-r	16.00	48.00	110.00
2	10.00	30.00	70.00
3,4	8.00	24.00	56.00
5-10	6.50	19.50	45.00
11-14,16-21	5.50	16.50	38.00
15-Used in SOTI, pg. 389	8.00	24.00	56.00

NOTE: Kamenish, headlight'-a most issues. Robinson a-10.

JOURNEY INTO MYSTERY (1st Series) (Thor No. 126 on)
6/52 - No. 48, 8/57; No. 49, 11/58 - No. 125, 2/66
Atlas(CPS No.1-48/AMI No.49-68/Marvel No.69(6/61) on)

	Good	Fine	N-Mint
1	54.00	161.00	375.00
2	26.00	80.00	185.00
3,4	21.50	64.00	150.00
5-11	13.00	40.00	90.00
12-20,22: 22-Davisesque-a; last pre-code issue (2/55)	10.00	30.00	70.00
21-Kubert-a; Tothish by Andru	11.00	32.00	75.00
23-32,35-38,40: 24-Torres?-a	5.70	17.00	40.00
33-Williamson-a	8.00	24.00	55.00
34,39: 34-Krigstein-a. 39-Wood-a	7.00	21.00	50.00
41-Crandall-a; Frazettaesque-a by Morrow	5.00	15.00	35.00
42,48-Torres-a	5.00	15.00	35.00
43,44-Williamson/Mayo-a in both	5.00	15.00	35.00
45,47,52,53	4.30	1300	30.00

Jon Sable. Freelance #3. First Comics

Journey Into Fear #8. SUPR

Journey Into Mystery #16. MEG

Journey Into Mystery #89. © MEG   Journey Into Unknown Worlds #12. © MEG   Judge Dredd #2 (12/83). © Quality Comics

JOURNEY INTO MYSTERY (continued)	Good	Fine	N-Mint
46-Torres & Krigstein-a	5.00	15.00	35.00
49-Matt Fox, Check-a	5.00	15.00	35.00
50,54: 50-Davis-a. 54-Williamson-a	4.50	14.00	32.00
51-Kirby/Wood-a	4.50	14.00	32.00
55-61,63-73: 66-Return of Xemnu	4.00	12.00	28.00
62-1st app. Xemnu (Titan) called "The Hulk"	5.70	17.00	40.00
74-82-Fantasy content #74 on. 75-Last 10 cent issue. 80-Anticommunist propaganda story by Ditko	3.50	10.50	24.00
83-Origin & 1st app. The Mighty Thor by Kirby (8/62)	107.00	320.00	750.00
83-R-/from the Golden Record Comic Set	3.60	11.00	25.00
with the record. . . .	7.00	21.00	50.00
84-2nd app. Thor	28.00	84.00	200.00
85-1st app. Loki & Heimdall	19.00	57.00	135.00
86-1st app. Odin	14.00	42.00	100.00
87-89: 89-Origin Thor reprint/#83	13.00	40.00	90.00
90-No Kirby-a: Aunt May proto-type	8.00	24.00	55.00
91,92,94-96-Sinnott-a	6.50	19.50	45.00
93,97-Kirby-a; Tales of Asgard series begins #97(Origin which concludes #99)	8.50	25.50	60.00
98-100-Kirby/Heck-a. 98-Origin/1st app. The Human Cobra. 99-1st app. Surtur & Mr. Hyde	6.50	19.50	45.00
101-104,110: 102-Intro Sif	3.60	11.00	25.00
105-109-Ten extra pages Kirby-a. 107-1st app. Grey Gargoyle	3.60	11.00	25.00
111,113,114,116-125: 119-Intro Hogun, Fandrall, Volstagg	2.85	8.50	20.00
112-Thor Vs. Hulk; origin Loki begins; ends #113	5.70	17.00	40.00
115-Detailed origin Loki	3.60	11.00	25.00
Annual 1('65)-1st app. Hercules; Kirby c/a	6.50	19.50	45.00

NOTE: *Ayers a-14, 39. Bailey a-43. Briefer a-5, 12. Check a-17. Colan a-23, 81. Ditko a-33, 38, 50-96; c-71, 88i. Ditko/Kirby a-50-83. Everett a-20, c-4-7, 9, 37, 39, 40-42, 44, 45, 47. Forte a-19, 40. Heath a-4, 5, 11, 14; c-1, 11, 15, 51. Kirby a(p)-60, 66, 76, 80, 83-89, 93, 97, 98, 100(w/Heck), 101-125; c-50-82(w/Ditko), 83-152p. Leiber/Fox a-93, 98-102. Maneely c-21, 22. Morrow a-41, 42. Orlando a-30, 45, 57. Mac Pakula (Tothish) a-9. Powell a-20, 27, 34. Reinman a-39, 87, 92, 96i. Robinson a-9. Roussos a-39. Robert Sale a-14. Severin a-27. Sinnott c-50. Tuska a-11. Wildey a-16.*

JOURNEY INTO MYSTERY (2nd Series)
Oct. 1972 - No. 19, Oct. 1975
Marvel Comics Group

	Good	Fine	N-Mint
1-Robert Howard adaptation; Starlin/Ploog-a		.40	.80
2,3,5-Bloch adaptation; 5-Last new story		.30	.60
4,6-19: 4-H. P. Lovecraft adaptation		.30	.60

NOTE: *Adams a-2i. Ditko a(r)-7, 10, 12, 14, 15, 19; c-10. Everett a-9r, 14r. G. Kane a-1p. 2p; c-13p. Kirby a-7r, 13r, 18r, 19r; c-7. Mort Lawrence a-2r. Maneely a-3r. Orlando a-16r. Reese a-1, 2i. Starlin a-3p. Torres a-16r. Wildey a-9r, 14r.*

JOURNEY INTO UNKNOWN WORLDS (Formerly Teen)
No. 36, 9/50 - No. 38, 2/51; No. 4, 4/51 - No. 59, 8/57
Atlas Comics (WFP)

	Good	Fine	N-Mint
36(#1)-Science fiction/weird; 'End Of The Earth' c/story	36.00	107.00	250.00
37(#2)-Science fiction; 'When Worlds Collide' c/story; Everett-c/a	27.00	81.00	190.00
38(#3)-Science fiction	21.50	64.00	150.00
4-6,8,10-Science fiction/weird	14.00	42.00	100.00
7-Wolverton-a-"Planet of Terror," 6 pgs; electric chair c-inset/story	25.00	75.00	175.00
9-Giant eyeball story	14.00	42.00	100.00
11,12-Krigstein-a	10.00	30.00	70.00
13,16,17,20	7.00	21.00	50.00
14-Wolverton-a-"One of Our Graveyards Is Missing," 4 pgs; Tuska-a	21.50	64.00	150.00
15-Wolverton-a-"They Crawl By Night," 5 pgs.	21.50	64.00	150.00
18,19-Matt Fox-a	8.50	25.50	60.00

	Good	Fine	N-Mint
21-26,28-33-Last pre-code (2/55). 21-Decapitation-c. 24-Sci/fic story.			
26-Atom bomb panel	4.30	13.00	30.00
27-Sid Check-a	4.50	14.00	32.00
34-Kubert, Torres-a	4.50	14.00	32.00
35-Torres-a	3.70	11.00	26.00
36-42	3.50	10.50	24.00
43,44: 43-Krigstein-a. 44-Davis-a	4.00	12.00	28.00
45,55,59-Williamson-a in all; with Mayo #55,59. Crandall-a, #55,59	5.70	17.00	40.00
46,47,49,52,56-58	2.65	8.00	18.00
48,53-Crandall-a; Check-a, #48	5.50	16.50	38.00
50-Davis, Crandall-a	5.00	15.00	35.00
51-Ditko, Wood-a	4.30	13.00	30.00
54-Torres-a	3.50	10.50	24.00

NOTE: *Ayers a-24, 43. Berg a-38(#3), 43. Lou Cameron a-33. Colan a-37(#2), 6, 17, 19, 20, 23, 39. Ditko a-45, 51. Evans a-20. Everett a-37(#2), 11, 14, 41, 55, 56; c-11, 13, 14, 17, 22, 47, 48, 50, 53-55, 59. Forte a-49. Fox a-21i. Heath a-38(#1), 4, 6-8, 17, 20, 22, 36i. Mort Lawrence a-38, 39. Maneely a-7, 8, 15, 16, 22, 49; c-25, 52. Morrow a-48. Orlando a-44, 57. Powell a-42, 53, 54. Reinman a-38. Rico a-21. Robert Sale a-24, 49. Sekowsky a-4, 5, 9. Severin a-38, 51; c-38, 48i, 56. Sinnott a-9, 21, 24. Tuska a-38(#3). Wildey a-25, 44.*

JOURNEY OF DISCOVERY WITH MARK STEEL (See Mark Steel)

JOURNEY TO THE CENTER OF THE EARTH (See 4-Color No. 1060)

JOURNEY: WARDRUMS
Aug, 1987 ($1.75, B&W)
Fantagraphics Books

1	.30	.90	1.75

JUDE, THE FORGOTTEN SAINT
1954 (16 pgs.; 8x11''; full color; paper cover)
Catechetical Guild Education Society

nn	1.50	4.50	10.00

JUDGE COLT
Oct, 1969 - No. 4, Sept, 1970
Gold Key

1	.85	2.50	6.00
2-4	.70	2.00	4.00

JUDGE DREDD (See The Law of Dredd & 2000 A.D. Monthly)
Nov, 1983 - No. 35, 1986; V2#1, Oct. 1986 - Present
Eagle Comics/IPC Magazines Ltd./Quality Comics No. 34 on

	Good	Fine	N-Mint
1-Bolland c/a begins	1.00	3.00	6.00
2,3	.60	1.80	3.60
4-10	.50	1.50	3.00
11-20	.40	1.20	2.40
21-35	.35	1.00	2.00
V2#1-('86)-New look begins	.35	1.00	2.00
V2#2-6	.25	.75	1.50
V2#7-20: 14-Bolland-a. 20-Begin $1.50-c	.65		1.30
V2#21,22, 23/24-Two issue numbers in one	.25	.75	1.50
25-40: 28-1st app. Megaman (super-hero)	.25	.75	1.50
Special 1		.70	1.40

NOTE: *Guice c-V2#23/24, 26, 27.*

JUDGE DREDD'S CRIME FILE
Aug, 1985 - No. 6, Feb, 1986 ($1.25, color, Mini-series)
Eagle Comics

1-6: 1-Byrne-a		.65	1.30

JUDGE DREDD'S CRIME FILE
Aug, 1989 - Vol. 4, Oct, 1989 ($5.95, color, high quality, 52 pgs.)
Quality Comics

Volume 1-4: Bolland-c	1.00	3.00	6.00

JUDGE DREDD: THE EARLY CASES
Feb, 1986 - No. 6, July, 1986 ($1.25, Mega-series, Mando paper)
Eagle Comics

	Good	Fine	N-Mint
JUDGE DREDD: THE EARLY CASES (cont.)			
1-6: 2000 A.D.-r		.65	1.30
JUDGE DREDD: THE JUDGE CHILD QUEST			
Aug, 1984 - No. 5, Oct, 1984 ($1.25, Limited series, Baxter paper)			
Eagle Comics			
1-5: 2000 A.D.-r; Bolland c/a		.65	1.30
JUDGE PARKER			
Feb, 1956 - No. 2, 1956			
Argo			
1	2.85	8.50	20.00
2	1.60	4.80	11.00
JUDO JOE			
Aug, 1953 - No. 3, Dec, 1953			
Jay-Jay Corp.			
1-Drug ring story	3.50	10.50	24.00
2,3: 3-Hypo needle story	2.00	6.00	14.00
JUDOMASTER (Gun Master No. 84-89) (Also see Crisis on Infinite Earths & Special War Series)			
No. 89, May-June, 1966 - No. 98, Dec, 1967 (two No. 89's)			
Charlton Comics			
89-98: 91-Sarge Steel begins. 93-Intro. Tiger	.85	2.60	6.00
93,94,96,98(Modern Comics reprint, 1977)		.15	.30
NOTE: **Morisi** Thunderbolt No. 90.			
JUDY CANOVA (Formerly My Experience) (Stage, screen, radio)			
No. 23, May, 1950 - No. 3, Sept, 1950			
Fox Features Syndicate			
23(#1)-Wood-c.a(p)?	9.30	28.00	65.00
24-Wood-a(p)	9.30	28.00	65.00
3-Wood-c; Wood/Orlando-a	11.00	32.00	75.00
JUDY GARLAND (See Famous Stars)			
JUDY JOINS THE WAVES			
1951 (For U.S. Navy)			
Toby Press			
nn	2.30	7.00	16.00
JUGHEAD (Formerly Archie's Pal...)			
No. 127, Dec, 1965 - No. 352, 1987			
Archie Publications			
127-130	1.00	3.00	6.00
131,133,135-160	.70	2.00	4.00
132-Shield-c; The Fly & Black Hood app.; Shield cameo	1.00	3.00	6.00
134-Shield-c	1.00	3.00	6.00
161-200	.40	1.25	2.50
201-240		.60	1.20
241-352: 300-Anniversary issue		.30	.60
JUGHEAD			
Aug, 1987 - Present			
Archie Enterprises			
1-10: 4-X-Mas issue		.40	.75
JUGHEAD AS CAPTAIN HERO			
Oct, 1966 - No. 7, Nov, 1967			
Archie Publications			
1	2.85	8.50	20.00
2	1.70	5.00	12.00
3-7	1.00	3.00	7.00
JUGHEAD JONES COMICS DIGEST, THE (...Magazine No. 10-on)			
June, 1977 - Present (Digest-size)			
Archie Publications			
1-Adams-a; Capt. Hero-r	.70	2.00	4.00
2(9/77)-Adams-a	.35	1.00	2.00

	Good	Fine	N-Mint
3-62: 7-Origin Jaguar-r; Adams-a. 13-r-/1957 Jughead's Folly			
		.60	1.20
JUGHEAD'S DOUBLE DIGEST			
Oct, 1989 - Present ($2.25, quarterly, 256 pgs.)			
Archie Comics			
1,2	.40	1.15	2.30
JUGHEAD'S EAT-OUT COMIC BOOK MAGAZINE (See Archie Giant Series Mag. No. 170)			
JUGHEAD'S FANTASY			
Aug, 1960 - No. 3, Dec, 1960			
Archie Publications			
1	11.50	34.00	80.00
2	8.50	25.50	60.00
3	6.50	19.50	45.00
JUGHEAD'S FOLLY			
1957			
Archie Publications (Close-Up)			
1-Jughead a la Elvis (Rare)	25.00	75.00	175.00
JUGHEAD'S JOKES			
Aug, 1967 - No. 78, Sept, 1982			
(No. 1-8, 38 on: reg. size; No. 9-23: 68 pgs.; No. 24-37: 52 pgs.)			
Archie Publications			
1	3.70	11.00	26.00
2	2.00	6.00	14.00
3-5	1.00	3.00	7.00
6-10	.70	2.00	4.00
11-30	.25	.75	1.50
31-50		.45	.90
51-78		.30	.60
JUGHEAD'S PAL HOT DOG			
Jan, 1990 ($1.00, color)			
Archie Comics			
1		.50	1.00
JUGHEAD'S SOUL FOOD			
1979 (49 cents)			
Spire Christian Comics (Fleming H. Revell Co.)			
nn		.30	.60
JUGHEAD WITH ARCHIE DIGEST (...Plus Betty & Veronica & Reggie Too No. 1,2; ...Magazine No. 33 on)			
March, 1974 - Present (Digest Size: $1.00-$1.25-$1.35-$1.50)			
Archie Publications			
1	1.15	3.50	7.00
2	.50	1.50	3.00
3-10	.25	.75	1.50
11-20: Capt. Hero r-in #14-16; Pureheart the Powerful #18,21,22;			
Capt. Pureheart #17,19		.50	1.00
21-98: 29-The Shield-r. 30-The Fly-r		.50	1.00
JUKE BOX COMICS			
March, 1948 - No. 6, Jan, 1949			
Famous Funnies			
1-Toth c/a; Hollingsworth-a	21.50	64.00	150.00
2-Transvestism story	11.00	32.00	75.00
3-6	9.30	28.00	65.00
JUMBO COMICS (Created by S.M. Iger)			
Sept, 1938 - No. 167, Apr, 1953 (No.1-3: 68 pgs.; No.4-8: 52 pgs.)			
(No. 1-8 oversized-10½x14½"; black & white)			
Fiction House Magazines (Real Adv. Publ. Co.)			
1-(Rare)-Sheena Queen of the Jungle by Meskin, The Hawk by Eisner, The Hunchback by Dick Briefer(ends #8) begin; 1st			

Judomaster #92.   CC   Judy Canova #23.   FOX   Jughead's Fantasy #2.   AP

Jumbo Comics #75.   FH

Jungle Action #6 (8/55).   MEG

Jungle Comics #2.   FH

	Good	Fine	N-Mint

JUMBO COMICS (continued)
comic art by Jack Kirby (Count of Monte Cristo & Wilton of the West); Mickey Mouse appears (1 panel) with brief biography of Walt Disney. **Note:** Sheena was created by Iger for publication in England as a newspaper strip. The early issues of Jumbo contain Sheena strip-r 550.00 1375.00 3300.00

2-(Rare)-Origin Sheena. Diary of Dr. Hayward by Kirby (also #3) plus 2 other stories; contains strip from Universal Film featuring Edgar Bergen & Charlie McCarthy 250.00 625.00 1500.00

3-Last Kirby issue 200.00 500.00 1200.00

4-(Scarce)-Origin The Hawk by Eisner; Wilton of the West by Fine (ends #14)(1st comic work); Count of Monte Cristo by Fine (ends #15); The Diary of Dr. Hayward by Fine (cont'd. #8,9)
.... 200.00 500.00 1200.00

5 .... 125.00 315.00 750.00

6-8-Last B&W issue. #8 was a N. Y. World's Fair Special Edition 108.00 270.00 650.00

9-Stuart Taylor begins by Fine; Fine-c; 1st color issue(8-9/39)-8¼x10¼″(oversized in width only) 117.00 295.00 700.00

10-13: 10-Regular size 68 pg. issues begin; Sheena dons new costume #10 .... 58.00 145.00 350.00

14-Lightning begins (Intro.) 43.00 130.00 300.00

15-20 .... 28.50 86.00 200.00

21-30: 22-1st Tom, Dick & Harry; origin The Hawk retold
.... 26.00 77.00 180.00

31-40: 35 shows V2#11 (correct number does not appear)
.... 23.00 70.00 160.00

41-50 .... 19.00 58.00 135.00

51-60: 52-Last Tom, Dick & Harry 16.50 50.00 115.00

61-70: 68-Sky Girl begins, ends #130; not in #79
.... 11.50 34.00 80.00

71-80 .... 10.00 30.00 70.00

81-93,95-99: 89-ZX5 becomes a private eye 10.00 30.00 70.00

94-Used in **Love and Death** by Legman 10.00 30.00 70.00

100 .... 11.50 34.00 80.00

101-110: 103-Lingerie panel 8.50 25.50 60.00

111-140 .... 7.00 21.00 50.00

141-149-Two Sheena stories. 141-Long Bow, Indian Boy begins, ends #160 .... 8.50 25.50 60.00

150-154,156-158 .... 7.00 21.00 50.00

155-Used in **POP**, pg. 98 .... 7.00 21.00 50.00

159-163: Space Scouts serial in all; 163-Suicide Smith app.
.... 7.00 21.00 50.00

164-The Star Pirate begins, ends #165 .... 7.00 21.00 50.00

165-167: 165,167-Space Rangers app. 7.00 21.00 50.00

NOTE: Bondage covers, negligee panels, torture, etc. are common in this series. Hawks of the Seas, Inspector Dayton, Spies in Action, Sports Shorts & Uncle Otto by Eisner, #1-7. Hawk by Eisner-#10-15, 114?. Eisner c-1, 3-6, 12, 13, 15. 1pg. Patsy pin-ups in 92-97, 99-101. Sheena by Meskin-#1, 4; by Powell-#2, 3, 5-28. Powell c-14, 16, 17, 19. Sky Girl by Matt Baker-#69-78, 80-124. Bailey a-1-8. Briefer a-1-8, 10. Fine c-8-11. Kamen a-101, 105, 123, 132, c-105. Bob Kane a-1-8.

JUMPING JACKS PRESENTS THE WHIZ KIDS
1978 (In 3-D) with glasses (4 pages)
Jumping Jacks Stores giveaway

nn .... .40 .80

JUNGLE ACTION
Oct. 1954 - No. 6, Aug, 1955
Atlas Comics (IPC)

1-Leopard Girl begins; Maneely c/a-all 10.00 30.00 70.00

2-(3-D effect cover) 11.50 34.00 80.00

3-6: 3-Last precode (2/55) 6.50 19.50 45.00

NOTE: Romita a-3, 6. Shores a-3, 6.

JUNGLE ACTION (& Black Panther #18-21?)
Oct. 1972 - No. 24, Nov, 1976
Marvel Comics Group

1-Lorna, Jann-r .... .40 .80

2-5: 5-Black Panther begins (new-a) .... .30 .60

6-18-All new stories. 8-Origin Black Panther .... .30 .60

19-23-KKK x-over. 23-r-/#22 .... .30 .60

24-1st Wind Eagle .... .30 .60

NOTE: Buckler a-6-9p, 22; c-8p, 12p. Buscema a-5p; c-22. Byrne c-23. Gil Kane c-2, 4, 10p, 11p, 13-17, 19, 24. G. Kane a-8p. Kirby c-18. Maneely r-1. Russell a-13i. Starlin c-3p.

JUNGLE ADVENTURES
1963 - 1964 (Reprints)
Super Comics

10,12(Rulah), 15(Kaanga/Jungle #152) 1.35 4.00 9.00

17(Jo-Jo) 1.35 4.00 9.00

18-Reprints/White Princess of the Jungle #1; no Kinstler-a; origin of both White Princess & Cap'n Courage 1.75 5.25 12.00

JUNGLE ADVENTURES
March, 1971 - No. 3, June, 1971
Skywald Comics

1-Zangar origin; reprints of Jo-Jo, Blue Gorilla(origin)/White Princess #3, Kinstler-a/White Princess #2 .... .50 1.50 3.00

2-Zangar,Sheena/Sheena #17 & Jumbo #162, Jo-Jo, origin Slave Girl Princess-r .... .50 1.50 3.00

3-Zangar, Jo-Jo, White Princess-r .... .50 1.50 3.00

JUNGLE BOOK, THE (See Movie Comics & Walt Disney Showcase #45)

JUNGLE CAT (See 4-Color No. 1136)

JUNGLE COMICS
Jan, 1940 - No. 163, Summer, 1954
Fiction House Magazines

1-Origin The White Panther, Kaanga, Lord of the Jungle, Tabu, Wizard of the Jungle; Wambi, the Jungle Boy, Camilla & Capt. Terry Thunder begin 142.00 355.00 850.00

2-Fantomah, Mystery Woman of the Jungle begins
.... 57.00 170.00 400.00

3,4 .... 49.00 148.00 345.00

5 .... 38.00 115.00 265.00

6-10: 7,8-Powell-c 33.00 100.00 235.00

11-20: 13-Tuska-c 23.00 70.00 165.00

21-30: 25 shows V2#1 (correct number does not appear). #27-New origin Fantomah, Daughter of the Pharoahs; Camilla dons new costume 19.00 60.00 135.00

31-40 .... 16.00 48.00 110.00

41,43-50 .... 12.00 36.00 85.00

42-Kaanga by Crandall, 12 pgs. 15.00 45.00 105.00

51-60 .... 11.00 32.00 75.00

61-70 .... 9.30 28.00 65.00

71-80: 79-New origin Tabu 8.50 25.50 60.00

81-97,99,101-110 .... 7.00 21.00 50.00

98-Used in **SOTI**, pg. 185 & illo-"In ordinary comic books, there are pictures within pictures for children who know how to look"; used by N.Y. Legis. Comm. 13.00 40.00 90.00

100 .... 8.50 25.50 60.00

111-142,144,146-150: 118-Clyde Beatty app. 135-Desert Panther begins in Terry Thunder (origin), not in #137; ends (dies) #138
.... 7.00 21.00 50.00

143,145-Used in **POP**, pg. 99 .... 7.00 21.00 50.00

151-157,159-163: 152-Tiger Girl begins 7.00 21.00 50.00

158-Sheena app. 8.50 25.50 60.00

I.W. Reprint #1,9: 9-r-/#151 .... 1.00 3.00 6.00

NOTE: Bondage covers, negligee panels, torture, etc. are common to this series. Camilla by Fran Hopper-#73, 78, 80-90; by Baker-#101, 103, 106, 107, 109, 111-113. Kaanga by John Celardo-#80-110; by Maurice Whitman-#124-163. Tabu by Whitman-#93-110. Astarita c-46. Celardo a-78; c-98-100, 103, 106, 109, 112. Eisner c-2, 5, 6. Fine c-1. Larsen a-65, 66, 72, 74, 75, 79, 83, 84, 87-90. Morisi a-51.

JUNGLE COMICS
May, 1988 - Present ($2.00, color; B&W #2 on?)

221

JUNGLE COMICS (continued)
Blackthorne Publishing

	Good	Fine	N-Mint
1-6: 1-Dave Stevens-c. B. Jones scripts in all	.35	1.00	2.00

JUNGLE GIRL (See Lorna   )

JUNGLE GIRL (Nyoka, Jungle Girl No. 2 on)
Fall, 1942 (No month listed) (Based on film character)
Fawcett Publications

	Good	Fine	N-Mint
1-Bondage-c: photo of Kay Aldridge who played Nyoka in movie serial app. on-c	50.00	150.00	350.00

JUNGLE JIM (Also see Ace Comics)
No. 11, Jan. 1949 - No. 20, Apr. 1951
Standard Comics (Best Books)

	Good	Fine	N-Mint
11	3.70	11.00	26.00
12-20	2.15	6.50	15.00

JUNGLE JIM
No. 490, 8/53 - No. 1020, 8-10/59 (Painted-c)
Dell Publishing Co.

4-Color 490	2.65	8.00	18.00
4-Color 565(6/54)	2.00	6.00	14.00
3(10-12/54)-5	1.70	5.00	12.00
6-19(1-3/59)	1.50	4.50	10.00
4-Color 1020(#20)	1.70	5.00	12.00

JUNGLE JIM
No. 5, December, 1967
King Features Syndicate

5-Reprints Dell #5; Wood-c	.85	2.60	6.00

JUNGLE JIM (Continued from Dell series)
No. 22, Feb. 1969 - No. 28, Feb, 1970 (No. 21 was an overseas edition only)
Charlton Comics

22-Dan Flagg begins; Ditko/Wood-a	1.70	5.00	12.00
23-28: 23-Last Dan Flagg; Howard-c. 24-Jungle People begin. 27-Ditko/Howard-a. 28-Ditko-a	1.15	3.50	8.00

JUNGLE JO
Mar, 1950 - No. 6, Mar, 1951
Fox Feature Syndicate (Hero Books)

nn-Jo-Jo blanked out, leaving Congo King; came out after Jo-Jo #29 (intended as Jo-Jo #30?)	13.00	40.00	90.00
1-Tangi begins; part Wood-a	14.00	42.00	100.00
2	11.00	32.00	75.00
3-6	10.00	30.00	70.00

JUNGLE LIL (Dorothy Lamour #2 on; Also see Feat. Stories Mag.)
April, 1950
Fox Feature Syndicate (Hero Books)

1	12.00	36.00	84.00

JUNGLE TALES (Jann of the Jungle No. 8 on)
Sept. 1954 - No. 7, Sept, 1955
Atlas Comics (CSI)

1-Jann of the Jungle	10.00	30.00	70.00
2-7: 3-Last precode (1/55)	7.00	21.00	50.00

NOTE: *Heath c-5. Heck a-6, 7. Maneely a-2; c-1, 3. Shores a-5-7. Tuska a-2.*

JUNGLE TALES OF TARZAN
Dec. 1964 - No. 4, July, 1965
Charlton Comics

1	2.00	6.00	14.00
2-4	1.50	4.50	10.00

NOTE: *Giordano c-3p. Glanzman a-1-3. Montes/Bache a-4.*

JUNGLE TERROR (See Harvey Comics Hits No. 54)

JUNGLE THRILLS (Terrors of the Jungle No. 17)
No. 16, Feb, 1952; Dec, 1953; No. 7, 1954
Star Publications

	Good	Fine	N-Mint
16-Phantom Lady & Rulah story-reprint/All Top No. 15; used in POP. pg. 98,99; L. B. Cole-c	16.00	48.00	110.00
3-D 1(12/53)-Jungle Lil & Jungle Jo appear; L. B. Cole-c	20.00	60.00	140.00
7-Titled 'Picture Scope Jungle Adventures';(1954, 36 pgs, 15 cents)-3-D effect c/stories; story & coloring book; Disbrow-a/script: L.B. Cole-c	14.00	43.00	100.00

JUNGLE TWINS, THE (Tono & Kono)
4/72 - No. 17, 11/75; No. 18, 5/82
Gold Key/Whitman No. 18 on

1	.30	.90	1.80
2-5		.60	1.20
6-18: 18-r		.40	.80

NOTE: *UFO c/story No. 13. Painted-c No. 1-17. Spiegle c-18.*

JUNGLE WAR STORIES (Guerrilla War No. 12 on)
July-Sept. 1962 - No. 11, Apr.-June, 1965 (Painted-c)
Dell Publishing Co.

01-384-209	.85	2.60	6.00
2-11	.70	2.00	4.00

JUNIE PROM
Winter, 1947-48 - No. 7, Aug. 1949
Dearfield Publishing Co.

1-Teen-age	4.65	14.00	32.00
2	2.30	7.00	16.00
3-7	1.50	4.50	10.00

JUNIOR CARROT PATROL
May, 1989 ($2.00, B&W)
Dark Horse Comics

1-Flaming Carrot spin-off; Bob Burden-c(i)	.35	1.00	2.00

JUNIOR COMICS
No. 9, Sept, 1947 - No. 16, July, 1948
Fox Feature Syndicate

9-Feldstein c/a; headlights-c	36.00	110.00	250.00
10-16-Feldstein c/a; headlights-c	31.50	95.00	220.00

JUNIOR FUNNIES (Formerly Tiny Tot Funnies No. 9)
No. 10, Aug. 1951 - No. 13, Feb, 1952
Harvey Publications (King Features Synd.)

10-Partial reprints in all-Blondie, Dagwood, Daisy, Henry, Popeye, Felix, Katzenjammer Kids	1.50	4.50	10.00
11-13	1.20	3.50	8.00

JUNIOR HOPP COMICS
Feb, 1952 - No. 3, July, 1952
Stanmor Publ.

1	3.70	11.00	26.00
2,3: 3-Dave Berg-a	2.00	6.00	14.00

JUNIOR MEDICS OF AMERICA, THE
1957 (15 cents)
E. R. Squire & Sons

1359	1.50	4.50	10.00

JUNIOR MISS
Winter, 1944; No. 24, April, 1947 - No. 39, Aug. 1950
Timely/Marvel Comics (CnPC)

1-Frank Sinatra & June Allyson life story	8.00	24.00	56.00
24	3.70	11.00	26.00
25-38	2.00	6.00	14.00
39-Kurtzman-a	2.65	8.00	18.00

NOTE: *Painted-c 35-37. 37-all romance. 35,36,38-mostly teen humor.*

Jungle Girl #1.   FAW

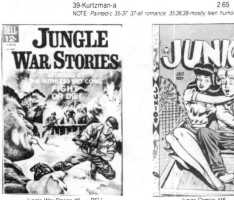

Jungle War Stories #8.   DELL

Junior Comics #16.   FOX

Justice Comics #16, © MEG

Justice League International #7, © DC

Justice League Of America #1, © DC

JUNIOR PARTNERS (Formerly Oral Roberts' True Stories)
No. 120, Aug, 1959 - V3No.12, Dec, 1961
Oral Roberts Evangelistic Assn.

	Good	Fine	N-Mint
120(#1)	1.70	5.00	12.00
2(9/59)	1.15	3.50	8.00
3-12(7/60)	.60	1.80	4.00
V2#1(8/60)-5(12/60)	.50	1.50	3.00
V3#1(1/61)-12	.35	1.00	2.00

JUNIOR TREASURY (See Dell Junior. . .)

JUNIOR WOODCHUCKS (See Huey, Dewey & Louie. . .)

JUSTICE
Nov. 1986 - No. 32, June, 1989
Marvel Comics Group

		Fine	N-Mint
1-31: 26-32-$1.50-c		.50	1.00
32-Unauthorized Joker app.	.50	1.50	3.00

JUSTICE COMICS (Tales of Justice #53 on; formerly Wacky Duck)
No. 7, Fall/47 - No. 9, 6/48; No. 4, 8/48 - No. 52, 3/55
Marvel/Atlas comics (NPP 7-9,4-19/CnPC 20-23/MjMC 24-38/Male 39-52

	Good	Fine	N-Mint
7 (#1, 1947)	7.00	21.00	50.00
8-Kurtzman-a-''Giggles 'N' Grins,'' (3)	5.00	15.00	35.00
9 (#3, 6/48)	4.30	13.00	30.00
4	3.50	10.50	24.00
5-9: 8-Anti-Wertham editorial	2.65	8.00	18.00
10-15-Photo-c	2.65	8.00	18.00
16-30	2.00	6.00	14.00
31-40,42-47,49-52-Last precode	1.70	5.00	12.00
41-Electrocution-c	4.30	13.00	30.00
48-Pakula & Tuska-a	1.70	5.00	12.00

NOTE: *Maneely c-44. Pakula a-43, 45. Louis Ravielli a-39. Robinson a-22, 25, 41. Wildey a-52.*

JUSTICE, INC. (The Avenger)
May-June, 1975 - No. 4, Nov-Dec, 1975
National Periodical Publications

		Fine	N-Mint
1-McWilliams-a; origin		.40	.80
2-4		.25	.50

NOTE: *Kirby c-2, 3p; a-2-4p. Kubert c-1, 4.*

JUSTICE, INC.
1989 - #2, 1989 ($3.95, color, squarebound, mature readers, 52 pgs.)
DC Comics

		Fine	N-Mint
1,2-Re-intro The Avenger	.70	2.00	4.00

JUSTICE LEAGUE (. . . International #7-25; . . . America #26 on)
May, 1987 - Present (Also see Legends #6)
DC Comics

		Fine	N-Mint
1-Batman, Gr. Lantern, Blue Beetle, others begin	2.00	6.00	12.00
2	1.15	3.50	7.00
3-Regular cover (white background)	.85	2.50	5.00
3-Limited cover (yellow background, Superman logo)	11.50	34.00	80.00
4-Booster Gold joins	.70	2.00	4.00
5,6: 5-Origin Gray Man	.40	1.25	2.50
7-Double size ($1.25); Capt. Marvel & Dr. Fate resign; Capt. Atom, Rocket Red join	.50	1.50	3.00
8-10: 9,10-Millennium x-over	.35	1.00	2.00
11-23		.60	1.20
24-($1.50)-Intro/1st app. Justice League Europe	.25	.75	1.50
25-36: 31,32-Justice League Europe x-over		.50	1.00
Annual 1 (9/87)	.50	1.50	3.00
Annual 2 ('88)-Joker c/story	.70	2.00	4.00
Annual 3 ('89, $1.75, 68 pgs.)	.30	.90	1.75
Special 1 ('90, $1.50)	.25	.75	1.50

	Good	Fine	N-Mint
A New Beginning Trade Paperback ($12.95, 1989)-r/1-7	2.15	6.50	12.95

NOTE: *Austin c/a-1(i). Giffen a-8-10; c-21p. Willingham a-30p. Annual 2.*

JUSTICE LEAGUE EUROPE
April, 1989 - Present (75 cents, color)
DC Comics

		Fine	N-Mint
1-Giffen plots/breakdowns #1-8 (plots only #9)	.35	1.10	2.20
2-12: 7-9, Batman app. 7,8-JLA x-over	.50		1.00

JUSTICE LEAGUE OF AMERICA (See Brave & the Bold, Mystery In Space #75 & Official. . .Index)
Oct-Nov, 1960 - No. 261, Apr, 1987 (91-99,139-157: 52 pgs.)
National Periodical Publications/DC Comics

	Good	Fine	N-Mint
1-Origin Despero; Aquaman, Batman, Flash, Green Lantern, J'onn J'onzz, Superman & Wonder Woman continue from Brave and the Bold	130.00	390.00	900.00
2	40.00	120.00	275.00
3-Origin/1st app. Kanjar Ro	27.00	81.00	190.00
4-Green Arrow joins JLA	23.00	70.00	160.00
5-Origin Dr. Destiny	16.00	48.00	110.00
6-8,10: 6-Origin Prof. Amos Fortune. 7-Last 10 cent issue. 10-Origin Felix Faust; 1st app. Time Lord	13.00	40.00	90.00
9-Origin J.L.A.	22.00	65.00	150.00
11-15: 12-Origin & 1st app. Dr. Light. 13-Speedy app. 14-Atom joins JLA	8.00	24.00	56.00
16-20: 17-Adam Strange flashback	5.70	17.00	40.00
21,22: 21-Re-intro. of JSA. 22-JSA x-over	12.00	36.00	85.00
23-28: 24-Adam Strange app. 28-Robin app.	3.60	11.00	25.00
29,30-JSA x-over; 1st Silver Age app. Starman	13.00	30.00	30.00
31-Hawkman joins JLA, Hawkgirl cameo	1.70	5.00	12.00
32-Intro & Origin Brain Storm	1.70	5.00	12.00
33,35,40,41: 41-Intro & origin The Key	1.50	4.50	10.00
34-Joker-c/story	2.65	8.00	18.00
36-1st Silver Age app. Mr. Terrific	1.70	5.00	12.00
37,38-JSA x-over	2.85	8.50	20.00
39-Giant G-16	2.30	7.00	16.00
42-45: 42-Metamorpho app. 43-Intro. Royal Flush Gang	1.35	4.00	8.00
46,47-JSA x-over	1.50	4.50	10.00
48-Giant G-29	1.50	4.50	10.00
49-57,59,60: 55-Intro. Earth 2 Robin	1.15	3.50	7.00
58-Giant G-41	1.35	4.00	8.00
61-66,68-72: 64-Intro/origin Red Tornado. 69-Wonder Woman quits; 71-Manhunter leaves. 72-Last 12 cent issue	.85	2.50	5.00
67-Giant G-53	1.00	3.00	6.00
73,74,77-80: 74-Black Canary joins. 78-Re-intro Vigilante	.70	2.00	4.00
75-2nd app. Green Arrow in new costume	.90	2.75	5.50
76-Giant G-65	.75	2.25	4.50
81-84,86-92: 83-Death of Spectre	.70	2.00	4.00
85,93-(Giant G-77,G-89; 68 pgs.)	.85	2.50	5.00
94-R/origin/1st app. Sandman (Adv. #40) & origin/1st app. Starman (Adv. #61); Deadman x-over; Adams-a	2.00	6.00	12.00
95-Origin Dr. Fate & Dr. Midnight reprint (More Fun #67, All-American #25)	.70	2.00	4.00
96-Origin Hourman (Adv. #48); Wildcat-r	.70	2.00	4.00
97-Origin JLA retold; Sargon, Starman-r	.70	2.00	4.00
98,99: 98-G.A. Sargon, Starman-r. 99-G.A. Sandman, Starman, Atom-r	.50	1.50	3.00
100	.85	2.50	5.00
101,102: 102-Red Tornado dies	.85	2.50	5.00
103-106: 103-Phantom Stranger joins. 105-Elongated Man joins. 106-New Red Tornado joins	.50	1.50	3.00
107,108-G.A. Uncle Sam, Black Condor, The Ray, Dollman, Phantom Lady, & The Human Bomb x-over	.85	2.50	5.00

JUSTICE LEAGUE OF AMERICA (continued)

	Good	Fine	N-Mint
109-116: 109-Hawkman resigns. 110-116: All 100 pg. issues. 111-Shining Knight, Green Arrow-r. 112-Crimson Avenger, Vigilante, origin Starman-r	.50	1.50	3.00
117-190: 117-Hawkman rejoins. 128-Wonder Woman rejoins. 129-Death of Red Tornado. 135-37-G.A. Bulletman, Bulletgirl, Spy Smasher, Mr. Scarlet, Pinky & Ibis x-over. 137-Superman battles G.A. Capt. Marvel. 144-Origin retold; origin J'onn J'onnz. 145-Red Tornado resurrected. 161-Zatanna joins & new costume. 171-Mr. Terrific murdered. 179-Firestorm joins. 181-Gr. Arrow leaves	.35	1.00	2.00
191-199: 192,193-Real origin Red Tornado. 193-1st app. All-Star Squadron as 16 pg. insert	.25	.75	1.50
200-Anniversary issue (76pgs., $1.50); origin retold; Green Arrow rejoins	.50	1.50	3.00
201-220: 203-Intro/origin new Royal Flush Gang. 208-All-Star Squadron app. 219,220-Origin Black Canary	.25	.75	1.50
221-249 (75 cents): 228-Re-intro Martian Manhunter. 233-New J.L.A. begins. 243-Aquaman leaves. 244,245-Crisis x-over. 253-Origin Despero. 258-Death of Vibe. 260-Death of Steel	.25	.75	1.50
250-Batman rejoins	.25	.75	1.50
251-260		.50	1.00
261-Last issue	.60	1.75	3.50
Annual 1(7/83)	.40	1.25	2.50
Annual 2(10/84)-Intro new J.L.A.	.25	.75	1.50
Annual 3(11/85)-Crisis x-over	.25	.75	1.50

NOTE: Adams a-63, 66, 67, 70, 74, 79, 81, 82, 86-89, 91, 92, 94, 96-98, 138, 139. Aparo a-200. Austin a-200i. Baily a-96r. Burnley a-94r, 98r, 99r. Greene a-46-61i, 64-73i, 110(r). Grell c-117, 122. Kaluta c-154p. Gil Kane a-200. Krigstein a-96(r-Sensation #84.) Kubert a-200; c-72, 73. Nino a-228i, 230i. Orlando a-151i. Perez a-184-86p, 192-97p, 200p; c-184p, 186, 192-195, 196p, 197p, 199, 200, 201p, 202, 203-05p, 207-09, 212-15, 217, 219, 220. Reinman a-97r. Roussos a-62i. Sekowsky a-44-63p, 110-12p(r); c-46-48p, 51p. Smith c-185i. Starlin c-178-80, 183, 185p. Staton a-244p; c-157p, 244p. Toth a-110r. Tuska a-153, 228p, 241-243p. JSA x-over-55, 56, 64, 65, 73, 74, 82, 83, 91, 92, 101, 102, 107, 108, 110, 113, 115, 123, 124, 135-37, 147, 148, 159, 160, 171, 172, 183-85, 195-97, 207, 208, 209, 219, 220, 231, 232.

JUSTICE MACHINE, THE
June, 1981 - No. 5, Nov, 1983 ($2.00, No. 1-3, Magazine size)
Noble Comics

1-Byrne-c(p)	3.35	10.00	20.00
2-Austin-c(i)	1.70	5.00	10.00
3	1.50	4.50	9.00
4,5	.85	2.50	5.00
Annual 1 (1/84, 68 pgs.)(published by Texas Comics); 1st app. The Elementals; Golden-c(p)	2.00	6.00	12.00

JUSTICE MACHINE (Also see The New Justice Machine)
Jan, 1987 - No. 29, May, 1989 ($1.50-1.75, color)
Comico/Innovation Publishing

1-29	.30	.90	1.75
Annual 1(6/89, $2.50, 36 pgs.)-Last Comico ish.	.40	1.25	2.50
Summer Spectacular 1 ('89, $2.75)-Innovation Publ.; Byrne/Gustovich cover	.45	1.40	2.75

JUSTICE MACHINE FEATURING THE ELEMENTALS
May, 1986 - No. 4, Aug, 1986 (mini-series)
Comico

1	.40	1.25	2.50
2-4	.30	.90	1.80

JUSTICE TRAPS THE GUILTY (Fargo Kid V11No.3 on)
Oct-Nov, 1947 - V11No.2(No.92), Apr-May, 1958
Prize/Headline Publications

V2#1-S&K c/a; electrocution-c	16.00	48.00	110.00
2-S&K-c/a	8.50	25.50	60.00
3-5-S&K c/a	7.00	21.00	50.00
6-S&K c/a; Feldstein-a	8.00	24.00	56.00
7,9-S&K c/a	5.70	17.00	40.00

	Good	Fine	N-Mint
8,10-Krigstein-a; S&K-c. 10-S&K-a	7.00	210	5.00
11,19-S&K-c	3.00	9.00	21.00
12,14-17,20-No S&K	2.00	6.00	14.00
13-Used in SOTI, pg. 110-111	4.65	14.00	32.00
18-S&K-c, Elder-a	2.30	7.00	16.00
21-S&K c/a	2.65	8.00	18.00
22,23,27-S&K-c	2.00	6.00	14.00
24-26,28-50	1.30	4.00	9.00
51-57,59-70	1.15	3.50	8.00
58-Illo. in SOTI, "Treating police contemptuously"(top left); text on heroin	10.00	30.00	70.00
71-75,77-92	1.15	3.50	8.00
76-Orlando-a	1.15	3.50	8.00

NOTE: Bailey a-12, 13. Elder a-8. Kirby a-19p. Meskin a-22, 27, 63, 64; c-45, 46. Robinson/Meskin a-5, 19. Severin a-8, 11p. Photo-c #12, 15, 16.

JUST KIDS
1932 (16 pages; 9½x12''; paper cover)
McLoughlin Bros.

283-Three-color text, pictures on heavy paper	6.50	19.50	45.00

JUST MARRIED
January, 1958 - No. 114, Dec, 1976
Charlton Comics

1	1.50	4.50	10.00
2	.75	2.25	5.00
3-10	.45	1.35	3.00
11-30	.25	.80	1.60
31-50		.40	.80
51-114		.20	.40

JUSTY
Dec 6, 1988 - No. 9, 1989 ($1.75, B&W, bi-weekly mini-series)
Viz Comics

1-9: Japanese manga	.30	.90	1.80

KA'A'NGA COMICS (. . .Jungle King)(See Jungle Comics)
Spring, 1949 - No. 20, Summer, 1954
Fiction House Magazines (Glen-Kel Publ. Co.)

1-Ka'a'nga, Lord of the Jungle begins	24.00	73.00	170.00
2 (Wint., '49-'50)	12.00	36.00	84.00
3,4	9.30	28.00	65.00
5-Camilla app.	6.50	19.50	45.00
6-9: 7-Tuska-a. 9-Tabu, Wizard of the Jungle app.	4.50	14.00	32.00
10-Used in POP, pg. 99	4.85	14.50	34.00
11-15	3.70	11.00	26.00
16-Sheena app.	4.00	12.00	28.00
17-20	3.15	9.50	22.00
I.W. Reprint #1 (r-/#18) Kinstler-c	.70	2.00	4.00
I.W. Reprint #8 (reprints #10)	.70	2.00	4.00

KAMANDI, THE LAST BOY ON EARTH (Also see Brave and the Bold No. 120 & Cancelled Comic Cavalcade)
Oct-Nov, 1972 - No. 59, Sept-Oct, 1978
National Periodical Publications/DC Comics

1-Origin	.60	1.75	3.50
2-59: 4-Intro. Prince Tuftan of the Tigers. 29-Superman x-over. 31-Intro Pyra. 32-68 pgs.; origin from #1	.25	.75	1.50

NOTE: Ayers a(p)-48-59 (most). Kirby a-1-40p; c-1-33. Kubert c-34-41. Nasser a-45p, 46p. Starlin a-59p; c-57, 59p.

KAMUI (Legend Of. . .#2 on)
May 12, 1987 - Present ($1.50, B&W, Bi-weekly)
Eclipse Comics/VIZ Comics #38 on

1	.50	1.50	3.00
2	.35	1.00	2.00
3	.25	.75	1.50

The Justice Machine #1 (6/81), © Noble Comics

Justice Traps The Guilty V2#1, © PRIZE

Ka'a'nga Comics #3, © FH

Kathy #1, ≅ STD

Katy Keene Pinup Parade #1, ≅ AP

Ka-Zar #1 (8/70), ≅ MEG

	Good	Fine	N-Mint
KAMUI (continued)			
1-3-2nd print		.60	1.20
4-10	.25	.70	1.40
11-38		.60	1.20

KARATE KID (See Action, Adventure, Legion of Super-Heroes, & Superboy)
Mar-Apr, 1976 - No. 15, July-Aug, 1978
National Periodical Publications/DC Comics

		Good	Fine
1-Meets Iris Jacobs; Estrada/Staton-a		.40	.80
2-15: 2-Major Disaster app. 15-Continued into Kamandi #58		.30	.60

NOTE: *Grell c-1-4, 5p, 6p, 7, 8. Staton a-1-9i. Legion x-over-No. 1, 2, 4, 6, 10, 12, 13. Princess Projectra x-over-#8, 9*

KASCO KOMICS
1945; No. 2, 1949 (regular size; paper cover)
Kasko Grainfeed (Giveaway)

	Good	Fine	N-Mint
1(1945)-Similar to Katy Keene; Bill Woggon-a; 28 pgs.;			
6-7/8''x9-7/8''	9.35	28.00	65.00
2(1949)-Woggon-a	8.00	24.00	55.00

KATHY
September, 1949 - No. 16, 1953
Standard Comics

	Good	Fine	N-Mint
1	3.50	10.50	24.00
2-Schomburg-c	1.70	5.00	12.00
3-5	1.30	4.00	9.00
6-16	.85	2.50	6.00

KATHY
Oct, 1959 - No. 27, Feb, 1964
Atlas Comics/Marvel (ZPC)

	Good	Fine	N-Mint
1-Teen-age	2.65	8.00	18.00
2	1.30	4.00	9.00
3-15	.90	2.75	5.50
16-27	.45	1.25	2.50

KAT KARSON
No date (Reprint)
I. W. Enterprises

	Good	Fine	N-Mint
1-Funny animals	.50	1.50	3.00

KATY AND KEN VISIT SANTA WITH MISTER WISH
1948 (16 pgs.; paper cover)
S. S. Kresge Co. (Giveaway)

	Good	Fine	N-Mint
nn	2.35	7.00	14.00

KATY KEENE (Also see Kasco Komics, Laugh, Pep, Suzie, & Wilbur)
1949 - No. 4, 1951; No. 5, 3/52 - No. 62, Oct, 1961
Archie Publ./Close-Up/Radio Comics

	Good	Fine	N-Mint
1-Bill Woggon-a begins	65.00	195.00	455.00
2	32.00	95.00	225.00
3-5	27.00	81.00	190.00
6-10	22.00	65.00	154.00
11,13-20	19.00	57.00	132.00
12-(Scarce)	21.00	62.00	146.00
21-40	13.00	40.00	90.00
41-62	10.00	30.00	70.00
Annual 1('54)	35.00	105.00	245.00
Annual 2-6('55-59)	18.00	54.00	125.00
3-D 1(1953-Large size)	28.00	84.00	195.00
Charm 1(9/58)	16.00	48.00	110.00
Glamour 1(1957)	16.00	48.00	110.00
Spectacular 1('56)	16.00	48.00	110.00

KATY KEENE COMICS DIGEST MAGAZINE
1987 - Present ($1.25-$1.35-$1.50, digest size, annual)
Close-Up, Inc. (Archie Ent.)

		Fine	N-Mint
1-10		.70	1.35

KATY KEENE FASHION BOOK MAGAZINE
1955 - No. 13, Sum, '56 - N. 23, Wint, '58-59 (nn 3-10)
Radio Comics/Archie Publications

	Good	Fine	N-Mint
1	32.00	95.00	225.00
2	18.00	54.00	125.00
11-18: 18-Photo Bill Woggon	14.00	42.00	100.00
19-23	11.00	32.00	75.00

KATY KEENE HOLIDAY FUN (See Archie Giant Series Mag. No. 7,12)

KATY KEENE PINUP PARADE
1955 - No. 15, Summer, 1961 (25 cents)
Radio Comics/Archie Publications

	Good	Fine	N-Mint
1	32.00	95.00	225.00
2	18.00	54.00	125.00
3-5	15.00	45.00	105.00
6-10,12-14: 8-Mad parody. 10-Photo Bill Woggon	12.00	36.00	84.00
11-Story of how comics get CCA approved, narrated by Katy	15.00	45.00	105.00
15(Rare)-Photo artist & family	32.00	95.00	225.00

KATY KEENE SPECIAL (Katy Keene No. 7 on)
Sept, 1983 - Present (Later issues published quarterly)
Archie Enterprises

		Fine	N-Mint
1-Woggon-r; new Woggon-c		.50	1.00
2-34: 3-Woggon-r		.30	.60

KATZENJAMMER KIDS, THE (Also see Hans Und Fritz)
1903 (50 pgs.; 10x15¼''; in color)
New York American & Journal

(by Rudolph Dirks, strip 1st appeared in 1898)

	Good	Fine	N-Mint
1903 (Rare)	30.00	90.00	210.00
1905-Tricks of. . . (10x15)	22.00	65.00	154.00
1906-Stokes-10x16'', 32 pgs. in color	22.00	65.00	154.00
1910-The Komical . . .(10x15)	22.00	65.00	154.00
1921-Embee Dist. Co., 10x16'', 20 pgs. in color	19.00	57.00	132.00

KATZENJAMMER KIDS, THE (See Giant Comic Album)
1945-1946; Summer, 1947 - No. 27, Feb-Mar, 1954
David McKay Publ./Standard No. 12-21(Spring/'50 - 53)/Harvey No. 22, 4/53 on

	Good	Fine	N-Mint
Feature Books 30	9.30	28.00	65.00
Feature Books 32,35('45),41,44('46)	7.00	21.00	50.00
Feature Books 37-Has photos & biog. of Harold Knerr	8.50	25.50	60.00
1(1947)	8.50	25.50	60.00
2	4.30	13.00	30.00
3-11	3.00	9.00	21.00
12-14(Standard)	2.15	6.50	15.00
15-21(Standard)	1.50	4.50	10.00
22-25,27(Harvey): 22-24-Henry app.	1.15	3.50	8.00
26-½ in 3-D	11.00	33.00	76.00

KAYO (Formerly Jest?)
No. 12, March, 1945
Harry 'A' Chesler

	Good	Fine	N-Mint
12-Green Knight, Capt. Glory, Little Nemo (not by McCay)	5.50	16.50	38.00

KA-ZAR (Also see Savage Tales #6 & X-Men #10)
Aug, 1970 - No. 3, Mar, 1971 (Giant-Size, 68 pgs.)
Marvel Comics Group

	Good	Fine	N-Mint
1-Reprints earlier Ka-Zar stories; Avengers x-over in Hercules; Daredevil, X-Men app; hidden profanity-c	.60	1.75	3.50
2,3-Daredevil app., Ka-Zar origin #2	.50	1.50	3.00

NOTE: *Kirby c/a-all. Colan a-1p(r).*

KA-ZAR
Jan, 1974 - No. 20, Feb, 1977 (Regular Size)
Marvel Comics Group

	Good	Fine	N-Mint
1	.25	.75	1.50
2-20		.50	1.00

NOTE: *Alcala a-6i, 8i. Brunner c-4. J. Buscema a-6-10p; c-1, 5, 7. Heath a-12. Gil Kane c(p)-3; 5, 8-11, 15, 20. Kirby c-12p. Reinman a-1p.*

KA-ZAR THE SAVAGE (See Marvel Fanfare)
4/81 - No. 34, 10/84 (Regular size) (Mando paper No. 10 on)
Marvel Comics Group

1-34: 11-Origin Zabu. 12-Two versions: With & without panel missing			
(1600 printed with panel). 29-Double size; Ka-Zar & Shanna wed			
		.50	1.00

NOTE: *B. Anderson a-1p-15p, 18, 19; c-1-17, 18p, 20(back-c). Gil Kane a-11, 12, 14. Photo-c #26.*

KEEN DETECTIVE FUNNIES (Formerly Detective Picture Stories?)
No. 8, July, 1938 - No. 24, Sept, 1940
Centaur Publications

	Good	Fine	N-Mint
V1#8-The Clock continues-r/Funny Picture Stories 1			
	83.00	210.00	500.00
9-Tex Martin by Eisner	43.00	130.00	300.00
10,11: 11-Dean Denton story (begins?)	37.00	110.00	260.00
V2#1,2-The Eye Sees by Frank Thomas begins; ends #23(Not in			
V2#3&5). 2-Jack Cole-a	33.00	100.00	235.00
3-TNT Todd begins	33.00	100.00	235.00
4-6,9-11: 4-Gabby Flynn begins. 5-Dean Denton story			
	33.00	100.00	235.00
7-The Masked Marvel by Ben Thompson begins			
	64.00	193.00	450.00
8-Nudist ranch panel w/four girls	37.00	110.00	260.00
12(12/39)-Origin The Eye Sees by Frank Thomas; death of			
Masked Marvel's sidekick ZL	43.00	130.00	300.00
V3#1,2	37.00	110.00	260.00
18,19,21,22: 18-Bondage/torture-c	37.00	110.00	260.00
20-Classic Eye Sees-c by Thomas	43.00	130.00	300.00
23-Air Man begins (intro)	43.00	130.00	300.00
24-Air Man-c	43.00	130.00	300.00

NOTE: *Burgos a-V2#2. Jack Cole a-V2#2. Eisner a-V2#6r. Ken Ernst a-V2#4-7, 9, 10, 19, 21. Everett a-V2#6, 7, 9, 11, 12, 20. Guardineer a-V2#5, 66. Gustavson a-V2#4-6. Simon c-V3#1.*

KEEN KOMICS
V2#1, May, 1939 - V2#3, Nov, 1939
Centaur Publications

V2#1(Large size)-Dan Hastings (s/f), The Big Top, Bob Phantom the			
Magician, The Mad Goddess app.	54.00	135.00	325.00
V2#2(Reg. size)-The Forbidden Idol of Machu Picchu; Cut Carson by			
Burgos begins	28.50	85.00	200.00
V2#3-Saddle Sniffl by Jack Cole, Circus Pays, Kings Revenge app.			
	28.50	85.00	200.00

NOTE: *Binder a-V2/2. Burgos a-V2/2,3. Ken Ernst a-V2/3. Gustavson a-V2/2. Jack Cole a-V2/3.*

KEEN TEENS
1945 - No. 6, Sept, 1947
Life's Romances Publ./Leader/Magazine Enterprises

nn-14 pgs. Claire Voyant (cont'd. in other nn issue) movie photos,			
Dotty Dripple, Gertie O'Grady & Sissy; Van Johnson, Frank			
Sinatra photo-c	10.00	30.00	70.00
nn-16 pgs. Claire Voyant & 16 pgs. movie photos			
	10.00	30.00	70.00
3-6: 4-Glenn Ford-c. 5-Perry Como-c	3.50	10.50	24.00

KEEPING UP WITH THE JONESES
1920 - No. 2, 1921 (52 pgs.; 9¼x9¼''; B&W daily strip reprints)
Cupples & Leon Co.

1,2-By Pop Momand	9.00	27.00	62.00

KELLYS, THE (Formerly Rusty Comics; Spy Cases No. 26 on)
No. 23, Jan, 1950 - No. 25, June, 1950
Marvel Comics (HPC)

	Good	Fine	N-Mint
23	5.00	15.00	35.00
24,25: 24-Margie app.	2.85	8.50	20.00

KELVIN MACE
1986 - No. 2, 1986 ($2.00, B&W)
Vortex Publications

1	.70	2.00	4.00
1-2nd print (1/87, $1.75)	.30	.85	1.70
2-Color	.70	2.00	4.00

KEN MAYNARD WESTERN (Movie star)(See Wow Comics, '36)
Sept, 1950 - No. 8, Feb, 1952 (All-36pgs; photo front/back-c)
Fawcett Publications

1-Ken Maynard & his horse Tarzan begin	26.00	77.00	180.00
2	17.00	51.00	120.00
3-8	13.50	41.00	95.00

KEN SHANNON (Gabby #11) (Also see Police Comics #103)
Oct, 1951 - No. 15, 1953 (a private eye)
Quality Comics Group

1-Crandall-a	11.50	34.00	80.00
2-Crandall c/a(2); text on narcotics	10.00	30.00	70.00
3-5-Crandall-a	6.50	19.50	45.00
6	3.70	11.00	26.00
7,9,10-Crandall-a	5.50	16.50	38.00
8-Opium den drug use story	5.50	16.50	38.00
11-15 (Exist?)	2.65	8.00	18.00

NOTE: *Jack Cole a-1-9. No. 11-15 published after title change to Gabby.*

KEN STUART
Jan, 1949 (Sea Adventures)
Publication Enterprises

1-Frank Borth-c/a	3.70	11.00	26.00

KENT BLAKE OF THE SECRET SERVICE (Spy)
May, 1951 - No. 14, 1953
Marvel/Atlas Comics(20CC)

1-Injury to eye, bondage, torture	6.50	19.50	45.00
2-Drug use w/hypo scenes	3.50	10.50	24.00
3-14	2.00	6.00	14.00

NOTE: *Heath c-5, 7. Infantino c-12. Maneely c-3. Sinnott a-2(3).*

KERRY DRAKE
Jan, 1956 - No. 2, March, 1956
Argo

1,2-Newspaper-r	2.85	8.50	20.00

KERRY DRAKE DETECTIVE CASES (. . .Racket Buster No. 32,33)
(Also see Chamber of Clues & Green Hornet Comics #42-47)
1944 - No. 5, 1944; No. 6, Jan, 1948 - No. 33, Aug, 1952
Life's Romances/Compix/Magazine Ent. No.1-5/Harvey No.6 on

nn(1944)(A-1 Comics)(slightly over-size)	12.00	36.00	84.00
2	8.00	24.00	56.00
3-5(1944)	6.00	18.00	42.00
6,8(1948): 8-Bondage-c	3.50	10.50	24.00
7-Kubert-a; biog of Andriola	4.00	12.00	28.00
9,10-Two-part marijuana story; Kerry smokes marijuana-No. 10			
	6.75	20.00	47.00
11-15	3.00	9.00	21.00
16-33	2.35	7.00	16.00
. . .in the Case of the Sleeping City-(1951-Publishers Synd.)-16 pg.			
giveaway for armed forces; paper cover	2.35	7.00	16.00

NOTE: *Berg a-5. Powell a-10-23, 28, 29.*

KEWPIES
Spring, 1949

Keen Detective Funnies #18, © CEN

Ken Maynard Western #8, © FAW

Kerry Drake Detective Cases #3, © HARV

Kid Colt Outlaw #42, © MEG

Kid Eternity #1, © QUA

The Kid From Texas #1, © MEG

KEWPIES (continued)
Will Eisner Publications

	Good	Fine	N-Mint
1-Feiffer-a; used in **SOTI** in a non-seductive context, pg. 35			
	25.00	75.00	175.00

KEY COMICS
Jan, 1944 - No. 5, Aug, 1946
Consolidated Magazines

1-The Key, Will-O-The-Wisp begin	11.00	32.00	75.00
2	5.70	17.00	40.00
3,4	4.30	13.00	30.00
5-4pg. Faust Opera adapt; Kiefer-a; back-c adv. "Masterpieces III." by Lloyd Jacquet after he left Classic Comics (no copies of MI known)	6.00	18.00	42.00

KEY COMICS
1951 - 1956 (32 pages) (Giveaway)
Key Clothing Co./Peterson Clothing

Contains a comic from different publishers bound with new cover. Cover changed each year. Many combinations possible. Distributed in Nebraska, Iowa, & Kansas. Contents would determine price, 40-60 percent of original.

KEY RING COMICS
1941 (16 pgs., two colors) (sold 5 for 10 cents)
Dell Publishing Co.

1-Sky Hawk	2.00	6.00	12.00
1-Viking Carter	2.00	6.00	12.00
1-Features Sleepy Samson	2.00	6.00	12.00
1-Origin Greg Gilday r-/War Comics No. 2	2.35	7.00	14.00
1-Radior(Super hero)	2.35	7.00	14.00

NOTE: Each book has two holes in spine to put in binder.

KICKERS, INC.
Nov. 1986 - No. 12, Oct, 1987
Marvel Comics Group

1-12		.50	1.00

KID CARROTS
September, 1953
St. John Publishing Co.

1-Funny animal	2.00	6.00	14.00

KID COLT OUTLAW (Kid Colt #1-4; . . .Outlaw #5-on)(Also see All Western Winners, Best Western, Black Rider, Two-Gun Kid, Two-Gun Western, Western Winners, Wild Western, & Wisco)
8/48 - No. 139, 3/68; No. 140, 11/69 - No. 229, 4/79
Marvel Comics(LCC) 1-16; Atlas(LMC) 17-102; Marvel 103-on

1-Kid Colt & his horse Steel begin; Two-Gun Kid app.			
	32.00	95.00	225.00
2	16.00	48.00	110.00
3-5: 4-Anti-Wertham editorial; Tex Taylor app. 5-Blaze Carson app.			
	10.00	30.00	70.00
6-8: 6-Tex Taylor app; 7-Nimo the Lion begins, ends #10			
	7.00	21.00	50.00
9,10 (52pgs.)	8.00	24.00	56.00
11-Origin	8.50	25.50	60.00
12-20	5.00	15.00	35.00
21-32	4.00	12.00	28.00
33-45: Black Rider in all	3.00	9.00	21.00
46,47,49,50	2.65	8.00	18.00
48-Kubert-a	3.50	10.50	24.00
51-53,55,56	2.00	6.00	14.00
54-Williamson/Maneely-c	2.85	8.50	20.00
57-60,66: 4-pg. Williamson-a in all. 59-Reprint Rawhide Kid #79			
	4.00	12.00	28.00
61-63,67-78,80-86: 86-Kirby-a(r)	1.30	4.00	9.00
64,65-Crandall-a	1.70	5.00	12.00
79,87: 79-Origin retold. 87-Davis-a(r)	1.70	5.00	12.00
88,89-Williamson-a in both (4 pgs.). 89-Redrawn Matt Slade #2			

	Good	Fine	N-Mint
	2.65	8.00	18.00
90-99,101-Last 10 cent issues	.70	2.00	5.00
100	1.00	3.00	7.00
101-120	.50	1.50	3.00
121-140: 121-Rawhide Kid x-over. 125-Two-Gun Kid x-over. 130-132-68pg. issues with one new story each; 130-Origin. 140-Reprints begin	.25	.75	1.50
141-160: 156-Giant; reprints		.50	1.00
161-229: 170-Origin retold		.30	.60
. . .Album (no date; 1950's; Atlas Comics)-132 pgs.; random binding, cardboard cover, B&W stories; contents can vary (Rare)			
	16.00	48.00	110.00
Giant Size 1(1/75), 2(4/75), 3(7/75)		.50	1.00

NOTE: Ayers a-many. Colan a-52, 53; c(p)-223, 228, 229. Crandall a-140r, 167r. Everett a-137r, 225i(r). Heath c-34, 35, 39, 44, 46, 48, 49, 57. Jack Keller a-25(2), 26-68(3-4), 78, 94p, 98, 99, 108, 110, 132. Kirby a-86r; 93, 96, 119, 176(part); c-87, 92-95, 97, 99-112, 114-117, 121-123, 197r. Maneely a-12, 68, 81; c-17, 19, 40-43, 47, 52, 53, 62, 65, 68, 78, 81. Morrow a-173r, 216r. Rico a-13, 18. Severin c-58. Shores a-39, 41-43; c-4, 24. Sutton a-137p, 225p(r). Wildey a-82. Williamson a-147r, 170r, 172r, 216r. Woodbridge a-64, 81. Black Rider a#33-45, 74, 86. Iron Mask in #110, 114, 121, 127. Sam Hawk in #84, 101, 111, 121, 146, 174, 181, 188.

KID COWBOY (Also see Approved Comics #4)
1950 - No. 14, 1954 (painted covers)
Ziff-Davis Publ./St. John (Approved Comics)

1-Lucy Belle & Red Feather begin	5.00	15.00	35.00
2	2.65	8.00	18.00
3-14: 11-Bondage-c	2.00	6.00	14.00

NOTE: Berg a-5. Maneely c-2.

KIDDIE KAPERS
1945?(nd); Oct, 1957; 1963 - 1964
Kiddie Kapers Co., 1945/Decker Publ. (Red Top-Farrell)

1(nd, 1945-46?)-Infinity-c; Funny animal, 36 pgs.			
	3.00	9.00	21.00
1(10/57)(Decker)-Little Bit reprints from Kiddie Karnival			
	1.30	4.00	9.00
Super Reprint #7, 10('63), 12, 14('63), 15,17('64), 18('64)			
	.35	1.00	2.00

KIDDIE KARNIVAL
1952 (100 pgs., 25 cents) (One Shot)
Ziff-Davis Publ. Co. (Approved Comics)

nn-Rebound Little Bit #1,2	10.00	30.00	70.00

KID ETERNITY (Becomes Buccaneers) (See Hit Comics)
Spring, 1946 - No. 18, Nov, 1949
Quality Comics Group

1	34.00	100.00	235.00
2	16.00	48.00	110.00
3-Mac Raboy-a	16.50	50.00	115.00
4-10	9.30	28.00	65.00
11-18	6.00	18.00	42.00

KID FROM DODGE CITY, THE
July, 1957 - No. 2, Sept, 1957
Atlas Comics (MMC)

1	3.00	9.00	21.00
2-Everett-c	1.70	5.00	12.00

KID FROM TEXAS, THE (A Texas Ranger)
June, 1957 - No. 2, Aug, 1957
Atlas Comics (CSI)

1-Powell-a; Severin-c	3.50	10.50	24.00
2	1.70	5.00	12.00

KID KOKO
1958
I. W. Enterprises

		Good	Fine	N-Mint

KID KOKO (continued)
Reprint #1,2-(r/M.E.'s Koko & Kola #4, 1947) .50 1.50 3.00

KID KOMICS (. . . Movie Komics No. 11)
Feb, 1943 - No. 10, Spring, 1946
Timely Comics (USA 1,2/FCI 3-10)

1-Origin Captain Wonder & sidekick Tim Mullrooney, & Subbie;
intro the Sea-Going Lad, Pinto Pete, & Trixie Trouble; Knuckles &
White-Wash Jones only app.; Wolverton art, 7 pgs.
129.00 325.00 775.00
2-The Young Allies, Red Hawk, & Tommy Tyme begin; last Captain
Wonder & Subbie 73.00 185.00 440.00
3-The Vision & Daredevils app. 50.00 125.00 300.00
4-The Destroyer begins; Sub-Mariner app.; Red Hawk & Tommy
Tyme end 43.00 110.00 260.00
5,6 31.00 78.00 185.00
7-10: The Whizzer app. 7; Destroyer not in #7,8; 10-Last Destroyer,
Young Allies & Whizzer 27.00 70.00 160.00
NOTE: *Schomburg c-2-10. Shores c-1.*

KID MONTANA (Formerly Davy Crockett Frontier Fighter; The Gun-
fighters No. 51 on)
V2#9, Nov, 1957 - No. 50, Mar, 1965
Charlton Comics

V2#9 2.65 8.00 18.00
10 1.30 4.00 9.00
11,12,14-20 .85 2.60 6.00
13-Williamson-a 2.00 6.00 14.00
21-35 .60 1.75 3.50
36-50 .25 .75 1.50
NOTE: *Title change to Montana Kid on cover only on No. 44; remained Kid Montana on
inside.*

KID MOVIE KOMICS (Formerly Kid Komics; Rusty Comics #12 on)
No. 11, Summer, 1946
Timely Comics

11-Silly Seal & Ziggy Pig; 2 pgs. Kurtzman "Hey Look" plus 6 pg.
"Pigtales" story 11.00 32.00 75.00

KIDNAPPED (See 4-Color No. 1101 & Movie Comics)

KIDNAP RACKET (See Harvey Comics Hits No. 57)

KID SLADE GUNFIGHTER (Formerly Matt Slade . . .)
No. 5, Jan, 1957 - No. 8, July, 1957
Atlas Comics (SPI)

5-Maneely, Roth, Severin-a in all; Maneely-c 3.50 10.50 24.00
6,8: 8-Severin-c 1.70 5.00 12.00
7-Williamson/Mayo-a, 4 pgs. 4.00 12.00 28.00

KID ZOO COMICS
July, 1948 (52 pgs.)
Street & Smith Publications

1-Funny Animal 8.00 24.00 55.00

KILLER
March, 1985 ($1.75, One-shot, color, Baxter paper)
Eclipse Comics

1-Timothy Truman c/a .30 .90 1.80

KILLERS, THE
1947 - No. 2, 1948 (No month)
Magazine Enterprises

1-Mr. Zin, the Hatchet Killer; mentioned in SOTI, pgs. 179,180;
Used by N.Y. Legis. Comm. L. B. Cole-c 43.00 130.00 300.00
2-(Scarce)-Hashish smoking story; "Dying, Dying, Dead" drug story;
Whitney, Ingels-a; Whitney hanging-c 43.00 130.00 300.00

KILLING JOKE, THE (See Batman: The Killing Joke)

KILROYS, THE
June-July, 1947 - No. 54, June-July, 1955

B&I Publ. Co. No. 1-19/American Comics Group

1 9.00 27.00 62.00
2 4.50 14.00 32.00
3-5: 5-Gross-a 3.50 10.50 24.00
6-10: 8-Milt Gross's Moronica 2.65 8.00 18.00
11-20: 14-Gross-a 2.15 6.50 15.00
21-30 1.60 4.80 11.00
31-47,50-54 1.15 3.50 8.00
48,49-(3-D effect) 8.50 25.50 60.00

KING CLASSICS
1977 (85 cents each) (36 pages. cardboard covers)
King Features (Printed in Spain for U.S. distr.)

1-Connecticut Yankee, 2-Last of the Mohicans, 3-Moby Dick, 4-Robin Hood, 5-Swiss
Family Robinson, 6-Robinson Crusoe, 7-Treasure Island, 8-20,000 Leagues, 9-Christmas
Carol, 10-Huck Finn, 11-Around the World in 80 Days, 12-Davy Crockett, 13-Don Quixote,
14-Gold Bug, 15-Ivanhoe, 16-Three Musketeers, 17-Baron Munchausen, 18-Alice in
Wonderland, 19-Black Arrow, 20-Five Weeks in a Balloon, 21-Great Expectations,
22-Gulliver's Travels, 23-Prince & Pauper, 24-Lawrence of Arabia

(Originals, 1977-78) each 1.15 3.50 8.00
Reprints, 1979; HRN-24) 1.00 3.00 6.00
NOTE: *The first eight issues were not numbered. Issues No. 25-32 were advertised but
not published. The 1977 originals have HRN 32a; the 1978 originals have HRN 32b.*

KING COLT (See 4-Color No. 651)

KING COMICS (Strip reprints)
Apr, 1936 - No. 159, Feb, 1952 (Winter on cover)
David McKay Publications/Standard No. 156-on

1-Flash Gordon by Alex Raymond; Brick Bradford, Mandrake the
Magician & Popeye begin 333.00 835.00 2000.00
2 150.00 375.00 900.00
3 108.00 270.00 650.00
4 66.00 200.00 465.00
5 50.00 150.00 350.00
6-10: 9-X-Mas-c 33.00 100.00 230.00
11-20 25.00 75.00 175.00
21-30 21.00 62.00 145.00
31-40: 33-Last Segar Popeye 18.50 56.00 130.00
41-50: 46-Little Lulu, Alvin & Tubby app. as text illos by Marge Buell
50-The Lone Ranger begins 16.50 50.00 115.00
51-60: 52-Barney Baxter begins? 12.00 36.00 85.00
61-The Phantom begins 11.00 32.00 75.00
62-80: 76-Flag-c 9.00 27.00 62.00
81-99: 82-Blondie begins? 7.00 21.00 50.00
100 9.50 28.00 65.00
101-115-Last Raymond issue 6.50 19.50 45.00
116-145: 117-Phantom origin retold 5.00 15.00 35.00
146,147-Prince Valiant in both 3.70 11.00 26.00
148-155-Flash Gordon ends 3.70 11.00 26.00
156-159 2.85 8.50 24.00
NOTE: *Marge Buell text illos in No. 24-46 at least.*

KING CONAN (Conan The King No. 20 on)
March, 1980 - No. 19, Nov, 1983 (52 pgs.)
Marvel Comics Group

1 .40 1.25 2.50
2-6: 4-Death of Thoth Amon .30 .90 1.80
7-19: 7-1st Paul Smith-a, 2 pgs. (9/81) .30 .90 1.80
NOTE: *Buscema a-1p-9p, 17p; c(p)1-5, 7-9, 14, 17. Kaluta c-19. Nebres a-17i, 18, 19i.
Severin c-18. Simonson c-6.*

KING KONG (See Movie Comics)

KING LEONARDO & HIS SHORT SUBJECTS (TV)
Nov-Jan, 1961-62 - No. 4, Sept, 1963
Dell Publishing Co./Gold Key

4-Color 1242,1278 5.00 15.00 35.00
01390-207(5-7/62)(Dell) 4.30 13.00 30.00

Kid Komics #9. / MEG

The Kilroys #1. / ACG

King Comics #4. / KING

King Of The Royal Mounted #15, © Zane Grey

King Solomon's Mines #1, © AVON

Kitty Pryde And Wolverine #5, © MEG

	Good	Fine	N-Mint
KING LEONARDO (continued)			
1 (10/62)	4.30	13.00	30.00
2-4	2.85	8.50	20.00

KING LOUIE & MOWGLI
May, 1968 (Disney)
Gold Key

1 (10223-805). Characters from Jungle Book	1.50	4.50	10.00

KING OF DIAMONDS (TV)
July-Sept, 1962
Dell Publishing Co.

01-391-209-Photo-c	2.00	6.00	14.00

KING OF KINGS (See 4-Color No. 1236)

KING OF THE BAD MEN OF DEADWOOD
1950 (See Wild Bill Hickok #16)
Avon Periodicals

nn-Kinstler-c; Kamen/Feldstein-a r-/Cowpuncher 2			
	9.50	28.00	65.00

KING OF THE ROYAL MOUNTED (See Feature Books #1 (McKay), Large Feature Comic #9, Red Ryder #3 & Super Book #2,6)

KING OF THE ROYAL MOUNTED (Zane Grey's)
No. 207, Dec, 1948 - No. 935, Sept-Nov, 1958
Dell Publishing Co.

4-Color 207('48)	11.50	34.00	80.00
4-Color 265,283	8.00	24.00	56.00
4-Color 310,340	5.00	15.00	35.00
4-Color 363,384	4.00	12.00	28.00
8(6-8/52)-10	4.00	12.00	28.00
11-20	3.50	10.50	24.00
21-28(3-5/58)	3.00	9.00	21.00
4-Color 935(9-11/58)	3.00	9.00	21.00

NOTE: 4-Color No. 207,265,283,310,340,363,384 are all newspaper reprints with **Jim Gary** art. No. 8 on are all Dell originals. Painted c-No. 9-on.

KING RICHARD & THE CRUSADERS (See 4-Color No. 588)

KINGS OF THE NIGHT
May, 1989 - No. 2, June, 1989 ($2.25, color, 2 issue series)
Dark Horse Comics

1,2-Robert E. Howard adaptation; Bolton-c	.40	1.15	2.30

KING SOLOMON'S MINES
1951 (Movie)
Avon Periodicals

nn(#1 on 1st page)	20.00	60.00	140.00

KISS (See Howard the Duck #12, 13 & Marvel Comics Super Special #1, 5)

KISSYFUR (TV)
1989 (Sept.) ($2.00, color, 52 pgs.)
DC Comics

1-Based on Saturday morning cartoon	.35	1.00	2.00

KIT CARSON (See Frontier Fighters)

KIT CARSON (Formerly All True Detective Cases No. 4; Fighting Davy Crockett No. 9; see Blazing Sixguns)
1950; No. 2, 8/51 - No. 3, 12/51; No. 5, 11-12/54 - No. 8, 9/55
Avon Periodicals

nn(#1) (1950)	6.50	19.50	45.00
2(8/51)	3.70	11.00	26.00
3(12/51)	3.00	9.00	21.00
5-6,8('54-'55)	2.65	8.00	18.00
7-Kinstler-a(2)	3.00	9.00	21.00
I.W. Reprint #10('63)-Severin-c	.85	2.50	5.00

NOTE: Kinstler c-1-3,5-8.

KIT CARSON & THE BLACKFEET WARRIORS
1953

	Good	Fine	N-Mint
Realistic			
nn-Reprint; Kinstler-c	4.60	14.00	32.00

KIT KARTER
May-July, 1962
Dell Publishing Co.

1	1.15	3.50	8.00

KITTY
October, 1948
St. John Publishing Co.

1-Lily Renee-a	3.50	10.50	24.00

KITTY PRYDE AND WOLVERINE
Nov, 1984 - No. 6, April, 1985 (6 issue mini-series)
Marvel Comics Group

1 (From X-Men)	.75	2.25	4.50
2-6	.60	1.75	3.50

KLARER GIVEAWAYS (See Wisco)

KNIGHTS OF THE ROUND TABLE (See 4-Color No. 540)

KNIGHTS OF THE ROUND TABLE
No. 10, April, 1957
Pines Comics

10	1.70	5.00	12.00

KNIGHTS OF THE ROUND TABLE
Nov-Jan, 1963/64 (Painted-c)
Dell Publishing Co.

1 (12-397-401)	2.30	7.00	16.00

KNOCK KNOCK (...Who's There?)
1936 (52 pages) (8x9'', B&W)
Whitman Publ./Gerona Publications

801-Joke book; Bob Dunn-a	5.00	15.00	35.00

KNOCKOUT ADVENTURES
Winter, 1953-54
Fiction House Magazines

1-Reprints/Fight Comics #53	5.70	17.00	40.00

KNOW YOUR MASS
1958 (100 Pg. Giant) (35 cents) (square binding)
Catechetical Guild

303-In color	2.30	7.00	16.00

KOBRA (See DC Special Series No. 1)
Feb-Mar, 1976 - No. 7, Mar-Apr, 1977
National Periodical Publications

1-Art plotted by Kirby		.40	.80
2-7: 3-Giffen-a		.25	.50

NOTE: **Austin** a-3i. **Buckler** a-5p; c-5p. **Kubert** c-4. **Nasser** a-6p, 7; c-7.

KOKEY KOALA
May, 1952
Toby Press

1	2.85	8.50	20.00

KOKO AND KOLA (Also see Tick Tock Tales)
Fall, 1946 - No. 5, May, 1947; No. 6, 1950
Compix/Magazine Enterprises

1-Funny animal	4.00	12.00	28.00
2	2.00	6.00	14.00
3-5,6(A-1 28)	1.50	4.50	10.00

KO KOMICS
October, 1945
Gerona Publications

1-The Duke of Darkness & The Menace (hero); Kirby-c			
	11.50	34.00	80.00

KOMIC KARTOONS
Fall, 1945 - No. 2, Winter, 1945
Timely Comics (EPC)

	Good	Fine	N-Mint
1,2-Andy Wolf, Bertie Mouse	7.00	21.00	50.00

KOMIK PAGES
April, 1945 (All-r)
Harry 'A' Chesler, Jr. (Our Army, Inc.)

	Good	Fine	N-Mint
10(#1 on inside)-Land O' Nod by Rick Yager (2 pgs.), Animal Crackers, Foxy GrandPa, Tom, Dick & Mary, Cheerio Minstrels, Red Starr plus other 1-2 pg. strips; Cole-a	8.00	24.00	56.00

KONA (. . . Monarch of Monster Isle)
Feb-Apr, 1962 - No. 21, Jan-Mar, 1967 (Painted-c)
Dell Publishing Co.

4-Color 1256 (#1)	2.85	8.50	20.00
2-10: 4-Anak begins	1.30	4.00	9.00
11-21	.70	2.00	5.00
NOTE: *Glanzman a-all issues.*

KONGA (Fantastic Giants No. 24) (See Return of . . .)
1960; No. 2, Aug, 1961 - No. 23, Nov, 1965
Charlton Comics

1(1960)-Based on movie	16.00	48.00	110.00
2	8.00	24.00	55.00
3-5	5.70	17.00	40.00
6-15	4.00	12.00	28.00
16-23	2.65	8.00	18.00
NOTE: *Ditko a-1, 3-15; c-4, 6-9. Glanzman a-12. Montes & Bache a-16-23.*

KONGA'S REVENGE (Formerly Return of . . .)
No. 2, Summer, 1963 - No. 3, Fall, 1964; Dec, 1968
Charlton Comics

2,3: 2-Ditko c/a	2.65	8.00	18.00
1('68)-Reprints Konga's Revenge No. 3	1.30	4.00	9.00

KONG THE UNTAMED
June-July, 1975 - No. 5, Feb-Mar, 1976
National Periodical Publications

1		.40	.80
2-5		.25	.50
NOTE: *Alcala a-1-3. Wrightson c-1,2.*

KOOKIE
Feb-Apr, 1962 - No. 2, May-July, 1962
Dell Publishing Co.

1,2-Written by John Stanley; Bill Williams-a	5.70	17.00	40.00

K. O. PUNCH, THE (Also see Lucky Fights It Through)
1948 (Educational giveaway)
E. C. Comics

Feldstein-splash; Kamen-a	117.00	340.00	700.00

KORAK, SON OF TARZAN (Edgar Rice Burroughs)
Jan, 1964 - No. 45, Jan, 1972 (Painted-c No. 1-?)
Gold Key

1-Russ Manning-a	3.50	10.50	24.00
2-11-Russ Manning-a	1.70	5.00	12.00
12-21: 14-Jon of the Kalahari ends. 15-Mabu, Jungle Boy begins.			
21-Manning-a	1.15	3.50	8.00
22-30	.70	2.00	5.00
31-45	.60	1.75	3.50
NOTE: *Warren Tufts a-12, 13.*

KORAK, SON OF TARZAN (Tarzan Family #60 on; see Tarzan #230)
No. 46, May-June, 1972 - No. 56, Feb-Mar, 1974; No. 57, May-June, 1975 - No. 59, Sept-Oct, 1975 (Edgar Rice Burroughs)
National Periodical Publications

46-(52 pgs.)-Carson of Venus begins (origin); Pellucidar feature

	Good	Fine	N-Mint
		.50	1.00
47-50: 49-Origin Korak retold		.35	.70
51-59: 56-Last Carson of Venus		.25	.50
NOTE: *Kaluta a-46-56. All have covers by Joe Kubert. Manning strip reprints-No. 57-59. Frank Thorn a-46-51.*

KOREA MY HOME (Also see Yalta to Korea)
nd (1950s)
Johnstone and Cushing

nn-Anti-communist; Korean War	15.00	45.00	105.00

KORG: 70,000 B. C. (TV)
May, 1975 - No. 9, Nov, 1976 (Hanna-Barbera)
Charlton Publications

1	.25	.75	1.50
2-9: 2-Byrne text illos		.50	1.00

KORNER KID COMICS
1947
Four Star Publications

1	3.70	11.00	26.00

KRAZY KAT
1946 (Hardcover)
Holt

Reprints daily & Sunday strips by Herriman	26.00	78.00	180.00
with dust jacket (Rare)	54.00	162.00	380.00

KRAZY KAT (See Ace Comics & March of Comics No. 72,87)

KRAZY KAT COMICS (. . . & Ignatz the Mouse early issues)
May-June, 1951 - F.C. #696, Apr, 1956; Jan, 1964 (None by Herriman)
Dell Publishing Co./Gold Key

1(1951)	4.30	13.00	30.00
2-5 (#5, 8-10/52)	3.00	9.00	21.00
4-Color 454,504	2.30	7.00	16.00
4-Color 548,619,696 (4/56)	2.00	6.00	14.00
1(10098-401)(1/64-Gold Key)(TV)	2.00	6.00	14.00

KRAZY KOMICS (1st Series) (Cindy Comics No. 27 on)
July, 1942 - No. 26, Spr, 1947 (Also see Ziggy Pig)
Timely Comics (USA No. 1-21/JPC No. 22-26)

1-Ziggy Pig & Silly Seal begins	19.00	58.00	135.00
2	9.30	28.00	65.00
3-10	5.00	15.00	35.00
11,13,14	3.70	11.00	26.00
12-Timely's entire art staff drew themselves into a Creeper story			
	5.70	17.00	40.00
15-Has "Super Soldier" by Pfc. Stan Lee	3.70	11.00	26.00
16-24,26	2.65	8.00	18.00
25-Kurtzman-a, 6 pgs.	4.30	13.00	30.00

KRAZY KOMICS (2nd Series)
Aug, 1948 - No. 2, Nov, 1948
Timely/Marvel Comics

1-Wolverton (10 pgs.) & Kurtzman (8 pgs.)-a; Eustice Hayseed begins, Li'l Abner swipe	19.00	57.00	135.00
2-Wolverton-a, 10 pgs.; Powerhouse Pepper cameo			
	11.50	34.00	80.00

KRAZY KROW (Also see Dopey Duck, Film Funnies, Funny Frolics & Movie Tunes)
Summer, 1945 - No. 3, Wint, 1945/46
Marvel Comics (ZPC)

1	5.70	17.00	40.00
2,3	3.50	10.50	24.00
I.W. Reprint #1('57), 2('58), 7	.35	1.00	2.00

KRAZYLIFE
1945 (no month)

Korak, Son Of Tarzan #3, © ERB

Krazy Kat Comics #3, © Herriman

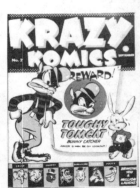
Krazy Komics #2 (9/42), © MEG

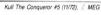
Kull The Conqueror #5 (11/72). © MEG

Lady Luck #86. © QUA

Lana #3. © MEG

KRAZYLIFE (continued)
Fox Feature Syndicate

	Good	Fine	N-Mint
1-Funny animal	5.70	17.00	40.00

KREE/SKRULL WAR STARRING THE AVENGERS, THE
Sept, 1983 - No. 2, Oct, 1983 ($2.50, 68 pgs.; Baxter paper)
Marvel Comics Group

1,2	.40	1.25	2.50

NOTE: *Adams* p-1r, 2. *Buscema* a-1r, 2r. *Simonson* c(p)/a(p)-1.

KRIM-KO KOMICS
5/18/35 - No. 6, 6/22/35; 1936 - 1939 (Giveaway) (weekly)
Krim-ko Chocolate Drink

1-(16 pgs., soft-c, Dairy giveaways)-Tom, Mary & Sparky Advs. by Russell Keaton, Jim Hawkins by Dick Moores, Mystery Island! by Rick Yager begin	5.00	15.00	35.00
2-6 (6/22/35)	2.35	7.00	16.00
Lola, Secret Agent; 184 issues, 4 pg. giveaways - all original stories each....	1.35	4.00	8.00

KROFFT SUPERSHOW (TV)
April, 1978 - No. 6, Jan, 1979
Gold Key

1		.60	1.20
2-6		.35	.70

KRULL
Nov, 1983 - No. 2, Dec, 1983
Marvel Comics Group

1,2-Film adapt. r/Marvel Super Spec.		.25	.50

KRYPTON CHRONICLES
Sept, 1981 - No. 3, Nov, 1981
DC Comics

1-Buckler-c(p)		.40	.80
2,3		.30	.60

KULL & THE BARBARIANS (Magazine)
May, 1975 - No. 3, Sept, 1975 (B&W) ($1.00)
Marvel Comics Group

1-Andru/Wood-r/Kull #1; 2 pgs. Adams; Gil Kane, Severin-a	.40	1.25	2.50
2-Red Sonja by Chaykin begins; Adams-i; Gil Kane-a	.30	.90	1.80
3-Origin Red Sonja by Chaykin; Adams-a; Solomon Kane app.	.30	.90	1.80

KULL IN 3-D (See Blackthorne 3-D Series #51)

KULL THE CONQUEROR (...the Destroyer #11 on; see Marvel Preview)
June, 1971 - No. 2, Sept, 1971; No. 3, July, 1972 - No. 15, Aug, 1974; No. 16, Aug, 1976 - No. 29, Oct, 1978
Marvel Comics Group

1-Andru/Wood-a; origin Kull	.60	1.75	3.50
2-29: 11-15-Ploog-a	.60	1.25	

NOTE: *No. 1,2,7,9,11* are based on Robert E. Howard stories. *Alcala* a-17p, 18-20i; c-24. *Ditko* a-12r, 15r. *Gil Kane* c-15p, 21. *Nebres* a-22i-27i; c-25i, 27i. *Ploog* c-11, 12p, 13. *Severin* a-2-9i; c-2-10i, 19. *Starlin* c-14.

KULL THE CONQUEROR
Dec, 1982 - No. 2, Mar, 1983 (52 pgs., printed on Baxter paper)
Marvel Comics Group

1,2: 1-Buscema-a(p)	.35	1.00	2.00

KULL THE CONQUEROR (No. 9,10 titled 'Kull')
5/83 - No. 10, 6/85 (52 pgs.; $1.25-60 cents; Mando paper)
Marvel Comics Group

V3#1-10		.50	1.00

KUNG FU (See Deadly Hands of..., & Master of...)

KUNG FU FIGHTER (See Richard Dragon...)

LABOR IS A PARTNER
1949 (32 pgs. in color; paper cover)
Catechetical Guild Educational Society

	Good	Fine	N-Mint
nn-Anti-communism	17.00	51.00	120.00
Confidential Preview-(B&W, 8½x11", saddle stitched)-only one known copy; text varies from color version, advertises next book on secularism (If the Devil Would Talk)	35.00	100.00	200.00

LABYRINTH
Nov, 1986 - No. 3, Jan, 1987 (mini-series, movie adaptation)
Marvel Comics Group

1-3: R-/Marv. Super Spec. #40		.40	.80

LAD: A DOG
1961 - No. 2, July-Sept, 1962
Dell Publishing Co.

4-Color 1303 (movie), 2	2.65	8.00	18.00

LADY AND THE TRAMP (See Dell Giants, 4-Color No. 629, 634, & Movie Comics)

LADY AND THE TRAMP IN "BUTTER LATE THAN NEVER"
1955 (16 pgs., 5x7¼", soft-c) (Walt Disney)
American Dairy Association (Premium)

nn	3.00	9.00	21.00

LADY BOUNTIFUL
1917 (10¼x13½"; 24 pgs.; B&W; cardboard cover)
Saalfield Publ. Co./Press Publ. Co.

nn-By Gene Carr; 2 panels per page	8.00	24.00	56.00

LADY COP (See First Issue Special)

LADY FOR A NIGHT (See Cinema Comics Herald)

LADY LUCK (Formerly Smash #1-85) (Also see Spirit Sections #1)
No. 86, Dec, 1949 - No. 90, Aug, 1950
Quality Comics Group

86(#1)	35.00	105.00	245.00
87-90	27.00	81.00	190.00

LAFF-A-LYMPICS (TV)(See The Funtastic World of Hanna-Barbera)
Mar, 1978 - No. 13, Mar, 1979
Marvel Comics Group

1		.30	.60
2-13		.25	.50

LAFFIN' GAS (See Adolescent Radioactive Blackbelt Hamsters)
June, 1986 - No. 12, 1988 ($2.00, B&W)
Blackthorne Publishing

1-5,7-12: 5-Boris The Bear app.	.35	1.00	2.00
6 (3-D issue; see Blackthorne 3-D Series #16)			

LAFFY-DAFFY COMICS
Feb, 1945 - No. 2, March, 1945
Rural Home Publ. Co.

1,2	3.00	9.00	21.00

LANA (Little Lana No. 8 on)
Aug, 1948 - No. 7, Aug, 1949 (Also see Annie Oakley)
Marvel Comics (MjMC)

1-Rusty, Millie begin	5.00	15.00	35.00
2-Kurtzman's "Hey Look" (1); last Rusty	3.70	11.00	26.00
3-7: 3-Nellie begins	2.00	6.00	14.00

LANCELOT & GUINEVERE (See Movie Classics)

LANCELOT LINK, SECRET CHIMP (TV)
April, 1971 - No. 8, Feb, 1973
Gold Key

1-Photo-c	1.35	4.00	8.00
2-8: 2-Photo-c	.85	2.50	5.00

LANCELOT STRONG (See The Shield)

LANCE O'CASEY (See Mighty Midget & Whiz Comics)
Spring, 1946 - No. 3, Fall, 1946; No. 4, Summer, 1948
Fawcett Publications

	Good	Fine	N-Mint
1-Captain Marvel app. on-c	10.00	30.00	70.00
2	5.50	16.50	38.00
3,4	4.30	13.00	30.00

LANCER (TV)(Western)
Feb, 1969 - No. 3, Sept, 1969 (All photo-c)
Gold Key

1	2.30	7.00	16.00
2,3	1.70	5.00	12.00

LAND OF THE GIANTS (TV)
Nov, 1968 - No. 5, Sept, 1969
Gold Key

1-Photo-c	2.00	6.00	14.00
2-5: 4,5-Photo-c	1.50	4.50	10.00

LAND OF THE LOST COMICS (Radio)
July-Aug, 1946 - No. 9, Spring, 1948
E. C. Comics

1	18.00	54.00	125.00
2	11.50	34.00	80.00
3-9	10.00	30.00	70.00

LAND UNKNOWN, THE (See 4-Color No. 845)

LARAMIE (TV)
Aug, 1960 - July, 1962 (All photo-c)
Dell Publishing Co.

4-Color 1125	5.50	16.50	38.00
4-Color 1223,1284	4.30	13.00	30.00
01-418-207	4.30	13.00	30.00

LAREDO (TV)
June, 1966
Gold Key

1 (10179-606)-Photo-c	2.00	6.00	14.00

LARGE FEATURE COMIC (Formerly called Black & White)
1939 - No. 13, 1943
Dell Publishing Co.

1 (Series I)-Dick Tracy Meets the Blank	86.00	257.00	600.00
2-Terry & the Pirates (#1)	43.00	130.00	300.00
3-Heigh-Yo Silver! The Lone Ranger (text & ill.)(76 pgs.). Also exists as a Whitman #710	43.00	130.00	300.00
4-Dick Tracy Gets His Man	46.00	140.00	325.00
5-Tarzan (#1) by Harold Foster (origin); reprints 1st dailies from '29	84.00	250.00	585.00
6-Terry & the Pirates & The Dragon Lady; reprints dailies from 1936	41.00	122.00	285.00
7-(Scarce)-52 pgs.; The Lone Ranger-Hi-Yo Silver the Lone Ranger to the Rescue. Also exists as a Whitman #715	53.00	160.00	370.00
8-Dick Tracy Racket Buster	42.00	125.00	295.00
9-King of the Royal Mounted	20.00	60.00	140.00
10-(Scarce)-Gang Busters (No. appears on inside front cover); first slick cover	29.00	87.00	205.00
11-Dick Tracy Foils the Mad Doc Hump	42.00	125.00	295.00
12-Smilin' Jack	27.00	81.00	190.00
13-Dick Tracy & Scotty	42.00	125.00	295.00
14-Smilin' Jack	27.00	81.00	190.00
15-Dick Tracy & the Kidnapped Princes	42.00	125.00	295.00
16-Donald Duck-1st app. Daisy Duck on back cover (6/41-Disney)	157.00	470.00	1100.00
(Prices vary widely on this book)			
17-Gang Busters (1941)	19.00	56.00	130.00

	Good	Fine	N-Mint
18-Phantasmo	16.50	50.00	115.00
19-Dumbo Comic Paint Book (Disney); partial-r 4-Color 17	105.00	315.00	735.00
20-Donald Duck Comic Paint Book (Rarer than #16) (Disney)	215.00	645.00	1500.00
(Prices vary widely on this book)			
21-Private Buck	7.00	21.00	50.00
22-Nuts & Jolts	7.00	21.00	50.00
23-The Nebbs	9.00	27.00	62.00
24-Popeye (Thimble Theatre) ½ by Segar	37.00	110.00	260.00
25-Smilin' Jack-1st issue to show title on-c	27.00	81.00	190.00
26-Smitty	16.00	48.00	110.00
27-Terry & the Pirates; Caniff-c/a	30.00	90.00	210.00
28-Grin & Bear It	6.50	19.50	45.00
29-Moon Mullins	14.00	42.00	100.00
30-Tillie the Toiler	13.00	40.00	90.00
1 (Series II)-Peter Rabbit by Cady; arrival date-3/27/42	28.00	84.00	195.00
2-Winnie Winkle (#1)	11.00	32.00	75.00
3-Dick Tracy	40.00	120.00	280.00
4-Tiny Tim (#1)	20.00	60.00	140.00
5-Toots & Casper	6.50	19.50	45.00
6-Terry & the Pirates; Caniff-a	30.00	90.00	210.00
7-Pluto Saves the Ship (#1)(Disney) written by Carl Barks, Jack Hannah, & Nick George. (Barks' 1st comic book work)	65.00	195.00	455.00
8-Bugs Bunny (#1)('42)	56.00	167.00	390.00
9-Bringing Up Father	9.30	27.00	65.00
10-Popeye (Thimble Theatre)	31.00	92.00	215.00
11-Barney Google & Snuffy Smith	13.00	40.00	90.00
12-Private Buck	6.50	19.50	45.00
13-(nn)-1001 Hours Of Fun; puzzles & games; by A. W. Nugent. This book was bound as #13 with Large Feature Comics in publishers files	7.00	21.00	50.00

NOTE: The Black & White Feature Books are oversized 8½x11-3/8" comics with color covers and black and white interiors. The first nine issues all have rough, heavy stock covers and, except for #7, all have 76 pages, including covers. #7 and #10-on all have 52 pages. Beginning with #10 the covers are slick and thin and, because of their size, are difficult to handle without damaging. For this reason, they are seldom found in fine to mint condition. The paper stock, unlike Wow #1 and Capt. Marvel #1, is itself not unstable . . . just thin.

LARRY DOBY, BASEBALL HERO
1950 (Cleveland Indians)
Fawcett Publications

nn-Bill Ward-a; photo-c	30.00	90.00	210.00

LARRY HARMON'S LAUREL AND HARDY (. . .Comics)
July-Aug, 1972 (Regular size)
National Periodical Publications

1	.45	1.25	2.50

LARS OF MARS
No. 10, Apr-May, 1951 - No. 11, July-Aug, 1951 (Painted-c)
Ziff-Davis Publishing Co.

10-Origin; Anderson-a(3) in each	29.00	87.00	205.00
11-Gene Colan-a	25.00	75.00	175.00

LARS OF MARS 3-D
Apr, 1987 ($2.50)
Eclipse Comics

1-r-/Lars of Mars #10,11 in 3-D + new story	.40	1.25	2.50
2-D limited edition	.85	2.50	5.00

LASER ERASER & PRESSBUTTON (See Axel Pressbutton & Miracleman 9)
Nov, 1985 - No. 6, 1987 (6 issue series, color)
Eclipse Comics

Lance O'Casey #1, © FAW

Large Feature Comic #19 (Series I), © WDC

Large Feature Comic #8 (Series II), © Warner Bros.

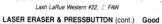
Lash LaRue Western #22, © FAW

Lassie #6, © M.G.M.

Laugh Comics #38, © AP

LASER ERASER & PRESSBUTTON (cont.)

	Good	Fine	N-Mint
1-6: 5,6-(95 cents)		.40	.80
. . .In 3-D 1 (8/86, $2.50)	.40	1.25	2.50
2-D 1 (B&W, limited to 100 copies signed & numbered)			
	.40	1.25	2.50

LASH LARUE WESTERN (Movie star; king of the bullwhip)(See Six-Gun Heroes)
Sum, 1949 - No. 46, Jan, 1954 (36pgs., 1-7,9,13,16-on)
Fawcett Publications

	Good	Fine	N-Mint
1-Lash & his horse Black Diamond begin; photo front/back-c begin			
	55.00	165.00	385.00
2(11/49)	28.00	84.00	195.00
3-5	25.00	75.00	175.00
6,7,9: 6-Last photo back-c; intro. Frontier Phantom (Lash's twin brother)	18.00	54.00	125.00
8,10 (52pgs.)	18.50	56.00	130.00
11,12,14,15 (52pgs.)	11.50	34.00	80.00
13,16-20 (36pgs.)	11.00	32.00	75.00
21-30: 21-The Frontier Phantom app.	9.30	28.00	65.00
31-45	8.00	24.00	55.00
46-Last Fawcett issue & photo-c	8.50	25.50	60.00

LASH LARUE WESTERN (Continues from Fawcett series)
No. 47, Mar-Apr, 1954 - No. 84, June, 1961
Charlton Comics

	Good	Fine	N-Mint
47-Photo-c	7.00	21.00	50.00
48	5.70	17.00	40.00
49-60	4.50	14.00	32.00
61-66,69,70: 52-r/#8; 53-r/#22	4.00	12.00	28.00
67,68-(68 pgs.). 68-Check-a	4.30	13.00	30.00
71-83	2.65	8.00	18.00
84-Last issue	3.50	10.50	24.00

LASSIE (TV)(M-G-M's . . . No. 1-36)
June, 1950 - No. 70, July, 1969
Dell Publishing Co./Gold Key No. 59 (10/62) on

	Good	Fine	N-Mint
1: (52 pgs.)-Photo-c; inside lists One Shot #282 in error			
	4.50	14.00	32.00
2-Painted-c begin	2.65	8.00	18.00
3-10	2.00	6.00	14.00
11-19: 12-Rocky Langford (Lassie's master) marries Gerry Lawrence.			
15-1st app. Timbu	1.60	4.80	11.00
20-22-Matt Baker-a	2.15	6.50	15.00
23-40: 33-Robinson-a. 39-1st app. Timmy as Lassie picks up her TV family	1.00	3.00	7.00
41-70: 63-Last Timmy. 64-r/#19. 65-Forest Ranger Corey Stuart begins, ends #69. 70-Forest Rangers Bob Ericson & Scott Turner app. (Lassie's new masters)	.75	2.25	4.50
11193(1978-Golden Press)-224 pgs.; $1.95; Baker-a(r), 92 pgs.			
	.55	1.65	4.00
The Adventures of. . .(Red Heart Dog Food giveaway, 1949)-16 pgs., soft-c	3.50	10.50	24.00
Kite Fun Book('73)-(16 pgs.; 5x7'')	2.00	6.00	14.00

NOTE: *Photo c-57. (See March of Comics #210, 217, 230, 254, 266, 278, 296, 308, 324, 334, 346, 358, 370, 381, 394, 411, 432)*

LAST DAYS OF THE JUSTICE SOCIETY SPECIAL
1986 (One shot, 68 pgs.)
DC Comics

	Good	Fine	N-Mint
1	.50	1.50	3.00

LAST GENERATION, THE
1986 - No. 5, 1989 ($1.95, B&W, high quality paper)
Black Tie Studios

	Good	Fine	N-Mint
1	1.15	3.50	7.00
2	.70	2.00	4.00
3-5	.50	1.50	3.00

	Good	Fine	N-Mint
Book 1 (1989, $6.95)-By Caliber Press	1.15	3.50	7.00

LAST HUNT, THE (See 4-Color No. 678)

LAST KISS
1988 ($3.95, B&W, squarebound, 52 pgs.)
ACME Press (Eclipse)

	Good	Fine	N-Mint
1-One story adapts E.A. Poe's The Black Cat	.70	2.00	4.00

LAST OF THE COMANCHES (See Wild Bill Hickok #28)
1953 (Movie)
Avon Periodicals

	Good	Fine	N-Mint
nn-Kinstler c/a, 21pgs.; Ravielli-a	8.50	25.50	60.00

LAST OF THE ERIES, THE (See American Graphics)

LAST OF THE FAST GUNS, THE (See 4-Color No. 925)

LAST OF THE MOHICANS (See King Classics & White Rider and. . .)

LAST OF THE VIKING HEROES, THE (Also see Silver Star #1)
Mar, 1987 - Present ($1.50-$1.95, color)
Genesis West Comics

	Good	Fine	N-Mint
1-4: 4-Intro The Phantom Force	.40	1.25	2.50
5A-Kirby/Stevens-c	.50	1.50	3.00
5B,6	.35	1.00	2.00
7-Art Adams-c	.50	1.50	3.00
8-Kirby back-c	.35	1.00	1.95
Summer Special 1(1988)-Frazetta-c	.50	1.50	3.00

NOTE: *Art Adams c-7. Byrne c-3. Kirby c-1p, 5p. Perez c-2i. Stevens c-5Ai.*

LAST STARFIGHTER, THE
Oct, 1984 - No. 3, Dec, 1984 (75 cents, movie adaptation)
Marvel Comics Group

	Good	Fine	N-Mint
1-3: R/Marvel Super Special; Guice-c		.40	.80

LAST TRAIN FROM GUN HILL (See 4-Color No. 1012)

LATEST ADVENTURES OF FOXY GRANDPA (See Foxy . . .)

LATEST COMICS (Super Duper No. 3?)
March, 1945 - No. 2
Spotlight Publ./Palace Promotions (Jubilee)

	Good	Fine	N-Mint
1-Super Duper	5.00	15.00	35.00
2-Bee-29 (nd)	3.50	10.50	24.00

LAUGH
June, 1987 - Present
Archie Enterprises

	Good	Fine	N-Mint
V2#1-20: 5-X-Mas issue		.40	.75

LAUGH COMICS (Formerly Black Hood #1-19) (Laugh #226 on)
No. 20, Fall, 1946 - No. 400, 1987
Archie Publications (Close-Up)

	Good	Fine	N-Mint
20-Archie begins; Katy Keene & Taffy begin by Woggon			
	38.00	115.00	265.00
21-23,25	18.00	54.00	125.00
24-''Pipsy'' by Kirby, 6 pgs.	18.00	54.00	125.00
26-30	10.00	30.00	70.00
31-40	8.00	24.00	50.00
41-60: 41,54-Debbi by Woggon. 57-Spanking panel			
	4.50	13.50	30.00
61-80: 67-Debbi by Woggon	2.85	8.50	20.00
81-99	2.00	6.00	14.00
100	3.00	9.00	21.00
101-126: 125-Debbi app.	1.35	4.00	9.00
127-144: Super-hero app. in all	1.35	4.00	9.00
145-160: 157-Josie app.	.75	2.25	4.50
161-165,167-200	.50	1.50	3.00
166-Beatles-c	.85	2.50	5.00
201-240	.25	.75	1.50
241-280		.40	.80

LAUGH COMICS (continued)   **Good**   **Fine**   **N-Mint**
281-400: 381-384-Katy Keene app.; by Woggon-381,382

		.30	.60

NOTE: *The Fly app. in 128, 129, 132, 134, 138, 139. Flygirl app. in 136, 137, 143. Flyman app. in 137. The Jaguar app. in 127, 130, 131, 133, 135, 140-142, 144. Josie app. in 145, 160, 164. Katy Keene app. in 20-125, 129, 130, 133. Many issues contain paper dolls.*

LAUGH COMICS DIGEST (. . .Magazine No. 23 on)
8/74; No. 2, 9/75; No. 3, 3/76 - Present (Digest-size)
Archie Publications (Close-Up No. 1, 3 on)

	Good	Fine	N-Mint
1-Adams-a	.70	2.00	4.00
2,7,8,19-Adams-a	.35	1.00	2.00
3-6,9,10		.50	1.00
11-18,20-88: Later issues $1.35,$1.50-c		.50	1.00

NOTE: **Katy Keene** *in 23, 25, 27, 32-38, 40, 45-48, 50.* **The Fly**-r *in 19, 20.* **The Jaguar**-r *in 25.* **Mr. Justice**-r *in 21.* **The Web**-r *in 23.*

LAUGH COMIX (Formerly Top Notch Laugh; Suzie No. 49 on)
No. 46, Summer, 1944 - No. 48, Winter, 1944-45
MLJ Magazines

46-Wilbur & Suzie in all	9.00	27.00	62.00
47,48	6.50	19.50	45.00

LAUGH-IN MAGAZINE (Magazine)
Oct., 1968 - No. 12, Oct, 1969 (50 cents) (Satire)
Laufer Publ. Co.

V1#1	1.00	3.00	7.00
2-12	.70	2.00	4.00

LAUREL & HARDY (See Larry Harmon's. . . & March of Comics No. 302,314)

LAUREL AND HARDY (. . .Comics)
March, 1949 - No. 28, March, 1956
St. John Publishing Co.

1	30.00	90.00	210.00
2	17.00	51.00	120.00
3,4	13.00	40.00	90.00
5-10	11.00	32.00	75.00
11-28; 26,28-r	8.50	25.50	60.00

LAUREL AND HARDY (TV)
Oct, 1962 - No. 4, Sept-Nov, 1963
Dell Publishing Co.

12-423-210 (8-10/62)	2.30	7.00	16.00
2-4 (Dell)	2.00	6.00	14.00

LAUREL AND HARDY
Jan, 1967 - No. 2, Oct, 1967 (Larry Harmon's)
Gold Key

1,2: 1-Photo back-c	1.70	5.00	12.00

LAUREL AND HARDY IN 3-D (See Blackthorne 3-D Series #23 & 34)

LAW AGAINST CRIME (Law-Crime on cover)
April, 1948 - No. 3, Aug, 1948
Essenkay Publishing Co.

1-(#1-3: ½ funny animal, ½ crime)-L. B. Cole electrocution-c/a

	26.00	77.00	180.00
2-L. B. Cole c/a	18.00	54.00	125.00

3-L. B. Cole c/a; used in **SOTI**, pg. 180,181 & illo-"The wish to hurt or kill couples in lovers' lanes;" reprinted in All-Famous Crime #9

	25.00	75.00	175.00

LAWBREAKERS (. . .Suspense Stories No. 10 on)
Mar, 1951 - No. 9, Oct-Nov, 1952
Law and Order Magazines (Charlton Comics)

1	8.50	25.50	60.00
2	4.30	13.00	30.00
3,5,6,8,9	3.00	9.00	21.00
4-"White Death" junkie story	5.00	15.00	35.00
7-"The Deadly Dopesters" drug story	4.30	13.00	30.00

LAWBREAKERS ALWAYS LOSE!
Spring, 1948 - No. 10, Oct, 1949
Marvel Comics (CBS)

	Good	Fine	N-Mint
1-2pg. Kurtzman-a, 'Giggles 'n Grins'	9.30	28.00	65.00
2	5.00	15.00	35.00
3-5: 4-Vampire story	3.50	10.50	24.00

6(2/49)-Has editorial defense against charges of Dr. Wertham

	4.30	13.00	30.00

7-Used in **SOTI**, illo-"Comic-book philosophy"

	11.00	32.00	75.00
8-10: 9,10-Photo-c	2.30	7.00	16.00

LAWBREAKERS SUSPENSE STORIES (Formerly Lawbreakers; Strange Suspense Stories No. 16 on)
No. 10, Jan, 1953 - No. 15, Nov, 1953
Capitol Stories/Charlton Comics

10	5.70	17.00	40.00

11 (3/53)-Severed tongues c/story & woman negligee scene

	22.00	65.00	154.00
12-14	3.50	10.50	24.00

15-Acid-in-face c/story; hands dissolved in acid story

	10.00	30.00	70.00

LAW-CRIME (See Law Against Crime)

LAWMAN (TV)
No. 970, Feb, 1959 - No. 11, Apr-June, 1962 (All photo-c)
Dell Publishing Co.

4-Color 970(#1)	6.50	19.50	45.00
4-Color 1035('60)	4.30	13.00	30.00
3(2-4/60)-Toth-a	5.00	15.00	35.00
4-11	3.50	10.50	24.00

LAW OF DREDD, THE (Also see Judge Dredd)
1989 - Present ($1.50, color)
Quality Comics

1-10: Bolland-a in 1-5	.25	.75	1.50

LAWRENCE (See Movie Classics)

LEADING COMICS (. . .Screen Comics No. 42 on)
Winter, 1941-42 - No. 41, Feb-Mar, 1950
National Periodical Publications

1-Origin The Seven Soldiers of Victory; Crimson Avenger, Green Arrow & Speedy, Shining Knight, The Vigilante, Star Spangled Kid & Stripesy begin. The Dummy (Vigilante villain) app.

	175.00	440.00	1050.00
2-Meskin-a	64.00	193.00	450.00
3	50.00	150.00	350.00
4,5	43.00	130.00	300.00
6-10	37.00	110.00	260.00
11-14(Spring, 1945)	26.00	77.00	180.00
15-(Sum,'45)-Content change to funny animal	11.00	32.00	75.00
16-22,24-30	4.50	14.00	32.00
23-1st app. Peter Porkchops by Otto Feur	11.00	32.00	75.00
31,32,34-41	3.50	10.50	24.00
33-(Scarce)	6.00	18.00	42.00

NOTE: **Rube Grossman**-a(Peter Porkchops)-most #15-on; c-15-41. **Post** a-23-37, 39, 41.

LEADING SCREEN COMICS (Formerly Leading Comics)
No. 42, Apr-May, 1950 - No. 77, Aug-Sept, 1955
National Periodical Publications

42	4.50	14.00	32.00
43-77	2.85	8.50	20.00

NOTE: **Grossman** a-most. **Mayer** a-45-48, 50, 54-57, 60, 62-74, 75(3), 76, 77.

LEATHERNECK THE MARINE (See Mighty Midget Comics)

LEAVE IT TO BEAVER (TV)
No. 912, June, 1958 - May-July, 1962 (All photo-c)

Lawbreakers #4, © CC

Lawman #7, © Warner Bros.

Leading Comics #6, © DC

Leave It To Binky #2, © DC

Legends #6, © DC

Legion Of Super-Heroes #3 (1973). © DC

LEAVE IT TO BEAVER (continued)
Dell Publishing Co.

	Good	Fine	N-Mint
4-Color 912	12.00	36.00	84.00
4-Color 999,1103,1191,1285, 01-428-207	11.00	32.00	75.00

LEAVE IT TO BINKY (Binky No. 72 on) (See Showcase and Super DC Giant) (No. 1-22: 52 pgs.)
2-3/48 - No. 60, 10/58; No. 61, 6-7/68 - No. 71, 2-3/70
National Periodical Publications

1	14.00	42.00	100.00
2	7.00	21.00	50.00
3-5: 5-Superman cameo	5.00	15.00	35.00
6-10	4.00	12.00	28.00
11-20	3.00	9.00	21.00
21-28,30-45: 45-Last pre-code (2/55)	2.00	6.00	14.00
29-Used in **POP**, pg. 78	2.00	6.00	14.00
46-60	1.00	3.00	7.00
61-71	.70	2.00	4.00

NOTE: **Drucker** a-28. **Mayer** a-1, 2, 15.

LEE HUNTER, INDIAN FIGHTER (See 4-Color No. 779, 904)

LEFT-HANDED GUN, THE (See 4-Color No. 913)

LEGEND OF CUSTER, THE (TV)
January, 1968
Dell Publishing Co.

1	1.15	3.50	8.00

LEGEND OF JESSE JAMES, THE (TV)
February, 1966
Gold Key

10172-602-Photo-c	1.70	5.00	12.00

LEGEND OF KAMUI, THE (See Kamui)

LEGEND OF LOBO, THE (See Movie Comics)

LEGEND OF WONDER WOMAN, THE
May, 1986 - No. 4, Aug, 1986 (mini-series)
DC Comics

1-4		.60	1.20

LEGEND OF YOUNG DICK TURPIN, THE (TV)
May, 1966 (Disney TV episode)
Gold Key

1 (10176-605)-Photo/painted-c	1.15	3.50	8.00

LEGENDS
Nov, 1986 - No. 6, Apr, 1987 (mini-series)
DC Comics

1-Byrne c/a(p) begins. 1st new Capt. Marvel	.35	1.00	2.00
2	.25	.80	1.60
3-5: 3-Intro new Suicide Squad; death of Blockbuster	.25	.70	1.40
6-Intro/1st app. New Justice League	1.00	3.00	6.00

LEGENDS OF DANIEL BOONE, THE
Oct-Nov, 1955 - No. 8, Dec-Jan, 1956-57
National Periodical Publications

1 (Scarce)	23.00	70.00	160.00
2 (Scarce)	17.00	51.00	120.00
3-8 (Scarce)	14.00	43.00	100.00

LEGENDS OF THE DARK KNIGHT (Batman)
Nov, 1989 - Present ($1.50, color)
DC Comics

1-"The Shaman of Gotham" begins, ends #5; outer cover has four different color variations, all worth same	.40	1.25	2.50
2-5	.25	.75	1.50

LEGENDS OF THE STARGRAZERS (See Vanguard Illustrated #2)
Aug, 1989 - No. 6, 1990 ($1.95, color, mini-series)
Innovation Publishing

	Good	Fine	N-Mint
1-6: 1-N. Redondo part inks	.35	1.00	2.00

L.E.G.I.O.N. '89 (Becomes L.E.G.I.O.N. '90 #11 on)
Feb, 1989 - Present ($1.50, color)
DC Comics

1-Giffen plots/breakdowns in all	.35	1.00	2.00
2-14	.25	.75	1.50

LEGIONNAIRES THREE
Jan, 1986 - No. 4, May, 1986 (Mini-series)
DC comics

1-4		.50	1.00

LEGION OF MONSTERS (Magazine)(Also see Marvel Premiere #28 & Marvel Preview #8)
September, 1975 (black & white)
Marvel Comics Group

1-Origin & 1st app. Legion of Monsters; Adams-c; Morrow-a; origin & only app. The Manphibian	.35	1.00	2.00

LEGION OF SUBSTITUTE HEROES SPECIAL
July, 1985 (One Shot)
DC Comics

1-Giffen c/a(p)	.25	.75	1.50

LEGION OF SUPER-HEROES (See Action, Adventure, All New Collectors Ed., Limited Collectors Ed., New Legion..., Secrets of the..., Superboy, & Superman)
Feb, 1973 - No. 4, July-Aug, 1973
National Periodical Publications

1-Legion & Tommy Tomorrow reprints begin	.85	2.50	5.00
2-4: 3-r/Adv. 340, Action 240. 4-r/Adv. 341, Action 233	.40	1.25	2.50

LEGION OF SUPER-HEROES, THE (Formerly Superboy; Tales of The Legion No. 314 on)
No. 259, Jan, 1980 - No. 313, July, 1984
DC Comics

259(#1)-Superboy leaves Legion	.45	1.40	2.80
260-270: 265-Contains 28pg. insert 'Superman & the TR5-80 Computer;' Origin Tyroc; Tyroc leaves Legion	.25	.80	1.60
271-284: 272-Blok joins; origin; 20pg. insert-Dial 'H' For Hero. 277-Intro Reflecto. 280-Superboy re-joins legion. 282-Origin Reflecto		.60	1.20
285,286-Giffen back up story	.35	1.00	2.00
287-Giffen-a on Legion begins	.45	1.40	2.80
288-290: 290-Great Darkness saga begins, ends #294	.35	1.00	2.00
291-293		.60	1.20
294-Double size (52 pgs.); Giffen-a(p)	.25	.70	1.40
295-299,301-305: 297-Origin retold. 304-Karate Kid & Princess Projectra resign		.50	1.00
300-Double size, 64 pgs., Mando paper; c/a by almost everyone at DC	.35	1.00	2.00
306-313 (75 cent-c): 306-Brief origin Star Boy	.35		.70
Annual 1(1982)-Giffen c/a; 1st app./origin new Invisible Kid who joins Legion	.25	.80	1.60
Annual 2(10/83)-Giffen-c; Karate Kid & Princess Projectra wed		.60	1.20
Annual 3('84)		.60	1.20
...The Great Darkness Saga (1989, $17.95, 196 pgs.)-r/LSH #287, 290-294 & Annual #3; Giffen-c/a	3.00	9.00	18.00

NOTE: **Aparo** c-282, 283. **Austin** c-268i. **Buckler** c-273p, 274p, 276p. **Colan** a-311p. **Ditko** a(p)-267, 268, 272, 274, 276, 281. **Giffen** a-285p-313p. Annual 1p; c-287p, 288p, 289, 290p, 291p, 292, 293, 294-299p, 300, 301p-313p, Annual 1p, 2p. **Perez** c-268p. 277-80, 281p. **Starlin** a-265. **Staton** a-259p, 260p, 280. **Tuska** a-308p.

LEGION OF SUPER-HEROES
Aug, 1984 - No. 63, Aug, 1989 ($1.25-$1.75, deluxe format)
DC Comics

	Good	Fine	N-Mint
1	.40	1.20	2.40
2-5: 4-Death of Karate Kid. 5-Death of Nemesis Kid			
	.35	1.00	2.00
6-10	.25	.80	1.60
11-14: 12-Cosmic Boy, Lightning Lad, & Saturn Girl resign. 14-Intro			
new members: Tellus, Sensor Girl, Quislet	.60	1.20	
15-18-Crisis x-over	.25	.80	1.60
19-25: 25-Sensor Girl i.d. revealed as Princess Projectra			
	.60	1.20	
26-36,39-44: 35-Saturn Girl rejoins. 40-$1.75 cover price begins. 42,			
43-Millennium tie-ins	.55	1.10	
37,38-Death of Superboy	.60	1.80	3.60
45 ($2.95, 68 pgs.)	.40	1.20	2.40
46-49,51-62	.55	1.10	
50-Double size, $2.50	.35	1.00	2.00
63-Final issue	.25	.70	1.40
Annual 1 (10/85)-Crisis x-over	.30	.90	1.80
Annual 2 (10/86), 3 (10/87)	.25	.80	1.60
Annual 4(11/88, $2.50)	.35	1.00	2.00

NOTE: *Byrne c-36p. Giffen a(p)-1, 2, 50-55, 57-63, Annual 1p, 2; c-1-5p, 54p, Annual 1. Orlando a-6p. Steacy c-45-50, Annual 3.*

LEGION OF SUPER-HEROES
Nov, 1989 - Present ($1.75, color)
DC Comics

	Good	Fine	N-Mint
1-Giffen-c/a(p), scripts begin	.35	1.00	2.00
2-6	.30	.90	1.80

LENNON SISTERS LIFE STORY, THE (See 4-Color No. 951,1014)

LEONARDO (Also see Teenage Mutant Ninja Turtles)
Dec, 1986 ($1.50, B&W, One shot)
Mirage Studios

1	.75	2.25	4.50

LEO THE LION
No date (10 cents)
I. W. Enterprises

1-Reprint	.50	1.50	3.00

LEROY (Teen-age)
Nov, 1949 - No. 6, Nov, 1950
Standard Comics

1	2.65	8.00	18.00
2-Frazetta text illo.	2.85	8.50	20.00
3-6: 3-Lubbers-a	1.50	4.50	10.00

LET'S PRETEND (CBS radio)
May-June, 1950 - No. 3, Sept-Oct, 1950
D. S. Publishing Co.

1	7.00	21.00	50.00
2,3	5.00	15.00	35.00

LET'S READ THE NEWSPAPER
1974
Charlton Press

Features Quincy by Ted Sheares		.30	.60

LET'S TAKE A TRIP (TV) (CBS TV Presents)
Spring, 1958
Pines Comics

1-Marv Levy c/a	1.50	4.50	10.00

LETTERS TO SANTA (See March of Comics No. 228)

LEX LUTHOR: THE UNAUTHORIZED BIOGRAPHY
1989 ($3.95, one-shot, squarebound, 52 pgs.)
DC Comics

	Good	Fine	N-Mint
1-Painted-c; Clark Kent app.	.75	2.25	4.50

LIBBY ELLIS
7/87 - No. 4, 1987; 6/88 - No. 4, 1988 ($1.95, B&W)
Malibu Graphics/Eternity Comics

1-4 (Malibu)	.35	1.00	2.00
1-4 (2nd series by Eternity)	.35	1.00	2.00
Graphic Novel ($7.95; B&W)	1.35	4.00	8.00

LIBERTY COMICS (Miss Liberty No. 1)
No. 4, 1945 - No. 15, 1946 (MLJ & other reprints)
Green Publishing Co.

4	8.50	25.50	60.00
5 (5/46)-The Prankster app; Starr-a	6.00	18.00	42.00
10-Hangman & Boy Buddies app.; Suzie & Wilbur begin; reprint of			
Hangman #8	8.00	24.00	56.00
11(V2/2, 1/46)-Wilbur in women's clothes	8.00	24.00	56.00
12-Black Hood & Suzie app.	6.50	19.50	45.00
14,15-Patty of Airliner; Starr-a in both	3.70	11.00	26.00

LIBERTY GUARDS
No date (1946?)
Chicago Mail Order

nn-Reprints Man of War #1 with cover of Liberty Scouts #1;			
Gustavson-c	18.00	54.00	125.00

LIBERTY PROJECT, THE
June, 1987 - No. 8, May, 1988 ($1.75, color, Baxter paper)
Eclipse Comics

1	.35	1.10	2.20
2-8	.30	.90	1.80

LIBERTY SCOUTS (See Liberty Guards & Man of War)
June, 1941 - No. 3, Aug, 1941
Centaur Publications

2(#1)-Origin The Fire-Man, Man of War; Vapo-Man & Liberty			
Scouts begin; Gustavson-c/a	75.00	225.00	525.00
3(#2)-Origin & 1st app. The Sentinel; Gustavson-c/a			
	54.00	160.00	375.00

LICENCE TO KILL (James Bond 007. . .)
1989 ($7.95, color, slick paper, 52 pgs.)
Eclipse Comics

nn-Movie adaptation; Timothy Dalton photo-c	1.35	4.00	8.00
Limited Hardcover ($24.95)	4.15	12.50	25.00

LIDSVILLE (TV)
Oct, 1972 - No. 5, Oct, 1973
Gold Key

1	1.15	3.50	7.00
2-5	.70	2.00	4.00

LIEUTENANT, THE (TV)
April-June, 1964
Dell Publishing Co.

1-Photo-c	1.15	3.50	8.00

LT. ROBIN CRUSOE, U.S.N. (See Movie Comics and Walt Disney Showcase 26)

LIFE OF CAPTAIN MARVEL, THE
Aug, 1985 - No. 5, Dec, 1985 ($2.00 cover; Baxter paper)
Marvel Comics Group

1-5: r-/Starlin issues of Capt. Marvel	.35	1.00	2.00

LIFE OF CHRIST, THE
1949 (100 pages) (35 cents)
Catechetical Guild Educational Society

301-Reprints from Topix(1949)-V5#11,12	2.30	7.00	16.00

Leroy #5, © STD

Lex Luthor: The Unauthorized Biography #1, © DC

Liberty Scouts #2 (#1), © CEN

Life With Archie #50, © AP

Lightning Comics V2#2, © ACE

Limited Collectors' Edition C-25, © DC

LIFE OF CHRIST VISUALIZED
1942 - No. 3, 1943
Standard Publishers

	Good	Fine	N-Mint
1-3: All came in cardboard case	2.30	7.00	16.00

LIFE OF CHRIST VISUALIZED
1946? (48 pgs. in color)
The Standard Publ. Co.

nn	1.00	3.00	6.00

LIFE OF ESTHER VISUALIZED
1947 (48 pgs. in color)
The Standard Publ. Co.

2062	1.00	3.00	6.00

LIFE OF JOSEPH VISUALIZED
1946 (48 pgs. in color)
The Standard Publ. Co.

1054	1.00	3.00	6.00

LIFE OF PAUL (See The Living Bible)

LIFE OF POPE JOHN PAUL II, THE
Jan, 1983
Marvel Comics Group

1	.25	.75	1.50

LIFE OF RILEY, THE (See 4-Color No. 917)

LIFE OF THE BLESSED VIRGIN
1950 (68 pages) (square binding)
Catechetical Guild (Giveaway)

nn-Contains "The Woman of the Promise" & "Mother of Us All" rebound	2.30	7.00	16.00

LIFE'S LIKE THAT
1945 (68 pgs.; B&W; 25 cents)
Croyden Publ. Co.

nn-Newspaper Sunday strip-r by Neher	2.65	8.00	18.00

LIFE'S LITTLE JOKES
No date (1924) (52 pgs.; B&W)
M.S. Publ. Co.

By Rube Goldberg	14.00	42.00	100.00

LIFE STORIES OF AMERICAN PRESIDENTS (See Dell Giants)

LIFE STORY
4/49 - V8#46, 1/53; V8#47, 4/53 (All have photo-c?)
Fawcett Publications

V1#1	4.30	13.00	30.00
2	2.15	6.50	15.00
3-6	1.70	5.00	12.00
V2#7-12	1.60	4.80	11.00
V3#13-Wood-a	6.50	19.50	45.00
V3#14-18, V4#19-21,23,24	1.50	4.50	10.00
V4#22-Drug use story	1.60	4.80	11.00
V5#25-30, V6#31-35	1.30	4.00	9.00
V6#36-"I sold drugs" on-c	1.60	4.80	11.00
V7#37,40-42, V8#44,45	1.00	3.00	7.00
V7#38, V8#43-Evans-a	2.00	6.00	14.00
V7#39-Drug Smuggling & Junkie story	1.50	4.50	10.00
V8#46,47 (Scarce)	1.15	3.50	8.00

NOTE: *Powell a-13, 23, 24, 26, 28, 30, 32, 39.*

LIFE WITH ARCHIE
Sept. 1958 - Present
Archie Publications

1	21.50	65.00	150.00
2	11.00	32.00	75.00
3-5	8.00	24.00	55.00
6-10	3.70	11.00	26.00
11-20	2.00	6.00	14.00
21-30	1.50	4.50	10.00
31-41	1.00	3.00	7.00
42-45: 42-Pureheart begins	.85	2.50	5.00
46-Origin Pureheart	.85	2.60	6.00
47-50: 50-United Three begin; Superteen, Capt. Hero app.	.60	1.75	3.50
51-59-Pureheart ends	.60	1.75	3.50
60-100: 60-Archie band begins	.35	1.00	2.00
101-150		.50	1.00
151-278: Later issues 95 cents & $1.00	.40	.80	

LIFE WITH MILLIE (Formerly A Date With Millie) (Modeling With Millie No. 21 on)
No. 8, Dec, 1960 - No. 20, Dec, 1962
Atlas/Marvel Comics Group

8	2.65	8.00	18.00
9-11	1.70	5.00	12.00
12-20	1.15	3.50	8.00

LIFE WITH SNARKY PARKER (TV)
August, 1950
Fox Feature Syndicate

1	10.00	30.00	70.00

LIGHT AND DARKNESS WAR, THE
Oct, 1988 - No. 6, Dec, 1989 ($1.95, color, limited series)
Epic Comics (Marvel)

1	.50	1.50	3.00
2-6	.35	1.00	2.00

LIGHT IN THE FOREST (See 4-Color No. 891)

LIGHTNING COMICS (Formerly Sure-Fire No. 1-3)
No. 4, Dec, 1940 - No. 13(V3No.1), June, 1942
Ace Magazines

4-Characters continue from Sure-Fire	36.00	107.00	250.00
5,6: 6-Dr. Nemesis begins	24.00	73.00	170.00
V2#1-6: 2-"Flash Lightning" becomes "Lash..."	22.00	65.00	154.00
V3#1-Intro. Lightning Girl & The Sword	22.00	65.00	154.00

NOTE: *Anderson a-V2#6. Mooney c-V1#6, V2#2. Bondage c-V2#6.*

LI'L (See Little)

LILY OF THE ALLEY IN THE FUNNIES
No date (1920's?) (10¼x15½''; 28 pgs. in color)
Whitman Publishers

W936 - by T. Burke	8.00	24.00	56.00

LIMITED COLLECTORS' EDITION (See Famous First Edition & Rudolph the Red Nosed Reindeer; becomes All-New Collectors' Edition) (#21-34,51:59: 84 pgs.; #35-41: 68 pgs.; #42-50: 60 pgs.)
C-21, Summer, 1973 - No. C-59, 1978 ($1.00) (10x13½'')
National Periodical Publications/DC Comics

nn(C-20)-Rudolph	.70	2.00	4.00
C-21: Shazam (TV); Captain Marvel Jr. reprint by Raboy	.50	1.50	3.00
C-22: Tarzan; complete origin reprinted from #207-210; all Kubert	.50	1.50	3.00
C-23: House of Mystery; Wrightson, Adams, Wood, Toth, Orlando-a	.35	1.00	2.00
C-24: Rudolph The Red-nosed Reindeer	.35	1.00	2.00
C-25: Batman; Adams-c/a	1.00	3.00	6.00
C-27: Shazam (TV)	.35	1.00	2.00
C-29: Tarzan; reprints "Return of Tarzan" from #219-223 by Kubert	.50	1.50	3.00
C-31: Superman; origin-r; Adams-a	.50	1.50	3.00

LIMITED COLLECTORS' EDITION (cont.)	Good	Fine	N-Mint
C-32: Ghosts (new-a)	.35	1.00	2.00
C-33: Rudolph The Red-nosed Reindeer(new-a)	.35	1.00	2.00
C-34: Xmas with the Super-Heroes; unpublished Angel & Ape story by Oksner & Wood	.50	1.50	3.00
C-35: Shazam; cover features TV's Captain Marvel, Jackson Bostwick (TV)	.35	1.00	2.00
C-36: The Bible; all new adaptation beginning with Genesis by Kubert, Redondo & Mayer	.50	1.50	3.00
C-37: Batman; r-1946 Sundays	1.00	3.00	6.00
C-38: Superman; 1 pg. Adams	.35	1.00	2.00
C-39: Secret Origins/Super Villains; Adams-a(r)	.35	1.00	2.00
C-40: Dick Tracy by Gould featuring Flattop; newspaper-r from 12/21/43 - 5/17/44	.70	2.00	4.00
C-41: Super Friends; Toth-c/a	.35	1.00	2.00
C-42: Rudolph	.35	1.00	2.00
C-43: Christmas with the Super-Heroes; Wrightson, S&K, Adams-a	.50	1.50	3.00
C-44: Batman; Adams-r; painted-c	1.00	3.00	6.00
C-45: Secret Origins/Super Villains; Flash-r/105	.35	1.00	2.00
C-46: Justice League of America; 3 pg. Toth-a	.50	1.50	3.00
C-47: Superman Salutes the Bicentennial (Tomahawk interior); 2 pgs. new-a	.25	.75	1.50
C-48: The Superman-Flash Race; 6 pgs. Adams-a	.35	1.00	2.00
C-49: Superboy & the Legion of Super-Heroes	.35	1.00	2.00
C-50: Rudolph The Red-nosed Reindeer	.25	.75	1.50
C-51: Batman; Adams-c/a	1.00	3.00	6.00
C-52: The Best of DC; Adams-c/a; Toth, Kubert-a	.50	1.50	3.00
C-57: Welcome Back, Kotter-r(TV)(5/78)	.25	.75	1.50
C-59: Batman's Strangest Cases; Adams, Wrightson-r;Adams/Wrightson-c	1.00	3.00	6.00

NOTE: All-r with exception of some special features and covers. **Aparo** a-52r; c-37. **Giordano** a-39. 45. **Grell** c-49. **Infantino** a-25, 39, 44, 45, 52.

LINDA (Phantom Lady No. 5 on)
Apr-May, 1954 - No. 4, Oct-Nov, 1954
Ajax-Farrell Publ. Co.

	Good	Fine	N-Mint
1-Kamenish-a	7.00	21.00	50.00
2-Lingerie panel	4.65	14.00	32.00
3,4	4.30	13.00	30.00

LINDA CARTER, STUDENT NURSE
Sept, 1961 - No. 9, Jan, 1963
Atlas Comics (AMI)

1-Al Hartley-c	2.00	6.00	14.00
2-9	1.15	3.50	8.00

LINDA LARK
Oct-Dec, 1961 - No. 8, Aug-Oct, 1963
Dell Publishing Co.

1	1.00	3.00	7.00
2-8	.55	1.65	4.00

LINUS, THE LIONHEARTED (TV)
September, 1965
Gold Key

1 (10155-509)	3.00	9.00	21.00

LION, THE (See Movie Comics)

LION OF SPARTA (See Movie Classics)

LIPPY THE LION AND HARDY HAR HAR (TV)
March, 1963 (Hanna-Barbera)
Gold Key

1 (10049-303)	3.00	9.00	21.00

LI'L ABNER (See Comics on Parade, Sparkle, Sparkler Comics, Tip Top Comics & Tip Topper)
1939 - 1940
United Features Syndicate

	Good	Fine	N-Mint
Single Series 4 ('39)	35.00	105.00	245.00
Single Series 18 ('40) (#18 on inside, #2 on cover)	27.00	81.00	190.00

LI'L ABNER (Al Capp's) (See Oxydol-Dreft)
No. 61, Dec, 1947 - No. 97, Jan, 1955
Harvey Publ. No. 61-69 (2/49)/Toby Press No. 70 on

61(#1)-Wolverton-a	15.00	45.00	105.00
62-65	11.00	32.00	75.00
66,67,69,70	8.50	25.50	60.00
68-Full length Fearless Fosdick story	9.30	28.00	65.00
71-74,76,80	6.50	19.50	45.00
75,77-79,86,91-All with Kurtzman art; 91 reprints #77	8.00	24.00	55.00
81-85,87-90,92-94,96,97: 93-reprints #71	5.50	16.50	38.00
95-Full length Fearless Fosdick story	7.00	21.00	50.00
...& the Creatures from Drop-Outer Space-nn (Job Corps giveaway; 36pgs., in color	6.00	18.00	42.00
...Joins the Navy (1950) (Toby Press Premium)	5.50	16.50	38.00
...by Al Capp Giveaway (Circa 1955, nd)	5.50	16.50	38.00

NOTE: **Powell** a-61, 65.

LI'L ABNER
1951
Toby Press

1	9.30	28.00	65.00

LI'L ABNER'S DOGPATCH (See Al Capp's ...)

LITTLE AL OF THE F.B.I.
No. 10, 1950 (no month) - No. 11, Apr-May, 1951
Ziff-Davis Publications (Saunders painted-c)

10(1950)	5.50	16.50	38.00
11(1951)	4.00	12.00	28.00

LITTLE AL OF THE SECRET SERVICE
No. 10, 7-8/51; No, 2, 9-10/51; No. 3, Wint., 1951
Ziff-Davis Publications (Saunders painted-c)

10(#1)-Spanking panel	8.00	24.00	56.00
2,3	4.00	12.00	28.00

LITTLE AMBROSE
September, 1958
Archie Publications

1-Bob Bolling-c	8.50	25.50	60.00

LITTLE ANGEL
No. 5, Sept, 1954; No. 6, Sept, 1955 - No. 16, Sept, 1959
Standard (Visual Editions)/Pines

5	2.65	8.00	18.00
6-16	1.30	4.00	9.00

LITTLE ANNIE ROONEY
1935 (48 pgs.; B&W dailies) (25 cents)
David McKay Publications

Book 1-Daily strip-r by Darrell McClure	9.30	28.00	65.00

LITTLE ANNIE ROONEY (See Treasury of Comics)
1938; Aug, 1948 - No. 3, Oct, 1948
David McKay/St. John/Standard

Feature Books 11 (McKay, 1938)	19.00	58.00	135.00
1 (St. John)	6.50	19.50	45.00
2,3	3.70	11.00	26.00

Li'l Abner #67, © UFS

Little Al Of The F.B.I. #10, © Z-D

Little Angel #13, © PINE

Little Archie #1, © AP

Little Beaver #4, © DELL

Little Dot #4, © HARV

LITTLE ARCHIE (The Adventures of . . . #13-on) (Also see Archie
Giant Series #527,534,538,545,549,556,566,570,583,596,607)
1956 - No. 180, Feb, 1983 (Giants No. 3-84)
Archie Publications

	Good	Fine	N-Mint
1-(Scarce)	26.50	80.00	185.00
2	13.00	42.00	90.00
3-5	8.50	25.50	60.00
6-10	5.50	16.50	38.00
11-20	3.50	10.50	24.00
21-30	2.15	6.50	15.00
31-40: Little Pureheart apps. #40-42,44	1.00	3.00	7.00
41-60: 42-Intro. The Little Archies. 59-Little Sabrina begins			
	.50	1.50	3.00
61-80	.35	1.00	2.00
81-100		.50	1.00
101-180		.40	.80
. . .In Animal Land 1('57)	9.20	27.50	64.00
. . .In Animal Land 17(Winter, 1957-58)-19(Summer,'58)-Formerly Li'l			
Jinx	4.50	13.50	31.00

LITTLE ARCHIE CHRISTMAS SPECIAL (See Archie Giant Series 581)
LITTLE ARCHIE COMICS DIGEST ANNUAL (. . .Magazine #5 on)
Oct, 1977 - Present (Digest-size)
Archie Publications

1(10/77)-Reprints	.35	1.00	2.00
2(4/78)-Adams-a		.60	1.20
3(11/78)-The Fly-r by S&K; Adams-a		.60	1.20
4(4/79) - 42('90): 28,40-Christmas-c, ½ Little Jinx		.60	1.20

LITTLE ARCHIE MYSTERY
Aug, 1963 - No. 2, Oct, 1963
Archie Publications

1	7.50	22.50	45.00
2	3.35	10.00	20.00

LITTLE ASPIRIN (See Wisco)
July, 1949 - No. 3, Dec, 1949 (52 pages)
Marvel Comics (CnPC)

1-Kurtzman-a, 4 pgs.	6.50	19.50	45.00
2-Kurtzman-a, 4 pgs.	3.50	10.50	24.00
3-No Kurtzman	1.60	4.70	11.00

LITTLE AUDREY (Also see Playful . . .)
April, 1948 - No. 24, May, 1952
St. John Publ.

1-1st app. Little Audrey	17.00	51.00	120.00
2	9.00	27.00	62.00
3-5	7.00	21.00	50.00
6-10	4.00	12.00	28.00
11-20	2.00	6.00	14.00
21-24	1.30	4.00	9.00

LITTLE AUDREY (See Harvey Hits #11,19)
No. 25, Aug, 1952 - No. 53, April, 1957
Harvey Publications

25 (Paramount Pictures Famous Star)	4.35	13.00	30.00
26-30: 26-28-Casper app.	2.00	6.00	14.00
31-40: 32-35-Casper app.	1.50	4.50	10.00
41-53	1.00	3.00	7.00
. . .Clubhouse 1 (9/61, 68 pg. Giant) w/reprints	3.00	9.00	18.00

LITTLE AUDREY (. . .Yearbook)
1950 (260 pages) (50 cents)
St. John Publishing Co.

Contains 8 complete 1949 comics rebound; Casper, Alice in Wonderland, Little Audrey, Abbott & Costello, Pinocchio, Moon Mullins, Three Stooges (from Jubilee), Little Annie
Rooney app. (Rare)   49.00   148.00   345.00

(Also see All Good & Treasury of Comics)

NOTE: This book contains remaindered St. John comics; many variations possible.

LITTLE AUDREY & MELVIN (Audrey &. . . No. 62)
May, 1962 - No. 61, Dec, 1973
Harvey Publications

	Good	Fine	N-Mint
1	5.35	16.00	32.00
2-5	2.75	8.00	16.00
6-10	1.70	5.00	10.00
11-20	1.00	3.00	6.00
21-40	.70	2.00	4.00
41-50,54-61	.50	1.50	3.00
51-53: All 52 pg. Giants	.70	2.00	4.00

LITTLE AUDREY TV FUNTIME
Sept, 1962 - No. 33, Oct, 1971 (#1-31: 68 pgs.; #32,33: 52 pgs.)
Harvey Publications

1-Richie Rich app.	3.35	10.00	20.00
2,3: Richie Rich app.	2.00	6.00	12.00
4,5: 5-25 & 35 cent-c exists	1.70	5.00	10.00
6-10	.85	2.50	5.00
11-20	.70	2.00	4.00
21-33	.50	1.50	3.00

LITTLE BAD WOLF (See 4-Color #403,473,564, Walt Disney's C&S #52, Walt
Disney Showcase #21 & Wheaties)
LITTLE BEAVER
No. 211, Jan, 1949 - No. 870, Jan, 1958 (All painted-c)
Dell Publishing Co.

4-Color 211('49)-All Harman-a	3.00	9.00	21.00
4-Color 267,294,332(5/51)	2.00	6.00	14.00
3(10-12/51)-8(1-3/53)	1.70	5.00	12.00
4-Color 483(8-10/53),529	1.70	5.00	12.00
4-Color 612,660,695,744,817,870	1.30	4.00	9.00

LITTLE BIT
March, 1949 - No. 2, 1949
Jubilee/St. John Publishing Co.

1,2	1.70	5.00	12.00

LITTLE DOT (See Blackthorne 3-D Series #59, Humphrey, Li'l Max,
Sad Sack, and Tastee-Freez Comics)
Sept, 1953 - No. 164, April, 1976
Harvey Publications

1-Intro./1st app. Richie Rich & Little Lotta	45.00	135.00	320.00
2-1st app. Freckles & Pee Wee (Richie Rich's poor friends)			
	21.00	64.00	150.00
3	15.00	45.00	105.00
4	11.00	32.50	75.00
5-Origin dots on Little Dot's dress	12.50	37.50	85.00
6-Richie Rich, Little Lotta, & Little Dot all on cover; 1st Richie Rich			
cover featured	12.50	37.50	85.00
7-10	5.00	15.00	35.00
11-20	4.00	12.00	28.00
21-40	2.00	6.00	14.00
41-60	1.00	3.00	7.00
61-80	.70	2.00	4.00
81-100	.50	1.50	3.00
101-141	.35	1.00	2.00
142-145: All 52 pg. Giants	.40	1.20	2.40
146-164		.50	1.00
Shoe store giveaway 2	4.00	12.00	28.00

NOTE: Richie Rich & Little Lotta in all.

LITTLE DOT DOTLAND (Dot Dotland No. 62,63)
July, 1962 - No. 61, Dec, 1973
Harvey Publications

1-Richie Rich begins	4.00	12.00	28.00
2,3	2.00	6.00	14.00

LITTLE DOT DOTLAND (continued)	Good	Fine	N-Mint
4,5	1.50	4.50	10.00
6-10	1.15	3.50	8.00
11-20	.85	2.50	6.00
21-30	.50	1.50	3.00
31-50,55-61	.35	1.00	2.00
51-54: All 52 pg. Giants	.40	1.20	2.40

LITTLE DOT'S UNCLES & AUNTS (See Harvey Hits No. 4,13,24)
Oct. 1961; No. 2, Aug, 1962 - No. 52, April, 1974
Harvey Enterprises

1-Richie Rich begins; 68 pgs. begin	4.00	12.00	28.00
2,3	2.00	6.00	14.00
4,5	1.50	4.50	10.00
6-10	1.15	3.50	8.00
11-20	.85	2.50	6.00
21-37: Last 68 pg. issue	.50	1.50	3.00
38-52: All 52 pg. Giants	.35	1.00	2.00

LITTLE EVA
May, 1952 - No. 31, Nov, 1956
St. John Publishing Co.

1	5.70	17.00	40.00
2	2.65	8.00	18.00
3-5	2.00	6.00	14.00
6-10	1.30	4.00	9.00
11-31	1.15	3.50	8.00
3-D 1,2(10/53-11/53); 1-Infinity-c	12.00	36.00	84.00
I.W. Reprint #1-3,6-8	.30	.90	1.80
Super Reprint #10,12('63),14,16,18('64)	.30	.90	1.80

LITTLE FIR TREE, THE
1942 (8½x11'') (12 pgs. with cover)
W. T. Grant Co. (Christmas giveaway)

8 pg. Kelly-a reprint/Santa Claus Funnies not signed.
(One copy in Mint sold for $1750.00 in 1986)

LI'L GENIUS (Summer Fun No. 54) (See Blue Bird)
1954 - No. 52, 1/65; No. 53, 10/65; No. 54, 10/85 - No. 55, 1/86
Charlton Comics

1	2.85	8.50	20.00
2	1.50	4.50	10.00
3-15,19,20	1.15	3.50	8.00
16,17-(68 pgs.)	1.50	4.50	10.00
18-(100 pgs., 10/58)	2.30	7.00	16.00
21-35	.85	2.60	6.00
36-53	.50	1.50	3.00
54,55	.25	.75	1.50

LI'L GHOST
Feb. 1958 - No. 3, Mar, 1959
St. John Publishing Co./Fago No. 1 on

1(St. John)	2.65	8.00	18.00
1(Fago)	2.00	6.00	14.00
2,3	1.15	3.50	8.00

LITTLE GIANT COMICS
7/38 - No. 3, 10/38; No. 4, 2/39 (132 pgs.) (6¾x4½'')
Centaur Publications

1-B&W with color-c	26.00	77.00	180.00
2,3-B&W with color-c	21.00	62.00	145.00
4 (6-5/8x9-3/8'')(68 pgs., B&W inside)	22.00	65.00	155.00
NOTE: **Gustavson** a-1. **Pinajian** a-4. **Bob Wood** a-1.

LITTLE GIANT DETECTIVE FUNNIES
Oct. 1938 - No. 4, Jan, 1939 (132 pgs., B&W) (6¾x4½'')
Centaur Publications

1-B&W with color-c	26.00	77.00	180.00
2,3	21.00	62.00	145.00

	Good	Fine	N-Mint
4(1/39)-B&W; color-c; 68 pgs., 6½x9½''; Eisner-r	22.00	65.00	155.00

LITTLE GIANT MOVIE FUNNIES
Aug, 1938 - No. 2, Oct, 1938 (132 pgs., B&W) (6¾x4½'')
Centaur Publications

1-Ed Wheelan's ''Minute Movies''-r	26.00	77.00	180.00
2-Ed Wheelan's ''Minute Movies''-r	19.00	58.00	135.00

LITTLE GROUCHO (. . .Grouchy No. 2) (See Tippy Terry)
No. 16; Feb-Mar, 1955 - No. 2, June-July, 1955
Reston Publ. Co.

16, 1 (2-3/55)	2.30	7.00	16.00
2(6-7/55)	1.50	4.50	10.00

LITTLE HIAWATHA (See 4-Color #439,787,901,988 & Walt Disney's C&S #143)

LITTLE IKE
April, 1953 - No. 4, Oct, 1953
St. John Publishing Co.

1	3.15	9.50	22.00
2	1.60	4.80	11.00
3,4	1.15	3.50	8.00

LITTLE IODINE (See Giant Comic Album)
April, 1949 - No. 56, Apr-June, 1962 (1-4: 52pgs.)
Dell Publishing Co.

4-Color 224-By Jimmy Hatlo	4.30	13.00	30.00
4-Color 257	3.50	10.50	24.00
1(3-5/50)	3.50	10.50	24.00
2-5	1.70	5.00	12.00
6-10	1.15	3.50	8.00
11-20	1.00	3.00	7.00
21-30: 27-Xmas-c	.85	2.50	6.00
31-40	.55	1.65	4.00
41-56	.45	1.35	3.00

LITTLE JACK FROST
1951
Avon Periodicals

1	3.50	10.50	24.00

LI'L JINX (Formerly Ginger?) (Little Archie in Animal Land #17)
(Also see Pep Comics #62)
No. 11(#1), Nov, 1956 - No. 16, Sept, 1957
Archie Publications

11 (#1)	5.50	16.50	38.00
12-16	3.50	10.50	24.00

LI'L JINX (See Archie Giant Series Magazine No. 223)

LI'L JINX CHRISTMAS BAG (See Archie Giant Series Mag. No. 195,206,219)

LI'L JINX GIANT LAUGH-OUT
No. 33, Sept, 1971 - No. 43, Nov, 1973 (52 pgs.)
Archie Publications

33-43	.35	1.00	2.00
(See Archie Giant Series Mag. No. 176,185)			

LITTLE JOE (See 4-Color #1, Popular & Super Comics)

LITTLE JOE
April, 1953
St. John Publishing Co.

1	1.50	4.50	10.00

LITTLE JOHNNY & THE TEDDY BEARS
1907 (10x14'') (32 pgs. in color)
Reilly & Britton Co.

By J. R. Bray	19.00	57.00	132.00

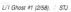

Li'l Ghost #1 (2/58). © STJ

Little Giant Comics #4. © CEN

Little Iodine #12. © DELL

Little Lizzie #4, © MEG

Li'l Menace #1, © Fago Mag. Co.

Little Miss Muffet #13, © KING

LI'L KIDS
8/70 - No. 2, 10/70; No. 3, 11/71 - No. 12, 6/73
Marvel Comics Group

	Good	Fine	N-Mint
1	.50	1.50	3.00
2-12: 10,11-Calvin app.	.25	.75	1.50

LITTLE KING (See 4-Color No. 494,597,677)

LITTLE KLINKER
Nov, 1960 (20 pgs.) (slick cover)
Little Klinker Ventures (Montgomery Ward Giveaway)

nn	.50	1.50	3.00

LITTLE LANA (Formerly Lana)
No. 8, Nov, 1949 - No. 9, Mar, 1950
Marvel Comics (MjMC)

8,9	2.00	6.00	14.00

LITTLE LENNY
June, 1949 - No. 3, Nov, 1949
Marvel Comics (CDS)

1	3.50	10.50	24.00
2,3	1.70	5.00	12.00

LITTLE LIZZIE
6/49 - No. 5, 4/50; 9/53 - No. 3, Jan, 1954
Marvel Comics (PrPI)/Atlas (OMC)

1	3.50	10.50	24.00
2-5	1.70	5.00	12.00
1 (1953, 2nd series)	2.65	8.00	18.00
2,3	1.30	4.00	9.00

LITTLE LOTTA (See Harvey Hits No. 10)
11/55 - No. 110, 11/73; No. 111, 9/74 - No. 121, 5/76
Harvey Publications

1-Richie Rich (r) & Little Dot begin	17.00	51.00	120.00
2,3	8.00	24.00	56.00
4,5	4.35	13.00	30.00
6-10	3.00	9.00	21.00
11-20	1.70	5.00	12.00
21-40	1.15	3.50	8.00
41-60	.85	2.50	6.00
61-80	.50	1.50	3.00
81-99	.35	1.00	2.00
100-103: All 52 pg. Giants	.40	1.20	2.40
104-121	.25	.75	1.50

LITTLE LOTTA FOODLAND
9/63 - No. 14, 10/67; No. 15, 10/68 - No. 29, Oct, 1972
Harvey Publications

1: 68 pgs. begin, end #26	5.00	15.00	35.00
2,3	2.30	7.00	16.00
4,5	1.70	5.00	12.00
6-10	1.30	4.00	9.00
11-20	1.00	3.00	6.00
21-26	.85	2.50	5.00
27,28: Both 52 pgs.	.70	2.00	4.00
29: 36 pgs.	.50	1.50	3.00

LITTLE LULU (Formerly Marge's. . .)
No. 207, Sept, 1972 - No. 268, April, 1984
Gold Key 207-257/Whitman 258 on

207,209,220-Stanley-r. 207-1st app. Henrietta	.60	1.75	3.50
208,210-219: 208-1st app. Snobbly, Wilbur's brother	.40	1.25	2.50
221-240,242-249, 250(r/166), 251-254(r/206)	.25	.80	1.60
241,263,268-Stanley-r	.25	.80	1.60
255-262,264-267: 256 r/212		.50	1.00

LITTLE MARY MIXUP (See Comics On Parade & Single Series #10,26)

LITTLE MAX COMICS (Joe Palooka's Pal; see Joe Palooka)
Oct, 1949 - No. 73, Nov, 1961
Harvey Publications

	Good	Fine	N-Mint
1-Infinity-c; Little Dot begins	7.00	21.00	50.00
2-Little Dot app.	3.50	10.50	24.00
3-Little Dot app.	2.75	8.00	19.00
4-10: 5-Little Dot app., 1pg.	1.50	4.50	10.00
11-20	1.00	3.00	7.00
21-68,70-72: 23-Little Dot app. 38-r/20	.75	2.25	5.00
69,73-Richie Rich app.	.85	2.50	6.00

LI'L MENACE
Dec, 1958 - No. 3, May, 1959
Fago Magazine Co.

1-Peter Rabbit app.	2.30	7.00	16.00
2-Peter Rabbit (Vincent Fago's)	1.50	4.50	10.00
3	1.15	3.50	8.00

LITTLE MISS MUFFET
No. 11, Dec, 1948 - No. 13, March, 1949
Best Books (Standard Comics)/King Features Synd.

11-Strip reprints; Fanny Cory-a	4.00	12.00	28.00
12,13-Strip reprints; Fanny Cory-a	2.30	7.00	16.00

LITTLE MISS SUNBEAM COMICS
June-July, 1950 - No. 4, Dec-Jan, 1950-51
Magazine Enterprises/Quality Bakers of America

1	5.50	16.50	38.00
2	2.85	8.50	20.00
3,4	2.35	7.00	16.00
. . .Advs. In Space ('55)	1.70	5.00	12.00
Bread Giveaway 1-4(Quality Bakers, 1949-50)-14 pgs. each	1.50	4.50	10.00
Bread Giveaway (1957,61; 16pgs, reg. size)	1.15	3.50	8.00

LITTLE MONSTERS, THE (See March of Comics No. 423 & Three Stooges No. 17)
Nov, 1964 - No. 44, Feb, 1978
Gold Key

1	1.50	4.50	10.00
2	.85	2.50	5.00
3-10	.70	2.00	4.00
11-20	.35	1.00	2.00
21-44: 20,34-39,43-reprints		.40	.80

LITTLE MONSTERS
1989 - Present ($1.75, color, movie adaptation)
Now Comics

1-5: 1,2-Photo-c from movie	.30	.90	1.80

LITTLE NEMO (See Cocomalt, Future Comics, Help, Jest, Kayo, Punch, Red Seal, & Superworld; mostly Winsor McCay Jr, son of famous artist) (Other McCay books: see Little Sammy Sneeze & Dreams of the Rarebit Fiend)

LITTLE NEMO (. . .in Slumberland)
1906, 1909 (Sunday strip reprints in color) (cardboard covers)
Doffield & Co.(1906)/Cupples & Leon Co.(1909)

1906-11x16½" in color by Winsor McCay; 30 pgs. (Very Rare)			
	143.00	430.00	1000.00
1909-10x14" in color by Winsor McCay (Very Rare)			
	115.00	345.00	800.00

LITTLE NEMO (. . .in Slumberland)
1945 (28 pgs.; 11x7¼"; B&W)
McCay Features/Nostalgia Press('69)

1905 & 1911 reprints by Winsor McCay	4.00	12.00	28.00
1969-70 (exact reprint)	1.50	4.00	8.00

LITTLE NEMO IN SLUMBERLAND IN 3-D (See Blackthorne 3-D Series 13)

LITTLE ORPHAN ANNIE (See Annie, Feature Books #7, Marvel Super Special, Merry Christmas. . . , Popular Comics, Super Book #7, 11, 23 & Super Comics)

LITTLE ORPHAN ANNIE (See Treasure Box of Famous Comics)
1926 - 1934 (Daily strip reprints) (7x8¾'') (B&W)
Cupples & Leon Co.

	Good	Fine	N-Mint
(Hardcover Editions, 100 pages)			
1(1926)-Little Orphan Annie	17.00	51.00	120.00
2('27)-In the Circus	13.00	40.00	90.00
3('28)-The Haunted House	13.00	40.00	90.00
4('29)-Bucking the World	13.00	40.00	90.00
5('30)-Never Say Die	13.00	40.00	90.00
6('31)-Shipwrecked	13.00	40.00	90.00
7('32)-A Willing Helper	10.00	30.00	70.00
8('33)-In Cosmic City	10.00	30.00	70.00
9('34)-Uncle Dan	13.00	40.00	90.00

NOTE: Hardcovers with dust jackets are worth 20-50 percent more; the earlier the book, the higher the percentage. Each book reprints dailies from the previous year.

LITTLE ORPHAN ANNIE
No. 7, 1937 - No. 3, Sept-Nov, 1948; No. 206, Dec, 1948
David McKay Publ./Dell Publishing Co.

	Good	Fine	N-Mint
Feature Books(McKay) 7-('37) (Rare)	75.00	225.00	525.00
4-Color 12(1941)	34.00	100.00	235.00
4-Color 18('43)-Flag-c	25.00	75.00	175.00
4-Color 52('44)	19.00	57.00	135.00
4-Color 76('45)	16.00	48.00	110.00
4-Color 107('46)	13.00	40.00	90.00
4-Color 152('47)	9.30	28.00	65.00
1(3-5/48)	12.00	36.00	84.00
2,3	7.00	21.00	50.00
4-Color 206(12/48)	5.70	17.00	40.00
Junior Commandos Giveaway(same cover as 4-Color #18, K.K. Publ.)			
(Big Shoe Store); same back cover as '47 Popped Wheat			
giveaway; 16 pgs; flag-c	14.50	43.50	100.00
Popped Wheat Giveaway('47)-16 pgs. full color; '40 reprints			
	.85	2.50	6.00
Quaker Sparkies Giveaway(1940)	6.50	19.50	45.00
Quaker Sparkies Giveaway(1941, Full color-20 pgs.); ''LOA and the			
Rescue,'' ''LOA and the Kidnappers,''	5.70	17.00	40.00
Quaker Sparkies Giveaway(1942, Full color-20 pgs..); ''LOA and Mr.			
Grudge'' and ''LOA and the Great Am''	4.30	13.00	30.00

LI'L PALS
Sept, 1972 - No. 5, May, 1973
Marvel Comics Group

1-5		.40	.80

LI'L PAN
No. 6, Dec-Jan, 1947 - No. 8, Apr-May, 1947
Fox Features Syndicate

6	2.65	8.00	18.00
7,8	1.70	5.00	12.00

LITTLE PEOPLE (See 4-Color #485, 573, 633, 692, 753, 809, 868, 908, 959, 1024, 1062)

LITTLE RASCALS (See 4-Color #674, 778, 825, 883, 936, 974, 1030, 1079, 1137, 1174, 1224, 1297)

LI'L RASCAL TWINS (Formerly Nature Boy)
No. 6, 1957 - No. 18, Jan, 1960
Charlton Comics

6-Li'l Genius & Tomboy in all	2.00	6.00	14.00
7-18	1.00	3.00	7.00

LITTLE ROQUEFORT COMICS
June, 1952 - No. 9, Oct, 1953; No. 10, Summer, 1958
St. John Publishing Co./Pines No. 10

1	3.50	10.50	24.00

	Good	Fine	N-Mint
2	1.70	5.00	12.00
3-10	1.30	4.00	9.00

LITTLE SAD SACK (See Harvey Hits No. 73,76,79,81,83)
Oct, 1964 - No. 19, Nov, 1967
Harvey Publications

1-Richie Rich app. on cover only	1.35	4.00	9.00
2-19	.35	1.00	2.00

LITTLE SAMMY SNEEZE
1905 (28 pgs. in color; 11x16½'')
New York Herald Co.

By Winsor McCay (Rare)	150.00	450.00	1050.00

NOTE: Rarely found in fine to mint condition.

LITTLE SCOUTS
No. 321, Mar, 1951 - No. 587, Oct, 1954
Dell Publishing Co.

4-Color #321 (#1, 3/51)	1.30	4.00	9.00
2(10-12/51) - 6(10-12/52)	.85	2.50	6.00
4-Color #462,506,550,587	.85	2.50	6.00

LITTLE SHOP OF HORRORS SPECIAL
Feb, 1987 ($2.00, 68 pgs.) (Movie adaptation)
DC Comics

1-Colan-a	.35	1.00	2.00

LITTLE SPUNKY
No date (19637) (10 cents)
I. W. Enterprises

1-Reprint	.30	.80	1.60

LITTLE STOOGES, THE (The Three Stooges' Sons)
Sept, 1972 - No. 7, Mar, 1974
Gold Key

1-Norman Maurer cover/stories in all	.70	2.00	4.00
2-7	.35	1.00	2.00

LITTLEST OUTLAW (See 4-Color #609)

LITTLEST SNOWMAN, THE
No. 755, 12/56; No. 864, 12/57; 12-2/1963-64
Dell Publishing Co.

4-Color #755,864, 1(1964)	2.15	7.00	16.00

LI'L TOMBOY (Formerly Fawcett's Funny Animals)
V14No.92, 10/56; No. 93, 3/57 - No. 107, 2/60
Charlton Comics

V14#92	1.70	5.00	12.00
93-107: 97-Atomic Bunny app.	1.15	3.50	8.00

LITTLE TREE THAT WASN'T WANTED, THE
1960, (Color, 28 pgs.)
W. T. Grant Co. (Giveaway)

nn-Christmas giveaway	.50	1.50	3.00

LI'L WILLIE COMICS (Formerly & becomes Willie Comics #22 on)
No. 20, July, 1949 - No. 21, Sept, 1949
Marvel Comics (MgPC)

20,21: 20-Little Aspirin app.	2.00	6.00	14.00

LIVE IT UP
1973, 1976 (39-49 cents)
Spire Christian Comics (Fleming H. Revell Co.)

nn		.40	.80

LIVING BIBLE, THE
Fall, 1945 - No. 3, Spring, 1946
Living Bible Corp.

1-Life of Paul	10.00	30.00	70.00

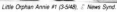

Little Orphan Annie #1 (3-5/48), © News Synd.

Little Scouts #2, © DELL

Li'l Willie Comics #21, © MEG

Lonely Heart #10, AJAX

The Lone Ranger #123, © Lone Ranger

The Lone Ranger's Companion Tonto #7, © Lone Ranger

	Good	Fine	N-Mint
THE LIVING BIBLE (continued)			
2-Joseph & His Brethren	5.70	17.00	40.00
3-Chaplains At War (classic-c)	12.00	36.00	84.00
NOTE: All have **L. B. Cole** -c.			
LOBO			
Dec, 1965; No. 2, Oct, 1966			
Dell Publishing Co.			
1,2	.85	2.50	6.00
LOCKE!			
1987 - No. 3? ($1.25, color)			
Blackthorne Publishing			
1-3		.60	1.25
LOCO (Magazine) (Satire)			
Aug, 1958 - V1No.3, Jan, 1959			
Satire Publications			
V1#1-Chic Stone-a	1.50	4.50	10.00
V1#2,3-Severin-a, 2 pgs. Davis; 3-Heath-a	.85	2.60	6.00
LOGAN'S RUN			
Jan, 1977 - No. 7, July, 1977			
Marvel Comics Group			
1		.40	.80
2-7		.25	.50
NOTE: Austin a-6i. Gulacy c-6. Kane c-7p. Perez a-1-5p; c-1-5p. Sutton a-6p, 7p.			
LOIS LANE (Also see Superman's Girlfriend . . .)			
Aug, 1986 - No. 2, Sept, 1986 (52 pgs.)			
DC Comics			
1,2-Morrow c/a	.25	.75	1.50
LOLLY AND PEPPER			
No. 832, Sept, 1957 - July, 1962			
Dell Publishing Co.			
4-Color 832	1.70	5.00	12.00
4-Color 940,978,1086,1206	1.30	4.00	9.00
01-459-207 (7/62)	1.30	4.00	9.00
LOMAX (See Police Action)			
LONE EAGLE (The Flame No. 5 on)			
Apr-May, 1954 - No. 4, Oct-Nov, 1954			
Ajax/Farrell Publications			
1	4.00	12.00	28.00
2-4: 3-Bondage-c	2.65	8.00	18.00
LONELY HEART (Formerly Dear Lonely Hearts; Dear Heart #15 on)			
No. 9, March, 1955 - No. 14, Feb, 1956			
Ajax/Farrell Publ. (Excellent Publ.)			
9-Kamenesca-a; (Last precode)	3.00	9.00	21.00
10-14	1.50	4.50	10.00
LONE RANGER, THE (See Ace Comics, Aurora, Dell Giants, Feature Books #21, 24(McKay), Future Comics, King Comics, Magic Comics & March of Comics #165, 174, 193, 208, 225, 238, 310, 322, 338, 350)			
LONE RANGER, THE			
No. 3, 1939 - No. 167, Feb, 1947			
Dell Publishing Co.			
Large Feat. Comic 3('39)-Heigh-Yo Silver; text with ill. by Robert Weisman; also exists as a Whitman #710	43.00 130.00 300.00		
Large Feat. Comic 7('39)-Ill. by Henry Valleley; Hi-Yo Silver the Lone Ranger to the Rescue; also exists as a Whitman #715			
	53.00	160.00	370.00
4-Color 82('45)	28.50	86.00	200.00
4-Color 98('45),118('46)	23.50	71.00	165.00
4-Color 125('46),136('47)	17.00	51.00	120.00
4-Color 151,167('47)	14.00	42.00	100.00

LONE RANGER, THE (Movie, radio & TV; Clayton Moore starred as L. Ranger in the movies; No. 1-37: strip reprints)(See Dell Giants)
Jan-Feb, 1948 - No. 145, May-July, 1962
Dell Publishing Co.

	Good	Fine	N-Mint
1 (36pgs.)-The L. Ranger, his horse Silver, companion Tonto & his horse Scout begin	49.00	148.00	345.00
2 (52pgs. begin, end #41)	24.00	73.00	170.00
3-5	20.00	60.00	140.00
6,7,9,10	17.00	51.00	120.00
8-Origin retold; Indian back-c begin, end #35	22.00	65.00	155.00
11-20: 11-"Young Hawk" Indian boy serial begins, ends #145	11.50	34.00	80.00
21,22,24-31: 51-Reprint. 31-1st Mask logo	9.30	28.00	65.00
23-Origin retold	13.00	40.00	90.00
32-37: 32-Painted-c begin. 36-Animal photo back-c begin, end #49. 37-Last newspaper-r issue; new outfit	7.00	21.00	50.00
38-41 (All 52pgs.)	5.00	15.00	35.00
42-50 (36pgs.)	3.70	11.00	26.00
51-74 (52pgs.): 71-Blank inside-c	3.70	11.00	26.00
75-99: 76-Flag-c. 79-X-mas-c	3.00	9.00	21.00
100	4.50	14.00	32.00
101-111: Last painted-c	2.65	8.00	18.00
112-Clayton Moore photo-c begin, end #145	13.00	40.00	90.00
113-117	7.00	21.00	50.00
118-Origin Lone Ranger, Tonto, & Silver retold; Special anniversary issue	12.00	36.00	85.00
119-145: 139-Last issue by Fran Striker	5.70	17.00	40.00
Cheerios Giveaways (1954, 16 pgs., 2½x7", soft-c) #1-"The Lone Ranger, His Mask & How He Met Tonto". #2-"The Lone Ranger & the Story of Silver" each	5.70	17.00	40.00
Doll Giveaways (Gabriel Ind.)(1973, 3¼x5")-"The Story of The L.R." & The Carson City Bank Robbery"	1.00	3.00	7.00
How the L. R. Captured Silver Book(1936)-Silvercup Bread giveaway	33.00	100.00	230.00
. . . In Milk for Big Mike(1955, Dairy Association giveaway), soft-c 5x7¼", 16 pgs.	9.30	28.00	65.00
Merita Bread giveaway('54; 16 pgs.; 5x7¼")-"How to Be a Lone Ranger Health & Safety Scout"	9.30	28.00	65.00

NOTE: **Hank Hartman** painted c(signed)-65, 66, 70, 75, 82; unsigned-64?, 67-69?, 71, 72, 73?, 74?, 76-78, 80, 81, 83-91, 92?, 93-111. **Ernest Nordli** painted c(signed)-42, 50, 52, 53, 56, 59, 60; unsigned-39-41, 44-49, 51, 54, 55, 57, 58, 61-63?

LONE RANGER, THE
9/64 - No. 16, 12/69; No. 17, 11/72; No. 18, 9/74 - No. 28, 3/77
Gold Key (Reprints #13-20)

1-Retells origin	2.85	8.50	20.00
2	1.50	4.50	10.00
3-10: Small Bear-r in #6-10	1.00	3.00	7.00
11-17: Small Bear-r in #11,12	2.50	5.50	6.00
18-28	.55	1.65	4.00
Golden West 1(30029-610)-Giant, 10/66-r/most Golden West #3-including Clayton Moore photo front/back-c	5.00	15.00	35.00

LONE RANGER COMICS, THE (10 cents)
1939(inside) (shows 1938 on-c) (68 pgs. in color; regular size)
Lone Ranger, Inc. (Ice cream mail order)

nn-(Scarce)-not by Vallely	50.00	150.00	350.00

LONE RANGER'S COMPANION TONTO, THE (TV)
No. 312, Jan, 1951 - No. 33, Nov-Jan/58-59 (All painted-c)
Dell Publishing Co.

4-Color 312(1951)	8.00	24.00	56.00
2(8-10/51),3: (#2 titled 'Tonto')	4.00	12.00	28.00
4-10	2.30	7.00	16.00
11-20	1.85	5.50	13.00
21-33	1.50	4.50	10.00

243

NOTE: *Ernest Nordli* painted c(signed)-2, 7; unsigned-3-6, 8-11, 12?, 13, 14, 18?, 22-24? See Aurora Comic Booklets.

LONE RANGER'S FAMOUS HORSE HI-YO SILVER, THE (TV)
No. 369, Jan, 1952 - No. 36, Oct-Dec, 1960 (All painted-c)
Dell Publishing Co.

	Good	Fine	N-Mint
4-Color 369-Silver's origin as told by The L.R.	5.50	16.50	38.00
4-Color 392(#2, 4/52)	2.85	8.50	20.00
3(7-9/52)-10(4-6/52)	1.60	4.80	11.00
11-36	1.15	3.50	8.00

LONE RIDER (Also see The Rider)
April, 1951 - No. 26, July, 1955 (36pgs., 3-on)
Superior Comics(Farrell Publications)

1 (52pgs.)-The Lone Rider & his horse Lightnin' begin; Kamenish-a begins	7.00	21.00	50.00
2 (52pgs.)-The Golden Arrow begins (origin)	4.00	12.00	28.00
3-6: 6-Last Golden Arrow	3.15	9.50	22.00
7-G. Arrow becomes Swift Arrow; origin of his shield	3.70	11.00	26.00
8-Origin Swift Arrow	4.50	14.00	32.00
9,10	2.30	7.00	16.00
11-14	2.00	6.00	14.00
15-Golden Arrow origin-r from #2, changing name to Swift Arrow	2.30	7.00	16.00
16-20,22-26: 23-Apache Kid app.	1.70	5.00	12.00
21-3-D effect-c	6.00	18.00	42.00

LONE WOLF AND CUB
May, 1987 - Present ($1.95-$2.50-$2.95, B&W, deluxe size)
First Comics

1	2.00	6.00	12.00
1-2nd print, 3rd print	.35	1.00	2.00
2	1.10	3.25	6.50
2-2nd print	.35	1.00	2.00
3	.70	2.00	4.00
4-12: 6-72 pg. origin issue. 8-$2.50-c begins	.45	1.30	2.60
13-25	.40	1.25	2.50
26-30,32-34: 26-Begin $2.95-c	.50	1.50	3.00
31 ($3.25, 92 pgs.)	.55	1.65	3.25
Deluxe Edition ($19.95; B&W)	3.35	10.00	19.95

NOTE: *Miller* c-1-12; intro-1-12. *Sienkiewicz* c-13-24.

LONG BOW (. . .Indian Boy)(See Indians & Jumbo Comics #141)
1951 - No. 9, Wint, 1952/53
Fiction House Magazines (Real Adventures Publ.)

1	6.50	19.50	45.00
2	3.70	11.00	26.00
3-9	2.65	8.00	18.00

LONG JOHN SILVER & THE PIRATES (Formerly Terry & the Pirates)
No. 30, Aug, 1956 - No. 32, March, 1957 (TV)
Charlton Comics

30-32: Whitman-c	2.85	8.50	20.00

LONGSHOT
Sept, 1985 - No. 6, Feb, 1986 (Limited-series)
Marvel Comics Group

1-Arthur Adams-c/a in all	3.35	10.00	20.00
2	2.50	7.50	15.00
3-5	2.00	6.00	12.00
6-Double size	2.70	8.00	16.00
Trade Paperback (1989, $16.95)-r/1-6	2.85	8.50	17.00

LOONEY TUNES (2nd Series)
April, 1975 - No. 47, July, 1984
Gold Key/Whitman

1		.50	1.00

	Good	Fine	N-Mint
2-47: Reprints: #1-4,16; 38-46(⅓r)		.30	.60

LOONEY TUNES AND MERRIE MELODIES COMICS ("Looney Tunes" #166 (8/55) on)
1941 - No. 246, July-Sept, 1962
Dell Publishing Co.

1-Porky Pig, Bugs Bunny, Daffy Duck, Elmer Fudd, Mary Jane & Sniffles, Pat, Patsy and Pete begin (1st comic book app. of each). Bugs Bunny story by Win Smith (early Mickey Mouse artist)	121.00	365.00	850.00
2 (11/41)	54.00	163.00	380.00
3-Kandi the Cave Kid begins by Walt Kelly; also in #4-6,8,11,15	48.00	145.00	340.00
4-Kelly-a	43.00	130.00	300.00
5-Bugs Bunny The Super Rabbit app. (1st funny animal super hero?); Kelly-a	32.00	95.00	225.00
6,8-Kelly-a	24.00	70.00	165.00
7,9,10: 9-Painted-c. 10-Flag-c	18.50	56.00	130.00
11,15-Kelly-a; 15-X-Mas-c	18.50	56.00	130.00
12-14,16-19	16.00	48.00	110.00
20-25: Pat, Patsy & Pete by Kelly in all	16.00	48.00	110.00
26-30	11.00	32.00	75.00
31-40	8.00	24.00	56.00
41-50	5.50	16.50	38.00
51-60	3.60	11.00	25.00
61-80	2.15	7.00	16.00
81-99: 87-X-Mas-c	2.00	6.00	14.00
100	2.15	7.00	16.00
101-120	1.60	4.80	11.00
121-150	1.30	4.00	9.00
151-200	1.00	3.00	7.00
201-246	.70	2.00	5.00

LOONEY TUNES MAGAZINE
Jan, 1990 - Present ($1.95, magazine size)
DC Comics

1-Bugs Bunny, Daffy Duck & Porky Pig; contains jokes, puzzles & mini poster	.35	1.00	2.00

LOONY SPORTS (Magazine)
Spring, 1975 (48 pages)
3-Strikes Publishing Co.

1-Sports satire	.25	.80	1.60

LOOY DOT DOPE (See Single Series No. 13)

LORD JIM (See Movie Comics)

LORDS OF THE ULTRA-REALM
June, 1986 - No. 6, Nov, 1986 (mini-series)
DC Comics

1	.50	1.50	3.00
2-6	.30	.85	1.70
Special 1(12/87, $2.25)	.40	1.15	2.30

LORNA THE JUNGLE GIRL (. . .Jungle Queen #1-5)
July, 1953 - No. 26, Aug, 1957
Atlas Comics (NPI 1/OMC 2-11/NPI 12-26)

1-Origin	11.00	32.00	75.00
2-Intro. & 1st app. Greg Knight	6.00	18.00	42.00
3-5	5.00	15.00	35.00
6-11: 11-Last pre-code (1/55)	3.70	11.00	26.00
12-17,19-26	2.85	8.50	20.00
18-Williamson/Colletta-c	4.30	13.00	30.00

NOTE: *Everett* c-21, 23-26. *Heath* c-6, 7. *Maneely* c-12, 15. *Romita* a-20, 22. *Shores* a-16; c-13, 16. *Tuska* a-6.

LOSERS SPECIAL (Also see G.I. Combat #138)
Sept, 1985 ($1.25 cover) (One Shot)(See Our Fighting Forces #123)

Lone Rider #10, © SUPR

Looney Tunes And Merrie Melodies #31, © Warner Bros.

Lorna The Jungle Girl #7, © MEG

Lost Planet #1, © Eclipse

Love At First Sight #1, © ACE

Love Diary #1, © Our Publ.

	Good	Fine	N-Mint

LOSERS SPECIAL (continued)
DC Comics

	Good	Fine	N-Mint
1-Capt. Storm, Gunner & Sarge; Crisis x-over	.65		1.30

LOST IN SPACE (Space Family Robinson . . ., on Space Station One)(Formerly Space Family Robinson; see Gold Key Champion)
No. 37, 10/73 - No. 54, 11/78; No. 55, 3/81 - No. 59, 5/82
Gold Key

37-48	.40	1.20	2.40
49-59: Reprints-#49,50,55-59	.60		1.20

NOTE: *Spiegle a-37-59. All have painted-c.*

LOST PLANET
5/87 - No. 5, 2/88; No. 6, 3/89 (mini-series, $1.75-$2.00, color, Baxter)
Eclipse Comics

1,2 ($1.75)-Bo Hampton c/a in all	.30	.90	1.80
3-6 ($2.00)	.35	1.00	2.00

LOST WORLD, THE (See 4-Color #1145)

LOST WORLDS
No. 5, Oct, 1952 - No. 6, Dec, 1952
Standard Comics

5-"Alice in Terrorland" by Toth; J. Katz-a	14.00	42.00	100.00
6-Toth-a	11.00	32.00	75.00

LOTS 'O' FUN COMICS
1940's? (5 cents) (heavy stock; blue covers)
Robert Allen Co.

nn-Contents can vary; Felix, Planet Comics known; contents would determine value.
Similar to Up-To-Date Comics. Remainders - re-packaged.

LOU GEHRIG (See The Pride of the Yankees)

LOVE ADVENTURES (Actual Confessions #13)
10/49; No. 2, 1/50; No. 3, 2/51 - No. 12, 8/52
Marvel (IPS)/Atlas Comics (MPI)

1-Photo-c	3.50	10.50	24.00
2-Powell-a; Tyrone Power, Gene Tierney photo-c			
	3.50	10.50	24.00
3-8,10-12: 8-Robinson-a	1.70	5.00	12.00
9-Everett-a	2.30	7.00	16.00

LOVE AND MARRIAGE
March, 1952 - No. 16, Sept, 1954
Superior Comics Ltd.

1	4.30	13.00	30.00
2	2.15	6.50	15.00
3-10	1.50	4.50	10.00
11-16	1.15	3.50	8.00
I.W. Reprint #1,2,8,11,14	.25	.80	1.60
Super Reprint #10('63),15,17('64)	.25	.80	1.60

NOTE: *All issues have Kamenish art.*

LOVE AND ROCKETS
July, 1982 - Present (Adults only)
Fantagraphics Books

1-B&W-c ($2.95; small size, publ. by Hernandez Bros.)(800 printed)			
	20.85	62.50	125.00
1 (Fall, '82; color-c)	11.70	35.00	70.00
1-2nd printing	.50	1.50	3.00
2	3.35	10.00	20.00
3-5	2.00	6.00	12.00
6-10	1.00	3.00	6.00
11-15	.40	1.25	2.50
16-32: 30($2.95, 52 pgs.). 31-on: $2.50-c	.30	.90	1.80

LOVE AND ROMANCE
Sept, 1971 - No. 24, Sept, 1975
Charlton Comics

1		.30	.60

	Good	Fine	N-Mint
2-24		.15	.30

LOVE AT FIRST SIGHT
Oct, 1949 - No. 42, Aug, 1956 (Photo-c: 21-42)
Ace Magazines (RAR Publ. Co./Periodical House)

1-Painted-c	4.00	12.00	28.00
2-Painted-c	2.00	6.00	14.00
3-10: 4-Painted-c	1.50	4.50	10.00
11-20	1.15	3.50	8.00
21-33: 33-Last pre-code	1.00	3.00	7.00
34-42	.85	2.50	6.00

LOVE BUG, THE (See Movie Comics)

LOVE CLASSICS
Nov, 1949 - No. 2, Feb, 1950 (Photo-c)
A Lover's Magazine/Marvel Comics

1,2: 2-Virginia Mayo photo-c; 30 pg. story 'I Was a Small Town Flirt'			
	4.30	13.00	30.00

LOVE CONFESSIONS
Oct, 1949 - No. 54, Dec, 1956 (Photo-c: 6,11-18,21)
Quality Comics Group

1-Ward c/a, 9 pgs; Gustavson-a	14.00	42.00	100.00
2-Gustavson-a	5.00	15.00	35.00
3	3.50	10.50	24.00
4-Crandall-a	4.65	14.00	32.00
5-Ward-a, 7 pgs.	5.50	16.50	38.00
6,7,9	1.70	5.00	12.00
8-Ward-a	4.65	14.00	32.00
10-Ward-a(2)	4.65	14.00	32.00
11-13,15,16,18	1.70	5.00	12.00
14,17,19,22-Ward-a; 17-Faith Domergue photo-c	3.85	11.50	27.00
20-Baker-a, Ward-a(2)	4.65	14.00	32.00
21,23-28,30-38,40-42: Last precode, 4/55	1.15	3.50	8.00
29-Ward-a	3.65	11.00	25.00
39-Matt Baker-a	1.70	5.00	12.00
43,44,46-48,50-54: 47-Ward-c?	1.00	3.00	7.00
45-Ward-a	2.15	6.50	15.00
49-Baker c/a	2.65	8.00	18.00

LOVE DIARY
July, 1949 - No. 48, Oct, 1955 (Photo-c: 1-24,27,29) (52 pgs. #1-11?)
Our Publishing Co./Toytown/Patches

1-Krigstein-a	6.50	19.50	45.00
2,3-Krigstein & Mort Leav-a in each	4.30	13.00	30.00
4-8	1.85	5.50	13.00
9,10-Everett-a	2.15	6.50	15.00
11-20: 16,20-Mort Leav-a	1.30	4.00	9.00
21-30,32-48: 45-Ward-a. 47-Last precode(12/54)	1.00	3.00	7.00
31-J. Buscema headlights-c	1.15	3.50	8.00

LOVE DIARY (Diary Loves #2 on)
September, 1949
Quality Comics Group

1-Ward-c, 9 pgs.	11.50	34.50	80.00

LOVE DIARY
July, 1958 - No. 102, Dec, 1976
Charlton Comics

1	2.00	6.00	14.00
2	1.00	3.00	7.00
3-5,7-10	.55	1.65	4.00
6-Torres-a	1.15	3.50	8.00
11-20	.35	1.00	2.50
21-40	.25	.75	1.50
41-60		.60	1.20
61-102		.20	.40

NOTE: *Photo c-10, 20.*

LOVE DOCTOR (See Dr. Anthony King . . .)

LOVE DRAMAS (True Secrets No. 3 on?)
Oct, 1949 - No. 2, Jan, 1950
Marvel Comics (IPS)

	Good	Fine	N-Mint
1-Jack Kamen-a; photo-c	6.00	18.00	42.00
2	3.50	10.50	24.00

LOVE EXPERIENCES (Challenge of the Unknown No. 6)
10/49 - No. 5, 6/50; No. 6, 4/51 - No. 38, 6/56
Ace Periodicals (A.A. Wyn/Periodical House)

1-Painted-c	3.50	10.50	24.00
2	1.70	5.00	12.00
3-5: 5-Painted-c	1.30	4.00	9.00
6-10	1.00	3.00	7.00
11-30: 30-Last pre-code (2/55)	.85	2.50	6.00
31-38: 38-Indicia date-6/56; c-date-8/56	.75	2.25	5.00
NOTE: *Anne Brewster a-15. Photo c-4,15-35,38.*

LOVE JOURNAL
No. 10, Oct, 1951 - No. 25, July, 1954
Our Publishing Co.

10	2.85	8.50	20.00
11-25: 19-Mort Leav-a	1.50	4.50	10.00

LOVELAND
Nov, 1949 - No. 2, Feb, 1950
Mutual Mag./Eye Publ. (Marvel)

1,2-Photo-c	3.00	9.00	21.00

LOVE LESSONS
Oct, 1949 - No. 5, June, 1950
Harvey Comics/Key Publ. No. 5

1-Metallic silver-c printed over the cancelled covers of Love Letters			
#1; indicia title is 'Love Letters'	3.50	10.50	24.00
2-Powell-a	1.50	4.50	10.00
3-5: 3-Photo-c	1.15	3.50	8.00

LOVE LETTERS (10/49, Harvey; advertised but never published; covers were printed before cancellation and were used as the cover to Love Lessions #1)

LOVE LETTERS (Love Secrets No. 32 on)
11/49 - #6, 9/50; #7, 3/51 - #31, 6/53; #32, 2/54 - #51, 12/56
Quality Comics Group

1-Ward-c, Gustavson-a	9.30	28.00	65.00
2-Ward-c, Gustavson-a	8.50	25.50	60.00
3-Gustavson-a	5.00	15.00	35.00
4-Ward-a, 9 pgs.	8.50	25.50	60.00
5-8,10	1.70	5.00	12.00
9-One pg. Ward-''Be Popular with the Opposite Sex''; Robert			
Mitchum photo-c	3.50	10.50	24.00
11-Ward-r/Broadway Romances #2 & retitled	3.50	10.50	24.00
12-15,18-20	1.30	4.00	9.00
16,17-Ward-a; 16-Anthony Quinn photo-c. 17-Jane Russell photo-c			
	4.60	14.00	32.00
21-29	1.15	3.50	8.00
30,31(6/53)-Ward-a	2.65	8.00	18.00
32(2/54) - 39: Last precode (4/55)	1.00	3.00	7.00
40-48	.70	2.00	5.00
49,50-Baker-a	2.65	8.00	18.00
51-Baker-c	2.15	6.50	15.00
NOTE: *Photo-c on most 3-28.*

LOVE LIFE
Nov, 1951
P. L. Publishing Co.

1	2.85	8.50	20.00

LOVELORN (Confessions of the Lovelorn #52 on)
Aug-Sept, 1949 - No. 51, July, 1954 (No. 1-26, 52 pgs.)
American Comics Group (Michel Publ./Regis Publ.)

	Good	Fine	N-Mint
1	3.50	10.50	24.00
2	1.70	5.00	12.00
3-10	1.30	4.00	9.00
11-20,22-48: 18-Drucker-a(2pgs.). 46-Lazarus-a	.85	2.50	6.00
21-Prostitution story	1.65	5.00	11.50
49-51-Has 3-D effect	6.50	19.50	45.00

LOVE MEMORIES
1949 (no month) - No. 4, July, 1950 (All photo-c)
Fawcett Publications

1	3.70	11.00	26.00
2-4	2.00	6.00	14.00

LOVE MYSTERY
June, 1950 - No. 3, Oct, 1950 (All photo-c)
Fawcett Publications

1-George Evans-a	8.50	25.50	60.00
2,3-Evans-a. 3-Powell-a	5.70	17.00	40.00

LOVE PROBLEMS (See Fox Giants)

LOVE PROBLEMS AND ADVICE ILLUSTRATED (Becomes Romance Stories of True Love No. 45 on)
June, 1949 - No. 6, Apr, 1950; No. 7, Jan, 1951 - No. 44, Mar, 1957
McCombs/Harvey Publ./Home Comics

V1#1	3.00	9.00	21.00
2	1.50	4.50	10.00
3-10	1.15	3.50	8.00
11-13,15-23,25-31: 31-Last pre-code (1/55)	.70	2.00	5.00
14,24-Rape scene	.85	2.50	6.00
32-37,39-44	.60	1.80	4.00
38-S&K-c	1.35	4.00	9.00
NOTE: *Powell a-1,2,7-14,17-25,28.29,33,40,41. #3 has True Love... on inside.*

LOVE ROMANCES (Formerly Ideal #5?)
No. 6, May, 1949 - No. 106, July, 1963
Timely/Marvel/Atlas(TCI No. 7-71/Male No. 72-106)

6-Photo-c	3.50	10.50	24.00
7-Kamen-a	2.30	7.00	16.00
8-Kubert-a; photo-c	3.15	9.50	22.00
9-20: 9-12-Photo-c	1.50	4.50	10.00
21,24-Krigstein-a	2.85	8.50	20.00
22,23,25-35,37,39,40	1.15	3.50	8.00
36,38-Krigstein-a	2.30	7.00	16.00
41-44,46,47: Last precode (2/55)	1.00	3.00	7.00
45,57-Matt Baker-a	1.70	5.00	12.00
48,50-52,54-56,58-74	.85	2.50	6.00
49,53-Toth-a, 6 & ? pgs.	2.30	7.00	16.00
75,77,82-Matt Baker-a	1.65	5.00	11.50
76,78-81,84,86-95: Last 10 cent issue?	.75	2.25	4.50
83-Kirby-c, Severin-a	1.50	4.50	10.00
85,96-Kirby c/a	1.50	4.50	10.00
97,100-104	.50	1.50	3.00
98-Kirby-a(4)	2.65	8.00	18.00
99,105,106-Kirby-a	1.15	3.50	8.00
NOTE: *Anne Brewster a-67, 72. Colletta a-37, 40, 42, 44, 67(2); c-42, 44, 49, 80. Everett c-70. Kirby c-80, 85, 88. Robinson a-29.*

LOVERS (Formerly Blonde Phantom)
No. 23, May, 1949 - No. 86, Aug?, 1957
Marvel Comics No. 23,24/Atlas No. 25 on (ANC)

23-Photo-c	3.50	10.50	24.00
24-Tothish plus Robinson-a; photo-c	1.70	5.00	12.00
25,30-Kubert-a; 7, 10 pgs.	2.65	8.00	18.00
26-29,31-36,39,40: 26,27-photo-c	1.15	3.50	8.00
37,38-Krigstein-a	2.65	8.00	18.00
41-Everett-a(2)	2.00	6.00	14.00
42,44-65: 65-Last pre-code (1/55)	1.00	3.00	7.00

Love Lessons #1, © HARV

Lovelorn #17, © ACG

Love Romances #12, © MEG

Love Trails #1, © MEG   Lucky Star #1, © Nation Wide   Lucy, The Real Gone Gal #1, © STJ

	Good	Fine	N-Mint
LOVERS (continued)			
43-1pg. Frazetta ad	1.30	4.00	9.00
66,68-86	.85	2.60	6.00
67-Toth-a	2.65	8.00	18.00

NOTE: *Anne Brewster a-86. Colletta a-54, 59, 62, 64, 69; c-64, 75. Powell a-27, 30. Robinson a-54, 56.*

LOVERS' LANE
Oct, 1949 - No. 41, June, 1954 (No. 1-18: 52 pgs.)
Lev Gleason Publications

1-Biro-c	3.50	10.50	24.00
2	1.70	5.00	12.00
3-10	1.30	4.00	9.00
11-19	1.00	3.00	7.00
20-Frazetta 1 pg. ad	1.30	4.00	9.00
21-38,40,41	.85	2.50	6.00
39-Story narrated by Frank Sinatra	2.00	6.00	14.00

NOTE: *Briefer a-6, 21. Fuje a-4, 16; c-many. Guardineer a-1. Kinstler c-41. Tuska a-6. Painted-c 2-18. Photo-c 19-22, 26-28.*

LOVE SCANDALS
Feb, 1950 - No. 5, Oct, 1950 (Photo-c #2-5) (All 52 pgs.)
Quality Comics Group

1-Ward c/a, 9 pgs.	11.50	34.00	80.00
2,3; 2-Gustavson-a	3.65	11.00	25.00
4-Ward-a, 18 pgs; Gil Fox-a	10.00	30.00	70.00
5-C. Cuidera-a; tomboy story 'I Hated Being a Woman'			
	3.65	11.00	25.00

LOVE SECRETS (Formerly Love Letters #31)
No. 32, Aug, 1953 - No. 56, Dec, 1956
Quality Comics Group

32	2.65	8.00	18.00
33,35-39	1.30	4.00	9.00
34-Ward-a	3.75	11.25	26.00
40-Matt Baker-c	2.50	7.50	17.00
41-43: 43-Last precode (3/55)	1.15	3.50	8.00
44,47-50,53,54	.85	2.50	6.00
45,46-Ward-a. 46-Baker-a	2.85	8.50	20.00
51,52-Ward(r). 52-r/Love Confessions #17	1.65	5.00	11.50
55,56-Baker-a; cover-#56	1.65	5.00	11.50

LOVE SECRETS
Oct, 1949 - No. 2, Jan, 1950 (52 pgs., photo-c)
Marvel Comics(IPC)

1	3.50	10.50	24.00
2	2.65	8.00	18.00

LOVE STORIES
No. 6, 1950 - No. 18, Aug, 1954
Fox Feature Syndicate/Star Publ. No. 13 on

6,8-Wood-a	8.00	24.00	56.00
7,9-12	2.85	8.50	20.00
13-18-L. B. Cole-a	3.35	10.00	23.00

LOVE STORIES (Formerly Heart Throbs)
No. 147, Nov, 1972 - No. 152, Oct-Nov, 1973
National Periodical Publications

147-152		.40	.80

LOVE STORIES OF MARY WORTH (See Harvey Comics Hits #55 & Mary Worth)
Sept, 1949 - No. 5, May, 1950
Harvey Publications

1-1940's newspaper reprints-#1-4	3.50	10.50	24.00
2	2.50	7.50	17.00
3-5: 3-Kamen/Baker-a?	2.35	7.00	16.00

LOVE TALES (Formerly The Human Torch #35)
No. 36, 5/49 - No. 58, 8/52; No. 59, date? - No. 75, Sept, 1957

	Good	Fine	N-Mint
Marvel/Atlas Comics (ZPC No. 36-50/MMC No. 67-75)			
36-Photo-c	3.50	10.50	24.00
37	1.70	5.00	12.00
38-44,46-50: 40,41-Photo-c	1.15	3.50	8.00
45-Powell-a	1.30	4.00	9.00
51,69-Everett-a	2.00	6.00	14.00
52-Krigstein-a	2.30	7.00	16.00
53-60: 60-Last pre-code (2/55)	1.00	3.00	7.00
61-68,70-75	.70	2.00	5.00

LOVE THRILLS (See Fox Giants)

LOVE TRAILS
Dec, 1949 - No. 2, Mar, 1950 (52 pgs.)
A Lover's Magazine (CDS)(Marvel)

1,2: 1-Photo-c	3.50	10.50	24.00

LOWELL THOMAS' HIGH ADVENTURE (See 4-Color #949,1001)

LT. (See Lieutenant)

LUCKY COMICS
Jan, 1944; No. 2, Summer, 1945 - No. 5, Summer, 1946
Consolidated Magazines

1-Lucky Starr, Bobbie	6.50	19.50	45.00
2-5	3.00	9.00	21.00

LUCKY DUCK
No. 5, Jan, 1953 - No. 8, Sept, 1953
Standard Comics (Literary Ent.)

5-Irving Spector-a	3.50	10.50	24.00
6-8-Irving Spector-a	2.30	7.00	16.00

LUCKY FIGHTS IT THROUGH (Also see The K. O. Punch)
1949 (16 pgs. in color; paper cover) (Giveaway)
Educational Comics

(Very Rare)-1st Kurtzman work for E. C.; V.D. prevention
	142.00	425.00	1000.00

(Prices vary widely on this book)
NOTE: *Subtitled "The Story of That Ignorant, Ignorant Cowboy." Prepared for Communications Materials Center, Columbia University.*

LUCKY "7" COMICS
1944 (No date listed)
Howard Publishers Ltd.

1-Congo Raider, Punch Powers; bondage-c	12.00	36.00	84.00

LUCKY STAR (Western)
1950 - No. 7, 1951; No. 8, 1953 - No. 14, 1955 (5x7¼"; full color)
Nation Wide Publ. Co.

1-Jack Davis-a; 52 pgs., 5 cents	5.00	15.00	35.00
2,3-(52 pgs.)-Davis-a	3.00	9.00	21.00
4-7-(52 pgs.)-Davis-a	2.65	8.00	18.00
8-14-(36 pgs.)	1.70	5.00	12.00

Given away with Lucky Star Western Wear by the Juvenile Mfg. Co.
	1.70	5.00	12.00

LUCY SHOW, THE (TV) (Also see I Love Lucy)
June, 1963 - No. 5, June, 1964 (Photo-c: 1,2)
Gold Key

1	5.70	17.00	40.00
2	4.00	12.00	28.00
3-5: Photo back-c,1,2,4,5	3.70	10.50	24.00

LUCY, THE REAL GONE GAL (Meet Miss Pepper #5 on)
June, 1953 - No. 4, Dec, 1953
St. John Publishing Co.

1-Negligee panels	3.70	11.00	26.00
2	2.00	6.00	14.00
3,4: 3-Drucker-a	1.70	5.00	12.00

LUDWIG BEMELMAN'S MADELEINE & GENEVIEVE (See 4-Color #796)

LUDWIG VON DRAKE (TV)(Disney)(See Walt Disney's C&S #256)
Nov-Dec, 1961 - No. 4, June-Aug, 1962
Dell Publishing Co.

	Good	Fine	N-Mint
1	2.00	6.00	14.00
2-4	1.30	4.00	9.00
. . . Fish Stampede (1962, Fritos giveaway)-16 pgs., 3¼x7'', soft-c; also see Donald Duck & Mickey Mouse	2.00	6.00	14.00

LUGER
Oct, 1986 - No. 3, Feb, 1987 ($1.75, color, mini-series, Baxter paper)
Eclipse Comics

1-3	.30	.90	1.80

LUKE CAGE (See Hero for Hire)

LUKE SHORT'S WESTERN STORIES
No. 580, Aug, 1954 - No. 927, Aug, 1958
Dell Publishing Co.

4-Color 580(8/54)	2.30	7.00	16.00
4-Color 651(9/55)-Kinstler-a	3.00	9.00	21.00
4-Color 739,771,807,875,927	2.30	7.00	16.00
4-Color 848	3.00	9.00	21.00

LUM
1989 - Present ($2.95, B&W, squarebound, 52 pgs.)
Viz Comics

1-6,8: Japanese manga	.50	1.50	3.00
7 ($3.25, 60 pgs.)	.55	1.65	3.30

LUNATIC FRINGE, THE
July, 1989 - No. 2?, 1989 ($1.75, color, deluxe format)
Innovation Publishing

1,2	.30	.90	1.80

LUNATICKLE (Magazine) (Satire)
Feb, 1956 - No. 2, Apr, 1956
Whitstone Publ.

1,2-Kubert-a	1.50	4.50	9.00

LYNDON B. JOHNSON
March, 1965
Dell Publishing Co.

12-445-503-Photo-c	1.50	4.50	10.00

MACHINE MAN (Also see 2001, A Space Odyssey)
4/78 - No. 9, 12/78; No. 10, 8/79 - No.19, 2/81
Marvel Comics Group

1	.35	1.00	2.00
2-17,19: 19-Intro Jack O'Lantern		.50	1.00
18-Wendigo, Alpha Flight-ties into X-Men #140	.85	2.50	5.00

NOTE: *Austin* c-7i, 19i. *Buckler* c-17p, 18p. *Byrne* c-14p. *Ditko* a-10-19; c-10-13, 14i, 15, 16. *Kirby* a-1-9p; c-1-5, 7-9p. *Layton* c-7i. *Miller* c-19p. *Simonson* c-6.

MACHINE MAN
Oct, 1984 - No. 4, Jan, 1985 (Limited-series)
Marvel Comics Group

1-Barry Smith-c/a(i) in all	.25	.75	1.50
2-4		.60	1.20

MACKENZIE'S RAIDERS (See 4-Color #1093)

MACO TOYS COMIC
1959 (36 pages; full color) (Giveaway)
Maco Toys/Charlton Comics

1-All military stories featuring Maco Toys	1.00	3.00	6.00

MACROSS (Robotech: The Macross Saga #2 on)
Dec, 1984 ($1.50)
Comico

1	2.50	7.50	15.00

MAD
Oct-Nov, 1952 - Present (No. 24 on are magazine format)
(Kurtzman editor No. 1-28, Feldstein No. 29 - No. ?)
E. C. Comics

	Good	Fine	N-Mint
1-Wood, Davis, Elder start as regulars	93.00	280.00	650.00
2-Davis-c	42.00	125.00	295.00
3	27.00	81.00	190.00
4-Reefer mention story ''Flob Was a Slob'' by Davis	27.00	81.00	190.00
5-Low distribution; Elder-c	52.00	155.00	365.00
6-10	19.00	57.00	135.00
11-Wolverton-a	19.00	57.00	135.00
12-15	17.00	51.00	120.00
16-23(5/55): 21-1st app. Alfred E. Neuman on-c in fake ad. 22-all by Elder. 23-Special cancel announcement	13.00	40.00	90.00
24(7/55)-1st magazine issue (25 cents); Kurtzman logo & border on-c	27.00	80.00	185.00
25-Jaffee starts as regular writer	14.00	42.00	100.00
26	10.00	30.00	70.00
27-Davis-c; Jaffee starts as story artist; new logo	10.00	30.00	70.00
28-Elder-c; Heath back-c; last issue edited by Kurtzman; (three cover variations exist with different wording on contents banner on lower right of cover; value of each the same)	8.00	24.00	56.00
29-Wood-c; Kamen-a; Don Martin starts as regular; Feldstein editing begins	8.00	24.00	56.00
30-1st A. E. Neuman cover by Mingo; Crandall inside-c; last Elder-a; Bob Clarke starts as regular; Disneyland spoof	11.00	32.00	75.00
31-Freas starts as regular; last Davis art until #99	7.00	21.00	50.00
32-Orlando, Drucker, Woodbridge start as regulars; Wood back-c	6.50	19.50	45.00
33-Orlando back-c	6.50	19.50	45.00
34-Berg starts as regular	5.50	16.50	38.00
35-Mingo wraparound-c; Crandall-a	5.50	16.50	38.00
36-40	3.70	11.00	26.00
41-50	2.85	8.50	20.00
51-60: 60-Two Clarke-c; Prohias starts as reg.	1.70	5.00	12.00
61-70: 64-Rickard starts as regular. 68-Martin-c	1.50	4.50	10.00
71-80: 76-Aragones starts as regular	1.30	4.00	9.00
81-90: 86-1st Fold-in. 89-One strip by Walt Kelly. 90-Frazetta back-c	1.15	3.50	8.00
91-100: 91-Jaffee starts as story artist. 99-Davis-a resumes	.85	2.60	6.00
101-120: 101-Infinity-c. 105-Batman TV show take-off. 106-Frazetta back-c	.70	2.00	4.00
121-140: 122-Drucker & Mingo-c. 128-Last Orlando. 130-Torres begins as regular. 135,139-Davis-c	.50	1.50	3.00
141-170: 165-Martin-c. 169-Drucker-c	.35	1.00	2.00
171-200: 173,178-Davis-c. 176-Drucker-c. 182-Bob Jones starts as regular. 186-Star Trek take-off. 187-Harry North starts as regular. 196-Star Wars take-off	.25	.75	1.50
201-295: 203-Star Wars take-off. 204-Hulk TV show take-off. 208-Superman movie take-off. 286-Drucker-c. 289-Batman parody. 291-TMNT parody	.25	.75	1.50

NOTE: *Jules Feiffer* a(r)-42. *Freas*-most-c and back covers-40-74. *Heath* a-14, 27. *Kamen* a-29. *Krigstein* a-12, 17, 24, 26. *Kurtzman* c-1, 3, 4, 6-10, 13, 14, 16, 18. *Mingo* c-30-37, 75-111. *John Severin* a-1-6, 9, 10. *Wolverton* c-11; a-11, 17, 29, 31, 36, 40, 82, 137. *Wood* a-24-45, 59; c-26, 29. *Woodbridge* a-43.

MAD (See . . . Follies, . . . Special, More Trash from . . . , and The Worst from . . .)

MAD ABOUT MILLIE
April, 1969 - No. 17, Dec, 1970
Marvel Comics Group

1-Giant issue	1.00	3.00	7.00
2-17: 16,17-r	.70	2.00	4.00

The Lunatic Fringe #1, © Innovation

Mad #1, © WMG

Mad #32, © WMG

Mage #9, © Comico

Magic Agent #1, © ACG

Magic Comics #18, © DMP

MAD ABOUT MILLIE (continued)	Good	Fine	N-Mint
Annual 1(11/71)	.35	1.00	2.00

MADAME XANADU
July, 1981 (No ads; $1.00; 32 pgs.)
DC Comics

1-Marshall Rogers-a(25 pgs.); Kaluta-c/a(2 pgs.); pin-up of Madame Xanadu		.50	1.00

MADBALLS
9/86 - No. 3, 11/86; No. 4, 6/87 - No. 10, June, 1988
Star Comics/Marvel Comics #9 on

1-10: Based on toys. 9-Post-a		.50	1.00

MAD FOLLIES (Special)
1963 - No. 7, 1969
E. C. Comics

nn(1963)-Paperback book covers	8.00	24.00	56.00
2(1964)-Calendar	5.00	15.00	35.00
3(1965)-Mischief Stickers	3.70	11.00	26.00
4(1966)-Mobile; Frazetta-r/back-c Mad #90	4.30	13.00	30.00
5(1967)-Stencils	3.50	10.50	24.00
6(1968)-Mischief Stickers	2.00	6.00	14.00
7(1969)-Nasty Cards	2.00	6.00	14.00

NOTE: *Clarke* c-4. *Frazetta* r-4, 6 (1 pg. ea.). *Mingo* c-1-3. *Orlando* a-5.

MAD HATTER, THE (Costume Hero)
Jan-Feb, 1946; No. 2, Sept-Oct, 1946
O. W. Comics Corp.

1-Freddy the Firefly begins; Giunta-c/a	20.00	60.00	140.00
2-Has ad for E.C.'s Animal Fables #1	14.00	42.00	100.00

MADHOUSE
3-4/54 - No. 4, 9-10/54; 6/57 - No. 4, Dec?, 1957
Ajax/Farrell Publ. (Excellent Publ./4-Star)

1(1954)	9.30	28.00	65.00
2,3	4.50	14.00	32.00
4-Surrealistic-c	7.00	21.00	50.00
1(1957, 2nd series)	3.70	11.00	26.00
2-4	2.30	7.00	16.00

MADHOUSE (Formerly Madhouse Glads; . . .Comics #104? on)
No. 95, 9/74 - No. 97, 1/75; No. 98, 8/75 - No. 130, 10/82
Red Circle Productions/Archie Publications

95-Horror stories through #97		.60	1.20
96		.60	1.20
97-Intro. Henry Hobson; Morrow, Thorne-a		.40	.80
98-130-Satire/humor stories		.30	.60
Annual 1(1970-71)- 12(1974-75)-Formerly Madhouse Ma-ad Annual.			
11-Wood-a(r)		.40	.80
. . .Comics Digest 1(1975-76)- 8(8/82)(. . .Mag. #5 on)			
		.50	1.00

NOTE: *B. Jones* a-96. *McWilliams* a-97. *Morrow* a-96; c-95-97. *Wildey* a-95, 96. See *Archie Comics Digest #1, 13.*

MADHOUSE GLADS (Formerly . . . Ma-ad; Madhouse #95 on)
No. 73, May, 1970 - No. 94, Aug, 1974 (No. 78-92: 52 pgs.)
Archie Publications

73		.50	1.00
74-94		.30	.60

MADHOUSE MA-AD (. . .Jokes #67-70; . . .Freak-Out #71-74)
(Formerly Archie's Madhouse) (Becomes Madhouse Glads #75 on)
No. 67, April, 1969 - No. 72, Jan, 1970
Archie Publications

67-72		.60	1.20
. . .Annual 7(1969-70)-Formerly Archie's Madhouse Annual; becomes Madhouse Annual		.50	1.00

MAD MONSTER PARTY (See Movie Classics)

MAD SPECIAL (. . .Super Special)
Fall, 1970 - Present (84 - 116 pages)
E. C. Publications, Inc.

	Good	Fine	N-Mint
Fall 1970(#1)-Bonus-Voodoo Doll; contains 17 pgs. new material			
	3.50	10.50	24.00
Spring 1971(#2)-Wall Nuts; 17 pgs. new material			
	2.30	7.00	16.00
3-Protest Stickers	2.30	7.00	16.00
4-8: 4-Mini Posters. 5-Mad Flag. 7-Presidential candidate posters, Wild Shocking Message posters. 8-TV Guise			
	1.70	5.00	12.00
9(1972)-Contains Nostalgic Mad #1 (28pp)	1.50	4.50	10.00
10,11,13: 10-Nonsense Stickers (Don Martin). 11-33⅓ RPM record.			
13-Sickie Stickers; 3 pgs. new Wolverton	1.50	4.50	10.00
12-Contains Nostalgic Mad #2 (36 pgs.); Davis, Wolverton-a			
	1.50	4.50	10.00
14-Vital Message posters & Art Depreciation paintings			
	1.15	3.50	8.00
15-Contains Nostalgic Mad #3 (28 pgs.)	1.50	4.50	10.00
16,17,19,20: 16-Mad-hesive Stickers. 17-Don Martin posters.			
20-Martin Stickers	1.00	3.00	7.00
18-Contains Nostalgic Mad #4 (36 pgs.)	1.15	3.50	8.00
21,24-Contains Nostalgic Mad #5 (28 pgs.) & #6 (28 pgs.)			
	1.15	3.50	8.00
22,23,25-27,29,30: 22-Diplomas. 23-Martin Stickers. 25-Martin Posters			
26-33⅓ RPM record. 27-Mad Shock-Sticks. 29-Mad Collectable-Correctables Posters. 30-The Movies	.55	1.65	4.00
28-Contains Nostalgic Mad #7 (36 pgs.)	.75	2.25	5.00
31,33-60	.55	1.65	4.00
32-Contains Nostalgic Mad #8	.85	2.50	6.00
61-72: 71-Batman parody-r by Wood	.50	1.50	3.00

NOTE: *#28-30: no number on cover. Mingo c-9, 11, 15, 19, 23.*

MAGE (The Hero Discovered . . .)
2/84 (no month) - No. 15, 12/86 ($1.50; 36 pgs; Mando paper)
Comico

1-Violence; Comico's 1st color comic	2.15	6.50	13.00
2	1.70	5.00	10.00
3-5: 3-Intro Edsel	1.00	3.00	6.00
6-Grendel begins (1st in color)	3.35	10.00	20.00
7-1st new Grendel story	1.50	4.50	9.00
8-14: 13-Grendel dies. 14-Grendel ends	.70	2.00	4.00
15-$2.95, Double size w/pullout poster	.85	2.50	5.00

MAGIC AGENT (See Forbidden Worlds & Unknown Worlds)
Jan-Feb, 1962 - No. 3, May-June, 1962
American Comics Group

1-Origin & 1st app. John Force	.85	2.50	5.00
2,3	.60	1.75	3.50

MAGIC COMICS
Aug, 1939 - No. 123, Nov-Dec, 1949
David McKay Publications

1-Mandrake the Magician, Henry, Popeye (not by Segar), Blondie, Barney Baxter, Secret Agent X-9 (not by Raymond), Bunky by Billy DeBeck & Thornton Burgess text stories illustrated by Harrison Cady begin	108.00	270.00	650.00
2	43.00	130.00	300.00
3	33.00	100.00	230.00
4	27.00	81.00	190.00
5	22.00	65.00	154.00
6-10	17.00	51.00	120.00
11-16,18-20	14.00	42.00	100.00
17-The Lone Ranger begins	16.00	48.00	110.00
21-30	10.00	30.00	70.00
31-40	8.00	24.00	56.00
41-50	6.50	19.50	45.00

MAGIC COMICS (continued)	Good	Fine	N-Mint
51-60	5.00	15.00	35.00
61-70	3.70	11.00	26.00
71-99	3.00	9.00	21.00
100	3.70	11.00	26.00
101-106,109-123	2.30	7.00	16.00
107,108-Flash Gordon app; not by Raymond	3.70	11.00	26.00

MAGICA DE SPELL (See Walt Disney Showcase #30)

MAGIC OF CHRISTMAS AT NEWBERRYS, THE
1967 (20 pgs.; slick cover; B&W inside)
E. S. London (Giveaway)

nn		.60	1.20

MAGIC SWORD, THE (See Movie Classics)

MAGIK
Dec, 1983 - No. 4, Mar, 1984 (mini-series)
Marvel Comics Group

1-Illyana & Storm from X-Men; Inferno begins	.40	1.25	2.50
2-4	.35	1.00	2.00

NOTE: *Buscema* a-1p. 2p; c-1p.

MAGILLA GORILLA (TV) (Hanna-Barbera)
May, 1964 - No. 10, Dec, 1968
Gold Key

1	3.00	9.00	21.00
2-10: 3-Vs. Yogi Bear for President	1.50	4.50	10.00
Kite Fun Book ('64, 16 pgs., 5x7¼'', soft-c)	2.00	6.00	14.00

MAGILLA GORILLA (TV)(See Spotlight #4)
Nov, 1970 - No. 5, July, 1971 (Hanna-Barbera)
Charlton Comics

1-5	.85	2.60	6.00

MAGNUS, ROBOT FIGHTER (. . .4000 A.D.)(See Doctor Solar)
Feb, 1963 - No. 46, Jan, 1977 (Painted-covers)
Gold Key

1-Origin Magnus; Aliens series begins	8.50	25.50	60.00
2,3	4.00	12.00	28.00
4-10	2.65	8.00	18.00
11-20	2.00	6.00	14.00
21,22,24-28: 22-Origin-r/#1. 28-Aliens ends	1.30	4.00	9.00
23 (12 cent and 15 cent editions exist)	1.30	4.00	9.00
29-46-Reprints	.70	2.00	5.00

NOTE: *Manning* a-1-22, 29-43(r). *Spiegle* a-23, 44r.

MAID OF THE MIST (See American Graphics)

MAI, THE PSYCHIC GIRL
May 19, 1987 - No. 28 (Bi-weekly, $1.50, B&W, 44pgs)
Eclipse Comics

1	.40	1.25	2.50
1,2-2nd print		.60	1.20
2-5	.30	.85	1.70
6-10	.25	.75	1.50
11-20	.25	.70	1.40
21-28		.65	1.30

MAJOR HOOPLE COMICS (See Crackajack Funnies)
nd (Jan, 1943)
Nedor Publications

1-Mary Worth, Phantom Soldier by Moldoff app.	17.00	51.00	120.00

MAJOR INAPAK THE SPACE ACE
1951 (20 pages) (Giveaway)
Magazine Enterprises (Inapac Foods)

1-Bob Powell-c/a	.25	.80	1.60

NOTE: *Many warehouse copies surfaced in 1973.*

MAJOR VICTORY COMICS (Also see Dynamic Comics)
1944 - No. 3, Summer, 1945
H. Clay Glover/Service Publ./Harry 'A' Chesler

	Good	Fine	N-Mint
1-Origin Major Victory by C. Sultan (reprint from Dynamic #1);			
Spider Woman 1st app.	27.00	80.00	185.00
2-Dynamic Boy app.	16.50	50.00	115.00
3-Rocket Boy app.	13.00	40.00	90.00

MALTESE FALCON (See Feature Books No. 48 (McKay))

MALU IN THE LAND OF ADVENTURE
1964 (See White Princess of Jungle #2)
I. W. Enterprises

1-R/Avon's Slave Girl Comics #1; Severin-c	4.75	14.00	28.00

MAMMOTH COMICS
1938 (84 pages) (Black & White, 8½x11½'')
Whitman Publishing Co.(K. K. Publications)

1-Alley Oop, Terry & the Pirates, Dick Tracy, Little Orphan Annie,			
Wash Tubbs, Moon Mullins, Smilin' Jack, Tailspin Tommy & other			
reprints	64.00	193.00	450.00

MAMMY YOKUM & THE GREAT DOGPATCH MYSTERY
1951 (Giveaway)
Toby Press

Li'l Abner	12.00	36.00	84.00

MAN-BAT (See Batman Family, Brave & the Bold, & Detective #400)
Dec-Jan, 1975-76 - No. 2, Feb-Mar, 1976; Dec, 1984
National Periodical Publications/DC Comics

1-Ditko-a(p); Aparo-c; She-Bat app.	1.00	3.00	6.00
2-Aparo-c	.50	1.50	3.00
. . .Vs. Batman 1 (12/84)-Adams-a(r)	.70	2.00	4.00

MAN COMICS
Dec, 1949 - No. 28, Sept, 1953 (#1-6: 52 pgs.)
Marvel/Atlas Comics (NPI)

1-Tuska-a	5.00	15.00	35.00
2-Tuska-a	2.65	8.00	18.00
3-5	2.00	6.00	14.00
6-8	1.70	5.00	12.00
9-13,15: 9-Format changes to war	1.30	4.00	9.00
14-Krenkel (3pgs), Pakula-a	2.30	7.00	16.00
16-21,23-28: 28-Crime issue	1.15	3.50	8.00
22-Krigstein-a, 5 pgs.	3.50	10.50	24.00

NOTE: *Berg* a-14, 15, 19. *Colan* a-21. *Everett* a-8, 22; c-22, 25. *Heath* a-11, 17. *Kuberlish* a-by *Bob Brown*-3. *Maneely* c-10, 11. *Robinson* a-10, 14. *Sinnott* a-22, 23. *Tuska* a-14, 23.

MANDRAKE THE MAGICIAN (See Defenders Of The Earth, Feature Books #18,19,23,46,52,55, King Comics, Magic Comics, The Phantom #21, Tiny Tot Funnies & Wow Comics, '36)

MANDRAKE THE MAGICIAN (See Harvey Comics Hits #53)
No. 752, Nov, 1956; Sept, 1966 - No. 10, Nov, 1967
Dell Publishing Co./King Comics

4-Color 752('56)	4.00	12.00	28.00
1(King)-Begin S.O.S. Phantom, ends #3	1.70	5.00	12.00
2-5: 4-Girl Phantom app. 5-Brick Bradford app., also #6			
	1.00	3.00	7.00
6,7,9: 7-Origin Lothar. 9-Brick Bradford app.	.85	2.60	6.00
8-Jeff Jones-a	1.50	4.50	10.00
10-Rip Kirby app.; Raymond-a (14 pgs.)	2.00	6.00	14.00

MANDRAKE THE MAGICIAN GIANT COMIC ALBUM
1972 (48 pgs.); 11x14''; B&W; cardboard covers)
Modern Promotions

nn-Strip reprints by Lee Falk	1.70	5.00	12.00

MAN FROM ATLANTIS (TV)
Feb, 1978 - No. 7, Aug, 1978

Major Victory #1, © CHES

Man-Bat #1 (12-1/75-76), © DC

Mandrake The Magician 2, © KING

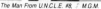
The Man From U.N.C.L.E. #8, © M.G.M.

Man O' Mars #1, © FH

Man-Thing #1, © MEG

MAN FROM ATLANTIS (continued)
Marvel Comics Group

	Good	Fine	N-Mint
1-(84 pgs.; $1.00)-Sutton-a(p), Buscema-c; origin		.30	.60
2-7		.25	.50

MAN FROM PLANET X, THE
1987 (no price, color, probably unlicensed)
Planet X Productions

1-Reprints Fawcett Movie Comic	.50	1.50	3.00

MAN FROM U.N.C.L.E., THE (TV) (Also see The Girl From . . .)
Feb, 1965 - No. 22, April, 1969 (All photo covers)
Gold Key

1	6.50	19.50	45.00
2-Photo back c-2-8	3.60	11.00	25.00
3-10: 7-Jet Dream begins (all new stories)	2.65	8.00	18.00
11-22: 21,22-Reprint #10 & 7	2.15	6.50	15.00

MAN FROM U.N.C.L.E., THE (TV)
1987 - No. 10? ($1.50/$1.75, B&W)
Entertainment Publishing

1-7 ($1.50)	.25	.75	1.50
8-10 ($1.75)	.30	.90	1.80

MAN FROM WELLS FARGO (TV)
No. 1287, Feb-Apr, 1962 - May-July, 1962 (Photo-c)
Dell Publishing Co.

4-Color 1287, #01-495-207	3.70	11.00	26.00

MANGLE TANGLE TALES
1990 ($2.95, color, deluxe format)
Innovation Publishing

1-Intro by Harlan Ellison	.50	1.50	3.00

MANHUNT! (Becomes Red Fox #15 on)
Oct, 1947 - No. 14, 1953
Magazine Enterprises

1-Red Fox by L. B. Cole, Undercover Girl by Whitney, Space Ace begin; negligee panels	19.00	57.00	132.00
2-Electrocution-c	14.00	42.00	100.00
3-6	12.00	36.00	84.00
7-9: 7-Space Ace ends. 8-Trail Colt begins	10.00	30.00	70.00
10-G. Ingels-a	10.00	30.00	70.00
11(8/48)-Frazetta-a, 7 pgs.; The Duke, Scotland Yard begin	19.00	57.00	132.00
12	7.00	21.00	50.00
13(A-1 63)-Frazetta, r-/Trail Colt #1, 7 pgs.	17.00	51.00	120.00
14(A-1 77)-Bondage/hypo-c; last L. B. Cole Red Fox; Ingels-a	11.00	32.00	75.00

NOTE: *Guardineer* a-1-5; c-8. *Whitney* a-2-14; c-1-6,10. Red Fox by *L. B. Cole*-#1-14. #15 was advertised but came out as Red Fox #15. Bondage c-6.

MANHUNTER (See Brave & the Bold, Detective Comics, First Issue Special, House of Mystery #143 and Justice League of America)
May, 1984 ($2.50, 76 pgs; high quality paper)
DC Comics

1-Simonson c/a(r)/Detective; Batman app.	.50	1.50	3.00

MANHUNTER
July, 1988 - Present ($1.00, color)
DC Comics

1-22: 9-Invasion; Flash app. 17-Batman-c/story	.60	1.20	

MAN IN BLACK (See Thrill-O-Rama) (Also see All New Comics, Front Page, Green Hornet #31, Strange Story & Tally-Ho Comics)
Sept, 1957 - No. 4, Mar, 1958
Harvey Publications

1-Bob Powell c/a	6.00	18.00	42.00
2-4: Powell c/a	5.00	15.00	35.00

MAN IN FLIGHT (See 4-Color #836)

MAN IN SPACE (See Dell Giant #27 & 4-Color #716,954)

MAN OF PEACE, POPE PIUS XII
1950 (See Pope Pius XII . . . & Topix V2#8)
Catechetical Guild

	Good	Fine	N-Mint
nn-All Powell-a	3.00	9.00	21.00

MAN OF STEEL, THE
1986 (June) - No. 6, 1986 (mini-series)
DC Comics

1 (silver logo)-Byrne-c/a/scripts in all; origin	.30	.90	1.80
1-Alternate-c for newsstand sales	.30	.85	1.70
1-Distr. to toy stores by So Much Fun		.60	1.25
2-6: 2-Intro. Lois Lane, Jimmy Olsen. 3-Intro/origin Magpie. 4-Intro. new Lex Luthor		.50	1.00
. . .The Complete Saga-Contains #1-6, given away in contest	.35	1.00	2.00
Limited Edition, softcover	5.00	15.00	30.00

MAN OF WAR (See Liberty Guards & Liberty Scouts)
Nov, 1941 - No. 2, Jan, 1942
Centaur Publications

1-The Fire-Man, Man of War, The Sentinel, Liberty Guards, & Vapo-Man begin; Gustavson-c/a; Flag-c	80.00	240.00	560.00
2-Intro The Ferret; Gustavson-c/a	64.00	193.00	450.00

MAN OF WAR
Aug, 1987 - No. 3, Feb, 1988 ($1.75, color, Baxter paper)
Eclipse Comics

1-3	.30	.90	1.80

MAN O' MARS
1953; 1964
Fiction House Magazines

1-Space Rangers	16.00	48.00	110.00
I.W. Reprint #1/Man O'Mars #1; Murphy Anderson-a	2.65	8.00	18.00

MANTECH ROBOT WARRIORS
Sept, 1984 - No. 4, April, 1985
Archie Enterprises, Inc.

1-4		.40	.80

MAN-THING (See Fear, Marvel Comics Presents, Marvel Fanfare, Monsters Unleashed & Savage Tales)
Jan, 1974 - No. 22, Oct, 1975; Nov, 1979 -V2No. 11, July, 1981
Marvel Comics Group

1-Howard the Duck cont./Fear 19(2nd app.)	1.00	3.00	6.00
2-4	.25	.75	1.50
5-11-Ploog-a		.60	1.25
12-22: 19-1st app. Scavenger. 21-Origin Scavenger & Man-Thing. 22-Howard the Duck cameo		.50	1.00
V2#1(1979) - 11: 6-Golden-c		.50	1.00
Giant Size 1(8/74)-Ploog c/a	.35	1.00	2.00
Giant Size 2(1974), 3(2/75)		.50	1.00
Giant Size 4(5/75)-Howard the Duck by Brunner; Ditko-a(r)	.85	2.50	5.00
Giant Size 5(8/75)-Howard the Duck by Brunner (p)	.85	2.50	5.00

NOTE: *Alcala* a-14, Gnt Size 3. *Brunner* c-1, Gnt Size 4. *J. Buscema* a-12p, 13p, 16p, Gnt Size 2p, 5p; c-Gnt Size 2. *Ditko* a-Gnt Size 1r, 3r, 4r. *Gil Kane* c-4p, 10p, 12-20p, 21, Gnt-Size 3p, 5p. *Kirby* a-Gnt Size 1-3r. *Mooney* a-17, 18, 19p, 20-22. V2#1-3p. *Ploog* Man-Thing-5p, 6p, 7, 8, 9-11p, Gnt Size 1p; c-5, 6, 8, 9, 11. *Powell* a-Gnt Size 2r. *Sutton* a-13i, Gnt-Size 3r, 5i.

MAN WITH THE X-RAY EYES, THE (See X. . . . under Movie Comics)

MANY GHOSTS OF DR. GRAVES, THE (Doctor Graves #73 on)
5/67 - No. 60, 12/76; No. 61, 9/77 - No. 62, 10/77; No. 63, 2/78 - No. 65, 4/78; No. 66, 6/81 - No. 72, 5/82

THE MANY GHOSTS OF DR. GRAVES (continued)
Charlton Comics

	Good	Fine	N-Mint
1	.70	2.00	4.00
2-10	.30	1.00	2.00
11-20	.25	.75	1.50
21-44,46-72: 47,49-Newton-a		.40	.80
45-1st Newton comic book work, 8pgs.	.35	1.00	2.00
Modern Comics Reprint 12,25 ('78)		.20	.40

NOTE: *Aparo* a-66r, 69r; c-66, 67. *Byrne* c-54. *Ditko* a-1, 7, 9, 11-13, 15-18, 20-22, 24, 26, 35, 37, 38, 40-44, 47, 48, 51-54, 58, 60r-65r, 70, 72; c-11-13, 16-18, 22, 24, 26-35, 38, 40, 55, 58, 62-65. *Howard* c-48. *Newton* a-45, 47p, 49p; c-49, 52. *Sutton* c/a-42, 49.

MANY LOVES OF DOBIE GILLIS (TV)
May-June, 1960 - No. 26, Oct, 1964
National Periodical Publications

	Good	Fine	N-Mint
1	12.00	36.00	85.00
2-5	5.70	17.00	40.00
6-10	4.50	14.00	32.00
11-26	3.60	11.00	25.00

MARAUDER'S MOON (See 4-Color #848)

MARCH OF COMICS (Boys' and Girls'. . .#3-353)
1946 - No. 488, Apr, 1982 (#1-4 are not numbered)
(K.K. Giveaway) (Founded by Sig Feuchtwanger)
K. K. Publications/Western Publishing Co.

Early issues were full size, 32 pages, and were printed with and without an extra cover of slick stock, just for the advertiser. The binding was stapled if the slick cover was added; otherwise, the pages were glued together at the spine. Most 1948 - 1951 issues were full size, 24 pages, pulp covers. Starting in 1952 they were half-size and 32 pages with slick covers. 1959 and later issues had only 16 pages plus covers. 1952 -1959 issues read oblong; 1960 and later issues read upright.

	Good	Fine	N-Mint
1(nn)(1946)-Goldilocks; Kelly back-c; 16pgs., stapled	24.00	72.00	170.00
2(nn)(1946)-How Santa Got His Red Suit; Kelly-a(11 pgs., r-/4-Color 61)('44); 16pgs., stapled	24.00	72.00	170.00
3(nn)(1947)-Our Gang (Walt Kelly)	40.00	110.00	235.00
4(nn)Donald Duck by Carl Barks, "Maharajah Donald," 28 pgs.; Kelly-c? (Disney)	428.00	1285.00	3000.00
5-Andy Panda	13.00	40.00	90.00
6-Popular Fairy Tales; Kelly-c; Noonan-a(2)	17.00	50.00	120.00
7-Oswald the Rabbit	17.00	50.00	120.00
8-Mickey Mouse, 32 pgs. (Disney)	50.00	150.00	330.00
9(nn)-The Story of the Gloomy Bunny	8.00	24.00	56.00
10-Out of Santa's Bag	6.75	20.00	47.00
11-Fun With Santa Claus	5.35	16.00	37.00
12-Santa's Toys	5.35	16.00	37.00
13-Santa's Surprise	5.35	16.00	37.00
14-Santa's Candy Kitchen	5.35	16.00	37.00
15-Hip-It-Ty Hop & the Big Bass Viol	5.35	16.00	37.00
16-Woody Woodpecker (1947)	8.50	25.00	60.00
17-Roy Rogers (1948)	20.00	60.00	140.00
18-Popular Fairy Tales	10.00	30.00	70.00
19-Uncle Wiggily	7.50	22.50	52.00
20-Donald Duck by Carl Barks, "Darkest Africa," 22 pgs.; Kelly-c (Disney)	257.00	770.00	1800.00
21-Tom and Jerry	7.50	22.50	52.00
22-Andy Panda	7.50	22.50	52.00
23-Raggedy Ann; Kerr-a	12.00	35.00	84.00
24-Felix the Cat, 1932 daily strip reprints by Otto Messmer	20.00	60.00	140.00
25-Gene Autry	20.00	60.00	140.00
26-Our Gang; Walt Kelly	20.00	60.00	140.00
27-Mickey Mouse; r/in M. M. #240 (Disney)	34.00	100.00	238.00
28-Gene Autry	20.00	60.00	140.00
29-Easter Bonnet Shop	4.00	12.00	28.00
30-Here Comes Santa	3.35	10.00	22.00
31-Santa's Busy Corner	3.35	10.00	22.00
32-No book produced			

	Good	Fine	N-Mint
33-A Christmas Carol	3.35	10.00	22.00
34-Woody Woodpecker	5.85	17.50	40.00
35-Roy Rogers (1948)	19.00	57.00	135.00
36-Felix the Cat(1949)-by Messmer; '34 daily strip-r	15.00	45.00	105.00
37-Popeye	12.50	37.50	87.00
38-Oswald the Rabbit	5.85	17.50	40.00
39-Gene Autry	19.00	57.00	135.00
40-Andy and Woody	5.85	17.50	40.00
41-Donald Duck by Carl Barks, "Race to the South Seas," 22 pgs.; Kelly-c; on Disney's reprint band list	200.00	600.00	1400.00
42-Porky Pig	5.85	17.50	40.00
43-Henry	3.75	11.00	26.00
44-Bugs Bunny	5.85	17.50	40.00
45-Mickey Mouse (Disney)	27.00	80.00	190.00
46-Tom and Jerry	5.85	17.50	40.00
47-Roy Rogers	17.00	51.00	120.00
48-Greetings from Santa	2.75	8.00	19.00
49-Santa Is Here	2.75	8.00	19.00
50-Santa Claus' Workshop (1949)	2.75	8.00	19.00
51-Felix the Cat (1950) by Messmer	13.00	40.00	90.00
52-Popeye	10.00	30.00	70.00
53-Oswald the Rabbit	5.85	17.50	40.00
54-Gene Autry	16.00	48.00	110.00
55-Andy and Woody	5.00	15.00	35.00
56-Donald Duck-not by Barks; Barks art on back-c (Disney)	22.00	65.00	140.00
57-Porky Pig	5.00	15.00	35.00
58-Henry	3.00	9.00	21.00
59-Bugs Bunny	5.00	15.00	35.00
60-Mickey Mouse (Disney)	18.00	55.00	125.00
61-Tom and Jerry	4.35	13.00	30.00
62-Roy Rogers	16.00	48.00	110.00
63-Welcome Santa; ½-size, oblong	2.75	8.00	19.00
64(nn)-Santa's Helpers; ½-size, oblong	2.75	8.00	19.00
65(nn)-Jingle Bells (1950)-½-size, oblong	2.75	8.00	19.00
66-Popeye (1951)	9.00	27.00	62.00
67-Oswald the Rabbit	4.00	12.00	28.00
68-Roy Rogers	14.00	42.00	100.00
69-Donald Duck; Barks-a on back-c (Disney)	19.00	57.00	125.00
70-Tom and Jerry	4.00	12.00	28.00
71-Porky Pig	4.00	12.00	28.00
72-Krazy Kat	6.00	18.00	42.00
73-Roy Rogers	12.00	36.00	84.00
74-Mickey Mouse (1951)(Disney)	14.00	42.50	96.00
75-Bugs Bunny	4.00	12.00	28.00
76-Andy and Woody	4.00	12.00	28.00
77-Roy Rogers	13.00	40.00	80.00
78-Gene Autry(1951)-Last regular size issue	13.00	40.00	80.00
79-Andy Panda (1952)-5x7'' size	2.75	8.00	19.00
80-Popeye	8.00	24.00	56.00
81-Oswald the Rabbit	3.00	9.00	21.00
82-Tarzan; Lex Barker photo-c	14.00	42.00	100.00
83-Bugs Bunny	3.00	9.00	21.00
84-Henry	2.35	7.00	16.00
85-Woody Woodpecker	2.35	7.00	16.00
86-Roy Rogers	10.00	30.00	70.00
87-Krazy Kat	4.75	14.00	33.00
88-Tom and Jerry	2.35	7.00	16.00
89-Porky Pig	2.35	7.00	16.00
90-Gene Autry	10.00	30.00	70.00
91-Roy Rogers & Santa	10.00	30.00	70.00
92-Christmas with Santa	2.00	6.00	14.00
93-Woody Woodpecker (1953)	2.35	7.00	16.00
94-Indian Chief	5.50	16.50	40.00
95-Oswald the Rabbit	2.35	7.00	16.00

Many Loves Of Dobie Gillis #1, © DC

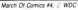
March Of Comics #4, © WDC

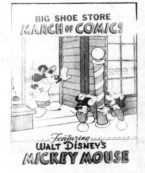
March Of Comics #45, © WDC

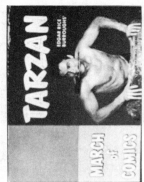

March Of Comics #98, © ERB

March Of Comics #133, © KING

March Of Comics #208, © Lone Ranger

MARCH OF COMICS (continued)	Good	Fine	N-Mint
96-Popeye	7.00	20.00	50.00
97-Bugs Bunny	2.35	7.00	16.00
98-Tarzan; Lex Barker photo-c	14.00	42.00	100.00
99-Porky Pig	2.35	7.00	16.00
100-Roy Rogers	8.00	24.00	56.00
101-Henry	2.00	6.00	14.00
102-Tom Corbett (TV)-Painted-c	11.50	34.00	80.00
103-Tom and Jerry	2.00	6.00	14.00
104-Gene Autry	8.00	24.00	56.00
105-Roy Rogers	8.00	24.00	56.00
106-Santa's Helpers	2.00	6.00	14.00
107-Santa's Christmas Book - not published			
108-Fun with Santa (1953)	2.00	6.00	14.00
109-Woody Woodpecker (1954)	2.00	6.00	14.00
110-Indian Chief	3.50	10.50	24.00
111-Oswald the Rabbit	2.00	6.00	14.00
112-Henry	1.70	5.00	12.00
113-Porky Pig	2.00	6.00	14.00
114-Tarzan; Russ Manning-a	14.00	42.00	100.00
115-Bugs Bunny	2.00	6.00	14.00
116-Roy Rogers	8.00	24.00	56.00
117-Popeye	7.00	20.00	50.00
118-Flash Gordon-Painted-c	10.00	30.00	70.00
119-Tom and Jerry	2.00	6.00	14.00
120-Gene Autry	8.00	24.00	56.00
121-Roy Rogers	8.00	24.00	56.00
122-Santa's Surprise (1954)	1.50	4.50	10.00
123-Santa's Christmas Book	1.50	4.50	10.00
124-Woody Woodpecker (1955)	1.70	5.00	12.00
125-Tarzan; Lex Barker photo-c	13.00	40.00	90.00
126-Oswald the Rabbit	1.70	5.00	12.00
127-Indian Chief	3.00	9.00	21.00
128-Tom and Jerry	1.70	5.00	12.00
129-Henry	1.50	4.50	10.00
130-Porky Pig	1.70	5.00	12.00
131-Roy Rogers	8.00	24.00	56.00
132-Bugs Bunny	1.70	5.00	12.00
133-Flash Gordon-Painted-c	8.50	25.50	60.00
134-Popeye	4.00	12.00	28.00
135-Gene Autry	7.00	21.00	50.00
136-Roy Rogers	7.00	21.00	50.00
137-Gifts from Santa	1.35	4.00	9.00
138-Fun at Christmas (1955)	1.35	4.00	9.00
139-Woody Woodpecker (1956)	1.70	5.00	12.00
140-Indian Chief	3.00	9.00	21.00
141-Oswald the Rabbit	1.70	5.00	12.00
142-Flash Gordon	8.50	25.50	60.00
143-Porky Pig	1.70	5.00	12.00
144-Tarzan; Russ Manning-a; Painted-c	12.00	36.00	84.00
145-Tom and Jerry	1.70	5.00	12.00
146-Roy Rogers-Photo-c	8.00	24.00	56.00
147-Henry	1.35	4.00	9.00
148-Popeye	4.00	12.00	28.00
149-Bugs Bunny	1.70	5.00	12.00
150-Gene Autry	7.00	21.00	50.00
151-Roy Rogers	7.00	21.00	50.00
152-The Night Before Christmas	1.35	4.00	9.00
153-Merry Christmas (1956)	1.35	4.00	9.00
154-Tom and Jerry (1957)	1.70	5.00	12.00
155-Tarzan-Photo-c	12.00	36.00	84.00
156-Oswald the Rabbit	1.70	5.00	12.00
157-Popeye	3.00	9.00	21.00
158-Woody Woodpecker	1.70	5.00	12.00
159-Indian Chief	3.00	9.00	21.00
160-Bugs Bunny	1.70	5.00	12.00
161-Roy Rogers	5.70	17.00	40.00

	Good	Fine	N-Mint
162-Henry	1.35	4.00	9.00
163-Rin Tin Tin (TV)	3.00	9.00	21.00
164-Porky Pig	1.70	5.00	12.00
165-The Lone Ranger	6.50	19.50	45.00
166-Santa and His Reindeer	1.35	4.00	9.00
167-Roy Rogers and Santa	5.70	17.00	40.00
168-Santa Claus' Workshop (1957)	1.35	4.00	9.00
169-Popeye (1958)	3.00	9.00	21.00
170-Indian Chief	3.00	9.00	21.00
171-Oswald the Rabbit	1.50	4.50	10.00
172-Tarzan	10.00	30.00	70.00
173-Tom and Jerry	1.50	4.50	10.00
174-The Lone Ranger	6.50	19.50	45.00
175-Porky Pig	1.50	4.50	10.00
176-Roy Rogers	5.50	16.50	38.00
177-Woody Woodpecker	1.50	4.50	10.00
178-Henry	1.35	4.00	9.00
179-Bugs Bunny	1.50	4.50	10.00
180-Rin Tin Tin (TV)	3.00	9.00	21.00
181-Happy Holiday	1.20	3.50	8.00
182-Happi Tim	1.50	4.50	10.00
183-Welcome Santa (1958)	1.20	3.50	8.00
184-Woody Woodpecker (1959)	1.50	4.50	10.00
185-Tarzan-Photo-c	10.00	30.00	70.00
186-Oswald the Rabbit	1.50	4.50	10.00
187-Indian Chief	3.00	9.00	21.00
188-Bugs Bunny	1.50	4.50	10.00
189-Henry	1.20	3.50	8.00
190-Tom and Jerry	1.50	4.50	10.00
191-Roy Rogers	5.50	16.50	38.00
192-Porky Pig	1.50	4.50	10.00
193-The Lone Ranger	6.50	19.50	45.00
194-Popeye	3.00	9.00	21.00
195-Rin Tin Tin (TV)	3.00	9.00	21.00
196-Sears Special - not published			
197-Santa Is Coming	1.20	3.50	8.00
198-Santa's Helpers (1959)	1.20	3.50	8.00
199-Huckleberry Hound (TV)(1960)	2.15	6.50	15.00
200-Fury (TV)	3.50	10.50	24.00
201-Bugs Bunny	1.35	4.00	9.00
202-Space Explorer	4.60	14.00	32.00
203-Woody Woodpecker	1.35	4.00	9.00
204-Tarzan	7.00	21.00	50.00
205-Mighty Mouse	2.50	7.50	17.50
206-Roy Rogers-Photo-c	5.50	16.50	38.00
207-Tom and Jerry	1.35	4.00	9.00
208-The Lone Ranger-Clayton Moore photo-c	10.00	30.00	70.00
209-Porky Pig	1.35	4.00	9.00
210-Lassie (TV)	3.00	9.00	21.00
211-Sears Special - not published			
212-Christmas Eve	1.20	3.50	8.00
213-Here Comes Santa (1960)	1.20	3.50	8.00
214-Huckleberry Hound (TV)(1961)	2.30	7.00	16.00
215-Hi Yo Silver	4.00	12.00	28.00
216-Rocky & His Friends (TV)	5.00	15.00	35.00
217-Lassie (TV)	2.35	7.00	16.00
218-Porky Pig	1.35	4.00	9.00
219-Journey to the Sun	3.00	9.00	21.00
220-Bugs Bunny	1.35	4.00	9.00
221-Roy and Dale-Photo-c	5.00	15.00	35.00
222-Woody Woodpecker	1.35	4.00	9.00
223-Tarzan	7.00	21.00	50.00
224-Tom and Jerry	1.35	4.00	9.00
225-The Lone Ranger	5.00	15.00	35.00
226-Christmas Treasury (1961)	1.20	3.50	8.00
227-Sears Special - not published?			

	Good	Fine	N-Mint
228-Letters to Santa (1961)	1.20	3.50	8.00
229-The Flintstones (TV)(1962)	4.30	13.00	30.00
230-Lassie (TV)	2.35	7.00	16.00
231-Bugs Bunny	1.20	3.50	8.00
232-The Three Stooges	6.50	19.50	45.00
233-Bullwinkle (TV)	5.70	17.00	40.00
234-Smokey the Bear	1.35	4.00	9.00
235-Huckleberry Hound (TV)	2.30	7.00	16.00
236-Roy and Dale	3.65	11.00	25.00
237-Mighty Mouse	2.00	6.00	14.00
238-The Lone Ranger	5.00	15.00	35.00
239-Woody Woodpecker	1.35	4.00	9.00
240-Tarzan	5.70	17.00	40.00
241-Santa Claus Around the World	1.20	3.50	8.00
242-Santa's Toyland (1962)	1.20	3.50	8.00
243-The Flintstones (TV)(1963)	4.00	12.00	28.00
244-Mister Ed (TV)-Photo-c	3.00	9.00	21.00
245-Bugs Bunny	1.35	4.00	9.00
246-Popeye	2.50	7.50	17.50
247-Mighty Mouse	2.00	6.00	14.00
248-The Three Stooges	6.50	19.50	45.00
249-Woody Woodpecker	1.35	4.00	9.00
250-Roy and Dale	3.65	11.00	25.00
251-Little Lulu & Witch Hazel	13.50	41.00	95.00
252-Tarzan-Painted-c	5.50	16.50	40.00
253-Yogi Bear (TV)	2.65	8.00	18.00
254-Lassie (TV)	2.35	7.00	16.00
255-Santa's Christmas List	1.20	3.50	8.00
256-Christmas Party (1963)	1.20	3.50	8.00
257-Mighty Mouse	2.00	6.00	14.00
258-The Sword in the Stone (Disney)	5.70	17.00	40.00
259-Bugs Bunny	1.35	4.00	9.00
260-Mister Ed (TV)	2.30	7.00	16.00
261-Woody Woodpecker	1.35	4.00	9.00
262-Tarzan	5.50	16.50	40.00
263-Donald Duck-not by Barks (Disney)	6.00	18.00	36.00
264-Popeye	2.50	7.50	17.50
265-Yogi Bear (TV)	2.00	6.00	14.00
266-Lassie (TV)	2.00	6.00	14.00
267-Little Lulu; Irving Tripp-a	11.00	32.00	75.00
268-The Three Stooges	5.70	17.00	40.00
269-A Jolly Christmas	1.20	3.50	8.00
270-Santa's Little Helpers	1.20	3.50	8.00
271-The Flintstones (TV)(1965)	4.00	12.00	28.00
272-Tarzan	5.50	16.50	40.00
273-Bugs Bunny	1.35	4.00	9.00
274-Popeye	2.50	7.50	17.50
275-Little Lulu-Irving Tripp-a	9.00	27.00	62.00
276-The Jetsons (TV)	6.50	19.50	45.00
277-Daffy Duck	1.35	4.00	9.00
278-Lassie (TV)	2.00	6.00	14.00
279-Yogi Bear (TV)	2.00	6.00	14.00
280-The Three Stooges-Photo-c	5.70	17.00	40.00
281-Tom and Jerry	1.00	3.00	7.00
282-Mister Ed (TV)	2.30	7.00	16.00
283-Santa's Visit	1.20	3.50	8.00
284-Christmas Parade (1965)	1.20	3.50	8.00
285-Astro Boy (TV)	20.00	60.00	140.00
286-Tarzan	5.00	15.00	35.00
287-Bugs Bunny	1.00	3.00	7.00
288-Daffy Duck	1.00	3.00	7.00
289-The Flintstones (TV)	3.00	9.00	21.00
290-Mister Ed (TV)-Photo-c	2.00	6.00	14.00
291-Yogi Bear (TV)	1.70	5.00	12.00
292-The Three Stooges-Photo-c	5.70	17.00	40.00
293-Little Lulu; Irving Tripp-a	7.00	21.00	50.00

	Good	Fine	N-Mint
294-Popeye	2.50	7.50	17.50
295-Tom and Jerry	.85	2.50	6.00
296-Lassie (TV)-Photo-c	1.70	5.00	12.00
297-Christmas Bells	1.20	3.50	8.00
298-Santa's Sleigh (1966)	1.20	3.50	8.00
299-The Flintstones (TV)(1967)	3.00	9.00	21.00
300-Tarzan	5.00	15.00	35.00
301-Bugs Bunny	.85	2.50	6.00
302-Laurel and Hardy (TV)-Photo-c	3.50	10.50	24.00
303-Daffy Duck	.70	2.00	5.00
304-The Three Stooges-Photo-c	5.00	15.00	35.00
305-Tom and Jerry	.70	2.00	5.00
306-Daniel Boone (TV)-Fess Parker photo-c	3.00	9.00	21.00
307-Little Lulu; Irving Tripp-a	5.70	17.00	40.00
308-Lassie (TV)-Photo-c	1.50	4.50	10.00
309-Yogi Bear (TV)	1.00	3.00	7.00
310-The Lone Ranger-Clayton Moore photo-c	10.00	30.00	70.00
311-Santa's Show	1.00	3.00	7.00
312-Christmas Album (1967)	1.00	3.00	7.00
313-Daffy Duck (1968)	.70	2.00	5.00
314-Laurel and Hardy (TV)	3.00	9.00	21.00
315-Bugs Bunny	.85	2.50	6.00
316-The Three Stooges	4.30	13.00	30.00
317-The Flintstones (TV)	2.65	8.00	18.00
318-Tarzan	4.65	13.00	32.00
319-Yogi Bear (TV)	1.50	4.50	10.00
320-Space Family Robinson (TV); Spiegle-a	6.50	19.50	45.00
321-Tom and Jerry	.70	2.00	5.00
322-The Lone Ranger	4.35	13.00	30.00
323-Little Lulu-not Stanley	3.50	10.50	24.00
324-Lassie (TV)-Photo-c	1.50	4.50	10.00
325-Fun with Santa	1.00	3.00	7.00
326-Christmas Story (1968)	1.00	3.00	7.00
327-The Flintstones (TV)(1969)	2.65	8.00	18.00
328-Space Family Robinson (TV); Spiegle-a	6.50	19.50	45.00
329-Bugs Bunny	.85	2.50	6.00
330-The Jetsons (TV)	5.00	15.00	35.00
331-Daffy Duck	.70	2.00	5.00
332-Tarzan	3.65	11.00	25.00
333-Tom and Jerry	.70	2.00	5.00
334-Lassie (TV)	1.15	3.50	8.00
335-Little Lulu	3.50	10.50	24.00
336-The Three Stooges	4.30	13.00	30.00
337-Yogi Bear (TV)	1.50	4.50	10.00
338-The Lone Ranger	4.35	13.00	30.00
339-(Did not come out)			
340-Here Comes Santa (1969)	1.00	3.00	7.00
341-The Flintstones (TV)	2.65	8.00	18.00
342-Tarzan	3.65	11.00	25.00
343-Bugs Bunny	.70	2.00	5.00
344-Yogi Bear (TV)	1.15	3.50	8.00
345-Tom and Jerry	.70	2.00	5.00
346-Lassie (TV)	1.15	3.50	8.00
347-Daffy Duck	.70	2.00	5.00
348-The Jetsons (TV)	4.30	13.00	30.00
349-Little Lulu-not Stanley	3.00	9.00	21.00
350-The Lone Ranger	3.65	11.00	25.00
351-Beep-Beep, the Road Runner (TV)	1.35	4.00	9.00
352-Space Family Robinson (TV)-Spiegle-a	6.50	19.50	45.00
353-Beep-Beep, the Road Runner (1971) (TV)	1.35	4.00	9.00
354-Tarzan (1971)	3.00	9.00	21.00
355-Little Lulu-not Stanley	3.00	9.00	21.00
356-Scooby Doo, Where Are You? (TV)	2.00	6.00	14.00
357-Daffy Duck & Porky Pig	.70	2.00	5.00
358-Lassie (TV)	1.15	3.50	8.00
359-Baby Snoots	1.35	4.00	9.00

March Of Comics #252, © ERB

March Of Comics #294, © KING

March Of Comics #349, © WEST

March Of Comics #391, © Hanna Barbera   March Of Comics #416, © Warner Bros.   March Of Comics #472, © Viacom Int.

MARCH OF COMICS (continued)	Good	Fine	N-Mint
360-H. R. Pufnstuf (TV)-Photo-c	1.30	4.00	9.00
361-Tom and Jerry	.70	2.00	5.00
362-Smokey the Bear (TV)	.70	2.00	5.00
363-Bugs Bunny & Yosemite Sam	.70	2.00	5.00
364-The Banana Splits (TV)-Photo-c	.85	2.50	6.00
365-Tom and Jerry (1972)	.70	2.00	5.00
366-Tarzan	3.00	9.00	21.00
367-Bugs Bunny & Porky Pig	.70	2.00	5.00
368-Scooby Doo (TV)(4/72)	1.70	5.00	12.00
369-Little Lulu-not Stanley	2.30	7.00	16.00
370-Lassie (TV)-Photo-c	1.15	3.50	8.00
371-Baby Snoots	1.00	3.00	7.00
372-Smokey the Bear (TV)	.70	2.00	5.00
373-The Three Stooges	3.70	11.00	26.00
374-Wacky Witch	.70	2.00	5.00
375-Beep-Beep & Daffy Duck (TV)	.70	2.00	5.00
376-The Pink Panther (1972) (TV)	1.35	4.00	9.00
377-Baby Snoots (1973)	1.00	3.00	7.00
378-Turok, Son of Stone	7.00	21.00	50.00
379-Heckle & Jeckle New Terrytoons (TV)	.50	1.50	3.00
380-Bugs Bunny & Yosemite Sam	.50	1.50	3.00
381-Lassie (TV)	.85	2.50	6.00
382-Scooby Doo, Where Are You? (TV)	1.50	4.50	10.00
383-Smokey the Bear (TV)	.50	1.50	3.00
384-Pink Panther (TV)	1.00	3.00	7.00
385-Little Lulu	2.00	6.00	14.00
386-Wacky Witch	.50	1.50	3.00
387-Beep-Beep & Daffy Duck (TV)	.50	1.50	3.00
388-Tom and Jerry (1973)	.50	1.50	3.00
389-Little Lulu-not Stanley	2.00	6.00	14.00
390-Pink Panther (TV)	.70	2.00	5.00
391-Scooby Doo (TV)	1.30	4.00	9.00
392-Bugs Bunny & Yosemite Sam	.50	1.50	3.00
393-New Terrytoons (Heckle & Jeckle) (TV)	.50	1.50	3.00
394-Lassie (TV)	.70	2.00	5.00
395-Woodsy Owl	.50	1.50	3.00
396-Baby Snoots	.70	2.00	5.00
397-Beep-Beep & Daffy Duck (TV)	.50	1.50	3.00
398-Wacky Witch	.50	1.50	3.00
399-Turok, Son of Stone	5.70	17.00	40.00
400-Tom and Jerry	.50	1.50	3.00
401-Baby Snoots (1975) (r-/No. 371)	.70	2.00	5.00
402-Daffy Duck (r-/No. 313)	.50	1.50	3.00
403-Bugs Bunny (r-/No. 343)	.50	1.50	3.00
404-Space Family Robinson (TV)(r-/No. 328)	5.00	15.00	35.00
405-Cracky	.50	1.50	3.00
406-Little Lulu (r-/No. 355)	1.70	5.00	12.00
407-Smokey the Bear (TV)(r-/No. 362)	.50	1.50	3.00
408-Turok, Son of Stone	5.00	15.00	35.00
409-Pink Panther (TV)	.50	1.50	3.00
410-Wacky Witch	.35	1.00	2.00
411-Lassie (TV)(r-/No. 324)	.70	2.00	5.00
412-New Terrytoons (1975) (TV)	.35	1.00	2.00
413-Daffy Duck (1976)(r-/No. 331)	.35	1.00	2.00
414-Space Family Robinson (r-/No. 328)	3.50	10.50	24.00
415-Bugs Bunny (r-/No. 329)	.35	1.00	2.00
416-Beep-Beep, the Road Runner (r-/#353)(TV)	.35	1.00	2.00
417-Little Lulu (r-/No. 323)	1.70	5.00	12.00
418-Pink Panther (r-/No. 384) (TV)	.35	1.00	2.00
419-Baby Snoots (r-/No. 377)	.50	1.50	3.00
420-Woody Woodpecker	.35	1.00	2.00
421-Tweety & Sylvester	.35	1.00	2.00
422-Wacky Witch (r-/No. 386)	.35	1.00	2.00
423-Little Monsters	.50	1.50	3.00
424-Cracky (12/76)	.35	1.00	2.00
425-Daffy Duck	.35	1.00	2.00

	Good	Fine	N-Mint
426-Underdog (TV)	1.15	3.50	8.00
427-Little Lulu (r/No. 335)	1.15	3.50	8.00
428-Bugs Bunny	.35	1.00	2.00
429-The Pink Panther (TV)	.35	1.00	2.00
430-Beep-Beep, the Road Runner (TV)	.35	1.00	2.00
431-Baby Snoots	.50	1.50	3.00
432-Lassie (TV)	.50	1.50	3.00
433-Tweety & Sylvester	.35	1.00	2.00
434-Wacky Witch	.35	1.00	2.00
435-New Terrytoons (TV)	.35	1.00	2.00
436-Wacky Advs. of Cracky	.35	1.00	2.00
437-Daffy Duck	.35	1.00	2.00
438-Underdog (TV)	1.15	3.50	8.00
439-Little Lulu (r/#349)	1.15	3.50	8.00
440-Bugs Bunny	.35	1.00	2.00
441-The Pink Panther (TV)	.35	1.00	2.00
442-Beep-Beep, the Road Runner (TV)	.35	1.00	2.00
443-Baby Snoots	.50	1.50	3.00
444-Tom and Jerry	.35	1.00	2.00
445-Tweety and Sylvester	.35	1.00	2.00
446-Wacky Witch	.35	1.00	2.00
447-Mighty Mouse	.50	1.50	3.00
448-Cracky	.35	1.00	2.00
449-Pink Panther (TV)	.35	1.00	2.00
450-Baby Snoots	.35	1.00	2.00
451-Tom and Jerry	.35	1.00	2.00
452-Bugs Bunny	.35	1.00	2.00
453-Popeye	.35	1.00	2.00
454-Woody Woodpecker	.35	1.00	2.00
455-Beep-Beep, the Road Runner (TV)	.35	1.00	2.00
456-Little Lulu (r/#369)	.85	2.50	6.00
457-Tweety & Sylvester	.35	1.00	2.00
458-Wacky Witch	.35	1.00	2.00
459-Mighty Mouse	.50	1.50	3.00
460-Daffy Duck	.35	1.00	2.00
461-The Pink Panther (TV)	.35	1.00	2.00
462-Baby Snoots	.35	1.00	2.00
463-Tom and Jerry	.35	1.00	2.00
464-Bugs Bunny	.35	1.00	2.00
465-Popeye	.35	1.00	2.00
466-Woody Woodpecker	.35	1.00	2.00
467-Underdog (TV)	.85	2.50	6.00
468-Little Lulu (r/#385)	.70	2.00	4.00
469-Tweety & Sylvester	.35	1.00	2.00
470-Wacky Witch	.35	1.00	2.00
471-Mighty Mouse	.50	1.50	3.00
472-Heckle & Jeckle(12/80)	.35	1.00	2.00
473-Pink Panther(1/81) (TV)	.35	1.00	2.00
474-Baby Snoots	.35	1.00	2.00
475-Little Lulu (r/#323)	.50	1.50	3.00
476-Bugs Bunny	.35	1.00	2.00
477-Popeye	.35	1.00	2.00
478-Woody Woodpecker	.35	1.00	2.00
479-Underdog (TV)	.85	2.50	6.00
480-Tom and Jerry	.35	1.00	2.00
481-Tweety and Sylvester	.35	1.00	2.00
482-Wacky Witch	.35	1.00	2.00
483-Mighty Mouse	.50	1.50	3.00
484-Heckle & Jeckle	.35	1.00	2.00
485-Baby Snoots	.35	1.00	2.00
486-The Pink Panther (TV)	.35	1.00	2.00
487-Bugs Bunny	.35	1.00	2.00
488-Little Lulu (r/#335)	.50	1.50	3.00

MARCH OF CRIME (My Love Affair #1-6) (See Fox Giants)
No. 7, July, 1950 - No. 2, Sept, 1950; No. 3, Sept, 1951

MARCH OF CRIME (continued)
Fox Features Syndicate

	Good	Fine	N-Mint
7(#1)(7/50)-Wood-a	14.00	42.00	100.00
2(9/50)-Wood-a (exceptional)	14.00	42.00	100.00
3(9/51)	5.00	15.00	35.00

MARCO POLO
1962 (Movie classic)
Charlton Comics Group

nn (Scarce)-Glanzman-c/a, 25pgs.	9.00	27.00	62.00

MARC SPECTOR: MOON KNIGHT (Also see Moon Knight)
June, 1989 - Present ($1.50, color, direct sale only)
Marvel Comics

1	.50	1.50	3.00
2-12: 4-Intro new Midnight. 8,9-Punisher app.	.25	.75	1.50

MARGARET O'BRIEN (See The Adventures of...)

MARGE'S LITTLE LULU (Little Lulu #207 on)
No. 74, 6/45 - No. 164, 7-9/62; No. 165, 10/62 - No. 206, 8/72
Dell Publishing Co./Gold Key #165-206

Marjorie Henderson Buell, born in Philadelphia, Pa., in 1904, created *Little Lulu*, a cartoon character that appeared weekly in the *Saturday Evening Post* from Feb. 23, 1935 through Dec. 30, 1944. She was not responsible for any of the comic books. John Stanley did pencils only on all *Little Lulu* comics through at least #135 (1959). He did pencils and inks on *Four Color #74 & 97*. Irving Tripp began inking stories from #1 on, and remained the comic's illustrator throughout its entire run. Stanley did storyboards (layouts), pencils, and scripts in all cases and inking only on covers. His word balloons were written in cursive. Tripp and occasionally other artists at Western Publ. in Poughkeepsie, N.Y. blew up the pencilled pages, inked the blowups, and lettered them. Arnold Drake did storyboards, pencils and scripts starting with #197 (1970), amidst reprinted issues. Buell sold her rights exclusively to Western Publ. in Dec., 1971. The earlier issues had to be approved by Buell prior to publication.

	Good	Fine	N-Mint
4-Color 74('45)-Intro Lulu, Tubby & Alvin	90.00	270.00	630.00
4-Color 97(2/46)	47.00	140.00	330.00
(Above two books are all John Stanley - cover, pencils, and inks.)			
4-Color 110('46)-1st Alvin Story Telling Time; 1st app. Willy	33.00	100.00	230.00
4-Color 115-1st app. Boys' Clubhouse	33.00	100.00	230.00
4-Color 120, 131: 120-1st app. Eddie	30.00	90.00	210.00
4-Color 139('47),146,158	27.00	81.00	190.00
4-Color 165 (10/47)-Smokes doll hair & has wild hallucinations. 1st Tubby detective story	27.00	81.00	190.00
1(1-2/48)-Lulu's Diary feat. begins	56.00	168.00	390.00
2-1st app. Gloria; 1st Tubby story in a L.L. comic; 1st app. Miss Feeny	29.00	87.00	200.00
3-5	25.00	75.00	175.00
6-10: 7-1st app. Annie; Xmas-c	18.00	54.00	125.00
11-20: 19-1st app. Wilbur. 20-1st app. Mr. McNabbem	15.00	45.00	105.00
21-30: 26-r/F.C. 110. 30-Xmas-c	11.50	34.00	80.00
31-38,40: 35-1st Mumday story	10.00	30.00	70.00
39-Intro. Witch Hazel in "That Awful Witch Hazel"	11.00	32.00	76.00
41-60: 42-Xmas-c. 45-2nd Witch Hazel app. 49-Gives Stanley & others credit	8.50	25.50	60.00
61-80: 63-1st app. Chubby (Tubby's cousin). 68-1st app. Prof. Cleff. 78-Xmas-c. 80-Intro. Little Itch (2/55)	6.50	19.50	45.00
81-99: 90-Xmas-c	4.00	12.00	30.00
100	4.60	14.00	35.00
101-130: 123-1st app. Fifi	3.50	10.50	24.00
131-164: 135-Last Stanley-p	2.65	8.00	20.00
165-Giant; ...In Paris ('62)	4.00	12.00	32.00
166-Giant; ...Christmas Diary ('62-'63)	4.00	12.00	32.00
167-169	2.15	6.50	15.00
170,172,175,176,178-196,198-200-Stanley-r. 182-1st app. Little Scarecrow Boy	1.30	4.00	9.00
171,173,174,177,197	.85	2.50	6.00

	Good	Fine	N-Mint
201,203,206-Last issue to carry Marge's name	.55	1.65	4.00
202,204,205-Stanley-r	1.00	3.00	7.00
...& Tubby in Japan (12 cents)(5-7/62) 01476-207	5.70	17.00	40.00
...Summer Camp 1(8/67-G.K.-Giant) '57-58-r	4.65	14.00	32.00
...Trick 'N' Treat 1(12-)(12/62-Gold Key)	5.00	15.00	35.00

NOTE: See *Dell Giant Comics* #23, 29, 36, 42, 50, & *Dell Giants* for annuals. All Giants not by *Stanley* from L.L. on Vacation (7/54) on. *Irving Tripp* a-#1-on. Christmas c-7, 18, 30, 42, 78, 90, 126, 166, 250. Summer Camp issues #173, 177, 181, 189, 197, 201, 206.

MARGE'S LITTLE LULU (See Golden Comics Digest #19, 23, 27, 29, 33, 36, 40, 43, 46 & March of Comics #251, 267, 275, 293, 307, 323, 335, 349, 355, 369, 385, 406, 417, 427, 439, 456, 468, 475, 488)

MARGE'S TUBBY (Little Lulu)(See Dell Giants)
No. 381, Aug, 1952 - No. 49, Dec-Feb, 1961-62
Dell Publishing Co./Gold Key

	Good	Fine	N-Mint
4-Color 381 (#1)-Stanley script; Irving Tripp-a	12.00	36.00	84.00
4-Color 430,444-Stanley-a	7.00	21.00	50.00
4-Color 461 (4/53)-1st Tubby and Men From Mars story; Stanley-a	6.50	19.50	45.00
5 (7-9/53)-Stanley-a	5.00	15.00	35.00
6-10	3.50	10.50	24.00
11-20	2.85	8.50	20.00
21-30	2.35	7.00	16.00
31-49	2.00	6.00	14.00
...& the Little Men From Mars No. 30020-410(10/64-G.K.)-25 cents; 68 pgs.	5.00	15.00	40.00

NOTE: *John Stanley* did all storyboards & scripts through at least #35 (1959). *Lloyd White* did all art except F.C. 381, 430, 444, 461 & #5.

MARGIE (See My Little...)

MARGIE (TV)
No. 1307, Mar-May, 1962 - No. 2, July-Sept, 1962 (Photo-c)
Dell Publishing Co.

4-Color 1307, 2	2.30	7.00	16.00

MARGIE COMICS (Formerly Comedy Comics; Reno Browne #50 on) (Also see Cindy Comics & Teen Comics)
No. 35, Winter, 1946-47 - No. 49, Dec, 1949
Marvel Comics (ACI)

35	4.00	12.00	28.00
36-38,42,45,47-49	2.00	6.00	14.00
39,41,43(2),44,46-Kurtzman's "Hey Look"	2.85	8.50	20.00
40-Three "Hey Looks," three "Giggles & Grins" by Kurtzman	4.00	12.00	28.00

MARINES (See Tell It to the...)

MARINES ATTACK
Aug, 1964 - No. 9, Feb-Mar, 1966
Charlton Comics

1	.35	1.00	2.00
2-9	.25	.75	1.50

MARINES AT WAR (Formerly Tales of the Marines #4)
No. 5, April, 1957 - No. 7, Aug, 1957
Atlas Comics (OPI)

5-7	.70	2.00	5.00

NOTE: *Colan* a-5. *Drucker* a-5. *Everett* a-5. *Maneely* a-5. *Orlando* a-7. *Severin* c-5.

MARINES IN ACTION
June, 1955 - No. 14, Sept, 1957
Atlas News Co.

1-Rock Murdock, Boot Camp Brady begin	2.00	6.00	14.00
2-14	1.00	3.00	7.00

NOTE: *Berg* a-2, 8, 9, 11, 14. *Heath* c-2, *Maneely* c-1. *Severin* a-4; c-7-11, 14.

Marge's Little Lulu #19, © WEST

Marge's Tubby #13, © WEST

Marines In Action #1, © MEG

M.A.R.S. Patrol Total War #3, © GK

Martian Manhunter #1, © DC

Marvel Boy #2, © MEG

MARINES IN BATTLE
Aug, 1954 - No. 25, Sept, 1958
Atlas Comics (ACI No. 1-12/WPI No. 13-25)

	Good	Fine	N-Mint
1-Heath-c; Iron Mike McGraw by Heath; history of U.S. Marine Corps. begins	3.70	11.00	26.00
2-Heath-c	1.70	5.00	12.00
3-6,8-10: 4-Last precode (2/55)	1.50	4.50	10.00
7-Six pg. Kubert/Moskowitz-a	2.30	7.00	16.00
11-16,18-22,24	1.00	3.00	7.00
17-Williamson-a, 3 pgs.	3.00	9.00	21.00
23-Crandall-a; Mark Murdock app.	2.00	6.00	14.00
25-Torres-a	1.70	5.00	12.00

NOTE: Berg a-22. Drucker a-6. Everett a-4, 15; c-21. Heath c-1, 2. Maneely c-24. Orlando a-14. Pakula a-6. Powell a-16. Severin c-12.

MARINE WAR HEROES (Charlton Premiere #19 on)
Jan, 1964 - No. 18, Mar, 1967
Charlton Comics

	Good	Fine	N-Mint
1	.35	1.00	2.00
2-18	.25	.75	1.50

NOTE: Montes/Bache a-1,14,18; c-1.

MARK, THE (Also see Mayhem)
Sept, 1987 - Present ($1.75, $1.95, color)
Dark Horse Comics

1,3-7 ($1.75)	.30	.90	1.80
2 ($1.95)	.35	1.00	2.00

MARK HAZZARD: MERC
Nov, 1986 - No. 12, Oct, 1987 (75 cents, color)
Marvel Comics Group

1-12: Morrow-a		.40	.80
Annual 1(11/87)		.60	1.20

MARK OF ZORRO (See 4-Color #228)

MARKSMAN, THE (Also see Champions)
Jan, 1988 - No. 5, 1988 ($1.95, color)
Hero Comics

1-5: 1-Origin The Marksman, Rose begins	.35	1.00	2.00
Annual 1 (1988, $2.75, 52 pgs.)	.45	1.40	2.80

MARK STEEL
1967, 1968, 1972 (24 pgs.) (Color)
American Iron & Steel Institute (Giveaway)

1967,1968-''Journey of Discovery with. . .''; Neal Adams art	2.35	7.00	16.00
1972-''. . .Fights Pollution;'' Adams-a	1.35	4.00	8.00

MARK TRAIL
Oct, 1955 - No. 5, Summer, 1959
Standard Magazines (Hall Syndicate)/Fawcett Publ. No. 5

1-Sunday strip-r	4.00	12.00	28.00
2-5	2.00	6.00	14.00
. . .Adventure Book of Nature 1(Summer, 1958; Pines)-100 pg. Giant; contains 78 Sunday strip-r	5.00	15.00	35.00

MARMADUKE MONK
No date; 1963 (10 cents)
I. W. Enterprises/Super Comics

1-I.W. Reprint, 14-(Super Reprint)('63)	.35	1.00	2.00

MARMADUKE MOUSE
Spring, 1946 - No. 65, Dec, 1956 (All 52 pgs.?)
Quality Comics Group (Arnold Publ.)

1-Funny animal	5.70	17.00	40.00
2	2.85	8.50	20.00
3-10	2.30	7.00	16.00
11-30	1.60	4.80	11.00
31-65	1.00	3.00	7.00

	Good	Fine	N-Mint
Super Reprint #14(1963)	.35	1.00	2.00

MARS
Jan, 1984 - No. 12, Jan, 1985 ($1.00, Mando paper)
First Comics

1-12: 2-The Black Flame begins. 10-Dynamo Joe begins		.50	1.00

MARS & BEYOND (See 4-Color #866)

MARSHAL LAW (Also see Crime And Punishment: Marshall Law. . .)
Oct, 1987 - No. 6, May, 1989 ($1.95, color, adults)
Epic Comics (Marvel)

1	.85	2.50	5.00
2	.50	1.50	3.00
3-6	.35	1.00	2.00

M.A.R.S. PATROL TOTAL WAR (Formerly Total War #1,2)
No. 3, Sept, 1966 - No. 10, Aug, 1969 (All-Painted-c)
Gold Key

3-Wood-a	2.00	6.00	14.00
4-10	1.00	3.00	7.00

MARTHA WAYNE (See The Story of . . .)

MARTIAN MANHUNTER
May, 1988 - No. 4, Aug., 1988 ($1.25, color, limited series)
DC Comics

1-4: 1-Batman app. 2-Batman cameo	.25	.75	1.50

MARTIN KANE (Formerly My Secret Affair) (Radio-TV)(Private Eye)
No. 4, June, 1950 - No. 2, Aug, 1950
Fox Features Syndicate (Hero Books)

4(#1)-Wood-c/a(2); used in SOTI, pg. 160; photo back cover	14.00	42.00	100.00
2-Orlando-a, 5pgs; Wood-a(2)	10.00	30.00	70.00

MARTY MOUSE
No date (1958?) (10 cents)
I. W. Enterprises

1-Reprint	.35	1.00	2.00

MARVEL ACTION UNIVERSE (TV)
Jan, 1989 ($1.00, color, one-shot)
Marvel Comics

1-R/Spider-Man And His Amazing Friends		.50	1.00

MARVEL ADVENTURES (. . .Adventure #4 on)
Dec, 1975 - No. 6, Oct, 1976
Marvel Comics Group

1-#1-6 r-/Daredevil 22-27		.25	.50
2-6		.20	.40

MARVEL AND DC PRESENT (Featuring the Uncanny X-Men and the New Teen titans)
Nov, 1982 (One Shot, 68pgs, $2.00 cover, printed on Baxter paper)
Marvel Comics Group/DC Comics

1-Simonson/Austin c/a; Perez-a(p)	1.40	4.25	8.50

MARVEL BOY (Astonishing #3 on; see Marvel Super Action #4)
Dec, 1950 - No. 2, Feb, 1951
Marvel Comics (MPC)

1-Origin Marvel Boy by Russ Heath	30.00	90.00	210.00
2-Everett-a	25.00	75.00	175.00

MARVEL CHILLERS
Oct, 1975 - No. 7, Oct, 1976
Marvel Comics Group

1-Intro. Modred the Mystic; Kane-c(p)		.30	.60
2-5,7: 3-Tigra, the Were-Woman begins (origin), ends #7. Chaykin/ Wrightson-c. 7-Kirby-c, Tuska-p		.25	.50

MARVEL CHILLERS (continued)	Good	Fine	N-Mint
6-Byrne-a(p); Buckler-c(p)		.50	1.00

MARVEL CLASSICS COMICS SERIES FEATURING. . . (Also see
Pendulum Illustrated Classics)
1976 - No. 36, Dec, 1978 (52 pgs., no ads)
Marvel Comics Group

	Good	Fine	N-Mint
1-Dr. Jekyll and Mr. Hyde	.35	1.00	2.00
2-27,29-36: 2-Time Machine, 3-Hunchback of Notre Dame, 4-20,000			
Leagues Under the Sea, 5-Black Beauty, 6-Gulliver's Travels, 7-			
Tom Sawyer, 8-Moby Dick, 9-Dracula, 10-Red Badge of Courage,			
11-Mysterious Island, 12-The Three Musketeers, 13-Last of the Mo-			
hicans, 14-War of the Worlds, 15-Treasure Island, 16-Ivanhoe, 17-			
The Count of Monte Cristo, 18-The Odyssey, 19-Robinson Crusoe,			
20-Frankenstein, 21-Master of the World, 22-Food of the Gods, 23-			
The Moonstone, 24-She, 25-The Invisible Man, 26-The Illiad, 27-			
Kidnapped, 28-Prisoner of Zenda, 30-Arabian Nights, 31-First Man			
in the Moon, 32-White Fang, 33-The Prince and the Pauper, 34-			
Robin Hood, 35-Alice in Wonderland, 36-A Christmas Carol			
each. . . .	.25	.75	1.50
28-1st M. Golden-a; The Pit and the Pendulum	.90	2.75	5.50

NOTE: **Adkins** c-1i, 4i, 12i. **Alcala** a-34i; c-34. **Bolle** a-35. **Buscema** c-17p, 19p, 26p.
Golden a-28. **Gil Kane** c-16p, 21p, 22p, 24p, 32p. **Nebres** a-5; c-24i. **Nino** a-2, 8, 12.
Redondo a-1, 9. No. 1-12 were reprinted from Pendulum Illustrated Classics.

MARVEL COLLECTORS ITEM CLASSICS
Feb, 1965 - No. 22, Aug, 1969 (Marvel's Greatest #23 on)(68 pgs.)
Marvel Comics Group(ATF)

	Good	Fine	N-Mint
1-Fantastic Four, Spider-Man, Thor, Hulk, Iron Man-r begin; all are			
25 cent cover price	3.60	11.00	25.00
2 (4/66) - 4	1.70	5.00	12.00
5-22	.70	2.00	4.00

NOTE: All reprints; **Ditko, Kirby** art in all.

MARVEL COMICS (Marvel Mystery Comics #2 on)
October, November, 1939
Timely Comics (Funnies, Inc.)

NOTE: The first issue was originally dated October 1939. Most copies have a black circle
stamped over the date (on cover and inside) with "November" printed over it. However, some
copies do not have the November overprint and could have a higher value. Most No. 1's
have printing defects, i.e., tilted pages which caused trimming into the panels usually on right
side and bottom. Covers exist with and without gloss finish.

1-Origin Sub-Mariner by Bill Everett(1st newsstand app.); 1st 8 pgs. were
produced for *Motion Picture Funnies Weekly* #1 which was probably not
distributed outside of advance copies; Human Torch by Carl Burgos, Kazar
the Great, & Jungle Terror (only app.); intro. The Angel by Gustavson, The
Masked Raider (ends #12); cover by sci/fi pulp illustrator Frank

R. Paul	Good	Fine	VF-NM
	5000.00	12,600.00	27,500.00

(Only one known copy exists in Mint condition which traded twice in 1986
for $69,000 & later for $82,000, & once in 1987 for $82,000. Two other copies
are known in NM-M condition & their value would vary beyond the VF-NM
price)

MARVEL COMICS PRESENTS
Early Sept, 1988 - Present ($1.25, color, bi-weekly)
Marvel Comics

	Good	Fine	N-Mint
1-Wolverine by Buscema in #1-10	.50	1.50	3.00
2-10: 6-Sub-Mariner app. 10-Colossus begins	.25	.75	1.50
11-24,26-37,39-44: 17-Cyclops begins. 19-1st app. Damage Control.			
24-Havok begins. 26-Hulk begins by Rogers. 29-Quasar app. 31-			
Excalibur begins by Austin (i). 33-Capt. America. 37-Devil-Slayer			
app. (1st?). 39-Spider-Man story	.60	1.25	
25-Origin & 1st app. Nth Man	.35	1.00	2.00
38-Wolverine begins by Buscema; Hulk app.	.25	.75	1.50

NOTE: **Austin** a-31-37i. **Buscema** a-1-10, 38, 39; c-6. **Colan** a-37p. **Ditko** a-7p.
McFarlane c-32. **Russell** c-4i. **Simonson** c-1, 7. **Smith** c-34. **Sparling** a-33.

MARVEL COMICS SUPER SPECIAL (Marvel Super Special #5 on)
September, 1977 - No. 41(?), Nov, 1986 (nn 7) (Magazine; $1.50)

Marvel Comics Group

	Good	Fine	N-Mint
1-Kiss, 40 pgs. comics plus photos & features; Simonson-a(p); also			
see Howard the Duck #12	3.50	10.50	24.00
2-Conan (3/78)	.50	1.50	3.00
3-Close Encounters of the Third Kind (6/78); Simonson-a			
	.35	1.00	2.00
4-The Beatles Story (8/78)-Perez/Janson-a	1.00	3.00	7.00
5-Kiss (12/78)	2.85	8.50	20.00
6-Jaws II (12/78)	.25	.75	1.50
8-Battlestar Galactica-tabloid size	.35	1.00	2.00
8-Battlestar Galactica publ. in reg. magazine format; low distribu-			
tion ($1.50)8½x11''	.85	2.50	5.00
9-Conan	.35	1.00	2.00
10-Star Lord	.35	1.00	2.00
11-13-Weirdworld begins #11; 25 copy special press run of each with			
gold seal and signed by artists (Proof quality), Spring-June, 1979			
	10.00	30.00	60.00
11-Weirdworld (regular issue)	.70	2.00	4.00
12-Weirdworld (regular issue)	.40	1.25	2.50
13-Weirdworld (regular issue)	.30	.90	1.80
14-Adapts movie 'Meteor'		.60	1.20
15-Star Trek with photos & pin-ups($1.50)		.60	1.20
15-with $2.00 price(scarce); the price was changed at tail end of a			
200,000 press run	.70	2.00	4.00
16-20: 16-'Empire Strikes Back'-Williamson-a, 17-Xanadu, 18-Raid-			
ers of the Lost Ark, 19-For Your Eyes Only (James Bond), 20-			
Dragonslayer	each. . . .	.30	.90	1.80
21-40 (Movie adaptations): 21-Conan, 22-Bladerunner; Williamson-a;			
Steranko-c, 23-Annie, 24-The Dark Crystal, 25-Rock and Rule-w/			
photos, 26-Octopussy (James Bond), 27-Return of the Jedi, 28-			
Krull, 29-Tarzan of the Apes (Greystoke movie), 30-Indiana Jones			
and the Temple of Doom, 31-The Last Star Fighter, 32-The Mup-			
pets Take Manhattan, 33-Buckaroo Bonzai, 34-Sheena, 35-Conan			
The Destroyer, 36-Dune, 37-2010, 38-Red Sonja, 39-Santa Claus:			
The Movie. 40-Labyrinth			
each. . . .	.35	1.00	2.00
41-Howard The Duck-movie adapt.(11/86)	.45	1.25	2.50

NOTE: **J. Buscema** a-1, 2, 9, 11-13, 18p, 21, 35, 40; c-11(part). 12. **Chaykin** a-9. 19p:
c-18, 19. **Colan** a(p)-6, 10, 14. **Spiegle** a-29. **Stevens** a-27. **Williamson** a-7.

MARVEL DOUBLE FEATURE
Dec, 1973 - No. 21, Mar, 1977
Marvel Comics Group

	Good	Fine	N-Mint
1-Captain America & Iron Man-r begin		.30	.60
2-21: 17-r/Iron Man & Sub-Mariner #1. 18,19-r/Iron Man #1			
		.25	.50

NOTE: **Colan** a-1-19p(r). **Gil Kane** a-15p(r). **Kirby** a-1r, 2-8p(r), 17p(r); c-17-20.

MARVEL FAMILY (Also see Captain Marvel Adventures No. 18)
Dec, 1945 - No. 89, Jan, 1954
Fawcett Publications

	Good	Fine	N-Mint
1-Origin Captain Marvel, Captain Marvel Jr., Mary Marvel, & Uncle			
Marvel retold; Origin/1st app. Black Adam	65.00	195.00	455.00
2	35.00	105.00	245.00
3	25.00	75.00	175.00
4,5	19.00	57.00	135.00
6-10: 7-Shazam app.	16.00	48.00	110.00
11-20	11.00	32.00	75.00
21-30	8.50	25.50	60.00
31-40	7.00	21.00	50.00
41-46,48-50	5.70	17.00	40.00
47-Flying Saucer c/story	7.00	21.00	50.00
51-76,79,80,82-89	5.00	15.00	35.00
77-Communist Threat-c	7.00	21.00	50.00
78,81-Used in POP, pgs. 92,93	5.00	15.00	35.00

MARVEL FANFARE
March, 1982 - Present ($1.25-$1.95, slick paper) (Direct Sale only)

Marvel Collectors Item Classics #6, © MEG

Marvel Comics #1, © MEG

Marvel Family #1, © FAW

Marvel Fanfare #3, © MEG

Marvel Feature #10, © MEG

Marvel Graphic Novel #5, © MEG

MARVEL FANFARE (continued)
Marvel Comics Group

	Good	Fine	N-Mint
1-Spider-Man/Angel team-up; 1st Paul Smith story	1.35	4.00	8.00
2-Spider-Man, Ka-Zar, The Angel. F.F. origin retold	1.50	4.50	9.00
3-X-Men & Ka-Zar	.85	2.50	5.00
4-X-Men & Ka-Zar	1.00	3.00	6.00
5-Dr. Strange, Capt. America	.50	1.50	3.00

6-15: 6-Spider-Man, Scarlet Witch. 7-Incredible Hulk. 8-Dr. Strange; Wolf Boy begins. 9-Man-Thing. 10-13-Black Widow. 14-The Vision.

| 15-The Thing by Barry Smith, c/a | .35 | 1.00 | 1.95 |

16-32,34-49: 16,17-Skywolf. 18-Capt. America. 19-Cloak and Dagger. 20,21-The Thing/Incr. Hulk. 22,23-Iron Man vs. Dr. Octopus. 24-26-Weirdworld. 27-Daredevil/Spider-Man. 28-Alpha Flight. 29-Hulk. 30-Moon Knight. 31,32-Capt. America. 34-37-Warriors Three. 38-Moon Knight/Dazzler. 39-Moon Knight/Hawkeye. 40-Angel/Rogue & Storm. 41-Doc. Strange. 42-Spider-Man. 43-Sub-Mariner/Human Torch. 44-Iron Man Vs. Dr. Doom by Ken Steacy. 45-All pin-up issue by Steacy, Art Adams & others. 46-Fantastic Four. 47-Hulk.

| 48-She-Hulk/Vision. 49-Dr. Strange/Nick Fury | .35 | 1.00 | 1.95 |
| 33-X-Men & Wolverine app. | .40 | 1.25 | 2.50 |

NOTE: *Art Adams* c-13. *Austin* a-1i, 4i, 33i, 38i; c-8i, 33i. *Byrne* a-1p, 29, 48; c-29. *Golden* a-1, 2, 4p, 47; c-1, 2. *Infantino* c/a(p)-8. *Gil Kane* a-8-11p. *Miller* a-18; c-1(Back-c). 18. *Perez* a-10, 11p, 12, 13p; c-10p-13p. *Rogers* a-5p; c-5p. *Russell* a-5i, 6i, 8-11i, 43i; c-5i, 6. *Paul Smith* a-1p, 32, 4p; c-4p. *Williamson* a-30i.

MARVEL FEATURE (See Marvel Two-In-One)
Dec, 1971 - No. 12, Nov, 1973 (No. 1,2: 25 cents)
Marvel Comics Group

1-Origin The Defenders; Sub-Mariner, The Hulk & Dr. Strange; G.A. Sub-Mariner-r, Adams-c	1.70	5.00	12.00
2-G.A. 1950s Sub-Mariner-r	1.00	3.00	6.00
3-Defender series ends	1.00	3.00	6.00

4-12: 4-Begin Ant-Man series; brief origin. 8-Origin Antman & The Wasp. 9-Iron Man app. 10-Last Ant-Man. 11,12-Thing team-ups. 11-Origin Fantastic-4 retold

| | .35 | 1.00 | 2.00 |

NOTE: *Bolle* a-9i. *Everett* a-1i, 3i. *Kane* c-3p, 7p. *Russell* a-7-10p. *Starlin* a-8, 11, 12; c-8.

MARVEL FEATURE (Also see Red Sonja)
Nov, 1975 - No. 7, Nov, 1976
Marvel Comics Group

| 1-Red Sonja begins; Adams r/Savage Sword of Conan #1 | .40 | 1.25 | 2.50 |
| 2-7: Thorne-c/a in #2-7 | .25 | .75 | 1.50 |

MARVEL FUMETTI BOOK
April, 1984 (One shot) ($1.00 cover price)
Marvel Comics Group

| 1-Art Adams-a | | .40 | .80 |

MARVEL GRAPHIC NOVEL
1982 - Present ($5.95-$6.95)
Marvel Comics Group (Epic Comics)

1 (First Printing)-Death of Captain Marvel	2.50	7.50	15.00
1 (2nd & 3rd Printing)	1.00	3.00	6.00
2-Elric: The Dreaming City	1.35	4.00	8.00
3-Dreadstar: Starlin-a, 48pgs.	1.20	3.50	7.00
4-The New Mutants-Origin	1.70	5.00	10.00
4-2nd Print	1.00	3.00	5.95
5-X-Men; book-length story	2.00	6.00	12.00
5-2nd Print	1.00	3.00	5.95

6-18: 6-The Star Slammers, 7-Killraven, 8-Super Boxers, 9-The Futurians. 10-Heartburst, 11-Void Indigo, 12-The Dazzler, 13-Star-struck, 14-The Swords Of The Swashbucklers, 15-The Raven Banner (Asgard), 16-The Aladdin Effect, 17-Revenge Of The Living Monolith, 18-She Hulk

| | 1.00 | 3.00 | 6.00 |

	Good	Fine	N-Mint

19-31: 19-The Witch Queen of Acheron (Conan). 20-Greenberg the Vampire. 21-Marada The She-Wolf. 22-Amaz. Spider-Man in Hooky by Wrightson. 23-Dr. Strange. 24-Love And War (Daredevil) by Miller. 25-Alien Legion. 26-Dracula. 27-Avengers. 28-Conan The Reaver. 29-The Big Chance (Thing vs. Hulk). 30-A Sailor's Story. 31-Wolfpack

| 32-Death of Groo ($5.95) | 1.15 | 3.50 | 7.00 |

33,34,36,37: 33-Thor. 34-Predator & Prey (Cloak & Dagger). 36-Willow (movie adapt.). 37-Hercules

	1.15	3.50	7.00
35-Hitler's Astrologer (The Shadow, $12.95)	2.15	6.50	13.00
38-Silver Surfer ($14.95)	3.00	8.75	17.50
nn-Inhumans (1988, $7.95)-Williamson-i	1.35	4.00	8.00
nn-Who Framed Roger Rabbit (1989, $6.95)	1.15	3.50	7.00

nn-Roger Rabbit In The Resurrection Of Doom (1989, $8.95)

| | 1.50 | 4.50 | 9.00 |
| nn-Arena by Bruce Jones ($5.95) | 1.00 | 3.00 | 6.00 |

NOTE: *Aragones* a-27, 32. *Byrne* c/a-18. *Kaluta* a-13, 35p; c-13. *Miller* a-24p. *Simonson* a-6; c-6. *Starlin* c/a-1,3. *Williamson* a-34. *Wrightson* c-29i.

MARVEL MASTERWORKS
Nov, 1987 - Present ($29.95, color-r, hard-c w/dust jackets)
Marvel Comics

| 1-Spiderman, r/AF 15 & AS 1-10; 1st & 2nd printings | | 5.00 | 15.00 | 29.95 |

2-Fantastic-4 r/1-10; 1st printing has pages out of order; 2nd printing has pages corrected	5.00	15.00	29.95
3-X-Men, r/1-10; 1st & 2nd printings	5.00	15.00	29.95
4-Avengers, r/1-10	5.00	15.00	29.95
5-Spider-Man, r/11-20	5.00	15.00	29.95
6-Fantastic Four, r/11-20	5.00	15.00	29.95
7-X-Men, r/11-21	5.00	15.00	29.95
8-Incredible Hulk, r/1-6 ($24.95)	4.15	12.50	24.95
9-Avengers, r/11-20 ($29.95)	5.00	15.00	30.00
10-Spider-Man, r/21-30 & Annual #1 ($29.95)	5.00	15.00	30.00
11-X-Men, r/94-100 & Giant Size #1 ($29.95)	5.00	15.00	30.00

MARVEL MINI-BOOKS
1966 (50 pgs., B&W; 5/8"x7/8") (6 different issues)
Marvel Comics Group (Smallest comics ever published)

Captain America, Spider-Man, Sgt. Fury, Hulk, Thor

| | .35 | 1.00 | 2.00 |
| Millie the Model | .50 | 1.00 | |

NOTE: Each came in six different color covers, usually one color: Pink, yellow, green, etc.

MARVEL MOVIE PREMIERE (Magazine)
Sept, 1975 (One Shot) (Black & White)
Marvel Comics Group

| 1-Burroughs "The Land That Time Forgot" adaptation | .35 | 1.00 | 2.00 |

MARVEL MOVIE SHOWCASE
Nov, 1982 - No. 2, Dec, 1982 (68 pgs.)
Marvel Comics Group

| 1,2-Star Wars movie adaptation r/Star Wars #1-6 | | .60 | 1.20 |

MARVEL MOVIE SPOTLIGHT
Nov, 1982 (68 pgs.)
Marvel Comics Group

| 1-Edited r/Raiders of the Lost Ark #1-3; Buscema-c/a(p) | | .40 | .80 |

MARVEL MYSTERY COMICS (Formerly Marvel Comics) (Marvel Tales No. 93 on)
No. 2, Dec, 1939 - No. 92, June, 1949
Timely /Marvel Comics (TP 2-17/TCI 18-54/MCI 55-92)

2-American Ace begins, ends #3; Human Torch (blue costume) by

MARVEL MYSTERY COMICS (continued)	Good	Fine	N-Mint

Burgos, Sub-Mariner by Everett continues; 2pg. origin recap of
Human Torch 750.00 1890.00 4500.00
3-New logo from Marvel pulp begins 433.00 1085.00 2600.00
4-Intro. Electro, the Marvel of the Age (ends #19), The Ferret, Mystery Detective (ends #9) 350.00 875.00 2100.00
5 (Scarce) 533.00 1365.00 3200.00
6,7 217.00 545.00 1300.00
8-Human Torch & Sub-Mariner battle 283.00 710.00 1700.00
9-(Scarce)-Human Torch & Sub-Mariner battle
350.00 875.00 2100.00
10-Human Torch & Sub-Mariner battle, conclusion; Terry Vance, the Schoolboy Sleuth begins, ends #57 190.00 475.00 1140.00
11 140.00 350.00 840.00
12-Classic Kirby-c 140.00 350.00 840.00
13-Intro. & 1st app. The Vision by S&K; Sub-Mariner dons new costume, ends #15 158.00 395.00 950.00
14-16 97.00 245.00 580.00
17-Human Torch/Sub-Mariner team-up by Everett/Burgos; pin-up on back-c 112.00 280.00 670.00
18 92.00 230.00 550.00
19-Origin Toro in text 94.00 235.00 565.00
20-Origin The Angel in text 90.00 225.00 540.00
21-Intro. & 1st app. The Patriot; not in #46-48; pin-up on back-c
81.00 205.00 485.00
22-25: 23-Last Gustavson Angel; origin The Vision in text. 24-Injury-to-eye story 72.00 180.00 430.00
26-30: 27-Ka-Zar ends; last S&K Vision who battles Satan. 28-Jimmy Jupiter in the Land of Nowhere begins, ends #48; Sub-Mariner vs. The Flying Dutchman 63.00 160.00 380.00
31-Sub-Mariner by Everett ends, begins again #84
62.00 155.00 370.00
32-1st app. The Boboes 62.00 155.00 370.00
33,35-40: 40-Zeppelin-c 62.00 155.00 370.00
34-Everett, Burgos, Martin Goodman, Funnies, Inc. office appear in story & battles Hitler; last Burgos Human Torch
72.00 180.00 430.00
41-43,45-48-Last Vision & Flag-c 56.00 140.00 335.00
44-Classic Super Plane-c 56.00 140.00 335.00
49-Origin Miss America 72.00 180.00 430.00
50-Mary becomes Miss Patriot (origin) 56.00 140.00 335.00
51-60: 53-Bondage-c 50.00 125.00 300.00
61,62,64-Last German War-c 47.00 120.00 280.00
63-Classic Hitler War-c; The Villainess Cat-Woman only app.
50.00 125.00 300.00
65,66-Last Japanese War-c 47.00 120.00 280.00
67-75: 74-Last Patriot. 75-Young Allies begin 43.00 110.00 260.00
76-78: 76-10 Chapter Miss America serial begins, ends #85
43.00 110.00 260.00
79-New cover format; Super Villains begin on cover; last Angel
39.00 100.00 235.00
80-1st app. Capt. America in Marvel Comics 50.00 125.00 300.00
81-Captain America app. 39.00 100.00 235.00
82-Origin Namora; 1st Sub-Mariner/Namora team-up; Captain America app. 67.00 170.00 400.00
83,85: 83-Last Young Allies. 85-Last Miss America; Blonde Phantom app. 39.00 100.00 235.00
84-Blonde Phantom, Sub-Mariner by Everett begins; Captain America app. 50.00 125.00 300.00
86-Blonde Phantom i.d. revealed; Captain America app.; last Bucky app. 44.00 110.00 265.00
87-1st Capt. America/Golden Girl team-up 50.00 125.00 300.00
88-Golden Girl, Namora, & Sun Girl (1st in Marvel Comics) x-over; Captain America, Blonde Phantom app.; last Toro
44.00 110.00 265.00
89-1st Human Torch/Sun Girl team-up; 1st Captain America solo; Blonde Phantom app. 47.00 120.00 280.00

	Good	Fine	N-Mint

90-Blonde Phantom un-masked; Captain America app.
47.00 120.00 280.00
91-Capt. America app.; intro Venus; Blonde Phantom & Sub-Mariner end 47.00 120.00 280.00
92-Feature story on the birth of the Human Torch and the death of Professor Horton (his creator); 1st app. The Witness in Marvel Comics; Captain America app. 77.00 195.00 460.00
(Very rare) 132 Pg. issue, B&W, 25 cents (1943-44)-printed in N. Y.; square binding, blank inside covers; has Marvel No. 33-c in color; contains 2 Capt. America & 2 Marvel Mystery Comics-r (Less than ten copies known) 300.00 750.00 1800.00
NOTE: Crandall a-26i. Everett c-7-9, 27, 84. Schomburg c-3-11, 13-15, 18, 19, 22-33, 35, 36, 39-48, 50-57, 59, 63-66. Shores c-77, 82, 83. Bondage covers-3, 4, 7, 12, 28, 29, 49, 50, 52, 56, 57, 58, 59, 65. Remember Pearl Harbor issues-#30, 31.

MARVEL NO-PRIZE BOOK, THE
Jan, 1983 (One Shot, Direct Sale only)
Marvel Comics Group

1-Golden-c .50 1.00

MARVEL PREMIERE
April, 1972 - No. 61, Aug, 1981
Marvel Comics Group

1-Origin Warlock by Gil Kane/Adkins; origin Counter-Earth
1.15 3.50 7.00
2-Warlock ends; Kirby Yellow Claw-r .85 2.50 5.00
3-Dr. Strange series begins, Smith-a(p) 1.25 3.75 7.50
4-Smith/Brunner-a .70 2.00 4.00
5-10: 10-Death of the Ancient One .35 1.00 2.00
11-14: 11-Origin-r by Ditko. 14-Intro. God; last Dr. Strange
.25 .80 1.60
15-Iron Fist begins (origin), ends #25 .85 2.50 5.00
16-20 .35 1.00 2.00
21-24,26-28: 26-Hercules. 27-Satana. 28-Legion of Monsters
.25 .80 1.60
25-Byrne's 1st Iron Fist .85 2.50 5.00
29-56,61: 35-Origin/1st app. 3-D Man. 47-Origin new Ant-Man. 61-Star Lord .40 .80
57-Dr. Who (1st U.S. app.) .35 1.00 2.00
58-60-Dr. Who .25 .75 1.50
NOTE: N. Adams part inks-10, 12, 13. Austin a-50i, 56i; c-46i, 50i, 56i, 58. Brunner a-4i, 6p, 9-14p; c-9-14. Byrne a-47p, 48p. Giffen a-31p, 44p; c-44. Gil Kane a-1p, 2p, 15p; c-1p, 22-24p, 27p, 36p, 37p. Kirby a-26, 29-31, 35. Layton a-47i, 48i; c-47. McWilliams a-25i. Miller c-49p, 53p, 58p. Nebres a-44i; c-38i. Nino a-38i. Perez c/a-38p, 45p, 46p. Ploog a-38; c-5-7. Russell a-7p. Simonson a-60i; c-57. Starlin a-8p; c-8. Sutton a-31; 43, 50p, 61; c-50p, 61. #57-60 published with two different prices on-c.

MARVEL PRESENTS
October, 1975 - No. 12, Aug, 1977
Marvel Comics Group

1-Bloodstone app. .40 .80
2-Origin Bloodstone; Kirby-c .30 .60
3-Guardians of the Galaxy .50 1.00
4-7,9,11,12-Guardians of the Galaxy .40 .80
8-Reprints Silver Surfer #2 .40 .80
10-Starlin-a(p) .40 .80
NOTE: Austin a-6i. Kane c-1p.

MARVEL PREVIEW (Magazine) (Bizarre Adventures #25 on)
Feb, 1975 - No. 24, Winter, 1980 (B&W) ($1.00)
Marvel Comics Group

1-Man Gods From Beyond the Stars; Adams-a(i) & cover; Nino-a
.35 1.00 2.00
2-Origin The Punisher (see Amaz. Spider-Man 129); 1st app. Dominic Fortune; Morrow-c 17.00 50.00 120.00
3-Blade the Vampire Slayer .35 1.00 2.00
4-Star-Lord & Sword in the Star (origins & 1st app.)
.35 1.00 2.00

Marvel Mystery Comics #12, © MEG

Marvel Mystery Comics #30, © MEG

Marvel Premiere #15, © MEG

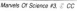

Marvels Of Science #3, © CC

Marvel Super Action #12, © MEG

Marvel Super-Heroes #12, © MEG

	Good	Fine	N-Mint
MARVEL PREVIEW (continued)			
5,6-Sherlock Holmes	.35	1.00	2.00
7-9: 7-Satana, Sword in the Star app. 8-Legion of Monsters. 9-Man-God; origin Star Hawk, ends #20	.35	1.00	2.00
10-24: 10-Thor the Mighty; Starlin-a. 11-Star-Lord; Byrne-a. 12-Haunt of Horror. 15-Star-Lord. 16-Detectives. 17-Black Mark by G. Kane. 18-Star-Lord. 19-Kull. 20-Bizarre Advs. 21-Moon Knight; Ditko-a. 22-King Arthur. 23-Bizarre Advs.; Miller-a. 24-Debut Paradox	.35	1.00	2.00

NOTE: **Adams** a-20i(r). **Buscema** a-22, 23. **Byrne** a-11. **Colan** a-16p, 18p, 23p; c-16p. **Giffen** a-7. **Infantino** a-14. **Kaluta** a-12; c-15. **Miller** a-23. **Morrow** a-8i; c-2-4. **Perez** a-20p. **Ploog** a-8. **Starlin** c-13, 14.

MARVEL SAGA, THE
Dec, 1985 - No. 25, Dec, 1987
Marvel Comics Group

1	.40	1.25	2.50
2-25		.60	1.20

NOTE: **Williamson** a-9i, 10i; c-10-12i, 14i, 16i.

MARVEL'S GREATEST COMICS (Marvel Coll. Item Classics #1-22)
No. 23, Oct, 1969 - No. 96, Jan, 1981
Marvel Comics Group

23-30	.25	.75	1.50
31-34,38-96		.50	1.00
35-37-Silver Surfer-r/Fantastic Four #48-50		.50	1.00

NOTE: Dr. Strange, Fantastic-4, Iron Man, Watcher-#23,24. Capt. America, Dr. Strange, Iron Man, Fantastic-4-#25-28. Fantastic Four-#38-96. **Buscema** a-85-92r; c-87-92r. **Ditko** a-23-28r. **Kirby** a(r)-1-82; c-75, 77p, 80p.

MARVELS OF SCIENCE
March, 1946 - No. 4, June, 1946
Charlton Comics

1-(1st Charlton comic)-A-Bomb story	7.00	21.00	50.00
2-4	3.70	11.00	26.00

MARVEL SPECIAL EDITION (Also see Special Collectors' Edition)
1975 - 1978 (84 pgs.) (Oversized)
Marvel Comics Group

1-Spider-Man(r); Ditko-a(r)	.25	.75	1.50
1-Star Wars ('77); r-Star Wars #1-3	.25	.75	1.50
2-Star Wars ('78); r-Star Wars #4-6		.50	1.00
3-Star Wars ('78, 116 pgs.); r-Star Wars #1-6		.50	1.00
3-Close Encounters ('78, 56 pgs., movie)		.50	1.00
V2#2(Spr. '80, $2.00, oversized)-"Star Wars: The Empire Strikes Back;" r-/Marvel Comics S. Special 16		.50	1.00

NOTE: **Chaykin** c/a-1(1977), 2, 3. **Stevens** a-2i(r), 3i(r).

MARVEL SPECTACULAR
Aug, 1973 - No. 19, Nov, 1975
Marvel Comics Group

1-Thor-r begin by Kirby		.30	.60
2-19		.25	.50

MARVEL SPOTLIGHT
11/71 - No. 33, 4/77; V2No. 1, 7/79 - V2No. 11, 3/81
Marvel Comics Group

1-Origin Red Wolf; Wood inks, Adams-c	.70	2.00	4.00
2-(Giant, 52pgs.)-Venus-r by Everett; origin/1st app. Werewolf By Night by Ploog; Adams-c	.35	1.00	2.00
3,4-Werewolf By Night ends #4		.60	1.20
5-Origin/1st app. Ghost Rider	1.35	4.00	8.00
6-8-Last Ploog issue	.50	1.50	3.00
9-11-Last Ghost Rider	.25	.75	1.50
12-27,30-33: 12-The Son of Satan begins (Origin). 25-Sinbad. 26-Scarecrow. 27-Sub-Mariner. 30-The Warriors Three, 31-Nick Fury. 32-Intro/partial origin Spider-Woman. 33-Deathlok	.25	.75	1.50
28,29-1st solo app. Moon Knight	.40	1.25	2.50

	Good	Fine	N-Mint
V2#1-11: Capt. Marvel #1-4. 5-Dragon Lord. 6,7-StarLord; origin #6. 9-11-Capt. Universe app.	.40		.80

NOTE: **Austin** c-V2#2i, 8. **J. Buscema** c/a-30p. **Ditko** a-V2#4, 5, 9-11; c-V2#4, 9-11. **Kane** c-21p, 32p. **Kirby** c-29. **McWilliams** a-20i. **Miller** a-V2#8p; c-V2#2, 5p, 7p, 8p. **Mooney** a-8i, 10i, 14-17p, 24p, 27, 32i. **Nasser** a-33p. **Ploog** a-2-5, 6-8p; c-3-9. **Sutton** a-9-11p, V2#6, 7. #29-25 cent & 30 cent issues exist.

MARVEL SUPER ACTION (Magazine)
January, 1976 (One Shot) (76 pgs.; black & white)
Marvel Comics Group

1-Origin & 2nd app. Dominic Fortune; The Punisher app., Weird World & The Huntress; Evans & Ploog-a	8.50	25.50	60.00

MARVEL SUPER-ACTION
May, 1977 - No. 37, Nov, 1981
Marvel Comics Group

1-Reprints Capt. America #100 by Kirby		.50	1.00
2,3,5-13: R/Capt. America #101,102,103-111. 11-Origin-r. 12,13-Classic Steranko-c/a(r)		.25	.50
4-Marvel Boy-r(origin)/M. Boy #1		.25	.50
14-37-Avengers-r in all (14,15-r/Avengers 55,56)		.25	.50

NOTE: **Buscema** a(r)-14p, 15p; c-18-20, 22, 35r-37. **Evans** a-1. **Everett** a-4. **Heath** a-4r. **Kirby** r-1-3, 5-11. **Ploog** a-1. **Smith** a-27r, 28r. **Steranko** a(r)-12p, 13p; c-12r, 13r.

MARVEL SUPER-HERO CONTEST OF CHAMPIONS
June, 1982 - No. 3, Aug, 1982 (Mini-Series)
Marvel Comics Group

1-3: Features nearly all Marvel characters currently appearing in their comics	.90	2.75	5.50

MARVEL SUPER HEROES
October, 1966 (25 cents, 68 pgs.) (1st Marvel One-shot)
Marvel Comics Group

1-r-origin Daredevil from D.D. #1; r-Avengers #2; G.A. Sub-Mariner-r/ Marvel Mystery No. 8 (H. Torch app.)	4.30	13.00	30.00

MARVEL SUPER-HEROES (Fantasy Masterpieces #1-11)
(Also see Giant-Size Super Heroes) (#12-20: 25 cents, 68 pgs.)
No. 12, 12/67 - No. 31, 11/71; No. 32, 9/72 - No. 105, 1/82
Marvel Comics Group

12-Origin & 1st app. Capt. Marvel of the Kree; G.A. H. Torch, Destroyer, Capt. America, Black Knight, Sub-Mariner-r	4.30	13.00	30.00
13-2nd app. Capt. Marvel; G.A. Black Knight, Torch, Vision, Capt. America, Sub-Mariner-r	2.15	6.50	15.00
14-Amazing Spider-Man (new-a); G.A. Sub-Mariner, Torch, Mercury, Black Knight, Capt. America reprints	.35	1.00	2.00
15-Black Bolt cameo in Medusa; G.A. Black Knight, Sub-Mariner, Black Marvel, Capt. America-r	.35	1.00	2.00
16-Origin & 1st app. Phantom Eagle; G.A. Torch, Capt. America, Black Knight, Patriot, Sub-Mariner-r	.35	1.00	2.00
17-Origin Black Knight; G.A. Torch, Sub-Mariner, All-Winners Squad reprints	.35	1.00	2.00
18-Origin Guardians of the Galaxy; G.A. Sub-Mariner, All-Winners Squad-r	.50	1.50	3.00
19-Ka-Zar; G.A. Torch, Marvel Boy, Black Knight, Sub-Mariner-r; Smith-c(p); Tuska-a(r)	.35	1.00	2.00
20-Capt. Marvel; G.A. Torch; r/Young Men #24 w/-c	.35	1.00	2.00
21-31: All-r issues. 31-Last Giant issue	.35	1.00	2.00
32-105: All-r issues	.50		1.00

NOTE: **Austin** a-104. **Colan** a-12p, 13p, 15p, 18p; c-12, 13, 15, 18. **Everett** a-14i, 15i(r), 18r, 19r, 33r; c-85(r). **New Kirby** c-22, 27. **Maneely** a-15r, 19r. **Severin** a-83-85i(r), 100-02r; c-100-02r. **Starlin** c-47. **Tuska** a-19p.

MARVEL SUPER-HEROES SECRET WARS (See Secret Wars II)
May, 1984 - No. 12, Apr, 1985 (Limited series)
Marvel Comics Group

1	.60	1.75	3.50
2-12: 6-The Wasp dies. 7-Intro. new Spider-Woman 8-Spider-Man's			

MARVEL SUPER-HEROES SECRET WARS (continued)

	Good	Fine	N-Mint
new costume explained	.35	1.00	2.00

MARVEL SUPER SPECIAL (See Marvel Comics Super . . .)

MARVEL TAILS STARRING PETER PORKER THE SPECTACULAR SPIDER-HAM
Nov., 1983 (One Shot)
Marvel Comics Group

	Good	Fine	N-Mint
1-Peter Porker, the Spectacular Spider-Ham, Captain Americat, Goose Rider, Hulk Bunny app.	.25	.75	1.50

MARVEL TALES (Formerly Marvel Mystery #1-92)
No. 93, Aug, 1949 - No. 159, Aug, 1957
Marvel/Atlas Comics (MCI)

	Good	Fine	N-Mint
93	34.00	103.00	240.00
94-Everett-a	28.50	86.00	200.00
95,96,99,101,103,105	16.00	48.00	110.00
97-Sun Girl, 2 pgs; Kirbyish-a; one story used in N.Y. State Legislative document	23.00	70.00	160.00
98-Krigstein-a	17.00	51.00	120.00
100	17.00	51.00	120.00
102-Wolverton-a "The End of the World," 6 pgs.	29.00	87.00	205.00
104-Wolverton-a "Gateway to Horror," 6 pgs; Heath-c	26.50	80.00	185.00
106,107-Krigstein-a. 106-Decapitation story	14.00	42.00	100.00
108-120: 118-Hypo-c/panels in End of World story. 120-Jack Katz-a	8.50	25.50	60.00
121,123-131: 128-Flying Saucer-c. 131-Last precode (2/55)	7.00	20.00	48.00
122-Kubert-a	7.50	22.00	52.00
132,133,135-141,143,145	4.00	12.00	28.00
134-Krigstein, Kubert-a; flying saucer-c	5.00	15.00	35.00
142-Krigstein-a	4.65	14.00	32.00
144-Williamson/Krenkel-a, 3 pgs.	5.00	15.00	35.00
146,148-151,154,155,158	2.85	8.50	20.00
147-Ditko-a	3.70	11.00	26.00
152-Wood, Morrow-a	4.00	12.00	28.00
153-Everett End of World c/story	4.00	12.00	28.00
156-Torres-a	3.50	10.50	24.00
157,159-Krigstein-a	4.65	14.00	32.00

NOTE: *Andru* a-103. *Briefer* a-118. *Check* a-147. *Colan* a-105, 107, 118, 120, 121, 127, 131. *Drucker* a-127, 135, 141, 146, 150. *Everett* a-98, 104, 106(2), 108(2), 131, 148, 151, 153, 155; c-109, 111, 114, 117, 127, 143, 147-151, 153, 155, 156. *Forte* a-125, 130. *Heath* a-110, 113, 118, 119; c-104-106, 130. *Gil Kane* a-117. *Lawrence* a-130. *Maneely* a-111, 126, 129; c-108, 116, 120, 129, 152. *Mooney* a-114. *Morrow* a-150, 152, 156. *Orlando* a-149, 151, 157. *Pakula* a-121, 144, 150, 152. *Powell* a-136, 137, 150, 154. *Ravielli* a-117. *Rico* a-97, 99. *Romita* a-108. *Sekowsky* a-96-98. *Shores* a-110. *Sinnott* a-105, 116. *Tuska* a-114. *Whitney* a-107. *Wildey* a-126, 138.

MARVEL TALES (. . . Annual #1,2; . . . Starring Spider-Man #123 on)
1964 - Present (No. 1-32: 72 pgs.)
Marvel Comics Group

	Good	Fine	N-Mint
1-Origin Spider-Man, Hulk, Ant/Giant Man, Iron Man, Thor, & Sgt. Fury; all-r	14.00	42.00	100.00
2 ('65)-r-X-Men #1(origin), Avengers #1(origin) & origin Dr. Strange/Str. Tales #115	6.50	19.50	45.00
3 (7/66)-Spider-Man-r begin	2.85	8.50	20.00
4,5	1.15	3.50	7.00
6-10	.85	2.50	5.00
11-32: 13-Origin Marvel Boy-r/M: Boy #1. 30-New Angel story. 32-Last 72 pg. issue	.35	1.00	2.00
33-76,80-97: 75-Origin Spider-Man-r		.50	1.00
77-79-Drug issues-r/Spider-Man No. 96-98		.50	1.00
98-Death of Gwen Stacy-r/A. Spider-Man #121		.50	1.00
99-Death Green Goblin-r/A. Spider-Man #122		.50	1.00
100-(52 pgs.)-New Hawkeye/Two Gun Kid story		.50	1.00

	Good	Fine	N-Mint
101-105-All Spider-Man-r		.50	1.00
106-1st Punisher-r/A. Spider-Man #129	1.15	3.50	7.00
107-133-All Spider-Man-r		.40	.80
134-136-Dr. Strange-r begin; SpM stories continue. 134-Dr. Strange r/Strange Tales #110		.40	.80
137-Origin-r Dr. Strange; shows original unprinted-c & origin Spider-Man/Amazing Fantasy #15	.40	1.25	2.50
137-Nabisco giveaway		.50	1.00
138-Reprints all Amazing Spider-Man #1; begin reprints of Spider-Man with covers similar to originals	.40	1.25	2.50
139-144: r/Amazing Spider-Man #2-7		.60	1.20
145-149,151-190: Spider-Man-r continue w/#8 on		.50	1.00
150 ($1.00, 52 pgs.)-Miller-r/Amaz. Spider-Man Annual #14			
191 (68 pgs., $1.50)-r/Spider-Man 96-98		.50	1.00
192 (52 pgs., $1.25)-r-Spider-Man 121,122		.50	1.00
193-199: 193-Byrne-r/Marvel Team-up begin		.50	1.00
200-Double size ($1.25)-Miller c/a(p)		.65	1.30
201-208,210-221: 208-Last Byrne-r		.40	.80
209-Reprints 1st app. The Punisher/Amazing Spider-Man #129; Punisher reprints begin (not in #210)	.35	1.00	2.00
222-Reprints origin Punisher/Spectacular Spider-Man #83; last Punisher reprint		.40	.80
223-McFarlane-a		.60	1.20
224-234		.50	1.00

NOTE: All are reprints with some new art. *Austin* a-100i. *Byrne* a(r)-193-198p, 201-208p. *Ditko* a-1-30, 83, 100, 137-155. *G. Kane* a-71, 81, 98-101p; c-125-127p, 130p. 137-155. *McFarlane* c-223-232. *Mooney* a-63, 95-97i, 103(i). *Nasser* a-100p.

MARVEL TEAM-UP (See Marvel Treasury Edition #18 & Official Marvel Index To . . .)
March, 1972 - No. 150, Feb, 1985
Marvel Comics Group

NOTE: Spider-Man team-ups in all but Nos. 18,23,26,29,32,35,97,104,105,137.

	Good	Fine	N-Mint
1-H-T	3.60	11.00	25.00
2,3-H-T	1.35	4.00	8.00
4-X-Men	2.15	6.50	15.00
5-10: 5-Vision. 6-Thing. 7-Thor. 8-The Cat. 9-Iron Man. 10-H-T	.70	2.00	4.00
11-20: 11-Inhumans. 12-Werewolf. 13-Capt. America. 14-Sub-Mariner. 15-Ghost Rider (new). 16-Capt. Marvel. 17-Mr. Fantastic. 18-H-T/Hulk. 19-Ka-Zar. 20-Black Panther	.25	.75	1.50
21-30: 21-Dr. Strange. 22-Hawkeye. 23-H-T/Iceman (X-Men app.). 24-Brother Voodoo. 25-Daredevil. 26-H-T/Thor. 27-Hulk. 28-Hercules. 29-H-T/Iron Man. 30-Falcon	.25	.75	1.50
31-40: 31-Iron Fist. 32-H-T/Son of Satan. 33-Nighthawk. 34-Valkyrie. 35-H-T/Dr. Strange. 36-Frankenstein. 37-Man-Wolf. 38-Beast. 39-H-T. 40-Sons of the Tiger/H-T	.25	.75	1.50
41-50: 41-Scarlet Witch. 42-The Vision. 43-Dr. Doom; retells origin. 44-Moondragon. 45-Killraven. 46-Deathlok. 47-Thing. 48-Iron Man. 49,50-Dr. Strange/Iron Man	.25	.75	1.50
51,52,56-58: 51-Dr. Strange/Iron Man. 52-Capt. America. 56-Daredevil. 57-Black Widow. 58-Ghost Rider		.50	1.00
53-Woodgod/Hulk; new X-Men app., 1st by Byrne (1/77)	1.00	3.00	6.00
54-Hulk/Woodgod; Byrne-a(p)	.60	1.75	3.50
55,59,60: 55-Warlock. 59-Yellowjacket/The Wasp. 60-The Wasp-All Byrne-a	.60	1.75	3.50
61-70: 61-H-T. 62-Ms. Marvel. 63-Iron Fist. 64-Daughters of the Dragon. 65-Capt. Britain (1st U.S. app.). 66-Capt. Britain; 1st app. Arcade. 67-Tigra. 68-Man-Thing. 69-Havock. 70-Thor-All Byrne-a	.25	.75	1.50
71-74,76-78,80: 71-Falcon. 72-Iron Man. 73-Daredevil. 74-Not Ready for Prime Time Players (Belushi). 76-Dr. Strange. 77-Ms. Marvel. 78-Wonder Man. 80-Dr. Strange/Clea	.25	.75	1.50
75,79: 75-Power Man. 79-Mary Jane Watson as Red Sonja. Both Byrne-a(p)	.40	1.25	2.50

Marvel Tales #98 (1st series), © MEG

Marvel Tales #5 (2nd series), © MEG

Marvel Team-Up #4, © MEG

Marvel Team-Up #89, © MEG

Marvel Triple Action #45, © MEG

Marvel Two-In-One #84, © MEG

	Good	Fine	N-Mint
MARVEL TEAM-UP (continued)			

81-88,90: 81-Satana. 82-Black Widow. 83-Nick Fury. 84-Shang-Chi.
85-Shang-Chi/Black Widow/Nick Fury. 86-Guardians of the
Galaxy. 87-Black Panther. 88-The Invisible Girl. 90-Beast

	.40		.80
89-Nightcrawler	.25	.75	1.50

91-99: 91-Ghost Rider. 92-Hawkeye. 93-Werewolf by Night. 94-SpM
vs. The Shroud. 95-Nick Fury/Shield; intro. Mockingbird. 96-
Howard The Duck. 97-Spider-Woman/Hulk. 98-Black Widow. 99-

Machine Man	.40		.80
100-Fantastic-4(Double size); origin/1st app. Karma, one of the New			

Mutants; origin Storm; X-Men x-over; Miller-a/c(p); Byrne-a on

new X-Men	1.00	3.00	6.00

101-116: 101-Nighthawk(Ditko-a). 102-Doc Samson. 103-Ant-Man. 104-
Hulk/Ka-Zar. 105-Hulk/Powerman/Iron Fist. 106-Capt. America.
107-She-Hulk. 108-Paladin; Dazzler cameo. 109-Paladin/Dazzler.
110-Iron Man. 111-Devil-Slayer. 112-King Kull. 113-Quasar. 114-

Falcon. 115-Thor. 116-Valkyrie	.40		.80
117-Wolverine	.50	1.50	3.00
118-Professor X (Double-size)	.25	.75	1.50

119-149: 119-Gargoyle. 120-Dominic Fortune. 121-Human Torch. 122-
Man-Thing. 123-Daredevil. 124-The Beast. 125-Tigra. 126-Hulk &
Powerman/Son of Satan. 127-The Watcher. 128-Capt. America.
129-The Vision. 130-Scarlet Witch. 131-Frogman. 132-Mr. Fantas-
tic. 133-Fantastic-4. 134-Jack of Hearts. 135-Kitty Pryde; X-Men
cameo. 136-Wonder Man. 137-Aunt May/Franklin Richards. 138-
Sandman. 139-Nick Fury, 140-Black Widow. 141-Daredevil; new
SpM/Black Widow app. 142-Captain Marvel. 143-Starfox. 144-
Moon Knight. 145-Iron Man. 146-Nomad. 147-Human Torch; SpM

old costume. 148-Thor. 149-Cannonball	.40		.80
150-X-Men ($1.00); B. Smith-c	.50	1.50	3.00
Annual 1(1976)-New X-Men app.	1.35	4.00	8.00
Annual 2(12/79)-SpM/Hulk	.25	.75	1.50
Annual 3(11/80)-Hulk/Power Man/Machine Man/Iron Fist; Miller-c(p)			
	.25	.75	1.50
Annual 4(10/81)-SpM/Daredevil/Moon Knight/Power Man/Iron Fist;			
brief origin of each; Miller-c(p)/a	.25	.75	1.50
Annual 5(1982)-SpM/The Thing/Scarlet Witch/Dr. Strange/Quasar			
	.25	.75	1.50
Annual 6(10/83)-New Mutants, Cloak & Dagger app.			
	.25	.75	1.50
Annual 7(10/84)-Alpha Flight; Byrne-c(i)	.25	.75	1.50

NOTE: *Art Adams* c-141p. *Austin* a-79i; c-76i, 79i, 96i, 101i, 112i, 130i. *Bolle* a-9i. *Byrne*
a(p)-53-55, 59-70, 75, 79, 100; c-69p, 70p, 72p, 75, 76p, 79p, 129i, 133i. *Colan* a-87p.
Ditko a-101. *Kane* a(p)-4-6, 13, 14, 16-19, 23; c(p)-4, 13, 14, 17-19, 23, 25, 26, 32-35, 37,
41, 44, 45, 47, 53, 54. *Miller* c-95p, 99p, 102p, 106. *Mooney* a-2i, 7i, 8, 10p, 11p, 16i,
24p, 29p, 72, 93i; Annual 5. *Nasser* a-89p; c-101p. *Simonson* c-99i, 148. *Paul Smith*
c-131, 132. *Starlin* c-27. *Sutton* a-93p. "H-T" means Human Torch; "SpM" means
Spider-Man; "S-M" means Sub-Mariner.

MARVEL TREASURY EDITION ($1.50-$2.50)
Sept, 1974 - No. 28, 1981 (100 pgs.; oversized, reprints)
Marvel Comics Group

1-Spectacular Spider-Man	.50	1.50	3.00
2-Fantastic Four, Silver Surfer	.25	.75	1.50
3-The Mighty Thor	.25	.75	1.50
4-Conan the Barbarian; Smith-c/a	.25	.75	1.50
5-14,16,17: 5-The Hulk (origin), 6-Doctor Strange, 7-Avengers, 8-			

Christmas stories; Spider-Man, Hulk, Nick Fury, 9-Giant; Super-
hero Team-up, 10-Thor, 11-Fantastic Four, 12-Howard the Duck,
13-Giant Super-hero Holiday Grab-Bag, 14-Spider-Man, 16-
Super-hero Team-up; The Defenders (origin) & Valkyrie, 17-

The Hulk	.60		1.20
15-Conan; Smith, Adams-i	.35	1.00	2.00
18-The Astonishing Spider-Man; Spider-Man's 1st team-ups with the			
X-Men, Ghost Rider & Werewolf by Night	.25	.75	1.50
19-28: 19-Conan the Barbarian, 20-Hulk, 21-Fantastic Four, 22-			

Spider-Man, 23-Conan, 24-Rampaging Hulk, 25-Spider-Man vs.

	Good	Fine	N-Mint

The Hulk, 26-The Hulk; Wolverine app., 27-Spider-Man, 28-

Spider-Man/Superman; (origin of each)	.60		1.20

NOTE: *Reprints-2,3,5,7-9,13,14,16,17. Adams* a(i)-6, 15. *Brunner* a-6, 12; c-6. *Buscema*
a-15, 19, 28; c-28. *Colan* c-12p. *Ditko* a-1, 6. *Kirby* a-2, 10, 11; c-7. *Smith* a-4, 15, 19;
c-4, 19.

MARVEL TREASURY OF OZ (See MGM's Marvelous . . .)
1975 (oversized) ($1.50)
Marvel Comics Group

1-The Marvelous Land of Oz; Buscema-a	.60		1.20

MARVEL TREASURY SPECIAL (Also see 2001: A Space Odyssey)
1974; 1976 (84 pgs.; oversized) ($1.50)
Marvel Comics Group

Vol. 1-Spider-Man, Torch, Sub-Mariner, Avengers "Giant Superhero

Holiday Grab-Bag"	.50		1.00
Vol. 1-Capt. America's Bicentennial Battles (6/76)-Kirby-a; Smith			
inks, 11 pgs.	.50		1.00

MARVEL TRIPLE ACTION
2/72 - No. 24, 3/75; No. 25, 8/75 - No. 47, 4/79
Marvel Comics Group

1-Giant (52 pgs.)	.25	.75	1.50
2-47: 7-Starlin-c. 45,46-X-Men-r	.50		1.00
Giant-Size 1(5/75), 2(7/75)	.50		1.00

NOTE: Fantastic Four reprints-#1-4; Avengers reprints-#5 on. *Buscema* a(r)-35p, 36p,
38p, 39p, 41, 42, 43p, 44p, 46p, 47p. *Ditko* a-2r; c-47. *Kirby* a(r)-1-4p. *Tuska* a(r)-40p,
43i, 46i, 47i.

MARVEL TWO-IN-ONE (See The Thing)
January, 1974 - No. 100, June, 1983
Marvel Comics Group

1-Thing team-ups begin	1.25	3.75	7.50
2-4: 3-Daredevil app.	.60	1.75	3.50
5-Guardians of the Galaxy	.70	2.00	4.00
6-10	.50	1.50	3.00
11-20	.35	1.10	2.20
21-40: 29-2nd app. Spider-Woman	.25	.70	1.40
41,42,44-49		.50	1.00
43,50,53-55-Byrne-a. 54-Death of Deathlok	.40	1.25	2.50
51-Miller-a(p)	.50	1.50	3.00
52-Moon Knight app.	.35	1.00	2.00
56-82: 60-Intro. Impossible Woman. 61-63-Warlock app.			
		.40	.80
83,84-Alpha Flight app.	.50	1.50	3.00
85-99: 93-Jocasta dies. 96-X-Men cameo		.30	.60
100-Double size, Byrne scripts	.25	.75	1.50
Annual 1(6/76)-Liberty Legion x-over	.25	.80	1.60
Annual 2(2/77)-Starlin c/a; Thanos dies	1.25	3.75	7.50
Annual 3(7/78), 4(9/79)		.50	1.00
Annual 5(9/80), 6(10/81)		.40	.80
Annual 7(10/82)-The Thing/Champion; Sasquatch, Colossus app.			
		.50	1.00

NOTE: *Austin* a-52i, 54i, 56i, 58i, 61i, 63i, 66i. *John Buscema* a-30p, 45; c-30p. *Byrne*
a-43p, 50p, 53-55p; c-43, 53p, 56p, 58i, 99i. *Gil Kane* a-1p, 2p; c(p)-1-3, 9, 11, 14, 28.
Kirby c-10, 12, 19p, 20, 25, 27. *Mooney* a-18i, 38i, 90i. *Nasser* a-70p. *Perez* a-56-58p,
60p, 64p, 65p; c-32p, 33p, 42p, 50-52p, 54p, 55p, 57p, 58p, 61-66p, 70p. *Roussos* a-
Annual 1. *Simonson* c-43i; Annual 6i. *Starlin* c-6. Annual 1. *Tuska* a-6p.

MARVEL UNIVERSE (See Official Handbook Of The . . .)

MARVIN MOUSE
September, 1957
Atlas Comics (BPC)

1-Everett c/a; Maneely-a	3.00	9.00	21.00

MARY JANE & SNIFFLES (See 4-Color #402, 474 & Looney Tunes)
MARY MARVEL COMICS (Monte Hale #29 on) (Also see Captain
Marvel #18, Marvel Family, Shazam, & Wow)
Dec, 1945 - No. 28, Sept, 1948

MARY MARVEL COMICS (continued)
Fawcett Publications

	Good	Fine	N-Mint
1-Captain Marvel intro. Mary on-c; intro/origin Georgia Sivana	59.00	178.00	415.00
2	28.00	84.00	195.00
3	20.00	60.00	140.00
4	16.00	48.00	110.00
5-8: 8-Bulletgirl x-over in Mary Marvel	13.00	40.00	90.00
9,10	10.00	30.00	70.00
11-20	7.50	22.00	52.00
21-28	6.50	19.50	45.00

MARY POPPINS (See Movie Comics & Walt Disney Showcase No. 17)

MARY'S GREATEST APOSTLE (St. Louis Grignion de Montfort)
No date (16 pages; paper cover)
Catechetical Guild (Topix) (Giveaway)

nn	1.70	5.00	12.00

MARY WORTH (See Harvey Comics Hits #55 & Love Stories of . . .)
March, 1956
Argo

1	3.50	10.50	24.00

MASK (TV)
Dec, 1985 - No. 4, Mar, 1986; Feb, 1987 - No. 9, Oct, 1987
DC Comics

1-(Mini-series) (Sat. morning TV show)	.35	1.00	2.00
2-4	.25	.70	1.40
1-(2nd series)		.60	1.20
2-9		.45	.90

MASK COMICS
Feb-Mar, 1945 - No. 2, Apr-May, 1945; No. 2, Fall, 1945
Rural Home Publications

1-Classic L. B. Cole Satan-c/a; Palais-a	74.00	223.00	520.00
2-(Scarce)Classic L. B. Cole Satan-c; Black Rider, The Boy Magician, & The Collector app.	38.00	114.00	265.00
2(Fall, 1945)-No publ.-same as regular #2; L. B. Cole-c	27.00	81.00	190.00

MASKED BANDIT, THE
1952
Avon Periodicals

nn-Kinstler-a	8.50	25.50	60.00

MASKED MAN, THE
12/84 - No. 10, 4/86; No. 11, 10/87; No. 12, 4/88 ($1.75-$2.00; Baxter)
Eclipse Comics

1-Origin retold	.35	1.00	2.00
2-8: 3-Origin Aphid-Man	.30	.90	1.80
9-12 ($2.00; B&W)	.30	.90	1.80

MASKED MARVEL (See Keen Detective Funnies)
Sept, 1940 - No. 3, Dec, 1940
Centaur Publications

1-The Masked Marvel begins	83.00	250.00	585.00
2,3: 2-Gustavson, Tarpe Mills-a	53.00	160.00	375.00

MASKED RAIDER, THE (Billy The Kid #9 on; Frontier Scout, Daniel Boone #10-13; also see Blue Bird)
6/55 - No. 8, 7/57; No. 14, 8/58 - No. 30, 6/61
Charlton Comics

1-Painted-c	4.00	12.00	28.00
2	2.30	7.00	16.00
3-8: 8-Billy The Kid app.	1.70	5.00	12.00
14,16-30: 22-Rocky Lane app.	1.15	3.50	8.00
15-Williamson-a, 7 pgs.	2.35	7.00	16.00

MASKED RANGER
April, 1954 - No. 9, Aug, 1955
Premier Magazines

	Good	Fine	N-Mint
1-The M. Ranger, his horse Streak, & The Crimson Avenger (origin) begin, end #9; Woodbridge/Frazetta-a	16.00	48.00	110.00
2,3	4.00	12.00	28.00
4-8-All Woodbridge-a. 5-Jesse James by Woodbridge. 6-Billy The Kid by Woodbridge. 7-Wild Bill Hickok by Woodbridge. 8-Jim Bowie's Life Story	5.50	16.50	38.00
9-Torres-a; Wyatt Earp by Woodbridge	6.00	18.00	42.00

NOTE: **Check** a-1. **Woodbridge** c/a-1, 4-9.

MASK OF DR. FU MANCHU, THE (See Dr. Fu Manchu)
1951
Avon Periodicals

1-Sax Rohmer adapt.; Wood c/a, 26 pgs., Hollingsworth-a	60.00	180.00	420.00

MASQUE OF THE RED DEATH (See Movie Classics)

MASTER, THE (Also see Young Master)
1989 - Present ($1.95, B&W)
New Comics

1-5: Val Mayerik painted-c/a in all	.35	1.00	2.00

MASTER COMICS (Combined with Slam Bang Comics #7 on)
Mar, 1940 - No. 133, Apr, 1953 (No. 1-6: oversized issues)
(#1-3: 15 cents, 52pgs.; #4-6: 10 cents, 36pgs.)
Fawcett Publications

1-Origin Master Man; The Devil's Dagger, El Carim, Master of Magic, Rick O'Say, Morton Murch, White Rajah, Shipwreck Roberts, Frontier Marshal, Streak Sloan, Mr. Clue begin (all features end #6)	208.00	520.00	1250.00
2	100.00	250.00	600.00
3-5	67.00	170.00	400.00
6-Last Master Man	75.00	190.00	450.00

NOTE: #1-6 rarely found in near mint to mint condition due to large-size format.

7-(10/40)-Bulletman, Zoro, the Mystery Man (ends #22), Lee Granger, Jungle King, & Buck Jones begin; only app. The War Bird & Mark Swift & the Time Retarder	125.00	315.00	750.00
8-The Red Gaucho (ends #13), Captain Venture (ends #22) & The Planet Princess begin	50.00	150.00	350.00
9,10: 10-Lee Granger ends	45.00	135.00	315.00
11-Origin Minute-Man	100.00	300.00	600.00
12	53.00	160.00	375.00
13-Origin Bulletgirl	92.00	275.00	550.00
14-16: 14-Companions Three begins, ends #31	45.00	135.00	315.00
17-20: 17-Raboy-a on Bulletman begins. 20-Captain Marvel cameo app. in Bulletman	45.00	135.00	315.00
21-(Scarce)-Captain Marvel x-over in Bulletman; Capt. Nazi origin	182.00	545.00	1275.00
22-Captain Marvel Jr. x-over in Bulletman; Capt. Nazi app; bondage-c	150.00	450.00	1050.00
23-Capt. Marvel Jr. begins, vs. Capt. Nazi	121.00	365.00	850.00
24,25,29	45.00	135.00	315.00
26-28,30-Captain Marvel Jr. vs. Capt. Nazi. 30-Flag-c	45.00	135.00	315.00
31,32: 32-Last El Carim & Buck Jones; Balbo, the Boy Magician intro. in El Carim	31.00	92.00	215.00
33-Balbo, the Boy Magician (ends #47), Hopalong Cassidy (ends #49) begins	31.00	92.00	215.00
34-Capt. Marvel Jr. vs. Capt. Nazi	31.00	92.00	215.00
35	31.00	92.00	215.00
36-40: 40-Flag-c	27.00	81.00	190.00
41-Bulletman, Capt. Marvel Jr. & Bulletgirl x-over in Minute-Man; only app. Crime Crusaders Club (Capt. Marvel Jr., Minute-Man,			

Mary Marvel Comics #1, © FAW

The Mask Of Dr. Fu Manchu #1, © AVON

Master Comics #22, © FAW

Master Of Kung Fu #17, © MEG

Matt Slade Gunfighter #1, © MEG

Maverick #7, © Warner Bros.

	Good	Fine	N-Mint
MASTER COMICS (continued)			
Bulletman & Bulletgirl)-only team in Fawcett Comics	31.00	92.00	215.00
42-47,49: 47-Hitler becomes Corpl. Hitler Jr. 49-Last Minute-Man	17.00	51.00	120.00
48-Intro. Bulletboy; Capt. Marvel cameo in Minute-Man	19.00	58.00	135.00
50-Radar, Nyoka the Jungle Girl begin; Capt. Marvel x-over in Radar; origin Radar	13.00	40.00	90.00
51-58	8.50	25.50	60.00
59-62: Nyoka serial ''Terrible Tiara'' in all; 61-Capt. Marvel Jr. 1st meets Uncle Marvel	10.00	30.00	70.00
63-80	6.50	19.50	45.00
81-92,94-99: 88-Hopalong Cassidy begins (ends #94). 95-Tom Mix begins (ends #133)	5.70	17.00	40.00
93-Krigstein-a	6.00	18.00	42.00
100	6.50	19.50	45.00
101-106-Last Bulletman	4.30	13.00	30.00
107-131	3.70	11.00	26.00
132-B&W and color illos in **POP**	4.30	13.00	30.00
133-Bill Battle app.	5.70	17.00	40.00

NOTE: **Mac Raboy** a-15-39, 40 in part, 42, 58; c-21-49, 51, 52, 54, 56, 58, 59.

MASTER DETECTIVE
1964 (Reprints)
Super Comics

10,17,18: 17-Young King Cole; McWilliams-a	.40	1.20	2.40

MASTER OF KUNG FU (Formerly Special Marvel Edition; see Deadly Hands of Kung Fu & Marvel Comics Presents)
No. 17, April, 1974 - No. 125, June, 1983
Marvel Comics Group

17-Starlin-a; intro Black Jack Tarr	.60	1.75	3.50
18-20: 19-Man-Thing app.	.35	1.00	2.00
21-23,25-30		.60	1.20
24-Starlin, Simonson-a	.25	.75	1.50
31-99: 33-1st Leiko Wu		.50	1.00
100-(Double size)		.60	1.20
101-117,119-124: 104-Cerebus cameo		.50	1.00
118,125-(Double size)		.60	1.20
Giant Size 1(9/74)-Russell-a; Yellow Claw-r	.35	1.00	2.00
Giant Size 2-r/Yellow Claw #1	.25	.75	1.50
Giant Size 3,4(6/75)-r/Yellow Claw		.60	1.20
Annual 1(4/76)-Iron Fist		.60	1.20

NOTE: **Austin** c-63i, 74i. **Buscema** c-44p. **Gulacy** a(p)-18-20, 22, 25, 29-31, 33-35, 38, 39, 40(p&i), 42-50. Giant Size #1, 2; c-51, 55, 64, 67. **Gil Kane** c(p)-20, 38, 39, 42, 45, 59, 63. **Nebres** c-73i. **Starlin** a-17p; c-54. **Sutton** a-42i.

MASTER OF THE WORLD (See 4-Color #1157)

MASTERS OF TERROR (Magazine)
July, 1975 - No. 2, Sept, 1975 (Black & White) (All Reprints)
Marvel Comics Group

1-Brunner, Smith-a; Morrow-c; Adams-a(i)(r); Starlin-a(p); Gil Kane-a	.30	.90	1.80
2-Reese, Kane, Mayerik-a; Steranko-c	.60	1.20	

MASTERS OF THE UNIVERSE
Dec, 1982 - No. 3, Feb, 1983 (mini-series)
DC Comics

1	.60	1.20	
2,3: 2-Origin He-Man & Ceril	.50	1.00	

NOTE: **Alcala** a-1i, 2i. **Tuska** a-1-3p; c-1-3p. #2 has 75 & 95 cent cover price.

MASTERS OF THE UNIVERSE (Comic Album)
1984 (8½x11''; $2.95; 64 pgs.)
Western Publishing Co.

11362-Based on Mattel toy & cartoon	.50	1.50	2.95

MASTERS OF THE UNIVERSE (TV)
May, 1986 - No. 12, March, 1988
Star Comics/Marvel #? on

	Good	Fine	N-Mint
1		.55	1.10
2-7		.40	.80
8-12 ($1.00)		.50	1.00
...The Motion Picture (11/87, $2.00)-Tuska-p	.35	1.00	2.00

MASTERWORKS SERIES OF GREAT COMIC BOOK ARTISTS, THE
May, 1983 - No. 3, Dec, 1983 (Baxter paper)
Sea Gate Distributors/DC Comics

1,2-Shining Knight by Frazetta r-/Adventure. 2-Tomahawk by Frazetta-r	.35	1.00	2.00
3-Wrightson-c/a(r)	.35	1.00	2.00

MATT SLADE GUNFIGHTER (Kid Slade Gunfighter #5 on?; See Western Gunfighters)
May, 1956 - No. 4, Nov, 1956
Atlas Comics (SPI)

1-Williamson/Torres-a; Maneely-c/a	7.00	21.00	50.00
2-Williamson-a	5.00	15.00	35.00
3,4: 4-Maneely-c	2.65	8.00	18.00

NOTE: **Maneely** a-1-4; c-1, 4. **Roth** a-2-4. **Severin** a-1-4.

MAUD
1906 (32 pgs. in color; 10x15½'') (cardboard covers)
Frederick A. Stokes Co.

By Fred Opper	15.00	45.00	105.00

MAVERICK (TV)
No. 892, 4/58 - No. 19, 4-6/62 (All have photo-c)
Dell Publishing Co.

4-Color 892 (#1): James Garner/Jack Kelly photo-c begin	7.00	21.00	50.00
4-Color 930,945,962,980,1005 (6-8/59)	5.00	15.00	35.00
7 (10/12/59) - 14: Last Garner/Kelly-c	4.00	12.00	28.00
15-18: Jack Kelly/Roger Moore photo-c	4.00	12.00	28.00
19-Jack Kelly photo-c	4.00	12.00	28.00

MAVERICK MARSHAL
Nov, 1958 - No. 7, May, 1960
Charlton Comics

1	1.60	4.80	11.00
2-7	.90	2.75	6.50

MAX BRAND (See Silvertip)

MAYA (See Movie Classics)
March, 1968
Gold Key

1 (10218-803)(TV)	1.15	3.50	8.00

MAYHEM
May, 1989 - No. 4, 1989 ($2.50, B&W, 52 pgs.)
Dark Horse Comics

1-4: The Mark, The Mask & Mecha in all	.40	1.25	2.50

MAZE AGENCY, THE
Dec, 1988 - Present ($1.95-$2.50, color)
Comico/Innovation Publishing #8 on

1-6 ($1.95)	.35	1.00	2.00
7 ($2.50)-Last Comico issue	.40	1.25	2.50
8-10 ($1.95)	.35	1.00	2.00
Special 1 (89?, $2.75)-Staton-p	.45	1.40	2.80

MAZIE (...& Her Friends) (See Mortie, Stevie & Tastee-Freez)
1953 - #12, 1954; #13, 12/54 - #22, 9/56; #23, 9/57 - #28, 8/58
Mazie Comics(Magazine Publ.)/Harvey Publ. No. 13-on

1-(Teen-age)-Stevie's girl friend	1.60	4.80	11.00

MAZIE (continued)	Good	Fine	N-Mint
2	.85	2.60	6.00
3-10	.70	2.00	5.00
11-28	.50	1.50	3.00

MAZIE
1950 - No. 7, 1951 (5 cents) (5x7¼"-miniature)(52 pgs.)
Nation Wide Publishers

	Good	Fine	N-Mint
1-Teen-age	1.70	5.00	12.00
2-7	.85	2.60	6.00

MAZINGER (See First Comics Graphic Novel #17)

'MAZING MAN
Jan, 1986 - No. 12, Dec, 1986
DC Comics

1		.50	1.00
2-11: 7,8-Hembeck-a		.40	.80
12-Dark Knight part-c by Miller		.40	.80
Special 1('87), 2(4/88) (both $2.00)	.30	.90	1.80

McCRORY'S CHRISTMAS BOOK
1955 (36 pgs.; slick cover)
Western Printing Co. (McCrory Stores Corp. giveaway)

nn-Painted-c	1.35	4.00	8.00

McCRORY'S TOYLAND BRINGS YOU SANTA'S PRIVATE EYES
1956 (16 pgs.)
Promotional Publ. Co. (Giveaway)

Has 9 pg. story plus 7 pg. toy ads	1.00	3.00	6.00

McCRORY'S WONDERFUL CHRISTMAS
1954 (20 pgs.; slick cover)
Promotional Publ. Co. (Giveaway)

nn	1.35	4.00	8.00

McHALE'S NAVY (TV) (See Movie Classics)
May-July, 1963 - No. 3, Nov-Jan, 1963-64 (Photo-c)
Dell Publishing Co.

1	2.00	6.00	14.00
2,3	1.70	5.00	12.00

McKEEVER & THE COLONEL (TV)
Feb-Apr, 1963 - No. 3, Aug-Oct, 1963
Dell Publishing Co.

1-Photo-c	2.30	7.00	16.00
2,3	1.70	5.00	12.00

McLINTOCK (See Movie Comics)

MD
Apr-May, 1955 - No. 5, Dec-Jan, 1955-56
E. C. Comics

1-Not approved by code	6.50	19.50	45.00
2-5	5.00	15.00	35.00

NOTE: *Crandall, Evans, Ingels, Orlando* art in all issues; *Craig c-1-5.*

MECHA (Also see Mayhem)
June, 1987 - No. 6, 1988 ($1.50-$1.95, color, B&W #3 on)
Dark Horse Comics

1,2 ($1.95, color)	.35	1.00	2.00
3,4 ($1.75, B&W)	.30	.90	1.80
5,6 ($1.50, B&W)	.25	.75	1.50

MECHANICS
Oct, 1985 - No. 3, Dec, 1985 ($2.00 cover; adults only)
Fantagraphics Books

1-3: Love & Rockets in all	.35	1.00	2.00

MEDAL FOR BOWZER, A
No date (1948-50?)
Will Eisner Giveaway

	Good	Fine	N-Mint
nn-Eisner-c/script	15.00	45.00	105.00

MEDAL OF HONOR COMICS
Spring, 1946
A. S. Curtis

1	5.00	15.00	35.00

MEDIA STARR
July, 1989 - No. 3, Sept, 1989 ($1.95, color, mini-series, 28 pgs.)
Innovation Publishing

1-3: Deluxe format	.35	1.00	2.00

MEET ANGEL (Formerly Angel & the Ape)
No. 7, Nov-Dec, 1969
National Periodical Publications

7-Wood-a(i)	.60	1.75	3.50

MEET CORLISS ARCHER (Radio/Movie)(My Life #4 on)
March, 1948 - No. 3, July, 1948
Fox Features Syndicate

1-(Teen-age)-Feldstein c/a	28.50	85.00	200.00
2-Feldstein-c only	21.50	64.00	150.00
3-Part Feldstein-c only	16.00	48.00	110.00

NOTE: *No. 1-3 used in Seduction of the Innocent, pg. 39.*

MEET HERCULES (See Three Stooges)

MEET HIYA A FRIEND OF SANTA CLAUS
1949 (18 pgs.?) (paper cover)
Julian J. Proskauer/Sundial Shoe Stores, etc. (Giveaway)

nn	3.00	9.00	18.00

MEET MERTON
Dec, 1953 - No. 4, June, 1954
Toby Press

1-(Teen-age)-Dave Berg-a	2.65	8.00	18.00
2-Dave Berg-a	1.50	4.50	10.00
3,4-Dave Berg-a. 3-Berg-c	1.00	3.00	7.00
I.W. Reprint #9		.60	1.20
Super Reprint #11('63), 18		.60	1.20

MEET MISS BLISS (Becomes Stories Of Romance #5 on)
May, 1955 - No. 4, Nov., 1955
Atlas Comics (LMC)

1-Al Hartley-a	4.00	12.00	28.00
2-4	2.30	7.00	16.00

MEET MISS PEPPER (Formerly Lucy, The Real Gone Gal)
No. 5, April, 1954 - No. 6, June, 1954
St. John Publishing Co.

5-Kubert/Maurer-a	12.00	36.00	84.00
6-Kubert/Maurer-a; Kubert-c	10.00	30.00	70.00

MEET THE NEW POST GAZETTE SUNDAY FUNNIES
3/12/49 (16 pgs.; paper covers) (7¼x10¼")
Commercial Comics (insert in newspaper)
Pittsburgh Post Gazette

Dick Tracy by Gould, Gasoline Alley, Terry & the Pirates, Brenda Starr, Buck Rogers by Yager, The Gumps, Peter Rabbit by Fago, Superman, Funnyman by Siegel & Shuster, The Saint, Archie, & others done especially for this book. A fine copy sold at auction in 1985 for $276.00.

Estimated value. . . .			$150—$300

MEGALITH (Also see The Revengers & Zero Patrol)
Mar, 1985 - No. 2, 1985; No. 1, 1989 ($2.00, color)
Continuity Comics

1,2 (1985)-Neal Adams-a	.35	1.00	2.00
1-('89)-Adams-c(i), Nebres-i (r/earlier issues?)	.35	1.00	2.00

MEGATON
11/83; No. 2, 10/85 - V2#3 (B&W, color V2#1 on)

McCrory's Christmas Book, © WEST

Meet Corliss Archer #1, © FOX

Megalith #1 (1989), © Continuity Comics

Melvin Monster #2, © DELL

Men Against Crime #4, © ACE

Men's Adventures #5, © MEG

MEGATON (continued)
Megaton Publ.

	Good	Fine	N-Mint
1,2 ($2.00, 68 pgs.)	.35	1.00	2.00
3-8 ($1.50/#3, 44 pgs.; #4, 52 pgs.)	.25	.75	1.50
V2#1-3 ($1.50, color)	.25	.75	1.50
Special 1 ($2.00, '87)	.35	1.00	2.00
X-Mas 2 ('87)	.35	1.00	2.00

MEGATON MAN (Also see The Return Of...)
Dec, 1984 - No. 10, 1986 ($2.00, color, Baxter paper)
Kitchen Sink Enterprises

1-Silver-Age heroes parody	1.15	3.50	7.00
1-2nd printing (1989, $2.00)	.35	1.00	2.00
2	.45	1.40	2.80
3-10: 6-Border Worlds begins	.40	1.25	2.50
...Meets the Uncategorizable X+Thems 1 (4/89, $2.00, B&W)			
	.35	1.00	2.00

MEL ALLEN SPORTS COMICS
No. 5, Nov, 1949; No. 6, June, 1950
Standard Comics

5(#1 on inside)-Tuska-a	6.50	19.50	45.00
6(#2)	4.00	12.00	28.00

MELVIN MONSTER (See Peter, the Little Pest)
Apr-June, 1965 - No. 10, Oct, 1969
Dell Publishing Co.

1-By John Stanley	8.00	24.00	56.00
2-10-All by Stanley. #10 r-/#1	5.00	15.00	35.00

MELVIN THE MONSTER (Dexter The Demon #7)
July, 1956 - No. 6, July, 1957
Atlas Comics (HPC)

1-Maneely-c/a	3.50	10.50	24.00
2-6: 4-Maneely c/a	2.00	6.00	14.00

MENACE
March, 1953 - No. 11, May, 1954
Atlas Comics (HPC)

1-Everett-a	12.00	36.00	85.00
2-Post-atom bomb disaster by Everett; anti-Communist propaganda/ torture scenes	8.00	24.00	56.00
3,4,6-Everett-a	5.70	17.00	40.00
5-Origin & 1st app. The Zombie by Everett (reprinted in Tales of the Zombie #1)(7/53)	10.00	30.00	70.00
7,8,10,11: 7-Frankenstein story. 8-End of world story. 10-H-Bomb panels	5.00	15.00	35.00
9-Everett-a r-in Vampire Tales #1	5.70	17.00	40.00

NOTE: Colan a-6. Everett a-1-6, 9; c-1-6. Heath a-1-8; c-10. Katz a-11. Maneely a-3, 7, 8. Powell a-11. Romita a-3, 6, 11. Shelly a-10. Sinnott a-2, 7. Tuska a-1, 2, 5.

MEN AGAINST CRIME (Formerly Mr. Risk; Hand of Fate #8 on)
No. 3, Feb, 1951 - No. 7, Oct, 1951
Ace Magazines

3-Mr. Risk app.	3.50	10.50	24.00
4-7: 4-Colan-a; entire book reprinted as Trapped! #4			
	1.85	5.50	13.00

MEN, GUNS, & CATTLE (See Classics Illustrated Special Issue)

MEN IN ACTION (Battle Brady #10 on)
April, 1952 - No. 9, Dec, 1952
Atlas Comics (IPS)

1-Berg, Pakula, Reinman-a	3.50	10.50	24.00
2	1.50	4.50	10.00
3-6,8,9: 3-Heath-c/a. 6-Pakula-a	1.30	4.00	9.00
7-Krigstein-a	3.00	9.00	21.00

MEN IN ACTION
April, 1957 - No. 9, 1958

Ajax/Farrell Publications

	Good	Fine	N-Mint
1	2.65	8.00	18.00
2	1.30	4.00	9.00
3-9	1.00	3.00	7.00

MEN INTO SPACE (See 4-Color No. 1083)

MEN OF BATTLE (See New...)

MEN OF COURAGE
1949
Catechetical Guild
Contains bound Topix comics-V7#2,4,6,8,10,16,18,20

	1.70	5.00	12.00

MEN OF WAR
August, 1977 - No. 26, March, 1980
DC Comics, Inc.

1-Origin Gravedigger, cont'd. in #2		.30	.60
2-26		.25	.50

NOTE: Chaykin a-9, 10, 12-14, 19, 20. Evans c-25. Kubert c-2-23, 24p, 26.

MEN'S ADVENTURES (Formerly True Adventures)
No. 4, Aug, 1950 - No. 28, July, 1954
Marvel/Atlas Comics (CCC)

4(#1)(52 pgs.)	7.00	21.00	50.00
5-Flying Saucer story	4.00	12.00	28.00
6-8: 8-Sci/fic story	3.00	9.00	21.00
9-20: All war format	1.70	5.00	12.00
21,22,24-26: All horror format	2.00	6.00	14.00
23-Crandall-a; Fox-a(i)	3.50	10.50	24.00
27,28-Captain America, Human Torch, & Sub-Mariner app. in each			
	21.00	62.00	145.00

NOTE: Berg a-15, 16. Burgos a-27. Colan a-14. Everett a-10, 14, 22, 25, 28; c-14, 21-23. Heath a-8, 24; c-20. Lawrence a-23, 27. Maneely a-24. Mac Pakula a-15, 25. Post a-23. Powell a-27. Reinman a-12. Robinson c-19. Romita a-22. Sinnott a-21. Tuska a-24. Adventure-#4-8; War-#9-20; Horror-#21-26.

MEN WHO MOVE THE NATION
(Giveaway) (Black & White)
Publisher unknown
Neal Adams-a

	2.65	8.00	16.00

MEPHISTO VERSUS... (See Silver Surfer #3)
Apr, 1987 - No. 4, July, 1987 ($1.50, mini-series)
Marvel Comics Group

1-Fantastic Four; Austin-i	.35	1.00	2.00
2-4: 2-X-Factor. 3-X-Men. 4-Avengers	.25	.80	1.60

MERC (See Mark Hazzard: Merc)

MERCHANTS OF DEATH
July, 1988 - No. 4, Nov, 1988 ($3.50, B&W/16pgs. color, 44pg. mag.)
Acme Press (Eclipse)

1-4: 4-Toth-c	.60	1.75	3.50

MERLIN JONES AS THE MONKEY'S UNCLE (See Movie Comics and The Misadventures of... under Movie Comics)

MERLINREALM 3-D (See Blackthorne 3-D Series #2)

MERRILL'S MARAUDERS (See Movie Classics)

MERRY CHRISTMAS (See A Christmas Adv., Donald Duck..., Dell Giant #39, & March of Comics #153)

MERRY CHRISTMAS, A
1948 (nn) (Giveaway)
K. K. Publications (Child Life Shoes)

nn	2.75	8.00	16.00

MERRY CHRISTMAS
1956 (7¼x5¼")
K. K. Publications (Blue Bird Shoes Giveaway)

nn	1.00	3.00	6.00

MERRY CHRISTMAS FROM MICKEY MOUSE
1939 (16 pgs.) (Color & B&W)
K. K. Publications (Shoe store giveaway)

	Good	Fine	N-Mint
nn-Donald Duck & Pluto app.; text with art (Rare); c-reprint/Mickey Mouse Mag. V3/3 (12/37)	70.00	200.00	400.00

MERRY CHRISTMAS FROM SEARS TOYLAND
1939 (16 pgs.) (In color)
Sears Roebuck Giveaway

nn-Dick Tracy, Little Orphan Annie, The Gumps, Terry & the Pirates	15.00	45.00	90.00

MERRY COMICS
December, 1945 (No cover price)
Carlton Publishing Co.

nn-Boogeyman app.	5.70	17.00	40.00

MERRY COMICS
1947
Four Star Publications

1	3.70	11.00	26.00

MERRY-GO-ROUND COMICS
1944 (132 pgs.; 25 cents); 1946; 9-10/47 - No. 2, 1948
LaSalle Publ. Co./Croyden Publ./Rotary Litho.

nn(1944)(LaSalle)	8.00	24.00	56.00
21	2.30	7.00	16.00
1(1946)(Croyden)	3.70	11.00	26.00
V1#1,2('47-'48; 52 pgs.)(Rotary Litho. Co. Ltd., Canada); Ken Hultgren-a	2.65	8.00	18.00

MERRY MAILMAN (See Funny Animals)

MERRY MOUSE (Also see Space Comics)
June, 1953 - No. 4, Jan-Feb, 1954
Avon Periodicals

1	3.70	11.00	26.00
2-4	2.00	6.00	14.00

METAL MEN (See Brave & the Bold, DC Comics Presents, and Showcase)
4-5/63 - No. 41, 12-1/69-70; No. 42, 2-3/73 - No. 44, 7-8/73; No. 45, 4-5/76 - No. 56, 2-3/78
National Periodical Publications/DC Comics

1	14.00	42.00	100.00
2	3.70	17.00	40.00
3-5	3.60	11.00	25.00
6-10	2.65	8.00	18.00
11-20	1.70	5.00	12.00
21-26,28-30	1.35	4.00	8.00
27-Origin Metal Men	1.50	4.50	10.00
31-41(1968-70)	1.00	3.00	6.00
42-44(1973)-Reprints	.70	2.00	4.00
45('76)-49-Simonson-a in all	.70	2.00	4.00
50-56: 50-Part-r. 54,55-Green Lantern x-over	.70	2.00	4.00

NOTE: Aparo c-53-56. Giordano c-45, 46. Kane a-30, 31p; c-31. Simonson a-45-49; c-47-52. Staton a-50-56.

METAMORPHO (See Action, Brave & the Bold, First Issue Special, & World's Finest)
July-Aug, 1965 - No. 17, Mar-Apr, 1968
National Periodical Publications

1	5.00	15.00	35.00
2,3	2.85	8.50	20.00
4-6	1.70	5.00	12.00
7-9	1.35	4.00	8.00
10-Origin & 1st app. Element Girl (1-2/67)	1.70	5.00	12.00
11-17	.85	2.50	5.00

NOTE: Ramona Fraden a-1-4. Orlando a-5, 6; c-5-9, 11. Sal Trapani a-7-16.

METEOR COMICS
November, 1945
L. L. Baird (Croyden)

	Good	Fine	N-Mint
1-Captain Wizard, Impossible Man, Race Wilkins app.; origin Baldy Bean, Capt. Wizard's sidekick; Bare-breasted mermaids story	13.00	40.00	90.00

MGM'S MARVELOUS WIZARD OF OZ
November, 1975 (84 pgs.; oversize) ($1.50)
Marvel Comics Group/National Periodical Publications

1-Adaptation of MGM's movie (See Marvel Treasury of Oz)	.70	2.00	4.00

M.G.M'S MOUSE MUSKETEERS (Formerly M.G.M.'s The Two Mouseketeers)
No. 670, Jan, 1956 - No. 1290, Mar-May, 1962
Dell Publishing Co.

4-Color 670 (#4)	1.00	3.00	7.00
4-Color 711,728,764	.85	2.50	6.00
8 (4-6/57) - 21 (3-5/60)	.75	2.25	5.00
4-Color 1135,1175,1290	.85	2.50	6.00

M.G.M.'S SPIKE AND TYKE
No. 499, Sept, 1953 - No. 1266, Dec-Feb, 1961-62
Dell Publishing Co.

4-Color 499 (#1)	1.30	4.00	9.00
4-Color 577,638	1.00	3.00	7.00
4(12-2/55-56)-10	.85	2.50	6.00
11-24(12-2/60-61)	.75	2.25	5.00
4-Color 1266	.85	2.50	6.00

M.G.M.'S THE TWO MOUSEKETEERS (See 4-Color 475,603,642)

MICHAELANGELO, TEENAGE MUTANT NINJA TURTLE
1986 (One shot) ($1.50, B&W)
Mirage Studios

1	1.70	5.00	10.00
1-2nd printing	.25	.75	1.50

MICKEY AND DONALD (Walt Disney's...#3 on)
Mar, 1988 - Present (95 cents, color)
Gladstone Publishing

1-Don Rosa-a; r-/1949 Firestone giveaway	.90	2.75	5.50
2	.40	1.25	2.50
3-Infinity-c	.35	1.00	2.00
4-8: Barks-r		.60	1.20
9-15: 9-r/1948 Firestone giveaway; X-Mas-c		.50	1.00
16 ($1.50, 52 pgs.)-r/FC #157	.25	.75	1.50
17 ($1.95, 68 pgs.)-Barks M.M.-r/FC #79 plus Barks D.D.-r; Rosa-a; X-Mas-c	.35	1.00	2.00

NOTE: Barks reprints in 1-15,17. Kelly c-13r, 14 (r/Walt Disney's C&S #58).

MICKEY AND DONALD IN VACATIONLAND (See Dell Giant No. 47)

MICKEY & THE BEANSTALK (See Story Hour Series)

MICKEY & THE SLEUTH (See Walt Disney Showcase #38,39,42)

MICKEY FINN (Also see Feature Funnies)
Nov?, 1942 - V3No. 2, May, 1952
Eastern Color 1-4/McNaught Synd. No. 5 on (Columbia)/Headline
V3No.2

1	16.00	48.00	110.00
2	8.00	24.00	56.00
3-Charlie Chan app.	5.50	16.50	38.00
4	3.70	11.00	26.00
5-10	2.65	8.00	18.00
11-15(1949): 12-Sparky Watts app.	2.00	6.00	14.00
V3#1,2(1952)	1.30	4.00	9.00

MICKEY MOUSE
1931 - No. 4, 1934 (52 pgs.; 10x9¾''; cardboard covers)

Metal Men #1, © DC

Metamorpho #3, © DC

Meteor Comics #1, © Croyden

Mickey Mouse Series 1 (1931, McKay), ⓒ WDC   Mickey Mouse Four Color #116, ⓒ WDC   Mickey Mouse #226, ⓒ WDC

MICKEY MOUSE (continued)
David McKay Publications

	Good	Fine	N-Mint
1(1931)	85.00	257.00	600.00
2(1932)	64.00	192.00	450.00
3(1933)-All color Sunday reprints; page #'s 5-17, 32-48 reissued in			
Whitman #948	107.00	320.00	750.00
4(1934)	57.00	170.00	400.00

NOTE: *Each book reprints strips from previous year - dailies in black and white in #1,2,4; Sundays in color in No. 3. Later reprints exist; i.e., #2 (1934).*

MICKEY MOUSE
1933 (Copyright date, printing date unknown)
(30 pages; 10x8¾''; cardboard covers)
Whitman Publishing Co.

948-(1932 Sunday strips in color)	85.00	257.00	600.00

NOTE: *Some copies were bound with a second front cover upside-down instead of the regular back cover; both covers have the same art, but different right and left margins. The above book is an exact, but abbreviated reissue of David McKay No. 3 but with ½-inch of border trimmed from the top and bottom.*

MICKEY MOUSE (See The Best of Walt Disney Comics, Cheerios giveaways, Dynabrite Comics, 40 Big Pages . . . , Gladstone Comic Album, Merry Christmas From . . . , Walt Disney's C&S & Wheaties)

MICKEY MOUSE (. . . See The New Mickey Mouse . . .)(See Dell Giants for annuals)
No. 16, 1941 - No. 84, 7-9/62; No. 85, 11/62 - No. 218, 7/84;
No. 219, 10/86 - Present
Dell Publ. Co./Gold Key No. 85-204/Whitman No. 205-218/
Gladstone No. 219 on

	Good	Fine	VF-NM
4-Color 16(1941)-1st M.M. comic book-''vs. the Phantom Blot'' by			
Gottfredson	343.00	1030.00	2400.00
(Prices vary widely on this book)			

	Good	Fine	N-Mint
4-Color 27(1943)-''7 Colored Terror''	50.00	150.00	350.00
4-Color 79(1945)-By Carl Barks (1 story)	64.00	193.00	450.00
4-Color 116(1946)	17.00	51.00	120.00
4-Color 141,157(1947)	16.00	48.00	110.00
4-Color 170,181,194('48)	13.00	40.00	90.00
4-Color 214('49),231,248,261	10.00	30.00	70.00
4-Color 268-Reprints/WDC&S #22-24 by Gottfredson (''Surprise			
Visitor'')	10.00	30.00	70.00
4-Color 279,286,296	8.50	25.50	60.00
4-Color 304,313(#1),325(#2),334	5.70	17.00	40.00
4-Color 343,352,362,371,387	4.30	13.00	30.00
4-Color 401,411,427(10-11/52)	3.50	10.50	24.00
4-Color 819-Mickey Mouse in Magicland	2.00	6.00	14.00
4-Color 1057,1151,1246(1959-61)-Album	1.70	5.00	12.00
28(12-1/52-53)-32,34	1.70	5.00	12.00
33-(Exists with 2 dates, 10-11/53 & 12-1/54)	1.70	5.00	12.00
35-50	1.15	3.50	8.00
51-73,75-80	.85	2.50	6.00
74-Story swipe-''The Rare Stamp Search''/4-Color 422-''The Gilded			
Man''	1.15	3.50	8.00
81-99: 93,95-titled ''Mickey Mouse Club Album''			
	.85	2.50	6.00
100-105: Reprints 4-Color 427,194,279,170,343,214 in that order			
	1.00	3.00	7.00
106-120	.75	2.25	5.00
121-130	.70	2.00	4.00
131-146	.50	1.50	3.00
147-Reprints ''The Phantom Fires'' from WDC&S 200-202			
	.85	2.50	5.00
148-Reprints ''The Mystery of Lonely Valley'' from WDC&S 208-210			
	.85	3.50	5.00
149-158	.35	1.00	2.00
159-Reprints ''The Sunken City'' from WDC&S 205-207			
	.70	2.00	4.00
160-170: 162-170-r	.35	1.00	2.00

	Good	Fine	N-Mint
171-178,180-199	.50	1.00	
179-(52 pgs.)	.60	1.20	
200-r-Four Color 371	.40	.80	
201-218	.40	.80	
219-1st Gladstone issue; The Seven Ghosts serial-r begins by			
Gottfredson	.85	2.50	5.00
220,221	.50	1.50	3.00
222-225: 222-Editor-in Grief strip-r	.40	1.25	2.50
226-230	.25	.75	1.50
231-243,245-254: 240-r/March of Comics #27. 245-r/F.C. #279. 250-r/			
F.C. #248	.50	1.00	
244 (1/89, $2.95, 100 pgs.)-60th anniversary	.60	1.75	3.50
255 ($1.95, 68 pgs.)	.35	1.00	2.00

NOTE: *Reprints #195-97, 198(2⁄3), 199(1⁄3), 200-208, 211(1⁄2), 212, 213, 215(1⁄3), 216-on.*

Album 01-518-210(Dell), 1(10082-309)/9/63-Gold Key			
	.85	2.50	6.00
. . .& Goofy ''Bicep Bungle''(1952, 16 pgs., 3¼x7'') Fritos giveaway,			
soft-c (also see Donald Duck & Ludwig Von Drake)			
	2.35	7.00	14.00
. . .& Goofy Explore Business(1978)	.40	.80	
. . .& Goofy Explore Energy(1976-1978) 36 pgs.; Exxon giveaway in			
color; regular size	.40	.80	
. . .& Goofy Explore Energy Conservation(1976-1978)-Exxon			
	.40	.80	
. . .& Goofy Explore The Universe of Energy(1985) 20pgs.; Exxon			
giveaway in color; regular size	.40	.80	
Club 1(1/64-G.K.)(TV)	1.75	5.25	12.00
Mini Comic 1(1976)(3¼x6½'')-Reprints 158			.15
New Mickey Mouse Club Fun Book 11190 (Golden Press, $1.95;			
224pgs, 1977)	.40	1.20	2.40
Surprise Party 1(30037-901, G.K.)(1/69)-40th Anniversary (see Walt			
Disney Showcase #47)	2.35	7.00	16.00
Surprise Party 1(1979)-r-/'69 issue	.35	1.00	2.00

MICKEY MOUSE BOOK
1930 (4 printings, 20pgs., magazine size, paperbound)
Bibo & Lang

nn-Very first Disney book with games, cartoons & songs; only Disney book to offer the origin of Mickey (based on a story originated by 11 yr. old Bobette Bibo). First app. Mickey & Minnie Mouse. Clarabelle Cow & Horace Horsecollar app. on back cover. Walt Disney, so the story goes, named him 'Mickey Mouse' after the green color of Ireland because he ate old green cheese. The book was printed in black & green to reinforce the Irish theme.

NOTE: *The first printing has a daily Win Smith M. Mouse strip at bottom of back cover; the reprints are blank in this area. Some copies are missing pages 9 & 10 which contain a puzzle to be cut out. Ub Iwerks-c*

	Good	Fine	VF-NM
First Printing (complete)	400.00	1200.00	2400.00
First Printing (Pgs. 9&10 missing)	140.00	420.00	840.00
2nd-4th Printings (complete)	200.00	600.00	1200.00
2nd-4th Printings (pgs. 9&10 missing)	90.00	270.00	540.00

MICKEY MOUSE CLUB MAGAZINE (See Walt Disney . . .)

MICKEY MOUSE CLUB SPECIAL (See The New Mickey Mouse . . .)

MICKEY MOUSE COMICS DIGEST
1986 - No. 6, 1987 (96 pgs.)
Gladstone Publishing

	Good	Fine	N-Mint
1-3 ($1.25)	.60	1.25	
4-6 ($1.50)	.25	.75	1.50

MICKEY MOUSE MAGAZINE
V1No.1, Jan, 1933 - V1No.9, Sept, 1933 (5¼x7¼'')
No. 1-3 published by Kamen-Blair (Kay Kamen, Inc.)
Walt Disney Productions

MICKEY MOUSE MAGAZINE (continued)
(Scarce)-Distributed by dairies and leading stores through their local theatres. First few issues had 5 cents listed on cover, later ones had no price.

	Good	Fine	VF-NM
V1#1	200.00	600.00	1200.00
2-9	85.00	257.00	600.00

MICKEY MOUSE MAGAZINE
V1No.1, Nov, 1933 - V2No.12, Oct, 1935
Mills giveaways issued by different dairies
Walt Disney Productions

	Good	Fine	N-Mint
V1#1	45.00	135.00	315.00
2-12: 2-X-mas issue	19.00	58.00	135.00
V2#1-12: 2-X-mas issue. 4-St. Valentine-c	13.00	40.00	90.00

MICKEY MOUSE MAGAZINE (Becomes Walt Disney's Comics & Stories) (No V3/1, V4/6)
Summer, 1935 (June-Aug, indicia) - V5/12, Sept, 1940
V1/1-5, V3/11,12, V4/1-3 are 44 pgs; V2/3-100 pgs; V5/12-68 pgs; rest are 36 pgs.
K. K. Publications/Western Publishing Co.

	Good	Fine	VF-NM
V1#1 (Large size, 13¼x10¼")-25 cents)-Contains puzzles, games, cels, stories and comics of Disney characters. Promotional magazine for Disney cartoon movies and paraphernalia	200.00	500.00	1200.00

Note: Some copies were autographed by the editors & given away with all early one year subscriptions.

	Good	Fine	N-Mint
2 (Size change, 11½x8½"; 10/35; 10 cents)-High quality paper begins; Messmer-a	93.00	280.00	650.00
3,4: 3-Messmer-a	54.00	160.00	375.00
5-1st Donald Duck solo-c; last 44pg. & high quality paper issue	57.00	170.00	400.00
6-9: 6-36 pg. issues begin; Donald becomes editor. 8-2nd Donald solo-c. 9-1st Mickey/Minnie-c	43.00	130.00	300.00
10-12, V2#1,2: 11-1st Pluto/Mickey-c; Donald fires himself and appoints Mickey as editor	39.00	118.00	275.00
V2#3-Special 100 pg. Christmas issue (25 cents); Messmer-a; Donald becomes editor of Wise Quacks	78.00	235.00	545.00
4-Mickey Mouse Comics & Roy Ranger (adventure strip) begin; both end V2#9; Messmer-a	34.00	100.00	235.00

	Good	Fine	N-Mint
5-Ted True (adventure strip, ends V2#9) & Silly Symphony Comics (ends V3#3) begin	27.00	81.00	190.00
6-9: 6-1st solo Minnie-c. 6-9-Mickey Mouse Movies cut-out in each	27.00	81.00	190.00
10-1st full color issue; Mickey Mouse (by Gottfredson; ends V3#12) & Silly Symphony (ends V3/3) full color Sunday-r, Peter The Farm Detective (ends V5#8) & Ole Of The North (ends V3#3) begins	38.00	115.00	265.00
11-13: 12-Hiawatha-c & feature story	27.00	81.00	190.00
V3#2-Big Bad Wolf Halloween-c	27.00	81.00	190.00
3 (12/37)-1st app. Snow White & The Seven Dwarfs (before release of movie)(possibly 1st in print); Mickey Christmas-c	38.00	115.00	265.00
4 (1/38)-Snow White & The Seven Dwarfs serial begins (on stands before release of movie); Ducky Symphony (ends V3#11) begins	31.00	92.00	215.00
5-1st Snow White & Seven Dwarfs-c (St. Valentine's Day)	31.00	92.00	215.00
6-Snow White serial ends; Lonesome Ghosts app. (2 pp.)	27.00	81.00	190.00
7-Seven Dwarfs Easter-c	25.00	75.00	175.00
8-10: 9-Dopey-c. 10-1st solo Goofy-c	23.00	70.00	165.00
11,12 (44 pgs; 8 more pages color added). 11-Mickey The Sheriff serial (ends V4#3) & Donald Duck strip-r (ends V3#12) begin. Color feature on Snow White's Forest Friends	27.00	81.00	190.00

	Good	Fine	N-Mint
V4#1 (10/38; 44 pgs.)-Brave Little Tailor-c/feature story, nominated for Academy Award; Bobby & Chip by Otto Messmer (ends V4#2) & The Practical Pig (ends V4#2) begin	27.00	81.00	190.00
2 (44 pgs.)-1st Huey, Dewey & Louie-c	25.00	75.00	175.00
3 (12/38, 44 pgs.)-Ferdinand The Bull-c/feature story, Academy Award winner; Mickey Mouse & The Whalers serial begins, ends V4#12	27.00	81.00	190.00
4-Spotty, Mother Pluto strip-r begin, end V4#8	23.00	70.00	160.00
5-St. Valentine's day-c. 1st Pluto solo-c	27.00	81.00	190.00
7 (3/39)-The Ugly Duckling-c/feature story, Academy Award winner	27.00	81.00	190.00
7 (4/39)-Goofy & Wilbur The Grasshopper classic-c/feature story from 1st Goofy cartoon movie; Timid Elmer begins, ends V5#5	27.00	81.00	190.00
8-Big Bad Wolf-c from Practical Pig movie poster; Practical Pig feature story	27.00	81.00	190.00
9-Donald Duck & Mickey Mouse Sunday-r begin; The Pointer feature story, nominated for Academy Award	27.00	81.00	190.00
10-Classic July 4th drum & fife-c; last Donald Sunday-r	30.00	90.00	210.00
11-1st slick-c; last over-sized issue	23.00	70.00	165.00
12 (9/39; format change, 10¼x8¼")-1st full color, cover to cover issue. Donald's Penguin-c/feature story	30.00	90.00	210.00
V5#1-Black Pete-c; Officer Duck-c/feature story; Autograph Hound feature story; Robinson Crusoe serial begins	30.00	90.00	210.00
2-Goofy-c; 1st app. Pinocchio (cameo)	30.00	90.00	210.00
3 (12/39)-Pinocchio Christmas-c (Before movie release). Pinocchio serial begins; 1st app. Jiminy Cricket	38.00	115.00	265.00
4,5: 5-Jiminy Crickett-c; Pinocchio serial ends; Donald's Dog Laundry feature story	30.00	90.00	210.00
6-Tugboat Mickey feature story; Rip Van Winkle feature begins, ends V5#8	28.50	85.00	200.00
7-2nd Huey, Dewey & Louie-c	28.50	85.00	200.00
8-Last magazine size issue; 2nd solo Pluto-c; Figaro & Cleo feature story	28.50	85.00	200.00
9 (44 pgs)-change to comic book size)-Jiminy Crickett feature story; Donald-c & Sunday-r begin	35.00	100.00	245.00
10-Special Independence Day issue	35.00	100.00	245.00
11-Hawaiian Holiday & Mickey's Trailor feature stories; last 36 pg. issue	35.00	100.00	245.00
12 (Format change)-The transition issue (68 pgs.) becoming a comic book. With only a title change to follow, becomes Walt Disney's Comics & Stories #1 with the next issue	130.00	390.00	910.00
V4#1 (Giveaway)	20.00	60.00	140.00

NOTE: Otto Messmer-a is in many issues of the first two-three years. The following story titles and issues have gags created by Carl Barks: V4#3(12/38)-'Donald's Better Self' & 'Donald's Golf Game;' V4#4(1/39)-'Donald's Lucky Day;' V4#7(3/39)-'Hockey Champ;' V4#7(4/39)-'Donald's Cousin Gus;' V4#9(6/39)-'Sea Scouts;' V4#12(9/39)-'Donald's Penguin;' V5#9(6/40)-'Donald's Vacation;' V5#10(7/40)-'Bone Trouble;' V5#12(9/40)-'Window Cleaners.'

MICKEY MOUSE MARCH OF COMICS
1947 - 1951 (Giveaway)
K. K. Publications

8(1947)-32 pgs.	50.00	150.00	330.00
27(1948)	34.00	100.00	238.00
45(1949)	27.00	80.00	190.00
60(1950)	18.00	55.00	125.00
74(1951)	14.00	42.50	96.00

MICKEY MOUSE SUMMER FUN (See Dell Giants)

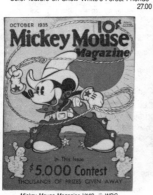
Mickey Mouse Magazine V1#2, © WDC

Mickey Mouse Magazine V3#3, © WDC

Mickey Mouse Magazine V5#7, © WDC

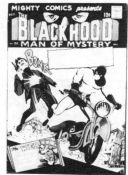

Micronauts #37, © MEG   Mighty Bear #14, © STAR   Mighty Comics #50, © AP

MICKEY MOUSE'S SUMMER VACATION (See Story Hour Series)

MICROBOTS, THE
December, 1971 (One Shot)
Gold Key

	Good	Fine	N-Mint
1 (10271-112)	.85	2.50	5.00

MICRONAUTS
Jan, 1979 - No. 59, Aug, 1984 (Mando paper #53 on)
Marvel Comics Group

	Good	Fine	N-Mint
1-Intro/1st app. Baron Karza	.35	1.00	2.00
2-5		.60	1.20
6-10: 7-Man-Thing app. 8-1st app. Capt. Universe. 9-1st app. Cilicia		.45	.90
11-20: 13-1st app. Jasmine. 15-Death of Microtron. 15-17-Fantastic-4 app. 17-Death of Jasmine. 20 Ant-Man app.		.45	.90
21-30: 21-Microverse series begins. 25-29-Nick Fury app. 27-Death of Biotron		.45	.90
31-36,39-59: 34,35-Dr. Strange app. 35-Double size; origin Microverse; intro Death Squad. 40-Fantastic Four app. 57-Double size		.45	.90
37-New X-Men app.; Giffen-a(p)	.35	1.00	2.00
38-First direct sale	.25	.80	1.60
nn-Reprints #1-3; blank UPC; diamond on top		.20	.40
Annual 1(12/79)-Ditko c/a	.30	.90	1.80
Annual 2(10/80)-Ditko c/a		.50	1.00

NOTE: #38-on distributed only through comic shops. *Adams* c-7i. *Chaykin* a-13-18p. *Ditko* a-39p. *Giffen* a-36p, 37p. *Golden* a-1-12p; c-2-6p, 7-23, 24p, 38, 39. *Guice* a-48-58p; c-49-58. *Gil Kane* a-38, 40p-45p; c-40-45. *Layton* c-33-37. *Miller* c-31.

MICRONAUTS
Oct, 1984 - No. 20, May, 1986
Marvel Comics Group

V2#1-20	.35	.70

NOTE: *Golden* a-1; c-1, 6. *Guice* a-4p; c-2p.

MICRONAUTS SPECIAL EDITION
Dec, 1983 - No. 5, Apr, 1984 ($2.00; mini-series; Baxter paper)
Marvel Comics Group

1-5: r-/original series 1-12; Guice-c(p)-all	.70	1.40

MIDGET COMICS (Fighting Indian Stories)
Feb, 1950 - No. 2, Apr, 1950 (5-3/8''x7-3/8'')
St. John Publishng Co.

1-Matt Baker-c	5.00	15.00	35.00
2-Tex West, Cowboy Marshal	2.65	8.00	18.00

MIDNIGHT
April, 1957 - No. 6, June, 1958
Ajax/Farrell Publ. (Four Star Comic Corp.)

1-Reprints from Voodoo & Strange Fantasy with some changes	4.00	12.00	28.00
2-5	2.00	6.00	14.00
6-Baker-r/Phantom Lady	3.70	11.00	26.00

MIDNIGHT MYSTERY
Jan-Feb, 1961 - No. 7, Oct, 1961
American Comics Group

1-Sci/Fic story	2.85	8.50	20.00
2-7: 7-Gustavson-a	1.70	5.00	12.00

NOTE: *Reinman* a-1, 3. *Whitney* a-1, 4-6; c-1-3, 5, 7.

MIDNIGHT TALES
Dec, 1972 - No. 18, May, 1976
Charlton Press

V1#1	.60	1.20
2-10,15-18	.40	.80
11-14-Newton-a	.40	.80
12,17(Modern Comics reprint, 1977)	.15	.30

NOTE: *Adkins* a-12i, 13i. *Ditko* a-12. *Howard* (Wood imitator) a-1-15, 17, 18; c-1-18.

Staton a-1, 3-11, 13. *Sutton* a-3-5, 7-10.

MIGHTY ATOM, THE (. . . & the Pixies #6) (Formerly The Pixies #1-5)
No. 6, 1949; 11/57 - No. 6, 8-9/58
Magazine Enterprises

	Good	Fine	N-Mint
6(1949-M.E.)-no month (1st Series)	2.30	7.00	16.00
1-6(2nd Series)-Pixies-r	1.00	3.00	7.00
I.W. Reprint #1(nd)	.30	.90	1.80
Giveaway(1959, '63, Whitman)-Evans-a	1.35	4.00	8.00
Giveaway ('65r, '67r, '68r, '73r, '76r)		.50	1.00

MIGHTY BEAR (Formerly Fun Comics; Mighty Ghost #4)
No. 13, Jan, 1954 - No. 14, Mar, 1954; 9/57 - No. 3, 2/58
Star Publ. No. 13,14/Ajax-Farrell (Four Star)

13,14-L. B. Cole-c	3.50	10.50	24.00
1-3('57-'58)Four Star (Ajax)	1.15	3.50	8.00

MIGHTY COMICS (. . . Presents) (Formerly Flyman)
No. 40, Nov, 1966 - No. 50, Oct, 1967
Radio Comics (Archie)

40-Web	1.15	3.50	8.00
41-50: 41-Shield, Black Hood. 42-Black Hood. 43-Shield, Web & Black Hood. 44-Black Hood, Steel Sterling & The Shield. 45-Shield & Hangman; origin Web retold. 46-Steel Sterling, Web & Black Hood. 47-Black Hood & Mr. Justice. 48-Shield & Hangman; Wizard x-over in Shield. 49-Steel Sterling & Fox; Black Hood x-over in Steel Sterling50-Black Hood & Web; Inferno x-over in Web	.85	2.60	6.00

NOTE: *Paul Reinman* a-40-50.

MIGHTY CRUSADERS, THE (Also see Advs. of the Fly & Fly Man)
Nov, 1965 - No. 7, Oct, 1966
Mighty Comics Group (Radio Comics)

1-Origin The Shield	1.70	5.00	12.00
2-Origin Comet	1.15	3.50	8.00
3-Origin Fly-Man	.85	2.60	6.00
4-Fireball, Inferno, Firefly, Web, Fox, Bob Phantom, Blackjack, Hangman, Zambini, Kardak, Steel Sterling, Mr. Justice, Wizard, Capt. Flag, Jaguar x-over	1.00	3.00	7.00
5-Intro. Ultra-Men (Fox, Web, Capt. Flag) & Terrific Three (Jaguar, Mr. Justice, Steel Sterling)	.85	2.60	6.00
6,7: 7-Steel Sterling feature; origin Fly-Girl	.85	2.60	6.00

NOTE: *Reinman* a-6.

MIGHTY CRUSADERS, THE (All New Advs. of . . .#2)
3/83 - No. 13, 9/85 ($1.00, 36 pgs, Mando paper)
Red Circle Prod./Archie Ent. No. 6 on

1-Origin Black Hood, The Fly, Fly Girl, The Shield, The Wizard, The Jaguar, Pvt. Strong & The Web	.45	.90
2-13: 2-Mister Midnight begins. 4-Darkling replaces Shield. 5-Origin Jaguar, Shield begins. 7-Untold origin Jaguar	.45	.90

NOTE: *Buckler* a-1-3, 4i, 5p, 7p, 8i, 9i; c-1-10p.

MIGHTY GHOST (Formerly Mighty Bear)
No. 4, June, 1958
Ajax/Farrell Publ.

4	1.15	3.50	8.00

MIGHTY HERCULES, THE (TV)
July, 1963 - No. 2, Nov, 1963
Gold Key

1,2(10072-307,311)	3.50	10.50	24.00

MIGHTY HEROES, THE (TV) (Funny)
Mar, 1967 - No. 4, July, 1967
Dell Publishing Co.

1-1957 Heckle & Jeckle-r	.85	2.50	6.00
2-4: 4-Two 1958 Mighty Mouse-r	.60	1.80	4.00

MIGHTY MARVEL WESTERN, THE
10/68 - No. 46, 9/76 (#1-14: 68 pgs.; #15,16: 52 pgs.)
Marvel Comics Group

	Good	Fine	N-Mint
1-Begin Kid Colt, Rawhide Kid, Two-Gun Kid-r	.35	1.00	2.00
2-10		.60	1.25
11-20		.50	1.00

21-46: 24-Kid Colt-r end. 25-Matt Slade-r begin. 31-Baker-r. 32-Origin-r/Ringo Kid #23; Williamson-r/Kid Slade #7. 37-Williamson, Kirby-r/Two-Gun Kid 51

		.30	.60

NOTE: *Jack Davis a(r)-21-24. Kirby a(r)-1-3, 6, 9, 12, 14, 16, 26, 29, 32, 36, 41, 43, 44; c-29. Maneely a(r)-22. No Matt Slade-r#43.*

MIGHTY MIDGET COMICS, THE (Miniature)
No date; circa 1942-1943 (36 pages) (Approx. 5x4'')
(Black & White & Red) (Sold 2 for 5 cents)
Samuel E. Lowe & Co.

	Good	Fine	N-Mint
Bulletman #11(1943)-R-/cover/Bulletman #3	3.50	10.50	24.00
Captain Marvel #11	3.50	10.50	24.00
Captain Marvel #11 (Same as above except for full color ad on back cover; this issue was glued to cover of Captain Marvel #20 and is not found in fine-mint condition)	3.50	10.50	24.00
Captain Marvel Jr. #11	3.50	10.50	24.00
Captain Marvel Jr. #11 (Same as above except for full color ad on back-c; this issue was glued to cover of Captain Marvel #21 and is not found in fine-mint condition)	3.50	10.50	24.00
Golden Arrow #11	2.30	7.00	16.00
Ibis the Invincible #11(1942)-Origin; r-/cover/Ibis #1	3.50	10.50	24.00
Spy Smasher #11(1942)	3.50	10.50	24.00

NOTE: *The above books came in a box called "box full of books" and was distributed with other Samuel Lowe puzzles, paper dolls, coloring books, etc. They are not titled Mighty Midget Comics. All have a war bond seal on back cover which is otherwise blank; These books came in a "Mighty Midget" flat cardboard counter display rack.*

	Good	Fine	N-Mint
Balbo, the Boy Magician #12	1.70	5.00	12.00
Bulletman #12	3.50	10.50	24.00
Commando Yank #12	2.30	7.00	16.00
Dr. Voltz the Human Generator	1.70	5.00	12.00
Lance O'Casey #12	1.70	5.00	12.00
Leatherneck the Marine	1.70	5.00	12.00
Minute Man #12	3.50	10.50	24.00
Mister Q	1.70	5.00	12.00
Mr. Scarlet & Pinky #12	3.50	10.50	24.00
Pat Wilton & His Flying Fortress	1.70	5.00	12.00
The Phantom Eagle #12	2.30	7.00	16.00
State Trooper Stops Crime	1.70	5.00	12.00
Tornado Tom; r-/from Cyclone 1-3; origin	2.00	6.00	14.00

MIGHTY MOUSE (See Adventures of . . ., Dell Giant #43, Giant Comics Edition, March of Comics #205, 237, 247, 257, 459, 471, 483, Oxydol-Dreft, Paul Terry's &, Terry-Toons Comics)

MIGHTY MOUSE (1st Series)
Fall, 1946 - No. 4, Summer, 1947
Timely/Marvel Comics (20th Century Fox)

	Good	Fine	N-Mint
1	50.00	150.00	350.00
2	24.00	73.00	170.00
3,4	17.00	51.00	120.00

MIGHTY MOUSE (2nd Series) (Paul Terry's. . . #62-71)
Aug., 1947 - No. 67, 11/55; No. 68, 3/56 - No. 83, 6/59
St. John Publishing Co./Pines No. 68 (3/56) on (TV issues #72 on)

	Good	Fine	N-Mint
5(#1)	17.00	51.00	120.00
6-10	8.00	24.00	56.00
11-19	5.00	15.00	35.00
20 (11/50) - 25-(52 pgs.)	4.00	12.00	28.00
20-25-(36 pg. editions)	3.70	11.00	26.00
26-37: 35-Flying saucer-c	2.85	8.50	20.00
38-45-(100 pgs.)	6.50	19.50	45.00
46-83: 62,64,67-Painted-c. 82-Infinity-c	2.00	6.00	14.00

	Good	Fine	N-Mint
Album 1(10/52)-100 pgs.	13.00	40.00	90.00
Album 2(11/52-St. John) - 3(12/52) (100 pgs.)	11.00	32.00	75.00
Fun Club Magazine 1(Fall, 1957-Pines, 100 pgs.) (CBS TV-Tom Terrific)	7.00	21.00	50.00
Fun Club Magazine 2-6(Winter, 1958-Pines)	4.00	12.00	28.00
3-D 1-(1st printing-9/53)(St. John)-stiff covers	20.00	60.00	140.00
3-D 1-(2nd printing-10/53)-slick, glossy covers, slightly smaller	16.50	50.00	115.00
3-D 2(11/53), 3(12/53)-(St. John)	14.00	42.00	100.00

MIGHTY MOUSE (3rd Series)(Formerly Advs. of Mighty Mouse)
No. 161, Oct, 1964 - No. 172, Oct, 1968
Gold Key/Dell Publishing Co. No. 166-on
161(10/64)-165(9/65)-(Becomes Advs. of . . . No. 166 on)

	Good	Fine	N-Mint
	1.50	4.50	10.00
166(3/66), 167(6/66)-172	1.15	3.50	8.00

MIGHTY MOUSE (TV)
1987 - No. 2, 1987 ($1.50, color)
Spotlight Comics

	Good	Fine	N-Mint
1,2: New stories	.25	.75	1.50
. . .And Friends Holiday Special (11/87, $1.75)	.30	.90	1.75

MIGHTY MOUSE ADVENTURES (Adventures of. . . #2 on)
November, 1951
St. John Publishing Co.

	Good	Fine	N-Mint
1	16.00	48.00	110.00

MIGHTY MOUSE ADVENTURE STORIES
1953 (384 pgs.) (50 Cents)
St. John Publishing Co.

	Good	Fine	N-Mint
Rebound issues	27.00	81.00	190.00

MIGHTY SAMSON (Also see Gold Key Champion)
7/64 - No.20, 11/69?; No.21, 8/72; No.22, 12/73 - No.31, 3/76;
No. 32, 8/82 (Painted-c #1-31)
Gold Key

	Good	Fine	N-Mint
1-Origin; Thorne-a begins	1.50	4.50	10.00
2-5	.85	2.60	6.00
6-10: 7-Tom Morrow begins, ends #20	.70	2.00	4.00
11-20	.50	1.50	3.00
21-32: 21,22,32-r	.25	.75	1.50

MIGHTY THOR (See Thor)

MIKE BARNETT, MAN AGAINST CRIME (TV)
Dec, 1951 - No. 6, 1952
Fawcett Publications

	Good	Fine	N-Mint
1	5.70	17.00	40.00
2	3.50	10.50	24.00
3,4,6	2.65	8.00	18.00
5-''Market for Morphine'' cover/story	4.00	12.00	28.00

MIKE GRELL'S SABLE (Also see Jon Sable & Sable)
March, 1990 - Present ($1.75, color)
First Comics

	Good	Fine	N-Mint
1-5: r/Jon Sable Freelance #1-5	.30	.90	1.80

MIKE MIST MINUTE MIST-ERIES (See Ms. Tree/Mike Mist in 3-D)
April, 1981 ($1.25, B&W, one-shot)
Eclipse Comics

	Good	Fine	N-Mint
1		.65	1.30

MIKE SHAYNE PRIVATE EYE
Nov-Jan, 1962 - No. 3, Sept-Nov, 1962
Dell Publishing Co.

	Good	Fine	N-Mint
1	1.50	4.50	10.00
2,3	1.15	3.50	8.00

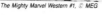
The Mighty Marvel Western #1, © MEG

Mighty Mouse #5 (St. John), © Terry Toons

Mike Barnett, Man Against Crime #1, © FAW

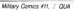

Military Comics #11, © QUA

Millie The Model #5, © MEG

Miracle Comics #4, © HILL

MILITARY COMICS (Becomes Modern Comics #44 on)
Aug, 1941 - No. 43, Oct, 1945
Quality Comics Group

	Good	Fine	N-Mint
1-Origin/1st app. Blackhawk by C. Cuidera; Miss America, The Death Patrol by Jack Cole (also #2-7,27-30), & The Blue Tracer by Guardineer; X of the Underground, The Yankee Eagle, Q-Boat & Shot & Shell, Archie Atkins, Loops & Banks by Bud Ernest (Bob Powell) ends #13) begin	300.00	750.00	1800.00
2-Secret War News begins (by McWilliams #2-16); Cole-a	125.00	375.00	875.00
3-Origin/1st app. Chop Chop	94.00	282.00	660.00
4	86.00	257.00	600.00
5-The Sniper begins; Miss America in costume #4-7	68.00	205.00	475.00
6-9: 8-X of the Underground begins (ends #13). 9-The Phantom Clipper begins (ends #16)	55.00	165.00	385.00
10-Classic Eisner-c	60.00	180.00	420.00
11-Flag-c	43.00	130.00	305.00
12-Blackhawk by Crandall begins, ends #22	60.00	180.00	420.00
13-15: 14-Private Dogtag begins (ends #83)	41.00	122.00	285.00
16-20: 16-Blue Tracer ends. 17-P.T. Boat begins	33.00	100.00	230.00
21-31: 22-Last Crandall Blackhawk. 27-Death Patrol revived	30.00	90.00	210.00
32-43	26.50	80.00	185.00

NOTE: *Berg* a-6. *J. Cole* a-1-3, 27-32. *Crandall* a-12-22; c-13-22. *Eisner* c-1, 9, 10. *McWilliams* a-2-16. *Powell* a-1-13. *Ward* Blackhawk-30, 31(15 pgs. each); c-29, 30.

MILITARY WILLY
1907 (14 pgs.; ½ in color (every other page))
(regular comic book format)(7x9½")(stapled)
J. I. Austen Co.

	Good	Fine	N-Mint
By F. R. Morgan	13.00	40.00	90.00

MILLENNIUM
Jan, 1988 - No. 8, Feb, 1988 (nd) (Weekly mini-series)
DC Comics

1-Staton c/a(p) begins	.40	1.25	2.50
2-8	.25	.80	1.60

MILLENNIUM INDEX
Mar, 1988 - No. 2, Mar, 1988 ($2.00)
Independent Comics Group

1,2	.35	1.00	2.00

MILLIE, THE LOVABLE MONSTER
Sept-Nov, 1962 - No. 6, Jan, 1973
Dell Publishing Co.

12-523-211, 2(8-10/63)	1.00	3.00	7.00
3(8-10/64)	.85	2.50	6.00
4(7/72), 5(10/72), 6(1/73)	.70	2.00	4.00

NOTE: *Woggon* a-3-6; c-3-6. 4 reprints 1; 5 reprints 2; 6 reprints 3.

MILLIE THE MODEL (See Comedy Comics, A Date With . . ., Gay Comics, Life With . . . & Modeling With . . .)
1945 - No. 207, December, 1973
Marvel/Atlas/Marvel Comics (SPI/Male/VPI)

1	21.50	64.00	150.00
2 (10/46)-Millie becomes The Blonde Phantom to sell Blonde Phantom perfume; a pre-Blonde Phantom app. (see All-Select #11, Fall, '46)	13.00	40.00	90.00
3-7: 5- Willie app. 7-Willie smokes extra strong tobacco	7.00	21.00	50.00
8,10-Kurtzman's ''Hey Look''	7.00	21.00	50.00
9-Powerhouse Pepper by Wolverton, 4 pgs.	10.00	30.00	70.00
11-Kurtzman-a, 'Giggles 'n Grins	4.65	14.00	32.00
12,15,17-20	3.00	9.00	21.00
13,14,16-Kurtzman's ''Hey Look''	3.70	11.00	26.00

	Good	Fine	N-Mint
21-30	2.30	7.00	16.00
31-60	1.50	4.50	10.00
61-99	.85	2.60	6.00
100	1.15	3.50	8.00
101-190: 107-Jack Kirby app. in story. 154-New Millie begins (10/67).			
192-(52 pgs.)	.40	1.25	2.50
191-207		.60	1.25
Annual 1(1962)	3.50	10.50	24.00
Annual 2-10(1963-11/71)	1.50	4.50	10.00
Queen-Size 11(9/74), 12(1975)	.70	2.00	4.00

MILLION DOLLAR DIGEST (Also see Richie Rich . . .)
11/86 - No. 7, 11/87; No. 8, 4/88 - Present ($1.25-$1.75, digest size)
Harvey Publications

1-8		.60	1.25
9-14	.30	.90	1.75

MILT GROSS FUNNIES (Also see Picture News #1)
Aug, 1947 - No. 2, Sept, 1947
Milt Gross, Inc. (ACG?)

1,2	4.30	13.00	30.00

MILTON THE MONSTER & FEARLESS FLY (TV)
May, 1966
Gold Key

1 (10175-605)	3.50	10.50	24.00

MINUTE MAN (See Master Comics & Mighty Midget Comics)
Summer, 1941 - No. 3, Spring, 1942
Fawcett Publications

1	70.00	210.00	485.00
2,3	53.00	160.00	375.00

MINUTE MAN
No date (B&W; 16 pgs.; paper cover blue & red)
Sovereign Service Station giveaway

American history	1.00	3.00	6.00

MINUTE MAN ANSWERS THE CALL, THE
1942 (4 pages)
By M. C. Gaines (War Bonds giveaway)

Sheldon Moldoff-a	6.00	18.00	42.00

MIRACLE COMICS
Feb, 1940 - No. 4, March, 1941
Hillman Periodicals

1-Sky Wizard, Master of Space, Dash Dixon, Man of Might, Dusty Doyle, Pinkie Parker, The Kid Cop, K-7, Secret Agent, The Scorpion, & Blandu, Jungle Queen begin; Masked Angel only app.	55.00	165.00	385.00
2	33.00	100.00	230.00
3,4: 3-Bill Colt, the Ghost Rider begins. 4-The Veiled Prophet & Bullet Bob app.	30.00	90.00	210.00

MIRACLEMAN
Aug, 1985 - No. 15, Nov, 1988 ($1.25-$1.75, Mando paper: 7-10)
Eclipse Comics

1-r-/of British Marvelman series; Alan Moore scripts in 1-15	.50	1.50	3.00
1-Gold edition	1.70	5.00	10.00
1-Silver edition	.70	2.00	4.00
2-12: 9,10-Origin Miracleman. 9-Shows graphic scenes of childbirth		.60	1.25
13-15 ($1.75)	.30	.90	1.75
3-D 1 (12/85)	.40	1.25	2.50
2-D 1 ($5.00, B&W, 100 copy limited signed & numbered edition)	.40	1.25	2.50

MIRACLEMAN FAMILY
May, 1988 - No. 2, Sept, 1988 ($1.95, color, mini-series, Baxter paper)
Eclipse Comics

	Good	Fine	N-Mint
1,2: 2-Gulacy-c	.35	1.00	2.00

MIRACLE OF THE WHITE STALLIONS, THE (See Movie Comics)

MIRACLE SQUAD, THE
Aug, 1986 - No. 4, 1987 ($2.00, color, mini-series)
Upshot Graphics (Fantagraphics Books)

1-4	.35	1.00	2.00

MIRACLE SQUAD: BLOOD AND DUST, THE
Jan, 1989 - No. 4, July, 1989 ($1.95, B&W, mini-series)
Apple Comics

1-4	.35	1.00	2.00

MISADVENTURES OF MERLIN JONES, THE (See Movie Comics & Merlin Jones as the Monkey's Uncle under Movie Comics)

MISCHIEVOUS MONKS OF CROCODILE ISLE, THE
1908 (8½x11½''; 4 pgs. in color; 12 pgs.)
J. I. Austen Co., Chicago

By F. R. Morgan; reads longwise	8.00	24.00	56.00

MISS AMERICA COMICS (Miss America Magazine #2 on; also see Blonde Phantom & Marvel Mystery Comics)
1944 (One Shot)
Marvel Comics (20CC)

1-2 pgs. pin-ups	50.00	150.00	350.00

MISS AMERICA MAGAZINE (Formerly Miss America) (Miss America #51 on)
V1#2, Nov, 1944 - No. 93, Nov, 1958
Miss America Publ. Corp./Marvel/Atlas (MAP)

V1#2: Photo-c of teenage girl in Miss America costume; Miss America, Patsy Walker (intro.) comic stories plus movie reviews & stories; intro. Buzz Baxter & Hedy Wolfe	43.00	130.00	300.00
3,5-Miss America & Patsy Walker stories	16.00	48.00	110.00
4-Betty Page photo-c (See Cupid #2, My Love #4); Miss America & Patsy Walker story	21.50	64.00	150.00
6-Patsy Walker only	4.30	13.00	30.00
V2#1(4/45)-6(9/45)-Patsy Walker continues	2.15	6.50	15.00
V3#1(10/45)-6(4/46)	2.15	6.50	15.00
V4#1(5/46),2,5(9/46)	1.70	5.00	12.00
V4#3(7/46)-Liz Taylor photo-c	3.50	10.50	24.00
V4#4 (8/46; 68pgs.)	1.70	5.00	12.00
V4#6 (10/46; 92pgs.)	1.70	5.00	12.00
V5#1(11/46)-6(4/47), V6#1(5/47)-3(7/47)	1.70	5.00	12.00
V7#1(8/47)-14,16-23(6/49)	1.30	4.00	9.00
V7#15-All comics	1.70	5.00	12.00
V7#24(7/49)-Kamen-a	1.50	4.50	10.00
V7#25(8/49), 27-44(3/52), VII,nn(5/52)	1.30	4.00	9.00
V7#26(9/49)-All comics	1.70	5.00	12.00
V1,nn(7/52)-V1,nn(1/53)(#46-49)	1.30	4.00	9.00
V7#50(Spring '53), V1#51-V7?#54(7/53)	1.15	3.50	8.00
55-93	1.15	3.50	8.00

NOTE: Photo-c #1, V2#4, 5, V3#5, V4#3, 4, 6, V7#15, 16, 24, 26, 34, 37, 38. *Powell a-V7#31.*

MISS BEVERLY HILLS OF HOLLYWOOD
Mar-Apr, 1949 - No. 9, July-Aug, 1950 (52 pgs.)
National Periodical Publications

1 (Meets Alan Ladd)	21.50	64.00	150.00
2-William Holden photo-c	16.50	50.00	115.00
3-5: 3,4-Part photo-c	13.00	40.00	90.00
6,7,9	11.50	34.00	80.00
8-Reagan photo on-c	16.50	50.00	115.00

MISS CAIRO JONES
1945

Croyden Publishers	Good	Fine	N-Mint
1-Bob Oksner daily newspaper-r (1st strip story); lingerie panels	12.00	36.00	84.00

MISS FURY COMICS (Newspaper strip reprints)
Winter, 1942-43 - No. 8, Winter, 1946
Timely Comics (NPI 1/CmPI 2/MPC 3-8)

1-Origin Miss Fury by Tarpe' Mills (68 pgs.) in costume w/pin-ups	167.00	420.00	1000.00
2-(60 pgs.)-In costume w/pin-ups	64.00	193.00	450.00
3-(60 pgs.)-In costume w/pin-ups	54.00	160.00	375.00
4-(52 pgs.)-Costume, 2 pgs. w/pin-ups	44.00	132.00	310.00
5-(52 pgs.)-In costume w/pin-ups	39.00	118.00	275.00
6-(52 pgs.)-Not in costume in inside stories, w/pin-ups	35.00	105.00	245.00
7,8-(36 pgs.)-In costume 1 pg. each, no pin-ups	35.00	105.00	245.00

NOTE: *Schomburg* c-1, 5, 6.

MISSION IMPOSSIBLE (TV)
5/67 - No. 4, 10/68; No. 5, 10/69 (All have photo-c)
Dell Publishing Co.

1	4.00	12.00	28.00
2-5: 5-reprints #1	3.00	9.00	21.00

MISS LIBERTY (Becomes Liberty Comics)
1945 (MLJ reprints)
Burten Publishing Co.

1-The Shield & Dusty, The Wizard, & Roy, the Super Boy app.; r-/Shield-Wizard #13	13.50	41.00	95.00

MISS MELODY LANE OF BROADWAY
Feb-Mar, 1950 - No. 3, June-July, 1950 (52 pgs.)
National Periodical Publications

1	21.50	64.00	150.00
2,3	17.00	51.00	120.00

MISS PEACH
Oct-Dec, 1963; 1969
Dell Publishing Co.

1-Jack Mendelsohn-a/script	5.00	15.00	35.00
...Tells You How to Grow(1969; 25 cents)-Mel Lazarus-a; also given away (36 pgs.)	3.00	9.00	21.00

MISS PEPPER (See Meet Miss Pepper)

MISS SUNBEAM (See Little Miss . . .)

MISS VICTORY (See Captain Fearless #1,2, Holyoke One-Shot #3, Veri Best Sure Fire & Veri Best Sure Shot Comics)

MR. & MRS.
1922 (52 & 28 pgs.) (9x9½'', cardboard-c)
Whitman Publishing Co.

By Briggs (B&W, 52pgs.)	8.00	24.00	56.00
28 pgs.-(9x9½'')-Sunday strips-r in color	14.00	42.00	100.00

MR. & MRS. BEANS (See Single Series #11)

MR. & MRS. J. EVIL SCIENTIST (TV)(See The Flintstones)
Nov, 1963 - No. 4, Sept, 1966 (Hanna-Barbera)
Gold Key

1-From The Flintstones	1.70	5.00	12.00
2-4	1.15	3.50	8.00

MR. ANTHONY'S LOVE CLINIC (Based on radio show)
Nov, 1949 - No. 5, Mar-May, 1950 (52 pgs.)
Hillman Periodicals

1-Photo-c	4.30	13.00	30.00
2	2.65	8.00	18.00
3-5: 5-Photo-c	2.15	6.50	15.00

Miracleman Family #1, © Eclipse   Miss Fury #4, © MEG   Mr. & Mrs. J. Evil Scientist #2, © Hanna-Barbera

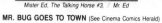
Mister Ed, The Talking Horse #3. © Mr. Ed

Mister Miracle #1 (1971). © DC

Mister Mystery #11. © Stanmore

MR. BUG GOES TO TOWN (See Cinema Comics Herald)

MR. DISTRICT ATTORNEY (Radio/TV)
Jan-Feb, 1948 - No. 67, Jan-Feb, 1959 (1-23: 52 pgs.)
National Periodical Publications

	Good	Fine	N-Mint
1	25.00	75.00	175.00
2	12.00	36.00	85.00
3-5	9.30	28.00	65.00
6-10	7.00	21.00	50.00
11-20	5.70	17.00	40.00
21-43: 43-Last pre-code (1-2/55)	4.30	13.00	30.00
44-67	3.00	9.00	21.00

MR. DISTRICT ATTORNEY (See 4-Color #13 & The Funnies #35)

MISTER ED, THE TALKING HORSE (TV)
Mar-May, 1962 - No. 6, Feb, 1964 (All photo-c; photo back-c: 1-6)
Dell Publishing Co./Gold Key

4-Color 1295	5.70	17.00	40.00
1(11/62) (Gold Key)-Photo-c	3.50	10.50	24.00
2-6-Photo-c	1.70	5.00	12.00

(See March of Comics #244,260,282,290)

MR. MAGOO (TV) (The Nearsighted . . . .& Gerald McBoing Boing
1954 issues; formerly Gerald McBoing-Boing And . . .)
No. 6, Nov-Jan, 1953-54; 5/54 - 3-5/62; 9-11/63 - 3-5/65
Dell Publishing Co.

6	5.00	15.00	35.00
4-Color 561(5/54),602(11/54)	5.00	15.00	35.00
4-Color 1235,1305(3-5/62)	4.00	12.00	28.00
3(9-11/63) - 5	3.50	10.50	24.00
4-Color 1235(12-536-505)(3-5/65)-2nd Printing	2.35	7.00	16.00

MISTER MIRACLE (See Brave & the Bold & Cancelled Comic Cav.)
3-4/71 - No. 18, 2-3/74; No. 19, 9/77 - No. 25, 8-9/78; 1987
National Periodical Publications/DC Comics (#7,8: 52 pgs.)

1	.60	1.75	3.50
2	.30	.90	1.75
3-10: 4-Boy Commandos-r begin. 9-Origin Mr. Miracle			
	.25	.75	1.50
11-25: 15-Intro/1st app. Shilo Norman. 18-Barda & Scott Free wed;			
New Gods app.	.60	1.25	
Special 1(1987, 52 pgs., $1.25)	.25	.75	1.50

NOTE: **Austin** a-19i. **Ditko** a-6r. **Golden** a-23-25p; c-25p. **Heath** a-24i, 25i; c-25i. **Kirby** a(p)/c-1-18. **Nasser** a-19i. **Rogers** a-19-22p; c-19, 20p, 21p, 22-24. **Wolverton** a-6r. 4-8 contain **Simon & Kirby** Boy Commandos reprints from Detective 82,76, Boy Commandos 1,3. Detective 64 in that order.

MISTER MIRACLE
Jan, 1989 - Present (1.00, color)
DC Comics

1-Spin-off from Justice League International	.25	.75	1.50
2-12: 9-Intro Maxi-Man		.50	1.00

MR. MIRACLE (See Capt. Fearless #1, Holyoke One-Shot! #4 & Super Duck #3)

MR. MONSTER (Doc Stearn... #7 on; See Airboy-Mr. Monster Special, Dark Horse Presents, Super Duper Comics & Vanguard Ill. #7)
Jan, 1985 - No. 10, June, 1987 ($1.75, color, Baxter paper)
Eclipse Comics

1	1.50	4.50	9.00
2-Dave Stevens-c	.65	1.90	3.75
3-9: 3-Alan Moore scripts	.50	1.50	3.00
10-6-D issue	.30	.90	1.80
. . .In 3-D #1	.35	1.00	2.00

MR. MONSTER
Feb. 1988 - Present ($1.75-$1.95, B&W)
Dark Horse Comics

1: 1,2-Origin	.40	1.25	2.50
2-6	.35	1.00	2.00

MR. MONSTER'S...
May, 1986 - No. 8, July, 1987 ($1.75, color)
Eclipse Comics

	Good	Fine	N-Mint
1 (5/86, $2.50)-Mr. Monster's Three Dimensional High Octane Horror			
#1; Kubert/Powell-r	.40	1.25	2.50
1. . .in 2-D: 100 copies signed & #'d (B&W)	1.00	3.00	6.00
2 (8/86). . .High Octane Horror #1; Grandenetti, Wolverton, Evans-r			
	.30	.90	1.80
3 (9/86). . .True Crime #1; Cole-r	.30	.90	1.80
4 (11/86). . .True Crime #2	.30	.90	1.80
5 (1/87). . .Hi-Voltage Super Science #1; r-/Vic Torry & His Flying			
Saucer #1 by Powell	.30	.90	1.80
6 (3/87). . .High Shock Schlock #1	.30	.90	1.80
7 (5/87). . .High Shock Schlock #2; Wolverton-r			
	.30	.90	1.80
8 (7/87). . .Weird Tales of the Future #1; Wolverton-r			
	.30	.90	1.80

MR. MUSCLES (Formerly Blue Beetle #18-21)
No. 22, Mar, 1956 - No. 23, Aug, 1956
Charlton Comics

22,23	2.15	6.50	15.00

MISTER MYSTERY
Sept, 1951 - No. 19, Oct, 1954
Mr. Publ. (Media Publ.) No. 1-3/SPM Publ./Stanmore (Aragon)

1-Kurtzmanesque horror story	19.00	57.00	135.00
2,3-Kurtzmanesque story	13.00	40.00	90.00
4,6: Bondage-c; 6-Torture	13.00	40.00	90.00
5,8,10	11.50	34.00	80.00
7-"The Brain Bats of Venus" by Wolverton; partially re-used in			
Weird Tales of the Future #7	41.00	122.00	285.00
9-Nostrand-a	12.00	36.00	84.00
11-Wolverton "Robot Woman" story/Weird Mysteries #2, cut up,			
rewritten & partially redrawn	21.50	64.00	150.00
12-Classic injury to eye-c	30.00	90.00	210.00
13,14,17,19	8.00	24.00	56.00
15-"Living Dead" junkie story	11.00	32.00	75.00
16-Bondage-c	11.00	32.00	75.00
18-"Robot Woman" by Wolverton reprinted from Weird Mysteries #2;			
decapitation, bondage-c	18.50	56.00	130.00

NOTE: **Andru** c/a-1, 2p. **Bailey** c-10-19(most). Bondage c-7. Some issues have graphic dismemberment scenes.

MISTER Q (See Mighty Midget Comics & Our Flag Comics #5)

MR. RISK (Formerly All Romances; Men Against Crime #3 on)
No. 7, Oct, 1950 - No. 2, Dec, 1950
Ace Magazines

7,2	2.30	7.00	16.00

MR. SCARLET & PINKY (See Mighty Midget Comics)

MISTER UNIVERSE (Professional wrestler)
July, 1951 - No. 2, Oct, 1951 - No. 5, April, 1952
Mr. Publications Media Publ. (Stanmor, Aragon)

1	8.00	24.00	56.00
2-'Jungle That Time Forgot', 24pg. story	5.50	16.50	38.00
3-Marijuana story	5.50	16.50	38.00
4,5-"Goes to War"	2.85	8.50	20.00

MISTER X (See Vortex)
6/84 - No. 14, 8/88 ($1.50-$2.25, direct sales, Coated paper, color)
V2#1, Apr, 1989 - Present ($2.00, B&W, newsprint)
Mr. Publications/Vortex Comics

1	1.25	3.75	7.50
2	.75	2.25	4.50
3-5	.60	1.75	3.50
6-10	.40	1.25	2.50
11-14: 13-Kaluta-c; 14-$2.25	.35	1.10	2.25

MR. X (continued)	Good	Fine	N-Mint
V2#1-9 (Second Coming, B&W)	.35	1.00	2.00
Graphic Novel, Return of. . . ($11.95)-r/1-4	2.00	6.00	12.00
Hardcover Limited Edition ($34.95)	5.85	17.50	35.00

MISTY
Dec. 1985 - No. 6, May, 1986 (mini-series)
Star Comics (Marvel)

	Good	Fine	N-Mint
1-Millie The Model's niece		.35	.70
2-6		.40	.80

MITZI COMICS (. . .Boy Friend #2 on)(See All Teen)
Spring, 1948 (One Shot)
Timely Comics

	Good	Fine	N-Mint
1-Kurtzman's "Hey Look" plus 3 pgs. "Giggles 'n' Grins"	7.00	21.00	50.00

MITZI'S BOY FRIEND (Formerly Mitzi; becomes Mitzi's Romances)
No. 2, June, 1948 - No. 7, April, 1949
Marvel Comics

	Good	Fine	N-Mint
2	3.00	9.00	21.00
3-7	2.00	6.00	14.00

MITZI'S ROMANCES (Formerly Mitzi's Boy Friend)
No. 8, June, 1949 - No. 10, Dec, 1949
Timely/Marvel Comics

	Good	Fine	N-Mint
8	3.00	9.00	21.00
9,10: 10-Painted-c	2.00	6.00	14.00

MOBY DICK (See Feature Presentations #6, Four Color #717, and King Classics)

MOBY DUCK (See Donald Duck #112 & W. D. Showcase #2,11)
10/67 - No. 11, 10/70; No. 12, 1/74 - No. 30, 2/78
Gold Key (Disney)

	Good	Fine	N-Mint
1	.85	2.50	6.00
2-5	.70	2.00	4.00
6-11	.35	1.00	2.00
12-30: 21,30-r		.60	1.20

MODEL FUN (With Bobby Benson)
No. 3, Winter, 1954-55 - No. 5, July, 1955
Harle Publications

	Good	Fine	N-Mint
3-Bobby Benson	2.85	8.50	20.00
4,5-Bobby Benson	1.70	5.00	12.00

MODELING WITH MILLIE (Formerly Life With Millie)
No. 21, Feb, 1963 - No. 54, June, 1967
Atlas/Marvel Comics Group (Male Publ.)

	Good	Fine	N-Mint
21	1.30	4.00	9.00
22-30	1.00	3.00	7.00
31-54	.70	2.00	5.00

MODERN COMICS (Formerly Military Comics #1-43)
No. 44, Nov, 1945 - No. 102, Oct, 1950
Quality Comics Group

	Good	Fine	N-Mint
44-Blackhawk continues	26.00	77.00	180.00
45-52: 49-1st app. Fear, Lady Adventuress	16.00	48.00	110.00
53-Torchy by Ward begins (9/46)	20.00	60.00	140.00
54-60: 55-J. Cole-a	14.00	42.00	100.00
61-77,79,80: 73-J. Cole-a	13.00	40.00	90.00
78-1st app. Madame Butterfly	14.00	42.00	100.00
81-99,101: 82,83-One pg. J. Cole-a	13.00	40.00	90.00
100	13.00	40.00	90.00
102-(Scarce)-J. Cole-a; Spirit by Eisner app.	16.00	48.00	110.00

NOTE: *Crandall* Blackhawk-#46-51, 54, 56, 58-60, 64, 67-70, 73, 82, 83. *Jack Cole* a-73. *Gustavson* a-47. *Ward* Blackhawk-#52, 53, 55 (15 pgs. each). Torchy in #53-102; by *Ward* only in #53-89(9/49); by *Gil Fox* #93, 102.

MODERN LOVE
June-July, 1949 - No. 8, Aug-Sept, 1950
E. C. Comics

	Good	Fine	N-Mint
1	41.50	125.00	290.00
2-Craig/Feldstein-c	33.00	100.00	230.00
3-Spanking panels	27.00	81.00	190.00
4-6 (Scarce): 4-Bra/panties panels	39.00	118.00	275.00
7,8	29.00	88.00	205.00

NOTE: *Feldstein* a-in most issues: c-1. 2). 3-8. *Ingels* a-1. 2. 4-7. *Wood* a-7. (Canadian reprints known; see Table of Contents.)

MOD LOVE
1967 (36 pages) (50 cents)
Western Publishing Co.

	Good	Fine	N-Mint
1	1.50	4.50	10.00

MODNIKS, THE
Aug, 1967 - No. 2, Aug, 1970
Gold Key

	Good	Fine	N-Mint
10206-708(#1), 2	.75	2.25	5.00

MOD SQUAD (TV)
Jan, 1969 - No. 3, Oct, 1969 - No. 8, April, 1971
Dell Publishing Co.

	Good	Fine	N-Mint
1-Photo-c	1.50	4.50	10.00
2-8: 8 reprints #2. 2-4-Photo-c	1.00	3.00	7.00

MOD WHEELS
March, 1971 - No. 19, Jan, 1976
Gold Key

	Good	Fine	N-Mint
1	1.00	3.00	6.00
2-19: 11,15-Extra 16pgs. ads	.50	1.50	3.00

MOE & SHMOE COMICS
Spring, 1948 - No. 2, Summer, 1948
O. S. Publ. Co.

	Good	Fine	N-Mint
1	3.50	10.50	24.00
2	2.30	7.00	16.00

MOEBIUS
Oct, 1987 - No. 6, 1988 ($9.95, $12.95, graphic novel, adults)
Epic Comics (Marvel)

	Good	Fine	N-Mint
1,2,4-6: (#2, 2nd printing, $9.95)	1.70	5.00	10.00
3 (1st & 2nd printings, $12.95)	2.15	6.50	13.00
Moebius I-Signed & numbered hard-c ($45.95, Graphitti Designs, 1,500 copies)-r/1-3	7.70	23.00	46.00

MOLLY MANTON'S ROMANCES (Romantic Affairs #3)
Sept, 1949 - No. 2, Dec, 1949 (52 pgs.)
Marvel Comics (SePl)

	Good	Fine	N-Mint
1-Photo-c	4.00	12.00	28.00
2-Titled 'Romances of. . .'; photo-c	2.85	8.50	20.00

MOLLY O'DAY (Super Sleuth)
February, 1945 (1st Avon comic)
Avon Periodicals

	Good	Fine	N-Mint
1-Molly O'Day, The Enchanted Dagger by Tuska (r-/Yankee #1), Capt'n Courage, Corporal Grant app.	30.00	90.00	210.00

MONKEES, THE (TV)(Also see Circus Boy, Groovy, Not Brand Echh #3, Teen-Age Talk, Teen Beam & Teen Beat)
March, 1967 - No. 17, Oct, 1969 (#1-4,6,7,10 have photo-c)
Dell Publishing Co.

	Good	Fine	N-Mint
1	4.30	13.00	30.00
2-17: 17 reprints #1	2.15	6.50	15.00

MONKEY & THE BEAR, THE
Sept, 1953 - No. 3, Jan, 1954
Atlas Comics (ZPC)

	Good	Fine	N-Mint
1-Howie Post-a	2.30	7.00	16.00
2,3	1.30	4.00	9.00

Mitzi Comics #1. © MEG

Modern Comics #73. © QUA

Molly O'Day #1. © AVON

Monte Hale Western #44, © FAW

Monty Hall Of The U.S. Marines #8, © TOBY

A Moon, A Girl... Romance #11, © WMG

MONKEYSHINES COMICS
Summer, 1944 - No. 27, July, 1949
Ace Periodicals/Publishers Specialists/Current Books/Unity Publ.

	Good	Fine	N-Mint
1	4.00	12.00	28.00
2	2.00	6.00	14.00
3-10	1.50	4.50	10.00
11-27: 23,24-Fago-c/a	1.15	3.50	8.00

MONKEY SHINES OF MARSELEEN
1909 (11½x17") (28 pages in two colors)
Cupples & Leon Co.

By Norman E. Jennett	11.00	32.00	75.00

MONKEY'S UNCLE, THE (See Merlin Jones As... under Movie Comics)

MONROES, THE (TV)
April, 1967
Dell Publishing Co.

1-Photo-c	1.70	5.00	12.00

MONSTER
1953 - No. 2, 1953
Fiction House Magazines

1-Dr. Drew by Grandenetti; reprint from Rangers Comics	17.00	51.00	120.00
2	14.00	42.00	100.00

MONSTER CRIME COMICS (Also see Crime Must Stop)
October, 1952 (52 pgs., 15 cents)
Hillman Periodicals

1-(Scarce)	38.00	115.00	265.00

MONSTER HOWLS (Magazine)
December, 1966 (Satire) (35 cents) (68 pgs.)
Humor-Vision

1	.85	2.50	5.00

MONSTER HUNTERS
8/75 - No. 9, 1/77; No. 10, 10/77 - No. 18, 2/79
Charlton Comics

1-Howard-a, Newton-c	.40	.80
2-Ditko-a	.40	.80
3-11	.30	.60
12,13,15-18-All reprints	.25	.50
14-Special all-Ditko issue	.50	1.00
1,2(Modern Comics reprints, 1977)	.15	.30

NOTE: Ditko a-6, 8, 10, 13-15r, 18r; c-13-15, 18. Howard r-13. Morisi a-1,13. Staton a-1,13. Sutton a-2, 4; c-2, 4.

MONSTER OF FRANKENSTEIN (See Frankenstein)

MONSTERS ON THE PROWL (Chamber of Darkness #1-8)
No. 9, 2/71 - No. 27, 11/73; No. 28, 6/74 - No. 30, 10/74
Marvel Comics Group (No. 13,14: 52 pgs.)

9-Smith inks	.50	1.00
10-30	.30	.60

NOTE: Ditko a-9r, 14r, 16r. Kirby r-10-17, 21, 23, 25, 27, 28, 30; c-9, 25. Kirby/Ditko r-14, 17-20, 22, 24, 26, 29. Marie/John Severin a-16(Kull). 9-13, 15-contain one new story. Woodish art by Reese-11.

MONSTERS UNLEASHED (Magazine)
July, 1973 - No. 11, April, 1975; Summer, 1975 (B&W)
Marvel Comics Group

1	.35	1.00	2.00
2-The Frankenstein Monster begins	.60	1.20
3-Adams-c; The Man-Thing begins (origin-r)-Adams-a			
	.25	.75	1.50
4-Intro. Satana, the Devil's daughter; Krigstein-r			
	.25	.75	1.50
5-7: 7-Williamson-a(r)		.60	1.20
8,10,11: 8-Adams-r. 10-Origin Tigra		.50	1.00

	Good	Fine	N-Mint
9-Wendigo app.	.40	1.25	2.50
Annual 1(Summer,'75)-Kane-a		.50	1.00

NOTE: Boris c-2, 6. Brunner a-2; c-11. J. Buscema a-2p, 4p, 5p. Colan a-1, 4r. Davis a-3r. Everett a-2r. G. Kane a-3. Morrow a-3; c-1. Perez a-8. Ploog a-6. Reese a-1, 2. Tuska a-3p. Wildey a-1r.

MONTANA KID, THE (See Kid Montana)

MONTE HALE WESTERN (Movie star; Formerly Mary Marvel #1-28; also see Picture News, Real Western Hero, Six-Gun Heroes, Western Hero & XMas Comics)
No. 29, Oct. 1944 - No. 88, Jan, 1956
Fawcett Publications/Charlton No. 83 on

	Good	Fine	N-Mint
29-(#1, 52pgs.)-Photo-c begin, end #82; Monte Hale & his horse Pardner begin	21.50	64.00	150.00
30-(52 pgs.)-Big Bow and Little Arrow begin, end #34; Captain Tootsie by Beck	13.00	40.00	90.00
31-36,38-40-(52 pgs.): 34-Gabby Hayes begins, ends #80. 39-Captain Tootsie by Beck	11.00	32.00	75.00
37,41,45,49-(36 pgs.)	7.00	19.50	45.00
42-44,46-48,50-(52 pgs.): 47-Big Bow & Little Arrow app.	7.00	21.00	50.00
51,52,54-56,58,59-(52 pgs.)	5.70	17.00	40.00
53,57-(36 pgs.): 53-Slim Pickens app.	4.30	13.00	30.00
60-81: 36pgs. #60-on. 80-Gabby Hayes ends	4.30	13.00	30.00
82-Last Fawcett issue (6/53)	5.50	16.50	38.00
83-1st Charlton issue (2/55); B&W photo back-c begin. Gabby Hayes returns, ends #86	5.50	16.50	38.00
84 (4/55)	4.30	13.00	30.00
85-86	4.00	12.00	28.00
87-Wolverton-r, ½pg.	4.30	13.00	30.00
88-Last issue	4.30	13.00	30.00

NOTE: Gil Kane a-33?, 34? Rocky Lane ½-1 pg. (Carnation ad)-38, 40, 41, 43, 44, 46, 55.

MONTY HALL OF THE U.S. MARINES (See With the Marines...)
Aug, 1951 - No. 11, 1953
Toby Press

1	4.00	12.00	28.00
2	2.85	8.50	20.00
3-5	2.50	7.50	17.00
6-11	1.85	5.50	13.00

NOTE: 3-5 have full page pin-ups (Pin-Up Pete) by Jack Sparling in all.

MOON, A GIRL...ROMANCE, A (Becomes Weird Fantasy #13 on; formerly Moon Girl #1-8)
No. 9, Sept-Oct, 1949 - No. 12, Mar-Apr, 1950
E. C. Comics

9-Moon Girl cameo; spanking panels	54.00	160.00	375.00
10,11	41.50	125.00	290.00
12-(Scarce)	57.00	170.00	400.00

NOTE: Feldstein, Ingels art in all. Canadian reprints known; see Table of Contents.

MOON GIRL AND THE PRINCE (#1) (Moon Girl #2-6; Moon Girl Fights Crime #7,8; becomes A Moon, A Girl, Romance #9 on)
Fall, 1947 - No. 8, Summer, 1949
E. C. Comics (Also see Happy Houlihans)

1-Origin Moon Girl	63.00	190.00	445.00
2	37.00	110.00	260.00
3,4: 4-Moon Girl vs. a vampire	31.50	94.00	220.00
5-E.C.'s 1st horror story, "Zombie Terror"	65.00	200.00	465.00
6-8 (Scarce): 7-Origin Star (Moongirl's sidekick)	36.00	107.00	250.00

NOTE: #2 & #3 are 52 pgs., #4 on, 36 pgs. Canadian reprints known; (see Table of Contents.)

MOON KNIGHT (Also see The Hulk, Marc Spector..., Marvel Preview #21, Marvel Spotlight & Werewolf by Night #32)
November, 1980 - No. 38, July, 1984 (Mando paper No. 33 on)

MOON KNIGHT (continued)
Marvel Comics Group

	Good	Fine	N-Mint
1-Origin resumed in #4	.40	1.25	2.50
2-34,36-38: 4-Intro Midnight Man. 25-Double size			
		.50	1.00
35-($1.00, 52 pgs.)-X-men app. Ploog back-c	.25	.75	1.50

NOTE: *Austin c-27i, 31i. Kaluta c-36-38. Miller c-9, 12p, 13p, 27p.*

MOON KNIGHT
June, 1985 - No. 6, Dec, 1985
Marvel Comics Group

V2#1-6: 1-Double size; new costume		.50	1.00

MOON KNIGHT SPECIAL EDITION
Nov, 1983 - No. 3, Jan, 1984 ($2.00, mini-series, Baxter paper)
Marvel Comics Group

1-3: 1-Hulk-r	.25	.75	1.50

MOON MULLINS
1927 - 1933 (52 pgs.) (daily B&W strip reprints)
Cupples & Leon Co.

Series 1('27)-By Willard	13.00	40.00	90.00
Series 2('28), Series 3('29), Series 4('30)	10.00	30.00	70.00
Series 5('31), 6('32), 7('33)	8.00	24.00	56.00
Big Book 1('30)-B&W	16.00	48.00	110.00

MOON MULLINS (See Popular, Super Book #3 & Super Comics)
1941 - 1945
Dell Publishing Co.

4-Color 14(1941)	21.00	62.00	145.00
Large Feature Comic 29(1941)	14.00	42.00	100.00
4-Color 31(1943)	12.00	36.00	84.00
4-Color 81(1945)	6.50	19.50	45.00

MOON MULLINS
Dec-Jan, 1947-48 - No. 8, 1949 (52 pgs.)
Michel Publ. (American Comics Group)

1-Alternating Sunday & daily strip-r	8.50	25.50	60.00
2	4.50	14.00	32.00
3-8	3.50	10.50	24.00

NOTE: *Milt Gross a-2, 4-6, 8. Willard r-all.*

MOON PILOT (See 4-Color #1313)

MOONSHADOW
5/85 - No. 12, 2/87 ($1.50-$1.75)(Adults only)
Epic Comics (Marvel)

1-Origin	.85	2.50	5.00
2-12: 11-Origin	.50	1.50	3.00
Trade paperback (1987?)-reprints	2.35	7.00	14.00
Signed & numbered hard-c ($39.95, 1,200 copies)-r/1-12			
	6.70	20.00	40.00

MOON-SPINNERS, THE (See Movie Comics)

MOONWALKER IN 3-D (See Blackthorne 3-D Series #75)

MOPSY (See Pageant of Comics & TV Teens)
Feb, 1948 - No. 19, Sept, 1953
St. John Publ. Co.

1-Part-r; r-/"Some Punkins" by Neher	11.00	32.00	75.00
2	5.50	16.50	38.00
3-10(1953): 8-Lingerie panels	4.30	13.00	30.00
11-19: 19-Lingerie-c	3.50	10.50	24.00

NOTE: *#1, 4-6, 8, 13, 19 have paper dolls.*

MORE FUN COMICS (Formerly New Fun Comics #1-6)
No. 7, Jan, 1936 - No. 127, Nov-Dec, 1947 (No. 7,9-11 paper-c)
National Periodical Publications

	Good	Fine	VF-NM
7(1/36)-Oversized, paper-c; 1 pg. Kelly-a	300.00	750.00	1800.00

	Good	Fine	VF-NM
8(2/36)-Oversized (10x12"), slick-c; 1 pg. Kelly-a			
	267.00	670.00	1600.00
9(3-4/36)(Very Rare)-Last Henri Duval by Siegel & Shuster			
	267.00	670.00	1600.00
10,11(7/36): 11-1st 'Calling All Cars' by Siegel & Shuster			
	175.00	440.00	1050.00
12(8/36)-Slick-c begin	154.00	385.00	925.00
V2#1(9/36, #13)	154.00	385.00	925.00
2(10/36, #14)-Dr. Occult in costume (Superman prototype) begins, ends #17; see The Comics Magazine	175.00	440.00	1050.00
V2#3(11/36, #15), 16(V2#4), 17(V2#5)-Cover numbering begins #16.			
16-Xmas-c	114.00	285.00	685.00
18-20(V2#8, 5/37)	87.00	220.00	525.00

	Good	Fine	N-Mint
21(V2#9)-24(V2#12, 9/37)	60.00	150.00	360.00
25(V3#1, 10/37)-27(V3#3, 12/37): 27-Xmas-c	60.00	150.00	360.00
28-30: 30-1st non-funny cover	60.00	150.00	360.00
31-35: 32-Last Dr. Occult	51.00	130.00	305.00
36-40: 36-The Masked Ranger begins, ends #41. 39-Xmas-c			
	47.00	120.00	285.00
41-50	43.00	110.00	260.00
51-1st app. The Spectre (in costume) in one panel ad at end of Buccaneer story	108.00	270.00	650.00
52-Origin The Spectre (out of costume), Part 1 by Bernard Baily; last Wing Brady (Rare)	1600.00	4000.00	9600.00
53-Origin The Spectre (out of costume), Part 2; Capt. Desmo begins (Scarce)	1035.00	2600.00	6200.00
(Prices vary widely on above two books)			
54-The Spectre in costume; last King Carter	417.00	1050.00	2500.00
55-(Scarce)-Dr. Fate begins (Intro & 1st app.); last Bulldog Martin	450.00	1125.00	2700.00
56-60: 56-Congo Bill begins	192.00	480.00	1150.00
61-66: 63-Last St. Bob Neal. 64-Lance Larkin begins	133.00	335.00	800.00
67-(Scarce)-Origin Dr. Fate; last Congo Bill & Biff Bronson	200.00	500.00	1200.00
68-70: 68-Clip Carson begins. 70-Last Lance Larkin	118.00	295.00	710.00
71-(Scarce)-Origin & 1st app. Johnny Quick by Mort Wysinger	200.00	500.00	1200.00
72-Dr. Fate's new helmet; last Sgt. Carey, Sgt. O'Malley & Captain Desmo	102.00	255.00	615.00
73-(Rare)-Origin & 1st app. Aquaman; intro. Green Arrow & Speedy	300.00	750.00	1800.00
74-2nd Aquaman	117.00	295.00	700.00
75-80: 76-Last Clip Carson; Johnny Quick by Meskin begins, ends #97. 80-1st small logo	100.00	250.00	600.00
81-88: 87-Last Radio Squad	73.00	185.00	440.00
89-Origin Green Arrow & Speedy Team-up	83.00	210.00	500.00
90-99: 93-Dover & Clover begin. 97-Kubert-a. 98-Last Dr. Fate	46.00	115.00	275.00
100	64.00	160.00	385.00
101-Origin & 1st app. Superboy (not by Siegel & Shuster); last Spectre issue	300.00	750.00	1800.00
102-2nd Superboy	79.00	200.00	475.00
103-3rd Superboy	58.00	145.00	350.00
104-107: 104-1st Superboy-c. 105-Superboy-c. 107-Last J. Quick & Superboy	48.00	120.00	290.00
108-120: 108-Genius Jones begins	7.00	21.00	50.00
121-124,126: 121-123,126-Post-c	5.70	17.00	40.00
125-Superboy on cover	30.00	90.00	210.00
127-(Scarce)-Post c/a	14.00	42.00	100.00

NOTE: *Cover features: The Spectre-#52-55, 57-60, 62-67. Dr. Fate-#55, 56, 61, 68-76. The Green Arrow & Speedy-#77-85, 88-97, 99, 101; w/Dover & Clover-#98. Johnny Quick-#86, 87, 100. Genius Jones-#108-127. Baily a-45, 52-on; c-52-55, 57-60, 62-67. Al Capp a-45(signed Koppy). Guardineer c-47. Kiefer a-20. Moldoff c-51.*

Moon Knight #36, © MEG

More Fun Comics #55, © DC

More Fun Comics #74, © DC

Motion Picture Comics #101, © FAW

Motion Picture Funnies Weekly #1, © MEG

Movie Classics (David Ladd), © David Ladd

MORE SEYMOUR (See Seymour My Son)
October, 1963
Archie Publications

	Good	Fine	N-Mint
1	1.35	4.00	8.00

MORE TRASH FROM MAD (Annual)
1958 - No. 12, 1969
E. C. Comics

nn(1958)-8 pgs. color Mad reprint from #20	10.00	30.00	70.00
2(1959)-Market Product Labels	7.00	21.00	50.00
3(1960)-Text book covers	5.70	17.00	40.00
4(1961)-Sing Along with Mad booklet	5.70	17.00	40.00
5(1962)-Window Stickers; r-/from Mad #39	3.50	10.50	24.00
6(1963)-TV Guise booklet	4.00	12.00	28.00
7(1964)-Alfred E. Neuman commemorative stamps	2.30	7.00	16.00
8(1965)-Life size poster-A. E. Neuman	2.30	7.00	16.00
9,10(1966-67)-Mischief Sticker	1.70	5.00	12.00
11(1968)-Campaign poster & bumper sticker	1.70	5.00	12.00
12(1969)-Pocket medals	1.70	5.00	12.00

NOTE: *Kelly Freas* c-1, 2, 4. *Mingo* c-3, 5-9, 12.

MORGAN THE PIRATE (See 4-Color #1227)

MORLOCK 2001
Feb, 1975 - No. 3, July, 1975
Atlas/Seaboard Publ.

1-Origin & 1st app.		.50	1.00
2		.30	.60
3-Ditko/Wrightson-a; origin The Midnight Man & The Midnight Men		.60	1.20

MORTIE (Mazie's Friend)
Dec, 1952 - No. 4, June, 1953?
Magazine Publishers

1	2.65	8.00	18.00
2	1.50	4.50	10.00
3,4	1.00	3.00	7.00

MORTY MEEKLE (See 4-Color #793)

MOSES & THE TEN COMMANDMENTS (See Dell Giants)

MOTHER GOOSE (See Christmas With Mother Goose & 4-Color #41, 59, 68, 862)

MOTHER OF US ALL
1950? (32 pgs.)
Catechetical Guild Giveaway

nn	1.15	3.50	8.00

MOTHER TERESA OF CALCUTTA
1984
Marvel Comics Group

1		.60	1.25

MOTION PICTURE COMICS (See Fawcett Movie Comics)
No. 101, 1950 - No. 114, Jan, 1953 (All-photo-c)
Fawcett Publications

101-"Vanishing Westerner"-Monte Hale (1950)	24.00	73.00	170.00
102-"Code of the Silver Sage"-Rocky Lane (1/51)	22.00	65.00	155.00
103-"Covered Wagon Raid"-Rocky Lane (3/51)	22.00	65.00	155.00
104-"Vigilante Hideout"-Rocky Lane (5/51)-book length Powell-a	22.00	65.00	155.00
105-"Red Badge of Courage"-Audie Murphy; Bob Powell-a (7/51)	27.00	81.00	190.00
106-"The Texas Rangers"-George Montgomery (9/51)	21.00	64.00	150.00
107-"Frisco Tornado"-Rocky Lane (11/51)	20.00	60.00	140.00

	Good	Fine	N-Mint
108-"Mask of the Avenger"-John Derek	14.00	42.00	100.00
109-"Rough Rider of Durango"-Rocky Lane	20.00	60.00	140.00
110-"When Worlds Collide"-George Evans-a (1951); Williamson & Evans drew themselves in story; (Also see Famous Funnies No. 72-88)	69.00	208.00	485.00
111-"The Vanishing Outpost"-Lash LaRue	24.00	73.00	170.00
112-"Brave Warrior"-Jon Hall & Jay Silverheels	13.00	40.00	90.00
113-"Walk East on Beacon"-George Murphy; Shaffenberger-a	9.30	28.00	65.00
114-"Cripple Creek"-George Montgomery (1/53)	11.00	32.00	75.00

MOTION PICTURE FUNNIES WEEKLY (Amazing Man #5 on?)
1939 (36 pgs.)(Giveaway)(Black & White)
No month given; last panel in Sub-Mariner story dated 4/39
(Also see Colossus, Green Giant & Invaders No. 20)
First Funnies, Inc.

1-Origin & 1st printed app. Sub-Mariner by Bill Everett (8 pgs.); Fred Schwab-c; reprinted in Marvel Mystery #1 with color added over the craft tint which was used to shade the black & white version; Spy Ring, American Ace (reprinted in Marvel Mystery No. 3) app. (Rare)-only seven (7) known copies, all with brown pages.	2500.00	5000.00	—
Covers only to #2-4 (set)			600.00

NOTE: The only seven known copies (with an eighth suspected) were discovered in 1974 in the estate of the deceased publisher. Covers only to issues No. 2-4 were also found which evidently were printed in advance along with #1. #1 was to be distributed only through motion picture movie houses. However, it is believed that only advanced copies were sent out and the motion picture houses not going for the idea. Possible distribution at local theaters in Boston suspected. The last panel of Sub-Mariner contains a rectangular box with "Continued Next Week" printed in it. When reprinted in Marvel Mystery, the box was left in with lettering omitted.

MOUNTAIN MEN (See Ben Bowie)

MOUSE MUSKETEERS (See M.G.M.'s...)

MOUSE ON THE MOON, THE (See Movie Classics)

MOVIE CLASSICS
Jan, 1953 - Dec, 1969
Dell Publishing Co.
(Before 1962, most movie adapt. were part of the 4-Color Series)

Around the World Under the Sea 12-030-612 (12/66)	1.50	4.50	10.00
Bambi 3(4/56)-Disney; r-/4-Color 186	1.50	4.50	10.00
Battle of the Bulge 12-056-606 (6/66)	1.50	4.50	10.00
Beach Blanket Bingo 12-058-509	4.30	13.00	30.00
Bon Voyage 01-068-212 (12/62)-Disney; photo-c	1.50	4.50	10.00
Castilian, The 12-110-401	2.30	7.00	16.00
Cat, The 12-109-612 (12/66)	1.30	4.00	9.00
Cheyenne Autumn 12-112-506 (4-6/65)	4.00	12.00	28.00
Circus World, Samuel Bronston's 12-115-411; John Wayne app. John Wayne photo-c	6.50	19.50	45.00
Countdown 12-150-710 (10/67); James Caan photo-c	1.50	4.50	10.00
Creature, The 1 (12-142-302) (12-2/62-63)	2.65	8.00	18.00
Creature, The 12-142-410 (10/64)	1.50	4.50	10.00
David Ladd's Life Story 12-173-212 (10-12/62)-Photo-c	6.00	18.00	42.00
Die, Monster, Die 12-175-603 (3/66)-Photo-c	2.00	6.00	14.00
Dirty Dozen 12-180-710 (10/67)	2.85	8.50	20.00
Dr. Who & the Daleks 12-190-612 (12/66)-Photo-c	11.00	33.00	75.00
Dracula 12-231-212 (10-12/62)	2.00	6.00	14.00
El Dorado 12-240-710 (10/67)-John Wayne; photo-c	10.00	30.00	70.00
Ensign Pulver 12-257-410 (8-10/64)	1.70	5.00	12.00

MOVIE CLASSICS (continued)

	Good	Fine	N-Mint
Frankenstein 12-283-305 (3-5/63)	2.00	6.00	14.00
Great Race, The 12-299-603 (3/66)-Natallie Wood, Tony Curtis			
photo-c	2.85	8.50	20.00
Hallelujah Trail, The 12-307-602 (2/66) (Shows 1/66 inside); Burt			
Lancaster, Lee Remick photo-c	3.70	11.00	26.00
Hatari 12-340-301 (1/63)-John Wayne	5.70	17.00	40.00
Horizontal Lieutenant, The 01-348-210 (10/62)	1.50	4.50	10.00
Incredible Mr. Limpet, The 12-370-408; Don Knotts photo-c			
	2.00	6.00	14.00
Jack the Giant Killer 12-374-301 (1/63)	5.00	15.00	35.00
Jason & the Argonauts 12-376-310 (8-10/63)-Photo-c			
	5.70	17.00	40.00
Lancelot & Guinevere 12-416-310 (10/63)	5.00	15.00	35.00
Lawrence 12-426-308 (8/63)-Story of Lawrence of Arabia; movie ad			
on back-c; not exactly like movie	3.70	11.00	26.00
Lion of Sparta 12-439-301 (1/63)	1.70	5.00	12.00
Mad Monster Party 12-460-801 (9/67)	4.50	14.00	32.00
Magic Sword, The 01-496-209 (9/62)	3.50	10.50	24.00
Masque of the Red Death 12-490-410 (8-10/64)-Vincent Price photo-c			
	2.65	8.00	18.00
Maya 12-495-612 (12/66)-Clint Walker part photo-c			
	2.65	8.00	18.00
McHale's Navy 12-500-412 (10-12/64)	2.00	6.00	14.00
Merrill's Marauders 12-510-301 (1/63)-Photo-c	1.70	5.00	12.00
Mouse on the Moon, The 12-530-312 (10/12/63)-Photo-c			
	2.00	6.00	14.00
Mummy, The 12-537-211 (9-11/62) 2 different back-c issues			
	2.30	7.00	16.00
Music Man, The 12-538-301 (1/63)	1.70	5.00	12.00
Naked Prey, The 12-545-612 (12/66)-Photo-c	4.30	13.00	30.00
Night of the Grizzly, The 12-558-612 (12/66)-Photo-c			
	2.30	7.00	16.00
None But the Brave 12-565-506 (4-6/65)	3.50	10.50	24.00
Operation Bikini 12-597-310 (10/63)-Photo-c	2.30	7.00	16.00
Operation Crossbow 12-590-512 (10-12/65)	2.30	7.00	16.00
Prince & the Pauper, The 01-654-207 (5-7/62)-Disney			
	2.30	7.00	16.00
Raven, The 12-680-309 (9/63)-Vincent Price photo-c			
	2.65	8.00	18.00
Ring of Bright Water 01-701-910 (10/69) (inside shows #12-701-909)			
	2.65	8.00	18.00
Runaway, The 12-707-412 (10-12/64)	1.30	4.00	9.00
Santa Claus Conquers the Martians 12-725-603 (3/60)-Regular issue			
with number & price; photo-c	5.00	15.00	35.00
Another version given away with a Golden Record, SLP 170, nn,			
no price (3/66) Complete with record	10.00	30.00	70.00
Six Black Horses 12-750-301 (1/63)-Photo-c	2.00	6.00	14.00
Ski Party 12-743-511 (9-11/65)-Frankie Avalon photo-c			
	3.50	10.50	24.00
Smoky 12-746-702 (2/67)	1.30	4.00	9.00
Sons of Katie Elder 12-748-511 (9-11/65); John Wayne app., Photo-c			
	11.00	32.00	75.00
Tales of Terror 12-793-302 (2/63)-Evans-a	1.30	4.00	9.00
Three Stooges Meet Hercules 01-828-208 (8/62)-Photo-c			
	5.00	15.00	35.00
Tomb of Ligeia 12-830-506 (4-6/65)	1.50	4.50	10.00
Treasure Island 01-845-211 (7-9/62)-Disney; r-/4-Color 624			
	1.15	3.50	8.00
Twice Told Tales (Nathaniel Hawthorne) 12-840-401 (11-1/63-64);			
Vincent Price photo-c	2.00	6.00	14.00
Two on a Guillotine 12-850-506 (4-6/65)	1.50	4.50	10.00
Valley of Gwangi 01-880-912 (12/69)	5.00	15.00	35.00
War Gods of the Deep 12-900-509 (7-9/65)	1.50	4.50	10.00
War Wagon, The 12-533-709 (9/67); John Wayne app.			
	8.00	24.00	56.00
Who's Minding the Mint? 12-924-708 (8/67)-Jerry Lewis photo-c			

	Good	Fine	N-Mint
Wolfman, The 12-922-308 (6-8/63)	1.50	4.50	10.00
Wolfman, The 1(12-922-410)(8-10/64)-2nd printing; 4-/#12-922-308			
	1.50	4.50	10.00
Zulu 12-950-410 (8-10/64)-Photo-c	5.70	17.00	40.00

MOVIE COMICS (See Cinema Comics Herald & Fawcett Movie Comics)

MOVIE COMICS
April, 1939 - No. 6, Sept, 1939 (Most all photo-c)
National Periodical Publications/Picture Comics

	Good	Fine	N-Mint
1-"Gunga Din,""Son of Frankenstein,""The Great Man Votes,"			
"Fisherman's Wharf,"&"Scouts to the Rescue part 1; Wheelan			
"Minute Movies" begin	183.00	460.00	1100.00
2-"Stagecoach,""The Saint Strikes Back,""King of the Turf,"			
"Scouts to the Rescue" part 2, "Arizona Legion"			
	100.00	300.00	700.00
3-"East Side of Heaven,""Mystery in the White Room,""Four			
Feathers,""Mexican Rose" with Gene Autry, "Spirit of Culver,"			
"Many Secrets,""The Mikado"	82.00	245.00	575.00
4-"Captain Fury," Gene Autry in "Blue Montana Skies,""Streets			
of N.Y." with Jackie Cooper, "Oregon Trail" part 1 with Johnny			
Mack Brown, "Big Town Czar" with Barton MacLane, & "Star			
Reporter" with Warren Hull	73.00	220.00	510.00
5-"Man in the Iron Mask,""Five Came Back,""Wolf Call,""The			
Girl & the Gambler,""The House of Fear,""The Family Next			
Door,""Oregon Trail" part 2	73.00	220.00	510.00
6-"The Phantom Creeps,""Chumps at Oxford,"&"The Oregon			
Trail" part 3	97.00	290.00	675.00

NOTE: Above books contain many original movie stills with dialogue from movie scripts.
All issues are scarce.

MOVIE COMICS
Dec, 1946 - No. 4, 1947
Fiction House Magazines

	Good	Fine	N-Mint
1-Big Town & Johnny Danger begin; Celardo-a			
	27.00	81.00	190.00
2-"White Tie & Tails" with William Bendix; Mitzi of the Movies be-			
gins by Matt Baker, ends #4	18.50	56.00	130.00
3-Andy Hardy	18.50	56.00	130.00
4-Mitzi In Hollywood by Matt Baker	21.50	64.00	150.00

MOVIE COMICS
Oct, 1962 - March, 1972
Gold Key/Whitman

	Good	Fine	N-Mint
Alice in Wonderland 10144-503 (3/65)-Disney; partial reprint of			
4-Color 331	1.75	5.25	12.00
Aristocats, The 1 (30045-103)(3/71)-Disney; with pull-out poster			
(25 cents)	4.30	13.00	30.00
Bambi 1 (10087-309)(9/63)-Disney; reprints 4-Color 186			
	2.00	6.00	14.00
Bambi 2 (10087-607)(7/66)-Disney; reprints 4-Color 186			
	1.70	5.00	12.00
Beneath the Planet of the Apes 30044-012 (12/70)-with pull-out			
poster; photo-c	3.50	10.50	24.00
Big Red 10026-211 (11/62)-Disney-Photo-c	1.15	3.50	8.00
Big Red 10026-503 (3/65)-Disney; reprints 10026-211-Photo-c			
	1.15	3.50	8.00
Blackbeard's Ghost 10222-806 (6/68)-Disney	1.50	4.50	10.00
Bullwhip Griffin 10181-706 (6/67)-Disney; Manning-a; photo-c			
	2.35	7.00	16.00
Captain Sindbad 10077-309 (9/63)-Manning-a; photo-c			
	3.50	10.50	24.00
Chitty Chitty Bang Bang 1 (30038-902)(2/69)-with pull-out poster;			
Disney; photo-c	3.50	10.50	24.00
Cinderella 10152-508 (8/65)-Disney; reprints 4-Color 786			
	1.50	4.50	10.00
Darby O'Gill & the Little People 10251-001(1/70)-Disney; reprints			

Movie Classics (Jason and the Argonauts), © Columbia Pic.   Movie Classics (Twice Told Tales), © Universal Pic.   Movie Comics (Beneath the Planet...), © 20th Century Fox

280

Movie Comics (Fantastic Voyage), © 20th Century Fox

Movie Comics (The Moon-Spinners), © WDC

Movie Comics (P.T. 109), © Warner Bros.

MOVIE COMICS (continued)	Good	Fine	N-Mint
4-Color 1024 (Toth-a)-Photo-c	3.00	9.00	21.00
Dumbo 1 (10090-310)(10/63)-Disney; reprints 4-Color 668			
	1.50	4.50	10.00
Emil & the Detectives 10120-502 (2/65)-Disney; photo-c			
	2.35	7.00	16.00
Escapade in Florence 1 (10043-301)(1/63)-Disney; starring Annette Funicello	5.00	15.00	35.00
Fall of the Roman Empire 10118-407 (7/64); Sophia Loren photo-c			
	2.00	6.00	14.00
Fantastic Voyage 10178-702 (2/67)-Wood/Adkins-a; photo-c			
	2.65	8.00	18.00
55 Days at Peking 10081-309 (9/63)-Photo-c	2.30	7.00	16.00
Fighting Prince of Donegal, The 10193-701 (1/67)-Disney			
	1.70	5.00	12.00
First Men in the Moon 10132-503 (3/65)-Fred Fredericks-a; photo-c			
	2.30	7.00	16.00
Gay Purr-ee 30017-301(1/63, 84pgs.)	3.50	10.50	24.00
Gnome Mobile, The 10207-710 (10/67)-Disney	2.30	7.00	16.00
Goodbye, Mr. Chips 10246-006 (6/70)-Peter O'Toole photo-c			
	2.00	6.00	14.00
Happiest Millionaire, The 10221-804 (4/68)-Disney			
	1.30	4.00	9.00
Hey There, It's Yogi Bear 10122-409 (9/64)-Hanna-Barbera			
	2.30	7.00	16.00
Horse Without a Head, The 10109-401 (1/64)-Disney			
	1.50	4.50	10.00
How the West Was Won 10074-307 (7/63)-Tufts-a			
	3.50	10.50	24.00
In Search of the Castaways 10048-303 (3/63)-Disney; Haley Mills photo-c	4.00	12.00	28.00
Jungle Book, The 1 (6022-801)(1/68-Whitman)-Disney; large size (10x13½"); 59 cents	2.00	6.00	14.00
Jungle Book, The 1 (30033-803)(3/68, 68 pgs.)-Disney; same contents as Whitman #1	1.30	4.00	9.00
Jungle Book 1 (6/78, $1.00 tabloid)	.60	1.20	
Jungle Book ('84)-r-/Giant		.40	.80
Kidnapped 10080-306 (6/63)-Disney; reprints 4-Color 1101; photo-c			
	1.15	3.50	8.00
King Kong 30036-809(9/68-68 pgs.)-painted-c	2.35	7.00	16.00
King Kong nn-Whitman Treasury($1.00,88pgs.,1968), same cover as Gold Key issue	.70	2.00	4.00
King Kong 11299(#1-786, 10x13¼", 68pgs., $1.00, 1978)			
	.50	1.00	
Lady and the Tramp 10042-301 (1/63)-Disney; r-4-Color 629			
	1.50	4.50	10.00
Lady and the Tramp 1 (1967-Giant; 25 cents)-Disney; r-part of Dell #1			
	2.50	7.50	20.00
Lady and the Tramp 2 (10042-203)(3/72)-Disney; r-4-Color 629			
	1.15	3.50	8.00
Legend of Lobo, The 1 (10059-303)(3/63)-Disney; photo-c			
	1.15	3.50	8.00
Lt. Robin Crusoe, U.S.N. 10191-610 (10/66)-Disney; Dick Van Dyke photo-c	1.50	4.50	10.00
Lion, The 10035-301 (1/63)-Photo-c	1.15	3.50	8.00
Lord Jim 10156-509 (9/65)-Photo-c	1.70	5.00	12.00
Love Bug, The 10237-906 (6/69)-Disney-Buddy Hackett photo-c			
	1.50	4.50	10.00
Mary Poppins 10136-501 (1/65)-Disney; photo-c 3.00	9.00	21.00	
Mary Poppins 30023-501 (1/65-68 pgs.)-Disney; photo-c			
	4.00	12.00	28.00
McLintock 10110-403 (3/64); John Wayne app.-c			
	10.00	30.00	70.00
Merlin Jones as the Monkey's Uncle 10115-510 (10/65)-Disney; Annette Funicello front/back photo-c	2.65	8.00	18.00
Miracle of the White Stallions, The 10065-306 (6/63)-Disney			
	1.70	5.00	12.00

	Good	Fine	N-Mint
Misadventures of Merlin Jones, The 10115-405 (5/64)-Disney; Annette Funicello photo front/back-c	3.00	9.00	21.00
Moon-Spinners, The 10124-410 (10/64)-Disney; Haley Mills photo-c	4.00	12.00	28.00
Mutiny on the Bounty 1 (10040-302)(2/63)-Marlon Brando photo-c			
	2.00	6.00	14.00
Nikki, Wild Dog of the North 10141-412 (12/64)-Disney; reprints 4-Color 1226	1.15	3.50	8.00
Old Yeller 10168-601 (1/66)-Disney; reprints 4-Color 869; photo-c			
	1.15	3.50	8.00
One Hundred & One Dalmations 1 (10247-002) (2/70)-Disney; reprints 4-Color 1183	1.50	4.50	10.00
Peter Pan 1 (10086-309)(9/63)-Disney; reprints 4-Color 442			
	1.70	5.00	12.00
Peter Pan 2 (10086-909)(9/69)-Disney; reprints 4-Color 442			
	1.15	3.50	8.00
Peter Pan 1 ('83)-r/4-Color 442		.40	.80
P.T. 109 10123-409 (9/64)-John F. Kennedy	3.00	9.00	21.00
Rio Conchos 10143-503(3/65)	3.00	9.00	21.00
Robin Hood 10163-506 (6/65)-Disney; reprints 4-Color 413			
	1.50	4.50	10.00
Shaggy Dog & the Absent-Minded Professor 30032-708 (8/67-Giant, 68 pgs.)-Disney; reprints 4-Color 985,1199	3.50	10.50	24.00
Sleeping Beauty 1 (30042-009)(9/70)-Disney; reprints 4-Color 973; with pull-out poster	3.00	9.00	21.00
Snow White & the Seven Dwarfs 1 (10091-310)(10/63)-Disney; reprints 4-Color 382	1.70	5.00	12.00
Snow White & the Seven Dwarfs 10091-709 (9/67)-Disney; reprints 4-Color 382	1.50	4.50	10.00
Snow White & the Seven Dwarfs nn(2/84)-r-/4-Color 382			
		.40	.80
Son of Flubber 1 (10057-304)(4/63)-Disney; sequel to "The Absent-Minded Professor"	1.70	5.00	12.00
Summer Magic 10076-309 (9/63)-Disney; Haley Mills; Manning-a			
	4.65	14.00	32.00
Swiss Family Robinson 10236-904 (4/69)-Disney; reprints 4-Color 1156; photo-c	1.70	5.00	12.00
Sword in the Stone, The 30019-402 (2/64-Giant, 84 pgs.)-Disney			
	3.50	10.50	24.00
That Darn Cat 10171-602 (2/66)-Disney; Haley Mills photo-c			
	4.00	12.00	28.00
Those Magnificent Men in Their Flying Machines 10162-510 (10/65); photo-c	1.70	5.00	12.00
Three Stooges in Orbit 30016-211 (11/62-Giant, 32 pgs.)-All photos from movie; stiff-photo-c	6.50	19.50	45.00
Tiger Walks, A 10117-406 (6/64)-Disney; Torres, Tufts-a; photo-c			
	2.65	8.00	18.00
Toby Tyler 10142-502 (2/65)-Disney; reprints 4-Color 1092; photo-c			
	1.50	4.50	10.00
Treasure Island 1 (10200-703)(3/67)-Disney; reprints 4-Color 624; photo-c	1.15	3.50	8.00
20,000 Leagues Under the Sea 1 (10095-312)(12/63)-Disney; reprints 4-Color 545	1.15	3.50	8.00
Wonderful Adventures of Pinocchio, The 1 (10089-310)(10/63)-Disney; reprints 4-Color 545	1.15	3.50	8.00
Wonderful Adventures of Pinocchio, The 10089-109 (9/71)-Disney; reprints 4-Color 545	1.15	3.50	8.00
Wonderful World of the Brothers Grimm 1 (10008-210)(10/62)			
	2.65	8.00	18.00
X, the Man with the X-Ray Eyes 10083-309 (9/63)-Ray Milland photo on-c	3.50	10.50	24.00
Yellow Submarine 35000-902 (2/69-Giant, 68 pgs.)-with pull-out poster; The Beatles cartoon movie	7.00	21.00	50.00

MOVIE LOVE (Also see Personal Love)
Feb, 1950 - No. 22, Aug, 1953

NOTE: *Miller pin-up-1-4, 6. Johnny Dynamite-r begin #36 by Morisi.*

MOVIE LOVE (continued)
Famous Funnies

	Good	Fine	N-Mint
1-Dick Powell photo-c	5.50	16.50	38.00
2	2.85	8.50	20.00
3-7,9	2.35	7.00	16.00
8-Williamson/Frazetta-a, 6 pgs.	26.00	78.00	180.00
10-Frazetta-a, 6 pgs.	32.00	95.00	225.00
11,12,14-16	2.15	6.50	15.00
13-Ronald Reagan photo-c with 1 pg. bio.	12.00	36.00	84.00
17-One pg. Frazetta ad	3.15	9.50	22.00
18-22	2.00	6.00	14.00

NOTE: *Each issue has a full-length movie adaptation with photo covers.*

MOVIE THRILLERS
1949 (Movie adaptation; photo-c)
Magazine Enterprises

	Good	Fine	N-Mint
1-"Rope of Sand" with Burt Lancaster	18.00	54.00	125.00

MOVIE TOWN ANIMAL ANTICS (Formerly Animal Antics; Raccoon Kids #52 on)
No. 24, Jan-Feb, 1950 - No. 51, July-Aug, 1954
National Periodical Publications

	Good	Fine	N-Mint
24-Raccoon Kids continue	4.50	14.00	32.00
25-51	3.50	10.50	24.00

NOTE: *Sheldon Mayer a-28-33, 35, 37-41, 43, 44, 47, 49-51.*

MOVIE TUNES COMICS (Formerly Animated...; Frankie No. 4 on)
No. 3, Fall, 1946
Marvel Comics (MgPC)

	Good	Fine	N-Mint
3-Super Rabbit, Krazy Krow, Silly Seal & Ziggy Pig	4.30	13.00	30.00

MOWGLI JUNGLE BOOK (See 4-Color #487, 582, 620)

MR. (See Mister)

MS. MARVEL (Also see The Avengers #183)
Jan, 1977 - No. 23, Apr, 1979
Marvel Comics Group

		Good	Fine	N-Mint
1,2: 2-Origin			.50	1.00
3-23: 5-Vision app. 20-New costume			.50	1.00

NOTE: *Austin c-14i, 16i, 17i, 22i. Buscema a-1-3p; c(p)-2, 4, 6, 7, 15. Infantino a-14p, 19p. Gil Kane c-8. Mooney a-4-8p, 13p, 15-18p. Starlin c-12.*

MS. MYSTIC (Also see Captain Victory...)
10/82; No. 2, 2/84 ($1.00, color)
Pacific Comics

	Good	Fine	N-Mint
1-Origin; intro Erth, Ayre, Fyre & Watr; Adams script/a/c	.35	1.00	2.00
2 ($1.50)-Adams c/a & script	.25	.75	1.50

MS. MYSTIC
1987 - Present ($2.00, color, Baxter paper)
Continuity Comics

	Good	Fine	N-Mint
1-4: Adams-c/a; #1,2-r/Pacific #1,2	.35	1.00	2.00

MS. TREE'S THRILLING DETECTIVE ADVENTURES (Ms. Tree #4 on; also see The Best of Ms. Tree) (Baxter paper #4-9)
2/83 - #9, 7/84; #10, 8/84 - #18, 5/85; #19, 6/85 - #50, 6/89
Eclipse Comics/Aardvark-Vanaheim 10-18/Renegade Press 19 on

	Good	Fine	N-Mint
1	.60	1.75	3.50
2-8: 2-Scythe begins	.35	1.00	2.00
9-Last Eclipse & last color issue	.30	.90	1.80
10,11 (Aardvark-Vanaheim) 2-tone	.30	.90	1.80
12-49 ($1.70; $2.00 #34 on).	.35	1.00	2.00
50-Contains flexi-disc ($3.95, 52 pgs.)	.70	2.00	4.00
Summer Special 1(8/86)	.50	1.50	3.00
...1950s 3-D Crime (7/87, no glasses)-Johnny Dynamite in 3-D	.40	1.25	2.50
...Mike Mist in 3-D (8/85)-With glasses	.50	1.50	3.00

MS. VICTORY SPECIAL (Also see Capt. Paragon & Femforce)
Jan, 1985 (nd)
Americomics

	Good	Fine	N-Mint
1	.30	.85	1.70

MUGGSY MOUSE (Also see Tick Tock Tales)
1951 - No. 3, 1951; No. 4, 1954 - No. 5, 1954; 1963
Magazine Enterprises

	Good	Fine	N-Mint
1(A-1 33)	2.15	6.50	15.00
2(A-1 36)	4.30	13.00	30.00
3(A-1 39), 4(A-1 95), 5(A-1 99)	1.15	3.50	8.00
Super Reprint #14(1963)	.25	.80	1.60
I.W. Reprint #1,2 (nd)	.25	.80	1.60

MUGGY-DOO, BOY CAT
July, 1953 - No. 4, Jan, 1954
Stanhall Publ.

	Good	Fine	N-Mint
1-Irving Spector-a	2.65	8.00	18.00
2-4	1.50	4.50	10.00
Super Reprint #12('63), 16('64)		.60	1.20

MUMMY, THE (See Movie Classics)

MUNDEN'S BAR ANNUAL
April, 1988 (52pgs.; $2.95; color)
First Comics

	Good	Fine	N-Mint
1-r/from Grimjack; Fish Police story	.50	1.50	3.00

MUNSTERS, THE (TV)
Jan, 1965 - No. 16, Jan, 1968
Gold Key

	Good	Fine	N-Mint
1 (10134-501)-Photo-c	9.00	27.00	62.00
2	5.00	15.00	35.00
3-5: 4-Photo-c	4.30	13.00	30.00
6-16	3.50	10.50	24.00

MUPPET BABIES, THE (TV)(See Star Comics Magazine)
Aug, 1985 - No. 26, July, 1989 (Children's book)
Star Comics/Marvel #18 on

	Good	Fine	N-Mint
1-13 (75 cents)		.40	.80
14-26 ($1.00)		.50	1.00

MUPPETS TAKE MANHATTAN, THE
Nov, 1984 - No. 3, Jan, 1985
Star Comics (Marvel)

	Good	Fine	N-Mint
1-3-Movie adapt. r-/Marvel Super Special		.30	.60

MURDER, INCORPORATED (My Private Life #16 on)
1/48 - No. 15, 12/49; (2 No.9's); 6/50 - No. 3, 8/51
Fox Feature Syndicate

	Good	Fine	N-Mint
1 (1st Series)	16.00	48.00	110.00
2-Transvestism, electrocution story; #1,2 have 'For Adults Only' on-c	12.00	36.00	84.00
3-7,9(4/49),10(5/49),11-15	5.70	17.00	40.00
8-Used in SOTI, pg. 160	8.00	24.00	55.00
9(3/49)-Possible use in SOTI, pg. 145; r-Blue Beetle #56('48)	7.00	21.00	50.00
5(6/50)(2nd Series)-Formerly My Desire	4.30	13.00	30.00
2(8/50)-Morisi-a	3.50	10.50	24.00
3(8/51)-Used in POP, pg. 81; Rico-a; lingerie-c/panels	4.30	13.00	30.00

MURDEROUS GANGSTERS
July, 1951; No. 2, Dec, 1951 - No. 4, June, 1952
Avon Periodicals/Realistic No. 3 on

	Good	Fine	N-Mint
1-Pretty Boy Floyd, Leggs Diamond; 1 pg. Wood	18.00	54.00	125.00
2-Baby-Face Nelson; 1 pg. Wood-a	11.00	32.00	76.00

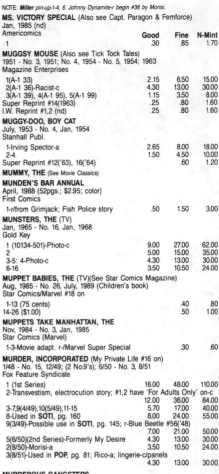

Ms. Mystic #1 (10/82), © Pacific

The Munsters #4, © Kayro-Vue Prod.

Murderous Gangsters #1, © AVON

Mutiny #3, © Aragon Mag.

Mutt And Jeff #17, © Ball Synd.

My Experience #22, © FOX

MURDEROUS GANGSTERS (continued)

	Good	Fine	N-Mint
3-Painted-c	9.50	28.00	65.00
4-"Murder by Needle" drug story; Mort Lawrence-a; Kinstler-c			
	11.00	32.00	76.00

MURDER TALES (Magazine)
V1#10, Nov, 1970 - V1#11, Jan, 1971 (52 pages)
World Famous Publications

V1#10-One pg. Frazetta ad	.70	2.00	4.00
11-Guardineer-r; bondage-c	.35	1.00	2.00

MUSHMOUSE AND PUNKIN PUSS (TV)
September, 1965 (Hanna-Barbera)
Gold Key

1 (10153-509)	3.00	9.00	21.00

MUTANT MISADVENTURES OF CLOAK AND DAGGER
Oct, 1988 - Present (#1: $1.25; #2-on: $1.50, color)
Marvel Comics

1-X-Factor app.	.35	1.00	2.00
2-10: 2-Russell-i. 4-Austin-c(i)	.25	.75	1.50

MUTANTS & MISFITS
1987 - No. 3? ($1.95, color)
Silverline Comics (Solson)

1-3	.35	1.00	2.00

MUTINY (Stormy Tales of Seven Seas)
Oct, 1954 - No. 3, Feb, 1955
Aragon Magazines

1	6.50	19.50	45.00
2,3: 2-Capt. Mutiny. 3-Bondage-c	3.50	10.50	24.00

MUTINY ON THE BOUNTY (See Classics Illustrated 100 & Movie Comics)

MUTT & JEFF (...Cartoon, The)
1910 - No. 5, 1916 (5¾x15½") (Hardcover-B&W)
Ball Publications

	Good	Fine	V. Fine
1(1910)(68 pgs., 50 cents)	30.00	90.00	210.00
2(1911), 3(1912)(68 pgs.)	30.00	90.00	210.00
4(1915)(68 pgs., 50 cents) (Rare)	35.00	105.00	245.00
5(1916)(84 pages, 60 cents) (Rare)	40.00	120.00	280.00

NOTE: Cover variations exist showing Mutt & Jeff reading various newspapers; i.e., The Oregon Journal, The American, and The Detroit News. Reprinting of each issue began soon after publication. No. 5 may not have been reprinted. Values listed include the reprints.

MUTT & JEFF
No. 6, 1916 - No. 22, 1933? (B&W dailies) (9½x9½"; stiff-c; 52 pgs.)
Cupples & Leon Co.

6-22-By Bud Fisher	17.00	51.00	120.00

NOTE: Later issues are somewhat rarer.

nn(1920)-(Advs. of...) 16x11"; 20 pgs.; reprints 1919 Sunday strips			
	30.00	90.00	210.00
Big Book nn(1926, 144pgs., hardcovers)	24.00	73.00	170.00
w/dust jacket....	35.00	105.00	245.00
Big Book 1(1928)-Thick book (hardcovers)	24.00	73.00	170.00
w/dust jacket....	35.00	105.00	245.00
Big Book 2(1929)-Thick book (hardcovers)	24.00	73.00	170.00
w/dust jacket....	35.00	105.00	245.00

NOTE: The Big Books contain three previous issues rebound.

MUTT & JEFF
1921 (9x15")
Embee Publ. Co.

Sunday strips in color (Rare)	52.00	155.00	365.00

MUTT AND JEFF (See All-American, All-Flash #18, Comic Cavalcade, The Funnies, Popular & Xmas Comics)

Summer, 1939 (nd) - No. 148, Nov, 1965
All American/National 1-103(6/58)/Dell 104(10/58)-115 (10-12/59)/Harvey 116(2/60)-148

	Good	Fine	N-Mint
1(nn)-Lost Wheels	78.00	235.00	550.00
2(nn)-Charging Bull (Summer 1940, nd; on sale 6/20/40)			
	43.00	130.00	300.00
3(nn)-Bucking Broncos (Summer 1941, nd)	30.00	90.00	210.00
4(Winter,'41), 5(Summer,'42)	22.00	65.00	155.00
6-10	13.00	40.00	90.00
11-20	8.50	25.50	60.00
21-30	6.50	19.50	45.00
31-50	3.70	11.00	26.00
51-75-Last Fisher issue. 53-Last 52pgs.	2.30	7.00	16.00
76-99,101-103: 76-Last precode issue(1/55)	1.50	4.50	10.00
100	1.70	5.00	12.00
104-148: 117,118,120-131-Richie Rich app.	.85	2.50	6.00
...Jokes 1-3(8/60-61, Harvey)-84 pgs.; Richie Rich in all; Little Dot in #2,3	1.50	4.50	10.00
...New Jokes 1-4(10/63-11/65, Harvey)-68 pgs.; Richie Rich in #1-3; Stumbo in #1	.75	2.25	5.00

NOTE: Issues 1-74 by Bud Fisher. 86 on by Al Smith. Issues from 1963 on have Fisher reprints. Clarification: early issues signed by Fisher are mostly drawn by Smith.

MY BROTHERS' KEEPER
1973 (36 pages) (35-49 cents)
Spire Christian Comics (Fleming H. Revell Co.)

nn		.50	1.00

MY CONFESSIONS (My Confession #7&8; formerly Western True Crime; A Spectacular Feature Magazine #11)
No. 7, Aug, 1949 - No. 10, Jan-Feb, 1950
Fox Feature Syndicate

7-Wood-a, 10 pgs.	10.00	30.00	70.00
8-Wood-a, 18 pgs.	8.00	24.00	56.00
9,10	3.50	10.50	24.00

MY DATE COMICS
July, 1947 - V1No.4, Jan, 1948 (1st Romance comic)
Hillman Periodicals

1-S&K-c/a	12.00	36.00	84.00
2-4-S&K, Dan Barry-a	7.00	21.00	50.00

MY DESIRE (Formerly Jo-Jo) (Murder, Inc. #5 on)
No. 30, Aug, 1949 - No. 4, April, 1950
Fox Feature Syndicate

30(#1)	4.35	13.00	30.00
31 (#2), 3,4	2.85	8.50	20.00
31 (Canadian edition)	1.50	4.50	10.00
32(12/49)-Wood-a	8.00	24.00	56.00

MY DIARY
Dec, 1949 - No. 2, Mar, 1950
Marvel Comics (A Lovers Mag.)

1,2-Photo-c	4.00	12.00	28.00

MY DOG TIGE (Buster Brown's Dog)
1957 (Giveaway)
Buster Brown Shoes

nn	1.70	5.00	10.00

MY EXPERIENCE (Formerly All Top; Judy Canova #23 on)
No. 19, Sept, 1949 - No. 22, Mar, 1950
Fox Feature Syndicate

19-Wood-a	10.00	30.00	70.00
20	2.85	8.50	20.00
21-Wood-a(2)	11.00	33.00	76.00
22-Wood-a, 9 pgs.	8.00	24.00	56.00

	Good	Fine	N-Mint

MY FAVORITE MARTIAN (TV)
1/64; No.2, 7/64 - No. 9, 10/66 (No. 1,3-9 have photo-c)
Gold Key

	Good	Fine	N-Mint
1-Russ Manning-a	5.00	15.00	35.00
2	2.65	8.00	18.00
3-9	2.30	7.00	16.00

MY FRIEND IRMA (Radio/TV) (Formerly Western Life Romances)
No. 3, June, 1950 - No. 47, Dec, 1954; No. 48, Feb, 1955
Marvel/Atlas Comics (BFP)

3-52 pgs.	5.70	17.00	40.00
4-Kurtzman-a, 10 pgs.	6.50	19.50	45.00
5-"Egghead Doodle" by Kurtzman, 4 pgs.	4.50	14.00	32.00
6,8-10: 9-paper dolls, 1pg; Millie app.	2.65	8.00	18.00
7-One pg. Kurtzman	2.85	8.50	20.00
11-22	1.70	5.00	12.00
23-One pg. Frazetta	1.70	5.00	12.00
24-48	1.15	3.50	8.00

MY GIRL PEARL
4/55 - #4, 10/55; #5, 7/57 - #6, 9/57; #7, 8/60 - #11, ?/61
Atlas Comics

1	3.70	11.00	26.00
2	1.85	5.50	13.00
3-6	1.15	3.50	8.00
7-11	.70	2.00	5.00

MY GREATEST ADVENTURE (Doom Patrol #86 on)
Jan-Feb, 1955 - No. 85, Feb, 1964
National Periodical Publications

1-Before CCA	43.00	130.00	300.00
2	19.00	57.00	135.00
3-5	15.00	45.00	105.00
6-10	8.00	24.00	55.00
11-15,19	5.00	15.00	35.00
16-18,20,21,28-Kirby-a; 18-Kirby-c	5.70	17.00	40.00
22-27,29,30	3.50	10.50	24.00
31-40	2.65	8.00	18.00
41-57,59	1.50	4.50	10.00
58,60,61-Toth-a; Last 10 cent issue	2.15	6.50	15.00
62-76,78,79	1.15	3.50	7.00
77-Toth-a	1.30	4.00	9.00
80-(6/63)-Intro/origin Doom Patrol and begin series; origin Robotman, Negative Man, & Elasti-Girl	18.00	54.00	125.00
81-85: 81,85-Toth-a	7.00	21.00	50.00

NOTE: **Anderson** a-42. **Colan** a-77. **Meskin** a-25, 26, 32, 39, 45, 50, 56, 57, 61, 64, 70, 73, 74, 76, 79; c-76. **Moreira** a-11, 17, 20, 23, 25, 27, 37, 40-43, 46, 48, 55-57, 59, 60, 62-65, 67, 69, 70. **Roussos** c/a-71-73.

MY GREATEST THRILLS IN BASEBALL
Date? (16 pg. Giveaway)
Mission of California

By Mickey Mantle	25.00	75.00	175.00

MY GREAT LOVE
Oct, 1949 - No. 4, Apr, 1950
Fox Feature Syndicate

1	5.00	15.00	35.00
2-4	2.85	8.50	20.00

MY INTIMATE AFFAIR (Inside Crime #3)
Mar, 1950 - No. 2, May, 1950
Fox Feature Syndicate

1	5.00	15.00	35.00
2	2.85	8.50	20.00

MY LIFE (Formerly Meet Corliss Archer)
No. 4, Sept, 1948 - No. 15, July, 1950
Fox Feature Syndicate

	Good	Fine	N-Mint
4-Used in **SOTI**, pg. 39; Kamen/Feldstein-a	16.00	48.00	110.00
5-Kamen-a	8.00	24.00	56.00
6-Kamen/Feldstein-a	8.00	24.00	56.00
7-Wash cover	4.65	14.00	32.00
8,9,11-15	2.85	8.50	20.00
10-Wood-a	8.00	24.00	56.00

MY LITTLE MARGIE (TV)
July, 1954 - No. 54, Nov, 1964
Charlton Comics

1-Photo front/back-c	8.00	24.00	56.00
2-Photo front/back-c	4.00	12.00	28.00
3-7,10	2.15	6.50	15.00
8,9-Infinity-c	2.65	8.00	18.00
11-13: part-photo-c (#13, 8/56)	1.70	5.00	12.00
14-19	1.30	4.00	9.00
20-(100 page issue)	3.50	10.50	24.00
21-35-Last 10 cent issue?	.85	2.50	6.00
36-53	.60	1.75	3.50
54-Beatles on cover; lead story spoofs the Beatle haircut craze of the 1960's	5.00	15.00	35.00

NOTE: Doll cut-outs in 32, 33, 40, 45, 50.

MY LITTLE MARGIE'S BOY FRIENDS (TV) (Freddy V2#12 on)
Aug, 1955 - No. 11, Apr?, 1958
Charlton Comics

1-Has several Archie swipes	4.00	12.00	28.00
2	2.15	6.50	15.00
3-11	1.15	3.50	8.00

MY LITTLE MARGIE'S FASHIONS (TV)
Feb, 1959 - No. 5, Nov, 1959
Charlton Comics

1	3.15	9.50	22.00
2-5	1.60	4.80	11.00

MY LOVE
July, 1949 - No. 4, Apr, 1950 (All photo-c)
Marvel Comics (CLDS)

1	3.50	10.50	24.00
2,3	1.70	5.00	12.00
4-Betty Page photo-c (See Cupid #2, Miss. America #4)			
	7.00	21.00	50.00

MY LOVE
Sept, 1969 - No. 39, Mar, 1976
Marvel Comics Group

1		.60	1.20
2-9		.40	.80
10-Williamson-r/My Own Romance #71; Kirby-a		.60	1.20
11-20: 14-Morrow-c/a; Kirby/Colletta-r		.30	.60
21,22,24-39: 38,39-Reprints		.30	.60
23-Steranko-r/Our Love Story #5	.35	1.00	2.00
Special(12/71)		.30	.60

MY LOVE AFFAIR (March of Crime #7 on)
July, 1949 - No. 6, May, 1950
Fox Feature Syndicate

1	5.50	16.50	38.00
2	3.00	9.00	21.00
3-6-Wood-a	8.00	24.00	56.00

MY LOVE LIFE (Formerly Zegra)
No. 6, June, 1949 - No. 13, Aug, 1950; No. 13, Sept, 1951
Fox Feature Syndicate

6-Kamenish-a	6.50	19.50	45.00
7-13	3.00	9.00	21.00
13 (9/51)	2.30	7.00	16.00

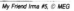

My Friend Irma #5, © MEG

My Greatest Adventure #6, © DC

My Love Affair #1, © FOX

My Love Story #3, © FOX   My Own Romance #16, © MEG   My Romantic Adventures #100, © ACG

MY LOVE MEMOIRS (Formerly Women Outlaws; Hunted #13 on)
No. 9, Nov, 1949 - No. 12, May, 1950
Fox Feature Syndicate

	Good	Fine	N-Mint
9,11,12-Wood-a	8.00	24.00	56.00
10	2.85	8.50	20.00

MY LOVE SECRET (Formerly Phantom Lady) (Animal Crackers #31)
No. 24, June, 1949 - No. 30, June, 1950; No. 53, 1954
Fox Feature Syndicate/M. S. Distr.

24-Kamen/Feldstein-a	7.00	21.00	50.00
25-Possible caricature of Wood on-c?	3.50	10.50	24.00
26,28-Wood-a	8.00	24.00	56.00
27,29,30: 30-photo-c	2.65	8.00	18.00
53-(Reprint, M.S. Distr.) 1954? nd given; formerly Western Thrillers (Crimes by Women #54). Photo-c	1.70	5.00	11.50

MY LOVE STORY (Hoot Gibson Western #5 on)
Sept, 1949 - No. 4, Mar, 1950
Fox Feature Syndicate

1	5.50	16.50	38.00
2	3.00	9.00	21.00
3,4-Wood-a	8.00	24.00	56.00

MY LOVE STORY
April, 1956 - No. 9, Aug, 1957
Atlas Comics (GPS)

1	2.65	8.00	18.00
2	1.30	4.00	9.00
3-Matt Baker-a	2.30	7.00	16.00
4-6,8,9	1.00	3.00	7.00
7-Matt Baker, Toth-a	2.30	7.00	16.00

NOTE: *Colletta a 1(2), 4(2), 5.*

MY ONLY LOVE
July, 1975 - No. 9, Nov, 1976
Charlton Comics

1,2,4-9		.20	.40
3-Toth-a	.35	1.00	2.00

MY OWN ROMANCE (Formerly My Romance; Teen-Age Romance #77 on)
No. 4, Mar, 1949 - No. 76, July, 1960
Marvel/Atlas (MjPC/RCM No. 4-59/ZPC No. 60-76)

4-Photo-c	3.70	11.00	26.00
5-10: 5,9,10-Photo-c	2.00	6.00	14.00
11-20: 14-Powell-a	1.50	4.50	10.00
21-42: 42-Last precode (2/55)	1.15	3.50	8.00
43-54,56-60	.85	2.60	6.00
55-Toth-a	2.65	8.00	18.00
61-70,72-76	.70	2.00	5.00
71-Williamson-a	3.75	11.25	26.00

NOTE: *Colletta a-45(2), 48, 50, 55; c-58i, 61. Everett a-25; c-58p. Morisi a-18. Orlando a-61. Romita a-36. Tuska a-10.*

MY PAL DIZZY (See Comic Books, Series I)

MY PAST (. . .Confessions) (Formerly Western Thrillers)
No. 7, Aug, 1949 - No. 11, April, 1950 (Crimes Inc. #12)
Fox Feature Syndicate

7	4.35	13.00	30.00
8-10	3.00	9.00	21.00
11-Wood-a	8.00	24.00	56.00

MY PERSONAL PROBLEM
11/55; No. 2, 2/56; No. 3, 9/56 - No. 4, 11/56; 10/57 - No. 3, 5/58
Ajax/Farrell/Steinway Comic

1	2.85	8.50	20.00
2-4	1.70	5.00	12.00
1-3('57-'58)-Steinway	1.30	4.00	9.00

MY PRIVATE LIFE (Formerly Murder, Inc.)
No. 16, Feb, 1950 - No. 17, April, 1950
Fox Feature Syndicate

	Good	Fine	N-Mint
16,17	3.50	10.50	24.00

MYRA NORTH (See The Comics, Crackajack Funnies, 4-Color #3 & Red Ryder)

MY REAL LOVE
No. 5, June, 1952
Standard Comics

5-Toth-a, 3 pgs.; Tuska, Cardy, Vern Greene-a; photo-c	4.35	13.00	30.00

MY ROMANCE (My Own Romance #4 on)
Sept, 1948 - No. 3, Jan, 1949
Marvel Comics (RCM)

1	3.70	11.00	26.00
2,3: 2-Anti-Wertham editorial (11/48)	2.00	6.00	14.00

MY ROMANTIC ADVENTURES (Formerly Romantic Adventures)
No. 68, 8/56 - No. 115, 12/60; No. 116, 7/61 - No. 138, 3/64
American Comics Group

68	2.30	7.00	16.00
69-85	1.15	3.50	8.00
86-Three pg. Williamson-a (2/58)	2.85	8.50	20.00
87-100	.70	2.00	5.00
101-138	.50	1.50	3.00

NOTE: *Whitney art in most.*

MY SECRET (Our Secret #4 on)
Aug, 1949 - No. 3, Oct, 1949
Superior Comics, Ltd.

1	4.00	12.00	28.00
2,3	2.85	8.50	20.00

MY SECRET AFFAIR (Martin Kane #4)
Dec, 1949 - No. 3, April, 1950
Hero Book (Fox Feature Syndicate)

1-Harrison/Wood-a, 10 pgs.	9.50	28.50	65.00
2-Wood-a (poor)	5.50	16.50	38.00
3-Wood-a	8.00	24.00	56.00

MY SECRET CONFESSION
September, 1955
Sterling Comics

1-Sekowsky-a	2.00	6.00	14.00

MY SECRET LIFE (Formerly Western Outlaws; Romeo Tubbs #26 on)
No. 22, July, 1949 - No. 27, May, 1950
Fox Feature Syndicate

22	3.70	11.00	26.00
23,26-Wood-a, 6 pgs.	8.00	24.00	56.00
24,25,27	2.30	7.00	16.00

NOTE: *The title was changed to Romeo Tubbs after #25 even though #26 & 27 did come out.*

MY SECRET LIFE (Formerly Young Lovers; Sue & Sally Smith #48)
No. 19, Aug, 1957 - No. 47, Sept, 1962
Charlton Comics

19	1.15	3.50	8.00
20-35	.70	2.00	4.00
36-47: 44-Last 10 cent issue	.35	1.00	2.00

MY SECRET MARRIAGE
May, 1953 - No. 24, July, 1956
Superior Comics, Ltd.

1	3.70	11.00	26.00
2	1.85	5.50	13.00
3-24	1.30	4.00	9.00

MY SECRET MARRIAGE (continued)	Good	Fine	N-Mint
I.W. Reprint #9	.30	.90	1.80

NOTE: Many issues contain Kamenish art.

MY SECRET ROMANCE (A Star Presentation #3)
Jan, 1950 - No. 2, March, 1950
Hero Books (Fox Feature Syndicate)

1-Wood-a	9.00	27.00	62.00
2-Wood-a	8.00	24.00	56.00

MY SECRET STORY (Formerly Captain Kidd #25; Sabu #30 on)
No. 26, Oct, 1949 - No. 29, April, 1950
Fox Feature Syndicate

26	4.00	12.00	28.00
27-29	3.00	9.00	21.00

MYSTERIES (. . .Weird & Strange)
May, 1953 - No. 11, Jan, 1955
Superior/Dynamic Publ. (Randall Publ. Ltd.)

1	10.00	30.00	70.00
2-A-Bomb blast story	5.00	15.00	35.00
3-9,11	3.50	10.50	24.00
10-Kamenish c/a r-/Strange Mysteries #2; cover from a panel in Strange Mysteries #2	4.00	12.00	28.00

MYSTERIES OF SCOTLAND YARD (See A-1 Comics #121)

MYSTERIES OF UNEXPLORED WORLDS (See Blue Bird) (Son of Vulcan V2#49 on)
Aug, 1956 - No. 48, Sept, 1965
Charlton Comics

1	13.00	40.00	90.00
2-No Ditko	5.00	15.00	35.00
3,4,6,8,9-Ditko-a	7.00	21.00	50.00
5-Ditko c/a (all)	8.00	24.00	56.00
7-(68 pgs., 2/58); Ditko-a(4)	8.50	25.50	60.00
10-Ditko-c/a(4)	8.00	24.00	56.00
11-Ditko-c/a(3)-signed J. Kotdi	8.00	24.00	56.00
12,19,21-24,26-Ditko-a	5.70	17.00	40.00
13-18,20	1.70	5.00	12.00
25,27-30	1.15	3.50	8.00
31-45	.70	2.00	4.00
46(5/65)-Son of Vulcan begins (origin)	.85	2.50	6.00
47,48	.70	2.00	4.00

NOTE: Ditko c-3-6, 10, 11, 19, 21-24.

MYSTERIOUS ADVENTURES
March, 1951 - No. 24, Mar, 1955; No. 25, Aug, 1955
Story Comics

1	14.00	42.00	100.00
2	7.00	21.00	50.00
3,4,6,10	5.00	15.00	35.00
5-Bondage-c; torture	7.00	21.00	50.00
7-Daggar in eye panel; dismemberment	11.00	32.00	75.00
8-Eyeball story	8.50	25.50	60.00
9-Extreme violence, gore, ax murder	6.50	19.50	45.00
11(12/52)-Used in SOTI, pg. 84	11.00	32.00	75.00
12-Dismemberment, eyes ripped out	11.50	34.00	80.00
13-Dismemberment	11.00	32.00	75.00
14-E.C. Old Witch swipe; extreme violence, decapitation, etc.	6.50	19.50	45.00
15-Violence; beheading, acid in face, face carved with knife	11.50	34.00	80.00
16-Violence, dismemberment, injury to eye	11.50	34.00	80.00
17-Violence, dismemberment	11.50	34.00	80.00
18-Used in Senate Investigative report, pgs. 5,6; E.C. swipe/T.F.T.C #35; extreme violence, dismemberment, severed heads, etc.	11.50	34.00	80.00
19	5.00	15.00	35.00

	Good	Fine	N-Mint
20-Violence, head split open, fried body organs-used by Wertham in the Senate hearings	11.50	34.00	80.00
21-Blood drainage story, hanging panels, intestines pulled out; bondage/beheading-c	11.50	34.00	80.00
22-'Cinderella' parody	5.70	17.00	40.00
23-Disbrow-a	6.00	18.00	42.00
24,25	5.00	15.00	35.00

NOTE: Tothish art by Ross Andru-#22, 23. Bache a-8. Cameron a-5-7. Harrison a-12. Hollingsworth a-3-8, 12. Schaffenberger a-24, 25. Wildey a-15, 17.

MYSTERIOUS ISLAND (See 4-Color #1213)

MYSTERIOUS ISLE
Nov-Jan, 1963/64 (Jules Verne)
Dell Publishing Co.

1	1.00	3.00	7.00

MYSTERIOUS STORIES (Horror From the Tomb #1)
No. 2, Dec-Jan, 1954-1955 - No. 7, Dec, 1955
Premier Magazines

2-Woodbridge-c	9.00	27.00	62.00
3-Woodbridge c/a	6.50	19.50	45.00
4-7: 5-Cinderella parody. 6-Woodbridge-c	5.70	17.00	40.00

NOTE: Hollingsworth a-2, 4.

MYSTERIOUS SUSPENSE
October, 1968
Charlton Comics

1-The Question app. by Ditko-c/a	2.30	7.00	16.00

MYSTERIOUS TRAVELER (See Tales of the . . .)

MYSTERIOUS TRAVELER COMICS (Radio)
Nov, 1948
Trans-World Publications

1-Powell-c/a(2); Poe adaptation, 'Tell Tale Heart'	21.50	64.00	150.00

MYSTERY COMICS
1944 - No. 4, 1944 (No months given)
William H. Wise & Co.

1-The Magnet, The Silver Knight, Brad Spencer, Wonderman, Dick Devins, King of Futuria, & Zudo the Jungle Boy begin; Schomburg-c on all	31.50	94.00	220.00
2-Bondage-c	21.00	62.00	145.00
3-Lance Lewis, Space Detective begins	18.00	56.00	130.00
4(V2No.1 inside)	18.00	56.00	130.00

MYSTERY COMICS DIGEST
March, 1972 - No. 26, Oct, 1975
Gold Key

1-Ripley's; reprint of Ripley's #1 origin Ra-Ka-Tep the Mummy; Wood-a	.85	2.50	5.00
2-Boris Karloff; Wood-a; 1st app. Werewolf Count Wulfstein	.40	1.25	2.50
3-Twilight Zone (TV); Crandall, Toth & George Evans-a; 1st app. Tragg & Simbar the Lion Lord; 2 Crandall/Frazetta-a r-Twilight Zone #1	.40	1.25	2.50
4-Ripley's Believe It or Not; 1st app. Baron Tibor, the Vampire	.35	1.00	2.00
5-Boris Karloff Tales of Mystery; 1st app. Dr. Spektor	.35	1.00	2.00
6-Twilight Zone (TV); 1st app. U.S. Marshal Reid & Sir Duane	.35	1.00	2.00
7-Ripley's Believe It or Not; origin The Lurker in the Swamp; 1st app. Duroc	.60	1.20	
8-Boris Karloff Tales of Mystery; McWilliams-r	.60	1.20	
9-Twilight Zone (TV); Williamson, Crandall, McWilliams-a; 2nd Tragg app.	.40	1.25	2.50

Mysteries Of Unexplored Worlds #7, © CC

Mysterious Adventures #20, © Story Comics

Mysterious Traveler Comics #1, © Trans-World

Mystery In Space #53, © DC   Mystery Men Comics #2, © FOX   Mystery Tales #1, © MEG

MYSTERY COMICS DIGEST (continued)	Good	Fine	N-Mint
10,13-Ripley's Believe It or Not	.50	1.00	
11,14-Boris Karloff Tales of Mystery. 14-1st app. Xorkon			
	.40	.80	
12,15-Twilight Zone (TV)	.40	.80	
16,19,22,25-Ripley's Believe It or Not	.40	.80	
17-Boris Karloff Tales of Mystery; Williamson-r	.25	.75	1.50
18,21,24-Twilight Zone (TV)	.40	.80	
20,23,26-Boris Karloff Tales of Mystery	.40	.80	

NOTE: Dr. Spektor app.-#5,10-12,21. Durak app.-#15. Duroc app.-#14 (later called Durak). King George 1st app.-#8.

MYSTERY IN SPACE
Apr-May, 1951 - No. 110, Sept, 1966; (#1-3: 52 pgs.)
No. 111, Sept, 1980 - No. 117, March, 1981
National Periodical Publications

	Good	Fine	N-Mint
1-Frazetta-a, 8 pgs.; Knights of the Galaxy begins, ends #8			
	136.00	407.00	950.00
2	55.00	165.00	385.00
3	43.00	130.00	300.00
4,5	30.00	90.00	210.00
6-10: 7-Toth-a	24.00	71.00	165.00
11-15: 13-Toth-a	17.00	51.00	120.00
16-18,20-25: Interplanetary Insurance feature by Infantino in all.			
24-Last precode issue	16.00	48.00	110.00
19-Virgil Finlay-a	17.00	51.00	120.00
26-34,36-40: 26-Space Cabbie begins	11.00	32.00	75.00
35-Kubert-a	11.50	34.00	80.00
41-52: 47-Space Cabbie feature ends	8.50	25.50	60.00
53-Adam Strange begins (8/59) (1st app. in Showcase)			
	52.00	155.00	360.00
54	21.00	63.00	145.00
55	14.00	42.00	100.00
56-60	11.00	32.00	75.00
61-71: 61-1st app. Adam Strange foe Ulthoon. 62-1st app. A.S. foe			
Mortan. 63-Origin Vandor. 66-Star Rovers begin. 68-Dust Devils			
app. 71-Last 10 cent issue	6.50	19.50	45.00
72-74,76-80	5.00	15.00	35.00
75-JLA x-over in Adam Strange (5/62)	5.70	17.00	40.00
81-86	2.65	8.00	18.00
87-90-Hawkman in all	2.85	8.50	20.00
91-102: 91-End Infantino art on Adam Strange. 92-Space Ranger			
begins. 94,98-Adam Strange/Space Ranger team-up. 102-Adam			
Strange ends	1.00	3.00	6.00
103-Origin Ultra, the Multi-Alien; Space Ranger ends			
	.35	1.15	2.30
104-110(9/66)	.35	1.15	2.30
111(9/80)-117		.65	1.30

NOTE: Anderson a-2, 4, 8-10, 12-17, 19, 45-48, 51, 57, 61-64, 70, 76, 87-98; c-9, 10, 15-25, 87, 89, 105-108, 110. Aparo a-111. Austin a-112i. Craig a-114, 116. Ditko a-111, 114-116. Drucker a-13, 14. Golden a-113b. Sid Greene a-78, 91. Infantino a-1-8, 11, 14-25, 27-46, 48, 49, 51, 53-91, 103, 117; c-60-86, 88, 90, 91, 105, 107. Gil Kane a-18, 100-102; c-52, 101. Kubert a-113; c-111-15. Newton a-117p. Rogers a-111. Sekowsky a-52. Simon & Kirby a-4(2 pgs.). Spiegle a-111, 114. Starlin c-116. Sutton a-112. Tuska a-115p, 117p.

MYSTERY MEN COMICS
Aug, 1939 - No. 31, Feb, 1942
Fox Features Syndicate

	Good	Fine	N-Mint
1-Intro. & 1st app. The Blue Beetle, The Green Mask, Rex Dexter			
of Mars by Briefer, Zanzibar by Tuska, Lt. Drake, D-13-Secret			
Agent by Powell, Chen Chang, Wing Turner, & Captain Denny			
Scott	162.00	405.00	975.00
2	64.00	193.00	450.00
3 (10/39)	54.00	160.00	375.00
4-Capt. Savage begins	48.00	145.00	340.00
5	38.00	115.00	265.00
6-8	32.00	95.00	225.00

	Good	Fine	N-Mint
9-The Moth begins	28.00	84.00	195.00
10-Wing Turner by Kirby	28.00	84.00	195.00
11-Intro. Domino	22.00	65.00	155.00
12,14-18	20.00	60.00	140.00
13-Intro. Lynx & sidekick Blackie	22.00	65.00	155.00
19-Intro. & 1st app. Miss X (ends #21)	22.00	65.00	155.00
20-25,27-31	18.00	54.00	125.00
26-The Wraith begins	18.00	54.00	125.00

NOTE: Briefer a-1-15, 20, 24; c-9. Cuidera a-22. Lou Fine c-1-8. Powell a-1-15, 24. Simon c-10-12. Tuska a-1-15, 22, 24, 27. Bondage-c 1, 3, 7, 8, 25, 27-29, 31.

MYSTERY TALES
March, 1952 - No. 54, Aug, 1957
Atlas Comics (20CC)

	Good	Fine	N-Mint
1	17.00	51.00	120.00
2-Krigstein-a	9.30	28.00	65.00
3-9: 6-A-Bomb panel	5.70	17.00	40.00
10-Story similar to 'The Assassin' from Shock SuspenStories			
	6.50	19.50	45.00
11,13-17,19,20: 20-Electric chair issue	4.30	13.00	30.00
12-Matt Fox-a	5.00	15.00	35.00
18-Williamson-a	5.70	17.00	40.00
21-Matt Fox-a; decapitation story	5.00	15.00	35.00
22-Forte/Matt Fox c; a(i)	5.70	17.00	40.00
23-26 (2/55)-Last precode issue	3.70	11.00	26.00
27,29-32,34,35,37,38,41-43,48,49	2.30	7.00	16.00
28-Jack Katz-a	3.00	9.00	21.00
33-Crandall-a	3.65	11.00	26.00
36,39-Krigstein-a	3.65	11.00	26.00
40,45-Ditko-a	3.65	11.00	26.00
44,51-Williamson/Krenkel-a	4.65	14.00	32.00
46-Williamson/Krenkel-a; Crandall text illos	4.65	14.00	32.00
47-Crandall, Ditko, Powell-a	4.00	12.00	28.00
50-Torres, Morrow-a	3.50	10.50	24.00
52,53	2.00	6.00	14.00
54-Crandall, Check-a	3.00	9.00	21.00

NOTE: Ayers a-18, 49, 52. Berg a-17, 51. Colan a-1, 3, 18, 35, 43. Everett a-2, 29, 33, 35, 41, 43; c-8-11, 14, 38, 39, 41, 43, 44, 46, 48-51, 53. Fass a-16. Forte a-21, 22. Matt Fox a-127, 21, 22; c-22. Heath a-3; c-3, 15, 17, 26. Heck a-25. Kinstler a-15. Mort Lawrence a-26, 32, 34. Maneely a-1, 9, 14, 22; c-12, 23, 24, 27. Mooney a-3, 40. Morisi a-43, 49, 52. Morrow a-50. Pakula a-16. Powell a-21, 29, 37, 38, 47. Reinman a-1, 14. Robinson a-7p, 42. Romita a-37. Roussos a-4, 44. R.Q. Sale a-49. Severin c-52. Tuska a-10, 12, 14. Whitney a-2. Wildey a-37.

MYSTERY TALES
1964
Super Comics

	Good	Fine	N-Mint
Super Reprint #16,17('64)	.50	1.50	3.00
Super Reprint #18-Kubert art/Strange Terrors #4			
	.50	1.50	3.00

MYSTIC (3rd Series)
March, 1951 - No. 61, Aug, 1957
Marvel/Atlas Comics (CLDS 1/CSI 2-21/OMC 22-35/CSI 35-61)

	Good	Fine	N-Mint
1-Atom bomb panels	18.50	56.00	130.00
2	10.00	30.00	70.00
3-Eyes torn out	7.00	21.00	50.00
4-"The Devil Birds" by Wolverton, 6 pgs.	21.50	64.00	150.00
5,7-10	5.70	17.00	40.00
6-"The Eye of Doom" by Wolverton, 7 pgs.	21.50	64.00	150.00
11-20: 16-Bondage/torture c/story	5.00	15.00	35.00
21-25,27-30,32-36-Last precode (3/55). 25-E.C. swipe. 35-Al Hartley-a			
	4.30	13.00	30.00
26-Atomic War, severed head stories	5.00	15.00	35.00
31-Sid Check-a	4.50	14.00	32.00
37-51,53-57,61	2.85	8.50	20.00
52-Wood, Crandall-a	5.00	15.00	35.00
58,59-Krigstein-a	3.50	10.50	24.00

MYSTIC (continued)	Good	Fine	N-Mint
60-Williamson/Mayo-a, 4 pgs.	3.85	11.50	27.00

NOTE: Andru a-23, 25. Ayers a-35, 53; c-8. Cameron a- 51. Check a-60. Colan a-3, 7, 12, 21, 37. Colletta a-29. Drucker a-46, 52, 56. Everett a-8, 9, 17, 40, 44, 57; c-18, 21, 42, 47, 49, 51-55, 58, 59, 61. Forte a-35, 52. Fox a-24i. Heath a-10; c-10, 20, 22, 23, 25, 30. Infantino a-12. Kane a-8, 24p. Jack Katz a-31, 33. Mort Lawrence a-19, 37. Maneely a-22, 24, 58; c-15, 28, 29, 31. Moldoff a-29. Morisi a- 52. Morrow a-51. Orlando a-57, 61. Pakula a-52. Powell a-52, 54-56. Robinson a-5. Romita a-11, 15. Sale a-35, 53. Sekowsky a-1, 2, 4, 5. Severin c-56. Tuska a-15. Whitney a-33. Wildey a-28, 30. Ed Win a-20. Canadian reprints known-title 'Startling'.

MYSTICAL TALES
June, 1956 - No. 8, Aug, 1957
Atlas Comics (CCC 1/EPI 2-8)

1-Everett c/a	11.00	32.00	75.00
2,4: 2-Berg-a	5.50	16.50	38.00
3-Crandall-a	6.00	18.00	42.00
5-Williamson-a, 4 pgs.	6.50	19.50	45.00
6-Torres, Krigstein-a	5.00	15.00	35.00
7-Torres, Orlando, Crandall, Everett-a	4.30	13.00	30.00
8-Krigstein, Check-a	5.00	15.00	35.00

NOTE: Everett a-1, 7; c-1-4, 6, 7. Orlando a-1, 2. Pakula a-3. Powell a-1, 4.

MYSTIC COMICS (1st Series)
March, 1940 - No. 10, Aug, 1942
Timely Comics (TPI 1-5/TCI 8-10)

1-Origin The Blue Blaze, The Dynamic Man, & Flexo the Rubber Man; Zephyr Jones, 3X's & Deep Sea Demon app.; The Magician begins; c-from Spider pulp V18#1, 6/39	442.00	1105.00	2650.00
2-The Invisible Man & Master Mind Excello begin; Space Rangers, Zara of the Jungle, Taxi Taylor app.	177.00	443.00	1065.00
3-Origin Hercules, who last appears in #4	141.00	353.00	845.00
4-Origin The Thin Man & The Black Widow; Merzak the Mystic app.; last Flexo, Dynamic Man, Invisible Man & Blue Blaze. (Some issues have date sticker on cover; others have July w/August overprint in silver color); Roosevelt assassination-c	164.00	410.00	985.00
5-Origin The Black Marvel, The Blazing Skull, The Sub-Earth Man, Super Slave & The Terror; The Moon Man & Black Widow app.	156.00	390.00	935.00
6-Origin The Challenger & The Destroyer	133.00	332.00	800.00
7-The Witness begins (origin); origin Davey & the Demon; last Black Widow; Simon & Kirby-c	108.00	270.00	650.00
8	93.00	232.00	550.00
9-Gary Gaunt app.; last Black Marvel, Mystic & Blazing Skull; Hitler-c	93.00	232.00	550.00
10-Father Time, World of Wonder, & Red Skeleton app.; last Challenger & Terror	93.00	232.00	550.00

NOTE: Rico a-9. Schomburg a-1-4; c-4. Sekowsky a-9. Bondage c-1, 2, 9.

MYSTIC COMICS (2nd Series)
Oct, 1944 - No. 4, Winter, 1944-45
Timely Comics (ANC)

1-The Angel, The Destroyer, The Human Torch, Terry Vance the Schoolboy Sleuth, & Tommy Tyme begin	79.00	198.00	475.00
2-Last Human Torch & Terry Vance; bondage-hypo-c	43.00	129.00	300.00
3-Last Angel (two stories) & Tommy Tyme	39.00	118.00	275.00
4-The Young Allies app.	34.00	103.00	240.00

MY STORY (. . .True Romances in Pictures #5,6) (Formerly Zago)
No. 5, May, 1949 - No. 12, Aug, 1950
Hero Books (Fox Features Syndicate)

5-Kamen/Feldstein-a	7.00	21.00	50.00
6-8,11,12: 12-Photo-c	3.00	9.00	21.00
9,10-Wood-a	8.00	24.00	56.00

MYTHADVENTURES
Mar, 1984 - No. 12, 1986 ($1.50-$1.75, B&W)
WaRP Graphics/Apple Comics #11, 12

	Good	Fine	N-Mint
1-11: ($1.50)-Early issues mag. size	.25	.75	1.50
12 ($1.75)	.30	.90	1.80

MYTH CONCEPTIONS
Nov, 1987 - No. 8, Jan, 1989 ($1.75/$1.95, B&W)
Apple Comics

1-3 ($1.75)	.30	.90	1.80
4-8 ($1.95)	.35	1.00	2.00

MY TRUE LOVE (Formerly Western Killers #64; Frank Buck #70 on)
No. 65, July, 1949 - No. 69, March, 1950
Fox Features Syndicate

65	4.35	13.00	30.00
66-69: 69-Morisi-a	3.00	9.00	21.00

NAKED PREY, THE (See Movie Classics)

'NAM, THE (See Savage Tales #1, 2nd series)
Dec, 1986 - Present
Marvel Comics Group

1-Golden a(p)/c begins, ends #13	2.35	7.00	14.00
1 (2nd printing)	.60	1.75	3.50
2	1.50	4.50	9.00
3,4	1.00	3.00	6.00
5-7	.75	2.25	4.50
8-10	.40	1.25	2.50
11-20: 12-Severin-a	.30	.90	1.80
21-42: 25-begin $1.50-c. 32-Death R. Kennedy	.25	.75	1.50
Trade Paperback 1-r/1-4	.75	2.25	4.50
Trade Paperback 2-r/5-8	1.10	3.25	6.50

'NAM MAGAZINE, THE
August, 1988 - No. 10, May, 1989 ($2.00, B&W, 52 pgs)
Marvel Comics

1-10: Each issue reprints two of the comic	.35	1.00	2.00

NAMORA (See Marvel Mystery & Sub-Mariner Comics)
Fall, 1948 - No. 3, Dec, 1948
Marvel Comics (PrPI)

1-Sub-Mariner x-over in Namora; Everett, Rico-a	63.00	190.00	440.00
2-The Blonde Phantom & Sub-Mariner story; Everett-a	52.00	156.00	365.00
3-(Scarce)-Sub-Mariner app.; Everett-a	46.00	139.00	325.00

NAMOR THE SUB-MARINER (See Prince Namor & Sub-Mariner)
Apr, 1990 - Present ($1.00, color)
Marvel Comics

1,2: Byrne-a(p)/scripts		.50	1.00

NANCY AND SLUGGO (See Comics On Parade & Sparkle Comics)
No. 16, 1949 - No. 23, 1954
United Features Syndicate

16(#1)	3.70	11.00	26.00
17-23	2.15	6.50	15.00

NANCY & SLUGGO (Nancy #146-173; formerly Sparkler Comics)
No. 121, Apr, 1955 - No. 192, Oct, 1963
St. John/Dell No. 146-187/Gold Key No. 188 on

121(4/55)(St. John)	3.15	9.50	22.00
122-145(7/57)(St. John)	2.15	6.50	15.00
146(9/57)-Peanuts begins, ends #192 (Dell)	1.85	5.50	13.00
147-161 (Dell)	1.60	4.80	11.00
162-165,177-180-John Stanley-a	3.70	11.00	26.00
166-176-Oona & Her Haunted House series; Stanley-a	4.00	12.00	28.00
181-187(3-5/62)(Dell)	1.50	4.50	10.00
188(10/62)-192 (Gold Key)	1.50	4.50	10.00

Mystic Comics #9, © MEG

Namora #3, © MEG

Nancy And Sluggo #16 (#1), © UFS

National Comics #21, © QUA   National Velvet #01-556-207, © M.G.M.   Navy Action #11, © MEG

	Good	Fine	N-Mint
NANCY & SLUGGO (continued)			
4-Color 1034(9-11/59)-Summer Camp	1.70	5.00	12.00
(See Dell Giant #34,45 & Dell Giants)			

NANNY AND THE PROFESSOR (TV)
Aug, 1970 - No. 2, Oct, 1970 (Photo-c)
Dell Publishing Co.

	Good	Fine	N-Mint
1(01-546-008), 2	2.30	7.00	16.00

NAPOLEON (See 4-Color No. 526)

NAPOLEON & SAMANTHA (See Walt Disney Showcase No. 10)

NAPOLEON & UNCLE ELBY (See Clifford McBride's. . .)
July, 1942 (68 pages) (One Shot)
Eastern Color Printing Co.

	Good	Fine	N-Mint
1	14.00	42.00	100.00
1945-American Book-Strafford Press (128 pgs.) (8x10½''-B&W re-			
prints; hardcover)	7.00	21.00	50.00

NATHANIEL DUSK
Feb, 1984 - No. 4, May, 1984 (mini-series; Baxter paper)
DC Comics (Direct Sale only)

	Good	Fine	N-Mint
1-Intro/origin		.60	1.20
2-4 ($1.25): Colan c/a		.60	1.20

NATHANIEL DUSK II
Oct, 1985 - No. 4, Jan, 1986 (mini-series; Baxter paper)
DC Comics

	Good	Fine	N-Mint
1 ($2.00 cover); Colan c/a	.25	.75	1.50
2-4		.55	1.10

NATIONAL COMICS
July, 1940 - No. 75, Nov, 1949
Quality Comics Group

	Good	Fine	N-Mint
1-Uncle Sam begins; Origin sidekick Buddy by Eisner; origin Won-			
der Boy & Kid Dixon; Merlin the Magician (ends #45); Cyclone,			
Kid Patrol, Sally O'Neil Policewoman, Pen Miller (ends #22), Prop			
Powers (ends #26), & Paul Bunyan (ends #22) begin			
	168.00	504.00	1175.00
2	78.00	235.00	550.00
3-Last Eisner Uncle Sam	63.00	188.00	440.00
4-Last Cyclone	45.00	135.00	315.00
5-(11/40)-Quicksilver begins (3rd w/lightning speed?); origin Uncle			
Sam	58.00	174.00	405.00
6-11: 8-Jack & Jill begins (ends #22). 9-Flag-c			
	43.00	130.00	300.00
12	31.50	94.00	220.00
13-16-Lou Fine-a	39.00	118.00	275.00
17,19-22	28.50	86.00	200.00
18-(12/41)-Shows orientals attacking Pearl Harbor; on stands one			
month before actual event	34.00	103.00	240.00
23-The Unknown & Destroyer 171 begin	31.50	94.00	220.00
24-26,28,30: 26-Wonder Boy ends	22.00	65.00	155.00
27-G-2 the Unknown begins (ends #46)	22.00	65.00	155.00
29-Origin The Unknown	22.00	65.00	155.00
31-33: 33-Chic Carter begins (ends #47)	19.00	57.00	135.00
34-40: 35-Last Kid Patrol. 39-Hitler-c	11.50	34.00	80.00
41-47,49,50: 42-The Barker begins (1st app?)	9.00	27.00	62.00
48-Origin The Whistler	9.00	27.00	62.00
51-Sally O'Neil by Ward, 8 pgs. (12/45)	11.50	34.50	80.00
52-60	6.50	19.50	45.00
61-67: 67-Format change; Quicksilver app.	4.65	14.00	32.00
68-75: The Barker ends	3.00	9.00	21.00

NOTE: *Cole* Quicksilver-13; Barker-43; c-43, 46, 47, 49, 50. *Crandall* Uncle Sam-11-13 (with *Fine*), 25, 26; c-24-26, 30-33, 43. *Crandall* Paul Bunyan-10-13. *Fine* Uncle Sam-13 (w/*Crandall*), 17, 18; c-1-14, 16, 18, 21. *Guardineer* Quicksilver-27. *Gustavson* Quicksilver-14-26. *McWilliams* a-23-28, 55, 57. Uncle Sam-c in #41. Bondage c-5.

NATIONAL CRUMB, THE (Magazine-Size)
August, 1975 (52 pages) (Satire)

Mayfair Publications

	Good	Fine	N-Mint
1	.70	2.00	4.00

NATIONAL VELVET (TV)
May-July, 1961 - No. 2, March, 1963 (All photo-c)
Dell Publishing Co./Gold Key

	Good	Fine	N-Mint
4-Color 1195	2.65	8.00	18.00
4-Color 1312	2.30	7.00	16.00
01-556-207, 12-556-210	2.00	6.00	14.00
1(12/62), 2(3/63)-Gold Key	2.00	6.00	14.00

NATURE BOY (Formerly Danny Blaze; Li'l Rascal Twins #6 on)
No. 3, March, 1956 - No. 5, Feb, 1957
Charlton Comics

	Good	Fine	N-Mint
3-Origin; Blue Beetle story; Buscema-c/a	12.00	36.00	84.00
4,5	9.30	28.00	65.00

NOTE: *Buscema* a-3, 4p, 5; c-3. *Powell* a-4.

NATURE OF THINGS (See 4-Color No. 727,842)

NAUSICAA OF THE VALLEY OF WIND
1988 - No. 7, 1989; 1989 - No. 5, 1990 ($2.50-$2.95, B&W, 68 pgs.)
Viz Comics

	Good	Fine	N-Mint
Book 1-7: ($2.50) 1-Contains Moebius poster	.40	1.25	2.50
Part I, Book 1-5 ($2.95)	.50	1.50	3.00

NAVY ACTION (Sailor Sweeney #12-14)
Aug, 1954 - No. 11, Apr, 1956; No. 15, 1/57 - No. 18, 8/57
Atlas Comics (CDS)

	Good	Fine	N-Mint
1-Powell-a	3.70	11.00	26.00
2-Lawrence-a	2.00	6.00	14.00
3-11: 4-Last precode (2/55)	1.30	4.00	9.00
15-18	.85	2.50	6.00

NOTE: *Berg* a-9. *Colan* a-8. *Drucker* a-7, 17. *Everett* a-3, 7, 16; c-16, 17. *Heath* c-2, 6. *Maneely* a-8, 18; c-1, 9, 11. *Pakula* a-2, 3, 9. *Reinman* a-7.

NAVY COMBAT
June, 1955 - No. 20, Oct, 1958
Atlas Comics (MPI)

	Good	Fine	N-Mint
1-Torpedo Taylor begins by Don Heck	3.70	11.00	26.00
2	2.00	6.00	14.00
3-10	1.30	4.00	9.00
11,13,15,16,18-20	1.00	3.00	7.00
12-Crandall-a	2.00	6.00	14.00
14-Torres-a	2.00	6.00	14.00
17-Williamson-a, 4 pgs.	2.75	8.00	18.00

NOTE: *Berg* a-10, 11. *Drucker* a-7, 11. *Everett* a-3, 20; c-8 & 9 w/*Tuska*, 10, 13-16. *Maneely* c-1, 11. *Pakula* a-7. *Powell* a-20.

NAVY HEROES
1945
Almanac Publishing Co.

	Good	Fine	N-Mint
1-Heavy in propaganda	4.00	12.00	28.00

NAVY: HISTORY & TRADITION
1958 - 1961 (nn) (Giveaway)
Stokes Walesby Co./Dept. of Navy

	Good	Fine	N-Mint
1772-1778, 1778-1782, 1782-1817, 1817-1865, 1865-1936, 1940-1945			
	2.00	6.00	14.00
1861: Naval Actions of the Civil War: 1865	2.00	6.00	14.00

NAVY PATROL
May, 1955 - No. 4, Nov, 1955
Key Publications

	Good	Fine	N-Mint
1	2.00	6.00	14.00
2-4	1.00	3.00	7.00

NAVY TALES
Jan, 1957 - No. 4, July, 1957
Atlas Comics (CDS)

NAVY TALES (continued)	Good	Fine	N-Mint
1-Everett-c; Berg, Powell-a	3.50	10.50	24.00
2-Williamson/Mayo-a, 5 pgs; Crandall-a	3.70	11.00	26.00
3,4-Reinman-a; Severin-c. 4-Colan, Crandall, Sinnott-a			
	2.65	8.00	18.00

NAVY TASK FORCE
Feb, 1954 - No. 8, April, 1956
Stanmor Publications/Aragon Mag. No. 4-8

1	2.30	7.00	16.00
2	1.15	3.50	8.00
3-8	.85	2.50	6.00

NAVY WAR HEROES
Jan, 1964 - No. 7, Mar-Apr, 1965
Charlton Comics

1	.40	1.25	2.50
2-7	.25	.75	1.50

NAZA (Stone Age Warrior)
Nov-Jan, 1963/64 - No. 9, March, 1966
Dell Publishing Co.

1 (12-555-401)-Painted-c	1.00	3.00	7.00
2-9: 2-4-Painted-c	.70	2.00	5.00

NEAT STUFF
July, 1985 - No. 15, 1989 ($1.95/$2.25/$2.50, B&W, adults)
Fantagraphics Books

1	.60	1.75	3.50
2-10	.45	1.40	2.75
11-15 ($2.50)	.40	1.25	2.50

NEBBS, THE
1928 (Daily B&W strip reprints; 52 pages)
Cupples & Leon Co.

By Sol Hess; Carlson-a	7.00	21.00	50.00

NEBBS, THE (Also see Crackajack Funnies)
1941; 1945
Dell Publishing Co./Croydon Publishing Co.

Large Feat. Comic 23(1941)	9.00	27.00	62.00
1(1945, 36 pgs.)-Reprints	5.00	15.00	35.00

NECROMANCER: THE GRAPHIC NOVEL
1989 ($9.95, color)
Epic Comics (Marvel)

nn	1.70	5.00	10.00

NEGRO (See All-Negro)

NEGRO HEROES (Calling All Girls, Real Heroes, & True Comics-r)
Spring, 1947 - No. 2, Summer, 1948
Parents' Magazine Institute

1	27.00	81.00	190.00
2-Jackie Robinson story	30.00	90.00	210.00

NEGRO ROMANCE (Negro Romances #4)
June, 1950 - No. 3, Oct, 1950 (All photo-c)
Fawcett Publications

1-Evans-a	65.00	195.00	455.00
2,3	50.00	150.00	350.00

NEGRO ROMANCES (Formerly Negro Romance)
No. 4, May, 1955   (Romantic Secrets #5 on)
Charlton Comics

4-Reprints Fawcett #2	35.00	105.00	245.00

NEIL THE HORSE (See Charlton Bullseye #2)
2/83 - No. 10, 12/84; No. 11, 4/85 - Present (B&W)
Aardvark-Vanaheim #1-10/Renegade Press #11 on

1 ($1.40)	.70	2.00	4.00

	Good	Fine	N-Mint
1-2nd print	.25	.75	1.50
2	.40	1.25	2.50
3-13: 13-Double size.; 11,13-w/paperdolls	.35	1.00	2.00
14,15-Double size ($3.00)	.50	1.50	3.00

NELLIE THE NURSE (Also see Gay Comics)
1945 - No. 36, Oct, 1952; 1957
Marvel/Atlas Comics (SPI/LMC)

1	11.00	32.00	75.00
2	5.00	15.00	35.00
3,4	4.00	12.00	28.00
5-Kurtzman's "Hey Look"	4.50	14.00	32.00
6-8,10: 7,8-Georgie app. 10-Millie app.	2.85	8.50	20.00
9-Wolverton-a, 1 pg.	3.15	9.50	22.00
11,14-16,18-Kurtzman's "Hey Look"	4.00	12.00	28.00
12-"Giggles 'n' Grins" by Kurtzman	3.15	9.50	22.00
13,17,19,20: 17-Annie Oakley app.	2.65	8.00	18.00
21-27,29,30	2.30	7.00	16.00
28-Kurtzman's Rusty reprint	2.65	8.00	18.00
31-36: 36-Post-c	1.70	5.00	12.00
1('57)-Leading Mag. (Atlas)-Everett-a, 20pgs.	1.50	4.50	10.00

NELLIE THE NURSE (See 4-Color No. 1304)

NEMESIS THE WARLOCK (Also see Spellbinders)
Sept, 1984 - No. 7, Mar, 1985 (Limited series; 36 pgs.)
Eagle Comics (Baxter paper)

1-7: 2000 A.D. reprints	.25	.75	1.50

NEMESIS THE WARLOCK
1989 - Present ($1.95, color)
Quality Comics

1-5	.35	1.00	2.00

NEUTRO
January, 1967
Dell Publishing Co.

1-Jack Sparling c/a (super hero)	1.00	3.00	7.00

NEVADA (See Zane Grey's Stories of the West #1)

NEVER AGAIN (War stories; becomes Soldier & Marine V2#9)
Aug, 1955 - No. 2, Oct?, 1955; No. 8, July, 1956 (No #3-7)
Charlton Comics

1	3.50	10.50	24.00
2 (Becomes Fightin' Air Force #3), 8(Formerly Foxhole?)			
	1.70	5.00	12.00

NEW ADVENTURE COMICS (Formerly New Comics; becomes Adventure Comics #32 on)
V1#12, Jan, 1937 - No. 31, Oct, 1938

National Periodical Publications	Good	Fine	VF-NM
V1#12-Federal Men by Siegel & Shuster continues; Jor-L mentioned			
	140.00	350.00	840.00
V2#1(2/37, #13), V2#2 (#14)	100.00	250.00	600.00

	Good	Fine	N-Mint
15(V2#3)-20(V2#8): 15-1st Adventure logo. 16-1st Shuster-c; 1st non-funny cover. 17-Nadir, Master of Magic begins, ends #30			
	100.00	250.00	600.00
21(V2#9),22(V2#10, 2/37)	83.00	208.00	500.00
23-31	67.00	168.00	400.00

NEW ADVENTURE OF WALT DISNEY'S SNOW WHITE AND THE SEVEN DWARFS, A (See Snow White Bendix Giveaway)

NEW ADVENTURES OF CHARLIE CHAN, THE (TV)
May-June, 1958 - No. 6, Mar-Apr, 1959
National Periodical Publications

1 (Scarce)-Gil Kane/Sid Greene-a in all	23.50	71.00	165.00
2 (Scarce)	14.00	42.00	100.00

Nellie The Nurse #15, © MEG

Neutro #1, © DELL

New Adventure Comics #20, © DC

The New Adventures of Superboy #1, © DC

New Comics #1, © DC

New Funnies #87, © DELL

	Good	Fine	N-Mint
NEW ADVS. OF CHARLIE CHAN (continued)			
3-6 (Scarce)	12.00	36.00	85.00

NEW ADVENTURES OF HUCK FINN, THE (TV)
December, 1968 (Hanna-Barbera)
Gold Key

1-''The Curse of Thut''; part photo-c	1.30	4.00	9.00

NEW ADVENTURES OF PETER PAN (Disney)
1953 (36 pgs.; 5x7¼'') (Admiral giveaway)
Western Publishing Co.

nn	4.65	14.00	32.00

NEW ADVENTURES OF PINOCCHIO (TV)
Oct-Dec, 1962 - No. 3, Sept-Nov, 1963
Dell Publishing Co.

12-562-212	5.00	15.00	35.00
2,3	4.00	12.00	28.00

NEW ADVENTURES OF ROBIN HOOD (See Robin Hood)

NEW ADVENTURES OF SHERLOCK HOLMES (See 4-Color #1169, 1245)

NEW ADVENTURES OF SUPERBOY, THE
Jan, 1980 - No. 54, June, 1984
DC Comics

1		.60	1.20
2-5		.50	1.00
6-10		.40	.80
11-47: 11-Superboy gets new power. 15-Superboy gets new parents.			
28-Dial ''H'' For Hero begins, ends #49. 45-47-1st app. Sunburst			
		.30	.60
48,49,51-54 (75 cent-c)		.40	.80
50 ($1.25, 52 pgs.)-Legion app.		.60	1.25
NOTE: *Buckler a-9p; c-36p. Giffen a-50; c-50. 40i. Gil Kane c-32p, 33p, 35, 39, 41-49.			
Miller c-51. Starlin a-7.			

NEW ADVS. OF THE PHANTOM BLOT, THE (See The Phantom Blot)

NEW AMERICA
Nov, 1987 - No. 4, Feb, 1988 (Color, $1.75, Baxter paper)
Eclipse Comics

1-4-Scout mini-series	.30	.90	1.80

NEW ARCHIES, THE
Oct, 1987 - Present (75 cents)
Archie Comic Publications

1-16: 3-Xmas issue		.40	.80
17-22 (.95-$1.00)		.50	1.00

NEW ARCHIES DIGEST
1988 - Present ($1.35-$1.50, digest size)
Archie Comics

1-10	.25	.70	1.35

NEW BOOK OF COMICS (Also see Big Book Of Fun)
1937; No. 2, Spring, 1938 (100 pgs. each) (Reprints)
National Periodical Publications

1(Rare)-1st regular size comic annual; 2nd DC annual; contains			
r-/New Comics #1-4 & More Fun #9; r-Federal Men (8pgs.), Henri			
Duval (1pg.), & Dr. Occult in costume (1pg.) by Siegel & Shuster;			
Moldoff, Sheldon Mayer (15pgs.)-a	400.00	1000.00	2400.00
2-Contains r-/More Fun #15 & 16; r-/Dr. Occult in costume (a			
Superman proto-type), & Calling All Cars (4pgs.) by Siegel &			
Shuster	233.00	582.00	1400.00

NEW CHAMPIONS (Also see Champions)
1989 - Present? ($2.95, color)
Hero Comics

1-4: 4-Southern Knights x-over	.50	1.50	3.00

NEW COMICS (New Adventure #12 on)
12/35 - No. 11, 12/36 (No. 1-6: paper cover) (No. 1-5: 84 pgs.)

National Periodical Publications

	Good	Fine	N-Mint
V1#1-Billy the Kid, Sagebrush 'n' Cactus, Jibby Jones, Needles, The			
Vikings, Sir Loin of Beef, Now-When I Was a Boy, & other 1-2			
pg. strips; 2 pgs. Kelly art(1st)-(Gulliver's Travels); Sheldon			
Mayer-a(1st)	500.00	1250.00	3000.00
2-Federal Men by Siegel & Shuster begins (Also see The Comics			
Magazine #2); Sheldon Mayer, Kelly-a. (Rare)	267.00	670.00	1600.00
3-6: 3,4-Sheldon Mayer-a which continues in The Comics Mag-			
azine #1; 5-Kiefer-a	154.00	385.00	925.00
7-11: 11-Christmas-c	121.00	302.00	725.00
NOTE: #1-6 rarely occur in mint condition.			

NEW DEFENDERS (See Defenders)

NEW DNAGENTS, THE (Formerly DNAgents)
Oct, 1985 - No. 17, Mar, 1987 (Mando paper)
Eclipse Comics

V2#1-Origin recap		.50	1.00
2-6		.40	.80
7-12: (95 cent-c). 9,10-Airboy app.		.50	1.00
13-17 ($1.25-c)		.60	1.20
3-D 1 (1/86)	.40	1.15	2.30
2-D 1 (1/86)-Limited ed. (100 copies)	.85	2.50	5.00

NEW FUN COMICS (More Fun #7 on; see Big Book of Fun Comics)
Feb, 1935 - No. 6, Oct, 1935 (10x15'', No. 1-4,6: slick covers)
(No. 1-5: 36 pgs; 68 pgs. No. 6-on)

National Periodical Publications	Good	Fine	V. Fine
V1#1 (1st DC comic); 1st app. Oswald The Rabbit. Jack Woods			
(cowboy) begins	1200.00	3000.00	7200.00
2(3/35)-(Very Rare)	840.00	2100.00	5040.00
3-5(8/35): 5-Soft-c	375.00	937.00	2250.00
6(10/35)-1st Dr. Occult (Superman proto-type) by Siegel &			
Shuster (Leger & Reughts); last ''New Fun'' title. ''New Comics			
#1 begins in Dec. which is reason for title change to More Fun;			
Henri Duval (ends #9) by Siegel & Shuster begins; paper-c			
	450.00	1125.00	2700.00

NEW FUNNIES (The Funnies #1-64; Walter Lantz . . . #109 on;
#259,260,272,273-New TV. . .; #261-271-TV Funnies)
No. 65, July, 1942 - No. 288, Mar-Apr, 1962

Dell Publishing Co.	Good	Fine	N-Mint
65(#1)-Andy Panda in a world of real people, Raggedy Ann & Andy,			
Oswald the Rabbit (with Woody Woodpecker x-overs), Li'l Eight			
Ball & Peter Rabbit begin	37.00	110.00	260.00
66-70: 67-Billy & Bonnie Bee by Frank Thomas & Felix The Cat			
begin. 69-2pg. Kelly-a; The Brownies begin (not by Kelly)			
	17.00	51.00	120.00
71-75: 72-Kelly illos. 75-Brownies by Kelly?	11.00	32.00	75.00
76-Andy Panda (Carl Barks & Pabian-a); Woody Woodpecker x-over			
in Oswald ends	57.00	171.00	400.00
77,78: 78-Andy Panda in a world with real people ends			
	11.00	32.00	75.00
79-81	8.00	24.00	56.00
82-Brownies by Kelly begins; Homer Pigeon begins			
	9.50	28.50	65.00
83-85-Brownies by Kelly in ea. 83-X-mas-c. 85-Woody Woodpecker,			
1pg. strip begins	9.50	28.50	65.00
86-90: 87-Woody Woodpecker stories begin	4.30	13.00	30.00
91-99	2.85	8.50	20.00
100 (6/45)	3.50	10.50	24.00
101-110	2.15	6.50	15.00
111-120: 119-X-mas-c	1.60	4.80	11.00
121-150: 143-X-mas-c	1.15	3.50	8.00
151-200: 155-X-mas-c. 168-X-mas-c, 182-Origin & 1st app. Knothead			
& Splinter. 191-X-mas-c	.85	2.50	6.00
201-240	.70	2.00	5.00

NEW FUNNIES (continued) | **Good** | **Fine** | **N-Mint**
241-288: 270-Walter Lantz c-app. 281-1st story swipe/WDC&S #100
| | .60 | 1.80 | 4.00

NOTE: *Early issues written by* **John Stanley.**

NEW GODS, THE (New Gods #12 on)(See Adventure #459, First Issue
Special & Super-Team Family)
2-3/71 - No. 11, 10-11/72; No. 12, 7/77 - No. 19, 7-8/78
National Periodical Publications/DC Comics

	Good	Fine	N-Mint
1-Intro/1st app. Orion	.85	2.50	5.00
2	.40	1.25	2.50
3-19: 4-Origin Manhunter-r. 5,7,8-Young Gods feature. 7-Origin			
Orion. 9-1st app. Bug		.60	1.20

NOTE: #4-9(52 pgs.) contain Manhunter-r by **Simon & Kirby** from Adventure #73, 74, 75, 76, 77, 78 with covers in that order. **Adkins** i-12-14, 17-19. **Kirby** c/a-1-11p. **Newton** p-12-14, 16-19. **Starlin** c-17. **Staton** c-19p.

NEW GODS, THE
May, 1984 - No. 6, Nov,1984 ($2.00; direct sale; Baxter paper)
DC Comics

1-New Kirby-c begin; r-/New Gods 1&2	.35	1.00	2.00
2-6: 6-Original art by Kirby	.35	1.00	2.00

NEW GODS
Feb, 1989 - Present ($1.50, color)
DC Comics

1-Russell-i	.35	1.00	2.00
2-14: 2-4-Starlin scripts	.25	.75	1.50

NEW GUARDIANS, THE
Sept, 1988 - No. 12, Sept, 1989 ($1.25, color)
DC Comics

1-Double size ($2.00)-Staton-c/a in #1-9	.35	1.10	2.25
2-12		.60	1.25

NEW HEROIC (See Heroic)

NEW HUMANS, THE
Dec, 1987 - No. 15, 1989 ($1.95, B&W)
Eternity Comics

1-15: 1-Origin	.30	.90	1.80
Annual 1 (1988, $2.95, B&W)	.50	1.50	3.00

NEW JUSTICE MACHINE, THE (Also see The Justice Machine)
1989 - No. 3, 1989 ($1.95, color, mini-series)
Innovation Publishing

1-3	.35	1.00	2.00

NEWLYWEDS
1907; 1917 (cardboard covers)
Saalfield Publ. Co.

...& Their Baby' by McManus; Saalfield, 1907, 13x10,'' 52pgs.
daily strips in full color | 28.00 | 84.00 | 195.00
...& Their Baby's Comic Pictures, The, by McManus, Saalfield,
1917, 14x10,'' 22pgs, oblong, cardboard-c, reprints 'Newlyweds'
(Baby Snookums stips) mainly from 1916; blue cover; says for
painting & crayoning, but some pages in color. (Scarce)
| | 22.00 | 65.00 | 154.00

NEW MEN OF BATTLE, THE
1949 (nn) (Carboard covers)
Catechetical Guild

nn(V8#1-V8#6)-192pgs.; contains 6 issues of Topix rebound
| | 2.00 | 6.00 | 14.00
nn(V8#7-V8#11)-160pgs.; contains 5 issues of Topix
| | 2.00 | 6.00 | 14.00

NEW MUTANTS, THE (Also see Marvel Graphic Novel #4)
March, 1983 - Present
Marvel Comics Group

1	1.25	3.75	7.50

	Good	Fine	N-Mint
2,3	.60	1.75	3.50
2-Limited test cover (75 cents)	8.35	25.00	50.00
4-10: 10-1st app. Magma	.50	1.50	3.00
11-20: 18-Intro. Warlock	.40	1.25	2.50
21-Double size; new Warlock origin	.50	1.50	3.00
22-30: 23-25-Cloak & Dagger app.	.40	1.25	2.50
31-40	.35	1.00	2.00
41-49	.25	.75	1.50
50-58: 50-Double size	.35	1.00	2.00
59-Fall of The Mutants begins, ends #61	.40	1.25	2.50
60-Double size, $1.25	.30	.90	1.80
61-Fall of The Mutants ends	.30	.90	1.80
62,64-72,74-86: 68-Intro Spyder. 76-X-Factor & X-Terminator app. 86-			
Ditko/McFarlane-c		.50	1.00
63-X-Men & Wolverine app.; $1.00-c begins	.25	.75	1.50
73-Double size, $1.50	.25	.75	1.50
Annual 1 (1984)	.85	2.50	5.00
Annual 2 (10/86; $1.25)	.35	1.00	2.00
Annual 3(9/87, $1.25)	.25	.75	1.50
Annual 4('88, $1.75)	.60	1.75	3.50
Annual 5('89, $2.00, 68 pgs.)-Atlantis Attacks	.35	1.00	2.00
Special 1-Special Edition ('85; 64 pgs.)-ties in with X-Men Alpha			
Flight mini-series; A. Adams/Austin-a	1.00	3.00	6.00

NOTE: **Art Adams** c-38, 39. **Austin** c-57i. **Byrne** c/a-75p. **Russell** a-48i. **Sienkiewicz** c/a-18-31, 35-38i; c-35i, 37i. **Simonson** c-11p. **B. Smith** c-36, 40-48. **Williamson** a(i)-69, 71-73, 75, 78, 79-83; c-69, 72, 73.

NEW PEOPLE, THE (TV)
Jan, 1970 - No. 2, May, 1970
Dell Publishing Co.

1,2	1.15	3.50	8.00

NEW ROMANCES
No. 5, May, 1951 - No. 21, Apr?, 1954
Standard Comics

5	3.70	11.00	26.00
6-9: 6-Barbara Bel Geddes, Richard Basehart ''Fourteen Hours'';			
	2.00	6.00	14.00
10,14,16,17-Toth-a	4.30	13.00	30.00
11-Toth-a; Liz Taylor, Montgomery Cliff photo-c	5.50	16.50	38.00
12,13,15,18-21	1.30	4.00	9.00

NOTE: *Celardo a-9. Moreira a-6. Tuska a-7, 20. Photo c-6-16.*

NEW STATESMEN, THE
1990 - No. 5, 1990 ($3.95, color, mini-series)
Quality Comics

1-5: Futuristic	.70	2.00	4.00

NEWSTRALIA
July, 1989 - Present ($1.75-$2.25, color, deluxe format)
Innovation Publishing

1-3: Timothy Truman-c/a; Gustovich-i	.35	1.00	2.00
4 ($2.25-c)	.40	1.15	2.30

NEW TALENT SHOWCASE (Talent Showcase No. 16 on)
Jan, 1984 - No. 19, Oct, 1985 (Direct sales only)
DC Comics

1-10: Features new strips & artists		.35	.70
11-19 ($1.25): 18-Williamson c(i)		.35	.70

NEW TEEN TITANS, THE (See DC Comics Presents 26, Marvel and
DC Present & Teen Titans; Tales of the Teen Titans #41 on)
November, 1980 - No. 40, March, 1984
DC Comics

1-Robin, Kid Flash, Wonder Girl, The Changeling, Starfire, The			
Raven, Cyborg begin; partial origin	2.00	6.00	12.00
2	1.10	3.25	6.50
3-Origin Starfire; Intro The Fearsome 5	.85	2.50	5.00

The New Gods #1 (2-3/71), © DC

The New Mutants #2, © MEG

Newstralia #1, © Innovation

The New Teen Titans #20 (1986), © DC

New York World's Fair, 1939, © DC

Next Man #4, © Comico

	Good	Fine	N-Mint

THE NEW TEEN TITANS (continued)
4-Origin continues; J.L.A. app. .85 2.50 5.00
5-10: 6-Origin Raven. 7-Cyborg origin. 8-Origin Kid Flash retold.
10-Origin Changeling retold .50 1.50 3.00
11-20: 13-Return of Madame Rouge & Capt. Zahl; Robotman revived.
14-Return of Mento; origin Doom Patrol. 15-Death of Madame
Rouge & Capt. Zahl; intro. new Brotherhood of Evil 16-1st app.
Carrot (free 16 pg. preview). 18-Return of Starfire. 19-Hawkman
teams-up .25 .75 1.50
21-30: 21-Intro Night Force in free 16 pg. insert; intro Brother Blood.
23-1st app. Vigilante (not in costume), & Blackfire. 24-Omega Men
app. 25-Omega Men cameo. 26-1st Terra. 29-The New Brotherhood
of Evil & Speedy app. 30-Terra joins the Titans
.60 1.20
31-38,40: 38-Origin Wonder Girl .40 .75
39-Last Dick Grayson as Robin; Kid Flash quits .35 1.00 2.00
Annual 1(11/82)-Omega Men app. .25 .70 1.40
Annual 2(9/83)-1st app. Vigilante in costume .45 .90
Annual 3(1984)-Death of Terra .45 .90
nn(11/83-Keebler Co. Giveaway)-In cooperation with "The President's
Drug Awareness Campaign" .60 1.20
nn-(re-issue of above on Mando paper for direct sales market);
American Soft Drink Ind. version; I.B.M. Corp. version
.50 1.00
NOTE: Perez a-1-4p, 6-40p, Annual 1p, 2p; c-1-12, 13-17p, 18-21, 22p, 23p, 24-37, 38,
39(painted), 40, Annual 1, 2.

NEW TEEN TITANS, THE (The New Titans #50 on)
Aug, 1984 - No. 49, Nov, 1988 ($1.25-$1.75; deluxe format)
DC Comics
1-New storyline; Perez c/a .85 2.50 5.00
2,3: 2-Re-intro Lilith .50 1.50 3.00
4-10: 5-Death of Trigon. 7-9-Origin Lilith. 8-Intro Kole. 10-Kole joins
.30 .90 1.80
11-19: 13,14-Crisis x-over .60 1.20
20-Robin (Jason Todd) joins; original Teen Titans return
.35 1.00 2.00
21-49: 37-Begin $1.75-c. 47-Origin all Titans. 48-1st app. Red Star
.25 .70 1.40
Annual 1 (9/85)-Intro. Vanguard .35 1.00 2.00
Annual 2 (8/86; $2.50): Byrne c/a(p); origin Brother Blood; intro new
Dr. Light .40 1.25 2.50
Annual 3 (11/87)-Intro. Danny Chase .35 1.00 2.00
Annual 4 ('88, $2.50)-Perez-c .40 1.15 2.30
NOTE: Orlando c-33p. Perez c/a 1-6; c-20, 22, 23. Perez a-1-6; c-1-6, 19-23, 43. Steacy
c-47.

NEW TERRYTOONS (TV)
6-8/60 - No. 8, 3-5/62; 10/62 - No. 54, 1/79
Dell Publishing Co./Gold Key
1('60-Dell)-Deputy Dawg, Dinky Duck & Hashimoto San begin
1.70 5.00 12.00
2-8('62) 1.00 3.00 7.00
1(30010-210)(10/62-G.Key, 84 pgs.)-Heckle & Jeckle begins
3.00 9.00 24.00
2(30010-301)-84 pgs. 2.50 7.50 20.00
3-10 .85 2.50 6.00
11-20 .60 1.75 3.50
21-30 .25 .75 1.50
31-54 .40 .80
NOTE: Reprints: #4-12, 38, 40, 47. (See March of Comics #379, 393, 412, 435)

NEW TESTAMENT STORIES VISUALIZED
1946 - 1947
Standard Publishing Co.
"New Testament Heroes—Acts of Apostles Visualized, Book I"
"New Testament Heroes—Acts of Apostles Visualized, Book II"
"Parables Jesus Told" Set.... 10.00 30.00 60.00

NOTE: All three are contained in a cardboard case, illustrated on front and info about
the set.

NEW TITANS, THE (Formerly The New Teen Titans)
No. 50, Dec, 1988 - Present ($1.75, color)
DC Comics

	Good	Fine	N-Mint
50-Perez-c/a begins; new origin Wonder Girl .75 2.25 4.50
51-59,62-64: 50-55-Painted-c. 55-Nightwing (Dick Grayson) forces
Danny Chase to resign; Batman app. in flashback
.40 1.25 2.50
60-A Lonely Place of Dying-Part 2/Batman .70 2.00 4.00
61-A Lonely Place of Dying-Part 4/Batman .35 1.00 2.00
Annual 5 (1989, $3.50, 68 pgs.) .60 1.75 3.50
NOTE: Perez a-50-55p, 57-60p; 61(layouts); c-50-61, Annual 5i.

NEW TV FUNNIES (See New Funnies)

NEW WAVE, THE
6/10/86 - No. 13, 3/87 (#1-8: bi-weekly, 20 pgs.; #9-13: monthly)
Eclipse Comics
1-8: 1-Origin 6-Origin Megabyte .30 .60
9-13 ($1.50) .25 .75 1.50
...Versus the Volunteers 3-D #1,2(4/87) .40 1.25 2.50

NEW WORLD (See Comic Books, series I)

NEW YORK GIANTS (See Thrilling True Story of the Baseball Giants)

**NEW YORK STATE JOINT LEGISLATIVE COMMITTEE TO STUDY
THE PUBLICATION OF COMICS, THE**
1951, 1955
N.Y. State Legislative Document

This document was referenced by Wertham for Seduction of the Innocent. Contains
numerous repros from comics showing violence, sadism, torture, and sex.
1955 version (196p, No. 37, 2/23/55)-Sold for $180 in 1986.

NEW YORK WORLD'S FAIR
1939, 1940 (100pgs.; cardboard covers) (DC's 4th & 5th annuals)
National Periodical Publications
1939-Scoop Scanlon, Superman (blonde haired Superman on-c),
Sandman, Zatara, Slam Bradley, Ginger Snap by Bob Kane begin
400.00 1200.00 2450.00
1940-Batman, Hourman, Johnny Thunderbolt app.
250.00 750.00 1500.00
NOTE: The 1939 edition was published at 25 cents. All other comics were 10 cents,
it didn't sell. Remaining copies were repriced with 15 cents stickers placed over the 25 cents
price. Four variations on the 15 cents stickers known. It was advertised in other DC comics
at 25 cents. Everyone who sent a quarter through the mail for it received a free Superman
#1 or#2 to make up the dime difference. The 1940 edition was priced at 15 cents.

NEW YORK: YEAR ZERO
Aug, 1988 - No. 3, Sept, 1988 ($2.00, B&W, mini-series)
Eclipse Comics
1-3 .35 1.00 2.00

NEXT MAN
Mar, 1985 - No. 5, Oct, 1985 ($1.50, color; Baxter paper)
Comico
1 .40 1.25 2.50
2-5 .25 .75 1.50

NEXT NEXUS, THE
Jan, 1989 - No. 4, April, 1989 ($1.95, mini-series, color, Baxter)
First Comics
1-4: By Baron & Rude .35 1.00 1.95

NEXUS (See First Comics Graphic Novel #4, 19 & The Next Nexus)
6/81 - No. 6, 3/84; No. 7, 4/85 - Present
(Direct sales only, 36 pgs.; V2/1('83)-printed on Baxter paper
Capital Comics/First Comics No. 7 on
1-B&W version; magazine size 5.00 15.00 30.00
1-B&W 1981 limited edition; 500 copies printed and signed; same

NEXUS (continued)	Good	Fine	N-Mint
as above except this version has a 2-pg. poster & a pencil sketch			
on paperboard by Rude	7.00	20.00	40.00
2-B&W, magazine size	2.00	6.00	12.00
3-B&W, magazine size; contains 33⅓ rpm record ($2.95 price)			
	1.25	3.75	7.50
V2#1-Color version	.60	1.75	3.50
2-49,51-68: 2-Nexus' origin begins	.35	1.00	2.00
50 ($3.50, 52 pgs.)	.60	1.75	3.50

NOTE: Bissette c-29. Rude c-3(B&W), V2#1-22, 24-27, 33-36, 39-42, 45-48, 50, 58-60; a-1-3, 8p-16p, 18p-22p, 24p-27p, 33p-36p, 39p-42p, 45p-48p, 50, 58, 59p, 60. Paul Smith a-37, 38, 43, 44, 51-55p; c-37, 38, 43, 44, 51-55.

NEXUS FILES
1989 ($4.50, color/16 pgs. B&W, One-shot, squarebound, 52 pgs.)
First Comics

1-New Rude-a; info on Nexus	.75	2.25	4.50

NEXUS LEGENDS
May, 1989 - Present ($1.50, color, Baxter)
First Comics

1-12: R/1-3(Capital) & early First Comics issues w/new Rude covers			
#1-6,9,10	.25	.75	1.50

NICKEL COMICS
1938 (Pocket size - 7½x5½")(132 pgs.)
Dell Publishing Co.

1-"Bobby & Chip" by Otto Messmer, Felix the Cat artist. Contains			
some English reprints	24.00	73.00	170.00

NICKEL COMICS
May, 1940 - No. 8, Aug, 1940 (36 pgs.; Bi-Weekly; 5 cents)
Fawcett Publications

1-Origin/1st app. Bulletman	100.00	300.00	700.00
2	45.00	135.00	315.00
3	40.00	120.00	280.00
4-The Red Gaucho begins	34.00	102.00	235.00
5-7	30.00	90.00	210.00
8-World's Fair-c; Bulletman moved to Master Comics #7 in Oct.			
	30.00	90.00	210.00

NOTE: Beck c-5-8. Jack Binder c-1-4. Bondage c-5.

NICK FURY, AGENT OF SHIELD (See Marv. Spotlight #31 & Shield)
6/68 - No. 15, 11/69; No. 16, 11/70 - No. 18, 3/71
Marvel Comics Group

1	3.60	11.00	25.00
2-4: 4-Origin retold	1.70	5.00	12.00
5-Classic-c	2.15	6.50	15.00
6,7	1.15	3.50	8.00
8-11: 9-Hate Monger begins (ends #11). 11-Smith-c			
	.70	2.00	4.00
12-Smith c/a	.85	2.50	5.00
13-18: 16-18, all-r	.40	1.25	2.50

NOTE: Adkins a-3i. Craig a-10i. Sid Greene a-12i. Kirby a-16-18r. Springer a-4, 6, 7, 8p, 9, 10p, 11; c-8, 9. Steranko a(p)-1-3, 5; c-1-7.

NICK FURY, AGENT OF SHIELD (Also see Strange Tales #135)
Dec, 1983 - No. 2, Jan, 1984 ($2.00; 52 pgs.; Baxter paper)
Marvel Comics Group

1,2-Nick Fury-r; Steranko-c/a	.35	1.00	2.00

NICK FURY, AGENT OF S.H.I.E.L.D.
Sept, 1989 - Present ($1.50, color)
Marvel Comics

V2#1-8	.25	.75	1.50

NICK FURY VS. SHIELD
June, 1988 - No. 6, Dec, 1988 ($3.50, 52pgs, color, deluxe format)
Marvel Comics

1-Steranko-c	2.35	7.00	14.00

	Good	Fine	N-Mint
2	3.50	10.50	21.00
3	1.25	3.25	6.50
4-6	.70	2.00	4.00

NICK HALIDAY
May, 1956
Argo

1-Daily & Sunday strip-r by Petree	4.00	12.00	28.00

NIGHT AND THE ENEMY (Graphic Novel)
1988 (8½x11") (color; 80pgs.; $11.95)
Comico

1-Harlan Ellison scripts/Ken Steacy-c/a; r/Epic Illustrated & new-a			
	2.00	6.00	11.95
1-2nd print	2.00	6.00	11.95
1-Limited edition ($39.95)	7.00	20.00	39.95

NIGHT BEFORE CHRISTMAS, THE (See March of Comics No. 152)

NIGHTBREED
Jan, 1990 - Present ($1.95, color, adults)
Epic Comics (Marvel)

1-5: 1-4-Adapts Clive Barker horror movie	.35	1.00	2.00

NIGHTCRAWLER
Nov, 1985 - No. 4, Feb, 1986 (mini-series from X-Men)
Marvel Comics Group

1-Cockrum c/a	.50	1.50	3.00
2-4	.35	1.00	2.00

NIGHT FORCE, THE (See New Teen Titans #21)
Aug, 1982, No. 14, Sept, 1983
DC Comics

1		.40	.80
2-14: 13-Origin The Baron. 14-Nudity panels		.30	.60

NOTE: Colan c/a-1-14p. Giordano c-1i, 2i, 4i, 5i, 7i, 12i.

NIGHTINGALE, THE
1948 (14 pgs., 7¼x10¼", ½B&W) (10 cents)
Henry H. Stansbury Once-Upon-A-Time Press, Inc.

(Very Rare)-Low distribution; distributed to Westchester County & Bronx, N.Y. only; used in Seduction of the Innocent, pf. 312,313 as the 1st and only "good" comic book ever published. Ill. by Dong Kingman; 1,500 words of text, printed on high quality paper & no word balloons. Copyright registered 10/22/48, distributed week of 12/5/48. (By Hans Christian Andersen)   Estimated value $135

NIGHTMARE
Summer, 1952 - No. 2, Fall, 1952; No. 3, 4, 1953 (Painted-c)
Ziff-Davis (Approved Comics)/St. John No. 3,4

1-1pg. Kinstler-a; Tuska-a(2)	16.50	50.00	115.00
2-Kinstler-a-Poe's "Pit & the Pendulum"	12.00	36.00	84.00
3-Kinstler-a	10.00	30.00	70.00
4	8.00	24.00	56.00

NIGHTMARE (Weird Horrors #1-9) (Amazing Ghost Stories #14 on)
No. 10, Dec, 1953 - No. 13, Aug, 1954
St. John Publishing Co.

10-Reprints Ziff-Davis Weird Thrillers #2 with new Kubert-c plus			
2 pgs. Kinstler, & Toth-a	18.00	54.00	125.00
11-Krigstein-a; Poe adapt., "Hop Frog"	13.00	40.00	90.00
12-Kubert bondage-c; adaptation of Poe's 'The Black Cat;'			
Cannibalism story	11.00	32.00	75.00
13-Reprints Z-D Weird Thrillers 3 with new cover; Powell-a(2),			
Tuska-a; Baker-c	6.50	19.50	45.00

NOTE: Anderson a-10. Colan a-10.

NIGHTMARE (Magazine)
Dec, 1970 - No. 23, Feb, 1975 (B&W) (68 pages)
Skywald Publishing Corp.

1-Everett-a	1.15	3.50	8.00

Nexus V2#1, © Capital   Nickel Comics #8, © FAW

Nick Fury, Agent Of Shield #4 (9/68), © MEG

Night Rider #1, © MEG

Noman #2, © TC

Normalman #1, © A-V

NIGHTMARE (continued)	Good	Fine	N-Mint
2-5: 4-Decapitation story	.85	2.50	5.00
6-Kaluta-a	.85	2.50	5.00
7,9,10	.70	2.00	4.00
8-Features E. C. movie ''Tales from the Crypt;'' reprints some E.C.			
comics panels	1.30	4.00	9.00
11-20: 12-Excessive gore, severed heads. 20-Severed head-c			
	.40	1.25	2.50
21-(1974 Summer Special)-Kaluta-a	.40	1.25	2.50
22-Tomb of Horror issue	.40	1.25	2.50
23-(1975 Winter Special)	.40	1.25	2.50
Annual 1(1972)-B.Jones-a	.60	1.80	3.50
Winter Special 1(1973)	.60	1.80	3.50
Yearbook-nn(1974)	.60	1.80	3.50

NOTE: *Adkins* a-5. *Boris* c-2, 3, 5 (#4 is not by Boris). *Byrne* a-20p. *Everett* a-4, 5. *Jones* a-6, 21; c-6. *Katz* a-5. *Reese* a-4, 5. *Wildey* a-5, 6, 21, '74 Yearbook. *Wrightson* a-9.

NIGHTMARE (Alex Nino's)
1989 ($1.95, color)
Innovation Publishing

1-Alex Nino-a	.35	1.00	2.00

NIGHTMARE & CASPER (See Harvey Hits #71) (Casper & Night-mare #6 on)(See Casper The Friendly Ghost #19)
Aug, 1963 - No. 5, Aug, 1964 (25 cents)
Harvey Publications

1-All reprints?	5.35	16.00	32.00
2-5: All reprints?	2.35	7.00	14.00

NIGHTMARE ON ELM STREET
Nov, 1989 - No. 2, Dec, 1989 ($2.25, B&W, mag., movie adaptation)
Marvel Comics

1,2: Origin Freddy Krueger; Buckler/Alcala-a	.40	1.15	2.30

NIGHTMARES (See Do You Believe in Nightmares)

NIGHTMARES
May, 1985 - No. 2, May, 1985 ($1.75, color, Baxter paper)
Eclipse Comics

1,2	.30	.90	1.80

NIGHTMASK
Nov, 1986 - No. 12, Oct, 1987
Marvel Comics Group

1		.45	.90
2-12		.40	.80

NIGHT MUSIC (See Eclipse Graphic Album Series)
Dec, 1984 - No. 7, Feb, 1988 ($1.75, color, Baxter paper)
Eclipse Comics

1-3: 3-Russell's Jungle Book adapt.	.30	.90	1.80
4,5-Pelleas And Melisande (double titled)	.30	.90	1.80
6-Salome' (double titled)	.30	.90	1.80
7-Red Dog #1	.30	.90	1.80

NIGHT NURSE
Nov, 1972 - No. 4, May, 1973
Marvel Comics Group

1-4		.40	.80

NIGHT OF MYSTERY
1953 (no month) (One Shot)
Avon Periodicals

nn-1pg. Kinstler-a, Hollingsworth-c	13.00	42.00	100.00

NIGHT OF THE GRIZZLY, THE (See Movie Classics)

NIGHT RIDER
Oct, 1974 - No. 6, Aug, 1975
Marvel Comics Group

	Good	Fine	N-Mint
1-#1-6 reprints Ghost Rider #1-6		.50	1.00
2-6		.30	.60

NIGHTVEIL (See Femforce)
Nov, 1984 - No. 7, 1985 ($1.75, color)
Americomics/AC Comics

1	.50	1.50	3.00
2-7	.35	1.00	2.00
Nightveil's Cauldron Of Horror 1 (1989, $2.50, B&W)-Kubert, Powell,			
Wood-r plus new Nightveil story	.40	1.25	2.50
Special 1 ('88, $1.95)-Kaluta-c	.35	1.00	2.00

NIGHTWINGS (See DC Science Fiction Graphic Novel)

NIKKI, WILD DOG OF THE NORTH (See 4-Color 1226 & Movie Comics)

1984 (Magazine) (1994 #11 on)
June, 1978 - No. 10, Jan, 1980 ($1.50)
Warren Publishing Co.

1	.50	1.50	3.00
2-10	.30	.90	1.80

NOTE: *Alacla* a-1-3, 5i. *Corben* a-1-8; c-1, 2. *Nino* a-1-10. *Thorne* a-7-10. *Wood* a-1,2,5i.

1994 (Formerly 1984) (Magazine)
No. 11, Feb, 1980 - No. 29, Feb, 1983
Warren Publishing Co.

11-29: 27-The Warhawks return	.35	1.00	2.00

NOTE: *Corben* c-26. *Nino* a-11-19, 20(2), 21, 25, 26, 28; c-21. *Redondo* c-20. *Thorne* a-11-14, 17-21, 25, 26, 28, 29.

NIPPY'S POP
1917 (Sunday strip reprints-B&W) (10½x13½'')
The Saalfield Publishing Co.

32 pages	7.00	21.00	50.00

NOAH'S ARK
1973 (35-49 Cents)
Spire Christian Comics/Fleming H. Revell Co.

By Al Hartley		.40	.80

NOID IN 3-D, THE (See Blackthorne 3-D Series #74)

NOMAN (See Thunder Agents)
Nov, 1966 - No. 2, March, 1967 (68 pgs.)
Tower Comics

1-Wood/Williamson-c; Lightning begins; Dynamo cameo; Kane-a(p)			
	3.00	9.00	21.00
2-Wood-c only; Dynamo x-over; Whitney-a-#1,2			
	1.70	5.00	12.00

NONE BUT THE BRAVE (See Movie Classics)

NOODNIK COMICS (See Pinky the Egghead)
1953; No. 2, Feb, 1954 - No. 5, Aug, 1954
Comic Media/Mystery/Biltmore

3-D(1953-Comic Media)(#1)	21.50	64.00	150.00
2-5	2.30	7.00	16.00

NORMALMAN
Jan, 1984 - No. 12, Dec, 1985 ($1.70-$2.00, B&W)
Aardvark-Vanaheim/Renegade Press

1-5 ($1.70)	.35	1.10	2.20
6-12 ($2.00)	.40	1.20	2.40
3-D 1(Annual,1986, $2.25)	.40	1.25	2.50
...The Novel (Published by Slave Labor Graphics)($12.95)-R/all			
issues	2.15	6.50	12.95

NORTH AVENUE IRREGULARS (See Walt Disney Showcase #49)

NORTH TO ALASKA (See 4-Color No. 1155)

NORTHWEST MOUNTIES (Also see Approved Comics)
Oct, 1948 - No. 4, July, 1949

NORTHWEST MOUNTIES (continued)
Jubilee Publications/St. John

	Good	Fine	N-Mint
1-Rose of the Yukon by Matt Baker; Walter Johnson-a; Lubbers-c			
	18.00	54.00	125.00
2-Baker-a; Lubbers-c. Ventrilo app.	13.00	40.00	90.00
3-Bondage-c, Baker-a; Sky Chief, K-9 app.	13.50	41.00	95.00
4-Baker-c, 2 pgs.; Blue Monk app.	13.50	41.00	95.00

NO SLEEP 'TIL DAWN (See 4-Color #831)

NOT BRAND ECHH (Brand Echh #1-4; See Crazy, 1973)
Aug, 1967 - No. 13, May, 1969 (No. 9-13: 68 pages)
Marvel Comics Group

1	2.15	6.50	15.00
2-4: 3-Origin Thor, Hulk & Capt. America; Monkees, Alfred E. Neuman cameo. 4-X-Men app.	1.00	3.00	7.00
5-8: 5-Origin/intro. Forbush Man. 7-Origin Fantastical-4 & Stuporman. 8-Beatles cameo; X-Men satire	1.00	3.00	7.00
9-13-All Giants. 9-Beatles cameo. 10-All-r; The Old Witch, Crypt Keeper & Vault Keeper cameos. 12,13-Beatles cameo, Avengers satire #12	1.00	3.00	7.00

NOTE: *Colan* a-4p, 5p, 8p. *Everett* a-1i. *Kirby* a(p)-1,3,5-7,10; c-1. *Severin* a-1; c-3, 7, 8. *Sutton* a-4, 5i, 7i, 8; c-5. Archie satire-No. 9.

NO TIME FOR SERGEANTS (TV)
No. 914, July, 1958 - No. 3, Aug-Oct, 1965
Dell Publishing Co.

4-Color 914 (Movie)-Toth-a	6.00	18.00	42.00
1(2-4/65)-3 (TV): Photo-c	2.30	7.00	16.00

NOVA (The Man Called. . .No. 22-25)
Sept, 1976 - No. 25, May, 1979
Marvel Comics Group

1-Origin	.35	1.00	2.00
2-25		.50	1.00

NOTE: *Austin* c-21i, 23i. *John Buscema* a(p)-1, 2, 3p, 8p, 21; c-1p, 2, 15. *Infantino* a(p)-15-20, 22-25; c-17-20, 21p, 23p, 24p. *Kirby* c-4p, 5, 7. *Nebres* c-25i. *Simonson* a-23i.

NOW AGE ILLUSTRATED (See Pendulum Illustrated Classics)

NTH MAN (. . .The Ultimate Ninja) (See Marvel Comics Presents 25)
Aug, 1989 - Present ($1.00, color)
Marvel Comics

1-Ninja mercenary	.35	1.00	2.00
2-10		.50	1.00

NUCLEUS (Also see Cerebus)
May, 1979 ($1.50, B&W, adult fanzine)
Heiro-Graphic Publications

1-Contains "Demonhorn" by Dave Sim; Cerebus The Aardvark, 4 pg. story	7.00	21.00	50.00

NUKLA
Oct-Dec, 1965 - No. 4, Sept, 1966
Dell Publishing Co.

1-Origin Nukla (super hero)	1.50	4.50	10.00
2,3	.85	2.60	6.00
4-Ditko-a, c(p)	1.00	3.00	7.00

NURSE BETSY CRANE (Formerly Teen Secret Diary)
V2#12, Aug, 1961 - V2#27, Mar, 1964 (See Soap Opera Romances)
Charlton Comics

V2#12-27	.35	1.00	2.00

NURSE HELEN GRANT (See The Romances of. . .)

NURSE LINDA LARK (See Linda Lark)

NURSERY RHYMES
No. 2, 1950 - No. 10, July-Aug, 1951 (Painted-c)
Ziff-Davis Publ. Co. (Approved Comics)

	Good	Fine	N-Mint
2	7.00	21.00	50.00
3-10: 10-Howie Post-a	4.50	14.00	32.00

NURSES, THE (TV)
April, 1963 - No. 3, Oct, 1963 (Photo-c: #1,2)
Gold Key

1	1.50	4.50	10.00
2,3	.85	2.50	6.00

NUTS! (Satire)
March, 1954 - No. 5, Nov, 1954
Premiere Comics Group

1-Hollingsworth-a	8.00	24.00	56.00
2,4,5: 5-Capt. Marvel parody	5.70	17.00	40.00
3-Drug "reefers" mentioned	6.50	19.50	45.00

NUTS (Magazine) (Satire)
Feb, 1958 - No. 2, April, 1958
Health Knowledge

1	2.85	8.50	20.00
2	2.00	6.00	14.00

NUTS & JOLTS (See Large Feature Comic #22)

NUTSY SQUIRREL (Formerly Hollywood Funny Folks)
(Also see Comic Cavalcade)
#61, 9-10/54 - #69, 1-2/56; #70, 8-9/56 - #71, 10-11/56; #72, 11/57
National Periodical Publications

61-Mayer-a; Grossman-a in all	3.50	10.50	24.00
62-72: Mayer a-62,65,67-72	2.00	6.00	14.00

NUTTY COMICS
Winter, 1946 (Funny animal)
Fawcett Publications

1-Capt. Kidd story; 1pg. Wolverton-a	7.00	21.00	50.00

NUTTY COMICS
1945 - No. 8, June-July, 1947
Home Comics (Harvey Publications)

nn-Helpful Hank, Bozo Bear & others	3.00	9.00	21.00
2-4	2.00	6.00	14.00
5-8: 5-Rags Rabbit begins (1st app.); infinity-c	1.50	4.50	10.00

NUTTY LIFE
No. 2, Summer, 1946
Fox Features Syndicate

2	3.70	11.00	26.00

NYOKA, THE JUNGLE GIRL (Formerly Jungle Girl; see The Further Adventures of. . ., Master Comics #50 & XMas Comics)
No. 2, Winter, 1945 - No. 77, June, 1953 (Movie serial)
Fawcett Publications

2	34.00	103.00	240.00
3	19.00	57.00	135.00
4,5	16.00	48.00	110.00
6-10	11.50	34.00	80.00
11,13,14,16-18-Krigstein-a	11.50	34.00	80.00
12,15,19,20	9.30	28.00	65.00
21-30: 25-Clayton Moore photo-c?	5.70	17.00	40.00
31-40	4.30	13.00	30.00
41-50	3.15	9.50	22.00
51-60	2.30	7.00	16.00
61-77	1.70	5.00	12.00

NOTE: Photo-c from movies 25, 27, 28, 30-70. Bondage c-4, 5, 7, 8, 14, 24.

NYOKA, THE JUNGLE GIRL (Formerly Zoo Funnies; Space Adventures #23 on)
No. 14, Nov, 1955 - No. 22, Nov, 1957
Charlton Comics

Not Brand Echh #4, © MEG

Nukla #1, © DELL

Nyoka, The Jungle Girl #30, © FAW

	Good	Fine	N-Mint
NYOKA, THE JUNGLE GIRL (continued)			
14	3.15	9.50	22.00
15-22	2.15	6.50	15.00

OAKY DOAKS
July, 1942 (One Shot)
Eastern Color Printing Co.

1	14.00	42.00	100.00

OAKLAND PRESS FUNNYBOOK, THE
9/17/78 - 4/13/80 (16 pgs.) (Weekly)
Full color in comic book form; changes to tabloid size 4/20/80-on
The Oakland Press

Contains Tarzan by Manning, Marmaduke, Bugs Bunny, etc. (low
distribution); 9/23/79 - 4/13/80 contain Buck Rogers by Gray Morrow

& Jim Lawrence	.25	.80	1.60

OBIE
1953 (6 cents)
Store Comics

1	.70	2.00	4.00

OBNOXIO THE CLOWN
April, 1983 (One Shot) (Character from Crazy Magazine)
Marvel Comics Group

1-Vs. the X-Men		.30	.60

OCCULT FILES OF DR. SPEKTOR, THE
4/73 - No. 24, 2/77; No. 25, 5/82 (Painted-c #1-24)
Gold Key/Whitman No. 25

1-1st app. Lakota; Baron Tibor begins	.85	2.50	5.00
2-5	.40	1.25	2.50
6-10	.35	1.00	2.00
11-13: 11-1st app. Spektor as Werewolf		.60	1.20
14-Dr. Solar app.		.60	1.20
15-25: 25-Reprints		.60	1.20
9(Modern Comics reprint, 1977)		.15	.30

NOTE: Also see Dan Curtis, Golden Comics Digest 33, Gold Key Spotlight, Mystery
Comics Digest 5, & Spine Tingling Tales.

ODELL'S ADVENTURES IN 3-D (See Adventures in 3-D)

OFFICIAL CRISIS ON INFINITE EARTHS INDEX, THE
March, 1986 ($1.75, color)
Independent Comics Group (Eclipse)

1	.30	.90	1.80

OFFICIAL CRISIS ON INFINITE EARTHS CROSSOVER INDEX, THE
July, 1986 ($1.75, color)
Independent Comics Group (Eclipse)

1	.30	.90	1.80

OFFICIAL DOOM PATROL INDEX, THE
Feb, 1986 - No. 2, Mar, 1986 ($1.50, color, 2 part series)
Independent Comics Group (Eclipse)

1,2	.25	.75	1.50

OFFICIAL HANDBOOK OF THE CONAN UNIVERSE
June, 1985 ($1.25, color, One Shot)
Marvel Comics

1-Indicia title is Handbook of the...		.65	1.30

OFFICIAL HANDBOOK OF THE MARVEL UNIVERSE, THE
Jan, 1983 - No. 15, May, 1984
Marvel Comics Group

1-Lists Marvel heroes & villains (letter A)	1.00	3.00	6.00
2 (B-C)	.85	2.50	5.00
3-5: 3-(C-D). 4-(D-G). 5-(H-J)	.70	2.00	4.00
6-9: 6-(K-L). 7-(M). 8-(N-P). 9-(Q-S)	.50	1.50	3.00
10-15: 10-(S). 11-(S-U). 12-(U-Z). 13,14-Book of the Dead. 15-Weaponry catalogue	.40	1.25	2.50

NOTE: **Byrne** c/a(p)-1-14; c-15p. **Grell** a-9. **Layton** a-2, 5, 7. **Miller** a-2, 3. **Nebres** a-3, 4,
8. **Simonson** a-11. **Paul Smith** a-1-3, 6, 7, 9, 10, 12. **Starlin** a-7. **Steranko** a-8p.

OFFICIAL HANDBOOK OF THE MARVEL UNIVERSE, THE
Dec, 1985 - No. 20, April?, 1987 ($1.50 cover; maxi-series)

Marvel Comics Group	Good	Fine	N-Mint
V2#1	.70	2.00	4.00
2-5	.50	1.50	3.00
6-10	.40	1.25	2.50
11-20	.35	1.00	2.00
Trade paperback Vol. 1-9	1.15	3.50	7.00

OFFICIAL HANDBOOK OF THE MARVEL UNIVERSE, THE
July, 1989 - No. 8, Mid-Dec, 1990 ($1.50, color, mini-series, 52 pgs.)
Marvel Comics

V3#1-8: 1-McFarlane-a(2 pgs.)	.25	.75	1.50

OFFICIAL HAWKMAN INDEX, THE
Nov, 1986 - No. 2, Dec, 1986 ($2.00)
Independent Comics Group

1,2	.35	1.00	2.00

OFFICIAL JUSTICE LEAGUE OF AMERICA INDEX, THE
April, 1986 - No. 8, Mar, 1987 ($2.00, Baxter)
Independent Comics Group (Eclipse)

1-8	.35	1.00	2.00

OFFICIAL LEGION OF SUPER-HEROES INDEX, THE
Dec, 1986 - No. 5, 1987 ($2.00, color)(No Official in title #2 on)
Independent Comics Group (Eclipse)

1-5: 4-Mooney-c	.35	1.00	2.00

OFFICIAL MARVEL INDEX TO MARVEL TEAM-UP
Jan, 1986 - No. 6?, 1986 ($1.25, color)
Marvel Comics Group

1-6		.65	1.30

OFFICIAL MARVEL INDEX TO THE AMAZING SPIDER-MAN
Apr, 1985 - No. 9, Dec, 1985 ($1.50?, color)
Marvel Comics Group

1	.40	1.25	2.50
2-9: 5-Punisher app.	.35	1.00	2.00

OFFICIAL MARVEL INDEX TO THE AVENGERS, THE
June, 1987 - No. 7, Oct, 1988 ($2.95, color, squarebound, 52 pgs.)
Marvel Comics Group

V5#1-7: All have wraparound-c	.50	1.50	3.00

OFFICIAL MARVEL INDEX TO THE FANTASTIC FOUR
Dec, 1985 - No. 5, 1986 ($1.25, color)
Marvel Comics Group

1-5	.25	.75	1.50

OFFICIAL MARVEL INDEX TO THE X-MEN, THE
May, 1987 - No. 8, 1988? ($2.95, color, squarebound, 52 pgs.)
Marvel Comics Group

V4#1-8: All have wraparound-c	.50	1.50	3.00

OFFICIAL SOUPY SALES COMIC (See Soupy Sales)

OFFICIAL TEEN TITANS INDEX, THE
Aug, 1985 - No. 5, 1986 ($1.50, color)
Independent Comics Group (Eclipse)

1-5	.25	.75	1.50

OFFICIAL TRUE CRIME CASES (Formerly Sub-Mariner #23; All-True
Crime Cases #26 on)
No. 24, Fall, 1947 - No. 25, Winter, 1947-48
Marvel Comics (OCI)

24(#1)-Burgos-a; Syd Shores-c	7.00	21.00	50.00
25-Kurtzman's "Hey Look"	5.70	17.00	40.00

OF SUCH IS THE KINGDOM
1955 (36 pgs., 15 cents)
George A. Pflaum

	Good	Fine	N-Mint
nn-R-/1951 Treasure Chest	1.15	3.50	8.00

O.G. WHIZ (See Gold Key Spotlight #10)
2/71 - No. 6, 5/72; No. 7, 5/78 - No. 11, 1/79 (No. 7: 52 pgs.)
Gold Key

1,2-John Stanley scripts	5.00	15.00	35.00
3-6(1972)	2.00	6.00	14.00
7-11('78-'79)-Part-r: 9-Tubby app.	.60	1.75	3.50

OH, BROTHER! (Teen Comedy)
Jan, 1953 - No. 5, Oct, 1953
Stanhall Publ.

1-By Bill Williams	2.30	7.00	16.00
2-5	1.30	4.00	9.00

OH SKIN-NAY!
1913 (8½x13'')
P.F. Volland & Co.

nn-The Days Of Real Sport by Briggs	10.00	30.00	70.00

OH SUSANNA (See 4-Color #1105)

OKAY COMICS
July, 1940
United Features Syndicate

1-Captain & the Kids & Hawkshaw the Detective reprints	20.00	60.00	140.00

OK COMICS
July, 1940 - No. 2, Oct, 1940
United Features Syndicate

1-Little Giant, Phantom Knight, Sunset Smith, & The Teller Twins begin	30.00	90.00	210.00
2 (Rare)-Origin Mister Mist	30.00	90.00	210.00

OKLAHOMA KID
June, 1957 - No. 4, 1958
Ajax/Farrell Publ.

1	3.50	10.50	24.00
2-4	1.70	5.00	12.00

OKLAHOMAN, THE (See 4-Color #820)

OLD GLORY COMICS
1944 (Giveaway)
Chesapeake & Ohio Railway

nn-Capt. Fearless reprint	2.35	7.00	16.00

OLD IRONSIDES (See 4-Color #874)

OLD YELLER (See 4-Color #869, Movie Comics, and Walt Disney Showcase #25)

OMAC (One Man Army, . . . Corps. #4 on; also see Warlord)
Sept-Oct, 1974 - No. 8, Nov-Dec, 1975
National Periodical Publications

1-Origin		.50	1.00
2-8: 8-2pg. Adams ad		.35	.70

NOTE: *Kirby* a-1-8p; c-1-7p. *Kubert* c-8. See Kamandi No. 59 & Cancelled Comic Cavalcade.

OMAHA THE CAT DANCER
1984 (no month) - Present (B&W, adults)
Steeldragon/Kitchen Sink #2 on

1-Preview (Steeldragon)	1.70	5.00	10.00
1 (Kitchen Sink)	1.15	3.50	7.00
1-2nd print	.35	1.00	2.00
2-Steeldragon ($1.75-c)	.70	2.00	4.00
2-Kitchen Sink ($2.00-c)	.50	1.50	3.00
3,4	.50	1.50	3.00

	Good	Fine	N-Mint
3,4-2nd print	.35	1.00	2.00
5-13	.35	1.00	2.00

O'MALLEY AND THE ALLEY CATS
April, 1971 - No. 9, Jan, 1974 (Disney)
Gold Key

1	1.50	4.50	10.00
2-9	.85	2.60	6.00

OMEGA ELITE
1987 ($1.25, color)
Blackthorne Publishing

1-Starlin-c		.60	1.25

OMEGA MEN, THE (See Green Lantern #141)
Dec, 1982 - No. 38, May, 1986 ($1.00-$1.50; Baxter paper)
DC Comics

1		.25	.75	1.50
2-38: 2-Origin Broot. 7-Origin The Citadel. 26,27-Alan Moore scripts. 30-Intro new Primus. 31-Crisis x-over. 34,35-Teen Titans x-over			
			.50	1.00
Annual 1(11/84, 52 pgs.), 2(11/85)	.25	.75	1.50

NOTE: *Giffen* c/a-1-6p. *Morrow* a-24r. *Nino* a-16, 21; c-16, 21.

OMEGA THE UNKNOWN
March, 1976 - No. 10, Oct, 1977
Marvel Comics Group

1		.60	1.20
2-10: 2-Hulk app. 3-Electro app.		.50	1.00

NOTE: *Kane* c/p-3, 5, 8, 9. *Mooney* a-1-3. 4p, 5, 6p, 7, 8i, 9, 10.

OMNI MEN
1987 - No. 3? ($1.25, color)
Blackthorne Publishing

1-3		.60	1.25

ONE, THE
July, 1985 - No. 6, Feb, 1986 (Mini-series; adults only)
Epic Comics (Marvel)

1-Post nuclear holocaust super-hero	.25	.75	1.50
2-6: 2-Intro. The Other	.25	.75	1.50

ONE-ARM SWORDSMAN, THE
1987 - Present? ($2.75-$1.80, color, 52 pgs.)
Victory Prod./Lueng's Publications #4 on

1-3 ($2.75)	.45	1.40	2.80
4-6 ($1.80)	.30	.90	1.80

ONE HUNDRED AND ONE DALMATIANS (See 4-Color #1183, Movie Comics, and Walt Disney Showcase #9,51)

100 PAGES OF COMICS
1937 (Stiff covers; square binding)
Dell Publishing Co.

101(Found on back cover)-Alley Oop, Wash Tubbs, Capt. Easy, Og Son of Fire, Apple Mary, Tom Mix, Dan Dunn, Tailspin Tommy, Doctor Doom	55.00	165.00	385.00

100-PAGE SUPER SPECTACULAR (See DC. . .)

$1,000,000 DUCK (See Walt Disney Showcase #5)

ONE MILLION YEARS AGO (Tor #2 on)
September, 1953
St. John Publishing Co.

1-Origin; Kubert-c/a	13.00	40.00	90.00

ONE SHOT (See 4-Color. . .)

1001 HOURS OF FUN (See Large Feature Comic #13)

ON STAGE (See 4-Color #1336)

OK Comics #2, © UFS

Omega The Unknown #3, © MEG

One Million Years Ago #1, © STG

Operation Peril #1, © ACG

The Original Black Cat #2, © HARV

Our Army At War #17, © DC

ON THE AIR
1947 (Giveaway) (paper cover)
NBC Network Comic

	Good	Fine	N-Mint
nn-(Rare)	10.00	30.00	70.00

ON THE DOUBLE (See 4-Color #1232)

ON THE LINKS
December, 1926 (48 pages) (9x10'')
Associated Feature Service

	Good	Fine	N-Mint
Daily strip-r	8.00	24.00	56.00

ON THE ROAD WITH ANDRAE CROUCH
1973, 1977 (39 cents)
Spire Christian Comics (Fleming H. Revell)

nn		.50	1.00

ON THE SPOT (Pretty Boy Floyd . . .)
Fall, 1948
Fawcett Publications

nn-Bondage-c	13.00	42.00	90.00

OPEN SPACE
Mid-Dec, 1989 - Present ($4.95, color, bi-monthly, 68 pgs.)
Marvel Comics

1-Bill Wray-a; Freas-c	.85	2.50	5.00

OPERATION BIKINI (See Movie Classics)

OPERATION BUCHAREST (See The Crusaders)

OPERATION CROSSBOW (See Movie Classics)

OPERATION PERIL
Oct-Nov, 1950 - No. 16, Apr-May, 1953 (52 pgs.): #1-5)
American Comics Group (Michel Publ.)

1-Time Travelers, Danny Danger (by Leonard Starr) & Typhoon Tyler			
(by Ogden Whitney) begin	11.00	32.00	75.00
2	6.50	19.50	45.00
3-5: 3-Horror story. 5-Sci/fi story	5.70	17.00	40.00
6-12-Last Time Travelers	5.00	15.00	35.00
13-16: All war format	2.00	6.00	14.00

NOTE: *Starr* a-2, 5. *Whitney* a-1, 2, 5-10, 12; c-1, 3, 5, 8, 9.

ORAL ROBERTS' TRUE STORIES (Junior Partners #120 on)
1956 (no month) - No. 119, 7/59 (15 cents)(No #102: 25 cents)
TelePix Publ. (Oral Roberts' Evangelistic Assoc./Healing Waters)

V1No.1(1956)-(Not code approved)-"The Miracle Touch"	7.00	21.00	50.00
102-(only issue approved by code)(10/56)	3.50	10.50	24.00
103-119: 115-(114 on inside)	2.30	7.00	16.00

NOTE: Also see Happiness & Healing For You.

ORANGE BIRD, THE
No date (1980) (36 pgs.) in color; slick cover)
Walt Disney Educational Media Co.

Included with educational kit on foods		.30	.60

ORIENTAL HEROES
Aug, 1988 - Present ($1.50-$1.95, color, 64 pgs.)
Jademan Comics

1-9 ($1.50)	.25	.75	1.50
10-20 ($1.95)	.35	1.00	2.00

ORIGINAL ASTRO BOY, THE (See Astro Boy)
Sept, 1987 - No. 19, 1989 ($1.50 - $1.75, color)
Now Comics

1-Ken Steacy painted-c/a in all	.60	1.80	3.60
2	.40	1.20	2.40
3: $1.75 cover begins		.55	1.10
4-10	.30	.90	1.80
11-19	.25	.80	1.60

ORIGINAL BLACK CAT, THE
Oct. 6, 1988 - Present ($2.00, color)
Recollections

	Good	Fine	N-Mint
1-3: Elias-r; 1-Bondage-c. 2-M. Anderson-c	.35	1.00	2.00

ORIGINAL E-MAN AND MICHAEL MAUSER, THE
Oct, 1985 - No. 7, April, 1986 ($1.75 cover; Baxter paper)
First Comics

1-Has r-/Charlton's E-Man, Vengeance Squad	.35	1.00	2.00
2-6	.30	.90	1.80
7 ($2.00; 44 pgs.)-Staton-a	.35	1.00	2.00

ORIGINAL NEXUS GRAPHIC NOVEL (See First Comics Graphic Novel #19)

ORIGINAL SHIELD, THE
April, 1984 - No. 4, Oct, 1984
Archie Enterprises, Inc.

1-4: 1-Origin Shield		.35	.70

ORIGINAL SWAMP THING SAGA, THE (See DC Spec. Series #2,14,17,20)

OSCAR COMICS (Formerly Funny Tunes; Awful . . . #11 & 12)
(Also see Cindy Comics)
No. 24, Spring, 1947 - No. 10, Apr, 1949; No. 13, Oct, 1949
Marvel Comics

24(#1, 1947)	4.00	12.00	28.00
25(#2, Sum, '47)-Wolverton-a plus Kurtzman's "Hey Look"			
	6.50	19.50	45.00
3-9,13: 8-Margie app.	2.85	8.50	20.00
10-Kurtzman's "Hey Look"	3.70	11.00	26.00

OSWALD THE RABBIT (Also see New Fun Comics #1)
No. 21, 1943 - No. 1268, 12-2/61-62 (Walter Lantz)
Dell Publishing Co.

4-Color 21(1943)	22.00	65.00	154.00
4-Color 39(1943)	16.00	48.00	110.00
4-Color 67(1944)	11.00	32.00	75.00
4-Color 102(1946)-Kelly-a, 1 pg.	9.50	28.50	65.00
4-Color 143,183	4.30	13.00	30.00
4-Color 225,273	2.65	8.00	18.00
4-Color 315,388	1.70	5.00	12.00
4-Color 458,507,549,593	1.15	3.50	8.00
4-Color 623,697,792,894,979,1268	.85	2.50	6.00

OSWALD THE RABBIT (See The Funnies, March of Comics #7, 38. 53, 67, 81, 95, 111, 126, 141, 156, 171, 186, New Funnies & Super Book #8, 20)

OUR ARMY AT WAR (Sgt. Rock #302 on; Also see Army At War)
Aug., 1952 - No. 301, Feb, 1977
National Periodical Publications

1	40.00	120.00	280.00
2	19.00	58.00	135.00
3,4: 4-Krigstein-a	18.50	56.00	130.00
5-7	9.30	28.00	65.00
8-11,14-Krigstein-a	10.00	30.00	70.00
12,15-20	7.00	21.00	50.00
13-Krigstein c/a; flag-c	9.30	28.00	65.00
21-31: Last precode (2/55)	5.00	15.00	35.00
32-40	4.00	12.00	28.00
41-60	3.50	10.50	24.00
61-70	1.30	7.00	16.00
71-80	1.70	5.00	12.00
81-1st Sgt. Rock app. by Andru & Esposito in Easy Co. story			
	37.00	110.00	260.00
82-Sgt. Rock cameo in Easy Co. story (6 panels)			
	11.00	32.00	75.00
83-1st Kubert Sgt. Rock (6/59)	12.00	36.00	85.00
84,86-90	4.50	14.00	32.00
85-1st app. & origin Ice Cream Soldier	5.00	15.00	35.00
91-All Sgt. Rock issue	8.00	24.00	55.00

OUR ARMY AT WAR (continued)	Good	Fine	N-Mint
92-100: 92-1st app. Bulldozer. 95-1st app. Zack	2.15	6.50	15.00
101-120: 101-1st app. Buster. 111-1st app. Wee Willie & Sunny. 113-1st app. Jackie Johnson. 118-Sunny dies. 120-1st app. Wildman	1.15	3.50	7.00
121-127,129-150: 126-1st app. Canary. 139-1st app. Little Sure Shot	1.00	3.00	6.00
128-Training & origin Sgt. Rock	2.15	6.50	15.00
151-Intro. Enemy Ace by Kubert	1.35	4.00	8.00
152-157,159-163,165-170: 153,155-Enemy Ace stories. 157-2 pg. pin-up. 162,163-Viking Prince x-over in Sgt. Rock	.85	2.50	5.00
158-1st app. & origin Iron Major(1965), formerly Iron Captain	1.00	3.00	6.00
164-Giant G-19	1.00	3.00	6.00
171-176,178-181	.50	1.50	3.00
177-(80 pg. Giant G-32)	.70	2.00	4.00
182,183,186-Adams-a; 186-Origin retold	.85	2.50	5.00
184,185,187-189,191-199: 184-Wee Willie dies. 189-Intro. The Teen-age Underground Fighters of Unit 3	.35	1.00	2.00
190-(80 pg. Giant G-44)	.50	1.50	3.00
200-12 pg. Rock story told in verse; Evans-a	.35	1.00	2.00
201-Krigstein-r/No. 14	.35	1.00	2.00
202,204-215: 204,205-All-r, no Sgt. Rock	.25	.75	1.50
203-(80 pg. Giant G-56)-All-r, no Sgt. Rock	.35	1.00	2.00
216,229-(80 pg. Giants G-68, G-80)	.35	1.00	2.00
217-228,230-239,241,243-301: 249-Wood-a	.25	.75	1.50
240-Adams-a	.30	.90	1.80
242-(50 cent issue DC-9)-Kubert-c	.25	.75	1.50

NOTE: *Alcala* a-251. *Drucker* a-47, 67, 68, 79, 82, 83, 96, 164, 177, 203, 212, 243r, 244, 269r, 275r, 280r. *Evans* a-165-175, 200, 266, 269, 270, 274, 276, 278, 280. *Glanzman* a-218, 220, 222, 223, 225, 227, 230-32, 238, 240, 241, 244, 247, 248, 256-59, 261, 265-67, 271, 282, 283, 298. *Grell* a-287. *Heath* a-50. & most 176-271. *Kubert* a-38,59, 67, 68 & most issues from 83-165. *Maurer* a-233, 237, 239, 240, 280, 284, 288, 290, 291, 295. *Severin* a-252, 265, 267, 269r, 272. *Toth* a-235, 241, 254. *Wildey* a-283-85, 287p.

OUR FIGHTING FORCES
Oct-Nov, 1954 - No. 181, Sept-Oct, 1978
National Periodical Publications/DC Comics

	Good	Fine	N-Mint
1-Grandenetti c/a	28.00	84.00	200.00
2	14.00	42.00	100.00
3-Kubert-c; last precode (3/55)	12.00	36.00	85.00
4,5	9.30	28.00	65.00
6-9	8.00	24.00	55.00
10-Wood-a	10.00	30.00	70.00
11-20	5.70	17.00	40.00
21-30	3.60	11.00	25.00
31-40	3.15	9.50	22.00
41-44: 41-Unknown Soldier tryout	2.30	7.00	16.00
45-Gunner & Sarge begin (ends #94)	8.50	25.50	60.00
46-50	1.70	5.00	12.00
51-64: 64-Last 10 cent issue	1.15	3.50	8.00
65-90	.70	2.00	4.00
91-100: 95-Devil-Dog begins, ends 98. 99-Capt. Hunter begins, ends #106	.40	1.25	2.50
101-122: 106-Hunters Hellcats begin. 116-Mlle. Marie app. 121-Intro. Heller	.25	.75	1.50
123-181: 123-Losers (Capt. Storm, Gunner/Sarge, Johnny Cloud) begin. 134,146-Toth-a	.25	.75	1.50

NOTE: *Adams* c-147. *Drucker* a-28, 37, 39, 42-44, 49, 53, 133r. *Evans* a-149, 164-74, 177-181. *Glanzman* a-125-28, 132, 134, 138-141, 143, 144. *Heath* a-2, 16, 18, 28, 41, 44, 49, 114, 135r-136r. *Kirby* a-151-162p; c-152-159. *Kubert* c/a in many issues. *Maurer* a-135. *Redondo* a-166. *Severin* a-123-130, 131l, 132-150.

OUR FIGHTING MEN IN ACTION (See Men In Action)

OUR FLAG COMICS
Aug, 1941 - No. 5, April, 1942
Ace Magazines

1-Captain Victory, The Unknown Soldier & The Three Cheers begin

	Good	Fine	N-Mint
	96.00	290.00	675.00
2-Origin The Flag (patriotic hero); 1st app?	46.00	140.00	325.00
3-5: 5-Intro & 1st app. Mr. Risk	41.00	122.00	285.00

NOTE: *Anderson* a-1, 4. *Mooney* a-1, 2; c-2.

OUR GANG COMICS (With Tom & Jerry #39-59; becomes Tom & Jerry #60 on; based on film characters)
Sept-Oct, 1942 - No. 59, June, 1949
Dell Publishing Co.

	Good	Fine	N-Mint
1-Our Gang & Barney Bear by Kelly, Tom & Jerry, Pete Smith, Flip & Dip, The Milky Way begin	60.00	180.00	420.00
2	27.00	81.00	190.00
3-5: 3-Benny Burro begins	18.00	54.00	125.00
6-Bumbazine & Albert only app. by Kelly	31.00	92.00	220.00
7-No Kelly story	14.00	42.00	100.00
8-Benny Burro begins by Barks	31.00	92.00	215.00
9-Barks-a(2): Benny Burro & Happy Hound; no Kelly story	25.00	75.00	175.00
10-Benny Burro by Barks	20.00	60.00	140.00
11-1st Barney Bear & Benny Burro by Barks; Happy Hound by Barks	20.00	60.00	140.00
12-20	12.00	36.00	84.00
21-30	9.00	27.00	63.00
31-36-Last Barks issue	6.50	19.50	45.00
37-40	2.65	8.00	18.00
41-50	2.00	6.00	14.00
51-57	1.70	5.00	12.00
58,59-No Kelly art or Our Gang story	1.50	4.50	10.00

NOTE: *Barks* art in part only. *Barks* did not write Barney Bear stories #30-34. (See March of Comics #3,26). Early issues have photo back-c.

OUR LADY OF FATIMA
3/11/55 (15 cents) (36 pages)
Catechetical Guild Educational Society

	Good	Fine	N-Mint
395	1.70	5.00	12.00

OUR LOVE (True Secrets #3 on)
Sept, 1949 - No. 2, Jan, 1950
Marvel Comics (SPC)

	Good	Fine	N-Mint
1	4.00	12.00	28.00
2-Photo-c	2.00	6.00	14.00

OUR LOVE STORY
Oct, 1969 - No. 38, Feb, 1976
Marvel Comics Group

	Good	Fine	N-Mint
1	.70	2.00	5.00
2-4,6-13: 2,9-J. Buscema-a	.50	1.50	3.00
5-Steranko-a	1.50	4.50	10.00
14-New story by Gary Fredrich & Tarpe' Mills	.55	1.65	4.00
15-38		.40	.80

OUR MISS BROOKS (See 4-Color #751)

OUR SECRET (Formerly My Secret)
No. 4, Dec, 1949 - No. 8, Jun, 1950
Superior Comics Ltd.

	Good	Fine	N-Mint
4-Kamen-a; spanking scene	4.30	13.00	30.00
5,6,8	2.85	8.50	20.00
7-Contains 9 pg. story intended for unpublished Ellery Queen #5	3.15	9.50	22.00

OUTBURSTS OF EVERETT TRUE
1921 (32 pages) (B&W)
Saalfield Publ. Co.

	Good	Fine	N-Mint
1907 (2-panel strips reprint)	9.00	27.00	62.00

OUTCASTS
Oct, 1987 - No. 12, Sept, 1988 ($1.75, mini-series, color)
DC Comics

Our Fighting Forces #1, © DC   Our Flag Comics #1, © ACE   Our Gang Comics #2, © M.G.M.

Outer Space #19, © CC

Outlanders #1, © Dark Horse

The Outlaw Kid #5, © MEG

	Good	Fine	N-Mint
OUTCASTS (continued)			
1-12	.30	.90	1.80

OUTER LIMITS, THE (TV)
Jan-Mar, 1964 - No. 18, Oct, 1969 (All painted-c)
Dell Publishing Co.

	Good	Fine	N-Mint
1	3.50	10.50	24.00
2	1.70	5.00	12.00
3-10	1.15	3.50	8.00
11-18: 17 reprints #1; 18-r-#2	.85	2.60	6.00

OUTER SPACE (Formerly This Magazine Is Haunted, 2nd Series)
May, 1958 - No. 25, Dec, 1959; Nov, 1968
Charlton Comics

	Good	Fine	N-Mint
17-Williamson/Wood style art; not by them (Sid Check?)	4.50	14.00	32.00
18-20-Ditko-a	6.50	19.50	45.00
21-25: 21-Ditko-c	3.15	9.50	22.00
V2#1(11/68)-Ditko-a, Boyette-c	1.15	3.50	8.00

OUTLANDERS
Dec, 1988 - Present ($2.00-$2.25, B&W, 44 pgs.)
Dark Horse Comics

	Good	Fine	N-Mint
1-7: Japanese Sci-fi manga	.35	1.00	2.00
8-10 ($2.25)	.40	1.15	2.30

OUTLAW (See Return of the . . .)

OUTLAW FIGHTERS
Aug, 1954 - No. 5, April, 1955
Atlas Comics (IPC)

	Good	Fine	N-Mint
1-Tuska-a	4.30	13.00	30.00
2-5: 5-Heath-c/a, 7pgs.	2.65	8.00	18.00

NOTE: *Heath a-5; c-5. Maneely c-2. Pakula a-2. Reinman a-2. Tuska a-1, 2.*

OUTLAW KID, THE (1st Series; see Wild Western)
Sept, 1954 - No. 19, Sept, 1957
Atlas Comics (CCC No. 1-11/EPI No. 12-29)

	Good	Fine	N-Mint
1-Origin; The Outlaw Kid & his horse Thunder begin; Black Rider app.	8.50	25.50	60.00
2-Black Rider app.	4.30	13.00	30.00
3-Woodbridge/Williamson-a	4.30	13.00	30.00
4-7,9	2.65	8.00	18.00
8-Williamson/Woodbridge-a, 4 pgs.	4.00	12.00	28.00
10-Williamson-a	4.00	12.00	28.00
11-17,19	2.00	6.00	14.00
18-Williamson-a	3.70	11.00	26.00

NOTE: *Berg a-4, 7, 13. Maneely c-1-3, 5-8, 11, 12, 18. Pakula a-3. Severin c-10. Shores a-1. Wildey a-1(3), 2-8, 10-18; c-4.*

OUTLAW KID, THE (2nd Series)
Aug, 1970 - No. 30, Oct, 1975
Marvel Comics Group

	Good	Fine	N-Mint
1,2-Reprints; 1-Orlando-r, Wildey-r(3)	.35	1.00	2.00
3,9-Williamson-a(r)		.60	1.20
4-8: 8-Crandall-r		.40	.80
10-Origin; new material begins, ends #16		.25	.50
11-30: 27-Origin r-/No. 10		.25	.50

NOTE: *Ayers a-10, 27r. Berg a-7, Gil Kane c-10, 11, 15, 27r; 28. Roussos a-10i, 27i(r). Severin c-1, 9, 20. Wildey r-1, 3, 6, 7, 9, 19-22, 25, 26. Williamson a-28r. Woodbridge a(p)-9r.*

OUTLAWS
Feb-Mar, 1948 - No. 9, June-July, 1949
D. S. Publishing Co.

	Good	Fine	N-Mint
1	11.00	32.00	75.00
2-Ingels-a	11.00	32.00	75.00
3,5,6: 3-Not Frazetta	4.30	13.00	30.00
4-Orlando-a	5.70	17.00	40.00
7,8-Ingels-a in each	8.00	24.00	56.00

	Good	Fine	N-Mint
9-(Scarce)-Frazetta-a, 7 pgs.	27.00	81.00	190.00

NOTE: *Another #3 was printed in Canada with Frazetta art "Prairie Jinx," 7 pgs. McWilliams a-6.*

OUTLAWS, THE (Formerly Western Crime Cases?)
No. 10, May, 1952 - No. 13, Sept, 1953; No. 14, April, 1954
Star Publishing Co.

	Good	Fine	N-Mint
10-L. B. Cole-c	3.70	11.00	26.00
11-14-L. B. Cole-c. 14-Kamen, Feldstein-a	2.65	8.00	18.00

OUTLAWS OF THE WEST (Formerly Cody of the Pony Express #10)
No. 11, 7/57 - No. 81, 5/70; No. 82, 7/79 - No. 88, 4/80
Charlton Comics

	Good	Fine	N-Mint
11	3.50	10.50	24.00
12,13,15-17,19,20	1.60	4.80	11.00
14-(68 pgs., 2/58)	2.00	6.00	14.00
18-Ditko-a	4.00	12.00	28.00
21-30	.85	2.60	6.00
31-50	.70	2.00	4.00
51-70: 54-Kid Montana app. 64-Captain Doom begins (1st app.)	.35	1.00	2.00
71-81: 73-Origin & 1st app. The Sharp Shooter, last app. #74. 75-Last Capt. Doom. 80,81-Ditko-a	.60		1.20
82-88	.35		.70
64,79(Modern Comics-r, 1977, '78)	.15		.30

OUTLAWS OF THE WILD WEST
1952 (132 pages) (25 cents)
Avon Periodicals

	Good	Fine	N-Mint
1-Wood back-c; Kubert-a (3 Jesse James-r)	16.50	50.00	115.00

OUT OF SANTA'S BAG (See March of Comics #10)

OUT OF THE NIGHT (The Hooded Horseman #18 on)
Feb-Mar, 1952 - No. 17, Oct-Nov, 1954
American Comics Group (Creston/Scope)

	Good	Fine	N-Mint
1-Williamson/LeDoux-a, 9 pgs	21.50	64.00	150.00
2-Williamson-a, 5 pgs.	18.00	54.00	125.00
3,5-10: 9-Sci/Fic story	5.70	17.00	40.00
4-Williamson-a, 7 pgs.	18.00	54.00	125.00
11,12,14-16	4.30	13.00	30.00
13-Nostrand-a; lingerie panels	5.00	15.00	35.00
17-E.C. Wood swipe; lingerie panels	4.50	14.00	32.00

NOTE: *Landau a-14, 16, 17. Shelly a-12.*

OUT OF THE PAST A CLUE TO THE FUTURE
1946? (16 pages) (paper cover)
E. C. Comics (Public Affairs Comm.)

Based on public affairs pamphlet-"What Foreign Trade Means to You"

	Good	Fine	N-Mint
	11.50	34.00	80.00

OUT OF THE SHADOWS
No. 5, July, 1952 - No. 14, Aug, 1954
Standard Comics/Visual Editions

	Good	Fine	N-Mint
5-Toth-p; Moreira, Tuska-a	10.00	30.00	70.00
6-Toth/Celardo-a	8.50	25.50	60.00
7-Jack Katz-a(2)	5.00	15.00	35.00
8,10	3.70	11.00	26.00
9-Crandall-a(2)	5.50	16.50	38.00
11-Toth-a, 2 pgs.	4.50	14.00	32.00
12-Toth/Peppe-a(2)	8.50	25.50	60.00
13,14: 13-Cannabalism story. 14-Toth-a	5.50	16.50	38.00

NOTE: *Katz a-6(2), 7(2), 11, 12. Sekowsky a-10, 13.*

OUT OF THIS WORLD
June, 1950 (One Shot)
Avon Periodicals

	Good	Fine	N-Mint
1-Kubert-a(2) (one reprint/Eerie #1-'47) plus Crom the Barbarian by Giunta (origin); Fawcette-c	35.00	105.00	245.00

OUT OF THIS WORLD
Aug, 1956 - No. 16, Dec, 1959
Charlton Comics

	Good	Fine	N-Mint
1	7.00	21.00	50.00
2	3.50	10.50	24.00
3-6-Ditko-a(4) each	9.50	28.50	65.00
7-(68 pgs., 2/58; 15 cents)-Ditko-c/a(4)	9.50	28.50	65.00
8-(68 pgs., 5/58)-Ditko-a(2)	7.00	21.00	50.00
9-12,16-Ditko-a	5.70	17.00	40.00
13-15	2.00	6.00	14.00

NOTE: *Ditko* c-3-7, 11, 12, 16. *Reinman* a-10.

OUT OUR WAY WITH WORRY WART (See 4-Color No. 680)

OUTPOSTS
June, 1987 - No. 4? ($1.25, color)
Blackthorne Publishing

		Good	Fine
1-4: 1-Kaluta-c(p)		.60	1.20

OUTSIDERS, THE (Also see Adventures of . . . & Batman & the . . .)
Nov, 1985 - No. 28, Feb, 1988
DC Comics

1	.30	.85	1.70
2-28: 21-Intro. Strike Force Kobra. 22-E.C. parody; Orlando-a. 21-1st app. Clayface IV. 25-Atomic Knight app. 27,28-Millennium tie-ins			
	.25	.70	1.40
Annual 1 (12/86; $2.50)	.40	1.25	2.50
Special 1 (7/87, $1.50)	.25	.75	1.50

OUTSTANDING AMERICAN WAR HEROES
1944 (16 pgs.) (paper cover)
The Parents' Institute

	Good	Fine	N-Mint
nn-Reprints from True Comics	2.30	7.00	16.00

OVERSEAS COMICS (Also see G.I. & Jeep Comics)
1944 (7¼x10¼''; 16 pgs. in color)
Giveaway (Distributed to U.S. armed forces)

	Good	Fine	N-Mint
23-65-Bringing Up Father, Popeye, Joe Palooka, Dick Tracy, Superman, Gasoline Alley, Buz Sawyer, Li'l Abner, Blondie, Terry & the Pirates, Out Our Way	3.00	9.00	21.00

OWL, THE
April, 1967; No. 2, April, 1968
Gold Key

	Good	Fine	N-Mint
1,2-Written by Jerry Siegel	1.15	3.50	8.00

OXYDOL-DREFT
1950 (Set of 6 pocket-size giveaways; distributed through the mail as a set) (Scarce)
Oxydol-Dreft

	Good	Fine	N-Mint
1-Li'l Abner, 2-Daisy Mae, 3-Shmoo	7.00	21.00	50.00
4-John Wayne; Williamson/Frazetta-c from John Wayne #3	10.00	30.00	70.00
5-Archie	6.00	18.00	42.00
6-Terrytoons Mighty Mouse	4.00	12.00	28.00

NOTE: *Set is worth more with original envelope.*

OZ (See First Comics Graphic Novel, Marvel Treaury Of Oz & MGM's Marvelous . . .)

OZARK IKE
Feb, 1948; Nov, 1948 - No. 24, Dec, 1951; No. 25, Sept, 1952
Dell Publishing Co./Standard Comics

	Good	Fine	N-Mint
4-Color 180(1948-Dell)	5.75	17.25	40.00
B11, B12, 13-15	4.35	13.00	30.00
16-25	3.50	10.50	24.00

OZ-WONDERLAND WARS, THE
Jan, 1986 - No. 3, March, 1986 (mini-series)
DC Comics

1-3	.35	1.00	2.00

OZZIE & BABS (TV Teens #14 on)
1947 - No. 13, Fall, 1949
Fawcett Publications

	Good	Fine	N-Mint
1-Teen-age	4.30	13.00	30.00
2	2.15	6.50	15.00
3-13	1.70	5.00	12.00

OZZIE & HARRIET (See The Adventures of . . .)

PACIFIC COMICS GRAPHIC NOVEL
Sept, 1984
Pacific Comics

	Good	Fine	N-Mint
1-The Seven Samuroid; Brunner-a	1.00	3.00	6.00

PACIFIC PRESENTS
10/82 - No. 2, 4/83; No. 3, 3/84 - No. 4, 6/84
Pacific

	Good	Fine	N-Mint
1-The Rocketeer app.; Stevens-c/a	.70	2.10	4.20
2-The Rocketeer app.; nudity; Stevens-c/a	.55	1.65	3.30
3,4: 1st Vanity	.35	1.00	2.00

NOTE: *Conrad* a-3, 4; c-3. *Ditko* a-1-3. *Stevens* c/a-1, 2.

PADRE OF THE POOR
nd (Giveaway) (16 pgs.; paper cover)
Catechetical Guild

	Good	Fine	N-Mint
nn	1.50	4.50	10.00

PAGEANT OF COMICS (See Jane Arden & Mopsy)
Sept, 1947 - No. 2, Oct, 1947
Archer St. John

	Good	Fine	N-Mint
1-Mopsy strip-r	5.00	15.00	35.00
2-Jane Arden strip-r	5.00	15.00	35.00

PANCHO VILLA
1950
Avon Periodicals

	Good	Fine	N-Mint
nn-Kinstler-c	12.00	36.00	84.00

PANDA KHAN (See Chronicles Of Panda Khan)

PANHANDLE PETE AND JENNIFER (TV)
July, 1951 - No. 3, Nov, 1951
J. Charles Laue Publishing Co.

	Good	Fine	N-Mint
1	3.50	10.50	24.00
2,3	2.30	7.00	16.00

PANIC (Companion to Mad)
Feb-Mar, 1954 - No. 12, Dec-Jan, 1955-56
E. C. Comics (Tiny Tot Comics)

	Good	Fine	N-Mint
1-Used in Senate Investigation hearings; Elder draws entire E. C. staff	8.00	24.00	56.00
2	6.00	18.00	42.00
3-Senate Subcommittee parody; Davis draws Gaines, Feldstein & Kelly, 1 pg.; Old King Cole smokes marijuana	4.00	12.00	28.00
4-Infinity-c	4.00	12.00	28.00
5-11	3.70	11.00	26.00
12 (Low distribution; many thousands were destroyed)	4.60	14.00	32.00

NOTE: *Davis* a-1-12; c-12. *Elder* a-1-12. *Feldstein* c-1-3,5. *Kamen* a-1. *Orlando* a-1-9. *Wolverton* c-4, panel-3. *Wood* a-2-9, 11, 12.

PANIC (Magazine) (Satire)
7/58 - No. 6, 7/59; V2No.10, 12/65 - V2No.12, 1966
Panic Publications

	Good	Fine	N-Mint
1	2.30	7.00	16.00
2-6	1.30	4.00	9.00
V2#10-12: Reprints earlier issues	.70	2.00	5.00

NOTE: *Davis* a-3(2 pgs.), 4, 5, 10; c-10. *Elder* a-5. *Powell* a-V2#10, 11. *Torres* a-V2#11. *Tuska* a-V2#11.

Out Of This World #7, © CC   The Owl #1, © GK   Panic #2, © WMG

Parole Breakers #2, © REAL *Patches #1, © RH* *Patsy Walker #30, © MEG*

PARADAX (Also see Strange Days)
1986 (One shot)
Eclipse Comics

	Good	Fine	N-Mint
1	.35	1.00	2.00

PARADAX
April, 1987 - No. 2, August, 1987 ($1.75, color, mature readers)
Vortex Comics

1,2-nudity, adult language	.30	.90	1.80

PARADE (See Hanna-Barbera . . .)

PARADE COMICS (Frisky Animals on Parade #2 on)
Sept, 1957
Ajax/Farrell Publ. (World Famous Publ.)

1	1.50	4.50	10.00

NOTE: Cover title: Frisky Animals on Parade.

PARADE OF PLEASURE
1954 (192 pgs.) (Hardback book)
Derric Verschoyle Ltd., London, England

By Geoffrey Wagner. Contains section devoted to the censorship of
American comic books with illustrations in color and black and white.
(Also see **Seduction of the Innocent**). Distributed in USA by
Library Publishers, N. Y.

	30.00	90.00	210.00
with dust jacket. . . .	55.00	165.00	385.00

PARAMOUNT ANIMATED COMICS (See Harvey Comics Hits #60,62)
Feb, 1953 - No. 22, July, 1956
Harvey Publications

	Good	Fine	N-Mint
1-Baby Huey, Herman & Katnip, Buzzy the Crow begin	10.00	30.00	70.00
2	6.00	18.00	42.00
3-6	5.00	15.00	35.00
7-Baby Huey becomes permanent cover feature; cover title becomes Baby Huey with #9	10.00	30.00	70.00
8-10: 9-Infinity-c	4.00	12.00	28.00
11-22	2.65	8.50	18.00

PARENT TRAP, THE (See 4-Color #1210)

PAROLE BREAKERS
Dec, 1951 - No. 3, July, 1952
Avon Periodicals/Realistic #2 on

1(#2 on inside)-c/-Avon paperback 283	15.00	45.00	105.00
2-Kubert-a; c/-Avon paperback 114	12.00	36.00	84.00
3-Kinstler-c	10.00	30.00	70.00

PARTRIDGE FAMILY, THE (TV)
March, 1971 - No. 21, Dec, 1973
Charlton Comics

1	1.15	3.50	8.00
2-4,6-21	.70	2.00	4.00
5-Partridge Family Summer Special (52 pgs.); The Shadow, Lone Ranger, Charlie McCarthy, Flash Gordon, Hopalong Cassidy, Gene Autry & others app.	1.50	4.50	10.00

PASSION, THE
1955
Catechetical Guild

394	1.70	5.00	12.00

PAT BOONE (TV)(Also see Superman's Girlfriend Lois Lane #9)
Sept-Oct, 1959 - No. 5, May-Jun, 1960
National Periodical Publications

1-Photo-c	18.00	54.00	125.00
2-5: 4-Previews 'Journey To The Center Of The Earth'. 2,5-Photo-c	12.00	36.00	84.00

PATCHES
Mar-Apr, 1945 - No. 11, Nov, 1947

Rural Home/Patches Publ. (Orbit)

	Good	Fine	N-Mint
1-L. B. Cole-c	10.00	30.00	70.00
2	5.00	15.00	35.00
3-8,10,11: 5-L.B. Cole-c. 11-Red Skelton story	4.00	12.00	28.00
9-Leav/Krigstein-a, 16 pgs.	4.50	14.00	32.00

PATHWAYS TO FANTASY
July, 1984
Pacific Comics

1-Barry Smith-c/a; J. Jones-a	.25	.75	1.50

PATORUZU (See Adventures of . . .)

PATSY & HEDY
Feb, 1952 - No. 110, Feb, 1967
Atlas Comics/Marvel (GPI/Male)

1	5.50	16.50	38.00
2	2.85	8.50	20.00
3-10	2.30	7.00	16.00
11-20	1.50	4.50	10.00
21-40	1.10	3.30	7.50
41-60	.70	2.00	5.00
61-110: 88-Lingerie panel	.40	1.25	2.50
Annual 1('63)	2.00	6.00	14.00

PATSY & HER PALS
May, 1953 - No. 29, Aug, 1957
Atlas Comics (PPI)

1	4.50	14.00	32.00
2	2.30	7.00	16.00
3-10	1.85	5.50	13.00
11-29: 24-Everett-c	1.30	4.00	9.00

PATSY WALKER (Also see All Teen, A Date With Patsy, Girls' Life,
Miss America Magazine & Teen Comics)
1945 (no month) - No. 124, Dec, 1965
Marvel/Atlas Comics (BPC)

1	18.00	54.00	125.00
2	8.50	25.50	60.00
3-10: 5-Injury-to-eye-c	5.70	17.00	40.00
11,12,15,16,18	3.50	10.50	24.00
13,14,17,19-22-Kurtzman's ''Hey Look''	4.50	14.00	32.00
23,24	2.65	8.00	18.00
25-Rusty by Kurtzman; painted-c	4.50	14.00	32.00
26-29,31: 26-31: 52 pgs.	2.30	7.00	16.00
30-Egghead Doodle by Kurtzman, 1pg. (52 pgs.)			
	3.50	10.50	24.00
32-57: Last precode (3/55)	1.50	4.50	10.00
58-80	.85	2.60	6.00
81-99: 92,98-Millie x-over	.60	1.80	4.00
100	.70	2.00	5.00
101-124	.40	1.25	2.50
Fashion Parade 1('66)-68 pgs.	2.00	6.00	14.00

NOTE: Painted c-25-28. 21-Anti-Wertham editorial. **Al Jaffee** c-57, 58.

PAT THE BRAT (Adventures of Pipsqueak #34 on)
June, 1953; Summer, 1955 - No. 33, July, 1959
Archie Publications (Radio)

nn(6/53)	6.50	19.50	45.00
1(Summer, 1955)	4.30	13.00	30.00
2-4-(5/56) (#5-14 not published)	2.30	7.00	16.00
15-(7/56)-33	1.15	3.50	8.00

PAT THE BRAT COMICS DIGEST MAGAZINE
October, 1980
Archie Publications

1		.50	1.00

PATTY POWERS (Formerly Della Vision #3)
No. 4, Oct, 1955 - No. 7, Oct, 1956

PATTY POWERS (continued)
Atlas Comics

	Good	Fine	N-Mint
4	2.65	8.00	18.00
5-7	1.50	4.50	10.00

PAT WILTON (See Mighty Midget Comics)

PAUL
1978 (49 cents)
Spire Christian Comics (Fleming H. Revell Co.)

		Good	Fine	N-Mint
nn			.40	.80

PAULINE PERIL (See The Close Shaves of...)

PAUL REVERE'S RIDE (See 4-Color #822 & Walt Disney Showcase #34)

PAUL TERRY'S ADVENTURES OF MIGHTY MOUSE (See Adventures of...)

PAUL TERRY'S COMICS (Formerly Terry-Toons Comics; becomes Adventures of Mighty Mouse No. 126 on)
No. 85, Mar, 1951 - No. 125, May, 1955
St. John Publishing Co.

	Good	Fine	N-Mint
85,86-Same as Terry-Toons #85, & 86 with only a title change; published at same time?	4.00	12.00	28.00
87-99: 89-Mighty Mouse begins, ends #125	2.65	8.00	18.00
100	3.15	9.50	22.00
101-104,107-125: 121-Painted-c	2.30	7.00	16.00
105,106-Giant Comics Edition, 100pgs. (9/53, ?)	7.00	21.00	50.00

PAUL TERRY'S HOW TO DRAW FUNNY CARTOONS
1940's (14 pages) (Black & White)
Terrytoons, Inc. (Giveaway)

	Good	Fine	N-Mint
Heckle & Jeckle, Mighty Mouse, etc.	6.00	18.00	42.00

PAUL TERRY'S MIGHTY MOUSE (See Mighty Mouse)

PAUL TERRY'S MIGHTY MOUSE ADVENTURE STORIES
1953 (384 pgs.) (50 cents) (cardboard covers)
St. John Publishing Co.

	Good	Fine	N-Mint
nn	36.00	107.00	250.00

PAWNEE BILL
Feb, 1951 - No. 3, July, 1951
Story Comics

	Good	Fine	N-Mint
1-Bat Masterson, Wyatt Earp app.	5.00	15.00	35.00
2,3: 3-Origin Golden Warrior; Cameron-a	2.30	7.00	16.00

PAY-OFF (This Is the..., ...Crime, ...Detective Stories)
July-Aug, 1948 - No. 5, Mar-Apr, 1949 (52 pages)
D. S. Publishing Co.

	Good	Fine	N-Mint
1	5.70	17.00	40.00
2	3.70	11.00	26.00
3-5	2.85	8.50	20.00

PEACEMAKER, THE (Also see Fightin' 5)
Mar, 1967 - No. 5, Nov, 1967
Charlton Comics

	Good	Fine	N-Mint
1-Fightin' Five begins	.70	2.00	4.00
2,3,5	.35	1.00	2.00
4-Origin The Peacemaker	.40	1.25	2.50
1,2(Modern Comics reprint, 1978)		.15	.30

PEACEMAKER (Also see Crisis On Infinite Earths)
Jan, 1988 - No. 4, April, 1988 ($1.25, mini-series)
DC Comics

			Fine	N-Mint
1-4			.60	1.25

PEANUTS (Charlie Brown) (See Fritzi Ritz, Nancy & Sluggo, Tip Top, Tip Topper & United Comics)
No. 878, 2/58 - No. 13, 5-7/62; 5/63 - No. 4, 2/64
Dell Publishing Co./Gold Key

	Good	Fine	N-Mint
4-Color 878(#1)	5.70	17.00	40.00
4-Color 969,1015('59)	5.00	15.00	35.00
4(2-4/60)	3.50	10.50	24.00
5-13	2.30	7.00	16.00
1(G.Key)	2.85	8.50	20.00
2-4	2.00	6.00	14.00
1(1953-54)-Reprints United Features' Strange As It Seems, Willie, Fernand	4.65	14.00	32.00

PEBBLES & BAMM BAMM (TV)
Jan, 1972 - No. 36, Dec, 1976 (Hanna-Barbera)
Charlton Comics

	Good	Fine	N-Mint
1	1.50	4.50	10.00
2-10	.85	2.50	5.00
11-36	.70	2.00	4.00

PEBBLES FLINTSTONE (TV)
Sept, 1963 (Hanna-Barbera)
Gold Key

	Good	Fine	N-Mint
1 (10088-309)	3.50	10.50	24.00

PECKS BAD BOY
1906 - 1908 (Strip reprints) (11¼x15¾'')
Thompson of Chicago (by Walt McDougal)

	Good	Fine	N-Mint
...& Cousin Cynthia(1907)-In color	18.00	54.00	125.00
...& His Chums(1908)-Hardcover; in full color; 16 pgs.	18.00	54.00	125.00
Advs. of...And His Country Cousins (1906)-In color, 18 pgs., oblong	18.00	54.00	125.00
Advs. of...in Pictures(1908)-In color; Stanton & Van V. Liet Co.	18.00	54.00	125.00

PEDRO (Also see Romeo Tubbs)
No. 18, June, 1950 - No. 2, Aug, 1950?
Fox Features Syndicate

	Good	Fine	N-Mint
18(#1)-Wood c/a(p)	11.00	32.00	75.00
2-Wood-a	8.50	25.50	60.00

PEE-WEE PIXIES (See The Pixies)

PELLEAS AND MELISANDE (See Night Music #4,5)

PENALTY (See Crime Must Pay the...)

PENDULUM ILLUSTRATED BIOGRAPHIES
1979 (B&W)
Pendulum Press

19-355x-George Washington/Thomas Jefferson, 19-3495-Charles Lindbergh/Amelia Earhart, 19-3509-Harry Houdini/Walt Disney, 19-3517-Davy Crockett/Daniel Boone-Redondo-a, 19-3525-Elvis Presley/Beatles, 19-3533-Benjamin Franklin/Martin Luther King Jr, 19-3541-Abraham Lincoln/Franklin D. Roosevelt, 19-3568-Marie Curie/Albert Einstein-Redondo-a, 19-3576-Three Musketeers-Nino art, 19-3584-Vince Lombardi/Pele, 19-3592-Babe Ruth/Jackie Robinson, 19-3606-Jim Thorpe/Althea Gibson

		Fine
Softback		1.50
Hardback		4.50

NOTE: Above books still available from publisher.

PENDULUM ILLUSTRATED CLASSICS (Now Age Illustrated)
1973 - 1978 (62pp, B&W, 5-3/8x8'') (Also see Marvel Classics)
Pendulum Press

64-100x(1973)-Dracula-Redondo art, 64-131x-The Invisible Man-Nino art, 64-0968-Dr Jekyll and Mr Hyde-Redondo art, 64-1005-Black Beauty, 64-1010-Call of the Wild, 64-1020-Frankenstein, 64-1025-Hucklebury Finn, 64-1030-Moby Dick-Nino-a, 64-1040-Red Badge of Courage, 64-1045-The Time Machine-Nino-a, 64-1050-Tom Sawyer, 64-1055-Twenty Thousand Leagues Under the Sea, 64-1069-Treasure Island, 64-1328(1974)-Kidnapped, 64-1336-Three Musketeers-Nino art, 64-1344-A Tale of Two Cities, 64-1352-Journey to the Center of the Earth, 64-1360-The War of the Worlds-Nino-a, 64-1379-The Greatest Advs of Sherlock Holmes-Redondo art, 64-1387-Mysterious Island, 64-1395-Hunchback of Notre Dame, 64-1409-Helen Keller-story of my life, 64-1417-Scarlet Letter, 64-1425-Gulliver's Travels, 64-2618(1977)-Around the World in Eighty Days, 64-2626-Captains Courageous, 64-2634-Connecticut Yankee, 64-2642-The Hound of the Baskervilles, 64-2650-The House of Seven Gables, 64-2669-Jane Eyre,

Paul Terry's Comics #121, © M.G.M.   Pay-Off #1, © DS   Peanuts #5, © Charles Schulz

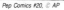

Pep Comics #20, © AP

The Perfect Crime #3, © Cross Publ.

Perfect Love #9, © STJ

PENDULUM ILLUSTRATED CLASSICS (continued)

64-2677-The Last of the Mohicans, 64-2685-The Best of O'Henry, 64-2693-The Best of Poe-Redondo-a, 64-2707-Two Years Before the Mast, 64-2715-White Fang, 64-2723-Wuthering Heights, 64-3126(978)-Ben Hur-Redondo art, 64-3134-A Christmas Carol, 64-3142-The Food of the Gods, 64-3150-Ivanhoe, 64-3169-The Man in the Iron Mask, 64-3177-The Prince and the Pauper, 64-3185-The Prisoner of Zenda, 64-3193-The Return of the Native, 64-3207-Robinson Crusoe, 64-3215-The Scarlet Pimpernel, 64-3223-The Sea Wolf, 64-3231-The Swiss Family Robinson, 64-3851-Billy Budd, 64-386x-Crime and Punishment, 64-3878-Don Quixote, 64-3886-Great Expectations, 64-3894-Heidi, 64-3908-The Iliad, 64-3916-Lord Jim, 64-3924-The Mutiny on Board H.M.S. Bounty, 64-3932-The Odyssey, 64-3940-Oliver Twist, 64-3959-Pride and Prejudice, 64-3967-The Turn of the Screw

Softback		1.45
Hardback		4.50

NOTE: All of the above books can be ordered from the publisher; some were reprinted as Marvel Classic Comics #1-12. In 1972 there was another brief series of 12 titles which contained Classics III. artwork. They were entitled **Now Age Books Illustrated**, but can be easily distinguished from later series by the small Classics Illustrated logo at the top of the front cover. The format is the same as the later series. The 48 pg. C.I. art was stretched out to make 62 pgs. After Twin Circle Publ. terminated the Classics III. series in 1971, they made a one year contract with Pendulum Press to print these twelve titles of C.I. art. Pendulum was unhappy with the contract, and at the end of 1972 began their own art series, utilizing the talents of the Filipino artist group. One detail which makes this rather confusing is that when they redid the art in 1973, they gave it the same identifying no. as the 1972 series. All 12 of the 1972 C.I. editions have new covers, taken from internal art panels. In spite of their recent age, all of the 1972 C.I. series are very rare. Mint copies would fetch at least $50. Here is a list of the 1972 series, with C.I. title no. counterpart:

64-1005 (CI60-A2) 64-1010 (CI#91) 64-1015 (CI-Jr #503) 64-1020 (CI#26)
64-1025 (CI#19-A2) 64-1030 (CI#5-A2) 64-1035 (CI#169) 64-1040 (CI#98)
64-1045 (CI#133) 64-1050 (CI#50-A2) 64-1055 (CI#47) 64-1060 (CI-Jr#535)PS6

PENDULUM ILLUSTRATED ORIGINALS

1979 (in color)
Pendulum Press

	Good	Fine	N-Mint
94-4254-Solarman: The Beginning	.25	.80	1.60

PENNY

1947 - No. 6, Sept-Oct,1949 (Newspaper reprints)
Avon Comics

1-Photo & biography of creator	5.50	16.50	38.00
2-5	2.85	8.50	20.00
6-Perry Como photo on-c	3.50	10.50	24.00

PEP COMICS (See Archie Giant Series Magazine #576,589,601)

Jan, 1940 - No. 411?, 1987
MLJ Magazines/Archie Publications No. 56 (3/46) on

1-Intro. The Shield by Irving Novick (1st patriotic hero); origin The Comet by Jack Cole, The Queen of Diamonds & Kayo Ward; The Rocket, The Press Guardian (The Falcon #1 only), Sergeant Boyle, Fu Chang, & Bentley of Scotland Yard			
	200.00	500.00	1200.00
2-Origin The Rocket	75.00	225.00	525.00
3	59.00	175.00	410.00
4-Wizard cameo	50.00	150.00	350.00
5-Wizard cameo in Shield story	50.00	150.00	350.00
6-10: 6-Transvestite story in Sgt. Boyle. 8-Last Cole Comet, no Cole art in #6,7	50.00	150.00	350.00
11-Dusty, Shield's sidekick begins; last Press Guardian, Fu Chang	37.00	110.00	260.00
12-Origin Fireball; last Rocket & Queen of Diamonds	50.00	150.00	350.00
13-15	34.00	103.00	240.00
16-Origin Madam Satan; blood drainage-c	50.00	150.00	350.00
17-Origin The Hangman; death of The Comet	100.00	300.00	700.00
18-20-Last Fireball	32.00	95.00	225.00
21-Last Madam Satan	32.00	95.00	225.00
22-Intro. & 1st app. Archie, Betty, & Jughead(12/41); (also see Jack-pot)	221.00	665.00	1550.00

(Prices vary widely on this book.)

	Good	Fine	N-Mint
23	61.00	182.00	425.00
24,25	51.00	152.00	355.00
26-1st app. Veronica Lodge	59.00	175.00	410.00
27-30: 30-Capt. Commando begins	41.00	122.00	285.00
31-35: 34-Bondage/Hypo-c	30.00	90.00	210.00
36-1st Archie-c	50.00	150.00	350.00
37-40	23.50	71.00	165.00
41-50: 41-Archie-c begin. 47-Last Hangman issue; infinity-c. 48-Black Hood begins (5/44); ends #51,59,60	17.00	51.00	120.00
51-60: 52-Suzie begins. 56-Last Capt. Commando. 59-Black Hood not in costume; spanking & lingerie panels; Archie dresses as his aunt; Suzie ends. 60-Katy Keene begins, ends #154	12.00	36.00	84.00
61-65-Last Shield. 62-1st app. Li'l Jinx	9.30	28.00	65.00
66-80: 66-G-Man Club becomes Archie Club (2/48)	6.50	19.50	45.00
81-99	4.35	13.00	30.00
100	5.00	15.00	35.00
101-130	2.00	6.00	14.00
131-149	1.00	3.00	7.00
150-160-Super-heroes app. in each	.85	2.60	6.00
161-167,169-200	.35	1.00	2.50
168-Jaguar app.	.70	2.00	5.00
201-260	.25	.75	1.50
261-411: 383-Marvelous Maureen begins (Sci/fi). 393-Thunderbunny begins		.35	.70

NOTE: Biro a-2, 4, 5. Jack Cole a-1-5, 8. Fuje a-39, 45, 47. Meskin a-2, 4, 5, 11(2). Novick c-1-10, 20, 22, 23, 25. Schomburg c-38. Bob Wood a-2, 4-6, 11. The Fly app. in 151, 154, 160. Flygirl app. in 153, 155, 156, 158. Jaguar app. in 150, 152, 157, 159. Katy Keene by Bill Woggon in many later issues. Bondage c-7, 12, 13, 15, 18, 21, 31, 32.

PEPE (See 4-Color #1194)

PERCY & FERDIE

1921 (52 pages) (B&W dailies, 10x10", cardboard-c)
Cupples & Leon Co.

By H. A. MacGill	8.00	24.00	56.00

PERFECT CRIME, THE

Oct, 1949 - No. 33, May, 1953 (#2-12, 52 pgs.)
Cross Publications

1-Powell-a(c)	7.00	21.00	50.00
2 (4/50)	4.50	14.00	32.00
3-7,9,10: 7-Steve Duncan begins, ends #30	4.00	12.00	28.00
8-Heroin drug story	5.50	16.50	38.00
11-Used in SOTI, pg. 159	6.00	18.00	42.00
12-14	2.65	8.00	18.00
15-"The Most Terrible Menace"-2 pg. drug editorial	3.85	11.50	27.00
16,17,19-25,27-29,31-33	2.00	6.00	14.00
18-Drug cover, heroin drug propaganda story, plus 2 pg. drug editorial	8.50	25.50	60.00
26-Drug-c with hypodermic; drug propaganda story	10.00	30.00	70.00
30-Strangulation cover	7.00	21.00	50.00

NOTE: Powell a-No. 1,2,4. Wildey a-1,5. Bondage c-11.

PERFECT LOVE

No. 10, 8-9/51 (cover date; 5-6/51 indicia date); No. 2, 10-11/51 -No. 10, 12/53
Ziff-Davis(Approved Comics)/St. John No. 9 on

10(#1)(8-9/51)	5.70	17.00	40.00
2(10-11/51)	3.50	10.50	24.00
3,6,7: 3-Painted-c	2.65	8.00	18.00
4,8 (Fall, '52)-Kinstler-a; last Z-D issue	2.85	8.50	20.00
5-Woodbridge-a? Photo-c	2.65	8.00	18.00
9,10 (10/53, 12/53, St. John): 9-Kinstler painted-c. 10-Photo-c	2.65	8.00	18.00

PERRI (See 4-Color #847)

PERRY MASON (See Feature Books #49,50 (McKay))

PERRY MASON MYSTERY MAGAZINE (TV)
June-Aug, 1964 - No. 2, Oct-Dec, 1964
Dell Publishing Co.

	Good	Fine	N-Mint
1,2: 2-Raymond Burr photo-c	1.70	5.00	12.00

PERSONAL LOVE (Also see Movie Love)
Jan, 1950 - No. 33, June, 1955
Famous Funnies

1	6.50	19.50	45.00
2	3.50	10.50	24.00
3-7,10	3.00	9.00	21.00
8,9-Kinstler-a	3.50	10.50	24.00
11-Toth-a	5.50	16.50	38.00
12,16,17-One pg. Frazetta	3.50	10.50	24.00
13-15,18-23	2.30	7.00	16.00
24,25,27,28-Frazetta-a in all-8,7&8&6 pgs.	24.00	73.00	170.00
26,29-31,33: 31-Last pre-code (2/55)	1.85	5.50	13.00
32-Classic Frazetta-a, 8 pgs.; Kirk Douglas/Bella Darvi photo-c			
	41.00	124.00	290.00

NOTE: *All have photo-c. Everett a-5, 9, 10, 24.*

PERSONAL LOVE (Going Steady V3#3 on)
V1No.1, Sept, 1957 - V3No.2, Nov-Dec, 1959
Prize Publ. (Headline)

V1#1	2.30	7.00	16.00
2	1.30	4.00	9.00
3-6(7-8/58)	1.00	3.00	7.00
V2#1(9-10/58)-V2#6(7-8/59)	.85	2.60	6.00
V3#1-Wood/Orlando-a	1.70	5.00	12.00
2	.70	2.00	5.00

NOTE: *Photo covers on most issues.*

PETER COTTONTAIL
Jan, 1954; Feb, 1954 - No. 2, Mar, 1954
Key Publications

1(1/54)-Not 3-D	3.70	11.00	26.00
1(2/54)-(3-D); written by Bruce Hamilton	14.00	42.00	100.00
2-Reprints 3-D #1 but not in 3-D	2.65	8.00	18.00

PETER GUNN (See 4-Color #1087)

PETER PAN (See 4-Color #442,446,926, Movie Classics & Comics, New Adventures of . . . & Walt Disney Showcase #36)

PETER PANDA
Aug-Sept, 1953 - No. 31, Aug-Sept, 1958
National Periodical Publications

1-Grossman-c/a in all	16.00	48.00	110.00
2	7.00	21.00	50.00
3-10	5.00	15.00	35.00
11-31	2.30	7.00	16.00

PETER PAN TREASURE CHEST (See Dell Giants)

PETER PARKER (See The Spectacular Spider-Man)

PETER PAT (See Single Series #8)

PETER PAUL'S 4 IN 1 JUMBO COMIC BOOK
No date (1953)
Capitol Stories

1-Contains 4 comics bound; Space Adventures, Space Western, Crime & Justice, Racket Squad in Action	17.00	51.00	120.00

PETER PENNY AND HIS MAGIC DOLLAR
1947 (16 pgs.; paper cover; regular size)
American Bankers Association, N. Y. (Giveaway)

nn-(Scarce)-Used in **SOTI**, pg. 310, 311	7.00	21.00	50.00

	Good	Fine	N-Mint
Another version (7¼x11'')-redrawn, 16 pgs., paper-c	5.00	15.00	35.00

PETER PIG
No. 5, May, 1953 - No. 6, Aug, 1953
Standard Comics

5,6	1.50	4.50	10.00

PETER PORKCHOPS (See Leading Comics #23)
11-12/49 - #61, 9-11/59; #62, 10-12/60 (1-5: 52 pgs.)
National Periodical Publications

1	16.00	48.00	110.00
2	8.00	24.00	56.00
3-10	5.50	16.50	38.00
11-30	3.70	11.00	26.00
31-62	2.30	7.00	16.00

NOTE: *Otto Feur a-all. Sheldon Mayer a-30-38, 40-44, 46-52, 61.*

PETER PORKER, THE SPECTACULAR SPIDER-HAM
May, 1985 - No. 17, Sept, 1987 (Also see Marvel Tails)
Star Comics (Marvel)

1	.35	1.00	2.00
2-17: 13-Halloween issue	.50	1.00	

PETER POTAMUS (TV)
January, 1965 (Hanna-Barbera)
Gold Key

1	2.30	7.00	16.00

PETER RABBIT (See Large Feature Comic #1, New Funnies #65 & Space Comics)

PETER RABBIT
1922 - 1923 (9¼x6¼'') (paper cover)
John H. Eggers Co. The House of Little Books Publishers

B1-B4-(Rare)-(Set of 4 books which came in a cardboard box)-Each book reprints ½ of a Sunday page per page and contains 8 B&W and 2 color pages; by Harrison Cady each. . . .	18.00	54.00	125.00

PETER RABBIT (Adventures of . . .; New Advs. of . . .later issues)
1947 - No. 34, Aug-Sept, 1956
Avon Periodicals

1(1947)-Reprints 1943-44 Sunday strips; contains a biography & drawing of Cady	23.00	70.00	160.00
2 (4/48)	18.00	54.00	125.00
3 ('48) - 6(7/49)-Last Cady issue	16.50	50.00	115.00
7-10(1950-8/51)	3.00	9.00	21.00
11(11/51)-34('56)-Avon's character	1.85	5.50	13.00
. . .Easter Parade (132 pgs., 1952)	10.00	30.00	70.00
. . .Jumbo Book(1954-Giant Size, 25 cents)-6 pgs. Jesse James by Kinstler	15.00	45.00	105.00

PETER RABBIT
1958
Fago Magazine Co.

1	3.00	9.00	21.00

PETER, THE LITTLE PEST (#4 titled Petey)
Nov, 1969 - No. 4, May, 1970
Marvel Comics Group

1	.50	1.50	3.00
2-4-Reprints Dexter the Demon & Melvin the Monster	.35	1.00	2.00

PETER WHEAT (The Adventures of . . .)
1948 - 1956? (16 pgs. in color) (paper covers)
Bakers Associates Giveaway

nn(No.1)-States on last page, end of 1st Adventure of . . .; Kelly-a	22.00	65.00	140.00

Perry Mason Mystery Magazine #2, © DELL

Peter Cottontail 3-D #1, © Key Publ.

Peter Panda #3, © DC

Petticoat Junction #2, © DELL

Phantom Lady #13 (#1), © FOX

The Phantom Stranger #4 (2-3/53), © DC

	Good	Fine	N-Mint
PETER WHEAT (continued)			
nn(4 issues)-Kelly-a	17.00	50.00	100.00
6-10-All Kelly-a	12.00	36.00	72.00
11-20-All Kelly-a	10.00	30.00	60.00
21-35-All Kelly-a	8.00	24.00	48.00
36-66	5.00	15.00	30.00
. . . Artist's Workbook ('54, digest size)	4.50	13.50	27.00
. . . Four-In-One Fun Pack (Vol. 2, '54), oblong, comics w/puzzles			
	5.00	15.00	30.00
. . . Fun Book ('52, 32pgs., paper-c, B&W & color, 8¼''x10¾''),			
contains cut-outs, puzzles, games, magic & pages to color			
	7.00	21.00	50.00

NOTE: *Al Hubbard* art #36 on; written by Del Connell.

PETER WHEAT NEWS
1948 - No. 30, 1950 (4 pgs. in color)
Bakers Associates

	Good	Fine	N-Mint
Vol. 1-All have 2 pgs. Peter Wheat by Kelly	20.00	60.00	140.00
2-10	13.00	40.00	80.00
11-20	6.75	20.00	40.00
21-30	4.00	12.00	24.00

NOTE: Early issues have no date & Kelly art.

PETE'S DRAGON (See Walt Disney Showcase #43)

PETE THE PANIC
November, 1955
Stanmor Publications

	Good	Fine	N-Mint
nn-Code approved	1.30	4.00	9.00

PETEY (See Peter, the Little Pest)

PETTICOAT JUNCTION (TV)
Oct-Dec, 1964 - No. 5, Oct-Dec, 1965 (Photo-c)
Dell Publishing Co.

	Good	Fine	N-Mint
1	4.00	12.00	28.00
2-5	2.30	7.00	16.00

PETUNIA (See 4-Color #463)

PHANTASMO (See Large Feature Comic #18)

PHANTOM, THE
1939 - 1949
David McKay Publishing Co.

	Good	Fine	N-Mint
Feature Books 20	43.00	130.00	300.00
Feature Books 22	36.00	107.00	250.00
Feature Books 39	26.00	77.00	180.00
Feature Books 53,56,57	20.00	60.00	140.00

PHANTOM, THE (See Ace Comics, Defenders Of The Earth, Eat Right to Work and Win, Future Comics, Harvey Comics Hits #51,56, Harvey Hits #1, 6, 12, 15, 26, 36, 44, 48 & King Comics)

PHANTOM, THE (nn 29-Published overseas only) (Also see Comics Reading Library)
Nov., 1962 - No. 17, July, 1966; No. 18, Sept, 1966 - No. 28, Dec, 1967; No. 30, Feb, 1969 - No. 74, Jan, 1977
Gold Key (No.1-17)/King (No.18-28)/Charlton (No.30 on)

	Good	Fine	N-Mint
1-Manning-a	5.00	15.00	35.00
2-King, Queen & Jack begins, ends #11	2.30	7.00	16.00
3-10	1.70	5.00	12.00
11-17: 12-Track Hunter begins	1.15	3.50	8.00
18-Flash Gordon begins; Wood-a	1.50	4.50	10.00
19,20-Flash Gordon ends	1.00	3.00	7.00
21-24,26,27: 21-Mandrake begins. 20,24-Girl Phantom app. 26-Brick Bradford app.	.85	2.60	6.00
25-Jeff Jones-a; 1 pg. Williamson ad	1.30	4.00	9.00
28(nn)-Brick Bradford app.	.85	2.60	6.00
30-40: 36,39-Ditko-a	.55	1.65	4.00
41-66: 46-Intro. The Piranha. 62-Bolle-c	.35	1.00	2.00
67-71,73-Newton c/a; 67-Origin retold	.35	1.00	2.00

	Good	Fine	N-Mint
72	.25	.75	1.50
74-Newton Flag-c; Newton-a	.35	1.00	2.00

NOTE: *Aparo* a-36-38; c-35-38, 60, 61. Painted c-1-17.

PHANTOM, THE
May, 1988 - No. 4, Aug, 1988 ($1.25, color)
DC Comics

	Good	Fine	N-Mint
1: Orlando-c/a in all	.35	1.00	2.00
2-4	.25	.75	1.50

PHANTOM, THE
Mar, 1989 - Present ($1.50, color)
DC Comics

	Good	Fine	N-Mint
1-Brief origin	.35	1.00	2.00
2-12	.25	.75	1.50

PHANTOM BLOT, THE (#1 titled New Adventures of . . .)
Oct, 1964 - No. 7, Nov, 1966 (Disney)
Gold Key

	Good	Fine	N-Mint
1 (Meets The Beagle Boys)	2.00	6.00	14.00
2-1st Super Goof	1.50	4.50	10.00
3-7	1.15	3.50	8.00

PHANTOM EAGLE (See Mighty Midget, Marvel Super Heroes #16 & Wow #6)

PHANTOM LADY (1st Series) (My Love Secret #24 on) (Also see All Top, Daring Advs., Freedom Fighters, Jungle Thrills, & Wonder Boy)
No. 13, Aug, 1947 - No. 23 April, 1949
Fox Features Syndicate

	Good	Fine	N-Mint
13(#1)-Phantom Lady by Matt Baker begins; The Blue Beetle app.			
	115.00	345.00	800.00
14(#2)	72.00	215.00	500.00
15-P.L. injected with experimental drug	61.00	182.00	425.00
16-Negligee-c, panels	61.00	182.00	425.00
17-Classic bondage cover; used in **SOTI**, illo-"Sexual stimulation by combining 'headlights' with the sadist's dream of tying up a woman"	145.00	435.00	1015.00
18,19	55.00	165.00	385.00
20-23: 23-Bondage-c	46.00	140.00	325.00

NOTE: *Matt Baker* a-in all; c-13, 15-21. *Kamen* a-22, 23.

PHANTOM LADY (2nd Series) (See Terrific Comics) (Formerly Linda)
Dec-Jan, 1954/1955 - No. 4, June, 1955
Ajax/Farrell Publ.

	Good	Fine	N-Mint
V1#5(#1)-by Matt Baker	30.00	90.00	210.00
V1#2-Last pre-code	23.50	71.00	165.00
3,4-Red Rocket	19.00	58.00	135.00

PHANTOM PLANET, THE (See 4-Color No. 1234)

PHANTOM STRANGER, THE (1st Series)(See Saga of Swamp Thing)
Aug-Sept, 1952 - No. 6, June-July, 1953
National Periodical Publications

	Good	Fine	N-Mint
1 (Scarce)	57.00	171.00	400.00
2 (Scarce)	43.00	130.00	300.00
3-6 (Scarce)	34.00	103.00	240.00

PHANTOM STRANGER, THE (2nd Series) (See Showcase)
May-June, 1969 - No. 41, Feb-Mar, 1976
National Periodical Publications

	Good	Fine	N-Mint
1-Last 12 cent issue	2.15	6.50	15.00
2,3	.85	2.50	5.00
4-Adams-a	1.15	3.50	8.00
5-10	.70	2.00	4.00
11-20	.35	1.00	2.00
21-41: 22-Dark Circle begins. 23-Spawn of Frankenstein begins by Kaluta; series ends #30. 31-The Black Orchid begins. 39-41-Deadman app.	.25	.75	1.50

NOTE: *Adams* a-4; c-3-19. *Aparo* a-7-26; c-20-24, 33-41. *B. Bailey* a-27-30. *DeZuniga*

THE PHANTOM STRANGER (continued)

a-14-16, 19-22, 31, 34. **Grell** a-33. **Kaluta** a-23-25; c-26. **Meskin** r-15, 16, 18. **Redondo** a-32, 35, 36. **Sparling** a-20. **Starr** a-17r. **Toth** a-15r. Black Orchid by **Carrilo**-38-41. Dr. 13 solo in-13, 18, 20. Frankenstein by **Kaluta**-23-25; by **Baily**-27-30. No Black Orchid-33, 34, 37.

PHANTOM STRANGER (See Justice League of America #103)
Oct, 1987 - No. 4, Jan, 1988 (mini-series, 75 cents, color)
DC Comics

	Good	Fine	N-Mint
1	.25	.75	1.50
2-4		.50	1.00

PHANTOM WITCH DOCTOR
1952 (Also see Eerie No. 8)
Avon Periodicals

	Good	Fine	N-Mint
1-Kinstler-c, 7 pgs.	20.00	60.00	140.00

PHANTOM ZONE, THE (See Adventure #283 & Superboy #100, 104)
January, 1982 - No. 4, April, 1982
DC Comics

1-Superman app. in all		.40	.80
2-4: Batman, Gr. Lantern app.		.30	.60

NOTE: **Colan** a-1-4p; c-1-4p. **Giordano** c-1-4i.

PHAZE
Apr, 1988 - No. 2, Oct, 1988 ($2.25, color)
Eclipse Comics

1,2: 2-Gulacy painted-c	.35	1.10	2.25

PHIL RIZZUTO (Baseball Hero)(See Sport Thrills, Accepted reprint)
1951 (New York Yankees)
Fawcett Publications

nn-Photo-c	25.00	75.00	175.00

PHOENIX
Jan, 1975 - No. 4, Oct, 1975
Atlas/Seaboard Publ.

1-Origin		.30	.60
2,3: 3-Origin & only app. The Dark Avenger		.25	.50
4-New origin/costume The Protector (formerly Phoenix)		.25	.50

NOTE: **Infantino** appears in #1,2. **Austin** a-3i. **Thorne** c-3.

PHOENIX (...The Untold Story)
April, 1984 ($2.00, One shot)
Marvel Comics Group

1-Byrne/Austin-r/X-Men 137 with original unpublished ending	1.35	4.00	8.00

PICNIC PARTY (See Dell Giants)

PICTORIAL CONFESSIONS (Pictorial Romances #4 on)
Sept, 1949 - No. 3, Dec, 1949
St. John Publishing Co.

1-Baker-c/a(3)	12.00	36.00	84.00
2-Baker-a; photo-c	6.00	18.00	42.00
3-Kubert, Baker-a; part Kubert-c	8.50	25.50	60.00

PICTORIAL LOVE STORIES (Formerly Tim McCoy)
No. 22, Oct, 1949 - No. 26, July, 1950
Charlton Comics

22-26-"Me-Dan Cupid" in all	5.00	15.00	35.00

PICTORIAL LOVE STORIES
October, 1952
St. John Publishing Co.

1-Baker c/a	10.00	30.00	70.00

PICTORIAL ROMANCES (Formerly Pictorial Confessions)
No. 4, Jan, 1950; No. 5, Jan, 1951 - No. 24, Mar, 1954
St. John Publishing Co.

4-All Baker	9.50	28.50	65.00

	Good	Fine	N-Mint
5,10-All Matt Baker issues	7.00	21.00	50.00
6-9,12,13,15,16-Baker-c, 2-3 stories	5.00	15.00	35.00
11-Baker c/a(3); Kubert-a	6.00	18.00	42.00
14,21-24-Baker-c/a each	3.70	11.00	26.00
17-20(7/53)-100 pgs. each; Baker-c/a	10.00	30.00	70.00

NOTE: **Matt Baker** art in most issues. **Estrada** a-19(2).

PICTURE NEWS
Jan, 1946 - No. 10, Jan-Feb, 1947
Lafayette Street Corp.

1-Milt Gross begins, ends No. 6; 4 pg. Kirby-a; A-Bomb-c/story	13.00	40.00	90.00
2-Atomic explosion panels; Frank Sinatra, Perry Como stories	5.70	17.00	40.00
3-Atomic explosion panels; Frank Sinatra, June Allyson stories	4.50	14.00	32.00
4-Atomic explosion panels; "Caesar and Cleopatra" movie adaptation; Jackie Robinson story	5.00	15.00	35.00
5-7: 5-Hank Greenberg story. 6-Joe Louis c/story	3.00	9.00	21.00
8-Monte Hale story(9-10/46; 1st?)	5.00	15.00	35.00
9-A-Bomb story; "Crooked Mile" movie adaptation; Joe DiMaggio story	5.00	15.00	35.00
10-A-Bomb story; Krigstein, Gross-a	4.50	14.00	32.00

PICTURE PARADE (Picture Progress #5 on)
Sept, 1953 - V1/4, Dec, 1953 (28 pages)
Gilberton Company (Also see A Christmas Adventure)

V1#1-Andy's Atomic Adventures-A-bomb blast-c; (Teachers version distributed to schools exists)	5.70	17.00	40.00
2-Around the World with the United Nations	5.00	15.00	35.00
3-Adventures of the Lost One(The Amer. Indian), 4-A Christmas Adventure (r-under same title in '69)	5.00	15.00	35.00

PICTURE PROGRESS (Formerly Picture Parade)
V1No.5, Jan, 1954 - V3No.2, Oct, 1955 (28-36 pgs.)
Gilberton Corp.

V1#5-News in Review 1953, 6-The Birth of America, 7-The Four Seasons, 8-Paul Revere's Ride, 9-The Hawaiian Islands(5/54), V2#1-The Story of Flight(9/54), 2-Vote for Crazy River(The Meaning of Elections), 3-Louis Pasteur, 4-The Star Spangled Banner, 5-News in Review 1954, 6-Alaska: The Great Land, 7-Life in the Circus, 8-The Time of the Cave Man, 9-Summer Fun(5/55) each...	2.30	7.00	16.00
V3#1-The Man Who Discovered America, 2-The Lewis & Clark Expedition each...	2.30	7.00	16.00

PICTURE SCOPE JUNGLE ADVENTURES (See Jungle Thrills)

PICTURE STORIES FROM AMERICAN HISTORY
1945 - No. 4, 1947 (#1,2: 56 pgs.; #3: 52pgs.)
National/All-American/E. C. Comics

1	8.00	24.00	56.00
2-4	5.00	15.00	35.00

PICTURE STORIES FROM SCIENCE
Spring, 1947 - No. 2, Fall, 1947
E.C. Comics

1,2	8.50	25.50	60.00

PICTURE STORIES FROM THE BIBLE
Fall, 1942-3 & 1944-46
National/All-American/E.C. Comics

1-4('42-Fall,'43)-Old Testament (DC)	8.00	24.00	56.00
Complete Old Testament Edition, 232pgs.(12/43-DC);-1st printing; contains #1-4. 2nd & 3rd printings exists	11.00	32.00	75.00
Complete Old Testament Edition (1945-publ. by Bible Pictures Ltd.)-			

Phantom Witch Doctor #1, © AVON

Pictorial Love Stories #1, © STJ

Picture Stories From American History #3, © WMG

Picture Stories From The Bible #2 (old test.), '46), © EC   Pinhead & Foodini #2, © FAW   Piracy #4, © WMG

	Good	Fine	N-Mint
PICTURE STORIES FROM THE BIBLE (cont.)			
232 pgs., hardbound, in color w/dust jacket	11.00	32.00	75.00

NOTE: Both Old and New Testaments published in England by Bible Pictures Ltd. in hardback, 1943, in color, 376 pages, and were also published by Scarf Press in 1979 (Old Test., $9.95) and in 1980 (New Test., $7.95)

1-3(New Test.)-1944-46, DC)-52pgs. ea.	6.50	19.50	45.00
The Complete Life of Christ Edition (1945)-96pgs.; contains #1&2 of			
the New Testament Edition	8.50	25.50	60.00
1,2(Old Testament-r in comic book form)(E.C., 1946; 52pgs.)			
	6.50	19.50	45.00
1-3(New Testament-r in comic book form)(E.C., 1946; 52pgs.)			
	6.50	19.50	45.00
Complete New Testament Edition (1946-E.C.)-144 pgs.; contains #1-3			
	9.30	28.00	65.00

NOTE: Another British series entitled **The Bible Illustrated** from 1947 has recently been discovered, with the same internal artwork. This eight edition series (5-OT, 3-NT) is of particular interest to Classics Ill. collectors because it exactly copied the C.I. logo format. The British publisher was Thorpe & Porter, who in 1951 began publishing the British Classics Ill. series. All editions of The Bible Ill. have new British painted covers. While this market is still new, and not all editions have as yet been found, current market value is about the same as the first U.S. editions of Picture Stories From The Bible.

PICTURE STORIES FROM WORLD HISTORY
Spring, 1947 - No. 2, Summer, 1947 (52,48 pgs.)
E.C. Comics

1,2	8.50	25.50	60.00

PINEAPPLE ARMY
Dec. 6, 1988 - No. 10, 1989 ($1.75, B&W, bi-weekly mini-series)
Viz Comics

1-10: Japanese manga	.30	.90	1.80

PINHEAD & FOODINI (TV)(Also see Foodini)
July, 1951 - No. 4, Jan, 1952
Fawcett Publications

1-Photo-c; 52 pgs.	7.00	21.00	50.00
2-Photo-c	5.00	15.00	35.00
3,4: 3-Photo-c	3.50	10.50	24.00

PINK LAFFIN
1922 (9x12'')(strip-r)
Whitman Publishing Co.

...the Lighter Side of Life,...He Tells 'Em,...and His Family, ...Knockouts; Ray Gleason-a (All rare)

each...	9.00	27.00	62.00

PINK PANTHER, THE (TV)
April, 1971 - No. 87, 1984
Gold Key

1-The Inspector begins	1.20	3.50	8.00
2-10	.70	2.00	4.00
11-30: Warren Tufts-a #16-on	.40	1.20	2.50
31-60	.25	.75	1.50
61-87		.50	1.00
Kite Fun Book(1972)-16pgs.	.70	2.00	4.00
Mini-comic No. 1(1976)(3¼x6½'')		.50	1.00

NOTE: Pink Panther began as a movie cartoon. (See Golden Comics Digest #38, 45 and March of Comics #376, 384, 390, 409, 418, 429, 441, 449, 461, 473, 486); #37, 72, 80-85 contain reprints.

PINKY LEE (See Adventures of...)

PINKY THE EGGHEAD
1963 (Reprints from Noodnik)
I.W./Super Comics

I.W. Reprint #1,2(nd)		.60	1.20
Super Reprint #14		.60	1.20

PINOCCHIO (See 4-Color #92.252,545,1203, Mickey Mouse Mag. V5#3, Movie Comics under Wonderful Advs. of..., New Advs. of..., Thrilling Comics #2, Wonderful Advs. of..., & World's Greatest Stories #2)

PINOCCHIO
1940 (10 pages; linen-like paper)
Montgomery Ward Co. (Giveaway)

	Good	Fine	N-Mint
nn	12.00	36.00	84.00

PINOCCHIO AND THE EMPEROR OF THE NIGHT
Mar, 1988 (52 pgs., $1.25)
Marvel Comics

1-Adapts film		.60	1.25

PINOCCHIO LEARNS ABOUT KITES (Also see Brer Rabbit & Donald Duck) (Disney)
1954 (8 pages) (Premium)
Pacific Gas & Electric Co./Florida Power & Light

nn	20.00	60.00	130.00

PIN-UP PETE (Also see Great Lover Romances & Monty Hall...)
1952
Toby Press

1-Jack Sparling pin-ups	9.00	27.00	62.00

PIONEER MARSHAL (See Fawcett Movie Comics)

PIONEER PICTURE STORIES
Dec, 1941 - No. 9, Dec, 1943
Street & Smith Publications

1	11.50	34.00	80.00
2	6.50	19.50	45.00
3-9	5.00	15.00	35.00

PIONEER WEST ROMANCES (Firehair #1,2,7-11)
No. 3, Spring, 1949 - No. 6, Winter, 1949-50
Fiction House Magazines

3-(52 pgs.)-Firehair continues	8.50	25.50	60.00
4-6	6.50	19.50	45.00

PIPSQUEAK (See The Adventures of...)

PIRACY
Oct-Nov, 1954 - No. 7, Oct-Nov, 1955
E. C. Comics

1-Williamson/Torres-a	13.00	40.00	90.00
2-Williamson/Torres-a	9.30	28.00	65.00
3-7	8.00	24.00	55.00

NOTE: Crandall a-in all; c-2-4. Davis a-1, 2, 6. Evans a-3-7; c-7. Ingels a-3-7. Krigstein a-3-5, 7; c-5, 6. Wood a-1, 2; c-1.

PIRANA (See Thrill-O-Rama #2,3)

PIRATE CORPS, THE
1987 - No. 5, 1988 ($1.95, color #3 on)
Eternity Comics/Slave Labor Graphics

1-5	.35	1.00	2.00
Special 1 ('89, $1.95, B&W)-Slave Labor publ.	.35	1.00	2.00

PIRATE OF THE GULF, THE (See Superior Stories #2)

PIRATES COMICS
Feb-Mar, 1950 - No. 4, Aug-Sept, 1950 (All 52 pgs.)
Hillman Periodicals

1	8.50	25.50	60.00
2-Berg-a	4.50	14.00	32.00
3,4-Berg-a	3.50	10.50	24.00

P.I.'S: MICHAEL MAUSER AND MS. TREE, THE
Jan, 1985 - No. 3, May, 1985 ($1.25, color, mini-series)
First Comics

1-3: Staton c/a(p)		.65	1.30

PITT, THE (Also see The Draft)
Mar, 1988 (one shot, $3.25, 52 pgs.)
Marvel Comics

1-Ties into Starbrand, D.P. 7	.70	2.00	4.00

PIUS XII MAN OF PEACE
No date (12 pgs.; 5½x8½'') (B&W)
Catechetical Guild Giveaway

	Good	Fine	N-Mint
nn	3.00	9.00	21.00

PIXIE & DIXIE & MR. JINKS (TV)(See Jinks, Pixie, and Dixie & Whitman Comic Books)
July-Sept, 1960 - Feb, 1963 (Hanna-Barbera)
Dell Publishing Co./Gold Key

4-Color 1112	3.00	9.00	21.00
4-Color 1196,1264	2.30	7.00	16.00
01-631-207 (Dell)	2.00	6.00	14.00
1(2/63-G.K.)	2.00	6.00	14.00

PIXIE PUZZLE ROCKET TO ADVENTURELAND
November, 1952
Avon Periodicals

1	5.00	15.00	35.00

PIXIES, THE (Advs. of . . .) (The Mighty Atom and . . .#6 on)
Winter, 1946 - No. 4, Fall?, 1947; No. 5, 1948
Magazine Enterprises

1-Mighty Atom	3.50	10.50	24.00
2-5-Mighty Atom	1.70	5.00	12.00
I.W. Reprint #1(1958), 8-(Pee-Wee Pixies), 10-I.W. on cover, Super on inside	.50	1.50	3.00

P. J. WARLOCK
Nov, 1986 - No. 3, March, 1987 ($2.00, B&W)
Eclipse Comics

1-3	.35	1.00	2.00

PLANET COMICS
Jan, 1940 - No. 73, Winter, 1953
Fiction House Magazines

1-Origin Auro, Lord of Jupiter; Flint Baker & The Red Comet begin; Eisner/Fine-c	433.00	1085.00	2600.00
2-(Scarce)	217.00	545.00	1300.00
3-Eisner-c	174.00	435.00	1045.00
4-Gale Allen and the Girl Squadron begins	150.00	375.00	900.00
5,6-(Scarce)	135.00	340.00	810.00
7-11	100.00	300.00	700.00
12-The Star Pirate begins	100.00	300.00	700.00
13-14: 13-Reff Ryan begins	75.00	225.00	525.00
15-(Scarce)-Mars, God of War begins	80.00	240.00	560.00
16-20,22	71.00	215.00	500.00
21-The Lost World & Hunt Bowman begins	75.00	225.00	525.00
23-26: 26-The Space Rangers begin	71.00	215.00	500.00
27-30	52.00	156.00	365.00
31-35: 33-Origin Star Pirates Wonder Boots, reprinted in #52.			
35-Mysta of the Moon begins	41.00	133.00	310.00
36-45: 41-New origin of ''Auro, Lord of Jupiter.'' 42-Last Gale Allen.			
43-Futura begins	37.00	112.00	260.00
46-60: 53-Used in SOTI, pg. 32	28.50	86.00	200.00
61-64	19.00	57.00	135.00
65-68,70: 65-70-All partial-r of earlier issues	19.00	57.00	135.00
69-Used in POP, pgs. 101,102	19.00	57.00	135.00
71-73-No series stories	16.00	48.00	110.00
I.W. Reprint #1(nd)-r-/#70; c-from Attack on Planet Mars	3.50	10.50	24.00
I.W. Reprint #8 (r-/#72), 9-r-/#73	3.50	10.50	24.00

NOTE: Anderson a-33-38, 40-51 (Star Pirate). Matt Baker a-53-59 (Mysta of the Moon). Celardo c-12. Elias c-70. Evans a-50-64 (Lost World). Fine c-2, 5. Ingels a-24-31, 56-61 (Auro, Lord of Jupiter). Lubbers c-40, 41. Renee a-40 (Lost World); c-33, 35, 39. Tuska a-30 (Star Pirate). M. Whitman a-51, 52 (Mysta of the Moon), 54-56 (Star Pirate). Starr a-59. 53-Bondage-c.

PLANET COMICS
1988 - Present? (2.00, color; B&W #3 on)

PLANET OF THE APES (Magazine) (Also see Advs. on the. . .)
Aug, 1974 - No. 29, Feb, 1977 (B&W) (Based on movies)
Marvel Comics Group

	Good	Fine	N-Mint
1-Ploog-a	.40	1.25	2.50
2-Ploog-a	.35	1.00	2.00
3-10	.25	.70	1.40
11-20		.50	1.00
21-29		.40	.80

NOTE: Alcala a-7-11, 17-22, 24. Ploog a-1-8, 11, 13, 14, 19. Sutton a-11, 12, 15, 17, 19, 20, 23, 24, 29. Tuska a-1-6.

PLANET OF VAMPIRES
Feb, 1975 - No. 3, July, 1975
Seaboard Publications (Atlas)

1-Adams-c(i); 1st Broderick c/a(p)		.40	.80
2-Adams-c, 3-Heath-c/a		.30	.60

PLANET TERRY
April, 1985 - No. 12, March, 1986 (Children's comic)
Star Comics/Marvel

1-12		.35	.70

PLASTIC MAN (Also see Police Comics & Smash Comics #17)
Sum, 1943 - No. 64, Nov, 1956
Vital Publ. No. 1,2/Quality Comics No. 3 on

nn(#1)-'In The Game of Death;' Jack Cole-c/a begins; ends-#64?	129.00	385.00	900.00
2(nn, 2/44)-'The Gay Nineties Nightmare'	79.00	235.00	550.00
3 (Spr, '46)	51.00	152.00	355.00
4 (Sum, '46)	45.00	135.00	315.00
5 (Aut, '46)	37.00	110.00	260.00
6-10	26.00	79.00	185.00
11-20	24.00	71.00	165.00
21-30: 26-Last non-r issue?	19.00	58.00	135.00
31-39	14.00	42.00	100.00
40-Used in POP, pg. 91	14.00	42.00	100.00
41-64: 53-Last precode issue	11.50	34.00	80.00
Super Reprint 11('63, r-/#16), 16 (r-#21, Cole-a), 18('64-Spirit app. by Eisner/Police #95)	2.30	7.00	16.00

NOTE: Cole r-44, 49, 56, 58, 59 at least.

PLASTIC MAN (See Brave & the Bold and DC Special #15)
11-12/66 - No. 10, 5-6/68; No. 11, 2-3/76 - No. 20, 10-11/77
National Periodical Publications/DC Comics

1	1.70	5.00	12.00
2-5: 4-Infantino-c	.85	2.50	5.00
6-10('68)	.70	2.00	4.00
11('76)-20: 17-Origin retold	.25	.75	1.50

NOTE: Gil Kane c/a-1. Mortimer a-4. Sparling a-10.

PLASTIC MAN
Nov, 1988 - No. 4, Feb, 1989 ($1.00, mini-series)
DC Comics

1-4: 1-Origin; Woozy Winks app		.50	1.00

PLAYFUL LITTLE AUDREY (TV)(Also see Little Audrey #25)
6/57 - No. 110, 11/73; No. 111, 8/74 - No. 121, 4/76
Harvey Publications

1	11.50	34.50	80.00
2	5.70	17.00	40.00
3-5	5.00	15.00	35.00
6-10	3.35	10.00	23.00
11-20	1.70	5.00	12.00
21-40	1.35	4.00	9.00
41-60	.85	2.50	5.00
61-80	.50	1.50	3.00

Planet Comics #35, © FH

Plastic Man #27, © QUA

Plastic Man #1 (11-12/66), © DC

Plop! #3, © DC

Pogo Possum #7, © Walt Kelly

Police Comics #1, © QUA

	Good	Fine	N-Mint
PLAYFUL LITTLE AUDREY (continued)			
81-99	.40	1.25	2.50
100: 52 pg. Giant	.70	2.00	4.00
101-103: 52 pg. Giants	.50	1.50	3.00
104-121	.35	1.00	2.00

PLAYFUL LITTLE AUDREY IN 3-D (See Blackthorne 3-D Series #66)

PLOP!
Sept-Oct, 1973 - No. 24, Nov-Dec, 1976
National Periodical Publications

	Good	Fine	N-Mint
1-22,24: Sergio Aragones-a. 1,5-Wrightson-a. 21-24 are 52 pgs.	.40	1.25	2.50
23-No Aragones-a	.50	1.00	

NOTE: *Alcala* a-1-3. *Anderson* a-5. *Aragones* a-1-22, 24. *Ditko* a-16p. *Evans* a-1. *Mayer* a-1. *Orlando* a-21, 22; c-21. *Sekowsky* a-5, 6p. *Toth* a-11. *Wolverton* a-4, 22, 23(1 pg.); c-1-12, 14, 17, 18. *Wood* a-14, 16i, 18-24; c-13, 15, 16, 19.

PLUTO (See Cheerios Premiums, Four Color #537, Mickey Mouse Magazine, Walt Disney Showcase #4,7,13,20,23,33 & Wheaties)
No. 7, 1942; No. 429, 10/52 - No. 1248, 11-1/61-62 (Walt Disney)
Dell Publishing Co.

	Good	Fine	N-Mint
Large Feature Comic 7(1942)	65.00	195.00	455.00
4-Color 429,509	3.00	9.00	21.00
4-Color 595,654	2.30	7.00	16.00
4-Color 736,853,941,1039,1143,1248	1.70	5.00	12.00

POCAHONTAS
1941 - No. 2, 1942
Pocahontas Fuel Company

	Good	Fine	N-Mint
nn(#1), 2	4.35	13.00	30.00

POCKET COMICS (Also see Double Up)
Aug, 1941 - No. 4, Jan, 1942 (Pocket size; 100 pgs.)
Harvey Publications (1st Harvey comic)

	Good	Fine	N-Mint
1-Origin The Black Cat, Cadet Blakey the Spirit of '76, The Red Blazer, The Phantom, Sphinx, & The Zebra; Phantom Ranger, British Agent #99, Spin Hawkins, Satan, Lord of Evil begin	41.00	122.00	285.00
2	27.00	81.00	190.00
3,4	21.00	62.00	145.00

POGO PARADE (See Dell Giants)

POGO POSSUM (Also see Animal Comics & Special Delivery)
No. 105, 4/46 - No. 148, 5/47; 10-12/49 - No. 16, 4-6/54
Dell Publishing Co.

	Good	Fine	N-Mint
4-Color 105(1946)-Kelly-c/a	57.00	171.00	400.00
4-Color 148-Kelly-c/a	47.00	141.00	330.00
1-(10-12/49)-Kelly c/a in all	45.00	135.00	315.00
2	24.00	70.00	165.00
3-5	17.00	51.00	120.00
6-10: 10-Infinity-c	14.00	42.00	100.00
11-16: 11-X-mas-c	12.00	36.00	84.00

NOTE: #1-4, 9-13: 52 pgs.; #5-8, 14-16: 36 pgs.

POINT BLANK
May, 1989 - No. 2, 1989 ($2.95, B&W, magazine)
Acme Press (Eclipse)

	Good	Fine	N-Mint
1,2-European-r	.50	1.50	3.00

POLICE ACADEMY (TV)
Nov, 1989 - Present ($1.00, color)
Marvel Comics

	Good	Fine	N-Mint
1-6: Based on TV cartoon; Post-c/a in all	.50	1.00	

POLICE ACTION
Jan, 1954 - No. 7, Nov, 1954
Atlas News Co.

	Good	Fine	N-Mint
1-Violent-a by Robert Q. Sale	5.50	16.50	38.00
2	2.65	8.00	18.00

	Good	Fine	N-Mint
3-7: 7-Powell-a	2.30	7.00	16.00

NOTE: *Ayers* a-4, 5. *Colan* a-1. *Forte* a-1, 2. *Mort Lawrence* a-5. *Maneely* a-3; c-1, 5. *Reinman* a-6, 7.

POLICE ACTION
Feb, 1975 - No. 3, June, 1975
Atlas/Seaboard Publ.

	Good	Fine	N-Mint
1-Lomax, N.Y.P.D., Luke Malone begin; McWilliams-a; bondage-c	.40	.80	
2,3: 2-Origin Luke Malone, Manhunter	.30	.60	

NOTE: *Ploog* art in all. *Sekowsky/McWilliams* a-1-3. *Thorne* c-3.

POLICE AGAINST CRIME
April, 1954 - No. 9, Aug, 1955
Premiere Magazines

	Good	Fine	N-Mint
1-Disbrow-a; extreme violence - man's face slashed with knife; Hollingsworth-a	6.50	19.50	45.00
2-Hollingsworth-a	3.50	10.50	24.00
3-9	2.30	7.00	16.00

POLICE BADGE #479 (Formerly Spy Thrillers #1-4)
No. 5, Sept, 1955
Atlas Comics (PrPI)

	Good	Fine	N-Mint
5-Maneely-c	2.30	7.00	16.00

POLICE CASE BOOK (See Giant Comics Editions)

POLICE CASES (See Authentic... & Record Book of...)

POLICE COMICS
Aug, 1941 - No. 127, Oct, 1953
Quality Comics Group (Comic Magazines)

	Good	Fine	N-Mint
1-Origin/1st app. Plastic Man (begins) by Jack Cole, The Human Bomb by Gustavson, & No. 711; intro. Chic Carter by Eisner, The Firebrand by R. Crandall, The Mouthpiece, Phantom Lady, & The Sword; r-in DC Special #15	308.00	770.00	1850.00
2-Plastic Man smuggles opium	130.00	390.00	910.00
3	108.00	325.00	755.00
4	93.00	280.00	650.00
5-Plastic Man forced to smoke marijuana	93.00	280.00	650.00
6,7	83.00	250.00	580.00
8-Manhunter begins (origin)	98.00	295.00	685.00
9,10	77.00	230.00	540.00
11-The Spirit strip-r begin by Eisner(Origin-strip #1)	125.00	375.00	875.00
12-Intro. Ebony	80.00	240.00	560.00
13-Intro. Woozy Winks; last Firebrand	80.00	240.00	560.00
14-19: 19-Last Firebrand; Destiny begins	52.00	155.00	365.00
20-The Raven x-over in Phantom Lady; features Jack Cole himself	52.00	155.00	365.00
21,22-Raven & Spider Widow x-over in Phantom Lady #21; cameo in Phantom Lady #22	39.00	118.00	275.00
23-30: 23-Last Phantom Lady. 24-Chic Carter becomes The Sword, only issue. 24-26-Flatfoot Burns by Kurtzman in all	35.00	105.00	245.00
31-41-Last Spirit-r by Eisner	25.00	75.00	175.00
42,43-Spirit-r by Eisner/Fine	21.50	64.00	150.00
44-Fine Spirit-r begin, end #88,90,92	18.00	54.00	125.00
45-50-(#50 on-c, #49 on inside)(1/46)	18.00	54.00	125.00
51-60: 58-Last Human Bomb	14.00	42.00	100.00
61,62,64-88	12.00	36.00	84.00
63-(Some issues have #65 printed on cover, but #63 on inside) Kurtzman-a, 6pgs.	12.00	36.00	84.00
89,91,93-No Spirit	11.00	32.00	75.00
90,92-Spirit by Fine	12.00	36.00	84.00
94-99,101,102: Spirit by Eisner in all; 101-Last Manhunter. 102-Last Spirit & Plastic Man by Jack Cole	16.50	49.00	115.00
100	18.50	56.00	130.00

	Good	Fine	N-Mint

POLICE COMICS (continued)

	Good	Fine	N-Mint
103-Content change to crime - Ken Shannon begins (1st app.)			
	8.50	25.50	60.00
104-111,114-127-Crandall-a most issues	6.00	18.00	42.00
112-Crandall-a	6.00	18.00	42.00
113-Crandall-c/a(2), 9 pgs. each	6.50	19.50	45.00

NOTE: *Most Spirit stories signed by Eisner are not by him; all are reprints. Cole c-17, 19-21, 24-26, 28-31, 36-38, 40-42, 45-48, 65-68, 69, 73, 75. Crandall Firebrand-1-8. Spirit by Eisner 1-41, 94-102; by Eisner/Fine-42, 43; by Fine-44-88, 90, 92, 103, 109, Bondage c-103, 109, 125.*

POLICE LINE-UP
Aug, 1951 - No. 4, July, 1952 (Painted-c)
Realistic Comics/Avon Periodicals

	Good	Fine	N-Mint
1-Wood-a, 1 pg. plus part-c; spanking panel-r/Saint #5			
	15.00	45.00	105.00
2-Classic story "The Religious Murder Cult," drugs, perversion			
r-/Saint #5; c-/Avon paperback 329	13.00	40.00	90.00
3-Kubert-a(r)/part-c, Kinstler-a	8.00	24.00	56.00
4-Kinstler-a	8.00	24.00	56.00

POLICE THRILLS
1954
Ajax/Farrell Publications

	Good	Fine	N-Mint
1	3.50	10.50	24.00

POLICE TRAP (Public Defender In Action #7 on)
8-9/54 - No. 4, 2-3/55; No. 5, 7/55 - No. 6, 9/55
Mainline No. 1-4/Charlton No. 5,6

	Good	Fine	N-Mint
1-S&K covers-all issues	6.50	19.50	45.00
2-4	3.50	10.50	24.00
5,6-S&K-c/a	6.50	19.50	45.00

POLICE TRAP
No. 11, 1963; No. 16-18, 1964
Super Comics

	Good	Fine	N-Mint
Reprint #11,16-18	.50	1.50	3.00

POLL PARROT
Poll Parrot Shoe Store/International Shoe
1950 - 1951; 1959 - 1962
K. K. Publications (Giveaway)

	Good	Fine	N-Mint
1 ('50)-Howdy Doody; small size	2.65	8.00	18.00
2-4('50)-Howdy Doody	1.70	5.00	12.00
2('59)-16('61): 2-The Secret of Crumbley Castle. 5-Bandit Busters. 7-The Make-Believe Mummy. 8-Mixed Up Mission('60). 10-The Frightful Flight. 11-Showdown at Sunup. 12-Menace at Mubu Island. 13-. . .and the Runaway Genie. 14-Bully for You. 15-Trapped In Tall Timber. 16-. . .& the Rajah's Ruby('62)			
	.50	1.50	3.00

POLLY & HER PALS (See Comic Monthly #1)

POLLYANNA (See 4-Color #1129)

POLLY PIGTAILS (Girls' Fun & Fashion Magazine #44 on)
Jan, 1946 - V4No.43, Oct-Nov, 1949
Parents' Magazine Institute/Polly Pigtails

	Good	Fine	N-Mint
1-Infinity-c; photo-c	5.50	16.50	38.00
2	2.65	8.00	18.00
3-5	2.00	6.00	14.00
6-10: 7-Photo-c	1.50	4.50	10.00
11-30: 22-Photo-c	1.15	3.50	8.00
31-43	1.00	3.00	7.00

PONY EXPRESS (See Four Color #942)

PONYTAIL
7-9/62 - No. 12, 10-12/65; No. 13, 11/69 - No. 20, 1/71
Dell Publishing Co./Charlton No. 13 on

	Good	Fine	N-Mint
12-641-209(#1)	.75	2.25	5.00

	Good	Fine	N-Mint
2-12	.50	1.50	3.00
13-20	.35	1.00	2.00

POP COMICS (7 cents)
1955 (36 pgs.; 5x7"; in color)
Modern Store Publ.

	Good	Fine	N-Mint
1-Funny animal	.50	1.50	3.00

POPEYE (See Comic Album #7,11,15, Comics Reading Libraries, Eat Right to Work and Win, Giant Comic Album, King Comics, Magic Comics, March of Comics #37, 52, 66, 80, 96, 117, 134, 148, 157, 169, 194, 246, 264, 274, 294, 453, 465, 477 & Wow Comics, 1st series)

POPEYE (See Thimble Theatre)
1935 (25 cents; 52 pgs.; B&W) (By Segar)
David McKay Publications

	Good	Fine	N-Mint
1-Daily strip serial reprints-"The Gold Mine Thieves"			
	47.00	141.00	330.00
2-Daily strip-r	38.00	114.00	265.00

NOTE: *Popeye first entered Thimble Theatre in 1929.*

POPEYE
1937 - 1939 (All by Segar)
David McKay Publications

	Good	Fine	N-Mint
Feature Books nn (100 pgs.) (Very Rare)	467.00	1400.00	2800.00
Feature Books 2 (52 pgs.)	54.00	150.00	350.00
Feature Books 3 (100 pgs.)-r-/nn issue with a new-c			
	45.00	135.00	315.00
Feature Books 5,10 (76 pgs.)	37.00	110.00	260.00
Feature Books 14 (76 pgs.) (Scarce)	50.00	150.00	350.00

POPEYE (Strip reprints through 4-Color #70)
1941 - 1947; #1, 2-4/48 - #65, 7-9/62; #66, 10/62 - #80, 5/66; #81, 8/66 - #92, 12/67; #94, 2/69 - #138, 1/77; #139, 5/78 - #171, 7/84 (no #93,160,161)
Dell #1-65/Gold Key #66-80/King #81-92/Charlton #94-138/Gold Key #139-155/Whitman #156 on

	Good	Fine	N-Mint
Large Feat. Comic 24('41)-½ by Segar	37.00	110.00	260.00
4-Color 25('41)-by Segar	41.00	122.00	285.00
Large Feature Comic 10('43)	31.00	92.00	215.00
4-Color 17('43)-by Segar	34.00	100.00	235.00
4-Color 26('43)-by Segar	31.00	92.00	215.00
4-Color 43('44)	21.00	62.00	145.00
4-Color 70('45)-Title: . . .& Wimpy	17.00	51.00	120.00
4-Color 113('46-original strips begin),127,145('47),168			
	9.30	28.00	65.00
1(2-4/48)(Dell)	21.50	64.00	150.00
2	11.00	32.00	75.00
3-10	9.30	28.00	65.00
11-20	7.00	21.00	50.00
21-40	5.00	15.00	35.00
41-45,47-50	3.70	11.00	26.00
46-Origin Swee' Pee	5.50	16.50	38.00
51-60	2.85	8.50	20.00
61-65 (Last Dell issue)	2.30	7.00	16.00
66,67-Both 84 pgs. (Gold Key)	4.00	12.00	32.00
68-80	1.85	5.50	13.00
81-92,94-100	1.00	3.00	7.00
101-130	.70	2.00	5.00
131-143,145-159,162-171	.55	1.65	4.00
144-50th Anniversary issue	.55	1.65	4.00

NOTE: *Reprints-#145, 147, 149, 151, 153, 155, 157, 163-68(½), 170.*

	Good	Fine	N-Mint
Bold Detergent giveaway (Same as regular issue #49)			
	.35	1.00	2.00
. . .Kite Fun Book ('77, 5x7¼", 16p., soft-c)	1.00	3.00	6.00

POPEYE
1972 - 1974 (36 pgs. in color)
Charlton (King Features) (Giveaway)

Police Trap #1, © PRIZE   *Popeye, Book 1 (1935), © KING*   *Popeye #4 (Dell), © KING*

Popeye Special #1, © KING

Popular Comics #38, © DELL

Popular Teen-Agers #5, © STAR

POPEYE (continued)	Good	Fine	N-Mint
E-1 to E-15 (Educational comics)	.25	.75	1.50
nn-Popeye Gettin' Better Grades-4 pgs. used as intro. to above			
giveaways (in color)	.25	.75	1.50

POPEYE CARTOON BOOK
1934 (40 pgs. with cover)(8½x13'')(cardboard covers)
The Saalfield Publ. Co.

2095-(Rare)-1933 strip reprints in color by Segar; each page contains a vertical half of a Sunday strip, so the continuity reads row by row completely across each double page spread. If each page is read by itself, the continuity makes no sense. Each double page spread reprints one complete Sunday page (from 1933)

	Good	Fine	N-Mint
	85.00	255.00	595.00
12 Page Version	50.00	150.00	350.00

POPEYE SPECIAL
Summer, 1987 - No. 2, Sept, 1988 ($1.75-$2.00, color)
Ocean Comics

	Good	Fine	N-Mint
1-Origin ($1.75)	.30	.90	1.80
2 ($2.00)	.35	1.00	2.00

POPPLES (TV, Movie)
Dec, 1986 - No. 5, Aug, 1987
Star Comics (Marvel)

		Fine	N-Mint
1-3-Based on toys		.35	.70
4,5 ($1.00)		.50	1.00

POPPO OF THE POPCORN THEATRE
10/29/55 - No. 13, 1956 (published weekly)
Fuller Publishing Co. (Publishers Weekly)

1	2.65	8.00	18.00
2-5	1.50	4.50	10.00
6-13	1.15	3.50	8.00

NOTE: By **Charles Biro**. 10 cent cover, given away by supermarkets such as IGA.

POP-POP COMICS
No date (Circa 1945) (52 pgs.)
R. B. Leffingwell Co.

1-Funny animal	4.30	13.00	30.00

POPSICLE PETE FUN BOOK (See All-American Comics #6)
1947, 1948
Joe Lowe Corp.

nn-36 pgs. in color; Sammy 'n' Claras, The King Who Couldn't Sleep & Popsicle Pete stories, games, cut-outs; hats ad, pg. 20, to order Classics III. by sending wrappers 5.00 15.00 35.00
Adventure Book ('48) 3.70 11.00 26.00

POPULAR COMICS
Feb, 1936 - No. 145, July-Sept, 1948
Dell Publishing Co.

1-Dick Tracy, Little Orphan Annie, Terry & the Pirates, Gasoline Alley, Don Winslow, Harold Teen, Little Joe, Skippy, Moon Mullins, Mutt & Jeff, Tailspin Tommy, Smitty, Smokey Stover, Winnie Winkle & The Gumps begin (all strip-r) 167.00 420.00 1000.00

2	70.00	210.00	490.00
3	54.00	163.00	380.00
4,5: 5-Tom Mix begins	43.00	130.00	300.00
6-10: 8,9-Scribbly, Reglar Fellers app.	35.00	105.00	245.00
11-20: 12-Xmas-c	27.00	81.00	190.00
21-27-Last Terry & the Pirates, Little Orphan Annie, & Dick Tracy	19.00	58.00	135.00
28-37: 28-Gene Autry app. 31,32-Tim McCoy app. 35-Christmas-c; Tex Ritter app.	16.50	50.00	115.00
38-43-Tarzan in text only. 38-Gang Busters (radio) & Zane Grey's Tex Thorne begins?	18.50	55.00	130.00
44,45: 45-Tarzan-c	13.00	40.00	90.00
46-Origin Martan, the Marvel Man	17.00	51.00	120.00

	Good	Fine	N-Mint
47-50	12.00	36.00	84.00
51-Origin The Voice (The Invisible Detective) strip begins	13.00	40.00	90.00
52-59: 55-End of World story	11.00	32.00	75.00
60-Origin Professor Supermind and Son	11.50	34.00	80.00
61-71: 63-Smilin' Jack begins	9.30	28.00	65.00
72-The Owl & Terry & the Pirates begin; Smokey Stover reprints begin	14.00	42.00	100.00
73-75	11.50	34.00	80.00
76-78-Capt. Midnight in all	13.00	40.00	90.00
79-85-Last Owl	10.00	30.00	70.00
86-99: 98-Felix the Cat, Smokey Stover-r begin	8.00	24.00	56.00
100	9.30	28.00	65.00
101-130: 114-Last Dick Tracy-r?	5.00	15.00	35.00
131-145: 142-Last Terry & the Pirates	4.30	13.00	30.00

POPULAR FAIRY TALES (See March of Comics #6,18)

POPULAR ROMANCE
No. 5, Dec, 1949 - No. 29, July, 1954
Better-Standard Publications

5	3.50	10.50	24.00
6-9: 7-Palais-a; lingerie panels	2.15	6.50	15.00
10-Wood-a, 2 pgs.	3.65	11.00	25.00
11,12,14-21,28,29	1.70	5.00	12.00
13-Severin/Elder-a, 3 pgs.	2.00	6.00	14.00
22-27-Toth-a	4.60	14.00	32.00

NOTE: All have photo-c. **Tuska** art in most issues.

POPULAR TEEN-AGERS (Secrets of Love) (Formerly School Day Romances)
No. 5, Sept, 1950 - No. 23, Nov, 1954
Star Publications

5-Toni Gay, Honey Bunn, etc.; L. B. Cole-c	11.00	32.00	75.00
6-8 (7/51)-Toni Gay, Honey Bunn, etc.; all have L. B. Cole-c; 6-Negligee panels	9.30	28.00	65.00
9-(. . .Romances; 1st romance issue, 10/51)	3.70	11.00	26.00
10-(. . .Secrets of Love)	3.70	11.00	26.00
11,16,18,19,22,23	2.85	8.50	20.00
12,13,17,20,21-Disbrow-a	3.50	10.50	24.00
14-Harrison/Wood-a; 2 spanking scenes	11.50	34.50	80.00
15-Wood?, Disbrow-a	8.00	24.00	55.00
Accepted Reprint 5,6 (nd); L.B. Cole-c	2.00	6.00	14.00

NOTE: All have **L. B. Cole** covers.

PORE LI'L MOSE
1902 (30 pgs.; 10½x15''; in full color)
New York Herald Publ. by Grand Union Tea
Cupples & Leon Co.

nn-By R. F. Outcault; 1 pg. strips about early Negroes 40.00 120.00 280.00

PORKY PIG (. . .& Bugs Bunny #40-69)
No. 16, 1942 - No. 81, Mar-Apr, 1962; Jan, 1965 - No. 109, July, 1984
Dell Publishing Co./Gold Key No. 1-93/Whitman No. 94 on

4-Color 16(#1, 1942)	38.00	114.00	265.00
4-Color 48(1944)-Carl Barks-a	70.00	210.00	490.00
4-Color 78(1945)	14.00	42.00	100.00
4-Color 112(7/46)	8.50	25.50	60.00
4-Color 156,182,191('49)	6.50	19.50	45.00
4-Color 226,241('49),260,271,277,284,295	4.30	13.00	30.00
4-Color 303,311,322,330	3.00	9.00	21.00
4-Color 342,351,360,370,385,399,410,426	2.30	7.00	16.00
25 (11-12/52)-30	1.30	4.00	9.00
31-50	.70	2.00	4.50
51-81(3-4/62)	.45	1.35	3.00
1(1/65-G.K.)(2nd Series)	.75	2.25	5.00

PORKY PIG (continued) — Good / Fine / N-Mint
2,4,5-Reprints 4-Color 226,284 & 271 in that order

	Good	Fine	N-Mint
	.45	1.35	3.00
3,6-10	.35	1.00	2.00
11-50		.50	1.00
51-109		.30	.60
Kite Fun Book (1960, 16pgs., 5x7¼", soft-c)	2.00	6.00	12.00

NOTE: Reprints-#1-8, 9-35(⅔); 36-46, 58, 67, 69-74, 76, 78, 102-109(½-109).

PORKY PIG (See Bugs Bunny & . . ., March of Comics #42, 57, 71, 89, 99, 113, 130, 143, 164, 175, 192, 209, 218, 367, and Super Book #6, 18, 30)

PORKY'S BOOK OF TRICKS
1942 (48 pages) (8½x5½")
K. K. Publications (Giveaway)

nn-7 pg. comic story, text stories, plus games & puzzles
25.00 / 75.00 / 175.00

PORTIA PRINZ OF THE GLAMAZONS
Dec, 1986 - No. 6, Oct, 1987 ($2.00, B&W, Baxter paper)
Eclipse Comics

1-6	.35	1.00	2.00

POST GAZETTE (See Meet the New. . .)

POWDER RIVER RUSTLERS (See Fawcett Movie Comics)

POWER COMICS
1944 - No. 4, 1945
Holyoke Publ. Co./Narrative Publ.

1-L. B. Cole-c	16.50	50.00	115.00
2-4: 2-Dr. Mephisto begins. 3,4-L. B. Cole-c; Miss Espionage app. each	14.00	42.00	100.00

POWER COMICS
1977 - No. 5, Dec, 1977 (B&W)
Power Comics Co.

1-A Boy And His Aardvark app. by Dave Sims; first Dave Sims aardvark (not Cerebus)	4.15	12.50	25.00
1-Reprint (3/77, black-c)	1.35	4.00	8.00
2-Cobalt Blue app.	2.00	6.00	12.00
3-Nightwitch app.	.35	1.00	2.00
4,5: 4-Northern Light. 5-Bluebird app.	.35	1.00	2.00

POWER FACTOR
May, 1987 - No. 3, 1987? ($1.95, color)
Wonder Color Comics

1-3: Super team	.35	1.00	2.00

POWER GIRL (See Infinity, Inc. & Showcase #97-99)
June, 1988 - No. 4, Sept, 1988 ($1.00, mini-series)
DC Comics

1-4		.50	1.00

POWERHOUSE PEPPER COMICS (See Gay Comics, Joker Comics & Tessie the Typist)
No. 1, 1943; No. 2, May, 1948 - No. 5, Nov, 1948
Marvel Comics (20CC)

1-(60 pgs.)-Wolverton-c/a in all	57.00	170.00	400.00
2	35.00	105.00	245.00
3,4	34.00	100.00	235.00
5-(Scarce)	39.00	118.00	275.00

POWER LINE
May, 1988 - No. 8, Sept, 1989 ($1.25, $1.50 #4 on, color)
Epic Comics (Marvel)

1-3: 2-Williamson-i; 3-Austin-i, Dr. Zero app.	.60		1.25
4-8: 4-7-Morrow-a. 8-Williamson-i	.25	.75	1.50

POWER LORDS
Dec, 1983 - No. 3, Feb, 1984 (mini-series; Mando paper)
DC Comics

1-3-Based on Revell toys — .40 / .80

POWER MAN (Formerly Hero for Hire; . . .& Iron Fist #68 on)
No. 17, Feb, 1974 - No. 125, Sept, 1986
Marvel Comics Group

17-20: 17-Iron Man app.	.40	1.20	2.40
21-31: 31-Part Adams-i		.60	1.20
32-47: 36-Reprint. 45-Starlin-c		.50	1.00
48-Byrne-a; Powerman/Iron Fist 1st meet	.50	1.50	3.00
49,50-Byrne-a(p); 50-Iron Fist joins Cage	.50	1.50	3.00
51-56,58-60: 58-Intro El Aguila		.40	.80
57-New X-Men app.	.85	2.50	5.00
61-65,67-83,85-125: 75-Double size. 87-Moon Knight app. 90-Unus app. 109-The Reaper app. 100-Double size; origin K'un L'un. 125-Double size		.40	.80
66,84-Sabretooth app.	.35	1.00	2.00
Giant-Size 1('75)	.25	.80	1.60
Annual 1(11/76)-Punisher cameo in flashback		.50	1.00

NOTE: Austin c-102i. Byrne a-48-50; c-102, 104, 106, 107. Kane c(p)-24, 25, 28, 48. Miller a-68; c-66-68, 70-74, 80i. Mooney a-53i, 55i. Nebres a-76p. Nino a-42i, 43i. Perez a-27. Tuska a-17p, 20p, 24p.

POWERMOWERMAN AND POWER MOWER SAFETY
1966 (16 pgs.) (Giveaway)
Frank Burgmeier Co. (Outdoor Power Equipment Inst.)

nn-Vaughn Bode'-a	22.00	65.00	130.00

POWER OF STRONGMAN, THE (Also see Strongman)
1989 ($2.95, color)
AC Comics

1-Powell G.A.-r	.50	1.50	3.00

POWER OF THE ATOM (See Secret Origins #29)
Aug, 1988 - No. 18, Nov, 1989 ($1.00, color)
DC Comics

1-18: 6-Byrne-p. 9-Justice League Int. app.		.50	1.00

POWER PACHYDERMS
Sept, 1989 ($1.25, color, one-shot)
Marvel Comics

1-Elephant super-heroes		.60	1.25

POWER PACK
Aug, 1984 - Present
Marvel Comics Group

1-($1.00)	.70	2.00	4.00
2-5	.45	1.35	2.70
6-8-Cloak & Dagger app.	.35	1.00	2.00
9-18	.25	.75	1.50
19-Dbl. size; Cloak & Dagger, Wolverine app.	.85	2.50	5.00
20-24		.60	1.25
25-Double size	.30	.90	1.80
26-Begin direct sale; Cloak & Dagger app.		.60	1.25
27-Mutant massacre, Wolverine app.	.85	2.50	5.00
28-43: 42-1st Inferno tie-in		.60	1.25
44,45,47-49,51-56: 44-Begin $1.50-c	.25	.75	1.50
46-Punisher app.	.35	1.10	2.20
50-Double size ($1.95)	.35	1.00	2.00

NOTE: Morrow a-51. Williamson a-52i.

POW MAGAZINE (Bob Sproul's) (Satire Magazine)
Aug, 1966 - No. 3, Feb, 1967 (30 cents)
Humor-Vision

1-3: 2-Jones-a. 3-Wrightson-a	1.15	3.50	8.00

PREDATOR
May, 1989 - No. 4, 1990 ($2.25, color, mini-series)
Dark Horse Comics

1: Based on movie	1.00	3.00	6.00

Power Comics #3, © HOKE

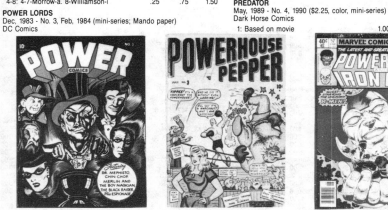

Powerhouse Pepper #3, © MEG

Power Man #57, © MEG

Primer #6, © Comico

Prison Break! #3, © REAL

POWER NELSON The FUTUREMAN
Prize Comics #2, © PRIZE

	Good	Fine	N-Mint
PREDATOR (continued)			
2	.45	1.40	2.75
3,4	.40	1.15	2.25

PREHISTORIC WORLD (See Classics Illustsrated Special Issue)

PREMIERE (See Charlton Premiere)

PRESTO KID, THE (See Red Mask)

PRETTY BOY FLOYD (See On the Spot)

PREZ (See Cancelled Comic Cavalcade & Supergirl #10)
Aug-Sept, 1973 - No. 4, Feb-Mar, 1974
National Periodical Publications

1-Origin		.30	.60
2-4		.25	.50

PRICE, THE (See Eclipse Graphic Album Series)

PRIDE AND THE PASSION, THE (See 4-Color #824)

PRIDE AND THE PASSION, THE (See Real Heroes & Sport Comics)
1949 (The Life of Lou Gehrig)
Magazine Enterprises

nn-Photo-c; Ogden Whitney-a	28.50	86.00	200.00

PRIMAL MAN (See The Crusaders)

PRIMER (Comico...)
Oct, 1982 - No. 6, Feb, 1984 (B&W)
Comico

1 (52 pgs.)	1.00	3.00	6.00
2-1st app. Grendel & Argent by Wagner	8.35	25.00	50.00
3-5	.70	2.00	4.00
6-Intro & 1st app. Evangeline	2.50	7.50	15.00

PRIMUS (TV)
Feb, 1972 - No. 7, Oct, 1972
Charlton Comics

1-5,7-Staton-a in all	.35	1.00	2.00
6-Drug propaganda story	.35	1.00	2.00

PRINCE & THE PAUPER, THE (See Movie Classics)

PRINCE NAMOR, THE SUB-MARINER
Sept, 1984 - No. 4, Dec, 1984 (mini-series)
Marvel Comics Group

1	.30	.90	1.75
2-4		.50	1.00

PRINCE NIGHTMARE
1987 ($2.95, color, 68 pgs.)
Aaaargh! Associated Artists

Book 1	.50	1.50	3.00

PRINCE VALIANT (See Ace Comics, Comics Reading Libraries, Feature Books #26, McKay, and 4-Color #567, 650, 699, 719, 788, 849, 900)

PRIORITY WHITE HEAT
1987 - No. 2, 1987 ($1.75, color, mini-series)
AC Comics

1,2-Bill Black-a	.30	.90	1.80

PRISCILLA'S POP (See 4-Color #569,630,704,799)

PRISON BARS (See Behind...)

PRISON BREAK!
1951 (Sept) - No. 5, Sept, 1952
Avon Periodicals/Realistic No. 3 on

1-Wood-c & 1 pg.; has r-/Saint #7 retitled Michael Strong Private Eye	17.00	51.00	120.00
2-Wood-c/Kubert-a plus 2 pgs. Wood-a	12.00	36.00	84.00
3-Orlando, Check-a; c-/Avon paperback 179	10.00	30.00	70.00
4,5: Kinstler-c. 5-Infantino-a	9.00	27.00	62.00

PRISONER, THE (TV)
1988 - No. 4, Jan, 1989 ($3.50, mini-series, squarebound)
DC Comics

	Good	Fine	N-Mint
1-Book A	.70	2.00	4.00
2-4: Book B-D	.60	1.75	3.50

PRISON RIOT
1952
Avon Periodicals

1-Marijuana Murders-1 pg. text; Kinstler-c	13.00	40.00	90.00

PRISON TO PRAISE
1974 (35 cents)
Logos International

True Story of Merlin R. Carothers		.30	.60

PRIVATE BUCK (See Large Feature Comic #12 & 21)

PRIVATEERS
Aug, 1987 - No. 2, 1987 ($1.50, color)
Vanguard Graphics

1,2	.25	.75	1.50

PRIVATE EYE (Cover title: Rocky Jordan...#6-8)
Jan, 1951 - No. 8, March, 1952
Atlas Comics (MCI)

1-Cover title: Crime Cases... #1-5	5.70	17.00	40.00
2,3-Tuska a(3)	3.70	11.00	26.00
4-8	2.85	8.50	20.00

NOTE: *Henkel a-6(3), 7; c-7. Sinnott a-6.*

PRIVATE EYE (See Mike Shayne...)

PRIVATE SECRETARY
Dec-Feb, 1962-63 - No. 2, Mar-May, 1963
Dell Publishing Co.

1,2	1.00	3.00	7.00

PRIVATE STRONG (See The Double Life of...)

PRIZE COMICS (...Western #69 on) (Also see Treasure Comics)
March, 1940 - No. 68, Feb-Mar, 1948
Prize Publications

1-Origin Power Nelson, The Futureman & Jupiter, Master Magician; Ted O'Neil, Secret Agent M-11, Jaxon of the Jungle, Bucky Brady & Storm Curtis begin	78.00	235.00	550.00
2-The Black Owl begins	37.00	110.00	260.00
3,4	30.00	90.00	210.00
5,6: Dr. Dekkar, Master of Monsters app. in each	27.00	81.00	190.00
7-(Scarce)-Black Owl by S&K; origin/1st app. Dr. Frost & Frankenstein; The Green Lama, Capt. Gallant, The Great Voodini & Twist Turner begin; Kirby-c	58.00	175.00	410.00
8,9-Black Owl & Ted O'Neil by S&K	32.00	95.00	225.00
10-12,14-20: 11-Origin Bulldog Denny. 16-Spike Mason begins	27.00	81.00	190.00
13-Yank & Doodle begin (origin)	32.00	95.00	225.00
21-24	18.00	54.00	125.00
25-30	12.00	36.00	84.00
31-33	9.00	27.00	62.00
34-Origin Airmale, Yank & Doodle; The Black Owl joins army, Yank & Doodle's father assumes Black Owl's role	10.00	30.00	70.00
35-40: 35-Flying Fist & Bingo begin. 37-Intro. Stampy, Airmale's sidekick; Hitler-c	8.00	24.00	56.00
41-50: 45-Yank & Doodle learn Black Owl's I.D. (their father). 48-Prince Ra begins	5.70	17.00	40.00
51-62,64-68: 53-Transvestism story. 55-No Frankenstein. 64-Black Owl retires. 65,66-Frankenstein-c by Briefer	5.00	15.00	35.00
63-Simon & Kirby c/a	7.00	21.00	50.00

NOTE: *Briefer a 7-on; c-65, 66. J. Binder a-16; c-22, 26, 29. Guardineer a-62. Kiefer*

315

PRIZE COMICS (continued)
c-62.

PRIZE COMICS WESTERN (Formerly Prize Comics #1-68)
No. 69(V7No.2), Apr-May, 1948 - No. 119, Nov-Dec, 1956
Prize Publications (Feature) (No. 69-84: 52 pgs.)

	Good	Fine	N-Mint
69(V7#2)	7.00	21.00	50.00
70-75	5.00	15.00	35.00
76-Randolph Scott photo-c; "Canadian Pacific" movie adaptation	7.00	21.00	50.00
77-Photo-c; Severin, Mart Bailey-a; "Streets of Laredo" movie adapt.	5.70	17.00	40.00
78-Photo-c; Kurtzman-a, 10 pgs.; Severin, Mart Bailey-a; "Bullet Code," & "Roughshod" movie adapt.	9.00	27.00	62.00
79-Photo-c; Kurtzman-a, 8 pgs.; Severin & Elder, Severin, Mart Bailey-a; "Stage To Chino" movie adapt.	9.00	27.00	62.00
80,81-Photo-c; Severin/Elder-a(2)	5.70	17.00	40.00
82-Photo-c; 1st app. The Preacher by Mart Bailey; Severin/Elder-a(3)	5.70	17.00	40.00
83,84	4.30	13.00	30.00
85-American Eagle by John Severin begins (1-2/50)	12.00	36.00	84.00
86,92,95,101-105	5.50	16.50	38.00
87-91,93,94,96-99,110,111-Severin/Elder a(2-3) each	5.70	17.00	40.00
100	7.00	21.00	50.00
106-108,112	3.70	11.00	26.00
109-Severin/Williamson-a	6.00	18.00	42.00
113-Williamson/Severin-a(2)	6.50	19.50	45.00
114-119: Drifter series in all; by Mort Meskin 114-118	2.65	8.00	18.00

NOTE: *Fass* a-81. *Severin & Elder* c-84, 88, 92, 94-96, 98. *Severin* a-72, 75, 77-79, 83-86, 96, 97, 100-105; c-most 85-109. *Simon & Kirby* c-75, 83.

PRIZE MYSTERY
May, 1955 - No. 3, Sept, 1955
Key Publications

1	3.15	9.50	22.00
2,3	2.15	6.50	15.00

PROFESSIONAL FOOTBALL (See Charlton Sport Library)

PROFESSOR COFFIN
No. 19, Oct, 1985 - No. 21, Feb, 1986
Charlton Comics

19-21: Wayne Howard-a(r)		.40	.80

PROJECT: HERO
Aug, 1987 ($1.50, color)
Vanguard Graphics (Canadian)

1	.25	.75	1.50

PROWLER (Also see Revenge of the...)
July, 1987 - No. 4, Oct, 1987 ($1.75, color)
Eclipse Comics

1-4	.30	.90	1.80

PROWLER IN "WHITE ZOMBIE", THE
Oct, 1988 ($2.00, B&W, Baxter paper)
Eclipse Comics

1-Adapts Bela Lugosi movie White Zombie	.35	1.00	2.00

PSI FORCE
Nov, 1986 - No. 32, June, 1989 (.75-$1.25-$1.50, color)
Marvel Comics Group

1-32: 11-13-Williamson-i		.65	1.30
Annual 1 (10/87)		.65	1.30

PSI-JUDGE ANDERSON
1989 - Present ($1.95, color)

Quality Comics

	Good	Fine	N-Mint
1-5	.35	1.00	2.00

PSYCHO (Magazine)
Jan, 1971 - No. 24, Mar, 1975 (68 pgs.; B&W) (no No.22?)
Skywald Publishing Corp.

1-All reprints	.85	2.50	6.00
2-Origin & 1st app. The Heap, & Frankenstein series by Adkins	.70	2.00	4.00
3-24: 13-Cannabalism. 18-Injury to eye-c. 20-Severed Head-c.			
24-1975 Winter Special	.40	1.25	2.50
Annual 1('72)	.60	1.75	3.50
Fall Special('74)-Reese, Wildey-a(r)	.40	1.25	2.50
Yearbook(1974-nn)	.40	1.25	2.50

NOTE: *Boris* c-3, 5. *Buckler* a-4, 5. *Everett* a-3-6. *J. Jones* a-6, 7, 9; c-12. *Kaluta* a-13. *Katz/Buckler* a-3. *Morrow* a-1. *Reese* a-5. *Sutton* a-3. *Wildey* a-5.

PSYCHOANALYSIS
Mar-Apr, 1955 - No. 4, Sept-Oct, 1955
E. C. Comics

1-All Kamen c/a; not approved by code	6.50	19.50	45.00
2-4-Kamen-c/a in all	5.00	15.00	35.00

PSYCHOBLAST
Nov, 1987 - No. 9, July, 1988 ($1.75, color)
First Comics

1-9	.30	.90	1.80

P.T. 109 (See Movie Comics)

PUBLIC DEFENDER IN ACTION (Formerly Police Trap)
No. 7, Mar, 1956 - No. 12, Oct, 1957
Charlton Comics

7	3.50	10.50	24.00
8-12	2.00	6.00	14.00

PUBLIC ENEMIES
1948 - No. 9, June-July, 1949
D. S. Publishing Co.

1	7.00	21.00	50.00
2-Used in SOTI, pg. 95	8.00	24.00	56.00
3-5: 5-Arrival date of 10/1/48	4.00	12.00	28.00
6,8,9	3.50	10.50	24.00
7-McWilliams-a; injury to eye panel	4.60	14.00	32.00

PUDGY PIG
Sept, 1958 - No. 2, Nov, 1958
Charlton Comics

1,2	1.15	3.50	8.00

PUMA BLUES
1986 - Present ($1.70-$2.00, B&W)
Aardvark One International/Mirage Studios #21 on

1	.70	2.00	4.00
1-2nd print	.30	.85	1.70
2	.35	1.00	2.00
3-19,21-26: 21-Begin $2.00-c?	.30	.85	1.70
20 ($2.25)-By Alan Moore, Miller, Grell, others	.40	1.15	2.30
Trade Paperback (12/88, $14.95)	2.50	7.50	14.95

PUNCH & JUDY COMICS
1944; No. 2, Fall, 1948 - V3No.9, Dec, 1951
Hillman Periodicals

V1#1-(1944, 60 pgs.)	7.00	21.00	50.00
2 (Fall, '48)	3.50	10.50	24.00
3-12(7/46)	2.30	7.00	16.00
V2#1,3-9	1.70	5.00	12.00
V2#2,10-12, V3#1-Kirby-a(2) each	8.00	24.00	56.00
V3#2-Kirby-a	7.00	21.00	50.00
3-9	1.50	4.50	10.00

Prize Comics Western #71, © PRIZE

Public Enemies #1, © DS

Pudgy Pig #1, © CC

Punch Comics #13, © CHES

Punisher Annual #2, © MEG

The Purple Claw #1, © TOBY

PUNCH COMICS
Dec, 1941 - No. 26, Dec, 1947
Harry 'A' Chesler

	Good	Fine	N-Mint
1-Mr. E, The Sky Chief, Hale the Magician, Kitty Kelly begin			
	43.00	130.00	300.00
2-Captain Glory app.	22.00	65.00	155.00
3	19.00	58.00	135.00
4	16.50	50.00	115.00
5	13.00	40.00	90.00
6-8	11.00	32.00	75.00
9-Rocketman & Rocket Girl & The Master Key begin			
	13.50	40.00	95.00
10-Sky Chief app.; J. Cole-a; Master Key r-/Scoop 3			
	11.00	32.00	75.00
11-Origin Master Key-r/Scoop 1; Sky Chief, Little Nemo app.; Jack Cole-a; Fineish art by Sultan	11.50	34.00	80.00
12-Rocket Boy & Capt. Glory app; Skull-c	10.00	30.00	70.00
13-17,19: 13-Cover has list of 4 Chesler artists' names on tombstone			
	9.30	28.00	65.00
18-Bondage-c; hypodermic panels	11.50	34.00	80.00
20-Unique cover with bare-breasted women	19.00	57.00	135.00
21-Hypo needle story	10.00	30.00	70.00
22-26: 22,23-Little Nemo-not by McCay	8.50	25.50	60.00

PUNCHY AND THE BLACK CROW
No. 10, Oct, 1985 - No. 12, Feb, 1986
Charlton Comics

10-12: Al Fago funny animal-r		.40	.80

PUNISHER (See Amazing Spider-Man #129, Captain America #241, Classic Punisher, Daredevil #182-184, 257, Daredevil and the . . . , Marvel Preview #2, Marvel Super Action, Marvel Tales, Power Pack #46, Spectacular Spider-Man #81-83, 140, 141, 143 & new Strange Tales #13,14)

PUNISHER
Jan, 1986 - No. 5, May, 1986 (mini-series)
Marvel Comics Group

1-Double size	5.00	15.00	35.00
2	3.00	9.00	18.00
3-Has 2 cover prices, 75 & 95(w/UPC) cents	1.70	5.00	10.00
4,5	1.35	4.00	8.00
Trade Paperback-r/1-5 (1988)	1.70	5.00	10.00

PUNISHER
July, 1987 - Present
Marvel Comics Group

V2#1	1.85	5.50	11.00
2	.70	2.00	4.00
3-5	.60	1.75	3.50
6-8	.50	1.50	3.00
9	.60	1.75	3.50
10-15: 10-Daredevil app.	.50	1.50	3.00
16-20: 13-18-Kingpin app.	.35	1.00	2.00
21-24,26-30: 24-1st app. Shadowmasters		.60	1.20
25-Double size ($1.50)-Shadowmasters app.	.30	.90	1.80
Annual 1(8/88)-Evolutionary War app.	1.00	3.00	6.00
Annual 2('89, $2.00, 68 pgs.)-Atlantis Attacks x-over; Moon Knight app.	.40	1.25	2.50
Hardcover ($16.95)-New story/art	4.15	12.50	25.00

NOTE: Heath a-26, 27. Williamson a-25i.

PUNISHER MAGAZINE
Oct, 1989 - Present ($2.25, B&W, Magazine, 52 pgs.)
Marvel Comics

1-3: 1-r/Punisher #1('86). 2,3-r/Punisher 2-5	.40	1.15	2.25
4-7: r/Punisher V2#1-8	.40	1.15	2.25

PUNISHER MOVIE COMIC
Nov, 1989 - No. 3, Dec, 1989 ($1.00, color, mini-series)

Marvel Comics

	Good	Fine	N-Mint
1-3: Movie adaptation		.50	1.00
1 (1989, $4.95, squarebound)-contains #1-3	.85	2.50	5.00

PUNISHER VS. WOLVERINE
1990 ($5.95, color)
Marvel Comics

1-r/Punisher War Journal #6 & 7	1.00	3.00	6.00

PUNISHER WAR JOURNAL
Nov, 1988 - Present ($1.50, color)
Marvel Comics

1: Origin The Punisher; Matt Murdock cameo	.75	2.25	4.50
2-5: 2,3-Daredevil x-over	.35	1.00	2.00
6-Two part Wolverine story begins	.90	2.75	5.50
7-Wolverine story ends	.60	1.75	3.50
8-16	.25	.75	1.50

PUPPET COMICS
Spring, 1946 - No. 2, Summer, 1946
George W. Dougherty Co.

1,2-Funny animal	3.70	11.00	26.00

PUPPETOONS (See George Pal's . . .)

PURE OIL COMICS (Also see Salerno Carnival of Comics, 24 Pages of Comics, & Vicks Comics)
Late 1930's (24 pgs.; regular size) (paper cover)
Pure Oil Giveaway

nn-Contains 1-2 pg. strips; i.e., Hairbreadth Harry, Skyroads, Buck Rogers by Calkins & Yager, Olly of the Movies, Napoleon, S'Matter Pop, etc.	25.00	75.00	175.00
Also a 16 pg. 1938 giveaway with Buck Rogers			
	20.00	60.00	140.00

PURPLE CLAW, THE (Also see Tales of Horror)
Jan, 1953 - No. 3, May, 1953
Minoan Publishing Co./Toby Press

1-Origin	11.00	32.00	75.00
2,3: 1-3 r-in Tales of Horror #9-11	6.50	19.50	45.00
I.W. Reprint #8-Reprints #1	.80	2.40	4.80

PUSSYCAT (Magazine)
Oct, 1968 (B&W reprints from Men's magazines)
Marvel Comics Group

1-(Scarce)-Ward, Everett, Wood-a; Everett-c	13.00	40.00	90.00

PUZZLE FUN COMICS (Also see Jingle Jangle)
Spring, 1946 - No. 2, Summer, 1946 (52 pgs.)
George W. Dougherty Co.

1(1946)-Gustavson-a	9.00	27.00	62.00
2	6.50	19.50	45.00

NOTE: #1,2('46) each contain a George Carlson cover plus a 6 pg. story "Alec in Fumbleland;" also many puzzles in each.

QUADRANT
1983 - No. 7, 1986 (B&W, nudity, adult)
Quadrant Publications

1-Peter Hsu-c/a in all	9.15	27.50	55.00
2	2.50	7.50	15.00
3	1.35	4.00	8.00
4	1.00	3.00	6.00
5	.70	2.00	4.00
6,7	.35	1.00	2.00

QUAKER OATS (Also see Cap'n Crunch)
1965 (Giveaway) (2½x5½") (16 pages)
Quaker Oats Co.

"Plenty of Glutton," "Lava Come-Back," "Kite Tale," "A Witch in Time"		.50	1.00

QUASAR (See Avengers #302 & Marvel Team-Up #113)
Oct, 1989 - Present ($1.00, color)
Marvel Comics

	Good	Fine	N-Mint
1-Origin; formerly Marvel Boy; Ryan-c/a in all	.25	.75	1.50
2-8: 3-Human Torch app. 7-Cosmic Spidey app.	.60		1.20

QUEEN OF THE WEST, DALE EVANS (TV)(See Western Roundup under Dell Giants)
No. 479, 7/53 - No. 22, 1-3/59 (All photo-c; photo back c-4-8, 15)
Dell Publishing Co.

	Good	Fine	N-Mint
4-Color 479('53)	7.00	21.00	50.00
4-Color 528('54)	5.00	15.00	35.00
3(4-6/54)-Toth-a	5.70	17.00	40.00
4-Toth, Manning-a	5.70	17.00	40.00
5-10-Manning-a. 5-Marsh-a	4.00	12.00	28.00
11,19,21-No Manning 21-Tufts-a	3.00	9.00	21.00
12-18,20,22-Manning-a	3.50	10.50	24.00

QUENTIN DURWARD (See 4-Color #672)

QUESTAR ILLUSTRATED SCIENCE FICTION CLASSICS
1977 (224 pgs.) ($1.95)
Golden Press

	Good	Fine	N-Mint
11197-Stories by Asimov, Sturgeon, Silverberg & Niven; Starstream-r	.50	1.50	3.00

QUESTION, THE (See Americomics, Blue Beetle (1967), Charlton Bullseye & Mysterious Suspense)

QUESTION, THE (Also see Crisis on Infinite Earths)
Feb, 1987 - No. 36, Mar, 1990 ($1.50-$1.75, color, mature readers)
DC Comics

	Good	Fine	N-Mint
1-Sienkiewicz painted-c #1-19,21,22	.75	2.25	4.50
2	.60	1.75	3.50
3-5	.50	1.50	3.00
6-15: 8-Intro. The Mikado	.40	1.15	2.30
16-36: 16-Begin $1.75-c	.35	1.00	2.00
Annual 1(9/88)	.45	1.40	2.75
Annual 2('89, $3.50, 68 pgs.)-Green Arrow app.	.60	1.75	3.50

QUESTPROBE
8/84; No. 2, 1/85; No. 3, 11/85 - No. 4, 12/85 (Limited series)
Marvel Comics Group

	Good	Fine	N-Mint
1-4: 1-The Hulk app. by Romita	.40		.80

QUICK-DRAW McGRAW (TV) (Hanna-Barbera)
No. 1040, 12-2/59-60 - No. 11, 7-9/62; No. 12, 11/62; No. 13, 2/63; No. 14, 4/63; No. 15, 6/69
Dell Publishing Co./Gold Key No. 12 on

	Good	Fine	N-Mint
4-Color 1040	3.70	11.00	26.00
2(4-6/60)-6	2.65	8.00	18.00
7-11	1.70	5.00	12.00
12,13-Title change to . . .Fun-Type Roundup (84 pgs.)	3.50	10.50	28.00
14,15	1.50	4.50	10.00

(See Whitman Comic Books)

QUICK-DRAW McGRAW (TV)(See Spotlight #2)
Nov, 1970 - No. 8, Jan, 1972 (Hanna-Barbera)
Charlton Comics

	Good	Fine	N-Mint
1	1.15	3.50	8.00
2-8	.70	2.00	4.50

QUICK-TRIGGER WESTERN (. . .Action #12; Cowboy Action #5-11)
No. 12, May, 1956 - No. 19, Sept, 1957
Atlas Comics (ACI No. 12/WPI No. 13-19)

	Good	Fine	N-Mint
12-Baker-a	4.30	13.00	30.00
13-Williamson-a, 5 pgs.	5.00	15.00	35.00
14-Everett, Crandall, Torres-a; Heath-c	4.30	13.00	30.00
15-Torres, Crandall-a	3.50	10.50	24.00

	Good	Fine	N-Mint
16-Orlando, Kirby-a	2.85	8.50	20.00
17,18: 17-Crandall-a. 18-Baker-a	2.65	8.00	18.00
19	1.70	5.00	12.00

NOTE: *Colan* a-16. *Maneely* a-15, 17; c-15, 18. *Morrow* a-18. *Powell* a-14. *Severin* c-12, 13, 16, 17, 19. *Shores* a-16. *Tuska* a-17.

QUINCY (See Comics Reading Libraries)

RACCOON KIDS, THE (Formerly Movietown Animal Antics)
No. 52, Sept-Oct, 1954 - No. 64, Nov, 1957
National Periodical Publications (Arleigh No. 63,64)

	Good	Fine	N-Mint
52-Doodles Duck by Mayer	4.00	12.00	28.00
53-64: 53-62-Doodles Duck by Mayer	2.65	8.00	18.00

RACE FOR THE MOON
March, 1958 - No. 3, Nov, 1958
Harvey Publications

	Good	Fine	N-Mint
1-Powell-a(5); ½-pg. S&K-a; c-redrawn from Galaxy Science Fiction pulp (5/53)	5.70	17.00	40.00
2-Kirby/Williamson c(r)/a(3)	13.50	40.50	95.00
3-Kirby/Williamson c/a(4)	14.50	43.50	100.00

RACER-X
8/88 - No. 11, 8/89; V2#1, 9/89 - Present ($1.75, color)
Now Comics

	Good	Fine	N-Mint
0-Deluxe ($3.50)	.60	1.75	3.50
1 (9/88) - 11	.30	.90	1.80
V2#1-7	.30	.90	1.80

RACKET SQUAD IN ACTION
May-June, 1952 - No. 29, March, 1958
Capitol Stories/Charlton Comics

	Good	Fine	N-Mint
1	8.50	25.50	60.00
2-4	3.50	10.50	24.00
5-Dr. Neff, Ghost Breaker app; headlights-c	5.00	15.00	35.00
6-Dr. Neff, Ghost Breaker app.	3.50	10.50	24.00
7-10: 10-Explosion-c	2.85	8.50	20.00
11-Ditko c/a	9.30	28.00	65.00
12-Ditko explosion-c (classic); Shuster-a(2)	18.50	56.00	130.00
13-Shuster c(p)/a; acid in woman's face	3.00	9.00	21.00
14-"Shakedown"-marijuana story	5.00	15.00	35.00
15-28	2.30	7.00	16.00
29-(68 pgs.)(15 cents)	2.85	8.50	20.00

RADIANT LOVE (Formerly Daring Love #1)
No. 2, Dec, 1953 - No. 6, Aug, 1954
Gilmor Magazines

	Good	Fine	N-Mint
2	2.65	8.00	18.00
3-6	1.70	5.00	12.00

RAGAMUFFINS
Jan, 1985 ($1.75, One Shot)
Eclipse Comics

	Good	Fine	N-Mint
1-Eclipse Magazine-r, w/color	.30	.90	1.80

RAGGEDY ANN AND ANDY (See Dell Giants, March of Comics #23 & New Funnies)
No. 5, 1942 - No. 533, 2/54; 10-12/64 - No. 4, 3/66
Dell Publishing Co.

	Good	Fine	N-Mint
4-Color 5(1942)	34.00	100.00	235.00
4-Color 23(1943)	24.00	73.00	170.00
4-Color 45(1943)	20.00	60.00	140.00
4-Color 72(1945)	16.50	50.00	115.00
1(6/46)-Billy & Bonnie Bee by Frank Thomas	16.50	50.00	115.00
2,3: 3-Egbert Elephant by Dan Noonan begins	8.00	24.00	56.00
4-Kelly-a, 16 pgs.	8.50	25.50	60.00
5-10: 7-Little Black Sambo, Black Mumbo & Black Jumbo only app; Christmas-c	6.50	19.50	45.00

Quasar #1, © MEG

Quick-Trigger Western #12, © MEG

Race For The Moon #3, © HARV

Ralph Snart Adventures #1 (6/86), © Now Comics Ramar Of The Jungle #4, © CC Rangers Comics #11, © FH

	Good	Fine	N-Mint
RAGGEDY ANN AND ANDY (continued)			
11-20	5.00	15.00	35.00
21-Alice In Wonderland cover/story	5.00	15.00	35.00
22-27,29-39(8/49), 4-Color 262(1/50)	3.70	11.00	26.00
28-Kelly-c	4.30	13.00	30.00
4-Color 306,354,380,452,533	3.00	9.00	21.00
1(10-12/64-Dell)	1.15	3.50	8.00
2,3(10-12/65), 4(3/66)	.75	2.25	5.00

NOTE: **Kelly** art ("Animal Mother Goose")-#1-34, 36, 37; c-28. Peterkin Pottle by **John Stanley** in 32-38.

RAGGEDY ANN AND ANDY
Dec, 1971 - No. 6, Sept, 1973
Gold Key

1	.70	2.00	4.00
2-6	.35	1.00	2.00

RAGGEDY ANN & THE CAMEL WITH THE WRINKLED KNEES (See Dell Jr. Treasury #8)

RAGMAN (See Batman Family #20, Brave & The Bold #196 & Cancelled Comic Cavalcade)
Aug-Sept, 1976 - No. 5, June-July, 1977
National Periodical Publications/DC Comics No. 5

1-Origin		.40	.80
2-Origin concludes; Kubert-c		.30	.60
3-5: 4-Drug use story		.25	.50

NOTE: **Kubert** a-4 .5; c-1-5. **Redondo** studios a-1-4.

RAGS RABBIT (See Harvey Hits #2, Harvey Wiseguys & Tastee Freez)
No. 11, June, 1951 - No. 18, March, 1954
Harvey Publications

11-(See Nutty Comics #5 for 1st app.)	1.15	3.50	8.00
12-18	1.00	3.00	7.00

RAIDERS OF THE LOST ARK
Sept, 1981 - No. 3, Nov, 1981 (Movie adaptation)
Marvel Comics Group

1-r/Marvel Comics Super Special #18		.40	.80
2,3		.30	.60

NOTE: **Buscema** a(p)-1-3; c(p)-1. **Simonson** a-2i, 3i.

RAINBOW BRITE AND THE STAR STEALER
1985
DC Comics

nn-Movie adaptation		.40	.80

RALPH KINER, HOME RUN KING
1950 (Pittsburgh Pirates)
Fawcett Publications

nn-Photo-c	23.00	70.00	160.00

RALPH SNART ADVENTURES
June, 1986 - V2#9, 1987; V3#1, Sept, 1988 - Present ($1.25, B&W)
Now Comics

1 ($1.00)	.60	1.75	3.50
2,3	.40	1.25	2.50
V2#1 (11/86)-Origin Rodent Ralph	.35	1.00	2.00
V2#2-9	.25	.75	1.50
V3#1 (9/88, $1.75, begin color series)	.35	1.00	2.00
V3#2-20: 16-Halloween issue	.30	.90	1.80
Book 1	1.35	4.00	8.00

RAMAR OF THE JUNGLE (TV)
1954 (no month); No. 2, 9/55 - No. 5, 9/56
Toby Press No. 1/Charlton No. 2 on

1-Jon Hall photo-c	6.50	19.50	45.00
2-5	5.00	15.00	35.00

RAMBO IN 3-D (See Blackthorne 3-D Series #49)

RAMPAGING HULK, THE (Magazine) (The Hulk #10 on; see Marvel Treasury Edition)
Jan, 1977 - No. 9, June, 1978
Marvel Comics Group

	Good	Fine	N-Mint
1-Bloodstone featured	.50	1.50	3.00
2-Old X-Men app; origin old & new X-Men in text w/Rogers illos	.85	2.50	5.00
3-9	.35	.75	1.50

NOTE: **Alcala** a-1-3i, 5i, 8i. **Buscema** a-1. **Giffen** a-4. **Nino** a-4i. **Simonson** a-1-3p. **Starlin** a-4(w/Nino), 7; c-4, 5, 7.

RANGE BUSTERS
Sept, 1950 - No. 8, 1951
Fox Features Syndicate

1	7.00	21.00	50.00
2	4.00	12.00	28.00
3-8	3.50	10.50	24.00

RANGE BUSTERS (Formerly Cowboy Love?; Wyatt Earp, Frontier Marshall #11 on)
No. 8, May, 1955 - No. 10, Sept, 1955
Charlton Comics

8	3.50	10.50	24.00
9,10	1.70	5.00	12.00

RANGELAND LOVE
Dec, 1949 - No. 2, Mar, 1950
Atlas Comics (CDS)

1,2	4.30	13.00	30.00

RANGER, THE (See 4-Color #255)

RANGE RIDER (See The Flying A's. . .)

RANGE RIDER, THE (See 4-Color #404)

RANGE ROMANCES
Dec, 1949 - No. 5, Aug, 1950 (#5: 52 pgs.)
Comic Magazines (Quality Comics)

1-Gustavson-c/a	11.50	34.00	80.00
2-Crandall-c/a; "spanking" scene	16.00	48.00	110.00
3-Crandall, Gustavson-a; photo-c	9.00	27.00	62.00
4-Crandall-a; photo-c	7.00	21.00	50.00
5-Gustavson-a; Crandall-a(p); photo-c	8.00	24.00	56.00

RANGERS COMICS (. . .of Freedom #1-7)
Oct, 1941 - No. 69, Winter, 1952-53
Fiction House Magazines (Flying stories)

1-Intro. Ranger Girl & The Rangers of Freedom; ends #7, cover app. only-#5	92.00	230.00	550.00
2	36.00	107.00	250.00
3	30.00	90.00	210.00
4,5	26.00	77.00	180.00
6-10: 8-U.S. Rangers begin	21.50	64.00	150.00
11,12-Commando Rangers app.	19.00	57.00	135.00
13-Commando Ranger begins-not same as Commando Rangers			
	19.00	57.00	135.00
14-20	14.00	42.00	100.00
21-Intro/origin Firehair (begins)	18.50	56.00	130.00
22-30: 23-Kazanda begins, ends #28. 28-Tiger Man begins (origin). 30-Crusoe Island begins, ends #40	13.00	40.00	90.00
31-40: 33-Hypodermic panels	11.50	34.00	80.00
41-46	8.50	25.50	60.00
47-56-"Eisnerish" Dr. Drew by Grandenetti	9.50	28.50	65.00
57-60-Straight Dr. Drew by Grandenetti	6.50	19.50	45.00
61,62,64-66: 64-Suicide Smith begins	5.70	17.00	40.00
63-Used in POP, pgs. 85, 99	5.70	17.00	40.00
67-69: 67-Space Rangers begin, end #69	5.70	17.00	40.00

NOTE: Bondage, discipline covers, lingerie panels are common. **Baker** a-36-38. **John Celardo** a-36-39. **Lee Elias** a-21-28. **Evans** a-19, 38-45, 47, 52. **Ingels** a-13-16. **Larsen**

RANGERS COMICS (continued)
a-34. **Bob Lubbers** *a-30-38, 40, 42, 44; c-42, 44.* **Moreira** *a-44, 45.* **Tuska** *a-16, 17, 19, 22.* **Zolne** *c-1-17.*

RANGO (TV)
August, 1967
Dell Publishing Co.

	Good	Fine	N-Mint
1-Tim Conway photo-c	1.75	5.25	12.00

RAPHAEL (See Teenage Mutant Ninja Turtles)
1985 (One shot, $1.50, B&W)
Mirage Studios

1	1.00	3.00	6.00
1-2nd print. (11/87)-New-c & 8pgs.-a	.50	1.50	3.00

RATFINK (See Frantic & Zany)
October, 1964
Canrom, Inc.

1-Woodbridge-a	2.35	7.00	14.00

RAT PATROL, THE (TV)
March, 1967 - No. 5, Nov, 1967; No. 6, Oct, 1969
Dell Publishing Co.

1-Christopher George photo-c	3.70	11.00	26.00
2	2.65	8.00	18.00
3-6: 3-6-Photo-c	2.00	6.00	14.00

RAVEN, THE (See Movie Classics)

RAVENS AND RAINBOWS
Dec, 1983 (Baxter paper)
Pacific Comics

1-Jeff Jones-c/a(r); nudity scenes	.25	.75	1.50

RAWHIDE (TV)
Sept-Nov, 1959 - June-Aug, 1962; July, 1963 - No. 2, Jan, 1964
Dell Publishing Co./Gold Key

4-Color 1028	14.00	42.00	100.00
4-Color 1097,1160,1202,1261,1269	11.00	32.00	75.00
01-684-208(8/62-Dell)	10.00	30.00	70.00
1(10071-307, G.K.), 2	7.00	21.00	50.00

NOTE: *All have Clint Eastwood photo-c.* **Tufts** *a-1028.*

RAWHIDE KID
3/55 - No. 16, 9/57; No. 17, 8/60 - No. 151, 5/79
Atlas/Marvel Comics (CnPC No. 1-16/AMI No. 17-30)

1-Rawhide Kid, his horse Apache & sidekick Randy begin; Wyatt Earp app.	21.50	64.00	150.00
2	10.00	30.00	70.00
3-5	5.70	17.00	40.00
6,8-10	4.50	14.00	32.00
7-Williamson-a, 4 pgs.	5.70	17.00	40.00
11-15	2.85	8.50	20.00
16-Torres-a	3.15	9.50	22.00
17-Origin by J. Kirby	5.00	15.00	35.00
18-22,24-30	2.30	7.00	16.00
23-Origin by J. Kirby	4.30	13.00	30.00
31,32,36-44: 40-Two-Gun Kid x-over. 42-1st Larry Lieber issue	1.70	5.00	12.00
33-35-Davis-a. 35-Intro & death of The Raven	2.30	7.00	16.00
45-Origin retold	2.30	7.00	16.00
46-Toth-a	2.30	7.00	16.00
47-70: 50-Kid Colt x-over. 64-Kid Colt story. 66-Two-Gun Kid story.			
67-Kid Colt story	1.00	3.00	7.00
71-85: 79-Williamson-a(r)	.70	2.00	4.00
86-Origin-r; Williamson-a r-/Ringo Kid #13, 4 pgs.	.70	2.00	4.00
87-99,101-115: Last new story	.40	1.25	2.50
100-Origin retold & expanded	.50	1.50	3.00
116-151	.40	1.25	2.50

	Good	Fine	N-Mint
Special 1(9/71)-All Kirby/Ayers reprints	.40	1.25	2.50

NOTE: **Ayers** *a-13, 14, 16.* **Colan** *a-5, 35, 37; c-145p, 148p.* **Davis** *a-125r.* **Everett** *a-54i, 65, 66, 88, 96i, 148i(r).* **Gulacy** *c-147.* **Heath** *c-4.* **G. Kane** *c-101, 144.* **Keller** *a-5.* **Kirby** *a-17-32, 34, 42, 43, 84, 86, 92, 109r, 112r; Spec. 1; c-17-35, 37, 40, 41, 43-47, 137.* **Maneely** *c-1, 2, 5, 14.* **Morisi** *a-13.* **Severin** *a-16; c-8, 13.* **Torres** *a-99r.* **Tuska** *a-14.* **Williamson** *a-95r, 111r.*

RAWHIDE KID
Aug, 1985 - No. 4, Nov, 1985 (mini-series)
Marvel Comics Group

1-4		.50	1.00

REAGAN'S RAIDERS
Aug, 1986 - No. 3, 1987? ($1.95, B&W)
Solson Publications

1-3-Ayers-a	.35	1.00	2.00

REAL ADVENTURE COMICS (Action Adventure #2 on)
April, 1955
Gilmor Magazines

1	1.50	4.50	10.00

REAL CLUE CRIME STORIES (Formerly Clue Comics)
V2#4, June, 1947 - V8No.3, May, 1953
Hillman Periodicals

V2#4(#1)-S&K c/a(3); Dan Barry-a	13.00	40.00	90.00
5-7-S&K c/a(3-4); 7-Iron Lady app.	11.00	32.00	75.00
8-12	2.30	7.00	16.00
V3#1-8,10-12, V4#1-3,5-8,11,12	2.00	6.00	14.00
V3#9-Used in **SOTI**, pg. 102	5.00	15.00	35.00
V4#4-S&K-a	3.50	10.50	24.00
V4#9,10-Krigstein-a	3.70	11.00	26.00
V5#1-5,7,8,10,12	1.50	4.50	10.00
6,9,11-Krigstein-a	2.85	8.50	20.00
V6#1-5,8,9,11	1.30	4.00	9.00
6,7,10,12-Krigstein-a. 10-Bondage-c	2.65	8.00	18.00
V7#1-3,5,7-11, V8#1-3	1.30	4.00	9.00
4,12-Krigstein-a	2.65	8.00	18.00
6-1 pg. Frazetta ad	1.30	4.00	9.00

NOTE: **Barry** *a-9, 10; c-V2#8.* **Briefer** *a-V6#6.* **Fuje** *a- V2#7(2), 8, 11.* **Infantino** *a-V2#8; c-V2#11.* **Lawrence** *a-V3#8, V5#7.* **Powell** *a-V4#11, 12. V5#4, 5, 7 are 68 pgs.*

REAL EXPERIENCES (Formerly Tiny Tessie)
No. 25, January, 1950
Atlas Comics (20CC)

25	1.70	5.00	12.00

REAL FACT COMICS
Mar-Apr, 1946 - No. 21, July-Aug, 1949
National Periodical Publications

1-S&K-a; Harry Houdini story; Just Imagine begins (not by Finlay)	21.50	64.00	150.00
2-S&K-a; Rin-Tin-Tin story	13.50	40.00	95.00
3-H.G. Wells, Lon Chaney story	8.00	24.00	55.00
4-Virgil Finlay-a on 'Just Imagine' begins, ends #12 (2 pgs. ea.); Jimmy Stewart story	13.50	40.00	95.00
5-Batman/Robin-c; 5pg. story about creation of Batman & Robin; Tom Mix story	68.00	205.00	480.00
6-Origin & 1st app. Tommy Tomorrow by Finlay; Flag-c; 1st writing by Harlan Ellison (letter column, non-professional); 1st man to reach Mars story	50.00	150.00	350.00
7-(No. 6 on inside)-Roussos-a	6.00	18.00	42.00
8-2nd app. Tommy Tomorrow by Finlay	25.00	75.00	175.00
9-S&K-a; Glenn Miller story	11.00	32.00	75.00
10-Vigilante by Meskin	10.00	30.00	70.00
11,12: 11-Kinstler-a	6.00	18.00	42.00
13-Dale Evans and Tommy Tomorrow cover/stories	21.50	64.00	150.00

Rawhide Kid #2, © MEG

Real Clue Crime Stories V2#6, © HILL

Real Fact Comics #13, © DC

Real Life Comics #2, © STD

Real Love #46, © ACE

Real Screen Comics #16, © DC

	Good	Fine	N-Mint
REAL FACT COMICS (continued)			
14,17,18: 14-Will Rogers story	5.50	16.50	38.00
15-Nuclear Explosion part-c	6.00	18.00	42.00
16-Tommy Tomorrow app.; 1st Planeteers?	21.50	64.00	150.00
19-Sir Arthur Conan Doyle story	5.70	17.00	40.00
20-Kubert-a, 4 pgs; Daniel Boone story	9.30	28.00	65.00
21-Kubert-a, 2 pgs; Kit Carson story	5.50	16.50	38.00

NOTE: *Roussos a-1-4.*

REAL FUN OF DRIVING!!, THE
1965, 1967 (Regular size)
Chrysler Corp.

	Good	Fine	N-Mint
Shaffenberger-a, 12pgs.	.85	2.50	5.00

REAL FUNNIES
Jan, 1943 - No. 3, June, 1943
Nedor Publishing Co.

	Good	Fine	N-Mint
1-Funny animal, humor; Black Terrier app. (clone of The Black Terror)	11.50	34.00	80.00
2,3	5.70	17.00	40.00

REAL GHOSTBUSTERS, THE (Also see Slimer and. . .)
Aug, 1988 - Present ($1.75, color)
Now Comics

	Good	Fine	N-Mint
1-Based on Ghostbusters movie	.50	1.50	3.00
2-22	.35	1.00	2.00

REAL HEROES COMICS
Sept, 1941 - No. 16, Oct, 1946
Parents' Magazine Institute

	Good	Fine	N-Mint
1-Roosevelt c/story	12.00	36.00	84.00
2	4.50	14.00	32.00
3-5,7-10	3.50	10.50	24.00
6-Lou Gehrig c/story	5.70	17.00	40.00
11-16: 13-Kiefer-a	2.30	7.00	16.00

REAL HIT
1944 (Savings Bond premium)
Fox Features Publications

	Good	Fine	N-Mint
1-Blue Beetle-r	8.50	25.50	60.00

NOTE: *Two versions exist, with and without covers. The coverless version has the title, No. 1 and price printed at top of splash page.*

REALISTIC ROMANCES
July-Aug, 1951 - No. 17, Aug-Sept, 1954 (no No. 9-14)
Realistic Comics/Avon Periodicals

	Good	Fine	N-Mint
1-Kinstler-a; c/Avon paperback 211	8.50	25.50	60.00
2	4.00	12.00	28.00
3,4	3.35	10.00	23.00
5,8-Kinstler-a	3.65	11.00	25.00
6-c-/Diversey Prize Novels 6; Kinstler-a	4.00	12.00	28.00
7-Evans-a?; c/Avon paperback 360	4.00	12.00	28.00
15,17	2.65	8.00	18.00
16-Kinstler marijuana story-r/Romantic Love #6	5.00	15.00	35.00
I.W. Reprint #1,8,9	.30	.90	1.80

NOTE: *Astarita a-2-4, 7, 8.*

REAL LIFE COMICS
Sept, 1941 - No. 59, Sept, 1952
Nedor/Better/Standard Publ./Pictorial Magazine No. 13

	Good	Fine	N-Mint
1-Uncle Sam c/story	13.50	40.00	95.00
2	6.50	19.50	45.00
3-Hitler cover	10.00	30.00	70.00
4,5: 4-Story of American flag "Old Glory"	4.00	12.00	28.00
6-10	3.50	10.50	24.00
11-20: 17-Albert Einstein story.	2.65	8.00	18.00
21-23,25,26,28-30: 29-A-Bomb story	2.00	6.00	14.00
24-Story of Baseball	3.50	10.50	24.00

	Good	Fine	N-Mint
27-Schomburg A-Bomb-c; story of A-Bomb	4.30	13.00	30.00
31-33,35,36,42-44,48,49	1.50	4.50	10.00
34,37-41,45-47: 34-Jimmy Stewart story. 37-Story of motion pictures; Bing Crosby story. 38-Jane Froman story. 39-"1,000,000 A.D." story. 40-Bob Feller story. 41-Jimmie Foxx story; "Home Run" Baker story. 45-Story of Olympic games; Burl Ives story. 46-Douglas Fairbanks Jr. & Sr. story. 47-George Gershwin story	2.00	6.00	14.00
50-Frazetta-a, 5 pgs.	11.50	34.00	80.00
51-Jules Verne "Journey to the Moon" by Evans	5.70	17.00	40.00
52-Frazetta-a, 4 pgs.; Severin/Elder-a(2); Evans-a	12.00	36.00	84.00
53-57-Severin/Elder-a	3.50	10.50	24.00
58-Severin/Elder-a(2)	3.70	11.00	26.00
59-1pg. Frazetta; Severin/Elder-a	3.50	10.50	24.00

NOTE: *Some issues had two titles. Guardineer a-40(2), 44. Schomburg c-1, 2, 4, 5, 7, 11, 13-21, 23, 24, 26, 28, 30-32, 34-40, 42, 44-47. Photo-c 5, 6.*

REAL LIFE SECRETS (Real Secrets #2 on)
Sept, 1949 (One shot)
Ace Periodicals

	Good	Fine	N-Mint
1-Painted-c	3.00	9.00	21.00

REAL LIFE STORY OF FESS PARKER (Magazine)
1955
Dell Publishing Co.

	Good	Fine	N-Mint
1	5.70	17.00	40.00

REAL LIFE TALES OF SUSPENSE (See Suspense)

REAL LOVE (Formerly Hap Hazard)
No. 25, April, 1949 - No. 76, Nov, 1956
Ace Periodicals (A. A. Wyn)

	Good	Fine	N-Mint
25	3.50	10.50	24.00
26	1.70	5.00	12.00
27-L. B. Cole-a	3.00	9.00	21.00
28-35	1.15	3.50	8.00
36-66: 66-Last pre-code (2/55)	1.00	3.00	7.00
67-76	.75	2.25	5.00

NOTE: *Photo-c No. 50-76. Painted-c No. 46.*

REALM, THE
Feb, 1986 - No. 20? ($1.50-$1.95, B&W)
Arrow Comics/WeeBee Comics #13/Caliber Press #14 on

	Good	Fine	N-Mint
1	.85	2.50	5.00
2		.65	1.30
3-20: 13-Begin $1.95-c	.25	.75	1.50
Book 1 ($4.95, B&W)	.85	2.50	4.95

REAL McCOYS, THE (TV)
No. 1071, 1-3/60 - 5- 5-7/1962 (Photo-c)
Dell Publishing Co.

	Good	Fine	N-Mint
4-Color 1071-Toth-a	7.00	21.00	50.00
4-Color 1134-Toth-a	7.00	21.00	50.00
4-Color 1193,1265	5.70	17.00	40.00
01-689-207 (5-7/62)	5.00	15.00	35.00

REAL SCREEN COMICS (#1 titled Real Screen Funnies; TV Screen Cartoons #129-138)
Spring, 1945 - No. 128, May-June, 1959 (#1-40: 52 pgs.)
National Periodical Publications

	Good	Fine	N-Mint
1-The Fox & the Crow, Flippity & Flop, Tito & His Burro begin	55.00	165.00	385.00
2	26.50	79.00	185.00
3-5	14.00	42.00	100.00
6-10 (2-3/47)	10.00	30.00	70.00
11-20 (10-11/48): 13-Crow x-over in Flippity & Flop	8.00	24.00	55.00

REAL SCREEN COMICS (continued)

	Good	Fine	N-Mint
21-30 (6-7/50)	5.50	16.50	38.00
31-50	3.70	11.00	26.00
51-99	2.65	8.00	18.00
100	3.50	10.50	24.00
101-128	2.00	6.00	14.00

REAL SECRETS (Formerly Real Life Secrets)
No. 2, Nov, 1950 - No. 5, May, 1950
Ace Periodicals

2	3.00	9.00	21.00
3-5: 3-Photo-c	1.60	4.80	11.00

REAL SPORTS COMICS (All Sports Comics #2 on)
Oct-Nov, 1948 (52 pgs.)
Hillman Periodicals

1-12 pg. Powell-a	14.00	42.00	100.00

REAL WAR STORIES
July, 1987 (52 pgs., $2.00, color)
Eclipse Comics

1-Bolland, Bissette, Totleben-a	.35	1.00	2.00
1-2nd print (2/88)	.35	1.00	2.00

REAL WESTERN HERO (Formerly Wow #1-69; becomes Western Hero #76 on)
No. 70, Sept, 1948 - No. 75, Feb, 1949 (All 52 pgs.)
Fawcett Publications

70(#1)-Tom Mix, Monte Hale, Hopalong Cassidy, Young Falcon begin			
	18.50	56.00	130.00
71-Gabby Hayes begins; Captain Tootsie by Beck			
	11.50	34.00	80.00
72-75: 72-Captain Tootsie by Beck. 75-Big Bow and Little Arrow app.			
	11.50	34.00	80.00

NOTE: *Painted/photo c-70-73; painted c-74,75.*

REAL WEST ROMANCES
4-5/49 - V1#6, 3/50; V2/1, Apr-May, 1950 (All 52 pgs. & photo-c)
Crestwood Publishing Co./Prize Publ.

V1#1-S&K-a(p)	8.00	24.00	56.00
2-Spanking panel	7.00	21.00	50.00
3-Kirby-a(p) only	3.50	10.50	24.00
4-S&K-a; Whip Wilson, Reno Browne photo-c			
	5.70	17.00	40.00
5-Audie Murphy, Gale Storm photo-c; S&K-a			
	4.50	14.00	32.00
6-S&K-a	4.50	14.00	32.00
V2#1-Kirby-a(p)	3.50	10.50	24.00

NOTE: *Meskin a-V1#5. Severin & Elder a-V1#3-6, V2#1. Leonard Starr a-1-3. Photo-c V1#1-5, V2#1.*

REAP THE WILD WIND (See Cinema Comics Herald)

REBEL, THE (See 4-Color #1076,1138,1207,1262)

RECORD BOOK OF FAMOUS POLICE CASES
1949 (132 pages) (25 cents)
St. John Publishing Co.

nn-Kubert-a(3) r-/Son of Sinbad; Baker-c	18.00	54.00	125.00

RED ARROW
May-June, 1951 - No. 3, Oct, 1951
P. L. Publishing Co.

1	3.70	11.00	26.00
2,3	2.30	7.00	16.00

RED BALL COMIC BOOK
1947 (Red Ball Shoes giveaway)
Parents' Magazine Institute

Reprints from True Comics	1.50	4.50	10.00

RED BAND COMICS
Feb, 1945 - No. 4, May, 1945
Enwil Associates

	Good	Fine	N-Mint
1	11.00	32.00	75.00
2-Origin Bogeyman & Santanas	9.30	28.00	65.00
3,4-Captain Wizard app. in both; each has identical contents/cover			
	8.00	24.00	55.00

RED CIRCLE COMICS
Jan, 1945 - No. 4, April, 1945
Rural Home Publications (Enwil)

1-The Prankster & Red Riot begin	11.00	32.00	75.00
2-Starr-a; The Judge (costumed hero) app.	8.00	24.00	56.00
3,4-Starr-c/a. 3-The Prankster not in costume	5.70	17.00	40.00
4-(dated 4/45)-Leftover covers to #4 were later restapled over early 1950s coverless comics. Variations in the coverless comics used are endless; Woman Outlaws, Dorothy Lamour, Crime Does Not Pay, Sabu, Diary Loves, Love Confessions & Young Love V3/3 known	5.00	15.00	35.00

RED CIRCLE SORCERY (Chilling Adventures in Sorcery #1-5)
No. 6, Apr, 1974 - No. 11, Feb, 1975
Red Circle Productions (Archie)

6-11: 8-Only app. The Cobra		.40	.80

NOTE: *Chaykin a-6, 10. B. Jones a-7(w/Wrightson, Kaluta, J. Jones). McWilliams a-10. Morrow a-6, 8, 11; c-6-11. Thorne a-8, 10. Toth a-8, 9. Wood a-10.*

RED DOG (See Night Music #7)

RED DRAGON COMICS (1st Series) (Formerly Trail Blazers; see Super Magician V5#7, 8)
No. 5, Jan, 1943 - No. 9, Jan, 1944
Street & Smith Publications

5-Origin Red Rover, the Crimson Crimebuster; Rex King, Man of Adventure, Captain Jack Commando, & The Minute Man begin; text origin Red Dragon; Binder-a	35.00	105.00	245.00
6-Origin The Black Crusader & Red Dragon (3/43)			
	26.00	77.00	180.00
7,8: 8-The Red Knight app.	20.00	60.00	140.00
9-Origin Chuck Magnon, Immortal Man	20.00	60.00	140.00

RED DRAGON COMICS (2nd Series)(See Super Magician V2#8)
Nov, 1947 - No. 6, Jan, 1949; No. 7, July, 1949
Street & Smith Publications

1-Red Dragon begins; Elliman, Nigel app.; Ed Cartier-c/a			
	34.00	102.00	240.00
2-Cartier-c	27.00	81.00	190.00
3-1st app. Dr. Neff by Powell; Elliman, Nigel app.			
	21.50	64.00	150.00
4-Cartier c/a	24.00	73.00	170.00
5-7	17.00	51.00	120.00

NOTE: *Maneely a-5, 7. Powell a-2-7; c-3, 5, 7.*

REDDY GOOSE
No. 2, Jan, 1959 - No. 16, July, 1962 (Giveaway)
International Shoe Co. (Western Printing)

nn,2-16	.50	1.50	3.00

REDDY KILOWATT (5 cents) (Also see Story of Edison)
1946 - No. 2, 1947; 1956 - 1960 (no month) (16 pgs.; paper cover)
Educational Comics (E. C.)

nn-Reddy Made Magic	12.00	35.00	70.00
nn-Reddy Made Magic (1958)	5.35	16.00	32.00
2-Edison, the Man Who Changed the World (¾ smaller than #1)			
	12.00	35.00	70.00
...Comic Book 2 (1954)-"Light's Diamond Jubilee"			
	6.75	20.00	40.00
...Comic Book 2 (1958)-"Wizard of Light," 16 pgs.			
	5.35	16.00	32.00

Real Western Hero #70, © FAW

Record Book Of Famous Police Cases nn, © STJ

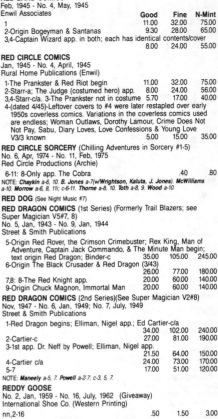

Reddy Kilowatt nn (1946), © WMG

The Red Iceberg, © CG

Red Mask #54, © Sussex

Red Ryder Comics #1, © DELL

	Good	Fine	N-Mint
REDDY KILOWATT (continued)			
...Comic Book 3 (1956)-"The Space Kite," 8 pgs.; Orlando story;			
regular size	5.35	16.00	32.00
...Comic Book 3 (1960)-"The Space Kite," 8 pgs.; Orlando story;			
regular size	4.75	14.00	28.00

NOTE: *Several copies surfaced in 1979.*

REDDY MADE MAGIC
1956, 1958 (16 pages) (paper cover)
Educational Comics (E. C.)

1-Reddy Kilowatt-r (splash panel changed)	8.00	24.00	48.00
1 (1958 edition)	5.00	15.00	30.00

RED EAGLE (See Feature Books #16, McKay)

REDEYE (See Comics Reading Libraries)

RED FOX (Formerly Manhunt! #1-14)
No. 15, 1954
Magazine Enterprises

15(A-1 108)-Undercover Girl app.; L.B. Cole c/a (Red Fox); r-from			
Manhunt; Powell-a	8.50	25.50	60.00

REDFOX
Jan, 1986 - No. 20? ($1.75-$2.00, B&W)
Harrier Comics/Valkyrie Press #11 on

1	1.00	3.00	6.00
1-2nd print	.25	.75	1.50
2	.40	1.25	2.50
3	.35	1.00	2.00
4	.25	.75	1.50
5-20: 11-Begin $2.00-c?		.65	1.30

RED GOOSE COMIC SELECTIONS (See Comic Selections)

RED HAWK (See A-1 Comics #90, Bobby Benson's . . . #14-16 & Straight Arrow #2)

RED HEAT IN 3-D See Blackthorne 3-D Series #45)

RED ICEBERG, THE
1960 (10 cents) (16 pgs.) (Communist propaganda)
Impact Publ. (Catechetical Guild)

(Rare)-'We The People'-back-c	37.00	110.00	240.00
2nd version-'Impact Press'-back-c	43.00	130.00	280.00

NOTE: *This book was the Guild's last anti-communist propaganda book and had very limited circulation. 3 - 4 copies surfaced in 1979 from the defunct publisher's files. Other copies do turn up.*

RED MASK (Formerly Tim Holt; see Best Comics, Blazing Six-Guns)
No. 42, 6-7/1954 - No. 53, 5/56; No. 54, 9/57
Magazine Enterprises No. 42-53/Sussex No. 54

42-Ghost Rider by Ayers continues, ends #50; Black Phantom			
continues; 3-D effect c/stories begin	13.00	40.00	90.00
43-3-D effect-c/stories	11.00	32.00	75.00
44-50: 3-D effect stories only. 50-Last Ghost Rider			
	10.00	30.00	70.00
51-The Presto Kid begins by Ayers (1st app.); Presto Kid-c begins,			
ends #54; last 3-D effect story	10.00	30.00	70.00
52-Origin The Presto Kid	10.00	30.00	70.00
53,54-Last Black Phantom	7.00	21.00	50.00
I.W. Reprint #1 (r-/#52), 2,3 (r-/#51), 8 (nd; Kinstler-c)			
	.80	2.40	4.80

NOTE: *Ayers art on Ghost Rider & Presto Kid. Bolle art in all (Red Mask); c-43, 44, 49. Guardineer a-52. Black Phantom in #42-44, 47-50, 53, 54.*

RED MOUNTAIN FEATURING QUANTRELL'S RAIDERS
1952 (Movie) (Also see Jesse James #28)
Avon Periodicals

nn-Alan Ladd; Kinstler c/a	14.00	42.00	100.00

"RED" RABBIT COMICS
Jan, 1947 - No. 22, Aug-Sept, 1951
Dearfield Comic/J. Charles Laue Publ. Co.

	Good	Fine	N-Mint
1	5.00	15.00	35.00
2	2.65	8.00	18.00
3-10	2.00	6.00	14.00
11-22: 18-Flying Saucer-c (1/51)	1.50	4.50	10.00

RED RAVEN COMICS (Human Torch #2 on)
August, 1940 (Also see Sub-Mariner #26, 2nd series)
Timely Comics

1-Origin Red Raven; Comet Pierce & Mercury by Kirby, The Human			
Top & The Eternal Brain; intro. Magar, the Mystic & only app.;			
Kirby-c	457.00	1150.00	3200.00
(Prices vary widely on this book)			

RED RYDER COMICS (Hi Spot #2)(Movies, radio)
(Also see Crackajack Funnies)
9/40; No. 3, 8/41 - No. 5, 12/41; No. 6, 4/42 - No. 151, 4-6/57
Hawley Publ. No. 1-5/Dell Publishing Co.(K.K.) No. 6 on

1-Red Ryder, his horse Thunder, Little Beaver & his horse Papoose			
strip reprints begin by Fred Harman; 1st meeting of Red & Little			
Beaver; Harman line-drawn-c #1-85	84.00	253.00	590.00
3-(Scarce)-Alley Oop, King of the Royal Mtd., Capt. Easy, Freckles			
& His Friends, Myra North & Dan Dunn strip-r begin			
	53.00	160.00	370.00
4,5	28.50	86.00	200.00
6-1st Dell issue	28.50	86.00	200.00
7-10	21.50	64.00	150.00
11-20	16.00	48.00	110.00
21-32-Last Alley Oop, Dan Dunn, Capt. Easy, Freckles			
	10.00	30.00	70.00
33-40 (52 pgs.)	6.50	19.50	45.00
41 (52 pgs.)-Rocky Lane photo back-c; photo back-c begin, end #57			
	7.00	21.00	50.00
42-46 (52 pgs.). 46-Last Red Ryder strip-r	5.70	17.00	40.00
47-53 (52 pgs.). 47-New stories on Red Ryder begin			
	4.30	13.00	30.00
54-57 (36 pgs.)	3.70	11.00	26.00
58-73 (36 pgs.). 73-Last King of the Royal Mtd. strip-r by Jim Gary			
	3.50	10.50	24.00
74-85,93 (36 pgs.)-Harman line-drawn-c	3.70	11.00	26.00
86-92 (52 pgs.)-Harman painted-c	3.70	11.00	26.00
94-96 (36 pgs.)-Harman painted-c	2.65	8.00	18.00
97,98,107,108 (36 pgs.)-Harman line-drawn-c	2.65	8.00	18.00
99,101-106 (36 pgs.)-Jim Bannon Photo-c	2.65	8.00	18.00
100 (36 pgs.)-Bannon photo-c	3.00	9.00	21.00
109-118 (52 pgs.)-Harman line-drawn-c	2.00	6.00	14.00
119-129 (52 pgs.). 119-Painted-c begin, not by Harman, end #151			
	1.70	5.00	12.00
130-144 (36 pgs., #130-on)	1.50	4.50	10.00
145-148: 145-Title change to Red Ryder Ranch Magazine with photos			
	1.30	4.00	9.00
149-151: 149-Title changed to Red Ryder Ranch Comics			
	1.30	4.00	9.00
4-Color 916 (7/58)	1.60	4.80	11.00
Buster Brown Shoes Giveaway (1941, 32pgs., color, soft-c)			
	19.00	57.00	132.00
Red Ryder Super Book Of Comics 10 (1944; paper-c; 32 pgs.; blank			
back-c)-Magic Morro app.	19.00	57.00	132.00
Red Ryder Victory Patrol-nn(1944, 32 pgs.)-r-/#43,44; comic has a			
paper-c & is stapled inside a triple cardboard fold-out-c; contains			
membership card, decoder, map of R.R. home range, etc. Herky			
app. (Langendorf Bread giveaway; sub-titled 'Super Book of			
Comics')	35.00	105.00	245.00
Wells Lamont Corp. giveaway (1950)-16 pgs. in color; regular size;			
paper-c; 1941-r	17.00	52.00	120.00

NOTE: *Fred Harman a-1-99; c-1-98, 107-118. Don Red Barry, Allan Rocky Lane, Wild Bill Elliott & Jim Bannon starred as Red Ryder in the movies. Robert Blake starred as Little Beaver.*

RED RYDER PAINT BOOK
1941 (148 pages) (8½x11½'')
Whitman Publishing Co.

	Good	Fine	N-Mint
Reprints 1940 daily strips	14.00	42.00	100.00

RED SEAL COMICS
No. 14, 10/45 - No. 18, 10/46; No. 19, 6/47 - No. 22, 12/47
Harry 'A' Chesler/Superior Publ. No. 19 on

14-The Black Dwarf begins; Little Nemo app; bondage/hypo-c; Tuska-a	20.00	60.00	140.00
15-Torture story	16.00	48.00	110.00
16-Used in **SOTI**, pg. 181, illo-"Outside the forbidden pages of de Sade, you find draining a girl's blood only in children's comics;" drug club story r-later in Crime Reporter #1; Veiled Avenger & Barry Kuda app; Tuska-a	22.00	65.00	154.00
17-Lady Satan, Yankee Girl & Sky Chief app; Tuska-a	13.00	40.00	90.00
18,20-Lady Satan & Sky Chief app.	13.00	40.00	90.00
19-No Black Dwarf-on cover only; Zor, El Tigre app.	10.00	30.00	70.00
21-Lady Satan & Black Dwarf app.	10.00	30.00	70.00
22-Zor, Rocketman app. (68 pgs.)	10.00	30.00	70.00

REDSKIN (Famous Western Badmen #13 on)
Sept, 1950 - No. 12, Oct, 1952
Youthful Magazines

1	4.50	14.00	32.00
2	2.65	8.00	18.00
3-12: 6,12-Bondage-c	2.15	6.50	15.00

RED SONJA (Also see Conan #23, Kull & The Barbarians, Marvel Feature & Savage Sword Of Conan #1)
1/77 - No. 15, 5/79; V1/1, 2/83 - V2/2, 3/83; V3/1, 8/83 - V3/4, 2/84; V3/5, 1/85 - V3/13, 1986
Marvel Comics Group

1	.50	1.50	3.00
2-5	.35	1.00	2.00
6-15, V1#1,2		.50	1.00
V3#1-4 ($1.00)		.60	1.20
5-13 (65-75 cents)		.50	1.00

NOTE: **Brunner** c-12-14. **J. Buscema** a(p)-12, 13, 15; c-V1No.1. **Nebres** a-V3/3i. **N. Redondo** a-8i, V3/2i, 3i. **Simonson** a-V3No.1. **Thorne** a-1-11; c-1-11.

RED SONJA: THE MOVIE
Nov, 1985 - No. 2, Dec, 1985 (limited-series)
Marvel Comics Group

1,2-Movie adapt-r/Marvel Super Spec. #38		.40	.80

RED TORNADO (See Justice League of America #64)
July, 1985 - No. 4, Oct, 1985 (mini-series)
DC Comics

1-4		.50	1.00

RED WARRIOR
Jan, 1951 - No. 6, Dec, 1951
Marvel/Atlas Comics (TCI)

1-Tuska-a	5.70	17.00	40.00
2-Tuska-c	3.50	10.50	24.00
3-6: 4-Origin White Wing, his horse	2.65	8.00	18.00

RED WOLF (See Avengers #80 & Marvel Spotlight #1)
May, 1972 - No. 9, Sept, 1973
Marvel Comics Group

1-Kane/Severin-c		.30	.60
2-9: 9-Origin sidekick, Lobo (wolf)		.25	.50

NOTE: **G. Kane** c-1p, 2.

REESE'S PIECES
Oct, 1985 - No. 2, Oct, 1985 ($1.75, color, Baxter)

Eclipse Comics

	Good	Fine	N-Mint
1,2-B&W-r in color	.30	.90	1.80

REFORM SCHOOL GIRL!
1951
Realistic Comics

nn-Used in **SOTI**, pg. 358, & cover ill. with caption "Comic books are supposed to be like fairy tales"	85.00	255.00	600.00
(Prices vary widely on this book)			

NOTE: *The cover and title originated from a digest-sized book published by Diversey Publishing Co. of Chicago in 1948. The original book "House of Fury," Doubleday, came out in 1941. The girl's real name which appears on the cover of the digest and comic is Marty Collins, Canadian model and ice skating star who posed for this special color photograph for the Diversey novel.*

REGENTS ILLUSTRATED CLASSICS
1981 (Plus more recent reprintings)
(48 pgs., b&w-a with 14 pages of teaching helps)
Prentice Hall Regents, Englewood Cliffs, NJ 07632

NOTE: This series contains Classics Ill. art, and was produced from the same illegal source as **Cassette Books**. But when Twin Circle sued to stop the sale of the Cassette Books, they decided to permit this series to continue. This series was produced as a teaching aid. The 20 title series is divided into four levels based upon number of basic words used therein. There is also a teacher's manual for each level. All of the titles are still available from the publisher for about $5 each retail. The number to call for mail order purchases is (201)767-5937. Almost all of the issues have new covers taken from some interior art panel. Here is a list of the series by Regents ident. no. and the Classics Ill. counterpart.

16770(CI#24-A2) 18333(CI#3-A2) 21668(CI#13-A2) 32224(CI#21) 33051(CI#26) 35788(CI#84) 37153(CI#16) 44460(CI#19-A2) 44808(CI#18-A2) 52395(CI#4-A2) 58627(CI#5-A2) 60067(CI#30) 68405(CI#23-A1) 70302(CI#29) 78192(CI#7-A2) 78193(CI#10-A2) 79679(CI#85) 92046(CI#1-A2) 93062(CI#64) 93512(CI#25)

REGGIE (Formerly Archie's Rival... ; Reggie & Me #19 on)
No. 15, Sept, 1963 - No. 18, Nov, 1965
Archie Publications

15(9/63), 16(10/64)	4.50	13.50	32.00
17(8/65), 18(11/65)	4.50	13.50	32.00

NOTE: *Cover title No. 15,16 is Archie's Rival....*

REGGIE AND ME (Formerly Reggie)
No. 19, 8/66 - No. 126, 9/80 (No. 50-68: 52 pgs.)
Archie Publications

19-Evilheart app.	2.00	6.00	12.00
20-23-Evilheart app.; with Pureheart #22	1.00	3.00	6.00
24-40	.35	1.00	2.00
41-60		.40	.80
61-126		.25	.50

REGGIE'S JOKES (See Reggie's Wise Guy Jokes)

REGGIE'S WISE GUY JOKES
Aug, 1968 - No. 60, Jan, 1982 (#5 on are Giants)
Archie Publications

1	1.70	5.00	12.00
2-4	.70	2.00	5.00
5-10	.35	1.00	2.00
11-28		.40	.80
29-60		.25	.50

REGISTERED NURSE
Summer, 1963
Charlton Comics

1-R/Nurse Betsy Crane & Cynthia Doyle	.35	1.00	2.00

REG'LAR FELLERS (See All-American Comics, Popular Comics & Treasure Box of Famous Comics)
1921 - 1929
Cupples & Leon Co./MS Publishng Co.

1(1921)-52 pgs. B&W dailies (Cupples & Leon, 10x10'')	10.00	30.00	70.00
1925, 48 pgs. B&W dailies (MS Publ.)	10.00	30.00	70.00

Red Seal Comics #14, © CHES

Red Sonja #10, © MEG

Reg'lar Fellers, 1929 Soft-c, © C & L

The Return Of Gorgo #3, © CC

Return Of The Outlaw #6, © TOBY

Rex Dexter Of Mars #1, © FOX

	Good	Fine	N-Mint
REG'LAR FELLERS (continued)			
Softcover (1929, nn, 36 pgs.)	10.00	30.00	70.00
Hardcover (1929)-B&W reprints, 96 pgs.	11.00	32.00	75.00

REG'LAR FELLERS
No. 5, Nov, 1947 - No. 6, Mar, 1948
Visual Editions (Standard)

	Good	Fine	N-Mint
5,6	3.70	11.00	26.00

REG'LAR FELLERS HEROIC (See Heroic Comics)

REID FLEMING, WORLD'S TOUGHEST MILKMAN
8/86; V2#1, 12/86 - V2#3, 12/88; V2#4, 11/89 (B&W)
Eclipse Comics

	Good	Fine	N-Mint
1 (3rd print, large size, 8/86, $2.50)	1.00	3.00	6.00
V2#1 (12/86, regular size, $2.00)	.50	1.50	3.00
1-2nd print, 3rd print ($2.00, 2/89)	.40	1.25	2.50
1-4th printing ($2.00, 1990)	.35	1.00	2.00
2,3 ($2.00)	.40	1.25	2.50
V2#2-2nd print	.35	1.00	2.00
4	.35	1.00	2.00

RELUCTANT DRAGON, THE (See 4-Color #13)

REMEMBER PEARL HARBOR
1942 (68 pages)
Street & Smith Publications

	Good	Fine	N-Mint
nn-Uncle Sam-c	21.50	64.00	150.00

RENO BROWNE, HOLLYWOOD'S GREATEST COWGIRL (Formerly
Margie Comics; Apache Kid #53 on)
No. 50, April, 1950 - No. 52, Sept, 1950 (52 pgs.)
Marvel Comics (MPC)

	Good	Fine	N-Mint
50-Photo-c	11.50	34.00	80.00
51,52: 51-Photo-c	10.00	30.00	70.00

REPTILICUS (Reptisaurus #3 on)
Aug, 1961 - No. 2, Oct, 1961
Charlton Comics

	Good	Fine	N-Mint
1 (Movie)	5.70	17.00	40.00
2	4.30	13.00	30.00

REPTISAURUS (Reptilicus #1,2)
Jan, 1962 - No. 8, Dec, 1962; Summer, 1963
Charlton Comics

	Good	Fine	N-Mint
V2#3-8: 8-Montes/Bache c/a	2.00	6.00	14.00
Special Edition 1 (1963)	2.00	6.00	14.00

RESCUERS, THE (See Walt Disney Showcase #40)

RESTLESS GUN (See 4-Color #934,986,1045,1089,1146)

RETIEF (Keith Laumer's)
April, 1987 - No. 6, 1988 ($1.75, B&W)
Mad Dog Graphics

	Good	Fine	N-Mint
1-6	.30	.90	1.80

RETIEF OF THE C.D.T.
1988 ($2.00, B&W)
Mad Dog Graphics

	Good	Fine	N-Mint
1	.35	1.00	2.00

RETURN FROM WITCH MOUNTAIN (See Walt Disney Showcase #44)

RETURN OF GORGO, THE (Formerly Gorgo's Revenge)
No. 2, Aug, 1963 - No. 3, Fall, 1964
Charlton Comics

	Good	Fine	N-Mint
2,3-Ditko-a, c-#3; based on M.G.M. movie	3.50	10.50	24.00

RETURN OF KONGA, THE (Konga's Revenge #2 on)
1962
Charlton Comics

	Good	Fine	N-Mint
nn	3.00	9.00	21.00

RETURN OF MEGATON MAN (Also see Megaton Man)
July, 1988 - No. 3, 1988? ($2.00, color, mini-series)
Kitchen Sink Press

	Good	Fine	N-Mint
1-3: Simpson-c/a	.35	1.00	2.00

RETURN OF THE OUTLAW
Feb, 1953 - No. 11, 1955
Toby Press (Minoan)

	Good	Fine	N-Mint
1-Billy the Kid	3.70	11.00	26.00
2	2.00	6.00	14.00
3-11	1.50	4.50	10.00

REVEALING LOVE STORIES (See Fox Giants)

REVEALING ROMANCES
Sept, 1949 - No. 6, Aug, 1950
Ace Magazines

	Good	Fine	N-Mint
1	3.00	9.00	21.00
2	1.50	4.50	10.00
3-6	1.15	3.50	8.00

REVENGE OF THE PROWLER (Also see The Prowler)
Feb, 1988 - No. 4, June, 1988 ($1.75/$1.95, color)
Eclipse Comics

	Good	Fine	N-Mint
1 ($1.75)	.30	.90	1.80
2 ($2.50)-Contains flexidisc	.40	1.25	2.50
3,4 ($1.95)	.35	1.00	2.00

REVENGERS, THE (Featuring Armor And Silverstreak)
Sept, 1985; 1987 - Present ($2.00, color, Baxter)
Continuity Comics

	Good	Fine	N-Mint
1-Origin; Adams c/a	.35	1.00	2.00
1-(1987, newsstand) - 8	.35	1.00	2.00

REVENGERS STARRING MEGALITH (Also see Megalith)
Sept, 1985; 1987 - Present ($2.00, color, Baxter)
Continuity Comics

	Good	Fine	N-Mint
1 (1985)-Adams c/a, scripts	.35	1.00	2.00
1 (1987, newsstand) - 5	.35	1.00	2.00

REX ALLEN COMICS (Movie star)(Also see 4-Color #877 & Western
Roundup under Dell Giants)
No. 316, Feb, 1951 - No. 31, Dec-Feb, 1958-59 (All-photo-c)
Dell Publishing Co.

	Good	Fine	N-Mint
4-Color 316(#1)(52 pgs.)-Rex Allen & his horse Koko begin; Marsh-a	11.50	34.00	80.00
2 (9-11/51, 36 pgs.)	5.70	17.00	40.00
3-10	4.65	14.00	32.00
11-20	3.70	11.00	26.00
21-23,25-31	3.50	10.50	24.00
24-Toth-a	4.30	13.00	30.00

NOTE: *Manning* a-20, 27-30. Photo back-c 316, 2-12, 20, 21.

REX DEXTER OF MARS (See Mystery Men Comics)
Fall, 1940
Fox Features Syndicate

	Good	Fine	N-Mint
1-Rex Dexter, Patty O'Day, & Zanzibar (Tuska-a) app.; Briefer-c/a	82.00	245.00	575.00

REX HART (Formerly Blaze Carson; Whip Wilson #9 on)
No. 6, Aug, 1949 - No. 8, Feb, 1950 (All photo-c)
Timely/Marvel Comics (USA)

	Good	Fine	N-Mint
6-Rex Hart & his horse Warrior begin; Black Rider app; Captain Tootsie by Beck	9.30	28.00	65.00
7,8: 18pg. Thriller in each. 8-Blaze the Wonder Collie app. in text	7.00	21.00	50.00

REX MORGAN, M.D. (Also see Harvey Comics Library)
Dec, 1955 - No. 3, 1956
Argo Publ.

REX MORGAN, M.D. (continued)	Good	Fine	N-Mint
1-Reprints Rex Morgan daily newspaper strips & daily panel-r of "These Women" by D'Alessio & "Timeout" by Jeff Keate			
	5.50	16.50	38.00
2,3	3.50	10.50	24.00

REX THE WONDER DOG (See The Adventures of . . .)

RHUBARB, THE MILLIONAIRE CAT (See 4-Color #423,466,563)

RIBIT!
Jan, 1989 - No. 4, April?, 1989 ($1.95, color, mini-series)
Comico

1-4: Created, written, & art by F. Thorne	.35	1.00	2.00

RIBTICKLER (Also see Fox Giants)
1945 - No. 9, Aug, 1947; 1957; 1959
Fox Feature Synd./Green Publ. (1957)/Norlen (1959)

1	4.50	14.00	32.00
2	2.30	7.00	16.00
3-9: 3,7-Cosmo Cat app.	1.70	5.00	12.00
3,7,8 (Green Publ.-1957)	1.00	3.00	7.00
3,7,8 (Norlen Mag.-1959)	1.00	3.00	7.00

RICHARD DRAGON, KUNG-FU FIGHTER (See Brave & the Bold)
Apr-May, 1975 - No. 18, Nov-Dec, 1977
National Periodical Publications/DC Comics

1,2: 2-Starlin-a(p). 3-Kirby-c; a(p)		.45	.90
3-18: 4-8-Wood inks		.30	.60

RICHARD THE LION-HEARTED (See Ideal a Classical Comic)

RICHIE RICH (See Harvey Collectors Comics, Harvey Hits, Little Dot, Little Lotta, Little Sad Sack, Million Dollar Digest, Mutt & Jeff, Super Richie, and 3-D Dolly)

RICHIE RICH (. . .the Poor Little Rich Boy) (See Harvey Hits #3, 9)
11/60 - No. 218, 10/82; No. 219, 10/86 - Present
Harvey Publications

1-(See Little Dot for 1st app.)	90.00	250.00	440.00
2	40.00	100.00	180.00
3-5	20.00	60.00	120.00
6-10: 8-Christmas-c	12.50	37.50	75.00
11-20	5.35	16.00	32.00
21-40	3.00	9.00	18.00
41-60	2.00	6.00	12.00
61-80: 65-1st app. Dollar the Dog	1.20	3.50	7.00
81-100	.70	2.00	4.00
101-111,117-120	.50	1.50	3.00
112-116: All 52 pg. Giants	.60	1.80	3.60
121-140	.40	1.25	2.50
141-160: 145-Infinity-c	.35	1.00	2.00
161-180	.25	.75	1.50
181-246		.50	1.00

RICHIE RICH AND. . .
Oct, 1987 - Present
Harvey Comics

1 (75 cents)-Diff. character apps. each issue		.40	.75
2-10 ($1.00)		.50	1.00

RICHIE RICH AND BILLY BELLHOPS
October, 1977 (One Shot) (52pgs.)
Harvey Publications

1		.50	1.50	3.00

RICHIE RICH AND CADBURY
10/77; No. 2, 9/78 - No. 23, 7/82 (#1-10: 52pgs.)
Harvey Publications

1	.70	2.00	4.00
2-5	.35	1.00	2.00
6-10		.50	1.00
11-23		.40	.80

RICHIE RICH AND CASPER (Also see Blackthorne 3-D Series #32)
Aug, 1974 - No. 45, Sept, 1982
Harvey Publications

	Good	Fine	N-Mint
1	1.15	3.50	7.00
2-5	.50	1.50	3.00
6-10: 10-Xmas-c	.35	1.00	2.00
11-20		.50	1.00
21-40: 22-Xmas-c		.40	.80
41-45		.30	.60

RICHIE RICH AND DOLLAR THE DOG (See Richie Rich #65)
9/77 - No. 24, 8/82 (#1-10: 52pgs.)
Harvey Publications

1	.70	2.00	4.00
2-10	.35	1.00	2.00
11-24		.50	1.00

RICHIE RICH AND DOT
October, 1974 (One Shot)
Harvey Publications

1	1.00	3.00	6.00

RICHIE RICH AND GLORIA
Sept, 1977 - No. 25, Sept, 1982 (#1-11: 52pgs.)
Harvey Publications

1	.70	2.00	4.00
2-5	.35	1.00	2.00
6-25		.40	.80

RICHIE RICH AND HIS GIRLFRIENDS
April, 1979 - No. 16, Dec, 1982
Harvey Publications

1: 52 pg. Giant	.50	1.50	3.00
2: 52 pg. Giant	.40	1.20	2.40
3-10	.35	1.00	2.00
11-16		.40	.80

RICHIE RICH AND HIS MEAN COUSIN REGGIE
April, 1979 - No. 3, 1980 (50 cents) (#1,2: 52pgs.)
Harvey Publications

1	.35	1.00	2.00
2-3: (#4 was advertised, but never released)	.25	.75	1.50

RICHIE RICH AND JACKIE JOKERS
Nov, 1973 - No. 48, Dec, 1982
Harvey Publications

1: 52 pg. Giant	1.70	5.00	10.00
2,3: 52 pg. Giants	1.00	3.00	6.00
4,5	.85	2.50	5.00
6-10	.50	1.50	3.00
11-20	.35	1.00	2.00
21-40		.50	1.00
41-48		.40	.80

RICHIE RICH AND TIMMY TIME
Sept, 1977 (50 Cents) (One Shot) (52 pages)
Harvey Publications

1	.50	1.50	3.00

RICHIE RICH BANK BOOKS
Oct, 1972 - No. 59, Sept, 1982
Harvey Publications

1	2.65	8.00	16.00
2-5	1.00	3.00	6.00
6-10	.70	2.00	4.00
11-20	.50	1.50	3.00
21-30	.35	1.00	2.00
31-40		.50	1.00
41-59		.40	.80

Rex Morgan, M.D. #1, © Argo Publ.

Richard Dragon, Kung-Fu Fighter #1, © DC

Richie Rich #13, © HARV

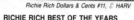

Richie Rich Dollars & Cents #11, © HARV

Richie Rich Millions #22, © HARV

Richie Rich Success Stories #17, © HARV

RICHIE RICH BEST OF THE YEARS
Oct, 1977 - No. 6, June, 1980 (Digest) (128 pages)
Harvey Publications

	Good	Fine	N-Mint
1(10/77)-Reprints, #2(10/78)-Reprints, #3(6/79-75 cents)	.35	1.00	2.00
4-6(11/79-6/80-95 cents)		.50	1.00

RICHIE RICH BILLIONS
10/74 - No. 48, 10/82 (#1-33: 52pgs.)
Harvey Publications

1	1.70	5.00	10.00
2-5	.85	2.50	5.00
6-10	.70	2.00	4.00
11-20	.35	1.00	2.00
21-33 (Last 52 pgs.)		.50	1.00
34-48		.40	.80

RICHIE RICH CASH
Sept, 1974 - No. 47, Aug, 1982
Harvey Publications

1	1.70	5.00	10.00
2-5	.85	2.50	5.00
6-10	.50	1.50	3.00
11-20	.35	1.00	2.00
21-30		.50	1.00
31-47		.40	.80

RICHIE RICH, CASPER & WENDY NATIONAL LEAGUE
June, 1976 (52 pages)
Harvey Publications

1	.50	1.50	3.00

RICHIE RICH COLLECTORS COMICS (See Harvey Collectors Comics)

RICHIE RICH DIAMONDS
8/72 - No. 59, 8/82 (#1, 23-45: 52pgs.)
Harvey Publications

1: 52 pg. Giant	2.65	8.00	16.00
2-5	1.00	3.00	6.00
6-10	.70	2.00	4.00
11-22	.50	1.50	3.00
23-30	.35	1.00	2.00
31-45: 39-Origin Little Dot		.50	1.00
46-50		.40	.80
51-59		.30	.60

RICHIE RICH DIGEST
Oct, 1986 - Present ($1.25-$1.75, digest-size)
Harvey Publications

1-21		.60	1.25

RICHIE RICH DIGEST STORIES (. . . Magazine #?-on)
10/77 - No. 17, 10/82 (Digest) (132 pages) (75-95 cents)
Harvey Publications

1-Reprints	.25	.80	1.60
2-17: 4-Infinity-c		.40	.80

RICHIE RICH DIGEST WINNERS
12/77 - No. 16, 9/82 (Digest) (132 pages) (75-95 Cents)
Harvey Publications

1	.25	.80	1.60
2-16		.40	.80

RICHIE RICH DOLLARS & CENTS
8/63 - No. 109, 8/82 (#1-43: 68 pgs.; 44-60, 71-94: 52pgs.)
Harvey Publications

1: (#1-64 are all reprint issues)	8.00	24.00	56.00
2	4.00	12.00	24.00
3-5: 5-r/1st app. R.R. from Little Dot #1	2.35	7.00	14.00
6-10	1.70	5.00	10.00

	Good	Fine	N-Mint
11-20	1.35	4.00	8.00
21-30	.85	2.50	5.00
31-43: Last 68 pg. issue	.50	1.50	3.00
44-60: All 52 pgs.	.40	1.20	2.40
61-70	.35	1.00	2.00
71-94: All 52 pgs.		.50	1.00
95-109: 100-Anniversary issue		.40	.80

RICHIE RICH FORTUNES
Sept, 1971 - No. 63, July, 1982 (#1-15: 52pgs.)
Harvey Publications

1	2.35	7.00	16.00
2-5	1.15	3.50	7.00
6-10	.85	2.50	5.00
11-15: Last 52 pg. Giant	.70	2.00	4.00
16-30	.35	1.00	2.00
31-40		.50	1.00
41-63		.40	.80

RICHIE RICH GEMS
Sept, 1974 - No. 43, Sept, 1982
Harvey Publications

1	1.70	5.00	10.00
2-5	.85	2.50	5.00
6-10	.50	1.50	3.00
11-20	.35	1.00	2.00
21-30		.50	1.00
31-43		.40	.80

RICHIE RICH GOLD AND SILVER
Sept, 1975 - No. 42, Oct, 1982 (#1-27: 52pgs.)
Harvey Publications

1	1.35	4.00	8.00
2-5	.70	2.00	4.00
6-10	.35	1.00	2.00
11-27		.50	1.00
28-42		.40	.80

RICHIE RICH HOLIDAY DIGEST MAGAZINE (. . . Digest #4)
1/80 - No. 3, 1/82; No. 4, 3/88 - Present (Published annually)
Harvey Publications

1-3: All X-Mas-c		.50	1.00
4-(3/88, $1.25), 5-(2/89, $1.75)		.60	1.25

RICHIE RICH INVENTIONS
Oct, 1977 - No. 26, Oct, 1982 (#1-11: 52pgs.)
Harvey Publications

1	.70	2.00	4.00
2-5	.35	1.00	2.00
6-11		.50	1.00
12-26		.40	.80

RICHIE RICH JACKPOTS
Oct, 1972 - No. 58, Aug, 1982 (#41-43: 52pgs.)
Harvey Publications

1	2.65	8.00	16.00
2-5	1.00	3.00	6.00
6-10	.70	2.00	4.00
11-20	.35	1.00	2.00
21-30	.25	.75	1.50
31-50		.50	1.00
51-58		.40	.80

RICHIE RICH MILLION DOLLAR DIGEST (. . . Magazine #?-on)(Also see Million Dollar Digest)
October, 1980 - No. 10, Oct, 1982
Harvey Publications

1-10		.50	1.00

RICHIE RICH MILLIONS
9/61; #2, 9/62 - #113, 10/82 (#1-48: 68 pgs.; 49-64, 85-97: 52 pgs.)
Harvey Publications

	Good	Fine	N-Mint
1: (#1-5 are all reprint issues)	10.00	30.00	70.00
2	5.00	15.00	35.00
3-10: (All other giants are new & reprints)	3.35	10.00	23.00
11-20	1.70	5.00	12.00
21-30	1.00	3.00	6.00
31-48: Last 68 pg. Giant	.75	2.30	4.60
49-64: 52 pg. Giants	.50	1.50	3.00
65-74	.35	1.00	2.00
75-94: 52 pg. Giants	.40	1.20	2.40
95-100		.50	1.00
101-113		.40	.80

RICHIE RICH MONEY WORLD
Sept, 1972 - No. 59, Sept, 1982
Harvey Publications

1: 52 pg. Giant	2.65	8.00	16.00
2-5	1.00	3.00	6.00
6-10: 9,10-R. Rich mistakenly named Little Lotta on covers	.50	1.50	3.00
11-20	.35	1.10	2.20
21-30	.25	.75	1.50
31-50		.50	1.00
51-59		.40	.80

RICHIE RICH PROFITS
Oct, 1974 - No. 47, Sept, 1982
Harvey Publications

1	2.00	6.00	12.00
2-5	1.00	3.00	6.00
6-10	.50	1.50	3.00
11-20	.35	1.00	2.00
21-30		.50	1.00
31-47		.40	.80

RICHIE RICH RELICS
Jan, 1988 - No. 5?, Aug, 1989 (All reprints, .75-$1.00)
Harvey Comics

1-5		.50	1.00

RICHIE RICH RICHES
7/72 - No. 59, 8/82 (#1, 2, 41-45: 52pgs.)
Harvey Publications

1: 52 pg. Giant	2.00	6.00	12.00
2: 52 pg. Giant	1.15	3.50	7.00
3-5	1.00	3.00	6.00
6-10	.50	1.50	3.00
11-20	.35	1.00	2.00
21-40		.50	1.00
41-45: 52 pg. Giants		.60	1.20
46-59		.40	.80

RICHIE RICH SUCCESS STORIES
11/64 - No. 105, 9/82 (#1-38: 68 pgs., 39-55, 67-90: 52pgs.)
Harvey Publications

1	8.00	24.00	56.00
2-5	3.00	9.00	21.00
6-10	2.00	6.00	12.00
11-30: 27-1st Penny Van Dough (8/69)	1.00	3.00	6.00
31-38: Last 68 pg. Giant	.85	2.50	5.00
39-55: 52 pgs.	.50	1.50	3.00
56-66	.35	1.00	2.00
67-90: 52 pgs. (Early issues are reprints)		.60	1.20
91-105		.40	.80

RICHIE RICH TREASURE CHEST DIGEST (. . . Magazine #3)
4/82 - No. 3, 8/82 (95 Cents, Digest Magazine)

Harvey Publications	Good	Fine	N-Mint
1-3		.50	1.00

RICHIE RICH VACATIONS DIGEST
11/77; No. 2, 10/78 - No. 7, 10/81; No. 8, 8/82 (Digest, 132 pgs.)
Harvey Publications

1-Reprints	.25	.80	1.60
2-8		.50	1.00

RICHIE RICH VAULTS OF MYSTERY
Nov, 1974 - No. 47, Sept, 1982
Harvey Publications

1	1.50	4.50	9.00
2-10	.70	2.00	4.00
11-20	.35	1.00	2.00
21-30	.25	.75	1.50
31-47		.40	.80

RICHIE RICH ZILLIONZ
10/76 - No. 33, 9/82 (#1-4: 68pgs.; #5-18: 52pgs.)
Harvey Publications

1	1.35	4.00	8.00
2-4: Last 68 pg. Giant	.70	2.00	4.00
5-10	.35	1.00	2.00
11-18: Last 52 pg. Giant		.50	1.00
19-33		.40	.80

RICK GEARY'S WONDERS AND ODDITIES
Dec, 1988 ($2.00, B&W, one-shot)
Dark Horse Comics

1	.35	1.00	2.00

RICKY
No. 5, September, 1953
Standard Comics (Visual Editions)

5	1.50	4.50	10.00

RICKY NELSON (TV)(See Sweethearts V2#42)
No. 956, 12/58 - No. 1192, 6/61 (All photo-c)
Dell Publishing Co.

4-Color 956,998	12.00	36.00	84.00
4-Color 1115,1192-Manning-a	12.00	36.00	84.00

RIDER, THE (Frontier Trail #6)
March, 1957 - No. 5, 1958
Ajax/Farrell Publ. (Four Star Comic Corp.)

1-Swift Arrow, Lone Rider begin	3.50	10.50	24.00
2-5	1.70	5.00	12.00

RIFLEMAN, THE (TV)
No. 1009, 7-9/59 - No. 12, 7-9/62; No. 13, 11/62 - No. 20, 10/64
Dell Publ. Co./Gold Key No. 13 on

4-Color 1009	8.50	25.50	60.00
2 (1-3/60)	6.50	19.50	45.00
3-Toth-a, 4 pgs.	7.00	21.00	50.00
4,5,7-10	5.00	15.00	35.00
6-Toth-a, 4pgs.	5.70	17.00	40.00
11-20	4.30	13.00	30.00

NOTE: *Warren Tufts a-2-9. All have Chuck Connors photo-c. Photo back-c, #13-15.*

RIMA, THE JUNGLE GIRL (TV)
Apr-May, 1974 - No. 7, Apr-May, 1975
National Periodical Publications

1-Origin, part 1		.60	1.20
2-4-Origin, part 2,3,&4		.40	.80
5-7: 7-Origin & only app. Space Marshal		.30	.60

NOTE: *Kubert c-1-7. Nino a-1-5. Redondo a-1-6.*

RING OF BRIGHT WATER (See Movie Classics)

The Rider #1, © AJAX

The Rifleman #4, © Four Star

Rima, The Jungle Girl #1, © DC

Rin Tin Tin #9, © Screen Gems

Riot #4, © MEG

Roachmill #1, © Blackthorne

RING OF THE NIBELUNG, THE
1989 - No. 4, 1990 ($4.95, squarebound, mature readers, 52 pgs.)
DC Comics

	Good	Fine	N-Mint
1-4: Adapts novel; G. Kane-a; nudity	.85	2.50	5.00

RINGO KID, THE (2nd Series)
1/70 - No. 23, 11/73; No. 24, 11/75 - No. 30, 11/76
Marvel Comics Group

1(1970)-Williamson-a r-from #10, 1956		.50	1.00
2-30: 13-Wildey-r. 20-Williamson-r/#1		.30	.60

RINGO KID WESTERN, THE (1st Series)(See Wild Western & Western Trails)
Aug, 1954 - No. 21, Sept, 1957
Atlas Comics (HPC)/Marvel Comics

	Good	Fine	N-Mint
1-Origin; The Ringo Kid & his horse Arab begin	9.30	28.00	65.00
2-Black Rider app.; origin Arab	4.50	14.00	32.00
3-5	2.85	8.50	20.00
6-8-Severin-a(3) each	3.70	11.00	26.00
9,11,14-21	2.00	6.00	14.00
10,13-Williamson-a, 4 pgs.	3.70	11.00	26.00
12-Orlando-a, 4 pgs.	2.30	7.00	16.00

NOTE: Berg a-8. Maneely a-1-5, 15, 16, 18, 20, 21; c-1-6, 8, 13, 15, 16, 18, 20. J. Severin c-10, 11. Sinnott a-1. Wildey a-16-18.

RIN TIN TIN (See March of Comics #163,180,195)

RIN TIN TIN (TV) (...& Rusty #21 on; see Western Roundup under Dell Giants)
Nov, 1952 - No. 38, May-July, 1961; Nov, 1963 (All Photo-c)
Dell Publishing Co./Gold Key

4-Color 434 (#1)	5.00	15.00	35.00
4-Color 476,523	3.70	11.00	26.00
4(3-5/54)-10	3.00	9.00	21.00
11-20	2.30	7.00	16.00
21-38	2.00	6.00	14.00
... & Rusty 1 (11/63-Gold Key)	2.00	6.00	14.00

RIO
June, 1987 ($8.95, color, 64 pgs.)
Comico

1-Wildey-c/a	1.50	4.50	9.00

RIO BRAVO (See 4-Color #1018)

RIO CONCHOS (See Movie Comics)

RIOT (Satire)
Apr, 1954 - No. 3, Aug, 1954; No. 4, Feb, 1956 - No. 6, June, 1956
Atlas Comics (ACI No. 1-5/WPI No. 6)

1-Russ Heath-a	7.00	21.00	50.00
2-Li'l Abner satire by Post	5.70	17.00	40.00
3-Last precode (8/54)	4.30	13.00	30.00
4-Infinity-c; Marilyn Monroe '7 Year Itch' movie satire; Mad Rip-off ads	6.50	19.50	45.00
5-Marilyn Monroe, John Wayne parody; part photo-c	7.00	21.00	50.00
6-Lorna of the Jungle satire by Everett; Dennis the Menace satire cover/story	4.30	13.00	30.00

NOTE: Berg a-3. Burgos c-1, 2. Colan a-1. Everett a-1, 4, 6. Heath a-1. Maneely a-1, 2, 4-6; c-3, 4, 6. Post a-1-4. Reinman a-2. Severin a-4-6.

RIPCORD (See 4-Color #1294)

RIP HUNTER TIME MASTER (See Showcase #20, 21, 25, 26 & Time Masters)
Mar-Apr, 1961 - No. 29, Nov-Dec, 1965
National Periodical Publications

1	18.00	54.00	125.00
2	9.30	28.00	65.00

	Good	Fine	N-Mint
3-5: 5-Last 10 cent issue	5.70	17.00	40.00
6,7-Toth-a in each	5.00	15.00	35.00
8-15	3.60	11.00	25.00
16-29: 29-G. Kane-c	2.15	6.50	15.00

RIP IN TIME
Aug, 1986 - No. 5, 1987 ($1.50, B&W)
Fantagor Press

1-5: Corben-c/a	.25	.75	1.50

RIP KIRBY (See Feature Books #51, 54, Harvey Comics Hits #57, & Street Comix)

RIPLEY'S BELIEVE IT OR NOT!
Sept, 1953 - No. 4, March, 1954
Harvey Publications

1-Powell-a	5.70	17.00	40.00
2-4	3.00	9.00	21.00
J. C. Penney giveaway (1948)	4.00	12.00	28.00

RIPLEY'S BELIEVE IT OR NOT! (Formerly ...True War Stories)
No. 4, April, 1967 - No. 94, Feb, 1980
Gold Key

4-McWilliams-a	1.70	5.00	12.00
5-Subtitled "True War Stories;" Evans-a	1.00	3.00	7.00
6-9: 6-McWilliams-a. 8-Orlando-a	1.00	3.00	7.00
10-Evans-a(2)	1.00	3.00	7.00
11-14,16-20	.70	2.00	5.00
15-Evans-a	.70	2.00	5.00
21-30	.60	1.75	3.50
31-38,40-60	.35	1.00	2.00
39-Crandall-a	.40	1.25	2.50
61-94: 74,77-83 (52 pgs.)	.25	.75	1.50
Story Digest Mag. 1(6/70)-4¾x6½''	.50	1.50	3.00

NOTE: Evanish art by Luiz Dominguez #22-25, 27, 30, 31, 40. McWilliams a-65, 70, 89. Sparling c-68. Reprints-#74,77-84,87 (part); 91,93 (all). Williamson, Wood-a-80r/#1.

RIPLEY'S BELIEVE IT OR NOT! (See Ace Comics, All-American Comics, Mystery Comics Digest #1, 4, 7, 10, 13, 16, 19, 22, 25)

RIPLEY'S BELIEVE IT OR NOT TRUE GHOST STORIES (Becomes ...True War Stories) (See Dan Curtis)
June, 1965 - No. 2, Oct, 1966
Gold Key

1-Williamson, Wood & Evans-a; photo-c	2.65	8.00	18.00
2-Orlando, McWilliams-a	1.50	4.50	10.00
Mini-Comic 1(1976-3¼x6½'')		.30	.60
11186(1977)-Golden Press; 224 pgs. ($1.95)-Reprints	.50	1.50	3.00
11401(3/79)-Golden Press; 96 pgs. ($1.00)-Reprints		.60	1.20

RIPLEY'S BELIEVE IT OR NOT TRUE WAR STORIES (Formerly ...True Ghost Stories; becomes Ripley's Believe It or Not #4 on)
Nov, 1966
Gold Key

1(#3)-Williamson-a	2.00	6.00	14.00

RIPLEY'S BELIEVE IT OR NOT! TRUE WEIRD
June, 1966 - No. 2, Aug, 1966 (B&W Magazine)
Ripley Enterprises

1,2-Comic stories & text	.50	1.50	3.00

RIVETS (See 4-Color #518)

RIVETS (A dog)
Jan, 1956 - No. 3, May, 1956
Argo Publ.

1-Reprints Sunday & daily newspaper strips	2.65	8.00	18.00
2,3	1.50	4.50	10.00

ROAD RUNNER, THE (See Beep Beep....)

ROACHMILL (1st series)
Dec, 1986 - No. 8, 1987 ($1.75, B&W)
Blackthorne Publishing

	Good	Fine	N-Mint
1	.70	2.10	4.20
2-8	.50	1.50	3.00

ROACHMILL (2nd series)
May, 1988 - Present ($1.75, B&W)
Dark Horse Comics

1	.50	1.50	3.00
2-8	.30	.90	1.75

ROBERT E. HOWARD'S CONAN THE BARBARIAN
1983 (No month) ($2.50, printed on Baxter paper)
Marvel Comics Group

1-r-/Savage Tales No. 2,3 by Smith; c-r/Conan No. 21 by Smith			
	.45	1.25	2.50

ROBIN (See Aurora, Detective Comics #38, New Teen Titans, Star Spangled Comics #65 & Teen Titans)

ROBIN HOOD (See The Advs. of . . . , Brave and the Bold, 4-Color #413,669, King Classics, & Movie Comics)

ROBIN HOOD (. . .& His Merry Men, The Illustrated Story of . . .) (See Classic Comics #7 & Classics Giveaways, 12/44)

ROBIN HOOD (New Adventures of . . .)
1952 (36 pages) (5x7¼'')
Walt Disney Productions (Flour giveaways)

"New Adventures of Robin Hood," "Ghosts of Waylea Castle," & "The Miller's Ransom" each. . . .	1.70	5.00	12.00

ROBIN HOOD (Adventures of . . . #7, 8)
No. 52, Nov, 1955 - No. 6, June, 1957
Magazine Enterprises (Sussex Publ. Co.)

52 (#1)-Origin Robin Hood & Sir Gallant of the Round Table			
	4.50	14.00	32.00
53, 3-6	3.00	9.00	21.00
I.W. Reprint #1,2 (r-#4), 9 (r-#52)(1963)	.50	1.50	3.00
Super Reprint #10 (r-#53?), 11,15 (r-#5), 17('64)	.50	1.50	3.00

NOTE: *Bolle* a-in all; c-52. *Powell* a-6.

ROBIN HOOD (Not Disney)
May-July, 1963 (One shot)
Dell Publishing Co.

1	1.00	3.00	7.00

ROBIN HOOD ($1.50)
1973 (Disney) (8½x11''; cardboard covers) (52 pages)
Western Publishing Co.

96151-"Robin Hood," based on movie, 96152-"The Mystery of Sherwood Forest," 96153-"In King Richard's Service," 96154-"The Wizard's Ring" each. . . .	.70	2.00	4.00

ROBIN HOOD AND HIS MERRY MEN (Formerly Danger & Adv.)
No. 28, April, 1956 - No. 38, Aug, 1958
Charlton Comics

28	2.65	8.00	18.00
29-37	1.50	4.50	10.00
38-Ditko-a, 5 pgs.	4.30	13.00	30.00

ROBIN HOOD'S FRONTIER DAYS (. . .Western Tales)
No date (Circa 1955) 20 pages, slick-c (Seven issues?)
Shoe Store Giveaway (Robin Hood Stores)

nn	2.30	7.00	16.00
nn-Issues with Crandall-a	3.50	10.50	24.00

ROBIN HOOD TALES (Published by National Periodical #7 on)
Feb, 1956 - No. 6, Nov-Dec, 1956
Quality Comics Group (Comic Magazines)

1	4.50	14.00	32.00

	Good	Fine	N-Mint
2-5-Matt Baker-a	5.00	15.00	35.00
6	2.30	7.00	16.00
Frontier Days giveaway (1956)	2.30	7.00	16.00

ROBIN HOOD TALES (Continued from Quality series)
No. 7, Jan-Feb, 1957 - No. 14, Mar-Apr, 1958
National Periodical Publications

7	11.00	32.00	75.00
8-14	8.50	25.50	60.00

ROBINSON CRUSOE (Also see King Classics)
Nov-Jan, 1963-64
Dell Publishing Co.

1	1.00	3.00	7.00

ROBOCOP
1989 ($2.25, B&W, magazine, one-shot)
Marvel Comics

1-Movie adaptation	.40	1.15	2.25

ROBOCOP
May, 1990 - Present ($1.50, color)
Marvel Comics

1-Based on movie	.25	.75	1.50

ROBO-HUNTER (Also see Sam Slade. . .)
April, 1984 - No. 6, 1984 ($1.00, color)
Eagle Comics

1-6-2000 A.D.-r		.50	1.00

R.O.B.O.T. BATTALION 2050
March, 1988 ($2.00, B&W, one-shot)
Eclipse Comics

1	.35	1.00	2.00

ROBOT COMICS
June, 1987 (One shot, $2.00, B&W)
Renegade Press

0-Bob Burden story/art	.35	1.10	2.20

ROBOTECH DEFENDERS
Mar, 1985 - No. 2, Apr, 1985 (mini-series)
DC Comics

1,2	.40	1.25	2.50

ROBOTECH IN 3-D
Aug, 1987 ($2.50)
Comico

1-Adapts TV show; Steacy-c	.40	1.25	2.50

ROBOTECH MASTERS (TV)
July, 1985 - No. 23, Apr, 1988
Comico

1	.50	1.50	3.00
2,3	.35	1.00	2.00
4-23 (#23, $1.75)	.25	.75	1.50

ROBOTECH SPECIAL
May, 1988 ($2.50, color, one shot, 44pgs.)
Comico

1-Ken Steacy wraparound-c; part photo-c	.40	1.25	2.50

ROBOTECH THE GRAPHIC NOVEL
Aug, 1986 ($5.95, 8½x11'', 52 pgs.)
Comico

1-Origin SDF-1; intro T.R. Edwards; Ken Steacy c/a; 2nd printing also exists (12/86)	1.00	3.00	6.00

ROBOTECH: THE MACROSS SAGA (Formerly Macross)(TV)
No. 2, Feb, 1985 - No. 36, Feb, 1989

Robin Hood Tales #1, © QUA

Robo-Hunter #2, © Eagle

Robotech Defenders #1, © DC

Rocket Comics #1, © HILL

Rock 'N' Roll Comics #1, © Revolutionary Comics

Rocky And His Fiendish Friends #5, © Jay Ward

ROBOTECH: THE MACROSS SAGA (continued)
Comico

	Good	Fine	N-Mint
2	1.15	3.50	7.00
3-5	.50	1.50	3.00
6,7	.40	1.25	2.50
8-25	.25	.75	1.50
26-36: 26-34-$1.75. 35,36-$1.95-c	.30	.90	1.75

ROBOTECH: THE NEW GENERATION (TV)
July, 1985 - No. 25, July, 1988
Comico

1	.50	1.50	3.00
2-4	.35	1.00	2.00
5-21	.25	.75	1.50
22-25 ($1.75)	.30	.90	1.75

ROBOTIX
Feb, 1986 (75 cents, one Shot)
Marvel Comics Group

1-Based on toy		.40	.80

ROBOTMEN OF THE LOST PLANET (Also see Space Thrillers)
1952   (Also see Strange Worlds #19)
Avon Periodicals

1-3pg. Kinstler-a	56.00	170.00	390.00

ROB ROY (See 4-Color #544)

ROCK AND ROLLO (Formerly TV Teens)
V2No.14, Oct, 1957 - No. 19, Sept, 1958
Charlton Comics

14-19	1.15	3.50	8.00

ROCKET COMICS
Mar, 1940 - No. 3, May, 1940
Hillman Periodicals

1-Rocket Riley, Red Roberts the Electro Man(Origin), The Phantom
  Ranger, The Steel Shark, The Defender, Buzzard Barnes, Lefty
  Larson, & Man With a Thousand Faces begin

	71.00	215.00	500.00
2,3	45.00	135.00	315.00

ROCKETEER, THE (See Eclipse Graphic Album Series, Pacific Presents & Starslayer #2)

ROCKETEER ADVENTURE MAGAZINE, THE
July, 1988 - Present ($2.00, color)
Comico

1-Dave Stevens-c/a in all; Kaluta back-up-a	.70	2.00	4.00
2 ($2.75)	.50	1.50	3.00

ROCKETEER SPECIAL EDITION, THE
Nov, 1984 ($1.50, color, Baxter paper)
Eclipse Comics

1-Dave Stevens-c/a; Kaluta back-c	1.00	3.00	6.00

ROCKET KELLY (See The Bouncer & Green Mask #10)
1944; Fall, 1945 - No. 5, 10-11/46
Fox Feature Syndicate

nn (1944)	10.00	30.00	70.00
1	10.00	30.00	70.00
2-The Puppeteer app. (costumed hero)	7.00	21.00	50.00
3-5-(#5 on cover, #4 inside)	5.70	17.00	40.00

ROCKETMAN (See Hello Pal & Scoop Comics)
June, 1952
Ajax/Farrell Publications

1-Rocketman & Cosmo	13.00	40.00	90.00

ROCKET RACCOON
May, 1985 - No. 4, Aug, 1985 (mini-series)

Marvel Comics Group

	Good	Fine	N-Mint
1-4	.25	.75	1.50

ROCKETS AND RANGE RIDERS
May, 1957 (16 pages, soft-c) (Giveaway)
Richfield Oil Corp.

Toth-a	10.50	30.00	70.00

ROCKET SHIP X
September, 1951; 1952
Fox Features Syndicate

1	35.00	105.00	245.00
1952 (nn, nd, no publ.)-Edited '51-c	22.00	65.00	154.00

ROCKET TO ADVENTURE LAND (See Pixie Puzzle...)

ROCKET TO THE MOON
1951
Avon Periodicals

nn-Orlando c/a; adapts Otis Adelbert Kline's "Maza of the Moon"

	55.00	165.00	385.00

ROCK HAPPENING (Harvey Pop Comics:...)(See Bunny)
Sept, 1969 - No. 2, Nov, 1969
Harvey Publications

1,2: Featuring Bunny	1.15	3.50	8.00

ROCK N' ROLL COMICS
June, 1989 - Present ($1.50-$1.95, B&W)
Revolutionary Comics

1-Guns N' Roses	1.15	3.50	7.00
1-2nd thru 5th printings	.25	.75	1.50
2-Metallica	.50	1.50	3.00
2-2nd thru 4th printings	.25	.75	1.50
3-12: 3-Bon Jovi. 4-Motley Crue. 6-Who. 9-Kiss	.35	1.00	2.00

ROCKY AND HIS FIENDISH FRIENDS (TV)(Bullwinkle)
Oct, 1962 - No. 5, Sept, 1963 (Jay Ward)
Gold Key

1 (84 pgs.)	9.50	28.50	76.00
2,3 (84 pgs.)	7.50	22.50	60.00
4,5 (Regular size)	5.00	15.00	35.00
Kite Fun Book ('63, 16p, soft-c, 5x7¼")	6.50	19.50	45.00
Kite Fun Book ('70, 16p, soft-c, 5x7¼")	4.30	13.00	30.00

ROCKY AND HIS FRIENDS (See 4-Color #1128, 1152, 1166, 1208, 1275, 1311 and March of Comics No. 216)

ROCKY JONES SPACE RANGER (See Space Adventures #15-18)

ROCKY JORDAN PRIVATE EYE (See Private Eye)

ROCKY LANE WESTERN (Rocky Allan Lane starred in Republic movies (for a short time as Red Ryder) & TV)(See Black Jack & Six Gun Heroes)
May, 1949 - No. 87, Nov, 1959
Fawcett Publications/Charlton No. 56 on

1 (36 pgs.)-Rocky, his stallion Black Jack, & Slim Pickens begin; photo-c begin, end #57; photo back-c	44.00	133.00	310.00
2 (36 pgs.)-Last photo back-c	16.50	50.00	115.00
3-5 (52 pgs.). 4-Captain Tootsie by Beck	13.00	40.00	90.00
6,10 (36 pgs.)	10.00	30.00	70.00
7-9 (52 pgs.)	11.50	34.00	80.00
11-13,15-17 (52 pgs.): 15-Black Jack's Hitching Post begins, ends #25	8.50	25.50	60.00
14,18 (36 pgs.)	7.00	21.00	50.00
19-21,23,24 (52 pgs.): 20-Last Slim Pickens. 21-Dee Dickens begins, ends #55,57,65-68	7.00	21.00	50.00
22,25-28,30 (36 pgs. begin)	6.50	19.50	45.00
29-Classic complete novel "The Land of Missing Men,"-hidden land of ancient temple ruins (r-in #65)	8.00	24.00	56.00

ROCKY LANE WESTERN (continued)	Good	Fine	N-Mint
31-40	6.00	18.00	42.00
41-54	5.00	15.00	35.00
55-Last Fawcett issue (1/54)	5.50	16.50	38.00
56-1st Charlton issue (2/54)-Photo-c	6.50	19.50	45.00
57,60-Photo-c	4.30	13.00	30.00
58,59,61-64: 59-61-Young Falcon app. 64-Slim Pickens app.			
	3.50	10.50	24.00
65-R-/#29, "The Land of Missing Men"	3.70	11.00	26.00
66-68: Reprints #30,31,32	2.65	8.00	18.00
69-78,80-86	2.65	8.00	18.00
79-Giant Edition, 68 pgs.	3.70	11.00	26.00
87-Last issue	3.50	10.50	24.00

NOTE: **Complete novels** in #10, 14, 18, 22, 25, 30-32, 36, 38, 39, 49. **Captain Tootsie** in #4, 12, 20. **Big Bow and Little Arrow** in #11, 28, 63. **Black Jack's Hitching Post** in #15-25, 64, 73.

ROD CAMERON WESTERN (Movie star)
Feb, 1950 - No. 20, April, 1953
Fawcett Publications

	Good	Fine	N-Mint
1-Rod Cameron, his horse War Paint, & Sam The Sheriff begin; photo front/back-c begin	28.50	86.00	200.00
2	14.00	42.00	100.00
3-Novel length story "The Mystery of the Seven Cities of Cibola"			
	12.00	36.00	84.00
4-10: 9-Last photo back-c	10.00	30.00	70.00
11-19	8.50	25.50	60.00
20-Last issue & photo-c	9.30	28.00	65.00

NOTE: **Novel length stories** in No. 1-8, 12-14.

RODEO RYAN (See A-1 Comics #8)

ROGER BEAN, R. G. (Regular Guy)
1915 - 1917 (34 pgs.; B&W; 4¾x16"; cardboard covers)
(No. 1 & 4 bound on side, No. 3 bound at top)
The Indiana News Co.

1-By Chic Jackson (48 pgs.)	8.00	24.00	56.00
2-4	5.50	16.50	38.00

ROGER DODGER (Also in Exciting Comics #57 on)
No. 5, Aug, 1952
Standard Comics

5-Teen-age	1.30	4.00	9.00

ROGER RABBIT (See Marvel Graphic Novel)

ROG 2000
June, 1982 ($2.95)
Pacific Comics

nn-Byrne c/a-r	.50	1.50	3.00

ROG 2000
1987 - No. 2, 1987 ($2.00, color, mini-series)
Fantagraphics Books

1,2-Byrne-r	.35	1.00	2.00

ROGUE TROOPER
Oct, 1986 - Present ($1.25-$1.50, color)
Quality Comics

1-19: ($1.25) 6-Double size		.60	1.25
20,21/22,23/24,25-40 ($1.50)	.25	.75	1.50

ROLY POLY COMIC BOOK
1944 - No. 15, 1946 (MLJ reprints)
Green Publishing Co.

1-Red Rube & Steel Sterling begin	12.00	36.00	84.00
6-The Blue Circle & The Steel Fist app.	6.00	18.00	42.00
10-Origin Red Rube retold; Steel Sterling story (Zip #41)			
	6.50	19.50	45.00
11,12,14: 11,14-The Black Hood app.	6.50	19.50	45.00
15-The Blue Circle & The Steel Fist app.; cover exact swipe from Fox			

	Good	Fine	N-Mint
Blue Beetle #1	16.50	50.00	115.00

ROM
December, 1979 - No. 75, Feb. 1986
Marvel Comics Group

1-Based on a Parker Bros. toy-origin	.35	1.00	2.00
2-5		.60	1.20
6-16: 13-Saga of the Space Knights begins		.50	1.00
17,18-X-Men app.	.40	1.25	2.50
19-24,26-30: 19-X-Men cameo		.45	.90
25-Double size		.60	1.20
31-49: 32-X-Men cameo		.40	.80
50-Double size		.50	1.00
51-56,58-75: 65-X-Men & Beta Ray Bill app.		.40	.80
57-Alpha Flight app.		.60	1.20
Annual 1(11/82)		.60	1.20
Annual 2(11/83), 3(1984)		.50	1.00
Annual 4(1985)		.60	1.20

NOTE: **Austin** c-3i, 18i, 61i. **Byrne** a-74i; c-56, 57, 74. **Ditko** a-59-75p. **Golden** c-7-12, 19. **Guice** a-61i; c-55, 58, 60p. **Layton** a-59i; c-15, 59i. **Miller** c-3p, 17p, 18p. **Russell** a(i)-64, 65, 67, 69; c-64, 65i, 66, 71, 75. **P. Smith** c-59p. **Starlin** c-67.

ROMANCE (See True Stories of . . .)

ROMANCE AND CONFESSION STORIES (See Giant Comics Ed.)
No date (1949) (100pgs.)
St. John Publishing Co.

1-Baker c/a; remaindered St. John love comics			
	20.00	60.00	140.00

ROMANCE DIARY
December, 1949 - No. 2, March, 1950
Marvel Comics (CDS)(CLDS)

1,2	4.00	12.00	28.00

ROMANCE OF FLYING, THE (See Feature Books #33)

ROMANCES OF MOLLY MANTON (See Molly Manton)

ROMANCES OF NURSE HELEN GRANT, THE
August, 1957
Atlas Comics (VPI)

1	1.70	5.00	12.00

ROMANCES OF THE WEST
Nov, 1949 - No. 2, Mar, 1950 (52 pgs.)
Marvel Comics (SPC)

1-Movie photo of Calamity Jane/Sam Bass	7.00	21.00	50.00
2	5.00	15.00	35.00

ROMANCE STORIES OF TRUE LOVE (Formerly Love Problems & Advice)
No. 45, 5/57 - No. 50, 3/58; No. 51, 9/58 - No. 52, 11/58
Harvey Publications

45-51	1.00	3.00	7.00
52-Matt Baker-a	2.35	7.00	16.00

NOTE: **Powell** a-45, 46, 48-50.

ROMANCE TALES
No. 7, Oct, 1949 - No. 9, March, 1950 (7,8: photo-c)
Marvel Comics (CDS)

7	3.00	9.00	21.00
8,9: 8-Everett-a	2.00	6.00	14.00

ROMANCE TRAIL
July-Aug, 1949 - No. 6, May-June, 1950
National Periodical Publications

1-Kinstler, Toth-a; Jimmy Wakely photo-c	17.00	51.00	120.00
2-Kinstler-a; photo-c	8.50	25.50	60.00
3-Photo-c; Kinstler, Toth-a	8.50	25.50	60.00
4-Photo-c; Toth-a	7.00	21.00	50.00

Rod Cameron Western #5, © FAW

Rom #17, © MEG

Romances Of The West #1, © MEG

Romantic Confessions #1, © HILL

Romantic Marriage #1, © Z-D

Romantic Story #1, © FAW

	Good	Fine	N-Mint

ROMANCE TRAIL (continued)
5,6: 5-Photo-c — 6.50 19.50 45.00

ROMAN HOLIDAYS, THE (TV)
Feb, 1973 - No. 4, Nov, 1973 (Hanna-Barbera)
Gold Key

	Good	Fine	N-Mint
1	1.35	4.00	8.00
2-4	1.00	3.00	6.00

ROMANTIC ADVENTURES (My. . . #49-67, covers only)
Mar-Apr, 1949 - No. 67, July, 1956 (My. . . No. 68 on)
American Comics Group (B&I Publ. Co.)

1	4.30	13.00	30.00
2	2.30	7.00	16.00
3-10	1.30	4.00	9.00
11-20 (4/52)	1.00	3.00	7.00
21-46,48-52: 52-Last Pre-code (2/55)	.70	2.00	5.00
47-3-D effect	2.00	6.00	14.00
53-67	.60	1.80	4.00

NOTE: #1-23, 52 pgs. **Shelly** a-40. **Whitney** c/art in many issues.

ROMANTIC AFFAIRS (Formerly Molly Manton's Romances #2)
No. 3, March, 1950
Marvel Comics (Select Publications)

3-Photo-c; from Molly Manton's Romances #2
— 2.00 6.00 14.00

ROMANTIC CONFESSIONS
Oct, 1949 - V3#1, April-May, 1953
Hillman Periodicals

V1#1-McWilliams-a	4.50	14.00	32.00
2-Briefer-a; negligee panels	2.30	7.00	16.00
3-12	1.70	5.00	12.00
V2#1,2,4-8,10-12: 2-McWilliams-a	1.30	4.00	9.00
3-Krigstein-a	2.85	8.50	20.00
9-One pg. Frazetta ad	1.50	4.50	10.00
V3#1	1.15	3.50	8.00

ROMANTIC HEARTS
Mar, 1951 - No. 9, Aug, 1952; July, 1953 - No. 12, July, 1955
Story Comics/Master/Merit Pubs.

1(3/51) (1st Series)	4.00	12.00	28.00
2	2.00	6.00	14.00
3-9	1.70	5.00	12.00
1(7/53) (2nd Series)	2.30	7.00	16.00
2	1.50	4.50	10.00
3-12	1.00	3.00	7.00

ROMANTIC LOVE
9-10/49 - #3, 1-2/50; #4, 2-3/51 - #13, 10/52; #20, 3-4/54 - #23, 9-10/54
Avon Periodicals/Realistic (No #14-19)

1-c-/Avon paperback 252	10.00	30.00	70.00
2	5.00	15.00	35.00
3-c-/paperback Novel Library 12	5.00	15.00	35.00
4-c-/paperback Diversey Prize Novel 5	5.00	15.00	35.00
5-c-/paperback Novel Library 34	5.00	15.00	35.00
6-"Thrill Crazy"-marijuana story; c-/Avon paperback 207; Kinstler-a	7.00	21.00	50.00
7,8: 8-Astarita-a(2)	4.35	13.00	30.00
9-c-/paperback/Novel Library 41; Kinstler-a	5.00	15.00	35.00
10-c-/Avon paperback 212	5.00	15.00	35.00
11-c-/paperback Novel Library 17; Kinstler-a	5.00	15.00	35.00
12-c-/paperback Novel Library 13	5.00	15.00	35.00
13,21,22: 22-Kinstler-c	4.35	13.00	30.00
20-Kinstler-c/a	4.35	13.00	30.00
23-Kinstler-c	3.65	11.00	25.00
nn(1-3/53)(Realistic-r)	2.85	8.50	20.00

NOTE: **Astarita** a-7, 10, 11, 21. Painted c-7, 9, 10, 11.

ROMANTIC LOVE
No. 4, June, 1950
Quality Comics Group

	Good	Fine	N-Mint
4 (6/50)(Exist?)	2.00	6.00	14.00
I.W. Reprint #2,3,8		.60	1.20

ROMANTIC MARRIAGE (Cinderella Love #25 on)
#1-3 (1950, no months); #4, 5-6/51 - #17, 9/52; #18, 9/53 - #24, 9/54
Ziff-Davis/St. John No. 18 on (#1-8: 52 pgs.)

1-Photo-c	6.50	19.50	45.00
2-Painted-c	3.50	10.50	24.00
3-9: 3,4,8,9-Painted-c; 5-7-Photo-c	2.65	8.00	18.00
10-Unusual format; front-c is a painted-c; back-c is a photo-c complete with logo, price, etc.	4.50	14.00	32.00
11-17 (9/52); last Z-D issue): 13-Photo-c	2.30	7.00	16.00
18-22,24: 20-Photo-c	2.30	7.00	16.00
23-Baker-c	2.65	8.00	18.00

ROMANTIC PICTURE NOVELETTES
1946
Magazine Enterprises

1-Mary Worth-r — 7.00 21.00 50.00

ROMANTIC SECRETS (Becomes Time For Love)
Sept, 1949 - No. 39, 4/53; No. 5, 10/55 - No. 52, 11/64 (#1-5: photo-c)
Fawcett/Charlton Comics No. 5 (10/55) on

1	4.00	12.00	28.00
2,3	2.00	6.00	14.00
4,9-Evans-a	2.85	8.50	20.00
5-8,10	1.70	5.00	12.00
11-23	1.30	4.00	9.00
24-Evans-a	2.65	8.00	18.00
25-39	1.00	3.00	7.00
5 (Charlton, 2nd series)(10/55, formerly Negro Romances #4)	2.00	6.00	14.00
6-10	1.00	3.00	7.00
11-20	.45	1.35	3.00
21-35: Last 10 cent issue?	.35	1.00	2.50
36-52('64)	.25	.75	1.50

NOTE: **Bailey** a-20. **Powell** a(1st series)-5, 7, 10, 12, 16, 17, 20, 26, 29, 33, 34, 36, 37. **Sekowsky** a-26. Photo c(1st series)-1-5, 16, 25, 27, 33.

ROMANTIC STORY (Cowboy Love #28 on)
11/49 - #22, Sum, 1953; #23, 5/54 - #27, 12/54; #28, 8/55 - #130, 11/73
Fawcett/Charlton Comics No. 23 on

1-Photo-c begin, end #22,24	5.00	15.00	35.00
2	2.30	7.00	16.00
3-5	2.00	6.00	14.00
6-14	1.70	5.00	12.00
15-Evans-a	2.65	8.00	18.00
16-22(Sum, '53; last Fawcett issue). 21-Toth-a?	1.30	4.00	9.00
23-39: 26,29-Wood swipes	1.30	4.00	9.00
40-(100 pgs.)	3.50	10.50	24.00
41-50	.85	2.60	6.00
51-56,58-80	.45	1.35	3.00
57-Hypo needle story	.70	2.00	4.00
81-100		.60	1.20
101-130		.40	.80

NOTE: **Powell** a-7, 8, 16, 20, 30.

ROMANTIC THRILLS (See Fox Giants)

ROMANTIC WESTERN
Winter, 1949 - No. 3, June, 1950 (All Photo-c)
Fawcett Publications

1	6.50	19.50	45.00
2-Williamson, McWilliams-a	8.50	25.50	60.00
3	4.30	13.00	30.00

ROMEO TUBBS (Formerly My Secret Life)
No. 26, 5/50 - No. 28, 7/50; No. 1, 1950; No. 27, 12/52
Fox Feature Syndicate/Green Publ. Co. #27

	Good	Fine	N-Mint
26-Teen-age	5.00	15.00	35.00
27-Contains Pedro on inside; Wood-a	7.00	21.00	50.00
28, 1	3.70	11.00	26.00

RONALD McDONALD (TV)
Sept, 1970 - No. 4, March, 1971
Charlton Press (King Features Synd.)

1	.35	1.00	2.00
2-4		.50	1.00

RONIN
July, 1983 - No. 6, Apr, 1984 (mini-series) (52 pgs., $2.50)
DC Comics

1-Miller script, c/a in all	1.00	3.00	6.00
2	.85	2.50	5.00
3-5	.70	2.00	4.00
6-Scarcer	1.35	4.00	8.00
Trade paperback-Reprints 1-6	2.50	7.50	15.00

ROOK (See Eerie Magazine & Warren Presents: The Rook)
November, 1979 - No. 14, April, 1982
Warren Publications

1-Nino-a		.40	.80
2-14: 3,4-Toth-a		.30	.60

ROOKIE COP (Formerly Crime and Justice?)
No. 27, Nov, 1955 - No. 33, Aug, 1957
Charlton Comics

27	2.85	8.50	20.00
28-33	1.70	5.00	12.00

ROOM 222 (TV)
Jan, 1970; No. 2, May, 1970 - No. 4, Jan, 1971
Dell Publishing Co.

1,2,4: 2,4-Photo-c. 4 r-/#1	2.30	7.00	16.00
3-Marijuana story	2.30	7.00	16.00

ROOTIE KAZOOTIE (TV)(See 3-D-ell)
No. 415, Aug, 1952 - No. 6, Oct-Dec, 1954
Dell Publishing Co.

4-Color 415	4.30	13.00	30.00
4-Color 459,502	3.50	10.50	24.00
4(4-6/54)-6	3.50	10.50	24.00

ROOTS OF THE SWAMPTHING
July, 1986 - No. 5, Nov, 1986 ($2.00, Baxter paper)
DC Comics

1-5: All Wrightson-r. 4-Batman-c/story	.40	1.25	2.50

ROUND THE WORLD GIFT
No date (mid 1940's) (4 pages)
National War Fund (Giveaway)

nn	10.00	30.00	70.00

ROUNDUP (Western Crime)
July-Aug, 1948 - No. 5, Mar-Apr, 1949 (52 pgs.)
D. S. Publishing Co.

1-1pg. Frazetta on 'Mystery of the Hunting Lodge'?; Ingels-a?	7.00	21.00	50.00
2-Marijuana drug mention story	5.70	17.00	40.00
3-5	4.00	12.00	28.00

ROYAL ROY
May, 1985 - No. 6, Mar, 1986 (Children's book)
Star Comics (Marvel)

1-6		.35	.70

ROY CAMPANELLA, BASEBALL HERO
1950
Fawcett Publications

	Good	Fine	N-Mint
nn-Photo-c	23.50	71.00	165.00

ROY ROGERS (See March of Comics #17, 35, 47, 62, 68, 73, 77, 86, 91, 100, 105, 116, 121, 131, 136, 146, 151, 161, 167, 176, 191, 206, 221, 236, 250)

ROY ROGERS AND TRIGGER
April, 1967
Gold Key

1-Photo-c; reprints	2.30	7.00	16.00

ROY ROGERS COMICS (See Western Roundup under Dell Giants)
No. 38, 4/44 - No. 177, 12/47 (#38-166: 52 pgs.)
Dell Publishing Co.

4-Color 38 (1944)-49pg. story; photo front/back-c on all 4-Color issues	50.00	150.00	350.00
4-Color 63 (1945)-Color photos inside-c	34.00	100.00	235.00
4-Color 86,95 (1945)	25.00	7500	175.00
4-Color 109 (1946)	19.00	57.00	135.00
4-Color 117,124,137,144	14.00	42.00	100.00
4-Color 153,160,166: 166-48pg. story	11.50	34.00	80.00
4-Color 177 (36 pgs.)-32pg. story	11.50	34.00	80.00

ROY ROGERS COMICS (. . .& Trigger #92(8/55)-on)(Roy starred in Republic movies, radio & TV) (Singing cowboy) (Also see Dale Evans, It Really Happened #8, Queen of the West . . ., & Roy Rogers' Trigger)
Jan, 1948 - No. 145, Sept-Oct, 1961 (#1-19: 36 pgs.)
Dell Publishing Co.

1-Roy, his horse Trigger, & Chuck Wagon Charley's Tales begin; photo-c begin, end #145	39.00	118.00	275.00
2	19.00	58.00	135.00
3-5	16.00	48.00	110.00
6-10	11.50	34.00	80.00
11-19: 19- . . .Charley's Tales ends	8.00	24.00	55.00
20 (52 pgs.)-Trigger feature begins, ends #46	8.00	24.00	55.00
21-30 (52 pgs.)	6.50	19.50	45.00
31-46 (52 pgs.): 37-X-mas-c	5.00	15.00	35.00
47-56 (36 pgs.): 47-Chuck Wagon Charley's Tales returns, ends #133			
49-X-mas-c. 55-Last photo back-c	4.00	12.00	28.00
57 (52 pgs.)-Heroin drug propaganda story	4.60	14.00	32.00
58-70 (52 pgs.): 61-X-mas-c	3.50	10.50	24.00
71-80 (52 pgs.): 73-X-mas-c	2.85	8.50	20.00
81-91 (36 pgs. #81-on): 85-X-mas-c	2.65	8.00	18.00
92-Title changed to Roy Rogers and Trigger (8/55)	2.65	8.00	18.00
93-99,101-110,112-118	2.65	8.00	18.00
100-Trigger feature returns, ends #133?	4.00	12.00	28.00
111,119-124-Toth-a	4.35	13.00	30.00
125-131	3.00	9.00	21.00
132-144-Manning-a. 144-Dale Evans feat.	3.50	10.50	24.00
145-Last issue	4.00	12.00	28.00
. . .& the Man From Dodge City (Dodge giveaway, 16 pgs., 1954)-Frontier, Inc. (5x7¼'')	10.00	30.00	70.00
Official R.R. Riders Club Comics (1952; 16 pgs., reg. size, paper-c)	11.00	32.00	75.00

NOTE: **Buscema** a-2 each-74-108. **Manning** a-123, 124, 132-144. **Marsh** a-110. Photo back-c No. 1-9, 11-35, 38-55.

ROY ROGERS' TRIGGER (TV)
No. 329, May, 1951 - No. 17, June-Aug, 1955
Dell Publishing Co.

4-Color 329-Painted-c	7.00	21.00	50.00
2 (9-11/51)-Photo-c	4.00	12.00	28.00
3-5: Painted-c #3-on	1.70	5.00	12.00
6-17	1.15	3.50	8.00

Ronin #3, © DC

Roots Of The Swampthing #2, © DC

Roy Rogers Comics #11, © Roy Rogers

Ruff & Reddy #7, © Hanna-Barbera   Saari #1, © P.L. Publ.   Sabu, "Elephant Boy" #2, © FOX

RUDOLPH, THE RED NOSED REINDEER (See Limited Collectors' Edition #20,24,33,42,50)

RUDOLPH, THE RED NOSED REINDEER
1939 (2,400,000 copies printed); Dec, 1951
Montgomery Ward (Giveaway)

	Good	Fine	N-Mint
Paper cover - 1st app. in print; written by Robert May; ill. by Denver			
Gillen	8.35	25.00	50.00
Hardcover version	10.00	30.00	70.00
1951 version (Has 1939 date)-36 pgs., illos in three colors; red-c	3.00	9.00	21.00

RUDOLPH, THE RED-NOSED REINDEER
1950 - No. 13?, Winter, 1962-63 (Issues are not numbered)
National Periodical Publications

1950 issue; Grossman-c/a begins	5.00	15.00	35.00
1951-54 issues (4 total)	3.50	10.50	24.00
1955-62 issues (8 total)	1.70	5.00	12.00

NOTE: The 1962-63 issue is 84 pages. 13 total issues published.

RUFF & REDDY (TV)
No. 937, 9/58 - No. 12, 1-3/62 (Hanna-Barbera)
Dell Publishing Co./Gold Key

4-Color 937(1st Hanna-Barbera book)	3.00	9.00	21.00
4-Color 981,1038	2.00	6.00	14.00
4(1-3/60)-12	1.50	4.50	10.00

RUGGED ACTION (Strange Stories of Suspense #5 on)
Dec, 1954 - No. 4, June, 1955
Atlas Comics (CSI)

1	3.70	11.00	26.00
2-4: 2-Last precode (2/55)	2.00	6.00	14.00

NOTE: Ayers a-2. 3. Maneely c-2. 3. Severin a-2.

RULAH JUNGLE GODDESS (Formerly Zoot; I Loved #28 on) (Also see All Top Comics & Terrors of the Jungle)
No. 17, Aug, 1948 - No. 27, June, 1949
Fox Features Syndicate

17	30.00	90.00	210.00
18-Classic girl-fight interior splash	26.00	79.00	185.00
19,20	23.50	70.00	165.00
21-Used in **SOTI**, pg. 388,389	26.00	78.00	180.00
22-Used in **SOTI**, pg. 22,23	23.50	70.00	165.00
23-27	17.00	51.00	120.00

NOTE: Kamen c-17-19, 21, 22.

RUNAWAY, THE (See Movie Classics)

RUN BABY RUN
1974 (39 cents)
Logos International

By Tony Tallarico from Nicky Cruz's book		.30	.60

RUN, BUDDY, RUN (TV)
June, 1967 (Photo-c)
Gold Key

1 (10204-706)	1.50	4.50	10.00

RUST
7/87 - No. 15, 1988; V2#1, 2/89 - No. 7, 1989 ($1.50-$1.75, color)
Now Comics

1-3 ($1.50)	.25	.75	1.50
4-15, V2#1-7 ($1.75)	.30	.90	1.80

RUSTY, BOY DETECTIVE
Mar-April, 1955 - No. 5, Nov, 1955
Good Comics/Lev Gleason

1-Bob Wood, Carl Hubbell-a begins	2.85	8.50	20.00
2-5	1.70	5.00	12.00

RUSTY COMICS (Formerly Kid Movie Comics; Rusty and Her Family #21, 22; The Kelleys #23 on; see Millie The Model)
No. 12, Apr, 1947 - No. 22, Sept, 1949
Marvel Comics (HPC)

	Good	Fine	N-Mint
12-Mitzi app.	6.50	19.50	45.00
13	3.50	10.50	24.00
14-Wolverton's Powerhouse Pepper (4 pgs.) plus Kurtzman's "Hey			
Look"	6.50	19.50	45.00
15-17-Kurtzman's "Hey Look"	5.50	16.50	38.00
18,19	2.30	7.00	16.00
20-Kurtzman, 5 pgs.	5.50	16.50	38.00
21,22-Kurtzman, 17 & 22 pgs.	8.50	25.50	60.00

RUSTY DUGAN (See Holyoke One-Shot #2)

RUSTY RILEY (See 4-Color #418,451,486,554)

SAARI (The Jungle Goddess)
November, 1951
P. L. Publishing Co.

1	17.00	51.00	120.00

SABLE (Formerly Jon Sable, Freelance; also see Mike Grell's Sable)
Mar, 1988 - Present ($1.75-$1.95, color)
First Comics

1-26 ($1.95 #10 on)	.30	.90	1.75

SABOTAGE (See The Crusaders)

SABRE (See Eclipse Graphic Album Series)
10/78; 1/79; 8/82 - No. 14, 8/85 (Color, Baxter paper #4 on)
Eclipse Comics

1-($1.00)-Sabre & Morrigan Tales begin		.50	1.00
2-14: 4-6-Origin Incredible Seven		.50	1.00

NOTE: Colan c-11p. Gulacy c/a-1, 2.

SABRINA'S CHRISTMAS MAGIC (See Archie Giant Series Magazine #196, 207, 220, 231, 243, 455, 467, 479, 491, 503, 515)

SABRINA, THE TEEN-AGE WITCH (TV)(See Archie Giant Series #544, Archie's Madhouse, Archie's TV..., Chilling Advs. In Sorcery)
April, 1971 - No. 77, Jan, 1983 (Giants No. 1-17)
Archie Publications

1	2.15	6.50	15.00
2	1.00	3.00	7.00
3-5: 3,4-Archie's Group x-over	.50	1.50	3.00
6-10	.35	1.00	2.00
11-20		.60	1.20
21-77		.30	.60

SABU, "ELEPHANT BOY" (Movie; formerly My Secret Story)
No. 30, June, 1950 - No. 2, Aug, 1950
Fox Features Syndicate

30(#1)-Wood-a; photo-c	10.00	30.00	70.00
2-Photo-c; Kamen-a	6.00	18.00	45.00

SACRAMENTS, THE
October, 1955 (25 cents)
Catechetical Guild Educational Society

304	2.00	6.00	12.00

SACRED AND THE PROFANE, THE (See Eclipse Graphic Album Series #9)

SAD CASE OF WAITING ROOM WILLIE, THE
1950? (nd) (14 pgs. in color; paper covers; regular size)
American Visuals Corp. (For Baltimore Medical Society)

By Will Eisner (Rare)	27.00	81.00	190.00

SADDLE JUSTICE (Happy Houlihans #1,2; Saddle Romances #9 on)
No. 3, Spring, 1948 - No. 8, Sept-Oct, 1949
E. C. Comics

3-The 1st E. C. by Bill Gaines to break away from M. C. Gaines' old

SADDLE JUSTICE (continued)

	Good	Fine	N-Mint
Educational Comics format. Craig, Feldstein, H. C. Kiefer, & Stan Asch-a. Mentioned in **Love and Death**	27.00	81.00	190.00
4-1st Graham Ingels E. C.-a	27.00	81.00	190.00
5-8-Ingels-a in all	25.00	75.00	175.00

NOTE: **Craig** and **Feldstein** art in most issues. Canadian reprints known; see Table of Contents. **Craig** c-3, 4. **Ingels** c-5-8.

SADDLE ROMANCES (Saddle Justice #3-8; Weird Science #12 on)
No. 9, Nov-Dec, 1949 - No. 11, Mar-Apr, 1950
E. C. Comics

	Good	Fine	N-Mint
9-Ingels-c/a	30.00	90.00	210.00
10-Wood's 1st work at E. C.; Ingels-a	32.00	95.00	225.00
11-Ingels-a	30.00	90.00	210.00

NOTE: Canadian reprints known; see Table of Contents. **Feldstein** c-10.

SADIE SACK (See Harvey Hits #93)

SAD SACK AND THE SARGE
Sept, 1957 - No. 155, June, 1982
Harvey Publications

	Good	Fine	N-Mint
1	5.00	15.00	35.00
2	2.00	6.00	14.00
3-10	1.70	5.00	12.00
11-20	1.00	3.00	6.00
21-50	.40	1.20	2.40
51-90,97-100		.50	1.00
91-96: All 52 pg. Giants		.60	1.20
101-155		.25	.50

SAD SACK COMICS (See Harvey Collector's Comics #16, Little Sad Sack, Tastee Freez Comics #4 & True Comics #55)
Sept, 1949 - No. 287, Oct, 1982
Harvey Publications

	Good	Fine	N-Mint
1-Infinity-c; Little Dot begins (1st app.); civilian issues begin, end #21	20.00	60.00	140.00
2-Flying Fool by Powell	9.50	28.50	65.00
3	5.70	17.00	40.00
4-10	3.50	10.50	24.00
11-21	2.35	7.00	16.00
22-("Back In The Army Again" on covers #22-36). "The Specialist" story about Sad Sack's return to Army	1.35	4.00	8.00
23-50	.85	2.50	5.00
51-100	.50	1.50	3.00
101-150	.25	.75	1.50
151-222		.40	.80
223-228 (25 cent Giants, 52 pgs.)	.25	.75	1.50
229-287: 286,287 had limited distribution		.40	.80
3-D 1 (1/54-titled "Harvey 3-D Hits")	10.00	30.00	70.00
Armed Forces Complimentary copies, HD #1-40 ('57-'62)	.50	1.50	3.00

NOTE: The **Sad Sack** Comics comic book was a spin-off from a Sunday Newspaper strip launched through John Wheeler's Bell Syndicate. The previous Sunday page had to be discontinued in the early '50s. Unpopularity caused the Sunday page to be discontinued in the early '50s. Meanwhile Sad Sack returned to the Army, by popular demand, in issue No. 22, remaining there ever since. Incidentally, relatively few of the first 21 issues were ever collected and remain scarce due to this.

SAD SACK FUN AROUND THE WORLD
1974 (no month)
Harvey Publications

		Fine	N-Mint
1-About Great Britain		.40	.80

SAD SACK GOES HOME
1951 (16 pgs. in color)
Harvey Publications

	Good	Fine	N-Mint
nn-by George Baker	3.50	10.50	24.00

SAD SACK IN 3-D (See Blackthorne 3-D Series #49)

SAD SACK LAUGH SPECIAL
Winter, 1958-59 - No. 93, Feb, 1977 (#1-60: 68 pgs.; #61-76: 52 pgs.)
Harvey Publications

	Good	Fine	N-Mint
1	3.00	9.00	21.00
2	1.50	4.50	10.00
3-10	1.35	4.00	8.00
11-30	.70	2.00	4.00
31-60: Last 68 pg. Giant	.40	1.20	2.40
61-76: 52 pg. issues	.35	1.00	2.00
77-93		.50	1.00

SAD SACK NAVY, GOBS 'N' GALS
Aug, 1972 - No. 8, Oct, 1973
Harvey Publications

		Fine	N-Mint
1: 52 pg. Giant		.50	1.00
2-8		.30	.60

SAD SACK'S ARMY LIFE (See Harvey Hits #8, 17, 22, 28, 32, 39, 43, 47, 51, 55, 58, 61, 64, 67, 70)

SAD SACK'S ARMY LIFE (...Parade #1-57, ...Today #58 on)
Oct, 1963 - No. 60, Nov, 1975; No. 61, May, 1976
Harvey Publications

	Good	Fine	N-Mint
1: 68 pg. issues begin	2.00	6.00	14.00
2-10	1.00	3.00	6.00
11-20	.40	1.20	2.40
21-34: Last 68 pg. issue	.35	1.00	2.00
35-51: All 52 pgs.		.50	1.00
52-61		.30	.60

SAD SACK'S FUNNY FRIENDS (See Harvey Hits #75)
Dec, 1955 - No. 75, Oct, 1969
Harvey Publications

	Good	Fine	N-Mint
1	3.50	10.50	24.00
2-10	1.70	5.00	10.00
11-20	.85	2.50	5.00
21-30	.40	1.20	2.40
31-50		.50	1.00
51-75		.30	.60

SAD SACK'S MUTTSY (See Harvey Hits #74, 77, 80, 82, 84, 87, 89, 92, 96, 99, 102, 105, 108, 111, 113, 115, 117, 119, 121)

SAD SACK USA (...Vacation #8)
Nov, 1972 - No. 7, Nov, 1973; No. 8, Oct, 1974
Harvey Publications

		Fine	N-Mint
1		.50	1.00
2-8		.25	.50

SAD SACK WITH SARGE & SADIE
Sept, 1972 - No. 8, Nov, 1973
Harvey Publications

		Fine	N-Mint
1: 52 pg. Giant		.50	1.00
2-8		.25	.50

SAD SAD SACK WORLD
Oct, 1964 - No. 46, Dec, 1973 (#1-31: 68 pgs.; #32-38: 52 pgs.)
Harvey Publications

	Good	Fine	N-Mint
1	.85	2.50	6.00
2-10	.40	1.20	2.40
11-31: Last 68 pg. issue	.35	1.00	2.00
32-38: All 52 pgs.	.25	.75	1.50
39-46		.50	1.00

SAGA OF BIG RED, THE
Sept, 1976 ($1.25) (In color)
Omaha World-Herald

	Good	Fine	N-Mint
nn-by Win Mumma; story of the Nebraska Cornhuskers (sports)	.25	.80	1.60

Saddle Justice #7, © WMG

Sad Sack And The Sarge #11, © HARV

Sad Sack Comics #19, © HARV

The Saga Of Ra's Al Ghul #2, © DC

The Saga Of Swamp Thing #34, © DC

The Saint #9, © AVON

SAGA OF CRYSTAR, CRYSTAL WARRIOR, THE
May, 1983 - No. 11, Feb, 1985
Marvel Comics Group

	Good	Fine	N-Mint
1-($2.00; Baxter paper)-Remco toy tie-in	.35	1.00	2.00
2-5,7-11: 7-9,11-Golden-c. 10,11($1.00). 11-Alpha Flight app.			
		.30	.60
6-Nightcrawler app. Golden-c	.25	.75	1.50

SAGA OF RA'S AL GHUL, THE (See Batman #232)
Jan, 1988 - No. 4, Apr, 1988 ($2.50, color, mini-series)
DC Comics

	Good	Fine	N-Mint
1-Batman reprints; Neal Adams-c/a (r) in all	.75	2.25	4.50
2-4	.65	1.90	3.75

SAGA OF SWAMP THING, THE (Swamp Thing #39-41,46 on)
May, 1982 - Present (Later issues for mature readers; #86 on: $1.50)
DC Comics

	Good	Fine	N-Mint
1-Origin retold; Phantom Stranger series begins; ends #13; movie adaptation	.25	.75	1.50
2-15: 2-Photo-c from movie		.50	1.00
16-19: Bissette-a	.35	1.00	2.00
20-1st Alan Moore issue	3.15	9.50	22.00
21-New origin	2.85	8.50	20.00
22-25: 24-JLA x-over	1.30	4.00	8.00
26-30	.90	2.75	5.50
31-33	.50	1.50	3.00
34	1.50	4.50	9.00
35,36,38-40	.35	1.10	2.25
37-1st app. John Constantine	.85	2.50	5.00
41-45		.90	1.75
46-52: 46-Crisis x-over. 50-Double-size ($1.25)	.25	.75	1.50
53-Double size ($1.25)-Batman app.	.35	1.00	2.00
54-64: 64-Last Alan Moore issue		.60	1.25
65,66: Direct only begins		.50	1.00
67-92: 79-Superman-c/story. 85-Jonah Hex app.	.25	.75	1.50
Annual 1(11/82)-Movie Adaptation		.50	1.00
Annual 2(1/85)-Alan Moore scripts, Bissette-a(p)	.50	1.50	3.00
Annual 3(10/87, $2.00)	.35	1.00	2.00
Annual 4(10/88)-Batman c/story	.50	1.50	3.00
Annual 5('89, $2.95, 68 pgs.)-Batman cameo; re-intro Brother Power, 1st app. since 1968	.50	1.50	3.00
Saga of the Swamp Thing ($10.95, '87)-reprints #20-26			
	1.85	5.50	10.95

NOTE: *Bissette* a(p)-16-19, 21-27, 29, 30, 34-36, 39-42, 44, 46, 50, 64; c-17i; 24-32p, 35-37p, 40p, 44p, 46-50p, 51-56, 57i, 58, 61, 62, 63p. *Kaluta* c/a-74. *Spiegle* a-1-3, 6. *Totleben* a(i)-10, 16-27, 29, 31, 34-40, 42, 44, 46, 48, 50, 53, 55i; c-25-32i, 33, 35-40i, 42i, 44i, 46-50i, 53, 55i, 59p, 64, 65, 68, 73, 76, 80, 82, 84, 89, Annual 4, 5. *Williamson* 86i. *Wrightson* a-18i(r), 33r; c-57p.

SAGA OF THE SUB-MARINER, THE
Nov, 1988 - No. 12, Oct, 1989 ($1.25-$1.50 #9 on, limited series)
Marvel Comics

	Good	Fine	N-Mint
1-12: Buckler-c/a. 9-Original X-Men app.	.25	.75	1.50

SAILOR ON THE SEA OF FATE (See First Comics Graphic Novel #11)

SAILOR SWEENEY (Navy Action #1-11, 15 on)
No. 12, July, 1956 - No. 14, Nov, 1956
Atlas Comics (CDS)

	Good	Fine	N-Mint
12-14: 12-Shores-a. 13-Severin-c	2.65	8.00	18.00

SAINT, THE(Also see Movie Comics(DC) #2 & Silver Streak #18)
Aug, 1947 - No. 12, Mar, 1952
Avon Periodicals

	Good	Fine	N-Mint
1-Kamen bondage c/a	28.00	84.00	195.00
2	15.00	45.00	105.00
3,4: 4-Lingerie panels	12.00	36.00	84.00
5-Spanking panel	18.00	54.00	125.00
6-Miss Fury app., 14 pgs.	20.00	60.00	140.00

	Good	Fine	N-Mint
7-c-/Avon paperback 118	11.00	32.00	76.00
8,9(12/50): Saint strip-r in #8-12; 9-Kinstler-c	9.00	27.00	62.00
10-Wood-a, 1 pg; c-/Avon paperback 289	9.00	27.00	62.00
11	6.50	19.50	45.00
12-c-/Avon paperback 123	8.50	25.50	60.00

NOTE: *Lucky Dale, Girl Detective* in #1,2,4,6. *Hollingsworth* a-4, 6. *Painted-c* 8,10,11.

ST. GEORGE
June, 1988 - No. 8, Oct, 1989 ($1.25-$1.50, color)
Epic Comics (Marvel)

	Good	Fine	N-Mint
1-Sienkiewicz-c	.30	.90	1.80
2-8: 3-Begin $1.50-c	.25	.75	1.50

SALERNO CARNIVAL OF COMICS (Also see Pure Oil Comics, 24 Pages of Comics, & Vicks Comics)
Late 1930s (16 pgs.) (paper cover) (Giveaway)
Salerno Cookie Co.

	Good	Fine	N-Mint
nn-Color reprints of Calkins' Buck Rogers & Skyroads, plus other strips from Famous Funnies	25.00	75.00	175.00

SALIMBA IN 3-D (See Blackthorne 3-D Series #6 & 9)

SALOME' (See Night Music #6)

SAM AND MAX, FREELANCE POLICE SPECIAL
1987 ($1.75, B&W); Jan, 1989 ($2.75, color, 44 pgs.)
Fishwrap Productions/Comico

	Good	Fine	N-Mint
1 ($1.75, B&W)-Fishwrap	.30	.90	1.80
1 ($2.75, color)-Comico	.45	1.40	2.80

SAM HILL PRIVATE EYE
1950 - No. 7, 1951
Close-Up (Archie)

	Good	Fine	N-Mint
1-Negligee panel	5.70	17.00	40.00
2	3.50	10.50	24.00
3-7	2.65	8.00	18.00

SAM SLADE ROBOHUNTER (Also see Robo-Hunter)
Oct, 1986 - No. 31, 1989 ($1.25-$1.50, color)
Quality Comics

	Good	Fine	N-Mint
1-19 ($1.25)		.65	1.30
20,21/22,23/24,25-31 ($1.50): 26,27-Guice-c	.25	.75	1.50

SAMSON (1st Series) (Capt. Aero #7 on; see Big 3 Comics)
Fall, 1940 - No. 6, Sept, 1941 (See Fantastic Comics)
Fox Features Syndicate

	Good	Fine	N-Mint
1-Powell-a, signed 'Rensie;' Wing Turner by Tuska app; Fine-c?			
	59.00	178.00	415.00
2-Dr. Fung by Powell; Fine-c?	28.00	84.00	195.00
3-Navy Jones app.; Simon-c	23.00	70.00	160.00
4-Yarko the Great, Master Magician by Eisner begins; Fine-c?			
	18.50	56.00	130.00
5,6: 6-Origin The Topper	18.50	56.00	130.00

SAMSON (2nd Series) (Formerly Fantastic Comics #10, 11)
No. 12, April, 1955 - No. 14, Aug, 1955
Ajax/Farrell Publications (Four Star)

	Good	Fine	N-Mint
12-Wonder Boy	9.00	27.00	62.00
13,14: 13-Wonder Boy, Rocket Man	6.50	19.50	45.00

SAMSON (See Mighty Samson)

SAMSON & DELILAH (See A Spectacular Feature Magazine)

SAMUEL BRONSTON'S CIRCUS WORLD (See Circus World under Movie Comics)

SAMURAI (Also see Eclipse Graphic Album Series #14)
1985 - No. 23, 1987 ($1.70, B&W); V2#1, 1988 - No. 3, 1988 (color); V3#1, 1988 - No. 7, 1989 ($1.95, B&W)
Aircel Publishing

	Good	Fine	N-Mint
1	1.50	4.50	9.00

SAMURAI (continued)	Good	Fine	N-Mint
1-2nd print (1/86)	.40	1.25	2.50
1-3rd print	.30	.85	1.70
2	.40	1.25	2.50
2-2nd print	.30	.85	1.70
3-23	.35	1.00	2.00
V2#1-3 ('88, color, $2.00, mini-series, 28 pgs.)	.35	1.00	2.00
V3#1-7 (B&W, $1.95)	.35	1.00	1.95

SAMUREE
May, 1987 - Present ($2.00, color, Baxter)
Continuity Comics

1-6	.35	1.00	2.00

SANDMAN, THE (See Adventure Comics #40 & World's Finest #3)
Winter, 1974; No. 2, Apr-May, 1975 - No. 6, Dec-Jan, .1975-76
National Periodical Publications

1-Kirby-a	.40	1.25	2.50
2-6: 6-Kirby/Wood c/a	.25	.75	1.50
NOTE: Kirby a-1p, 4-6p; c-1-5.

SANDMAN
Jan, 1989 - Present ($1.50, color, mature readers)
DC Comics

1 ($2.00, 52 pgs.)	.70	2.00	4.00
2-13 ($1.50)	.35	1.00	2.00
14-Double size ($2.50)	.40	1.25	2.50

SANDS OF THE SOUTH PACIFIC
January, 1953
Toby Press

1	10.00	30.00	70.00

SANTA AND HIS REINDEER (See March of Comics #166)

SANTA AND POLLYANNA PLAY THE GLAD GAME
Aug, 1960 (16 pages) (Disney giveaway)
Sales Promotion

nn	1.00	3.00	6.00

SANTA AND THE ANGEL (See Dell Junior Treasury #7 & 4-Color #259)

SANTA & THE BUCCANEERS
1959
Promotional Publ. Co. (Giveaway)

nn-Reprints 1952 Santa & the Pirates	.50	1.50	3.00

SANTA & THE CHRISTMAS CHICKADEE
1974 (20 pgs.)
Murphy's (Giveaway)

nn		.50	1.00

SANTA & THE PIRATES
1952
Promotional Publ. Co. (Giveaway)

nn-Marv Levy c/a	.85	2.50	5.00

SANTA AT THE ZOO (See 4-Color #259)

SANTA CLAUS AROUND THE WORLD (See March of Comics #241)

SANTA CLAUS CONQUERS THE MARTIANS (See Movie Classics)

SANTA CLAUS FUNNIES
No date (1940s) (Color & B&W; 8x10''; 12pgs., heavy paper)
W. T. Grant Co. (Giveaway)

nn-March Of Comics-r?	6.75	20.00	40.00

SANTA CLAUS FUNNIES (Also see Dell Giants)
Dec?, 1942 - No. 1274, Dec, 1961
Dell Publishing Co.

nn(#1)(1942)-Kelly-a	30.00	90.00	210.00
2(12/43)-Kelly-a	20.00	60.00	140.00

	Good	Fine	N-Mint
4-Color 61(1944)-Kelly-a	20.00	60.00	140.00
4-Color 91(1945)-Kelly-a	14.00	42.00	100.00
4-Color 128('46),175('47)-Kelly-a	12.00	36.00	84.00
4-Color 205,254-Kelly-a	11.00	32.00	76.00
4-Color 302,361	2.30	7.00	16.00
4-Color 525,607,666,756,867	1.70	5.00	12.00
4-Color 958,1063,1154,1274	1.50	4.50	10.00
NOTE: Most issues contain only one Kelly story.

SANTA CLAUS PARADE
1951; No. 2, Dec, 1952; No. 3, Jan, 1955 (25 cents)
Ziff-Davis (Approved Comics)/St. John Publishing Co.

nn(1951-Ziff-Davis)-116 pgs. (Xmas Special 1,2)	8.50	25.50	60.00
2(12/52-Ziff-Davis)-100 pgs.; Dave Berg-a	7.00	21.00	50.00
V1#3(1/55-St. John)-100 pgs.	6.50	19.50	45.00

SANTA CLAUS' WORKSHOP (See March of Comics #50,168)

SANTA IS COMING (See March of Comics #197)

SANTA IS HERE (See March of Comics #49)

SANTA ON THE JOLLY ROGER
1965
Promotional Publ. Co. (Giveaway)

Marv Levy c/a	.50	1.50	3.00

SANTA! SANTA!
1974 (20 pgs.)
R. Jackson (Montgomery Ward giveaway)

nn		.50	1.00

SANTA'S BUSY CORNER (See March of Comics #31)

SANTA'S CANDY KITCHEN (See March of Comics #14)

SANTA'S CHRISTMAS BOOK (See March of Comics #123)

SANTA'S CHRISTMAS COMICS
December, 1952 (100 pages)
Standard Comics (Best Books)

nn-Supermouse, Dizzy Duck, Happy Rabbit, etc.	5.70	17.00	40.00

SANTA'S CHRISTMAS COMIC VARIETY SHOW
1943 (24 pages)
Sears Roebuck & Co.

Contains puzzles & new comics of Dick Tracy, Little Orphan Annie,
Moon Mullins, Terry & the Pirates, etc. 10.00 30.00 70.00

SANTA'S CHRISTMAS LIST (See March of Comics #255)

SANTA'S CHRISTMAS TIME STORIES
nd (late 1940s) (16 pgs.; paper cover)
Premium Sales, Inc. (Giveaway)

nn	2.00	6.00	12.00

SANTA'S CIRCUS
1964 (half-size)
Promotional Publ. Co. (Giveaway)

Marv Levy c/a	.50	1.50	3.00

SANTA'S FUN BOOK
1951, 1952 (regular size, 16 pages, paper-c)
Promotional Publ. Co. (Murphy's giveaway)

nn	1.70	5.00	10.00

SANTA'S GIFT BOOK
No date (16 pgs.)
No Publisher

Puzzles, games only	1.00	3.00	6.00

SANTA'S HELPERS (See March of Comics #64,106,198)

SANTA'S LITTLE HELPERS (See March of Comics #270)

Samurai V1#2, © Aircel Publ.

Sandman #1 (1/89), © DC

Santa Claus Funnies #1 (1942), © DELL

Sarge Steel #1, © CC

The Savage She-Hulk #25, © MEG

Savage Tales #1 (5/71), © MEG

SANTA'S NEW STORY BOOK
1949 (16 pgs.; paper cover)
Wallace Hamilton Campbell (Giveaway)

	Good	Fine	N-Mint
nn	3.00	9.00	18.00

SANTA'S REAL STORY BOOK
1948, 1952 (16 pgs.)
Wallace Hamilton Campbell/W. W. Orris (Giveaway)

nn	2.35	7.00	14.00

SANTA'S RIDE
1959
W. T. Grant Co. (Giveaway)

nn	1.35	4.00	8.00

SANTA'S RODEO
1964 (half-size)
Promotional Publ. Co. (Giveaway)

nn-Marv Levy-a	.70	2.00	4.00

SANTA'S SECRETS
1951, 1952? (16 pgs.; paper cover)
Sam B. Anson Christmas giveaway

nn	2.00	6.00	12.00

SANTA'S SHOW (See March of Comics #311)

SANTA'S SLEIGH (See March of Comics #298)

SANTA'S STORIES
1953 (regular size; paper cover)
K. K. Publications (Klines Dept. Store)

nn-Kelly-a	12.00	36.00	84.00

SANTA'S SURPRISE (See March of Comics #13)

SANTA'S SURPRISE
1947 (36 pgs.; slick cover)
K. K. Publications (Giveaway)

nn	2.75	8.00	16.00

SANTA'S TINKER TOTS
1958
Charlton Comics

1-Based on "The Tinker Tots Keep Christmas"

	1.30	4.00	8.00

SANTA'S TOYLAND (See March of Comics #242)

SANTA'S TOYS (See March of Comics #12)

SANTA'S TOYTOWN FUN BOOK
1952, 1953?
Promotional Publ. Co. (Giveaway)

nn-Marv Levy-c	1.00	3.00	6.00

SANTA'S VISIT (See March of Comics #283)

SANTIAGO (See 4-Color #723)

SARGE SNORKEL (Beetle Bailey)
Oct, 1973 - No. 17, Dec, 1976
Charlton Comics

1		.50	1.00
2-17		.30	.60

SARGE STEEL (Becomes Secret Agent #9 on; see Judomaster)
Dec, 1964 - No. 8, Mar-Apr, 1966
Charlton Comics

1-Origin	.50	1.50	3.00
2-8: 6-Judo Master app.	.35	1.00	2.00

SAVAGE COMBAT TALES
Feb, 1975 - No. 3, July, 1975
Atlas/Seaboard Publ.

	Good	Fine	N-Mint
1-3: 1-Sgt. Stryker's Death Squad begins (origin). 2-Only app. Warhawk		.30	.60

NOTE: *McWilliams* a-1-3; c-1. *Sparling* a-1, 3. *Toth* a-2.

SAVAGE HENRY
Jan, 1987 - Present ($1.75-$2.00, B&W, mature readers)
Vortex Comics

1-9 ($1.75)	.30	.90	1.80
10-14 ($2.00)	.35	1.00	2.00

SAVAGE RAIDS OF GERONIMO (See Geronimo #4)

SAVAGE RANGE (See 4-Color #807)

SAVAGE SHE-HULK, THE (See The Avengers, Marvel Graphic Novel #18 & The Sensational She-Hulk)
Feb, 1980 - No. 25, Feb, 1982
Marvel Comics Group

1-Origin & 1st app. She-Hulk	.40	1.25	2.50
2-25: 52-52 pgs.	.25	.75	1.50

NOTE: *Austin* a-25i; c-23i-25i. *J. Buscema* a-1p; c-1, 2p. *Golden* c-8-11.

SAVAGE SWORD OF CONAN, THE (Magazine)
Aug, 1974 - Present (B&W)(Mature readers)
Marvel Comics Group

1-Smith-r; Buscema/Adams/Krenkel-a; origin Blackmark by Gil Kane (part 1) & Red Sonja (3rd app.)	5.70	17.00	40.00
2-Adams-c; Chaykin/Adams-a	2.15	6.50	15.00
3-Severin/Smith-a; Adams-a	1.50	4.50	9.00
4-Adams/Kane-a(r)	1.35	4.00	8.00
5-10: 5-Jeff Jones frontispiece (r)	1.15	3.50	7.00
11-20	1.00	3.00	6.00
21-50	.85	2.50	5.00
51-100: 70-Article on movie. 83-Red Sonja-r by Adams from #1	.70	2.00	4.00
101-172: Later issues $2.00. 163-on: $2.25-c. 170-Solomon Kane by Williamson (i)	.50	1.50	3.00
Annual 1('75)-B&W, Smith-r (Conan #10,13)	.85	2.50	5.00

NOTE: *Adams* a-14p, 60, 83p(r). *Alcala* a-2, 4, 7, 12, 15-20, 23, 24, 28, 59, 67, 69, 75, 76i, 80i, 82i, 83i, 89. *Austin* a-78i. *Boris* c-1, 4, 5, 7, 9, 10, 12, 15. *Brunner* a-30; c-8, 30. *Buscema* a-1-5, 7, 10-12, 15-24, 26-28, 31, 32, 36-43, 45, 47-58p, 60-67p, 70, 71-74p, 76-81p, 87-96p, 98, 99p-101p; c-40. *Corben* a-4, 16, 29. *Finlay* a-16. *Golden* a-98, 101; c-150. *Kaluta* a-11, 18; c-3, 91, 93. *Gil Kane* a-2, 3, 8, 18r, 29, 47, 64, 65, 67, 85p, 86p. *Krenkel* a-9, 11, 14, 16, 24. *Morrow* a-7. *Nebres* a-93i, 101i, 107, 114. *Newton* a-6. *Nino* a/c-6. *Redondo* c-48, 50, 52, 56, 57, 85i, 90, 96i. *Simonson* a-7, 8, 12, 15-17. *Smith* a-7, 16, 24, 82r. *Starlin* c-26. *Toth* a-64. *Williamson* a-162i. No. 8 & 10 contain a Robert E. Howard Conan adaptation.

SAVAGE TALES (Magazine) (B&W)
May, 1971; No. 2, 10/73; No. 3, 2/74 - No. 12, Summer, 1975
Marvel Comics Group

1-Origin & 1st app. The Man-Thing by Morrow; Conan the Barbarian by Barry Smith, Femizons by Romita begin; Ka-Zar app.	7.00	21.00	50.00
2-Smith, Brunner, Morrow, Williamson, Wrightson-a (reprint/Creatures on the Loose #10); King Kull app.	3.60	11.00	25.00
3-Smith, Brunner, Steranko, Williamson-a	2.15	6.50	15.00
4,5-Adams-c; last Conan (Smith-r/#4) plus Kane/Adams-a. 5-Brak the Barbarian begins, ends #8	1.50	4.50	10.00
6-8: 6-Ka-Zar begins; Williamson-r; Adams-c. 7-Adams-i. 8-Shanna, the She-Devil app. thru #10; Williamson-r	.70	2.00	4.00
9,11	.50	1.50	3.00
10-Adams-a(i), Williamson-r	.70	2.00	4.00
Annual 1(Summer'75)(#12 on inside)-Ka-Zar origin by G. Kane; B&W; Smith-r/Astonishing Tales	.70	2.00	4.00

NOTE: *Boris* c-7,10. *Buscema* a-5r, 6p, 8p; c-2. *Fabian* c-8. *Heath* a-10p, 11p. *Kaluta* c-9. *Maneely* a-2r. *Morrow* a-7. *Reese* a-2. *Severin* a-7. *Starlin* a-5. Robert E. Howard adaptations-1-4.

SAVAGE TALES (Magazine size)
Nov, 1985 - No. 9, Mar, 1987 ($1.50, B&W, mature readers)

SAVAGE TALES (continued)
Marvel Comics Group

	Good	Fine	N-Mint
1-1st app. The Nam; Golden-a	1.50	4.50	9.00
2-9: Golden-a	.25	.75	1.50

SCAMP (Walt Disney)(See Walt Disney's Comics & Stories #204)
No. 703, 5/56 - No. 1204, 8-10/61; 11/67 - No. 45, 1/79
Dell Publishing Co./Gold Key

4-Color 703(No. 1)	1.70	5.00	12.00
4-Color 777,806('57),833	1.15	3.50	8.00
5(3-5/58)-10(6-8/59)	.85	2.50	6.00
11-16(12-2/60-61)	.70	2.00	5.00
4-Color 1204(1961)	.85	2.50	6.00
1(12/67-Gold Key)-Reprints begin	.55	1.65	4.00
2(3/69)-10	.35	1.00	2.00
11-20	.25	.75	1.50
21-45		.40	.80

NOTE: *New stories-#20(in part), 22-25, 27, 29-31, 34, 36-40, 42-45. New covers-#11, 12, 14, 15, 17-25, 27, 29-31, 34, 36-38.*

SCAR FACE (See The Crusaders)

SCARECROW OF ROMNEY MARSH, THE (See W.D. Showcase #53)
April, 1964 - No. 3, Oct, 1965 (Disney TV Show)
Gold Key

10112-404 (#1)	2.65	8.00	18.00
2,3	1.70	5.00	12.00

SCARLET IN GASLIGHT
Nov, 1987 - No. 4, 1988 ($1.95, B&W)
Eternity Comics

1-4	.35	1.00	2.00
Graphic Novel 1 (r/#1-4)	1.35	4.00	7.95

SCARLET O'NEIL (See Harvey Comics Hits #59 & Invisible . . .)

SCARY TALES
8/75 - #9, 1/77; #10, 9/77 - #20, 6/79; #21, 8/80 - #46, 10/84
Charlton Comics

1-Origin/1st app. Countess Von Bludd, not in #2	.40	.80
2-11	.30	.60
12-36,39,46-All reprints	.30	.60
37,38,40-45-New-a. 38-Mr. Jigsaw app.	.30	.60
1(Modern Comics reprint, 1977)	.15	.30

NOTE: *Adkins a-31i; c-31i. Ditko a-3, 5, 7, 8(2), 11, 12, 14-16r, 18(3)r, 19r, 21r, 30r, 32, 39r; c-5, 11, 14, 18, 30, 32. Newton a-31p; c-31p. Powell a-18r. Staton a-1(2 pgs.), 4, 20r; c-1, 20. Sutton a-9; c-4, 9.*

SCAVENGERS
Feb, 1988 - No. 14, 1989 ($1.25-1.50, color)
Quality Comics

1-7 ($1.25)		.60	1.25
8-10: ($1.50) 9-13-Guice-c	.25	.75	1.50

SCHOOL DAY ROMANCES (. . .of Teen-Agers #4) (Popular Teen-Agers #5 on)
Nov-Dec, 1949 - No. 4, May-June, 1950
Star Publications

1-Tony Gayle (later Gay), Gingersnap	8.00	24.00	56.00
2,3	4.30	13.00	30.00
4-Ronald Reagan photo-c	12.00	36.00	84.00

NOTE: *All have L. B. Cole covers.*

SCHWINN BICYCLE BOOK (. . . Bike Thrills, 1959)
1949; 1952; 1959 (10 cents)
Schwinn Bicycle Co.

1949	2.30	7.00	16.00
1952-Believe It or Not type facts; comic format; 36 pgs.	1.35	4.00	8.00
1959	1.00	3.00	6.00

SCIENCE COMICS (1st Series)
Feb, 1940 - No. 8, Sept, 1940
Fox Features Syndicate

	Good	Fine	N-Mint
1-Origin Dynamo (called Electro in #1), The Eagle (1st app.), & Navy Jones; Marga, The Panther Woman (1st app.), Cosmic Carson & Perisphere Payne, Dr. Doom begin; bondage/hypo-c	128.00	385.00	900.00
2	64.00	193.00	450.00
3,4; 4-Kirby-a	54.00	160.00	375.00
5-8	37.00	110.00	260.00

NOTE: *Cosmic Carson by Tuska-#1-3; by Kirby-#4. Lou Fine c-1-3 only.*

SCIENCE COMICS (2nd Series)
January, 1946 - No. 5, 1946
Humor Publications (Ace Magazines?)

1-Palais c/a in No. 1-3; A-Bomb-c	4.50	14.00	32.00
2	2.65	8.00	18.00
3-Feldstein-a, 6 pgs.	6.00	18.00	42.00
4,5	2.30	7.00	16.00

SCIENCE COMICS
May, 1947 (8 pgs. in color)
Ziff-Davis Publ. Co.

nn-Could be ordered by mail for 10 cents; like the nn Amazing Advs. (1950)-used to test the market	24.00	73.00	170.00

SCIENCE COMICS
March, 1951
Export Publication Ent., Toronto, Canada
Distr. in U.S. by Kable News Co.

1-Science Adventure stories plus some true science features	2.30	7.00	16.00

SCIENCE FICTION SPACE ADVENTURES (See Space Adventures)

SCOOBY DOO (. . .Where are you? #1-16,26; . . .Mystery Comics #17-25,27 on) (TV) (See March Of Comics #356,368,382,391)
March, 1970 - No. 30, Feb, 1975 (Hanna-Barbera)
Gold Key

1	2.85	8.50	20.00
2-5	1.50	4.50	10.00
6-10	1.00	3.00	7.00
11-20: 11-Tufts-a	.70	2.00	5.00
21-30	.50	1.50	3.00

SCOOBY DOO (TV)
April, 1975 - No. 11, Dec, 1976 (Hanna Barbera)
Charlton Comics

1	1.15	3.50	8.00
2-5	.70	2.00	4.00
6-11	.50	1.50	3.00

SCOOBY-DOO (TV)
Oct, 1977 - No. 9, Feb, 1979 (Hanna-Barbera)
Marvel Comics Group

1-Dyno-Mutt begins	.40	1.25	2.50
2-9		.50	1.00

SCOOP COMICS
November, 1941 - No. 8, 1946
Harry 'A' Chesler (Holyoke)

1-Intro. Rocketman & Rocketgirl; origin The Master Key; Dan Hastings begins; Charles Sultan c/a	38.00	115.00	270.00
2-Rocket Boy app; Injury to eye story (Same as Spotlight #3)	22.00	65.00	155.00
3-Injury to eye story-r from #2; Rocket Boy	17.00	51.00	120.00
4-8	13.00	40.00	90.00

SCOOTER (See Swing with . . .)

Scamp #11 (Dell), © WDC

Science Comics #2, © FOX

Scoop Comics #1, © CHES

Scooter Comics #1, © Rucker Publ.

Scout Handbook #1, © Eclipse

Sea Devils #16, © DC

SCOOTER COMICS
April, 1946
Rucker Publ. Ltd. (Canadian)

	Good	Fine	N-Mint
1-Teen-age/funny animal	3.00	9.00	21.00

SCORE, THE
1989 - No. 4, 1990 ($4.95, color, squarebound, adults, 52 pgs.)
Piranha Press (DC Comics)

Book One - Four: Mark Badger painted-c/a	.85	2.50	5.00

SCORPION
Feb, 1975 - No. 3, July, 1975
Atlas/Seaboard Publ.

1-Intro.; bondage-c by Chaykin	.40	.80	
2,3: 2-Wrightson, Kaluta, Simonson-a(i)	.30	.60	

NOTE: *Chaykin a-1, 2. **Mooney** a-3i.*

SCORPIO ROSE
Jan, 1983; No. 2, Oct, 1983 ($1.25, color, Baxter paper)
Eclipse Comics

1,2: 1-Dr. Orient back-up story begins. 2-Origin	.65	1.30	

NOTE: *Rogers c/a 1, 2.*

SCOTLAND YARD (Inspector Farnsworth of...) (Texas Rangers in Action #5 on?)
June, 1955 - No. 4, March, 1956
Charlton Comics Group

1-Tothish-a	5.50	16.50	38.00
2-4: 2-Tothish-a	3.50	10.50	24.00

SCOUT (See Eclipse Graphic Album #16, New America & Swords of Texas)(Becomes Scout: War Shaman)
Dec, 1985 - No. 24, Oct, 1987 ($1.25 - $1.75, color, Baxter)
Eclipse Comics

1	1.25	3.75	7.50
2-8,11,12: 11-Monday: The Eliminator begins	.40	1.25	2.50
9,10: 9-Airboy app. 10-Bissette-a	.35	1.00	2.00
13-15,17,18,20-24 ($1.75)	.35	1.00	2.00
16-Scout 3-D Special ($2.50)	.40	1.25	2.50
16-Scout 2-D Limited Edition	.40	1.25	2.50
19-Contains Flexidisk ($2.50)	.50	1.50	3.00
...Handbook 1 (8/87, $1.75, B&W)	.30	.90	1.75

SCOUT: WAR SHAMAN (Formerly Scout)
March, 1988 - No. 16, Oct, 1989 ($1.95, color)
Eclipse Comics

1-16	.35	1.00	2.00

SCREAM (...Comics) (Andy Comics #20 on)
Fall, 1944 - No. 19, April, 1948
Humor Publications/Current Books(Ace Magazines)

1	5.50	16.50	38.00
2	2.85	8.50	20.00
3-15: 11-Racist humor (Indians)	2.30	7.00	16.00
16-Intro. Lily-Belle	2.30	7.00	16.00
17,19	2.00	6.00	14.00
18-Transvestism, hypo needle story	3.70	11.00	26.00

SCREAM (Magazine)
Aug, 1973 - No. 11, Feb, 1975 (68 pgs.) (B&W)
Skywald Publishing Corp.

1	.70	2.00	4.00
2-5: 2-Origin Lady Satan. 3 (12/73)-#3 found on pg. 22	.35	1.00	2.00
6-11: 6-Origin The Victims. 9-Severed head-c	.25	.75	1.50

SCRIBBLY (See All-American Comics, Buzzy, The Funnies & Popular Comics)
8-9/48 - No. 13, 8-9/50; No. 14, 10-11/51 - No. 15, 12-1/51-52
National Periodical Publications

	Good	Fine	N-Mint
1-Sheldon Mayer-a in all; 52pgs. begin	48.00	144.00	335.00
2	28.00	85.00	200.00
3-5	24.00	73.00	170.00
6-10	17.00	51.00	120.00
11-15: 13-Last 52 pgs.	13.00	40.00	90.00

SEA DEVILS (See DC Special #10,19, DC Super-Stars #14,17, Limited Collectors' Edition #39,45, & Showcase #27-29)
Sept-Oct, 1961 - No. 35, May-June, 1967
National Periodical Publications

1	14.00	42.00	100.00
2-Last 10 cent issue	5.70	17.00	40.00
3-5	3.60	11.00	25.00
6-10	2.15	6.50	15.00
11,12,14-20	1.50	4.50	10.00
13-Kubert, Colan-a	1.70	5.00	12.00
21,23-35	1.15	3.50	8.00
22-Intro. International Sea Devils; origin & 1st app. Capt. X & Man Fish	1.15	3.50	8.00

NOTE: *Heath a-1-10; c-1-10,14-16. Moldoff a-16i.*

SEADRAGON (Also see The Epsilon Wave)
May, 1986 - No. 8, 1987 ($1.75, color)
Elite Comics

1-8: 1-First & second printings exist	.30	.90	1.80

SEA HOUND, THE (Capt. Silver's Log Of The...)
1945 (no month) - No. 4, Jan-Feb, 1946
Avon Periodicals

nn	5.70	17.00	40.00
2-4 (#2, 9-10/45)	4.00	12.00	28.00

SEA HOUND, THE (Radio)
No. 3, July, 1949 - No. 4, Sept, 1949
Capt. Silver Syndicate

3,4	3.50	10.50	24.00

SEA HUNT (TV)
#928, 8/58; #994, 5-7/59; #1041, 10-12/59; #4, 1-3/60 - #13, 4-6/62
Dell Publishing Co. (All have Lloyd Bridges photo-c)

4-Color 928 (#1)	5.70	17.00	40.00
4-Color 994 (#2), 4-13: Manning-a #4-6,8-11,13	4.50	14.00	32.00
4-Color 1041 (#3)-Toth-a	6.50	19.50	45.00

SEARCH FOR LOVE
Feb-Mar, 1950 - No. 2, Apr-May, 1950 (52 pgs.)
American Comics Group

1	3.70	11.00	26.00
2,3(6-7/50): 3-Exist?	2.00	6.00	14.00

SEARCHERS (See 4-Color #709)

SEARS (See Merry Christmas From...)

SEASON'S GREETINGS
1935 (6¼x5¼'') (32 pgs. in color)
Hallmark (King Features)

Cover features Mickey Mouse, Popeye, Jiggs & Skippy. ''The Night Before Christmas'' told one panel per page, each panel by a famous artist featuring their character. Art by Alex Raymond, Gottfredson, Swinnerton, Segar, Chic Young, Milt Gross, Sullivan (Messmer), Herriman, McManus, Percy Crosby & others (22 artists in all)

Estimated value....	$200.00 — $400.00	

SECRET AGENT (Formerly Sarge Steel)
V2#9, Oct, 1966; V2No.10, Oct, 1967
Charlton Comics

V2#9-Sarge Steel part-r begins	.50	1.50	3.00
10-Tiffany Sinn, CIA app. (from Career Girl Romances #39); Aparo-a	.35	1.00	2.00

SECRET AGENT (TV)
Nov, 1966 - No. 2, Jan, 1968
Gold Key

	Good	Fine	N-Mint
1,2-Photo-c	2.65	8.00	18.00

SECRET AGENT X-9 (See Flash Gordon #4 by King)
1934 (Book 1: 84 pgs.; Book 2: 124 pgs.) (8x7½")
David McKay Publications

Book 1-Contains reprints of the first 13 weeks of the strip by Alex
Raymond; complete except for 2 dailies 38.00 115.00 265.00
Book 2-Contains reprints immediately following contents of Book 1,
for 20 weeks by Alex Raymond; complete except for two dailies.
Note: Raymond mis-dated the last five strips from 6/34, and
while the dating sequence is confusing, the continuity is correct
32.00 95.00 225.00

SECRET AGENT X-9 (See Feature Books #8, McKay & Magic Comics)

SECRET AGENT Z-2 (See Holyoke One-Shot No. 7)

SECRET DIARY OF EERIE ADVENTURES
1953 (One Shot) (25 cent giant-100 pgs.)
Avon Periodicals

nn-(Rare) Kubert-a; Hollingsworth-c; Check back-c
82.00 246.00 575.00

SECRET HEARTS
9-10/49 - No. 6, 7-8/50; No. 7, 12-1/51-52 - No. 153, 7/71
(No. 1-6, photo-c; all 52 pgs.)
National Periodical Publications (Beverly)(Arleigh No. 50-113)

	Good	Fine	N-Mint
1	16.00	48.00	110.00
2-Toth-a	7.00	21.00	50.00
3,6 (1950)	5.70	17.00	40.00
4,5-Toth-a	7.00	21.00	50.00
7(12-1/51-52) (Rare)	7.00	21.00	50.00
8-10 (1952)	4.00	12.00	28.00
11-20	3.00	9.00	21.00
21-26: 26-Last precode (2-3/55)	2.65	8.00	18.00
27-40	2.00	6.00	14.00
41-50	1.30	4.00	9.00
51-60	.85	2.60	6.00
61-75: Last 10 cent issue	.70	2.00	4.00
76-109	.50	1.50	3.00
110-"Reach for Happiness" serial begins, ends #138	.35	1.00	2.00
111-119,121-126,128-133,135-138	.60	1.20	
120,134-Adams-c	.35	1.00	2.00
127 (4/68)-Beatles cameo	.35	1.00	2.00
139,140	.60	1.20	
141,142-"20 Miles to Heartbreak," Chapter 2 & 3 (See Young Love for Chapter 1 & 4); Toth, Colletta-a	.50	1.00	
143-148,150-153: 144-Morrow-a. 153-Kirby-i	.25	.50	
149-Toth-a	.50	1.00	

SECRET ISLAND OF OZ, THE (See First Comics Graphic Novel)

SECRET LOVE (See Fox Giants & Sinister House of . . .)

SECRET LOVE
12/55 - No. 3, 8/56; 4/57 - No. 5, 2/58; No. 6, 6/58
Ajax-Farrell/Four Star Comic Corp. No. 2 on

	Good	Fine	N-Mint
1(12/55-Ajax, 1st series)	2.65	8.00	18.00
2,3	1.50	4.50	10.00
1(4/57-Ajax, 2nd series)	2.00	6.00	14.00
2-6: 5-Bakerish-a	1.30	4.00	9.00

SECRET LOVES
Nov, 1949 - No. 6, Sept, 1950 (#5: photo-c)
Comic Magazines/Quality Comics Group

	Good	Fine	N-Mint
1-Ward-c	9.00	27.00	62.00
2-Ward-c	8.50	25.50	60.00

	Good	Fine	N-Mint
3-Crandall-a	5.50	16.50	38.00
4,6	2.85	8.50	20.00
5-Suggestive art-"Boom Town Babe"	4.35	13.00	30.00

SECRET LOVE STORIES (See Fox Giants)

SECRET MISSIONS
February, 1950
St. John Publishing Co.

	Good	Fine	N-Mint
1-Kubert-c	8.50	25.50	60.00

SECRET MYSTERIES (Formerly Crime Mysteries & Crime Smashers)
No. 16, Nov, 1954 - No. 19, July, 1955
Ribage/Merit Publications No. 17 on

	Good	Fine	N-Mint
16-Horror, Palais-a	5.70	17.00	40.00
17-19-Horror; #17-mis-dated 3/54?	4.00	12.00	28.00

SECRET ORIGINS (See 80 Page Giant #8)
Aug-Oct, 1961 (Annual) (Reprints)
National Periodical Publications

1('61)-Origin Adam Strange (Showcase #17), Green Lantern (G.L.
#1), Challs (partial/Showcase #6, 6 pgs. Kirby-a). J'onn J'onzz
(Det. #225), New Flash (Showcase #4). Green Arrow (1pg. text).
Superman-Batman team (W. Finest #94). Wonder Woman (W.
Woman #105). 18.00 54.00 125.00

SECRET ORIGINS
Feb-Mar, 1973 - No. 6, Jan-Feb, 1974; No. 7, Oct-Nov, 1974
National Periodical Publications (All origin reprints)

	Good	Fine	N-Mint
1-Origin Superman-r/Action #1(1st time since G.A.), Batman, The Ghost, The Flash (Showcase #4)	.25	.75	1.50
2-4: 2-New Green Lantern, the new Atom, & Supergirl. 3-Wonder Woman, Wildcat. 4-Vigilante by Meskin, Kid Eternity		.50	1.00
5-7: 5-The Spectre. 6-Blackhawk & Legion of Super-Heroes. 7-Robin, Aquaman		.45	.90

NOTE: *Colan c-5p. Infantino a-1. Kane a-2. Kubert a-1.*

SECRET ORIGINS
April, 1986 - Present (All origins)(52 pgs. #6 on)
DC Comics

	Good	Fine	N-Mint
1-Origin Superman	.50	1.50	3.00
2-Blue Beetle	.35	1.10	2.25
3-5: 3-Shazam. 4-Firestorm. 5-Crimson Avenger/Shadow/Doll Man	.35	1.00	2.00
6-G.A. Batman	.70	2.00	4.00
7-10: 7-Green Lantern/G.A. Sandman. 8-Doll Man. 9-G.A. Flash/Skyman. 10-Phantom Stranger	.30	.90	1.75
11,12,14-20: 11-G.A. Hawkman/Power Girl. 12-Challs of Unknown/G.A. Fury. 14-Suicide Squad. 15-Spectre/Deadman. 16-G.A. Hourman/Warlord. 17-Adam Strange/Dr. Occult. 18-G.A. Gr. Lantern/The Creeper. 19-Uncle Sam/The Guardian. 20-Batgirl/G.A. Dr. Mid-Nite	.25	.75	1.50
13-Origin Nightwing; Johnny Thunder app.	.50	1.50	3.00
21-38,40: 21-Jonah Hex/Black Condor. 22-Manhunters. 23-Floronic Man/Guardians of the Universe. 24-Blue Devil/Dr. Fate. 25-L.S.H./Atom. 26-Bl. Lightning/Miss America. 27-Zatara/Zatanna. 28-Midnight/Nightshade. 29-Power-Atom/Mr. America. 30-Plastic Man/Elongated Man. 31-J.S.A. 32-J.L.A. 33-35-Justice League Inter. 36-Green Lantern/Poison Ivy. 37-Legion Of Substitute Heroes/Doctor Light. 38-Green Arrow/Speedy; Grell scripts. 40-All Ape issue	.25	.75	1.50
39,44-Batman app.	.35	1.00	2.00
41-48: 41-Rogues Gallery of Flash. 42-Phantom Girl/Grim Ghost. 43-Original Hawk & Dove/Cave Carson/Chris KL-99. 45-Blackhawk/El Diablo. 46-JLA/LSH/New Titans. 47-LSH. 48-Ambush Bug/Stanley & His Monster/Rex the Wonder Dog	.25	.75	1.50
Annual 1 (8/87)-Doom Patrol by Byrne c/a	.35	1.00	2.00

Secret Diary Of Eerie Adventures, © AVON

Secret Mysteries #19, © Merit

Secret Origins #1 (2-3-/73), © DC

Secret Origins Special #1, © DC

Secret Six #1, © DC

Secret Society Of Super-Villains #1, © DC

SECRET ORIGINS (continued)	Good	Fine	N-Mint
Annual 2 ('88, $2.00)-Origin Flash	.35	1.00	2.00
Annual 3 ('89, $2.95, 84 pgs.)-Teen Titans	.50	1.50	2.95
Special 1 (10/89, $2.00)-Batman villains: Penguin, Riddler, & Two-Face; Bolland-c	.40	1.25	2.50

NOTE: **Art Adams** a-33i. **Bolland** a-33i. **Bolland** c-7. **Colan** a-5. **Forte** a-37. **Giffen** a-18p, 44p. **Kaluta** c-39. **Gil Kane** a-2, 28; c-2p. **Morrow** a-21. **Orlando** a-10. **Perez** c-Annual 3. **Rogers** a-6p. **Russell** a-27i. **Steacy** a-35. **Staton** a-36. **Tuska** a-9p.

SECRET ORIGINS OF SUPER-HEROES (See DC Special Series #10,19)

SECRET ROMANCE
10/68 - No. 41, 11/76; No. 42, 3/79 - No. 48, 2/80
Charlton Comics

1	.40	1.25	2.50
2-10: 9-Reese-a		.60	1.20
11-48		.30	.60

NOTE: *Beyond the Stars app.-No. 9, 11, 12, 14.*

SECRET ROMANCES
April 1951 - No. 27, July, 1955
Superior Publications Ltd.

1	5.00	15.00	35.00
2	2.85	8.50	20.00
3-10	2.65	8.00	18.00
11-13,15-18,20-27	1.85	5.50	13.00
14,19-Lingerie panels	2.85	8.50	20.00

SECRET SERVICE (See Kent Blake of the. . .)

SECRET SIX (See Action Comics Weekly)
Apr-May, 1968 - No. 7, Apr-May, 1969
National Periodical Publications

1-Origin	1.50	4.50	10.00
2-7	.85	2.60	6.00

SECRET SOCIETY OF SUPER-VILLAINS
May-June, 1976 - No. 15, June-July, 1978
National Periodical Publications/DC Comics

1-Origin; JLA cameo		.65	1.30
2-5: 2-Re-intro/origin Capt. Comet; Gr. Lantern x-over		.30	.60
6-15: 9,10-Creeper x-over. 11-Capt. Comet app.; Orlando-i. 15-G.A. Atom, Dr. Midnite, & JSA app.		.25	.50

SECRET SOCIETY OF SUPER-VILLAINS SPECIAL (See DC Special Series #6)

SECRETS OF HAUNTED HOUSE
4-5/75 - #5, 12-1/75-76; #6, 6-7/77 - #14, 10-11/78; #15, 8/79 - #46, 3/82
National Periodical Publications/DC Comics

1		.50	1.00
2-46: 31-Mr. E series begins, ends #41		.25	.50

NOTE: **Bissette** a-46. **Buckler** c-32-40p. **Ditko** a-9, 12, 41, 45. **Golden** a-10. **Howard** a-13i. **Kaluta** c-8, 10, 11, 14, 16, 29. **Kubert** c-41, 42. **Sheldon Mayer** a-43p. **McWilliams** a-35. **Nasser** a-24. **Newton** a-30p. **Nino** a-1, 13, 19. **Orlando** c-13, 30, 43, 45i. **Redondo** a-4, 5, 29. **Rogers** c-26. **Spiegle** a-31-41. **Wrightson** c-5, 44.

SECRETS OF HAUNTED HOUSE SPECIAL (See DC Special Series #12)

SECRETS OF LIFE (See 4-Color #749)

SECRETS OF LOVE (See Popular Teen-Agers. . .)

SECRETS OF LOVE AND MARRIAGE
V2#1, Aug, 1956 - V2#25, June, 1961
Charlton Comics

V2#1	1.50	4.50	10.00
V2#2-6	.70	2.00	5.00
V2#7-9(All 68 pgs.)	.60	1.75	3.50
10-25	.40	1.25	2.50

SECRETS OF MAGIC (See Wisco)

SECRETS OF SINISTER HOUSE (Sinister H. of Secret Love #1-4)
No. 5, June-July, 1972 - No. 18, June-July, 1974
National Periodical Publications

	Good	Fine	N-Mint
5-9: 7-Redondo-a		.30	.60
10-Adams-a(i)	.50	1.50	3.00
11-18: 17-Barry-a		.25	.50

NOTE: **Alcala** a-6, 13, 14. **Kaluta** c-6, 7. **Nino** a-8, 11-13. Ambrose Bierce adapt.-#14.

SECRETS OF THE LEGION OF SUPER-HEROES
Jan, 1981 - No. 3, March, 1981 (mini-series)
DC Comics

1-Origin of the Legion		.50	1.00
2,3: 2-Retells origins of Brainiac 5, Shrinking Violet, Sun-Boy, Bouncing Boy, Ultra-Boy, Matter-Eater Lad, Mon-El, Karate Kid, & Dream Girl		.40	.80

SECRETS OF TRUE LOVE
February, 1958
St. John Publishing Co.

1	1.50	4.50	10.00

SECRETS OF YOUNG BRIDES
No. 5, 9/57 - No. 44, 10/64; 7/75 - No. 9, 11/76
Charlton Comics

5	1.50	4.50	10.00
6-10: 8-Negligee panel	.70	2.00	5.00
11-20	.60	1.80	4.00
21-30: Last 10 cent issue?	.50	1.50	3.00
31-44	.25	.75	1.50
1-9 (2nd series)		.25	.50

SECRET SQUIRREL (TV)
October, 1966 (Hanna-Barbera)
Gold Key

1	2.85	8.50	20.00
Kite Fun Book (1966, 16p, 5x7¼", soft-c)	2.65	8.00	18.00

SECRET STORY ROMANCES (Becomes True Tales of Love)
Nov, 1953 - No. 21, Mar, 1956
Atlas Comics (TCI)

1-Everett-a	3.50	10.50	24.00
2	1.70	5.00	12.00
3-11: 11-Last pre-code (2/55)	1.30	4.00	9.00
12-21	1.15	3.50	8.00

NOTE: **Colletta** a-10, 14, 15, 17, 21; c-10, 14, 17.

SECRET VOICE, THE (See Great American Comics Presents. . .)

SECRET WARS II (Also see Marvel Super Heroes. . .)
July, 1985 - No. 9, Mar, 1986 (maxi-series)
Marvel Comics Group

1-Byrne/Austin-c	.30	.90	1.80
2-9: 9-Double sized (75 cents)		.65	1.30

SECTAURS
June, 1985 - No. 10?, 1986 (75 cents, color)
Marvel Comics Group

1-10: Based on Coleco Toys		.40	.80
1-Coleco giveaway; diff-c		.40	.80

SEDUCTION OF THE INNOCENT (Also see N. Y. State Joint Legis. Committee to Study. . .)
1953, 1954 (399 pages) (Hardback)
Rinehart & Co., Inc., N. Y. (Also printed in Canada by Clarke, Irwin & Co. Ltd., Toronto)

Written by Dr. Fredric Wertham

	Good	Fine
(1st Version)-with bibliographical note intact (several copies got out before the comic publishers forced the removal of this page)	70.00	150.00
with dust jacket....	150.00	300.00

SEDUCTION OF THE INNOCENT (continued)

	Good	Fine	N-Mint
(2nd Version)-without bibliographical note	42.00		90.00
with dust jacket....	65.00		140.00
(3rd Version)-Published in England by Kennikat Press, 1954, 399pp.			
has bibliographical page	30.00		60.00
1972 r-/of 3rd version; 400pgs w/bibliography page; Kennikat Press			
	12.00		24.00

NOTE: Material from this book appeared in the November, 1953(Vol.70, pp50-53,214) issue of the **Ladies' Home Journal** under the title "What Parents Don't Know About Comic Books." With the release of this book, Dr. Wertham reveals seven years of research attempting to link juvenile delinquency to comic books. Many illustrations showing excessive violence, sex, sadism, and torture are shown. This book was used at the Kefauver Senate hearings which led to the Comics Code Authority. Because of the influence this book had on the comic industry and the collector's interest in it, we feel this listing is justified. Also see **Parade of Pleasure**.

SEDUCTION OF THE INNOCENT!
Nov, 1985 - No. 6, April, 1986 ($1.75, color)
Eclipse Comics

1-6: Double listed under cover title #7 on	.30	.90	1.80
...3-D 1(10/85; $2.25 cover)-Contains unpub. Advs. Into Darkness			
#15 (pre-code) (36 pgs.); Dave Stevens-c	.40	1.15	2.30
2-D 1 (100 copy limited signed & numbered edition)(B&W)			
	.85	2.50	5.00
...3-D 2 (4/86)-Baker, Toth-r; Wrightson-c	.40	1.25	2.50
2-D 2 (100 copy limited signed & numbered edition)(B&W)			
	.85	2.50	5.00

SELECT DETECTIVE
Aug-Sept, 1948 - No. 3, Dec-Jan, 1948-49
D. S. Publishing Co.

1-Matt Baker-a	8.00	24.00	56.00
2-Baker, McWilliams-a	5.50	16.50	38.00
3	4.50	14.00	32.00

SEMPER FI (Tales of the Marine Corps)
Dec, 1988 - No. 9, Aug, 1989 (75 cents, color)
Marvel Comics

1-Severin-c/a, Glanzman back-up-a in all	.35	1.00	2.00
2-9	.25	.75	1.50

SENSATIONAL POLICE CASES (Becomes Captain Steve Savage, 2nd series)
1952; 1954 - No. 4, 1954
Avon Periodicals

nn-100 pg. issue (1952, 25 cents)-Kubert & Kinstler-a			
	17.00	51.00	120.00
1 (1954)	5.70	17.00	40.00
2,3: 2-Kirbyish-a	4.35	13.00	30.00
4-Reprint/Saint #5	4.35	13.00	30.00

SENSATIONAL POLICE CASES
No date (1963?)
I. W. Enterprises

Reprint #5-Reprints Prison Break #5(1952-Avon); Infantino-a			
	1.00	3.00	7.00

SENSATIONAL SHE-HULK, THE (Also see She-Hulk)
May, 1989 - Present ($1.50, color, deluxe format)
Marvel Comics

1-Byrne-c/a(p)/scripts begin, end #8	.35	1.00	2.00
2-8: 4-Reintro G.A. Blonde Phantom	.30	.90	1.75
9-12	.25	.75	1.50

SENSATIONAL SPIDER-MAN
April, 1989 ($5.95, color, squarebound, 80 pgs.)
Marvel Comics

1-r/Amaz. Spider-Man Annual #14,15 by Miller and Annual #8 by Kirby/Ditko	1.00	3.00	6.00

SENSATION COMICS (Sensation Mystery #110 on)
Jan, 1942 - No. 109, May-June, 1952
National Periodical Publ./All-American

	Good	Fine	N-Mint
1-Origin Mr. Terrific, Wildcat, The Gay Ghost, & Little Boy Blue; Wonder Woman(cont'd from All Star #8), The Black Pirate begin; intro. Justice & Fair Play Club	383.00	960.00	2300.00

1-Reprint, Oversize 13½"x10." **WARNING:** This comic is an exact duplicate reprint of the original except for its size. DC published it in 1974 with a second cover titling it as a Famous First Edition. There have been many reported cases of the outer cover being removed and the interior sold as the original edition. The reprint with the new outer cover removed is practically worthless.

2	135.00	407.00	950.00
3-W. Woman gets secretary's job	80.00	240.00	560.00
4-1st app. Stretch Skinner in Wildcat	71.00	215.00	500.00
5-Intro. Justin, Black Pirate's son	54.00	160.00	375.00
6-Origin/1st app. Wonder Woman's magic lasso			
	46.00	137.00	320.00
7-10	43.00	130.00	300.00
11-20: 13-Hitler, Tojo, Mussolini-c	37.00	110.00	260.00
21-30	27.00	81.00	190.00
31-33	21.00	62.00	145.00
34-Sargon, the Sorcerer begins, ends #36; begins again #52			
	21.00	62.00	145.00
35-40: 38-Xmas-c	17.00	51.00	120.00
41-50: 43-The Whip app.	14.00	42.00	100.00
51-60: 51-Last Black Pirate. 56,57-Sargon by Kubert			
	13.00	40.00	90.00
61-80: 63-Last Mr. Terrific. 65,66-Wildcat by Kubert. 68-Origin Huntress	13.00	40.00	90.00
81-Used in **SOTI**, pg. 33,34; Krigstein-a	15.00	45.00	105.00
82-90: 83-Last Sargon. 86-The Atom app. 90-Last Wildcat			
	11.00	32.00	75.00
91-Streak begins by Alex Toth	11.00	32.00	75.00
92,93: 92-Toth-a, 2 pgs.	10.00	30.00	70.00
94-1st all girl issue	12.00	36.00	84.00
95-99,101-106: Wonder Woman ends. 99-1st app. Astra, Girl of the Future, ends 106. 105-Last 52 pgs.	12.00	36.00	84.00
100	16.00	48.00	110.00
107-(Scarce)-1st mystery issue; Toth-a	24.00	70.00	165.00
108-(Scarce)-Johnny Peril by Toth(p)	21.00	62.00	145.00
109-(Scarce)-Johnny Peril by Toth(p)	24.00	70.00	165.00

NOTE: **Krigstein** a-(Wildcat)-81, 83, 84. **Moldoff** Black Pirate-1-25; Black Pirate not in 34-36, 43-48. Wonder Woman by H. G. Peter, all issues except #8, 17-19. 21. **Toth** a-91, 98.

SENSATION MYSTERY (Sensation #1-109)
No. 110, July-Aug, 1952 - No. 116, July-Aug, 1953
National Periodical Publications

110-Johnny Peril continues	12.00	36.00	84.00
111-116-Johnny Peril in all	11.00	32.00	75.00

NOTE: **Colan** a-114p. **Giunta** a-112. **G. Kane** c-112, 113, 115.

SENSEI
Aug, 1989 - No. 4, Dec, 1989 ($2.75, color, mini-series, deluxe)
First Comics

1-4: 1-Mayerik painted-c	.45	1.40	2.80

SENTINELS OF JUSTICE, THE (See Americomics & Captain Paragon & . . .)

SERGEANT BARNEY BARKER (G. I. Tales #4 on)
Aug, 1956 - No. 3, Dec, 1956
Atlas Comics (MCI)

1-Severin-a(4)	6.50	19.50	45.00
2,3-Severin-a(4)	3.70	11.00	26.00

SERGEANT BILKO (Phil Silvers) (TV)
May-June, 1957 - No. 18, Mar-Apr, 1960
National Periodical Publications

1	17.00	51.00	120.00

The Sensational She-Hulk #1, © MEG

Sensation Comics #107, © DC

Sergeant Bilko #1, © DC

Sgt. Fury #1, © MEG   Sgt. Rock Special #1, © DC   The Shadow #2 (Archie), © Conde Nast Publ.

	Good	Fine	N-Mint
SERGEANT BILKO (continued)			
2	12.00	36.00	84.00
3-5	10.00	30.00	70.00
6-18: 11,12,15-Photo-c	8.00	24.00	56.00

SGT. BILKO'S PVT. DOBERMAN (TV)
June-July, 1958 - No. 11, Feb-Mar, 1960
National Periodical Publications

1	13.50	40.00	95.00
2	8.50	25.50	60.00
3-5: 5-Photo-c	6.50	19.50	45.00
6-11: 6,9-Photo-c	5.00	15.00	35.00

SGT. DICK CARTER OF THE U.S. BORDER PATROL (See Holyoke One-Shot)

SGT. FURY (& His Howling Commandos)(See Special Marvel Ed.)
May, 1963 - No. 167, Dec, 1981
Marvel Comics Group

1-1st app. Sgt. Fury; Kirby/Ayers c/a	28.00	84.00	200.00
2-Kirby-a	11.00	32.00	75.00
3-5: 3-Reed Richards x-over. 4-Death of Junior Juniper. 5-1st Baron			
Strucker app.; Kirby-a	5.70	17.00	40.00
6-10: 8-Baron Zemo, 1st Percival Pinkerton app. 10-1st app. Capt.			
Savage (the Skipper)	3.60	11.00	25.00
11,12,14-20: 14-1st Blitz Squad. 18-Death of Pamela Hawley			
	1.70	5.00	12.00
13-Captain America app.; Kirby-a	5.00	15.00	35.00
21-50: 25-Red Skull app. 27-1st Eric Koenig app., origin Fury's eye			
patch. 34-Origin Howling Commandos. 35-Eric Koeing joins			
Howlers. 43-Bob Hope, Glen Miller app. 44-Flashback-Howlers 1st			
mission	1.00	3.00	7.00
51-100: 64-Capt. Savage & Raiders x-over. 76-Fury's Father app. in			
WWI story. 98-Deadly Dozen x-over. 100-Captain America, Fantas-			
tic Four cameos; Stan Lee, Martin Goodman & others app.			
	.70	2.00	4.00
101-167: 101-Origin retold. 167-reprints #1	.50	1.50	3.00
Annual 1('65, 25 cents, 72 pgs.)	2.15	6.50	15.00
Special 2-7('66-11/71)	.70	2.00	4.00

NOTE: *Ditko a-15i. Gil Kane c-37, 96. Kirby a-1-8, 13p, 167p. Special 5; c-120, 25, 167p. Severin a-44-46, 48, 162, 164; inks-4, 6, 49-79; c-4i, 5, 6, 44, 46, 110, 149i, 155i, 162-166. Sutton a-57p. Reprints in #80, 82, 85, 87, 89, 91, 93, 95, 99, 101, 103, 105, 107, 109, 111, 145.*

SGT. FURY AND HIS HOWLING DEFENDERS (See The Defenders)

SERGEANT PRESTON OF THE YUKON (TV)
No. 344, Aug, 1951 - No. 29, Nov-Jan, 1958-59
Dell Publishing Co.

4-Color 344(#1)-Sergeant Preston & his dog Yukon King begin;			
painted-c begin, end #18	5.70	17.00	40.00
4-Color 373,397,419('52)	3.70	11.00	26.00
5(11-1/52-53)-10(2-4/54)	3.00	9.00	21.00
11,12,14-17	2.30	7.00	16.00
13-Origin S. Preston	3.00	9.00	21.00
18-Origin Yukon King; last painted-c	3.00	9.00	21.00
19-29: All photo-c	3.00	9.00	21.00

SERGEANT PRESTON OF THE YUKON
1956 (4 comic booklets) (Soft-c, 16p, 7x2½" & 5x2½")
Giveaways with Quaker Cereals

"How He Found Yukon King, The Case That Made Him A Sergeant,
How Yukon King Saved Him From The Wolves, How He Became A
Mountie"   each... | 4.00 | 12.00 | 28.00 |

SGT. ROCK (Formerly Our Army at War; see Brave & the Bold #52)
No. 302, March, 1977 - No. 422, July, 1988
National Periodical Publications/DC Comics

302	.50	1.50	3.00
303-350: 318-Reprints	.25	.75	1.50

	Good	Fine	N-Mint
351-422		.50	1.00
Annual 2(9/82), 3(8/83), 4(8/84)		.50	1.00

NOTE: *Estrada a-322, 327, 331, 336, 337, 341, 342i. Glanzman a-384, 421. Kubert a-302, 303, 305r, 306, 328, 351, 356, 368, 373; c-317, 318r, 319-323, 325-333-on, Annual 2, 3. Spiegle a-382, Annual 2, 3. Thorne a-384. Toth a-385r.*

SGT. ROCK SPECIAL (Also see DC Special Series #3)
Oct, 1988 - Present ($2.00, color, quarterly, 52 pgs.)
DC Comics

1-7: All reprints; 5-Reprints 1st Sgt. Rock/Our Army At War #81.
  7-Tomahawk-r by Thorne | .35 | 1.00 | 2.00 |

NOTE: *Adams r-1. Chaykin r-3; c-3. Drucker r-6. Heath r-5. Krigstein r-4. Kubert r-1-7; c-1p, 2. Miller r-6p. Severin r-3, 6. Simonson r-2, 4; c-4. Thorne r-7. Toth r-2. Wood r-4.*

SGT. ROCK SPECTACULAR (See DC Special Series #13)

SGT. ROCK'S PRIZE BATTLE TALES (See DC Special Series #18)
Winter, 1964 (One Shot) (Giant - 80 pgs.)
National Periodical Publications

1-Kubert, Heath-r; new Kubert-c | 1.30 | 4.00 | 9.00 |

SGT. STRYKER'S DEATH SQUAD (See Savage Combat Tales)

SERGIO ARAGONES' GROO THE WANDERER (See Groo . . .)

SEVEN DEAD MEN (See Complete Mystery #1)

SEVEN DWARFS (See 4-Color #227, 382)

SEVEN SEAS COMICS
Apr, 1946 - No. 6, 1947 (no month)
Universal Phoenix Features/Leader No. 6

1-South Sea Girl by Matt Baker, Capt. Cutlass begin; Tugboat			
Tessie by Baker app.	30.00	90.00	210.00
2	25.00	75.00	175.00
3-6: 3-Six pg. Feldstein-a	23.00	70.00	165.00

NOTE: *Baker a-1-6; c-3,6.*

1776 (See Charlton Classic Library)

7TH VOYAGE OF SINBAD, THE (See 4-Color #944)

77 SUNSET STRIP (TV)
No. 1066, 1-3/60 - No. 2, 2/63 (All photo-c)
Dell Publ. Co./Gold Key

4-Color 1066-Toth-a	6.50	19.50	45.00
4-Color 1106,1159-Toth-a	5.70	17.00	40.00
4-Color 1211,1263,1291, 01-742-209(7-9/62)-Manning-a in all			
	4.50	14.00	32.00
1(11/62-G.K.), 2-Manning-a in each	4.00	12.00	28.00

77TH BENGAL LANCERS, THE (See 4-Color #791)

SEYMOUR, MY SON (See More Seymour)
September, 1963
Archie Publications (Radio Comics)

1 | 2.85 | 8.50 | 20.00 |

SHADE, THE CHANGING MAN (See Cancelled Comic Cavalcade)
June-July, 1977 - No. 8, Aug-Sept, 1978 (also see Suicide Squad #16)
National Periodical Publications/DC Comics

1-Ditko c/a in all		.40	.80
2-8		.30	.60

SHADOW, THE
Aug, 1964 - No. 8, Sept, 1965
Archie Comics (Radio Comics)

1	1.70	5.00	12.00
2-8-The Fly app. in some issues	1.15	3.50	8.00

SHADOW, THE
Oct-Nov, 1973 - No. 12, Aug-Sept, 1975
National Periodical Publications

1-Kaluta-a begins | 1.15 | 3.50 | 7.00 |

THE SHADOW (continued)	Good	Fine	N-Mint
2	.70	2.00	4.00
3-Kaluta/Wrightson-a	.85	2.50	5.00
4,6-Kaluta-a ends	.50	1.50	3.00
5,7-12: 11-The Avenger (pulp character) x-over	.25	.75	1.50

NOTE: *Craig* a-10. *Cruz* a-10-12. *Kaluta* a-1, 2, 3p, 4, 6; c-1-4, 6, 10-12. *Kubert* c-9. *Robbins* a-5, 7-9; c-5, 7.

SHADOW, THE
May, 1986 - No. 4, Aug, 1986 (mini-series) (mature readers)
DC Comics

	Good	Fine	N-Mint
1-Chaykin-a in all	1.15	3.50	7.00
2-4	.75	2.25	4.50
. . . Blood & Judgement (1987, $12.95)-r/Shadow #1-4, 1986			
	2.15	6.50	13.00

SHADOW, THE (Also see Marvel Graphic Novel #35)
Aug, 1987 - No. 19, Jan, 1989 ($1.50, mature readers)
DC Comics

1	.50	1.50	3.00
2-19: 13-Death of The Shadow	.35	1.00	2.00
Annual 1 (12/87, $2.25)-Orlando-a	.40	1.25	2.50
Annual 2 (12/88, $2.50)	.40	1.25	2.50

SHADOW COMICS (Pulp, radio)
March, 1940 - V9No.5, Aug, 1949
Street & Smith Publications

NOTE: The Shadow first appeared in Fame & Fortune Magazine, 1929, began on radio the same year, and was featured in pulps beginning in 1931. The early covers of this series were reprinted from the pulp covers.

V1#1-Shadow, Doc Savage, Bill Barnes, Nick Carter, Frank Merriwell, Iron Munro, the Astonishing Man begin	167.00	420.00	1000.00
2-The Avenger begins, ends #6; Capt. Fury only app.			
	62.00	185.00	435.00
3(nn-5/40)-Norgil the Magician app. (also #9)			
	48.00	145.00	335.00
4,5: 4-The Three Musketeers begins, ends #8. 5-Doc Savage ends	39.00	118.00	275.00
6,8,9	30.00	90.00	210.00
7-Origin & 1st app. Hooded Wasp & Wasplet; series ends V3#8			
	34.00	100.00	235.00
10-Origin The Iron Ghost, ends #11; The Dead End Kids begins, ends #14	30.00	90.00	210.00
11-Origin The Hooded Wasp & Wasplet retold			
	30.00	90.00	210.00
12-Dead End Kids app.	26.00	77.00	180.00
V2#1,2(11/41): 2-Dead End Kid story	24.00	73.00	170.00
3-Origin & 1st app. Supersnipe; series begins; Little Nemo story			
	30.00	90.00	210.00
4,5: 4-Little Nemo story	21.50	64.00	150.00
6-9: 6-Blackstone the Magician app.	20.00	60.00	140.00
10-12: 10-Supersnipe app.	20.00	60.00	140.00
V3#1-12: 10-Doc Savage begins, not in V5#5, V6#10-12, V8#4			
	18.50	56.00	130.00
V4#1-12	17.00	51.00	120.00
V5#1-12	16.00	47.00	110.00
V6#1-11: 9-Intro. Shadow, Jr.	14.00	42.00	100.00
12-Powell-c/a; atom bomb panels	16.00	48.00	110.00
V7#1,2,5,7,9,12: 2,5-Shadow, Jr. app.; Powell-a	16.00	48.00	110.00
3,6,11-Powell c/a	17.00	51.00	120.00
4-Powell c/a; Atom bomb panels	18.50	56.00	130.00
10(1/48)-Flying Saucer issue; Powell c/a (2nd of this theme; see The Spirit 9/28/47)	21.50	64.00	150.00
V8#1-12-Powell-a	17.00	51.00	120.00
V9#1,5-Powell c/a	16.00	48.00	110.00
2-4-Powell c/a	17.00	51.00	120.00

NOTE: *Powell* art in most issues beginning V6#12.

SHADOWMASTERS (See Punisher #24)
10/89 - No. 4, 1/90 ($3.95, squarebound, limited series, 52pgs.)
Marvel Comics

	Good	Fine	N-Mint
1-4: 1-Heath-i; story cont'd from Punisher	.70	2.00	4.00

SHADOW OF THE BATMAN
Dec, 1985 - No. 5, Apr, 1986 ($1.75 cover; mini-series)
DC Comics

1-Detective-r	1.70	5.00	10.00
2,3,5	1.15	3.50	7.00
4-Joker-c/story	1.50	4.50	9.00

NOTE: *Austin* a-2-4i. *Rogers* c/a-1-5.

SHADOW PLAY
June, 1982
Whitman Publications

1		.30	.60

SHADOWS FROM BEYOND (Formerly Unusual Tales)
V2#50, October, 1966
Charlton Comics

V2#50-Ditko-c	.60	1.75	3.50

SHADOW STRIKES!, THE
Sept, 1989 - Present ($1.75, color)
DC Comics

1-6	.30	.90	1.75
Annual 1('89, $3.50, 68pgs.)-Spiegle-a; Kaluta-c	.60	1.75	3.50

SHADOW WAR OF HAWKMAN
May, 1985 - No. 4, Aug, 1985 (mini-series)
DC Comics

1-4: 1-Alcala inks		.50	1.00

SHAGGY DOG & THE ABSENT-MINDED PROFESSOR (See 4-Color #985, Movie Comics & Walt Disney Showcase #46)

SHANNA, THE SHE-DEVIL (See Savage Tales #8)
Dec, 1972 - No. 5, Aug, 1973
Marvel Comics Group

1-Steranko-c; Tuska-a		.40	.80
2-5: 2-Steranko-c		.30	.60

SHARK FIGHTERS, THE (See 4-Color No. 762)

SHARP COMICS (Slightly large size)
Winter, 1945-46 - V1No.2, Spring, 1946 (52 pgs.)
H. C. Blackerby

V1#1-Origin Dick Royce Planetarian	14.00	42.00	100.00
2-Origin The Pioneer; Michael Morgan, Dick Royce, Sir Gallagher, Planetarian, Steve Hagen, Weeny and Pop app.			
	11.50	34.00	80.00

SHARPY FOX (See Comic Capers & Funny Frolics)
1958; 1963
I. W. Enterprises/Super Comics

1,2-I.W. Reprint (1958)	.35	1.00	2.00
14-Super Reprint (1963)	.35	1.00	2.00

SHATTER (See Jon Sable #25-30)
June, 1985 (One Shot; Baxter paper, color)
First Comics

1-1st computer-generated artwork in a comic book			
	.50	1.50	3.00
1-2nd printing	.30	.85	1.70

NOTE: *1st printings have the number "1" included in the row of numbers at the bottom of the indicia.*

SHATTER
Dec, 1985 - No. 14, April, 1988 ($1.75 cover; deluxe paper)
First Comics

Shadow Comics V7#3, © Conde Nast Publ.

Shadow Of The Batman #2, © DC

The Shadow Strikes #1, © Conde Nast Publ.

Sheena, Queen Of The Jungle #1, © FH   Shield #1, © MEG   Shield Wizard Comics #8, © AP

	Good	Fine	N-Mint
SHATTER (continued)			
1-Computer-generated art and lettering	.50	1.50	3.00
2-14	.35	1.00	2.00

SHAZAM (See Giant Comics to Color & Limited Collectors' Edition)

SHAZAM! (TV)(See World's Finest #253)
Feb, 1973 - No. 35, May-June, 1978
National Periodical Publications/DC Comics

1-1st revival of original Captain Marvel(origin retold), by Beck;			
Captain Marvel Jr. & Mary Marvel x-over		.60	1.25
2-7,9,10: 2-Infinity-c; re-intro Mr. Mind & Tawney. 4-Origin retold.			
10-Last Beck issue		.50	1.00
8-100 pgs.; reprints Capt. Marvel Jr. by Raboy; origin/C.M. #80;			
origin Mary Marvel/C.M. #18		.50	1.00
11-Shaffenberger-a begins		.50	1.00
12-17-All 100 pgs.; 15-Lex Luthor x-over		.50	1.00
18-35: 25-1st app. Isis. 30-1st DC app. 3 Lt. Marvels. 31-1st DC app.			
Minuteman. 34-Origin Capt. Nazi & Capt. Marvel Jr. retold			
		.50	1.00

NOTE: Reprints in #1-8, 10, 12-17, 21-24. Beck a-1-10, 12-17r, 21-24r; c-1, 3-9. Nasser c-35p. Newton a-35p. Raboy a-5r, 8r, 17r. Shaffenberger a-11, 14-20, 25, 26, 27p, 28, 29-31p, 33i, 35i; c-20, 22, 23, 25, 26i, 27i, 28-33.

SHAZAM: THE NEW BEGINNING
Apr, 1987 - No. 4, July, 1987 (mini-series)
DC Comics

1-New origin Capt. Marvel	.25	.75	1.50
2-4		.60	1.20

SHEA THEATRE COMICS
No date (1940's) (32 pgs.)
Shea Theatre

Contains Rocket Comics; MLJ cover in mono color

	10.00	20.00	30.00

SHEENA
Dec, 1984 - No. 2, Feb, 1985 (Limited series, movie adaptation)
Marvel Comics Group

1,2-r/Marvel Comics Super Special		.40	.80

SHEENA, QUEEN OF THE JUNGLE (See Jerry Iger's Classic . . . ,
Jumbo Comics, & 3-D Sheena)
Spring, 1942 - No. 18, Winter, 1952-53 (#1,2: 68 pgs.)
Fiction House Magazines

1-Sheena begins	107.00	321.00	750.00
2 (Winter, 1942/43)	54.00	160.00	375.00
3 (Spring, 1943)	37.00	110.00	260.00
4, 5 (Fall, 1948 - Sum., '49)	21.50	64.00	150.00
6,7 (Spring, '50 - '50, 52 pgs.)	19.00	58.00	135.00
8-10('50, 36 pgs.)	17.00	51.00	120.00
11-17	14.00	42.00	100.00
18-Used in POP, pg. 98	14.00	42.00	100.00
I.W. Reprint #9-Reprints #17	2.50	7.50	15.00

SHEENA 3-D (Also see Blackthorne 3-D Series #1)
Jan, 1985 ($2.00)
Eclipse Comics

1-Dave Stevens-c	.50	1.50	3.00

SHE-HULK (See The Savage She-Hulk & The Sensational She-Hulk)

SHERIFF BOB DIXON'S CHUCK WAGON (TV)
November, 1950 (See Wild Bill Hickok #22)
Avon Periodicals

1-Kinstler c/a(3)	7.00	21.00	50.00

SHERIFF OF COCHISE, THE
1957 (16 pages) (TV Show)
Mobil Giveaway

Shaffenberger-a	1.00	3.00	7.00

SHERIFF OF TOMBSTONE
Nov, 1958 - No. 17, Sept, 1961
Charlton Comics

	Good	Fine	N-Mint
V1#1-Williamson/Severin-c	3.70	11.00	26.00
2	2.00	6.00	14.00
3-17	1.15	3.50	8.00

SHERLOCK HOLMES (See Cases of . . . , 4-Color #1169,1245, Marvel Preview & Spectacular Stories)

SHERLOCK HOLMES (All New Baffling Advs. of . . .)
Oct, 1955 - No. 2, Mar, 1956 (Young kEagle #3 on?)
Charlton Comics

1-Dr. Neff, Ghost Breaker app.	22.00	65.00	155.00
2	19.00	58.00	135.00

SHERLOCK HOLMES (Also see The Joker)
Sept-Oct, 1975
National Periodical Publications

1-Cruz-a; Simonson-c		.50	1.00

SHERRY THE SHOWGIRL (Showgirls #4)
7/56 - No. 3, 12/56; No. 5, 4/57 - No. 7, 8/57
Atlas Comics

1	3.70	11.00	26.00
2	2.30	7.00	16.00
3,5-7	1.70	5.00	12.00

SHIELD (Nick Fury & His Agents of . . .) (Also see Nick Fury)
Feb, 1973 - No. 5, Oct, 1973
Marvel Comics Group

1-Steranko-c	.40	1.25	2.50
2-Steranko flag-c	.35	1.00	2.00
3-5: 1-5 all contain-r from Strange Tales #146-155. 3-5-are cover-r;			
3-Kirby/Steranko-c(r). 4-Steranko-c(r)	.35	1.00	2.00

NOTE: Buscema a-3p(r). Kirby layouts 1-5; c-3 (w/Steranko). Steranko a-3r, 4r(2).

SHIELD, THE (Becomes Shield-Steel Sterling #3; #1 titled 'Lancelot Strong;' also see Advs. of the Fly, Double Life of Private Strong, Fly Man, Mighty Comics, The Mighty Crusaders & The Original . . .)
June, 1983 - No. 2, Aug, 1983
Archie Enterprises, Inc.

1,2: Steel Sterling app.		.45	.90

SHIELD-STEEL STERLING (Formerly The Shield)
No. 3, Dec, 1983 (Becomes Steel Sterling No. 4)
Archie Enterprises, Inc.

3-Nino-a		.45	.90

SHIELD WIZARD COMICS (Also see Pep & Top-Notch Comics)
Summer, 1940 - No. 13, Spring, 1944
MLJ Magazines

1-(V1#5 on inside)-Origin The Shield by Irving Novick & The Wizard			
by Ed Ashe, Jr; Flag-c	125.00	375.00	875.00
2-Origin The Shield retold; intro. Wizard's sidekick, Roy			
	57.00	171.00	400.00
3,4	37.00	110.00	260.00
5-Dusty, the Boy Detective begins	33.00	100.00	230.00
6-8: 6-Roy the Super Boy begins	28.50	86.00	200.00
9,10	25.00	75.00	175.00
11-13: 13-Bondage-c	23.50	70.00	165.00

SHIP AHOY
November, 1944 (52 pgs.)
Spotlight Publishers

1-L. B. Cole-c	6.00	18.00	42.00

SHMOO (See Al Capp's . . . & Washable Jones & . . .)

SHOCK (Magazine)
(Reprints from horror comics) (Black & White)

SHOCK (continued)
May, 1969 - V3No.4, Sept, 1971
Stanley Publications

	Good	Fine	N-Mint
V1#1-Cover-r/Weird Tales of the Future #7 by Bernard Baily	1.15	3.50	8.00
2-Wolverton-r/Weird Mysteries 5; r-Weird Mysteries 7 used in SOTI; cover r-/Weird Chills #1	1.00	3.00	7.00
3,5,6	.70	2.00	4.00
4-Harrison/Williamson-r/Forbidden Worlds #6	.85	2.60	6.00
V2#2, V1#8, V2#4-6, V3#1-4	.60	1.75	3.50

NOTE: *Disbrow* r-V2#4; bondage c-V1#4, V2#6, V3#1.

SHOCK DETECTIVE CASES (Formerly Crime Fighting Detective)
(Becomes Spook Detective Cases No. 22)
No. 20, Sept, 1952 - No. 21, Nov, 1952
Star Publications

20,21-L.B. Cole-c	4.50	14.00	32.00

NOTE: *Palais* a-20. No. 21-*Fox*-r.

SHOCK ILLUSTRATED (Magazine format)
Sept-Oct, 1955 - No. 3, Spring, 1956
E. C. Comics

1-All by Kamen; drugs, prostitution, wife swapping	3.50	10.50	24.00
2-Williamson-a redrawn from Crime SuspenStories #13 plus Ingels, Crandall, & Evans	4.00	12.00	28.00
3-Only 100 known copies bound & given away at E.C. office; Crandall, Evans-a	100.00	300.00	700.00
(Prices vary widely on this book)			

SHOCKING MYSTERY CASES (Formerly Thrilling Crime Cases)
No. 50, Sept, 1952 - No. 60, Oct, 1954
Star Publications

50-Disbrow "Frankenstein" story	12.00	36.00	84.00
51-Disbrow-a	5.70	17.00	40.00
52-55,57-60	5.00	15.00	35.00
56-Drug use story	5.50	16.50	38.00

NOTE: *L. B. Cole* covers on all; a-60(2 pgs.). *Hollingsworth* a-52. *Morisi* a-55.

SHOCKING TALES DIGEST MAGAZINE
Oct, 1981 (95 cents)
Harvey Publications

1-1957-58-r; Powell, Kirby, Nostrand-a	.50		1.00

SHOCK SUSPENSTORIES
Feb-Mar, 1952 - No. 18, Dec-Jan, 1954-55
E. C. Comics

1-Classic Feldstein electrocution-c. Bradbury adaptation	45.00	135.00	315.00
2	27.00	81.00	190.00
3	18.50	56.00	130.00
4-Used in SOTI, pg. 387,388	18.50	56.00	130.00
5-Hanging-c	17.00	51.00	120.00
6,7: 6-Classic bondage-c. 7-Classic face melting-c	21.50	64.00	150.00
8-Williamson-a	18.50	56.00	130.00
9-11: 9-Injury to eye panel. 10-Junkie story	14.00	42.00	100.00
12-"The Monkey"-classic junkie cover/story; drug propaganda issue	18.00	54.00	125.00
13-Frazetta's only solo story for E.C., 7 pgs.	23.00	70.00	160.00
14-Used in Senate Investigation hearings	11.00	32.00	75.00
15-Used in 1954 Reader's Digest article, "For the Kiddies to Read"	11.00	32.00	75.00
16-"Red Dupe" editorial; rape story	11.00	32.00	75.00
17,18	11.00	32.00	75.00

NOTE: *Craig* a-11; c-11. *Crandall* a-9-13, 15-18. *Davis* a-1-5. *Evans* a-7, 8, 14-18; c-16-18. *Feldstein* c-1, 7-9, 12. *Ingels* a-1, 2, 6. *Kamen* a-in all; c-10. *Krigstein* a-14, 18. *Orlando*

SHOGUN WARRIORS
Feb, 1979 - No. 20, Sept, 1980
Marvel Comics Group

	Good	Fine	N-Mint
1-Raydeen, Combatra, & Dangard Ace begin	.40	.80	
2-20		.25	.50

SHOOK UP (Magazine) (Satire)
November, 1958
Dodsworth Publ. Co.

V1#1	1.00	3.00	6.00

SHORT RIBS (See 4-Color #1333)

SHORT STORY COMICS (See Hello Pal,...)

SHORTY SHINER
June, 1956 - No. 3, Oct, 1956
Dandy Magazine (Charles Biro)

1	2.30	7.00	16.00
2,3	1.50	4.50	10.00

SHOTGUN SLADE (See 4-Color #1111)

SHOWCASE (See Cancelled Comic Cavalcade & New Talent...)
3-4/56 - No. 93, 9/70; No. 94, 8-9/77 - No. 104, 9/78
National Periodical Publications/DC Comics

1-Fire Fighters	70.00	210.00	485.00
2-King of the Wild; Kubert-a	27.00	81.00	185.00
3-The Frogmen	22.00	65.00	155.00
4-Origin The Flash (1st DC Silver Age Hero, Sept.-Oct., 1956) & The Turtle; Kubert-a	320.00	1200.00	3000.00
5-Manhunters	24.00	72.00	165.00
6-Origin Challengers (1st app.) by Kirby, partly r-/in Secret Origins #1 & Challengers of the Unknown #64,65	72.00	215.00	500.00
7-Challengers by Kirby r-in/Challengers of the Unknown #75	40.00	120.00	275.00
8-The Flash; intro/origin Capt. Cold	130.00	390.00	900.00
9,10-Lois Lane. 9-(Pre-#1, 7-8/57)	36.00	108.00	250.00
11,12-Challengers by Kirby	32.00	95.00	225.00
13-The Flash; origin Mr. Element	87.00	260.00	600.00
14-The Flash; origin Dr. Alchemy, former Mr. Element	87.00	260.00	600.00
15-Space Ranger (1st app.)	21.00	65.00	150.00
16-Space Ranger	17.00	51.00	120.00
17-Adventures on Other Worlds; origin/1st app. Adam Strange (11-12/58)	48.00	145.00	335.00
18,19-Adam Strange	28.00	85.00	200.00
20-1st app/origin Rip Hunter (5-6/59); Moriera-a	21.00	63.00	145.00
21-Rip Hunter; Sekowsky c/a	11.50	34.50	80.00
22-Origin & 1st app. Silver Age Green Lantern by Gil Kane (9-10/59)	104.00	312.00	725.00
23,24-Green Lantern. 23-Nuclear explosion-c	43.00	129.00	300.00
25,26-Rip Hunter by Kubert	6.50	19.50	45.00
27-1st app. Sea Devils (7-8/60); Heath c/a	14.00	42.00	100.00
28,29-Sea Devils by Heath, c/a	11.50	34.50	80.00
30-Origin Silver Age Aquaman (see Adventure #260 for 1st app.)	18.00	54.00	125.00
31-33-Aquaman	7.00	21.00	50.00
34-Origin & 1st app. Silver Age Atom by Kane & Anderson (9-10/61)	37.00	110.00	260.00
35-The Atom by Gil Kane; last 10 cent issue	11.00	32.00	75.00
36-The Atom by Gil Kane	7.00	21.00	50.00
37-1st app. Metal Men (3-4/62)	18.00	54.00	125.00
38-40-Metal Men	7.00	21.00	50.00
41,42-Tommy Tomorrow	2.15	6.50	15.00
43-Dr. No (James Bond); Nodel-a; originally published as British Classics III. #158A, and as #6 in a European Detective series, all			

Shock Illustrated #3, © WMG

Shock Suspenstories #5, © WMG

Showcase #9, © DC

Showcase #60, © DC

Showcase #73, © DC

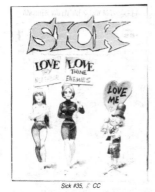
Sick #35, © CC

	Good	Fine	N-Mint
SHOWCASE (continued)			
with a diff. painted-c. This Showcase #43 version is actually			
censored, deleting all racial skin color, and dialogue thought to			
be racially demeaning	21.50	64.00	150.00
44-Tommy Tomorrow	1.70	5.00	12.00
45-Sgt. Rock; origin retold; Heath-c	2.85	8.50	20.00
46,47-Tommy Tomorrow	1.15	3.50	8.00
48,49-Cave Carson	1.15	3.50	8.00
50,51-I Spy (Danger Trail-r by Infantino), King Farady story (#50 is not			
a reprint)	1.15	3.50	8.00
52-Cave Carson	1.15	3.50	8.00
53,54-G.I. Joe; Heath-a	1.15	3.50	8.00
55,56-Dr. Fate & Hourman	1.15	3.50	8.00
57,58-Enemy Ace by Kubert	1.15	3.50	8.00
59-Teen Titans (3rd app., 11-12/65)	4.30	13.00	30.00
60-1st Silver Age app. The Spectre; Anderson-a (1-2/66)			
	2.85	8.50	20.00
61,64-The Spectre by Anderson	1.00	3.00	6.00
62-Origin/1st app. Inferior Five (5-6/66)	2.15	6.50	15.00
63,65-Inferior Five	1.00	3.00	7.00
66,67-B'wana Beast	.50	1.50	3.00
68,69,71-Maniaks	.50	1.50	3.00
70-Binky	.50	1.50	3.00
72-Top Gun (Johnny Thunder-r)-Toth-a	.50	1.50	3.00
73-Origin/1st app. Creeper; Ditko c/a (3-4/67)	1.70	5.00	12.00
74-Intro/1st app. Anthro; Post c/a (5-6/67)	1.70	5.00	12.00
75-1st app/origin Hawk & the Dove; Ditko c/a	1.70	5.00	12.00
76-Bat Lash	1.00	3.00	6.00
77-Angel & Ape	1.15	3.50	8.00
78-Jonny Double	.50	1.50	3.00
79-Dolphin; Aqualad origin-r	.85	2.50	5.00
80-Phantom Stranger-r; Adams-c	.85	2.50	5.00
81-Windy & Willy	.50	1.50	3.00
82-Nightmaster by Grandenetti & Giordano; Kubert-c			
	.50	1.50	3.00
83,84-Nightmaster by Wrightson/Jones/Kaluta in each; Kubert-c.			
84-Origin retold	2.15	6.50	15.00
85-87-Firehair; Kubert-a	.85	2.50	5.00
88-90-Jason's Quest: 90-Manhunter 2070 app.	.35	1.00	2.00
91-93-Manhunter 2070: origin-92	.35	1.00	2.00
94-Intro/origin new Doom Patrol & Robotman	.50	1.50	3.00
95,96-The Doom Patrol. 95-Origin Celsius	.35	1.00	2.00
97-99-Power Girl; origin-97,98; JSA cameos	.35	1.00	2.00
100-(52 pgs.)-Most Showcase characters feat.	.35	1.00	2.00
101-103-Hawkman; Adam Strange x-over	.35	1.00	2.00
104-(52 pgs.)-O.S.S. Spies at War	.35	1.00	2.00

NOTE: *Anderson* a-22-24i, 34-36i, 55, 56, 60, 61, 64, 101-03i; c-50i, 51i, 55, 56, 60, 61, 64. *Aparo* c-94-96. *Estrada* a-104. *Infantino* a/c-4, 8, 13, 14; c-50p, 51p. *Gil Kane* a-22-24p, 34-36p; c-17-19, 22-24, 31, 34-36. *Kirby* c-6, 7, 11, 12. *Kubert* a-2, 4i, 25, 26, 45, 53, 54, 72; c-25, 26, 53, 54, 57, 58, 82-87, 101-04. *Orlando* a-62p, 63p, 97i; c-62, 63, 97i. *Sekowsky* a-65p. *Sparling* a-78. *Staton* a-94, 95-99p, 100; c-97-100p.

SHOWGIRLS (Formerly Sherry the Showgirl #3)
No. 4, 1-2/57?; June, 1957 - No. 2, Aug, 1957
Atlas Comics (MPC No. 2)

	Good	Fine	N-Mint
4	2.30	7.00	16.00
1-Millie, Sherry, Chili, Pearl & Hazel begin	4.00	12.00	28.00
2	2.30	7.00	16.00

SHROUD OF MYSTERY
June, 1982
Whitman Publications

1		.30	.60

SHURIKEN (Also see Blade Of . . .)
Summer, 1985 - No. 7, May, 1987 ($1.50, B&W)
Victory Productions

1		.75	2.25	4.50

	Good	Fine	N-Mint
1-Reprint (Wint./86)	.25	.75	1.50
2 (Fall/85) - 7	.25	.75	1.50
Graphic Novel ($7.95, Blackthorne Publ.)	1.35	4.00	8.00

SICK (Magazine) (Satire)
Aug, 1960 - No. 140?, 1980?
Feature Publ./Headline Publ./Crestwood Publ. Co./Hewfred Publ./
Pyramid Comm./Charlton Publ. No. 109 (4/76) on

	Good	Fine	N-Mint
V1#1-Torres-a	7.00	21.00	50.00
2-5-Torres-a in all	3.50	10.50	24.00
6	2.00	6.00	14.00
V2#1-8(#7-14)	1.50	4.50	10.00
V3#1-8(#15-22)	1.15	3.50	8.00
V4#1-5(#23-27)	1.00	3.00	7.00
28-40	.70	2.00	5.00
41-140: 45 has #44 on-c & #45 on inside	.50	1.50	3.00
Annual 1969, 1970, 1971	1.00	3.00	7.00
Annual 2-4('80)	.60	1.75	3.50
Special 2 ('78)	.35	1.00	2.00

NOTE: *Davis* c/a in most issues of #16-27, 30-32, 34, 35. *Simon* a-1-3. *Torres* a-V2#7, V4#2, V6#1-3. Civil War Blackouts-23, 24.

SIDESHOW
1949 (One Shot)
Avon Periodicals

	Good	Fine	N-Mint
1-(Rare)-Similar to Bachelor's Diary	16.00	48.00	110.00

SIEGEL AND SHUSTER: DATELINE 1930s
11/84 - No. 2, 9/85 (Baxter paper #1; $1.50-$1.75)
Eclipse Comics

	Good	Fine	N-Mint
1-Unpubbed samples of strips from 1935; includes 'Interplanetary			
Police;' Shuster-c	.25	.75	1.50
2 ($1.75, B&W)-Unpubbed strips	.30	.90	1.80

SILENT INVASION, THE
April, 1986 - No. 12, March, 1988 ($1.70/$2.00, B&W)
Renegade Press

	Good	Fine	N-Mint
1-UFO sightings of '50s	.60	1.75	3.50
2	.50	1.50	3.00
3-12	.40	1.25	2.50
Book 1	1.35	4.00	7.95

SILK HAT HARRY'S DIVORCE SUIT
1912 (5¾x15½'') (B&W)
M. A. Donoghue & Co.

	Good	Fine	N-Mint
Newspaper reprints by Tad (Thomas Dorgan)	9.00	27.00	62.00

SILLY PILLY (See Frank Luther's . . .)

SILLY SYMPHONIES (See Dell Giants)

SILLY TUNES
Fall, 1945 - No. 7, June, 1947
Timely Comics

	Good	Fine	N-Mint
1-Silly Seal, Ziggy Pig begin	6.50	19.50	45.00
2	3.50	10.50	24.00
3-7	2.65	8.00	18.00

SILVER (See Lone Ranger's Famous Horse . . .)

SILVERBACK
1989 - No. 3, 1990 ($2.50, color, mini-series, adults)
Comico

	Good	Fine	N-Mint
1-3: Character from Grendel; Matt Wagner-a	.40	1.25	2.50

SILVERBLADE
Sept, 1987 - No. 12, Sept, 1988
DC Comics

	Good	Fine	N-Mint
1-12: Colan c/a(p) in all	.25	.75	1.50

SILVERHAWKS
Aug, 1987 - No. 6, June, 1988 ($1.00)
Star Comics/Marvel #6

	Good	Fine	N-Mint
1-6		.50	1.00

SILVERHEELS (See Eclipse Graphic Album #12)
Dec, 1983 - No. 3, May, 1984 ($1.50, color)
Pacific Comics

1-3	.25	.75	1.50

SILVER KID WESTERN
Oct, 1954 - No. 5, 1955
Key/Stanmor Publications

1	3.50	10.50	24.00
2	1.70	5.00	12.00
3-5	1.30	4.00	9.00
I.W. Reprint #1,2	.50	1.50	3.00

SILVER STAR
Feb, 1983 - No. 6, Jan, 1984 ($1.00, color)
Pacific Comics

1-6: 1-1st app. Last of the Viking Heroes		.50	1.00

NOTE: *Kirby* a-1-5p.

SILVER STREAK COMICS (Crime Does Not Pay #22 on)
Dec, 1939 - May, 1942; 1946 (Silver logo-#1-5)
Your Guide Publs. No. 1-7/New Friday Publs. No. 8-17/Comic House
Publ./Newsbook Publ.

1-Intro. The Claw by Cole (r-/in Daredevil #21), Red Reeves, Boy
Magician & Captain Fearless; The Wasp, Mister Midnight begin;
Spirit Man app. Silver metallic-c begin, also end #5 (Scarce)

	Good	Fine	N-Mint
	329.00	985.00	2300.00

2-The Claw by Cole; Simon c/a

	143.00	430.00	1000.00

3-1st app. & origin Silver Streak (2nd with lightning speed); Dickie
Dean the Boy Inventor, Lance Hale, Ace Powers, Bill Wayne, &
The Planet Patrol begin

	129.00	385.00	900.00

4-Sky Wolf begins; Silver Streak by Jack Cole (new costume);
intro. Jackie, Lance Hale's sidekick

	68.00	204.00	475.00

5-Jack Cole c/a(2)

	79.00	235.00	550.00

6-(Scarce)-Origin & 1st app. Daredevil (blue & yellow costume) by
Jack Binder; The Claw returns; classic Cole Claw-c

	271.00	815.00	1900.00
(Prices vary widely on this book)			

7-Claw vs. Daredevil (new costume-blue & red) by Jack Cole & 3
other Cole stories (38 pgs.)

	179.00	535.00	1250.00

8-Claw vs. Daredevil by Cole; last Cole Silver Streak

	107.00	321.00	750.00

9-Claw vs. Daredevil by Cole

	76.00	230.00	535.00

10-Origin Captain Battle; Claw vs. Daredevil by Cole

	71.00	212.00	495.00

11-Intro. Mercury by Bob Wood, Silver Streak's sidekick; conclusion
Claw vs. Daredevil by Rico; in 'Presto Martin,' 2nd pg., news
paper says 'Roussos does it again'

	49.00	147.00	340.00

12-14: 13-Origin Thun-Dohr

	40.00	120.00	280.00

15-17-Last Daredevil issue

	37.00	110.00	260.00

18-The Saint begins; by Leslie Charteris (See Movie Comics #4-7, DC)

	31.00	92.00	215.00

19-21(1942): 20,21 have Wolverton's Scoop Scuttle

	19.00	58.00	135.00

22,24(1946)-Reprints

	13.00	40.00	90.00

23-Reprints?; bondage-c

	13.00	40.00	90.00

nn(11/46)(Newsbook Publ.)-R-/S.S. story from #4-7 plus 2 Captain
Fearless stories, all in color; bondage/torture-c

	24.00	70.00	170.00

NOTE: *Binder* c-3, 4, 13-15, 17. *Jack Cole* a-(Daredevil)-#6-10, (Dickie Dean)-#3-10,
(Pirate Prince)-#7, (Silver Streak)-#4-8, nn; c-5 (Silver Streak), 6-8 (Daredevil). *Everett*
Red Reed begins #20. *Guardineer* a-#8-13. *Don Rico* a-11-17 (Daredevil); c-11, 12, 16.
Simon a-3 (Silver Streak). *Bob Wood* a-9 (Silver Streak); c-9, 10. Claw c-#1, 2, 6-8.

SILVER SURFER (See Fantastic Four, Fantasy Masterpieces V2/1, Marvel Comics
Presents, Marvel Graphic Novel, Marvel Presents #8, Marvel's Greatest Comics & Tales
To Astonish)

SILVER SURFER, THE
Aug, 1968 - No. 18, Sept, 1970; June, 1982 (No. 1-7: 68 pgs.)
Marvel Comics Group

	Good	Fine	N-Mint
1-Origin by John Buscema (p); Watcher begins (origin), ends #7	13.50	40.00	95.00
2	5.15	15.50	36.00
3-1st app. Mephisto	4.50	14.00	32.00
4-Low distribution; Thor app.	9.30	28.00	65.00
5-7-Last giant size. 5-The Stranger app. 6-Brunner inks. 7-Brunner-c	3.15	9.50	22.00
8-10	2.15	6.50	15.00
11-18: 14-Spider-Man x-over. 18-Kirby c/a	1.50	4.50	10.00
V2#1 (6/82, 52 pgs.)-Byrne-c/a	1.00	3.00	6.00

NOTE: *Adkins* a-8-15i. *Brunner* a-6i. *J. Buscema* a-1-17p. *Colan* a-1-3p. *Reinman*
a-1-4i.

SILVER SURFER, THE (See Marvel Graphic Novel #38)
July, 1987 - Present
Marvel Comics Group

1-Double size ($1.25)	.70	2.00	4.00
2	.40	1.25	2.50
3-10	.30	.90	1.80
11-20: 19-Rogers-a		.60	1.20
21-24,26-30,32-34: 34-Thanos returns		.50	1.00
25,31 ($1.50, 52 pgs.): 25-Skrulls app.	.25	.75	1.50
Annual 1 (8/88, $1.75)-Evolutionary War app.	.40	1.25	2.50
Annual 2 ('89, 2.00, 68 pgs.)-Atlantis Attacks	.35	1.00	2.00

SILVER SURFER, THE
Dec, 1988 - No. 2, Jan, 1989 ($1.00, limited series)
Epic Comics (Marvel)

1,2: By Stan Lee & Moebius	.30	.90	1.75

SILVERTIP (Max Brand)
No. 491, Aug, 1953 - No. 898, May, 1958
Dell Publishing Co.

4-Color 491	4.00	12.00	24.00
4-Color 572,608,637,667,731,789,898-Kinstler-a; all painted-c	3.00	9.00	21.00
4-Color 835	2.30	7.00	16.00

SINBAD, JR (TV Cartoon)
Sept-Nov, 1965 - No. 3, May, 1966
Dell Publishing Co.

1	1.70	5.00	12.00
2,3	1.00	3.00	7.00

SINBAD (See Movie Comics: Capt. Sinbad, and Fantastic Voyages of Sinbad)

SINGING GUNS (See Fawcett Movie Comics)

SINGLE SERIES (Comics on Parade #30 on)(Also see John Hix . . .)
1938 - No. 28, 1942 (All 68 pgs.)
United Features Syndicate

1-Captain and the Kids (#1)	40.00	120.00	280.00
2-Broncho Bill (1939) (#1)	24.00	70.00	170.00
3-Ella Cinders (1939)	22.00	65.00	154.00
4-Li'l Abner (1939) (#1)	35.00	105.00	245.00
5-Fritzi Ritz (#1)	14.00	42.00	100.00
6-Jim Hardy by Dick Moores (#1)	20.00	60.00	140.00
7-Frankie Doodle	14.00	42.00	100.00
8-Peter Pat (On sale 7/14/39)	14.00	42.00	100.00
9-Strange As It Seems	14.00	42.00	100.00
10-Little Mary Mixup	14.00	42.00	100.00
11-Mr. and Mrs. Beans	14.00	42.00	100.00
12-Joe Jinks	13.00	40.00	90.00

Silver Kid Western #1, © Key Publ.

Silver Streak Comics #1, © LEV

The Silver Surfer #7 (8/69)

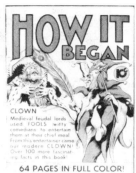

64 PAGES IN FULL COLOR!

Single Series #15, © UFS

Six-Gun Heroes #35, © CC

Skeleton Hand #2, © ACG

SINGLE SERIES (continued)	Good	Fine	N-Mint
13-Looy Dot Dope	12.00	36.00	84.00
14-Billy Make Believe	12.00	36.00	84.00
15-How It Began (1939)	14.00	42.00	100.00
16-Illustrated Gags (1940)-Has ad for Captain and the Kids #1 reprint			
listed below	8.00	24.00	56.00
17-Danny Dingle	11.00	32.00	75.00
18-Li'l Abner (#2 on-c)	27.00	81.00	190.00
19-Broncho Bill (#2 on-c)	20.00	60.00	140.00
20-Tarzan by Hal Foster	75.00	225.00	525.00
21-Ella Cinders (#2 on-c; on sale 3/19/40)	17.00	51.00	120.00
22-Iron Vic	14.00	42.00	100.00
23-Tailspin Tommy by Hal Forrest (#1)	17.00	51.00	120.00
24-Alice in Wonderland (#1)	20.00	60.00	140.00
25-Abbie and Slats	19.00	57.00	135.00
26-Little Mary Mixup (#2 on-c, 1940)	14.00	42.00	100.00
27-Jim Hardy by Dick Moores (1942)	14.00	42.00	100.00
28-Ella Cinders and Abbie and Slats (1942)	17.00	51.00	120.00
1-Captain and the Kids (1939 reprint)-2nd Edition			
	23.00	70.00	160.00
1-Fritzi Ritz (1939 reprint)-2nd edition	12.00	36.00	84.00

NOTE: Some issues given away at the 1939-40 New York World's Fair (#6).

SINISTER HOUSE OF SECRET LOVE, THE (Secrets of Sinister House No. 5 on)
Oct-Nov, 1971 - No. 4, Apr-May, 1972
National Periodical Publications

1		.50	1.00
2-4: 3-Toth-a, 36 pgs.		.35	.70

SINNERS, THE
1989 - Present ($9.95, color, mature readers, 8-1/8 x 10-7/8'', 52 pgs.)
Piranha Press (DC Comics)

nn-By Alec Stevens	1.70	5.00	10.00

SIR LANCELOT (See 4-Color #606,775)

SIR WALTER RALEIGH (See 4-Color #644)

SISTERHOOD OF STEEL (See Eclipse Graphic Album #13)
12/84 - No. 8, 2/86 ($1.50, Baxter paper) (Adults only)
Epic Comics (Marvel)

1-(Women mercenaries)	.35	1.10	2.20
2-8	.30	.90	1.80

6 BLACK HORSES (See Movie Classics)

SIX FROM SIRIUS
July, 1984 - No. 4, Oct, 1984 ($1.50, mini-series)
Epic Comics (Marvel)

1-Gulacy c/a in all	.35	1.00	2.00
2-4	.30	.90	1.80

SIX FROM SIRIUS II
Feb, 1986 - No. 4, May, 1986 ($1.50, color, Adults only)
Epic Comics (Marvel)

1-4	.25	.75	1.50

SIX-GUN HEROES
March, 1950 - No. 23, Nov, 1953 (Photo-c #1-23)
Fawcett Publications

1-Rocky Lane, Hopalong Cassidy, Smiley Burnette begin			
	24.00	73.00	170.00
2	14.00	42.00	100.00
3-5	11.00	32.00	75.00
6-15: 6-Lash LaRue begins	8.00	24.00	56.00
16-22: 17-Last Smiley Burnette. 18-Monte Hale begins			
	7.00	21.00	50.00
23-Last Fawcett issue	8.00	24.00	56.00

SIX-GUN HEROES (Continued from Fawcett; Gunmasters #84 on)
No. 24, Jan, 1954 - No. 83, Mar-Apr, 1965 (All Vol. 4)(See Blue Bird)
Charlton Comics

	Good	Fine	N-Mint
24-Tom Mix, Lash LaRue	6.50	19.50	45.00
25	3.70	11.00	26.00
26-30	3.15	9.50	22.00
31-40-Tom Mix, Lash LaRue, Rocky Lane, Tex Ritter			
	2.30	7.00	16.00
41-46,48,50	2.00	6.00	14.00
47-Williamson-a, 2 pgs; Torres-a	2.85	8.50	20.00
49-Williamson-a, 5 pgs.	2.85	8.50	20.00
51-60: 58-Gunmaster app.	1.30	4.00	9.00
61-70: 62-Origin, Gunmaster	1.00	3.00	7.00
71-83: 76-Gunmaster begins	.70	2.00	5.00

SIXGUN RANCH (See 4-Color #580)

SIX-GUN WESTERN
Jan, 1957 - No. 4, July, 1957
Atlas Comics (CDS)

1-Crandall-a; two Williamson text illos	6.50	19.50	45.00
2,3-Williamson-a in both	5.50	16.50	38.00
4-Woodbridge-a	2.65	8.00	18.00

NOTE: Ayers a-2, 3. Maneely c-2. 3. Orlando a-2. Pakula a-2. Powell a-3. Romita a-1, 4. Severin c-1, 4. Shores a-2.

SIX MILLION DOLLAR MAN (TV)(Magazine)
June, 1976 - No. 7, Nov, 1977 (B&W)
Charlton Comics

1-Adams c/a	.50	1.50	3.00
2-Adams-c	.25	.80	1.60
3-7: 3-Adams part inks		.60	1.20

SIX MILLION DOLLAR MAN (TV)
6/76 - No. 4, 1/77; No. 5, 10/77; No. 6, 2/78 - No. 9, 6/78
Charlton Comics

1-Staton c/a	.25	.80	1.60
2-Adams-c; Staton-a		.50	1.00
3-9		.30	.60

SKATEMAN
Nov, 1983 (One Shot) (Baxter paper)
Pacific Comics

1-Adams c/a	.25	.75	1.50

SKATING SKILLS
1957 (36 & 12 pages; 5x7'', two versions) (10 cents)
Custom Comics, Inc./Chicago Roller Skates

Resembles old ACG cover plus interior art	.50	1.50	3.00

SKEEZIX (Also see Gasoline Alley)
1925 - 1928 (Strip reprints) (soft covers) (pictures & text)
Reilly & Lee Co.

...and Uncle Walt (1924)-Origin	9.30	28.00	65.00
...and Pal (1925)	6.50	19.50	45.00
...at the Circus (1926)	6.50	19.50	45.00
...& Uncle Walt (1927)	6.50	19.50	45.00
...Out West (1928)	6.50	19.50	45.00
Hardback Editions...	10.00	30.00	70.00

SKELETON HAND (...In Secrets of the Supernatural)
Sept-Oct, 1952 - No. 6, July-Aug, 1953
American Comics Group (B&M Dist. Co.)

1	11.50	34.00	80.00
2	7.00	21.00	50.00
3-6	5.70	17.00	40.00

SKI PARTY (See Movie Classics)

SKIPPY'S OWN BOOK OF COMICS (See Popular Comics)
1934 (52 pages) (Giveaway)
No publisher listed

	Good	Fine	N-Mint
nn-(Rare)-Strip-r by Percy Crosby	275.00	690.00	1650.00

Published by Max C. Gaines for Phillip's Dental Magnesia to be advertised on the Skippy Radio Show and given away with the purchase of a tube of Phillip's Tooth Paste. This is the first four-color comic book of reprints about one character.

SKREEMER
May, 1989 - No. 6, Oct, 1989 ($2.00, color, mini-series, adults)
DC Comics

1-6: Contains graphic violence	.35	1.00	2.00

SKULL, THE SLAYER
August, 1975 - No. 8, Nov, 1976
Marvel Comics Group

1-Origin; Gil Kane-c	.40	.80	
2-8: 2-Gil Kane-c. 8-Kirby-c	.30	.60	

SKY BLAZERS (Radio)
Sept, 1940 - No. 2, Nov, 1940
Hawley Publications

1-Sky Pirates, Ace Archer, Flying Aces begin	19.00	58.00	135.00
2	14.00	42.00	100.00

SKY KING "RUNAWAY TRAIN" (TV)
1964 (16 pages) (regular size)
National Biscuit Co.

nn	1.30	4.00	9.00

SKYMAN (See Big Shot Comics & Sparky Watts)
Fall?, 1941 - No. 2, 1941; No. 3, 1948 - No. 4, 1948
Columbia Comics Group

1-Origin Skyman, The Face, Sparky Watts app.; Whitney-a; 3rd story r-/Big Shot #1	34.00	100.00	235.00
2 (1941)-Yankee Doodle	19.00	58.00	135.00
3,4 (1948)	11.00	32.00	75.00

SKY PILOT
No. 10, 1950(nd) - No. 11, Apr-May, 1951 (Saunders painted-c)
Ziff-Davis Publ. Co.

10,11-Frank Borth-a	4.30	13.00	30.00

SKY RANGER (See Johnny Law...)

SKYROCKET
1944
Harry 'A' Chesler

nn-Alias the Dragon, Dr. Vampire, Skyrocket app.	10.00	30.00	70.00

SKY SHERIFF (Breeze Lawson...) (Also see Exposed)
Summer, 1948
D. S. Publishing Co.

1-Edmond Good-a	5.00	15.00	35.00

SKY WOLF (Also see Airboy)
Mar, 1988 - No. 3, Oct, 1988 ($1.75-$1.95, color, limited series)
Eclipse Comics

1,2 ($1.75)	.30	.90	1.80
3 ($1.95)	.35	1.00	2.00

SLAINE, THE BERSERKER (Slaine the King #21 on)
July, 1987 - No. 28, 1989 ($1.25; $1.50 #13 on, color)
Quality Comics

1-12 ($1.25)		.65	1.30
13,14/15,16/17,18-28	.25	.75	1.50

SLAM BANG COMICS (Western Desperado #8)
March, 1940 - No. 7, Sept, 1940 (Combined with Master Comics #7)
Fawcett Publications

	Good	Fine	N-Mint
1-Diamond Jack, Mark Swift & The Time Retarder, Lee Granger, Jungle King begin	57.00	171.00	400.00
2	28.50	86.00	200.00
3-Classic-c	28.50	86.00	200.00
4-7: 7-Bondage-c	21.50	64.00	150.00

SLAM BANG COMICS
No date
Post Cereal Giveaway

9-Dynamic Man, Echo, Mr. E, Yankee Boy app.	1.70	5.00	12.00

SLAPSTICK COMICS
nd (1946?) (36 pages)
Comic Magazines Distributors

nn-Firetop feature; Post-a(2)	8.00	24.00	56.00

SLASH-D DOUBLECROSS
1950 (132 pgs.) (pocket size)
St. John Publishing Co.

Western comics	7.00	21.00	50.00

SLASH MARAUD
Nov, 1987 - No. 6, April, 1988 ($1.75, mini-series)
DC Comics

1-6	.35	1.00	2.00

SLAUGHTERMAN (See Primer #1 for 1st app.)
Feb, 1983 - No. 2, 1983 ($1.50, B&W)
Comico

1,2	.25	.75	1.50

SLAVE GIRL COMICS (See Malu... & White Princess of/Jungle #2)
Feb, 1949 - No. 2, Apr, 1949 (52 pgs.)
Avon Periodicals/Eternity Comics

1-Larsen c/a	50.00	150.00	350.00
2-Larsen-a	35.00	105.00	245.00
1 (3/89, $2.25, B&W, 44 pgs., Eternity)-r/#1	.40	1.15	2.30

SLEDGE HAMMER (TV)
Feb, 1988 - No. 2, Mar, 1988 ($1.00, color)
Marvel Comics

1,2		.50	1.00

SLEEPING BEAUTY (See Dell Giants, 4-Color #973,984, Movie Comics)

SLEEZE BROTHERS
Aug, 1989 - Present ($1.75, color, mature readers, direct sale only)
Marvel Comics

1-6: Private eyes; 4-(11/89-c, 9/89 indicia)	.30	.90	1.80

SLICK CHICK COMICS
1947(nd) - No. 3, 1947(nd)
Leader Enterprises

1	5.50	16.50	38.00
2,3	3.70	11.00	26.00

SLIMER AND THE REAL GHOSTBUSTERS (TV) (Also see The Real Ghostbusters)
1989 - Present ($1.75, color)
Now Comics

1-12: Based on animated TV cartoon	.30	.90	1.80

SLIM MORGAN (See Wisco)

SLUGGER (of the Little Wise Guys)
April, 1956
Lev Gleason Publications

1-Biro-c	2.00	6.00	14.00

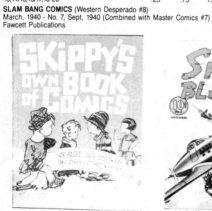

Skippy's Own Book Of Comics, © Percy Crosby

Sky Blazers #1, © Hawley Publ.

Slick Chick Comics #1, © Leader Ent.

Smash Comics #9, © QUA

Smiley Burnette Western #2, © FAW

Smilin' Jack #2, © N.Y. News Synd.

SMASH COMICS (Lady Luck #86 on)
Aug, 1939 - No. 85, Oct, 1949
Quality Comics Group

	Good	Fine	N-Mint
1-Origin Hugh Hazard & His Iron Man, Bozo the Robot, Espionage, Starring Black X by Eisner, & Invisible Justice; Chic Carter & Wings Wendall begin	71.00	215.00	500.00
2-The Lone Star Rider app; Invisible Hood gains power of invisibility	34.00	100.00	235.00
3-Captain Cook & John Law begin	23.00	70.00	160.00
4,5: 4-Flash Fulton begins	21.00	62.00	145.00
6-12: 12-One pg. Fine-a	16.00	48.00	115.00
13-Magno begins; last Eisner issue; The Ray app. in full page ad; The Purple Trio begins	16.00	48.00	115.00
14-Intro. The Ray by Lou Fine & others	110.00	330.00	770.00
15,16	55.00	165.00	385.00
17-Wun Cloo becomes plastic super-hero by Jack Cole (9-months before Plastic Man)	55.00	165.00	385.00
18-Midnight by Jack Cole begins (origin)	65.00	195.00	455.00
19-22: Last Fine Ray; The Jester begins-#22	38.00	115.00	265.00
23,24: 24-The Sword app.; last Chic Carter; Wings Wendall dons new costume #24,25	30.00	90.00	210.00
25-Origin Wildfire	35.00	105.00	245.00
26-30: 28-Midnight-c begin	26.00	77.00	180.00
31,32,34: Ray by Rudy Palais; also #33	20.00	60.00	140.00
33-Origin The Marksman	24.00	73.00	170.00
35-37	20.00	60.00	140.00
38-The Yankee Eagle begins; last Midnight by Jack Cole	20.00	60.00	140.00
39,40-Last Ray issue	16.00	48.00	110.00
41,43-50	7.00	21.00	50.00
42-Lady Luck begins by Klaus Nordling	9.50	28.50	65.00
51-60	6.00	18.00	42.00
61-70	5.00	15.00	35.00
71-85	4.65	14.00	32.00

NOTE: Cole a-17-38, 68, 69, 72, 73, 78, 80, 83, 85; c-38, 60-62, 69, 75, 80. Crandall a-(Ray)-23-29, 35-38; c-36, 39, 40, 43, 44, 46. Fine a(Ray)-14, 15, 16(w/Tuska), 17-22. Fuje Ray-30. Gil Fox a-6-7, 9, 11-13. Guardineer a-(The Marksman)-39-?, 49, 52. Gustavson a-4-7, 9, 11-13 (The Jester)-22-46: (Magno)-13-21; (Midnight)-39(Cole inks), 49, 52, 63-65. Kotzky a-(Espionage)-33-38; c-45, 47. Nordling a-49, 52, 63-65. Powell a-11,12, (Abdul the Arab)-13-24.

SMASH HIT SPORTS COMICS
V2#1, Jan, 1949
Essankay Publications

	Good	Fine	N-Mint
V2#1-L.B. Cole c/a	7.00	21.00	50.00

S'MATTER POP?
1917 (44 pgs.; B&W; 10x14''; cardboard covers)
Saalfield Publ. Co.

By Charlie Payne; ½ in full color; pages printed on one side

	8.00	24.00	56.00

SMILE COMICS (Also see Gay Comics, Tickle, & Whee)
1955 (52 pages; 5x7¼'') (7 cents)
Modern Store Publ.

1	.50	1.50	3.00

SMILEY BURNETTE WESTERN (See Six-Gun Heroes)
March, 1950 - No. 4, Oct, 1950 (All photo-c)
Fawcett Publications

1	16.00	48.00	110.00
2-4	11.00	32.00	75.00

SMILIN' JACK (See Popular Comics, Super Book #1,2,7,19 & Super)
No. 5, 1940 - No. 8, Oct-Dec, 1949
Dell Publishing Co.

4-Color 5	42.00	125.00	290.00
4-Color 10 (1940)	39.00	116.00	270.00
Large Feature Comic 12,14,25 (1941)	27.00	81.00	190.00

	Good	Fine	N-Mint
4-Color 4 (1942)	31.00	92.00	215.00
4-Color 14 (1943)	25.00	75.00	175.00
4-Color 36,58 (1943-44)	14.00	42.00	100.00
4-Color 80 (1945)	11.50	34.00	80.00
4-Color 149 (1947)	8.50	25.50	60.00
1 (1-3/48)	8.50	25.50	60.00
2	4.65	14.00	32.00
3-8 (10-12/49)	3.50	10.50	24.00
Popped Wheat Giveaway(1947)-1938 reprints; 16 pgs. in full color	.80	2.40	4.80
Shoe Store Giveaway-1938 reprints; 16 pgs.	2.65	8.00	18.00
Sparked Wheat Giveaway(1942)-16 pgs. in full color	2.30	7.00	16.00

SMILING SPOOK SPUNKY (See Spunky)

SMITTY (See Treasure Box of Famous Comics)
1928 - 1933 (B&W newspaper strip reprints)
(cardboard covers; 9½x9½'', 52 pgs.; 7x8¼'', 36 pgs.)
Cupples & Leon Co.

1928-(96pgs. 7x8¾'')	11.00	32.00	75.00
1928-(Softcover, 36pgs., nn)	12.00	36.00	84.00
1929-At the Ball Game, 1930-The Flying Office Boy, 1931-The Jockey, 1932-In the North Woods....each....	8.50	25.50	60.00
1933-At Military School	8.50	25.50	60.00
Mid-1930s issue (reprint of 1928 Treasure Box issue)-36 pgs.; 7x8¾''	7.00	21.00	50.00
Hardback Editions (100 pgs., 7x8¼'') with dust jacket each....	14.00	42.00	100.00

SMITTY (See Popular Comics, Super Book #2,4 & Super Comics)
No. 11, 1940 - No. 7, Aug-Oct, 1949; Apr, 1958
Dell Publishing Co.

4-Color 11 (1940)	24.00	71.00	165.00
Large Feature Comic 26 (1941)	16.00	48.00	110.00
4-Color 6 (1942)	13.00	40.00	90.00
4-Color 32 (1943)	11.00	32.00	76.00
4-Color 65 (1945)	8.50	25.50	60.00
4-Color 99 (1946)	7.00	21.00	50.00
4-Color 138 (1947)	6.50	19.50	45.00
1 (11-1/47-48)	6.50	19.50	45.00
2	3.50	10.50	24.00
3 (8-10/48), 4 (1949)	2.30	7.00	16.00
5-7	1.70	5.00	12.00
4-Color 909	1.50	4.50	10.00

SMOKEY BEAR (TV) (See March Of Comics #362,372,383,407)
Feb, 1970 - No. 13, Mar, 1973
Gold Key

1	.70	2.00	4.00
2-13	.40	1.25	2.50

SMOKEY STOVER (See Popular Comics, Super Book #5,17,29 & Super Comics)
No. 7, 1942 - No. 827, Aug, 1957
Dell Publishing Co.

4-Color 7 (1942)-Reprints	22.00	65.00	155.00
4-Color 35 (1943)	11.50	34.00	80.00
4-Color 64 (1944)	8.50	25.50	60.00
4-Color 229 (1949)	3.00	9.00	21.00
4-Color 730,827	1.70	5.00	12.00
General Motors giveaway (1953)	3.00	9.00	21.00
National Fire Protection giveaway('53 & '54)-16 pgs., paper-c	3.00	9.00	21.00

SMOKEY THE BEAR (See Forest Fire for 1st app.)
No. 653, 10/55 - No. 1214, 8/61 (See March Of Comics #234)
Dell Publishing Co.

SMOKEY THE BEAR (continued)

	Good	Fine	N-Mint
4-Color 653	2.65	8.00	18.00
4-Color 708,754,818,932	2.00	6.00	14.00
4-Color 1016,1119,1214	1.50	4.50	10.00

True Story of. . ., The('59)-U.S. Forest Service giveaway-Publ. by
Western Printing Co. (reprinted in '64 & '69)-Reprints 1st 16 pgs.

of 4-Color 932	.85	2.50	6.00

SMOKY (See Movie Classics)

SMURFS (TV)
Dec, 1982 (No month given) - No. 3, Feb, 1983
Marvel Comics Group

1-3		.30	.60
. . .Treasury Edition 1(64pgs.)-r/#1-3	.40	1.25	2.50

SNAFU (Magazine)
Nov, 1955 - V2#2, Mar, 1956 (B&W)
Atlas Comics (RCM)

V1#1-Heath/Severin-a	4.65	14.00	32.00
V2#1,2-Severin-a	3.00	9.00	21.00

SNAGGLEPUSS (TV)(See Spotlight #4)
Oct, 1962 - No. 4, Sept, 1963 (Hanna-Barbera)
Gold Key

1	2.30	7.00	16.00
2-4	1.50	4.50	10.00

SNAP (Jest #10?)
No. 9, 1944
Harry 'A' Chesler

9-Manhunter, The Voice	5.70	17.00	40.00

SNAPPY COMICS
1945
Cima Publ. Co. (Prize Publ.)

1-Airmale app; 9pg. Sorcerer's Apprentice adapt; Kiefer-a			
	5.00	15.00	35.00

SNARKY PARKER (See Life with. . .)

SNIFFY THE PUP
No. 5, Nov, 1949 - No. 18, Sept, 1953
Standard Publications (Animated Cartoons)

5-Two Frazetta text illos	3.50	10.50	24.00
6-10	1.30	4.00	9.00
11-18	.70	2.00	5.00

SNOOPER AND BLABBER DETECTIVES (TV)
Nov, 1962 - No. 3, May, 1963 (Hanna-Barbera)
Gold Key

1 (See Whitman Comic Books)	2.30	7.00	16.00
2,3	1.70	5.00	12.00

SNOW FOR CHRISTMAS
1957 (16 pages) (Giveaway)
W. T. Grant Co.

nn	1.20	3.50	7.00

SNOW WHITE (See Christmas With. . ., 4-Color #49,227,382, Mickey Mouse Mag.,
& Movie Comics)

SNOW WHITE AND THE SEVEN DWARFS
1952 (32 pgs.; 5x7¼'', soft-c) (Disney)
Bendix Washing Machines

nn	5.00	15.00	35.00

SNOW WHITE AND THE SEVEN DWARFS
April, 1982 (60 cent cover price)
Whitman Publications

nn-r/4-Color #49		.30	.60

SNOW WHITE AND THE 7 DWARFS IN ''MILKY WAY''
1955 (16 pgs., 5x7¼'', soft-c) (Disney premium)
American Dairy Association

	Good	Fine	N-Mint
nn	5.00	15.00	35.00

SNOW WHITE AND THE SEVEN DWARFS
1957 (small size)
Promotional Publ. Co.

nn	2.75	8.00	19.00

SNOW WHITE AND THE SEVEN DWARFS
1958 (16 pgs, 5x7¼'', soft-c) (Disney premium)
Western Printing Co.

''Mystery of the Missing Magic''	3.50	10.50	24.00

SOAP OPERA LOVE
Feb, 1983 - No. 3, June, 1983
Charlton Comics

1-3		.25	.50

SOAP OPERA ROMANCES
July, 1982 - No. 5, March, 1983
Charlton Comics

1-5-Nurse Betsy Crane-r		.25	.50

SOJOURN ($1.50)
9/77 - No. 2, 1978 (Full tabloid size) (Color & B&W)
White Cliffs Publ. Co.

1-Tor by Kubert, Eagle by Severin, E. V. Race, Private Investigator
by Doug Wildey, T. C. Mars by S. Aragones begin plus other

strips	.25	.80	1.60
2	.25	.80	1.60

SOLARMAN
Jan, 1989 ($1.00, color, one-shot)
Marvel Comics

1		.50	1.00

SOLDIER & MARINE COMICS (Fightin' Army #16 on)
No. 11, 12/54 - No. 15, 8/55; V2No.9, 12/56
Charlton Comics (Toby Press of Conn. V1No.11)

V1#11 (12/54)-Bob Powell-a	1.15	3.50	8.00
V1#12(2/55)-15	.60	1.80	4.00
V2#9(Formerly Never Again; Jerry Drummer V2#10 on)			
	.60	1.80	4.00

SOLDIER COMICS
Jan, 1952 - No. 11, Sept, 1953
Fawcett Publications

1	3.15	9.50	22.00
2	1.60	4.80	11.00
3-5	1.35	4.00	9.00
6,7,9-11	1.00	3.00	7.00
8-Illo. in POP	1.15	3.50	8.00

SOLDIERS OF FORTUNE
Feb-Mar, 1951 - No. 13, Feb-Mar, 1953
American Comics Group (Creston Publ. Corp.)

1-Capt. Crossbones by Shelly, Ace Carter, Lance Larson begin

	8.00	24.00	56.00
2	5.00	15.00	35.00
3-10: 6-Bondage-c	3.70	11.00	26.00
11-13 (War format)	1.15	3.50	8.00

NOTE: **Shelly** a-1-3, 5. **Whitney** a-6, 8-11, 13; c-1-3, 5, 6. Most issues are 52 pages.

SOLDIERS OF FREEDOM
1987 - No. 2? ($1.75, color)
Americomics

1,2		.30	.90	1.80

Snagglepuss #3, © Hanna-Barbera

Soldier Comics #1, © FAW

Soldiers Of Fortune #1, © ACG

Soulquest #1, © Innovation

Space Action #1, © ACE

Space Adventures #33, © CC

SOLO AVENGERS (Becomes Avengers Spotlight #21 on)
Dec, 1987 - No. 20, July, 1989
Marvel Comics

	Good	Fine	N-Mint
1	.35	1.10	2.20
2-5	.25	.70	1.40
6-20: 11-Intro Bobcat		.50	1.00

SOLO EX-MUTANTS
Jan, 1988 - No. 6, 1988 ($1.95, B&W)
Eternity Comics

1-6	.35	1.00	2.00

SOLOMON AND SHEBA (See 4-Color #1070)

SOLOMON KANE (Also see Blackthorne 3-D Series #60)
Sept, 1985 - No. 6, Mar, 1986 (mini-series)
Marvel Comics Group

1		.50	1.00
2-6: 3,4-Williamson-a		.45	.90

SOMERSET HOLMES (See Eclipse Graphic Album Series)
9/83 - No. 4, 4/84; No. 5, 11/84 - No. 6, 12/84 ($1.50; Baxter)
Pacific Comics/Eclipse Comics No. 5, 6

1-B. Anderson c/a; Cliff Hanger by Williamson begins, ends #6	.40	1.25	2.50
2-6	.35	1.00	2.00

SONG OF THE SOUTH (See Brer Rabbit & 4-Color #693)

SONIC DISRUPTORS
12/87 - No. 7, 7/88 ($1.75, limited series; mature readers)
DC Comics

1-7	.30	.90	1.80

SON OF AMBUSH BUG (Also see Ambush Bug)
July, 1986 - No. 6, Dec, 1986 (75 cents, color)
DC Comics

1-6: Giffen c/a(p) in all		.40	.80

SON OF BLACK BEAUTY (See 4-Color #510,566)

SON OF FLUBBER (See Movie Comics)

SON OF SATAN (Also see Marvel Spotlight #12)
Dec, 1975 - No. 8, Feb, 1977
Marvel Comics Group

1-Mooney-a		.40	.80
2-Origin The Possessor		.25	.50
3-8: 4,5-Russell-a(p). 8-Heath-a		.20	.40

SON OF SINBAD (Also see Abbott & Costello & Daring Adventures)
February, 1950
St. John Publishing Co.

1-Kubert c/a	26.00	78.00	180.00

SON OF TOMAHAWK (See Tomahawk)

SON OF VULCAN (Mysteries of Unexplored Worlds #1-48; Thunderbolt, V3#51 on)
No. 49, Nov, 1965 - V2No. 50, Jan, 1966
Charlton Comics

49,50	.70	2.00	4.00

SONS OF KATIE ELDER (See Movie Classics)

SORCERY (See Chilling Adventures in . . . & Red Circle . . .)

SORORITY SECRETS
July, 1954
Toby Press

1	2.85	8.50	20.00

SOULQUEST (See Againts Blackshard 3-D)
April, 1989 ($3.95, color, squarebound, 52 pgs.)
Innovation Publishing

	Good	Fine	N-Mint
1-Blackshard app.	.70	2.00	4.00

SOUPY SALES COMIC BOOK (TV)(The Official . . .)
1965
Archie Publications

1	5.50	16.50	38.00

SOUTHERN KNIGHTS, THE (Formerly Crusaders No. 1)
No. 2, 1983 - No. 7, 9/84; No. 8, 1984 - Present ($1.75, B&W)
Guild Publ./Fictioneer Books(Comics Interview) No. 8 on

2-Magazine size	1.70	5.00	10.00
3	.85	2.50	5.00
4,5	.70	2.00	4.00
6-10	.50	1.50	3.00
11-15	.40	1.25	2.50
16-33: 28-Begin $1.95-c	.35	1.00	2.00
34-Christmas issue ($2.25)	.40	1.15	2.25
. . .Dread Halloween Special 1	.35	1.10	2.25
Special 1 (Spring, 1989, $2.25)	.35	1.10	2.25
Graphic Novels #1-4	.85	2.50	5.00

SPACE ACE (Also see Manhunt!)
No. 5, 1952
Magazine Enterprises

5(A-1 61)-Guardineer-a	17.00	51.00	120.00

SPACE ACTION
June, 1952 - No. 3, Oct, 1952
Ace Magazines (Junior Books)

1	25.00	75.00	175.00
2,3	21.00	62.00	145.00

SPACE ADVENTURES (War At Sea #22 on)
7/52 - No. 21, 5/56; No. 23, 5/58 - No. 59, 11/64; V3/60,
10/67; V1/2, 7/68 - V1No.8, 7/69; No. 9, 5/78 - No. 13, 3/79
Capitol Stories/Charlton Comics

1	14.00	42.00	100.00
2	7.00	21.00	50.00
3-5	5.70	17.00	40.00
6,8,9	5.00	15.00	35.00
7-Transvestism story	6.00	18.00	42.00
10-Ditko c/a	17.00	51.00	120.00
11-Ditko c/a(2)	17.00	51.00	120.00
12-Ditko-c (Classic)	20.00	60.00	140.00
13-(Fox-r, 10-11/54); Blue Beetle story	5.70	17.00	40.00
14-Blue Beetle story (Fox-r, 12-1/54-55)	4.65	14.00	32.00
15,17-19: 15-18-Rocky Jones app.(TV)	4.00	12.00	28.00
16-Krigstein	9.50	28.50	65.00
20-Reprints Fawcett's "Destination Moon"	11.00	32.00	76.00
21-(8/56) (no #22)	5.00	15.00	35.00
23-(5/58; formerly Nyoka, The Jungle Girl)-Reprints Fawcett's "Destination Moon"	9.50	28.50	65.00
24,25,31,32-Ditko-a	6.50	19.50	45.00
26,27-Ditko-a(4) each	8.00	24.00	56.00
28-30	2.30	7.00	16.00
33-1st app./origin Captain Atom by Ditko (3/60)	18.00	54.00	125.00
34-40,42-All Captain Atom by Ditko	7.00	21.00	50.00
41,43,46-59	.85	2.60	6.00
44,45-Mercury Man in each	.85	2.60	6.00
V3#60(10/67)-Origin Paul Mann & The Saucers From the Future	.70	2.00	4.00
2-8('68-'69)-1,2,5,6,8-Ditko-a; 2,4-Aparo-c/a	.35	1.00	2.00
9-13('78-'79)-Capt. Atom-r/Space Advs. by Ditko; 9-Origin-r		.40	.80

NOTE: *Aparo* a-V3#60. c-V3#8. *Ditko* c-12, 31-42. *Shuster* a-11.

SPACE BUSTERS
Spring/52 - No. 3, Fall/52 (Painted covers by Norman Saunders)

SPACE BUSTERS (continued)
Ziff-Davis Publ. Co.

	Good	Fine	N-Mint
1-Krigstein-a(3)	32.00	95.00	225.00
2,3: 2-Kinstler-a(2pgs.); Krigstein-a(3)	26.00	79.00	185.00

NOTE: Anderson a-2. Bondage c-2.

SPACE CADET (See Tom Corbett, . . .)

SPACE COMICS
No. 4, Mar-Apr, 1954 - No. 5, May-June, 1954
Avon Periodicals

4,5-Space Mouse, Peter Rabbit, Super Pup, & Merry Mouse app.			
	2.30	7.00	16.00
I.W. Reprint #8 (nd)-Space Mouse-r	.50	1.50	3.00

SPACED
1985? - No. 13, 1988 ($1.50, B&W)
Unbridled Ambition/Eclipse Comics #10 on

1	8.30	25.00	50.00
2	5.00	15.00	30.00
3,4	3.35	10.00	20.00
5,6	1.00	3.00	6.00
7-13	.25	.75	1.50
Special Edition (1983, Mimeo)	1.70	5.00	10.00

SPACE DETECTIVE
July, 1951 - No. 4, July, 1952
Avon Periodicals

1-Rod Hathway, Space Det. begins, ends #4; Wood c/a(3)-23 pgs.; "Opium Smugglers of Venus" drug story; Lucky Dale-r/Saint #4			
	62.00	185.00	435.00
2-Tales from the Shadow Squad story; Wood/Orlando-c; Wood inside layouts	30.00	90.00	210.00
3-Kinstler-c	19.00	57.00	132.00
4-Kinstler-a	19.00	57.00	132.00
I.W. Reprint #1(Reprints #2), 8(Reprints cover #1 & part Famous Funnies #191)	1.35	4.00	8.00
I.W. Reprint #9	1.35	4.00	8.00

SPACE EXPLORER (See March of Comics #202)

SPACE FAMILY ROBINSON (TV)(. . . Lost in Space #15-36)(Lost in Space #37 on)
Dec, 1962 - No. 36, Oct, 1969 (All painted covers)
Gold Key

1-(low distr.); Spiegle-a in all	8.50	25.50	60.00
2(3/63)-Family becomes lost in space	4.50	14.00	32.00
3-10: 6-Captain Venture begins	2.30	7.00	16.00
11-20	1.50	4.50	10.00
21-36	.85	2.60	6.00

SPACE FAMILY ROBINSON (See March of Comics #320,328,352,404,414)

SPACE GHOST (TV) (Also see Golden Comics Digest #2 & Hanna Barbera Super TV Heroes #3-7)
March, 1967 (Hanna-Barbera) (TV debut was 9/10/66)
Gold Key

1 (10199-703)-Spiegle-a	11.00	32.00	75.00

SPACE GHOST (TV) (Graphic Novel)
12/87 (One Shot) (52pgs.; deluxe format; $3.50)
Comico

1-(Hanna-Barbera)-Rude c/a(p)	.85	2.50	5.00

SPACE GIANTS, THE
1979 (One shot, $1.00, B&W, TV)
FBN Publications

1-Based on Japanese TV series	1.50	4.50	10.00

SPACEHAWK (See Epic Illustrated, Target Comics & 3-D Zone #18)
1989 - No. 2, 1989 ($2.00, B&W)

Dark Horse Comics

	Good	Fine	N-Mint
1,2-Wolverton-c/a(r) plus new stories	.35	1.00	2.00

SPACE KAT-ETS (in 3-D)
Dec, 1953 (25 cents)
Power Publishing Co.

1	20.00	60.00	140.00

SPACEMAN (Speed Carter. . .)
Sept, 1953 - No. 6, July, 1954
Atlas Comics (CnPC)

1	21.50	64.00	150.00
2	14.00	42.00	100.00
3-6: 4-A-Bomb-c	11.50	34.00	80.00

NOTE: Everett c-1, 3. Maneely a-1-6?; c-6. Tuska a-5(3).

SPACE MAN
No. 1253, 1-3/62 - No. 8, 3-5/64; No. 9, 7/72 - No. 10, 10/72
Dell Publishing Co.

4-Color 1253 (1-3/62)	3.50	10.50	24.00
2,3	1.70	5.00	12.00
4-8	1.00	3.00	7.00
9-Reprints #1253	.40	1.25	2.80
10-Reprints #2	.35	1.00	2.00

SPACE MOUSE (Also see Space Comics)
April, 1953 - No. 5, Apr-May, 1954
Avon Periodicals

1	3.70	11.00	26.00
2	2.15	6.50	15.00
3-5	1.50	4.50	10.00

SPACE MOUSE (Walter Lantz. . . #1; see Comic Album #17)
No. 1132, 8-10/60 - No. 5, 11/63 (Walter Lantz)
Dell Publishing Co./Gold Key

4-Color 1132,1244	1.50	4.50	10.00
1(11/62)(G.K.)	1.50	4.50	10.00
2-5	1.00	3.00	7.00

SPACE MYSTERIES
1964 (Reprints)
I.W. Enterprises

1-r-/Journey Into Unknown Worlds #4 w/new-c	.50	1.50	3.00
8,9	.50	1.50	3.00

SPACE: 1999 (TV)
Nov, 1975 - No. 7, Nov, 1976
Charlton Comics

1-Staton-c/a; origin Moonbase Alpha		.60	1.20
2,7: 2-Staton-a		.50	1.00
3-6: All Byrne-a; c-5	.50	1.50	3.00

SPACE: 1999 (TV)(Magazine)
Nov, 1975 - No. 8, Nov, 1976 (B&W)
Charlton Comics

1-Origin Moonbase Alpha; Morrow c/a	.50	1.50	3.00
2,3-Morrow c/a	.30	.90	1.80
4-8 (#7 shows #6 on inside)	.25	.80	1.60

SPACE PATROL (TV)
Summer/52 - No. 2, Oct-Nov/52 (Painted-c by Norman Saunders)
Ziff-Davis Publishing Co. (Approved Comics)

1-Krigstein-a	38.00	115.00	265.00
2-Krigstein-a(3)	32.00	95.00	225.00
. . .'s Special Mission (8 pgs., B&W, Giveaway)	50.00	150.00	300.00

SPACE PIRATES (See Archie Giant Series #533)

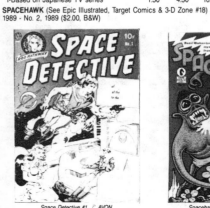

Space Detective #1, © AVON

Spacehawk #1, © Dark Horse

Space Patrol #1, © Z-D

Space Western #42, © CC   Sparkler Comics #6, © UFS   Sparkling Love #1, © AVON

SPACE SQUADRON (Becomes Space Worlds #6)
June, 1951 - No. 5, Feb, 1952
Marvel/Atlas Comics (ACI)

	Good	Fine	N-Mint
1	23.00	70.00	160.00
2	18.50	56.00	130.00
3-5	14.00	42.00	100.00

SPACE THRILLERS
1954 (Giant) (25 cents)
Avon Periodicals

nn-(Scarce)-Robotmen of the Lost Planet; contains 3 rebound comics of The Saint & Strange Worlds. Contents could vary			
	65.00	195.00	455.00

SPACE TRIP TO THE MOON (See Space Adventures #23)

SPACE WAR (Fightin' Five #28 on)
Oct, 1959 - No. 27, Mar, 1964; No. 28, Mar, 1978 - No. 34, 3/79
Charlton Comics

	Good	Fine	N-Mint
V1#1	6.50	19.50	45.00
2,3	2.65	8.00	18.00
4,5,8,10-Ditko c/a	7.00	21.00	50.00
6-Ditko-a	5.70	17.00	40.00
7,9,11-15: Last 10 cent issue?	1.70	5.00	12.00
16-27	1.15	3.50	8.00
28,29,33,34-Ditko c/a(r)	1.70	5.00	12.00
30-Ditko c/a(r); Staton, Sutton/Wood-a	2.15	6.50	15.00
31-Ditko c/a; atom-blast-c	2.15	6.50	15.00
32-r-/Charlton Premiere V2#2	.30	.90	1.80

NOTE: *Sutton a-30, 33.*

SPACE WESTERN (Formerly Cowboy Western Comics; becomes
Cowboy Western Comics #46 on)
No. 40, Oct, 1952 - No. 45, Aug, 1953
Charlton Comics (Capitol Stories)

40-Intro Spurs Jackson & His Space Vigilantes; flying saucer story			
	23.00	70.00	160.00
41,43-45: 41-Flying saucer-c	17.00	51.00	120.00
42-Atom bomb explosion-c	19.00	57.00	135.00

SPACE WORLDS (Formerly Space Squadron #1-5)
No. 6, April, 1952
Atlas Comics (Male)

6	11.50	34.00	80.00

SPANKY & ALFALFA & THE LITTLE RASCALS (See The Little Rascals)

SPANNER'S GALAXY
Dec, 1984 - No. 6, May, 1985 (mini-series)
DC Comics

1-6: Mandrake c/a in all. 2-Intro sidekick Gadg		.50	1.00

SPARKIE, RADIO PIXIE (Becomes Big John & Sparkie #4)
Winter, 1951 - No. 3, 1952 (Painted-c)
Ziff-Davis Publ. Co.

1	8.00	24.00	56.00
2,3	6.50	19.50	45.00

SPARKLE COMICS
Oct-Nov, 1948 - No. 33, Dec-Jan, 1953-54
United Features Syndicate

1-Li'l Abner, Nancy, Captain & the Kids	6.50	19.50	45.00
2	3.50	10.50	24.00
3-10	2.30	7.00	16.00
11-20	1.70	5.00	12.00
21-33	1.15	3.50	8.00

SPARKLE PLENTY (See 4-Color #215 & Harvey Comics Library #2)

SPARKLER COMICS (1st Series)
July, 1940 - No. 2, 1940

United Feature Comic Group

	Good	Fine	N-Mint
1-Jim Hardy	19.00	57.00	135.00
2-Frankie Doodle	13.00	40.00	90.00

SPARKLER COMICS (2nd Series)(Nancy & Sluggo #121 on)(Cover title becomes Nancy And Sluggo #101? on)
July, 1941 - No. 120, Jan, 1955
United Features Syndicate

1-Origin Sparkman; Tarzan (by Hogarth in all issues), Captain & the Kids, Ella Cinders, Danny Dingle, Dynamite Dunn, Nancy, Abbie & Slats, Frankie Doodle, Broncho Bill begin; Sparkman c-#1-12			
	71.00	215.00	500.00
2	31.50	94.00	220.00
3,4	27.00	81.00	190.00
5-10: 9-Sparkman's new costume	22.00	65.00	154.00
11-13,15-20: 12-Sparkman new costume-color change. 19-1st Race Riley	18.50	56.00	130.00
14-Hogarth Tarzan-c	21.50	64.00	150.00
21-24,26,27,29,30: 22-Race Riley & the Commandos strips begin, ends #44	14.00	42.00	100.00
25,28,31,34,37,39-Tarzan-c by Hogarth	18.00	54.00	125.00
32,33,35,36,38,40	8.50	25.50	60.00
41,43,45,46,48,49	6.00	18.00	42.00
42,44,47,50-Tarzan-c	11.00	32.00	75.00
51,52,54-70: 57-Li'l Abner begins (not in #58); Fearless Fosdick app.-#58	4.30	13.00	30.00
53-Tarzan-c by Hogarth	9.30	28.00	65.00
71-80	3.50	10.50	24.00
81,82,84-90: 85-Li'l Abner ends. 86-Lingerie panels	2.65	8.00	18.00
83-Tarzan-c	4.65	14.00	32.00
91-96,98-99	2.30	7.00	16.00
97-Origin Casey Ruggles by Warren Tufts	5.00	15.00	35.00
100	2.85	8.50	20.00
101-107,109-112,114-120	1.70	5.00	12.00
108,113-Toth-a	5.00	15.00	35.00

SPARKLING LOVE
June, 1950; 1953
Avon Periodicals/Realistic (1953)

1(Avon)-Kubert-a; photo-c	11.50	34.00	80.00
nn(1953)-Reprint; Kubert-a	5.00	15.00	35.00

SPARKLING STARS
June, 1944 - No. 33, March, 1948
Holyoke Publishing Co.

1-Hell's Angels, FBI, Boxie Weaver & Ali Baba begin			
	7.00	21.00	50.00
2	4.00	12.00	28.00
3-Actual FBI case photos & war photos	2.85	8.50	20.00
4-10: 7-X-mas-c	2.30	7.00	16.00
11-19: 13-Origin/1st app. Jungo The Man-Beast	2.00	6.00	14.00
20-Intro Fangs the Wolf Boy	2.30	7.00	16.00
21-29,32,33: 29-Bondage-c	2.00	6.00	14.00
31-Spanking panel; Sid Greene-a	2.30	7.00	16.00

SPARK MAN (See Sparkler Comics)
1945 (One Shot) (36 pages)
Frances M. McQueeny

1-Origin Spark Man; female torture story; cover redrawn from Sparkler No. 1	13.00	40.00	90.00

SPARKY WATTS (Also see Columbia Comics)
Nov?, 1942 - No. 10, 1949
Columbia Comic Corp.

1(1942)-Skyman & The Face app.; Hitler-c	16.00	48.00	110.00
2(1943)	7.00	21.00	50.00
3(1944)	6.50	19.50	45.00

SPARKY WATTS (continued)	Good	Fine	N-Mint
4(1944)-Origin	5.70	17.00	40.00
5(1947)-Skyman app.	4.50	14.00	32.00
6('47),7,8('48),9,10('49)	2.85	8.50	20.00

SPARTACUS (See 4-Color #1139)

SPECIAL AGENT (Steve Saunders...)(Also see True Comics #68)
Dec, 1947 - No. 8, Sept, 1949
Parents' Magazine Institute (Commended Comics No. 2)

1-J. Edgar Hoover photo-c	4.50	14.00	32.00
2	2.30	7.00	16.00
3-8	1.70	5.00	12.00

SPECIAL COLLECTORS' EDITION
Dec, 1975 (No month given) (10¼x13½'')
Marvel Comics Group

1-Kung Fu, Iron Fist & Sons of the Tiger	.30	.90	1.80

SPECIAL COMICS (Hangman #2 on)
Winter, 1941-42
MLJ Magazines

1-Origin The Boy Buddies (Shield & Wizard x-over); death of The Comet; origin The Hangman retold	97.00	290.00	675.00

SPECIAL DELIVERY
1951 (32 pgs.; B&W)
Post Hall Synd. (Giveaway)

Origin of Pogo, Swamp, etc.; 2 pg. biog. on Walt Kelly
(One copy sold in 1980 for $150.00)

SPECIAL EDITION (See Gorgo, Reptisaurus)

SPECIAL EDITION (U. S. Navy Giveaways)
1944 - 1945 (Regular comic format with wording simplified, 52pgs.)
National Periodical Publications

1-Action (1944)-reprints Action 80	70.00	210.00	490.00
2-Action (1944)-reprints Action 81	70.00	210.00	490.00
3-Superman (1944)-reprints Superman 33	70.00	210.00	490.00
4-Detective (1944)-reprints Det. 97	75.00	225.00	525.00
5-Superman (1945)-reprints Superman 34	70.00	210.00	490.00
6-Action (1945)-reprints Action 84	70.00	210.00	490.00

SPECIAL EDITION COMICS
1940 (Aug.) (One Shot, 68pgs.)
Fawcett Publications

1-1st book devoted entirely to Captain Marvel; C.C. Beck c/a; only app. of C. Marvel with belt buckle; C. Marvel appears with button-down flap, 1st story (came out before Captain Marvel #1)	271.00	815.00	1900.00

NOTE: Prices vary widely on this book. Since this book is all Captain Marvel stories, it is actually a pre-Captain Marvel #1. There is speculation that this book almost became **Captain Marvel #1**. After **Special Edition** was published, there was an editor change at Fawcett. The new editor commissioned Kirby to do a nn **Captain Marvel** book early in 1941. This book was followed by a 2nd book several months later. This 2nd book was advertised as a #3 (making Special Edition the #1, & the nn issue the #2). However, the 2nd book did come out as a #2.

SPECIAL EDITION X-MEN
Feb, 1983 (One Shot) (Baxter paper, $2.00)
Marvel Comics Group

1-r-/Giant-Size X-Men plus one new story	1.25	3.75	7.50

SPECIAL MARVEL EDITION (Master of Kung Fu #17 on)
Jan, 1971 - No. 16, Feb, 1974
Marvel Comics Group

1-4: Thor reprints; all 25 cent Giants	.25	.75	1.50
5-14: Sgt. Fury-r; 11 r-/Sgt. Fury #13 (Captain America app.)	.25	.75	1.50
15-Master of Kung Fu begins; Starlin-a; origin & 1st app. Nayland Smith & Dr. Petric	1.35	4.00	8.00
16-1st app. Midnight; Starlin-a	.70	2.00	4.00

SPECIAL MISSIONS (See G.I. Joe ...)

SPECIAL WAR SERIES (Attack V4#3 on?)
Aug, 1965 - No. 4, Nov, 1965
Charlton Comics

	Good	Fine	N-Mint
V4No.1-D-Day (See D-Day listing)	.50	1.50	3.00
2-Attack!	.35	1.00	2.00
3-War & Attack	.35	1.00	2.00
4-Judomaster (Intro/1st app.)	1.15	3.50	8.00

SPECTACULAR ADVENTURES (See Adventures)

SPECTACULAR FEATURE MAGAZINE, A (Formerly My Confessions)
(Spectacular Features Magazine #12 on)
No. 11, April, 1950
Fox Feature Syndicate

11 (#1)-Samson & Delilah	12.00	36.00	84.00

SPECTACULAR FEATURES MAGAZINE (Formerly A Spectacular Feature Magazine)
No. 12, June, 1950 - No. 3, Aug, 1950
Fox Feature Syndicate

12 (#2)-Iwo Jima; photo flag-c	12.00	36.00	84.00
3-True Crime Cases	8.50	25.50	60.00

SPECTACULAR SPIDER-MAN, THE (See Marvel Special Edition and Marvel Treasury Edition)

SPECTACULAR SPIDER-MAN, THE (Magazine)
July, 1968 - No. 2, Nov, 1968 (35 cents)
Marvel Comics Group

1-(Black & White)	2.15	6.50	15.00
2-(Color)-Green Goblin app.	2.85	8.50	20.00

SPECTACULAR SPIDER-MAN, THE (Peter Parker...#54-132,134)
Dec, 1976 - Present
Marvel Comics Group

1-Origin retold	1.70	5.00	10.00
2-5	.70	2.00	4.00
6-10	.60	1.75	3.50
11-20	.50	1.50	3.00
21,24-26	.40	1.25	2.50
22,23-Moon Knight app.	.45	1.40	2.80
27-Miller's 1st Daredevil	1.75	5.25	10.50
28-Miller Daredevil (p)	1.40	4.20	8.40
29-57,59: 33-Origin Iguana	.35	1.05	2.10
58-Byrne a(p)	.55	1.60	3.20
60-Double size; origin retold with new facts revealed	.35	1.10	2.20
61-63,65-68,71-74	.25	.80	1.60
64-1st Cloak & Dagger app.	1.60	4.75	9.50
69,70-Cloak & Dagger app.	.80	2.35	4.70
75-Double size	.35	1.05	2.10
76-80	.25	.80	1.60
81,82-Punisher app.	1.05	3.15	6.30
83-Origin Punisher retold	1.25	3.70	7.40
84-93,97-99: 98-Intro The Spot	.25	.80	1.60
94-96-Cloak & Dagger app.	.25	.80	1.60
100-Double size	.35	1.05	2.10
101-130: 107-Death of Jean DeWolff. 111-Secret Wars II tie-in. 128-Black Cat new costume. 130-Hobgoblin app.	.55		1.10
131-Six part Kraven tie-in	.70	2.00	4.00
132-Kraven tie-in	.50	1.50	3.00
133-139: 139-Origin Tombstone	.25	.80	1.60
140-Punisher cameo app.	.35	1.00	2.00
141-Punisher app.	.60	1.75	3.50
142,143-Punisher app.	.40	1.25	2.50
144-157,159-162: 147-Hobgoblin app. 151-Tombstone returns	.25	.80	1.60

158-Spider-Man gets new powers (1st Cosmic Spidey, continued in

The Spectre #5 (8/68), © DC

Speed Comics #38, © HARV

Speed Racer #6, © Now Comics

	Good	Fine	N-Mint
THE SPECTACULAR SPIDER-MAN (cont.)			
Web of Spider-Man #59	.35	1.00	2.00
Annual 1 (12/79)	.25	.80	1.60
Annual 2 (8/80)-1st app. & origin Rapier	.25	.80	1.60
Annual 3 (11/81)-Last Manwolf	.25	.80	1.60
Annual 4 (11/84), 5 (10/85), 6 ('85), 7 (11/87)	.25	.80	1.60
Annual 8 ('88, $1.75)-Evolutionary War x-over	.45	1.30	2.60
Annual 9 ('89, $2.00, 68 pgs.)-Atlantis Attacks	.35	1.00	2.00

NOTE: *Austin* c-21i. *Byrne* o(p)-17, 43, 58, 101, 102. *Giffen* a-120p. *Miller* c-46p, 48p, 50, 51p, 52p, 54p, 55, 56p, 57, 60. *Mooney* a-7i, 11i, 21p, 23p, 25p, 26p, 29-34p, 36p, 37p, 39i, 41, 42i, 49p, 50i, 51i, 53p, 54-57i, 59-66i, 68i, 71i, 73-79i, 81-83i, 85i, 87-99i, 102i, 125p. *Annual* 1i, 2p. *Nasser* c-37p. *Perez* c-10. *Simonson* c-54i.

SPECTACULAR STORIES MAGAZINE (Formerly A Star Presentation)
No. 4, July, 1950 - No. 3, Sept, 1950
Fox Feature Sydicate (Hero Books)

	Good	Fine	N-Mint
4-Sherlock Holmes	18.00	54.00	125.00
3-The St. Valentine's Day Massacre	11.00	32.00	75.00

SPECTRE, THE (See Adventure Comics, More Fun & Showcase)
Nov-Dec, 1967 - No. 10, May-June, 1969
National Periodical Publications

1-Anderson c/a	2.65	8.00	18.00
2-5-Adams c/a; 3-Wildcat x-over	2.15	6.50	15.00
6-8,10: 7-Hourman app.	.85	2.60	6.00
9-Wrightson-a	1.15	3.50	8.00

NOTE: *Anderson* inks-#6-8.

SPECTRE, THE (Also see Wrath of the . . .)
Apr, 1987 - No. 31, Oct, 1989 ($1.00, new format)
DC Comics

1-Colan-a(p) begins; Kaluta-c	.35	1.10	2.25
2-10: 3-Kaluta-c. 9-Nudity panels. 10-Morrow-a	.25	.75	1.50
11-31: 10,11-Millennium tie-ins	.60	1.20
Annual 1 ('88, $2.00)	.35	1.00	2.00

NOTE: *Art Adams* c-Annual #1. *Colan* a-1-6p. *Morrow* a-9-15.

SPEEDBALL (See Amazing Spider-Man Annual #12)
Sept, 1988(10/88-inside) - No. 11, July, 1989 (75 cents, color)
Marvel Comics

1-11: Ditko/Guice a-1-4, c-1; Ditko c-5,9		.40	.80

SPEED BUGGY (TV)(Also see Fun-In #12,15)
July, 1975 - No. 9, Nov, 1976 (Hanna-Barbera)
Charlton Comics

1-9		.25	.50

SPEED CARTER SPACEMAN (See Spaceman)

SPEED COMICS (New Speed)(Also see Double Up)
Oct, 1939 - No. 44, Jan-Feb, 1947 (No.14-16: pocket size, 100 pgs.)
Brookwood Publ./Speed Publ./Harvey Publications No. 14 on

1-Origin Shock Gibson; Ted Parrish, the Man with 1000 Faces begins; Powell-a	79.00	235.00	550.00
2-Powell-a	38.00	115.00	270.00
3	24.00	72.00	170.00
4-Powell-a?	21.00	62.00	145.00
5	19.00	57.00	135.00
6-11: 7-Mars Mason begins, ends #11	16.50	50.00	115.00
12 (3/41); shows #11 in indicia)-The Wasp begins; Major Colt app. (Capt. Colt #12)	20.00	60.00	140.00
13-Intro. Captain Freedom & Young Defenders; Girl Commandos, Pat Parker, War Nurse begins; Major Colt app.	24.00	73.00	170.00
14-16 (100 pg. pocket size, 1941): 14-2nd Harvey comic (See Pocket).			
15-Pat Parker dons costume, last in costume #23; no Girl Commandos	18.50	56.00	130.00
17-Black Cat begins (origin), r-/Pocket #1; not in #40,41	30.00	90.00	210.00
18-20	16.50	50.00	115.00
21,22,25-30: 26-Flag-c	14.00	42.00	100.00

	Good	Fine	N-Mint
23-Origin Girl Commandos	21.00	62.00	145.00
24-Pat Parker team-up with Girl Commandos	14.00	42.00	100.00
31-44: 38-Flag-c	11.50	34.00	80.00

NOTE: *Briefer* a-6, 7. *Kubert* a-7-11(Mars Mason), 37, 38, 42-44. *Powell* a-1, 2, 4-7, 28, 31, 44. *Schomburg* c-31-36. *Tuska* a-3, 6, 7. *Bondage* c-18, 35.

SPEED DEMONS (Formerly Frank Merriwell at Yale #1-4?; Submarine Attack #11 on)
No. 5, Feb, 1957 - No. 10, 1958
Charlton Comics

5-10	.60	1.80	4.00

SPEED RACER (See Dai Kamikaze! & Racer-X)
July, 1987 - Present (#1-3: $1.50, 4 on: $1.75; color)
Now Comics

1	.60	1.75	3.50
1-2nd printing	.25	.75	1.50
2-10	.35	1.00	2.00
11-30	.30	.90	1.75
Special 1 (3/88, $2.00)-Origin Mach 5	.35	1.00	2.00
Special 2 ('88, $3.50)	.60	1.75	3.50

NOTE: *Steacy* c-3, 4, 11-14, Special #1.

SPEED SMITH THE HOT ROD KING
Spring, 1952
Ziff-Davis Publishing Co.

1-Saunders painted-c	8.00	24.00	56.00

SPEEDY GONZALES (See 4-Color #1084)

SPEEDY RABBIT (See Television Puppet Show)
nd (1953); 1963
Realistic/I. W. Enterprises/Super Comics

nn (1953)-Realistic Reprint?	1.00	3.00	7.00
I.W. Reprint #1 (2 versions w/diff. c/stories exist)	.25	.80	1.60
Super Reprint #14(1963)	.25	.80	1.60

SPELLBINDERS
Dec, 1986 - No. 12, Jan, 1988 ($1.25, color)
Quality Comics

1-12: Nemesis The Warlock, Amadeus Wolf		.65	1.30

SPELLBOUND (See The Crusaders)

SPELLBOUND (Tales to Hold You . . . #1, Stories to Hold You . . .)
3/52 - No. 23, 6/54; No. 24, 10/55 - No. 34, 6/57
Atlas Comics (ACI 1-15/Male 16-23/BPC 24-34)

1	17.00	51.00	120.00
2-Edgar A. Poe app.	9.30	28.00	65.00
3-5: 3-Whitney-a; cannibalism story	7.00	21.00	50.00
6-Krigstein-a	7.00	21.00	50.00
7-10: 8-Ayers-a	5.00	15.00	35.00
11-16,18-20: 14-Ed Win-a	4.30	13.00	30.00
17-Krigstein-a	5.00	15.00	35.00
21-23-Last precode (6/54)	3.50	10.50	24.00
24,26-28,30,31,34	2.30	7.00	16.00
25-Orlando-a	2.30	7.00	16.00
29-Ditko-a	3.50	10.50	24.00
32,33-Torres-a	4.00	12.00	28.00

NOTE: *Colan* a-17. *Everett* a-2, 5, 7, 10, 16, 28, 31; c-2, 8, 9, 14, 17-19, 28, 30. *Forte/Fox* a-16. *Heath* a-2, 4, 8-10, 12, 14, 16; c-3, 4, 12, 16, 20, 21. *Infantino* a-15. *Maneely* a-7, 14, 27; c-10, 24, 31. *Mooney* a-5, 13, 18. *Mac Pakula* a-22, 32. *Post* a-8. *Powell* a-19, 20, 32. *Robinson* a-1. *Romita* a-24, 26, 27. *Severin* c-29. *Sinnott* a-8, 16.

SPELLBOUND
Jan, 1988 - No. 6, Apr, 1988 ($1.50, bi-weekly; Baxter paper)
Marvel Comics

1-5	.25	.75	1.50
6 ($2.25, 52 pgs.)	.35	1.10	2.25

SPENCER SPOOK (Formerly Giggle Comics; see Advs. of . . .)
No. 100, Mar-Apr, 1955 - No. 101, May-June, 1955
American Comics Group

	Good	Fine	N-Mint
100,101	1.70	5.00	12.00

SPIDER-MAN (See Amazing . . ., Marvel Tales, Marvel Team-Up, Spectacular . . ., Spidey Super Stories, & Web Of . . .)

SPIDER-MAN AND DAREDEVIL
March, 1984 (One-Shot; $2.00; deluxe paper)
Marvel Comics Group

1-r-/Spect. Spider-Man #'s 26-28 by Miller	.35	1.10	2.25

SPIDER-MAN AND HIS AMAZING FRIENDS
Dec, 1981 (One shot) (See Marvel Action Universe)
Marvel Comics Group

1-Adapted from TV cartoon show; Green Goblin app.; Spiegle-a(p)			
	.25	.75	1.50

SPIDER-MAN COMICS MAGAZINE
Jan, 1987 - No. 13, 1988 ($1.50, Digest-size)
Marvel Comics Group

1-13-Reprints	.25	.75	1.50

SPIDER-MAN GRAPHIC NOVEL
Summer, 1987 ($5.95)
Marvel Comics

1-Kingpin app.	1.00	3.00	5.95

SPIDER-MAN VS. WOLVERINE
Feb, 1987 (One-shot, 68 pgs.)
Marvel Comics Group

1-Williamson-i; intro Charlemagne	1.35	4.00	8.00

SPIDER-WOMAN (Also see The Avengers #240 & Marvel Spotlight #32)
April, 1978 - No. 50, June, 1983 (See Marvel Two-In-One)
Marvel Comics Group

1-New origin & mask added		.60	1.25
2-20: 20-Spider-Man app.		.60	1.25
21-36,39-49: 47-New look		.60	1.25
37,38-New X-Men x-over; 37-1st Siryn; origin retold; photo-c			
	.35	1.10	2.20
50-Double size; photo-c; Death of S-W		.60	1.25

NOTE: *Austin* a-37i. *Byrne* c-26p. *Layton* c-19. *Miller* c-32p.

SPIDEY SUPER STORIES (Spider-Man)
Oct, 1974 - No. 57, Mar, 1982 (35 cents) (no ads)
Marvel/Children's TV Workshop

1-(Stories simplified)		.30	.60
2-57		.25	.50

SPIKE AND TYKE (See M.G.M.'s . . .)

SPIN & MARTY (TV) (Walt Disney's)(See W. Disney Showcase #32)
No. 714, June, 1956 - No. 1082, Mar-May, 1960 (All photo-c)
Dell Publishing Co. (Mickey Mouse Club)

4-Color 714	4.00	12.00	28.00
4-Color 767,808	3.70	11.00	26.00
4-Color 826-Annette Funicello photo-c	8.50	25.50	60.00
5(3-5/58) - 9(6-8/59)	3.50	10.50	24.00
4-Color 1026,1082	3.50	10.50	24.00

SPINE-TINGLING TALES (Doctor Spektor Presents . . .)
May, 1975 - No. 4, Jan, 1976
Gold Key

1-1st Tragg r-/Mystery Comics Digest #3		.40	.80
2-Origin Ra-Ka-Tep r-/Mystery Comics Digest #1; Dr. Spektor #12			
		.40	.80
3-All Durak issue; (r)		.40	.80

	Good	Fine	N-Mint
4-Baron Tibor's 1st app. r-/Mystery Comics Digest #4			
		.40	.80

SPIRAL PATH, THE
7/86 - No. 2, 7/86 ($1.75, Baxter paper, color, mini-series)
Eclipse Comics

1,2	.30	.90	1.80

SPIRAL ZONE
2/88 - No. 4, 5/88 ($1.00, mini-series)
DC Comics

1-4-Based on Tonka toys		.50	1.00

SPIRIT, THE (Weekly Comic Book)
6/2/40 - 10/5/52 (16 pgs.; 8 pgs.) (no cover) (in color)
(Distributed through various newspapers and other sources)
Will Eisner

NOTE: *Eisner* script, pencils/inks for the most part from 6/2/40-4/26/42; a few stories assisted by Jack Cole, Fine, Powell and Kotsky.

6/2/40(#1)-Origin/1st app. The Spirit; reprinted in Police #11; Lady Luck (Brenda Banks)(1st app.) by Chuck Mazoujian & Mr. Mystic (1st. app.) by S. R. (Bob) Powell begin	60.00	180.00	420.00
6/9/40(#2)	26.00	78.00	180.00
6/16/40(#3)-Black Queen app. in Spirit	17.00	51.00	110.00
6/23/40(#4)-Mr. Mystic receives magical necklace	13.00	40.00	90.00
6/30/40(#5)	13.00	40.00	90.00
7/7/40(#6)-Black Queen app. in Spirit	13.00	40.00	90.00
7/14/40(#7)-8/4/40(#10)	10.00	30.50	70.00
8/11/40-9/22/40	9.00	27.00	62.00
9/29/40-Ellen drops engagement with Homer Creep			
	8.00	24.00	56.00
10/6/40-11/3/40	8.00	24.00	56.00
11/10/40-The Black Queen app.	8.00	24.00	56.00
11/17/40, 11/24/40	8.00	24.00	56.00
12/1/40-Ellen spanking by Spirit on cover & inside; Eisner-1st 3 pgs., J. Cole rest	11.50	34.00	80.00
12/8/40-3/9/41	5.70	17.00	40.00
3/16/41-Intro. & 1st app. Silk Satin	10.00	30.00	70.00
3/23/41-6/1/41: 5/11/41-Last Lady Luck by Mazoujian; 5/18/41-Lady Luck by Nick Viscardi begins, ends 2/22/42	5.70	17.00	40.00
6/8/41-2nd app. Satin; Spirit learns Satin is also a British agent			
	8.50	25.50	60.00
6/15/41-1st app. Twilight	7.00	21.00	50.00
6/22/41-Hitler app. in Spirit	5.00	15.00	35.00
6/29/41-1/25/42,2/8/42	5.00	15.00	35.00
2/1/42-1st app. Duchess	7.00	21.00	50.00
2/15/42-4/26/42-Lady Luck by Klaus Nordling begins 3/1/42			
	5.00	15.00	35.00
5/3/42-8/16/42-Eisner/Fine/Quality staff assists on Spirit			
	4.00	12.00	24.00
8/23/42-Satin cover splash; Spirit by Eisner/Fine although signed by Fine	8.00	24.00	56.00
8/30/42,9/27/42-10/11/42,10/25/42-11/8/42-Eisner/Fine/Quality staff assists on Spirit	4.00	12.00	24.00
9/6/42-9/20/42,10/18/42-Fine/Belfi art on Spirit; scripts by Manly Wade Wellman	2.75	8.00	16.00
11/15/42-12/6/42,12/20/42,12/27/42,1/17/43-4/18/43,5/9/43-8/8/43-Wellman/Woolfolk scripts, Fine pencils, Quality staff inks	2.75	8.00	16.00
12/13/42,1/3/43,1/10/43,4/25/43,5/2/43-Eisner scripts/layouts; Fine pencils, Quality staff inks	3.35	10.00	20.00
8/15/43-Eisner script/layout; pencils/inks by Quality staff; Jack Cole-a	2.00	6.00	12.00
8/22/43-12/12/43-Wellman/Woolfolk scripts, Fine pencils, Quality staff inks; Mr. Mystic by Guardineer-10/10/43-10/24/43			

Spider-Woman #3, © MEG

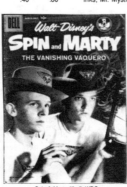

Spin & Marty #5, © WDC

The Spirit, 8/23/42, © Will Eisner

The Spirit, 4/21/46, © Will Eisner

The Spirit, 1/23/49, © Will Eisner

The Spirit, 8/10/52, © Will Eisner

THE SPIRIT (continued)	Good	Fine	N-Mint
	2.00	6.00	12.00

12/19/43-8/13/44-Wellman/Woolfolk/Jack Cole scripts; Cole, Fine &
  Robin King-a; Last Mr. Mystic-5/14/44 — 1.70 / 5.00 / 10.00
8/22/44-12/16/45-Wellman/Woolfolk scripts; Fine art with unknown
  staff assists — 1.70 / 5.00 / 10.00

NOTE: Scripts/layouts by Eisner, or Eisner/Nordling, Eisner/Mercer or Spranger/Eisner; inks by Eisner or Eisner/Spranger in issues 12/23/45-2/2/47.

	Good	Fine	N-Mint
12/23/45-1/6/46	4.00	12.00	28.00
1/13/46-Origin Spirit retold	6.00	18.00	42.00
1/20/46-1st postwar Satin app.	5.70	17.00	40.00
1/27/46-3/10/46: 3/3/46-Last Lady Luck by Nordling			
	4.00	12.00	28.00
3/17/46-Intro. & 1st app. Nylon	5.70	17.00	40.00
3/24/46,3/31/46,4/14/46	4.00	12.00	28.00
4/7/46-2nd app. Nylon	5.00	15.00	35.00
4/21/46-Intro. & 1st app. Mr. Carrion & His Buzzard Pet Julia			
	6.50	19.50	45.00
4/28/46-5/12/46,5/26/46-6/30/46: Lady Luck by Fred Schwab in			
issues 5/5/46-11/3/46	4.00	12.00	28.00
5/19/46-2nd app. Mr. Carrion	5.00	15.00	35.00
7/7/46-Intro. & 1st app. Dulcet Tone & Skinny	6.00	18.00	42.00
7/14/46-9/29/46	4.00	12.00	28.00
10/6/46-Intro. & 1st app. P'Gell	7.00	21.00	50.00
10/13/46-11/3/46,11/16/46-11/24/46	4.00	12.00	28.00
11/10/46-2nd app. P'Gell	5.00	15.00	35.00
12/1/46-3rd app. P'Gell	4.65	14.00	32.00
12/8/46-2/2/47	3.70	11.00	26.00

NOTE: Scripts, pencils/inks by Eisner except where noted in issues 2/9/47-12/19/48.

2/9/47-7/6/47: 6/8/47-Eisner self satire	3.70	11.00	26.00
7/13/47-"Hansel & Gretel" fairy tales	5.70	17.00	40.00
7/20/47-Li'L Abner, Daddy Warbucks, Dick Tracy, Fearless Fosdick			
parody; A-Bomb blast-c	5.70	17.00	40.00
7/27/47-9/14/47	3.70	11.00	26.00
9/21/47-Pearl Harbor flashback	3.70	11.00	26.00
9/28/47-1st mention of Flying Saucers in comics-3 months after 1st			
sighting in Idaho on 6/25/47	8.00	24.00	56.00
10/5/47-"Cinderella" fairy tales	5.70	17.00	40.00
10/12/47-11/30/47	3.70	11.00	26.00
12/7/47-Intro. & 1st app. Powder Pouf	6.00	18.00	42.00
12/14/47-12/28/47	3.70	11.00	26.00
1/4/48-2nd app. Powder Pouf	5.00	15.00	35.00
1/11/48-1st app. Sparrow Fallon; Powder Pouf app.			
	5.00	15.00	35.00
1/18/48-He-Man ad cover; satire issue	5.00	15.00	35.00
1/25/48-Intro. & 1st app. Castanet	5.70	17.00	40.00
2/1/48-2nd app. Castanet	4.00	12.00	28.00
2/8/48-3/7/48	3.70	11.00	26.00
3/14/48-Only app. Kretchma	4.00	12.00	28.00
3/21/48,3/28/48,4/11/48-4/25/48	3.70	11.00	26.00
4/4/48-Only app. Wild Rice	4.00	12.00	28.00
5/2/48-2nd app. Sparrow	3.70	11.00	26.00
5/9/48-6/27/48,7/11/48,7/18/48: 6/13/48-Television issue			
	3.70	11.00	26.00
7/4/48-Spirit by Andre Le Blanc	2.75	8.00	16.00
7/25/48-Ambrose Bierce's "The Thing" adaptation classic by			
Eisner/Grandenetti	8.00	24.00	56.00
8/1/48-8/15/48,8/29/48-9/12/48	3.70	11.00	26.00
8/22/48-Poe's "Fall of the House of Usher" classic by Eisner/			
Grandenetti	8.00	24.00	56.00
9/19/48-Only app. Lorelei	4.30	13.00	30.00
9/26/48-10/31/48	3.70	11.00	26.00
11/7/48-Only app. Plaster of Paris	5.00	15.00	35.00
11/14/48-12/19/48	3.70	11.00	26.00

NOTE: Scripts by Eisner or Feiffer or Eisner/Feiffer or Nordling. Art by Eisner with backgrounds by Eisner, Grandenetti, Le Blanc, Stallman, Nordling, Dixon and/or others

in issues 12/26/48-4/1/51 except where noted.

	Good	Fine	N-Mint
12/26/48-Reprints some covers of 1948 with flashbacks			
	3.70	11.00	26.00
1/2/49-1/16/49	3.70	11.00	26.00
1/23/49,1/30/49-1st & 2nd app. Thorne	6.75	20.00	35.00
2/6/49-8/14/49	3.70	11.00	26.00
8/21/49,8/28/49-1st & 2nd app. Monica Veto	6.75	20.00	35.00
9/4/49,9/11/49	3.70	11.00	26.00
9/18/49-Love comic cover; has gag love comic ads on inside			
	7.35	22.00	38.00
9/25/49-Only app. Ice	4.65	14.00	32.00
10/2/49,10/9/49-Autumn News appears & dies in 10/9 issue			
	4.65	14.00	32.00
10/16/49-11/27/49,12/18/49,12/25/49	3.70	11.00	26.00
12/4/49,12/11/49-1st & 2nd app. Flaxen	4.30	13.00	30.00
1/1/50-Flashbacks to all of the Spirit girls-Thorne, Ellen, Satin, &			
Monica	6.50	19.50	45.00
1/8/50-Intro. & 1st app. Sand Saref	9.00	27.00	62.00
1/15/50-2nd app. Saref	6.50	19.50	45.00
1/22/50-2/5/50	3.70	11.00	26.00
2/12/50-Roller Derby issue	4.00	12.00	28.00
2/19/50-Half Dead Mr. Lox - Classic horror	4.65	14.00	32.00
2/26/50-4/23/50,5/14/50,5/28/50,7/23/50-9/3/50	3.70	11.00	26.00
4/30/50-Script/art by Le Blanc with Eisner framing			
	1.70	5.00	10.00
5/7/50,6/4/50-7/16/50-Abe Kanegson-a	1.70	5.00	10.00
5/21/50-Script by Feiffer/Eisner, art by Blaisdell, Eisner framing			
	1.70	5.00	10.00
9/10/50-P'Gell returns	5.00	15.00	35.00
9/17/50-1/7/51	3.70	11.00	26.00
1/14/51-Life Magazine cover; brief biography of Comm. Dolan, Sand			
Saref, Silk Satin, P'Gell, Sammy & Willum, Darling O'Shea, &			
Mr. Carrion & His Pet Buzzard Julia, with pin-ups by Eisner			
	4.65	14.00	32.00
1/21/51,2/4/51-4/1/51	3.70	11.00	26.00
1/28/51-"The Meanest Man in the World" classic by Eisner			
	4.65	14.00	32.00
4/8/51-7/29/51,8/12/51-Last Eisner issue	3.70	11.00	26.00
8/5/51,8/19/51-7/20/52-Not Eisner	1.70	5.00	10.00
7/27/52-(Rare)-Denny Colt in Outer Space by Wally Wood; 7 pg. S/F			
story of E.C. vintage	40.00	120.00	280.00
8/3/52-(Rare)-"Mission...The Moon" by Wood			
	40.00	120.00	280.00
8/10/52-(Rare)-"A DP On The Moon" by Wood			
	40.00	120.00	280.00
8/17/52-(Rare)-"Heart" by Wood/Eisner	42.00	125.00	240.00
8/24/52-(Rare)-"Rescue" by Wood	40.00	120.00	280.00
8/31/52-(Rare)-"The Last Man" by Wood	40.00	120.00	280.00
9/7/52-(Rare)-"The Man in The Moon" by Wood			
	40.00	120.00	280.00
9/14/52-(Rare)-Eisner/Wenzel-a	8.00	24.00	56.00
9/21/52-(Rare)-"Denny Colt, Alias The Spirit/Space Report" by			
Eisner/Wenzel	14.00	42.00	100.00
9/28/52-(Rare)-"Return From The Moon" by Wood			
	40.00	120.00	280.00
10/5/52-(Rare)-"The Last Story" by Eisner	14.00	42.00	100.00
Large Tabloid pages from 1946 on (Eisner) - Price 30 percent over			
listed prices.			

NOTE: Spirit sections came out in both large and small format. Some newspapers went to the 8-pg. format months before others. Some printed the pages so they cannot be folded into a small comic book section; these are worth less. (Also see Three Comics & Spiritman).

SPIRIT, THE (Section)
January 9, 1966
N. Y. Sunday Herald Tribune

New 5-pg. Spirit story by Eisner; 2 pg. article on super-heroes; 2

THE SPIRIT (continued)	Good	Fine	N-Mint
pgs. color strips (BC, Miss Peach, Peanuts, Wizard of Id)			
	13.00	40.00	80.00

SPIRIT, THE (1st Series)(Also see Police Comics #11)
1944 - No. 22, Aug, 1950
Quality Comics Group (Vital)

	Good	Fine	N-Mint
nn(#1)-"Wanted Dead or Alive"	41.00	122.00	285.00
nn(#2)-"Crime Doesn't Pay"	26.00	77.00	180.00
nn(#3)-"Murder Runs Wild"	19.00	57.00	135.00
4,5	14.00	42.00	100.00
6-10	13.00	40.00	90.00
11	11.50	34.00	80.00
12-17-Eisner-c	20.00	60.00	140.00
18-21-Strip-r by Eisner; Eisner-c	28.50	86.00	200.00
22-Used by N.Y. Legis. Comm; Classic Eisner-c			
	44.00	133.00	310.00
Super Reprint #11-r-/Quality Spirit #19 by Eisner			
	1.35	4.00	8.00
Super Reprint #12-r-/Quality Spirit #17 by Fine	1.00	3.00	6.00

SPIRIT, THE (2nd Series)
Spring, 1952 - No. 5, 1954
Fiction House Magazines

1-Not Eisner	19.00	57.00	135.00
2-Eisner c/a(2)	21.50	64.00	150.00
3-Eisner/Grandenetti-c	14.00	42.00	100.00
4-Eisner/Grandenetti-c; Eisner-a	17.00	51.00	120.00
5-Eisner c/a(4)	22.00	65.00	154.00

SPIRIT, THE
Oct, 1966 - No. 2, Mar, 1967 (Giant Size, 25 cents, 68 pgs.)
Harvey Publications

1-Eisner-r plus 9 new pgs.(Origin Denny Colt, Take 3, plus 2 filler pages)	4.00	12.00	24.00
2-Eisner-r plus 9 new pgs.(Origin of the Octopus)			
	4.00	12.00	24.00

SPIRIT, THE (Underground)
Jan, 1973 - No. 2, Sept, 1973 (Black & White)
Kitchen Sink Enterprises (Krupp Comics)

1-New Eisner-c, 4 pgs. new Eisner-a plus-r (titled Crime Convention)	1.00	3.00	6.00
2-New Eisner-c, 4 pgs. new Eisner-a plus-r(titled Meets P'Gell)			
	1.35	4.00	8.00

SPIRIT, THE (Magazine)
4/74 - No. 16, 10/76; No. 17, Winter, 1977 - No. 41, 6/83
Warren Publ. Co./Krupp Comic Works No. 17 on

1-Eisner-r begin	.80	2.40	4.80
2-5	.50	1.50	3.00
6-9,11-16: 7-All Ebony issue. 8-Female Foes issue. 12-X-Mas issue			
	.40	1.20	2.40
10-Origin	.45	1.40	2.80
17,18(8/78)		.60	1.20
19-21-New Eisner-a plus Wood #20,21		.60	1.20
22,23-Wood-r		.60	1.20
24-35: 28-r-last story (10/5/52)		.60	1.20
36-Begin Spirit Section-r; 1-st story (6/2/40) in color; new Eisner-c/a (18 pgs.)($2.95)	.50	1.50	3.00
37-r-2nd story in color plus 18 pgs. new Eisner-a			
	.50	1.50	3.00
38-41: r-3rd through 6th story in color	.50	1.50	3.00
Special 1('75)-All Eisner-a	.30	.90	1.80

NOTE: Covers pencilled/inked by **Eisner** only #1-9,12-16; painted by Eisner & Ken Kelly #10 & 11; painted by Eisner #17-up; one color story reprinted in #1-10. **Austin** a-30i. **Byrne** a-30p. **Miller** a-30p.

SPIRIT, THE
Oct, 1983 - Present (Baxter paper) ($2.00)
Kitchen Sink Enterprises

	Good	Fine	N-Mint
1-Origin; r/12/23/45 Spirit Section	.70	2.00	4.00
2-4: 2-r/sections 1/20/46-2/10/46. 3-r/sections 2/17/46-3/10/46. 4-r/sec- tions 3/17/46-4/7/46	.70	2.00	4.00
5-11 ($2.95 cover)	.50	1.50	3.00
12-64 ($1.95-$2.00, B&W)-54-r/section 2/19/50	.35	1.00	2.00
. . . In 3-D #1 (11/85)-Eisner-r; new Eisner-c	.35	1.00	2.00

SPIRITMAN (Also see Three Comics)
No date (1944) (10 cents)
(Triangle Sales Co. ad on back cover)
No publisher listed

1-Three 16pg. Spirit sections bound together, (1944, 48 pgs., 10 cents)	12.00	35.00	84.00
2-Two Spirit sections (3/26/44, 4/2/44) bound together; by Lou Fine			
	9.20	27.50	64.00

SPIRIT WORLD (Magazine)
Fall, 1971 (Black & White)
National Periodical Publications

1-Kirby-a/Adams-c	.70	2.00	4.00

SPITFIRE
No. 132, 1944 (Aug) - No. 133, 1945 (Female undercover agent)
Malverne Herald (Elliot)(J. R. Mahon)

132,133: Both have Classics Gift Box ads on b/c with checklist to #20			
	8.50	25.50	60.00

SPITFIRE AND THE TROUBLESHOOTERS
Oct, 1986 - No. 9, June, 1987 (Codename: Spitfire #10 on)
Marvel Comics Group

1-3,5-9		.50	1.00
4-McFarlane-a	.25	.75	1.50

SPITFIRE COMICS (Also see Double Up)
Aug, 1941 - No. 2, Oct, 1941 (Pocket size; 100 pgs.)
Harvey Publications

1-Origin The Clown, The Fly-Man, The Spitfire & The Magician From Bagdad	28.50	85.00	200.00
2	23.00	70.00	160.00

SPOOF!
Oct, 1970; No. 2, Nov, 1972 - No. 5, May, 1973
Marvel Comics Group

1-Infinity-c		.30	.60
2-5		.25	.50

SPOOK (Formerly Shock Detective Cases)
No. 22, Jan, 1953 - No. 30, Oct, 1954
Star Publications

22-Sgt. Spook-r; acid in face story	8.00	24.00	56.00
23,25,27: 27-two Sgt. Spook-r	5.70	17.00	40.00
24-Used in SOTI, pg. 182,183-r/Inside Crime 2; Transvestism story			
	10.00	30.00	70.00
26-Disbrow-a	6.50	19.50	45.00
28,29-Rulah app.; Jo-Jo in #29	6.50	19.50	45.00
30-Disbrow c/a(2); only Star-c	6.50	19.50	45.00

NOTE: **L. B. Cole** covers-all issues; a-28(1pg.). **Disbrow** a-26(2), 28, 29(2), 30(2); No. 30 r-/Blue Bolt Weird Tales #114.

SPOOK COMICS
1946
Baily Publications/Star

1-Mr. Lucifer app.	10.00	30.00	70.00

SPOOKY (The Tuff Little Ghost; see Casper The Friendly Ghost)
11/55 - 139, 11/73; No. 140, 7/74 - No. 155, 3/77; No. 156, 12/77 -

The Spirit #3 (Quality), © Will Eisner

Spook #23, © STAR

Spook Comics #1, © Baily Publ.

Spooky Spooktown #19, © HARV

Sport Thrills #11, © STAR

Spy And Counterspy #2, © ACG

SPOOKY (continued)
No. 158, 4/78; No. 159, 9/78; No. 160, 10/79; No. 161, 9/80
Harvey Publications

	Good	Fine	N-Mint
1-Nightmare begins (See Casper #19)	13.00	40.00	90.00
2	6.00	18.00	42.00
3-10(1956-57)	3.00	9.00	21.00
11-20(1957-58)	1.50	4.50	10.00
21-40(1958-59)	.70	2.00	5.00
41-60	.50	1.50	3.00
61-80	.35	1.10	2.20
81-100	.30	.90	1.80
101-120	.25	.70	1.40
121-126,133-140		.60	1.20
127-132: All 52 pg. Giants	.25	.75	1.50
141-161		.40	.80

SPOOKY HAUNTED HOUSE
Oct, 1972 - No. 15, Feb, 1975
Harvey Publications

1	1.00	3.00	6.00
2-5	.50	1.50	3.00
6-10	.25	.80	1.60
11-15		.60	1.20

SPOOKY MYSTERIES
No date (1946) (10 cents)
Your Guide Publ. Co.

1-Mr. Spooky, Super Snooper, Pinky, Girl Detective app.			
	5.00	15.00	35.00

SPOOKY SPOOKTOWN
9/61; No. 2, 9/62 - No. 52, 12/73; No. 53, 10/74 - No. 66, Dec, 1976
Harvey Publications

1-Casper, Spooky; 68 pgs. begin	5.70	17.00	40.00
2	3.00	9.00	20.00
3-5	2.75	8.00	16.00
6-10	1.35	4.00	8.00
11-20	1.00	3.00	6.00
21-39: Last 68 pg. issue	.50	1.50	3.00
40-45: All 52 pgs.	.35	1.00	2.00
46-66	.25	.80	1.60

SPORT COMICS (True Sport Picture Stories #5 on)
Oct, 1940(No mo.) - No. 4, Nov, 1941
Street & Smith Publications

1-Life story of Lou Gehrig	20.00	60.00	140.00
2	10.00	30.00	70.00
3,4	8.50	25.50	60.00

SPORT LIBRARY (See Charlton Sport Library)

SPORTS ACTION (Formerly Sport Stars)
No. 2, Feb, 1950 - No. 14, Sept, 1952
Marvel/Atlas Comics (ACI No. 2,3/SAI No. 4-14)

2-Powell painted-c; George Gipp life story	8.00	24.00	56.00
3-Everett-a	5.70	17.00	40.00
4-11,14: Weiss-a. 9,10-Maneely-c	5.00	15.00	35.00
12-Everett-c	5.70	17.00	40.00
13-Krigstein-a	5.70	17.00	40.00

NOTE: Title may have changed after No. 3, to Crime Must Lose No. 4 on, due to
publisher change.

SPORT STARS
2-3/46 - No. 4, 8-9/46 (½ comic, ½ photo magazine)
Parents' Magazine Institute (Sport Stars)

1-"How Tarzan Got That Way" story of Johnny Weissmuller			
	13.00	40.00	90.00
2-Baseball greats	9.30	28.00	65.00
3,4	6.50	19.50	45.00

SPORT STARS (Becomes Sports Action #2 on)
Nov, 1949 (52 pgs.)
Marvel Comics (ACI)

	Good	Fine	N-Mint
1-Knute Rockne; painted-c	13.00	40.00	90.00

SPORT THRILLS (Formerly Dick Cole)
No. 11, Nov, 1950 - No. 15, Nov, 1951
Star Publications

11-Dick Cole app; Ted Williams & Ty Cobb life stories			
	6.50	19.50	45.00
12-L. B. Cole c/a	4.30	13.00	30.00
13-15-All L. B. Cole-c; 13-Dick Cole app.	4.30	13.00	30.00
Accepted Reprint #11 (#15 on-c, nd); L.B. Cole-c			
	1.70	5.00	12.00
Accepted Reprint #12 (nd); L.B. Cole-c; Joe DiMaggio & Phil Rizzuto			
life stories	1.70	5.00	12.00

SPOTLIGHT (TV)
Sept, 1978 - No. 4, Mar, 1979 (Hanna-Barbera)
Marvel Comics Group

1-Huckleberry Hound, Yogi Bear, 2-Quick Draw McGraw, Augie			
Doggie, 3-The Jetsons, Yakky Doodle, 4-Magilla Gorilla,			
Snagglepuss		.25	.50

SPOTLIGHT COMICS
Nov, 1944 - No. 3, 1945
Harry 'A' Chesler (Our Army, Inc.)

1-The Black Dwarf, The Veiled Avenger, & Barry Kuda begin;			
Tuska-c	21.50	64.00	150.00
2	17.00	51.00	120.00
3-Injury to eye story(Same as Scoop #3)	19.00	57.00	135.00

SPOTTY THE PUP (Becomes Super Pup? or Space Comics?)(Also
see Television Puppet Show)
No. 2, Oct-Nov?, 1953 - No. 3, Dec-Jan, 1953-54
Avon Periodicals/Realistic Comics

2,3	1.50	4.50	10.00
nn (1953, Realistic-r)	.85	2.50	6.00

SPUNKY (...Junior Cowboy)(...Comics #2 on)
April, 1949 - No. 7, Nov, 1951
Standard Comics

1,2-Text illos by Frazetta	3.50	10.50	24.00
3-7	1.70	5.00	12.00

SPUNKY THE SMILING SPOOK
Aug, 1957 - No. 4, May, 1958
Ajax/Farrell (World Famous Comics/Four Star Comic Corp.)

1-Reprints from Frisky Fables	2.30	7.00	16.00
2-4	1.50	4.50	10.00

SPY AND COUNTERSPY (Spy Hunters #3 on)
Aug-Sept, 1949 - No. 2, Oct-Nov, 1949 (52 pgs.)
American Comics Group

1-Origin, 1st app. Jonathan Kent, Counterspy	6.50	19.50	45.00
2	4.50	14.00	32.00

SPY CASES (Formerly The Kellys)
No. 26, Sept, 1950 - No. 19, Oct, 1953
Marvel/Atlas Comics (Hercules Publ.)

26 (#1)	5.70	17.00	40.00
27,28(2/51): 27-Everett-a; bondage-c	3.70	11.00	26.00
4(4/51) - 7,9,10: 7-Tuska-a	2.30	7.00	16.00
8-A-Bomb-c/story; Maneely-a	3.00	9.00	21.00
11-19: 11-14-War format	2.00	6.00	14.00

SPY FIGHTERS
March, 1951 - No. 15, July, 1953
Marvel/Atlas Comics (CSI)

SPY FIGHTERS (continued)	Good	Fine	N-Mint
1	7.00	21.00	50.00
2-Tuska-a	3.00	9.00	21.00
3-13	2.30	7.00	16.00
14,15-Pakula-a(3), Ed Win-a	2.65	8.00	18.00

SPY-HUNTERS (Formerly Spy & Counterspy)
No. 3, Dec-Jan, 1949-50 - No. 24, June-July, 1953 (#3-11: 52 pgs.)
American Comics Group

	Good	Fine	N-Mint
3-Jonathan Kent continues, ends #10	6.50	19.50	45.00
4-10: 4,8,10-Starr-a	3.70	11.00	26.00
11-15,17-22,24	2.30	7.00	16.00
16-Williamson-a (9 pgs.)	5.50	16.50	38.00
23-Graphic torture, injury to eye panel	6.00	18.00	42.00
NOTE: *Whitney a-many issues; c-7, 8, 10-12, 16.*

SPYMAN (Top Secret Adventures on cover)
Sept, 1966 - No. 3, Feb, 1967 (12 cents)
Harvey Publications (Illustrated Humor)

1-Steranko-a(p)-1st pro work; 1pg. Adams ad; Tuska c/a, Crandall-a(i)	.50	1.50	3.00
2,3: Simon-c. 2-Steranko-a(p)	.35	1.00	2.00

SPY SMASHER (See Mighty Midget, Whiz & XMas Comics)
Fall, 1941 - No. 11, Feb, 1943 (Also see Crime Smasher)
Fawcett Publications

1-Spy Smasher begins; silver metallic-c	121.00	362.00	845.00
2-Raboy-c	60.00	180.00	420.00
3,4: 3-Bondage-c	50.00	150.00	350.00
5-7: Raboy-a; 6-Raboy c/a. 7-Part photo-c	43.00	130.00	300.00
8-11: 9-Hitler, Tojo, Mussolini-c. 10-Hitler-c	38.00	115.00	265.00
Well Known Comics (1944, 12 pgs.), 8½x10½'', paper-c, glued binding, printed in green; Bestmaid/Samuel Lowe giveaway	15.00	45.00	90.00

SPY THRILLERS (Police Badge No. 479 #5)
Nov, 1954 - No. 4, May, 1955
Atlas Comics (PrPI)

1	5.00	15.00	35.00
2-Last precode (1/55)	3.00	9.00	21.00
3,4	2.00	6.00	14.00

SQUADRON SUPREME
Sept, 1985 - No. 12, Aug, 1986 (maxi-series)
Marvel Comics Group

1	.30	.90	1.80
2-11		.50	1.00
12-Double size ($1.25)	.25	.75	1.50

SQUALOR
Dec, 1989 - No. 4, Mar, 1990 ($2.75, color, mini-series)
First Comics

1-4: Sutton-a	.45	1.40	2.80

SQUEEKS
Oct, 1953 - No. 5, June, 1954
Lev Gleason Publications

1-Funny annual; Biro-c	3.00	9.00	21.00
2-Biro-c	1.50	4.50	10.00
3-5: 3-Biro-c	1.15	3.50	8.00

STAINLESS STEEL RAT
Oct, 1985 - No. 6, Mar, 1986 (limited-series)
Eagle Comics

1 (52 pgs.; $2.25 cover)	.35	1.10	2.20
2-6 (36 pgs.)	.25	.75	1.50

STALKER
June-July, 1975 - No. 4, Dec-Jan, 1975-76
National Periodical Publications

	Good	Fine	N-Mint
1-Origin & 1st app; Ditko/Wood c/a	.40	.80
2-4-Ditko/Wood c/a	.30	.60

STAMP COMICS (Stamps. . . on-c; Thrilling Advs. In . . .#8)
Oct, 1951 - No. 7, Oct, 1952 (No. 1: 15 cents)
Youthful Magazines/Stamp Comics, Inc.

1('Stamps' on indicia No. 1)	12.00	36.00	84.00
2	7.00	21.00	50.00
3-6: 3,4-Kiefer, Wildey-a	5.70	17.00	40.00
7-Roy Krenkel-a 9 pgs.	8.50	25.50	60.00
NOTE: *Promotes stamp collecting; gives stories behind various commemorative stamps. No. 2, 10 cents printed over 15 cents c-price. Kiefer a-1-7. Kirkel a-1-6. Napoli a-2-7. Palais a-2-4, 7.*

STANLEY & HIS MONSTER (Formerly The Fox & the Crow)
No. 109, Apr-May, 1968 - No. 112, Oct-Nov, 1968
National Periodical Publications

109-112	1.00	3.00	7.00

STAR BLAZERS
Apr, 1987 - No. 4, July, 1987 (mini-series, color, $1.75)
Comico

1-4	.30	.90	1.80

STAR BLAZERS
1989 - No. 5, 1989 ($1.95-$2.50, color, mini-series)
Comico

1,2 ($1.95)-Steacy wraparound painted-c on all	.35	1.00	2.00
2-5 ($2.50)	.40	1.25	2.50

STAR BRAND
Oct, 1986 - No. 19, May, 1989 (.75-$1.50 #17 on, color)
Marvel Comics Group

1-13: 3-Williamson-a		.50	1.00
14-19 ($1.25): 16-19-Byrne-c/a, scripts		.50	1.00
Annual 1 (10/87)		.65	1.30

STAR COMICS
Feb, 1937 - V2No.7 (No. 23), Aug, 1939 (#1-6: large size)
Ultem Publ. (Harry 'A' Chesler)/Centaur Publications

V1#1-Dan Hastings (s/f) begins	71.00	215.00	500.00
2	36.00	108.00	250.00
3-6 (#6, 9/37): 5-Little Nemo	31.00	92.00	215.00
7-9: 8-Severed head centerspread; Impy & Little Nemo by Winsor McCay Jr, Popeye app. by Bob Wood; Mickey Mouse-c app.	27.00	81.00	190.00
10 (1st Centaur; 3/38)-Impy by Winsor McCay Jr; Don Marlow by Guardineer begins	43.00	130.00	300.00
11-1st Jack Cole comic-a, 1 pg. (4/38)	27.00	81.00	190.00
12-15: 12-Border of the Golden West begins; Little Nemo app.	27.00	81.00	190.00
15-Speed Silvers by Gustavson & The Last Pirate by Burgos begins	27.00	81.00	190.00
16 (12/38)-The Phantom Rider begins, ends V2#6	27.00	81.00	190.00
V2#1(#17, 2/39)	27.00	81.00	190.00
2-7(#18-23): 2-Diana Deane by Tarpe Mills app. 3-Drama of Hollywood by Mills begins. 7-Jungle Queen app.	24.00	73.00	170.00
NOTE: *Biro c-9, 10. Burgos a-15, 16. V2#1-7. Ken Ernst a-10, 12, 14. Gill Fox c-V2#2. Guardineer a-6, 8-14. Gustavson a-13-16, V2#1-7. Tarpe Mills a-15, V2#1-7. Bob Wood a-10, 12, 13; c-8.*

STAR COMICS MAGAZINE
Dec, 1986 - No. 13, 1988 ($1.50, Digest-size)
Star Comics (Marvel)

1-13: Heathcliff, Muppet Babies, Ewoks, Carebears, Top Dog, Alf, Flintstone Kids app.	.25	.75	1.50

Spyman #1, © HARV

Spy Smasher #9, © FAW

Star Comics V1#15, © CEN

Starman #1, © DC

A Star Presentation #3, © FOX

Stars And Stripes #2 (#1), © CEN

STAR FEATURE COMICS
1963
I. W. Enterprises

	Good	Fine	N-Mint
Reprint #9-Stunt-Man Stetson app.	.50	1.50	3.00

STARFIRE (See New Teen Titans & Teen Titans)
Aug-Sept, 1976 - No. 8, Oct-Nov, 1977
National Periodical Publications/DC Comics

1-Origin & 1st app; (CCA stamp fell off cover art; so it **was** approved by code)		.50	1.00
2-8		.30	.60

STAR HUNTERS (See DC Super Stars #16)
Oct-Nov, 1977 - No. 7, Oct-Nov, 1978
National Periodical Publications/DC Comics

1-Newton-a(p)		.30	.60
2-6		.25	.50
7-Giant		.30	.60

NOTE: *Buckler* a-4p-7p; c-1p-7p. *Layton* a-1i-5i; c-1i-6i. *Nasser* a-3p. *Sutton* a-6i.

STARK TERROR (Magazine)
Dec, 1970 - No. 5, Aug, 1971 (52 pages) (B&W)
Stanley Publications

1-Bondage, torture-c	1.00	3.00	7.00
2-4 (Gillmor/Aragon-r)	.70	2.00	4.00
5 (ACG-r)	.50	1.50	3.00

STARLET O'HARA IN HOLLYWOOD (Teen-age)
Dec, 1948 - No. 4, Sept, 1949
Standard Comics

1-Owen Fitzgerald-a in all	8.00	24.00	56.00
2	5.50	16.50	38.00
3,4	4.30	13.00	30.00

STAR-LORD THE SPECIAL EDITION (Also see Marvel Comics Super
Special #10, Marvel Premiere & Preview & Marvel Spotlight V2#6,7)
Feb, 1982 (One Shot) (Direct sale, 1st Baxter paper comic)
Marvel Comics Group

1-Byrne/Austin-a; Austin-c, Golden-a(p)	.50	1.50	3.00

STARMAN (See Adventure #467, Brave & the Bold, First Issue
Special, Justice League & Showcase)
Oct, 1988 - Present ($1.00, color)
DC Comics

1-Origin		.50	1.50	3.00
2-18: 4-Intro The Power Elite. 9,10-Batman app. 14-Superman app. 17-Power Girl app.		.50	1.00

STARMASTERS
Mar, 1984 (Color)
Americomics

1-The Women of W.O.S.P. & Breed begin	.25	.75	1.50

STAR PRESENTATION, A (Formerly My Secret Romance #1,2;
Spectacular Stories #4 on) (Also see This Is Suspense)
No. 3, May, 1950
Fox Features Syndicate (Hero Books)

3-Dr. Jekyll & Mr. Hyde by Wood & Harrison (reprinted in Startling Terror Tales #10); 'The Repulsing Dwarf' by Wood; Wood-c			
	30.00	90.00	210.00

STAR QUEST COMIX (Warren Presents . . . on cover)
October, 1978
Warren Publications

1		.50	1.00

STAR RAIDERS (See DC Graphic Novel #1)

STAR RANGER (Cowboy Comics #13 on)
Feb, 1937 - No. 12, May, 1938 (Large size: No. 1-6)
Ultem Publ./Centaur Publications

	Good	Fine	N-Mint
1-(1st Western comic)-Ace & Deuce, Air Plunder; Flessel-a			
	80.00	240.00	560.00
2	37.00	110.00	260.00
3-6	33.00	100.00	230.00
7-9: 8-Christmas-c	28.50	86.00	200.00
V2#10 (1st Centaur; 3/38)	43.00	130.00	300.00
11,12	33.00	100.00	230.00

NOTE: *J. Cole* a-10, 12; c-12. *Ken Ernst* a-11. *Gill Fox* a-8(illo), 9, 10. *Guardineer* a-1, 3, 6, 7, 8(illos), 9, 10, 12. *Gustavson* a-8-10, 12. *Bob Wood* a-8-10.

STAR RANGER FUNNIES (Formerly Cowboy Comics?)
V1#15, Oct, 1938 - V2#5, Oct, 1939
Centaur Publications

V1#15-Eisner, Gustavson-a	47.00	140.00	325.00
V2#1 (1/39)	34.00	100.00	235.00
2-5: 2-Night Hawk by Gustavson. 4-Kit Carson app.			
	27.00	81.00	190.00

NOTE: *Jack Cole* a-V2#1,3; c-V2#1. *Guardineer* a-V2#3. *Gustavson* a-V2#2. *Pinajian* c/a-V2#5.

STAR REACH CLASSICS
Mar, 1984 - No. 6, Aug, 1984 ($1.50; color; Baxter paper)
Eclipse Comics

1-6: Adams-r/Star Reach #1	.25	.75	1.50

NOTE: *Brunner* c/a-4r. *Nino* a-3r. *Russell* c/a-3r.

STARR FLAGG, UNDERCOVER GIRL (See Undercover . . .)

STARRIORS
Aug, 1984 - No. 4, Feb, 1985 (limited-series)
Marvel Comics Group

1-Based on Tomy Toy robots		.60	1.20
2-4		.50	1.00

STARS AND STRIPES COMICS
No. 2, May, 1941 - No. 6, Dec, 1941
Centaur Publications

2(#1)-The Shark, The Iron Skull, Aman, The Amazing Man, Mighty Man, Minimidget begin; The Voice & Dash Dartwell, the Human Meteor, Reef Kinkaid app.; Gustavson Flag-c			
	100.00	300.00	700.00
3-Origin Dr. Synthe; The Black Panther app.	68.00	205.00	475.00
4-Origin/1st app. The Stars and Stripes; injury to eye-c			
	57.00	171.00	400.00
5(#5 on cover & inside)	43.00	130.00	300.00
5(#6)-(#5 on cover, #6 on inside)	43.00	130.00	300.00

NOTE: *Gustavson* c/a-3. *Myron Strauss* c-5.

STARSLAYER
9/81 - No. 6, 4/83; No. 7, 8/83 - No. 34, 11/85
Pacific Comics/First Comics No. 7 on

1-Origin; excessive blood & gore	.50	1.50	3.00
2-Intro & origin the Rocketeer by Dave Stevens			
	1.15	3.50	7.00
3-Rocketeer continues	.85	2.50	5.00
4	.35	1.00	2.00
5-2nd app. Groo the Wanderer by Aragones	1.25	3.75	7.50
6,7: 7-Grell-a ends	.35	1.00	2.00
8-34: 10-Intro Grimjack (ends #17). 19-Starslayer meets Grimjack; 20-The Black Flame begins, ends #33		.50	1.00

NOTE: *Grell* a-1-7; c-1-8. *Sutton* a-17p, 20-22p.

STAR SPANGLED COMICS (. . . War Stories #131 on)
Oct, 1941 - No. 130, July, 1952
National Periodical Publications

1-Origin Tarantula; Captain X of the R.A.F., Star Spangled Kid(See Action #40) & Armstrong of the Army begin			
	158.00	395.00	950.00
2	61.00	182.00	425.00

...

STAR SPANGLED COMICS (continued)

	Good	Fine	N-Mint
3-5	41.00	122.00	285.00
6-Last Armstrong of the Army	27.00	81.00	190.00
7-Origin/1st app. The Guardian by S&K, & Robotman by Paul Cassidy; The Newsboy Legion & TNT begin; last Captain X	192.00	480.00	1150.00
8-Origin TNT & Dan the Dyna-Mite	82.00	245.00	575.00
9,10	71.00	215.00	500.00
11-17	57.00	171.00	400.00
18-Origin Star Spangled Kid	71.00	215.00	500.00
19-Last Tarantula	57.00	171.00	400.00
20-Liberty Belle begins	57.00	171.00	400.00
21-29-Last S&K issue; 23-Last TNT. 25-Robotman by Jimmy Thompson begins	43.00	130.00	300.00
30-40	20.00	60.00	140.00
41-50	16.50	50.00	115.00
51-64: Last Newsboy Legion & The Guardian; 53 by S&K	16.00	48.00	110.00
65-Robin begins with cover app.	40.00	120.00	280.00
66-68,70-80	18.50	55.00	130.00
69-Origin Tomahawk	22.00	65.00	154.00
81-Origin Merry, Girl of 1000 Gimmicks	16.00	48.00	110.00
82,83,85,86: 83-Capt. Compass begins, ends #130	16.00	48.00	110.00
84,87 (Rare)	20.00	60.00	140.00
88-94: Batman-c/stories in all. 88-Last Star Spangled Kid. 91-Federal Men begin, end #93. 94-Manhunters Around the World begin, end #121	20.00	60.00	140.00
95-99	12.00	36.00	84.00
100	15.00	45.00	105.00
101-112,114,115,117-121: 114-Retells Robin's origin. 120-Last 52 pgs.	10.00	30.00	70.00
113-Frazetta-a, 10 pgs.	26.50	80.00	185.00
116-Flag-c	10.00	30.00	70.00
122-Ghost Breaker begins (origin), ends #130	9.00	27.00	62.00
123-129	7.00	21.00	50.00
130	11.50	34.00	80.00

NOTE: Most all issues after #29 signed by **Simon & Kirby** are not by them. **Batman** c/stories-88-94.

STAR SPANGLED WAR STORIES (Star Spangled Comics #1-130; The Unknown Soldier #205 on) (See Showcase)
No. 131, 8/52 - No. 133, 10/52; No. 3, 11/52 - No. 204, 2-3/77
National Periodical Publications

	Good	Fine	N-Mint
131(#1)	24.00	72.00	170.00
132	16.00	48.00	110.00
133-Used in POP, Pg. 94	16.00	48.00	110.00
3-5: 4-Devil Dog Dugan app.	11.50	34.00	80.00
6-Evans-a	9.30	28.00	65.00
7-10	7.00	21.00	50.00
11-20	5.70	17.00	40.00
21-30: Last precode (2/55)	4.30	13.00	30.00
31-33,35-40	3.15	9.50	22.00
34-Krigstein-a	5.00	15.00	35.00
41-50	2.85	8.50	20.00
51-83: 67-Easy Co. story w/o Sgt. Rock	2.30	7.00	16.00
84-Origin Mlle. Marie	5.00	15.00	35.00
85-89-Mlle. Marie in all	2.85	8.50	20.00
90-1st Dinosaur issue & begin series	11.50	34.00	80.00
91-2nd Dinosaur issue	5.70	17.00	40.00
92-100	4.30	13.00	30.00
101-133,135-137-Last Dinosaur story; Heath Birdman-#129,131	2.85	8.50	20.00
134-Adams-a	3.60	11.00	25.00
138-Enemy Ace begins by Joe Kubert	.85	2.50	5.00
139-143,145-148,152,153,155	.70	2.00	4.00
144-Adams & Kubert-a	1.00	3.00	6.00

	Good	Fine	N-Mint
149,150-Viking Prince by Kubert	.70	2.00	4.00
151-1st Unknown Soldier	.85	2.50	5.00
154-Origin Unknown Soldier	.85	2.50	5.00
156-1st Battle Album	.25	.75	1.50
157-161-Last Enemy Ace	.25	.75	1.50
162-204: 181-183-Enemy Ace vs. Balloon Buster serial app.	.50	1.00	

NOTE: **Drucker** a-59, 61, 64, 66, 67, 73-84. **Estrada** a-149. **John Giunta** a-72. **Glanzman** a-167, 171, 172, 174. **Heath** c-67. **Kaluta** a-197/; c-167. **Kubert** a-6-162(most later issues), 200. **Maurer** a-160. **Severin** a-65. **Simonson** a-170, 172, 174, 180. **Sutton** a-168. **Thorne** a-183. **Toth** a-164. **Wildey** a-161. Suicide Squad in 110, 116-18, 120, 121, 127.

STARSTREAM (Adventures in Science Fiction)(See Questar Illustr.)
1976 (68 pgs.; cardboard covers) (79 cents)
Whitman/Western Publishing Co.

	Good	Fine	N-Mint
1-Bolle-a	.25	.80	1.60
2-4-McWilliams & Bolle-a		.60	1.20

STARSTRUCK
Mar, 1985 - No. 6, Feb, 1986 ($1.50; adults only)
Epic Comics (Marvel)

	Good	Fine	N-Mint
1-6: Kaluta-c/a; nudity & strong language	.25	.75	1.50

STAR STUDDED
1945 (25 cents; 132 pgs.); 1945 (196 pgs.)
Cambridge House/Superior Publishers

	Good	Fine	N-Mint
1-Captain Combat by Giunta, Ghost Woman, Commandette, & Red Rogue app.	12.00	36.00	84.00
nn-The Cadet, Edison Bell, Hoot Gibson, Jungle Lil (196 pgs.); copies vary - Blue Beetle in some	10.00	30.00	70.00

STAR TEAM
1977 (20 pgs.) (6½x5'')
Marvel Comics Group (Ideal Toy Giveaway)

	Good	Fine	N-Mint
nn		.15	.30

STARTLING COMICS
June, 1940 - No. 53, May, 1948
Better Publications (Nedor)

	Good	Fine	N-Mint
1-Origin Captain Future-Man Of Tomorrow, Mystico (By Eisner/Fine), The Wonder Man; The Masked Rider begins; drug use story	71.00	212.00	495.00
2	30.00	90.00	210.00
3	23.00	70.00	160.00
4	17.00	51.00	120.00
5-9	13.00	40.00	90.00
10-The Fighting Yank begins (origin & 1st app.)	55.00	165.00	385.00
11-15: 12-Hitler, Hirohito, Mussolini-c	16.50	50.00	115.00
16-Origin The Four Comrades; not in #32,35	18.50	56.00	130.00
17-Last Masked Rider & Mystico	12.00	36.00	84.00
18-Pyroman begins (origin)	30.00	90.00	210.00
19	13.00	40.00	90.00
20-The Oracle begins; not in #26,28,33,34	13.00	40.00	90.00
21-Origin The Ape, Oracle's enemy	12.00	36.00	84.00
22-33	11.00	32.00	75.00
34-Origin The Scarab & only app.	11.50	34.00	80.00
35-Hypodermic syringe attacks Fighting Yank in drug story	11.50	34.00	80.00
36-43: 36-Last Four Comrades. 40-Last Capt. Future & Oracle. 41-Front Page Peggy begins. 43-Last Pyroman	11.00	32.00	75.00
44-Lance Lewis, Space Detective begins; Ingels-c	17.00	51.00	120.00
45-Tygra begins (Intro/origin)	17.00	51.00	120.00
46-Ingels c/a	17.00	51.00	120.00
47-53: 49-Last Fighting Yank. 50,51-Sea-Eagle app.	13.00	40.00	90.00

Star Spangled Comics #14, © DC

Star Spangled Comics #66, © DC

Startling Comics #12, © BP

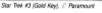

Star Trek #3 (Gold Key), © Paramount

Star Trek: The Next Generation #3 ('88), © Paramount

Star Wars #1 (30 cent ed.), © Lucasfilms

STARTLING COMICS (continued)
NOTE: *Ingels* c-44, 46(Wash). *Schomburg (Xela)* c-21-43; 47-53 (airbrush). *Tuska* c-45? Bondage c-16, 21, 37, 46-49.

STARTLING TERROR TALES
No. 10, 5/52 - No. 14, 2/53; No. 4, 4/53 - No. 11, 1954
Star Publications

	Good	Fine	N-Mint
10-(1st Series)-Wood/Harrison-a (r-A Star Presentation #3) Disbrow/ Cole-c	21.50	64.00	150.00
11-L. B. Cole Spider-c; r-Fox's "A Feature Presentation #5"	11.00	32.00	75.00
12,14	4.00	12.00	28.00
13-Jo-Jo-r; Disbrow-a	4.30	13.00	30.00
4-7,9,11('53-54) (2nd Series)	3.50	10.50	24.00
8-Spanking scene; Palais-a(r)	5.00	15.00	35.00
10-Disbrow-a	4.00	12.00	28.00

NOTE: *L. B. Cole* covers-all issues. *Palais* a-V2#11r.

STAR TREK (TV) (See Dan Curtis & Dynabrite Comics)
7/67; No. 2, 6/68; No. 3, 12/68; No. 4, 6/69 - No. 61, 3/79
Gold Key

	Good	Fine	N-Mint
1: 1-9-photo-c	14.00	42.00	100.00
2-5	8.50	25.50	60.00
6-9	5.70	17.00	40.00
10-20	3.60	11.00	25.00
21-30	2.65	8.00	18.00
31-40	1.50	4.50	10.00
41-61: 52-Drug propaganda story	1.00	3.00	7.00
...the Enterprise Logs nn(8/76)-Golden Press, 224 pgs. ($1.95)-Re- prints #1-8 plus 7 pgs. by McWilliams (#11185)	1.15	3.50	8.00
...the Enterprise Logs Vol.2('76)-Reprints #9-17 (#11187)	1.00	3.00	7.00
...the Enterprise Logs Vol.3('77)-Reprints #18-26 (#11188); McWilliams-a (4 pgs.)	.85	2.60	6.00
Star Trek Vol.4(Winter '77)-Reprints #27,28,30-34,36,38 (#11189) plus 3 pgs. new art	.85	2.60	6.00

NOTE: *McWilliams* a-38, 40-44, 46-61. #29 reprints #1; #35 reprints #4; #37 reprints #5; #45 reprints #7. The tabloids all have photo covers and blank inside covers. Painted covers #10-44, 46-59.

STAR TREK
April, 1980 - No. 18, Feb, 1982
Marvel Comics Group

	Good	Fine	N-Mint
1-r/Marvel Super Special; movie adapt.	.50	1.50	3.00
2-18	.35	1.00	2.00

NOTE: *Austin* c-18i. *Buscema* a-13. *Gil Kane* a-15. *Miller* c-5. *Nasser* c/a-7. *Simonson* c-17.

STAR TREK
Feb, 1984 - No. 56, Nov, 1988 (Mando paper)
DC Comics

	Good	Fine	N-Mint
1-Sutton-a(p) begin	1.05	3.15	6.50
2-5	.70	2.10	4.20
6-10 (75 cent cover)	.55	1.60	3.20
11-20	.35	1.05	2.10
21-32	.25	.80	1.60
33 ($1.25)-20th Anniversary issue	.35	1.05	2.10
34-49		.55	1.10
50 ($1.50, 52 pgs.)	.25	.80	1.60
51-56		.55	1.10
Annual 1 (10/85), 2 (9/86), 3 ('88, $1.50)	.35	1.05	2.10

NOTE: *Morrow* a-28, 35, 36. *Orlando* c-8i. *Perez* c-1-3. *Spiegle* a-19. *Starlin* c-24, 25. *Sutton* a-1-6p, 8-18p, 20-27p, 29p, 31-34p, 39-52p, 55p; c-4-6p, 8-22p, 46p.

STAR TREK
Oct, 1989 - Present ($1.50, color)
DC Comics

	Good	Fine	N-Mint
1-Capt. Kirk and crew	.35	1.00	2.00
2-6	.25	.75	1.50

STAR TREK MOVIE SPECIAL
June, 1984 - No. 2, 1987 (68pgs; $1.50); 1989 ($2.00, 52 pgs.)
DC Comics

	Good	Fine	N-Mint
1-Adapts Star Trek III; Sutton-a(p)	.35	1.00	2.00
2-Adapts Star Trek IV; Sutton-a	.35	1.00	2.00
1-Adapts Star Trek V; painted-c	.35	1.00	2.00

STAR TREK: THE NEXT GENERATION (TV)
Feb, 1988 - No. 6, July, 1988 (Mini series)
DC Comics

	Good	Fine	N-Mint
1 (52 pgs.)-Based on TV show	.65	1.90	3.80
2-6 ($1.00)	.45	1.40	2.80

STAR TREK: THE NEXT GENERATION (TV)
Oct, 1989 - Present ($1.50, color)
DC Comics

	Good	Fine	N-Mint
1-Capt. Picard and crew from TV show	.35	1.00	2.00
2-6	.25	.75	1.50

STAR WARS (Movie) (See Contemporary Motivators, The Droids, The Ewoks, Marvel Movie Showcase & Marvel Special Edition)
July, 1977 - No. 107, Sept, 1986
Marvel Comics Group

	Good	Fine	N-Mint
1-(Regular 30 cent edition)-Price in square w/UPC code	1.70	5.00	10.00
1-(35 cent cover; limited distribution - 1500 copies?)- Price in square w/UPC code	43.00	130.00	300.00
2-4	.70	2.00	4.00
5-10	.50	1.50	3.00
11-20	.35	1.00	2.00
21-37	.25	.75	1.50
38-44: 39-The Empire Strikes Back r-begin, ends #44	.35	1.00	2.00
45-107: 100-Dbl. size	.50	1.00	
1-9-Reprints; has "reprint" in upper lefthand corner of cover or on inside or price and number inside a diamond with no date or UPC on cover; 30 cents and 35 cents issues published	.25	.50	
Annual 1 (12/79)	.35	1.00	2.00
Annual 2 (11/82), 3(12/83)	.60	1.20	

NOTE: *Austin* c-11-15i, 21i, 38; c-12-15i, 21i. *Byrne* c-13p. *Chaykin* a-1-10p; c-1. *Golden* c/a-38. *Miller* c-47p. *Nebres* c/a-Annual 2i. *Simonson* a-16p, 49p, 51-63p, 65p, 66p; c-16, 49-51, 52p, 53-62, Annual 1. *Williamson* a-39-44p, 50p; c-39, 40, 41-44p, 98.

STAR WARS IN 3-D (See Blackthorne 3-D Series #30, 47, 48)

STAR WARS: RETURN OF THE JEDI
Oct, 1983 - No. 4, Jan, 1984 (Mini-series, movie adaptation)
Marvel Comics Group

	Good	Fine	N-Mint
1-4-Williamson-a(p) in all		.50	1.00
Oversized issue ('83; 10¾x8¼"; 68 pgs.; cardboard-c)-Reprints above 4 issues	.50	1.50	2.95

STATIC (Also see Ditko's World)
No. 11, Oct, 1985 - No. 12, Dec, 1985
Charlton Comics

	Good	Fine	N-Mint
11,12: Ditko c/a		.40	.80

STEEL CLAW, THE
Dec, 1986 - No. 4, Mar, 1987 (.75-$1.50, color, mini-series)
Quality Comics

	Good	Fine	N-Mint
1-3 (75 cents)		.40	.80
4 ($1.50)	.25	.75	1.50

STEELGRIP STARKEY
July, 1986 - No. 6, June, 1987 ($1.50, mini-series, Baxter paper)
Epic Comics (Marvel)

	Good	Fine	N-Mint
STEELGRIP STARKEY (continued)			
1-6	.25	.75	1.50

STEEL STERLING (Formerly Shield-Steel Sterling; see Blue Ribbon, Jackpot, Mighty Comics, Mighty Crusaders, Roly Poly & Zip Comics)
No. 4, Jan, 1984 - No. 7, July, 1984
Archie Enterprises, Inc.

4-7: 6-McWilliams-a		.40	.80

STEEL, THE INDESTRUCTIBLE MAN
March, 1978 - No. 5, Oct-Nov, 1978
DC Comics, Inc.

1		.30	.60
2-5: 5-Giant		.25	.50

STEVE CANYON (See 4-Color #519, 578, 641, 737, 804, 939, 1033, and Harvey Comics Hits #52)

STEVE CANYON
1959 (96 pgs.; no text; 6¾x9''; hardcover)(B&W inside)
Grosset & Dunlap

100100-Reprints 2 stories from strip (1953, 1957)	3.00	9.00	21.00
100100 (softcover edition)	2.50	7.50	17.00

STEVE CANYON COMICS
Feb, 1948 - No. 6, Dec, 1948 (Strip reprints) (No. 4,5: 52pgs.)
Harvey Publications

1-Origin; has biog of Milton Caniff; Powell-a, 2pgs.; Caniff-a	13.50	40.50	95.00
2-Caniff, Powell-a	10.00	30.00	70.00
3-6: Caniff, Powell-a in all. 6-Intro Madame Lynx	8.50	25.50	60.00
Dept. Store giveaway #3(6/48, 36pp)	8.50	25.50	60.00
. . .'s Secret Mission (1951, 16 pgs., Armed Forces giveaway); Caniff-a	8.00	24.00	56.00
Strictly for the Smart Birds-16 pgs., 1951; Information Comics Div. (Harvey) Premium	8.00	24.00	56.00

STEVE CANYON IN 3-D
June, 1986 (One shot, $2.25)
Kitchen Sink Press

1-Contains unpublished story from 1954	.40	1.15	2.30

STEVE DONOVAN, WESTERN MARSHAL (TV)
No. 675, Feb, 1956 - No. 880, Feb, 1958 (All photo-c)
Dell Publishing Co.

4-Color 675-Kinstler-a	4.00	12.00	28.00
4-Color 768-Kinstler-a	3.50	10.50	24.00
4-Color 880	2.30	7.00	16.00

STEVE ROPER
April, 1948 - No. 5, Dec, 1948
Famous Funnies

1-Contains 1944 daily newspaper-r	5.00	15.00	35.00
2	2.65	8.00	18.00
3-5	2.30	7.00	16.00

STEVE SAUNDERS SPECIAL AGENT (See Special Agent)

STEVE SAVAGE (See Captain. . .)

STEVE ZODIAC & THE FIRE BALL XL-5 (TV)
January, 1964
Gold Key

1 (10108-401)	4.50	14.00	32.00

STEVIE (Also see Mazie & Mortie)
Nov, 1952 - No. 6, April, 1954
Mazie (Magazine Publ.)

1	2.00	6.00	14.00
2-6	1.15	3.50	8.00

STEVIE MAZIE'S BOY FRIEND (See Harvey Hits #5)

STEWART THE RAT (See Eclipse Graphic Album Series)

ST. GEORGE (See listing under Saint. . .)

STIGG'S INFERNO
1985 - No. 7, Mar, 1987 ($2.00, B&W)

Vortex Publs./Eclipse Comics #6 on	Good	Fine	N-Mint
1 ($1.95)	.85	2.50	5.00
2-4	.50	1.50	3.00
5-7	.35	1.00	2.00
Graphic Album ($6.95, B&W, 100 pgs.)-reprints	1.15	3.50	7.00

STONEY BURKE (TV)
June-Aug, 1963 - No. 2, Sept-Nov, 1963
Dell Publishing Co.

1,2	1.15	3.50	8.00

STONY CRAIG
1946 (No #)
Pentagon Publishing Co.

Reprints Bell Syndicate's ''Sgt. Stony Craig'' newspaper strips	3.70	11.00	26.00

STORIES BY FAMOUS AUTHORS ILLUSTRATED (Fast Fiction #1-5)
No. 6, Aug, 1950 - No. 13, March, 1951
Seaboard Publ./Famous Authors III.

1-Scarlet Pimpernel-Baroness Orczy	16.00	48.00	115.00
2-Capt. Blood-Raphael Sabatini	16.00	48.00	115.00
3-She, by Haggard	19.00	57.00	135.00
4-The 39 Steps-John Buchan	11.00	32.00	75.00
5-Beau Geste-P. C. Wren	11.00	32.00	75.00

NOTE: *The above five issues are exact reprints of Fast Fiction #1-5 except for the title change and new Kiefer covers on #1 and 2. The above 5 issues were released before Famous Authors #6.*

6-Macbeth, by Shakespeare; Kiefer art (8/50); used in **SOTI**, pg. 22,143. Kiefer-c	13.00	42.00	90.00
7-The Window; Kiefer-c/a; 52p	11.00	32.00	75.00
8-Hamlet, by Shakespeare; Kiefer-c/a; 36p	13.00	40.00	90.00
9-Nicholas Nickleby, by Dickens; G. Schrotter-a; 52p	11.00	32.00	75.00
10-Romeo & Juliet, by Shakespeare; Kiefer-c/a; 36p	11.00	32.00	75.00
11-Ben-Hur; Schrotter-a; 52p	11.50	34.00	80.00
12-La Svengali; Schrotter-a; 36p	11.50	34.00	80.00
13-Scaramouche; Kiefer-c/a; 36p	11.50	34.00	80.00

NOTE: *Artwork was prepared/advertised for #14, The Red Badge Of Courage. Gilberton bought out Famous Authors, Ltd. and used that story as C.I. #98. Famous Authors, Ltd. then published the regular Classics Junior series. The Famous Authors titles were published as part of the regular Classics III. Series in Brazil starting in 1952.*

STORIES OF CHRISTMAS
1942 (32 pages; paper cover) (Giveaway)
K. K. Publications

nn-Adaptation of ''A Christmas Carol;'' Kelly story- ''The Fir Tree;'' Infinity-c	40.00	100.00	200.00

STORIES OF ROMANCE (Formerly Meet Miss Bliss)
No. 5, Mar, 1956 - No. 13, Aug, 1957
Atlas Comics (LMC)

5-Baker-a?	2.30	7.00	16.00
6-13	1.30	4.00	9.00

NOTE: **Ann Brewster** a-13. **Colletta** a-9(2); c-5.

STORMWATCHER
April, 1989 - No. 4, 1989 ($2.00, B&W, mini-series)
Eclipse Comics (Acme Press)

1-4	.35	1.00	2.00

STORMY (See 4-Color #537)

Steve Canyon #6, © Milton Caniff

Steve Roper #1, © FF

Stories By Famous Authors #1, © Seaboard

Straight Arrow #1, © ME
Strange Adventures #18, © DC
Strange Adventures #206, © DC

STORY HOUR SERIES (Disney)
1948, 1949; 1951-1953 (36 pgs., paper-c) (4½x6¼'')
Given away with subscription to Walt Disney's Comics & Stories
Whitman Publishing Co.

	Good	Fine	N-Mint
nn(1948)-Mickey Mouse and Boy Thursday	5.00	15.00	35.00
nn(1948)-Mickey Mouse Miracle Maker	5.00	15.00	35.00
nn(1948)-Minnie Mouse and Antique Chair	5.00	15.00	35.00
nn(1949)-The Three Orphan Kittens(B&W & color)			
	2.35	7.00	16.00
nn(1949)-Danny-The Little Black Lamb	2.35	7.00	16.00
800-Donald Duck in "Bringing Up the Boys;" 1948			
	8.00	24.00	56.00
1953 edition	4.00	12.00	28.00
801-Mickey Mouse's Summer Vacation; 1948	4.00	12.00	28.00
1951, 1952 edition	2.00	6.00	14.00
802-Bugs Bunny's Adventures; 1948	3.00	9.00	21.00
803-Bongo; 1948	2.75	8.00	18.00
804-Mickey and the Beanstalk; 1948	3.35	10.00	23.00
805-15-Andy Panda and His Friends; 1949	3.00	9.00	21.00
806-15-Tom and Jerry; 1949	3.00	9.00	21.00
808-15-Johnny Appleseed; 1949	2.75	8.00	18.00
1948, 1949 Hard Cover Edition of each....$2.00 - $3.00 more.			

STORY OF EDISON, THE
1956 (16 pgs.) (Reddy Killowatt)
Educational Comics

Reprint of Reddy Killowatt #2(1947)	4.75	14.00	30.00

STORY OF HARRY S. TRUMAN, THE
1948 (16 pgs.) (in color, regular size)(Soft-c)
Democratic National Committee (Giveaway)
Gives biography on career of Truman; used in **SOTI**, pg. 311

	10.00	30.00	70.00

STORY OF JESUS (See Classics Illustrated Special Issue)

STORY OF MANKIND, THE (See 4-Color #851)

STORY OF MARTHA WAYNE, THE
April, 1956
Argo Publ.

1-Newspaper-r	1.70	5.00	12.00

STORY OF RUTH, THE (See 4-Color #1144)

STORY OF THE COMMANDOS, THE (Combined Operations)
1943 (68 pgs.; B&W) (15 cents)
Long Island Independent (Distr. by Gilberton)

nn-All text (no comics); photos & illustrations; ad for Classic Comics on back cover (Rare)	12.00	36.00	84.00

STORY OF THE GLOOMY BUNNY, THE (See March of Comics #9)

STRAIGHT ARROW (Radio)(See Best of the West & Great Western)
Feb-Mar, 1950 - No. 55, Mar, 1956 (all 36 pgs.)
Magazine Enterprises

1-Straight Arrow (alias Steve Adams) & his palomino Fury begin; 1st mention of Sundown Valley & the Secret Cave; Whitney-a			
	21.50	64.00	150.00
2-Red Hawk begins (1st app?) by Powell (Origin), ends #55			
	10.00	30.00	70.00
3-Frazetta-c	14.00	42.00	100.00
4,5: 4-Secret Cave-c	6.00	18.00	42.00
6-10	4.65	14.00	32.00
11-Classic story "The Valley of Time," with an ancient civilization made of gold	5.00	15.00	35.00
12-19	3.50	10.50	24.00
20-Origin S. Arrow's Shield	5.00	15.00	35.00
21-Origin Fury	5.70	17.00	40.00
22-Frazetta-c	10.00	30.00	70.00
23,25-30: 25-Secret Cave-c. 28-Red Hawk meets The Vikings			

	Good	Fine	N-Mint
	3.00	9.00	21.00
24-Classic story "The Dragons of Doom!" with prehistoric pteradactyls	4.65	14.00	32.00
31-38	2.65	8.00	18.00
39-Classic story "The Canyon Beast," with a dinosaur egg hatching a Tyranosaurus Rex	3.50	10.50	24.00
40-Classic story "Secret of The Spanish Specters," with Conquista-dors' lost treasure	3.50	10.50	24.00
41,42,44-54: 45-Secret Cave-c	2.15	6.50	15.00
43-Intro & 1st app. Blaze, Straight Arrow's Warrior dog			
	2.65	8.00	18.00
55-Last issue	3.00	9.00	21.00

NOTE: **Fred Meagher** a 1-55; c-1, 2, 4-21, 23-55. **Powell** a 2-55. Many issues advertise the radio premiums associated with Straight Arrow.

STRAIGHT ARROW'S FURY (See A-1 Comics #119)

STRANGE
March, 1957 - No. 6, May, 1958
Ajax-Farrell Publ. (Four Star Comic Corp.)

1	5.70	17.00	40.00
2	2.85	8.50	20.00
3-6	2.30	7.00	16.00

STRANGE ADVENTURES
Aug-Sept, 1950 - No. 244, Oct-Nov, 1973 (No. 1-12: 52 pgs.)
National Periodical Publications

1-Adaptation of "Destination Moon;" Kris KL-99 & Darwin Jones begin; photo-c	115.00	345.00	800.00
2	54.00	161.00	375.00
3,4	34.00	100.00	235.00
5-8,10: 7-Origin Kris KL-99	30.00	90.00	210.00
9-Captain Comet begins (6/51, Intro/origin)	81.00	242.00	565.00
11,14,15	25.00	75.00	175.00
12,13,17-Toth-a	27.00	81.00	190.00
16,18-20	18.00	54.00	125.00
21-30	15.00	45.00	105.00
31,34-38	13.00	40.00	90.00
32,33-Krigstein-a	14.00	42.00	100.00
39-Ill. in SOTI-"Treating police contemptuously" (top right)			
	20.00	60.00	140.00
40-49-Last Capt. Comet; not in 45,47,48	11.50	34.00	80.00
50-53-Last precode issue (2/55)	8.50	25.50	60.00
54-70	5.00	15.00	35.00
71-99	3.70	11.00	26.00
100	5.70	17.00	40.00
101-110: 104-Space Museum begins by Sekowsky			
	2.85	8.50	20.00
111-116: 114-Star Hawkins begins, ends #185; Heath-a in Wood E.C. style	2.30	7.00	16.00
117-1st app./Origin Atomic Knights	13.50	40.00	95.00
118-120	3.60	11.00	25.00
121-134: 124-Origin Faceless Creature. 134-Last 10 cent issue			
	2.85	8.50	20.00
135-145	1.70	5.00	12.00
146-160: 159-Star Rovers app. 160-Last Atomic Knights			
	1.70	5.00	12.00
161-179: 161-Last Space Museum. 163-Star Rovers app. 170-Infinity-c. 177-Origin Immortal Man	.70	2.00	4.00
180-Origin Animal Man	2.15	6.50	15.00
181-186,188-204: 201-Last Animal Man	.40	1.25	2.50
187-Origin The Enchantress	.40	1.25	2.50
205-Intro/origin Deadman by Infantino (10/67)	4.00	12.00	28.00
206-Adams-a begins	2.15	6.50	15.00
207-210	1.50	4.50	10.00
211-216-Last Deadman	1.15	3.50	8.00
217-230: 217-Adam Strange & Atomic Knights-r begin. 226-236-(68-52			

STRANGE ADVENTURES (continued)	Good	Fine	N-Mint
pgs.)	.50	1.50	3.00
231-244: 231-Last Atomic Knights-r		.50	1.00

NOTE: **Adams** a-206-216; c-207-216, 228, 235. **Anderson** a-8-52, 94, 96, 97, 99, 115, 117, 119-163, 217r, 218r, 222-25r, 222, 226, 242(r); c/r-157i, 190i, 217-224, 228-31, 233, 235-39, 241-43. **Ditko** a-188, 189. **Drucker** a-42, 43, 45. **Finlay** a-2, 3, 6, 7, 210r, 229i. **Infantino** a-10-101, 106-151, 154, 157-163, 180, 190, 223-25p(r), c/r-190p, 197, 199-211, 219-221, 223-244. **Kaluta** c-238, 240. **Gil Kane** a-8-116, 124, 125, 130, 138, 146-157, 173-186, 204r, 222r, 227-231r; c-154p, 157p. **Kubert** a-55(2 pgs.), 226; c-219, 220, 225-227, 232, 234. **Moriera** c-230. **Powell** a-4. **Mike Sekowsky** a-71p, 97-162p, 217p(r), 218p(r); c-206, 217-219r. **Simon & Kirby** a-2r (2 pg.) **Sparling** a-201. **Toth** a-8, 12, 13, 17-19. **Wood** a-154i. Chris KL99 in 1-3, 5, 7, 9, 11, 15. Capt. Comet covers-9-14, 17-19, 24, 26, 27, 32-44.

STRANGE AS IT SEEMS (See Famous Funnies-A Carnival of Comics, Feature Funnies #1, The John Hix Scrap Book & Peanuts)

STRANGE AS IT SEEMS
1932 (64 pgs.; B&W; square binding)
Blue-Star Publishing Co.

1-Newspaper-r	13.00	40.00	90.00

NOTE: Published with and without No. 1 and price on cover.
Ex-Lax giveaway(1936,24pgs,5x7'',B&W)-McNaught Synd.

	2.00	6.00	14.00

STRANGE AS IT SEEMS
1939
United Features Syndicate

Single Series 9, 1, 2	14.00	42.00	100.00

STRANGE CONFESSIONS
Jan-Mar, 1952 - No. 4, Fall, 1952
Ziff-Davis Publ. Co. (Approved)

1(Scarce)-Photo-c; Kinstler-a	20.00	60.00	140.00
2(Scarce)	13.00	40.00	90.00
3(Scarce)-#3 on-c, #2 on inside; Reformatory girl story; photo-c	13.00	40.00	90.00
4(Scarce)-Reformatory girl story	13.00	40.00	90.00

STRANGE DAYS
Oct., 1984 - No. 3, Apr, 1985 ($1.75, color, Baxter paper)
Eclipse Comics

1-3-Freakwave & Johnny Nemo & Paradax from Vanguard III.; nudity, violence, strong language	.30	.90	1.80

STRANGE FANTASY
Aug., 1952 - No. 14, Oct-Nov, 1954
Harvey Publ./Ajax-Farrell No. 2 on

2(#1, 8/52)-Jungle Princess story; no Black Cat; Kamenish-a; r/ Ellery Queen #1	9.00	27.00	62.00
2(10/52)-No Black Cat or Rulah; Bakerish, Kamenish-a; hypo/meat-hook-c	8.00	24.00	56.00
3-Rulah story, called Pulah	8.00	24.00	56.00
4-Rocket Man app.	6.50	19.50	45.00
5,6,8,10,12,14	5.00	15.00	35.00
7-Madam Satan/Slave story	6.00	18.00	42.00
9(w/Black Cat), 9(w/Boy's Ranch; S&K-a)	7.00	21.00	50.00
9-Regular issue	5.00	15.00	35.00
11-Jungle story	6.00	18.00	42.00
13-Bondage-c; Rulah (Kolah) story	8.00	24.00	56.00

STRANGE GALAXY (Magazine)
V1#8, Feb, 1971 - No. 11, Aug, 1971 (B&W)
Eerie Publications

V1#8-Cover-r/from Fantastic V19#3 (2/70) (a pulp)	1.00	3.00	7.00
9-11	.70	2.00	4.00

STRANGE JOURNEY
Sept., 1957 - No. 4, June, 1958 (Farrell reprints)
America's Best (Steinway Publ.) (Ajax/Farrell)

	Good	Fine	N-Mint
1	6.50	19.50	45.00
2-4	3.70	11.00	26.00

STRANGE LOVE (See Fox Giants)

STRANGE MYSTERIES
Sept, 1951 - No. 21, Jan, 1955
Superior/Dynamic Publications

1-Kamenish-a begins	17.00	51.00	120.00
2	9.30	28.00	65.00
3-5	6.50	19.50	45.00
6-8	5.70	17.00	40.00
9-Bondage 3-D effect-c	8.00	24.00	56.00
10-Used in SOTI, pg. 181	5.70	17.00	40.00
11-18	4.00	12.00	28.00
19-r/Journey Into Fear #1; cover is a splash from one story; Baker-a(2)(r)	6.50	19.50	45.00
20,21-Reprints; 20-r-/#1 with new-c	3.50	10.50	24.00

STRANGE MYSTERIES
1963 - 1964
I. W. Enterprises/Super Comics

I.W. Reprint #9; Rulah-r	.60	1.80	3.60
Super Reprint #10-12,15-17('63-'64): #12-reprints Tales of Horror #5 (3/53) less-c. #15,16-reprints The Dead Who Walk	.60	1.80	3.60
Super Reprint #18-R-/Witchcraft #1; Kubert-a	.60	1.80	3.60

STRANGE PLANETS
1958; 1963-64
I. W. Enterprises/Super Comics

I.W. Reprint #1(nd)-E. C. Incred. S/F #30 plus-c/Strange Worlds #3	5.00	15.00	35.00
I.W. Reprint #8	2.00	6.00	14.00
I.W. Reprint #9-Orlando/Wood-a (Strange Worlds #4); c-from Flying Saucers #1	6.50	19.50	45.00
Super Reprint #10-22 pg. Wood-a from Space Detective #1; c-/Attack on Planet Mars	6.50	19.50	45.00
Super Reprint #11-25 pg. Wood-a from An Earthman on Venus	10.00	30.00	70.00
Super Reprint #12-Orlando-a from Rocket to the Moon	6.50	19.50	45.00
Super Reprint #15-Reprints Atlas stories; Heath, Colan-a	1.70	5.00	12.00
Super Reprint #16-Avon's Strange Worlds #6; Kinstler, Check-a	2.30	7.00	16.00
Super Reprint #17	1.35	4.00	9.00
Super Reprint #18-Reprints Daring Adventures; Space Busters, Explorer Joe, The Son of Robin Hood; Krigstein-a	2.00	6.00	14.00

STRANGE SPORTS STORIES (See Brave & the Bold, DC Special, and DC Super Stars #10)
Sept-Oct, 1973 - No. 6, July-Aug, 1974
National Periodical Publications

1		.30	.60
2-6: 3-Swan/Anderson-a		.25	.50

STRANGE STORIES FROM ANOTHER WORLD (Unknown World #1)
No. 2, Aug, 1952 - No. 5, Feb, 1953
Fawcett Publications

2-Saunders painted-c	14.00	42.00	100.00
3-5-Saunders painted-c	11.00	32.00	75.00

STRANGE STORIES OF SUSPENSE (Rugged Action #1-4)
No. 5, Oct, 1955 - No. 16, Aug, 1957
Atlas Comics (CSI)

5(#1)	8.50	25.50	60.00

Strange Fantasy #3, © AJAX

Strange Mysteries #2, © SUPR

Strange Stories From Another World #4, © FAW

Strange Stories Of Suspense #14, © MEG | Strange Suspense Stories #75, © CC | Strange Tales #116, © MEG

	Good	Fine	N-Mint
STRANGE STORIES OF SUSPENSE (cont.)			
6,9	5.00	15.00	35.00
7-E. C. swipe cover/Vault of Horror #32	5.50	16.50	38.00
8-Williamson/Mayo-a; Pakula-a	6.00	18.00	42.00
10-Crandall, Torres, Meskin-a	6.00	18.00	42.00
11	3.00	9.00	21.00
12-Torres, Pakula-a	3.50	10.50	24.00
13-E.C. art swipes	3.00	9.00	21.00
14-Williamson-a	4.30	13.00	30.00
15-Krigstein-a	3.70	11.00	26.00
16-Fox, Powell-a	4.30	13.00	30.00

NOTE: *Everett* a-6, 7, 13; c-9, 11-14. *Heath* a-5. *Maneely* c-5. *Morrow* a-13. *Powell* a-8. *Severin* c-7. *Wildey* a-14.

STRANGE STORY (Also see Front Page)
June-July, 1946 (52 pages)
Harvey Publications

1-The Man in Black Called Fate by Powell	10.00	30.00	70.00

STRANGE SUSPENSE STORIES (Lawbreakers Suspense Stories
#10-15; This Is Suspense #23-26; Captain Atom V1#78 on)
6/52 - No. 5, 2/53; No. 16, 1/54 - No. 22, 11/54; No. 27, 10/55 - No. 77,
10/65; V3No.1, 10/67 - V1No.9, 9/69
Fawcett Publications/Charlton Comics No. 16 on

1-(Fawcett)-Powell, Sekowsky-a	20.00	60.00	140.00
2-George Evans horror story	13.00	40.00	90.00
3-5 (2/53)-George Evans horror stories	11.00	32.00	75.00
16(1-2/54)	6.50	19.50	45.00
17,21	5.00	15.00	35.00
18-E.C. swipe/HOF 7; Ditko c/a(2)	11.00	32.00	75.00
19-Ditko electric chair-c; Ditko-a	13.00	40.00	90.00
20-Ditko c/a(2)	11.00	32.00	75.00
22(11/54)-Ditko-c, Shuster-a; last pre-code issue; becomes This Is			
Suspense	8.50	25.50	60.00
27(10/55)-(Formerly This Is Suspense #26?)	2.00	6.00	14.00
28-30,38	1.70	5.00	12.00
31-33,35,37,40,51-Ditko c/a(2-3)	5.70	17.00	40.00
34-Story of ruthless business man, Wm. B. Gaines; Ditko-c/a			
	8.00	24.00	56.00
36-(68 pgs.); Ditko-a	7.00	21.00	50.00
39,41,52,53-Ditko-a	5.00	15.00	35.00
42-44,46,49,54-60	1.50	4.50	10.00
45,47,48,50-Ditko c/a	4.00	12.00	28.00
61-74	.50	1.50	3.00
75(6/65)-Origin Captain Atom by Ditko-r/Space Advs.			
	8.50	25.50	60.00
76,77-Ditko Captain Atom-r/Space Advs.	3.50	10.50	24.00
V3#1(10/67)-4	.50	1.50	3.00
V1#2-9: 2-Ditko-a, atom bomb-c	.35	1.00	2.00

NOTE: *Alascia* a-19. *Aparo* a-V3/1, 2. *Bailey* a-1-3; c-5. *Evans* c-4. *Montes/Bache* c-66.
Powell a-4. *Shuster* a-19, 21.

STRANGE TALES (Becomes Doctor Strange #169 on)
6/51 - No. 168, 5/68; No. 169, 9/73 - No. 188, 11/76
Atlas (CCPC #1-67/ZPC #68-79/VPI #80-85)/Marvel #86(7/61) on

1	80.00	240.00	560.00
2	36.00	107.00	250.00
3,5: 3-Atom bomb panels	26.00	80.00	185.00
4-"The Evil Eye," cosmic eyeball story	28.50	86.00	200.00
6-9	18.50	56.00	130.00
10-Krigstein-a	20.00	60.00	140.00
11-14,16-20	10.00	30.00	70.00
15-Krigstein-a	11.00	32.00	75.00
21,23-27,29-32,34-Last precode issue(2/55): 27-Atom bomb panels			
	8.00	24.00	56.00
22-Krigstein, Forte/Fox-a	8.50	25.50	60.00
28-Jack Katz story used in Senate Investigation report, pgs. 7 & 169			
	8.50	25.50	60.00

	Good	Fine	N-Mint
33-Davis-a	8.00	24.00	56.00
35-41,43,44	5.00	15.00	35.00
42,45,59,61-Krigstein-a; #61 (2/58)	5.70	17.00	40.00
46-52,54,55,57,60: 60 (8/57)	4.30	13.00	30.00
53-Torres, Crandall-a	5.70	17.00	40.00
56-Crandall-a	5.00	15.00	35.00
58,64-Williamson-a in each, with Mayo-#58	5.70	17.00	40.00
62-Torres-a	4.50	14.00	32.00
63,65	4.30	13.00	30.00
66-Crandall-a	4.50	14.00	32.00
67-80-Ditko/Kirby-a. 79-Dr. Strange proto-type app.			
	4.00	12.00	28.00
81-92-Last 10 cent issue. Ditko/Kirby-a	3.70	11.00	26.00
93-100-Kirby-a	3.50	10.50	24.00
101-Human Torch begins by Kirby (10/62)	40.00	120.00	275.00
102	16.00	48.00	110.00
103-105	13.00	40.00	90.00
106,108,109	8.50	25.50	60.00
107-Human Torch/Sub-Mariner battle	11.00	32.00	75.00
110-Intro Dr. Strange (begin series), Ancient One & Wong by Ditko			
	28.00	85.00	200.00
111-2nd Dr. Strange	7.00	21.00	50.00
112,113	5.00	15.00	35.00
114-Acrobat disguised as Captain America, 1st app. since the G.A.;			
intro. & 1st app. Victoria Bentley	11.00	32.00	75.00
115-Origin Dr. Strange; Sandman (villain) app.	15.00	45.00	105.00
116-120: 116-Thing/Torch battle	3.60	11.00	25.00
121-129,131-133: Thing/Torch team-up in all; 126-Intro Clea			
	2.15	6.50	15.00
130-The Beatles cameo	2.85	8.50	20.00
134-Last Human Torch; Wood-a(i)	2.15	6.50	15.00
135-Nick Fury, Agent of Shield begins (origin) by Kirby, ends #167			
	4.00	12.00	28.00
136-147,149: 146-Last Ditko Dr. Strange who is in consecutive stories			
since No. 113	1.50	4.50	10.00
148-Origin Ancient One	1.70	5.00	12.00
150(11/66)-John Buscema's 1st work at Marvel	1.50	4.50	10.00
151-1st Marvel work by Steranko (w/Kirby)	1.70	5.00	12.00
152,153-Kirby/Steranko-a	1.50	4.50	10.00
154-158-Steranko-a/script	1.50	4.50	10.00
159-Origin Nick Fury; Intro Val; Captain America app; Steranko-a			
	1.70	5.00	12.00
160-162-Steranko-a/scripts; Cap. America app.	1.50	4.50	10.00
163-166,168-Steranko-a(p)	1.50	4.50	10.00
167-Steranko pen/script; classic flag-c	1.70	5.00	12.00
169,170-Brother Voodoo origin in each; series ends #173			
	.50		1.00
171-177: 174-Origin Golem. 177-Brunner-c	.50		1.00
178-Warlock by Starlin with covers; origin Warlock & Him			
	1.50	4.50	9.00
179-181-Warlock by Starlin with covers. 179-Intro/1st app. Pip the			
Troll. 180-Intro Gamora	.85	2.50	5.00
182-188	.50		1.00
Annual 1(1962)-Reprints from Str. Tales #73,76,78, Tales of Suspense			
#7,9, Tales to Astonish #1,6,7, & Journey Into Mystery #53,55,59			
	21.50	64.00	150.00
Annual 2(1963)-r-/from Str. Tales #67, Str. Worlds (Atlas) #1-3, World			
of Fantasy #16, Human Torch vs. Spider-Man by Kirby/Ditko;			
Kirby-c	14.00	42.00	100.00

NOTE: *Briefer* a-17. *Burgos* a-123p. *J. Buscema* a-174p. *Colan* a-11, 20, 53, 169-73p.
188p. *Davis* c-71. *Ditko* a-46, 50, 67-122, 123-25p, 126-146, 175r, 182-88r; c-33, 51, 93,
115, 121, 146. *Everett* a-4, 21, 40-42, 73, 147-52, 164i; c-8, 10, 11, 13, 24, 45, 49-54, 56,
58, 60, 61, 63, 148, 150, 152, 158i. *Forte* a-27, 43, 50, 53, 60. *Heath* c-20. *Kamen* a-45.
G. Kane c-170-72-, 173, 182p. *Kirby* Human Torch-101-105, 108, 109, 114, 120; Nick
Fury-135p, 141-43p; (Layouts)-135-153; other *Kirby* a-67-100p; c-68-70, 72-92, 94, 95,
101-114, 115-23, 125-130, 132-135, 136p, 138-145, 147, 149, 151p. *Lawrence* a-29.
Leiber/Fox a-110, 111, 113. *Maneely* a-3, 42; c-33. *Moldoff* a-20. *Mooney* a-174i. *Morisi*

STRANGE TALES (continued)
a-53. Orlando a-41, 44, 46, 49, 52. Powell a-42, 44, 49, 54, 130-34p; c-131p. Reinman a-50, 74, 88, 91, 95, 104, 106, 112i, 124-127i. Robinson a-17. Sekowski a-3, 11. Starlin a-178, 179, 180p, 181p; c-178-80, 181p. Steranko a-151-61, 162-68p; c-151i, 153, 155, 157, 159, 161, 163, 165, 167. Tuska a-14, 166p. Wildey a-42. Woodbridge a-59. Fantastic Four cameo-101-134. Jack Katz app.-26.

STRANGE TALES
Apr, 1987 - No. 19, Oct, 1988
Marvel Comics Group

	Good	Fine	N-Mint
V2#1		.50	1.00
2-12,15-19: 10-Austin-c		.40	.80
13,14-Punisher app.	.25	.75	1.50

NOTE: Austin c-10, 12i, 13i. Williamson a-3i.

STRANGE TALES OF THE UNUSUAL
Dec, 1955 - No. 11, Aug, 1957
Atlas Comics (ACI No. 1-4/WPI No. 5-11)

1-Powell-a	10.00	30.00	70.00
2	5.00	15.00	35.00
3-Williamson-a, 4 pgs.	5.70	17.00	40.00
4,6,8,11	2.85	8.50	20.00
5-Crandall, Ditko-a	5.00	15.00	35.00
7-Kirby, Orlando-a	3.70	11.00	26.00
9-Krigstein-a	3.70	11.00	26.00
10-Torres, Morrow-a	3.50	10.50	24.00

NOTE: Baily a-6. Everett a-2, 6; c-6, 9, 11. Heck a-1. Maneely c-1. Orlando a-7. Pakula a-10. Romita a-1.

STRANGE TERRORS
June, 1952 - No. 7, Mar, 1953
St. John Publishing Co.

1-Bondage-c; Zombies spelled Zoombies on-c; Fineesque-a	13.00	40.00	90.00
2	7.00	21.00	50.00
3-Kubert-a; painted-c	10.00	30.00	70.00
4-Kubert-a(r-/in Mystery Tales #18); Ekgren-c; Fineesque-a; Jerry Iger caricature	18.00	54.00	125.00
5-Kubert-a; painted-c	10.00	30.00	70.00
6-Giant, 100 pgs.(1/53); bondage-c	14.00	42.00	100.00
7-Giant, 100 pgs.; Kubert c/a	18.50	56.00	130.00

NOTE: Cameron a-6, 7. Morisi a-6.

STRANGE WORLD OF YOUR DREAMS
Aug, 1952 - No. 4, Jan-Feb, 1953
Prize Publications

1-Simon & Kirby-a	21.50	64.00	150.00
2,3-Simon & Kirby-a. 2-Meskin-a	16.00	48.00	110.00
4-S&K-c; Meskin-a	13.00	40.00	90.00

STRANGE WORLDS (#18 continued from Avon's Eerie #1-17)
Nov, 1950 - No. 22, Sept-Oct, 1955 (no no. 11-17)
Avon Periodicals

1-Kenton of the Star Patrol by Kubert (r-/Eerie #1-'47); Crom the Barbarian by John Giunta	38.00	115.00	265.00
2-Wood-a; Crom the Barbarian by Giunta; Dara of the Vikings app.; used in SOTI, pg. 112; injury to eye panel	33.00	100.00	230.00
3-Wood/Orlando-a(Kenton), Wood/Williamson/Frazetta/Krenkel/ Orlando-a (7 pgs.); Malu Slave Girl Princess app.; Kinstler-c	68.00	205.00	485.00
4-Wood c/a (Kenton); Orlando-a; origin The Enchanted Daggar; Sultan-a	32.00	95.00	225.00
5-Orlando/Wood-a (Kenton); Wood-c	27.00	81.00	190.00
6-Kinstler-a(2); Orlando/Wood-c, Check-a	17.00	51.00	120.00
7-Kinstler, Fawcette & Becker/Alascia-a	13.00	40.00	90.00
8-Kubert, Kinstler, Hollingsworth & Lazarus-a; Lazarus-c	14.00	42.00	100.00
9-Kinstler, Fawcette, Alascia-a	13.00	40.00	90.00
10-Exist?	12.00	36.00	84.00

	Good	Fine	N-Mint
18-Reprints "Attack on Planet Mars" by Kubert	13.50	40.00	95.00
19-Reprints Avon's "Robotmen of the Lost Planet"	13.50	40.00	95.00
20-War stories; Wood-c(r)/U.S. Paratroops #1	3.65	11.00	25.00
21,22-War stories	3.35	10.00	23.00
I.W. Reprint #5-Kinstler-a(r)/Avon's #9	1.35	4.00	8.00

STRANGE WORLDS
Dec, 1958 - No. 5, Aug, 1959
Marvel Comics (MPI No. 1,2/Male No. 3,5)

1-Kirby & Ditko-a; flying saucer issue	18.00	54.00	130.00
2-Ditko c/a	11.00	32.00	75.00
3-Kirby-a(2)	8.50	25.50	60.00
4-Williamson-a	10.00	30.00	70.00
5-Ditko-a	8.00	24.00	56.00

NOTE: Buscema a-3. Ditko a-1-5; c-2. Kirby a-1, 3; c-1, 3-5.

STRAWBERRY SHORTCAKE
June, 1985 - No. 7, April, 1986 (Children's comic)
Star Comics (Marvel)

1-7: Howie Post-a		.35	.70

STRAY TOASTERS
Jan, 1988 - No. 4, April, 1989 ($3.50, squarebound, color, mini-series)
Epic Comics (Marvel)

1-4: Sienkiewicz story & art	.60	1.75	3.50

STREET COMIX (50 cents)
1973 (36 pgs.; B&W) (20,000 print run)
Street Enterprises/King Features

1-Rip Kirby		.40	.80
2-Flash Gordon		.60	1.20

STREETFIGHTER
Aug, 1986 - No. 4, Spr, 1987 ($1.75, color, mini-series)
Ocean Comics

1-4: 2-Origin begins	.30	.85	1.70

STRICTLY PRIVATE
July, 1942 (#1 on sale 6/15/42)
Eastern Color Printing Co.

1,2	11.00	32.00	75.00

STRIKE!
Aug, 1987 - No. 6, Jan, 1988 ($1.75, color)
Eclipse Comics

1-6	.30	.90	1.80
. . .Vs. Sgt. Strike Special 1 (5/88, $1.95)	.35	1.00	2.00

STRIKEFORCE: MORITURI
Dec, 1986 - No. 31, July, 1989
Marvel Comics Group

1	.40	1.25	2.50
2-5	.30	.90	1.80
6-12,14		.60	1.20
13-Double size	.25	.75	1.50
15-23 ($1.00-$1.25)		.60	1.25
24-31 ($1.50): 25-Heath-c	.25	.75	1.50

STRIKEFORCE MORITURI: ELECTRIC UNDERTOW
Dec, 1989 - No. 5, Apr, 1990 ($3.95, color, mini-series, 52 pgs.)
Marvel Comics

1-5: Squarebound	.70	2.00	4.00

STRONG MAN (Also see Complimentary Comics & Power of. . .)
Mar-Apr, 1955 - No. 4, Sept-Oct, 1955
Magazine Enterprises

1(A-1 130)-Powell-c/a	9.30	28.00	65.00

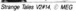

Strange Tales V2#14, © MEG

Strange World Of Your Dreams #3, © PRIZE

Strange Worlds #3, © AVON

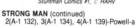
Stuntman Comics #1, © HARV

The Sub-Mariner #2, © MEG

Sub-Mariner Comics #1, © MEG

	Good	Fine	N-Mint
STRONG MAN (continued)			
2(A-1 132), 3(A-1 134), 4(A-1 139)-Powell-a	8.00	24.00	56.00

STRONTIUM DOG
Dec, 1985 - No. 4, Mar, 1986 ($1.25, mutie series)
Eagle Comics

1-4		.65	1.30
Special 1 ('86)-Moore scripts	.25	.75	1.50

STRONTIUM DOG
July, 1987 - Present ($1.25-$1.50, color)
Quality Comics

1-12 ($1.25)		.65	1.30
13,14/15,16-24 ($1.50): 13,18,20-Guice-c	.25	.75	1.50

STUMBO THE GIANT (See Harvey Hits #49, 54, 57, 60, 63, 66, 69, 72, 78, 88 & Hot Stuff #2)

STUMBO TINYTOWN
Oct, 1963 - No. 13, Nov, 1966
Harvey Publications

1	9.50	28.50	65.00
2	5.00	15.00	35.00
3-5	3.50	10.50	24.00
6-13	2.65	8.00	18.00

STUNTMAN COMICS (Also see Thrills Of Tomorrow)
Apr-May, 1946 - No. 2, June-July, 1946; No. 3, Oct-Nov, 1946
Harvey Publications

1-Origin Stuntman by S&K reprinted in Black Cat #9	57.00	171.00	400.00
2-S&K-a	36.50	110.00	255.00

3-Small size (5½x8½''); B&W; 32 pgs.); distributed to mail subscribers only; S&K-a; Kid Adonis by S&K reprinted in Green Hornet #37   Estimated value . . . $250.00-$400.00
(Also see All-New #15, Boy Explorers #2, Flash Gordon #5 & Thrills of Tomorrow)

SUBMARINE ATTACK (Formerly Speed Demons)
No. 11, May, 1958 - No. 54, Feb-Mar, 1966
Charlton Comics

11	.85	2.60	6.00
12-20	.60	1.75	3.50
21-54	.35	1.00	2.00

NOTE: Glanzman c/a-25. Montes/Bache a-38, 40, 41.

SUB-MARINER (See All-Select, All-Winners, Blonde Phantom, Daring, The Defenders, Fantastic Four #4, Human Torch, The Invaders, Iron Man, Marvel Mystery, Marvel Spotlight #27, Men's Adventures, Motion Picture Funnies Weekly, Namora, Namor, The. . . , Prince Namor, The Sub-Mariner, Saga Of The. . . , Tales to Astonish #70 & 2nd series, USA & Young Men)

SUB-MARINER, THE (2nd Series)(Sub-Mariner #31 on)
May, 1968 - No. 72, Sept, 1974 (No. 43: 52 pgs.)
Marvel Comics Group

1-Origin Sub-Mariner	8.50	25.50	60.00
2-Triton app.	2.85	8.50	20.00
3-10: 5-1st Tiger Shark. 7-Photo-c	1.50	4.50	10.00
11-13	1.15	3.50	7.00
14-Sub-Mariner vs. G.A. Human Torch; death of Toro	1.50	4.50	10.00
15-20: 19-1st Sting Ray	1.00	3.00	6.00
21-40: 37-Death of Lady Dorma. 35-Ties into 1st Defenders story;			
38-Origin	.70	2.00	4.00

41-72: 44,45-Sub-Mariner vs. H. Torch. 50-1st app. Nita, Namor's niece. 61-Last artwork by Everett; 1st 4 pgs. completed by Mortimer; pgs. 5-20 by Mooney. 62-1st Tales of Atlantis, ends #66

	.50	1.50	3.00
Special 1(1/71), Special 2(1/72)-Everett-a	.50	1.50	3.00

NOTE: Bolle a-67i. Buscema a(p)-1-8, 20, 24. Colan a-10p, 11p, 40p, 43p, 46-49p. Spec. 1p, 2; c(p)-10, 11, 40. Craig a-17, 19-23i. Everett a-45r, 50-55, 57, 58, 59-61(plot), 63(plot); c-47, 48i, 55, 57-59i, 61, Spec. 2. G. Kane c(p)-42-52, 58, 66, 70, 71. Mooney

a-24i, 25i, 32-35i, 39i, 42i, 44i, 45i, 60i, 61i, 65p, 66p, 68i. Severin c/a-38i. Starlin c-59p. Tuska a-41p, 42p, 69-71p. Wrightson a-36i.

SUB-MARINER COMICS (1st Series) (The Sub-Mariner #1,2,33-42)
(Official True Crime Cases #24 on; Amazing Mysteries #32 on; Best Love #33 on)
Spring, 1941 - No. 23, Sum, '47; No. 24, Wint, '47 - No. 31, 4/49; No. 32, 7/49; No. 33, 4/54 - No. 42, 10/55
Timely/Marvel Comics (TCI 1-7/SePI 8/MPI 9-32/Atlas Comics (CCC 33-42))

	Good	Fine	N-Mint
1-The Sub-Mariner by Everett & The Angel begin	467.00	1170.00	2800.00
2-Everett-a	220.00	550.00	1320.00
3-Churchill assassination-c; 40 pg. Sub-Mariner story	150.00	375.00	900.00
4-Everett-a, 40 pgs.; 1 pg. Wolverton-a	138.00	345.00	830.00
5	100.00	250.00	600.00
6-10: 9-Wolverton-a, 3 pgs.; flag-c	75.00	190.00	450.00
11-15	52.00	130.00	315.00
16-20	47.00	120.00	280.00
21-Last Angel; Everett-a	36.00	90.00	215.00
22-Young Allies app.	36.00	90.00	215.00
23-The Human Torch, Namora app.	36.00	90.00	215.00
24-Namora x-over	36.00	90.00	215.00
25-The Blonde Phantom begins, ends No. 31; Kurtzman-a; Namora x-over	43.00	110.00	260.00
26,27	40.00	100.00	240.00
28-Namora cover; Everett-a	40.00	100.00	240.00
29-31 (4/49): 29-The Human Torch app. 31-Capt. America app.	40.00	100.00	240.00
32 (7/49, Scarce)-Origin Sub-Mariner	62.00	155.00	370.00
33 (4/54)-Origin Sub-Mariner; The Human Torch app.; Namora x-over in Sub-Mariner #33-42	36.00	90.00	215.00
34,35-Human Torch in each	25.00	62.00	150.00
36,37,39-41: 36,39-41-Namora app.	25.00	62.00	150.00
38-Origin Sub-Mariner's wings; Namora app.	32.00	80.00	195.00
42-Last issue	28.00	70.00	170.00

NOTE: Angel by Gustavson-#1. Everett a-1-4, 22-24, 26-42; c-32, 33, 40. Maneely a-38i. Rico c-27, 28, 30. Schomburg c-1-4, 6, 8-18, 20. Sekowsky c-24. 25. Shores c-21-23, 38. Bondage c-13, 22, 24, 25, 34.

SUBURBAN HIGH LIFE
June, 1987 - No. 4?, 1988 ($1.75, B&W)
Slave Labor Graphics

1-4	.30	.90	1.80

SUE & SALLY SMITH (Formerly My Secret Life)
V2No. 48, 11/62 - No. 54, 11/63 (Flying Nurses)
Charlton Comics

V2#48	.35	1.00	2.00
49-54		.60	1.20

SUGAR & SPIKE (Also see The Best of DC)
Apr-May, 1956 - No. 98, Oct-Nov, 1971
National Periodical Publications

1 (Scarce)	61.00	182.00	425.00
2	30.00	90.00	210.00
3-5	27.00	81.00	190.00
6-10	17.00	51.00	120.00
11-20	13.00	40.00	90.00
21-29,31-40: 26-XMas-c	7.00	21.00	50.00
30-Scribbly x-over	8.50	25.50	60.00
41-60	3.50	10.50	24.00
61-80: 72-Origin & 1st app. Bernie the Brain	2.30	7.00	16.00
81-98: 85-68 pgs.; r-#72. #96-68 pgs. #97,98-52 pgs.	1.70	5.00	12.00

NOTE: All written and drawn by Sheldon Mayer.

SUGAR BEAR
No date (16 pages) (2½x4½'')
Post Cereal Giveaway

	Good	Fine	N-Mint
"The Almost Take Over of the Post Office," "The Race Across the Atlantic," "The Zoo Goes Wild" each. . .		.40	.80

SUGAR BOWL COMICS (Teen-age)
May, 1948 - No. 5, Jan, 1949
Famous Funnies

	Good	Fine	N-Mint
1-Toth-c/a	7.00	21.00	50.00
2,4,5	2.30	7.00	16.00
3-Toth-a	5.00	15.00	35.00

SUGARFOOT (See 4-Color #907,992,1059,1098,1147,1209)

SUICIDE SQUAD (See Brave & the Bold, Doom Patrol and Suicide Squad Special & Legends #3)
May, 1987 - Present (Direct sale only #32 on)
DC Comics

1	.30	.90	1.80
2	.25	.75	1.50
3-38: 16-Re-intro Shade The Changing Man		.50	1.00
Annual 1 ('88, $1.50)	.25	.75	1.50

SUMMER FUN (See Dell Giants)

SUMMER FUN (Formerly Li'l Genius; Holiday Surprise #55)
No. 54, Oct, 1966 (Giant)
Charlton Comics

54	.40	1.25	2.50

SUMMER LOVE (Formerly Brides in Love?)
V2#46, 10/65; V2#47, 10/66; V2#48, 11/68
Charlton Comics

V2#46-Beatles c/story	2.85	8.50	20.00
47-Beatles story	2.85	8.50	20.00
48	.35	1.00	2.00

SUMMER MAGIC (See Movie Comics)

SUNDANCE (See 4-Color #1126)

SUNDANCE KID (Also see Blazing Six-Guns)
June, 1971 - No. 3, Sept, 1971 (52 pages)
Skywald Publications

1-Durango Kid; 2 Kirby Bullseye-r		.60	1.20
2-Swift Arrow, Durango Kid, Bullseye by S&K; Meskin plus 1 pg. origin		.40	.80
3-Durango Kid, Billy the Kid, Red Hawk-r		.30	.60

SUNDAY FUNNIES
1950
Harvey Publications

1	1.50	4.50	10.50

SUN DEVILS
July, 1984 - No. 12, June, 1985 (12-issue series; $1.25)
DC Comics

1-12: 6-Death of Sun Devil		.60	1.20

SUN FUN KOMIKS
1939 (10 cents; black, white & red)
Sun Publications

1-Satire on comics	13.00	40.00	90.00

SUN GIRL (See The Human Torch & Marvel Mystery Comics #88)
Aug, 1948 - No. 3, Dec, 1948
Marvel Comics (CCC)

1-Sun Girl begins; Miss America app.	53.00	160.00	370.00
2,3: 2-The Blonde Phantom begins	39.00	118.00	275.00

SUNNY, AMERICA'S SWEETHEART
No. 11, Dec, 1947 - No. 14, June, 1948

Fox Features Syndicate

	Good	Fine	N-Mint
11-Feldstein c/a	27.00	81.00	190.00
12-14-Feldstein c/a; 14-Lingerie panels	23.50	70.00	165.00
I.W. Reprint #8-Feldstein-a; r-Fox issue	4.30	13.00	30.00

SUN-RUNNERS (Also see Tales of the. . .)
2/84 - No. 3, 5/84; No. 4, 11/84 - No. 6, '86 (Baxter paper)
Pacific Comics/Eclipse Comics/Amazing Comics

1-6: P. Smith-a	.25	.80	1.60
Christmas Special 1 (1987, $1.95)-Amazing	.35	1.00	2.00

SUNSET CARSON (Also see Cowboy Western)
Feb, 1951 - No. 4, 1951
Charlton Comics

1-Photo/retouched-c (Scarce, all issues)	62.00	185.00	435.00
2	41.00	122.00	285.00
3,4	30.00	90.00	210.00

SUPER ANIMALS PRESENTS PIDGY & THE MAGIC GLASSES
Dec, 1953
Star Publications

3-D 1-L. B. Cole-c	24.00	73.00	170.00

SUPER BOOK OF COMICS
nd (1943?) (32 pgs., soft-c) (Pan-Am/Gilmore Oil/Kelloggs premiums)
Western Publishing Co.

nn-Dick Tracy (Gilmore)-Magic Morro app.	30.00	90.00	210.00
1-Dick Tracy & The Smuggling Ring; Stratosphere Jim app. (Rare) (Pan-Am)	26.00	78.00	180.00
2-Smitty, Magic Morro	5.00	15.00	35.00
3-Moon Mullins?	4.00	12.00	28.00
4-Red Ryder, Magic Morro	4.00	12.00	28.00
5-Don Winslow, Magic Morro (Gilmore)	4.00	12.00	28.00
5-Don Winslow, Stratosphere Jim (Pan-Am)	4.00	12.00	28.00
5-Terry & the Pirates	9.00	27.00	62.00
6-Don Winslow, McWilliams-a	5.00	15.00	35.00
7-Little Orphan Annie	5.00	15.00	35.00
8-Dick Tracy?	10.00	30.00	70.00
9-Terry & the Pirates	8.00	24.00	56.00

SUPER-BOOK OF COMICS
(Omar Bread & Hancock Oil Co. giveaways)
1944 - No. 30, 1947 (Omar); 1947 - 1948 (Hancock) (16 pgs.)
Western Publishing Co.

Note: The Hancock issues are all exact reprints of the earlier Omar issues. The issue numbers were removed in some of the reprints.

1-Dick Tracy (Omar, 1944)	16.00	48.00	110.00
1-Dick Tracy (Hancock, 1947)	12.00	36.00	84.00
2-Bugs Bunny (Omar, 1944)	3.50	10.50	24.00
2-Bugs Bunny (Hancock, 1947)	2.65	8.00	18.00
3-Terry & the Pirates (Omar, 1944)	8.00	24.00	56.00
3-Terry & the Pirates (Hancock, 1947)	6.00	18.00	42.00
4-Andy Panda (Omar, 1944)	3.50	10.50	24.00
4-Andy Panda (Hancock, 1947)	2.65	8.00	18.00
5-Smokey Stover (Omar, 1945)	2.65	8.00	18.00
5-Smokey Stover (Hancock, 1947)	1.70	5.00	12.00
6-Porky Pig (Omar, 1945)	3.50	10.50	24.00
6-Porky Pig (Hancock, 1947)	2.65	8.00	18.00
7-Smilin' Jack (Omar, 1945)	3.50	10.50	24.00
7-Smilin' Jack (Hancock, 1947)	2.65	8.00	18.00
8-Oswald the Rabbit (Omar, 1945)	2.65	8.00	18.00
8-Oswald the Rabbit (Hancock, 1947)	1.70	5.00	12.00
9-Alley Oop (Omar, 1945)	8.50	25.50	60.00
9-Alley Oop (Hancock, 1947)	7.00	21.00	50.00
10-Elmer Fudd (Omar, 1945)	2.65	8.00	18.00
10-Elmer Fudd (Hancock, 1947)	1.70	5.00	12.00
11-Little Orphan Annie (Omar, 1945)	4.35	13.00	30.00
11-Little Orphan Annie (Hancock, 1947)	3.00	9.00	21.00

Suicide Squad #1, © DC

Sunny, America's Sweetheart #12, © FOX

Super Animals Presents . . . #1, © STAR

Super-Book Of Comics #13 (Omar), © N.Y. News Synd.   *Superboy #11, © DC*   *Superboy #123, © DC*

	Good	Fine	N-Mint
SUPER-BOOK OF COMICS (continued)			
12-Woody Woodpecker (Omar, 1945)	2.65	8.00	18.00
12-Woody Woodpecker (Hancock, 1947)	1.70	5.00	12.00
13-Dick Tracy (Omar, 1945)	9.00	27.00	62.00
13-Dick Tracy (Hancock, 1947)	7.00	21.00	50.00
14-Bugs Bunny (Omar, 1945)	2.65	8.00	18.00
14-Bugs Bunny (Hancock, 1947)	1.70	5.00	12.00
15-Andy Panda (Omar, 1945)	2.30	7.00	16.00
15-Andy Panda (Hancock, 1947)	1.70	5.00	12.00
16-Terry & the Pirates (Omar, 1945)	7.00	21.00	50.00
16-Terry & the Pirates (Hancock, 1947)	5.00	15.00	35.00
17-Smokey Stover (Omar, 1946)	2.65	8.00	18.00
17-Smokey Stover (Hancock, 1948?)	1.70	5.00	12.00
18-Porky Pig (Omar, 1946)	2.30	7.00	16.00
18-Porky Pig (Hancock, 1948?)	1.70	5.00	12.00
19-Smilin' Jack (Omar, 1946)	2.65	8.00	18.00
nn-Smilin' Jack (Hancock, 1948)	1.70	5.00	12.00
20-Oswald the Rabbit (Omar, 1946)	2.30	7.00	16.00
nn-Oswald the Rabbit (Hancock, 1948)	1.70	5.00	12.00
21-Gasoline Alley (Omar, 1946)	4.00	12.00	28.00
nn-Gasoline Alley (Hancock, 1948)	3.00	9.00	21.00
22-Elmer Fudd (Omar, 1946)	2.30	7.00	16.00
nn-Elmer Fudd (Hancock, 1948)	1.70	5.00	12.00
23-Little Orphan Annie (Omar, 1946)	3.50	10.50	24.00
nn-Little Orphan Annie (Hancock, 1948)	2.65	8.00	18.00
24-Woody Woodpecker (Omar, 1946)	2.30	7.00	16.00
nn-Woody Woodpecker (Hancock, 1948)	1.70	5.00	12.00
25-Dick Tracy (Omar, 1946)	7.00	21.00	50.00
nn-Dick Tracy (Hancock, 1948)	5.00	15.00	35.00
26-Bugs Bunny (Omar, 1946))	2.30	7.00	16.00
nn-Bugs Bunny (Hancock, 1948)	1.70	5.00	12.00
27-Andy Panda (Omar, 1946)	2.30	7.00	16.00
27-Andy Panda (Hancock, 1948)	1.70	5.00	12.00
28-Terry & the Pirates (Omar, 1946)	7.00	21.00	50.00
28-Terry & the Pirates (Hancock, 1947)	5.00	15.00	35.00
29-Smokey Stover (Omar, 1947)	2.30	7.00	16.00
29-Smokey Stover (Hancock, 1948)	1.70	5.00	12.00
30-Porky Pig (Omar, 1947)	2.30	7.00	16.00
30-Porky Pig (Hancock, 1948)	1.70	5.00	12.00
nn-Bugs Bunny (Hancock, 1948)-Does not match any Omar book			
	1.70	5.00	12.00

SUPERBOY (See Adventure, Aurora, DC Comics Presents, DC 100 Page Super Spect. #15, DC Super Stars, 80 Page Giant #10, More Fun, The New Advs. of . . . & Superman Family #191)

SUPERBOY (. . .& the Legion of Super Heroes with #231)
(Becomes The Legion of Super Heroes No. 259 on)
Mar-Apr, 1949 - No. 258, Dec, 1979 (#1-16: 52 pgs.)
National Periodical Publications/DC Comics

	Good	Fine	N-Mint
1-Superman cover	250.00	750.00	1750.00
2-Used in SOTI, pg. 35-36,226	96.00	290.00	675.00
3	70.00	210.00	490.00
4,5: 5-Pre-Supergirl tryout	59.00	178.00	415.00
6-10: 8-1st Superbaby. 10-1st app. Lana Lang			
	43.00	130.00	300.00
11-15	32.00	95.00	225.00
16-20	22.00	65.00	155.00
21-26,28-30	17.00	51.00	120.00
27-Low distribution	18.00	54.00	125.00
31-38: 38-Last pre-code issue	12.00	36.00	84.00
39-48,50 (7/56)	8.30	28.00	65.00
49 (6/56)-1st app. Metallo (Jor-El's robot)	11.00	32.00	75.00
51-60: 55-Spanking-c	6.50	19.50	45.00
61-67	5.00	15.00	35.00
68-Origin/1st app. original Bizarro (10-11/58)	18.00	54.00	125.00
69-77,79: 75-Spanking-c. 76-1st Supermonkey. 77-Pre-Pete Ross tryout	4.30	13.00	30.00

	Good	Fine	N-Mint
78-Origin Mr. Mxyzptlk & Superboy's costume	8.00	24.00	55.00
80-1st meeting Superboy/Supergirl (4/60)	4.30	13.00	30.00
81-85,87,88: 82-1st Bizarro Krypto. 83-Origin & 1st app. Kryptonite Kid			
	3.15	9.50	22.00
86(1/61)-4th Legion app; Intro Pete Ross	9.30	28.00	65.00
89(6/61)-Mon-el 1st app.	12.00	36.00	85.00
90-92: 90-Pete Ross learns Superboy's I.D. 92-Last 10 cent issue			
	2.85	8.50	20.00
93(12/61)-10th Legion app; Chameleon Boy app.			
	3.50	10.50	24.00
94-97,99	1.70	5.00	12.00
98(7/62)-19th Legion app; Origin & intro. Ultra Boy; Pete Ross joins Legion	2.85	8.50	20.00
100-Ultra Boy app; 1st app. Phantom Zone villains, Dr. Xadu & Erndine. 2 pg. map of Krypton; origin Superboy retold; r-cover of Superman 1; Pete Ross joins Legion	11.00	32.00	75.00
101-120: 104-Origin Phantom Zone. 115-Atomic bomb-c. 117-Legion app.	1.00	3.00	6.00
121-128: 124(10/65)-1st app. Insect Queen (Lana Lang). 125-Legion cameo. 126-Origin Krypto the Super Dog retold with new facts			
	.50	1.50	3.00
129 (80-pg. Giant G-22)-Reprints origin Mon-el	.60	1.75	3.50
138 (80-pg. Giant G-35)	.60	1.75	3.50
130-137,139,140: 131-Legion cameo (statues). 132-1st app. Supremo	.40	1.25	2.50
141-146,148-155,157-164,166-173,175,176: 145-Superboy's parents re-gain their youth. 172,173,176-Legion app.; 172-Origin Yango (Super Ape)	.35	1.00	2.00
147(6/68)-Giant G-47; origin Saturn Girl, Lightning Lad, Cosmic Boy; origin Legion of Super-Pets-r/Adv. 293?	.85	2.50	5.00
156,165,174 (Giants G-59,71,83)	.50	1.50	3.00
177-184,186,187 (All 52 pgs.): 184-Origin Dial H for Hero-r			
		.50	1.00
185-100 pg. Super Spec. #12; Legion app.-c, story; Teen Titans, Kid Eternity, Star Spangled Kid-r	.25	.75	1.50
188-196: 188-Origin Karkan. 191-Origin Sunboy retold; Legion app. 193-Chameleon Boy & Shrinking Violet get new costumes. 195-1st app. Erg/Wildfire; Phantom Girl gets new costume. 196-Last Superboy solo story		.50	1.00
197-Legion begins; Lightning Lad's new costume			
	.75	2.25	4.50
198,199: 198-Element Lad & Princess Projectra get new costumes	.35	1.00	2.00
200-Bouncing Boy & Duo Damsel marry; Jonn' Jonzz' cameo			
	.75	2.25	4.50
201,204,206,207,209: 201-Re-intro Erg as Wildfire. 204-Supergirl resigns from Legion. 206-Ferro Lad & Invisible Kid app. 209-Karate Kid new costume	.35	1.00	2.00
202,205-(100 pgs.): 202-Light Lass gets new costume			
	.45	1.25	2.50
203-Invisible Kid dies	.50	1.50	3.00
208-(68 pgs.)	.45	1.25	2.50
210-Origin Karate Kid	.45	1.25	2.50
211-220: 212-Matter-Eater Lad resigns. 216-1st app. Tyroc who joins Legion in #218	.30	.90	1.80
221-249: 226-Intro. Dawnstar. 228-Death of Chemical King. 240-Origin Dawnstar	.60		1.20
250-258: 253-Intro Blok	.50		1.00
Annual 1(Sum/64, 84 pgs.)-Origin Krypto-r	6.50	19.50	45.00
. . .Spectacular 1(1980, Giant)-Distr. through comic stores; mostly-r			
		.50	1.00

NOTE: *Adams* c-143, 145, 146, 148-155, 157-161, 163, 164, 166-168, 172, 173, 175, 176, 178. *Ditko* a-257p. *Grell* a-202; 203-219, 220-24p, 235p; c-207-232, 235, 236p, 237, 239p, 240p, 243p, 246, 258. *Nasser* a(p)-222, 225, 226, 230, 231, 233, 236. *Simonson* a-237p. *Starlin* a(p)-239, 250, 251; c-238. *Staton* a-227p, 243-249p, 252-258p; c-247-251p. *Tuska* a-172, 173, 176, 235p. *Wood* inks-152-155, 157-161. Legion app.-172, 173,

SUPERBOY (continued)
176, 177, 183, 184, 188, 190, 191, 193, 195.

SUPERBOY (TV)
Feb, 1990 - Present ($1.00, color)
DC Comics

	Good	Fine	N-Mint
1-4: Mooney-a(p); 1-photo-c from TV show		.50	1.00

SUPER BRAT
January, 1954 - No. 4, July, 1954
Toby Press

1 (1954)	2.00	6.00	14.00
2-4: 4-Li'l Teevy by Mel Lazarus	1.00	3.00	7.00
I.W. Reprint #1,2,3,7,8('58)		.40	.80
I.W. (Super) Reprint #10('63)		.40	.80

SUPERCAR (TV)
Nov, 1962 - No. 4, Aug, 1963 (All painted covers)
Gold Key

1	4.30	13.00	30.00
2-4	3.00	9.00	21.00

SUPER CAT (Also see Animal Crackers & Frisky Animals)
Sept, 1957 - No. 4, May, 1958
Ajax/Farrell Publ. (Four Star Comic Corp.)

1('57-Ajax)	2.00	6.00	14.00
2-4	1.15	3.50	8.00

SUPER CIRCUS (TV)
January, 1951 - No. 5, 1951 (Mary Hartline)
Cross Publishing Co.

1-Cast photos on-c	3.70	11.00	26.00
2-Cast photos on-c	2.65	8.00	18.00
3-5	2.00	6.00	14.00

SUPER CIRCUS (TV)
No. 542, March, 1954 - No. 694, Mar, 1956 (Feat. Mary Hartline)
Dell Publishing Co.

4-Color 542,592,694: Mary Hartline photo-c	2.65	8.00	18.00

SUPER COMICS
May, 1938 - No. 121, Feb-Mar, 1949
Dell Publishing Co.

1-Terry & The Pirates, The Gumps, Dick Tracy, Little Orphan Annie, Gasoline Alley, Little Joe, Smilin' Jack, Smokey Stover, Smitty, Tiny Tim, Moon Mullins, Harold Teen, Winnie Winkle begin			
	103.00	260.00	615.00
2	43.00	130.00	300.00
3	38.00	115.00	270.00
4,5	30.00	90.00	210.00
6-10	24.00	73.00	170.00
11-20	19.00	57.00	135.00
21-29: 21-Magic Morro begins (Origin, 2/40)	16.00	48.00	115.00
30-"Sea Hawk" movie adaptation-c/story with Errol Flynn			
	16.00	48.00	115.00
31-40	13.00	40.00	90.00
41-50: 43-Terry & The Pirates ends	11.00	32.00	75.00
51-60	8.00	24.00	56.00
61-70: 65-Brenda Starr-r begin? 67-X-mas-c	6.50	19.50	45.00
71-80	5.50	16.50	40.00
81-99	4.50	14.00	32.00
100	5.50	16.50	40.00
101-115-Last Dick Tracy (moves to own title)	3.70	11.00	26.00
116,118-All Smokey Stover	3.00	9.00	21.00
117-All Gasoline Alley	3.00	9.00	21.00
119-121: 119-121-Terry & The Pirates app.	3.00	9.00	21.00

SUPER COPS, THE
July, 1974 (One Shot)
Red Circle Productions (Archie)

	Good	Fine	N-Mint
1-Morrow-c/a		.30	.60

SUPER CRACKED (See Cracked)

SUPER DC GIANT (25 cents)
No. 13, 9-10/70 - No. 26, 7-8/71; No. 27, Summer, 1976 (No #1-12)
National Periodical Publications

S-13-Binky	.35	1.00	2.00
S-14-Top Guns of the West; Kubert-c; Trigger Twins, Johnny Thunder, Wyoming Kid-r	.35	1.00	2.00
S-15-Western Comics; Kubert-c; Pow Wow Smith, Vigilante, Buffalo Bill-r	.35	1.00	2.00
S-16-Best of the Brave & the Bold; Kubert-a	.35	1.00	2.00
S-17-Love 1970	.25	.75	1.50
S-18-Three Mouseketeers; Dizzy Dog, Doodles Duck, Bo Bunny-r; Sheldon Mayer-a	.25	.75	1.50
S-19-Jerry Lewis; no Adams-a	.25	.75	1.50
S-20-House of Mystery; Adams-c; Kirby-a(3)(r)	.25	.75	1.50
S-21-Love 1971		.50	1.00
S-22-Top Guns of the West	.25	.75	1.50
S-23-The Unexpected		.50	1.00
S-24-Supergirl		.50	1.00
S-25-Challengers of the Unknown; all Kirby/Wood-r			
	.25	.75	1.50
S-26-Aquaman (1971)		.50	1.00
27-Strange Flying Saucers Adventures (Fall, '76)		.50	1.00

NOTE: *Sid Greene a-27p(r), Heath a-27r. G. Kane a-14r, 15r, 27p(r).*

SUPER-DOOPER COMICS
1946 (10 cents)(32 pages)(paper cover)
Able Manufacturing Co.

1-The Clock, Gangbuster app.	6.50	19.50	45.00
2	3.00	9.00	21.00
3,4,6	2.30	7.00	16.00
5,7-Capt. Freedom & Shock Gibson	3.70	11.00	26.00
8-Shock Gibson, Sam Hill	3.70	11.00	26.00

SUPER DUCK COMICS (The Cockeyed Wonder) (See Jolly Jingles)
Fall, 1944 - No. 94, Dec, 1960
MLJ Mag. No. 1-4(9/45)/Close-Up No. 5 on (Archie)

1-Origin	19.00	58.00	135.00
2	8.50	25.50	60.00
3-5: 3-1st Mr. Monster	6.50	19.50	45.00
6-10	4.50	14.00	32.00
11-20	2.85	8.50	20.00
21,23-40	2.30	7.00	16.00
22-Used in **SOTI**, pg. 35,307,308	3.50	10.50	24.00
41-60	1.50	4.50	10.00
61-94	1.15	3.50	8.00

SUPER DUPER
No. 5, 1941 - No. 11, 1941
Harvey Publications

5-Captain Freedom & Shock Gibson app.	12.00	36.00	84.00
8,11	6.50	19.50	45.00

SUPER DUPER COMICS (Formerly Latest Comics?)
No. 3, May-June, 1947
F. E. Howard Publ.

3-Mr. Monster app.	3.70	11.00	26.00

SUPER FRIENDS (TV) (Also see Best of DC & Limited Coll. Ed.)
Nov, 1976 - No. 47, Aug, 1981
National Periodical Publications/DC Comics

1-Superman, Batman, Wonder Woman, Aquaman, Atom, Robin, Wendy, Marvin & Wonder Dog begin		.30	.60
2-10: 7-1st app. Wonder Twins, & The Seraph. 8-1st app. Jack O'Lantern. 9-1st app. Icemaiden		.25	.50

Super Comics #3, ⓔ DELL   Super DC Giant #S-14, ⓔ DC   Super Duck #4, ⓔ AP

Super Heroes #1, © DELL

Super Magician Comics V2#9, © S & S

Superman #1, © DC

SUPER FRIENDS (continued)

	Good	Fine	N-Mint
11-47: 13-1st app. Dr. Mist. 14-Origin Wonder Twins. 25-1st app. Green Fury. 31-Black Orchid app. 47-Origin Green Fury		.25	.50
...Special 1 (1981, giveaway, no ads, no code or price)-r/Super Friends #19 & 36		.30	.60

NOTE: *Estrada a-1p, 2p. Orlando a-1p. Staton a-43, 45.*

SUPER FUN
January, 1956 (By A.W. Nugent)
Gillmor Magazines

	Good	Fine	N-Mint
1-Comics, puzzles, cut-outs	1.50	4.50	10.00

SUPER FUNNIES (...Western Funnies #3,4)
Dec, 1953 - No. 4, June, 1954
Superior Comics Publishers Ltd. (Canada)

	Good	Fine	N-Mint
1-(3-D)-Dopey Duck; make your own 3-D glasses cut-out inside front-c; did not come w/glasses	25.00	75.00	175.00
2-Horror a satire	2.85	8.50	20.00
3-Geronimo, Billy The Kid app.	2.00	6.00	14.00
4-(Western-Phantom Ranger)	2.00	6.00	14.00

SUPERGEAR COMICS
1976 (4 pages in color) (slick paper)
Jacobs Corp. (Giveaway)

	Good	Fine	N-Mint
(Rare)-Superman, Lois Lane; Steve Lombard app.	1.00	3.00	6.00

NOTE: *500 copies printed, over half destroyed?*

SUPERGIRL (See Action, Adventure, Brave & the Bold, Crisis on Infinite Earths #7, Daring New Advs. of..., Super DC Giant, Superman Family, & Super-Team Family)

SUPERGIRL
11/72 - No. 9, 12-1/73-74; No. 10, 9-10/74
National Periodical Publications

	Good	Fine	N-Mint
1-Zatanna begins; ends #5		.50	1.00
2-5: 5-Zatanna origin-r		.40	.80
6-10: 8-JLA x-over		.30	.60

NOTE: *Zatanna in #1-5, 7(Guest); Prez-#10.*

SUPERGIRL (Formerly Daring New Advs. of...)
No. 14, Dec, 1983 - No. 23, Sept, 1984
DC Comics

	Good	Fine	N-Mint
14,15,17-23: 20-New Teen Titans app.		.40	.80
16-Ambush Bug app.		.60	1.20
Movie Special (1985)-Adapts movie		.60	1.20
Giveaway ('84, '86 Baxter, nn)(American Honda/U.S. Dept. Transportation)-Torres-a		.60	1.20

SUPER GOOF (Walt Disney) (See Dynabrite & The Phantom Blot)
Oct, 1965 - No. 74, 1982
Gold Key No. 1-57/Whitman No. 58 on

	Good	Fine	N-Mint
1	1.15	3.50	8.00
2-10	.55	1.65	4.00
11-20	.45	1.35	3.00
21-30	.35	1.00	2.00
31-50		.50	1.00
51-74		.30	.60

NOTE: *Reprints in #16, 24, 28, 29, 37, 38, 43, 45, 46, 54(½), 56-58, 65(½), 72(r-#2).*

SUPER GREEN BERET (Tod Holton...)
April, 1967 - No. 2, June, 1967 (68 pages)
Lightning Comics (Milson Publ. Co.)

	Good	Fine	N-Mint
1,2	.85	2.60	6.00

SUPER HEROES (See Giant-Size... & Marvel...)

SUPER HEROES
Jan, 1967 - No. 4, June, 1967
Dell Publishing Co.

	Good	Fine	N-Mint
1-Origin & 1st app. Fab 4	1.50	4.50	10.00

	Good	Fine	N-Mint
2-4	1.00	3.00	7.00

SUPER-HEROES BATTLE SUPER-GORILLAS (See DC Special #16)
Winter, 1976-77 (One Shot, 52 pgs.)
National Periodical Publications

	Good	Fine	N-Mint
1-Superman, Batman, Flash stories; Infantino-a(p); all-r		.30	.60

SUPER HEROES PUZZLES AND GAMES
1979 (32 pgs.) (regular size)
General Mills Giveaway (Marvel Comics Group)

	Good	Fine	N-Mint
Four 2-pg. origin stories of Spider-Man, Captain America, The Hulk, & Spider-Woman	.50	1.50	3.00

SUPER-HEROES VERSUS SUPER-VILLAINS
July, 1966 (no month given)(68 pgs.)
Archie Publications

	Good	Fine	N-Mint
1-Flyman, Black Hood, The Web, Shield-r; Reinman-a	2.00	6.00	14.00

SUPERICHIE (Formerly Super Richie)
No. 5, Oct, 1976 - No. 18, Jan, 1979
Harvey Publications

	Good	Fine	N-Mint
5-18: All 52 pg. Giants		.25	.50

SUPERIOR STORIES
May-June, 1955 - No. 4, Nov-Dec, 1955
Nesbit Publishing Co.

	Good	Fine	N-Mint
1-Invisible Man app.	7.00	21.00	50.00
2-The Pirate of the Gulf by J.H. Ingrahams	3.70	11.00	26.00
3-Wreck of the Grosvenor	3.70	11.00	26.00
4-O'Henry's "The Texas Rangers"	4.30	13.00	30.00

NOTE: *Morisi c/a in all.*

SUPER MAGIC (Super Magician Comics #2 on)
May, 1941
Street & Smith Publications

	Good	Fine	N-Mint
V1#1-Blackstone the Magician app.; origin & 1st app. Rex King (Black Fury); not Eisner-c	38.00	115.00	265.00

SUPER MAGICIAN COMICS (Super Magic #1)
No. 2, Sept, 1941 - V5No.8, Feb-Mar, 1947
Street & Smith Publications

	Good	Fine	N-Mint
V1#2-Rex King, Man of Adventure app.	16.00	48.00	110.00
3-Tao-Anwar, Boy Magician begins	9.30	28.00	65.00
4-Origin Transo	8.50	25.50	60.00
5-7,9-12: 8-Abbott & Costello story. 11-Supersnipe app.	8.50	25.50	60.00
8-Abbott & Costello story	10.00	30.00	70.00
V2#1-The Shadow app.	11.50	34.00	80.00
2-12: 5-Origin Tigerman. 8-Red Dragon begins	4.50	14.00	32.00
V3#1-12: 5-Origin Mr. Twilight	4.50	14.00	32.00
V4#1-12: 11-Nigel Elliman begins	4.00	12.00	28.00
V5#1-6	4.00	12.00	28.00
7,8-Red Dragon by Cartier	12.00	36.00	84.00

SUPERMAN (See Action Comics, Advs. of..., All-New Coll. Ed., All-Star Comics, Best of DC, Brave & the Bold, Cosmic Odyssey, DC Comics Presents, Heroes Against Hunger, Krypton Chronicles, Limited Coll. Ed., Man of Steel, Special Edition, Super Friends, Taylor's Christmas Tabloid, Three-Dimension Advs., World Of Krypton, World Of Metropolis, World Of Smallville & World's Finest Comics)

SUPERMAN (Becomes Adventures Of...#424 on)
Summer, 1939 - No. 423, Sept, 1986
National Periodical Publications/DC Comics

	Good	Fine	VF-NM
1(nn)-1st four Action stories reprinted; origin Superman by Siegel & Shuster; has a new 2 pg. origin plus 4 pgs. omitted in Action story	4,000.00	11,000.00	26,000.00
(No known copy exists beyond Vf-NM condition)			

SUPERMAN (continued)

1-Reprint, Oversize 13½"x10." WARNING: This comic is an exact duplicate reprint of the original except for its size. DC published it in 1978 with a second cover titling it as a Famous First Edition. There have been many reported cases of the outer cover being removed and the interior sold as the original edition. The reprint with the new outer cover removed is practically worthless.

	Good	Fine	N-Mint
2-All daily strip-r	567.00	1420.00	3400.00
3-2nd story-r from Action #5; 3rd story-r from Action #6	417.00	1050.00	2500.00
4-1st mention of Daily Planet? (Spr/40)-Also see Action #23	300.00	750.00	1800.00
5	242.00	605.00	1450.00
6,7: 7-1st Perry White?	175.00	440.00	1050.00
8-10: 10-1st bald Luthor	142.00	355.00	850.00
11-13,15: 13-Jimmy Olsen app.	108.00	270.00	650.00
14-Patriotic Shield-c by Fred Ray	129.00	325.00	775.00
16-20: 17-Hitler, Hirohito-c	92.00	230.00	550.00
21-23,25	72.00	180.00	430.00
24-Flag-c	83.00	210.00	500.00
26-29: 28-Lois Lane Girl Reporter series begins, ends #40,42	65.00	165.00	390.00
28-Overseas edition for Armed Forces; same as reg. #28	65.00	165.00	390.00
30-Origin 1st app. Mr. Mxyztplk (pronounced "Mix-it-plk"); name later became Mxyzptlk ("Mix-yez-pit-l-ick"); the character was inspired by a combination of the name of Al Capp's Joe Blyfstyk (the little man with the black cloud over his head) & the devilish antics of Bugs Bunny	91.00	275.00	640.00
31,32,34-40	48.00	145.00	340.00
33-(3-4/45)-3rd app. Mxyztplk	48.00	145.00	340.00
41-50: 45-Lois Lane as Superwoman (see Action #60 for 1st app.)	36.00	108.00	250.00
51,52	29.00	87.00	205.00
53-Origin Superman retold	71.00	215.00	500.00
54,56-60	30.00	90.00	210.00
55-Used in SOTI, pg. 33	32.00	95.00	225.00
61-Origin Superman retold; origin Green Kryptonite (1st Kryptonite story)	54.00	160.00	375.00
62-65,67-70: 62-Orson Welles app. 65-1st Krypton Tales: Mala, K120, & U-Ban	30.00	90.00	210.00
66-2nd Superbaby story	31.00	92.00	215.00
71-75: 75-Some have #74 on-c	27.00	81.00	190.00
72-Giveaway(9-10/51)-(Rare)-Price blackened out; came with banner wrapped around book	35.00	105.00	245.00
76-Batman x-over; Superman & Batman learn each other's I.D.	71.00	215.00	500.00
77-80: 78-Last 52 pgs.	24.00	73.00	170.00
81-Used in POP, pg. 88	24.00	73.00	170.00
82-90	22.00	65.00	155.00
91-95: 95-Last precode issue	21.00	62.00	145.00
96-99	17.00	51.00	120.00
100 (9-10/55)	57.00	171.00	400.00
101-110	14.00	42.00	100.00
111-120	12.00	35.00	80.00
121-130: 123-Pre-Supergirl tryout. 127-Origin/1st app. Titano. 128-Red Kryptonite used (4/59). 129-Intro/origin Lori Lemaris, The Mermaid	9.30	28.00	65.00
131-139: 139-Lori Lemaris app.	7.00	21.00	50.00
140-1st Blue Kryptonite & Bizarro Supergirl; origin Bizarro Jr. #1	7.00	21.00	50.00
141-145,148: 142-2nd Batman x-over	5.00	15.00	35.00
146-Superman's life story	6.50	19.50	45.00
147(8/61)-7th Legion app; 1st app. Legion of Super-Villains; intro. Adult Legion	7.00	21.00	50.00
149(11/61)-9th Legion app. (cameo); last 10 cent issue	7.00	21.00	50.00
150-162: 152(4/62)-15th Legion app. 155(8/62)-20th Legion app; Light-			

	Good	Fine	N-Mint
ning Man & Cosmic Man, & Adult Legion app. 156,162-Legion app. 157-Gold Kryptonite used (see Adv. 299); Mon-el app.; Lightning Lad cameo (11/62). 158-1st app. Flamebird & Nightwing & Nor-Kan of Kandor. 161-1st told death of Ma and Pa Kent	3.15	9.50	22.00
163-166,168-180: 169-Last Sally Selwyn. 172,173-Legion cameo	2.15	6.50	15.00
167-New origin Braniac & Brainiac 5; intro Tixarla (Later Luthor's wife)	3.60	11.00	25.00
181,182,184-186,188-192,194-196,198-200: 181-1st 2965 story/series 189-Origin/destruction of Krypton II. 199-1st Superman/Flash race	1.30	4.00	9.00
183,187,193,197 (Giants G-18,G-23,G-31,G-36)	1.50	4.50	10.00
201,203-206,208-211,213-216,218-221,223-226,228-231,234-238: 213-Brainiac-5 app.	1.00	3.00	6.00
202 (80-pg. Giant G-42)-All Bizarro issue	1.15	3.50	7.00
207,212,217,222,227,239 (Giants G-48,G-54,G-60,G-66,G-72,G-84): 207-Legion app.; 30th anniversary Superman	1.15	3.50	7.00
232(Giant, G-78)-All Krypton issue	1.15	3.50	7.00
233-1st app. Morgan Edge, Clark Kent switch from newspaper reporter to TV newscaster	1.00	3.00	6.00
240-Kaluta-a	.45	1.40	2.75
241-244 (52 pgs.). 243-G.A.-r/#38	.40	1.25	2.50
245-DC 100 pg. Super Spec. #7; Air Wave, Kid Eternity, Hawkman, Atom-r	.50	1.50	3.00
246-248,250,251,253 (All 52 pgs.): 246-G.A.-r/#40. 248-World of Krypton story. 253-Finlay-a, 2pgs., G.A.-r/#13	.55		1.10
249,254-Adams-a. 249-(52 pgs.); origin & 1st app. Terra-Man by Adams (inks)	.90	2.75	5.50
252-DC 100 pg. Super Spec. #13; Ray, Black Condor, Starman, Dr. Fate, Hawkman, Spectre app.; Adams-c	.75	2.20	4.40
255-263: 263-Photo-c		.55	1.10
264-1st app. Steve Lombard	.30	.85	1.65
265-271,273-277,279-283,285-299: 276-Intro Capt. Thunder. 289-Photo-c. 292-Origin Lex Luthor retold		.55	1.10
272,278,284-All 100 pgs. G.A.-r in all	.30	.85	1.65
300-Retells origin	.55	1.65	3.30
301-399: 301,320-Solomon Grundy app. 323-Intro. Atomic Skull. 327-329-(44 pgs.). 330-More facts revealed about I. D. 338-The bottled city of Kandor enlarged. 372-Superman 2021 app. 376-Free 16 pg. preview of Daring, New Advs. of Supergirl		.55	1.10
400 (10/84, $1.50, 68 pgs.)-Many top artists featured		.35	1.10	2.20
401-410,412-422: 415-Crisis x-over		.55	1.10
411-Special Julius Schwartz tribute issue	.50	1.50	3.00
423	1.00	3.00	6.00
Annual 1(10/60)-Reprints 1st Supergirl/Action #252; r-/Lois Lane #1	28.00	84.00	200.00
Annual 2(1960)-Brainiac, Titano, Metallo, Bizarro origin-r	18.00	54.00	125.00
Annual 3(1961)	13.00	40.00	90.00
Annual 4(1961)-11th Legion app; 1st Legion origins-text & pictures	11.00	32.00	75.00
Annual 5(Sum, '62)-All Krypton issue	8.00	24.00	55.00
Annual 6(Wint, '62-'63)-Legion-r/Adv. #247	6.50	19.50	45.00
Annual 7(Sum/'63)-Origin-r/Superman-Batman team/Adv. 275; r-1955 Superman dailies	5.00	15.00	35.00
Annual 8(Wint, '63-'64), 9(8/64)	3.60	11.00	25.00
Annual 9(9/83)-Toth/Austin-a	.35	1.10	2.20
Annual 10(11/84, $1.25)-M. Anderson inks	.35	1.10	2.20
Annual 11(9/85)-Moore scripts	.35	1.10	2.20
Annual 12(8/86)	.35	1.10	2.20
Special 1(3/83)-G. Kane c/a; r-that appeared in Germany	.35	1.10	2.20

Superman #17, © DC

Superman #170, © DC

Superman #245, © DC

Superman #2 (2/87), © DC   The Superman Family #195, © DC   Superman's Girlfriend Lois Lane #44, © DC

	Good	Fine	N-Mint
SUPERMAN (continued)			
Special 2(3/84, 48pgs.), 3(4/85, $1.25)	.35	1.10	2.20
The Amazing World of Superman "Official Metropolis Edition"			
($2.00; 1973, 14x10½")-Origin retold	1.35	4.00	8.00
Kelloggs Giveaway-(⅔ normal size, 1954)-r-two stories/Superman #55			
	30.00	90.00	200.00
. . . Meets the Quik Bunny ('87, Nestles Quik premium, 36 pgs.)			
	.50		1.00
. . . Movie Special-(9/83)-Adaptation of Superman III			
	.50		1.00
Pizza Hut Premium(12/77)-Exact-r of #97,113	.25	.75	1.50
Radio Shack Giveaway-36pgs. (7/80) 'The Computers That Saved			
Metropolis;' Starlin/Giordano-a; advertising insert in Action 509,			
New Advs. of Superboy 7, Legion of Super-Heroes 265, & House			
of Mystery 282. (All comics were 64 pgs.) Cover of inserts printed			
on newsprint. Giveaway contains 4 extra pgs. of Radio Shack ad-			
vertising that inserts do not	.25	.75	1.50
Radio Shack Giveaway-(7/81) 'Victory by Computer'			
	.25	.75	1.50
Radio Shack Giveaway-(7/82) 'Computer Masters of Metropolis'			
	.50		1.00
11195(2/79,224pp,$1.95)-Golden Press	.40	1.20	2.40

NOTE: *Adams* a-249i, 254p; c-204-208, 210, 212-215, 219, 231, 233-237, 240-243, 249-252, 254, 263, 307, 308, 313, 314, 317. *Adkins* a-323i. *Austin* c-368i. *Wayne Boring* art-late 1940's to early 1960's. *Buckler* a-352p, 363p, 364p, 369p; c(p)-324-327, 356, 363, 368, 369, 373, 376, 378. *Burnley* a-252r. *Fine* a-252r. *Gil Kane* a-272r, 367, 372, 375, Special 2; c-374p, 375p, 377, 381, 382, 384-390, 392. *Anual 9. Kubert* c-216. *Morrow* a-238. *Perez* c-364p. *Starlin* c-355. *Staton* a-354i, 355i. *Williamson* a-408-410i, 412i, 416i; c-408i, 409i. *Wrightson* a-416.

SUPERMAN (2nd series)			
Jan, 1987 - Present (.75-$1.00, bi-weekly #19-?)			
DC Comics			
1-Byrne c/a begins; intro Metallo	.35	1.00	2.00
2-8,10: 7-Origin/1st app. Rampage		.60	1.20
9-Joker-c	.50	1.50	3.00
11-40: 11-1st app. Mr. Mxyzptlk. 12-Lori Lemaris app.			
Toyman. 13,14-Millennium x-over. 20-Doom Patrol app.; Supergirl			
revived in cameo. 28-Steranko-c(p). 31-Mr. Mxyzptlk app. 37-Kirby-			
c(p); Newsboy Legion app.	.40		.80
Annual 1 (8/87)-No Byrne-a	.25	.75	1.50
Annual 2 ('88)-Byrne-a; Newsboy Legion	.25	.75	1.50
SUPERMAN & THE GREAT CLEVELAND FIRE (Giveaway)			
1948 (4 pages, no cover)(Hospital Fund)			
National Periodical Publications			
nn-In full color	43.00	130.00	300.00
SUPERMAN FAMILY, THE (Formerly Superman's Pal Jimmy Olsen)			
No. 164, Apr-May, 1974 - No. 222, Sept, 1982			
National Periodical Publications/DC Comics			
164-Jimmy Olsen, Supergirl, Lois Lane begin	.60	1.20	
165-176 (100-68 pgs.)	.45	.90	
177-181 (52 pgs.)	.40	.80	
182-$1.00 issues begin; Marshall Rogers-a; Krypto begins, ends #192			
	.25	.75	1.50
183-193,195-222: 183-Nightwing-Flamebird begins, ends #194. 189-			
Brainiac 5, Mon-el app. 191-Superboy begins, ends #198. 200-			
Book length story. 211-Earth II Batman & Catwoman marry			
	.40		.80
194-Rogers-a	.25	.75	1.50

NOTE: *Adams* c-182-185. *Anderson* a-186i. *Buckler* c-190p, 191p, 209p, 210p, 215p, 217p, 220p. *Jones* a-191-193. *Gil Kane* c-221p, 222p. *Mortimer* a-191-93p, 199p, 201-22p. *Orlando* a-186i, 187i. *Rogers* a-182, 194. *Staton* a-191-194i, 196p. *Tuska* a-203p, 207-209p.

SUPERMAN IV MOVIE SPECIAL			
1987 ($2.00, color, one-shot)			
DC Comics			
1-Movie adaptation; Heck-a	.35	1.00	2.00

	Good	Fine	N-Mint
SUPERMAN (Miniature)			
1942; 1955 - 1956 (3 issues; no #'s; 32 pgs.)			
The pages are numbered in the 1st issue: 1-32; 2nd: 1A-32A, and			
3rd: 1B-32B			
National Periodical Publications			
No date-Py-Co-Pay Tooth Powder giveaway (8 pgs.; circa 1942)			
	45.00	135.00	315.00
1-The Superman Time Capsule (Kellogg's Sugar Smacks)(1955)			
	22.00	65.00	154.00
1A-Duel in Space	17.00	51.00	120.00
1B-The Super Show of Metropolis (also #1-32, no B)			
	17.00	51.00	120.00

NOTE: *Numbering variations exist. Each title could have any combination-No. 1, 1A, or 1B.*

SUPERMAN RECORD COMIC			
1966 (Golden Records)			
National Periodical Publications			
(with record)-Record reads origin of Superman from comic; came			
with iron-on patch, decoder, membership card & button; comic			
r-/Superman 125, 146	4.65	14.00	32.00
comic only	2.00	6.00	14.00
SUPERMAN'S BUDDY (Costume Comic)			
1954 (4 pgs.) (One Shot) (Came in box w/costume; slick-paper/c)			
National Periodical Publications			
1-(Rare)-w/box & costume	65.00	195.00	455.00
Comic only	35.00	105.00	245.00
SUPERMAN'S CHRISTMAS ADVENTURE			
1940, 1944 (16 pgs.) (Giveaway)			
Distr. by Nehi drinks, Bailey Store, Ivey-Keith Co., Kennedy's Boys			
Shop, Macy's Store, Boston Store			
National Periodical Publications			
1(1940)-by Burnley	75.00	225.00	525.00
nn(1944)	60.00	180.00	420.00
SUPERMAN SCRAPBOOK (Has blank pages; contains no comics)			
SUPERMAN'S GIRLFRIEND LOIS LANE (See 80 Page Giant #3,14,			
Showcase #9,10 & Superman Family)			
SUPERMAN'S GIRLFRIEND LOIS LANE (Also see Lois Lane)			
Mar-Apr, 1958 - No. 136, Jan-Feb, 1974; No. 137, Sept-Oct, 1974			
National Periodical Publications			
1	57.00	171.00	400.00
2	22.00	65.00	155.00
3	16.50	50.00	115.00
4,5	13.50	40.00	95.00
6-10: 9-Pat Boone app.	8.50	25.50	60.00
11-20: 14-Supergirl x-over	5.00	15.00	35.00
21-29: 23-1st app. Lena Thorul, Lex Luthor's sister. 29-Aquaman,			
Batman, Green Arrow cameo; last 10 cent issue			
	2.85	8.50	20.00
30-32,34-49: 47-Legion app.	1.15	3.50	8.00
33(5/62)-Mon-el app.	1.70	5.00	12.00
50-Triplicate Girl, Phantom Girl & Shrinking Violet app.			
	1.30	4.00	9.00
51-55,57-67,69,70	.50	1.50	3.00
56-Saturn Girl app.	.85	2.50	5.00
68-(Giant G-26)	.85	2.50	5.00
71-76,78: 74-1st Bizarro Flash	.35	1.00	2.00
77-(Giant G-39)	.50	1.50	3.00
79-Adams-c begin, end No. 95,108	.35	1.00	2.00
80-85,87-94: 89-Batman x-over; all Adams-c	.35	1.00	2.00
86-(Giant G-51)-Adams-c	.50	1.00	3.00
95-(Giant G-63)-Wonder Woman x-over; Adams-c	.50	1.50	3.00
96-103,105-111: 105-Origin/1st app. The Rose & the Thorn.			
108-Adams-c	.35	1.00	2.00

	Good	Fine	N-Mint
104-(Giant G-75)	.50	1.50	3.00
112,114-123 (52 pgs.): 111-Morrow-a. 122-G.A.-r/Superman #30.			
123-G.A. Batman-r	.35	1.00	2.00
113-(Giant G-87)	.50	1.50	3.00
124-137: 130-Last Rose & the Thorn. 132-New Zatanna story. 136-			
Wonder Woman x-over	.35	1.00	2.00
Annual 1(Sum,'62)	5.00	15.00	35.00
Annual 2(Sum,'63)	2.85	8.50	20.00

NOTE: *Buckler a-117-121p. Curt Swan a-1-50(most).*

SUPERMAN'S PAL JIMMY OLSEN (Superman Family #164 on)
(See 80 Page Giant)
Sept-Oct, 1954 - No. 163, Feb-Mar, 1974
National Periodical Publications

	Good	Fine	N-Mint
1	87.00	260.00	610.00
2	36.00	108.00	250.00
3-Last pre-code issue	23.00	70.00	160.00
4,5	16.50	50.00	115.00
6-10	12.00	36.00	85.00
11-20	8.00	24.00	55.00
21-30: 29-1st app. Krypto in Jimmy Olsen	6.00	18.00	30.00
31-40: 31-Origin Elastic Lad. 33-One pg. biography of Jack Larson			
(TV Jimmy Olsen). 36-Intro Lucy Lane	2.65	8.00	18.00
41-47,49,50: 41-1st J.O. Robot	1.70	5.00	12.00
48-Intro/origin Superman Emergency Squad	1.70	5.00	12.00
51-56: 56-Last 10 cent issue	1.15	3.50	7.00
57-61,64-70: 57-Olsen marries Supergirl. 70-Element Lad app.			
	.70	2.00	4.00
62(7/62)-18th Legion app.; Mon-el, Elastic Lad app.			
	1.35	4.00	8.00
63(9/62)-Legion of Super-Villains app.	.85	2.50	5.00
71,74,75,78,80-84,86,89,90: 86-J.O. Robot becomes Congorilla			
	.50	1.50	3.00
72(10/63)-Legion app; Elastic Lad (Olsen) joins	.70	2.00	4.00
73-Ultra Boy app.	.70	2.00	4.00
76,85-Legion app.	.70	2.00	4.00
77-Olsen with Colossal Boy's powers & costume; origin Titano retold			
	.50	1.50	3.00
79(9/64)-Titled The Red-headed Beatle of 1000 B.C.			
	.50	1.50	3.00
87-Legion of Super-Villains app.	.70	2.00	4.00
88-Star Boy app.	.50	1.50	3.00
91-94,96-98,101-103,105-110: 106-Legion app. 110-Infinity-c			
	.35	1.00	2.00
95,104 (Giants G-25,G-38)	.50	1.50	3.00
99-Legion app; Olsen with powers/costumes of Lightning Lad, Sun			
Boy, & Star Boy	.50	1.50	3.00
100-Legion cameo app.	.50	1.50	3.00
111,112,114-121,123-130,132	.35	1.00	2.00
113,122,131 (Giants G-50,G-62,G-74)	.35	1.00	2.00
133-Newsboy Legion by Kirby begins	.50	1.50	3.00
134-140: 135-G.A. Guardian app. 136-Origin new Guardian. 140-			
(Giant G-86)	.35	1.00	2.00
141-148: 141-Newsboy Legion reprints by S&K begin (52 pg. issues			
begin). 142-148-Newsboy Legion-r	.35	1.00	2.00
149,150-G.A. Plastic Man reprint in both; last 52 pg. issue. 150-			
Newsboy Legion app.	.35	1.00	2.00
151-163	.35	1.00	2.00

NOTE: *Issues #141-148 contain Simon & Kirby Newsboy Legion reprints from Star Spangled #7, 8, 9, 10, 11, 12, 13, 14 in that order. Adams c-109-112, 115, 117, 118, 120, 121, 132, 134-136, 147, 148. Kirby a-133-139p, 141-148p; c-133, 139, 145p. Kirby/Adams c-137, 138, 141-144, 146.*

SUPERMAN SPECTACULAR (Also see DC Special Series #5)
1982 (Magazine size)(Square binding)
DC Comics

	Good	Fne	N-Mint
1	.35	1.00	2.00

SUPERMAN: THE EARTH STEALERS
1988 (one-shot, $2.95, 52pgs, prestige format)
DC Comics

1-Byrne scripts; painted-c	.60	1.75	3.50
1-2nd printing	.50	1.50	2.95

SUPERMAN: THE SECRET YEARS
Feb, 1985 - No. 4, May, 1985 (Mini-series)
DC Comics

1-Miller-c on all	.25	.75	1.50
2-4		.50	1.00

SUPERMAN 3-D (See Three-Dimension Adventures)

SUPERMAN-TIM (Becomes Tim)
Aug, 1942 - May, 1950 (½-size) (B&W Giveaway)
Superman-Tim Stores/National Periodical Publications

8/42, 2/43, 3/43, 6/43, 8/43, 9/43, 3/44, 2/45, 11/49 issues-Two pg.			
Superman illos	8.50	25.50	60.00
10/43, 12/43, 2/44, 4/44-1/45, 3/45, 4/45, 4/46, 6/46, 8/46 issues-no			
Superman	6.50	19.50	45.00
9/46-1st app. stamp album issue (worth more if complete with Superman			
stamps)	7.00	21.00	50.00
10/46-1st Superman story	14.00	42.00	100.00
11/46, 12/46, 1/47, 2/47, 3/47, 4/47, 5/47-8/47 issues-Superman story			
	14.00	42.00	100.00
9/47-Stamp album issue & Superman story	16.00	48.00	110.00
10/47, 11/47, 12/47-Superman stories	14.00	42.00	100.00
1/48, 2/48, 6/48, 8/48, 10/48, 11/48, 2/49-4/49, 12/49-5/50 issues-no			
Superman	5.50	16.50	40.00
9/48-Stamp album issue	6.50	19.50	45.00

NOTE: *16 pgs. through 9/47; 8 pgs. 10/47 on? The stamp album issues (3) may contain Superman stamps that were made to glue in these books. Books with the stamps included would be worth more, and the value would depend upon completeness of the album. There is no stamp album in the 9/49 issue.*

SUPERMAN VS. THE AMAZING SPIDER-MAN (Also see Marvel Treasury Edition No. 28)
April, 1976 (100 pgs.) ($2.00) (Over-sized)
National Periodical Publications/Marvel Comics Group

1	.50	1.50	3.00
1-2nd printing; 5000 numbered copies signed by Stan Lee & Car-			
mine Infantino on front cover & sold through mail			
	.85	2.50	5.00

SUPERMAN WORKBOOK
1945 (One Shot) (68 pgs; reprints) (B&W)
National Periodical Publ./Juvenile Group Foundation

c-r/Superman #14	65.00	195.00	455.00

SUPERMOUSE (...the Big Cheese; see Coo Coo Comics)
12/48 - No. 34, 9/55; No. 45, 4/56, Fall, 1958
Standard Comics/Pines No. 35 on (Literary Ent.)

1-Frazetta text illos (3)	16.00	48.00	110.00
2-Frazetta text illos	8.50	25.50	60.00
3,5,6-Text illos by Frazetta in all	6.50	19.50	45.00
4-Two pg. text illos by Frazetta	7.00	21.00	50.00
7-10	2.30	7.00	16.00
11-20: 13-Racist humor (Indians)	1.70	5.00	12.00
21-45	1.15	3.50	8.00
1-Summer Holiday issue (Summer,'56-Pines)-100 pgs.			
	5.00	15.00	35.00
2-Giant Summer issue (Summer,'58-Pines)-100 pgs.			
	4.00	12.00	28.00

SUPER-MYSTERY COMICS
July, 1940 - V8#6, July, 1949

Superman's Pal Jimmy Olsen #12, © DC

Superman: The Secret Years #1, © DC

Supermouse #1, © STD

Super-Mystery Comics V4#5, © ACE

Supersnipe Comics V2#1, © S & S

Super-Villain Team-Up #2, © MEG

SUPER-MYSTERY COMICS (continued)
Ace Magazines (Periodical House)

	Good	Fine	N-Mint
V1#1-Magno, the Magnetic Man & Vulcan begin	71.00	215.00	500.00
2	34.00	100.00	240.00
3-The Black Spider begins	27.00	81.00	190.00
4-Origin Davy	24.00	73.00	170.00
5-Intro. The Clown; begin series	24.00	73.00	170.00
6(2/41)	21.00	62.00	145.00
V2#1(4/41)-Origin Buckskin	21.00	62.00	145.00
2-6(2/42)	18.50	56.00	130.00
V3#1(4/42),2: 1-Vulcan & Black Ace begin	16.00	48.00	115.00
3-Intro. The Lancer; Dr. Nemesis & The Sword begin; Kurtzman c/a(2) (Mr. Risk & Paul Revere Jr.)	23.00	70.00	160.00
4-Kurtzman-a	18.50	56.00	130.00
5-Kurtzman-a(2); L.B. Cole-a; Mr. Risk app.	19.00	57.00	135.00
6(10/43)-Mr. Risk app.; Kurtzman's Paul Revere Jr.; L.B. Cole-a	19.00	57.00	135.00
V4#1(1/44)-L.B. Cole-a	14.00	42.00	100.00
2-6(4/45): 2,5,6-Mr. Risk app.	11.50	34.00	80.00
V5#1(7/45)-6	9.30	28.00	65.00
V6#1-6: 3-Torture story. 4-Last Magno. Mr. Risk app. in #2,4-6	8.00	24.00	56.00
V7#1-6, V8#1-4,6	8.00	24.00	56.00
V8#5-Meskin, Tuska, Sid Greene-a	9.30	28.00	65.00

NOTE: *Sid Greene a-V7#4. Mooney c-V1#5, 6, V2#1-6. Palais c/a-V5#3,4. Bondage c-V2#5, 6, V3#2, 5.*

SUPERNATURAL THRILLERS
12/72 - No. 6, 11/73; No. 7, 7/74 - No. 15, 10/75
Marvel Comics Group

	Good	Fine	N-Mint
1-It!-Sturgeon adaptation, 2-The Invisible Man, 3-The Valley of the Worm		.40	.80
4-15: 4-Dr. Jekyll & Mr. Hyde. 5-The Living Mummy. 6-The Headless Horseman. 7-The Living Mummy begins		.25	.50

NOTE: *Brunner c-11. Buckler a-5p. Ditko a-8r, 9r. G. Kane a-3p; c-3, 9p, 15p. Mayerik a-2p, 7, 8, 9p, 10p, 11. McWilliams a-14i. Mortimer a-4. Steranko c-1, 2. Sutton a-15. Tuska a-6p. Robert E. Howard story-#3.*

SUPER POWERS
7/84 - No. 5, 11/84; 9/85 - No. 6, 2/86; 9/86 - No. 4, 12/86
DC Comics

	Fine	N-Mint
1 (1st series)-Kirby-c	.60	1.20
2-5	.45	.90
1 ('85, 2nd series)-Kirby c/a in all; Capt. Marvel & Firestorm join	.50	1.00
2-6	.45	.90
1-4 ('86, 3rd series): 1-Cyborg joins; 1st app. Samurai from Super Friends TV show	.40	.80

SUPER PUP (Formerly Spotty The Pup?) (See Space Comics)
No. 4, Mar-Apr, 1954 - No. 5, 1954
Avon Periodicals

	Good	Fine	N-Mint
4,5	1.50	4.50	10.00

SUPER RABBIT (See All Surprise, Animated Movie Tunes, Comedy Comics, Comic Capers, Ideal Comics, It's A Duck's Life, Movie Tunes & Wisco)
Fall, 1944 - No. 14, Nov, 1948
Timely Comics (CmPI)

	Good	Fine	N-Mint
1-Hitler-c	32.00	95.00	225.00
2	16.00	48.00	115.00
3-5	9.00	27.00	62.00
6-Origin	7.00	21.00	50.00
7-10; 9-Infinity-c	5.00	15.00	35.00
11-Kurtzman's "Hey Look"	5.70	17.00	40.00
12-14	4.00	12.00	28.00

	Good	Fine	N-Mint
I.W. Reprint #1,2('58),7,10('63)	.70	2.00	4.00

SUPER RICHIE (Superichie #5 on)
Sept, 1975 - No. 4, Mar, 1976 (All 52 pg. Giants)
Harvey Publications

	Good	Fine	N-Mint
1	.35	1.00	2.00
2-4		.50	1.00

SUPERSNIPE COMICS (Formerly Army & Navy #1-5)
V1#6, Oct, 1942 - V5#1, Aug-Sept, 1949 (See Shadow Comics V2/3)
Street & Smith Publications

	Good	Fine	N-Mint
V1#6-Rex King Man of Adventure(costumed hero) by Jack Binder begins; Supersnipe by George Marcoux continues from Army & Navy #5; Bill Ward-a	34.00	100.00	235.00
7,8,10-12: 11-Little Nemo app.	19.00	56.00	130.00
9-Doc Savage x-over in Supersnipe; Hitler-c	22.00	65.00	155.00
V2#1-12: 1-Huck Finn by Clare Dwiggins begins, ends V3#5	13.00	40.00	90.00
V3#1-12: 8-Bobby Crusoe by Dwiggins begins, ends V3#12	10.00	30.00	70.00
V4#1-12, V5#1: V4#10-Xmas-c	7.00	21.00	50.00

NOTE: *Doc Savage in some issues.*

SUPERSPOOK (Formerly Frisky Animals on Parade)
No. 4, June, 1958
Ajax/Farrell Publications

	Good	Fine	N-Mint
4	1.70	5.00	12.00

SUPER SPY (See Wham Comics)
Oct, 1940 - No. 2, Nov, 1940 (Reprints)
Centaur Publications

	Good	Fine	N-Mint
1-Origin The Sparkler	70.00	210.00	490.00
2-The Inner Circle, Dean Denton, Tim Blain, The Drew Ghost, The Night Hawk by Gustavson, & S.S. Swanson by Glanz app.	50.00	150.00	350.00

SUPER STAR HOLIDAY SPECIAL (See DC Special Series #21)

SUPER-TEAM FAMILY
10-11/75 - No. 15, 3-4/78 (#1-4: 68 pgs.; #5 on: 52 pgs.)
National Periodical Publications/DC Comics

	Fine	N-Mint
1-Reprints; Adams, Kane/Wood	.40	.80
2-7: 4-7-Reprints	.25	.50
8-15-New stories; Chall. of the Unknown in #8-10	.25	.50

NOTE: *Adams a-1r-3r. Brunner c-3. Buckler c-8p. Estrada a-2. Tuska a-7r. Wood a-1i(r), 3.*

SUPER TV HEROES (See Hanna-Barbera ...)

SUPER-VILLAIN CLASSICS
May, 1983 (One Shot)
Marvel Comics Group

	Fine	N-Mint
1-"Galactus the Origin"	.50	1.00

SUPER-VILLAIN TEAM-UP (Also see Fantastic Four #6)
8/75 - No. 14, 10/77; No. 15, 11/78; No. 16, 5/79; No. 17, 6/80
Marvel Comics Group

	Good	Fine	N-Mint
1-Sub-Mariner app.	.35	1.00	2.00
2-17: 1st Shroud. 7-Origin The Shroud	.60	1.20	
Giant-Size 1(3/75, 68 pgs.)-Craig inks-r	.25	.75	1.50
Giant-Size 2(6/75, 68 pgs.)-Dr. Doom, Sub-Mariner app.		.50	1.00

NOTE: *Buckler c-4p, 5p, 7p. Buscema c-1. Byrne/Austin c-14. Ditko a-Gnt-Size 2r. Evans a-1p, 3p. Everett a-1p. Giffen a-8p, 13p; c-13p. Kane c-2p, 9p. Mooney a-4i. Sekowsky a-Gnt-size 2p. Starlin c-6. Tuska a-1p, 15p(r). Wood a-15p(r).*

SUPER WESTERN COMICS (Also see Buffalo Bill)
Aug, 1950 - No. 4, Mar, 1951
Youthful Magazines

SUPER WESTERN COMICS (continued)

	Good	Fine	N-Mint
1-Buffalo Bill begins; Calamity Jane app; Powell-c/a			
	4.00	12.00	28.00
2-4	2.30	7.00	16.00

SUPER WESTERN FUNNIES (See Super Funnies)

SUPERWORLD COMICS
April, 1940 - No. 3, Aug, 1940 (All have 68 pgs.)
Hugo Gernsback (Komos Publ.)

	Good	Fine	N-Mint
1-Origin Hip Knox, Super Hypnotist; Mitey Powers & Buzz Allen, the Invisible Avenger, Little Nemo begin; cover by Frank R. Paul			
	130.00	390.00	910.00
2-Marvo 1,2 Go+, the Super Boy of the Year 2680			
	91.00	275.00	640.00
3	71.00	215.00	500.00

SURE-FIRE COMICS (Lightning Comics #4 on)
June, 1940 - No. 4, Oct, 1940 (Two No. 3's)
Ace Magazines

	Good	Fine	N-Mint
V1#1-Origin Flash Lightning; X-The Phantom Fed, Ace McCoy, Buck Steele, Marvo the Magician, The Raven, Whiz Wilson (Time Traveler) begin	61.00	182.00	425.00
2	37.00	110.00	260.00
3(9/40)	30.00	90.00	210.00
3(#4)(10/40)-nn on-c, #3 on inside	30.00	90.00	210.00

SURF 'N' WHEELS
Nov, 1969 - No. 6, Sept, 1970
Charlton Comics

	Good	Fine	N-Mint
1	.35	1.00	2.00
2-6	.25	.75	1.50

SURGE
July, 1984 - No. 4, Jan, 1985 (mini-series) ($1.50; Baxter paper)
Eclipse Comics

	Good	Fine	N-Mint
1-4-Ties into DNAgents series	.25	.75	1.50

SURPRISE ADVENTURES (Formerly Tormented)
No. 3, Mar, 1955 - No. 5, July, 1955
Sterling Comic Group

	Good	Fine	N-Mint
3-5: 3,5-Sekowsky-a	1.70	5.00	12.00

SUSIE Q. SMITH (See Four Color #323,377,453,553)

SUSPENSE (Radio/TV; Real Life Tales of . . . #1-4) (Amazing
Detective Cases #3 on? . . .)
Dec, 1949 - No. 29, Apr, 1953 (#1-8,17-23: 52 pgs.)
Marvel/Atlas Comics (CnPC No. 1-10/BFP No. 11-29)

	Good	Fine	N-Mint
1-Powell-a; Peter Lorre, Sidney Greenstreet photo-c from Hammett's 'The Maltese Falcon'	18.00	54.00	125.00
2-Crime stories; photo-c	9.30	28.00	65.00
3-Change to horror	9.30	28.00	65.00
4,7-10	6.00	18.00	42.00
5-Krigstein, Tuska, Everett-a	7.00	21.00	50.00
6-Tuska, Everett, Morisi-a	6.50	19.50	45.00
11-17,19,20: 14-Hypo-c; A-Bomb panels	5.00	15.00	35.00
18,22-Krigstein-a	5.70	17.00	40.00
21,23,26-29	4.00	12.00	28.00
24-Tuska-a	4.50	14.00	32.00
25-Electric chair c/a	7.00	21.00	50.00

NOTE: *Ayers a-20. Briefer a-5, 7, 27. Colan a-8(2), 9. Everett a-5, 6(2), 19, 23, 28; c-21-23, 26. Fuje a-29. Heath a-5, 6, 8, 10, 12, 14; c-14, 19, 24. Maneely a-24, 28, 29; c-10, 15. Mooney a-24, 28. Morisi a-6. Palais a-10. Rico a-7-9. Robinson a-29. Romita a-20(2), 25. Sekowsky a-11, 13, 14. Sinnott a-23, 25. Tuska a-5, 6, 12; c-12. Whitney a-15, 16, 22. Ed Win a-27.*

SUSPENSE COMICS
Dec, 1943 - No. 12, Dec?, 1946
Continental Magazines

	Good	Fine	N-Mint
1-The Grey Mask begins; bondage/torture-c; L. B. Cole-a, 7pgs.			

	Good	Fine	N-Mint
	38.00	115.00	270.00
2-Intro. The Mask; Rico, Giunta, L. B. Cole-a, 7pgs.			
	23.00	70.00	160.00
3-L.B. Cole-a; Schomburg-c	23.00	70.00	160.00
4-6: 5-Schomburg-c	21.00	62.00	145.00
7,9,10	19.00	58.00	135.00
8-Classic L. B. Cole spider-c	43.00	130.00	300.00
11-Classic Devil-c	30.00	90.00	210.00
12-r-#7-c	19.00	58.00	135.00

NOTE: *L. B. Cole c-6-12. Larsen a-11. Palais a-10, 11. Bondage c-1, 3, 4.*

SUSPENSE DETECTIVE
June, 1952 - No. 5, Mar, 1953
Fawcett Publications

	Good	Fine	N-Mint
1-Evans-a, 11 pgs; Baily c/a	12.00	36.00	84.00
2-Evans-a, 10 pgs.	7.00	21.00	50.00
3,5	5.70	17.00	40.00
4-Bondage-c	6.50	19.50	45.00

NOTE: *Baily a-4, 5. Sekowsky a-2, 4, 5; c-5.*

SUSPENSE STORIES (See Strange Suspense Stories)

SUZIE COMICS (Formerly Laugh Comix; see Pep Comics & Top-
Notch Comics #28)
No. 49, Spring, 1945 - No. 100, Aug, 1954
Close-Up No. 49,50/MLJ Mag./Archie No. 51 on

	Good	Fine	N-Mint
49-Ginger begins	12.00	36.00	84.00
50-55: 54-Transvestism story	9.00	27.00	62.00
56-Katy Keene begins by Woggon	8.00	24.00	56.00
57-65	5.70	17.00	40.00
66-80	5.00	15.00	35.00
81-87,89-99	4.30	13.00	30.00
88-Used in POP, pg. 76,77; Bill Woggon draws himself in story			
	5.00	15.00	35.00
100-Last Katy Keene	4.30	13.00	30.00

NOTE: *Katy Keene in 53-82, 85-100.*

SWAMP FOX, THE (See 4-Color #1179 & Walt Disney Presents #2)

SWAMP FOX, THE
1960 (14 pgs, small size) (Canada Dry Premiums)
Walt Disney Productions

	Good	Fine	N-Mint
Titles: (A)-Tory Masquerade, (B)-Rindau Rampage, (C)-Turnabout Tactics; each came in paper sleeve, books 1,2 & 3;			
Set with sleeves	3.50	10.50	24.00
Comic only	1.00	3.00	6.00

SWAMP THING (See Brave & the Bold, Challengers of the Unknown
#82, DC Comics Presents #8 & 85, DC Special Series #2, 14, 17, 20,
House of Secrets #92, Roots of the . . ., & The Saga of . . .)
Oct-Nov, 1972 - No. 24, Aug-Sept, 1976
National Periodical Publications/DC Comics

	Good	Fine	N-Mint
1-Wrightson-c/a begin	1.30	4.00	9.00
2	.85	2.50	5.00
3-Intro. Patchworkman	.70	2.00	4.00
4-6,8-10: 10-Last Wrightson issue	.50	1.50	3.00
7-Batman-c/story	.85	2.50	5.00
11-24-Redondo-a; 23-Swamp Thing reverts back to Dr. Holland			
	.50	1.00	

NOTE: *J. Jones a-9i. Kaluta a-9i. Redondo c-12-19, 21.*

SWAT MALONE
Sept, 1955
Swat Malone Enterprises

	Good	Fine	N-Mint
V1#1-Hy Fleishman-a	4.30	13.00	30.00

SWEENEY (Buz Sawyer's Pal, Roscoe . . .)
No. 4, 1949 - No. 5, 1949
Standard Comics

Sure-Fire Comics #4, © ACE

Suzie Comics #58, © AP

Swamp Thing #7, © DC

Sweethearts #76, © FAW

Swift Arrow #1 (2-3/54), © AJAX

Swords Of Texas #1, © Eclipse

	Good	Fine	N-Mint
SWEENEY (continued)			
4,5-Crane-a #5	3.70	11.00	26.00
SWEE'PEA (See 4-Color #219)			

SWEETHEART DIARY (Cynthia Doyle #66-on)
Wint, 1949; #2, Spr, 1950; #3, 6/50 - #5, 10/50; #6, 1951(nd); #7,
9/51 - #14, 1/53; #32, 10/55; #33, 4/56 - #65, 8/62 (#1-14: photo-c)
Fawcett Publications/Charlton Comics No. 33 on

1	5.70	17.00	40.00
2	3.15	9.50	22.00
3,4-Wood-a	8.00	24.00	56.00
5-10: 8-Bailey-a	2.35	7.00	16.00
11-14-Last Fawcett issue	1.30	4.00	9.00
32 (10/55; 1st Charlton issue)(Formerly Cowboy Love #31)			
	1.15	3.50	8.00
34-40	.85	2.50	6.00
41-60	.50	1.50	3.00
61-65	.25	.75	1.50

SWEETHEARTS (Formerly Captain Midnight)
#68, 10/48 - #121, 5/53; #122, 3/54; #23, 5/54 - #137, 12/73
Fawcett Publications/Charlton No. 122 on

68-Robert Mitchum photo-c	5.00	15.00	35.00
69-80: 72-Baker-a?	2.15	6.50	15.00
81-84,86-93,95-99	1.60	4.80	11.00
85,94,103,105,110,117-George Evans-a	2.65	8.00	18.00
100	2.00	6.00	14.00
101-Powell-a	1.70	5.00	12.00
102,104,106-109,112-116,118,121	1.15	3.50	8.00
111-1 pg. Ronald Reagan biography	3.50	10.50	24.00
119-Marilyn Monroe photo-c; also appears in story; part Wood-a			
	11.50	34.00	80.00
120-Atom Bomb story	4.00	12.00	28.00
122-(1st Charlton? 3/54)-Marijuana story	2.15	6.50	15.00
V2/23 (5/54)-28: Last precode issue (2/55)	.85	2.50	6.00
29-39,41,43-45,47-50	.60	1.80	4.00
40-Photo-c; Tommy Sands story	1.00	3.00	7.00
42-Ricky Nelson photo-c/story	2.00	6.00	14.00
46-Jimmy Rodgers photo-c/story	1.00	3.00	7.00
51-60	.70	2.00	5.00
61-80	.50	1.50	3.00
81-100	.25	.75	1.50
101-110		.60	1.20
111-137		.25	.50

NOTE: *Photo c-68-121.*

SWEETHEART SCANDALS (See Fox Giants)

SWEETIE PIE (See 4-Color #1185,1241)

SWEETIE PIE
Dec, 1955 - No. 15, Fall, 1957
Ajax-Farrell/Pines (Literary Ent.)

1-By Nadine Seltzer	2.65	8.00	18.00
2 (5/56; last Ajax?)	1.50	4.50	10.00
3-15 (#3-10, exist?)	1.00	3.00	7.00

SWEET LOVE
Sept, 1949 - No. 5, May, 1950
Home Comics (Harvey)

1-Photo-c	2.00	6.00	14.00
2-Photo-c	1.50	4.50	10.00
3,4: 3-Powell-a; 4-Photo-c	1.35	4.00	9.00
5-Kamen, Powell-a; photo-c	2.65	8.00	18.00

SWEET ROMANCE
October, 1968
Charlton Comics

1	.25	.75	1.50

SWEET SIXTEEN
Aug-Sept, 1946 - No. 13, Jan, 1948
Parents' Magazine Institute

	Good	Fine	N-Mint
1-Van Johnson's life story; Dorothy Dare, Queen of Hollywood Stunt			
Artists begins in all issues); part photo-c	5.70	17.00	40.00
2-Jane Powell, Roddy McDowall "Holiday in Mexico" photo-c			
	3.70	11.00	26.00
3-6,8-11: 6-Dick Haymes story	2.65	8.00	18.00
7-Ronald Reagan's life story	10.00	30.00	70.00
12-Bob Cummings, Vic Damone story	3.50	10.50	24.00
13-Robert Mitchum's life story	4.00	12.00	28.00

SWIFT ARROW (Also see Lone Rider & The Rider)
2-3/54 - No. 5, 10-11/54; 4/57 - No. 3, 9/57
Ajax/Farrell Publications

1(1954) (1st Series)	5.00	15.00	35.00
2	2.30	7.00	16.00
3-5: 5-Lone Rider story	2.00	6.00	14.00
1 (2nd Series) (Swift Arrow's Gunfighters #4)	2.00	6.00	14.00
2,3: 2-Lone Rider begins	1.70	5.00	12.00

SWIFT ARROW'S GUNFIGHTERS (Formerly Swift Arrow)
No. 4, Nov, 1957
Ajax/Farrell Publ. (Four Star Comic Corp.)

4	2.00	6.00	14.00

SWING WITH SCOOTER
6-7/66 - No. 35, 8-9/71; No. 36, 10-11/72
National Periodical Publications

1	1.15	3.50	8.00
2-10	.70	2.00	5.00
11-20	.50	1.50	3.00
21-32,35,36	.35	1.00	2.00
33-Interview with David Cassidy	.35	1.00	2.00
34-Interview with Ron Ely (Doc Savage)	.35	1.00	2.00

NOTE: *Orlando a-1-11; c-1-11, 13. #20, 33, 34: 68 pgs.; #35: 52 pgs.*

SWISS FAMILY ROBINSON (See 4-Color #1156, King Classics, & Movie Comics)

SWORD & THE DRAGON, THE (See 4-Color #1118)

SWORD & THE ROSE, THE (See 4-Color #505,682)

SWORD IN THE STONE, THE (See March of Comics #258 & Movie Comics)

SWORD OF LANCELOT (See Movie Comics)

SWORD OF SORCERY
Feb-Mar, 1973 - No. 5, Nov-Dec, 1973
National Periodical Publications

1-Leiber Fafhrd & The Grey Mouser; Adams/Bunkers inks; also #2;			
Kaluta-c	.35	1.00	2.00
2-Wrightson-c(i); Adams-a(i)	.25	.75	1.50
3-5: 5-Starlin-a; Conan cameo	.60	1.20	

NOTE: *Chaykin a-1p, 2-4; c-2p, 3-5. Kaluta a-3i. Simonson a-1i, 3p, 4, 5p; c-5. Starlin a-5p.*

SWORD OF THE ATOM
Sept, 1983 - No. 4, Dec, 1983 (Mini-series)
DC Comics

1-4: Kane c/a in all		.50	1.00
Special 1(7/84), 2(7/85): Kane c/a each		.65	1.30
Special 3(6/88, $1.50)		.65	1.30

SWORDS OF TEXAS
Oct, 1987 - No. 4, Jan, 1988 ($1.75, color, Baxter paper)
Eclipse Comics

1-4: Scout app.	.30	.90	1.80

SWORDS OF THE SWASHBUCKLERS (See Marvel Graphic Novel)
May, 1985 - No. 12, June,1987 ($1.50; Mature readers)
Epic Comics (Marvel)

SWORDS OF THE SWASHBUCKLERS (cont.) | Good | Fine | N-Mint
1-12-Butch Guice-c/a cont'd from Marvel Graphic Novel
.25 .80 1.60

SYPHONS
July, 1986 - No. 7, 1987 ($1.50, $1.75, color)
Now Comics

1-7	.25	.75	1.50

TAFFY COMICS
Mar-Apr, 1945 - No. 12, 1948
Rural Home/Orbit Publ.

1-L.B. Cole-c; origin of Wiggles The Wonderworm plus 7 chapter
 WWII funny animal adventures 6.50 19.50 45.00
2-L.B. Cole-c 4.00 12.00 28.00
3,4,6-12: 6-Perry Como c/story. 7-Duke Ellington, 2pgs.
  3.00 9.00 21.00
5-L.B. Cole-c; Van Johnson story 3.70 11.00 26.00

TAILGUNNER JO
Sept, 1988 - No. 6, Jan, 1989 ($1.25, color)
DC Comics

1-6 .60 1.25

TAILSPIN
November, 1944
Spotlight Publishers

nn-Firebird app.; L.B. Cole-c 7.00 21.00 50.00

TAILSPIN TOMMY STORY & PICTURE BOOK
1931? (nd) (Color stip reprints; 10½x10'')
McLoughlin Bros.

266-by Forrest 14.00 42.00 100.00

TAILSPIN TOMMY (Also see The Funnies)
1932 (100 pages)(hardcover)
Cupples & Leon Co.

(Rare)-B&W strip reprints from 1930 by Hal Forrest & Glenn Claffin
  17.00 51.00 120.00

TAILSPIN TOMMY (Also see Popular Comics)
1940; 1946
United Features Syndicate/Service Publ. Co.

Single Series 23('40) 17.00 51.00 120.00
Best Seller (nd, '46)-Service Publ. Co. 8.50 25.50 60.00

TALENT SHOWCASE (See New Talent Showcase)

TALES CALCULATED TO DRIVE YOU BATS
Nov, 1961 - No. 7, Nov, 1962; 1966
Archie Publications

1 4.00 12.00 28.00
2 2.00 6.00 14.00
3-6 1.30 4.00 9.00
7-Storyline change .85 2.60 6.00
1('66)-25 cents 1.00 3.00 7.00

TALES FROM THE CRYPT (Formerly The Crypt Of Terror; see Three
Dimensional . . .)
No. 20, Oct-Nov, 1950 - No. 46, Feb-Mar, 1955
E.C. Comics

20 55.00 165.00 385.00
21-Kurtzman-r/Haunt of Fear #15/1 45.00 135.00 315.00
22-Moon Girl costume at costume party, one panel
  36.00 107.00 250.00
23-25 27.00 81.00 190.00
26-30 21.00 64.00 150.00
31-Williamson-a(1st at E.C.); B&W and color illos. in POP; Kamen
 draws himself, Gaines & Feldstein; Ingels, Craig & Davis draw
 themselves in his story 24.00 73.00 170.00

	Good	Fine	N-Mint
32,35-39	17.00	51.00	120.00
33-Origin The Crypt Keeper	30.00	90.00	210.00
34-Used in POP, pg. 83; lingerie panels	17.00	51.00	120.00

40-Used in Senate hearings & in Hartford Cournat anti-comics
 editorials-1954 17.00 51.00 120.00
41-45: 45-2pgs. showing E.C. staff 16.00 48.00 110.00
46-Low distribution; pre-advertised cover for unpublished 4th horror
 title 'Crypt of Terror' used on this book 20.00 60.00 140.00
NOTE: Craig a-20, 22-24; c-20. Crandall a-38, 44. Davis a-24-46; c-29-46. Elder a-37, 38. Evans a-32-34, 36, 40, 41, 43, 46. Feldstein a-20-23; c-21-25, 28. Ingels a-in all. Kamen a-20, 22, 25, 27-31, 33-36, 39, 41-45. Krigstein a-40, 42, 45. Kurtzman a-21. Orlando a-27-30, 35, 37, 39, 41-45. Wood a-21, 24, 25; c-26, 27. Canadian reprints known; see Table of Contents.

TALES FROM THE CRYPT (Magazine)
No. 10, July, 1968 (35 cents)(B&W)
Eerie Publications

10-Contains Farrell reprints from 1950s .85 2.60 6.00

TALES FROM THE GREAT BOOK
Feb, 1955 - No. 4, Jan, 1956
Famous Funnies

1-Story of Samson 3.70 11.00 26.00
2-4-Lehti-a in all 2.00 6.00 14.00

TALES FROM THE TOMB
Oct, 1962 - No. 2, Dec, 1962
Dell Publishing Co.

1(02-810-210)(25 cent Giant)-All stories written by John Stanley
  2.30 7.00 16.00
2 1.50 4.50 10.00

TALES FROM THE TOMB (Magazine)
V1#6, July, 1969 - V7#1, Feb, 1975 (52 pgs.)
Eerie Publications

V1#6-8 1.15 3.50 8.00
V2#1-3,5,6: 6-Rulah-r .60 1.80 4.00
 4-LSD story-r/Weird V3#5 .85 2.50 6.00
V3#1-Rulah-r .70 2.00 5.00
 2-6('70),V4#1-5('72),V5#1-6('73),V6#1-6('74),V7#1('75)
  .50 1.50 3.00

TALES OF ASGARD
Oct, 1968 (68 pages); Feb, 1984 ($1.25, 52 pgs.)
Marvel Comics Group

1-Thor r-/from Journey into Mystery #97-106; new Kirby-c
  1.50 4.50 10.00
V2#1 (2/84)-Thor-r; Simonson-c .40 .80

TALES OF DEMON DICK & BUNKER BILL
1934 (78 pgs; 5x10½''; B&W)(hardcover)
Whitman Publishing Co.

793-by Dick Spencer 9.00 27.00 62.00

TALES OF EVIL
Feb, 1975 - No. 3, July, 1975
Atlas/Seaboard Publ.

1 .30 .60
2-Intro. The Bog Beast .25 .50
3-Origin The Man-Monster .25 .50
NOTE: Lieber c-1. Sekowsky a-1. Sutton a-2. Thorne c-2.

TALES OF GHOST CASTLE
May-June, 1975 - No. 3, Sept-Oct, 1975
National Periodical Publications

1-3: 1,3-Redondo-a. 2-Nino-a .25 .50

TALES OF G.I. JOE
Jan, 1988 - No. 14, 1989 (Color)
Marvel Comics

Tales From The Crypt #33, © WMG

Tales From The Great Book #4, © FF

Tales Of Asgard #1 (10/68), © MEG

Tales Of Suspense #63, © MEG
Tales Of Terror #1 (1952), © TOBY
Tales Of The Green Beret #1, © Chicago Tribune

	Good	Fine	N-Mint
TALES OF G.I. JOE (continued)			
1 ($2.25)	.40	1.15	2.30
2-14 ($1.50)(#1-4-r/G.I. Joe #1-4)	.25	.75	1.50

TALES OF HORROR
June, 1952 - No. 13, Oct, 1954
Toby Press/Minoan Publ. Corp.

1	10.00	30.00	70.00
2-Torture scenes	7.00	21.00	50.00
3-8,13	5.00	15.00	35.00
9-11-Reprints Purple Claw #1-3	5.50	16.50	38.00
12-Myron Fass c/a; torture scenes	5.70	17.00	40.00

NOTE: *Andru a-5. Bailey a-5. Myron Fass a-2, 3, 12; c-1-3, 12. Hollingsworth a-2. Sparling a-6, 9; c-9.*

TALES OF JUSTICE
No. 53, May, 1955 - No. 67, Aug, 1957
Atlas Comics(MjMC No. 53-66/Male No. 67)

53	5.00	15.00	35.00
54-57	3.00	9.00	21.00
58,59-Krigstein-a	3.70	11.00	26.00
60-63,65	2.00	6.00	14.00
64,67-Crandall-a	3.00	9.00	21.00
66-Torres, Orlando-a	3.00	9.00	21.00

NOTE: *Everett a-53, 60. Orlando a-65, 66. Powell a-54. Severin c-58, 60, 65.*

TALES OF SUSPENSE (Captain America #100 on)
Jan, 1959 - No. 99, March, 1968
Atlas (WPI No. 1,2/Male No. 3-12/VPI No. 13-18)/Marvel No. 19 on

1-Williamson-a, 5 pgs.	47.00	140.00	325.00
2,3	20.00	60.00	140.00
4-Williamson-a, 4 pgs; Kirby/Everett c/a	20.00	60.00	140.00
5-10	12.00	36.00	85.00
11,13-20: 14-Intro. Colossus. 16-Intro Metallo (Pre-Iron Man prototype)	8.50	25.50	60.00
12-Crandall-a	9.30	28.00	65.00
21-25: 25-Last 10 cent issue	5.70	17.00	40.00
26-38: 32-Sazzik The Sorcerer app. (Dr. Strange proto-type)	4.30	13.00	30.00
39 (3/63)-Origin & 1st app. Iron Man; 1st Iron Man story-Kirby layouts	87.00	350.00	875.00
40-Iron Man in new armor	57.00	171.00	400.00
41	32.00	95.00	225.00
42-45: 45-Intro. & 1st app. Happy & Pepper	13.00	40.00	90.00
46,47	7.00	21.00	50.00
48-New Iron Man armor	8.50	25.50	60.00
49-51: 49-X-Men x-over. 50-1st app. Mandarin	4.30	13.00	30.00
52-1st app. The Black Widow	6.50	19.50	45.00
53-Origin The Watcher (5/64); 2nd app.); Black Widow app.	4.50	14.00	32.00
54-56	2.85	8.50	20.00
57-1st app./Origin Hawkeye (9/64)	7.00	21.00	50.00
58-Captain America battles Iron Man (10/64)-Classic-c; 2nd Kraven app.	8.50	25.50	60.00
59-Iron Man plus Captain America double feature begins (11/64); intro Jarvis, Avenger's butler; Classic-c	5.70	17.00	40.00
60,61,64	2.85	8.50	20.00
62-Origin Mandarin (2/65)	2.85	8.50	20.00
63-1st Silver Age origin Captain America(3/65)	5.70	17.00	40.00
65-1st Silver-Age Red Skull (6/65)	4.30	13.00	30.00
66-Origin Red Skull	4.30	13.00	30.00
67-94,96-98: 69-1st app. Titanium Man. 75-Intro/1st app. Agent 13 later named Sharon Carter. 76-Intro Batroc & Sharon Carter, Agent 13 of Shield. 79-Intro Cosmic Cube. 94-Intro Modok. 95-Capt. America's i.d. revealed	1.70	5.00	12.00
99-Becomes Captain America with #100	2.85	8.50	20.00

NOTE: *Colan a-39, 73-99p; c(p)-73, 75, 77, 79, 81, 83, 85-87, 89, 91, 93, 95, 97, 99. Craig a-99i. Crandall a-12. Davis a-38. Ditko/Kirby art in most issues #1-15, 17-49. Everett*

a-8. *Forte a-5, 9. Heath a-10. Gil Kane a-88p, 89-91; c-88, 89-91p. Kirby a(p)-40, 41, 43, 59-75, 77-86, 92-99; layouts-69-75, 77; c(p)-29-56, 58-72, 74, 76, 78, 80, 82, 84, 86, 92, 94, 96, 98. Leiber/Fox a-42, 43, 45, 51. Reinman a-26, 44i, 49i, 52i, 53i. Tuska a-58, 70-74. Wood c/a-71i.*

TALES OF SWORD & SORCERY (See Dagar)

TALES OF TERROR
1952 (no month)
Toby Press Publications

	Good	Fine	N-Mint
1-Fawcette-c; Ravielli-a	5.50	16.50	38.00

NOTE: *This title was cancelled due to similarity to the E.C. title.*

TALES OF TERROR (See Movie Classics)

TALES OF TERROR (Magazine)
Summer, 1964
Eerie Publications

1	1.70	5.00	12.00

TALES OF TERROR
July, 1985 - No. 13, July, 1987 ($2.00, Baxter paper, mature readers)
Eclipse Comics

1	.40	1.25	2.50
2-13: 3-Morrow-a. 7-Bissette, Bolton-a	.35	1.00	2.00

TALES OF TERROR ANNUAL
1951 - No. 3, 1953 (25 cents) (132 pgs.)
E.C. Comics

nn(1951)(Scarce)-Feldstein infinity-c	200.00	600.00	1400.00
2(1952)-Feldstein-c	100.00	300.00	700.00
3(1953)	72.00	215.00	500.00

No. 1 contains three horror and one science fiction comic which came out in 1950. No. 2 contains a horror, crime, and science fiction book which generally had cover dates in 1951, and No. 3 had horror, crime, and shock books that generally appeared in 1952. All E.C. annuals contain four complete books that did not sell on the stands which were re-bound in the annual format, minus the covers, and sold from the E.C. office and on the stands in key cities. The contents of each annual may vary in the same year.

TALES OF TERROR ILLUSTRATED (See Terror Illustrated)

TALES OF TEXAS JOHN SLAUGHTER (See 4-Color #997)

TALES OF THE BEANWORLD
Feb, 1985 - Present ($1.50/$2.00, B&W)
Beanworld Press/Eclipse Comics

1	1.70	5.00	10.00
2	.70	2.00	4.00
3-14	.35	1.00	2.00

TALES OF THE GREEN BERET
Jan, 1967 - No. 5, Oct, 1969
Dell Publishing Co.

1	1.00	3.00	7.00
2-5: 5 reprints #1	.75	2.25	5.00

NOTE: *Glanzman a 1-4, 5r.*

TALES OF THE GREEN LANTERN CORPS
May, 1981 - No. 3, July, 1981
DC Comics

1-Origin of G.L. & the Guardians; Staton-a(p)		.45	.90
2,3-Staton-a(p)		.30	.60
Annual 1 (1/85)-G. Kane c/a		.65	1.30

TALES OF THE INVISIBLE SCARLET O'NEIL (See Harvey Comics Hits #59)

TALES OF THE KILLERS (Magazine)
V1#10, Dec, 1970 - V1#11, Feb, 1971 (52pgs.)(B&W)
World Famous Periodicals

V1#10-One pg. Frazetta	1.50	4.50	10.00
11	.70	2.00	5.00

TALES OF THE LEGION (Formerly The Legion of Super-Heroes)
No. 314, Aug, 1984 - No. 354, Dec, 1987

385

TALES OF THE LEGION (continued)
DC Comics

	Good	Fine	N-Mint
314-320: 314-Origin The White Witch		.40	.80
321-354: r-/Legion of S.H. (Baxter series)		.40	.80
Annual 4 ('86), 5 (10/87)		.60	1.20

TALES OF THE MARINES (Formerly Devil-Dog Dugan #1-3)
No. 4, Feb, 1957 (Marines At War #5 on)
Atlas Comics (OPI)

4-Powell-a	1.30	4.00	9.00

TALES OF THE MYSTERIOUS TRAVELER (See Mysterious. . .)
8/56 - No. 13, 6/59; V2#14, 10/85 - No. 15, 12/85
Charlton Comics

1-No Ditko-a	14.00	42.00	100.00
2-Ditko-a(1)	12.00	36.00	84.00
3-Ditko c/a(1)	11.00	32.00	75.00
4-6-Ditko c/a(3-4)	15.00	45.00	105.00
7-9-Ditko-a(1-2)	11.00	32.00	75.00
10,11-Ditko-c/a(3-4)	12.00	36.00	84.00
12,13	4.50	14.00	32.00
V2#14,15 (1985)-Ditko c/a		.40	.80

TALES OF THE NEW TEEN TITANS
June, 1982 - No. 4, Sept, 1982 (mini-series)
DC Comics

1-Origin Cyborg-book length story	.35	1.00	2.00
2-4: 2-Origin Raven. 3-Origin Changeling. 4-Origin Starfire			
	.25	.75	1.50

NOTE: *Perez c/a-1-4p.*

TALES OF THE PONY EXPRESS (See 4-Color #829, 942)

TALES OF THE SUN RUNNERS
V2#1, July, 1986 - V2#3, 1986? ($1.50, color)
Sirius Comics/Amazing Comics No. 3

V2#1	.25	.75	1.50
V2#2,3 ($1.95)	.35	1.00	2.00
Christmas Special 1(12/86)	.25	.75	1.50

TALES OF THE TEENAGE MUTANT NINJA TURTLES
May, 1987 - No. 7, Apr, 1989 (B&W, $1.50)(See Teenage Mutant. . .)
Mirage Studios

1	.70	2.00	4.00
2-7: Title merges w/Teenage Mutant Ninja. . .	.35	1.00	2.00

TALES OF THE TEEN TITANS (Formerly The New Teen Titans)
No. 41, April, 1984 - No. 91, July, 1988
DC Comics

41-43,45-59: 43-1st app. Terminator. 46-Aqualad & Aquagirl join. 50-Double size. 53-Intro Azreal. 56-Intro Jinx. 57-Neutron app. 59-r/DC Comics Presents #26		.40	.80
44-Dick Grayson becomes Nightwing & joins Titans; Jericho joins also; origin Terminator	.50	1.50	3.00
60-91: r/New Teen Titans Baxter series. 68-B. Smith-c. 69-Origin Kole. #83-91 are $1.00 cover	.40	.80	
Annual 3('84; $1.25)-Death of Terra	.60	1.20	
Annual 4(11/86, reprints), 5('87)	.60	1.20	

TALES OF THE TEXAS RANGERS (See Jace Pearson. . .)

TALES OF THE UNEXPECTED (The Unexpected #105 on)(See Super DC Giant)
Feb-Mar, 1956 - No. 104, Dec-Jan, 1967-68
National Periodical Publications

1	36.00	107.00	250.00
2	16.00	48.00	110.00
3-5	10.00	30.00	70.00
6-10	7.00	21.00	50.00
11,12,14	4.00	12.00	28.00

	Good	Fine	N-Mint
13,15-18,21-23: Kirby-a. 16-Character named 'Thor' with a magic hammer - not like later Thor	5.00	15.00	35.00
19,20,24-39: 24-Cameron-c/a	2.85	8.50	20.00
40-Space Ranger begins, ends #82	18.00	54.00	125.00
41	4.30	13.00	30.00
42-50	3.15	9.50	22.00
51-67: 67-Last 10 cent issue	2.30	7.00	16.00
68-80	1.35	4.00	8.00
81-100: 91-1st Automan (also in #94,97)	.85	2.50	5.00
101-104	.50	1.50	3.00

NOTE: *Adams a-104. Anderson a-50. Brown a-50-82(Space Ranger). Heath a-31, 49. Bob Kane a-24, 48. Kirby a-12, 24; c-22. Meskin a-15, 18, 26, 27, 35, 66. Moreira a-16, 39, 38, 44, 62; c-38.*

TALES OF THE WEST (See 3-D. . .)

TALES OF THE WIZARD OF OZ (See 4-Color #1308)

TALES OF THE ZOMBIE (Magazine)
Aug, 1973 - No. 10, Mar, 1975 (75 cents)(B&W)
Marvel Comics Group

V1#1-Reprint/Menace #5; origin	1.15	3.50	8.00
2,3: 2-Everett biography & memorial	.70	2.00	5.00
V2#1(#4)-Photos & text of James Bond movie "Live & Let Die"			
	.70	2.00	5.00
5-10: 8-Kaluta-a	.70	2.00	5.00
Annual 1(Summer,'75)(#11)-B&W; Everett, Buscema-a			
	.70	2.00	5.00

NOTE: *Alcala a-7-9. Boris c-1-4. Colan a-2r, 6. Heath a-5r. Reese a-2. Tuska a-2r.*

TALES OF THUNDER
March, 1985
Deluxe Comics

1-Dynamo, Iron Maiden & Menthor app.; Giffen-a			
	.35	1.00	2.00

TALES OF VOODOO (Magazine)
V1#11, Nov, 1968 - V7#6, Nov, 1974
Eerie Publications

V1#11	1.30	4.00	9.00
V2#1(3/69)-V2#4(9/69)	.70	2.00	5.00
V3#1-6('70): 4-'Claws of the Cat' redrawn from Climax #1			
	.70	2.00	5.00
V4#1-6('71), V5#1-6('72), V6#1-6('73), V7#1-6('74)			
	.70	2.00	5.00
Annual 1	.75	2.25	5.25

NOTE: *Bondage-c-V1No.10, V2No.4, V3No.4.*

TALES OF WELLS FARGO (See 4-Color #876, 968, 1023,1075, 1113, 1167, 1215, & Western Roundup under Dell Giants)

TALES TO ASTONISH (Becomes The Incredible Hulk #102 on)
Jan, 1959 - No. 101, March, 1968
Atlas (MAP) No. 1/ZPC No. 2-14/VPI No. 15-21/Marvel No. 22 on

1-Jack Davis-a	46.00	138.00	325.00
2-Ditko-a	20.00	60.00	140.00
3-5: 5-Williamson-a, 4 pgs.	16.00	48.00	110.00
6-10	11.50	34.00	80.00
11-20	7.00	21.00	50.00
21-26,28-34	4.30	13.00	30.00
27-1st Antman app. (1/62); last 10 cent issue	118.00	354.00	825.00
35-(9/62)-2nd Antman, 1st in costume; begin series	72.00	215.00	500.00
36	28.00	84.00	200.00
37-40	12.00	36.00	85.00
41-43	7.00	21.00	50.00
44-Origin & 1st app. The Wasp	9.30	28.00	65.00
45-48: 46-1st Crimson Dynamo	5.70	17.00	40.00
49-Antman becomes Giant Man	9.30	28.00	65.00

Tales Of The Teen Titans #44, © DC

Tales Of The Unexpected #1, © DC

Tales To Astonish #44, © MEG

Tales To Astonish #88, © MEG

Target Comics V3#3, © NOVP

Target Western Romances #106, © STAR

	Good	Fine	N-Mint

TALES TO ASTONISH (continued)
50-58: 50-Origin/1st app. Human Top. 52-Origin/1st app. Black Knight

	Good	Fine	N-Mint
	3.15	9.15	22.00
59-Giant Man vs. Hulk feature story	6.50	19.50	45.00
60-Giant Man/Hulk double feature begins	8.50	25.50	60.00

61-69: 62-1st app./origin The Leader; new Wasp costume. 65-New
Giant Man costume. 68-New Human Top. 69-Last Giant

Man	2.85	8.50	20.00
70-Sub-Mariner & Incred. Hulk begins	4.30	13.00	30.00

71-101: 90-1st app. The Abomination. 92,93-Silver Surfer app. 100-
Hulk battles Sub-Mariner 2.15 6.50 15.00
NOTE: **Berg** a-1. **Burgos** a-62-64p. **Buscema** a-85-87p. **Colan** a(p)-70-76, 78-82, 84, 85,
101; c(p)-71-76, 78, 80, 82, 84, 86, 88, 90. **Ditko** a-5-most issues-1-48, 50i; 60-67. **Everett**
a-78, 79i, 80-84, 85-90i, 94i, 95, 96; c(i)-79-81, 83, 86, 88. **Forte** a-6. **Kane** a-76, 88-91;
c-89, 91. **Kirby** a(p)-1-34(most), 35-40, 44, 49-51, 68-70, 82, 83; layouts-71-84; c(p)-1-48,
50-70, 72, 73, 75, 77, 78, 79, 81, 85, 90. **Leiber/Fox** a-47, 48, 50, 51. **Powell** a-65-69p, 73,
74. **Reinman** a-6, 36, 45, 46, 54i, 56-60i.

TALES TO ASTONISH (2nd Series)
Dec, 1979 - No. 14, Jan, 1981
Marvel Comics Group

V1#1-Reprints Sub-Mariner #1 by Buscema		.30	.60
2-14: Reprints Sub-Mariner #2-14		.25	.50

TALES TO HOLD YOU SPELLBOUND (See Spellbound)

TALKING KOMICS
1957 (20 pages) (Slick covers)
Belda Record & Publ. Co.

Each comic contained a record that followed the story - much like the
Golden Record sets. Known titles: Chirpy Cricket, Lonesome Octopus,
Sleepy Santa, Grumpy Shark, Flying Turtle, Happy Grasshopper
with records. . . .80 2.40 4.80

TALLY-HO COMICS
December, 1944
Swappers Quarterly (Baily Publ. Co.)

nn-Frazetta's 1st work as Giunta's assistant; Man in Black horror
story; violence; Giunta-c 20.00 60.00 140.00

TALOS OF THE WILDERNESS SEA
Aug, 1987 ($2.00, color, One Shot)
DC Comics

1	.35	1.00	2.00

TALULLAH (See Comic Books Series I)

TAMMY, TELL ME TRUE (See 4-Color #1233)

TAPPING THE VEIN (Clive Barker's . . .)
1989 - Present ($6.95, color, adults, squarebound, 68 pgs.)
Eclipse Comics

Book 1-4: 1-Russell-a, Bolton-a. 2-Bolton-a	1.15	3.50	7.00

TARANTULA (See Weird Suspense)

TARGET: AIRBOY
Mar, 1988 ($1.95, color)
Eclipse Comics

1	.35	1.00	2.00

TARGET COMICS (. . .Western Romances #106 on)
Feb, 1940 - V10#3 (#105), Aug, Sept, 1949
Funnies, Inc./Novelty Publications/Star Publications

V1#1-Origin & 1st app. Manowar, The White Streak by Burgos, &
Bulls-Eye Bill by Everett; City Editor (ends #5), High Grass
Twins by Jack Cole(ends #4), T-Men by Joe Simon(ends #9),
Rip Rory (ends #4), Fantastic Feature Films by Tarpe Mills
(ends #39, & Calling 2-R(ends #14) begin; Marijuana use story

	168.00	505.00	1175.00
2	79.00	235.00	550.00
3,4	58.00	174.00	405.00

	Good	Fine	N-Mint

5-Origin The White Streak in text; Space Hawk by Wolverton begins (See Blue Bolt & Circus) 131.00 395.00 920.00
6-The Chameleon by Everett begins; White Streak origin cont'd.
in text 74.00 220.00 515.00

7-Wolverton Spacehawk-c (Scarce)	171.00	515.00	1200.00
8,9,12	55.00	165.00	385.00
10-Intro. & 1st app. The Target; Kirby-c	74.00	220.00	515.00
11-Origin The Target & The Targeteers	74.00	220.00	515.00
V2#1-Target by Bob Wood; flag-c	39.00	118.00	275.00

2-10-part Treasure Island serial begins; Harold Delay-a; reprinted
in Catholic Comics V3#1-10 (See Key Comics #5)

	39.00	118.00	275.00
3-5: 4-Kit Carter, The Cadet begins	29.00	86.00	200.00
6-9:Red Seal with White Streak in 6-10	29.00	86.00	200.00
10-Classic-c	32.00	95.00	225.00

11,12: 12-10-part Last of the Mohicans serial begins; Delay-a
29.00 86.00 200.00
V3#1-10-Last Wolverton issue. 8-Flag-c; 6-part Gulliver Travels serial
begins; Delay-a 29.00 86.00 200.00

11,12	5.00	15.00	35.00
V4#1-5,7-12	3.00	9.00	21.00
6-Targetoons by Wolverton, 1 pg.	3.00	9.00	21.00
V5#1-8	2.30	7.00	16.00
V6#1-10, V7#1-12	2.00	6.00	14.00
V8#1,3-5,8,9,11,12	1.70	5.00	12.00
2,6,7-Krigstein-a	2.30	7.00	16.00
10-L.B. Cole-c	5.00	15.00	35.00
V9#1,3,6,8,10,12, V10#2-L.B. Cole-c	5.00	15.00	35.00
V9#2,4,5,7,9,11, V10#1,3	1.70	5.00	12.00

NOTE: **Jack Cole** a-1-8. **Everett** a-1-9. **Tarpe Mills** a-1-4, 6, 8, 11, V3#1. **Rico** a-V7#4, 10,
V8#5, 6, V9#3. **Simon** a-1, 2.

TARGET: THE CORRUPTORS (TV)
No. 1306, Mar-May, 1962 - No. 3, Oct-Dec, 1962 (Photo-c)
Dell Publishing Co.

4-Color 1306, #2,3	2.30	7.00	16.00

TARGET WESTERN ROMANCES (Formerly Target Comics)
No. 106, Oct-Nov, 1949 - No. 107, Dec-Jan, 1949-50
Star Publications

106-Silhouette nudity panel; L.B. Cole-c	11.50	34.00	80.00
107-L.B. Cole-c; lingerie panels	8.50	25.50	60.00

TARGITT
March, 1975 - No. 3, July, 1975
Atlas/Seaboard Publ.

1-Origin; Nostrand-a in all		.30	.60
2,3: 2-1st in costume		.25	.50

TARZAN (See Aurora, Comics on Parade, Crackajack, DC 100-Page Super Spec.,
Famous Feat. Stories 1, Golden Comics Digest #4,9, Jeep Comics 1-29, Jungle Tales
of . . ., Limited Coll. Edition, Popular, Sparkler, Sport Stars 1, Tip Top & Top Comics)
TARZAN
No. 5, 1939 - No. 161, Aug, 1947
Dell Publishing Co./United Features Syndicate

Large Feature Comic 5('39)-(Scarce)-by Hal Foster; r-1st dailies from

1929	84.00	250.00	585.00
Single Series 20(:40)-by Hal Foster	75.00	225.00	525.00
4-Color 134(2/47)-Marsh-a	40.00	120.00	280.00
4-Color 161(8/47)-Marsh-a	35.00	105.00	245.00

TARZAN (. . .of the Apes #138 on)
1-2/48 - No. 131, 7-8/62; No. 132, 11/62 - No. 206, 2/72
Dell Publishing Co./Gold Key No. 132 on

1-Jesse Marsh-a begins	71.00	215.00	500.00
2	41.00	125.00	290.00
3-5	30.00	90.00	210.00

Tarzan #16 (Dell), © ERB

Tarzan #110 (Dell), © ERB

Tasmanian Devil & His Tasty Friends #1, © Warner Bros.

Teddy Roosevelt & His Rough Riders #1, © AVON Teenage Hotrodders #1, © CC Teenage Mutant Ninja Turtles Advs. #1 (8/88), © Mirage

	Good	Fine	N-Mint
TASTEE-FREEZ COMICS (continued)			
1-Little Dot, 3-Casper	3.35	10.00	23.00
2-Rags Rabbit, 5-Mazie	2.00	6.00	14.00
4-Sad Sack	2.00	6.00	14.00
6-Dick Tracy	4.00	12.00	28.00

TAYLOR'S CHRISTMAS TABLOID
Mid 1930s, Cleveland, Ohio
Dept. Store Giveaway (Tabloid size; in color)

nn-(Very Rare)-Among the earliest pro work of Siegel & Shuster; one full color page called "The Battle in the Stratosphere," with a pre-Superman look; Shuster art thoughout. (Only 1 known copy)
Estimated value. . . $900.00

TEAM AMERICA (See Captain America #269)
June, 1982 - No. 12, May, 1983
Marvel Comics Group

	Good	Fine	N-Mint
1-Origin; Ideal Toy motorcycle characters	.40		.80
2-12: 11-Ghost Rider app. 12-Double size	.30		.60

TEAM YANKEE
Jan, 1989 - No. 6, Feb, 1989 ($1.95, weekly limited series, color)
First Comics

1-6	.35	1.00	2.00

TEDDY ROOSEVELT & HIS ROUGH RIDERS (See Real Heroes #1)
1950
Avon Periodicals

1-Kinstler-c; Palais-a; Flag-c	10.00	30.00	70.00

TEDDY ROOSEVELT ROUGH RIDER (See Battlefield #22 & Classics Illustrated Special Issue)

TEE AND VEE CROSLEY IN TELEVISION LAND COMICS
(Also see Crosley's House of Fun)
1951 (52 pgs.; 8x11"; paper cover; in color)
Crosley Division, Avco Mfg. Corp. (Giveaway)

Many stories, puzzles, cut-outs, games, etc.	2.65	8.00	18.00

TEENA
No. 11, 1948 - No. 15, 1948; No. 20, 8/49 - No. 22, 10/50
Magazine Enterprises/Standard Comics

A-1 #11-Teen-age	2.65	8.00	18.00
A-1 #12, 15	2.00	6.00	14.00
20-22 (Standard)	1.15	3.50	8.00

TEEN-AGE BRIDES (True Bride's Experiences #8 on)
Aug, 1953 - No. 7, Aug, 1954
Harvey/Home Comics

1-Powell-a	2.00	6.00	14.00
2-Powell-a	1.50	4.50	10.00
3-7: 3,6-Powell-a	1.35	4.00	9.00

TEEN-AGE CONFESSIONS (See Teen Confessions)

TEEN-AGE CONFIDENTIAL CONFESSIONS
July, 1960 - No. 22, 1964
Charlton Comics

1	.65	1.90	4.50
2-10	.40	1.25	2.50
11-22	.25	.75	1.50

TEEN-AGE DIARY SECRETS (Formerly Blue Ribbon Comics; becomes Diary Secrets #10 on)
No. 4, 9/49; nn (#5), 9/49 - No. 7, 11/49; No. 8, 2/50; No. 9, 8/50
St. John Publishing Co.

4(9/49)-oversized; part mag., part comic	9.50	28.50	65.00
nn(#5),6,8: 8-Photo-c; Baker-a(2-3) in each	6.50	19.50	45.00
7,9-Digest size	8.00	24.00	56.00

TEEN-AGE DOPE SLAVES (See Harvey Comics Library #1)

TEENAGE HOTRODDERS (Top Eliminator #25 on; see Blue Bird)
April, 1963 - No. 24, July, 1967
Charlton Comics

	Good	Fine	N-Mint
1	.85	2.60	6.00
2-10	.50	1.50	3.00
11-24	.35	1.00	2.00

TEEN-AGE LOVE (See Fox Giants)

TEEN-AGE LOVE (Formerly Intimate)
V2#4, July, 1958 - No. 96, Dec, 1973
Charlton Comics

V2#4	1.15	3.50	8.00
5-9	.60	1.80	4.00
10(9/59)-20	.50	1.50	3.00
21-35	.35	1.00	2.00
36-70		.60	1.20
71-96: 61&62-Jonnie Love begins (origin)	.25		.50

TEENAGE MUTANT NINJA TURTLES (Also see Anything Goes, Donatello, First Comics Graphic Novel, Grimjack #26, Leonardo, Michaelangelo, Raphael & Tales Of The. . .)
1984 - Present ($1.50, B&W)
Mirage Studios

1-1st printing (3000 copies)-Only printing to have ad for Gobbledygook #1 & 2	31.00	92.50	185.00
1-2nd printing (6/84, 15,000 copies)	5.50	16.50	33.00
1-3rd printing (36,000 copies)	1.70	5.00	10.00
1-4th printing (50,000 copies)	.85	2.50	5.00
1-5th printing, new-c (8/88-c, 11/88 inside)	.35	1.00	2.00
2-1st printing (15,000 copies)	9.15	27.50	55.00
2-2nd printing	1.35	4.00	8.00
2-3rd printing; new Corben-c/a (2/85)	.60	1.75	3.50
3-1st printing	4.50	13.50	27.00
3-Variant, 500 copies, given away in NYC. Has 'Laird's Photo' in white rather than light blue	6.70	20.00	40.00
3-2nd printing	.70	2.00	4.00
4-1st printing	2.00	6.00	12.00
4-2nd printing (5/87)	.35	1.05	2.10
5-1st printing	1.70	5.00	10.00
5-2nd printing (11/87)	.35	1.00	2.00
6-1st printing	1.35	4.00	8.00
6-2nd printing	.35	1.00	2.00
7-4pg. Corben color insert; 1st color TMNT	1.00	3.00	6.00
7-2nd printing (1/89)	.25	.75	1.50
8-Rion 2990 begins	.85	2.50	5.00
9,10	.70	2.00	4.00
11-15	.55	1.65	3.25
16-18	.50	1.50	3.00
19-28: 19-Begin $1.75-c. 24,25-Veitch-c/a	.30	.90	1.75
Book 1,2($1.50, B&W): 2-Corben-c	.25	.75	1.50

TEENAGE MUTANT NINJA TURTLES ADVENTURES (TV)
8/88 - No. 3, 12/88; 3/89 - Present ($1.00, color, mini-series)
Archie Comics

1-Adapts TV cartoon; not by Eastman/Laird	.35	1.00	2.00
2,3	.25	.75	1.50
1 (2nd series)	.25	.75	1.50
2-10: 5-Begins original stories not based on TV	.50		1.00

TEEN-AGE ROMANCE (Formerly My Own Romance)
No. 77, Sept, 1960 - No. 86, March, 1962
Marvel Comics (ZPC)

77-86	.60	1.80	4.00

TEEN-AGE ROMANCES
Jan, 1949 - No. 45, Dec, 1955
St. John Publ. co. (Approved Comics)

1-Baker c/a(1)	13.00	40.00	90.00

TEEN-AGE ROMANCES (continued)	Good	Fine	N-Mint
2-Baker c/a	8.00	24.00	56.00
3-Baker c/a(3); spanking panel	8.50	25.50	60.00
4,5,7,8-Photo-c; Baker-a(2-3) each	5.70	17.00	40.00
6-Slightly large size; photo-c; part magazine; Baker-a (10/49)	5.70	17.00	40.00
9-Baker c/a; Kubert-a	8.50	25.50	60.00
10-12,20-Baker c/a(2-3) each	5.70	17.00	40.00
13-19,21,22-Complete issues by Baker	9.00	27.00	62.00
23-25-Baker c/a(2-3) each	4.85	14.50	34.00
26,27,33,34,36-42-Last Precode, 3/55; Baker-a. 38-Suggestive-c	3.50	10.50	24.00
28-30-No Baker-a	1.70	5.00	12.00
31-Baker-c	2.15	6.50	15.00
32-Baker c/a, 1pg.	2.15	6.50	15.00
35-Baker c/a, 16pgs.	3.65	11.00	25.00
43-45-Baker-a	2.50	7.50	17.00

TEEN-AGE TALK
1964
I.W. Enterprises

Reprint #1-Monkees photo-c	1.00	3.00	6.00
Reprint #5,8,9	.25	.80	1.60

TEEN-AGE TEMPTATIONS (Going Steady #10 on)(See True Love Pic.)
Oct, 1952 - No. 9, Aug, 1954
St. John Publishing co.

	Good	Fine	N-Mint
1-Baker c/a; has story ''Reform School Girl'' by Estrada	15.00	45.00	105.00
2-Baker-c	5.00	15.00	35.00
3-7,9-Baker c/a	8.50	25.50	60.00
8-Teenagers smoke reefers; Baker c/a	9.00	27.00	62.00

NOTE: *Estrada a-1, 4, 5.*

TEEN BEAM (Formerly Teen Beat #1)
No. 2, Jan-Feb, 1968 (Monkees photo-c)
National Periodical Publications

2-Orlando, Drucker-a(r)	1.00	3.00	7.00

TEEN BEAT (Becomes Teen Beam #2)
Nov-Dec, 1967
National Periodical Publications

1-Photos & text only; Monkees photo-c	1.30	4.00	9.00

TEEN COMICS (Formerly All Teen; Journey Into Unknown Worlds #36 on)
No. 21, April, 1947 - No. 35, May, 1950
Marvel comics (WFP)

21-Kurtzman's ''Hey Look''; Patsy Walker, Cindy, Georgie, Margie app.	4.30	13.00	30.00
22,23,25,27,29,31-35	2.65	8.00	18.00
24,26,28,30-Kurtzman's ''Hey Look''	3.70	11.00	26.00

TEEN CONFESSIONS
Aug, 1959 - No. 97, Nov, 1976
Charlton Comics

1	3.00	9.00	21.00
2	1.50	4.50	10.00
3-10	.95	2.80	6.50
11-30	.50	1.50	3.00
31-Beatles-c	2.65	8.00	18.00
32-36,38-55	.25	.75	1.50
37 (1/66)-Beatles Fan Club story; Beatles-c	2.65	8.00	18.00
56-97: 89,90-Newton-c		.20	.40

TEENIE WEENIES, THE
No. 10, 1950 - No. 11, 1951 (Newspaper reprints)
Ziff-Davis Publishing Co.

10,11	6.50	19.50	45.00

TEEN-IN (Tippy Teen)
Summer, 1968 - No. 4, Fall, 1969

Tower Comics	Good	Fine	N-Mint
nn(#1, Summer,'68), nn(#2, Spring,'69),3,4	.70	2.00	5.00

TEEN LIFE (Formerly Young Life)
No. 3, Winter, 1945 - No. 5, Fall, 1945
New Age/Quality Comics Group

3-June Allyson photo-c	3.50	10.50	24.00
4-Duke Ellington story	2.30	7.00	16.00
5-Van Johnson, Woody Herman & Jackie Robinson articles	3.50	10.50	24.00

TEEN ROMANCES
1964
Super Comics

10,11,15-17-Reprints		.30	.60

TEEN SECRET DIARY (Nurse Betsy Crane #12 on)
Oct, 1959 - No. 11, June, 1961; No. 1, 1972
Charlton Comics

1	1.30	4.00	9.00
2	.55	1.65	4.00
3-11	.50	1.50	3.00
1 (1972)		.30	.60

TEEN TALK (See Teen)

TEEN TITANS (See Brave & the Bold, DC Super-Stars #1, Marvel & DC Present, New Teen Titans, Official . . . Index and Showcase)
1-2/66 - No. 43, 1-2/73; No. 44, 11/76 - No. 53, 2/78
National Periodical Publications/DC Comics

1-Titans join Peace Corps; Batman, Flash, Aquaman, Wonder Woman cameos	12.00	36.00	85.00
2	5.70	17.00	40.00
3-5: 4-Speedy app.	2.85	8.50	20.00
6-10: 6-Doom Patrol app.	1.70	5.00	12.00
11-18: 11-Speedy app. 18-1st app. Starfire	1.50	4.50	10.00
19-Wood-i; Speedy begins as regular	1.50	4.50	10.00
20-22: All Adams-a. 21-Hawk & Dove app. 22-Origin Wonder Girl	1.70	5.00	12.00
23-30: 23-Wonder Girl dons new costume. 25-Flash, Aquaman, Batman, Green Arrow, Green Lantern, Superman, & Hawk & Dove guests; 1st app. Lilith who joins T.T. West in #50. 29-Hawk & Dove & Ocean Master app. 30-Aquagirl app.	1.15	3.50	7.00
31-43: 31-Hawk & Dove app. 36,37-Superboy-r. 38-Green Arrow/Speedy-r; Aquaman/Aqualad story. 39-Hawk & Dove-r. (36-39: 52 pgs.)	1.00	3.00	6.00
44,45,47,49,51,52: 44-Mal becomes the Guardian. 50-Intro. Teen Titans West; 1st revival original Bat-Girl	.70	2.00	4.00
46-Joker's daughter begins	1.15	3.50	7.00
48-Intro Bumblebee; Joker's daughter becomes Harlequin	1.35	4.00	8.00
50-1st revival original Bat-Girl	1.00	3.00	6.00
53-Origin retold	.85	2.50	5.00

NOTE: *Aparo a-36. Buckler c-46-53. Kane a(p)-19,22-24, 39r. Tuska a(p)-31,36,38,39.*

TEEN TITANS SPOTLIGHT
Aug, 1986 - No. 21, Apr, 1988
DC Comics

1	.25	.75	1.50
2,3		.50	1.00
4-10: 7-Guice's 1st work at DC		.40	.80
11-21: 21-$1.00-c		.35	.70

TEEPEE TIM (Formerly Ha Ha Comics)
No. 100, Feb-Mar, 1955 - No. 102, June-July, 1955
American Comics Group

100-102		.85	2.60	6.00

Teen-Age Romances #5, © STJ

Teen Comics #30, © MEG

Teen Titans #16, © DC

Tell It To The Marines #7, © TOBY

Terrific Comics #2, © Continental

Terrifying Tales #13, © STAR

	Good	Fine	N-Mint

TEGRA JUNGLE EMPRESS (Zegra Jungle Empress #2 on)
August, 1948
Fox Features Syndicate

	Good	Fine	N-Mint
1-Blue Beetle, Rocket Kelly app.; used in SOTI, pg. 31	20.00	60.00	140.00

TELEVISION (See TV)

TELEVISION COMICS
No. 5, Feb, 1950 - No. 8, Nov, 1950
Standard Comics (Animated Cartoons)

5-1st app. Willy Nilly	2.65	8.00	18.00
6-8: 6 has #2 on inside	1.70	5.00	12.00

TELEVISION PUPPET SHOW
1950 - No. 2, Nov, 1950
Avon Periodicals

1,2: Speedy Rabbit, Spotty The Pup	5.70	17.00	40.00

TELEVISION TEENS MOPSY (See TV Teens)

TELL IT TO THE MARINES
Mar, 1952 - No. 15, July, 1955
Toby Press Publications

1-Lover O'Leary and His Liberty Belles (with Pin-ups), ends #6	5.50	16.50	40.00
2-Madame Cobra app. c/story	3.70	11.00	26.00
3,5	2.85	8.50	20.00
4-Transvestism story	4.35	13.00	30.00
6-12,14,15: 7-9,14-Photo-c	1.70	5.00	12.00
13-John Wayne photo-c	2.65	8.00	18.00
I.W. Reprint #1,9	.30	.90	1.80
Super Reprint #16('64)	.30	.90	1.80

TEN COMMANDMENTS (See Moses & the...and Classics Illustrated Special)

TENDER LOVE STORIES
Feb, 1971 - No. 4, July, 1971 (All 52pgs.)(25 cents)
Skywald Publ. Corp.

1-4	.25	.80	1.60

TENDER ROMANCE (Ideal Romance #3 on)
Dec, 1953 - No. 2, Feb, 1954
Key Publications (Gilmour Magazines)

1-Headlight & lingerie panels	5.50	16.50	38.00
2	2.65	8.00	18.00

TENNESSEE JED (Radio)
nd (1945) (16 pgs.; paper cover; regular size; giveaway)
Fox Syndicate? (Wm. C. Popper & Co.)

nn	7.00	21.00	50.00

TENNIS (...For Speed, Stamina, Strength, Skill)
1956 (16 pgs.; soft cover; 10 cents)
Tennis Educational Foundation

Book 1-Endorsed by Gene Tunney, Ralph Kiner, etc. showing how tennis has helped them	2.00	6.00	14.00

TENSE SUSPENSE
Dec, 1958 - No. 2, Feb, 1959
Fago Publications

1,2	2.00	6.00	14.00

TEN STORY LOVE (Formerly a pulp magazine with same title)
V29#3, June-July, 1951 - V36#5(#209), Sept, 1956 (#3-6: 52 pgs.)
Ace Periodicals

V29#3(#177)-Part comic, part text	3.00	9.00	21.00
4-6(1/52)	1.50	4.50	10.00
V30#1(3/52)-6(1/53)	1.15	3.50	8.00
V31#1(2/53),V32#2(4/53)-6(12/53)	.85	2.50	6.00
V33#1(1/54)-3(5#54, #195), V34#4(7/54, #196)-6(10/54, #198)			

	Good	Fine	N-Mint
	.80	2.40	5.50
V35#1(12/54, #199)-3(4/55, #201)-Last precode	.75	2.25	5.00
V35#4-6(9/55, #201-204), V36#1(11/55, #205)-3, 5(9/56, #209)	.55	1.65	4.00
V36#4-L.B. Cole-a	1.15	3.50	8.00

TEN WHO DARED (See 4-Color #1178)

TERMINATOR, THE
Sept, 1988 - No. 17?, 1989 ($1.75, color, Baxter paper)
Now Comics

1-Based on movie	1.70	5.00	10.00
2	.85	2.50	5.00
3-11,13-17	.35	1.00	2.00
12 ($1.75, 52pgs.)-Intro. John Connor	.40	1.25	2.50

TERMINATOR: THE BURNING EARTH
1989 - No. 5, 1990 ($1.75, color, mini-series)
Now Comics

1-5	.30	.90	1.80

TERRAFORMERS
April, 1987 - No. 2?, 1987 ($1.95, color)
Wonder Color Comics

1,2	.35	1.00	2.00

TERRANAUTS
Aug, 1986 - No. 2, 1986? ($1.75, color)
Fantasy General Comics

1,2	.30	.90	1.80

TERRIFIC COMICS
Jan, 1944 - No. 6, Nov, 1944
Continental Magazines

1-Kid Terrific; opium story	30.00	90.00	210.00
2-The Boomerang by L.B. Cole & Ed Wheelan's "Comics" McCormick, called the world's #1 comic book fan begins; Schomburg-c	25.00	75.00	175.00
3,4: 3-Diana becomes Boomerang's costumed aide	23.00	70.00	175.00
5-The Reckoner begins; Boomerang & Diana by L.B. Cole; Schomburg bondage-c	25.00	75.00	175.00
6-L.B. Cole c/a	27.00	80.00	185.00

NOTE: L.B. Cole a-1, 2(2), 3-6. Fuje a-5, 6. Rico a-2.

TERRIFIC COMICS (Formerly Horrific; Wonder Boy #17 on)
No. 14, Dec, 1954 - No. 16, Mar, 1955
Mystery Publ.(Comic Media)/(Ajax/Farrell)

14-Art swipe/Advs. into Unknown 37; injury-to-eye-c; page-2, panel 5 swiped from Phantom Stranger #4; surrealistic Palais-a; Human Cross story	6.50	19.50	45.00
15,16-No Phantom Lady. 16-Wonder Boy app. (precode)	5.00	15.00	35.00

TERRIFYING TALES
No. 11, Jan, 1953 - No. 15, Apr, 1954
Star Publications

11-Used in POP, pgs. 99,100; all Jo-Jo-r	17.00	51.00	120.00
12-All Jo-Jo-r; L.B. Cole splash	13.00	40.00	90.00
13-All Rulah-r; classic devil-c	19.00	56.00	130.00
14-All Rulah reprints	13.00	40.00	90.00
15-Rulah, Zago-r; used in SOTI-r/Rulah #22	13.00	40.00	90.00

NOTE: All issues have L.B. Cole covers; bondage covers-No. 12-14.

TERROR ILLUSTRATED (Adult Tales of...)
Nov-Dec, 1955 - No. 2, Spring, 1956 (Magazine)
E.C. Comics

1	5.70	17.00	40.00
2	5.00	15.00	35.00

TERROR ILLUSTRATED (continued)
NOTE: Craig, Evans, Ingels, Orlando art in each. Crandall c-1, 2.

TERRORS OF THE JUNGLE (Formerly Jungle Thrills)
No. 17, May, 1952 - No. 10, Sept, 1954
Star Publications

	Good	Fine	N-Mint
17-Reprints Rulah #21, used in **SOTI**; L.B. Cole bondage-c			
	16.50	50.00	115.00
18-Jo-Jo-r	11.00	32.00	75.00
19,20(1952)-Jo-Jo-r; Disbrow-a	9.30	28.00	65.00
21-Jungle Jo, Tangi, r; used in **POP**, pg. 100 & color illos.			
	11.50	34.00	80.00
4,6,7-Disbrow-a	9.30	28.00	65.00
5,8,10: All Disbrow-a. 5-Jo-Jo-r. 8-Rulah, Jo-Jo-r. 10-Rulah-r			
	9.30	28.00	65.00
9-Jo-Jo-r; Disbrow-a; Tangi by Orlando	9.30	28.00	65.00
NOTE: L.B. Cole c-all; bondage c-17, 19, 21, 5, 7.

TERROR TALES (See Beware Terror Tales)

TERROR TALES (Magazine)
V1#7, 1969 - V6#6, Dec, 1974; V7#1, Apr, 1976 - V10, 1979?
(V1-V6: 52 pgs.; V7 on: 68 pgs.)
Eerie Publications

V1#7	1.15	3.50	8.00
V1#8-11('69): 9-Bondage-c	.70	2.00	5.00
V2#1-6('70), V3#1-6('71), V4#1-7('72), V5#1-6('73), V6#1-6('74)			
	.60	1.75	3.50
V7#1,4(no V7#2), V8#1-3('77), V9, V10	.60	1.75	3.50
V7#3-LSD story-r/Weird V3#5	.60	1.75	3.50

TERRY AND THE PIRATES (See Merry Christmas From Sears Toyland, Popular Comics, Super Book #3,5,9,16,28, & Super Comics)

TERRY AND THE PIRATES
1939 - 1953 (By Milton Caniff)
Dell Publishing Co.

Large Feat. Comic 2('39)	43.00	130.00	300.00
Large Feat. Comic 6('39)-1936 dailies	41.00	122.00	285.00
4-Color 9(1940)	43.00	130.00	300.00
Large Feature Comic 27('41), 6('42)	30.00	90.00	210.00
4-Color 44('43)	26.00	78.00	185.00
4-Color 101('45)	17.00	51.00	120.00
Buster Brown Shoes giveaway(1938)-32 pgs.; in color			
	20.00	60.00	140.00
Canada Dry Premiums-Books #1-3(1953-Harvey)-2x5''; 36 pgs.			
	5.00	15.00	35.00
Family Album(1942)	8.50	25.50	60.00
Gambles Giveaway ('38)-16 pgs.	4.35	13.00	26.00
Gillmore Giveaway('38)-24 pgs.	5.00	15.00	30.00
Popped Wheat Giveaway('38)-Reprints in full color; 24 pgs.			
	.85	2.50	5.00
Shoe Store giveaway('38, 16pp, soft-c)(2-diff.)	3.00	9.00	18.00
Sparked Wheat Giveaway('42)-16 pgs. in full color			
	4.60	14.00	32.00

TERRY AND THE PIRATES
1941 (16 pgs.; regular size)
Libby's Radio Premium

''Adventure of the Ruby of Genghis Khan'' - Each pg. is a puzzle that must be completed to read the story	8.50	25.50	60.00

TERRY AND THE PIRATES (Formerly Boy Explorers; Long John Silver & the Pirates #30 on) (Daily strip-r) (Two #26's)
No. 3, 4/47 - No. 26, 4/51; No. 26, 6/55 - No. 28, 10/55
Harvey Publications/Charlton No. 26-28

3(#1)-Boy Explorers by S&K; Terry & the Pirates begin by Caniff			
	20.00	60.00	140.00
4-S&K Boy Explorers	13.00	40.00	90.00
5-10	7.00	21.00	50.00

	Good	Fine	N-Mint
11-Man in Black app. by Powell	7.00	21.00	50.00
12-20: 16-Girl threatened with red hot poker	5.35	16.00	37.00
21-26(4/51)-Last Caniff issue	4.75	14.00	33.00
26-28('55)(Formerly This Is Suspense)-Not by Caniff			
	3.70	11.00	26.00
NOTE: Powell a (Tommy Tween)-5-10,12,14; 15-17(½-2 pgs.).

TERRY BEARS COMICS (TerryToons, The... #4)
June, 1952 - No. 3, Oct, 1952
St. John Publishing Co.

1	1.70	5.00	12.00
2,3	1.60	4.80	11.00

TERRY-TOONS COMICS (1st Series) (Becomes Paul Terry's Comics #85 on; later issues titled ''Paul Terry's. . .) (See Giant Comics Ed.)
Oct, 1942 - No. 86, May, 1951 (Two #60s exist)
Timely/Marvel No. 1-60 (8/47)(Becomes Best Western No. 58 on?, Marvel)/St. John No. 60 (9/47) on

1 (Scarce)-feat. characters that 1st app. on movie screen; Gandy Goose begins	50.00	150.00	350.00
2	25.00	75.00	175.00
3-5	15.00	45.00	105.00
6-10	10.00	30.00	70.00
11-20	6.50	19.50	45.00
21-37	4.30	13.00	30.00
38-Mighty Mouse begins (1st app.)(11/45)	38.00	115.00	270.00
39-2nd Mighty Mouse app.	13.00	40.00	90.00
40-49: 43-Infinity-c	5.50	16.50	38.00
50-1st app. Heckle & Jeckle	12.00	36.00	84.00
51-60(8/47): 55-Infinity-c. 60(9/47)-Atomic explosion panel			
	4.00	12.00	28.00
61-84	2.65	8.00	18.00
85,86-Same book as Paul Terry's Comics #85,86 with only a title change; published at same time?	2.65	8.00	18.00

TERRY-TOONS COMICS (2nd Series)
June, 1952 - No. 9, Nov, 1953
St. John Publishing Co./Pines

1	4.30	13.00	30.00
2	2.85	8.50	20.00
3-9	2.30	7.00	16.00
Giant Summer Fun Book 101,102(Summer,'57-Summer,'58)(TV, Tom Terrific app.)	3.00	9.00	21.00

TERRYTOONS, THE TERRY BEARS (Formerly Terry Bears)
No. 4, Summer, 1958
Pines Comics

4	1.50	4.50	10.00

TESSIE THE TYPIST (Tiny Tessie #24; see Comedy Comics, Gay & Joker Comics)
Summer, 1944 - No. 23, Aug, 1949
Timely/Marvel Comics (20CC)

1-Doc Rockblock & others by Wolverton	22.00	65.00	155.00
2-Wolverton's Powerhouse Pepper	13.00	40.00	90.00
3-No Wolverton	4.00	12.00	28.00
4,5,7,8-Wolverton-a	8.00	24.00	56.00
6-Kurtzman's ''Hey Look,'' 2 pgs. Wolverton	8.50	25.50	60.00
9-Wolverton's Powerhouse Pepper (8 pgs.) & 1 pg. Kurtzman's ''Hey Look''	10.00	30.00	70.00
10-4 pgs. Wolverton's Powerhouse Pepper	8.30	28.00	65.00
11-8 pgs. Wolverton's Powerhouse Pepper	10.00	30.00	70.00
12-4 pgs. Wolverton's Powerhouse Pepper & 1 pg. Kurtzman's ''Hey Look''	9.30	28.00	65.00
13-4 pgs. Wolverton's Powerhouse Pepper	8.50	25.50	60.00
14-1 pg. Wolverton's Dr. Whackyhack, 1½ pgs. Kurtzman's ''Hey Look''	5.70	17.00	40.00

Terry And The Pirates #11, © News Syndicate

Terry-Toons Comics #38, © Paul Terry

Tessie The Typist #9, © MEG

Texas Kid #8, © MEG

Tex Granger #24, © PMI

Tex Morgan #6, © MEG

TESSIE THE TYPIST (continued)

	Good	Fine	N-Mint
15-3 pgs. Kurtzman's "Hey Look" & 3 pgs. Giggles 'n' Grins	5.70	17.00	40.00
16-18-Kurtzman's "Hey Look" (?, 2 & 1 pg.)	3.70	11.00	26.00
19-Eight pg. Annie Oakley story	2.65	8.00	18.00
20-23: 20-Anti-Wertham editorial (2/49)	2.00	6.00	14.00

NOTE: *Lana app.-21. Millie The Model app.-13,15,17,21. Rusty app.-10,11,13,15,17.*

TEXAN, THE (Fightin' Marines #15 on; Fightin' Texan #16 on)
Aug, 1948 - No. 15, Oct, 1951
St. John Publishing Co.

1-Buckskin Belle	7.00	21.00	50.00
2	3.70	11.00	26.00
3,5,10: 10-Oversized issue	3.00	9.00	21.00
4,7,15-Baker c/a	5.70	17.00	40.00
6,9-Baker-c	3.50	10.50	24.00
8,11,13,14-Baker c/a(2-3) each	5.70	17.00	40.00
12-All Matt Baker; Peyote story	8.00	24.00	56.00

NOTE: *Matt Baker c-6-15. Larsen a-6. Tuska a-1, 2, 8.*

TEXAN, THE (See 4-Color #1027,1096)

TEXAS JOHN SLAUGHTER (See 4-Color #997,1181 & W. Disney Presents #2)

TEXAS KID (See Two-Gun Western, Wild Western)
Jan, 1951 - No. 10, July, 1952
Marvel/Atlas Comics (LMC)

1-Origin; Texas Kid (alias Lance Temple) & his horse Thunder begin	7.00	21.00	50.00
2	3.50	10.50	24.00
3-10	2.65	8.00	18.00

NOTE: *Maneely a-1-4; c-3, 5-10.*

TEXAS RANGERS, THE (See Jace Pearson of... ans Superior Stories #4)

TEXAS RANGERS IN ACTION (Formerly Captain Gallant or Scotland Yard?) (See Blue Bird Comics)
No. 5, July, 1956 - No. 79, Aug, 1970
Charlton Comics

5	2.65	8.00	18.00
6-10	1.30	4.00	9.00
11-Williamson-a(5,5,&8 pgs.); Torres-a	4.35	13.00	30.00
12,14-20	.85	2.60	6.00
13-Williamson-a, 5 pgs; Torres-a	3.35	10.00	23.00
21-30: 30-Last 10 cent issue?	.70	2.00	5.00
31-59	.50	1.50	3.00
60-Rileys Rangers begin	.25	.75	1.50
61-70: 65-1st app. The Man Called Loco, origin-#67			
	.60	1.20	
71-79	.40	.80	
76(Modern Comics-r, 1977)	.15	.30	

TEXAS SLIM (See A-1 Comics #2-8,10)

TEX DAWSON, GUN-SLINGER (Gunslinger #2 on)
January, 1973 (Also see Western Kid, 1st series)
Marvel Comics Group

1-Steranko-c; Williamson-a(r); Tex Dawson-r		.30	.60

TEX FARNUM (See Wisco)

TEX FARRELL
Mar-Apr, 1948
D. S. Publishing Co.

1-Tex Farrell & his horse Lightning; Shelly-c	5.50	16.50	38.00

TEX GRANGER (Formerly Calling All Boys; see True Comics)
No. 18, June, 1948 - No. 24, Sept, 1949
Parents' Magazine Institute/Commended

18-Tex Granger & his horse Bullet begin	4.30	13.00	30.00
19	2.85	8.50	20.00
20-24: 22-Wild Bill Hickok story	2.30	7.00	16.00

TEX MORGAN (See Blaze Carson and Wild Western)
Aug, 1948 - No. 9, Feb, 1950
Marvel Comics (CCC)

	Good	Fine	N-Mint
1-Tex Morgan, his horse Lightning & sidekick Lobo begin	10.00	30.00	70.00
2	7.00	21.00	50.00
3-6: 4-Arizona Annie app.	5.00	15.00	35.00
7-9: All photo-c. 7-Captain Tootsie by Beck. 8-18pg. story "The Terror of Rimrock Valley;" Diablo app.	7.00	21.00	50.00

NOTE: *Tex Taylor app.-6, 7, 9.*

TEX RITTER WESTERN (Movie star; singing cowboy; see Six-Gun Heroes and Western Hero)
Oct, 1950 - No. 46, May, 1959 (Photo-c: 1-21)
Fawcett No. 1-20 (1/54)/Charlton No. 21 on

1-Tex Ritter, his stallion White Flash & dog Fury begin; photo front/back-c begin	30.00	90.00	210.00
2	15.00	45.00	105.00
3-5: 5-Last photo back-c	13.00	40.00	90.00
6-10	11.00	32.00	75.00
11-19	7.00	21.00	50.00
20-Last Fawcett issue (1/54)	8.00	24.00	56.00
21-1st Charlton issue; photo-c (3/54)	8.00	24.00	56.00
22	4.50	14.00	32.00
23-30: 23-25-Young Falcon app.	3.50	10.50	24.00
31-38,40-45	2.85	8.50	20.00
39-Williamson-c/a (1/58)	4.35	13.00	30.00
46-Last issue	3.15	9.50	22.00

NOTE: *B&W photo back-c #23-32.*

TEX TAYLOR (See Blaze Carson, Kid Colt, Tex Morgan, Wild West, Wild Western, & Wisco)
Sept, 1948 - No. 9, March, 1950
Marvel Comics (HPC)

1-Tex Taylor & his horse Fury begin	11.00	32.00	75.00
2	6.50	19.50	45.00
3	5.70	17.00	40.00
4-6: All photo-c. 4-Anti-Wertham editorial. 5,6-Blaze Carson app.	6.50	19.50	45.00
7-Photo-c; 18pg. Movie-Length Thriller "Trapped in Time's Lost Land!" with sabre toothed tigers, dinosaurs; Diablo app.	8.00	24.00	56.00
8-Photo-c; 18pg. Movie-Length Thriller "The Mystery of Devil-Tree Plateau!" with dwarf horses, dwarf people & a lost miniature Inca type village; Diablo app.	8.00	24.00	56.00
9-Photo-c; 18pg. Movie-Length Thriller "Guns Along the Border!" Captain Tootsie by Schreiber; Nimo The Mountain Lion app.	8.00	24.00	56.00

THANE OF BAGARTH
No. 24, Oct, 1985 - No. 25, Dec, 1985
Charlton Comics

24,25		.40	.80

THAT DARN CAT (See Movie Comics & Walt Disney Showcase No. 19)

THAT'S MY POP! GOES NUTS FOR FAIR
1939 (76 pages) (B&W)
Bystander Press

nn-by Milt Gross	8.00	24.00	56.00

THAT THE WORLD MAY BELIEVE
No date (16 pgs.) (Graymoor Friars distr.)
Catechetical Guild Giveaway

nn	1.15	3.50	8.00

THAT WILKIN BOY (Meet Bingo. . .)
Jan, 1969 - No. 52, Oct, 1982
Archie Publications

THAT WILKIN BOY (continued)	Good	Fine	N-Mint
1	1.35	4.00	8.00
2-10	.70	2.00	4.00
11-26 (last Giant issue)	.35	1.00	2.00
27-52		.50	1.00

T.H.E. CAT (TV)
Mar, 1967 - No. 4, Oct, 1967 (All have photo-c)
Dell Publishing Co.

1	1.70	5.00	12.00
2-4	1.15	3.50	8.00

THERE'S A NEW WORLD COMING
1973 (35-49 Cents)
Spire Christian Comics/Fleming H. Revell Co.

nn		.50	1.00

THEY ALL KISSED THE BRIDE (See Cinema Comics Herald)

THEY RING THE BELL
1946
Fox Feature Syndicate

1	6.00	18.00	42.00

THIEF OF BAGHDAD (See 4-Color #1229)

THIMBLE THEATRE STARRING POPEYE
1931 - No. 2, 1932 (52 pgs.; 25 cents; B&W)
Sonnet Publishing Co.

1-Daily strip serial-r in both by Segar	52.00	156.00	365.00
2	47.00	140.00	325.00

NOTE: Probably the first Popeye reprint book. Popeye first entered Thimble Theatre in 1929.

THIMK (Magazine) (Satire)
May, 1958 - No. 6, May, 1959
Counterpart

1	2.65	8.00	18.00
2-6	1.50	4.50	10.00

THING!, THE (Blue Beetle #18 on)
Feb, 1952 - No. 17, Nov, 1954
Song Hits No. 1,2/Capitol Stories/Charlton

1	25.00	75.00	175.00
2,3: 3-Drug mention (several panels)	18.00	54.00	125.00
4-6,8,10	13.00	40.00	90.00
7-Injury to eye-c & inside panel. E.C. swipes from Vault of Horror			
#28	26.00	77.00	180.00
9-Used in **SOTI**, pg. 388 & illo-"Stomping on the face is a form of brutality which modern children learn early"			
	29.00	86.00	200.00
11-Necronomicon story; Hansel & Gretel parody; Injury-to-eye panel; Check-a	23.00	70.00	160.00
12-"Cinderella" parody; Ditko-c/a; lingerie panels			
	35.00	105.00	245.00
13,15-Ditko c/a(3 & 5); 13-Ditko E.C. swipe/Haunt of Fear #15(#1)-"House of Horror"	35.00	105.00	245.00
14-Extreme violence/torture; Rumpelstiltskin story; Ditko c/a(4)			
	35.00	105.00	245.00
16-Injury to eye panel	17.00	51.00	120.00
17-Ditko-c; classic parody-"Through the Looking Glass;" Powell-a(r)			
	27.00	81.00	190.00

NOTE: Excessive violence, severed heads, injury to eye are common No. 5 on.

THING, THE (See Fantastic Four, Marvel Fanfare, Marvel Two-In-One)
July, 1983 - No. 36, June, 1986
Marvel Comics Group

1-Byrne scripts 1-13,18 on; life story of Ben Grimm			
		.60	1.20
2-36		.50	1.00

NOTE: Byrne a-2i, 7; c-1, 7.

THIRTEEN (. . .Going on 18)
11-1/61-62 - No. 25, 12/67; No. 26, 7/69 - No. 29, 1/71
Dell Publishing Co.

	Good	Fine	N-Mint
1	3.50	10.50	24.00
2-10	2.65	8.00	18.00
11-29: 26-29-r	2.00	6.00	14.00

NOTE: John Stanley script-No. 3-29; art?

THIRTY SECONDS OVER TOKYO (Also see Guadacanal Diary)
1943 (Movie) (Also see American Library)
David McKay Co.

nn(B&W, text & pictures)	18.00	54.00	125.00

THIS IS SUSPENSE! (Formerly Strange Suspense Stories; Strange
Suspense Stories #27 on)
No. 23, Feb, 1955 - No. 26, Aug, 1955
Charlton Comics

23-Wood-a(r)/A Star Presentation #3-"Dr. Jekyll & Mr. Hyde"			
	11.00	32.00	75.00
24-Evans-a	4.50	14.00	32.00
25,26	2.85	8.50	20.00

THIS IS THE PAYOFF (See Pay-Off)

THIS IS WAR
No. 5, July, 1952 - No. 9, May, 1953
Standard Comics

5-Toth-a	5.70	17.00	40.00
6,9-Toth-a	4.30	13.00	30.00
7,8	1.30	4.00	9.00

THIS IS YOUR LIFE, DONALD DUCK (See 4-Color #1109)

THIS MAGAZINE IS CRAZY (Crazy V3#3 on)
V3#2, July, 1957 (68 pgs.) (25 cents) (Satire)
Charlton Publ. (Humor Magazines)

V3#2	1.15	3.50	8.00

THIS MAGAZINE IS HAUNTED (Danger and Adventure #22 on)
Oct, 1951 - No. 14, 12/53; No. 15, 2/54 - V3/#21, Nov, 1954
Fawcett Publications/Charlton No. 15(2/54) on

1-Evans-a(i?)	18.00	54.00	125.00
2,5-Evans-a	12.00	36.00	84.00
3,4	6.50	19.50	45.00
6-9,11,12,14	5.00	15.00	35.00
10-Severed head-c	8.00	24.00	56.00
13-Severed head c/story	7.00	21.00	50.00
15,20	4.30	13.00	30.00
16,19-Ditko-c. 19-Injury-to-eye panel; story r-/#1	9.50	28.50	65.00
17-Ditko-c/a(3); blood drainage story	13.00	40.00	100.00
18-Ditko-c/a; E.C. swipe/Haunt of Fear 5; injury-to-eye panel			
	12.00	36.00	84.00
21-Ditko-c, Evans-a	9.50	28.50	65.00

NOTE: Bailey a-1, 3, 4, 21r/#1. Powell a-3-5, 11, 12, 17. Shuster a-18-20.

THIS MAGAZINE IS HAUNTED (2nd Series) (Formerly Zaza the
Mystic; Outer Space #17 on)
V2#12, July, 1957 - V2#16, April, 1958
Charlton Comics

V2#12-14-Ditko c/a in all	11.00	32.00	75.00
15-No Ditko-c/a	1.70	5.00	12.00
16-Ditko-a	7.00	21.00	50.00

THIS MAGAZINE IS WILD (See Wild)

THIS WAS YOUR LIFE (Religious)
1964 (3½x5½") (40 pgs.) (Black, white & red)
Jack T. Chick Publ.

nn		.40	.80

T.H.E. Cat #2, © NBC

The Thing! #15, © CC

This Magazine Is Haunted #1, © FAW

Thor #151, © MEG

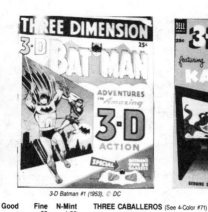

3-D Batman #1 (1953), © DC

3-D-Ell #1, © DELL

	Good	Fine	N-Mint
THIS WAS YOUR LIFE (continued)			
Another version (5x2¾'', 26pgs.)	.60		1.20

THOR (See Avengers #1, Marvel Collectors Item Classics, Marvel Graphic Novel 33, Marvel Preview, Marvel Spectacular, Marvel Treasury Ed., Special Marvel Ed. & Tales of Asgard)

THOR (Formerly Journey Into Mystery)
March, 1966 - Present
Marvel Comics Group

126	5.00	15.00	35.00
127-133,135-140	2.15	6.50	15.00
134-Intro High Evolutionary	3.60	11.00	25.00
141-145,150: 146-Inhumans begin, end #151	1.50	4.50	10.00
146,147-Origin The Inhumans	1.50	4.50	10.00
148,149-Origin Black Bolt in each; 149-Origin Medusa, Crystal, Maximus, Gorgon, Kornak	1.50	4.50	10.00
151-157,159,160	1.50	4.50	10.00
158-Origin-r/No. 83; origin Dr. Blake, concludes #159	4.30	13.00	30.00
161,163,164,167,170-179-Last Kirby issue	1.15	3.50	8.00
162,168,169-Origin Galactus	2.15	6.50	15.00
165,166-Warlock(Him) app.	1.15	3.50	8.00
180,181-Adams-a	1.15	3.50	8.00
182-192,194-200	.70	2.00	4.00
193-(52 pgs.); Silver Surfer x-over	1.70	5.00	12.00
201-299: 225-Intro. Firelord. 294-Origin Asgard & Odin	.25	.75	1.50
300-End of Asgard; origin of Odin & The Destroyer	.40	1.25	2.50
301-336	.50		1.00
337-Simonson-a begins; Beta Ray Bill becomes new Thor	1.15	3.50	7.00
338	.50	1.50	3.00
339,340: 340-Donald Blake returns as Thor	.25	.75	1.50
341-373,375-381,383: 373-X-Factor tie-in		.50	1.00
374-Mutant massacre; X-Factor app.	1.00	3.00	6.00
382-Anniversary issue ($1.25)	.35	1.00	2.00
384-Intro. new Thor	.35	1.00	2.00
385-399,401-414: 395-Intro The Earth Force. 411-New Warriors cameo.			
412-Intro New Warriors (Marvel Boy, Kid Nova, Namorita, Night Thrasher, Firestar & Speedball)	.50		1.00
400 ($1.75, 68 pgs.)-Origin Loki	.40	1.25	2.50
Giant-Size 1('75)	.35	1.00	2.00
Special 2(9/66)	2.15	6.50	15.00
King Size Special 3(1/71)-See Journey Into Mystery for 1st annual	.85	2.50	5.00
Special 4(12/71)	.50	1.50	3.00
Annual 5(11/76), 6(10/77), 7(9/78), 8(11/79)	.50	1.50	3.00
Annual 9(11/81), 10(11/82), 11(11/83), 12(11/84)	.50	1.50	3.00
Annual 13(12/85)	.35	1.00	2.00
Annual 14(1989, $2.00, 68 pgs.)-Atlantis Attacks	.35	1.00	2.00

NOTE: *Adams* c-179-181. *Austin* a-342i, 346i; c-312i. *Buscema* a(p)-178, 182-213, 215-226, 231-238, 241-253, 254r; 256-259, 272-278, 283-285, 370, Annual 6, 8; c(p)-175, 182-196, 198-200, 202-204, 206, 211, 212, 215, 219, 221, 226, 256, 259, 261, 262, 272-278, 283, 289, 370, Annual 6. *Everett* a(i)-143, 170-175; c(i)-171, 172, 174, 176, 241. *Gil Kane* a-318p; c(p)-201, 205, 207-10, 216, 220, 222, 223, 231, 233-40, 242, 243, 318. *Kirby* a(p)-126-177, 179, 194, 254r; c(p)-126-169, 171-174, 176-178, 249-253, 255, 257, 258, Annual 5, Special 1-4. *Mooney* a(i)-201, 204, 214-216, 218, 322i, 324i, 325i, 327i. *Simonson* a-260-271p, 337-354, 357-367, 380, Annual 7p; c-260, 263-271, 337-355, 357-369, 371, 373-382, Annual 7. *Starlin* c-213.

THOSE ANNOYING POST BROS.
Jan, 1985 - Present ($1.75-$2.00, B&W)
Vortex Comics

1-14 ($1.75)	.30	.90	1.80
15-17 ($2.00)	.35	1.00	2.00

THOSE MAGNIFICENT MEN IN THEIR FLYING MACHINES (See Movie Comics)

THREE CABALLEROS (See 4-Color #71)

THREE CHIPMUNKS, THE (See 4-Color #1042)

THREE COMICS (Also see Spiritman)
1944 (10 cents, 48pgs.) (2 different covers exist)
The Penny King Co.

	Good	Fine	N-Mint
1,3,4-Lady Luck, Mr. Mystic, The Spirit app. (3 Spirit sections bound together)-Lou Fine-a	13.00	40.00	90.00

NOTE: *No. 1 contains Spirit Sections 4/9/44 - 4/23/44, and No. 4 is also from 4/44.*

3-D (NOTE: The prices of all the 3-D comics listed include glasses. Deduct 40-50 percent if glasses are missing, and reduce slightly if glasses are loose.)

3-D ACTION
Jan, 1954 (Oversized) (15 cents)(2 pairs glasses included)
Atlas Comics (ACI)

1-Battle Brady	24.00	73.00	170.00

3-D ADVENTURE COMICS
Aug, 1986 (One shot)
Stats, Etc.

1-Promo material	.25	.75	1.50

3-D ALIEN TERROR
June, 1986 ($2.50)
Eclipse Comics

1-Morrow-a; Old Witch, Crypt-Keeper, Vault Keeper cameo	.40	1.25	2.50
. . .in 2-D: 100 copies signed & numbered (B&W)	.85	2.50	5.00

3-D ANIMAL FUN (See Animal Fun)

3-D BATMAN
1953, Reprinted in 1966
National Periodical Publications

1953-Reprints Batman #42 & 48; Tommy Tomorrow app.	71.00	215.00	500.00
1966-Tommy Tomorrow app.	22.00	65.00	150.00

3-D CIRCUS
1953 (25 cents)
Fiction House Magazines

1	24.00	73.00	170.00

3-D COMICS (See Mighty Mouse and Tor)

3-D DOLLY
December, 1953 (2 pairs glasses included)
Harvey Publications

1-Richie Rich story redrawn from his 1st app. in Little Dot #1	12.00	36.00	84.00

3-D-ELL
1953 - No. 3, 1953 (3-D comics) (25 cents)
Dell Publishing Co.

1,2-Rootie Kazootie	24.00	73.00	170.00
3-Flukey Luke	22.00	65.00	150.00

3-D FEATURES PRESENT JET PUP
Oct-Dec, 1953
Dimensions Public

1-Irving Spector-a(2)	24.00	71.00	165.00

3-D FUNNY MOVIES
1953 (25 cents)
Comic Media

1-Bugsey Bear & Paddy Pelican	22.00	65.00	150.00

3-D HEROES (See Blackthorne 3-D Series #3)

THREE-DIMENSION ADVENTURES (Superman)
1953 (Large size)

THREE-DIMENSION ADVENTURES (continued)

	Good	Fine	N-Mint
National Periodical Publications			
nn-Origin Superman (new art)	75.00	225.00	525.00

THREE DIMENSIONAL ALIEN WORLDS (See Alien Worlds)
July, 1984 (One-Shot)
Pacific Comics

1-Bolton/Stevens, Art Adams-a	.85	2.50	5.00

THREE DIMENSIONAL DNAGENTS (See New DNAgents)

THREE DIMENSIONAL E. C. CLASSICS (Three Dimensional Tales
From the Crypt No. 2)
Spring, 1954 (Prices include glasses; came with 2 pairs)
E. C. Comics

1-Reprints: Wood (Mad #3), Krigstein (W.S. #7), Evans (F.C. #13), & Ingels (CSS #5); Kurtzman-c	43.00	130.00	300.00

NOTE: *Stories redrawn to 3-D format. Original stories not necessarily by artists listed.*
CSS: Crime SuspenStories; F.C.: Frontline Combat; W.S.: Weird Science.

THREE DIMENSIONAL TALES FROM THE CRYPT (Formerly Three
Dimensional E. C. Classics)
No. 2, Spring, 1954 (Prices include glasses; came with 2 pair)
E. C. Comics

2-Davis (TFTC #25), Elder (VOH #14), Craig (TFTC #24), & Orlando (TFTC #22) stories; Feldstein-c	46.00	140.00	325.00

NOTE: *Stories redrawn to 3-D format. Original stories not necessarily by artists listed.*
TFTC: Tales From the Crypt; VOH: Vault of Horror.

3-D LOVE
December, 1953 (25 cents)
Steriographic Publ. (Mikeross Publ.)

1	24.00	71.00	165.00

3-D NOODNICK (See Noodnick)

3-D ROMANCE
January, 1954 (25 cents)
Steriographic Publ. (Mikeross Publ.)

1	24.00	71.00	165.00

3-D SHEENA, JUNGLE QUEEN (Also see Sheena 3-D)
1953
Fiction House Magazines

1	38.00	115.00	265.00

3-D TALES OF THE WEST
Jan, 1954 (Oversized) (15 cents)(2 pair glasses included)
Atlas Comics (CPS)

1 (3-D)	25.00	75.00	175.00

3-D THREE STOOGES (Also see Three Stooges)
Sept, 1986 - No. 2, Nov, 1986; No. 3, Oct, 1987; No. 4, 1989 ($2.50)
Eclipse Comics

1-3 (10/87)-Maurer-r	.40	1.25	2.50
4 ('89, $3.50)-Reprints "Three Missing Links"	.60	1.75	3.50
5 (2-D)	.85	2.50	5.00

3-D WHACK (See Whack)

3-D ZONE, THE
Feb, 1987 - Present ($2.50)
The 3-D Zone(Renegade Press)/Ray Zone

1-10: 1-Wolverton-r. 2-Wolverton-r, 3-Picture Scope Jungle Advs., 4-Electric Fear, 5-Krazy Kat-r, 6-Ratfink, 7-Hollywood 3-D; Jayne Mansfield photo-c, 8-High Seas 3-D, 9-Redmask-r, 10-Jet 3-D; Powell & Williamson-r	.40	1.25	2.50
11-20: 11-Danse Macabre; Matt Fox c/a(r). 12-3-D Presidents. 13-Flash 13-Gordon. 14-Tyranostar. 15-3-Dementia Comics; Kurtzman-c, Kubert, Maurer-a. 16-Space Vixens; Dave Stevens-c/a. 17-Thrilling Love. 18-Spacehawk; Wolverton-r. 19-Cracked Classics. 20-Commander Battle and His Atomic Submarine	.40	1.25	2.50

21-26: 21-The Deep, Deep Sleep. 22-Mr. Monster 3-D Pin-Up Spect.; Alan Moore-a, D. Stevens-a. 23-God's Man. 24-3-D War; photos of wars. 25-Exotic Beauties. 26-Robot Love	.40	1.25	2.50

NOTE: *Anderson r-26; c-26. L. B. Cole c-25(new). Davis r-19. Ditko r-19. Elder r-19. Everett r-19. Feldstein r-17. Frazetta r-17. Heath r-19. Kamen r-17. Kinstler r-26. Kubert r-26. Severin r-19. Ward r-17, 19. Wolverton r-2, 18, 19. Wood r-1, 17, 26. Photo c-12.*

3 FUNMAKERS, THE
1908 (64 pgs.) (10x15'')
Stokes and Company

Maude, Katzenjammer Kids, Happy Hooligan (1904-06 Sunday strip reprints in color)	27.00	81.00	190.00

3 LITTLE PIGS (See 4-Color #218)

3 LITTLE PIGS, THE (See Walt Disney Showcase #15 & 21)
May, 1964; No. 2, Sept, 1968 (Walt Disney)
Gold Key

1-Reprints 4-Color 218	1.00	3.00	7.00
2	.75	2.25	5.00

THREE MOUSEKETEERS, THE (1st Series)
3-4/56 - No. 24, 9-10/59; No. 25, 8-9/60 - No. 26, 10-12/60
National Periodical Publications

1	8.00	24.00	56.00
2	4.00	12.00	28.00
3-10	2.85	8.50	20.00
11-26	2.00	6.00	14.00

NOTE: *Rube Grossman a-1-26. Sheldon Mayer a-1-8; c-1, 3, 4, 6, 7.*

THREE MOUSEKETEERS, THE (2nd Series) (See Super DC Giant)
May-June, 1970 - No. 7, May-June, 1971
National Periodical Publications

1-Mayer-a	.35	1.00	2.00
2-7-Mayer-a (68 pgs. #5-7)		.50	1.00

THREE NURSES (Formerly Confidential Diary; Career Girl
Romances #24 on)
V3#18, May, 1963 - V3#23, Mar, 1964
Charlton Comics

V3#18-23	.25	.75	1.50

THREE RASCALS
1958; 1963
I. W. Enterprises

I.W. Reprint #1 (Says Super Comics on inside)-(M.E.'s Clubhouse Rascals), #2('58)	.25	.80	1.60
10('63)-Reprints #1	.25	.80	1.60

THREE RING COMICS
March, 1945
Spotlight Publishers

1	3.50	10.50	24.00

THREE ROCKETEERS (See Blast-Off)

THREE STOOGES (See Comic Album #18, The Little Stooges, March of Comics #232, 248, 268, 280, 292, 304, 316, 336, 373, Movie Classics & Comics & 3-D Three Stooges)

THREE STOOGES
Feb, 1949 - No. 2, May, 1949; Sept, 1953 - No. 7, Oct, 1954
Jubilee No. 1,2/St. John No. 1 (9/53) on

1-(Scarce, 1949)-Kubert-a; infinity-c	50.00	150.00	350.00
2-(Scarce)-Kubert, Maurer-a	38.00	115.00	265.00
1(9/53)-Hollywood Stunt Girl by Kubert, 7 pgs.	34.00	100.00	235.00
2(3-D, 10/53)-Stunt Girl story by Kubert	24.00	71.00	165.00
3(3-D, 11/53)	21.00	64.00	150.00
4(3/54)-7(10/54)	14.00	42.00	100.00

Three Dimensional Tales From The Crypt #2, © WMG

The 3-D Zone #1, © Ray Zone

The Three Mousketeers #24, © DC

Three Stooges #8, © Norman Maurer Prod.

Thrilling Comics #2, © STD

Thrills Of Tomorrow #19, © HARV

THREE STOOGES (continued)
NOTE: All issues have Kubert-Maurer art. Maurer c-1, 2('49), 1('53).

THREE STOOGES
No. 1043, Oct-Dec, 1959 - No. 55, June, 1972
Dell Publishing Co./Gold Key #10 (10/62) on

	Good	Fine	N-Mint
4-Color 1043 (#1)	7.00	21.00	50.00
4-Color 1078,1127,1170,1187	5.00	15.00	35.00
6(9-11/61) - 10: 6-Professor Putter begins; ends #16	3.70	11.00	26.00
11-14,16-20: 17-The Little Monsters begin (5/64)(1st app.?)	3.50	10.50	24.00
15-Go Around the World in a Daze (movie scenes)	3.70	11.00	26.00
21,23-30	2.65	8.00	18.00
22-Movie scenes/'The Outlaws Is Coming'	3.70	11.00	26.00
31-55	2.00	6.00	14.00

NOTE: All Four Colors, 6-50, 52-55 have photo-c.

3 WORLDS OF GULLIVER (See 4-Color #1158)

THRILL COMICS (See Flash Comics, Fawcett)

THRILLER
Nov, 1983 - No. 12, Nov, 1984 ($1.25; Baxter paper)
DC Comics

		Good	Fine	N-Mint
1-9,11,12: 1-Intro Seven Seconds. 2-Origin. 5,6-Elvis satire			.65	1.30
10-($2.00)		.35	1.00	2.00

THRILLING ADVENTURES IN STAMPS COMICS
V1#8, Jan, 1953 (25 cents) (100 pages) (Formerly Stamp Comics)
Stamp Comics, Inc. (Very Rare)

	Good	Fine	N-Mint
V1#8-Harrison, Wildey, Kiefer, Napoli-a	25.00	75.00	175.00

THRILLING ADVENTURE STORIES (See Tigerman)
Feb, 1975 - No. 2, July-Aug, 1975 (B&W) (68 pgs.)
Atlas/Seaboard Publ.

	Good	Fine	N-Mint
1-Tigerman, Kromag the Killer begin; Heath, Thorne-a	.40	1.20	2.40
2-Toth, Severin, Simonson-a; Adams-c	.40	1.20	2.40

THRILLING COMICS
Feb, 1940 - No. 80, April, 1951
Better Publ./Nedor/Standard Comics

	Good	Fine	N-Mint
1-Origin Doc Strange (37 pgs.); Nickie Norton of the Secret Service begins	64.00	193.00	450.00
2-The Rio Kid, The Woman in Red, Pinocchio begins	29.00	86.00	200.00
3-The Ghost & Lone Eagle begin	26.00	79.00	185.00
4-10	17.00	51.00	120.00
11-18,20	13.00	40.00	90.00
19-Origin The American Crusader, ends #39,41	19.00	56.00	130.00
21-30: 24-Intro. Mike, Doc Strange's sidekick. 29-Last Rio Kid	11.50	34.00	80.00
31-40: 36-Commando Cubs begin	9.30	28.00	65.00
41-52: 41-Hitler bondage-c. 44-Hitler-c. 52-The Ghost ends	7.00	21.00	50.00
53-The Phantom Detective begins; The Cavalier app.; no Commando Cubs	7.00	21.00	50.00
54-The Cavalier app.; no Commando Cubs	7.00	21.00	50.00
55-Lone Eagle ends	7.00	21.00	50.00
56-Princess Pantha begins	14.00	42.00	100.00
57-60	13.00	40.00	90.00
61-65: 61-Ingels-a; The Lone Eagle app. 65-Last Phantom Detective & Commando Cubs	13.00	40.00	90.00
66-Frazetta text illo	13.00	40.00	90.00
67,70-73: Frazetta-a(5-7 pgs.) in each. 72-Sea Eagle app.	18.00	54.00	125.00
68,69-Frazetta-a(2), 8 & 6 pgs.; 9 & 7 pgs.	19.00	57.00	132.00
74-Last Princess Pantha; Tara app. Buck Ranger, Cowboy Detective begins	6.50	19.50	45.00
75-78: 75-Western format begins	3.70	11.00	26.00
79-Krigstein-a	5.00	15.00	35.00
80-Severin & Elder, Celardo, Moreira-a	5.00	15.00	35.00

NOTE: Bondage c-5, 9, 13, 20, 22, 27-30, 38, 41, 52, 54, 70. Kinstler a-45, 48. Leo Morey a-7. Schomburg (Xela) c-7, 11-18, 36-71; airbrush 62-71. Tuska a-63. Woman in Red not in #19, 23, 31-33, 39-45. No. 72 exists as a Canadian reprint with no Frazetta story.

THRILLING CRIME CASES (Shocking Mystery Cases #50 on)
No. 41, June-July, 1950 - No. 49, 1952
Star Publications

	Good	Fine	N-Mint
41	5.50	16.50	38.00
42-44-Chameleon story-Fox-r	4.50	14.00	32.00
45-48: 47-Used in POP, pg. 84	4.30	13.00	30.00
49-Classic L. B. Cole-c	11.50	34.00	80.00

NOTE: All have L. B. Cole-c; a-43p, 45p, 46p, 49(2pgs.). Disbrow a-48. Hollingsworth a-48.

THRILLING ROMANCES
No. 5, Dec, 1949 - No. 26, June, 1954
Standard Comics

	Good	Fine	N-Mint
5	3.50	10.50	24.00
6,8	1.70	5.00	12.00
7-Severin/Elder-a, 7 pgs.	3.00	9.00	21.00
9,10-Severin/Elder-a	2.35	7.00	16.00
11,14-21,26	1.15	3.50	8.00
12-Wood-a, 2 pgs.; photo-c	4.35	13.00	30.00
13-Severin-a	2.00	6.00	14.00
22-25-Toth-a	3.70	11.00	26.00

NOTE: All photo-c. Celardo a-9, 16. Colletta a-23, 24(2). Tuska a-9.

THRILLING SCIENCE TALES
1989 ($3.50, color)
AC Comics

	Good	Fine	N-Mint
1-Frazetta, Guardineer, Krenkel, Orlando, Williamson & Wood-r; Kaluta-c	.60	1.75	3.50

THRILLING TRUE STORY OF THE BASEBALL....
1952 (Photo-c, each)
Fawcett Publications

	Good	Fine	N-Mint
...Giants-photo-c; has Willie Mays rookie photo-biography	30.00	90.00	210.00
...Yankees-photo-c	27.00	81.00	190.00

THRILLOGY
Jan, 1984 (One-shot, color)
Pacific Comics

	Good	Fine	N-Mint
1-Conrad-c/a		.50	1.00

THRILL-O-RAMA
Oct, 1965 - No. 3, Dec, 1966
Harvey Publications (Fun Films)

	Good	Fine	N-Mint
1-Fate (Man in Black) by Powell app.; Doug Wildey-a; Simon-c; Williamson-a (5 pgs.)	.85	2.50	6.00
2-Pirana begins; Williamson 2 pgs.; Fate (Man in Black) app.; Tuska/Simon-c	.85	2.50	6.00
3-Fate (Man in Black) app.; Sparling-c	.50	1.50	3.00

THRILLS OF TOMORROW (Formerly Tomb of Terror)
No. 17, Oct, 1954 - No. 20, April, 1955
Harvey Publications

	Good	Fine	N-Mint
17-Powell-a (horror); r/Witches Tales #7	2.35	7.00	16.00
18-Powell-a (horror); r/Tomb of Terror #1	2.00	6.00	14.00
19,20-Stuntman by S&K (r/from Stuntman 1 & 2); 19 has origin & is last pre-code (2/55)	13.50	40.50	95.00

NOTE: Palais a-17.

THROBBING LOVE (See Fox Giants)

THROUGH GATES OF SPLENDOR
1973, 1974 (36 pages) (39-49 cents) **Good Fine N-Mint**
Spire Christian Comics (Fleming H. Revell Co.)

nn	.40	.80

THUMPER (See 4-Color #19 & 243)

THUN'DA (. . . King of the Congo)
1952 - No. 6, 1953
Magazine Enterprises

	Good	Fine	N-Mint
1(A-1 47)-Origin; Frazetta c/a; only comic done entirely by Frazetta; All Thun'da stories, no Cave Girl	83.00	250.00	580.00
2(A-1 56)-Powell-c/a begins, ends #6; Intro/1st app. Cave Girl in filler strip (also app. in 3-6)	12.00	36.00	84.00
3(A-1 73), 4(A-1 78)	9.00	27.00	62.00
5(A-1 83), 6(A-1 86)	8.00	24.00	56.00

THUN'DA TALES (See Frank Frazetta's . . .)

THUNDER AGENTS (See Tales Of Thunder)
11/65 - No. 17, 12/67; No. 18, 9/68, No. 19, 11/68, No. 20, 11/69
(No. 1-16: 68 pgs.; No. 17 on: 52 pgs.)(All are 25 cents)
Tower Comics

	Good	Fine	N-Mint
1-Origin & 1st app. Dynamo, Noman, Menthor, & The Thunder Squad; 1st app. The Iron Maiden	7.00	21.00	50.00
2-Death of Egghead	3.60	11.00	25.00
3-5: 4-Guy Gilbert becomes Lightning who joins Thunder Squad; Iron Maiden app.	2.85	8.50	20.00
6-10: 7-Death of Menthor. 8-Origin & 1st app. The Raven	1.70	5.00	12.00
11-15: 13-Undersea Agent app.; no Raven story	1.15	3.50	8.00
16-19	1.00	3.00	6.00
20-Special Collectors Edition; all reprints	.70	2.00	4.00

NOTE: Crandall a-1, 4p, 5p, 18, 20r; c-18. Ditko a-6, 7p, 12p, 13, 14p, 16, 18. Kane a-1, 5p, 6p, 14, 16p; c-14, 15. Tuska a-1p, 7, 8, 10, 13-17, 19. Whitney a-9p, 10, 13, 15, 17, 18; c-17. Wood a-1-11, 15(w/Ditko-12,18), (inks-#9, 13, 14, 16, 17), 19r, 20r; c-1-8, 9i, 10-13(#10 w/Williamson(p)), 16.

T.H.U.N.D.E.R. AGENTS (See Blue Ribbon Comics, Hall of Fame Featuring the . . ., JCP Features & Wally Wood's . . .)
May, 1983 - No. 2, Jan, 1984
JC Comics (Archie Publications)

1,2-New material	.35	1.00	2.00

THUNDER BIRDS (See Cinema Comics Herald)

THUNDERBOLT (See The Atomic . . .)

THUNDERBOLT (Peter Cannon . . .; see Crisis on Infinite Earths)
Jan, 1966; No. 51, Mar-Apr, 1966 - No. 60, Nov, 1967
Charlton Comics

1-Origin	.85	2.60	6.00
51-(Formerly Son of Vulcan #50)	.50	1.50	3.00
52-58: 54-Sentinels begin. 58-Last Thunderbolt & Sentinels	.40	1.25	2.50
59,60: 60-Prankster app.	.35	1.00	2.00
Modern Comics-r. 57,58('77)		.15	.30

NOTE: Aparo a-60. Morisi a-1, 51-56, 58; c-1, 51-56, 58, 59.

THUNDERBUNNY (Also see Blue Ribbon Comics #13, Charlton Bullseye & Pep Comics #393)
Jan, 1984 (Direct sale only)
Red Circle Comics

1-Origin	.60	1.20

THUNDERCATS (TV)
Dec, 1985 - No. 24, June, 1988
Star Comics/Marvel #22 on

1-Mooney c/a begins	.35	1.00	2.00
2-(65 & 75 cent cover exist)	.25	.75	1.50

	Good	Fine	N-Mint
3-24: 12-Begin $1.00-c; 20-Williamson-i		.50	1.00

THUNDERMACE
Mar, 1986 - No. 5? ($1.50-$1.75, B&W)
RAK Graphics

1-Two color-c	1.70	5.00	10.00
1-2nd print, multi-color-c	.25	.75	1.50
2-5 ($1.75)	.25	.80	1.60
Graphic Novel 1 (B&W-r)	.85	2.50	5.00

THUNDER MOUNTAIN (See 4-Color #246)

TICK, THE
June, 1988 - Present ($1.75-$1.95-$2.25; B&W)
New England Comics Press

Special Edition 1-1st comic book app. serially numbered & limited to 5000 copies	3.70	11.00	22.00
Special Edition 2-Serially numbered and limited to 3000 copies	2.85	8.50	17.00
1-Reprints Spec. Ed. 1 w/minor changes	3.00	9.00	18.00
1-2nd, 3rd printing ($1.95); 3rd-(6/89)	.35	1.00	2.00
2-Reprints Spec. Ed. 2 w/minor changes	1.15	3.50	7.00
2-2nd printing ($1.95)	.35	1.00	2.00
3-5 ($1.95)	.50	1.50	3.00
6,7 ($2.25)	.40	1.15	2.30

TICKLE COMICS (Also see Gay, Smile, & Whee Comics)
1955 (52 pages) (5x7¼'') (7 cents)
Modern Store Publ.

1	.40	1.20	2.40

TICK TOCK TALES
Jan, 1946 - No. 34, 1951
Magazine Enterprises

1-Koko & Kola begin	5.00	15.00	35.00
2	2.65	8.00	18.00
3-10	2.00	6.00	14.00
11-34: 19-Flag-c. 23-Muggsy Mouse, The Pixies & Tom-Tom The Jungle Boy app.	1.30	4.00	9.00

TIGER (Also see Comics Reading Libraries)
March, 1970 - No. 6, Jan, 1971 (15 cents)
Charlton Press (King Features)

1	.25	.80	1.60
2-6		.50	1.00

TIGER BOY (See Unearthly Spectaculars)

TIGER GIRL
September, 1968
Gold Key

1 (10227-809)	1.75	5.25	12.00

NOTE: Sparling c/a; written by Jerry Siegel.

TIGERMAN (Also see Thrilling Adventure Stories)
April, 1975 - No. 3, Sept, 1975
Seaboard Periodicals (Atlas)

1	.40	.80
2,3-Ditko-p in each	.30	.60

TIGER WALKS, A (See Movie Comics)

TILLIE THE TOILER
1925 - No. 8, 1933 (52 pgs.) (B&W daily strip reprints)
Cupples & Leon Co.

nn (#1)	10.00	30.00	70.00
2-8	6.50	19.50	45.00

NOTE: First strip app. was January, 1921.

TILLIE THE TOILER (See Comic Monthly)
No. 15, 1941 - No. 237, July, 1949

Thun'da #3, © ME

Thunder Agents #10, © TC

Thunderbolt #51, © CC

Time Twisters #2, © Quality Comics   Tim Holt #25, © ME   Tim McCoy #18, © CC

TILLIE THE TOILER (continued)
Dell Publishing Co.

	Good	Fine	N-Mint
4-Color 15(1941)	21.00	62.00	145.00
Large Feature Comic 30(1941)	13.00	40.00	90.00
4-Color 8(1942)	13.00	40.00	90.00
4-Color 22(1943)	10.00	30.00	70.00
4-Color 55(1944)	8.00	24.00	56.00
4-Color 89(1945)	7.00	21.00	50.00
4-Color 106('45),132('46)	5.70	17.00	40.00
4-Color 150,176,184	4.30	13.00	30.00
4-Color 195,213,237	3.70	11.00	26.00

TILLY AND TED-TINKERTOTLAND
1945 (Giveaway) (20 pgs.)
W. T. Grant Co.

nn-Christmas comic	2.00	6.00	14.00

TIM (Formerly Superman-Tim; becomes Gene Autry-Tim)
June, 1950 (Half-size, B&W)
Tim Stores

4 issues	2.50	7.50	15.00

TIME BANDITS
Feb, 1982 (One shot)
Marvel Comics Group

1-Movie adaptation		.50	1.00

TIME BEAVERS (See First Comics Graphic Novel #2)

TIME FOR LOVE (Formerly Romantic Secrets)
V2#53, Oct, 1966 - No. 47, May, 1976
Charlton Comics

V2#53(10/66), 1(10/67), 2(12/67)-20	.25	.75	1.50
21-47		.20	.40

TIMELESS TOPIX (See Topix)

TIME MACHINE, THE (See 4-Color #1085)

TIME MASTERS
Feb, 1990 - No. 8, Sept, 1990 ($1.75, mini-series)
DC Comics

1-4: New Rip Hunter series	.30	.90	1.80

TIMESPIRITS
Jan, 1985 - No. 8, Mar, 1986 ($1.50, Baxter paper; adults only)
Epic Comics (Marvel)

1	.30	.90	1.80
2-8: 4-Williamson-a	.25	.75	1.50

TIME TO RUN
1973 (39, 49 cents)
Spire Christian Comics (Fleming H. Revell Co.)

nn-by Al Hartley (from Billy Graham movie)		.40	.80

TIME TUNNEL, THE (TV)
Feb, 1967 - No. 2, July, 1967
Gold Key

1,2-Photo back-c	2.30	7.00	16.00

TIME TWISTERS
Sept, 1987 - No. 21, 1989 ($1.25-$1.50, color)
Quality Comics

1-10: Alan Moore scripts in 1-4, 6-9,14(2pg.)		.60	1.25
11-21 ($1.50): 14-Bolland-a(2pg.). 15,16-Guice-c		.60	1.25

TIME 2: THE EPIPHANY (See First Comics Graphic Novel #9)

TIME WARP
Oct-Nov, 1979 - No. 5, June-July, 1980 ($1.00)
DC Comics, Inc.

1		.40	.80
2-5		.30	.60

NOTE: *Aparo* a-1. *Buckler* a-1p. *Chaykin* a-2. *Ditko* a-1-4. *Kaluta* c-1-5. *G. Kane* a-2. *Nasser* a-4. *Newton* a-1-5p. *Orlando* a-2. *Sutton* a-1-3.

TIME WARRIORS THE BEGINNING
1986 (Aug) - No. 2, 1986? ($1.50, color)
Fantasy General Comics

	Good	Fine	N-Mint
1-Alpha Track/Skellon Empire	.25	.75	1.50
2		.40	.75

TIM HOLT (Movie star) (Becomes Red Mask #42 on; also see Crack Western #72, & Great Western)
1948 - No. 41, April-May, 1954 (All 36 pgs.)
Magazine Enterprises

1(A-1 14)-Photo-c begin, end No. 18, 29; Tim Holt, His horse Lightning & sidekick Chito begin	35.00	105.00	245.00
2(A-1 17)(9-10/48)	22.00	65.00	155.00
3(A-1 19)-Photo back-c	15.00	45.00	105.00
4(1-2/49),5: 5-Photo back-c	11.50	34.00	80.00
6-1st app. The Calico Kid (alias Rex Fury), his horse Ebony & Sidekick Sing-Song (begin series); photo back-c	13.00	40.00	90.00
7-10: 7-Calico Kid by Ayers. 8-Calico Kid by Guardineer (r-/in Great Western 10). 9-Map of Tim's Home Range	9.30	28.00	65.00
11-The Calico Kid becomes The Ghost Rider (Origin & 1st app.) by Dick Ayers (r-/in Great Western 8); his horse Spectre & sidekick Sing-Song begin series	25.00	75.00	175.00
12-16,18-Last photo-c	6.50	19.50	45.00
17-Frazetta Ghost Rider-c	25.00	75.00	175.00
19,22,24: 19-Last Tim Holt-c; Bolle line-drawn-c begin	5.00	15.00	35.00
20-Tim Holt becomes Redmask (Origin); begin series; Redmask-c #20-on	9.50	28.50	65.00
21-Frazetta Ghost Rider/Redmask-c	21.50	65.00	150.00
23-Frazetta Redmask-c	17.00	51.00	120.00
25-1st app. Black Phantom	10.00	30.00	70.00
26-30: 28-Wild Bill Hickok, Bat Masterson team up with Redmask. 29-B&W photo-c	5.00	15.00	35.00
31-33-Ghost Rider ends	4.30	13.00	30.00
34-Tales of the Ghost Rider begins (horror)-Classic "The Flower Women" & "Hard Boiled Harry!"	5.00	15.00	35.00
35-Last Tales of the Ghost Rider	4.30	13.00	30.00
36-The Ghost Rider returns, ends No. 41; liquid hallucinogenic drug story	5.50	16.50	38.00
37-Ghost Rider classic "To Touch Is to Die!," about Inca treasure	5.50	16.50	38.00
38-The Black Phantom begins; classic Ghost Rider "The Phantom Guns of Feather Gap!"	5.50	16.50	38.00
39-41: All 3-D effect c/stories	12.00	36.00	84.00

NOTE: *Dick Ayers* a-7, 9-41. *Bolle* a-1-41; c-19, 20, 22, 24-28, 30-41.

TIM IN SPACE (Formerly Gene Autry Tim; becomes Tim Tomorrow)
1950 (½-size giveaway) (B&W)
Tim Stores

nn	1.70	5.00	10.00

TIM McCOY (Formerly Zoo Funnies; Pictorial Love Stories #22 on)
No. 16, Oct, 1948 - No. 21, Aug-Sept, 1949 (Western Movie Stories)
Charlton Comics

16-John Wayne, Montgomery Clift app. in 'Red River;' photo back-c	17.00	51.00	120.00
17-21: 17-Rod Cameron guest stars	13.00	40.00	90.00

TIM McCOY, POLICE CAR 17
1934 (32 pgs.) (11x14¾'') (B&W) (Like Feature Books)
Whitman Publishing Co.

674-1933 movie ill.	12.00	36.00	84.00

TIMMY (See 4-Color #715, 823, 923, 1022)

TIMMY THE TIMID GHOST (Formerly Win-A-Prize?; see Blue Bird)
No. 3, 2/56 - No. 44, 10/64; No. 45, 9/66; 10/67 - No. 23, 7/71; V4/24,
9/85 - No. 26, 1/86
Charlton Comics

	Good	Fine	N-Mint
3(1956) (1st Series)	2.30	7.00	16.00
4,5	1.15	3.50	8.00
6-10	.60	1.80	4.00
11,12(4/58,10/58)(100pgs.)	1.70	5.00	12.00
13-20	.60	1.75	3.50
21-45('66)	.25	.80	1.60
1(10/67, 2nd series)	.35	1.00	2.00
2-23		.60	1.20
24-26 (1985-86): Fago-r		.40	.80

TIM TOMORROW (Formerly Tim In Space)
8/51, 9/51, 10/51, Christmas, 1951 (5x7¾")
Tim Stores

	Good	Fine	N-Mint
Prof. Fumble & Captain Kit Comet in all	1.35	4.00	8.00

TIM TYLER (See Harvey Comics Hits #54)

TIM TYLER (Also see Comics Reading Libraries)
1942
Better Publications

	Good	Fine	N-Mint
1	6.00	18.00	42.00

TIM TYLER COWBOY
No. 11, Nov, 1948 - No. 18, 1950
Standard Comics (King Features Synd.)

	Good	Fine	N-Mint
11	4.00	12.00	28.00
12-18	2.65	8.00	18.00

TINKER BELL (See 4-Color #896,982, & Walt Disney Showcase #37)

TINY FOLKS FUNNIES (See 4-Color #60)

TINY TESSIE (Tessie #1-23; Real Experiences #25)
No. 24, Oct, 1949
Marvel Comics (20CC)

	Good	Fine	N-Mint
24	2.00	6.00	14.00

TINY TIM (Also see Super Comics)
No. 4, 1941 - No. 235, July, 1949
Dell Publishing Co.

	Good	Fine	N-Mint
Large Feature Comic 4('41)	20.00	60.00	140.00
4-Color 20(1941)	21.00	62.00	145.00
4-Color 42(1943)	11.50	34.00	80.00
4-Color 235	3.70	11.00	26.00

TINY TOT COMICS
Mar, 1946 - No. 10, Nov-Dec, 1947 (For younger readers)
E. C. Comics

	Good	Fine	N-Mint
1(nn) (52 pgs.)	14.00	42.00	100.00
2 (5/46, 52 pgs.)	11.00	32.00	75.00
3-10: 10-Christmas-c	9.30	28.00	65.00

TINY TOT FUNNIES (Formerly Family Funnies)
No. 9, June, 1951 (Becomes Junior Funnies)
Harvey Publ. (King Features Synd.)

	Good	Fine	N-Mint
9-Flash Gordon, Mandrake	2.50	7.50	17.00

TINY TOTS COMICS
1943 (Not reprints)
Dell Publishing Co.

	Good	Fine	N-Mint
1-Kelly-a(2); fairy tales	30.00	90.00	210.00

TIPPY & CAP STUBBS (See 4-Color #210,242 & Popular Comics)

TIPPY'S FRIENDS GO-GO & ANIMAL
July, 1966 - No. 15, Oct, 1969 (25 cents)
Tower Comics

	Good	Fine	N-Mint
1	1.00	3.00	7.00

	Good	Fine	N-Mint
2-7,9-15: 12-15 titled "Tippy's Friend Go-Go"	.70	2.00	5.00
8-Beatles on front/back-c	2.65	8.00	18.00

TIPPY TEEN (See Vicki)
Nov, 1965 - No. 27, Feb, 1970 (25 cents)
Tower Comics

	Good	Fine	N-Mint
1	.85	2.60	6.00
2-27: 5-1pg. Beatles pin-up	.50	1.50	3.00
Special Collectors' Editions('69-nn)(25 cents)	.50	1.50	3.00

TIPPY TERRY
1963
Super/I. W. Enterprises

	Good	Fine	N-Mint
Super Reprint #14('63)-Little Grouchy reprints		.60	1.20
I.W. Reprint #1 (nd)		.60	1.20

TIP TOP COMICS
4/36 - No. 210, 1957; No. 211, 11-1/57-58 - No. 225, 5-7/61
United Features #1-187/St. John #188-210/Dell Publishing Co. #211 on

	Good	Fine	N-Mint
1-Tarzan by Hal Foster, Li'l Abner, Broncho Bill, Fritzi Ritz, Ella Cinders, Capt. & The Kids begin; strip-r	180.00	450.00	1080.00
2	82.00	205.00	490.00
3	55.00	165.00	385.00
4	41.00	125.00	290.00
5-10: 7-Photo & biography of Edgar Rice Burroughs. 8-Christmas-c	33.00	100.00	230.00
11-20: 20-Christmas-c	24.00	73.00	170.00
21-40: 36-Kurtzman panel (1st published comic work)	22.00	65.00	155.00
41-Has 1st Tarzan Sunday	22.00	65.00	155.00
42-50: 43-Mort Walker panel	19.00	56.00	130.00
51-53	16.00	48.00	110.00
54-Origin Mirror Man & Triple Terror, also featured on cover	20.00	60.00	140.00
55,56,58,60: Last Tarzan by Foster	13.00	40.00	90.00
57,59,61,62-Tarzan by Hogarth	17.00	51.00	120.00
63-80: 65,67-70,72-74,77,78-No Tarzan	9.00	27.00	62.00
81-90	8.00	24.00	56.00
91-99	5.70	17.00	40.00
100	6.50	19.50	45.00
101-140: 110-Gordo story. 111-Li'l Abner app. 118, 132-no Tarzan	3.70	11.00	26.00
141-170: 145,151-Gordo story. 157-Last Li'l Abner; lingerie panels	2.65	8.00	18.00
171-188-Tarzan reprints by B. Lubbers in all. #177?-Peanuts by Schulz begins; no Peanuts in #178,179,181-183	2.85	8.50	20.00
189-225	1.70	5.00	12.00

Bound Volumes (Very Rare) sold at 1939 World's Fair; bound by
publ. in pictorial comic boards. (Also see Comics on Parade)

	Good	Fine	N-Mint
Bound issues 1-12	171.00	515.00	1200.00
Bound issues 13-24	115.00	345.00	800.00
Bound issues 25-36	93.00	280.00	650.00

NOTE: Tarzan covers-#3, 9, 11, 13, 16, 18, 21, 24, 27, 30, 32-34, 36, 37, 39, 41, 43, 45, 47,
50, 52 (all worth 10-20 percent more). Tarzan by Foster-#1-40, 44-50; by Rex
Maxon-#41-43; by Byrne Hogarth-#57, 59, 62.

TIP TOPPER COMICS
Oct-Nov, 1949 - No. 28, 1954
United Features Syndicate

	Good	Fine	N-Mint
1-Li'l Abner, Abbie & Slats	4.30	13.00	30.00
2	2.65	8.00	18.00
3-5: 5-Fearless Fosdick app.	2.15	6.50	15.00
6-10: 6-Fearless Fosdick app.	1.70	5.00	12.00
11-25: 17-22,24,26-Peanuts app. (2 pgs.)	1.50	4.50	10.00
26-28-Twin Earths	3.50	10.50	24.00

NOTE: Many lingerie panels in Fritzi Ritz stories.

Timmy The Timid Ghost #2 (12/67), © CC   Tim Tyler Cowboy #12, © STD   Tip Top Comics #13, © UFS

T-Man #26, © QUA   Tomahawk #30, © DC   Tomb Of Dracula #4 (9/72), © MEG

T-MAN
Sept, 1951 - No. 38, Dec, 1956
Quality Comics Group

	Good	Fine	N-Mint
1-Jack Cole-a	12.00	36.00	84.00
2-Crandall-c	7.00	21.00	50.00
3,6-8: Crandall-c	5.70	17.00	40.00
4,5-Crandall c/a each; 5-Drug test	6.50	19.50	45.00
9-Crandall-c	5.00	15.00	35.00
10,12	2.85	8.50	20.00
11-Used in POP, pg. 95 & color illo.	5.00	15.00	35.00
13-19,21-24,26	2.65	8.00	18.00
20-H-Bomb explosion-c/story	5.50	16.50	38.00
25-All Crandall-a	4.65	14.00	32.00
27-38	2.00	6.00	14.00

NOTE: Anti-communist stories are common. Bondage c-15.

TNT COMICS
Feb, 1946 (36 pgs.)
Charles Publishing Co.

1-Yellowjacket app.	8.50	25.50	60.00

TOBY TYLER (See 4-Color #1092 and Movie Comics)

TODAY'S BRIDES
11/55; No. 2, 2/56; No. 3, 9/56; No. 4, 11/56
Ajax/Farrell Publishing Co.

1	3.00	9.00	21.00
2-4	1.50	4.50	10.00

TODAY'S ROMANCE
No. 5, March, 1952 - No. 8, Sept, 1952
Standard Comics

5	2.65	8.00	18.00
6-Toth-a	3.50	10.50	24.00
7,8	1.30	4.00	9.00

TO DIE FOR IN 3-D (See Blackthorne 3-D Series #64)

TOKA (Jungle King)
Aug-Oct, 1964 - No. 10, Jan, 1967 (Painted-c)
Dell Publishing Co.

1	.60	1.80	4.00
2	.40	1.25	2.50
3-10	.35	1.00	2.00

TOMAHAWK (Son of . . . #131-140 on-c; see Star Spangled Comics & World's Finest Comics #65)
Sept-Oct, 1950 - No. 140, May-June, 1972
National Periodical Publications

1	46.00	137.00	320.00
2-Frazetta/Williamson-a, 4 pgs.	26.00	77.00	180.00
3-5	13.00	40.00	90.00
6-10: 7-Last 52 pgs.	10.00	30.00	70.00
11-20	6.50	19.50	45.00
21-27,30: 1st precode (2/55)	5.00	15.00	35.00
28-1st app. Lord Shilling (arch-foe)	6.50	19.50	45.00
29-Frazetta-r/Jimmy Wakely #3 (3 pgs.)	12.00	36.00	84.00
31-40	3.50	10.50	24.00
41-50	2.65	8.00	18.00
51-56,58-60	2.00	6.00	14.00
57-Frazetta-r/Jimmy Wakely #6 (3 pgs.)	6.50	19.50	45.00
61-77: 77-Last 10 cent issue	1.15	3.50	8.00
78-85: 81-1st app. Miss Liberty. 83-Origin Tomahawk's Rangers	.60	1.80	4.00
86-100: 96-Origin/1st app. The Hood, alias Lady Shilling	.35	1.00	2.00
101-110: 107-Origin/1st app. Thunder-Man	.60	1.20	
111-130,132-138,140		.50	1.00
131-Frazetta-r/Jimmy Wakely #7 (3 pgs.); origin Firehair retold			

	Good	Fine	N-Mint
	.35	1.00	2.00
139-Frazetta-r/Star Spangled #113		.60	1.20

NOTE: Adams c-116-119, 121, 123-130. Firehair by Kubert-131-134, 136. Maurer a-138. Severin a-135.

TOM AND JERRY (See Comic Album #4, 8, 12, Dell Giant #21, Dell Giants, Golden Comics Digest #1, 5, 8, 13, 15, 18, 22, 25, 28, 35, & March of Comics #21, 46, 61, 70, 88, 103, 119, 128, 145, 154, 173, 190, 207, 224, 281, 295, 305, 321, 333, 345, 361, 365, 388, 400, 444, 451, 463, 480)

TOM AND JERRY (. . .Comics, early issues) (M.G.M.)
(Formerly Our Gang No. 1-59) (See Dell Giants for annuals)
No. 193, 6/48; No. 60, 7/49 - No. 212, 7-9/62; No. 213, 11/62 - No. 291, 2/75; No. 292, 3/77 - No. 342, 5/82 - No. 344, 1982?
Dell Publishing Co./Gold Key No. 213-327/Whitman No. 328 on

4-Color 193 (#1)	8.00	24.00	56.00
60	4.30	13.00	30.00
61	3.50	10.50	24.00
62-70: 66-X-mas-c	2.65	8.00	18.00
71-80: 77-X-mas-c	2.00	6.00	14.00
81-99: 90-X-mas-c	1.70	5.00	12.00
100	2.00	6.00	14.00
101-120	1.30	4.00	9.00
121-140: 126-X-mas-c	1.00	3.00	7.00
141-160	.75	2.25	5.00
161-200	.55	1.65	4.00
201-212(7-9/62)(Last Dell issue)	.45	1.35	3.00
213,214-(84 pgs.)-titled ". . .Funhouse"	1.50	4.50	12.00
215-240: 215-titled ". . .Funhouse"	.45	1.35	3.00
241-270	.35	1.00	2.00
271-300: 286 "Tom & Jerry"	.25	.75	1.50
301-344		.40	.80
Mouse From T.R.A.P. 1(7/66)-Giant, G. K.	1.75	5.25	14.00
Summer Fun 1(7/67, 68pgs.)(Gold Key)-R-/Barks' Droopy/Summer Fun No. 1	1.75	5.25	14.00
. . .Kite Fun Book (1958, 5x7¼", 16pgs.)	1.50	4.50	12.00

NOTE: #60-87, 98-121, 268, 277, 289, 302 are 52 pages. Reprints-#225, 241, 245, 247, 252, 254, 266, 268, 270, 292-327, 329-342, 344.

TOMB OF DARKNESS (Formerly Beware)
No. 9, July, 1974 - No. 23, Nov, 1976
Marvel Comics Group

9-23: 17-Woodbridge-r/Astonishing #62. 20-Everett Venus r-/Venus #19. 23-Everett-a(r)		.25	.50

NOTE: Ditko a-15r, 19r.

TOMB OF DRACULA (See Giant-Size Dracula & Dracula Lives)
April, 1972 - No. 70, Aug, 1979
Marvel Comics Group

1-Colan-p in all	1.35	4.00	8.00
2-10: 3-Intro. Dr. Rachel Van Helsing & Inspector Chelm. 6-Adams-c. 10-1st app. Blade the Vampire Slayer	.70	2.00	4.00
11,12,14-20: 12-Brunner-c(p)	.40	1.25	2.50
13-Origin Blade the Vampire Slayer	.40	1.25	2.50
21-70: 43-Wrightson-c. 70-Double size	.35	1.00	2.00

NOTE: Colan a-1-70p; c(p)-8, 38-42, 44-56, 58-70.

TOMB OF DRACULA (Magazine)
Nov, 1979 - No. 6, Sept, 1980 (B&W)
Marvel Comics Group

1,4-6		.60	1.20
2-Ditko-a (36 pgs.)	.35	1.00	2.00
3-Miller-a	.35	1.00	2.00

NOTE: Buscema a-4p, 5p. Chaykin c-5. 6. Colan a(p)-1, 3-6. Miller a-3.

TOMB OF LIGEIA (See Movie Classics)

TOMB OF TERROR (Thrills of Tomorrow #17 on)
June, 1952 - No. 16, July, 1954

TOMB OF TERROR (continued)
Harvey Publications

	Good	Fine	N-Mint
1	7.00	21.00	50.00
2	4.50	14.00	32.00
3-Bondage-c; atomic disaster story	5.50	16.50	38.00
4-7: 4-Heart ripped out	4.50	14.00	32.00
8-12-Nostrand-a	4.50	14.00	32.00
13-Special S/F issue	7.00	21.00	50.00
14-Check-a; special S/F issue	7.00	21.00	50.00
15-S/F issue; c-shows head exploding; Nostrand-a(r)			
	10.00	30.00	70.00
16-Special S/F issue; Nostrand-a	7.00	21.00	50.00

NOTE: *Kremer a-1, 7, c-1. Palais a-2, 3, 5-7. Powell a-1, 3, 5, 9-16. Sparling a-12, 13, 15.*

TOMBSTONE TERRITORY (See 4-Color #1123)

TOM CAT (Formerly Bo; Atom The Cat #9 on)
No. 4, Apr, 1956 - No. 8, July, 1957
Charlton Comics

	Good	Fine	N-Mint
4-Al Fago c/a	1.60	4.80	11.00
5-8	1.00	3.00	7.00

TOM CORBETT, SPACE CADET (TV)
No. 378, 1-2/52 - No. 11, 9-11/54 (All painted covers)
Dell Publishing Co.

	Good	Fine	N-Mint
4-Color 378-McWilliams-a	7.00	21.00	50.00
4-Color 400,421,McWilliams-a	5.70	17.00	40.00
4(11-1/53) - 11	3.50	10.50	24.00

TOM CORBETT SPACE CADET (See March of Comics #102)

TOM CORBETT SPACE CADET (TV)
V2#1, May-June, 1955 - V2#3, Sept-Oct, 1955
Prize Publications

	Good	Fine	N-Mint
V2#1	10.00	30.00	70.00
2,3: 3-Meskin-c	8.00	24.00	56.00

TOM, DICK & HARRIET (See Gold Key Spotlight)

TOM LANDRY AND THE DALLAS COWBOYS
1973 (35-49 cents)
Spire Christian Comics/Fleming H. Revell Co.

nn	.25	.75	1.50

TOM MIX (...Commandos Comics #10-12)
Sept, 1940 - No. 12, Nov, 1942 (36 pages); 1983 (One-shot)
Given away for two Ralston box-tops; in cereal box, 1983
Ralston-Purina Co.

	Good	Fine	N-Mint
1-Origin (life) Tom Mix; Fred Meagher-a	71.00	215.00	500.00
2	40.00	120.00	280.00
3-9	34.00	100.00	240.00
10-12: 10-Origin Tom Mix Commando Unit; Speed O'Dare begins.			
12-Sci/fi-c	27.00	81.00	190.00
1983-'Taking of Grizzly Grebb,' Toth-a; 16 pg. miniature			
	1.00	3.00	6.00

TOM MIX WESTERN (Movie, radio star) (Also see The Comics, Crackajack Funnies, Master Comics, 100 Pages Of Comics, Popular Comics, Real Western Hero, Six Gun Heroes, Western Hero & XMas Comics)
Jan, 1948 - No. 61, May, 1953 (1-17: 52 pgs.)
Fawcett Publications

	Good	Fine	N-Mint
1 (Photo-c, 52 pgs.)-Tom Mix & his horse Tony begin; Tumbleweed Jr begins, ends #52,54,55	43.00	130.00	300.00
2 (Photo-c)	24.00	73.00	170.00
3-5 (Painted/photo-c): 5-Billy the Kid & Oscar app.			
	19.00	57.00	135.00
6,7 (Painted/photo-c)	16.00	48.00	110.00
8-Kinstler tempera-c	16.00	48.00	110.00
9,10 (Painted/photo-c)-Used in **SOTI**, pgs. 323-325			

	Good	Fine	N-Mint
	14.00	42.00	100.00
11-Kinstler oil-c	13.00	40.00	90.00
12 (Painted/photo-c)	11.50	34.00	80.00
13-17 (Painted-c, 52 pgs.)	11.50	34.00	80.00
18,22 (Painted-c, 36 pgs.)	9.30	28.00	65.00
19 (Photo-c, 52 pgs.)	11.50	34.00	80.00
20,21,23 (Painted-c, 52 pgs.)	9.30	28.00	65.00
24,25,27-29 (52 pgs.): 24-Photo-c begin, end #61. 29-Slim Pickens app.	9.30	28.00	65.00
26,30 (36 pgs.)	8.50	25.50	60.00
31-33,35-37,39,40,42 (52 pgs.): 39-Red Eagle app.			
	8.00	24.00	56.00
34,38 (36 pgs. begin)	6.50	19.50	45.00
41,43-60	4.50	14.00	32.00
61-Last issue	5.70	17.00	40.00

NOTE: *Photo-c from 1930s Tom Mix movies (he died in 1940). Many issues contain ads for Tom Mix, Rocky Lane, Space Patrol and other premiums. Captain Tootsie by C.C. Beck in No. 6-11, 20.*

TOM MIX WESTERN
1988 - Present ($2.95, B&W w/16 pgs. color, 44 pgs.)
AC Comics

	Good	Fine	N-Mint
1-Tom Mix-r/Master #124,128,131,102 plus Billy the Kid-r by Severin; photo front/back-c	.50	1.50	3.00
2-($2.50, B&W)-G.A. reprints	.40	1.25	2.50

TOMMY OF THE BIG TOP
No. 10, Sept, 1948 - No. 12, Mar, 1949
King Features Syndicate/Standard Comics

	Good	Fine	N-Mint
10-By John Lehti	3.00	9.00	21.00
11,12	1.70	5.00	12.00

TOM SAWYER (See Adventures of... & Famous Stories)

TOM SAWYER & HUCK FINN
1925 (52 pgs.) (10¾x10'') (stiff covers)
Stoll & Edwards Co.
By Dwiggins; reprints 1923, 1924 Sunday strips in color

	10.00	30.00	70.00

TOM SAWYER COMICS
1951? (paper cover)
Giveaway
Contains a coverless Hopalong Cassidy from 1951; other combinations possible 1.00 3.00 6.00

TOM SKINNER-UP FROM HARLEM (See Up From Harlem)

TOM TERRIFIC! (TV)(See Mighty Mouse Fun Club Mag. #1)
Summer, 1957 - No. 6, Fall, 1958
Pines Comics (Paul Terry)

	Good	Fine	N-Mint
1	8.50	25.50	60.00
2-6	6.50	19.50	45.00

TOM THUMB (See 4-Color #972)

TOM-TOM, THE JUNGLE BOY (See Tick Tock Tales)
1947 - No. 3, 1947; Nov, 1957 - No. 3, Mar, 1958
Magazine Enterprises

	Good	Fine	N-Mint
1-Funny animal	3.70	11.00	26.00
2,3(1947)	2.30	7.00	16.00
1(1957)(& Itchi the Monk), 2,3('58)	1.15	3.50	8.00
I.W. Reprint No. 1,2,8,10		.40	.80

TONKA (See 4-Color #966)

TONTO (See The Lone Ranger's Companion...)

TONY TRENT (The Face #1,2)
No. 3, 1948 - No. 4, 1949
Big Shot/Columbia Comics Group

	Good	Fine	N-Mint
3,4: 3-The Face app. by Mart Bailey	5.50	16.50	40.00

Tom Cat #7, © CC

Tom Corbett Space Cadet V2#3, © PRIZE

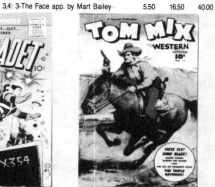

Tom Mix Western #11, © FAW

Top Cat #4 (Gold Key), © Hanna-Barbera   Topix V10#13, © CG   Top Love Stories #17, © STAR

TOODLE TWINS, THE
1-2/51 - No. 10, 7-8/51; 1956 (Newspaper reprints)
Ziff-Davis (Approved Comics)/Argo

	Good	Fine	N-Mint
1	4.00	12.00	28.00
2	2.65	8.00	18.00
3-9	2.30	7.00	16.00
10-Painted-c, some newspaper-r	2.30	7.00	16.00
1(Argo, 3/56)	2.00	6.00	14.00

TOONERVILLE TROLLEY
1921 (Daily strip reprints) (B&W) (52 pgs.)
Cupples & Leon Co.

1-By Fontaine Fox	14.00	42.00	100.00

TOOTS & CASPER (See Large Feature Comic #5)

TOP ADVENTURE COMICS
1964 (Reprints)
I. W. Enterprises

1-Reprints/Explorer Joe #2; Krigstein-a	.70	2.00	4.00
2-Black Dwarf	.80	2.40	4.80

TOP CAT (TV) (Hanna-Barbera)
12-2/61-62 - No. 3, 6-8/62; No. 4, 10/62 - No. 31, 9/70
Dell Publishing Co./Gold Key No. 4 on

1	2.85	8.50	20.00
2-5	1.70	5.00	12.00
6-10	1.30	4.00	9.00
11-20	.85	2.50	6.00
21-31: 21,24,25,29-Reprints	.60	1.80	4.00
Kite Fun Book (1963, 16pgs., 5x7¼", soft-c)	1.15	3.50	8.00

TOP CAT (TV) (Hanna-Barbera)(See TV Stars #4)
Nov, 1970 - No. 20, Nov, 1973
Charlton Comics

1	1.00	3.00	7.00
2-10	.60	1.75	3.50
11-20	.35	1.00	2.00

NOTE: #8 (1/72) went on sale late in 1972 between #14 and #15 with the January 1973 issues.

TOP COMICS
July, 1967 (All rebound issues)
K. K. Publications/Gold Key

nn-The Gnome-Mobile (Disney-movie)	.50	1.50	3.00
1-Beagle Boys (#7), Bugs Bunny, Chip 'n' Dale, Daffy Duck (#50), Flintstones, Flipper, Huckleberry Hound, Huey, Dewey & Louie, Junior Woodchucks, Lassie, The Little Monsters (#71), Moby Duck, Porky Pig (has Gold Key label - says Top Comics on inside), Scamp, Super Goof, Tarzan of the Apes (#169), Three Stooges (#35), Tom & Jerry, Top Cat (#21), Tweety & Sylvester (#7), Walt Disney C&S (#322), Woody Woodpecker, Yogi Bear, Zorro known; each character given own book	.30	.90	1.80
1-Uncle Scrooge (#70)	1.00	3.00	6.00
1-Donald Duck (not Barks), Mickey Mouse	.70	2.00	4.00
1-The Jetsons	1.50	4.50	10.00
2-Bugs Bunny, Daffy Duck, Donald Duck (not Barks), Mickey Mouse (#114), Porky Pig, Super Goof, Three Stooges, Tom & Jerry, Tweety & Sylvester, Uncle Scrooge (#71)-Barks-c, Walt Disney's C&S (r-/#325), Woody Woodpecker, Yogi Bear (#30), Zorro (r-#8; Toth-a)	.30	.90	1.80
2-Snow White & 7 Dwarfs(6/67)(1944-r)	.80	2.40	4.80
3-Donald Duck	.50	1.50	3.00
3-Uncle Scrooge (#72)	1.00	3.00	6.00
3-The Flintstones, Mickey Mouse (r-/#115), Tom & Jerry, Woody Woodpecker, Yogi Bear	.35	1.00	2.00
4-The Flintstones, Mickey Mouse, Woody Woodpecker	.35	1.00	2.00

NOTE: Each book in this series is identical to its counterpart except for cover, and came out at same time. The number in parentheses is the original issue it contains.

TOP DETECTIVE COMICS
1964 (Reprints)
I. W. Enterprises

	Good	Fine	N-Mint
9-Young King Cole & Dr. Drew (not Grandenetti)	.40	1.20	2.40

TOP DOG (See Star Comics Mag.)
Apr, 1985 - No. 14, June, 1987 (Children's book)
Star Comics (Marvel)

1-13 (75 cents)		.35	.70
14 ($1.00)		.50	1.00

TOP ELIMINATOR (Formerly Teenage Hotrodders; Drag 'n' Wheels #30 on)
No. 25, Sept, 1967 - No. 29, July, 1968
Charlton Comics

25-29	.35	1.00	2.00

TOP FLIGHT COMICS
1947; July, 1949
Four Star Publications/St. John Publishing Co.

1	3.70	11.00	26.00
1(7/49)-Hector the Inspector	2.65	8.00	18.00

TOP GUN (See 4-Color #927 & Showcase #72)

TOP GUNS OF THE WEST (See Super DC Giant)

TOPIX (...Comics) (Timeless Topix-early issues) (Also see Men of Courage & Treasure Chest)(V1-V5#1,V7#1-20-paper-c)
11/42 - V10No.15, 1/28/52 (Weekly - later issues)
Catechetical Guild Educational Society

V1#1(8pgs.,8x11")	7.00	21.00	42.00
2,3(8pgs.,8x11")	4.00	12.00	24.00
4-8(16pgs.,8x11")	2.70	8.00	16.00
V2#1-10(16pgs.,8x11"): V2#8-Pope Pius XII	2.70	8.00	16.00
V3#1(16pgs.,8x11")	2.15	6.50	13.00
V4#1-10	2.15	6.50	13.00
V5#1(10/46,52pgs.)-9,12-15(12/47)-#13 shows V5#4			
	1.15	3.50	7.00
10,11-Life of Christ editions	2.35	7.00	14.00
V6#1-14	.70	2.00	4.00
V7#1(9/1/48)-20(6/15/49), 32pgs.	.70	2.00	4.00
V8#1(9/19/49)-3,5-11,13-30(5/15/50)	.70	2.00	4.00
4-Dagwood Splits the Atom(10/10/49)-Magazine format			
	1.35	4.00	8.00
12-Ingels-a	2.75	8.00	16.00
V9#1(9/25/50)-11,13-30(5/14/51)	.50	1.50	3.00
12-Special 36pg. Xmas issue, text illos format			
	.85	2.50	5.00
V10#1(10/1/51)-15: 14-Hollingsworth-a	.50	1.50	3.00

TOP JUNGLE COMICS
1964 (Reprint)
I. W. Enterprises

1(nd)-Reprints White Princess of the Jungle #3, minus cover			
	.80	2.40	4.80

TOP LOVE STORIES
No. 8, 11-12/49 - No. 9, 1950?; No. 3, 5/51 - No. 19, 3/54
Star Publications

8 (#1)	4.30	13.00	30.00
9 (#2), 3-5,7-9	3.50	10.50	24.00
6-Wood-a	7.00	21.00	50.00
10-16,18,19-Disbrow-a	3.70	11.00	26.00
17-Wood art (Fox-r)	5.00	15.00	35.00

NOTE: All have L. B. Cole covers.

TOP-NOTCH COMICS (. . . Laugh #28-45; Laugh Comix #46 on)
Dec, 1939 - No. 45, June, 1944
MLJ Magazines

	Good	Fine	N-Mint
1-Origin The Wizard; Kardak the Mystic Magician, Swift of the Secret Service (ends No. 3), Air Patrol, The Westpointer, Manhunters (by J. Cole), Mystic (ends #2) & Scott Rand (ends #3) begin	100.00	300.00	700.00
2-Dick Storm (ends #8), Stacy Knight M.D. (ends #4) begin; Jack Cole-a	49.00	148.00	345.00
3-Bob Phantom, Scott Rand on Mars begin; J. Cole-a	39.00	115.00	270.00
4-Origin/1st app. Streak Chandler on Mars; Moore of the Mounted only app.; J. Cole-a	34.00	100.00	235.00
5-Flag-c; origin/1st app. Galahad; Shanghai Sheridan begins (ends #8); Shield cameo	27.00	81.00	190.00
6-Meskin-a	24.00	73.00	170.00
7-The Shield x-over in Wizard; The Wizard dons new costume	36.00	107.00	250.00
8-Origin The Firefly & Roy, the Super Boy	40.00	120.00	280.00
9-Origin & 1st app. The Black Hood; Fran Frazier begins	100.00	300.00	700.00
10	41.00	125.00	290.00
11-20	27.00	81.00	185.00
21-30: 23,24-No Wizard, Roy app. in each. 25-Last Bob Phantom, Roy app. 26-Roy app. 27-Last Firefly. 28-Suzie begins. 29-Last Kardak	23.00	70.00	160.00
31-44: 33-Dotty & Ditto by Woggon begins. 44-Black Hood series ends	12.00	36.00	84.00
45-Last issue	7.00	21.00	50.00

NOTE: **J. Binder** a-1-3. **Meskin** a-2, 3, 6, 15. **Woggon** a-33-40, 42. Bondage c-17, 19. Black Hood also appeared on radio in 1944.

TOPPER & NEIL (See 4-Color #859)

TOPPS COMICS
1947
Four Star Publications

	Good	Fine	N-Mint
1-L. B. Cole-c	4.50	14.00	32.00

TOPS
July, 1949 - No. 2, Sept, 1949 (68 pgs, 25 cents) (10¼x13¼")
(Large size-magazine format; for the adult reader)
Tops Magazine, Inc. (Lev Gleason)

	Good	Fine	N-Mint
1 (Rare)-Story by Dashiell Hammett; Crandall/Lubbers, Tuska, Dan Barry, Fuje-a; Biro painted-c	62.00	185.00	435.00
2 (Rare)-Crandall/Lubbers, Biro, Kida, Fuje, Guardineer-a	54.00	160.00	375.00

TOPS COMICS (See Tops in Humor)
1944 (Small size, 32 pgs.) (7¼x5")
Consolidated Book Publ. (Lev Gleason)

	Good	Fine	N-Mint
2001-The Jack of Spades	10.00	30.00	70.00
2002-Rip Raider	5.00	15.00	35.00
2003-Red Birch (gag cartoons)	1.00	3.00	7.00

TOPS COMICS
1944 (132 pages) (10 cents)
Consolidated Book Publishers

	Good	Fine	N-Mint
nn(Color-c, inside in red shade & some in full color)-Ace Kelly by Rick Yager, Black Orchid, Don on the Farm, Dinky Dinkerton (Rare)	16.00	48.00	110.00

NOTE: This book is printed in such a way that when the staple is removed, the strips on the left side of the book correspond with the same strips on the right side. Therefore, if strips are removed from the book, each strip can be folded into a complete comic section of its own.

TOP SECRET
January, 1952
Hillman Publ.

	Good	Fine	N-Mint
1	8.00	24.00	56.00

TOP SECRET ADVENTURES (See Spyman)

TOP SECRETS (. . . of the F.B.I.)
Nov, 1947 - No. 10, July-Aug, 1949
Street & Smith Publications

	Good	Fine	N-Mint
1-Powell c/a	12.00	36.00	84.00
2-Powell-c/a	8.50	25.50	60.00
3-6,8,10-Powell-a	8.00	24.00	56.00
7-Used in **SOTI**, pg. 90 & illo.-"How to hurt people;" used by N.Y. Legis. Comm.; Powell c/a	12.00	36.00	84.00

NOTE: **Powell** c-1-3, 5-10.

TOPS IN ADVENTURE
Fall, 1952 (132 pages, 25 cents)
Ziff-Davis Publishing Co.

	Good	Fine	N-Mint
1-Crusader from Mars, The Hawk, Football Thrills, He-Man; Powell-a; painted-c	23.00	70.00	160.00

TOPS IN HUMOR (See Tops Comics?)
1944 (Small size) (7¼x5")
Consolidated Book Publ. (Lev Gleason)

	Good	Fine	N-Mint
2001(#1)-Origin The Jack of Spades, Ace Kelly by Rick Yager, Black Orchid (female crime fighter) app.	11.00	32.00	75.00
2	5.70	17.00	40.00

TOP SPOT COMICS
1945
Top Spot Publ. Co.

	Good	Fine	N-Mint
1-The Menace, Duke of Darkness app.	10.00	30.00	70.00

TOPSY-TURVY
April, 1945
R. B. Leffingwell Publ.

	Good	Fine	N-Mint
1-1st app. Cookie	3.70	11.00	26.00

TOR (Formerly One Million Years Ago)
No. 2, Oct, 1953; No. 3, May, 1954 - No. 5, Oct, 1954
St. John Publishing Co.

	Good	Fine	N-Mint
3-D 2(10/53)-Kubert-a	10.00	30.00	70.00
3-D 2(10/53)-Oversized, otherwise same contents	9.00	27.00	62.00
3-D 2(11/53)-Kubert-a	9.00	27.00	62.00
3-5-Kubert-a; 3-Danny Dreams by Toth	10.00	30.00	70.00

NOTE: The two October 3-D's have same contents and Powell art; the Nov. issue is titled 3-D Comics.

TOR (See Sojourn)
May-June, 1975 - No. 6, Mar-Apr, 1976
National Periodical Publications

	Good	Fine	N-Mint
1-New origin by Kubert		.30	.60
2-6: 2-Origin-r/St. John #1		.25	.50

NOTE: **Kubert** a-1; 2-6r; c-1-6. **Toth** a(p)-3r.

TOR (3-D)
July, 1986 - No. 2, Aug, 1987 ($2.50)
Eclipse Comics

	Good	Fine	N-Mint
1-r/One Million Years Ago	.40	1.25	2.50
2-D 1-Limited signed & numbered edition	.40	1.25	2.50
2-r-/Tor 3-D #2	.40	1.25	2.50
2-D 2-Limited signed & numbered edition	.40	1.25	2.50

TORCHY (. . . Blonde Bombshell) (See Dollman, Military, & Modern)
Nov, 1949 - No. 6, Sept, 1950
Quality Comics Group

	Good	Fine	N-Mint
1-Bill Ward-c, Gil Fox-a	75.00	225.00	525.00
2,3-Fox c/a	32.00	95.00	225.00
4-Fox c/a(3), Ward-a, 9pgs.	42.00	125.00	295.00

Top-Notch Comics #2, © AP

Tops In Adventure #1, © Z-D

Torchy #3, © QUA

The Tormented #1, © Sterling Comics

Tower Of Shadows #5, © MEG

Transformers: Headmasters #1, © MEG

	Good	Fine	N-Mint
TORCHY (continued)			
5,6-Ward c/a, 9 pgs; Fox-a(3) each	52.00	155.00	365.00
Super Reprint #16('64)-R-/#4 with new-c	6.00	18.00	36.00
TORMENTED, THE (Surprise Adventures #3 on)			
July, 1954 - No. 2, Sept, 1954			
Sterling Comics			
1,2	5.00	15.00	35.00
TORNADO TOM (See Mighty Midget Comics)			
TOTAL ECLIPSE			
May, 1988 - No. 5, Apr, 1989 ($3.95, color, deluxe size, 52 pgs.)			
Eclipse Comics			
Book 1-5: 3-Intro/1st app. new Black Terror	.70	2.00	3.95
TOTAL ECLIPSE: THE SERAPHIM OBJECTIVE			
Nov, 1988 ($1.95, color, one-shot, Baxter paper)			
Eclipse Comics			
1-Airboy, Valkyrie, The Heap app.	.35	1.00	2.00
TOTAL WAR (M.A.R.S. Patrol #3 on)			
July, 1965 - No. 2, Oct, 1965 (Painted covers)			
Gold Key			
1,2-Wood-a	1.70	5.00	12.00
TOUGH KID SQUAD COMICS			
March, 1942			
Timely Comics (TCI)			
1-(Scarce)-Origin The Human Top & The Tough Kid Squad; The Flying Flame app.	310.00	775.00	1850.00
TOWER OF SHADOWS (Creatures on the Loose #10 on)			
Sept, 1969 - No. 9, Jan, 1971			
Marvel Comics Group			
1-Steranko, Craig-a		.60	1.20
2-4: 2-Neal Adams-a. 3-Smith-a. 4-Kirby/Everett-c		.50	1.00
5,7-Smith(p), Wood-a (Wood draws himself-1st pg., 1st panel-#5)	.25	.75	1.50
6,8: Wood-a; 8-Wrightson-c		.50	1.00
9-Wrightson-c; Roy Thomas app.		.50	1.00
Special 1(12/71)-Adams-a		.50	1.00

NOTE: *J. Buscema a-1p, 2p. Colan a-3p, 6p. J. Craig a-1. Ditko a-6, 8, 9r, Special 1. Everett a-9(i)r; c-5i. Kirby a-9(p)r. Severin c-5i, 6. Steranko a-1. Tuska a-3. Wood a-5-8. Issues 1-9 contain new stories with some pre-Marvel age reprints in 6-9. H. P. Lovecraft adaptation-9.*

	Good	Fine	N-Mint
TOWN & COUNTRY			
May, 1940			
Publisher?			
Origin The Falcon	24.00	73.00	170.00
TOWN THAT FORGOT SANTA, THE			
1961 (24 pages) (Giveaway)			
W. T. Grant Co.			
nn	1.35	4.00	9.00
TOYBOY			
Oct, 1986 - Present ($2.00, color, Baxter paper)			
Continuity Comics			
1-8; 1,2-Adams-c. 1-Adams-a. 1,2-Nebres-i	.35	1.00	2.00
TOYLAND COMICS			
Jan, 1947 - No. 4, July?, 1947			
Fiction House Magazines			
1	9.30	28.00	65.00
2-4: 3-Tuska-a	5.70	17.00	40.00
148 pg. issue	11.50	34.00	80.00

NOTE: *All above contain strips by Al Walker.*

	Good	Fine	N-Mint
TOY TOWN COMICS			
1945 - No. 7, May, 1947			
Toytown/Orbit Publ./B. Antin/Swapper Quarterly			
1-Mertie Mouse; L. B. Cole-c/a	9.30	28.00	65.00
2-L. B. Cole-a	5.00	15.00	35.00
3-7-L. B. Cole-a	3.70	11.00	26.00
TRAGG AND THE SKY GODS (See Gold Key Spotlight, Mystery Comics Digest #3,9 & Spine Tingling Tales) (Painted-c #3-8)			
June, 1975 - No. 8, Feb, 1977; No. 9, May, 1982			
Gold Key/Whitman No. 9			
1-Origin		.60	1.20
2-9: 4-Sabre-Fang app. 8-Ostellon app.; 9-r #1		.40	.80
NOTE: *Santos a-1, 2, 9r; c-3-7. Spiegel a-3-8.*			
TRAIL BLAZERS (Red Dragon #5 on)			
1941 - No. 4, 1942			
Street & Smith Publications			
1-True stories of American heroes	14.00	42.00	100.00
2	9.30	28.00	65.00
3,4	8.00	24.00	56.00
TRAIL COLT (Also see Manhunt!)			
1949 - No. 2, 1949			
Magazine Enterprises			
nn(A-1 24)-7 pg. Frazetta r-in Manhunt #13; Undercover Girl app.; The Red Fox by L. B. Cole; Ingels-c; Whitney-a (Scarce)	27.00	81.00	190.00
2(A-1 26)-Undercover Girl; Ingels-c; L. B. Cole-a, 6pgs.	22.00	65.00	150.00
TRANSFORMERS, THE (TV)(Also see G.I. Joe and...)			
Sept, 1984 - Present (75 cents, $1.00)			
Marvel Comics Group			
1-Based on Hasbro toy	.60	1.75	3.50
2,3	.35	1.00	2.00
4-10	.25	.75	1.50
11-64: 21-Intro Aerialbots. 54-Intro Micromasters		.50	1.00
NOTE: *Second and third printings of all issues exist and are worth less than originals.*			
TRANSFORMERS COMICS MAGAZINE, THE			
Oct, 1986 - No. 11, 1988 ($1.50, Digest-size)			
Marvel Comics Group			
1-11	.25	.75	1.50
TRANSFORMERS: HEADMASTERS, THE			
July, 1987 - No. 4, Jan, 1988 (mini-series)			
Marvel Comics Group			
1	.35	1.00	2.00
2-4	.25	.75	1.50
TRANSFORMERS IN 3-D See Blackthorne 3-D Series #25, 29, 37)			
TRANSFORMERS, THE MOVIE			
Dec, 1986 - No. 3, Feb, 1987 (mini-series)			
Marvel Comics Group			
1-Adapts animated movie	.25	.75	1.50
2,3		.50	1.00
TRANSFORMERS UNIVERSE, THE			
Dec, 1986 - No. 4, March, 1987 ($1.25, mini-series)			
Marvel Comics Group			
1-A guide to all characters	.35	1.00	2.00
2-4		.65	1.30
TRAPPED			
1951 (Giveaway) (16 pages) (soft cover)			
Harvey Publications (Columbia University Press)			
Drug education comic (30,000 printed?) distributed to schools. Mentioned in SOTI, pgs. 256,350	2.00	6.00	12.00

TRAPPED (continued)
NOTE: Many copies surfaced in 1979 causing a setback in price; beware of trimmed edges, because many copies have a brittle edge.

TRAPPED!
Oct, 1954 - No. 5, June?, 1955
Periodical House Magazines (Ace)

	Good	Fine	N-Mint
1 (All-r)	3.70	11.00	26.00
2-5: 4-r/Men Against Crime #4 in it's entirety	2.00	6.00	14.00

NOTE: Colan a-1, 4. Sekowsky a-1.

TRAVELS OF HAPPY HOOLIGAN, THE
1906 (10¼"x15¾", 32 pgs., cardboard covers)
Frederick A. Stokes Co.

	Good	Fine	N-Mint
1905-r	22.00	65.00	154.00

TRAVELS OF JAIMIE McPHEETERS, THE (TV)
December, 1963
Gold Key

	Good	Fine	N-Mint
1-Kurt Russell	2.00	6.00	14.00

TREASURE BOX OF FAMOUS COMICS
Mid 1930's (36 pgs.) (6-7/8"x8½") (paper covers)
Cupples & Leon Co.

Box plus 5 titles: Reg'lar Fellers(1928), Little Orphan Annie(1926), Smitty(1928), Harold Teen(1931), How D. Tracy & D. Tracy Jr. Caught The Racketeers (1933) (These are abbreviated versions of hardcover editions) (Set). . . . 71.00 215.00 500.00

NOTE: Dates shown are copyright dates; all books actually came out in 1934 or later.

TREASURE CHEST (Catholic Guild; also see Topix)
3/12/46 - V27#8, July, 1972 (Educational comics)
George A. Pflaum (not publ. during Summer)

	Good	Fine	N-Mint
V1#1	7.00	21.00	50.00
2-6 (5/21/46): 5-Dr. Styx app. by Baily	3.00	9.00	21.00
V2#1 (9/3/46) - 6	1.50	4.50	10.00
V3#1-5,7-20 (1st slick cover)	1.50	4.50	10.00
V3#6-Jules Verne's "Voyage to the Moon"	3.35	10.00	22.00
V4#1-20 (9/9/48-5/31/49)	1.35	4.00	8.00
V5#1-20 (9/6/49-5/31/50)	1.00	3.00	6.00
V6#1-20 (9/14/50-5/31/51)	1.00	3.00	6.00
V7#1-20 (9/13/51-6/5/52)	.70	2.00	4.00
V8#1-20 (9/11/52-6/4/53)	.70	2.00	4.00
V9#1-20 ('53-'54)	.50	1.50	3.00
V10#1-20 ('54-'55)	.50	1.50	3.00
V11('55-'56), V12('56-'57)	.50	1.50	3.00
V13#1,3-5,7,9-V17#1 ('57-'63)	.35	1.00	2.00
V13#2,6,8-Ingels-a	2.00	6.00	14.00

V17#2-'This Godless Communism' series begins (Not in odd numbered issues); Cover shows hammer & sickle over Statue of Liberty; 8pg. Crandall-a of family life under communism 9.00 27.00 62.00

	Good	Fine	N-Mint
V17#3,5,7,9,11,13,15,17,19	.25	.80	1.60
V17#4,6,14-'This Godless Communism' stories	6.00	18.00	42.00

V17#8-Shows red octopus encompassing Earth, firing squad; 8pg. Crandall-a 6.50 19.50 45.00
V17#10-'This Godless Communism'-how Stalin came to power, part I; Crandall-a 6.00 18.00 42.00
V17#12-Stalin in WWII, forced labor, death by exhaustion; Crandall-a 6.00 18.00 42.00
V17#16-Kruschev takes over; de-Stalinization 6.00 18.00 42.00
V17#18-Kruschev's control; murder of revolters, brainwash, space race by Crandall 6.00 18.00 42.00
V17#20-End of series; Kruschev-people are puppets, firing squads hammer & sickle over Statue of Liberty, snake around communist manifesto by Crandall 6.00 18.00 42.00

	Good	Fine	N-Mint
V18#1-20,V19#11-20,V20#1-20('64-'65)	.40	.80	

V18#5-'What About Red China?'-describes how communists took over China 2.75 8.00 16.00
V19#1-10-'Red Victim' anti-communist series in all 2.75 8.00 16.00

	Good	Fine	N-Mint
V21-V25('65-'70)-(two V24#5's 11/7/68 & 11/21/68) (no V24#6)		.30	.60
V26, V27#1-8 (V26,27-68 pgs.)		.30	.60
Summer Edition V1#1-6('66), V2#1-6('67)		.20	.40

NOTE: **Anderson** a-V18/13. **Borth** a-V7/10-19 (serial), V8/8-17 (serial), V9/1-10 (serial), V13/2, 6, 11, V14-V25 (except V22/1-3, 11-13), Summer Ed. V1/3-6. **Crandall** a-V16/7, 9, 12, 14, 16-18, 20; V17/1, 2, 4-6, 10, 12, 14, 16-18, 20; V18/1, 2, 3(2pg.), 7, 9-20; V19/4, 11, 13, 16, 19, 20; V20/1, 2, 4, 8-10, 12, 14-16, 18, 20; V21/1-5, 8-11, 13, 16-18; V22/3, 7, 9-11, 14; V23/3, 6, 9, 16, 18; V24/7, 8, 10, 13; 16; V25/8, 16; V27/1, 2, 3-6r, 8(2 pg.), Summer Ed. V1/3-5, V2/3; c-V16/7; V18/2(part), 7, 11, V19/4, 19, 20. V20/15, V21/5, 9, V22/3, 7, 9, 11, V23/9, 16?, V24/13, 16, V25/8. **Powell** a-V10/11, V19/11, 15, V10/13, V13/6, 8 all have wraparound covers. All the above Crandall issues should be priced by condition from $4-8.00 in mint unless already priced.

TREASURE CHEST OF THE WORLD'S BEST COMICS
1945 (500 pgs.) (hardcover)
Superior, Toronto, Canada

Contains Blue Beetle, Captain Combat, John Wayne, Dynamic Man, Nemo, Li'l Abner; contents can vary - represents random binding of extra books; Capt. America on-c 38.00 115.00 265.00

TREASURE COMICS
No date (1943) (324 pgs.; cardboard covers) (50 cents)
Prize Publications? (no publisher listed)

1-(Rare)-Contains Prize Comics #7-11 from 1942 (blank inside-c) 136.00 407.00 950.00

TREASURE COMICS
June-July, 1945 - No. 12, Fall, 1947
Prize Publications (American Boys' Comics)

	Good	Fine	N-Mint
1-Paul Bunyan & Marco Polo begin; Highwayman & Carrot Topp only app.; Kiefer-a	11.00	32.00	75.00
2-Arabian Knight, Gorilla King, Dr. Styx begin	5.50	16.50	38.00
3,4,9,12: 9-Kiefer-a	3.70	11.00	26.00
5-Marco Polo-c; Kirby a(p); Krigstein-a	8.00	24.00	56.00
6,11-Krigstein-a; 11-Krigstein-c	6.50	19.50	45.00
7,8-Frazetta-a, 5 pgs. each	22.00	65.00	154.00
10-Kirby-c/a	10.00	30.00	70.00

NOTE: **Barry** a-9, 11. **Roussos** a-11.

TREASURE ISLAND (See 4-Color #624, King Classics, & Movie Classics & Movie Comics)

TREASURY OF COMICS
1947; No. 2, July, 1947 - No. 4, Sept, 1947; No. 5, Jan, 1948
St. John Publishing Co.

	Good	Fine	N-Mint
nn(#1)-Abbie 'n' Slats (nn on-c, #1 on inside)	8.50	25.50	60.00
2-Jim Hardy	6.00	18.00	42.00
3-Bill Bumlin	4.30	13.00	30.00
4-Abbie 'n' Slats	5.50	16.50	38.00
5-Jim Hardy Comics #1	5.50	16.50	38.00

TREASURY OF COMICS
Mar, 1948 - No. 5, 1948; 1948-1950 (Over 500 pgs., $1.00)
St. John Publishing Co.

	Good	Fine	N-Mint
1	11.00	32.00	75.00
2(#2 on-c, #1 on inside)	6.50	19.50	45.00
3-5	5.50	16.50	38.00

1-(1948, 500 pgs., hard-c)-Abbie & Slats, Abbott & Costello, Casper, Little Annie Rooney, Little Audrey, Jim Hardy, Ella Cinders (16 books bound together) (Rare) 90.00 270.00 630.00
1(1949, 500pgs.)-Same format as above 90.00 270.00 630.00
1(1950, 500pgs.)-Same format as above; different-c; (Also see Little Audrey Yearbook) (Rare) 90.00 270.00 630.00

TREASURY OF DOGS, A (See Dell Giants)
TREASURY OF HORSES, A (See Dell Giants)

Trapped! #1, © ACE

Treasure Comics #5, © PRIZE

Treasury Of Comics #2 (7/47), © STJ

The Trouble With Girls V2#1, © Comico

True Comics #31, © PMI

True Comics And Adventure Stories #1, © PMI

TREKKER (See Dark Horse Presents #6)
May, 1987 - No. 9?, 1988 ($1.50, B&W)
Dark Horse Comics

	Good	Fine	N-Mint
1-9: Sci/Fi stories	.25	.75	1.50
Color Special 1 (1989, $2.95, 52 pgs.)	.50	1.50	3.00
. . .Collection ($5.95, B&W)	1.00	3.00	5.95

TRIALS OF LULU AND LEANDER, THE
1906 (32 pgs. in color) (10x16")
William A. Stokes Co.

By F. M. Howarth	15.00	45.00	105.00

TRIGGER (See Roy Rogers. . .)

TRIGGER TWINS
Mar-Apr, 1973 (One Shot)
National Periodical Publications

1-Trigger Twins & Pow Wow Smith-r; Infantino-a(p)		.40	.80

TRIPLE GIANT COMICS (See Archie All-Star Spec. under Archie Comics)

TRIPLE THREAT
Winter, 1945
Special Action/Holyoke/Gerona Publ.

1-Duke of Darkness, King O'Leary	6.00	18.00	42.00

TRIP WITH SANTA ON CHRISTMAS EVE, A
No date (early 50's) (16 pgs.; full color; paper cover)
Rockford Dry Goods Co. (Giveaway)

nn	2.00	6.00	12.00

TROLLORDS
2/86 - No. 15, 1988; V2#1, 11/88 - V2#4, 1989 (1-15: $1.50, B&W)
Tru Studios/Comico V2#1 - on

1	1.00	3.00	6.00
1-2nd print	.35	1.00	2.00
2	.50	1.50	3.00
3-15: 6-Christmas issue; silver logo	.25	.75	1.50
V2#1 ($1.75, color, Comico)	.30	.90	1.80
V2#2,3 ($1.95, color)	.35	1.00	2.00
V2#4 ($2.50, color)	.40	1.25	2.50
Special 1($1.75, 2/87, color)-Jerry's Big Fun Bk.	.35	1.00	2.00

TROLLORDS: DEATH AND KISSES
July, 1989 - No. 6, 1990 ($2.25, B&W, mini-series)
Apple Comics

1-6: 1-"The Big Batman Movie Parody"	.40	1.15	2.30

TROUBLE SHOOTERS, THE (See 4-Color #1108)

TROUBLE WITH GIRLS, THE
Aug, 1987 - No. 14, 1988; V2#1, Feb, 1989 - Present ($1.95, B&W)
Malibu Comics/Eternity Comics #7-14/Comico V2#1-4/Eternity #5 on

1-14 ($1.95, B&W)	.35	1.00	2.00
V2#1-4 ($1.95, color, Comico)	.35	1.00	2.00
5-10 ($1.95, B&W, Eternity)	.35	1.00	2.00
Annual 1 ($2.95, '88)	.50	1.50	2.95
Graphic Novel 1 (7/88, $6.95, B&W)-r/1-3	1.15	3.50	7.00
Graphic Novel 2 (1989, $7.95, B&W)-r/4-6	1.35	4.00	8.00

TRUE ADVENTURES (Formerly True Western)(Men's Advs. #4 on)
No. 3, May, 1950 (52 pgs.)
Marvel Comics (CCC)

3-Powell, Sekowsky-a	5.70	17.00	40.00

TRUE ANIMAL PICTURE STORIES
Winter, 1947 - No. 2, Spr-Summer, 1947
True Comics Press

1,2	3.50	10.50	24.00

TRUE AVIATION PICTURE STORIES (Aviation Adventures & Model Building #16)
1942 - No. 15, Sept-Oct, 1946
Parents' Magazine Institute

	Good	Fine	N-Mint
1-(#1 & 2 titled . . .Aviation Comics Digest)(not digest size)			
	8.00	24.00	56.00
2	4.00	12.00	28.00
3-14	3.50	10.50	24.00
15-(titled "True Aviation Adventures & Model Building")			
	2.65	8.00	18.00

TRUE BRIDE'S EXPERIENCES (Formerly Teen-Age Brides)
(True Bride-To-Be Romances No. 17 on)
No. 8, Oct, 1954 - No. 16, Feb, 1956
True Love (Harvey Publications)

8	1.70	5.00	12.00
9,10: 10-Last pre-code (2/55)	1.35	4.00	9.00
11-15	1.00	3.00	7.00
16-Spanking issue	5.00	15.00	35.00

NOTE: **Powell** a-8-10, 12, 13.

TRUE BRIDE-TO-BE ROMANCES (Formerly True Bride's Exp.)
No. 17, Apr, 1956 - No. 30, Nov, 1958
Home Comics/True Love (Harvey)

17-S&K-c, Powell-a	2.00	6.00	14.00
18-20,22,25-28,30	1.00	3.00	7.00
21,23,24-Powell-a	1.20	3.50	8.00
29-Powell, 1 pg. Baker-a	1.35	4.00	9.00

TRUE COMICS (Also see Outstanding American War Heroes)
April, 1941 - No. 84, Aug, 1950
True Comics/Parents' Magazine Press

1-Marathon run story	14.00	42.00	100.00
2-Everett-a	7.00	21.00	50.00
3-Baseball Hall of Fame story	8.00	24.00	56.00
4,5: 4-Story of American flag "Old Glory." 5-Life story of Joe Louis			
	6.00	18.00	42.00
6-Baseball World Series story	5.70	17.00	40.00
7-10	4.30	13.00	30.00
11-17,18-20: 13-Harry Houdini story. 14-Charlie McCarthy story. 15-Flag-c; Bob Feller story. 18-Story of America begins, ends #26			
	3.70	11.00	26.00
17-Brooklyn Dodgers story	4.30	13.00	30.00
21-30	3.50	10.50	24.00
31-Red Grange story	2.85	8.50	20.00
32-45: 39-FDR story	2.30	7.00	16.00
46-George Gershwin story	2.30	7.00	16.00
47-Atomic bomb issue	4.30	13.00	30.00
48-67: 55(12/46)-1st app. Sad Sack by Baker, ½ pg. 58-Jim Jeffries (boxer) story; Harry Houdini story. 59-Bob Hope story. 66-Will Rogers story			
	1.70	5.00	12.00
68-1st oversized issue?; Steve Saunders, Special Agent begins			
	2.65	8.00	18.00
69-72,74-79: 69-Jack Benny story. 71-Joe DiMaggio story. 78-Stan Musial story	1.50	4.50	10.00
73-Walt Disney's life story	2.35	7.00	16.00
80-84 (Scarce)-All distr. to subscribers through mail only; paper-c; 81-Red Grange story	14.30	43.00	100.00
(Prices vary widely on these books)			

NOTE: **Bob Kane** a-7. **Palais** a-80. **Powell** c/a-80. #80-84 have soft covers and combined with Tex Granger, Jack Armstrong, and Calling All Kids. #68-78 featured true FBI adventures.

TRUE COMICS AND ADVENTURE STORIES
1965 (Giant) (25 cents)
Parents' Magazine Institute

1,2-Fighting Hero of Viet Nam; LBJ on-c	.70	2.00	4.50

TRUE COMPLETE MYSTERY (Formerly Complete Mystery)
No. 5, April, 1949 - No. 8, Oct, 1949
Marvel Comics (PrPl)

	Good	Fine	N-Mint
5	8.00	24.00	56.00
6-8: 6,8-Photo-c	6.50	19.50	45.00

TRUE CONFIDENCES
1949 (Fall) - No. 4, June, 1950 (All photo-c)
Fawcett Publications

1-Has ad for Fawcett Love Adventures #1, but publ. as Love Memoirs #1 as Marvel publ. the title first	5.70	17.00	40.00
2-4: 4-Powell-a	2.65	8.00	18.00

TRUE CRIME CASES
1944; V1No.6, June-July 1949 - V2No.1, Aug-Oct, 1949
St. John Publishing Co.

1944-(100 pgs.)	20.00	60.00	140.00
V1#6, V2#1	4.50	14.00	32.00

TRUE CRIME COMICS (Also see Complete Book of. . .)
No. 2, May, 1947; No. 3, Jul-Aug, 1948 - No. 6, June-Jul, 1949;
V2No.1, Aug-Sept, 1949 (52 pgs.)
Magazine Village

2-Jack Cole c/a; used in SOTI, pg. 81,82 plus illo.-"A sample of the injury-to-eye motif" & illo.-"Dragging living people to death;" used in POP, pg. 105; "Murder, Morphine and Me" classic drug propaganda story used by N.Y. Legis. Comm.	75.00	225.00	525.00
3-Classic Cole c/a; drug sty with hypo, opium den & withdrawing addict	50.00	150.00	350.00
4-Jack Cole c/a; c-taken from a story panel in #3; r-(2) SOTI & POP stories/#2	45.00	135.00	315.00
5-Jack Cole-c; Marijuana racket story	21.50	65.00	150.00
6	10.00	30.00	70.00
V2#1-Used in SOTI, pgs. 81,82 & illo.-"Dragging living people to death;" Toth, Wood (3 pgs.), Roussos-a; Cole-r from #2	32.00	95.00	225.00

NOTE: V2#1 was reprinted in Canada as V2#9 (12/49); same cover & contents minus Wood-a.

TRUE GHOST STORIES (See Ripley's. . .)

TRUE LIFE ROMANCES (. . .Romance on cover)
Dec, 1955 - No. 3, Aug, 1956
Ajax/Farrell Publications

1	3.50	10.50	24.00
2	1.70	5.00	12.00
3-Disbrow-a	2.65	8.00	18.00

TRUE LIFE SECRETS
Mar-April, 1951 - No. 28, Sept, 1955; No. 29, Jan, 1956
Romantic Love Stories/Charlton

1	4.35	13.00	30.00
2	2.65	8.00	18.00
3-12,15-19: 17-Headlights-c/a	2.00	6.00	14.00
13-Headlight-a	5.35	16.00	37.00
14-Drug mention story(marijuana)	3.15	9.50	22.00
20-22,24-29: 25-Last precode (3/55)	1.50	4.50	10.00
23-Suggestive-c	2.65	8.00	18.00

TRUE LIFE TALES
No. 8, Oct, 1949 - No. 2, Jan, 1950
Marvel Comics (CCC)

8(10/49), 2(1/50)-Photo-c	3.50	10.50	24.00

TRUE LOVE
Jan, 1986 - No. 2, Jan, 1986 ($2.00, color, Baxter paper)
Eclipse Comics

1,2-Love stories-r from pre-code Standard Comics; Toth-a(p) in both; 1-Dave Stevens-c. 2-Mayo-a	.35	1.00	2.00

TRUE LOVE CONFESSIONS
May, 1954 - No. 11, Jan, 1956
Premier Magazines

	Good	Fine	N-Mint
1-Marijuana story	4.30	13.00	30.00
2	2.00	6.00	14.00
3-11	1.30	4.00	9.00

TRUE LOVE PICTORIAL
1952 - No. 11, Aug, 1954
St. John Publishing Co.

1	6.00	18.00	42.00
2	3.00	9.00	21.00
3-5(All 100 pgs.): 5-Formerly Teen-Age Temptations (4/53); Kubert-a-#3,5; Baker-a-#3-5	15.00	45.00	105.00
6,7-Baker c/a	6.00	18.00	42.00
8,10,11-Baker c/a	5.00	15.00	35.00
9-Baker-c	4.00	12.00	28.00

TRUE MOVIE AND TELEVISION (Part magazine)
Aug, 1950 - No. 3, Nov, 1950 (52 pgs.) (10 cents)
Toby Press

1-Liz Taylor photo-c; Gene Autry, Shirley Temple, Li'l Abner app.	21.00	62.00	145.00
2-Frazetta John Wayne illo	13.00	40.00	90.00
3-June Allyson-c; Montgomery Cliff, Esther Williams, Andrews Sisters app; Li'l Abner feat.	13.00	40.00	90.00

NOTE: 16 pages in color, rest movie material in black & white.

TRUE SECRETS (Formerly Our Love)
No. 3, Mar, 1950; No. 4, Feb, 1951 - No. 40, Sept, 1956
Marvel (IPS)/Atlas Comics (MPI)

3 (52 pgs.)	4.00	12.00	28.00
4,5,7-10	2.00	6.00	14.00
6,22-Everett-a	2.65	8.00	18.00
11-20	1.50	4.50	10.00
21,23-28: 28-Last pre-code (2/55)	1.15	3.50	8.00
29-40	1.00	3.00	7.00

NOTE: Colletta a-34, 36; c-24.

TRUE SPORT PICTURE STORIES (Formerly Sport Comics)
V1#5, Feb, 1942? - V5/#2, July-Aug, 1949
Street & Smith Publications

V1#5	12.00	36.00	84.00
6-12 (1942-43)	6.50	19.50	45.00
V2#1-12 (1944-45)	5.70	17.00	40.00
V3#1-12 (1946-47)	4.30	13.00	30.00
V4#1-12 (1948-49), V5/1,2	3.50	10.50	24.00

NOTE: Powell a-V3#10, V4#1-4, 6-8, 10-12; V5#1, 2; c-V4#5-7, 9, 10.

TRUE STORIES OF ROMANCE
Jan, 1950 - No. 3, May, 1950 (All photo-c)
Fawcett Publications

1	4.35	13.00	30.00
2,3	2.65	8.00	18.00

TRUE STORY OF JESSE JAMES, THE (See 4-Color #757)

TRUE SWEETHEART SECRETS
5/50; No. 2, 7/50; No. 3, 1951(nd); No. 4, 9/51 - No. 11, 1/53
Fawcett Publications (All photo-c)

1-Photo-c; Debbie Reynolds?	5.00	15.00	35.00
2-Wood-a, 11 pgs.	8.00	24.00	56.00
3-11: 4,5-Powell-a	2.35	7.00	16.00

TRUE TALES OF LOVE (Formerly Secret Story Romances)
No. 22, April, 1956 - No. 31, Sept, 1957
Atlas Comics (TCI)

22	2.00	6.00	14.00
23-31-Colletta-a in most	1.00	3.00	7.00

True Crime Comics #2, © Magazine Village

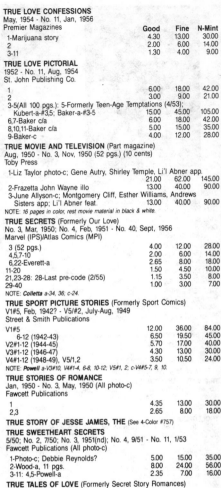

True Movie And Television #3, © TOBY

True Secrets #16, © MEG

True Western #1, © MEG

Turok, Son Of Stone #7, © DELL

Turtle Soup #1, © Mirage Studios

TRUE TALES OF ROMANCE
No. 4, June, 1950
Fawcett Publications

	Good	Fine	N-Mint
4	2.85	8.50	20.00

TRUE 3-D
Dec, 1953 - No. 2, Feb, 1954
Harvey Publications

1-Nostrand, Powell-a	5.70	17.00	40.00
2-Powell-a	10.00	30.00	70.00

NOTE: *Many copies of #1 surfaced in 1984.*

TRUE-TO-LIFE ROMANCES
#8, 11-12/49; #9, 1-2/50; #3, 4/50 - #5, 9/50; #6, 1/51 - #23, 10/54
Star Publications

8 (#1, 1949)	5.70	17.00	40.00
9,3-10: 3-Janet Leigh/Glenn Ford photo on-c	4.50	14.00	32.00
11,22,23	4.30	13.00	30.00
12-14,17-21-Disbrow-a	5.50	16.50	38.00
15,16-Wood & Disbrow-a in each	8.35	25.00	58.00

NOTE: *Kamen a-13. Kamen/Feldstein a-14. All have L.B. Cole covers.*

TRUE WAR EXPERIENCES
Aug, 1952 - No. 4, Dec, 1952
Harvey Publications

1	2.35	7.00	16.00
2-4	1.35	4.00	9.00

TRUE WAR ROMANCES
Sept, 1952 - No. 21, June, 1955
Quality Comics Group

1-Photo-c	5.00	15.00	35.00
2	2.65	8.00	18.00
3-10: 9-Whitney-a	2.00	6.00	14.00
11-21: 20-Last precode (4/55). 14-Whitney-a	1.60	4.80	11.00

TRUE WAR STORIES (See Ripley's . . .)

TRUE WESTERN (True Adventures #3)
Dec, 1949 - No. 2, March, 1950
Marvel Comics (MMC)

1-Photo-c; Billy The Kid story	7.00	21.00	50.00
2: Alan Ladd photo-c	8.00	24.00	56.00

TRUE WEST ROMANCE
No. 21, 1952
Quality Comics Group

21 (Exist?)	2.65	8.00	18.00

TRUMP (Magazine format)
Jan, 1957 - No. 2, Mar, 1957
HMH Publishing Co.

1-Harvey Kurtzman satire	9.30	28.00	65.00
2-Harvey Kurtzman satire	8.00	24.00	56.00

NOTE: *Davis, Elder, Heath, Jaffee art-#1,2; Wood a-1. Article by Mel Brooks in #2.*

TRUMPETS WEST (See 4-Color #875)

TRUTH ABOUT CRIME (See Fox Giants)

TRUTH ABOUT MOTHER GOOSE (See 4-Color #862)

TRUTH BEHIND THE TRIAL OF CARDINAL MINDSZENTY, THE (See Cardinal Mindszenty)

TRUTHFUL LOVE (Formerly Youthful Love)
No. 2, July, 1950
Youthful Magazines

2-Ingrid Bergman's true life story	2.65	8.00	18.00

TRY-OUT WINNER BOOK
Mar, 1988
Marvel Comics

	Good	Fine	N-Mint
1-Spider-Man vs. Doc. Octopus		.60	1.25

TUBBY (See Marge's . . .)

TUFF GHOSTS STARRING SPOOKY
7/62 - No. 39, 11/70; No. 40, 9/71 - No. 43, 10/72
Harvey Publications

1	4.00	12.00	24.00
2-5	2.00	6.00	12.00
6-10	1.35	4.00	8.00
11-20	.70	2.00	4.00
21-30	.50	1.50	3.00
31-39,43		.50	1.00
40-42: 52 pg. Giants		.60	1.20

TUFFY
1949 - No. 10, 1950
Standard Comics

1-All by Sid Hoff	2.65	8.00	18.00
2	1.30	4.00	9.00
3-10	1.15	3.50	8.00

TUFFY TURTLE
No date
I. W. Enterprises

1-Reprint	.25	.80	1.60

TUROK, SON OF STONE (See Dan Curtis, Golden Comics Digest #31, and March of Comics #378,399,408)
No. 596, 12/54 - No. 29, 9/62; No. 30, 12/62 - No. 91, 7/74; No. 92, 9/74 - No. 125, 1/80; No. 126, 3/81 - No. 130, 4/82
Dell Publ. Co. No. 1-29/Gold Key No. 30-91/Gold Key or Whitman No. 92-125/Whitman No. 126 on

4-Color 596 (12/54)(#1)-1st app./origin Turok & Andar			
	24.00	73.00	170.00
4-Color 656 (10/55)(#2)-1st mention of Lanok	17.00	50.00	120.00
3(3-5/56)-5	12.00	36.00	84.00
6-10	8.00	24.00	56.00
11-20: 17-Prehistoric pygmies	4.00	12.00	28.00
21-30: 30-Back-c pin-ups begin. 30-33-Painted back-c pin-ups			
	2.30	7.00	16.00
31-50: 31-Drug use story	1.15	3.50	8.00
51-60: 58-Flying Saucer c/sty	.70	2.00	5.00
61-83: 62-12 & 15 cent-c. 63-Only line drawn-c	.35	1.00	2.00
84-Origin & 1st app. Hutec	.35	1.00	2.00
85-130: 114,115-(52 pgs.)		.50	1.00
Giant 1(30031-611) (11/66)	4.50	13.50	36.00

NOTE: *Most painted-c; line-drawn #63 & 130. Alberto Gioletti painted-c No. 30-129. Sparling a-117-120,122,124,126,129,130. Reprints-#36, 54, 57, 75, 112, 114(½), 115(½), 118, 125, 127(½), 128, 129(½), 130(½), Giant 1.*

TURTLE SOUP
Sept, 1987 ($2.00, B&W, one shot, 76 pgs.)
Mirage Studios

1-Feat. Teenage Mutant Ninja Turtles	.50	1.50	3.00

TV CASPER & COMPANY
Aug, 1963 - No. 46, April, 1974 (25 cent Giants)
Harvey Publications

1: 68 pg. Giants begin	4.30	13.00	30.00
2-5	2.00	6.00	14.00
6-10	1.35	4.00	8.00
11-20	.70	2.00	4.00
21-31: Last 68 pg. issue	.50	1.50	3.00
32-46: All 52 pgs.		.50	1.00

NOTE: *Many issues contain reprints.*

TV FUNDAY FUNNIES (See Famous TV . . .)

TV FUNNIES (See New Funnies)

TV FUNTIME (See Little Audrey)

TV LAUGHOUT (See Archie's...)

TV SCREEN CARTOONS (Formerly Real Screen)
No. 129, July-Aug, 1959 - No. 138, Jan-Feb, 1961
National Periodical Publications

	Good	Fine	N-Mint
129-138 (Scarce)	2.30	7.00	16.00

TV STARS (TV)(Hanna-Barbera)
Aug, 1978 - No. 4, Feb, 1979
Marvel Comics Group

1-Great Grape Ape app.	.40	1.25	2.50
2,4: 4-Top Cat app.		.50	1.00
3-Toth-c/a	.60	1.75	3.50

TV TEENS (Formerly Ozzie & Babs; Rock and Rollo #14 on)
V1#14, Feb, 1954 - V2#13, July, 1956
Charlton Comics

V1#14-Ozzie & Babs	3.50	10.50	24.00
15	1.85	5.50	13.00
V2#3(6/54) - 7-Don Winslow	2.15	6.50	15.00
8(7/55)-13-Mopsy	1.85	5.50	13.00

TWEETY AND SYLVESTER (1st Series)
No. 406, June, 1952 - No. 37, June-Aug, 1962
Dell Publishing Co.

4-Color 406	1.70	5.00	12.00
4-Color 489,524	1.00	3.00	7.00
4 (3-5/54) - 20	.85	2.50	6.00
21-37	.55	1.65	4.00

(See March of Comics #421,433,445,457,469,481)

TWEETY AND SYLVESTER (2nd Series)
Nov, 1963; No. 2, Nov, 1965 - No. 121, July, 1984
Gold Key No. 1-102/Whitman No. 103 on

1	.85	2.50	6.00
2-10	.45	1.35	3.00
11-30	.25	.75	1.50
31-70		.50	1.00
71-121: 99,119-r(⅓)		.30	.60
Kite Fun Book (1965, 16pgs., 5x7¼'', soft-c)	.50	1.50	3.00
Mini Comic No. 1(1976)-3¼x6½''		.30	.60

12 O'CLOCK HIGH (TV)
Jan-Mar, 1965 - No. 2, Apr-June, 1965 (Photo-c)
Dell Publishing Co.

1,2	2.30	7.00	16.00

24 PAGES OF COMICS (No title) (Also see Pure Oil Comics, Salerno Carnival of Comics, & Vicks Comics)
Late 1930s
Giveaway by various outlets including Sears
Contains strip reprints-Buck Rogers, Napoleon, Sky Roads, War on Crime

	20.00	60.00	140.00

20,000 LEAGUES UNDER THE SEA (See 4-Color #614, King Classics, and Movie Comics)

TWICE TOLD TALES (See Movie Classics)

TWILIGHT AVENGER, THE
July, 1986 - No. 2, 1987 ($1.75, color, mini-series)
Elite Comics

1,2	.30	.90	1.80

TWILIGHT MAN
June, 1989 - No. 4, Sept, 1989 ($2.75, color, mini-series)
First Publishing

1-4	.45	1.40	2.80

TWILIGHT ZONE, THE (TV) (See Dan Curtis)
No. 1173, 3-5/61 - No. 91, 4/79; No. 92, 5/82
Dell Publishing Co./Gold Key/Whitman #92

	Good	Fine	N-Mint
4-Color 1173-Crandall/Evans-c/a	5.70	17.00	40.00
4-Color 1288-Crandall/Evans-c/a	4.50	14.00	32.00
01-860-207 (5-7/62-Dell)	3.70	11.00	26.00
12-860-210 on-c; 01-860-210 on inside(8-10/62-Dell)-Evans c/a; Crandall/Frazetta-a(2)	3.70	11.00	26.00
1(11/62-Gold Key)-Crandall,Evans-a	3.50	10.50	24.00
2	1.70	5.00	12.00
3,4,9-Toth-a, 11,10 & 15 pgs.	2.00	6.00	14.00
5-8,10,11	1.30	4.00	9.00
12-Williamson-a	1.70	5.00	12.00
13,15-Crandall-a	1.70	5.00	12.00
14-Williamson/Orlando/Crandall/Torres-a	2.00	6.00	14.00
16-20	1.00	3.00	7.00
21-Crandall-a(r)	.70	2.00	5.00
22-27: 25-Evans/Crandall-a(r). 26-Crandall, Evans-a(r). 27-Evans-r(2)	.60	1.80	4.00
28-32: 32-Evans-a(r)	.35	1.00	2.00
33-42,44-50,52-70	.25	.75	1.50
43,51: 43-Crandall-a. 51-Williamson-a	.30	.90	1.80
71-92: 71-Reprint. 83,84-(52 pgs.)		.50	1.00
Mini Comic #1(1976-3¼x6½'')		.30	.60

NOTE: *Bolle* a-13(w/*McWilliams*), 50, 57, 59. *McWilliams* a-59. *Orlando* a-19, 20, 22, 23. *Sekowsky* a-3. (See Mystery Comics Digest 3, 6, 9, 12, 15, 18, 21, 24). Reprints-26(⅓), 71, 73, 79, 83, 84, 86, 92. Painted-c 1-91.

TWINKLE COMICS
May, 1945
Spotlight Publishers

1	7.00	21.00	50.00

TWIST, THE
July-September, 1962
Dell Publishing Co.

01-864-209-painted-c	3.00	9.00	21.00

TWISTED TALES (See Eclipse Graphic Album Series #15)
11/82 - No. 8, 5/84; No. 9, 11/84; No. 10, 12/84 (Baxter paper)
Pacific Comics/Independent Comics Group (Eclipse) #9, 10

1-Nudity/Violence in all	.60	1.75	3.50
2-10	.35	1.00	2.00

NOTE: *Alcala* a-1. *Bolton* painted c-4, 6, 7; a-7. *Conrad* a-1. *Corben* a-1, 3, 5; c-1, 3, 5. *Guice* a-8. *Morrow* a-10. *Ploog* a-2. *Wildey* a-3. *Wrightson* a(Painted)-10; c-2.

TWISTED TALES IN 3-D (See Blackthorne 3-D Series #7)

TWISTED TALES OF BRUCE JONES, THE
Feb, 1986 - No. 4, Mar, 1986 ($1.75, Baxter paper)
Eclipse Comics

1-4	.30	.90	1.80

TWO BIT THE WACKY WOODPECKER (See Wacky...)
1951 - No. 3, May, 1953
Toby Press

1	2.30	7.00	16.00
2,3	1.30	4.00	9.00

TWO FACES OF COMMUNISM (Also see Double Talk)
1961 (36 pgs.; paper cover) (Giveaway)
Christian Anti-Communism Crusade, Houston, Texas

nn	10.00	30.00	70.00

TWO-FISTED TALES (Formerly Haunt of Fear #15-17)
No. 18, Nov-Dec, 1950 - No. 41, Feb-Mar, 1955
E. C. Comics

18(#1)-Kurtzman-c	64.00	193.00	450.00
19-Kurtzman-c	47.00	140.00	325.00

Tweety And Sylvester #2 (Gold Key), © Warner Bros.

The Twilight Zone #14, © Cayuga Prod.

Twisted Tales #1, © Pacific

Two-Fisted Tales #22, © WMG

Two-Gun Kid #26, © MEG

UFO Flying Saucers #7, © GK

TWO-FISTED TALES (continued)	Good	Fine	N-Mint
20-Kurtzman-c	27.00	81.00	190.00
21,22-Kurtzman-c	21.00	62.00	145.00
23-25-Kurtzman-c	15.00	45.00	105.00
26-35: 33-"Atom Bomb" by Wood	12.00	36.00	80.00
36-41	7.35	22.00	50.00
Two-Fisted Annual, 1952	61.00	182.00	430.00
Two-Fisted Annual, 1953	45.00	135.00	315.00

NOTE: Berg a-29. Craig a-18, 19, 32. Crandall a-35, 36. Davis a-20-36, 40; c-30, 34, 35, 41, Annual 2. Evans a-34, 40, 41; c-40. Feldstein a-18. Krigstein a-41. Kubert a-32, 33. Kurtzman a-18-25; c-18-29, 31, Annual 1. Severin a-26, 28, 29, 31, 34-41 (No.37-39 are all-Severin issues); c-36-39. Severin/Elder a-19-29, 31, 33, 36. Wood a-18-28, 30-35, 41; c-32, 33. Special issues: #26 (ChanJin Reservoir), 31 (Civil War), 35 (Civil War). Canadian reprints known; see Table of Contents.

TWO-GUN KID (Also see All Western Winners, Best Western, Black Rider, Blaze Carson, Kid Colt, Western Winners, Wild West, & Wild Western)
3/48(No mo.) - No. 10, 11/49; No. 11, 12/53 - No. 59, 4/61; No. 60, 11/62 - No. 92, 3/68; No. 93, 7/70 - No. 136, 4/77
Marvel/Atlas (MCI No. 1-10/HPC No. 11-59/Marvel No. 60 on)

1-Two-Gun Kid & his horse Cyclone begin; The Sheriff begins	34.00	100.00	240.00
2	14.00	42.00	100.00
3,4: 3-Annie Oakley app.	10.00	30.00	70.00
5-Pre-Black Rider app. (Wint. 48/49); Spanking panel. Anti-Wertham editorial (1st?)	13.00	40.00	90.00
6-10 (11/49)	8.00	24.00	56.00
11 (12/53)-Black Rider app.	6.50	19.50	45.00
12-Black Rider app.	6.50	19.50	45.00
13-20	5.00	15.00	35.00
21-24,26-29	3.70	11.00	26.00
25,30-Williamson-a in both, 5 & 4 pgs.	4.50	14.00	32.00
31-33,35,37-40	2.85	8.50	20.00
34-Crandall-a	3.50	10.50	24.00
36,41,42,48-Origin in all	3.15	9.50	22.00
43,44,47	2.00	6.00	14.00
45,46-Davis-a	2.85	8.50	20.00
49,50,52,55,57-Severin-a(3) in each	2.00	6.00	14.00
51-Williamson-a, 5pgs.	3.00	9.00	21.00
53,54,56	1.00	3.00	7.00
58,60-New origin. 58-Last 10 cent issue	1.00	3.00	7.00
59,61-80: 64-Intro. Boom-Boom	.50	1.50	3.00
81-92: 92-Last new story; last 12 cent issue	.25	.75	1.50
93-100,102-136		.40	.80
101-Origin retold/#58		.30	.60

NOTE: Ayers a-26, 27. Davis c-45-47. Everett a-82, 91. Fuje a-13. Heath c-13, 21, 23. Keller a-16, 19, 28. Kirby a-54, 55, 57-62, 75-77, 90, 95, 101, 119, 120, 129; c-10, 52, 54-65, 67-72, 74-76, 116. Maneely a-20; c-16, 19, 20, 25-28, 49. Powell a-38, 102, 104. Severin a-29, 51. Tuska a-12. Whitney a-87, 89-91, 98-113, 124, 129; c-87, 89, 91, 113. Wildey a-21. Williamson a-110r. Kid Colt in #13, 14, 16-21.

TWO GUN WESTERN (1st Series) (Casey Crime Photographer #1-4)
No. 5, Nov, 1950 - No. 14, June, 1952
Marvel/Atlas Comics (MPC)

5-The Apache Kid (Intro & origin) & his horse Nightwind begin by Buscema	8.50	25.50	60.00
6-10: 8-Kid Colt, The Texas Kid & his horse Thunder begin?	5.00	15.00	35.00
11-14: 13-Black Rider app.	4.00	12.00	28.00

NOTE: Maneely a-6, 7, 9; c-6, 11-13. Romita a-8. Wildey a-8.

2-GUN WESTERN (2nd Series) (Formerly Billy Buckskin; Two-Gun Western #5 on)
No. 4, May, 1956
Atlas Comics (MgPC)

4-Apache Kid; Ditko-a	6.50	19.50	45.00

TWO-GUN WESTERN (Formerly 2-Gun Western)
No. 5, July, 1956 - No. 12, Sept, 1957

Atlas Comics (MgPC)	Good	Fine	N-Mint
5-Apache Kid, Kid Colt Outlaw, Doc Holiday begin; Black Rider app.	4.50	14.00	32.00
6,7,10	2.30	7.00	16.00
8,12-Crandall-a	3.50	10.50	24.00
9,11-Williamson-a in both, 5 pgs. each	4.00	12.00	28.00

NOTE: Ayers a-9. Everett c-12. Kirby a-12. Maneely a-6, 8, 12; c-5, 6, 8. Morrow a-9, 10. Powell a-7, 11. Severin c-10.

TWO MOUSEKETEERS, THE (See 4-Color #475,603,642 under M.G.M.'s...; becomes M.G.M.'s Mouse Musketeers)

TWO ON A GUILLOTINE (See Movie Classics)

2000 A.D. MONTHLY/PRESENTS (...Showcase #25 on)
4/85 - No. 6, 9/85; 4/86 - Present ($1.25-$1.50, color, Mando paper)
Eagle Comics/Quality Comics No. 5 on

1-6 ($1.25): 1-4-r/British series featuring Judge Dredd; Alan Moore			
scripts begin		.65	1.30
1-25 ($1.25)		.65	1.30
26,27/28,29/30,31-45: 27/28,29/30,31-Guice-c	.25	.75	1.50

2001: A SPACE ODYSSEY (Marvel Treasury Special)
Oct, 1976 (One Shot) (Over-sized)
Marvel Comics Group

1-Kirby, Giacoia-a	.35	1.00	2.00

2001, A SPACE ODYSSEY
Dec, 1976 - No. 10, Sept, 1977 (Regular size)
Marvel Comics Group

1-Kirby c/a in all		.30	.60
2-10: 8-Origin/1st app. Machine Man (called Mr. Machine)		.25	.50
Howard Johnson giveaway(1968, 8pp); 6pg. movie adaptation, 2pg. games, puzzles		.25	.50

2010
Apr, 1985 - No. 2, May, 1985
Marvel Comics Group

1,2-r/Marvel Super Special; movie adapt.		.40	.80

UFO & ALIEN COMIX
Jan, 1978 (One Shot)
Warren Publishing Co.

Toth, Severin-a(r)	.25	.80	1.60

UFO & OUTER SPACE (Formerly UFO Flying Saucers)
No. 14, June, 1978 - No. 25, Feb, 1980 (all painted covers)
Gold Key

14-Reprints UFO Flying Saucers #3	.35	1.00	2.00
15,16-Reprints		.60	1.20
17-20-New material	.25	.75	1.50
21-25: 23-McWilliams-a. 24-3 pg.-r. 25-r-UFO Flying Saucers #2 w/cover		.50	1.00

UFO ENCOUNTERS
May, 1978 (228 pages) ($1.95)
Western Publishing Co.

11192-Reprints UFO Flying Saucers	.70	2.00	4.00
11404-Vol.1 (128 pgs.)-See UFO Mysteries for Vol.2	.35	1.00	2.00

UFO FLYING SAUCERS (UFO & Outer Space #14 on)
Oct, 1968 - No. 13, Jan, 1977 (No. 2 on, 36 pgs.)
Gold Key

1(30035-810) (68 pgs.)	1.15	3.50	8.00
2(11/70), 3(11/72), 4(11/74)	1.00	3.00	6.00
5(2/75)-13: Bolle-a No. 4 on	.70	2.00	4.00

UFO MYSTERIES
1978 (96 pages) ($1.00) (Reprints)

411

UFO MYSTERIES (continued)
Western Publishing Co.

	Good	Fine	N-Mint
11400(96 pgs., $1.00)	.25	.75	1.50
11404(Vol.2)-Cont'd from UFO Encounters, pgs. 129-224			
	.25	.75	1.50

ULTRA KLUTZ
1981; 6/86 - #27, 1/89 ($1.50, B&W); #18-22: $1.75, #23-27: $2.00)
Onward Comics

1 (1981)-re-released after 2nd #1	.25	.75	1.50
1 (6/86)	.35	1.00	2.00
2-27-Photo back-c	.25	.75	1.50

UNBIRTHDAY PARTY WITH ALICE IN WONDERLAND (See 4-Color #341)

UNCANNY TALES
June, 1952 - No. 56, Sept, 1957
Atlas Comics (PrPI/PPI)

	Good	Fine	N-Mint
1-Heath-a	21.00	62.00	145.00
2	10.00	30.00	70.00
3-5	8.50	25.50	60.00
6-Wolvertonish-a by Matt Fox	8.50	25.50	60.00
7,8,10: 8-Tothish-a	8.00	24.00	56.00
9-Crandall-a	8.00	24.00	56.00
11-20: 17-Atom bomb panels; anti-communist story. 19-Krenkel-a			
	6.00	18.00	42.00
21-27: 25-Nostrand-a?	5.00	15.00	35.00
28-Last precode issue (1/55); Kubert-a; #1-28 contain 2-3 sci/fic			
stories each	6.50	19.50	45.00
29-41,43-49,52	2.30	7.00	16.00
42,54,56-Krigstein-a	3.50	10.50	24.00
50,53,55-Torres-a	3.00	9.00	21.00
51,57-Williamson-a (#57, exist?)	4.00	12.00	28.00

NOTE: *Andru a-15, 27. Ayers a-22. Bailey a-51. Briefer a-19, 20. Cameron a-47. Colan a-11, 16, 17. Drucker a-37, 42, 45. Everett a-2, 7, 12, 32, 36, 39, 47, 48; c-7, 11, 17, 39, 41, 50, 52, 53. Fass a-9, 10, 15, 24. Forte a-18, 27, 34. Heath a-13, 14; c-10. Keller a-3. Lawrence a-14, 17, 19, 23, 27, 28, 35. Maneely a-4, 8, 10, 16, 29, 35; c-2, 22, 26, 33, 38. Moldoff a-23. Morisi a-48. Morrow a-46, 51. Orlando a-49, 50, 53. Powell a-12, 18, 34, 38, 43, 50, 53, 56. Robinson a-3, 13. Reinman a-12. Romita a-10. Roussos a-8. Sale a-47. Sekowsky a-25. Sinnott a-15. Tothish-a by Andru-27. Wildey a-22, 48.*

UNCANNY TALES
Dec, 1973 - No. 12, Oct, 1975
Marvel Comics Group

1-Crandall-a(r-'50s #9)		.30	.60
2-12		.25	.50

NOTE: Ditko reprints-#4, 6-8, 10-12.

UNCANNY X-MEN, THE (See X-Men)

UNCANNY X-MEN AND THE NEW TEEN TITANS (See Marvel and DC Present)

UNCANNY X-MEN AT THE STATE FAIR OF TEXAS, THE
1983 (36 pgs.)(One-Shot)
Marvel Comics Group

nn	1.70	5.00	10.00

UNCANNY X-MEN IN DAYS OF FUTURE PAST, THE
1989 ($3.95, color, squarebound, 52 pgs.)
Marvel Comics Group

nn-Byrne/Austin-r (2 stories); Guice-c(p)	.70	2.00	4.00

UNCENSORED MOUSE, THE
1989 - No. 2, 1989 ($1.95, B&W)
Eternity Comics

1-Early Gottfredson strip-r in plastic bag	1.15	3.50	7.00
2-Both contain racial stereotyping & violence	1.70	5.00	10.00

UNCLE CHARLIE'S FABLES
Jan, 1952 - No. 5, Sept, 1952

Lev Gleason Publications

	Good	Fine	N-Mint
1-Norman Maurer-a; has Biro's picture	4.00	12.00	28.00
2-Fuje-a; Biro photo; Biro painted-c	3.00	9.00	21.00
3-5: 4-Biro-c	2.30	7.00	16.00

UNCLE DONALD & HIS NEPHEWS DUDE RANCH (See Dell Giant #52)

UNCLE DONALD & HIS NEPHEWS FAMILY FUN (See Dell Giant #38)

UNCLE JOE'S FUNNIES
1938 (B&W)
Centaur Publications

1-Games/puzzles, some interior art; Bill Everett-c			
	24.00	71.00	165.00

UNCLE MILTY (TV)
Dec, 1950 - No. 4, July, 1951 (52 pgs.)
Victoria Publications/True Cross

1-Milton Berle	20.00	60.00	140.00
2	11.00	32.00	75.00
3,4	9.30	28.00	65.00

UNCLE REMUS & HIS TALES OF BRER RABBIT (See 4-Color #129, 208, 693)

UNCLE SAM QUARTERLY (Blackhawk #9 on)(See Freedom Fighters)
Autumn, 1941 - No. 8, Fall, 1943 (Also see National Comics)
Quality Comics Group

1-Origin Uncle Sam; Fine/Eisner-a, chapter headings, 2 pgs. by			
Eisner. (2 versions: dark cover, no price; light cover with price);			
Jack Cole-a	112.00	335.00	785.00
2-Cameos by The Ray, Black Condor, Quicksilver, The Red Bee,			
Alias the Spider, Hercules & Neon the Unknown; Eisner, Fine-c/a			
	54.00	160.00	375.00
3-Tuska-c/a	39.00	115.00	270.00
4	33.00	100.00	230.00
5-8	27.00	81.00	190.00

NOTE: *Kotzky or Tuska a-4-8.*

UNCLE SAM'S CHRISTMAS STORY
1958
Promotional Publ. Co. (Giveaway)

nn-Reprints 1956 Christmas USA	1.00	3.00	7.00

UNCLE SCROOGE (Disney)(See Dell Giants 33,55, Dynabrite, Four Color #178, Gladstone Comic Album & Walt Disney's C&S #98)
No. 386, 3/52 - No. 39, 8/10/62; No. 40, 12/62 - No. 209, 1984; No. 210, 10/86 - Present
Dell #1-39/Gold Key #40-173/Whitman #174-209/Gladstone #210 on

4-Color 386(#1)-in "Only a Poor Old Man" by Carl Barks; r-in Uncle			
Scrooge & Donald Duck #1('65) & The Best of Walt Disney			
Comics('74)	60.00	180.00	420.00
4-Color 456(#2)-in "Back to the Klondike" by Carl Barks; r-in Best of			
U.S. & D.D. #1('66) & Gladstone C.A. #4	29.00	86.00	200.00
4-Color 495(No.3)-r-in #105	26.00	77.00	180.00
4(12-2/53-54)-r-Gladstone Comic Album #11	20.00	60.00	140.00
5-r-in Gladstone Spec. #2 & W.D. Digest #1	16.00	48.00	110.00
6-r-in U.S. #106,165,233 & Best of U.S. & D.D. #1('66)			
	15.00	45.00	105.00
7-The Seven Cities of Cibola by Barks; r-in #217 & Best of D.D. &			
U.S. #2('67)	11.50	34.00	80.00
8-10: 8-r-in #111,222. 9-r-in #104,214. 10-r-in #67			
	9.30	28.00	65.00
11-20: 11-r-in #237. 17-r-in #215. 19-r-in Gladstone C.A. #1. 20-r-in 213			
	8.00	24.00	56.00
21-30: 26-r-in #211	6.50	19.50	45.00
31-40: 34-r-in #228	5.50	16.50	38.00
41-50	4.00	12.00	28.00
51-60	3.70	11.00	26.00

Uncle Scrooge #224, © WDC   Uncle Scrooge Adventures #3, © WDC   Underworld #1, © DS

UNCLE SCROOGE (continued)

	Good	Fine	N-Mint
61-66,68-70: 70-Last Barks issue with original story			
	2.85	8.50	20.00
67,72,73-Barks-r	1.85	5.50	13.00
71-Written by Barks only	1.85	5.50	13.00
74-One pg. Barks-r	1.15	3.50	8.00
75-81,83-Not by Barks	1.15	3.50	8.00
82,84-Barks-r begin	1.15	3.50	8.00
85-100	1.00	3.00	6.00
101-110	.85	2.50	5.00
111-120	.70	2.00	4.00
121-141,143-152,154-157	.60	1.75	3.50
142-Reprints 4-Color 456 with-c	.70	2.00	4.00
153,158,162-164,166,168-170,178,180: No Barks		.50	1.00
159-160,165,167,172-176-Barks-a	.25	.75	1.50
161(r-#14), 171(r-#11), 177(r-#16), 179(r-#9), 183(r-#6)-Barks-r			
	.25	.75	1.50
181(r-4-Color 495), 195(r-4-Color 386)	.25	.70	1.40
182,186,191-194,197-202,204-206: No Barks		.40	.80
184,185,187,188-Barks-a		.50	1.00
189(r-#5), 190(r-#4), 196(r-#13), 203(r-#12), 207(r-#93,92), 208(r-US #18), 209(r-U.S. #21)-Barks-r		.60	1.20
210-1st Gladstone issue; r-WDC&S #134 (1st Beagle Boys)			
	.85	2.50	5.00
211-218	.40	1.25	2.50
219-Son Of The Sun by Rosa	1.70	5.00	10.00
220-Don Rosa story/a	.50	1.50	3.00
221-230: 224-Rosa c/a. 226,227-Rosa-a	.25	.75	1.50
231-240: 235-Rosa story/art		.50	1.00
241-($1.95, 68 pgs.)-Rosa finishes over Barks-r	.35	1.00	2.00
242-($1.95, 68 pgs.)-Barks-r	.35	1.00	2.00
Uncle Scrooge & Money(G.K.)-Barks-r/from WDC&S #130 (3/67)			
	4.00	12.00	24.00
Mini Comic #1(1976)(3¼x6½'')-R-/U.S. #115; Barks-c			
			.20

NOTE: **Barks** c-4-Color 386, 456, 495, #4-37, 39, 40, 43-71. **Barks** r-210-218, 220-223, 224(2pg.), 225-234, 236-242; c(r)-210, 212, 221, 228, 229, 232, 233. **Rosa** a-219, 220, 224, 226, 227, 235; c-219, 224, 231; scripts-219, 220, 224, 235.

UNCLE SCROOGE ADVENTURES (Walt Disney's. . .#4 on)
Nov, 1987 - Present
Gladstone Publishing

1-Barks-r begin	.70	2.00	4.00
2-5: 5-Rosa c/a	.25	.75	1.50
6-19: 9,14-Rosa-a. 10-r/U.S. #18(all Barks)		.50	1.00
20,21 ($1.95, 68 pgs.) 20-Rosa-c/a	.35	1.00	2.00

NOTE: **Barks** r-1-4, 6-8, 10-13, 15-21; c-15r, 16r, 17r. **Rosa** a-5, 9, 14, 20; c-5, 13, 14, 17(finishes), 20; scripts-5, 9, 14.

UNCLE SCROOGE & DONALD DUCK
June, 1965 (25 cents) (Paper cover)
Gold Key

1-Reprint of 4-Color 386(#1) & lead story from 4-Color 29			
	8.35	25.00	50.00

UNCLE SCROOGE COMICS DIGEST
Dec, 1986 - No. 5, Aug, 1987 ($1.25, Digest-size)
Gladstone Publishing

1-5		.60	1.25

UNCLE SCROOGE GOES TO DISNEYLAND (See Dell Giants)
Aug, 1985 ($2.50)
Gladstone Publishing Ltd.

1-r/Dell Giant w/new-c by Mel Crawford, based on old cover			
	.40	1.25	2.50
Comics Digest 1 ($1.50, digest size)	.25	.75	1.50

UNCLE WIGGILY (See 4-Color #179, 221, 276, 320, 349, 391, 428, 503, 543, & March of Comics #19)

UNDERCOVER GIRL (Starr Flagg) (Also see Manhunt!)
No. 5, 1952 - No. 7, 1954
Magazine Enterprises

	Good	Fine	N-Mint
5(#1)(A-1 62)	20.00	60.00	140.00
6(A-1 98), 7(A-1 118)-All have Starr Flagg	18.00	54.00	125.00

NOTE: **Powell** c-6, 7. **Whitney** a-5-7.

UNDERDOG (TV) (See March of Comics 426,438,467,479)
July, 1970 - No. 10, Jan, 1972; Mar, 1975 - No. 23, Feb, 1979
Charlton Comics/Gold Key

1	2.30	7.00	16.00
2-10	.85	2.60	6.00
1 (G.K.)	1.50	4.50	10.00
2-10	.60	1.80	4.00
11-23: 13-1st app. Shack of Solitude	.50	1.50	3.00
Kite Fun Book('74)-5x7''; 16 pgs.	.70	2.00	4.00

UNDERDOG
1987 - No. 3?, 1987 ($1.50, color)
Spotlight Comics

1-3	.25	.75	1.50

UNDERDOG IN 3-D (See Blackthorne 3-D Series #43)

UNDERSEA AGENT
Jan, 1966 - No. 6, Mar, 1967 (68 pages)
Tower Comics

1-Davy Jones, Undersea Agent begins	2.00	6.00	14.00
2-6: 2-Jones gains magnetic powers. 5-Origin & 1st app. of Merman. 6-Kane?/Wood-c(r)	1.15	3.50	8.00

NOTE: **Gil Kane** a-3-6; c-4, 5. **Moldoff** a-2i.

UNDERSEA FIGHTING COMMANDOS (See Fighting Undersea. . .)
May, 1952 - No. 5, Jan, 1953; 1964
Avon Periodicals

1-Ravielli-c	4.30	13.00	30.00
2	2.65	8.00	18.00
3-5	2.30	7.00	16.00
I.W. Reprint #1,2('64): 2-Severin-c	.85	2.00	4.00

UNDERWATER CITY, THE (See 4-Color #1328)

UNDERWORLD (True Crime Stories)
Feb-Mar, 1948 - No. 9, June-July, 1949 (52 pgs.)
D. S. Publishing Co.

1-Moldoff-c; excessive violence	15.00	45.00	105.00
2-Moldoff-c; Ma Barker story used in **SOTI**, pg. 95; female electrocution panel; lingerie art	16.00	48.00	110.00
3-McWilliams c/a; extreme violence, mutilation	12.00	36.00	84.00
4-Used in **Love and Death** by Legman; Ingels-a	9.30	28.00	65.00
5-Ingels-a	6.50	19.50	45.00
6-9: 8-Ravielli-a	5.00	15.00	35.00

UNDERWORLD
Dec, 1987 - No. 4, Mar, 1988 ($1.00, mini-series, adults)
DC Comics

1-4		.50	1.00

UNDERWORLD CRIME
June, 1952 - No. 9, Oct, 1953
Fawcett Publications

1	11.00	32.00	75.00
2	5.70	17.00	40.00
3-6,8,9 (8,9-exist?)	5.00	15.00	35.00
7-Bondage/torture-c	10.00	30.00	70.00

UNDERWORLD STORY, THE
1950 (Movie)

THE UNDERWORLD STORY (continued)
Avon Periodicals

	Good	Fine	N-Mint
nn-(Scarce)-Ravielli-c	13.00	40.00	90.00

UNEARTHLY SPECTACULARS
Oct, 1965 - No. 3, Mar, 1967
Harvey Publications

1-Tiger Boy; Simon-c	.50	1.50	3.00
2-Jack Q. Frost app.; Wood, Williamson, Kane art; r-1 story/ Thrill-O-Rama #2	1.70	5.00	10.00
3-Jack Q. Frost app.; Williamson/Crandall-a; r-from Alarming Advs. No. 1, 1962	1.70	5.00	10.00

NOTE: *Crandall a-3r. G. Kane a-2. Orlando a-3. Simon, Sparling, Wood c-2. Simon/Kirby a-3r. Torres a-1. Wildey a-1(3). Williamson a-2, 3r. Wood a-2(2).*

UNEXPECTED, THE (Formerly Tales of the . . .)
No. 105, Feb-Mar, 1968 - No. 222, May, 1982
National Periodical Publications/DC Comics

105	.50	1.50	3.00
106-115,117,118,120,122-127	.35	1.00	2.00
116,119,121,128-Wrightson-a	.40	1.25	2.50
129-162: 132-136-(52 pgs.) 157-162-(100 pgs.)	.50	1.00	
163-188		.30	.60
189,190,192-195 ($1.00 size)		.40	.80
191-Rogers-a(p) ($1.00 size)		.50	1.00
196-221: 205-213-Johnny Peril app. 210-Time Warp app.		.30	.60

NOTE: *Adams c-110, 112-118, 121, 124. J. Craig a-195. Ditko a-189, 221p, 222p; c-222. Drucker a-107. Giffen a-219, 222. Kaluta c-203, 212. Kirby a-127, 162. Kubert c-204, 214-216, 219-221. Mayer a-217p, 220, 221p. Moldoff a-136r. Moreira a-133 Mortimer a-212p. Newton a-204p. Orlando a-202; c-191. Perez a-217p. Redondo a-155, 195. Reese a-145. Sparling a-107, 205-209p, 212p. Spiegle a-217. Starlin c-198. Toth a-126r, 127r. Tuska a-132, 136, 139, 152, 180, 200p. Wildey a-193. Wood a-122i, 133i, 137i, 138i. Wrightson a-161r(2 pgs.). Johnny Peril in #106-117, 205-213.*

UNEXPECTED ANNUAL, THE (See DC Special Series #4)

UNIDENTIFIED FLYING ODDBALL (See Walt Disney Showcase #52)

UNIDENTIFIED COMICS
Aug, 1940 - No. 26, Jan-Feb, 1953
United Features Syndicate

1-Fritzi Ritz & Phil Fumble	13.00	40.00	90.00
2-Fritzi Ritz, Abbie & Slats	7.00	21.00	50.00
3-9-Fritzi Ritz, Abbie & Slats	4.00	12.00	28.00
10-26: 22, 25-Peanuts app.	2.30	7.00	16.00

NOTE: *Abbie & Slats reprinted from Tip Top.*

UNITED NATIONS, THE (See Classics Illustrated Special Issue)

UNITED STATES AIR FORCE PRESENTS: THE HIDDEN CREW
1964 (36 pages) (full color)
U.S. Air Force

nn-Shaffenberger-a	.50	1.50	3.00

UNITED STATES FIGHTING AIR FORCE
Sept, 1952 - No. 29, Oct, 1956
Superior Comics Ltd.

1	3.70	11.00	26.00
2	1.85	5.50	13.00
3-10	1.00	3.00	7.00
11-29	.85	2.50	6.00
I.W. Reprint #1,9(nd)	.35	1.10	2.20

UNITED STATES MARINES
1943 - No. 4, 1944; No. 5, 1952 - No. 11, 1953
William H. Wise/Life's Romances Publ. Co./Magazine Enterprises No. 5-8/Toby Press No. 7-11

nn-Mart Bailey-a	4.00	12.00	28.00
2-Bailey-a	3.00	9.00	21.00
3,4	2.65	8.00	18.00

	Good	Fine	N-Mint
5(A-1 55), 6(A-1 60), 7(A-1 68), 8(A-1 72)	2.35	7.00	16.00
7-11 (Toby)	1.00	3.00	7.00

NOTE: *Powell a-5-7.*

UNIVERSAL PRESENTS DRACULA (See Dell Giants)

UNKEPT PROMISE
1949 (24 pages)
Legion of Truth (Giveaway)

nn-Anti-alcohol	5.00	15.00	35.00

UNKNOWN MAN, THE
1951 (Movie)
Avon Periodicals

nn-Kinstler-c	13.00	40.00	90.00

UNKNOWN SOLDIER (Formerly Star-Spangled War Stories)
No. 205, Apr-May, 1977 - No. 268, Oct, 1982
National Periodical Publications/DC Comics

205-268: 251-Enemy Ace begins. 268-Death of Unknown Soldier. 248,249-Origin		.30	.60

NOTE: *Evans a-265-267; c-235. Kubert c-Most. Miller a-219p. Severin a-251-253, 260, 261, 265-267. Simonson a-254-256. Spiegle a-258, 259, 262-264.*

UNKNOWN SOLDIER, THE (Also see Brave & the Bold #146)
Winter, 1988-'89 - No. 12, Dec, 1989 ($1.50, maxi-series, adults)
DC Comics

1-12	.25	.75	1.50

UNKNOWN WORLD (Strange Stories From Another World #2 on)
June, 1952
Fawcett Publications

1-Norman Saunders painted-c	13.00	40.00	90.00

UNKNOWN WORLDS (See Journey Into . . .)

UNKNOWN WORLDS
Aug, 1960 - No. 57, Aug, 1967
American Comics Group/Best Synd. Features

1	5.70	17.00	40.00
2-5	2.65	8.00	18.00
6-11: 11-Last 10 cent issue?	1.70	5.00	12.00
12-19	1.30	4.00	9.00
20-Herbie cameo	1.50	4.50	10.00
21-35	1.00	3.00	7.00
36-"The People vs. Hendricks" by Craig; most popular ACG story ever	1.15	3.50	8.00
37-46	.70	2.00	5.00
47-Williamson-a r-from Adventures Into the Unknown #96, 3 pgs.; Craig-a	.85	2.60	6.00
48-57	.50	1.50	3.00

NOTE: *Ditko a-49, 50p, 54. Forte a-3, 6, 11. Landau a-56(2). Reinman a-3, 9, 36. Whitney c/a-most issues. John Force, Magic Agent app.-No. 35, 36, 48, 50, 52, 54, 56.*

UNKNOWN WORLDS OF FRANK BRUNNER
Aug, 1985 - No. 2, Aug, 1985 ($1.75 cover)
Eclipse Comics

1,2-B&W-r in color	.30	.90	1.80

UNKNOWN WORLDS OF SCIENCE FICTION
1/75 - No. 6, 11/75; 12/76 (B&W Magazine) ($1.00)
Marvel Comics Group

1-Williamson/Wood/Torres/Frazetta r-/Witzend #1, Adams-r/Phase 1; Brunner & Kaluta-r	.50	1.50	3.00
2-6	.40	1.20	2.40
Special 1(12/76)-100 pgs.; Newton-c; Nino-a	.40	1.20	2.40

NOTE: *Brunner a-2; c-4. Chaykin a-5. Colan a(p)-1, 3, 5. Corben a-4. Kaluta a-2; c-2. Morrow a-3, 5. Nino a-3, 6. Perez a-2, 3.*

UNSANE
No. 15, June, 1954

Unearthly Spectaculars #1, © HARV

United States Marines #3, © WHW

Unknown Worlds #13, © ACG

The Untold Legend Of The Batman #1, © DC   Unusual Tales #11, © CC   USA Comics #5, © MEG

INSANE (continued)
Star Publications

	Good	Fine	N-Mint
15-Disbrow-a(2); L. B. Cole-c	12.00	36.00	84.00

UNSEEN, THE
No. 5, 1952 - No. 15, July, 1954
Visual Editions/Standard Comics

5-Toth-a	9.30	28.00	65.00
6,7,9,10-Jack Katz-a	6.50	19.50	45.00
8,11,13,14	4.30	13.00	30.00
12,15-Toth-a. 12-Tuska-a	7.00	21.00	50.00

NOTE: *Fawcette a-13, 14. Sekowsky a-7, 8(2), 10, 13.*

UNTAMED LOVE (Also see Frank Frazetta's Untamed Love)
Jan, 1950 - No. 5, Sept, 1950
Quality Comics Group (Comic Magazines)

1-Ward-c, Gustavson-a	11.50	34.00	80.00
2,4: 2-Photo-c	6.50	19.50	45.00
3,5-Gustavson-a	7.00	21.00	50.00

UNTOLD LEGEND OF THE BATMAN, THE
July, 1980 - No. 3, Sept, 1980 (mini-series)
DC Comics

1-Origin; Joker-c	.70	2.00	4.00
2,3	.50	1.50	3.00

NOTE: *Aparo a-1i, 2, 3. Byrne a-1p.*

UNTOUCHABLES, THE (TV)
No. 1237, 10-12/61 - No. 4, 8-10/62 (Robert Stack photo-c)
Dell Publishing Co.

4-Color 1237,1286	5.00	15.00	35.00
01-879-207, 12-879-210(01879-210 on inside)	4.00	12.00	28.00

Topps Bubblegum premiums-2½x4½'', 8 pgs. (3 different issues)
''The Organization, Jamaica Ginger, The Otto Frick Story (drug),
3000 Suspects, The Antidote, Mexican Stakeout, Little Egypt,
Purple Gang, Bugs Moran Story, & Lily Dallas Story''

	1.70	5.00	12.00

UNUSUAL TALES (Blue Beetle & Shadow From Beyond #50 on)
Nov, 1955 - No. 49, Mar-Apr, 1965
Charlton Comics

1	7.00	21.00	50.00
2	3.00	9.00	21.00
3-5	2.30	7.00	16.00
6-8-Ditko c/a	8.00	24.00	56.00
9-Ditko c/a, 20 pgs.	9.00	27.00	62.00
10-Ditko c/a(4)	10.00	30.00	70.00
11-(68 pgs., 3/58); Ditko-a(4)	10.00	30.00	70.00
12,14-Ditko-a	5.50	16.50	38.00
13,16-20	1.50	4.50	10.00
15-Ditko c/a	6.00	18.00	42.00
21,24,28	1.00	3.00	7.00
22,25-27,29-Ditko-a	3.50	10.50	24.00
23-Ditko-c	1.50	4.50	10.00
30-49	.70	2.00	5.00

NOTE: *Colan a-11. Ditko c-22, 23, 25-27, 31(part).*

UP FROM HARLEM (Tom Skinner...)
1973 (35-49 Cents)
Spire Christian Comics (Fleming H. Revell Co.)

nn		.50	1.00

UP-TO-DATE COMICS
No date (1938) (36 pgs.; B&W cover) (10 cents)
King Features Syndicate

nn-Popeye & Henry cover; The Phantom, Jungle Jim & Flash
Gordon by Raymond, The Katzenjammer Kids, Curley Harper &

others	17.00	51.00	120.00

(Variations to above contents exist.)

UP YOUR NOSE AND OUT YOUR EAR (Magazine)
April, 1972 - No. 2, June, 1972 (52 pgs.) (Satire)
Klevart Enterprises

	Good	Fine	N-Mint
V1#1,2	.30	.90	1.80

USA COMICS
Aug, 1941 - No. 17, Fall, 1945
Timely Comics (USA)

1-Origin Major Liberty (called Mr. Liberty #1), Rockman by Wolverton, & The Whizzer by Avison; The Defender with sidekick Rusty
& Jack Frost begin; The Young Avenger only app.; S&K-c plus

1 pg. art	350.00	875.00	2100.00

2-Origin Captain Terror & The Vagabond; last Wolverton Rockman

	183.00	460.00	1100.00
3-No Whizzer	142.00	355.00	850.00

4-Last Rockman, Major Liberty, Defender, Jack Frost, & Capt. Ter-

ror; Corporal Dix app.	117.00	295.00	700.00

5-Origin American Avenger & Roko the Amazing; The Blue Blade,
The Black Widow & Victory Boys; Gypo the Gypsy Giant & Hills
of Horror only app.; Sergeant Dix begins; no Whizzer. Hitler-c

	97.00	245.00	580.00

6-Captain America, The Destroyer, Jap Buster Johnson, Jeep Jones

begin; Terror Squad only app.	108.00	270.00	650.00

7-Captain Daring, Disk-Eyes the Detective by Wolverton app.;
origin & only app. Marvel Boy; Secret Stamp begins; no Whizzer,

Sergeant Dix	90.00	225.00	540.00

8-10: 9-Last Secret Stamp. 10-The Thunderbird only app.

	65.00	165.00	390.00
11,12: 11-No Jeep Jones	53.00	135.00	320.00

13-17: 13-No Whizzer; Jeep Jones ends. 15-No Destroyer; Jap

Buster Johnson ends	39.00	98.00	235.00

NOTE: *Schomburg c-6-10, 12, 13, 15-17. Shores c-11.*

U.S. AGENT (See Jeff Jordan...)

USAGI YOJIMBO (See Albedo & Doomsday Squad #3)
July, 1987 - Present ($2.00, B&W)
Fantagraphics Books

1	.70	2.00	4.00
1-2nd print	.35	1.00	2.00
2-20: 10-Leonardo app.(TMNT). 11-Aragones-a	.35	1.00	2.00
Color Special 1 (11/89, $2.95, 68 pgs.)-new & r	.50	1.50	3.00

Summer Special 1 (1986, B&W, $2.75)-r/early Albedo issues

	2.00	6.00	12.00

U.S. AIR FORCE COMICS (Army Attack #38 on)
Oct, 1958 - No. 37, Mar-Apr, 1965
Charlton Comics

1	1.30	4.00	9.00
2	.65	1.90	4.50
3-10	.50	1.50	3.00
11-20	.35	1.00	2.00
21-37	.25	.75	1.50

NOTE: *Glanzman c/a-9, 10, 12. Montes/Bache a-33.*

USA IS READY
1941 (68 pgs.) (One Shot)
Dell Publishing Co.

1-War propaganda	19.30	58.00	135.00

U.S. BORDER PATROL COMICS (Sgt. Dick Carter of the...) (See Holyoke
One Shot)

U.S. FIGHTING MEN
1963 - 1964 (Reprints)
Super Comics

10-Avon's With the U.S. Paratroops	.50	1.50	3.00
11,12,15-18	.25	.80	1.60

415

U.S. JONES (Also see Wonderworld Comics #28)
Nov, 1941 - No. 2, Jan, 1942
Fox Features Syndicate

	Good	Fine	N-Mint
1-U.S. Jones & The Topper begin	54.00	160.00	375.00
2	39.00	118.00	275.00

U.S. MARINES
Fall, 1964 (One shot)
Charlton Comics

1	.35	1.00	2.00

U.S. MARINES IN ACTION!
Aug, 1952 - No. 3, Dec, 1952
Avon Periodicals

1-Louis Ravielli c/a	3.35	10.00	23.00
2,3: 3-Kinstler-c	1.70	5.00	12.00

U.S. 1
May, 1983 - No. 12, Oct, 1984
Marvel Comics Group

1		.30	.60
2-12		.25	.50

NOTE: **Golden** c-5-7, 9, 10, 12.

U.S. PARATROOPS (See With the . . .)

U.S. PARATROOPS
1964?
I. W. Enterprises

1-Wood-c r/With the. . . #1	.50	1.50	3.00
8-Kinstler-c	.50	1.50	3.00

U.S. TANK COMMANDOS
June, 1952 - No. 4, March, 1953
Avon Periodicals

1-Kinstler-c	3.75	11.25	26.00
2-4: 2-Kinstler-c	2.15	6.50	15.00
I.W. Reprint #1,8	.35	1.10	2.20

NOTE: **Kinstler** a-3, 4, I.W. #1; c-1-4, I.W. #1, 8.

"V" (TV)
Feb, 1985 - No. 18, July, 1986
DC Comics

1-Based on TV movie & series (Sci/Fi)	.25	.75	1.50
2-18		.45	.90

VACATION COMICS (See A-1 Comics #16)

VACATION DIGEST
Sept, 1987 ($1.25, digest size)
Harvey Comics

1		.60	1.25

VACATION IN DISNEYLAND (Also see Dell Giants)
Aug-Oct, 1959; May, 1965 (Walt Disney)
Dell Publishing Co./Gold Key (1965)

4-Color 1025-Barks-a	6.00	18.00	42.00
1(30024-508)(G.K.)-Reprints Dell Giant #30 & cover to #1('58)	1.50	4.50	12.00

VACATION PARADE (See Dell Giants)

VALKYRIE (See Airboy)
May, 1987 - No. 3, July, 1987 ($1.75, color, mini-series)
Eclipse Comics

1-3: 2-Holly becomes new Black Angel	.50	1.50	3.00

VALKYRIE!
July, 1988 - No. 3, Sept, 1988 ($1.95, color, mini-series)
Eclipse Comics

1-3	.35	1.00	2.00

VALLEY OF THE DINOSAURS (TV)
April, 1975 - No. 11, Dec, 1976 (Hanna-Barbara)
Charlton Comics

	Good	Fine	N-Mint
1-Howard inks		.40	.80
2-11: 2-Howard inks		.30	.60

VALLEY OF GWANGI (See Movie Classics)

VALOR
Mar-Apr, 1955.- No. 5, Nov-Dec, 1955
E. C. Comics

1-Williamson/Torres-a; Wood c/a	16.50	50.00	115.00
2-Williamson c/a; Wood-a	14.00	42.00	100.00
3,4: 3-Williamson, Crandall-a. 4-Wood-c	10.00	30.00	70.00
5-Wood c/a; Williamson/Evans-a	8.50	25.50	60.00

NOTE: **Crandall** a-3, 4. **Ingels** a-1, 2, 4, 5. **Krigstein** a-1-5. **Orlando** a-3, 4; c-3. **Wood** a-1, 2, 5; c-1, 4, 5.

VALOR THUNDERSTAR AND HIS FIREFLIES
Dec, 1986 ($1.50, color)
Now Comics

1-Ordway-c(p)	.25	.75	1.50

VAMPIRE LESTAT, THE
Jan, 1990 - No. 12 ($2.50, painted color, mini-series)
Innovation Publishing

1-4: Adapts novel; Bolton painted-c on all	.40	1.25	2.50

VAMPIRELLA (Magazine)(See Warren Presents)
Sept, 1969 - No. 112, Feb, 1983; No. 113, Jan, 1988? (B&W)
Warren Publishing Co./Harris Publications #113

1-Intro. Vampirella	10.00	30.00	70.00
2-Amazonia series begins, ends #12	3.60	11.00	25.00
3 (Low distribution)	12.00	36.00	85.00
4-7	2.85	8.50	20.00
8-Vampi begins by Tom Sutton as serious strip (early issues-gag line)	2.15	6.50	15.00
9-Smith-a	2.85	8.50	20.00
10-No Vampi story	1.60	4.80	11.00
11-15: 10-Origin, 1st app. Pendragon. 12-Vampi by Gonzales begins	1.70	5.00	12.00
16-18,20-25: 17-Tomb of the Gods begins, ends #22	1.15	3.50	8.00
19 (1973 Annual)	1.50	4.50	10.00
26,28-36,38-40: 30-on contain some color; intro. Pantha. 31-Origin Luana, the Beast Girl. 33-Pantha ends	.85	2.60	6.00
27 (1974 Annual)	1.15	3.50	8.00
37 (1975 Annual)	1.00	3.00	7.00
41-45,47-50: 50-Spirit cameo	.50	1.50	3.00
46-Origin retold	.60	1.75	3.50
51-99: 93-Cassandra St. Knight begins, ends #103; new Pantha series begins, ends 108	.35	1.00	2.00
100 (96pg. r-special)-Origin retold	.40	1.25	2.50
101-112: 108-Torpedo series by Toth begins	.30	.90	1.75
113 (1988)	.25	.75	1.50
Annual 1('72)-New origin Vampirella by Gonzales; reprints by Adams (from #1), Wood(from #9)	9.30	28.00	65.00
Special 1 ('77; large-square bound)	1.00	3.00	6.00

NOTE: **Adams** a-1, 10p, 19p. **Alcala** a-90, 93i. **Bode'/Todd** c-3. **Bode'/Jones** c-4. **Boris** c-9. **Brunner** a-10. **Corben** a-30, 31, 33, 54. **Crandall** a-1, 19. **Frazetta** c-1, 5, 7, 11, 31. **Jones** a-5, 9, 12, 27, 32, 33, 34, 50i. **Nino** a-59i, 61i, 67, 76, 85, 90. **Ploog** a-14. **Smith** a-9. **Sutton** a-11. **Toth** a-90i, 108, 110. **Wood** a-9, 10, 12, 19, 27; c-9. **Wrightson** a-33, 63. All reprint issues-37, 74, 83, 87, 91, 105, 107, 109, 111. Annuals from 1973 on are included in regular numbering. Later annuals are same format as regular issues.

VAMPIRE TALES (Magazine)
Aug, 1973 - No. 11, June, 1975 (B&W) (75 cents)
Marvel Comics Group

1-Morbius, the Living Vampire begins by Pablo Marcos	.35	1.00	2.00

U.S. Marines In Action #1, © AVON

"V" #1, © DC

Vampirella #17, © WP

Vault Of Horror #23, © WMG   Venus #18, © MEG   Veronica #1, © AP

	Good	Fine	N-Mint
VAMPIRE TALES (continued)			
2-Intro. Satana; Steranko-r	.25	.75	1.50
3-11: 3-Satana app. 5-Origin Morbius. 6-1st Lilith app. 8-1st Blade app.		.60	1.20
Annual 1(10/75)	.25	.75	1.50

NOTE: Alcala a-6, 8, 9i. Boris c-4, 6. Chaykin a-7. Everett a-1r. Gulacy a-7p. Heath a-9. Infantino a-3r. Gil Kane a-4, 5r.

VANGUARD ILLUSTRATED
Nov, 1983 - No. 11, Oct., 1984 (Color, Baxter paper)
Pacific Comics

1-6,8,11: 1-Nudity scenes. 2-1st app. Stargrazers	.25	.75	1.50
7-1st app. Mr. Monster	1.15	3.50	7.00

NOTE: Evans a-7. Kaluta c-5, 7p. Perez a-6; c-6. Rude a-3-5; c-4.

VANITY (See Pacific Presents)
Jun, 1984 - No. 2, Aug, 1984 ($1.50, color)
Pacific Comics

1,2-Origin	.25	.75	1.50

VARIETY COMICS
1944 - No. 2, 1945; No. 3, 1946 - No. 5, 1946?
Rural Home Publications/Croyden Publ. Co.

1-Origin Captain Valiant	8.00	24.00	56.00
2-Captain Valiant	4.30	13.00	30.00
3(1946-Croyden)-Captain Valiant	3.70	11.00	26.00
4,5	2.85	8.50	20.00

VARIETY COMICS (See Fox Giants)

VARSITY
1945
Parents' Magazine Institute

1	2.65	8.00	18.00

VAUDEVILLE AND OTHER THINGS
1900 (10½x13'') (in color) (18+ pgs.)
Isaac H. Blandiard Co.

nn-By Bunny	20.00	60.00	140.00

VAULT OF EVIL
Feb, 1973 - No. 23, Nov, 1975
Marvel Comics Group

1 (Reprints begin)		.35	.70
2-23: 3,4-Brunner-c		.25	.50

NOTE: Ditko a-14r, 15r, 20-22r. Drucker a-10r(Mystic #52), 13r(Uncanny Tales #42). Everett a-11r(Menace #2), 13r(Menace #4); c-10. Heath a-5r. Krigstein a-20r(Uncanny Tales #54). Tuska a-6r.

VAULT OF HORROR (War Against Crime #1-11)
No. 12, Apr-May, 1950 - No. 40, Dec-Jan, 1954-55
E. C. Comics

12	116.00	348.00	810.00
13-Morphine story	54.00	160.00	375.00
14	46.00	140.00	325.00
15	39.00	118.00	275.00
16	30.00	90.00	210.00
17-19	23.00	70.00	160.00
20-22,24,25	17.00	51.00	120.00
23-Used in POP, pg. 84	17.00	51.00	120.00
26-B&W & color illos in POP	17.00	51.00	120.00
27-35: 35-X-Mas-c	13.00	40.00	90.00
36-''Pipe Dream''-classic opium addict story by Krigstein; 'Twin Bill' cited in articles by T.E. Murphy & Wertham	13.00	40.00	90.00
37-Williamson-a	13.00	40.00	90.00
38-39: 39-Bondage-c	11.00	32.00	75.00
40-Low distribution	13.00	40.00	90.00

NOTE: Craig art in all but No. 13 & 33; c-12-40. Crandall a-33, 34, 39. Davis a-17-38. Evans a-27, 28, 30, 32, 33. Feldstein a-12-16. Ingels a-13-20, 22-40. Kamen a-15-22, 25,

29, 35. Krigstein a-36, 38-40. Kurtzman a-12, 13. Orlando a-24, 31, 40. Wood a-12-14.

V. . .-COMICS (Morse code for ''V'' - 3 dots, 1 dash)
Jan, 1942 - No. 2, Mar-Apr, 1942
Fox Features Syndicate

	Good	Fine	N-Mint
1-Origin V-Man & the Boys; The Banshee & The Black Fury, The Queen of Evil, & V-Agents begin	54.00	160.00	375.00
2-Bondage/torture-c	43.00	130.00	300.00

VECTOR
1986 - No. 4, 1986? ($1.50; 1st color comic by Now Comics)
Now Comics

1-4: Computer-generated art		.70	1.40

VEGAS KNIGHTS
1989 ($1.95, color)
Pioneer Comics

1	.35	1.00	2.00

VENGEANCE SQUAD
July, 1975 - No. 6, May, 1976
Charlton Comics

1-Mike Mauser, Private eye begins by Staton		.40	.80
2-6: Morisi-a in all		.25	.50
5,6(Modern Comics-r, 1977)		.15	.30

VENTURE
Aug, 1986 - No. 3, 1986? ($1.75, color)
AC Comics (Americomics)

1-3: 1-3-Bolt. 1-Astron. 2-Femforce. 3-Fazers	.30	.90	1.80

VENUS (See Marvel Spotlight #2 & Weird Wonder Tales)
August, 1948 - No. 19, April, 1952
Marvel/Atlas Comics (CMC 1-9/LCC 10-19)

1-Venus & Hedy Devine begin; Kurtzman's ''Hey Look''	43.00	130.00	300.00
2	25.00	75.00	175.00
3,5	22.00	65.00	150.00
4-Kurtzman's ''Hey Look''	23.00	70.00	160.00
6-9: 6-Loki app. 7,8-Painted-c	20.00	60.00	140.00
10-S/F-horror issues begin (7/50)	22.00	65.00	150.00
11-S/F end of the world(11/50)	26.00	77.00	180.00
12	19.00	58.00	135.00
13-19-Venus by Everett, 2-3 stories each; covers-#13,15-19; 14-Everett part cover (Venus)	29.00	86.00	200.00

NOTE: #3-5-content changes to teen-age. Bondage c-17. Colan a-12.

VERI BEST SURE FIRE COMICS
No date (circa 1945) (Reprints Holyoke One-Shots)
Holyoke Publishing Co.

1-Captain Aero, Alias X, Miss Victory, Commandos of the Devil Dogs, Red Cross, Hammerhead Hawley, Capt. Aero's Sky Scouts, Flagman app.	13.00	40.00	90.00

VERI BEST SURE SHOT COMICS
No date (circa 1945) (Reprints Holyoke One-Shots)
Holyoke Publishing Co.

1-Capt. Aero, Miss Victory by Quinlan, Alias X, The Red Cross, Flagman, Commandos of the Devil Dogs, Hammerhead Hawley, Capt. Aero's Sky Scouts	13.00	40.00	90.00

VERONICA
April, 1989 - Present (75 & 95 cents, color)
Archie Comics

1,2 (75 cents)		.40	.80
3-8 (95 cents)		.50	1.00

VERY BEST OF DENNIS THE MENACE, THE
July, 1979 - No. 2, Apr, 1980 (132 pgs., Digest, 95 cents, $1.00)
Fawcett Publications

417

THE VERY BEST OF DENNIS THE MENACE (continued)

	Good	Fine	N-Mint
1,2-Reprints		.50	1.00

VERY BEST OF DENNIS THE MENACE, THE
April, 1982 - No. 3, Aug, 1982 (Digest Size) ($1.25)
Marvel Comics Group

		Good	Fine	N-Mint
1-3-Reprints			.65	1.25

NOTE: **Hank Ketcham** c-all. A few thousand of #1 & 2 were printed with DC emblem.

V FOR VENDETTA
9/88 - No. 10, 5/89 ($2.00, color, maxi-series, mature readers)
DC Comics

	Good	Fine	N-Mint
1-Alan Moore scripts in all	.85	2.50	5.00
2-5	.50	1.50	3.00
6-10	.40	1.25	2.50

VIC AND BLOOD
Oct, 1987 - No. 2, 1988 ($2.00, B&W)
Mad Dog Graphics

	Good	Fine	N-Mint
1,2-Harlan Ellison adapt., Corben-a	.40	1.25	2.50

VIC BRIDGES FAZERS SKETCHBOOK AND FACT FILE
Nov, 1986 ($1.75, color)
AC Comics

	Good	Fine	N-Mint
1	.30	.90	1.80

VIC FLINT (Crime Buster. . .)(See Authentic Police Cases #10-14 &
Fugitives From Justice #2)
August, 1948 - No.5, April, 1949 (Newspaper reprints; NEA Service)
St. John Publishing Co.

	Good	Fine	N-Mint
1	5.50	16.50	38.00
2	3.50	10.50	24.00
3-5	2.65	8.00	18.00

VIC FLINT
Feb, 1956 - No. 2, May, 1956 (Newspaper reprints)
Argo Publ.

	Good	Fine	N-Mint
1,2	2.85	8.50	20.00

VIC JORDAN (Also see Big Shot Comics #32)
April, 1945
Civil Service Publ.

	Good	Fine	N-Mint
1-1944 daily newspaper-r	5.70	17.00	40.00

VICKI (Humor)
Feb, 1975 - No. 4, July, 1975 (No. 1,2: 68 pgs.)
Atlas/Seaboard Publ.

	Good	Fine	N-Mint
1-Reprints Tippy Teen	.50	1.50	3.00
2-4	.30	.80	1.60

VICKI VALENTINE (. . .Summer Special #1)
July, 1985 - No. 4, July, 1986 ($1.70 cover; B&W)
Renegade Press

	Good	Fine	N-Mint
1-4: Woggon, Rausch-a; all have paper dolls. 2-Christmas issue	.30	.85	1.70

VICKS COMICS (Also see Pure Oil Comics, Salerno Carnival of Comics, & 24 Pages of Comics)
nd (circa 1938) (68 pgs. in color) (Giveaway)
Eastern Color Printing Co. (Vicks Chemical Co.)

	Good	Fine	N-Mint
nn-Famous Funnies-r (before #40). Contains 5 pgs. Buck Rogers (4 pgs. from F.F. #15, & 1 pg. from #16) Joe Palooka, Napoleon, etc. app.	55.00	165.00	385.00
nn-16 loose, untrimmed page giveaway; paper-c; r-/Famous Funnies #14; Buck Rogers, Joe Palooka app.	20.00	60.00	140.00

VICKY
Oct, 1948 - No. 5, June, 1949
Ace Magazine

	Good	Fine	N-Mint
nn(10/48)	2.65	8.00	18.00
4(12/48), nn(2/49), 4(4/49), 5(6/49)	2.00	6.00	14.00

VIC TORRY & HIS FLYING SAUCER (Also see Mr. Monster's. . .#5)
1950 (One Shot)
Fawcett Publications

	Good	Fine	N-Mint
Book-length saucer story by Powell; photo/painted-c	27.00	81.00	190.00

VICTORY COMICS
Aug, 1941 - No. 4, Dec, 1941
Hillman Periodicals

	Good	Fine	N-Mint
1-The Conqueror by Bill Everett, The Crusader, & Bomber Burns begin; Conqueror's origin in text; Everett-c; #1 by Funnies, Inc.	90.00	270.00	625.00
2-Everett-c/a	49.00	145.00	340.00
3,4	35.00	105.00	245.00

VIC VERITY MAGAZINE
1945 - No. 7, Sept, 1946 (A comic book)
Vic Verity Publications

	Good	Fine	N-Mint
1-C. C. Beck-c/a	6.50	19.50	45.00
2	4.30	13.00	30.00
3-7: 6-Beck-a. 7-Beck-c	3.50	10.50	24.00

VIDEO JACK
Nov, 1987 - No. 6, Nov, 1988 ($1.25, color)
Epic Comics (Marvel)

	Good	Fine	N-Mint
1-6: 6-N. Adams, Wrightson, others-a		.65	1.30

VIETNAM JOURNAL
Nov, 1987 - Present ($1.75/$1.95, B&W)
Apple Comics

	Good	Fine	N-Mint
1-Don Lomax-c/a/scripts in all	.70	2.00	4.00
1-2nd print	.35	1.00	1.95
2	.40	1.25	2.50
3-14	.35	1.00	1.95
. . .: Indian Country Vol. 1 (1990, $12.95)-r/1-4 plus one new story	2.15	6.50	13.00

VIGILANTE, THE (Also see Action Comics #42, Justice League of
America, Leading Comics, New Teen Titans & World's Finest #244)
Oct, 1983 - No. 50, Feb, 1988 ($1.25; Baxter paper)
DC Comics

	Good	Fine	N-Mint
1-Origin	.90	2.75	5.50
2	.60	1.75	3.50
3-10: 3-Cyborg app. 6,7-Origin	.40	1.25	2.50
11-50: 20,21-Nightwing app. 35-Origin Mad Bomber	.30	.90	1.75
Annual 1 (10/85)	.40	1.25	2.50
Annual 2 (11/86)	.35	1.10	2.25

NOTE: **Newton** a-4p. **Steacy** c-50.

VIGILANTES, THE (See 4-Color #839)

VIKINGS, THE (See 4-Color #910)

VILLAINS AND VIGILANTES
Dec, 1986 - No. 4, May, 1987 ($1.50, color, mini-series, Baxter)
Eclipse Comics

	Good	Fine	N-Mint
1-4: Based on role-playing game	.30	.90	1.75

VIRGINIAN, THE (TV)
June, 1963
Gold Key

	Good	Fine	N-Mint
1(10060-306)-Part photo-c	2.00	6.00	14.00

VISION AND THE SCARLET WITCH, THE (See Marvel Fanfare)
Nov, 1982 - No. 4, Feb, 1983 (mini-series)
Marvel Comics Group

V For Vendetta #4, © DC

Vic Verity Magazine #1, © Vic Verity Publ.

Vietnam Journal #3, © Apple Comics

The Vision And The Scarlet Witch #1 (11/82), © MEG

Voyage To The Deep #3, © DELL

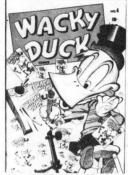

Wacky Duck #4, © MEG

	Good	Fine	N-Mint
VISION AND THE SCARLET WITCH (cont.)			
1	.30	.90	1.75
2-4: 2-Nuklo & Future Man app.		.60	1.25
VISION AND THE SCARLET WITCH, THE			
Oct, 1985 - No. 12, Sept, 1986 (maxi-series)			
Marvel Comics Group			
V2#1-Origin; 1st app. in Avengers #57	.30	.90	1.75
2-5: 2-West Coast Avengers x-over	.25	.75	1.50
6-12		.60	1.25
VISIONARIES			
Nov, 1987 - No. 6, Sept, 1988			
Star Comics/Marvel #3 on			
1	.25	.75	1.50
2-6		.50	1.00
VISIONS			
1979 - No. 5, 1983 (B&W, fanzine)			
Vision Publications			
1-Flaming Carrot begins	20.00	60.00	120.00
2	5.85	17.50	35.00
3	2.50	7.50	15.00
4-Flaming Carrot-c & info.	3.35	10.00	20.00
5-1 pg. Flaming Carrot	1.70	5.00	10.00

NOTE: *After #4, Visions became an annual publication of The Atlanta Fantasy Fair.*

	Good	Fine	N-Mint
VOID INDIGO (Also see Marvel Graphic Novel)			
Nov, 1984 - No. 2, Mar, 1985 ($1.50, Baxter paper)			
Epic Comics (Marvel)			
1-Continues from Graphic Novel	.25	.75	1.50
2-Sex, violence shown	.25	.75	1.50
VOLTRON (TV)			
1985 - No. 3, 1985 (75 cents, color, limited series)			
Modern Publishing			
1-3: Ayers-a		.40	.80
VOODA (Jungle Princess) (Formerly Voodoo)			
No. 20, April, 1955 - No. 22, Aug, 1955			
Ajax-Farrell (Four Star Publications)			
20-Baker c/a; Baker-r/Seven Seas #4	9.00	27.00	62.00
21,22-Baker-a plus Kamen/Baker story, Kimbo Boy of Jungle, &			
Baker-c (p) in all	8.00	24.00	56.00
VOODOO (Vooda #20 on)			
May, 1952 - No. 19, Jan-Feb, 1955			
Ajax-Farrell (Four Star Publ.)			
1-South Sea Girl by Baker	17.00	51.00	120.00
2-Rulah story-r plus South Sea Girl from Seven Seas #2 by Baker			
(name changed from Alani to El'nee)	13.00	40.00	90.00
3-Bakerish-a; man stabbed in face	10.00	30.00	70.00
4,8-Baker-r. 8-Severed head panels	10.00	30.00	70.00
5-7,9,10: 5-Nazi flaying alive. 6-Severed head panels			
	8.00	24.00	56.00
11-14,16-18: 14-Zombies take over America. 17-Electric chair panels			
	6.50	19.50	45.00
15-Opium drug story-r/Ellery Queen #3	7.00	21.00	50.00
19-Bondage-c; Baker-a(2)(r)	10.00	30.00	70.00
Annual 1(1952)(25 cents); Baker-a	26.00	78.00	180.00
VOODOO (See Tales of . . .)			
VORTEX			
Nov, 1982 - No. 15, 1988(No month) ($1.50-$1.75, B&W)			
Vortex Publs.			
1 ($1.95)-Peter Hsu-a; Ken Steacy-c; nudity	3.60	11.00	25.00
2-1st app. Mister X (on-c only)	1.25	3.75	7.50
3	1.00	3.00	6.00
4-8	.50	1.50	3.00

	Good	Fine	N-Mint
9-15	.35	1.00	2.00
VOYAGE TO THE BOTTOM OF THE SEA (TV)			
No. 1230, 9-11/61 - No. 16, 4/70 (Painted covers)			
Dell Publishing Co./Gold Key			
4-Color 1230(Movie-1961)	4.00	12.00	28.00
10133-412(G.K.-12/64)	2.65	8.00	18.00
2(7/65) - 5: Photo back-c, 1-5	1.70	5.00	12.00
6-14	1.15	3.50	8.00
15,16-Reprints	.70	2.00	5.00
VOYAGE TO THE DEEP			
Sept-Nov, 1962 - No. 4, Nov-Jan, 1964 (Painted-c)			
Dell Publishing Co.			
1	2.00	6.00	14.00
2-4	1.30	4.00	9.00
WACKY ADVENTURES OF CRACKY (Also see Gold Key Spotlight)			
Dec, 1972 - No. 12, Sept, 1975			
Gold Key			
1	.70	2.00	4.00
2	.35	1.00	2.00
3-12		.50	1.00
(See March of Comics #405,424,436,448)			
WACKY DUCK (Formerly Dopey Duck?; Justice Comics #7 on)			
No. 3, Fall, 1946 - No. 6, Summer, 1947; 8/48 - No. 2, 10/48			
Marvel Comics (NPP)			
3	6.00	18.00	42.00
4-Infinity-c	8.00	24.00	56.00
5,6('46-47)	5.00	15.00	35.00
1,2(1948)	3.70	11.00	26.00
I.W. Reprint #1,2,7('58)	.30	.90	1.80
Super Reprint #10(I.W. on-c, Super-inside)	.30	.90	1.80
WACKY QUACKY (See Wisco)			
WACKY RACES (TV)			
Aug, 1969 - No. 7, Apr, 1972 (Hanna-Barbera)			
Gold Key			
1	1.50	4.50	10.00
2-7	.85	2.50	6.00
WACKY SQUIRREL (Also see Dark Horse Presents)			
Oct, 1987 - No. 4, 1988 ($1.75, B&W)			
Dark Horse Comics			
1-4: 4-Superman parody	.30	.90	1.75
Halloween Adventure Special 1 (1987, $2.00)	.30	.90	1.75
Summer Fun Special 1 (1988, $2.00)	.35	1.00	2.00
WACKY WITCH (Also see Gold Key Spotlight)			
March, 1971 - No. 21, Dec, 1975			
Gold Key			
1	1.00	3.00	6.00
2	.60	1.75	3.50
3-21	.35	1.00	2.00
(See March of Comics #374,398,410,422,434,446,458,470,482)			
WACKY WOODPECKER (See Two Bit . . .)			
1958; 1963			
I. W. Enterprises/Super Comics			
I.W. Reprint #1,2,7(nd-r-/Two Bit . . .)	.30	.90	1.80
Super Reprint #10('63)	.30	.90	1.80
WAGON TRAIN (1st Series) (TV) (See Western Roundup under Dell Giants)			
No. 895, Mar, 1958 - No. 13, Apr-June, 1962 (All photo-c)			
Dell Publishing Co.			
4-Color 895 (#1)	5.70	17.00	40.00

Wagon Train #8 (1st series), © Revue Prod.

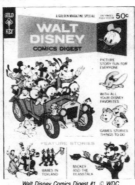

Walt Disney Comics Digest #1, © WDC

Walt Disney's Comics And Stories #1, © WDC

Walt Disney's Comics And Stories #161, © WDC   Walt Disney's Comics And Stories #518, © WDC   Walt Disney Showcase #30, © WDC

WALT DISNEY'S COMICS & STORIES (cont.)

	Good	Fine	N-Mint
107-Barks-a; Taliaferro-c. Donald acquires super powers			
	6.50	19.50	45.00
111,114,117-All Barks	5.00	15.00	35.00
112-Drug (ether) issue (Donald Duck)	5.50	16.50	38.00
113,115,116,118-123: Not by Barks. 116-Dumbo x-over. 121-Grandma Duck begins, ends #168; not in #135,142,146,155			
	2.15	6.50	15.00
124,126-130-All Barks. 124-X-Mas-c	4.35	13.00	30.00
125-Intro. & 1st app. Junior Woodchucks; Barks-a			
	7.00	21.00	50.00
131,133,135-139-All Barks	4.35	13.00	30.00
132-Barks-a(2) (D. Duck & Grandma Duck)	5.15	15.50	36.00
134-Intro. & 1st app. The Beagle Boys	8.50	25.50	60.00
140-1st app. Gyro Gearloose by Barks	8.50	25.50	60.00
141-150-All Barks. 143-Little Hiawatha begins, ends #151,159			
	2.65	8.00	18.00
151-170-All Barks	2.35	7.00	16.00
171-200-All Barks	2.00	6.00	14.00
201-240: All Barks. 204-Chip 'n' Dale & Scamp begin			
	1.70	5.00	12.00
241-283: Barks-a. 241-Dumbo x-over. 247-Gyro Gearloose begins, ends #274. 256-Ludwig Von Drake begins, ends #274			
	1.50	4.50	9.00
284,285,287,290,295,296,309-311-Not by Barks	.85	2.50	5.00
286,288,289,291-294,297,298,308-All Barks stories; 293-Grandma Duck's Farm Friends. 297-Gyro Gearloose. 298-Daisy Duck's Diary-r	1.35	4.00	8.00
299-307-All contain early Barks-r (#43-117). 305-Gyro Gearloose			
	1.50	4.50	9.00
312-Last Barks issue with original story	1.35	4.00	8.00
313-315,317-327,329-334,336-341	.70	2.00	4.00
316-Last issue published during life of Walt Disney			
	.70	2.00	4.00
328,335,342-350-Barks-r	.85	2.50	5.00
351-360-w/posters inside; Barks reprints (2 versions of each with & without posters)-without posters. . .	.75	2.25	4.50
351-360-With posters	1.15	3.50	8.00
361-400-Barks-r	.75	2.25	4.50
401-429-Barks-r	.50	1.50	3.00
430,433,437,438,441,444,445,466,506,509,510-No Barks			
	.35		.70
431,432,434-436,439,440,442,443-Barks-r	.25	.75	1.50
446-465,467-505,507,508-510: All Barks-r. 494-r/WDC&S #98 (1st Uncle Scrooge)	.50		1.00
511-Wuzzles by Disney studio	.85	2.50	5.00
512	.50	1.50	3.00
513-520: 518-Infinity-c	.30	.90	1.80
521-540: 522-r/1st app. Huey, Dewey & Louie from D. Duck Sunday page. 535-546-Barks-r	.60		1.20
541-545: (All $1.50, 52 pgs.)	.25	.75	1.50
546 ($1.95, 68 pgs.)-Kelly-r	.35	1.00	2.00

NOTE: (#1-38, 68 pgs.; #39-42, 60 pgs.; #43-57, 61-134, 143-168, 446, 447, 52 pgs.; #58-60, 135-142, 169-540, 36 pgs.)

NOTE: **Barks** art in all issues #31 on, except where noted; c-95, 96, 104, 108, 109, 130-172, 174-178, 183, 198-200, 204, 206-209, 212-216, 218, 220, 226, 228-233, 235-238, 240-243, 247, 250, 253, 256, 260, 261, 276-283, 288-292, 295-298, 301, 303, 304, 306, 307, 309, 310, 313-316, 319, 321, 322, 324, 326, 328, 329, 331, 332, 334, 341, 342, 350, 351, 540(never before published). Kelly a-546r; covers(most)-34-94, 97-103, 105, 106, 110-123, 537; 538; 541r, 543r, 544r. Walt Disney's Comics & Stories featured Mickey Mouse serials which were in practically every issue from #1 through #394. The titles of the serials, along with the issues they are in, are listed in previous editions of this price guide. **Floyd Gottfredson** Mickey Mouse serials in issues #1-61, 63-74, 77-92 plus ''Mickey Mouse in a Warplant'' (3 pgs.), and ''Pluto Catches a Nazi Spy'' (4 pgs.) in #62; ''Mystery Next Door,'' #93; ''Sunken Treasure,'' #94; ''Aunt Marissa,'' #95; ''Gangland,'' #98; ''Thanksgiving Dinner,'' #99; and ''The Talking Dog,'' #100. Mickey Mouse by **Paul Murry** #152 on except 155-57 (**Dick Moore**), 327-29 (**Tony Strobl**), 348-50 (**Jack Manning**). **Don Rosa** story/a-523, 524, 526, 528, 531. Al Taliaferro Silly Symphonies in #5-''Three Little Pigs;'' #13-''Birds of a Feather;'' #14-''The Boarding School Mystery;'' #15-''Cookieland'' and ''Three Little Kittens;'' #16-''Three Little Pigs;'' #17-''The

Ugly Duckling'' and ''The Robber Kitten;'' #19-''Penguin Isle'' and ''Bucky Bug'' in #20-23, 25, 26, 28 (one continuous story from 1932-34; first 2 pgs. not Taliaferro).

WALT DISNEY'S COMICS & STORIES
1943 (36 pgs.) (Dept. store Xmas giveaway)
Walt Disney Productions

	Good	Fine	N-Mint
nn	45.00	135.00	300.00

WALT DISNEY'S COMICS & STORIES
Mid 1940's ('45-48), 1952 (4 pgs. in color) (slick paper)
Dell Publishing Co.(Special Xmas offer)

1940's version - subscription form for WDC&S - (Reprints two different WDC&S covers with subscription forms printed on inside covers)	8.50	25.50	60.00
1952 version	5.00	15.00	35.00

WALT DISNEY'S COMICS DIGEST
Dec, 1986 - No. 7, Sept, 1987
Gladstone Publishing

1-7		.60	1.25

WALT DISNEY SHOWCASE
Oct, 1970 - No. 54, Jan, 1980 (No. 44-48: 68pgs., 49-54: 52pgs.)
Gold Key

	Good	Fine	N-Mint
1-Boatniks (Movie)-Photo-c	1.00	3.00	6.00
2-Moby Duck	.50	1.50	3.00
3,4,7: 3-Bongo & Lumpjaw-r. 4,7-Pluto-r	.35	1.00	2.00
5-$1,000,000 Duck (Movie)-Photo-c	.70	2.00	4.00
6-Bedknobs & Broomsticks (Movie)	.70	2.00	4.00
8-Daisy & Donald	.35	1.00	2.00
9-101 Dalmatians (cartoon feature); r-4-Color 1183			
	.50	1.50	3.00
10-Napoleon & Samantha (Movie)-Photo-c	.70	2.00	4.00
11-Moby Duck-r	.25	.75	1.50
12-Dumbo-r/4-Color 668	.35	1.00	2.00
13-Pluto-r	.30	.90	1.80
14-World's Greatest Athlete (Movie)-Photo-c	.70	2.00	4.00
15-3 Little Pigs-r	.25	.75	1.50
16-Aristocats (cartoon feature); r-Aristocats #1	.70	2.00	4.00
17-Mary Poppins; r-M.P. #10136-501-Color	.70	2.00	4.00
18-Gyro Gearloose; Barks-r/4-Color #1047,1184	.70	2.00	4.00
19-That Darn Cat; r-T.D.C. #10171-602-Haley Mills photo-c			
	.50	1.50	3.00
20,23-Pluto-r	.25	.75	1.50
21-Li'l Bad Wolf & The Three Little Pigs	.30	.90	1.80
22-Unbirthday Party with Alice in Wonderland; r-4-Color #341			
	.50	1.50	3.00
24-26: 24-Herbie Rides Again (Movie); sequel to ''The Love Bug;'' Photo-c. 25-Old Yeller (Movie); r-4-Color #869; Photo-c. 26-Lt. Robin Crusoe USN (Movie); r-Lt. Robin Crusoe USN #10191-601; Photo-c	.35	1.00	2.00
27-Island at the Top of the World (Movie)-Photo-c			
	.40	1.25	2.50
28-Brer Rabbit, Bucky Bug/WDC&S 58	.25	.75	1.50
29-Escape to Witch Mountain (Movie)-Photo-c	.50	1.50	3.00
30-Magica De Spell; Barks-r/Uncle Scrooge #36 & WDC&S #258			
	1.00	3.00	6.00
31-Bambi (cartoon feature); r-4-Color #186	.50	1.50	3.00
32-Spin & Marty-r/F.C. 1026; Mickey Mouse Club (TV)-Photo-c			
	.70	2.00	4.00
33-39: 33-Pluto-r/F.C. #1143. 34-Paul Revere's Ride with Johnny Tremain (TV); 4-Color #822-r. 35-Goofy-r/F.C. #952. 36-Peter Pan-r/ F.C. #442. 37-Tinker Bell & Jiminy Cricket-r/FC #982,989. 38,39-Mickey & the Sleuth, Parts 1 & 2	.25	.75	1.50
40-The Rescuers (cartoon feature)	.40	.90	1.80
41-Herbie Goes to Monte Carlo (Movie); sequel to ''Herbie Rides Again''-Photo-c	.35	1.00	2.00
42-Mickey & the Sleuth	.25	.75	1.50

421

	Good	Fine	N-Mint

WALT DISNEY SHOWCASE (continued)

	Good	Fine	N-Mint
43-Pete's Dragon (Movie)-Photo-c	.70	2.00	4.00
44-Return From Witch Mountain (new) & In Search of the Castaways			
-r(Movies)-Photo-c; 68 pg. giants begin	.50	1.50	3.00
45-The Jungle Book (Movie); r-#30033-803	.50	1.50	3.00
46-The Cat From Outer Space (Movie)(new), & The Shaggy Dog			
(Movie)-r/F.C. 985-Photo-c	.50	1.50	3.00
47-Mickey Mouse Surprise Party-r	.50	1.50	3.00
48-The Wonderful Advs. of Pinocchio-r/F.C. 1203; last 68 pg. issue			
	.50	1.50	3.00
49-54: 49-North Avenue Irregulars (Movie); Zorro-r/Zorro 11; 52 pgs.			
begin; photo-c. 50-Bednobs & Broomsticks-r/#6; Mooncussers-r/			
World of Adv. #1; photo-c. 51-101 Dalmatians-r. 52-Unidentified Fly-			
ing Oddball (Movie); r-/Picnic Party #8-Photo-c. 53-The Scarecrow-r			
(TV). 54-The Black Hole (Movie)-Photo-c	.25	.75	1.50

WALT DISNEY'S MAGAZINE (TV)(Formerly Walt Disney's Mickey
Mouse Club Magazine) (50 cents) (Bi-monthly)
V2No.4, June, 1957 - V4No.6, Oct, 1959
Western Publishing Co.

	Good	Fine	N-Mint
V2#4-Stories & articles on the Mouseketeers, Zorro, & Goofy and			
other Disney characters & people	3.50	10.50	24.00
V2#5, V2#6(10/57)	3.50	10.50	24.00
V3#1(12/57), V3#3-6(10/58)	2.00	6.00	14.00
V3#2-Annette photo-c	5.00	15.00	35.00
V4#1(12/58) - V4#2-4,6(10/59)	2.00	6.00	14.00
V4#5-Annette photo-c	4.00	12.00	28.00

NOTE: V2#4-V3#6 were 11½x8½''; 48 pgs.; V4#1 on were 10x8''; 52 pgs. (Peak circulation of 400,000).

WALT DISNEY'S MERRY CHRISTMAS (See Dell Giant #39)

WALT DISNEY'S MICKEY MOUSE CLUB MAGAZINE (TV)(Becomes
Walt Disney's Magazine) (Quarterly)
Winter, 1956 - V2#3, April, 1957 (11½x8½'') (48 pgs.)
Western Publishing Co.

	Good	Fine	N-Mint
V1#1	10.00	30.00	70.00
2-4	5.00	15.00	35.00
V2#1-3	4.00	12.00	28.00
Annual(1956)-Two different issues; ($1.50-Whitman); 120 pgs., card-			
board covers, 11¾x8¾''; reprints	10.00	30.00	70.00
Annual(1957)-Same as above	7.00	21.00	50.00

WALT DISNEY'S WHEATIES PREMIUMS (See Wheaties)

WALTER LANTZ ANDY PANDA (Also see Andy Panda)
Aug, 1973 - No. 23, Jan, 1978 (Walter Lantz)
Gold Key

1-Reprints	.35	1.00	2.00
2-10-All reprints	.40	.80	
11-23: 15,17-19,22-Reprints	.15	.30	

WALT KELLY'S...
Dec, 1987; April, 1988 ($1.75-$2.50, color, Baxter)
Eclipse Comics

...Christmas Classics 1 ('87, $1.75)-Kelly-r/Peter Wheat & Santa			
Claus Funnies	.30	.90	1.75
...Springtime Tales 1 (4/88, $2.50)-Kelly-r	.40	1.25	2.50

WALT SCOTT'S CHRISTMAS STORIES (See 4-Color #959,1062)

WAMBI, JUNGLE BOY (See Jungle Comics)
Spring, 1942 - No. 3, Spring, 1943; No. 4, Fall, 1948 - No. 18,
Winter, 1952-53 (#1-3, 68 pgs.)
Fiction House Magazines

	Good	Fine	N-Mint
1-Wambi, the Jungle Boy begins	30.00	90.00	210.00
2 (1942)-Kiefer-c	16.00	48.00	110.00
3 (1943)-Kiefer c/a	11.50	34.00	80.00
4 (1948)-Origin in text	7.00	21.00	50.00
5 (Fall, '49, 36pgs.)-Kiefer c/a	6.00	18.00	42.00

	Good	Fine	N-Mint
6-10: 7-52 pgs.	5.00	15.00	35.00
11-18	3.70	11.00	26.00
I.W. Reprint #8('64)-R-/#12 with new-c	1.00	3.00	6.00

WANDERERS (See Adventure Comics 375, 376)
June, 1988 - No. 13, April, 1989 ($1.25, color)
DC Comics

1-13: 1-Steacy-a; 3-Legion app.		.65	1.30

WANTED COMICS
No. 9, Sept-Oct, 1947 - No. 53, April, 1953 (#9-33: 52 pgs.)
Toytown Publications/Patches/Orbit Publ.

	Good	Fine	N-Mint
9	5.70	17.00	40.00
10,11: 10-Giunta-a; radio's Mr. D. A. app.	3.50	10.50	24.00
12-Used in SOTI, pg. 277	4.30	13.00	30.00
13-Heroin drug propaganda story	4.65	14.00	32.00
14-Marijuana drug mention story, 2 pgs.	2.65	8.00	18.00
15-17,19,20	2.30	7.00	16.00
18-Marijuana story, 'Satan's Cigarettes'; r-in #45 and retitled			
	10.00	30.00	70.00
21-Krigstein-a	3.00	9.00	21.00
22-Extreme violence	3.00	9.00	21.00
23,25-34,36-38,40-44,46-48,53	1.50	4.50	10.00
24-Krigstein-a; 'The Dope King,' marijuana mention story			
	4.65	14.00	32.00
35-Used in SOTI, pg. 160	4.00	12.00	28.00
39-Drug propaganda story ''The Horror Weed''	5.50	16.50	38.00
45-Marijuana story from #18	5.50	16.50	38.00
49-Has unstable pink-c that fades easily; rare in mint condition			
	2.00	6.00	14.00
50-Has unstable pink-c like #49; surrealist-c; horror stories			
	5.00	15.00	35.00
51-''Holiday of Horror''-junkie story; drug-c	5.00	15.00	35.00
52-Classic ''Cult of Killers'' opium use story	5.00	15.00	35.00

NOTE: Buscema c-50. 51. Lawrence and Leav c/a most issues. Syd Shores c/a-48.

WANTED: DEAD OR ALIVE (See 4-Color #1102,1164)

WANTED, THE WORLD'S MOST DANGEROUS VILLAINS
July-Aug, 1972 - No. 9, Aug-Sept, 1973 (All reprints)
National Periodical Publications (See DC Special)

	Good	Fine	N-Mint
1-Batman, Green Lantern (story r-from G.L. #1), & Green Arrow			
	.35	1.00	2.00
2-Batman/Joker/Penguin-c/story r-from Batman #25; plus Flash			
story r-from Flash #121	.50	1.50	3.00
3-9: 3-Dr. Fate, Hawkman(r/Flash #100), & Vigilante. 4-Gr. Lantern &			
Kid Eternity. 5-Dollman/Green Lantern. 6-Burnley Starman; Wild-			
cat/Sargon. 7-Johnny Quick/Hawkman/Hourman by Baily. 8-Dr.			
Fate/Flash(r/Flash #114). 9-S&K Sandman/Superman			
	.40		.80

NOTE: Kane r-1, 5. Kubert r-3i, 6, 7. Meskin r-3. 7. Reinman r-4. 6.

WAR
7/75 - No. 9, 11/76; No. 10, 9/78 - No. 49?, 1984
Charlton Comics

1-49: 47-r		.15	.30
7,9(Modern Comics-r, 1977)		.15	.30

WAR, THE
1989 - No. 4, 1989 ($3.50, color, squarebound, 52 pgs.)
Marvel Comics

1-4: Sequel to The Draft & The Pitt	.60	1.75	3.50

WAR ACTION
April, 1952 - No. 14, June, 1953
Atlas Comics (CPS)

	Good	Fine	N-Mint
1	5.00	15.00	35.00
2	2.30	7.00	14.00

Wambi, Jungle Boy #1, © FH

Wanted: The World's Most Dangerous Villains #2, © DC

The War #1, © MEG

War Against Crime! #11, © WMG

War Battles #1, © HARV

War Heroes #3, © DELL

WAR ACTION (continued)	Good	Fine	N-Mint
3-10,14: 7-Pakula-a	1.50	4.50	10.00
11-13-Krigstein-a	3.00	9.00	21.00

NOTE: Heath a-1; c-7, 14. Keller a-6. Maneely a-1. Tuska a-2, 8.

WAR ADVENTURES
Jan, 1952 - No. 13, Feb, 1953
Atlas Comics (HPC)

1-Tuska-a	4.30	13.00	30.00
2	2.00	6.00	14.00
3-7,9-13	1.50	4.50	10.00
8-Krigstein-a	3.00	9.00	21.00

NOTE: Heath a-5; c-4, 5, 9, 13. Pakula a-3. Robinson a-3; c-10.

WAR ADVENTURES ON THE BATTLEFIELD (See Battlefield)

WAR AGAINST CRIME! (Vault of Horror #12 on)
Spring, 1948 - No. 11, Feb-Mar, 1950
E. C. Comics

1	39.00	118.00	275.00
2,3	22.00	65.00	155.00
4-9: 9-Morphine drug use story	21.50	64.00	150.00
10-1st Vault Keeper app.	55.00	165.00	385.00
11-2nd Vault Keeper app.	48.00	144.00	335.00

NOTE: All have Craig covers. Feldstein a-4, 7-9. Ingels a-1, 2, 8.

WAR AND ATTACK (Also see Special War Series #3)
Fall, 1964; V2#54, June, 1966 - V2#63, Dec, 1967
Charlton Comics

1-Wood-a	.85	2.50	5.50
V2#54(6/66)-#63 (Formerly Fightin' Air Force)	.35	1.00	2.00

NOTE: Montes/Bache a-55, 56, 60, 63.

WAR AT SEA (Formerly Space Adventures)
No. 22, Nov, 1957 - No. 42, June, 1961
Charlton Comics

22	1.15	3.50	8.00
23-30	.60	1.80	4.00
31-42	.40	1.25	2.50

WAR BATTLES
Feb, 1952 - No. 9, Dec, 1953
Harvey Publications

1	2.75	8.00	18.00
2	1.50	4.50	10.00
3-5,7-9	1.35	4.00	9.00
6-Nostrand-a	2.35	7.00	16.00

NOTE: Powell a-1-3, 7.

WAR BIRDS
1952 - No. 7?, 1952?
Fiction House Magazines

1	5.50	16.50	38.00
2	2.85	8.50	20.00
3-7 (4-7 exist?)	2.65	8.00	18.00

WAR COMBAT (Combat Casey #6 on)
March, 1952 - No. 5, Nov, 1952
Atlas Comics (LBI 1/SAI 2-5)

1	3.50	10.50	24.00
2	1.70	5.00	12.00
3-5	1.50	4.50	10.00

NOTE: Berg a-2, 4, 5. Henkel a-5. Maneely a-1, 4; c-3.

WAR COMICS (War Stories #5 on)(See Key Ring Comics)
May, 1940 (No mo. given) - No. 4?, 1942
Dell Publishing Co.

1-Sikandur the Robot Master, Sky Hawk, Scoop Mason, War Correspondent begin	24.00	71.00	165.00
2-Origin Greg Gilday	11.50	34.00	80.00

	Good	Fine	N-Mint
3-Joan becomes Greg Gilday's aide	8.00	24.00	56.00
4-Origin Night Devils	9.30	28.00	65.00
5-8: Exist?	5.70	17.00	40.00

WAR COMICS
Dec, 1950 - No. 49, Sept, 1957
Marvel/Atlas (USA No. 1-41/JPI No. 42-49)

1	6.50	19.50	45.00
2	3.00	9.00	21.00
3-10	2.30	7.00	16.00
11-20	1.50	4.50	10.00
21,23-32: Last precode (2/55). 26-Valley Forge story			
	1.30	4.00	9.00
22-Krigstein-a	3.00	9.00	21.00
33-37,39-42,44,45,47,48	1.15	3.50	8.00
38-Kubert/Moskowitz-a	2.30	7.00	16.00
43,49-Torres-a. 43-Davis E.C. swipe	2.00	6.00	14.00
46-Crandall-a	2.30	7.00	16.00

NOTE: Colan a-4, 48, 49. Drucker a-37, 43, 48. Everett a-17 Heath a-7-9, 19; c-11, 26, 29, 31. G. Kane a-19 Maneely c-37. Orlando a-42, 48. Pakula a-26. Reinman a-26. Robinson a-15; c-13. Severin a-26; c-48.

WAR DOGS OF THE U.S. ARMY
1952
Avon Periodicals

1-Kinstler c/a	6.35	19.00	44.00

WARFRONT
9/51 - #35, 11/58; #36, 10/65; #37, 9/66 - #38, 12/66; #39, 2/67
Harvey Publications

1	3.50	10.50	24.00
2	1.70	5.00	12.00
3-10	1.35	4.00	9.00
11,12,14,16-20	.85	2.50	6.00
13,15,22-Nostrand-a	2.75	8.00	18.00
21,23-27,29,31-33,35	.70	2.00	5.00
28,30,34-Kirby-c	1.35	4.00	9.00
36-Dynamite Joe begins, ends #39; Williamson-a			
	1.35	4.00	9.00
37-Wood-a, 17pgs.	1.35	4.00	9.00
38,39-Wood-a, 2-3 pgs.; Lone Tiger app.	.85	2.50	6.00

NOTE: Powell a-1-6, 9-11, 14, 17, 20, 23, 25-28, 30, 31, 34, 36. Powell/Nostrand a-12, 13, 15. Simon c-36?, 38.

WAR FURY
Sept, 1952 - No. 4, March, 1953
Comic Media/Harwell (Allen Hardy Associates)

1-Heck c/a in all; Bullet hole in forehead-c	3.00	9.00	21.00
2-4: 4-Morisi-a	1.50	4.50	10.00

WAR GODS OF THE DEEP (See Movie Classics)

WAR HEROES (See Marine War Heroes)

WAR HEROES
July-Sept, 1942 (no month); No. 2, Oct-Dec, 1942 - No. 10, Oct-Dec, 1944; No. 11, Mar, 1945
Dell Publishing Co.

1	9.30	28.00	65.00
2	4.50	14.00	32.00
3,5: 3-Pro-Russian back-c	3.50	10.50	24.00
4-Disney's Gremlins app.	8.50	25.50	60.00
6-11: 6-Tothish-a by Discount	2.85	8.50	20.00

NOTE: No. 1 was to be released in July, but was delayed. Cameron a-6.

WAR HEROES
May, 1952 - No. 8, April, 1953
Ace Magazines

1	2.65	8.00	18.00

	Good	Fine	N-Mint
WAR HEROES (continued)			
2	1.35	4.00	9.00
3-8	1.20	3.50	8.00

WAR HEROES (Also see Blue Bird Comics)
Feb, 1963 - No. 27, Nov, 1967
Charlton Comics

	Good	Fine	N-Mint
1	.60	1.80	4.00
2-10	.35	1.00	2.00
11-27: 27-1st Devils Brigade by Glanzman		.60	1.20

NOTE: **Montes/Bache** a-3-7, 21, 25, 27; c-3-7.

WAR IS HELL
Jan, 1973 - No. 15, Oct, 1975
Marvel Comics Group

	Good	Fine	N-Mint
1-Williamson-a(r), 3 pgs.		.40	.80
2-9-All reprints		.30	.60
10-15		.15	.30

NOTE: **Bolle** a-3r. **Powell, Woodbridge** a-1. Sgt. Fury reprints-7, 8.

WARLOCK (The Power of...)(See Marvel Premiere & Strange Tales)
Aug, 1972 - No. 8, Oct, 1973; No. 9, Oct, 1975 - No. 15, Nov, 1976
Marvel Comics Group

	Good	Fine	N-Mint
1-Origin by Kane	.85	2.50	5.00
2,3	.40	1.20	2.40
4-8: 4-Death of Eddie Roberts	.35	1.00	2.00
9-15-Starlin-c/a in all. 10-Origin Thanos & Gamora. 14-Origin Star Thief	.35	1.00	2.00

NOTE: **Buscema** a-2p; c-8p. **G. Kane** a-1p, 3-5p; c-1p, 2, 3, 4p, 5p, 7p. **Starlin** a-9-14p, 15; c-12p, 13-15. **Sutton** a-1-8i.

WARLOCK
12/82 - No. 6, 5/83 ($2.00) (slick paper) (Direct Sales only)
Marvel Comics Group

	Good	Fine	N-Mint
1-Starlin Warlock r-/Str. Tales #178-180; Starlin-c	.35	1.00	2.00
2(1/83)-Starlin Warlock r-/Str. Tales #180,181 & Warlock #9; Starlin-c	.35	1.00	2.00
3-6: Starlin-a(r) in all. 3-r/Warlock #10-12. 4-r/Warlock #12-15.			
5-r/Warlock #15	.35	1.00	2.00
Special Edition #1(12/83)	.35	1.00	2.00

NOTE: **Byrne** a-5r. **Starlin** a-1-6r; c-1-4.

WARLOCK 5
11/86 - No, 22, 5/89; V2#1, June, 1989 - Present ($1.70-$1.95, B&W)
Aircel Publishing

	Good	Fine	N-Mint
1-All issues by Barry Blair	1.10	3.25	6.50
2	.75	2.25	4.50
3	1.40	4.25	8.50
4-6: 5-Green Cyborg on-c. 6-Misnumbered; Blue Girl on-c			
	1.10	3.25	6.50
7-9	.90	2.75	5.50
10,11	.60	1.75	3.50
12-22: 18-Begin $1.95-c	.35	1.00	2.00
V2#1-5 ($2.00, B&W)	.35	1.00	2.00
Compilation 1-r/#1-5 (1988, $5.95)	1.00	3.00	5.95
Compilation 2-r/#6-9 ($5.95)	1.00	3.00	5.95

WARLORD (See First Issue Special)
1-2/76; No.2, 3-4/76; No.3, 10-11/76 - No. 133, Wint, 1988-89
National Periodical Publications/DC Comics #123 on

	Good	Fine	N-Mint
1-Story cont'd. from First Issue Special #8	2.35	7.00	14.00
2-Intro. Machiste	1.00	3.00	6.00
3-5	.85	2.50	5.00
6-10: 6-Intro Mariah. 7-Origin Machiste. 9-Dons new costume			
	.70	2.00	4.00
11-20: 11-Origin-r. 12-Intro Aton. 15-Tara returns; Warlord has son			
	.50	1.50	3.00
21-40: 27-New facts about origin. 28-1st app. Wizard World. 32-Intro			

	Good	Fine	N-Mint
Shakira. 37,38-Origin Omac by Starlin. 38-Intro Jennifer Morgan, Warlord's daughter. 39-Omac ends. 40-Warlord gets new costume			
	.35	1.00	2.00
41-47,49-52: 42-47-Omac back-up series. 49-Claw The Unconquered app. 50-Death of Aton. 51-r-/No.1		.50	1.00
48-(52pgs.)-1st app. Arak; contains free 16pg. Arak Son of Thunder; Claw The Unconquered app.	.35	1.00	2.00
53-99,101-122: 55-Arion Lord of Atlantis begins, ends #62. 63-The Barren Earth begins; contains free 16pg. Masters of the Universe			
91-Origin w/new facts		.50	1.00
100-Double size ($1.25)		.65	1.30
123-133: 125-Death of Tara. 133-($1.50, 52 pgs.)		.50	1.00
Remco Toy Giveaway (2¾x4'')		.50	1.00
Annual 1(11/82)-Grell-c, a(p)	.35	1.00	2.00
Annual 2(10/83)		.50	1.00
Annual 3(9/84), 4(8/85), 5(9/86), 6(10/87)		.50	1.00

NOTE: **Grell** a-1-15, 16-50p, 51r, 52p, 59p, Annual 1p; c-1-70, 100-104, 112, 116, 117, Annual 1, 5. **Wayne Howard** a-64i. **Starlin** a-37-39p.

WARLORDS (See DC Graphic Novel #2)

WARP
March, 1983 - No. 19, Feb, 1985 ($1.00-$1,25, Mando paper)
First Comics

	Good	Fine	N-Mint
1-Sargon-Mistress of War app.	.30	.90	1.80
2-5: 2-Faceless Ones begins		.65	1.30
6-10: 10-New Warp advs., & Outrider begin		.50	1.00
11-19		.45	.90
Special 1(7/83, 36 pgs.)-Origin Chaos-Prince of Madness; origin of Warp Universe begins, ends #3		.50	1.00
Special 2(1/84)-Lord Cumulus vs. Sargon Mistress of War ($1.00)			
		.50	1.00
Special 3(6/84)-Chaos-Prince of Madness		.50	1.00

NOTE: **Brunner** a-1-9p; c-1-9. **Chaykin** a(p)-Special 1; c-Special 1. **Ditko** a-2-4. **Staton** a-1i. No. 1-9 are adapted from the Warp plays.

WARPATH
Nov, 1954 - No. 3, April, 1955
Key Publications/Stanmor

	Good	Fine	N-Mint
1	3.50	10.50	24.00
2,3	2.00	6.00	14.00

WARP GRAPHICS ANNUAL
Dec, 1985; 1988 ($2.50 cover)
WaRP Graphics

	Good	Fine	N-Mint
1-Elfquest, Blood of the Innocent, Thunderbunny & Mythadventures app.	.50	1.50	3.00
1 ('88)	.50	1.50	3.00

WARREN PRESENTS
Jan, 1979 - No. 14, Nov, 1981
Warren Publications

	Good	Fine	N-Mint
1-14-Eerie, Creepy, & Vampirella-r		.50	1.00
...The Rook 1 (5/79)-r/Eerie #82-85		.50	1.00

WAR REPORT
Sept, 1952 - No. 5, May, 1953
Ajax/Farrell Publications (Excellent Publ.)

	Good	Fine	N-Mint
1	3.00	9.00	21.00
2	1.50	4.50	10.00
3,5	1.20	3.50	8.00
4-Used in **POP**, pg. 94	1.20	3.50	8.00

WARRIOR COMICS
1945 (1930s DC reprints)
H.C. Blackerby

	Good	Fine	N-Mint
1-Wing Brady, The Iron Man, Mark Markon	5.00	15.00	35.00

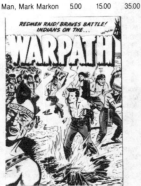

Warlock #4 (2/73), © MEG   Warlord #1, © DC   Warpath #1, © Key Publ.

Warworld! #1, © Dark Horse

Watchmen #9, © DC

Web Of Evil #6, © QUA

WARRIORS
1987 - No. 7, 1988 ($1.95, B&W)
Adventure Publications

	Good	Fine	N-Mint
1-Hsu painted-c	.60	1.75	3.50
2-7	.35	1.00	2.00

WAR ROMANCES (See True . . .)

WAR SHIPS
1942 (36 pgs.)(Similar to Large Feature Comics)
Dell Publishing Co.
Cover by McWilliams; contains photos & drawings of U.S. war ships

	7.00	21.00	50.00

WAR STORIES (Formerly War Comics?)
No. 5, 1942 - No. 8, Feb-Apr, 1943
Dell Publishing Co.

1-Exist?	8.00	24.00	56.00
2-4: Exist?	4.35	13.00	30.00
5-Origin The Whistler	7.00	21.00	50.00
6-8: 6-8-Night Devils app.	6.00	18.00	42.00

WAR STORIES (Korea)
Sept, 1952 - No. 5, May, 1953
Ajax/Farrell Publications (Excellent Publ.)

1	3.00	9.00	21.00
2	1.50	4.50	10.00
3-5	1.20	3.50	8.00

WAR STORIES (See Star Spangled . . .)

WART AND THE WIZARD
Feb, 1964 (Walt Disney)
Gold Key

1 (10102-402)	1.75	5.25	12.00

WARTIME ROMANCES
July, 1951 - No. 18, Nov, 1953
St. John Publishing co.

1-All Baker-a	11.00	32.00	75.00
2-All Baker-a	6.50	19.50	45.00
3,4-All Baker-a	5.75	17.25	40.00
5-8-Baker c/a(2-3) each	5.15	15.50	36.00
9-12,16,18-Baker c/a each	3.75	11.25	26.00
13-15,17-Baker-c only	2.85	8.50	20.00

WAR VICTORY ADVENTURES (#1 titled War Victory Comics)
Summer, 1942 - No. 3, Winter, 1943-44 (5 cents)
U.S. Treasury Dept./War Victory/Harvey Publ.

1-(Promotion of Savings Bonds)-Featuring America's greatest comic art by top syndicated cartoonists; Blondie, Joe Palooka, Green Hornet, Dick Tracy, Superman, Gumps, etc.; (36 pgs.); All profits contributed to U.S.O.	19.00	57.00	135.00
2-Powell-a	10.00	30.00	70.00
3-Capt. Red Cross (cover & text only); Powell-a	8.00	24.00	56.00

WAR WAGON, THE (See Movie Classics)

WAR WINGS
October, 1968
Charlton Comics

1	.25	.75	1.50

WARWORLD!
Feb, 1989 ($1.75, B&W, One-shot)
Dark Horse Comics

1-Gary Davis sci/fi art in Moebius style	.30	.90	1.80

WASHABLE JONES & SHMOO
June, 1953
Harvey Publications

	Good	Fine	N-Mint
1	11.00	32.00	75.00

WASH TUBBS (See The Comics, Crackajack Funnies & 4-Color #11, 28, 53)

WASTELAND
Dec, 1987 - No. 18, May, 1989 ($1.75-$2.00 #13 on, color, adults)
DC Comics

1-5(4/88), 5(5/88), 6(5/88)-18: 13,15-Orlando-a	.30	.90	1.80

WATCHMEN
Sept, 1986 - No. 12, Oct, 1987 (12 issue maxi-series)
DC Comics

1-Alan Moore scripts in all	1.15	3.50	7.00
2,3	.85	2.50	5.00
4-10	.65	1.90	3.75
11,12	.50	1.50	3.00
Trade paperback ('87, $14.95)	2.65	8.00	16.00
Hardcover (SF Book Club, $15)	4.15	12.50	25.00
Hardcover (Limited, Graphitti Designs, $50)	10.00	30.00	60.00
Hardcover (French #1-6, word balloons in French)	2.50	7.50	15.00
DC Portfolio (24 plate, $20)	4.15	12.50	25.00
Signed/Limited French Portfolio (2000 copies, $50)	25.00	75.00	150.00
Limited/Numbered Button set ($4.95)	2.50	7.50	15.00

WATCH OUT FOR BIG TALK
1950
Giveaway

nn-Dan Barry-a (about crooked politicians)	2.35	7.00	16.00

WATER BIRDS AND THE OLYMPIC ELK (See 4-Color #700)

WAXWORK IN 3-D (See Blackthorne 3-D Series #55)

WEASEL PATROL SPECIAL, THE
April, 1989 ($2.00, B&W, one-shot)
Eclipse Comics

1-Funny animal	.35	1.00	2.00

WEATHER-BIRD (See Comics From . . . & Free Comics to You . . .)
1958 - No. 16, July, 1962 (Giveaway)
International Shoe Co./Western Printing Co.

1	.70	2.00	4.00
2-16	.45	1.25	2.50

NOTE: *The numbers are located in the lower bottom panel. pg. 1. All feature a character called Weather-Bird.*

WEATHER BIRD COMICS (See Comics From Weather Bird)
1957 (Giveaway)
Weather Bird Shoes

nn-Contains a comic bound with new cover. Several combinations possible; contents determines price (40 - 60 percent of contents).

WEB OF EVIL
Nov, 1952 - No. 21, Dec, 1954
Comic Magazines/Quality Comics Group

1-Used in SOTI, pg. 388. Jack Cole-a; morphine use story	18.00	54.00	125.00
2,3-Jack Cole-a	10.00	30.00	70.00
4,6,7-Jack Cole c/a	11.00	32.00	75.00
5-Electrocution-c; Jack Cole-c/a	13.00	40.00	90.00
8-11-Jack Cole-a	7.00	21.00	50.00
12,13,15,16,19-21	3.70	11.00	26.00
14-Part Crandall-c; Old Witch swipe	4.65	14.00	32.00
17-Opium drug propaganda story	4.00	12.00	28.00
18-Acid-in-face story	5.00	15.00	35.00

NOTE: *Jack Cole a(2 each)-2, 6, 8, 9. Ravielli a-13.*

WEB OF HORROR (Magazine)
Dec, 1969 - No. 3, Apr, 1970

WEB OR HORROR (continued)

Major Magazines

	Good	Fine	N-Mint
1-Jones-c; Wrightson-a	3.00	9.00	18.00
2-Jones-c; Wrightson-a(2), Kaluta-a	2.00	6.00	12.00
3-Wrightson-c; Brunner, Kaluta, Bruce Jones, Wrightson-a			
	2.00	6.00	12.00

WEB OF MYSTERY

Feb, 1951 - No. 29, Sept, 1955
Ace Magazines (A. A. Wyn)

	Good	Fine	N-Mint
1	13.00	40.00	90.00
2-Bakerish-a	8.00	24.00	56.00
3-10	6.50	19.50	45.00
11-18,20-26: 13-Surrealistic-c. 20-r/The Beyond #1			
	5.50	16.50	38.00
19-r/Challenge of the Unknown #6 used in N.Y. Legislative			
Committee	5.70	17.00	40.00
27-Bakerish-a(r-/The Beyond #2); last pre-code issue			
	4.50	14.00	32.00
28,29: 28-All-r	3.50	10.50	24.00

NOTE: This series was to appear as "Creepy Stories," but title was changed before publication. **Cameron** a-6, 8, 12, 13, 17-20, 22, 24, 25, 27; c-8, 13, 17. **Colan** a-4. **Palais** a-28r. **Sekowsky** a-1-3, 7, 8, 11, 14, 21, 29. **Toothish** a-by **Bill Discount** #16. #29-all-r, 19-28-partial-r.

WEB OF SPIDER-MAN, THE

Apr, 1985 - Present
Marvel Comics Group

1	1.15	3.50	7.00
2,3	.70	2.00	4.00
4-8: 7-Hulk x-over	.50	1.50	3.00
9-13	.45	1.40	2.80
14-28,30: 19-Intro Humbug & Solo. 30-Origin The Rose			
	.35	1.10	2.20
29-Wolverine app.	.75	2.25	4.50
31-Six part Kraven storyline	.85	2.50	5.00
32-Kraven storyline continues	.75	2.25	4.50
33,34	.25	.70	1.40
35-49: 38-Hobgoblin app.; begin $1.00-c. 48-Hobgoblin, Kingpin app.			
	.55	1.10	
50-($1.50, 52 pgs.)	.30	.90	1.80
51-62: 59-Cosmic Spidey cont./Spect. Spider-Man	.50	1.00	
Annual 1 (9/85)	.40	1.20	2.40
Annual 2 (9/86)-New Mutants; Art Adams-a	.85	2.50	5.00
Annual 3 (10/87)	.35	1.00	2.00
Annual 4 ($1.75, 68 pgs.)-Evolutionary War x-over	.50	1.50	3.00
Annual 5 (1989, $2.00, 68 pgs.)-Atlantis Attacks; Captain Universe by Ditko (p) & Silver Sable stories; F.F. app.	.35	1.00	2.00

WEDDING BELLS

Feb, 1954 - No. 19, Nov, 1956
Quality Comics Group

1-Whitney-a	5.70	17.00	40.00
2	2.85	8.50	20.00
3-9: 8-Last precode (4/55)	1.85	5.50	13.00
10-Ward-a, 9 pgs.	6.85	20.50	48.00
11-14,17	1.50	4.50	10.00
15-Baker-c	2.00	6.00	14.00
16-Baker-c/a	3.15	9.50	22.00
18,19-Baker-a each	2.65	8.00	18.00

WEEKENDER, THE

V1#4, 1945 - V2#1, 1946 (52 pages)
Rucker Publ. Co.

V1#4(1945)	9.30	28.00	65.00
V2#1-36 pgs. comics, 16 in newspaper format with photos; partial Dynamic Comics reprints; 4 pgs. of cels from the Disney film Pinocchio; Little Nemo story by Winsor McCay, Jr.; Jack Cole-a			

	Good	Fine	N-Mint
	11.50	34.00	80.00

WEEKLY COMIC MAGAZINE

May 12, 1940 (16 pgs.) (Full Color)
Fox Publications

(1st Version)-8 pg. Blue Beetle story, 7 pg. Patty O'Day story; two copies known to exist. Estimated value....			$500.00
(2nd Version)-7 two-pg. adventures of Blue Beetle, Patty O'Day, Yarko, Dr. Fung, Green Mask, Spark Stevens, & Rex Dexter; one copy known to exist Estimated value....			$400.00

Discovered with business papers, letters and exploitation material promoting **Weekly Comic Magazine** for use by newspapers in the same manner of **The Spirit** weeklies. Interesting note: these are dated three weeks before the first **Spirit** comic. Letters indicate that samples may have been sent to a few newspapers. These sections were actually 15½x22" pages which will fold down to an approximate 8x10" comic booklet. Other various comic sections were found with the above, but were more like the Sunday comic sections in format.

WEIRD (Magazine)

V1#10, 1/66 - V8#6, 12/74; V9#1, 1/75 - V10#3, 1977
(V1-V8: 52 pgs.; V9 on: 68 pgs.)
Eerie Publications

V1#10(#1)-Intro. Morris the Caretaker of Weird (ends V2#10); Burgos-a			
	1.15	3.50	8.00
11,12	.60	1.80	4.00
V2#1-4(10/67), V3#1(1/68), V2#6(4/68)-V2#7,9,10(12/68), V3#1(2/69)-			
V3#4	.60	1.80	4.00
V2#8-Reprints Ditko's 1st story/Fantastic Fears #5			
	.70	2.00	5.00
5(12/69)-Rulah reprint; "Rulah" changed to "Pulah;" LSD story reprinted in Horror Tales V4#4, Tales From the Tomb V2#4, & Terror Tales V7#3	.60	1.75	3.50
V4#1-6('70), V5#1-6('71), V6#1-7('72), V7#1-7('73), V8#1-6('74), V9#1-4(1/75-'76)(no V9#1), V10#1-3('77)	.60	1.75	3.50

WEIRD, THE

Apr, 1988 - No. 4, July, 1988 ($1.50, color, mini-series)
DC Comics

1-Wrightson c/a in all	.40	1.25	2.50
2-4	.35	1.00	2.00

WEIRD ADVENTURES

May-June, 1951 - No. 3, Sept-Oct, 1951
P. L. Publishing Co. (Canada)

1-"The She-Wolf Killer" by Matt Baker, 6 pgs.			
	13.50	41.00	95.00
2-Bondage/hypodermic panel; opium den text story			
	10.00	30.00	70.00
3-Male bondage/torture-c; severed head story	8.50	25.50	60.00

WEIRD ADVENTURES

No. 10, July-Aug, 1951
Ziff-Davis Publishing Co.

10-Painted-c	10.00	30.00	70.00

WEIRD CHILLS

July, 1954 - No. 3, Nov, 1954
Key Publications

1-Wolverton-a r-/Weird Mysteries No. 4; blood transfusion-c by Baily			
	20.00	60.00	140.00
2-Injury to eye-c	23.00	70.00	160.00
3-Bondage E.C. swipe-c	11.00	32.00	75.00

WEIRD COMICS

April, 1940 - No. 20, Jan, 1942
Fox Features Syndicate

1-The Birdman, Thor, God of Thunder (ends #5), The Sorceress of Zoom, Blast Bennett, Typhon, Voodoo Man, & Dr. Mortal begin; Fine bondage-c	107.00	321.00	750.00
2-Lou Fine-c	52.00	156.00	365.00

The Web Of Spider-Man Annual #2, © MEG

Weird Adventures #1, © P.L. Publ.

Weird Comics #1, © FOX

Weird Fantasy #11, © WMG

Weird Mysteries #2, © Gillmore

Weird Science #14 (#3), © WMG

	Good	Fine	N-Mint
WEIRD COMICS (continued)			
3,4: 3-Simon-c. 4-Torture-c	36.00	107.00	250.00
5-Intro. Dart & sidekick Ace (ends #20); bondage/hypo-c			
	38.00	115.00	265.00
6,7-Dynamite Thor app. in each	35.00	105.00	245.00
8-Dynamo, the Eagle (1st app.) & sidekick Buddy & Marga, the Panther Woman begin	35.00	105.00	245.00
9	28.00	85.00	200.00
10-Navy Jones app.	28.00	85.00	200.00
11-16: 16-Flag-c	24.00	70.00	165.00
17-Origin The Black Rider	24.00	70.00	165.00
18-20: 20-Origin The Rapier; Swoop Curtis app; Churchill, Hitler-c	24.00	70.00	165.00

WEIRD FANTASY (Formerly A Moon, A Girl, Romance; becomes Weird Science-Fantasy #23 on)
No. 13, May-June, 1950 - No. 22, Nov-Dec, 1953
E. C. Comics

	Good	Fine	N-Mint
13(#1) (1950)	84.00	250.00	585.00
14-Necronomicon story; atomic explosion-c	46.00	137.00	320.00
15,16: 16-Used in SOTI, pg. 144	37.00	110.00	260.00
17 (1951)	31.00	92.00	215.00
6-10	23.00	70.00	160.00
11-13 (1952)	17.00	51.00	120.00
14-Frazetta/Williamson(1st team-up at E.C.)/Krenkel-a, 7 pgs.; Orlando draws E.C. staff	30.00	90.00	210.00
15-Williamson/Evans-a(3), 4,3,&7 pgs.	19.00	57.00	135.00
16-19-Williamson/Krenkel-a in all. 18-Williamson/Feldstein-c			
	17.00	51.00	120.00
20-Frazetta/Williamson-a, 7 pgs.	19.00	57.00	135.00
21-Frazetta/Krenkel-c & Williamson/Krenkel-a			
	30.00	90.00	210.00
22-Bradbury adaptation	13.00	40.00	90.00

NOTE: *Crandall* a-22. *Elder* a-17. *Feldstein* a-13(#1)-8; c-13(#1)-18 (#18 w/Williamson), 20. *Kamen* a-13(#1)-16, 18-22. *Krigstein* a-22. *Kurtzman* a-13(#1)-17(#5), 6. *Orlando* a-9-22 (2 stories in #16); c-19, 22. *Severin/Elder* a-18-21. *Wood* a-13(#1)-14, 17(2 stories ea. in #10-13). Canadian reprints exist; see Table of Contents.

WEIRD HORRORS (Nightmare #10 on)
June, 1952 - No. 9, Oct, 1953
St. John Publishing Co.

	Good	Fine	N-Mint
1-Tuska-a	14.00	42.00	100.00
2,3: 3-Hashish story	7.00	21.00	50.00
4,5	6.50	19.50	45.00
6-Ekgren-a	13.00	40.00	90.00
7-Ekgren-c; Kubert, Cameron-a	14.00	42.00	100.00
8,9-Kubert c/a	10.00	30.00	70.00

NOTE: *Cameron* a-7, 9. *Finesque* a-1-5. *Morisi* a-3. Bondage c-8.

WEIRD MYSTERIES
Oct, 1952 - No. 14, Jan, 1955
Gillmore Publications

	Good	Fine	N-Mint
1-Partial Wolverton-c swiped from splash page "Flight to the Future" in Weird Tales of the Future #2; "Eternity" has an Ingels swipe	20.00	60.00	140.00
2-"Robot Woman" by Wolverton; Bernard Baily-c-reprinted in Mister Mystery #18; acid in face panel	38.00	115.00	265.00
3,6: Both have decapitation-c	13.00	40.00	90.00
4-"The Man Who Never Smiled" (3 pgs.) by Wolverton; B. Baily skull-c	29.00	90.00	205.00
5-Wolverton story "Swamp Monster", 6 pgs.	34.00	100.00	235.00
7-Used in SOTI, illo-"Indeed" & illo-"Sex and blood"			
	21.50	65.00	150.00
8-Wolverton-c panel reprint/No. 5; used in a 1954 Readers Digest anti-comics article by T. E. Murphy entitled "For the Kiddies to Read"	12.00	36.00	85.00
9-Excessive violence, gore & torture	11.00	32.00	75.00
10-Silhouetted nudity panel	10.00	30.00	70.00

	Good	Fine	N-Mint
11-14 (#13,14-Exist?)	7.00	21.00	50.00

NOTE: *Baily* c-2-8, 10-12.

WEIRD MYSTERIES (Magazine)
Mar-Apr, 1959 (68 pages) (35 cents) (B&W)
Pastime Publications

	Good	Fine	N-Mint
1-Torres-a; E. C. swipe from TFTC No. 46 by Tuska-"The Ragman"	2.00	6.00	14.00

WEIRD MYSTERY TALES (See DC 100 Page Super Spectacular)

WEIRD MYSTERY TALES (See Cancelled Comic Cavalcade)
Jul-Aug, 1972 - No. 24, Nov, 1975
National Periodical Publications

	Good	Fine	N-Mint
1-Kirby-a		.50	1.00
2-24		.20	.40

NOTE: *Alcala* a-5, 10, 13, 14. *Aparo* c-4. *Bolle* a-8. *Howard* a-4. *Kaluta* a-24; c-1. *G. Kane* a-10. *Kirby* a-1, 2p, 3p. *Nino* a-5, 6, 9, 13, 16, 21. *Redondo* a-9. *Starlin* a-2-4. *Wood* a-23. *Wrightson* c-21.

WEIRD SCIENCE (Formerly Saddle Romances) (Becomes Weird Science-Fantasy #23 on)
No. 12, May-June, 1950 - No. 22, Nov-Dec, 1953
E. C. Comics

	Good	Fine	N-Mint
12(#1) (1950)	86.00	257.00	600.00
13	49.00	146.00	340.00
14,15 (1950)	43.00	130.00	305.00
5-10: 5-Atomic explosion-c	27.00	81.00	185.00
11-14 (1952)	17.00	51.00	120.00
15-18-Williamson/Krenkel-a in each; 15-Williamson-a. 17-Used in POP, pgs. 81,82	20.00	60.00	140.00
19,20-Williamson/Frazetta-a, 7 pgs each. 19-Used in SOTI, illo-"A young girl on her wedding night stabs her sleeping husband to death with a hatpin..."	27.00	80.00	185.00
21-Williamson/Frazetta-a, 6 pgs.; Wood draws E.C. staff; Gaines & Feldstein app. in story	27.00	80.00	185.00
22-Williamson/Frazetta/Krenkel-a, 8 pgs.; Wood draws himself in his story - last pg. & panel	27.00	80.00	185.00

NOTE: *Elder* a-14, 19. *Evans* a-22. *Feldstein* a-12(#1)-8; c-12(#1)-8. 11. *Ingels* a-15. *Kamen* a-12(#1)-13, 15-18, 20, 21. *Kurtzman* a-12(#1)-7. *Orlando* a-10-22. *Wood* a-12(#1), 13(#2), 5-22 (#9, 10, 12, 13 all have 2 Wood stories); c-9, 10, 12-22. Canadian reprints exist; see Table of Contents.

WEIRD SCIENCE-FANTASY (Formerly Weird Science & Weird Fantasy) (Becomes Incredible Science Fiction #30)
No. 23 Mar, 1954 - No. 29, May-June, 1955
E. C. Comics

	Good	Fine	N-Mint
23-Williamson & Wood-a	19.00	57.00	135.00
24-Williamson & Wood-a; Harlan Ellison's 1st professional story, 'Upheaval!,' later adapted into a short story as 'Mealtime,' and then into a TV episode of Voyage to the Bottom of the Sea as 'The Price of Doom'	19.00	57.00	135.00
25-Williamson-c; Williamson/Torres/Krenkel-a plus Wood-a	23.00	70.00	165.00
26-Flying Saucer Report; Wood, Crandall, Orlando-a	18.50	56.00	130.00
27	19.00	57.00	135.00
28-Williamson/Krenkel/Torres-a; Wood-a	22.00	65.00	154.00
29-Frazetta-c; Williamson/Krenkel & Wood-a	42.00	125.00	295.00

NOTE: *Crandall* a-26, 27, 29. *Evans* a-26. *Feldstein* c-24, 26, 28. *Kamen* a-27, 28. *Krigstein* a-23-25. *Orlando* a-in all. *Wood* a-in all; c-23, 27.

WEIRD SCIENCE-FANTASY ANNUAL
1952, 1953 (Sold thru the E. C. office & on the stands in some major cities) (25 cents, 132 pgs.)
E. C. Comics

	Good	Fine	N-Mint
1952-Feldstein-c	100.00	300.00	700.00
1953	63.00	190.00	440.00

NOTE: The 1952 annual contains books cover-dated in 1951 & 1952, and the 1953 an

WEIRD SCIENCE-FANTASY ANNUAL (continued)

nual from 1952 & 1953. Contents of each annual may vary in same year.

WEIRD SUSPENSE
Feb, 1975 - No. 3, July, 1975
Atlas/Seaboard Publ.

	Good	Fine	N-Mint
1-Tarantula begins		.30	.60
2,3: 3-Buckler-c		.25	.50

WEIRD SUSPENSE STORIES (Canadian reprint of Crime SuspenStories #1-3; see Table of Contents)

WEIRD TALES OF THE FUTURE
March, 1952 - No. 8, July, 1953
S.P.M. Publ. No. 1-4/Aragon Publ. No. 5-8

	Good	Fine	N-Mint
1-Andru-a(2)	26.00	77.00	180.00
2,3-Wolverton-c/a(3) each. 2-''Jumpin Jupiter'' satire by Wolverton			
begins, ends #5	48.00	145.00	335.00
4-''Jumpin Jupiter'' satire by Wolverton; partial Wolverton-c			
	24.00	73.00	170.00
5-Wolverton-c/a(2)	48.00	145.00	335.00
6-Bernard Baily-c	13.00	40.00	90.00
7-''The Mind Movers'' from the art to Wolverton's ''Brain Bats of Venus'' from Mr. Mystery #7 which was cut apart, pasted up, partially redrawn, and rewritten by Harry Kantor, the editor; Bernard Baily-c	24.00	72.00	170.00
8-Reprints Weird Mysteries #1(10/52) minus cover; gory cover showing heart ripped out	12.00	36.00	84.00

WEIRD TALES OF THE MACABRE (Magazine)
Jan, 1975 - No. 2, Mar, 1975 (B&W) (75 cents)
Atlas/Seaboard Publ.

	Good	Fine	N-Mint
1-Jones-c	.35	1.00	2.00
2-Boris Vallejo-c, Severin-a	.25	.80	1.60

WEIRD TERROR (Also see Horrific)
Sept, 1952 - No. 13, Sept, 1954
Allen Hardy Associates (Comic Media)

	Good	Fine	N-Mint
1-''Portrait of Death,'' adapted from Lovecraft's ''Pickman's Model;'' lingerie panels, Hitler story	12.00	36.00	84.00
2-Text on Marquis DeSade, Torture, Demonology, & St. Elmo's Fire	6.50	19.50	45.00
3-Extreme violence, whipping, torture; article on sin eating, dowsing	5.70	17.00	40.00
4-Dismemberment, decapitation, article on human flesh for sale, Devil, whipping	9.30	28.00	65.00
5-Article on body snatching, mutilation; cannibalism story	5.70	17.00	40.00
6-Dismemberment, decapitation, man hit by lightning	9.30	28.00	65.00
7,9,10	5.70	17.00	40.00
8-Decapitation story; Ambrose Bierce adapt.	8.00	24.00	56.00
11-End of the world story with atomic blast panels; Tothish-a by Bill Discount	8.00	24.00	56.00
12-Discount-a	5.00	15.00	35.00
13-Severed head panels	5.70	17.00	40.00

NOTE: *Don Heck* c/a-most issues. *Landau* a-6. *Morisi* a-2-5, 7, 9, 12. *Palais* a-1, 5, 6, 8(2), 10, 12. *Powell* a-10. *Ravielli* a-11, 20.

WEIRD THRILLERS
Sept-Oct, 1951 - No. 5, Oct-Nov, 1952 (#2-4: painted-c)
Ziff-Davis Publ. Co. (Approved Comics)

	Good	Fine	N-Mint
1-Ron Hatton photo-c	17.00	51.00	120.00
2-Toth, Anderson, Colan-a	13.00	40.00	90.00
3-Two Powell, Tuska-a	10.00	30.00	70.00
4-Kubert, Tuska-a	11.50	34.00	80.00
5-Powell-a	10.00	30.00	70.00

NOTE: *Anderson* a-2. *Roussos* a-4. #2, 3 reprinted in Nightmare #10 & 13; #4,5 r-/in Amazing Ghost Stories #16 & #15.

WEIRD WAR TALES
Sept-Oct, 1971 - No. 124, June, 1983
National Periodical Publications/DC Comics

	Good	Fine	N-Mint
1	.25	.75	1.50
2-7,9,10: 5,6,10-Toth-a. 7-Krigstein-a		.30	.60
8-Adams c/a(i)	.30	.90	1.80
11-50: 36-Crandall, Kubert r-/No.2		.25	.50
51-63,65-67,69-124: 69-Sci-Fic issue. 93-Origin Creature Commandos. 101-Origin G.I. Robot		.20	.40
64,68-Miller-a		.40	.80

NOTE: *Austin* a-51i, 52i. *Bailey* a-21, 33. *Crandall* a-2r, 36r. *Ditko* a-46p, 49p, 95, 99, 104-106. *Drucker* a-2, 3. *Evans* a-17, 22, 35, 46, 74, 82; c-73, 74, 82, 83, 85. *Giffen* a-124p. *Grell* a-67. *Heath* a-3, 59. *Howard* a-53r. *Kaluta* c-12. *Gil Kane* c-115, 116, 118. *Kubert* a-1-4, 7, 36, 68, 69; c-51, 60, 62-69, 72, 75-81, 84, 86-88, 90-96, 100, 103, 104, 106, 107, 123, 124. *Lopez* a-108. *Maurer* a-5. *Meskin* a-4r. *Morrow* c-54. *Newton* a-82p, 122p. *Nino* a-9. *Redondo* a-10, 13, 30, 38, 42, 52. *Rogers* a-51p, 52p. *Sekowsky* a-75p. *Simonson* a-10, 72. *Sparling* a-86p. *Spiegle* a-96, 97, 107, 109-112. *Starlin* c-89. *Staton* a-106p; c-108p. *Sutton* a-66, 87, 91, 92, 103. *Tuska* a-103p, 122p.

WEIRD WESTERN TALES (Formerly All-Star Western)
No. 12, June-July, 1972 - No. 70, Aug, 1980 (No. 12: 52 pgs.)
National Periodical Publications/DC Comics

	Good	Fine	N-Mint
12-Bat Lash, Pow Wow Smith reprints; El Diablo by Adams/ Wrightson	.35	1.00	2.00
13,15-Adams-a. 15-Adams-c	.35	1.00	2.00
14,29: 14-Toth-a. 29-Origin Jonah Hex		.50	1.00
16-28,30-70: 39-Origin/1st app. Scalphunter		.30	.60

NOTE: *Ditko* a-99. *Evans* inks-39-48; c-39i, 40, 47. *G. Kane* a-15. *Kubert* c-12, 33. *Starlin* c-44, 45. *Wildey* a-26.

WEIRD WONDER TALES
Dec, 1973 - No. 22, May, 1977
Marvel Comics Group

	Good	Fine	N-Mint
1-Wolverton r-from Mystic #6		.40	.80
2-22: 16-18-Venus r-by Everett/Venus #19,18 & 17. 19-22-Dr. Druid (Droom)-r		.25	.50

NOTE: *All Reprints: Check* a-1. *Colan* a-17r. *Ditko* a-4, 5, 10-13, 19-21. *Drucker* a-12, 20. *Everett* a-3(Spellbound #16), 6(Astonishing #10), 9(Adv. Into Mystery #5). *Kirby* a-6, 11, 13, 16-22; c-17, 19, 20. *Krigstein* a-19. *Kubert* a-22. *Maneely* a-8. *Mooney* a-7p. *Powell* a-3r, 7. *Torres* a-7. *Wildey* a-2.

WEIRD WORLDS (See Adventures Into...)

WEIRD WORLDS (Magazine)
V1#10(12/70), V2#1(2/71) - No. 4, Aug, 1971 (52 pgs.)
Eerie Publications

	Good	Fine	N-Mint
V1#10	.70	2.00	4.00
V2#1-4	.50	1.50	3.00

WEIRD WORLDS
Aug-Sept, 1972 - No. 9, Jan-Feb, 1974; No. 10, Oct-Nov, 1974
National Periodical Publications

	Good	Fine	N-Mint
1-Edgar Rice Burrough's John Carter of Mars & David Innes begin; Kubert-c		.50	1.00
2-7: 7-Last John Carter		.40	.80
8-10: 8-Iron Wolf begins by Chaykin		.30	.60

NOTE: *Adams* a-2i, 3i. *John Carter by Anderson*-No. 1-3. *Chaykin* c-7, 8. *Kaluta* a-4; c-5, 6, 10. *Orlando* a-4i; c-2-4. *Wrightson* a-2i.

WELCOME BACK, KOTTER (TV) (See Limited Collectors' Ed. #57)
Nov, 1976 - No. 10, Mar-Apr, 1978
National Periodical Publications/DC Comics

	Good	Fine	N-Mint
1-Sparling a(p)		.40	.80
2-10: 3-Estrada-a		.30	.60

WELCOME SANTA (See March of Comics #63,183)

WELLS FARGO (See Tales of...)

WENDY IN 3-D (See Blackthorne 3-D Series #70)

WENDY PARKER COMICS
July, 1953 - No. 8, July, 1954

Weird Tales Of The Future #5, © Aragon Publ.

Weird Terror #10, © Comic Media

Weird War Tales #93, © DC

West Coast Avengers Annual #4, © MEG

Western Bandits #1, © AVON

Western Comics #3, © DC

WENDY PARKER COMICS (continued)
Atlas Comics (OMC)

	Good	Fine	N-Mint
1	3.70	11.00	26.00
2	2.00	6.00	14.00
3-8	1.50	4.50	10.00

WENDY, THE GOOD LITTLE WITCH (TV)
8/60 - No. 82, 11/73; No. 83, 8/74 - No. 93, 4/76
Harvey Publications

1	8.35	25.00	50.00
2	4.00	12.00	24.00
3-5	3.35	10.00	20.00
6-10	2.50	7.50	15.00
11-20	1.70	5.00	10.00
21-30	.85	2.50	5.00
31-50	.50	1.50	3.00
51-69	.40	1.20	2.40
70-74: All 52 pg. Giants	.50	1.50	3.00
75-93	.25	.75	1.50

NOTE: (See Casper the Friendly Ghost #20 & Harvey Hits #7, 16, 21, 23, 27, 30, 33)

WENDY WITCH WORLD
10/61; No. 2, 9/62 - No. 52, 12/73; No. 53, 9/74
Harvey Publications

1: 68 pg. Giants begin	5.35	16.00	32.00
2-5	2.75	8.00	16.00
6-10	1.70	5.00	10.00
11-20	1.00	3.00	6.00
21-30	.50	1.50	3.00
31-39: Last 68 pg. issue	.35	1.00	2.00
40-45: 52 pg. issues	.25	.75	1.50
46-53		.60	1.20

WEREWOLF (Super Hero)
Dec, 1966 - No. 3, April, 1967
Dell Publishing Co.

1	.50	1.50	3.00
2,3	.25	.75	1.50

WEREWOLF BY NIGHT (See Marvel Spotlight #2-4)
Sept, 1972 - No. 43, Mar, 1977
Marvel Comics Group

1-Ploog-a-cont'd./Marvel Spotlight #4	.50	1.50	3.00
2-31: 15-New origin Werewolf		.50	1.00
32-Origin & 1st app. Moon Knight	1.50	4.50	9.00
33-Moon Knight app.	.85	2.50	5.00
34-36,38-43: 35-Starlin/Wrightson-c		.50	1.00
37-Moon Knight app; part Wrightson-c	.40	1.25	2.50
Giant Size 2(10/74, 68 pgs.)(Formerly G-S Creatures)-Frankenstein app; Ditko-a(r)		.50	1.00
Giant Size 3-5(7/75, 68 pgs.); 4-Morbius the Living Vampire app.		.50	1.00

NOTE: Bolle a-6i. Ditko a-Gnt. Size 2r. G. Kane a-11p, 12p; c-21, 22, 24-30, 34p, Gnt. Size 3-5. Mooney a-7i. Ploog 1-4p, 5, 6p, 7p, 13-16p; c-5-8, 13-16. Reinman a-8i. Sutton a(i)-9, 11, 16, 35.

WEREWOLF IN 3-D (See Blackthorne 3-D Series #61)

WEREWOLVES & VAMPIRES (Magazine)
1962 (One Shot)
Charlton Comics

1	3.00	9.00	21.00

WEST COAST AVENGERS
Sept, 1984 - No. 4, Dec, 1984 (mini-series; Mando paper)
Marvel Comics Group

1-Hawkeye, Iron Man, Mockingbird, Tigra	1.15	3.50	7.00
2-4	.75	2.25	4.50

WEST COAST AVENGERS (Becomes Avengers West Coast #48 on)
Oct, 1985 - No. 47, Aug, 1989 (On-going series)
Marvel Comics Group

	Good	Fine	N-Mint
V2#1	.85	2.50	5.00
2,3	.60	1.75	3.50
4-6	.45	1.40	2.75
7-10	.35	1.10	2.25
11-20	.35	1.00	2.00
21-30		.60	1.25
31-41		.50	1.00
42-Byrne-a(p)/scripts begin	.35	1.00	2.00
43-47: 46,46-Byrne-c. 46-1st app. Great Lakes Avengers		.50	1.00
Annual 1 (10/86)	.35	1.00	2.00
Annual 2 (9/87)	.30	.90	1.75
Annual 3 (10/88, $1.75)-Evolutionary War app.	.40	1.25	2.50
Annual V2#4 ('89, $2.00, 68 pgs.)-Atlantis Attacks; Byrne/Austin-a	.35	1.00	2.00

WESTERN ACTION
1964
I. W. Enterprises

7-Reprint	.30	.90	1.80

WESTERN ACTION
February, 1975
Atlas/Seaboard Publ.

1-Kid Cody by Wildey & The Comanche Kid stories; intro. The Renegade		.30	.60

WESTERN ACTION THRILLERS
April, 1937 (100 pages)(Square binding)
Dell Publishers

1-Buffalo Bill, The Texas Kid, Laramie Joe, Two-Gun Thompson, & Wild West Bill app.	40.00	120.00	280.00

WESTERN ADVENTURES COMICS (Western Love Trails #7 on)
Oct, 1948 - No. 6, Aug, 1949
Ace Magazines

nn(#1)-Sheriff Sal, The Cross-Draw Kid, Sam Bass begin	10.00	30.00	70.00
nn(#2)(12/48)	5.00	15.00	35.00
nn(#3)(2/49)-Used in SOTI, pgs. 30,31	5.70	17.00	40.00
4-6	4.00	12.00	28.00

WESTERN BANDITS
1952 (Painted-c)
Avon Periodicals

1-Butch Cassidy, The Daltons by Larsen; Kinstler-a; c-part r-/paperback Avon Western Novel 1	8.00	24.00	56.00

WESTERN BANDIT TRAILS (See Approved Comics)
Jan, 1949 - No. 3, July, 1949
St. John Publishing Co.

1-Tuska-a; Baker-c; Blue Monk, Ventrilo app.	10.00	30.00	70.00
2-Baker-c	6.50	19.50	45.00
3-Baker c/a, Tuska-a	8.00	24.00	56.00

WESTERN COMICS (See Super DC Giant)
Jan-Feb, 1948 - No. 85, Jan-Feb, 1961 (1-27: 52pgs.)
National Periodical Publications

1-The Wyoming Kid & his horse Racer, The Vigilante (Meskin-a), The Cowboy Marshal, & Rodeo Rick begin	29.00	86.00	200.00
2	16.50	50.00	115.00
3,4-Last Vigilante	13.00	40.00	90.00
5-Nighthawk & his horse Nightwind begin (not in #6); Captain Tootsie by Beck	11.50	34.00	80.00
6,7,9,10	9.30	28.00	65.00

WESTERN COMICS (continued)	Good	Fine	N-Mint
8-Origin Wyoming Kid; 2pg. pin-ups of rodeo queens			
	11.50	34.00	80.00
11-20	6.50	19.50	45.00
21-40: 27-Last 52 pgs.	5.00	15.00	35.00
41-49: Last precode (2/55). 43-Pow Wow Smith begins, ends #85			
	4.00	12.00	28.00
50-60	4.00	12.00	28.00
61-85-Last Wyoming Kid. 77-Origin Matt Savage Trail Boss. 82-1st app. Fleetfoot, Pow Wow's girlfriend	2.30	7.00	16.00

NOTE: *Gil Kane, Infantino* art in most. *Meskin a-1-4. Moreira a-35, 37, 39. Post a-3-5.*

WESTERN CRIME BUSTERS
Sept, 1950 - No. 10, Mar-Apr, 1952
Trojan Magazines

	Good	Fine	N-Mint
1-Six-Gun Smith, Wilma West, K-Bar-Kate, & Fighting Bob Dale begin; headlight-a	11.50	34.00	80.00
2	7.00	21.00	50.00
3-5: 3-Myron Fass-c	6.50	19.50	45.00
6-Wood-a	19.00	56.00	130.00
7-Six-Gun Smith by Wood	19.00	56.00	130.00
8	5.70	17.00	40.00
9-Tex Gordon & Wilma West by Wood; Lariat Lucy app.	19.00	56.00	130.00
10-Wood-a	16.50	50.00	115.00

WESTERN CRIME CASES (The Outlaws #10 on?)
No. 9, Dec, 1951
Star Publications

9-White Rider & Super Horse; L. B. Cole-c	3.00	9.00	21.00

WESTERN DESPERADO COMICS (Formerly Slam Bang Comics)
No. 8, 1940 (Oct.?)
Fawcett Publications

8-(Rare)	30.00	90.00	210.00

WESTERNER, THE (Wild Bill Pecos)
No. 14, June, 1948 - No. 41, Dec, 1951 (#14-31: 52 pgs.)
"Wanted" Comic Group/Toytown/Patches

14	4.50	14.00	32.00
15-17,19-21: 19-Meskin-a	2.30	7.00	16.00
18,22-25-Krigstein-a	3.70	11.00	26.00
26(4/50)-Origin & 1st app. Calamity Kate, series ends #32; Krigstein-a	4.65	14.00	32.00
27-Krigstein-a(2)	5.50	16.50	38.00
28-41: 33-Quest app. 37-Lobo, the Wolf Boy begins	1.70	5.00	12.00

NOTE: *Mort Lawrence c-19, 27. Leav c-14, 31. Syd Shores c-35, 40.*

WESTERNER, THE
1964
Super Comics

Super Reprint #15,16(Crack West. #65), 17	.25	.75	1.50

WESTERN FIGHTERS
Apr-May, 1948 - V4No.7, Mar-Apr, 1953 (#1-V3#2: 52 pgs.)
Hillman Periodicals/Star Publ.

V1#1-Simon & Kirby-c	12.00	36.00	84.00
2-Kirby-a(p?)	4.50	14.00	32.00
3-Fuje-c	3.70	11.00	26.00
4-Krigstein, Ingels, Fuje-a	4.50	14.00	32.00
5,6,8,9,12	2.85	8.50	20.00
7,10-Krigstein-a	4.50	14.00	32.00
11-Williamson/Frazetta-a	16.00	48.00	110.00
V2#1-Krigstein-a	4.50	14.00	32.00
2-12: 4-Berg-a	1.70	5.00	12.00
V3#1-11	1.50	4.50	10.00
12-Krigstein-a	4.00	12.00	28.00
V4#1,4-7	1.50	4.50	10.00

	Good	Fine	N-Mint
2,3-Krigstein-a	3.50	10.50	24.00
3-D 1(12/53, Star Publ.)-L. B. Cole-c	18.00	54.00	125.00

NOTE: *Kinstlerish a-V2#6, 8, 9, 12; V3#2, 5-7, 11, 12; V4#1(plus cover). McWilliams a-11. Powell a-V2#2. Reinman a-1-11. Rowich c-6i.*

WESTERN FRONTIER
Apr-May, 1951 - No. 7, 1952
P. L. Publishers

1	4.00	12.00	28.00
2	2.30	7.00	16.00
3-7	1.70	5.00	12.00

WESTERN GUNFIGHTERS (1st Series) (Apache Kid #11-19)
No. 20, June, 1956 - No. 27, Aug, 1957
Atlas Comics (CPS)

20	4.00	12.00	28.00
21,25-27	2.30	7.00	16.00
22-Wood & Powell-a	7.00	21.00	50.00
23-Williamson-a	5.00	15.00	35.00
24-Toth-a	4.00	12.00	28.00

NOTE: *Colan a-27. Heath a-25. Maneely a-25; c-22, 23, 25. Pakula a-23. Severin c-27. Woodbridge a-27.*

WESTERN GUNFIGHTERS (2nd Series)
Aug, 1970 - No. 33, Nov, 1975 (#1-6: 68 pgs.) (#7: 52 pgs.)
Marvel Comics Group

1-Ghost Rider begins; Fort Rango, Renegades & Gunhawk app.		.50	1.00
2-33: 2-Origin Nightwind (Apache Kid's horse). 7-Origin Rider retold. 10-Origin Black Rider. 12-Origin Matt Slade		.25	.50

NOTE: *Baker a-2r. Everett a-6i. G. Kane c-29, 31. Kirby a-1p(r), 10, 11. Kubert a-2r. Maneely a-2, 10r. Morrow a-29r. Severin c-10. Smith a-4. Steranko c-14. Sutton a-1, 2i, 3, 4. Torres a-26('57). Wildey a-8r; 9r. Williamson a-2r, 18r. Woodbridge a-27('57). Renegades in #4, 5; Ghost Rider-#1-7.*

WESTERN HEARTS
Dec, 1949 - No. 10, Mar, 1952
Standard Comics

1-Severin-a, Whip Wilson & Reno Browne photo-c	7.00	21.00	50.00
2-Williamson/Frazetta-a, 2 pgs; photo-c	11.50	34.00	80.00
3	2.65	8.00	18.00
4-7,10-Severin & Elder, Al Carreno-a. 5,6-Photo-c	2.85	8.50	20.00
8-Randolph Scott/Janis Carter photo-c/'Santa Fe;' Severin & Elder-a	3.70	11.00	26.00
9-Whip Wilson & Reno Browne photo-c; Severin & Elder-a	4.30	13.00	30.00

WESTERN HERO (Wow Comics #1-69; Real Western Hero #70-75)
No. 76, Mar, 1949 - No. 112, Mar, 1952
Fawcett Publications

76(#1, 52 pgs.)-Tom Mix, Hopalong Cassidy, Monte Hale, Gabby Hayes, Young Falcon (ends #78,80), & Big Bow and Little Arrow (ends #102,105) begin; painted-c begin	14.00	42.00	100.00
77 (52 pgs.)	10.00	30.00	70.00
78,80-82 (52 pgs.): 81-Capt. Tootsie by Beck	10.00	30.00	70.00
79,83 (36 pgs.): 83-Last painted-c	7.00	21.00	50.00
84-86,88-90 (52 pgs.): 84-Photo-c begin, end #112. 86-Last Hopalong Cassidy	8.00	24.00	56.00
87,91,95,99 (36 pgs.): 87-Bill Boyd begins, ends #95	6.50	19.50	45.00
92-94,96-98,101 (52 pgs.): 96-Tex Ritter begins. 101-Red Eagle app.	7.00	21.00	50.00
100 (52 pgs.)	8.00	24.00	56.00
102-111 (36pgs. begin)	6.50	19.50	45.00
112-Last issue	7.00	21.00	50.00

Western Crime Busters #1, © TM

Western Hearts #9, © STD

Western Hero #80, © FAW

Western Life Romances #1, © MEG

Western Outlaws & Sheriffs #65, © MEG

Western Picture Stories #4, © CM

WESTERN HERO (continued)
NOTE: ½-1 pg. Rocky Lane (Carnation) in 80-83, 86, 88, 97.

WESTERN KID (1st Series)
Dec, 1954 - No. 17, Aug, 1957
Atlas Comics (CPC)

	Good	Fine	N-Mint
1-Origin; The Western Kid (Tex Dawson), his stallion Whirlwind & dog Lightning begin	7.00	21.00	50.00
2	3.50	10.50	24.00
3-8	2.65	8.00	18.00
9,10-Williamson-a in both, 4 pgs. each	4.00	12.00	28.00
11-17	2.00	6.00	14.00

NOTE: Ayers a-6, 7. Maneely c-2-7, 10, 14. Romita a-1-17; c-1, 12. Severin c-17.

WESTERN KID, THE (2nd Series)
Dec, 1971 - No. 5, May, 1972
Marvel Comics Group

1-Reprints; Romita-c		.25	.50
2,4,5: 2-Severin-a. 4-Everett-r		.20	.40
3-Williamson-r		.25	.50

WESTERN KILLERS
No. 60, 1948 - No. 64, May, 1949; No. 6, July, 1949
Fox Features Syndicate

nn(nd, F&J Trading Co.)-Range Busters	5.70	17.00	40.00
60 (9/48)-Extreme violence; lingerie panel	8.00	24.00	56.00
61-64, 6: 61-J. Cole-a	5.00	15.00	35.00

WESTERN LIFE ROMANCES (My Friend Irma #3?)
Dec, 1949 - No. 2, Mar, 1950 (52 pgs.)
Marvel Comics (IPP)

1-Whip Wilson & Reno Browne photo-c	5.70	17.00	40.00
2-Spanking scene	5.00	15.00	35.00

WESTERN LOVE
July-Aug, 1949 - No. 5, Mar-Apr, 1950 (All photo-c & 52 pgs.)
Prize Publications

1-S&K-a; Randolph Scott "Canadian Pacific" photo-c (see Prize #76)	8.50	25.50	60.00
2,5-S&K-a: 2-Whip Wilson & Reno Browne photo-c	6.50	19.50	45.00
3,4	4.50	14.00	32.00

NOTE: Meskin & Severin/Elder a-2-5.

WESTERN LOVE TRAILS (Formerly Western Adventures)
No. 7, Nov, 1949 - No. 9, Mar, 1950
Ace Magazines (A. A. Wyn)

7	4.65	14.00	32.00
8,9	3.00	9.00	21.00

WESTERN MARSHAL (See Steve Donovan . . . & Ernest Haycox's 4-Color 534, 591, 613, 640 [based on Haycox's "Trailtown"])

WESTERN OUTLAWS (My Secret Life #22 on)
No. 17, Sept, 1948 - No. 21, May, 1949
Fox Features Syndicate

17-Kamen-a; Iger shop-a in all; 1 pg. 'Death and the Devil Pills' r-in Ghostly Weird #122	10.00	30.00	70.00
18-21	5.70	17.00	40.00

WESTERN OUTLAWS
Feb, 1954 - No. 21, Aug, 1957
Atlas Comics (ACI No. 1-14/WPI No. 15-21)

1-Heath, Powell-a; Maneely hanging-c	6.50	19.50	45.00
2	3.00	9.00	21.00
3-10: 7-Violent-a by R.Q. Sale	2.65	8.00	18.00
11,14-Williamson-a in both, 6 pgs. each	4.00	12.00	28.00
12,18,20,21: Severin covers	2.00	6.00	14.00
13-Baker-a	2.65	8.00	18.00
15-Torres-a	2.85	8.50	20.00

	Good	Fine	N-Mint
16-Williamson text illo	2.00	6.00	14.00
17-Crandall-a, Williamson text illo	3.00	9.00	21.00
19-Crandall-a	2.65	8.00	18.00

NOTE: Ayers a-7, 10, 18, 20. Bolle a-21. Colan a-5, 17. Everett a-9, 10. Heath a-1; c-3, 4, 8, 16. Kubert a-9p. Maneely a-13, 16, 17; c-5, 7, 9, 10, 12, 13. Morisi a-18. Powell a-3, 15, 16. Romita a-7, 13. Severin a-8, 16; c-17, 18, 20, 21. Tuska a-6.

WESTERN OUTLAWS & SHERIFFS (Formerly Best Western)
No. 60, Dec, 1949 - No. 73, June, 1952
Marvel/Atlas Comics (IPC)

60 (52 pgs.)	6.50	19.50	45.00
61-65: 61-Photo-c	4.50	14.00	32.00
66,68-73: 66-story contains 5 hangings	3.00	9.00	21.00
67-Cannibalism story	4.50	14.00	32.00

NOTE: Maneely a-62, 67; c-62, 69, 70, 73. Robinson a-68. Sinnott a-70. Tuska a-69, 70.

WESTERN PICTURE STORIES (1st Western comic)
Feb, 1937 - No. 4, June, 1937
Comics Magazine Company

1-Will Eisner-a	87.00	260.00	600.00
2-Will Eisner-a	55.00	165.00	385.00
3,4: 3-Eisner-a	43.00	130.00	300.00

WESTERN PICTURE STORIES (See Giant Comics Edition #6,11)

WESTERN ROMANCES (See Target . . .)

WESTERN ROUGH RIDERS
Nov, 1954 - No. 4, May, 1955
Gillmor Magazines No. 1,4 (Stanmor Publications)

1	2.85	8.50	20.00
2-4	1.70	5.00	12.00

WESTERN ROUNDUP (See Dell Giants & Fox Giants)

WESTERN TALES (Formerly Witches . . .)
No. 31, Oct, 1955 - No. 33, July-Sept, 1956
Harvey Publications

31,32-All S&K-a; Davy Crockett app. in ea.	5.70	17.00	40.00
33-S&K-a; Jim Bowie app.	5.70	17.00	40.00

NOTE: #32 & 33 contain Boy's Ranch reprints.

WESTERN TALES OF BLACK RIDER (Formerly Black Rider; Gunsmoke Western #32 on)
No. 28, May, 1955 - No. 31, Nov, 1955
Atlas Comics (CPS)

28 (#1): The Spider dies	6.00	18.00	42.00
29-31	4.30	13.00	30.00

NOTE: Lawrence a-30. Maneely c-28-30. Severin a-28. Shores c-31.

WESTERN TEAM-UP
November, 1973
Marvel Comics Group

1-Origin & 1st app. The Dakota Kid; Rawhide Kid-r; Gunsmoke Kid-r by Jack Davis		.25	.50

WESTERN THRILLERS (My Past Confessions #7 on)
Aug, 1948 - No. 6, June, 1949; No. 52, 1954?
Fox Features Syndicate

1-"Velvet Rose"-Kamenish-a; "Two-Gun Sal," "Striker Sisters" (all women outlaws issue)	19.00	57.00	135.00
2	6.50	19.50	45.00
3,6: 3-Tuska-a, Heath-c	5.00	15.00	35.00
4,5-Bakerish-a; Butch Cassidy app. #5	7.00	21.00	50.00
52-(Reprint, M.S. Dist.)-1954? No date given (Becomes My Love Secret #53)	2.30	7.00	16.00

WESTERN THRILLERS (Cowboy Action #5 on)
Nov, 1954 - No. 4, Feb, 1955 (All-r/ Western Outlaws & Sheriffs)
Atlas Comics (ACI)

1-Ringo Kid. Severin-c?	5.70	17.00	40.00

431

WESTERN THRILLERS (continued)

	Good	Fine	N-Mint
2-4	3.00	9.00	21.00

NOTE: *Heath* c-3. *Maneely* a-1; c-2. *Powell* a-4. *Robinson* a-4. *Romita* c-4. *Tuska* a-2.

WESTERN TRAILS
May, 1957 - No. 2, July, 1957
Atlas Comics (SAI)

	Good	Fine	N-Mint
1-Ringo Kid app.; Severin-c	3.50	10.50	24.00
2-Severin-c	2.30	7.00	16.00

NOTE: *Bolle* a-1, 2. *Maneely* a-1, 2. *Severin* c-1, 2.

WESTERN TRUE CRIME (Becomes My Confessions)
No. 15, Aug, 1948 - No. 6, June, 1949
Fox Features Syndicate

	Good	Fine	N-Mint
15(#1)-Kamenish-a	11.00	32.00	75.00
16-Kamenish-a	5.70	17.00	40.00
3,5,6	3.50	10.50	24.00
4-Johnny Craig-a	9.30	28.00	65.00

WESTERN WINNERS (Formerly All-West. Winners; Black Rider #8)
No. 5, June, 1949 - No. 7, Dec, 1949
Marvel Comics

	Good	Fine	N-Mint
5-Two-Gun Kid, Kid Colt, Black Rider	12.00	36.00	85.00
6-Two-Gun Kid, Black Rider, Heath Kid Colt story; Captain Tootsie By Beck	10.00	30.00	70.00
7-Randolph Scott Photo-c w/true stories about the West	10.00	30.00	70.00

WEST OF THE PECOS (See 4-Color #222)

WESTWARD HO, THE WAGONS (See 4-Color #738)

WHACK (Satire)
Oct, 1953 - No. 3, May, 1954
St. John Publishing Co.

	Good	Fine	N-Mint
1-(3-D)-Kubert-a; Maurer-c	18.00	54.00	125.00
2,3-Kubert-a in each; 3-Maurer-c	7.00	21.00	50.00

WHACKY (See Wacky)

WHAM COMICS (See Super Spy)
Nov, 1940 - No. 2, Dec, 1940
Centaur Publications

	Good	Fine	N-Mint
1-The Sparkler, The Phantom Rider, Craig Carter and the Magic Ring Detector, Copper Slug, Speed Silvers by Gustavson, Speed Centaur & Jon Linton (s/f) begin	72.00	215.00	500.00
2-Origin Blue Fire & Solarman; The Buzzard app.	53.00	160.00	375.00

WHAM-O GIANT COMICS (98 cents)
1967 (Newspaper size) (One Shot) (Full Color)
Wham-O Mfg. Co.

	Good	Fine	N-Mint
1-Radian & Goody Bumpkin by Wally Wood; 1 pg. Stanley-a; Lou Fine, Tufts-a; wraparound-c	2.85	8.50	20.00

WHAT DO YOU KNOW ABOUT THIS COMICS SEAL OF APPROVAL?
nd (1955) (4pgs.; color; slick paper-c)
No publisher listed (DC Comics Giveaway)

	Good	Fine	N-Mint
nn-(Rare)	45.00	135.00	315.00

WHAT IF. . .? (1st series)
Feb, 1977 - No. 47, Oct, 1985; June, 1988 (All 52 pgs.)
Marvel Comics Group

	Good	Fine	N-Mint
1-Brief origin Spider-Man, Fantastic Four	1.25	3.75	7.50
2-Origin The Hulk retold	.85	2.50	5.00
3-5	.70	2.00	4.00
6-10: 9-Origins Venus, Marvel Boy, Human Robot, 3-D Man	.50	1.50	3.00
11,12	.40	1.25	2.50
13-Conan app.	.70	2.00	4.00

	Good	Fine	N-Mint
14-26,29,30: 22-Origin Dr. Doom retold	.35	1.00	2.00
27-X-Men app.; Miller-c	1.00	3.00	6.00
28-Daredevil by Miller	1.00	3.00	6.00
31-X-Men app.; death of Hulk, Wolverine & Magneto	1.00	3.00	6.00
32,36-Byrne-a	.25	.75	1.50
33,34: 34-Marvel crew each draw themselves	.25	.75	1.50
35-What if Elektra had lived?; Miller/Austin-a	.25	.75	1.50
37-47: 37-Old X-Men app.	.25	.75	1.50
Special 1 ($1.50, 6/88)-Iron Man, F.F., Thor app.	.25	.75	1.50

NOTE: *Austin* a-27p, 32i, 34, 35i; c-35i, 36i. *J. Buscema* a-13p, 15p; c-10, 13p, 23p. *Byrne* a-32i, 36; c-36p. *Colan* a-21p; c-17p, 18p, 21p. *Ditko* a-35, Special 1. *Golden* c-29, 40, 42. *Guice* a-40p. *Gil Kane* a-3p, 24p; c-2-4p, 7p, 8p. *Kirby* a-11p; c-9p, 11p. *Layton* a-32i, 33i; c-30, 32p, 33i, 34. *Miller* a-28p, 32i, 35p; c-27, 28p. *Mooney* a-8i, 30i. *Perez* a-15p. *Simonson* a-15p, 32i. *Starlin* a-32i. *Stevens* a-16i. *Sutton* a-2i, 18p, 28. *Tuska* a-5p.

WHAT IF. . .? (2nd series)
July, 1989 - Present ($1.25 color)
Marvel Comics

	Good	Fine	N-Mint
V2#1- . . .The Avengers Had Lost the Evol. War	.35	1.00	2.00
2-5: 2-Daredevil, Punisher app.		.65	1.25
6-12: 6-X-Men. 7-Wolverine. 10-Punisher	.25	.75	1.50

WHAT'S BEHIND THESE HEADLINES
1948 (16 pgs.)
William C. Popper Co.

	Good	Fine	N-Mint
nn-Comic insert-"The Plot to Steal the World"	1.35	4.00	8.00

WHAT THE-?!
Aug, 1988 - Present ($1.25-$1.50, color; semi-annually #5 on; #6-$1.00)
Marvel Comics

	Good	Fine	N-Mint
1	.35	1.00	2.00
2,4,6: 6-Alpha Flight parody; Byrne/Austin-a	.25	.75	1.50
3-X-Men parody; McFarlane-a	.50	1.50	3.00
5-Punisher/Wolverine parody	.25	.75	1.50

WHEATIES (Premiums) (32 titles)
1950 & 1951 (32 pages) (pocket size)
Walt Disney Productions

(Set A-1 to A-8, 1950)
A-1 Mickey Mouse & the Disappearing Island, A-2 Grandma Duck, Homespun Detective, A-3 Donald Duck & the Haunted Jewels, A-4 Donald Duck & the Giant Ape, A-5 Mickey Mouse, Roving Reporter, A-6 Li'l Bad Wolf, Forest Ranger, A-7 Goofy, Tightrope Acrobat, A-8 Pluto & the Bogus Money

	Good	Fine	N-Mint
each. . . .	2.00	6.00	12.00

(Set B-1 to B-8, 1950)
B-1 Mickey Mouse & the Pharoah's Curse, B-2 Pluto, Canine Cowpoke, B-3 Donald Duck & the Buccaneers, B-4 Mickey Mouse & the Mystery Sea Monster, B-5 Li'l Bad Wolf in the Hollow Tree Hideout, B-6 Donald Duck, Trail Blazer, B-7 Goofy & the Gangsters, B-8 Donald Duck, Klondike Kid

	Good	Fine	N-Mint
each. . . .	1.70	5.00	10.00

(Set C-1 to C-8, 1951)
C-1 Donald Duck & the Inca Idol, C-2 Mickey Mouse & the Magic Mountain, C-3 Li'l Bad Wolf, Fire Fighter, C-4 Gus & Jaq Save the Ship, C-5 Donald Duck in the Lost Lakes, C-6 Mickey Mouse & the Stagecoach Bandits, C-7 Goofy, Big Game Hunter, C-8 Donald Duck Deep-Sea Diver

	Good	Fine	N-Mint
each. . . .	1.70	5.00	10.00

(Set D-1 to D-8, 1951)
D-1 Donald Duck in Indian Country, D-2 Mickey Mouse and the Abandoned Mine, D-3 Pluto & the Mysterious Package, D-4 Bre'r Rabbit's Sunken Treasure, D-5 Donald Duck, Mighty Mystic, D-6 Mickey Mouse & the Medicine Man, D-7 Li'l Bad Wolf and the Secret of the Woods, D-8 Minnie Mouse, Girl Explorer

	Good	Fine	N-Mint
each. . . .	1.70	5.00	10.00

NOTE: Some copies lack the Wheaties ad.

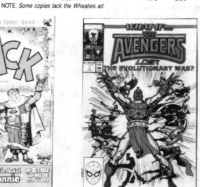

Western True Crime #4, © FOX   Whack #3, © STJ   What If. . .? V2#1, © MEG

Whirlwind Comics #3, © Nita Publ.

White Indian #15, © ME

White Princess Of The Jungle #3, © AVON

WHEE COMICS (Also see Gay, Smile & Tickle Comics)
1955 (52 pgs.) (5x7¼'') (7 cents)
Modern Store Publications

	Good	Fine	N-Mint
1-Funny animal	.40	1.20	2.40

WHEELIE AND THE CHOPPER BUNCH (TV)
July, 1975 - No. 7, July, 1976 (Hanna-Barbera)
Charlton Comics

1,2-Byrne-a (see Flintstones for 1st art)	.85	2.50	5.00
3-7-Staton-a	.40	1.25	2.50

WHEN KNIGHTHOOD WAS IN FLOWER (See 4-Color #505, 682)

WHEN SCHOOL IS OUT (See Wisco)

WHERE CREATURES ROAM
July, 1970 - No. 8, Sept, 1971
Marvel Comics Group

1-Kirby/Ayers-r		.25	.50
2-8-Kirby-r		.20	.40

NOTE: *Ditko* r-1, 2, 4, 6, 7.

WHERE MONSTERS DWELL
Jan, 1970 - No. 38, Oct, 1975
Marvel Comics Group

1-Kirby/Ditko-a(r)		.40	.80
2-10,12: 4-Crandall-a(r). 12-Giant issue		.30	.60
11,13-37		.20	.40
38-Williamson-r/World of Suspense #3		.30	.60

NOTE: *Ditko* a(r)-4, 8, 10, 12, 17-19, 23-25, 37. *Reinman* a-4r. *Severin* c-15.

WHERE'S HUDDLES? (TV) (See Fun-In #9)
Jan, 1971 - No. 3, Dec, 1971 (Hanna-Barbera)
Gold Key

1	.85	2.50	5.00
2,3: 3 r-most #1	.50	1.50	3.00

WHIP WILSON (Movie star) (Formerly Rex Hart; Gunhawk #12 on;
see Western Hearts, Western Life Romances, Western Love)
No. 9, April, 1950 - No. 11, Sept, 1950 (52pgs., 9,10; 36pgs., 11)
Marvel Comics

9-Photo-c; Whip Wilson & his horse Bullet begin; origin Bullet;
issue #23 listed on splash page; cover changed to #9

	19.50	60.00	135.00
10,11-Photo-c	16.00	48.00	110.00
I.W. Reprint #1('64)-Kinstler-c; r-Marvel #11	1.15	3.50	8.00

WHIRLWIND COMICS (Also see Cyclone Comics)
June, 1940 - No. 3, Sept, 1940
Nita Publication

1-Cyclone begins (origin)	43.00	130.00	300.00
2,3	27.00	81.00	190.00

WHIRLYBIRDS (See 4-Color #1124,1216)

WHISPER (Female Ninja)
Dec, 1983 - No. 2, 1984 ($1.50; Baxter paper)
Capital Comics

1-Origin; Golden-c	1.50	4.50	9.00
2	.70	2.00	4.00

WHISPER (Also see First Adventures)
June, 1986 - No. 37, June, 1990 ($1.25, $1.75, $1.95, color, Baxter)
First Comics

V2#1	.50	1.50	3.00
2	.35	1.00	2.00
3-9		.65	1.30
10-16 ($1.75)	.30	.90	1.80
17-32 ($1.95)	.35	1.00	2.00
Special 1 (11/85, First Comics)	.40	1.25	2.50

WHITE CHIEF OF THE PAWNEE INDIANS
1951
Avon Periodicals

	Good	Fine	N-Mint
nn-Kit West app.; Kinstler-c	7.00	21.00	50.00

WHITE EAGLE INDIAN CHIEF (See Indian Chief)

WHITE INDIAN
No. 11, July, 1953 - No. 15, 1954
Magazine Enterprises

11(A-1 94), 12(A-1 101), 13(A-1 104)-Frazetta-r(Dan Brand) in all from			
Durango Kid. 11-Powell-c	16.00	48.00	110.00
14(A-1 117), 15(A-1 135)-Check-a; Torres-a/#15	6.50	19.50	45.00

NOTE: #11 contains reprints from Durango Kid #1-4; #12 from #5, 9, 10, 11; #13 from #7, 12, 13, 16.

WHITE PRINCESS OF THE JUNGLE (Also see Jungle Adventures &
Top Jungle Comics)
July, 1951 - No. 5, Nov, 1952
Avon Periodicals

1-Origin of White Princess (Taanda) & Capt'n Courage (r); Kinstler-c

	23.00	70.00	160.00
2-Reprints origin of Malu, Slave Girl Princess from Avon's Slave			
Girl Comics #1 w/Malu changed to Zora; Kinstler c/a(2)			
	17.00	51.00	120.00
3-Origin Blue Gorilla; Kinstler c/a	13.00	40.00	90.00
4-Jack Barnum, White Hunter app.; r-/Sheena #9			
	11.00	32.00	75.00
5-Blue Gorilla by Kinstler	11.00	32.00	75.00

WHITE RIDER AND SUPER HORSE (Indian Warriors #7 on; also see
Blue Bolt #1, Four Most & Western Crime Cases)
Dec, 1950 - No. 6, Mar, 1951
Novelty-Star Publications/Accepted Publ.

1	5.00	15.00	35.00
2,3	2.85	8.50	20.00
4-6-Adapt. ''The Last of the Mohicans''	3.15	9.50	22.00
Accepted Reprint #5(r/#5),6 (nd); L.B. Cole-c	2.00	6.00	14.00

NOTE: All have L. B. Cole covers.

WHITE WILDERNESS (See 4-Color #943)

WHITMAN COMIC BOOKS
1962 (136 pgs.; 7¾x5¾''; hardcover) (B&W)
Whitman Publishing Co.

1-7: 1-Yogi Bear. 2-Huckleberry Hound. 3-Mr. Jinks and Pixie &
Dixie. 4-The Flintstones. 5-Augie Doggie & Loopy de Loop. 6-
Snooper & Blabber Fearless Detectives/Quick Draw McGraw of
the Wild West. 7-Bugs Bunny-(r)-/from #47,51,53,54 & 55

each	.50	1.50	3.00
8-Donald Duck-reprints most of WDC&S #209-213. Includes 5 Barks			
stories, 1 complete Mickey Mouse serial & 1 Mickey Mouse serial			
missing the 1st episode	7.75	22.00	44.00

NOTE: Hanna-Barbera #1-6(TV), original stories. Dell reprints-#7, 8.

WHIZ COMICS (Formerly Flash Comics & Thrill Comics #1)
No. 2, Feb, 1940 - No. 155, June, 1953
Fawcett Publications

	Good	Fine	VF-NM
1-(nn on cover, #2 inside)-Origin & 1st newsstand app. Captain			

Marvel (formerly Captain Thunder) by C. C. Beck (created by Bill
Parker), Spy Smasher, Golden Arrow, Ibis the Invincible, Dan
Dare, Scoop Smith, Sivana, & Lance O'Casey begin

	3,000.00	8,400.00	18,200.00

(Only one known copy exists in Mint condition which has not sold)
1-Reprint, oversize 13½''x10''. **WARNING:** This comic is an exact duplicate reprint
of the original except for its size. DC published it in 1974 with a second cover titling it as
a Famous First Edition. There have been many reported cases of the outer cover being removed and the interior sold as the original edition. The reprint with the new outer cover removed
is practically worthless.

433

WHIZ COMICS (continued)

	Good	Fine	N-Mint
2-(nn on cover, #3 inside); cover to Flash #1 redrawn, pg. 12, panel 4; Spy Smasher reveals I.D. to Eve	300.00	900.00	2100.00
3-(#3 on cover, #4 inside)-1st app. Beautia	185.00	557.00	1300.00
4-(#4 on cover, #5 inside)	153.00	460.00	1070.00
5-Captain Marvel wears button-down flap on splash page only	114.00	343.00	800.00
6-10: 7-Dr. Voodoo begins (by Raboy-#9-22)	93.00	280.00	650.00
11-14	61.00	182.00	425.00
15-Origin Sivana; Dr. Voodoo by Raboy	78.00	232.00	545.00
16-18-Spy Smasher battles Captain Marvel	78.00	232.00	545.00
19,20	43.00	130.00	300.00
21-Origin & 1st app. Lt. Marvels	45.00	135.00	315.00
22-24: 23-Only Dr. Voodoo by Tuska	35.00	105.00	245.00
25-Origin/1st app. Captain Marvel Jr., x-over in Capt. Marvel; Capt. Nazi app.; origin Old Shazam in text	104.00	312.00	730.00
26-30	29.00	86.00	200.00
31,32: 32-1st app. The Trolls	21.50	64.00	150.00
33-Spy Smasher, Captain Marvel x-over on cover and inside	26.50	79.00	185.00
34,36-40-The Trolls in #37	19.00	57.00	135.00
35-Captain Marvel & Spy Smasher-c	21.50	64.00	150.00
41-50: 43-Spy Smasher, Ibis, Golden Arrow x-over in Capt. Marvel. 44-Flag-c. 47-Origin recap (1pg.)	12.00	36.00	84.00
51-60: 52-Capt. Marvel x-over in Ibis. 57-Spy Smasher, Golden Arrow, Ibis cameo	9.30	28.00	65.00
61-70	8.00	24.00	56.00
71,77-80	6.00	18.00	42.00
72-76-Two Captain Marvel stories in each; 76-Spy Smasher becomes Crime Smasher	6.50	19.50	45.00
81-99: 86-Captain Marvel battles Sivana Family. 91-Infinity-c	6.00	18.00	42.00
100	8.50	25.50	60.00
101,103-105	5.00	15.00	35.00
102-Commando Yank app.	5.00	15.00	35.00
106-Bulletman app.	5.00	15.00	35.00
107-141,143-152: 107-White House photo-c. 108-Brooklyn Bridge photo-c. 112-photo-c. 139-Infinity-c	4.30	13.00	30.00
142-Used in POP, pg. 89	4.35	13.00	30.00
153-155-(Scarce)	8.50	25.50	60.00
Wheaties Giveaway(1946, Miniature)-6½x8¼'', 32 pgs.; all copies were taped at each corner to a box of Wheaties and are never found in fine or mint condition; "Capt. Marvel & The Water Thieves," Golden Arrow, Ibis stories	13.00	40.00	80.00

NOTE: *Krigstein* Golden Arrow-No. 75, 78, 91, 95, 96, 98-100. *Wolverton* ½ pg. "Culture Corner"-No. 65-68, 70-85, 87-96, 98-100, 102-109, 112-121, 123, 125, 126, 128-131, 133, 134, 136, 142, 143, 146.

WHODUNIT

Aug-Sept, 1948 - No. 3, Dec-Jan, 1948-49 (#1: 52 pgs.)
D.S. Publishing Co.

1-Baker-a, 7pgs.	6.50	19.50	45.00
2-Morphine story	3.70	11.00	26.00
3	2.85	8.50	20.00

WHODUNNIT?

June, 1986 - No. 3, April, 1987 (Color, $2.00)
Eclipse Comics

1-3	.35	1.00	2.00

WHO FRAMED ROGER RABBIT (See Marvel Graphic Novel)

WHO IS NEXT?

No. 5, January, 1953
Standard Comics

5-Toth, Sekowsky, Andru-a	8.50	25.50	60.00

WHO'S MINDING THE MINT? (See Movie Classics)

WHO'S WHO IN STAR TREK

March, 1987 - No. 2, April, 1987
DC Comics

	Good	Fine	N-Mint
1,2-Chaykin-c	.85	2.50	5.00

WHO'S WHO IN THE LEGION OF SUPER-HEROES

Apr, 1987 - No. 7, Nov, 1988 ($1.25, color index)
DC Comics

1-7		.65	1.30

WHO'S WHO: THE DEFINITIVE DIRECTORY OF THE DC UNIV.

3/85 - No. 26, 4/87 (26 issue maxi-series, no ads)
DC Comics

1-DC heroes from A-Z	.35	1.00	2.00
2-26		.60	1.20

NOTE: *Kane* a-1,3. *Kirby* a-3. *Perez* c-1, 2, 3-5p, 13, 14p, 15, 16p, 17, 18p.

WHO'S WHO UPDATE '87

Aug, 1987 - No. 5, Dec, 1987 ($1.25, color)
DC Comics

1-5	.25	.75	1.50

WHO'S WHO UPDATE '88

Aug, 1988 - No. 4, Nov, 1988 ($1.25)
DC Comics

1-4		.60	1.25

WILBUR COMICS (Also see Zip Comics)(Teen-age)

Sum', 1944 - No. 87, 11/59; No. 88, 9/63; No. 89, 10/64; No. 90, 10/65 (No. 1-46: 52 pgs.)
MLJ Magazines/Archie Publ. No. 8, Spr.'46 on

1	24.00	73.00	170.00
2(Fall,'44)	12.00	36.00	84.00
3,4(Wint,'44-'45; Spr,'45)	10.00	30.00	70.00
5-1st app. Katy Keene-begin series; Wilbur story same as Archie story in Archie #1 except that Wilbur replaces Archie	37.00	110.00	260.00
6-10(Fall,'46): 7-Transvestism issue	9.50	28.50	65.00
11-20	5.00	15.00	35.00
21-30(1949)	4.00	12.00	28.00
31-50	2.00	6.00	14.00
51-69: 59-Last 10 cent issue?	1.15	3.50	8.00
70-90	.85	2.50	5.00

NOTE: Katy Keene in No. 5-56, 58-69.

WILD

Feb, 1954 - No. 5, Aug, 1954
Atlas Comics (IPC)

1	7.00	21.00	50.00
2	4.30	13.00	30.00
3-5	3.70	11.00	26.00

NOTE: *Berg* a-5; c-4. *Burgos* c-3. *Colan* a-4. *Everett* a-1-3. *Heath* a-2, 3, 5. *Maneely* a-1-3, 5; c-1, 5. *Post* a-2, 5. *Ed Win* a-1, 3.

WILD (This Magazine Is . . .) (Magazine)

Jan, 1968 - No. 3, 1968 (52 pgs.) (Satire)
Dell Publishing Co.

1-3	.85	2.50	5.00

WILD ANIMALS

Dec, 1982 ($1.00, color) (One-Shot)
Pacific Comics

1-Funny animal; Sergio Aragones-a; Shaw-c/a		.50	1.00

WILD BILL ELLIOTT (Also see Western Roundup under Dell Giants)

No. 278, 5/50 - No. 643, 7/55 (No #11,12) (All photo-c)
Dell Publishing Co.

4-Color 278(#1, 52pgs.)-Titled "Bill Elliott;" Bill & his horse Stormy begin; photo front/back-c begin	10.00	30.00	70.00

Whiz Comics #21, Ⓔ FAW

Wilbur Comics #9, Ⓔ AP

Wild Animals #1, Ⓔ Pacific

Wild Bill Elliott #15, © DELL

Wild Bill Hickok #4, © AVON

Wild Frontier #1, © CC

	Good	Fine	N-Mint
WILD BILL ELLIOTT (continued)			
2 (11/50), 3 (52 pgs.)	5.00	15.00	35.00
4-10(10-12/52)		4.00	12.00	28.00
4-Color 472(6/53),520(12/53)-Last photo back-c	4.00	12.00	28.00
13(4-6/54) - 17(4-6/55)	3.50	10.50	24.00
4-Color 643	3.50	10.50	24.00

WILD BILL HICKOK (Also see Blazing Sixguns)
Sept-Oct, 1949 - No. 28, May-June, 1956
Avon Periodicals

	Good	Fine	N-Mint
1-Ingels-c	11.50	34.00	80.00
2-Painted-c; Kit West app.	5.70	17.00	40.00
3,5-Painted-c	3.00	9.00	21.00
4-Painted-c by Howard Winfield	3.00	9.00	21.00
6-10,12: 8-10-Painted-c; 9-Ingels-a?	3.00	9.00	21.00
11,14-Kinstler c/a	3.65	11.00	25.00
13,15,17,18,20,23	2.15	6.50	15.00
16-Kamen-a; r-3 stories/King of the Badmen of Deadwood			
	3.00	9.00	21.00
19-Meskin-a	2.15	6.50	15.00
21-Reprints 2 stories/Chief Crazy Horse	2.15	6.50	15.00
22-Kinstler-a; r-/Sheriff Bob Dixon's. . .	2.15	6.50	15.00
24-27-Kinstler-c/a(r)	2.85	8.50	20.00
28-Kinstler-c/a (new); r-/Last of the Comanches			
	2.85	8.50	20.00
I.W. Reprint #1-Kinstler-c	.50	1.50	3.00
Super Reprint #10-12	.50	1.50	3.00

NOTE: #23, 25 contain numerous editing deletions in both art and script due to code.
Kinstler c-6, 7, 11-14, 17, 18, 20-22, 24-28. **Howard Larsen** a-1, 2(3), 4(4), 5(3), 7(3), 9(3), 11(4), 12(4), 17, 18, 21(2), 22, 24(3), 26. **Meskin** a-7. **Reinman** a-17.

WILD BILL HICKOK & JINGLES (TV)(Formerly Cowboy Western)
No. 68, March, 1958 - No. 76?, 1960 (Also see Blue Bird)
Charlton Comics

	Good	Fine	N-Mint
68,69-Williamson-a	3.70	11.00	26.00
70-Two pgs. Williamson-a	2.00	6.00	14.00
71-76 (#75,76, exist?)	1.15	3.50	8.00

WILD BILL PECOS (See The Westerner)

WILD BOY OF THE CONGO (Also see Approved Comics)
No. 10, Feb-Mar, 1951 - No. 15, June, 1955
Ziff-Davis No. 10-12,4-6/St. John No. 7? on

	Good	Fine	N-Mint
10(#1, 2-3/51)-Origin; bondage-c by Saunders; used in SOTI, pg. 189			
	8.00	24.00	56.00
11(4-5/51),12(8-9/51)-Norman Saunders-c	4.30	13.00	30.00
4(10-11/51)-Saunders bondage-c	4.30	13.00	30.00
5(Winter) St.-Saunders-c	3.70	11.00	26.00
6,8,9(10/53),10: 6-Saunders-c	3.50	10.50	24.00
7(8-9/52)-Baker-c; Kinstler-a	4.00	12.00	28.00
11-13-Baker-c(St. John)	4.00	12.00	28.00
14(4/55)-Baker-c; r-#12('51)	4.00	12.00	28.00
15(6/55)	2.65	8.00	18.00

WILD DOG
Sept, 1987 - No. 4, Dec, 1987 (Mini-series)
DC Comics

	Good	Fine	N-Mint
1-4		.40	.80
Special 1 (1989, $2.50, 52 pgs.)	.40	1.25	2.50

WILD FRONTIER (Cheyenne Kid #8 on)
Oct, 1955 - No. 7, April, 1957
Charlton Comics

	Good	Fine	N-Mint
1-Davy Crockett	2.85	8.50	20.00
2-6-Davy Crockett in all	1.50	4.50	10.00
7-Origin Cheyenne Kid	1.50	4.50	10.00

WILD KINGDOM (TV)
1965 (Giveaway) (regular size) (16 pgs., slick-c)
Western Printing Co.

	Good	Fine	N-Mint
Mutual of Omaha's. . .	1.00	3.00	7.00

WILD WEST (Wild Western #3 on)
Spring, 1948 - No. 2, July, 1948
Marvel Comics (WFP)

	Good	Fine	N-Mint
1-Two-Gun Kid, Arizona Annie, & Tex Taylor begin; Shores-c			
	10.00	30.00	70.00
2-Captain Tootsie by Beck; Shores-c	8.50	25.50	60.00

WILD WEST (Black Fury #1-57)
V2#58, November, 1966
Charlton Comics

	Good	Fine	N-Mint
V2#58		.60	1.20

WILD WESTERN (Wild West #1,2)
No. 3, 9/48 - No. 57, 9/57 (3-11: 52pgs; 12-on: 36pgs)
Marvel/Atlas Comics (WFP)

	Good	Fine	N-Mint
3(#1)-Tex Morgan begins; Two-Gun Kid, Tex Taylor, & Arizona Annie continue from Wild West	11.00	32.00	75.00
4-Last Arizona Annie; Captain Tootsie by Beck; Kid Colt app.			
	8.00	24.00	56.00
5-2nd app. Black Rider (1/49); Blaze Carson, Captain Tootsie by Beck app.	8.50	25.50	60.00
6-8: 6-Blaze Carson app; Anti-Wertham editorial			
	6.00	18.00	42.00
9-Photo-c; Black Rider begins, ends #19	7.00	21.00	50.00
10-Charles Starrett photo-c	8.50	25.50	60.00
11-(Last 52 pg. issue)	4.70	17.00	40.00
12-14,16-19: All Black Rider-c/stories. 12-14-The Prairie Kid & his horse Fury app.	4.30	13.00	30.00
15-Red Larabee, Gunhawk (Origin), his horse Blaze, & Apache Kid begin, end #22; Black Rider c/story	5.70	17.00	40.00
20-29: 20-Kid Colt-c begin	3.70	11.00	26.00
30-Katz-a	4.30	13.00	30.00
31-40	2.65	8.00	18.00
41-47,49-51,53,57	1.70	5.00	12.00
48-Williamson/Torres-a, 4 pgs; Drucker-a	4.00	12.00	28.00
52-Crandall-a	3.00	9.00	21.00
54,55-Williamson-a in both, 5 & 4 pgs., #54 with Mayo plus 2 text illos	3.50	10.50	24.00
56-Baker-a?	2.00	6.00	14.00

NOTE: **Annie Oakley** in #46, 47. **Apache Kid** in #15-22, 39. **Arizona Kid** in #21, 23. **Arrowhead** in #34-39. **Black Rider** in #5, 9-19, 33-44. **Fighting Texan** in #17. **Kid Colt** in #4-6, 9-11, 20-47, 52, 54-56. **Outlaw Kid** in #43. **Red Hawkins** in #13, 14. **Ringo Kid** in #26, 39, 41, 43, 44, 46, 47, 50, 52-56. **Tex Morgan** in #3, 4, 6, 9, 11. **Tex Taylor** in #3-6, 9, 11. **Texas Kid** in #23-25. **Two-Gun Kid** in #3-6, 9, 11, 12, 33-39, 41. **Wyatt Earp** in #47. **Ayers** a-41. **Berg** a-26; c-24. **Colan** a-49. **Forte** a-28, 30. **Heath** a-4, 5, 8; c-34, 44. **Keller** a-24, 26, 29-40, 44-46, 52. **Maneely** a-10, 12, 15, 16, 28, 35, 38, 40, 41, 43-45; c-18-22, 33, 35, 36, 38, 39, 41, 45. **Morisi** a-23, 52. **Pakula** a-52. **Powell** a-51. **Severin** a-46, 47. **Shores** a-3, 5, 30, 31, 33, 35, 36, 38, 41; c-4, 5. **Sinnott** a-34-39. **Wildey** a-43. Bondage c-19.

WILD WESTERN ACTION (Also see The Bravados)
March, 1971 - No. 3, June, 1971 (Reprints, 52 pgs.)
Skywald Publishing Corp.

	Good	Fine	N-Mint
1-Durango Kid, Straight Arrow; with all references to "Straight" in story relettered to "Swift;" Bravados begin		.50	1.00
2-Billy Nevada, Durango Kid		.30	.60
3-Red Mask, Durango Kid		.30	.60

WILD WESTERN ROUNDUP
Oct, 1957; 1960-'61
Red Top/Decker Publications/I. W. Enterprises

	Good	Fine	N-Mint
1(1957)-Kid Cowboy-r	1.15	3.50	8.00
I.W. Reprint #1('60-61)	.25	.75	1.50

WILD WEST RODEO
1953 (15 cents)
Star Publications

	Good	Fine	N-Mint

WILD WEST RODEO (continued)
1-A comic book coloring book with regular full color cover & B&W
inside — 2.30 / 7.00 / 16.00

WILD WILD WEST, THE (TV)
June, 1966 - No. 7, Oct, 1969
Gold Key

	Good	Fine	N-Mint
1,2-McWilliams-a	4.00	12.00	28.00
3-7	3.00	9.00	21.00

WILKIN BOY (See That . . .)

WILLIE COMICS (Formerly Ideal #1-4; Crime Cases #24 on; Li'l Willie
#20 & 21) (See Gay Comics, Millie The Model & Wisco)
#5, Fall, 1946 - #19, 4/49; #22, 1/50 - #23, 5/50 (No #20 & 21)
Marvel Comics (MgPC)

	Good	Fine	N-Mint
5(#1)-Nellie The Nurse & Margie begin	5.00	15.00	35.00
6,8,9	2.30	7.00	16.00
7(1),10,11-Kurtzman's "Hey Look"	3.50	10.50	24.00
12,14-18,22,23	2.00	6.00	14.00
13,19-Kurtzman's "Hey Look"	3.00	9.00	21.00

NOTE: Cindy app.-14. Jeanie app.-17. Little Lizzie app.-22.

WILLIE MAYS (See The Amazing. . .)

WILLIE THE PENGUIN
April, 1951 - No. 6, April, 1952
Standard Comics

	Good	Fine	N-Mint
1	1.70	5.00	12.00
2-6	.85	2.60	6.00

WILLIE THE WISE-GUY (Also see Cartoon Kids)
Sept, 1957
Atlas Comics (NPP)

	Good	Fine	N-Mint
1-Kida, Maneely-a	1.70	5.00	12.00

WILLIE WESTINGHOUSE EDISON SMITH THE BOY INVENTOR
1906 (36 pgs. in color) (10x16")
William A. Stokes Co.

	Good	Fine	N-Mint
By Frank Crane	18.00	54.00	125.00

WILLOW
Aug, 1988 - No. 3, Oct, 1988 ($1.00, color)
Marvel Comics

	Good	Fine	N-Mint
1-3-R/Marvel Graphic Novel 36 (movie adapt.)		.50	1.00

WILL ROGERS WESTERN (See Blazing & True Comics #66)
No. 5, June, 1950 - No. 2, Aug, 1950
Fox Features Syndicate

	Good	Fine	N-Mint
5,2: Photo-c	10.00	30.00	70.00

WILL-YUM (See 4-Color #676,765,902)

WIN A PRIZE COMICS (Timmy The Timid Ghost #3 on?)
Feb, 1955 - No. 2, Apr, 1955
Charlton Comics

	Good	Fine	N-Mint
V1#1-S&K-a; Poe adapt; E.C. Swipe	22.00	65.00	150.00
2-S&K-a	16.50	50.00	115.00

WIND RAGE
1987 ($1.25, color)
Blackthorne Publishing

	Good	Fine	N-Mint
1-Exist?		.60	1.25

WINDY & WILLY
May-June, 1969 - No. 4, Nov-Dec, 1969
National Periodical Publications

	Good	Fine	N-Mint
1-4: r-/Dobie Gillis with some art changes	.25	.75	1.50

WINGS COMICS
Sept, 1940 - No. 124, 1954
Fiction House Magazines

	Good	Fine	N-Mint
1-Skull Squad, Clipper Kirk, Suicide Smith, Jane Martin, War Nurse, Phantom Falcons, Greasemonkey Griffin, Parachute Patrol & Powder Burns begin	72.00	215.00	500.00
2	35.00	105.00	245.00
3-5	27.00	80.00	185.00
6-10	22.00	65.00	154.00
11-15	19.00	57.00	135.00
16-Origin Captain Wings	21.00	62.00	145.00
17-20	14.00	42.00	100.00
21-30	13.00	40.00	90.00
31-40	11.00	32.00	75.00
41-50	8.50	25.50	60.00
51-60: 60-Last Skull Squad	7.00	21.00	50.00
61-67: 66-Ghost Patrol begins (becomes Ghost Squadron #71)	7.00	21.00	50.00
68,69: 68-Clipper Kirk becomes The Phantom Falcon-origin, Part 1; Part 2-#69	7.00	21.00	50.00
70-72: 70-1st app. The Phantom Falcon in costume, origin-Part 3; Capt. Wings battles Col. Kamikaze in all	5.50	16.50	38.00
73-99	5.50	16.50	38.00
100	6.50	19.50	45.00
101-114,116-124: 111-Last Jane Martin. 112-Flying Saucer c/story	4.00	12.00	28.00
115-Used in POP, pg. 89	4.60	14.00	32.00

NOTE: Bondage covers are common. Captain Wings battles Sky Hag-#75, 76; Mr. Atlantis-#85-92; . . . Mr. Pupin(Red Agent)-#98-103. Capt. Wings by Elias-#52-64; by Lubbers-#29-32,70-103; by Renee-#33-46. Evans a-85-103, 108(Jane Martin). Larsen a-52, 59, 64, 73-77. Jane Martin by Fran Hopper-#68-84; Suicide Smith by John Celardo-#76-103; by Hollingsworth-#105-109; Ghost Patrol by Maurice Whitman-#83-103; Skull Squad by M. Baker-#52-60; Clipper Kirk by Baker-#60, 61; Ghost Squadron by Whitman-#72-77, 104-110. Elias c-61-69. Fawcette c-6, 7, 10, 11, 17, 24-27, 30, 32. Lubbers c-75-100. Tuska a-5.

WINGS OF THE EAGLES, THE (See 4-Color #790)

WINKY DINK (Adventures of . . .)
No. 75, March, 1957 (One Shot)
Pines Comics

	Good	Fine	N-Mint
75-Marv Levy c/a	1.70	5.00	12.00

WINKY DINK (See 4-Color #663)

WINNIE-THE-POOH (Also see Dynabrite Comics)
January, 1977 - No. 33, 1984 (Walt Disney)
(Winnie-The-Pooh began as Edward Bear in 1926 by Milne)
Gold Key No. 1-17/Whitman No. 18 on

	Good	Fine	N-Mint
1-New art	.25	.75	1.50
2-4,6-11		.40	.80
5,12-33-New material		.35	.70

WINNIE WINKLE
1930 - No. 4, 1933 (52 pgs.) (B&W daily strip reprints)
Cupples & Leon Co.

	Good	Fine	N-Mint
1	8.50	25.50	60.00
2-4	6.00	18.00	42.00

WINNIE WINKLE (See Popular Comics & Super Comics)
1941 - No. 7, Sept-Nov, 1949
Dell Publishing Co.

	Good	Fine	N-Mint
Large Feature Comic 2('41)	11.00	32.00	75.00
4-Color 94('45)	8.50	25.50	60.00
4-Color 174	5.00	15.00	35.00
1(3-5/48)-Contains daily & Sunday newspaper-r from 1939-1941	4.00	12.00	28.00
2 (6-8/48)	2.65	8.00	18.00
3-7	1.70	5.00	12.00

WINTERWORLD
Sept, 1987 - No. 3, Mar, 1988 ($1.75, color, mini-series)
Eclipse Comics

Willie Comics #18, © MEG

Win A Prize Comics #1, © CC

Wings Comics #1, © FH

Witchcraft #4, © AVON

Witches Tales #6, © HARV

The Witching Hour #4, © DC

	Good	Fine	N-Mint
WINTERWORLD (continued)			
1-3	.30	.90	1.80

WISCO/KLARER COMIC BOOK (Miniature)
1948 - 1964 (24 pgs.) (3½x6¾")
Given away by Wisco "99" Service Stations, Carnation Malted Milk, Klarer Health Wieners, Fleers Dubble Bubble Gum, Rodeo All-Meat Wieners, Perfect Potato Chips, & others; see ad in Tom Mix #21
Marvel Comics/Vital Publications/Fawcett Publications

Blackstone & the Gold Medal Mystery(1948)	2.65	8.00	16.00
Blackstone "Solves the Sealed Vault Mystery"(1950)			
	2.65	8.00	16.00
Blaze Carson in "The Sheriff Shoots It Out"(1950)			
	2.65	8.00	16.00
Captain Marvel & Billy's Big Game (r-/Capt. Marvel Adv. #76)			
	24.00	70.00	155.00
(Prices vary widely on this book)			
China Boy in "A Trip to the Zoo" #10	.85	2.50	5.00
Indoors-Outdoors Game Book	.85	2.50	5.00
Jim Solar Space Sheriff in "Battle for Mars," "Between Two Worlds," "Conquers Outer Space," "The Creatures on the Comet," "Defeats the Moon Missile Men," "Encounter Creatures on Comet," "Meet the Jupiter Jumpers," "Meets the Man From Mars," "On Traffic Duty," "Outlaws of the Spaceways," "Pirates of the Planet X," "Protects Space Lanes," "Raiders From the Sun," "Ring Around Saturn," "Robots of Rhea," "The Sky Ruby," "Spacetts of the Sky," "Spidermen of Venus," "Trouble on Mercury")			
	2.35	7.00	14.00
Johnny Starboard & the Underseas Pirates('48)	.70	2.00	4.00
Kid Colt in "He Lived by His Guns"('50)	3.00	9.00	18.00
Little Aspirin as "Crook Catcher" #2('50)	.60	1.80	3.60
Little Aspirin in "Naughty But Nice" #6(1950)	.60	1.80	3.60
Return of the Black Phantom (not M.E. character)(Roy Dare)			
	1.00	3.00	6.00
Secrets of Magic	1.00	3.00	6.00
Slim Morgan "Brings Justice to Mesa City" #3	1.30	4.00	8.00
Super Rabbit(1950)-Cuts Red Tape, Stops Crime Wave!			
	1.20	3.50	7.00
Tex Farnum, Frontiersman(1948)	1.50	4.50	9.00
Tex Taylor in "Draw or Die, Cowpoke!"('50)	2.65	8.00	16.00
Tex Taylor in "An Exciting Adventure at the Gold Mine"('50)			
	2.35	7.00	14.00
Wacky Quacky in "All-Aboard"	.50	1.50	3.00
When School Is Out	.50	1.50	3.00
Willie in a "Comic-Comic Book Fall" #1	.50	1.50	3.00
Wonder Duck "An Adventure at the Rodeo of the Fearless Quacker!" (1950)	.50	1.50	3.00
Rare uncut version of three; includes Capt. Marvel, Tex Farnum, Black Phantom Estimated value. . . .			$300.00

WISE GUYS (See Harvey. . .)

WISE LITTLE HEN, THE
1934 (48 pgs.); 1935; 1937 (Story book)
David McKay Publ./Whitman

2nd book app. Donald Duck; Donald app. on cover with Wise Little Hen & Practical Pig; painted cover; same artist as the B&W's from Silly Symphony Cartoon, The Wise Little Hen (1934)(McKay)			
	29.00	87.00	200.00
1935 Edition with dust jacket; 44 pgs. with color, 8¾x9¾" (Whitman)	23.00	70.00	160.00
888(1937)-9½x13", 12 pgs. (Whitman) Donald Duck app.			
	16.00	48.00	110.00

WITCHCRAFT (See Strange Mysteries, Super Reprint #18)
Mar-Apr, 1952 - No. 6, Mar, 1953
Avon Periodicals

1-Kubert-a; 1pg. Check-a	25.00	75.00	175.00

	Good	Fine	N-Mint
2-Kubert & Check-a	15.00	45.00	105.00
3,6: 3-Kinstler, Lawrence-a	11.00	32.00	75.00
4-People cooked alive c/story	11.50	34.00	80.00
5-Kelly Freas-c	16.00	48.00	110.00

NOTE: *Hollingsworth a-4-6; c-4, 6.*

WITCHES TALES (Witches Western Tales #29,30)
Jan, 1951 - No. 28, Dec, 1954 (date misprinted as 4/55)
Witches Tales/Harvey Publications

1-1pg. Powell-a	13.00	40.00	90.00
2-Eye injury panel	5.00	15.00	35.00
3-7,9,10	3.70	11.00	26.00
8-Eye injury panels	4.30	13.00	30.00
11-13,15,16: 12-Acid in face story	3.50	10.50	24.00
14,17-Powell/Nostrand-a. 17-Atomic disaster story			
	5.00	15.00	35.00
18-Nostrand-a; E.C. swipe/Shock S.S.	5.00	15.00	35.00
19-Nostrand-a; E.C. swipe/"Glutton"	5.00	15.00	35.00
20-24-Nostrand-a. 21-E.C. swipe; rape story. 23-Wood E.C. swipes/ Two-Fisted Tales #34	5.00	15.00	35.00
25-Nostrand-a; E.C. swipe/Mad Barber	5.00	15.00	35.00
26-28: 27-r-/#6 with diff.-c. 28-r-/#8 with diff.-c	2.65	8.00	18.00

NOTE: *Check a-24. Kremer a-18; c-25. Nostrand a-17-25; 14, 17(w/Powell). Palais a-1, 2, 4(2), 5(2), 7-9, 12, 14, 15, 17. Powell a-3-7, 10, 11, 19-27. Bondage-c 1, 3, 5, 6, 8, 9.*

WITCHES TALES (Magazine)
V1No.7, July, 1969 - V7No.1, Feb, 1975 (52 pgs.) (B&W)
Eerie Publications

V1#7(7/69) - 9(11/69)	.85	2.60	6.00
V2#1-6('70), V3#1-6('71)	.60	1.80	4.00
V4#1-6('72), V5#1-6('73), V6#1-6('74), V7#1	.60	1.80	4.00

NOTE: *Ajax/Farrell reprints in early issues.*

WITCHES' WESTERN TALES (Formerly Witches Tales) (Western Tales #31 on)
No. 29, Feb, 1955 - No. 30, April, 1955
Harvey Publications

29,30-S&K-r/from Boys' Ranch including-c	8.00	24.00	56.00

WITCHING HOUR, THE
Feb-Mar, 1969 - No. 85, Oct, 1978
National Periodical Publications/DC Comics

1-Toth plus Adams, 3 pgs.	.70	2.00	4.00
2,6	.30	1.00	2.00
3,5-Wrightson-a; Toth-a(p)	.40	1.25	2.50
4,7,9-12: Toth-a in all	.25	.75	1.50
8-Adams-a	.50	1.50	3.00
13-Adams c/a, 2pgs.	.35	1.00	2.00
14-Williamson/Garzon, Jones-a; Adams-c	.35	1.00	2.00
15-20		.50	1.00
21-85: 38-(100 pgs.)		.25	.50

NOTE: *Combined with The Unexpected with No. 189. Adams c-7-11, 13, 14. Alcala a-24, 27, 33, 41, 43. Anderson a-9, 38. Cardy c-4, 5. Kaluta a-12p. Kane a-12p. Morrow a-10, 13, 15, 16. Nino a-31, 40, 45, 47. Redondo a-20, 23, 24, 34, 65. Reese a-23. Toth a-38r. Tuska a-12. Wood a-12i, 15.*

WITH THE MARINES ON THE BATTLEFRONTS OF THE WORLD
1953 (no month) - No. 2, March, 1954 (photo covers)
Toby Press

1-John Wayne story	13.00	40.00	90.00
2-Monty Hall in #1,2	2.30	7.00	16.00

WITH THE U.S. PARATROOPS BEHIND ENEMY LINES (Also see U.S. Paratroops. . . ; #2-5 titled U.S. Paratroops. . .)
1951 - No. 6, Dec, 1952
Avon Periodicals

1-Wood-c & inside-c	8.50	25.50	60.00
2	4.50	14.00	32.00

	Good	Fine	N-Mint
3-6	3.70	11.00	26.00

NOTE: *Kinstler a-2, 5, 6; c-2, 4, 5.*

WITNESS, THE (Also see Amazing Mysteries, Captain America #71, Ideal #4, Marvel Mystery #92 & Mystic #7)
Sept, 1948
Marvel Comics (MjMe)

1(Scarce)-No Everett-c	43.00	130.00	300.00

WITTY COMICS
1945 - No. 7, 1945
Irwin H. Rubin Publ./Chicago Nite Life News No. 2

1-The Pioneer, Junior Patrol	5.00	15.00	35.00
2-The Pioneer, Junior Patrol	3.00	9.00	21.00
3-7-Skyhawk	2.30	7.00	16.00

WIZARD OF FOURTH STREET, THE
Dec, 1987 - No. 2, 1988 ($1.75, B&W, mini-series)
Dark Horse Comics

1,2: Adapts novel by S/F author Simon Hawke	.30	.90	1.80

WIZARD OF OZ (See Classics Illustrated Jr. 535, Dell Jr. Treasury No. 5, First Comics Graphic Novel, 4-Color No. 1308, Marvelous . . . , & Marvel Treasury of Oz)

WOLF GAL (See Al Capp's . . .)

WOLFMAN, THE (See Movie Classics)

WOLFPACK
2/88 ($7.95); 8/88 - No. 12, 7/89 (limited series)
Marvel Comics

1-1st app./origin (Marvel Graphic Novel #31)	1.35	4.00	8.00
1-12		.40	.80

WOLVERINE (See Alpha Flight, Daredevil #196, 249, Havok & . . . , Incredible Hulk #180, Incredible Hulk & . . . , Kitty Pryde And . . . , Marvel Comics Presents, Power Pack, Punisher Vs . . . , Spider-Man vs . . . & X-Men #94)

WOLVERINE
Sept, 1982 - No. 4, Dec, 1982 (mini-series)
Marvel Comics Group

1-Frank Miller-c/a(p)	2.50	7.50	15.00
2,3-Miller-c/a(p)	1.70	5.00	10.00
4-Miller-c/a(p)	2.00	6.00	12.00

WOLVERINE
Nov, 1988 - Present ($1.50, color, Baxter paper)
Marvel Comics

1-Buscema a-1-16, c-1-10; Williamson i-1,4-8	1.00	3.00	6.00
2,3	.50	1.50	3.00
4-8: 6-McFarlane back-c. 7,8-Hulk app.	.35	1.10	2.25
9-22: 11-New costume. 17-Byrne-c/a begins	.25	.75	1.50

WOLVERINE SAGA
Sept, 1989 - No. 4, Dec, 1989 ($3.95, color, mini-series, 52 pgs.)
Marvel Comics

1-4: 1-Austin-c(i); art w/text; gives history	.70	2.00	3.95

WOLVERINE: THE JUNGLE ADVENTURE
1990 ($4.50, color, squarebound)
Marvel Comics

nn-Simonson scripts; Mignola-c/a(p)	.75	2.25	4.50

WOMAN OF THE PROMISE, THE
1950 (General Distr.) (32 pgs.) (paper cover)
Catechetical Guild

nn	2.15	6.50	15.00

WOMEN IN LOVE (A Feature Presentation #5)
* Aug, 1949 - No. 4, Feb, 1950
Fox Features Synd./Hero Books

	Good	Fine	N-Mint
1	11.00	32.00	76.00
2-Kamen/Feldstein-c	8.50	25.50	60.00
3	5.70	17.00	40.00
4-Wood-a	8.00	24.00	56.00

WOMEN IN LOVE
Winter, 1952 (100 pgs.)
Ziff-Davis Publishing Co.

nn-Kinstler-a (Scarce)	21.50	64.00	150.00

WOMEN OUTLAWS (My Love Memories #9 on)
July, 1948 - No. 8, Sept, 1949 (Also see Red Circle)
Fox Features Syndicate

1-Used in SOTI, illo-''Giving children an image of American womanhood''; negligee panels	27.00	81.00	190.00
2-Spanking panel	23.00	70.00	160.00
3-Kamen-a	20.00	60.00	140.00
4-8	14.00	42.00	100.00
nn(nd)-Contains Cody of the Pony Express; same cover as #7	11.00	32.00	75.00

WOMEN TO LOVE
No date (1953)
Realistic

nn-(Scarce)-Reprint/Complete Romance No. 1; c-/Avon paperback			
165	20.00	60.00	140.00

WONDER BOY (Formerly Terrific Comics) (See Bomber Comics)
No. 17, May, 1955 - No. 18, July, 1955 (Also see Blue Bolt)
Ajax/Farrell Publ.

17-Phantom Lady app. Bakerish c/a	11.50	34.00	80.00
18-Phantom Lady app.	11.00	32.00	75.00

NOTE: *Phantom Lady not by Matt Baker.*

WONDER COMICS (Wonderworld #3 on)
May, 1939 - No. 2, June, 1939
Fox Features Syndicate

1-(Scarce)-Wonder Man only app. by Will Eisner; Dr. Fung (by Powell), K-51 begins; Bob Kane-a; Eisner-c	358.00	900.00	2150.00
2-(Scarce)-Yarko the Great, Master Magician by Eisner begins; 'Spark' Stevens by Bob Kane, Patty O'Day, Tex Mason app. Lou Fine's 1st-c; a(2pgs.)	200.00	500.00	1200.00

WONDER COMICS
May, 1944 - No. 20, Oct, 1948
Great/Nedor/Better Publications

1-The Grim Reaper & Spectro, the Mind Reader begin; Hitler/ Hirohito bondage-c	32.00	95.00	225.00
2-Origin The Grim Reaper; Super Sleuths begin, end #8,17	19.00	58.00	135.00
3-5	17.00	51.00	120.00
6-10: 6-Flag-c. 8-Last Spectro. 9-Wonderman begins	14.00	42.00	100.00
11-14-Dick Devens, King of Futuria begins #11, ends #14	17.00	51.00	120.00
15-Tara begins (origin), ends #20	19.00	56.00	130.00
16,18: 16-Spectro app.; last Grim Reaper. 18-The Silver Knight begins	16.50	50.00	115.00
17-Wonderman with Frazetta panels; Jill Trent with all Frazetta inks	18.00	54.00	125.00
19-Frazetta panels	17.00	51.00	120.00
20-Most of Silver Knight by Frazetta	21.50	65.00	150.00

NOTE: *Ingels c-11, 12. Schomburg (Xela) c-1-10; (airbrush)-13-20. Bondage-c 12, 13, 15.*

WONDER DUCK (See Wisco)
Sept, 1949 - No. 3, Mar, 1950
Marvel Comics (CDS)

The Witness #1, © MEG

Wolverine #1 (9/82), © MEG

Wonder Comics #1 (5/39), © FOX

Wonder Woman #3 (2-3/43), © DC

Wonder Woman #4 (5/87), © DC

Wonderworld Comics #3, © FOX

	Good	Fine	N-Mint
WONDER DUCK (continued)			
1	4.00	12.00	28.00
2,3	2.85	8.50	20.00

WONDERFUL ADVENTURES OF PINOCCHIO, THE (See Movie Comics & Walt Disney Showcase #48)
No. 3, April, 1982 (Walt Disney)
Whitman Publishing Co.

3-(Cont. of Movie Comics?); r-/FC #92		.30	.60

WONDERFUL WORLD OF DUCKS (See Golden Picture Story Book)
1975
Colgate Palmolive Co.

1-Mostly-r		.30	.60

WONDERFUL WORLD OF THE BROTHERS GRIMM (See Movie Comics)

WONDERLAND COMICS
Summer, 1945 - No. 9, Feb-Mar, 1947
Feature Publications/Prize

1	3.70	11.00	26.00
2-Howard Post-c/a(2)	2.00	6.00	14.00
3-9: 4-Post-c	1.50	4.50	10.00

WONDER MAN (See The Avengers #9 & 151)
Mar, 1986 ($1.25, color, One-Shot, 52 pgs.)
Marvel Comics Group

1		.65	1.30

WONDERS OF ALADDIN, THE (See 4-Color #1255)

WONDER WOMAN (See Adventure, All-Star Comics, Brave & the Bold, DC Comics Presents, Justice League of America, Legend of . . ., Sensation Comics, Super Friends and World's Finest)

WONDER WOMAN
Summer, 1942 - No. 329, Feb, 1986
National Periodical Publications/All-American Publ./DC Comics

	Good	Fine	N-Mint
1-Origin Wonder Woman retold (see All-Star #8); r-in/Famous 1st			
Edition; H. G. Peter-a begins	307.00	921.00	2150.00
2-Origin & 1st app. Mars; Duke of Deception app.			
	100.00	300.00	700.00
3	74.00	220.00	515.00
4,5: 5-1st Dr. Psycho app.	55.00	165.00	385.00
6-10: 6-1st Cheetah app.	43.00	130.00	300.00
11-20	33.00	100.00	230.00
21-30	24.00	73.00	170.00
31-40	18.00	54.00	125.00
41-44,46-48	14.00	42.00	100.00
45-Origin retold	24.00	73.00	170.00
49-Used in SOTI, pgs. 234,236; Last 52 pg. issue			
	14.00	42.00	100.00
50-(44 pgs.)-Used in POP, pg. 97	13.00	40.00	90.00
51-60	10.00	30.00	70.00
61-72: 62-Origin of W.W. i.d. 64-Story about 3-D movies. 70-1st Angle			
Man app. 72-Last pre-code	8.50	25.50	60.00
73-90: 80-Origin The Invisible Plane	6.50	19.50	45.00
91-94,96-99: 97-Last H. G. Peter-a. 98-Origin W.W. i.d. with new facts			
	4.30	13.00	30.00
95-A-Bomb-c	5.00	15.00	35.00
100	5.50	16.50	38.00
101-104,106-110: 107-1st advs. of Wonder Girl; 1st Merboy; tells how			
Wonder Woman won her costume	3.60	11.00	25.00
105-(Scarce)-Wonder Woman's secret origin; W. Woman appears as			
a girl (not Wonder Girl)	8.00	24.00	55.00
111-120	2.00	6.00	14.00
121-126: 122-1st app. Wonder Tot. 124-1st app. Wonder Woman			
Family. 126-Last 10 cent issue	1.30	4.00	9.00
127-130: 128-Origin The Invisible Plane retold	1.15	3.50	8.00
131-150	.85	2.50	5.00
151-158,160-170	.70	2.00	4.00

	Good	Fine	N-Mint
159-Origin retold	.85	2.50	5.00
171-178	.50	1.50	3.00
179-195: 179-Wears no costume to issue #203. 180-Death of Steve			
Trevor. 195-Wood inks?	.45	1.25	2.50
196 (52 pgs.)-Origin r-/All-Star 8	.50	1.50	3.00
197,198 (52 pgs.)-r	.50	1.50	3.00
199,200-Jones-c; 52 pgs.	.85	2.50	5.00
201-210: 204-Return to old costume; death of I Ching. 202-The			
Grey Mouser debut		.60	1.20
211-240: 211,214-(100 pgs.), 217-(68 pgs.). 220-Adams assist. 223-			
Steve Trevor revived as Steve Howard & learns W.W.'s I.D. 228-			
Both W. Women team up & new World War II stories begin, end			
#243. 237-Origin retold		.50	1.00
241-286: 241-Intro Bouncer. 248-Steve Trevor Howard dies. 250-Intro/			
origin Orana, the new W. Woman. 251-Orana dies. 269-Last			
Wood a(i) for DC? (7/80). 271-Huntress & 3rd Life of Steve Trevor			
begin		.50	1.00
287-New Teen Titans x-over	.25	.75	1.50
288-299: 288-New costume, logo. 291-93-Three part epic with			
Super-Heroines		.50	1.00
300-($1.50, 76 pgs.)-Anniversary issue; Giffen-a; New Teen Titans,			
JLA app.	.25	.75	1.50
301-328: 308-Huntress begins		.50	1.00
329-Double size	.25	.75	1.50
Pizza Hut Giveaways (12/77)-Reprints #60, 62		.40	.80

NOTE: *Colan a-288-305p; c-288-290p. Giffen a-300p. Grell c-217. Kaluta c-297. Gil Kane c-294p, 303-305, 307, 312, 314. Miller c-298p. Morrow c-233. Nasser a-232p; c-231p, 232p. Perez c-283p, 284p. Spiegle a-312. Staton a-241p, 271-287p, 289p, 290p, 294-299p; c-241p, 245p, 246p.*

WONDER WOMAN
Feb, 1987 - Present
DC Comics

	Good	Fine	N-Mint
1-New origin; Perez c/a begins	.50	1.50	3.00
2-5	.25	.75	1.50
6-10: 8-Origin Cheetah		.65	1.30
11-20: 18,26-Free 16 pg. story		.55	1.10
21-40: 24-Last Perez-a; c/scripts continue		.50	1.00
Annual 1 ('88, $1.50)-Art Adams-a(p&i)	.25	.75	1.50
Annual 2 ('89, $2.00, 68 pgs.)-All women artists issue; Perez-c(i)			
	.35	1.00	2.00

WONDER WOMAN SPECTACULAR (See DC Special Series #9)

WONDER WORKER OF PERU
No date (16 pgs.) (B&W) (5x7'')
Catechetical Guild (Giveaway)

nn	1.70	5.00	10.00

WONDERWORLD COMICS (Formerly Wonder Comics)
No. 3, July, 1939 - No. 33, Jan, 1942
Fox Features Syndicate

3-Intro The Flame by Fine; Dr. Fung (Powell-a), K-51 (Powell-a?),			
& Yarko the Great, Master Magician (Eisner-a) continues; Eisner/			
Fine-c	130.00	325.00	780.00
4	55.00	165.00	385.00
5-10	50.00	150.00	350.00
11-Origin The Flame	59.00	175.00	410.00
12-20: 13-Dr. Fung ends	30.00	90.00	210.00
21-Origin The Black Lion & Cub	27.00	81.00	190.00
22-27: 22,25-Dr. Fung app.	21.50	64.00	150.00
28-1st app/origin U.S. Jones; Lu-Nar, the Moon Man begins			
	26.00	77.00	180.00
29,31-33: 32-Hitler-c	16.50	50.00	115.00
30-Origin Flame Girl	30.00	90.00	210.00

NOTE: *Yarko by Eisner-No. 3-11. Eisner text illos-3. Lou Fine c/a-3-11; c-12, 13, 15; text illos-4. Nordling a-4-14. Powell a-3-12. Tuska a-5-9. Bondage-c 14, 15, 28, 31, 32.*

WOODSY OWL (See March of Comics #395)
Nov, 1973 - No. 10, Feb, 1976
Gold Key

	Good	Fine	N-Mint
1	.25	.75	1.50
2-10		.50	1.00

WOODY WOODPECKER (Walter Lantz... #73 on?)(See Dell Giants for annuals) (Also see The Funnies, Jolly Jingles & New Funnies)
No. 169, 10/47 - No. 72, 5-7/62; No. 73, 10/62 - No. 201, 4/84 (nn 192)
Dell Publishing Co./Gold Key No. 73-187/Whitman No. 188 on

	Good	Fine	N-Mint
4-Color 169-Drug turns Woody into a Mr. Hyde	7.00	21.00	50.00
4-Color 188	5.00	15.00	35.00
4-Color 202,232,249,264,288	3.00	9.00	21.00
4-Color 305,336,350	2.00	6.00	14.00
4-Color 364,374,390,405,416,431('52)	1.70	5.00	12.00
16 (12-1/52-53) - 30('55)	1.15	3.50	8.00
31-50	.75	2.25	5.00
51-72 (Last Dell)	.55	1.65	4.00
73-75 (Giants, 84 pgs., Gold Key)	1.75	5.25	14.00
76-80	.50	1.50	3.00
81-100	.35	1.00	2.00
101-120		.60	1.20
121-191,193-201		.40	.80
Christmas Parade 1(11/68-Giant)(G.K.)	1.70	3.50	12.00
Clover Stamp-Newspaper Boy Contest('56)-9 pg. story-(Giveaway)	.85	2.50	6.00
In Chevrolet Wonderland(1954-Giveaway)(Western Publ.)-20 pgs., full story line; Chilly Willy app.	3.00	9.00	21.00
Kite Fun Book (1956, 5x7¼'', 16p, soft-c)	4.00	12.00	28.00
Meets Scotty McTape(1953-Scotch Tape giveaway)-16 pgs., full size	2.30	7.00	16.00
Summer Fun 1(6/66-G.K.)(84 pgs.)	2.25	6.75	18.00

NOTE: 15 cent editions exist. Reprints-No. 92, 102, 103, 105, 106, 124, 125, 152, 153, 157, 162, 165, 194(½)-200(½).

WOODY WOODPECKER (See Comic Album #5,9,13, Dell Giant #24, 40, 54, Dell Giants, The Funnies, Golden Comics Digest #1, 3, 5, 8, 15, 16, 20, 24, 32, 37, 44, March of Comics #16, 34, 85, 93, 109, 124, 139, 158, 177, 184, 203, 222, 239, 249, 261, 420, 454, 466, 478, New Funnies & Super Book #12, 24)

WOOLWORTH'S CHRISTMAS STORY BOOK
1952 - 1954 (16 pgs., paper-c) (See Jolly Christmas Book)
Promotional Publ. Co.(Western Printing Co.)

	Good	Fine	N-Mint
nn	2.00	6.00	14.00

NOTE: 1952 issue-Marv Levy c/a.

WOOLWORTH'S HAPPY TIME CHRISTMAS BOOK
1952 (Christmas giveaway, 36 pgs.)
F. W. Woolworth Co.(Whitman Publ. Co.)

	Good	Fine	N-Mint
nn	2.00	6.00	14.00

WORLD AROUND US, THE (Illustrated Story of...)
Sept, 1958 - No. 36, Oct, 1961 (25 cents)
Gilberton Publishers (Classics Illustrated)

	Good	Fine	N-Mint
1-Dogs	2.30	7.00	16.00
2-Indians-Crandall-a	2.00	6.00	14.00
3-Horses; L. B. Cole-c	2.00	6.00	14.00
4-Railroads	2.00	6.00	14.00
5-Space; Ingels-a	3.50	10.50	24.00
6-The F.B.I.; Disbrow, Evans, Ingels-a	2.65	8.00	18.00
7-Pirates; Disbrow, Ingels-a	3.00	9.00	21.00
8-Flight; Evans, Ingels, Crandall-a	3.00	9.00	21.00
9-Army; Disbrow, Ingels, Orlando-a	2.65	8.00	18.00
10-Navy; Disbrow, Kinstler-a	2.00	6.00	14.00
11-Marine Corps.	2.00	6.00	14.00
12-Coast Guard	2.00	6.00	14.00
13-Air Force; L.B. Cole-c	2.00	6.00	14.00
14-French Revolution; Crandall, Evans-a	3.50	10.50	24.00
15-Prehistoric Animals; Al Williamson-a, 6 & 10 pgs. plus Morrow-a			

	Good	Fine	N-Mint
	3.70	11.00	26.00
16-Crusades	3.00	9.00	21.00
17-Festivals-Evans, Crandall-a	3.00	9.00	21.00
18-Great Scientists; Crandall, Evans, Torres, Williamson, Morrow-a	3.00	9.00	21.00
19-Jungle; Crandall, Williamson, Morrow-a	4.00	12.00	28.00
20-Communications; Crandall, Evans-a	4.00	12.00	28.00
21-American Presidents	3.00	9.00	21.00
22-Boating; Morrow-a	2.00	6.00	14.00
23-Great Explorers; Crandall, Evans-a	2.30	7.00	16.00
24-Ghosts; Morrow, Evans-a	3.00	9.00	21.00
25-Magic; Evans, Morrow-a	3.00	9.00	21.00
26-The Civil War	3.70	11.00	26.00
27-Mountains (High Advs.); Crandall/Evans, Morrow, Torres-a	2.65	8.00	18.00
28-Whaling; Crandall, Evans, Morrow-a; L.B. Cole-c	2.30	7.00	16.00
29-Vikings; Crandall, Evans, Torres, Morrow-a	2.65	8.00	18.00
30-Undersea Adventure; Crandall/Evans, Kirby-a	3.70	11.00	26.00
31-Hunting; Crandall/Evans, Ingels, Kinstler, Kirby-a	3.00	9.00	21.00
32-For Gold & Glory; Morrow, Kirby, Crandall, Evans-a	2.65	8.00	18.00
33-Famous Teens; Torres, Crandall, Evans-a	2.65	8.00	18.00
34-Fishing; Crandall/Evans, Ingels-a	2.30	7.00	16.00
35-Spies; Kirby, Evans, Morrow-a	2.30	7.00	16.00
36-Fight for Life (Medicine); Kirby-a	2.30	7.00	16.00

NOTE: See Classics Illustrated Special Edition. Another World Around Us issue entitled The Sea had been prepared in 1962 but was never published in the U.S. It was published in the British/European World Around Us series. Those series then continued with seven additional WAU titles not in the U.S. series.

WORLD FAMOUS HEROES MAGAZINE
Oct, 1941 - No. 4, Apr, 1942 (a comic book)
Comic Corp. of America (Centaur)

	Good	Fine	N-Mint
1-Gustavson-c; Lubbers, Glanzman-a; Davy Crockett story; Flag-c	40.00	120.00	280.00
2-Lou Gehrig life story; Lubbers-a	20.00	60.00	140.00
3,4-Lubbers-a; 4-Wild Bill Hickok app.	17.00	51.00	120.00

WORLD FAMOUS STORIES
1945
Croyden Publishers

	Good	Fine	N-Mint
1-Ali Baba, Hansel & Gretel, Rip Van Winkle, Mid-Summer Night's Dream	5.70	17.00	40.00

WORLD IS HIS PARISH, THE
1953 (15 cents)
George A. Pflaum

	Good	Fine	N-Mint
The story of Pope Pius XII	3.50	10.50	22.00

WORLD OF ADVENTURE (Walt Disney's...)(TV)
April, 1963 - No. 3, Oct, 1963
Gold Key

	Good	Fine	N-Mint
1-3-Disney TV characters; Savage Sam, Johnny Shiloh, Capt. Nemo, The Mooncussers	.75	2.25	5.00

WORLD OF ARCHIE, THE (See Archie Giant Series Mag. #148, 151, 156, 160, 165, 171, 177, 182, 188, 193, 200, 208, 213, 225, 232, 237, 244, 249, 456, 461, 468, 473, 480, 485, 492, 497, 504, 509, 516, 521, 532, 543, 554, 565, 574, 587, 599)

WORLD OF FANTASY
May, 1956 - No. 19, Aug, 1959
Atlas Comics (CPC No. 1-15/ZPC No. 16-19)

	Good	Fine	N-Mint
1	10.00	30.00	70.00
2-Williamson-a, 4 pgs.	7.00	21.00	50.00
3-Sid Check, Roussos-a	4.30	13.00	30.00
4-7	3.50	10.50	24.00

The World Around Us #18, © GIL

World Famous Stories #1, © Croyden

World Of Fantasy #1, © MEG

World Of Mystery #1, © MEG

Worlds Beyond #1, © FAW

World's Finest Comics #3, © DC

	Good	Fine	N-Mint
WORLD OF FANTASY (continued)			
8-Matt Fox, Orlando, Berg-a	5.00	15.00	35.00
9-Krigstein-a	4.30	13.00	30.00
10,12-15: 12-Everett-c	2.85	8.50	20.00
11-Torres-a	3.70	11.00	26.00
16-Williamson-a, 4 pgs.; Ditko, Kirby-a	5.00	15.00	35.00
17-19-Ditko, Kirby-a	4.50	14.00	32.00

NOTE: *Ayers a-3. Berg a-5, 6, 8. Check a-3. Ditko a-17, 19. Everett c-4-7, 9, 13. Kirby c-15, 17-19. Krigstein a-9. Maneely c-14. Morrow a-7, 8, 14. Orlando a-8, 13, 14. Powell a-4, 6. Sale a-3.*

WORLD OF GIANT COMICS, THE (See Archie All-Star Specials under Archie Comics)

WORLD OF GINGER FOX, THE (Also see Ginger Fox)
Nov, 1986 ($6.95, 68 pgs, mature readers, 8½ x 11'')
Comico

Graphic Novel ($6.95)	1.15	3.50	7.00
Hardcover ($27.95)	4.70	14.00	28.00

WORLD OF JUGHEAD, THE (See Archie Giant Series Mag. #9, 14, 19, 24, 30, 136, 143, 149, 152, 157, 161, 166, 172, 178, 183, 189, 194, 202, 209, 215, 227, 233, 239, 245, 251, 457, 463, 469, 475, 481, 487, 493, 499, 505, 511, 517, 523, 531, 542, 553, 564, 577, 590, 602)

WORLD OF KRYPTON, THE (World of . . .#3; see Superman #248)
7/79 - No. 3, 9/79; 12/87 - No. 4, 3/88 (Both are mini-series)
DC Comics, Inc.

1 ('79)-Jor-El marries Lara		.50	1.00
2,3: 3-Baby Superman sent to Earth; Krypton explodes; Mon-el app.		.50	1.00
1-4 (2nd series)-Byrne scripts; Byrne/Simonson-c		.50	1.00

WORLD OF METROPOLIS, THE
Aug, 1988 - No. 4, July, 1988 (Mini-series)
DC Comics

1-4: Byrne scripts		.50	1.00

WORLD OF MYSTERY
June, 1956 - No. 7, July, 1957
Atlas Comics (GPI)

1-Torres, Orlando-a	8.50	25.50	60.00
2-Woodish-a	2.85	8.50	20.00
3-Torres, Davis, Ditko-a	5.00	15.00	35.00
4-Davis, Pakula, Powell-a; Ditko-c	5.00	15.00	35.00
5,7: 5-Orlando-a	2.85	8.50	20.00
6-Williamson/Mayo-a, 4 pgs.; Ditko-a; Crandall text illo	5.50	16.50	38.00

NOTE: *Colan a-7. Everett c-1-3. Romita a-2. Severin c/a-7.*

WORLD OF SMALLVILLE
Apr, 1988 - No. 4, July, 1988 (75 cents, color, mini-series)
DC Comics

1-4: Byrne scripts		.60	1.20

WORLD OF SUSPENSE
April, 1956 - No. 8, July, 1957
Atlas News Co.

1-Orlando-a	8.50	25.50	60.00
2-Ditko-a	4.50	14.00	32.00
3,7-Williamson-a in both, 4 pgs. each; #7-with Mayo	5.00	15.00	35.00
4-6,8	2.85	8.50	20.00

NOTE: *Berg a-6. Ditko a-2. Everett a-1, 5; c-6. Heck a-5. Orlando a-5. Powell a-6. Reinman a-4. Roussos a-6.*

WORLD OF WHEELS (Formerly Dragstrip Hotrodders)
No. 17, Oct, 1967 - No. 32, June, 1970
Charlton Comics

17-20-Features Ken King	.35	1.00	2.00
21-32-Features Ken King	.25	.75	1.50

	Good	Fine	N-Mint
Modern Comics Reprint 23('78)		.15	.30

WORLD OF WOOD
1986 - No. 4, 1987?; No. 5, Feb, 1989 ($1.75, color, mini-series)
Eclipse Comics

1-4: 1-Dave Stevens-c. 2-Wood/Stevens-c	.30	.90	1.80
5 ($2.00, B&W)-r/Avon's Flying Saucers	.35	1.00	2.00

WORLD'S BEST COMICS (World's Finest #2 on)
Spring, 1941 (Cardboard-c)(DC's 6th annual format comic)
National Periodical Publications (100 pgs.)

1-The Batman, Superman, Crimson Avenger, Johnny Thunder, The King, Young Dr. Davis, Zatara, Lando, Man of Magic, & Red, White & Blue begin (inside-c blank)	415.00	1040.00	2500.00

WORLDS BEYOND (Worlds of Fear #2 on)
Nov, 1951
Fawcett Publications

1-Powell, Bailey-a	12.00	36.00	84.00

WORLD'S FAIR COMICS (See New York. . . .)

WORLD'S FINEST COMICS (Formerly World's Best Comics #1)
No. 2, Sum, 1941 - No. 323, Jan, 1986 (early issues have 100 pgs.)
National Periodical Publ./DC Comics (#1-17 have cardboard covers)

2 (100 pgs.)	196.00	490.00	1175.00
3-The Sandman begins; last Johnny Thunder; origin & 1st app. The Scarecrow	167.00	420.00	1000.00
4-Hop Harrigan app.; last Young Dr. Davis	117.00	295.00	700.00
5-Intro. TNT & Dan the Dyna-Mite; last King & Crimson Avenger	117.00	295.00	700.00
6-Star Spangled Kid begins; Aquaman app.; S&K Sandman with Sandy in new costume begins, ends #7	92.00	230.00	550.00
7-Green Arrow begins; last Lando, King, & Red, White & Blue; S&K art	92.00	230.00	550.00
8-Boy Commandos begin	83.00	210.00	500.00
9-Batman cameo in Star Spangled Kid; S&K-a; last 100pg. issue; Hitler, Mussolini, Tojo-c	75.00	190.00	450.00
10-S&K-a	75.00	190.00	450.00
11-17-Last cardboard cover issue	65.00	165.00	390.00
18-20: 18-Paper covers begin; last Star Spangled Kid	59.00	150.00	355.00
21-30: 30-Johnny Peril app.	43.00	110.00	260.00
31-40: 33-35-Tomahawk app.	37.00	95.00	225.00
41-50: 41-Boy Commandos end. 42-Wyoming Kid begins, ends #63. 43-Full Steam Foley begins, ends #48. 48-Last square binding. 49-Tom Sparks, Boy Inventor begins	29.00	75.00	175.00
51-60: 51-Zatara ends. 59-Manhunters Around the World begins, ends #62	29.00	75.00	175.00
61-64: 63-Capt. Compass app.	25.00	65.00	150.00
65-Origin Superman; Tomahawk begins, ends #101	32.00	80.00	190.00
66-70-(15 cent issues)(Scarce)-Last 68pg. issue	24.00	65.00	165.00
71-(10 cent issue)(Scarce)-Superman & Batman begin as team	30.00	90.00	210.00
72,73-(10 cent issues)(Scarce)	21.50	64.00	150.00
74-80: 74-Last pre-code issue	11.50	34.00	80.00
81-90: 88-1st Joker/Luthor team-up. 90-Batwoman's 1st app. in World's Finest	8.00	24.00	55.00
91-93,95-99: 96-99-Kirby Green Arrow	5.00	15.00	35.00
94-Origin Superman/Batman team retold	22.00	65.00	155.00
100	12.00	36.00	85.00
101-121: 102-Tommy Tomorrow begins, ends. #124. 113-Intro. Miss Arrowette in Green Arrow; 1st Batmite/ Mxyzptlk team-up. 121-Last 10 cent issue	3.60	11.00	25.00
122-128,130-141: 125-Aquaman begins, ends #139. 140-Last Green Arrow	1.70	5.00	12.00

441

WORLD'S FINEST COMICS (continued)	Good	Fine	N-Mint
129-Joker-c/story	2.85	8.50	20.00
142-Origin The Composite Superman(Villain); Legion app.			
	1.70	5.00	12.00
143-150: 143-1st Mailbag	1.15	3.50	8.00
151-155,157-160	1.00	3.00	6.00
156-1st Bizarro Batman; Joker-c/story	2.85	8.50	20.00
161,170 (80-Pg. Giants G-28,G-40)	1.00	3.00	7.00
162-165,167-169,171-174: 168,172-Adult Legion app.			
	.70	2.00	4.00
166-Joker-c/story	1.15	3.50	8.00
175,176-Adams-a; both r-J'onn J'onzz origin/Detective 225,226			
	.85	2.50	5.00
177,178,180-187,189-196,198-204: 182-Silent Knight-r/Brave & Bold #6. 186-Johnny Quick-r. 187-Green Arrow origin-r/Adv. #256. 190-193-Robin-r. 198,199-3rd Superman/Flash race	.35	1.00	2.00
179,188,197 (80-Pg. Giant G-52,G-64,G-76)	.50	1.50	3.00
205-6 pgs. Shining Knight by Frazetta/Adv. #153; 52 pgs.; Teen Titans x-over	.35	1.00	2.00
206 (80-Pg. Giant G-88)	.35	1.00	2.00
207-212 (52 pgs.)	.25	.75	1.50
213-222: 215-Intro. Batman Jr. & Superman Jr. 217-Metamorpho begins, ends #220; Batman/Superman team-ups begin			
	.25	.75	1.50
223,226-Adams-a(r); 100 pgs.; 223-Deadman origin; 226-S&K, Toth-r; Manhunter part origin-r/Detective 225,226	.25	.75	1.50
224,225,227,228-(100 pgs.)	.25	.75	1.50
229-243: 229-r/origin Superman-Batman team	.25	.75	1.50
244-246: 244-Green Arrow, Black Canary, Wonder Woman, Vigilante begin; $1.00 size begins. 246-Death of Stuff in Vigilante; origin Vigilante retold. 248-Last Vigilante	.25	.75	1.50
249-The Creeper begins by Ditko, ends #255	.50	1.50	3.00
250-282-The Creeper origin retold by Ditko. 253-Capt. Marvel begins. 255-Last Creeper. 256-Hawkman begins. 257-Black Lightning begins. 268-Capt. Marvel Jr. origin retold. 271-Origin Superman/Batman team retold. 274-Zatanna begins. 279,280-Capt. Marvel Jr. & Kid Eternity learn they are brothers	.25	.75	1.50
283-297 (36 pgs.) 284-Legion app.	.25	.75	1.50
298,299 (75 cent issues begin)	.25	.75	1.50
300-(52pgs., $1.25)-New Teen Titans app. by Perez			
	.35	1.00	2.00
301-323: 304-Origin Null and Void	.25	.75	1.50
Giveaway (c. 1944-45, 8 pgs., in color, paper-c)-Johnny Everyman-r/ World's Finest	11.50	34.00	80.00

NOTE: **Adams** a-230r; c-174-176, 178-180, 182, 183, 185, 186, 199-205, 208-211, 244-246, 258. **Austin** a-244-246i. **Burnley** a-8, 10; c-7-9, 12. **Colan** a-274p. **Ditko** a-249-255. **Giffen** c-284p. **G. Kane** a-38, 174r; 282, 283; c-281, 282, 289. **Kirby** a-187. **Kubert** Zatara-40-44. **Miller** c-285p. **Morrow** a-245-248. **Nasser** a(p)-244-246, 259, 260. **Robinson** a-253-281p. **Orlando** a-224r. **Perez** a-300i; c-271, 276, 277p, 278p. **Robinson** a-2, 9, 13-15; c-2-4, 6. **Rogers** a-259p. **Roussos** a-212r. **Simonson** c-291. **Spiegle** a-275-78, 284. **Staton** a-262p, 273p. **Toth** a-228r. **Tuska** a-250p, 250p, 252p, 254p, 257p, 283p, 284p, 308p.

(Also see 80 Page Giant #15)

WORLD'S FINEST COMICS DIGEST (See DC Special Series #23)

WORLD'S GREATEST ATHLETE (See Walt Disney Showcase #14)

WORLD'S GREATEST SONGS
Sept, 1954
Atlas Comics (Male)

1-(Scarce) Heath & Harry Anderson-a; Eddie Fisher life story			
	14.00	42.00	100.00

WORLD'S GREATEST STORIES
Jan, 1949 - No. 2, May, 1949
Jubilee Publications

1-Alice in Wonderland	10.00	30.00	70.00
2-Pinocchio	8.50	25.50	60.00

WORLD'S GREATEST SUPER HEROES			
1977 (3¾x3¾'') (24 pgs. in color) (Giveaway)	Good	Fine	N-Mint
DC Comics (Nutra Comics) (Child Vitamins, Inc.)			
Batman & Robin app.; health tips	.25	.75	1.50

WORLDS OF FEAR (Formerly Worlds Beyond #1)
V1No.2, Jan, 1952 - V2No.10, June, 1953
Fawcett Publications

V1#2	10.00	30.00	70.00
3-Evans-a	8.00	24.00	56.00
4-6(9/52)	7.00	21.00	50.00
V2#7-9	5.70	17.00	40.00
10-Saunders Painted-c; man with no eyes surrounded by eyeballs-c			
	12.00	36.00	85.00

NOTE: **Powell** a-2, 4, 5. **Sekowsky** a-4.

WORLDS UNKNOWN
May, 1973 - No. 8, Aug, 1974
Marvel Comics Group

1-R-/from Astonishing #54; Torres, Reese-a	.30	.60
2-8	.20	.40

NOTE: **Adkins/Mooney** a-5. **Buscema** a/c-4p. **W. Howard** c/a-3i. **Kane** a(p)-1,2; c(p)-5, 6, 8. **Sutton** a-2. **Tuska** a(p)-7, 8; c-7p. No. 7, 8 has Golden Voyage of Sinbad movie adaptation.

WORLD WAR STORIES
Apr-June, 1965 - No. 3, Dec, 1965
Dell Publishing Co.

1	1.30	4.00	9.00
2,3: 1-3-Glanzman-a	.70	2.00	5.00

WORLD WAR II (See Classics Illustrated Special Issue)

WORLD WAR III
Mar, 1953 - No. 2, May, 1953
Ace Periodicals

1-(Scarce)-Atomic bomb-c	30.00	90.00	210.00
2-Used in POP, pg. 78 and B&W & color illos.			
	24.00	73.00	170.00

WORST FROM MAD, THE (Annual)
1958 - No. 12, 1969 (Each annual cover is reprinted from the cover of the Mad issues being reprinted)
E. C. Comics

nn(1958)-Bonus; record labels & travel stickers; 1st Mad annual; r-/Mad #29-34	12.00	36.00	84.00
2(1959)-Bonus is small 33⅓ rpm record entitled ''Meet the Staff of Mad;'' r-/Mad #35-40	16.50	50.00	115.00
3(1960)-20''x30''campaign poster ''Alfred E. Neuman for President;'' r-/Mad #41-46	9.00	27.00	62.00
4(1961)-Sunday comics section; r-/Mad #47-54			
	9.00	27.00	62.00
5(1962)-Has 33⅓ record; r-/Mad #55-62	13.00	40.00	90.00
6(1963)-Has 33⅓ record; r-/Mad #63-70	14.00	42.00	100.00
7(1964)-Mad protest signs; r-/Mad #71-76	5.70	17.00	40.00
8(1965)-Build a Mad Zeppelin	6.50	19.50	45.00
9(1966)-33⅓ rpm record	10.00	30.00	70.00
10(1967)-Mad bumper sticker	3.50	10.50	24.00
11(1968)-Mad cover window stickers	3.50	10.50	24.00
12(1969)-Mad picture postcards; Orlando-a	3.50	10.50	24.00

NOTE: Covers: **Bob Clarke**-#8. **Mingo**-#7, 9-12.

WOTALIFE COMICS
No. 3, Aug-Sept, 1946 - No. 12, July, 1947; 1959
Fox Features Syndicate/Norlen Mag.

3-Cosmo Cat	3.50	10.50	24.00
4-12-Cosmo Cat	2.00	6.00	14.00
1('59-Norlen)-Atomic Rabbit, Atomic Mouse	1.50	4.50	10.00

World's Finest Comics #201, © DC

World's Greatest Stories #1, © Jubilee

World War III #2, © ACE

Wow Comics #21, © FAW

Wyatt Earp #4 (Dell), © Wyatt Earp Ent.

X-Factor Annual #1, © MEG

WOTALIFE COMICS
1957 - No. 5, 1957
Green Publications

	Good	Fine	N-Mint
1	1.50	4.50	10.00
2-5	1.00	3.00	7.00

WOW COMICS
July, 1936 - No. 4, Nov, 1936 (52 pgs., magazine size)
Henle Publishing Co.

	Good	Fine	N-Mint
1-Fu Manchu; Eisner-a	167.00	420.00	1000.00
2-Ken Maynard, Fu Manchu, Popeye by Segar; Eisner-a	115.00	285.00	685.00
3-Eisner-c/a(3); Popeye by Segar, Fu Manchu, Hiram Hick by Bob Kane, Space Limited app.	115.00	285.00	685.00
4-Flash Gordon by Raymond, Mandrake, Popeye by Segar, Tillie The Toiler, Fu Manchu, Hiram Hick by Bob Kane; Eisner-a(3), Briefer-c	145.00	365.00	875.00

WOW COMICS (Real Western Hero #70 on)(See XMas Comics)
Winter, 1940-41; No. 2, Summer, 1941 - No. 69, Fall, 1948
Fawcett Publications

	Good	Fine	N-Mint
nn(#1)-Origin Mr. Scarlet by S&K; Atom Blake, Boy Wizard, Jim Dolan, & Rick O'Shay begin; Diamond Jack, The White Rajah, & Shipwreck Roberts, only app.; the cover was printed on unstable paper stock and is rarely found in fine or mint condition; blank inside-c; bondage-c by Beck (Rare)	625.00	1875.00	5000.00
(Prices vary widely on this book)			
2 (Scarce)-The Hunchback begins	64.00	193.00	450.00
3 (Fall, 1941)	40.00	120.00	280.00
4-Origin Pinky	46.00	137.00	320.00
5	33.00	100.00	230.00
6-Origin The Phantom Eagle; Commando Yank begins	27.00	81.00	190.00
7,8,10	25.00	75.00	175.00
9 (1/6/43)-Capt. Marvel, Capt. Marvel Jr., Shazam app.; Scarlet & Pinky x-over; Mary Marvel c/stories begins (cameo #9)	36.00	107.00	250.00
11-17,19,20: 15-Flag-c	16.00	48.00	110.00
18-1st app. Uncle Marvel (10/43); infinity-c	17.00	51.00	120.00
21-30: 28-Pinky x-over in Mary Marvel	9.30	28.00	65.00
31-40	6.50	19.50	45.00
41-50	5.00	15.00	35.00
51-58: Last Mary Marvel	4.00	12.00	28.00
59-69: 59-Ozzie begins. 62-Flying Saucer gag-c (1/48). 65-69-Tom Mix stories	3.50	10.50	24.00

WRATH OF THE SPECTRE, THE
May, 1988 - No. 4, Aug, 1988 ($2.50, color, mini-series)
DC Comics

	Good	Fine	N-Mint
1-4	.40	1.25	2.50

WRECK OF GROSVENOR (See Superior Stories #3)

WRINGLE WRANGLE (See 4-Color #821)

WULF THE BARBARIAN
Feb, 1975 - No. 4, Sept, 1975
Atlas/Seaboard Publ.

	Good	Fine	N-Mint
1-Origin	.40		.80
2-Intro. Berithe the Swordswoman; Adams, Wood, Reese-a	.30		.60
3,4	.25		.50

WYATT EARP (Hugh O'Brian Famous Marshal)
No. 860, 11/57 - No. 13, 12-2/1960-61 (Photo-c)
Dell Publishing Co.

	Good	Fine	N-Mint
4-Color 860 (#1)-Manning-a	7.00	21.00	50.00
4-Color 890,921(6/58)-All Manning-a	4.00	12.00	28.00
4 (9-11/58) - 12-Manning-a	3.50	10.50	24.00

	Good	Fine	N-Mint
13-Toth-a	4.30	13.00	30.00

WYATT EARP
11/55 - No. 29, 6/60; No. 30, 10/72 - No. 34, 6/73
Atlas Comics/Marvel No. 23 on (IPC)

	Good	Fine	N-Mint
1	7.00	21.00	50.00
2-Williamson-a, 4 pgs.	5.00	15.00	35.00
3-6,8-11: 3-Black Bart app. 8-Wild Bill Hickok app.	2.85	8.50	20.00
7,12-Williamson-a, 4pgs. ea.; #12 with Mayo	4.00	12.00	28.00
13-19: 17-1st app. Wyatt's deputy, Grizzly Grant	2.30	7.00	16.00
20-Torres-a	2.65	8.00	18.00
21-Davis-c	2.30	7.00	16.00
22-24,26-29: 22-Ringo Kid app. 23-Kid From Texas app. 29-Last 10 cent issue	1.50	4.50	10.00
25-Davis-a	1.70	5.00	12.00
30-Williamson-r ('72)		.40	.80
31,33,34-Reprints		.25	.50
32-Torres-a(r)		.30	.60

NOTE: *Ayers* a-8, 17. *Everett* c-6. *Kirby* c-25, 29. *Maneely* a-1; c-1, 3, 4, 8, 12, 17, 20. *Maurer* a-3(4), 4(4), 8(4). *Severin* a-4, 10; c-10, 14. *Wildey* a-5, 17, 24, 28.

WYATT EARP FRONTIER MARSHAL (Formerly Range Busters)
No. 12, Jan, 1956 - No. 72, Dec, 1967 (Also see Blue Bird)
Charlton Comics

	Good	Fine	N-Mint
12	2.30	7.00	16.00
13-19	1.15	3.50	8.00
20-Williamson-a(4), 8,5,5,& 7 pgs.; 68 pgs.	5.50	16.50	38.00
21-30	.70	2.00	5.00
31-50: 31-Crandall-r	.50	1.50	3.00
51-72	.25	.75	1.50

XANADU COLOR SPECIAL
Dec, 1988 ($2.00, color, one-shot)
Eclipse Comics

	Good	Fine	N-Mint
1-R/Xanadu from Thoughts & Images	.35	1.00	2.00

XENON
Dec, 1987 - No. 23, Nov 1, 1988 ($1.50, Bi-weekly, B&W)
Eclipse Comics

	Good	Fine	N-Mint
1-23	.25	.75	1.50

XENOZOIC TALES
Feb, 1987 - No. 7, 1988 ($2.00, B&W)
Kitchen Sink Press

	Good	Fine	N-Mint
1	.50	1.50	3.00
2	.40	1.25	2.50
3-7	.35	1.00	2.00

X-FACTOR (Also see The Avengers #263 & Fantastic Four #286)
Feb, 1986 - Present
Marvel Comics Group

	Good	Fine	N-Mint
1-Double size; Layton/Guice-a	1.35	4.00	8.00
2,3	.85	2.50	5.00
4,5	.75	2.25	4.50
6-10	.50	1.50	3.00
11-20	.40	1.25	2.50
21-23	.30	.90	1.80
24-26: Fall Of The Mutants. 26-New outfits	.40	1.25	2.50
27-30	.25	.70	1.40
31-37,39-49,51-54: 35-Origin Cyclops. 44-P. Smith-a begins		.50	1.00
38,50-Double size ($1.50)	.25	.75	1.50
Annual 1 (10/86), 2 (10/87)	.40	1.25	2.50
Annual 3 ('88, $1.75)-Evolutionary War app.	.50	1.50	3.00
Annual 4 ('89, $2.00, 68 pgs.)-Atlantis Attacks; Byrne/Simonson-a, Byrne-c	.35	1.00	2.00

X-FACTOR (continued)
NOTE: *Art Adams* a-41p, 42p. *Paul Smith* a-44-48; c-43. *Simsonson* c/a-38 & others.

XMAS COMICS
12?/1941 - No. 2, 12?/1942 (324 pgs.) (50 cents)
No. 3, 12?/1943 - No. 7, 12?/1947 (132 pgs.)
Fawcett Publications

	Good	Fine	N-Mint
1-Contains Whiz #21, Capt. Marvel #3, Bulletman #2, Wow #3, & Master #18; Raboy back-c. Not rebound, remaindered comics printed at same time as originals	130.00	390.00	900.00
2-Capt. Marvel, Bulletman, Spy Smasher	65.00	195.00	455.00
3-7-Funny animals	17.00	51.00	120.00

XMAS COMICS
No. 4, Dec, 1949 - No. 7, Dec, 1952 (196 pgs.)
Fawcett Publications

4-Contains Whiz, Master, Tom Mix, Captain Marvel, Nyoka, Capt. Video, Bob Colt, Monte Hale, Hot Rod Comics, & Battle Stories. Not rebound, remaindered comics—printed at the same time as originals	26.00	78.00	180.00
5-7-Same as above	23.00	70.00	160.00

XMAS FUNNIES
No date (paper cover) (36 pgs.?)
Kinney Shoes (Giveaway)

Contains 1933 color strip-r; Mutt & Jeff, etc.	10.00	30.00	70.00

X-MEN, THE (See Amazing Adventures, Capt. America #172, Classic X-Men, Heroes For Hope . . ., Kitty Pryde & . . ., Marvel & DC Present, Marvel Fanfare, Marvel Graphic Novel, Marvel Masterworks, Marvel Team-up, Marvel Triple Action, Nightcrawler, Official Marvel Index To . . ., Special Edition . . ., The Uncanny . . ., X-Factor & X-Terminators)

X-MEN, THE (The Uncanny . . . #142 on)
Sept, 1963 - Present
Marvel Comics Group

	Good	Fine	N-Mint
1-Origin/1st app. X-Men; 1st app. Magneto	110.00	415.00	990.00
2-1st app. The Vanisher	54.00	162.00	380.00
3-1st app. The Blob	28.00	84.00	200.00
4-1st Quick Silver & Scarlet Witch & Brotherhood of the Evil Mutants	23.00	70.00	160.00
5	19.00	57.00	130.00
6-10: 8-1st Unus the Untouchable. 9-Avengers app. 10-1st Silver-Age app. Ka-Zar	14.00	42.00	100.00
11,13-15: 11-1st app. The Stranger. 14-1st app. Sentinels. 15-Origin Beast	9.30	28.00	65.00
12-Origin Prof. X	11.00	32.00	75.00
16-20: 19-1st app. The Mimic	6.50	19.50	45.00
21-27,29,30	5.00	15.00	35.00
28-1st app. The Banshee	5.70	17.00	40.00
31-37	3.60	11.00	25.00
38-Origin The X-Men feat. begins, ends #57	4.30	13.00	30.00
39,40- 39-New costumes	3.60	11.00	25.00
41-49: 42-Death of Prof. X (Changeling disguised as). 44-Red Raven app. (G.A.) 49-Steranko-c; 1st Polaris	2.85	8.50	20.00
50,51-Steranko c/a	3.60	11.00	25.00
52	2.30	7.00	16.00
53-Smith c/a; 1st Smith comic book work	3.60	11.00	25.00
54,55-Smith-c	2.85	8.50	20.00
56-63,65-Adams-a(p). 56-Intro Havoc without costume. 65-Return of Professor X. 58-1st app. Havoil	4.00	12.00	28.00
64-1st Sunfire app.	2.85	8.50	20.00
66	1.70	5.00	12.00
67-80: 67-All-r. 67-70,72-(52 pgs.)	1.70	5.00	12.00
81-93-r-/#39-45 with-c	1.70	5.00	12.00
94(8/75)-New X-Men begin; Colossus, Nightcrawler, Thunderbird, Storm, Wolverine, & Banshee join; Angel, Marvel Girl, & Iceman resign	18.00	54.00	125.00
95-Death Thunderbird	5.70	17.00	40.00
96-99	4.00	12.00	28.00

	Good	Fine	N-Mint
98,99 (30 cent cover)	4.50	14.00	32.00
100-Old vs. New X-Men; part origin Phoenix	4.30	13.00	30.00
101-Phoenix origin concludes	4.00	12.00	28.00
102-107: 102-Origin Storm. 104-Intro. Star Jammers. 106-Old vs. New X-Men	1.85	5.50	13.00
108-Byrne-a begins (See Marvel Team-Up 53)	4.35	13.00	30.00
109-1st Vindicator	3.70	11.00	25.00
110,111: 110-Phoenix joins	2.15	6.50	15.00
112-119: 117-Origin Professor X	1.70	5.00	12.00
120-1st app. Alpha Flight (cameo), story line begins	4.00	12.00	28.00
121-1st Alpha Flight (full story)	4.35	13.00	30.00
122-128: 124-Colossus becomes Proletarian	1.85	5.50	11.00
129-Intro Kitty Pryde	2.15	6.50	13.00
130-1st app. The Dazzler by Byrne	2.35	7.00	14.00
131-135: 131-Dazzler app. 133-Wolverine app. 134-Phoenix becomes Dark Phoenix	1.70	5.00	10.00
136,138: 138-Dazzler app.	1.45	4.25	8.50
137-Giant; death of Phoenix	1.85	5.50	11.00
139-Alpha Flight app.; Kitty Pryde joins	2.15	6.50	13.00
140-Alpha Flight app.	3.00	9.00	18.00
141-Intro Future X-Men & The New Brotherhood of Evil Mutants; death of Frank Richards	1.75	5.25	10.50
142,143: 142-Deaths of Wolverine, Storm & Colossus. 143-Last Byrne issue	1.05	3.15	6.30
144-150: 145-Old X-Men app. 148-Spider-Woman, Dazzler app. 150-Double size	.90	2.65	5.30
151-157,159-161,163,164: 161-Origin Magneto. 163-Origin Binary. 164-1st app. Binary as Carol Danvers	.60	1.85	3.70
158-1st app. Rogue in X-Men (See Avengers Annual #10)	.70	2.10	4.20
162-Wolverine solo story	.75	2.25	4.50
165-Paul Smith-a begins	.90	2.65	5.30
166-Double size; Paul Smith-a	.70	2.10	4.20
167-170: 167-New Mutants x-over. 168-1st app. Madeline Pryor in X-Men (See Avengers Annual #10)	.55	1.60	3.20
171-Rogue joins X-Men	1.00	3.00	6.00
172-174: 174-Phoenix cameo	.55	1.60	3.20
175-Double size; anniversary issue; Phoenix returns? Last P. Smith-c/a	.70	2.00	4.00
176-185: 181-Sunfire app.	.45	1.30	2.60
186-Double-size; Barry Smith/Austin-a	.60	1.75	3.50
187-192,194-199	.40	1.25	2.50
193-Double size; 100th app. New X-Men	.70	2.00	4.00
200-Double size	.85	2.50	5.00
201-209	.50	1.50	3.00
210-213-Mutant Massacre	1.30	4.00	8.00
214-224	.35	1.00	2.00
225-227: Fall Of The Mutants. 226-Double size	1.00	3.00	6.00
228-241: 229-$1.00 begin	.30	.90	1.75
242-Double size, X-Factor app., Inferno tie-in	.35	1.00	2.00
243-252,254-260		.50	1.00
253-All new X-men begin	.25	.75	1.50
Annual 3(2/80)	1.25	3.75	7.50
Annual 4(11/80)	1.00	3.00	6.00
Annual 5(10/81)	.70	2.10	4.25
Annual 6(11/82)	.50	1.50	3.00
Annual 7(1/84), 8(12/84)	.40	1.25	2.50
Annual 9(1985)-New Mutants; Art Adams-a	1.50	4.50	9.00
Annual 10(1/87)-Art Adams-a	1.50	4.50	9.00
Annual 11(11/87)	.35	1.00	2.00
Annual 12('88, $1.75)-Evolutionary War app.	.50	1.50	3.00
Annual 13('89, $2.00, 68 pgs.)-Atlantis Attacks	.35	1.00	2.00
Giant-Size 1(Summer,'75, 50 cents)-1st app. new X-Men; Intro Nightcrawler, Storm, Colossus & Thunderbird; Wolverine app.	13.50	34.00	95.00

The X-Men #5, © MEG

The X-Men #100, © MEG

The X-Men Special #1, © MEG

X-Venture #1, © Victory Mag.

Yankee Comics #1, © CHES

Yellow Claw #3, © MEG

	Good	Fine	N-Mint
X-MEN (continued)			
Giant-Size 2(11/75)-51 pgs. Adams-a(r)	2.85	9.00	20.00
Special 1(12/70)-Kirby-c/a; origin The Stranger	2.85	9.00	20.00
Special 2(11/71)	2.85	9.00	20.00

NOTE: **Art Adams** a-56-63p, 65p, Annual 9, 10p, 12p. **Neal Adams** c-56-63. **Adkins** c-34. **Austin** a-108i, 109i, 111-17i, 119-43i, 196i, 204i, 228i, Annual 3i, 7i, 9i, 13; c-109-111i, 114-22i, 123, 124-41i, 142, 143, 228i, Annual 3i. **Buscema** c-42, 43p, 45p. **Byrne** a-108p, 109p, 111-43p; c-113-16p, 127p, 129p, 131-41p. **Ditko** a-90r. **Everett** c-73. **Golden** a-Annual 7p. **G. Kane** c(p)-33, 74-76, 79, 80, 94, 95. **Kirby** a(p)-1-17 (#12-17, 24, 27-29, 32, 67-layouts); c(p)-1-22, 25, 26, 30, 31, 35. **Layton** a-105i; c-112i, 113i. **Miller** c-Annual 3. **Perez** c/a-Annual 3p; c-112p, 128p, Annual 3p. **Roussos** a-84i. **Simonson** a-171p; c-171. **B. Smith** a-198, 205, 214; c-186, 198. **Paul Smith** a-165-70p, 172-75p; c-165-70, 172-75. **Sparling** a-78p. **Steranko** a-50p, 51p; c-49-51. **Sutton** a-106i. **Toth** a-12p, 67p(r). **Tuska** a-40-42i, 44-46p, 88i(r); c-39-41, 77p, 78p. **Williamson** a-202i, 203i, 211i; c-202i, 203i, 206i. **Wood** c-14i. 25 cent & 30 cent issues of #98 & 99 exist.

X-MEN/ALPHA FLIGHT
Jan, 1986 - No. 2, Jan, 1986 ($1.50, mini-series)
Marvel Comics Group

1,2: 1-Intro The Berserkers; Paul Smith-a	.60	1.75	3.50

X-MEN AND THE MICRONAUTS, THE
Jan, 1984 - No. 4, April, 1984 (mini-series)
Marvel Comics Group

1-4: Guice-c/a(p) in all	.25	.75	1.50

X-MEN CLASSICS
Dec, 1983 - No. 3, Feb, 1984 ($2.00; Baxter paper)
Marvel Comics Group

1-3: Adams-r/X-Men	.50	1.50	3.00

X-MEN VS. THE AVENGERS
Apr, 1987 - No. 4, July, 1987 ($1.50, mini-series, Baxter paper)
Marvel Comics Group

1	.60	1.75	3.50
2-4	.40	1.25	2.50

X-TERMINATORS
Oct, 1988 - No. 4, Jan, 1989 ($1.00, color, mini-series)
Marvel Comics

1-X-Men/X-Factor tie-in; Williamson-i	.50	1.50	3.00
2	.30	.90	1.75
3,4		.60	1.25

X, THE MAN WITH THE X-RAY EYES (See Movie Comics)

X-VENTURE
July, 1947 - No. 2, Nov, 1947 (Super heroes)
Victory Magazines Corp.

1-Atom Wizard, Mystery Shadow, Lester Trumble begin			
	26.00	77.00	180.00
2	17.00	51.00	120.00

XYR (See Eclipse Graphic Album series #21)

YAK YAK (See 4-Color #1186,1348)

YAKKY DOODLE & CHOPPER (TV) (Also see Spotlight #3)
Dec, 1962 (Hanna-Barbera)
Gold Key

1	2.35	7.00	16.00

YALTA TO KOREA (Also see Korea My Home)
1952 (8 pgs.) (Giveaway) (paper cover)
M. Phillip Corp. (Republican National Committee)

Anti-communist propaganda book	15.00	45.00	90.00

YANG (See House of Yang)
11/73 - No. 13, 5/76; V14/23, 9/85 - No. 17, 1/86
Charlton Comics

1-Origin		.50	1.00
2-5		.30	.60
6-13(1976)		.20	.40

	Good	Fine	N-Mint
14-17(1986)		.40	.80
3,10,11(Modern Comics-r, 1977)		.15	.30

YANKEE COMICS
Sept, 1941 - No. 4, Mar, 1942
Harry 'A' Chesler

1-Origin The Echo, The Enchanted Dagger, Yankee Doodle Jones, The Firebrand, & The Scarlet Sentry; Black Satan app.

	42.00	125.00	290.00

2-Origin Johnny Rebel; Major Victory app.; Barry Kuda begins

	25.00	75.00	175.00
3,4	21.00	62.00	145.00

4 (nd, '40s; 7¼x5'', 68pgs. distr. to the service)-Foxy Grandpa, Tom, Dick & Harry, Impy, Ace & Deuce, Dot & Dash, Ima Slooth by Jack Cole (Remington Morse publ.)

	1.70	5.00	12.00

YANKS IN BATTLE
Sept, 1956 - No. 4, Dec, 1956
Quality Comics Group

1	2.65	8.00	18.00
2-4	1.30	4.00	9.00

YANKS IN BATTLE
1963
I. W. Enterprises

Reprint #3	.25	.75	1.50

YARDBIRDS, THE (G. I. Joe's Sidekicks)
Summer, 1952
Ziff-Davis Publishing Co.

1-By Bob Oskner	3.70	11.00	26.00

YARNS OF YELLOWSTONE
1972 (36 pages) (50 cents)
World Color Press

Illustrated by Bill Chapman	.50	1.50	3.00

YELLOW CLAW
Oct, 1956 - No. 4, April, 1957
Atlas Comics (MjMC)

1-Origin by Joe Maneely	29.00	86.00	200.00
2-Kirby-a	23.00	70.00	160.00
3,4-Kirby-a; 4-Kirby/Severin-a	20.00	60.00	140.00

NOTE: **Everett** c-3. **Maneely** c-1. **Reinman** a-2i, 3. **Severin** c-2, 4.

YELLOWJACKET COMICS (Jack in the Box #11 on)(See TNT Comics)
Sept, 1944 - No. 10, June, 1946
E. Levy/Frank Comunale

1-Origin Yellowjacket; Diana, the Huntress begins

	17.00	51.00	120.00
2	10.00	30.00	70.00
3,5	8.50	25.50	60.00

4-Poe's 'Fall Of The House Of Usher' adaptation; Palais-a

	10.00	30.00	70.00

6-10: 7,8-Has stories narrated by old witch in 'Tales of Terror'

	8.00	24.00	56.00

YELLOWSTONE KELLY (See 4-Color #1056)

YELLOW SUBMARINE (See Movie Comics)

YIN FEI THE CHINESE NINJA
1988 - Present ($1.80, color, 52 pgs.)
Leung's Publications

1-6	.30	.90	1.80

YOGI BEAR (TV) (Hanna-Barbera)
No. 1067, 12-2/59-60 - No. 9, 7-9/62; No. 10, 10/62 - No. 42, 10/70
Dell Publishing Co./Gold Key No. 10 on

4-Color 1067 (#1)	4.00	12.00	28.00

YOGI BEAR (continued)	Good	Fine	N-Mint
4-Color 1104,1162 (5-7/61)	3.00	9.00	21.00
4(8-9/61) - 6(12-1/61-62)	2.30	7.00	16.00
4-Color 1271(11/61), 1349(1/62)	2.30	7.00	16.00
7(2-3/62) - 9(7-9/62)-Last Dell	2.00	6.00	14.00
10(10/62-G.K.), 11(1/63)-titled ''Yogi Bear Jellystone Jollies''-80 pgs.;			
11-Xmas-c	2.50	7.50	20.00
12(4/63), 14-20	1.70	5.00	12.00
13(7/63)-Surprise Party, 68 pgs.	2.50	7.50	20.00
21-30	1.00	3.00	7.00
31-42	.60	1.80	4.00
. . . Kite Fun Book('62, 16 pgs., soft-c)	1.50	3.50	8.00

YOGI BEAR (See Dell Giant #41, March of Comics #253, 265, 279, 291, 309, 319, 337, 344, Movie Comics under "Hey There It's. . ." & Whitman Comic Books)

YOGI BEAR (TV)
Nov, 1970 - No. 35, Jan, 1976 (Hanna-Barbera)
Charlton Comics

1	.70	2.00	5.00
2-6,8-35: 28-31-partial-r	.50	1.50	3.00
7-Summer Fun (Giant); 52 pgs.	.50	1.50	3.00

YOGI BEAR (TV)(See The Flintstones, 3rd series & Spotlight #1)
Nov, 1977 - No. 9, Mar, 1979 (Hanna-Barbera)
Marvel Comics Group

1-Flintstones begin		.40	.80
2-9		.20	.40

YOGI BEAR'S EASTER PARADE (See The Funtastic World of Hanna- Barbera #2)

YOGI BERRA (Baseball hero)
1951 (Yankee catcher)
Fawcett Publications

nn-Photo-c	30.00	90.00	210.00

YOSEMITE SAM (. . .& Bugs Bunny)
Dec, 1970 - No. 81, Feb, 1984
Gold Key/Whitman

1	.70	2.00	4.00
2-10	.40	1.25	2.50
11-30		.60	1.20
31-81: 81-r(⅓)		.30	.60

(See March of Comics #363,380,392)

YOUNG ALLIES COMICS (All-Winners #21; see Kid Komics #2)
Summer, 1941 - No. 20, Oct, 1946
Timely Comics (USA 1-7/NPI 8,9/YAI 10-20)

1-Origin/1st app. The Young Allies; 1st meeting of Capt. America & Human Torch; Red Skull app.; S&K c/splash; Hitler-c			
	250.00	625.00	1500.00
2-Captain America & Human Torch app.; Simon & Kirby-c			
	117.00	290.00	700.00
3-Fathertime, Captain America & Human Torch app.			
	92.00	230.00	550.00
4-The Vagabond & Red Skull, Capt. America, Human Torch app.			
	88.00	220.00	525.00
5-Captain America & Human Torch app.	53.00	130.00	315.00
6-10: 9-Hitler, Tojo, Mussolini-c. 10-Origin Tommy Tyme & Clock of Ages; ends #19	41.00	105.00	245.00
11-20: 12-Classic decapitation story; Schomburg-c			
	32.00	80.00	190.00

NOTE: *Schomburg c-5-13, 15, 17-19.*

YOUNG ALL-STARS
June, 1987 - No. 31, Nov, 1989 ($1.00, deluxe format, color)
DC Comics

1-1st app. Iron Munro & The Flying Fox	.70	2.00	4.00
2,3	.35	1.00	2.00

	Good	Fine	N-Mint
4-31: 7-18-$1.25. 8,9-Millennium tie-ins. 19-23-$1.50. 24-Begin $1.75-c			
	.30	.90	1.75
Annual 1 ('88, $2.00)	.35	1.00	2.00

YOUNG BRIDES
Sept-Oct, 1952 - No. 29, Jul-Aug, 1956 (Photo-c: 1-3)
Feature/Prize Publications

V1#1-Simon & Kirby-a	7.00	21.00	50.00
2-S&K-a	3.50	10.50	24.00
3-6-S&K-a	2.85	8.50	20.00
V2#1,3-7,10-12 (#7-18)-S&K-a	2.30	7.00	16.00
2,8,9-No S&K-a	1.15	3.50	8.00
V3#1-3(#19-21)-Last precode (3-4/55)	1.00	3.00	7.00
4,6(#22,24), V4#1,3(#25,27)	.85	2.60	6.00
V3#5(#23)-Meskin-c	1.30	4.00	9.00
V4#2(#26-All S&K issue	2.30	7.00	16.00
V4#4(#28)-S&K-a, V4#5(#29)	1.30	4.00	9.00

YOUNG DR. MASTERS (See The Adventures of Young Dr. Masters)

YOUNG DOCTORS, THE
January, 1963 - No. 6, Nov, 1963
Charlton Comics

V1#1	.50	1.50	3.00
2-6	.25	.75	1.50

YOUNG EAGLE
12/50 - No. 10, 6/52; No. 3, 7/56 - No. 5, 4/57 (Photo-c: 1-10)
Fawcett Publications/Charlton

1	8.00	24.00	56.00
2	4.30	13.00	30.00
3-9	3.50	10.50	24.00
10-Origin Thunder, Young Eagle's Horse	2.65	8.00	18.00
3-5(Charlton)-Formerly Sherlock Holmes?	1.30	4.00	9.00

YOUNG HEARTS
Nov, 1949 - No. 2, Feb, 1950
Marvel Comics (SPC)

1-Photo-c	3.50	10.50	24.00
2	2.00	6.00	14.00

YOUNG HEARTS IN LOVE
1964
Super Comics

17,18: 17-r/Young Love V5#6, 4-5/62	.25	.75	1.50

YOUNG HEROES (Formerly Forbidden Worlds #34)
No. 35, Feb-Mar, 1955 - No. 37, June-July, 1955
American Comics Group (Titan)

35-37-Frontier Scout	2.00	6.00	14.00

YOUNG KING COLE (Becomes Criminals on the Run)
Fall, 1945 - V3#12, July, 1948
Premium Group/Novelty Press

V1#1-Toni Gayle begins	7.00	21.00	50.00
2	5.00	15.00	35.00
3-6	3.70	11.00	26.00
V2#1-7(7/47)	3.00	9.00	21.00
V3#1,3-6,12: 5-McWilliams-c/a	2.30	7.00	16.00
2-L.B. Cole-a	3.00	9.00	21.00
7-L.B. Cole-c/a	4.50	14.00	32.00
8-11-L.B. Cole-c	3.70	11.00	26.00

YOUNG LAWYERS, THE (TV)
Jan, 1971 - No. 2, April, 1971
Dell Publishing co.

1,2	1.15	3.50	8.00

YOUNG LIFE (Teen Life #3 on)
Spring, 1945 - No. 2, Summer, 1945

Yogi Bear #13 (Dell), © Hanna-Barbera

Young Allies Comics #4, © MEG

Young Hearts #1, © MEG

Young Lovers #18, © CC

Young Master #1, © New Comics Group

Young Men #25, © MEG

YOUNG LIFE (continued)
New Age Publ./Quality Comics Group

	Good	Fine	N-Mint
1-Skip Homeier, Louis Prima stories	4.00	12.00	28.00
2-Frank Sinatra c/story	3.50	10.50	24.00

YOUNG LOVE
2-3/49 - No. 73, 12-1/56-57; V3#5, 2-3/60 - V7#1, 6-7/63
Prize(Feature)Publ.(Crestwood)

	Good	Fine	N-Mint
V1#1-S&K c/a(2)	12.00	36.00	84.00
2-Photo-c begin; S&K-a	5.70	17.00	40.00
3-S&K-a	4.00	12.00	28.00
4-5-Minor S&K-a	2.65	8.00	18.00
V2#1(#7)-S&K-a	4.00	12.00	28.00
2-5(#8-11)-Minor S&K-a	2.00	6.00	14.00
6,8(#12,14)-S&K-c only	2.65	8.00	18.00
7,9-12(#13,15-18)-S&K c/a	4.00	12.00	28.00
V3#1-4(#19-22)-S&K c/a	2.65	8.00	18.00
5-7,9-12(#23-25,27-30)-Photo-c resume; S&K-a			
	2.00	6.00	14.00
8(#26)-No S&K	1.50	4.50	10.00
V4#1,6(#31,36)-S&K-a	2.00	6.00	14.00
2-5,7-12(#32-35,37-42)-Minor S&K-a	1.70	5.00	12.00
V5#1-12(#43-54), V6#1-9(#55-63)-Last precode; S&K-a-some			
	1.30	4.00	9.00
V6#10-12(#64-66)	1.00	3.00	7.00
V7#1-7(#67-73)	.70	2.00	5.00
V3#5(2-3/60),6(4-5/60)(Formerly All For Love)	.60	1.75	3.50
V4#1(6-7/60)-6(4-5/61)	.60	1.75	3.50
V5#1(6-7/61)-6(4-5/62)	.60	1.75	3.50
V6#1(6-7/62)-6(4-5/63), V7#1	.40	1.25	2.50

NOTE: *Severin/Elder* a-V1#3. S&K art not in #53, 57, 58, 61, 63-65. *Meskin* a-27. Photo c-V3#5-V5#11.

YOUNG LOVE
#39, 9-10/63 - #120, Wint./75-76; #121, 10/76 - #126, 7/77
National Periodical Publ.(Arleigh Publ. Corp #49-60)/DC Comics

39	.70	2.00	5.00
40-50	.60	1.80	3.50
51-70: 64-Simon & Kirby-a	.40	1.25	2.50
71,72,74-77,80	.35	1.00	2.00
73,78,79-Toth-a	.25	.75	1.50
81-126: 107-114 (100 pgs.). 122-Toth-a		.30	.60

YOUNG LOVER ROMANCES (Formerly & becomes Great Lover. . .)
No. 4, June, 1952 - No. 5, Aug, 1952
Toby Press

4,5-Photo-c	1.70	5.00	12.00

YOUNG LOVERS (My Secret Life #19 on)(Formerly Brenda Starr?)
No. 16, 7/56 - No. 18, 5/57
Charlton Comics

16,17('56)	1.30	4.00	9.00
18-Elvis Presley picture-c, text story (biography)			
	20.00	60.00	140.00

YOUNG MARRIAGE
June, 1950
Fawcett Publications

1-Powell-a; photo-c	4.30	13.00	30.00

YOUNG MASTER (Also see The Master)
Nov, 1987 - No. 9, 1989 ($1.75, B&W)
New Comics Group

1-9: Val Mayerik-c/a	.35	1.00	2.00

YOUNG MEN (Formerly Cowboy Romances)(. . .on the Battlefield
#12-20(4/53); . . .In Action #21)
No. 4, 6/50 - No. 11, 10/51; No.12, 12/51 - No. 28, 6/54
Marvel/Atlas Comics (IPC)

	Good	Fine	N-Mint
4-(52 pgs.)	5.00	15.00	35.00
5-11	2.85	8.50	20.00
12-23	2.30	7.00	16.00
24-Origin Captain America, Human Torch, & Sub-Mariner which are			
revived w/#28. Red Skull app.	32.00	95.00	225.00
25-28: 25-Romita-c/a	24.00	71.00	165.00

NOTE: *Berg* a-7, 17, 20; c-17. *Colan* a-15. Human Torch by *Burgos*-#25, 27, 28. Sub-Mariner by *Everett*-#24-28. *Everett* a-18-20. *Heath* a-13, 14. *Maneely* c-12, 15.

YOUNG REBELS, THE (TV)
January, 1971
Dell Publishing Co.

1-Photo-c	1.00	3.00	6.00

YOUNG ROMANCE COMICS (The 1st romance comic)
Sept-Oct, 1947 - V16#4, June-July, 1963 (#1-33: 52 pgs.)
Prize/Headline (Feature Publ.)

V1#1-S&K c/a(2)	13.00	40.00	90.00
2-S&K c/a(2-3)	7.00	21.00	50.00
3-6-S&K c/a(2-3) each	5.70	17.00	40.00
V2#1-6(#7-12)-S&K c/a(2-3) each	5.00	15.00	35.00
V3#1-3(#13-15)-Last line drawn-c; S&K c/a	2.65	8.00	18.00
4-12(#16-24)-Photo-c; S&K-a	2.65	8.00	18.00
V4#1-11(#25-35)-S&K-a	2.30	7.00	16.00
12(#36)-S&K, Toth-a	4.00	12.00	28.00
V5#1-12(#37-48), V6#4-12(#52-60)-S&K-a	2.30	7.00	16.00
V6#1-3(#49-51)-No S&K-a	1.70	5.00	12.00
V7#1-11(#61-71)-S&K-a in most	2.30	7.00	16.00
V7#12(#72), V8#1-3(#73-75)-Last precode (12-1/54-55)-No S&K-a			
	1.15	3.50	8.00
V8#4(#76, 4-5/55), 5(#77)-No S&K	1.00	3.00	7.00
V8#6-8(#78-80, 12-1/55-56)-S&K-a	1.50	4.50	10.00
V9#3,5,6(#81, 2-3/56, 83,84)-S&K-a	1.30	4.00	9.00
4, V10#1(#82,85)-All S&K-a	1.70	5.00	12.00
V10#2-6(#86-90, 10-11/57)-S&K-a	1.30	4.00	9.00
V11#1,2,5,6(#91,92,95,96)-S&K-a	1.30	4.00	9.00
3,4(#93,94), V12#2,4,5(#98,100,101)-No S&K	.85	2.50	6.00
V12#1,3,6(#97,99,102)-S&K-a	1.30	4.00	9.00
V13#1(#103)-S&K, Powell-a	1.50	4.50	10.00
2-6(#104-108)	.60	1.75	3.50
V14#1-6, V15#1-6, V16#1-4(#109-124)	.40	1.25	2.50

NOTE: *Meskin* a-16, 24(2); 47. *Robinson/Meskin* a-6. *Leonard Starr* a-11. Photo c-16-32, 34-65.

YOUNG ROMANCE COMICS (Continued from Prize series)
No. 125, Aug-Sept, 1963 - No. 208, Nov-Dec, 1975
National Periodical Publ.(Arleigh Publ. Corp. No. 127)

125	.70	2.00	5.00
126-153,155-162	.50	1.50	3.00
154-Adams-c	.60	1.75	3.50
163,164-Toth-a		.60	1.20
165-196: 170-Michell from Young Love ends; Lily Martin, the			
Swinger begins		.40	.80
197 (100 pgs.)-208		.25	.50

YOUR DREAMS (See Strange World of. . .)

YOUR TRIP TO NEWSPAPERLAND
June, 1955 (12 pgs.; 14x11½'')
Philadelphia Evening Bulletin (Printed by Harvey Press)
Joe Palooka takes kids on tour through newspaper

	2.65	8.00	18.00

YOUR UNITED STATES
1946
Lloyd Jacquet Studios

Used in SOTI, pg. 309,310; Sid Greene-a	13.00	40.00	90.00

447

YOUTHFUL HEARTS (Daring Confessions #4 on)
May, 1952 - No. 3, 1952
Youthful Magazines

	Good	Fine	N-Mint
1-"Monkey on Her Back" swipes E.C. drug story from SuspenStories #12	10.00	30.00	70.00
2,3	5.70	17.00	40.00

NOTE: *Doug Wildey* art in all.

YOUTHFUL LOVE (Truthful Love #2)
May, 1950
Youthful Magazines

	Good	Fine	N-Mint
1	3.50	10.50	24.00

YOUTHFUL ROMANCES
8-9/49 - #14, 10/52; #15, 1/53 - #18, 7/53; #5, 9/53 - #8, 5/54
Pix-Parade #1-14/Ribage #15 on

	Good	Fine	N-Mint
1-(1st series)-Titled Youthful Love-Romances	8.00	24.00	56.00
2	4.50	14.00	32.00
3-5	3.70	11.00	26.00
6,7,9-14(10/52, Pix-Parade; becomes Daring Love #15); 7-Tony Martin photo on-c	2.65	8.00	18.00
8-Wood-c	8.50	25.50	60.00
15-18 (Ribage)	2.65	8.00	18.00
5(9/53, Ribage)	2.00	6.00	14.00
6,7(#7, 2/54)	1.70	5.00	12.00
8(5/54)	1.70	5.00	12.00

YUPPIES FROM HELL
1989 ($2.95, B&W, one-shot, direct sale only, 52 pgs.)
Marvel Comics

	Good	Fine	N-Mint
1-Satire	.50	1.50	3.00

ZAGO, JUNGLE PRINCE (My Story #5 on)
Sept, 1948 - No. 4, March, 1949
Fox Features Syndicate

	Good	Fine	N-Mint
1-Blue Beetle app.-partial r-/Atomic #4 (Toni Luck)	17.00	51.00	120.00
2,3-Kamen-a	13.00	40.00	90.00
4-Baker-c	12.00	36.00	84.00

ZANE GREY'S STORIES OF THE WEST
No. 197, 9/48 - No. 996, 5-7/59; 11/64 (All painted-c)
Dell Publishing Co./Gold Key 11/64

	Good	Fine	N-Mint
4-Color 197(9/48)	6.00	18.00	42.00
4-Color 222,230,236('49)	5.00	15.00	35.00
4-Color 246,255,270,301,314,333,346	3.70	11.00	26.00
4-Color 357,372,395,412,433,449,467,484	3.00	9.00	21.00
4-Color 511-Kinstler-a	3.50	10.50	24.00
4-Color 532,555,583,604,616,632(5/55)	3.00	9.00	21.00
27(9-11/55) - 39(9-11/58)	2.30	7.00	16.00
4-Color 996(5-7/59)	2.30	7.00	16.00
10131-411-(11/64-G.K.)-Nevada; r-4-Color #996	1.30	4.00	9.00

ZANY (Magazine)(Satire)(See Frantic & Ratfink)
Sept, 1958 - No. 4, May, 1959
Candor Publ. Co.

	Good	Fine	N-Mint
1-Bill Everett-c	3.50	10.50	24.00
2-4	2.00	6.00	14.00

ZATANNA SPECIAL (See Adventure Comics #413, Justice League of America #161, Supergirl #1 & World's Finest Comics #274)
1987 ($2.00, One shot)
DC Comics

	Good	Fine	N-Mint
1	.35	1.00	2.00

ZAZA, THE MYSTIC (Formerly Charlie Chan; This Magazine Is Haunted V2#12 on)
No. 10, April, 1956 - No. 11, Sept, 1956
Charlton Comics

	Good	Fine	N-Mint
10,11	3.50	10.50	24.00

ZEGRA JUNGLE EMPRESS (Formerly Tegra)(My Love Life #6 on)
No. 2, Oct, 1948 - No. 5, April, 1949
Fox Features Syndicate

	Good	Fine	N-Mint
2	20.00	60.00	140.00
3-5	14.00	42.00	100.00

ZERO PATROL, THE
Nov, 1984 - No. 2; 1987 - Present ($2.00, color)
Continuity Comics

	Good	Fine	N-Mint
1,2: Adams c/a; Megalith begins	.35	1.00	2.00
1-5 (#1,2-reprints above, 1987)	.25	.75	1.50

ZIGGY PIG-SILLY SEAL COMICS (See Animated Movie-Tunes, Comic Capers, Krazy Komics & Silly Tunes)
Fall, 1944 - No. 6, Fall, 1946
Timely Comics (CmPL)

	Good	Fine	N-Mint
1-Vs. the Japs	8.00	24.00	56.00
2	4.00	12.00	28.00
3-5	3.50	10.50	24.00
6-Infinity-c	5.70	17.00	40.00
I.W. Reprint #1('58)-r/Krazy Komics	.50	1.50	3.00
I.W. Reprint #2,7,8	.25	.75	1.50

ZIP COMICS
Feb, 1940 - No. 47, Summer, 1944
MLJ Magazines

	Good	Fine	N-Mint
1-Origin Kalathar the Giant Man, The Scarlet Avenger, & Steel Sterling; Mr. Satan, Nevada Jones & Zambini, the Miracle Man, War Eagle, Captain Valor begins	117.00	295.00	700.00
2	50.00	150.00	350.00
3	39.00	115.00	270.00
4,5	33.00	100.00	230.00
6-9: 9-Last Kalathar & Mr. Satan	29.00	86.00	200.00
10-Inferno, the Flame Breather begins, ends #13	26.00	77.00	180.00
11,12: 11-Inferno without costume	24.00	73.00	170.00
13-17,19: 17-Last Scarlet Avenger	24.00	73.00	170.00
18-Wilbur begins (1st app.)	27.00	81.00	190.00
20-Origin Black Jack (1st app.)	36.00	107.00	250.00
21-26: 25-Last Nevada Jones. 26-Black Witch begins; last Captain Valor	23.00	70.00	160.00
27-Intro. Web	35.00	105.00	245.00
28-Origin Web	35.00	105.00	245.00
29,30	19.00	57.00	135.00
31-38: 34-1st Applejack app. 35-Last Zambini, Black Jack. 38-Last Web issue	14.00	42.00	100.00
39-Red Rube begins (origin, 8/43)	14.00	42.00	100.00
40-47: 45-Wilbur ends	10.00	30.00	70.00

NOTE: *Biro* a-5, 9, 17; c-4-7, 9, 11, 12, 14, 17. *Meskin* a-1-3, 5-7, 9, 10, 12, 13, 15, 16 at least. *Novick* c-19, 20, 24, 25, 31. Bondage c-8, 9, 33, 34.

ZIP-JET (Hero)
Feb, 1953 - No. 2, Apr-May, 1953
St. John Publishing Co.

	Good	Fine	N-Mint
1,2-Rocketman-r/Punch Comics; #1-c from splash in Punch #10	17.00	50.00	120.00

ZIPPY THE CHIMP (CBS TV Presents...)
No. 50, March, 1957 - No. 51, Aug, 1957
Pines (Literary Ent.)

	Good	Fine	N-Mint
50,51	1.70	5.00	12.00

ZODY, THE MOD ROB
July, 1970
Gold Key

	Good	Fine	N-Mint
1	.70	2.00	4.00

Zane Grey's Stories Of The West #37, © DELL

Zaza, The Mystic #10, © CC

Zip Comics #23, © AP

Zooniverse #1, © Eclipse

Zoot #2, © FOX

Zorro #4 (Gold Key), © WDC

ZOO ANIMALS
No. 8, 1954 (36 pages; 15 cents)
Star Publications

	Good	Fine	N-Mint
8-(B&W for coloring)	1.50	4.50	10.00

ZOO FUNNIES (Tim McCoy #16 on)
Nov, 1945 - No. 15, 1947
Charlton Comics/Children Comics Publ.

101(#1)(1945)-Funny animal; Al Fago-c	5.70	17.00	40.00
2(12/45, 52 pgs.)	2.85	8.50	20.00
3-5	2.30	7.00	16.00
6-15: 8-Diana the Huntress app.	1.70	5.00	12.00

ZOO FUNNIES (Becomes Nyoka, The Jungle Girl #14 on?)
July, 1953 - No. 13, Sept, 1955; Dec, 1984
Capitol Stories/Charlton Comics

1-1st app.? Timothy The Ghost; Fago-c/a	3.70	11.00	26.00
2	2.00	6.00	14.00
3-7 (8/46)	1.50	4.50	10.00
8-13-Nyoka app.	3.70	11.00	26.00
1('84)		.40	.80

ZOONIVERSE
8/86 - No. 6, 6/87 ($1.25-$1.75, color, mini-series, Mando paper)
Eclipse Comics

1-5 ($1.25)		.65	1.30
6 ($1.75)	.30	.90	1.80

ZOO PARADE (See 4-Color #662)

ZOOM COMICS
December, 1945 (One Shot)
Carlton Publishing Co.

nn-Dr. Mercy, Satannas, from Red Band Comics; Capt. Milksop origin retold	17.00	51.00	120.00

ZOOT (Rulah Jungle Goddess #17 on)
nd (1946) - No. 16, July, 1948 (Two #13s & 14s)
Fox Features Syndicate

nn-Funny animal only	8.50	25.50	60.00
2-The Jaguar app.	7.00	21.00	50.00
3(Fall,'46) - 6-Funny animals & teen-age	4.00	12.00	28.00
7-Rulah, Jungle Goddess begins (6/47); origin & 1st app.			
	33.00	100.00	230.00
8-10	24.00	72.00	165.00
11-Kamen bondage-c	25.00	75.00	175.00

	Good	Fine	N-Mint
12-Injury-to-eye panels	16.00	48.00	110.00
13(2/48)	16.00	48.00	110.00
14(3/48)-Used in SOTI, pg. 104, "One picture showing a girl nailed by her wrists to trees with blood flowing from the wounds, might be taken straight from an ill. ed. of the Marquis deSade"			
	19.00	57.00	135.00
13(4/48), 14(5/48)	16.00	48.00	110.00
15,16	16.00	48.00	110.00

ZORRO (Walt Disney with #882)(TV)(See Eclipse Graphic Album)
May, 1949 - No. 15, Sept-Nov, 1961 (Photo-c 882 on)
Dell Publishing Co.

4-Color 228	16.00	48.00	110.00
4-Color 425,497	8.50	25.50	60.00
4-Color 538-Kinstler-a	9.30	28.00	65.00
4-Color 574,617,732	8.50	25.50	60.00
4-Color 882-Photo-c begin; Toth-a	7.00	21.00	50.00
4-Color 920,933,960,976-Toth-a in all	7.00	21.00	50.00
4-Color 1003('59)	5.70	17.00	40.00
4-Color 1037-Annette Funicello photo-c	8.00	24.00	56.00
8(12-2/59-60)	4.00	12.00	28.00
9,12-Toth-a	4.30	13.00	30.00
10,11,13-15-Last photo-c	3.00	9.00	21.00

NOTE: *Warren Tufts a-4-Color 1037, 8, 9, 13.*

ZORRO (Walt Disney)(TV)
Jan, 1966 - No. 9, March, 1968 (All photo-c)
Gold Key

1-Toth-a	3.00	9.00	21.00
2,4,5,7-9-Toth-a	2.30	7.00	16.00
3,6-Tufts-a	2.00	6.00	14.00

NOTE: *#1-9 are reprinted from Dell stories. Tufts a-3,4. #3-r/#12-c & #8 inside; #4-r/#9-c & insides; #6-r/#11(all); #7a-r/#14-c.*

ZOT! (Also see Adventures of Zot)
4/84 - No. 10, 7/85; No. 11, 1/87 - Present ($1.50, Baxter paper)
Eclipse Comics

1	1.15	3.50	7.00
2,3	.65	1.90	3.75
4-10: 4-Origin. 10-Last color issue	.35	1.00	2.00
11-30 ($2.00, B&W)	.35	1.00	2.00

Z-2 COMICS (Secret Agent. . .)(See Holyoke One-Shot #7)

ZULU (See Movie Classics)

451

456

COMICS:
MARVEL,
DC &
INDEPENDENTS,
GOLDEN AGE,
SILVER AGE,
UNDER-
GROUNDS,
& GRAPHIC
NOVELS.

FORBIDDEN PLANET
THE SCIENCE FICTION
MEGASTORE

SCIENCE
FICTION,
FANTASY
& HORROR
BOOKS,
ROBOTS,
TOYS,
GAMES,
MASKS,
POSTERS,
MODELS
& MORE.

227 E. 59TH ST. BETWEEN 2ND & 3RD AVE.
NEW YORK CITY 10022, 212-751-4386

821 BROADWAY AT 12TH STREET
NEW YORK CITY 10003, 212-473-1576

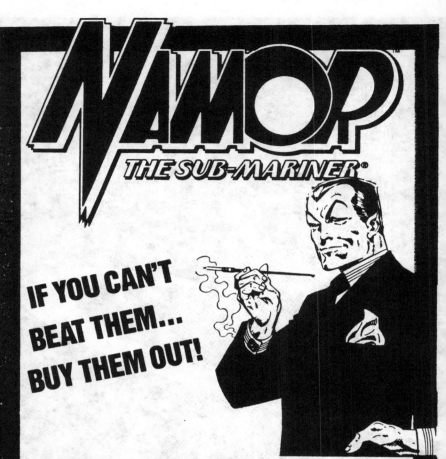

NAMOR™
THE SUB-MARINER®

IF YOU CAN'T
BEAT THEM...
BUY THEM OUT!

The Marvel° Comics hero from the 40's
becomes the corporate raider of the 90's!

Available at:
LEE TENNANT ENTERPRISES INC.
6963 W. 111th. St. P.O.Box 296
Worth, IL. 60482
708- 532-1771
NEW COMICS AT 40% off!

WHEN IT COMES TO DISTRIBUTION HERE AND ABROAD, COMICS UNLIMITED HAS TAKEN THE WORLD BY STORM.

- **Low freight rates from New York**
- **Competitive discounts**
- **Faster service**

These are just some of the benefits of choosing Comics Unlimited for your wholesale distribution. Every week we ship to England, France, Germany and Australia. And we're shipping now, so when it comes to experience and a long history of customer satisfaction, we can make a world of difference. It's simple. We know how to do it. So put the whole world in your reach. Comics Unlimited.

COMICS UNLIMITED
6833 Amboy Rd.
Staten Island, NY 10309
(718) 948-2223
Fax 718-356-1173
(United States outside of N.Y. City) 1-800-729-5704

473

476

477

CONGRATULATIONS

OVERSTREET COMIC BOOK PRICE GUIDE

on your...

20th EDITION!

Archie

Dan DeCarlo

Look for our exciting new titles in 1990!

JOIN THE PARADE TO....

Master Comics #7, 1940, © FAW. 1st comic-size issue.

Mystery In Space #53, 1959, © DC. Adam Strange series begins.

...omics #2, 1939,

The Phantom Stranger #1, 1952, © DC

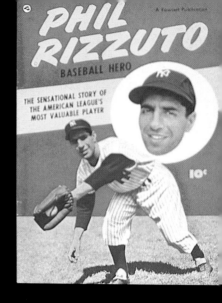

Phil Rizzuto nn, 1951, © FAW

Prize Comics #7, 1940, © PRIZE. Origin

Real Clue Crime Stories V2#4, 1947, © HILL

Four Color #1134, 1960, © Brennan-Westgate Prod.

Reno Browne #51, 1950, © MCG

Science Comics #4, 194

Scoop Comics #2, 1942, © CHES

Secret Origins #1, 1961, © DC

Showcase #4, 1956, © DC. The Silver
Age begins with this book, 1st app. the Silver

Showcase #23, 1959, © DC. The 2nd app.
Silver Age Green Lantern

Showcase #34, 1961, © DC. 1st app. The Atom.

Showcase #37, 1962, © DC. 1st app. Metal Men.

Sports Action #2, 1950, © MCG

Strange Adventures #50, 1954, © DC

Strange Tales #114, 1963, © MCG. 1st

Strange Tales Annual #1, 1962, © MCG

Tales Of Suspense #39, 1963, © MCG. 1st app. Iron Man.

Tales Of Suspense #58, 1964, © MCG. Iron Man, Captain America battle issue.

Tales To Astonish #27, 1962, © MCG. 1st

The Three Stooges #1, 1949, © Jubilee

Thrilling Comics #6, 1940, © BP

Uncle Sam #3, 1942, © QUA

Voodoo #16, 1954, © Four Star Publ.

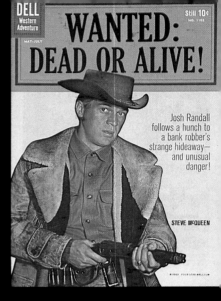

Four Color #1102, 1960, © Four Star-Malcolm.

Wonderworld Comics #7, 1939, © FOX. Lou Fine cover art.

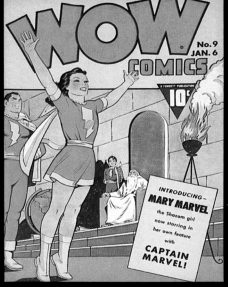

Wow Comics #9, 1943, © FAW. Mary Marvel begins.

Young Men #24, 1953, © MCG

Zip Comics #9, 1940, © MLJ

486

491

COLLECTORS - DON'T BE LEFT OUT!

Three of the most important publications available are being produced *exclusively* for you!

Now featuring a
full color slick cover
and
full color insert
every month!

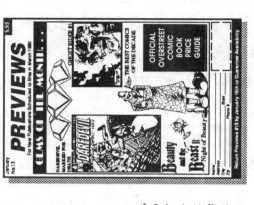

Get the latest information in every issue of **PREVIEWS**. Each issue gives you a look at what's going to be on sale two months in advance! Every issue also features plot and character information on hundreds of DC, Marvel, and Independent titles— a virtual "crystal ball" for comics! Plus, you'll see the latest book releases, magazines, games, toys, and more! Let **PREVIEWS** be your guide to the exciting world of collecting every month! Each issue includes an easy to use order form.

dave's
comics and collectibles

HUGE SELECTION OF BACK ISSUE COMICS, MOVIE/TV MAGS AND MEMORABILIA, CHARACTER TOYS, LUNCH BOXES, MODEL KITS, COLLECTORS SUPPLIES AND MUCH MORE !!!!
SORRY, NO LISTS, BUT YOUR WANT LISTS WELCOME WITH SASE.

907 S. WASHINGTON
ROYAL OAK, MI. 98067
313-548-1230

623 WILLIAM (at STATE)
ANN ARBOR, MI. 98109
313-665-6969

501

Los Angeles has great weather, terrific beaches, Disneyland and 16 of the BEST COMIC BOOK SPECIALTY STORES IN THE WORLD!!

CULVER CITY:
GRAPHITTI
4325 OVERLAND AVE, 90230
(213) 559-2058

EAGLE ROCK:
ANOTHER WORLD
1615 COLORADO BLVD, 90041
(213) 257-7757

GARDEN GROVE:
COMICS UNLIMITED
12913 HARBOR BLVD, 92640
(714) 638-2040

GARDENA:
GEOFFREY'S COMICS
15530 CRENSHAW BLVD, 90249
(213) 538-3198

HAWAIIAN GARDENS:
COMICS UNLIMITED
21505 NORWALK BLVD, 90716
(213) 865-4474

HOLLYWOOD:
GOLDEN APPLE
7711 MELROSE AVE, 90046
(213) 658-6047

LONG BEACH:
PACIFIC COMICS
5622 E. SECOND ST, 90803
(213) 434-5136

NORTH RIDGE:
GOLDEN APPLE COMICS
8958 & 8960 RESEDA BLVD, 91324
(818) 993-7804

SANTA MONICA:
HI De HO COMICS & FANTASY
525 SANTA MONICA BLVD, 90401
(213) 394-2820

STUDIO CITY:
GRAPHITTI
12080 VENTURA PLACE #3, 91604
(818) 980-4976

VENICE:
HI De HO COMICS & FANTASY
64 WINDWARD AVE, 90291
(213) 399-6206

WEST LOS ANGELES:
GOLDEN APPLE COMICS
8934 W. PICO BLVD, 90035
(213) 274-2008

WESTCHESTER:
GRAPHITTI
8639 LINCOLN BLVD, #102 (REAR)
(213) 641-8661   90045

WESTMINSTER:
COMICS UNLIMITED
16344 BEACH BLVD, 92683
(714) 841-6646

WESTWOOD:
GRAPHITTI
960 GAYLEY AVE, 90024
(213) 824-3656

WHITTIER:
COMICS UNLIMITED
14153 E. WHITTIER BLVD, 90605
(213) 945-1733

Visit, call or write individual stores and see for yourself!

A project of LA-Orange County COBRA (Comic Book Retailers Assoc.) and Dark Horse Comics.

"THE FINAL BID"

1990 COMIC BOOK AUCTION

TOMORROW'S TREASURES

GOLDEN AGE • SILVER AGE • DC • TIMELY •
EC • DISNEY • EARLY MARVEL • (1933-1969)

1,000,000 COMIX INC.
THE LEADING INTERNATIONAL FRANCHISOR OF COMIC BOOK STORES OFFERS YOU A UNIQUE OPPORTUNITY

1,000,000 COMIX INC.
presents COMIC BOOK STORE COMPONENTS

1,000,000 Comix inc. constructs stores. As a byline we are now offering to the dealer community the opportunity to make an investment in their store by purchasing highly functional, attractively crafted store fixtures. Make no mistake about it, as competition in the retail industry, heats up, collectors will choose the store they feel most comfortable in.

NEW COMIC BOOK DISPLAY RACKS (NCD)

62" high x 50" across x 30" deep
Each row pocket holds approx. 10-20 comics deep
11 rows, 7 comics across / row.
(As pictured). Each NCD rack is built to withstand the pounding that small children and others can administer. Built of solid pre-finished melamine, of the type found on counter tops. Hammer blows bounce off. THICK plexiglass allows each reader to view a majority of the comic cover thereby increasing sales potential. As the ENTIRE 10" height of the comic is protected from bending, fingerprints, etc., the comic stays in high grade, thereby increasing future profits. It cannot be stressed enough that most retailers will tell you that many comics get bent, creased, etc., from people bending through a stack to find that one "mint" book. Rack is approx. 62" high x 50" across, depth 30". Each of the 11 rows holds 7 titles across with a depth of 15-20 comics per cover.

The entire comic is prevented from bending and is about 60% visible. Rack is in white melamine with red trim. Very solidly and professionally built.

$895.00 plus shipping and handling

BACK ISSUE COMIC BINS (BICB)

Bin 8 ft long x 50" across, height is 38"
row height 8"
11 rows each side (300 comics / row)
base 5' x 3'

What always turned us off about comic stores was when you had to look through boxes on tables, or cabinets for back issues. The height of the comic (10") comes to the top of the box so the only way to see it was to BEND the comic. Boxes also get beat on as they are made of cardboard. As comics move away from the image of the second hand book store, stores MUST present back issues in a professional, organized manner. Also, back issues are usually the profit maker in any store - another reason to present them to their maximum potential.

Each BICB is constructed of pre-finished melamine (usually white). Melamine is a wood with a plastic coating baked into the wood. Thus it has the finish of arborite with none of the negatives. It can't be peeled off. It is strong, virtually chip proof. Each bin has 11 rows per side, holding about 300 comics per row (6600 back issues per bin or about 22 long white comic boxes). Row height is about 8" so the comic title is usually seen, thus the dreaded bending of the book is avoided. Constructed on a heavy duty base of 5' x 3' which provides an immovable solid anchor. Each BICB is 8 feet long by 50" across. Height is 38" from ground. This unit maximizes back issue sales.

$1275.00 plus shipping and handling

CUSTOM STORE PRODUCTION. In addition to above we construct specifically for comic stores, custom designed upper wall display units, Graphic Novel display units, Comic wall showcases, etc... **Call for details.**

CALL **(514) 630-4518** or write to **1,000,000 COMIC INC.**
P.O. Box 4953, St-Laurent, Montreal, Quebec, Canada   H4L 4Z6

Attention Comic Collectors!!!

Here are just a few reasons why you should consider Gryphon Books Ltd for your comic needs:

EVERYTHING DISCOUNTED
Every item in our monthly order pack is available at a discount (color comics are usually 25% off).

LARGE SELECTION EVERY MONTH
Choose from Marvel, DC, Eclipse, Dark Horse, Viz, Eternity, Fantagraphics and many others.

HASSLE-FREE ORDERING
You are sent a newsletter and order form listing all items available each month. The order can be mailed or called in. Our order line is available **24 hours a day,** seven days a week at **(818) 705-0720.**

LOW MINIMUM ORDER
Our minimum is just 10 items per month.

FREE SHIPPING ON MONTHLY ORDERS
Monthly orders are shipped *FREE.* Biweekly orders are charged $4.00 shipping. These rates apply anywhere in the continental US.

WE SHIP WITH PROTECTION IN MIND
We use sturdy shipping boxes. New comics and magazines are sealed in a poly bag to keep dust and moisture away from the contents. All back-issues are shipped with bags and boards.

OUR BACK-ISSUE POLICY
Back-issues up to 6 months old are available at cover price. Our prices are also very competitive on issues older than 6 months.

WE ALSO CARRY BAGS, BOARDS AND OTHER SUPPLIES

Send $1.00 for catalogue refundable with first order.

COLLECT COMICS!!

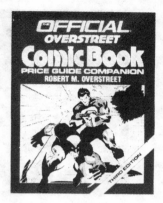

The *Official®* Overstreet Comic Book Price Guide *Companion,* in its *third* edition, written by expert ROBERT OVERSTREET, *tells us how!*

✶ This portable, easy-to-carry treasure includes the *complete* guide to BIG LITTLE BOOKS . . . lists today's prices of the *most* collectible comic books . . . features a comic book convention calendar . . . with cover art by artist John Buscema!

This is a treasure chest of all your favorite comics!

Fourth edition coming soon!

IT'S A HIT!

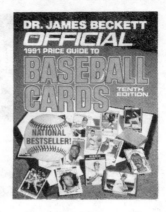

ATTENTION
STAR TREK AND STAR WARS FANS!

THE SECOND LARGE-SIZE EDITION OF THE BESTSELLING PRICE GUIDE TO STAR TREK AND STAR WARS COLLECTIBLES IS NOW AVAILABLE—WITH EXCLUSIVE NEW INFORMATION THAT IS OUT OF THIS WORLD!

Published by the House of Collectibles, this book is the most complete and official guide available!

Over 10,000 current prices for Action Figures, Calendars, Ceramics, Clothing, Comic Books, Toys, and much more!

All-new material for *Voyage Home* and specialty items expressly designed for the 20th-year celebration, *plus* a detailed history of the TV show and behind-the-scenes facts on all four movies!

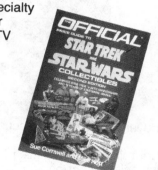

Celebrate ten years of Star Wars with inside information on all three films in the trilogy, *plus* fascinating facts on their special effects!

PLUS, many new photographs of the hottest items!

"OPENING THIS BOOK IS LIKE DISCOVERING A GOLD MINE!"
Filmfax

HOUSE OF COLLECTIBLES
201 East 50th Street
New York, New York 10022

Please send me *The Official® Price Guide to Star Trek® and Star Wars® Collectibles*, 2nd Ed....0-876-37358-9...$8.95. I am enclosing $_____ (add $2.00 for the first book and 50¢ for each additional book to cover postage and handling). Send check or money order—no cash or C.O.D.'s, please. Prices and numbers are subject to change without notice.

Name_____

Address_____

City_____ State_____ Zip Code_____

Allow at least 4 weeks for delivery.

TOYS ARE *NOT* JUST FOR KIDS!

The Official® Identification and Price Guide to Collectible Toys is a *must* for the beginning and expert collector!

RICHARD FRIZ* explores the wide range of collectible toys, from Disneyana, military miniatures, and transportation vehicles to riding toys and world's fair toys.

● Over 100 photos . . . 8 pages of dramatic color . . . fully indexed!

THIS USEFUL GUIDE PROVES TOYS ARE NOT ONLY FUN, THEY'RE BIG BU$INESS, TOO!

*Richard Friz is the author of *The Official® Price Guide to Political Memorabilia* and *The Official® Price Guide to World's Fair Memorabilia* (House of Collectibles: New York).

527

ARION COLLECTOR'S ARCHIVE

New and innovative. Simply put, that is what Arion is. Arion Collector's Archive is about to introduce a new concept that will enable collectors to achieve their desired goals. Arion is a company which will strive to provide collectors a service never before available. This new service is so innovative, that it is bound to change the nature of the comic book industry. Firstly, a question to the collector. Certainly, you take your hobby seriously. The dollars you have invested in your collection proves this. Yet the most likely forum to realise a return on your investment (when you want to sell) is a dealer. And most dealers have to show a profit, most of which is gained by buying comics at a "market" discount, and selling at a "market" premium. This is a fact we all face as serious collectors. Let us follow up this question, with another. When you desperately want a book, regardless of how much you are willing to pay, despite the fact that it may be for sale somewhere, you may miss the opportunity time and again. Firstly your local dealer may not have access to it. Secondly, conventions that you may frequent may not have it, or may not have it in the condition you want. Thirdly, you may see the opportunity too late, and the book that you wanted was sold "yesterday" or even moments before you got to the source. Does this sound familiar? Yes, we have experienced it first hand too. Arion proposes to end this. We are offering a unique solution. A solution where buyers and sellers can meet without having to go through the current sources. And yes, our service is completely computerized. Here is how it works:

I - As a buyer: you purchase an exclusive membership to the Arion group. The cost is $50 U.S. per annum. This membership entitles you to the following:

- Enables you to send in a list of the titles you currently seek. These are entered into our data base.
- If a title becomes available, you will be notified and asked to respond with a bid. The bid request letter will indicate a "floor" price, which should be deemed as a "minimum" asking price. The book will be described completely, and its condition will be certified according to the Overstreet rules of grading. Additional questions will be answered by simply placing a call to us. All bids must be accompanied by a 10% certified deposit (U.S. funds). Responses must be received by a specific deadline, which will be specified.

- All bids will be open, and you will be able to call up 48 hours prior to the deadline to find out the current bid, in case you wish to revise yours.
- At the specified time deadline, the highest bidder will have purchased the title, and will be notified immediately. At this time a transfer of funds for the title will be arranged. If for any reason the successful purchaser withdraws from buying the title, he/she forgoes the deposit and the second highest bid becomes the successful bid. All deposits of other unsuccessful bidders will be refunded immediately in full.

II - As a seller: You must hold a valid and currently active membership with the Arion Group.

- You contact us with all required information about the book, its condition, and the price you seek. We will need to have the book's condition verified for your protection and that of the prospective buyer.
- You will be sent a contract which will bind you from selling the book to anyone during the time of its "marketing". In some cases we may also request that the book be placed in trust.
- You will be subject to paying a fee (to be negotiated) if and only if the book is sold.
- If and when the book is sold, we will arrange transfer of funds to you, the seller, and the book (fully insured) to the purchaser.

Using this method, we hope to open the market for all collectors across North America. Our innovative service means full disclosure of availability immediately to all interested parties. Finally, we intend to provide sellers with a forum within which everyone can realize the dramatic investment returns our industry has proven.
Yes, there is one restriction. A book, in order to qualify for this service, must have a current buyers guide value of at least $750.00. (This floor is subject to change). That is the only restriction. The market awaits you...

ARION COLLECTOR'S ARCHIVE INC.
60 Columbia Way, Suite 220
Markham, Ontario (Canada) L3R 0C9
TEL: (416) 940-8100 FAX: (416) 940-6629

Announcing

CENTRAL JERSEY'S NEWEST, LARGEST, & FINEST FULL-LINE COMICS SHOP

★★★★★★★★★★★★★★★★★★★★★★★★

Star Spangled

COMICS

King George Plaza, Route 22 & Green Brook Rd.
Green Brook, New Jersey

★★★★★★★★★★★★★★★★★★★★★★★★

"Over 100,000 Back Issues in Stock from Golden Age to Present – Plus All Your Current Favorites"

533

JIMMY OLSEN
1 . . . . 45.00
2-5 . . . . 10.00
6-20 . . . . 4.00
21-65 . . . . 1.50

JIMMY WAKELY
all issues 2.50

JOHNNY MACK BROWN
all issues 2.50

JOHN WAYNE
all issues 12.00

JOURNEY INTO MYSTERY
1-82 . . . . 2.50
83 Thor 55.00
84 Thor 15.00
85-89 Thor 10.00
90-95 Thor 6.00
96-112 Thor 2.50

**JOURNEY INTO UNKNOWN
WORLDS**, all issues . . . 2.50

JUMBO COMICS
all issues 4.50

JUNGLE COMICS
all issues 4.50

JUNGLE JIM
1949-1959, all 2.00

**JUSTICE LEAGUE OF
AMERICA**
1 . . . . 60.00
2,3 . . . . 15.00
4-10 . . . . 7.00
11-20 . . . . 4.00
21-29 . . . . 2.50

KAANGA COMICS
1949-1954, all 4.00

KATZENJAMMER KIDS
all issues 5.00

KEEN DETECTIVE FUNNIES
all issues 15.00

KEN MAYNARD WESTERN
all issues 8.00

KID COLT OUTLAW
1948-1964, all 1.00

KID ETERNITY
all issues 4.00

KING COMICS
all issues 2.50

**KING OF THE ROYAL
MOUNTED**, all issues . . 2.00

KRAZY KAT
all issues 2.00

LASH LARUE WESTERN
1-47 . . . . 4.50
48-84 . . . . 1.00

LASSIE
all issues 1.00

LAUGH COMICS
20-60 . . . . 2.00

LAUREL AND HARDY
St. John, all 5.00

LAWMAN
all issues 3.00

LEAVE IT TO BEAVER
all issues 3.00

LIGHTNING COMICS
all issues 10.00

LI'L ABNER
all issues 2.50

LITTLE LULU (Dell)
all issues 1.50

LOIS LANE
1 . . . . 30.00
2-5 . . . . 7.00
6-10 . . . . 5.00
11-20 . . . . 2.00
21-38 . . . . 1.50

LONE RANGER (Dell)
with photo covers 3.00
without photo covers . . 1.50

LORNA THE JUNGLE GIRL
all issues 2.00

MAD COMICS
1 . . . . 60.00
2-5 . . . . 15.00
6-23 . . . . 10.00

MAGIC COMICS
all issues 1.50

MARVEL FAMILY
all issues 4.50

**MARVEL MYSTERY
COMICS**, all issues . . . 30.00

MARVEL TALES
1949-1957, all 2.50

MARY MARVEL
all issues 5.00

MASTER COMICS
all issues 4.00

MAVERICK
all issues 2.50

MD (EC)
all issues 4.00

MICKEY MOUSE (Dell)
all titles/issues 1.00

MILITARY COMICS
all issues 15.00

MODERN COMICS
all issues 7.00

MONTE HALE WESTERN
all issues 4.00

MORE FUN
1936-1937, all 30.00
28-107 . . . . 30.00
108-127 . . . . 5.00

MOTION PICTURE COMICS
101-114 . . . . 5.00

MY GREATEST ADV.
1955-1964, all 4.00

MYSTERY IN SPACE
1951-1961, all 4.00
1962-1964, all 1.50

MYSTERY MEN COMICS
all issues 10.00

MYSTERY TALES
Atlas, all 2.50

MYSTIC
all issues 2.50

NATIONAL COMICS
all issues 3.00

NICKEL COMICS
all issues 16.00

NYOKA THE JUNGLE GIRL
all issues 2.00

OUR ARMY AT WAR
1952-1959, all 1.00

OUR FIGHTING FORCES
1954-1959, all 1.00

PANIC
1954-1956, all 3.00

PAT BOONE
all issues 5.00

PEP COMICS
1940-1943, all 12.00
1944-1948, all 3.00

PHANTOM LADY
all issues 12.00

PHANTOM STRANGER
all issues 15.00

PIRACY
all issues 6.00

PLANET COMICS
10-45 . . . . 18.00
46-73 . . . . 10.00

POGO POSSUM
all issues 4.00

POLICE COMICS
1941-1946, all 9.00
1947-1953, all 4.00

POPEYE (Dell)
all issues 1.00

POPULAR COMICS
all issues 3.00

PRIZE COMICS
all issues 4.00

PRIZE COMICS WESTERN
all issues 3.00

PSYCHOANALYSIS
all issues 4.00

PUNCH COMICS
all issues 5.00

RANGERS COMICS
all issues 4.50

RAWHIDE
all issues 4.00

RAWHIDE KID
1955-1964, all 1.00

REAL FACT COMICS
all issues 4.00

REAL MCCOYS
all issues 2.00

REAL WESTERN HERO
all issues 4.00

THE REBEL
all issues 3.00

RED DRAGON COMICS
all issues 8.00

RED RYDER
all issues 2.00

REX ALLEN
all issues 2.50

RIFLEMAN
all issues 3.00

RIN TIN TIN
all issues 1.50

ROCKY LANE WESTERN
1949-1953, all 4.00
1954-1959, all 1.50

ROD CAMERON WESTERN

all issues 4.00

ROY ROGERS (Dell)
all issues 2.00

RULAH JUNGLE GODDESS
all issues 10.00

THE SAINT
all issues 7.00

SCIENCE COMICS (1940)
all issues 22.00

SEA HUNT
all issues 2.50

SENSATION COMICS
4-20 . . . . 22.00
21-34 . . . . 14.00
35-109 . . . . 8.00

SGT. FURY
1 . . . . 20.00
2-5 . . . . 3.00
6-13 . . . . 1.50

**SGT. PRESTON OF THE
YUKON**, all issues 2.00

77 SUNSET STRIP
all issues 3.00

SHADOW COMICS
1940-1949, all 7.00

SHEENA
1942-1953, all 6.00

SHIELD WIZARD
all issues 15.00

SHOCK SUSPENSTORIES
all issues 10.00

SHOWCASE
1-19,22-24,43 . . . . write
20,21,25-40 . . . . 3.00
41,42,44-59 . . . . 1.50

SILLY SYMPHONIES
all issues 2.50

SILVER STREAK
1939-1942, all 14.00

SIX GUN HEROES
Fawcett, all 5.00

SMASH COMICS
all issues 4.00

SPARKLER COMICS
all issues 2.00

SPEED COMICS
all issues 8.00

SPELLBOUND (Atlas)
all issues 2.50

SPIDER-MAN (see Amazing)

THE SPIRIT (Quality, Fiction
House), all 8.00

SPY SMASHER
1941-1943, all 22.00

STAR COMICS
all issues 12.00

STAR SPANGLED COMICS
9-29 . . . . 25.00
30-80 . . . . 9.00
81-100 . . . . 7.00
101-130 . . . . 5.00

**STAR SPANGLED WAR
STORIES** 1952-59, all . 1.00

STARTLING COMICS
all issues 6.00

STEVE CANYON
all issues 1.00

**STORIES BY FAMOUS
AUTHORS ILLUSTRATED**
all issues 5.00

STRAIGHT ARROW
all issues 2.00

STRANGE ADVENTURES
1950-1963, all 3.00

STRANGE TALES
1951-1962, all 2.50
101,110 . . . . 20.00
102-105,115 . . . . 5.00
106-109,111-114 . . . . . 4.00
116-130 . . . . 1.50
Annual 1,2 . . . . 5.00

STRANGE WORLDS
1950-1959, all 3.00

SUB-MARINER COMICS
1941-1955, all 30.00

SUGARFOOT
all issues 2.50

SUPERBOY
3-15 . . . . 20.00
16-30 . . . . 9.00
31-50 . . . . 5.00
51-68 . . . . 3.00
69-100 . . . . 1.50

SUPER COMICS
all issues 2.00

SUPERMAN
21-40 . . . . 30.00
41-70 . . . . 20.00
71-95 . . . . 12.00
96-120 . . . . 7.00
121-169 . . . . 3.00
Annual 1-8 . . . . 2.50

SUPER MYSTERY COMICS
all issues 4.00

SUPERSNIPE COMICS
all issues 4.00

SUSPENSE
1943-1953, all 2.50

TALES FROM THE CRYPT
1950-1955, all 12.00

TALES OF SUSPENSE
1959-1963, all 2.50
39 . . . . 60.00
40 . . . . 16.00
41 . . . . 10.00
42-45 . . . . 6.50
46-50 . . . . 3.00
51-69 . . . . 2.00

**TALES OF THE UNEXPEC-
TED**, 1956-1963, all . . . 1.00

TALES TO ASTONISH
1959-1963, all 2.50
27 . . . . 50.00
35 . . . . 17.00
36 . . . . 10.00
37-40 . . . . 5.00
41-49 . . . . 3.00
50-70 . . . . 1.50

TARGET COMICS
all issues 2.00

TARZAN (Dell)
all issues 1.00

**TARZAN'S JUNGLE
ANNUAL**, all issues . . . 2.00

TEX RITTER
1-21 . . . . 4.00
22-46 . . . . 1.00

THOR (See Journey Into
Mystery)

THREE STOOGES
1949-1962, all 2.50

THRILLING COMICS
all issues 2.50

TIM HOLT
all issues 4.00

TOMAHAWK
1950-1955, all 2.50
1956-1959, all 1.50

**TOM CORBETT, SPACE
CADET**, all issues 2.50

TOM MIX WESTERN
all issues 4.00

TONTO
all issues 1.50

TOP NOTCH/LAUGH
1954-1964, all 5.00

TUROK, SON OF STONE
all issues 2.00

TWO FISTED TALES
all issues 9.00

TWO GUN KID
1948-1962, all 1.50

UNCANNY TALES (Atlas)
all issues 2.50

UNCLE SAM QUARTERLY
all issues 15.00

UNCLE SCROOGE (Dell)
all issues 3.00

USA COMICS
all issues 25.00

VALOR
all issues 7.00

VAULT OF HORROR
all issues 10.00

VENUS
all issues ssssssssssss . 10.00

VOODOO/VOODA
all issues 3.00

WAGON TRAIN
all issues 2.50

**WALT DISNEY'S COMICS &
STORIES** (Dell), all . . . 1.00

WAMBI, THE JUNGLE BOY
1942-1953, all 3.00

WAR AGAINST CRIME!
all issues 10.00

WEIRD COMICS
all issues 15.00

WEIRD FANTASY
all issues 14.00

WEIRD SCIENCE
all issues 14.00

WEIRD SCIENCE FANTASY
all issues 14.00

WESTERN COMICS (DC)
all issues 1.50

WESTERN HERO
all issues 4.00

WESTERN ROUNDUP
all issues 2.50

WHIZ COMICS
all issues 5.00

WILD BILL ELLIOTT
all issues 2.50

WILD BOY OF THE CONGO
all issues 3.00

WINGS COMICS
all issues 4.00

WONDER COMICS
all issues 9.00

WONDER WOMAN
4-20 . . . . 20.00
21-40 . . . . 10.00
41-72 . . . . 6.00
73-90 . . . . 4.00
91-139 . . . . 2.00

WONDERWORLD COMICS
all issues 11.00

WORLD OF FANTASY
all issues 2.50

WORLD'S FINEST COMICS
8-20 . . . . 35.00
21-40 . . . . 20.00
41-73 . . . . 14.00
74-90 . . . . 4.00
91-139 . . . . 2.00

WOW COMICS
1940-1943, all 8.00
1944-1948, all 4.00

WYATT EARP (Dell)
all issues 2.50

X-MEN
1 . . . . 60.00
2 . . . . 20.00
3,4 . . . . 15.00
5 . . . . 8.00
6-10 . . . . 5.00
11-20 . . . . 2.00

YELLOWJACKET COMICS
all issues 6.00

YOUNG ALLIES COMICS
all issues 27.00

YOUNG MEN
all issues 1.50

**ZANE GREY'S STORIES OF
THE WEST**, all issues . 1.00

ZIP COMICS
all issues 6.00

ZORRO (Dell)
all issues 2.50

For comic titles not listed,
please see following for additional prices we pay:

Atlas/Marvel - All Horror,
Mystery, Terror, Fantasy,
Jungle & related
1950-1963 . . . . 2.50
Atlas/Marvel - All Western &
related titles, 1946-1964 1.00
Atlas/Marvel - All War &
related titles, 1950-1960 1.00
Atlas/Marvel - All Crime,
Spy, Humor, 1946-1960 . 1.50
DC Comics - All with photo
covers, 1946-1960 . . . . 1.00
Dell Comics - All with photo
covers 1.00
All Pre 1955 comic titles per-
taining to Adventure, Chills,
Crime, Fantasy, Fear, For-
bidden, Haunted, Horror,
Journey, Jungle, Justice,
Mystery, Police, Space,
Spook, Science, Spy, Star,
Strange, Tales, Terror, 3-D,
Thrilling, Tomb, Unknown,
Web, Weird, Witches . . 1.50

SALES
CATALOG
AVAILABLE
$1.00

COMIC BOOK CABINETS

...The **VALUE** of your comic book collection is **Rising!! ...Protect, store and organize** your valuable comics in a modern attractive comic cabinet.

The white laminated cabinets are available in two compact sizes, and can be ordered <u>with</u> and <u>without</u> doors.

The double unit is 22" wide x 32" high x 14" deep. Comes with 16 fully adjustable shelves and will hold up to **600 comics.**

The triple unit is 33" wide x 32" high x 14" deep. Comes with 24 fully adjustable shelves and will hold up to **900 comics.**

- -

ORDER FORM

Description	Qty	Price	Total
double unit without doors, 16 shelves		$99.50	
double unit with doors, 16 shelves		119.50	
triple unit without doors, 24 shelves		119.00	
triple unit with doors, 24 shelves		139.50	
		TOTAL ORDER	

make check or money order payable to:

Habitat Group Ltd.
mail to: Habitat Group Ltd.
          10 Lucon Drive
          Deer Park, N.Y. 11729
Upon receipt of payment your order will be promptly shipped.
All units ship K.D. and Freight Collect
N.Y. State residents...add tax.
Allow 4 to 6 weeks for delivery.

Shipping Information

NAME _____

STREET _____

CITY _____ State _____

ZIP CODE _____

542

Classified Advertising (continued)

SALE: pre-'62 all Ducks, Superman, ½-size, etc. Tom Sheridan, 845 5th, San Rafael, CA 94901

BEATLES!!! BEATLES!!! BEATLES!!! I want items on the Beatles like concert tickets, toys, dolls, Yellow Submarine items, records, movie posters, magazines, etc. Monkees items also wanted! Rick Rann, P. O. Box 877, Oak Park, IL 60303

CASH IN AT COMIC CONVENTIONS. Learn the secrets of making a whole lot more than $300-$500 every weekend selling your comics at shows. Secrets revealed for the first time. Results guaranteed! Free details. Collins Publishing, Box 803-A, Glenwood, IL 60425.

SUPPLIES FOR CANADA. Mylars, boards, boxes, polypro's, polyeth's. All acid-free. Largest selection in Canada (24 different mylars). Send $1 for list. Refunded 1st order. 416-251-1659. D. FARRELL, 2 DALSTON RD., TORONTO, CAN. M8W 4R3.

Selling comic books from 1930's to present, Most items discounted 25-50%, prices as low as 10 cents ...please send $1 for my latest list to James Haack, 11149 West Meinecke #2, Wauwatosa, WI 53226. Ph (414) 771-5209.

ORIGINAL ART WANTED—DITKO, KUBERT, ADAMS, WRIGHTSON, AND MANY OTHERS. CONTACT SCOTT DUNBIER, P.O. BOX 1446, GRACIE STATION, NEW YORK, NY 10028. TEL. (212) 666-0982.

Complete Collections Purchased We won't cherry pick only key books! Fast nationwide service. We'll come to you! SPARKLE CITY COMICS, P. O. Box 67, Sewell, NJ 08080. Ph 609-881-4847.

FOR SALE: Thousands of Marvels and DCs. 1960s to present. 10% off all first orders, so hurry!!! Send $2.00 for catalog. D. W. Comix INTERNATIONAL, P. O. Box 750025, Petaluma, CA 94975-0025.

• VIDEO MOVIES & POSTERS • MOVIES, POSTERS, CARTOONS, STANDEES, AD/PROMO PACKS, COUNTER CARDS & MORE! SEND 50 CENTS & S.A.S.E. FOR CURRENT LIST OR $2.50 FOR SAMPLE COLOR MOVIE CATALOG & FREE 18"x24" POSTER. J.C. VIDEO, P. O. BOX 161341, FORT WORTH, TX 76161.

SHADOW PULPS WANTED! ALSO ANY SHADOW RELATED ITEMS LIKE RING, CLUB PIN, BLBs, ETC. TIM ISAACSON, 1002 CLINTON, OAK PARK, IL 60304.

CEREAL BOXES: paying over $100 for certain boxes (1920s-1980s). DAVID WELCH, RR 2 BOX 233, MURPHYSBORO, IL 62966. (618) 687-2282.

DISNEY/POGO/OZ Specialty lists $2 each; LULU/STAR TREK/BEATLES lists $1 each. Extensive Search Service, Squaw Rock, Danielson, CT 06239. (203) 774-1203.

Batman, Detective and other silver and golden age comics. Single issues or partial/full collections. Please write with list & prices, or phone. John Whissell, 612 Wahstao Road, Edmonton, Alberta, Canada T5T 2Y4 or (403) 487-5081.

Attention comic/baseball card fans & dealers. Selling my 25,000 comics, Beatles, Playboy, golden age collection, etc. Want coins, baseball, football, basketball, hockey cards, & old sports items! Complete line of all 1990 baseball products, old star cards, wax boxes, etc. Supplies: storage boxes, 9-pocket pages albums, plastic boxes, holders, sleeves. 25 cents for list. LOWEST PRICES ANYWHERE!! (509)943-6547. Coin House, 777 Stevens, Richland, WA 99352.

COMICS—Thousands of Marvels, DCs & Independents, mid 70s to present, for sale! Many Superhero role playing games available as well!! For list, send SASE to: A. Christians, 75 Wynford Heights Cres. Apt.#1507, Don Mills, Ontario, Canada M3C 3H9.

DCs Disorganized?

MARVELs in a Mess?

It's time for the Doctor!